24th International Conference on Computational Linguistics

(COLING 2012)

Posters

Mumbai, India
8-15 December 2012

Volume 1 of 2

Editors:

Martin Kay
Christian Boitet

ISBN: 978-1-62748-390-2

Printed from e-media with permission by:

Curran Associates, Inc.
57 Morehouse Lane
Red Hook, NY 12571

proceedings.com

Some format issues inherent in the e-media version may also appear in this print version.

Printed by Curran Associates, Inc. (2013)

Association for Computational Linguistics
209 N. Eighth Street
Stroudsburg, Pennsylvania 18360

Phone: 1-570-476-8006
Fax: 1-570-476-0860

acl@aclweb.org

Additional copies of this publication are available from:

Curran Associates, Inc.
57 Morehouse Lane
Red Hook, NY 12571 USA
Phone: 845-758-0400
Fax: 845-758-2634
Email: curran@proceedings.com
Web: www.proceedings.com

COLING 2012

24th International Conference on Computational Linguistics

Proceedings of COLING 2012: Posters

Program chairs:
Martin Kay and Christian Boitet

8-15 December 2012
Mumbai, India

Diamond sponsors

Tata Consultancy Services
Linguistic Data Consortium for Indian Languages (LDC-IL)

Gold Sponsors

Microsoft Research
Beijing Baidu Netcon Science Technology Co. Ltd.

Silver sponsors

IBM, India Private Limited
Crimson Interactive Pvt. Ltd.
Yahoo
Easy Transcription & Software Pvt. Ltd.

Table of Contents

Author Index

K-Best Spanning Tree Dependency Parsing With Verb Valency Lexicon Reranking

Željko AGIĆ
Department of Information and Communication Sciences
Faculty of Humanities and Social Sciences, University of Zagreb
Ivana Lučića 3, 10000 Zagreb, Croatia
zeljko.agic@ffzg.hr

ABSTRACT
A novel method for hybrid graph-based dependency parsing of natural language text is proposed. It is based on k-best maximum spanning tree dependency parsing and evaluation of the spanning trees by using a verb valency lexicon for a given language as a reranking knowledge base. The approach is compared with existing state-of-the-art transition-based and graph-based approaches to dependency parsing. As the proposed generic method was developed specifically for improving the accuracy of Croatian dependency parsing, Croatian Dependency Treebank and CROVALLEX verb valency lexicon are used in the experiment. The suggested approach scored approximately 77.21% LAS, outperforming the tested state-of-the-art approaches by at least 2.68% LAS.

TITLE AND ABSTRACT IN CROATIAN

Ovisnosno parsanje pomoću *k* najboljih razapinjućih stabala i ponovnoga vrjednovanja valencijskim rječnikom glagola

Predlaže se novi pristup hibridnom ovisnosnom parsanju tekstova prirodnoga jezika temeljenom na teoriji grafova. Pristup je zasnovan na ovisnosnom parsanju pomoću *k* najboljih razapinjućih stabala i uporabi valencijskog rječnika glagola parsanoga jezika kao baze znanja za ponovno vrjednovanje tih stabala. Pristup je uspoređen s najboljim postojećim pristupima ovisnosnom parsanju temeljenima na teoriji grafova i na prijelazničkim sustavima. Budući da je predložena metoda razvijana sa specifičnim ciljem povećanja točnosti ovisnosnoga parsanja hrvatskih tekstova, u eksperimentu je korištena Hrvatska ovisnosna banka stabala i valencijski rječnik glagola hrvatskoga jezika CROVALLEX. Predloženi pristup postigao je ukupnu točnost od otprilike 77.21% LAS, što predstavlja povećanje točnosti od oko 2.68% LAS u odnosu na testirane najbolje postojeće sustave.

KEYWORDS: dependency parsing, k-best spanning trees, verb valency lexicon.

KEYWORDS IN CROATIAN: ovisnosno parsanje, razapinjuća stabla, valencijski rječnik glagola.

Proceedings of COLING 2012: Posters, pages 1–12,
COLING 2012, Mumbai, December 2012.

1 Condensed version of the paper in Croatian

Kvaliteta parsanja u paradigmi ovisnosnoga parsanja temeljenog na podatcima ovisi u najvećoj mjeri o svojstvima parsanoga jezika. Budući da su svojstva jezika u tome teorijskom okviru implicitno sadržana u banci ovisnosnih stabala, kaže se da je kvaliteta parsanja ovisna o svojstvima banke ovisnosnih stabala (Kübler et al., 2009). Ovdje se nastoji — koristeći postojeće spoznaje o ovisnosnomu parsanju različitih razreda prirodnih jezika parserima temeljenim na podatcima (Buchholz and Marsi, 2006; Nivre et al., 2007) — unaprijediti kvalitetu ovisnosnoga parsanja tekstova pisanih hrvatskim jezikom koristeći postojeće metode ovisnosnoga parsanja, Hrvatsku ovisnosnu banku stabala (HOBS) (Tadić, 2007) i valencijski rječnik glagola hrvatskoga jezika CROVALLEX (Mikelić Preradović, 2008; Mikelić Preradović et al., 2009).

Prikazana su dva skupa eksperimenata. U prvome se skupu na hrvatskim tekstovima iz HOBS-a testiraju najbolji od postojećih javno dostupnih ovisnosnih parsera temeljenih na podatcima, kako bi se utvrdila najveća točnost parsanja koja se može postići njihovom uporabom. S obzirom na točnost postignutu pri parsanju srodnih jezika, poput češkoga i slovenskoga, u sklopu natjecanja u ovisnosnome parsanju CoNLL 2006 (Buchholz and Marsi, 2006) i 2007 (Nivre et al., 2007), za vrjednovanje je odabran MaltParser (Nivre et al., 2007) kao najbolji predstavnik prijelazničkih parsera i MSTParser (McDonald et al., 2006) kao najbolji među ovisnosnim parserima temeljenima na teoriji grafova. Za testiranje je korištena najnovija inačica HOBS-a, koja je sadržavala ukupno 88,045 pojavnica u 3,465 rečenica. Osnovni statistički podatci o HOBS-u i skupovima za treniranje i testiranje ovisnosnih parsera izloženi su u Tablici 1. Sva mjerenja su ponovljena deset puta, i to podjelom HOBS-a na deset nepreklapajućih dijelova, korištenjem devet od tih deset dijelova za postupak treniranja i desetoga dijela, veličine oko 5,000 pojavnica, za postupak testiranja. Uporabljeno je sedam algoritama za prijelazničko parsanje iz sustava MaltParser i četiri algoritma za parsanje temeljeno na teoriji grafova iz sustava MSTParser. Slika 1 i Tablica 2 i 3 prikazuju rezultate prvoga skupa eksperimenata. Parser MstCle2 (neprojektivni ovisnosni parser temeljen na grafovima, jezičnome modelu s parovima ovisnosnih relacija i algoritmu za pronalaženje najvećega prostirućeg stabla Chu-Liu/Edmonds) postigao je najveću točnost pri parsanju tekstova iz HOBS-a prema svim odabranim mjerama za vrjednovanje. Testiranje statističke značajnosti pokazalo je da su razlike u točnostima svih parsera temeljenih na grafovima u odnosu na prijelazničke parsere statistički značajne. S druge

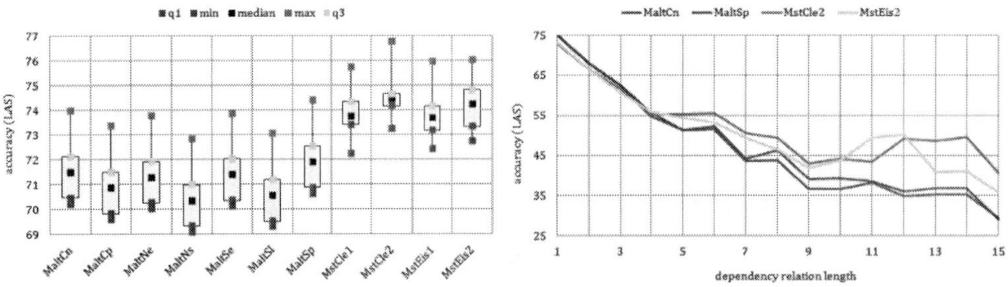

Figure 1: Overall parsing accuracy boxplot and parsing accuracy with respect to dependency relation length for the top-performing algorithms of the standard dependency parsers (Croatian: Ukupna točnost parsanja algoritmima postojećih ovisnosnih parsera i točnost parsanja s obzirom na duljinu ovisnosne relacije za najbolje od tih algoritama)

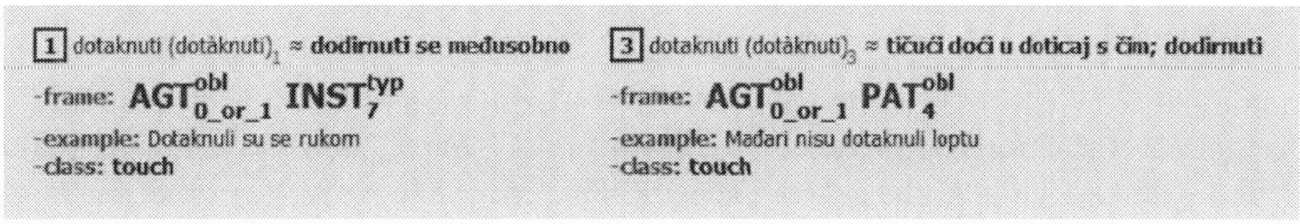

Figure 2: Two CROVALLEX valency frames for the verb *dotaknuti* (en. *to touch*) (Croatian: Dva valencijska okvira glagola *dotaknuti* u CROVALLEX-u)

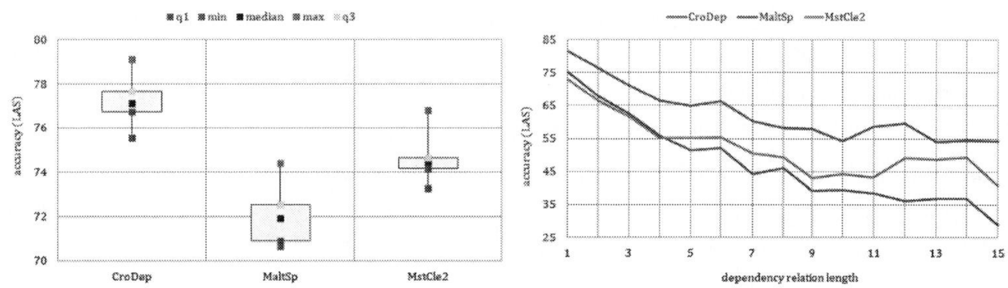

Figure 3: Overall parsing accuracy boxplot and parsing accuracy with respect to dependency relation length for CroDep, MaltSp and MstCle2 algorithm (Croatian: Ukupna točnost parsanja i točnost parsanja s obzirom na duljinu ovisnosne relacije za algoritme CroDep, MaltSp i MstCle2)

strane, točnosti među parserima unutar skupine prijelazničkih parsera nisu različite u statistički značajnoj mjeri. Razlike u postignutoj točnosti parsanja nisu statistički značajne ni u skupini parsera temeljenih na grafovima, no u njoj se po postignutoj točnosti izdvajaju parseri MstCle2 (74.53% LAS) i MstEis2 (74.17% LAS), odnosno parseri s jezičnim modelima temeljenim na parovima ovisnosnih relacija.

U drugome se skupu eksperimenata uspoređuje parser CroDep s najboljim parserima iz prvoga skupa eksperimenata. Parser CroDep (Agić, 2012) novopredloženi je hibridni ovisnosni parser koji se sastoji od tri međuovisne komponente: (1) ovisnosnoga parsera temeljenog na teoriji grafova u skladu s izvedbom iz (McDonald et al., 2005) i algoritmu za parsanje pronalaženjem k najboljih parsanja ulazne rečenice u skladu s izvedbom iz (Hall, 2007), (2) vrjednovatelja predloženih k ovisnosnih stabala pomoću valencijskoga rječnika glagola hrvatskoga jezika CROVALLEX i (3) modula za ponovno vrjednovanje tih stabala povezivanjem vrjednovanja iz dviju prethodnih komponenata, koji daje konačni izlaz iz sustava u vidu jednoga ovisnosnog stabla kojem je dodijeljena najviša zbirna ocjena. Slika 3 i Tablica 5 i 6 prikazuju rezultate drugoga skupa eksperimenata. Zabilježena je točnost parsera CroDep od 77.21% prema mjeri LAS, što predstavlja porast od 2.68% u odnosu najbolji parser iz prethodnoga skupa eksperimenata. Razlika između njihovih točnosti statistički je značajna s obzirom na sve korištene mjere. Za porast ukupne točnosti zaslužan je statistički značajan porast točnosti parsanja imenica i glagola. Prema mjerama LAS i UAS parser CroDep u usporedbi s parserom MstCle2 bilježi povećanje točnosti od preko 10% za predikate, subjekte i objekte, što potvrđuje smislenost povezivanja CROVALLEX-a i parsera temeljenoga na grafovima. Detaljniji prikaz izvedbe parsera CroDep i rezultata pojedinih ekperimenata izložen je dalje u tekstu.

2 Introduction

The quality of data-driven dependency parsing — as expressed by the *de facto* standard dependency parsing evaluation metrics such as LAS and UAS (Nivre, 2006) — is repeatedly shown to be highly language-dependent. More specifically, being that syntactic properties of a given language are implicitly encoded by dependency treebanks in the framework of data-driven dependency parsing, it is seen as treebank-dependent (Kübler et al., 2009). The CoNLL 2006 and 2007 shared tasks on multilingual data-driven dependency parsing (Buchholz and Marsi, 2006; Nivre et al., 2007) separate the tested languages into three classes on the basis of observed dependency parsing accuracy scores: low, medium and high. It is specifically noted in (Nivre et al., 2007) that "the classes are more easily definable via language characteristics than via characteristics of the data sets" and that the "most difficult[-to-parse] languages are those that combine a relatively free word order with a high degree of inflection," modified to an extent only by the respective treebank sizes.

The research presented here was conducted with a goal of improving the baseline for dependency parsing of Croatian texts. Croatian is a highly inflected Slavic language with a relatively free word order, similar to Czech and Slovene, which were included in the CoNLL shared tasks on dependency parsing. With respect to the results of the shared tasks, it was expected that the scores for state-of-the-art parsers on the Croatian Dependency Treebank (Tadić, 2007; Agić, 2012; Berović et al., 2012) would place Croatian in the low accuracy class, i.e., the class of most difficult-to-parse languages. After conducting these preliminary experiments, various courses of action were considered in order to improve the baseline. Parsing baselines in data-driven dependency parsing are usually topped by feature reselection (Passarotti and Dell'Orletta, 2010), merging parser outputs — as in parser voting (Sagae and Lavie, 2006) and stacking (Nivre and McDonald, 2008) — and by using external sources of linguistic knowledge, such as subcategorization information (Zeman, 2002), possibly introducing rule-based (language-dependent) modules into data-driven (language-independent) parsers. The presented approach deals with implementing an interaction between a graph-based dependency parser and a valency lexicon of Croatian verbs, producing in turn a parsing model requiring only a dependency treebank and a machine-readable verb valency lexicon to operate.

In the paper, the baseline experiment in dependency parsing of Croatian using existing state-of-the-art data-driven dependency parsers is first described, including a description of the current state of development of the Croatian Dependency Treebank. Second, the valency lexicon reranking parser is introduced, along with a short description of the verb valency lexicon of Croatian verbs used in this experiment — CROVALLEX (Mikelić Preradović, 2008; Mikelić Preradović et al., 2009). The newly-developed parser is evaluated within the testing framework of the existing parsers and the obtained results are presented in comparison. Future work plans for improving the parser and for improving dependency parsing of Croatian texts in general are sketched in the closing section.

3 Baseline experiment

At the time of conducting the experiments within the CoNLL shared tasks of 2006 and 2007, no treebanks for Croatian were available, for any syntactic formalism. More precisely, the development of the Croatian Dependency Treebank started in January 2007 and only a 100-sentence prototype of the treebank existed when the CoNLL 2007 task was initiated. Being that both shared tasks required a training and testing set and that the minimum size of the testing set was fixed at 5,000 tokens, the prototype was insufficient for participation. Once

Feature	Entire treebank	Training sets	Testing sets
Sentences	3,465	3,261.18 ± 4.20	203.82 ± 4.20
Tokens	88,045	82,865.88 ± 6.87	5,179.12 ± 6.87
Types (wordforms)	20,703	19,927.06 ± 15.71	2,594.06 ± 12.26
Lemmas	10,481	10,166.00 ± 9.19	1,909.00 ± 14.12
POS/MSD tags	828	817.94 ± 1.40	368.35 ± 4.41
Analytical functions	26	26.00 ± 0.00	23.24 ± 0.43

Table 1: Basic stats for Croatian Dependency Treebank and its tenfold sets

the treebank had finally matured in size, the shared task experiments could be recreated for Croatian texts in order to establish a baseline. This section briefly presents this experiment by presenting the treebank, parser selection, experimental setup and the obtained results.

3.1 Treebank

Quoting (Tadić, 2007) and (Agić et al., 2010), the Croatian Dependency Treebank (hr. *Hrvatska ovisnosna banka stabala*, HOBS further in the text) is a dependency treebank built along the principles of Functional Generative Description (Sgall et al., 1986), a multistratal model of dependency grammar developed for Czech. This formalism was further adapted in the Prague Dependency Treebank (PDT) (Hajič et al., 2000) project and applied in sentence analysis and annotation on the levels of morphology, syntax and tectogrammatics. The ongoing construction of HOBS closely follows the guidelines set by PDT, with their simultaneous adaptation to the specifics of Croatian. More detailed account of the HOBS project plan is given in (Tadić, 2007). Currently, HOBS consists of 3,465 sentences in the form of dependency trees that were manually annotated with syntactic functions using TrEd (Pajas, 2000) as the annotation tool. These sentences, encompassing approximately 88,000 tokens, stem from the CW100 newspaper sub-corpus of the Croatian National Corpus (Tadić, 2002, 2009). The CW100 sub-corpus was previously XCES-encoded, sentence-delimited, tokenized, lemmatized and morphosyntactically annotated by linguists. Thus, each of the analyzed sentences contains the manually assigned information on part-of-speech, morphosyntactic category, lemma, dependency and analytical function for each of the tokens. Such a course of action was taken in order to enable the training procedures of state-of-the-art dependency parsers to choose from a wide selection of different features in experiments with stochastic dependency parsing of Croatian texts. Basic stats for HOBS and the experiment sets are given in Table 1. Sentences in HOBS are annotated according to the PDT annotation manual for the analytical level of annotation, with respect to differing properties of Croatian and consulting the Slovene Dependency Treebank (SDT) project (Džeroski et al., 2006). The utilized analytical functions are thus compatible with those of PDT. HOBS is available via META-SHARE (Federmann et al., 2012; Piperidis, 2012).

The experiment was envisioned as a tenfold cross-validated run of several parsing algorithms on the Croatian Dependency Treebank respecting the rules of the CoNLL 2006 and 2007 shared tasks. Training and testing set stats are also given in Table 1. They are indicative of the high morphological complexity of Croatian, as tokens in HOBS are annotated by using 828 different morphosnytactic tags (out of the 1,405 existing in the Croatian Morphological Lexicon (Tadić and Fulgosi, 2003)). As to the syntactic complexity inherent in HOBS, 1,801 of dependency relations (2.06%) were found to be non-projective in 761 different sentences

System	Algorithm	LA	LAS	UAS
MaltParser	Nivre eager	83.74 ± 0.46	71.29 ± 0.74	77.13 ± 0.71
	Nivre standard	83.16 ± 0.47	70.35 ± 0.73	76.44 ± 0.70
	Covington projective	83.46 ± 0.48	70.87 ± 0.73	76.80 ± 0.69
	Stack projective	84.05 ± 0.44	71.91 ± 0.74	77.59 ± 0.73
MaltParser	**Covington non-projective**	83.88 ± 0.46	71.50 ± 0.74	77.30 ± 0.72
	Stack eager	83.75 ± 0.42	71.39 ± 0.73	77.23 ± 0.72
	Stack lazy	83.28 ± 0.48	70.56 ± 0.73	76.54 ± 0.71
MSTParser	Eisner 1st	85.57 ± 0.36	73.73 ± 0.65	80.92 ± 0.61
	Eisner 2nd	85.64 ± 0.39	74.17 ± 0.64	81.27 ± 0.59
MSTParser	Chu-Liu/Edmonds 1st	85.76 ± 0.35	73.88 ± 0.58	80.99 ± 0.50
	Chu-Liu/Edmonds 2nd	85.87 ± 0.38	74.53 ± 0.57	81.69 ± 0.44

Table 2: Overall parsing accuracy of the standard dependency parsing algorithms

(21.96%), indicating an expectedly high presence of non-projectivity, similar to what is observed in PDT (Nivre and Nilsson, 2005). All selected parsers were thus evaluated as non-projective parsers, regardless of their need for treebank (de)projectivization that may be present as a pre- or post-processing step in certain workflows.

3.2 Parsers

Parser selection was based on the results of the CoNLL 2006 and 2007 shared tasks for languages similar to Croatian, i.e., the observed LAS scores for Czech and especially Slovene (being that PDT is substantially larger than both HOBS and SDT). Two standalone parser generators — MaltParser (Nivre et al., 2007) and MSTParser (McDonald et al., 2006) — were shown to be predominant in scores for parsing morphologically complex languages, with the graph-based MSTParser systems slightly outperforming the transition-based MaltParser systems for both emphasized languages. Based on these results, MaltParser and MSTParser were chosen among the publicly available CoNLL 2006 and 2007 parser generators for inclusion in the baseline testing on HOBS. MaltParser was configured by using MaltOptimizer (Ballesteros and Nivre, 2012) and seven projective and non-projective parsing algorithms were tested, while four different configurations of MSTParser were tested: first- and second-order arc-factored language model with Eisner's (projective) and Chu-Liu/Edmonds (non-projective) parsing algorithms.

3.3 Results

Labeled (LAS) and unlabeled (UAS) attachment score was observed, as well as linear label attachment (LA), both overall and for specific syntactic functions and parts of speech. The first set of results is given in Table 2. Systems are grouped into four classes by the way parsing algorithms handle non-projectivity — as pseudo-projective and non-projective MaltParsers and projective and non-projective MSTParsers. Boldfaced names indicate the top performing algorithms for the four classes. Statistical significance of the observed scores is indicated by Figure 1 as it shows that the MSTParser systems are consistently and significantly outperforming MaltParser systems. The top-scorer of the experiment is the MSTParser system that used a second-order arc-factored language model and the non-projective Chu-Liu/Edmonds maximum

Algorithm	Adv	Atr	AuxC	AuxP	Coord	Obj	Pnom	Pred	Sb
MaltSp	70.67	83.77	74.36	71.99	46.28	67.40	66.55	36.45	69.14
MaltCn	71.31	83.98	75.68	72.08	46.96	68.15	66.35	37.33	70.12
MstEis2	69.01	81.80	71.94	74.35	56.49	69.38	65.18	68.10	72.51
MstCle2	68.38	81.46	73.21	74.15	55.05	68.29	62.47	69.09	72.63

Table 3: Accuracy of the top-performing standard dependency parsing algorithms for specific syntactic functions

spanning tree (MST) algorithm. The results are consistent with the ones recorded for Czech and Slovene in CoNLL 2006 and 2007. Figure 1 also shows how graph-based top-performing systems handle long-range dependencies better than their transition-based counterparts.

From another perspective, the top-performing MSTParser system with a second-order arc-factored language model and the Chu-Liu/Edmonds MST parsing algorithm scored approximately 74.53% LAS, a result that places Croatian in the group of languages with low parsing accuracy, as expected. Table 3 additionally indicates that the parsing scores are even lower for the most important syntactic functions with respect to information extraction – subjects (Sb), predicates (Pred) and objects (Obj). This supported the initial estimation that a compound approach to dependency parsing should be implemented in order to increase overall parsing accuracy for Croatian. The method is presented and evaluated in the following section.

4 Valency lexicon reranking parser

The suggested parsing method draws on the fact that verb valency lexicons, such as VALLEX (Lopatková et al., 2006) and the VALLEX-inspired valency lexicon of Croatian verbs CROVALLEX (Mikelić Preradović et al., 2009), explicitly encode obligatory and optional constraints on the number and morphosyntactic properties of dependents that the verbs contained in the lexicon impose. While rule-based dependency parsers might use such information on (predicate) verbs at parser runtime, a post-processing reranking approach is presented here. Namely, a parser is developed that provides k-best dependency trees sorted by adequacy for an input sentence and this parser is then linked to the valency lexicon through a reranking module that reorders the suggested k-best trees by using the lexicon to evaluate them. The evaluation and subsequent reranking is done by weighting dependency relations whose heads are verbs contained within the valency lexicon and adding up the weights to provide overall scores for the suggested dependency trees.

In this section, the CROVALLEX valency lexicon is briefly presented and followed by a presentation of the reranking parser CroDep. The parser is then evaluated in the same testing environment as in the baseline experiment and the obtained results are discussed.

4.1 Valency lexicon

CROVALLEX is a verb valency lexicon created following the FGD guidelines (Sgall et al., 1986) and is accordingly compatible with HOBS with respect to the syntactic theory of choice. The utilized version of CROVALLEX (v2.008) contained 1,797 verb lemmas with 5,188 valency frames. Each valency frame is defined by stating the number, obligatoriness and morphological properties of sentence elements that a given verb introduces. An example is given in Figure 2

Sb 19.87%	AuxP 16.38%	AuxV 15.47%	Obj 12.17%	Adv 10.00%	AuxC 5.34%	Pnom 4.27%
Coord 3.93%	AuxR 2.01%	AuxY 2.00%	AuxX 2.00%	AuxT 1.61%	AuxG 1.42%	Apos 1.19%
AtvV 0.82%	Pred 0.65%	ExD 0.40%	AuxZ 0.35%	AuxK 0.05%	AuxO 0.05%	Atr 0.03%

Table 4: Distribution of direct predicate dependents in HOBS

for the verb *dotaknuti* (en. *to touch*). In the first frame, the agent (AGT) is obligatory (obl) and the instrument (INST) is optional and has to be in the instrumental case (case number 7). In the second frame, the patient (PAT) is obligatory and has to be in the accusative case (4).

The lexicon was adapted to the requirements of data-driven dependency parsing by filtering all multiword lemmas and entries with frequency of 0 denoted in the lexicon. 1,455 verbs and 4,090 respective frames were held. HOBS was then tested using CROVALLEX in order to observe the overlaps. HOBS contained a total of 1,525 verb lemmas and 12,952 verb tokens (ca 14.55% of all lemmas and 14.72% of all tokens), out of which a total of 791 verb lemmas was found in CROVALLEX (ca 51.87%). On the other hand, 664 of the CROVALLEX verbs were not represented by HOBS (ca 45.64% of all CROVALLEX verbs). Even though the measurement of static coverage of verb lemmas itself implicitly supports the course of action with interacting CROVALLEX with a HOBS-trained dependency parser, the dynamic coverage, i.e., the coverage of verb tokens provides an even stronger justification. Only 9.24% of all the verb tokens in HOBS were not covered by CROVALLEX, i.e., for 90.76% of verb tokens in HOBS, at least a single valency frame was found in CROVALLEX.

Another CROVALLEX-related viewpoint on HOBS is given in Table 4. It shows the relative frequency of dependents attached to verbal predicates by their syntactic function. It can be seen that a place in the sentence is most frequently opened by predicates to subjects (almost 20%), prepositions introducing prepositional phrases (16.38%), auxiliary verbs (15.47%), objects (12.17%) and adverbials (10%). The distribution indicates that the properties of verbs encoded in CROVALLEX are readily instantiated in HOBS.

4.2 Parser

Within the suggested framework, parsing is envisioned as a three-step procedure. First, k-best dependency trees sorted by confidence are provided by a language-independent data-driven parsing algorithm. Second, these k dependency trees are scored by a valency-lexicon-based scoring module. Third and final, the trees are re-sorted by combining the scores from the previous steps.

The data-driven component is a dependency parser based on both MSTParser (McDonald et al., 2006) and kMSTParser (Hall, 2007). Graph-based dependency parsing was chosen as a starting point in prototype development on basis of the results obtained in the baseline experiment, showing that graph-based dependency parsers consistently outperform transition-based dependency parsers on Croatian texts. The prototype uses the perceptron training algorithm implemented in MSTParser (McDonald et al., 2005) and the parsing algorithm based on (Camerini et al., 1980) for detecting k-best maximum spanning trees adapted to dependency parsing in kMSTParser. This prototype parser is called CroDep0. Currently it supports only first-order arc-factored language models. It was evaluated on HOBS within the baseline testing framework to provide a reference point and it scored 73.27% LAS, 1.26% lower than the top-performing second-order Chu-Liu/Edmonds MSTParser.

The verb valency lexicon reranking component prototype was developed in what could be considered the simplest possible form of validating dependency relations with respect to valency frames. Namely, the reranking component takes a dependency tree as input. It searches the tree for verbal predicates. When a verbal predicate is encountered, its lemma is matched with the valency lexicon. If it exists as an entry in the lexicon, each of the first-level dependents introduced to the sentence by the verbal predicate is matched with the predicted slots in the valency frames on basis of its morphosyntactic properties: if the properties match and if the element is defined as obligatory, the tree score is incremented. The final score of the tree is defined as the sum of scores of all dependency relations having a verbal predicate as relation head. Each of the k-best trees provided by CroDep0 is given a score by the reranking component.

Finally, the re-sorting component combines the two lists — confidence scores for the k-best trees provided by CroDep0 and valency scores provided by the valency reranker — into a single list averaging the scores while favoring the stochastic component in case of ties. Being that the dependency tree scores from the valency reranker are positive integers representing overall counts of dependency relation confirmations extracted from the valency lexicon, they are normalized for comparison with the CroDep0 confidence scores. The normalization is done by using the maximum confidence score of CroDep0 as ceiling for the valency reranker scores. More formally, let $S_p = \{c_p(t_i)\}_{i=1}^k, \forall i, c_p(t_i) \in [0,1]$ represent the confidence scores for the k dependency trees t_i from the k-best parser module and let $S_v = \{c_v(t_i)\}_{i=1}^k, \forall i, c_v(t_i) \in \mathbb{N}$ be a list of trees and respective integer scores obtained from the valency reranker. The normalized valency reranker scores $\hat{S}_v$ and finally the overall dependency tree scores S_o are provided by the re-sorting component as follows.

$$\hat{S}_v = \{\hat{c}_v(t_i)\}_{i=1}^k, \forall i, \hat{c}_v(t_i) \in [0,1] \qquad \hat{c}_v(t_i) = \max_i(c_p(t_i)) \cdot \frac{c_v(t_i)}{\max_i(c_v(t_i))}$$

$$S_o = \{c_o(t_i)\}_{i=1}^k, \forall i, c_o(t_i) \in [0,1] \qquad c_o(t_i) = \frac{2 \cdot c_p(t_i) \cdot \hat{c}_v(t_i)}{c_p(t_i) + \hat{c}_v(t_i)}$$

The final output of the parser is always $\arg\max_i(c_o(t_i))$. If there are multiple dependency trees with the same overall score c_o, the ordering is decided by selecting the tree with the highest relative score in the k-best parser ranking, i.e., S_p. The resulting parser prototype is called CroDep. It inherits the properties of CroDep0 stochastic module, has the value of k fixed to 10 and additionally requires a verb valency lexicon in VALLEX-XML format for operation.

4.3 Results

Table 5 shows the overall accuracy of CroDep and its accuracy on selected parts of speech. CroDep outperforms the top-performing baseline parser by 2.68% LAS and the difference is shown to be statistically significant. The difference is also indicated graphically by the confidence intervals in Figure 3 (left side), where CroDep is compared to the top-performing graph-based system (second-order Chu-Liu/Edmonds MSTParser) and the top-performing transition-based

metric	Noun	Verb	Adj	Adp	Pro	Adv	overall
LA	85.34	87.89	92.67	98.64	84.38	80.14	88.27 ± 0.30
LAS	80.10	82.85	86.40	71.20	76.04	65.77	77.21 ± 0.59
UAS	90.16	86.84	89.13	71.92	84.84	75.30	83.05 ± 0.50

Table 5: Overall accuracy and accuracy on specific parts of speech for CroDep

metric	Adv	Atr	AuxC	AuxP	Coord	Obj	Pnom	Pred	Sb
LAS	70.69	83.94	69.80	70.59	49.41	83.17	71.46	82.12	85.01
UAS	84.81	88.90	71.53	71.48	50.87	93.12	79.92	86.81	91.35
P(LA)	78.96	91.21	91.96	97.86	89.72	84.12	77.06	84.36	86.78
R(LA)	74.11	90.94	87.77	97.74	81.60	94.75	49.73	97.21	97.50

Table 6: CroDep accuracy on specific syntactic functions

system (MaltParser stack projective). Table 6 shows the CroDep LAS and UAS scores on selected syntactic functions, as well as precision and recall with respect to label attachment for these functions, similar to linear morphosyntactic tagging evaluation. Compared to Table 3 which listed the scores on these syntactic functions for the top-performing baseline parsers, it can be clearly seen that the overall increase of CroDep accuracy by 2.68% LAS on MSTParser is caused by a substantial increase in LAS for predicates, subjects and objects (more than 10.00% LAS for each of the functions). Figure 3 (right side) shows that CroDep also handles long-distance dependencies better than the best baseline parsers and that its footprint is very similar to the one of the graph-based parser.

Conclusion and perspectives

A method is presented for hybrid language-independent dependency parsing by combining data-driven k-best maximum spanning tree parsing and rule-based reranking guided by a verb valency lexicon. It was tested in the form of prototype parser CroDep on the Croatian Dependency Treebank by using the CROVALLEX lexicon of Croatian verbs and it scored 77.21% LAS, topping the top-performing baseline parser by 2.68% LAS. Future work plans include testing the method on other languages, combining CroDep with other parsers and using methods of automatic valency frame extraction to enrich existing resources. Introduction of valency features to standard parsers might be considered. A preliminary experiment with parsing Czech was conducted by using PDT and VALLEX in compliance with the CoNLL 2007 shared task. CroDep scored 80.51% LAS, topping CroDep0 by 1.73% LAS, thus indicating method applicability across languages and outlining the influence of resource properties on method performance. Further research in language-independent k-best spanning tree parsing with valency lexicon reranking is required to support these preliminary results.

Acknowledgments

The presented results were partially obtained from research within project CESAR (ICT-PSP, grant 271022) funded by the European Commission, and partially from research within projects 130-1300646-0645 and 130-1300646-1776 funded by the Ministry of Science, Education and Sports of the Republic of Croatia.

References

Agić Ž, Šojat K, Tadić M. (2010). An Experiment in Verb Valency Frame Extraction from Croatian Dependency Treebank. In *Proceedings of ITI 2010*, Zagreb, SRCE University Computer Centre, University of Zagreb, 2010, pp. 55–60.

Agić Ž. (2012). *Pristupi ovisnosnom parsanju hrvatskih tekstova*. PhD thesis, University of Zagreb, Faculty of Humanities and Social Sciences, 2012.

Ballesteros M, Nivre J. (2012). MaltOptimizer: A System for MaltParser Optimization. In *Proceedings of LREC 2012*, ELRA, 2012.

Berović D, Agić Ž, Tadić M. (2012). Croatian Dependency Treebank: Recent Development and Initial Experiments. In *Proceedings of LREC 2012*, ELRA, 2012, pp. 1902–1906.

Buchholz S, Marsi E. (2006). CoNLL-X Shared Task on Multilingual Dependency Parsing. In *Proceedings of the 10th Conference on Computational Natural Language Learning (CoNLL-X)*, New York, NY, pp. 149–164.

Camerini P M, Fratta L, Maffioli F. (1980). The k-Best Spanning Arborescences of a Network. *Networks*, 10, 1980, pp. 91–110.

Džeroski S, Erjavec T, Ledinek N, Pajas P, Žabokrtský Z, Žele A. (2006). Towards a Slovene Dependency Treebank. In *Proceedings of LREC 2006*, ELRA, 2006.

Federmann C, Giannopoulou I, Girardi C, Hamon O, Mavroeidis D, Minutoli S, Schröder M. (2012). META-SHARE v2: An Open Network of Repositories for Language Resources including Data and Tools. In *Proceedings of LREC 2012*, ELRA, 2012, pp. 3300–3303. See URL http://www.meta-share.eu (accessed 2012-10-27).

Hajič J, Böhmová A, Hajičová E, Vidová Hladká B. (2000). The Prague Dependency Treebank: A Three-Level Annotation Scenario. In *Treebanks: Building and Using Parsed Corpora*, Amsterdam, Kluwer, 2000.

Hall K. (2007). K-Best Spanning Tree Parsing. In *Proceedings of the 45th Annual Meeting of the Association of Computational Linguistics*, 2007, pp. 392–399.

Kübler S, McDonald R, Nivre J. (2009). *Dependency Parsing*. Synthesis Lectures on Human Language Technologies, Morgan&Claypool Publishers, 2009.

Lopatková M, Žabokrtský Z, Skwarska K. (2006). Valency Lexicon of Czech Verbs: Alternation-Based Model. In *Proceedings of LREC 2006*, pp. 1728–1733.

McDonald R, Crammer K, Pereira F. (2005). Online Large-Margin Training of Dependency Parsers. In *Proceedings of the 43rd Annual Meeting of the Association for Computational Linguistics*, ACL, 2005.

McDonald R, Lerman K, Pereira F. (2006). Multilingual Dependency Parsing with a Two-Stage Discriminative Parser. In *Proceedings of the Tenth Conference on Computational Natural Language Learning (CoNLL-X)*, 2006.

Mikelić Preradović N. (2008). *Pristupi izradi strojnog tezaurusa za hrvatski jezik*. PhD thesis, University of Zagreb, Faculty of Humanities and Social Sciences, 2008.

Mikelić Preradović N, Boras D, Kišiček S. (2009). CROVALLEX: Croatian Verb Valence Lexicon. In *Proceedings of ITI 2009*, SRCE, Zagreb, 2009, pp. 533–538.

Nivre J, Nilsson J. (2005). Pseudo-Projective Dependency Parsing. In *Proceedings of the 43rd Annual Meeting of the Association for Computational Linguistics*, ACL, 2005, pp. 99–106.

Nivre J. (2006). *Inductive Dependency Parsing*. Springer, 2006.

Nivre J, Hall J, Kübler S, McDonald R, Nilsson J, Riedel S, Yuret D. (2007). The CoNLL 2007 Shared Task on Dependency Parsing. In *Proceedings of the CoNLL Shared Task of EMNLP-CoNLL 2007*, Prague, Czech Republic, pp. 915–932.

Nivre J, Hall J, Nilsson J, Chanev A, Eryigit G, Küble S, Marinov S, Marsi E. (2007). MaltParser: A Language-Independent System for Data-Driven Dependency Parsing. *Natural Language Engineering*, 13(2), 2007, pp. 95–135.

Nivre J, McDonald R. (2008). Integrating Graph-Based and Transition-Based Dependency Parsers. In *Proceedings of ACL 2008: HLT*, ACL, 2008, pp. 950–958.

Pajas P. (2000). Tree Editor TrEd, Prague Dependency Treebank, Charles University, Prague. See URL http://ufal.mff.cuni.cz/tred/ (accessed 2012-10-27).

Passarotti M, Dell'Orletta F. (2010). Improvements in Parsing the Index Thomisticus Treebank: Revision, Combination and a Feature Model for Medieval Latin. In *Proceedings of LREC 2010*, ELRA, 2010, pp. 1964–1971.

Piperidis S. (2012). The META-SHARE Language Resources Sharing Infrastructure: Principles, Challenges, Solutions. In *Proceedings of LREC 2012*, ELRA, 2012, pp. 36–42. See URL http://www.meta-share.eu (accessed 2012-10-27).

Sagae K, Lavie A. (2006). Parser Combination by Reparsing. In *Proceedings of HLT/NAACL*, 2006.

Sgall P, Hajičová E, Panevová J. (1986). *The Meaning of the Sentence in Its Semantic and Pragmatic Aspects*. Dordrecht, D. Reidel Publishing Company, 1986.

Tadić M. (2002). Building the Croatian National Corpus. In *Proceedings LREC 2002*, ELRA, pp. 441–446.

Tadić M, Fulgosi S. (2003). Building the Croatian Morphological Lexicon. In *Proceedings of the EACL2003 Workshop on Morphological Processing of Slavic Languages*, ACL, 2003, pp. 41–46. See URL http://hml.ffzg.hr (accessed 2012-10-27).

Tadić M. (2007). Building the Croatian Dependency Treebank: The Initial Stages. *Suvremena lingvistika*, 63, pp. 85–92.

Tadić M. (2009). New Version of the Croatian National Corpus. *After Half a Century of Slavonic Natural Language Processing*, Masaryk University, Brno, 2009, pp. 199–205. See URL http://hnk.ffzg.hr (accessed 2012-10-27).

Zeman D. (2002). Can Subcategorization Help a Statistical Dependency Parser? In *Proceedings of COLING 2002*, volume 1, pp. 1–7.

A best-first anagram hashing filter for approximate string matching with generalized edit distance

Malin AHLBERG Gerlof BOUMA
Språkbanken / Department of Swedish
University of Gothenburg
`malin.ahlberg@gu.se, gerlof.bouma@gu.se`

ABSTRACT
This paper presents an efficient method for approximate string matching against a lexicon. We define a filter that for each source word selects a small set of target lexical entries, from which the best match is then selected using generalized edit distance, where edit operations can be assigned an arbitrary weight. The filter combines a specialized hash function with best-first search. Our work extends and improves upon a previously proposed hash-based filter, developed for matching with uniform-weight edit distance. We evaluate an approximate matching system implemented with the new best-first filter, by conducting several experiments on a historical corpus and a set of weighted rules taken from the literature. We present running times and discuss how performance varies using different stopping criteria and target lexica. The results show that the filter is suitable for large rule sets and million word corpora, and encourage further development.

KEYWORDS: Approximate string matching, generalized edit distance, anagram hash, spelling variation, historical corpora.

Proceedings of COLING 2012: Posters, pages 13–22,
COLING 2012, Mumbai, December 2012.

1 Introduction

A common task in text processing is to match tokens in running text to a dictionary, for instance to see if we recognize a token as an existing word or to retrieve further information about the token, like part-of-speech or distributional statistics. Such matching may be approximate: the dictionary entry that we are looking for might use a slightly different spelling than the token at hand. Examples include words containing typos, but also errors introduced by optical character recognition or spelling variation due to the lack of a standardized orthography. Historical corpora, which have gained a lot of interest recently, are an example application where spelling variation is the rule rather than the exception.

A much researched family of approaches to the approximate matching task is based on edit distance, that is, the number of string manipulation operations needed to change a source into a target. For instance, we could count that dictionary entry as a match, whose edit distance from the source token is minimal. If we allow single character insertion, deletion and substitution as edit operations, we end up with the well-known Levenshtein distance. Edit distance calculation is relatively costly, but there is a wide range of literature on efficient algorithms for approximate dictionary matching with Levenshtein and similar distances (Boytsov, 2011, for an overview).

Generalized edit distance refers to a variant in which we allow arbitrary costs for edits. For instance, for processing historical text, we may wish to make the substitution *þ→th* cheaper than *e→th*. The costs can be linguistically motivated, come from empirically estimated probabilities, etcetera. Instead of minimization of the number of operations. the goal is now minimization of the sum of edit costs. In this paper, we propose an adaptation of the *anagram hashing filter* (Reynaert, 2011), an algorithm for efficient matching with the minimum edit distance criterion. Our proposal facilitates approximate matching with minimum *generalized* edit distance. In a short case study on real world material, we highlight different performance aspects of the filter, demonstrate improvement over the original, and show that under reasonable parameter settings our experimental implementation is able to process corpora fast enough for off-line tasks.

2 Anagram hashing

Edit distance calculation with dynamic programming takes time proportional to the product of the source and target lengths. Approximately matching all tokens in a corpus to a fixed lexicon using edit distance is thus potentially very expensive. The naive approach calculates the edit distance for each word in the corpus to each word in the lexicon, which quickly becomes infeasible. To improve this situation, Reynaert (2011) proposes an *anagram hashing filter* to prefilter the lexicon. For each source word, the filter removes target entries that are guaranteed to lie beyond a certain edit distance. Expensive exact calculations then only need to be performed on a small selection of lexical entries. The technique is efficient enough to support spelling correction of multi-million token corpora in a few hours.

The anagram hashing algorithm assigns hash values to strings using a character based function. Characters in the alphabet are assigned an integer value and the hash value of a string is simply the sum of its character values each raised to some predefined constant. Conveniently, edit operations can be performed directly on these hash values: deleting a character means subtracting its hash value from the source's hash value, insertion corresponds to addition and substitution is a combination of both. This carries over to more general operations involving n-grams rather than just single characters. To illustrate, given *kamel* and the substitution *ka* → *ca* we can obtain the anagram hash value of *camel*. We pick 5 as the power constant.

kamel	$11^5 + 1^5 + 13^5 + 5^5 + 12^5$	784302	
ka $\rightarrow$ *ca*	$-(11^5 + 1^5) + (3^5 + 1^5)$	-160808 +	
camel		623494	$(= 3^5 + 1^5 + 13^5 + 5^5 + 12^5)$

Hash values for the target vocabulary and all edit operations are precalculated. Given a source string, the anagram hashing filter then creates all permutations up to a small number of edits. Only target entries whose hash values occur in this set of permutations are submitted for exact edit distance calculation. The anagram hash loses information about the order of characters in a string. Therefore, the actual edit distance between source and candidate target may be higher than estimated by the filter. This optimism is what necessitates performing exact calculations.

In the past, researchers have shown the need for approximate matching with weighted edits (Brill and Moore 2000; Toutanova and Moore 2002 for spelling correction, Hauser et al. 2007; Jurish 2010; Adesam et al. 2012 for historical document processing). As said, we then minimize the sum of edit weights rather than the number of edits. Although these two quantities correlate, there are bound to be divergences. Used in this context, the anagram hashing filter may wrongly exclude good targets when they involve many cheap edits. That is, the filter is no longer optimistic with respect to the exact distance. An approximate solution would be to increase the number of permutations the filter goes through, but given the exponential growth of the permutation set for each added numerical edit, this is ineffective, especially when dealing with thousands of weighted rules.

Given a fixed maximum edit distance and rules that have positive cost, the space of hash permutations that has to be explored is finite but possibly extremely large. A proper adaptation of the anagram hash filter should move information about the cost of each individual edit into the filter, so that as little of this permutation space as possible is explored.

3 Best-first anagram hashing

We incorporate weighted rules into the anagram hashing filter by performing a best-first search of the hash permutation space up to a certain cost cutoff – rather than an exhaustive search of all possible hashes up to a given number of edits – returning a stream of anagram hash permutations of ever increasing cost. The cost estimate is based upon the weights of the substitution rules. As before, this estimate is optimistic. The search stops when the search tree is empty because the cutoff point is reached. Alternatively, we may collect top k lists, in which case we can stop when the cost of the current hash permutation as estimated by the filter is higher than the exact cost of the kth-best match found thus far.

We will assume that all edits have the form of n-gram substitutions (but see Sect. 5). The filter estimates so called *restricted* generalized edit distance (Boytsov, 2011), where substitutions never overlap. Pseudocode for the search algorithm is given in Fig. 1. Three further specifications of the procedure outlined in the preceding paragraph where implemented to constrain search space. These are:

1. Although each vertex in the search tree can have as many children as there are applicable substitution rules, we keep the frontier of active vertices to a minimum by **implicitly binarizing the search tree**. At each iteration, we expand the vertex with the lowest cost. Instead of creating a whole new generation at once, we only add the best child (a conjunctive expansion, lines 8–12 in Fig. 1). In addition, we add the best younger sibling (disjunctive expansion, lines 13–18). Each vertex holds a pointer into the sorted list of

Given an anagram hash H for the input word, a maximal cost C, and an ordered list of substitution rules R with associated hash updates, costs and bitmaps.
Returns a stream of anagram hash permutations of increasing cost.

1 $q \leftarrow$ new priority queue
2 $u \leftarrow \langle \ldots, \text{rule} = \text{after last rule in} R, \ldots \rangle$ (an infertile dummy vertex)
3 $v \leftarrow \langle \text{cost} = 0, \text{hash} = H, \text{bitmaps} = \{0\}, \text{rule} = \text{first rule in} R, \text{parent} = u \rangle$
4 add v to q with priority v_{cost}
5 **while not** q is empty **do**
6 $\quad v \leftarrow$ next item from q
7 $\quad$ **yield** v_{hash} and v_{cost}
8 $\quad$ **if** $r \leftarrow$ next rule from v_{rule} where $v_{\text{cost}} + r_{\text{cost}} \leq C$ and $\exists x \in v_{\text{bitmaps}} y \in r_{\text{bitmaps}} [x \text{ AND } y = 0]$ **then**
9 $\quad\quad$ point v_{rule} at the position in R behind r
10 $\quad\quad w \leftarrow \langle v_{\text{cost}} + r_{\text{cost}}, v_{\text{hash}} + r_{\text{hash}}, \{x \text{ OR } y \mid x \in v_{\text{bitmaps}} \land y \in r_{\text{bitmaps}} \land x \text{ AND } y = 0\}, r, v \rangle$
11 $\quad\quad$ add w to q with priority w_{cost}
12 $\quad$ **end if**
13 $\quad u \leftarrow v_{\text{parent}}$
14 $\quad$ **if** $r \leftarrow$ next rule from u_{rule} where $u_{\text{cost}} + r_{\text{cost}} \leq C$ and $\exists x \in u_{\text{bitmaps}} y \in r_{\text{bitmaps}} [x \text{ AND } y = 0]$ **then**
15 $\quad\quad$ point u_{rule} at the position in R behind r
16 $\quad\quad w \leftarrow \langle u_{\text{cost}} + r_{\text{cost}}, u_{\text{hash}} + r_{\text{hash}}, \{x \text{ OR } y \mid x \in u_{\text{bitmaps}} \land y \in r_{\text{bitmaps}} \land x \text{ AND } y = 0\}, r, u \rangle$
17 $\quad\quad$ add w to q with priority w_{cost}
18 $\quad$ **end if**
19 **end while**

Figure 1: Best first exploration of the anagram hashing search space

rules to know what the next rule to consider is. A fertile vertex is one whose rule pointer is not at the end of the rule list. In order to create siblings, we keep around and update parent vertices for as long as they are fertile.

2. We compact the rule set by **fusing substitutions with identical anagram hash updates.** The same substitution can target several positions in the same source (*e*→*a* in *theatre*), two substitutions may be the same but for unchanged context material (*e*→*a* and *tre*→*tra*), substitutions can be anagrams of each other (*th*→*t*, *ht*→*t*), or two substitutions may accidentally give the same hash update. All such cases are gathered into one effective rule. The associated cost is that of the cheapest constituting substitution, so that substitution fusion does not lead to overestimation of the actual edit distance.

3. We prune the search tree by **keeping track of overlap between substitutions.** In restricted edit distance, substitutions that target the same source characters cannot be combined. Thus, when creating a vertex, we need not consider the more expensive rules that overlap with any of the cheaper rules used for vertex' ancestors. We use bitmaps to record which source characters have been used in the creation of a vertex and to mark the characters appearing in a substitution's left hand side. Substitution fusing means that vertices and rules have sets of bitmaps, which represent disjunctions of substitutions. A rule's overlap with previous substitutions is checked using bitwise AND (line 8 respectively

line 14). Updating the bitmap set uses bitwise OR (line 10 respectively line 16). To illustrate this update (we show strings rather than hashes for readability):

start with *theatre*: {0000000}
apply $e \rightarrow a$: {0010000,0000001} to get *thaatre*, *theatra*: {0010000,0000001}
apply *tre*→*te*: {0000111} to get *thaate*: {0010111}.

When fusing substitutions into one rule, only the most general bitmaps are included in its bitmap set, because they determine its combinatorial possibilities. For instance, putting two substitutions 01100 and 00100 into one rule gives {00100}.[1]

4 Experiments

To get an impression of the effectiveness of the best first anagram hash filter, we performed approximate string matching experiments using a real world data set (Adesam et al., 2012). In total, there are 6045 weighted substitution rules of the form $n \rightarrow m$, where n and m are uni-, bi- or trigrams, possibly of unequal length. The corpus is made up of a collection of Old Swedish texts, comprising 162k types in 3Mln tokens. As lexicon we first use a combination of three Old Swedish dictionaries with 54k entries in total and later the corpus itself.

The approximate matching program is implemented in Python, including the dynamic programming code for the exact edit distance calculations, but excluding the search algorithm given in Fig. 1, which was implemented in Cython (Bradshaw et al.). The experiments ran on a single core of 2.7 Ghz Intel CoreT i7, with 4 GByte of memory running 32-bit Linux. Across experiments, the implementation used about 1GByte at most for the search space.

We used an integer representation of the cost of a vertex during search, corresponding to 6 decimal places precision. This, in combination with the fixed cutoff point and the fact that vertex cost never decreases during the search, allows us to use a very simple implementation of the priority queue based on an array of linked lists. Each index in the array points to the vertices of that cost. Profiling suggests that the filter accounts for 20–60% of running time, depending on the experiment.

We ran the whole corpus against the dictionaries of Old Swedish, with different stopping criteria. The dictionary experiments are summarized in Table 1. Since the substitution costs are in the 0.2–0.9 range, cutoff levels of 1.5 and 2.0 respectively allow matches that require more than just 1 or 2 edits. The number of rules submitted to the filter is fixed by the corpus and the set of substitutions. On average, 194 rules, fused from 450 applicable substitutions, per type were input to the filter.

With cutoff 1.5 and stopping after the best match, matching all 162k types against the 54k entry dictionary takes 106m49s, a throughput of 25 types/s, or 85 tokens/s.[2] The top slice in Table 1 gives the distribution of matches. We find 0.7 matches per type, taking up to 6 edits, but most of them occurring 1 or 2 edits away. On average, the filter produces 21k hash permutations (including possible duplicates), of which an average of 22 hashes (no duplicates) are found in the lexicon's hash table and thus trigger exact edit distance calculation. Looking for the top 3

[1] One might consider doing the same during the search process, for each vertex expansion. Testing has shown that the overhead incurred is too high to increase performance

[2] We matched the corpus by type. To give an impression of speeds when applied to running text, token throughput is calculated by taking the weighted average over per type processing times, with weights corresponding to token occurrences of that type.

	Edits								
	0	1	2	3	4	5	6	7	Total
cutoff 1.5, best match									
#	8887	41020	46173	19279	2216	86	2		117663
%	7.6	34.9	39.2	16.4	1.9	0.1	<.1		
Σ%	7.6	42.4	81.7	98.0	99.9	100.0	100.0		
cutoff 1.5, top 3									
#	8887	81153	140298	67638	7547	258	6		305787
%	2.9	26.5	45.9	22.1	2.5	0.1	<.1		
Σ%	2.9	29.4	75.3	97.4	99.9	100.0	100.0		
cutoff 1.5, full search									
#	8887	129517	1294345	1339331	97440	1826	7		2871353
%	0.3	4.5	45.1	46.6	3.4	<.1	<.1		
Σ%	0.3	4.8	49.9	96.5	99.9	100.0	100.0		
cutoff 2.0, top 3									
#	8887	81199	140388	103580	37492	4035	162	1	375744
%	2.4	21.6	37.4	27.6	10.0	1.1	<.1	<.1	
Σ%	2.4	24.0	61.3	88.9	98.9	100.0	100.0	100.0	

Table 1: Matching against the dictionary with different stopping criteria. Distribution in terms of number of required edits per cutoff. #: counts, %: proportion, Σ%: cumulative proportion.

matches at cutoff 1.5 takes 209m36s (13 types/s, 41 tokens/s). As the second slice in table 1 shows, we now find 1.8 matches per type. The filter returns 32k hash permutations, of which 51 are found in the lexicon's hash table, on average.

We also asked for all matches at cutoff 1.5. Running time now more than doubles to 491m52s, or 5.5 types/s. The filter only accounts for about 1/5th of the running time. The filter creates 46k permutations, of which 219 trigger exact edit distance calculations, on average. These exact calculations dominate running time completely in this experiment and explain the slow down. The impact of the exact calculation cost is most clearly seen in the token throughput, which counter-intuitively is *lower* than the type throughput at 4.4 tokens/s. We can explain this from the high lexical neighbourhood density of short words, which also are frequent words. For instance, for types of length 3 and 4, we submit on average over 500 targets for exact calculation, more than double the total average, even though the number of hash permutations generated is below average for these words.

The distribution of matches for this exhaustive run is in the third slice in Table 1. The exhaustive search finds almost 18 matches per type at this cutoff level. The greater proportion of matches is found at a higher number of edits compared to earlier experiments. This is expected, because there is some correlation between cost and the number of edits. Note that to capture 99% of the matches under cutoff 1.5, an exhaustive run with the original anagram hashing filter would have to examine up to four edits; in the order of $194^4 \approx 1.4 \cdot 10^9$ hash permutations on our rule set. Merely generating this number of permutations would be prohibitively expensive, let alone considering the subset of lexicon matches for exact calculation.

We ran two further experiments with higher cutoff points. First, we looked for the top 3 matches with cutoff 2.0. Processing took 1992m27s, giving a throughput of 1.4 types/s, 7.9 tokens/s – a dramatic slow down compared to the cutoff 1.5, top 3 experiment, considering we only find about 25% more matches (bottom slice, Table 1). The explanation lies in the number of hash permutations returned by the filter, which increased 20-fold to 640k,[3] of which 217 hashes per type are found in the lexicon, on average. At these cost levels, the density of the search space increases as the estimated cost increases. That is, there are many more hash permutations in the 1.5–2.0 range than there are in the 1.0–1.5 range.

Secondly and finally, we used the corpus itself as the vocabulary, to study the impact of a larger lexicon size on performance. There is no direct effect on the filter itself, but we can expect a higher proportion of hash permutations to exist in the lexicon. On the one hand, this will trigger more of the expensive exact calculations. On the other, this also means we may be able to stop earlier on average if we use the top 3 stopping criterion. With cutoff 2.0, top 3,[4] running time shows that the early stopping effect dominates: 823m46s, 3.3 types/s, 30 tokens/s.

We have seen that the best-first anagram hash filter allows us to efficiently search for approximate matches in a fixed vocabulary when the distance function is defined by weighted substitution rules rather than by the number of edit operations. Even in our experimental implementation, which has important bottlenecks in the Python code, we are able to achieve throughput high enough to enable the processing of medium-large corpora using a large rule set. Although the filter itself is fixed by the source string, the number of applicable substitutions and the cutoff point, we note that overall performance is very dependent on the size of, and distribution of items in, the lexicon.

5 Comparison to related work

There is a very rich literature on approximate matching against a fixed vocabulary, but work on approximate matching using edit distance tends to focus on unweighted edits (Boytsov, 2011). We will briefly compare our proposal against the implementations used by the research mentioned in Sect. 2, that motivated the use of generalized edit distance.

As mentioned, in its original form the anagram hashing filter only considers hash permutations within a fixed number of edits, irrespective the weight of the operation. Reynaert (2011), however, does apply a more fine-grained ranking to candidate targets that pass the anagram hashing filter, in a way simulating weighted edits. Although effective in that case, the limits to this approach were explained in Sec.2. Until now, we have focused on substitutions, but like the original anagram hash filter, our best-first adaptation can easily incorporate insertions and deletions. Like with substitutions, the bitmap for deletions (substitution with ϵ) marks the deleted characters as used. The bitmap for insertions would be 0, as they always apply (0 AND $x = 0$) and do not change the source bitmap (0 OR $x = x$).

The spelling correction method presented in Brill and Moore (2000) relies on weighted substitution rules much like the ones we used in our case study. The authors report best-match

[3]The maximum number of examined permutations was 40Mln, incurred for a falsely segmented token. Such false tokens are long and almost guaranteed to lead to a search through the whole space up to the cutoff point as they do not have any suitable matches. As we do not look at the *quality* of the matches in this paper, we have left these pathological cases in.

[4]We ignored the first match, effectively running top 4, since the first and best match is now always the word itself. To compare, only 2.4 of matches against the dictionary are at 0 edits distance (see Table 1, bottom slice).

processing speeds of 20 types/s from an implementation using trie-based precompilation of the lexicon and the weighted substitutions. An interesting aspect to this work is the differential weighting of substitution rules depending on where they apply in the string. A quick way to incorporate this into our setup is to use the lowest weight for a rule in the filter, and differentiate according to position in the exact distance calculation stage.

A more recent proposal using approximate matching with weighted edits is Jurish (2010, and refs. therein). Formally, the matching is defined as a composition of three weighted finite state transducers, representing the input word, the edit operations and the lexicon. Instead of actually compiling the resulting transducer – which would be too resource intensive – cheapest paths through the pipeline are calculated on-line using an adapted Dijkstra-algorithm. The author reports processing speeds of 50 tokens/s for Levenshtein distance-based approximate matching. Considerably faster processing is reported for smaller sets of specialized rewrite rules, although it is unclear how the technique would scale when using a very large rule set like in our experiments. However, a real advantage of representing the vocabulary as an automaton is the ability to handle vocabularies of non-finite size, by modeling productive compounding in the automaton. As far as we can see, an anagram hash filter-based approach is not able to accommodate non-finite target vocabularies.

A well-known application for computer-supported orthographic normalization is VARD2, which employs an ensemble of techniques to match tokens against a fixed vocabulary. The authors also use Levenshtein distance, although they consider it to be too computationally expensive to apply to the whole dictionary (Baron and Rayson, 2009, Sect. 3). As Reynaert's (2011) and our work shows, this need not be the case. Of course, if a hybrid approach improves the accuracy of the automatic normalization, our method could well be part of such an ensemble.

Conclusions

We have presented a best first anagram hashing filter for generalized edit distance matching. The algorithm prefilters a lexicon to narrow down the search for a best match given a set of weighted edit operations. Several experiments have shown the efficiency of the filter and the way it interacts with the rest of the system, such as the size and layout of the lexicon, and parameters setting the maximum cost and the number of matches desired. Even though the system's bottleneck is implemented in Python and we tested using a large rule set, we achieve throughput at reasonable parameter settings good enough for off-line processing of million word corpora. At the most advantageous settings, we are able to process 25 types/s, corresponding to 85 tokens/s. The fact that there are enough opportunities left for easy improvements in running time makes these results especially encouraging.

Algorithmic improvements on the filter itself to be researched include the way dependencies between rules are tracked. As it is, the calculation of the Cartesian product of bitmap sets when checking for rule applicability causes considerable overhead. A further topic for investigation is ways to extend the filter to unrestricted edit distance, so that edits on the source string may feed each other, or, similarly, to allow edits with a context specification that is not formally part of the substitution.

Acknowledgments

This work was carried out in the context of the Center for Language Technology, of Gothenburg University and Chalmers University of Technology. The authors thank Yvonne Adesam for feedback and for collaboration on the Old Swedish data.

References

Adesam, Y., Ahlberg, M., and Bouma, G. (2012). *bokstaffua, bokstaffwa, bokstafwa, bokstaua, bokstawa…* Towards lexical link-up for a corpus of Old Swedish. In Declerck, T., Krenn, B., and Mörth, K., editors, *Proceedings of LTHist 2012*.

Baron, A. and Rayson, P. (2009). Automatic standardisation of texts containing spelling variation: How much training data do you need? In *Proceedings of the Corpus Linguistics Conference*, Lancaster.

Boytsov, L. (2011). Indexing methods for approximate dictionary searching: Comparative analysis. *Journal Experimental Algorithmics*, 16(1):1–91.

Bradshaw, R., Behnel, S., Seljebotn, D. S., Ewing, G., et al. The Cython compiler. Software. `http://cython.org`.

Brill, E. and Moore, R. C. (2000). An improved error model for noisy channel spelling correction. In *Proceedings of the 38th Annual Meeting of the Association for Computational Linguistics*, pages 286–293, Hong Kong. Association for Computational Linguistics.

Hauser, A., Heller, M., Leiss, E., Schulz, K., and Wanzeck, C. (2007). Information access to historical documents from the early new high german period. In *Proceedings of the International Joint Conference on Artificial Intelligence (IJCAI-2007) Workshop on Analytics for Noisy Unstructured Text Data*, Hyderabad, India.

Jurish, B. (2010). Comparing canonicalizations of historical German text. In *Proceedings of the 11th Meeting of the ACL Special Interest Group on Computational Morphology and Phonology*, pages 72–77, Uppsala, Sweden. Association for Computational Linguistics.

Reynaert, M. (2011). Character confusion versus focus word-based correction of spelling and OCR variants in corpora. *International Journal on Document Analysis and Recognition*, 14:173–187. 10.1007/s10032-010-0133-5.

Toutanova, K. and Moore, R. (2002). Pronunciation modeling for improved spelling correction. In *Proceedings of 40th Annual Meeting of the Association for Computational Linguistics*, pages 144–151, Philadelphia, Pennsylvania, USA. Association for Computational Linguistics.

Automatic bilingual phrase extraction from comparable corpora

Ahmet Aker Yang Feng Robert Gaizauskas
University of Sheffield
{ahmet.aker,y.feng, r.gaizauskas}@sheffield.ac.uk

ABSTRACT
In this work we present an approach for extracting parallel phrases from comparable news articles to improve statistical machine translation. This is particularly useful for under-resourced languages where parallel corpora are not readily available. Our approach consists of a phrase pair generator that automatically generates candidate parallel phrases and a binary SVM classifier that classifies the candidate phrase pairs as parallel or non-parallel. The phrase pair generator is also used to automatically create training and testing data for the SVM classifier from parallel corpora. We evaluate our approach using English-German, English-Greek and English-Latvian language pairs. The performance of our classifier on the test sets is above 80% precision and 97% accuracy for all language pairs. We also perform an SMT evaluation by measuring the impact of phrases extracted from comparable corpora on SMT quality using BLEU. For all language pairs we obtain significantly better results compared to the baselines.

KEYWORDS: SMT for under-resourced languages, phrase extraction from comparable corpora.

Proceedings of COLING 2012: Posters, pages 23–32,
COLING 2012, Mumbai, December 2012.

1 Introduction

Statistical machine translation (SMT) relies on the availability of rich parallel resources (corpora). However, in many cases, such as for under-resourced languages or in narrow domains, sufficient parallel resources are not readily available. This leads to machine translation systems under-performing relative to those for better resourced languages and domains. To overcome the scarcity of parallel resources the machine translation community has recognized the potential of using comparable corpora as training data. As a result different methods for extracting parallel sentences or smaller text units such as phrases from comparable corpora have been investigated (Munteanu and Marcu, 2006; Sharoff et al., 2006; Kumano et al., 2007; Marcu and Wong, 2002; Barzilay and McKeown, 2001; Kauchak and Barzilay, 2006; Callison-Burch et al., 2006; Nakov, 2008; Zhao et al., 2008; Marton et al., 2009; Skadiņa et al., 2012; Ion, 2012).

A common idea in this related work is the use of some heuristics to pair target and source phrases. By contrast we approach the task of parallel phrase extraction as a classification task and use feature extraction on the training data to train an SVM classifier to distinguish between parallel and non-parallel phrases. Our method is fully automatic and is essentially a "generate and test" approach. In the generate phase, given source and target language sentences S and T, we first generate all possible phrases of a given length for S and for T and then compute all possible phrase pairings consisting of one phrase from S and one phrase from T. In the test phase we use a binary SVM classifier to determine for each generated phrase pair whether it is or is not parallel. The SVM classifier is trained using phrase pairs taken from parallel data word aligned using Giza++ (Och and Ney, 2000, 2003).

We have tested our approach on the English-German, English-Greek and English-Latvian language pairs. Latvian is an under-resourced language, while for Greek and German text resources are more readily available. Considering all three languages allows us to directly compare our method's performance on resource-rich and under-resourced languages. We perform two different tests. First, we evaluate the performance of the classifier on phrases extracted from held-out parallel data using standard measures such as recall, precision and accuracy. Secondly, we test whether the phrases extracted by our method from comparable corpora lead to improved SMT quality, as measured using BLEU (Papineni et al., 2002) .

Hewavitharana and Vogel (2011) also adopt a classification approach for phrase extraction. However, their approach requires manual intervention in data preparation, whereas we perform the preparation of training and testing data fully automatically. In addition, Hewavitharana and Vogel (2011) do not report any SMT performance evaluation of their approach, so it is difficult to estimate how useful their approach is for the actual task it is meant to improve. We test the impact of our extracted phrases on the performance of an SMT system, which allows us to draw conclusions about the likely utility of our approach for SMT in practice.

In Section 2 we present our phrase pair generation method. In Section 3 we describe our classification approach and list the features used within the classifier. Section 4 describes our experimental set-up and results.

2 Phrase Pair Generation

Phrase pairs are generated under two different conditions. During training of the SVM phrase pair classifier, positive and negative instances of aligned phrase pairs are generated from existing parallel resources for the source and target languages. During testing candidate phrase pairs are generated from arbitrary source and target language sentence pairs.

2.1 Training Example Extraction

We use whatever parallel data is available for a language pair to extract training examples for the SVM classifier. To get positive training examples (parallel phrases), we first align the parallel sentence pairs using the Giza++ toolkit (Och and Ney, 2000, 2003) in both directions and then refine the alignments using a "grow-diag-final-and" strategy. Then, we extract all phrases, as defined in the statistical machine translation literature (Koehn et al., 2003; Och and Ney, 2004; Chiang, 2005), and take these phrases as positive examples.

Let S denote a sentence, S_i the i-th word in S and S_i^j the subsequence of words in S from position i to j. Given a word-aligned sentence pair $\langle S, T\rangle$, $\langle S_i^j, T_{i'}^{j'}\rangle$ is a phrase iff:

- S_k is aligned to $T_{k'}$ for some $k \in [i, j]$ and $k' \in [i', j']$
- S_k is not aligned to $T_{k'}$ for all $k \in [i, j]$ and $k' \notin [i', j']$
- S_k is not aligned to $T_{k'}$ for all $k \notin [i, j]$ and $k' \in [i', j']$

To get negative training examples (non-parallel phrases), for each sentence pair, we enumerate all segments on the source side and on the target side, the length of which falls in the range $[minSrcLen..maxSrcLen]$ and $[minTrgLen..maxTrgLen]$, respectively. Then we pair each source segment with each target segment to get all possible training examples. Next, we leave out the positive examples and label the rest as negative examples.

A training example may be discovered many times during extraction process. We do not keep duplicate occurrences but keep all the training examples unique. As the alignment of the parallel corpus inevitably introduces some errors, we do some processing to remove the noise. For instance, a training example may appear both as a positive example and as a negative example, but in our approach, a training example can only have one label, positive or negative. For a training example, assume the number of occurrences as a positive example is N_p and the number of occurrences as a negative example is N_n. We check the following conditions in order:

- If N_p is smaller than a count threshold τ, then we label this example as negative.
- If the ratio N_n/N_p is below a ratio threshold π, then we label it as positive.

2.2 Test Instance Generation

To generate candidate parallel phrase pairs from unseen comparable text pairs we proceed as follows. First we generate all sentence pairs $\langle S, T\rangle$ where S is from the source language text and T is from the target language text. For each such pair we generate all phrase pairs $\langle s, t\rangle$ where s is a word subsequence of S of length i $minSrcLen \leq i \leq maxSrcLen$ and t is a word subsequence of T of length j, $minTrgLen \leq j \leq maxTrgLen$.

3 SVM Classifier

For classifying phrase pairs as parallel or non-parallel we use an SVM classifier. Within the classifier we use the following features as reported in previous work (Munteanu and Marcu, 2005; Hewavitharana and Vogel, 2011):

- ***lengthDifferenceInChar*** is the difference in number of characters in the source and target phrases. We consider duplicates in the phrases when counting the characters.
- ***lengthDifferenceInWords*** is similar to the first feature but use words instead of characters.
- ***sameEnding*** is *1* if source and target phrase have the same ending otherwise *0*.
- ***numberOfWordsInPhrase*** is number of words in the source phrase.
- ***firstWordTranslationScore*** indicates whether the first word in the source phrase is a translation of the first word in the target phrase. If this is the case, the translation probability is returned.
- ***lastWordTranslationScore*** indicates whether the last word in the source phrase is a translation of the last word in the target phrase. If this is the case, the translation probability is returned.
- ***translationCount*** is number of source phrase words which have translations in the target one.
- ***translationRatio*** is ratio of the count of source phrase words which have translations in the target phrase and the number of words in the source language.

- ***isHalfTranslated*** is *1* if at least half of the source phrase words have translations in the target phrase, otherwise *0*.
- ***longestTranslatedUnit*** is count of words within the longest sequence of words which have all translations in the target phrase.
- ***longestNotTranslatedUnit*** similar to the previous one but considers words which do not have translations.
- ***translationPositionDistance*** captures the distance between the source words positions and the position of their maximum likely translations in the target side. E.g. if the first word in the source phrase is the translation of the first word in the target phrase then they have a translation position distance of *0*. For each word in the source phrase we compute its translation position distance, sum all the distances together and return it.

The first three features are independent of which language is taken as source and which as target. The feature *numberOfWordsInPhrase* is computed once for the source and once for the target phrase. The remaining nine features are direction-dependent and are computed in both directions, reversing which language is taken as the source and which as the target. Thus in total we have 21 features. To perform the translation of phrase words we use GIZA++ dictionaries trained on parallel data (see Section 4.2).

3.1 Cognate-based Methods for Translation Purposes

Dictionaries mostly fail to return translation entries for named entities (NEs) or specialized terminology. Because of this we also use cognate-based methods to perform the mapping between source and target words or vice versa. We only apply the cognate-based methods for the *firstWordTranslationScore* and *lastWordTranslationScore* features. For these two features it is easy to compare the first or the last words from both the source and target phrases. The score of the cognate methods becomes the translation score for the features. We adopt several string similarity measures described in Aswani and Gaizauskas (2010): (1) Longest Common Subsequence Ratio, (2) Longest Common Substring, (3) Dice Similarity, (4) Needleman-Wunsch Distance and (5) Levenshtein Distance. Each of these measures returns a score between 0 and 1. We use a weighted linear combination of the scores to compute the final score. We learn the weights using linear regression over training data consisting of pairs of truely and falsely aligned city names available from Wikipedia[1]. For the truely aligned named entities we assign a score of *1* and for the falsely aligned ones a score of *0*. We take the cognate similarity score as the translation score only if it is above 0.7, a threshold which we set experimentally.

The cognate methods assume that the source and target language strings being compared are drawn from the same character set. However, this is not the case for English and Greek. To be able to apply our cognate-based approach to Greek we first map the Greek characters into English characters and apply the cognate metrics on the mapped characters. To learn the mappings we used a list of Greek-English place name variants[2] and the Giza++ tool. The input to Giza++ is a list of aligned NEs (Greek and English) where each NE is split into single characters. The output of the tool is a dictionary with character mappings. We use these mappings to transliterate a Greek word into English characters and use the transliterated version for the cognate comparison. Note, since GIZA++ lists multiple entries as translation variants we always select the one with the highest probability value.

4 Experiments

4.1 Data Sources

Our experiments involve the English-Greek (EN-EL), English-Latvian (EN-LV) and English-German (EN-DE) language pairs. We train a separate classifier for each language pair. Therefore, for each language pair a data set consisting of parallel phrases is needed to train and test the

[1]http://en.wikipedia.org/wiki/Names_of_European_cities_in_different_languages.

[2]http://en.wikipedia.org/wiki/List_of_Greek_place_names

SVM classifier. A second data source needed for our experiments is comparable corpora for the above mentioned language pairs. From these we generate pairs of phrases and judge them for parallelism using the trained classifier. Finally, the phrases judged as parallel by the classifier are used to attempt to improve a baseline SMT system.

4.1.1 Parallel Corpora

We used the JRC-Acquis[3] parallel corpora to prepare the parallel phrases used to train and test the SVM classifier. For each language pair we split the corpus into two parts: a training set and a test set. The test set contains 10K parallel sentences. The training set contains 99K sentences for EN-DE, 423K for EN-EL and 53K sentences for EN-LV.

4.1.2 Comparable Corpora

We used comparable corpora in English-Greek, English-Latvian and English-German language pairs. These corpora were collected from news articles using a light weight approach that only compares titles and date of publication of two articles to judge them for comparability (Aker et al., 2012). The corpora are aligned at the document level and are detailed in Table 1.

language pair	document pairs	EN sentences	target sentences	EN words	target words
EN-DE	66K	623K	533K	14837K	6769K
EN-EL	122K	1600K	313K	27300K	8258K
EN-LV	87K	1122K	285K	18704K	5356K

Table 1: Size of comparable corpora.

4.2 Phrase Extraction for Classifier Training and Testing

On both parallel training and testing data sets (see Section 4.1.1) we separately applied GIZA++ to obtain the word alignment information used in our parallel phrase extraction method (see Section 2.1). Then we ran the training example extraction method on each data set to extract phrase pairs, setting $minSrcLen = minTrgLen = 2$ and $maxSrcLen = maxTrgLen = 7$. To train the classifier we used 20K parallel and 20K non-parallel phrase pairs extracted from the training data. In testing we used 500 parallel and 10K non-parallel phrase pairs extracted from the testing data. Note that the test set contains substantially more non-parallel than parallel data. This is to simulate the real-world scenario where the data from which parallel phrases have to be extracted will necessarily contain more non-parallel entries than parallel ones. It is also important to note that in both the training and testing parallel phrase extraction steps we used GIZA++ dictionaries obtained from the parallel training data which excludes the 10K parallel sentences used in testing. We did this to ensure that feature extraction is testing is performed using a dictionary that has been built by a process which is blind to the test data.

4.3 Phrase Extraction from Comparable Corpora

We used the comparable corpora described in the previous section and for each language and each aligned document pair we extracted phrase pairs as described above in Section 2.2. As when generating training instances we set $minSrcLen = minTrgLen = 2$ and $maxSrcLen = maxTrgLen = 7$. As in the training and testing steps described in previous section, in feature extraction from the phrase pairs generated from the comparable corpora we used the GIZA++

[3]http://langtech.jrc.it/JRC-Acquis.html

dictionary created from parallel sentences in the training data. Table 2 gives details about the phrases extracted from the comparable corpora.

language pair	analysed sentence pairs	analysed phrase pairs	extracted phrase pairs
EN-DE	39659	852327K	248K
EN-EL	33844K	1499169K	125K
EN-LV	30788K	1919128K	106K

Table 2: Phrase pairs extracted from comparable corpora.

We also ran a performance test to evaluate the speed of parallel phrase extraction. We took 1000 comparable document pairs from the EN-DE data and recorded the time it took to process them. We recorded ~ 44 minutes processing time on a single desktop machine with a 2.4GHz processor and 4GB memory. 99% of the processing time was spent on feature extraction and the remaining 1% for phrase pairing and SVM classifier. Note that since the document pairs are independent from each other, multiple processes could be run in parallel on different sets of document pairs which could significantly reduce processing time.

4.4 Results

To test the performance of our approach we performed two different evaluations: classifier evaluation using Information Retrieval (IR) metrics and SMT performance using BLEU.

4.4.1 Classifier Evaluation

In this evaluation we measure the performance of our classifier using precision, recall, F-measure and accuracy (Manning et al., 2008). Note that we use $F_{0.5}$ which puts more emphasis on precision than recall. We sought to optimize SVM classifier performance for our task by finding the SVM-margin distance boundary that maximizes $F_{0.5}$. During training the SVM classifier determines a maximum margin hyperplane between the positive and negative examples. During classification the distance to this boundary is used to classify instances: any instance that has negative distance ($distance < 0$) to the boundary is treated as a negative example, otherwise as positive ($distance >= 0$). We shift the boundary between negative and positive examples to a new value which maximizes the $F_{0.5}$ metric. To do this we determine the maximal negative and maximal positive distance from the classification results, go from the negative value towards the maximal positive value in increments of 0.1 and record the boundary value that leads to the maximum $F_{0.5}$. To learn the new boundary we used held out training data containing 500 parallel and 10K non-parallel phrases. Note that this held out training data is different from the testing data (see Section 4.1.1) but has the same size. Finally, we run the classifier with the new boundary on the testing data. The results are shown in Table 3.

language pair	recall	precision	$F_{0.5}$-measure	accuracy
EN-DE	45	86	73	97
EN-EL	63	81	77	97
EN-LV	59	84	77	97

Table 3: Classifier's performance on phrases extracted from the test data.

From Table 3 we can see that the classifiers for each language pair perform reasonably well on the testing data. They all achieve an accuracy score above 97%, though note that always picking the majority class (non-parallel) gives 95% accuracy given the deliberate skew in the test data. The precision score obtained from each classifier is above 81% showing good performance in identifying correct parallel phrases. In general the recall scores are low, in the neighborhood of

50%. However, given the potentially very large quantities of comparable text pairs available recall is not a primary concern.

To identify the sources of misclassifications we manually checked the EN-DE phrases from the test set which were classified incorrectly. The first source of problems is due to the existence of productive compounds in German and negatively affects recall. For example, the classifier classifies the following parallel phrases as non-parallel. The features we use within the classifier do not capture morphological elements within compound words and thus fail to match, e.g. *tiergesundheitszeugnisse* with *veterinary certificates* or *umweltkriterien* with *ecological criteria*.

(1) *der tiergesundheitszeugnisse für die — veterinary certificates for the*

(2) *zur festlegung überarbeiteter umweltkriterien — establishing revised ecological criteria*

The second problem is due to feature extraction and causes a decrease in precision. The following phrases are non-parallel examples classified by the classifier as parallel. The reason for the misclassification is that while the words in the English phrase can be entirely mapped to those in the German phrase, the phrases are not parallel because they differ either in the number or in the order of constituents.

(3) *parlaments und des rates zur einführung — the council and the*

(4) *die kommission erstattet dem europäischen parlament und — european parliament and of the council*

In (3) all words of the English phrase have translations in the German phrase (both *the*'s are mapped to *des*, *council* is mapped to *rates* or *parlaments* and *and* is mapped to *und*). In (4) we have a similar picture. The words *european parliament* are mapped to *europäischen parlament*, *and* to *und*, *the* to *die* or *dem* and *council* to *kommision*. The problem arises from the fact that in (3) the English word *council* translates into both German *Rat* and *Parlament*. Thus, two German noun phrases (NPs) are covered by one in English, so that the English phrase is not an adequate translation of the German one. In (4), the problem lies in the order of the constituents which results in the two phrases not being parallel. The English phrase contains a coordination of two NPs, while in the German phrase, the coordinating conjunction *und* is at the end of the phrase and serves to link either the entire phrase or the second NP (*dem europäischen parlament*) to a further constituent not extracted as a part of this phrase.

4.4.2 BLEU Evaluation for SMT

In the BLEU evaluation we tested the impact of the phrases extracted from the comparable corpora on improving the performance of the baseline SMT systems. We trained a baseline decoder for each language pair using the entire JRC-Acquis corpus for that language pair, which consists of the training and test data used for our phrase extraction system. We then injected the extracted phrases[4] into the baseline training data and re-trained a new decoder which we call an *extended* decoder. As SMT test data we used 612 parallel sentences manually generated from news articles. The English and the German sentences have both in total 14K words. The Latvian sentences contain around 13K and the Greek ones 15K words. To construct these test sets we used English as the pivot language. We selected from different news articles 612 English sentences and then manually translated them into German, Greek and Latvian. For each language pair a professional translator was hired to perform the translation. Note that these articles are not included in the comparable corpora summarized in Table 1.

From the results shown in Table 4 we can see that all extended decoders significantly outperform the baseline systems[5]. This shows that the phrases extracted from the comparable corpora are

[4] These phrases are extracted with the SVM margin that maximizes the F-measure, see for details Section 4.4.1

[5] Koehn (2004) reports that increase of 1% in BLEU score is a significant improvement.

language pair	baseline BLEU score	extended BLEU score
EN-DE	15.97	**18.05**
EN-EL	28.30	**29.37**
EN-LV	10.24	**12.23**

Table 4: BLEU scores on the SMT testing data.

indeed of usable quality. In the table we also see that the EN-EL BLEU scores are much higher than the others. We think that this is a result of the large size of the EN-EL parallel training data made available by JRC which we used to train the EN-EL decoder. As described in Section 4.1.1 the EN-EL parallel corpus is more than 4 times bigger than the EN-DE corpus and 8 times bigger than the EN-LV parallel corpus. For the language with least training data Latvian, the classifier still significantly outperforms the baseline. This is an encouraging result which shows that although the amount of parallel data is important for SMT performance, our method for phrase extraction from comparable data provides a viable way to significantly improve SMT performance in cases where parallel data is sparse.

Conclusions

In this paper we presented a fully automated approach to extract parallel phrases from comparable corpora using a classifier. The data used to train the classifier is automatically derived from parallel corpora. We measured the performance of our classifier using IR metrics but also performed an SMT evaluation using BLEU. We performed the evaluations EN-DE, EN-EL and EN-LV language pairs. In the IR evaluation we tested our approach on pairs of phrases extracted automatically from parallel corpora. The results of this evaluation show that our approach is precise and accurate in identifying parallel phrases. The SMT evaluation was performed by comparing the translation performance of two decoders on a set of parallel sentences manually collected from news articles. The first decoder is a baseline system trained on the JRC-Acquis parallel corpus. In the second decoder we again use the same parallel corpus but extend it with phrases extracted from a comparable corpus. The results show that the extended decoder performs significantly better than the baselines for all language pairs.

A number of questions remain for further research. First, how much can SMT system performance be improved using this approach? The number of comparable text pairs available is in principle virtually unlimited; however, it is unlikely indefinite improvements to SMT systems can be made using our approach. But how much improvement can be made? Second, the relation between the amount of parallel data initially available, from which dictionaries are derived and parallel phrase pairs are extracted for training the SVM classifier, and the improvement obtainable through use of our approach needs to be better understood. Second, can we bootstrap? – in particular can we use Giza++ to extract a new dictionary from the original parallel data plus the phrase pairs extracted by our classifier during an initial round of phrase extraction and then use this new dictionary to retrain the classifier? Third, more detailed failure analysis needs to be carried out on all of our test languages as well as an analysis of the role of particular features in the classifier. This should provide insights, such as those mentioned in Section 4.4 above, that may allow performance of the classifier to be improved further.

Acknowledgement

The research reported was funded by the ACCURAT and the TaaS projects, European Union Seventh Framework Programme, grant agreements no. 248347 and 296312 respectively. The authors would like to thank Accurat partners and Trevor Cohn for helpful inputs.

References

Aker, A., Kanoulas, E., and Gaizauskas, R. (2012). A light way to collect comparable corpora from the web. *Proceedings of the 8th International Conference on Language Resources and Evaluation (LREC), Istanbul, Turkey*, pages 21–27.

Aswani, N. and Gaizauskas, R. (2010). English-Hindi transliteration using multiple similarity metrics. In *7th Language Resources and Evaluation Conference (LREC), La Valletta, Malta.*

Barzilay, R. and McKeown, K. R. (2001). Extracting paraphrases from a parallel corpus. In *ACL '01: Proceedings of the 39th Annual Meeting on Association for Computational Linguistics*, pages 50–57, Morristown, NJ, USA. Association for Computational Linguistics.

Callison-Burch, C., Koehn, P., and Osborne, M. (2006). Improved statistical machine translation using paraphrases. In *Proceedings of the main conference on Human Language Technology Conference of the North American Chapter of the Association of Computational Linguistics*, pages 17–24, Morristown, NJ, USA. Association for Computational Linguistics.

Chiang, D. (2005). A hierarchical phrase-based model for statistical machine translation. In *Proceedings of the 43rd Annual Meeting on Association for Computational Linguistics*, pages 263–270. Association for Computational Linguistics.

Hewavitharana, S. and Vogel, S. (2011). Extracting parallel phrases from comparable data. In *Proceedings of the 4th Workshop on Building and Using Comparable Corpora: Comparable Corpora and the Web*, pages 61–68. Association for Computational Linguistics.

Ion, R. (2012). Pexacc: A parallel sentence mining algorithm from comparable corpora. *Proceedings of the 8th International Conference on Language Resources and Evaluation (LREC), Istanbul, Turkey.*

Kauchak, D. and Barzilay, R. (2006). Paraphrasing for automatic evaluation. In *Proceedings of the main conference on Human Language Technology Conference of the North American Chapter of the Association of Computational Linguistics*, pages 455–462, Morristown, NJ, USA. Association for Computational Linguistics.

Koehn, P. (2004). Statistical significance tests for machine translation evaluation. In *Proceedings of EMNLP*, volume 4, pages 388–395.

Koehn, P., Och, F., and Marcu, D. (2003). Statistical phrase-based translation. In *Proceedings of the 2003 Conference of the North American Chapter of the Association for Computational Linguistics on Human Language Technology-Volume 1*, pages 48–54. Association for Computational Linguistics.

Kumano, T., Tanaka, H., and Tokunaga, T. (2007). Extracting phrasal alignments from comparable corpora by using joint probability SMT model. In *Proceedings of the 11th International Conference on Theoretical and Methodological Issues in Machine Translation (TMI-07)*, pages 95–103.

Manning, C., Raghavan, P., and Schutze, H. (2008). *Introduction to information retrieval*, volume 1. Cambridge University Press Cambridge.

Marcu, D. and Wong, W. (2002). A phrase-based, joint probability model for statistical machine translation. In *Proceedings of the ACL-02 conference on Empirical methods in natural language processing*, volume 10, pages 133–139.

Marton, Y., Callison-Burch, C., and Resnik, P. (2009). Improved statistical machine translation using monolingually-derived paraphrases. In *Proceedings of the 2009 Conference on Empirical Methods in Natural Language Processing*, pages 381–390. Association for Computational Linguistics.

Munteanu, D. S. and Marcu, D. (2005). Improving machine translation performance by exploiting non-parallel corpora. *Computational Linguistics*, 31(4):477–504.

Munteanu, D. S. and Marcu, D. (2006). Extracting parallel sub-sentential fragments from non-parallel corpora. In *ACL-44: Proceedings of the 21st International Conference on Computational Linguistics and the 44th annual meeting of the Association for Computational Linguistics*, pages 81–88, Morristown, NJ, USA. Association for Computational Linguistics.

Nakov, P. (2008). Paraphrasing verbs for noun compound interpretation. In *Proc. of the Workshop on Multiword Expressions, LREC-2008.*

Och, F. and Ney, H. (2004). The alignment template approach to statistical machine translation. *Computational Linguistics*, 30(4):417–449.

Och, F. J. and Ney, H. (2000). A comparison of alignment models for statistical machine translation. In *Proceedings of the 18th conference on Computational linguistics*, pages 1086–1090, Morristown, NJ, USA. Association for Computational Linguistics.

Och, F. J. O. and Ney, H. (2003). A systematic comparison of various statistical alignment models. *Computational Linguistics*, 29(1):19–51.

Papineni, K., Roukos, S., Ward, T., and Zhu, W. (2002). BLEU: a method for automatic evaluation of machine translation. In *Proceedings of the 40th annual meeting on association for computational linguistics*, pages 311–318. Association for Computational Linguistics.

Sharoff, S., Babych, B., and Hartley, A. (2006). Using comparable corpora to solve problems difficult for human translators. In *Proceedings of the COLING/ACL on Main conference poster sessions*, pages 739–746, Morristown, NJ, USA. Association for Computational Linguistics.

Skadiņa, I., Aker, A., Mastropavlos, N., Su, F., Tufis, D., Verlic, M., Vasiļjevs, A., Babych, B., Clough, P., Gaizauskas, R., et al. (2012). Collecting and using comparable corpora for statistical machine translation. In *Proceedings of the 8th International Conference on Language Resources and Evaluation (LREC), Istanbul, Turkey.*

Zhao, S., Niu, C., Zhou, M., Liu, T., and Li, S. (2008). Combining multiple resources to improve SMT-based paraphrasing model. In *Proceedings of ACL-08: HLT*, pages 1021–1029, Columbus, Ohio. Association for Computational Linguistics.

A Formalized Reference Grammar for UNL-based Machine Translation between English and Arabic

Sameh Alansary [1,2]
(1) Bibliotheca Alexandrina, Alexandria, Egypt
(2) Faculty of Arts, Department of Phonetics and Linguistics, Alexandria University
El Shatby, Alexandria, Egypt
Sameh.alansary@bibalex.org

ABSTRACT

The Universal Networking Language (UNL) is an artificial language that can replicate human language functions in cyberspace in terms of hyper semantic networks. This paper aims to: a) design a reference grammar capable of dealing with the basic linguistic structures in order to act as a test-bed in automating translation between English and Arabic in both directions through UNL; b) evaluate the current state of the UNL system as an Interlingua in analyzing and generating English and Arabic as far as the reference structures are concerned. A reference parallel corpus of 500 structures was used. Results are promising; precision and recall of analyzing English to UNL (UNLization) are 0.979 and 0.96 respectively, while precision and recall of analyzing Arabic to UNL are 0.98 and 0.96 respectively. Precision and recall of generating English from UNL (NLization) are 0.97 and 0.96 respectively, while precision and recall of generating Arabic from UNL are 0.989 and 0.96 respectively.

KEYWORDS: Reference Grammar, Formal Grammar, Interlingua, UNL, UNL-ization Grammar, NL-ization Grammar, Machine Translation, Universal Networking Language, UNL system.

Proceedings of COLING 2012: Posters, pages 33–42,
COLING 2012, Mumbai, December 2012.

Introduction

While languages differ greatly in their "surface structures", they all share a common "deep structure"; hence came the idea of creating a universal representation capable of conveying this deep structure while enjoying the regularity and predictability natural languages lack. Although interlingua is a promising idea, the number of interlinguas created is still very limited. Examples of well-known interlinguas are DLT (Witkam 2006), UNITRAN (Dorr (1987, 1990) and (Dorr et al. (2004)), KANT (Nyberg and Mitamura (1992), Nyberg et al. (1997)) and UNL (Uchida 1996, Uchida and Zhu (1993, 2005), Alansary et al. (2010)). The first three of these interlinguas lack standardization, however, the fourth, UNL, has succeeded in standardizing its tools, tagset and methodology as well as rely on meaning as an intermediate representation (Alansary 2011). UNL is a kind of mark-up language which represents the core information of a text. The UNDL Foundation, the founder of UNL, has created a wrapper application for development of various UNL tools and applications (Martins 2012, Martins and Avatesyan 2009). All engines, resources and tools are available through the UNLweb (www.unlweb.net) that contains many tools designed for linguists, computational linguists as well as non-professionals. These tools are used in analysing and generating natural languages. IAN, the Interactive ANalyzer, it employs the analysis grammar rules to analyze input and finally generate its corresponding UNL expressions. It operates semi-automatically; word-sense disambiguation is still carried out by a language specialist, nevertheless, the system can filter the candidates using an optional set of disambiguation rules. EUGENE (the dEep-to-sUrface natural language GENErator) is a fully automatic engine, it simply uses the target language grammar rules in order to decode the incoming UNL document and generate it in natural languages. IAN and Eugene use two types of Natural language dictionaries; enumerative and generative. The enumerative dictionary of IAN contains all inflected word forms of a language together with their corresponding Universal Words (concepts) and a set of linguistic features covering different linguistic levels. The generative dictionary, on the other hand, is the same as the 'enumerative' one but it contains all lexemes of language as bases together with a morphological paradigm number that controls the generative morphological behaviour (e.g. agreement and inflected forms) of words in natural language (Martins and Avetisyan 2009). It might be a fact that all languages have classical reference grammars in grammar books. Such a reference grammar maybe defined as a description of the grammar of a language, with explanations of the principles governing the construction of words, phrases, clauses, and sentences. It is designed to give someone a reference tool for looking up specific details of the language. In Natural Language Processing, computers should also learn a language in order to give a comprehensive and objective test-bed that enables us to evaluate, compare and follow up the performance of different grammars. A formalized reference grammar is needed in order to synchronize different languages; the UNL is initiating this idea as it utilizes a standardized environment. The current paper is limited to English and Arabic only; it is organized as follows: Section 1 discusses the design and compilation of the reference corpus. Section 2 discusses the design and implementation of the analysis grammar. Section 3 discusses the design and implementation of the generation grammar. Section 4 evaluates the analysis and generation results in English and Arabic. And finally section 5 is a conclusion and future work.

1 Reference corpus

Corpora are considered essential language resources necessary when building grammars. A reference corpus has been compiled as an experimental English corpus in order to prepare the initial version of analysis and generation grammars. An Arabic parallel Corpus has been compiled by translating the English reference corpus into Arabic, this corpus consists of 500 sentences collected from English grammar books. It is supposed to cover the basic and common linguistic phenomena between all languages that may be encountered in the process of building grammars within the UNL framework such as: temporary entries (e.g. URLs, nonsense words, symbols etc.), words that are not found in the dictionary (a grammar in NLP may face a set of words that might not be found in the dictionary), numerals, determiners, prepositions, conjunctions, noun phrase structures, expressions of time, verb forms, pronouns and sentence structures. The English reference corpus is manually annotated to make a standard version of UNL reference corpus. Both versions; English reference and UNL corpora, are available on the UNL web (http://www.unlweb.net/wiki/Corpus500).The Arabic UNL language centre has translated the English reference corpus into Arabic.

2 Building the UNLization (analysis) Grammar

UNLization is the process of representing the content of a natural language structure using UNL. In order to UNLize any Natural language text, the UNLization (analysis) grammar for that natural language should be, first, developed. The UNLization reference grammars for English and Arabic reference corpora have been already built to represent the content of both corpora. English and Arabic grammars have common modules such as; the tokenization, numeral, attribute, syntactic and syntax-semantic modules; however, the Arabic analysis grammar has an extra module; namely, the transliteration module which was developed in order to transliterate words that are not found in the Arabic Analysis dictionary into Latin characters. The following sub-sections will describe each of the aforementioned modules.

2.1 The Tokenization module

The tokenization algorithm is strictly dictionary-based; the system tries to match the strings of the natural language input against the entries existing in the dictionary. In case it does not succeed, the string is considered a temporary entry. There are no predefined tokens: spaces and punctuation marks have to be inserted in the dictionary in order to be treated as non-temporary entries. The tokenization algorithm goes from left to right trying to match the longest possible string with dictionary entries, and it assigns the feature **TEMP** (temporary) to strings that are not found in the dictionary. For instance, any URL such as "www.undlfoundation.org" should be considered TEMP; however, it is tokenized according to the entries found in the dictionary as [www] [.] [u] [nd] [l] [foundation] [.] [or] [g], which is incorrect since we expect the whole string to be treated as a single temporary entry. In order to avoid that, a disambiguation rule applies to consider any string a single node if followed by blank space or a full stop (is at the end of the sentence). The tokenization algorithm blocks the segmentation of tokens or sequences of tokens prohibited by disambiguation rules. Disambiguation rules are not only responsible for the segmentation of the input, but also responsible for choosing the word senses most appropriate to the context. For instance, "you" have two different realizations in the dictionary; the singular second person pronoun and the plural second person pronoun. In the sentence "you love yourself", disambiguation rules should prevent the choice of the plural pronoun, thus, causing the engine to choose the singular pronoun if the verb is followed by a singular personal possessive pronoun.

2.2 The Numerals Module

Numerals in UNL are temporary UWs and should be represented in UNL as Digits between quotes. There are two cases in Numerals; they may be present in the input as digits in which case the engine will consider them as TEMP automatically, or, they may be written in letters, in the latter case the numerals module is activated. In order to handle numerals in both English and Arabic, both a dictionary and analysis rules are required. The numerals module is part of both the English and Arabic grammars. There are 4 types of numerals to be covered in this module: cardinal, ordinal, partitive and multiplicative. We will examine cardinal numbers first as they constitute the base for other types of numerals. There are many subsets of cardinal numbers such as units, tens, hundreds, thousands, millions...etc. The first step towards analyzing them is compiling a small dictionary that will enable rules to convert numbers in both English and Arabic into digits. Some cardinal numbers will be inserted in the dictionary as is such as the numbers from one to nineteen. Other numbers will be inserted incomplete in the dictionary to be later completed by rules; for example, tens are inserted without their zeros, "twenty" is inserted as "2"....etc. The second step is to develop the required rules; units and numbers from ten to nineteen are retrieved from the dictionary without any modification by rules. Tens starting from the number twenty have two possibilities in analysis: the first is adding tens to units; for instance in the case of "twenty one", "twenty" which is stored in the dictionary as "2' and "one" which is stored as "1" will be joined by a rule and will be treated as a single number "21". The second is not adding tens to units as in "twenty", a zero will be added to "2" and joined together by a rule to become "20". The analysis of partitive numerals depends on their existence in the dictionary. In ordinal and multiplicative numbers; after converting the numbers in letters into digital numbers, an attribute "@ordinal" will be assigned to the number. If the number is followed by the word "times" such as "four times", the attribute "@times" will be assigned to "4"to be "4.@times".

2.3 Attributes module

In UNL, attributes have been used to represent information conveyed by natural language grammatical categories (such as tense, mood, aspect, number, etc). The set of attributes, which is claimed to be universal, is defined in the UNL Specs (http://www.unlweb.net/wiki/Attributes). The attributes module can handle determiners, pronouns, prepositions and verb forms. It is responsible for substituting certain words or morphemes with attributes, as in the case of quantity quantifiers ("a lot of", "several", "few", "all", "any...etc.) which will be deleted and substituted by the attributes "@multal, @paucal, @any, @all ..etc." to be assigned to the following word. In UNL, pronouns are "empty concepts" represented semantically as "00". The person, number and gender of the pronoun are described by UNL attributes.

2.4 Syntactic module

After assigning the necessary attributes, the syntactic module should start drawing the syntactic trees for noun phrases, verb phrases and sentence structures that are part of the corpus, according to the X- bar theory (http://www.unlweb.net/wiki/X-bar_theory). The syntactic modules for Arabic and English grammars both follow the same methodology, thus, the following subsections will present and discuss only English examples since they will be easier to understand. The syntactic module is divided into two phases; the list–to-tree phase and the tree-to-tree phase.

2.4.1 The list-to-tree phase

In this phase, rules are used to parse the tokenized input sentences into a tree structure. It starts by composing small trees for the small phrases in the sentence and then combining these small trees together to form a bigger tree. List-to-tree rules are responsible for building the trees for language structures; ordering of rules is required; rules for building noun phrase trees should be followed by rules for building verb phrase trees. The sentence "he buys books about cars from Paris" after being processed by the attribute module will be "he.@3.@male buy.@present book.@pl about car.@pl from Paris". This sentence has two noun phrases, rules will start to project all nouns and pronouns in the sentence to the intermediate constituent "NB" and link the NBs to form a higher constituent from right to left. "cars" and "Paris" will be firstly linked together under the intermediate constituent "NB" (A decision to link "from Paris" to the nearest head " car " was taken to solve the structural ambiguity concerning the PP attachment " from Paris ".) and projected to the maximal projection NP by linking it to an empty node which will act as the specifier. The preposition "from" between the two NBs will be deleted leaving the semantic feature "frm" to be assigned to "Paris". This feature will help later in the process of linking them with a semantic relation as will be shown in sub-section 2.6. then the NB "book" and the NP "cars from Paris" will be linked together under the bigger intermediate constituent "NB" and the preposition "about" will be deleted leaving the semantic feature "cnt" assigned to the NP "cars from Paris". Then, rules will project the NB "book about cars from Paris" to the maximal projection NP by linking it with an empty node which will act as the specifier, and the NB of the pronoun "he" will also be projected to an NP since a pronoun does not need a specifer, as shown in figure 1.

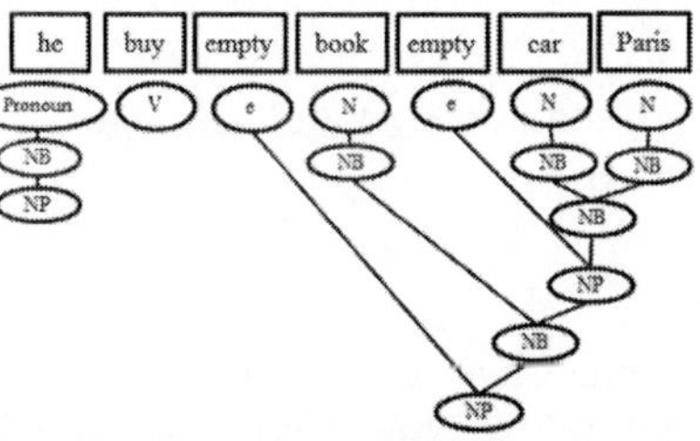

FIGURE1 – The syntactic tree for "books about cars from Paris".

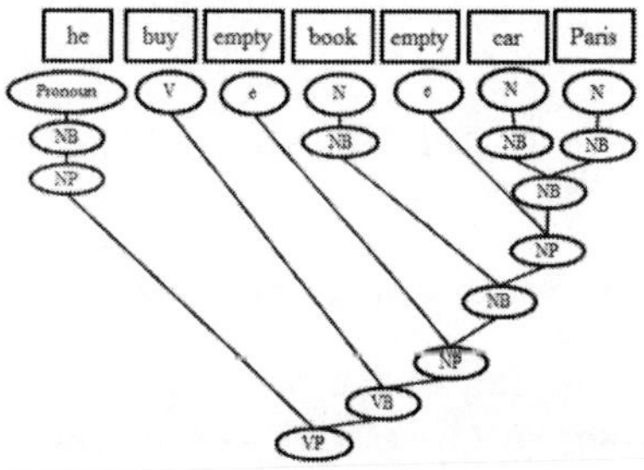

FIGURE2 – The syntactic tree for "he buys books about cars from Paris".

After building the tree of the noun phrase "books about cars from Paris", rules will start to form a bigger tree that contains this noun phrase and the verb "buy" by combining them under the intermediate constituent "VB". The transitive verb "buy" is carrying the feature "TSTD" in the dictionary; this means that it needs two syntactic arguments: a subject which is the doer of the action, and a single direct object. These two arguments are mapped semantically to an agent and an object. The two arguments should be "NPs", thus, the semantic feature "obj" will be assigned to the NP "books about cars from Paris". The biggest tree will be formed by combining the "VB" with the NP "he" under the maximal projection "VP" as in figure 2 and the semantic feature "agt" will be assigned to the pronoun "he".

2.4.2 The tree-to-tree phase

The constituents "NB, NB, NP, VB and VP" will be mapped onto their syntactic roles. The methodology used in this phase is to start decomposing constituents from the biggest to the smallest. Ordering of rules is required; rules for decomposing verb phrase trees should be followed by rules for decomposing noun phrase trees. VP is the last constituent to be composed, hence, it will be the first one to be decomposed. A key assumption of X-bar theory is that branching is always binary, thus, the decomposition of any constituent will affect the tree. A constituent is decomposed into a syntactic role between a node and the head of the adjacent constituent to make the binary relation. In the present example, the decomposition of "VP" will affect the tree; a "VS" or a Verb Specifier relation will be constructed between the verb and the pronoun as shown in figure 3. The second branch to be decomposed is the "VB" which will be decomposed into a Verb Complement relation "VC" constructed between the verb and the head of the NP "book about cars from Paris", "book", as shown in figure 3. After first decomposing the biggest constituents in the tree, the VP and the VB, decomposing the smaller NPs and NBs starts. Because the specifier slot in the noun phrase is empty, the NP syntactic relations between the empty nodes and the NBs will be deleted. The bigger NB "book about cars from Paris" will be decomposed into "book" and the head "cars" of the smaller NB "cars from Paris", and the syntactic relation "NA" or Noun Adjunct will be established between them as shown in figure 4. Finally, the smallest constituent in the tree will be decomposed into the two nouns "car" and "Paris", and the syntactic relation "NA" will be constructed between them as shown in figure 4. The output of the tree-to-tree phase; the four syntactic relations: VS, VC, NA and NA will be the input of the tree to Network phase.

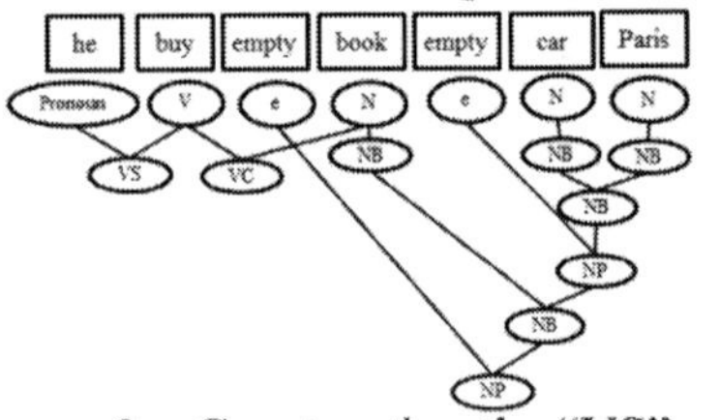

FIGURE3 – Constructing the "VS" and "VC"

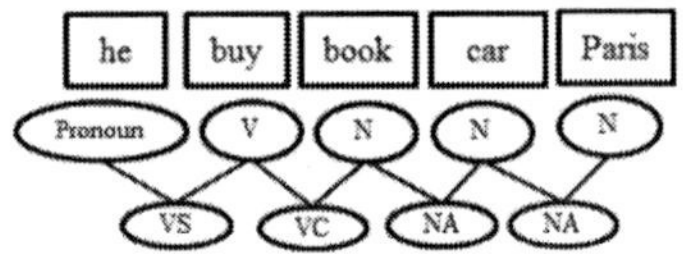

FIGURE4 – Constructing the "NAs"

2.5 Syntax – semantic module

In this module, rules have been built to derive the semantic network from the syntactic graph. Order of rules in this module are not necessary since the semantic features assigned to nodes from the list-to-tree phase (see section 2.4.1) constrain the rules enough to be carried out in their context. In the present example, the output of the tree-to-tree phase will be the input of this module. In this module, the VC, VS, NA and NA will be mapped with their corresponding semantic relations: "obj", "agt", "cnt" and "frm" respectively .

3 Building the NLization (Generation) Grammar

This section discusses the NL-ization of the reference corpus from the interlingua representation (UNL) into both Arabic and English. To achieve this purpose, Arabic and English linguistic resources have been developed. These resources are Arabic and English specialized dictionaries in addition to Arabic and English NL-ization grammars. The process of generation may be seen to some extent as a mirror image of the analysis process; generating well-formed sentences has to pass through a set of grammar modules which are: the semantic-syntactic module, the syntactic module, the attributes module, the numerals module and also a transliteration module that is responsible for to transliterating temporary UWs that are not found in the Arabic generative dictionary into Arabic characters.

3.1 The Semantic-Syntactic Module (Network-to-Tree Phase)

This module is responsible for mapping the semantic relations onto their syntactic equivalents. As an example, the semantic graph generated in section 2.5 representing a verbal phrase requires mapping rules to map the semantic relations agt, obj, cnt, and frm onto their counterpart syntactic relations; Verb specifier (VS), Verb Complement (VC), Noun Adjunct (NA) and another Noun Adjunct (NA) respectively. Moreover, in case the semantic relations "cnt" and "frm" are the counterpart of the syntactic relation noun adjunct (NA), mapping rules should also take into consideration whether the noun adjunct requires a preposition or not. The generated syntactic relations will be processed in the following section 3.2.

3.2 The Syntactic Module

The syntactic module is the second module of the NL-ization grammar, it is responsible for transforming the deep syntactic structure generated from the semantic-syntactic module into a surface syntactic structure. The Syntactic module is divided into two phases; the tree-to-tree phase and the tree-to-list phase. The tree-to-tree phase is responsible for gathering individual syntactic relations and forming higher constituents while the tree-to-list phase is responsible for linearizing the surface tree structure into a list structure. The following two subsections will explain these two phases in more detail.

3.2.1 The tree-to-tree phase

In the tree-to-tree phase, rules are responsible for building the surface syntactic structure of the sentence by building the intermediate constituents (XBs) which are combined to form the maximal projections (XPs) and finally combined to form the sentence structure. For example, the syntactic relations VS, VC, and the two NAs will be combined to form the maximal projection VP according to the schema of X-bar theory. The NA between "كتاب" and " سيارة" will be transformed gradually to the maximal projection NP passing through the intermediate projection NB as shown in figure 5, the second NA between " سيارة" and "باريس" will also become a NP as shown in figure 6. In figure 5, the preposition (P) "عن" was inserted in the tree as the adjunct of the noun "كتاب", "كتاب"in the current example needs a preposition which is predicted by means of the semantic – syntactic module. Similarly, the preposition "من" was inserted in figure 6. The NP in figure 5 is combined with the NP in figure 6 to constitute the complement of the main verb "اشترى" as shown in figure 7.

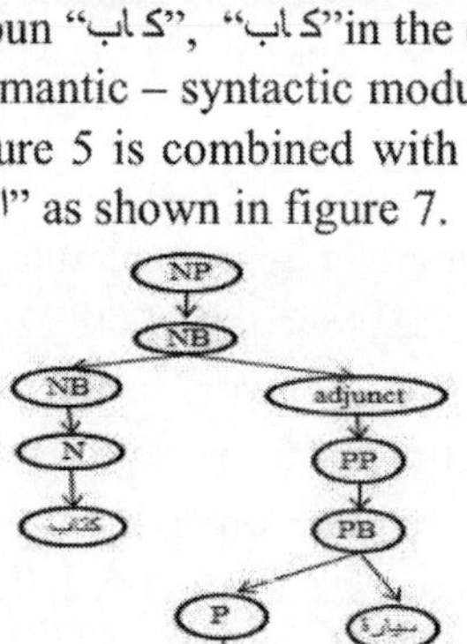

FIGURE 5 – The maximal projection for NA

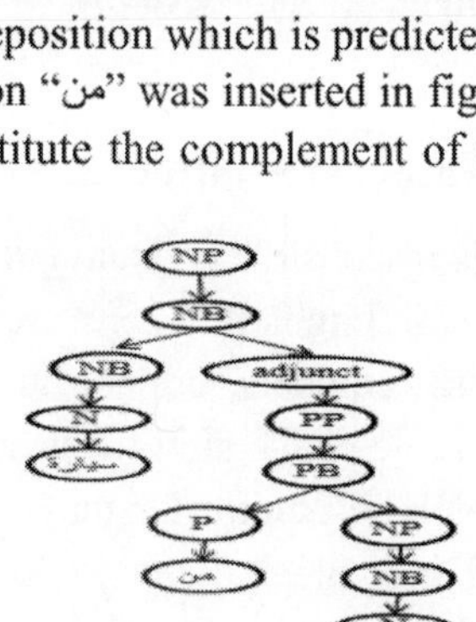

FIGURE 6 – The maximal projection for NA

The verb complement will in turn be combined with the verb "اشترى" to form the intermediate projection VB "اشترى كتاب عن سيارة من باريس". Finally, the resulting VB is combined with the specifier (VS) to build the final maximal projection of the phrase VP as shown in figure 8.

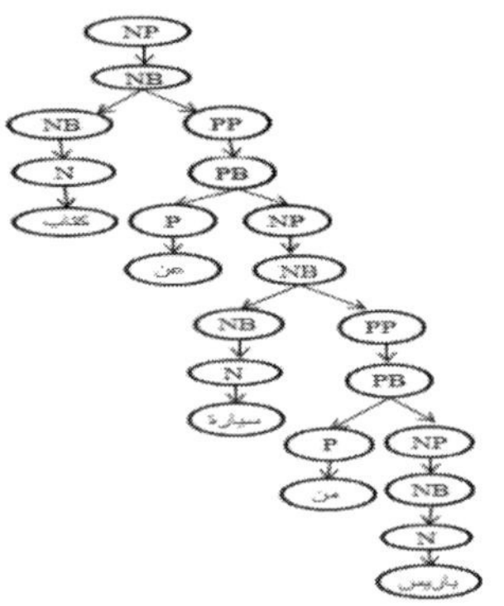

FIGURE 7 – combined the two NPs

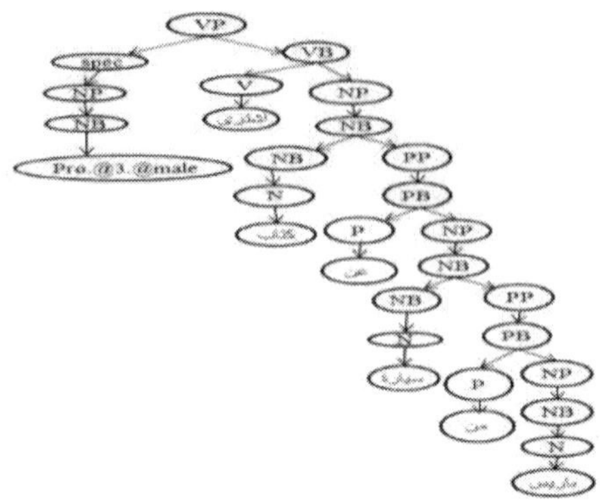

FIGURE 8 – the syntactic tree of the final VP

3.2.2 The tree-to-list phase

In the tree-to-list phase, rules are responsible for transferring the surface syntactic structure into a list structure and also adding the required spaces. Thus, the syntactic tree in figure 8 will be transformed into the natural language list “هو ا رى كـ ب عن السا ارات من باريس”. “كـ ب” and “سا ارات” were generated as plural forms since they carried the attribute “@pl” in the semantic network. Attribute assigning will be discussed in subsection 3.3.

3.3 The Attributes Module

This module is responsible for converting the attributes represented in the interlingua into the suitable natural language words or affixes. For example, pronouns are represented in UNL as "00" nodes along with some attributes to reflect their number, gender....etc. The pronoun in figure 9 will be replaced by “هو”[1] in the list structure as shown in section 3.2.2. Moreover, there are many types of attributes represented in the UNL framework; all are handled during the NLization process. For example, an attribute expressing definiteness such as “@def” will be realized as the prefix “ال”, and an attribute expressing number such as “@pl” may be realized as a suffix such as “ات”.

3.4 The Numeral Module

This module is responsible for converting digital numbers onto their counterpart natural language string (Arabic or English). There are four types of numerals to be covered in the numerals module; cardinal numbers, ordinal numbers, partitive numbers and multiplicatives. For cardinal numbers, the basic conversion mechanism is converting individual digits from (0 to 9) directly onto the counterpart natural language string, and then converting multiple digits by combining the converted individual digits to form bigger numbers. The numerals module handles also ordinals, multiplicatives and partitive numbers.

4. Evaluation

The output of the UNLization process for both Arabic and English languages has been evaluated based on a corpus that is annotated manually semantically in order to figure out the quality and

[1] A decision was taken to generate an overt pronoun to make the structure more explicit.

accuracy of the automatically generated semantic networks. The output of the NLization process has been evaluated based on a manually translated corpus. The F-measure (F1-score) is used to measure of the grammar accuracy, according to the formula: F-measure = 2 x ((precision x recall) / (precision + recall)). Precision measurement of the UNL-ized Arabic sentences was 0.98 while recall measurement was 0.96. Precision measurement of the UNL-ized English sentences was 0.979 while recall measurement was 0.96. Also, the same measurement was applied to figure out the correctness of the automatically generated Arabic and English languages from the UNL-ized documents; the precision measurement of the generated Arabic was 0.989 while recall measurement was 0.96. The precision measurement for the generated English was 0.97 while the recall measurement was 0.96. Accordingly, the F-measure of English-UNL is 0.969, Arabic-UNL is 0.974, UNL-English is 0.964 and UNL-Arabic is 0.974. The values report a very high similarity between the actual output and the expected output.

5 Conclusion and Future Work

This paper presented a formalized reference grammar for analyzing and generating Arabic and English within the UNL framework. The design of the reference grammar depended on linguistic phenomenon common to all languages in order to support the idea of an Interlingua. The evaluation of the current state reflected very high accuracy which can: first, be the base of a more robust system of machine translation; second, a support for other languages in the UNL system in order to synchronize themselves by building parallel corpora and analysis and generation grammars. This would also constitute objective criteria to compare results. UNL as an Interlingua is expected to be used in several different tasks such as text mining, multilingual document generation, summarization, text simplification, information retrieval and extraction, sentiment analysis etc. Future work will be mainly directed to the reference corpus. It is planned to increase the number of structures from 500 to 1000, 5 sentences at least for every structure. Therefore, the minimal number of sentences to be processed in the next stage is expected to be 5000.

References

Alansary, S. (2010). A Practical Application of the UNL+3 Program on the Arabic Language. In Proceedings of the 10th International Conference on Language Engineering, Cairo, Egypt.

Alansary, S. (2011). Interlingua-based Machine Translation Systems: UNL versus Other Interlinguas. In Proceedings of the 11th International Conference on Language Engineering, Cairo, Egypt.

Alansary, S., Nagi, M., Adly, N. (2011). Understanding Natural Language through the UNL Grammar Work-bench , Conference on Human Language Technology for Development (HLTD 2011), Bibliotheca Alexandrina, Alexandria, Egypt.

Alansary, S., Nagi, M., Adly, N. (2010). UNL+3: The Gateway to a Fully Operational UNL System , 10th International Conference on Language Engineering, Ain Shams University, Cairo, Egypt.

AlAnsary, S. (2011), Interlingua-based Machine Translation Systems: UNL versus Other

Interlinguas. 11th International Conference on Language Engineering , Ain Shams University, Cairo, Egypt.

Alansary, S. (2012). A UNL-based approach for building an Arabic computational lexicon, the 8th international conference on informatics and system (infos2012), Cairo, Egypt.

Boitet C. (2002). A rationale for using UNL as an interlingua and more in various domains. Proc. LREC-02 First International Workshop on UNL, other Interlinguas, and their Applications, Las Palmas, 26-31/5/2002, ELRA/ELDA, J. Cardeñosa ed., pp. 23—26.

Dorr, Bonnie J. (1987). UNITRAN: An Interlingua Approach to Machine Translation. Proceedings of the 6th Conference of the American Association of Artificial Intelligence, Seattle, Washington.

Dorr, Bonnie J. (1990). "A cross-linguistic approach to translation". Proceedings of 3rd International Conference on Theoretical and Methodological Issues in Machine Translation of Natural Language, Linguistics Research Center, University of Texas, Texas.

Dorr, Bonnie J., Hovy, E., Levin, L. (2004). Machine Translation: Interlingual Methods, Encyclopedia of Language and Linguistics. 2nd ed., Brown, Keith (ed.).

Nyberg E.H., Mitamura T. (1992). The KANT System: Fast, Accurate, High-Quality Translation in Practical Domains, in Proceedings of the International Conference on Computation Linguistics, (COLING 1992), Nantes, France.

Nyberg E. H., Mitamura T., Carbonell J. (1997). The KANT Machine Translation System: From R&D to Initial Deployment, in Proceedings of LISA (The Library and Information Services in Astronomy) Workshop on Integrating Advanced Translation Technology, Hyatt Regency Crystal City, Washington D.C.

Martins, R., Avetisyan, V. (2009). Generative and Enumerative Lexicons in the UNL Framework, the seventh international conference on computer science and information technologies (CSIT 2009), 28 September – 2 October, 2009, Yerevan, Armenia.

Martins, R. (2012). Le Petit Prince in UNL, the 8th international conference on language resources and evaluation (LREC'12), 23-25 May 2012, Istanbul, Turkey.

Uchida .H , Zhu .M. (2005). UNL2005 for Providing Knowledge Infrastructure, in Proceedings of the Semantic Computing Workshop (SeC2005), Chiba, Japan, 2005

Uchida H., Zhu M., (1993). Interlingua for Multilingual Machine Translation, in Proceedings of the Machine Translation Summit IV, Kobe, Japan.

Uchida H. and M. Zhu (2005). UNL2005 for Providing Knowledge Infrastructure, in Proceedings of the Semantic Computing Workshop (SeC2005), Chiba, Japan.

Uchida H. (1996). UNL: Universal Networking Language – An Electronic Language for Communication, Understanding, and Collaboration, UNU/IAS/UNL Center, Tokyo, Japan.

Witkam T. (2006). History and Heritage of the DLT (Distributed Language Translation) project, Utrecht, The Netherlands: private publication.

Mapping Arabic Wikipedia into the Named Entities Taxonomy

Fahd Alotaibi and Mark Lee
School of Computer Science, University of Birmingham, UK
{fsa081|m.g.lee}@cs.bham.ac.uk

ABSTRACT

This paper describes a comprehensive set of experiments conducted in order to classify Arabic Wikipedia articles into predefined sets of Named Entity classes. We tackle using four different classifiers, namely: Naïve Bayes, Multinomial Naïve Bayes, Support Vector Machines, and Stochastic Gradient Descent. We report on several aspects related to classification models in the sense of feature representation, feature set and statistical modelling. The results reported show that, we are able to correctly classify the articles with scores of 90% on Precision, Recall and balanced F-measure.

KEYWORDS: Arabic Named Entity, Wikipedia, Arabic Document Classification, Supervised Machine Learning.

Proceedings of COLING 2012: Posters, pages 43–52,
COLING 2012, Mumbai, December 2012.

1 Introduction

Relying on supervised machine learning technologies to recognize Named Entities (NE) in the text requires the development of a reasonable volume of data for the training phase. Manually developing a training dataset that goes beyond the news-wire domain is a non-trivial task.

Examination of online and freely available resources, such as the Arabic Wikipedia (AW) offers promise because the underlying scheme of AW can be exploited in order to automatically identify NEs in context. To utilize this resource and develop a NEs corpus from AW means two different tasks should be addressed: 1) Identifying the NEs in the context regardless of assigning those into NEs semantic classes. 2) Classifying AW articles into predefined NEs taxonomy.

The first task has already been addressed in Alotaibi and Lee (2012) where they present a novel approach to identify the NEs in AW by transforming the news-wire domain to facilitate binary NEs classification and to extract contextual and language-specific features, which are then compiled into a classifier.

In this study we investigated the problem of classifying AW articles into NEs categories, exploiting both the Wikipedia-specific format and Arabic language features. We modelled this problem as a document classification task in order to assign each AW article into a particular NEs class. We decided to apply the coarse-grained NEs classes provided by ACE (2008).

After conducting a comprehensive set of experiments, we were able to identify the three-tuples {Feature representation, Features set, Statistical model} for best performance. We found that the 3-tuples {TF-IDF, FF, SGD} gave the highest results with scores of 90% in all metrics.

2 Mapping Wikipedia into NEs Taxonomy

2.1 Selecting Named Entities Classes

For the purpose of this study, we decided to adopt the ACE (2008) taxonomy of named entities for our corpus. However, some ACE (2008) classes required slight amendments in order to be better suited for use in an open domain corpus, such as Wikipedia. For example, we found that there are many articles in Wikipedia related to products and therefore, we decided to add a "Product" class. In addition, we used a "Not-Named-Entity" class to indicate that the article does not reference a named entity.

This procedure resulted in eight coarse-grained classes: Person (PER), Organisation (ORG), Location (LOC), Geo-Political (GPE), Facility (FAC), Vehicle (VEH), Weapon (WEA), Product (PRO) and Not-Named-Entity (NOT).

2.2 Annotation Strategy and Evaluation[1]

Two Arabic native speakers were involved in the annotation process, using the modified NEs taxonomy in Section 2.1. It was decided that a reasonable goal would be to annotate 4,000 documents and the annotators used a self-developed annotation tool to facilitate the annotation process and both annotators were given guidelines, which clearly defined the distinguishing features of each class, including a practical method to pursue the annotation.

[1] The annotated dataset of Arabic Wikipedia articles is freely available at http://www.cs.bham.ac.uk/~fsa081/

The annotators were initially given the first 500 articles to annotate as a training session, in order to evaluate and identify limitations that might then be expected to manifest during the annotation process. It was expected that there would be a lower level of agreement between them in this round. In order to evaluate the inter-annotator agreement between the annotators we used the Kappa Statistic (Carletta, 1996).

The overall annotation task, including the training session, was divided into three cycles to ensure the resolution of any difficulties the annotators might encounter. After each cycle, the Kappa was calculated and reported. Table 1 summarises the results when evaluating the inter-annotator agreement for each coarse-grained level.

Class	Kappa n = 500	Kappa n = 2000	Kappa n = 4000
PER	98	99	99
ORG	76	94	97
LOC	76	92	97
GPE	97	99	99
FAC	54	88	96
VEH	100	100	100
WEA	85	85	99
PRO	91	97	98
NOT	91	98	98

TABLE 1 - Inter-annotator agreement in coarse-grained level.

The percentage of the coverage of the articles referring to named entities in the annotated documents is 74%.

2.3 Features Representation

The features representation affected the way the classification process was modelled in order to classify given Wikipedia articles and to then produce the mapped named entity class for this article; otherwise the article would not relate to a named entity. In this research, we conducted a comprehensive investigation to evaluate different methods of representing features in order to evaluate those most suitable to our task.

- **Term Presence (TP):** For each given document, the feature representation was simply counted by examining the presence of the tokens in the document. There was no consideration given regarding the frequency of the tokens.
- **Term Frequency (TF):** This represents how many times the tokens in our corpus were found in a given document.

  For a given set of documents $D = \{d_1, d_2, \dots, d_n\}$ where n is the number of documents. The term frequency (TF) for a given token (t) is calculated thus

  $$TF(t, D) = \sum_{d \in D} frequency(d, t)$$

- **Term Frequency-Inverse Document Frequency (TF-IDF):** This reveals how important a given token is to a document within the corpus. It involves scaling down the most frequent words across the documents while scaling up rare ones. The (TF-IDF) is then calculated by multiplying the (TF) with the inverse document frequency (IDF) as follows:

$$TF - IDF(t) = TF(t,d) \times IDF(t)$$

where:

$$idf(t) = log \frac{|D|}{1 + |\{d: t \in d\}|}$$

where $|\{d: t \in d\}|$ is the number of documents the term (t) appears in.

2.4 Features Engineering

The nature of AW articles differs compared with traditional newswire documents, as newswire articles have a tendency to be of a particular length and size due to certain externally imposed conditions. This does not apply to AW, and so some articles are very short while others are very long. Therefore, this necessitates a careful extraction of the most useful textual elements of offer a good representation of the article. Moreover, being able to minimise the size of the dataset, while maintaining representation of semantic knowledge can also accelerate the classification running time.

We believe that using complete tokens in articles contributed surplus noisy data to the model. Therefore, we manually investigated several AW articles of different types in order to define appropriate locations. We decided to compile our raw dataset based on four different locations, based on specific aspects of the AW articles. These are the articles title (t), the first sentence (f), category links (c) and infobox parameters (p).

Although the dataset was modelled as a bag-of-words, we were interested in investigating the optimum features set used within this representation, so as to yield the highest performance for our classification model. The feature sets presented below either involve eliminating or augmenting data, i.e. features, which have been defined as either language-dependent or independent:

- **Simple Features (SF):** This represents the raw dataset as a simple bag of words without further processing. The idea in this case is to evaluate the nature of the full word representation of the AW articles in this task.
- **Filtered Features (FF):** In this version, the following heuristic has been applied in order to obtain a filtered version of the dataset:
    1. Removing the punctuation and symbols (none alphabetical tokens).
    2. Filtering stop words.
    3. Normalising digits where each number has been converted into a letter (d). If we have a date such as 1995, this will be normalised to "dddd".
- **Language-dependent Features (LF):** Both Syiam et al. (2006) and El-Halees (2007) report the usefulness of the stem representation of the token, in reference to news-wire corpora. This value would not apply to AW. Therefore, we aimed to investigate the effect of applying shallow morphological processing. We relied on the NLTK::ISRIStemmer package (Bird et al., 2009) which is based on the algorithm proposed by Taghva et al. (2005).
- **Enhanced Language-dependent Features (ELF):** This features set was processed in several steps, which are explained below:

1. Tokenising all tokens within the data set using the AMIRA tokeniser developed by Diab (2009), applying the tokenisation scheme of (Conjunction + Preposition + Prefix) instead of stemming. Tokenisation then revealed valuable information such as (Det) and valuable proclitic data, such as the plural noun phrases in AW articles' categories.
2. Using the same tool to assign the part of speech (POS) for each token would allow filtering of the dataset by involving only nouns (for instance) in the classifier.
3. Isolation of tokens based on their locations: this is a novel idea for representing the dataset. The intent in this case being to isolate similar tokens, which appear in different locations on a given document. The intuition behind this is that some tokens that appear in a particular location, i.e. title, first sentence, categories and infobox, of the AW articles, are more discriminative in certain location rather than the whole article. The idea with isolation would be to attach to each token an identifier, i.e. (t) for title, (f) for first sentence, (c) for category and (i) for infobox, to act as a header based on the location in which the token appears. The results of the isolation process are shown in Figure 1.

t_القوات t_الجوية t_المصرية
f_القوات f_الجوية f_المصرية f_هي f_فرع f_الطيران f_العسكري f_في f_القوات f_المسلحة f_المصرية f_.
c_القوات c_الجوية c_المصرية c_الطيران c_في c_مصر c_قوات c_جوية c_عربية
i_الاسم i_صورة i_عنوان i_الصورة i_تاريخ i_الإنشاء i_الدولة

Figure 1: The isolated representation of the article titled "Egyptian Air Force"

In this case example, the feature representation of the token (المصرية /AlmSryħ/ 'The Egyptian')[2] presented in the first sentence does not affect, and is not affected by, the same token in the category links or title, even though they have identical glyphs. Surprisingly, the implementation of this idea contributed significant improvements to the classification process.

4. For term presence (TP) only, we applied the most informative features for the top 1000 informative features. To calculate the most informative features we used a Chi Square test (Yang and Pedersen, 1997).

3 Experimentation and Results:

We conducted the experiments by splitting the annotated dataset into training and test sets of 80% and 20% respectively. To the best of our knowledge, there is no similar comparable work for the target language and dataset; therefore we will instead analyse our findings as comprising a comparative study of several properties.

The experiment was designed to evaluate three factors; the features representation, features sets and the probabilistic models. Therefore we extensively use this 3-touple representation to facilitate analysis of the results.

Several text classifiers were applied in order to evaluate performance: Naïve Bayes (NB), Multinomial Naïve Bayes (MNB), and Support Vector Machine (SVM). Since we expected to

[2] Throughout this paper and where appropriate, Arabic words are represented in three variants: (Arabic word /HSB transliteration scheme (Habash et al., 2007)/ 'English translation')

have a sparse representation of the features, we examined the Stochastic Gradient Descent (SGD) classifier (Bottou, 1991). Moreover, we were not aware of the possibility of applying this classifier to Arabic textual data previously. The experimentation was conducted relying on both Scikit-learn (Pedregosa et al. 2011) and NLTK (Bird et al., 2009).

Since the traditional Naïve Byes classifier relies on term presence we started by evaluating those factors alone. The following table presents the features sets used, in conjunction with three standard metrics, i.e. Precision, Recall and balanced F-measure.

Classifier	Features set	precision	Recall	f1-score
NB	SF	0.60	0.54	0.56
	FF	**0.62**	0.62	0.62
	LF	0.59	0.69	0.63
	ELF	**0.62**	**0.81**	**0.70**

TABLE 2 - The classification results when using Naive Bayes across different features sets where (TP) is applied

Although both FF and ELF have scored identical points, ELF shows significant improvements in the recall and F-measure. This gives the impression that, the enhanced features, i.e. ELF, have boosted the model so as to recall more documents. Table 3 shows the result when applying the remaining classifiers in the case of the TF as the feature representing the backbone.

Features set	MNB			SGD			SVM		
	P	R	F	P	R	F	P	R	F
SF	0.82	0.82	0.81	0.81	0.79	0.77	0.86	**0.87**	0.86
FF	0.82	0.82	0.82	0.87	0.87	0.87	**0.87**	0.86	0.86
LF	0.77	0.76	0.76	0.83	0.83	0.83	0.83	0.83	0.83
ELF	**0.88**	**0.88**	**0.88**	**0.88**	**0.88**	**0.88**	**0.87**	**0.87**	**0.87**

TABLE 3 - The classification results using MNB, SGD and SVM over different features sets where (TF) is applied

The tuples {TF, ELF, SGD} and {TF, ELF, MNB} achieved the best result of all the metrics. It is also shown that, MNB has been affected by the feature set used, as it performs slightly better than NB, where LF was used. {TF, SF, SVM} has proven to perform very well by merely using a simple features set. An important point to notice is that, using ELF leads to the highest performance across all classifiers. However, relying on stemming only, as with LF illustrates that there are no such improvements when comparing with other features sets, with the exception of SGD. The results of applying TF-IDF for features representation are shown in Table 4.

Features set	MNB			SGD			SVM		
	P	R	F	P	R	F	P	R	F
SF	0.85	0.85	0.85	0.89	0.89	0.89	0.89	**0.89**	**0.89**
FF	0.86	0.86	0.85	**0.9**	**0.9**	**0.9**	**0.9**	**0.89**	**0.89**
LF	0.79	0.78	0.78	0.86	0.86	0.86	0.85	0.85	0.85
ELF	**0.88**	**0.88**	**0.88**	0.89	0.89	0.89	0.89	0.89	**0.89**

TABLE 4 - The classification results when using MNB, SGD and SVM over different features sets where (TF-IDF) is applied

In the main, all classifiers showed improvements; although this was not the case with {TF-IDF, ELF, MNB} despite MNB scoring better compared with reliance on TF for other features sets. The tuple {TF-IDF, FF, SGD} outperforms all other models where this shows the ability for SGD to generalise the optimum model in order to achieve the highest performance. {TF-IDF, FF, SVM} scored 0.9 on precision, while slightly missing one point on both the recall and F-measures.

4 Discussion:

It was proven that carefully selecting the 3-tuple i.e. {Feature representation, Features set, Statistical model}, yields significant benefits in the sense of overall performance. This can be achieved, in this study, by empirically evaluating the effects of each tuple. Otherwise, closely inspecting the dataset is mandatory but this seems unfeasible in most practical applications.

We have demonstrated that it is possible to achieve a high level performance by compiling parts of the raw dataset as explained in Section 2.4; it is therefore beneficial in minimising the running time of the whole classification process. We doubt, however, if similar heuristics would be valid over a news-wire based corpus.

Due to the nature of AW, it is evident that TP is not the right choice for feature representation. To understand this point, see Figure 1 where the words (القوات /AlqwAt/ 'The Troop') and (قوات /qwAt/ 'Troop') have been repeated four and two times respectively. Meanwhile, (TF) and (TF-IDF) representation have exploited the redundancy of tokens and showed dramatic improvements of all features and sets.

Language-dependent features have the tendency to cause different affects. Shallow morphological analysis of tokens, i.e. stemming, show no further improvements across features representation and classifiers. Unlike stemming, tokenisation and filtering the analysis POS of the type "Nouns" is superior.

5 Related Work

An early contribution to Arabic NER was made by Maloney and Niv (1998). This involved a combination of a morphological analyser and a pattern recognition engine, the former being responsible for identifying the start and the end of a token, and the latter for identifying the corresponding pattern applied.

Abuleil (2004) developed an NE tagger for QA systems. The aim of this being to eventually acquire a database of names by utilising keywords and specific verbs to identify potential NE. Once this was achieved a directed graph could then be used to delineate the relationship between words contextualised in phrases. Finally, the verification step is accomplished by applying rules to the names.

Shaalan and Raza (2007) compiled a large lexicon list dedicated to personal names forming a gazetteer, extracted from different resources. The gazetteer contained over 472000 entries, including first, middle and last names, job titles and country names. They applied a regular expression rule to identify the availability of personal names in the selected context. Given that Arabic is a highly inflectional language and has relatively free word ordering, designing generic hand-crafted rules is challenging. Traboulsi (2009) partially utilised contextual clues to identify personal names, by identifying reporting verbs as keywords preceding a personal name. Building a reasonably large gazetteer requires, in addition to time and effort, various additional resources to assure a wide coverage of entities. Elsebai et al. (2009) took a different approach; merging parts of speech with manually created keywords and heuristic rules, without using a gazetteer.

A slightly wider granular NER was later proposed by Shaalan and Raza (2009), with the ability to identify ten different types of named entities. This extended the work of Shaalan and Raza (2007), which relied on gazetteers and lists of rules derived from large resources. A disambiguation method was used to resolve the inevitability of lexical overlap.

Four different machine learning methods have been utilised: Maximum Entropy (Benajiba and Rosso, 2007), Structured Perceptrons (Farber et al., 2008), Support Vector Machines (Benajiba et al., 2008) and Conditional Random Fields (AbdelRahman et al., 2010). It is difficult to judge which approach is the most effective, as the results are inevitably affected by the set of features used. Thus, researchers tend to empirically test different sets of features using various approaches, aiming to achieve an optimum result, for instance as in the work of Benajiba et al. (2008).

In terms of detecting named entities and delimiting their boundaries in Arabic Wikipedia, the work presented by Attia et al. (2010) relies on multilingual interlinks by utilising capitalisation as well as a specific set of heuristics. Recently, Mohit et al. (2012) developed a semi-supervised approach to detect named entities in the Arabic Wikipedia. A self-training algorithm combined with cost function was presented to solve the issue regarding low recall when training on out of domain data. Alotaibi and Lee (2012) presented an approach to identify the NEs in AW. The idea is centred on transforming the news-wire domain for binary NEs detection. A CRF sequence model has been used in order to perform the classification.

Dakka and Cucerzan (2008) presented the first work in which Wikipedia was exploited for a NE task. Their goal was to classify Wikipedia articles into traditional NE semantic classes. For this purpose a set of 800 random articles was manually annotated in order for use with the classifier. Naïve Bayes and the Support Vector Machine (SVM) were chosen as the statistical interface exploiting a specific set of features; such as bag-of-words, structured data, unigram and bigram context. Recently, Saleh et al. (2010) proposed a similar approach to classifying multilingual Wikipedia articles into traditional NE classes. The assumption in that case was that most Wikipedia articles relate to a named entity. Therefore, sets of structured and unstructured data have been extracted so as to be used as a features set when using a support vector machine. Among these features are bag-of-words, category links and infobox attributes. Thus multilingual links are exploited in order to map classified articles for different languages.

6 Conclusion

In the study detailed in this paper we tackled the problem of mapping Arabic Wikipedia articles into a predefined set of NEs classes. We modelled this problem as a document classification issue and comprehensive experiments were empirically conducted in order to evaluate several properties concerning the classification task. Despite our prior assumptions, the use of enhanced language-dependent features did not always lead the best performance especially when combined with the TDF-IDF statistic. More generally we showed that automatic named entity classification can be done on the Arabic Wikipedia with reasonable accuracy.

References

AbdelRahman, S., Elarnaoty, M., Magdy, M., and Fahmy, A. (2010). Integrated machine learning techniques for Arabic named entity recognition. IJCSI International Journal of Computer Science, 7(4):27–36.

Abuleil, S. (2004). Extracting names from Arabic text for question-answering systems. In Proceedings of Coupling Approaches, Coupling Media and Coupling Languages for Information Retrieval (RIAO 2004), pages 638–647, Avignon, France.

ACE (2008). Ace (automatic content extraction) English annotation guidelines for entities. [accessed 12 June 2012].

Alotaibi, F. and Lee, M. (2012). Using Wikipedia as a resource for Arabic named entity recognition. pages 27–34, Rabat, Morocco. In Proceeding of the 4th International Conference on Arabic Language Processing (CITALA12).

Attia, M., Toral, A., Tounsi, L., Monachini, M., and van Genabith, J. (2010). An automatically built named entity lexicon for Arabic. In Proceedings of the Seventh conference on International Language Resources and Evaluation (LREC10), Valletta, Malta. European Language Resources Association (ELRA).

Benajiba, Y., Diab, M., and Rosso, P. (2008). Arabic named entity recognition: An svm-based approach. In Proceedings of 2008 Arab International Conference on Information Technology (ACIT), pages 16–18, Amman, Jordan. Association of Arab Universities.

Benajiba, Y. and Rosso, P. (2007). Anersys 2.0: Conquering the NER task for the Arabic language by combining the maximum entropy with POS-tag information. In Proceedings of the Workshop on Natural Language-Independent Engineering, 3rd Indian Int. Conf. on Artificial Intelligence, IICAI-2007, Pune, India.

Bird, S., Klein, E., and Loper, E. (2009). Natural language processing with Python. O'Reilly Media.

Bottou, L. (1991). Stochastic gradient learning in neural networks. Proceedings of Neuro-*Nımes*, 91.

Carletta, J. (1996). Assessing agreement on classification tasks: the kappa statistic. Computational linguistics, 22(2):249–254.

Dakka, W. and Cucerzan, S. (2008). Augmenting Wikipedia with named entity tags. In

Proceedings of the 3rd International Joint Conference on Natural Language Processing, pages 545–552, Hyderabad, India. Asian Federation of Natural Language Processing.

Diab, M. (2009). Second generation AMIRA tools for Arabic processing: Fast and robust tokenization, POS tagging, and base phrase chunking. In 2nd International Conference on Arabic Language Resources and Tools.

El-Halees, A. (2007). Arabic text classification using maximum entropy. The Islamic University Journal (Series of Natural Studies and Engineering) Vol, 15:157–167.

Elsebai, A., Meziane, F., and Belkredim, F. Z. (2009). A rule based persons names Arabic extraction system. Communications of the IBIMA, 11(6):53–59.

Farber, B., Freitag, D., Habash, N., and Rambow, O. (2008). Improving NER in Arabic using a morphological tagger. In Proceedings of the Sixth International Language Resources and *Evaluation (LREC'08)*, pages 2509–2514, Marrakech, Morocco. European Language Resources Association (ELRA).

Habash, N., Soudi, A., and Buckwalter, T. (2007) On Arabic Transliteration. In A. van den Bosch and A. Soudi, editors, Arabic Computational Morphology: Knowledge-based and Empirical Methods. Springer.

Maloney, J. and Niv, M. (1998). Tagarab, a fast, accurate Arabic name recognizer using high-precision morphological analysis. In Proceedings of the Workshop on Computational Approaches to Semitic Languages, pages 8–15, Montreal, Quebec, Canada. Association for Computational Linguistics.

Mohit, B., Schneider, N., Bhowmick, R., Oflazer, K., and Smith, N. (2012). Recall-oriented learning of named entities in Arabic Wikipedia. In Proceedings of the 13th Conference of the European Chapter of the Association for Computational Linguistics (EACL 2012), pages 162–173. Citeseer.

Pedregosa, F., Varoquaux, G., Gramfort, A., Michel, V., Thirion, B., Grisel, O., Blondel, M., Prettenhofer, P., Weiss, R., Dubourg, V., Vanderplas, J., Passos, A., Cournapeau, D., Brucher, M., Perrot, M. and Duchesnay, E. (2011) Scikit-learn: Machine Learning in Python. Journal of Machine Learning Research, 12:2825-2830.

Saleh, I., Darwish, K., and Fahmy, A. (2010). Classifying Wikipedia articles into NE's using SVM's with threshold adjustment. In Proceedings of the 2010 Named Entities Workshop, pages 85–92, Uppsala, Sweden. Association for Computational Linguistics.

Shaalan, K. and Raza, H. (2007). Person name entity recognition for Arabic. In Proceedings of the 2007 Workshop on Computational Approaches to Semitic Languages: Common Issues and Resources, pages 17–24, Prague, Czech Republic. Association for Computational Linguistics.

Shaalan, K. and Raza, H. (2009). NERA: Named entity recognition for Arabic. Journal of the American Society for Information Science and Technology, 60:1652–1663.

Syiam, M., Fayed, Z., and Habib, M. (2006). An intelligent system for Arabic text categorization. International Journal of Intelligent Computing and Information Sciences, 6(1):1–19.

Taghva, K., Elkhoury, R., and Coombs, J. (2005). Arabic stemming without a root dictionary. In Information Technology: Coding and Computing, 2005. ITCC 2005. International Conference on, volume 1, pages 152–157. IEEE.

Traboulsi, H. (2009). Arabic named entity extraction: A local grammar-based approach. In Proceedings of the 2009 International Multiconference on Computer Science and Information Technology (IMCSIT 2009), pages 139–143, Mragowo, Polland.

Yang, Y. and Pedersen, J. (1997). A comparative study on feature selection in text categorization. In Machine Learning-International Workshop Then Conference, pages 412–420. Morgan Kaufmann Publishers, INC.

Probabilistic Refinement Algorithms for the Generation of Referring Expressions

Romina Altamirano[1] *Carlos Areces*[1,2] *Luciana Benotti*[1]
(1) FaMAF, Universidad Nacional de Córdoba, Argentina
(2) Consejo Nacional de Investigaciones Científicas y Técnicas, Argentina
{ialtamir,areces,benotti}@famaf.unc.edu.ar

ABSTRACT
We propose an algorithm for the generation of referring expressions (REs) that adapts the approach of Areces et al. (2008, 2011) to include overspecification and probabilities learned from corpora. After introducing the algorithm, we discuss how probabilities required as input can be computed for any given domain for which a suitable corpus of REs is available, and how the probabilities can be adjusted for new scenes in the domain using a machine learning approach. We exemplify how to compute probabilities over the GRE3D7 corpus of Viethen (2011). The resulting algorithm is able to generate different referring expressions for the same target with a frequency similar to that observed in corpora. We empirically evaluate the new algorithm over the GRE3D7 corpus, and show that the probability distribution of the generated referring expressions matches the one found in the corpus with high accuracy.

KEYWORDS: Generation of referring expressions, refinement algorithms, machine-learning.

Proceedings of COLING 2012: Posters, pages 53–62,
COLING 2012, Mumbai, December 2012.

1 Generation of referring expressions

In linguistics, a *referring expression* (RE) is an expression that unequivocally identifies the intended target to the interlocutor, from a set of possible distractors. The generation of referring expressions (GRE) is a key task of most natural language generation (NLG) systems (Reiter and Dale, 2000, Section 5.4). Depending on the information available to the NLG system, certain objects might not be associated with an identifier which can be easily recognized by the user. In those cases, the system will have to generate a, possibly complex, description that contains enough information so that the interlocutor will be able to identify the intended referent.

The generation of referring expressions is a well developed field in automated natural language generation. Building upon GRE foundational work (Winograd, 1972; Dale, 1989; Dale and Reiter, 1995), various proposals have investigated the generation of different kinds of referring expressions such as relational expressions ("the blue ball next to the cube" (Dale and Haddock, 1991)), reference to sets ("the two small cubes" (Stone, 2000)), or more expressive logical connectives ("the blue ball not on top of the cube" (van Deemter, 2002)). REs involving relations, in particular, have received increasing attention recently. However, the classical algorithm by Dale and Haddock (1991) was shown to be unable to generate satisfying REs in practice (see the analysis over the *cabinet corpus* in (Viethen and Dale, 2006)). Furthermore, the Dale and Haddock algorithm and many of its successors (such as (Kelleher and Kruijff, 2006)) are vulnerable to the problem of *infinite regress*, where the algorithm enters an infinite loop, jumping back and forth between descriptions for two related individuals, as in "the book on the table which supports a book on the table ..."

Areces et al. (2008, 2011) have proposed low complexity algorithms for the generation of relational REs that eliminate the risk of infinite regression. These algorithms are based on variations of the partition refinement algorithms of Paige and Tarjan (1987). The information provided by a given scene is interpreted as a relational model whose objects are classified into sets that fit the same description. This classification is successively *refined* till the target is the only element fitting the description of its class. The existence of an RE depends on the information available in the input scene, and on the expressive power of the formal language used to describe elements of the different classes in the refinement. Refinement algorithms effectively compute REs for all individuals in the domain, at the same time. The algorithms always terminate returning a formula of the formal language chosen that uniquely describes the target (if the formal language is expressive enough to identify the target in the input model). Refinement algorithms require an ordered list of properties that can be used to described the objects in the scene, and the naturalness of the generated REs strongly depends on this ordering. The goal of this paper is twofold. First we show how we can add non-determinism and overspecification to the refinement algorithms, by replacing the fixed ordering over properties of the input scene by a *probability of use* for each property, and modifying the algorithm accordingly. In this way, each call to the algorithm can produce different REs for the same input scene and target. We will then show that given suitable corpora of REs (like the GRE3D7 corpora discussed in (Viethen, 2011)) we can estimate these probabilities of use so that REs are generated with a probability distribution that matches the one found in corpora.

2 Adding non-determinism and overspecification

Refinement algorithms for GRE are based on the following basic idea: given a scene S, the objects appearing in S are successively classified according to their properties into finer and finer classes. A description (in some formal language $\mathscr{L}$) of each class is computed every time a class is refined. The procedure always stops when the set of classes stabilizes, i.e., no further refinement is possible with the information available in the scene[1]. If the target element is in a singleton class, then the formal description of that class is a referring expression; otherwise the target cannot be unequivocally described (in $\mathscr{L}$).

We present a modification of the algorithm in (Areces et al., 2008) where the fixed order of properties in the input scene is replaced by a finite probability distribution. The resulting algorithm (see Figure 3) is now non-deterministic: two runs of the algorithm with the same input might result in different REs for objects in the scene. The input to the algorithm will be a relational model $\mathscr{M} = \langle \Delta, \| \cdot \| \rangle$, where Δ is the non-empty domain of objects in the scene, and $\| \cdot \|$ is an interpretation function that assigns to all properties in the scene its intended extension. For example, the scene shown in Figure 1 could be represented by the model $\mathscr{M} = \langle \Delta, \| \cdot \| \rangle$ shown in Figure 2; where $\Delta = \{e_1, \ldots, e_7\}$, and $\|green\|$, for example, is $\{e_3, e_4, e_6\}$.

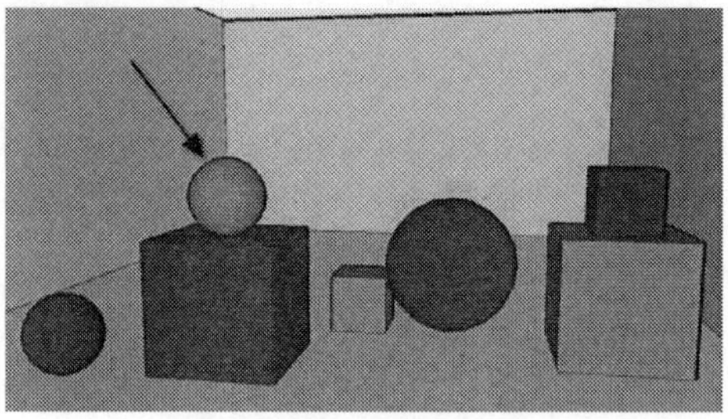

Figure 1: Input scene

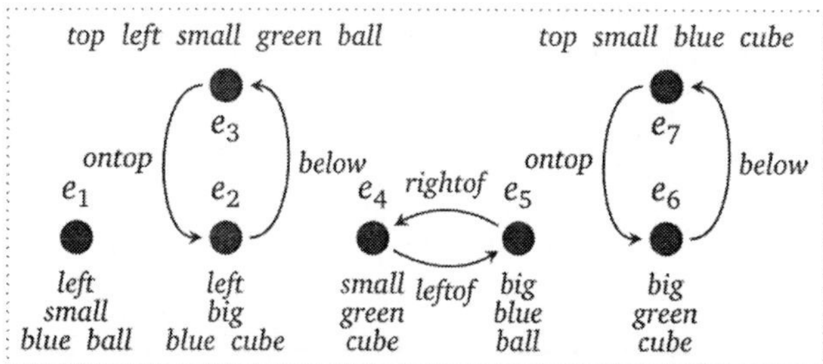

Figure 2: Scene as a relational model

On termination, the algorithm computes what are called the $\mathscr{L}$-similarity classes of the input model $\mathscr{M}$. Intuitively, if two elements in the model belong to the same $\mathscr{L}$-similarity class, then $\mathscr{L}$ is not expressive enough to tell them appart (i.e, no formula in $\mathscr{L}$ can distinguish them).

The algorithm we discuss uses formulas of the $\mathscr{EL}$ description logic language (Baader et al., 2003) to describe refinement classes[2]. The interpretation of the $\mathscr{EL}$ formula $\psi \sqcap \exists R.\varphi$ is the set of all elements that satisfy ψ and that are related by relation R to some element that satisfy φ.

Algorithm 1 takes as input a model and a list Rs of pairs (R,R.p_{use}) that links each relation R $\in$ REL, the set of all relation symbols in the model, to some probability of use R.p_{use}. The set RE will contain the formal description of the refinement classes and it is initialized by the most general description $\top$. For each R, we first compute R.rnd_{use}, a random number in [0,1]. If R.$rnd_{use} \leq$ R.p_{use} then we will use R to refine the set of classes. The value of R.p_{use} will be incremented by R.inc_{use} in each main loop, to ensure that all relations are, at some point, considered by the algorithm. This ensures that a referring expression will be found if it exists; but gives higher probability to expressions using relations with a high R.p_{use}. While RE contains descriptions that can be refined (i.e., classes with at least two elements) we will call the refinement function $add_{\mathscr{L}}$(R,φ,RE) successively with each relation in Rs. A change in one of the classes, can trigger changes in others. For that reason, if RE changes, we exit the **for** loop to start again with the relations of higher R.p_{use}. If after trying to refine the set with all relations in Rs, the set RE has not changed, then we have reached a stable state (i.e., the classes described in RE cannot be further refined with the current R.p_{use} values). We will then increment all

[1]Of course, if we are only interested in a referring expression for a given target we can stop the procedure as soon as the target is the only element of some of the classes.

[2]Notice, though, that the particular formal language used is independent of the main algorithm, and different $add_{\mathscr{L}}$(R,φ,RE) functions can be used depending on the language involved.

```
Algorithm 1: Computing ℒ-similarity classes
Input: A model ℳ and a list Rs ∈ (REL × [0,1])* of relation symbols with their p_use values, ordered by p_use
Output: A set of formulas RE such that {‖φ‖ | φ ∈ RE} is the set of ℒ-similarity classes of ℳ
RE ← {⊤}          // the most general description ⊤ applies to all elements in the scene
for (R,R.p_use) ∈ Rs do
    R.rnd_use = Random(0,1)                     // R.rnd_use is the probability of using R
    R.inc_use = (1 − R.p_use) / MaxIterations   // R.p_use are incremented by R.inc_use in each loop

repeat
    while ∃(φ ∈ RE).(#‖φ‖ > 1) do          // while some class has at least two elements
        RE' ← RE                            // make a copy for future comparison
        for (R, R.p_use) ∈ Rs do
            if R.rnd_use ≤ R.p_use then          // R will be used in the expression
                for φ ∈ RE do add_ℰℒ(R, φ, RE)     // refine all classes using R

            if RE ≠ RE' then                // the classification has changed
                exit                        // exit for-loop to try again highest R.p_use

        if RE = RE' then                    // the classification has stabilized
            exit                            // exit while-loop to increase R.p_use

    for (R,R.p_use) ∈ Rs do R.p_use ← R.p_use + R.inc_use     // increase R.p_use
until ∀((R,R.p_use) ∈ Rs).(R.p_use ≥ 1)          // R.p_use are incremented until they reach 1
```

```
Algorithm 2: add_ℰℒ(R, φ, RE)
if FirstLoop? then                          // are we in the first loop?
    Informative ← TRUE                      // allow overspecification

else Informative ← ‖ψ ⊓ ∃R.φ‖ ≠ ‖ψ‖;        // informative: smaller than the original?
for ψ ∈ RE with #‖ψ‖ > 1 do
    if ψ ⊓ ∃R.φ is not subsumed in RE and   // non-redundant: can't be obtained from RE?
      ‖ψ ⊓ ∃R.φ‖ ≠ ∅ and                    // non-trivial: has elements?
      Informative then
        add ψ ⊓ ∃R.φ to RE                  // add the new class to the classification
        remove subsumed formulas from RE    // remove redundant classes
```

Figure 3: Refinement algorithm with probabilities and overspecification for the $\mathcal{EL}$-language

the R.p_{use} values and start the procedure again. Algorithm 2 almost coincides with the one in (Areces et al., 2008). The **for** loop will refine each descriptions in RE using the relation R and the other descriptions already in RE, under certain conditions. The new description should be *non-redundant* (it cannot be obtained from classes already in RE), *non-trivial* (it is not empty), and *informative* (it does not coincide with the original class). If these conditions are met, the new description is added to RE, and redundant descriptions created by the new description are eliminated. The **if** statement at the beginning of Algorithm 2 disregards the informativity test during the first loop of the algorithm allowing overspecification.

3 Learning to describe new objects from corpora

The algorithm presented in the previous section assumes that each relation R used in a referring expression has a known probability of use R.p_{use}. In this section, we describe how to learn these probabilities from corpora. We use the GRE3D7 corpus to illustrate our learning set up.

The REs in the corpus were produced by 294 participants, each producing 16 referring expressions for 16 scenes. In this way, 140 descriptions for 32 different scenes were obtained, resulting in a corpus of 4480 REs describing a target in a 3D scene containing seven objects. Each description was elicited in the absence of a preceding discourse. A sample scene is shown in Figure 1 (the target is marked with an arrow). For more details on the corpus see (Viethen, 2011, Chapter 5). Importantly for our purposes, the corpus not only contains propositional REs (as other benchmark corpora in the area, e.g., (Gatt et al., 2008)) but also relational REs naturally produced by people. For example, the RE "small ball on top of cube" is used to describe the target in Figure 1. As our algorithm is one of the few that can generate relational REs in an efficient and reliable way, a corpus of relational REs is needed to test its full potential. It is worth mentioning that, although people only used 16 propositional properties and 4 relational properties in their REs, and converged to between 10 and 30 different descriptions of the same target, the possible different correct *relational REs* for a generation algorithm are in the order of several hundred. Hence, reproducing the corpus distribution is a complex task.

We calculate R.p_{use} values for each training scene in the corpus in the following way. First, we use the REs in the corpus C to define the relational model $\mathcal{M}$ used by the algorithm. Then we calculate the value of p_{use} for each relation R in the model as the percentage of REs in which the relation appears. I.e., R.p_{use}= (# of REs in C in which R appears)/(# of REs in C). The values R.p_{use} obtained in this way should be interpreted as the probability of using R to describe the target in model $\mathcal{M}$, and we could argue that they are correlated to the *saliency* of R in the scene. For that reason, for example, in the scene in Figure 1 the value of *ball*.p_{use} is 1, while the value of *cube*.p_{use} is 0.178. These probabilities will not be useful to describe different targets in different scenes. We will now see how we can use them to obtain values for new targets and scenes using a machine learning approach.

We selected eight different scenes for testing from the GRE3D7 corpus, and for each, we used the rest of the corpus for training. We used linear regression (Hall et al., 2009) to learn a function estimating the value of p_{use} for each relation in the domain. We used simple, domain independent features that can be extracted automatically from the relational model:

target-has(R)	:= true if the target is in R
#relations	:= number of relations the target is in
#bin-relations	:= number of the binary relations the target is in
landmark-has(R)	:= true if a landmark (i.e., an object directly related to the target) is in R
discrimination(R)	:= 1 divided the number of objects in the model that are in R

Despite its simplicity, the functions obtained by linear regression are able to learn interesting characteristics of the domain. E.g., they correctly model that the saliency of a color depends strongly on whether the target object is of that color, and it does not depend on its discrimination power in the model. They also correctly predict that the *ontop* relation is used more frequently than the horizontal relations (*leftof* and *rightof*), as reported in (Viethen, 2011). Interestingly, they also indicate a characteristic of the GRE3D7 corpus not mentioned in previous work: size is more frequently used for overspecification when the target and landmark have the same size (it is used in overspecified REs in 49% of the descriptions for scenes where target and landmark have the same size, and only 25% of the time when target and landmark have different size).

4 Evaluation

We present a quantitative evaluation of the algorithm proposed. In particular, we show that the probabilistic refinement algorithm with overspecification is able to generate a distribution of REs similar to that observed in corpora. We discuss in detail the experiments we run for the

Referring Expressions	Corpus		Algorithm		Accuracy
	#Cor	%Cor	#Alg	%Alg	%Acc
ball,green	91	65.00	6376	63.76	63.76
ball,green,small	23	16.43	3440	34.40	16.43
ball,green,small,on-top(blue,cube,large)	8	5.71	0	0.00	0.00
ball,green,on-top(blue,cube)	5	3.57	0	0.00	0.00
ball,green,on-top(blue,cube,large)	5	3.57	0	0.00	0.00
ball,green,small,on-top(blue,cube)	2	1.43	0	0.00	0.00
ball,on-top(cube)	1	0.71	27	0.27	0.27
ball,green,small,on-top(blue,cube,large,left)	1	0.71	0	0.00	0.00
ball,small,on-top(cube,large)	1	0.71	2	0.02	0.02
ball,green,top	1	0.71	0	0.00	0.00
ball,small,on-top(cube)	1	0.71	3	0.03	0.03
ball,green,on-top(cube)	1	0.71	0	0.00	0.00
ball,front,green	0	0.00	97	0.97	0.00
ball,front,green,small	0	0.00	13	0.13	0.00
ball,front,top	0	0.00	12	0.12	0.00
ball,green,left	0	0.00	11	0.11	0.00
ball,top	0	0.00	10	0.10	0.00
ball,green,left,small	0	0.00	5	0.05	0.00
ball,left,top	0	0.00	2	0.02	0.00
ball,small,top	0	0.00	1	0.01	0.00
ball,front,on-top(cube,left)	0	0.00	1	0.01	0.00
Total	140	100.00	10000	100	80.51

Table 1: REs in the corpus and those produced by our algorithm for Figure 1

scene shown in Figure 1 (Scene 3 in the GRE3D7 corpus), then summarize the results for the other seven scenes we used for testing.

Using p_{use} learned as described in Section 3 and running our algorithm 10000 times, we obtain 14 different referring expressions for Figure 1. It is already interesting to see that with the p_{use} values learned from the corpus the algorithm generates only a small set of RE with a high probability. Of these 14 different REs, 5 are the most frequent REs found in the corpus of 140 REs associated to the Scene; indeed, 98% of the utterances generated by the algorithm for this scene appear in the corpus. The remaining 9 REs generated by the algorithm, not present in the corpora, are very natural as can be observed in Table 1. The table lists the REs in the corpus and the REs generated by the algorithm using the learned p_{use}. For each RE, we indicate the number of times it appears in the corpus (#Cor), the proportion it represents (%Cor), the number of times it is generated by our algorithm (#Alg) and the proportion it represents (%Alg). Finally, the accuracy (%Acc) column compares the REs in the corpus with the REs generated by the algorithm. The accuracy is the proportion of perfect matches between the algorithm output and the human REs from the corpus. The accuracy metric has been used in previous work for comparing the output of an RE generation algorithm with the REs found in corpora (van der Sluis et al., 2007; Viethen, 2011) and it is considered a strict comparison metric for this task.

To put our results in perspective we compare in Table 2 our algorithm with a number of possible variations. All numbers shown in the table represent accuracy with the corresponding corpus. The first column shows the values obtained when we run the algorithm over the scene with the values of p_{use} obtained *from the scene itself*. As we could expect, this column has the highest average accuracy. The second column shows the results of the algorithm runs with p_{use} learned

	Scene p_{use}	Learned p_{use}	Random p_{use}	Uniform p_{use}
Scene 1	85.75%	84.49%	17.95%	5.37%
Scene 3	82.81%	80.51%	9.89%	4.40%
Scene 6	90.11%	83.30%	4.13%	4.16%
Scene 8	86.52%	64.06%	16.32%	9.75%
Scene 10	89.49%	75.80%	7.56%	3.70%
Scene 12	80.21%	81.29%	57.09%	6.68%
Scene 13	89.98%	50.79%	9.30%	3.59%
Scene 21	92.13%	80.01%	8.45%	6.77%
Average	87.13%	75.03%	16.34%	5.55%

Table 2: Accuracy between the REs in the corpus and those generated using p_{use} values computed from the scene, machine learned, random and uniform.

from corpora as explained in Section 3. In most cases the accuracy is rather high and the average accuracy is still high. The relatively low accuracy obtained in Scene 13 is explained mostly by the poor estimation of the p_{use} value for the *large* relation. In the corpus, relations *small* and *large* are used much more when the target cannot be uniquely identified using taxonomical (*ball* and *cube*) and absolute (*green* and *blue*) properties, but the features we used for machine learning do not capture such dependencies. In spite of this limitation, the average of the second column is 75%, indicating that p_{use} values learned from the corpus are good enough to be used to generate REs for new scenes from the domain. The last two columns can be considered as baselines. In the first one we generate random values for p_{use}. The accuracy obtained is in most cases poor, but with a noticeable variation due to chance. In addition to poor accuracy, when random p_{use} values were used many of the generated REs where unnaturally sounding like "small on the top of a blue cube that is below of something that is small." In the last column we present the accuracy for an artificial run, where all the REs generated in any of the previous columns were assigned the same probability.

We also computed the entropy of the probability distribution of REs found in the corpus, and the cross-entropy between the corpus distribution of REs and the execution of each algorithm we just described (see (Jurafsky and Martin, 2008) for details on cross-entropy evaluation). Figure 4 shows the results for the eight scenes we are considering. The cross-entropies from the first two runs (*scene* and *learned*) are, in general, much closer to the corpus entropy than *random*'s and *uniform*'s cross-entropies, and to each other. Only in Scene 12 *random* approaches, by chance, the other two.

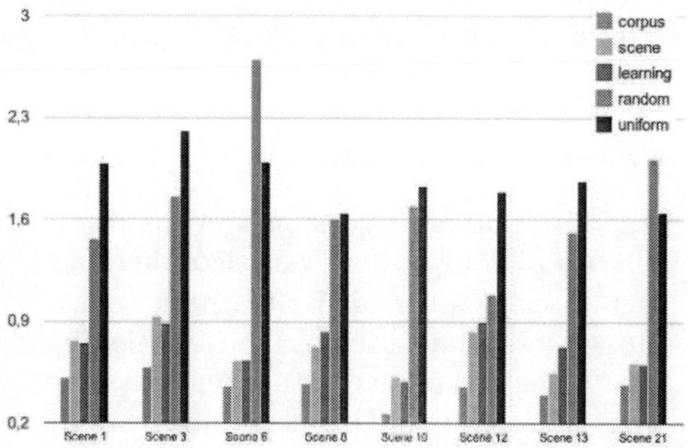

Figure 4: Cross-entropy between the corpus distribution and different runs of the algorithm

5 Discussion and Conclusions

We extend Areces et al. (2008) algorithm to generate REs similar to those produced by humans. The modifications we proposed are based on two observations. First, it has been argued that no fixed ordering of properties is able to generate all REs produced by humans and, second, humans frequently overspecify their REs (Engelhardt et al., 2006; Arts et al., 2011; Viethen, 2011). We tested the proposed algorithm on the GRE3D7 corpus and found that it is able to generate a large proportion of the overspecified REs found in the corpus without generating trivially redundant referring expressions. Viethen (2011) trains decision trees that achieve 65% average accuracy on the GRE3D7 corpus. This approach is able to generate overspecified relational descriptions, but they might fail to be referring expressions. Indeed, because the method does not verify the extension of the generated expression over a model of the scene, the generated descriptions might not uniquely identify the target. As we have already discussed, our algorithm ensures termination and it always finds a referring expression if one exists. Moreover, it achieves an average of 75% of accuracy over the 8 scenes used in our tests.

Different algorithms for the generation of overspecified referring expressions have been recently proposed (de Lucena and Paraboni, 2008; Ruud et al., 2012). To our knowledge, they have not been evaluated on the GRE3D7 corpus and, hence, comparison is difficult. de Lucena and Paraboni (2008) and Ruud et al. (2012) algorithms have been evaluated on the TUNA-AR corpus (Gatt et al., 2008) where they have achieved a 33% and 40% accuracy respectively. As the TUNA-AR corpus includes only propositional REs, it would be interesting future work to evaluate how these algorithms perform in corpora with relational REs such as GRE3D7.

The way we introduce overspecification is inspired by the work of Keysar et al. (1998) on egocentrism and natural language production. Keysar et al. argue that when producing language, considering hearers point of view is not done from the outset but it is rather an afterthought; adult speakers produce REs egocentrically, just like children do, but then adjust REs so that the addressee is able to identify the target unequivocally. The first, egocentric, step is a heuristic process based in a model of saliency of the scene that contains the target. Our definition of p_{use} is intended to capture the saliences of the properties for different scenes and targets. The p_{use} of a relation changes according to the scene. This is in contrast with previous work where the saliency of a property is constant in a domain. Keysar et al. argue that the reason for this generate-and-adjust procedure may have to do with information processing limitations of the mind: if the heuristic that guides the egocentric phase is well tunned, it succeeds with a suitable RE in most cases and seldom requires adjustments. Interestingly, we observe a similar behavior with our algorithm: when p_{use} values learned from the domain are used, the algorithm is not only more accurate but also much faster than when using random p_{use}values.

Besides testing our algorithm over the rest of the scenes in the GRE3D7 corpus, as future work we plan to evaluate our algorithm on more complex domains like those provided by Open Domain Folksonomies (Pacheco et al., 2012). We will also explore corpora obtained through interaction such as the GIVE Corpus (Gargett et al., 2010) where it is common to observe multi shot REs. Under time pressure, subjects will first produce an underspecified expression that includes salient properties of the target (e.g., "the red button"). And then, in a following utterance, they add additional properties (e.g., "to the left of the lamp") to make the expression a proper RE identifying the target uniquely. The source code and the documentation for the algorithm are distributed under the GNU Lesser GPL and can be obtained at `http://code.google.com/p/bisimulation-gre`.

Acknowledgments. This work was partially supported by grants ANPCyT-PICT-2008-306, ANPCyT-PICT-2010-688, the FP7-PEOPLE-2011-IRSES Project "Mobility between Europe and Argentina applying Logics to Systems" (MEALS) and the Laboratoire Internationale Associé "INFINIS".

References

Areces, C., Figueira, S., and Gorín, D. (2011). Using logic in the generation of referring expressions. In Pogodalla, S. and Prost, J., editors, *Proceedings of the 6th International Conference on Logical Aspects of Computational Linguistics (LACL 2011)*, volume 6736 of *Lecture Notes in Computer Science*, pages 17–32, Montpelier. Springer.

Areces, C., Koller, A., and Striegnitz, K. (2008). Referring expressions as formulas of description logic. In *Proceedings of the 5th International Natural Language Generation Conference (INLG'08)*, pages 42–49, Morristown, NJ, USA. Association for Computational Linguistics.

Arts, A., Maes, A., Noordman, L., and Jansen, C. (2011). Overspecification facilitates object identification. *Journal of Pragmatics*, 43(1):361–374.

Baader, F., McGuiness, D., Nardi, D., and Patel-Schneider, P., editors (2003). *The Description Logic Handbook: Theory, implementation and applications*. Cambridge University Press.

Dale, R. (1989). Cooking up referring expressions. In *Proceedings of the 27th annual meeting on Association for Computational Linguistics*, pages 68–75.

Dale, R. and Haddock, N. (1991). Generating referring expressions involving relations. In *Proceedings of the 5th conference of the European chapter of the Association for Computational Linguistics (EACL'91)*, pages 161–166.

Dale, R. and Reiter, E. (1995). Computational interpretations of the Gricean maxims in the generation of referring expressions. *Cognitive Science*, 19(2):233–263.

de Lucena, D. J. and Paraboni, I. (2008). USP-EACH frequency-based greedy attribute selection for referring expressions generation. In *Proceedings of the 5th International Conference on Natural Language Generation (INLG 2008)*, pages 219–220. Association for Computational Linguistics.

Engelhardt, P., Bailey, K., and Ferreira, F. (2006). Do speakers and listeners observe the gricean maxim of quantity? *Journal of Memory and Language*, 54(4):554–573.

Gargett, A., Garoufi, K., Koller, A., and Striegnitz, K. (2010). The give-2 corpus of giving instructions in virtual environments. In *Proceedings of the 7th International Conference on Language Resources and Evaluation (LREC)*, Malta.

Gatt, A., Belz, A., and Kow, E. (2008). The tuna challenge 2008: Overview and evaluation results. In *Proceedings of the 5th International Conference on Natural Language Generation (INLG 2008)*, pages 198–206. Association for Computational Linguistics.

Hall, M., Frank, E., Holmes, G., Pfahringer, B., Reutemann, P., and Witten, I. H. (2009). The WEKA data mining software: an update. *ACM SIGKDD Explorations Newsletter*, 11(1):10–18.

Jurafsky, D. and Martin, J. (2008). *Speech and Language Processing*. Pearson Prentice Hall, second edition.

Kelleher, J. and Kruijff, G.-J. (2006). Incremental generation of spatial referring expressions in situated dialog. In *Proceedings of the 21st International Conference on Computational Linguistics and the 44th annual meeting of the Association for Computational Linguistics*, pages 1041–1048.

Keysar, B., Barr, D. J., and Horton, W. S. (1998). The Egocentric Basis of Language Use. *Current Directions in Psychological Science*, 7(2):46–49.

Pacheco, F., Duboue, P., and Domínguez, M. (2012). On the feasibility of open domain referring expression generation using large scale folksonomies. In *Proceedings of the 2012 Conference of the North American Chapter of the Association for Computational Linguistics: Human Language Technologies*, pages 641–645, Montréal, Canada. Association for Computational Linguistics.

Paige, R. and Tarjan, R. (1987). Three partition refinement algorithms. *SIAM Journal on Computing*, 16(6):973–989.

Reiter, E. and Dale, R. (2000). *Building Natural Language Generation Systems*. Cambridge University Press, Cambridge.

Ruud, K., Emiel, K., and Mariët, T. (2012). Learning preferences for referring expression generation: Effects of domain, language and algorithm. In *INLG 2012 Proceedings of the Seventh International Natural Language Generation Conference*, pages 3–11, Utica, IL. Association for Computational Linguistics.

Stone, M. (2000). On identifying sets. In *Proceedings of the 1st International Natural Language Generation Conference (INLG'00)*, pages 116–123.

van Deemter, K. (2002). Generating referring expressions: Boolean extensions of the incremental algorithm. *Computational Linguistics*, 28(1):37–52.

van der Sluis, I., Gatt, A., and van Deemter., K. (2007). Evaluating algorithms for the generation of referring expressions: Going beyond toy domains. In *Proceedings of Recent Advances in Natural Language Processing*.

Viethen, H. A. E. (2011). *The Generation of Natural Descriptions: Corpus-Based Investigations of Referring Expressions in Visual Domains*. PhD thesis, Macquarie University, Sydney, Australia.

Viethen, J. and Dale, R. (2006). Algorithms for generating referring expressions: Do they do what people do? In *Proceedings of the 4th International Natural Language Generation Conference (INLG'06)*, pages 63–70.

Winograd, T. (1972). Understanding natural language. *Cognitive Psychology*, 3(1):1–191.

Measuring the adequacy of cross-lingual paraphrases in a Machine Translation setting

Marianna APIDIANAKI
LIMSI-CNRS
BP 133, 91403 Orsay Cedex
France
marianna@limsi.fr

ABSTRACT
Following the growing trend in the semantics community towards models adapted to specific applications, the SemEval-2 Cross-Lingual Lexical Substitution and Word Sense Disambiguation tasks address the disambiguation needs of Machine Translation (MT). The experiments conducted in this study aim at assessing whether the proposed evaluation protocol and methodology provide a fair estimate of the adequacy of cross-lingual predictions in translations. For this purpose, the gold SemEval paraphrases are fed into a state-of-the-art MT system and the obtained translations are compared to paraphrase quality judgments based on the source context. The results show the strong dependence of cross-lingual paraphrase adequacy on the translation context and cast doubt on the contribution that systems performing well in existing evaluation schemes would have on MT. These empirical findings highlight the importance of complementing the current evaluation schemes with translation information to allow a more accurate estimation of the systems impact on end-to-end applications.

KEYWORDS: Cross-Lingual Word Sense Disambiguation, Cross-Lingual Lexical Substitution, paraphrasing, Machine Translation.

Proceedings of COLING 2012: Posters, pages 63–72,
COLING 2012, Mumbai, December 2012.

1 Introduction

An important trend in computational semantics in recent years is the adaptation of inventories, models and evaluations to specific applications. In this vein, the Cross-Lingual Lexical Substitution (CLLS) and Word Sense Disambiguation (CL-WSD) tasks of SemEval-2 address the disambiguation needs of multilingual applications: what is being evaluated is the capacity of the participating systems to provide semantically correct translations for words in context that could, among others, constitute the input of Machine Translation (MT) systems (Mihalcea et al., 2010; Lefever and Hoste, 2010).[1] The underlying assumption is that the closer the output of a CLLS/CL-WSD system is to a manually built gold standard of cross-lingual paraphrases, the higher its contribution in a real application will be.

Paraphrasing is highly useful in MT as is shown by the substantial amount of research undertaken on the subject.[2] It permits to deal with out-of-vocabulary words (Callison-Burch et al., 2006; Marton et al., 2009), capture lexical variation during evaluation (Zhou et al., 2006; Owczarzak et al., 2006), expand the set of reference translations for minimum error rate training (Madnani et al., 2007) and improve the general performance of MT systems (Max, 2010). It is however interesting that in spite of the MT orientation of the CL SemEval-2 tasks, translation selection and evaluation are carried out by reference solely to the source language. The target language context which plays an important role in lexical selection in statistical MT systems, as highlighted by the strong influence of the language model on word choice, is not considered.

In this work, we explore the role of the target language in CLLS and CL-WSD by measuring the adequacy of CL paraphrases in translations. Our goal is not to estimate the impact of semantics in MT, as was the case in previous works on the subject (Carpuat and Wu, 2007; Chan et al., 2007), but to empirically test the adequacy of the sense descriptions provided in the CL evaluation tasks in an MT setting. The paper is organized as follows. The CL SemEval-2 tasks are described in Section 2. The adopted experimental methodology and evaluation setup are presented in Section 3. The analysis of the obtained results, in Section 4, highlights the importance of the target language context for CLLS and CL-WSD, and the implications of these findings for CL semantic evaluations.

2 Translation context in cross-lingual semantic evaluations

2.1 The SemEval-2 Cross-Lingual tasks

In the CLLS and CL-WSD tasks of the SemEval-2 evaluation campaign, the participating systems had to predict semantically correct translations in different languages for English target words in context (Mihalcea et al., 2010; Lefever and Hoste, 2010). The performance of the systems was measured by comparing their output to a manually built gold standard (GS) of cross-lingual paraphrases. For example, the instance of the target word *fresh* in sentence #952 of the CLLS test set: "*At first the user is impressed by the* ***fresh*** *clean smell coming out of the machine and how nice it makes their home smell.*", was tagged by the following set of translations which express the sense of *fresh* in Spanish: *fresco 4; puro 1; flamante 1; limpio 1; nuevo 1*. GS translations are lemmatized and the frequency counts indicate the number of annotators that proposed each substitute.

The differences between the two tasks mainly lie in the targeted lexical samples and the involved

[1] These systems can also help human translators in their work and assist language learners.

[2] See (Madnani and Dorr, 2010) for a comprehensive survey of data-driven methods for paraphrase generation.

language pairs. CLLS addresses words of all open-class parts of speech in one language pair (English-Spanish) while CL-WSD focuses on the translation of English nouns in five languages (French, Spanish, German, Dutch and Italian).[3] Another point of variation concerns the definition of senses. In CL-WSD, target word senses were described by means of clusters of their semantically similar translations (Ide et al., 2002; Apidianaki, 2008). More precisely, the translations of the target words in the Europarl corpus (Koehn, 2005) were manually clustered and the obtained clusters served for tagging. On the contrary, CLLS did not involve a clustering step and the annotators could propose translations found in any external resource. The CLLS test set was built from the English Internet Corpus (Sharoff, 2005) while CL-WSD test sentences were extracted from the BNC[4] and the JRC-ACQUIS corpus (Steinberger et al., 2006).

2.2 Translation context: a neglected parameter

Although the CL SemEval tasks are clearly oriented towards MT, annotator judgments and system suggestions are made on the basis of source language information. Translations are selected so as to express the meaning of the target words in the target language but the translation context in which they would be used has no influence on the selection process. This lack of target language information would have a minimal impact in settings where CLLS/CL-WSD systems serve to assist human users, but becomes more important in the context of MT where the proposed CL paraphrases have to be automatically filtered to select the most adequate translation. This selection is not straightforward for several reasons.

Words that seem interchangeable on the basis of formal criteria, such as distributional similarity, might not be substitutable in real texts because of other parameters preventing the substitution (e.g. syntactic structure, collocations). In a translation setting where the substitution is done cross-lingually, it is important that the paraphrases preserve both the sense of the original word (or phrase) and the fluency of the translated text. However, clustered translations are usually near-synonyms translating the same sense, but almost never absolute synonyms interchangeable in translations (Edmonds and Hirst, 2002; Apidianaki, 2009). Consequently, although CLLS and CL-WSD could greatly contribute in MT by enhancing the semantic relevance of translations, the existing evaluations do not provide a fair estimate of the systems' capacity to propose translations that would also fit well in the translated texts.

We conduct a series of experiments to assess the adequacy of CL paraphrases in translations by exploiting the CLLS and CL-WSD test sets. As the two test sets were mainly built from monolingual corpora, no reference translations are available against which the quality of the CL paraphrases could be measured using standard MT evaluation metrics (BLEU, METEOR, etc.). So, we adopt a variation of the *substitution-based* approach used in works on paraphrasing (Bannard and Callison-Burch, 2005) for validating candidate paraphrases, based on the assumption that items deemed to be paraphrases may behave as such only in some contexts and not in others. We translate the CLLS and CL-WSD test sets with a state-of-the-art MT system by exploiting the manually-defined GS paraphrases. Once the set of translations for each test sentence is produced, we measure the substitutability of the GS paraphrases using an automatic and a human ranking, as explained in the next section.

[3]The CLLS lexical sample is composed of 300 noun, 310 verb, 280 adjective and 110 adverb instances with approximately 5 Spanish substitutes per target word and a pairwise inter-annotator agreement of 0.2777. The CL-WSD test data contains 50 instances of 20 target nouns and their substitutes in five languages.

[4]`http://www.natcorp.ox.ac.uk/`

3 Experimental setup

3.1 Systems and data

The CLLS and CL-WSD test sets are translated into Spanish and French, respectively, using the baseline system of the WMT-2011 shared task (Moses) (Koehn et al., 2007). The two MT systems are trained on the data released for WMT-2011 for the two language pairs, namely the French-English and Spanish-English parts of Europarl (version 6) (Koehn, 2005). The language models used during decoding are trained on the monolingual Spanish and French parts of Europarl. For each test sentence, we constrain the decoder to produce translations by using all GS paraphrases. These are plugged into Moses using its 'XML Markup' feature which allows to specify translations for parts of the input sentence. The 'exclusive' mode is activated which forces the decoder to use the XML-specified translations and ignore any phrases from the phrase table that overlap with that span.[5] In total, 4,791 unique Spanish translations are produced for the CLLS test set and 4,220 French translations for the CL-WSD test set.

The GS paraphrases are lemmatized, so we first produce translations at the lemma level without dealing with inflections. At this stage, the test sentences are lemmatized and the MT systems are trained on lemmatized bi-texts. The CL-WSD test set is also translated into French using inflections. We gather all the inflectional variants of each paraphrase found in the training bi-text and provide them to Moses through the XML markup. For instance, to translate the test sentence: "*Taking with determination this road leading to a dynamic European Union on the world* ***scene*** *will yield further substantial benefits to all parties involved in the EU and beyond.*" we provide all inflected forms of each GS paraphrase found in Europarl: *scène/scènes, niveau/niveaux, marché/marchés*, etc. The MT system then selects the best inflection depending on the surrounding context, as shown in Table 1.

3.2 Automatic ranking

The set of lemmatized translations produced by Moses for each test sentence is ranked by a target language model (lm). Language model scores reflect the probability of the sentences formed by substituting paraphrases and are useful for ranking candidate paraphrases in automatic paraphrasing tasks. Bannard and Callison-Burch (2005), for example, combine a language model probability with a paraphrase probability to rank candidate paraphrases produced by the *pivot* method.[6] The use of a language model allows to account for the fact that the best paraphrase might vary depending on information about the sentence it appears in and lets the surrounding words in the sentence influence paraphrase ranking and selection.

We build two extended lms (in Spanish and French) using additional monolingual data compared to that used for training the lms used by Moses. The training data comprises Europarl, the News Commentary corpus and the 2009, 2010 and 2011 News Crawl data provided at the WMT-11 shared task for the two languages. We employ the SRILM toolkit (Stolcke, 2002) to compute two 5-gram language models and, subsequently, to score and rank the translations produced by Moses. As the use of different GS paraphrases may alter the context of the translated sentences normalized lm scores are used, defined as $\frac{1}{n} - \log(P)$, where n is the length of the translation

[5] The 'inclusive' mode allows phrase table entries to compete with the XML entry. This configuration permits to define probabilities for the provided translation choices and leave the final selection to the target language model.

[6] In the pivot method, phrases in one language are considered to be potential paraphrases of each other if they share a translation in another language. The paraphrase probability is defined in terms of the translation model probabilities that the original phrase translates as a particular phrase in the other language.

GS	Translation	lm score
scène (3)	prendre avec détermination cette voie conduisant à une dynamique de l' union européenne sur la **scène** mondiale enregistre encore des avantages substantiels pour toutes les parties concernées dans l' ue et au-delà .	2
niveau (2)	... menant à une union européenne dynamique au **niveau** mondial engendrera davantage des avantages substantiels pour toutes les parties concernées ...	2.13
vie (2)	... conduisant à une dynamique de l' union européenne sur la **vie** apportera des avantages substantiels pour toutes les parties impliquées ...	1.8
marché (1)	... conduisant à une dynamique de l' union européenne sur le **marché** mondial engendrera davantage des avantages substantiels pour toutes les parties concernées ...	1.96
plan (1)	... menant à une union européenne dynamique sur le **plan** mondial engendrera davantage des avantages substantiels pour toutes les parties concernées ...	2.09

Table 1: Ranking of Moses translations using GS paraphrases and lm scores.

and P the language model probability. Table 1 shows the normalized lm scores of the set of translations produced for the test sentence given in the previous section.[7] The lm ranking is compared to the GS one which reflects the semantic relevance of the paraphrases as estimated by reference to the source context. Our hypothesis is that a high correlation between the two rankings would indicate that translations privileged in the GS (i.e. with a high frequency) would serve to produce fluent translations (i.e. with better lm scores). Given the important role of lms in lexical selection, the low ranking of paraphrases could be interpreted as denoting their lower chances of being used in translations. However, this judgment cannot be absolute as the language model is one among other components that determine lexical choice in MT systems.

3.3 Human ranking

Although the lm scoring yields interesting results, we consider that it is not reliable enough to lead to safe conclusions as to the adequacy of CL paraphrases in translations. So, we also conduct a human evaluation. The annotators are asked to rank the set of Moses translations produced for each target word instance on a 3-point scale, according to the adequacy of the paraphrases and the fluency of the translated text.[8] Good quality paraphrases (i.e. the highest ranked ones, assigned a '1' value) should preserve both the meaning of the source word and the grammaticality of the target sentence. This experiment can be viewed as a substitution test (Callison-Burch, 2008) with the difference that the paraphrases are not just substituted in the translated sentences but fed into the MT system which exploits them during translation. Consequently, the context surrounding the paraphrase might be altered as well, as shown in the examples given in Table 1.

The human ranking covers 538 instances of the CL-WSD test set with an average of 4.17 French paraphrases per instance. The 538 translation sets produced by Moses contain a total of 1821

[7]Normalized scores are rounded to two decimal places. Translations with lower scores are considered as more fluent.
[8]The annotators are native and highly proficient French speakers working on MT and paraphrasing.

unique translations and each translation is annotated twice. We calculate the inter-annotator agreement using Cohen's kappa coefficient for three different annotation configurations: the ranking performed using the 3-point scale and two coarser-grained rankings obtained by interpreting intermediate ('2') values as denoting good or low quality translations (i.e. converting them into '1's or '3's). As shown by the kappa values given in Table 2, agreement on the 3-point ranking is rather low ($K = 0.35$) but it gets higher when the intermediate values are interpreted as 'good' or 'bad'. In the first case kappa is 0.57, which is considered as substantial agreement, but it reaches its highest value ($K = 0.72$) when medium-ranked translations are considered as low quality ones (2→3). This practically means that in most cases both annotators perceive a problem in the translated texts but have a different estimate of its severity. The increase of the kappa value when a scale with fewer points is used is natural and has been observed in other works on paraphrasing.[9]

rating scale	kappa
3-point scale	0.35
2-point scale (2 → 1)	0.57
2-point scale (2 → 3)	**0.72**

Table 2: Inter-annotator agreement.

Examples of human-ranked translation sets are given in Table 3. We observe that medium-ranked CL paraphrases, such as the translation ***charge*** of the target word *strain* (assigned values '2' and '3') or the translation ***parties*** of the noun *side*, do not fit well in the translated texts. However, the annotators give some credit to paraphrases that may seem awkward in the translated texts but still carry some of the semantic load of the source word, reserving the lowest values to erroneous translations from both points of view. Given the inadequacy of medium-ranked paraphrases in translations, we consider these judgments as low quality ones and distinguish between two categories. The $K = 0.72$ agreement obtained in this case is very high, especially for a semantics task like this one.

4 Results

4.1 Gold standard judgments *vs* language model scores

We calculate the correlation of the two rankings with the GS frequency ranking. We first compute the correlation between the semantic relevance of CL paraphrases, as reflected in the GS frequencies, and their adequacy in translated texts, as measured by the lm. We use the Spearman's rank order correlation coefficient (ρ), a non-parametric test, because the data does not seem to be normally distributed. The Spearman coefficient is defined as the Pearson correlation between ranked variables. To compute the correlation of two random variables X and Y, Pearson's coefficient divides their covariance by the product of their standard deviations.

$$\rho(X,Y) = \frac{cov(X,Y)}{\sigma_X \sigma_Y} \quad (1)$$

To compute Spearman's ρ, absolute values are transformed into ranks.[10] The correlation

[9]Callison-Burch (2008) reports a kappa agreement of 0.33 when a 5-point scale is used and an agreement of 0.61 with a 2-point scale. The scale conversion is performed by measuring agreement in terms of how often the annotators assigned a value higher or lower than a pre-defined threshold.

Word	Source	Translations	Ranks
strain	Exposure both in working life and everyday living to different sets of values, assumptions, expectations, and behaviour patterns places a severe **strain** on the individual.	l' exposition à la fois dans la vie professionnelle et de la vie de tous les jours à différents ensembles de valeurs , des hypothèses , de leurs attentes et leurs comportements accorde une très forte **pression** sur les individus	1|1
		... lieux de graves **tensions** sur les individus	2|2
		... peser une **charge** sur les individus	2|3
		... peser une grave **pesant** sur les individus	3|3
		... peser une grave **serrée** sur l' individu	3|3
		... peser une grave **grevée** sur l' individu	3|3
side	Many American students working in British drama schools find the answer to this question by using what is called "standard American", and this approach is being used now in training on both **sides** of the Atlantic.	bon nombre des étudiants américains travaillent dans les écoles du drame , trouver la réponse à cette question , en utilisant ce qui est appelé " norme américaine " , et cette approche est utilisé dans la formation sur les deux **rives** de l' atlantique	1|1
		... des deux **côtés** de l' atlantique	1|1
		... des deux **bords** de l' atlantique	1|3
		... des deux **parties** de l ' atlantique	2|3
		... des deux **transatlantique** de l' atlantique	2|3
		... des deux **outre** de l' atlantique	3|3

Table 3: Manually ranked translations.

between the GS annotations in the French data set and the lm scores on the lemmatized translation dataset is $\rho = 0.067$ and highly significant with $p = 1.361e{-}05$ (< 0.05). Spearman correlation with the normalized lm scores is $-.014$ with a p-value of .363. As the dataset with the normalized scores contains *ties*, we also calculate the Kendall's tau-b non-parametric correlation. Let $(x_1, y_1), (x_2, y_2), ..., (x_n, y_n)$ be a set of joint observations from two random variables X and Y, the Kendall's tau coefficient is defined as

$$\tau = \frac{(|\text{concordant pairs}| - |\text{discordant pairs}|)}{\frac{1}{2}n(n-1)} \qquad (2)$$

Concordant is any pair of observations (x_i, y_i) (x_j, y_j) where the ranks for both elements agree (e.g. $x_i > x_j$ and $y_i > y_j$), otherwise it is discordant. Kendall's tau-a requires all the values of x_i and y_i to be unique for the p-value to be accurate, but Kendall's tau-b accounts for ties (i.e. pairs of observations where $x_i = x_j$ or $y_i = y_j$) .[11] The Kendall's tau-b correlation between the GS ranking and the normalized lm scores is low: $-.011$ ($p = .363$). This lack of correlation could mean in practical terms that the best paraphrases from a semantics point of view would not lead to more fluent translations. To draw safer conclusions we present in the next section the results obtained by the human ranking.

The correlation between GS estimates and the unnormalized lm scores for Spanish is $\rho = 0.0242$, with lower significance than in French ($p = 0.09$). Given the similar size of the test sets in the two languages, this divergence might be due to the higher homogeneity of the French dataset

[10]The analysis is done using the R package: `http://www.r-project.org`

[11]Kendall's tau-b correlation is calculated using the IBM SPSS statistics environment.

which contains only nouns. Words of different parts of speech, found in the Spanish test set, are handled differently by the annotators and their paraphrases have a varying impact on translation fluency. The correlation computed between the Spanish GS scores and the normalized lm scores is low as well, with $\rho = .005$ ($p = .726$) and a Kendall's tau-b value of .004 ($p = .723$).

4.2 Gold standard *vs* target language human judgments

The dataset that consists of the GS frequency estimates and the human judgments of translation adequacy contains ties, so we calculate the Kendall's tau-b correlation. We use the values assigned in the first annotation pass. The obtained correlation is $-.271$, for the 3-point scale (negative because the values in the two rankings are inverted), and $-.26$ for the 2-point scale (conversion 2→3). Both correlations are significant at the 0.01 level. The 3-point scale judgments correlate slightly better with the GS ones because they are rated on the same scale.[12] These results show that paraphrases privileged in the GS do not fit well in the translated texts, while translations ranked low in the GS might be preferred in translations.

We finally calculate the correlation between the human ranking and the normalized lm scores on unlemmatized translations. Kendall's tau-b correlation is .018 and .033, for the 3 and the 2-point scale respectively, but the p-values are quite high (.334 and .091). It would be interesting to repeat this correlation experiment once more annotated examples will be available. A detailed analysis of this discordance would provide valuable hints on the capacity of lms to measure fluency and paraphrase adequacy. We observe, for instance, that the annotators often base their judgments on the context surrounding the paraphrases although lm scores are computed on the entire sentences that might be altered during translation. Nevertheless, the fact that these correlation results are not yet safe does not influence the conclusions that can be drawn from the low correlation observed between the gold standard ranking and the human ranking of translation adequacy, which is highly significant.

Conclusion

The findings of this study reveal that the results of the CL SemEval-2 tasks are not indicative of the contribution that the participating systems would have in MT. It has been shown that although the proposed evaluation metrics address the semantic relevance of CL paraphrases, they do not account for their suitability in translations. These empirical results highlight the importance of integrating translation information in CL semantic evaluations by resorting either to simplified translation tasks (Vickrey et al., 2005) or to full-fledged MT systems. Evaluation metrics capable of rewarding semantically correct translations that do not distort the fluency of the translations are much needed in the field of MT for evaluating the output of MT systems and the contribution of disambiguation modules. Another perspective worth exploring is the set up of all-words CL evaluation tasks, in addition to the lexical sample ones, allowing to assess the global capacities of CLLS and CL-WSD systems and the coverage they can attain in real-life applications. This setting would also permit to explore the potential of collaboration between CL-WSD modules and MT systems for correct lexical selection.

Acknowledgments

We would like to thank the annotators for the time and effort they put into this task. This work was partly funded by the Cap Digital SAMAR project.

[12] GS paraphrases were assigned frequencies from '1' to '3'; only two cases were assigned a '4' value.

References

Apidianaki, M. (2008). Translation-oriented sense induction based on parallel corpora. In *Proceedings of the 6th International Conference on Language Resources and Evaluation (LREC-08)*, pages 3269–3275, Marrakech, Morocco.

Apidianaki, M. (2009). Data-driven semantic analysis for multilingual WSD and lexical selection in translation. In *Proceedings of the 12th Conference of the European Chapter of the ACL (EACL 2009)*, pages 77–85, Athens, Greece. Association for Computational Linguistics.

Bannard, C. and Callison-Burch, C. (2005). Paraphrasing with bilingual parallel corpora. In *Proceedings of the 43rd Annual Meeting of the Association for Computational Linguistics (ACL'05)*, pages 597–604, Ann Arbor, Michigan. Association for Computational Linguistics.

Callison-Burch, C. (2008). Syntactic Constraints on Paraphrases Extracted from Parallel Corpora. In *Proceedings of the 2008 Conference on Empirical Methods in Natural Language Processing*, pages 196–205, Honolulu, Hawaii. Association for Computational Linguistics.

Callison-Burch, C., Koehn, P., and Osborne, M. (2006). Improved statistical machine translation using paraphrases. In *Proceedings of the Human Language Technology Conference of the NAACL, Main Conference*, pages 17–24, New York City, USA. Association for Computational Linguistics.

Carpuat, M. and Wu, D. (2007). Improving Statistical Machine Translation using Word Sense Disambiguation. In *Proceedings of the Joint EMNLP-CoNLL Conference*, pages 61–72, Prague, Czech Republic.

Chan, Y. S., Ng, H. T., and Chiang, D. (2007). Word sense disambiguation improves statistical machine translation. In *Proceedings of the 45th Annual Meeting of the Association of Computational Linguistics*, pages 33–40, Prague, Czech Republic. Association for Computational Linguistics.

Edmonds, P. and Hirst, G. (2002). Near-synonymy and lexical choice. *Computational Linguistics*, 28:105–144.

Ide, N., Erjavec, T., and Tufiş, D. (2002). Sense discrimination with parallel corpora. In *Proceedings of the ACL Workshop on Word Sense Disambiguation: Recent Successes and Future Directions*, pages 54–60, Philadelphia.

Koehn, P. (2005). Europarl: A Parallel Corpus for Statistical Machine Translation. In *Proceedings of MT Summit X*, pages 79–86, Phuket, Thailand.

Koehn, P., Hoang, H., Birch, A., Callison-Burch, C., Federico, M., Bertoldi, N., Cowan, B., Shen, W., Moran, C., Zens, R., Dyer, C., Bojar, O., Constantin, A., and Herbst, E. (2007). Moses: Open source toolkit for statistical machine translation. In *Proceedings of the 45th Annual ACL Meeting, Companion Volume Proceedings of the Demo and Poster Sessions*, pages 177–180, Prague, Czech Republic. Association for Computational Linguistics.

Lefever, E. and Hoste, V. (2010). Semeval-2010 task 3: Cross-lingual word sense disambiguation. In *Proceedings of the 5th International Workshop on Semantic Evaluation*, pages 15–20, Uppsala, Sweden. Association for Computational Linguistics.

Madnani, N., Ayan, N. F., Resnik, P., and Dorr, B. J. (2007). Using Paraphrases for Parameter Tuning in Statistical Machine Translation. In *Proceedings of the Workshop on Statistical Machine Translation*, Prague, Czech Republic. Association for Computational Linguistics.

Madnani, N. and Dorr, B. J. (2010). Generating Phrasal and Sentential Paraphrases: A Survey of Data-driven Methods. *Computational Linguistics*, 36:341–387.

Marton, Y., Callison-Burch, C., and Resnik, P. (2009). Improved Statistical Machine Translation Using Monolingually-Derived Paraphrases. In *Proceedings of the 2009 Conference on Empirical Methods in Natural Language Processing*, pages 381–390, Singapore.

Max, A. (2010). Example-based paraphrasing for improved phrase-based statistical machine translation. In *Proceedings of the 2010 Conference on Empirical Methods in Natural Language Processing*, pages 656–666, Cambridge, MA. Association for Computational Linguistics.

Mihalcea, R., Sinha, R., and McCarthy, D. (2010). Semeval-2010 task 2: Cross-lingual lexical substitution. In *Proceedings of the 5th International Workshop on Semantic Evaluation*, pages 9–14, Uppsala, Sweden. Association for Computational Linguistics.

Owczarzak, K., Groves, D., Van Genabith, J., and Way, A. (2006). Contextual bitext-derived paraphrases in automatic mt evaluation. In *Proceedings on the Workshop on Statistical Machine Translation*, pages 86–93, New York City. Association for Computational Linguistics.

Sharoff, S. (2005). Open-source corpora: Using the net to fish for linguistic data. *International Journal of Corpus Linguistics*, 11:435–462.

Steinberger, R., Pouliquen, B., Widiger, A., Ignat, C., Erjavec, T., and Tufiş, D. (2006). The jrc-acquis: A multilingual aligned parallel corpus with 20+ languages. In *Proceedings of the 5th International Conference on Language Resources and Evaluation (LREC'2006)*, pages 2142–2147, Genoa, Italy.

Stolcke, A. (2002). SRILM - an extensible language modeling toolkit. In *Proceedings of the 7th International Conference on Spoken Language Processing (ICSLP-02)*, pages 901–904, Denver, CO.

Vickrey, D., Biewald, L., Teyssier, M., and Koller, D. (2005). Word-Sense Disambiguation for Machine Translation. In *Proceedings of the Joint Conference on Human Language Technology / Empirical Methods in Natural Language Processing (HLT-EMNLP)*, pages 771–778, Vancouver, Canada.

Zhou, L., Lin, C.-Y., and Hovy, E. (2006). Re-evaluating machine translation results with paraphrase support. In *Proceedings of the 2006 Conference on Empirical Methods in Natural Language Processing*, pages 77–84, Sydney, Australia. Association for Computational Linguistics.

Cross-Lingual Sentiment Analysis for Indian Languages using Linked WordNets

Balamurali A R[1,2] *Aditya Joshi*[1] *Pushpak Bhattacharyya*[1]
(1) Indian Institute of Technology, Mumbai, India 400076
(2) IITB-Monash Research Academy, Mumbai, India 400076
balamurali@iitb.ac.in, aditya.jo@iitb.ac.in, pb@iitb.ac.in

Abstract

Cross-Lingual Sentiment Analysis (CLSA) is the task of predicting the polarity of the opinion expressed in a text in a language L_{test} using a classifier trained on the corpus of another language L_{train}. Popular approaches use Machine Translation (MT) to convert the test document in L_{test} to L_{train} and use the classifier of L_{train}. However, MT systems do not exist for most pairs of languages and even if they do, their translation accuracy is low. So we present an alternative approach to CLSA using WordNet senses as features for supervised sentiment classification. A document in L_{test} is tested for polarity through a classifier trained on *sense marked* and polarity labeled corpora of L_{train}. The crux of the idea is to use the linked WordNets of two languages to bridge the language gap. We report our results on two widely spoken Indian languages, Hindi (450 million speakers) and Marathi (72 million speakers), which do not have an MT system between them. The sense-based approach gives a CLSA accuracy of 72% and 84% for Hindi and Marathi sentiment classification respectively. This is an improvement of 14%-15% over an approach that uses a bilingual dictionary.

Keywords: Sentiment Analysis, Cross Lingual Sentiment Analysis, Linked Wordnets, Semantic Features, Sense Space.

Proceedings of COLING 2012: Posters, pages 73–82,
COLING 2012, Mumbai, December 2012.

1 Introduction

Sentiment Analysis (SA) is the task of inferring polarity of an opinion in a text. Though the majority of the work in SA is for English, there has been work in other languages as well such as Chinese, Japanese, German and Spanish (Seki et al., 2007; Nakagawa et al., 2010; Schulz et al., 2010). To perform SA on these languages, cross-lingual approaches are often used due to the lack of annotated content in these languages. In Cross-Lingual Sentiment Analysis (CLSA), the training corpus in one language (call it L_{train}) is used to predict the sentiment of documents in another language (call it L_{test}). Machine Translation is often employed for CLSA (Wan, 2009; Wei and Pal, 2010). A document in L_{test} is translated into L_{train} and is checked for polarity using the classifier trained on the polarity marked documents of L_{train}. However, MT is resource-intensive and does not exist for most pairs of languages.

WordNet (Fellbaum, 1998) is a widely used lexical resource in the NLP community and is present in many languages.[1] Most of the WordNets are developed using the expansion based approach (Vossen, 1998; Bhattacharyya, 2010) wherein a new WordNet for a target language (L_t) is created by adding words which represent the corresponding synsets in the source language (L_s) WordNet. As a consequence, corresponding concepts in L_s and L_t have the same synset (concept) identifier. Our work leverages this fact, and uses WordNet senses as features for building a classifier in L_{train}. The document to be tested for polarity is preprocessed by replacing words in this document with the corresponding synset identifiers. This step eliminates the distinction between L_{train} and L_{test} as far as the document is concerned. The document vector created from the sense-based features could belong to any language. The preprocessed document is then given to the classifier coming from L_{train} for polarity detection.

This work is an extension our sense-based SA work on English (Balamurali et al., 2011) where we showed that *WordNet synset-based features perform better than word-based features for sentiment analysis*. Here, we carry out our study on two widely spoken Indian languages: *Hindi* and *Marathi*. These languages belong to the Indo-Aryan subgroup of the Indo-European language family. For these two languages, we first verify the superiority of sense-based features over word-based features for SA. Thereafter we proceed to verify the efficacy of the sense-based approach for cross-lingual sentiment analysis for these two languages. This work differs from existing works(Brooke et al., 2009; Wan, 2009; Wei and Pal, 2010; Banea et al., 2008) on CLSA in two aspects: (i) our focus is not necessarily to use a resource-rich language to help a resource-scarce language but *can be applied to any two languages which share a common sense space* (by using WordNets with matching synset identifiers); (ii) our work is an alternative to *MT-based cross-lingual sentiment analysis* for languages which do not have an MT system between them.

2 Background Study: Word Senses for SA

In our previous work (Balamurali et al., 2011), we showed that word senses act as better features than lexeme-based features for document level SA. We termed this feature space as *synset space* or *sense space*. In the sense space, the semantics of document is represented in a compact way using synset identifiers.

Different variants of a travel review domain corpus are generated by using automatic/manual sense disambiguation techniques. Thereafter, classification accuracy of classifiers based on

[1] http://www.globalWordNet.org/gwa/WordNet_table.html

different sense-based and word-based features were compared. The experimental results show that *WordNet senses act as better features compared to words alone.*

The following subsection validates this hypothesis for Hindi and Marathi. Since the documents for training and testing belong to the same language, we refer to this set of classification experiments as *in-language sentiment classification*.

2.1 WordNet Senses as Better Features: Approach

A classifier is trained for each of the following feature representations: Words (*W*), Manually annotated word senses (*M*), Automatically annotated word senses (*I*), Words and *manually* annotated word senses (*W+S(M)*) and Words and *automatically* annotated word senses (*W+S(I)*). At present, the development of Hindi and Marathi WordNets is not complete. Thus, a number of words belonging to open POS categories (*e.g.* nouns) do not have corresponding synsets created. We used W+S(M) and W+S(I) representations in order to alleviate problems that can arise due to these missing synsets.

We perform our experiments on the above feature representations for *in-language sentiment classification* and compare their performance. The results are discussed in section 6.1.

3 Word Senses for Cross-Lingual SA

We now describe our approach to cross-lingual SA, which is the focus of this work. This approach harnesses word senses to build a supervised sentiment classifier in a cross-lingual setting (*i.e.,* when the L_{train} and L_{test} are different).

Our baseline as well as sense-based approach center around the WordNets of the two languages *viz.,* Hindi and Marathi. WordNets of Hindi and Marathi have been developed using an expansion approach. This approach involves expanding the Marathi WordNet by adding concept definition for concepts from Hindi WordNet. Subsequently, corresponding related terms are added and mapped. Thus, corresponding concepts/synsets in WordNets of both languages have the same synset identifier. Once this mapping is completed, concepts found only in the target language are added.

An instance of WordNets which are collectively developed for multiple languages is referred to as Multidict (Mohanty et al., 2008). In a Multidict, each row constitutes a concept, identified by a synset identifier.

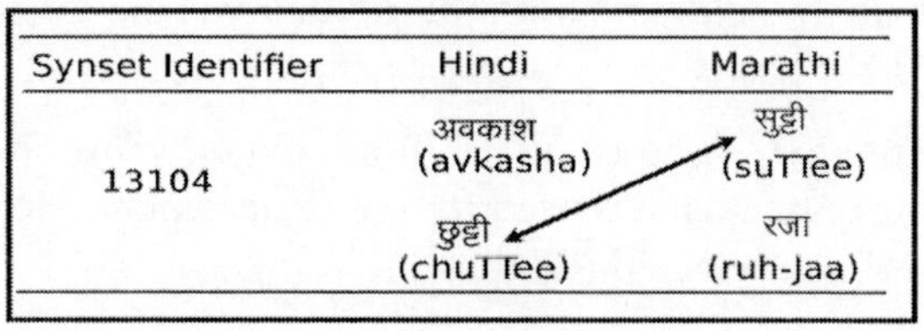

Figure 1: An example entry *(concept: holiday)* in Multidict for Hindi and Marathi

Each column contains synonymous terms representing these concepts in different languages. Further, a manual cross link is provided between words in one language to another based on their lexical preference.

The words in the corresponding synsets are thus translations of each other in specific contexts. For example, an entry pertaining to Marathi and Hindi can be explained as follows (Figure 1):

13104 (Synset identifier) pertains to the concept of *holiday* and its related terms are *suTTee* and *ruh-jaa* in Marathi and *chuTTee* and *avkasha* in Hindi. The cross links shown in the above entry indicates that when the Marathi word *suTTee* is used in the sense represented by the synset identifier *13104*, its exact Hindi translation is *chuTTee* (*i.e.,* this translation is more preferred over the other related Hindi words of the same synset).

3.1 Our Approach: Sense-based Representation

Following the fact that the Hindi and Marathi WordNet have the same synset identifier for the same concept, we represent words in the two languages by corresponding synset identifiers.

Thus, in a cross-lingual setting for a given target language, we map the words of the training as well as the test corpus to their WordNet synset identifiers. A classification model is learnt on the training corpus and tested on the test corpus. Both corpora consists of synset identifiers. This experiment is performed for two variants of the corpora: one with manually annotated senses and another with automatically annotated senses. Thus, in the context of using senses as features for cross-lingual sentiment analysis, we evaluate the following approaches: 1. A group of word senses that have been manually annotated (*M*), 2. A group of word senses that have been annotated by an automatic Word Sense Disambiguation (WSD) engine (*I*).

The replacement of a word by its synset identifier is carried out for all documents in the training corpus and the test corpus. The representation of the new corpora is in a common feature space, *i.e.,* the sense space.

3.2 Baseline: Naïve Translation Using Lexeme Replacement

MT-based techniques have been the main way of performing cross-lingual SA (Wan, 2009; Wei and Pal, 2010). The obvious choice for a baseline to compare our approach would have been a MT based CLSA approach. However, at present, there exists no Hindi-Marathi MT system. Hence we develop a strategy for obtaining a naïve translation of the corpus-based on lexical transfer which forms the baseline for comparing sentiment classification accuracy of the proposed cross-lingual SA based on synset representation.

Our approach consists of converting a document from the L_{test} to the L_{train} so that a classifier modeled on documents from the training language can be used. The words in the test documents are mapped to the corresponding words in the training language to obtain a naïve translation. No semantic/syntactic transfer is maintained. We use Multidict to translate synonymous terms in different languages, namely Hindi and Marathi (Mohanty et al., 2008). We offer two versions which differ from each other based on the *replacement lexeme chosen.*

Exact word replacement (E): Based on the disambiguated sense identifier, the exact cross-linked word from the source language is used for the replacement. Hence, for the word *suTTee*, the translation *chuTTee* will be selected (Figure 1).

Random word replacement (R): Based on the disambiguated sense identifier, the cross linked word from the source language is used for the replacement. This word in Figure 1 is not necessarily the exact (*preferred*) translation as mentioned above. For example, for the word *suTTee*, some random translation from the same synset will be selected, for example *ruh-jaa*, instead of the preferred translation *chuTTee* (Figure 1) will be selected.

The replacement is carried out for all documents in the test corpus (originally in L_{test}) to generate a new test corpus (containing words in L_{train}). We understand this naïve translation may not give as strong a baseline as a statistical MT-based approach, but given the state of these languages, we believe the results obtained are fairly comparable.

4 Datasets

The dataset we created for Hindi and Marathi consists of user-written travel destination reviews. We collected them from various blogs and Sunday travel editorials. A review consists of approximately 4-5 sentences of 10-15 words each. The Hindi corpus consists of approximately 100 positive and 100 negative reviews while the Marathi corpus consists of approximately 75 positive and 75 negative reviews. The documents are labeled with polarity (positive/negative) by a native speaker.

To create the manual sense-annotated corpus, the words were manually annotated by a native speaker. Based on the word and POS category, the annotation tool shows all possible sense entries for that word in the WordNet. The lexicographer then chooses the right sense based on the context. Hindi corpora contains 11038 words whereas Marathi corpora contains 12566 words. To generate automatic sense-annotated corpus, we use the engine based on the IWSD algorithm, which is trained on the tourism domain and can operate on Hindi, Marathi and English. We chose the travel review domain for our analysis because the IWSD engine was trained on this domain.

POS	#Words	Precision	Recall	F-score
Noun	2601	73.26%	70.59%	71.90%
Adverb	506	80.08%	79.45%	79.76%
Adjective	700	56.65%	54.14%	55.37%
Verb	1487	54.11%	51.78%	52.92%
Overall	5294	66.41%	63.98%	65.17%

Table 1: Annotation statistics for Hindi

POS	#Words	Precision	Recall	F-score
Noun	1628	76.60%	75.80%	76.20%
Adverb	204	73.53%	73.53%	73.53%
Adjective	583	76.27%	74.96%	75.61%
Verb	363	82.35%	80.99%	81.67%
Overall	2778	77.05%	76.13%	76.59%

Table 2: Annotation statistics for Marathi

Tables 1 and 2 show the evaluation of sense disambiguation statistics for IWSD for Hindi and Marathi respectively.

5 Experimental Setup

The experiments are performed using C-SVM (linear kernel with default parameters; C=0.0, ϵ=0.0010) available as a part of LibSVM package.[2] We chose SVM as its known to be a good learner for sentiment classification (Pang and Lee, 2002).

To conduct experiments on words as features, we perform stop-word removal and word stemming. For synset-based experiments, words in the corpus are substituted with synset identifiers along with POS categories, which are used as features. To create automatically sense-annotated corpora, we use the state-of-the-art domain specific word sense disambiguation (IWSD) algorithm by Khapra et al. (2010) for sense disambiguating our datasets in the two languages.

The results are evaluated using commonly used classification metrics: classification accuracy, Fscore, recall and precision. Recall and precision for each polarity label is also calculated for analysis.

For our background study experiments pertaining to the in-language sentiment classification, a two-fold validation of five repeats is carried out. Each repeat consists of a random configuration

[2]http://www.csie.ntu.edu.tw/čjlin/libsvm

of test/train documents maintained across different representations for a given run. Such a cross-fold validation is taken to minimize the variance between the classification results of different folds since the sizes of the corpus are not that large (Dietterich, 1998).

6 Results and Discussions

Our results are divided into two parts. Section 6.1 shows the results related to our background study pertaining to in-language sentiment classification. In section 6.2, we compare the approaches for cross-lingual sentiment analysis.

6.1 In-language Classification

The results of in-language classification for Marathi and Hindi are shown in Table 3[3]. We consider unigram words as the baseline (Words) for comparison. Note that since cross-lingual SA using 'perfect' translation from target to source language is identical to in-language sentiment classification, these results act as an *upper bound/skyline* to the performance of cross-lingual SA. While using sense-based features, we also use the POS information and hence to have a fair comparison, we use an additional baseline which include the POS information in addition to unigram features (represented as *Words + POS)*.

L_{train} & L_{test} : Marathi							
Feature Representation	Accuracy	PF	NF	PP	NP	PR	NR
Words(Baseline)	86.53	85.13	86.96	96.68	80.25	76.05	94.90
Words + POS (Baseline)	83.32	79.91	85.42	97.00	76.92	69.33	97.00
Sense (M)	97.45	97.38	97.62	100.00	95.36	94.89	100.00
Sense + Words (M)	**97.87**	97.82	97.94	100.00	95.97	95.74	100.00
Sense(I)	93.44	93.97	92.94	89.25	99.19	99.21	87.43
Sense + Words (I)	92.78	93.35	92.32	88.14	99.17	99.20	86.36
L_{train} & L_{test} : Hindi							
Feature Representation	Accuracy	PF	NF	PP	NP	PR	NR
Words(Baseline)	65.64	61.65	64.83	71.38	62.29	54.25	67.60
Words+POS(Baseline)	76.34	70.18	79.92	89.42	70.34	58.27	92.80
Sense(M)	82.57	78.55	84.45	89.68	78.34	69.88	91.60
Words+Sense(M)	**83.06**	79.48	85.09	92.11	77.86	69.90	93.80
Sense(I)	81.92	78.00	83.25	88.63	78.98	69.65	88.00
Words+Sense(I)	81.21	78.03	83.50	89.35	77.29	69.26	90.80

Table 3: Background study: In-language sentiment classification showing the skyline performance for Marathi and Hindi; PF-Positive F-score, NF-Negative F-score, PP-Positive Precision(%), NP-Negative Precision(%), PR-Positive Recall (%), NR-Negative Recall (%)

Overall Sentiment Classification:

All sense-based features give a higher overall accuracy than the baseline for both Marathi and Hindi. The baseline for Hindi is lower than that for Marathi. However, manually annotated sense-based features perform better than the baseline by 11.3% for Marathi and 6.7% for Hindi. The classification accuracy of the combination of manually annotated synsets and words is comparable to that of manually annotated synsets for both the languages.

As expected, automatic sense disambiguation-based features perform better than the baseline but lower than manually annotated features. For Marathi, the classification accuracy for

[3]All results statistically significant (paired-T test, confidence=95%) with respect to the baseline. 3. For Marathi, Sense (M) and Words + Sense (M) results are not significant. Same is the case for Sense (I) and Words + Sense (I) for Hindi.

automatic sense disambiguation-based representation degrades by 4% below the manually annotated counterpart. This degradation is less significant in case of Hindi as the overall accuracy of Hindi sense disambiguation engine is only 66% (refer to Table 1). This suggests that even a low accuracy sense disambiguation may be sufficient to obtain better results than word based features.

6.2 CLSA Accuracy

L_{train} : Hindi & L_{test} : Marathi							
Feature Representation	**Accuracy**	**PF**	**NF**	**PP**	**NP**	**PR**	**NR**
Words(E) Baseline 1	71.64	72.22	62.86	75.36	67.69	69.33	58.67
Words(R) Baseline 2	70.15	71.23	60.87	73.24	66.67	69.33	56.00
Senses(M)	84.00	81.54	85.88	96.36	76.84	70.67	97.33
Senses(I)	**84.50**	83.33	85.51	96.15	76.62	73.53	96.72
L_{train} : Marathi & L_{test} : Hindi							
Feature Representation	**Accuracy**	**PF**	**NF**	**PP**	**NP**	**PR**	**NR**
Words(E) Baseline 1	56.42	29.31	64.37	94.44	52.17	17.35	84.00
Words(R) Baseline 2	57.69	30.77	66.16	94.74	53.37	18.37	87.00
Senses(M)	**72.08**	62.82	77.18	87.50	65.96	49.00	93.00
Senses(I)	68.11	61.04	72.81	77.05	63.71	50.54	84.95

Table 4: Cross-Lingual sentiment classification for target languages Marathi and Hindi; PF-Positive F-score, NF-Negative F-score, PP-Positive Precision(%), NP-Negative Precision(%), PR-Positive Recall (%), NR-Negative Recall (%)

Sense based CLSA accuracy along with the baseline accuracy is shown in Table 4[4].

L_{test} - **Marathi:** In-language classification accuracy for Marathi using words as features is only 86.53% (refer to Table 3). In a way, this forms the upper bound for a perfectly translated document. In the case of the naïve translation-based approach, an accuracy of 71.64% and 70.15% for Words (E) and Words (R) is obtained respectively. Both the manually and the automatically annotated sense-based features show an improvement of 12% (approximately) over both the baselines.

L_{test} - **Hindi:** When Hindi is the target language, the baseline using lexeme replacement is lower than the baseline for Marathi. An approximate 15% improvement over the baseline is observed for manually annotated sense-based features (which has an accuracy of 72%). Sense-based features developed using automatic sense disambiguation work with a lower accuracy with respect to manually annotated synsets.

A considerable improvement in the positive recall can be seen for Hindi as the target language. The same can be said about the negative precision. These results highlight the effectiveness of synsets as features for negative sentiment detection in a cross-lingual setup.

As most of the Indian languages do not have MT systems between them, we believe this approach can be an alternative to MT based CLSA approaches. Our approach is at par with MT based CLSA approach as our results are not far behind the in-language classification results. Hence MT based CLSA approaches are comparable with our approach as they too fall behind in-language classification results (based on the results of an independent study).

[4] All results are statistically significant with respect to the baseline. However, baseline 1 and baseline 2 are not statistically significant and so is the case for Sense (M) and Sense(I) accuracy figures for Marathi (as L_{test})

Effect of Automatic WSD on Classification Accuracy

Sense annotation accuracy (Fscore) of the WSD engine used for annotating the words with their respective sense is 65% and 76% (Tables 1 and 2) for Hindi and Marathi respectively. Annotation accuracy is less for Hindi as there are more finer senses in Hindi WordNet than in Marathi WordNet. Thus, there is a higher chance of assigning an incorrect sense for a word in Hindi than compared to a word in Marathi. However, the fall in classification accuracy due to this reason is not reflected on the in-language sentiment classification accuracy of Hindi and Marathi respectively. Nevertheless, there is a drop in the cross lingual accuracy when L_{test} is Hindi, which may be due to relatively small training corpora size of Marathi when compared to Hindi. Marathi corpus is half the size of Hindi corpus and hence contain less training samples where L_{test} is Hindi. As both the manually and the automatically assigned sense based features give almost similar cross lingual accuracy for the case when L_{test} is Hindi, we strongly believe that classification accuracy can be improved by adding more Marathi documents.

7 Error Analysis

Two possible reasons for errors in the existing approach that we found are:

1. **Missing Concepts:** As the Marathi WordNet is created using the expansion approach from the Hindi WordNet, almost all concepts present in the Marathi WordNet are derived from the Hindi WordNet. In contrast, there are many concepts present in the Hindi WordNet but not yet included in the Marathi WordNet. This leads to a low cross-lingual sentiment classification accuracy using sense-based features with target language as Hindi.

2. **Hindi Morph Analyzer Defect:** The accuracy of sense-based in-language classification for Hindi is comparatively lower than that for Marathi. We traced the problem to the sense annotation tool used by the manual annotator. The morphological analyzer used to find the root word (for verbs) did not match Hindi WordNet entries for verb synsets in many cases, thus reducing the coverage of the annotation.

8 Conclusion and Future Work

We presented an approach to cross-lingual SA that uses WordNet synset identifiers as features of a supervised classifier. Our sense-based approach provides a cross-lingual classification accuracy of 72% and 84% for Hindi and Marathi respectively, which is an improvement of 14% - 15% over the baseline based on a cross-lingual approach using a naïve translation of the training and test corpus. We also performed experiments based on a sense marked corpora using an automatic WSD engine. Results suggest that even a low quality word sense disambiguation leads to an improvement in the performance of sentiment classification. In summary, we have shown that WordNet synsets can act as good features for cross-lingual SA.

In future, we would like to perform sentiment analysis in a multilingual setup. Training data belonging to multiple languages can be leveraged to perform SA for some specific target language. Additionally, we would like to compare our CLSA approach with a MT based approach. For this, we plan to perform same set of experiments for languages (like English and Romanian) which have a linked wordnet as well a MT system between them.

References

Balamurali, A., Joshi, A., and Bhattacharyya, P. (2011). Harnessing wordnet senses for supervised sentiment classification. In *Proc. of EMNLP-11*, pages 1081–1091.

Banea, C., Mihalcea, R., Wiebe, J., and Hassan, S. (2008). Multilingual subjectivity analysis using machine translation. In *Proc. of EMNLP-08*, pages 127–135.

Bhattacharyya, P. (2010). Indowordnet. In *Proc. of LREC-10*, Valletta, Malta. European Language Resources Association (ELRA).

Brooke, J., Tofiloski, M., and Taboada, M. (2009). Cross-Linguistic Sentiment Analysis: From English to Spanish. In *Proc. of RANLP-09*.

Dietterich, T. G. (1998). Approximate statistical tests for comparing supervised classification learning algorithms. *Neural Computation*, 10:1895–1923.

Fellbaum, C. (1998). *WordNet: An Electronic Lexical Database*. Bradford Books.

Khapra, M., Shah, S., Kedia, P., and Bhattacharyya, P. (2010). Domain-specific word sense disambiguation combining corpus basedand wordnet based parameters. In *Proceedings of GWC-10*.

Mohanty, R., Bhattacharyya, P., Pande, P., Kalele, S., Khapra, M., and Sharma, A. (2008). Synset based multilingual dictionary: Insights, applications and challenges. In *Proc. of GWC-08*.

Nakagawa, T., Inui, K., and Kurohashi., S. (2010). Dependency tree-based sentiment classification using crfs with hidden variables. In *Proc. of NAACL/HLT-10*.

Pang, B. and Lee, L. (2002). Thumbs up? sentiment classification using machine learning techniques. In *Proc. of EMNLP-02*, pages 79–86.

Schulz, J. M., Womser-Hacke, C., and Mandl, T. (2010). Multilingual corpus development for opinion mining. In *Proc. of LREC-10*.

Seki, Y., Evans, D. K., Ku, L.-W., Sun, L., Chen, H.-H., and Kando, N. (2007). Overview of multilingual opinion analysis task at ntcir-7. In *Proc. of NTCIR-7 Workshop*.

Vossen, P. (1998). Eurowordnet: a multilingual database with lexical semantic networks. In *International Conference on Computational Linguistics*.

Wan, X. (2009). Co-training for cross-lingual sentiment classification. In *Proc. of ACL-AFNLP-09*, pages 235–243.

Wei, B. and Pal, C. (2010). Cross lingual adaptation: an experiment on sentiment classifications. In *Proc. of ACL-10*, pages 258–262.

THE CREATION OF LARGE-SCALE ANNOTATED CORPORA OF MINORITY LANGUAGES USING UNIPARSER AND THE EANC PLATFORM

Timofey ARKHANGELSKIY[1] *Oleg BELYAEV*[2,3] *Arseniy VYDRIN*[4]
(1) National Research University Higher Scool of Economics,
Moscow, Myasnitskaya St. 20
(2) Institute of Linguistics of the Russian Academy of Sciences,
Moscow, Bolshoy Kislovskiy Lane 1/1
(3) Sholokhov Moscow State University for the Humanities,
Moscow, 3-ya Vladimirskaya St. 5, room 35
(4) Institute for Linguistic Research of the Russian Academy of Sciences,
St. Petersburg, Tuchkov per. 9
tarkhangelskiy@hse.ru, belyaev@iling-ran.ru, senjacom@gmail.com

ABSTRACT

This paper is devoted to the use of two tools for creating morphologically annotated linguistic corpora: UniParser and the EANC platform. The EANC platform is the database and search framework originally developed for the Eastern Armenian National Corpus (www.eanc.net) and later adopted for other languages. UniParser is an automated morphological analysis tool developed specifically for creating corpora of languages with relatively small numbers of native speakers for which the development of parsers from scratch is not feasible. It has been designed for use with the EANC platform and generates XML output in the EANC format.

UniParser and the EANC platform have already been used for the creation of the corpora of several languages: Albanian, Kalmyk, Lezgian, Ossetic, of which the Ossetic corpus is the largest (5 million tokens, 10 million planned for 2013), and are currently being employed in construction of the corpora of Buryat and Modern Greek languages. This paper will describe the general architecture of the EANC platform and UniParser, providing the Ossetic corpus as an example of the advantages and disadvantages of the described approach.

KEYWORDS : corpus linguistics, automated morphological analysis, language documentation, Iranian languages, Ossetic

Proceedings of COLING 2012: Posters, pages 83–92,
COLING 2012, Mumbai, December 2012.

1 Corpus technologies and minority languages

Corpus lingustics is currently a rapidly developing area of study. Corpora created for such large languages as English, Czech, or Russian are being increasingly used for analyzing the grammatical phenomena of these languages drawing on more empirical material than could ever be possible before in the history of linguistics. Using corpus data as a basis for linguistic research has become a new "philosophical approach" rather than just one of possible methodologies (Leech 1991) and is widely considered to be superior to the classical approaches of introspection/elicitation, since it draws on real language use instead of artificially constructed examples.

Unfortunately, the creation of a reasonably large annotated corpus (with 1 million tokens or more), especially for a morphologically rich language, is a complicated task that few languages can "afford". The prerequisites for creating a successful corpus are: (1) the availability of digitized texts in that language; (2) the existence of an automatic morphological analyzer. Both of these tasks require considerable investment of time and money, even when a language has a reasonably developed literary tradition (like e.g. Ossetic does, having had literature since the late 1800s).

Therefore, the linguistic community ends up in a situation when large corpora suitable for efficiently studying grammatical phenomena are available only for the major languages of the world. This creates a strong typological bias in favour of these languages.

Our work on Ossetic is an attempt to overcome this limitation, producing a large corpus of a minority language of Russia. Ossetic is an Iranian (Indo-European) language spoken by about 500,000 people mainly in the Russian Federation, in the Republic of North Ossetia situated in the North Caucasus. Digitized versions of Ossetic literature (written in the literary Iron dialect) are readily available from publishers in Vladikavkaz[1]. However, problematic was the creating of an automatic morphological analyzer for Ossetic, a language with a relatively rich inflectional morphology (9 nominal cases and a large number of verbal forms), and the choice of a web platform to be used for accessing the corpus. The solution was reached by developing a universal morphological parser. It operates using rules provided by linguists (and can thus be applied to different languages) and produces XML output that is accepted by the Eastern Armenian National Corpus (EANC) platform, which was adapted for use with the Ossetic language. The final result is the Ossetic National Corpus, which is freely available online (http://corpus.ossetic-

[1]We are thankful to the editors of the *Max dug* literary journal, as well as to the personnel of the *Ir* publishing house, for providing us with electronic versions of their publications and approving of them being used in the corpus.

studies.org) and contains about 5 million morphologically analyzed tokens (with 10 million planned for 2013).

2 The EANC platform

The platform we used for the Ossetic corpus was initially developed by CorpusTechnologies for the Eastern Armenian National Corpus in 2007 (see e. g. Khurshudian et al. 2009). It includes a search engine and a web interface. Although the interface was designed specifically for the Armenian language, the search engine itself is language-independent and is suitable for a great variety of languages. To use the platform with Ossetic, we had to produce parsed texts in the format supported by the EANC platform and make some corrections to the user interface.

2.1 General architecture and features

Parsed data are stored in a number of datafiles. The text itself is stored in XML form in these datafiles. There is a number of index files which list positions of all occurrences of specific wordforms, lemmas and combinations of grammatical tags in the texts. The texts can be equipped with metadata, such as the name of the text, the name of the author, the date of creation, etc. The datafiles are produced by the indexer written in Python which takes parsed texts as its input.

The user interface is written in PHP and HTML. When the user initiates a new search, the interface collects the data entered by the user and sends them to the client written in PHP which, in turn, transmits the query to the server. The server is a program written in C++ which is constantly running and waiting for requests. The server performs the search and sends the result back to the client. Then the result is transformed according to the specified display options and displayed in the browser.

The main query types offered by the EANC interface are wordform, lemma, and grammatical tags queries. When searching for a particular wordform, lemma, or a set of grammatical tags, the platform displays all sentences containing the requested wordforms.

There are a number of special characters for enhanced queries. Specifically, one can use "*" for arbitrary number of characters, "|" for disjunction, "&" for conjunction, and "~" for negation. For example, if "*тты|*тыл" is typed into the Wordform box in the Ossetic corpus, the platform will find all wordforms ending with either *тты* or *тыл*. In the case more than one operator is used, their order can be specified by means of parentheses.

There are also other restrictions one may impose on the words one wants to find. They include specifying a subcorpus, restrictions on the positions of the words being searched relative to each other, etc. The output can be displayed in several ways, including KWIC (Key Word In Context), and supports transliteration mode.

2.2 Adopting the platform for other languages

To use the EANC platform with another corpus, we had to rewrite the language-specific parts of the user interface. These include, for example, a form where one can specify grammar query with the help of checkboxes, every checkbox corresponding to one of the grammatical tags used in the corpus, such as "inessive case". To do that in a more efficient way, we wrote a Python script which takes a simple csv table with all grammatical features of the language and transforms it into the PHP file used in the interface. Parts concerning the writing system were also rewritten, namely the transliteration system and the virtual keyboard. The indexer and the datafile system remained intact and works fine with languages other than Armenian without additional adjustments, provided one doesn't need any additional features.

3 UniParser

A corpus of texts without annotation is effectively a mere electronic library with quite limited applicability for linguistic research. Annotation can include different kinds of data - among others, it can include text-level information such as the name of the author and the time of creation of the text, sentence-level, or word-level information.

The most widely used type of word-by-word annotation used in general purpose corpora, such as the one under consideration, is lemmatization and grammatical markup. Lemmatization means that for every wordform in the corpus, its lemma (dictionary form) is provided, and grammatical markup of a wordform means that all or some subset of grammatical values expressed in it are explicitly shown. (The "lighter" variant of the latter is part-of-speech tagging.) While for languages with poor morphology, such as English, the absence of grammatical markup might not constitute a big obstacle, for morphologically rich languages such as Ossetic it would make any corpus research involving searches for all instances of a given lexeme or all wordforms with a given morphosyntactic feature virtually impossible.

While for small corpora whose size doesn't exceed several hundred thousand tokens it is feasible to annotate them manually, with corpus size going in the millions, automatic tagging is the only possible way of performing this task. Ossetic corpus being approximately 5 million tokens in size at the beginning with even more on the way, we needed an automated utility to annotate with. In the same time, we also were in contact with several other related groups working on other corpora of morphologically rich and diverse languages, namely Albanian, Greek, Kalmyk, and Lezgian, who were also in need of such a tool, so rather than creating a program designed specifically for morphological parsing of Ossetic language, it was deemed more feasible to build a general parser with capability of parsing any of those languages provided their lexicons and grammars are described in some suitable format.

After considering several existing resources, we decided to develop a new system from scratch. The resulting tool, UniParser, is suitable for parsing large amounts of texts in structurally different languages. We are going to make UniParser freely available in 2013. The tool and the format it utilizes to store the information about the language, are the subject of the description below.

3.1 The requirements

When designing a parsing tool for middle-sized and large corpora in different languages, we had in mind several requirements it should conform to.

First, it should work fast enough to cope with big amounts of texts. This is one of the reasons why we couldn't use tools aimed at parsing small corpora. For example, one of the parsers used in the Fieldworks Language Explorer, XAMPLE, and its predecessor, AMPLE, can process tens to hundreds wordforms per second (see Black, Simons 2006), which would require at least half a day for parsing the entire Ossetic Corpus.

Second, the files should have simple enough format to be edited with the help of an ordinary plain text processor by a linguist without programming or other technical skills. The only specific piece of knowledge which might be required for describing some fragments of grammar in UniParser format is regular expressions.

Third, it should be flexible enough to be used with structurally different languages, addressing a wide range of various morphological phenomena.

Other requirements, namely limitation imposed on the morpological model and the output format of the parsed text are presented in more detail below.

3.2 The morphological model

The basic approach taken in the UniParser format can be roughly described as Word-And-Paradigm morphology (see e. g. (Matthews, 1972) for thorough description of this model). Here by this term we mean that wordforms in the parsed corpus should be labelled with grammatical tags like "Noun" or "genitive case", and provided with lemmata, but the researchers who compile the corpus shouldn't be obliged to overtly mark morpheme boundaries when making a description of the grammar. This is contrary to the approach taken e. g. in the parsers used in the Fieldworks Language Explorer where the user first has to create a dictionary of morphemes and then define templates describing the ways these morphemes can be assembled together producing wordforms. However, if the user wants their corpus to be glossed and displayed with interlinears, the UniParser format offers a possibility of doing that. We adhere to this approach to facilitate the annotation of corpora in flective languages where division into morphemes may be not that straightforward, so that providing accurate information about individual morphemes in the grammatical description would be time-consuming and often subjective.

The word inflection in the UniParser format is described, first of all, through the notions of stem, inflexion, paradigm, and productive derivation model. All data in the description of the lexicon and the grammar is concerned only with the graphical representations of wordforms, without appealing to their phonemic or any other "deep" levels.

A lexeme is thought of as a set of wordforms. In the vast number of cases, all these forms have some letters in common. Thus every wordform of a lexeme can be divided into the part common for the entire lexeme and the part that is unique for the given form (or several forms). These units are called a stem and an inflexion. If a unit is disjoint, the places where parts of another units can appear are marked with dots. The dot also appears at the beginning or at the end of a unit if it can be, respectively, preceded or followed by a part of another unit. So, in Ossetic (and in most other IE languages) most stems would have a dot at the end meaning that they can take inflectional markers on the right. Accordingly, most inflexions would look like a contiguous block of letters with a dot at the beginning. A stem and an inflexion can be combined into a wordform by inserting parts of one of them into the dot-marked slots of the other. To take an extreme example, in Arabic wordform *katabtu* 'I wrote' with the stem KTB, the stem would be written as ".k.t.b.", and the inflexion as ".a.a.tu".

A complete set of inflexions a lexeme can take is called a paradigm. Different lexemes of the same part of speech can belong to different paradigms and use different markers for expressing the same grammatical values. Every inflexion in the UniParser format belongs to one of the paradigms.

Another feature of UniParser format is productive derivation models. By derivation we understand the process whereby new lexemes are created on the basis of existing ones according to some rules; a productive derivation model is such a rule which is applicable to a large and open set of lexemes (say, to all lexemes of a particular paradigm type). For example, many Ossetic verbs have perfectivized forms with different preverbs which are considered separate lexemes. A productive derivation model was set up for every preverb, which automatically adds all the derivatives to the lexicon.

3.3 Dictionary format

All the information about the lexicon and the grammar of a language is stored in a number of files, the core files being stem.txt (lexicon), paradigm.txt (inflexions) and derivation.txt (productive derivation models).

The format of description is based on YAML, which was preferred over XML because the former is more human-readable, so that the files can be edited by hand. All files contain "objects" which are collections of parameter-value pairs, values being strings or another objects.

The basic object of the file stem.txt is a lexeme, which is described as a list of parameter-value pairs. This list is open in principle, with only several fields being obligatory, namely lex (the lemma), stem, paradigm, and gramm (grammatical tags which should be assigned to every wordform of that lexeme in the parsed text). In the Ossetic dictionary, the two additional fields contain Russian and English translations of the lemma.

In the case of suppletivism or stem alternations, several stems (allomorphs of the stem) can be stipulated instead of one. Another case when several stems can be stipulated is free variation. As an example of a lexeme with both of these phenomena, we will take the Ossetic word æххормаг 'hunger' which has three stem allomorphs, each allomorph possessing two variants:

```
-lexeme
 lex: æххормаг
 stem: æххормаг.//ххормаг.|æххормадж.//ххормадж.|
æххормæг.//ххормæг.
 paradigm: Nct
 gramm: N-ADJ,inanim,nonhuman
```

The basic object of the file paradigm.txt is a paradigm which is a collection of inflexions. A fragment of Ossetic nominal paradigm Nctt is presented below:

```
-paradigm: Nctt
 -flex: <1>.ы
  gramm: sg,gen
  gloss: GEN
 -flex: <0>.æн
  gramm: sg,dat
  gloss: DAT
```

The number in angle brackets defines the stem allomorph a given inflexion can be used with. In inflexions, the only obligatory field is gramm which contains grammatical tags assigned to all wordforms with that inflexion by the parser. If the user wants the text to be glossed, she may optionally specify the division of the inflexion into morphemes and add the gloss field.

3.4 Technical details

The UniParser tool consists of a simple user interface, the preprocessing module and the analysis module. The user interface allows to load description files, view full paradigms of the lexemes in the lexicon (which is crucial for error-checking), and launch preprocessing or analysis. The preprocessing module transforms the description of the language into a datafile to be used in the course of parsing. The analysis module uses a finite-state automaton with hashtables. The analysis module of the UniParser tool was implemented in C++, and the user interface and the preprocessing module were written in C#.

The parsing speed for Ossetic texts reached approximately 7000 wordforms per second on an AMD Athlon 64X2 (2x2,20 GHz) system with 2 GB RAM. By using a relatively short list of pre-analyzed high-frequency wordforms, we could increase the speed some 30% further. Although the speed can be considered sufficiently high for our purposes (12 minutes for the whole corpus), there is evidently room for improvement (for example, by introducing multithreading). Another parameter which should be optimised is memory usage, as in the current version more than 1 GB of memory was used.

No statistical disambiguation techniques were used because, despite their high accuracy rates, there is a risk of systematically distorting some linguistically peculiar information. Therefore any token was assigned all parses that were possible on the basis of the language description. The quality of analysis can be estimated by parsed tokens rate and the average number of parses per parsed token. Among all the tokens of the corpus, more than 85% were assigned at least one parse, the dictionary size being about 15,000 entries. The average number of parses per parsed token is approximately 1.7. The figure is quite high, so addressing this problem with the help of deterministic disambiguation rules is planned.

The parser takes plain text files encoded in UTF-8 as its input and produces an XML file with the parsed text. The XML we use is similar to that used in the Russian National Corpus.

Conclusion and perspectives

As a result of developing a universal morphological parser and a set of rules for this parser, as well as adopting an existing search engine (the EANC platform) for being used with the Ossetic language, we have successfully created a corpus of literary Ossetic consisting of 5 million tokens, which is one of the first corpora of such scale having been developed for a minority language. Our next aim is to reach 10 million tokens, as well as develop the parser further in order to allow for analyzing compounds and verbs with incorporated nouns, which are quite widespread in Ossetic. This will allow us to reach higher percentages of analyzed tokens than the current 85%. A further possible area of inquiry is developing mechanisms for automatic resolution of ambiguity, at least in those cases where the function of the wordform is clear from its immediate context.

References

Black, H. A. and Simons, G. F. (2006). The SIL FieldWorks Language Explorer Approach to Morphological Parsing. In *Computational Linguistics for Less-studied Languages: Proceedings of Texas Linguistics Society 10, 3–5 November 2006*, Austin, TX

Khurshudian, V. G., Daniel, M. A., Levonian D. V., Plungian V. A., Polyakov A. E., Rubakov S. V. (2009). Eastern Armenian National Corpus. In *Computational Linguistics and Intellectual Technologies (Papers from the Annual International Conference "Dialogue 2009")*, 8 (15), pages 509-518, Moscow, RGGU

Leech, G. (1992). Corpora and theories of linguistic performance. In *J. Svartvik (ed)., Directions in Corpus Linguistics: Proceedings of the Nobel Symposium 82, Stockholm, 4–8 August 1991*, pages 105-122, Berlin, Mouton de Gruyter

Matthews, P. H. (1972). *Inflectional Morphology (a Theoretical Study based on Aspects of Latin Verb Conjugation).* Cambridge, Cambridge University Press

Collocation Extraction Using Parallel Corpus

Kavosh Asadi Atui[1] *Heshaam Faili*[1] *Kaveh Assadi Atuie*[2]
(1)NLP Laboratory, Electrical and Computer Engineering Dept., University of Tehran, Iran
(2)Electrical Engineering Dept., Sharif University of Technology, Iran
kavosh.asadi@ece.ut.ac.ir, hfaili@ut.ac.ir, kassadi@ee.sharif.ir

ABSTRACT

This paper presents a novel method to extract the collocations of the Persian language using a parallel corpus. The method is applicable having a parallel corpus between a target language and any other high-resource one. Without the need for an accurate parser for the target side, it aims to parse the sentences to capture long distance collocations and to generate more precise results. A training data built by bootstrapping is also used to rank the candidates with a log-linear model. The method improves the precision and recall of collocation extraction by 5 and 3 percent respectively in comparison with the window-based statistical method in terms of being a Persian multi-word expression.

KEYWORDS: Information and Content Extraction, Parallel Corpus, Under-resourced Languages

Proceedings of COLING 2012: Posters, pages 93–102,
COLING 2012, Mumbai, December 2012.

1 Introduction

Collocation is usually interpreted as the occurrence of two or more words within a short space in a text (Sinclair, 1987). This definition however is not precise, because it is not possible to define a short space. It also implies the strategy that all traditional models had. They were looking for co-occurrences rather than collocations (Seretan, 2011). Consider the following sentence and its Persian translation[1]:

"Lecturer issued a major and also impossible to solve problem."

مدرس یک مشکل بزرگ و غیر قابل حل را عنوان کرد.

"مدرس"/modarres/"lecturer"

"یک"/yek/"a"

"مشکل"/moshkel/"problem"

"بزرگ"/bozorg/"major"

"و"/va/"and"

"غیر قابل حل"/gheyreghabelehal/"impossible to solve"

"عنوان کرد"/onvankard/"issued"

This sentence emphasizes the action of "issuing a problem" which is a collocation, because it is a common way of saying that someone warned about a problem. Figure 1 shows that a verb-object relation between "issued" and "problem" and the alignments between the sentences imply that there is a corresponding relation between "مشکل" /moshkel/"problem" and "عنوان کرد"/onvan kard/"issued" in the Persian language.

FIGURE1 – Example of a collocation: The relation between مشکل and عنوان کرد in the Persian sentence corresponds to the relation between issued and problem in English sentence.

Noticeably, window-based method cannot extract the collocation, because of the vagueness in the definition of short space. Moreover, the window cannot be expanded to include the words constructing the collocation. It is proved that expanding the window to more than 5 words is impractical (Dias, 2003). Besides, another flaw of the classical methods is that many false positive samples are mistakenly classified as collocation. This problem occurs especially in pairs having a small number of occurrences in the corpus (Seretan, 2011). While the latter problem can be solved (Basili et al.,1994), what this paper presents is another strategy which does not insist on classical approaches.

Recent improvements on the accuracy of parsers motivate modern approaches to analyze the sentences first (Seretan, 2006). Although that is the case in many languages like English, a lot of

[1] Persian uses Arabic script as its writing formalism which is written from right to left direction.

efforts have to be done in order to obtain an admissible accuracy in parsing the sentences of under-resourced languages like Persian.

This study accepts an alternative definition for collocation: "an expression consisting of two or more words that corresponds some conventional way of saying things" (Manning & Schütze, 1999). This definition does not have the vagueness the window-based method has.

Collocation has a deep influence on many other tasks of NLP such as MT systems (Orliac & Dillinger, 2003) and Text Summarization (Seretan, 2011) which makes it essential to find an alternative solution. From the next part of the paper, a process of extracting the collocations of Persian language will be presented.

The parallel corpus used in this study is Tehran English-Persian Parallel Corpus (Pilevar et al., 2011). The Corpus is comprised of more than 500000 pairs of sentences. The sentences are aligned by the IBM model3 using Giza++. In IBM model3 it is possible to have many to many alignments. This model is selected because it provides the extraction of collocations including more than two words.

In this method, by having a parallel aligned corpus and also parsed sentences of the source language, dependencies between the words of the target language are extracted initially. Direct Projection Algorithm (Hwa et al., 2005) is employed. It uses the alignments between the source and target sentences and the dependencies of the source language. In order to rank pairs of words by a log-linear classifier, a reasonable training data is then provided using bootstrapping with a small initial training set. Afterwards, the log-linear model is trained to sort and classify the candidates. Finally, the validation phase is implemented by the means of mutual dependency of two constituents to validate them based on their frequency of occurrence in another Persian corpus. Figure 2 demonstrates the architecture of this system.

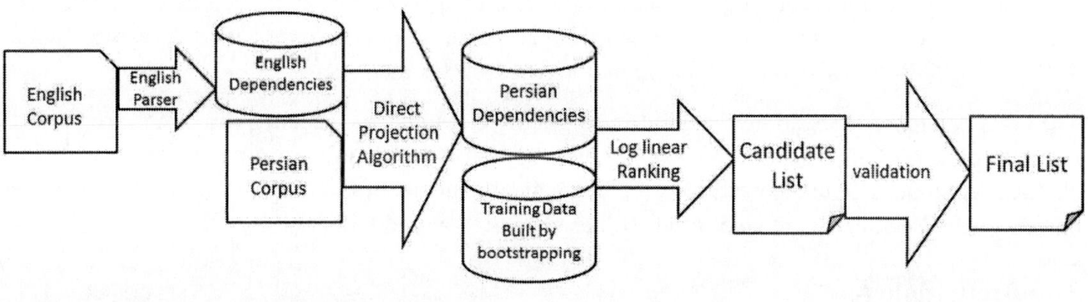

FIGURE 2 – Simplified architecture of system.

Briefly, the contribution of the paper is as follows:

- Employing the initial syntactical analysis without a parser for target language
- Using bootstrapping to build up a training data for log-linear classifier
- Developing the first dependency-based collocation extraction approach for Persian language.

In the next section, previous work related to this study is discussed. Section 3 consists of 4 separate parts and explains the method. Section 4 reports a comparative evaluation between our method and a classical window-based method as a baseline.

2 Related work

In the past decades, many studies regarding the collocation extraction have been undertaken. Classically, all approaches are consisted of two parts: Candidate Identification and Candidate Ranking. All earliest approaches devoted most of their efforts to find a suitable association measure (AM) in order to perform the ranking phase. One of the earliest measures is the z-score (Smadja, 1993) which assumes the data to be normally distributed. Log likelihood ratio (LLR) is another measure that is used in the recent efforts (Orliac & Dilinger, 2003). Still, the most common measure of collocation extraction is Pointwise Mutual Information (Church & Hanks, 1990). There is not an agreement on the best AM, but recent studies suggest that Mutual Information is the best possible measure (Pecina, 2010).

As mentioned above, the first phase of the architecture is identifying possible candidates. This phase is consisted of a linguistic preprocessing of the sentences (Seretan, 2011). The phase could be varied from lemmatization to deep parsing. Obviously, collocation deals with lemmas, not with word surface. Combining all inflected forms of a unique lemma leads to more competitive results (Evert, 2004). POS tagging is another preprocessing attempt to identify the potential candidates more precisely. There is a considerable improvement in the results of the system by performing POS tagging (Church & Hanks, 1990).

The common drawback of all these approaches is that they are not able to capture long distance dependencies. There is a solution to overcome this problem (Charest et al.,2007; Pecina,2010). Although less convenient to apply for under-resourced languages, deep parsing could be used to preprocess the text (Lu & Zhou, 2004).

Using monolingual corpora and word alignment is another recently common approach. In this approach, the monolingual corpus is replicated to generate a parallel corpus of the same sentences. Then, the aligned words are ranked, and pairs with higher scores are extracted as collocation (Liu et al., 2011). Another option is to use a multilingual parser to obtain more accurate results (Seretan & Wehrli, 2006). It is also unavailable in under-resourced languages.

The classical approaches do not lead to the competitive results, and recent approaches are based on accurate parsers. This paper introduces a novel method that not only eliminates the drawbacks of classical approaches, but also employs the syntactical analysis of the corpus without the need for a parser for the Persian (target side) or any other under-resourced language.

3 Methodology

This section introduces the novel method of extraction of the collocations of the Persian language. The method is divided into four steps: dependency projection, candidate generation, candidate ranking, and validation. Each step is explained in the following parts.

3.1 Dependency projection

Having a parsed English corpus, a list of relations between pairs of words is provided. In this method Dependency Parsing is used. It provides the relations between pairs of constituents. An algorithm is needed to transfer these relations to the target language.

Direct Projection Algorithm (Hwa et al., 2005) is employed in this step. This algorithm needs a list of the alignments between source and target words. Having a pair of sentences formed by an arbitrary number of words named e_1 through e_N in the source language and f_1 through f_M in the target language and also alignments between the words, five different scenarios are possible:

1. one to one: if two words of the source sentence named e_i and e_j are aligned to unique words f_i and f_j in the target language, relation (e_i,e_j) results in a new relation between f_i and f_j in the target language.
2. unaligned: if there is no corresponding word for e_i, a new null node is created. Relations including the unaligned word form relations having that null node in one part of the relation in the target language.
3. one to many: if more than one word i.e. f_x ,..., f_y are aligned to a unique word in the source language, a new node as the parent of these words is created and the alignment is modified to form a one to one alignment.
4. many to one: if e_i ,..., e_j are all aligned to a single word in the target language, all the alignments between them and the unique target word is eliminated except for the alignment containing the head of these words (which could be extracted from the set of the dependencies).
5. many to many: in this case, first one to many and then many to one scenario happen.

Importantly, in order to extract the collocations with more than two words, many to many alignments are necessary. The next step is generation of the candidates.

3.2 Candidate generation

In this step, a list of the potential collocations is generated. Dependency parser provides the relations between pairs of the constituents and their directions. Dependencies listed in Table 1 are primary candidates to construct collocation if they satisfy the following conditions:

1. not having a proper noun in one of its two parts.
2. not containing a null node created by Direct Projection.
3. not being an erroneous dependency e.g. dependency between a verb and an object without having any verbs at the both sides of the relation.
4. not including an auxiliary or modal verb.
5. not including uncommon constituents between the source and target languages. An example is a dependency having "را"/ra/ in the Persian language. This word indicates that there is an object right before it, while there is no such word in the English language.

Type	Example
Verb - Adverb	Sleep – Deeply
Verb - Object	Issue – Problem
Verb - Subject	Shine – Gold
Noun - Adjective	Game – Full
Adjective - Adverb	Fully – Optimistic

TABLE 1 – List of types of collocations accepted in this paper and their corresponding examples.

After identifying potential pairs, candidate ranking is performed. The next part describes the method of sorting the candidates.

3.3 Candidate ranking

In this phase the method of ranking the candidates is introduced. This ranking is based on a set of features and a log linear model. As mentioned earlier, sorting the pairs depends on some set of features. Importantly, the type of the dependency and two phrases are not the only information used to perform the ranking. It is crucial to include the results of Direct Projection Algorithm to better define discriminative features.
Following is the list of the features:

- Length of the target sentence
- Difference between the length of two sentences
- Total number of null nodes created by Direct Projection Algorithm in the sentence
- Type of the dependency
- Relation-specific features. An example is whether the verb imposes an object in a verb-object relation

Having these features, a training data is needed. This is provided by bootstrapping. This is obtained by having only a small initial training data. In each step of the algorithm best decisions made by the algorithm are selected and are added to the initial training data. This process results in a large training data which is necessary to train the log-linear model. The most important requirement of this phase is to have a measure to evaluate each decision made by the algorithm in all iterations.

It is now possible to build up a log linear model and estimate the weights for each one of the features form the training data derived from bootstrapping. Equation 1 denotes the possibility of each class.

$$p(c|x) = \frac{e^{\sum_{i=0}^{N}(w_i f_i)}}{\sum_{c=1}^{2}(e^{\sum_{i=0}^{N} w_i f_i})} \qquad (1)$$

Here, $p(c|x)$ denotes the probability of constructing a collocation for every pairs of words x or belonging to other class. In the next step the validation phase is discussed.

3.4 Validation

In order to exclude outliers and noisy samples that remained in the list after the two previous sections, validation is essential. We should note that this step is equally applied to the window-based method which is selected as the baseline for collocation extraction. For validation, an association measure (AM) is needed. AM is interpreted as a formula that computes an association score in a pair type's contingency table (Evert, 2004).Among many measures defined to test the dependency between pairs of words or more generally pairs of constituents of a sentence, mutual dependency (MD) is used. As a notification, the measure is defined as equation 2.

$$D(w1,w2) = \log_2 \frac{p(w1,w2)^2}{P(w1)\,P(w2)} \qquad (2)$$

The measure is maximized for the pairs that are dependent. Note that this measure could be replaced by any other measure estimating the probability of co-occurrence within a sentence. Since the candidates that this measure is trying to test their co-occurrence are the result of Min Direct Algorithm, unrelated pairs are not verified.

4 Evaluation

In order to evaluate this method we performed a comparison between our method and the classical baseline for Collocation Extraction which is the window-based method. Our evaluation approach obviates the necessity of setting a threshold. To have a better baseline, we performed a part of speech tagging to eliminate some noisy pairs from the list of collocations resulted at the end of the process. Maximum size of the window is 5 with expansion to 7 words based on part of speech of the two outmost words in the rare cases. The final results of both two methods are judged manually by three different referees. Every pair not verified by two or three of our referees was not counted as a true sample. Table 2 shows the agreement rate for 500 best results.

	Window method	Our method
Referees 1 and 2	85.0	82.1
Referees 2 and 3	76.5	77.3
Referees 1 and 3	89.2	88.5
Referees 1 and 2 and 3	70.6	69.8

TABLE 2 – Agreement Rate among referees.

At each level, N best pairs are picked and the precision is calculated. Every pair is required to be validated by two out of the three referees. Table 3 shows the precision of both methods in terms of being a sub-part of a Persian MWE.

N	Window Method	Our method
100	77.0	82.0
200	73.5	76.5
300	62.3	69.0
400	61.7	66.5
500	60.2	64.2

TABLE 3 – Precision for N best samples: Each raw shows the precision for N best results of both methods.

To compare the recall of these methods, 200 pairs validated by all of our three referees and 500 pairs validated by two out of the three referees are selected. Table 4 shows the results of the comparison.

	Window Method	Our method
Accepted by two referees	68.3	71.4
Accepted by All referees	69.1	72.9

TABLE 4 – Recall of the methods in each condition. First raw considers the pairs that are accepted by minimum of two judges and the second raw shows the recall in pairs accepted by 3 referees.

Table 5 shows why our method has a better recall in comparison to the window-based method. The results are showed for 100 best results picked by our method. The method is able to capture long distance dependencies. Hence, a noticeable improvement in the recall of the system is occurred. Besides, our method generates less false positive samples.

Distance between pairs	1 or 2	2 or 3	4 or 5	More than 5
Total number of collocations	42	35	14	9

TABLE 5 – 23 out of 100 best pairs are 3 words away from each other and 9 of them more than 5 which makes it impossible for window-based methods to have a reasonable recall.

Conclusion

This paper introduced a method to extract the collocations of the Persian language with a preprocessing phase by means of a dependency parser for the English language. The results suggested that syntactical analysis makes the method more accurate, even if it is implemented in a novel approach. What is important tough is that the accuracy of whole system tightly depends on the accuracy of the parser as well as the alignments between words. Having a noisy parser makes it impossible to achieve competitive results. In other words, it can diminish the benefits of employing the syntactical analysis.

It was concluded that although it is still impossible to have an accurate parser for many languages such as Persian, initial syntactical analysis of corpus is such indispensable that it can lead to a better precision and recall in extracting the collocations even in this kind of implementation.

With no doubt, preprocessing is both essential and beneficial in collocation extraction. Achieving more accurate results is not hindered by the fact that many languages such as the Persian language are under-resourced. The method presented in this paper simultaneously solved the problem of missing long-distance collocations and generation of false positive samples in the earlier methods.

Acknowledgements

We would like to express our deepest gratitude towards Professor Maryam S. Mirian for her valuable advice on our research.

References

Hwa, R. , Resnik, P. , Weinberg, A. , Cabezas, C., and Kolak, O. (2005). Bootstrapping parsers via syntactic projection across parallel texts. *Nat. Lang. Eng.,* 11(3): 311-325.

Pilevar, M. T., Faili, H., and Pilevar, A. H. (2011). TEP: Tehran English-Persian parallel corpus. In *Proceedings of the 12th international conference on Computational linguistics and intelligent text processing* - Volume Part II, Tokyo, Japan.

Manning, C. D., and Schèutze, H. (1999). *Foundations of Statistical Natural Language Processing*. Cambridge, Mass.: MIT Press.

Liu, Z., Wang, H., Wu, H., and Li, S. (2011). Two-word collocation extraction using monolingual word alignment method. *ACM Trans. Intell. Syst. Technol., 3*(1): 1-29.

Seretan, V., and Wehrli, E. (2006). Accurate collocation extraction using a multilingual parser. In *Proceedings of the 21st International Conference on Computational Linguistics and the 44th annual meeting of the Association for Computational Linguistics*, Sydney, Australia.

Rasooli, M. S. , Faili, H. , and Minaei-Bidgoli, B. (2011). Unsupervised identification of persian compound verbs. In *Proceedings of the 10th Mexican international conference on Advances in Artificial Intelligence*, Puebla, Mexico.

Sinclair, J.M. (1987). Collocation: a progress report. In R. Steele and T. Treadgold (eds.), Essays in honour of Michael Halliday, (pp. 319-331). Amsterdam: John Benjamins.

Seretan, V. (2011). *Syntax-based collocation extraction,*Berlin: Spriger.

Basili, R. , Pazienza, M. T. and Velardi, P. (1993). Semi-automatic extraction of linguistic information for syntactic disambiguation. *Applied Artificial Intelligence,* 7, 339-364.

Orliac, B., and Dillinger, M. (2003). Collocation extraction for machine translation. *Machine Translation Summit., 9*: 292-298.

Smadja, F. (1993). Retrieving collocations from text: Xtract. *Computational Linguistics* 19(1): 143–177.

Evert, S., and Krenn, B. (2001). Methods for the qualitative evaluation of lexical association measures. In *Proceedings of the 39th Annual Meeting on Association for Computational Linguistics*, Toulouse, France.

Church, K. , and Hanks, P. (1990). Word association norms, mutual information, and lexicography. *Computational Linguistics, 16*(1): 22–29.

Pecina, P., and Schlesinger, P. (2006). Combining association measures for collocation extraction. In *Proceedings of the COLING/ACL*, Sydney, Australia.

LU, Y., and ZHOU, M. (2004). Collocation translation acquisition using monolingual corpora. In *Proceedings of the 42nd Annual Meeting on Association for Computational Linguistics*, Barcelona, Spain.

Liu, Z., Wang, H., Wu, H., and Li, S. (2009). Collocation extraction using monolingual word alignment method. In *Proceedings of the 2009 Conference on Empirical Methods in Natural Language Processing*, Singapore.

Liu, Z., Wang, H., Wu, H., and Li, S. (2010). Improving statistical machine translation with monolingual collocation. In *Proceedings of the 48th Annual Meeting of the Association for Computational Linguistics*, Uppsala, Sweden.

Dias, G. (2003). Multiword unit hybrid extraction. In *Proceedings of the ACL 2003 workshop on Multiword expressions: analysis, acquisition and treatment*, Sapporo, Japan.

Improved Spelling Error Detection and Correction for Arabic

Mohammed Attia[1, 4] *Pavel Pecina*[2] *Younes Samih*[3]
Khaled Shaalan[1] *Josef van Genabith*[4]
(1) The British University in Dubai, UAE
(2) Institute of Formal and Applied Linguistics,
Faculty of Mathematics and Physics,
Charles University in Prague, Czech Republic
(3) Heinrich-Heine-Universität, Germany
(4) School of Computing, Dublin City University, Ireland
{mattia,josef}@computing.dcu.ie, pecina@ufal.mff.cuni.cz,
samih@phil.uni-duesseldorf.de, khaled.shaalan@buid.ac.ae

ABSTRACT

A spelling error detection and correction application is based on three main components: a dictionary (or reference word list), an error model and a language model. While most of the attention in the literature has been directed to the language model, we show how improvements in any of the three components can lead to significant cumulative improvements in the overall performance of the system. We semi-automatically develop a dictionary of 9.3 million fully inflected Arabic words using a morphological transducer and a large corpus. We improve the error model by analysing error types and creating an edit distance based re-ranker. We also improve the language model by analysing the level of noise in different sources of data and selecting the optimal subset to train the system on. Testing and evaluation experiments show that our system significantly outperforms Microsoft Word 2010, OpenOffice Ayaspell and Google Docs.

TITLE IN ARABIC

تحسين اكتشاف وتصحيح الأخطاء الإملائية في اللغة العربية

ABSTRACT IN ARABIC

تقوم تطبيقات اكتشاف وتصحيح الأخطاء الإملائية على ثلاث مكونات رئيسية وهي: قاموس (أو قائمة كلمات مرجعية)، ونموذج الخطأ ونموذج اللغة. وبينما ينصب الاهتمام في الأبحاث العلمية على نموذج اللغة، فإننا نبين أن التحسينات التي يتم إدخالها على المكونات الثلاثة يمكن أن تؤدي إلى تحسينات تراكمية في النتائج النهائية لأداء البرنامج. وقد قمنا في هذا البحث بتطوير قاموس يتكون من 9.3 مليون مصرفة تصريفا كاملا كلمة بشكل شبه آلي باستخدام محلل صرفي وذخيرة نصوص كبيرة. وقمنا بتحسين نموذج الخطأ عن طريق تحليل أنواع الأخطاء الإملائية وتطوير وسيلة لإعادة ترتيب المقترحات الناتجة عن خوارزمية مسافة التحرير. وقمنا كذلك بتحسين نموذج اللغة عن طريق تحليل نسبة الأخطاء في مصادر البيانات المختلفة واختيار الجزء المثالي لتدريب البرنامج عليه. وتبين تجارب الاختبار والتقييم أن البرنامج يتفوق بشكل كبير على مايكروسوفت أوفيس 2010 وأوبن أوفيس وملفات جوجل.

KEYWORDS : Arabic, spelling error detection and correction, finite state morphological generation, Arabic spell checker, spelling error model, Arabic word list
KEYWORDS IN ARABIC:
اللغة العربية، اكتشاف وتصحيح الأخطاء الإملائية، التوليد الصرفي باستخدام آلات الحالة المحدودة، التدقيق الإملائي، قائمة كلمات اللغة العربية

Proceedings of COLING 2012: Posters, pages 103–112,
COLING 2012, Mumbai, December 2012.

1 Introduction

Spelling correction solutions have significant importance for a variety of applications and NLP tools including text authoring, OCR, pre-editing or post-editing for parsing and machine translation, intelligent tutoring systems, etc.

The spelling correction problem is formally defined (Brill, and Moore, 2000) as: given an alphabet Σ, a dictionary D consisting of strings in Σ^*, and a spelling error s, where $s \notin D$ and $s \in \Sigma^*$, find the correction c, where $c \in D$, and c is most likely to have been erroneously typed as s. This is treated as a probabilistic problem formulated as (Kernigan, 1990; Norvig, 2009; Brill, and Moore, 2000):

$$argmax_c \; P(s \mid c) \, P(c)$$

Here c is the correction, s is the spelling error, $P(c)$ is the probability that c is the correct word (or the language model), and $P(s \mid c)$ is the probability that s is typed when c is intended (the error model or noisy channel model), $argmax_c$ is the scoring mechanism that computes all plausible values of the correction c and maximizes its probability.

The definition shows that a good spelling correction system needs a balanced division of labour between the three main components: the dictionary, error model and language model. In this paper we show that in the error model there is a direct relationship between the number of correction candidates and the likelihood of finding the correct correction: the larger the number of candidates generated by the error model, the more likely is to include the best correction. At the same time, in the language model there is an inverse relationship between the number of candidates and the ability of the model to decide on the right correction: the larger the number of candidates, the less likely the language model will be successful in making the correct choice. A language model is negatively affected by a high dimensional search space. A language model is also negatively affected by noise in the data when the size of the data is not very large.

In this paper we deal with Modern Standard Arabic as used in official and edited news web sites. Dialectal Arabic is beyond the scope of this research. Furthermore, we deal with non-word errors; real word errors are not handled in this paper. The problem of spell checking and spelling error correction for Arabic has been investigated in a number of papers. Shaalan et. al. (2003) provide a characterization and classification of spelling errors in Arabic. Haddad and Yaseen (2007) propose a hybrid approach that utilizes morphological knowledge to formulate morphographemic rules to specify the word recognition and non-word correction process. Shaalan et. al. (2012) use the Noisy Channel Model trained on word-based unigrams for spelling correction, but their system performs poorly against the Microsoft Spell Checker.

Our research differs in that we use an n-gram language model (mainly bigrams) trained on the largest available corpus to date, the Arabic Gigaword Corpus 5th Edition. In addition, we classify spelling errors by comparing the errors with the gold correction, and, based on this classification, we develop knowledge-based re-ranking rules for reordering and constraining the number of candidates generated though the Levenshtein edit distance (Levenshtein, 1966) and integrate them into the overall model. Furthermore, we show that careful selection of the language model training data based on the amount of noise present in the data, has the potential to further improve overall results. We also highlight the importance of the dictionary (or reference word list) in the processes of spell checking and candidate generation.

In order to evaluate the system, we create a test corpus of 400,000 running words (tokens) consisting of news articles collected from various sources on the web (and not included in the corpus used in the development phase). From this test corpus, we extract 2,027 spelling errors (naturally occurring and not automatically generated), and we manually provide each spelling error with its gold correction. We test our system against this gold standard and compare it to Microsoft Word 2010, OpenOffice Ayaspell, and Google Docs. Our system performs significantly better than the three other systems both in the tasks of spell checking and automatic correction (or 1st order ranking).

The remainder of this paper is structured as follows: Section 2 shows how the dictionary (or word list) is created from the AraComLex finite-state morphological generator (Attia et al., 2011), and how spelling errors are detected. Section 3 explains how the error model is improved by developing rules to improve the ranking produced through finite-state edit distance. Section 4 shows how the language model is improved by selecting the right type of data to be trained on. Various data sections are analysed to detect the amount of noise they have, then some subsets of data are chosen for the n-gram language model training and the evaluation experiments. Finally Section 5 concludes.

2 Improving the Dictionary

The dictionary (or word list) is an essential component of a spell checker/corrector, as it is the reference against which the decision can be made whether a given word is correct or misspelled. It is also the reference against which correction candidates are filtered. There are various options for creating a word list for spell checking. It can be created from a corpus, a morphological analyser/generator, or both. The quality of the word list will inevitably affect the quality of the application whether in checking errors or generating valid and plausible candidates.

We use the AraComLex Extended word list for Arabic described in Shaalan et. al. (2012) further enhancing it by matching its word list against the Gigaword corpus. Words found in the Gigaword corpus and not included in the AraComLex Extended are double-checked by a second morphological analyser, the Buckwalter Arabic Morphological Analyser (Buckwalter, 2004), and the mismatches are manually revised, ultimately creating a dictionary of 9.3 million fully inflected Arabic word types.

For spelling error detection, we use two methods, the direct method, that is matching against the dictionary (or word list), and a character-based language modelling method in case such a word list is not available. The direct way for detecting spelling errors is to match words in an input text against a dictionary. Such a dictionary for Arabic runs into several million word types, therefore it is more efficient to use finite state automata to store words in a more compact manner. An input string is then compared against the valid word list paths and spelling errors will show as the difference between the two word lists (Hassan et al., 2008, Hulden, 2009a).

Shaalan et. al. (2012) implement error detection through language modelling. They build a character-based tri-gram language model using SRILM[1] (Stolcke et al., 2011) in order to classify words as valid and invalid. They split each word into characters, and create two language models: one for the total list of words pre-classified as valid (9,306,138 words), and one for a list of words classified as invalid (5,841,061 words). Their method yields a precision of 98.2 % at a recall of 100 %.

1 http://www.speech.sri.com/projects/srilm/

3 Improving the Error Model: Candidate Generation

Having detected a spelling error, the next step is to generate possible and plausible corrections for that error. For a spelling error s and a dictionary D, the purpose of the error model is to generate the correction c, or list of corrections c_1^n where $c_1^n \in D$, and c_1^n are most likely to have been erroneously typed as s. In order to do this, the error model generates a list of candidate corrections $c_1, c_2, \ldots, c_n$ that bear the highest similarity to the spelling error s.

We use a finite-state transducer to propose candidate corrections within edit distance 1 and 2 measured by Levenshtein Distance (Levenshtein, 1966) from the misspelled word (Oflazer, 1996; Hulden, 2009b; Norvig, 2009; Mitton, 1996). The transducer works basically as a character-based generator that replaces each character with all possible characters in the alphabet as well as deleting, inserting, and transposing neighbouring characters. There is also the problem of merged (or run-on) words that need to be split, such as أوأي '>w>y' "or any".

Candidate generation using edit distance is a brute-force process that ends up with a huge list of candidates. Given that there are 35 alphabetic letters in Arabic, for a word of length n, there will be n deletions, $n-1$ transpositions, $35n$ replaces, $35(n+1)$ insertions and $n-3$ splits, totaling $73n+31$. For example, a misspelt word consisting of 6 characters will have 469 candidates (with possible repetitions). This large number of candidates needs to be filtered and reordered in such a way that the correct correction comes top or near the top of the list. To filter out unnecessary words, candidates that are not found in the dictionary (or word list) are discarded. The ranking of the candidates is explained in the following sub-section.

3.1 Candidate Ranking

The ranking of candidates is initially based on a simple edit distance measure where the cost assignment is based on arbitrary letter change. In order to improve the ranking, we analyse error types in our gold standard of 2,027 misspelt words with their corrections to determine how they are distributed in order to devise ranking rules for the various edit operations.

```
Insert 2
Substitute 2
Delete 2
```

FIGURE 1 – Simple edit distance measure

```
Insert 3
Substitute 3
Delete 3
Cost 2
&:> r: :r }:y j:p :t :A :w t:n b:y :h :d ':} s:$ :' w: |:A d: :Y p:h v:t :l w:A :n v:t t:v T: :T
$:s b: l: >:| y:} q: :q >:' y:d z:s m: n:t x:H n: t: }:> x: :E >:& }:& :w f:k S: :S :b d:*
Y:A |:< w:r q:f :m j:k :& g:j T:t h:d :p p: ':> }:' :} q: l: :y y: l:S A:
Cost 1
>:A <:A |:A A:| A:> A:< <:> >:< |:> >:| >:& y:Y Y:y h:p h:p &:' H:j j:H S:l y ':} y ':y
```

FIGURE 2 – Re-ranked edit distance

Based on these facts we use a re-ranker to order edit distance operations according to their likelihood to generate the most plausible correction. Our analysis shows that *hamzahs* (>, <, &,

A, }, {, ' and |), the pair of *yaa* (y) and *alif maqsoura* (Y), and the pair of *taa marboutah* (p) and *haa* (h) contribute to the largest amount of spelling errors. Our re-ranker is sensitive to these facts and primes the edit distance scoring mechanism with different rules following the error patterns for Arabic. It assigns a lower cost score to the most-frequently confused character sets (which are often graphemically similar), and a higher score to other operations. We use the foma (Hulden, 2009b) "apply med <string>" command to find approximate matches to the string in the top network by minimum edit distance. Figure 1 and 2 show the different configuration files for the simple and re-ranked edit distance.

We also notice that split words constitute 16 % of the spelling errors in the Arabic data. These are cases where two words are joined together and the space is omitted, such as عبدالدايم 'EbdAldAym' "Abdul-Dayem". The problem with split words is that they are not handled by the edit distance operation. Therefore we add a process for automatically inserting spaces between the various parts of the string. This will create more candidates: a word of length n will have $n - 3$ candidates, given that the minimum word length in Arabic is two characters.

3.2 Evaluation of the Candidate Ranking Technique

Our purpose in ranking generated candidates is to see the correct candidate (the gold correction) at or near the top of the list, so that when we reduce the list of candidates we do not lose so many of the correct ones. We test the ranking mechanism using our gold standard of 2,027 misspelt words with their gold correction.

Cut-off limit	Simple edit distance score gold found in candidates		Re-ranked edit distance score gold found in candidates	
	without split words %	after adding split words %	without split words %	after adding split words %
100	79.97	90.97	82.09	93.09
90	79.87	90.87	82.04	93.04
80	79.72	90.73	82.04	93.04
70	79.33	90.33	82.04	93.04
60	78.93	89.94	81.85	92.85
50	78.34	89.34	81.85	92.85
40	77.16	88.16	81.65	92.65
30	75.04	86.04	81.55	92.55
20	71.88	82.88	81.01	92.01
10	64.58	75.58	79.92	90.92
9	62.90	73.90	79.72	90.73
8	61.77	72.77	79.63	90.63
7	59.60	70.60	79.13	90.13
6	56.83	67.83	78.93	89.94
5	53.33	64.33	78.59	89.59
4	48.99	59.99	78.10	89.10
3	44.06	55.06	77.70	88.70
2	37.15	48.15	75.78	86.78
1	23.88	34.88	65.66	76.67

TABLE 1 – Comparing simple edit distance with re-ranked edit distance

We compare the simple edit distance measure to our revised edit distance re-ranking scorer. As Table 1 shows, the re-ranking scorer performs better at all levels. We notice that when the number of candidates is large the difference between the simple edit distance and the re-ranked edit distance is not big (about 2 % absolute at the 100 cut-off limit without splits), but when the limit for the number of candidate is lowered the difference increases quite considerably (about 42 % absolute at 1 cut-off limit without splits). This indicates that our knowledge-based edit distance re-ranker has been successful in pushing good candidates up the top of the list. We also notice that adding splits for merged words has a beneficial effect on all counts.

4 Spelling Correction

Having generated correction candidates and improved their ranking based on the study of the frequency of the error types, we now use language models trained on different corpora to finally choose the single best correction. We compare the results against the Microsoft Spell Checker in Office 2010, Ayaspell used in OpenOffice, and Google Docs.

4.1 Correction Procedure

For automatic spelling correction (or first order ranking) we use n-gram language models. Language modelling assumes that the production of a human language text is characterized by a set of conditional probabilities, $P(w_k|w_1^{k-1})$, where w_1^{k-1} is the history and w_k is the prediction, so that the probability of a sequence of k words $P(w_1, \ldots, w_k)$ is formulated as a product (Brown et al., 1992):

$$P(w_1^k) = P(w_1)P(w_2 \mid w_1) \ldots P(w_k|w_1^{k-1})$$

We use the SRILM toolkit[2] (Stolcke et al., 2011) to train 2-, 3- and 4-gram language models on our data sets. As we have two types of candidates, normal words and split words, we use two SRILM tools: *disambig* and *ngram*. We use the *disambig* tool to choose among the normal candidates. Handling split words is done as a posterior step where we use the *ngram* tool to score the chosen candidate from the first round and the various split-word options. Then the candidate with the least perplexity score is selected. The *perplexity* of a language model is the reciprocal of the geometric average of the probabilities. If a sample text S has $|S|$ words, then the perplexity is $P(S)^{-1/|S|}$ (Brown et al., 1992). This is why the language model with the smaller perplexity is in fact the one with the higher probability with respect to S.

4.2 Analysing the Training Data

Our language model is based on raw data from two sources: the Arabic Gigaword Corpus 5th Edition and a corpus of news articles crawled from the Al-Jazeera web site. The Gigaword corpus is a collection of news articles from nine news sources: Agence France-Presse, Xinhua News Agency, An Nahar, Al-Hayat, Al-Quds Al-Arabi, Al-Ahram, Assabah, Asharq Al-Awsat and Ummah Press.

Before we start using our available corpora in training the language model, we analyse the data to measure the amount of noise in each subset of the data. In order to do this, we create a list of the most common spelling errors. This list of spelling errors is created by analysing the data using MADA (Habash et al., 2005; Roth et al., 2008) and checking instances where words have been normalized. In this case the original word is considered to be a suboptimal variation of the spelling of the diacritized form. We collect these suboptimal forms and sort them by frequency.

[2] http://www.speech.sri.com/projects/srilm/

Then we take the top 100 misspelt forms and see how frequent they are in the different subsets of data in relation to the word count in each data set.

The analysis shows that the data has a varying degree of cleanness, ranging from the very clean to the very noisy. Data in the Agence France-Presse (AFP) is the noisiest while Ummah Press is the cleanest, and Al-Jazeera is the second cleanest. Due to the fact that the Ummah Press data is small in size compared to the AFP data we ignore it in our experiments and use instead the Al-Jazeera data for representing the cleanest data set.

4.3 Automatic Correction Evaluation

For comparison, we first evaluate the automatic correction (or first order ranking) of three industrial text authoring applications: Google Docs[3], Open-Office Ayaspell, and Microsoft Word. We use our test set of 2,027 spellings errors. We test the automatic correction on two levels: at the word type level (that is unique words without repetition) and the word token level (that is words as they are found in the corpus with possible repetition). The results in Table 2 are reported in terms of accuracy (number of correct corrections divided by the number of all errors).

	Google Docs Accuracy %	**OpenOffice Ayaspell Accuracy %**	**MS Word Accuracy %**
Tested on word types	17.02	41.88	71.24
Tested on word tokens	9.32	41.86	57.15

TABLE 2 – Evaluation of spelling correction of Google Docs, Ayaspell and MS Word 2010

cut-off limit	**normal candidates accuracy 2-gram**			**normal candidates + splitword accuracy 2-gram**		
	AFP	**Jazeera**	**Gigaword**	**AFP**	**Jazeera**	**Gigaword**
100	44.58	59.75	61.27	50.75	67.34	68.98
90	44.85	60.32	61.64	51.03	67.90	69.30
80	45.66	60.95	62.19	51.58	68.54	69.76
70	47.46	62.40	64.05	53.39	69.97	71.62
60	47.90	62.92	64.58	53.88	70.43	72.10
50	48.88	63.87	65.34	54.75	71.39	72.82
40	50.50	64.67	66.05	56.29	72.18	73.49
30	51.90	66.10	67.43	57.58	73.53	74.82
20	53.85	67.90	69.20	59.13	74.94	76.37
10	60.94	70.82	72.11	64.95	77.05	78.87
9	61.79	71.21	72.43	65.31	77.33	79.12
8	62.90	71.88	73.07	66.17	77.82	79.58
7	63.87	72.17	73.69	67.04	78.07	80.12
6	66.42	72.79	74.39	69.23	78.51	80.73
5	67.60	73.78	74.91	69.97	79.10	81.03
4	69.37	75.21	75.95	71.21	80.05	81.79
3	72.73	76.48	**77.24**	73.93	80.97	**82.86**
2	70.68	72.47	73.33	70.72	76.37	78.39

TABLE 3 – Correction accuracy with 2-gram LM trained on AFP, Al-Jazeera and Gigaword

[3] Tested in June 2012

Next we evaluate our approach using language models trained on the AFP data (as representing the noisiest type of data), the Al-Jazeera data (as representing the cleanest subset of data) and the entire Gigaword corpus (as representing a huge data set with a moderate amount of noise). We run our experiments on the candidates generated through the re-ranked edit distance processing explained in Section 3 with varying candidate cut-off limits. We test the normal candidates using the SRILM *disambig* tool and the split words using *ngram* tool.

As Table 3 shows, the best score achieved for the automatic correction is 82.86 % using the bigram language model with a candidate cut-off limit of 3, and with the split words added. Table 3 shows that when there are too many candidates (above 10 candidates) the n-gram language model performs poorly and with too few candidates (2 candidates) the performance also deteriorates considerably. Therefore a reasonable range for the number of candidates for the n-gram language model is between 7 and 3, with optimal performance at 3.

Comparing the two data sets which are comparable in size, the AFP and Al-Jazeera, we find that the best score achieved with the AFP data is 73.93 % that is 7.04 % absolute less than the best score achieved with the Al-Jazeera data (80.97 %). The quality of the data is a crucial factor here. The Al-Jazeera data is relatively clean while the AFP data is full of noise and misspellings. This emphasizes the point in language modelling that clean data is better than noisy data when they are comparable in size.

Table 3 also shows that the extremely large corpus ameliorates the effect of the noise and produces the best results among all the data sets. The best score achieved for the language model trained on the Gigaword corpus is 82.86 %, which is 1.89 % absolute better than the score for Al-Jazeera (80.97 %). This could be a further indication in favour of the argument that more data is better than clean data. However, we must notice that the Gigaword data is one order of magnitude larger than the Al-Jazeera data, and in some applications, for efficiency reasons, it could be better to work with the language model trained on Al-Jazeera. We notice that the addition of the split word component has a positive effect on all test results.

Compared to other spelling error detection and correction systems we notice that our best accuracy score (82.86 %) is significantly higher than that for Google Docs (9.32 %), Ayaspell for OpenOffice (41.86 %) and Microsoft Word 2010 (57.15 %).

Conclusion

We have developed methods for improving the main three components in a spelling error correction application: the dictionary (or word list), the error model and the language model. These three components are highly interconnected and interrelated. Without the dictionary being an exhaustive and accurate representation of the language words space, without an error model being able to generate a plausible and compact list of candidates, and without a language model being trained on either clean data or an extremely large amount of data, no high quality correction results can be expected. Our spelling correction methodology significantly outperforms the three industrial applications of Ayaspell, MS Word, and Google Docs in first order ranking of candidates.

Acknowledgments

This research is funded by the Irish Research Council for Science Engineering and Technology (IRCSET), the UAE National Research Foundation (NRF) (Grant No. 0514/2011), the Czech Science Foundation (grant no. P103/12/G084), and the Science Foundation Ireland (Grant No. 07/CE/I1142) as part of the Centre for Next Generation Localisation (www.cngl.ie) at Dublin City University.

References

Attia, Mohammed, Pavel Pecina, Lamia Tounsi, Antonio Toral, Josef van Genabith. (2011). An Open-Source Finite State Morphological Transducer for Modern Standard Arabic. International Workshop on Finite State Methods and Natural Language Processing (FSMNLP). Blois, France.

Beesley, K. R., and Karttunen, L. (2003). *Finite State Morphology*: CSLI studies in computational linguistics. Stanford, Calif.: CSLI.

Ben Othmane Zribi C. and Ben Ahmed M. (2003). Efficient Automatic Correction of Misspelled Arabic Words Based on Contextual Information, *Lecture Notes in Computer Science*, Springer, 2003, Vol. 2773, pp.770–777.

Brill, Eric and Robert C. Moore. (2000). An improved error model for noisy channel spelling correction. ACL '00 Proceedings of the 38th Annual Meeting on Association for Computational Linguistics.

Brown, P. F., V. J. Della Pietra, P. V. deSouza, J. C. Lai and R. L. Mercer. (1992). Class-Based n-gram Models of Natural Language, ' *Computational Linguistics* 18(4), 467-479.

Buckwalter, T. (2004). Buckwalter Arabic Morphological Analyzer (BAMA) Version 2.0. Linguistic Data Consortium (LDC) catalogue number: LDC2004L02, ISBN1-58563- 324-0

Choudhury, Monojit, Rahul Saraf, Vijit Jain, Animesh Mukherjee, Sudeshna Sarkar and Anupam Basu. (2007). Investigation and modeling of the structure of texting language. *International Journal on Document Analysis and Recognition*. Volume 10, Numbers 3-4, 157-174, DOI: 10.1007/s10032-007-0054-0

Haddad, Bassam and Mustafa Yaseen. (2007). Detection and Correction of Non-Words in Arabic: A Hybrid Approach. International Journal of Computer Processing of Oriental Languages. Vol. 20, No. 4

Hajič, J., Smrž, O., Buckwalter, T., and Jin, H. (2005). Feature-Based Tagger of Approximations of Functional Arabic Morphology. In: The 4th Workshop on Treebanks and Linguistic Theories (TLT 2005), Barcelona, Spain.

Habash, Nizar and Rambow, Owen. (2005). Arabic Tokenization, Part-of-Speech Tagging and Morphological Disambiguation in One Fell Swoop. Proceedings of the 43rd Annual Meeting of the Association for Computational Linguistics (ACL'05), pp. 573—580

Hassan, Ahmed, Sara Noeman and Hany Hassan. (2008). Language Independent Text Correction using Finite State Automata. IJCNLP. Hyderabad, India

Hulden, Mans. (2009a). Fast Approximate String Matching with Finite Automata. Proceedings of the 25th Conference of the Spanish Society for Natural Language Processing (SEPLN).

Hulden, Mans. (2009b). Foma: a Finite-state compiler and library. EACL '09 Proceedings of the 12th Conference of the European Chapter of the Association for Computational Linguistics. Association for Computational Linguistics Stroudsburg, PA, USA

Kernigan, M., Church, K., Gale W. (1990). A Spelling Correction Program Based on a Noisy Channel Model. AT & T Laboratories, 600 Mountain Ave., Murray Hill, NJ.

Kiraz, G. A. (2001). *Computational Nonlinear Morphology: With Emphasis on Semitic Languages*. Cambridge University Press.

Levenshtein, V. I. (1966). Binary codes capable of correcting deletions, insertions, and reversals. In: Soviet Physics Doklady, pp. 707-710.

Magdy, Walid and Kareem Darwish. (2006). Arabic OCR error correction using character segment correction, language modeling, and shallow morphology. EMNLP '06 Proceedings of the 2006 Conference on Empirical Methods in Natural Language Processing.

Mitton, Roger (1996). *English spelling and the computer*. Harlow, Essex: Longman Group

Norvig, Peter. (2009). Natural language corpus data. In Beautiful Data, edited by Toby Segaran and Jeff Hammerbacher, pp. 219–242. Sebastopol, Calif.: O'Reilly

Oflazer, K. (1996) Error-tolerant finite-state recognition with applications to morphological analysis and spelling correction. Computational Linguistics 22(1): 73-90

Parker, Robert, David Graff, Ke Chen, Junbo Kong, and Kazuaki Maeda. (2011). Arabic Gigaword Fifth Edition. LDC Catalog No.: LDC2011T11, ISBN: 1-58563-595-2.

Roth, Ryan and Rambow, Owen and Habash, Nizar and Diab, Mona and Rudin, Cynthia. (2008). Arabic Morphological Tagging, Diacritization, and Lemmatization Using Lexeme Models and Feature Ranking. Proceedings of ACL-08: HLT, Short Papers, pp. 117--120.

Shaalan, Khaled,Younes Samih, Mohammed Attia, Pavel Pecina, and Josef van Genabith. (2012). Arabic Word Generation and Modelling for Spell Checking. Language Resources and Evaluation (LREC). Istanbul, Turkey. Pages: 719-725

Shaalan K., Allam A., Gomah A. (2003). Towards Automatic Spell Checking for Arabic, In Proceedings of the 4th Conference on Language Engineering, Egyptian Society of Language Engineering (ELSE), PP. 240-247, Oct. 21-22, Cairo, Egypt.

Stolcke, A., J. Zheng, W. Wang, and V. Abrash, (2011). SRILM at sixteen: Update and outlook. in Proc. IEEE Automatic Speech Recognition and Understanding Workshop. Waikoloa, Hawaii.

Watson, J. (2002). *The Phonology and Morphology of Arabic*, New York: Oxford University Press.

Wintner, Shuly. (2008). Strengths and weaknesses of finite-state technology: a case study in morphological grammar development Natural Language Engineering 14(4):457-469, October 2008.

Heloise — A reengineering of Ariane-G5 SLLPs for application to π-languages

Vincent Berment[1] *Christian Boitet*[2]
(1) INaLCO, Place du Maréchal de Lattre de Tassigny - 75775 Paris cedex 16
(2) GETALP, LIG-campus, 385, avenue de la Bibliothèque - 38041 Grenoble cedex 9

Vincent.Berment@imag.fr, Christian.Boitet@imag.fr

ABSTRACT

Heloise is a reengineering of the specialised languages for linguistic programming (SLLPs) of Ariane-G5 running both Linux and Windows. Heloise makes the core of Ariane-G5 available to anyone willing to develop "expert" (i.e. relying on linguistic expertise) operational machine translation (MT) systems in that framework, used with success since the 80's to build many prototypes and a few systems of the "multilevel transfer" and "interlingua" architecture. This initiative is part of the movement to reduce the digital divide by providing easily understandable tools that allow the development of lingware for poorly-resourced languages (π-languages). This paper shows how Heloise can contribute to the democratisation of quality MT, describes some technical aspects of it, and provides elements of comparison with Ariane-G5.

KEYWORDS: machine translation, specialised languages for linguistic programming, SLLP, MT lingware, online lingware building, collaborative lingware building, Ariane-G5, Ariane-Y, Heloise, under-resourced languages

TITRE ET RÉSUMÉ EN FRANÇAIS

Héloïse — une réingénierie des LSPL d'Ariane-G5 pour application aux langues-π

Héloïse est une réingénierie des langages spécialisés (LSPL) d'Ariane-G5 tournant sous Linux et Windows. Héloïse rend le cœur d'Ariane-G5 accessible à toute personne désirant réaliser par elle-même des systèmes de traduction automatique (TA) experts (s'appuyant sur une expertise linguistique) opérationnels dans cet environnement, qui a été utilisé avec succès depuis les années 80 pour construire de nombreux prototypes et quelques systèmes adoptant une architecture de "transfert multiniveau" et d'"interlingua". Cette démarche s'inscrit dans le mouvement visant réduire la fracture numérique par la mise à disposition d'outils facilement appropriables, et permettant de développer des linguiciels pour des langues peu dotées (langues-π). Cet article montre comment Héloïse peut participer à la démocratisation de la TA de qualité, en décrit quelques aspects techniques, et donne des éléments de comparaison avec Ariane-G5.

MOTS-CLÉS EN FRANÇAIS : traduction automatique, langages spécialisés pour la programmation linguistique, LSPL, linguiciels de TA, construction collaborative de linguiciels, Ariane-G5, Ariane-Y, Heloise, langues peu dotées.

Proceedings of COLING 2012: Posters, pages 113–124,
COLING 2012, Mumbai, December 2012.

1 Héloïse : des compilateurs de LSPL et des interfaces utilisateurs

1.1 Compilateurs

Fonctionnellement, Héloïse offre un service équivalent aux compilateurs d'Ariane-G5 : il permet de transformer des linguiciels en programmes exécutables. Contrairement à Ariane-G5, Héloïse produit cependant un exécutable qui est l'image des linguiciels, ne recourant pas à des interpréteurs, supposés trop lents, bien que pouvant présenter des avantages comme la facilité de réaliser un débogueur symbolique. Les compilateurs d'Héloïse réalisent successivement :

- un arbre d'analyse à partir des différentes parties des linguiciels (déclarations de variables, formats, dictionnaires, grammaires, procédures...),
- une structure d'interprétation à partir de chacun de ces arbres ou directement une base de données dans le cas des dictionnaires,
- du code C++ réalisant la part d'algorithme associé,
- la compilation du code de la phase et son édition de liens.

Héloïse fait appel à deux bibliothèques ouvertes :

- `saint-jean` (Claude Del Vigna), un générateur d'analyseurs syntaxiques dans le formalisme duquel ont été écrits les analyseurs des LSPL et des arbres décorés,
- `sqlite` (http://www.sqlite.org/), un gestionnaire de bases de données léger, utilisé pour les dictionnaires.

Les traces d'exécution d'Héloïse et d'Ariane-G5 sont strictement équivalentes, sans amélioration ni modification des fonctionnalités d'Ariane-G5. Les compilateurs d'Héloïse présentent cependant quelques limitations par rapport à ceux d'Ariane-G5 ainsi que quelques différences.

- Il y a quatre compilateurs, dans Héloïse, et non dix (REFORM/TRACOMPL y est traité comme un cas particulier d'EXPANS qui n'a que les fichiers spécifiquement TRACOMPL ; voir [Boitet et al, 1985] et [Guillaume, 1989]).
- Le LSPL ATEF d'Héloïse est limité aux sorties sans homographes (voir [Boitet, 1982]).
- L'ensemble constitué des quatre compilateurs, de la bibliothèque HCL et du moniteur Win32 est écrit en C++, l'interface Web est écrite en HTML, AJAX et PHP, et fait appel à des petits programmes C/C++ pour le calcul des arbres affichés en SVG.
- Les compilateurs et les programmes compilés fonctionnent à la fois sous Windows et sous Linux.
- Le traitement des erreurs est (provisoirement) assez limité dans Héloïse.

1.2 Interfaces utilisateurs

L'interface utilisateur est simplifiée (mais plus moderne) par rapport au moniteur Ariane. Il existe deux versions d'Héloïse : une application Win32 et un service Web.

L'application Win32 a été développée sous Visual C++. En haut à gauche de l'application, un champ de saisie est destiné au texte à traduire et un autre à la traduction. Dans la partie droite, un premier onglet concerne la traduction et permet, en particulier, de visualiser les phases à exécuter. Les autres onglets sont spécifiques aux différentes phases et permettent de gérer les fichiers, lancer les compilations et visualiser les résultats et les traces. Le couple de langues est choisi dans une liste déroulante située dans le bas de l'application.

L'interface Web est agencée différemment de l'interface Windows mais offre les mêmes fonctionnalités. On retrouve la gestion de la traduction et les deux champs de saisie dans la partie droite, la sélection du couple de langues en haut à gauche, et la gestion des phases (compilation, traces…) en bas à gauche. Un affichage graphique des arbres de sortie au format SVG est aussi disponible dans cette interface. La copie d'écran ci-dessous montre l'arbre (technologie SVG) obtenu par Héloïse avec le linguiciel FR3 d'analyse du français pour la phrase « *Le chat voit la souris.* ». L'encadré, qui s'affiche quand la souris passe sur un nœud, présente les décorations portées par le nœud (ici, le nœud correspondant au mot « *voit* »).

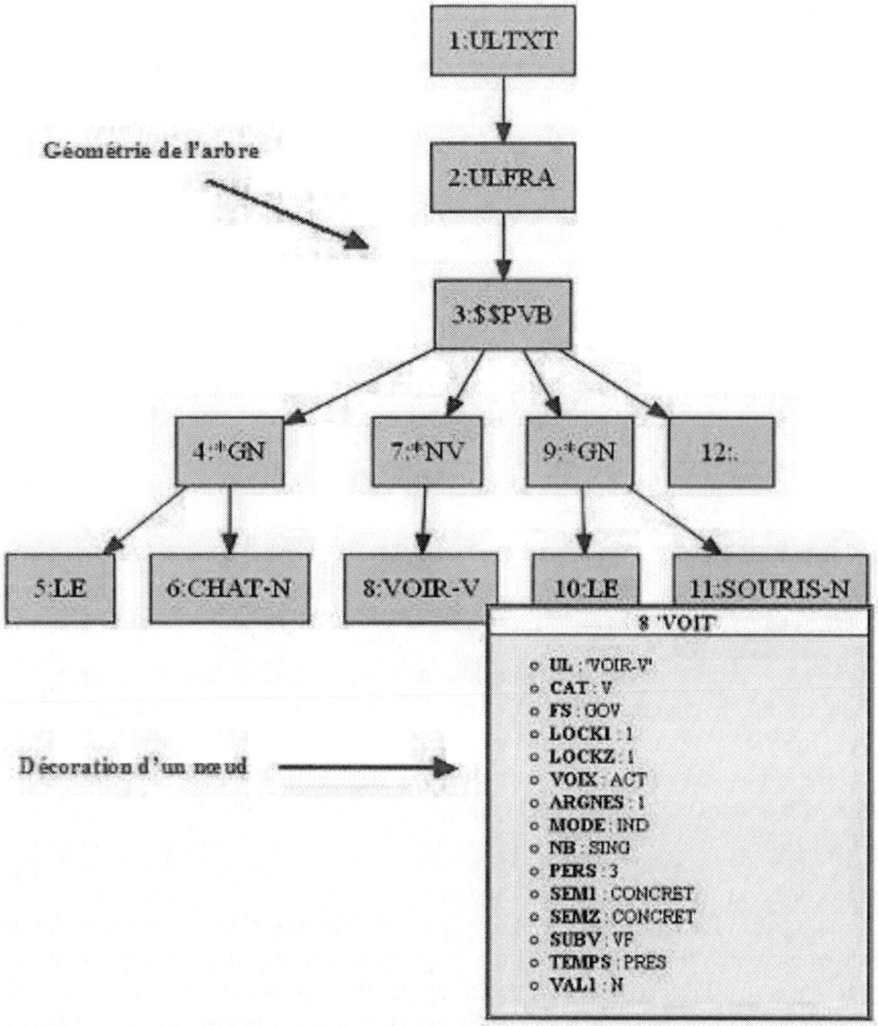

FIGURE 1 – Visualisation de la géométrie et des décorations dans Héloïse

2 Introduction

Ariane-G5 is a generator of machine translation systems developed and improved by the GETA group[1] during the years 1970 and 1980. This framework, despite the numerous publications and cooperative projects that made it widely known, remains of difficult access because of the "mainframe" environment under which it runs (zVM/CMS on z390). Ariane-G5 can be accessed either natively through a 3270 terminal emulator or using CASH, a portable "meta-environment" (written in Revolution) which contains the source files (lingware, corpus), and which communicates with Ariane-G5 that performs all the treatments (compilations and executions of "translation chains").

Heloise is a reengineering of compilers and "engines" of Ariane-G5's Specialized Languages for Linguistic Programming (SLLPs), running both Linux and Windows. The aim of its author when he developed this new version of Ariane-G5 SLLPs, was to make this system available to anyone wishing to design his own operational expert MT system (i.e. an MT system relying on linguistic expertise, as opposed to systems based on statistical properties of languages). This approach is part of the movement aiming at reducing the digital divide through the provision of tools, usable by non-specialists, and enabling them to develop their own language services.

This article shows how Ariane-G5 can significantly contribute to the democratization of quality machine translation and to its usability to under-resourced languages (π-languages), and especially to under-resourced languages pairs (not only pairs of π-languages!). It then describes some technical aspects of Heloise and provides a comparison with Ariane-G5 as well as with Ariane-Y, another software developed within the GÉTALP and also deriving from Ariane-G5. The need for complementary tools in addition to the SLLPs is discussed in the conclusion.

3 Ariane-G5

3.1 General principles

Ariane-G5 is a generator of machine translation systems. It uses an expert approach (including a description of the languages handled) and the generated systems are generally based on a multilevel transfer linguistic architecture, and developed using a heuristic programming approach. It has also been used for "abstract pivot" approaches (IF semantico-pragmatic formulas for speech MT in the CSTAR and Nespole! projects in 1995-2003, and UNL linguistic-semantic graphs since 1997).

Ariane-G5 relies on five Specialized Languages for Linguistic Programming (SLLPs) operating on decorated trees. Each of these languages is compiled and the internal tables produced are given as parameters to the "engines" of the languages. The specificity of an SLLP is that it offers high-level data structures (decorated trees or graphs, grammars, dictionaries) and high-level control structures (1-ary or N-ary non-determinism, pattern-matching in trees, guarded iteration).

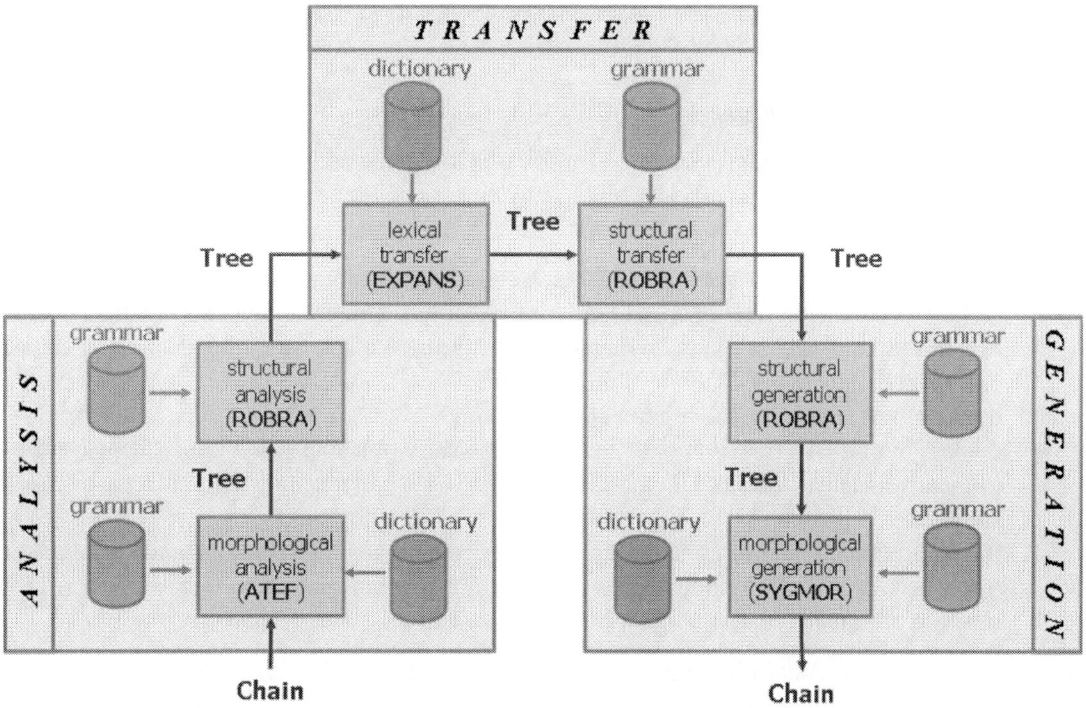

FIGURE 2 – Ariane: analysis, transfer et generation.

3.2 Programming languages for L-developers

From the beginning, Ariane has offered high-level programming languages — specialized languages for linguistic programming (LSPL) — thus simplifying the work of the L-developers:

- ATEF (string-to-tree transformations) allows writing morphological and morphosyntactic analyzers producing decorated trees encoding the remaining ambiguities, with the possibility of treating inflectional derivational and compositional morphology, connected uninflected idioms, and of performing sophisticated treatment of "unknown words".
- ROBRA (tree-to-tree transformations) allows writing transformational systems operating on decorated trees. It offers parallel rewriting, guarded iteration and recursion, and 1-ary non-determinism (by backtracking) at the level of the control graph.
- TRANSF/EXPANS (tree-to-tree transformations) allows writing transformation phases of lexical items, where one node can be transformed into a large subtree;
- REFORM/TRACOMP [3] (tree-to-tree transformations) can perform conversions of decoration sets between phases;
- SYGMOR (tree-to-string transformations) allows writing morphological and morphotactic generators.

[3] REFORM/TRACOMPL, which is a sub-language of the ROBRA, TRANSF/EXPANS, and SYGMOR SLLPs, only appears implicitly in figure 1.

These languages were designed in order to free the L-developers of the need to use conventional programming languages to write the rules and dictionaries.

3.3 Architecture principles and limitations of Ariane-G5

Although it received many improvements from Pierre Guillaume and Maurice Quézel-Ambrunaz between 1985 and 2003, Ariane-G5 retains many historical limitations. These limitations are mainly:

- the size of decorations (limited to 32 bytes, 2 for the lexical unit (UL) and 2 for the form), and therefore the number of lexical units active at the same time must be less than 65,536 (32,768 "static" and as many "dynamic"), and the size of the source text of a translation unit must be less than 64K or 46.8 full standard pages[4], or 11,700 words),
- the length of an occurrence (up to 256 characters);
- the length of a UL[5] (maximum 34 characters, because of a syntax in tabular format, which is inconvenient to take as UL the UWs of the UNL project: they are replaced by small subtrees);
- the maximum number of nodes in a tree (64K), more than enough for a standard linguistic tree (there are 2.5 to 3 nodes per word), but not for multiple parse trees (in the LIDIA mockup of interactive disambiguation MT, there can be 400 nodes per word).

The new developments that are Ariane-Y ([Nguyen, 2009], pp. 70—74, 93—100) and Heloise free the user of these limitations.

3.4 The usefulness of a reengineering of Ariane-G5 for π-languages

Until the arrival of operational statistical solutions (Pharaoh, Moses, Joshuah, and especially Google, which reached an advanced stage of maturity), the cost and difficulty of development of machine translation systems restricted to about twenty — the main languages the world — the number of languages benefitting from this type of service, i.e. the languages that allowed a rapid return on investment.

This situation lasted until about 2007. Since then, things have considerably progressed: for example, more than 60 languages are already available as source and as target language on Google Translation (http://translate.google.fr). However, the quality of translations obtained remains low for the reasons cited in [Boitet, 2008]. This paper shows in particular that the systems obtained by an expert approach are unavoidable — and also more economical — to open under-resourced languages (π-languages) and under-resourced language pairs (π-pairs of languages) to quality automated translation systems.

To democratize machine translation quality, it is also desirable to have efficient and open solutions. To limit the cost of building translation systems, generators must allow non-specialists — spontaneous groups (often diasporas) collaborating over the Internet, linguists having lexical resources... — to develop themselves a significant portion of an initial system and then to enrich and to maintain it on their own.

---

[4] A "standard page" has 1,400 alphabetical characters / 250 words in French or in English, or 400 characters in Chinese, Japanese or Korean.

[5] UL = Lexical Unit (French acronym), often not a lemma, but a symbol denoting a whole derivational family.

Besides its scientific interest, Ariane-G5 has several interesting features that make it a serious candidate for this purpose:

1. It is a generic generator of machine translation systems.

- It has been used to make mockups and prototypes for language pairs including a wide variety of European and Asian languages, in all about ten languages (Arabic, Chinese, English, French, German, Japanese, Malay, Portuguese, Russian, Thai), thus proving its usability for the most varied languages and language pairs.
- It takes as input linguistic resources described in specialized languages accessible to non-programmers.

2. In September 2010, the LIG has put under the BSD license[6] the existing lingware base, greatly facilitating the implementation of new systems[7].
3. Systems produced by Ariane-G5 are all made of three steps — analysis, transfer and generation — exchanging clearly defined hybrid multi-level structures. Accordingly:

- the analysis step only depends on the source language,
- the generation step only depends on the target language,
- that choice of language architecture allows to:

  - reuse totally the analyzers and generators made for a language (2*N if there are N languages),
  - limit to the transfer the effort to build a new language pair[8].

From the point of view of the democratization of machine translation quality, Ariane-G5 also has several disadvantages.

- The generated systems do not run natively on operating systems that are the most common: Windows, MacOS and Linux.
- No generated system yet reached or approached the level of commercial products (e.g., the transfer dictionary (dictionary of lexical units (UL)) of the Russian-French system, which is one of the largest, does not exceed 12,000 UL, the equivalent of 40,000 lemmas). The capacity of Ariane-G5 to go full scale (dictionaries of more than 1 million UL...) remains to be demonstrated.
- Lingware programming remains difficult and requires close collaboration between L-developers (linguists who develop grammars and dictionaries), and Ariane experts ([Vauquois, 1979] indicated that the correct composition for a team developing a grammar is one computer scientist and three linguists).
- The native monitor (human-machine interface via an IBM 3270 terminal) no longer meets current standards, and the meta-CASH environment, although very friendly and portable, designed by E. Blanc, can only be used if a zVM system administrator creates a virtual machine for each potential developer. Therefore, the only L-developments made for the

---

[6] See http://en.wikipedia.org/wiki/BSD_licenses.

[7] These lingware modules will soon be available for download.

[8] Contrary to a widespread but erroneous idea, the number of transfers for getting N(N-1) translation systems between N languages is not necessarily quadratic. For example, if we take as a "pivot" the linguistic trees of one of the N languages and write the 2(N-1) transfers between this language and the others, then 2(N-1) translations will be done with only one transfer and (N-1)(N-2) with two transfers. We can also use as pivot "UNL trees" equivalent to the "UNL graphs" (abstract structures, eventually under-specified, of English utterances), so all the translations will then be made with a double lexical and structural transfer.

last 15 years are limited to lingware written for GÉTA projects (CSTAR and Nespole! for speech translation, 1995-2003, and UNL enconverter/deconverter for French, since 1997).

- Ariane is a system designed in the 1970s so its designers have almost all left the laboratory. The L-developer community created during the ESOPE project (active between 1982 and 1992) fell apart when B'VITAL was purchased by SITE/Eurolang, thus complicating recruiting and training new L-developers.

The development of Heloise (and of course of Ariane-Y) had as main goals to transmit specific skill of Ariane and to create a PC version of its SLLPs. Work is underway to further facilitate the task of the L-developers.

3.5 Ariane-Y

The Ariane-Y project is a response to this need for reengineering of Ariane-G5. Started in 2000, this project driven by GETALP aims to achieve high performance version (removal of limitations), free (LGPL license), open (user-friendly interface) and incremental (dictionaries can change during treatment) of Ariane-G5. The software, having recently received additional funding from the ANR (Traouïéro project), should be available within one year. This project is described in [Nguyen, 2009].

4 Heloise, a reengineering of Ariane-G5

Heloise is essentially a reengineering of the Ariane-G5 compilers, except that the code generated by Heloise is directly executable code, when Ariane-G5 generates an intermediate compact code interpreted by "engines". The development of Heloise [9] was performed in the technical perspective described in [Berment, 2004]. The objective defended in this PhD thesis is to provide non-computer specialists, with an amount of training as limited as possible, the possibility to enrich the language services offered by standard host platforms. For Heloise, the targeted service is machine translation and the host platform is, for example, a commercial word processor (Microsoft Word, Open Office ...) or an Internet browser. The linguistic complements in figure 3 are then machine translation systems, produced by Heloise for a given language pair.

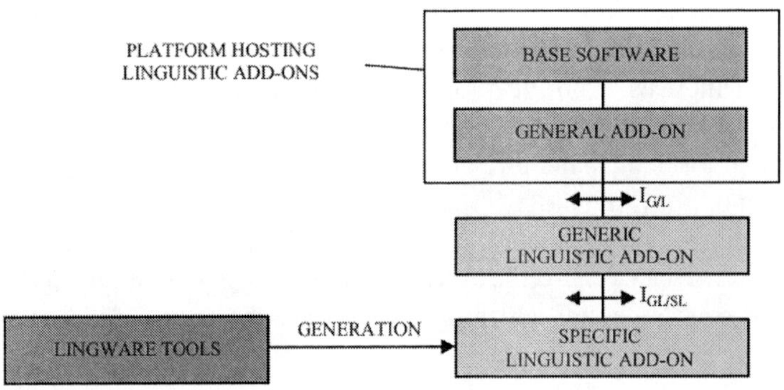

FIGURE 3 – Modular organization of the developments

Please refer to section 1 (in French) for technical details about Heloise, especially for a description of its SLLP compilers and of its users' interfaces.

[9] This development, done in 2009, followed a theoretical study ([Del Vigna et al]).

5 Comparisons and performances

5.1 Comparison between Heloise, Ariane-G5 and Ariane-Y

The table below provides some comparisons between Heloise, Ariane-G5 and Ariane-Y.

	Ariane-G5	**Ariane-Y**	**Heloise**
Number of SLLPs	5	5	4
Programming languages used to implement the SLLPs			
SLLP Compilers	ASM360, PL360, PL/I, EXEC/XEDIT, REXX	C/C++ et REXX	C/C++
SLLP engines or « interpreters »	ASM360, PL360	C/C++	No interpreter (executable code)
Techniques used for SLLPs			
Implementation architecture	Compilation directly producing loadable bytecode	Compiler calling a « loader » producing a bytecode	Double compilation: SLLP → C++, C++ → executable code
Development of SLLP compilers	Direct writing in ASM360 and PL/I (only SYGMOR)	`ANTLR`	`saint-jean` (Claude Del Vigna)
Standard compilers used	ASM360, PL360, PL/I	`gcc/g++`	`Visual C++` (Win32) `gcc/g++` (Linux)
Internal management of dictionaries	Compressed form allowing a binary search	`TabFich` (infinite tables) and AVL (almost balanced trees)	`sqlite`
Human-machine interfaces			
HMI	Command line and parameters files editor (IBM 3270) Hypertext stacks (CASH/RunRev for PC)	Web demo interface[13]	Web (Linux) Application (Windows)

TABLE 1 – Elements of comparison between Ariane-G5, Ariane-Y and Heloise.

[13] Several interfaces are planned (command line and graphical dialogs like in CASH).

5.2 Performance

5.2.1 Execution time

In morphological analysis of French (FR3 lingware), the analysis of 30 pages of text (Word pages in Times New Roman 12 points, 15,858 words, generating a tree of 37,729 nodes in AM output) takes approximately 42 seconds (the tests give at least 40,326 ms and a maximum of 43,402 ms) and 431,653 database accesses only contribute for ~5.7 seconds (exact figures: min. 5,672 ms, max. 5,906 ms), about 14%.

As a comparison, the morphological analysis of the same 30 pages by SYGFRAN, the analyser of French created by Jacques Chauché (LIRMM), takes about 2 seconds on the site http://www.lirmm.fr/~chauche/ExempleAnl.html, at the « *liste lemmes* » item. Ariane-G5, for the same text, takes 23 seconds, measure that must be weighted against the lower power of the H30 machine (42 to 126 times less).

The table below (Table 2) provides the computation times used by the server (a PC under Linux 2.6, CentOS release 5.3) for analysing a text of 480 words in French (from Victor Hugo's "*Les Misérables*", as were the 30 pages mentioned before). Several trials were done to study the dispersion of the results, which is finally rather low (< 2.5 % of the total).

Phase	Time (trial 1)	Time (trial 2)	Time (trial 3)
AM	1 813 ms	1 686 ms	1 679 ms
AS 1	1 845 ms	1 524 ms	1 485 ms
AS 2	10 770 ms	10 468 ms	10 475 ms
AS 3	1 814 ms	1 744 ms	1 722 ms
AS 4	39 029 ms	39 253 ms	39 675 ms
AS 5	962 ms	984 ms	977 ms
Total	**57 033 ms**	**55 659 ms**	**56 013 ms**

TABLE 2 – Computation times for analysing a text of 480 words.

The linearity with the data was evaluated with a longer text (~5 Word pages in Times New Roman 12 points, 2,880 words, thus 6 times longer). The parse trees contain 6,499 nodes at the output of AM and 5,629 nodes at the output of AS5. The results are summarized below (Table 3):

Phase	Time (480 words)	Time (2,880 words)	Ratio (x 6)
AM	1 813 ms	10 344 ms	x 5,7
AS 1	1 845 ms	26 998 ms	x 14,6
AS 2	10 770 ms	76 851 ms	x 7
AS 3	1 814 ms	23 581 ms	x 13
AS 4	39 029 ms	247 300 ms	x 6,3
AS 5	962 ms	22 698 ms	x 24
Total	**57 033 ms**	**407 772 ms**	**x 7**

TABLE 3 – Relationship between text size and computation time.

The order of magnitude is still the same, but important disparities can be noted in three ROBRA phases: AS1, AS3 and more especially AS5.

5.2.2 Data size

With the technique used in Heloise, the generated code (formats, dictionaries…) can reach sizes that dramatically exceed the compilers capacities (g++, Microsoft), thus making a problem for scalability. The strategy selected in Heloise to solve this problem is a "divide and conquer" approach: the code to compile is split into several files of controlled size (for example, a file can contain the image of 1,000 formats).

Note that this problem does not exist in Ariane-G5, which compilers can process up to 8,000 formats and 30,000 lexical entries dictionaries in one time. As for Ariane-Y, ANTLR allows to process files of more than one million lines.

Conclusion and future work

Several works and research axes are under way around Heloise, including:

- the study of tools even more "appropriable" and easily understandable by L-developers and of a simpler development platform (graphical programming...);
- the evaluation of the effort needed for creating a system for a new language pair with at least one of them under-resourced;
- the study of performances and of translation quality improvement, including, for example, the addition of new SLLPs (dependency analyzer, Q-systems...), statistical treatments or the introduction of learning techniques.

Conclusion

The development of Heloise was the occasion to evaluate the behaviour and performances of Ariane-G5 outside its "mainframe" environment. The result appeared to be good enough to decide to make Heloise being used for developing operational MT systems. However, it remains for that aim to:

- develop more user-friendly tools (graphical programming, Q-systems...) such that non-specialists can easily become L-developers and develop new lingware by themselves, in particular for π-couples of languages,
- demonstrate Heloise capacity (so also Ariane-G5 and Ariane-Y) to produce operational systems with similar performances to current commercial systems (dictionaries of several millions of entries, low translation delays, good translation quality…).

A modified version of Ariane-G5 could also be developed, as that was foreseen with the Ariane-X project. This could for example consist in adding a dependency analyser or some statistical processing. The use of the HCL library would ease that development.

Other ideas for democratizing quality machine translation remain to be explored. They can be technological (use of translation memories [Boitet, 1999], translation through a UNL pivot [Boitet, 2002]…), legal (license policy) or methodological (collaborative project, involvement o the diasporas, software reuse... [Berment, 2004]).

References

Bachut D., Le projet EUROLANG : *une nouvelle perspective pour les outils d'aide à la traduction*, Actes de TALN 1994, journées du PRC-CHM, Université de Marseille, 7-8 avril 1994.

Bachut D., Verastegui N., *Software tools for the environment of a computer aided translation system*, COLING-1984, Stanford University, pages 330 à 333, 2-6 juillet 1984.

Berment V., *Méthodes pour informatiser les langues et les groupes de langues peu dotés*, Thèse de doctorat, Grenoble, 18 mai 2004.

Boitet C., *Le point sur Ariane-78 début 1982 (DSE-1), vol. 1, partie 1, le logiciel*, rapport de la convention ADI n° 81/423, avril 1982.

Boitet C., Guillaume P., Quézel-Ambrunaz M., *A case study in software evolution: from Ariane-78.4 to Ariane-85*, Proceedings of the Conference on Theoretical and Methodological Issues in Machine Translation of Natural Languages, Colgate University, Hamilton, New York, 14-16 août 1985.

Boitet C., *Current machine translation systems developed with GETA's methodology and software tools*, conférence Translating and the Computer 8, 13-14 novembre 1986.

Boitet C., *La TAO à Grenoble en 1990, 1980-90 : TAO du réviseur et TAO du traducteur*, partie des supports de l'école d'été de Lannion organisée en 1990 par le LATL et le CNET, 1990.

Boitet C., *A research perspective on how to democratize machine translation and translation aids aiming at high quality final output*, MT Summit VII, Kent Ridge Digital Labs, Singapour, pages 125 à 133, 13-17 septembre 1999.

Boitet C., *A roadmap for MT: four « keys » to handle more languages, for all kinds of tasks, while making it possible to improve quality (on demand)*, International Conference on Universal Knowledge and Language (ICUKL 2002), Goa, 25-29 novembre 2002.

Boitet C., *Les architectures linguistiques et computationnelles en traduction automatique sont indépendantes*, TALN 2008, Avignon, 9-13 juin 2008.

Del Vigna C., Berment V., Boitet C., *La notion d'occurrence de formes de forêt (orientée et ordonnée) dans le langage ROBRA pour la traduction automatique, Approches algébrique, logique et algorithmique*, Journée thématique ATALA sur la traduction automatique, ENST Paris, 1er décembre 2007.

Guillaume P., Ariane-G5 : *Les langages spécialisés TRACOMPL et EXPANS*, document GÉTA, juin 1989.

Guilbaud J.-P., Ariane-G5 : *Environnement de développement et d'exécution de systèmes (linguiciels) de traduction automatique*, Journée du GDR I3 co-organisée avec l'ATALA, Paris, novembre 1999.

Nguyen H.-T., *Des systèmes de TA homogènes aux systèmes de TAO hétérogènes*, Thèse de doctorat, Grenoble, 18 décembre 2009.

Vauquois B., *Aspects of mechanical translation in 1979*, Conference for Japan IBM Scientific program, juillet 1979.

Vauquois B., *Computer aided translation and the Arabic language*, First Arab school on science and technology, Rabat, octobre 1983.

Machine translation for language preservation

Steven BIRD[1,2] *David CHIANG*[3]
(1) Department of Computing and Information Systems, University of Melbourne
(2) Linguistic Data Consortium, University of Pennsylvania
(3) Information Sciences Institute, University of Southern California
sbird@unimelb.edu.au, chiang@isi.edu

ABSTRACT
Statistical machine translation has been remarkably successful for the world's well-resourced languages, and much effort is focussed on creating and exploiting rich resources such as treebanks and wordnets. Machine translation can also support the urgent task of documenting the world's endangered languages. The primary object of statistical translation models, bilingual aligned text, closely coincides with interlinear text, the primary artefact collected in documentary linguistics. It ought to be possible to exploit this similarity in order to improve the quantity and quality of documentation for a language. Yet there are many technical and logistical problems to be addressed, starting with the problem that – for most of the languages in question – no texts or lexicons exist. In this position paper, we examine these challenges, and report on a data collection effort involving 15 endangered languages spoken in the highlands of Papua New Guinea.

KEYWORDS: endangered languages, documentary linguistics, language resources, bilingual texts, comparative lexicons.

Proceedings of COLING 2012: Posters, pages 125–134,
COLING 2012, Mumbai, December 2012.

1 Introduction

Most of the world's 6800 languages are relatively unstudied, even though they are no less important for scientific investigation than major world languages. For example, before Hixkaryana (Carib, Brazil) was discovered to have object-verb-subject word order, it was assumed that this word order was not possible in a human language, and that some principle of universal grammar must exist to account for this systematic gap (Derbyshire, 1977). In spite of the scientific importance of the world's languages, computational linguistics research has only touched about 1%. In 100 years, 90% will be extinct or on the way out (Krauss, 2007). Linguists are addressing this problem by *documenting* the world's endangered languages (Woodbury, 2010). What can computational linguistics offer to support this urgent task?

Machine translation (MT) is directly relevant to the process of language documentation (Abney and Bird, 2010). First, when source texts are translated into a major world language, we guarantee that the language documentation will be interpretable even after the language has fallen out of use. Second, when a surviving speaker can identify errors in the output of an MT system, we have timely evidence of those areas of grammar and lexicon that need better coverage while there is still time to collect more. These tasks of producing and correcting translations can be performed by speakers of the language without depending on the intervention of outside linguists. Furthermore, we sidestep the need for linguistic resources like treebanks and wordnets, which are expensive to create and which depend on the existence of morphological, syntactic, and semantic analyses of the language.

For over a century, an early task in describing a new language has been to collect and translate texts, where a "text" could be a written document or a transcribed recording. Despite the documentary value of such data and its usefulness for linguistic research, for most languages there is no collection of texts and translations. Now, transcribing and translating audio recordings takes upwards of ten times real time. It is evidently not practical for an expatriate linguist to do such work, based on the track record of past language documentation projects in which the text collection only amounts to a few thousand words. We would need a thousand times as much primary data in order to support wide-ranging investigations of a language once it is no longer spoken, equivalent to 10 million words, or 1,000 hours of speech (Liberman, 2006) Yet a small team of bilingual speakers should be able to transcribe and translate a substantial collection of texts in a few months. The questions then shift to the following: (a) how can we harness the efforts of minimally trained bilingual speakers to create and share bilingual texts? (b) how can we maximise the consistency of the data in the absence of an orthography or a dictionary? (c) how can we tell when enough of the right kind of data has been collected?

These are difficult questions to answer. In this paper we point a way forward. After a background discussion, we discuss a simplified workflow for language documentation and the role that MT can play in that workflow, then we report on our experience of collecting bilingual spoken and written texts in Papua New Guinea.

This work represents a new approach to language preservation. It begins with the observation that linguists will probably not be able to collect an adequate sized corpus. It leverages local capacity to get started on the work rather than waiting until outside linguists to arrive. It puts the work in the hands of locals, who can make their own decisions about what should be preserved. And it offers a plausible way to limit the "observer effect" which occurs when an outsider comes into a language situation and starts eliciting data (Himmelmann, 1998, 184ff).

2 Background

A statistical translation model is simply a model of parallel text, that is, a model that knows what sentence pairs are more likely than others to occur as translations of each other. Accordingly, a prerequisite for building a statistical MT system for any language pair is to collect texts and their translations into a reference language. However, this coincides with a key activity in documentary linguistics, and harks back to the early days of 19th century descriptive linguistics in which text collection is a major component.

A *language documentation* consists of "a comprehensive and representative sample of communicative events as natural as possible" (Himmelmann, 1998, 168), or "comprehensive and transparent records supporting wide ranging scientific investigations of the language" (Woodbury, 2010). The ideal form of the primary data is video, though audio is a good second-best, and requires less expertise and less expensive equipment, and produces smaller data files. To facilitate access, the raw data is usually transcribed and translated. It should be clear that language documentation is not the same as linguistic description, which calls for linguistic expertise and which produces systematic presentations of the phonology, morphology, syntax, and semantics of the language. Nevertheless, the descriptive work cannot proceed without the language documentation. This documentation – the bilingual text collection – is the same as what is needed for statistical MT and we can expect to apply MT algorithms to the data from linguistic fieldwork (Xia and Lewis, 2007; Palmer et al., 2010).

The workflow for language documentation and description has never been standardised, but there is general agreement that it involves at least the following activities: (a) recording communicative events; (b) transcribing and translating the recordings; (c) performing basic morphosyntactic analysis leading to a lexicon and to a collection of morphologically-glossed text; (d) eliciting paradigms, i.e. systematic tabulations of linguistic forms designed to reveal underlying patterns; (e) preparing descriptive reports to show how the language is structured. These activities are well understood and widely practiced, and provide the empirical foundation for linguistic theory and for the preparation of language resources such as treebanks and wordnets. However this workflow does not scale up. Languages are falling out of use before linguists can get to them.

This leaves the question of what quantity and quality of documentation is required. Here the only consensus amongst linguists is that more is better. Yet linguist-driven documentation projects only produce a tiny fraction of the quantity required for corpus-based studies. Linguists stress the importance of quality, which includes the accuracy and consistency of transcriptions and glosses, but do not report explicit measures of transcription quality (e.g. the Kappa coefficient, widely used for inter-annotator agreement). Since the documentary linguistics community does not provide objective methods and measures of quantity and quality, we need to develop these ourselves.

Note that the agenda is not to remove linguists from the language documentation process. Without specialised training, speakers of endangered languages will never produce the lexicons, morphologically glossed text, treebanks, and wordnets that we would like to have. Instead, we want to capture enough bilingual text to enable documentation and description even after the language has fallen out of use and only the archived documentation is available.

3 A simplified workflow for language documentation

How could minimally-trained speakers of a language create a useful corpus for their language? From the earliest days of corpus construction for English, the first step was to have a digital text collection, from which a balanced corpus could be selected and further annotations applied. However, most endangered languages lack any kind of text collection. Thus, we would like to find a way to produce a substantial text collection for a language without external staffing and resourcing. We envisage that members of the speech community could create documentary artefacts – recordings and transcriptions – using locally available technology, even if it is only a pen and exercise book, or an inexpensive recording device.

The first step is to create a text, either by recording then transcribing, or by composing directly onto paper. Chances are that the speaker will have no experience at IPA transcription and that no standardised orthography for the language exists. Thus, transcription needs to use whatever orthography people know. This practice has some documentary value, for it shows meaningful sound contrasts and word boundaries, and serves as a rough finding aid. In cases where more than one speaker transcribes content in a language, we can try to clean up the transcriptions automatically (Foda and Bird, 2011).

The second step is to translate the text, providing word by word glosses plus a phrasal translation. The correspondence between this literal and "free" translation amounts to training data for an alignment model, and does not require a separate translation model. The final step is to prepare a lexicon, in order to help fix the inconsistencies in spelling and glossing between. SIL's *Fieldworks Language Explorer* (FLEx) software is ideal for this purpose, though it currently lacks support for synchronisation and conflict resolution between databases.

An important refinement is to conduct the above workflow within a cluster of closely related languages. Speakers often produce a wealth of information about lexical correspondences with neighboring languages, as illustrated in Figure 1. Armed with these correspondences, we can pool knowledge about all the languages in the cluster (Nakov and Tiedemann, 2012). We can also try to guess word translations by leveraging regular sound correspondences.

eng	aso	bef	gah	ino	kbq	snp	yby	zuh
sun	ho	yege	ho	yake	zge	fo	homa	ho
water	noso	nagami	nagami	tina	tina	no	noma	nosa
fire	olo	logo	lo	ata	teve	soo	iizo	olo
earth	misumbo	mei	mikasi	mopa	mo'pa	mika	mika	mikesupa
tree	ya	yafa	za	yosa	zafa	yaa	yah	yah
mountain	golo	kosa	agoka	akoya	agona	obura	bora	gola
house	numuno	nohi	numuni	nona	nona	numuna	numuda	numuna
food	nosonite	nosena	nosa'neta	neya	ne'zane	aáwa'a	nodenesa	nosaneta
pig	ije	yaga	iza	afu	afu	savu	izah	iza
man	we	bo	ve	ve	ve'nene	wee	we	vemoha
woman	vene	amo	vena	a'ne	a're	wena	mena	vena
father	meneho'we	afonifu	ahono	afo nimo'e	nenfa	wemeteuo	ahone	meneho
mother	ijeneho	itonifu	izo'no	ita	anta'nimo	wena otevo	idone	izeneho

Figure 1: Comparative wordlist for the languages spoken near Goroka. Languages are identified by ISO 639-3 code. It is likely that, for some language pairs (e.g. aso-zuh, ino-kbq), many wordforms are related to one another by regular sound correspondences.

4 Collecting parallel and comparable texts in Papua New Guinea

Papua New Guinea (PNG) is home to the greatest number of languages and the greatest diversity of language families in the world (Nettle, 1999), including many languages with only a few hundred speakers. Although there is a long history of linguistic description in PNG (Foley, 1986), few of these languages have been comprehensively documented. There is no up-to-date picture of language vitality across PNG, and no systematic efforts to preserve them on the kind of scale that would be required. Some small languages are clearly vital: for example, the Nen language, spoken in the Morehead District, has a population of just 300, and the language is reportedly being transmitted completely to the younger generation (Nicholas Evans, pers. comm.). Nevertheless, many languages – perhaps even the majority – are already moribund and are quickly being overtaken by Tok Pisin, an English-based creole. In the face of this language shift, there is almost no local capacity for language documentation.

Bird trained university staff and students, adult literacy workers, and retired professionals, to collect oral literature using 100 digital voice recorders (Bird, 2010). Participants learned the technique of "respeaking", which involves listening to an original recording and repeating what was heard carefully and slowly (Woodbury, 2003), resulting in a secondary recording which is much easier to transcribe later on. The respoken version plus a phrase-by-phrase spoken interpretation are captured on a second voice recorder. Each voice recorder comes with an A5 exercise book which is used for logging recordings, and keeping track of the different linguistic genres that have been collected. Genres included dialogue, narrative, procedural discourse, oratory, and singing (Johnson and Aristar Dry, 2002).

The result of that work has been a set of phrase-aligned audio files for approximately 50 languages. One significant shortcoming of this approach is that it is virtually impossible to manage files that are collected on 100 voice recorders. Instead, we have developed a mobile phone interface, as shown in Figure 2. It can be used for audio collection and sharing, and for respeaking and interpreting (Hanke and Bird, 2012).

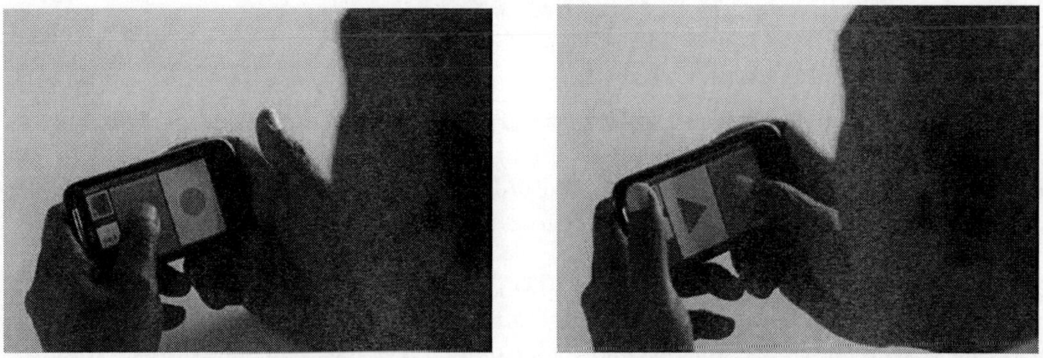

(a) Audio playback

(b) Respeaking and Interpretating

Figure 2: Mobile phone interface: (a) press and hold the play button to hear the original recording (b) press and hold the record button to record the respeaking or interpreting

However, voice recorders and mobile phones can only collect bilingual audio, while machine translation technologies require bilingual text. We organised a two week workshop at the University of Goroka involving approximately 40 speakers of 15 undocumented languages (Bird et al., 2012). We elicited comparable texts across the languages with a variety of tasks, for example: (a) write about the national election or about a traditional legend; (b) listen to someone's story and put it in your own words, e.g. the *Rabaul Queen* disaster; (c) listen to dictation in English and Tok Pisin, but translate each sentence into your language, e.g. a story about a visit to the chicken market. Each text was set out using the format shown in Figure 3.

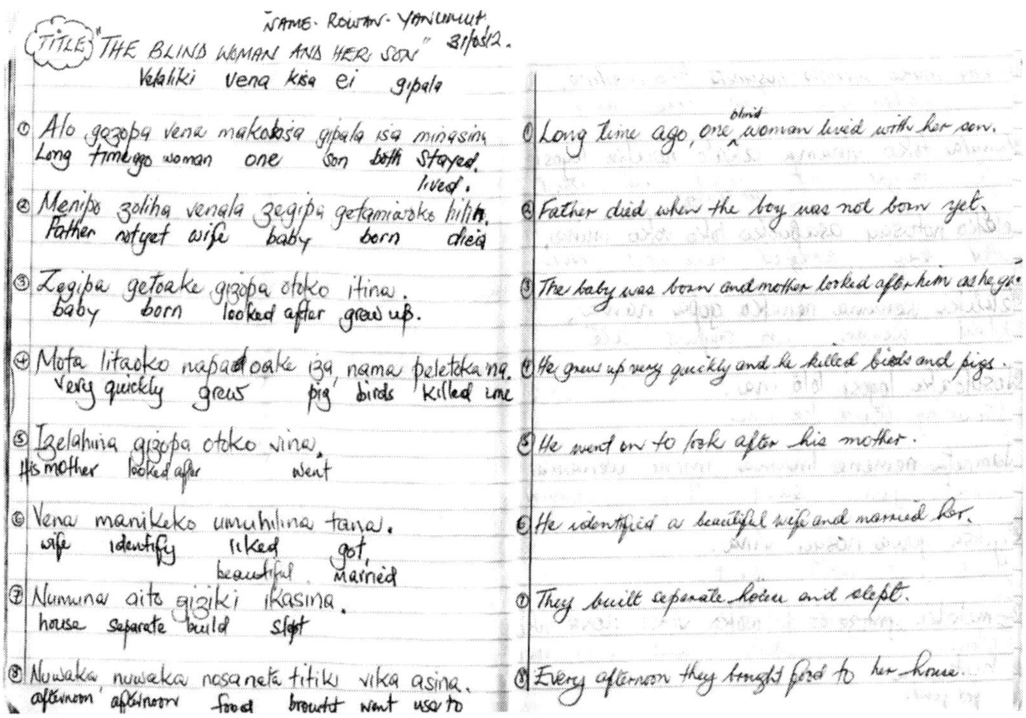

Figure 3: Interlinear Text Layout: (a) the title, translated title, author, and date are written at the top; (b) the source text is written on the left page, with three-line spacing, numbering each sentence; (c) the gloss is written beneath each word (omitted if no simple gloss is possible); (d) the phrasal translation is written on the right page, and coindexed with the source.

We were able to categorise the speakers into four types based on linguistic and technical capabilities. The first category, *monolinguals*, consisted of elders with no functional knowledge of Tok Pisin, who probably have good knowledge of their oral literature but who are so culturally different that it is difficult to tap their knowledge; they are not particularly comfortable in the university setting. The second category, *village-based bilinguals*, consisted of elders with basic literacy in Tok Pisin or English, and no formal education beyond primary school. The third category, *retired professionals*, consisted of bilingual speakers with post-secondary education who have moved around the country and held various professional roles, with solid literacy in English. Finally, the fourth category, *young professionals*, consisted of bilingual speakers who are studying or are employed in town, with English literacy, computer literacy, but limited fluency in their ancestral language and almost no knowledge of oral literature.

Texts and translations were keyboarded by people working in pairs, as illustrated in Figure 4. Once it was finalised, each text and translation was printed and displayed on a wall. This served three purposes: (a) participants were publicly recognised for completing a text; (b) corrections could be marked for later editing; and (c) ideas for writing topics were shared. On the last day, we published a booklet containing all the texts.

Figure 4: Interlinear Text Entry: an Adzera speaker who is a competent typist (left) enters interlinear text for the Asaro speaker (right) who dictates the words and glosses and checks that they are correctly entered. (The handwritten source text is shown in Figure 3.)

A sample of the interlinear text is shown in (1).

(1) Velaliki veena kisa ei gipala (The blind woman and her son)
Alo gozopa vena makokisa gipala isa minasina.
long time ago woman one son both lived.
A long time ago, a blind woman lived with her son.

Menipo zoliha venala zegipa getamiwoko hilina.
father not yet wife baby born died.
The father died when the boy was not yet born.

Zegipa getoake gizopa otoko itina.
baby born looked after grew up.
The baby was born and the mother looked after him as he grew.

Mota litaoko napaoake iza, nama peletoka ana.
very quickly grew pig, birds killed came.
He grew up very quickly and he killed birds and pigs.

Izelahina gizopa otoko vina.
his mother looked after went.

He went on to look after his mother.

In the two weeks of the workshop, we only managed to collect a total of 20k words of source text (16k translated) for the 15 languages. Many participants found it relatively difficult to compose directly into the written form, and so they did not produce much writing. For the languages where we had more than one speaker, there was some dialect variation and this was reflected in spelling. There was also some variation in the marking of word boundaries, and with the writing of glottal stop (apostrophe, *q*, or omitted). We lacked the time and the language-specific information required to perform morphological glossing, and this would have been quite challenging given the systems of switch reference, serial verbs, and clause chaining in many of these languages (Foley, 1986; Payne, 1997). Perhaps because of these morphological issues, word-level glossing was slower than phrase-level translation. In any case, for these reasons it proved impossible to construct useful translation models for the languages.

In order to scale up the work to generate a quantity of data that would be more useful for machine translation experiments, the following steps would be required. First, the primary textual sources should be audio recordings, and transcribed using a tool that preserves the audio alignment (for later verification) and which links wordforms to lexemes (for consistency in spelling, word breaks, and glosses). Second, the transcription and glossing software should operate in tandem with curating a shared n-language lexicon to speed up the process and encourage consistency across speakers, possibly using the structures described in (Baldwin et al., 2010; Abney and Bird, 2011).

5 Conclusion

Most of the world's languages will fall out of use before the world's linguists and computational linguists are able to collect sufficient data. However, we have been investigating simple methodologies and supporting software that are helping speakers of endangered languages in Papua New Guinea to produce usable documentation on their own. The primary data type is bilingual text – or interlinear glossed text – which serves the dual purpose of documenting a language and developing translation models.

Once the translation models reach an adequate level, they could be usable as the basis for post-editing work, and may speed the translation process. More importantly, system errors will draw attention to those areas of the grammar and lexicon that are not yet well represented in the data. They may prompt speakers to provide more data of the required kind, without requiring the intervention of an outside linguist. While is still difficult to imagine being able to do this work on the required scale, it represents a promising approach for shaping the effort of non-specialist language speakers in creating a documentary record of their languages while there is still time.

Acknowledgements

We are grateful to the many colleagues and students who helped run the workshop discussed in section 4. This research is sponsored by NSF 1144167 *Machine Translation for Language Preservation* and ARC 120101712 *Language Engineering in the Field*.

References

Abney, S. and Bird, S. (2010). The Human Language Project: building a universal corpus of the world's languages. In *Proceedings of the 48th Meeting of the Association for Computational Linguistics*, pages 88–97. Association for Computational Linguistics.

Abney, S. and Bird, S. (2011). Towards a data model for the Universal Corpus. In *Proceedings of the 4th Workshop on Building and Using Comparable Corpora: Comparable Corpora and the Web*, pages 120–127. Association for Computational Linguistics.

Baldwin, T., Pool, J., and Colowick, S. (2010). PanLex and LEXTRACT: Translating all words of all languages of the world. In *Proceedings of the 23rd International Conference on Computational Linguistics, Demonstrations Volume*, pages 37–40. Tsinghua University Press.

Bird, S. (2010). A scalable method for preserving oral literature from small languages. In *Proceedings of the 12th International Conference on Asia-Pacific Digital Libraries*, pages 5–14.

Bird, S., Chiang, D., Frowein, F., Eby, M., Hanke, F., Shelby, R., Vaswani, A., and Wan, A. (2012). Language preservation in Papua New Guinea: Report from a workshop at the University of Goroka. Unpublished.

Derbyshire, D. C. (1977). Word order universals and the existence of OVS languages. *Linguistic Inquiry*, 8:590–99.

Foda, A. and Bird, S. (2011). Normalising audio transcriptions for unwritten languages. In *Proceedings of 5th International Joint Conference on Natural Language Processing*, pages 527–535, Chiang Mai, Thailand. Asian Federation of Natural Language Processing.

Foley, W. A. (1986). *The Papuan Languages of New Guinea*. Cambridge University Press.

Hanke, F. and Bird, S. (2012). Preserving endangered oral culture: speech annotation on mobile devices. Unpublished.

Himmelmann, N. P. (1998). Documentary and descriptive linguistics. *Linguistics*, 36:161–195.

Johnson, H. and Aristar Dry, H. (2002). OLAC discourse type vocabulary. `http://www.language-archives.org/REC/discourse.html`.

Krauss, M. E. (2007). Mass language extinction and documentation: the race against time. In Miyaoka, O., Sakiyama, O., and Krauss, M. E., editors, *The Vanishing Languages of the Pacific Rim*. Oxford University Press.

Liberman, M. (2006). The problems of scale in language documentation. Plenary talk at TLSX Texas Linguistics Society 10: Computational Linguistics for Less-Studied Languages, `http://uts.cc.utexas.edu/~tls/2006tls/`.

Nakov, P. and Tiedemann, J. (2012). Combining word-level and character-level models for machine translation between closely-related languages. In *Proceedings of the 50th Annual Meeting of the Association for Computational Linguistics*, pages 301–305. Association for Computational Linguistics.

Nettle, D. (1999). *Linguistic Diversity*. Oxford University Press.

Palmer, A., Moon, T., Baldridge, J., Erk, K., Campbell, E., and Can, T. (2010). Computational strategies for reducing annotation effort in language documentation. *Linguistic Issues in Language Technology*, 3(4):1–42.

Payne, T. E. (1997). *Describing Morphosyntax*. Cambridge University Press.

Woodbury, A. C. (2003). Defining documentary linguistics. In Austin, P., editor, *Language Documentation and Description*, volume 1, pages 35–51. London: SOAS.

Woodbury, A. C. (2010). Language documentation. In Austin, P. K. and Sallabank, J., editors, *The Cambridge Handbook of Endangered Languages*. Cambridge University Press.

Xia, F. and Lewis, W. D. (2007). Multilingual structural projection across interlinearized text. In *Proceedings of the Meeting of the North American Chapter of the Association for Computational Linguistics*, pages 452–459. Association for Computational Linguistics.

Comparing Non-projective Strategies for Labeled Graph-based Dependency Parsing

Anders Björkelund Jonas Kuhn
Institut für Maschinelle Sprachverarbeitung
University of Stuttgart
{anders,jonas}@ims.uni-stuttgart.de

ABSTRACT
We fill a gap in the systematically analyzed space of available techniques for state-of-the-art dependency parsing by comparing non-projective strategies for graph-based parsers. Using three languages with varying frequency of non-projective constructions, we compare the non-projective approximation algorithm with pseudo-projective parsing. We also analyze the differences between different encoding schemes for pseudo-projective parsing. We find only minor differences between the encoding schemes for pseudo-projective parsing, and that the non-projective approximation algorithm is superior to pseudo-projective parsing.

KEYWORDS: Multilingual Dependency Parsing, Non-projective Parsing, Pseudo-projective Parsing.

Proceedings of COLING 2012: Posters, pages 135–144,
COLING 2012, Mumbai, December 2012.

1 Introduction

One common justification for dependency syntax is that it, in contrast to constituent syntax, can represent long-distance dependencies between words through non-projective dependencies in a more straightforward way, without the use of traces or secondary edges. Informally, a dependency tree is said to be non-projective if it cannot be drawn without crossing edges. An example is shown in Figure 1.

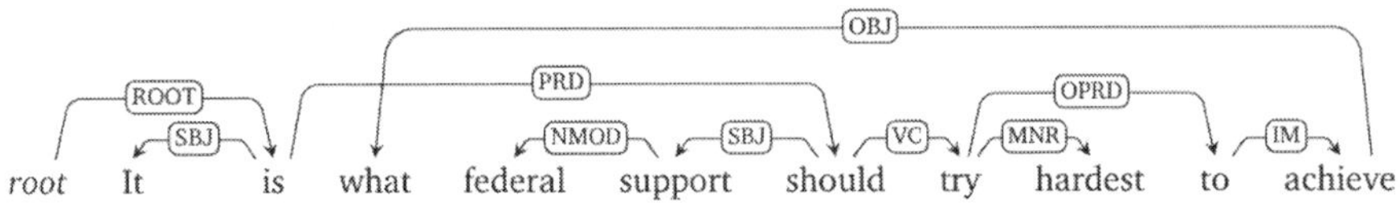

Figure 1: A non-projective sentence

Although there are decoding algorithms for graph-based parsers that are able to output non-projective trees directly (e.g. spanning tree algorithms (McDonald et al., 2005b) and ILP-based parsers (Riedel and Clarke, 2006, *inter alia*)), the chart-based algorithm of Eisner (1996), which is restricted to projective output, has shown very promising results in recent years. It typically outperforms the non-projective algorithms since it allows access to features involving pairs of edges.

A notable extension to the chart-based parsing algorithm that is able to output non-projective dependencies while still including edge-pair features is the non-projective approximation algorithm of McDonald and Pereira (2006).

Non-projective edges have also been handled by applying pre- and post-processing steps to the training and test data, allowing for the use of any labeled projective parsing algorithm, only to recover the non-projective edges after parsing, e.g. pseudo-projective parsing (Nivre and Nilsson, 2005).

In the CoNLL 2008 and 2009 Shared Tasks (Surdeanu et al., 2008; Hajič et al., 2009), some of the best systems used the chart-based parsing algorithm. Besides using slightly different feature sets, non-projective edges were handled differently – Bohnet (2009) used the non-projective approximation algorithm, while Johansson and Nugues (2008) and Che et al. (2009) used pseudo-projective parsing. Handling non-projective edges is unarguably an important aspect of a parser, however, little is known about whether one of the methods mentioned above is better than the other. With a fixed feature set, we compare pseudo-projective parsing with non-projective approximation using a state-of-the-art chart-based dependency parser (Bohnet, 2010). We also evaluate different encoding schemes for pseudo-projective parsing. More recently, highly accurate parsers that model non-projective edges directly in the parsing algorithm have been proposed, such as the ILP-based parser of Martins et al. (2010) as well as algorithms relying on non-projective head automata (Koo et al., 2010). It would be interesting to include these parsers in our study, however they only provide unlabeled trees. For now, we leave the extension of these parsers to the labeled case and the comparison to future work.

All experiments are performed on three languages that exhibit different typological properties and frequency of non-projective dependencies: Czech, English, and German. We find that non-projective approximation performs better than pseudo-projective parsing, although both methods clearly outperform a projective baseline. While similar studies have been carried out for transition-based parsers (Kuhlmann and Nivre, 2010), this is the first time non-projective strategies for graph-based algorithms are compared in a multilingual setting.

2 Background

We consider single-rooted dependency trees with one head per token, such as the one in Figure 1. We use the notation $x = x_0 \dots x_n$ to denote a sentence with n tokens, where x_0 is a special *root* node. A labeled head-dependent relation (or edge) between a head h and dependent c with the label l is denoted $(h \xrightarrow{l} c)$. We omit the label when this is not relevant. A dependency tree for a sentence x is a set $y = \{(p_1 \xrightarrow{l_1} x_1), \dots, (p_n \xrightarrow{l_n} x_n)\}$ of edges, such that each node except the root has exactly one head, and the graph is acyclic (i.e., it forms a single-rooted tree). A node x_i *dominates* another node x_j if x_i is an ancestor of x_j. An edge $(x_i \rightarrow x_j)$ is defined to be *projective* iff x_i dominates all words between x_i and x_j. Otherwise it is *non-projective*. Moreover, a dependency tree y is projective iff every edge is projective. Otherwise it is non-projective.

Graph-based Dependency Parsing algorithms solve the parsing problem by finding the highest scoring dependency tree for a sentence: $\hat{y} = \arg\max_y F(x, y)$, given a scoring function F. To make the search for the optimal tree tractable, the scoring function is decomposed into a sum over *factors* of the tree (McDonald et al., 2005a):

$$F(x,y) = \sum_{f \in factors(x,y)} \psi(f) \cdot w$$

where ψ is a feature-mapping function that maps a factor f to a vector in high-dimensional feature space and w a weight vector.

The chart-based algorithm of Eisner (1996) has the advantage that it can incorporate second-order factors while still remaining computationally feasible. The version we use is due to Carreras (2007) and makes use of second-order factors including sibling and grandchild relations. This factorization offers access to valuable features but comes at the cost of a time complexity of $O(Ln^4)$, where L is the number of edge labels. To reduce the impact of the factor L, edge filters are applied (Bohnet, 2010), constraining the search of edge labels to those observed in training for the same head and dependent POS-tags; this reduces execution time considerably.

The **Non-projective Approximation** algorithm (McDonald and Pereira, 2006) exploits the observation that, although the chart-based parsing algorithm is only able to output projective structures, the weight vector used to score the factors of the tree is not limited in this respect. Hence, starting from the highest scoring projective tree output by the chart-based algorithm, it iteratively tries to reattach all tokens, one at a time, everywhere in the sentence as long as the tree property holds. In each iteration, the highest scoring move, i.e., the move that increases the total score of the tree the most is executed. The process terminates when the increase is below a certain threshold.

Pseudocode[1] for the algorithm is given in Figure 2. The auxiliary function ALLOWED-LABELS(h, c, x) returns the labels permitted by the edge filters and TREE(y) returns true if y is a tree, and false otherwise. The notation $y[j \xrightarrow{k} i]$ denotes a tree identical to y, except that the head of x_i is replaced by x_j, and its label by k. This process could potentially take exponential time, although this is not a problem in practice, and the algorithm typically halts after a few moves (McDonald and Pereira, 2006).

Pseudo-projective Parsing can be used with any labeled projective parsing algorithm. The training data is pre-processed by applying lifting operations to the non-projective edges while

[1]From McDonald and Pereira (2006), but adapted to the labeled case.

```
input Sentence x, tree y, scoring function F, threshold t
returns (Non-)projective tree y'
  score ← F(x, y)
  while true
    m ← −∞, c ← −1, p ← −1, l ← null
    for i : 1..n
      for j : 0..n
        y' ← y[j → i]
        if ¬TREE(y') continue
        for k ∈ ALLOWED-LABELS(i, j)
          y' ← y[j -k-> i]
          s ← F(x, y')
          if s > m
            m ← s, c ← i, p ← j, l ← k
    if m − score > t
      score ← m, y ← y[p -l-> c]
    else return y
```

Figure 2: Non-projective approximation

encoding information about the lifts into the edge labels in the tree. The parser is then trained on these projective trees and learns the encoding of the liftings. An inverse transformation that recovers the non-projective edges is then applied to the parser output (Nivre and Nilsson, 2005). This way, non-projective edges are introduced in a post-processing step allowing for the use of any projective parsing algorithm.

Nivre and Nilsson (2005) propose three label encoding schemes differing in terms of the granularity in the marking of lifts: **Head** - each lifted edge is marked as lifted, and additionally receives the label of its original head; **Path** - the lifted edge is marked as lifted, and all heads along the path it was lifted through get marked as having had a dependent lifted; **HeadPath** - a combination of Head and Path, where the lifted edge is marked as in the Head scheme *and* all heads along the path it was lifted get marked as in the Path scheme. Figure 3 shows the dependency tree from Figure 1 when the edge of *what* has been lifted using the HeadPath scheme.

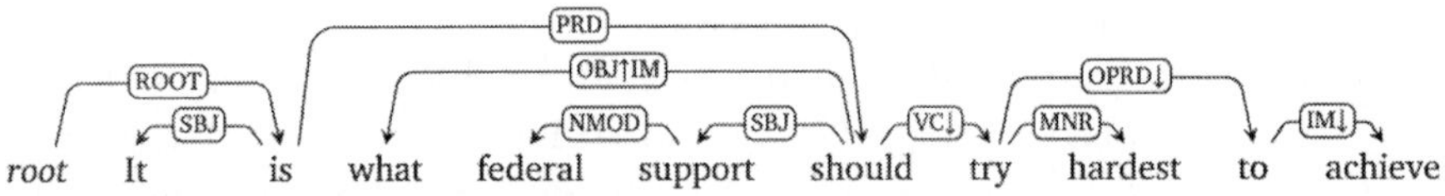

Figure 3: The same sentence as in Figure 1, but the non-projective edge has been lifted using the HeadPath scheme

Each of the encoding schemes leads to an increase in the set of edge labels (up to $2n(n+1)$ new labels for HeadPath (Nivre and Nilsson, 2005)), and thus to an increase in parsing time. Additionally, there is a possible data sparsity issue as a result of very infrequent lifted edges. It has therefore been proposed to cap the number of newly introduced labels and retain only the m most frequent new labels in the training data (Johansson and Nugues, 2008).

The inverse transformation looks for edges that are marked as lifted (i.e. of the form $l\uparrow$ or $l\uparrow l_{np}$). It then does a breadth-first search, starting from the head of this edge, looking for a new head for the dependent. Details depend on the encoding scheme: For Head, search halts at the first token whose edge label matches the lifted edge (i.e. the first token with the label l_{np}); for Path, only the subtrees marked with $\downarrow$ are considered, and search halts at the deepest edge marked with $\downarrow$; for HeadPath the edge is reattached at the deepest token that matches $l_{np}\downarrow$. Additionally, for HeadPath, the inverse transformation of Head is used as a fallback in case the search fails (Nivre and Nilsson, 2005).

3 Experiments and Results

The parser we employ (Bohnet, 2010)[2] uses non-projective approximation by default.[3] In the experiments involving pseudo-projective parsing, we switched off the non-projective approximation.

We use the three data sets from the CoNLL 2009 Shared Task (Hajič et al., 2009) that contain non-projective edges, namely Czech, English, and German. We use the standard data split. Since the frequency of non-projective edges is relatively small, we resort to a 10-fold cross-validation on the training set in order to get more reliable figures. A breakdown of the training sets for each language is shown in Table 1. We use the "predicted" layers of annotation, i.e. output of standard POS-taggers etc., for a realistic evaluation. We report labeled attachment score (LAS), i.e. the percentage of correctly assigned heads and edge labels, and labeled exact match (LEM) for complete sentences. The scores are micro-averaged, i.e., the parser output for all folds are concatenated and compared against the whole training set.

Following Kuhlmann and Nivre (2010) we also compute precision and recall for non-projective edges. They define recall as the percentage of tokens that have a non-projective dependency in the gold standard and receive the correct head and label in the parser output. Precision is defined as the percentage of tokens getting a non-projective dependency in the parser output receiving the correct head and label. As Kuhlmann and Nivre (2010) point out, these definitions are somewhat unusual since they have different numbers of true positives, and combining them through the unweighted harmonic mean is not meaningful. Hence we do not present any F-measures in the tables.

	Sentences	#NP edges (%)	% NP sentences
Czech	38,727	12,112 (1.86%)	22.42%
English	39,279	3,724 (0.39%)	7.63%
German	36,020	15,123 (2.33%)	28.10%

Table 1: Breakdown of the training sets of each language. NP means non-projective.

In the experiments we want to investigate three questions: (1) Are pseudo-projective parsing and non-projective approximation equally good, or is one better than the other? (2) What is the difference between the different label encoding schemes for pseudo-projective parsing? (3) How badly does label capping for pseudo-projective parsing degrade performance?

We also trained a baseline parser on trees that were projectivized, but received no augmented edge labels. All results are shown in Table 2. The rows with subscripted pseudo-projective encodings denote parsers that used a label cap (of 30). As an indication of how often the different parsers produce non-projective edges, the total number of non-projective edges are given in the last column.

[2] `http://code.google.com/p/mate-tools`

[3] The threshold t has already been tuned to 0.3 by Bohnet (2010), and we keep this fixed throughout the experiments.

During training and testing we experienced that the capped parsers required about as much time as the parsers that use the non-projective approximation, while the uncapped HeadPath parsers took about twice as much time. This is because the increase in decoding time due to the increased set of labels for the pseudo-projective parsers is roughly canceled out by the call to the non-projective approximation algorithm. When the cap is dropped, however, the pseudo-projective parsers are overwhelmed by the number of new labels and consequently need more time for decoding.

	All		Non-projective		
Czech	LAS	LEM	P	R	#NP
Baseline	81.10	25.90		5.40	0
Path_{30}	81.75	27.28	**76.86**	40.13	5,748
Head_{30}	**81.86**	**27.67**	71.23	**44.23**	6,868
HeadPath_{30}	81.73	27.51	71.64	39.28	5,973
Path	81.78	27.35	**76.48**	41.03	5,868
Head	**81.94**	27.87	70.10	48.18	7,716
HeadPath	**81.94**	**27.94**	70.40	**48.82**	7,727
NPA	**82.11**	**28.40**	68.95	**65.72**	11,394
English	LAS	LEM	P	R	#NP
Baseline	89.73	28.95		7.44	0
Path_{30}	89.74	29.08	**75.42**	23.58	834
Head_{30}	**89.80**	**29.37**	61.47	**39.02**	1,983
HeadPath_{30}	**89.80**	29.27	63.21	38.94	1,911
Path	89.77	29.41	**75.85**	23.85	824
Head	**89.83**	**29.44**	61.33	39.98	2,061
HeadPath	89.82	29.40	60.55	**40.44**	2,066
NPA	89.80	**29.52**	49.46	**43.77**	3,787
German	LAS	LEM	P	R	#NP
Baseline	86.01	30.94		4.74	0
Path_{30}	86.60	33.44	**70.36**	36.05	6,778
Head_{30}	**86.74**	**33.77**	62.45	40.12	8,741
HeadPath_{30}	86.64	33.58	64.32	**40.24**	8,416
Path	86.61	33.62	**69.78**	36.53	6,885
Head	**86.79**	**33.74**	60.27	41.65	9,424
HeadPath	86.75	33.66	60.78	**42.14**	9,359
NPA	**87.05**	**34.99**	65.37	**58.47**	14,208

Table 2: Results for pseudo-projective parsing and non-projective approximation (NPA). P and R denote precision and recall for non-projective edges. #NP denotes the total number of predicted non-projective edges.

Not surprisingly, our results indicate that handling non-projective edges is much more important in Czech and German. In these languages, the baseline is clearly outperformed by all other parsers. In English, non-projective approximation, and uncapped Head, HeadPath ($p < 0.001$), and Path ($p < 0.05$) are all significantly better than the baseline (using a paired t-test).

The non-projective approximation has a considerably higher recall and the amount of non-projective edges is closer to the real number (cf. Table 1), yet the precision does not seem to be severely penalized. The low recall for the pseudo-projective parsers is explained by the fact that these transformations rely on predicting corresponding labels (depending on encoding scheme) in *two* places – the predicted projective head, with an augmented label, and the reattachment location. Since the parser as such is not aware of this interdependency, it is possible that it predicts a tree with a lifted edge, but no appropriate place to reattach it, in which case the edge is left in place. The non-projective approximation algorithm does not have the same limitation as it simply moves single edges around as long as it increases the overall scores.

Pseudo-projective parsing vs Non-projective approximation. Comparing non-projective approximation with the uncapped pseudo-projective parsers, we find that in Czech and German the non-projective approximation is significantly better than all the pseudo-projective parsers ($p < 0.001$). The difference in LAS, compared to the best pseudo-projective encoding, is roughly 0.25. Although this may seem tiny, the increase in exact match (LEM) is more than a point for German and about half a point for Czech. This improvement is important since, ultimately, a correct analysis of an entire tree is what we aim for. For English, the scores are much closer and only the improvement for the non-projective approximation over Path is significant ($p < 0.05$). The improvements in exact match are also rather small.

Pseudo-projective parsing. Considering pseudo-projective parsing alone, Path consistently predicts the fewest non-projective edges, leading to the highest precision but almost always the lowest recall. This is reasonable, as the requirement for Path to induce a non-projective edge is that it predicts both a lifted edge, *and* a path of edges from the head to an appropriate place to reattach it. Since these augmented labels are rather rare, it seems like the parser suffers from sparsity issues during training and underpredicts these edges.

The recall figures are highest for HeadPath, although it lags a bit behind Head for the capped version in Czech and English. This is because some of the most frequent labels in the HeadPath scheme are of the form $l\downarrow$, which means that the parser learns only very few lifted edges (i.e. edges of the form $l\uparrow l_{np}$).

Besides the slightly lower scores for Path, the overall difference between the encoding schemes appear very small. With the cap, the Head encoding appears to be a bit better, but HeadPath catches up when the cap is dropped.

Capping the number of new labels leads to slightly lower results in Czech and German, however only the increases for HeadPath against its capped counterpart in Czech ($p < 0.001$) and German ($p < 0.01$) are statistically significant.

4 Conclusion

We presented a comparative analysis of the non-projective approximation algorithm and pseudo-projective parsing using a graph-based parser. Our experimental results indicate that the non-projective approximation algorithm outperforms pseudo-projective parsing in overall accuracy for Czech and German. For English, where non-projective dependencies are relatively infrequent, the strategies are rather tied, albeit better than the baseline. In conclusion, the non-projective approximation algorithm is clearly superior for languages that more often exhibit long-distance dependencies.

Our evaluation of the different encoding schemes for pseudo-projective parsing reveals that the schemes are roughly equivalent in overall performance, and that capping the number of labels results only in a slight performance degradation.

In the future, we aim to extend our study to include parsers that handle non-projective edges in the immediate parsing process. We also intend to look more closely at the underlying phenomena that give rise to the non-projective edges.

Acknowledgments

This work was funded by the Deutsche Forschungsgemeinschaft (DFG) via the SFB 732 "Incremental Specification in Context", project D8.

References

Bohnet, B. (2009). Efficient parsing of syntactic and semantic dependency structures. In *Proceedings of the Thirteenth Conference on Computational Natural Language Learning (CoNLL 2009): Shared Task*, pages 67–72, Boulder, Colorado. Association for Computational Linguistics.

Bohnet, B. (2010). Top accuracy and fast dependency parsing is not a contradiction. In *Proceedings of the 23rd International Conference on Computational Linguistics (Coling 2010)*, pages 89–97, Beijing, China. Coling 2010 Organizing Committee.

Carreras, X. (2007). Experiments with a higher-order projective dependency parser. In *Proceedings of the CoNLL Shared Task Session of EMNLP-CoNLL 2007*, pages 957–961, Prague, Czech Republic. Association for Computational Linguistics.

Che, W., Li, Z., Li, Y., Guo, Y., Qin, B., and Liu, T. (2009). Multilingual dependency-based syntactic and semantic parsing. In *Proceedings of the Thirteenth Conference on Computational Natural Language Learning (CoNLL 2009): Shared Task*, pages 49–54, Boulder, Colorado. Association for Computational Linguistics.

Eisner, J. (1996). Three new probabilistic models for dependency parsing: An exploration. In *Proceedings of the 16th International Conference on Computational Linguistics (Coling 1996)*, pages 340–345, Copenhagen, Denmark.

Hajič, J., Ciaramita, M., Johansson, R., Kawahara, D., Martí, M. A., Màrquez, L., Meyers, A., Nivre, J., Padó, S., Štěpánek, J., Straňák, P., Surdeanu, M., Xue, N., and Zhang, Y. (2009). The conll-2009 shared task: Syntactic and semantic dependencies in multiple languages. In *Proceedings of the Thirteenth Conference on Computational Natural Language Learning (CoNLL 2009): Shared Task*, pages 1–18, Boulder, Colorado. Association for Computational Linguistics.

Johansson, R. and Nugues, P. (2008). Dependency-based syntactic–semantic analysis with propbank and nombank. In *CoNLL 2008: Proceedings of the Twelfth Conference on Computational Natural Language Learning*, pages 183–187, Manchester, England. Coling 2008 Organizing Committee.

Koo, T., Rush, A. M., Collins, M., Jaakkola, T., and Sontag, D. (2010). Dual decomposition for parsing with non-projective head automata. In *Proceedings of the 2010 Conference on Empirical Methods in Natural Language Processing*, pages 1288–1298, Cambridge, MA. Association for Computational Linguistics.

Kuhlmann, M. and Nivre, J. (2010). Transition-based techniques for non-projective dependency parsing. *Northern European Journal of Language Technology*, 2(1):1–19.

Martins, A., Smith, N., Xing, E., Aguiar, P., and Figueiredo, M. (2010). Turbo parsers: Dependency parsing by approximate variational inference. In *Proceedings of the 2010 Conference on Empirical Methods in Natural Language Processing*, pages 34–44, Cambridge, MA. Association for Computational Linguistics.

McDonald, R., Crammer, K., and Pereira, F. (2005a). Online large-margin training of dependency parsers. In *Proceedings of the 43rd Annual Meeting of the Association for Computational Linguistics (ACL'05)*, pages 91–98, Ann Arbor, Michigan. Association for Computational Linguistics.

McDonald, R. and Pereira, F. (2006). Online learning of approximate dependency parsing algorithms. In *Proceedings of the 11th Conference of the European Chapter of the ACL (EACL 2006)*, pages 81–88, Trento, Italy. Association for Computational Linguistics.

McDonald, R., Pereira, F., Ribarov, K., and Hajic, J. (2005b). Non-projective dependency parsing using spanning tree algorithms. In *Proceedings of Human Language Technology Conference and Conference on Empirical Methods in Natural Language Processing*, pages 523–530, Vancouver, British Columbia, Canada. Association for Computational Linguistics.

Nivre, J. and Nilsson, J. (2005). Pseudo-projective dependency parsing. In *Proceedings of the 43rd Annual Meeting of the Association for Computational Linguistics (ACL'05)*, pages 99–106, Ann Arbor, Michigan. Association for Computational Linguistics.

Riedel, S. and Clarke, J. (2006). Incremental integer linear programming for non-projective dependency parsing. In *Proceedings of the 2006 Conference on Empirical Methods in Natural Language Processing*, pages 129–137, Sydney, Australia. Association for Computational Linguistics.

Surdeanu, M., Johansson, R., Meyers, A., Màrquez, L., and Nivre, J. (2008). The conll 2008 shared task on joint parsing of syntactic and semantic dependencies. In *CoNLL 2008: Proceedings of the Twelfth Conference on Computational Natural Language Learning*, pages 159–177, Manchester, England. Coling 2008 Organizing Committee.

Phrase Structures and Dependencies for End-to-End Coreference Resolution

Anders Björkelund *Jonas Kuhn*
Institut für Maschinelle Sprachverarbeitung
University of Stuttgart
{anders,jonas}@ims.uni-stuttgart.de

ABSTRACT
We present experiments in data-driven coreference resolution comparing the effect of different syntactic representations provided as features in the coreference classification step: no syntax, phrase structure representations, dependency representations, and combinations of the representation types. We compare the end-to-end performance of a parametrized state-of-the-art coreference resolution system on the English data from the CoNLL 2012 shared task. On their own, phrase structures are more useful than dependencies, but the combinations yield highest performance and a significant improvement on the resolution of pronouns.
Enriching phrase structure with dependency trees obtained from an independent parser is most helpful, but an extension of the predicted phrase structure using just pattern-based phrase-to-dependency conversion seems to provide signals for the machine learning that cannot be distilled from phrase structure alone (despite intense feature selection). This is an interesting result for a highly configurational language: It is easier to learn generalizations over grammatical constraints on coreference when grammatical relations are explicitly provided.

KEYWORDS: Coreference Resolution, Dependency Parsing vs. Phrase-structure Parsing.

Proceedings of COLING 2012: Posters, pages 145–154,
COLING 2012, Mumbai, December 2012.

1 Introduction

Data-driven coreference resolution has received a lot of recent attention, including the 2011 and 2012 CoNLL shared tasks (Pradhan et al., 2011, 2012). To a greater or lesser extent, most coreference systems make use of syntax. For the subtask of mention detection, i.e., identifying referential phrases (substrings) for which coreference relations are subsequently determined, a phrase structure representation is useful for obvious reasons – in particular for the standard coreference task focusing on noun phrase (NP) and pronoun resolution. But also for the subsequent subtask, coreference resolution, syntactic information has proven useful in data-driven approaches – as one might expect from the rich linguistic work on Binding Theory, which targets the grammatical constraints on possible interpretations of referential phrases. It is this second subtask that we will parametrize systematically in this paper.

Most coreference work has built on phrase structure syntax, although dependency syntax was, for instance, used in the SemEval 2010 Task 1 (Recasens et al., 2010). To our knowledge, effects of the two main alternatives have not been studied systematically. The choice typically seems to be driven by external factors (such as availability in shared task data). The fact that mention detection is so straightforward with phrase structure input also creates a practical bias affecting the full pipeline, but since both the phrase structure and the dependency parsing research paradigms are at mature stages, with parsers available for many languages, a more informed decision would be desirable.

We here intend to shed some initial light on how the two different syntactic representations fare comparatively in end-to-end coreference resolution: What is the best basis for machine learning to pick up the (sometimes subtle) grammatical constraints influencing coreference resolution? Starting from a state-of-the-art system, we compare a phrase-structure-based resolver with a dependency-based counterpart and combinations of the two syntactic information sources on the English data from the CoNLL 2012 Shared Task. In a nutshell, the main results are that as a single source of information, phrase structures are more useful than dependencies, but experiments indicate that the two might be complementary: combined feature information from both sources outperform the phrase-structure-based system, particularly with respect to pronouns.

2 Grammatical Factors in Coreference Relations

For decades, coreference data have been at the core of many considerations (and debates) in Generative Linguistics, because grammatical configurations influence the availability of certain readings and hence make coreference tests a useful (albeit mostly theory-dependent) diagnostic for many linguistic purposes. Typical examples of facts addressed by Binding Theory are the following:

(1) a. John$_i$ thinks that Bill$_j$ hurt himself$_{*i/j}$.

b. John$_i$ thinks that Bill$_j$ hurt him$_{i/*j}$.

c. He$_i$ hurt John$_{*i/j}$.

Roughly speaking, (A) reflexives like *himself* have to be coreferent with an element inside of their local clause, whereas (B) non-reflexive pronouns like *him* must have an antecedent outside of their local clause. (C) Full NPs, such as proper names, must not be preceded by a coreferent NP in the same sentence. Chomsky (1981) describes the grammatical constraints over possible coreference interpretations by three Binding Principles (A, B, C), which have been discussed, extended and criticized in countless contributions in the linguistic literature.

Given that there are grammatical constraints of this kind, one may expect that hard-coding some of the Binding Principles should help in practical coreference systems. However, the treatment of more subtle cases is quite controversial in the literature and sometimes involves fairly involved assumptions about phrase structure; in addition, there are a number of contextually driven or construction-specific exceptions to the grammar-driven principles, such as so-called logophoric usages of reflexives (2), and plain pronouns in contexts where one would expect reflexives (3) (examples due to (König and Gast, 2002)).

(2) Ronni$_i$ suspected that was probably true [...] [S]omething else [...] had provoked her$_i$ own furious outburst [...] Some more personal resentment that had come from within herself$_i$. [BNC JXT 2086]

(3) John did not have any money on him (/*himself).

In this light, a somewhat less committed but practically effective way is to provide the relevant "building blocks" of the Binding Principles as features for machine learning of the coreference relation, so the general principles (and possibly even some of the systematic exceptions) can be picked up from the training data. One may assume that this is in effect what happens when the inclusion of syntactic features in coreference classification leads to an improvement in accuracy. (Additionally, a trained system will react more gracefully to parsing errors.)

But what are the relevant building blocks of the Binding Principles that should be provided as syntactic features in coreference classification? Chomsky's original formulation relies on phrase-structural configurations, making reference to the so-called *governing category* of an anaphoric element: reflexive pronouns must be bound[1] within their governing category, whereas non-reflexive pronouns must be free (not bound) within their governing category. The governing category of some element X is defined as the minimal domain that includes X, X's governor (typically the element that subcategorize for X) and an accessible SUBJECT.[2] Any details are beyond the scope of this paper, suffice it to note that all relevant notions are ultimately defined with respect to phrase structure (following the full-fledged representations of Government-and-Binding Theory, in this case). So, in theory, phrase structure features alone should be sufficient input to machine learning.

Yet it is probably clear even from the brief exposition that the conditions underlying the principles are highly complex, so it is quite possible that even in an expressive machine learning paradigm with powerful feature selection, the relevant notions may be hard to pick up. We note that certain relational notions like subject play a central role. So, could it be helpful to offer a simple labeling of the grammatical relations as additional building blocks for the machine learning – even though it is in principle possible to derive these notions from the syntax tree?

In constraint-based approaches to syntax, Chomsky's purely phrase-structure-based approach has been criticized, and (Pollard and Sag, 1992) and (Dalrymple, 1993), among others, argue for alternative statements of the Binding Principles, using relational notions and referring to various prominence hierarchies.[3] So, according to these approaches, phrase structural configurations

[1]Binding is also defined with respect to phrase structure configuration: X **binds** Y, if X and Y are co-indexed (i.e., interpreted as coreferent), and X c-commands Y. (X is again defined to **c-command** Y, if X and Y do not dominate each other in the tree, and the first branching node dominating X also dominates Y).

[2]The notion of "accessible SUBJECT", as opposed to the plain notion of subject, takes care of subtle distinctions between tensed and untensed clauses and the role that possessives play; however it is ultimately defined configurationally as well.

[3]In (Dalrymple, 1993), e.g., Binding Principles are stated as a combination of an abstraction over grammatical function paths (following Lexical-Functional Grammar) and conditions on the ranking of the antecedent and the anaphor within a hierarchy of thematic roles.

are not the (only) relevant building blocks one should consider – even from the theoretical perspective. The results from an end-to-end evaluation of real-life coreference systems using off-the-shelf phrase structure and dependency parsers will of course by no means allow us to differentiate between the theoretical paradigms; but we believe that a systematic comparison will help increase awareness of how different syntactic paradigms emphasize different syntactic properties in their core representations and how this may affect downstream processing tasks.

3 Coreference System

We use our in-house coreference resolver (Björkelund and Farkas, 2012), which obtained the second best result in the CoNLL 2012 shared task. At the core, the system is similar to the pair-wise model proposed by Soon et al. (2001), which has become a *de facto* standard in coreference research during the last decade. However, the system features some extensions, including the use of multiple decoders that are combined through stacking. It also uses a rich feature set that includes both lexical information and syntax paths. The system is parametrized to allow for flexible experimentation with different feature sets. Since the system relies on a linear classifier, the parametrization also supports conjunctions between basic features.

The system works in thee stages: First, mentions are extracted by a set of rules that work on a phrase structure tree and extract all pronouns and noun phrases. Additionally, a statistical classifier is applied to filter out non-referential instances of certain pronouns (such as expletive *it*). The second stage is a cluster-based coreference algorithm that relies on a pairwise classifier. This resolver gives relatively small, but consistent clusters. The third stage is a standard best-first resolver (Ng and Cardie, 2002) that, in addition to the features used by the previous resolver, also encodes the *output* of the previous resolver into its feature space. For a more detailed description we refer to (Björkelund and Farkas, 2012).

The system relies on a phrase structure tree for two purposes: 1) For mention extraction; 2) As features for the pair-wise classifier. Since our systematic comparison focuses on the latter, we keep a phrase-structure-based mention extraction module fixed throughout the experiments.

Syntax-based features. To provide the "building blocks" for picking up machine-learned variants of the Binding Principles, we provide two types of feature templates building on the output of the parser: the first represents the *syntax path* in the phrase structure tree between two mentions. For example, consider the mentions "Kofi Annan" and "himself" in Figure 1. Here the path would be represented as PRP↑NP↑VP↑VP↑S↓NP from the anaphor to the antecedent.

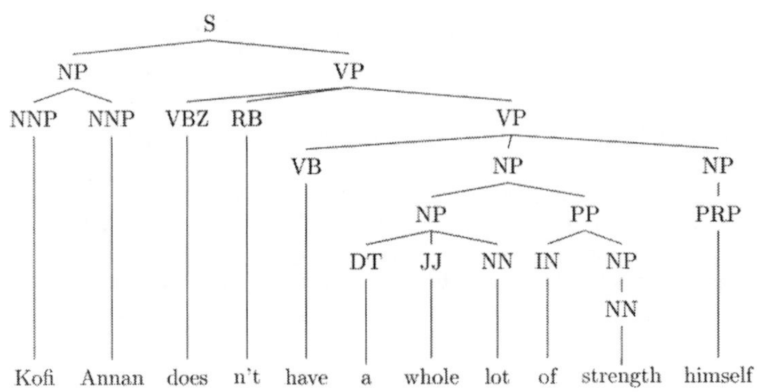

Figure 1: An example phrase structure tree.

Note that the path may provide some relevant characteristics of the structural "domain" that includes the reflexive and its (candidate) antecedent to mimic the Binding Principles: a reflexive needs to be bound within its *governing category*, and indeed the given path includes no major clause boundaries (no S) – but is there an accessible SUBJECT? The sub-path ↑S↓NP does reflect the subject configuration in English, but note that it will also occur for additional NPs like temporal ones as in *Last year, he left* or for topicalized NPs. Moreover, the tree paths aid the resolution algorithm in two ways: On the one hand, it may convince the pairwise classifier that two mentions in the same sentence are coreferent. On the other hand, it may also disallow coreference and prohibit false positive links when the antecedent is in a preceding sentence.

Now consider the dependency representation of the same sentence in Figure 2. With the dependency tree a corresponding path from the head of the anaphor to the head of the antecedent can be computed, i.e., ↑ADV↑VC↓SBJ. In this case, the grammatical function of the antecedent is explicitly captured in the syntax path. (Yet, from the dependency label path alone it may be hard to reliably identify the categorical characteristics of binding domains.)

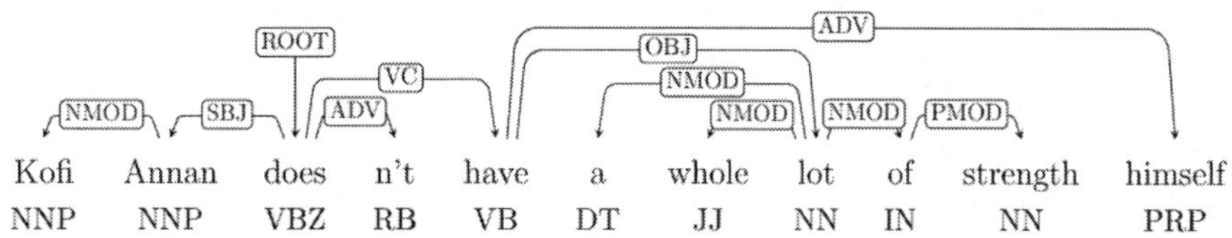

Figure 2: Dependency representation of the example from Figure 1.

Besides the path features, we also have feature templates that capture the local syntactic context of the mentions under consideration and of their immediate ancestors in the phrase structure tree. This can mimic a certain amount of subcategorization information or may indicate certain subclasses of mentions. For example, the local tree context of the antecedent NP can be described as NP → NNP NNP, and its ancestor tree context as S → NP VP. So for this example, configurationality of English actually indicates (implicitly) that the antecedent is, in fact, a subject. The local tree expansion of the NP mention alone is also helpful, for instance to detect bare plurals.

Similarly to how the idea of syntax paths can be transferred to the dependency representation, we also transfer the local tree context features. For instance, the dependency-based local tree context of the antecedent in Figure 2 can be described as SBJ → NMOD. And the local dependency tree context of the ancestor of the antecedent can be derived from the head of the head noun, i.e., ROOT → SBJ ADV VC.

Feature selection. Given the set of newly generated dependency-based feature templates, we perform an automatic feature selection procedure that evaluates new feature templates and conjunctions thereof. Specifically, we start from a seed set of templates and a pool of candidate templates (including conjunctions). We then run a greedy forward selection, where we evaluate the combination of the seed set with each of the templates from the candidate pool. In every iteration the template that contributes the most (according to some metric) is removed from the pool an inserted in the seed set. This process is repeated until the contribution of adding new feature templates is below a certain threshold. For the feature selection we optimized towards the CoNLL average (cf. Section 5 for details on evaluation metrics).

4 Data sets and Dependency conversion

In the experiments we use the English data from this year's CoNLL Shared Task (Pradhan et al., 2012). The data set comes from the OntoNotes project (Hovy et al., 2006) and features a multi-layer annotation that includes, among other things, syntax, named entities, and coreference. In the shared task, these additional annotation layers were available during training and testing as well. In the testing case, *only predicted* versions of the additional layers are provided, based on off-the-shelf tools that were trained on the training portion.

Since the official test set has not yet been released, we use the development set as test set. In order to do feature engineering, we partitioned the documents in the training set into two sets – 75% used for training and 25% used for evaluation of new features.

To study the role of dependency information vs. phrase structure information in coreference classification, we added two variants of dependency annotations to the training and development sets. In the first variant, we use the dependency parser by Bohnet (2010), trained on the OntoNotes parse trees run through the phrase-to-dependency conversion of Choi and Palmer (2010). This conversion (henceforth Choi) takes advantage of the function labels in the phrase structure annotation and produces a rich label set. For instance, subjects and objects are distinguished by distinct dependency relations. In the same manner that the shared task data was prepared, we created predicted dependency trees for both the training (using 10-fold cross-validation) and the development sets using the Bohnet dependency parser (Bohnet, 2010).[4]

For the second variant, we created dependency trees automatically by converting the *predicted* phrase structure trees that are provided in the CoNLL data set using the Stanford conversion (de Marneffe et al., 2006), which uses rules for identifying phrase structure patterns for particular grammatical relations, taking advantage of the configurationality of English. Since these trees are converted from the predicted phrase structure trees, they are more likely to be synchronized with the NPs that are used as mentions, i.e., NPs are more likely to form proper subtrees in the dependency tree.

In conclusion, we experiment with three different syntactic annotations that are all predicted on the test set: 1) Predicted phrase structure trees from the CoNLL 2012 Shared Task; 2) Dependency trees obtained via the Stanford conversion when applied to the parse trees from 1); 3) Dependency trees obtained from the Bohnet parser that was trained on the Choi conversion of the OntoNotes parse trees.

5 Experimental Setup and Results

For the experiments we built 5 different systems that differ only in their feature representation:

1. Baseline (BL) – Our system (Björkelund and Farkas, 2012) stripped of all syntax-based features;
2. Reference (BL+PS) – Same as above, but including the syntax-based features, i.e., the same system as in (Björkelund and Farkas, 2012);
3. Choi dependencies (BL+DT_{Choi}) – The Baseline feature set, extended with dependency features from a dependency parser (Choi-style);
4. Choi dependencies and phrase structures (BL+PS+DT_{Choi}) – The Reference feature set, extended with Choi-style dependency features;

[4] Downloaded from `http://code.google.com/p/mate-tools/`

5. Stanford dependencies and phrase structures (BL+PS+DT$_{Stanf}$) – The Reference feature set, extended with dependency features from the rule-based Stanford conversion.

For systems 3, 4, and 5, the extended feature sets were computed by the automatic feature selection procedure describe above. The baseline provides a lower bound on how well coreference resolution can be accomplished without syntax-based features. Besides the baseline, system 3 is the only one that does not make use of phrase-structure-based features. Hence, this system will reveal the importance of phrase-structure-based features. Systems 4 and 5 allow us to measure if the combination of features from both syntactic paradigms improves the performance of the system. Finally, system 2 is a purely phrase-structure-based system with an already optimized feature set. This is the *reference system*, and it provides an upper bound for using the standard CoNLL annotation layers alone (i.e., not using any dependency-based features).[5]

Results. To evaluate the systems we use the official CoNLL scorer,[6] which computes several metrics including MUC (Vilain et al., 1995), BCUB (Bagga and Baldwin, 1998), and CEAF (Luo, 2005). For completeness we also present end-to-end mention detection (MD) F-measure and the CoNLL average, i.e., the unweighted arithmetic mean of MUC, BCUB and the entity-based CEAF (CEAFE). To avoid clutter, and since precision and recall do not provide additional insights for the discussion at hand, we only present the F-measures of the corresponding metrics. The results of all systems on the CoNLL development set are presented in Table 1.

Sys.	Feature set	MD	MUC	BCUB	CEAFE	CoNLL
1	BL	73.64	65.64	70.45	45.43	60.51
2	BL+PS	74.96	67.12	71.18	46.84	61.71
3	BL+DT$_{Choi}$	74.54	66.74	70.98	46.50	61.42
4	BL+PS+DT$_{Choi}$	75.23	67.69	71.48	47.02	62.07
5	BL+PS+DT$_{Stanf}$	75.23	67.46	71.22	47.18	61.96

Table 1: Results on coreference task when varying the feature set.

The results indicate that syntax-based features play an important role when it comes to resolving coreference. The baseline system, which does not use syntax in its feature set at all, is outperformed by the all other systems by more than a point in almost all metrics. The difference for all metrics is significant ($p < 0.005$).[7] Systems 2, 4, and 5 are all also significantly better than system 3 ($p < 0.05$). The systems that use a combination of both phrase-structure-based and dependency-based features obtain the highest scores, however compared to system 2, only the improvement in MUC for system 4 is significant ($p < 0.05$).

Error analysis. General quantitative error analysis for end-to-end coreference resolution is difficult, owing to the fact that the problem is ultimately a matter of evaluating partitionings over sets that do not necessarily contain the same elements. However, manual inspection of the alternative system outputs indicated that the systems using the combined feature set appeared to be better at finding the correct antecedent for pronouns. A crude quantitative analysis is to look at the links between a pronoun mention and its closest antecedent in the system output vs. the gold standard. While link-based metrics for coreference resolution have been criticized (see e.g. Luo (2005)), we believe that for pronouns they can still be an analytical device, since their antecedents tend to be close.

[5]The system and feature templates are available at `http://www.ims.uni-stuttgart.de/~anders`

[6]Downloaded from `http://conll.cemantix.org/2012/`

[7]Using a paired t-test over the documents

Specifically, for every pronoun in the gold standard, we regard the system output to be correct if (i) the nearest predicted antecedent to the left belongs to the same cluster as the mention in the gold standard; or (ii) if the mention is not part of a cluster in both the gold standard and the system output.[8] Otherwise the system prediction is regarded as incorrect. Based on these definitions, we computed the pronoun accuracy and broke down the results by by pronoun type, as shown in Table 2. The bottom-most row shows the total number of occurrences of each type.

System	Feature set	Standard	Possessive	Reflexive	All
1	BL	68.47	68.65	69.07	68.51
2	BL+PS	69.35	71.00	68.04	69.64
3	BL+DT_{Choi}	68.95	69.86	65.98	69.09
4	BL+PS+DT_{Choi}	70.00	71.63	74.23	70.35
5	BL+PS+DT_{Stanf}	69.51	71.69	69.07	69.91
Total		7,497	1,745	97	9,339

Table 2: Accuracy on pronouns.

The trends are similar to the improvement in the general coreference metrics. The difference between the non-syntax-based baseline system (1) and the reference system (2) is for all pronouns about 1% absolute. Note however that the improvement from system 2 to system 4 is not far behind with 0.7% absolute. This improvement is statistically significant ($p < 0.005$), as well as the improvement of system 5 over system 2 ($p < 0.05$). Our interpretation is that the small improvement in the coreference metrics (cf. Table 1) stems mostly from improved handling of pronouns.

6 Discussion and Conclusion

Starting out from a state-of-the-art coreference system for English, we experimented with phrase structure vs. dependency features for coreference resolution, studying effects on end-to-end performance (as shown in Table 1). On their own, dependencies (as in system 3) are a significantly weaker source of information than phrase structure (as in system 2) for coreference resolution in English. This is not too surprising since certain characteristics of grammatical binding domains are not captured in the latter system's dependency path information.

It also seems like like information from phrase structure and dependencies is orthogonal: although not significant overall, a combination yields better results (as in systems 4 and 5) than using phrase structures alone (system 2). System 4, with its independently obtained phrase structure and dependency structure, has the best performance overall according to most end-to-end metrics, and significantly so for the accuracies on pronoun links (compare Table 2).

It is worth noting that system 5, which uses "just" configurational patterns to identify and label grammatical relations in the predicted phrase structures already present in system 2, outperforms the latter according to all metrics. This means that the phrase-to-dependency conversion seems to add signals to the data that the system's machine learning cannot distill from phrase structure alone – despite intense feature selection. This is an interesting result for English as a highly configurational language: It is easier to learn generalizations over grammatical constraints on coreference when grammatical relations are explicitly provided. It can be expected that for other, less configurational languages, an even more pronounced difference can be observed. We plan to study this in future work.

[8] We ignore cataphoric pronouns since they do not have any antecedents to the left and it is not obvious how to include these in the evaluation. These cases are, however, rare and account for only about 3% of the pronouns in the test set.

Acknowledgments

This work was funded by the Deutsche Forschungsgemeinschaft (DFG) via the SFB 732 "Incremental Specification in Context", project D8.

References

Bagga, A. and Baldwin, B. (1998). Algorithms for scoring coreference chains. In *In The First International Conference on Language Resources and Evaluation Workshop on Linguistics Coreference*, pages 563–566.

Björkelund, A. and Farkas, R. (2012). Data-driven multilingual coreference resolution using resolver stacking. In *Joint Conference on EMNLP and CoNLL - Shared Task*, pages 49–55, Jeju Island, Korea. Association for Computational Linguistics.

Bohnet, B. (2010). Top accuracy and fast dependency parsing is not a contradiction. In *Proceedings of the 23rd International Conference on Computational Linguistics (Coling 2010)*, pages 89–97, Beijing, China. Coling 2010 Organizing Committee.

Choi, J. D. and Palmer, M. (2010). Robust Constituent-to-Dependency Conversion for English. In *Proceedings of 9th Treebanks and Linguistic Theories Workshop (TLT)*, pages 55–66.

Chomsky, N. (1981). *Lectures on Government and Binding*. Foris Publications, Dordrecht.

Dalrymple, M. (1993). *The Syntax of Anaphoric Binding*. CSLI Publications, Stanford, CA.

de Marneffe, M.-C., MacCartney, B., and Manning, C. D. (2006). Generating typed dependency parses from phrase structure parses. In *Proceedings of LREC-2006*, pages 449–454, Genoa, Italy.

Hovy, E., Marcus, M., Palmer, M., Ramshaw, L., and Weischedel, R. (2006). Ontonotes: The 90% solution. In *Proceedings of the Human Language Technology Conference of the NAACL, Companion Volume: Short Papers*, pages 57–60, New York City, USA. Association for Computational Linguistics.

König, E. and Gast, V. (2002). Reflexive pronouns and other uses of self-forms in English. *Zeitschrift für Anglistik und Amerikanistik*, 50(3):1–14.

Luo, X. (2005). On coreference resolution performance metrics. In *Proceedings of Human Language Technology Conference and Conference on Empirical Methods in Natural Language Processing*, pages 25–32, Vancouver, British Columbia, Canada. Association for Computational Linguistics.

Ng, V. and Cardie, C. (2002). Improving machine learning approaches to coreference resolution. In *Proceedings of 40th Annual Meeting of the Association for Computational Linguistics*, pages 104–111, Philadelphia, Pennsylvania, USA. Association for Computational Linguistics.

Pollard, C. and Sag, I. A. (1992). Anaphors in English and the scope of binding theory. *Linguistic Inquiry*, 23(2):261–303.

Pradhan, S., Moschitti, A., Xue, N., Uryupina, O., and Zhang, Y. (2012). Conll-2012 shared task: Modeling multilingual unrestricted coreference in ontonotes. In *Joint Conference on EMNLP and CoNLL - Shared Task*, pages 1–40, Jeju Island, Korea. Association for Computational Linguistics.

Pradhan, S., Ramshaw, L., Marcus, M., Palmer, M., Weischedel, R., and Xue, N. (2011). Conll-2011 shared task: Modeling unrestricted coreference in ontonotes. In *Proceedings of the Fifteenth Conference on Computational Natural Language Learning: Shared Task*, pages 1–27, Portland, Oregon, USA. Association for Computational Linguistics.

Recasens, M., Màrquez, L., Sapena, E., Martí, M. A., Taulé, M., Hoste, V., Poesio, M., and Versley, Y. (2010). Semeval-2010 task 1: Coreference resolution in multiple languages. In *Proceedings of the 5th International Workshop on Semantic Evaluation*, pages 1–8, Uppsala, Sweden. Association for Computational Linguistics.

Soon, W. M., Ng, H. T., and Lim, D. C. Y. (2001). A machine learning approach to coreference resolution of noun phrases. *Computational Linguistics*, 27(4):521–544.

Vilain, M., Burger, J., Aberdeen, J., Connolly, D., and Hirschman, L. (1995). A model theoretic coreference scoring scheme. In *Proceedings of the Sixth Conference on Message Understanding (MUC-6)*, Columbia, Maryland.

The Language of Power and its Cultural Influence

David B. Bracewell and Marc T. Tomlinson
Language Computer Corporation
Richardson, TX
{david,marc}@languagecomputer.com

Abstract

In this paper, we investigate whether the social goals of an individual can be recognized through analysis of the social actions indicated by their use of language. Specifically, we focus on recognizing when someone is pursuing power within a web forum. Individuals pursue power in order to increase their control over the actions and goals of the group. We cast the problem as social conversational entailment where we determine if a dialogue entails a hypothesis which states a dialogue participant is in pursuit of power. In the social conversational entailment framework the hypothesis is decomposed into a series of social commitments which define series of actions and responses that are indicative of the hypothesis. The social commitments are modeled as social acts which are pragmatic speech acts. We identify nine culturally neutral psychologically-motivated social acts that can be detected in language and are indicative of whether an individual is pursuing power. Our best results using social conversational entailment achieve an overall F-measure of 79.7% for predicting pursuit of power for English speakers and 78.3% for Chinese speakers.

Keywords: dialogue, power, social actions, entailment, online communication, culture, norms.

Proceedings of COLING 2012: Posters, pages 155–164,
COLING 2012, Mumbai, December 2012.

1 Introduction

Social media has empowered the masses by allowing individuals to participate in a variety of group projects which impact the future of society. Sites like Wikipedia allow anyone to edit content that is used the world over for resolving debates and informing science. Because of the influence of these sites, many contributors pursue a high-power role giving them control over the site's content and the goals and actions of other contributors. Traditionally research has focused on inferring whether individuals are already in power through such means as social network analysis or more recently through the language those in power employ (Bramsen et al., 2011; Danescu-Niculescu-Mizil et al., 2012). However, the dialogue taking place on these sites provide a richer source of observations on the interaction patterns of individuals and in particular how individuals pursue power. By analyzing and characterizing these observations, models of these pursuits of power can be built which can provide important information about the dynamics of the group and its evolving leadership structure. To accurately infer if an individual is pursuing power, we must address three main questions:

(1) *What characterizes the language of individuals pursuing power?*
(2) *Can these characterizations be captured automatically?*
(3) *What impact does culture have on the characterization of pursuit of power?*

In order to answer these questions, we must first define what it means for an individual to pursue power. Power is a nebulous topic whose meaning differs depending on the domain and the context. For the purposes of this paper, we have defined the pursuit of power for online discussions, such as those on Wikipedia, as repeated attempts by an individual to increase their status and to control the actions and goals of others. As an example let us examine the dialogue in Figure 1 which illustrates a pursuit of power by participant B.

A) B ... contrary to your edit summary, your deletion of over 4,000 bytes of material is not explained on the talk page. Please cease and desist. It is vandalism to delete sourced information relevant to the topic at hand. As an editor states directly above, it is more beneficial to add to the article than to delete material that is reliably sourced. Please do so.
B) The explanation is right above - read it, and stop claiming this is vandalism when it is not.
A) There is no explanation from you above, only (with regret) some hyperbole. As the editor writes above: "It goes without saying that examples of use should be included. It can be expanded later. Add more material rather than deleting." Please cease deleting this material without consensus.
B) Please read more carefully. The explanation is there. Your repeated claims of vandalism are uncivil - stop them.
C) I tend to agree with B this article is not from a neutral point of view.

Figure 1: Example conversation in which participant B is pursuing power.

As the dialogue in Figure 1 illustrates the understanding of social phenomena is less about the content of the information exchanged and more about the social actions and intentions of the participants. Building on the work done in textual entailment (Bar-Haim et al., 2006; Dagan et al., 2005; Giampiccolo et al., 2007; Hickl, 2008) and conversation entailment (Zhang and Chai, 2010), we cast the problem of implying the social phenomena, e.g. pursuit of power, exhibited by participants in a dialogue as *social conversational entailment*. Textual entailment has focused mainly on the information, often factual, distilled in monologue. Conversation entailment extended this to the information exchanged in conversation. In contrast, social conversational entailment focuses on the social phenomena exhibited by the participants in the conversation through examination of their social intentions and goals which are captured through social acts. The intentions and goals informs the *why* and constrains the *how* information is exchanged. For example, in Figure 1 the information exchanged by B was to support his desire to gain power and control the content of the Wikipedia article. Additionally, B's actions influenced A to communicate in such a way as to try to stave off B's potential gain in power.

In this paper, we explore building social conversational entailment models to entail hypotheses about whether or not an individual is pursuing power. We focus on groups communicating in English and Chinese on Wikipedia talk forums. We then turn our focus to how cultural differences exhibit themselves in the characterization of pursuit of power.

2 Related Work

Work in the area of social relationship extraction can be divided into several areas. The field of socio-linguistics boasts well-established studies of interpersonal relationships. For example, Eggins and Slade (1997) present a thorough linguistic analysis on causal conversations that covers topics such as humor, attitude, friendliness, and gossip. Other studies have examined how individuals vie for power in meetings and the work place (Keller, 2009; Owens and Sutton, 2001). These studies have shown that status differences can have a large effect on how a particular individual will seek power. Further, work on the effects of power on cognition has shown that individuals with power use language differently than lower status individuals (Smith and Trope, 2006) has provided insights on how pursuits of power may be characterized.

Recently work in natural language processing has been conducted to identify the relative status of individuals through automated analysis of their language. Bramsen et al. (2011) looked for the presence of *upspeak* (speech directed towards individuals of higher status) and *downspeak* (speech directed towards individuals of lower status) within the Enron email corpus using an n-gram based approach combined with human-engineered features. They achieved an accuracy of 78.1% for detecting the relative status difference between individuals. Additionally, Danescu-Niculescu-Mizil et al. (2012) examined the use of coordination, often referred to as mimicry, for inferring power relationships. In contrast to identifying a static social relationship between individuals, we look at detecting an individual's intentions to manipulate an existing social relationship.

There is a long history of work in discourse understanding that focuses on understanding the pragmatics of the discourse. More recent work has focused on inferring information, such as conversational intent, about the discourse participants. Zhang and Chai (2010) introduced conversation entailment, which is designed to answer a variety of hypotheses about dialogue participants. The hypotheses can be about factual information, beliefs and opinions, desires, or communicative intentions. Additionally, work in textual entailment has used discourse commitments, which are general beliefs held by the author of the text and hypothesis (Hickl, 2008). In contrast, we focus on social conversational entailment, which uses social commitments, for inferring the social roles, relationships, and intentions of dialogue participants through analysis of their social acts as signaled through the dialogue.

3 Social Conversational Entailment for Pursuit of Power

Power is exhibited in many forms, through physical intimidation, wealth (money, physical resources, or knowledge), or position within a hierarchy. There are variety of methods to pursue power. Moreover, because of the shear variety of methods to pursue power, it is difficult to develop a robust cross-domain text-based recognition approach to identify those who are in pursuit. Instead, we focus on detecting differences in the way people use language when they are attempting to pursue power. We look to mimic human understanding of power and follow the non-conscious cues provided within a dialogue. We model social conversational entailment for pursuits of power after work in speech act recognition (Stolcke et al., 1998) and language modeling (Niederhoffer and Pennebaker, 2002) using *social conversational entailment*. The task of social conversational entailment is defined as follows:

Given a dialogue (D) and a hypothesis (H) about one ore more participants, the goal is to determine if D entails H.

Hypotheses in social conversational entailment describe the *role* (e.g. leader) or *action* (e.g. pursuing power) of a participant whom we label the central individual or the *relationship* (e.g. collegial) between two or more participants whom we label the central group. In this paper, we focus solely on the action of pursuing power for a single central individual. A pursuit of power hypothesis is in the form of: ***Person A is pursing power***.

A pursuit of power hypothesis is decomposable into a number of social commitments. These social commitments represent patterns of action that individuals pursuing power are likely to perform as well as the responses elicited by those actions from others towards those in pursuit. We capture the actions performed by participants as social acts. Social acts are pragmatic speech acts that signal a dialogue participant's social intentions. The social acts used to identify pursuits of power are discussed in section 4.

The model for social conversational entailment is based on the social commitments and social actions. More formally, given a dialogue D which is represented as a series of social acts $s_1, \ldots, s_m$, performed by the central individual and others directed toward the central individual, and a hypothesis H which is represented as a number of social commitments $c_1, \ldots, c_n$, the prediction of whether D entails H is approximated as:

$$\begin{aligned}
&P(D \models H \mid D,\ H) \\
&\quad = P(D \models c_1, \ldots, c_n | D, c_1, \ldots, c_n) \\
&\quad = \textstyle\prod_{i=1}^{n} P(D \models c_i | D = s_1, \ldots, s_m, c_i) \\
&\quad = \textstyle\prod_{i=1}^{n} P(s_1, \ldots, s_m \models c_i | s_1, \ldots, s_m, c_i)
\end{aligned}$$

One way in which we can model the social commitments is a Markov process over the social acts. Social commitments then become chains of social actions which represent prominent patterns associated with individuals pursuing power. Assuming the Markov process, we can approximate the probability of D entailing H as:

$$P(D \models H \mid D,\ H) \propto \prod_{i=1}^{m} P(s_i | s_{i+m-1}, \ldots, s_{i-1})$$

We can further simplify the model by making a first order Markov assumption, which results in:

$$P(D \models H \mid D,\ H) \propto \prod_{i=1}^{m} P(s_i | s_{i-1})$$

The entailment model is then built from a corpora of positive entailments, i.e. where D entails H, using Kneser-Ney smoothing (Chen and Goodman, 1996). Dialogues with probabilities over some threshold τ given the entailment model have a sufficient alignment with the social commitments to entail the hypothesis One potential problem is that the model can be overwhelmed by repeated exhibition of social and cultural norms which participants follow through the normal course of a conversation. The conflation of these norms with true social commitments hinder the accuracy of the inference as the norms are not a sign of pursuit of power.

3.1 Social and Cultural Norms

In order to accurately infer social phenomena it is critical to take into account social and cultural norms. It is often through the violations of these norms that social phenomena, such as pursuing power, are witnessed. The accurate depiction of social and cultural norms is an entire field of research upon its own. Instead of completely addressing this complex topic, we look to only roughly determine the norms as portrayed by participants in a corpus.

By building a model around the actions of participants who do not entail the pursuit of power hypothesis, we can capture aspects of the social and cultural norms. We call this the *background model*. The background model is built in the same manner as entailment using the following equation:

$$P(D \quad H \mid D, H) \propto \prod_{i=1}^{m} P(s_i | s_{i-1})$$

The data used for building the model are negative entailment examples, i.e. dialogue D in which the central individual is not pursuing power. As the diversity of genre and amount of conversations used for training the background model increases it will more accurately portray the social and cultural norms. By combining the entailment and background models, we can more accurately model the characteristics of pursuit of power and better infer if a participant is pursuing power.

3.2 Inference

We combine the entailment and background model in order to determine if a dialogue D entails a hypothesis H. We predict D entails H when:

$$\beta_0 + \beta_1 \cdot P(D \models H \mid D,\ H) + \beta_2 \cdot P(D \quad H \mid D,\ H) + \beta_3 \cdot \frac{P(D \models H \mid D,\ H)}{P(D \quad H \mid D,\ H)} > 0.5$$

where $\beta_0, \cdots, \beta_3$ are weights controlling the effect that the entailment and background model have in predicting if an individual is in pursuit of power. The β_0 weight is the bias and acts as a prior on the likelihood of a participant to pursue power in the training data. The weights are learned using a linear regression model over the training data. Examples of entailment are assigned the value of 1 and examples of non-entailment are assigned the value of 0 making the final equation result in a probability.

4 The Social Actions of those who Pursue Power

Because individuals rarely explicitly state their intent to pursue power in text, we must look for reflections of their social intentions through their language. We use social acts which are pragmatic speech acts to capture the dialogue participants' social intentions. Social acts are specifically designed to take into account participants' social cognition which constrains their dialogue facilitating the inference of their social goals from their communication.

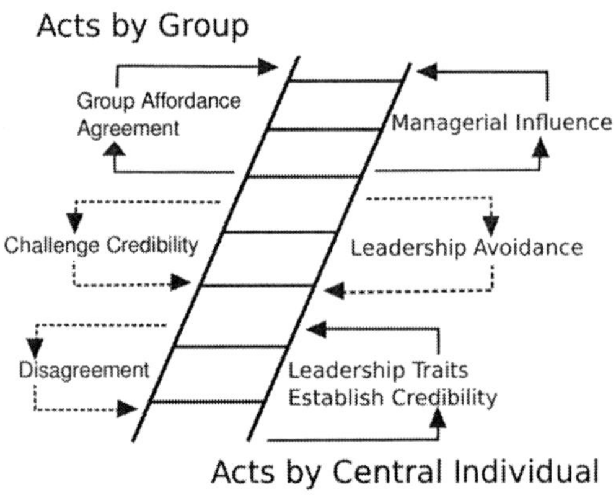

(a) Ladder model of the path to power. Social acts on the left are directed towards the individual and those on the right are made by the individual.

Agreement	Statements made to indicate a sharing of view about something another member has said or done.
Challenge Credibility	Attempts to discredit or raise doubt about another group member's qualifications or abilities.
Disagreement	Statements made to indicate differences in view about something another member has said or done.
Establish Credibility	Statements made demonstrate knowledge or personal experience in order to look better in the eyes of the group.
Group Affordance	Use of honorifics and deference to show respect and esteem for another group member.
Leadership Avoidance	Attempts to avoid being in a position of control over the group.
Leadership Traits	Common linguistic signs that a person is in power, such as extroversion and locus of control.
Managerial Influence	Statements made to control the discussion with the goal of increasing sway over the group.
Solidarity	Statements made to strengthen the group's sense of community and unity.

(b) The set of nine social acts that capture social moves by individuals pursuing power.

We base our list of nine social acts on the reciprocal influence model of power developed by Keltner et al. (2008), shown in Figure 2a. The employment of social acts by the central individual and the group facilitate a change in the central individual's level of power within the group. For example, the use of Leadership Traits by the central individual moves her up the ladder, i.e. increasing her level of power, whereas if a member of the group employs Challenge Credibility it lessens the central individual's level of power. The complete set of nine social acts with their definition is shown in Figure 2b. A more in-depth discussion on social acts and these in particular can be found in Bracewell et al. Bracewell et al. (2012).

5 Data Collection

We constructed a corpus consisting of English and Chinese Wikipedia talk pages. Each Wikipedia talk page is a threaded discussion and is associated with a Wikipedia article. The talk pages provide a forum for users to discuss and debate the content of the target article as well as propose, vote, an denounce changes to the content. We collected a total of 149 English and 401 Chinese Wikipedia talk discussions whose associated articles covered a wide domain of topics. Within these discussions there were a total of 778 and 3,476 participants respectively for English and Chinese. Each discussion was annotated by three to five annotators, which included annotation of every individual in the discussion as either pursuing or not pursing power.

We employed both in-house and Mechanical Turk annotators. Annotator training consisted of the definition for pursuit of power and example questions to test understanding of the definition. The Mechanical Turk annotators were further tested to judge their language ability. An annotation was said to have agreement when all or all but one annotator chose the same answer, i.e. 2 out of 3, 3 out of 4, or 4 out of 5 chose yes for pursuit of power. For English, we had agreement rates of 76.0% for our in-house annotators, 67.5% for our Mechanical Turk annotators, and 70.0% combined. For Chinese, we had agreement rates of 85.6% for our in-house annotators, 80.0% for our Mechanical Turk annotators, and 82.8% combined.

6 Experimental Results

For experimentation, we used a standard 80/20 split over the data discussed in section 5, where 80% of the participants were used for training and 20% of the participants were used for testing. We focused our experiments to determine the validity of the social conversational entailment model and of using social acts over a purely lexical approach.

As an alternative to the social conversational entailment model, we examined the use of a Support Vector Machine (SVM) classifier using a linear kernel. SVMs have shown promise for such related tasks as the recognition of dialogue acts (Hu et al., 2009) and the identification of social status (Bramsen et al., 2011). We compared the effectiveness of the social acts for inferring pursuits of power to a purely lexical approach. For the SVM model we extracted n-grams from the utterances of the central individual[1]. We pruned the list of n-grams using information gain. We tested with different size n-grams, but report here only the best results which were obtained using a combination of unigrams and bigrams. For conversational entailment, a text was generated based on the utterances of the central individual and others in the group responding to the central individual. The origin, i.e. central individual or other, was denoted using a special symbol prepended to the words. For both models punctuation and symbols were removed and cardinals and proper nouns replaced with generic tags (<CARDINAL> AND <PROPERNOUN>). The results of the experiments are presented in Table 1 for English and Table 2 for Chinese.

English	SVM		SCE	
	N-Gram	Social Acts	N-Gram	Social Acts
Pursuing Power	66.2%	79.6%	53.1%	81.4%
Not Pursuing Power	72.7%	63.6%	64.7%	77.8%
Micro-Avg.	69.8%	73.8%	59.7%	79.7%

Table 1: Resulting F-measure for entailing pursuits of power in English using support vector machines (SVM) and social conversational entailment (SCE) with either word-based n-grams (N-Gram) or social acts as features.

Chinese	SVM		SCE	
	N-Gram	Social Acts	N-Gram	Social Acts
Pursuing Power	42.7%	87.2%	1.1%	75.6%
Not Pursuing Power	60.2%	78.8%	28.0%	80.6%
Micro-Avg.	53.0%	84.0%	16.6%	78.3%

Table 2: Resulting F-measure for entailing pursuits of power in Chinese using support vector machines (SVM) and social conversational entailment (SCE) with either word-based n-grams (N-Gram) or social acts as features.

As can be seen in Tables 1 and 2 using social acts performed better than n-grams for SVM and social conversational entailment. This suggests that social acts capture an intermediate-level concept between words and the social phenomena which provide better evidence for entailing pursuit of power. Chinese saw the biggest boost where the use of social acts brought increases in F-measure of 31% and 61.7% respectively for SVM and social conversational entailment. For English the use of social acts brought increases of 4% for the SVM and 20% for the social conversational entailment model. For both models n-grams worked better for inferring pursuits of power in English than for pursuits of power in Chinese (similar findings are seen in text categorization, see Suzuki et al. (2010)).

[1]We tried to incorporate information from the other speakers who were replying to the central individual, as is done with social acts, but this resulted in an inability to identify any positive instances of pursuit of power.

7 Discussion

The pursuit of power is a social construct that embodies significant cultural differences, and thus it is exhibited differently across cultures and languages. In order to judge the cultural impact on pursuits of power in Wikipedia discussions, we examined the differences in social acts. The first social act by individuals in pursuit of power is strikingly different between the Wikitalk discussions in Chinese and those in English. For discussions in Chinese an individual who starts the conversation with group affordance, such as honorifics and respectful sentiments, is most likely pursuing power. Also of interest is that Leadership Avoidance is seen as more likely to entail pursuit of power in Chinese and English. The difference, however, is in how Leadership Avoidance is employed with respects to other social acts. In discussions communicated Chinese, an individual normally exhibits Leadership Avoidance after establishing credibility or through a managerial act. Both of these previous social acts are generally strong indicators that an individual is not pursuing power, however the act of Leadership Avoidance, often manifested through order negation, makes it more likely that the individual is pursuing power.

While we cannot draw any strong conclusions on the exact path individuals follow when pursuing power or make overarching statements about the cultural differences, we can state that there are clearly differences in pursuing power in Wikipedia between groups communicating in English and Groups communicating in Chinese. We leave for future research a deeper study on how to accurately capture these differences through improvements in social act identification and the social conversational entailment model. The cultural differences need not be across language, but also exist within a single language, e.g. mainland China vs. Taiwan. By capturing these cultural differences, we believe we can improve the social conversational entailment model as we can better identify the social cultural norms for each individual in the dialogue.

Conclusion

We have shown that is possible to model pursuits of power by individuals in Wikipedia discussions using social conversational entailment. Social conversational entailment answers hypotheses around social roles, relationships, and intentions of individuals in a dialogue. The entailment is validated by fulfilling social commitments, which are culturally dependent mappings of social acts onto social phenomena, such as pursuit of power. The social acts are pragmatic speech acts that capture the social cognition of dialogue participants and are detected through language usage. We have studied the cultural differences in how pursuit of power is exhibited in English and Chinese Wikipedia discussions. We have found that the entailment models of pursuit of powers differ greatly between the two cultures.

Acknowledgment

This research was funded by the Office of the Director of National Intelligence (ODNI), Intelligence Advanced Research Projects Activity (IARPA), and through the U.S. Army Research Lab. All statements of fact, opinion or conclusions contained herein are those of the authors and should not be construed as representing the official views or policies of IARPA, the ODNI or the U.S. Government.

References

Bar-Haim, R., Dagan, I., Dolan, B., Ferro, L., Giampiccolo, D., Magnini, B., and Szpektor, I. (2006). The second PASCAL recognising textual entailment challenge. In *Proceedings of the Second PASCAL Challenges Workshop on Recognising Textual Entailment*.

Bracewell, D. B., Tomlinson, M., Brunson, M., Plymale, J., Bracewell, J., and Boerger, D. (2012). Annotation of adversarial and collegial social actions in discourse. In *The 6th Linguistics Annotation Workshop (LAW VI)*.

Bramsen, P., Escobar-Molana, M., Patel, A., and Alonso, R. (2011). Extracting social power relationships from natural language. *Proceedings of ACL HLT*, pages 773–782.

Chen, S. F. and Goodman, J. (1996). An empirical study of smoothing techniques for language modeling. In *Proceedings of the 34th annual meeting on Association for Computational Linguistics*, ACL '96, pages 310–318, Stroudsburg, PA, USA. Association for Computational Linguistics.

Dagan, I., Glickman, O., and Magnini, B. (2005). The pascal recognising textual entailment challenge. In *MLCW*, pages 177–190.

Danescu-Niculescu-Mizil, C., Lee, L., Pang, B., and Kleinberg, J. (2012). Echoes of power: language effects and power differences in social interaction. In *Proceedings of the 21st international conference on World Wide Web*, WWW '12, pages 699–708, New York, NY, USA. ACM.

Eggins, S. and Slade, D. (1997). *Analysing casual conversation*. Cassell.

Giampiccolo, D., Magnini, B., Dagan, I., and Dolan, B. (2007). The third pascal recognizing textual entailment challenge. In *In Proceedings of the ACLPASCAL Workshop on Textual Entailment and*.

Hickl, A. (2008). Using discourse commitments to recognize textual entailment. *Proceedings of the 22nd International Conference on Computational Linguistics - COLING '08*, (August):337–344.

Hu, J., Passonneau, R. J., and Rambow, O. (2009). Contrasting the interaction structure of an email and a telephone corpus: a machine learning approach to annotation of dialogue function units. In *Proceedings of the SIGDIAL 2009 Conference: The 10th Annual Meeting of the Special Interest Group on Discourse and Dialogue*, SIGDIAL '09, pages 357–366, Stroudsburg, PA, USA. Association for Computational Linguistics.

Keller, K. (2009). *Power Conflict: Struggles for Intragroup Control and Dominance*. PhD thesis, University of Maryland.

Keltner, D., Van Kleef, G. A., Chen, S., and Kraus, M. W. (2008). A reciprocal influence model of social power: Emerging principles and lines of inquiry. *Advances in experimental social psychology*, 40:151–192.

Niederhoffer, K. G. and Pennebaker, J. W. (2002). Linguistic Style Matching in Social Interaction. *Journal of Language and Social Psychology*, 21(4):337–360.

Owens, D. and Sutton, R. (2001). Status contests in meetings: Negotiating the informal order. *Groups at work: Theory and research*, 14:299–316.

Smith, P. K. and Trope, Y. (2006). You focus on the forest when you're in charge of the trees: power priming and abstract information processing. *Journal of personality and social psychology*, 90(4):578–96.

Stolcke, A., Shriberg, E., Bates, R., Coccaro, N., Jurafsky, D., Martin, R., Meteer, M., Ries, K., Taylor, P., and Ess-Dykema, C. V. (1998). Dialog Act Modeling for Conversational Speech. In *Applying Machine Learning to Discourse Processing*, pages 98–105. AAAI Press.

Suzuki, M., Yamagishi, N., Tsai, Y.-C., Ishida, T., and Goto, M. (2010). English and taiwanese text categorization using n-gram based on vector space model. In *ISITA'10*, pages 106–111.

Zhang, C. and Chai, J. (2010). Towards conversation entailment: an empirical investigation. In *Proceedings of the 2010 Conference on Empirical Methods in Natural Language Processing*, number October, pages 756–766. Association for Computational Linguistics.

Learning Opinionated Patterns for Contextual Opinion Detection

Caroline Brun[1]
(1) Xerox Research Centre Europe, 38240 Meylan, France
Caroline.Brun@xrce.xerox.com

ABSTRACT

This paper tackles the problem of polar vocabulary ambiguity. While some opinionated words keep their polarity in any context and/or across any domain (except for the ironic style that goes beyond the present article), some other have an ambiguous polarity which is highly dependent of the context or the domain: in this case, the opinion is generally carried by complex expressions ("patterns") rather than single words. In this paper, we propose and evaluate an original hybrid method, based on syntactic information extraction and clustering techniques, to learn automatically such patterns and integrate them into an opinion detection system.

TITLE AND ABSTRACT IN FRENCH

Apprentissage de patrons polarisés pour la détection contextuelle d'opinions

Cet article se penche sur le problème de l'ambiguïté du vocabulaire de polarité. Alors que certains mots conservent la même polarité dans n'importe quel contexte ou domaine (à l'exception du registre ironique qui va au-delà du présent article), d'autres ont une polarité ambiguë dépendante du contexte ou du domaine : dans ce cas l'opinion est portée par des expressions complexes (patrons) et non des mots isolés. Dans cet article, nous proposons et évaluons une méthode hybride originale, utilisant de l'information syntaxique et des techniques de « clusterisation », pour apprendre automatiquement de tels patrons et les intégrer à un système de détection d'opinions.

KEYWORDS: opinion detection, polar vocabulary ambiguity, hybrid method
KEYWORDS IN FRENCH: détection d'opinions, ambiguïté du vocabulaire de polarité, méthode hybride

Proceedings of COLING 2012: Posters, pages 165–174,
COLING 2012, Mumbai, December 2012.

Introduction

A fundamental task in opinion mining is classifying the polarity of a given text, sentence or feature/aspect level to find out whether it is positive, negative or neutral. Different methodologies using NLP and machine learning techniques are used for this purpose. The most fine grained analysis model is the feature based sentiment mining method. Feature based opinion mining aims at to determining the sentiments or opinions that are expressed on different features or aspects of entities (e.g. [Bloom et al. 2007]).

The context of this paper is the development of a feature-based opinion mining system, for French. One of the essential tasks in the course of this development is the acquisition of polar vocabulary, for which one encounters almost immediately the problem of polarity ambiguity. In the present paper, we try to address this particular problem: while some opinionated words keep their polarity in any context and/or across any domain (except for the ironic style that goes beyond the scope of the present article), some other have an ambiguous polarity and are highly dependent of the context or the domain. In this case, the opinion is generally carried by complex expressions rather than single words. Let's illustrate this problem with some French examples:

- An adjective like "hideux" (hideous) can be considered to have a negative polarity in any context and any domain;
- An adjective like "merveilleux" (wonderful) can be considered to have a positive polarity in any context and any domain
- On the contrary, an adjective like "frais" (fresh) in French might have different polarities depending on context and domain :
    - In the context "avoir le **teint** **frais**" (to have a healthy glow), "frais" has a positive connotation
    - In the context « un **accueil** plutôt **frais** » (a rather cool reception)… "frais" has a negative connotation
    - In the context un "**poisson** bien **frais** (a fresh fish) « frais » has a positive connotation
- An adjective like "rapide » (rapid, fast) in French might also have different polarities depending on context and domain :
    - In the context "l'**impression** est **rapide**" (the printing is fast), "rapide" has a positive connotation
    - In the context "un **résumé** **rapide**" (a short summary), "rapide" is rather neutral.
- Etc.

When building an opinion detection system, it is necessary to be able to disambiguate these polar expressions and associate them the adequate polarity, i.e. positive or negative, according to the context. In this paper, we focus on the extraction of contextual patterns that carry a given polarity. In other terms, we try to automatically detect the polarity of a term according to the context, i.e. learn contextual polarity patterns, for ambiguous polar adjectives.

After a short review of the related work, we briefly describe our feature based opinion detection system, and then we present the methodology we propose to acquire opinionated patterns, which is based on syntactic information extraction combined with simple clustering techniques. We then show how we have integrated the learned patterns into our opinion detection system, and finally evaluate the benefits of this integration.

Related Work

In the literature about opinion mining, there is a considerable number of works aiming at associating polarity to single words. For example SentiWordnet (Baccianella at al. 2010) is a resource aiming at associating polarity scores to WordNet synsets. Many works try to classify polar adjectives, like for example (Vegnaduzzo 2004) who proposes a distributional method to classify polarity adjective using a small seed of polar adjectives. For French, (Vernier and Monceaux 2010) present a learning method relying on the indexing of Web documents by a search engine and large number of linguistically motivated requests automatically sent. There is considerably less attempts to address the problem of associating polarities to larger expressions, and in particular pairs of words in a given syntactic relation, as we propose here. (Wilson et al. 2005), noticed that polar vocabulary have a "prior polarity" that can change according to the context (negation, diminishers such as "little", "less",etc). They learn such contexts by performing classification using various features and an annotated corpus. In the present paper, we focus on different kind of patterns (noun-adj) and also use a different methodology since we only use the marks given to reviews by users and data automatically annotated with our rule-based system to perform the clustering step. (Riloff et al. 2003) propose a bootstrapping process that learns linguistically rich extraction patterns for subjective (opinionated) expressions. High-precision classifiers label are used on un-annotated data to automatically create a large training set, which is then given to an extraction pattern learning algorithm. The learned patterns are then used to identify more subjective sentences. The bootstrapping process learns many subjective patterns and increases recall while maintaining high precision. While it as some similarities with the work proposed in this paper, is also quite different since they try to learn opinionated syntactic patterns while we try to learn opinionated pairs of words, contextually dependent in a given syntactic relation. They also make use of annotated data, while we only use the marks given to reviews by users and data automatically annotated with our rule-based system in order to perform the clustering step.

Our Opinion Detection System

The opinion detection system we build relies on a robust deep syntactic parser, c.f. (Ait-Mokhtar et al. 2002), as a fundamental component, from which semantic relations of opinion are calculated. Having syntactic relations already extracted by a general dependency grammar, we use the robust parser by combining lexical information about word polarities, sub categorization information and syntactic dependencies to extract the semantic relations. The polarity lexicon has been built using existing resources and also by applying classification techniques over large corpora, while the semantic extraction rules are handcrafted, see (Brun 2011) for the complete description of these different components. At this step of development of the system for the French language, we have built generic rules for extracting opinion relations and a generic polar lexicon containing elements that can be considered as non ambiguous in terms of polarity. The work described in this paper aims at enriching this system with patterns that disambiguate ambiguous polar terms according to their context of appearance.

Learning Opinionated Patterns

As said in introduction, our goal is to try to automatically detect the polarity of a term according to the context, i.e. learn contextual polarity patterns, for ambiguous polar adjectives. We focus on NOUN-ADJ expressions, where the adjective is qualifying the noun and that can be mainly found in texts within two types of expressions, adjectives in modifier (1) or attribute (2) position:

(1) « un **accueil sympathique** », ... "a sympathetic reception")
(2) « la **cuisine** est **inventive** », le **service** est **lent**, ... (« the cooking is inventive », « the service is slow »)

To perform this task, we first collect a large corpus of customer reviews from the web, where such opinionated patterns can be found. We then use a robust syntactic parser to extract the candidate patterns, i.e. the modifier and attribute relationships presented above. We apply clustering techniques to group automatically the pattern according to their polarities. These different steps are detailed in the remaining of this section.

Corpus Selection

We have extracted a large corpus of online user's reviews about restaurant in French, extracted from the web site (http://www.linternaute.com/restaurant/). The reviews in html format have been cleaned and converted into xml format. Here's an example of such review, which contains a title (the name of the restaurant), and one or more user reviews containing the user rating of the restaurant and a free text comment:

```
<review>
<title> Brasserie André, restaurant gastronomique à Lille</title>
<userreview>
<rating>3</rating>
<comment> Très bonne adresse, les salades sont copieuses, le coin retiré de la circulation, rapport qualité
prix très correct. </comment>
(Very good place, salads are substantial, the place is far from traffic, value for money quite correct.)
</userreview>
</review>
```

The corpus we have collected contains 99364 user's reviews about 15473 different restaurants, i.e. 260 082 sentences (3 337 678 words). The repartition of the reviews according to the rating given by the users is shown on table 1. We consider that reviews rated from 0 to 2 are negative and that reviews rated from 3 to 5 are positive.

User's rating	0/5	1/5	2/5	3/5	4/5	5/5	total
Number of reviews	2508	8810	7511	14142	41382	25011	99364

TABLE 1 – Repartition of reviews according to user's rating

Pattern Extraction

In order to extract the patterns we aim at classifying as positive or negative, we use the robust syntactic parser presented in section 2, which detects such relations (attribute modifier relations between noun and adjectives). Moreover, as this work aims at improving an opinion detection system, we also use the opinion detection component we have developed on top of this robust parser (see (anonymous_reference)). We filter out patterns that are already marked as positive and negative by the opinion detection system (because they contain single polar terms that are already encoded in the polar lexicon of the system) and keep only the patterns that do not carry any information about polarity. The parser outputs syntactic relations among which we select the noun-adj modifiers and noun-adj attributes. We then count the number of occurrences of these relations within reviews rated 0, 1, 2, 3, 4 and 5. Moreover, we use the existing opinion detection system presented previously in order to also count the number of time a given pattern co-occurs with positive opinions and with negative opinions, on the whole corpus of reviews. Some examples of the results are shown in table 2:

Review rating / Noun,adj patterns	0/5	1/5	2/5	3/5	4/5	5/5	Frequencies of co-occurring positive opinions	Frequencies of co-occurring negative opinions
	Frequencies of patterns within reviews							
addition, convenable	0	0	0	1	1	0	6	0
estomac, solide	2	0	0	0	0	0	5	0
service, minimum	1	4	5	3	0	0	21	11
service, lent	30	87	71	71	64	10	707	399
service, rapide	0	1	2	2	6	6	55	7

TABLE 2 – Frequency counting for some example noun-adj patterns

We end up with a list of 29543 different NOUN-ADJ patterns together with their number of occurrences per type of reviews as well as the number of co-occurring positive and negative opinions within the whole corpus.

Clustering

In this step, we aim at clustering together the patterns to group them according to their polarity. We use the frequencies per type of review and the number of co-occurring positive and negative opinions previously extracted as features for clustering algorithms. We use the Weka software (Hall et al. 2009) that embeds a collection of machine learning algorithms for data mining tasks, among which clustering algorithms. We tested several algorithms and choose to use the Kmeans [1] algorithm. We experimentally try several numbers of clusters as target for the algorithm, as we have a relatively large number of data to cluster (~30 000 patterns). We needed to have a trade-off between number of clusters and precision of the results: a too small number of clusters gives imprecise results, a too large number of clusters is difficult to evaluate and useless (for example starting from N=60 clusters, a lot of clusters contain only 1 element, which is not interesting). We found this trade-off with a number of 50 clusters, that we reorder from the smallest to the largest, since the smallest clusters are the more accurate and contain the most frequent elements. Here is the content of the very first clusters (with the associated numerical features):

Cluster1 (5 elements) :

prix,élevé,41,77,45,57,62,15,541,321	*(high,price)*
service,lent,33,107,92,95,80,13,707,399	*(service,slow)*
attente,long,31,69,70,50,60,14,521,342	*(wait,long)*
service,long,69,280,233,255,218,37,1637,1012	*(service,long)*
accueil,froid,35,95,53,33,29,3,297,223	*(reception,cool)*

Which is clearly a cluster of expressions with negative polarity;

Cluster2 (9 elements) :

cuisine,simple,4,25,56,225,362,109,1910,133	*(cooking,simple)*
restaurant,petit,8,26,32,213,608,244,2286,182	*(restaurant,small)*
produit,frais,7,24,45,246,1049,637,5138,324	*(product,fresh)*
prix,abordable,3,11,17,102,363,250,2117,101	*(price,affordable)*
service,rapide,22,72,117,478,1180,433,5920,514	*(service,fast)*
cuisine,original,2,10,23,115,451,210,1949,115	*(cooking,original)*
service,efficace,7,19,31,142,451,140,2337,177	*(service,efficient)*
resto,petit,4,7,30,152,404,187,1739,98	*(resto,small)*
cuisine,traditionnel,5,12,28,161,427,169,1814,108	*(cooking,traditional)*

Which is clearly a cluster of expressions with positive polarity;

Cluster3 (10 elements):

poisson,frais,2,5,8,44,155,82,775,71	*(fish,fresh)*
ambiance,familial,2,1,5,43,155,88,719,48	*(atmosphere,family)*
cuisine,fin,3,4,10,58,309,152,1336,61	*(cooking,delicate)*
oeil,fermé,1,3,1,13,119,170,1150,54	*(eyes,shut)~blindfolded*

[1] There might be alternative clustering algorithms, we use this one because it was accurate and fast and gave.

choix,grand,1,3,15,49,233,70,924,43	*(choice,large)*
plat,original,3,6,19,60,198,104,1067,85	*(dish,original)*
choix,large,3,10,9,59,194,66,865,50	*(choice,large)*
salle,petit,11,18,22,93,191,59,1129,180	*(room,small)*
service,discret,2,6,19,51,191,77,1143,74	*(service,discreet)*
carte,varié,1,13,18,82,288,123,1273,65	*(menu,varied)*

Which is clearly a cluster of expressions with positive polarity; etc.

We validated the first 14 clusters, by counting the number of elements of the cluster that have the polarity of the whole cluster. We stopped evaluating at this stage since the accuracy started to be low as well as the corpus frequencies of the elements of the clusters. Thanks to this validation, we end up with a list of 151 positive patterns and 118 negative patterns, i.e. a total of 269 opinionated frequent NOUN-ADJ patterns.

Integration within the Opinion Detection System

At the end of the previous step, we have collected and validated clusters of patterns and associated them a positive or negative polarity. We then inject these results in our rule-based opinion extractor by automatically converting these patterns into rules (in the dedicated format of our robust parser). For example a pattern like "service,lent", which belongs to a negative cluster (cluster1 showed before), is automatically converted into the following rule:

|#1[lemma:"lent", **negative**= + |
If (ATTRIB(#2[lemme : « service »],#1) | ADJMOD(#2[lemme : « service »],#1))
~

This rule assigns the semantic feature « negative » to the adjective "lent"(#1) ("*slow*"), **if and only if** this adjective is in attribute or modifier relation with the noun "service"(#2), ("*service*"). Then, the opinion detection component that is applied afterward benefits from these polar rules to extract opinion relations accordingly.

Using these rules, if the input sentence is: "Le service est lent." (*the service is slow*), the system extracts a negative opinion relation : OPINION[negative](service,lent). While if the input sentence is: "La cuisson doit etre lente." (*the cooking should be slow*), the system does not extract any opinion relation, because the association "cuisson, lente" is rather neutral.

It is quite straightforward to convert automatically the clustered validated patterns into this kind of rules that then can be applied on top of the parser, and integrated into the opinion detection module. This specific parsing component contains 269 such rules.

Evaluation

In order to evaluate the impact of the learned opinionated rules on the overall performance of the opinion detection system, we compare the application of the system to review's classification task, with and without including the new resource. The corpus we have collected can be considered as annotated in terms of classification, since the user gives an explicit mark: 0, 1, 2 = negative and 3, 4, 5 = positive. We use the relations of opinions extracted by our system to train a SVM binary classifier (SVMLight, Joachims 1999) in order to classify the reviews as positive or negative. The experimental setup[2] consists in 25000 reviews extracted randomly from the initial corpus to train the SVM classifier, 3500 reviews extracted randomly for validation and 3500 reviews extracted randomly for testing. The SVM features are the relations of opinion on a given *target concept* and their values are the frequencies of these relations within a given review, e.g. OPINION-POSITIVE-on-*SERVICE*:2, OPINION-NEGATIVE-on-*CUISINE*:1 , etc. Using this information, we evaluate the system ability to classify reviews according to an overall opinion, and we run exactly the same test with the same data, respectively with and without the integration of our new learned resource of opinionated patterns. The following table shows the results we obtain on the test set.

Test set	positive reviews	negative reviews	**Total reviews**
Number	1750	1750	**3500**
Accuracy of the classification : system **without** the learned resources (~baseline)	81,6%	78.6%	**80.1%**
Accuracy of the classification : system **including** the learned resources	85.7%	83.1%	84.4%

TABLE 3 – Results on review classification task

Both results are in line with state of the art results, obtained for similar classification tasks, cf. (Pang et al. 2002) or (Paroubek et al. 2007), but the patterns, once encoded into our system, improve the classification task accuracy of about 3.3%, which is a quite satisfying result.

Conclusion and Perspectives

In this paper, we propose an original hybrid method to cope with the problem of ambiguous polar vocabulary, by automatically learning contextual patterns and encode them into an opinion detection system. The learning step consists in syntactic pattern clustering using frequencies extracted thanks to the ratings given by the user in review's comments, and frequencies about co-occurring opinions extracted by an opinion detection system. This system is then enriched with the new learned patterns. The evaluation on the task of review classification provides encouraging results. We plan to pursue this work along three perspectives. This first one will be to investigate other types of syntactic patterns for example SUBJECT or OBJECT relations between verbs and nouns or MODIFIER relation between nouns and nouns, in order to enrich the opinion detection system new opinionated patterns. The second is to apply the methodology to opinion detection in English. The last perspective is to improve the clustering step by investigating methods to automatically detect the optimal number of cluster, as for example proposed in (Pham et al. 2005) or (Arthur 2007).

---

[2] We constrained a 50% repartition of positive and negative reviews on the train, validation and test corpora.

References

Ait-Mokthar, S., Chanod, J.P. (2002). Robustness beyond Shallowness: Incremental Dependency Parsing. *Special Issue of NLE Journal.*

Arthur, D. and Vassilvitskii, S. (2007). k-means++: the advantages of careful seeding. In *Proceedings of the eighteenth annual ACM-SIAM symposium on Discrete algorithms (SODA '07).* Society for Industrial and Applied Mathematics, Philadelphia, PA, USA, 1027-1035.

Baccianella, S., Esuli, A. and Sebastiani. (2010). SentiWordNet 3.0: An Enhanced Lexical Resource for Sentiment Analysis and Opinion Mining. *In Proceedings of the Seventh International Conference on Language Resources and Evaluation (LREC'10)*. ELRA.

Bloom, K. Navendu G., Argamon S. (2007). Extracting Appraisal Expressions. In *Proceedings of HLT-NAACL*, Rochester, USA.

Brun. C. (2011). Detecting Opinions using Deep Syntactic Analysis. *In Proceedings of RANLP 2011 (Recent Advances in Natural Language Processing).* Hissar, Bulgaria.

Hu, M. and Liu, B. (2004). Mining and summarizing customer reviews. In *Proceedings of ACM SIGKDD International Conference on Knowledge Discovery & Data Mining (KDD-2004)*, Seattle, Washington, USA.

Hall, M., Eibe, F., Holmes, G. , Pfahringer, B., Reutemann, P. and Witten I. H. (2009); The WEKA Data Mining Software: An Update. *SIGKDD Explorations, Volume 11, Issue 1.*

Joachims T. (1999). Making large-Scale SVM Learning Practical. Advances in Kernel Methods – Support Vector Learning, B. Schölkopf and C. Burges and A. Smola (ed.), MIT Press.

Paroubek, P., Berthelin J.B., El Ayari S., Grouin C., Heitz T., Hurault-Plantet M., Jardino M., Khalis Z., Lastes M. (2007). Résultats de l'édition 2007 du DÉfi Fouille de Textes, In *Proceedings of DEFT'07*, GRENOBLE.

Pang B., L. Lee, S. Vaithyanathan. (2002). Thumbs up? Sentiment classification using machine learning techniques. In *Proceedings of the Conference on Empirical Methods in Natural Language Processing (EMNLP)*, pages 79–86.

Pham, D. T., Dimov, S. S. and Nguyen C. D. (2005) Selection of K in K -means clustering. In *Proceedings of the I MECH E Part C Journal of Mechanical Engineering Science*, Vol. 219, No. 1. , pp. 103-119.

Riloff, E. and Wiebe J. Learning extraction patterns for subjective expressions. (2003) In Proceedings *of the 2003 conference on Empirical Methods in Natural Language Processing*, Morristown, NJ, USA: Association for Computational Linguistics, p. 105--112.

Vegnaduzzo, S. (2004). Acquisition of subjective adjectives with limited resources. In *Proceedings of the AAAI spring symposium on exploring attitude and affect in text: Theories and applications*, Stanford, US.

Vernier M. et Monceaux L. (2010) Enrichissement d'un lexique de termes subjectifs à partir de tests sémantiques. *Revue TAL volume 51 (1)*, pp. 125-149.

Wilson, T., Wiebe, J. and Hoffmann, P. (2005). Recognizing contextual polarity in phrase-level sentiment analysis. In *Proceedings of the conference on Human Language Technology and Empirical Methods in Natural Language Processing (HLT '05)*. Association for Computational Linguistics, Stroudsburg, PA, USA, 347-354.

Does *Similarity* Matter? The Case of Answer Extraction from Technical Discussion Forums

Rose Catherine[1] *Amit Singh*[1]
Rashmi Gangadharaiah[1] *Dinesh Raghu*[1] *Karthik Visweswariah*[1]
(1) IBM Research - India, Bangalore
{rosecatherinek, amitkumarsingh, rashgang, dinraghu, v-karthik}@in.ibm.com

ABSTRACT
Extracting question–answer pairs from social media discussions has garnered much attention in recent times. Several methods have been proposed in the past that pose this task as a post or sentence classification problem, which label each entry as an answer or not. This paper makes the first attempt at the following two–fold objectives: (a) In all classification based approaches towards this direction, one of the foremost signals used to identify answers is their *similarity* to the question. We study the contribution of content similarity specifically in the context of technical problem–solving domain. (b) We introduce hitherto unexplored features that aid in high–precision extraction of answers, and present a thorough study of the contribution of all features to this task. Our results show that, it is possible to extract answers using these features with high accuracy, when their similarity to the question is unreliable.

KEYWORDS: Question Answering, Information & Content Extraction, Text Mining.

Proceedings of COLING 2012: Posters, pages 175–184,
COLING 2012, Mumbai, December 2012.

1 Introduction

Online discussion forums are internet sites that provide a channel for users to discuss and share their views on various topics ranging from troubleshooting products to choosing holiday resorts. Over a period of time, they have accumulated huge amounts of data, thus making them excellent sources of information for future reference. Mining question–answer knowledge from these online forums, and social media discussions in general, has garnered much research and commercial interest of late. Such mined data can be used to provide enhanced access to the forum content, augment chatbot knowledge (Huang et al., 2007), supplement the data in Community Question Answering (CQA) sites (Cong et al., 2008) etc.

All answer extraction methods suggested in the past use a multitude of features that include similarity based and lexical features, structural features constructed from the organization of the discussion etc. Of these, similarity of the answer candidate to the question post has been a de facto standard feature, whose contribution to the accuracy of extraction have so far only been assumed, but never really measured.

The goals and contributions of this paper are as below:

- Study the characteristics of technical discussion forums and their points of difference from other domains, thus motivating the rest of the contributions of this paper.
- Analyze the effectiveness of similarity of candidates to the question, as a feature towards the task of identifying answers, specifically in the case of technical discussion forums. Unlike other domains, here, the answers have minimal lexical overlap with the question.
- Propose new features and study the contribution of all features to the overall goal of answer extraction. Particularly, we aim to test if similarity–independent features can act as an understudy to question similarity for this task, when the latter is unavailable/unreliable.

To the best of the authors' knowledge, this is the first paper which attempts the above objectives.

2 Related Work

Classification–based approaches proposed in the past for detecting answers in online discussion forums like (Ding et al., 2008), (Hong and Davison, 2009), (Yang et al., 2009), (Kim et al., 2010), and in email discussions like (Shrestha and McKeown, 2004) use similarity of the sentence or post to the question as one of the main features for identifying answers. Other approaches like graph based methods (Cong et al., 2008) and (Otterbacher et al., 2005) rely on similarity to construct the graph. However, none of these approaches test systematically, the inadequacy or indispensability, which ever is the case, of similarity to the task.

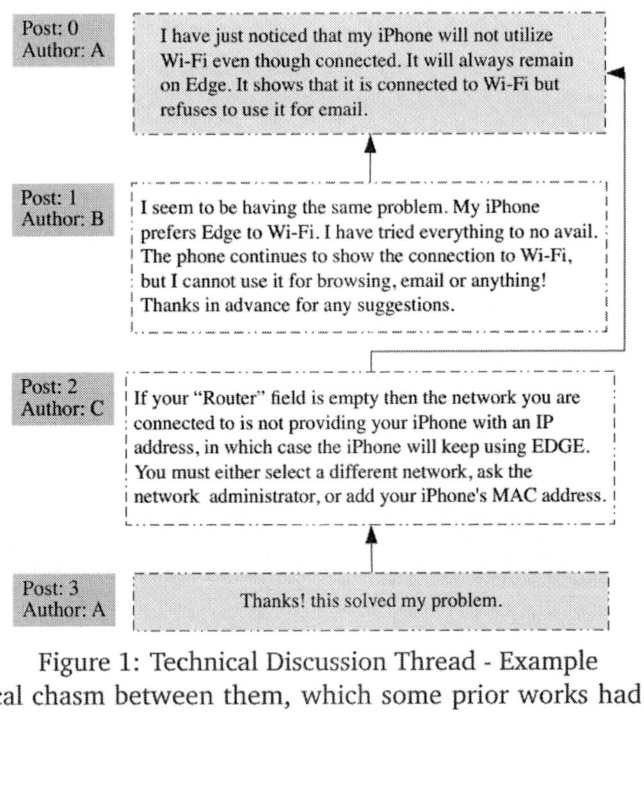

Figure 1: Technical Discussion Thread - Example

The low similarity between questions and answers is due to the lexical chasm between them, which some prior works had incidentally observed (Cong et al., 2008), (Ding et al., 2008), (Hong and Davison, 2009), and used external data like Yahoo! Answers[1] to either expand the content or learn a translation model. For learning such models, it should be noted that, such data may not always be available and is required in good amounts to train a decent model. Also, (Hong and Davison, 2009), while experimenting on technical discussions, reported that a combination of two non–similarity based features gave better accuracy than a language model. In Section 4.1, we show that, in addition to these features, with the aid of other non–similarity based features, the accuracy of the task can be greatly improved.

3 Does Question Similarity Matter for Answer Extraction?

Discussion forums provide an online medium for users to collaboratively solve a problem or answer a query. Figure 1 shows a typical discussion in an online forum – it starts with the first post, which we refer to as the `question` post. The directed edges show the `reply-to` relation, where the start node of the edge – child post, was posted in reply to the end node of the edge – parent post. In this paper, we use the term 'thread' interchangeably with 'discussion' to refer to a single multi–user conversation of the above form.

Discussions frequently have digressions, where new questions are posted and discussed within the same thread. We do not attempt to find these questions; question detection is a well researched area (Cong et al., 2008), and is outside the scope of this paper. We treat the first post as the main question and find answers to only this question. Answers to other questions within the same thread are not considered.

3.1 Characteristics of Technical Discussion Forums

Technical discussion forums differ from other forums like travel and shopping in that, they are characterized by low lexical overlap between the problem statement and the answer.

3.1.1 Lexical Overlap

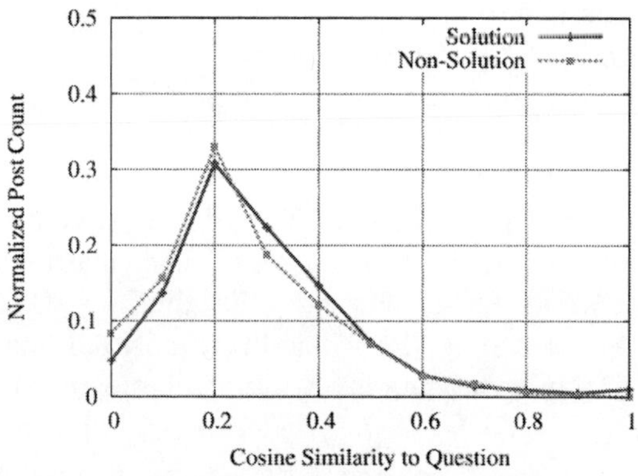

Figure 2: Similarity Histogram

To verify the above hypothesis about the overlap between answer posts and question posts, we studied about 450 threads which together have about 2000 reply posts, from Apple Discussions[2] (details about the dataset is in Section 4). Figure 2 plots a histogram (counts normalized) of cosine similarity (bucketized) of answers and non–answers to their respective question posts. The cosine similarity was computed on the *tf-idf* representation of the posts, after removing common English stopwords and stemming the words using a Porter Stemmer (Porter, 1980). It is clear from the figure that, a large fraction of answers have very minimal overlap with the question, and the fraction of answers with high overlap is very minimal. It is interesting to note that, the same trend is exhibited by non-answers too, thereby making it difficult to separate out the two using question similarity alone. In-depth inspection showed that, a large fraction of posts whose overlap with the question post is high, are in fact, other users complaining about facing the same or a similar problem, while the actual answer

[1]http://answers.yahoo.com
[2]https://discussions.apple.com/community/iphone

Forum	Avg. Spam %	Avg. Digression %
Apple Discussions (discussions.apple.com)	0	10.9
Ubuntu (ubuntuforums.org)	0	5.9
Photography (photography-on-the.net)	0	8.9
Avg. for Technical	0	8.5
Trip Advisor (www.tripadvisor.com)	4.1	25.2
Lonely Planet (www.lonelyplanet.com)	0	33.5
Vogue (forums.vogue.com.au)	0	21.3
Avg. for Non Technical	1.3	26.6

Table 1: Avg. Spam and Digressions per Thread

Statistics	Training	Test
No. of Threads	451	150
No. of Posts	2003	702
Avg. Replies	3.5	3.7
Avg. Answers per Thread	1.6	1.8

Table 2: Statistics of the Training and Test datasets

uses a different set of words, thus resulting in a low lexical overlap. This is also noticeable in the sample discussion of Figure 1. Here, similarity with the question post is actually misleading.

3.1.2 Spam and Digressions

When the similarity of answers to questions is low or unreliable, are there other properties of the post, the thread or its structure that we can rely on for accurate extraction? To explore such options, we conducted a small study to compare the amount of spam and digressions in technical forums versus other forums.

A spam is a completely off–topic post, while a digression is a post that is related to, but not discussing the same exact problem stated in the first post. Spam posts are usually advertisements generated automatically by spambots[3] and can be safely ignored without affecting the rest of the discussion. A digression, however, is still related to the overall discussion; at times, the result of this seemingly different problem might be useful in solving the main problem, and hence cannot be ignored completely. Nevertheless, for the purposes of this paper, we do not attempt to collate any of the sub–problems or their answers discussed within the thread.

Table 1 summarizes our findings on three technical and non-technical forums each. The numbers give the fraction (percentage) of the number of replies per thread, averaged over 15 randomly chosen threads from each of the forums. In the table, we note that the former has fewer spam and digressions, which suggests that it might be possible to find answers to the main question without regard to the question post or similarity to it, in a technical domain.

3.2 Features for Answer Extraction

The features that we study in this paper for the answer extraction task are detailed in Table 3. All Part-Of-Speech tags were generated using the Open NLP POS Tagger[4]. The column **Type** groups the features and **Availability** gives the fraction of forums in which each feature is publicly available, from 12 technical forums that we inspected. For example, the `Reply-to` structure of the thread may not always be displayed (Seo et al., 2009), and is usually flattened to their chronological order. Where the entry is `Always`, the data is always available, usually because it is computed from the text of the post.

Out of these, `Has_Link`, `Has_Navigation`, `Post_Belongs_to_First_N_Posts`, `In_Reply_to_Question_Author` and `Is_Replied_by_Question_Author` have not been proposed before, to the best of our knowledge.

4 Experiments

We crawled about 147,000 threads from Apple Discussions[5] of which we discarded those that had only 2 or fewer number of reply posts (88, 565 threads) and those that had more than 30

[3]http://en.wikipedia.org/wiki/Forum_spam

[4]http://opennlp.apache.org

[5]https://discussions.apple.com/community/iphone

	Feature	Description	Type	Availability
1	`Has Noun`	`True` or `False` depending on whether this post has nouns.	Lexical	Always
2	`Has Proper Noun`	`True` or `False` depending on whether this post has proper nouns.		
3	`Has Verb`	`True` or `False` depending on whether this post has verbs.		
4	`No. of Non-Stopwords`	The number of words in the post after discarding common English stopwords.		
5	`Has Link`	`True` if the post has a hyper–link, for example, to another thread or an online manual; else `False`.	Content	Always
6	`Has Navigation`	`True` if the post gives a navigational instruction like `'Settings→Sounds→Ringtone'`; else `False`.		
7	`Author Authority`	A forum specific value - numerical (e.g. 1000 points) or categorical (e.g. `Beginner`) - assigned to the author, and indicative of their level of expertise in the context of the forum.	Forum Specific	100%
8	`Post Rating`	Numerical (e.g. 5 votes) or categorical (e.g. `Helpful`) value assigned by the question author or other users, indicating the usefulness of the post in answering the question.		36.3%
9	`Relative Post Position in Thread`	Computed from the ordinal position of the post in the thread, which is usually chronological. This value is grouped into 3 buckets - `Beginning`, `Middle` and `End`.	Structural	Always
10	`Post Belongs to First N Posts`	`True` if the ordinal number of the post is less than N, which was set to 5 in our experiments. Else, `False`.		
11	`Post Author is Not Question Author`	`True` if the two authors are different; else `False`.		
12	`Time Difference to Question Post`	Difference between the time of posting of the question post and the reply post, bucketized into `hour`, `day` and `more`.		100%
13	`In Reply to Question Author`	`True` or `False` depending on whether this post was in reply to the Question Author.	Reply-to	75%
14	`Is Replied by Question Author`	`True` or `False` depending on whether this post was replied by the Question Author.		
15	`In Reply to Question Post`	`True` or `False` depending on whether this post was in reply to the first post.		
16	`No. of Replies to this Post`	Number of replies to this post, as a fraction of the total number of replies in the thread.		
17	`No. of Replies to Parent Post`	Number of replies to the parent post, as a fraction of the total number of replies in the thread.		

Table 3: Features generated for a post, their types and availability

reply posts (845 threads), which gave us 58, 356 threads. From this, about 600 threads were randomly chosen for manual tagging. Posts in these threads were tagged as 'Answer' if they proposed an answer to the question post, and as 'Other', otherwise. If there were more than one answer post, ALL were marked as 'Answer's. Answers to other questions within the thread (digressions) were marked as 'Other'. Table 2 gives statistics of the training and test datasets.

4.1 Classification Experiments

We trained LibSVM classifiers[6] (Chang and Lin, 2011) on different sets of features as listed below, to obtain classifiers that mark each post as an answer or not, the precision–recall plot[7] of which is given in Figure 3:

- `Question Similarity`: uses the cosine similarity of the answer candidate and its respective question post, after discarding English stopwords and Porter stemming. As expected, it fails to give good accuracy for the task.
- `Word`: the features of this classifier are the words of the post after stopword removal and stemming. This is to test if answer posts use similar terminology which can be leveraged,

[6]With default settings (svm-type: C-SVC, kernel-type: RBF) and no tuning of hyperparameters

[7]Precision–Recall Plot: To obtain this plot, for each post in the test set, the trained classifier was used to get the probability of it being an answer. Let t be a threshold where all posts whose predicted probability is greater than t are labeled as answers. Then, t was varied from 0 to 1 in steps of 0.05 to get the different precision–recall values.

but gives an unimpressive performance.

- `Hong and Davison` (Hong and Davison, 2009): this classifier uses `Relative Post Position in Thread` and `Author Authority` alone, as reported in their paper. As can be seen from the figure, it gives better performance than the above two classifiers.
- `Forum Features`: this is the classifier that uses all features listed in Table 3 and is able to show a significant improvement over `Hong and Davison`.
- `Forum Features and Question Similarity`: it uses question similarity in addition to `Forum Features`, but overlaps almost completely with it indicating that similarity does not give any value addition.

4.2 Feature Selection Experiments

To study the relative importance of features for the answer extraction task, we performed two sets of feature selection experiments – a permutation test (Section 4.2.1) and a feature ablation study (Section 4.2.2), discussed in the below sections. The latter technique gauges the importance based on the performance of a classifier, while the former uses a statistical measure and does not depend on an external classifier.

4.2.1 Permutation Test

Permutation test (Good, 2000) is a popular non-parametric technique for statistical analysis of data and provides an empirical estimate for the distribution of the statistic under the null hypothesis ($\mathscr{H}_0$). Let l, m be the number of class 0, 1 samples respectively. For each feature, a test statistic θ (like information gain, mutual information) indicating similarity between the two class conditional densities, is calculated. Next, the data for the feature is randomly permuted and partitioned into sets of size l and m, on which the test statistic θ_p is calculated. This procedure is repeated over all possible such partitions of the feature into sets of size l and m. p-value is then estimated as the fraction of times $\theta_p > \theta$ and is an indicator of feature importance. Table 4 shows the Mutual Information scores for all features along with p-value. As a standard practice, any feature with p-value $<$ 0.05 (marked with *) is deemed important and the ones with p-value $\gg$ 0.05 (marked with **) are suggestively weak. From Table 4, it can be seen that `Question_Similarity` ranks very low on mutual Information. More detailed analysis is in Section 4.2.3.

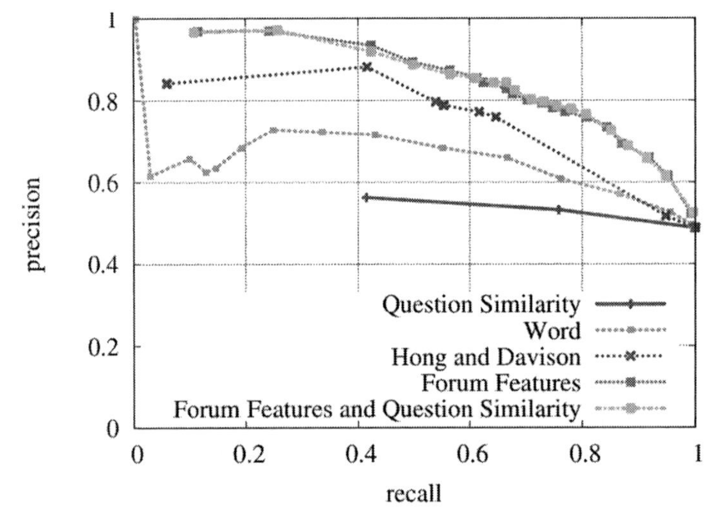

Figure 3: Precision Recall plots for answer classification

4.2.2 Feature Ablation Study

The goal of this study is to find the most reliable features that a classifier can use for the answer extraction task. In the feature ablation analysis (Arguello et al., 2009), at each step, each feature is individually omitted and the classifier is trained on the rest of the features. The importance of the feature is then measured as the classifier's percentage decrease in F-measure; higher the decrease, higher is the contribution. This process is repeated with the best feature of each step

Feature	Mutual Information
Relative Post Position in Thread	0.1256**
Post Author is Not Question Author	0.0977*
Has Link	0.0336**
Post Belongs to First N Posts	0.0299**
Time Difference to Question Post	0.0265**
Author Authority	0.0250**
Is Replied by Question Author	0.0223
No. of Replies to Parent Post	0.0201**
Has Proper Noun	0.0080*
Has Verb	0.0046*
No. of Non-Stopwords	0.0041*
Post Rating	0.0033
Has Noun	0.0027
Has Navigation	0.0019
In Reply to Question Post	0.0013
Question Similarity	0.0013
No. of Replies to Parent Post	0.0010*

Table 4: Permutation test results

Feature	Precision	Recall	F measure
Post Author is Not Question Author	0.82	0.69	0.75
Author Authority	0.81	0.65	0.72
Has Link	0.79	0.64	0.71
In Reply to Question Post	0.77	0.64	0.70
In Reply to Question Author	0.83	0.59	0.69
Relative Post Position in Thread	0.84	0.51	0.63
Is Replied by Question Author	0.70	0.46	0.55
Post Belongs to First N Posts	0.69	0.43	0.53
No. of Non-Stopwords	0.71	0.39	0.50
Has Verb	0.69	0.36	0.48
Has Navigation	0.70	0.35	0.46
Has Proper Noun	0.71	0.35	0.47
Post Rating	0.67	0.37	0.47
Has Noun	0.63	0.34	0.44
No. of Replies to this Post	0.63	0.34	0.44
Time Difference to Question Post	0.63	0.34	0.44
Question Similarity	0.63	0.34	0.44
No. of Replies to Parent Post	0.58	0.34	0.43

Table 5: Feature Ablation Study

progressively removed until all features are exhausted, to give them in their decreasing order of importance. For the experiment, we used a LibSVM classifier (Chang and Lin, 2011), and the results are in Table 5. The table lists the most helpful to the least helpful of features; the Precision, Recall and F-measure values (Chakrabarti, 2002) shown against each feature gives the accuracy numbers obtained when that feature and all those below it in the table were used to train the classifier. Detailed analysis is in Section 4.2.3.

4.2.3 Feature Selection Results Discussion

The results of permutation test in Table 4 and that of feature ablation study in Table 5 differ slightly because the latter is dependent on the performance of a classification algorithm while the former uses a statistical measure. However, it can be noted that, the following features show up as the best in both the tests:

- Post Author is Not Question Author
- Author Authority
- Has Link*
- Relative Post Position in Thread
- Is Replied by Question Author*
- Post Belongs to First N Posts*

Note that, out of the best 6 features, 3 were newly proposed in this paper (marked with *). Also note that, `Question_Similarity` ranks among the lowest in both the tests, thus showing its insignificance to this task. Another rather surprising observation is that `Post_Rating`, which gives the usefulness of the post, also does not contribute highly, which could be because, the number of posts that can be marked as `Helpful` is limited in the Apple discussions forum, thus missing out on useful suggestions that exceed the limit.

4.3 Feature Correlation Study

Correlation[8] refers to any of the broad class of statistical relationships between two random variables. In this paper, we use Pearson Product-Moment Correlation Coefficient[9] (Pearson's r), a widely used measure of correlation, defined as $\frac{cov(X,Y)}{\sigma_X \sigma_Y}$ for two variables X and Y, where cov and σ are the covariance and the standard deviation respectively.

[8]http://en.wikipedia.org/wiki/Correlation_and_dependence
[9]http://en.wikipedia.org/wiki/Pearson_product-moment_correlation_coefficient

Feature	Correlation to Answer
Time Difference to Question Post	58.92
Author Authority	57.41
Is Replied by Question Author	40.92
Has Link	39.81
Post Rating	32.17
Relative Post Position in Thread	30.89
In Reply to Question Post	19.08
No. of Non-Stopwords	18.16
In Reply to Question Author	12.22
Post Belongs to First N Posts	12.06
Has Navigation	10.47
Has Proper Noun	8.73
No. of Replies to Parent Post	8.21
Post Author is Not Question Author	5.47
Has Noun	4.18
Has Verb	3.80
No. of Replies to this Post	1.44

Table 6: Feature – Answer Correlation

Feature A	Feature B	Correlation
In Reply to Question Post	In Reply to Question Author	86.72
Post Belongs to First N Posts	Relative Post Position in Thread	63.68
In Reply to Question Author	Post Author is Not Question Author	58.14
Time Difference to Question Post	Author Authority	55.41
In Reply to Question Post	Post Author is Not Question Author	51.94
Time Difference to Question Post	In Reply to Question Post	43.91
No. of Replies to Parent Post	In Reply to Question Post	41.68
Post Belongs to First N Posts	In Reply to Question Author	40.75
Is Replied by Question Author	Author Authority	38.89
Time Difference to Question Post	In Reply to Question Author	37.61
In Reply to Question Author	No. of Replies to Parent Post	37.29
Time Difference to Question Post	Is Replied by Question Author	35.40

Table 7: Feature – Feature Correlation

Table 6 gives the correlation of all the features to the answer label of the post. Higher the score, higher is the influence of the feature on the label. However, a higher score alone does not imply that the feature is important. If the feature is also highly correlated to many other features, it introduces redundancy, thus reducing its significance. The top 12 inter–feature correlation are listed in Table 7. Though `Time_Difference_to_Question_Post` shows the highest correlation to the answer label (Table 6), Table 7 shows that it is also highly correlated to many other features. Another contradicting result is that, in Section 4.2.3, `Post_Rating` was not ranked high. But Tables 6 and 7 show that it is highly correlated to the answer label and at the same time, not correlated to other features, suggesting that it might still prove to be useful.

Some of the features chosen in Section 4.2.3 from the feature selection experiments show correlation amongst themselves, as shown in Table 7. However, `Has_Link` proves to be a high ranking feature according to both (a) Feature Selection, as well as, (b) Feature Correlation, since it highly correlates to the answer, but does not overlap with other features.

5 Conclusion

In this paper, we studied the contribution and importance of similarity to question in extracting answers from technical discussions, and showed that this feature does not contribute significantly towards the task of answer extraction, contrary to its perceived significance. We also presented the characteristics of technical discussion forums that distinguish them from other domains thus suggesting that it is possible to extract answers with high accuracy using other non-similarity based features when question similarity is unreliable, which was then demonstrated through experiments. We also presented a careful study of all features to determine which ones contributed highly to this task. The results of one set of experiments – Feature Selection – showed that out of the 6 best features, 3 were the ones newly proposed in this paper. Further analysis using Feature Correlation tests showed that all but one of the 6 best features from the former experiments were in fact highly correlated amongst themselves. The one feature that proved to be highly important in all the tests is `Has_Link`, proposed for the first time in this paper.

As part of future work, we aim to test the importance of the features proposed in this paper in other domains, and the marginal improvement in accuracy that they can provide even in the presence of high similarity of answers to question posts.

References

Arguello, J., Callan, J., and Diaz, F. (2009). Classification-based resource selection. In *Proceedings of the 18th ACM conference on Information and knowledge management*, CIKM '09, pages 1277–1286, New York, NY, USA. ACM.

Chakrabarti, S. (2002). *Mining the Web: Discovering Knowledge from Hypertext Data*. Morgan-Kauffman.

Chang, C. and Lin, C. (2011). LIBSVM: A library for support vector machines. *ACM Transactions on Intelligent Systems and Technology*, 2:27:1–27:27. http://www.csie.ntu.edu.tw/ cjlin/libsvm.

Cong, G., Wang, L., Lin, C.-Y., Song, Y.-I., and Sun, Y. (2008). Finding question-answer pairs from online forums. In *Proceedings of the 31st annual international ACM SIGIR conference on Research and development in information retrieval*, SIGIR '08, pages 467–474, New York, NY, USA. ACM.

Ding, S., Cong, G., Lin, C.-Y., and Zhu, X. (2008). Using conditional random fields to extract contexts and answers of questions from online forums. In *ACL*, pages 710–718.

Good, P. (2000). *Permutation Tests: A Practical Guide to Resampling Methods for Testing Hypotheses*. Springer, 2nd edition.

Hong, L. and Davison, B. D. (2009). A classification-based approach to question answering in discussion boards. In *Proceedings of the 32nd international ACM SIGIR conference on Research and development in information retrieval*, SIGIR '09, pages 171–178, New York, NY, USA. ACM.

Huang, J., Zhou, M., and Yang, D. (2007). Extracting chatbot knowledge from online discussion forums. In *Proceedings of the 20th international joint conference on Artifical intelligence*, IJCAI'07, pages 423–428, San Francisco, CA, USA. Morgan Kaufmann Publishers Inc.

Kim, S. N., Wang, L., and Baldwin, T. (2010). Tagging and linking web forum posts. In *Proceedings of the Fourteenth Conference on Computational Natural Language Learning*, CoNLL '10, pages 192–202, Stroudsburg, PA, USA. Association for Computational Linguistics.

Otterbacher, J., Erkan, G., and Radev, D. R. (2005). Using random walks for question-focused sentence retrieval. In *Proceedings of the conference on Human Language Technology and Empirical Methods in Natural Language Processing*, HLT '05, pages 915–922, Stroudsburg, PA, USA. Association for Computational Linguistics.

Porter, M. (1980). An algorithm for suffix stripping. In *Program*.

Seo, J., Croft, W. B., and Smith, D. A. (2009). Online community search using thread structure. In *Proceedings of the 18th ACM conference on Information and knowledge management*, CIKM '09, pages 1907–1910, New York, NY, USA. ACM.

Shrestha, L. and McKeown, K. (2004). Detection of question-answer pairs in email conversations. In *Proceedings of the 20th international conference on Computational Linguistics*, COLING '04, Stroudsburg, PA, USA. Association for Computational Linguistics.

Yang, W.-Y., Cao, Y., and Lin, C.-Y. (2009). A structural support vector method for extracting contexts and answers of questions from online forums. In *Proceedings of the 2009 Conference on Empirical Methods in Natural Language Processing: Volume 2 - Volume 2*, EMNLP '09, pages 514–523, Stroudsburg, PA, USA. Association for Computational Linguistics.

Chinese Noun Phrase Coreference Resolution: Insights into the State of the Art

Chen CHEN   Vincent NG
Human Language Technology Research Institute
University of Texas at Dallas
Richardson, TX 75083-0688, USA
{yzcchen,vince}@hlt.utdallas.edu

ABSTRACT

Compared to the amount of research on English coreference resolution, relatively little work has been done on Chinese coreference resolution. Worse still, it has been difficult to determine the state of the art in Chinese coreference resolution, owing in part to the lack of a standard evaluation dataset. The organizers of the CoNLL-2012 shared task, Modeling Unrestricted Multilingual Coreference in OntoNotes, have recently addressed this issue by providing standard training and test sets for developing and evaluating Chinese coreference resolvers. We aim to gain insights into the state of the art via extensive experimentation with our Chinese resolver, which is ranked first in the shared task on the Chinese test data.

TITLE AND ABSTRACT IN CHINESE

中文名词短语共指消解：探究研究现状

与大量的英文共指消解研究相比，针对中文的共指研究相对较少。更糟糕的是，中文共指消解很难确定当前的研究现状，部分原因是缺少标准的评测集。CoNLL-2012 共同任务（在 OntoNotes 上对无限制多语言共指消解的建模）的组织者解决了这个问题，他们提供了标准化的训练集和测试集供开发和评定中文共指消解系统。我们的系统在中文测试集的评测中排名第一。本文在原系统的基础上做了广泛的实验，以探究中文共指消解的研究现状。

KEYWORDS: coreference resolution, anaphora resolution, Chinese language processing, OntoNotes, CoNLL shared task.

KEYWORDS IN CHINESE: 共指消解, 指代消解, 中文语言处理, OntoNotes, CoNLL 共同任务.

Proceedings of COLING 2012: Posters, pages 185–194,
COLING 2012, Mumbai, December 2012.

1 Introduction

Coreference resolution is the task of determining which noun phrases (NPs) in a text refer to the same real-world entity. Compared to the amount of research on English coreference resolution, relatively little work has been done on Chinese coreference resolution. Worse still, it has been difficult to determine the state of the art in Chinese coreference resolution. The reason can be attributed in part to the lack of a standard evaluation dataset: while recently developed Chinese resolvers are typically evaluated on the ACE datasets, different researchers have used different splits of the ACE data for training and testing, making performance comparisons difficult.[1] The organizers of the CoNLL-2012 shared task, Modeling Unrestricted Multilingual Coreference in OntoNotes, have recently addressed this issue by providing free access to the training and test sets used in the official evaluation (Pradhan et al., 2012).

Our goal in this paper is to gain a better understanding of the state of the art in Chinese coreference resolution by providing an extensive empirical analysis of our Chinese resolver, which is ranked first on the Chinese subtask of the CoNLL-2012 shared task. Briefly, our resolver adopts a hybrid rule-based/machine learning approach to coreference resolution, extending the successful rule-based multi-pass sieve approach (Raghunathan et al., 2010; Lee et al., 2011) with lexical features that have proven useful in machine learning approaches (Rahman and Ng, 2011a, 2011b). Our analysis is focused on four issues.

1. **Mention detection.** Previous work has shown that the quality of the extracted *mentions* (i.e., the NPs participating in a coreference chain) plays an important role in the performance of a resolver. To what extent is the performance of our resolver limited by the *recall* and *precision* of our mention detector? To improve the precision of our mention detector, we need to improve its *mention pruning* strategy, but to what extent is its precision limited by our current mention pruning strategy? To improve the recall of our mention detector, we need to improve the extraction of mentions from syntactic parse trees, but to what extent is its recall limited by the *mention extraction* strategy versus the quality of the syntactic parses?
2. **Preprocessing.** After mention detection, we need to compute *features* based on the extracted mentions using preprocessing tools such as syntactic parsers and named entity (NE) recognizers. To what extent is the performance of our resolver limited by the correctness of the output produced by these tools?
3. **The coreference algorithm.** To better understand our hybrid approach, we focus on three questions. First, do we really need a hybrid approach? In other words, will our approach work equally well without the learning component? Second, how much does each sieve in the multi-pass sieve approach contribute to overall performance? Third, how important is the ordering of the sieves as far as performance is concerned?
4. **Comparison with classifier-based approaches.** In the shared task, our resolver outperformed those systems that adopted the popularly-used mention-pair (MP) model (Soon et al., 2001), a classifier trained to determine whether two given NPs are coreferent. However, we cannot claim that our coreference algorithm is superior to the MP model because we do not know which component(s) of our resolver (e.g., mention detection, feature computation, resolution) contributed to the superiority. In fact, much of the previous work focuses on comparing *systems* rather than *models/methods*. We determine whether our resolution *method* is better than the MP model if both are given the same set of mentions and features.

[1] One may wonder why researchers did not simply follow the same train-test split used in the official ACE evaluations. The reason is that only the training sets used in the official evaluations are released to the public.

	Docs	Mentions	Chains	Mentions/Chain
Train	1391	102854	28257	3.6
Development	172	3875	14183	3.7
Test	166	3559	12801	3.6

Table 1: Statistics of the training, development and test sets.

2 Datasets and Evaluation Measures

The training, development and test sets that we use in our experiments are the same as those in the official CoNLL-2012 shared task evaluation (see Table 1 for their statistics). As we will see in the next section, we use the training set for learning probabilities (e.g., how likely is it that two mentions are coreferent?), the development set for tuning thresholds, and the test set for evaluating our resolver.

We follow the method adopted by the shared task for evaluating a resolver. Specifically, the score of a resolver is the unweighted average of the F-measure scores computed by three scoring programs (MUC, B^3, and entity-based CEAF), whose implementation is provided by the shared task organizers. It is worth mentioning that (1) a resolver is not rewarded for correctly identifying singleton mentions; and (2) a mention is considered correctly extracted if and only if there is an exact phrase match between the gold mention and the extracted mention. In addition, elided pronouns, copulars, and appositive constructions are excluded in this (and the official shared task) evaluation.

3 Our Coreference Resolver

In this section, we give an overview of our two-step resolver as used for the shared task (see Chen and Ng (2012) for details). Note that linguistic annotations such as word segmentation and syntactic parses come with the shared task datasets and do not need to be computed separately.

Step 1: Mention Detection. To build a mention detector, we employ a two-step approach. First, in the *extraction* step, we extract mentions from all the NP and QP nodes in syntactic parse trees. Then, in the *pruning* step, we identify and filter erroneously extracted mentions by employing two types of pruning. In *heuristic pruning*, we use simple heuristics to prune erroneous mentions. For instance, we prune a candidate mention m_k if it is an interrogative pronoun or an NE that is a PERCENT or QUANTITY. In *learning-based pruning*, we prune m_k if the probability that it is a mention in the training data is less than t_C, where t_C is a threshold whose value is determined using the development set.

Step 2: Sieve-Based Coreference Resolution. A *sieve* is composed of one or more manually-designed rules for establishing the coreference relation between two mentions. A sieve-based resolver is composed of a set of *sieves* ordered by their precision, with the most precise sieves appearing first. When given a text, the resolver makes multiple passes over it: in the i-th pass, it uses only the rules in the i-th sieve to establish coreference relations.

Our resolver is composed of 10 sieves. The **Chinese Head Match** (CHM) sieve identifies the coreference relation between two same-head mentions where one is embedded within the other in newswire articles. The **Discourse Processing** (DP) sieve resolves mentions, especially first- and second-person pronouns, in dialogues. The **Exact String Match** (ESM) sieve resolves a non-pronominal mention to a mention with the same string. The **Precise Constructs** (PC) sieve posits two mentions as coreferent based on lexical and syntactic information, such as whether one is an acronym of the other and whether the mentions are in an appositive construction. In addition, we incorporated Chinese-specific rules for determining whether one mention is an abbreviation of the other based on NE information. **Strict Head Match A–C** (SHMA–C) are three head match sieves that contain progressively less precise coreference rules based on head matching. The **Proper Head Match** (PHM) is a relaxed version of Strict Head Match C applicable only to proper nouns. The **Pronouns** (Pro) sieve contains rules for resolving pronouns based on features that we learned from the training set, such as gender and number. Finally, the **Lexical Pair** (LP) sieve identifies coreference relations based on lexical features. For example, one rule specifies that two mentions are coreferent if the probability that their heads are coreferent according to the training data is greater than t_{HPU}, where t_{HPU} is a threshold determined using the development set.

Note that the usual linguistic constraints on non-coreference are applied before a rule in any of the sieves posits two mentions as coreferent. These constraints are implemented as a single *non-coreference* rule, which specifies that two mentions m_i and m_j cannot be coreferent if one of the following five conditions holds: (1) they satisfy the i-within-i constraint (Haghighi and Klein, 2009); (2) they refer to different speakers in a dialogue despite being the same string; (3) they are in a copular construction; (4) m_i is composed of two NPs connected by an "and" and m_j is one of the conjuncts; and (5) the probability that m_i and m_j are coreferent (as calculated from training data) falls below a certain threshold.

Step 3: Postprocessing. We postprocess the coreference partition before sending it to the scoring program. Specifically, we remove from it (1) all coreference links between two mentions in appositive constructions and (2) singleton clusters.

4 Evaluation

In this section, we conduct extensive experimentation with our resolver in an attempt to shed light on the four issues raised in the introduction.

4.1 Mention Detection and Preprocessing

We begin by describing the experimental setup related to the first two issues.

The first issue concerns how the performance of our resolver is affected by the quality of the mentions. Stoyanov et al. (2009) show that for English coreference, results obtained using gold mentions (i.e., mentions taken directly from gold-standard coreference annotations) are substantially better than those produced using system mentions (i.e., automatically extracted mentions). While we will explore gold mentions in our Chinese experiments, we seek to gain a better understanding of this issue by considering three types of system mentions. The first type, *system mentions from system parses with imperfect pruning*, is typically what researchers use to produce end-to-end coreference results. It is composed of mentions extracted from system parse trees (i.e., automatically generated parse trees) and pruned using the method described in Step 1 of Section 3. The second type, *system mentions from system parses with perfect pruning*, is the same as the first type except that an oracle is used to prune all the erroneous mentions. The third type, *system mentions from gold parses with imperfect pruning*, is the same as the first type except that the mentions are extracted from gold-standard parse trees. Experiments involving the last two types of mentions will enable us to determine the role of pruning and syntactic parsing in coreference resolution.

The second issue concerns the impact of preprocessing. In particular, we address two questions. First, to what extent will the performance of our resolver be affected if the linguistic features used to create the rules in the sieves are computed based on system rather than gold parse trees? Second, to what extent will its performance be affected if the features are computed based on system rather

	Feature Computation		MUC			B^3			$CEAF_e$			Avg
Mention Type	Parse Type	NE Type	R	P	F	R	P	F	R	P	F	F
System		System NEs	62.5	67.1	64.7	71.2	78.4	74.6	53.6	49.1	51.3	63.5
Mentions	System Parses	Gold NEs	62.2	67.0	64.5	71.0	78.6	74.6	53.5	48.9	51.1	63.4
from System		No NEs	59.9	64.7	62.2	69.7	77.8	73.6	53.4	48.7	51.0	62.2
Parses with		System NEs	62.4	67.2	64.8	71.0	78.4	74.6	53.8	49.0	51.3	63.5
Imperfect	Gold Parses	Gold NEs	62.2	67.2	64.6	70.8	78.7	74.5	53.7	48.8	51.1	63.4
Pruning		No NEs	60.0	65.0	62.4	69.6	77.9	73.5	53.5	48.7	51.0	62.3
System		System NEs	65.4	92.5	76.6	65.8	92.4	76.8	79.1	44.9	57.3	70.3
Mentions	System Parses	Gold NEs	65.4	92.6	76.7	65.6	92.7	76.8	79.2	44.9	57.3	70.3
from System		No NEs	64.3	91.6	75.6	64.3	92.2	75.8	78.8	44.4	56.8	69.4
Parses with		System NEs	65.5	92.6	76.7	65.9	92.4	76.9	79.2	45.0	57.4	70.3
Perfect	Gold Parses	Gold NEs	65.5	92.7	76.8	65.7	92.7	76.9	79.3	45.0	57.4	70.4
Pruning		No NEs	64.5	91.7	75.7	64.4	92.2	75.9	78.9	44.5	56.9	69.5
System		System NEs	73.5	74.3	73.9	76.3	80.5	78.3	58.2	57.3	57.8	70.0
Mentions	System Parses	Gold NEs	73.3	74.4	73.9	76.1	80.9	78.4	58.3	57.1	57.7	70.0
from Gold		No NEs	70.8	72.1	71.4	74.4	79.9	77.0	58.0	56.4	57.2	68.5
Parses with		System NEs	74.8	74.9	74.9	77.1	80.8	78.9	58.6	58.5	58.6	70.8
Imperfect	Gold Parses	Gold NEs	74.6	75.0	74.8	76.9	81.2	79.0	58.6	58.1	58.4	70.7
Pruning		No NEs	72.1	72.8	72.5	75.3	80.2	77.7	58.4	57.6	58.0	69.4
		System NEs	78.1	93.2	85.0	75.0	91.6	82.5	84.0	59.2	69.4	79.0
	System Parses	Gold NEs	78.1	93.4	85.0	74.8	92.0	82.5	84.2	59.1	69.4	79.0
Gold		No NEs	76.6	92.4	83.8	73.0	91.4	81.2	83.6	57.9	68.4	77.8
Mentions		System NEs	79.1	93.6	85.7	75.8	91.9	83.1	84.8	60.4	70.6	79.8
	Gold Parses	Gold NEs	79.2	93.7	85.8	75.7	92.3	83.2	84.9	60.5	70.6	79.9
		No NEs	77.9	92.9	84.7	74.0	91.7	81.9	84.3	59.5	69.7	78.8

Table 2: Impact of the quality of mentions, parse trees and NEs on coreference performance.

than gold NE information, and what if no NE information is used by the resolver?[2] We hypothesize that coreference performance will drop when gold parses and NEs are replaced with their system counterparts, since these two types of linguistic annotations are used extensively by the rules in our resolver: syntactic parses are used to identify copular and appositive constructions, find speakers in dialogue, and determine the modifier(s) of a mention, whereas NEs are used in the Chinese-specific abbreviation rules in the Precise Constructs sieve, the pronoun resolution rules (for computing the animacy of an NP), and some of the relaxed head matching rules in the Proper Head Match sieve.

Considering both issues together, we have 24 coreference experiments resulting from different combinations of four types of mentions (gold mentions and the three types of system mentions), two types of syntactic parse trees (gold and system), and three types of NE annotations (gold, system, and none). Table 2 shows the test results of these 24 experiments, which are organized as follows. There are four blocks of results corresponding to the four types of mentions (column 1); for each type of mentions, we conduct experiments using two types of parses (column 2) and three types of NEs (column 3). Hence, each row of the table corresponds to one of these 24 experiments. Results are reported in terms of the recall (R), precision (P), and F-score provided by three scoring programs (MUC, B^3, $CEAF_e$) as well as the unweighted average of their F-scores (Avg).

Comparing the first two blocks of results, which differ in terms of whether imperfect or perfect pruning is applied to system mentions extracted from system parses, we see that coreference results with perfect pruning surpass those with imperfect pruning by an Avg F-score of 6.8–7.2%. Not

[2]Two points concerning NE annotations deserve mention. First, when "no NE" is used, all the coreference rules that depend on NE information are removed from the sieves. We consider the "no NE" option because the use of NEs is not permitted in the official closed track evaluation in the shared task. Second, system NEs are not provided by the shared task organizers. To obtain system NEs for the development and test sets, we employ a CRF-based NE recognizer trained on the gold NEs in the training set using 18 lexical, semantic, and gazetteer-based features.

Mention Type	No Pruning R	No Pruning P	No Pruning F	Imperfect Pruning R	Imperfect Pruning P	Imperfect Pruning F	Perfect Pruning R	Perfect Pruning P	Perfect Pruning F
System mentions from system parses	86.1	33.0	47.7	83.5	43.7	57.4	86.1	100	92.5
System mentions from gold parses	98.7	36.6	53.4	96.3	48.9	64.8	98.7	100	99.3
Gold mentions	100	100	100	---	---	---	---	---	---

Table 3: Mention detection results.

surprisingly, improvements stem primarily from increases in precision according to MUC and B^3, since these pruned mentions will not be (erroneously) resolved.[3]

A related question is: how well does our pruning method perform at the mention detection level? To answer this question, we show in Table 3 the results of mention detection when different mention extraction methods are combined with different mention pruning methods. From row 1, we can see that our (imperfect) pruning method leaves a lot of room for improvement: currently it only yields a precision of 43.7%. However, row 1 also shows that our pruning method is somewhat useful: pruning increases precision by more than 10% with only a 3% drop in recall.

Conclusion 1: Improving the mention pruning algorithm can substantially improve coreference performance.

Comparing the first and third blocks of results, we see that coreference results obtained using mentions from gold parse trees surpass those obtained using mentions from system parse trees by an Avg F-score of 6.3−7.3%. Additional insights can be gained by considering the mention detection results in Table 3. From row 2, we can see that without pruning, we manage to recall 98.7% of the mentions from gold parse trees using our simple mention extraction heuristic. We believe that the high recall can be attributed to the fact that the manual coreference annotations in OntoNotes were performed on top of gold parse trees.

Conclusion 2: Improving the recall of mention detection can substantially improve coreference performance.

Note, however, that conclusion 2 does not necessarily hold true for other languages: Pradhan et al. (2012) found in their *gold mention boundaries* experiments that merely increasing the recall of mention detection does not lead to improvements in coreference performance for English and Arabic.[4] We hypothesize that this can be attributed to the failure of the resolution algorithm to find the correct antecedent in these languages despite the increase in the number of correct mentions. Additional experiments are needed to precisely determine the reason, however.

Comparing the third and fourth blocks of results, we see that coreference results obtained using gold mentions surpass those obtained using system mentions from gold parse trees by an Avg F-score of 9.0−9.4%. This improvement is accompanied by a simultaneous rise in recall and precision for MUC and B^3. This should not be surprising: precision increases because erroneous mentions are pruned and will not be resolved, and recall increases because mentions are more likely to be correctly resolved due to the reduction in the number of candidate antecedents.

Comparing the first and fourth blocks of results, the improvement is even more dramatic: coreference results obtained using gold mentions surpass those obtained using system mentions from system parse trees by an Avg F-score of 15.5−16.5%. An interesting question is: how much of this difference can be attributed to the *recall* versus the *precision* of our mention detector? We can answer this question by comparing the third and fourth blocks of results in Table 2 again. Row 2 of Table 3 says that 96.3% of the gold mentions are used when producing the third block of results

[3]Note that results obtained from $CEAF_e$ do not show the same trend as those from MUC and B^3 owing to the somewhat counterintuitive definitions of $CEAF_e$ recall and precision, but space limitations preclude further discussion.

[4]We repeated the experiments in Table 2 on the mentions with gold boundaries and obtained results that are identical to those of the system mentions obtained from system parses.

in Table 2. Hence, the difference between the third and fourth blocks of results in Table 2 can be attributed mostly to the *precision* of our mention detector. Returning to our question with this assumption, we can attribute approximately 58% of the difference (i.e., 9.0−9.4 of 15.5−16.5) to the precision of the mention detector and the remaining 42% to its recall.[5]

Conclusion 3: Improving both the recall and precision of mention detection can yield substantially better coreference performance than improving one of them.

Next, we examine how coreference performance varies when different types of parse trees and NEs are used for feature computations.[6] Regardless of which of the four types of mentions are used, we can see from Table 2 that (1) replacing gold parses with system parses and/or replacing gold NEs with system NEs for feature computations has little impact on coreference performance; (2) Avg F-score drops by 1.0−1.5% when NE information is not used. A closer examination of the results reveals that (1) NE information is particularly useful in establishing a mention and its abbreviated form; and (2) the insignificant difference between the results using gold NEs and those using system NEs can be attributed to the fact that our NE recognizer achieves reasonably good F-scores (80%) for PERSON and GPE, the NE classes that our resolver relies on.[7]

Conclusion 4: Improving syntactic parsing and NE recognition for the sake of feature computation is unlikely to improve coreference performance.

4.2 The Coreference Algorithm

Our next set of experiments aims to address three questions concerning our rule-based and learning-based coreference algorithm. All experiments in this subsection are performed with system mentions extracted from system parse trees, with features computed over system parses and NEs.

First, how important is the ordering of the sieves? Raghunathan et al. (2010) implicitly suggest that ordering matters by noting that the sieves should be arranged in decreasing order of precision, although they never show how important this particular ordering is to coreference performance. To answer this question, we randomly order the sieves in our resolver and measure the performance of the resulting resolver on the test set. Results averaged over five random orderings are shown in row 2 of Table 4. For convenience, the results of our unperturbed resolver are shown in row 1. As we can see, Avg F-score decreases significantly by 1.2% when the sieves are ordered randomly.

Conclusion 5: The ordering of the sieves in our resolver is important.

Second, how important is the learning component of our resolver? To answer this question, we remove all components of our resolver that are learning-based, including (1) the String Pair sieve; (2) the last condition of the non-coreference rule; and (3) learning-based mention pruning. Test results of the resulting resolver are shown in row 3 of Table 4. In comparison to row 1, Avg F-score drops significantly by 0.6%.

Conclusion 6: The learning component plays a significant role in our hybrid approach.

Finally, how much performance gain is provided by each sieve? To answer this question, we start with only the first sieve and then add the sieves incrementally to our resolver. The Avg F-score obtained after adding each sieve is shown in Table 5. As we can see, Chinese Head Match and Exact String Match contribute the most to performance, followed by Discourse Processing.

---

[5]Note that this estimation is very rough: it does not take into account the fact that it tends to be harder to get from, say, 80% F-score to 90% F-score than it is to get from 70% F-score to 80% F-score.

[6]Note that we distinguish between using parse trees for feature computations versus using them for mention extraction. Hence, we can compute features from system parses while extracting mentions from gold parses.

[7]All statistical significance test results in this paper are obtained using the paired t-test, with $p < 0.05$.

	MUC			B^3			$CEAF_e$			Avg
System Variation	R	P	F	R	P	F	R	P	F	F
Our resolver	62.5	67.1	64.7	71.2	78.4	74.6	53.6	49.1	51.3	63.5
With randomly ordered sieves	60.8	65.5	63.1	69.9	77.2	73.3	52.8	48.2	50.4	62.3
Without learning	61.6	66.7	64.1	70.4	78.2	74.1	53.2	48.3	50.6	62.9

Table 4: Results on perturbing the components of our resolver.

Sieve	CHM	DP	ESM	PC	SHMA	SHMB	SHMC	PHM	Pro	SP
Avg F	32.6	39.0	56.8	58.2	58.9	59.7	59.7	59.8	63.3	63.5

Table 5: Avg F-scores of our resolver as sieves are incrementally inserted.

	MUC			B^3			$CEAF_e$			Avg
	R	P	F	R	P	F	R	P	F	F
Our resolver	62.5	67.1	64.7	71.2	78.4	74.6	53.6	49.1	51.3	63.5
MP (atomic features)	56.7	54.2	55.4	71.2	70.0	70.6	41.9	44.0	42.9	56.3
MP (atomic features + non-coreference)	56.2	55.3	55.7	70.6	71.1	70.8	42.7	43.5	43.1	56.5
MP (rules as features)	55.1	62.8	58.7	66.4	78.4	71.9	52.3	45.2	48.5	59.7
MP (rules as features + non-coreference)	54.8	63.9	59.0	66.0	79.4	72.1	53.2	44.8	48.6	59.9

Table 6: Comparison of our resolver with the mention-pair model.

4.3 Comparison with the Mention-Pair Model

Our final set of experiments aims to compare our resolver with the MP model. To implement the MP model, we use SVM^{light} (Joachims, 1999) for classifier training with the instances created using Soon et al.'s (2001) method. We then apply the resulting classifier in combination with Soon et al.'s closest-first clustering algorithm to create a coreference partition for each test document.

For a fairer comparison, both models are given the same set of mentions (i.e., system mentions extracted from system parse trees). To ensure that they are given the same set of features, we experiment with two methods of creating features for the MP model from the coreference rules used by our resolver. In the first method, we create one binary feature from each rule used in the sieves, setting its value to 1 if and only if the corresponding rule was used to establish a coreference link between the two mentions in our resolver. In the second method, we create one binary feature from each distinct *rule condition*[8]; employing these *atomic* features will enable us to determine whether the difference in performance between our resolver and the MP model can be attributed to the way the SVM combines features. Recall that our resolver also employs lexical features and the non-coreference rule. To ensure fairness, we incorporate lexical features into the MP model's feature set by creating one binary feature from each head, head pair and string pair found in the training data. In addition, we employ the non-coreference rule as a hard constraint for the closest-first clustering algorithm: the clustering algorithm cannot posit two mentions as coreferent if they satisfy the non-coreference rule, even if the classifier posits them as coreferent.

Given two feature generation methods and a choice of whether the non-coreference constraint is applied in the clustering process, we have four experiments with the MP model. Their results are shown in rows 2–5 of Table 6, and the results of our resolver are shown in row 1 for convenience. As we can see, our resolver is significantly better than the MP models that use rules as features, which in turn are significantly better than those that use atomic features. However, the use of the non-coreference constraint has an insignificant impact on the performance of the MP model.

Conclusion 7: The SVM used to train the MP model is unable to combine features as well as a human.

[8]Recall that each rule is of the form $A_1 \wedge A_2 \wedge \cdots A_n$, where each A_i is a condition that needs to be satisfied in order for the rule to posit two mentions as coreferent. If A_i appears in multiple rules, only one binary feature will be created.

Acknowledgments

We thank the three anonymous reviewers for their invaluable comments on an earlier draft of the paper. This work was supported in part by NSF Grants IIS-1147644 and IIS-1219142.

References

Chen, C. and Ng, V. (2012). Combining the best of two worlds: A hybrid approach to multilingual coreference resolution. In *Proceedings of the 2012 Joint Conference on Empirical Methods in Natural Language Processing and Computational Natural Language Learning: Shared Task*, pages 56–63.

Haghighi, A. and Klein, D. (2009). Simple coreference resolution with rich syntactic and semantic features. In *Proceedings of the 2009 Conference on Empirical Methods in Natural Language Processing*, pages 1152–1161.

Joachims, T. (1999). Making large-scale SVM learning practical. In Scholkopf, B. and Smola, A., editors, *Advances in Kernel Methods - Support Vector Learning*, pages 44–56. MIT Press.

Lee, H., Peirsman, Y., Chang, A., Chambers, N., Surdeanu, M., and Jurafsky, D. (2011). Stanford's multi-pass sieve coreference resolution system at the CoNLL-2011 shared task. In *Proceedings of the Fifteenth Conference on Computational Natural Language Learning: Shared Task*, pages 28–34.

Pradhan, S., Moschitti, A., Xue, N., Uryupina, O., and Zhang, Y. (2012). CoNLL-2012 shared task: Modeling multilingual unrestricted coreference in OntoNotes. In *Proceedings of the 2012 Joint Conference on Empirical Methods in Natural Language Processing and Computational Natural Language Learning: Shared Task*, pages 1–40.

Raghunathan, K., Lee, H., Rangarajan, S., Chambers, N., Surdeanu, M., Jurafsky, D., and Manning, C. (2010). A multi-pass sieve for coreference resolution. In *Proceedings of the 2010 Conference on Empirical Methods in Natural Language Processing*, pages 492–501.

Rahman, A. and Ng, V. (2011a). Coreference resolution with world knowledge. In *Proceedings of the 49th Annual Meeting of the Association for Computational Linguistics: Human Language Technologies*, pages 814–824.

Rahman, A. and Ng, V. (2011b). Narrowing the modeling gap: A cluster-ranking approach to coreference resolution. *Journal of Artificial Intelligence Research*, 40:469–521.

Soon, W. M., Ng, H. T., and Lim, D. C. Y. (2001). A machine learning approach to coreference resolution of noun phrases. *Computational Linguistics*, 27(4):521–544.

Stoyanov, V., Gilbert, N., Cardie, C., and Riloff, E. (2009). Conundrums in noun phrase coreference resolution: Making sense of the state-of-the-art. In *Proceedings of the Joint Conference of the 47th Annual Meeting of the ACL and the 4th International Joint Conference on Natural Language Processing of the AFNLP*, pages 656–664.

Linguistic and Statistical Traits Characterising Plagiarism

Miranda Chong[1] *Lucia Specia*[2]
(1) University of Wolverhampton, Stafford Street, Wolverhampton, WV1 1SB UK
(2) University of Sheffield, 211 Portobello, Sheffield, S1 4DP UK
miranda.chong@wlv.ac.uk, l.specia@sheffield.ac.uk

ABSTRACT
This paper investigates the problem of distinguishing between original and rewritten text materials, with focus on the application of plagiarism detection. The hypothesis is that original texts and rewritten texts exhibit significant and measurable differences, and that these can be captured through statistical and linguistic indicators. We propose and analyse a number of these indicators (including language models, syntactic trees, etc.) using machine learning algorithms in two main settings: (i) the classification of individual text segments as original or rewritten, and (ii) the ranking of two or more versions of a text segment according to their "originality", thus rendering the rewriting direction. Different from standard plagiarism detection approaches, our settings do not involve comparisons between supposedly rewritten text and (a large number of) original texts. Instead, our work focuses on the sub-problem of finding segments that exhibit rewriting traits. Identifying such segments has a number of potential applications, from a first-stage filtering for standard plagiarism detection approaches, to intrinsic plagiarism detection and authorship identification. The corpus used in the experiments was extracted from the PAN-PC-10 plagiarism detection task, with two subsets containing manually and artificially generated plagiarism cases. The accuracies achieved are well above a by chance baseline across datasets and settings, with the statistical indicators being particularly effective.

KEYWORDS: Text Reuse, Plagiarism Detection, Plagiarism Direction.

Proceedings of COLING 2012: Posters, pages 195–204,
COLING 2012, Mumbai, December 2012.

1 Introduction

Current studies in plagiarism detection are mostly focused on the detection of plagiarised segments in a collection of documents or within a document. The direction of plagiarism is thus predetermined. Original documents and plagiarised documents are provided separately and the task is to determine which segments of plagiarised texts (if any) are copied or rewritten from which segments of original texts. This is generally done through a large number of pairwise comparisons: the "suspicious" text is compared against original texts using similarity metrics, which are mostly based on word overlap.

To date, very superficial metrics such as n-gram matching achieve the state of the art performance on verbatim plagiarism cases. While this is a perfectly reasonable approach for plagiarism detection, it has some limitations. Firstly, pairwise comparisons in large collections are computationally very expensive and in practice very simple filtering strategies are used to rule out most of the original texts. Secondly, for real-world, open data collections such as the web, pairwise comparisons may be less reliable. It is not uncommon to find multiple versions of a plagiarised material on the web, and thus the concept of an "original" text becomes less clear.

This study looks at the plagiarism practice from a novel perspective: instead of measuring the similarity between pairs of texts, the goal is to investigate traits that distinguish original from rewritten texts based on examples of both types of texts. We make use of machine learning algorithms and exploit a number of linguistically and statistically-motivated features – e.g. statistical language models, syntactic trees and features from *translationese* studies – to (i) determine whether an individual text segment is original or plagiarised, and (ii) determine the direction of plagiarism, that is, rank a pair of texts according to their originality. This approach requires observing patterns of features in individual texts, without any direct comparison between texts.

2 Related Work

Research on distinguishing original from plagiarised texts is very limited. The only existing work analyses character 16-grams on artificially generated plagiarised documents from the PAN-PC-10 corpus (Grozea and Popescu, 2010). These plagiarism cases are generated via automatic means with various obfuscation levels through the insertion, deletion, replacement of words, and other simple operations. At document level, overall accuracies reached about 75%. Tests on highly obfuscated artificial documents reached an accuracy of 69.77%. This analysis has indicated that there seem to be significant differences between original and plagiarised texts in the PAN corpus. However, given the way the artificial plagiarism cases were produced, this finding is somehow trivial. To the best of the authors' knowledge, no research has been done on the more challenging cases of manually plagiarised documents, nor at the level of segments, as opposed to documents.

Considering translation as a process of text rewriting (in a different language), studies on *translationese* (i.e. on distinguishing original from translated texts in a given language) and on detecting translation direction in a bilingual pair of texts are also relevant for this work. Most work in this area follows the *Translation Universals* theory (Gellerstam, 1986), which hypothesises that translated texts tend to exhibit characteristics that are different from non-translated texts. The theory was further explored by (Baker, 1993, 1996) and based on such a theory, research has been done for identifying specific properties that reflect these universals and using them to automatically test these universals. For example, on a corpus of original (non-translated) and translated texts in Italian, (Baroni and Bernardini, 2006) finds that features such as the distribution of function words, personal pronouns and adverbs are very relevant. (Pastor et al., 2008) explored the existence of the *simplification* universal – which states that translated texts are simpler than their source counterpart –, suggesting that this universal does affect Spanish translated texts. Also focusing on the simplification universal, the studies by (Ilisei et al., 2010; Ilisei and Inkpen, 2011) on Romanian and Spanish translationese use morphological and simplification-based features.

A six-lingual study by (Halteren, 2008) using frequencies of word n-grams shows that it is possible to distinguish between translated and non-translated texts down to their respective original languages. This is followed by the work of (Lembersky et al., 2011, 2012) which uses statistical language models for each language. Furthermore, a study by (Volansky et al., 2012) explores the differences between original, manually translated and machine translated texts.

The experiments on translation direction identification suggest that translated texts have lower lexical richness and higher number of frequent words. They point out that simplification-based features are very helpful, but alone they are not sufficient to distinguish original from translated texts. Although by nature plagiarised texts are very different from translated texts, we exploit insights gained from these and other related studies in the features we use, including many of the simplification-based features.

3 Methodology and Experimental Settings

A supervised machine learning approach is proposed to test the hypothesis that original and plagiarised texts exhibit significant and measurable differences. We build models based on various linguistically and statistically-motivated features. The models are tested on manually simulated and artificially generated plagiarism cases. Each case consists of a segment of text. Well-known machine learning algorithms are used for two tasks: binary classification and ranking. These two variations of the approach are evaluated in the same way: computing the accuracy of each algorithm in categorising segments as original or plagiarised.

3.1 Corpus

This study uses the PAN-PC-10 plagiarism detection task corpus (Potthast et al., 2010), which comprises books from the Project Gutenberg.[1] Two datasets were extracted from this corpus, as shown in Table 1. The segments are extracted according to the annotation provided in the corpus: pre-defined labels for manually simulated and artificial plagiarism sequences of words.

The *Artificial Dataset* is composed of a randomly selected subset of plagiarised texts that were generated automatically by three types of edits: (i) a set of text operations, which include replacing, shuffling, removing or inserting words at random, (ii) semantic word variations by replacing words by similar or related words (such as synonyms), and (iii) POS-preserving word shuffling, which shuffles words at random but keeps the same ordering of part-of-speech tags. The *Simulated Dataset* is composed of all the manually simulated plagiarised segments available in the corpus. The plagiarism cases were manually written using mechanical turks to simulate plagiarism by paraphrasing the original texts.

Given the way the artificial dataset was created, it is expected that our approach will perform significantly better on this dataset, while the simulated dataset represents a much more challenging, but more realistic, problem.

[1] http://www.gutenberg.org

	Statistics	Simulated Dataset	Artificial Dataset
Original texts	Number of segments	4067	4000
	Minimum length	74 words	46 words
	Maximum length	745 words	4506 words
	Average length	409.5 words	2276 words
Plagiarised texts	Number of segments	4067	4000
	Minimum length	21 words	38 words
	Maximum length	1190 words	3917 words
	Average length	605.5 words	1977.5 words

Table 1: Corpus statistics

3.2 Machine learning algorithms

In the **binary classification task** the goal is to assign each instance in the collection to one of the two classes: *original* or *plagiarised*. In the **ranking task**, the goal is to sort two (or potentially more) versions of a segment according to the order in which they were created, in other words, to identify the plagiarism direction.

The algorithms applied here are as follow: the rule-based learner Repeated Incremental Pruning to Produce Error Reduction (RIPPER) for binary classification and Support Vector Machines (SVM) for ranking. RIPPER[2] was selected as a good representative of symbolic classifiers: the rules produced can help identify relevant features for specific cases. SVM is one of the most robust and best performing algorithms in many language processing tasks. For ranking, the SVMrank algorithm[3] (Joachims, 2006) is used with a linear kernel. Both classification and ranking models are trained and tested using 4-fold cross-validation. In addition, a structured prediction version of SVM was applied as an alternative binary classifier: SVM-light-TK[4] (Moschitti, 2006), wich uses tree kernels with (partial) syntactic trees as features.

3.3 Feature extraction and selection

The datasets are pre-processed with sentence segmentation, tokenisation and lowercasing. The part-of-speech (POS) tags and lemmas of words and the syntactic trees of sentences are generated using the Stanford CoreNLP toolkit[5] (Klein and Manning, 2003). Pre-defined lists of function words (Koppel and Ordan, 2011) and stopwords[6] are used.

N-gram language models (with n = 3 & 5) are built using the KenLM toolkit[7] (Heafield, 2011). The corpus used to build such models consisted in a random selection of 1.7M segments extracted from the entire "original" collection of the PAN-PC-10 corpus, excluding all the documents containing one or more segments present in our two datasets. We then use these language models to calculate the scores for both plagiarised and original segments.

Features that capture simplification, morphological, statistical and syntactic aspects of texts are investigated. Based on the simplification universal, we extract the following **simplification-based features**:

[2]We used the Jrip Weka implementation of this algorithm: `http://www.cs.waikato.ac.nz/ml/weka/`
[3]`http://www.cs.cornell.edu/people/tj/svm_light/svm_rank.html`
[4]`http://disi.unitn.it/moschitti/Tree-Kernel.htm`
[5]`http://nlp.stanford.edu/software/corenlp.shtml`
[6]`http://nltk.org/`
[7]`http://kheafield.com/code/kenlm/`

1. Average token length: number of characters normalised by the number of tokens.
2. Average sentence length: average number of tokens in all sentences of the segment.
3. Information load: proportion of lexical words to tokens. Lexical words refer to nouns, verbs, adjectives, adverbs and numerals.
4. Lexical variety: type/token ratio obtained by normalising the word types over all words.
5. Lexical richness: proportion of type lemmas per tokens. Different from lexical variety, lexical richness considers the lemmatised word types normalised by all words.
6. Proportion of sentences without finite verbs.
7. Proportion of simple sentences: sentences that contain only one finite verb.
8. Proportion of complex sentences: sentences that contain more than one finite verb.

To capture plagiarism traits that may occur at the **morphological** level, the following features are extracted:

9. Proportion of nouns over tokens.
10. Proportion of prepositions over tokens.
11. Proportion of pronouns over tokens.
12. Proportion of stopwords over tokens.
13. Proportion of finite verbs over tokens.
14. Grammatical cohesion rate: proportion of grammatical words over lexical words. Grammatical words are determiners, articles, prepositions, auxiliary verbs, pronouns, conjunctions and interjections.
15. Individual function words: each function word in the pre-defined list is extracted as an individual feature, such as "the", "of", "and", "to", "be", "someone", "self" etc.
16. Proportion of function words in texts: number of function words over word tokens.

The following shallow **statistical features** are proposed:

17. Number of sentences in the segment.
18. Number of tokens in the segment.
19. Number of characters in the segment.
20. Language model 3-gram log probability.
21. Language model 3-gram perplexity (all tokens).
22. Language model 3-gram perplexity (without end of sentence tags).
23. Language model 5-gram log probability.
24. Language model 5-gram perplexity (all tokens).
25. Language model 5-gram perplexity (without end of sentence tags).

Finally, from a more linguistically motivated perspective, (partial) syntactic trees are used with the tree-kernel algorithm (the other algorithms do not allow structured features):

26. Syntactic trees: dependency-based parse trees for all sentences in the segments.

4 Results and Discussion

The baseline results are defined according to the distribution of the two classes in the datasets, which is 50:50. Therefore, the baseline accuracy is 50%. The machine learning algorithms described in Section 3.2 are used with different feature sets as shown in Table 2, along with the results for each combination of algorithm and feature set.

With respect to the algorithms, the comparison shows that the rule-based classification (RIPPER) and the ranking (SVM-rank) algorithms using pre-selected features perform very similarly, and well above the by chance classifier, with the rule-based algorithm doing slightly better. The precision, recall and f-score of the feature sets with RIPPER are given in Table 3.

The *pre-selected* feature set contains the top 12 features ranked according to their Information Gain computed on the training set: F2, F3, F6, F13, F14, F19, F20, F21, F22, F23, F24, F25. These features include some morphological, statistical and simplification indicators, showing that these feature families are complementary. The improvement using these features over the set of all features is not consistent across datasets.

Algorithm	Feature set	Simulated	Artificial
Baseline: by chance	-	50%	50%
RIPPER	All	74.67%	98.15%
RIPPER	Pre-selected	75.66%	97.94%
RIPPER	Simplification-based	59.81%	70.24%
RIPPER	Morphological	59.53%	68.08%
RIPPER	Statistical	74.17%	97.78%
SVM-rank	Pre-selected	74%	95%
SVM-tree kernels	Syntactic	56.17%	79.9%

Table 2: Accuracy of algorithms and feature sets in classifying cases as "original" or "plagiarised"

Dataset	Class	Feature set	Precision	Recall	F-score
Simulated	Original	Pre-selected	75.8%	75.4%	75.6%
		Statistical	73.6%	75.5%	74.5%
		Simplification-based	59.9%	59.4%	59.7%
		Morphological	59.8%	58.2%	59%
	Plagiarised	Pre-selected	75.5%	75.9%	75.7%
		Statistical	74.8%	72.9%	73.8%
		Simplification-based	59.7%	60.2%	60%
		Morphological	59.3%	60.8%	60%
Artificial	Original	Pre-selected	98.4%	97.5%	97.9%
		Statistical	97.8%	97.7%	97.8%
		Simplification-bases	67.8%	72.2%	72.2%
		Morphological	66.1%	74.1%	69.9%
	Plagiarised	Pre-selected	97.5%	98.4%	97.9%
		Statistical	97.7%	97.8%	97.8%
		Simplification-based	73.5%	63.3%	68%
		Morphological	70.5%	62.1%	66%

Table 3: Precision, recall and f-score of various feature sets using RIPPER

On the comparison between the features sets, it was observed that using statistical features alone yields nearly the same performance as using all features. Features involving language models are amongst the best performing. Statistical features performed significantly better in the Artificial Dataset. The relative improvement of these features in the Simulated Dataset over simplification or morphological features is 14%. In the Artificial Dataset, the relative improvement over the other features is 27%. Morphological, simplification and syntactic features are not as discriminative on their own, but their performance is well above the baseline. Interestingly, tree kernels on the Artificial Dataset performs significantly better than tree kernels on the Simulated Dataset with respect to the baseline. This may be a consequence of the fact that artificial cases consistently exhibit malformed syntax, which makes it easier for syntactic features to capture relevant distinctions.

4.1 Discussion and examples

Across all experiments with different algorithms and feature sets, the problem of identifying artificially generated plagiarism cases proved significantly easier than that of identifying manually plagiarised cases. Given the nature of the operations applied to generate artificial cases, this result is not surprising. Nevertheless, the near-100% performance for these cases is a very positive result. It shows that this approach can be used for the filtering of candidates in a real plagiarism detection system, one of the applications suggested in this paper.

It is arguable that the experiments above show only a marginal gain from using a combination of simplification, morphological and statistical methods with respect using simple statistical features. Although previous studies have also pointed out that statistical features are generally relevant for related problems, confirming this finding for the specific problem we address is an interesting contribution of this study.

With respect to the novel, linguistically motivated features suggested here, they perform well on artificially generated texts, which exhibit a considerable proportion of ungrammatical constructions. Along with statistical features, these may help future work in identifying not only the existence and direction of plagiarism, but also several types or levels of plagiarism.

We found no strong evidence that the simplification universal applies to plagiarism. Although some simplification-based features do seem relevant, they could be interpreted from different perspectives, which are not necessarily related to simplification.

A closer inspection on some examples of pairs of segments is given below.

Example 1: Correctly classified pair of cases by SVM-rank and SVM-tree kernels from the *Simulated Dataset*

Original: But a better idea of the journal can perhaps be given, by stating what it lacked than what it then contained. It had no leaders, no parliamentary reports, and very little indeed, in any shape, that could be termed political news.

Plagiarised: The journal could better be described by what was missing than what it contained. It lacked leaders, had no parliamentary reports and in no way could be described as political news.

In this example, we speculate that in addition to the strong features throughout all instances (the language model features), others contributed to classify this pair. They include the average sentence length, number of characters, and independent clause rate. For example, the average sentence length for the plagiarised text is lower than the original text. Also, the proportion of nouns is higher in the original text and the lexical richness is lower in the plagiarised text. These clues suggest that the simplification traits were good indicators in this particular case.

Example 2: Incorrectly classified pair of cases by SVM-rank and SVM-tree kernels from the *Simulated Dataset*

Original: There is a great gain in time of acceleration and for stopping, and for the Boston terminal it was estimated that with electricity 50 per cent, more traffic could be handled, as the headway could be reduced from three to two minutes.

Plagiarised: There is a huge profit in time of speeding up and for slowing down, and for the Boston extremity it was guessed that with current 50 percent, more movement could be lifted, as the headway could be minimised from three to two minutes.

Example 2 does not contain any simplification traits but only synonym substitution. The shallow statistical features failed to identify any differences between the two segments. The length of both texts is virtually the same and they are both equally fluent. Morphological and syntactic features did not perform well either. The proportion of grammatical and lexical words remains the same, and the word order and syntactic structure in both texts is the same.

Example 3: Incorrectly classified pair of cases by SVM-rank, but correctly classified by SVM-tree kernels from the *Artificial Dataset*

Original: "Giulietta," at last said the young man, earnestly, when he found her accidentally standing alone by the parapet, "I must be going to-morrow." "Well, what is that to me?" said Giulietta, looking wickedly from under her eyelashes.

Plagiarised: "well, what is that to me?" said Giulietta, standing alone under the parapet, earnestly, when he found her were accidentally looking wickedly from by her eyelashes. "Giulietta," at last young the man, "I must be going to-morrow.

Example 3 involves shuffling of sequences of words. As both texts kept the same words and length, none of the statistical, morphological and simplification features were able to distinguish the two. On the other hand, SVM-tree kernels correctly classified these cases according to their subtrees structure. This suggests that syntactic clues should be considered especially when all other features fail.

Conclusions

This paper presented a study on the underexplored area of distinguishing original from reused text segments, with application to plagiarism detection. A number of statistical and linguistic indicators were explored using a supervised machine learning approach to distinguish between original and plagiarised texts, as well as to rank pairs of original-plagiarised texts according to the order in which they were created. Overall, the study showed that original and reused texts exhibit distinguishable traits. It thus confirms our hypothesis that original texts and plagiarised texts exhibit significant differences and that these are measurable via computational means.

The findings of this study can be directly used to improve the filtering performed prior to more complex comparisons in plagiarism detection approaches. It can also be used to improve intrinsic plagiarism detection and authorship attribution. In addition, this study lays the foundation for further research on text reuse, as it can be expanded to cover multiple versions of the same text, as well as cross-lingual text reuse.

We plan to further investigate this problem in a number of directions, including the use of other types of rewritten texts, such as news, with potentially more than one version for each original text, as well as different levels of text reuse (as in (Clough et al., 2002)).

References

Baker, M. (1993). *Corpus Linguistics and Translation Studies: Implications and Applications*. John Benjamins, Amsterdam.

Baker, M. (1996). *Corpus-based Translation Studies: The Challenges that Lie Ahead*. John Benjamins, Amsterdam.

Baroni, M. and Bernardini, S. (2006). A new approach to the study of translationese: Machine-learning the difference between original and translated text. *Literary and Linguistic Computing*, 21(3):259–274.

Clough, P., Gaizauskas, R., Piao, S., and Wilks, Y. (2002). Meter: Measuring text reuse. In *Proceedings of the 40th Annual Meeting on Association for Computational Linguistics*, pages 152–159. Association for Computational Linguistics.

Gellerstam, M. (1986). *Translationese in Swedish novels translated from English*. CWK Gleerup.

Grozea, C. and Popescu, M. (2010). Who's the thief ? automatic detection of the direction of plagiarism. *Lecture Notes in Computer Science*, 6008:700–710.

Halteren, H. V. (2008). Source language markers in europarl translations. In *Proceedings of the 22nd International Conference on Computational Linguistics (Coling 2008)*, number August, pages 937–944, Manchester, UK.

Heafield, K. (2011). Kenlm: Faster and smaller language model queries. In *Proceedings of the EMNLP 2011 Sixth Workshop on Statistical Machine Translation*, number 2009, pages 187–197, Edinburgh, UK.

Ilisei, I. and Inkpen, D. (2011). Translationese traits in romanian newspapers: A machine learning approach. *International Journal of Computational Linguistics and Applications*, 2.

Ilisei, I., Inkpen, D., Pastor, G. C., and Mitkov, R. (2010). Identification of translationese: A machine learning approach. In *11th International Conference on Intelligent Text Processing and Computational Linguistics*, pages 503–511, Iaşi, Romania.

Joachims, T. (2006). Training linear svms in linear time. In *Proceedings of the 12th ACM SIGKDD international conference on Knowledge discovery and data mining - KDD '06*, pages 217–226, Philadelphia, USA. ACM Press.

Klein, D. and Manning, C. (2003). Accurate unlexicalized parsing. In *Proceedings of the 41st Meeting of the Association for Computational Linguistics*, pages 423–430, Sapporo, Japa.

Koppel, M. and Ordan, N. (2011). Translationese and its dialects. In *Proceedings of the 49th Annual Meeting of the Association for Computational Linguistics: Human Language Technologies*, volume 1, pages 1318–1326, Portland, USA.

Lembersky, G., Ordan, N., and Wintner, S. (2011). Language models for machine translation: original vs. translated texts. In *Proceedings of the 2011 Conference on Empirical Methods in Natural Language Processing (EMNLP 2011)*, pages 363–374, Edinburgh, Scotland.

Lembersky, G., Ordan, N., and Wintner, S. (2012). Adapting translation models to translationese improves smt. In *Proceedings of the 13th Conference of the European Chapter of the Association for Computational Linguistics (EACL 2012)*, pages 255–265, Avignon, France.

Moschitti, A. (2006). Making tree kernels practical for natural language learning. In *In Proceedings of the 11th Conference of the European Chapter of the Association for Computational Linguistics*, Trento, Italy.

Pastor, G., Mitkov, R., Afzal, N., and Pekar, V. (2008). Translation universals: do they exist? a corpus-based nlp study of convergence and simplification. In *Proceedings of the Eighth Conference of the Association for Machine Translation in the Americas (AMTA-08)*, number October, pages 21–25, Waikiki, Hawaii.

Potthast, M., Stein, B., Barrón-Cedeño, A., and Rosso, P. (2010). An evaluation framework for plagiarism detection. In *Proceedings of the 23rd International Conference on Computational Linguistics*, pages 997–1005, Beijing, China. Association for Computational Linguistics.

Volansky, V., Ordan, N., and Wintner, S. (2012). More human or more translated ? original texts vs . human and machine translations. In *11th Bar-Ilan Symposium on the Foundations of Artificial Intelligence*, Ramat Gan, Israel.

Impact of Less Skewed Distributions on Efficiency and Effectiveness of Biomedical Relation Extraction

Md. Faisal Mahbub Chowdhury[1,2] Alberto Lavelli[2]
(1) Fondazione Bruno Kessler (FBK-irst), via Sommarive 18, I-38100 Povo, Trento, Italy
(2) University of Trento, via Sommarive 5, I-38123 Povo, Trento, Italy
chowdhury@fbk.eu, lavelli@fbk.eu

Abstract

Like in other NLP tasks, it has been claimed that advances of machine learning (ML) based approaches to relation extraction (RE) are hampered by the imbalanced distribution of positive and negative instances in the annotated training data. Usually, the number of negative instances is much larger than that of the positive ones and such skewness also exists in the test data. In this paper, we aim at addressing the problem of imbalanced distribution by automatically curbing *less informative* negative instances. We propose some criteria for identifying such instances and incorporate them in an existing state-of-the-art RE approach. Empirical results on 5 benchmark biomedical corpora show that our proposed approach improves both recall and F_1 scores. At the same time, there is a large drop in the number of negative instances and in execution runtime as well.

Title and Abstract in Italian

L'Impatto di Distribuzioni Meno Squilibrate sull'Efficienza e l'Efficacia dell'Estrazione di Relazioni Biomediche

Come per altri compiti di Trattamento Automatico del Linguaggio, si è sostenuto che i progressi degli approcci all'estrazione di relazioni basati su apprendimento automatico sono ostacolati dalla distribuzione squilibrata dei casi positivi e negativi nei dati di addestramento annotati. Generalmente, il numero di istanze negative è molto più grande del numero di quelli positivi e tale squilibrio esiste anche nei dati di test. In questo articolo, ci si propone di affrontare il problema della distribuzione squilibrata eliminando automaticamente le istanze negative *meno informative*. Proponiamo alcuni criteri per individuare tali casi e inserirli in un approccio all'estrazione di relazioni con prestazioni allo stato dell'arte. I risultati empirici su 5 corpora biomedici di riferimento mostrano che l'approccio proposto migliora sia la recall sia il punteggio di F_1. Allo stesso tempo, c'è una diminuzione nel numero di istanze negative e anche nel tempo di esecuzione.

Keywords: Relation Extraction, Imbalanced Distribution, Skewed Distribution, Machine Learning, Biomedical Text Mining, Protein-Protein Interaction.

Keywords in Italian: Estrazione di Relazioni, Distribuzione non Equilibrata, Distribuzione Asimmetrica, Apprendimento Automatico, Text Mining Biomedico, Interazioni proteina-proteina.

Proceedings of COLING 2012: Posters, pages 205–216,
COLING 2012, Mumbai, December 2012.

1 Introduction

The imbalance between negative and positive annotated training instances in machine learning (ML) based approaches is a known issue. Previous studies have empirically shown that unbalanced datasets lead to poor performance for the minority class (Weiss and Provost, 2001). Apart from some exceptions, the number of negative instances is usually higher than that of the positive instances. As Gliozzo et al. (2005) argued, in most cases the error rate of a classifier trained on a skewed dataset is typically very low for the majority class and this results in biased estimation (Kotsiantis and Pintelas, 2003) and suboptimal classification performance (Chawla et al., 2004).

Some ML techniques have built-in mechanisms to deal with the skewness in somewhat limited scope[1]. But, according to the empirical results (obtained using SVM) presented in this paper, this might not guarantee to overcome completely the impact of skewness. Some ML algorithms (e.g. kNN) do instance pruning during training while maintaining the generalization accuracy. However, the main drawback of such techniques is the increased time complexity, which is generally quadratic in the data set size, without any guarantee of performance improvement (Gliozzo et al., 2005).

There exist some works in NLP that deal with the problem of skewed data distribution. For example, in the context of named entity recognition (NER), stopword filtering is used to reduce the number of candidate tokens to be considered as target entities (Gliozzo et al., 2005; Giuliano et al., 2006b). In the context of relation extraction (RE), recently Sun et al. (2011) adopted the strategy of discarding any pair of mentions proposed as candidate instance if they were separated by more than two other mentions. They conducted their experiments on news domain texts. However, the increment/decrement of performance due to such filtering was not reported.

In this paper to improve RE system's performance we have tried to reduce skewness in data by automatically identifying and removing what we call *"less informative"* instances[2]. In particular, we aim at explicitly addressing the following questions through empirical investigation:

1. Would reducing skewness in data distribution through negative instance reduction really lead to better RE results?
2. If the answer is 'yes', then can we achieve such goal by randomly discarding negative instances? Or, do we need to define an automatic methodology for singling out less informative instances?
3. To what extent could the data skewness and the efficiency (i.e. runtime) be reduced? Would the reduction of skewness help to train a better ML model/classifier?

The task chosen for our experiments is Protein–Protein Interaction (PPI) extraction from scientific papers, a widely investigated topic in biomedical RE. We adopt a state-of-the-art PPI extraction approach as a baseline system for our experiments and apply various techniques to reduce the number of negative instances being considered. We show that, by discarding less informative instances, it is possible to improve both efficiency and effectiveness of the system.

The remaining of this paper is organized as follows. First, Section 2 includes a brief discussion of the related work. Then in Section 3, we describe the data used in our experiments. Section 4 provides details about the baseline RE method used for the experiments. Following that, in Sections 5 and 6, we discuss our proposed approach. Empirical results are presented in Section 7. Finally, we summarize our work and discuss future directions.

[1] E.g., SVM allows to provide a cost-factor by which training errors on positive instances outweigh errors on the negatives.

[2] These are groups of instances that share some common characteristics and whose exclusion results in better performance.

2 Background

In Section 1, we have briefly discussed the problem of skewness of positive and negative instances in annotated data and mentioned some of the works in NLP on reducing such skewness. Due to space limitation, we cannot discuss other related NLP works not focussed on RE.[3] Previous studies (e.g. Sun et al. (2011)) hypothesized (without providing empirical evidence) that unbalanced distribution of instances is an obstacle for further improving the performance of RE.

Ideally, before reducing skewness of instances, informativeness of both positive and negative instances should be taken on account. In their seminal work regarding selection of features and instances Blum and Langley (1997) pointed out that as learning progresses and the learner's knowledge about certain parts of the training data increases, the remaining data which are similar to the already "well-understood" portion become less useful.

Our goal is to get rid of such instances from the training data prior to training the ML classifier to reduce imbalance in instance distribution and obtain a more accurately learned model/classifier. Ideally, a well trained classifier is expected to successfully identify all negative test instances. But, in practice, sometimes it would mistakenly label some of the negative instances as *(false) positives*. So, we also want to automatically get rid of as many (true) negative instances as possible from the test data (before applying the learned classifier) using the same knowledge used to reduce skewness in training data. Hopefully this would reduce the number of *false positives* produced by the classifier.

Different techniques are employed in open domain IE[4] for filtering irrelevant data to construct datasets. For example, whether the semantic type of the retrieved entity mentions and that of the target mentions are the same[5], or the number of words between the candidate mentions is greater than a certain limit, etc (Banko et al., 2007; Wu and Weld, 2010; Wang et al., 2011). However, such filtering is applied in a setting substantially different from ours.

Regarding the previous work on PPI extraction, several RE approaches have been reported to date. Most of them are based on kernel methods (Bunescu and Mooney, 2006; Giuliano et al., 2006a; Airola et al., 2008; Miwa et al., 2009a,b; Kim et al., 2010; Tikk et al., 2010; Chowdhury and Lavelli, 2012b). Among the state-of-the-art systems, Miwa et al. (2009a) proposed a hybrid kernel by combining graph, tree and bag-of-words kernel. They further boosted system performance by training on multiple PPI corpora and adopting a corpus weighting concept with SVM (Miwa et al., 2009b). Chowdhury and Lavelli (2012b) proposed an approach in which they combined different types of information and their different representations into a hybrid kernel and showed that they can complement each other to obtain state-of-the-art results.

3 Data

There are 5 frequently used benchmark PPI corpora: IEPA (Ding et al., 2002), LLL (Nédellec, 2005), AIMed (Bunescu et al., 2005), HPRD50 (Fundel et al., 2007) and BioInfer (Pyysalo et al., 2007). We use the common annotation format of these corpora provided by Pyysalo et al. (2008).

Although all these corpora are annotated for PPI extraction, the differences in performance of the same system on these corpora reported by previous studies are quite dramatic. This is due to the fact that there is no general consensus regarding PPI annotation. Furthermore, there are differences

[3]There exist many related ML studies (e.g. He and Garcia (2009)), apart from the ones discussed in this paper.

[4]Open domain IE has substantial differences with traditional RE some of which are discussed in Wang et al. (2011).

[5]In traditional RE, any pair of mentions to be considered as an instance must satisfy the already known argument types of the target relation. Hence, this technique does not qualify as a criterion for negative instance filtering in traditional RE.

in the entity types, too (i.e. the PPI annotations are not just restricted to proteins). Pyysalo et al. (2008) reported their findings of quantitative and qualitative analyses of the annotations and their differences. In a different study, Chowdhury and Lavelli (2012a) reported statistics of various characteristics of these five corpora and this study pointed out that they are quite distinct datasets.

4 Baseline RE System

As a starting point, we use the state-of-the-art system proposed by Chowdhury and Lavelli (2012b) (where more details about the system can be found). We made few minor changes in data pre-processing of the system. The main change concerns entity blinding. Originally, entity mentions were replaced by placeholders such as *Entity0*, *Entity1*, ... where the digits represent corresponding entity mention indices inside the given sentence. Such replacement did not include a co-reference mechanism when a particular entity is mentioned multiple times inside a given sentence (using exactly the same string). For the experiments in this paper, if it appears that two (or more) mentions consist of the same string, then we replace them with the same placeholder. In the remaining of the paper, we will refer to this system as the ***primary baseline system***.

5 Anti-positive Governors

The semantic roles of the entity mentions somehow contribute either to relate or not to relate them in a particular relation type (e.g. PPI) in the corresponding context. In other words, the semantic roles of two mentions in the same context could provide an indication whether the relation of interest does *not* hold between them. Interestingly, the word on which a certain entity mention is (syntactically) dependent (along with the dependency type) could often provide a clue of the semantic role of such mention in the corresponding sentence.

Our goal is to automatically identify the words (if there any) that tend to prevent mentions, which are directly dependent on those words, from participating in a certain relation of interest with any other mention in the same sentence. We call such words as ***anti-positive governors*** and assume that they could be exploited to identify negative instances (i.e. negative entity mention pairs) in advance. Below we describe our approach for the automatic identification of such words.

Let $\mathtt{EN}$ be the set of entity mentions such that if $\mathtt{e}^i{}_s \in \mathtt{EN}$ (where s indicates the corresponding training sentence and i indicates the corresponding entity mention index inside such sentence), then $\mathtt{e}^i{}_s$ does not have any relation of interest (i.e. PPI) with any other mention inside the same sentence.

Let $\mathtt{EP}$ be the set of entity mentions such that if $\mathtt{e}^k{}_s \in \mathtt{EP}$ (where s indicates the corresponding training sentence and k indicates the corresponding entity mention index inside such sentence), then $\mathtt{e}^k{}_s$ has at least one relation of interest with one of the mentions inside the same sentence.

For example, consider the following sentence (taken from the IEPA corpus) where there are three entity mention annotations – *oxytocin*^{1}, *oxytocin*^{2} and *IP3*^{3}.

These results indicate that oTP-1 may prevent luteolysis by inhibiting development of endometrial responsiveness to ***oxytocin***^{1} *and, therefore, reduce* ***oxytocin***^{2}*-induced synthesis of* ***IP3***^{3} *and PGF2 alpha.*

Here, the mention *oxytocin*^{1} does not participate in any PPI relation in this sentence. So, it would be included in $\mathtt{EN}$. The other two mentions would be added to $\mathtt{EP}$, because they are in PPI relation with each other. Note that, the two mentions of the entity *oxytocin* are treated separately.

Now, let $\mathtt{GV}$ be the set of governor words where for each $\mathtt{w} \in \mathtt{GV}$, *(i)* there is at least one mention $\mathtt{e}^i{}_s \in \mathtt{EN}$ which is syntactically dependent on $\mathtt{w}$ in the corresponding training sentence s, and *(ii)* there is *no* mention $e^k{}_s \in \mathtt{EP}$ which is syntactically dependent on w in the corresponding training sentence s. We call this set GV as the list of *anti-positive governors*.

6 Detection and Removal of Less Informative Negative Instances

We exploit static (i.e. already known, heuristically motivated) and dynamic (i.e. automatically collected from the data) knowledge for identifying less informative negative instances as described by the following criteria:

- **C1:** If two entity mentions in a sentence refer to the same entity, then it is unlikely that they would have a relation (for our experiments, PPI relation) between themselves.
- **C2:** If each of the two entity mentions (of a candidate pair) have *anti-positive governors* with respect to the type of the relation, then they are not likely to be in a given relation.
- **C3:** If a mention is the abbreviation of another mention (i.e. they refer to the same entity), then they are unlikely to be in a relation.

Criteria C1 and C3 (static knowledge) are quite intuitive. Criterion C2 is motivated by our analyses of some randomly selected sentences from the PPI corpora (and also by what we described at the beginning of Section 5). For criterion C1, we simply check whether two mentions have the same name and there is more than one character between them[6]. As for criterion C2, we construct a list of *anti-positive governors* (dynamic knowledge) from the training data on the fly and use them for detecting pairs that are unlikely to be in relation. For criterion C3, we look for any expression of the form *"Protein1 (Protein2)"* and consider *"Protein2"* as an abbreviation or alias of *"Protein1"*.

7 Results and Discussion

All experiments are conducted (on a computer having Intel(R) Xeon(R) CPU W3520 @ 2.67GHz processor and 4GB RAM) by doing 10-fold cross validation using exactly the same procedures and folds used by Tikk et al. (2010) and Chowdhury and Lavelli (2012b). SVM hyperparameters are tuned separately on 25% data of each dataset during each experiment. The ratio of negative and positive examples is used as value of the SVM parameter known as cost-factor.

7.1 Experiments using the Three Criteria Incrementally

In these experiments, we created another baseline system (henceforth, **2nd baseline system**) by applying the strategy of Sun et al. (2011) for limiting negative instances (see Section 1) in the *primary baseline system*. Also, we created three new different systems (henceforth, **new systems**) by incrementally incorporating the three criteria (see Section 6) into the *primary baseline system*.

The *2nd baseline system* and the three *new systems* use a less skewed distribution and a smaller number of training instances than the *primary baseline system*. They also consider a smaller number of candidate test instances since some of them are automatically discarded by their corresponding criteria for the exclusion of (possible) negative (candidate) instances.

To make sure that results of the *2nd baseline system* and the *new systems* are directly comparable with the *primary baseline system*, we simply consider all the discarded candidate test instances by these four systems as negatives. If the actual label of a discarded test instance is *true*, then we consider it as a *false negative (FN)* during the calculation of precision, recall and F_1 scores.

[6] In biomedical literature sometimes expressions such as *"Protein1-Protein1"* refer to PPI. We wanted to keep mention pairs of such expressions even if the mentions have the same name.

As Table 1 shows, the *2nd baseline system* performs almost similarly as the *primary baseline system*, except that it obtains quite lower F_1 score on BioInfer. On the contrary, all the *new systems* perform better than (or as effectively as) both the *primary baseline* and *2nd baseline* systems.

The improvement of F_1 scores for the *new system v3*, which integrates all the three criteria, with respect to the *primary baseline system* is as follows – LLL: **+1.3**, HPRD50: **+6.3**, IEPA: **+1.8**, AIMed: **+1.1**. The F_1 score for BioInfer remained the same (more on this in Section 7.4). The differences in F_1 scores (except on BioInfer) are statistically significant (verified using *Approximate Randomization Procedure* (Noreen, 1989); number of iterations = 1,000, confidence level = 0.05).

The improvement of F_1 scores for the *new system v3* with respect to the *2nd baseline system* is as follows – LLL: **+1.2**, HPRD50: **+5.5**, IEPA: **+1.8**, AIMed: **+1.6**, BioInfer: **+2.2**. These differences are statistically significant, too.

A noticeable observation is that the *new system v3* obtains better recall than the *primary baseline system* on each of the corpora except LLL. For LLL, the recall remains the same but precision increases by *1.9* points. Similarly, the *new system v3* obtains better recall than the *2nd baseline system* on each of the corpora except AIMed. Although the recall decreases on AIMed, the F_1 scores improves by *1.6* points due to a significant improvement in precision.

Table 1 also reports the *AUC* scores computed following the same way as Airola et al. (2008) did. It is hard to draw any conclusion from these *AUC* scores. It should be noted that the practical value of *AUC* has been called into question by some recent ML studies (Lobo et al., 2008; Hand, 2009).

LLL	**HPRD50**	**IEPA**	**AIMed**	**BioInfer**
AUC / P / R / F_1	**AUC / P / R / F_1**	**AUC / P / R / F_1**	**AUC / P / R / F_1**	**AUC / P / R / F_1**
Primary baseline system: Using all the instances				
88.1 / 69.6 / 96.3 / 80.8	77.2 / 55.7 / 81.0 / 66.0	86.0 / 76.1 / 75.8 / 75.9	88.1 / 63.3 / 58.0 / 60.5	92.9 / 78.0 / 74.7 / 76.3
2nd baseline system: Adding the approach proposed by Sun et al. (2011) in the *primary baseline system*				
88.0 / 72.5 / 91.5 / 80.9	77.8 / 57.5 / 79.8 / 66.8	85.9 / 76.1 / 75.8 / 75.9	87.2 / 55.2 / 65.6 / 60.0	93.2 / 79.0 / 69.8 / 74.1
New system v1: Adding criterion **C1** in the *primary baseline system*				
88.4 / 70.0 / 98.2 / **81.7**	79.0 / 60.3 / 82.8 / **69.8**	85.2 / 78.2 / 76.1 / **77.2**	87.4 / 64.0 / 58.7 / **61.2**	93.1 / 77.5 / 75.2 / **76.3**
New system v2: Adding criterion **C2** in the *new system v1*				
88.4 / 71.5 / 96.3 / **82.1**	80.8 / 65.0 / 81.0 / **72.1**	85.3 / 78.0 / 77.3 / **77.7**	87.3 / 63.6 / 58.9 / **61.2**	93.1 / 77.5 / 75.2 / **76.3**
New system v3: Adding criterion **C3** in the *new system v2*				
88.4 / 71.5 / 96.3 / **82.1**	80.1 / 64.9 / 81.6 / **72.3**	85.3 / 78.0 / 77.3 / **77.7**	86.7 / 63.3 / 59.9 / **61.6**	93.1 / 77.2 / 75.4 / **76.3**

Table 1: Results on the five corpora for the *primary baseline, 2nd baseline* and *new systems*. Note that discarded positive and negative test instances (for the *2nd baseline* and *new systems*) are automatically considered as *false negatives* and *true negatives* during the calculation of the scores.

As we can see, the improvement of F_1 scores (mentioned above) varies from corpus to corpus. One of the major differences among these corpora concerns their size. But since they also have other differences, e.g. different annotation guidelines regarding entity mentions and relations, these variations of F_1 scores cannot be exclusively attributed to the disparity of corpus size. To test the influence of data size on performance, we carried out a set of experiments on a single corpus using different proportions of training data. These experiments are done on AIMed, the largest corpus among the 5 corpora considered, having 1,955 sentences collected from 225 PubMed abstracts. The learning curve for the *primary baseline system* and the *new system v3* (not reported because of lack of space) using 25, 40, 50, 60, 75 and 100% data shows that our approach for reducing skewness obtains slightly better results when the size of the corpus gets bigger.

7.2 Random Removal of Negative Instances

We wanted to investigate what happens if one decides to reduce the skewed distribution by randomly removing instances of the majority class (i.e. negative instances). This would help to better understand the effectiveness of our idea of singling out less informative instances.

For each corpus, the number of randomly discarded negative instances from the training data was kept equal to that discarded by the *new system v3*. To put it differently, the ratio of positive and negative training instances of this *3rd baseline system* (which uses random sampling) is equal to that of the *new system v3*.

As shown in Table 2, in 3 out of the 5 corpora there was a slight increase of F_1 scores for the *3rd baseline system* with respect to those for the *primary baseline system*. There was no change on BioInfer but deteriorating F_1 score on LLL. Overall, the results of the *new system v3* are better than that obtained by exploiting random sampling.

7.3 Impact on Efficiency Improvement and Skewness Reduction

Table 3 shows how much the runtime and the distribution of positive and negative instances were reduced in the *new systems* with respect to those of the *primary baseline system*. All these systems are much faster than their original *primary baseline system*. The reduction of runtime for the final version (*new system v3*) ranges from 15% to 33% depending on the corpora.

As for the reduction of skewness in the instance distribution, the number of negative instances decreased quite sharply (>= 20%) for all the corpora except BioInfer. While positive instances also decreased, the percentage of such reduction is negligible with respect to that of the negative instances.

It is evident from the numbers in Table 3 that for LLL and IEPA the greater number of negative instances were discarded in *new systems v1* and *v2*. For HPRD50 and AIMed, a considerable decrease in negative instances can be observed in each of the new systems.

The decrease of negative instances for the *2nd baseline system* (see Table 3) is negligible, while the decrease of positive instances is worrying. This suggests that merely considering the number of entity mentions in between the target mentions (as in Sun et al. (2011)) is not an effective strategy.

7.4 Peculiarities of the BioInfer Corpus

Since the F_1 score on the BioInfer corpus did not change (Table 1), we wanted to understand why it is so. The first peculiarity that we observed in the BioInfer corpus is that 2.19% of its PPIs are between entity mentions having the same name. The only other corpus which has such annotations is AIMed, but only 0.20%. So, although the criterion *C1* discarded 6.69% negative instances in BioInfer (Table 3), that was perhaps not enough to counter the loss of information due to the discarded PPIs.

The second peculiarity is that the usage of *anti-positive governors* (criterion *C2*) actually discarded positive instances in BioInfer and failed to filter any negative instance. To check why it is so, we extracted the list of *anti-positive governors* from the whole BioInfer corpus (total 1,100 sentences) and found there are only 10 such words. By comparison, the number of *anti-positive governors* in AIMed (total 1,955 sentences) and IEPA (total 486 sentences) are 300 and 161 respectively. Further investigation revealed that there are startling differences for the concentration of PPIs/sentence between BioInfer and the other corpora. For BioInfer, it is 2.30 PPIs/sentence. If we compare this with AIMed and IEPA then the respective numbers are 0.51 PPIs/sentence and 0.70 PPIs/sentence. As a result, it is quite difficult to spot a word which is not governing any mention that participate in PPI, but only governing those mentions that are not in any PPI in the corresponding sentence.

LLL			HPRD50			IEPA			AIMed			BioInfer		
P	R	F_1	P	R	F_1	P	R	F_1	P	R	F_1	P	R	F_1
3rd baseline system (using random selection)														
66.0	98.2	78.9	57.8	77.3	66.1	75.5	77.3	76.4	60.3	61.7	61.0	76.5	76.2	76.3
New system v3: Implementing criteria **C1, C2,** and **C3** in the *primary baseline system*														
71.5	96.3	**82.1**	64.9	81.6	**72.3**	78.0	77.3	**77.7**	63.3	59.9	**61.6**	77.2	75.4	**76.3**

Table 2: Comparison between the results of the *3rd baseline system* (that randomly discards negative training instances) and the *new system v3*.

		LLL	HPRD50	IEPA	AIMed	BioInfer
2nd baseline system	*Reduction of runtime*	5.77%	4.84%	1.04%	6.05%	5.83%
	Reduction of positive instances	4.88%	2.45%	0.00%	4.20%	11.37%
	Reduction of negative instances	1.81%	0.37%	0.00%	1.67%	3.21%
New system v1	*Reduction of runtime*	7.69%	19.35%	19.69%	28.13%	10.80%
(criterion C1)	*Reduction of positive instances*	0.00%	0.00%	0.00%	0.20%	2.19%
	Reduction of negative instances	6.63%	12.59%	19.71%	12.83%	6.69%
New system v2	*Reduction of runtime*	17.31%	20.97%	23.32%	31.61%	13.23%
(criteria C1, C2)	*Reduction of positive instances*	1.83%	0.61%	0.60%	0.40%	2.19%
	Reduction of negative instances	19.88%	21.48%	24.07%	15.34%	6.69%
New system v3	*Reduction of runtime*	15.38%	20.97%	23.32%	33.24%	15.93%
(criteria C1, C2, C3)	*Reduction of positive instances*	1.83%	0.61%	0.60%	0.60%	2.46%
	Reduction of negative instances	19.88%	26.30%	24.07%	20.18%	9.22%

Table 3: Percentage of the decrease in runtime and number of instances for the *2nd baseline system* and for each of the *new systems* (shown in Table 1) with respect to the *primary baseline system.*

7.5 Effect of Excluding Negative Instances during Learning

An obvious question would be whether the exclusion of less informative negative instances provides any gain in learning, i.e. whether less skewed data provide a better trained model. To answer this, we performed two different sets of experiments. At first, we applied the *primary baseline system* and *New system v3* on the filtered (using the three criteria) test data. These results are reported in Table 4 which shows the recall of *New system v3* is always considerably higher than that of the *primary baseline system* for any of the corpora. As for the F_1 scores, *New system v3* obtains slightly better scores on all corpora apart from LLL (the smallest PPI corpus considered), even for BioInfer.

In a second set of experiments, we applied these two systems on the unfiltered test data. It is not possible to include details on these results in this paper for space limitation. Nevertheless, we found similar trend of better recall and slightly better F_1 scores for *New system v3* in these results. However, F_1 scores for both the systems degrades with respect to those of the previous set of experiments.

Some of the F_1 score differences in the above experiments are statistically significant, while others are not. So, the answer to the question posed above is inconclusive.

LLL			HPRD50			IEPA			AIMed			BioInfer		
P	R	F_1	P	R	F_1	P	R	F_1	P	R	F_1	P	R	F_1
Primary baseline system: Training using all the instances and testing only on the instances not filtered by the three criteria														
73.8	96.3	83.6	63.6	80.9	71.2	78.3	75.7	77.0	64.1	58.3	61.0	78.8	75.8	77.2
New system v3														
71.5	98.1	82.7	64.9	82.1	**72.5**	78.0	77.8	**77.9**	63.3	60.3	**61.8**	77.2	77.8	**77.5**

Table 4: Results obtained discarding the less informative test instances for the *primary baseline system* too.

	LLL	HPRD50	IEPA	AIMed	BioInfer
	P / R / F_1	P / R / F_1	P / R / F_1	P / R / F_1	P / R / F_1
Miwa et al. (2009a)	77.6 / 86.0 / 80.1	68.5 / 76.1 / 70.9	67.5 / 78.6 / 71.7	55.0 / 68.8 / 60.8	65.7 / 71.1 / 68.1
Miwa et al. (2009b)	– / – / 80.5	– / – / 69.7	– / – / 74.4	– / – / **64.2**	– / – / 67.6
Chowdhury and Lavelli (2012b)	70.4 / 95.7 / 81.1	72.9 / 59.5 / 65.5	81.1 / 69.3 / 74.7	64.2 / 58.2 / 61.1	80.0 / 71.4 / 75.5
Our proposed approach	71.5 / 96.3 / **82.1**	64.9 / 81.6 / **72.3**	78.0 / 77.3 / **77.7**	63.3 / 59.9 / 61.6	77.2 / 75.4 / **76.3**

Table 5: Comparison of our results with other state-of-the-art approaches.

8 Conclusion

In this paper, we have addressed the well known issue of skewed distribution, which has been hypothesized as one of the stumbling blocks for the advancement of ML based RE approaches (Sun et al., 2011). To the best of our knowledge, there are no existing studies showing that the reduction of skewed distribution could lead to better RE results. Since negative instances play important role for accurate ML training, only the less informative negative instances should be discarded.

To meet this challenge, we proposed three criteria for identifying less informative instances. We applied them on a state-of-the-art RE system and evaluated our approach on 5 different benchmark PPI corpora. Empirical outcome shows that our proposed approach performs better than 3 different *baseline systems* (which were created from an existing state-of-the-art RE approach) on 4 out of 5 corpora. Although the F_1 score remains the same on the 5th corpus, i.e. BioInfer, recall improves. In fact, the proposed approach boosts recall in 4 corpora (in LLL recall remains the same but precision increases) which is a desirable characteristic for biomedical RE. However, it is inconclusive whether less skewed distribution leads to a better trained model. Nonetheless, our approach significantly reduces the number of negatives instances and runtime. Comparison with previous studies shows that our approach provides state-of-the-art results for PPI extraction (see Table 5).

As for future work, we plan to investigate whether the proposed approach can also improve performance of RE from other genres of text such as news domain, since none of the criteria proposed for discarding less informative instances is domain specific.

Acknowledgements

The authors would like to thank the anonymous reviewers for their useful comments.

References

Airola, A., Pyysalo, S., Bjorne, J., Pahikkala, T., Ginter, F., and Salakoski, T. (2008). All-paths graph kernel for protein-protein interaction extraction with evaluation of cross-corpus learning. *BMC Bioinformatics*, 9(Suppl 11):S2.

Banko, M., Cafarella, M. J., Soderland, S., Broadhead, M., and Etzioni, O. (2007). Open information extraction from the web. In *Proceedings of the 20th international joint conference on Artifical intelligence (IJCAI 2007)*, pages 2670–2676, Hyderabad, India.

Blum, A. L. and Langley, P. (1997). Selection of relevant features and examples in machine learning. *Artificial Intelligence*, 97(1-2):245–271.

Bunescu, R., Ge, R., Kate, R., Marcotte, E., Mooney, R., Ramani, A., and Wong, Y. (2005). Comparative experiments on learning information extractors for proteins and their interactions. *Artificial Intelligence in Medicine (Special Issue on Summarization and Information Extraction from Medical Documents)*, 33(2):139–155.

Bunescu, R. and Mooney, R. (2006). Subsequence kernels for relation extraction. In *Proceedings of the 19th Conference on Neural Information Processing Systems (NIPS 2006)*, pages 171–178.

Chawla, N. V., Japkowicz, N., and Kotcz, A. (2004). Editorial: special issue on learning from imbalanced data sets. *SIGKDD Explor. Newsl.*, 6(1):1–6.

Chowdhury, M. and Lavelli, A. (2012a). An Evaluation of the Effect of Automatic Preprocessing on Syntactic Parsing for Biomedical Relation Extraction. In *Proceedings of the 8th conference on International Language Resources and Evaluation (LREC 2012)*, pages 544–551.

Chowdhury, M. F. M. and Lavelli, A. (2012b). Combining tree structures, flat features and patterns for biomedical relation extraction. In *Proceedings of the 13th Conference of the European Chapter of the Association for Computational Linguistics (EACL 2012)*, pages 420–429, Avignon, France. Association for Computational Linguistics.

Ding, J., Berleant, D., Nettleton, D., and Wurtele, E. (2002). Mining MEDLINE: abstracts, sentences, or phrases? *Pacific Symposium on Biocomputing*, pages 326–337.

Fundel, K., Küffner, R., and Zimmer, R. (2007). RelEx–relation extraction using dependency parse trees. *Bioinformatics*, 23(3):365–371.

Giuliano, C., Lavelli, A., and Romano, L. (2006a). Exploiting shallow linguistic information for relation extraction from biomedical literature. In *Proceedings of the 11th Conference of the European Chapter of the Association for Computational Linguistics (EACL 2006)*, pages 401–408.

Giuliano, C., Lavelli, A., and Romano, L. (2006b). Simple Information Extraction (SIE): A portable and effective IE system. In *Proceedings of the Workshop on Adaptive Text Extraction and Mining (ATEM 2006)*, pages 9–16.

Gliozzo, A. M., Giuliano, C., and Rinaldi, R. (2005). Instance filtering for entity recognition. *SIGKDD Explor. Newsl.*, 7(1):11–18.

Hand, D. J. (2009). Measuring classifier performance: a coherent alternative to the area under the ROC curve. *Machine Learning*, 77(1):103–123.

He, H. and Garcia, E. A. (2009). Learning from imbalanced data. *IEEE Transactions on Knowledge and Data Engineering*, 21(9):1263–1284.

Kim, S., Yoon, J., Yang, J., and Park, S. (2010). Walk-weighted subsequence kernels for protein-protein interaction extraction. *BMC Bioinformatics*, 11(1).

Kotsiantis, S. B. and Pintelas, P. E. (2003). Mixture of Expert Agents for Handling Imbalanced Data Sets. *Annals of Mathematics, Computing and Teleinformatics*, 1(1):46–55.

Lobo, J., Jimenez-Valverde, A., and Real, R. (2008). Auc: A misleading measure of the performance of predictive distribution models. *Global Ecology and Biogeography*, 17:145–151.

Miwa, M., Sætre, R., Miyao, Y., and Tsujii, J. (2009a). Protein-protein interaction extraction by leveraging multiple kernels and parsers. *International Journal of Medical Informatics*, 78.

Miwa, M., Sætre, R., Miyao, Y., and Tsujii, J. (2009b). A rich feature vector for protein-protein interaction extraction from multiple corpora. In *Proceedings of EMNLP 2009*, pages 121–130, Singapore.

Nédellec, C. (2005). Learning language in logic - genic interaction extraction challenge. In *Proceedings of the ICML 2005 workshop: Learning Language in Logic (LLL05)*, pages 31–37.

Noreen, E. W. (1989). *Computer-Intensive Methods for Testing Hypotheses : An Introduction*. Wiley-Interscience.

Pyysalo, S., Airola, A., Heimonen, J., Björne, J., Ginter, F., and Salakoski, T. (2008). Comparative analysis of five protein-protein interaction corpora. *BMC Bioinformatics*, 9(Suppl 3):S6.

Pyysalo, S., Ginter, F., Heimonen, J., Björne, J., Boberg, J., Jarvinen, J., and Salakoski, T. (2007). Bioinfer: a corpus for information extraction in the biomedical domain. *BMC Bioinformatics*, 8(1):50.

Sun, A., Grishman, R., and Sekine, S. (2011). Semi-supervised relation extraction with large-scale word clustering. In *Proceedings of the 49th Annual Meeting of the Association for Computational Linguistics: Human Language Technologies (ACL 2011)*, pages 521–529, Portland, Oregon, USA. Association for Computational Linguistics.

Tikk, D., Thomas, P., Palaga, P., Hakenberg, J., and Leser, U. (2010). A Comprehensive Benchmark of Kernel Methods to Extract Protein-Protein Interactions from Literature. *PLoS Computational Biology*, 6(7).

Wang, W., Besançon, R., Ferret, O., and Grau, B. (2011). Filtering and clustering relations for unsupervised information extraction in open domain. In *Proceedings of the 20th ACM international conference on Information and knowledge management (CIKM 2011)*, pages 1405–1414, New York, NY, USA. ACM.

Weiss, G. and Provost, F. (2001). The effect of class distribution on classifier learning: An empirical study. Technical report, Rutgers University.

Wu, F. and Weld, D. S. (2010). Open information extraction using wikipedia. In *Proceedings of the 48th Annual Meeting of the Association for Computational Linguistics (ACL 2010)*, pages 118–127, Uppsala, Sweden. Association for Computational Linguistics.

Lattice Rescoring for Speech Recognition Using Large Scale Distributed Language Models

Euisok Chung Hyung-Bae Jeon Jeon-Gue Park and Yun-Keun Lee
Speech Processing Research Team, ETRI, 138 Gajeongno, Daejeon, 305-700, KOREA
eschung@etri.re.kr, hbjeon@etri.re.kr, jgp@etri.re.kr and ykLee@etri.re.kr

ABSTRACT

In this paper, we suggest a lattice rescoring architecture that has features of a Trie DB based language model (LM) server and a naïve parameter estimation (NPE) to integrate distributed language models. The Trie DB LM server supports an efficient computation of LM score to re-rank the n-best sentences extracted from the lattice. In the case of NPE, it has a role of an integration of heterogeneous LM resources. Our approach distributes LM computations not only to distribute LM resources. This is simple and easy to implement and maintain the distributed lattice rescoring architecture. The experimental results show that the performance of the lattice rescoring has improved with the NPE algorithm that can find the optimal weights of the LM interpolation. In addition, we show that it is available to integrate n-gram LM and DIMI LM.

KEYWORDS : lattice rescoring, distributed language model, large scale language model

Proceedings of COLING 2012: Posters, pages 217–224,
COLING 2012, Mumbai, December 2012.

1 Introduction

The speech dictation with over multi-million words requires the large-scale language model. This need has a few problems such as a high computation time and a memory limitation. Automatic speech recognition for the multiple simultaneous accesses occupies the memory as multi-processes and uses multi-core capability of the CPU to guarantee high performance service. Hence, the limitation of the system resource requires the distributed approach for the large-scale language model. Previous researches have shown that the distributed modeling approach is available to avoid these problems.

In the case of language model researches, the distribution approach focuses on the client/server paradigm with splitting a training corpus as a technique of suffix array (Zhang, 2006 and Emami, 2007). These approaches depend on the distributed n-gram count servers; on the other hand, there is a more sophisticated technique to alleviate the burden of network communication. It uses MapReduce programming model to save and serve the smoothed probability of n-gram (Brants, 2007). These researches have presented the distributed architecture for the n-gram based language model. In the case of composite language model, there is a research, which simultaneously accounts for lexical information, syntactic structure and semantic content under a directed Markov random field paradigm (Tan, 2011). In addition, the composite language model approach showed the limitation in the training time, which takes 25.6 hours for the EM algorithm to build model of 230M corpus in the cloud environment.

In this paper, we suggest a lattice rescoring architecture that has features of a Trie DB based language model (LM) server and naïve parameter estimation (NPE) to integrate distributed language models. We use this architecture for speech recognition. Therefore, the multi-stage lattice rescoring approach is prerequisite. The Trie DB language model server has a role of efficient computation of LM score to re-rank the n-best sentences extracted from the lattice. In the case of NPE, it has a role of an integration of heterogeneous LM resources.

2 Lattice rescoring architecture

2.1 Lattice rescoring flow

The process of lattice rescoring begins with the automatic speech recognition (ASR) that recognizes the input speech and generates the lattice that is a weighted directed acyclic graph where represents the ASR results. With the lattice input, the am/lm decoupling step splits acoustic model (AM) and language model (LM) scores of the lattice for the lattice rescoring since in the LM rescoring stage, we only use AM scores of the input lattice. After that, it extracts the N-best list from the lattice. The rescoring step rescores the sentence scores of the N-best list with large scaled LM resources. Finally, it reorders the n-best list according to the new scores.

The rescoring step uses the AM scores of n-best sentences and new LM scores computed in distributed LM servers. The LM server and rescoring module communicates through stream sockets. The LM servers return each LM scores when it receives n-best sentences. The rescoring module re-ranks the n-best sentences after interpolating new LM scores received from the distributed LM servers.

The rescoring flow depends on two approaches, one is the LM interpolation parameter estimation and the other is the LM Trie DB. The step of the LM interpolation parameter estimation computes the interpolation weights in the back-end step with the correct ASR result scripts. We propose Naïve parameter estimation algorithm to estimate the LM interpolation weights. In the case of LM Trie DB, we build LM as a Trie DB that guarantees high performance and light footprint. Figure 1 describes the flow of lattice rescoring.

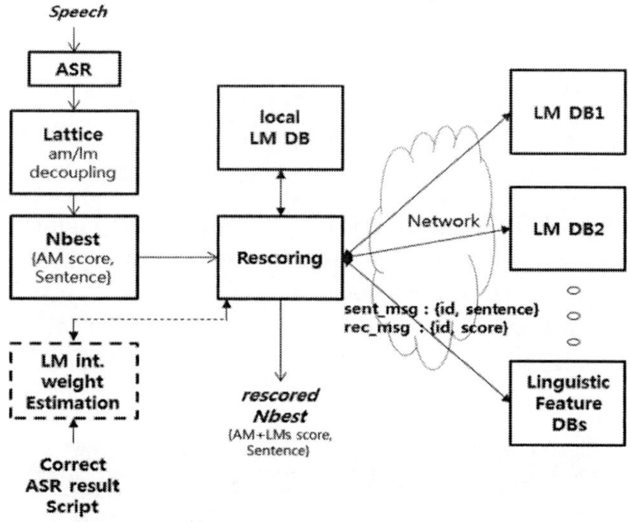

FIGURE 1 – System architecture for a lattice rescoring

2.2 Lattice Generation and AM/LM Decoupling

We implement the unit of generating lattices considering high performance. The lattice is built at the ASR decoding step without the increase of memory and computation. The decoder generates the lattice using the recognized word path at the backtracking step. It attaches completed word paths to the 1-best recognized word at the specific time according to the accumulated likelihood score.

The lattice link has the likelihood score that is a summation of AM and LM scores with the proportion determined empirically. We decouple the likelihood score with the original LM of the ASR decoder since we cannot improve the result of lattice rescoring when we maintain the original LM scores. Therefore, the basic step of the lattice rescoring is the replacement of the lattice LM score with other LM resources.

2.3 LM Trie DB Server

We propose LM Trie DB server. It consists of two components; one is the LM Trie DB and the other is the service function. The LM Trie DB is built by converting the ARPA format for language model representation into a Trie structure. In the case of the server function, it computes the LM scores for the n-best sentences in a style of dynamic programing. In runtime, the DB is loaded in the memory space to deal with the requests of LM value computation for the N-best sentence list. As a DB structure, we use a double-array Trie approach (Aoe, 1992).

The basic schema of LM Trie DB is a pair of key string and data string. The 1-gram entry has "word" as a key and "prob_backoff_winx" as a data; "word" is a unigram word string, "prob" is a

LM probability, "backoff" is a value of backoff and "winx" is the index of this entry which is used in n-gram entries. In the case of 2-gram entry, the key string is "winx_winx". It means that the key string is composed of two 1-gram word indexes. Also, it has "winx2" for a 2-gram index used in 3-gram entries. Table 1 shows the schema of LM Trie DB.

Key	Data
word	prob backoff winx
winx winx	prob backoff winx2
winx2 winx	prob backoff winx3
winx3 winx	prob backoff winx4
winx4 winx	prob backoff winx5
winx5 winx	prob backoff

TABLE 1 – Schema of LM Trie DB

The dynamic chart for the computation of LM score is described in Figure 2. This figure shows to compute LM score for the input string with 4-gram LM. First line shows input string. The LM values are presented from 2nd layer to 4th layer. The cell filled with backoff b_i and probability p_i. The arrow shows the computation with previous layer scores when there is no n-gram entry in LM DB. We denote a probability of a dynamic chart as a DC(n-gram, p_n) and a backoff value as a DC(n-gram, b_n).

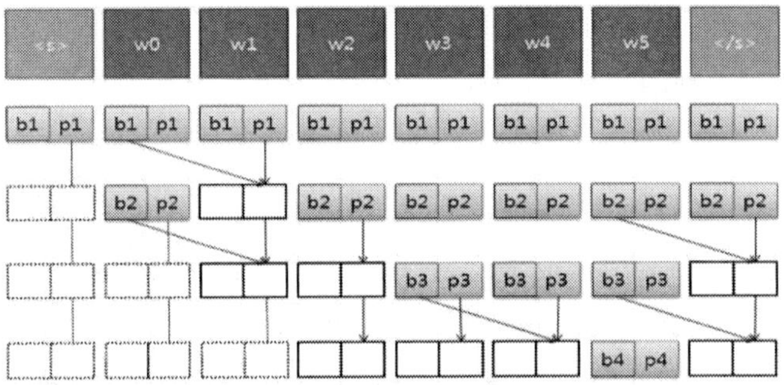

FIGURE 2 – Dynamic chart for the computation of LM score

When the LM Trie DB server receives the request of the computation of LM value, first, it searches 1-gram data in the LM Trie DB with input sentence <s> w_0 w_1 w_2 .. w_n </s>. Then, it searches 2-gram data. When it cannot find the 2-gram data, it fills the slot of the dynamic chart with the backoff and probability of each composed 1-gram; DC(w_0w_1, p_2) $\leftarrow$ DC(w_1, p_1) + DC(w_0, b_1). If there is no backoff value, the previous probability transfers to the current slot; DC($w_0w_1w_2$, p_3) $\leftarrow$ DC(w_1w_2, p_2). Finally, the summation of last slots is the LM value of the input sentence; $\sum$ DC(-, p_4). This procedure is same with a normal procedure for backoff in LM. The difference is that the DC computation depends on the schema of LM Trie DB. The higher n-gram DB search uses the "winx" of the lower n-grams.

2.4 Distributed LM interpolation

We propose naïve parameter estimation (NPE) algorithm for the integration of distributed LMs. The goal of NPE estimates the optimal interpolation weights of the distributed LMs to the evaluation set. Simply, NPE uses the accuracy of the ASR to the evaluation set with each LM. The idea is that the update of the weight of the LM is multiplicative (high change) when the accuracy of ASR decreases and the other is additive (small change) when the accuracy of ASR increases. Although we adopt simple approach to estimate LM interpolation weights, it can find the optimal weights of all LMs in a few iterations.

In addition, we can process the NPE in distributed environment since the ASR evaluation function only uses the network procedures. The evaluation function, do_eval(), sends the message of LM score computation and receives the message of LM score from each LM server. Although the NPE sends the network calls iteratively to the LM servers, it can efficiently process the task since the NPE uses not only the distributed LM resources but also the distributed LM computation.

```
 0: E := {e1..en}
 1: W ← initialize()   # W := {w1..wn}
 2: ΔW ← W * c         # 0 < c < 1
 3: acc_old ← do_eval(W, E)
 4: for itr = 0 to max_iteration do
 5:   W' ← W
 6:   for i = 0 to number of LMs do
 7:     w'i ← wi + Δwi
 8:     acc_new ← do_eval(W', E)
 9:     if (acc_old-acc_new > 0) then
10:       Δwi ← -Δwi * random()
11:     else
12:       Δwi ← Δwi + random()
13:     end if
14:   end for
15:   W ← W + ΔW
16:   acc_old ← do_eval(W, E)
17:   if (acc_old is max) then
18:     Wmax ← W
19:   end if
20: end for
21: return Wmax
```

FIGURE 3 – Naïve parameter estimation algorithm.

The NPE algorithm is described in Figure 3. Firstly, it initializes the interpolation weights W as many as the number of LMs (line1). In addition, it initializes ΔW which compute by multiplying constant value c ($0 < c < 1$) to the interpolation weight W (line2). The last stage of the initialization is to get the first accuracy with the initialized W (line3). At this time, do_eval() evaluates the evaluation set E that is the set of the lattice and correct script pairs.

The evaluation step, do_eval(), extracts n-best from the input lattice and then rescores the n-best with the distributed LMs. It sends the n-best sentences to the distributed LM servers and receives each LM scores computed by the LM servers. Then, it computes the score of LM interpolation with W to re-rank the n-bests. Finally, it can compare the correct scripts to find the accuracy.

The weight estimation step processes iteratively. It try to evaluate with the updated weight in each LMs (line7 ~ line8). If new updated weight cannot show the better accuracy, it processes a multiplicative decrease of the weight (line10). On the other hand, if new weight shows the better result, it processes an additive increase of the weight (line12). We use the random scale to change the weight value in order to avoid the stalled state, which is a repetition of two weight values.

After deciding all LM weights, NPE gets new evaluation value (line15 ~ line16). Then, if the value is the maximum, it saves the value as W_{max}(line18). Let the rescoring function for a sentence s be res(s). We define:

$$res(S) = am(S) + \sum_{i=1}^{n} w_{npe}(i) \cdot lm_i(S)$$

Where, $w_{npe}(i)$ is the NPE determined i^{th} weight of the distributed LM and $lm_i(s)$ is the result of ith distributed LM to the sentence s. am(s) is the decoupled AM score to the sentence s. These values are in the log domain so that we can add them as shown in the equation.

3 Evaluation

3.1 Evaluation Set and LMs

The evaluation set also consists of four domains such as email, news, Q&A and twitter. It has 2,000 clean Korean speeches independent of LM training corpus. We converts the speeches into HTK standard lattice format (SLF) files with wFST-based Korean speech recognizer, which uses small LM. We prepare two evaluation sets as described in Table 2. EVAL1 uses all sentences and EVAL2 divides the evaluation set into a train/development set and a test set.

# of speech		email	news	Q&A	twitter	All
EVAL1		200	400	400	1000	2000
EVAL2	train	150	300	300	750	1500
	Test	50	100	100	250	500

TABLE 2 – Preparation of two evaluation sets.

We select a vocabulary set for building language models. The vocabulary has 1.3 million entries which extracts from the corpus of 3.3 billion words with a coverage of 99.84% of the corpus. We use the 3.3 billion words corpus as a training set for language models in this evaluation. The domain of the corpus consists of twitter, news, community and Q&A. The training corpus is built by crawling from the web sites

We builds two n-gram language models for the evaluation; one is Small LM (1.3m 1gram, 4.5m 2gram, 2.3 3gram), and the other is Big LM (1.3m 1gram, 42.1m 2gram, 45.8m 3gram). In addition, we build the distance independent mutual information LM (DIMI LM) (GuoDong, 2004), which has 121 million pairs extracted from the training data within the 6 words distance.

3.2 Lattice Rescoring

We use EVAL1 to evaluate our distributed LM architecture. In this experiment, EVAL1 is a training set of the NPE algorithm to estimate interpolation weights for the LMs. Also, EVAL1 is a test set of this experiment. Table 3 shows the result of the lattice rescoring tests.

type		email	news	Q&A	twitter	All
1	AM	85.13	80.34	83.59	85.6	84.32
2	AM+Small LM	86.93	83.17	86.49	87.16	86.35
3	AM+Big LM	88.3	84.67	87.4	88.15	87.41
4	AM+Big LM+DIMI LM	88.41	85.81	87.59	88.28	87.73
5	Big LM+DIMI LM (no AM)	85.1	83.75	85.7	85.28	85.13

TABLE 3 – Evaluation with EVAL1 (accuracy %, top1)

The result of type1 is the ASR accuracy with only AM scores. The result of type2 is the baseline accuracy since it is the performance of ASR with small LM. We use the NPE algorithm from type3 to type5. The gain of the accuracy is 1.06% when we apply the Big LM to replace small LM in type3. The test type4, the accuracy of the all test sentences increases in small. However, in news domain, the gain of the accuracy is 1.14%. The result of type5 shows the importance of AM scores. The test cannot improve the result of lattice rescoring when we ignore AM scores in the input lattice.

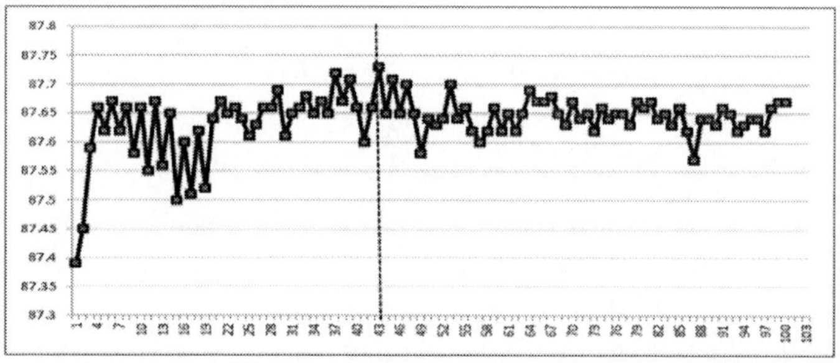

FIGURE 4 – Naïve parameter estimation algorithm.

Figure 4 shows the oscillation of the accuracy when NPE estimates the interpolation weights to the big LM and DIMI LM (type4). The NPE finds the optimal weights in the 43th iteration and the duration time is not over 20 minutes. Although the NPE cannot maintain the optimal accuracy, the result shows that it is available to find the appropriate interpolation weights in the short-term. This evaluation shows that the NPE can integrate a long-distance LM that is different with n-gram based LMs. In addition, the algorithm can estimate the interpolation weights to the multiple LM resources.

type			email	news	Q&A	twitter	All
Baseline	AM+Small LM	Train	86.15	83.71	86.26	87.23	86.29
		Test	87.84	82.01	85.57	86.48	85.97
Lattice Rescoring	AM+Big LM +DIMI LM	Train	87.65	86.28	87.83	88.23	87.63
		Test	88.87	83.61	86.21	88.18	87.37

TABLE 4 – Evaluation with EVAL2 (accuracy %, top1), NPE with Train Set

The evaluation with EVAL2 described in Table 4. In this experiment, we apply NPE only to the train set. The result shows that the gain of accuracy of test set is 1.4% when the gain of accuracy of train set is 1.34%. From this test, we find that the NPE cannot guarantee the optimal weight of test set with only train set because of the over-fitting problem; the accuracy of all test is 87.47 when we apply NPE to test set. However, the result shows consistency in the gain of accuracy in all domains.

	Distributed LM		Non-distributed LM	
	Acc. %	Time(sec)	Acc. %	Time(sec)
1st	88.44	180	88.44	206
2nd	88.33	164	88.47	249
3rd	88.36	184	88.36	193
Avg.	88.37	176	88.42	216

TABLE 5 – Distributed LM vs. Non-distributed LM

In addition, we test the email set of EVAL1 considering the comparison of distributed LM and non-distributed LM. We test it 3 times of NPE with 30 iterations. The total number of LM score computation is 394,581 in one NPE process. The type of experiment is same with type 4 in Table 4. From the Table 5, we find that the reduction of the time is 18%. In the case of accuracy, there is only marginal difference between two tests.

If the Non-distributed LM is 1st-pass big LM based ASR, then the result of this test, EVAL1 email set, is 89.16% accuracy; EVAL1 all set is 88.20%. The two-pass approach such as the lattice rescoring cannot overcome 1st pass approach of the big LM since the small LM based ASR cannot show the coverage of n-gram path of big LM. However, in this paper, our assumption is the case that it is not possible to use the approach of 1st pass big LM ASR.

The main feature of our approach is to distribute LM computations not only to distribute LM resources. The rescoring client sends the k numbers of n-best sentences to the k numbers of LM servers. The LM servers return LM scores of the n-best sentences to the client. The computation of a LM scoring is only occurred in the servers in parallel with each other. This is simple and easy to implement and maintain the distributed lattice rescoring architecture.

Conclusion and perspectives

In this paper, we proposed the lattice rescoring architecture for applying the large scale distributed language model to the speech recognition. AM/LM decoupling approach of a lattice is required to replace large scale LMs with first-pass small LM. In the distributed LM server, we adopted socket-streaming approach and the Trie-based memory DB for LM. Finally, we suggested the naïve parameter estimation algorithm for the interpolation of multiple LMs. The evaluation showed the appropriate gain using NPE algorithm that can find the optimal weights of the LM interpolation. Also, we showed the integration between n-gram LM and DIMI LM. In the future, we will improve the NPE algorithm in various domains. Domain adaptation technique can be one of them.

References

Aoe, J., Morimoto, K. and Sato, T. (1992). An efficient implementation of trie structures, Software Practice & Experiments, 22(9): 695-721.

Emami, A., Papineni, K. and Sorensen, J. (2007). Large-scale distributed language modeling. In Proceedings of the International Conference on Acoustics, Speech, and Signal Processing 2007.

Guodong, Z. (2004). Modeling of Long Distance Context Dependency. In Proceedings of the *20th international conference on computational linguistics, COLING '04*, page 92, 2004.

Tan, M., Zhou, W., Zheng, L. and Wang, S. (2011). A Large Scale Distributed Syntactic, Semantic and Lexical Language Model for Machine Translation. In 49th Annual Meeting of the Association for Computational Linguistics(ACL), 201-210.

Zhang, Y., Hildebrand, A. S. and Vogel, S. (2006). Distributed language modeling for Nbest list re-ranking. In Proceedings of the 2006 Conference on Empirical Methods in Natural Language Processing, pages 216–223.

Morphological Analyzer for Affix Stacking Languages: A Case Study of Marathi

Raj Dabre[1] Archana Amberkar[1] Pushpak Bhattacharyya[1]
(1) Indian Institute of Technology Bombay, Mumbai-400076, India
prajdabre@gmail.com, amberkararchanaa@gmail.com,
pb@cse.iitb.ac.in

ABSTRACT

In this paper we describe and evaluate a Finite State Machine (FSM) based Morphological Analyzer (MA) for Marathi, a highly inflectional language with agglutinative suffixes. Marathi belongs to the Indo-European family and is considerably influenced by Dravidian languages. Adroit handling of participial constructions and other derived forms (Krudantas and Taddhitas) in addition to inflected forms is crucial to NLP and MT of Marathi. We first describe Marathi morphological phenomena, detailing the complexities of inflectional and derivational morphology, and then go into the construction and working of the MA. The MA produces the root word and the features. A thorough evaluation against gold standard data establishes the efficacy of this MA. To the best of our knowledge, this work is the first of its kind on a systematic and exhaustive study of the Morphotactics of a suffix-stacking language, leading to high quality morph analyzer. The system forms part of a Marathi-Hindi transfer based machine translation system. The methodology delineated in the paper can be replicated for other languages showing similar suffix stacking behaviour as Marathi.

KEYWORDS: Marathi, Morphology, Derivational, Inflectional, Architecture, Finite State Transducer, Two-Level, Indian Language Technology.

Proceedings of COLING 2012: Posters, pages 225–234,
COLING 2012, Mumbai, December 2012.

1. Introduction

The number of Marathi speakers all over the world is close to 72 million[1]. Marathi uses agglutinative, inflectional and analytic forms. It displays abundant amount of both derivational (wherein attachment of suffixes to a word form changes its grammatical category) and inflectional morphology. About 15% of the word forms are participial forms known as Krudantas, which result from the influence of Dravidian languages. Traditional grammars of Marathi classify the derived forms in Marathi into two categories- Krudantas and Taddhitas. Krudantas are the adjectives, adverbs and nouns derived from verbs, while Taddhitas are nouns, adjectives and adverbs derived from words of any category other than verb. This is also accompanied by inflectional processes which help lend the words features of gender, number, person, case, tense, aspect and modality (the latter 3 for verbs only).

1.1. Related work

The first MA for Marathi used a very naïve suffix stripping approach propounded by Eryiğit and Adalı, (2004). This neither had the ability to handle the stacking of suffixes which might involve orthographic changes at morpheme boundaries, nor could it indicate spelling mistakes and thus was discarded. The need for a mechanism to handle both inflectional and derivational morphology was felt, and we adopted the Finite State Transducer (FST) based approach that allows specification of legal morpheme sequences of both inflectional and derivational kind. We thus used a two level morphological analysis model (Oflazer, 1993; Kim et al., 1994), including a Morphological Parser (Antworth, 1991). Dixit et al. (2006) implemented a Marathi spell-checker, which is an inherent part of our MA. Bapat et al. (2010) had developed a FST based MA which handled the derivational morphology of verbs, and Bhosale et al. (2011) showed that the inclusion of this MA helps improve the translation quality. We extended the work of Bapat et al. to other grammatical categories, thereby increasing the coverage of Marathi morphological phenomena.

2. Morphological phenomena in Marathi

We first describe inflectional morphology. Nouns in Marathi are inflected for gender, number and case; adjectives are inflected for gender and number, pronouns for gender, number, case and person. The noun आंबा {aambaa} {mango} is masculine. Its direct singular and plural forms are: आंबा and आंबे {aamb<u>e</u>} {mangoes} respectively. Its oblique singular and plural forms are: आंब्या {aamb**<u>yaa</u>**} and आंब्यां {aamb**<u>yaan</u>**} respectively. Verbs in Marathi are inflected for person, number and gender of the subject alone or that of both the subject the object of the verb and also for tense, aspect and mood. Marathi has three genders (masculine, feminine and neuter), two numbers (singular and plural), eight cases (nominative, accusative, instrumental, dative, ablative, genitive, locative and vocative) and three persons (first, second and third). Different linguists give different typologies for the tenses, aspects and moods in Marathi. We have followed the typology given by Damle, M.K. (1970). We have also followed the linguistic analyses in the book of Dhongde and Wali (2009).

[1] http://en.wikipedia.org/wiki/List of Indian languages by total speakers

2.1. Derivational Morphology:

In the derivational process, a derivational morpheme is affixed to the word stem (the form a root takes when a derivational morpheme is attached to it), in order to add meaning to it and thereby derive a new word. The resulting word may or may not be of the same grammatical category. For example, Marathi has a derivational morpheme- "पणा" {panaa}, which is attached to adjectives like "मूर्ख" {moorkh} {foolish}, in order to derive nouns like "मूर्खपणा" {moorkhapanaa} {foolishness}. Marathi has many such derivational morphemes.

Another important feature of Marathi is its set of participles, which are derived by attaching derivational morphemes to verbs. These participles indicate tense, aspect, voice, mood in addition to gender and number features. For e.g. "येणारा" {yenaaraa} {coming} is a masculine, singular present participle form, while "गेलेला" {gelelaa} {has gone} is a masculine, singular past participle. Most of these participles, in addition to infinitive forms are currently handled by our MA. It also handles the extraction of most of the derivational morphemes that attach to verbs and a few that attach to nouns, adjectives and adverbs. Handling Derivational Morphology is important as it requires only base forms to be stored thereby reducing the lexicon size. We now describe some of the morphological complexities and methods of handling them.

2.2. Complexities in handling Inflectional Morphology

1. When a genitive case marker is attached to a noun or a pronoun, the resulting form holds the gender and number information of both the base noun and the genitive case marker. For example, in the word "मुलींचा" {muleenchaa} {of the girls}, the stem "मुलीं" {muleen} has the features feminine, plural, while the suffix "चा" {chaa} has the features masculine, singular. Thus, the morphological analysis of this form should consist of two feature structures- one for the stem and the other for the genitive suffix. Currently, we obtain a selective combination of both.
2. Pronouns take all cases except the vocative. However in case of pronouns, all cases are not overtly marked. For example, the instrumental case is not overtly marked in case of first and second person pronouns ("मी" {mee} {I/me} and "तू" {tu} {you}). Marathi also has demonstrative pronouns which are same as third person pronouns. However, when these pronouns occur as demonstrative pronouns, they do not take case postpositions. Distinguishing between pronouns and demonstratives becomes difficult (a property of almost all Indo-Aryan languages). For instance, "त्या मुलाने" {tyaa mulaane} {that boy (did): ergative form}. We handle these by special entries in the repository of inflected forms (REPO) (see next section).
3. Spatial and temporal adverbs like "आता" {aata} {now}, which act as nouns, can take some case markers like "चा"{chaa} {of} to give "आताचा" {aataa-chaa} {now-of} for which the Marathi MA uses the type NST (Noun of Space and Time). We create special paradigms (Bapat et al., 2010) for NSTs.
4. There are morphemes that indicate a few features of the agent of the verb and a few features of the object of the verb. For example, the morpheme "लीस" {lees} in "खाल्लीस" {khallees} {eaten} in addition to indicating the perfective aspect, indicates that the agent of the verb is in singular and second person, while the object of the verb is feminine, singular and third

person. In such cases, the morphological output should ideally have two separate feature structures- one for the agent and the other for the object.

5. Stacking of two or more suffixes is very common. Consider the example, "जाणाऱ्यानेसुद्धा" {jaanaaryanesuddhaa} {the one going also (instrumental)} {जा + णारा + ने + सुद्धा}. The root is the verb "जा" {jaa} {go} attached with three suffixes "णाऱ्या" {naarya}, ने {ne} and "सुद्धा" {suddha} {also} respectively. Here "णाऱ्या" has "ने" as suffix which in turn has "सुद्धा" as suffix. The finite state approach (next section) for morphological analysis helps in solving this.
6. There are a few pairs of morphemes that have similar orthographical shape, and the stems to which these morphemes are attached are orthographically similar too. Thus, the resulting inflected/derived forms are orthographically similar, but have two different meanings. For example, there are two morphemes represented by the letter "त" {ta}, one of which denotes habitual past and the other, imperfective aspect. Thus, attached to a verbal root like "फिर" {fir} {to wander}, these two suffixes produce two similar forms- "फिरत" {phirat} {(they) used to wander} and "फिरत" {phirat} {wandering}. In such cases, the Morphological Analyzer should be able to produce both the analyses. Once again, the finite state approach helps.

2.3. Complexities in handling Derivational Morphology

1. Base roots may have multiple forms (called stems) depending on which derivational morpheme is attached to them. For example, the cardinal "पन्नास" {pannaas} {fifty}, when attached with the derivational morpheme "वा", takes the stem "पन्नासा" {pannaasaa}. However, when attached with the derivational morpheme "दा" {da}, the same cardinal takes the stem "पन्नास" {pannaas}. In such cases, we need separate Suffix Replacement Rules (SRRs) (Bapat et al., 2010) for each derivational morpheme.
2. Some of the derivational morphemes like "पणा" {panaa}, "दा" {daa} are highly productive, as they are attached to all members of a particular grammatical category like nouns. However, some derivational morphemes are attached to only some particular semantic classes within a grammatical category. For instance "भर" {bhar} is attached to only nouns, and to only those nouns which indicate places or containers- "देश" {desh} {country- a place}, "वाटी" {vaati} {bowl - a container}. The resultant form for "देश" is "देशभर" {deshbhar} {throughout the country}. For such nouns, we need to create special paradigms.

3. Architecture and Working of the Morphological Analyzer

The Marathi Morphological Analyzer is fully rule-based and thus relies on string manipulation and file lookup. It requires two main resources, namely, a FST (Finite State Transducer) and a REPO (Repository of Inflected Forms), generated using an Inflector and SFST[2] (Stuttgart Finite State Transducer) compiler, which are explained below. These are in turn generated by the basic resources; namely, the monolingual lexicon, the suffix replacement rules (SRRs), the special word forms repository, the verb suffix (for Krudantas) list (Bapat et al., 2010) and morphology rules (Morphotactics).

[2] http://www.ims.uni-stuttgart.de/projekte/gramotron/SOFTWARE/SFST.html

3.1. Tools and Resources

3.1.1. FST (Finite State Transducer)

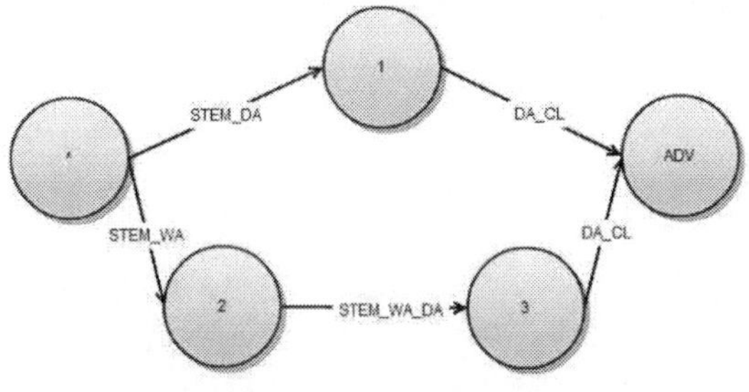

Figure 1 - FST for deriving Adverbs from Cardinal

The rules which specify the legal sequences of word-forming morphemes in Marathi are called Morphotactics. These rules constitute a Finite State Transducer. This helps identify incorrectly written words efficiently and allow for easy word segmentation. An example of a rule would be: "ADJ = ADJ_OF SSY?" This means that an adjective (ADJ) can be formed by a sequence of oblique form adjective (ADJ_OF) and an optional suffix (SSY). The question mark indicates optionality. This is a FSM rule. We thus work with parts instead of wholes. Here ADJ_OF and SSY are inflectional types. To understand this better consider the FST in figure 1 above.

The FST describes the derivation of adverbs from cardinals. The adverb "वीसदा "{veesdaa} {twenty times} is derived by suffixing "दा "{da} {time(s)} (which comes under DA_CL) to the cardinal "वीस "{vees} {twenty} (which comes under STEM_DA), while the adverb "विसाव्यांदा " {visaavyaandaa} {twentieth time} is derived by suffixing "दा "{da} {time(s)}to the stem "विसाव्यां" {visaavyaan} of the ordinal "विसावा" {visaavaa} {twentieth} where "वा" {vaa} becomes "व्यां" {vyaan} (which comes under STEM_WA_DA). Here the ordinal "विसावा " {visaavaa} {twentieth} is derived by suffixing "वा "to the cardinal "वीस "{vees} {twenty} (which comes under STEM_WA). DA_CL represents the derivational suffix "दा" which cannot be followed by any other suffix. STEM_DA is the cardinal stem and STEM_WA_DA is the ordinal stem deriving suffix "व्यां" to which the suffix "दा" is attached. STEM_WA is the cardinal stem to which the suffix "वा" is attached. There are close to a 100 rules. We add more rules to handle more complex forms.

We use Stuttgart University's SFST (Stuttgart Finite State Transducer) compiler which takes the categorised inflected forms (in files) and the Morphotactics to give the transducer file, an augmented Finite Automaton (FA) transition table, called the Morphotact file. We chose SFST as it enjoys the ease of specifying Morphotactics. Alternatives like HFST (Helsinki Finite State Transducer) and FOMA also exist.

3.1.2. Repository of Inflected Forms (REPO)

After undergoing inflection, using an Inflector, which applies SRR's to the words in the lexicon, all inflectional forms with their root words and features (gender, number, etc.) are stored in a single flat file called as the REPO file. Separate files for each inflectional type containing the inflected morphemes of that type are also created which are used for the generation of the FST. The format of this file is: <inflectional type>; <inflected word>; <root word-1, feature list-1#

root word-2, feature list-2#...# root word-n, feature list-n>. An example for "महाबळेश्वर" {mahabaleshwar} {the god of great strength} is <DF>; <महाबळेश्वर>; <महाबळेश्वर,n,n,sg,,,,,d# महाबळेश्वर,n,m,sg,,,,,d# महाबळेश्वर,n,m,pl,,,,,d>.

3.2. Morphological Processing

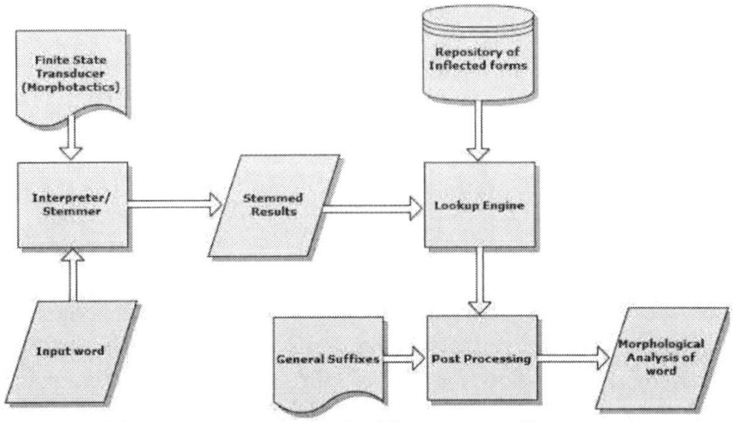

Figure 2 - Morphological Processing Flow

The flow of processing is in figure 2 above. There are 3 main components: the FST interpreter/Stemmer (level 1), a lookup engine and a post processing unit (level 2). An auxiliary support list of suffixes is also used.

3.2.1. FST interpreter / Stemmer / Segmenter

The interpreter (our Java equivalent of SFST interpreter) takes the input word and gives the morphemes it contains. As such this is a Stemmer or Segmenter. It uses the transition table of the FST and gives the output in the form: <input word>: morpheme-1 <category-1> morpheme-2 <category-2> ..... morpheme-n<category-n>. The first morpheme is the Stem. There is a possibility that a word may be stemmed in more than one way because it could be a direct form of a word or a morphologically complex word with a root and suffix(es). An example for "हलवा" {halawaa}:

1. हलवा: An inflected form with the imperative suffix "ा" is attached to the verbal root "हलव" {halaw} {to shake} .
2. हलवा: A direct form of a noun referring to a dessert.

3.2.2. Lookup engine / Parsing

This unit accepts stemmed results to give intermediate morphological analyses. This and the next stage constitute Morphological Parsing (MP). We currently perform MP for all inflectional morphemes and for the derivational morphemes that attach to verbs. First a hash table of the REPO file, by using the inflected form and the word form category as the joint index, is constructed. The first morpheme and its category are then used on this hash structure to obtain its root form and its features. This is followed by the most crucial- Krudanta processing. If the stemmer detects a Krudanta suffix, the lookup gets it from the hash table and modifies the features of the feature list using those of the Krudanta suffix. Otherwise the following suffixes (if any) are either case markers or postpositions or non Krudanta derivational morphemes which we append to the feature list.

Verbs have additional features namely "Krudanta Type" and "Krudanta Case Marker/Suffix". An example for "**धावणारा**" {dhaavnara} {runner}, an adjective, would be: **धावणारा**< fs af (feature structure abbreviated form)='**धाव**,v,m,sg,,d,**णारा**,**णारा**' tense='' aspect='' mood='' kridanta_type='nara' kridanta_cm='**णारा**'>.

3.2.3. Post Processing

A word can be stemmed in multiple ways and hence the resulting duplication of features that happens is eliminated in this unit. Some Marathi specific cases which cannot be handled by rules are also handled here. The final part of this is handling unrecognised words. A word will not be stemmed if either it was not entered in the lexicon or there is a spelling mistake or there are no rules to handle it. It is important to identify the suffix as it shows relations between words and must be translated even if the word it is attached to is unknown or unidentifiable. This is mostly for foreign words. The word is matched against the list of suffixes and the one identified is extracted. There will be no linguistic features associated with it.

Builders of Morphological Analyzers, especially, for Indian (and other similar) languages can use our framework effectively. Our Java based stemmer can completely stem/segment and parse around 50000 tokens in 8-10 seconds. The end result of all this processing is the minimally sufficient morphological analysis of the input word. In the next section we present the methods for evaluation of our MA and the results.

4. Evaluation

We have two measures of quality, namely, accuracy and usability. We prepared Gold Standard Data of 101 sentences with a total of 1341 tokens/words. We compared the outputs of our MA with the gold standard data. For analysis, each word is put into one of 6 different categories. Table1 below describes these categories and also gives the results of our evaluation.

Analysis number	Analysis category	Number of words	Percentage
1	Same analysis: Identical to gold	968	72.18
2	Spurious analysis: Extra analyses along with gold	161	12.00
3	Missing analysis: Missing analyses from gold	66	4.92
4	Missing and spurious analysis: Missing and extra analyses from gold	70	5.21
5	Completely spurious analysis: Totally incorrect	2	0.14
6	No output: No analysis given	74	5.51
	Total	1341	

Table 1- Distribution of Analysis types

Our formula for accuracy is:

$$Accuracy = (Number\ of\ type\ 1\ analyses)/(Total\ number\ of\ words)$$

This gives us an accuracy of 72.18%. This proportion of words is perfectly analyzed and their analyses were correct, complete and useful in terms of the root and features information. The analyses of words under type 2, 3 and 4 give at least one usable analysis (feature list including root and suffix), which is mostly sufficient for NLP applications. Analysis belonging to categories 5 and 6 are totally useless.

The formula for usability is:

$$Usability = Number\ of\ type\ 1,2,3\ and\ 4\ analyses/Total\ number\ of\ words$$

This brings our usability score to 94.33%. Out of 273 derivational morphemes, 265 (97.06%) were correctly segmented and 237 (86.81%) of them were correctly parsed. Our parsing of derivational morphemes needs more work, as only 237 (89.43%) out of 265 recognised are correctly parsed.

4.1. Error Analysis

Errors found in the MA output are of two types- errors of commission (false positives) and errors of omission (false negatives). Errors of commission which occur due to wrong entries and overgenerating rules in the lexicon grammatical rules list, respectively, are solved by modifying the entries and rules. Errors of omission which occur when necessary entries and rules are not made in the lexicon and grammatical rules list, respectively, are solved by adding the missing entries and rules.

Conclusions and Future work

We described the construction of a morphology analyzer for Marathi, which can be adapted for other languages that do suffix stacking. The Morphotactics have to be carefully captured- all generalities and exceptions included, after which standard FSM type tools can be harnessed to perform the analysis. The lexicon needs to be exhaustive and rich in morphosyntactic information. Our MA for Marathi has the ability to handle inflectional and derivational morphology for almost all of the grammatical categories. In future work, the parsing of derivational morphemes for categories other than verbs needs to be handled. We also need to adopt the suffix stripping approach where the FST approach fails, thereby leading to a hybrid MA. In the context of translation, the influence of derivational morphology needs to be investigated. Multiword and compounds form another area of investigation.

References

Damale, M. K. (1970). Shastriya Marathii Vyaakarana. Deshmukh and Company, Pune, India.

Koskenniemi, Kimmo (1983). Two-level Morphology: a general computational model for word-form recognition and production. University of Helsinki, Helsinki.

Antworth, E. L. (1990). PC-KIMMO: A Two level Processor for Morphological Analysis. Occasional Publications in Academic Computing. Summer Institute of Linguistics, Dallas, Texas.

Deok-Bong, Kim., Sung-Jin, Lee., Key-Sun, Choi and Gil-Chang, Kim (1994). A two level Morphological Analysis of Korean. In Conference on Computational Linguistics (COLING), pages 535–539.

Bharati, Akshar., Chaitanya, Vineet and Sanghal, Rajeev (1995). Natural Language Processing: A Paninian Perspective. Prentice Hall, India.

Eryiğit, Gülşen and Adalı, Eşref (2004). An Affix Stripping Morphological Analyzer for Turkish. In IASTED International Multi-Conference on Artificial Intelligence and Applications. Innsbruck, Austria, pages 299–304.

Dixit, Veena., Dethe, Satish and Joshi, Rushikesh K. (2006). Design and Implementation of a Morphology-based Spellchecker for Marathi, an Indian Language. In Special issue on Human Language Technologies as a challenge for Computer Science and Linguistics. Part I. 15, pages 309–316. Archives of Control Sciences.

Dhongde and Wali (2009). Marathi. John Benjamins Publishing Company, Amsterdam, Netherlands.

Bapat, Mugdha., Gune, Harshada and Bhattacharyya, Pushpak (2010). A Paradigm-Based Finite State Morphological Analyzer for Marathi. Proceedings of the 1st Workshop on South and Southeast Asian Natural Language Processing (WSSANLP), pages 26–34, the 23rd International Conference on Computational Linguistics (COLING), Beijing, August 2010

Bhosale, Ganesh., Kembhavi, Subodh., Amberkar, Archana., Mhatre, Supriya., Popale, Lata and Bhattacharyya, Pushpak (2011). Processing of Participle (Krudanta) in Marathi. In International Conference on Natural Language Processing (ICON 2011), Chennai, December, 2011.

Modelling the Organization and Processing of Bangla Polymorphemic Words in the Mental Lexicon: A Computational Approach

Tirthankar Dasgupta Manjira Sinha Anupam Basu
Indian Institute of Technology Kharagpur, Kharagpur 721302
iamtirthankar@gmail.com, manjira87@gmail.com, anupambas@gmail.com

ABSTRACT
In this paper we try to present psycholinguistically motivated computational model for the access and representation of Bangla polymorphemic words in the Mental Lexicon. We first conduct a series of masked priming experiment on a set of Bangla polymorphemic words. Our analysis indicates a significant number of words shows morphological decomposition during the processing stage. We further developed a computational model for the processing of Bangla polymorphemic words. The novelty of the new model over the existing ones are, the proposed model not only considers the frequency of the derived word but also considers the role of its constituent stem, suffix and the degree of affixation between the stem and the suffix. We have evaluated the new model with the results obtained from the priming experiment and then compare it with the state of the art. The proposed model has been found to perform better than the existing models.

KEYWORDS: Mental Lexicon, Morphology, Decomposition, Psycholinguistics, Masked Priming.

Proceedings of COLING 2012: Posters, pages 235–244,
COLING 2012, Mumbai, December 2012.

1 Introduction

The mental lexicon refers to the organization of words in the human mind and their interactions that facilitates fast retrieval and comprehension of a word in a context. One important goal of cognitive science is to understand the organization of mental lexicon as it will help to model how brain processes language. This knowledge will benefit the development various NLP applications that includes text comprehension, lexicon development, information retrieval, text summarization and question answering.

One of the key investigation areas in psycholinguistics is the representation and processing of morphologically complex words in the mental lexicon. That is, for a native speaker, whether a polymorphemic word like "unpreventable" will be processed as a whole (Bradley, 1980; Butterworth, 1983) or will it be decomposed into its individual morphemes "un", "prevent", and "able" and finally recognised by the representation of its stem (morphemic model)(Taft and Forster, 1975; MacKay, 1978). It has been argued that people do have the capability of such decomposition as they can understand novel words like "unsupportable". However, there has been a long standing debate whether such decomposition are obligatory or are they applicable to only those situations where the whole word access fails (Taft, 2004) (partial decomposition model) (Caramazza et al., 1988; Baayen et al., 1997; Baayen, 2000). An alternative to the morphemic and partial decomposition model is the full listing model that assumes decomposition is not at all an obligatory process and the initial processing of words are performed in terms of the whole word representation in the mental lexicon (Burani and Caramazza, 1987; Burani and Laudanna, 1992; Caramazza et al., 1988). Several computational models have been developed to predict the processing of polymorphemic words. The obligatory decomposition model (Taft, 2004) accounts for the fact that decomposition of a polymorphemic word depends on the frequency of its constituent stem (or the base word). Therefore, higher the stem frequency, easier is the decomposition. On the other hand, the full listing model (Burani and Laudanna, 1992) states that the whole word frequency facilitates the recognition of a polymorphemic word. The dual route access model (Baayen et al., 1997) argues that the decomposition of a polymorphemic word into its constituent morphemes depends on the surface frequency of that word; if the frequency crosses a threshold then the word is accessed as a whole otherwise it is accessed via its parts.

In spite of the plethora of work that has been done to understand the representation and processing of polymorphemic words in the mental lexicon, a coherent picture is yet to be emerged. Further, most of the existing studies have conducted experiments mainly in English; Hebrew, Italian, French, Dutch, and few other languages (Frost et al., 1997), (Forster and Davis, 1984; Grainger et al., 1991; Drews and Zwitserlood, 1995; Taft and Forster, 1975; Taft, 2004) have also been considered. Any such investigation for Indian languages has not been reported so far, though they are considered to be morphologically richer than many of their Indo-European cousins. On the other hand, several cross-linguistic experiments have indicated that mental representation and processing of polymorphemic words are not language independent (Taft, 2004). The conclusion drawn in one language cannot be generalized to the others without repeating the experiments on them. Bangla, in particular, supports stacking of inflectional suffixes and it has a rich derivational morphology inherited from Sanskrit and some borrowed from Persian, and Arabic, and shows abundance of compounding.

The objective of this paper is to understand the organization and processing of Bangla derivationally suffixed words in the mental lexicon. Our aim is to determine whether the mental lexicon decomposes morphologically complex words into its constituent morphemes or it represents the intact surface form of a word and subsequently develop a robust computational model. To achieve this, first we have conducted the masked priming experiment and gathered reaction time data for next level analysis. The experimental results show that priming occurs only for those cases where the prime is the derived form of the target and have a recognizable suffix (like, *sonA-sonAli* (GOLD-GOLDEN), and *bayasa-bayaska*(AGE-AGED). Weak or no priming is observed for cases where the prime is a derived form of the target but do not have a recognizable suffix or when the prime and the target is not morphologically related at all. These observations instigate the basic assumptions of the obligatory decomposition model (Taft and Forster, 1975; Taft, 2004) that polymorphemic words are always processed via decomposition. Deeper analysis of the experimental data reveals that processing of Bangla polymorphemic words may be explained by the dual route decomposition model proposed by (Baayen, 2000). However, unlike the dual route model, our proposed model not only considers the frequency of the derived word but also the role of its constituent stem, suffix and the degree of affixation between them. Our proposed model is the first ever attempt to computationally predict the processing mechanism of a polymorphemic word in any Indian language. We have evaluated our proposed model against the priming experiment results and also compared our performance with that of the existing models in other languages. We have found that our proposed model provides good accuracy for Bangla polymorphemic words which reinforces the language dependent nature of word processing phenomena.

The rest of the paper is organized as follows: section 2 presents related works; section 3 describes the masked priming experiment performed over a set of Bangla morphologically complex words; section 4 compares the performance of different frequency based models in predicting the processing mechanisms of Bangla polymorphemic words; section 5 describes the proposed models of word recognition in Bangla; the last concluding section contains the summary of the observations and discusses the findings.

2 Related Works

Their is a rich literature on representation, organization and accessing of polymorphemic words in the mental lexicon. Typically, priming experiments, and frequency models are used to address such issues. Priming is a process that results in increase in speed or accuracy of response to a stimulus, called the target, based on the occurrence of a prior exposure of another stimulus, called the prime. For details please refer to the literature (Caramazza et al., 1988; Bodner and Masson, 1997; Tulving et al., 1982). These experiments demonstrate that across the languages, recognition of a target word (say happy) is facilitated by a prior exposure of a morphologically related prime word (e.g., happiness). Since morphological relatedness often implies orthographic, phonological and semantic similarities between two words, several attempts have been made to factor out other priming effects from morphological priming (Bentin and Feldman, 1990; Drews and Zwitserlood, 1995)(Bodner and Masson, 1997)(Davis and Rastle, 2010)(Forster and Davis, 1984)(Frost et al., 1997)(Crepaldi et al., 2010)(Grainger et al., 1991)(Drews and Zwitserlood, 1995). A cross modal priming experiment has been conducted for Bangla derivationally suffixes words by (Dasgupta et al., 2010) where strong priming effects have been observed for morphologically and phonologically related prime-target pairs; weak priming is observed for morphologically related but phonologically opaque pairs and no priming is observed for morphologically unrelated pairs. Apart from this, we do not know of any other cognitive experiments on morphological priming in Bangla or other Indian languages.

Class	Examples
M+S+O+	nibAsa (residence)-nibAsi (resident)
M+S+O-	mitra (friend) - maitri (friendship)
M'+S-O+	Ama (Mango)- AmadAni (import)
M-S+O-	jantu (Animal)- bAgha (Tiger)
M-S-O+	ghaDi (watch)- ghaDiYAla (crocodile)

Table 1: Dataset for the Experiment. M=Morphology, S=Semantics, O=Orthography. + implies related, - implies unrelated.

In the frequency model analysis, (Taft and Forster, 1975) with his experiment on English inflected words, argued that lexical decision responses of polymorphemic words depends upon the base word frequency. In other words, higher the frequency of the stem is (called, base frequency), the shorter is the time to recognize the word (called, Reaction Time or RT). Previous experiments have shown such base frequency effects in most of the cases but not for all (Baayen et al., 1997; Bertram et al., 2000; Bradley, 1980; Burani and Caramazza, 1987; Burani et al., 1984; Colé et al., 1989; Schreuder and Baayen, 1997; Taft and Forster, 1975; Taft, 2004). (Baayen, 2000) proposed the dual processing race model where both the full-listing and morphemic path compete among each other and depending upon the frequency of base and the surface word any one of the paths are chosen.

3 Psycholinguistic Study of Bangla Polymorphemic Words through Masked Priming Experiments

We apply the masked priming experiment discussed in (Forster and Davis, 1984; Rastle et al., 2000) (Marslen-Wilson et al., 2008) for Bangla morphologically complex words. Here, the prime is placed between a forward pattern mask and the target stimulus, which acts as a backward mask. This is illustrated below.
$mask(500ms)\ \#\#\#\#\# \rightarrow prime(50ms)\ sonA(GOLD) \rightarrow target(500ms)\ sonAli(GOLDEN)$
After presenting the target probe, the subjects were asked to make a lexical decision whether the given target is a valid word in that language. The same target word is again probed but with a different visual probe called the control word. The control shows no relationship with the target. For example, baYaska (aged) and baYasa (age) is a prime-target pair, for which the corresponding control-target pair could be naYana (eye) and baYasa (age).

There were 171 prime-target and control-target pairs classified into five different classes. The prime is related to the target either in terms of morphology, semantics and orthography depending upon the class in which they belong. For example, class-I primes are morphologically, semantically as well as orthographically related where as class-V primes are related only in terms of semantics. The five different class along with their examples are discussed in Table 1.

The experiments were conducted on 14 highly educated native Bangla speakers. Nine of them have a graduate degree and five hold a post graduate degree. The age of the subjects varies between 22 to 35 years.
Results:
The RTs with extreme values and those for incorrect lexical decisions (about 3.2%) were excluded from the data[1]. Table 2 summarizes the average RTs for the prime and control sets for the five classes. The p-values for two-sample t-test and paired t-test are also indicated, where

[1]Any RT value that falls outside the range of $Average\ RT \pm 500ms$ is considered as extreme

the prime and corresponding control RTs have been considered as the two samples or items within a pair. We observe that, strong priming effects are observed when the target word is morphologically derived and has a recognizable suffix, semantically and orthographically related with respect to the prime; no priming effects are observed when the prime and target words are orthographically related but share no morphological or semantic relationship; although not statistically significant, but weak priming is observed for prime target pairs that are only semantically related. The results for [M+S+O+] and [M-S-O+] classes are statistically significant according to the t-statistics. However, we see no significant difference between the prime and control RTs for other classes.

Class	Avg RT (in ms)		p values		Sign Score Range		
	P	C	S	Pair	-14 to -4	-3 to +3	+4 to +14
$[M+S+O+]$	623	689	<0.00	<0.01	24	4	18
$[M+S+O-]$	658	660	<0.09	<0.06	6	14	19
$[M'+S-O+]$	545	549	<0.10	>0.20	5	7	19
$[M-S+O-]$	602	597	>0.20	<0.10	3	6	22
$[M-S-O+]$	590	569	<0.05	<0.08	2	5	21

Table 2: Average RT for the word classes, the p-values and the sign score ranges.

Analysis of RTs for Lexical Items:

We also looked at the RTs for each of the 171 target words. Since we had only 14 observations, one from each participant, we decided to conduct a sign test instead of the usual parametric tests of significance (e.g., t-test). The null hypothesis here is that the average or sum is 0 (i.e., there are equal number of cases where control RT is greater than prime RT and vice versa). The results are summarized in Table 2. Since, we subtracted the control RT from the prime RT, a negative sign indicates priming. Therefore, the smaller the value of the sum for a target word, the more significant is the priming effect. We consider a value less than or equal to -4 as significant. In other words, a target is considered to be significantly primed by the prime word if, out of 14 responses, RT for the prime-target was smaller than the RT for the corresponding control-target in at least 9 cases.

As explained earlier, the effect of priming with a morphologically derived word instigates decomposition, leading to reduced RT of the target. However, it is apparent from the above results that not all polymorphemic words tend to decompose during processing. This contradicts the obligatory decomposition model of (Taft and Forster, 1975; Taft, 2004). Naturally, the question that arises is, what are the other factors that are responsible for the decomposition of Bangla polymorphemic words. In order to answer this we need to further investigate the processing phenomena of Bangla derived words. One notable means is to identify whether the stem or suffix frequency of a polymorphemic word is involved in the processing stage of that word. For this, we apply the existing frequency based models to the Bangla polymorphemic words and try to evaluate their performance by comparing their predicted results with the result obtained through the priming experiment.

4 Applying Base Word and Derived Word Frequency Models

The *base word frequency model* (or, Model-1) states that a polymorphemic word that constitute a high frequency stem will be decomposed faster than a word having low stem frequency. In order to compare the results with respect to that of the masked priming experiment discussed in the previous section, we made a slight change to the original model. We propose that if the stem frequency of a polymorphemic word crosses a given threshold value τ, then the word will decomposed into its constituent morpheme. The model is formally represented as:

$$Decomposability(W_i) = \begin{cases} TRUE, & \text{if } \log_{10}(frequency(W_{stem})) \geq \tau \\ FALSE, & \text{if } \log_{10}(frequency(W_{stem})) \leq \tau \end{cases} \tag{1}$$

The *derived word frequency model* (or, Model-2) claims that, if a specific morphologically complex form is above a certain threshold of frequency, then the whole word access will be preferred and thus no priming effect will be observed in this case. On the other hand if the derived word frequency is below that same threshold of frequency, the parsing route will be preferred, and the word will be accessed via its parts. Here, the threshold value is computed as the log of average corpus frequency of words[2] which comes out to be 3 in our case. We apply model-1 and Model-2 to a set of 171 morphologically derived words. The predicted values of both the models are evaluated with respect to the results obtained from the priming experiment discussed in section. performances of the models are computed in terms of Precision, Recall, F-Measure and Accuracy. matrix along with the computed results is depicted in Table 4. We observed that Model-1 posses an accuracy of 62% where as Model-2 has an accuracy of 49%. Table 4 also shows that the false positive and false negative values to be around 11% and 26% respectively. This indicates for these 11% of the words, Model-1 predicts no morphological decomposition due to extremely low base word frequency (ranges between 1 to 7 out of 4 million) but the priming experiment shows high degree of morphological decomposition. On the other hand, model fails to explain why around 27% words (like, *ekShatama, juYADi and rAjakiYa*) having extremely low base word frequency (ranges between 1 to 7) shows high degree of priming. Moreover, the model also fails to explain the negative decomposability of 11% words (like, *laThiYAla, dAktArakhAnA, and Alokita*) despite having high root word frequencies (ranges between 100 to 1100). We observe that Model-2 can be used to explain the possible decomposition of low frequency derived words which the base word frequency model fails to explain. Thus, the false positive value for the present model is lower than that of the earlier one (21%). However, the present model performs poorly due to the high false negative value (28%). This implies the model fails to recognise the potentially decomposable words (like, *meghalA, pAkAmo and AkAShamandala*) properly.

From the above results we observed that, Model-1 predicts that the priming/decomposition will take place if the base word frequency is high, irrespective of the frequency of the prime. However, the prediction of the model was not validated when the prime as well as the target words are both having high frequency. On the other hand, Model-2 predicts that priming/decomposition will take place if the prime is of low frequency. However, the model was not validated from the experimental results for low frequency prime and low frequent target pairs. Hence, the two extremes of paring call for a newer model.

5 Combining the Base and the Derived Word Frequencies with Suffix Frequencies

In a pursuit towards an extended model, we combine the model 1 and 2 together to observe if and how their combination can predict the parsing phenomena. We further tried to analyse

[2]Computed by combining the CIIL, and Anandabazar corpus and literary works of Rabindranath Tagore, and Bankim Chandra available from (www.ciil.org, iitkgp.ernet.in and nltr.org)

the role of suffixes in determining the decomposability of Bangla derivationally suffixed words. Accordingly, we followed the same regression based technique discussed in (Hay and Baayen, 2001) to derive relationship between the base and surface word frequencies. We took the log of frequency of both the base and the derived words and plotted their values in a log-log scale. In order to get the best-fit curve over the given dataset we have used the least square fit regression method, the equation of the straight line being:

$$Log_{10}(Base\ Frequency) = 0.264 \times Log_{10}(Surface\ Frequency) + 1.822 \quad (2)$$

We propose that any point that falls above the regression line will be parsed into its constituent morphemes during processing. On the other hand, points situated below the regression line will be accessed as a whole. In other words, given the surface frequency of a derived word W, the equation above can predict the frequency of the corresponding base word. If the predicted frequency of the base word is greater than the actual frequency then the point lies above the regression line and thus, during processing these words will be accessed via the decomposition model. This is depicted in Figure 1 which illustrates the surface and base word frequency distribution of 171 Bangla polymorphemic words. The model predicts that those points that lie on or above the regression line will be parsed during processing where as points lying below the regression line will be accessed as a whole. Next, we compute the type and token

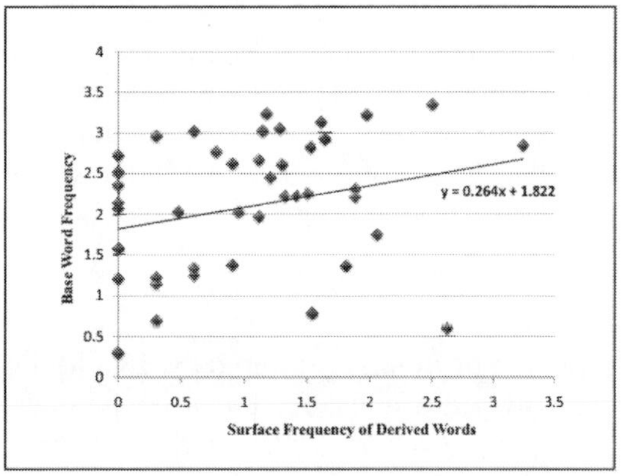

Figure 1: The relation between log derived frequency and log base frequency for 171 different Bangla polymorphemic words.

frequencies of the individual suffixes. The type frequency is defined as the total number of distinct words associated with an affix. On the other hand, token frequency of a suffix is the total number of times a suffix is attached with a word. The hypothesis can be given as, for a given Bangla polymorphemic word if the type/token ratio exceeds a predefined threshold τ, then the word will be accessed as a whole otherwise the derived word will be decomposed into the corresponding stem and suffix. In order to compute the threshold ratio, we follow the same approach as discussed above. Therefore, we draw a parsing line which is the linear regression line passing from the origin. The slope of the line thus computed is the value of the threshold frequency τ. Thus, the proposed model can be viewed as:

$$Type\ Frequency(S_i) = 0.09 * Token\ Frequency(S_i) \quad (3)$$

Finally, we combine equation 2 (E2) and equation 3 (E43) together to get a new enhanced model. The combination of the models were done by performing a logical OR operation on the

	False Positive	True Negative	True Positive	False Negative	P (%)	R (%)	F (%)	A (%)
BF	46	38	68	19	40	54	46	62
SF	38	30	53	49	41	55	47	49
Combined	20	39	51	17	72	75	73	71

Table 3: Summarising the comparative results of the frequency based models. BF= Base frequency model, SF= Surface frequency model, Combine= Combining all the models together. P= Precision, R=Recall, F=F-Measure, A=Accuracy

outputs of E2 and E3. This is represented as:

$$Decomposability(W) = \begin{cases} TRUE, & \text{if } (E3 \vee E4) = 1 \\ FALSE, & Otherwise \end{cases} \quad (4)$$

The enhanced model is evaluated over a set of 136 Bangla polymorphemic words where the stem and the suffixes are transparent (i.e the suffix is fully or partly recognizable). This is because, as automatic identification of opaque Bangla suffixes and computing the frequency is difficult. Thus, for the present model we have not considered the 39 Bangla derived words (belonging to the class [M+S+O-]) for which the stem and suffix is opaque. The results are depicted in Table 4. The performance of our final model shows an accuracy of 71% with a precision of 72% and a recall of 75%. This suppresses the performance of the other models discussed earlier. However, around 29% of the test words that includes words like, *rAShTrIya, nAchuni, nishThAbAna, and juyADi*, were wrongly classified which the model fails to justify.

Conclusion

In this paper we try to model the processing of Bangla words in the mental lexicon. Our aim is to determine whether such words are accessed as a whole or does it is decomposed into its constituent morphemes during recognition. We tried to answer this question through two different angles. First, we conduct a series of masked priming experiments. The reaction time of the subjects for recognizing various lexical items under appropriate conditioning reveals important facts about their organization and processing of words in the brain which are discussed in the paper. Next, we try to develop computational models that can predict the recognition process of Bangla words and validated the prediction through the results of priming experiment. We observed that appart from the surface and base word frequency, decomposition of a Bangla polymorphemic word depends upon the suffix with which the base is attached. The performance of our proposed model shows an improvement of 9% compared to the existing ones. However, further study is needed in order to concretize our claim. To the best of our knowledge there is no other work on computational modelling of Bangla polymorphemic words against which we could benchmark our results.

Acknowledgements

We thank Dr. Monojit Choudhury from Microsoft Research India for his valuable suggestions and SNLTR, Kolkata to support and sponsor our work. We also thank members of SNLTR, Kolkata and Communication Empowerment Lab, IIT Kharagpur for participating in our experiments.

References

Baayen, H. (2000). On frequency, transparency and productivity. *G. Booij and J. van Marle (eds), Yearbook of Morphology*, pages 181–208.

Baayen, R., Dijkstra, T., and Schreuder, R. (1997). Singulars and plurals in dutch: Evidence for a parallel dual-route model. *Journal of Memory and Language*, 37(1):94–117.

Bentin, S. and Feldman, L. (1990). The contribution of morphological and semantic relatedness to repetition priming at short and long lags: Evidence from hebrew. *The quarterly journal of experimental psychology*, 42(4):693–711.

Bertram, R., Schreuder, R., and Baayen, R. (2000). The balance of storage and computation in morphological processing: The role of word formation type, affixal homonymy, and productivity. *Journal of Experimental Psychology: Learning, Memory, and Cognition*, 26(2):489.

Bodner, G. and Masson, M. (1997). Masked repetition priming of words and nonwords: Evidence for a nonlexical basis for priming. *Journal of Memory and Language*, 37:268–293.

Bradley, D. (1980). Lexical representation of derivational relation. *Juncture*, pages 37–55.

Burani, C. and Caramazza, A. (1987). Representation and processing of derived words. *Language and Cognitive Processes*, 2(3-4):217–227.

Burani, C. and Laudanna, A. (1992). Units of representation for derived words in the lexicon. *Advances in psychology*, 94:361–376.

Burani, C., Salmaso, D., and Caramazza, A. (1984). Morphological structure and lexical access. *Visible Language*, 18(4):342–352.

Butterworth, B. (1983). Lexical representation. *Language production*, 2:257–294.

Caramazza, A., Laudanna, A., and Romani, C. (1988). Lexical access and inflectional morphology. *Cognition*, 28(3):297–332.

Colé, P., Beauvillain, C., and Segui, J. (1989). On the representation and processing of prefixed and suffixed derived words: A differential frequency effect. *Journal of Memory and Language*, 28(1):1–13.

Crepaldi, D., Rastle, K., Coltheart, M., and Nickels, L. (2010). 'fell'primes 'fall', but does 'bell'prime 'ball'? masked priming with irregularly-inflected primes. *Journal of memory and language*, 63(1):83–99.

Dasgupta, T., Choudhury, M., Bali, K., and Basu, A. (2010). Mental representation and access of polymorphemic words in bangla: Evidence from cross-modal priming experiments. In *International Conference on Natural LAnguage Processing*.

Davis, M. and Rastle, K. (2010). Form and meaning in early morphological processing: Comment on feldman, o'connor, and moscoso del prado martín (2009). *Psychonomic bulletin & review*, 17(5):749–755.

Drews, E. and Zwitserlood, P. (1995). Morphological and orthographic similarity in visual word recognition. *Journal of Experimental Psychology: Human Perception and Performance*, 21(5):1098.

Forster, K. and Davis, C. (1984). Repetition priming and frequency attenuation in lexical access. *Journal of experimental psychology: Learning, Memory, and Cognition*, 10(4):680.

Frost, R., Forster, K., and Deutsch, A. (1997). What can we learn from the morphology of hebrew? a masked-priming investigation of morphological representation. *Journal of Experimental Psychology: Learning, Memory, and Cognition*, 23(4):829.

Grainger, J., Colé, P., and Segui, J. (1991). Masked morphological priming in visual word recognition. *Journal of memory and language*, 30(3):370–384.

Hay, J. and Baayen, H. (2001). Parsing and productivity. *Yearbook of morphology*, 35.

MacKay, D. (1978). Derivational rules and the internal lexicon. *Journal of Verbal Learning and Verbal Behavior*, 17(1):61–71.

Marslen-Wilson, W., Bozic, M., and Randall, B. (2008). Early decomposition in visual word recognition: Dissociating morphology, form, and meaning. *Language and Cognitive Processes*, 23(3):394–421.

Rastle, K., Davis, M., Marslen-Wilson, W., and Tyler, L. (2000). Morphological and semantic effects in visual word recognition: A time-course study. *Language and Cognitive Processes*, 15(4-5):507–537.

Schreuder, R. and Baayen, R. (1997). How complex simplex words can be. *Journal of Memory and Language*, 37:118–139.

Taft, M. (2004). Morphological decomposition and the reverse base frequency effect. *Quarterly Journal of Experimental Psychology Section A*, 57(4):745–765.

Taft, M. and Forster, K. (1975). Lexical storage and retrieval of prefixed words. *Journal of verbal learning and verbal behavior*, 14(6):638–647.

Tulving, E., Schacter, D., and Stark, H. (1982). Priming effects in word-fragment completion are independent of recognition memory. *Journal of experimental psychology: learning, memory, and cognition*, 8(4):336–342.

Coreference Clustering Using Column Generation

Jan De Belder   Marie-Francine Moens
KU Leuven, Department of Computer Science
Celestijnenlaan 200A, 3001 Heverlee, Belgium
`jan.debelder@cs.kuleuven.be, sien.moens@cs.kuleuven.be`

ABSTRACT
In this paper we describe a novel way of generating an optimal clustering for coreference resolution. Where usually heuristics are used to generate a document-level clustering, based on the output of local pairwise classifiers, we propose a method that calculates an exact solution. We cast the clustering problem as an Integer Linear Programming (ILP) problem, and solve this by using a column generation approach. Column generation is very suitable for ILP problems with a large amount of variables and few constraints, by exploiting structural information. Building on a state of the art framework for coreference resolution, we implement several strategies for clustering. We demonstrate a significant speedup in time compared to state-of-the-art approaches of solving the clustering problem with ILP, while maintaining transitivity of the coreference relation. Empirical evidence suggests a linear time complexity, compared to a cubic complexity of other methods.

KEYWORDS: Coreference Resolution, Linear Programming, Column Generation.

Proceedings of COLING 2012: Posters, pages 245–254,
COLING 2012, Mumbai, December 2012.

1 Introduction

Coreference resolution is a well-studied problem in Natural Language Processing, and can be defined as the task of grouping mentions in a text based on which entities they correspond to. The goal is to have all mentions which refer to the same entity in the same group or cluster.

Generalizing research in this area, we can see there are two key aspects to coreference resolution. First, there is the identification of which mentions in a document are likely to be coreferent. For each two mentions a decision is made by a local pairwise classifier whether or not they are compatible. More generally, the classifier outputs a probability that reflects the degree to which the two mentions are coreferent. Second, the coreferent mentions need to be clustered to form coreference chains. Transitivity is an important aspect, since two coreferent pairs (m_1, m_2) and (m_2, m_3) entail that m_1 and m_3 are coreferent as well. In the beginning of the previous decade (Soon et al., 2001; Ng and Cardie, 2002), these two steps were done separately, and the latter rather naively. Later, more advanced Machine Learning approaches were proposed to solve the two tasks simultaneously (Daume III and Marcu, 2005; Haghighi and Klein, 2007; Poon and Domingos, 2008). Recently there has been a movement towards more conservative models, that employ very rich and accurate feature spaces (Raghunathan et al., 2010), but still the clustering method is understudied, and taking the transitive closure of the individual pairwise decision is still common (Haghighi and Klein, 2009).

In this paper we focus on the clustering aspect of coreference resolution. Previous work has solved this using heuristic approaches, most notable (Soon et al., 2001), who use the link-first decision, which links a mention to its closest candidate referent. (Ng and Cardie, 2002) consider instead the link-best decision, which links a mention to its most confident candidate referent. Both these clustering decisions are locally optimized. Several researchers have worked on generating a globally optimized clustering, but these suffer from a very large search space, and need to resort to heuristics to find an approximate solution. E.g. (Luo et al., 2004) uses a Bell tree representation to construct the space of all possible clusterings, although a complete search in it is intractable and partial and heuristic search strategies have to be employed. Other approaches are based on graph partitioning (Cai and Strube, 2010; Nicolae and Nicolae, 2006), to divide the fully-connected pairwise graph into smaller graphs that represent entities. Few have attempted to calculate an exact solution to the clustering problem. (Denis and Baldridge, 2009; Finkel and Manning, 2008; Chang et al., 2011) solve this with an Integer Linear Programming approach, but when enforcing transitivity on the pairwise decisions, they are faced with a cubic number of constraints, and solving large instances takes too long. Linear Programming techniques have many benefits (Roth and Yih, 2004), but efficiency is still an issue (Martins et al., 2009; Rush et al., 2010).

We also use Integer Linear Programming (ILP) to formulate the clustering problem, and to solve this exactly. Although previous approaches decide for every pair of mentions if they are in the same cluster, we instead decide on which clusters are in the optimal clustering. This leads to an ILP problem with an exponential amount of variables (i.e. one for every possible cluster of mentions), but few constraints. However, by using column generation, and exploiting the special structure of the clustering problem, we can efficiently find a solution. We show that we obtain a drastic decrease in time complexity by using this approach.

Column generation is well known for its application to the cutting stock problem (Gilmore and Gomory, 1961), but also other problems in operations research benefit from this technique, e.g. vehicle routing and crew scheduling (Desrosiers and Lubbecke, 2005).

In the next section we will provide a formal definition of the clustering problem in the context of coreference resolution, and cast it as an ILP problem. In section 3, we will show how to solve this problem using column generation. Related formulations are given in section 4, which we will also use as a baseline. The experimental setup is given in section 5, and the results in section 6. We end with our conclusions and directions for future work.

2 The clustering problem

2.1 Basic concepts

Suppose we are given a document with n mentions, $m_1..m_n$. As in most work on coreference resolution, we assume a mention can be a proper noun, a common noun, or a pronoun. The goal is to produce a single clustering, that consists of multiple clusters. Each cluster contains one or more mentions, that refer to the same real-world entity. A cluster containing exactly one mention is called a singleton cluster.

In the example in table 1 we can see six mentions. The first four form one cluster, and mentions 5 and 6 form two separate (singleton) clusters. The optimal clustering thus consists of three clusters: $\{cl_i = \{m_1, m_2, m_3, m_4\}, cl_2 = \{m_5\}, cl_3 = \{m_6\}\}$.

As a first and most import step in many methods, a pairwise classification is performed. With a trained model, the probability that m_i and m_j are coreferent is calculated. We call this classifier a pairwise classifier (PC). In general, the output is a value $p_{ij} \in [0,1]$, and can be easily obtained, e.g. by training a Maximum Entropy model on pairs of mentions.

It is not a secret that **Sony Corp.**$_1$ is looking at 8mm as an all-purpose format. More important to the future of 8mm is **Sony**$_2$'s success in the \$2.3 billion camcorder market. **The Japanese company**$_3$ already has 12% of the total camcorder market, ranking **it**$_4$ third behind the RCA$_5$ and Panasonic$_6$ brands.

Table 1: Example

For a document with n mentions, there are 2^n possible clusters: we can choose n times whether or not a mention is in the cluster. There are even more possible clusterings: having a subset of the mentions assigned in one cluster, we can still divide the remaining mentions in clusters in an exponential amount of ways. Clearly, clustering is a difficult problem, with an enormous search space of possible solutions.

2.2 Integer Linear Programming

The approach we take is based on an Integer Linear Programming (ILP) formulation. The goal of Linear Programming is to find values for a set of variables, so that the objective function (linear in these variables) is maximized (or, without loss of generality, minimized). The variables are further constrained: linear functions in the variables determine lower bounds, upper bounds, or exact values for linear combinations of the variables. Integer Linear Programming is an extension of Linear Programming. In the latter, the variables can take on any numerical value; in ILP, they are required to be integers.

In general, we can write a Linear Programming problem as follows:

$$\begin{aligned} \text{maximize:} \quad & z = cx \\ \text{subject to:} \quad & Ax = b, \ x \geq 0 \end{aligned} \tag{1}$$

in which x is a vector with values we are trying to determine, cx is the objective function. c is called the cost vector, and c_j is the cost for x_j, for $j = 1..n$. A is the constraint matrix or coefficient matrix. Given that there are m constraints, its size will be $m \times n$. b is a column vector, containing m elements (the right-hand side vector). Furthermore, we define $\mathbf{a}_j$ to be the column of matrix A that corresponds to variable x_j.

2.3 Clustering as an ILP

Given that there are n mentions, we can enumerate all possible clusters, using the integers from 0 to 2^n–1. 0 is the cluster without any mentions, 2^n–1 is that containing all mentions. Every integer is at most n bits long, and we can easily map integer i with binary value $b(i)$ to the cluster with the mentions for which their corresponding bit is set to 1. Let us define $b_j(i)$ to be the j-th order bit in cluster i, indicating whether or not mention j is in cluster x_i. For example, cluster x_{19}, with binary representation 10011, corresponds with the cluster containing mentions 4, 1 and 0, because $b_4(19) = 1, b_1(19) = 1$ and $b_0(19) = 1$. Finding a clustering thus entails finding a set of $x_{i_1}..x_{i_k}$, with $k \leq n$ the number of clusters.

To convert this to an ILP form, we require two more elements. First, not every cluster is equally good. Clusters which group mentions "he" and "she" together, obviously need a low score. For now, we will assume the score of cluster x_i to be c_i. Second, only valid clusterings must be generated. Every mention must be in exactly one cluster. We can enforce this by using constraints. For every j-th order bit, the sum across all clusters must be equal to 1. This leads to the ILP formulation in equation 2. The number of constraints is linear in n, but the number variables is exponential in n. In the section 3, we will show how to solve this efficiently.

$$\begin{aligned} \text{maximize: } & z = \sum_{i=1}^{2^n} c_i x_i \\ \text{subject to: } & \sum_{i=1}^{2^n} b_j(i) x_i = 1 \qquad 1 \leq j \leq n \\ & x_i \geq 0, \;\; x_i \text{ binary} \end{aligned} \tag{2}$$

2.4 Defining a cost for the clusters

Several options are possible for determining a cost, or score, for a cluster. Important is that clusters with mentions that do not belong together receive a low score, since we are trying to maximize the value of the objective function. A simple but effective strategy is to take the sum of the pairwise similarities of all mentions in a cluster. Formally we can write this as:

$$c_i = \sum_{j:b_j(i)=1} \sum_{k:b_k(i)=1} PC(m_j, m_k) \tag{3}$$

Note that we do not require the output of the pairwise classifier PC to be a probability, so it can take on negative values as well. We can also write it in terms of feature vectors $\phi(m_1, m_2)$ and a learned weight vector w:

$$c_i = \sum_{j:b_j(i)=1} \sum_{k:b_k(i)=1} w \cdot \phi(m_j, m_k) \tag{4}$$

2.4.1 Training

With the formulation given above, learning encompasses learning the pairwise classifier PC. For mentions that are possibly coreferent, this function should output a positive value, and for mentions that are not coreferent it should output a negative value. Simply using probabilities in the range of $[0, 1]$ would generate a single cluster with every mention in it.

There are several ways to estimate this pairwise classifier PC, and this is inherently related with the coreference resolution task. A straightforward approach is to generate training samples of the form (m_i, m_j), with a positive label if they are in the same cluster, and a negative label if they are in a different cluster. Using the perceptron algorithm it is possible to learn a vector w for eq. 4. An approach that exploits more structural information can also be used, for example with a modified version of the Margin Infused Relaxed Algorithm (Crammer and Singer, 2003).

3 Solving the ILP using Column Generation

3.1 Solving ILPs

Before going into the details of solving the problem in equation 2, we will briefly discuss how generic (I)LPs are solved. There are several algorithms to solve Linear Programming problems. Broadly, they can be separated in two classes. The simplex algorithm and its variants find an optimal solution by moving along the edges of the n-dimensional polytope created by the constraints, until no better value is found. Because the objective function is linear, a local optimum is also a global optimum, so the solution is guaranteed to be exact (Wayne, 1994). A different class of algorithms are interior point algorithms. These move inside the polygon, but never on the edge. The latter class of methods has a guaranteed polynomial runtime, whereas the simplex method has a worst case exponential complexity, although the expected runtime is polynomial. In practice, the simplex algorithm is able to find a solution equally fast, if not faster, for most LP problems.

An often used extension for many Natural Language Processing applications is obtained by limiting the variables x to take only integer values. This is called Integer Linear Programming (ILP). ILP problems are harder to solve. A typical approach is to relax the integer requirement and solve the *relaxed* LP problem. If there is a variable in the optimal solution that is not integer, but required to be one in the original problem, several approaches are possible, such as a branch-and-bound method, or a cutting plane approach.

A special case arises when the constraint matrix A is completely unimodular, i.e. all submatrices of A have determinant $-1, 0$, or 1. In this case, the optimal solution of the relaxed LP problem is always an integer solution. The clustering formulation in equation 2 has such a unimodular structure. This means that we can solve the problem with a standard LP approach, and the solution will be integer.

As mentioned before, the simplex algorithm operates by moving along the edges of the polytope. In each iteration of the algorithm, a new improving direction is to be chosen. When no such direction exists, the optimal solution is found, and the algorithm terminates. During the execution of the algorithm, a certain set of variables are "active". These are called basic variables, and are the only variables that have a value $\neq 0$. All non-basic variables have value 0. There are always m basic variables, as many as the number of constraints. To find the direction that maximally improves the objective function, we need to calculate the *reduced cost* for each non-basic variable. This maximally improving variable will then enter the basis, and another variable has to leave the basis. The reduced cost $\overline{c}_j$ for a non-basic variable x_j is defined as

$$\overline{c}_j = -c_j + \pi \mathbf{a}_j \tag{5}$$

in which c_j is the cost for variable j, and $\mathbf{a}_j$ is the column in the constraint matrix A for variable j. π is the vector of shadow prices, and is dependent on the current set of basic variables.[1] The size of π is $1 \times m$. The goal is to find the j for which $\overline{c}_j$ is minimal.

3.2 Finding the column with the highest reduced cost

The bottleneck for our ILP formulation of the clustering problem lies in finding the new variable with the lowest reduced cost. We have 2^n variables, which becomes quickly intractable for realistic values of n. However, like some other problems, the problem of finding the column with the highest reduced cost can be solved differently. For example, in the cutting stock problem (Gilmore and Gomory, 1961), there are also an exponential amount of variables. However, the problem of finding the column with the highest reduced cost can be rewritten, and a maximally improving column can be found by solving a knapsack problem.

In the remainder of this section we will define an efficient method for finding the column with the highest reduced cost. We start by rewriting the problem in equation 5 in function of the binary representation of j. Let us write j as $b_{n-1}b_{n-2}..b_1b_0$, from which we can see the inclusion of mentions in the clustering.

$$\begin{aligned} & min_j - c_j + \pi \mathbf{a}_j \\ = & min_{j=b_{n-1}..b_0} - c_{b_{n-1}..b_0} + \sum_{i=0}^{n-1} \pi_i b_i \end{aligned} \tag{6}$$

Instead of trying all possible combinations, we can find optimal values for variables b_i, by solving equation 6 as an Integer Linear Programming problem, in which the variables b_i are the decision variables. A more complex aspect is generating the cluster score for a certain assignment to the b_is. For this we introduce binary variables p_{kl}, which have value 1 if both b_k and b_l are in the cluster, and 0 otherwise. With these variables we can model the pairwise scores as in equation 3, and rewrite equation 6 as:

$$\begin{aligned} & min_{j=b_{n-1}..b_0} - \sum_{k=0}^{n-1}\sum_{l=0}^{n-1} p_{kl} PC(m_k, m_l) + \sum_{i=0}^{n-1} \pi_i b_i \\ & \text{with } p_{kl} \Leftrightarrow b_k \wedge b_l \end{aligned} \tag{7}$$

This is again an Integer Linear Programming problem, this time with $\mathcal{O}(n^2)$ variables and $\mathcal{O}(n^2)$ constraints. To model $p_{kl} \Leftrightarrow b_k \wedge b_l$, we use the following three constraints:

$$-p_{kl} + b_k \geq 0, \qquad -p_{kl} + b_l \geq 0, \qquad p_{kl} - b_k - b_l \geq -1$$

These ensure that the value of p_{kl} equals 1 if and only if b_k and b_l have value 1. The constraint matrix is totally unimodular, so solving the relaxed ILP problem yields an integer solution.

[1] Intuitively, the shadow prices reflect how much the objective value will change due to the increased value of the new x_j, because the constraints may prohibit some variables in the basis to keep their old value. Formally, $\pi = c_B B^{-1}$, with c_B the cost for the basic variables, and B^{-1} the matrix that holds the transformations done on the original system. Details regarding the (revised) simplex algorithm can be found in many textbooks, e.g. (Shapiro, 1979).

4 Alternative formulation

An alternative way of formulating the clustering problem, is by deciding for every two mentions whether or not they are in the same cluster. We can do so by defining a decision variable x_{ij} for every two mentions m_i and m_j. The score c_{ij} for these two mentions being in the same cluster can be defined as $PC(m_j, m_k)$. This is the approach taken in (Chang et al., 2011). The complete formulation is given in equation 8.

$$\begin{aligned} \text{maximize:} \quad & z = \sum_{i,j} c_{ij} x_{ij} \\ \text{subject to:} \quad & x_{ij} \geq x_{ik} + x_{kj} - 1 \qquad \forall i, j, k \\ & x_{ij} \geq 0, \quad x_{ij} \text{ binary} \end{aligned} \tag{8}$$

This formulation has $\mathcal{O}(n^2)$ variables, and $\mathcal{O}(n^3)$ constraints that enforce a transitive closure of the clustering. For large documents, this number of constraints becomes problematic.

5 Experimental Setup

As a baseline method, we use the ILP clustering formulation described in section 4. In essence, the method described in this paper calculates the same solution as that presented in (Chang et al., 2011). Therefore, and due to spatial constraints, we will focus on the speed of the methods, rather than the results of the clustering, which are the same.

As an evaluation measure, we use the time taken by the different ILP formulations to solve the clustering problem. Computationally, we use the time taken by the LP solver (lp_solve[2]), excluding file IO[3], including the time to start the process. For the baseline this entails a single call; for our algorithm several calls to the LP solver are made. The overhead associated with keeping track of the current basis is negligible. We group the documents by the number of mentions they contain, and put these in bins of 10 wide. So we have a set of documents with 11 to 20 mentions, a set with 21 to 30 mentions, etc. We take the average runtime of each bin.

In the experiments we used the CoNLL 2011 data, which contains documents with over one hundred mentions. We trained the pairwise classifier on the training set, and evaluated on the development set. In our implementation we use the RECONCILE framework (Stoyanov et al., 2010) to learn a pairwise classifier, using 76 state of the art features. We use default values for the classifier and training sample generation, and train a model to obtain pairwise similarity measures in the $[0, 1]$ range, and subtract 0.5. This is then used as the pairwise similarity.

6 Results

The results are in figure 1. The graphs shows the average runtime of the two methods in function of the number of mentions in the document. The baseline method, indicated with all-link, appears to have a cubic complexity. The method proposed in this paper, named all-link-colgen, appears to have a lower complexity, despite the exponential worst-case complexity.

At every step of the simplex algorithm an ILP with $\mathcal{O}(n^2)$ variables and $\mathcal{O}(n^2)$ constraints is solved. An interesting observation is the number of steps the simplex algorithm takes before the final solution is reached. Empirical evidence suggests that this is roughly linear in the number

[2]http://sourceforge.net/projects/lpsolve/

[3]In our implementation we write the LP problem to a file, but this could be optimized by using the API.

of mentions. Since the two approaches optimize the same objective function, and the generated clusters are identical, we will not report on the results of the coreference task itself.

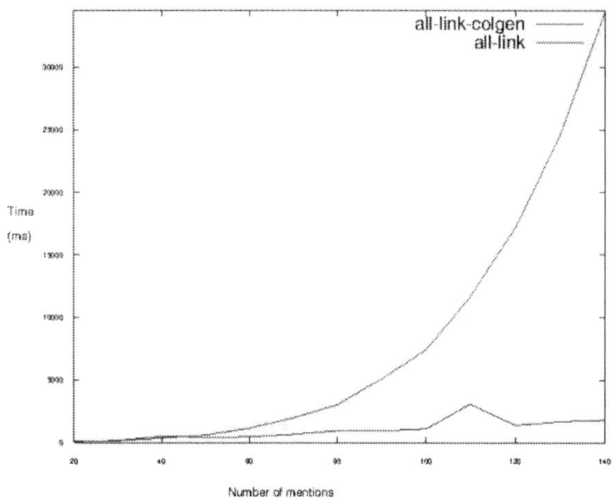

Figure 1: Comparison of the runtime for the two strategies for solving the coreference resolution clustering problem. In red is the baseline approach. In blue is our approach using column generation, that achieves a much more favourable runtime.

Conclusion and Perspectives

In this paper we have presented a new approach to solve the clustering problem for coreference resolution. Previous approaches for clustering are heuristic in nature or become intractable for large documents. By writing the clustering problem as an Integer Linear Programming problem, we obtain an exact solution. To overcome the bottleneck posed by transitivity constraints, we formulate the problem in terms of clusters, which leads to an ILP problem with an exponential amount of variables, but with few constraints. The key aspect of our approach is that this formulation has a special structure, and we can use column generation to solve it. Column generation is a technique from operations research, that has allowed solving combinatorially complex problems in an efficient way, by exploiting the structure of these problems. Using column generation circumvents dealing with the exponential amount of variables; instead we solve multiple subproblems, that corresponds to solving multiple smaller ILP problems.

Our results show that we achieve a drastic decrease in runtime, compared to an ILP formulation that calculates the same solutions, but with a quadratic number of variables, and a cubic number of constraints.

Next we will focus on ways of learning the pairwise classification function using more structured information. One direction of research is to learn this function in such a way that the most confident clusters are generated first, which could lead to additional increases in speed. We will also continue our research with finding different ways of defining scores for clusters, which might lead to different subproblems to be solved.

Acknowledgments

This research was funded by the TERENCE project (EU FP7-257410).

References

Cai, J. and Strube, M. (2010). End-to-end coreference resolution via hypergraph partitioning. In *Proceedings of the 23rd International Conference on Computational Linguistics*, pages 143–151. ACL.

Chang, K., Samdani, R., Rozovskaya, A., Rizzolo, N., Sammons, M., and Roth, D. (2011). Inference protocols for coreference resolution. In *Proceedings of the Fifteenth Conference on Computational Natural Language Learning: Shared Task*, pages 40–44. ACL.

Crammer, K. and Singer, Y. (2003). Ultraconservative online algorithms for multiclass problems. *Journal of Machine Learning Research*, 3:951–991.

Daume III, H. and Marcu, D. (2005). A large-scale exploration of effective global features for a joint entity detection and tracking model. In *Proceedings of the Conference on Human Language Technology and Empirical Methods in Natural Language Processing*, pages 97–104. ACL.

Denis, P. and Baldridge, J. (2009). Global joint models for coreference resolution and named entity classification. *Procesamiento del Lenguaje Natural*, 42:87–96.

Desrosiers, J. and Lubbecke, M. (2005). A primer in column generation. *Column Generation*, pages 1–32.

Finkel, J. and Manning, C. (2008). Enforcing transitivity in coreference resolution. In *Proceedings of the 46th Annual Meeting of the Association for Computational Linguistics on Human Language Technologies: Short Papers*, pages 45–48. ACL.

Gilmore, P. and Gomory, R. (1961). A linear programming approach to the cutting-stock problem. *Operations Research*, pages 849–859.

Haghighi, A. and Klein, D. (2007). Unsupervised coreference resolution in a nonparametric Bayesian model. In *Proceedings of the 45th Annual Meeting of the Association of Computational Linguistics*, pages 848–855, Prague, Czech Republic. ACL.

Haghighi, A. and Klein, D. (2009). Simple coreference resolution with rich syntactic and semantic features. In *Proceedings of the 2009 Conference on Empirical Methods in Natural Language Processing: Volume 3*, pages 1152–1161. ACL.

Luo, X., Ittycheriah, A., Jing, H., Kambhatla, N., and Roukos, S. (2004). A mention-synchronous coreference resolution algorithm based on the Bell tree. In *Proceedings of the 42nd Annual Meeting on Association for Computational Linguistics*, page 135. ACL.

Martins, A., Smith, N., and Xing, E. (2009). Concise integer linear programming formulations for dependency parsing. In *Proceedings of the Joint Conference of the 47th Annual Meeting of the ACL and the 4th International Joint Conference on Natural Language Processing of the AFNLP*, pages 342–350, Suntec, Singapore. ACL.

Ng, V. and Cardie, C. (2002). Improving machine learning approaches to coreference resolution. In *Proceedings of the 40th Annual Meeting on Association for Computational Linguistics*, pages 104–111. ACL.

Nicolae, C. and Nicolae, G. (2006). Bestcut: A graph algorithm for coreference resolution. In *Proceedings of the 2006 Conference on Empirical Methods in Natural Language Processing*, pages 275–283. ACL.

Poon, H. and Domingos, P. (2008). Joint unsupervised coreference resolution with markov logic. In *Proceedings of the Conference on Empirical Methods in Natural Language Processing*, pages 650–659. ACL.

Raghunathan, K., Lee, H., Rangarajan, S., Chambers, N., Surdeanu, M., Jurafsky, D., and Manning, C. (2010). A multi-pass sieve for coreference resolution. In *Proceedings of the 2010 Conference on Empirical Methods in Natural Language Processing*, pages 492–501. ACL.

Roth, D. and Yih, W. (2004). *A linear programming formulation for global inference in natural language tasks*. Defense Technical Information Center.

Rush, A. M., Sontag, D., Collins, M., and Jaakkola, T. (2010). On dual decomposition and linear programming relaxations for natural language processing. In *Proceedings of the 2010 Conference on Empirical Methods in Natural Language Processing*, pages 1–11, Cambridge, MA. ACL.

Shapiro, J. (1979). *Mathematical Programming: Structures and Algorithms*. Wiley New York, NY.

Soon, W., Ng, H., and Lim, D. (2001). A machine learning approach to coreference resolution of noun phrases. *Computational Linguistics*, 27(4):521–544.

Stoyanov, V., Cardie, C., Gilbert, N., Riloff, E., Buttler, D., and Hysom, D. (2010). Coreference resolution with reconcile. In *Proceedings of the ACL 2010 Conference Short Papers*, pages 156–161, Uppsala, Sweden. ACL.

Wayne, L. (1994). *Operations Research: Applications and Algorithms*. Duxbury Press.

Metric Learning for Graph-based Domain Adaptation

Paramveer S. Dhillon
Computer and Information Science, University of Pennsylvania, U.S.A
dhillon@cis.upenn.edu

Partha Pratim Talukdar
Machine Learning Department, Carnegie Mellon University, U.S.A
ppt@cs.cmu.edu

Koby Crammer
Department of Electrical Engineering, The Technion, Israel
koby@ee.technion.ac.il

Abstract

In many domain adaption formulations, it is assumed to have large amount of unlabeled data from the domain of interest (target domain), some portion of it may be labeled, and large amount of labeled data from other domains, also known as source domain(s). Motivated by the fact that labeled data is hard to obtain in any domain, we design algorithms for the settings in which there exists large amount of unlabeled data from all domains, small portion of which may be labeled.

We build on recent advances in graph-based semi-supervised learning and supervised metric learning. Given all instances, labeled and unlabeled, from all domains, we build a large similarity graph between them, where an edge exists between two instances if they are close according to some metric. Instead of using predefined metric, as commonly performed, we feed the labeled instances into metric-learning algorithms and (re)construct a data-dependent metric, which is used to construct the graph. We employ different types of edges depending on the domain-identity of the two vertices touching it, and learn the weights of each edge.

Experimental results show that our approach leads to significant reduction in classification error across domains, and performs better than two state-of-the-art models on the task of sentiment classification.

Keywords: Machine Learning, Domain Adaptation, Graph-based Semi-Supervised Learning, Sentiment Analysis.

Proceedings of COLING 2012: Posters, pages 255–264,
COLING 2012, Mumbai, December 2012.

1 Introduction

Domain adaptation is an important machine learning subtask where the goal is to perform well on a particular classification task on a *target domain*, especially when most of the resources are available from other different domains, called *source(s) domain(s)* (Pan and Yang, 2009), and only limited amount of supervision is available to the target domain. In the standard setting, most domain adaptation algorithms assume the availability of large amounts of labeled data for the source domain, with little or no labeled data from the target domain (Arnold et al., 2008; Dai et al., 2007; Wang et al., 2009). However, in many practical situations, obtaining labeled data from *any* domain is expensive and time consuming, while unlabeled data is easily available. This setting of domain adaptation, where there is only limited amount of labeled data and large amounts of unlabeled data, both from all domains, is relatively unexplored.

To address the issue of labeled data sparsity even within a single domain, recent research has focused on Semi-Supervised Learning (SSL) algorithms, which learn from limited amounts of labeled data combined with widely available unlabeled data. Examples of a few graph-based SSL algorithms include Gaussian Random Fields (GRF) (Zhu et al., 2003), Quadratic Criteria (QR) (Bengio et al., 2006), and Modified Adsorption (MAD) (Talukdar and Crammer, 2009). Given a set of instances that contain small amount of labeled instances and a majority that is unlabeled, most graph based SSL algorithms first construct a graph where each node corresponds to an instance. Similar nodes are connected by an edge, with edge weight encoding the degree of similarity. Once the graph is constructed, the nodes corresponding to labeled instances are injected with the corresponding label. Using this initial label information along with the graph structure, graph based SSL algorithms assign labels to all unlabeled nodes in the graph. Most of the graph based SSL algorithms are iterative and also parallelizable, making them suitable for large scale SSL setting where vast amounts of unlabeled data is usually available.

Most of the graph based SSL algorithms mentioned above concentrate primarily on the label inference part, i.e., assigning labels to nodes *once the graph has already been constructed*, with very little emphasis on construction of the graph itself. Only recently, the issue of graph construction has begun to receive attention (Wang and Zhang, 2006; Jebara et al., 2009; Daitch et al., 2009; Talukdar, 2009). Most of these methods emphasize on constructing graphs which satisfy certain structural properties (e.g., degree constraints on each node). Since our focus is on SSL, a certain number of labeled instances are available at our disposal. However, the graph construction methods mentioned above are all unsupervised in nature, i.e., they do not utilize available label information during the graph construction process. As recently proposed by (Dhillon et al., 2010), the available label information can be used to *learn* a distance metric, which can then be used to set the edge weights in the constructed graph.

In this paper, we bring together these three lines of work: domain adaptation, graph-based SSL, and metric learning for graph construction, and make the following contributions:

1. We consider an important setting for domain adaptation: one where most of the data is unlabeled and only limited amount of instances are labeled. This holds across *all* domains. This setting is relatively unexplored.

2. To the best of our knowledge, we are the first to employ graph-based non-parametric methods for domain adaptation.

2 Related Work

Several methods for domain adaptation have recently been proposed (Arnold et al., 2008; Blitzer et al., 2006; Dai et al., 2007; Pan and Yang, 2009; Eaton et al., 2008; Wang et al., 2009). In (Arnold et al., 2008), the labeled data comes entirely from the source domain, while certain amount of unlabeled target data is also used during transduction. Similar setting is also explored in (Dai et al., 2007; Wang et al., 2009). In contrast to these methods, we assume that limited amount of labeled data and large amounts of unlabeled data from both source and target domains are available. This is motivated by the fact that obtaining large amount of labeled data from any domain is expensive to prepare. The method presented by (Blitzer et al., 2006) also explores a similar setting, but our method is easier to implement and it does not make use of the high domain specific prior knowledge (i.e., for pivot selection) performed by (Blitzer et al., 2006).

All previously proposed methods mentioned above are parametric in nature. The graph-based adaptation method presented in this paper is non-parametric. To the best of our knowledge, it is novel in the context of domain adaptation.The method of (Wang et al., 2009) is similar in spirit as both employ graphs, yet they use a hybrid graph structure involving both instances and features for transfer learning, while we focus on domain adaptation and use homogeneous graph consisting of instance nodes only. Another important difference is that the graphs their algorithms build do *not* take available label information into account, while our algorithms do take such information into account. We will see below in Section 8, that this leads to significant improvement in performance. Another work similar in spirit to ours is of (Eaton et al., 2008). They build a graph over tasks (i.e., a node in such a graph is a task) to decide on the transferability among different tasks for transfer learning. In contrast, we focus on domain adaptation and build a graph over data instances, i.e., a node in our graph corresponds to a data instance.

3 Notation

We denote by n_l^s and n_u^s, the number of labeled and unlabeled instances (respectively) from the source domain. Similarly, n_l^t and n_u^t are the number of labeled and unlabeled instances from the target domain. Denote by n the total number of instances. Let X be the $d \times n$ matrix of n d-dimensional column instances (from source and target domains combined). We define the $n \times n$ diagonal label-indicator matrix S to be $S_{ii} = 1$ iff instance x_i is labeled, and zero otherwise. We denote by $\mathscr{L}$ the set of all possible labels of size $m = |\mathscr{L}|$. We define the $n \times m$ instance-label matrix by Y, where $Y_{i,j} = 1$ iff the ith instance is labeled by the jth label. Note, that the ith column of Y is undefined if $S_{i,i} = 0$, i.e., the data instance is not labeled. Similarly, we denote by $\hat{Y}$ the $n \times m$ matrix of estimated label information, i.e., output of a inference algorithm (e.g., see Section 5). Such algorithms assign a labeling score to all instances, including labeled and unlabeled.

4 Domain Adaptation

Formally, we consider the following problem. Given, a total of $n_l^s + n_l^t$ labeled instances from the source(s) and target domains combined, and in addition $n_u^s + n_u^t$ unlabeled instances from the same domains. Our goal is to label these n_u^t unlabeled instances from the target domain (domain of interest). The task is challenging and non-trivial since we assume that $n_l^s \ll n_u^s$, and similarly $n_l^t \ll n_u^t$. Our setting is different from previous approaches in two ways: First, we assume small amount of labeled data from all domains, as opposed to most previous work in domain adaption which have focused in the "asymmetric" case where there is large amount of labeled source instances, and only very few, if any, labeled target instances. Second, we compensate, this lack in labeled data by considering unlabeled data from all domains, source and target, as opposed to previous settings which assumed unlabeled data only from the target domain. We believe that our "symmetric" setting is very realistic, since labeled data is expensive in any domain.

In Section 8, we report the results of experiments using a sentiment dataset, which contains reviews on products from a few categories. We assume that only a few instances are hand-labeled with the correct sentiment for every category, and our goal is to exploit the labeled and *unlabeled* instances from all domains to perform well on a single pre-defined *target* domain. Our task is harder, since we have only few labeled examples from each domain, however, we exploit additional cheap resource, namely unlabeled data from all the domains.

5 Graph Construction & Inference

Given a set X of n instances, both from the source and target domains, we construct a graph where each instance is associated with a node. We add an edge between two nodes if the two nodes are similar and the edge's weight represents the degree of similarity between the corresponding instances. Denote the resulting graph by $G = (V, E, W)$ be this graph, where $V = V_l^s \cup V_u^s \cup V_l^t \cup V_u^t$ is the set of vertices with $|V| = n$, $|V_l^s| = n_l^s$, $|V_u^s| = n_u^s$, $|V_l^t| = n_l^t$, $|V_u^t| = n_u^t$; E is the set of edges, and W is the symmetric $n \times n$ matrix of edge weights. W_{ij} is the weight of edge (i, j) which is monotonic in the similarity between instances x_i and x_j. Additionally, $V^s = V_l^s \cup V_u^s$, and $V^t = V_l^t \cup V_u^t$ are the set of vertices associated with sources and target domain instances, respectively. Gaussian kernel (Zhu et al., 2003) is a widely used measure of similarity between data instances, which can be used to compute edge weights as shown in Eq. (1).

$$W_{ij} = \alpha_{ij} \times \exp\Big(-d_A(x_i, x_j)/(2\sigma^2)\Big) \qquad (1)$$

where $d_A(x_i, x_j)$ is the distance measure between instances x_i and x_j and A is a positive definite matrix of size $d \times d$, which parameterizes the (squared) Mahalanobis distance (Eq. (3)). Furthermore, σ is the kernel bandwidth parameter, and $\alpha_{ij} = \alpha$ $(0 \le \alpha \le 1)$ if the edge connects instances from two different domains, and $\alpha_{ij} = 1$, otherwise. In other words, the hyperparameter, α, controls the importance of cross domain edges. Setting edge weights directly using Eq. (1) results in a complete graph, where *any* two pair of nodes are connected, since the Gaussian kernel always attains strictly positive values by definition. This is undesirable as the graph is dense (and in fact complete) and thus all computation times are at least quadratic in the number of instances, which may be very large. We thus generate a sparse graph by retaining only edges to k nearest neighbors of each node, and dropping all other edges (i.e., setting corresponding edge weights to 0), a commonly used graph sparsification strategy. The number of edges in the resulting graph is linear in the number of instances.

With the graph $G = (V, E, W)$ constructed, we perform inference over this graph to assign labels to all n_u unlabeled nodes. This is done by propagating the label information from the labeled nodes to the unlabeled nodes. Any of the several graph based SSL algorithms mentioned in Section 1 may be used for this task. For the experiments in this paper, we use the GRF algorithm (Zhu et al., 2003) which minimizes the optimization problem shown in (2).

$$\min_{\hat{Y}} \sum_{i,j} \sum_{l \in \mathcal{L}} W_{i,j} (\hat{Y}_{il} - \hat{Y}_{jl})^2, \ \text{s.t.} \ SY = S\hat{Y} \qquad (2)$$

As outlined in (Zhu et al., 2003), this optimization can be efficiently and exactly solved to obtain $\hat{Y}$. The result, is a labeling of all instances, including the n_u^t unlabeled instances from the target domain.

In most previous graph-based SSL methods (e.g., (Zhu et al., 2003)), the matrix A is predefined to the identity $A = I$, in Eq. (1), resulting in the standard Euclidean distance in input space. This

Algorithm 1 Supervised Graph Construction (SGC) **Input**: instances X, training labels Y, training instance indicator S, neighborhood size k **Output**: Graph edge weight matrix, W

```
A ← MetricLearner(X, S, Y)
W ← ConstructKnnGraph(X, A, k)
return W
```

Algorithm 2 Iterative Graph Construction (IGC) **Input**: instances X, training labels Y, training instance indicator S, label entropy threshold β, neighborhood size k **Output**: Graph edge weight matrix, W

```
Ŷ ← Y, Ŝ ← S
repeat
    W ← SGC(X, Ŷ, k)
    Ŷ' ← GraphLabelInference(W, Ŝ, Ŷ)
    U ← SelectLowEntInstances(Ŷ', Ŝ, β)
    Ŷ ← Ŷ + UŶ'
    Ŝ ← Ŝ + U
until convergence (i.e., U_ii = 0, ∀i)
return W
```

method of unsupervised graph construction is *not* task dependent. Instead, we also learn the matrix A using the (small) set of labeled instances using metric learning algorithms. We add more detail below in Section 7. In a nutshell, we construct a similarity metric tailored to the current specific adaptation task.

6 Metric Learning Review

We now review a recently proposed *supervised* method for learning Mahalanobis distance between instance pairs. We shall concentrate on learning the PSD matrix $A \succeq 0$ which parametrizes the distance, $d_A(x_i, x_j)$, between instances x_i and x_j.

$$d_A(x_i, x_j) = (x_i - x_j)^\top A (x_i - x_j) \tag{3}$$

This is equivalent to finding a linear transformation P of the input space, and then applying Euclidean distance on the transformed instances Px_i.

Information-Theoretic Metric Learning (ITML) (Davis et al., 2007) assumes the availability of prior knowledge about inter-instance distances. In this scheme, similar instances should have low Mahalanobis distance between them, i.e., $d_A(x_i, x_j) \leq u$, for some non-trivial upper bound u. Similarly, dissimilar instances should have a large distance between them, that is, $d_A(x_i, x_j) \geq l$ for some l. Given a set of similar instances S and dissimilar instances D, the ITML algorithm chooses the matrix A that minimizes the following optimization problem:

$$\begin{aligned} \min_{A \succeq 0, \xi} \quad & D_{\text{ld}}(A, A_0) + \gamma \cdot D_{\text{ld}}(\xi, \xi_0) \\ \text{s.t.} \quad & \text{tr}\{A(x_i - x_j)(x_i - x_j)^\top\} \leq \xi_{c(i,j)}, \ \forall (i,j) \in S \\ & \text{tr}\{A(x_i - x_j)(x_i - x_j)^\top\} \geq \xi_{c(i,j)}, \ \forall (i,j) \in D \end{aligned} \tag{4}$$

where γ is a hyperparameter which determines the importance of violated constraints and A_0 is a Mahalanobis matrix provided using prior knowledge. To solve the optimization problem in (4), an algorithm involving repeated Bregman projections is presented in (Davis et al., 2007), which we use for the experiments reported in this paper.

7 Using Labeled Data for Graph Construction

We now describe how to incorporate labeled and unlabeled data during graph construction. We start with a review of a new graph construction framework (Dhillon et al., 2010) which combines existing *supervised* metric learning algorithms (such as ITML) with *transductive* graph-based label inference to learn a new distance metric from labeled as well as unlabeled data combined. In self-training styled iterations, IGC alternates between graph construction and label inference; with output of label inference used during next round of graph construction, and so on.

7.1 Iterative Graph Construction (IGC)

IGC builds on the assumption that supervised (metric) learning improves with more labeled data. Since we are focusing on the SSL setting with n_l labeled and n_u unlabeled instances, the algorithm automatically labels the unlabeled instances using some existing graph based SSL algorithm, and then includes a subset of the labeled instances in the training set for the next round of metric learning. Naturally, only examples with low assigned label entropy (i.e., high confidence label assignments) are used. Specifically, we use a threshold parameter $\beta > 0$ to determine which examples will be used for the next round. (In practice we set $\beta = 0.05$ and observed that indeed most of the low entropy instances which are selected for inclusion in next iteration of metric learning, are classified correctly.) This iterative process continues until no new instances are set of labeled instances. This occurs when either all the instances are already exhausted, or when none of the remaining unlabeled instances can be assigned labels with high confidence.

The IGC framework is presented in Algorithm 2. The algorithm iterates between the two main steps as follows. In Line 1, any supervised metric learner, such as ITML, may be used as the MetricLearner. Using the distance metric learned in Line 1, a new k-NN graph is constructed in Line 2, whose edge weight matrix is stored in W. In Line 4, GraphLabelInference optimizes over the newly constructed graph the GRF objective (Zhu et al., 2003) shown in Eq. (5).

$$\min_{\hat{Y}'} \ \mathrm{tr}\{\hat{Y}'^{\top} L \hat{Y}'\}, \ \text{s.t.} \ \hat{S}\hat{Y} = \hat{S}\hat{Y}' \tag{5}$$

where $L = D - W$ is the (unnormalized) Laplacian, and D is a diagonal matrix with $D_{ii} = \sum_j W_{ij}$. The constraint, $\hat{S}\hat{Y} = \hat{S}\hat{Y}'$, in (5) makes sure that labels on training instances are not changed during inference. In Line 5, a currently unlabeled instance x_i (i.e., $\hat{S}_{ii} = 0$) is considered a new labeled training instance, i.e., $U_{ii} = 1$, for next round of metric learning if the instance has been assigned labels with high confidence in the current iteration, i.e., if its label distribution has low entropy (i.e., Entropy$(\hat{Y}'_{i:}) \leq \beta$). Finally in Line 6, training instance label information is updated. This iterative process is continued till no new labeled instance can be added, i.e., when $U_{ii} = 0 \ \forall i$. IGC returns the learned matrix A which can be used to compute Mahalanobis distance using Eq. (3). The number of parameters estimated by IGC (i.e., dimensions of W) increases as the number data instances increase. Hence, we note that that IGC is non-parametric, just as other graph-based methods.

8 Experiments

Data: We use data from 12 domain pairs obtained from (Crammer et al., 2009), and preprocessed to keep only those features which occurred more than 20 times. The classification task is the following: given a product review, predict user's sentiment, i.e., whether it is positive or negative.

Domain Pairs	SVM	PCA	IGC
Electronics-DVDs	43.1 ± 0.3	41.4 ± 0.2	$\mathbf{38.3 \pm 0.3}$
DVDs-Electronics	37.1 ± 0.2	36.5 ± 0.3	$\mathbf{27.9 \pm 0.3}$
DVDs-Books	41.0 ± 0.3	40.3 ± 0.4	$\mathbf{31.9 \pm 0.4}$
Books-DVDs	43.9 ± 0.2	43.1 ± 0.3	$\mathbf{40.3 \pm 0.2}$
Music-Books	41.0 ± 0.3	39.9 ± 0.3	$\mathbf{30.1 \pm 0.3}$
Books-Music	36.7 ± 0.3	36.4 ± 0.2	$\mathbf{31.8 \pm 0.5}$
Video-Electronics	35.9 ± 0.2	35.5 ± 0.3	$\mathbf{28.4 \pm 0.3}$
Electronics-Video	37.4 ± 0.3	36.6 ± 0.4	$\mathbf{32.9 \pm 0.4}$
Video-DVDs	43.0 ± 0.2	42.0 ± 0.3	$\mathbf{40.1 \pm 0.3}$
DVDs-Video	38.1 ± 0.3	36.8 ± 0.2	$\mathbf{33.0 \pm 0.2}$
Kitchen-Apparel	35.0 ± 0.2	33.8 ± 0.3	$\mathbf{32.9 \pm 0.5}$
Apparel-Kitchen	38.2 ± 0.3	37.0 ± 0.4	$\mathbf{27.5 \pm 0.4}$

Table 1: Classification errors (lower is better, lowest marked in bold) comparing SVM, GRF (see Section 5) in PCA space, and GRF in IGC space. Total $n = 3000$ instances, with total 300 labeled instances ($n_l^s = 200$ and $n_l^t = 100$). The reported errors are on $n_u^t = 1400$ instances, with results averaged over 4 trials.

Hence, this is a binary classification problem with number of classes $m = 2$. A total of $1,500$ instances from each domain were sampled, i.e., $n = 3000$. We note that the goal is to label unlabeled target data (n_u^t), so in all experiments reported below we have at least $1,300$ instances to be labeled.

Experimental Setup: We used cosine similarity[1] (using appropriate A) to set edge weights, followed by k-NN graph sparsification, as described in Section 5. The hyperparameters $k \in \{2,5,10,50,100,200,500,1000\}$ and the Gaussian kernel bandwidth multiplier[2], $\rho \in \{1,2,5,10,50,100\}$, are tuned on a separate development set. The hyperparameter, α (see Eq. (1)) was tuned over the range $[0.1,1]$, with step size 0.1. The α value which gave the best GRF objective (Eq. (2)) was selected. Please note that this is an automatic parameter selection mechanism requiring no additional held out data. For all graph-based experiments, GRF (see Section 5) is used as the inference algorithm.

Setting The Mahalanobis Matrix A: We consider two methods to set the value of the matrix A. First, instances are projected into a lower dimensional space using Principal Components Analysis (PCA). For all experiments, dimensionality of the projected space was set at 250. We set $A = P^\top P$, where P is the projection matrix generated by PCA. We found the baseline algorithms to perform better in this space than the input d-dimensional space, and hence this is used as the original space. Second, the matrix A is learned by applying IGC (Algorithm 2) (see Section 7) on the PCA projected space (above); with ITML used as MetricLearner in IGC. We use standard implementations of ITML and IGC made available by respective authors.

8.1 Domain Adaptation Results

We experimented with a variety of settings in which we varied the amount of source and target labeled and unlabeled data (ranging from 0 labeled instances to 200 labeled instances). Due to

[1]We experimented with both Gaussian kernels and cosine similarity, and cosine similarity lead to better performance, and we use it in all experiments.

[2]$\sigma = \rho\ \sigma_0$, where ρ is the tuned multiplier, and σ_0 is set to average distance.

Domain Pairs	TSVM	EasyAdapt	IGC
Electronics-DVDS	40.1 ± 0.2	41.0 ± 0.4	$\mathbf{38.3 \pm 0.3}$
Books-Music	32.7 ± 0.3	33.4 ± 0.3	$\mathbf{31.8 \pm 0.5}$
DVDs-Videos	33.8 ± 0.4	34.9 ± 0.4	$\mathbf{33.0 \pm 0.2}$
Videos-Electronics	29.7 ± 0.2	30.1 ± 0.4	$\mathbf{28.4 \pm 0.3}$
Kitchen-Apparel	33.9 ± 0.3	33.7 ± 0.1	$\mathbf{32.9 \pm 0.5}$

Table 2: Classification errors for IGC comparison with TSVM and EasyAdapt. In all cases, we use $n_l^s = 200$ and $n_l^t = 100$ labeled instances. The reported errors are on $n_u^t = 1400$ instances, results averaged over four trials. Lowest errors are marked in bold.

paucity of space we can not describe the details of those experiments here; the interested reader is encouraged to refer to the longer version of this paper (Dhillon et al., 2012). The setting that performed the best was the one which used source unlabeled data, 200 source labeled instances, and 100 target labeled instances. So, for this setting, we compared the performance of GRF in IGC space to GRF in PCA space and a Support Vector Machine (SVM) classifier trained over the 300 training instances (200 from the source domain, and 100 from the target domain) using a polynomial kernel whose degree is tuned on a development set.

The results are summarized in Table 1. Clearly, for all domain pairs, GRF in PCA space is either comparable or better than SVM. This may not be surprising since SVM did not use the additional 1,300 source unlabeled data. Also, as already seen above, GRF in IGC space outperforms both SVM baseline and GRF in PCA space. This demonstrates the benefit of using a learned metric (in this case using IGC) during graph construction for graph-based domain adaptation.

8.2 Comparison with Other Methods

In previous sections, we have shown the superior performance of IGC over projections learnt using PCA and standard SVM (a state-of-the-art baseline which is also the top performing algorithm in the seminal sentiment classification work of (Pang et al., 2002)). However, a comparison with state-of-the-art semi-supervised learning and domain adaptation approaches was pending. So, in this section we compare the performance of IGC with TSVM (Transductive SVM) – a widely used large margin transductive model which has shown state-of-the-art performance on many text classification tasks (Joachims, 1999) and EasyAdapt (Daume III, 2007) which is a state-of-the-art domain adaptation algorithm. The results are shown in Table 2, where we observe that IGC outperforms TSVM and EasyAdapt.

9 Conclusion

We brought together three active directions of research: domain adaptation, graph-based learning, and metric learning, and made the following contributions: (1) investigated usage of unlabeled data from all domains and limited labeled data from all domains; and (2) employed graph-based non-parametric methods for domain adaptation. We plan to further investigate improved usage of graph-based techniques to adaptation. Here, we considered only two domains at once. We plan to extend these methods for multiple source domains.

Acknowledgment

This work is supported in part by European Union grant IRG-256479, DARPA (contract number FA8750-09-C-0179), and Google. Any opinions, findings, conclusions and recommendations expressed in this paper are the authors' and do not necessarily reflect those of the sponsors.

References

Arnold, A., Nallapati, R., and Cohen, W. (2008). A comparative study of methods for transductive transfer learning. In *ICDM Workshop on Mining and Management of Biological Data.*, pages 77–82. IEEE.

Bengio, Y., Delalleau, O., and Le Roux, N. (2006). Label propagation and quadratic criterion. *Semi-supervised learning*, pages 193–216.

Blitzer, J., McDonald, R., and Pereira, F. (2006). Domain adaptation with structural correspondence learning. In *EMNLP*, pages 120–128.

Crammer, K., Dredze, M., and Kulesza, A. (2009). Multi-Class Confidence Weighted Algorithms. In *EMNLP*.

Dai, W., Xue, G., Yang, Q., and Yu, Y. (2007). Co-clustering based classification for out-of-domain documents. In *KDD*, pages 210–219. ACM.

Daitch, S., Kelner, J., and Spielman, D. (2009). Fitting a graph to vector data. In *ICML*.

Daume III, H. (2007). Frustratingly easy domain adaptation. In *Proceedings of the 45th Annual Meeting of the Association of Computational Linguistics*, pages 256–263, Prague, Czech Republic. Association for Computational Linguistics.

Davis, J., Kulis, B., Jain, P., Sra, S., and Dhillon, I. (2007). Information-theoretic metric learning. In *ICML*.

Dhillon, P., Talukdar, P., and Crammer, K. (2010). Inference-driven metric learning for graph construction. Technical report, MS-CIS-10-18, CIS Department, University of Pennsylvania, May.

Dhillon, P., Talukdar, P., and Crammer, K. (Nov. 2012). Metric Learning for Graph-based Domain Adaptation. Technical report, MS-CIS-12-17, CIS Department, University of Pennsylvania, `http://repository.upenn.edu/cis_reports/975/`.

Eaton, E., Desjardins, M., and Lane, T. (2008). Modeling transfer relationships between learning tasks for improved inductive transfer. *Machine Learning and Knowledge Discovery in Databases*, pages 317–332.

Jebara, T., Wang, J., and Chang, S. (2009). Graph construction and b-matching for semi-supervised learning. In *ICML*.

Joachims, T. (1999). Transductive inference for text classification using support vector machines. In *Proceedings of the Sixteenth International Conference on Machine Learning*, ICML '99, pages 200–209, San Francisco, CA, USA.

Pan, S. and Yang, Q. (2009). A survey on transfer learning. *IEEE Transactions on Knowledge and Data Engineering*.

Pang, B., Lee, L., and Vaithyanathan, S. (2002). Thumbs up?: sentiment classification using machine learning techniques. In *Proceedings of the ACL-02 conference on Empirical methods in natural language processing - Volume 10*, EMNLP '02, pages 79–86. Association for Computational Linguistics.

Talukdar, P. (2009). Topics in graph construction for semi-supervised learning. Technical report, MS-CIS-09-13, CIS Department, University of Pennsylvania.

Talukdar, P. and Crammer, K. (2009). New Regularized Algorithms for Transductive Learning. In *ECML-PKDD*. Springer.

Wang, F. and Zhang, C. (2006). Label propagation through linear neighborhoods. In *ICML*.

Wang, Z., Song, Y., and Zhang, C. (2009). Knowledge transfer on hybrid graph. In *IJCAI*, pages 1291–1296.

Zhu, X., Ghahramani, Z., and Lafferty, J. (2003). Semi-supervised learning using Gaussian fields and harmonic functions. In *ICML*.

Automatic Hashtag Recommendation for Microblogs using Topic-specific Translation Model

Zhuoye Ding Qi Zhang XuanJing Huang
School of Computer Science, Fudan University,
825 Zhangheng Road, Shanghai, P.R. China
{09110240024,qi_zhang,xjhuang}@fudan.edu.cn

ABSTRACT
Microblogging services continue to grow in popularity, users publish massive instant messages every day through them. Many tweets are marked with hashtags, which usually represent groups or topics of tweets. Hashtags may provide valuable information for lots of applications, such as retrieval, opinion mining, classification, and so on. However, since hashtags should be manually annotated, only 14.6% tweets contain them (Wang et al., 2011). In this paper, we adopt topic-specific translation model(TSTM) to suggest hashtags for microblogs. It combines the advantages of both topic model and translation model. Experimental result on dataset crawled from real world microblogging service demonstrates that the proposed method can outperform some state-of-the-art methods.

TITLE AND ABSTRACT IN CHINESE

基于特定话题下翻译模型的微博标签推荐

微博服务变得越来越流行，用户可以通过微博提交大量的及时信息。很多条微博被用户通过标签标记，这些标签代表了微博的话题类别。标签可以为很多应用提供有价值的信息，比如检索，情感分析，分类等等。微博的标签本应该由用户自行标记，然而，根据统计只有14.6%的微博包含标签。在这篇论文中，我们提出了一种基于特定话题的翻译模型， 来为每条微博自动推荐标签。此模型综合了话题模型和翻译模型的优点。在基于真实微博语料的实验中，我们提出的方法超过了很多经典的方法。

KEYWORDS: Microblogs, Tag recommendation, Topic model.
KEYWORDS IN CHINESE: 微博，标签推荐，话题模型.

Proceedings of COLING 2012: Posters, pages 265–274,
COLING 2012, Mumbai, December 2012.

1 Introduction

Hashtags, which are usually prefixed with the symbol # in microblogging services, represent the relevance of a tweet to a particular group, or a particular topic (Kwak et al., 2010). Popularity of hashtags grows concurrently with the rise and popularity of microblogging services. Many microblog posts contain a wide variety of user-defined hashtags. It has been proven to be useful for many applications, including microblog retrieval (Efron, 2010), query expansion (A.Bandyopadhyay et al., 2011), sentiment analysis (Davidov et al., 2010; Wang et al., 2011), and many other applications. However, not all posts are marked with hashtags. How to automatically generate or recommend hashtags has become an important research topic.

The task of hashtag recommendation is to automatically generate hashtags for a given tweet. It is similar to the task of keyphrase extraction, but it has several different aspects. Keyphrases are defined as a short list of phrases to capture the main topics of a given document (Turney, 2000). Keyphrases are usually extracted from the given document. However, hashtags indicate where a tweet is about a particular topic or belong to a particular group. So words and hashtags of a tweet are usually diverse vocabularies, or even hashtags may not occur in the tweet. Take the tweet in Table 1 for instance, the word "Lion" is used in the tweet, while users annotate with the hashtag "Mac OS Lion". That is usually refered to as a *vocabulary gap* problem.

Tweet
At the WWDC conference 2012, Apple introduces its new operating system release-**Lion**.
Annotated tags
Apple Inc, WWDC, **MAC OS Lion**

Table 1: An example of a tweet with annotated hashtags.

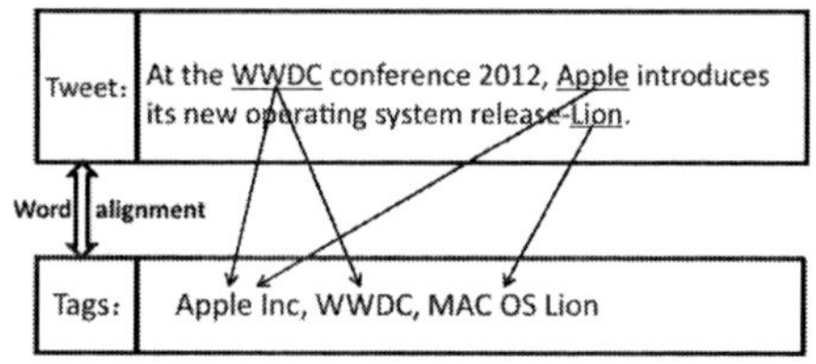

Figure 1: The basic idea of word alignment method for suggesting hashtags.

To solve the *vocabulary gap* problem, most researchers applied a statistic machine translation model to learn the word alignment probabilities(Zhou et al., 2011; Bernhard and Gurevych, 2009). Liu et al. (2011) proposed a simple word alignment method to suggest tags for book reviews and online bibliographies. In this work, tags are trigged by the important words of the resource. Figure 1 shows the basic idea of using word alignment method for tag suggestion.

Due to the open access in microblogs, topics tend to be more diverse in microblogs than in formal documents. However, all the existing models did not take into account any contextual information in modeling word translation probabilities. Beyond word-level, contextual-level topical information can help word-alignment choice because sometimes translation model is vague due to their reliance solely on word-pair co-occurrence statistics. For example, the word "apple" should be translated into "Apple Inc" in the topic of *technology*, or "juice" in the topic of *drink*. Thus the idea is using topic information to facilitate word alignment choice.

Based on this perspective, in this paper, we propose a topic-specific translation model(TSTM) to recommend hashtags for microblogs. This method regards hashtags and tweets as *parallel* description of a resource. We first investigate to combine topic model and word alignment model to estimate the topic-specific word alignment probabilities between the words and hashtags. After that, when given an unlabeled dataset, we first identify topics for each tweet and then compute importance scores for candidate tags based on the learned topic-specific word-

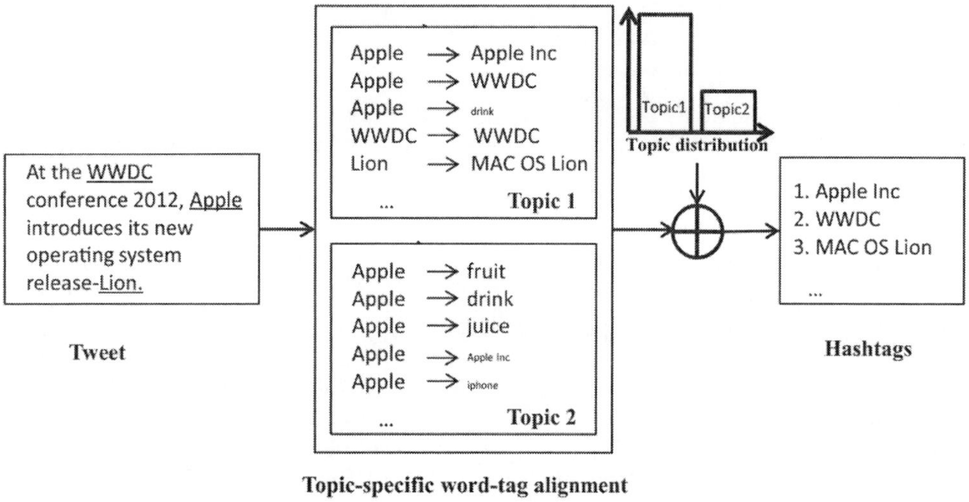

Figure 2: The basic idea of topic-specific word alignment for tag recommendation.

tag alignment probabilities and topic distribution. Figure 2 illustrates the basic idea of our model. In Figure 2, for simplicity, we suppose there are totally two topics, topic 1(information technology) and topic 2(food). We use the font size of tags to indicate the word-tag alignment probability for each specific topic. With the topic distribution and word-tag alignment probabilities for each topic, we can compute the importance score for each candidate tag.

The remainder of this paper is organized as follows: related work and state-of-the-art approaches are reviewed in Section 2. The proposed approach is detailed in Section 3. Experimental results and analysis are described and discussed in Section 4. The last section concludes the paper.

2 Related work

Our approach relates to two research areas: tag suggestion and keyphrase extraction. In this section, we discuss them in detail.

2.1 Tag suggestion

Previous work on tag suggestion can be roughly divided into three directions, including collaborative filtering(CF) (Rendle et al., 2009; Herlocker et al., 2004), discriminative models (Ohkura et al., 2006; Heymann et al., 2008), and generative models(Krestel et al., 2009; Iwata et al., 2009). Our proposal is complementary to these efforts, because microblogs differ from other media in some ways: (1) microblog posts are much shorter than traditional documents. (2) topics tend to be more diverse than in formal documents. So these methods cannot be directly applied to hashtag recommendation in microblogs.

2.2 Keyphrase extraction

Keyphrase extraction from documents is the most similar task to this research. Existing methods can be categorized into supervised and unsupervised approaches. Unsupervised approaches usually selected general sets of candidates and used a ranking step to select the

Symbol	Description
D	number of annotated tweets
W	number of unique words
T	number of unique hashtags
K	number of topics
N_d	number of words in the dth tweet
M_d	number of hashtags in the dth tweet
$w_d = \{w_{dn}\}_{n=1}^{N_d}$	words in the dth tweet
$z_d = \{z_{dn}\}_{n=1}^{N_d}$	topic of each word in the dth tweet
$t_d = \{t_{dm}\}_{m=1}^{M_d}$	hashtags in the dth tweet
$c_d = \{c_{dm}\}_{m=1}^{M_d}$	topic of each hashtag in the dth tweet

Table 2: Notations of our model.

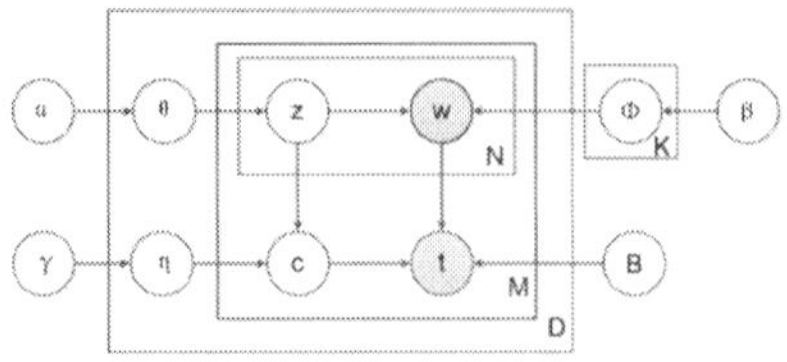

Figure 3: Graphical model representation of our model.

most important candidates (Mihalcea and Tarau, 2004; Wan and Xiao, 2008). Supervised approaches used a corpus of training data to learn a keyphrase extraction model that is able to classify candidates as keyphrases (Turney, 2003; Hulth., 2003).

3 Proposed method

3.1 Preliminaries

We assume an annotated corpus consisting of D tweets with a word vocabulary of size W and a hashtag vocabulary of size T. Suppose there are K topics embedded in the corpus. The dth tweet consists of a pair of words and assigned hashtags (w_d, t_d), where $w_d = \{w_{dn}\}_{n=1}^{N_d}$ are N_d words in the tweet that represent the content, and $t_d = \{t_{dm}\}_{m=1}^{M_d}$ are M_d assigned hashtags. Our notation is summarized in Table 2. Given an unlabeled data set, the task of hashtag recommendation is to discover a list of hashtags for each tweet.

The proposed topic-specific translation model is based on the following assumptions. When a user wants to write a tweet, he first generates the content, and then generates the hashtags. When starting the content, he first chooses some topics based on the topic distribution. Then he chooses a bag of words one by one based on the word distribution for each chosen topic. During the generative process for hashtags, a topic is first chosen from topics that have previously generated the content. And hashtags are chosen according to the chosen topic and important words in the content.

Formally, let θ denotes the topic distribution and ϕ_k denotes the word distribution for topic k. Let η_d denote the distribution of topic choice when assigning hashtags for the dth tweet and the choice probability of topic k is sampled randomly from topics of content, as follows, $\eta_{dk} = \frac{N_k^d+\gamma}{N_{(.)}^d+K\gamma}$, where N_k^d is the number of words that are assigned to topic k in the dth tweet. And then each hashtag t_{dm} is annotated according to topic-specific translation possibility $P(t_{dm}|w_d, c_{dm}, \mathbf{B})$, where $P(t_{dm}|w_d, c_{dm}, \mathbf{B}) = \sum_{n=1}^{N_d} P(t_{dm}|c_{dm}, w_{dn}, \mathbf{B})P(w_{dn}|w_d)$ and $\mathbf{B}$ presents the topic-specific word alignment table between a word and a hashtag, where $B_{i,j,k} = P(t = t_j|w = w_i, z = k)$ is the word alignment probability between the word w_i and the hashtag t_j for topic k, $P(w_{dn}|w_d)$ indicates the importance of the word in the dth tweet, which will be described in detail in section 3.4.2 .

In summary, the generation process of annotated tweets is described as follows:

1. Draw topic probability $\theta \sim$ Dirichlet (α);
2. Draw topic probability $\eta \sim$ Dirichlet (γ);
3. For each topic $k = 1, ..., K$
   Draw word probability $\phi_k \sim$ Dirichlet (β)
4. For each tweet $d = 1, ..., D$
   (a) For each word $n = 1, ..., N_d$
       Draw topic $z_{dn} \sim$ Multinomial (θ_d)
       Draw word $w_{dn} \sim$ Multinomial (Φz_{dn})
   (b) For each hashtag $m = 1, ..., M_d$
       Draw topic $c_{dm} \sim$ Multinomial (η_d)
       Draw hashtag $t_{dm} \sim P(t_{dm}|w_d, c_{dm}, \mathbf{B})$

where α, β and γ are Dirichlet distribution parameters.

Figure 3 shows a graphical model representation of the proposed model.

3.2 Learning and inference

We use collapsed Gibbs sampling(Griffiths and Steyvers, 2004) to find latent variables. The sampling probability of a latent topic for each word and hashtag in the tweet is sampled respectively. Due to the space limit, we leave out the derivation details and the sampling formulas.

After the topics of each word and hashtag become stable, we can estimate topic-specific word alignment table B by: $B_{t,w,c} = \frac{N^t_{c,w}}{N^{(.)}_{c,w}}$. where $N^t_{c,w}$ is a count of the hashtag t that co-occurs with the word w for topic c in tweet-hashtag pairs.

The possibility table $B_{t,w,c}$ have a potential size of WTK, assuming the vocabulary sizes for words, hashtags and topics are W, T and K. The data sparsity poses a more serious problem in estimating $B_{t,w,c}$ than the topic-free word alignment case. To reduce the data sparsity problem, we introduce the remedy in our model. We can employ a linear interpolation with topic-free word alignment probability to avoid data sparseness: $B^*_{t,w,c} = \lambda B_{t,w,c} + (1-\lambda)P(t|w)$, where $P(t|w)$ is topic-free word alignment probability from the word w and the hashtag t, λ is trade-off of two probabilities. Here we explore IBM model-1 (Brown et al., 1993), which is a widely used word alignment model, to obtain $P(t|w)$.

3.3 Tag recommendation using Topic-specific translation probabilities

3.3.1 Topic identification

Suppose given an unlabeled dataset $\mathbf{W}^* = \{w^*_d\}^U_{d=1}$ with U tweets, where the dth tweet $w^*_d = \{w^*_{dn}\}^{L_d}_{n=1}$ consists of L_d words. $z^*_d = \{z^*_{dn}\}^{L_d}_{n=1}$ denotes topics of words in dth tweet and $\mathbf{Z}^* = \{z^*_d\}^U_{d=1}$. we first identify topics for each tweet using the standard LDA model. The collapsed Gibbs sampling is also applied for inference. After the topics of each word become stable, we can estimate the distribution of topic choice for hashtags of the dth tweet in unlabeled data by: $\eta^*_{dk} = \frac{N^d_k+\gamma}{N^d_{(.)}+\gamma K}$, where N^d_k is a count of words that are assigned topic k in the dth tweet of unlabeled dataset.

3.3.2 Tag recommendation

With topic distribution η^* and topic-specific word alignment table $\mathbf{B}^*$, we can rank hashtags for the dth tweet in unlabeled data by computing the scores:

$$P(t^*_{dm}|w^*_d, \eta^*_d, \mathbf{B}^*) = \sum_{c^*_{dm}=1}^{K} \sum_{n=1}^{L_d} P(t^*_{dm}|c^*_{dm}, w^*_{dn}, \mathbf{B}^*) P(c^*_{dm}|\eta^*_d) P(w^*_{dn}|w^*_d)$$

Where $P(w^*_{dn}|w^*_d)$ indicates the importance of the words in the tweet. Here, we used IDF to compute this importance score. According to the ranking scores, we can suggest the top-ranked hashtags for each tweet to users.

4 Experiments

4.1 Data collection and analysis

In our experiments, we use a Microblog dataset collected from Sina-Weibo[1] for evaluation. Sina-Weibo is a Twitter-like microblogging system in China provided by Sina, one of the largest Chinese Internet content providers. It was launched in August, 2009 and quickly become the most popular microblogging service in China. We collected a dataset with totally **10,320,768** tweets. Among them, there are **551,479** tweets including hashtags annotated by users. We extracted these annotated tweets for training and evaluation. Some detailed statistical information is shown in Table 3. We divided them into a training set of 446,909 tweets and a test set of 104,570 tweets. The training set is applied for building topic-specific translation model, while the test set is for evaluation. We use hashtags annotated by users as the golden set.

#tweet	W	T	$\bar{N_w}$	$\bar{N_t}$
551,479	244,027	116,958	19.97	1.24

Table 3: Statistical information of dataset. W, T, $\bar{N_w}$ and $\bar{N_t}$ are the vocabulary of words, the vocabulary of hashtags, the average number of words in each tweet and the average number of hashtags in each tweet respectively.

4.2 Evaluation metrics and settings

We use Precision(P), Recall(R), and F-value(F) to evaluate the performance of hashtag recommendation methods. We ran topic-specific translation model with 1000 iterations of Gibbs sampling. After trying a few different numbers of topics, we empirically set the number of topics to 100. We use $\alpha = 50.0/K$ and $\beta = 0.1$ as (Griffiths and Steyvers, 2004) suggested. Parameter γ is also set to 0.1. We use IDF to indicate the importance of a word and set smoothing parameter λ to 0.8 which gives the best performance. The influence of smoothing to our model can be found in Section 4.5.

4.3 Comparison with other methods

In this subsection, we implement several methods for comparison, where Naive Bayes(NB) is a representative classification method, while LDA (Krestel et al., 2009) is selected to represent generative model for tag suggestion, IBM model-1 (Liu et al., 2011) is a novel translation-based model.

[1]http://weibo.com/

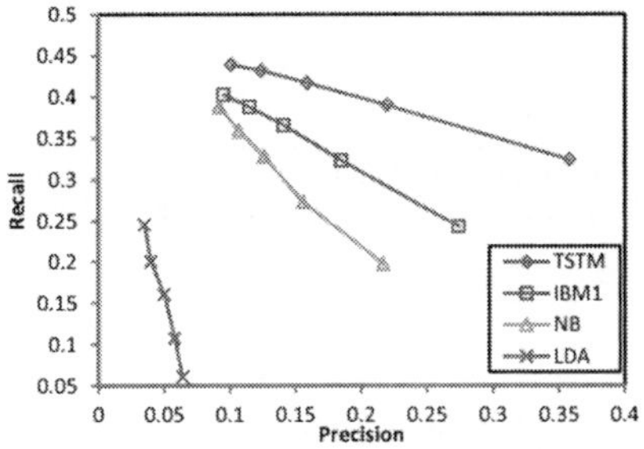

Figure 4: Performance comparison between NB, LDA-based, IBM1 and TSTM.

Method	Precision	Recall	F-measure
NB	0.217	0.197	0.203
LDA	0.064	0.060	0.062
IBM1	0.271	0.241	0.249
TSTM	**0.358**	**0.324**	**0.334**

Table 4: Comparison results of NB, LDA-based, IBM1 and TSTM when suggesting top-1 hashtag.

In Figure 4, we show the Precision-Recall curves of NB, LDA, IBM1 and TSTM on the data set. Each point of a Precision-Recall curve represents different numbers of suggested hashtags from M = 1(bottom right, with higher Precision and lower Recall) to M = 5(upper left, with higher Recall but lower Precision) respectively. The closer the curve to the upper right, the better the overall performance of the method. From the Figure, we have the following observations: (1)TSTM outperforms all the baselines. This indicates the robustness and effectiveness of our approach for hashtag recommendation. (2)IBM1 underperforms TSTM, because IBM1 relies solely on word-tag co-occurrence statistics. And contextual topical information can help to disambiguate word-alignment choices in TSTM. (3)LDA performs so poor, because it ranks the candidate hashtags by the hashtag distribution for each topic. So it can only suggest general hashtags.

To further demonstrate the performance of TSTM and other baseline methods, in Table 4, we show the Precision, Recall and F-measure of NB, LDA, IBM1 and TSTM suggesting top-1 hashtag, because the number is near the average number of hashtags in dataset. We find that the F-measure of TSTM comes to 0.334, outperforming all the baselines more than 8%.

4.4 Example

In Table 5, we show top-8 hashtags suggested by NB, LDA, IBM1 and TSTM for the tweet in Table 1[2]. The number in brackets after the name of each method is the count of correctly suggested hashtags. The correctly suggested hashtags are marked in bold face.

From Table 5, we observe that classification model NB suggests some unrelated hashtags. While LDA, as generative models, tends to suggest general hashtags, such as "Information News", "mobile phone" and "Technology leaders", and fail to generate the specific hashtags "WWDC", "MAC OS Lion". IBM1 method will suggest some topic-unrelated hashtags. For instance, "2012 Jinshan Inc cloud computing" and "2012 spring and summer men's week" are triggered by the word "2012". On the contrary, TSTM succeeds to suggest specific hashtags, and most of them are topic-related to the tweet.

4.5 Influences of smoothing

To validate the power of smoothing in TSTM on different sizes of datasets, the experiments were conducted on two datasets, including a small dataset(a training set of 100,000 tweets

[2]Hashtags are translated from Chinese

NB(+1): **MAC OS Lion**, 2012 wishes, OS, Smiles to the world, 2012 salary report, 2012 Jinshan Inc cloud computing, Lion, Noah's ark 2012
LDA(+1): Android, Information news, Japan earthquake, mobile phone, **Apple Inc**, Cloud computing, Tablet PC, Technology leaders
IBM1(+2): **WWDC**, Android, 2012 Jinshan Inc cloud computing, **Apple Inc**, 2012 spring and summer men's week, 2012, mobile phone OS, Information news
TSTM(+3): **Mac OS Lion**, **WWDC**, MAC, **Apple Inc**, Baidu union conference, Microsoft, Android, iphone

Table 5: Top-8 hashtags suggested by NB, LDA, IBM1 and TSTM.

and a test set of 10,000 tweets) and a large dataset(100% training set and 100% test set). Figure 5 and Figure 6 show the performance on both of the datasets when λ ranges from 0.0 to 1.0. We find that TSTM achieves the best performance when $\lambda = 0.8$ in both of the two Figures. Furthermore, the model cannot perform well without smoothing (when $\lambda = 1$) on the small data set. That indicates smoothing is more powerful on the small data set. While the model can still perform well without smoothing on the large data set. This is reasonable because large data set can help to solve the problem of data sparsity to some extent.

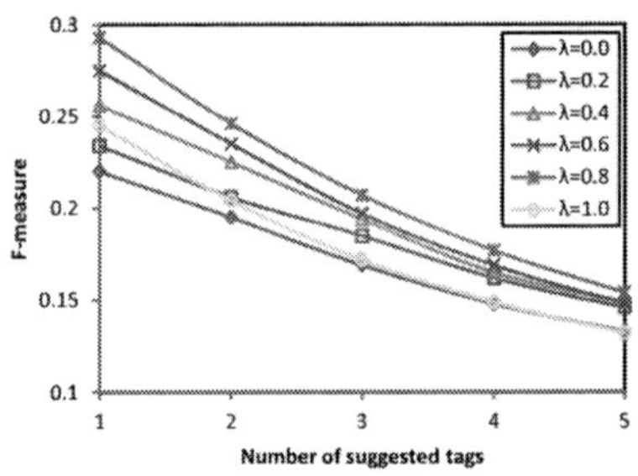

Figure 5: F-measure of TSTM on the small data set when smoothing parameter λ ranges from 0.0 to 1.0.

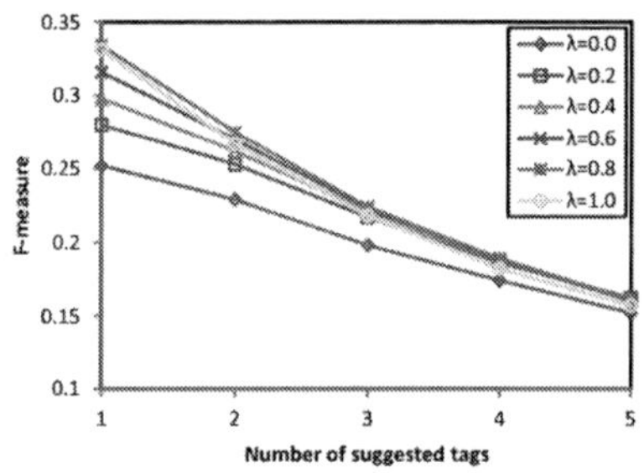

Figure 6: F-measure of TSTM on the large data set when smoothing parameter λ ranges from 0.0 to 1.0.

Conclusions

In this paper, we address the issue of suggesting hashtags for microblogs. The existing methods cannot be directly applied to this task due to the following challenges. (1) tweets are much shorter than traditional documents. (2) topics are more diverse in microblogs than other media. To solve these problems, we proposed a topic-specific translation model, which combines the advantages of both topic model and translation model. Experimental result on tweets crawled from real world service demonstrates that the proposed method can outperforms some state-of-the-art methods.

Acknowledgments

The author wishes to thank the anonymous reviewers for their helpful comments. This work was partially funded by 973 Program (2010CB327900), National Natural Science Foundation of China (61003092, 61073069), and "Chen Guang" project supported by Shanghai Municipal Education Commission and Shanghai Education Development Foundation (11CG05).

References

A.Bandyopadhyay, Mitra, M., and Majumder, P. (2011). Query expansion for microblog retrieval. In *Proceedings of The Twentieth Text REtrieval Conference*, TREC 2011.

Bernhard, D. and Gurevych, I. (2009). Combining lexical semantic resources with question & answer archives for translation-based answer finding. In *Proceeding of ACL*, pages 728–736.

Brown, P. F., Pietra, S. A. D., Pietra, V. J. D., and Mercer, R. L. (1993). The machematics of statistical machine translation: parameter estimation. *Computational linguistics*, 19(2):263–311.

Davidov, D., Tsur, O., and Rappoport, A. (2010). Enhanced sentiment learning using twitter hashtags and smileys. In *Proceedings of the 23rd International Conference on Computational Linguistics: Posters*, COLING '10, pages 241–249, Stroudsburg, PA, USA. Association for Computational Linguistics.

Efron, M. (2010). Hashtag retrieval in a microblogging environment. In *Proceedings of the 33rd international ACM SIGIR conference on Research and development in information retrieval*, SIGIR '10, pages 787–788, New York, NY, USA. ACM.

Griffiths, T. L. and Steyvers, M. (2004). Finding scientific topics. In *Proceedings of the National Academy of Sciences*, volume 101, pages 5228–5235.

Herlocker, J. L., Konstan, J. A., Terveen, L. G., and Riedl, J. T. (2004). Evaluating collaborative filtering recommender systems. *ACM Trans. Inf. Syst.*, 22(1):5–53.

Heymann, P., Ramage, D., and Garcia-Molina, H. (2008). Social tag prediction. In *Proceedings of the 31st annual international ACM SIGIR conference on Research and development in information retrieval*, SIGIR '08, pages 531–538, New York, NY, USA. ACM.

Hulth., A. (2003). Improved automatic keyword extraction given more linguistic knowledge. In *proceedings of EMNLP*.

Iwata, T., Yamada, T., and Ueda, N. (2009). Modeling social annotation data with content relevance using a topic model. In *Proceedings of NIPS*, pages 835–843.

Krestel, R., Fankhauser, P., and Nejdl, W. (2009). Latent dirichlet allocation for tag recommendation. In *RecSys*.

Kwak, H., Lee, C., Park, H., and Moon, S. (2010). What is twitter, a social network or a news media? In *Proceedings of the 19th international conference on World wide web*, WWW '10, pages 591–600, New York, NY, USA. ACM.

Liu, Z., Chen, X., and Sun, M. (2011). A simple word trigger method for social tag suggestion. In *Proceedings of EMNLP*.

Mihalcea, R. and Tarau, P. (2004). Textrank: Bringing order into texts. In *Proceedings of EMNLP*.

Ohkura, T., Kiyota, Y., and Nakagawa, H. (2006). Browsing system for weblog articles based on automated folksonomy. *Workshop on the Weblogging Ecosystem Aggregation Analysis and Dynamics at WWW*.

Rendle, S., Balby Marinho, L., Nanopoulos, A., and Schmidt-Thieme, L. (2009). Learning optimal ranking with tensor factorization for tag recommendation. In *Proceedings of the 15th ACM SIGKDD international conference on Knowledge discovery and data mining*, KDD '09, pages 727–736, New York, NY, USA. ACM.

Turney, P. D. (2000). Learning algorithms for keyphrase extraction. *Inf. Retr.*, 2(4):303–336.

Turney, P. D. (2003). Coherent keyphrase extraction via web mining. In *proceedings of IJCAI*.

Wan, X. and Xiao, J. (2008). Single document keyphrase extraction using neighborhood knowledge. In *Proceedings of AAAI*.

Wang, X., Wei, F., Liu, X., Zhou, M., and Zhang, M. (2011). Topic sentiment analysis in twitter: a graph-based hashtag sentiment classification approach. In *Proceedings of the 20th ACM international conference on Information and knowledge management*, CIKM '11, pages 1031–1040, New York, NY, USA. ACM.

Zhou, G., Cai, L., Zhao, J., and Liu, K. (2011). Phrase-based translation model for question retrieval in community question answer archives. In *Proceeding of ACL*, pages 653–662.

Unsupervised Feature-Rich Clustering

Vladimir Eidelman
Dept. of Computer Science and UMIACS, University of Maryland, College Park, MD
vlad@umiacs.umd.edu

ABSTRACT
Unsupervised clustering of documents is challenging because documents can conceivably be divided across multiple dimensions. Motivated by prior work incorporating expressive features into unsupervised generative models, this paper presents an unsupervised model for categorizing textual data which is capable of utilizing arbitrary features over a large context. Utilizing locally normalized log-linear models in the generative process, we offer straightforward extensions to the standard multinomial mixture model that allow us to effectively utilize automatically derived complex linguistic, statistical, and metadata features to influence the learned cluster structure for the desired task. We extensively evaluate and analyze the model's capabilities over four distinct clustering tasks: topic, perspective, sentiment analysis, and Congressional bill survival, and show that this model outperforms strong baselines and state-of-the-art models.

KEYWORDS: Unsupervised Learning, Text Clustering, Sentiment Analysis.

Proceedings of COLING 2012: Posters, pages 275–286,
COLING 2012, Mumbai, December 2012.

1 Introduction

Partitioning documents into categories based on some criterion is an essential research area in language processing and machine learning (Sebastiani, 2002). However, documents are inherently multidimensional, thus a given set of documents can be correctly partitioned along a number of dimensions, depending on the criterion. For instance, given a set of movie reviews, we may be interested in partitioning them by genre, with horror, comedy, drama, etc. in separate categories, or we may want to partition by sentiment, with positive and negative reviews in separate categories. However, it often proves difficult to adapt a model suited for one task, such as topic analysis, to another, such as sentiment analysis.

Supervised generative and discriminative approaches for text classification have achieved remarkable success across a variety of tasks (Joachims, 1998; Kotsiantis, 2007; Pang et al., 2002). Since the partition criterion for a supervised model is encoded in the data via the class labels, even the standard information retrieval representation of a document as a vector of term frequencies is sufficient for many state-of-the-art classification models. Furthermore, for tasks where term presence may not be adequate, discriminative models have the ability to incorporate complex features, allowing them to generalize and adapt to the specific domain.

In unsupervised clustering of documents, we try to partition the documents such that those in one partition are somehow more similar to each other than they are to documents in another partition. Probabilistic clustering models internally assess the quality of clusters via an objective function, $\mathscr{L}(\theta)$, which is commonly maximizing the log-likelihood of generating the data $\mathscr{D}$ under the current parameters of the model, θ. Clustering models rely almost exclusively on a simple bag-of-words vector representation, and therefore achieve an optimum $\mathscr{L}(\theta)$ when grouping documents with similar terms together. This performs well for topic analysis, but, unfortunately, since we do not inherently know the underlying distribution which generated our data, maximizing $\mathscr{L}(\theta)$ is not guaranteed to learn a posterior distribution that performs well for a different task. One method for influencing the objective towards a desired outcome is to include additional feature functions which are able to capture pertinent domain specific information.

Berg-Kirkpatrick et al. (2010) presented an effective framework for learning unsupervised models with expressive feature sets by re-parameterizing every local multinomial in a generative model as a locally normalized log-linear model. They showed that this method allowed them to incorporate arbitrary features of the observation and label pair, and led to competitive performance with more complex models for unsupervised tasks like part-of-speech and grammar induction.

Motivated by their work, we developed a feature-enhanced unsupervised model for clustering in this framework by re-parameterizing the multinomial mixture model. The proposed model, which will serve as our baseline, allows for the integration of arbitrary features of the observations within a document. While in generative models the observed context is usually a single unigram, we extend our re-parametrized baseline model to enable the extraction of features from a context of larger size and incorporate document-level information. After presenting the model, we explore the use of automatically derived linguistic and statistical features, many of which have not been applied to unsupervised clustering. We show that by introducing domain relevant features, we can guide the model towards the task-specific partition we want to learn across four practical tasks with different criterion: topic, perspective, sentiment analysis, and Congressional bill survival. For each task, our feature-enhanced model is highly competitive with or outperforms strong baselines.

2 Related Work

Research on selecting which dimension of the data to cluster can broadly be categorized into approaches which constrain the clustering via external information, and those which cluster along multiple dimensions and then select an appropriate one. Druck (2011) presented a semi-supervised approach that uses domain knowledge in the form of labeled features, which encode affinities between features and classes, to constrain a log-linear model on unlabeled data using generalized expectation criteria (GE-FL). Andrzejewski et al. (2009) and Mimno and McCallum (2008) both attempt to incorporate generalized domain knowledge into generative topic models using priors. The Latent Semantic Model (LSM) (Lin et al., 2010) is a Bayesian model for unsupervised sentiment classification, similar to LDA, but only modeling a mixture of three sentiment labels, positive, negative, and neutral. Another recent approach to guide clustering for sentiment analysis was introduced by Dasgupta and Ng (2009), where they incorporate user feedback into a spectral clustering algorithm (DN). Generalized Weighted Cluster Aggregation (GWCA) (Wang et al., 2009) is a consensus clustering method for topic analysis which utilizes a set of different K-Means clusterings of the same data to construct a similarity matrix, on which spectral clustering is performed to create a single consensus clustering. Iterative Double Clustering (El-Yaniv and Souroujon, 2001) (IDC) is an extension of the Double Clustering approach based on the Information Bottleneck method for topic analysis.

3 Model Description

In our probabilistic generative model for categorizing documents, we assume documents are generated according to a mixture model. The generative process begins by first selecting a class for each document according to the class prior probabilities, θ_j. Each class corresponds to a mixture component, and θ_j are the mixture weights. Next, we generate the contents of the document conditioned on the class according to the class-conditional density, $P_\theta(d_i|c_j)$. Following the Naive Bayes (NB) assumption, we treat all words in a document as conditionally independent given the class, and break $P_\theta(d_i|c_j)$ into its constituent word probabilities θ_{kj}. Under this model, the objective we would like to maximize is the marginal log-likelihood of generating the documents, given by: $\mathcal{L}(\theta) = \sum_{d_i \in \mathcal{D}} \log P_\theta(d_i) = \sum_{d_i \in \mathcal{D}} \log \sum_{c_j \in \mathcal{C}} \theta_j \prod_{w_k \in d_i} \theta_{kj}^{c_{ki}}$ where θ_{kj} is the probability of observing word w_k in class c_j, and c_{ki} is the frequency of w_k in document d_i. Thus, there are two sets of parameters we need to estimate: θ_j for each class and θ_{kj} for each mixture component. The standard instantiation of this model is known as the Multinomial Mixture (MM) model, which is a generalization of the NB classifier for unsupervised learning where θ_{kj} and θ_j are computed using multinomial distributions.

3.1 Unsupervised Feature-Rich (UFR) Model

In order to incorporate features beyond those of term frequency, we can follow the procedure presented in Berg-Kirkpatrick et al. (2010) and re-parameterize the multinomial distribution as a log-linear model based on a feature weight vector ψ_w. In this light, θ_{kj} is the output of a locally normalized logistic regression function that scores the word probability according to the active feature functions and weights for that context. Similarly, we can re-parameterize the class prior probability θ_j with a log-linear model with weights ψ_c:

$$\theta_{kj}(\psi_w) = \frac{\exp\langle \psi_w, \mathbf{f}(w_k, c_j)\rangle}{\sum_{w_p \in \mathcal{V}} \exp\langle \psi_w, \mathbf{f}(w_p, c_j)\rangle} \quad (1) \qquad \theta_j(\psi_c) = \frac{\exp\langle \psi_{c_j}\rangle}{\sum_{c_m \in \mathcal{C}} \exp\langle \psi_{c_m}\rangle} \quad (2)$$

Combining ψ_w and ψ_c into a single vector ψ, the objective function for this model remains the marginal log-likelihood, $\mathcal{L}(\psi) = \sum_{d_i \in \mathcal{D}} \log P_\psi(d_i) - \kappa||\psi||^2$, to which we also incorporate a ℓ_2-norm regularization term.

Conveniently, exactly the same generative story as before applies. Thus, optimizing this objective remains straightforward with the Expectation-Maximization (EM) (Dempster et al., 1977) algorithm. The E-step remains the same as the MM model, with the exception that the multinomial probabilities are now being computed with a log-linear model. In the M-step however, instead of simply normalizing, we need to perform an optimization procedure to recompute the weight vector ψ to optimize the complete log-likelihood objective. However, Berg-Kirkpatrick et al. (2010) suggest an alternative method of optimization, the direct gradient approach, which directly optimizes the regularized marginal log-likelihood using L-BFGS (Liu and Nocedal, 1989). The gradient of $\mathcal{L}(\psi)$ with respect to ψ has the form:

$$\nabla\mathcal{L}(\psi) = \sum_{w_k\in\mathcal{V},c_j\in\mathcal{C}} e_{kj}\cdot\Delta_{kj}(\psi) - 2\kappa\cdot\psi \quad (3) \qquad \Delta_{kj}(\psi) = \mathbf{f}(w_k,c_j) - \sum_{w_p\in\mathcal{V}} \theta_{pj}\mathbf{f}(w_p,c_j) \quad (4)$$

3.2 Event Context Expansion

As mentioned earlier, the observation, or event, for most generative models has predominantly been restricted to a single word; the one whose probability is being estimated. Due to the independence assumptions imposed by the naive structure of our UFR model, when computing θ_{kj}, we are only able to look at w_k. So although features can be shared among different observation and label pairs, such as a suffix 'ing' feature activating for both 'going' and 'trying', we are restricted to features of a single word. Thus, without modifying the model, we could not introduce a feature that considered a larger context around w_k, such as w_{k-1} and w_{k+1}. Intuitively, since we want to guide the model towards the partition of the data which we consider relevant for a specific task, it should be beneficial to utilize a larger context than a single word for feature extraction when estimating θ_{kj}. Therefore, we want to weaken the independence assumptions imposed by NB by introducing feature dependence - assuming independence between fewer words - while concurrently taking advantage of the tractable learning and inference that NB offers.

There has been a considerable amount of work in alleviating the independence assumptions of NB model by explicitly representing dependencies between attributes (i.e. words in our case), such as Lazy Bayesian Rules and Tree-Augmented NB (Friedman et al., 1997; Zheng and Webb, 2000). These approaches can be generally characterized as utilizing a less restrictive set of assumptions. First, they select a set of words $b\in\mathcal{N}_x(w_k)$ and then, w_k is allowed to depend on the words in b; such that $\theta_{kj}\rightarrow\theta_{kj|b} = p(w_k|c_j,b)$.

Our proposed extension to UFR, E-UFR, is similar in spirit to these approaches, as we will let each observation encompass the set of surrounding context words. At each position k in the document, instead of generating a single word event, w_k, according to θ_{kj}, we propose generating the entire context as the event, according to $\theta_{b_{k-r}^{k+q}j}$. Here, $b_{k-r}^{k+q}\in\mathcal{N}_{r+q}(w_k)$ is the context: the set of words centered at and including w_k, going q positions forward, and r positions back, and $\mathcal{N}_{r+q}(w_k)$ is the set of all possible contexts of size $(r+q)$ for all k. In another light, instead of having a single θ_{kj}, we now have a θ_{kj} for every different context of w_k. Since we now generate w_k along with its context, we modify the log-linear model from Eq. 1 to Eq. 5 and marginalize over the contexts, enabling feature extraction from its entirety. This will allow features to be active for more observations, thus tying more probability estimates together.

$$\theta_{b_{k-r}^{k+q}j}(\psi_w) = \frac{\exp\langle\psi_w,\mathbf{f}(b_{k-r}^{k+q},c_j)\rangle}{\sum_{b_p\in\mathcal{N}_{r+q}(w_k)}\exp\langle\psi_w,\mathbf{f}(b_{p-r}^{p+q},c_j)\rangle} \quad (5)$$

Table 1 shows an example of context generation. Crucially, the context is not treated as a bag-of-words, and by preserving word order, we are able to extract linguistic features that depend on structure. This method of computing $\theta_{b_{k-r}^{k+q}j}$ can be viewed as a form of contrastive estimation (Smith and Eisner, 2005), where we condition the probability on $\mathcal{N}(w_k)$, the neighborhood of possible contexts. In practice, to make parameter estimation tractable for increased context size, we restrict $\mathcal{N}(w_k)$ to observed contexts.

The United States is failing in its mission to implement the roadmap
the united states, the **united** states is, the united **states** is failing, united states **is** failing in, states is **failing** in its, is failing **in** its mission, failing in **its** mission to, in its **mission** to implement, its mission **to** implement the, mission to **implement** the roadmap

Table 1: Contexts generated when producing the sentence above with a 5-word context; $r=q=2$. Bold indicates the w_k being generated, with surrounding context available for feature extraction.

4 Experiments

To measure the effectiveness of the E-UFR clustering model, we applied it to text corpora with known labels used in supervised classification. Specifically, to topic, perspective, and sentiment analysis, as well as Congressional bill survival. The details of the datasets are summarized in Table 2. All data is preprocessed by performing tokenization, downcasing, and removing non alpha-numeric characters, and stopwords, unless otherwise noted. We compare E-UFR performance on each task with three baselines, UFR, MM and LDA, and where applicable, results taken from related work. The UFR and E-UFR baseline models incorporate only word indicator features, making their feature set identical to the MM model. As the observation context in the E-UFR model, we utilize a 5-word context with $q=2$ and $r=2$. The θ_{kj} parameters in the MM model are initialized with uniform MAP estimates across classes from the data, all weights in ψ are initialized to 0, and θ_j is slightly perturbed using a random seed in both cases to allow for learning. To evaluate the accuracy of our approach we compute the cluster purity (Zhao and Karypis, 2002). Since each document can only be assigned one label, and we have the same number of clusters as classes, the measure is directly comparable with micro-averaged precision, accuracy, and F1 (Xue and Zhou, 2009; Bekkerman et al., 2006). All results reported are averaged over 5 runs. Results in bold are statistically significant improvements over the other models and indistinguishable from each other at the $p < 0.05$ level, according to the p-test (Yang and Liu, 1999).

4.1 Topic Analysis

For topic analysis, we use several subsets of the 20-Newsgroup (NG20) (Lang, 1995), and WebKB (Craven et al., 1998) datasets. The NG20 corpus consists of messages posted to various Usenet newsgroups, of which we utilize the Politics, Sport, and Computer splits. The WebKB corpus consists of web pages from university computer science department websites, and has a skewed distribution of examples from each class. We use the WebKB4 split. We present two methods of introducing automatically derived features from LDA. In the first, LDA-A, we introduce a feature representing the per-word topic assignment for every term in the document. In the second, LDA-K, for each topic t_i, we sort terms w_k by $P(w_k|t_i)$ and introduce features for the top 100 terms. For example, given a context $generate_{14}$ a_7 $larger_7$ set_3 of_7 $data_{18}$ with subscripts representing the per-word topic assignments, possible features are $f(w{=}\text{data}, t{=}18)$ or $f(\#(t{=}7){=}3)$. We also incorporate linguistic features in the form of part-of-speech (POS) tags in the same manner, produced using a latent-variable POS tagger (Huang et al., 2009).

The results are presented in Table 3. On the NG20 set, the MM and UFR models exhibit strong performance, mostly outperforming the E-UFR model. With the addition of LDA-A features, however, the E-UFR becomes highly competitive. On WebKB4, the baseline E-UFR model is significantly better than the others. The introduction of LDA features does not enhance its performance, however, POS features reduce the error by 10% over the baseline. Also note, that in comparison to GE-FL, which is semi-supervised and uses LDA features, we achieve better performance. Interestingly, across all the sets, introducing either form of LDA feature results in significantly higher accuracies for the E-UFR model than the original LDA model from which the features are derived. In addition, the LDA-A features always outperform LDA-K.

Set	Task	Docs	Words
WebKB(4)	To	4199	1.3m
Pol(3)	To	2625	1.4m
Sprt(2)	To	1993	670k
Comp(2)	To	1943	480k
Mov(2)	Se	2000	1.5m
BL(2)	Pe	594	510k
Bills(2)	Su	1000	2.5m

Table 2: Description of datasets for Topic (To), Sentiment (Se), Perspective (Pe) analysis and Congressional bill survival (Su) tasks.

Model	Pol	Sprt	Comp	WebKB
MM	69.7	**98**	**83.9**	68.1
LDA	77.5	89.1	72.8	64.8
IDC	78	89	-	-
GWCA	-	-	-	67
UFR	71	**97.4**	69.2	60.6
GE-FL	-	91.5	81.7	61.5
E-UFR	69.3	93.9	63.4	71.2
+LDA-A	**84.1**	96.7	**82.7**	70.7
+LDA-K	77.3	95.7	76.3	68.3
+POS				**74.5**

Table 3: Results on Politics, Sport, Computer newsgroups and WebKB. Table cells marked with "-" for models from related work indicate result for that setting was not available in the literature for that model.

4.2 Perspective Analysis

The BitterLemons corpus Lin et al. (2006) is comprised of essays representing contrasting perspectives on the Israeli-Palestinian conflict, written by Editors and Guests. There are two clear partitions in this data. The first, IP, commonly applied and referred to as determining implicit sentiment, is the task of determining whether a document is written from the Israeli or Palestinian perspective. The second, EG, is whether the author of the article is a permanent Editor or Guest[1]. We extract complex linguistic information, in the form of OPUS (observable proxies for underlying semantics) features, which were shown to improve performance for supervised classification. OPUS features are meant to address implicit sentiment by focusing on syntactic framing in the form of grammatically relevant semantic properties (Greene and Resnik, 2009). We extracted these relations for a set of domain relevant verbs from parses of the corpus obtained with the Stanford parser (Klein and Manning, 2003). For example, sample features from the context *officially endorse the creation* would include f (w=endorse,*transitive*), f (dobj, w=creation), and f (w=endorse,dobj). Table 4 presents the results on these two tasks. As can be seen, the high performance of the UFR and MM models on topic analysis does not carry to the perspective task. The E-UFR model, on the other hand, achieves very impressive results on both tasks. Although the results are not directly comparable to supervised classifiers due to the training-test split, it is interesting to note that our unsupervised results are competitive with those of supervised classifiers on IP (Greene and Resnik, 2009). Unfortunately, the gain from OPUS features did not transfer to clustering. On the other hand, the fact that the performance

[1] As we are interested in differences in author writing style, we did not remove stopwords for this task.

did not degrade with the introduction is itself enticing, as the model was able to incorporate many complex linguistic features and not become obstructed by them. We further explored the use of POS information in EG, which led to a slight improvement. Table 5 presents the most highly weighted OPUS features.

Model	IP	EG
MM	51.4	55.1
LDA	54.4	62
UFR	51.1	52.3
E-UFR	**90.4**	**69.4**
+OPUS	**90.4**	**68.6**
+POS		**70.2**

Table 4: Results on IP and EG split of the BitterLemons dataset.

Weight	Feature
0.594	dobj(abandoned,n)/0
0.582	dobj(oppose,initiative)/0
0.574	subj(accept,israel)/1
0.525	dobj-failure/0
0.488	maintaining-subj/1
0.482	dobj-initiative/0
0.477	dobj(confront,them)/0

Table 5: Top OPUS features/class for IP split. Palestinian perspective class is 0, Israeli perspective is 1.

4.3 Sentiment Analysis

For sentiment analysis we use the Polarity v2.0 dataset (Pang and Lee, 2004), where we cluster movie reviews as negative or positive. We utilize the MPQA subjectivity lexicon (Wiebe and Cardie, 2005), where words which occur in the lexicon are associated with their prescribed polarity. For instance, *result is tepid and dull* would produce $f(w=\text{dull,neg})$ and $f(w=\text{tepid,neg})$, as well as total counts of negative and positive polarity carrying words. The results are presented in Table 6. As can be seen, the baseline UFR model is quite bad, but E-UFR outperforms MM, LDA, and LSM, and is comparable to DN, which uses user interaction. Incorporating the subjectivity lexicon provides a further significant gain. Table 7 presents the most highly weighted sentiment lexicon features. Examining the reviews alongside the lexicon, we noticed that terms that may generally be considered to convey a certain sentiment are inaccurate in their correlation with this domain. For instance, "war" is considered negative, but positive reviews are almost three times as likely to mention it. Thus, we created an alternative version of the lexicon, SUBJR, where we automatically filtered the lexicon to only include domain relevant terms. Impressively, the accuracy achieved with SUBJR is competitive with supervised approaches on this task.

Model	Movie
MM	68.1
LDA	66.6
UFR	51.1
DN	70.9
LSM	61.7
+MPQA	**74.1**
E-UFR	70.5
+MPQA	**72.4**
+SUBJR	79.7

Table 6: Results on Movie Review dataset.

Weight	Feature
0.2077	(pos,great)/1
0.168	(pos,love)/0
0.121	(neg,waste)/0
0.108	(neg,dull)/0
0.105	(neg,bland)/0
0.101	(pos,master/1
0.093	(neg,emotional)/1

Table 7: Top polarity features/class for Movie collection. Positive polarity class is 1, negative is 0.

4.4 Congressional Bill Survival

The recently introduced Congressional Bill Corpus (Yano et al., 2012) contains Congressional bills from the 103rd to 111th Congresses. The task is to predict whether a bill survived, i.e., was recommended by the Congressional committee, or died in committee. We randomly selected

1000 bills from the collection to evaluate our model. While features for the previous tasks are extracted from the content, for Congressional bill survival we incorporate document-level information, both from observable metadata and automatic predictions. The feature set is the one presented in Yano et al. (2012), and includes observable information about the bill (when it was proposed), the bill's sponsor (their party, etc.), the committee (is the sponsor on the committee, etc.), and automatically predicted urgency (trivial, recurring, and critical). Interestingly, our model replicates the results found in the supervised setting, where they found that the sponsor affiliations have the highest impact scores (Yano et al., 2012). The second set, *Spon*, is restricted to the highest weighted observable features describing the bill sponsor, namely, if the sponsor is on the committee and/or in the majority party. The restricted *Spon* set further outperforms all other models.

Model	Bills
MM	58.2
LDA	52.7
UFR	56.2
E-UFR	54.9
+All	60.4
+Spon	**64.1**

Table 8: Results on Congressional bill survival dataset.

Weight	Feature
2.051	sponsor-in-committee-majority/1
1.516	bill-cat4-function-CQ2-00/0
1.478	bill-cat4-function-RECUR-00/0
1.064	sponsor-in-committee/1
1.056	sponsor-in-majority/1

Table 9: Top features/class for Congressional bill survival. Bills which survived are class 1, those that died are class 0. bill-cat features indicate that the bill is not in the category of bills classified as CQ (critical) or RECUR (recurring).

5 Discussion

The results show that the E-UFR model is able to achieve strong performance across the four tasks. We believe this is due both to the increased context and additional features that can be leveraged. Both POS and LDA are a form of dimensionality reduction which can be viewed as categorizing words into distributional categories. As such, using them as features in our model allows us to incorporate information about a possible partition of the data. Since LDA is geared toward discovering topics, LDA features guide the E-UFR model into the correct space. Likewise, POS features assist with authorship because they relate to writing style. Extrapolating from this, any previous clustering of the data can be used as features within our model. In this work, we focused on using unsupervised learning to predict a certain externally imposed partition on the data. However, unsupervised learning is also useful as an exploratory technique for describing a document collection. In this setup, we can incorporate various features in our model to determine not whether they lead to a better accuracy, but what dimensions of the data we can discover. Previous studies on the use of linguistic features for supervised text classification have achieved mostly negative results (Moschitti and Basili, 2004), oftentimes finding that linguistic features do not improve classification accuracy. However, to the best of our knowledge no such analysis exists for the unsupervised treatment of text categorization. In this work, we have shown that linguistic features can be useful for clustering, while questions remain as to how best to incorporate these features.

6 Conclusion

We presented a feature-rich generative model for clustering. By extending the model to handle a wider context, we were able to utilize a rich set of automatically derived linguistic and statistical features, many of which have previously only been explored in supervised learning. We extensively analyzed and evaluated this model, showing that it is stable with respect to many arbitrary features. Applying the model to several challenging categorization domains, we showed that our model is able to adapt and achieve high clustering performance.

Acknowledgments

We would like to thank Chris Dyer, Zhongqiang Huang, and Philip Resnik for helpful comments and suggestions. This research was supported by a National Defense Science and Engineering Graduate Fellowship. Any opinions, findings, conclusions, or recommendations expressed are the author's and do not necessarily reflect those of the sponsors.

References

Andrzejewski, D., Zhu, X., and Craven, M. (2009). Incorporating domain knowledge into topic modeling via dirichlet forest priors. In *Proceedings of the 26th Annual International Conference on Machine Learning*, pages 25–32.

Bekkerman, R., Eguchi, K., and Allan, J. (2006). Unsupervised Non-topical Classification of Documents. Technical report.

Berg-Kirkpatrick, T., Bouchard-Côté, A., DeNero, J., and Klein, D. (2010). Painless Unsupervised Learning with Features. In *Human Language Technologies: The 2010 Annual Conference of the North American Chapter of the Association for Computational Linguistics*, Stroudsburg, PA, USA.

Craven, M., DiPasquo, D., Freitag, D., McCallum, A., Mitchell, T., Nigam, K., and Slattery, S. (1998). Learning to Extract Symbolic Knowledge from the World Wide Web. In *Proceedings of the fifteenth national/tenth conference on Artificial Intelligence/Innovative Applications of Artificial Intelligence*.

Dasgupta, S. and Ng, V. (2009). Topic-wise, Sentiment-wise, or Otherwise? Identifying the Hidden Dimension for Unsupervised Text Classification. In *Proceedings of the 2009 Conference on Empirical Methods in Natural Language Processing*.

Dempster, A. P., Laird, M. N., and Rubin, D. B. (1977). Maximum Likelihood from Incomplete Data via the EM Algorithm. *Journal of the Royal Statistical Society: Series B (Statistical Methodology)*, 39:1–22.

Druck, G. (2011). Generalized Expectation Criteria for Lightly Supervised Learning. In *Open Access Dissertations*.

El-Yaniv, R. and Souroujon, O. (2001). Iterative Double Clustering for Unsupervised and Semi-supervised Learning. In *Proceedings of the 12th European Conference on Machine Learning*.

Friedman, N., Geiger, D., and Goldszmidt, M. (1997). Bayesian network classifiers. *Mach. Learn.*, 29(2-3):131–163.

Greene, S. and Resnik, P. (2009). More than Words: Syntactic Packaging and Implicit Sentiment. In *Proceedings of Human Language Technologies: The 2009 Annual Conference of the North American Chapter of the Association for Computational Linguistics*.

Huang, Z., Eidelman, V., and Harper, M. (2009). Improving A Simple Bigram HMM Part-of-Speech Tagger by Latent Annotation and Self-Training. In *Proceedings of Human Language Technologies: The 2009 Annual Conference of the North American Chapter of the Association for Computational Linguistics*, Boulder, Colorado.

Joachims, T. (1998). Text Categorization with Support Vector Machines: Learning with Many Relevant Features. In Nédellec, C. and Rouveirol, C., editors, *European Conference on Machine Learning*, pages 137–142, Berlin. Springer.

Klein, D. and Manning, C. D. (2003). Accurate Unlexicalized Parsing. In *Proceedings of the 41st Annual Meeting of the Association for Computational LinguisticsS*, pages 423–430.

Kotsiantis, S. B. (2007). Supervised Machine Learning: A Review of Classification Techniques. Informatica 31:249268.

Lang, K. (1995). Newsweeder: Learning to filter netnews. In *Proceedings of the Twelfth International Conference on Machine Learning*, pages 331–339.

Lin, C., He, Y., and Everson, R. (2010). A Comparative Study of Bayesian Models for Unsupervised Sentiment Detection. In *Proceedings of the Fourteenth Conference on Computational Natural Language Learning*.

Lin, W. H., Wilson, T., Wiebe, J., and Hauptmann, A. (2006). Which Side are You on? Identifying Perspectives at the Document and Sentence Levels. In *Proceedings of the Tenth Conference on Computational Natural Language Learning*.

Liu, D. C. and Nocedal, J. (1989). On the Limited Memory BFGS Method for Large Scale Optimization. *Mathematical Programming*, 45:503–528.

Mimno, D. M. and McCallum, A. (2008). Topic models conditioned on arbitrary features with dirichlet-multinomial regression. In *UAI*, pages 411–418.

Moschitti, A. and Basili, R. (2004). Complex Linguistic Features for Text Classification: A Comprehensive Study. In *Proceedings of the 26th European Conference on Information Retrieval*.

Pang, B. and Lee, L. (2004). A Sentimental Education: Sentiment Analysis Using Subjectivity Summarization Based on Minimum Cuts. In *Proceedings of the 42nd Annual Meeting on Association for Computational Linguistics*.

Pang, B., Lee, L., and Vaithyanathan, S. (2002). Thumbs up? Sentiment classification using machine learning techniques. In *Proceedings of EMNLP*, pages 79–86.

Sebastiani, F. (2002). Machine Learning in Automated Text Categorization. *ACM Comput. Surv.*, 34:1–47.

Smith, N. A. and Eisner, J. (2005). Contrastive estimation: training log-linear models on unlabeled data. In *Proceedings of ACL*, pages 354–362, Stroudsburg, PA, USA. Association for Computational Linguistics.

Wang, F., Wang, X., and Li, T. (2009). Generalized Cluster Aggregation. In *Proceedings of the 21st international jont conference on Artifical intelligence*.

Wiebe, J. and Cardie, C. (2005). Annotating Expressions of Opinions and Emotions in Language. In *Language Resources and Evaluation*.

Xue, X.-B. and Zhou, Z.-H. (2009). Distributional Features for Text Categorization. *IEEE Transactions on Knowledge and Data Engineering*, 21.

Yang, Y. and Liu, X. (1999). A re-examination of text categorization methods. In *Proceedings of the ACM SIGIR*, pages 42–49, New York, NY, USA. ACM.

Yano, T., Smith, N. A., and Wilkerson, J. D. (2012). Textual predictors of bill survival in congressional committees. In *Proceedings of the 2012 Conference of the North American Chapter of the Association for Computational Linguistics: Human Language Technologies*, pages 793–802, Montréal, Canada. Association for Computational Linguistics.

Zhao, Y. and Karypis, G. (2002). Criterion Functions for Document Clustering: Experiments and Analysis. Technical report.

Zheng, Z. and Webb, G. I. (2000). Lazy learning of bayesian rules. *Machine Learning*, 41(1):53–84.

Token Level Identification of Linguistic Code Switching

Heba Elfardy[1] *Mona Diab*[2]

(1) Department of Computer Science, Columbia University, New York, NY

(2) Center for Computational Learning Systems, Columbia University, New York, NY

heba@cs.columbia.edu, mdiab@ccls.columbia.edu

Abstract

Typically native speakers of Arabic mix dialectal Arabic and Modern Standard Arabic in the same utterance. This phenomenon is known as linguistic code switching (LCS). It is a very challenging task to identify these LCS points in written text where we don't have an accompanying speech signal. In this paper, we address automatic identification of LCS points in Arabic social media text by identifying token level dialectal words. We present an unsupervised approach that employs a set of dictionaries, sound-change rules, and language models to tackle this problem. We tune and test the performance of our approach against human-annotated Egyptian and Levantine discussion fora datasets. Two types of annotations on the token level are obtained for each dataset: context sensitive and context insensitive annotation. We achieve a token level $F_{\beta=1}$ score of 74% and 72.4% on the context-sensitive development and test datasets, respectively. On the context insensitive annotated data, we achieve a token level $F_{\beta=1}$ score of 84.4% and 84.9% on the development and test datasets, respectively.

Keywords: Linguistic Code Switching, Dialect Identification, Modern Standard Arabic, Dialectal Arabic, Dictionaries, Language Models, Sound Change Rules.

Title and Abstract in Arabic:

تحديد نقاط التحول اللغوي على مستوي مفردات الجملة

عادة ما يمزج ناطقوا اللغة العربية بين الفصحى والعامية او اللهجات المختلفة في نفس الجملة وتعرف هذه الظاهرة بالتحول اللغوي. ويمثل تحديد نقاط التحول اللغوي تحدي بسبب عدم وجود الاشارات الصوتية الدالة علي اللهجة. في هذا البحث نهدف الى التعرف الياً على نقاط التحول اللغوي في النصوص من خلال تحديد لهجات الكلمات او مفردات الجملة. ولمعالجة هذه المشكلة نستخدم مجموعة من القواميس بالاضافة الى نماذج اللغة وقواعد لحصر تشابه الاصوات. وقد اختبرنا عدة اعدادات للنظام المقترح على مجموعتين من البيانات المرقمة لغوياً. الاولي تحدّد الفئة الخاصة بالكلمة بغض النظر عن السياق في حين ان الثانية تاخذ السياق في الاعتبار. وحقق النظام المقدم في هذا البحث معدلات وصلت الى ٧٤ % على مجموعة البيانات الخاصة بالظبط و ٧٢،٤ % على البيانات الخاصة بالاختبار في البيانات المعتمدة على السياق. و ٨٤،٤ % و ٨٤،٩ % على مجموعتي البيانات الغير معتمدة على السياق، تباعاً .

التحول اللغوي، تحديد اللهجة، اللغة العربية الفصحى، اللهجات العربية، نماذج اللغة، قواعد تغيّر الصوت

Proceedings of COLING 2012: Posters, pages 287–296,

COLING 2012, Mumbai, December 2012.

1 Introduction

Linguistic Code Switching (LCS) refers to the phenomenon where speakers switch between multiple languages within the same utterance (intra-utterance) or across utterances within the same conversation (inter-utterance). For an example of intra-utterance LCS, consider "Starting a sentence in English, *mais je finis* the same sentence *en Français*", where the italicized words are in French meaning 'but I finish... in French'. Intra-utterance LCS poses a significant challenge for language technologies since ideally one would need to use language processing for both languages simultaneously. In this paper we are mostly interested in intra-utterance LCS. Techniques trained for one language quickly break down when there is input from another. Intra-utterance LCS is quite pervasive in bilingual communities but it is quite pronounced in diglossic languages (Ferguson, 1959) where two forms of the language live side by side and are closely related. This is the case for Arabic where the official form of the language Modern Standard Arabic (MSA) and the dialects (DA), corresponding to the native tongue of the speakers of Arabic, are frequently used together within the same utterances/sentences. There are significant linguistic differences between MSA and DA phonologically, morphologically, lexically and syntactically; MSA is the only standardized written form of the language hence people have no standards for writing DA; and there is a pervasive presence of faux amis between MSA and DA, where words look the same (homographs or homophones) but have different semantic and pragmatic connotations. These differences lead to an exacerbation of the challenges posed by LCS – due to its pervasiveness – on processing informal textual Arabic sources such as news groups, tweets, blogs, and other social media, which are increasingly being studied as rich sources of social, commercial and political information. In this paper, we tackle the problem of identifying LCS points on the token level in a given Arabic text. We cast the problem as a token level dialect identification problem. We incorporate a variety of resources including dictionaries and language models to automatically identify the dialect id of a word in context. We adopt a classification perspective on the problem, hence each token is labeled with a class id (MSA/DA/UNKNOWN). We tune and test different settings of the system. Our approach also allows for producing MSA equivalents and English glosses for the identified DA words. Identifying the classes and sequences of MSA vs. DA words in an utterance can allow for better modeling of Arabic language usage and processing. Moreover the dialect id component can be used for smart filtering for various levels of domain adaptation and targeted document search in an Information Retrieval framework in a rapid process of identifying whether a document is predominantly MSA or DA.

2 Related Work

While there has been considerable interest in LCS from the theoretical and socio-linguistic communities, there has, with few exceptions (Joshi, 1985) (Chan et al., 2004), (Solorio and Liu, 2008a), (Solorio and Liu, 2008b) and (Manandise and Gdaniec, 2011), been little research in computational approaches to the problem. Predictive models of how and when LCS typically occurs, as well as how to interpret LCS items in the context of the matrix language, have yet to be developed. A major barrier to research on LCS has been the lack of large, consistently and accurately annotated corpora of LCS data. In fact, there has been very little discussion even of how such data should be collected and annotated to best support the interests of both the theoretical and the computational communities. (Diab and Kamboj, 2011), and (Elfardy and Diab, 2012) attempted to tackle this problem by annotating corpora of Hindi-English and MSA-DA code switched social media text.
For Chinese English LCS, (Lyu et al., 2006) found that building a unified acoustic model of the regional dialects to be detected, a bilingual pronunciation model, and a Chinese character-based tree-structured search strategy improved ASR performance significantly. For Spanish-English LCS,

Input	dh [1]	Al~y	byHSl	fy	Alwqt	AlrAhn
Eng-GL	that	what	-	in	time	current
MSA-GL	*lk	Al*y	-	fy	Alwqt	AlrAhn
No-Context	DA	DA	DA	MSA-DA	MSA-DA	MSA
Contextual	DA	DA	DA	MSA	MSA	MSA

Table 1: An example of the output of AIDA.

(Solorio and Liu, 2008b) found that LCS poses a serious challenge to part-of-speech tagging: while monolingual taggers reach >96% accuracy, English taggers tested on Spanish-English LCS data obtain only 65% accuracy. Moreover, (Manandise and Gdaniec, 2011) analyzed the effect on Machine Translation quality of borrowing and LCS of Spanish-English within the context of IBM's *"TranslateNow!"* email system. Their study showed that borrowing and LCS degrade the performance of the syntactic parser because these switched tokens are mostly treated as nouns, which results in erroneous analysis and in some cases incomplete parses. As mentioned earlier LCS is even more prominent in Arabic due to the *diglossic* nature of the language yet most of the research effort carried out to tackle Arabic NLP focuses on MSA. A significant exception in Arabic speech processing is work by (Biadsy et al., 2009). In this work, (Biadsy et al., 2009) present a system that identifies dialectal words in speech and their dialect of origin.

3 Approach

In this paper, we present a system, AIDA (Automatic Identification of Dialectal Arabic), that incorporates a set of Language Models, Dictionaries, MSA Morphological Analyzer and Sound-Change-Rules in order to perform Token-Level Dialect Identification. Table 1 shows a sample of the output produced when applying AIDA on a sample Arabic sentence that exhibits LCS. Two outputs are produced for each word in the given sentence. The first of which is a *context-insensitive* output while the second is a *context-sensitive* one. Moreover, AIDA also yields word level glossing in both English and MSA for the DA words.

3.1 Pre-processing

Both corpora used for language models and input text undergo a simple cleaning step. The cleaning process prunes out noisy data yet maintaining all the signals that can help in identifying DA content. This cleaning step: separates punctuation and numbers from words; handles speech effects such as 'goaaaaaaaal', it reduces it to 'goaaal', hence reducing the repeated characters to a maximum of three consecutive repeated characters thereby normalizing all the occurrences of these words to the same form but also maintaining the information that there is a speech effect – a potential clue to dialectalness. This module assigns tokens that have a speech effect a *speech-effect-score*; We also map Latin words, URLs, digits, and punctuation to LAT, URL, NUM, and PUNC class labels, respectively.

For the current implementation of AIDA, we only focus on Arabic written in Arabic script, hence we do not address the problem of romanized Arabic writing. Therefore, any text written using Latin script is replaced by the token LAT which could in principle include romanized Arabic.

In general written Arabic is underspecified for short vowels and consonantal gemination markers which are expressed via diacritics. We find more diacritized words in MSA text than in DA text. In social-media text, we rarely observe the use of diacritics except occasionally for MSA. Therefore, we remove diacritics from all the tokens (LM corpora, input text, and dictionaries) so as to reduce

[1] We use Buckwalter transliterated Arabic. www.qamus.org/transliteration.htm

the variation in forms of the tokens, thereby reducing sparseness. However we assign each token a *diacritization-score* based on the percentage of diacritics it had in the raw text.

3.2 Dialectal Dictionaries

For the DA data we use machine readable dictionaries (MRDs) that are developed for the system Tharwa (Diab et al., 2013). The dictionary, Tharwa, is a three way DA-MSA-English MRD. Tharwa is based on paper dictionaries combined with other resources obtained from the Linguistic Data Consortium (LDC). Tharwa comprises DA lemmas, some surface forms and their corresponding MSA and English equivalents. We have two DA dictionaries: Egyptian and Other-Dialects (mostly Lebanese and Iraqi Arabic). The *Egyptian* Dictionary comprises 33,955 unique DA entries; and the *Other-Dialects* Dictionary comprises 6,926 unique DA entries.[2] At this point we are not addressing Word Sense Disambiguation, hence we merged all the different senses of each word in one entry. However to improve the output of the MSA and English Equivalents for given tokens, the MSA equivalents (Lemmas) are sorted by their frequency of occurrence in the Arabic Gigaword (AGW4).[3]

3.3 ALMOR

We are interested in knowing if a token is MSA or not. We employ a system of MSA morphological analysis, ALMORGEANA (ALMOR) (Habash, 2007). ALMOR relies on the LDC SAMA (Maamouri et al., 2010) database to generate the list of all possible morphological analyses for a word out of context. Moreover, ALMOR provides the English glosses for the analyzed words. If a word has an analysis according to ALMOR, we assume it is MSA.[4] If an analysis is found and it doesn't belong to a predefined DA list then the word is assumed MSA and assigned a score of 1. If the word is analyzed by ALMOR and it belongs to the dialectal-entries' list we assume it is DA and it is assigned a score of 0.5. We limit the number of produced English glosses by having the internal MSA SAMA database entries ranked by their frequency of occurrence in the AGW4.

3.3.1 Using Sound Change Rules for OOVs

If the word isn't successfully analyzed by ALMOR and is not in our DA dictionaries, we attempt a relaxed match on the token using sound change rules (SCR) that model the possible phonological variants of the token. We use a subset of the SCR proposed by (Dasigi and Diab, 2011). Table 2 shows the SCR used. In this case, if the relaxed approximated phonological variant of the word is found by ALMOR, we tag the input word as DA not MSA, and assign it a DA score of 0.5; *and not 1 since the word might be a misspelled MSA word and not a DA variant*; but return the MSA relaxed variant as the MSA equivalent and the corresponding English gloss.

3.4 Language Models (LM)

3.4.1 Data Collection

Our data collection comprises various genres. For the MSA-LM we used a subset of the Arabic Gigaword (AGW4) (Parker et al., 2009), Broadcast News, Broadcast Conversations, and Web-Logs obtained from LDC as well a subset of a more formal MSA-corpus produced by (Rashwan et al.,

[2]The number of entries in these dictionaries reflects the number of undiacritized types (and not tokens) in the original sources.

[3]Detailed information about the dictionaries and their content can be found in (Diab et al., 2013)

[4]Out of the 42,334 lemma entries in the SAMA database, we manually identified 1,725 DA entries. Some of these DA entries could be found in MSA but with extremely low probability.

Letter(s)	Variants	Letter(s)	Variants	Letter(s)	Variants	Letter(s)	Variants
{ < > ' } |	A	t	T v	E	H	g	E x
v	s t S	j	q y $	H	h E	d	* D
*	d z Z	z	* Z d	s	$ S v	$	s v
S	s	D	Z d z *	T	S Z t	Z	T D z d *

Table 2: SCR rules used to expand the coverage of the MSA morphological Analyzer.

2011). We create a small highly dialectal lexicon of words that can rarely or never be used in MSA, we use it to filter out sentences from the MSA corpora thereby attempting to have a more homogeneously MSA collection.

For the DA-LM we use DA news-articles, users-commentaries, DA speech-transcriptions, DA wikipedia, DA poems as well as DA web-logs.

All the corpora undergo the same cleaning preprocessing as described in Subsection 3.1. The corpora DA and MSA comprise 13M tokens each.

3.4.2 Building the Language Models

We use the SRILM toolkit (Stolcke, 2002). We build two 3-gram LMs; (1) *MSA-LM* and (2) *DA-LM* using Kneser-Ney discounting. Using both LMs with the Mix-LM capability in SRILM we create a mixture LM, we allow equal weights for both LMs, thereby creating a third LM, *MSA-DA LM*, that incorporates the entries in both LMs.

3.4.3 Dialect Identification Using LM

From the DA-LM and MSA-LM we build three lists of n-grams, (1) Shared-MSA-DA, (2) MSA-Unique, and (3) DA-Unique Shared-MSA-DA contains the n-grams that are shared between the MSA and DA LMs, while the MSA-Unique and DA-Unique contain entries that exist only in either the MSA-LM or the DA-LM, respectively.

For the shared n-gram list each entry lists: (1) the n-gram, (2) its probability in the MSA-LM, and (3) its probability in the DA-LM. Using these probabilities, we rank the n-gram in each list, the higher the probability, the lower the rank. We then calculate the DA and MSA scores of each n-gram as follows:

$$MSA\_Score_1 = 1 - (MSA\_Rank/Size(Shared\_n - grams\_List))$$
$$DA\_Score_1 = 1 - (DA\_Rank/Size(Shared\_n - grams\_List))$$

We run each input sentence through the mixed-language model in order to divide the sentence into a set of n-grams. For each of the resulting n-grams we check whether it belongs to the Shared-MSA-DA, MSA-Unique or DA-Unique n-gram list.

If the n-gram belongs to the MSA-Unique list, each token in the given n-gram is assigned an MSA score of 1 and a DA score of 0. Conversely if it belongs to the DA-Unique list, then the n-gram tokens are assigned a DA score of 1 and and MSA score of 0.

When the n-gram belongs to the Shared-MSA-DA list, we calculate the difference between the MSA_Score_1 and DA_Score_1 of the n-gram. If the difference is above a certain threshold, we maintain the previously calculated scores, otherwise we update the MSA and DA scores as follows:

$$MSA\_Score_2 = DA\_Score_2 = Maximum(MSA\_Score_1, DA\_Score_1)$$

We experimented with different thresholds (0, 0.1, 0.2, ..., 0.9) on the development (tuning) dataset and got the best results with *0.4* and *0* for the context-insensitive and context-sensitive datasets, respectively.

4 Experiments and Results

We carried out five experimental conditions using the different resources for Dialect Identification.

4.1 Evaluation Dataset

Our approach is unsupervised hence we only annotated data for development and evaluation. We harvested the data from Egyptian and Levantine fora yet there was a significant number of Gulf posts. We annotated 1,170 forum posts corresponding to a total of 27,173 tokens; excluding punctuation, numbers and tokens written in romanized script, yielding 11,767 types. Half of the data comes from Egyptian fora while the other half comes from Levantine ones. Moreover, the data is chosen in a way so as to balance the DA and MSA content. We annotated the data in two different ways: on the word level without much attention to the context (context-insensitive), and contextually where the class of the word highly depends on the context of the text it occurred in (context-sensitive).

Context-Sensitive/Contextual Annotation The annotators are asked to consider the word in context and read it out aloud to themselves to make a decision on whether the word is deemed MSA or DA. For example If a word is used in both MSA and DA with the same sense but occurs in a DA context then it is deemed DA.

Context-Insensitive/No-Context Annotation The annotators perform a per-word annotation meaning that if a word is used in MSA and DA with the same sense then it is assigned a class-label of "MSA-DA".

The Contextual Annotation is more useful in evaluating how well our system is doing on detecting code-switch points while the No-Context helps in assessing the coverage of our MSA and DA resources. For our experiments we split both the Egyptian and Levantine datasets into development and test sets independently. We then merge the development sets from both dialects together and do the same for the test sets, resulting in an Egyptian-Levantine development set and an Egyptian-Levantine test set.

4.2 Dialect Identification Results

We have five Dialect Identification (DID) experimental conditions. Below is a detailed description of how we calculated the score of each token in each of the five experimental set ups. Table 3 shows the results obtained using each of these conditions on the no-context and contextual datasets. We exclude all tokens that are labeled *Named-Entities* or *Foreign* from the evaluation process and consider all tokens labeled as Typos to be *Unknown* words. For all experiments we initialize the DA-score to 1 if the word has consecutive repeated characters (speech-effects) and 0 otherwise, and for the MSA-Score initialization we are guided by the diacritics-scores as described earlier.

DID-1: (Using DICTs and ALMOR) We calculate the MSA score based on analysis retrieved by ALMOR and the DA score from both the dialectal dictionaries and ALMOR (as described earlier, recall that we identified the dialectal entries in the underlying dictionary used by ALMOR and assigned these entries a DA score as opposed to an MSA score). The two scores for DA are then summed and the class of the given token is chosen based on comparing the scores of the two class labels: MSA vs. DA.

DID-2: (Using DICTs, ALMOR and SCR) We use the DA Dictionaries, and attempt to increase the coverage of ALMOR based on Sound Change Rules (SCR). Scores for words that are identified using SCR relaxation are calculated using the approach described earlier (See subsection 3.3.1) and again the scores for the different components are summed prior to identifying the class of the token of interest.

	Dev No-Context						Dev Contextual					
	BL	1	2	3	4	5	BL	1	2	3	4	5
MSA	72.1	92.3	92.3	84.2	88.0	80.8	62.5	81.7	81.7	77.8	82.0	82.0
DA	72.1	62.3	64.6	87.7	73.6	73.9	48.5	45.6	49.5	62.6	64.1	64.6
UNK	2.1	21.2	22.0	18.1	26.2	23.3	2.1	21.2	22.0	18.1	26.2	23.3
All	71.4	77.2	78.6	**84.4**	80.4	80.8	55.6	66.3	68.0	68.5	73.8	**74.0**
	Test No-Context						Test Contextual					
	BL	1	2	3	4	5	BL	1	2	3	4	5
MSA	73.4	92.8	92.8	83.5	87.9	88.1	60.0	75.3	75.3	74.3	77.9	77.8
DA	72.6	62.7	64.3	88.8	74.0	74.3	52.1	50.3	52.7	67.0	66.4	66.7
UNK	0.0	16.7	17.7	14.2	24.6	22.5	0.0	16.7	17.7	14.2	24.6	22.5
All	72.6	78.3	79.3	**84.9**	80.8	81.1	55.8	64.1	65.3	68.8	72.2	**72.4**

Table 3: Token based $F_{\beta=1}$ scores of a random-baseline and the different experimental-conditions on both the context-insensitive and context-sensitive development and test datasets.

DID-3: (Using LMs only) In this condition we assign the score to each token based on the approach described in subsection 3.4.

DID-4: (Using DICTs, ALMOR, and LMs) In this condition, we combine the LMs, DA dictionaries and ALMOR scores.

DID-5: (Using DICTs, ALMOR, LMs, and SCR) In this condition we combine all the scores from all resources and the class for the word is based on the highest aggregate score per class We also calculate a random baseline (BL). We report all our results $F_{\beta=1}$ score metric.

5 Discussion

All the experimental conditions significantly beat the baseline BL. The language-model based approach (DID-3) yields better results than the Dictionary-based and hybrid conditions (DID-1, DID-2, DID-4, and DID-5) on the no-context dataset. Because currently we only use an MSA morphological analyzer (and not a DA one), the dictionary-based and hybrid approaches will bias the predicted class of "MSA-DA" surface tokens towards MSA. ALMOR will produce correct analyses for these tokens while the DA dictionaries won't be able to identify them due to lack of coverage of the different morphological forms – most of our DA entries in the Tharwa dictionary are lemmas – and moreover the problem is exacerbated by the inherent orthographic variance in the DA data yielding potential differences between the data used in the LM and the input data. An example of this is the word *"mdrsthm"* which means *"their school"*, that won't be identified by our DA dictionaries because of the inflection but will be identified by ALMOR.

On the other hand, the hybrid approach performs better on the contextual annotation since we have very few "MSA-DA" tokens in this case hence biasing the system towards choosing only one label is desirable.

While adding the SCR component always yields better results, the absolute magnitude of improvement is diminished when using SCR with LM since LMs increases the coverage of DA words. However SCR are still very useful in getting the MSA-Equivalent of a DA word without having to add more entries to the DA dictionary.

The percentage of OOVs (words that were unrecognized by our system) are much less on MSA tokens compared to DA tokens in the contextual case. The better performance on the MSA data is again attributed to the use of the MSA morphological analyzer that gives better coverage on surface form MSA words; a capability that we currently don't have for DA.

Table 4 shows the details of the confusability between different classes for the best experimental conditions on the no-context and contextual Test-datasets respectively.

No-Context					Contextual				
	P-MSA	P-DA	P-UNK	A-Tot.[5]		P-MSA	P-DA	P-UNK	G-Tot.
G-MSA	7818	1878	433	10190	G-MSA	5907	2176	14	6833
G-DA	634	9560	389	10036	G-DA	2385	3839	148	5413
G-UNK	52	40	61	153	G-UNK	45	68	40	153

Table 4: Confusion matrix for MSA, DA and UNK classes of Test for conditions that yielded best results. (DID-3 for the context-insensitive dataset and DID-5 for the context-sensitive dataset). The G-MSA/G-DA/G-UNK correspond to gold manual labels while P-MSA/P-DA/P-UNK correspond to the predicted labels (AIDA output)

Context-Insensitive [DID-3] For MSA words, we note that 18.4% of the words are confused for being DA while only 4.2% of the MSA words are classified as UNK reflecting the high-coverage level of our LMs. For DA words, we note that 6.3% of the words are misclassified as MSA and 3.9% of the DA words are classified as UNK. In general, this indicates that we have good coverage DA corpora for LM but more importantly it suggests that our MSA LMs include a residual significant amount of DA data.

Context-Sensitive [DID-5] For MSA words, we note that a significant percentage (31.8%) of the words are confused for being DA. A tiny percentage is confused for being UNK (0.2%). For DA words, we note that a similarly significant percentage, 44.1% of the words, are misclassified as MSA and 2.7% of the DA words are classified as UNK. It does make sense due to the nature of the data since the conditions of both MSA and DA are hard to tell apart. In the contextual annotation guidelines we almost force the annotator to choose between DA or MSA allowing for a "MSA-DA" interpretation only when there isn't enough context (mostly in extremely short phrases). The overall numbers indicate that DA was much harder to classify than MSA words.

Similar to the context-insensitive annotation condition, the majority of the UNK are classified as MSA. In general compared to the results of the context-insensitive condition confusion matrix, we note that there seems to be significantly more confusion among the classes for the contextual conditions.

6 Conclusion[6]

In this paper, we presented several combinations of resources to address the problem of automatic identification of token level dialectalness. The resources include Dictionaries, Morphological Analyzer, Sound Change Rules and Language Models . We evaluate the system performance against forum data pertaining to Egyptian and Levantine dialects. The dataset is annotated with two different sets of guidelines: context-sensitive and context-insensitive. Preliminary results show that using all the resources together perform better on the context-sensitive dataset while the language models perform better on the context-insensitive dataset. Adding Sound-Change-Rules never hurts the performance yet their added value depends on how dialectal the dataset is since they only affect dialectal tokens. These results are encouraging given the different challenges that written Arabic impose. We plan on further extending our approach by identifying LCS on the sentence as well as the document level in addition to classifying the dialects.

[5]Tokens that were annotated as "MSA-DA" are counted twice, hence the *G-Tot.* count differs across the No-Context and Contextual annotations (Since the no-context annotation has more "MSA-DA" tokens. Also if a token has an actual class of MSA and the system produces "MSA-DA", it is considered a true-positive for MSA and false-positive for DA.

[6]This work is supported by the Defense Advanced Research Projects Agency (DARPA) BOLT program under contract number HR0011-12-C-0014.

References

Biadsy, F., Hirschberg, J., and Habash., N. (2009). Spoken arabic dialect identification using phonotactic modeling. In *Proceedings of the Workshop on Computational Approaches to Semitic Languages at the meeting of the European Association for Computational Linguistics (EACL), Athens, Greece.*

Chan, J. Y. C., Ching, P. C., LEE, T., and Meng, H. M. (2004). Detection of language boundary in code-switching utterances by bi-phone probabilities. In *Proceedings of the International Symposium on Chinese Spoken Language Processing.*

Dasigi, P. and Diab, M. (2011). Codact: Towards identifying orthographic variants in dialectal arabic. In *Proceedings of the 5th International Joint Conference on Natural Language Processing (ICJNLP), Chiangmai, Thailand.*

Diab, M., Hawwari, A., Elfardy, H., Dasigi, P., Al-Badrashiny, M., Eskandar, R., and Habash, N. (2013). Tharwa: A multi-dialectal multi-lingual machine readable dictionary. In *Forthcoming.*

Diab, M. and Kamboj, A. (2011). Feasibility of leveraging crowd sourcing for the creation of a large scale annotated resource for hindi english code switched data: A pilot annotation. In *Proceedings of the 9th Workshop on Asian Language Resources, Chiangmai,Thailand.*

Elfardy, H. and Diab, M. (2012). Simplified guidelines for the creation of large scale dialectal arabic annotations. In *Proceedings of the 8th International Conference on Language Resources and Evaluation (LREC), Istanbul, Turkey.*

Ferguson (1959). *Diglossia. Word 15. 325340.*

Habash, N. (2007). *Arabic Morphological Representations for Machine Translation.*

Joshi, A. K. (1985). Processing of sentences with intrasentential code switching. In *R. Dowty, L. Karttunen, and A. M., Zwicky, eds., Natural Language Parsing: Psychological, Computational, and Theoretical Perspectives. Cambridge: Cambridge University Press. 190-205.*

Lyu, D.-C., yuan Lyu, R., chin Chiang, Y., and nan Hsu, C. (2006). Speech recognition on code-switching among the chinese dialects. In *Proceedings of the International Conference on nAcoustics, Speech and Signal Processing(ICASSP).*

Maamouri, M., Graff, D., Bouziri, B., Krouna, S., Bies, A., and Kulick, S. (2010). Ldc standard arabic morphological analyzer (sama) version 3.1.

Manandise, E. and Gdaniec, C. (2011). Morphology to the rescue redux: Resolving borrowings and code-mixing in machine translation. In *SFCM'11*, pages 86–97.

Parker, R., Graff, D., Chen, K., Kong, J., , and Maeda, K. (2009). Arabic gigaword fourth edition.

Rashwan, M., Al-Badrashiny, M., Attia, M., Abdou, S., and Rafea, A. (2011). A stochastic arabic diacritizer based on a hybrid of factorized and unfactorized textual features. In *Proceedings of the International Conference on Natural Language Processing and Knowledge Engineering.*

Solorio, T. and Liu, Y. (2008a). Learning to predict code-switching points. In *Proceedings of the Conference on Empirical Methods in Natural Language Processing (EMNLP), Honolulu, Hawaii.*

Solorio, T. and Liu, Y. (2008b). Part-of-speech tagging for english-spanish code-switched text. In *Proceedings of the Conference on Empirical Methods in Natural Language Processing (EMNLP), Honolulu, Hawaii.*

Stolcke, A. (2002). Srilm an extensible language modeling toolkit. In *Proceedings of the International Conference on Spoken Language Processing (ICSLP).*

Parenthetical Classification for Information Extraction

Ismail EL MAAROUF[1,2] *Jeanne VILLANEAU*[1]
(1) IRISA, Université Bretagne Sud, France
(2) RIILP, University of Wolverhampton, UK
elmaarouf.ismail@yahoo.fr, Jeanne.Villaneau@univ-ubs.fr

ABSTRACT
The article focuses on a rather unexplored topic in NLP: parenthetical classification. Parentheticals are defined as any text sequence between parentheses. They have been approached from isolated perspectives, like translation pairs extraction, but a full account of their syntactic and semantic properties is lacking. This article proposes a new comprehensive scheme drawn from corpus-based linguistic studies on French news. This research is part of a project investigating the structural aspects of punctuation signs and their usefulness for Information Extraction. Parenthetical classification is approached as a relation extraction problem split into three correlated subtasks: syntactic and semantic classification and head recognition. Corpus-based studies singled out 11 syntactic and 18 semantic relation subtypes. The article addresses automatic classification, using a combination of CRF and SVM. This baseline system reports 0.674 (head recognition), 0.908 (syntax), 0.734 (semantics), and 0.518 (end-to-end) of F1.

TITLE AND ABSTRACT IN ANOTHER LANGUAGE, FRENCH (FR)

Classification des parenthétiques pour l'extraction d'information

Définies dans cet article comme du texte entre parenthèses, les parenthétiques ont été jusqu'à présent peu étudiées en TALN. Si elles ont fait l'objet d'études particulières telles que l'extraction de paires de traduction, il manque une approche globale des relations syntaxiques et sémantiques qui les rattachent à leur contexte. Cet article propose un nouveau schéma de classification élaboré à partir d'études de corpus de presse. Cette recherche s'inscrit dans un projet explorant les aspects structurants des signes de ponctuation et leur utilité en Extraction d'Information. La classification des parenthétiques est abordée sous l'angle de l'extraction de relations et divisée en trois sous-tâches : classification syntaxique et sémantique et reconnaissances des têtes. Les études de corpus ont fait émerger 11 classes syntaxiques et 18 classes sémantiques. L'article propose d'évaluer un système combinant CRF et SVM. La baseline obtenue est de 0,674 (reconnaissance des têtes), 0,908 (syntaxe), 0,734 (sémantique) et 0,518 (toutes tâches confondues) de F-mesure.

KEYWORDS: Parentheticals, Punctuation, Information Extraction.

KEYWORDS IN FRENCH (FR): Parenthétiques, Ponctuation, Extraction d'information.

Proceedings of COLING 2012: Posters, pages 297–308,
COLING 2012, Mumbai, December 2012.

1 Condensed version in French (FR)

Cet article a pour objectif de contribuer à une meilleure connaissance des propriétés syntaxico-sémantiques des parenthétiques, définies comme des empans de texte entre parenthèses. La tâche y est abordée du point de vue de l'Extraction de Relations : (i) extraction des têtes externe et interne des parenthétiques, (ii) classifications syntaxique et sémantique des couples de têtes extraites.

La tête interne d'une parenthétique est son élément informationnel majeur. Sa tête externe est l'élément du contexte auquel l'information entre parenthèses doit préférentiellement être rattachée. Une particularité de ces têtes est de couvrir à peu près toutes les classes grammaticales : texte, phrase, Entités Nommées, noms, verbes, adjectifs, etc. Trois catégories spécifiques ont dû être définies pour les têtes externes : *a*, *p* renvoient respectivement aux cas où la tête externe est le texte entier et la phrase dans sa globalité alors que *n* renvoie au cas où il est impossible de spécifier un rattachement particulier. Dans les exemples de la Table 1, les têtes sont en caractères gras. La Table 2 (en bas à gauche) donne des précisions statistiques sur la nature des têtes dans le corpus étudié.

L'étude d'un corpus de la presse française (Le Monde) a permis d'identifier 11 classes syntaxiques, organisées suivant différents critères (voir détails section 4.2) : parenthétique de nature propositionnelle (inter-clause) ou non (intra-clause), apposition/adjonction (exemples (1, 4, 5, 8)/ (2, 3, 6, 7), présence ou absence de mots introductifs (soulignés dans les exemples), la parenthétique est (ou non) en coordination avec sa tête externe (exemples (3b), (7b)). La Table 1 donne un exemple de chacune des 10 principales classes ainsi définies.

	Inter-clause
(1)	le **produit intérieur brut** (**PIB**). [the **gross domestic product** (**GDP**).]
(2)	il est (**très**) **réussi**. [it is (**very**) **nice**.]
(3a)	son **taux** directeur (à 2,5%). [its reference **rate** (at 2.5%).]
(3b)	elle a connu la **liberté** (et les **pressions**). [She experienced **freedom** (and **pressure**).]
(4)	La cérémonie a **lieu** mercredi (cf. **page** 15) [Celebrations is **held** Wednesday (cf. **page** 15)]
	Intra-clause
(5)	elle est **partie** (Gustave **avait** 6 ans). [She **left** (Gustave **was** 6 years old).]
(6)	elle est **partie** ce jour-là (Gustave **ayant** 6 ans). [She **left** that day (Gustave **being** 6 years old).]
(7a)	elle est **partie** (alors que Gustave **avait** 6 ans). [She **left** (when Gustave **was** 6 years old).]
(7b)	elle est **partie** (et Gustave **avait** 6 ans). [She **left** (and Gustave **was** 6 years old).]
(8)	je ne **suis** pas (ici elle **baissa** la voix qui tremblait) de l'avis de sa majesté! [I **am** not (here she **lowered** her shaking voice) of your Highness's opinion!]

Table 1: Exemples pour la classification syntaxique. *(Examples for syntactic Classification.)*

La classification sémantique ne traite que d'une classe syntaxique particulièrement fréquente (82%) : les parenthétiques appositives non introduites et intra-propositionnelles (exemple (1) Table 1). Les études de corpus ont permis de mettre à jour 18 classes sémantiques génériques, comme l'ancrage spatial ou temporel (section 4.3).

Des conventions d'annotation ont été élaborées pour permettre l'annotation complète d'un corpus de 1000 parenthétiques. On pourra se reporter aux Tables 2 pour une description de ce corpus en termes de classes et à la Table 4 pour l'accord inter-annotateurs. Bien que, dans la classe des parenthétiques sémantiquement classées, la relation sémantique soit totalement implicite, le bon accord inter-annotateur montre, s'il en était besoin, que le lecteur décode sans difficultés la nature de l'information qui lui est donnée entre parenthèses.

Syntactic Class	Frequency
Intra App NI	801
Intra Adj IN Not-Coord	60
Inter App NI	27
Truncation	25
Intra Adj NI	21
Inter Adj IN NotCoord	22
Intra Adj IN Coord	21
Inter Adj NI	1
Total	978

Head Class	Frequency
ID	869
p	62
n	25
a	22
Total	978

Semantic Class	Frequency
NULL	177
CoRef-Abbreviation	150
Sit-SA	87
Cat-Instantiation	78
Sit-ArgVal	72
Sit-Affiliation	72
Ref-IR	55
CoRef-EntRef	49
Other	43
Sit-PS	43
Cat-ValPrec	28
CoRef-ValRef	27
Cat-Type	25
CoRef-Translation	22
Sit-TA-Date	21
Ref-PR	9
CoRef-Explanation	9
Sit-TA-Period	7
Ref-Coordinates	4
Total	978

Table 2: Fréquences des classes dans le corpus. *(Sample corpus class counts.)*

Le système proposé comme baseline (Section 6) combine les CRF (pour la détection des candidats) et les SVM (pour la classification), pour chaque tâche indépendamment et toutes tâches confondues. L'évaluation de ce système (Table 3) a permis tout d'abord d'observer que les ensembles de variables (formes, étiquettes morpho-syntaxiques, Entités Nommées, etc.) avaient un impact qui variait en fonction de la tâche : les étiquettes morpho-syntaxiques (T) sont par exemple les plus utiles à la classification syntaxique. De plus, la détection des candidats est une tâche cruciale, étant donné que le nombre de couples candidats aux frontières correctement délimitées est responsable d'une chute de la F-mesure globale du système (0,674, indépendamment, 0,518 toutes tâches confondues). Ces résultats sont confirmés par ceux obtenus par (Zhou et al., 2005) en Extraction de Relation à grand nombre de classes.

Feature	Pre-detection	Exact-Rec.	Soft-Rec	Syntax	Semantics
F	**0.965**	0.426	0.680	0.861	0.512
C	0.914	**0.499**	0.705	0.859	**0.637**
T	0.955	0.470	0.714	**0.908**	0.582
Ab	0.888	0.318	0.642	0.818	0.312
Pre-detection	-	0.349	**0.719**	-	-
Size	0.886	-	-	0.796	0.286
All	0.963	0.674	0.774	0.902	0.716
Baseline	0.888	0.3	0.649	0.818	0.182

Table 3: Résultats obtenus par le système en fonction des ensembles de variables utilisés. *(Independent task results on each feature set.)*

Les expériences à venir feront intervenir les informations syntaxiques pour évaluer leur apport. La robustesse du schéma d'annotation nécessite d'être également mise à l'épreuve; les expériences préliminaires menées en ce sens sur des corpus encyclopédiques, littéraires, juridiques et scientifiques n'ont jusqu'à présent donné lieu qu'à des modifications minimes.

2 Introduction

As Say and Akman (1996) point out, punctuation has not attracted much theoretical attention in Linguistics nor in NLP (see however (Briscoe, 1996; Jones, 1996; Nunberg, 1990)). Nevertheless, it is pervasive in written texts and commonly used in NLP systems: phrase boundaries, sentence boundaries, and so on.

This work is a part of a discourse-oriented project investigating how punctuation interacts with different linguistic levels such as syntax and semantics. It attempts to provide answers as to why and how punctuation helps comprehension, through the analysis of text segments between parentheses, named parentheticals. This punctuation structure should not be confused with the definition of parentheticals as optional embedded segments.

The article introduces a new scheme designed for robustness and large coverage from an Information Extraction perspective. The task is divided into three subtasks, Head recognition, Syntactic and Semantic classification. The choice of the classes is based on a linguistic corpus study on French news: 11 syntactic relations and 18 semantic relations have been defined, according to several levels of granularity or dimensions.

The article describes the application and results of an annotation experiment on a sampled corpus of a thousand parenthetical observations. It provides baselines for each subtask, using various feature sets. The results, along with an analysis of feature set impact, call for further experiments as well as for a generalization of the task to different corpora.

Section 3 discusses related work on parentheticals and section 4 introduces the classification scheme. Section 5 details the annotated corpus. The systems are described in section 6 and their evaluation is presented in section 6.3.

3 Parentheticals in Information Extraction (IE)

It is commonly stated that parentheticals provide optional information: they can be removed without affecting understanding. For instance, they are deleted in sentence compression applications (e.g. equation (31) in (Clarke and Lapata, 2008)). However, they have recently aroused interest in IE.

IE (Sundheim, 1991; Sarawagi, 2008) is the NLP field concerned with (i) the identification of Named Entities (NE) from text, (ii) their co-referring units (anaphora, acronyms), and (iii) their interactions (e.g. Affiliation, Location). Two text types have particularly been studied in IE: newswire and biomedical articles. In both types, parentheticals are pervasive. For instance, Bretonnel Cohen et al. (2010), report finding about 17,000 parentheses in a corpus of 97 scientific articles (about 600,000 words). Comparatively, we found more than 4 parentheses per article in newswire texts (136,000 on 17,000,000 words).

Parentheticals have mainly been studied under the topics of Abbreviation, Translation and Transliteration pairs extraction. Abbreviation recognition (extracting co-referring full and short forms) is a well-defined task which has both been conducted on biomedical literature (Pustejovsky et al., 2001; Schwartz and Hearst, 2003) and on newswire (Okazaki et al., 2008): systems generally record more than 0.9 in F1. Okazaki et al. (2008) analyzed 7,887 frequent parenthetical instances and classified them into *Acronym*, *Translated Acronym*, *Alias* and *Other*. In their study, the *Other* category covers 81.9% of all studied instances. The authors propose to split it into *alphabetic transcription*, *location*, or *affiliation*.

Parentheticals have also been studied in the field of Machine Translation. Cao et al. (2007)

observe that many terms (very frequently NE) are followed by their English translation inside parentheses on Chinese monolingual webpages. They use parentheticals to extract a bilingual dictionary automatically, and find that the majority of pairs are not covered by a standard lexicon. In a similar experiment, Kaji and Kitsuregawa (2011) propose to classify transliteration pairs in order to help segmenting complex katakana compounds.

A recent much larger scheme was proposed for the biomedical domain (Bretonnel Cohen et al., 2011). The authors propose to classify parenthetic content into 20 categories. They note that some categories are ambiguous if only the content inside parentheses is taken into account. The scheme introduced in the next section builds on previous works and aims to be generic and rich at the same time.

4 Annotation scheme

The annotation scheme is the result of an in-depth corpus-based linguistic study. It proposes to identify, when possible, the most prominent unit inside parentheses (internal head) and the word in the host sentence (external head) to which it is most preferably linked. This link is syntactically characterized. Besides, most of the time, deleting parentheses affects sentence grammaticality (cf. ex. (4)), so the relation between parenthetical and its environment needs to be inferred by the reader. In this case (and only in this case), the scheme provides semantic categories.

4.1 Head Detection

Internal heads are most straightforwardly detected, because they tend to correspond to the syntactic head of the first information group. When more than one head can be selected, only the first is kept.

External heads are very frequently multi-word units (cf. example (1), Table 1), but is not necessarily the head of its own syntactic phrase. In the following example (9), the relation holds between a color and its interpretation, but it is "niveau" which is the syntactic head of the prepositional phrase.

(9)...maintenir le niveau d'alerte antiterroriste au niveau **orange** *(très* **élevé***) [keeping the anti-terrorism threat level at level* **orange** *(very* **high***)]*

In some rarer cases, the external head may follow (and not precede) the parenthetical, as in ex. (2), Table 1. More examples can be found in bold type in Table 1.

Three labels are provided when no words can be singled out as head: *p* for the whole proposition, *n* for no head, for example in the case of truncation (cf. end of 4.2) and *a* is used when the parenthetical provides information on the whole document.

4.2 Syntactic classification

Ten syntactic categories were organized along four criteria. An example for each of them is given Table 1.

- The first criterion is the distinction between *intra*(-clause) and *inter*(-clause). A parenthetical is *inter* if its content can be viewed as a finite clause (cf. examples (5), (6), (7a), (7b) and (8) of Table 1.). In contrast, an *intra* corresponds to non-finite clauses (cf. (1), (2), (3a), (3b) and (4)).

- The second criterion discriminates between *adj*(-oined) and *app*(-ositionnal) (non-adjoined) parentheticals. In the case of *adj* parentheticals, the sentence remains correct when the brackets are removed (cf. (2), (3a), (3b), (6), (7a) and (7b), Table 1.). In *app* parentheticals, the deletion of the parentheses breaks the progression of the sentence (cf. (1), (4), (5) and (8)).
- The third criterion divides parentheticals into *intro*(-duced) (IN) and *not-intro*(duced) (NI) parentheticals. A parenthetical is *intro* when an expression introduces its head, and links it with the outer context (cf. (3a), (3b), (4), (7a), (7b) and (8) of Table 1, where introducing elements are underlined).

Eight classes are obtained by applying the previous three criteria. A fourth criterion splits *intro adj* parentheticals (*inter* or *intra*) and discriminates between *coord*(-inated) and *not-coord*(-inated) parentheticals. In *coord* parentheticals, the internal head has the same syntactic category as the external head (word or clause) (cf. (3b) and (7b)).

The last and eleventh class concerns the case of punctuation marks in brackets ((...), (!), etc.), called *truncation*. All cases have been found in corpus, though with high distribution differences (Table 2, left).

4.3 Semantic classification

Eighteen semantic categories, organized into four dimensions, were defined for *intra app NI (intra-clause appositional not-introduced)* parentheticals, which lack an explicit link. Classifying other syntactic classes was left for further investigation.

1. The first, *Co-reference (CoRef)*, corresponds to cases where both heads refer to the same entity, but use different names.
   (a) *Abbreviation*: the parenthetical contains an abbreviation of the external head (its full form; cf. example (1)).
   (b) *Explanation*: the definition of an acronym (the reverse of the previous relation).
   (c) *Translation*: it contains a translation of the external head in an other language.
   (d) *Reformulated Entity (RefEnt)*: other co-referential relations not covered by the previous classes; for example, the name an actor has in a movie.
   (e) *Reformulated Value (RefVal)*: it translates the value expressed by the external head in another unit of measurement.
2. The second broad class, *Categorization (Cat)*, refers to asymmetric relations between entities and categories.
   (a) *Type*: it provides the category of the entity of the external head (as hyponyms).
   (b) *Instantiation*: the reverse of the previous relation. It provides an instance of the category expressed by the external head.
   (c) *Value Precision (ValPrec)*: it precises the value of its external head, which is already a quantity category (drop, growth, etc.).
3. The third class relates to *Situational relations (Sit)*. Most correspond to standard semantic relations defined for relation extraction (ACE, 2008).
   (a) *Product Source (PS)*: it refers to the producer, editor, etc. of a product referred by the external head (e.g. book).

(b) *Affiliation*: it contains the organization to which its external head (person or organization) is affiliated.
(c) *Spatial Anchoring (SA)*: it sets the spatial location of an entity.
(d) *Temporal Anchoring (TA)* is split into *Date* and *Period* (of any kind of entity).
(e) *Argument Value (ArgVal)*: it gives a value related to its external head (as age).

4. The fourth class concerns *Referencing (Ref)*, where parentheticals attribute references or indexes to the external head.

   (a) *Inter-textual Reference (IR)*: it makes a reference to the journal, media as source of the external head (citation).
   (b) *Para-textual Reference (PR)*: it refers to para-textual elements of the document (figure, footnote, etc.)
   (c) *Coordinates*: It provides the code value indexing entities in a given coding scheme (phone number, postal address, etc.).
   (d) *Indexing*: it refers to the marks (numbers) indexing document elements (such as examples) and to which parentheticals may elsewhere refer to.

Contrary to Okazaki et al. (2008), translated acronyms are here considered as abbreviations. In principle, most classes defined by Bretonnel Cohen et al. (2011) could be fitted in this scheme, like *p-values* (*ArgVal*) or *Figure references* (*IR*).

5 Corpus Annotation

The scheme was tested on a sample of French news (114 parentheticals) by two highly-trained annotators. The results of inter-annotator agreement for the three tasks are illustrated in Table 4. Kappa indexes show that parenthetical syntactic (0.89) and semantic (0.79) categories could easily be recognized by annotators. The Kappa was not computed for Head recognition since head spans vary greatly. It is thus hard to approximate the random baseline on which the Kappa is based (Grouin et al., 2011).

Task	# agr.	# disagr.	Total	Kappa
Syntax	109	5	114	0.89
Semantics	88	13	101	0.79
Head	103	11	114	/

Table 4: Inter-annotator agreement synthesis.

As can be seen in Table 2 (left), the *intra app NI* class is the most frequent syntactic class. This validates the use of a semantic scheme designed especially for this class (other syntactic classes being semantically classified as *NULL*). Heads are mostly words, though the "p" class covers 6% of examples.

The counts of semantic classes (Table 2, right) shows that the semantic class *Other*, used for the examples of *intra app NI* parentheticals which don't match with the defined semantic categories covers less than 5% of examples.

At last, the annotated corpus was sampled (stratified sampling) according to the concatenated labels to build the training and testing corpora (half each).

6 System design and Evaluation

6.1 Overview

Relation Extraction (RE) systems typically (i) extract Named Entity (NE) pairs to filter positive targeted instances (recognition step), before (ii) they attribute a label to them (classification step). The recognition step is problematic since it requires that all possible NE instances be extracted: Sun et al. (2011) indicate that the number of negative instances is about 8 times higher than the number of positive ones. The current best classification systems on complex schemes rely on feature-based approaches (Zhou et al., 2005). Such methods typically use information on candidate NE pairs (such as NE tag, POS tag, form, etc.), along with information on the words in between (Zhou et al., 2005) for prediction.

In our case, candidate pairs (heads) do not correspond uniquely to NE, but also to whole sentences, quotations, verbs, adjectives, etc.: the number of candidate pairs is huge. This is why, instead of elaborating a preprocessing system, the recognition step was approached as a sequence labeling task (6.2).

What is more, annotators had the choice between using labels and select word spans to identify parenthetical heads. Therefore, the system first discriminates labeled instances (*a*, *p*, and *n*) from others (*ID* class). In a second step, it detects head boundaries from previously pre-detected *ID* instances. This first step (pre-detection), along with syntactic and semantic classification, is approached as a classification task performed on each parenthetical instance.

6.2 System

Two systems were used : CRF++ (Kudo, 2007) for head recognition and SVM (Hall et al., 2009) for parenthetical classification as they are recognized as very efficient algorithms [1]. The features used for CRF Recognition include:

- forms (F) without any processing.
- categories (C) provided by a linguistic analyzer, which includes NE recognition and semantic labels (Rosset et al., 2006). This tagset was transformed into BIO format (Tjong Kim Sang and De Meulder, 2003).
- POS tags (T) provided by the Tree-tagger (Schmid, 2003).
- Abbreviation pairs (Ab) from the system provided by Schwartz and Hearst (2003).
- pre-detection labels (*a*, *p*, *n*, *ID*) propagated on all the words,

Unigrams, bigrams, and label bigrams (Kudo, 2007) occurring in the most optimal window size (cf. 6.3.2) were used for all feature sets.

The same features were used for classification, except removing predetection labels and adding parenthetical size (*Size*). For the other sets (*F*, *C*, and *T*), each feature value was combined with positional parameters to distinguish between the first and second words before and after the opening brace.

6.3 Evaluation

Evaluation was performed on the test corpus (490 instances) using the standard metrics of precision, recall and F1 (F-measure). All results are displayed in Table 3.

[1] Different algorithms were tested to confirm this.

6.3.1 Head Label pre-detection

Pre-detection is a straightforward task: most corpus instances are annotated with one label (ID), which results in a high baseline of 0.888, just by assigning this label to all examples. The SVM beats this baseline with 0.963 of overall F1. Detailed feature analysis shows that the *Ab* and *Size* features do not individually help for this task since the resulting models behave like the baseline. The best feature set is F (forms): the SVM perfectly classifies *a* and *n* classes (1 in F-measure). This is due to the fact that the *a* class corresponds to a parenthetical which only contains punctuation signs such as "...". The *n* class instances generally occur at the end of an article and are immediately preceded by dashes. The real challenge is therefore to discriminate the *p* class (0.667) from the *ID* class (0.981).

6.3.2 Head recognition

Only external heads were evaluated for this task. The baseline selects the word immediately preceding the parenthetical as the head, because most heads occupy this position. An example can be considered correctly labeled if (i) all the labeled words need to be correct (exact evaluation), or if (ii) at least one word needs to be correctly labeled (soft evaluation). The baseline F1 is very low (0.3) in the first case, and reaches 0.649 in the second case. The best results (0.674) recorded for the CRF were obtained with a window size of 4 words [-1,2]. The best feature set is *C* (0.499), i.e. the categories provided by the linguistic analyzer, including Named Entities. These results are still much lower than the system using the combination of all feature sets (0.674 in F1 for exact matching; 0.774 for soft matching). The latter takes benefit of the pre-detection features (best feature set for *p* and *n* classes) but also largely improves exact head recognition (+0.146 compared to *C*).

The high difference between Soft and Exact head recognition across feature sets indicates that multi-word units management play a large part in system performances.

6.3.3 Classification

The Syntax and semantic tasks were first carried out independently. The Syntax task consists of 7 labels (4 rare *inter* categories are missing) and the semantic task, of 19 classes (*Indexing* is missing). The baseline model assigns the most frequent class to all examples (0.818 in F1 for syntax, 0.182 for semantics). Table 3 shows the superiority of the *T* set for syntax. *T* is composed of precise syntactic labels; for instance, it discriminates between various verb forms such as past and present participles (contrary to the *C* set which only divides between auxiliaries, modals, actions and gerunds).

Concerning Semantics, it is the *C* feature set which is the most effective. This said, the system reaches higher scores when all the features are taken together. It is also clear from the table that POS tags (*T*) have a greater impact than forms (*F*) on this task.

A second experiment was conducted to analyze the impact of syntax on semantics: only the examples predicted as *Intra App NI* (the most frequent class to be semantically labeled) by SVM-T were extracted for semantic classification (the rest being considered as *NULL*). This filtering method prove successful (0.734; +0.018 improvement): even if 8 examples are incorrectly filtered (semantically *NULL*), the system correctly classifies 31 semantic instances. Detailed class analysis indicate that improvements mostly affect *ValPrec* (+0.22), *NULL* (+0.2), and *Other* (+0.15).

6.3.4 End-to-end Evaluation

The aim of the end-to-end evaluation is to observe how Head recognition affects both syntactic and semantic classification. An example was considered correct when all task labels were correctly assigned. F1 significantly drops drops to 0.518 on exact matching, and to 0.586 on soft matching. These results are consistent with previous work in RE. Zhou et al. (2005) report 0.55 of F1 when recognition and classification are evaluated together on subtypes (0.68 on supertypes), and attribute 73% of errors to recognition (53% in our case).

It is interesting that the *Situational* dimension, which contains traditional RE broad categories (*SA* and *Affiliation*), obtains the best scores. These scores are even higher than reported in RE literature (Sun et al., 2011), though the dataset is barely comparable. *Abbreviation* experiences comparably lower results than reported in the literature: Okazaki et al. (2008) report 95.7% accuracy (0.887 of F1).

7 Conclusion and discussion

Parenthetical classification is a rather unexplored topic and this article aims at providing insights into this punctuation pattern. An annotation scheme was designed to cover most frequent cases for three tasks: syntactic and semantic classification and head recognition.

Corpus analyses revealed that most parentheticals lack an explicit link to the external context (the *App* syntactic class), but are nonetheless similarly understood by annotators. Only the *Intra App NI* class was semantically labeled (81% of instances) and tested. Analyzing *inter app* parentheticals was left for further investigation because it is believed that they must be studied on the discourse level (see for example (Marcu, 2000)): proposition links may be characterized as *causal* for instance.

Other annotation experiments have been started on different text types (encyclopedic, legal, scientific or fictional documents), to assess the robustness of the scheme across text types, and evaluate automatic systems in the light of domain adaptation. Preliminary results are encouraging in the sense that the same scheme can be used with little adaptation.

The evaluation proposed a baseline using CRF and SVM for each task separately, with various feature sets based on POS tags, Named Entities, Forms, etc. The best model reported 0.908 for syntax, 0.734 for semantics, and 0.674 for head recognition. It is interesting that different feature sets have had different impacts on classification tasks. All tasks except semantics have shown better performance on isolated feature sets. Besides, Zhou et al. (2005) have shown that chunking improves performances ACE Relation Extraction. Following evaluations should investigate the benefits of feature sets like chunking and semantic lexicons (as hyperonym lexicon for *Type* and *Instanciation* categories).

Since classification tasks such as syntax or semantics reported better results, it would also be interesting to investigate what gain results from their use as feature sets, much like what was done for pre-detection. Overall, it seems that improving recognition performances would rely on careful feature construction.

As suggested in section 6.3.4, the results obtained for *Affiliation* and *SA* are higher than usually reported on standard RE. This could simply be due to the fact that parenthetical structures impose strong constraints which facilitate classification. If these results are confirmed in subsequent evaluations, it would mean that parentheticals could be used as a small window to extract valuable seeds for general RE.

References

ACE (2008). Automatic content extraction 2008 evaluation plan. assessment of detection and recognition of entities and relations within and across documents.

Bretonnel Cohen, K., Christiansen, T., and Hunter, L. E. (2011). Parenthetically speaking: Classifying the contents of parentheses for text mining. In *AMIA annual symposium proceedings: 267.*

Bretonnel Cohen, K., Johnson, H. L., Verspoor, K., Roeder, C., and Hunter, L. E. (2010). The structural and content aspects of abstracts versus bodies of full text journal articles are different. *BMC Bioinformatics, 11:492.*

Briscoe, T. (1996). The syntax and semantics of punctuation and its use in interpretation. In *Proceedings of the ACL Workshop on Punctuation:1–7.*

Cao, G., Gao, J., and Nie, J.-Y. (2007). A system to mine large-scale bilingual dictionaries from monolingual web pages. In *MT summit XI proceedings: 57-64.*

Clarke, J. and Lapata, M. (2008). Global inference for sentence compression: An integer linear programming approach. *Journal of Artificial Intelligence Research (JAIR), 31:399–429.*

Grouin, C., Rosset, S., Zweigenbaum, P., Fort, K., Galibert, O., and Quintard, L. (2011). Proposal for an extension of traditional named entities: From guidelines to evaluation, an overview. In *Proceedings of the Fifth Linguistic Annotation Workshop (LAW-V)*, pages 92–100, Portland, OR. Association for Computational Linguistics.

Hall, M., Frank, E., Holmes, G., Pfahringer, B., Reutemann, P., and Witten, I. H. (2009). The weka data mining software: An update. *SIGKDD Explorations, 11(1).* `http://www.cs.waikato.ac.nz/ml/weka`.

Jones, B. (1996). *What's The Point? A (Computational) Theory of Punctuation.* PhD thesis, University of Pennsylvania.

Kaji, N. and Kitsuregawa, M. (2011). Splitting noun compounds via monolingual and bilingual paraphrasing: A study on japanese katakana words. In *EMNLP proceedings: 959–969.*

Kudo, T. (2007). Crf++: Yet another crf toolkit. `http://crfpp.sourceforge.net`.

Marcu, D. (2000). The rhetorical parsing of unrestricted texts: a surface-based approach. *Computational Linguistics, 26(3):395–448.*

Nunberg, G. (1990). *The Linguistics of Punctuation.* CSLI Lecture notes (18), CSLI publications, Stanford, CA.

Okazaki, N., Ishizuka, M., and Tsujii, J. (2008). A discriminative approach to japanese abbreviation extraction. In *IJCNLP proceedings: 889–894.*

Pustejovsky, J., Castaño, J., Cochran, B., Kotecki, M., and Morrell, M. (2001). Automatic extraction of acronym-meaning pairs from medline databases. *Studies in health technology and informatics, 84:371–375.*

Rosset, S., Galibert, O., Illouz, G., and Max, A. (2006). Integrating spoken dialog and question answering: the ritel project. In *Proceedings of InterSpeech'06.*

Sarawagi, S. (2008). Information extraction. *Foundations and Trends in Databases, 1(3):261–377.*

Say, B. and Akman, V. (1996). Current approaches to punctuation in computational linguistics. *Computers and the Humanities, 30(6):457–469.*

Schmid, H. (2003). Probabilistic part-of-speech tagging using decision trees. In *ICNMLP 1994 proceedings:44–49.*

Schwartz, A. S. and Hearst, M. A. (2003). A simple algorithm for identifying abbreviation definitions in biomedical text. In *Pacific Symposium on Biocomputing 84:451–462.*

Sun, A., Grishman, R., and Sekine, S. (2011). Semi-supervised relation extraction with large-scale word clustering. In *ACL 2011 proceedings: 521–529.*

Sundheim, B. M. (1991). Overview of the third message understanding evaluation and conference. In *Proceedings of MUC:3–16.*

Tjong Kim Sang, E. and De Meulder, F. (2003). Introduction to the conll-2003 shared task: Language-independent named entity recognition. In *CoNLL 2003 proceedings: 142–147.*

Zhou, G., Su, J., Zhang, J., and Zhang, M. (2005). Exploring various knowledge in relation extraction. In *ACL 2005 proceedings.*

A Dictionary-Based Approach to Identifying Aspects Implied by Adjectives for Opinion Mining

Geli Fei [1] *Bing Liu* [1] *Meichun Hsu* [2] *Malu Castellanos* [2] *Riddhiman Ghosh* [2]
(1) Department of Computer Science, University of Illinois at Chicago, Chicago, USA
(2) HP Labs, Palo Alto, California, USA
gfei2@uic.edu, liub@cs.uic.edu
{meichun.hsu, malu.castellanos, riddhiman.ghosh}@hp.com

ABSTRACT

One of the central problems of opinion mining is to extract aspects of entities or topics that have been evaluated in an opinion sentence or document. Much of the existing research focused on extracting explicit aspects which are nouns and nouns phrases that have appeared in sentences, e.g., *price* in "*The price of this bike is very high.*" However, in many cases, people do not explicitly mention an aspect in a sentence, but the aspect is implied, e.g., "*This bike is expensive,*" where *expensive* indicates the *price* aspect of the bike. Although there are some existing works dealing with the problem, they all used the corpus-based approach, which has several shortcomings. In this paper, we propose a dictionary-based approach to address these shortcomings. We formulate the problem as collective classification. Experimental results show that the proposed approach is effective and produces significantly better results than strong baselines based on traditional supervised classification.

KEYWORDS: Implied Aspects or Topics, Opinion Mining, Sentiment Analysis

Proceedings of COLING 2012: Posters, pages 309–318,
COLING 2012, Mumbai, December 2012.

1 Introduction

In sentiment analysis, the task of aspect extraction is to identify aspects of entities or topics on which opinions have been expressed (Hu and Liu 2004). For example, in the sentence *"The picture quality of this camera is great," picture quality* is an aspect of the camera. In most cases, aspects appear explicitly in sentences, e.g., *picture quality*. Such aspects are *called explicit aspects* (Hu and Liu 2004). However, in many other cases, they do not appear, but are implied. For instance, the sentence *"This is an expensive bike"* gives a negative opinion about the *price* aspect. However, *price* is not in the sentence, but it is clearly implied. *Price* is called an *implicit aspect* (Liu, 2010). Price is also called an attribute of *expensive* in lexical semantics (Almuhareb, 2006). In this paper, we will use the terms *aspect* and *attribute* interchangeably as they mean the same thing in our context. Since aspects or attributes used in this work are nouns, we also call them *aspects/attribute nouns.*

Implicit aspects can be indicated by many types of expressions, e.g., adjectives, adverbs, verbs and their phrases. This paper focuses on opinion adjectives. Although there are general opinion adjectives which can describe anything, e.g., *good* and *bad*, most adjectives describe some specific attributes of entities. The goal of this work is to identify attribute nouns of each adjective, e.g., to identify *price, cost*, etc., for adjective *expensive.*

There are some existing works that tried to find implicit aspects indicated by adjectives (Su et al., 2008; Hai et al., 2011). They all depend on co-occurrences of adjectives and explicit attribute nouns in sentences in a corpus. There are also some relevant works in lexical semantics, which also use corpus-based techniques (Almuhareb and Poesio 2004; Hartung and Frank, 2010; Hartung and Frank, 2011). The corpus-based approach is useful for finding context specific mappings of adjectives and attributes because an adjective can have multiple senses. In a specific domain or context, it takes only a specific sense (which needs to be discovered). However, the corpus-based approach alone also has some weaknesses:

1. It is hard to discover attributes that do not co-occur with their adjectives. For example, in English, people don't say *"The price of iPhone is expensive."* Instead, they say *"iPhone is expensive."* It is thus hard for a corpus-based approach to find *price* for *expensive.*
2. Even if an adjective and one of its attribute nouns do appear in a corpus, due to the limited corpus size, they may not co-occur in many sentences to be associated reliably.
3. If one wants to find all attribute nouns for each adjective, it is also difficult due to the corpus size limit because not all adjectives or all attributes may appear in a corpus.

In this work, we propose a dictionary-based approach which complements the corpus-based approach and can address these problems. The first and the second problems are tackled because dictionaries typically define adjectives using their attributes. For example, *expensive* is defined as *"Marked by high prices"* in thefreedictionary.com. The third problem is also addressed because dictionaries are not restricted by any specific corpus. We can work on every adjective in a dictionary. Since not all attribute nouns of an adjective may appear in a dictionary, we use multiple dictionaries for better coverage. To our knowledge, this is the first dictionary-based approach. It finds all attribute nouns for an adjective.

We propose to solve the problem using a relational learning method called *collective classification* (Sen et al. 2008), which can take advantage of rich lexical relationships of words (e.g., synonyms, antonyms, hyponym and hypernym) for classification. Our evaluation shows that collective classification outperforms traditional classification significantly.

2 The Proposed Approach

Our proposed method consists of three steps:

1. Given a set of adjectives $A = \{A_1, A_2, ..., A_r\}$, crawl the online dictionaries for their glosses.
2. For each adjective $A_i \in A$, perform POS tagging of its glosses and extract nouns from them. These nouns are regarded as the candidate attribute nouns C_i for adjective A_i.
3. Classify each candidate attribute noun $c_{ij} \in C_i$ to one of the two classes, *attribute noun* or *not attribute noun*, of A_i. This step uses a collective classification algorithm to exploit the lexical relationships of words in dictionaries to build more accurate classifiers.

Since the first two steps are straightforward, the rest of the paper focuses on step 3.

2.1 Problem Formulation and Solution

In traditional supervised learning, each instance is drawn independently of others (Mitchell, 1997). However, in many real-life data, instances are not independent of each other. Such data is often represented as a graph where nodes are instances and links are their relations. The classification of one node can influence its neighboring nodes. This type of classification is called *collective classification* (Sen et al., 2008) as opposed to the instance-based classification. We formulate the proposed problem as collective classification.

Each instance in our data denotes a pair with an adjective A_i and one of its candidate attribute nouns c_{ij}, i.e., (A_i, c_{ij}). Due to the relational features (which will be detailed later), we use a graph representation of instances, with a set of nodes (pairs), $V = \{(A_i, c_{ij}) \mid c_{ij} \in C_i, A_i \in A\}$, and a neighborhood function N, where $N_{ij} \subseteq V - \{(A_i, c_{ij})\}$. Each node (a pair (A_i, c_{ij})) in V is represented with a vector $\mathbf{x}_{ij}$ of features, $f_1, f_2, ..., f_n$, and is associated with a class label y_{ij} in the domain of {positive, negative}. The positive class means *attribute noun*, and the negative class means *not attribute noun*. V is further divided into two sets of nodes: L, labeled nodes, and U, unlabeled nodes. Our task is to predict the label for each node $u_{ij} \in U$.

A collective classification algorithm called the *iterative classification algorithm* (ICA) (Sen et al. 2008) is employed to solve this problem. ICA is given in Figure 1. Its training process (not in Figure 1) trains a classifier h just like traditional supervised learning, using the labeled set L with all features. The classification (or testing) step is the core of this algorithm.

In testing, the learned classifier h assigns a class label to each node $u_{ij} \in U$ in the test data (lines 1-4). Line 2 computes the feature vector $\mathbf{x}_{ij}$ for u_{ij}. This (and also line 8) is an important step of this algorithm which makes it different from the classic supervised learning. It computes all the relational features for u_{ij} using the neighbors of u_{ij}. However, line 2 is slightly different from line 8 as in line 2 not all nodes have been assigned class labels, so we compute $\mathbf{x}_{ij}$ based on the intersection of the labeled nodes (L) and u_{ij}'s neighbors. Line 3 uses h to assign a class (y_{ij}) to node u_{ij}. Lines 1-4 are considered as the initialization step.

After initialization, the classifier is run iteratively (lines 5-11) until the class labels of all nodes no longer change. The iterations are needed because some relational features of a node depend on the class labels of its neighbors. Such labels are assigned in each iteration and may change from one iteration to the next. In each iteration (lines 6-10), the algorithm first generates an ordering of nodes to be classified. We order them randomly in order to reduce bias as the random ordering makes the process stochastic. Line 8 does the same job as line 2. Line 9 does the same job as line 3. Classifier h does not change in the iterations.

Algorithm ICA - Iterative classification

for each node $u_{ij} \in U$ // each node is a pair
  compute $\mathbf{x}_{ij}$ using only $L \cap N_{ij}$
  $y_{ij} \leftarrow h(\mathbf{x}_{ij})$
endfor
repeat // iterative classification
  generate an ordering O over pairs in U
  for each node $o_{ij} \in O$ do
    compute $\mathbf{x}_{ij}$ using current assignments to N_{ij}
    $y_{ij} \leftarrow h(\mathbf{x}_{ij})$
  endfor
until all class labels do not change

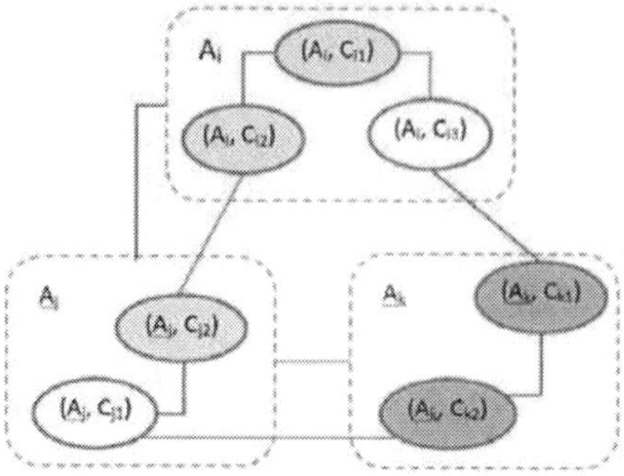

Figure 2. An example of a graph of word relations and an ICA iteration

Figure 2 shows a simplified example of a graph based on some relationships of words. It is also a snapshot of an iteration of ICA. Each oval node denotes an instance (an adjective and attribute pair). A dashed box encloses the pairs that belong to the same adjective. A link between two oval nodes denotes a relationship between two (candidate) attribute nouns, and a link between two dashed boxes denotes a relationship between two adjectives. Green lines denote synonym and red lines denote antonym. The green shaded nodes denote those labeled pairs, the grey shaded nodes denote those candidate attribute nouns whose labels have been predicted (unlabeled at the beginning), whereas un-shaded oval nodes denote those candidate attribute nouns whose labels are yet to be predicted in the iteration. In the figure, adjectives A_k and A_j are synonyms, attribute noun c_{k2} (labeled) and candidate attribute noun c_{j1} are synonyms, and candidate attribute nouns c_{j1} and c_{j2} are antonyms. In the previous iteration, ICA has predicted/labeled c_{j2} as an attribute noun of A_j. Since c_{j2}, c_{j1} and c_{k2} are related, the label of c_{j1} will be affected by the labels of c_{j2} and c_{k2} in this iteration.

2.2 Useful Relations

In this work, we consider two kinds of relations for adjectives: synonym and antonym, and four kinds of relations for nouns: synonym, antonym, hypernym and hyponym. Using them, we created two sets of relational features, *static* (relational) *features* and *dynamic* (relational) *features*. Static features are not affected by the classification process in testing. Dynamic features are affected by the classification process, i.e., the values of these features can change during the testing phase because they depend on the predicted labels of its neighbours (which are also candidate attribute noun and adjective pairs) (see Section 2.5). Finally, we have three sets of features: (1) local features (these are the traditional features about each instance itself), (2) static relational features, and (3) dynamic relational features.

2.3 Local Features

The local features (L1, ..., L6) are only about the adjective-noun pair (A_i, c_{ij}) itself:

L1. Word *n*-grams: These are traditional n-grams of words in the glosses of each adjective A_i.

L2. Part of speech (POS) *n*-grams: n-grams of POS tags. These are also traditional features.

L3. Number of times that candidate attribute noun c_{ij} appears in the glosses for adjective A_i in all dictionaries. Intuitively, the more times it appears, the more likely it is a true attribute.

L4. Diversity of candidate nouns in C_i for adjective A_i: The idea is that if the candidate words are too numerous and all different, then they are less likely to be true attribute nouns. Entropy is one of the methods for measuring diversity. Let n_{ij} be the frequency that the candidate attribute noun $c_{ij} \in C_i$, as well as c_{ij}'s synonyms and antonyms, occur in the glosses of A_i in all dictionaries. We call a set of words formed by c_{ij} and its synonyms and antonyms in C_i a *semantic group* for c_{ij}. Let m be the number of semantic groups formed by the words in C_i. Let T_i be the occurrence count of A_i's candidate attribute nouns in all dictionaries. Let p_{ij} (= n_{ij} / T_i) be the probability of occurrence of the candidate nouns in c_{ij}'s semantic group in the dictionaries. The diversity (entropy) of C_i is defined as:

$$diversity\ (C_i) = -\sum_{j=1}^{m} p_{ij} \log p_{ij} \tag{1}$$

L5. Similarity of candidate attribute noun c_{ij} and its adjective A_i. This is the number of same letters (m_{ij}) in their prefixes normalized by the maximum length (len(.)) of the two words,

$$sim\ (c_{ij}, A_i) = \frac{m_{ij}}{\max(\ len\ (c_{ij}), len\ (A_i))} \tag{2}$$

We use this feature because in some cases a noun is turned into an adjective with ending changes, e.g., *style* (c_{ij}) and *stylistic* (A_i) (their similarity is 4/9).

L6. Frequent POS sequence patterns mined from the POS tags of q (= 5) words right before each candidate attribute noun c_{ij} in a gloss, using a sequence pattern mining algorithm (Srikant and Agrawal, 1996). All the discovered patterns are used as features. Note that POS patterns are not POS n-grams because a pattern can skip POS tags but a POS n-gram is a sequence of consecutive POS tags. For pattern discovery, every gloss sentence containing c_{ij} generate a POS tag sequence for mining. For testing, when multiple glosses containing c_{ij} (we use multiple dictionaries), as long as the POS tags of the q word before one occurrence of c_{ij} satisfies the pattern, the feature for the pattern is set to 1; otherwise 0.

2.4 Static Relational Features

To define relational features, we first need to define some relations. Let R_s be a binary synonym function and R_a be a binary antonym function on the set of all adjectives or candidate attribute nouns. For w_i, $w_j \in A$ (all adjectives) or w_i, $w_j \in C$ (all candidate attribute nouns), if $R_s(w_i, w_j) = 1$, w_i and w_j are synonyms. If $R_s(w_i, w_j) = 0$, w_i and w_j are not synonyms. If $R_a(w_i, w_j) = 1$, w_i and w_j are antonyms. If $R_a(w_i, w_j) = 0$, w_i and w_j are not antonyms. Similarly, we have R_{hyper} (hypernym) and R_{hypo} (hyponym) on the set of all candidate attribute nouns C. We also assume that both R_s and R_a are symmetric, which means that for all w_i, $w_j \in A$ or w_i, $w_j \in C$, $R_s(w_i, w_j)$ implies $R_s(w_j, w_i)$, and $R_a(w_i, w_j)$ implies $R_a(w_j, w_i)$.

We now present the static relational features. Let g_{id} be the glosses in the *d-th* dictionary for adjective A_i. Let $E(c_{ij}, g_{id})$ be a function that returns the number of times that c_{ij} occurs in g_{id}. For each node (or pair) (A_i, c_{ij}), we have the following 7 static relational features:

S1-S4. These four features represent respectively the number of times that c_{ij}'s synonyms, antonyms, hypernyms and hyponyms appear in the glosses of A_i in the dictionaries,

$$\sum_{k=1}^{|S|} \sum_{d=1}^{H} R(c_{ik}, c_{ij}) E(c_{ik}, g_{id}) \tag{3}$$

where S is the set of synonyms, antonyms, hypernyms or hyponyms of $c_{ij} \in C_i$ and H is the number of dictionaries, $R \in \{R_s, R_a, R_{hyper}, R_{hypo}\}$. These relationships are extracted from the WordNet. These features are relational because they are related to other nodes in the graph as each synonym, antonym, hypernym or hyponym of c_{ij} in S that appears in the glosses of a dictionary also generates an instance (or a node) in the data. And the reason we call these relational features static is because they don't change during the testing phase. These features are used because the more times that c_{ij}'s synonyms, antonyms, hypernyms or hyponyms appear in the glosses of adjective A_i, the more likely c_{ij} is a true attribute noun of A_i.

S5-S6. These two features represent respectively the total number of times that c_{ij} appears in the glosses of A_i's synonyms and antonyms,

$$\sum_{k=1}^{|S|}\sum_{d=1}^{H} R(A_i, A_k)E(c_{ij}, g_{kd}) \tag{4}$$

where S is the set of synonyms or antonyms of A_i in set A, and $R \in \{R_s, R_a\}$.

S7. The number of times that c_{ij} appears in the glosses of other adjectives which are neither synonym nor antonym of A_i. This feature can be calculated as follows,

$$\sum_{k=1}^{|S|}\sum_{d=1}^{H} (1 - R_s(A_i, A_k))(1 - R_a(A_i, A_k))E(c_{ij}, g_{kd}) \tag{5}$$

where S is the set of all adjectives in the data. The intuition is that the more c_{ij} appears, the less likely it is a real attribute for A_i.

2.5 Dynamic Relational Features

Dynamic relational features mean that their values can change during the testing phase because they are calculated based on the classified labels of neighboring nodes. That is, these features let the system see how the neighboring nodes of the current node are classified, which affects the classification of the current node.

For each $c_{ij} \in C_i$ of adjective A_i, $Y(c_{ij}, A_i)$ denotes the class label of node (A_i, c_{ij}). If the node is classified as positive (we also say that c_{ij} is classified as an attribute noun of adjective A_i), $Y(c_{ij}, A_i) = 1$; otherwise $Y(c_{ij}, A_i) = 0$. We have the following 14 dynamic relational features:

D1-D4. These four features represent respectively the number of times that c_{ij}'s synonyms, antonyms, hypernyms and hyponyms are classified as attribute nouns for A_i,

$$\sum_{k=1}^{|S|} R(c_{ik}, c_{ij})Y(c_{ik}, A_i) \tag{6}$$

where S is the set of synonyms, antonyms, hypernyms or hyponyms of $c_{ij} \in C_i$, and $R \in \{R_s, R_a, R_{hyper}, R_{hypo}\}$. We use these features because if a synonym, antonym, hypernym or hyponym of c_{ij} is an attribute noun for A_i then c_{ij} is also likely to be such a noun for A_i.

D5-D6. These two features represent respectively the number of times that c_{ij} is classified as attributes for A_i's synonyms and antonyms,

$$\sum_{k=1}^{|S|} R(A_k, A_i)Y(c_{ij}, A_k) \tag{7}$$

where S is the set of synonyms or antonyms of $A_i \in A$ and $R \in \{R_s, R_a\}$.

D7-D14. These eight features represent respectively the number of times that c_{ij}'s synonyms, antonyms, hypernyms and hyponyms are classified as attribute nouns for A_i's synonyms and antonyms,

$$\sum_{p=1}^{|T|}\sum_{q=1}^{|S|} R_C(c_{ip}, c_{ij})R_A(A_q, A_i)Y(c_{ip}, A_q) \tag{8}$$

where S is the set of synonyms or antonyms of A_i, T is the set of synonyms, antonyms, hypernyms or hyponyms of $c_{ij} \in C_i$, and $R_C \in \{R_s, R_a, R_{hyper}, R_{hypo}\}$, $R_A \in \{R_s, R_a\}$. So we obtain a total of 8 dynamic features.

local features	Accuracy	F-score
Best local feature combination (L3, L4, L5, L6)	0.689	0.701

Table 1 – Usefulness of different local features

	Feature sets	Logistic Regression				SVM			
		Prec	Rec	F-score	Acc	Prec	Rec	F-score	Acc
Strategy 1	Local features (traditional learning)	0.689	0.723	0.701	0.689	0.731	0.616	0.654	0.695
	Local+static features	0.715	0.722	0.716	0.710	0.750	0.627	0.675	0.708
	Local+dynamic features	0.725	**0.783**	**0.746**	0.730	0.741	0.668	0.700	0.721
	All features	**0.747**	0.742	0.743	0.732	0.756	0.621	0.676	0.710
Strategy 2	ICA (all features)	**0.791**	0.675	0.725	0.736	0.823	0.518	0.624	0.700
	ICA (local+dynamic features)	0.750	**0.766**	**0.754**	**0.742**	0.792	0.594	0.670	0.717

Table 2 – Average Precision, Recall, F-score and Accuracy results over 10-fold cross-validations

3 Experimental Results

We now evaluate the proposed technique. First, we compare the results of different feature sets, i.e., local features, static relational features, and dynamic relational features, and also two learning strategies. Note that using only local features is the traditional supervised classification. Second, we compare our results with WordNet in terms of attribute coverage.

3.1 Experiment Settings

Datasets: Our data were extracted from 5 online dictionaries: *Dictionary.com*, *The Free Dictionary*, *Longman Dictionary of Contemporary English*, *Your Dictionary*, and *The Free Merriam-Webster Dictionary*. For opinion adjectives, we used a subset of 310 adjectives from the opinion lexicon of Hu and Liu (2004)[1]. From each dictionary, we extracted the glosses of these adjectives. The Stanford POS Tagger[2] (Toutanova et al., 2003) was used to find nouns. The nouns from each adjective's gloss were considered as its candidate attribute nouns.

Altogether 4410 adjective-noun pairs from 310 adjectives were annotated by two human labelers. Kappa (κ) gave κ = 0.77 (substantial agreement (Landis and Koch, 1977)). As a 2-class classification problem, we treat *attribute noun* as the positive class, and *not attribute noun* as the negative class. The distribution of the positive and negative classes is 48% and 52% respectively. All classification results were obtained through 10-fold cross-validations.

3.2 Results and Discussions

We first assess the usefulness of different local features. Traditional classification is applied to these features. Table 1 gives the best local feature combination (L3, L4, L5, and L6). Word n-grams and POS n-grams were found not so useful. POS n-grams also perform worse than POS patterns (due to space limitations, we cannot show the detailed results) because n-grams are consecutive POS tags, while POS patterns do not have to be consecutive. This makes POS patterns better able to capture the regularities in the text. Next we evaluate the collective classification based on the best set of local features and all static and dynamic features. Two classification strategies were examined.

[1] http://www.cs.uic.edu/~liub /FBS/sentiment-analysis.html
[2] http://nlp.stanford.edu/software/tagger.shtml

Strategy 1 (two stages): The first stage simply builds a local classifier using the local features or a combination of local and static relational features to classify each node. The results serve as the initialization for stage two. In the second stage, dynamic relational features are added to run the ICA algorithm in Figure 1 without the first 4 lines.

Strategy 2 (one stage): We simply train with both local and relational features. The trained classifier is then applied to classify the test data using the ICA algorithm in Figure 1.

Table 2 shows the results of for each strategy and each feature set for Logistic Regression (LR) and SVM. For LR, we used the Lingpipe system (http://alias-i.com/lingpipe/). For SVM, we used SVM^{light} (http://svmlight. joachims.org/). From the table, we can see that LR performs better than SVM in general. Our discussions and comparisons below are thus based on LR. Table 2 also allows us to make the following observations:

1. "Local" features perform the worst (traditional classification). With the addition of either the two sets of relational features, the results improve. The dynamic relational features are most useful. We can say that the results of collective classification are superior.
2. For strategy 1, we see that "local+static" outperforms "local" features. Using all features is even better. "local+dynamic" features gives us the best F-score.
3. For strategy 2, using all features again performs better than only "local" features. Using "local+dynamic" gives both the best F-score and accuracy among all experiments.

Compare with WordNet: We now compare our method with WordNet, which can retrieve attributes given an adjective. Table 3 shows the comparison results. Column 2 gives the average number of correct attributes found by our system over 3-fold cross validation and by WordNet respectively. Our method can find far more attribute nouns than WordNet. Although WordNet has 100% precision (as it was manually compiled), the recall is so low. Many adjectives have no attribute nouns in WordNet, e.g., it gives no attribute for *expensive*.

	No. of correct attributes found	Prec.	Rec.	F-score
WordNet	53	100%	7.9%	0.146
Our method	522	76.3%	77.3%	0.768

Table 3 – Comparison results of WordNet and our method (3-fold cross-validation)

5 Conclusion

This paper studied the problem of mining attribute nouns of opinion adjectives. A dictionary-based approach was proposed. To our knowledge, this is the first work using such an approach. Existing works are all based on corpuses. To solve the problem, we formulated it as collective classification as words are related through many lexical relations. Such relations can be exploited to produce better classifiers. Our evaluation showed that collective classification using dynamic relational features performed significantly better than traditional classification. It also performs dramatically better than WordNet. Finally, we note that there are two related approaches used in finding opinion words: the corpus-based approach (e.g., Hazivassiloglou and McKeown, 1997; Wilson et al., 2005; Kanayama and Nasukawa, 2006; Ding et al., 2008; Choi and Cardie, 2008; Wu and Wen, 2010) and the dictionary based approach (e.g., Hu and Liu 2004; Kim and Hovy, 2004; Kamps et al., 2004; Esuli and Sebastiani, 2005; Andreevskaia and Bergler, 2006; Blair-Goldensohn et al., 2008; Hassan and Radev, 2010). Although the two approaches are analogous to the two corresponding approaches for the attribute discovery of adjectives, the two tasks are entirely different.

References

Almuhareb, A. 2006. *Attributes in Lexical Acquisition.* Ph.D. *Dissertation,* Department of Computer Science, University of Essex.

Almuhareb, A and M. Poesio. 2004. Attribute-Based and Value-Based Clustering: An Evaluation. *Proceedings of the Conference on Empirical Methods in Natural Language Processing.*

Andreevskaia, A. and S. Bergler. 2006. Mining WordNet for fuzzy sentiment: Sentiment tag extraction from WordNet glosses. *Proceedings of Conference of the European Chapter of the Association for Computational Linguistics* (EACL-06). 2006.

Blair-Goldensohn, S., K. Hannan, and R. McDonald, Tyler Neylon, George A. Reis, and Jeff Reynar. 2008. Building a sentiment summarizer for local service reviews. *Proceedings of WWW-2008 Workshop on NLP in the Information Explosion Era.*

Choi, Y. and C. Cardie. Learning with compositional semantics as structural inference for subsentential sentiment analysis. *Proceedings of Conference on Empirical Methods in Natural Language Processing* (EMNLP-2008). 2008.

Ding, X., B. Liu, and P. S. Yu. 2008. A holistic lexicon-based approach to opinion mining. *Proceedings of the Conference on Web Search and Web Data Mining* (WSDM-2008).

Esuli, A. and F. Sebastiani. Determining the semantic orientation of terms through gloss classification. *Proceedings of ACM International Conference on Information and Knowledge Management* (CIKM-2005). 2005.

Hai, Z., K. Chang, and J. Kim. 2011. Implicit feature identification via co-occurrence association rule mining. *Computational Linguistics and Intelligent Text Processing,* 2011: p. 393-404.

Hartung, M and A. Frank, 2010. A Structured Vector Space Model for Hidden Attribute Meaning in Adjective-Noun Phrases. *Coling* 2010.

Hartung, M and A. Frank, 2011. Exploring Supervised LDA Models for Assigning Attributes to Adjective-Noun Phrases. *Proceedings of the Conference on Empirical Methods in Natural Language Processing.*

Hassan, A. and D. Radev. 2010. Identifying text polarity using random walks. *Proceedings of Annual Meeting of the Association for Computational Linguistics* (ACL-2010).

Hatzivassiloglou, V. and K. R. McKeown. 1997. Predicting the semantic orientation of adjectives. *Proceedings of Annual Meeting of the Association for Computational Linguistics* (ACL-1997).

Hu, M. and Liu, B. 2004. Mining and summarizing customer reviews. *Proceedings of SIGKDD International Conference and Knowledge Discovery and Data Mining.*

Kamps, J., M. Marx, R. J. Mokken, and M. De Rijke. 2004. Using WordNet to measure semantic orientation of adjectives. Proc. of LREC-2004.

Kanayama, H. and T. Nasukawa. 2006. Fully automatic lexicon expansion for domain-oriented sentiment analysis. *Proceedings of Conference on Empirical Methods in Natural Language Processing* (EMNLP-2006).

Kim, S-M and E. Hovy. 2004. Determining the sentiment of opinions. *Proceedings of International Conference on Computational Linguistics* (COLING-2004).

Landis, J. R. and G. G. Koch. 1977. The measurement of observer agreement for categorical data. *Biometrics.*

Liu, B. 2010. Sentiment analysis and subjectivity. In Handbook of Natural Language Processing, edited by Indurkhya, N and Damerau, F. J.

Mitchell, T. 1997. *Machine Learning,* McGraw Hill.

Sen, P., G. Namata, M. Bilgic and L. Getoor. 2008. Collective Classification in Network Data. *Technical Report* CS-TR-4905 and UMIACS-TR-2008-04.

Srikant, R and R. Agrawal. 1996. Mining sequential patterns: Generalization and performance improvements. *Advances in Database Technology.*

Su, Q., X. Xu, H. Guo, Z. Guo, X. Wu, X. Zhang, B. Swen, and Z. Su. 2008. Hidden sentiment association in chinese web opinion mining. *Proceedings of International Conference on World Wide Web.*

Toutanova, K., D. Klein, C. Manning, and Y. Singer. 2003. Feature-Rich Part-of-Speech Tagging with a Cyclic Dependency Network. *Proceedings of HLT-NAACL* 2003, pp. 252-259.

Wilson, T., J. Wiebe, and P. Hoffmann. 2005. Recognizing contextual polarity in phrase-level sentiment analysis. *Proceedings of the Human Language Technology Conference and the Conference on Empirical Methods in Natural Language Processing* (HLT/EMNLP-2005).

Wu, Y. and M. Wen. 2010. Disambiguating dynamic sentiment ambiguous adjectives. *Proceedings of the 23rd International Conference on Computational Linguistics* (Coling 2010).

Dealing with Input Noise in Statistical Machine Translation

Lluis Formiga[1] *Jose A. R. Fonollosa*[1]
(1) Universitat Politècnica de Catalunya
{lluis.formiga,jose.fonollosa}@upc.edu

ABSTRACT
Misspelled words have a direct impact on the final quality obtained by Statistical Machine Translation (SMT) systems as the input becomes noisy and unpredictable. This paper presents some improvement strategies for translating real-life noisy input. The proposed strategies are based on a preprocessing step consisting in a character-based translator (MT) from noisy into cleaned text. The use of a character-level translator allows us to provide various spelling alternatives in a lattice format to the final bilingual translator. Therefore, the final MT is the one that decides the best path to be translated. The different hypotheses are obtained under the assumption of a noisy channel model for this task. This paper shows the experiments done with real-life noisy input and a standard phrase-based SMT system from English into Spanish.

TITLE AND ABSTRACT IN ANOTHER LANGUAGE, SPANISH

Estudio de estrategias para tratar los errores ortográficos en la entrada de los sistemas de traducción automática estadística

Las palabras con errores ortográficos tienen un impacto directo en la calidad final obtenida por los sistemas de traducción automática estadística (TA) debido a que la entrada se vuelve ruidosa e impredecible. Este artículo presenta algunas estrategias de mejora a la hora de traducir textos de entrada con ruido del mundo real. Estas estrategias consisten en la adición de un paso de preproceso basado en un traductor a nivel de carácter de texto ruidoso a texto limpio. El uso de un traductor a nivel de carácter permite proporcionar diversas alternativas de ortografía en un formato de *lattice* como entrada del traductor bilingüe final. Por lo tanto, es el traductor final quien decide la mejor secuencia de palabras a traducir. Para esta tarea, las diferentes hipótesis se obtienen bajo suponiendo un modelo de distorsión del canal. En este trabajo presentamos los experimentos realizados con textos reales de entrada ruidosa y un sistema estándar de traducción auotmática estadística de inglés a español.

KEYWORDS: Noisy Text, Statistical Machine Translation, Social Media, Xat, SMS, Web2.0.

KEYWORDS IN SPANISH: Texto ruidoso, Traducción Automática Estadística, Medios Sociales, Chat, SMS, Web2.0.

Proceedings of COLING 2012: Posters, pages 319–328,
COLING 2012, Mumbai, December 2012.

1 Introduction

Internet and Social Media have changed the trends of written text communication during the last years providing a straightforward and informal scenario (Agichtein et al., 2008). Thus, the focus of written text has evolved from grammatically correct structures to a content centered scenario. Nowadays, human web readers do not get surprised of finding misspellings or low-profile language. The text of chats, comments, tweets or SMS's is usually full of misspelled words, slang or wrong abbreviations introducing noise into the text data (Subramaniam et al., 2009; Yvon, 2010) and affecting NLP tasks such as text-mining, machine translation or opinion classification (Dey and Haque, 2009).

The Machine Translation (MT) task, as a field related to Natural Language Processing (NLP), is not immune to this noise (Aikawa et al., 2007). Generally, misspelling problems can be addressed with a simple Levenshtein distance under a noisy channel model paradigm (Brill and Moore, 2000). On the other side, Bertoldi et al. (2010) presented a preliminary work focused on preserving all spelling alternatives to the input of MT system through Confusion Networks (CNs). However, this preliminary work was focused on an artificially generated noise that is not able to cover all the different properties of real-scenario weblog noise.

In this paper, we present a study of the performance of the aforementioned spelling correction strategies for real weblog translation requests. In addition, we present two new adaptive strategies based on obtaining the spelling alternatives from character-based translation models with multiple weighted cost functions.

2 Related work

Misspelling correction has been a recurrent issue to be resolved on NLP since its very first beginnings (Damerau, 1964). Good surveys of different types of noisy text and its related spell-correction programs can be found in Pedler (2007); Subramaniam et al. (2009); Kukich (1992) along with (Mitton, 1996).

According to Deorowicz and Ciura (2005), misspelling correction methods can be separated as *isolated-word error detection-correction* methods (Damerau, 1964; Philips, 2000; Toutanova and Moore, 2002), where isolated words are processed independently of their context and *context-dependent error detection-correction* methods where they feature their analysis in a more phrase-consistent manner(Deorowicz and Ciura, 2005; Pedler, 2007; Jacquemont et al., 2007). Usually Noisy-Channel model is assumed for this task.

Among other new strategies, in this paper we study two already existing spelling correction strategies based on the Noisy Channel Model (Mays et al., 1991). First, we study the performance of a simple edit-distance based strategy computed from a lexicon of words under a noisy channel model scenario. Secondly, we study a strategy specially designed for the MT framework (Bertoldi et al., 2010). We did not consider context-dependent strategies due to their dependency to several language-specific analysis tools, which are beyond the scope our study.

3 Adaptive spelling correction based on character-based translation models

The strategy presented by Bertoldi et al. (2010) consists in generating hypotheses from a sequence of characters by means of confusion networks heuristically defined. The best sequences are retrieved from the CN according to char based language model (6-gram). The novelty of

Source	Target	Probabilities			
		Ident.	Subst.	Del.	Add.
a	a	e^1	e^0	e^0	e^0
a	b	e^0	$e^{p(b\|a)}$	e^0	e^0
a	_	e^0	$e^{p(\_\|a)}$	e^0	e^0
a	NULL	e^0	e^0	e^1	e^0
a	_ a	e^0	e^0	e^0	e^1
a	a _	e^0	e^0	e^0	e^1
a	a b	e^0	e^0	e^0	e^1
a	b a	e^0	e^0	e^0	e^1
⋮	⋮	⋮	⋮	⋮	⋮

Table 1: Heuristic phrase table used for the spelling hypotheses generator (Moses decoder).

their work is the method employed to generate spelling alternatives, which it is a character-based decoder of heuristically defined CNs. Thus, the simplified decoder is based only on a single character-based LM without any phrase-based or distortion models. Hence, the strategy assumes that all editing operations are equally weighted at decoding stage since CNs are globally weighted (weight-i). However, state-of-the art decoders (e.g. Moses) may deal with multiple transformation models. We propose two new strategies that deal with multiple transformation models.

The first strategy works with a heuristic phrase-table containing different model scores depending on the type of transformation that is addressed (i.e. identity, substitution, deletion, addition), and also allows the reordering of chars according to a distance-based distortion model. The second strategy is based on the classical SMT training strategy but adapted to character level. These strategies allow weighting all the probability models independently. Thus, they are more suited for being adapted into training data by means of an optimization step as more functions take part into the final hypothesis. Analogously to the previous approach, the N-best hypotheses may be fused in a lattice or confusion network form and submitted as input to the final translator. In this paper we only work with lattices as input to the translator. The lattices are built from a three-step process (Formiga and Fonollosa, 2012); first each character-sequence of the N-best list is transformed into a single-path word-based lattice, then the different word lattices are aligned to the original sequence through a distance based algorithm. Once aligned, the single-path lattices are combined generating a single lattice containing all the spelling variations that have been seen on the N-best output of the character-based decoder.

3.1 Misspelling correction through a heuristic phrase-table

All the possible edit operations can be represented through phrase table transformations. Therefore, our first strategy designs a heuristic phrase table with all the probabilities of the possible transformations separated in different models according to their type. A fragment of the table is given in Table 1. The table is composed of 4 transformation models: Identity, Substitution, Deletion and Addition.

Probabilities are given on an exponential base as Moses works on the log-space and we are more interested in working in a linear space. We assign a binary probability (e^0,e^1) to identity, addition and deletion operations because they are not distance based. On the other side, since substitution operations might be based in a distance model, we assign the same probability defined on Bertoldi et al. (2010). It is important to highlight that each entry of the phrase table takes a single non-zero probability for its related operation, being all the others set to e^0. In addition, we also consider that transposition operations can be performed by the distance based reordering implemented in the Moses decoder. That approach contrasts with the CN decoding approach (Bertoldi et al., 2010), were transposition operations were performed by the sum of deletion and addition operations. In order to prevent big reorderings we limit the distortion up to three positions. Therefore, we consider 6 different probability models: character-based language model, distance based distortion, identity, substitution, deletion and addition.

3.2 Misspelling correction through character-based SMT models

With the strategies presented so far we have only addressed issues related to low-level misspellings. Unfortunately, the noise of chat/SMS domains concerns higher level errors. Within these errors we can distinguish two types: *i)* structural errors in the order of words within the sentence due to the lack of knowledge of the language and *ii)* on-purpose induced errors based on the economy of language consisting of abbreviations, acronyms, contraction or slang among others.

Similar to Contractor et al. (2010), our second improvement strategy learns a SMT at character-level in order to propose alternative spelling to the final translator. In this sense, we first clean manually a certain amount of noisy text (e.g 8000 sentences) gathered from web translation requests. Afterwards, both the noisy text and the clean text are converted to character sequences using a common alignment tool (e.g. GIZA++). Once aligned, the character level bicorpus is used to learn the typical probabilities of a phrase-based SMT. That is: *i)* $\varphi(f|e)$ inverse phrase translation, *ii)* $lex(f|e)$ inverse lexical weighting, *iii)* $\varphi(e|f)$ direct phrase translation and *iv)* $lex(e|f)$ direct lexical weighting along with a *v)* transformation penalty (which is e^1) inspired in the phrase penalty. The main difference of this strategy with respect to the one presented in Section 3.1 is the building of the phrase-table. While the previous strategy builds a heuristic phrase-table, the new one learns from the real proofreading. This approach also allows the use of a penalty model (based on word-based penalty of Moses). In that case, we consider 8 different probability models: character-based language model, distance based distortion, $\varphi(f|e)$, $lex(f|e)$, $\varphi(e|f)$, $lex(e|f)$, transformation-based penalty and character-based penalty.

4 Experiments

We based our experiments under the framework of a factored decoder (Moses – Koehn and Hoang (2007)) from English into Spanish (See details in Formiga et al. (2012)). In this experiments, we preprocessed the text to lowercase in order to overcome the casing problems, which are quite frequent under noisy scenarios. The weights of the system were optimized by MERT and a BLEU score with the help of a weblog development set consisting of 999 sentences, as explained in the next section.

We have conducted the experiments in three parts. Firstly we studied the properties of the real-life noisy scenario. Then, we compared the systems performance when generating spelling correction hypotheses and then we analyzed the actual performance of the systems as for the translation task.

4.1 Real-life scenario: dealing with actual noisy words

Most of the work mentioned in Section 2, deals with synthetic or controlled noisy scenarios. However, real-life texts are poorly related with this controlled scenario in terms of literary quality (Agichtein et al., 2008; Subramaniam et al., 2009).

	Perplexity		WER	
Data	DEV	TEST	DEV	TEST
Original Source (wr)	835.713	891.55	–	–
Clean Source 0 (w0)	541.58	533.74	13.54%	16.33%
Clean Source 1 (w1)	575.35	660.34	8.61%	6.51%
Combined Clean Sources (w0.w1)	558.39	594.03	6.67%	6.35%

Table 2: Perplexity and WER obtained between original and cleaned data.

As we wanted to deal with real data, we used weblog translations from the FAUST project (Pighin et al., 2012) for testing the translation performance with noisy texts. Regarding the weblog translations we considered 1997 translation requests submitted to Softissimo's portal [1].

Two independent human translators corrected the most obvious typos and provided reference translations into Spanish for all of them along with the clean versions of the input requests. Hence, there are three different test sets from this material: *i)* *Weblog Raw* (*wr*): The noisy weblog input, *ii)* *Weblog Clean$_i$* (*w0* and *w1*): the cleaned version of the input text provided by different humans on the source side. Cleaned versions may differ due to the interpretation of the translators and *iii)* *Weblog Clean0.1* (*w0.w1*): the cleaned versions with mixed up criteria. In that case the cleaned versions are concatenated (making up a set of 3994 sentences). In order to perform the different optimization tasks, we have divided the noisy set in development (999 sentences) and test (998 sentences) sets.

We analyzed through some indicators the presence of noise within the weblog data sets following the work performed by Subramaniam et al. (2009). Concretely we measured the level of noise on the real data computing *Word-Error-Rate* (WER) (Kobus et al., 2008) and Language Model Perplexity (Kothari et al., 2009).

Results are detailed on table 2. From the tables it can be observed that WER can vary up to 5% depending on the human translator who made the cleaning task. Still, considering all the test sets, the averaged WER is around 11%, and no notable differences are found between the development and the test sets. In that sense, the *w0* set takes higher edit modifications than *w1* compared to the original text. Consequently, as for the perplexity results, *w0* takes less perplexity regarding the character-based LM with respect to *w1*. This fact shows that strong changes (due to high-lever error fixing) on the edit distance (higher WER) lead to a more normalized input (lower perplexity).

4.2 Implemented Systems

In our study we compared the different strategies presented in Sections 2 and 3. They are named *i)* Distance (Levenshtein distance plus a LM), *ii)* Confusion (Bertoldi et al., 2010), *iii)* Heuristic PT (heuristically defined phrase-table) and *iv)* GIZA PT (monolingual char-based MT). In the latter case we post-edited manually 8000 noisy sentences submitted to the same portal (Softissimo), so they were similar to the dev/test sets. The number was chosen heuristically based on the previous work of Aw et al. (2006). The noisy and cleaned sentences were character-aligned with mGIZA and then the standard phrase-based SMT models were trained at character level. Distortion limit was set to the Moses standard 6-positions. It had 8 weights to be tuned (5 phrase-table model weights, language model, character penalty and distortion).

[1]http://www.reverso.net

The weights of the character-based strategies were tuned with the weblog development set already mentioned. We modified the MERT script to work with the Character Error Rate metric.

Regarding the N-best size for building the lattice, we studied different values on the low-range in order to obtain low-dimensionality lattices. Thus we studied building the lattice from the 1-best, 5-best and 10-best lists of the preprocessing step.

Additionally, the fact of providing a lattice to the Eng→Spa translator required to perform a retuning step in order to find the appropriate weight value for the edges of the lattice (w_l). We did this retuning step for each strategy only searching different values for the w_l weight and fixing all the others to the already tuned value.

4.3 Spelling Correction Strategies Performance

Before evaluating the performance in the translation task, we wanted to evaluate the suitability of each strategy for finding good spelling alternatives. We did this evaluation either in the development and test weblog sets using four different evaluation metrics: CER, WER, BLEU and METEOR (Denkowski and Lavie, 2011). We left out of our study Precision/Recall analyses as we are focused on the translation performance and not only the misspellings, they could be considered in future work. These results were obtained by comparing the automatically cleaned input with the two human post-edited references (being CER and WER evaluated through mCER and mWER). In case of CER, WER and BLEU this comparison was done considering only the 1-best spelling alternative of the strategy. In case of METEOR we computed the oracle results considering the best hypothesis from the obtained N-best list (1000-best for dev and 50-best for test).

Strategy	*dev*	*test*	*dev*	*test*	*dev*	*test*	*dev*	*test*
	CER		WER		BLEU		METEOR nbest oracle	
Baseline	3.41	3.09	6.67	6.35	90.62	90.24	63.10	63.17
Distance	3.47	3.19	6.92	6.96	89.87	89.02	64.63	63.62
Confusion	3.40	3.10	6.62	6.36	90.72	90.19	64.00	63.69
Heuristic PT	3.36	3.07	6.35	6.23	91.25	90.37	**65.81**	**64.92**
GIZA PT	**3.33**	**2.99**	**6.26**	**5.82**	**91.32**	**91.02**	64.02	64.24

Table 3: CER/WER/BLEU/METEOR scores obtained when cleaning the texts.

Results are detailed in table 3. Within these results "Baseline" refers to the case when no spelling correction strategy is applied at all. We observe that the GIZA PT strategy performs better when considering the 1-best output whereas the Heuristic PT strategy finds better alternatives within the N-best list, despite they are not the first hypothesis. In addition we can see that the Distance strategy worsens the baseline results for the 1-best tests whereas it can achieve a slightly improvement in the N-best based tests. These results seem to indicate that the language-model used for ranking the final hypothesis might not be fully functional for that purpose. We have to remember that the language model was built from the formal WMT12 data and thus the interpolation towards perplexity reduction may not be enough to obtain a good language model based on the open-domain of weblog requests.

4.4 Translation Task Performance

After evaluating the spelling correction strategies we evaluated the overall strategy involving the misspelling correction and translation tasks.

Strategy	N-best	w0	w0.w1	w1	wr	AVG
Baseline	1	30.61	37.44	29.86	33.62	32.88
Distance	1	30.20	36.99	29.41	33.54	32.54
Distance	5	29.84	36.67	29.21	33.40	32.28
Distance	10	29.83	36.65	29.20	33.42	32.28
Confusion	1	**30.77**	37.56	29.90	33.72	32.99
Confusion	5	30.65	37.44	29.74	33.68	32.88
Confusion	10	30.59	37.35	29.66	33.64	32.81
Heuristic PT	1	30.70	37.51	29.83	33.74	32.95
Heuristic PT	5	30.45	37.27	29.62	33.95	32.82
Heuristic PT	10	30.37	37.17	29.50	33.88	32.73
GIZA PT	1	**30.77**	37.61	29.97	33.97	33.08
GIZA PT	5	30.76	37.62	29.98	**33.98**	33.09
GIZA PT	10	30.76	**37.63**	**30.00**	**33.98**	**33.09**

Table 4: BLEU scores obtained applying different misspelling MT strategies

The detailed results (BLEU) are shown in Table 4. A more detailed analysis might be found in Formiga and Fonollosa (2012)

In general terms we observe that the GIZA PT strategy outperforms all the other strategies across all the metrics and test sets. Regarding the recovery from the noisy set (*wr*) we can see a maximum gain of 0.36 BLEU points. Also we can observe slightly improvements on the clean sets: ≈ 0.16 BLEU points,. The improvements on the clean sets are explained by some tokenization errors of Freeling that are fixed thanks to the misspelling correction step (e.g. I'll go $\rightarrow$ I will go or I 'll go). In that sense the misspelling correction step also performs a revision of the tokenization carried out beforehand. We can see also that the GIZA PT strategy is quite robust while increasing the N-best list to build the lattice. In contrast, the other strategies decrease the quality when the N-best list size is increased. As it has been explained, this might be motivated due to the high perplexities of the language model to the open domain text, making it not suitable for ranking the different hypotheses. The Confusion and Heuristic PT strategies perform slightly better than the baseline (no-processing at all) for the 1 and 5-best configurations in the noisy test sets. However, when it comes to the clean test sets they are not able to improve the baseline and worsening the result in case of increasing the n-best list size. The Distance based strategy is the worst, even compared to the baseline, across all the metrics and test sets. Making it not feasible for dealing with noisy input translations.

5 Discussion

The results of the experiments allow us to gain an in-depth specific understanding of how each strategy contributes to the misspelling correction when making MT from real-life texts.

The translation results obtained are coherent with the 1-best spelling correction results reported in table 3. However, the higher scores obtained in the METEOR N-best oracle case show that there may be scope for improvement if a more adecuate language model based on an open domain (e.g. Google N-grams) helps in the reranking of the proposed hypotheses.

In detail, we see that strategies based on a simple distance with respect to some closed lexicon worsen the baseline system. This is explained by the real-word errors corrections and the lack of a good language model (perplexities are over 500). Replacing a misspelled word with a correctly spelled word but senseless in that specific context usually leads to a worse automatic translation.

Secondly, the results of the heuristic strategies (Confusion and Heuristic PT) show that the translation scores improve with noisy input but can decrease the quality of clean input translations. This behavior had already been identified by Bertoldi et al. (2008) in two cases: when the noise level was lower than 2% or when the errors were caused mainly by real-word errors. In order to avoid the decrease of the MT quality on clean texts for the heuristic strategies, they (Bertoldi et al., 2010) reported that it would be necessary to incorporate a noisy-text detector step on the input data which would trigger the correction process.

However, the new GIZA PT strategy presented in this paper is also robust to clean text, avoiding the need of a clean / noisy-text detector. In fact, the GIZA PT strategy can partially correct both the noisy and cleaned text fixing low-level (e.g. thats fun → that is fun) as well as high-level errors (e.g. prove'em wrong → prove them wrong).

In addition, we want to highlight that the presented methodology is somewhat language independent since it does not need deep-language tools such as parsers or semantic role labelers. A small training corpus (or development corpus in case of the heuristic strategies) of about 8000 sentences might be enough to obtain a good spelling corrector, given a constant noise density ratio bounded to weblog translations.

6 Conclusions and Future work

We presented a detailed study of different spelling correction strategies for improving the quality of Machine Translation in real-life noisy scenarios. Real-life errors may be produced by different causes such as general misspelling (low-level errors) or informal text conventions (high-level errors) among others.

Apart from the basic strategy based on the Levenshtein distance, we also studied two strategies based on heuristic models and a strategy based on building a character-level translator. Regarding the heuristic methods, we adapted an existing strategy to take full advantage of standard feature functions such as distortion and we included a MERT-based tuning of the weights.

Whereas the distance-based strategy is not able to deal with real-life errors, the heuristic strategies show some improvement to the baseline translation and are easy to implement. However, the heuristic strategies are bounded to low-level misspelling errors and rely solely in the quality of the language model used for scoring the different alternatives.

In contrast, the trainable character-based strategy, namely GIZA PT, reports a significant and robust improvement across all the evaluated test sets and metrics. The GIZA PT offers a good trade-off between cost of implementation and quality improvement. Concretely it achieves an improvement of 0.36 BLEU points when translating noisy text.

However, oracle results show that there may be still margin for improvement on the heuristic strategies if a better ranking method for the hypotheses could be found. In the future we plan to study the behavior of bigger language models for open domain tasks (e.g. Google N-grams) and we will try to combine the heuristic and trained character-based phrase-tables in order to provide additional robustness to the proposed misspelling correction strategies.

Acknoweledgments

We would like to thank the anonymous reviewers for their insightful comments. This research has been partially funded by the European Community's Seventh Framework Programme (FP7/2007-2013) under grant agreement 247762 (FAUST project, FP7-ICT-2009-4-247762) and by the Spanish Government (Buceador, TEC2009-14094-C04-01)

References

Agichtein, E., Castillo, C., Donato, D., Gionis, A., and Mishne, G. (2008). Finding High-quality Content in Social Media. In *Proceedings of the International Conference on Web Search and Web Data Mining*, WSDM '08, pages 183–194, New York, NY, USA. ACM.

Aikawa, T., Schwartz, L., King, R., Corston-Oliver, M., and Lozano, C. (2007). Impact of Controlled Language on Translation Quality and Post-editing in a Statistical Machine Translation Environment. In *Proceedings of MT Summit XI*, pages 10–14.

Aw, A., Zhang, M., Xiao, J., and Su, J. (2006). A phrase-based statistical model for sms text normalization. In *Proceedings of the COLING/ACL on Main conference poster sessions*, pages 33–40. Association for Computational Linguistics.

Bertoldi, N., Cettolo, M., and Federico, M. (2010). Statistical Machine Translation of Texts with Misspelled Words. In *Human Language Technologies: The 2010 Annual Conference of the North American Chapter of the Association for Computational Linguistics*, HLT '10, pages 412–419, Stroudsburg, PA, USA. Association for Computational Linguistics.

Bertoldi, N., Zens, R., Federico, M., and Shen, W. (2008). Efficient Speech Translation Through Confusion Network Decoding. *IEEE Transactions on Audio, Speech, and Language Processing*, 16(8):1696 –1705.

Brill, E. and Moore, R. (2000). An Improved Error Model for Noisy Channel Spelling Correction. In *Proceedings of the 38th Annual Meeting on Association for Computational Linguistics*, ACL '00, pages 286–293, Stroudsburg, PA, USA. Association for Computational Linguistics.

Contractor, D., Faruquie, T., and Subramaniam, L. (2010). Unsupervised cleansing of noisy text. In *Proceedings of the 23rd International Conference on Computational Linguistics: Posters*, pages 189–196. Association for Computational Linguistics.

Damerau, F. (1964). A Technique for Computer Detection and Correction of Spelling Errors. *Communications of the ACM*, 7(3):171–176.

Denkowski, M. and Lavie, A. (2011). Meteor 1.3: Automatic metric for reliable optimization and evaluation of machine translation systems. In *Proc. of the 6th Workshop on Statistical Machine Translation*, pages 85–91. Association for Computational Linguistics.

Deorowicz, S. and Ciura, M. (2005). Correcting Spelling Errors by Modelling their Causes. *International Journal of Applied Mathematics and Computer Science*, 15(2):275.

Dey, L. and Haque, S. (2009). Studying the Effects of Noisy Text on Text Mining Applications. In *Proceedings of The 3rd Workshop on Analytics for Noisy Unstructured Text Data*, pages 107–114. ACM.

Formiga, L. and Fonollosa, J. A. R. (2012). Correcting input noise in SMT as a char-based translation problem. In *TALP internal report*, UPC, Barcelona. http://nlp.lsi.upc.edu/publications/papers/misspelling_techrep_oct2012.pdf

Formiga, L., Henríquez Q., C. A., Hernández, A., Mariño, J. B., Monte, E., and Fonollosa, J. A. R. (2012). The talp-upc phrase-based translation systems for wmt12: Morphology simplification and domain adaptation. In *Proceedings of the Seventh Workshop on Statistical Machine Translation*, pages 275–282, Montréal, Canada. Association for Computational Linguistics.

Jacquemont, S., Jacquenet, F., and Sebban, M. (2007). Correct your Text with Google. In *Proceedings of the IEEE/WIC/ACM International Conference on Web Intelligence*, pages 170–176. IEEE Computer Society.

Kobus, C., Yvon, F., and Damnati, G. (2008). Normalizing SMS: Are Two Metaphors Better than One? In *Proceedings of the 22nd International Conference on Computational Linguistics - Volume 1*, pages 441–448. Association for Computational Linguistics.

Koehn, P. and Hoang, H. (2007). Factored translation models. In *Proc. of the 2007 Joint Conf. on Empirical Methods in Natural Language Processing and Computational Natural Language Learning (EMNLP-CoNLL)*, pages 868–876, Prague, Czech Republic. ACL.

Kothari, G., Negi, S., Faruquie, T., Chakaravarthy, V., and Subramaniam, L. (2009). SMS based Interface for FAQ Retrieval. In *Proceedings of the Joint Conference of the 47th Annual Meeting of the ACL and the 4th International Joint Conference on Natural Language Processing of the AFNLP: Volume 2*, pages 852–860. Association for Computational Linguistics.

Kukich, K. (1992). Spelling Correction for the Telecommunications Network for the Deaf. *Commun. ACM*, 35:80–90.

Mays, E., Damerau, F. J., and Mercer, R. L. (1991). Context based spelling correction. *Information Processing & Management*, 27(5):517 – 522.

Mitton, R. (1996). *English Spelling and the Computer*. Longman Group.

Pedler, J. (2007). *Computer Correction of Real-word Spelling Errors in Dyslexic Text*. PhD thesis, Birkbeck, University of London.

Philips, L. (2000). The Double Metaphone Search Algorithm. *C/C++ Users J.*, 18:38–43.

Pighin, D., Màrquez, L., and Formiga, L. (2012). The faust corpus of adequacy assessments for real-world machine translation output. In *Proc. of the 8th International Conference on Language Resources and Evaluation (LREC'12)*, Istanbul, Turkey. European Language Resources Association (ELRA).

Subramaniam, L., Roy, S., Faruquie, T., and Negi, S. (2009). A Survey of Types of Text Noise and Techniques to Handle Noisy Text. In *Proceedings of The 3rd Workshop on Analytics for Noisy Unstructured Text Data*, AND '09, pages 115–122, New York, NY, USA. ACM.

Toutanova, K. and Moore, R. (2002). Pronunciation Modeling for Improved Spelling Correction. In *Proceedings of the 40th Annual Meeting on Association for Computational Linguistics*, pages 144–151. Association for Computational Linguistics.

Yvon, F. (2010). Rewriting the orthography of sms messages. *Nat. Lang. Eng.*, 16(2):133–159.

A Comparison of Knowledge-based Algorithms for Graded Word Sense Assignment

Annemarie Friedrich Nikos Engonopoulos Stefan Thater Manfred Pinkal
Department of Computational Linguistics
Saarland University
{afried, nikolaos, stth, pinkal}@coli.uni-saarland.de

ABSTRACT
Standard word sense disambiguation (WSD) data sets annotate each word instance in context with exactly one sense of a predefined inventory, and WSD systems are traditionally evaluated with regard to how good they are at picking this sense. Recently, the notion of graded word sense assignment (GWSA) has gained attention as a more natural view of the contextual specification of word meaning; multiple senses may apply simultaneously to one instance of a word, and they may be applicable to different degrees. In this paper, we apply three different WSD algorithms to the task of GWSA. The three models belong to the class of knowledge-based models in the WSD terminology; they are unsupervised in the sense that they do not depend on annotated training material. We evaluate the models on two recently published GWSA data sets. We find positive correlations with the human judgments for all models, and develop a metric based on the notion of accuracy that highlights differences in the behaviors of the models.

KEYWORDS: lexical semantics, graded word senses, knowledge-based disambiguation.

Proceedings of COLING 2012: Posters, pages 329–338,
COLING 2012, Mumbai, December 2012.

1 Introduction

The problem of *word sense disambiguation* (WSD) is a central topic in computational linguistics, with a long-standing, rich history of research (see McCarthy, 2009; Navigli, 2009). Typically, the WSD task is designed such that each target word in context is assigned a single word sense from a predefined sense inventory. However, several word senses may be simultaneously present in a contextual instance of a word, which holds in particular in connection with fine-grained sense inventories, like the one provided by WordNet (Fellbaum, 1998). The single-sense restriction typically leads to a somewhat arbitrary overspecification of word meaning, which may be detrimental to the use of WSD systems in practical applications. Moreover, both agreement between human annotators and accuracy of WSD systems tend to be rather low, which stands in contrast to the strong intuition that words in context generally have a well-understood meaning.

Recently, the notion of *graded word sense assignment* (GWSA) has been brought into discussion by Erk et al. (2009, 2012), and two closely related GWSA data sets are now available. The underlying assumption of GWSA is that a word in context may in fact evoke more than one sense, and the different senses may participate in the meaning of the word to different degrees. To produce the aforementioned data sets, annotators were presented target instances, i.e., lemmas in the context of a sentence, and asked to assign a value, which indicates the applicability of the sense in the context, on a scale from 1 to 5 to each WordNet sense of the lemma independently. The annotation method allows more than one word sense for a given target instance to be assigned a high applicability score, and it induces an ordering of the word senses on the level of single instances. Erk et al. (2009) give the example of "paper" occurring in a sentence which clearly identifies a scientific context. All three annotators agree that the WordNet sense *scholarly article* fully applies and consistently assign a score of 5. However, the senses *essay* and *medium for written communication* are also assigned high scores by some of the annotators. This reflects these annotators' intuitions that several senses apply simultaneously, and induces an ordering of the senses' applicabilities.

A first, supervised, computational model for GWSA is presented by Erk and McCarthy (2009). In this paper, we explore models that are unsupervised in the sense that they do not depend on annotated training material; in the WSD terminology, they belong to the class of knowledge-based WSD systems. More specifically, we address the task of ranking the WordNet senses of a lemma for each of its instances, according to the degree of applicability of the respective senses in context. We evaluate our models against the data sets provided by Erk et al. (2009, 2012), and use the ranking induced by the average scores for each word sense as a gold standard. We carry out the evaluation for three different systems: two related models, which are based on the individual similarity scores between the contextualized vector representation of a target word in context and vector representations computed for the respective word senses (Thater et al., 2011; Li et al., 2010), plus a reimplementation of the approach of Sinha and Mihalcea (2007), a representative of the larger class of graph-based approaches to WSD. Our major findings are first, that the knowledge-based systems show positive correlation with the human judgments, and second, that there are interesting differences in performance between the different types of systems according to our metric of Adjusted Accuracy.

2 Related Work

The only WSD system that has been evaluated on the full GWSA data set of Erk et al. (2009) so far is the supervised model of Erk and McCarthy (2009). Thater et al. (2010) describe an approach to unsupervised GWSA on the basis of a syntactically informed distributional similarity model. The evaluation was carried out for three selected verb lemmas, and therefore has the character of a case study only. The study of Jurgens (2012), which explores the application of word sense induction techniques to GWSA, has a similar status: Since he needs a large part of the GWSA data set as a sense mapping corpus, only a very small amount of data is left for evaluation.

3 Modeling

This section reviews the three knowledge-based WSD algorithms that we use in our study, and which we chose for the following reasons: (1) They are knowledge-lean, i.e., the only resource required is a semantic lexicon (such as WordNet), and they can be implemented quickly. (2) They exhibit state-of-the-art performance on the SemEval-2007 coarse-grained WSD task.

3.1 Vector Space-based WSD System

We use the vector-space model (VSM) of Thater et al. (2011), which is closely related to the models of Thater et al. (2010) and Erk and Padó (2008). The general idea behind VSMs of word meaning is to represent words by vectors in a high-dimensional space. These vectors record co-occurrence statistics with context words in a large unlabeled text corpus, and their relative directions are taken to indicate semantic similarity. The particular model used in our experiments is the one of Thater et al. (2011), which provides context-specific (contextualized) vectors for words in their syntactic context. It can be applied to WSD and GWSA in a straightforward way: given a target word in a sentential context, we extract a set of *sense paraphrases* for each sense of the target from WordNet. We then compute the cosine similarities of all sense paraphrases and the contextualized vector of the target word, and set the similarity of the sense to be the average of the best two sense paraphrases. In the case of standard WSD, the VSM predicts the sense with the highest score; in the case of GWSA, the scores assigned to the senses induce a ranking. In rare cases, the VSM fails to make predictions, i.e., when the dependency tree for the input sentence does not assign the correct POS to the target word, or when no useful sense paraphrases can be extracted from WordNet.

3.2 Topic Model-based WSD System

Li et al. (2010) use topic models (Blei et al., 2003), which represent text corpora using generative probability distributions, as the central component of their WSD system. Topics are distributions over words and each document is modeled as a mixture of latent topics. Li et al. (2010) extract one *sense paraphrase* per word sense from WordNet. The topic model is used to estimate a vector of the topic distribution for the context of the target word (usually the sentence in which it occurs) and a vector for the sense paraphrase of the candidate sense. The cosine between these vectors is taken as the final score for the word sense. This algorithm naturally produces a ranking of word senses. We closely follow the experimental settings (for Model II) reported by Li et al. (2010), but we were not able to fully reproduce their system. For SemEval-2007, Li et al. (2010) report an F1-measure of 79.99% for their Topic Model system. Our reimplementation achieved an F-measure of 71.7%. Hence, the Topic Models approach might yield better performance using different parameter settings. We noticed that due to the sampling step inside the algorithm, the results varied by small, but non-negligible, amounts. We thus sum up the scores produced by the system across multiple (ten) runs in order to predict a more reliable ranking. This results in a slight increase of performance.

3.3 Graph-based WSD System

To date, many graph-based WSD algorithms have been proposed, (among others by Sinha and Mihalcea, 2007; Agirre and Soroa, 2009; Navigli and Lapata, 2010; Tsatsaronis et al., 2010; Ponzetto and Navigli, 2010). We chose to reimplement the approach of Sinha and Mihalcea (2007) for several reasons. First, it is based on the PageRank algorithm, which is easy to understand and implement; second, a reference implementation was made available by the authors, which allowed for clarification in several issues; and third, its performance is robust. The algorithm consists of the following steps, which we illustrate using Figure 1. (1) *Construction of the graph.* When disambiguating a word (e.g. "order"), a graph is built using a context of N (2 in the example) content words on either side of the word. For each content word, the admissible word senses are added to the graph as nodes. Undirected edges are introduced between nodes that were not introduced for the same word and whose content words are not more than M (2 in the example) content words apart in the surface string. The edge weights are determined using the Extended Lesk Similarity (Banerjee, 2003) between the two synsets of the two nodes' word senses.[1] The setting we used for the SemEval-2007 experiments was N=6 and M=3; for the GWSA task, we report results for N=2 and M=2. The parameters were tuned on the respective data sets. (2) *Scoring using a graph-based centrality algorithm* (ten iterations of PageRank). (3) *Assignment of word senses.* In a standard WSD setting, the system picks the sense of the target word whose node has been assigned the highest score. In GWSA, we simply assign the scores of the respective nodes to the senses.

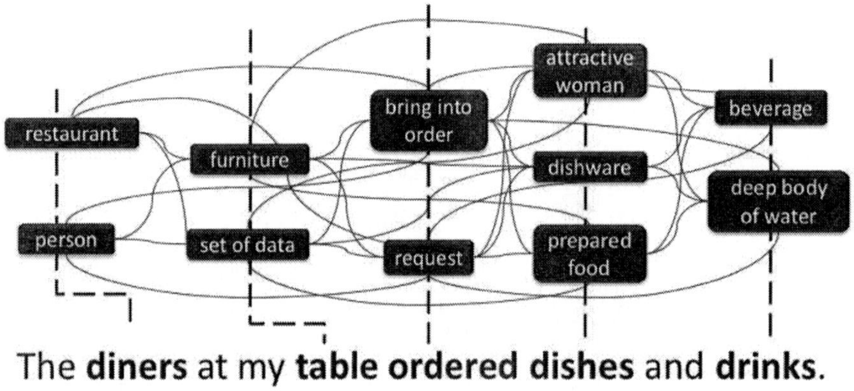

Figure 1: Example graph used in the PageRank algorithm.

4 Evaluation

4.1 Data Sets

WSsim-1: (Erk and McCarthy, 2009) present the first data set for the evaluation of GWSA. A total of 430 sentences for 11 different lemmas were extracted from SemCor and Senseval-3. Three untrained annotators provided judgments of the applicability of word senses of the lemmas in the context of the sentence on a scale from 1 to 5, where 1 means that the sense is not present at all in the sentence and 5 means that the sense totally matches the meaning of the word in the context. We refer to the task of ranking the senses of a word (lemma) in the context of a particular sentence as the *lemma-sentence ranking task*.

[1]We are using the WordNet::Similarity toolkit of (Pedersen et al., 2004). We also experimented with other sense similarity measures, but the method suggested by Sinha and Mihalcea (2007) worked best with PageRank.

WSsim-2: In this round of data collection, eight annotators judged the applicability of the senses of 26 lemmas in 10 sentences each, resulting in a set of 260 sentences (Erk et al., 2012). Otherwise, the annotation procedure was identical to WSsim-1.

4.2 Correlation Analysis of Sense Ranking

Erk and McCarthy (2009) propose Spearman's rank correlation coefficient (ρ) as a measure of a system's performance on the GWSA task. ρ compares two rankings while abstracting away from the absolute values of judgments. We used the R mathematical package to compute ρ for the rankings of the senses for each lemma-sentence task and then average across all sentences (see Table 1). As an upper bound, we report the correlations achieved by the human annotators (compare to Tables 9 and 10 of (Erk et al., 2012)). Significance is hard to show due to the small number of senses to be ranked (on average 6.1 senses per lemma in WSsim-1 and 10.6 in WSsim-2). The upper part of Table 1 shows the performance of the supervised system reported by Erk and McCarthy (2009), Prototype 2/N, as well as a sense frequencies baseline, whose sense frequencies have been estimated on SemCor and the training part of Senseval-3 (minus the sentences used in WSsim-1), while the lower part of the table shows the correlations achieved by our implementations of knowledge-based systems. Erk and McCarthy test their system only on the sentences for 8 out of the 11 lemmas of WSsim-1 and the numbers are therefore not directly comparable. The supervised system (Prototype 2/N) performs best, but the knowledge-based systems also show meaningful correlations with the human judgments. The VSM performs surprisingly well; the Topic Models system outperforms the PageRank system. It is worth noting that the sense frequencies baseline performs much better on WSsim-1 than on WSsim-2 for the lemma-sentence task, the reason being that the frequencies have been estimated in-domain for WSsim-1.

	WSsim-1		WSsim-2	
Model	ρ	sign.	ρ	sign.
Average of humans*	0.555	30.4	0.641	48.3
Prototype 2/N (E&K)	0.478	22.8	-	-
Sense Frequencies (SF)	0.357	10.7	0.245	14.2
VSM (Thater et al.)⋆	0.305	12.7	0.389	21.4
Topic Models (Li et al.)⋈†	0.241	11.6	0.256	15.0
PageRank (Sinha et al.)†	0.210	4.0	0.097	4.6

Table 1: Spearman's rank correlation coefficient (ρ) by lemma-sentence compared to the average scores of all human annotators. The columns labelled "sign." show the percentage of the sentences in which the sense ranking correlation was significant. *Correlation of scores of one annotator with the average scores of the other annotators (omitting cases where annotators did not produce valid rankings). ⋆Performance of the VSM is reported on the 99% (WSsim-1) and 93% (WSsim-2) of the sentences for which the model creates a ranking. †Our reimplementations.

5 Analysis

5.1 Analysis of Data

As we have seen in section 4.2, the correlation between the human annotators is by no means perfect: it is hard to quantify the actual degree of applicability on the scale proposed by Erk et al. (2012) in many cases. In order to gain some more understanding about how the human annotators use the scale and to what extent the (correlation) analysis of systems using the WSsim-2 data set is meaningful, we created the plot shown in Figure 2.

In the lemma-sentence task, two annotators define the same ranking for a pair of senses if one assigns the scores 3-4 and the other assigns 4-5. For this reason, we look at the scores given to a sense pair by one annotator, and whether the ranking of these two senses is concordant with the ranking of the average of all other annotators. Each pair of senses of the ranking of one annotator is sorted into one of the diagram's cells depending on the scores assigned to the two senses; if there is no tie, we find the position on the y-axis using the higher score and the position on the x-axis using the lower score, thus producing a diagonal matrix. We then compare the ranking of the first annotator to the ranking resulting from the average of the other annotators and increment the cell's count if the pair is concordant. In each cell, we add up the numbers of concordant pairs over all the annotators. Finally, we divide each cell's count by the total number of pairs that fell into the cell in order to decrease the bias caused by score combinations that occur more often. From this analysis, we can conclude that humans agree more often on the ordering of two senses if they assign scores at the two ends of the scale (the cell 5-1 has the highest proportion of concordant pairs), but that they use the intermediate scores rather interchangeably. There is high agreement for cell 1-1 (88.5%) out of the 100,217 pairs that fell into this cell. Cell 2-2 also shows high agreement, but note that only 1,684 pairs fell into this cell. However, we can see that in WSsim-2, annotators seem to make a clear distinction whether a sense applies to some extent (scores 2-5) or does not apply at all (score 1). Based on this analysis, we propose a new way of judging a system's performance from an application point of view in section 5.2.

	1	2	3	4	5
5	0.912 *16,914*	0.860 *2,034*	0.754 *1,480*	0.605 *1,084*	0.337 *838*
4	0.684 *6,984*	0.567 *1,283*	0.498 *963*	0.320 *394*	
3	0.482 *11,024*	0.347 *1,868*	0.435 *800*		
2	0.179 *14,433*	0.733 *1,684*			
1	0.885 *100,217*				

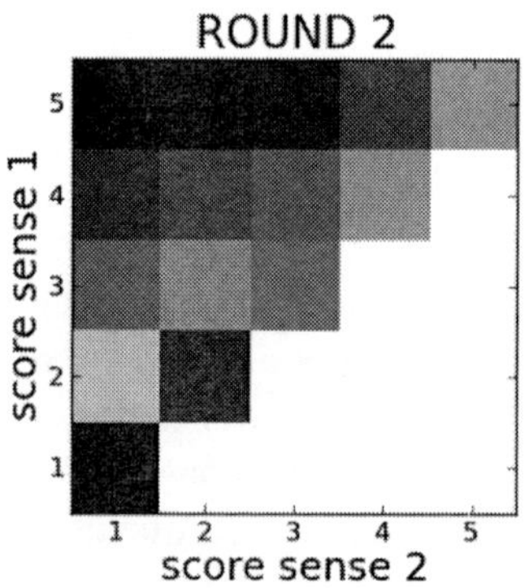

Figure 2: Analysis of the percentage of concordant pairs for sense pairs given particular scores in the data set for GWSA by (Erk et al., 2012). Normalized concordance matrix, summed over all annotators. The total counts of (concordant and discordant) pairs per cell, summed over all annotators, are reported in italic.

5.2 Accuracy-based Analysis using Graded Annotations

As we have seen above, human annotators use the scores 2-5 as an indicator that the sense is present at least to some extent in WSsim-2. Using fine-grained sense inventories such as WordNet, it is very hard even for humans to argue which of the senses is more present in a particular context. From a practical point of view, it may be sufficient if the sense to which a system assigned the highest score is present at least to some extent according to the humans' annotations. We propose to evaluate systems – in addition to the correlation analysis – according to this criterion. This analysis allows to treat the GWSA data set as the gold standard for an evaluation similar to the coarse-grained WSD task of SemEval-2007, with the difference that SemEval-2007 uses predefined sense clusters, while in the GWSA data set, clusters are formed per context. Erk et al. (2009) show that it is not possible to form clusters out of the GWSA annotations that are applicable across the instances. Hence, we believe that the GWSA data sets are a valuable resource for evaluating WSD system performance in a coarse-grained but context-sensitive way.

For each treshold from 2 to 5 (in steps of 0.5), we create a gold standard in which all senses that received an average score $\geq$ the threshold are counted as correct, and then we evaluate accuracy as the percentage of lemma-sentence tasks in which the sense scored highest by a system is in this set of correct senses. For lower thresholds, the probability of picking a correct sense is higher as the set of correct senses is larger. Hence, we adjust our measure of accuracy inspired by Cohen's κ (Cohen, 1960). For each threshold t and for each lemma-sentence task i, we partition the set of graded senses S_i into two sets $S_{i,score \geq t}$ and $S_{i,score<t}$. Then, the probability of choosing a correct sense by chance for this task becomes

$$P^{t,i}_{chance} = \frac{|S_{i,score \geq t}|}{|S_i|}.$$

The average chance of picking a correct sense at threshold t is

$$P^{t}_{chance} = \frac{\sum_{i=1}^{N^t} P^{t,i}_{chance}}{N^t}.$$

where N^t is the total number of lemma-sentence tasks at threshold t in which $P^{t,i}_{chance} > 0$. We exclude the cases where the set of true positives is empty because the system cannot possibly pick a "correct" sense. The accuracy of a system at threshold t is computed as

$$Acc^t = \frac{\sum_{i=1}^{N^t} \mathbf{1}_{s^i \in S_{i,score>=t}}}{N^t}$$

with $\mathbf{1}$ being the indicator function and s^i being the sense that was scored highest by the system for the lemma-sentence task i. We then compute the Adjusted Accuracy at threshold t, which is plotted in Figure 3 , as

$$AdjAcc^t = \frac{Acc^t - P^t_{chance}}{1 - P^t_{chance}}.$$

The threshold-accuracy plots show how much better than chance a system is at predicting a sense that has a score above a certain threshold. As an upper bound, for each annotator, we regard the average of the other annotators as the gold standard and compute the Adjusted Accuracies, which range from 62% (for $t = 4.5$) to 76% (for $t = 2$). For $t = 5$, humans achieve a remarkable average Adjusted Accuracy of 73%.

5.3 Discussion

Referring to Figure 3, it is interesting to note that the shape of the curve for PageRank is much lower for all $t < 5$ than the other systems' curves. It shows a sharp increase when setting $t = 5$, which suggests that unlike the other systems, the graph-based PageRank algorithm is better suited for the standard WSD task of picking one best-fitting sense[2], while its ranking ability is not as good past the top rank as the other systems'. These findings are also supported by the observation that PageRank outperforms our reimplementation of the Topic Models approach on

[2]Sinha and Mihalcea report an F1-measure of 52.55% on the fine-grained WSD task of Senseval-2, and our PageRank system achieves an F1-measure of 76.0% on the coarse-grained WSD task of SemEval-2007.

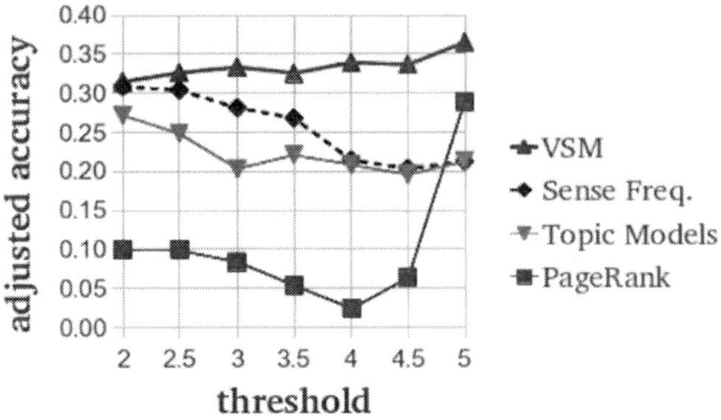

Figure 3: Adjusted Accuracy of picking a "correct" sense as the highest-ranked sense at various thresholds. Computed using the WSsim-2 data set. The numbers of sentences for which the set of "correct" senses $S_{i,score \geq t}$ is non-empty at the respective thresholds are 259, 256, 252, 238, 204, 150, and 46.

the SemEval-2007 coarse-grained task (F-measure of PageRank: 76% vs. Topic Models: 71.7%). A possible reason for this behavior might be the interaction of all the senses of the target word in one graph in PageRank. In contrast, the Topic Models and the VSM methods score only one sense at a time. When comparing to PageRank, the Topic Models system correlates more closely with the human average judgments per lemma-sentence. The same holds for a comparison using our metric of Adjusted Accuracy. We would like to note that none of the algorithms were tuned specifically for the GWSA task, with the exception of setting M and N of PageRank.

The VSM approach outperforms the two other knowledge-based systems of our study in all metrics presented in this paper. The VSM method has been developed mainly for tasks involving fine-grained lexical distinctions and has shown excellent performance on other lexical semantic tasks as well. Our comparison suggests that the model is good at capturing subtle distinctions between senses. It is also worth noting that the VSM is the only system that does not rely on WordNet's glosses, which in some cases contain examples that may be misleading for a system looking for topical information.

6 Conclusion

We explored the applicability of three knowledge-based WSD systems to the task of graded word sense assignment. We found a positive rank correlation between each of the systems' outputs and the human annotators' judgments. However, the performance levels of the individual systems were quite different. The most successful model (Thater et al., 2011) does not reach the supervised approach, but outperforms a sense frequencies baseline on the WSsim-2 data set. In addition, we showed that systems that are good at standard WSD (like the PageRank-based system) are not necessarily strong on the GWSA ranking task. We conclude that the use of the GWSA data sets with correlation and accuracy analyses as presented in this paper sheds a different light on the performance of WSD systems, by providing an in-depth analysis of their ranking behavior instead of treating WSD as a standard classification problem.

Acknowledgment

We are grateful to Diana McCarthy and Katrin Erk for providing us with the data and for clarifying several questions. We want to thank Alexis Palmer and the anonymous reviewers for their insightful comments. Thanks also go to Moinuddin Mushirul Haque. This work was supported by the Cluster of Excellence "Multimodal Computing and Interaction", funded by the German Excellence Initiative.

References

Agirre, E. and Soroa, A. (2009). Personalizing PageRank for word sense disambiguation. In *Proceedings of the 12th Conference of the European Chapter of the Association for Computational Linguistics*, EACL '09, pages 33–41, Stroudsburg, PA, USA. Association for Computational Linguistics.

Banerjee, S. (2003). Extended gloss overlaps as a measure of semantic relatedness. In *Proceedings of the Eighteenth International Joint Conference on Artificial Intelligence*, pages 805–810.

Blei, D. M., Ng, A. Y., and Jordan, M. I. (2003). Latent Dirichlet Allocation. *Journal of Machine Learning Research*, 3:993–1022.

Cohen, J. (1960). A Coefficient of Agreement for Nominal Scales. *Educational and Psychological Measurement*, 20(1):37.

Erk, K. and McCarthy, D. (2009). Graded Word Sense Assignment. In *Proceedings of the 2009 Conference on Empirical Methods in Natural Language Processing, EMNLP 2009, 6-7 August 2009, Singapore, A meeting of SIGDAT, a Special Interest Group of the ACL*, pages 440–449.

Erk, K., McCarthy, D., and Gaylord, N. (2009). Investigations on Word Senses and Word Usages. In Su, K.-Y., Su, J., and Wiebe, J., editors, *ACL/AFNLP*, pages 10–18. The Association for Computer Linguistics.

Erk, K., McCarthy, D., and Gaylord, N. (2012). Measuring word meaning in context. *Computational Linguistics (to appear)*.

Erk, K. and Padó, S. (2008). A structured vector space model for word meaning in context. In *Proceedings of the 2008 Conference on Empirical Methods in Natural Language Processing*, pages 897–906, Honolulu, Hawaii. Association for Computational Linguistics.

Fellbaum, C., editor (1998). *WordNet: An Electronic Lexical Database*. The MIT Press, Cambridge, MA ; London.

Jurgens, D. (2012). An Evaluation of Graded Sense Disambiguation using Word Sense Induction. In **SEM 2012: The First Joint Conference on Lexical and Computational Semantics – Volume 1: Proceedings of the main conference and the shared task, and Volume 2: Proceedings of the Sixth International Workshop on Semantic Evaluation (SemEval 2012)*, pages 189–198, Montréal, Canada. Association for Computational Linguistics.

Li, L., Roth, B., and Sporleder, C. (2010). Topic Models for Word Sense Disambiguation and Token-Based Idiom Detection. In Hajic, J., Carberry, S., and Clark, S., editors, *Proceedings of the 48th Annual Meeting of the Association for Computational Linguistics (ACL 2010), July 11-16, 2010, Uppsala, Sweden*, pages 1138–1147. The Association for Computational Linguistics.

McCarthy, D. (2009). Word sense disambiguation: An overview. *Language and Linguistics Compass*, 3(2):537–558.

Navigli, R. (2009). Word sense disambiguation: A survey. *ACM Comput. Surv.*, 41(2):10:1–10:69.

Navigli, R. and Lapata, M. (2010). An Experimental Study of Graph Connectivity for Unsupervised Word Sense Disambiguation. *IEEE Trans. Pattern Anal. Mach. Intell.*, 32(4):678–692.

Pedersen, T., Patwardhan, S., and Michelizzi, J. (2004). Wordnet::Similarity – Measuring the Relatedness of Concepts. In *Proceedings of the Nineteenth National Conference on Artificial Intelligence (AAAI-04)*, pages 1024–1025.

Ponzetto, S. P. and Navigli, R. (2010). Knowledge-Rich Word Sense Disambiguation Rivaling Supervised Systems. In Hajic, J., Carberry, S., and Clark, S., editors, *Proceedings of the 48th Annual Meeting of the Association for Computational Linguistics (ACL 2010), July 11-16, 2010, Uppsala, Sweden*, pages 1522–1531. The Association for Computer Linguistics.

Sinha, R. S. and Mihalcea, R. (2007). Unsupervised Graph-based Word Sense Disambiguation Using Measures of Word Semantic Similarity. In *ICSC*, pages 363–369. IEEE Computer Society.

Thater, S., Fürstenau, H., and Pinkal, M. (2010). Contextualizing semantic representations using syntactically enriched vector models. In Hajic, J., Carberry, S., and Clark, S., editors, *ACL*, pages 948–957. The Association for Computer Linguistics.

Thater, S., Fürstenau, H., and Pinkal, M. (2011). Word Meaning in Context: A Simple and Effective Vector Model. In *Proceedings of 5th International Joint Conference on Natural Language Processing (IJCNLP 2011)*.

Tsatsaronis, G., Varlamis, I., and Nørvåg, K. (2010). An Experimental Study on Unsupervised Graph-based Word Sense Disambiguation. In Gelbukh, A. F., editor, *CICLing*, volume 6008 of *Lecture Notes in Computer Science*, pages 184–198. Springer.

Leveraging Statistical Transliteration for Dictionary-Based English-Bengali CLIR of OCR'd Text

Utpal Garain[1] Arjun Das[1] David S. Doermann[2] Douglas D. Oard[2]
(1) INDIAN STATISTICAL INSTITUTE, 203, B. T. Road, Kolkata 700108, India.
(2) UNIVERSITY OF MARYLAND, College Park, MD USA
{utpal|arjundas}@isical.ac.in, {doermann|oard}@umd.edu

ABSTRACT

This paper describes experiments with transliteration of out-of-vocabulary English terms into Bengali to improve the effectiveness of English-Bengali Cross-Language Information Retrieval. We use a statistical translation model as a basis for transliteration, and present evaluation results on the FIRE 2011 RISOT Bengali test collection. Incorporating transliteration is shown to substantially and statistically significantly improve Mean Average Precision for both the text and OCR conditions. Learning a distortion model for OCR errors and then using that model to improve recall is also shown to yield a further substantial and statistically significant improvement for the OCR condition.

TITLE AND ABSTRACT IN BENGALI

OCR-কৃত নথি থেকে ইংরাজি-বাংলা অভিধান-ভিত্তিক CLIR-এর ক্ষেত্রে সংখ্যাতাত্বিক লিপ্যন্তর-এর প্রভাব

সারাংশ

এই গবেষণাপত্রে অভিধান-বহির্ভূত ইংরাজি শব্দের বাংলায় লিপ্যন্তর বা প্রতিবর্ণীকরণ বিষয়ে পরীক্ষা এবং তার মাধ্যমে ইংরাজি-বাংলা CLIR-এর কার্যকারিতায় উন্নতিসাধন দেখানো হয়েছে। আমরা লিপ্যন্তর করার জন্য একটি সংখ্যাতাত্বিক পদ্ধতি ব্যবহার করেছি এবং FIRE ২০১১ RISOT উপাত্ত বা ডাটা-এর সাহায্যে পদ্ধতিটির মূল্যায়ন করেছি। এটা দেখান হয়েছে যে এই লিপ্যন্তর-এর মাধ্যমে ইংরাজি-বাংলা CLIR-এর কার্যকারিতায় অনেকটাই উন্নতি পাওয়া যায়, যা পরিসংখ্যানগতভাবে উল্লেখযোগ্য। টাইপ অথবা OCR করা দু'ধরনের নথির ক্ষেত্রেই একই ধরনের ফল পাওয়া গেছে। পরিবর্তীকালে, OCR করা নথি থেকে CLIR করার ব্যাপারে OCR-এর ভুলগুলি থেকে একটি মডেল বানান হয়েছে ও দেখানো হয়েছে যে এই মডেল কিভাবে তথ্যোদ্ধারের ক্ষেত্রে আরও উন্নতি ঘটাতে পারে।

KEYWORDS: CLIR, OCR, English-Bengali, Dictionary based translation, Statistical transliteration, OCR error modeling, Stemming, Evaluation, FIRE-RISOT 2011.

KEYWORDS IN BENGALI: ভিন্ন ভাষায় তথ্যোদ্ধার, ছাপা অক্ষর/লেখা সনাক্তকরণ, ইংরাজি-বাংলা, অভিধান-ভিত্তিক অনুবাদ, সংখ্যাতাত্বিক পদ্ধতিতে লিপ্যন্তর, OCR-এর ভুলের মডেলিং, স্টেমিং, মূল্যায়ন।

Proceedings of COLING 2012: Posters, pages 339–348,
COLING 2012, Mumbai, December 2012.

1 Introduction

Research in Cross-Language Information Retrieval (CLIR) has a long history, resulting in the formation of evaluation venues such as CLEF [CLEF, undated] and NTCIR [NTCIR, undated]. European and Oriental languages received the initial focus, but in recent years the CLEF evaluation has included Indian languages [Jagarlamudi, 2007]. Beginning in 2008, the Forum for Information Retrieval Evaluation (FIRE) [FIRE, undated] focused specifically on Indian languages. Monolingual Bengali retrieval was introduced to FIRE in 2008, and the first reported experiments with an English-to-Bengali (E2B) CLIR experiment design (i.e., English queries and Bengali documents) were reported in 2010, but the lack of translation resources for Bengali limited those experiments to simulation of CLIR using human query translation [Leveling, 2010]. This paper reports on the first fully automated experiments with E2B CLIR.

In case of E2B CLIR, the major challenge is limited Bengali resources. Although there is now an English-to-Bengali machine-readable dictionary available, we are not aware of any English-Bengali parallel corpus that is available for research use, any prior work (which is available for reuse) on English-Bengali transliteration, or any other lexical resources (e.g., multilingual WordNets) from which such a bilingual E2B translation lexicon might be extracted. We have therefore created an E2B lexicon of about 32,000 entries by manually cleaning the one available English-Bengali machine readable dictionary and we have trained a statistical transliteration tool to perform E2B translation.

A second important challenge with providing access to Bengali information is that a relatively large percentage of sources are only found in printed rather than digital form. In FIRE 2011, the RISOT track introduced a CLIR test collection (with both English and Bengali queries) for which two versions of a Bengali document collection are available: one containing digital Unicode text (text collection) and a second containing text recognized from document images using Optical Character Recognition (OCR collection) [Garain, 2011a]. Two groups reported results at FIRE 2011 on monolingual (Bengali-to-Bengali) OCR'd document retrieval [Garain, 2011b; Ghosh, 2011]. In this paper we report the first CLIR results for OCR'd Bengali documents using English queries, which to the best of our knowledge is only the second OCR-based CLIR results for any language (the first being English-to-Chinese [Tseng, 2001]). Our results show large and statistically significant improvements from statistical transliteration, statistical OCR error modeling, and their combination.

2 Statistical Transliteration for English-Bengali

To begin we used the transliteration method described by Virga and Khudanpur [Virga and Khudanpur, 2003]. In this method, transliteration is viewed as a simple character translation task. We used the Joshua open source statistical machine translation system [Li et al., 2009] which is reconfigured in [Irvine et al., 2010] for transliteration. Pairs of transliterated words and character-based n-gram language models are used in place of parallel sentences and word n-grams models. The Berkeley aligner [DeNero and Klein, 2007] is used to automatically align characters in pairs of transliterations. The language models are then trained on 2- through 10-gram sequences of target language characters. The goal is to minimize the edit distance between the system's output and the reference transliterations. This optimization is done by using the Joshua's Minimum Error Rate Training (MERT) and a character based BLEU score objective function (BLEU-4).

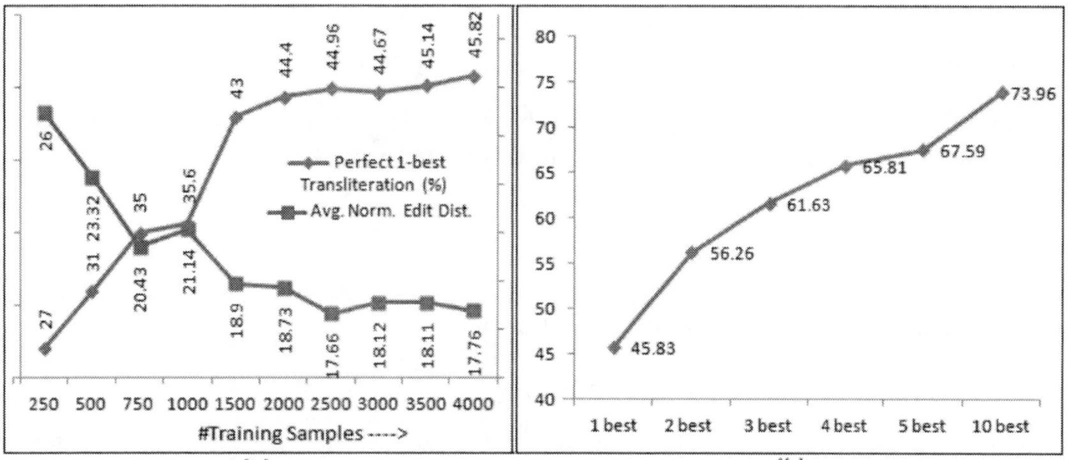

(a) (b)

FIGURE 1 - Plots of (a) transliteration accuracy (1 best) and average normalized edit distance with the number of training samples and (b) N-best transliteration accuracy.

2.1 Training Data

For training, name pairs are mined from Wikipedia following an approach similar to one used by Irvine et al. [Irvine et al., 2010]. We obtained about 3,000 name pairs by considering the firstHeading field of the English and corresponding Bengali Wikipedia pages. Another 3,000 pairs were collected from other sources that contain both English and Bengali names of famous personalities, significant places (including names of Indian states, state capitals, important cities, etc.), movies, and other named entities. A Bengali language model was then built by first tagging the full Bengali news corpus from the FIRE test collection. This was done using the Stanford Part of Speech (POS) tagger, which was trained on approximately 8,000 tagged Bengali sentences (collected from Linguistic Data Consortium (LDC), University of Pennsylvania and the NLP Tool Contest at [ICON, 2009]). A total of ~30,000 unique named entities were identified through this process. The resulting named entities were then used to construct a character n-gram language model that includes n-grams up to length ten.

2.2 Evaluation of the English-Bengali Transliteration Model

For evaluating the transliteration module, our list of 6,000 name pairs was divided into 6 sets to facilitate a 6-fold cross validation. The ratio of training, development and test data for each fold was 4:1:1. Each set was used once as a test data and once as a development data. We report the Levenshtein edit distance, optionally normalized by the length of the reference string, and the F1 measure as intrinsic evaluation measures. As Figure 1(a) shows, increasing the number of training pairs yields substantial improvement between 250 to 1,500 pairs, with less dramatic improvements beyond 1500 training pairs - the system performance shows slower change as more data is added to the training set. For our final system (trained on about 6,000 pairs) the edit distance is 1.22, the normalized edit distance is 0.1776, and the F1measure is 0.7919. As Figure 1(b) shows, in about 46% of the cases, our system produced exactly the same string as the reference in the top position, increasing to about 74% of the cases when we look for an exact match somewhere in the top 10 candidates generated by our transliteration system. This suggests that using multiple transliteration alternatives in our CLIR system may be helpful.

3 English-Bengali CLIR System

In our CLIR model, the query in a source language (English) is first translated into the target language (Bengali) using an English-Bengali Bilingual dictionary. The out-of-vocabulary terms are transliterated. The query in the target language is then expanded using a generative stemmer (i.e., a system that generates terms that would stem to the same Bengali term). We conducted our CLIR (English query and Bengali collection) experiment both on clean and OCR'd collections separately. We refer to experiments on the clean collection as the "text condition" and the experiment on the OCR as the "OCR condition." For the OCR condition, the query terms were further expanded using an OCR error modeling technique.

3.1 English-Bengali Bilingual Dictionary

A bilingual dictionary is available from the Ankur project [Dictionary, undated], but as distributed it contains many unedited entries. We elected to retain only the edited entries, repeated entries were also automatically removed. This yielded 31,267 unique English terms. Most of the English terms have more than one Bengali translation. Only 14,764 English terms have only one Bengali meaning and others have multiple (up to 16) different translations. In total, there are 70,808 total term pairs (English term - Bengali translation). Although all English terms are one word, many of the Bengali translations are multiple word expressions. Out of 70,808 term pairs, for 26,915 cases the Bengali translation includes more than one word.

3.2 OCR Error Modeling

A key problem that distinguishes document image retrieval from other information retrieval problems is that character confusability during Optical Character Recognition (OCR) can result in mismatches between the (undistorted) query representation and the (distorted) document representation. For example consider an English query word "cat". Because of OCR errors "cat" may be distorted to "cot" if 'a' is misrecognized as 'o' in the OCR'd documents. Therefore, documents containing "cat" or "cot" or both should perhaps be retrieved for the query word "cat." One way of doing this is to expand the query (e.g., to include the word "cot" in the query in addition to "cat" whenever "cat" appears in the query posed by the user). In our case, we are using Bengali search terms. In order to do this well, the system needs some model for how Bengali characters are affected by OCR errors.

Our OCR error probabilities are built by comparing 20,000 documents containing 37 million characters of clean text with the electronic text generated from OCR. These pages are part of the RISOT collection on which we have tested our error model (note that the collection has about 63,000 documents). We used a dynamic programming approach to compare each pair of documents and to report statistics of Unicode errors. The report details which Unicode glyphs have been inserted, deleted, or substituted in the OCR text, and with what frequency each error was observed. The error counts for these 20,000 pages are combined and global statistics, referred to as "translation errors," are computed. From this knowledge we build a table (E_t) of triplets $<t_i, o_i, p_i>$ where t_i is translated to o_i with probability p_i, referred to as the corruption probability. Note that both t_i and o_i refer to a single codepoint or a group of codepoints. Our further investigation reveals that though the table contains more than 200 such triplets, the 75 top most frequent entries cover 80% of the error cases and our error model considers only them.

```
<top>
<num>26</num>
<title>সিঙ্গুরে জমি অধিগ্রহণ সমস্যা</title>
<desc>সিঙ্গুরে বামফ্রন্ট সরকারের জমি অধিগ্রহণ কর্মসূচি এবং ভূমি উচ্ছেদ প্রতিরোধ কমিটির বিক্ষোভ সংক্রান্ত নথি খুঁজে বার করো।</desc>
<narr>শিল্পোন্নয়নের জন্য সিঙ্গুরে কৃষি জমি অধিগ্রহণ, বামপন্থী ও বিরোধী দলের মধ্যে সঙ্ঘর্ষ, সাধারণ মানুষকে নিষ্ঠুর ভাবে হত্যা, সমাজের বিভিন্ন স্তরের মানুষের প্রতিবাদ ও সমালোচনা প্রাসঙ্গিক নথিতে থাকা উচিত।</narr>
</top>
```

```
<top>
<num>26</num>
<title>Singur land dispute</title>
<desc>The land acquisition policies of the Left Parties in Singur and the protest of Bhumi Ucched Protirodh Committee against this policy.</desc>
<narr>Relevant documents should contain information regarding the acquisition of agricultural land for industrial growth in Singur, the territorial battle between the Left Parties and the opposition parties, the brutal killing of the innocent people and the protests and the criticism by people from different sections of society.</narr>
</top>
```

FIGURE 2- Same topic in Bengali (left) and English (right).

3.3 Formation of the Translated Query

RISOT 2011 actually provided topics in only in Bengali, but the corresponding English topics are available from the FIRE 2010 E2B CLIR task. Fig. 2 is a sample topic in Bengali and English. We used Lemur toolkit for our experiments [Lemur, undated]. Following the Indri 5.1 query syntax, a title-only (T) query for the above topic would be posed as:

```
<query>
      <number>26</number>
      <text> #combine(singur land dispute)</text>
</query>
```

3.3.1 Dictionary-based Query Translation (DQT)

For a query in English, the basic idea is to look up each query word in the E2B lexicon, and for Out-of-Vocabulary (OOV) terms (i.e., those not found in the E2B lexicon) to use transliteration. For example, for the above query, "singur" (the name of a place) was not found in the E2B lexicon and thus was transliterated. For the term "land," 10 different translations are available in the E2B lexicon while the term "dispute" has 6 available translations. Since we don't have translation preference information available, the best known approach is to treat each alternate translation for a single term as members of a synonym set. In the query, these are combined using Indri's '#syn' operator [Pirkola, 1998]. We process these multiple word expressions (on the Bengali side of our E2B lexicon) as ordered phrases using Indri's '#1' proximity operator to enforce exact matching (e.g., #1(পৃথিবীর স্থলভাগ) will match only পৃথিবীর স্থলভাগ together and in that order). Before insertion of transliterations for OOV terms, the resulting Bengali query for the example shown above would be:

```
<query>
  <number>26</number>
    <text>
      #combine(#syn(#1(কৃষিভূমি) #1(পৃথিবীর স্থলভাগ) #1(জমিদারি) #1(অবতরণ
      করা)  #1(জাহাজ) #1(গাড়ি থেকে নামা) #1(দেশ) #1(জমি) #1(স্থলবাহিনী) #1(জরিপ
      আমিন))  #syn(#1(তর্কাতর্কি) #1(প্রতিরোধ করা) #1(বিতর্ক) #1(প্রবল
      তর্ক) #1(সংঘাত) #1(বচসা করা)))
    </text>
</query>
```

3.3.2 Handling of OOVs

The English-Bengali transliteration module is used to generate one or more transliterated versions of each OOV term, returning the transliterations ranked in a best-first order. We then combine some number N of those transliterations, again using the #syn operator (as if they were alternative translations). When 10-best transliteration for the term "singur" in the above example is included, the Bengali query becomes:

```
<query>
  <number>26</number>
    <text>
      #combine(#syn(সিঙ্গুর সিনগুর সিনগর শিঙ্গুর সিংগুর সিংূর সীনগর সিনগুরে ◌সিঙ্গুর সিন্গুর) ...)
    </text>
</query>
```

3.3.3 OCR Error Modeling (OEM)

Let $W_t = w_1w_2 \ldots w_n$ be an n-codepoint query word. Note that we refer to codepoints (i.e., a single Unicode value) rather than characters to avoid confusion between the printed and digital representation; some Bengali glyphs are composed from more than one Unicode codepoint. We used the pruned set of 75 distortion probabilities learned in table E_t (see Section 3.2 above), treating all other Bengali code points as if they have zero distortion probability. Assuming that the codepoints of W_t are corrupted by OCR independently of each other, there may be many distorted versions of the word W_t. On average 27.5 variants are added for each term (minimum 0, maximum 128). We treat these distorted versions as synonyms, but this time we know the distortion probability and thus we use the Probabilistic Structured Query (PSQ) technique [Darwish and Oard, 2003], which is implemented by Indri's '#wsyn' operator. Let W_{ocr} be a possible distortion of query term W_{text}. We can then compute $P(W_{text} \mid W_{ocr})$ as

$$P(W_{text} \mid W_{ocr}) = \frac{P(W_{ocr} \mid W_{text}) P(W_{text})}{P(W_{ocr})}$$

where $P(W_{text})$ and $P(W_{ocr})$ are computed from the text and OCR collections. The term W_{ocr} is not considered in the expanded query if $P(W_{ocr}) = 0$. The third component, $P(W_{ocr}|W_{text})$ is basically $P(W_t \rightarrow W_s^i)$ which is computed from the error table E_t as discussed in Sec. 3.2.

4 Evaluation

The RISOT collection contains about 63,000 Bengali documents. We indexed both collections (Text and OCR) separately using the Lemur Toolkit and formed two types of queries: one from each topic's title field (T queries) and the other from each topic's title and description fields (TD queries). RISOT 2011 provides 92 topics for which one or more relevance judgments are available. We limited our evaluation to the 66 topics for which at least 5 relevant documents are known. Indri's default retrieval model [Ponte and Croft, 1998] is used.

4.1 Results

As a reference we report the monolingual MAP for the text condition using the original Bengali version of the topics. This yields 0.3205 for TD and 0.2649 for T queries (runs T1 and T6 in Table 1). When we perform CLIR without transliteration (the DQT technique alone), only 73%

of the query terms are found in the E2B lexicon. As a result, we get relatively poor results; a MAP of 0.1230 for TD queries and 0.0965 for T queries (runs T2 and T7). Translation ambiguity is not actually hurting us much in this case: manually selecting the best single-word Bengali translations from the alternatives available in the B2C lexicon (to eliminate both the '#1' and '#syn' operators) results in only small apparent improvements (runs T3 and T8) that are not statistically significant (runs T2:T3, T7:T8; $p>0.1$ by a two-tail t-test).

TABLE 1 – English-Bengali CLIR results for RISOT 2011 Collection, Text Condition

Run	Q	Retrieval Condition	Processing	MAP	MAP %	P@5	P@10	Rprec
T1	TD	Monolingual	--	0.3205	100%	0.3762	0.3182	0.3083
T2	TD	CLIR	DQT	0.1230	38%	0.1370	0.1167	0.1240
T3	TD	CLIR	DQT (Manual selection)	0.1269	40%	0.1665	0.1433	0.1410
T4	TD	CLIR	DQT + OOV	0.2645	83%	0.2887	0.2558	0.2605
T5	**TD**	**CLIR**	**DQT + OOV + Stemming**	**0.3306**	**103%**	**0.3609**	**0.3197**	**0.3204**
T6	T	Monolingual	---	0.2649	100%	0.3109	0.2630	0.2550
T7	T	CLIR	DQT	0.0965	36%	0.1114	0.1068	0.0980
T8	T	CLIR	DQT (Manual selection)	0.0969	37%	0.1271	0.1094	0.1080
T9	T	CLIR	DQT + OOV	0.2186	83%	0.2386	0.2114	0.2150
T10	**T**	**CLIR**	**DQT + OOV + Stemming**	**0.2689**	**102%**	**0.2935**	**0.2600**	**0.2648**

Incorporating the 10-best transliterations for OOV English query terms (with fully automatic E2B translation for all other English query terms) yields substantial and statistically significant improvement over DQT alone (runs T2:T4, T7:T9; $p<0.01$). Smaller values of N (not shown) do somewhat less well (MAP improvements from 1-best to 3-best, 3-best to 5-best and 5-best to 10-best are statistically significant at $p<0.05$), and larger values of N yield no further improvement.

As Bengali is a highly inflectional language, we then used a statistical stemmer [Paik et al., 2011]. Given a query term, it generates all possible variations of the words. The stemming yields a statistically significant improvements for both T and TD queries (runs T4:T5, T9:T10; $p<0.01$). The best CLIR results are thus obtained from combining dictionary based translation with transliteration of OOVs and generative stemming. Indeed, this combination achieved MAP values that slightly exceed those of monolingual retrieval (without stemming), demonstrating that the monolingual condition should be considered as a reference and not as an upper bound.

Table 2 shows comparable results for our experiments with the OCR condition. Again, DQT alone does relatively poorly (runs O2 and O8) and manual selection of single-word translations again does not yield a significant improvement (runs O2:O3, O8:O9; $p>0.1$). As with the text condition, transliteration yields significant improvements for the OCR condition (runs O2:O4, O8:O10; $p<0.01$). Further statistically significant improvement results from OCR error modeling (see Section 3.2.3) (runs O4:O5, O10:O11; $p<0.01$). Finally, the best overall results for the OCR condition resulted from combining transliteration of OOV terms, modeling of OCR errors, and stemming (runs O5:O6, O11:O12; $p<0.01$). For the OCR condition, this combination achieves MAP valued near, but below, the corresponding monolingual MAP for the text condition.

Note that stemmed monolingual retrieval yielded MAPs equal to 0.3929 (TD) and 0.3125 (T). If these MAPs are used as baselines, CLIR (text condition) best performance is only 84% (and 86% for T queries) of the best monolingual performance for TD queries and CLIR OCR condition MAPs are only 74% and 75% of the best monolingual results for TD and T queries.

TABLE 2 – English-Bengali CLIR results for RISOT 2011 OCR'd Collection
(The rows for Runs T1 and T6 are reference results from text condition)

Run	Q	Retrieval Condition	Processing	MAP	MAP%	P@5	P@10	Rprec
T1	TD	Mono+Text	--	0.3205	100%	0.3762	0.3182	0.3083
O1	TD	Monolingual	--	0.2689	84%	0.2420	0.2420	0.4166
O2	TD	CLIR	DQT	0.0813	25%	0.1025	0.0854	0.0679
O3	TD	CLIR	DQT (Manual selection)	0.0848	26%	0.1150	0.0938	0.0864
O4	TD	CLIR	DQT + OOV	0.1866	58%	0.2529	0.2063	0.1901
O5	TD	CLIR	DQT+OOV+OEM	0.2650	83%	0.3338	0.2723	0.2509
O6	**T**	**CLIR**	**DQT+OOV+OEM+Stem**	**0.2915**	**91%**	**0.3672**	**0.2996**	**0.2760**
T6	T	Mono+Text	--	0.2649	100%	0.3109	0.2630	0.2550
O7	T	Monolingual	---	0.2222	84%	0.2000	0.2000	0.3330
O8	T	CLIR	DQT	0.0672	25%	0.0847	0.0706	0.0560
O9	T	CLIR	DQT (Manual selection)	0.0701	26%	0.0950	0.0775	0.0710
O10	T	CLIR	DQT+OOV	0.1607	61%	0.1694	0.1494	0.1490
O11	T	CLIR	DQT + OOV + OEM	0.2121	80%	0.2236	0.1972	0.1965
O12	**T**	**CLIR**	**DQT+OOV+OEM+Stem**	**0.2333**	**88%**	**0.2460**	**0.2169**	**0.2162**

Conclusion and perspectives

We have described an English-to-Bengali CLIR system and showed that the basic dictionary-based method can be significantly improved by using transliteration to accommodate OOV terms. Our system has been evaluated using both a clean (digital) text and an OCR condition, and for the OCR condition modeling of OCR errors has also been shown to significantly improve retrieval effectiveness. Our reliance on affordable statistically trained techniques for stemming, transliteration, and OCR error modeling, suggests that similar techniques could reasonably be tried with any language for which a moderately large bilingual dictionary (and a suitable test collection) are available.

Several significant resources are resulted in from this research. A list of 6,000 English-Bengali proper names has been generated. An English-Bengali transliteration system is now available (the system can easily be modified to a B2E transliteration system). The English-Bengali cleaned dictionary consisting of about 32,000 entries is another sharable resource which is generated under this work. All these resources are made freely available for doing further research in NLP and CLIR involving Bengali. Comparison with stemmed monolingual retrieval suggests that further improvements might be possible in some cases where our present E2B lexicon has gaps. In these cases, our present transliteration system fails to find the correct transliteration. This suggests that continued work on tuning and robustness might be productive. As next steps, we plan to try (i) pre-translation and post-translation blind relevance feedback to improve robustness and (ii) mining comparable corpora to learn additional translation candidates as an additional way of filling lexical gaps.

Acknowledgments

One of the authors thanks the Indo-US Science and Technology Forum for providing him with a support to conduct a part of this research at the University of Maryland. Thanks to Ann Irvine of John Hopkins University and Jiaul Paik of ISI, Kolkata for their kind help.

References

CLEF: The Cross-Language Evaluation Forum. http://clef-campaign.org.

Darwish, K. and Oard, D. (2003). Probabilistic Structured Query Methods, In ACM-SIGIR, pages 338-344.

DeNero, J. and Klein, D. (2007). Tailoring word alignments to syntactic machine translation, In ACL, pages 17-24.

Dictionary: http://www.bengalinux.org/english-to-bengali-dictionary/

FIRE: The Forum for Information Retrieval Evaluation. http://www.isical.ac.in/~clia/

Garain, U., Paik, J., Pal, T., Majumder, P., Doermann, D. and Oard, D. (2011a). Overview of FIRE 2011 RISOT Task, In Forum for Information Retrieval Evaluation (FIRE), Mumbai, India.

Garain, U., Doermann, D. and Oard, D. (2011b). Maryland at FIRE 2011: Retrieval of OCR'd Bengali, In Forum for Information Retrieval Evaluation (FIRE) 2011, Mumbai, India.

Ghosh, K. and Parui, S.K. (2011). Retrieval from OCR text: RISOT track, In Forum for Information Retrieval Evaluation (FIRE) 2011, Mumbai, India.

ICON (2009). NLP Tool Contest: Parsing, In 7th International Conference on Natural Language Processing, Hyderabad, India.

Irvine, A., Callison-Burch, C. and Klementiev, A. (2010). Transliterating From All Languages, In AMTA 2010, Denver, Colorado.

Jagarlamudi, J. and Kumaran, A. (2007). Cross-lingual Information Retrieval System for Indian Languages, In CLEF Workshop.

Lemur: http://www.lemurproject.org/indri/

Leveling, J., Ganguly, D. and Jones, G.J.F. (2010). DCU@FIRE2010: Term Conflation, Blind Relevance Feedback, and Cross-Language IR with Manual and Automatic Query Translation, In Forum for Information Retrieval Evaluation (FIRE) 2010, Ghandhinagar, India.

Li, Z., Callison-Burch, C., Dyer, C., Ganitkevitch, J., Khudanpur, S., Schwartz, L. Thornton, W., Weese, J. and Zaidan, O. (2009). Joshua: An open source toolkit for parsing based machine translation, In EACL 4th Workshop on Statistical Machine Translation, Athens, Greece.

NTCIR: fttp://research.nii.ac.jp/ntcir.

Paik, J., Mitra, M., Parui, S., and Järvelin, K. (2011). GRAS: An Effective and Efficient Stemming Algorithm for Information Retrieval, In ACM Transactions on Information Systems, 29(4).

Pirkola, A. (1998). The Effects of Query Structure and Dictionary Setups in Dictionary-Based Cross-Language Information Retrieval. In ACM SIGIR, Pages 55-63.

Ponte, J.M. and Croft, W.B. (1998). A language modeling approach to information retrieval, In ACM SIGIR, Pages 275-281.

Tseng, Y.-H. and Oard, D.W. (2001). Document Image Retrieval Techniques for Chinese, In Symposium on Document Image Understanding Technology, pages 151-158, Columbia, MD.

Virga, P. and Khudanpur, S. (2003). Transliteration of Proper Names in Cross-Lingual Information Retrieval, In ACL Workshop on Multi-lingual Named Entity Recognition Combining Statistical and Symbolic Models, Sapporo , Japan.

RU-EVAL-2012: Evaluating dependency parsers for Russian

Anastasia Gareyshina[1], Maxim Ionov[1], Olga Lyashevskaya[2], Dmitry Privoznov[1], Elena Sokolova[3], Svetlana Toldova[1,3]

(1) MOSCOW STATE UNIVERSITY, Philological Faculty, Dept. of Theoretical and Applied Linguistics, Leninskie gory, GSP-1, 119991 Moscow, Russia

(2) NATIONAL RESEARCH UNIVERSITY HIGHER SCHOOL OF ECONOMICS, Faculty of Philology, Myasnitskaya 20, 101000 Moscow, Russia

(3) RUSSIAN STATE UNIVERSITY FOR THE HUMANITIES, Institute of Linguistics, Miusskaya pl. 6, GSP-3, 125993 Moscow, Russia

a.r.gare@gmail.com, max.ionov@gmail.com, olesar@gmail.com, dprivoznov@gmail.com, minegot@rambler.ru, toldova@yandex.ru

ABSTRACT

The paper reports on the recent forum RU-EVAL – a new initiative for evaluation of Russian NLP resources, methods and toolkits. It started in 2010 with evaluation of morphological parsers, and the second event RU-EVAL 2012 (2011-2012) focused on syntactic parsing. Eight participating IT companies and academic institutions submitted their results for corpus parsing. We discuss the results of this evaluation and describe the so-called "soft" evaluation principles that allowed us to compare output dependency trees, which varied greatly depending on theoretical approaches, parsing methods, tag sets, and dependency orientations principles, adopted by the participants.

TITLE AND ABSTRACT IN RUSSIAN

RU-EVAL-2012: Оценка парсеров грамматики зависимостей для русского языка

RU-EVAL – это форум по оценке русскоязычных ресурсов, методов и инструментов автоматической обработки текста. Первый этап форума состоялся в 2010 году и был посвящен оценке морфологических парсеров (Lyashevskaya et al. 2010), второй цикл (2011-2012) связан с оценкой синтаксического анализа текста (Toldova et al. 2012). На синтаксическом форуме результаты разметки тестового корпуса в формате синтаксиса зависимостей прислали 8 участников из коммерческих компаний и академических учреждений. В статье описываются принципы «мягкой» оценки, позволившие сравнивать ответы, которые весьма значительно различались как теоретическими подходами и методами парсинга, так и по конкретному составу тегов и направлению зависимостей. Обсуждаются результаты, сложные для оценки случаи, а также некоторые проблемные точки в работе русских синтаксических парсеров, которые выявила экспертиза результатов.

KEYWORDS : Parsing evaluation, dependency grammar, Russian, Russian treebank

KEYWORDS IN RUSSIAN : Оценка синтаксических парсеров, грамматика зависимостей, русский язык, русский трибанк

Proceedings of COLING 2012: Posters, pages 349–360,
COLING 2012, Mumbai, December 2012.

1 RU-EVAL-2012: Оценка парсеров грамматики зависимостей для русского языка

Статья посвящена первому опыту проведения в России форума по оценке методов автоматического синтаксического анализа текстов на русском языке. В задачи форума входило оценить общее положение дел в этой области: какие парсеры русского языка существуют, какие теоретические подходы представлены, каковы средние и максимальные показатели существующих разработок. В статье излагаются основные принципы и проблемы подготовки форума: создание тестовой коллекции и Золотого стандарта (ЗС), проработка заданий и мер оценки, подводятся итоги форума, анализируются результаты сравнения работы синтаксических парсеров, представленных на форуме. Тестовой коллекцией служил корпус из отдельных предложений и последовательностей предложений из художественной и научно-публицистической литературы, а также новостных сообщений общим объемом 1 млн. токенов.

В соревновании участвовали системы: SyntAutom, DictaScope Syntax, SemSin, ЭТАП-3, синтактико-семантический парсер SemanticAnalyzer Group, AotSoft, ABBYY Compreno (DIALOGUE 2012). Один участник, Russian Malt (С.Шаров, Лидс, Великобритания), участвовал вне конкурса, в то время как участник Link Grammar Parser (С. Протасов, Москва) не смог конвертировать результаты в адекватный формат грамматики зависимостей и отказался от участия в соревновании.

Предварительная оценка известных открытых систем синтаксического анализа показала, что большинство парсеров для русского языка базируются на грамматике зависимостей. Анализ пробного разбора 100 предложений, представленного разработчиками – потенциальными участниками форума 2011–2012, показал, что в России системы синтаксического анализа развивались автономно, без использования какого бы то ни было корпуса в качестве эталона. Поскольку расхождения между системами по составу тегов и по принципам установления связей оказались значительными, было принято решение о том, что на данном этапе оцениваться должно только правильное определение системами синтаксически связанных пар словоформ и установление «главного» элемента в паре. Оценивалась правильность приписывания вершины зависимой словоформе (однако, правильность разметки всего предложения не оценивалась).

Результаты, полученные от участников, сравнивались на корпусе ЗС: 800 предложений, случайным образом выбранных из тестовой коллекции и размеченных вручную. Принципы и средства синтаксической разметки, использованные при аннотировании ЗС были сформулированы в (Sokolova 2011; ср. также Hovy and Lavid 2010). Разметка производилась параллельно тремя аннотаторами. Была предпринята попытка свести результаты анализа к общему формату автоматически, однако, больша́я вариативность в сложных случаях не позволила обойтись без ручной проверки.

Использовалось так называемое «мягкое» оценивание: допускались отклонения от ЗС в ответах систем, обусловленные спецификой теоретических или производственных решений, если такие решения проводятся последовательно на всем тестовом корпусе. Для классификации расхождений с ЗС использовалась шкала оценок, включающая как «допустимые» расхождения (расхождения объясняются расхождением в принципиальных решениях системы и ЗС), так и семантически допустимую синтаксическую омонимию.

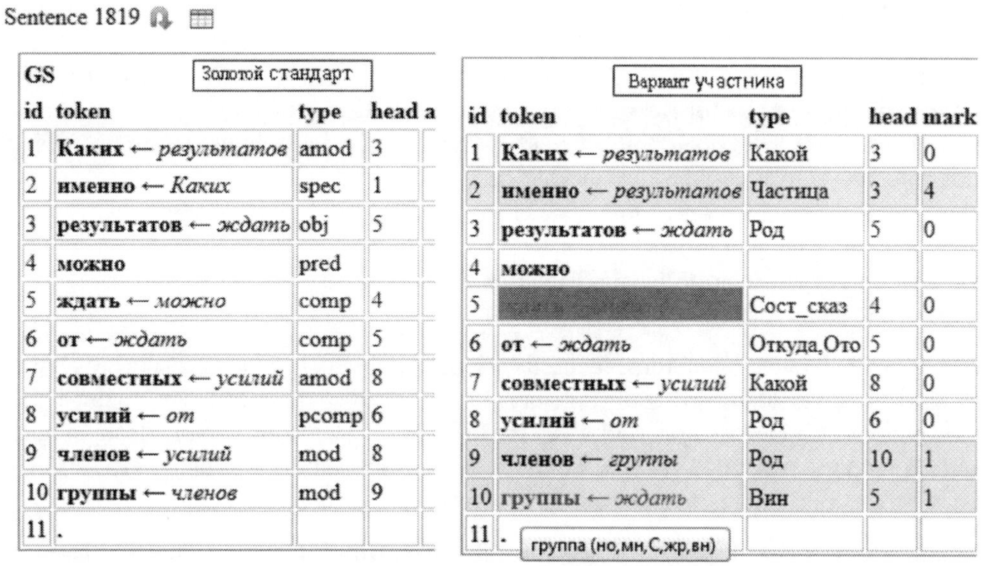

Sentence 1819

GS	Золотой стандарт			
id	token	type	head	a
1	**Каких** ← *результатов*	amod	3	
2	**именно** ← *Каких*	spec	1	
3	**результатов** ← *ждать*	obj	5	
4	**можно**	pred		
5	**ждать** ← *можно*	comp	4	
6	**от** ← *ждать*	comp	5	
7	**совместных** ← *усилий*	amod	8	
8	**усилий** ← *от*	pcomp	6	
9	**членов** ← *усилий*	mod	8	
10	**группы** ← *членов*	mod	9	
11	.			

Вариант участника				
id	token	type	head	mark
1	**Каких** ← *результатов*	Какой	3	0
2	**именно** ← *результатов*	Частица	3	4
3	**результатов** ← *ждать*	Род	5	0
4	**можно**			
5	[redacted]	Сост_сказ	4	0
6	**от** ← *ждать*	Откуда,Ото	5	0
7	**совместных** ← *усилий*	Какой	8	0
8	**усилий** ← *от*	Род	6	0
9	**членов** ← *группы*	Род	10	1
10	**группы** ← *ждать*	Вин	5	1
11	. группа (но,мн,С,жр,вн)			

Рис.1. Сопоставление разметки ЗС и ответа системы с градуальной оценкой (mark).

Результаты оценивались с использованием стандартных мер: точность (P), полнота (R) и F-мера. Точность оценивалась как отношение количества допустимых ответов системы. Результаты Unlabeled Attachment Score составили: Pmax – 0.952, F-мера – 0.967, Pmin – 0.789, F-мера = 0.872, средний результат по всем системам: Pav – 0.88.

Наилучшие результаты достигнуты системами, «обогащенными» семантическими и другими экспертными лингвистическими знаниями. Эти системы создавались большими коллективами высокопрофессиональных лингвистов в течение длительного периода времени. Третья по точности – система Russian Malt, основанная на машинном обучении (MALT). Обучение происходило на трибанке SynTagRus (http://ruscorpora.ru), который, таким образом, обеспечивает машинное обучение с высокими результатами по точности и полноте. Как свидетельствуют остальные результаты, менее дорогие и ресурсозатратные решения также имеют неплохую точность и полноту.

В ходе подготовки и проведения форума были выработаны принципы и методы оценки работы зависимостных парсеров, основанных на разных теоретических принципах. Также были созданы важные ресурсы: (а) ЗС объемом 800 предложений, размеченных вручную; (б) Паралелльный Трибанк, в котором представлена параллельная аннотация тестового корпуса (1 млн. токенов) четырьмя системами с визуализацией и возможностью поиска (оба ресурса представлены в свободном доступе на сайте http://testsynt.soiza.com).

Опыт проведения форума показал, что автоматический синтаксический анализ для языков типа русского имеет целый ряд особенностей, связанных с развитой морфологией и богатой омонимией на уровне форм, а также со свободным порядком слов. Эти обстоятельства существенным образом влияют не только на специфику разработки, но и на специфику проведения сравнения между системами. На сегодняшний день наиболее распространённые и успешные методы преодоления данных трудностей и методы борьбы с синтаксической омонимией – это учет ограничений на лексическую сочетаемость и усиление статистическими процедурами лингвистических компонентов, основанных на правилах.

2 Introduction

The NLP Evaluation forum RU–EVAL started in 2010 as a new initiative aimed at independent evaluation of NLP systems for Russian. The second evaluation campaign (2011–2012) is focused on syntactic parsing. It is open both to academic institutions and industrial companies, and its general objective is to assess the current state-of-the-art in the field and promote the development of syntactic technologies. The forum has also an educational component: the expert group includes students who plan to work in the field of computational linguistics. The forum provides a good opportunity for them to have a hands-on experience of how the NLP tools work, and to see their strong and weak sides.

The first NLP Evaluation forum focused on morphological taggers (see http://ru-eval.ru, Lyashevskaya et al. 2010), bringing together 15 participants from Moscow, Saint-Petersburg, Yekaterinburg, Ukraine, Belarus and UK. In 2011-2012, syntactic parsing technologies were evaluated (Toldova et al. 2012). It was the first time such evaluation was held in Russia. This task turned out to be much more complicated than morphological taggers evaluation.

The main features for Russian parsers are the following: they are mostly based on the dependency trees representation, they are rule-based, and there is no uniform annotation scheme for such systems. The controversial issues we faced while working out the evaluation routine for Russian parsers could be explained first of all by some peculiarities of Slavic languages: Russian is a morphologically rich language with a rather free word order. In fact, word order is mostly triggered by information flow (e.g. topic-focus hierarchy, prominence of participants in a profiled frame, emphasis etc.), though there exist some 'neutral word order' patterns, grounded in certain discourse registers (question, beginning of narrative, etc.) and individual morphosyntactic structures (such as Dative construction). Since frame relations are mainly encoded by grammatical case and prepositions, the role of word order in the recognition of semantic-syntactic relations shrinks dramatically. So, it is not surprising that a wide variety of formalisms and principles of syntactic structure representation are used for parsing Russian texts. There are considerable differences in parsing outputs, depending mainly on the end task of the NLP system.

Since the majority of potential participants develop the dependency parsers, only dependency trees were evaluated. The overall procedure was organized as follows: participants received a tokenized text collection, processed it in their systems and sent the result back in a unified format. Precision and recall was assessed by comparing the result against the manually tagged Gold Standard (GS). The expertise of the task output was performed semi-automatically with subsequent double manual check.

Section 3 presents possible approaches to evaluating Russian syntactic parsers and critical points that should be taken into consideration. Section 4 reports on track design, the board of participants, datasets for the training, task and test collections, evaluation measures and results. In Section 5, we discuss most systematic cases of variation in the output as well as some crucial points that still pose a problem for many Russian parsers.

3 Approaches to evaluating Russian syntactic parsing

A preliminary study on the current state of syntactic parsing for Russian has shown that most of the systems use the dependency grammar representation. Given this, dependency trees were chosen as an output format, and those participants who used mixed dependency-constituency representation or other formalisms, were asked to convert their results.

The general practice suggests that the organizers provide a syntactic treebank ready to use as a GS; this provides also a standard tag set, namely, names and types of relations. Moreover, most developers use these corpora for building their systems, especially if the system is ML-aided. For example, in EVALITA, Turin University Treebank (TUT) is used, that is tagged with respect to both formalisms: dependency grammar and phrase structure grammar. Using the sentences from such treebanks as a test corpus also simplifies the procedure of automatic assessment.

During the organization we relied upon similar evaluation events (EVALITA and other mentioned in Section 2). However, we could not simply use the main principles of EVALITA per se for the reasons mentioned below. We did not take into account morphological and syntactical tags (despite the fact that we included them into the output to make the manual evaluation easier).

For the dependency tree parsing tracks, participants got the text corpus split into sentences and tokens. The task was to mark the syntactic head and the type of syntactic relation for each word.

The analysis of the 100-sentence test sample, parsed by potential participants of the forum 2011–2012, showed that in Russia, syntactic parsing systems developed autonomously, without using any corpus as a GS. As a result, differences between the systems in both tag sets and principles of tagging were so significant that on several issues there could not be proposed any single solution for data output format. Therefore, at this point, we decided to assess only syntactic pairs detection and detection of their syntactic heads. In addition, we decided that theoretically motivated divergences should not be evaluated as errors.

The main assumption of the expertise was the following: there is no single 'correct' answer to complicated questions, and there is no 'correct' parsing algorithm. We tried to mark as wrong only those parses that were motivated neither by theoretical nor by practical decisions. In many cases, the solution to a complicated syntax problem depends on the end goal of the system. There were also some problematic cases which did not have a single solution. After a comparison of results, produced by different parsers, the list of problematic cases for syntactic analysis and methods for their processing were specified.

4 Participants, data sets and results

4.1 Participants

Eleven NLP groups from Moscow, St. Petersburg, Nizhniy Novgorod (Russia), Donetsk (Ukraine), and Leeds (UK) expressed their interest in participating in both tracks. These were systems that use dependency parsing, phrase structure parsing, link grammar and mixed approaches. The answers were submitted by eight groups: SyntAutom (A.Antonova and A.Misyurev, Moscow), DictaScope Syntax (Dictum, Nizhniy Novgorod), SemSin (K.Boyarsky, E.Kanevsky, St.Petersburg), ETAP-3 (Kharkevich Institute for Information Transmission Problems RAS, Moscow), syntactical-semantic analyzer from the SemanticAnalyzer Group (D.Kan, St.Petersburg), AotSoft (V.Vasilyev, Moscow), Compreno (ABBYY, Moscow), Russian Malt (S.Sharoff, Leeds; participated out of competition). One of the participants (namely, Link Grammar Parser (S.Protasov, Moscow)) had not succeeded in converting results to output format, thus there were seven participants involved in the final assessment.

4.2 Test collections and tasks

Evaluation corpus consisted of untagged texts of different types. Corpus for the main track consisted of fiction, news, non-fiction and texts from social networks (5%). There were both separate sentences (0.2 MW from the open collection of the Russian National Corpus) and text fragments. Corpus for news track consisted of text fragments from the ROMIP news collection. These were sequences of three sentences picked randomly. All sentences were tokenized and indexed.

Participants were to markup a syntactic head for each token. Correctness of parsing the whole sentence was irrelevant, only correctness of choosing the head was evaluated. Assessment was conducted on a GS subcorpus which included about 800 randomly selected sentences (500 for the main collection and 300 for the news collection) that had been manually tagged (see section 3.5).

4.3 Input and output format

Input data were in two different formats: plain-text without any markup, and XML with numeration and detailed tokenization. Tokenization and numeration allowed us to simplify the assessment procedure, making it semi-automatic. Plain-text was provided to the participants who take plain-text as the input.

Output format was also specified. Sentence and token numeration should match numeration in the input file, for each token there should be: a number of syntactic head token, relation type and, optionally, morphological tags (provided for experts so that they could analyze reasons of mismatches with GS).

4.4 Gold Standard

Before the assessment, the GS was tagged manually using the tagging tool created by Maxim Ionov. Each sentence was independently tagged by two experts, then divergences were discussed, if any, and the common decision was made. Then the result was checked by the third expert. Such procedure allowed us to achieve three aims. First, it helped to minimize the fraction of arguably tagged tokens. Second, organizers wanted to avoid 'overfitting': getting the experts used to common error of the specific system and omitting errors by not noticing them. Third, tagging was supposed to give the experts the basic knowledge about difficult cases and to help them form criteria for evaluating mismatches.

The group of experts developed the tag set and principles of manual annotation based on (Sokolova 2011; see also Hovy and Lavid 2010). Since uniformity of tagging performed by several people was the main concern, the annotators were asked to choose, among other possible decisions, the most natural one which would correspond to the most popular understanding of the sentence in a possible context. The simpler and clearer decisions are, the more inter-annotator agreement score they provide.

4.5 Evaluation measures

The common evaluation strategy is to compare the output of the parsers to the GS test set (cf. CONLL and EVALITA, Buchholz and Marsi 2006, Nivre et al. 2007, Bosco and Mazzei 2012). The test sets usually are based on a treebank used for the development of the parsers. As it was mentioned above, there is no comparable generally accepted treebank for Russian. Moreover, there is a great variation in labelling syntactic relations and even in the head-modifier relations through parsers. For these reasons the only Unlabeled Attachment Score measure was taken into account. In the dependency parsing each token in the sentence is assigned the only one Head ID. Thus, the precision could be measured as the percentage of tokens with correct or "admissible" heads. As noted above, we considered certain kinds of mismatches between the GS variant and the system response as acceptable.

The assessment assumed comparing the ID number on the tagged head for each token with the corresponding number in the GS. The match was automatically marked as 0. Mismatches (along with matches, however) were given to the experts for further examination. They could mark a mismatch as:

1 — system error
2 — GS error
3 — acceptable mismatch (theoretical difference between the system and the GS)
4 — acceptable mismatch (in case of homonymy)
5 — the response matches the GS, but they are both wrong
6 — syntactic head is not specified for the token, but it should be specified
7 — syntactic head is not specified for the token, and could be omitted
8 — uncertain
9 — other (cases that do not fall into categories 1–8).

There were a significant number of mismatches in choices of syntactic relation directions among parsers. These were not mistakes but decisions made during the systems' development, so they could not be qualified as errors. For the purpose of simplification of assessment, the participants agreed to unify relation directions in some cases, such as: (1) preposition – noun; (2) auxiliary verb – lexical verb; (3) relations in coordinating constructions.

However, the other dependencies had to be consistent with the decisions concerning such relation directions. For example, if auxiliary verbs were taken to be heads, then subjects had to be dependents of auxiliary verbs, whereas if main verbs were considered heads, then subjects had to be dependents of main verbs; in the case of coordination, it was the phrase heads established by a system that had to be conjoined, e.g. if noun (noun phrase) was considered a head of a prepositional phrase, then only nouns (noun phrases) could be conjoined, for prepositional phrases to form a coordinated structure. We did not penalize such decisions, should they be not unified, – again, provided that they (and the "outer" dependencies) were consistent throughout the output. When relation directions were unified and converted to the GS format, but there were still "old" mismatches with "outer" dependencies (i.e. relation directions were updated so as to fit the GS format, but their dependencies were not), such cases were treated as artifacts – conversion errors.

The number of such cases was significant, so they required further detailed assessment. After the developers got access to their intermediate scores, they sent some comments, which proved to be of great help in improving the assessment design. But even then we could not fully eliminate 'false positives', where penalty was assigned by mistake (see Section 5 for the discussion of some difficulties that we had to face).

4.6 Results

The results of the main track are shown in table 2. According to the "soft" evaluation measures the best result has been achieved by ABBYY Compreno (precision 0,952, F-measure 0,967). The results of the ETAP–3 system are slightly lower. The average precision was 88,8.

Mask name	P	R	F1	System Name
Trieste	0,952	0,983	0,967	Compreno
Marceille	0,933	0,981	0,956	ETAP–3
Barcelona	0,895	0,980	0,935	SyntAutom
Toulon	0,889	0,947	0,917	SemSyn
Brega	0,863	0,980	0,917	Dictum
Nice	0,856	0,860	0,858	SemanticAnalyzer Group
Napoli	0,789	0,975	0,872	AotSoft

TABLE 1 – Dependency parsing, main track evaluation.

The best results have been achieved by two systems that developed their parsers on the basis of manual rule-based approach, enriched with a thoroughly elaborated semantic component by teams of linguist experts. However, low-time-consuming systems, such as SyntAutom, have also proved to be reliable. One of the systems, Russian Malt, was based on the machine-learning technology. It used the SynTagRus Treebank (http://ruscorpora.ru) as a learning corpus and achieved the third-highest results (the results are not shown in the chart since the system participated out of competition). In the next section we will discuss in detail some questions touched upon during RU-EVAL 2012 and the difficulties that we had to face.

5 Discussion

5.1 Variation in parsing

As it has been mentioned above, the systems vary significantly with respect to tag sets and dependency assignment rules. It is only in the simplest cases (e.g. attributes that agree with nouns) that there is hardly any variation at all. More often, the systems process a particular construction in several different ways. For instance, while in some parsers simple clauses can be connected with each other by means of establishing a syntactic relation between their verbal heads, other analyzers parse a complex sentence by linking its simple clauses with a subordinating conjunction.

What is more important, there can be cases where there is no uniform theoretical decision within dependency formalism. Sometimes it generally remains unclear which one of the units of the syntactic relation is the head or dependent (Iomdin 1990, Gladkij 1973). Such ambiguities emerge when different criterions on head-dependent distinction yield different results (Testelets 2001), or not a single criterion is applicable.

(1) *(pol'zovat'sya)* velikimi(Adj1) i *udivitel'nymi*(Adj2) blagami(N)

(use) wonderful and great amenities

A. N → i; i → Adj1; i → Adj2; B. N → Adj1; Adj1 → i → Adj2;

C. N → Adj1; Adj1 → i; Adj1 → Adj2; D. N → Adj1; Adj1 → Adj2; Adj2 → i.

The coordinated structure in (1) can be parsed in several ways: a conjunction can be treated as a head itself (A); the coordinated group can form a linear dependent-head chain (B); it can be treated as a dependent on any element in the coordinated group (C and D). For this example, no parsing result can be argued to be a system error, as long as the whole coordinated structure is successfully parsed in a consistent way.

Further steps should be taken to reduce variation in dependency relations labels so that tag assignment evaluation could be performed. There is a considerable variation in classifications of dependency relations: some of them are based on morphological properties of the head or of the dependent while others rely upon general syntactic functions of a given word form. For example, one system has the tag 'card' (cardinal) for encoding the numeral-noun dependency; in other systems, quantifier is just an instance of a noun modifier. Merging different classifications is still a goal to be achieved.

5.2 Qualitative output analysis: some problem cases

After we had analyzed all systems' answers, we came to the conclusion that there were no 'universal problem cases' – cases that cannot be properly parsed with all systems, and that conclusion is a pleasant fact indeed. A special case example here would be prepositional dependents (it can have verb as a head irrespective of weather it is an argument or an adjunct or a noun as a dependent in an NP). If there are several head candidates in a sentence, the parsers choose either the first noun preceding prepositional dependent, or verbal head, or the closest finite verb in a tree. Yet many thus generated variants are not semantically admissible, compare acceptable examples (2A-C), (3A-B) to inacceptable ones (2D), (3C):

(2) Google prodolzhaet *ukrepljat'* pozicii na rynke
GoogleNOM.SG continues strengthen.INF position.ACC.PLon market.LOC.SG

prilozhenij dlja sovmestnoj raboty.
application.GEN.PL for collaborative.GEN.SG work.GEN.SG

"Google continues strengthening positions on the market of applications for collaborative work".

A. Ok pozicii 'position.ACC.PL' → na rynke 'on market.LOC.SG'
B. Ok ukrepljat' 'strengthen.INF' → na rynke 'on market.LOC.SG'
C. Ok prilozhenij 'application.GEN.PL' → dlja sovmestnoj raboty 'for collaborative.GEN.SG work.GEN.SG'
D. * *ukrepljat'* → dlja sovmestnoj raboty 'for collaborative.GEN.SG work.GEN.SG'

(3) chto mozhet *dobit'sja* svojej celi *lish'* pri
that can achieve.INF REFL.POSS.GEN.SG goal.GEN.SG only at

odnom uslovii...
one.LOC.SG condition.LOC.SG

'...that [he] can achieve his goal only on a single condition...'

A. Ok *dobit'sj*a 'achieve.INF' → pri uslovii 'on condition.LOC.SG'
B. Ok mozhet 'can' → pri uslovii 'on condition.LOC.SG'
C. * celi 'goal.GEN.SG' → pri uslovii 'on condition.LOC.SG'

There are certainly much more errors in complex sentences. Among the most typical problem cases is establishing the simple (dependent) clause head in a clause that precedes the dependent one. Similarly, nominal and copular heads may not be regarded as possible candidates for being a clause head. Finally, quite often are the cases when a distant dependent is connected to a hypothetical head across the clause boundary and the cases when heads remain undefined for words absent from the system dictionary (words and abbreviations like "OC", "Intel" etc.).

Conclusion

The RU-EVAL 2012 has brought together a considerable number of IT companies and academic groups that work on Russian syntax parsing, and made it possible to assess the state-of-the-art in the field (so far, mostly in Russia). The forum has shown that the majority of parsers for Russian are based on dependency formalism. They are rule-based.

The event has the following practical outcomes:

- A manually tagged standard set, consisting of 800 sentences, is made available through testsynt.soiza.com; the guidelines for tagging according to GS principles have been compiled and tested.
- Variations in theoretical and practical decisions between existing parsers have been registered.
- The treebank with parallel annotation (1 mln. tokens, annotated by four participants) is made available at http://testsynt.soiza.com; it is presumed that the treebank can enable reliable machine learning for parsing.

The RU-EVAL 2012 has shown that there are three basic approaches to parsing for Russian:

1. systems, manually enriched with expert linguistic knowledge (Compreno, ETAP-3);
2. automata-based systems (SyntAutom);
3. machine-learning systems.

The manually enriched with rules systems have shown the best results. However, low-time-consuming systems, such as SyntAutom, have also proved to be reliable. The results have also demonstrated that there exists at least one Russian treebank that enables reliable machine learning for parsing Russian (the Russian Malt system). Although Russian is a free-word order language with a rich morphology, the quality of syntactic parsing is quite high. The majority of Russian parsers override the difficulties due to lack of word order constraints by developing semantic components and integrating statistical approaches into the rule-based systems. The best result has been demonstrated by the system that heavily depended on semantic components and took into consideration the semantic constraints on lexeme co-occurrence.

Acknowledgments

The work was partly supported by Corpus Linguistics Program of the Presidium of Russian Academy of Sciences. We would like to thank Irina Astaf'eva, Anastasia Bonch-Osmolovskaya, Julia Grishina, Anna Koroleva, Pavel Koval', Anna Lityagina, Natalia Men'shikova, Alexandra Semenovskaya, Eugenia Sidorova, Lyubov' Tupikina who took part in all stages of evaluation routine as experts and annotators. We are also most grateful to the participants of the forum.

References

Bosco, C. and Mazzei, A. (2012). The EVALITA 2011 parsing task: the dependency track. In *EVALITA'11 Working Notes*, Roma.

Buchholz, S., Marsi E. (2006). CoNLL-X Shared Task on Multilingual Dependency Parsing. In Proceedings of the CoNLL-X. New York, NY, pages 149-164.

DIALOGUE (2012). Computational linguistics and intellectual technologies. Proceedings of the International Workshop Dialogue'2012. Vol. 11 (18). Part 2. Moscow, pages 77-131.

Gladkij, A.V. (1973). *Formal'nye grammatiki i jazyki* [Formal Grammars and Languages], Moscow, Nauka.

Hovy, E. and Lavid, Ju. (2010). Towards a 'science' of corpus annotation: a new methodological challenge for corpus linguistics. International journal of translation, 22 (1): 1–25.

Iomdin, L.L. (1990). Avtomaticheskaja obrabotka teksta na estestvennom jazyke: *model'soglasovanija* [Natural Language Processing: a Model of Agreement]. Moscow, Nauka.

Lyashevskaya, O., Astafeva, I., Bonch-Osmolovskaya, A., Garejshina, A., Grishina, Ju., D'jachkov, V., Ionov, M., Koroleva, A., Kudrinsky, M., Lityagina, A., Luchina, E., Sidorova, E., Toldova, S., Savchuk, S., and Koval', S. (2010). Ocenka metodov avtomaticheskogo analiza teksta: morfologicheskije parsery russkogo jazyka [NLP evaluation: Russian morphological parsers], in Computational linguistics and intellectual technologies. Proceedings of the International Workshop Dialogue'2010. Vol. 9 (16). Moscow, pages 318–326.

Toldova, S., Sokolova E., Astaf'eva I., Gareyshina A., Koroleva A., Privoznov D., Sidorova E., Tupikina L., and Lyashevskaya O. (2012). Ocenka metodov avtomaticheskogo analiza teksta 2011-2012: sintaksicheskie parsery russkogo jazyka [NLP evaluation 2011-2012: Russian syntactic parsers]. In Computational linguistics and intellectual technologies. Proceedings of the International Workshop Dialogue'2012. Vol. 11 (18). Moscow, pages 797-809.

Nivre, J., Hall, J., Kübler, S., McDonald, R., Nilsson, J., Riedel, S., and Yuret, D. (2007). The CoNLL 2007 Shared Task on Dependency Parsing. In Proceedings of EMNLP-CoNLL. Prauge, Czech Republic, pages 915-932.

ROMIP. (2009). Rossijskij seminar po ocenke metodov informacionnogo poiska. Trudy ROMIP 2009, Petrozavodsk, 16 sentjabrja 2009 [Russian Information Retrieval Evaluation Seminar. Proceedings of ROMIP 2009, Petrozavodsk, September 16, 2009]. Saint–Petersburg, NU CSI.

Sokolova, E. (2011). Sintaksicheskaja razmetka v terminax grammatiki zavisimostej i sintaksicheskix funkcij [Syntactic annotation in terms of dependency grammar and syntactic functions], Moscow, RGGU, available at: http://elib.lib.rsuh.ru/elib/000003603.pdf

Testelets Ja.G. (2001). Vvedenie v obshchij sintaksis [Introduction to general syntax], Moscow, RGGU.

Assessing Sentiment Strength in Words Prior Polarities

Lorenzo Gatti[1] *Marco Guerini*[1]
(1) TRENTO-RISE, 38123 Povo, Trento, Italy
lorenzo.gatti@trentorise.eu, marco.guerini@trentorise.eu

ABSTRACT
Many approaches to sentiment analysis rely on lexica where words are tagged with their prior polarity - i.e. if a word out of context evokes something positive or something negative. In particular, broad-coverage resources like SentiWordNet provide polarities for (almost) every word. Since words can have multiple senses, we address the problem of how to compute the prior polarity of a word starting from the polarity of each sense and returning its *polarity strength* as an index between -1 and 1. We compare 14 such formulae that appear in the literature, and assess which one best approximates the human judgement of prior polarities, with both regression and classification models.

TITLE AND ABSTRACT IN ITALIAN

Valutazione dell'intensità emotiva delle parole nelle polarità a-priori

Molti approcci alla sentiment analysis fanno affidamento su lessici in cui le parole sono contrassegnate con la loro polarità a-priori - ossia, se una parola fuori contesto evoca qualcosa di positivo o qualcosa di negativo. In particolare, risorse a copertura ampia come SentiWordNet forniscono le polarità per (quasi) ogni parola. Poiché le parole possono avere molteplici sensi, dobbiamo affrontare il problema di come calcolare la polarità a-priori di una parola partendo dalla polarità di ogni suo senso e restituendo la sua *intensità emotiva* sotto forma di un indice compreso tra -1 e 1. In questo articolo, confrontiamo 14 di queste formule, apparse nella letteratura, e stabiliamo quale di esse approssimi meglio il giudizio degli umani sulle polarità a-priori, sia con modelli di regressione che di classificazione.

KEYWORDS: Prior Polarities, Sentiment Analysis, SentiWordNet.
KEYWORDS IN ITALIAN: Polarità a-priori, Sentiment Analysis, SentiWordNet.

Proceedings of COLING 2012: Posters, pages 361–370,
COLING 2012, Mumbai, December 2012.

1 Introduction

Many approaches to sentiment analysis use bag of words resources - i.e. a lexicon of positive and negative words. In these lexica, words are tagged with their prior polarity, that represents how a word is perceived out of context, i.e. if it evokes something positive or something negative. For example, *wonderful* has a positive connotation - prior polarity -, and *horrible* has a negative prior polarity. The advantage of these approaches is that they don't need deep semantic analysis or word sense disambiguation to assign an affective score to a word and are domain independent (so, less precise but portable).

Unfortunately, many of these resources are manually built and have a limited coverage. To overcome this limitation and to provide prior polarities for (almost) every word, other broad-coverage resources - built in a semi-automatic way - have been developed, such as SentiWordNet (Esuli and Sebastiani, 2006). Since words can have multiple senses and SentiWordNet provides polarities for each sense, there is the need for "reconstructing" prior polarities starting from the various word senses polarities (also called 'posterior polarities'). For example, the adjective *cold* has a posterior polarity for the meaning "having a low temperature" - like in "*cold* beer" - that is different from the polarity in "*cold* person" that refers to "being emotionless". Different formulae have been used in the previous literature to compute prior polarities (e.g. considering the posterior polarity of the most frequent sense, averaging over the various posterior polarities, etc.), but no comparison or analysis has ever been tried among them. Furthermore, since such formulae are often used as baseline methods for sentiment classification, there is the need to define a state-of-the-art performance level for approaches relying on SentiWordNet.

The paper is structured as follows: in Section 2 we briefly describe our approach and how it differentiates from similar sentiment analysis tasks. Then, in Section 3 we present SentiWordNet and overview various formulae appeared in the literature, which rely on this resource to compute words prior polarity. In Section 4 we introduce the ANEW resource that will be used as a gold standard. From section 5 to 7 we present a series of experiments to asses how good SentiWordNet is for computing prior polarities and which formula, if any, best approximates human judgement. Finally in Section 8 we try to understand whether the findings about formulae performances can be extended from the regression framework to a classification task.

2 Proposed Approach

In this paper we face the problem of assigning affective scores (between -1 and 1) to words. This problem is harder than traditional binary classification tasks (assessing whether a word - or a fragment of text - is either *positive* or *negative*), see (Pang and Lee, 2008) or (Liu and Zhang, 2012) for an overview. We want to asses not only that *pretty*, *beautiful* and *gorgeous* are positive words, but also that *gorgeous* is more positive than *beautiful* which, in turn, is more positive than *pretty*. This is fundamental for tasks such as affective modification of existing texts, where not only words polarity, but also their strength, is necessary for creating multiple "graded" variations of the original text (Guerini et al., 2008). Some of the few works that address the problem of sentiment strength are presented in (Wilson et al., 2004; Paltoglou et al., 2010), however, their approach is modeled as a multi-class classification problem (*neutral*, *low*, *medium* or *high* sentiment) at the sentence level, rather than a regression problem at the word level. Other works, see for example (Neviarouskaya et al., 2011), use a fine grained classification approach too, but they consider emotion categories (*anger*, *joy*, *fear*, etc.), rather than sentiment strength categories.

On the other hand, even if approaches that go beyond pure prior polarities - e.g. using word bigram features (Wang and Manning, 2012) - are better for sentiment analysis tasks, there are tasks that are intrinsically based on the notion of words prior polarity. Consider for example the task of naming, where evocative names are a key element to a successful business (Ozbal and Strapparava, 2012; Ozbal et al., 2012). In such cases no context is given for the name and the brand name alone, with its perceived prior polarity, is responsible for stating the area of competition and evoking semantic associations.

3 SentiWordNet

One of the most widely used resources for sentiment analysis is SentiWordNet (Esuli and Sebastiani, 2006). SentiWordNet is a lexical resource in which each word is associated with three numerical scores: `Obj(s)`, `Pos(s)` and `Neg(s)`. These scores represent the objective, positive and negative valence of the entry respectively. Each entry takes the form `lemma#pos#sense-number`, where the first sense corresponds to the most frequent.

Obviously, different word senses can have different polarities. In Table 1, the first 5 senses of `cold#a` present all possible combinations: a negative score only (`cold#a#1` and `cold#a#2`), a positive and objective score only (`cold#a#5`, `cold#a#3`), and mixed scores (`cold#a#4`). Intuitively, mixed scores for the same sense are acceptable, like in "*cold* beer" vs. "*cold* pizza".

PoS	Offset	PosScore	NegScore	SynsetTerms
a	1207406	0.0	0.75	cold#a#1
a	1212558	0.0	0.75	cold#a#2
a	1024433	0.0	0.0	cold#a#3
a	2443231	0.125	0.375	cold#a#4
a	1695706	0.625	0.0	cold#a#5

Table 1: First five *SentiWordNet* entries for `cold#a`

3.1 Prior Polarities Formulae

In this section we review the main strategies for computing prior polarities from the previous literature. All the prior polarities formulae provided below come in two different versions (except *uni* and *rnd*). Given a lemma with n senses (`lemma#pos#n`), every formula f is applied - separately - to all the n `posScores` and `negScores` of the `lemma#pos`; once the prior polarities for positive and negative scores are computed according to that formula, to map the result to a single polarity score (that can be either positive or negative), the possibility is:

1. $f_m = MAX(|posScore|, |negScore|)$ - take the max of the two scores
2. $f_d = |posScore| - |negScore|$ - take the difference of the two scores

Both versions range from -1 to 1. So, considering the first 5 senses of `cold#a` in Table 1, the various formulae will compute `posScore(cold#a)` starting from the values $<0.0, 0.0, 0.0, 0.125, 0.625>$ and `negScore(cold#a)` starting from $<0.750, 0.750, 0.0, 0.375, 0.0>$. Then either f_m or f_d will be applied to `posScore(cold#a)` and `negScore(cold#a)` to compute the final polarity strength. For the sake of simplicity, we will describe how to compute the *posScore* of a given lemma, since *negScore* can be easily derived. In details *posScore* stands for `posScore(lemma#pos)`, while $posScore_i$ indicates the positive score for the ith sense of the `lemma#pos`.

rnd. This formula represents the baseline random approach. It simply returns a random number between -1 and 1 for any given `lemma#pos`.

swrnd. This formula represents an advanced random approach that incorporates some "knowledge" from SentiWordNet. It returns the `posScore` and `negScores` of a random sense of the `lemma#pos` under scrutiny. We believe this is a fairer baseline than *rnd* since SentiWordNet information can possibly constrain the values. A similar approach has been used in (Qu et al., 2008), even though the authors used the polarity information from the first match of the term in the SentiWordNet synsets list - i.e. ignoring senses order - rather than a pure random sense.

$$posScore = posScore_i \quad \text{where} \quad i = RANDOM(1, n) \tag{1}$$

fs. In this formula only the first (and thus most frequent) sense is considered for the given `lemma#pos`. This is equivalent to asking for `lemma#pos#1` SentiWordNet scores. Based on (Neviarouskaya et al., 2009), (Agrawal et al., 2009) and (Guerini et al., 2008) (that uses the fs_m approach), this is the most basic form of prior polarities.

$$posScore = posScore_1 \tag{2}$$

mean. It calculates the mean of the positive and negative scores for all the senses of the given `lemma#pos`, and then returns either the biggest or the difference of the two scores. Used for example in (Thet et al., 2009), (Denecke, 2009) and (Devitt and Ahmad, 2007). An approach explicitly based on $mean_d$ is instead presented in (Sing et al., 2012).

$$posScore = \frac{\sum_{i=1}^{n} posScore_i}{n} \tag{3}$$

senti. This formula is an advanced version of the simple mean, and concludes that only senses with a score $\neq 0$ should be considered in the mean:

$$posScore = \frac{\sum_{i=1}^{n} posScore_i}{numPos} \tag{4}$$

where $numPos$ and $numNeg$ are the number of senses that have, respectively, a $posScore > 0$ or $negScore < 0$ value. It is based on (Fahrni and Klenner, 2008) and (Neviarouskaya et al., 2009).

uni. This method, based on (Neviarouskaya et al., 2009) extends the previous formula, by choosing the MAX between $posScore$ and $negScore$. In case $posScore$ is equal to $negScore$ (modulus) the one with the highest weight is selected, where weights are defined as

$$posWeight = \frac{numPos}{n} \tag{5}$$

As mentioned before, this is the only method, together with *rnd*, for which we cannot take the difference of the two means, as it decides which mean ($posScore$ or $negScore$) to return according to the weight.

w1. This formula weighs each sense with a geometric series of ratio 1/2. The rationale behind this choice is based on the assumption that more frequent senses should bear more "affective weight" than very rare senses, when computing the prior polarity of a word. The system presented in (Chaumartin, 2007) uses a similar approach of weighted mean.

$$posScore = \frac{\sum_{i=1}^{n}(\frac{1}{2^{i-1}} \times posScore_i)}{n} \tag{6}$$

w2. Similar to the previous one, this formula weighs each lemma with a harmonic series, see for example (Denecke, 2008):

$$posScore = \frac{\sum_{i=1}^{n}(\frac{1}{i} \times posScore_i)}{n} \tag{7}$$

4 ANEW

To asses how well prior polarity formulae perform, a gold standard is needed, with word polarities provided by human annotators. Resources, such as sentiment-bearing words from the General Inquirer lexicon (Stone et al., 1966) are not suitable for our purpose since they provide only a binomial classification of words (either *positive* or *negative*). The resource presented in (Wilson et al., 2005) uses a similar binomial annotation for single words; another potentially useful resource is WordNetAffect (Strapparava and Valitutti, 2004) but it labels terms with affective dimensions (*anger*, *joy*, *fear*, etc.) rather than assigning a sentiment score.

We then choose ANEW (Bradley and Lang, 1999), a resource developed to provide a set of normative emotional ratings for a large number of words (roughly 1 thousand) in the English language. It contains a set of words that have been rated in terms of pleasure (affective valence), arousal, and dominance. In particular for our task we considered the valence dimension. Since words were presented to subjects in isolation (i.e. no context was provided) this resource represents a human validation of prior polarities strength for the given words, and can be used as a gold standard. For each word ANEW provides two main metrics: $anew_\mu$, which correspond to the average of annotators votes, and $anew_\sigma$ that gives the variance in annotators scores for the given word. In the same way these metrics are also provided for the male/female annotator groups.

5 Dataset pre-processing

In order to use the ANEW dataset to measure prior polarities formulae performance, we had to align words to the `lemma#pos` format that SentiWordNet uses. First we removed from ANEW those words that did not align with SentiWordNet. The adopted procedure was as follows: for each word, check if it is present among SentiWordNet lemmas; if this is not the case, lemmatize the word with TextPro (Pianta et al., 2008) and check again if the lemma is present[1]. If it is not found, remove the word from the list (this was the case for about 30 words of the 1034 present in ANEW).

The remaining 1004 lemmas were then associated with the PoS present in SentiWordNet to get the final `lemma#pos`. Note that a lemma can have more than one PoS, for example, 'writer' is

[1]We didn't lemmatize words in advance to avoid duplications (for example, if we lemmatize the ANEW entry 'addicted', we obtain 'addict', which is already present in ANEW).

present only as a noun (`writer#n`), while 'yellow' is present as a verb, a noun and an adjective (`yellow#v`, `yellow#n`, `yellow#a`). This gave us a list of 1494 words in the `lemma#pos` format. For each word, we tested the metrics described in Section 3.1 and annotated the results.

6 Evaluation Metrics

Given a formula for the prior polarities (f), we consider two different metrics to asses how well a formula performs on the ANEW dataset. The first metric is the Mean Absolute Error (*MAE*), that averages the error of the given formula on each ANEW entry. So given n words w, we compute *MAE* as follows:

$$MAE = \frac{\sum_{i=1}^{n} |f(w_i) - anew_\mu(w_i)|}{n} \tag{8}$$

In multi-class classification problems a similar approach, based on Mean Squared Error (MSE), is used (based on a fixed threshold): if the strength of a sentence is high, classifying it as neutral (off by 3) is a much worse error than classifying it as medium (off by 1), (Wilson et al., 2004). The second metric, instead, tries to asses the percentage of successes of a given formula in assigning correct values to a word:

$$success = \frac{\sum_{i=1}^{n} [|f(w_i) - anew_\mu(w_i)| < \frac{1}{2} anew_\sigma(w_i)]}{n} = \frac{\sum_{i=1}^{n} [-\frac{1}{2} < zscore(w_i) < \frac{1}{2}]}{n} \tag{9}$$

Success, for a given word, is obtained when its *z-score* is between -0.5 and 0.5, i.e. the value returned by the formula, for the given word w_i, falls within one standard deviation $anew_\sigma(w_i)$ centered on the ANEW value. Assessing success according to the ANEW variance has the advantage of taking into account whether the given word has a high degree of agreement among annotators or not: for words with low variance (high annotator agreement) we need formulae values to be more precise. This approach is in line with other approaches on affective annotation that either assume one standard deviation (Grimm and Kroschel, 2005) or two (Mohammad and Turney, 2011) as an acceptability threshold and we chose the strictest one.

Finally, to capture the idea that the best approach to prior polarities is the one that maximizes success and minimizes error at the same time, we created a simple metric:

$$s/e = \frac{success}{MAE} \tag{10}$$

We decided to model the problem using *MAE* and *success* - rather than simply MAE (or MSQ) - in a regression framework, because we believe that apart from classification and ranking procedures (see (Pang and Lee, 2008) for an overview) traditional regression frameworks also cannot properly handle annotator's variability over polarity strength judgement (i.e. there is not a "true" sentiment value for the given word, rather an acceptability interval defined by the variability in annotators perception of prior polarity).

7 Analysis and Discussion

In Table 2, we present the results of the prior formulae applied to the whole dataset (as described in Section 5). In the following tables we report *success* and *MAE* for every formula; all formulae are ordered according to the s/e metric. For the sake of readability, statistically significant differences in the data are reported in the discussion section. For *MAE* the significance is computed using Student's t-test. For *success* we computed significance using χ^2 test.

Metrics	$w2_m$	$w1_m$	$mean_m$	$senti_m$	fs_m	$senti_d$	uni	fs_d	$w2_d$	$mean_d$	$w1_d$	$swrnd_d$	$swrnd_m$	rnd
MAE	0.377	0.379	0.378	0.379	0.390	0.381	0.380	0.390	0.380	0.382	0.382	0.397	0.400	0.624
success	32.5%	32.5%	32.3%	32.3%	33.1%	31.7%	31.5%	32.1%	31.2%	30.9%	30.9%	30.5%	30.6%	19.9%
s/e	0.864	0.858	0.856	0.852	0.848	0.834	0.830	0.825	0.820	0.810	0.810	0.767	0.765	0.319

Table 2: Function performances for all `lemma#pos`

Metrics	$w2_m$	$w1_m$	$mean_m$	$senti_m$	fs_m	$senti_d$	uni	fs_d	$w2_d$	$mean_d$	$w1_d$	$swrnd_d$	$swrnd_m$	rnd
MAE	0.381	0.384	0.383	0.385	0.405	0.388	0.386	0.404	0.387	0.390	0.390	0.418	0.422	0.638
success	33.1%	32.9%	32.7%	32.6%	34.0%	31.6%	31.2%	32.3%	30.6%	30.2%	30.2%	29.3%	29.6%	21.1%
s/e	0.868	0.857	0.854	0.846	0.840	0.815	0.809	0.800	0.791	0.774	0.774	0.702	0.700	0.331

Table 3: Function performances for `lemma#pos` with at least 1 SWN score $\neq 0$

We also focused on a particular subset to reduce noise, by ruling out "non-affective" words, i.e. those `lemma#pos` that have `posScore` and `negScore` equal to 0 for all senses in SentiWordNet - and for which the various formulae $f(w)$ always returns 0. Ruling out such words reduced the dataset to 55% of the original size to a total of 830 words. Results are shown in Table 3.

SentiWordNet improves over Random: the first thing we note - in Tables 2 and 3 - is that rnd, as expected, is the worst performing metric, while all other metrics have statistically significant improvements in results for both *MAE* and *success* (p<0.001). So, using SentiWordNet information for computing prior polarities increases the performance above baseline, regardless of the prior formula used.

Picking up only one sense is not a good choice: Interestingly $swrnd$ and fs have very similar results which do not differ significantly (considering *MAE*). This means, surprisingly, that taking the first sense of a `lemma#pos` has no improvement over taking a random sense. This is also surprising since in many NLP tasks, such as word sense disambiguation, algorithms based on most frequent sense represent a very strong baseline[2]. In addition, *picking up one sense is also one of the worst performing strategies for prior polarities* and considering the mean error (*MAE*) the improvement over $swnrd_{m/d}$ and $fs_{m/d}$ is statistically significant for all other formulae (from p<0.05 to p<0.01).

Is it better to use f_m or f_d?: The tables suggest that there is a better performance of prior formulae using f_m over strategies using f_d (according to s/e such formulae rank higher). Still, on average, the *MAE* is almost the same (0.380 for f_m formulae vs. 0.383, see Table 3). According to *success*, using the maximum of the two scores rather than the difference yields slightly better results (32.5% vs. 31.4%).

Best performing formula, weighted average: Best performing formulae on the whole dataset (according to s/e) are $w2_m$ and $w1_m$ (both on all words, in Table 2, and affective words in Table 3). In details, focusing on *MAE* and *success* metrics, and comparing results against $swnrnd_d$ (the worst performing approach using SentiWordNet) we observe that: (i) considering *MAE*, significance level in Table 2 indicates that $w2_m$, $mean_m$, $w1_m$, $senti_m$ perform better than $swnrnd_d$ (p<0.01). For Table 3 the same holds true but also including uni (p<0.01).

[2]In SemEval 2010 competition, only 5 participants out of 29 performed better than the most frequent threshold (Agirre et al., 2010).

(ii) Considering *success* the significance levels are milder, with $p<0.05$ and only for the best performing function on this metric (fs_m).

8 Prior Polarities and Classification tasks

Given the findings of the previous sections we can conclude that not all approaches to prior polarities using SentiWordNet are equivalent, and we manage to define a state-of-the-art approach. Still, since we conducted our experiments in a regression framework, we have to check if such findings also hold true for sentiment classification tasks, which are the most widely used. In fact, it is not guaranteed that significant differences in *MAE* or *success* are relevant when it comes to assessing the polarity of a word. Two formulae can have very different error and success rates on polarity strength assessment, but if they both succeed in assigning the correct polarity to a word, from a classification perspective the two formulae are equivalent.

In Table 4 we present the results of prior polarities formulae performance over a two-class classification task (i.e. assessing whether a word in ANEW is *positive* or *negative*, regardless of the sentiment strength). We also considered a classifier committee (*cc*) with majority vote on the other formulae (random approaches not included). Significance is computed using an approximate randomization test (Yeh, 2000) and formulae are ordered according to F1 metric. Note that in this task the difference between f_m and f_d is not relevant since both versions always return the same classification answer.

	$w2$	$mean$	$w1$	cc	$sentiful$	uni	fs	$swrnd$	rnd
Precision	0.712	0.708	0.706	0.705	0.703	0.698	0.687	0.666	0.493
Recall	0.710	0.707	0.705	0.704	0.702	0.699	0.675	0.653	0.493
F1	0.711	0.707	0.706	0.705	0.702	0.698	0.681	0.659	0.493

Table 4: Precision, Recall and F1 in the classification task on positive and negative words.

Results are very similar to the regression case: all classifiers have a significant improvement over a random approach (rnd, $p<0.001$), and most of the formulae also over $swrnd$ with $p<0.05$. As before, fs has no improvement over the latter (i.e. also in this case choosing the most frequent sense has the same poor performances of picking up a random sense). Furthermore $w2$, $mean$ and $w1$ - the best performing formulae in the regression case -have a stronger significance over $swrnd$ with $p<0.01$. This means that also for the classification task we can define a state-of-the-art approach for prior polarities with SentiWordNet based on (weighted) averages.

9 Conclusions

In this paper we have presented a series of experiments in a regression framework that compare different approaches in computing prior polarities of a word starting from its posterior polarities. We have shown that a weighted average over word senses is the strategy that best approximates human judgment. We have further shown that similar results holds true for sentiment classification tasks, indicating that also in this case that a weighted average is the best strategy to be followed.

References

Agirre, E., De Lacalle, O., Fellbaum, C., Hsieh, S., Tesconi, M., Monachini, M., Vossen, P., and Segers, R. (2010). Semeval-2010 task 17: All-words word sense disambiguation on a specific domain. In *Proceedings of the 5th International Workshop on Semantic Evaluation*, pages 75–80. Association for Computational Linguistics.

Agrawal, S. et al. (2009). Using syntactic and contextual information for sentiment polarity analysis. In *Proceedings of the 2nd International Conference on Interaction Sciences: Information Technology, Culture and Human*, pages 620–623. ACM.

Bradley, M. and Lang, P. (1999). Affective norms for english words (anew): Instruction manual and affective ratings. *Technical Report C-1, University of Florida*.

Chaumartin, F. (2007). Upar7: A knowledge-based system for headline sentiment tagging. In *Proceedings of the 4th International Workshop on Semantic Evaluations*, pages 422–425.

Denecke, K. (2008). Accessing medical experiences and information. In *European Conference on Artificial Intelligence, Workshop on Mining Social Data*.

Denecke, K. (2009). Are sentiwordnet scores suited for multi-domain sentiment classification? In *Fourth International Conference on Digital Information Management (ICDIM)*, pages 1–6.

Devitt, A. and Ahmad, K. (2007). Sentiment polarity identification in financial news: A cohesion-based approach. In *Proceedings of the Association for Computational Linguistics (ACL)*, pages 984–991.

Esuli, A. and Sebastiani, F. (2006). SentiWordNet: A publicly available lexical resource for opinion mining. In *Proceedings of LREC-2006*, pages 417–422, Genova, IT.

Fahrni, A. and Klenner, M. (2008). Old wine or warm beer: Target-specific sentiment analysis of adjectives. In *Proceedings of the Symposium on Affective Language in Human and Machine, AISB*, pages 60–63.

Grimm, M. and Kroschel, K. (2005). Evaluation of natural emotions using self assessment manikins. In *Automatic Speech Recognition and Understanding*, pages 381–385. IEEE.

Guerini, M., Stock, O., and Strapparava, C. (2008). Valentino: A tool for valence shifting of natural language texts. In *Proceedings of LREC 2008*, Marrakech, Morocco.

Liu, B. and Zhang, L. (2012). A survey of opinion mining and sentiment analysis. *Mining Text Data*, pages 415–463.

Mohammad, S. and Turney, P. (2011). Crowdsourcing a word–emotion association lexicon. *Computational Intelligence*, 59:1–24.

Neviarouskaya, A., Prendinger, H., and Ishizuka, M. (2009). Sentiful: Generating a reliable lexicon for sentiment analysis. In *Affective Computing and Intelligent Interaction, ACII*, pages 1–6. Ieee.

Neviarouskaya, A., Prendinger, H., and Ishizuka, M. (2011). Affect analysis model: novel rule-based approach to affect sensing from text. *Natural Language Engineering*, 17(1):95.

Ozbal, G. and Strapparava, C. (2012). A computational approach to the automation of creative naming. *Proceedings of the 50th Annual Meeting of the Association for Computational Linguistics (ACL)*.

Ozbal, G., Strapparava, C., and Guerini, M. (2012). Brand pitt: A corpus to explore the art of naming. In *Proceedings of LREC-2012*.

Paltoglou, G., Thelwall, M., and Buckley, K. (2010). Online textual communications annotated with grades of emotion strength. In *Proceedings of the 3rd International Workshop of Emotion: Corpora for research on Emotion and Affect*, pages 25–31.

Pang, B. and Lee, L. (2008). Opinion mining and sentiment analysis. *Foundations and Trends in Information Retrieval*, 2(1-2):1–135.

Pianta, E., Girardi, C., and Zanoli, R. (2008). The textpro tool suite. In *Proceedings of LREC-2008*.

Qu, L., Toprak, C., Jakob, N., and Gurevych, I. (2008). Sentence level subjectivity and sentiment analysis experiments in ntcir-7 moat challenge. In *Proceedings of the 7th NTCIR Workshop Meeting on Evaluation of Information Access Technologies: Information Retrieval, Question Answering, and Cross-Lingual Information Access*, pages 210–217.

Sing, J., Sarkar, S., and Mitra, T. (2012). Development of a novel algorithm for sentiment analysis based on adverb-adjective-noun combinations. In *Emerging Trends and Applications in Computer Science (NCETACS)*, pages 38–40. IEEE.

Stone, P., Dunphy, D., and Smith, M. (1966). *The General Inquirer: A Computer Approach to Content Analysis*. MIT press.

Strapparava, C. and Valitutti, A. (2004). WordNet-Affect: an affective extension of WordNet. In *Proc. of 4th International Conference on Language Resources and Evaluation (LREC 2004)*, pages 1083 – 1086, Lisbon.

Thet, T., Na, J., Khoo, C., and Shakthikumar, S. (2009). Sentiment analysis of movie reviews on discussion boards using a linguistic approach. In *Proceedings of the 1st international CIKM workshop on Topic-sentiment analysis for mass opinion*, pages 81–84. ACM.

Wang, S. and Manning, C. (2012). Baselines and bigrams: Simple, good sentiment and topic classification. *Proceedings of the 50th Annual Meeting of the Association for Computational Linguistics (ACL)*.

Wilson, T., Wiebe, J., and Hoffmann, P. (2005). Recognizing contextual polarity in phrase-level sentiment analysis. In *Proceedings of the conference on Human Language Technology and Empirical Methods in Natural Language Processing*, pages 347–354.

Wilson, T., Wiebe, J., and Hwa, R. (2004). Just how mad are you? finding strong and weak opinion clauses. In *Proceedings of AAAI*, pages 761–769.

Yeh, A. (2000). More accurate tests for the statistical significance of result differences. In *Proceedings of the 18th conference on Computational linguistics-Volume 2*, pages 947–953. Association for Computational Linguistics.

Improving Dependency Parsing with Interlinear Glossed Text and Syntactic Projection

Ryan Georgi[1] Fei Xia[1] William D Lewis[2]
(1) University of Washington, Seattle, WA 98195, USA
(2) Microsoft Research, Redmond, WA 98052, USA
{rgeorgi, fxia}@uw.edu, wilewis@microsoft.com

ABSTRACT
Producing annotated corpora for resource-poor languages can be prohibitively expensive, while obtaining parallel, unannotated corpora may be more easily achieved. We propose a method of augmenting a discriminative dependency parser using syntactic projection information. This modification will allow the parser to take advantage of unannotated parallel corpora where high-quality automatic annotation tools exist for one of the languages. We use corpora of interlinear glossed text—short bitexts commonly found in linguistic papers on resource-poor languages with an additional gloss line that supports word alignment—and demonstrate this technique on eight different languages, including resource-poor languages such as Welsh, Yaqui, and Hausa. We find that incorporating syntactic projection information in a discriminative parser generally outperforms deterministic syntactic projection. While this paper uses small IGT corpora for word alignment, our method can be adapted to larger parallel corpora by using statistical word alignment instead.

KEYWORDS: Dependency Parsing, Syntactic Projection, Interlinear Glossed Text.

Proceedings of COLING 2012: Posters, pages 371–380,
COLING 2012, Mumbai, December 2012.

1 Introduction

The development of large-scale treebanks has significantly improved the performance of statistical parsers (e.g. Klein and Manning, 2001; Collins and Koo, 2005; de Marneffe et al., 2006) Unfortunately, resources such as these typically only exist for a handful of languages, because building large treebanks is very labor-intensive and often cost-prohibitive. As thousands of other languages have no such resources, other techniques are required to attain similar performance.

One way in which natural language tools might be created for resource-poor languages is by using resources containing translations between resource-rich and resource-poor languages and use the alignment information to transfer information to the resource-poor ones. Syntactic projection takes advantage of existing tools used to annotate a resource-rich language in a corpus, and transfers the analysis to the resource-poor language by means of syntactic projection using word-to-word alignment (Yarowsky and Ngai, 2001; Hwa et al., 2002).

While little annotated data typically exists for resource-poor languages, some work has been done examining the utility of interlinear glossed text (IGT) (Xia and Lewis, 2007; Lewis and Xia, 2008), a format used for illustrative examples in linguistic papers. An IGT instance includes a language line which is a phrase or sentence in a foreign language, a gloss line that shows word-to-word translation, and a translation line which is normally in English. We chose IGT for this study because the gloss line can serve as a bridge for aligning the words in the language line and the translation line. The method proposed in this paper can be easily extended when IGT is replaced by bitexts of sufficient size to train a high-quality word aligner.

In this paper, we investigate the possibility of using small corpora of interlinear text and syntactic projection to bootstrap a dependency parser and improve the resulting parses over projection alone.

2 Background

Before presenting our system, we will first describe previous studies on syntactic projection. Next, we will describe the phenomenon of linguistic divergence, and explain why this can affect projection performance. Finally, we will describe interlinear glossed text (IGT) in more detail and highlight the ways in which it is well-suited to this task.

2.1 Syntactic Projection

Syntactic projection via word alignment has shown promise in adapting resources between languages. Merlo et al. (2002) demonstrated a technique of classifying verb types via projection, while Yarowsky and Ngai (2001) worked on projecting POS taggers and NP bracketeers. Hwa et al. (2004) bootstrapped both phrase and dependency parsers. While these systems did not match the performance of supervised systems, they do succeed in demonstrating that even a small amount of information can significantly boost the performance of a baseline system.

Syntactic projection, however, suffers from a major flaw—using word alignment to transfer analyses between languages assumes that the language pair represents the similar sentences using similar structures. Hwa et al. (2002) referred to this as the Direct Correspondence Assumption, or DCA. As useful as this assumption may be, Dorr (1994) discussed how languages may be divergent in their representations of similar sentences in semantic, syntactic, or lexical representations.

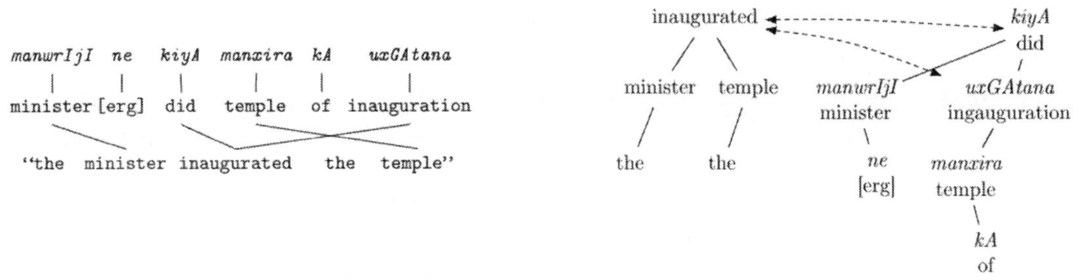

(a) Original IGT representation and word alignment between the three lines.

(b) The dependency trees for Hindi and English

Figure 1: An example of the light verb construction in Hindi.

2.2 Linguistic Divergence

Dorr (1994) defined several types of translation divergence. These variations, or linguistic divergence, can be problematic for projection algorithms, as the assumptions that projection relies on may not hold. One example which may affect projections is the light-verb construction. Take as an example the Hindi sentence in Figure 1, where an English verb ("inaugurated") is represented in Hindi as a light verb ("did") plus a noun ("inaugurate"). As a result, the dependency structures in English and Hindi are not identical, as illustrated in Figure 1(b).

In order to address some of the noise inherent in projection results, Ganchev et al. (2009) took an approach of using "soft" constraints to improve projection results. Rather than commit to a single parse, Ganchev et al. used statistical methods to disambiguate between multiple parse options, and showed significant improvements over a purely deterministic approach.

In our previous study, (Georgi et al., 2012), we looked at measuring forms of alignment between dependency structures to quantify the amount of divergence between languages. In this paper we will look at how performance varies among a set of typologically different languages. We hope to investigate the correlation between performance in these languages and these quantitative measures in future work.

2.3 Interlinear Glossed Text (IGT)

IGT is a resource well-suited to the task of adapting dependency parsing to new languages. As seen in Figure 1a, an IGT instance contains a foreign-language line, an English translation, and a gloss line, which provides additional annotation about the foreign language line. Xia and Lewis (2007) demonstrated that interlinear glossed text can be used to obtain high quality word-to-word alignments with a relatively small amount of data. Xia and Lewis further show

	Hindi	German	Irish	Hausa	Korean	Malagasy	Welsh	Yaqui
# IGT Instances	147	105	46	77	103	87	53	68
# of Words (F)	963	747	252	424	518	489	312	350
# of Words (E)	945	774	278	520	731	646	329	544

Table 1: Data set sizes for all languages. For the number of words, the number of words in the foreign (F) language are given first, followed by the number of English (E) words.

that these heuristics can be used to augment statistical methods to produce higher-quality alignments over statistical methods alone, suggesting that a small corpus of IGT may be able to provide a bootstrap for alignment on much larger parallel corpora.

Where does one find IGT corpora? The Online Database of INterlinear text (ODIN) (Lewis and Xia, 2010) is an online resource of IGT instances for that contains approximately two hundred thousand instances for 1274 languages. Lewis and Xia (2008) use ODIN data for 97 languages to perform syntactic projection and determine basic word order. They found that the languages in this sample with 40 or more instances could be used to predict basic word order with 99% accuracy. With such broad language coverage, ODIN is an ideal resource for providing information for resource-poor languages for which little other data exists.

3 Methodology

Given a set of IGT instances, our system works as follows (see Figure 2):

1. Align words in the language line and translation line (the translation lines are all English in our experiments)
2. Parse the translation lines using an English parser
3. Project the dependency structure of the translation line to the language line
4. Extract features from the projected structure and use them to train a parser.

If the input is a set of parallel sentences instead of IGT, the process will be exactly the same except that word alignment in step (1) will be done by training a statistical word aligner, instead of using the gloss line in IGTs as a bridge between the language lines and the translation lines.

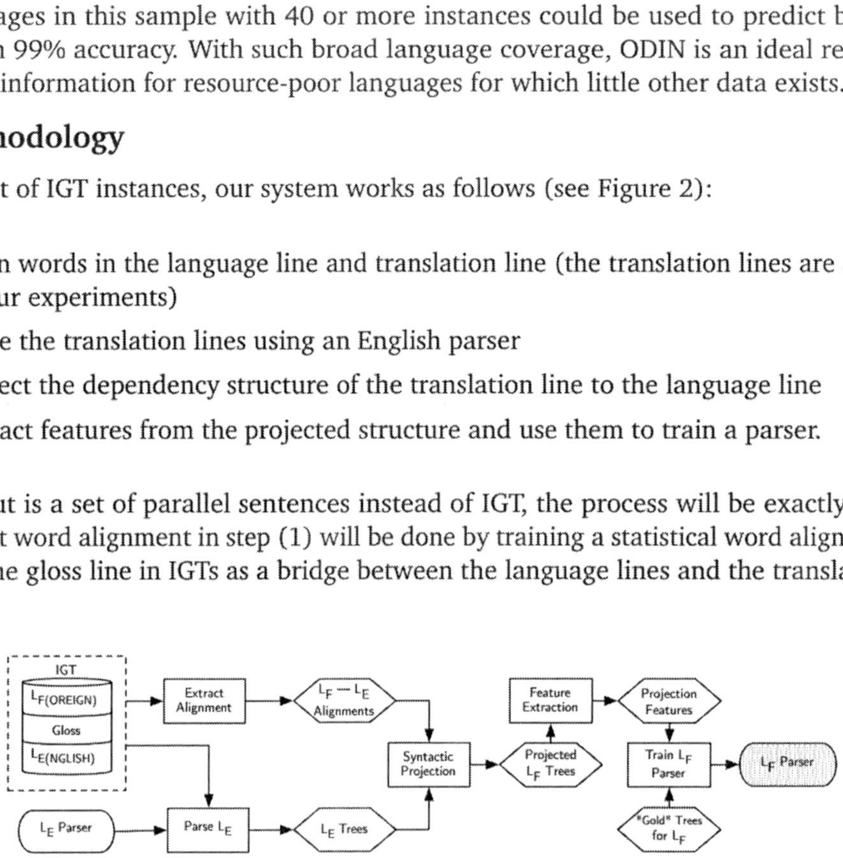

(a) Flowchart illustrating the training procedure for a given L_F–L_E language pair, where L_F is the foreign (non-English) language, and L_E is English.

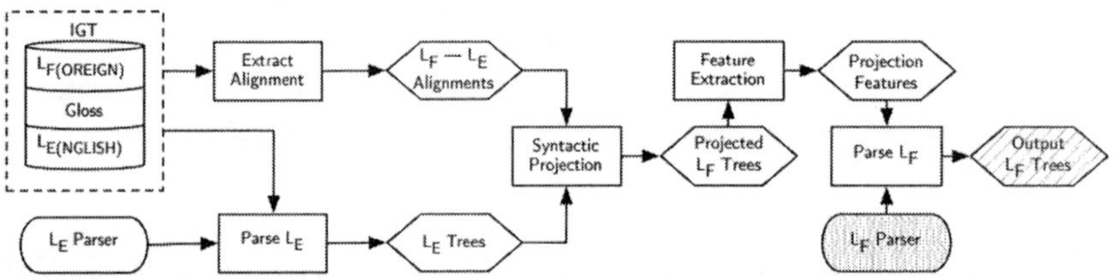

(b) A flowchart showing an overview of the testing procedure for the L_F–L_E language pair using the L_F parser produced in the training phase, and augmented by the information projected from the parsed L_E portion of the bitext. A Future system will include an augmented statistical aligner to produce the L_F–L_E alignments.

Figure 2: Flowcharts illustrating the training and testing phases of the proposed system.

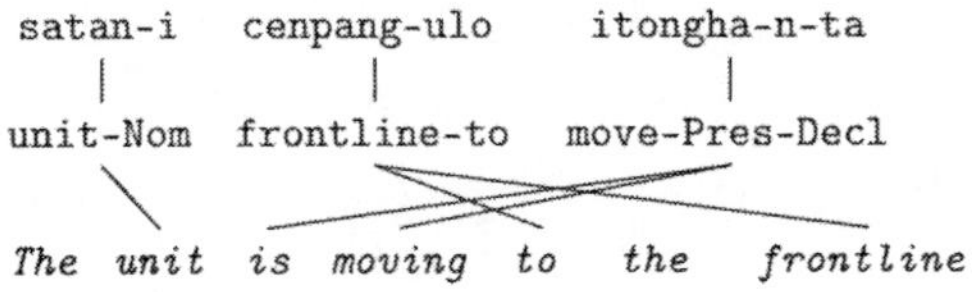

(a) An IGT example in Korean.

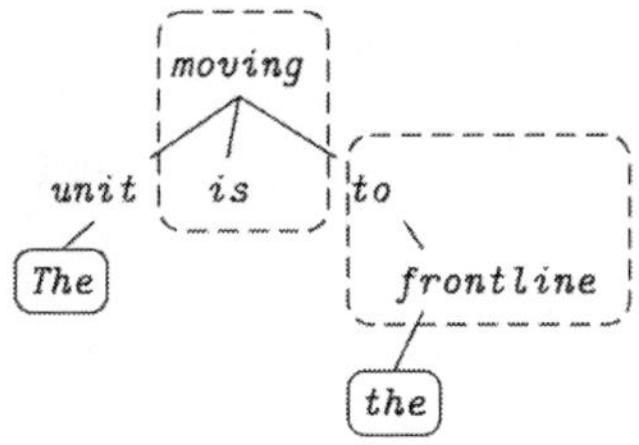

(b) The parse of the English translation from (a). The words in solid boxes do not align to any word in Korean, while the words in dotted boxes align to the same word in Korean.

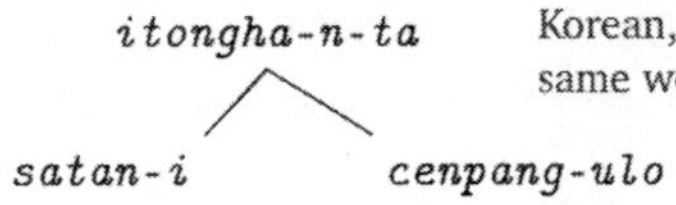

(c) The projected tree for the Korean sentence, after the English words are replaced by Korean counterparts, words in the solid boxes are removed and words in the dotted boxes are collapsed into a single node.

Figure 3: The steps of the projection process, as illustrated using an IGT instance from Korean.

In this study, we will focus the last two steps. Therefore, for the first two steps, we use word alignment and English parse trees from the gold standard. The last two steps and the evaluation corpora are explained below.

3.1 Corpora

We used two different sources of language data for our experiment. The first was a set of guideline sentences for the Hindi treebank (Bhatt et al., 2009). These sentences were provided both in the IGT format, as well as with gold-standard dependency trees in both English and Hindi. The second set was the IGT data used in Xia and Lewis (2007), which includes IGTs for seven languages, plus manually annotated word alignment and dependency trees for both English and the foreign language. In all, eight languages were used for our experiments: Hindi, German, Irish, Hausa, Korean, Malagasy, Welsh, and Yaqui. The size of each data set is given in Table 1. We use the pre-existing, manually annotated parse trees in these two data sets as our gold standard for evaluation.

For the Hindi data, which did not include word alignment, we first automatically aligned the Hindi sentences and the English translation via the gloss line as in Xia and Lewis (2007), then manually corrected the alignment errors. While this manual correction step creates alignments that are not fully automated, the amount of effort required to make these modifications are minimal, and still greatly reduces the costs involved in creating parallel annotated corpora.

3.2 The Projection Algorithm

For the projection algorithm, we follow the dependency projection algorithm described in Xia and Lewis (2007), an example of which can be seen in Figure 3. Given the word alignment L_E and L_F and the parse tree T_E for L_E, the projection algorithm works as follows. For each English node e_i that aligns with foreign word f_i, we replace the node for e_i with the foreign word. If a single English node e_i aligns with multiple foreign words (f_i, f_j), we make multiple copies of e_i as siblings in the tree for each source word, then replace the English words with those from the source. If multiple English nodes align to a single foreign word, the node highest up in the tree is kept, and all others removed. Finally, remaining unaligned words in L_F are attached heuristically, following (Quirk et al., 2005).

3.3 The Parser

Due to linguistic divergence, projected trees are error-prone. Instead of making hard decisions based on projection, we use information from projected trees as a feature in a discriminative parser. This feature will be highly predictive, but not result in a strictly deterministic method like projection alone. We modified the MST Parser (McDonald et al., 2006) by adding features that check whether certain edges considered by the parser appear in the projected tree. We define two types of features: BOOL, and TAG.

The first feature type, BOOL, looks at the current parent→child edge being considered by the parser and returns `true` if the edge matches one in the projected tree. While this feature was a logical starting point, we also wondered if certain word classes of English projected better than others, and so the second feature type, TAG, creates a feature for each $\left(POS_{parent}, POS_{child}\right)$ pair such that the feature is true if the current parent→child edge being considered matches the one in the projected tree, and the POS tags of the parent and child are POS_parent and POS_{child}, respectively.

4 Experiments

As shown in Figure 2a, the L_F parser is trained with two kinds of input: (1) projected L_F trees from which BOOL and TAG features are extracted, and (2) "Gold" trees for L_F from which the standard features used by the MST parser are extracted.

We ran two sets of experiments. In the first, the "Gold" trees are the same as the projected L_F trees. This is to replicate the case when no gold standard is available for L_F. In the second set of experiments, the "Gold" trees are indeed the manually-corrected trees for the L_F sentences. The results are shown in Tables 2a and 2b, respectively.

In each set, there are several individual experiments. The "projection" row shows the results of evaluating the projected L_F trees directly without training a parser. The "MST baseline (B)" row shows the results when we train the MST parser without part-of-speech (POS) tag features and features from projected L_F trees. The third to seventh rows show the results when features from the projected L_F trees are added when training the MST parser. Finally, we want to see how well the system works if the projected L_F trees are perfect, so in the first two rows, we replace the projected L_F trees with the L_F trees from the gold standard. Because our data sets are small, we ran ten-fold cross validation. The highest results in each column for rows 3–9 are shown in bold.

5 Discussion

There are several observations to make from Table 2. First, comparing Tables 2a and 2b, it is clear that using the gold standard trees for L_F improves performance. Second, the projected trees are error-prone, as shown by the last row of the two tables, indicating linguistic divergence is very common. Third, in Table 2a, adding projection-derived features helps the MST baseline, but the results are not better than the "projection" row because the parser is trained on the projected trees only. In contrast, when the parser is trained on the correct parse trees with

	Hindi	German	Gaelic	Hausa	Korean	Malagasy	Welsh	Yaqui
B + Oracle	75.69	95.05	79.76	84.49	98.55	94.19	87.50	96.26
B + Oracle + POS	67.01	90.65	72.62	80.32	95.65	90.87	86.11	89.53
B + POS + Bool + Tag	66.09	87.07	73.41	78.70	**90.27**	89.21	86.11	84.04
B + POS + Tag	56.48	77.17	59.92	69.91	81.37	77.80	69.10	78.05
B + POS + Bool	66.67	87.62	74.21	79.40	89.44	88.59	84.38	85.04
B + POS	56.02	76.07	60.71	70.60	80.75	76.97	65.97	76.31
B + Bool	66.90	**87.90**	76.19	**80.56**	**90.27**	**90.25**	87.85	**86.53**
MST Baseline (B)	49.54	61.21	49.21	51.85	80.33	73.03	38.54	71.32
Projection	**67.82**	**87.90**	**78.57**	79.40	89.65	89.63	**89.58**	84.79

(a) Parse accuracy results for experiments where the parser was trained on automatically-produced projected trees for each language.

	Hindi	German	Gaelic	Hausa	Korean	Malagasy	Welsh	Yaqui
B + Oracle	98.03	98.07	95.63	99.31	99.17	97.93	98.26	96.51
B + Oracle + POS	97.34	97.94	89.29	94.44	98.34	97.72	94.44	97.26
B + POS + Bool + Tag	**79.05**	90.23	70.24	**88.66**	87.78	89.63	88.89	**86.53**
B + POS + Tag	76.74	83.49	65.87	82.64	82.40	79.46	72.92	83.79
B + POS + Bool	79.51	**91.47**	69.84	88.43	87.37	**90.25**	89.24	86.28
B + POS	77.20	82.12	63.10	83.80	80.75	81.54	75.00	81.80
B + Bool	77.31	87.76	70.24	87.73	**92.34**	89.42	**91.32**	85.54
MST Baseline (B)	65.16	62.72	55.16	72.22	80.75	73.03	51.39	66.08
Projection	67.82	87.90	**78.57**	79.40	89.65	89.63	89.58	84.79

(b) Parse accuracy results for experiments where the parser was trained on manually-corrected trees for each language.

Table 2: Parse accuracy results for all experiments. In each table, projection and baseline parser ("B") results are shown at the bottom. Oracle results, where the gold-standard trees (rather than projected trees) were used for the BOOL/TAG features, rather than projection are at top. "POS" represents the experiments where part-of-speech tags were projected from the English side, and "Bool" and "Tag" are features as explained in §3.3. The best result for the non-oracle runs is shown in bold.

additional features derived from projection (see Table 2b), the results are much better than both the MST baseline and projection, and often outperforms the heuristics-based projection algorithm as well. This indicates that, although projected trees are error-prone, using features from them indeed improves parsing performance.

6 Conclusion and Future Work

Building large-scale treebanks is very labor-intensive and often cost-prohibitive. As thousands of languages do not have such resources, syntactic projection has been proposed to transfer syntactic structure from resource-rich languages to resource-poor languages and the projected structure is used to bootstrap NLP tools. However, the projected structure is error-prone due to linguistic divergence.

We propose to augmenting a discriminative dependency parser by adding features extracted from projected structures, and have evaluated our system on eight typologically diverse languages, most of which are extremely resource-poor. The experiments show that the augmented parser outperforms both the original parser without the projection-derived features and the parse trees produced by the projection algorithm only. While the corpora used here are very small, they nonetheless are working examples and show that despite the linguistic divergence, parsing performance can be improved by using features extracted from the dependency trees produced by syntactic projection. Using the IGT data found in the ODIN database and elsewhere on the web, it is conceivable that our method can be applied to bootstrap dependency parsers for hundreds of languages at a very low cost.

For future work, there are several avenues we would like to investigate further. First, the results in this study have all been obtained from very small sets of data. Extending one or more of these languages out to a larger data set may give us a better understanding of the effects of incorporating IGT information. Second, we plan to extend our system to take advantage of a large amount of bitext if it is available. For that, we will train statistical word aligners and test how word alignment errors affect system performance. Finally, while the features used in this study look solely at the result of the projected trees, we would like to add features that look at different divergence types as discussed in Georgi et al. (2012).

Acknowledgments

This work is supported by the National Science Foundation Grant BCS-0748919.

References

Bhatt, R., Narasimhan, B., Palmer, M., Rambow, O., Sharma, D. M., and Xia, F. (2009). A multi-representational and multi-layered treebank for Hindi/Urdu. In *The Third Linguistic Annotation Workshop (The LAW III) in conjunction with ACL/IJCNLP 2009*. Association for Computational Linguistics.

Collins, M. and Koo, T. (2005). Discriminative reranking for natural language parsing. *Computational Linguistics*, 31(1):25–70.

de Marneffe, M.-C., MacCartney, B., and Manning, C. D. (2006). Generating typed dependency parses from phrase structure parses. In *Fifth International Conference on Language Resources and Evaluation*.

Dorr, B. J. (1994). Machine translation divergences: a formal description and proposed solution. *Computational Linguistics*, 20:597–633.

Ganchev, K., Gillenwater, J., and Taskar, B. (2009). Dependency grammar induction via bitext projection constraints. In *Proceedings of the Joint Conference of the 47th Annual Meeting of the ACL and the 4th International Joint Conference on Natural Language Processing of the AFNLP*, pages 369–377.

Georgi, R., Xia, F., and Lewis, W. (2012). Measuring the divergence of dependency structures cross-linguistically to improve syntactic projection algorithms. In Chair), N. C. C., Choukri, K., Declerck, T., Doğan, M. U., Maegaard, B., Mariani, J., Odijk, J., and Piperidis, S., editors, *Proceedings of the Eight International Conference on Language Resources and Evaluation (LREC'12)*, Istanbul, Turkey. European Language Resources Association (ELRA).

Hwa, R., Resnik, P., Weinberg, A., Cabezas, C., and Kolak, O. (2004). Bootstrapping parsers via syntactic projection across parallel texts. *Natural Language Engineering*, 1(1):1–15.

Hwa, R., Resnik, P., Weinberg, A., and Kolak, O. (2002). Evaluating translational correspondence using annotation projection. In *Proceedings of the Annual Meeting of the Association for Computational Linguistics*.

Klein, D. and Manning, C. (2001). An O(n^3) agenda-based chart parser for arbitrary probabilistic context-free grammars. Technical report.

Lewis, W. and Xia, F. (2008). Automatically identifying computationally relevant typological features. In *Proceedings of the Third International Joint Conference on Natural Language Processing*.

Lewis, W. D. and Xia, F. (2010). Developing ODIN: A multilingual repository of annotated language data for hundreds of the world's languages. *Journal of Literary and Linguistic Computing (LLC)*, 25(3):303–319.

McDonald, R., Lerman, K., and Pereira, F. (2006). Multilingual dependency analysis with a two-stage discriminative parser. In *Proceedings of the Tenth Conference on Computational Natural Language Learning*, pages 216–220. Association for Computational Linguistics.

Merlo, P., Stevenson, S., Tsang, V., and Allaria, G. (2002). A multilingual paradigm for automatic verb classification. *Proceedings of the 40th Annual Meeting on Association for Computational Linguistics*, pages 207–214.

Quirk, C., Menezes, A., and Cherry, C. (2005). Dependency treelet translation: Syntactically informed phrasal SMT. In *Proceedings of the ACL 2005*. Microsoft Research.

Xia, F. and Lewis, W. D. (2007). Multilingual Structural Projection across Interlinear Text. In *Human Language Technologies: The Annual Conference of the North American Chapter of the Association for Computational Linguistics*.

Yarowsky, D. and Ngai, G. (2001). Inducing multilingual POS taggers and NP bracketers via robust projection across aligned corpora. In *Proceedings of NAACL*, Stroudsburg, PA. Johns Hopkins University.

Diachronic Variation in Grammatical Relations

Aaron Gerow *Khurshid Ahmad*
Trinity College Dublin, College Green, Dublin, Ireland.
`gerowa@tcd.ie, kahmad@scss.tcd.ie`

ABSTRACT
We present a method of finding and analyzing shifts in grammatical relations found in diachronic corpora. Inspired by the econometric technique of measuring return and volatility instead of relative frequencies, we propose them as a way to better characterize changes in grammatical patterns like nominalization, modification and comparison. To exemplify the use of these techniques, we examine a corpus of NIPS papers and report trends which manifest at the token, part-of-speech and grammatical levels. Building up from frequency observations to a second-order analysis, we show that shifts in frequencies overlook deeper trends in language, even when part-of-speech information is included. Examining token, POS and grammatical levels of variation enables a summary view of diachronic text as a whole. We conclude with a discussion about how these methods can inform intuitions about specialist domains as well as changes in language use as a whole.

KEYWORDS: Corpus Analysis, Diachronic Analysis, Language Variation, Text Classification.

Proceedings of COLING 2012: Posters, pages 381–390,
COLING 2012, Mumbai, December 2012.

1 Introduction

Language is both representative and constitutive of the world around us, which makes tracking changes in its use a central goal in understanding how people make sense of the world. Charting these changes is a two-part challenge: extracting meaningful, diachronic data and finding the best way to characterize it. Literature on visualizing themes in text (Havre et al., 2002), identifying topics (Kim & Sudderth, 2011; Rosen-Zvi et al., 2010) and analyzing the sentiment of financial news and social media (Tetlock, 2006; Kouloumpis et al., 2011) are examples of how changes in language are linked to changes in the world. The underlying assumption is that shifts in the distribution of words and phrases may indicate changes in a domain or community.

Language use in specific subjects is known to be productive: a relatively small set of words are not used repetitively, instead, they give rise to new words through inflectional and derivational processes (Halliday & Martin, 1993). This productivity, as genesis and obsolescence, suggests that by analyzing diachronic text we can gain insight into the ontological commitment of a domain (Ahmad, 2000; see McMahon, 1994 for general language and Geeraerts, 2002 for scientific language). Topic modeling has been shown to make use of frequency observations to build probabilistic models with which to infer clusters of representative words (Griffiths & Steyvers, 2004). However, word-frequency is only one level of linguistic variation. Other shifts, like part-of-speech and grammatical relations, are also important in understanding a domain's language. As we will see, some trends in frequency have consistent underlying trends in grammatical relations that signal changes not apparent at higher levels.

By organizing text diachronically, frequency data can be analyzed as a time-series. Enabled by an endless amount of text on the internet, corpus linguists have constructed large databases of such text to chart linguistic trends (for example Davies, 2010). Sentiment and opinion mining have developed nearly real-time methods of tracking sentiment in text (Tetlock, 2007). Other work has tracked shifts in parts-of-speech (Mair et al., 2003) and related fluctuations in verb-distributions to stock-markets (Gerow & Keane, 2011). Perhaps the boldest claim analysts of language-change have made, is that by analyzing the relative frequency of words over time, we gain a quantitative view of culture itself (Michel et al., 2010).

To find variation over time, we explore whether a time-series analysis can help uncover patterns of seemingly random movements in frequency. To do this, we use continuously compounded return and volatility. These measures are commonly used in econometrics where high prices tend to beget higher prices and low prices, lower still. This phenomenon of auto-correlation is also apparent in frequency-variations in text, which means an analysis of mean and variance can be misleading. Using return and volatility has been used in sentiment analysis, where it was found that negative-affect terms caused a larger, and longer-lasting deviation from the mean than positive terms (Ahmad, 2011). To our knowledge, these metrics have not been used to investigate trends in words with respect to the grammatical relations in which they are found. By looking at grammatical relations in particular, we get a picture *how* those words are used. This type of analysis may shed light on language-change and perhaps help predict trends in topics and key-terms which characterize a domain.

The driving question in this paper is whether second-order analyses of diachronic text can be used to find trends not apparent on the surface. Using return and volatility we get a synoptic picture of changes in a diachronic corpus which is informed by the *kind* of changes themselves. And by examining grammatical relations, we note specific shifts not apparent at the lexical token level. Our results offer some interesting findings about academic language: by analyzing key terms, we find discernible trends at varying levels of language as well as generalizations about the text as a whole.

2 Methods: Measuring Diachronic Shifts

A series, $f(t)$, is a discrete set of ordered data-points which typically exhibit a degree of auto-correlation, meaning that preceding values tend to have a discernible effect on subsequent values. Even in heteroskedastic series – the log-normal regression of which is non-linear – the values of the past, $f(t-n)$, tend to be good predictors of successive values. Measuring and making use of this relation is the focus of predictive econometric models, widely employed in economics and finance (Taylor, 2005). One common method used to measure the variation in a time-series is to calculate successive ratios of consecutive values, known as the *return* of a series. Unlike standard deviation in a sample or population, calculating the return series is order-aware and can be computed for varying segments of time and degrees of resolution. In our analysis we use the continuously compounded return defined as:

$$r(t) = \log \frac{f(t)}{f(t-1)} \tag{1}$$

Unlike the original series, returns are not serially correlated. This leads economists to consider variance in the return-series, or *volatility*, a better way to estimate the dispersion of values in the original. For a time-series, $f(t)$ of N ordered-points, volatility is defined as:

$$v = \sum_{t=0}^{N} \frac{(r(t) - \bar{t})^2}{N(N-1)} \tag{2}$$

We can combine equations 1 and 2 to gain a view of the overall variation in a corpus composed of an time-ordered set of documents, D, as the mean of continuously compounded returns, $\bar{r}$:

$$\bar{r} = \frac{1}{|D|} \sum_{d \in D} \log \frac{f_d}{f_{d-1}} \tag{3}$$

where f_d is a frequency observation of document d.

3 Results: Variation in the NIPS corpus

The NIPS corpus[1] consists of papers from thirteen volumes of Neural Information Processing Systems proceedings. It contains 6.7 million words in 1,740 documents published over 13 years from 1987 to 1999, with an average of 516,394 tokens per year. The mean return for yearly corpus-size was 4% with a volatility of 11% – exhibiting a relatively slow, steady growth.

[1] Available at http://www.cs.nyu.edu/˜roweis/data.html.

Sketch Engine (Kilgarriff et al., 2004) was used to clean, lemmatize, tag, divide the corpus into yearly sub-corpora and provide frequencies of grammatical relations (see Table 1). Sketch Engine uses a pre-trained version of TreeTagger (Shmid, 1994) and was also used to extract the grammatical relations by applying abstract tag templates or a "sketch grammar" to the tagged corpus. It should be noted that the NIPS corpus offers a uniformly diachronic corpus on which to test our methods, but any diachronically organized corpus would suffice. Moreover, though we rely on a POS tagger and subsequent POS-based grammatical relation extraction, the method, as such, is applicable to any language from which grammatical relationships can be extracted.

By comparing relative frequencies to the ACL Anthology Reference Corpus (ACL ARC)[2], we isolated five terms to analyze in detail: *network*, *learning*, *training*, *algorithm* and *neuron*. The relative frequency and return series are shown in Figure 1 and their respective mean frequency, standard deviation, mean of returns and volatility are given in Table 2. Taken together, we have an overview of how the use of these terms changed over the thirteen-year corpus. We can see that *algorithm* doubled in usage, while *neuron* showed a steady decline and *network* a turbulent decline from dominating the five words. Only *learning* was steady throughout. Also note how *network* dominates the plot of relative frequency, despite having a relatively steady return series. Alternatively, *algorithm* appears quiescent in the frequency series, but shows considerable fluctuations in return.

Relationship	**Example**
`subject_of`	Cooperative **training** *gives* a framework [...]
`object_of`	*Showing* that **training** increased the [...]
`modifier`	[...] with a single **training** *pattern*.
`a_modified`	[...] at *smaller* **training** set sizes.
`n_modified`	[...] using back *propagation* **training**.
`and/or`	[...] achieved during **training** *or* testing.

Table 1: Common grammatical relations found in our analysis. The defining feature of each is italicized in the example and the word-in-question is in bold.

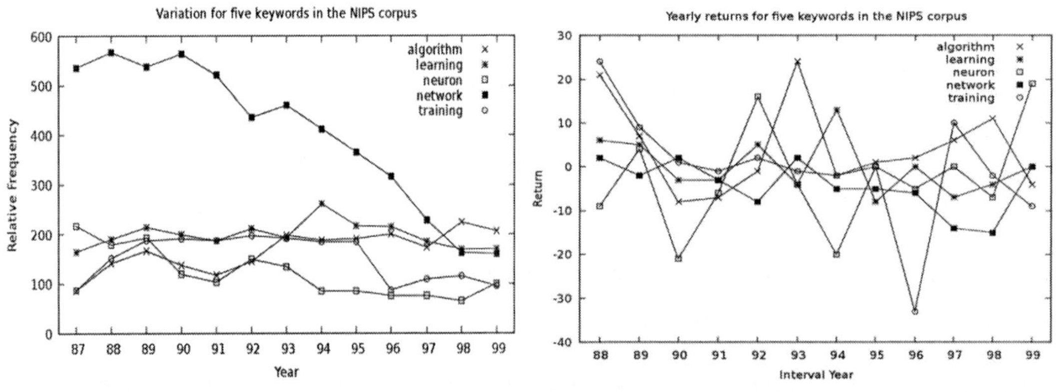

Figure 1: On the left are the relative frequencies (per 100,000 tokens) for five keywords (all forms) in the NIPS corpus. On the right are the return series for each keyword. Note how there is considerably more variance in the return series than in the relative frequencies – particularly for *neuron* and *training*.

[2]Available at http://acl-arc.comp.nus.edu.sg/.

	$\bar{f}$	SD(f)	$\bar{r}$	v
training-[n]	0.151%	30%	0.3%	13%
neuron-[n]	0.122%	40%	-3%	12%
algorithm-[n]	0.165%	27%	3%	10%
learning-[n]	0.198%	13%	0.1%	6%
network-[n]	0.405%	37%	-4%	6%

Table 2: Summary statistics for the relative frequency and return series of the five keywords we examined in the NIPS corpus, ordered by volatility. Shown are the relative frequency ($\bar{f}$; per 100,000 tokens), the standard deviation of the frequency, the mean of return ($\bar{r}$; Eq. 3) and the volatility (v; Eq. 2).

The key question in this paper is whether there is significant variation at the grammatical level. In Table 3, the nouns *learning* and *training* are presented with a breakdown of their occurrences and their most common grammatical relations. Note that although *learning*-[noun] appears steady (1-lag auto-correlation = 28%, $p = 0.18$), it exhibits relatively high volatility in its two most common relations: adjective modified and as a modifier. *Training*-[noun], which at 1-lag is 61% auto-correlated ($p < 0.1$), is also deceptively summarized by its frequencies being found in a number of a volatile relationships, the least volatile being the one which increased the most: as a modifier.

The remaining three terms, *network*, *algorithm* and *neuron*, are presented in Figure 2, which contains plots of the mean return against volatility for each POS-class and the five most common relations in which they occur, as well the plots of the relative frequency throughout the corpus. Consider *network* in Figure 2, which, despite showing a steady negative trend overall in Figure 1, is increasingly modified by both nouns and adjectives, appearing less frequently as a subject. Also consider forms of the word *neuron*, which include the two adjectives *neural* and *neuronal* both in stable states compared to its noun forms. Though *neuron* declined in use overall, it shows wide variation in two relations, `and/or` and `modifier`, in addition to an increase in *neuron*-[noun] being noun-modified.

Year:	87	88	89	90	91	92	93	94	95	96	97	98	99	$\bar{f}$	$\bar{r}$	v
***learning*-[n]**																
N	164	190	214	199	187	211	193	261	217	215	185	169	170	**198**	**0.1%**	**6%**
a_modified	14	23	24	28	25	26	19	42	29	31	27	23	25	**26**	**5%**	**32%**
modifier	19	20	19	20	18	19	18	24	27	23	16	15	22	**20**	**1%**	**20%**
n_modified	10	8	11	14	11	17	11	23	17	18	21	17	16	**15**	**2%**	**15%**
object_of	8	10	11	13	10	9	8	14	9	12	9	7	8	**10**	**0%**	**12%**
subject_of	7	6	8	14	20	18	12	19	15	16	13	9	10	**13**	**1%**	**15%**
***training*-[n]**																
N	87	151	187	191	187	197	192	185	185	87	109	115	95	**151**	**0.3%**	**13%**
a_modified	7	7	9	8	11	15	11	8	12	9	5	8	4	**9**	**-1%**	**42%**
modifier	34	57	71	88	103	95	91	95	164	167	111	96	74	**96**	**7%**	**25%**
n_modified	5	4	5	7	9	14	10	8	16	13	5	6	4	**8**	**-1%**	**44%**
object_of	9	9	8	13	14	17	16	17	33	24	15	14	7	**15**	**-1%**	**33%**
subject_of	10	10	14	15	18	15	22	25	40	25	15	12	9	**18**	**-1%**	**30%**

Table 3: Variation in the relative frequency of *training*-[noun] and *learning*-[noun] and occurrences in their five most common grammatical relationships. Here $\bar{f}$ is the mean relative frequency. Volatility (v) and mean return ($\bar{r}$) are calculated as in equations 2 and 3 respectively. Maximum values are underlined and summary statistics are shown in bold.

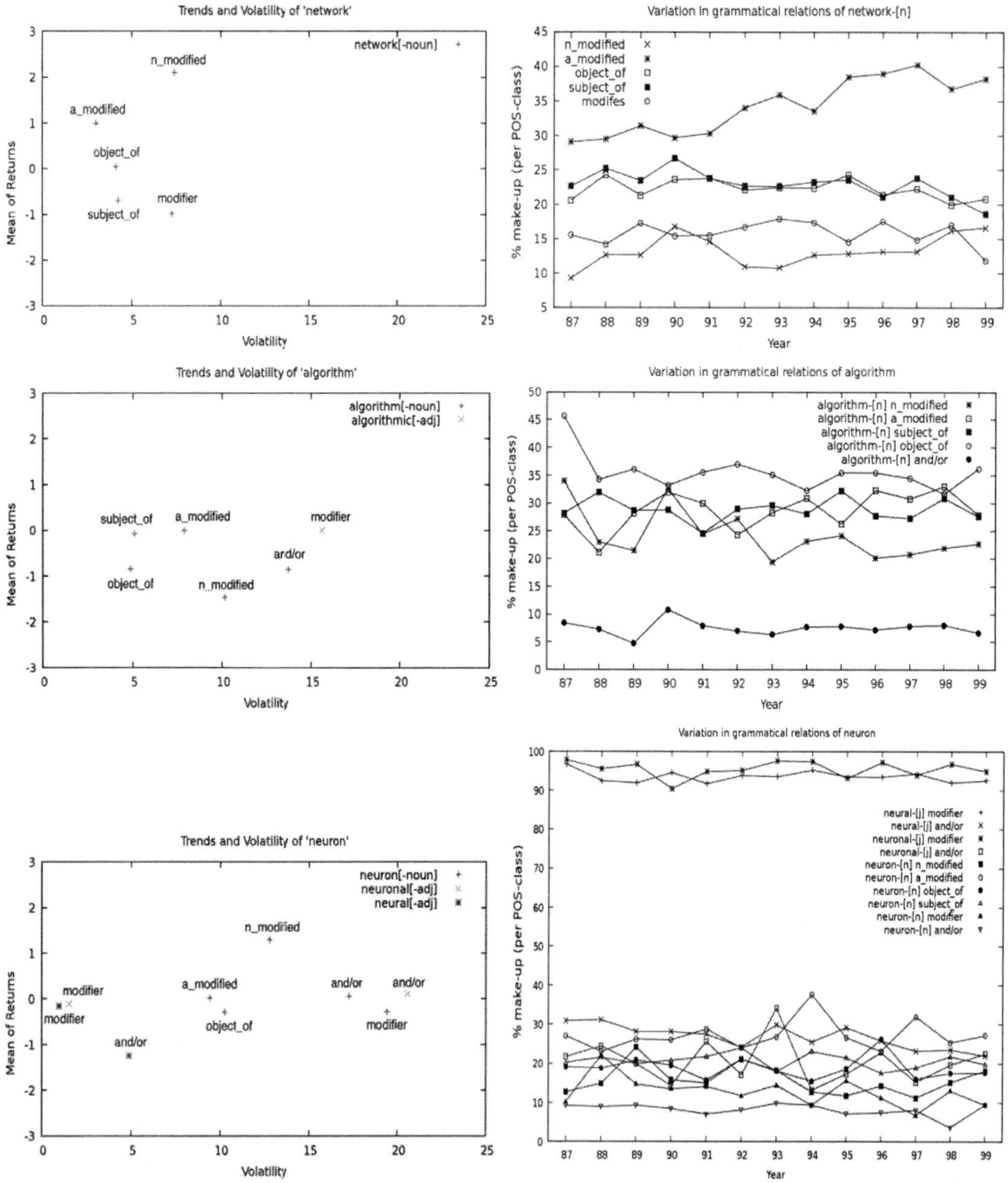

Figure 2: Grammatical shifts for the three keywords *network* (top), *algorithm* (middle) and *neuron* (bottom) are summarized in each pair of plots. On the left, the mean of returns (Eq. 3) is plotted using the word-form's relative frequency (per 100,000 tokens) against its volatility (Eq. 2) for each relationship in which it was found. In these plots, we expect clusters around the origin, where relations show little trend or volatility. On the right are plots showing the percentage make-up of each relationship over the NIPS corpus. Note that relationships which occurred less than 10 times per year are not shown but are factored into the percentage calculations.

Looking at individual words can tell us a lot about how their independent usage changes over time, but it is also useful to take a broad look at a corpus to. To this end, we extracted the top 200 noun keywords in the NIPS corpus, again by comparing their distributions to the ACL ARC. We excluded nouns that occurred less than 10 times per 100,000 tokens each year, and those that did not occur in at least two different grammatical relations every year. Because some commonly cited authors dominate the noun-distribution when compared to the reference corpus, we also removed proper nouns. In the end we were left with 43 nouns which were indicative of NIPS and consistent enough to ensure a complete analysis.

The most common relations were the same as those for *training*, *learning*, *neuron*, *algorithm* and *network*. For each noun we computed the mean return, volatility and the correlation between the relationship and the frequency of the overall word (all forms). For mean return, only `and/or` was significantly changing at 0.7% ($p < 0.1$). The most volatile relationship among the nouns was `n_modified` which had 27.5% volatility. However, the least volatile relationship, `subject_of`, showed 15.3% volatility. Lastly, no relationship consistently correlated with words' overall usage. In fact, the correlations themselves were highly variable (SD = 37.03%), implying that grammatical relationships are not independently indicative of word usage.

To further explore whether grammatical relationships could be indicative of a word's change in usage, we grouped words with positive trends and compared them to words with negative trends. Of the 43 nouns, 17 had a positive mean return ($\bar{r} \geq .5$), 21 had negative mean return ($\bar{r} \leq -.5$) and 5 were relatively steady ($-.5 < \bar{r} < .5$). We found that in negative trends `subject_of`, `object_of` and `a_modified` were more likely to peak *after* the word as a whole (`subject_of`: 11 proceeding the word's peak, 3 preceding; `object_of`: 13 and 6; `a_modified`: 15 and 3). The frequency of preceding and proceeding a word's peak were weighted by the number of positive to negative trends (40% positive and 49% negative). Using the weighted scores, we found that in negative trends `and/or` comparison was 7.4 times more likely to proceed the word's peak when compared to positive trends. On the other hand, in positive trends, both adjective and noun modification were 3.3 times more likely to peak before the word as a whole than in negative trends. Results of this analysis are presented in Table 4.

Relationship	Preceded	Simultaneous	Proceeded
Positive Trends (N=17)			
`subject`	2.8 (7)	0.0 (0)	1.2 (4)
`object`	5.5 (14)	0.0 (0)	2.8 (7)
`a_modified`	4.7 (12)	0.8 (2)	2.0 (5)
`n_modified`	3.2 (8)	0.8 (2)	2.0 (5)
`modifier`	3.6 (9)	0.0 (0)	2.0 (5)
`and/or`	4.0 (10)	0.0 (0)	0.8 (2)
Negative Trends (N=21)			
`subject`	1.5 (3)	0.0 (0)	5.4 (11)
`object`	2.9 (6)	0.0 (0)	6.3 (13)
`a_modified`	1.5 (3)	0.5 (1)	7.3 (15)
`n_modified`	1.0 (2)	1.0 (2)	4.9 (10)
`modifier`	1.5 (3)	0.5 (1)	5.4 (11)
`and/or`	2.0 (4)	0.0 (0)	5.9 (12)

Table 4: Of the 43 noun keywords, shown here are the weighted frequencies of how many times a given relationship's frequency peaked before, simultaneously and after the word's overall frequency. The weighting was done by the number of trends in each category (17 positive and 21 negative). Raw frequencies are shown in parentheses.

4 Analysis & Discussion

One example of how shifts in relations indicate changes in the domain is the increased noun modification of *neuron*. Since the beginning of the NIPS corpus in 1987, a great deal of research has been undertaken to discern and simulate the functions of various neurons in the brain. The increased noun modification of *neuron* may be due to increased attention to particular types and functions of neurons. The word *network* also exhibits this change to being increasingly noun-modified but has steadily decreased in use as a subject. This could be due to the ubiquity of the term in the NIPS community; no longer is a neural network a "network" as such, but something more specific, like a "self organizing map", a "connectionist model" or "multilayer perceptron." Lastly, recall that despite the overall steadiness of the word *training* (Table 2), its use as a modifier dominates its ascent. This could be because the concept of training became established midway through the corpus, enabling terms like "training sample" or "training data" without as much explanation of training specifically. Though these results are somewhat speculative in nature, we feel they go deeper than first-order analyses of frequencies, by measuring the changes through the corpus as a whole.

The broader analysis of 43 key-nouns exemplifies some techniques for uncovering how changes at different levels of language use may be interrelated. We did not find a grammatical relationship among the key nouns that consistently correlated with the term's use, which implies that grammatical variation is informed by the lexicon. Comparing rising and falling patterns, we found that words which are increasingly common tend to be preceded by increased modification, both adjectival and nominal. Perhaps this points to the need for authors to further specify concepts before the community adopts them. Conversely, terms which were decreasing in use were more likely to see a subsequent peak in `and/or` comparison. This may point to an explanatory transition from one term to another, that is, writers liken new terms to old terms fading from use.

The key observation in this paper is that academic language – which is used primarily used to explain complex, technical ideas – exhibits grammatical shifts not apparent in tokens or parts-of-speech. Our proposoal is that examining a time-series' second-order moments, which better quantifies changes in linguistic data, enables the investigation of deeper shifts in language. These shifts, like the grammatical relations explored here, show how language is put to use in explanation as well as in general communication.

Acknowledgments

Thanks to Sam Glucksberg for comments and advice on this research. This work was supported by Enterprise Ireland grant #CC-2011-2601-B for the GRCTC project and a Trinity College research studentship to the first author.

References

Ahmad, K. (2000). Neologisms, nonces and word formation. In Heid, U., Evert, S., Lehmann, E., and Rohrer, C., editors, *The 9th EURALEX International Congress, Volume II*, pages 711–730, Munich: Universitat Stuttgart.

Ahmad, K. (2011). The "return" and "volatility" of sentiments: An attempt to quantify the behaviour of the markets? In Ahmad, K., editor, *Affective Computing and Sentiment Analysis*. Springer.

Davies, M. (2010). The corpus of contemporary american english as the first reliable monitor corpus of english. *Literary and Linguistic Computing*, 25(4):447–464.

Geeraerts, D. (2002). The scope of diachronic onomasiology. In Agel, V., Gardt, A., Hass-Zumkehr, U., and Roelcke, T., editors, *Das Wort. Seine strukturelle und kulturelle Dimension. Festschrift für Oskar Reichmann zum 65*, pages 29–44. Geburtstag.

Gerow, A. and Keane, M. T. (2011). Mining the web for the "voice of the herd" to track stock market bubbles. In *Proceedings of the 22nd International Joint Conference on A.I.*, Barcelona, Spain.

Griffiths, T. and Steyvers, M. (2004). Finding scientific topics. *Proceedings of the National Academy of Sciences*, 101(1):5228–5235.

Halliday, M. A. K. and Martin, J. R. (1993). *Writing Science: Literacy and Discursive Power*. The Falmer Press, London and Washington DC.

Havre, S., Hetzler, E., Whitney, P., and Nowell, L. (2002). Themeriver: Visualizing thematic changes in large document collections. *IEEE Transactions on Visualization and Computer Graphics*, 8(1):9–20.

Kilgarriff, A., Rychlý, P., Smrž, P., and Tugwell, D. (2004). The sketch engine. In *Proceedings of EURALEX 2004*, pages 105–116.

Kim, D. I. and Sudderth, E. B. (2011). The doubly correlated nonparametric topic model. *Neural Information Processing Systems*, 24.

Kouloumpis, E., Wilson, T., and Moore, J. (2011). Twitter sentiment analysis: The good the bad and the omg! In *Proceedings of the Fifth International AAAI Conference on Weblogs and Social Media*, pages 538–541.

Mair, C., Hundt, M., Leech, G., and Smith, N. (2003). Short term diachronic shifts in part-of-speech frequencies: a comparison of the tagged lob and f-lob corpora. *International Journal of Corpus Linguistics*, 7(2):245–264.

McMahon, A. S. (1994). *Understanding Language Change*. Cambridge University Press, Cambridge and New York.

Michel, J.-B., Shen, Y. K., Aiden, A. P., Veres, A., Gray, M. K., Team, T. G. B., Pickett, J. P., Hoiberg, D., Clancy, D., Norvig, P., Orwant, J., Pinker, S., Nowak, M. A., and Aiden, E. L. (2011). Quantitative analysis of culture using millions of digitized books. *Science*, 331(6014):176–182.

Rosen-Zvi, M., Chemudugunta, C., Griffiths, T., Smyth, P., and Steyvers, M. (2010). Learning author-topic models from text corpora. *ACM Transactions on Information Systems*, 28(1).

Schmid, H. (1994). Probabilistic part-of-speech tagging using decision trees. In *Proceedings of International Conference on New Methods in Language Processing*, Manchester, UK.

Taylor, S. J. (2005). *Asset Price Dynamics, Volatility, and Prediction*. Princeton University Press, Cambridge, MA.

Tetlock, P. (2007). Giving content to investor sentiment: The role of media in the stock market. *The Journal of Finance*, 62(3):1139–1168.

Relation Classification using Entity Sequence Kernels

Debanjan Ghosh   Smaranda Muresan
School of Communication and Information
Rutgers University, New Jersey 08854, USA
{debanjan.ghosh,smuresan}@rutgers.edu

Abstract
This paper presents a novel gap weighted string kernel referred to as an entity sequence kernel for the task of relation extraction. Experiments classifying different relations on a standard dataset show that the entity sequence kernels achieve F1 scores on par with current state-of-the-art techniques. We also present a study of how the *order* of candidate entities influences the *relation directionality* and how various factors might contribute to the accuracy of results for each relation direction.

TITLE AND ABSTRACT IN Bengali (বাংলা)

নামাঙ্কিত সত্তার সম্পর্ক নিষ্কাশন করণ ক্রম কার্নেল

এই গবেষণা পত্রে সম্পর্ক নিষ্কাশনের জন্য একটি নতুন নামাঙ্কিত সত্তার ভারযুক্ত স্ট্রিং কার্নেল উপস্থাপন করা হয়েছে। পরীক্ষামূলক ভাবে নামাঙ্কিত সত্তা কার্নেল্স ব্যবহার করে বিভিন্ন সম্পর্কের উদাহরণগুলি শ্রেণীবদ্ধ করা হয়েছে যার ফলাফল খুবই সন্তোষজনক। কিভাবে বিভিন্ন স্থিতিমাপ এবং সত্তা-প্রার্থীদের অনুবর্তিতা, সম্পর্ক অভিমুখ বিচারে অবদান রাখে আমরা সেটিও এই প্রবন্ধে পরিবেশন করেছি।

Keywords: Relation Extraction, Entity Sequence Kernel, SVM.

Keywords in L_2: সম্পর্ক নিষ্কাশন,নামাঙ্কিত সত্তা কার্নেল, SVM.

Proceedings of COLING 2012: Posters, pages 391–400,
COLING 2012, Mumbai, December 2012.

1 Introduction

Information Extraction (IE) is the task of extracting structured information from unstructured text. Two major sub-tasks of IE are extracting entities such as [John Smith]$_{Pers}$, [New York]$_{Loc}$ and [Google Inc]$_{Org}$ and the relation between these entities, such as *Work_For* relation between [John Smith]$_{Pers}$ and [Google Inc.]$_{Org}$, and *Live_In* relation between [John Smith]$_{Pers}$ and [New York]$_{Loc}$. Extracting relations between entities is still a significantly harder task than recognizing entities, and current state-of-the-art systems achieve inferior results. Consider the following examples of a *Live_In* relation from the corpus introduced by (Roth and Yih, 2004):

(1) *[Actress Angie Dickinson]$_{Pers}$, who was born in [Kulm,N.D.]$_{Loc}$ donated a coat she wore to the 1966 [Academy Awards]$_{Other}$*

(2) *[Modesto]$_{Loc}$, native [George Lucas]$_{Per}$'s film was released...*

Our task is to extract the *Live_In* relation from the above sentences where the involved named entities are [Actress Angie Dickinson]$_{Per}$ and [Kulm, N.D.]$_{Loc}$ in example (1) and [George Lucas]$_{Per}$ and [Modesto]$_{Loc}$ in example (2). These two examples are illustrative of two key challenges: 1) a sentence can contain multiple entities (e.g., [Academy awards]$_{Other}$ is a named entity in sentence (1), but it is not part of the *Live_In* relation); and 2) each relation has a concept of *directionality*. This is because the arguments in a relation often take different roles and need to be distinguished (*Live_in*([Actress Angie Dickinson]$_{Pers}$, [Kulm,N.D.]$_{Loc}$] vs. *Live_in*([Modesto]$_{Loc}$,[George Lucas]$_{Pers}$). Identifying the right directionality is key to the task of relation extraction. While few recent work on relation extraction has modeled the directionality of relations (Roth and Yih, 2004; Giuliano et al., 2007; Kate and Mooney, 2010; Zhang et al., 2008), these studies have only reported averaged results. A key contribution of this paper is an in-depth study of relation directionality, showing how various factors might contribute to the accuracy of results for each relation direction.

In this paper, we explore a novel approach of creating substring sequences from corpora annotated with entities for relation extraction. We use intra-sentential information between the entities to create string sequences, which we call *entity sequences*. In our approach, we assume that entity boundaries are known, but the types of entities are unknown. We treat the relation extraction problem as a supervised learning (classification) problem. A modified string kernel is applied over *entity sequences*. This kernel in turn is augmented with SVM to find the decision hyperplane that can separate one relation from the other. We show that semantic and syntactic features (WordNet hypernyms and dependency relations) help the classifier to achieve better results. We also present a preliminary set of experiments using a shortest path dependency kernel similar to the one introduced by Bunescu and Mooney (2005b), which improves our results for three out of the five relations under study. We use the dataset created by Roth and Yih (2004)[1] for two main reasons: 1) it represents a challenging dataset for our task since there are often more than two entities in a sentence, unlike SemEval 2010 dataset[2] and 2) it has been widely used in recent relation extraction research (Roth and Yih, 2004, 2007; Giuliano et al., 2007; Kate and Mooney, 2010) allowing us to compare our results with prior work. This dataset is referred to as the RY dataset.

In Section 2 we describe the method of creating entity sequences for the relation extraction task. Section 3 formally presents our proposed kernel. We discuss the kernel performance in Section

[1]http://cogcomp.cs.illinois.edu/Data/ER/

[2]http://semeval2.fbk.eu/semeval2.php

4 including detailed experiments of relation directionality and comparison with state-of-the-art methods. In Section 5 we briefly review related work.

2 Entity Sequence Generation

Given a sentence S that contains a set of entities $e_1, \ldots e_n$ a relation R_{ij} exists between a pair of entities e_i and e_j, where e_i is the first entity and e_j is the second entity. Together e_i and e_j are considered *candidate entities*. For example, given the sentence:

(3) a reasonable doubt that $[\text{Oswald}]_{Pers}$ was the lone gunman who killed $[\text{President Kennedy}]_{Pers}$ and $[\text{Officer Tippit}]_{Pers}$ and that there was no coverup by the $[\text{Warren Commission}]_{Org}$

There are two *Kill* relations. The first one between $[\text{Oswald}]_{e_i}$ (first entity) and $[\text{President Kennedy}]_{e_j}$ (second entity) and the second one between $[\text{Oswald}]_{e_i}$ (first entity) and $[\text{Officer Tippit}]_{e_j}$ (second entity). In this paper, we introduce the concept of the *entity sequence* and describe how it represents entities and relations in a sentence. An entity sequence depends upon the position and occurrence of entities in a sentences. We introduce three terms to represent the word sequences related to a relation: 1) *pre-entity* (the word sequence before the first entity of a relation), 2) *intra-entities* (the word sequence between the two entities) and 3) *post-entity* (the word sequence after the second entity). Thus, an entity sequence (ES) is defined as:

$$ES = [pre] + entity1 + [intra] + entity2 + [post] \tag{1}$$

The pre/post entity word sequences have a maximum length of four words. Each entity sequence can contain a maximum of one relation between candidate entities *entity1* and *entity2*. If an entity sequence contains a relation, then the sequence is considered as a *positive* example for the given relation. Otherwise, it is a *negative* example. A single entity can take part in multiple relations. For example, in Figure 1, $[\text{Oswald}]_{Pers}$ is part of two *Kill* relations. In contrast, an entity in a given sentence might not take part in any relation (e.g., $[\text{Warren Commission}]_{Org}$). From a given sentence S, it is trivial to create the set of entity sequences by permuting the position of the entities (e.g., Figure 1). However, this has an unwanted consequence of producing an extremely large number of negative entity sequences. Thus, to balance the distribution of the positive and the negative examples in the training set, we selected only those negative entity sequences where at least one of the two entities is a gold standard entity. In Figure 1, we have a total of six entity sequences generated from the candidate sentence. The first ([Oswald]e_i ... killed [President Kennedy]e_j) and the second ([Oswald]e_i ... killed ... and [Officer Tippit]e_k) are positive examples for the *Kill* relation, where the rest are negative examples. Sentences in the RY dataset are taken from the TREC corpus and annotated with entities and relations. Our experiments used only the 1,437 sentences that contain at least one relation. There are four types of entities (*Person (Pers)*, *Location (Loc)*, *Organization (Org)* and *Other*) and five types of relations: *Kill*, *Live_In*, *Work_For*, *Located_In*, and *OrgBased_In*. Based on the algorithm of entity sequence generation we created 268 *Kill*, 521 *Live_in*, 401 *Work_For*, 405 *Located_In* and 452 *OrgBased_In* positive entity sequences. Each ES indicates a pair of candidate entities holding a binary relation. Table 1 depicts the relations in the RY dataset, as well as relation directionality. For each entity sequence the candidate entities have assigned a role. For three relations (*Work_For*, *OrgBased_In* and *Live_In*) the types of the candidate entities are different. For simplicity, we have defined a specific nomenclature for the

Entity Sequences Generated:
ES1= a reasonable doubt that [Oswald]e_i was the lone gunman who killed [President Kennedy]e_j and Officer Tippit and
ES2= a reasonable doubt that [Oswald]e_i was the lone gunman who killed President Kennedy and [Officer Tippit]e_k and that there was
ES3= a reasonable doubt that [Oswald]e_i was the lone gunman who killed President Kennedy and Officer Tippit and that there was no coverup by the [Warren Commission]e_l
ES4= gunman who killed [President Kennedy]e_j and [Officer Tippit]e_k and that there was
ES5= gunman who killed [President Kennedy]e_j and Officer Tippit and that there was no coverup by the [Warren Commission]e_l
ES6= killed President Kennedy and [Officer Tippit]e_k and that there was no coverup by the [Warren Commission]e_l

Figure 1: Example of entity sequences for a given sentence.

Relation	positive	negative	e_1	e_2	Example
Kill	191	962	Pers	Pers	*Oswald* killed *Kennedy*
	77		Pers	Pers	*Tippit* was killed by *Oswald*
Located_in	337	1234	Loc	Loc	*DisneyWorld* in *Florida*
	68		Loc	Loc	*China*'s agricultural producers, *Anhui*
Work_for	260	1280	Pers	Org	*Emmerich* vice president of *ABCcorp*
	141		Org	Pers	*Pepco* executive *SharonPrattDixon*
Orgbased_in	283	1338	Loc	Org	*USA* has leaped 34%... *FBI* reported
	169		Org	Loc	*leatherfactory* in *Caguasu*
Live_in	376	1549	Pers	Loc	*DavidAbernathy* is born in *Linden*
	145		Loc	Pers	*Illinois* born *CharltonHeston*

Table 1: Statistics of Entity Sequences in the RY dataset

order of the entities. In the case of *Work_For* relation, the *Pers* entity is e_1 and the *Org* entity is e_2. This ordering of entities is denoted as $e_1 \rightarrow e_2$. There are 260 examples of this ordering in Table 1. Conversely, there are 141 examples of type $e_2 \rightarrow e_1$ where *Org* is the first entity and *Pers* is the second entity. We have applied some heuristics for *Kill* and *Located_In* because the candidate entities are of the same type. In the first example, one *Pers* entity [Oswald]e_1 is acting upon another *Pers* entity [President Kennedy]e_2. According to our heuristic thus [Oswald] is denoted as e_1 and [President Kennedy] is e_2. So the order of the entities is $e_1 \rightarrow e_2$. Similarly, in *[Officer Tippit]* e_k*, the Dallas policeman who was killed by [Oswald]*e_i the order of the entities is $e_2 \rightarrow e_1$. For the *Located_in* relation, when a location entity is inside another location entity we denote the contained entity e_1 and the container entity as e_2. In the example *[Disney World]*e_i *in [Florida]*e_j, we have that [Disney World] is e_1 and [Florida] is e_2. Similarly, in the example *[China]*e_i*'s major agricultural producers, [Anhui]*e_j, [China] becomes e_2 and [Anhui] is e_1.

3 Entity Sequence Kernel and SVM

Once we generate *entity sequences* from the given sentences, the next task is to adopt the proper machine learning algorithm for the relation extraction task. Every relation is split into two *sub relations* ($e_1 \rightarrow e_2$ and $e_2 \rightarrow e_1$) depending upon the order of the candidate entities. All negative examples are categorized together in a single category. We utilize a modified version of the gap weighted sequence kernel (Lodhi et al., 2002) for the relation extraction task. Our data set (entity sequences) is nothing but a carefully selected sequences of words, where the order of the words is of prime importance. A conventional BoW feature vector representation (e.g., binary value features) is unaware of the word order and hence it will be difficult for a traditional classifier (e.g., a standard vector kernel) to classify entity sequences. Instead, gap weighted sequence kernels (Lodhi et al., 2002) are a perfect fit to handle instances where the order of the word sequences is essential. Thus, this kernel is a natural choice for our classification task.

Given two *entity sequences* s and t, an Entity Sequence Kernel K_{es} counts the number of subsequences of length n common to both s and t. Formally, let F_i be the feature space over the *words* in an ES. Similarly, we consider other disjoint feature spaces $F_j, F_k, ..., F_l$ (e.g., stem, POS tags, chunk tags) (Bunescu and Mooney, 2005a) where the set of all possible feature vectors $F_\times = F_i \times F_j \times F_k \times ... \times F_l$. For any two feature vectors $x, y \in F_\times$ let $sim(x, y)$ computes the number of similar (i.e., common) features between x and y. Given two entity sequences s and t over the finite set $F_\times$, let $|s|$ denote the length of $s = s_1...s_{|s|}$. Let $\mathbf{i} = (i_1, ..., i_{|i|})$ be a sequence of $|i|$ indices in s where the length l(**i**) is $i_{|\mathbf{i}|} - i_1 + 1$. Similarly, **j** is a sequence of $|j|$ indices in t. The kernel function $K_{es}(s, t, \lambda)$ that calculates the number of weighted sparse subsequences of length n (say, n=2:bigram) common to both s and t, is defined as:

$$K_{es}(s, t, \lambda) = \sum_{\mathbf{i}:|\mathbf{i}|=n} \sum_{\mathbf{j}:|\mathbf{j}|=n} \prod_{k=1}^{n} sim(s_{i_k}, t_{j_k}) \lambda^{l(\mathbf{i})+l(\mathbf{j})} \quad (2)$$

The recursive computation can be computed in $O(kn|s||t|)$ time. The gap between the words is penalized with a suitable decay factor λ $(0 < \lambda < 1)$. This decay factor in turn compensates for matches between lengthy word sequences. The design of the kernel K_{es} is created by the pre, $intra$, and $post$ patterns, which have already been found useful in previous work of relation extraction (Giuliano et al., 2007; Bunescu and Mooney, 2005a). We define two separate kernels to effectively use the candidate entities and the word sequence before and after them. The *relation kernel* K_{rel} measures the similarity between s and t by adding up the evidences of various sub kernels over the word sequences (pre, $post$ and $intra$): $K_{rel} = K_{prei} + K_{int} + K_{ipost}$, where K_{prei} consists of *pre-entity* and *intra-entity* substrings, K_{int} consists of *intra-entity* substring, and K_{ipost} consists of *intra-entity* and *post-entity* substrings. The *entity kernel*, K_{ent} measures the similarity between the candidate entities ($K_{ent} = K_{e_1} + K_{e_2}$) where K_{e_1} is the kernel for the first entity, and K_{e_2} is the kernel for the second entity. The final entity sequence kernel is $K_{es} = K_{rel} + K_{ent}$.

Several features are used in computing $sim(s, t)$ such as original word, stem, POS, chunk information, dependency and WordNet hypernym features. Various preprocessing steps (sentence detection, POS tagging, chunking) are performed using the JTextPro[3] package. Rita.WordNet[4] is used as the WordNet library to compute the similar hypernyms between words. Stanford Dependency Parser[5] is utilized to extract the dependency features. Often the entity sequences are just sequences of words which are non-grammatical as an utterance. Consequently, a parser will behave unexpectedly while parsing these sequences. Thus, we ran the Stanford Parser over the original sentences instead of the entity sequences. The grammatical relation with the *governing* token is used as a feature for the words. All the experiments are conducted using the LibSVM (Chang and Lin, 2001) package customized to augment the entity sequence kernel. The decay factor λ was set to 0.5 empirically. To reduce the data imbalance problem the cost factor W_i was set to be the ratio between the number of negative and positive examples.

We have also performed an initial set of experiments using the shortest path dependency

[3]http://jtextpro.sourceforge.net/

[4]http://www.rednoise.org/rita/wordnet/documentation/

[5]http://nlp.stanford.edu/software/lex-parser.shtml

Approach	Direction	Kill			Located In			Live In		
		Prec.	Rec.	F_1	Prec.	Rec.	F_1	Prec.	Rec.	F_1
BL	$e_1 \rightarrow e_2$	65.5	73.5	69.3	74.1	67.6	70.7	59.5	61.7	60.6
BL	$e_2 \rightarrow e_1$	87.1	70.1	77.6	68.0	32.4	43.9	80.5	40.9	54.2
BL + WN	$e_1 \rightarrow e_2$	68.8	76.7	72.5	82.5	79.4	80.9	60.8	62.2	61.5
BL + WN	$e_2 \rightarrow e_1$	92.6	64.6	76.6	71.0	29.7	41.7	84.5	41.2	55.4
BL + Dep + WN	$e_1 \rightarrow e_2$	75.0	76.7	75.9	81.6	79.3	80.4	60.5	60.7	60.7
BL + Dep + WN	$e_2 \rightarrow e_1$	94.6	66.7	78.1	73.3	29.6	42.2	85.9	41.3	55.8

Approach	Direction	OrgBased In			Work For		
		Prec.	Rec.	F_1	Prec.	Rec.	F_1
BL	$e_1 \rightarrow e_2$	56.1	42.7	48.5	70.2	72.6	71.4
BL	$e_2 \rightarrow e_1$	79.7	77.4	78.6	83.8	45.5	59.0
BL + WN	$e_1 \rightarrow e_2$	69.9	60.5	64.9	67.3	72.4	69.8
BL + WN	$e_2 \rightarrow e_1$	88.1	80.8	84.3	87.5	52.0	65.2
BL + Dep + WN	$e_1 \rightarrow e_2$	54.2	44.8	49.1	69.5	75.9	72.6
BL + Dep + WN	$e_2 \rightarrow e_1$	83.0	80.8	81.9	87.8	54.1	67.0

Table 2: Performance of entity sequence kernels (K_{es}) on both relation directions.

kernel of Bunescu and Mooney (2005b) modified for our settings. We have modified the Entity Sequence Kernel to use only those words that occur on the shortest dependency path between the mentioned entities. Using the Stanford Dependency Parser we create the shortest path between two entities (e_i and e_j) in the undirected version of the dependency graph. Thus an entity sequence - shortest path (ES_{SP}) is defined as $ES_{SP} = entity1 + [sp] + entity2$, where $[sp]$ represents the words which appear on the shortest dependency path between entity1 and entity2. We define the shortest path entity sequence kernel $K_{es\_sp} = K_{rel\_sp} + K_{ent}$, where K_{rel_sp} is based on the words present in $[sp]$. In Table 3, we notice that for three out of the five relations, K_{es_sp} kernel outperforms the original K_{es} kernel.

4 Results and Discussion

Table 2 presents the results for each of the five relations, including directionality ($e_1 \rightarrow e_2$ vs $e_2 \rightarrow e_1$). All scores are averaged over a 5-fold cross validation set. *BL* denotes baseline features (word, stem, chunk, POS), *Dep* is the dependency feature and *WN* is the WordNet hypernym similarity. For three relations (*Kill, Work_For* and *Live_In*) the $e_1 \rightarrow e_2$ relations have a higher recall but lower precision where the $e_2 \rightarrow e_1$ have significantly higher precision for all the relations. For the *Kill* relation, there are 191 examples of $e_1 \rightarrow e_2$ direction and only 77 examples of $e_2 \rightarrow e_1$ (Table 1). This imbalance in number explains the general trend to express a *Kill* relation in text. The entity order $e_1 \rightarrow e_2$ (*Oswald killed Kennedy*) is more common than $e_2 \rightarrow e_1$ (*Kennedy was killed by Oswald*).

In addition, a larger number of negative examples are created for $e_1 \rightarrow e_2$ relations than for the $e_2 \rightarrow e_1$ relations. For *Kill* relation there are around 650 negative examples for the direction $e_1 \rightarrow e_2$, i.e., 70% of all the negative sequences. These negative examples are similar in syntactic structure to the positive examples, which leads the classifier to misclassify the negative examples as $e_1 \rightarrow e_2$. This explains the low precision. In addition, from the perspective of a sequence kernel, it considers all possible subsequences for matching, implementing a partial (fuzzy) matching. Table 2 for $e_1 \rightarrow e_2$ represents the effect of disjoint feature scopes of every features (POS, Chunk, Dep, WordNet). Each features adds up and expands the feature scope of the sequence kernels by allowing fuzzy matching, which in turn improve the recall. For the $e_2 \rightarrow e_1$ direction, the number of negative examples is small and thus there are fewer false

Approach	Kill			Located In			Live In		
	Prec.	Rec.	F_1	Prec.	Rec.	F_1	Prec.	Rec.	F_1
K_{es} BL + WN	80.7	70.7	75.4	77.7	51.6	62.1	72.7	51.7	60.5
K_{es} BL + Dep + WN	84.8	71.7	77.8	77.4	54.5	64.0	73.2	52.0	61.0
$K_{es_{sp}}$ BL + WN	80.0	73.7	76.7	65.9	71.1	**68.4**	65.1	58.5	**61.6**
$K_{es_{sp}}$ BL + Dep + WN	82.0	75.1	**78.4**	65.5	69.6	67.5	64.9	56.3	60.3
KM10 Pipeline	91.1	61.2	73.1	71.5	57.0	62.3	68.1	56.6	61.7
KM10 CardPyramid	91.6	64.1	75.2	67.5	56.7	58.3	66.4	60.1	**62.9**
RY07 Pipeline	73.0	81.5	76.5	52.5	56.4	50.7	58.9	50.0	53.5
RY07 Joint	77.5	81.5	79.0	53.9	55.7	51.3	59.1	49.0	53.0
G10 $M_C\|K^*_{SL}$	82.5	77.2	**79.8**	78.1	59.0	**67.2**	71.8	53.4	61.2

Approach	OrgBased In			Work For		
	Prec.	Rec.	F_1	Prec.	Rec.	F_1
K_{es} BL + WN	79.0	70.7	**74.6**	77.4	62.2	69.0
K_{es} BL + Dep + WN	68.6	62.8	62.3	78.7	65.0	**71.2**
$K_{es_{sp}}$ BL + WN	68.4	69.1	68.7	71.7	65.2	68.3
$K_{es_{sp}}$ BL + Dep + WN	68.8	68.8	68.8	74.3	65.1	69.4
KM10 Pipeline	70.6	60.2	64.6	74.1	66.0	69.7
KM10 CardPyramid	66.2	64.1	64.7	73.5	68.3	70.7
RY07-Pipeline	77.8	42.1	54.3	60.8	44.4	51.2
RY07 Joint	79.8	41.6	54.3	72.0	42.3	53.1
G10 $M_C\|K^*_{SL}$	68.3	61.5	64.7	75.4	67.1	**71.0**

Table 3: Comparison with existing state-of-the-art systems (Average F1)

positives, which explains the higher precision. But since there are a small number of training examples (for a 5-fold cross validation, each fold has an average of 60 training instance), the recall is low. In the case of *OrgBased_In* and *Located_In* we observe two outcomes. First, for $e_1 \rightarrow e_2$ the precision is little higher than the recall, unlike the other three relations. Even if we add features in the sequence kernel the concept of fuzzy matching is not helping to improve the recall for these two relations. We notice that a lot of of positive examples for these two relations are connected either by a single word or by punctuation. Consider the following examples, a) *[Havana]e_i [Radio Rebelda Network]e_j in spanish GMT...*, and b) *[George Lucas]e_i , a [Modesto]e_j*. Even if we add POS, Chunk, Dep features besides the word features, it will not help the classifier to improve the recall as there is not much useful information available. A single letter token like *a* is like a stop-word and does not help in classification. Thus, the recall does not change for these cases. Second, we notice that the dependency feature is not contributing much to these two relations. Stanford Parser does not recognize punctuation as relation markers. To test our hypothesis we observe that for these two relations (containing shorter sequences) the original gap sequence word kernel performs close to the baseline kernel (around 58% F1 for *Located_In* and around 62.1% for *OrgBased_In*). However, for *OrgBased_In* we achieve a very high precision at the same time. WordNet hypernym help to match non-obvious terms like (*Federation* and *Nation*), (*Citizen* and *National*). In the case of $e_2 \rightarrow e_1$ for *Located_In*, entities are mostly linked via the "possession" type of dependency relation. However, a lot of negative examples are linked like that; so by adding the dependency feature for $e_2 \rightarrow e_1$, we observe that the precision slightly decreases.

In order to compare the results with state of the art systems (Kate and Mooney, 2010; Roth and Yih, 2007; Giuliano et al., 2007), Table 3 shows the average scores of the relation directions (however our folds of the 5-fold cross validation are not the same as their folds which were not available). For Entity Sequence Kernels we present the results of *BL+WN* and *BL+WN+Dep*.

For Roth and Yih (2007), we report the results they obtain using their most sophisticated model which they call "E $\leftrightarrow$ R" (RY07 in Table 3). For Kate and Mooney (2010) we show both the results of their card-pyramid method that performs joint modeling of entities and relations, and their pipeline approach (KM10 in Table 3). For (Giuliano et al., 2007) (G10 in Table 3) we use the results of their $M_C|K^*_{SL}$ model which is the closest to ours (it uses entity boundaries but no entity types during training). Our method performs the best for three out of the five relations (*OrgBased_In, Work_For, Located_In*). For the other two relations our average F1 is very close to the best results, being 3rd for *Kill*, 2nd for *Live_In*.

5 Related Work

Recently there has been a lot of research on relation extraction using kernel methods. In this section we review mainly two lines of work closely related to ours.

In Section 4 we have introduced several state-of-the-art approaches to relation extraction which have used the RY corpus. Roth and Yih (2007) have adopted an integer linear programming framework for joint extraction of entity and relations. Kate and Mooney (2010) have implemented a card-pyramid parsing technique where each candidate sentence is represented as a binary directed graph. The entities are placed on the leaf nodes and relations are on the higher levels in the graph. Giuliano et al. (2007) et al. have studied the relation extraction problem using a pipeline architecture, similar in nature to our approach but using linear kernel with only basic features. They ran an independent NER to recognize the entities in the sentences and used these new recognized entities as possible entity mentions for the relation extraction. However, we have not conducted any NER experiments to recognize entities and thus have used the available correct boundaries of entities in our research. Both Kate and Mooney (2010) and Giuliano et al. (2007) have mentioned the directionality issue of the relations but they only presented the micro-average F1 scores.

In terms of methodology, the closest approaches to ours are the ones using sequence kernels for relation extraction. Inspired by the string kernel of Lodhi et al. (2002), Bunescu and Mooney (2005a) created subsequence patterns between entities to extract top-level relations from the ACE dataset. In our work we use entity sequence kernes, and only consider the entity boundaries as given, and not entity types as in (Bunescu and Mooney, 2005a). Bunescu and Mooney (2005b) present a shortest path (between the entities) dependency tree kernel and evaluate it on the ACE 2002 dataset. However, as pointed out by (Giuliano et al., 2007) due to the varied datasets (e.g. ACE, SemEval) employed for these research it is a hard task to compare one against another. The generic trend is usually similar — sequence kernels have more flexibility and thus gap sequence kernels find similar subsequences and often results in a higher recall (Wang, 2008).

6 Conclusion

We have presented an approach for relation extraction using semantic and syntactic features augmented with an entity sequence kernel. To the best of our knowledge, this paper presents the first in depth study of how the *order* of the candidate entities influences *relation directionality* and how various factors might contribute to the accuracy of results for each relation direction. Our proposed entity sequence kernel outperforms state-of-the-art methods for three out of the five relations under study. We plan to further explore the shortest path dependency kernel with different kernel combination schemes in future work.

References

Bunescu, R. and Mooney, R. J. (2005a). Subsequence kernels for relation extraction. Proceedings of the 19th Conference on Neural Information Processing Systems (NIPS).

Bunescu, R. C. and Mooney, R. J. (2005b). A shortest path dependency kernel for relation extraction. Vancouver, BC. Proceedings of the Joint Conference on Human Language Technology / Empirical Methods in Natural Language Processing (HLT/EMNLP).

Chang, C.-C. and Lin, C.-J. (2001). Libsvm: a library for support vector machines.

Giuliano, C., Lavelli, A., and Romano, L. (2007). Relation extraction and the influence of automatic named-entity recognition. *ACM Transactions on Speech and Language Processing (TSLP)*, 5(2).

Kate, R. J. and Mooney, R. J. (2010). Joint entity and relation extraction using card-pyramid parsing. Number 203-212, Uppsala, Sweden. Proceedings of the Fourteenth Conference on Computational Natural Language Learning (CoNLL-2010).

Lodhi, H., Saunders, C., Taylor, J. S., Christianini, N., and Watkins, C. (2002). Text classification using string kernels. *Journal of Machine Learning Research*, 2:419–444.

Roth, D. and Yih, W. (2004). A linear programming formulation for global inference in natural language tasks. *Proc. of the Annual Conference on Computational Natural Language Learning (CoNLL)*, pages 1–8.

Roth, D. and Yih, W. (2007). Global inference for entity and relation identification via a linear programming formulation. *Introduction to Statistical Relational Learning.*

Wang, M. (2008). A re-examination of dependency path kernel for relation extraction. In Proceedings of IJCNLP.

Zhang, M., Zhoua, G., and Aw, A. (2008). Exploring syntactic structured features over parse trees for relation extraction using kernel methods. *Information Processing and Management*, 44(2):687–701.

Translating Questions to SQL Queries with Generative Parsers Discriminatively Reranked

Alessandra Giordani and Alessandro Moschitti
Computer Science and Engineering Department
University of Trento, Povo (TN), Italy
{giordani,moschitti}@disi.unitn.it

ABSTRACT

In this paper, we define models for automatically translating a factoid question in natural language to an SQL query that retrieves the correct answer from a target relational database (DB). We exploit the DB structure to generate a set of candidate SQL queries, which we rerank with an SVM-ranker based on tree kernels. In particular, in the generation phase, we use (i) lexical dependencies in the question and (ii) the DB metadata, to build a set of plausible SELECT, WHERE and FROM clauses enriched with meaningful joins. We combine the clauses by means of rules and a heuristic weighting scheme, which allows for generating a ranked list of candidate SQL queries. This approach can be recursively applied to deal with complex questions, requiring nested SELECT instructions. Finally, we apply the reranker to reorder the list of question and SQL candidate pairs, whose members are represented as syntactic trees. The F1 of our model derived on standard benchmarks, 87% on the first question, is in line with the best models using external and expensive hand-crafted resources such as the question meaning interpretation. Moreover, our system shows a Recall of the correct answer of about 94% and 98% on the first 2 and 5 candidates, respectively. This is an interesting outcome considering that we only need pairs of questions and answers concerning a target DB (no SQL query is needed) to train our model.

KEYWORDS: Natural Language Interface to Databases, Semantic Parsing, Reranking.

Proceedings of COLING 2012: Posters, pages 401–410,
COLING 2012, Mumbai, December 2012.

TABLES

TABLE_SCHEMA	TABLE_NAME	...
geoquery	state	
geoquery	city	
geoquery	river	
geoquery	border	
geoquery	highlow	
...	...	

COLUMNS

TABLE_SCHEMA	TABLE_NAME	COLUMN_NAME	DATA_TYPE	...
geoquery	state	state_name	varchar	
geoquery	state	population	float	
geoquery	city	city_name	varchar	
geoquery	city	state_name	varchar	
geoquery	river	traverse	varchar	
...			...	

KEY_COLUMN_USAGE

TABLE_SCHEMA	TABLE_NAME	COLUMN_NAME	REFERENCED_ TABLE_SCHEMA	REFERENCED_ TABLE_NAME	REFERENCED_ COLUMN_NAME	...
geoquery	city	state_name	geoquery	state	state_name	
geoquery	river	traverse	geoquery	state	state_name	
...						

Figure 1: A DBMS catalog containing GeoQuery database

1 Introduction

In the last decade, a variety of approaches have been developed to automatically convert natural language questions into machine-readable instructions. A considerable amount of research work has tackled such problem along the line of semantic parsing, e.g., (Ge and Mooney, 2005; Wong and Mooney, 2006) defined algorithms for mapping natural language questions to logical forms, (Minock et al., 2008) made use of a specific semantic grammar and (Zettlemoyer and Collins, 2005; Wong and Mooney, 2007) applied lambda calculus to the meaning representation of the questions.

In the perspective of question answering (QA) targeting the information of databases (DBs), the automatic system only needs to execute one or more Structured Query Language (SQL) queries that retrieve the answer to the posed natural language question. In our recent work (Giordani and Moschitti, 2009a,b, 2010, 2012), we have shown that machine learning algorithms, exploiting syntactic representations of both questions and queries, can be used to automatically associate a question with the corresponding SQL queries. One limitation of this approach is that the set of possible queries that a user would execute on the DB must be known in advance. This because such method cannot generate new queries, it can only verify if a given query probably retrieves the correct answer for the asked question. This limitation is critical as the design of a generative parser which, given a question, feeds the model above with a reasonable set of candidate queries seems inevitably to fall in the category of semantic parsers.

This paper will demonstrate that it is possible to avoid full-semantic interpretation by relying on (i) a simple SQL generator, which both exploits syntactic lexical dependencies in the questions along with the target DB metadata; and (ii) advanced machine learning such as kernel-based rerankers, which can improve the initial candidate list provided by the generative parser.

The idea of point (i) can be understood by noting that database designers tend to choose names for entities, relationships, tables and columns according to the semantics of the application domain. Such logic organization is referred to as *catalog*, and in SQL systems it is stored in a database called Information_Schema (IS for brevity). The values stored in IS along with their constraints and data types are important metadata, which is useful to decode a natural language question about the DB domain in a corresponding SQL query. For example, given the IS associated with a DB, shown in Figure 1 and 2, if we ask a related question, q_0:*Which rivers run through New York?*[1], a human being will immediately derive the semantic predicate

[1]GeoQueries (Tang and Mooney, 2001) is available at http://www.cs.utexas.edu/m̃l/geo.html

CITY

CITY_NAME	STATE_NAME	POPULATION	...
new york	new york	7071640	
newark	new jersey	329248	
...			

STATE

STATE_NAME	CAPITAL	POPULATION	...
new york	albany	17558000	
new jersey	trenton	7365000	
...			

RIVER

RIVER_NAME	TRAVERSE	...
delaware	new york	
delaware	new jersey	
allegheny	new york	
hudson	new york	
hudson	new jersey	
...		

Figure 2: GeoQuery database fragment

run_through(*rivers*, *New York*) from it. Then she/he will associate the argument *river*, which is also the question focus, with the table `RIVER`. Once the latter is targeted, she/he will select the column `TRAVERSE`, which, being a synonym of *run through*, provides the same predicative relation asked in the question. Finally, by instantiating the available argument, *New York*, in such predicate, she/he will retrieve the set {`Delaware`, `Allegheny`, `Hudson`} from the column `RIVER_NAME`, i.e., the missing argument (as they are in the same row of *New York*).

The above example shows that several inference steps must be performed to retrieve the correct answer. In particular, lexical relations must be extracted from the questions, e.g., using dependency syntactic parsing and predicate arguments must be expanded with their synonyms or related concepts, e.g., using Wordnet (Miller, 1995).

Additionally, ambiguity and noise play a critical role in deriving the interpretation of the question described above but we can exploit metadata to verify that the selected sense is correct, e.g., from the fact that *New York* in this database is in the column `TRAVERSE`, we can gather evidence that the sense of *running-through* matches the one of *traverse*. Therefore, the general idea is to generate all possible (even ambiguous) queries exploiting related metadata information (i.e., primary and foreign keys, constraints, datatypes, etc.) to select the most probable one using a ranking approach.

Last but no least, we deal with nested SQL queries and complex questions containing subordinates, conjunctions and negations. We designed a generative algorithm based on the matches between lexical dependencies and SQL structure, which allows for building a set of feasible queries. Starting from the general syntactic formulation of an SQL query, i.e.,:

$$\text{SELECT } column \text{ FROM } table \text{ [WHERE } condition\text{]}, \tag{1}$$

we generate the set of column, table and condition terms using the lexical relations in the questions. The relation arguments can be generalized using Wordnet and disambiguated using metadata and the execution of the resulting query candidates in the reference DB. Once the list of candidates is available, we can apply supervised rerankers to improve the accuracy of the system. For this step, we improved on the model, we proposed in (Giordani and Moschitti, 2009b), by designing a preference reranker based on structural kernels. The input of such model consists of pairs of syntactic trees of the questions and queries, where for the query we use their derivation tree provided by the SQL compiler.

We tested our model on three subsets of GeoQuery data (Tang and Mooney, 2001) such that we could compare with several systems of previous work. The results show that our generative model is robust and accurate achieving a Recall of 95.0% on the first 5 candidate answers. Additionally, when we apply our structural reranker to the generated list, we obtain state-of-the-art results, i.e., an F1 of 87.2 on the top answer and a Recall of about 98% on the top 5 answers. The major contribution of our approach is that it is simple and does not require any heavy annotation or handcrafted semantic resources. It just relies on the database and the availability of a training set of correct question and answer pairs targeting a DB.

2 Syntactic Dependencies and Relational Algebra

We extract lexical relations from the question using the Stanford Dependencies Parser (de Marneffe et al., 2006). This provides a set of binary grammar relations existing between a *governor* and a *dependent*, where each dependency has the format *abb_rel_name* (*gov*, *dep*), while *gov* and *dep* are words in the sentence associated with a number indicating the position of the word in the sentence. In particular, we consider collapsed representations, i.e., the dependencies, involving prepositions, conjuncts, as well as information about the referent of relative clauses, are collapsed to get direct dependencies between content words. For example, the Stanford Dependencies Collapsed (SDC) representation for the question,
q_1: "*What are the capitals of the states that border the most populated state?*"
is the following:

$$SDC_{q_1} = \big\{attr(\text{are-2, what-1}), root(\text{ROOT-0, are-2}), det(\text{capitals-4, the-3}), nsubj(\text{are-2, capitals-4}), nsubj(\text{border-9, states-7}), rcmod(\text{states-7, border-9}), det(\text{states-13, the-10}), advmod(\text{populated-12, most-11}), amod(\text{state-13, populated-12}), dobj(\text{borders-9, state-13})\big\}$$

A general SQL query structure is shown in Eq. 1. Its execution starts from the relation in the FROM clause by selecting DB tuples that satisfy the condition indicated in the WHERE clause (optional) and then projects the target attribute specified in the SELECT clause. In relational algebra, selection and projection are performed by σ and π operators respectively. The meaning of the SQL query above is the same as that of the relational expression:

$$\pi_{COLUMN}\left(\sigma_{CONDITION}(TABLE)\right) \tag{2}$$

It is worth noting that while relational algebra formally applies to sets of tuples (i.e. relations), in a DBMS relations are bags so it may contain duplicate tuples (Garcia-Molina et al., 2008). For our purposes the fact of having duplicates in the result adds noise[2]. In our QA task we expect that questions can be answered with a single result set (e.g., we can deal with "*Cities in Texas*" and "*Populations in Texas*" but not with the combined query "*Cities and their population in Texas*"). That is, even if in general $COLUMN$ could be a - possibly empty - list of attributes, in our system it just contains one attribute. We can apply aggregation operators to this attribute that summarize it by means of SUM, AVG, MIN, MAX and COUNT, always combined with DISTINCT keyword, e.g. `SELECT COUNT(DISTINCT state.state_name)`.

Instead, *CONDITION* is a logical expression where basic conditions e_L OP e_R, with OP=$\{<, >,$ LIKE, IN$\}$, are combined with AND, OR, NOT operators. While e_L is always in the form `table.column`, e_R could be:

- numerical value (e.g. `city.population > 15000`) or
- string value (e.g. `city.state_name LIKE "Texas"`) or
- nested query (e.g. `city.city_name IN (SELECT state.capital FROM state)`

An example of a complex WHERE condition could be the following, selecting "*major non-capital cities excluding texas*"): `city.population > 15000 AND city.city_name NOT IN (SELECT state.capital FROM state)) AND NOT city.state_name LIKE "Texas"`.

The meaning of $TABLE$ is more straightforward, since it should contain the table name(s) to which the other two clauses refer. This clause could just be a single relation or a JOIN operation, which selectively pairs tuples of two relations. In practice we take the Cartesian product of two relations and exclusively select those tuples that satisfy a condition C. We use the SQL keyword ON to keep this condition C separated from the other WHERE conditions since it reflects a database requirement and should not match any term of the question (e.g., `city JOIN state ON city.city_name = state.capital`). The

[2]We always delete multiple copies of a tuple by using the keyword DISTINCT in the *COLUMN* field

(1)*root*(ROOT, are),	$\Pi = \{\text{capital, state}\}$
(2)*nsubj*(are, capital),	$\Sigma = \{\text{are}\} \Rightarrow \Sigma = \phi$
(3)*prep_of*(capital, state),	
(4)*nsubj*(border, state),	$\Pi' = \{\text{state, border}\}$
(5)*rcmod*(state, border),	$\Sigma' = \{\text{border, state}\}$
(6)*advmod*(populat, most),	
(7)*amod*(state, populat),	$\Pi'' = \{\text{most, populat, state}\}$
(8)*dobj*(border, state)	$\Sigma'' = \phi$

Figure 3: Categorizing stems into projection and/or selection oriented sets

$$\mathcal{S} = \{state.capital^3, state.state\_name^2, border\_info.state\_name^1, ...\}$$
$$\mathcal{S}' = \{border\_info.state\_name^3, border\_info.border^2, state.state\_name^2, ...\}$$
$$\mathcal{S}'' = \left\{max(state.population)^4, max(city.population)^3, state.population^3, ...\right\}$$

Figure 4: A subset of SELECT clauses for q_1

complexity of generated queries is fairly high indeed, since we can deal with questions that require nesting, aggregation and negation in addition to basic projection, selection and joining (e.g. "*How many states have major non-capital cities excluding Texas*").

3 Automatic Generation of SQL Queries from a Question

The basic idea of our generative parser is to produce queries of the form:

$$\exists s \in \mathcal{S}, \exists f \in \mathcal{F}, \exists w \in \mathcal{W} \text{ s.t. } \pi_s\left(\sigma_w(f)\right) \text{ answers q,} \tag{3}$$

where q is the starting question represented by means of SDC_q and $\mathcal{S}, \mathcal{F}, \mathcal{W}$ are the three sets of clauses (argument of SELECT, FROM and WHERE, respectively). The query answering a question, $\pi_s\left(\sigma_w(f)\right)$, can be chosen among the set of all possible queries $\mathcal{A}$ ={SELECT $s\times$ FROM $f\times$ WHERE w} in a way that maximizes the probability of generating a result set answering q.

Clause set construction. To build $\mathcal{S}$ and $\mathcal{W}$ sets, we identify the stems that can most probably participate in the role of projection (i.e., composing the SELECT argument) and/or selection (composing the WHERE condition). Accordingly, we create two sets of terms Π and Σ. The main idea is that some terms can be used to choose the DB table and column where the answer is contained whereas others tend to indicate properties (i.e., table rows) useful to locate the answer in the column. For categorizing terms we use a heuristic based on the grammatical relations provided by a dependency parser[3]. For example, let us consider the list of preprocessed dependencies SDC_{q_1} in Fig. 3. At the first iteration, we use *ROOT* to add *are* to Σ. Then, the *nsubj(are,capital)* suggests that the subject *capital* may be a focus of a projection thus we included in Π. Additionally, given *prep_of(capital, state)*, *state* is a modifier of the subject thus it may have the same role and we include it in Π. We immediately verify this assumption by automatically checking that there is an occurrence of `state.capital` in IS.

We use the set Π to retrieve all the metadata terms that match with its elements: this will produce S according to our generative grammar[4]. For example, considering the IS scheme in Figure 1, the SELECT clauses that are generated from Π, whose elements are listed in the right side of Fig. 3, are shown in Fig. 4 [5]. For generating the WHERE clauses, we need to divide Σ in two distinct sets: Σ_L and Σ_R, for the left-and right-hand side of the condition, respectively. The set Σ_L contains stems matching the IS metadata terms. Σ_L is used to generate the left condition $\mathcal{W}_L$.

Query Generation. Since each clause set may contain up to ten items, the cartesian product between clause set can be very large. Thus, we verify some conditions during the generative process, e.g., tables

[3]For lack of space we cannot report such heuristics in this paper.

[4]Again for lack of space we cannot report it here.

[5]The superscript numbers just indicate the weight associated with each statement.

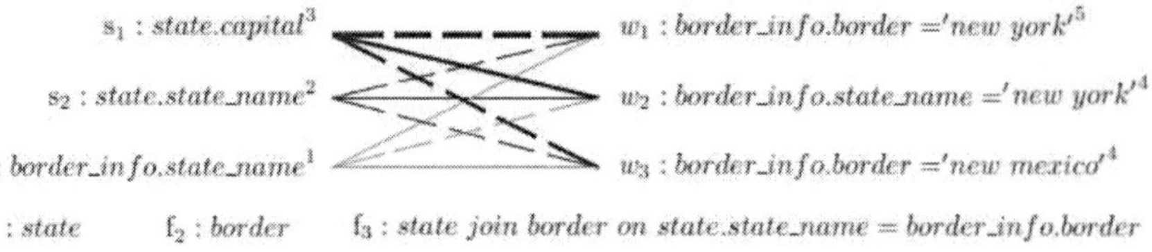

Figure 5: Possible pairing between clauses for q_2

appearing in SELECT and WHERE clauses must also appear in the FROM clause to avoid the failure of the execution of the query. As an example, Figure 5 shows generated clauses from the question q_2, together with possible combinations; the tuple $\langle s_1, f_1, w_1 \rangle$ is not correct as it leads to the MySQL error: `Unknown table: border_info`.

4 The Experiments

We ran several experiments to evaluate the accuracy of our approach for automatic generation and selection of correct SQL queries from questions. We experimented with a well-known dataset GeoQuery developed in the context of semantic parsing.

To generate the set of possible SQL queries we applied our algorithm described in Section 3 to the GEOQUERIES corpus. We considered the full GeoQuery annotation (GEO880) but we used the subset of 700 pairs (henceforth GEO700) since they are translated by (Popescu et al., 2003) from Prolog data to SQL queries. Additionally, to compare with latest systems (Clarke et al., 2010; Liang et al., 2011), which used a subset of 500 pairs, hereafter GEO500, we annotated the remaining 180 pairs as they were included in GEO500. The latter was randomly split by (Clarke et al., 2010) in 250 pairs for training and 250 pairs for testing. The data is slightly *easier* since the number of logical symbols per word are limited to an average of 13 logical symbols. It is worth noting that even if we manually annotated missing questions with their answering SQL queries, we only used them for extracting the answer from the database and evaluate the pair correctness (so we do not really use the SQL queries).

To learn the reranker, we used SVM-Light-TK[6], which extends the SVM-Light optimizer (Joachims, 1999) with tree kernels (Moschitti, 2006) as described in (Giordani and Moschitti, 2009b). We modeled many different combinations described in the next section. We used the default parameters, i.e. the cost and trade-off parameters = 1 (for normalized kernels) and $\lambda = 0.4$.

4.1 Generative Results

We carried out the first experiment on GEO700. Our algorithm could generate a correct SQL query in the first 25 candidates for 95.3% of the cases but could not answer to 33 questions. This was due to (i) empty clauses set $\mathscr{S}$ and/or $\mathscr{W}$, for example, *"How many square kilometers in the US?"* does not contain useful stems; and (ii) mismatching in nested queries, for example, *"Count the states which have elevations lower than what Alabama has"* contains an implicit reference to the missing information. In addition, there were incomplete questions like *"Which states does the Colorado?"* from which we retrieved an incomplete dependency set. When our algorithm can generate an ordered list of possible queries, the top query is correct for 82% of the cases. Additionally, the correct answer is contained in the first 10 candidates for 99% of the cases (excluding the 33 questions above). Note also that the correct query is found among the first three in 93% of the cases. This shows that our ranking based on heuristic weights is rather robust and produce high recall. The accuracy on the top candidate can then be promisingly increased with reranking.

We obtain similar results with the GEO500 subset: we fail to generate an answer in 18 out of the 250 pairs of the test set. We also found that the correct answer is 78% of the times in the top position while it can be retrieved among the first top seven in 98% of the cases.

---

[6] `http://disi.unitn.it/~moschitt/Tree-Kernel.htm`

Combination	Rec@1	Rec@2	Rec@3	Rec@4	Rec@5
NO RERANKING	81.4±5.8	87.6±3.8	90.8±3.1	94.0±2.4	95.0±2.0
STK + STK	83.5±3.6	90.4±3.5	94.2±2.9	95.8±2.0	96.7±1.7
STK × STK	86.5±4.0	92.6±3.7	95.3±3.2	97.0±1.8	97.7±1.4
BOW × STK	86.7±4.1	92.1±3.2	95.6±2.5	97.1±1.4	97.6±1.2
$(1+\text{STK} \times \text{STK})^2$	**87.2±3.9**	**94.1±3.4**	95.6±2.7	97.1±1.9	97.9±1.4

Table 1: Kernel combination recall (± Std. Dev) for GEO700 dataset

4.2 Reranking Results

To improve the accuracy of our generative model, we used a preference reranking approach (Moschitti et al., 2006, 2012; Severyn and Moschitti, 2012). The reranker uses the following kernels: $\text{STK}_n+\text{STK}_s$, $\text{STK}_n \times \text{STK}_s$, $\text{BOW}_n \times \text{STK}_s$ and $(1+\text{STK}_n \times \text{STK}_s)^2$, where n indicates kernels for questions and s for queries, respectively. We applied standard 10-fold cross validation and measured the average Recall in selecting a correct query for each question. The results for different models on GEO700 are reported in Table 1. The first column lists the kernel combination by means of product and sum between pairs of basic kernels used for the question and the query, respectively. The other columns show the Recall of at least 1 correct answer in the top k positions (more precisely the average of Recall@k over 10 folds ± Std. Dev). Additionally, we evaluated the same kernels for reranking pairs generated from the GEO500 dataset. Using $\text{STK}_n+\text{STK}_s$ we obtain a Recall of 84.77%, while if we exploit the product $\text{STK}_n \times \text{STK}_s$, we achieve 87.31%. These results are rather exciting since they compare favorably with the state-of-the-art.

5 Related Work and Discussion

Early work on semantic parsing (Tang and Mooney, 2001) required either the definition of rules and constrains in an ILP framework or manually produced meaning representations (Ge and Mooney, 2005; Wong and Mooney, 2006), which are costly to produce. Additionally, authoring systems where developed by specifying a semantic grammar (Minock et al., 2008), which requires large effort of human experts.

Table 2 shows the f-measure of some state-of-the-art systems to which we compare. Such systems were tested on GEOQUERIES, according to different experimental setups and data versions. The first half of the table reports on systems exploiting the annotated logical form (deriving the answer) whereas the last five rows show the f-measure of systems only exploiting the training pairs, questions and answers.

PRECISE (Popescu et al., 2003) is the only system evaluated on GEO700 in terms of correct SQL queries. The value reported in the table refers to the correctness of answering questions if the expected SQL query (i.e., one with equivalent result) is produced by one of the top k queries[7]. Also our system can provide multiple answers and if we select the first k candidates, we highly increase the Recall (within the first 2 we have an F1 of 90%). Note that (Popescu et al., 2003) needed to rephrase some queries to achieve their result. Another system similar to ours, which applies SVMs and string kernel is KRISP (Kate and Mooney, 2006). The major difference is that it requires meaning representations (following a user-defined MR grammar), instead of SQL queries.

Recent work has also explored learning to map sentences to meaning representations suitable for applying lambda-calculus (Zettlemoyer and Collins, 2005; Wong and Mooney, 2007). This kind of system require a large amount of supervision. In particular, the system in (Zettlemoyer and Collins, 2005) shows a Precision of 96.3% and a Recall of 79.3%, for an f-measure of 86.9%, while our system shows a Precision of 82.8% and a Recall of 87.2%, for an f-measure of 85.0%. Thus, our system trades-off 2 points of accuracy for avoiding large work for handcrafting resources, i.e., the semantic trees manually annotated for each question. Moreover, our system is much simpler to implement. A more recent work (Lu et al., 2008) does not rely on annotation and shows a Precision of 89.3% and a Recall of 81.5%, for an f-measure of 85.2%. Their generative model coupled with a discriminative reranking technique (MODELIII+R) is conceptually similar to our approach.

SEMRESP (Clarke et al., 2010) also learn a semantic parser from question-answer pairs. They achieve the

[7]Being k a small constant, not better defined by the authors.

System Name	Human Supervision	Geo500	Geo700	Geo880
Precise	Rephrase question	-	87%	-
Krisp	Specify the grammar	-	-	81%
ModelIII+R	-	-	-	85%
SemResp	Define a Lexicon	80%	-	-
UBL	Specify a CCG Lexicon	-	-	89%
SemResp	Define a Lexicon	73%	-	-
UBL	Specify a CCG Lexicon	-	-	85%
DCS	Define Lexical Triggers	79%	-	89%
DCS^+	Define an Augmented Lexicon	87%	-	91%
Our system/SQL*	-	**87%**	85%	-

Table 2: Comparison between state-of-the-art systems in terms of F1.

highest accuracy when tested on annotated logical forms whereas when tested on answers their accuracy is lower (80% vs. 73% in f-measure). In contrast, our system, evaluated on answers, outperforms their best system in all setting, e.g., (85% vs. 80%).

Another system evaluated both with logical forms and with answers is UBL (Kwiatkowski et al., 2010). Starting from a restricted set of lexical items and CCG combinatory rules, it is able to learn new lexical entries and achieves the best performance with Geo880 when trained with logical forms.

In contrast, the best performing system that does not exploit the annotation of the Geo880 is DCS (Liang et al., 2011). The comparison of the systems above with ours on Geo500 shows that ours largely outperforms DCS (87% vs. 78% in f-measure). Our system performs comparably to the version enriched with prototype triggers, DCS^+, even though we do not exploit such manual resources.

In summary, our system is competitive with other supervised parsers as it: (i) only relies on the answers, i.e., without using any annotated meaning representations (e.g. Prolog data, MR, Lambda calculus, SQL queries); and (ii) requires much less supervision since there is no need to build semantic representation. Our manual intervention only regards the definition of few synonym relations, i.e., *border* and *next to* as synonyms for *traverse*, since there are not such relations in Wordnet. The rest of the lexicon is induced by the database metadata or obtained exploiting Wordnet.

Finally, our system is competitive with the state-of-the-art defined in (Lu et al., 2008). This is not surprising since we use a very similar approach, i.e., a generative model coupled with discriminative reranking. However, while the system above learns a parser on meaning representations, we only need natural language questions their answers (of course targeting a DB).

6 Conclusion

In this paper, we have approached question answering targeting database information by automatically generating SQL queries in response of the posed question. Our method exploits grammatical dependencies and metadata matching. To our knowledge, our approach to build and combine clauses sets is novel. Additionally, we firstly experimented with a preference reranking kernel, which is able to boost the accuracy of our generative model.

Given the high accuracy, the simplicity and the practical usefulness of our approach, (e.g., we can generate the correct question in the first 5 candidates in 98% of the cases), we believe that it can be successfully used for real-world applications.

Acknowledgments

The research described in this paper has been partially supported by the European Community's Seventh Framework Programme (FP7/2007-2013) under the grants #247758: EternalS – Trustworthy Eternal Systems via Evolving Software, Data and Knowledge, and #288024: LiMoSINe – Linguistically Motivated Semantic aggregation engiNes

References

Clarke, J., Goldwasser, D., Chang, M., and Roth, D. (2010). Driving semantic parsing from the world's response. In *CoNLL*.

de Marneffe, M.-C., MacCartney, B., and Manning, C. D. (2006). Generating typed dependency parses from phrase structure parses. In *Proceedings LREC 2006*.

Garcia-Molina, H., Ullman, J. D., and Widom, J. (2008). *Database Systems: The Complete Book*. Prentice Hall Press, Upper Saddle River, NJ, USA, 2 edition.

Ge, R. and Mooney, R. (2005). A statistical semantic parser that integrates syntax and semantics. In *Proceedings of the Ninth Conference on Computational Natural Language Learning (CoNLL-2005)*, pages 9–16, Ann Arbor, Michigan. Association for Computational Linguistics.

Giordani, A. and Moschitti, A. (2009a). Semantic mapping between natural language questions and SQL queries via syntactic pairing. In *NLDB*, pages 207–221.

Giordani, A. and Moschitti, A. (2009b). Syntactic structural kernels for natural language interfaces to databases. In *Proceedings of the European Conference on Machine Learning and Knowledge Discovery in Databases: Part I*, ECML PKDD '09, pages 391–406, Berlin, Heidelberg. Springer-Verlag.

Giordani, A. and Moschitti, A. (2010). Corpora for automatically learning to map natural language questions into SQL queries. In *Proceedings of LREC'10)*, Valletta, Malta. European Language Resources Association (ELRA).

Giordani, A. and Moschitti, A. (2012). Generating SQL queries using natural language syntactic dependencies and metadata. In *NLDB*, pages 164–170.

Joachims, T. (1999). Making large-scale SVM learning practical. In Schölkopf, B., Burges, C., and Smola, A., editors, *Advances in Kernel Methods*.

Kate, R. J. and Mooney, R. J. (2006). Using string-kernels for learning semantic parsers. In *Proceedings of the 21st ICCL and 44th Annual Meeting of the ACL*, pages 913–920, Sydney, Australia. Association for Computational Linguistics.

Kwiatkowski, T., Zettlemoyer, L. S., Goldwater, S., and Steedman, M. (2010). Inducing probabilistic ccg grammars from logical form with higher order unification. In *EMNLP*, pages 1223–1233. ACL.

Liang, P., Jordan, M. I., and Klein, D. (2011). Learning dependency-based compositional semantics. In *Association for Computational Linguistics (ACL)*, pages 590–599.

Lu, W., Ng, H. T., Lee, W. S., and Zettlemoyer, L. S. (2008). A generative model for parsing natural language to meaning representations. In *Proceedings of the Conference on Empirical Methods in Natural Language Processing*, EMNLP '08, pages 783–792, Stroudsburg, PA, USA. Association for Computational Linguistics.

Miller, G. A. (1995). WordNet: A lexical database for English. *Communications of the ACM*.

Minock, M., Olofsson, P., and Näslund, A. (2008). Towards building robust natural language interfaces to databases. In *NLDB '08: Proceedings of the 13th international conference on Natural Language and Information Systems*, Berlin, Heidelberg.

Moschitti, A. (2006). Efficient convolution kernels for dependency and constituent syntactic trees. In *Proceedings of ECML'06*.

Moschitti, A., Ju, Q., and Johansson, R. (2012). Modeling topic dependencies in hierarchical text categorization. In *ACL (1)*, pages 759–767.

Moschitti, A., Pighin, D., and Basili, R. (2006). Semantic role labeling via tree kernel joint inference. In *Proceedings of CoNLL-X*, New York City.

Popescu, A.-M., A Etzioni, O., and A Kautz, H. (2003). Towards a theory of natural language interfaces to databases. In *Proceedings of the 2003 International Conference on Intelligent User Interfaces*, pages 149–157, Miami. Association for Computational Linguistics.

Severyn, A. and Moschitti, A. (2012). Structural relationships for large-scale learning of answer re-ranking. In *SIGIR*, pages 741–750.

Tang, L. R. and Mooney, R. J. (2001). Using multiple clause constructors in inductive logic programming for semantic parsing. In *Proceedings of the 12th European Conference on Machine Learning*, pages 466–477, Freiburg, Germany.

Wong, Y. W. and Mooney, R. (2006). Learning for semantic parsing with statistical machine translation. In *Proceedings of the Human Language Technology Conference of the NAACL, Main Conference*, pages 439–446, New York City, USA. Association for Computational Linguistics.

Wong, Y. W. and Mooney, R. (2007). Learning synchronous grammars for semantic parsing with lambda calculus. In *Proceedings of the 45th Annual Meeting of the Association of Computational Linguistics*, pages 960–967, Prague, Czech Republic. Association for Computational Linguistics.

Zettlemoyer, L. S. and Collins, M. (2005). Learning to map sentences to logical form: Structured classification with probabilistic categorial grammars. In *UAI*, pages 658–666.

Classifier-based Tense Model for SMT

GONG ZhengXian[1] *ZHANG Min*[2] *TAN ChewLim*[3] *ZHOU GuoDong*[1*]
(1) School of Computer Science and Technology, Soochow University, Suzhou, China 215006
(2) Human Language Technology, Institute for Infocomm Research, Singapore 138632
(3) School of Computing, National University of Singapore, Singapore 117417
{zhxgong, gdzhou}@suda.edu.cn, mzhang@i2r.a-star.edu.sg,
tancl@comp.nus.edu.sg

ABSTRACT

Tense of one sentence can indicate the time when an event takes place. Therefore, it is very useful for natural language processing tasks such as Machine Translation (MT). However, the mapping of tense in MT is a very challenging problem as the usage of tenses varies from one language to another. Aiming at translating one language (source) which lacks overt tense markers into another language (target) whose tense information is easily recognized, we propose to use a classifier-based tense model to keep the main tense in target side consistent with the one in source side. Furthermore, we present a simple and effective way to help this model by expanding more phrase pairs with different tenses. Experimental results demonstrate our methods significantly improve translation accuracy.

TITLE AND ABSTRACT IN ANOTHER LANGUAGE (CHINESE)

基于分类的时态模型在SMT里的应用

时态对一些自然语言处理任务来说特别重要, 比如机器翻译. 然而, 在翻译过程中要保持源、目标端的时态一致性是非常困难的, 尤其表现在对某些没有明显时态标记的源语言句子进行翻译的时候. 本文提出了一种基于分类技术的时态模型去帮助这类翻译. 此外, 本文还采用了一种简单有效的方法来获取更多时态的短语对. 实验表明我们的方法能够显著提高翻译质量.

KEYWORDS: Statistical Machine Translation(SMT), Tense Model, Verb Phrase .

KEYWORDS IN CHINESE: 统计机器翻译, 时态模型, 动词短语 .

*Corresponding author.

Proceedings of COLING 2012: Posters, pages 411–420,
COLING 2012, Mumbai, December 2012.

1 Introduction

Correct usage of tenses is important because they encode the temporal order of events in a text and odd tense can lead to confusion and misunderstanding in communication. However, there is a big difference in the usage of tenses in different languages. In inflectional languages like English, tense is often expressed by verb inflections and thus can be easily recognized. Whereas, some of the major Eastern Asian languages such as Chinese, Vietnamese and Thai, do not have the grammatical category of tense, and their tense is indicated by content words such as adverbs of time. So mapping a correct tense from source-side into target-side in this case is difficult and thus it poses challenges on current machine translation tasks.

In some Interlingua-based MT systems (Dorr, 1992; Olsen et al., 2001; Wang and Seneff, 2006), tense information of the source language can be firstly transformed into an abstract language-independent representation and passed to the target language. However, such research works have not been thoroughly studied since the definition of an Interlingua is already very difficult esp. for a wider domain. With the popularity of SMT, corpus-based methods of addressing tense problems for MT have been introduced (Ye and Zhang, 2005; Liu et al., 2011; Lee, 2011). However, these works just resolve tense recognition and do not address how to integrate their works into a realistic SMT system.

There is little work on resolving tense error for SMT. Gong et al. (2012) propose target N-gram-based tense models to improve translation performance. However, it is not reliable enough since they only consider the target-side tense information and SMT systems often generate abnormal outputs. For the source language with weak inflections or even without inflections, its contexts can provide valuable cues about tense. For example, some Chinese words, such as "经常(JinChang, often)" and "昨天(ZuoTian, yesterday)", can obviously indicate present tense and past tense respectively.

Our proposed SMT system, both source-side and target-side tense cues are employed. Aiming at translating one language (source) which lacks overt tense markers into another language (target) whose tense information is easily recognized, we first automatically construct two tense classifiers based on a Chinese-to-English parallel corpus. Then, two related features are specially designed for a phrase-based SMT system. Furthermore, since verb phrases have limited tense forms in our phrase table, we propose a simple and effective solution to expand phrase table. Experimental results on Chinese-to-English translation show that classifier-based tense model can obtain significant improvements over the baseline.

2 SMT with classifier-based tense model

2.1 Basic idea

In Chinese-to-English translation, the taxonomy of English tenses typically includes three basic tenses (present, past and future) plus their combination with the progressive and perfect grammatical aspects. Since Chinese sentences lack tense markers, it is natural to label them with correct tenses before translation. We treat this labeling task as a classification problem and train a multi-class SVM classifier to assign four labels: P_r- present tense; P_a-past tense; F-future tense; UNK-unknown tense. Given T_s is the major tense of one Chinese sentence f,

$$P(T_s|f) = \arg\max P(T_{s\_i}|f),\ \ i = 1\ to\ 4,\ \ T_{s\_i} \in \{P_r, P_a, F, UNK\}.$$

where $P(T_{s\_i}|f)$ is the probability that the major tense of f equals to T_{s_i}. Furthermore, given e_{best} is the most possible equivalent translation of f and T_g is the major tense of e_{best}, we confine our translation model to satisfy this condition: $T_g = T_s$. That means we assume hypothesis translations with good quality should keep the same tense with source-side sentence.

This idea is straightforward but its implementation is difficult. First of all, source sentences lack inflections and it brings difficulty in determining T_s . Furthermore, there exists the same degree of difficulty in determining T_g for SMT outputs because they are uncompleted texts with abnormal word ordering(Vilar et al., 2006). We treat such task of determining T_g and T_s as tense predication. Although our source-side tense predication is slightly similar to Liu et al. (2011), our predication is special in two aspects: (1) we only consider the major tense of source-side sentence and thus our classification accuracy is high enough; (2) we exploit more useful features for this task. Furthermore, we integrate our tense model into a popular SMT system and improve the translation results.

2.2 The system framework

The work described in this paper is based on a modified Moses, a state-of-the-art phrase-based SMT system. The major modified parts for Moses are input and output modules in order to translate using document-level information. Our SMT system follows Koehn et al. (2003) and adopts similar six groups of features. Besides, the log-linear model(Och and Ney, 2000) is employed to linearly interpolate these features according to formula(1):

$$e_{best} = \arg\max_{e} \sum_{m=1}^{M} \lambda_m h_m(e,f) \tag{1}$$

where $h_m(e,f)$ is a feature function, and λ_m is the weight of $h_m(e,f)$ optimized by a discriminative training method on a held-out development data (Och, 2003).

Classifier-based tense model can be easily integrated into the formula(1) by the following special features:

$$F_1 = \begin{cases} 1 & if(t_g = t_s) \\ 0 & else \end{cases} \qquad F_2 = P(T_{s\_i}|f)$$

F_1 is a binary feature which encourages the decoder to prefer hypothesis translations which have tense form conforming to the source-side contexts. Since tense of source-side sentence sometimes is not reliable enough, F_2 is introduced to inform the decoder to what extent it can trust F_1, it indicates the confidence of the source-side tense classifier. It is worth noting that we don't introduce the similar feature for the target side since the classification accuracy for hypothesis translation is low(see section 3.3).

Before translation, our decoder uses a trained source-side tense classifier to predict its major tense and obtains the value of F_2. During decoding, when a hypothesis translation covers the whole source-side words, the decoder will use a trained target classifier to predict its major tense and compute F_1. The two feature values with related tuned weights are used to re-rank all hypothesis translations.

3 Constructing tense classifiers

3.1 Prepare training data

The key of constructing tense classifiers is to obtain a collection of labelled data. Because of lack of annotated training data, we propose to generate reference tenses based on a Chinese-English parallel corpus (FBIS, see Section 5).

To English sentences in this parallel corpus, we first automatically identify their major tenses according to the morphology of their ***root word***. Here ***root word*** is the word with typed dependency of "root" in a dependency parsing tree obtained from the Stanford dependencies[1]. If ***root word*** is a verb with special POS tag[2] [3], the major tense can be easily recognized in most cases. If ***root word*** can not determine the specific tense, we will traverse the dependency tree forward and backward to find other verb governed by ***root word*** directly. The worst case is to use "UNK" as the major tense for an English sentence.

Since we use parallel corpus, it is reasonable that we treat such major tenses produced by English sentences as gold standards to train a classifier for their corresponding Chinese sentences.

3.2 Source-side tense classifier

After obtaining training data, we built a 4-class (p_r, p_a, F, UNK) tense classifier for source-side (Chinese) sentences with the tool of $SVM^{multiclass}$[4] accompanied by the following features:

(1) *Words and POS patterns (WP) features*: Combinations of word/POS tag for each of words in the whole sentence. These features are expected to capture some special expression patterns, for example, a Chinese verb followed by the word "了(Le)" often refers to past tense.

(2) *Temporal word feature*: The word with the typed dependency of "tmod" (means temporal modifier). A complicated sentence maybe contains multiple "tmod" words. We only consider such "tmod" word who is governed by its "major" verb directly. Here the major verb maybe a ***root word*** or a verb governed by ***root word*** directly. This feature can catch special temporal words, such as "近日(JinRi, recently)", "今年(JinNian, this year)".

(3) *History tense feature*: History tense means tense of previous sentence. We found some Chinese sentences have no temporal words or markers at all and thus their limited contexts at sentence level can not classify them with correct tense form by itself. Gong et al. (2012) and Lee (2011) show history tense has close relation to current sentence.

(4) *The category of document feature*: This feature is expected to control the feature of "history tense". For example, articles about products and laws like to use present tense and in this case history tense is important. However, the importance of history tense in other domains such as news reports may be reduced since they tend to use tense diversely. In order to obtain the category of documents, another SVM classifier is trained based on a public classification corpus[5], which only uses bag of words and TF/IDF (Salton et al., 1975) as feature/value.

The first two features refer to lexical information at sentence level and the latter two features reflect high-level semantic at document level.

After constructing a source-side classifier, we use classification accuracy to measure its performance. Table 1 shows the 5-fold cross validation results using different features for Chinese sentences from previous training set. The performance is improved incrementally by adding above features. When "WP" features are used, the accuracy is 75.44%. Adding "Temporal

[1]http://nlp.stanford.edu/software/lex-parser.shtml

[2]POS tags can distinguish five different forms of verbs: the base form (tagged as VB), and forms with overt endings D for past tense, G for present participle, N for past participle, and Z for third person singular present. It is worthy to note that VB, VBG and VBN cannot determine the specific tenses by themselves.

[3]special modal verbs with POS tag "MD", such as "will","shall","'ll", indicate future tense

[4]http://svmlight.joachims.org/svm_multiclass.html

[5]http://www.nlp.org.cn/docs/doclist.php?cat_id=16&type=15

word" feature obtains a gain of 3.06%. After introducing "history tense" feature, a slightly improvement with 1.59% is yielded. Finally, the classification accuracy reaches to 83.10% by adding "category of doc" feature. It is obvious that the "history tense" feature is largely affected by different document categories.

Table 1 also shows one result for Chinese sentences from a test set "NIST 2005"(see Section 5). There are 4 English references for NIST 2005, we choose one of them and determine their major tense using the method described in Section 3.1 and thus obtain the gold standards for "NIST 2005". we use the source-side tense classifier to predict tenses for NIST 2005, the accuracy of this 4-class classifier can reach to 78.26.

Data	Features	Accuracy(%)
Training Data	WP	75.44
	+Temporal word	78.50
	+History tense	80.09
	+Category of DOC	83. 10
NIST 2005	ALL	78.26

Table 1: Classification accuracy for Chinese sentence with different features

Data	Features	Accuracy(%)
Training Data	Words	81.46
	+POS	86.22
Reference of NIST 2005	Words	79.01
	+POS	81.00
1-best translation of NIST 2005	Words	59.07
	+POS	57.02
Oracle translation of NIST 2005	Words	66.40
	+POS	64.70

Table 2: Classification accuracy for English sentence with different features.

3.3 Target tense classifier for SMT outputs

Unlike normal English texts in previous training data, the SMT outputs are very noisy. So we can not determine their major tense using the method described in Section3.1. Similarly we try to build a tense classifier for these "special" English sentences based on the previous training set only according to two kinds of feature, words and POS tags.

We first measure the cross validation performance for this target-side tense classifier. We can obtain the classification accuracy of 81.46% (Shown on Table 2, 5-fold cross validation) only with "words" features. Then, we use this classifier to classify one reference in "NIST 2005" and the accuracy can still keep to 79.01%. However, when we measure on the translation results (1-best) produced by our baseline, the classification accuracy sharply drops to 59.07%. It is interesting that the classifier's accuracy on oracle translation texts (hypothesis translations with the highest BLEU score from the N-best lists) can rise to 66.40%. From these experimental results, we can conclude that the loss of target-side tense classification accuracy is due to the imperfect translations.

It is worth noting that POS tags can contribute to predict tense for normal English sentence but slightly harm the performance for SMT outputs since POS Tagger can give wrong POS tags by automatically adjusting to its current contexts (Och et al., 2004). In order to use more correct POS tags, we pass the original POS tags to our decoder by introducing an expanded phrase table described in Section 4.1.

4 Expanding verb phrases

Another important impact factor of employing tense model in a phrase-based SMT system is phrase pairs. The core of a phrase-based statistical machine translation system is a phrase table containing pairs of source and target language phrases, each weighted by a conditional translation probability. Koehn et al. (2003) showed that translation quality is very sensitive to this table. If the required phrase pairs with correct tense forms are not in phrase table, the tense model will never play an important role even it is effective in principle. The ideal way to address this problem is to build large parallel corpus but the cost is huge. In this section, we propose a simple and effective way to expand some special phrase pairs.

4.1 Expanding procedure

The detailed procedure is described as follows,

1. POS tagging the English sentences in parallel corpus. Then performing word alignment and phrase extraction between normal Chinese sentences and special Word/POS sentences. So one phrase table, denoted by **PT**, whose target phrases containing POS tags is generated;
2. Traversing each phrase pair whose target phrases contains verb (verb phrases in short). We denote such phrase pair by *ph*, the source phrase of *ph* by ph_{sc} , and the target phrase of *ph* by ph_{tg};
3. Searching verb word of ph_{tg}, and automatically generating new verbs with other tense forms according to serials of transformation rules. For each new verb, expanding a new target phrase by associating other words of ph_{tg}. Putting the new target phrase together with ph_{sc}, POS tags and some translation probabilities of *ph* into a new table **PA**.
4. Generating an expanded phrase table **PE** by merging **PA** and **PT**.

During translation, our decoder only employs the phrase pair and POS tags of **PE** and discard the translation probability parts of **PE** for reducing the influence of data sparsity.

4.2 Automatic transformation rules for verb phrases

The transformation rules described in Section 4.1 involve the following directions: past → present , present → past, base form → past and base form → future. For example, "was *" is evolved into "is *"; "referred to *" into "refer(s) to *"; "operate *" into "will operate *". When doing the transformation of past→ present, we need to specially consider the form of the third person singular. The transformation of present → past involves regular verbs and irregular verbs. To irregular past, we manually construct a special mapping file (put → put).

Some special source phrases containing words like " 正(Zheng)"," 过(Guo)","着(Zhe)"," 了(Le)" should not be expanded with a new tense form since they have already indicated certain tenses. Furthermore, if there are two or more verbs in one phrase and all of them have the same tense form, we assure to expand all of them with one kind of new tense form.

It is worth noting some useful verb phrases are produced by expanding rules, but at the same it also brings some noisy data. For example, we wrongly derive a new target phrase "yesterday night, they discuss" for the phrase pair of " 昨晚 商讨(ZuoWan ShangTao) ||| yesterday night, they discussed". Maybe we can rule out them by using previous target-side tense classifier but it will cost time since phrase tables are often huge.

5 Experimentation

5.1 Experimental setting for SMT

In our experiment, SRI language modeling toolkit (Stolcke et al., 2002) was used to train a 5-Gram general language model on the Xinhua portion of the Gigaword corpus. Word alignment

Corpus		Sentences	Documents
Role	Name		
Train	FBIS	228455	10000
Dev	NIST2003	919	100
Test	NIST2005	1082	100

Table 3: Corpus statistics

was performed on the training parallel corpus using GIZA++ (Och and Ney, 2000) in two directions. We use FBIS as the training data, the 2003 NIST MT evaluation test data as the development data, and the 2005 NIST MT test data as the test data. Table 3 shows the statistics of these data sets (with document boundaries annotated).

5.2 Translation results

For evaluation, the NIST BLEU script (version 13) with the default setting is used to calculate the BLEU score (Papineni et al., 2002), which measures case-insensitive matching of 4-grams. We conduct significance tests using the paired bootstrap method (Koehn, 2004)[6]. In this paper, "***" means significantly better with p-value of 0.05. In addition, we also evaluate translation quality with METEOR (Banerjee and Lavie, 2005) and three edit-distance style metrics, Word Error Rate(WER), Position independent word Error Rate(PER) (Tillmann et al., 1997), and Translation Edit Rate(TER) (Snover et al., 2006).

The main goal of this experiment is to testify the influence of integrating the proposed tense model. From the results shown on Table 4, the systems with tense model significantly outperform the ones without it. The system with tense model (Baseline+Tense Model) yields a gain of 0.74 in BLEU score compared to the baseline and the METEOR score rises to 53.11. In all cases, all edit-distance errors are reduced.

The other goal is to see whether expanded phrase table can contribute to SMT system or not. After being expanded, the size of phrase table has a rise of 35%. But such a big rise only bring a slight improvement with 0.16 in BLEU score in the system(Baseline+Ex_phrases). As our expectation, the new phrase table can help our proposed system (Baseline+Tense Model+Ex_phrases) to gain a rise about 1 point (0.97) in BLEU score. It seems our proposed system can give more chance to expanded phrase pairs.

System	BLEU	METEOR	WER	PER	TER
Moses_Md(Baseline)	28.30	52.07	65.66	43.25	59.76
Baseline+Ex_phrases	28.46	52.13	65.48	42.41	59.30
Baseline+Tense Model	29.04(***)	53.11	63.09	40.12	55.82
Baseline+Tense Model + Ex_phrases	29.27(***)	54.50	60.82	36.03	52.37

Table 4: Translation Results

5.3 Tense accuracy of SMT outputs

This experiment is designed to analyze quality of SMT outputs from a new viewpoint. We enforce the decoder to output the POS tag. Then we predict the major tense of the new SMT

[6]http://www.ark.cs.cmu.edu/MT

outputs with previous target-side tense classifier (see Section 3.3). We found the classification accuracy shown on table 5 is improved in both 1-best translation and oracle translation. It also shows the quality of translations has been improved due to our proposed tense model.

System	Data	Accuracy(%)
Baseline	1-best translation of NIST 2005	57.02
	Oracle translation of NIST 2005	64.70
Our best system	1-best translation of NIST 2005	68.59
	Oracle translation of NIST 2005	71.13

Table 5: Tense classification results for the best proposed system

5.4 Discussion

Our tense model is a discriminative model with rich features. The two tense features in our SMT system seem straightforward, but when the decoder uses these classifiers to keep target-side major tense consistent with source-side tense, all lexicon and shallow syntactic information in target side have been employed.

Table 6 shows an example produced by the baseline and our proposed system respectively. The source-side tense classifier predicts that the Chinese sentence has 84.39% probability to utilize past tense. The target-side tense classifier predicates the output of baseline and our system is in past tense with the probability of 53.01% and 78.11% respectively. We think both occurrence of "was" and "is" in the baseline confuses the classifier.

Src	这个 组织 当年 是 在 赫尔辛基 举行 的 会议 成立，对 结束 冷战 有 其 贡献 。
Ref	The organization was established at the Helsinki conference,which helped end the Cold War.
Baseline	the organization was held for years helsinki conference,is a contribution to end the cold war.
Ours	the organization in those days was held at the helsinki conference,a contribution to end the cold war.

Table 6: An example produced by the baseline and our proposed system respectively

Conclusion and perspectives

We have incorporated source-side and target-side tense knowledge into a phrase-based SMT system with two special features. We explore and capture more useful features to predict source-side tense. And the translation model is enhanced with an expanded phrase table which has more verb phrases with diverse tense forms. We evaluate translation results with multiple popular metrics, and especially with tense classification accuracy which can be introduced to current automatic evaluation metrics. All experimental results show our proposed system can obtain significant improvements over the baseline.

In the future, we will extend our wok to consider aspect information since it can indicate the situation of events and more semantics.

Acknowledgments

This research is supported partly by NUS FRC Grant R252-000-452-112,the National Natural Science Foundation of China under grant No.61273320 and 61003155, the National High Technology Research and Development Program of China (863 Program) under grant No.2012AA011102, and the Preliminary Research Project of Soochow University.

References

Banerjee, S. and Lavie, A. (2005). Meteor: An automatic metric for mt evaluation with improved correlation with human judgments. In *Proceedings of the ACL Workshop on Intrinsic and Extrinsic Evaluation Measures for Machine Translation and/or Summarization*, pages 65–72.

Dorr, B. (1992). A parameterized approach to integrating aspect with lexical-semantics for machine translation. In *Proceedings of the 30th annual meeting on Association for Computational Linguistics*, pages 257–264. Association for Computational Linguistics.

Gong, Z., Zhang, M., Tan, C., and Zhou, G. (2012). N-gram-based tense models for statistical machine translation. In *Proceedings of EMNLP*, pages 276–919.

Koehn, P., Och, F., and Marcu, D. (2003). Statistical phrase-based translation. In *Proceedings of the 2003 Conference of the North American Chapter of the Association for Computational Linguistics on Human Language Technology-Volume 1*, pages 48–54. Association for Computational Linguistics.

Lee, J. (2011). Verb tense generation. *Procedia-Social and Behavioral Sciences*, 27:122–130.

Liu, F., Liu, F., and Liu, Y. (2011). Learning from chinese-english parallel data for chinese tense prediction. In *Proceedings of IJCNLP*, pages 1116–1124, Chiang Mai, Thailand.

Och, F. (2003). Minimum error rate training in statistical machine translation. In *Proceedings of the 41st Annual Meeting on Association for Computational Linguistics-Volume 1*, pages 160–167. Association for Computational Linguistics.

Och, F., Gildea, D., Khudanpur, S., Sarkar, A., Yamada, K., Fraser, A., Kumar, S., Shen, L., Smith, D., Eng, K., et al. (2004). A smorgasbord of features for statistical machine translation. In *Proceedings of HLT-NAACL*, pages 161–168.

Och, F. and Ney, H. (2000). Improved statistical alignment models. In *Proceedings of the 38th Annual Meeting on Association for Computational Linguistics*, pages 440–447. Association for Computational Linguistics.

Olsen, M., Traum, D., Van Ess-Dykema, C., Weinberg, A., et al. (2001). Implicit cues for explicit generation: using telicity as a cue for tense structure in a chinese to english mt system.

Papineni, K., Roukos, S., Ward, T., and Zhu, W. (2002). Bleu: a method for automatic evaluation of machine translation. In *Proceedings of the 40th annual meeting on association for computational linguistics*, pages 311–318. Association for Computational Linguistics.

Salton, G., Wong, A., and Yang, C. (1975). A vector space model for automatic indexing. *Communications of the ACM*, 18(11):613–620.

Snover, M., Dorr, B., Schwartz, R., Micciulla, L., and Makhoul, J. (2006). A study of translation edit rate with targeted human annotation. In *Proceedings of association for machine translation in the Americas*, pages 223–231, Boston.

Stolcke, A. et al. (2002). Srilm-an extensible language modeling toolkit. In *Proceedings of the international conference on spoken language processing*, volume 2, pages 901–904.

Tillmann, C., Vogel, S., Ney, H., Zubiaga, A., and Sawaf, H. (1997). Accelerated dp based search for statistical translation. In *European Conf. on Speech Communication and Technology*, pages 2667–2670, Rhodes, Greece.

Vilar, D., Xu, J., d'Haro, L., and Ney, H. (2006). Error analysis of statistical machine translation output. In *Proceedings of LREC*, pages 697–702.

Wang, C. and Seneff, S. (2006). High-quality speech-to-speech translation for computer-aided language learning. *ACM Transactions on Speech and Language Processing (TSLP)*, 3(2):1–21.

Ye, Y. and Zhang, Z. (2005). Tense tagging for verbs in cross-lingual context: A case study. *Natural Language Processing–IJCNLP 2005*, pages 885–895.

Extracting and Normalizing Entity-Actions from Users' Comments

Swapna Gottipati, Jing Jiang
School of Information Systems, Singapore Management University, Singapore
swapnag.2010@smu.edu.sg, jingjiang@smu.edu.sg

ABSTRACT
With the growing popularity of opinion-rich resources on the Web, new opportunities and challenges arise and aid people in actively using such information to understand the opinions of others. Opinion mining process currently focuses on extracting the sentiments of the users on products, social, political and economical issues. In many instances, users not only express their sentiments but also contribute their ideas, requests and suggestions through comments. Such comments are useful for domain experts and are referred to as actionable content. Extracting actionable knowledge from online social media has attracted a growing interest from both academia and the industry. We define a new problem in this line which is extracting entity-actionable knowledge from the users' comments. The problem aims at extracting and normalizing the entity-action pairs. We propose a principled approach to solve this problem and detect exactly matched entities with 75.1% F-score and exactly matched actions with 76.43% F-score. We could achieve an average precision of 81.15% for entity-action normalization.

KEYWORDS: Information Extraction, Normalization, Clustering, Conditional Random Fields.

Proceedings of COLING 2012: Posters, pages 421–430,
COLING 2012, Mumbai, December 2012.

1 Introduction

Opinion mining generally refers to extracting, classifying, understanding, and assessing the opinions expressed in various forums, online news sources, review sites, social media comments, and other user-generated content. Many different aspects of opinions, such as opinion targets (Ma and Wan, 2010), opinion polarity (Pang and Lee, 2008), and opinion holders (Kim and Hovy, 2005, 2006), have been studied.

In general, 90% of user's intention to write product reviews is to talk about the quality of the product and help others in decision making to buy the products[1]. Different from product reviews, user's intention to write comments on non-product issues like social, economical and political issues is to express sentiments or suggestions to the issue. In this work, we focus on comments that contain suggestions. Following the work by (Whittle et al., 2010; Ferrario et al., 2012), we define *actionable comments* as expressions that contain the requests or suggestions that can be acted upon. While motivating our task based on the previous work, we further extend the definition of *an actionable comment as an expression with an entity such as person or organization and a suggestion that can be acted upon*. More formally, an *actionable comment* is an expression with an entity and action expression. For example, in the comment "the government should tighten immigration rules," "the government" is the entity and "tighten immigration rules" is the action expression.

Detecting actionable comments is an important subtask for various problems. First, actionable knowledge detection opens a new perspective to opinion mining such that it taps into the aspect of suggestion generation process currently missed by traditional content analysis approaches. Second, this task aids in finding the public's actionable sentiment towards the entity by exploiting the individual value of an opinion and aids domain experts (Ferrario et al., 2012). Third, when users intend to get the gist of the comments, this task aids in generating such well-structured entity-based summaries on suggestions.

Finding a piece of actionable knowledge in social media typically involves extensive human inspection, which is labor-intensive and time-consuming. To illustrate the nature of the task, let us examine the following examples:

[C1]*The government should lift diplomatic immunity of the ambassador.*

[C2]*Govt must inform the romanian government of what happened immediately.*

[C3]*SG government needs to cooperate closely with romania in persecuting this case.*

[C4]*Hope the government help the victims by at least paying the legal fees.*

[C5]*I believe that goverment will help the victims for legal expenses.*

The above comments are in response to the news about a car accident. First, all sentences consist of an action and the corresponding entity who should take the action. Second, users tend to express the actions in various sentence structures and hence extracting entities and actions is desired and challenging as well. Third, we observe that entities in all the above sentences refer to the same entity, Government, but expressed in various forms. This drives the need for normalizing the entities. Finally, similar actions are expressed differently which drives the need for normalizing the actions. We treat all the above expressions as actionable comments and here we study how to extract and normalize entities and actions from users' comments. Table 1 gives an example output of our task.

[1]http://www.bazaarvoice.com/about/press-room/keller-fay-group-and-bazaarvoice-study-finds-altruism-drives-online-reviewers

Entity	Action
government	lift diplomatic immunity of the ambassador and get him to face..
government	inform the romanian government of what happened immediately..
government	cooperate closely with romania in persecuting..
government	help victims by at least paying the legal fees

Table 1: Sample output of actionable comments extraction and normalization task.

2 Nature of actionable comments

How are actionable comments expressed in English sentences? In this section, we study the language aspects of actionable comments at sentence level and at phrase level. This study is important for motivating and designing our solution.

2.1 Sentence level study

First, to understand how frequently a user writes an actionable comment, we randomly selected 500 sentences from AsiaOne.com[2], a news forum site. These sentences are from users' comments and each comment contains one or more sentences. We manually labeled these sentences as actionable comments or non-actionable comments. Our first observation is that 13.6% of the sentences are actionable comments. This is a very small set of candidates and hence justifies the need for detecting actionable comments. Second, to understand how to filter the comments that are non-actionable using some patterns, we further analyzed actionable comments at sentence level and our second observation is that, 88.3% of the actionable comments use the keywords listed in the Table 2. These findings are very similar to (Ferrario et al., 2012).

Keyword	Frequency	Keyword	Frequency	Keyword	Frequency
should	54.24%	hope	8.47%	believe	3.39%
may be	5.08%	have to	5.08%	ought	1.69%
to be	3.39%	suggest	3.39%	suppose to	1.69%
need to	3.39%	must	3.39%	advise	3.39%
needs to	1.69%	request	1.69%		

Table 2: Keywords and their relative frequencies in actionable comments.

Using the above keywords we now study the accuracy of identifying the actionable comments. We randomly extracted 550 sentences with the actionable keywords defined in Table 2 and traced for actionable comments. We identified that 83.41% of the comments are actionable and others are non-actionable comments. This observation justifies the need for filtering the user comments using the keywords and generating the candidate set of sentences. For our solution, we rely on data pre-processing by leveraging on these language dynamics.

2.2 Phrase level study

Intuitively, given an actionable comment, the entities can be treated as noun phrases and actions as verb phrases. We observe the following challenges in extracting actionable comments:
Entity extraction: Users tend to express the suggestions either in active voice or passive voice. The first challenge is to identify the correct entity in the actionable comment.

[2]www.asiaone.com

Normalization: People may refer to the same entity using different expressions and ideally we should normalize them. The second challenge is to normalize the entity mentions to their canonical form.
Redundancy: Very similar actions can be expressed differently. The third challenge is to normalize similar actions to aid in redundancy elimination.
Overall, the first challenge motivates us to detect entity-action pairs as an information extraction task and the last two challenges motivate normalizing the entity-action pairs as a normalization task.

3 Task Definition

The goal of our task is to extract and normalize actionable comments from user generated content in response to a news article. The actionable comments will be represented as an entity-action pair. Our problem of detecting normalized actionable comment is defined as follows: Given a news article A and corresponding candidate comments $C = \{c_1, c_2, \ldots, c_n\}$ extracted using the keywords, our goal is to detect pairs of $\{ne_i, na_i\}$ where ne_i is a normalized entity and na_i is a normalized action.

4 Solution Method

In this section, we first describe our solution for entity-action extraction based on CRF model (Lafferty et al., 2001) and then our normalization model based on the clustering techniques for entity and action normalization.

4.1 Entity-action extraction

The entity-action extraction problem can be treated as a sequence labeling task. Let $x = (x_1, x_2, \ldots, x_n)$ denote a comment sentence where each x_i is a single token. We need to assign a sequence of labels or tags $y = (y_1, y_2, \ldots, y_n)$ to x. We define our tag set as {BE, IE, BA, IA, O}, following the commonly used BIO notation (Ramshaw and Marcus, 1995), where E stands for entity and A stands for action.

Features: To develop features, we consider three main properties of actionable comments. First, the entities of the actionable pairs are mostly nouns or pronouns. Second, the entities display the positional properties with respect to the keywords. Third, the entities should be grammatically related to the actions. For example the verb in the action phrase is related to the subject which is an entity of the actionable comment.

a. Parts-of-speech features: To capture the first property, we classify each word x_i into one of the POS tags using the Stanford POS tagger[3]. We combine this feature with the POS features of neighboring words in [-2, +2] window.

b. Positional features: To capture the second property, we find the position of each word, x_i with respect to the keyword in the given sentence. The feature is represented as positive numbers for words preceding the keyword and negative numbers for words succeeding the keyword in the sentence. We do the same for neighboring words in [-2, +2] window.

c. Dependency tree features: To capture the third property, for each word x_i, we check if it is nominal subject in the sentence and represent it by *nsubj*. The dependency tree features can be extracted using Stanford dependencies tool[4].

[3] http://nlp.stanford.edu/software/tagger.shtml
[4] http://nlp.stanford.edu/software/stanford-dependencies.shtml

The output of this task is $S = \{e_i, a_i\}$, a set of entity-action pairs. The next task is to normalize S which is described below.

4.2 Entity-action normalization

Given $S = \{e_i, a_i\}$, a set of entity-action pairs, the goal is to generate $NS = \{ne_i, na_i\}$, a set of normalized entity-action pairs.

4.2.1 Entity normalization

We use agglomerative clustering which is a hierarchical clustering method which works bottom-up (Olson, 1995) together with expanding the entity with the features from Google and Semantic-Similarity Sieves adopted from Stanford coreference algorithm (Raghunathan et al., 2010).

Features: Two types of features are used to expand an entity mention: first from Google and second from the parse tree structure. The representative of a cluster, n_e is chosen to be the entity mention which has the largest average similarity distance from the other entity mentions in the cluster.

a. Alias features: This sieve addresses name aliases, which are detected as follows: Given an entity mention, it is first expanded with the title of the news article and this query is fed to the Google API. Google outputs the ranked matching outputs. One option is to use the entire snippet as the features. Another option is use partial snippet. Google returns snippets that has bolded aliases. We use them as alias features for a given entity mention. For example, alias features for "Ionescu + *title*" are *Dr.Ionescu, Silvia Ionescu, Romanian Diplomat Ionescu* etc. This sieve also aids in solving the spell problems.

b. Semantic-similarity features: We follow the following steps from the relaxation algorithm from Stanford coreference resolution tool for both named and unnamed entities: (a) remove the text following the mention head word; (b) select the lowest noun phrase (NP) in the parse tree that includes the mention head word; (c) use the longest proper noun (NNP*) sequence that ends with the head word; (d) select the head word.

4.2.2 Action normalization

The main objective of normalizing the actions is to remove the redundant actions. We choose clustering same as above to normalize the actions associated with same normalized entity. The feature set for this task is simply bag-of-words with stop word removal. The representative action is also chosen similar to the above.

5 Dataset

Since the task of actionable comment extraction is new, we gathered and annotated our own dataset for evaluation. Our dataset consists of 5 contentious news articles and the corresponding comments from Asiaone.com, an online forum.

5.1 Pre-processing

For the dataset preparation, we use the keywords listed in Table 2 to extract the candidate sentences from all the comments (each comment has 1 or more sentences) in 5 news articles for the task. We use random 110 candidate sentences from each article and in total 550 candidates for experiments. We calculated the inter-annotator agreement level using Cohen's kappa. Cohen's kappa on actionable comments is 0.7679 which displays a strong agreement between the annotators.

6 Experiments

6.1 Experiments on entity-action extraction

To evaluate the entity-action extraction, we prepare the ground truth using the dataset described in Section 5. We first answer (Q1), how well the model performs in identifying actionable comments. We then evaluate the entity and action extraction from the actionable comments to answer (Q2). We experimented various combinations of features (not reported here) for CRF model and combined feature set gives the best results. We perform 10-fold cross validation for all our experiments. We use this pattern matching technique as a baseline.

Annotation: To prepare the ground truth, we engaged two annotators to label 550 candidate sentences for suggestion, entity and action. For this annotation task the judge should do the following:

1. Look for the person(s) or organization(s) who should execute the suggestion and label the entity with BE (beginning of an entity) and IE (inside an entity).
2. Look out for the action that should be performed by the entity and label it as an action: BA (beginning of an action), IA (inside an action). The others are labeled as O (other).
3. If both entity and action are found, sentence is a valid suggestion. Label it as 1. Otherwise, label it as 0.

6.1.1 Actionable knowledge detection results

Our model achieved precision of 88.26%, recall of 93.12% and F-score of 90.63% in classifying actionable comments and that answers our (Q1). In our analysis, we observed that the model failed in detecting the actionable comments when the sentences have poor grammatical structure. For example, "*Dont need to call the helpline..*", has a poor grammatical structure.

6.1.2 Entity extraction results

In Table 3, the baseline outperformed the CRF model on the overlap F-score and this is due to the relax mode of the overlap. But, for the exact match CRF has high F-score of 75.09% which is relatively 6.67% higher than the baseline. This answers our (Q2) for entity extraction evaluation.

	Exact Match		Overlap Match	
Metrics	**Baseline**	**CRF**	**Baseline**	**CRF**
Recall	**0.8799**	0.8352	0.9032	**0.9306**
Precision	0.5866	**0.6849**	**0.9597**	0.8578
F-score	0.7039	**0.7509**	**0.9306**	0.8927

Table 3: Entity Extraction Results

6.1.3 Action extraction results

From Table 4, we see that the baseline, which is the pattern matching technique, has high recall for both exact match and head match. But, for both exact match and head match CRF has high

F-score of 76.43% and 82.7%, respectively, which is relatively 11.9% and 0.03% higher than the baseline. Head match has generally high performance for both due to the property that an action is expressed as a verb. This answers our (Q2) for action extraction evaluation.

	Exact Match		Head Match	
Metrics	**Baseline**	**CRF**	**Baseline**	**CRF**
Recall	**0.8947**	0.8944	**0.9200**	0.9169
Precision	0.5519	**0.6741**	0.7468	**0.7544**
F-score	0.6827	**0.7643**	0.8244	**0.8270**

Table 4: Action Extraction Results

6.2 Experiments on entity-action normalization

We first answer (Q3), between single link and complete link, which technique is more suitable for this problem? We then answer (Q4), how does the clustering-based solution perform in normalizing the entity-action pairs?

6.2.1 Single Link Vs Complete Link

Annotation: The human annotator is given a set of entities from each article and asked to first group the similar entities together and then assign a label to each group.

	Single Link			Complete Link		
Article	**Precision**	**Recall**	**F-Score**	**Precision**	**Recall**	**F-Score**
A1	0.5161	0.5039	0.5100	**0.8462**	**0.6929**	**0.7619**
A2	**1.0000**	0.3333	0.5000	0.7143	**0.5238**	**0.6044**
A3	**0.7368**	0.3218	0.4480	0.5664	**0.7356**	**0.6400**
A4	**0.6258**	0.4567	0.5280	0.5328	**0.6689**	**0.5931**
A5	**0.9661**	0.4560	0.6196	0.7282	**0.6000**	**0.6579**

Table 5: F-score results comparison between single link and complete link

As shown in Table 5, even though the precision for single link is high, complete link out performs single link on recall and F-score and answers our Q3. For example, "*the ceo*" and "*ceo, smrt ceo ms saw*" are grouped into single cluster using complete link. Where as, for single link cluster, "*smrt ceo ms saw*" is a false negative.

6.2.2 Entity-Action Normalization Results

Annotation: We asked a human judge to validate the normalized entity-action pairs. Only if both entity and action are normalized (entity should be in canonical form and action should be non-redundant), the pair is labeled as valid. If we obtain (e1, a1), (e2, a2), and a1 and a2 refer to the same action, we label one of them as invalid.

From Figure 1, we notice that on all articles the precision is high for complete link measure. This can be justified due to high F-score from complete link measure.

We observed that for single link, the entities like *he*, *they* are not normalized into the correct clusters resulting in the lower precision. Complete link measure outperforms single link measure for all articles in normalizing task with an average precision of 81.15% and that answers

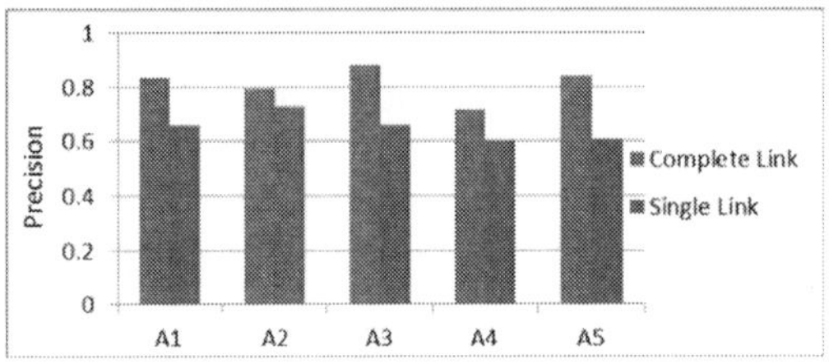

Figure 1: Entity-action normalization results

our Q4. We further analyzed the results for complete link. For article, A4 and the normalized entity *Ionescu*, the actionable comments have entity mentions like *asshole*, *dog* etc., which could not be normalized due to non-distinctive feature set.

7 Related Work

Opinion Mining: Opinion mining is a well studied research for the past ten years mainly focussing on the sentiment extraction and classification tasks (Turney, 2002; Pang et al., 2002). However, according to (Hu and Liu, 2004), fine-grained opinion mining and analysis is highly effective like feature identification by (Popescu and Etzioni, 2005), linking opinions to features by (Lin and He, 2009), and polarity classification by (Liu et al., 2005). Assessing the usefulness and quality of text has been well studied in natural language processing as quality plays a key role in online content (Agichtein et al., 2008) like helpfulness of reviews (Ghose and Ipeirotis, 2011), detecting low quality reviews (Liu et al., 2007) and detecting spam reviews (Lim et al., 2010).

Actionable content: (Zhang et al., 2009) attempted to discover the diagnostic knowledge and defined diagnostic data mining as, "a task to understand the data and/or to find causes of problems and actionable knowledge in order to solve the problems". Their work is more focussed towards manufacturing applications in which the problems are identified to aid the designers in the product design improvements. (Simm et al., 2010) analysed actionable knowledge in on-line social media conversation and the concept of actionability is defined as request or suggestion. (Ferrario et al., 2012) work aims at discovering aspects of actionable knowledge in the social media. To the best of our knowledge, our problem of extracting and normalizing entity-action pairs from users' comments is not studied.

Conclusion and perspectives

Actionable content extraction is a new direction in opinion mining process with many opportunities and challenges. With the increasing user generated content in micro blogs, detecting actionable knowledge in such media will be an interesting problem. For example, during Obama's state union address, apart from political and news forums, the public was asked to express opinions on Twitter using specific hashtags. This triggers the need for gathering actionable content in micro blogs. In the same line, diagnostic opinion detection that talks about what could have happened, who should be blamed, etc., is also an interesting problem.

Acknowledgments

This research/project is supported by the Singapore National Research Foundation under its International Research Centre@Singapore Funding Initiative and administered by the IDM Programme Office.

References

Agichtein, E., Castillo, C., Donato, D., Gionis, A., and Mishne, G. (2008). Finding high-quality content in social media. In *WSDM '08: Proceedings of the international conference on Web search and web data mining*, pages 183–194, New York, NY, USA. ACM.

Ferrario, M. A., Simm, W., Whittle, J., Rayson, P., Terzi, M., and Binner, J. (2012). Understanding actionable knowledge in social media: Bbc question time and twitter, a case study. In *ICWSM*.

Ghose, A. and Ipeirotis, P. G. (2011). Estimating the helpfulness and economic impact of product reviews: Mining text and reviewer characteristics. *IEEE Trans. Knowl. Data Eng.*, 23(10):1498–1512.

Hu, M. and Liu, B. (2004). Mining opinion features in customer reviews. In *Proceedings of the 19th national conference on Artifical intelligence*, AAAI'04, pages 755–760. AAAI Press.

Kim, S.-M. and Hovy, E. (2005). Identifying opinion holders for question answering in opinion texts. In *Proceedings of the AAAI Workshop on Question Answering in Restricted Domains*.

Kim, S.-M. and Hovy, E. (2006). Extracting opinions, opinion holders, and topics expressed in online news media text. In *Proceedings of ACL/COLING Workshop on Sentiment and Subjectivity in Text*, Sidney, AUS.

Lafferty, J. D., McCallum, A., and Pereira, F. C. N. (2001). Conditional random fields: Probabilistic models for segmenting and labeling sequence data. In *Proceedings of the Eighteenth International Conference on Machine Learning*, ICML '01, pages 282–289, San Francisco, CA, USA. Morgan Kaufmann Publishers Inc.

Lim, E.-P., Nguyen, V.-A., Jindal, N., Liu, B., and Lauw, H. W. (2010). Detecting product review spammers using rating behaviors. In *CIKM*, pages 939–948.

Lin, C. and He, Y. (2009). Joint sentiment/topic model for sentiment analysis. In *Proceedings of the 18th ACM conference on Information and knowledge management*, CIKM '09, pages 375–384, New York, NY, USA. ACM.

Liu, B., Hu, M., and Cheng, J. (2005). Opinion observer: analyzing and comparing opinions on the web. In *Proceedings of the 14th international conference on World Wide Web*, WWW '05, pages 342–351, New York, NY, USA. ACM.

Liu, J., Cao, Y., Lin, C.-Y., Huang, Y., and Zhou, M. (2007). Low-quality product review detection in opinion summarization. In *EMNLP-CoNLL*, pages 334–342.

Ma, T. and Wan, X. (2010). Opinion target extraction in chinese news comments. In *Coling 2010: Posters*, pages 782–790, Beijing, China. Coling 2010 Organizing Committee.

Olson, C. F. (1995). Parallel algorithms for hierarchical clustering. *Parallel Computing*, 21:1313–1325.

Pang, B. and Lee, L. (2008). Opinion mining and sentiment analysis. *Foundations and Trends in Information Retrieval*, 2(1-2):1–135.

Pang, B., Lee, L., and Vaithyanathan, S. (2002). Thumbs up?: sentiment classification using machine learning techniques. In *Proceedings of the ACL-02 conference on Empirical methods in natural language processing - Volume 10*, EMNLP '02, pages 79–86, Stroudsburg, PA, USA. Association for Computational Linguistics.

Popescu, A.-M. and Etzioni, O. (2005). Extracting product features and opinions from reviews. In *Proceedings of the conference on Human Language Technology and Empirical Methods in Natural Language Processing*, HLT '05, pages 339–346, Stroudsburg, PA, USA. Association for Computational Linguistics.

Raghunathan, K., Lee, H., Rangarajan, S., Chambers, N., Surdeanu, M., Jurafsky, D., and Manning, C. (2010). A multi-pass sieve for coreference resolution. In *Proceedings of the 2010 Conference on Empirical Methods in Natural Language Processing*, EMNLP '10, pages 492–501, Stroudsburg, PA, USA. Association for Computational Linguistics.

Ramshaw, L. A. and Marcus, M. P. (1995). Text chunking using transformation-based learning. *CoRR*, cmp-lg/9505040.

Simm, W., Ferrario, M. A., Piao, S. S., Whittle, J., and Rayson, P. (2010). Classification of short text comments by sentiment and actionability for voiceyourview. In *SocialCom/PASSAT'10*, pages 552–557.

Turney, P. D. (2002). Thumbs up or thumbs down?: semantic orientation applied to unsupervised classification of reviews. In *Proceedings of the 40th Annual Meeting on Association for Computational Linguistics*, ACL '02, pages 417–424, Stroudsburg, PA, USA. Association for Computational Linguistics.

Whittle, J., Simm, W., Ferrario, M. A., Frankova, K., Garton, L., Woodcock, A., Nasa, B., Binner, J., and Ariyatum, A. (2010). Voiceyourview: collecting real-time feedback on the design of public spaces. In *UbiComp*, pages 41–50.

Zhang, L., Liu, B., Benkler, J., and Zhou, C. (2009). Finding actionable knowledge via automated comparison. In *ICDE*, pages 1419–1430.

Expected Divergence based Feature Selection for Learning to Rank

Parth Gupta *Paolo Rosso*
Natural Language Engineering Lab - ELiRF
Department of Information Systems and Computation
Universidad Politecnica de Valencia, Spain
`http://www.dsic.upv.es/grupos/nle`
`pgupta,prosso@dsic.upv.es`

ABSTRACT

Feature selection methods are essential for learning to rank (LTR) approaches as the number of features are directly proportional to computational cost and sometimes, might lead to the over-fitting of the ranking model. We propose an expected divergence based approach to select a subset of highly discriminating features over relevance categories. The proposed method is evaluated in terms of performance of standard LTR algorithms when trained with reduced features over a set of standard LTR datasets. The proposed method leads to not significantly worse, and in some cases, significantly better performance compared to the baselines with as few features as less than 10%. The proposed method is scalable and can easily be parallelised.

TITLE AND ABSTRACT IN ANOTHER LANGUAGE, L_2 (OPTIONAL, AND ON SAME PAGE)

श्रेणी अधिगम के लिए अपेक्शित विचलन आधारित नक्श चयन

श्रेणी अधिगम (learning to rank) प्रक्रिया के लिए नक्श चयन पद्धतियाँ महत्वपूर्ण हैं, क्योंकि संगणात्मक मूल्य, नक्श संख्या से समानुपाती है और कभी कभी नक्श संख्या रेंकिंग मॉडल की ओवर-फ़िटिंग को प्रेरित करता है। हम नक्श चयन के लिए अपेक्शित विचलन आधारित पद्धति का प्रस्ताव करते हैं जो प्रासंगिक वर्गों में अति विवेकी नक्श उपगण का चयन करती है। प्रस्तावित पद्धति का मान्य श्रेणी अधिगम संग्रह पर अल्प नक्शों से प्रशिक्शित मान्य श्रेणी अधिगम कलन गणितों (algorithms) के संपादन से मूल्यांकन किया गया है। प्रस्तावित पद्धति आधार रेखाओं की तुलना में सिर्फ 10% नक्शों के उपयोग से not significantly worse और कुछ किस्सों में significantly बेहतर प्रदर्शन दिखा रही है। प्रस्तावित पद्धति स्केलेबल है और आसानी से समान्तर चलाई जा सकती है।

KEYWORDS: feature selection, ranking.

KEYWORDS IN L_2: नक्श चयन, रेंकिंग.

Proceedings of COLING 2012: Posters, pages 431–440,
COLING 2012, Mumbai, December 2012.

1 Introduction

Ranking is one of the most important modules of Information Retrieval (IR) systems. Unsupervised ranking models like BM25 okapi and language models have power to rank documents with limited number of features such as term frequency (TF), inverse document frequency (IDF), document length (DL). Although they can rank with speed and without the need of labeled relevance information, they are quite restrictive for the incorporation of more features such as age, link information in web graph, click information etcetera of the document. Elimination of such features from ranking might prove to be a big limitation in the rapidly increasing and annotation rich Web. To overcome this limitation, the research community has posed the ranking problem in machine learning framework and referred as learning to rank (LTR). LTR is a supervised setting of ranking in the IR system where, each document for the given query is represented as a feature vector to which, the ranking function assigns a score. The ranking function is trained on a prelabelled training data.

Over the time, the number of features used in the learning to rank has increased drastically. Although increasing number of features induces more information for the ranking algorithms, it is directly related to the computational complexity and to some extent the over-fitting of the ranking model in some cases. As a result, the attempts to reduce the dimensionality of the feature vector subsequently started (Geng et al., 2007; Pan et al., 2009; Dang and Croft, 2010).

Among a few approaches of feature selection for LTR, Geng et al. (2007) proposed an efficient greedy feature selection method for ranking that finds the features with maximum total importance scores and minimum total similarity scores. The greedy search algorithm over an undirected graph of features was employed to solve the optimization problem. In contrast, Dang and Croft (2010) used best first search to come up with subsets of features and coordinate ascent to learn the weights for those features. This approach, feature selection - best first search (FS-BFS), has recently shown to outperform the greedy approach, hence we use it as one of the baselines to compare with. Pan et al. (2009) used boosting trees with randomized and greedy approach, where th *wrapper* approach was taken with forward selection and backward elimination.

In our approach, the subset of features are selected based on their expected divergence over the relevance classes and the importance of features are estimated by the evaluation scores produced individually by the features. We use Kullback-Leibler (KL) divergence to estimate the divergence and adapt it to make it more suitable for the ranking. The results with the proposed method are reported on a set of standard LTR datasets with three state-of-the-art LTR algorithms RankSVM (Herbrich et al., 2000), RankBoost (Freund et al., 2003) and LamdaMart (Wu et al., 2010). We use the performance of LTR algorithms when learnt with all features (WAF) as another baseline. The performance achieved with the proposed feature selection method is statistically similar to the baselines and in some cases the performance is significantly improved with very few features as 10%. Moreover, the proposed algorithm can easily be parallelised.

We describe the details of the proposed method in Section 2. In Section 3 we describe the experimental setup and the results with analyses are presented subsequently in Section 4. Finally, we end the discussion with concluding remarks in Section 5.

2 Method

The feature selection methods of type *filter*, as defined in Guyon and Elisseeff (2003), computes the score of each feature as a preprocessing step and the subset of features are selected based on the scores assigned. In contrast to *filter* methods, *wrapper* methods use the learning algorithms to assign scores to the features. We opt for a *filter* approach and refer it as feature selection - expected divergence (FS-ED), while FS-BFS is a *wrapper* approach.

The proposed method has two components: (*i*) the importance of the features defined as $s(f_i)$ and, (*ii*) the expected divergence of the features defined as $d(f_i)$. The goal of the method is to score each feature $f_i \in F$, where F is the set of all features and $|F| = n$. We pose the feature selection method as a maximization problem of selecting top k features from F where, the score of a feature $\psi(\cdot)$ is calculated as shown in Eq. 1. For the simplicity, we combine the two objective functions linearly.

$$\psi(f_i) = s(f_i) + d(f_i) \tag{1}$$

As reported in Geng et al. (2007), the feature importance $s(f_i)$ derived from evaluation scores and learning algorithms lead to statistically similar results. Hence, we opt for the evaluation measure, NDCG@10, to estimate the importance of an individual feature. The evaluation score for the queries in the training data using a particular feature value individually to rank documents is considered as the importance score $s(f_i)$.

Usually, the features which can not better discriminate between relevance classes do not add more knowledge for the learning algorithm. This discrimination can be better captured by measuring the divergence of the feature on relevance classes. In order to estimate the divergence of a feature over the relevance classes, we use KL divergence. KL divergence has successfully been used for the feature selection methods for classification problems (Coetzee, 2005; Schneider, 2004). Because of the intuitive differences between the classification and ranking, we adapt and call it as expected divergence which, to the best of our knowledge, is novel. Classes in ranking are ordinal relevance levels, while they are unordered categories in case of classification. Hence, we boost the divergence of a feature over distant relevance classes by the expected divergence. For example, consider a 5-scale relevance system with relevance classes $r_i \in R$ where $i \in \{0, 1, .., 4\}$, the divergence of a feature over r_0 and r_4 is far more important than that over r_0 and r_1. The expected divergence of a feature is calculated as shown in Eq. 2.

$$d(f_i) = \sum_{m=0}^{|R|-1} \sum_{n=m+1}^{|R|-1} (n-m) * \mathrm{div}(f_i^{r_m}, f_i^{r_n}) \tag{2}$$

where,

$$\mathrm{div}(f_i^{r_m}, f_i^{r_n}) = \frac{1}{2} d_{KL}\left(\hat{f}_i^{r_m} || \hat{f}_i^{avg}\right) + \frac{1}{2} d_{KL}\left(\hat{f}_i^{r_n} || \hat{f}_i^{avg}\right) \tag{3}$$

Eq. 3 is the Jensen-Shannon divergence where, $\hat{f}_i^{r_m}$ is the estimated probability density function (PDF) using kernel density estimation (KDE) of ith feature over relevance class r_m learnt from the training data and estimated on the validation data as shown in Eq. 4, $\hat{f}_i^{avg}$ is an average over both relevance classes and d_{KL} is KL divergence.

$$\hat{f}_i = \frac{1}{Mh} \sum_{j=1}^{M} \phi\left(\frac{x - x_j}{h}\right) \tag{4}$$

where, M is the total number of samples in the training data, x_j and x refers to the value of ith feature in the training and validation data respectively , h is the bandwidth which is estimated using *Silverman's rule of thumb* (Bernard, 1986) and the kernel is chosen as standard normal distribution (ϕ). The complete feature selection method is described in Fig. 1.

```
T = training data
V = validation data
ψ⃗ = weight vector of features
F, F_k = feature sets, all and top-k respectively
for each f_i ∈ F
   ψ(f_i) = 0     /* Initialise the weights */
end for
for each f_i
   s(f_i) = evaluation score over T
   for each r_i ∈ R
      estimate PDF(f_i) over r_i from T using KDE
   end for
   for i = 0 to |R| − 1
      for j = i + 1 to |R| − 1
         estimate JS div. of f_i over r_i and r_j from V
      end for
   end for
   calculate d(f_i) as show in Eq. 2
   ψ(f_i) = s(f_i) + d(f_i)
end for
sort ψ⃗
for i = 1 to k
   add f_i in F_k
end for
RETURN F_k
```

Figure 1: Feature selection procedure.

3 Experimental Setup

In order to compare the proposed method with the baselines, we use the performance evaluation of three state-of-the-art LTR algorithms when trained with selected features on four standard LTR datasets. We use NDCG@10 as metric and five-fold cross valiadation. NDGC@10 estimates the quality of ranking especially in the graded multi-scale relevance level setting (Jarvelin and Kekalainen, 2002). Each ranking method is trained over training set and the model that performs best on validation set is used for testing in each fold.

3.1 Ranking Methods

3.1.1 RankSVM

RankSVM is a widely used pairwise LTR algorithm proposed in Herbrich et al. (2000). At first, the training data is transformed to make the pairs of correctly and incorrectly ranked documents, then an SVM model is trained to learn the weight vector $\vec{w}$. We used the publicly available implementation of RankSVM [1] to train the model on training data and choose the parameters which maximizes the performance on the validation data. We use linear kernel, $epsilon = 0.001$ and loop over [0.00001, 10] with step of x2 to estimate C.

3.1.2 RankBoost

RankBoost (Freund et al., 2003) is another popular pairwise LTR algorithm based on boosting technique. The boosting algorithm uses weak rankings to update the weights of the pairs. The weights of the correctly ranked instances are decreased and that of incorrectly ranked are increased to give them more importance in the next round. Finally, a linear combination of weak rankers is produced. We used a publicly available implementation of RankBoost[2] and train the model until no performance change is observed for 100 iterations.

3.1.3 LambdaMART

LambdaMART (Wu et al., 2010) uses gradient boosting, to optimize a ranking cost function, which produces an ensemble of regression trees. The final model can be seen as a weighted combination of such trees as shown in Eq. 5 where, N is the total number of regression trees and α_i is the weight associated with i^{th} tree.

$$F_N(x) = \sum_{i}^{N} \alpha_i * f_i(x) \tag{5}$$

More details, about LambdaMART can be found in Burges (2010). We used a publicly available implementation of LambdaMART[2] with following mentioned parameters, $\#\ of\ trees = 1000$, $learning\ rate = 0.1$ and $\#\ of\ tree\ leaves = 10$.

3.2 Datasets

We conduct the experiments on three standard LTR datasets: (i) OHSUMED, (ii) Letor 4.0 and (iii) Yahoo!. OHSUMED (Hersh et al., 1994) is a part of Letor 3.0 and contains documents from the MEDLINE, a corpus of medical publications. This corpus contains 106 queries, 3 levels and 45 features. The Letor 4.0 dataset is created from the Gov-2 document collection which contains roughly 25 million Web pages. It contains two query-sets MQ2007 and MQ2008 corresponding to years 2007 and 2008 editions of TREC Million Query track[3]. The Letor 4.0 has in total 2476 queries, 3 relevance levels and 46 features. We used Yahoo! SET 2 query-set which contains the LTR data of the commercial search engine and has 6330 queries, 5 relevance levels and 699 features.

Although the dimensionality of features in OHSUMED and Letor 4.0 is less than 50, we consider necessary to report results on these datasets. Based on the feature analysis presented in Geng et al. (2007), features importance in OHSUMED and .Gov datasets are highly different. Moreover, Information Gain and CHI based $filter$ approaches perform quite differently on them, hence we opt to investigate the stability of the proposed method on these datasets too.

[1] `http://www.cs.cornell.edu/people/tj/svm_light/svm_rank.html`
[2] RankLib-v2.0 `http://people.cs.umass.edu/~vdang/ranklib.html`
[3] `http://ciir.cs.umass.edu/research/million/`

3.3 FS-BFS

The FS-BFS is a *wrapper* based approach of feature selection for ranking (Dang and Croft, 2010). The method partitions the F into non-overlapping k subsets and learns a ranking model which maximizes the performance over that subset of features. Best first search is used on the undirected graph of features to extract subsets and the weights of the features are learnt using coordinate ascent. Each best subset will be a weighted combination of the original features in the subset and will represent a completely new feature. We use the parameters as defined in (Dang and Croft, 2010).

4 Results and Discussion

Fig. 2 represents the performance evaluation of RankSVM, RankBoost and LamdaMART when trained with FS-ED, FS-BFS and WAF. We did the significance TTest of the results where we consider the p-value < 0.05 for statistical significance. As can be noticed from the figures, FS-ED performs statistically similar to the baselines in all the cases and in some cases it significantly outperforms the baselines. FS-BFS is a very computation intensive model and it was impractical to optimize the best first search over 699 features graph of a large dataset on our server. Therefore, the the results on Yahoo! dataset are not available with FS-BFS[4]. Here, we would like to mention that, in FS-ED, the scoring of a feature does not depend on the other features' scores so it can easily be parallelised for individual features as can be noticed from Fig. 1. On the contrary, FS-BFS can not be parallelised as the optimization of the consecutive subset depends on the prior best subset. Just to mention, running FS-ED on our server with parallelisation on 8 processors produced results for Yahoo! dataset in ~1.5 hours under normal CPU load. We would also like to mention, the selection method of features presented in Geng et al. (2007) also depend on other features similarity with it, hence making it much computation intensive when running for large datasets like Yahoo!. Table 1 reflects the number of features used to produce the best results. It is noticeable that in some cases FS-ED was able to produce the best results using less than 10% of total features on all datasets.

FS Method	O	M7	M8	Y	R. Method
FS-ED	15	**3**	**3**	**50**	RankSVM
	4	15	15	75	RankBoost
	20	10	20	75	LambdaMART
FS-BFS	**6**	9	12	-	RankSVM
	12	**7**	**7**	-	RankBoost
	14	10	**7**	-	LambdaMART
WAF	45	46	46	699	ALL

Table 1: The number of features used to obtain the results reported in Fig. 2 with different feature selection strategies. O, M7, M8 and Y refer to OHSUMED, MQ2007, MQ2008 and Yahoo! respectively.

The proposed method exhibit similar behaviour on datasets like OHSUMED, MQ2007 and MQ2008 while, an interesting behaviour is noticed on Yahoo! dataset. FS-ED achieved more than 5 point gain in NDCG@10 for RankSVM with only 50 features while performed relatively worse with RankBoost and LambdaMART. To understand this phenomenon better, we analysed the distribution of the top and last features obtained using FS-ED over the relevance

[4]We used Intel Xeon CPU E5520 @ 2.27GHz with 4 cores, 8 processors and 12GiB memory. We ran FS-BFS for around 7 days but did not notice any progress.

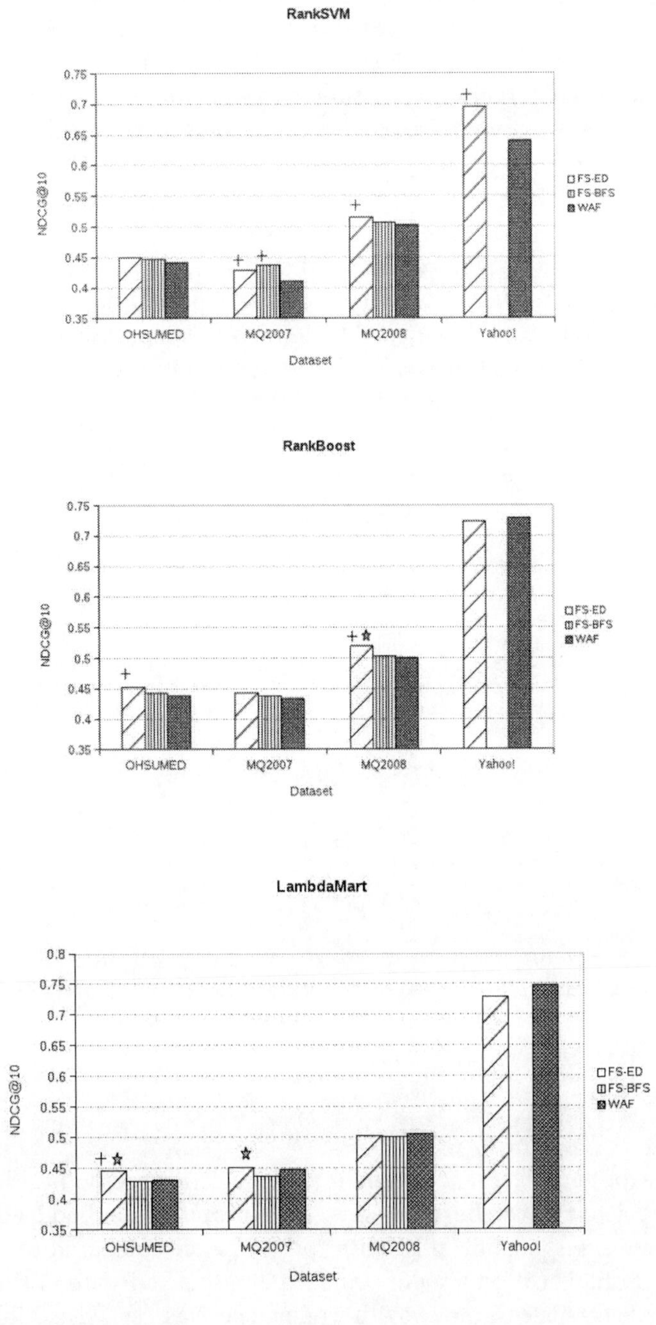

Figure 2: Performance evaluation of feature selection schemes on different datasets with RankSVM, RankBoost and LambdaMART. + and $\star$ indicate statistical significance with WAF and the other FS strategy respectively.

classes. The analysis is presented in Fig. 3. It is noticeable that, the top features better discriminate between the relevance classes and exhibit high divergence over distant relevance levels. Moreover, the expected divergence component minimizes the weight of those features which are least discriminative and in turn, might prove to be ambiguous for some of the ranking models. We consider this as the main reason where FS-ED performs better compared to WAF. Because of this characteristic, the large margin classifier based ranking models like RankSVM are benefited more compared to the weak learner based models like RankBoost and LambdaMART. The weak learner based models can easily minimise the importance of the less discriminative features by assigning less weight and hence the performance does not rapidly deteriorate as compared to large margin classifiers based models. This phenomenon makes the proposed method much efficient and important for the large-margin classifier based rankers which can clearly be noticed from statistical significance of FS-ED over WAF across the datasets for RankSVM. The method is quite robust, as the feature importance component captures the linearity of features over relevance classes while the expected divergence component enables the method to capture the non-linearity. Eventhough the experiments are carried for the document retrieval task of information retrieval, the observations remain intact when the feature selection is performed for a task where classes are ordinal.

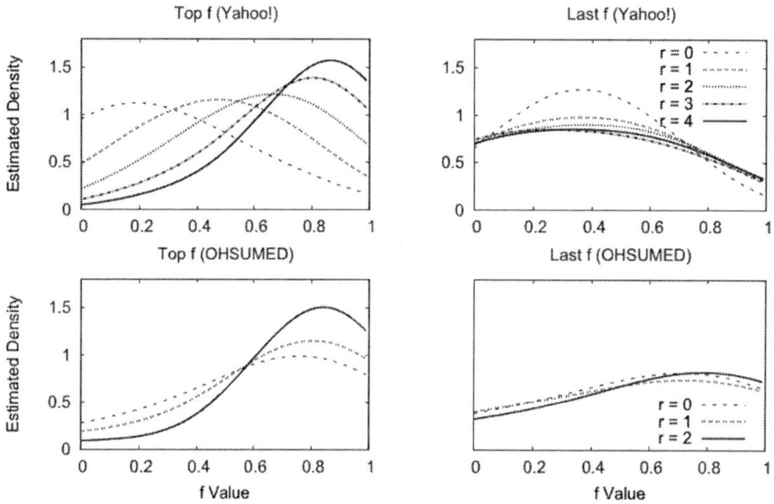

Figure 3: The estimated density of the top and last features according to FS-ED over relevance classes (r) on Yahoo! and OHSUMED. X-axis denote values a feature can take. The features having constant or zero value for all the queries are excluded.

5 Remarks

We proposed an expected divergence based feature selection method for learning to rank. The method is very efficient and can be parallelised. The proposed method leads to not significantly worse, and in some cases, significantly better performance compared to the baselines with as few features as less than 10% on a set of standard datasets and state-of-the-art LTR algorithms. We analysed the selected features over the relevance classes and exhibit that large margin classifier based ranking models can greatly benefit from the selection method.

6 Acknowledgement

This work has been done in the framework of the VLC/CAMPUS Microcluster on Multimodal Interaction in Intelligent Systems and it has been partially funded by the European Commission as part of the WIQ-EI IRSES project (grant no. 269180) within the FP 7 Marie Curie People Framework, and by the Text-Enterprise 2.0 research project (TIN2009-13391-C04-03).

References

Bernard, S. (1986). *Density estimation for statistics and data analysis (Chapman & Hall/CRC Monographs on Statistics & Applied Probability)*. Chapman and Hall/CRC, 1 edition.

Burges, C. J. (2010). From ranknet to lambdarank to lambdamart: An overview. In *Microsoft Research Technical Report MSR-TR-2010-82*.

Coetzee, F. M. (2005). Correcting the kullback-leibler distance for feature selection. *Pattern Recogn. Lett.*, 26(11):1675–1683.

Dang, V. and Croft, B. W. (2010). Feature selection for document ranking using best first search and coordinate ascent. In *SIGIR Workshop on Feature Generation and Selection for Information Retrieval,*, SIGIR '10.

Freund, Y., Iyer, R., Schapire, R. E., and Singer, Y. (2003). An efficient boosting algorithm for combining preferences. *J. Mach. Learn. Res.*, 4:933–969.

Geng, X., Liu, T.-Y., Qin, T., and Li, H. (2007). Feature selection for ranking. In *Proceedings of the 30th annual international ACM SIGIR conference on Research and development in information retrieval*, SIGIR '07, pages 407–414, New York, NY, USA. ACM.

Guyon, I. and Elisseeff, A. (2003). An introduction to variable and feature selection. *J. Mach. Learn. Res.*, 3:1157–1182.

Herbrich, R., Graepel, T., and Obermayer, K. (2000). *Large margin rank boundaries for ordinal regression*. MIT Press, Cambridge, MA.

Hersh, W., Buckley, C., Leone, T. J., and Hickam, D. (1994). Ohsumed: an interactive retrieval evaluation and new large test collection for research. In *Proceedings of the 17th annual international ACM SIGIR conference on Research and development in information retrieval*, SIGIR '94, pages 192–201, New York, NY, USA. Springer-Verlag New York, Inc.

Jarvelin, K. and Kekalainen, J. (2002). Cumulated gain-based evaluation of ir techniques. *ACM Trans. Inf. Syst.*, 20(4):422–446.

Pan, F., Converse, T., Ahn, D., Salvetti, F., and Donato, G. (2009). Feature selection for ranking using boosted trees. In *Proceedings of the 18th ACM conference on Information and knowledge management*, CIKM '09, pages 2025–2028, New York, NY, USA. ACM.

Schneider, K.-M. (2004). A new feature selection score for multinomial naive bayes text classification based on kl-divergence. In *Proceedings of the ACL 2004 on Interactive poster and demonstration sessions*, ACLdemo '04, Stroudsburg, PA, USA. Association for Computational Linguistics.

Wu, Q., Burges, C. J., Svore, K. M., and Gao, J. (2010). Adapting boosting for information retrieval measures. *Inf. Retr.*, 13(3):254–270.

LEPOR: A Robust Evaluation Metric for Machine Translation with Augmented Factors

Aaron L. F. HAN *Derek F. WONG* *Lidia S. CHAO*
Natural Language Processing & Portuguese-Chinese Machine Translation Laboratory
Department of Computer and Information Science
University of Macau
Macau S.A.R., China
hanlifengaaron@gmail.com, derekfw@umac.mo, lidiasc@umac.mo

ABSTRACT

In the conventional evaluation metrics of machine translation, considering less information about the translations usually makes the result not reasonable and low correlation with human judgments. On the other hand, using many external linguistic resources and tools (e.g. Part-of-speech tagging, morpheme, stemming, and synonyms) makes the metrics complicated, time-consuming and not universal due to that different languages have the different linguistic features. This paper proposes a novel evaluation metric employing rich and augmented factors without relying on any additional resource or tool. Experiments show that this novel metric yields the state-of-the-art correlation with human judgments compared with classic metrics BLEU, TER, Meteor-1.3 and two latest metrics (AMBER and MP4IBM1), which proves it a robust one by employing a feature-rich and model-independent approach.

KEYWORDS : Machine translation, Evaluation metric, Context-dependent *n*-gram alignment, Modified length penalty, Precision, Recall.

Proceedings of COLING 2012: Posters, pages 441–450,
COLING 2012, Mumbai, December 2012.

1 Introduction

Since IBM proposed and realized the system of BLEU (Papineni et al., 2002) as the automatic metric for Machine Translation (MT) evaluation, many other methods have been proposed to revise or improve it. BLEU considered the n-gram precision and the penalty for translation which is shorter than that of references. NIST (Doddington, 2002) added the information weight into evaluation factors. Meteor (Banerjee and Lavie, 2005) proposed an alternative way of calculating matched chunks to describe the n-gram matching degree between machine translations and reference translations. Wong and Kit (2008) introduced position difference in the evaluation metric. Other evaluation metrics, such as TER (Snover et al., 2006), the modified Meteor-1.3 (Denkowski and Lavie, 2011), and MP4IBM1 (Popovic et al., 2011) are also used in the literature. AMBER (Chen and Kuhn, 2011) declares a modified version of BLEU and attaches more kinds of penalty coefficients, combining the n-gram precision and recall with the arithmetic average of F-measure. In order to distinguish the reliability of different MT evaluation metrics, people used to apply the Spearman correlation coefficient for evaluation tasks in the workshop of statistical machine translation (WMT) for Association of Computational Linguistics (ACL) (Callison-Burch et al., 2011; Callison-Burch et al., 2010; Callison-Burch et al., 2009, 2008).

2 Related work

Some MT evaluation metrics are designed with the part-of-speech (POS) consideration using the linguistic tools, parser or POS tagger, during the words matching period between system-output and reference sentences. Machacek and Bojar (2011) proposed SemPOS metric, which is based on the Czech-targeted work by Kos and Bojar (2009). SemPOS conducts a deep-syntactic analysis of the target language with a modified version of similarity measure from the general overlapping method (Gimenez and Marquez, 2007). However, SemPOS only focuses on the English and Czech words and achieves no contribution for other language pairs.

To reduce the human tasks during the evaluation, the methodologies that do not need reference translations are growing up. MP4IBM1 (Popovic et al., 2011) used IBM1 model to calculate scores based on morphemes, POS (4-grams) and lexicon probabilities. MP4IBM1 is not a simple model although it is reference independent. For instance, it needs large parallel bilingual corpus, POS taggers (requesting the details about verb tenses, cases, number, gender, etc.) and other tools for splitting words into morphemes. It performed well on the corpus with English as source language following the metric TESLA (Dahlmeier et al., 2011) but got very poor correlation when English is the target language. For example, it gained the system-level correlation score 0.12 and 0.08 respectively on the Spanish-to-English and French-to-English MT evaluation tasks (Callison-Burch et al., 2011) and these two scores mean nearly no correlation with human judgments.

Reordering errors play an important role in the translation for distant language pairs (Isozaki et al., 2010). But BLEU and many other metrics are both insensitive to reordering phenomena and relatively time-consuming to compute (Talbot et al., 2011). Snover et al. (2006) introduced Translation Edit Rate (TER) and the possible edits include the insertion, deletion, and substitution of words as well as sequences allowing phrase movements without large penalties. Isozaki et al. (2010) paid attention to word order on the evaluation between Japanese and English. Wong and Kit (2008) designed position difference factor during the alignment of words between reference translations and candidate outputs, but it only selects the candidate word that has the nearest position in principle.

Different words or phrases can express the same meanings, so it is considered commonly in the literature to refer auxiliary synonyms libraries during the evaluation task. Meteor (Banerjee and Lavie, 2005) is based on unigram match on the words and their stems also with additional synonyms database. Meteor-1.3 (Denkowski and Lavie, 2011), an improved version of Meteor, includes ranking and adequacy versions and has overcome some weaknesses of previous version such as noise in the paraphrase matching, lack of punctuation handling and discrimination between word types (Callison-Burch et al., 2011).

3 Proposed metric

According to the analysis above, we see that in the previous MT evaluation metrics, there are mainly two problems: either presenting incomprehensive factors (e.g. BLEU focus on precision) or relying on many external tools and databases. The first aspect makes the metrics result in unreasonable judgments. The second weakness makes the MT evaluation metric complicated, time-consuming and not universal for different languages. To address these weaknesses, a novel metric LEPOR[1] is proposed in this research, which is designed to take thorough variables into account (including modified factors) and does not need any extra dataset or tool. These are aimed at both improving the practical performance of the automatic metric and the easily operating of the program. LEPOR focuses on combining two modified factor (sentence length penalty, *n*-gram position difference penalty) and two classic methodologies (precision and recall). LEPOR score is calculated by:

$$LEPOR = LP \times NPosPenal \times Harmonic(\alpha R, \beta P) \tag{1}$$

The detailed introductions and designs of the features are shown below.

3.1 Design of LEPOR metric

3.1.1 Length penalty:

In the Eq. (1), *LP* means Length penalty, which is defined to embrace the penalty for both longer and shorter system outputs compared with the reference translations, and it is calculated as:

$$LP = \begin{cases} e^{1-\frac{r}{c}} & if\ c < r \\ 1 & if\ c = r \\ e^{1-\frac{c}{r}} & if\ c > r \end{cases} \tag{2}$$

where c and r mean the sentence length of output candidate translation and reference translation respectively. As seen in Eq. (2), when the output length of sentence is equal to that of the reference one, *LP* will be one which means no penalty. However, when the output length c is larger or smaller than that of the reference one, *LP* will be little than one which means a penalty on the evaluation value of LEPOR. And according to the characteristics of exponential function mathematically, the larger of numerical difference between c and r, the smaller the value of *LP* will be.

[1] LEPOR: **L**ength **P**enalty, **P**recision, *n*-gram **Po**sition difference Penalty and **R**ecall.

3.1.2 N-gram position difference penalty:

In the Eq. (1), the $NPosPenal$ is defined as:

$$NPosPenal = e^{-NPD} \tag{3}$$

where NPD means n-gram position difference penalty. The $NPosPenal$ value is designed to compare the words order in the sentences between reference translation and output translation. The $NPosPenal$ value is normalized. Thus we can take all MT systems into account whose effective NPD value varies between 0 and 1, and when N equals 0, the $NPosPenal$ will be 1 which represents no penalty and is quite reasonable. When the NPD increases from 0 to 1, the $NPosPenal$ value decreases from 1 to $1/e$ based on the mathematical analysis. Consequently, the final LEPOR value will be smaller. According to this thought, the NPD is defined as:

$$NPD = \frac{1}{Length_{output}} \sum_{i=1}^{Length_{output}} |PD_i| \tag{4}$$

where $Length_{output}$ represents the length of system output sentence and PD_i means the n-gram position D-value (difference value) of aligned words between output and reference sentences. Every word from both output translation and reference should be aligned only once (one-to-one alignment). Case (upper or lower) is irrelevant. When there is no match, the value of PD_i will be zero as default for this output translation word.

Output Sentence: $W = \{w_1 w_2 w_3 \dots w_{m_1} | \, m_1 \in (1,\infty)\}$
Reference Sentence: $W^r = \{w_1^r w_2^r w_3^r \dots w_{m_2}^r | \, m_2 \in (1,\infty)\}$
$\forall x \in (1,\infty)$, The Alignment of word w_x:

if $\forall y \in (1,\infty): w_x \neq w_y^r$ *// $\forall$ means for each, $\exists$ means there is/are*
    $(w_x \rightarrow \emptyset)$;   *// $\rightarrow$ shows the alignment*
elseif $\exists! \, y \in (1,\infty): w_x = w_y^r$ *// $\exists!$ means there exists exactly one*
    $(w_x \rightarrow w_y^r)$;
elseif $\exists y_1, y_2 \in (1,\infty): (w_x = w_{y_1}^r) \wedge (w_x = w_{y_2}^r)$ *// $\wedge$ is logical conjunction, and*
    foreach $k \in (-n,-1) \cup (1,n)$
        foreach $j \in (-n,-1) \cup (1,n)$
            if $\exists k_1, k_2, j_1, j_2: (w_{x+k_1} = w_{y_1+j_1}^r) \wedge (w_{x+k_2} = w_{y_2+j_2}^r)$
                if $Distance(w_x, w_{y_1}^r) \leq Distance(w_x, w_{y_2}^r)$
                    $(w_x \rightarrow w_{y_1}^r)$;
                else
                    $(w_x \rightarrow w_{y_2}^r)$;
            elseif $\exists k_1, j_1: (w_{x+k_1} = w_{y_1+j_1}^r) \wedge (\forall k_2, j_2: (w_{x+k_2} \neq w_{y_2+j_2}^r))$
                $(w_x \rightarrow w_{y_1}^r)$;
            else *// i.e.* $\forall k_1, k_2, j_1, j_2: (w_{x+k_1} \neq w_{y_1+j_1}^r) \wedge (w_{x+k_2} \neq w_{y_2+j_2}^r)$
                if $Distance(w_x, w_{y_1}^r) \leq Distance(w_x, w_{y_2}^r)$
                    $(w_x \rightarrow w_{y_1}^r)$;
                else
                    $(w_x \rightarrow w_{y_2}^r)$;
else *// when more than two candidates, the selection steps are similar as above*

FIGURE 1 – Context-dependent n-gram word alignment algorithm

To calculate the NPD value, there are two steps: aligning and calculating. To begin with, the Context-dependent n-gram Word Alignment task: we take the context-dependent factor into consideration and assign higher priority on it, which means we take into account the surrounding context (neighbouring words) of the potential word to select a better matching pairs between the output and the reference. If there are both nearby matching or there is no matched context around the potential words pairs, then we consider the nearest matching to align as a backup choice. The alignment direction is from output sentence to the reference translations. Assuming that w_x represents the current word in output sentence and w_{x+k} (or w_{x+k_i}) means the kth word to the previous ($k < 0$) or following ($k > 0$). While w_y^r (or $w_{y_i}^r$) means the words matching w_x in the references, and w_{y+j}^r (or $w_{y_i+j_i}^r$) has the similar meaning as w_{x+k} but in reference sentence. $Distance$ is the position difference value between the matching words in outputs and references. The operation process and pseudo code of the context-dependent n-gram word alignment algorithm are shown in Figure 1 (with "→" as the alignment). Taking 2-gram ($n = 2$) as an example, let's see explanation in Figure 2. We label each word with its absolute position, then according to the context-dependent n-gram method, the first word "A" in the output sentence has no nearby matching with the beginning word "A" in reference, so it is aligned to the fifth word "a" due to their matched neighbor words "stone" and "on" within one (≤ 2) and two (≤ 2) steps respectively away from current position. Then the fourth word "a" in the output will align the first word "A" of the reference due to the one-to-one alignment. The alignments of other words in the output are obvious.

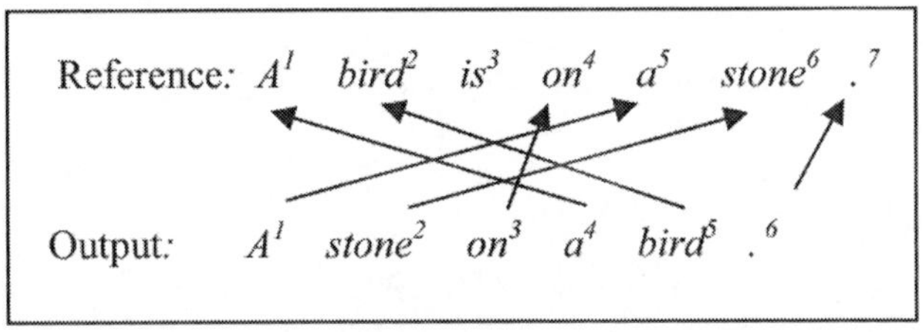

FIGURE 2 – Example of context-dependent n-gram word alignment

In the second step (calculating step), we label each word with its position number divided by the corresponding sentence length for normalization, and then using the Eq. (4) to finish the calculation. We also use the example in Figure 2 for the NPD introduction:

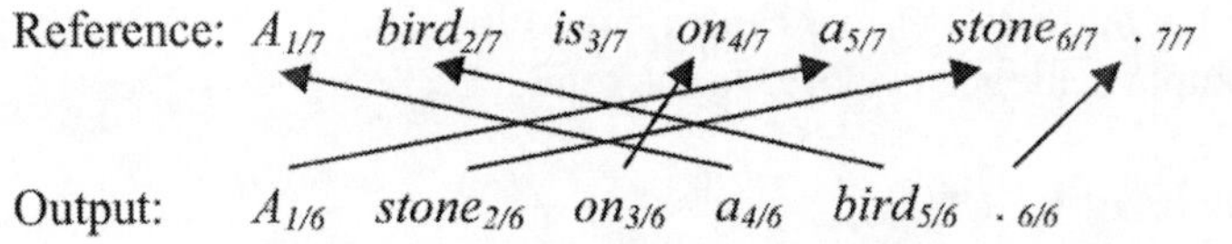

$$NPD = \frac{1}{6} \times [\left|\frac{1}{6} - \frac{5}{7}\right| + \left|\frac{2}{6} - \frac{6}{7}\right| + \left|\frac{3}{6} - \frac{4}{7}\right| + \left|\frac{4}{6} - \frac{1}{7}\right| + \left|\frac{5}{6} - \frac{2}{7}\right|] = \frac{2}{7}$$

In the example, when we label the word position of output sentence we divide the numerical position (from 1 to 6) of the current word by the reference sentence length 6. Similar way is applied in labeling the reference sentence. After we get the NPD value, using the Eq. (3), the values of $NPosPenal$ can be calculated.

When there is multi-references (more than one reference sentence), for instance 2 references, we take the similar approach but with a minor change. The alignment direction is reminded the same (from output to reference), and the candidate alignments that have nearby matching words also embrace higher priority. If the matching words from Reference-1 and Reference-2 both have the nearby matching with the output word, then we select the candidate alignment that makes the final NPD value smaller. See below (also 2-gram) for explanation:

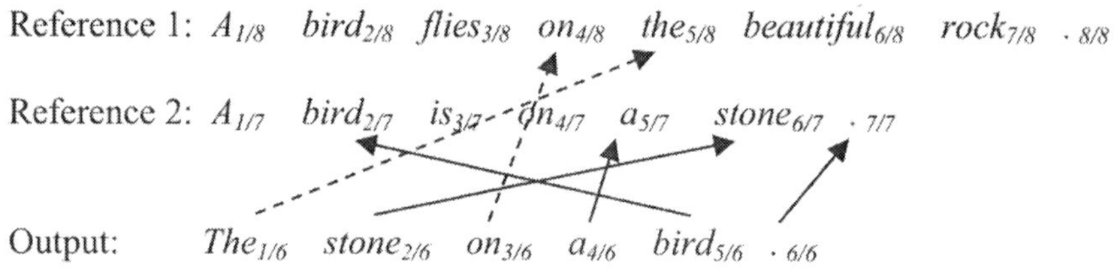

The beginning output words "the" and "stone" are aligned simply for the single matching. The output word "on" has nearby matching with the word "on" both in Reference-1 and Reference-2, due to the words "the" (second to previous) and "a" (first in the following) respectively. Then we should select its alignment to the word "on" in Reference-1, not Reference-2 for the further reason $\left|\frac{3}{6}-\frac{4}{8}\right| < \left|\frac{3}{6}-\frac{4}{7}\right|$ and this selection will obtain a smaller NPD value. The remaining two words "a" and "bird" in output sentence are aligned using the same principle.

3.1.3 Precision and recall:

Precision is designed to reflect the accurate rate of outputs while recall means the loyalty to the references. In the Eq. (1), $Harmonic(\alpha R, \beta P)$ means the Harmonic mean of αR and βP and is calculated as:

$$Harmonic(\alpha R, \beta P) = (\alpha + \beta)/(\frac{\alpha}{R} + \frac{\beta}{P}) \quad (5)$$

where α and β are two parameters we designed to adjust the weight of R (recall) and P (precision). The two metrics are calculated by:

$$P = \frac{common\_num}{system\_length} \quad (6)$$

$$R = \frac{common\_num}{reference\_length} \quad (7)$$

where $common\_num$ represents the number of aligned (matching) words and marks appearing both in translations and references, $system\_length$ and $reference\_length$ specify the sentence length of system output and reference respectively (Melamed et al., 2003). After we finish the above steps, taking all the variables into Eq. (1), we can calculate the final LEPOR score, and higher LEPOR value means the output sentence is closer to the references.

3.2 Two variants of system-level LEPOR

We have introduced the computation of LEPOR on single output sentence, and we should consider a proper way to calculate the LEPOR value when the cases turn into document (system) level. We perform the system-level LEPOR with two different variants LEPOR-A and LEPOR-B as follow.

$$\overline{LEPOR_A} = \frac{1}{SentNum} \sum_{i=1}^{SentNum} LEPOR_i \quad (8)$$

$$\overline{LEPOR_B} = \overline{LP} \times \overline{PosPenalty} \times \overline{Harmonic(\alpha R, \beta P)} \quad (9)$$

$$\overline{LP} = \frac{1}{SentNum} \sum_{i=1}^{SentNum} LP_i \quad (10)$$

$$\overline{PosPenalty} = \frac{1}{SentNum} \sum_{i=1}^{SentNum} PosPenalty_i \quad (11)$$

$$\overline{Harmonic(\alpha R, \beta P)} = \frac{1}{SentNum} \sum_{i=1}^{SentNum} Harmonic(\alpha R, \beta P)_i \quad (12)$$

where $\overline{LEPOR_A}$ and $\overline{LEPOR_B}$ in Eq. (8) and (9) both represent the system-level score of LEPOR, $SentNum$ specifies the sentence number of the test document, and $LEPOR_i$ in Eq. (8) means the LEPOR value of the ith sentence. As shown above, $\overline{LEPOR_A}$ is calculated by the arithmetic mean of LEPOR value of each sentence. On the other hand, $\overline{LEPOR_B}$ is designed from another perspective, which reflects the system-level values of three factors in LEPOR. To compute $\overline{LEPOR_B}$ using Eq. (9), we should firstly calculate the three system-level factors $\overline{LP}$, $\overline{PosPenalty}$ and $\overline{Harmonic(\alpha R, \beta P)}$ using Eq. (10) to Eq. (12), which are calculated in a similar way to that of $\overline{LEPOR_A}$ by the arithmetic mean.

4 Experiments and comparisons

We trained LEPOR on the public ACL WMT 2008[2] data (EN: English, ES: Spanish, DE: German, FR: French and CZ: Czech). The parameters α and β are set to 9 and 1 respectively for all languages pairs except that $\alpha = 1$ and $\beta = 9$ are used for Czech-English translations. For the context-dependent *n*-gram word alignment, we adjust *n* as 2 on all the corpora meaning that we consider both the proceeding and following two words as the context information.

We use the MT evaluation corpora from 2011 ACL WMT[3] for testing. The tested eight corpora are English-to-*other* (Spanish, German, French and Czech) and *other*-to-English news text. Following a common practice (e.g. the TER metric was proposed by the comparison with BLEU and Meteor, the AMBER metric compared with BLEU and Meteor-1.0, the MP4IBM1 compared with BLEU), we compare the scoring results by LEPOR against the three "gold standard" metrics BLEU (Papineni et al., 2002), TER (Snover et al., 2006) and Meteor (version 1.3) (Denkowski and Lavie, 2011). In addition, we select the latest AMBER (modified version of BLEU) (Chen and Kuhn, 2011) and MP4IBM1 (without reference translation) (Popovic et al., 2011) as representatives to examine the quality of LEPOR in this study. The correlation results are shown in Table 1.

Evaluation system	Correlation Score with Human Judgment								
	other-to-English				English-to-other				Mean score
	CZ-EN	DE-EN	ES-EN	FR-EN	EN-CZ	EN-DE	EN-ES	EN-FR	
LEPOR-B	0.93	0.62	0.96	0.89	0.71	0.36	0.88	0.84	**0.77**
LEPOR-A	0.95	0.61	0.96	0.88	0.68	0.35	0.89	0.83	**0.77**
AMBER	0.88	0.59	0.86	0.95	0.56	0.53	0.87	0.84	0.76
Meteor-1.3-RANK	0.91	0.71	0.88	0.93	0.65	0.30	0.74	0.85	0.75
BLEU	0.88	0.48	0.90	0.85	0.65	0.44	0.87	0.86	0.74
TER	0.83	0.33	0.89	0.77	0.50	0.12	0.81	0.84	0.64
MP4IBM1	0.91	0.56	0.12	0.08	0.76	0.91	0.71	0.61	0.58

TABLE 1 – Spearman correlation scores of the metrics on eight corpora.

[2] http://www.statmt.org/wmt08/
[3] http://www.statmt.org/wmt11/

The metrics are ranked by their mean (hybrid) performance on the eight corpora from the best to the worst. Table 1 shows that LEPOR-A and LEPOR-B obtained the highest scores among the metrics, and LEPOR-B yields the best results by mean scores. BLEU, AMBER (modified version of BLEU) and Meteor-1.3 perform unsteady with better correlation on some translation languages and worse on others, resulting in medium level generally. TER and MP4IBM1 get the worst scores by the mean correlation. The result proves that LEPOR is a robust metric in all cases by constructing augmented features and also a concise and independent model without using any external tool and database (e.g. AMBER using auxiliary tokenize tool for stem, prefix and suffix matching; Meteor using word stems and synonyms databases etc.). MP4IBM1 does not need the reference translations instead using the POS tagger and word morphemes, but the current correlation is low. Table 1 also releases the information that although the test metrics yield high system-level correlations with human judgments on certain language pairs (e.g. all correlations above 0.83 on Czech-to-English), they are far from satisfactory by synthetically mean scores on total eight corpora (currently spanning from 0.58 to 0.77 only) and there is clearly a potential for further improvement.

Conclusion and perspectives

As we know that better evaluation metrics will be helpful to leading to better machine translations (Liu et al., 2011). This paper proposes a novel automatic evaluation metric LEPOR, which employs rich and augmented evaluation factors such that the result is close to human assessments. From the empirical results, we found that LEPOR can achieve better results compared with the state-of-the-art MT evaluation metrics, including BLEU, TER, Meteor-1.3 and the recently proposed AMBER and MP4IBM1. LEPOR gives good outputs generally on all the testing languages, with the state-of-the-art performance on the Czech-to-English, Spanish-to-English, English-to-Spanish and the mean correlation score without relying on any extra tool and data sources. Actually the correlation coefficient value of LEPOR can be further improved through the adjustment of the parameters α (weighting of recall) and β (weighting of precision), as well as the number of words concurrences used in the context-dependent n-gram position difference penalty.

Some further works are worth doing in the future. First, test on synonym thesaurus: in most cases, translation of word can be re-expressed in different ways, such as multi-words or paraphrases. It will certainly be helpful to the correlation score if a synonym thesaurus is available during the matching of words (Wong et al., 2009). Secondly, evaluate the effectiveness on languages of different topologies: in this paper we use the corpora that cover five languages English, Spanish, Czech, French, and German. That will be good if proposed metric can be tested on more pairs of languages from different families such as Portuguese, Japanese and Chinese etc. Thirdly, employ the Multi-references: another way to replace the synonym is the use of multi-references for evaluation. This can reduce the deviation when calculating the mechanical translation quality. The results will be more reason if we use multi-references. Lastly, in this work, we focus on the lexical information and how can we go beyond this is another direction that worth for further studies.

Acknowledgments

This work is partially supported by the Research Committee of University of Macau, and Science and Technology Development Fund of Macau under the grants UL019B/09-Y3/EEE/LYP01/FST, and 057/2009/A2. The authors are also grateful to the ACL's special interest group in machine translation (SIGMT) association for the offering of the data.

References

Banerjee, S. and Lavie, A. (2005). Meteor: an automatic metric for MT evaluation with high levels of correlation with human judgments. In *Proceedings of the Workshop on Intrinsic and Extrinsic Evaluation Measures for Machine Translation and/or Summarization of the Association for Computational Linguistics*, pages 65-72, Prague, Czech Republic.

Callison-Bruch, C., Koehn, P., Monz, C. and Zaidan, O. F. (2011). Findings of the 2011 Workshop on Statistical Machine Translation. In *Proceedings of the Sixth Workshop on Statistical Machine translation of the Association for Computational Linguistics(ACL-WMT)*, pages 22-64, Edinburgh, Scotland, UK.

Callison-Burch, C., Koehn, P., Monz, C., Peterson, K., Przybocki, M. and Zaidan, O. F. (2010). Findings of the 2010 Joint Workshop on Statistical Machine Translation and Metrics for Machine Translation. In *Proceedings of the 5th Workshop on Statistical Machine Translation, Stroudsburg, Association for Computational Linguistics(ACL-WMT)*, pages 17-53, PA, USA.

Callison-Burch, C., Koehn, P., Monz,C. and Schroeder, J. (2008). Further meta-evaluation of machine translation. In *Proceedings of the Third Workshop on Statistical Machine Translation, Association for Computational Linguistics (ACL-WMT)*, pages 70-106, Columbus, Ohio, USA.

Callison-Burch, C., Koehn, P., Monz,C. and Schroeder, J. (2009). Findings of the 2009 Workshop on Statistical Machine Translation. In *Proceedings of the 4th Workshop on Statistical Machine Translation, the European Chapter of Association for Computational Linguistics (EACL-WMT)*, pages 1-28, Athens, Greece.

Chen, B. and Kuhn, R. (2011). Amber: A modified bleu, enhanced ranking metric. In *Proceedings of the Sixth Workshop on Statistical Machine translation of the Association for Computational Linguistics(ACL-WMT)*, pages 71-77, Edinburgh, Scotland, UK.

Dahlmeier, D., Liu, C. and Ng, H. T. (2011). TESLA at WMT2011: Translation evaluation and tunable metric. In *Proceedings of the Sixth Workshop on Statistical Machine Translation, Association for Computational Linguistics (ACL-WMT)*, pages 78-84, Edinburgh, Scotland, UK.

Denkowski, M. and Lavie, A. (2011). Meteor 1.3: Automatic metric for reliable optimization and evaluation of machine translation systems. In *Proceedings of the Sixth Workshop on Statistical Machine translation of the Association for Computational Linguistics(ACL-WMT)*, pages 85-91, Edinburgh, Scotland, UK.

Doddington, G. (2002). Automatic evaluation of machine translation quality using n-gram co-occurrence statistics. In *Proceedings of the second international conference on Human Language Technology Research(HLT 2002)*, pages 138-145, San Diego, California, USA.

Gimenez, J. and Marquez, L. (2007). Linguistic Features for Automatic Evaluation of Heterogenous MT Systems. In *Proceedings of the Second Workshop on Statistical Machine Translation, Association for Computational Linguistics (ACL-WMT)*, pages 256–264, Prague.

Isozaki, H., Hirao, T., Duh, K., Sudoh, K., Tsukada, H. (2010). Automatic Evaluation of Translation Quality for Distant Language Pairs, In *Proceedings of the Conference on Empirical Methods in Natural Language Processing, Association for Computational Linguistics(EMNLP)*, pages 944-952, MIT, Massachusetts, USA.

Kos, K. and Bojar, O. (2009). Evaluation of Machine Translation Metrics for Czech as the

Target Language. *Prague Bull. Math. Linguistics*, Vol. 92: 135-148.

Liu, C., Dahlmeier, D. and Ng, H. T. (2011). Better evaluation metrics lead to better machine translation. In *Proceedings of the Conference on Empirical Methods in Natural Language Processing, Association for Computational Linguistics(EMNLP)*, pages 375-384, Stroudsburg, PA, USA.

Melamed, I. D., Green, R., Turian, J. P. (2003). Precision and recall of machine translation. In *Proceedings of the Conference of the North American Chapter of the Association for Computational Linguistics on Human Language Technology (HLT-NAACL)*, pages 61-63, Edmonton, Canada.

Papineni, K., Roukos, S., Ward, T. and Zhu, W. J. (2002). BLEU: a method for automatic evaluation of machine translation. In *Proceedings of the 40th Annual Meeting of the Association for Computational Linguistics (ACL 2002)*, pages 311-318, Philadelphia, PA, USA.

Popovic, M., Vilar, D., Avramidis, E. and Burchardt, A. (2011). Evaluation without references: IBM1 scores as evaluation metrics. In *Proceedings of the Sixth Workshop on Statistical Machine Translation, Association for Computational Linguistics (ACL-WMT)*, pages 99-103, Edinburgh, Scotland, UK.

Snover, M., Dorr, B., Schwartz, R., Micciulla, L. and Makhoul, J. (2006). A study of translation edit rate with targeted human annotation. In *Proceedings of the Conference of the Association for Machine Translation in the Americas (AMTA)*, pages 223-231, Boston, USA.

Talbot, D., Kazawa, H., Ichikawa, H., Katz-Brown, J., Seno, M. and Och, F. (2011). A Lightweight Evaluation Framework for Machine Translation Reordering. In *Proceedings of the Sixth Workshop on Statistical Machine Translation, Association for Computational Linguistics (ACL-WMT)*, pages 12-21, Edinburgh, Scotland, UK.

Wong, B. T-M and Kit, C. (2008). Word choice and word position for automatic MT evaluation. In *Workshop: MetricsMATR of the Association for Machine Translation in the Americas (AMTA)*, short paper, 3 pages, Waikiki, Hawai'I, USA.

Wong, F., Chao, S., Hao, C. C. and Leong, K. S. (2009). A Maximum Entropy (ME) Based Translation Model for Chinese Characters Conversion, *Journal of Advances in Computational Linguistics, Research in Computer Science*, 41: 267-276.

Predicting Stance in Ideological Debate with Rich Linguistic Knowledge

Kazi Saidul HASAN   *Vincent NG*
Human Language Technology Research Institute
University of Texas at Dallas
Richardson, TX 75083-0688, USA
{saidul,vince}@hlt.utdallas.edu

ABSTRACT

Debate stance classification, the task of classifying an author's stance in a two-sided debate, is a relatively new and challenging problem in opinion mining. One of its challenges stems from the fact that it is not uncommon to find words and phrases in a debate post that are indicative of the *opposing* stance, owing to the frequent need for an author to re-state other people's opinions so that she can refer to and contrast with them when establishing her own arguments. We propose a machine learning approach to debate stance classification that leverages two types of rich linguistic knowledge, one exploiting contextual information and the other involving the determination of the author's stances on *topics*. Experimental results on debate posts involving two popular debate domains demonstrate the effectiveness of our two types of linguistic knowledge when they are combined in an integer linear programming framework.

TITLE AND ABSTRACT IN BENGALI

উন্নত ভাষাবিদ্যার সাহায্যে ভাবাদর্শিক বিতর্কের পক্ষ নির্ণয়

বিতর্কের পক্ষ নির্ণয় তথা একটি দ্বিপাক্ষিক বিতর্কে একজন তার্কিক কোন পক্ষ নিচ্ছেন সেটি নির্ধারণ করা ওপিনিয়ন মাইনিং-এ একটি অপেক্ষাকৃত নতুন এবং জটিল সমস্যা। এক্ষেত্রে একটি অন্যতম প্রতিবন্ধক হলো একজন তার্কিকের লেখায় প্রায়ই বিপক্ষের ব্যবহৃত শব্দ এবং বাক্যাংশ পাওয়া যায় যা ঐ তার্কিক অন্যপক্ষের যুক্তি পুনরুল্লেখ এবং খন্ডনের মাধ্যমে নিজ যুক্তি উপস্থাপনের জন্য ব্যবহার করেন। বিতর্কের পক্ষ নির্ণয়ের জন্য আমরা একটি মেশিন লার্নিং পদ্ধতি প্রস্তাব করছি যাতে দুই ধরণের উন্নত ভাষাবিদ্যা প্রয়োগ করা হয়েছে, প্রথমটি প্রাসংগিক তথ্য এবং অন্যটি বিভিন্ন আলোচ্য বিষয়ের ক্ষেত্রে তার্কিকের অভিমতের উপর ভিত্তি করে প্রতিষ্ঠিত। দুটি বহুল আলোচিত বিষয়ের পক্ষে-বিপক্ষে লেখা রচনার উপর চালানো পরীক্ষার ফলাফল ইন্টিজার লিনিয়ার প্রোগ্র্যামিং-এর সাথে যুক্তাবস্থায় এই দুই ধরণের উন্নত ভাষাবিদ্যার কার্যকারিতা প্রমাণ করে।

KEYWORDS: debate stance classification, opinion mining, sentiment analysis.
KEYWORDS IN BENGALI: বিতর্কের পক্ষ নির্ণয়, ওপিনিয়ন মাইনিং, মতামত বিশ্লেষণ।

Proceedings of COLING 2012: Posters, pages 451–460,
COLING 2012, Mumbai, December 2012.

1 Introduction

While much traditional work on opinion mining has involved determining the polarity expressed in a customer review (e.g., whether a review is "thumbs up" or "thumbs down") (Pang et al., 2002)), researchers have begun exploring new opinion mining tasks in recent years. One such task is *debate stance classification*: given a post written for a *two-sided* online debate topic (e.g., *"Should abortion be banned?"*), determine which of the two sides (i.e., *for* and *against*) its author is taking.

Debate stance classification is arguably a more challenging task than polarity classification. While in polarity classification sentiment-bearing words and phrases have proven to be useful (e.g., "excellent" correlates strongly with positive polarity), in debate stance classification it is not uncommon to find words and phrases in a debate post that are indicative of the *opposing* stance. For example, consider the two posts below:

Post 1: Do you really think that criminals won't have access to guns if the federal government bans guns? I don't think so. If guns cause death, that is only because of criminals, not because we carry them for our safety. A firearm ban will only cause deaths of innocent citizens.

Post 2: You said that guns should not be banned. Do you really believe guns can protect citizens from criminals? I don't think so.

It is clear that the author of Post 1 supports gun rights even though the post contains phrases that are indicative of the opposing stance, such as *"bans guns"* and *"guns cause death"*. It is similarly clear that Post 2's author opposes gun rights despite the fact that Post 2 contains phrases that support the opposing view, such as *"guns should not be banned"* and *"guns can protect citizens"*.

It is worth noting that these phrases do *not* represent the authors' opinions: they are merely re-statements of other people's opinions. However, re-stating other people's opinions is not uncommon in debate posts: it is a useful method allowing an author to contrast her own view or indicate which point raised by other people she is responding to. These phrases typically appear in sentences that express concession, as well as in rhetorical questions, where an author questions the validity of other people's arguments.

Hence, for debate stance classification, it is particularly important to interpret a phrase using its *context*. Unfortunately, existing work on this task has largely failed to take context into account, training a single classifier for stance prediction using shallow features computed primarily from n-grams and dependency parse trees (Somasundaran and Wiebe, 2010; Anand et al., 2011).

Motivated by the above discussion, our goal in this paper is to improve the performance of a learning-based debate stance classification system. As we will see below, our approach exploits rich linguistic knowledge that can be divided into two types: (1) knowledge that can be automatically computed and encoded as features for better exploiting contextual information, and (2) knowledge that is acquired from additional manual annotations on the debate posts. Briefly, our approach is composed of three steps:

1. **Employing additional linguistic features to train a post-stance classifier.** To improve the performance of a debate stance classifier (which we will refer to as the *post-stance* classifier), we augment an existing feature set, specifically the one employed by Anand et al. (2011), with novel linguistic features. These new features aim to better capture a word's *local context*, which we define to be the sentence in which the word appears. They include, for instance, the *type* of sentence in which a word occurs (e.g., whether it occurs in a question or a conditional sentence), as well as those that capture long-distance syntactic dependencies.

2. **Training a topic-stance classifier.** Intuitively, knowing the author's stance on the *topics* mentioned in a post would be useful for debate stance classification. For example, one of the topics mentioned in Post 1 is *firearm ban*, and being able to determine that the author holds a negative stance on this topic would help us infer that the author supports gun rights. Note that topic stances are a rich source of knowledge that cannot be adequately captured by the local contextual features employed in Step 1: understanding the author's stance on a topic may sometimes require information gathered from one or more sentences in a post. Since determining topic stances is challenging, we propose to tackle it using a machine learning approach, where we train a *topic-stance* classifier to determine an author's stance on a topic by relying on manual topic-stance annotations.

3. **Improving post stance prediction using topic stances.** Now that we have topic stances, we want to use them to improve the prediction of post stances. One way to do so is to encode topic stances as additional features for training the post-stance classifier. Another way, which we adopt in this paper, is to perform joint inference over the predictions made by the topic-stance classifier and the post-stance classifier using integer linear programming (ILP) (Roth and Yih, 2004).

We evaluate our approach on debate posts taken from two domains (Abortion and Gun Rights), and show that both sources of linguistic information we introduce (the additional linguistic features for training the post-stance classifier and the topic stances) significantly improve a baseline classifier trained on Anand et al.'s (2011) features.

The rest of the paper is structured as follows. We first discuss related work (Section 2) and our datasets (Section 3). Then we describe our three-step approach to debate stance classification (Section 4). Finally, we evaluate our approach (Section 5).

2 Related Work on Debate Stance Classification

Debate stance classification is a relatively new opinion mining task. To our knowledge, there have only been two major attempts at this task, both of which train a binary classifier for assigning a stance value (*for*/*against*) to a post (Somasundaran and Wiebe, 2010; Anand et al., 2011). Somasundaran and Wiebe (2010) examine two types of features, *sentiment* features and *arguing* features. In comparison to the unigrams features, the sentiment features consistently produced worse results whereas the arguing features yielded mixed results. Owing to space limitations, we will refer the reader to their work for details. On the other hand, since our approach extends the recent work by Anand et al. (2011), we will describe it in some detail in this section.

Anand et al. (2011) employ four types of features for debate stance classification, n-grams, document statistics, punctuation, and syntactic dependencies. We will collectively refer to these as the CRDD features.[1] Their n-gram features include both the unigrams and bigrams in a post, as well as its first unigram, first bigram, and first trigram. The features based on document statistics include the post length, the number of words per sentence, the percentage of words with more than six letters, and the percentage of words that are pronouns and sentiment words. The punctuation features are composed of the repeated punctuation symbols in a post. The dependency-based features have three variants. In the first variant, the pair of arguments involved in each dependency relation extracted by a dependency parser together with the relation type are used as a feature. The

[1] As we will see, we re-implemented Anand et al.'s features and used them as one of our baseline feature sets. Note that we excluded their context features (i.e., a rebuttal post has its parent post's features) in our re-implementation since we do not have the thread structure of posts in our dataset.

second variant is the same as the first except that the head (i.e., the first argument in a relation) is replaced by its part-of-speech tag. The features in the third variant, which they call *opinion dependencies*, are created by replacing each feature from the first two types that contains a sentiment word with the corresponding polarity label (i.e., + or −). For instance, the opinion dependencies <John,−,nsubj> and <guns,−,dobj> are generated from Post 3, since "hate" has a negative polarity and it is connected to "John" and "guns" via the *nsubj* and *dobj* relations, respectively.

Post 3: John hates guns.

At first glance, opinion dependencies seem to encode the kind of information that topic stances intend to capture. However, there are two major differences between opinion dependencies and topic stances. First, while opinion dependencies can be computed only when sentiment-bearing words are present, topic stances can be computed even in the absence of sentiment words, as shown in Post 4, in which the author holds a positive stance on the topic *fetus*:

Post 4: A fetus is still a life. One day it will grow into a human being.

Another difference between opinion dependencies and topic stances is that when computing opinion dependencies, the sentiment is linked to the corresponding word (e.g., associating a negative sentiment to *guns*) via a syntactic dependency relation and hence is "local". On the other hand, topic stances capture global information about a post in the sense that the stance of a topic may sometimes be inferred only from the entire post.

3 Datasets

For our experiments, we collected debate posts from two popular *domains*, Abortion and Gun Rights. Each post should receive one of two *domain labels*, *for* or *against*, depending on whether the author of the post is for or against abortion/gun rights. To see how we obtain these domain labels, let us first describe the data collection process in more detail.

We collect our debate posts for the two domains from various online debate forums[2]. In each domain, there are several two-sided debates. Each debate has a subject (e.g., "Abortion should be banned") for which a number of posts were written by different authors. Each post is manually tagged with its author's stance (i.e., *yes* or *no*) on the debate subject. Since the label of each post represents the subject stance but not the domain stance, we need to automatically convert the former to the latter. For example, for the subject "Abortion should be banned", the subject stance *yes* implies that the author opposes abortion, and hence the domain label for the corresponding label should be *against*.

We constructed one dataset for each domain. For the Abortion dataset, we have 1289 posts (52% *for* and 48% *against*) collected from 10 debates, with 153 words per post on average. For the Gun Rights dataset, we have 764 posts (55% *for* and 44% *against*) collected from 13 debates, with 130 words per post on average.

4 Our Approach

In this section, we describe the three steps of our approach in detail.

4.1 Step 1: Employing New Features to Train the Post-Stance Classifier

We introduce three types of features and train a post-stance classifier using a feature set composed of these and Anand et al.'s features.

[2] `http://www.convinceme.net`, `http://www.createdebate.com`, `http://www.opposingviews.com`, `http://debates.juggle.com`, `http://wiki.idebate.org`

4.1.1 Topic Features

Anand et al. employ unigrams and bigrams in their feature set, so they cannot represent topics that are longer than two words. While one can mitigate this problem by incorporating higher-order n-grams, doing so will substantially increase the number of n-gram-based features, many of which do not correspond to meaningful phrases. To capture the meaningful topics in a post, we extract from each post *topic features*, which are all the word sequences starting with zero or more adjectives followed by one or more nouns.

4.1.2 Cue Features

As noted in the introduction, certain types of sentences in a debate post often contain words and phrases that do not represent the stance of its author. In this work, we consider three such types of sentences. The Type-1 sentences are those containing the word "if", "but", or "however"; the Type-2 sentences are those ending with the '?' symbol; and the Type-3 sentences are those that have "you" as the subject of a reporting verb (e.g., "think", "say", "believe").

We hypothesize that features that encode not only the presence/absence of a word but also the type of sentences it appears in would be useful for debate stance classification. Consequently, we introduce *cue features*: for each unigram appearing in any of the three types of sentences, we create a new binary feature by attaching a type tag (i.e., Type-1, Type-2, Type-3) to the unigram. The feature value is 1 if and only if the corresponding unigram occurs in the specified type of sentence. Additionally, we assign another tag, Type-4, to the unigrams in sentences with "I" as the subject of a reporting verb to indicate that these unigrams are likely to represent the author's opinions.

4.1.3 Topic-Opinion Features

Recall that Anand et al. (2011) employ opinion dependencies, but their method of creating such features has several weaknesses. To see the weaknesses, consider the following posts:

Post 5: Mary does not like gun control laws.
Post 6: Guns can be used to kill people.

From Post 5, two of the opinion dependencies generated by Anand et al. would be <Mary,+,nsubj> and <laws,+,dobj>, since *like* has a positive polarity and is connected to *Mary* and *laws* via the *nsubj* and *dobj* relations, respectively. However, these two features could be misleading for a learner that uses them for several reasons. First, they fail to take into account negation (as signaled by *not*), assigning a positive polarity to *laws*. Second, they assign a polarity label to a word, not a topic, so the feature <laws,+,dobj> will be generated regardless of whether we are talking about *gun control laws* or *gun rights laws*. A further problem is revealed by considering Post 6: ideally, we should generate a feature in which guns are assigned a negative polarity because *kill* is negatively polarized, but Anand et al. would fail to do so because *guns* and *kill* are not involved in the same dependency relation.

We address these problems by creating *topic-polarity* features as follows. For each sentence, we (1) identify its topic(s) (see Section 4.1.1); (2) label each sentiment word with its polarity (+ or −) and strength (strong (S) or weak (W)) using the MPQA subjectivity lexicon[3]; and (3) generate the typed dependencies using the Stanford Parser[4]. For each dependency relation with arguments w and o, there are two cases to consider:

[3]`http://www.cs.pitt.edu/mpqa/`
[4]`http://nlp.stanford.edu/software/lex-parser.shtml`

Case 1: w appears within a topic and o is a sentiment word. In this case, we create a feature that attaches the polarity and the strength of o to the *topic* to which w belongs, flipping the polarity value if o is found in a negative relation (*neg*) or any relation with negation words (e.g., no, never, nothing). We define this relation as a *direct* (D) relation since the topic-opinion pair can be formed using one dependency relation. For Post 5, our method yields two topic-opinion features, <Mary,–,S,nsubj,D> and <gun control laws,–,S,dobj,D>. As we can see, each feature is composed of the topic, the associated polarity and strength, as well as the relation type.

Case 2: w appears within a topic but o is not a sentiment word. In this case, we check whether o is paired with any sentiment word via any dependency relation. In Post 6, for instance, *guns* is paired with *used*, which is not a sentiment word, but *used* is paired with the negative sentiment word *kill* via an *xcomp* (open clausal complement) relation. So we assign *kill*'s polarity and strength labels to *guns*, flipping the polarity as necessary. We define this connection as an *indirect* (IND) relation since the topic and the sentiment word are present in different relations. This method yields the feature <guns,–,S,nsubjpass,IND>.

4.2 Step 2: Learning Topic Stances

Next, we train a classifier for assigning stances to the topics mentioned in a post.

Manually annotating a post with topic stances. To train a topic-stance classifier, we need a training set in which each post is annotated with topic-stance pairs. We randomly selected 100 posts from each domain for annotation. Given a post, we first extract the topics automatically using the method outlined in Section 4.1.1. Since not all extracted topics are equally important, we save annotation effort by manually labeling only the *key* topics. We define a topic t as a key topic for a post d if (1) t is one of the 10 topics with the highest Tf-Idf value in d and (2) t appears in at least 10 posts. These conditions ensure that t is important for both d *and* the domain. We then ask two human annotators to annotate each key topic with one of three labels, *support*, *oppose*, or *neutral*, depending on the annotators' perception of the author's stance on a topic after reading the *entire* post. The kappa value computed over the two sets of manual annotations is 0.69, indicating substantial agreement (Carletta, 1996).

Training and applying a topic-stance classifier. For each key topic with a stance label in a training post, we create one training instance. Each instance is represented by the same set of features that we used to train the post-stance classifier, except that (1) the topic features (Section 4.1.1) and the topic-opinion features (Section 4.1.3) are extracted only for the topic under consideration; and (2) all the features are computed using only the sentences in which the topic appears. After training, we apply the resulting classifier to a test post. Test instances are generated the same way training instances are.

4.3 Step 3: Performing Joint Inference using Integer Programming

We hypothesize that debate stance classification performance could be improved if we leveraged the predictions made by both the post-stance classifier and the topic-stance classifier. Since these two classifiers are trained independently of each other, their predictions can be inconsistent. For example, a post could be labeled as "anti-gun rights" by the post-stance classifier but receive an incompatible topic-stance such as *gun control*^{oppose} from the topic-stance classifier. To make use of both classifiers and ensure that their predictions are consistent, we perform joint inference over their predictions using ILP.

Abortion			Gun Rights		
Topic	Rule		Topic	Rule	
abortion	S→F	O→A	gun control law	S→A	O→F
partial birth abortion	S→F	O→A	second amendment	S→F	O→A
fetus	S→A	O→F	gun/weapon/arms	S→F	O→A
pro choice	S→F	O→A	gun ownership	S→F	O→A
choice	S→F	O→A	gun control	S→A	O→F
life	S→A		gun violence	O→A	
unwanted pregnancy	O→F		gun owner	S→F	O→A

Table 1: Automatically acquired conversion rules. For a given topic, $x \rightarrow y$ implies that topic-stance label x (where x can be 'S' (support) or 'O' (oppose)) should be converted to domain-stance label y (where y can be 'F' (for) or 'A' (against)) for the topic.

Converting topic-stances to post-stances. To facilitate joint inference, we first convert the stance in each topic-stance pair to the corresponding domain-stance label. For example, given the gun rights domain, the topic-stance pairs *gun control law*^{oppose} and *gun ownership*^{support} will become *gun control law*^{for} and *gun ownership*^{for}, respectively, since people who support gun rights oppose to gun control laws and support gun ownership. Rather than hand-write the conversion rules, we derive them automatically from the posts manually annotated with both post-stance and topic-stance labels. Specifically, we learn a rule for converting a topic-stance label tsl to a post-stance label psl if tsl co-occurs with psl at least 90% of the time. Using this method, we obtain less than 10 conversion rules for each domain, all of which are shown in Table 1. Only those topic-stance labels that can be converted using these rules will be used in formulating ILP programs.

Formulating the ILP program. We formulate one ILP program for each debate post. Each ILP program contains two post-stance variables (x_{for} and $x_{against}$) and $3N_T$ topic-stance variables ($z_{t,for}$, $z_{t,against}$, and $z_{t,neutral}$ for a topic t), where N_T is the number of key topics in the post. Our objective is to maximize the linear combination of these variables and their corresponding probabilities assigned by their respective classifiers (see (1) below) subject to two types of constraints, the *integrity* constraints and the *post-topic* constraints. The integrity constraints ensure that each post is assigned exactly one stance and each topic in a post is assigned exactly one stance (see the two equality constraints in (2)). The post-topic constraints ensure consistency between the predictions made by the two classifiers. Specifically, (1) if there is at least one topic with a *for* label, the post must be assigned a *for* label; and (2) a *for*-post must have at least one *for*-topic. These constraints are defined for the *against* label as well (see the inequality constraints in (3)).

Maximize:

$$\sum_{i \in L_P} u_i x_i + \frac{1}{N_T} \sum_{t=1}^{N_T} \sum_{k \in L_T} w_{t,k} z_{t,k} \tag{1}$$

subject to:

$$\sum_{i \in L_P} x_i = 1, \forall_t \sum_{k \in L_T} z_{t,k} = 1, \text{where } \forall_i x_i \in \{0,\ 1\} \text{ and } \forall_k z_{t,k} \in \{0,\ 1\} \tag{2}$$

$$\forall_t x_i \geq z_{t,i}, \sum_{t=1}^{N_T} z_{t,i} \geq x_i, \text{where } i \in \{for,\ against\} \tag{3}$$

Note that (1) u and w are the probabilities assigned by the post-stance and topic-stance classifiers, respectively; (2) L_P and L_T denote the set of unique labels for post and topic, respectively; and (3) the fraction $\frac{1}{N_T}$ ensures that both classifiers are contributing equally to the objective function. We train all models using maximum entropy[5] and solve our ILP models using *lpsolve*[6].

5 Evaluation

In this section, we evaluate our approach to debate stance classification.

Train-test partition. Recall that 100 posts from each domain were labeled with both domain stance labels and topic stance labels. These posts constitute our training set, and the remaining posts are used for evaluation purposes.

Baseline systems. We employ two baselines. Both of them involve training a post-stance classifier, and they differ only with respect to the underlying feature set. The first one, which uses only unigrams as features, has been shown to be a competitive baseline by Somasundaran and Wiebe (2010). The second one uses the CRDD features (see Section 2). Results of the two baselines on the two domains are shown in Table 2. As we can see, Unigram is slightly better than CRDD for Gun Rights, whereas the reverse is true for Abortion. The differences in performance between the baselines are statistically insignificant for both domains (paired t-test, $p < 0.05$).

Datasets	**Baseline 1**	**Baseline 2**	**Our Approach**	
	Unigram	CRDD	CRDD+Ext1	CRDD+Both
Abortion	56.60	57.44	58.79	**61.14**
Gun Rights	53.31	53.16	55.72	**57.83**

Table 2: Results.

Our approach. Recall that our approach extends CRDD with (1) three types of new features for post-stance classification (Section 4.1) and (2) learned topic stances that are reconciled with post stances using ILP. We incorporate these two extensions incrementally into CRDD, and the corresponding results are shown under the "CRDD+Ext1" and "CRDD+Both" in Table 2, respectively. For both domains, we can see that performance improves significantly after each extension is added. Overall, our approach improves the better baseline by 3.96 and 4.52 percentage points in absolute F-measure for Abortion and Gun Rights, respectively. These results demonstrate the effectiveness of both extensions.

Conclusion and Perspectives

We proposed a machine learning approach to the debate stance classification task that extends Anand et al.'s (2011) approach with (1) three types of new features for post-stance classification and (2) learned topic stances that are reconciled with post stances using integer linear programming. Experimental results on two domains, Abortion and Gun Rights, demonstrate the effectiveness of both extensions. In future work, we plan to gain additional insights into our approach via extensive experimentation with additional domains.

Acknowledgments

We thank the two anonymous reviewers for their invaluable comments on an earlier draft of the paper. This work was supported in part by NSF Grant IIS-1147644.

[5] `http://nlp.stanford.edu/software/classifier.shtml`

[6] `http://sourceforge.net/projects/lpsolve/`

References

Anand, P., Walker, M., Abbott, R., Fox Tree, J. E., Bowmani, R., and Minor, M. (2011). Cats rule and dogs drool!: Classifying stance in online debate. In *Proceedings of the 2nd Workshop on Computational Approaches to Subjectivity and Sentiment Analysis*, pages 1–9.

Carletta, J. (1996). Assessing agreement on classification tasks: The kappa statistic. *Computational Linguistics*, 22(2):249–254.

Pang, B., Lee, L., and Vaithyanathan, S. (2002). Thumbs up? Sentiment classification using machine learning techniques. In *Proceedings of the 2002 Conference on Empirical Methods in Natural Language Processing*, pages 79–86.

Roth, D. and Yih, W.-T. (2004). A linear programming formulation for global inference in natural language tasks. In *Proceedings of the Eighth Conference on Computational Natural Language Learning*, pages 1–8.

Somasundaran, S. and Wiebe, J. (2010). Recognizing stances in ideological on-line debates. In *Proceedings of the NAACL HLT 2010 Workshop on Computational Approaches to Analysis and Generation of Emotion in Text*, pages 116–124.

FeatureForge: A Novel Tool for Visually Supported Feature Engineering and Corpus Revision

Florian Heimerl[1] *Charles Jochim*[2] *Steffen Koch*[1] *Thomas Ertl*[1]
(1) Institute for Visualization and Interactive Systems (VIS), University of Stuttgart
(2) Institute for Natural Language Processing (IMS), University of Stuttgart
`firstname.lastname@[vis|ims].uni-stuttgart.de`

ABSTRACT
In many fields of NLP, supervised machine learning methods reach the best performance results. Apart from creating new classification models, there are two possibilities to improve classification performance: (i) improve the comprehensiveness of feature representations of linguistic instances, and (ii) improve the quality of the training gold standard. While researchers in some fields can rely on standard corpora and feature sets, others have to create their own domain specific corpus and feature representations. The same is true for practitioners developing NLP-based applications. We present a software prototype that uses interactive visualization to support researchers and practitioners in two aspects: (i) spot problems with the feature set and define new features to improve classification performance, and (ii) find groups of instances hard to label or that get systematically mislabeled by annotators to revise the annotation guidelines.

TITLE AND ABSTRACT IN GERMAN

FeatureForge: Ein neues Werkzeug für visuell unterstütze Merkmalsoptimierung und Korpusüberarbeitung

In vielen Bereichen der maschinellen Sprachverarbeitung erzielen überwachte Lernmethoden die besten Ergebnisse. Neben dem Entwurf neuer Klassifikationsmodelle gibt es zwei Möglichkeiten die Klassifikationsleistung bestehender Modelle zu verbessern: (i) durch Verbessern des Informationsgehalts der Merkmalsrepräsentationen und (ii) durch Verbessern der Qualität des Goldstandards der Trainingsdaten. Während manche Forscher auf Standardkorpora und -merkmale zurückgreifen können, müssen andere eigene domänenspezifische Korpora und Merkmalsrepräsentationen erstellen. Gleiches gilt für NLP-basierte Anwendungen in der Praxis. Wir stellen einen Softwareprototyp vor, der Forscher und Entwickler mit interaktiver Visualisierung auf zwei Arten unterstützt: (i) beim Auffinden von durch die Merkmalsmenge erzeugten Problemen und der Definition von neuen Merkmalen zur Verbesserung der Klassifikationsleistung und (ii) bei der Überarbeitung der Annotationsrichtlinien durch Auffinden von Instanzengruppen die Problemfälle beim Labeln darstellen oder von Annotatoren systematisch falsch gelabelt werden.

KEYWORDS: Feature Engineering, Corpus Annotation, Interactive Visualization, Machine Learning, Citation Classification.

KEYWORDS IN L_2: Feature Engineering, Korpusannotation, Interaktive Visualisierung, Maschinelles Lernen, Zitationsklassifikation

Proceedings of COLING 2012: Posters, pages 461–470,
COLING 2012, Mumbai, December 2012.

1 Introduction

Supervised machine learning methods provide state-of-the-art performance in many fields of NLP. Researchers who want to advance the state-of-the-art either deal with the development of new classification methods that better model the linguistic data, or improve training data by developing clean and accurately labeled corpora and feature definitions that allow for an effective vector representation of linguistic entities and provide as much discriminatory information as possible for accurate classification. Guyon and Elisseeff (2003) identify the feature definition step as the one that should be tackled first when trying to improve classification performance. In this paper, we present the prototype of an interactive software system that helps researchers with the task of spotting problems with their vector representations as well as with the gold labels of their corpora. It is based on concepts from the field of Visual Analytics, which evolved from the field of visualization and incorporates methods from data mining, data representation, and human computer interaction. Visual Analytics systems (Cook and Thomas, 2005; Keim et al., 2008) typically employ automatic data aggregation and data mining methods that enable users to retrieve useful information out of vast and often unstructured amounts of data. Data aggregation and filtering methods are used to highlight relevant aspects of the data and the data mining models and visualizations can be steered and controlled through user interaction. Such an interactive system can support feature engineers in NLP, who need to get a comprehensive overview of the linguistic data at hand in order to derive meaningful linguistic features that describe the data accurately with respect to a specific classification problem. While interacting with the tool, a sensemaking (Russell et al., 1993) loop is established and new insights into the data, the usefulness of features and the interaction between feature representations and classification algorithms are created. The presented tool combines interactive visualization techniques with unsupervised clustering methods to effectively support researchers with the task of refining vector representations by creating new features, as well as finding systematic annotation errors in the corpus. It provides information about the effectiveness and discriminatory power (cf. Somol et al., 2010) of the current feature representation by displaying the current state of the classifier in combination with a hierarchical clustering of the instance space to easily identify problematic instances. Feature engineers can examine such instances, derive new features, implement and test them. When adding a new feature, the system updates all views instantaneously and thus gives much richer feedback about their impact than just the bare performance numbers of the resulting classifier. Apart from deriving new features, mislabeled instances can help updating annotation guidelines by refining or adding annotation rules. Some of the mislabeled instances can additionally be used as examples for annotation guidelines in order to convey labeling rules more effectively.

2 The FeatureForge System

The first part of this section presents the FeatureForge desktop, depicted in Figure 1. It describes what information is displayed in its views and how it is presented to the users. The second part concentrates on interaction with the views and their interplay. FeatureForge currently integrates the feature definition language of the *ColumnDataClassifier* which is part of the Stanford Classifier suite (Manning and Klein, 2003) and makes them available to users, with the restriction of only allowing Boolean feature definitions, resulting in Boolean instance vectors. The prototype supports the column-based file format of the *ColumnDataClassifier* for the primary data of instances. Primary data is the data on which features are defined, and which has been extracted from the linguistic classification entities in a previous step. Users are able to load an arbitrary number of files containing instance sets.

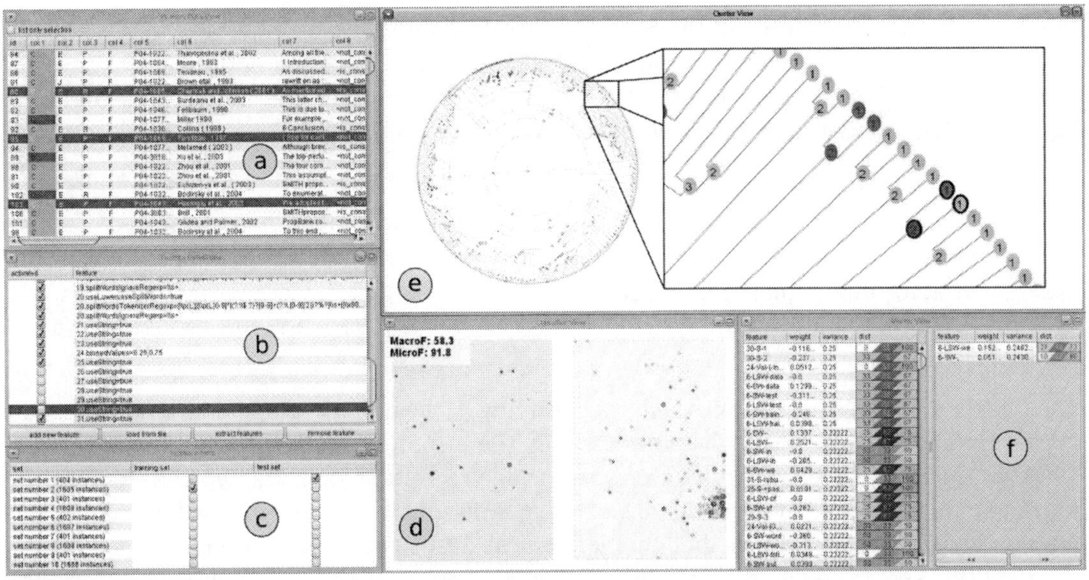

Figure 1: The FeatureForge desktop with (a) the Primary Data View, (b) the Feature Definition View, (c) the Instance Set View, (d) the Classifier View, (e) the Cluster View, and (f) the Vector Set View. The picture shows the cluster tree zoomed out and part of it enlarged for illustration.

2.1 Views and Visualizations

The Primary Data View (a) displays a table containing the instances from the loaded instance sets. Alternatively, by selecting the checkbox on top, the list of instances displayed can be restricted to the currently selected instances of other views. The column that contains the gold labels is highlighted by color. Users can select colors for each class in the dataset. The current prototype supports only data with binary labels (we chose the colors blue and ocher for them in Figure 1).

The Feature Definition View (b) shows a list of the currently defined features and allows the user to add, remove, activate and deactivate features at any time. Feature definitions can also be loaded from file. After users have modified the list of feature definitions in this view, the feature representations for the currently loaded instance sets are updated by clicking the *extract features* button.

The Instance Set View (c) holds a list of all the instance sets loaded. One training and one test set have to be selected from all available sets. The training set is used to train a classification model with one of the learning algorithms integrated into FeatureForge, while the test set is used for classifier evaluation and as a basis for the definition of new features.

The Classifier View (d) visualizes the classification model with the test set to give users an impression of the classifier's state and performance. Currently the classification methods integrated in the FeatureForge prototype are the *linear* and the *logistic* classifiers from the Stanford suite, and linear support vector machines (LibLinear, Fan et al., 2008). The decision boundary of a model is depicted as a white line separating the two instance half spaces. The instances of the test set are mapped on the 2D plane of the Classifier View. For the arrangement along the horizontal axis the classifier confidence (either geometric distance from decision boundary or probability estimate) is used. The position along the vertical axis is determined by the first principal component of the 50 most uncertain instances on each side of the decision boundary. We restrict the PCA to a subset of test instances to keep computational expense at a feasible level and guarantee interactivity. We chose examples with high uncertainty for this to keep the fidelity of their 2D representation highest. The vertical position of all other instances is determined by $v(d_i) = \frac{\sum_{d \in U_i} e(d_i,d)^{-1} \cdot v(d)}{\sum_{d \in U_i} e(d_i,d)^{-1}}$ where $v(d_i)$ gives the vertical position of an instance d_i, U_i are the ten instances from the PCA set closest to d_i, and e gives the Euclidean distance in the original vector space (cf. Heimerl et al., 2012). The Classifier View colors the instances from the test set according to their gold label to allow easy identification of misclassified instances. This view also includes a performance panel that evaluates micro- and macro-F scores (upper left corner).

The Cluster View (e) displays a hierarchical clustering of the test set computed by agglomorative clustering based on Euclidean distance between the instances. We use Ward's linkage (Ward, 1963) as the cluster similarity measure, which at each iteration joins the two clusters resulting in the minimal increase in the residual sum of squares with respect to the cluster centroids. A frequently used visualization method for hierarchical clusters are dendrograms (e.g. in Manning et al., 2008; Seo and Shneiderman, 2002). The Cluster View in the FeatureForge prototype uses a radial dendrogram to visualize the clustering of the test instances. The advantage of the radial layout is that it provides more space for the growing number of nodes towards the perimeter of the circle thus providing a better overview of the clustering tree. Instances with identical feature representations are joined before the clustering and form one leaf node in the tree. Each node is labeled with the number of instances that the respective cluster contains. The color of the nodes is chosen according to the signed homogeneity value, which we define as $(\frac{2 \cdot c_1}{c_1 + c_2} - 1)$, where c_1 and c_2 are the number of instances of the two classes in the cluster. The color of the node is the color of c_1 if signed homogeneity is $+1$, and the color of c_2 if its value is -1. If the homogeneity value reaches 0, the node color is red. For values in between ± 1 and 0, the color is interpolated between red and the color of c_1 or the color of c_2, respectively.

The Vector Set View (f) provides information about the attributes of selected instances. Each dimension[1] occupies a row of the table with the following information (in order of the columns): textual description, weights of the classification model, variance of values, occurrences of attribute. The last column is partitioned into three blocks. The middle one displays the fraction of instances that have the respective attribute, as a numerical value and with color being interpolated between white (0%) and black (100%). The left block displays the fraction of them that belong to c_1, and the right block those that belong to c_2. Both blocks are interpolated between white and the color of the respective class. By using the buttons on the bottom right, selected dimensions can be moved to the table on the right. If it contains dimensions, the left table is restricted to the set of instances that have the respective attributes, i.e. it shows the conditional distribution of attributes.

2.2 Interacting with the System

The instances in the views are highlighted (color changes to black) if hovered and selected (black edge color) if clicked by the mouse. Selection and highlight events are propagated from one to all other views. This is known as brushing and linking. The Classifier and the Cluster

[1]We use the term *feature* for the user defined units to describe the data, e.g. a bag-of-words representation for a sentence. *Dimension* describes a position of the resulting vector and *attribute* denotes the respective instance property. Examples for dimensions / attributes are e.g. single terms for a bag-of-words feature.

View also support panning and zooming. While the Primary Data View contains all instances available, the Classifier and the Cluster View only show those from the test set. They ignore highlight or selection events for other instances. If a node in the Cluster View is selected or hovered, all child nodes are highlighted and a selection event is triggered for all instances contained in the respective cluster. In all tables, columns can be sorted arbitrarily, and rows are sorted by any column when clicking on the column header.

The purpose of the Cluster View is to guide users' attention to nodes that are candidates for closer inspection. We hypothesize that instances very similar with respect to their vector representations having heterogeneous gold labels are a symptom of missing discriminatory information or a result of mislabelings. Such nodes have a high heterogeneity level (are colored red) and lie close to the perimeter of the radial tree. This means that the better the discriminatory power of the vector representation, the higher up in the cluster tree nodes with differently labeled instances are created. The heterogeneous nodes thus move higher up in the tree when improving discriminatory power of the vector representation and removing labeling errors. The Classifier View provides insight into how the classification model treats the similar yet heterogeneously labeled instances. If, e.g., the instances are scattered near the decision boundary, classification confidence for them is low which could indicate problems of data sparseness or missing discriminatory information. If they are classified with high confidence, this could be indicative of systematic labeling errors. In case they get assigned correct classes by the classifier, no intervention is necessary, but additional features could help to increase classification confidence. FeatureForge links clustering and classification on a visual and interaction level, but not at an algorithmic level. While this type of linkage is designed to help users explore the properties of a feature set and learn about its problems, we cannot guarantee that all feature or labeling problems can be identified with this approach.

The Vector Set View characterizes selected instances in terms of the defined features by showing in what dimensions they differ and how the attributes are distributed over the instances. This gives a hint about how well certain attributes are an indicator for a class in the selected set. By using the second table, interdependencies of the attributes can be explored, thus offering more fine-grained information about the distribution of attributes.

3 Case Study: Citation Classification

For our case study we concentrate on citation classification (Teufel et al., 2006), where each citation occurring in a scientific text constitutes a classification instance. We enumerate the problems we discovered during an example session and suggest solutions for those findings. The dataset comes from the ACL Anthology Reference Corpus (Bird et al., 2008) and has been annotated by NLP students. We use this corpus because we have developed it ourselves (including annotation guidelines) and are familiar with it. Citations are labeled following the classification scheme of Moravcsik and Murugesan (1975). It is comprised of four facets with two possible labels for each, resulting in four binary classification problems. For the purpose of this illustration we will focus on the facet *conceptual vs. operational*. Conceptual citations contain an idea or concept relevant to the citing paper, while operational citations contain a tool or programming library that the citing paper uses. The complete dataset contains 2009 citations, which we split into a training- and a test-set (80%/20%) on the granularity level of the documents containing the citations, resulting in 1605 training and 404 test instances. We used the Stanford logistic classifier for classification. We loaded an initial feature set containing 32 features of which some are standard features and some are self-developed. Examples of features are a bag-of-words representation for the sentence containing the citation, the position of the citation in that sentence, whether the citation is a constituent of this sentence, and whether the sentence contains any named entity that denotes an NLP tool.

By looking at the Cluster View with all initial features activated, we realized that a high number of citations in heterogeneous nodes on low variance levels occurred within the same sentence. The fact that one of the defined features was a bag-of-words representation of the sentence enclosing the citation and most of the other features also depend on the surrounding sentence resulted in this problem. The Classifier View showed that the classifier had problems separating those instances, even though we created the splits by separating the data on the granularity level of papers, thus citations with identical sentences did not occur in the training and the test set. This problem could be solved by splitting up sentences containing more than one citation as constituents. In the table of the Primary Data View, a parse tree containing the sentence of each citation is stored. It can be used to assign the largest constituent containing the respective citation as the basis for feature extraction. Unfortunately, we were not able to test it right away with the Stanford language, but we disabled the bag-of-words feature for the rest of the session.

The next finding was a cluster of four citations, of which two were labeled operational and two were labeled conceptual. By looking at the Primary Data View containing the sentences with the citations and the citation keys, we saw that one of the citations labeled operational was referring to datasets, the other one was referring to a specific type-hierarchy that the citing paper adopted from the cited paper. The citations labeled conceptual referred to aspects of two different QA systems. Although all of those labels were correct, we realized that it is generally not obvious where to draw the line between a tool borrowed and a concept adopted from another work. The next finding supported the assumption that such instances are problematic for annotators. It was a cluster with two citations, one citing a paper about a classification library and the other referring to a corpus. The citation to the classification library was correctly labeled operational, whereas the citation referring to the corpus was erroneously labeled conceptual. We will thus update the annotation guidelines with the instruction to label datasets used from other publications as operational, and emphasize that conceptual aspects of systems that are adopted by the citing paper are to be marked as conceptual. As examples we can use the citations just found.

Next, we discovered a node with three citations in the Cluster View. One was referring to a Prolog implementation and another was referring to a parser, both labeled correctly as operational. The third citation in the cluster was referring to a set of metrics and was labeled conceptual. This is also a borderline example, for which the annotation guidelines offered no clear guidance, but which should have been labeled operational. We will further refine the guidelines using this citation as an example.

The next cluster that attracted our attention contained three citations. Two of them were correctly labeled as conceptual, and were referring to the classification algorithm used in the work referred to. The third citation referred to the training set that was used in the cited paper. It was labeled correctly as operational. In the Classifier View, however, we could see that the classifier was not able to correctly separate these examples and all of them ended up on the conceptual side of the decision boundary. We realized that the annotation guidelines do not have clear instructions on how to label algorithms that the citing work builds on. They should be labeled as conceptual, and we will update the guidelines consequently. We then took a look at the main verbs of the sentences containing the citation, which were defined as features and thus visible in the Vector Set View. The two sentences that were labeled as conceptual had the main verbs 'describe' (with the cited classification algorithm as direct object) and 'build [on]' (with the classification algorithm as prepositional object), whereas the operational citation had the main verb 'use' (with the training set as the direct object). In the Vector Set View we saw that the classification model had weights pointing to the conceptual subspace for the two verbs 'describe' and 'build', and a weight pointing to the operational one for 'use', which was what we expected the classification algorithm to learn. However, we realized that single verbs were probably not features that offer the right granularity for classification, because they run into data sparseness problems. We thus expect to solve this particular classification problem by using verb classes as features. For this, we will build on verb classes from the VerbNet (Schuler, 2006) project.

4 Future Work

The FeatureForge software is currently under active development. This section presents the most important improvements we plan to implement. The first one is the integration of a more powerful feature definition language. We were not able to directly implement the ideas for new features that we had while exploring our citation data in Section 3. An example of such a more powerful language is the one sketched by (Kobdani et al., 2010). Like the language for the Stanford Classifiers, it is based on primary instance data in a tabular format, but offers much more flexibility to extract and define features based on this data. Furthermore, primary data should not be static during the runtime of the tool. We plan to make this data extensible during runtime with new data columns for each instance, as well as with linguistic tools that can directly be used as a data source. We also plan to support real-valued vectors in the future. Second, we want to develop a measure for the quality of the clustering reflecting the discriminatory power of the features. There exist measures for the quality of a flat clustering (Manning et al., 2008, chapter 16.3). We plan to extend those and derive a measure for the whole clustering tree. We further plan to analyze how our new measures are linked to the classification performance. Furthermore, we aim at a tighter integration of classification and clustering. In the current version of the system this integration takes place on a visual and interaction level, but we plan to explore possibilities to take the hypothesis about the data of the classifier into account for the clustering. Third, we aim at much broader evaluation of the prototype system. Since FeatureForge is tailored to a specific user group of NLP specialists, a quantitative study to investigate the usefulness of our approach will not be possible because it will be hard to find NLP-tasks and corpora with which a large number of NLP specialists are equally familiar. Nevertheless, we plan to conduct an informal study with NLP practitioners to learn about the benefits and deficiencies of the FeatureForge system.

5 Related Work

The contributions to the ACL Feature Engineering Symposium (Ringger, 2005) show that feature engineering plays an important role in many NLP tasks. Carefully and resourcefully engineered features are able to significantly improve classification performance. NLP problems tackled by the symposium contributions include, but are not limited to, text segmentation (Kauchak and Chen, 2005), shallow semantic parsing (Moschitti et al., 2005) and recognition of temporal expressions (Adafre and de Rijke, 2005). There is evidence (Scott and Matwin, 1999) that domain-specific feature engineering is also beneficial for a task such as text classification, where the bag-of-words model is established and shows good performance in many situations. Berend and Farkas (2010) present a set of new and effective features for automatic keyphrase extraction from scientific papers. Those examples all show the importance of linguistic feature creation for statistical NLP applications. Kobdani et al. (2010) identify the creation of feature representations for linguistic instances as the most crucial and costly step in the process of building an NLP application.

There are approaches to feature space examination that build on visualization to give users insight into the usefulness and discriminatory power of feature representations. Kienreich and Seifert (2012) apply matrix reordering algorithms on document-term matrices and classify and discuss typical emerging patterns. With the help of those patterns, users are able to judge the usefulness of certain terms for the discrimination of classes. Schreck and Keim (2006) create a 2D map of an instance space produced by a feature extractor for multimedia datasets. They hypothesize that the uniformity of distances between instances in different clusters and low variance between instances in one cluster correlates with the discriminatory power of a feature representation and provide visualization techniques that help users asses both characteristics. Dolfing (2007) developed a Visual Analytics system for feature engineering for the problem of optical character recognition based on an interactive clustering algorithm that, unlike our approach, directly incorporates user judgment in its clustering decisions. The popular machine learning system WEKA (Hall et al., 2009) offers user interfaces for clustering and classification including visualization to support the user in understanding the data better. WEKA also includes methods for feature selection. Contrary to FeatureForge, however, it does not offer any linking between clustering and classification to support the feature engineering process and offers no solution for corpus improvement.

Feature engineering is related to feature selection, which comprises a number of techniques to automatically reduce the number of dimensions of instance vectors in order to either produce more compact representations, or optimize the representations for a certain classification task. Liu and Yu (2005) provide an overview.

Conclusion

We have presented FeatureForge, a prototype system that offers a fresh approach to feature engineering and corpus improvement. It uses interactive visualization to support NLP researchers and practitioners in two aspects: (i) spot problems with the feature set and define new features to improve discriminatory power and thus classification performance, and (ii) find groups of instances that are hard to label or get systematically mislabeled by the annotators and revise the annotation guidelines accordingly and add newly found instances for better illustration of hard examples. An informal evaluation on a citation corpus showed that our approaches effectively help with those two aspects. By facilitating interactive exploration of corpora with a special focus on the labels of the instances for a specific classification task and the feature representation of the linguistic classification instances, users of FeatureForge are supported during the process of designing features and in addition they can easily spot annotation problems. We expect that future extensions of our approach will support the development of new and even better performing machine-learning based NLP applications.

Acknowledgments

The work presented here is supported by the DFG as part of the Priority Program 1335 *Scalable Visual Analytics*.

References

Adafre, S. F. and de Rijke, M. (2005). Feature engineering and post-processing for temporal expression recognition using conditional random fields. In *Proceedings of the ACL Workshop on Feature Engineering for Machine Learning in Natural Language Processing*, FeatureEng'05, pages 9–16.

Berend, G. and Farkas, R. (2010). Sztergak: Feature engineering for keyphrase extraction. In *Proceedings of the 5th International Workshop on Semantic Evaluation*, SemEval'10, pages 186–189.

Bird, S., Dale, R., Dorr, B., Gibson, B., Joseph, M., Kan, M.-Y., Lee, D., Powley, B., Radev, D., and Tan, Y. F. (2008). The ACL anthology reference corpus: A reference dataset for bibliographic research in computational linguistics. In *Proceedings of LREC*, pages 1755–1759.

Cook, K. A. and Thomas, J. J. (2005). *Illuminating the Path: The Research and Development Agenda for Visual Analytics*. IEEE Computer Society.

Dolfing, H. (2007). A Visual Analytics Framework for Feature and Classifier Engineering. Master's thesis, Department of Computer and Information Science, University of Konstanz, Konstanz, Germany.

Fan, R.-E., Chang, K.-W., Hsieh, C.-J., Wang, X.-R., and Lin, C.-J. (2008). LIBLINEAR: A library for large linear classification. *Journal of Machine Learning Research*, 9:1871–1874.

Guyon, I. and Elisseeff, A. (2003). An introduction to variable and feature selection. *Journal of Machine Learning Research*, 3:1157–1182.

Hall, M., Frank, E., Holmes, G., Pfahringer, B., Reutemann, P., and Witten, I. H. (2009). The weka data mining software: an update. *SIGKDD Exploration Newsletter*, 11(1):10–18.

Heimerl, F., Koch, S., Bosch, H., and Ertl, T. (2012). Visual classifier training for text document retrieval. In *IEEE VAST'2012*.

Kauchak, D. and Chen, F. (2005). Feature-based segmentation of narrative documents. In *Proceedings of the ACL Workshop on Feature Engineering for Machine Learning in Natural Language Processing*, FeatureEng'05, pages 32–39.

Keim, D., Mansmann, F., Schneidewind, J., Thomas, J., and Ziegler, H. (2008). Visual Analytics: Scope and Challenges Visual Data Mining. In *Visual Data Mining*, volume 4404 of *Lecture Notes in Computer Science*, chapter 6, pages 76–90. Springer.

Kienreich, W. and Seifert, C. (2012). Visual Exploration of Feature-Class Matrices for Classification Problems. In *International Workshop on Visual Analytics*, EuroVA'12, pages 37–41.

Kobdani, H., Schütze, H., Burkovski, A., Kessler, W., and Heidemann, G. (2010). Relational feature engineering of natural language processing. In *Proceedings of the 19th ACM international conference on Information and knowledge management*, CIKM'10, pages 1705–1708.

Liu, H. and Yu, L. (2005). Toward integrating feature selection algorithms for classification and clustering. *Knowledge and Data Engineering, IEEE Transactions on*, 17(4):491–502.

Manning, C. and Klein, D. (2003). Optimization, maxent models, and conditional estimation without magic. Tutorial at HLT-NAACL 2003 and ACL 2003.

Manning, C. D., Raghavan, P., and Schütze, H. (2008). *Introduction to information retrieval*. Cambridge University Press.

Moravcsik, M. J. and Murugesan, P. (1975). Some results on the function and quality of citations. *Social Studies of Science*, 5:86–92.

Moschitti, A., Coppola, B., Pighin, D., and Basili, R. (2005). Engineering of syntactic features for shallow semantic parsing. In *Proceedings of the ACL Workshop on Feature Engineering for Machine Learning in Natural Language Processing*, FeatureEng'05, pages 48–56.

Ringger, E., editor (2005). *Proceedings of the ACL Workshop on Feature Engineering for Machine Learning in Natural Language Processing*. Assiciation for Computational Linguistics.

Russell, D. M., Stefik, M. J., Pirolli, P., and Card, S. K. (1993). The cost structure of sensemaking. In *Proceedings of the INTERACT '93 and CHI '93 conference on Human factors in computing systems*, CHI'93, pages 269–276.

Schreck, T. and Keim, D. (2006). Visual feature space analysis for unsupervised effectiveness estimation and feature engineering. In *In IEEE International Conference on Multimedia and Expo*, ICME'06, pages 9–12.

Schuler, K. K. (2006). *VerbNet: A Broad-Coverage, Comprehensive Verb Lexicon*. PhD thesis, University of Pennsylvania.

Scott, S. and Matwin, S. (1999). Feature engineering for text classification. In *Proceedings of the 16th International Conference on Machine Learning*, ICML'99, pages 379–388.

Seo, J. and Shneiderman, B. (2002). Interactively exploring hierarchical clustering results. *Computer*, 35(7):80–86.

Somol, P., Novovičová, J., and Pudil, P. (2010). *Pattern Recognition Recent Advances*, chapter 4, pages 75–97. InTech.

Teufel, S., Siddharthan, A., and Tidhar, D. (2006). Automatic classification of citation function. In *Proceedings of EMNLP*, pages 103–110.

Ward, J. (1963). Hierarchical grouping to optimize an objective function. *Journal of the American Statistical Association*, 58:236–244.

Verb Temporality Analysis using Reichenbach's Tense System

André Kenji HORIE[1] *Kumiko TANAKA−ISHII*[2] *Mitsuru ISHIZUKA*[1]
(1) UNIVERSITY OF TOKYO, 7-3-1 Hongo, Bunkyo-ku, Tokyo, Japan
(2) KYUSHU UNIVERSITY, 744 Motooka, Nishi-ku, Fukuoka, Japan
andre@mi.ci.i.u-tokyo.ac.jp, kumiko@ait.kyushu-u.ac.jp,
ishizuka@i.u-tokyo.ac.jp

ABSTRACT
This paper presents the analysis process of verb temporality using Reichenbach's tense system, a language-independent system which describes tense as relations among linguistic and extra-linguistic temporal entities. Several difficulties arise from the deep analysis required for classification into Reichenbach's categories. They regard establishing the logical sequence of clauses in the skeletal structure of the discourse, and modeling the behavior of temporal markers according to this sequence. A dependency clause anchoring algorithm is then proposed and compared to other anchoring methods, and sequential supervised learning is used for abstracting surrounding context in order to determine temporal marker behavior. Experimental results show that the proposed approach is able to better abstract verb temporality than statistical ones, suggesting that analytical interlingual translation can complement existing SMT techniques by providing an additional layer of semantic information.

TITLE AND ABSTRACT IN PORTUGUESE

Análise de Tempo Verbal Utilizando o Sistema de Reichenbach

Este artigo apresenta o processo de análise de temporalidade de verbos utilizando o sistema proposto por Reichenbach, que descreve tempos verbais como relações entre entidades temporais linguísticas e extra-linguísticas. De tal análise, são observadas diversas dificuldades relacionadas ao estabelecimento de uma sequência lógica de orações na estrutura esquelética do texto e à modelagem do comportamento de marcadores temporais de acordo com esta sequência. Um algoritmo de ancoragem de orações é então proposto, sendo comparado com outros métodos de ancoragem, e aprendizado supervisionado sequencial é utilizado para abstrair o contexto de forma a determinar o posicionamento temporal desses marcadores. Resultados experimentais mostram que a abordagem proposta é capaz de melhor abstrair a temporalidade verbal quando comparada a abordagens estatísticas, o que sugere que tradução automática baseada em interlíngua pode complementar técnicas estatísticas já existentes, provendo uma camada adicional de informação semântica.

KEYWORDS: Verb tense, Interlingual Machine Translation.

KEYWORDS IN PORTUGUESE: Tempo verbal, Tradução Automática baseada em Interlíngua.

Proceedings of COLING 2012: Posters, pages 471–482,
COLING 2012, Mumbai, December 2012.

1 Synopsis in Portuguese

Tempo verbal é o aspecto da língua responsável por expressar a localização de uma eventualidade (evento, estado, processo ou ação) no tempo, sendo regida por regras gramaticais bem definidas. Em Tradução Automática Estatística, os modelos probabilísticos utilizados impõem diversas limitações quanto à abstração dessas regras. O uso de Tradução Automática baseada em Interlíngua provê uma ferramenta incremental para a descrição do texto de entrada por se utilizar de uma representação de conhecimento independente de linguagem, o que indica um melhor suporte para tradução no domínio de tempo verbal. Este trabalho propõe, portanto, usar como interlíngua o sistema de descrição de tempo verbal sistematicamente consolidado por (Reichenbach, 1947).

Neste sistema, os tempos verbais são descritos como relações entre três marcadores temporais: o tempo de referência R, o tempo da fala S e a eventualidade E. As relações possíveis são as de simultaneidade (,) ou precedência (–) e formam as categorias observadas na tabela 1.

Relations	Tense Category	Example
E-R-S	Anterior Past	He *had left* before I arrived
E,R-S	Simple Past	I *went* there yesterday
R–E–S	Posterior Past	I didn't know he *would come* yesterday
R-S,E	Posterior Past	I didn't know he *would be* here now
R-S–E	Posterior Past	I didn't know he *would come* tomorrow
E-S,R	Anterior Present	I *have* already *gone* there
S,R,E	Simple Present	I *go* there everyday
S,R–E	Posterior Present	I *shall go* there tomorrow
S–E–R	Anterior Future	He *will have fixed* the car by tomorrow (not fixed)
S,E–R	Anterior Future	He *will have fixed* the car by tomorrow (fixing)
E–S–R	Anterior Future	He *will have fixed* the car by tomorrow (already fixed)
S–R,E	Simple Future	I *will go* tomorrow
S–R–E	Posterior Future	I *will be going to go*

Table 1: Reichenbach's tense system / Sistema de tempos verbais de Reichenbach

Inerente aos métodos analíticos, esta representação semântica profunda também requer um processo de análise não trivial, com as principais dificuldades (Moulin and Dumas, 1994) descritas abaixo:

1. *Ancoragem de orações*: Determina a sequência de orações através da qual se observa continuidade do tempo verbal
2. *Composição de marcadores com expressões temporais*: Relaciona-se com o modo que expressões temporais modificam o tempo verbal
3. *Determinação e interpretação de R em relação a S*: Relaciona-se a como eventos são estruturados e compreendidos no eixo temporal de acordo com o ponto de referência

Essas dificuldades mostram a necessidade de técnicas relacionadas a: determinação de uma sequência textual de eventualidades, através de métodos de ancoragem de orações; extração de expressões temporais e outros aspectos linguísticos que regem a temporalidade na conjugação verbal, através de extração de atributos; e a modelagem da relação entre os diversos atributos e o comportamento dos marcadores temporais, utilizando-se de um classificador sequencial. A arquitetura do sistema proposto está na figura 1.

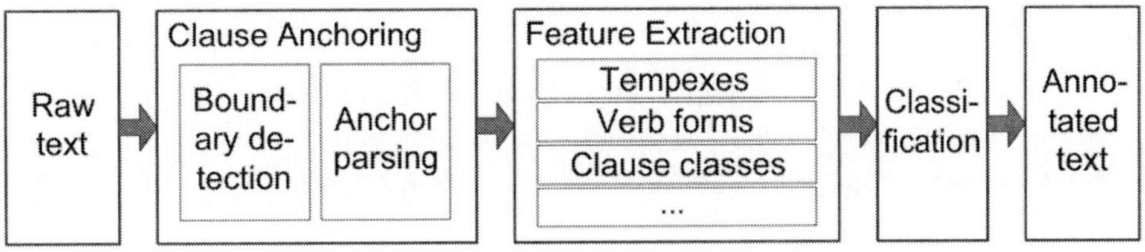

Figure 1: Components of the proposed system / Componentes do sistema proposto

Em relação à sequência de orações, sua determinação depende da construção sintática do discurso e de diversos fenômenos linguísticos tais como utilização plano de fundo (*backgrounding*). Dois esquemas de ancoragem são apresentados neste artigo: ancoragem linear, para a qual âncoras são formadas na ordem em que orações aparecem no texto, trocando acurácia por simplicidade de implementação; e ancoragem baseada em dependências, que utiliza coordenação e subordinação para formação de uma árvore de orações (figura 2). Um algoritmo baseado em análise de deslocamento e redução (*shift-reduce*) é proposto para tal esquema, sendo ele comparado com ancoragens linear e manual.

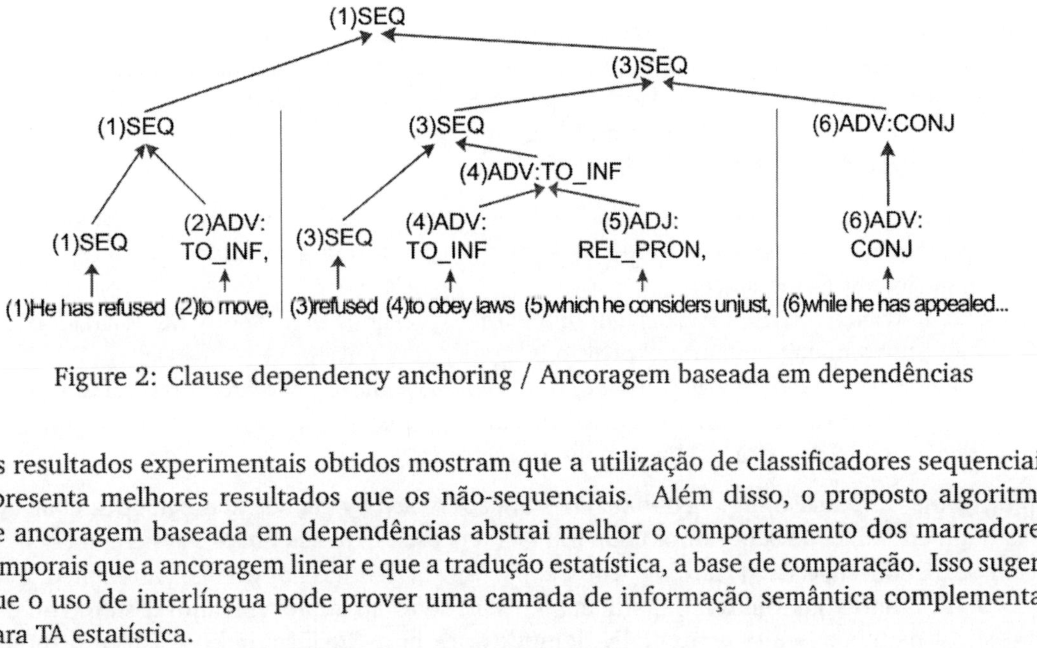

Figure 2: Clause dependency anchoring / Ancoragem baseada em dependências

Os resultados experimentais obtidos mostram que a utilização de classificadores sequenciais apresenta melhores resultados que os não-sequenciais. Além disso, o proposto algoritmo de ancoragem baseada em dependências abstrai melhor o comportamento dos marcadores temporais que a ancoragem linear e que a tradução estatística, a base de comparação. Isso sugere que o uso de interlíngua pode prover uma camada de informação semântica complementar para TA estatística.

Para finalizar, as principais contribuições deste trabalho são:

- Demonstrar como interlíngua pode complementar TA estatística no domínio de tempo verbal provendo uma camada de informação semântica adicional
- Propor o sistema de Reichenbach como essa interlíngua, com resultados que sugerem melhor acurácia se comparado a abordagens estatísticas
- Abordar as dificuldades resultantes da análise profunda baseada em interlíngua
- Apresentar e comparar métodos de ancoragem de orações, avaliando como formas diferentes de sequenciamento afetam a análise de tempo verbal

2 Introduction

Tense is the aspect of language responsible for expressing the location of an eventuality (event, state, process or action) in time. This paper studies the deep analysis of verb tense into a language independent representation, providing a proof of concept as to how Interlingual Machine Translation can support current statistical techniques.

In Statistical Machine Translation (SMT) (Koehn, 2010), highly grammatical aspects of language such as tense are not properly addressed due to its limitation in abstracting well-defined linguistic rules. The *translation model* may not be able to provide proper lexical disambiguation in cases in which there is a word form with very high probability, and the *language model* may not be able to penalize ungrammatical sentences if the error occurs outside of the n-gram window, as shown respectively in the following examples.

- "*He is running in tomorrow's race*". Futurate "is running" translated as the more probable present continuous
- "*I could have easily, although maybe more cumbersomely, made it*". The 5-gram model does not associate "could have" with "made", resulting in an incorrect simple past

The presented problems in tense translation can be alleviated by analyzing temporal semantics of verb. As a result, using Interlingual MT (Dorr et al., 2004), a paradigm that uses language-independent intermediate representation of knowledge, seems a natural approach. This research presents a study on the analysis of verb using as interlingua a representation of tense which has been systematically theorized by (Reichenbach, 1947). The resulting difficulties of the required deep analysis, observed by (Moulin and Dumas, 1994) and avoided in older transfer-based approaches, are described below:

1. *Clause anchoring*: Given an observed tendency of tense continuity across sequential clauses (unless there is an indication of change), the task of *clause anchoring* aims to determine this sequence
2. *Composition of tense markers with temporal expressions that modify the verb*: Concerns how surrounding temporal expressions modify verb tense
3. *Determination and interpretation of the temporal point of reference in respect to the point of speech*: Relates to how eventualities are structured and perceived in the time axis according to an extra-linguistic point of reference

In this work, the three mentioned difficulties are addressed by analyzing the linguistic phenomena that determine the behavior of temporal markers used in Reichenbach's system, modeling it using sequential supervised learning. This deep tense analysis has not yet been attempted, to the best of the authors' knowledge. Experimental results show an improvement over state-of-the-art statistical methods, which potentially demonstrates how SMT could co-exist with Interlingual MT by conceptualizing the interlingua as an additional information layer for improving translation in the tense domain. The main contributions of this work are the following:

- Showing how SMT can possibly be complemented by the interlingua in the verb tense domain by providing an additional information layer
- Proposing Reichenbach's tense system as this interlingua, with results suggesting an increase in accuracy for this task when compared to SMT
- Addressing difficulties arising from deep analysis required in the interlingual approach
- Presenting and comparing methods for clause anchoring, evaluating how different ways of sequencing clauses affect tense analysis

3 Reichenbach's Tense System

The proposed interlingua for the verb tense translation task is Reichenbach's system, the most widely accepted theory for describing tense. It provides a rich language-independent description of eventualities by logically structuring them in the time axis according to a reference point. These temporal interactions among semantic entities thus accomodate differences in culture-specific time perception of eventualities.

This system describes tense using relations among three temporal markers: S, E and R. The point of speech S indicates time of the utterance, the eventuality E represents the time location of the verb, and the reference point R is an extra-linguistic reference. There are 13 marker combinations considering concurrence (,) and precedence (–) relations, resulting in the 9 tense categories stated in table 1. It is observed that the semantic value of relation S::R defines if the tense category is a present, past or future – in the special case in which E::R is concurrent, R::S defines the absolute tense; and the semantic value of R::E defines if the tense is simple, anterior or posterior, being primarily responsible for defining relative tense.

Reichenbach's system has a number of extensions which try to better accomodate observed phenomena. To mention some, (Dowty, 1979) proposes R as an interval rather than a point, and (Comrie, 1985) proposes a second R. However, since there is no consensus as to the best representation of tense, the original system is used in this work.

In order to classify an eventuality into one of Reichenbach's categories, deeper semantic understanding of temporal structure is necessary. A variety of linguistic phenomena are used for interpreting the behavior of the markers according to surrounding context, and thus for inferring the relative positions of S, E and R. In the example, a grammaticaly correct sentence would employ the simple past "reached" in the second clause (c_2) because it maintains a *sequence of tense* (SOT); using "reach" disrupts the timely order of eventualities, abruptly changing R from R–S in c_1 to R,S in c_2.

"*The train had left* (E–R-S) | *before we* {*reach* (E,R,S) / *reached* (E,R-S) } *the station.*"

This behavior of R is explained by the *Temporal Discourse Interpretation Principle* (TDIP) (Dowty, 1979). Under this principle, R is (a) at a time consistent with the temporal expressions ('tempex' for short) related to the given verb. This indicates that tempexes have preference in determining changes in R, being directly related to previously mentioned difficulty (2). The extraction task for tempexes, as well as the modeling of how they affect R, is presented in section 4.2.

According to TDIP, in the absence of tempexes, R is (b) at a time which follows the reference time of the previous clause. This is further explained by the *Permanence of the Reference Point Principle* (PRPP) (Reichenbach, 1947), which states a tendency of R to remain unchanged across sequential clauses. Nevertheless, this clause sequence is not purely linear (i.e. in the order they appear in text), but instead depends on coordination and subordination, resulting in difficulty (1). Computational methods for clause anchoring are explained in section 4.1.

Finally, although PRPP properly explains the behavior of R in many situations, it has proven to fail in some cases, leading to difficulty (3). Two of these cases are presented:

- *Backgrounding* (Hopper, 1979): Background eventualities offer supporting information not in the chronologically sequential skeleton of the discourse. There is a strong correlation between backgrounding and adjective/noun clauses (Tomlin, 1985).

Ex.: In "*I talked to John, who is in charge of the event, and we agreed on the issue*", the adjective clause introduces a present between two past clauses, but is not ungrammatical.
- *Shift of perspective* (Binnick, 1991): Perspective is shifted from the speaker to that of a subject, implicating change in S. It is observed in quoted and free indirect speech.
  Ex.: In "*He said he is not talking to you*", S is moved by the free indirect speech.

The computational interpretation of R is done via supervised learning, as explained in section 4.2. By using features representing tempexes, among others, a sequential classifier is responsible for abstracting the behavior of R, outputting a Reichenbach category for each clause.

4 Interlingual Verb Tense Analysis

This section presents the analysis process (figure 1), which classifies each verb in text into a tense category. In contrast with traditional analytical approaches, which employed manually tailored rules, this work uses supervised learning for obtaining the interlingua.

4.1 Clause Anchoring

The process of *clause anchoring* determines the sequence of clauses in a text. By analyzing the anchoring structure, it is possible to model the behavior of temporal markers across a sequence of clauses which is consistent to SOT.

The first part of clause anchoring is boundary detection, which was the target of CoNLL-2001 (Tjong et al., 2001) and consists of finding the position that delimits two clauses. The proposed analysis process uses the best performing system of CoNLL-2001 (Carreras and Márquez, 2003) (F-value of 84.36%) with some rule-based post-processing.

The second part is the anchoring itself. A pre-processing step is first carried in order to identify the type of coordination/subordination. Using heuristics based on its first words and the last words of the previous clauses, each clause is categorized as coordinated (COORD), subordinated nominal (NOUN), subordinated adjective (ADJ), subordinated adverbial clause (ADV) or none (NONE), and then further subcategorized. For example, in the sentence below, the second clause is adverbial starting with a to-infinitive.

> *He has frequently refused* (NONE) | (...) *to obey local laws* (ADV:TO_INF) | *which he considers unjust (...)* (ADJ:REL_PRON)

Given separated and categorized clauses, two types of anchoring are then presented: linear and dependency anchoring. They propose different ways of establishing sequential clauses:

- *Linear anchoring*: Anchoring clauses in the order they appear in the text, not modeling backgrounding. Accuracy is traded off for simplicity, as most anchors are linear.
- *Dependency anchoring*: Parses a clause tree using coordination and subordination (figure 2). An automatic approach based on shift-reduce is detailed next.

Dependency Anchoring

Clause dependency anchoring aims to build a tree that identifies anchors according to coordination/subordination. This research proposes a bottom-up parsing algorithm which uses a grammar built upon head-tail relations between clauses for English. For the algorithm, anchors are first defined as production rules which directly represent coordinated/subordinated clauses. Given H the head clause of the anchor and T the tail, these rules are in the form:

- $H \rightarrow HT$ (direct order): *"He has refused | to move"*
- $H \rightarrow TH$ (reverse order): *"After the fruit is harvested, | it is sold at the market"*
- $H \rightarrow HT_1T_2$ (middle positioning): *"The car, | which was red, | belonged to him"*

Using these production rules, the clauses are then linked using a parsing algorithm. Shift-reduce has been applied for the extraction of temporal dependencies, such as in ordering events on the time axis (Kolomiyets et al., 2012). Given $C = (c_1 \ldots c_n)$ linear clauses from the text, this algorithm either pushes a clause onto the stack (shift) or inversely applies a production rule to the top of the the stack (reduce). This is done until only one symbol remains in this stack.

In the context of tense analysis, however, the problem of clause cascading is observed. If a sentence $(c_1c_2c_3c_4)$ is produced by $c_1 \rightarrow c_1c_2c_4$ and $c_2 \rightarrow c_2c_3$, the algorithm has to analyze if $c_3 \rightarrow c_3c_4$ is valid or not before reducing c_2, which is solved with n-lookahead. However, due to clause cascading, there is no formal limit to the growth of c_2 (no limit to n), resulting in difficulty in the decision between shifting or reducing. This motivates a modification in the algorithm, using a multiple pass approach as shown in algorithm 1.

Algorithm 1 Dependency anchoring algorithm for a group of clauses

```
Input: C = (c_1 ... c_n) linear clauses
function DEPENDENCY-ANCHORING(C)
    while true do
        for cursor ← 1 to n do
            if !Is-Linked(C, cursor) then Preferential-Link(C, cursor)
        Reduce-Farthest-Linked-Clauses(C)
        if size(C) = 1 then return C[0]
```

For each pass, the algorithm first moves a cursor to each position (shift), applying preferential linking in the clauses to the right of the cursor if they are not yet linked. Preferential linking removes ambiguities in the formation fules. When the cursor reaches the final position, the algorithm will have linked all adjacent clauses that should be linked (as in linear anchoring). Leaf reduction is then performed, removing the clauses that have already been linked and which stand farthest away from the root. This guarantees to completely reduce c_2, which may cascade, before reducing $c_1 \rightarrow c_1c_2c_4$. This process is iterated until only the root for this tree is left.

In order to further simplify the problem, clauses in a sentence are divided into groups, arranged according to punctuation symbols such as commas (figure 2), since clauses within the same group are usually anchored first. The algorithm is then applied to each group, obtaining a group root clause, and is then run again using these group roots, finally obtaining the sentence root. The backbone of the text is then formed by linking the last clause of the sentence which is connected to the root only by NONE and COORD anchors to the first clause of the next sentence.

4.2 Feature Selection and Tense Classification

Manually defining rules concerning difficulty (3) as observed in rule-based approaches is not feasible. The classification of a verb into one of Reichenbach's categories would then be better addressed by using supervised learning. The classifier used for this task is CRF, which performs sequential classification, considering the output class of the previous token for determining the current token. The quality of the classification, and consequently of the analysis process, depends largely on the feature selection, which must be able to address the linguistic phenomena presented in section 3, allowing the classifier to abstract the relations among tense markers.

The first feature type relates to difficulty (2), since R is primarily defined by surrounding tempexes. The extraction of such expressions has been extensively researched – it was the target of ACE 2004 TERN Evaluation and TARSQI, a project which addresses timestamping, ordering and reasoning of events, automatically annotating text under the TimeML (Pustejovsky et al., 2003) specification language. In this work, the TARSQI tempex extraction module (Mani and Wilson, 2000) is used. It is complemented with a CRF-based extractor, as some tense-related tempexes such as "often" and "ever" were not extracted.

Aside from tempexes, other extracted features are given below. They are extracted using TARSQI and Stanford CoreNLP, and are also illustrated by an example in figure 3.

- *Verb form*: English tense (present, past, future, infinitive, etc.), aspect (perfect, progressive, perfect progressive) and modality (modal verbs) provide information for determining Reichenbach's tense category
- *Verb POS*: Complementary information when verb form is not properly identified
- *Verb lemma*: Utterance verbs from surrounding clauses are useful for identifying indirect, quoted and free indirect speech clauses
- *Clause link*: Adjective and nominal clauses provide background information (section 4.1)
- *Eventuality type*: A break in the SOT by a eventuality of type 'state' is one indication of background independent clause
- *Quotation*: Verb between quotation marks indicate quoted speech

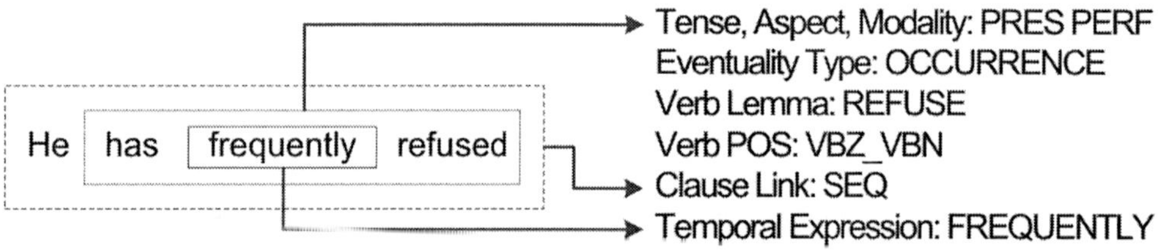

Figure 3: Example of extracted features for the clause "*He has frequently refused*"

In many cases, background independent clauses and free indirect speech have no apparent differentiation from regular clauses except for pragmatic information. The solution for these cases requires further investigation.

5 Verb Tense-Annotated Dataset

For this task, a dataset has been manually annotated according to Reichenbach's tense categories. The chosen corpus is a subset of the Brown Corpus (Kučera and Francis, 1967) and contains 8 texts from each of Reportage (news), Belles Lettres (essays, biographies) and Adventure (fiction) genres, totaling over 6,700 clauses. An example of annotation is given below:

> *Social Darwinism was able to stave off (...)* (SIMPLE PAST) | *However, in recent decades,* (NONE) | *for what doubtless are multiple reasons,* (SIMPLE PRESENT) | *(...) shift has occurred in both facets of national activity.* (ANTERIOR PRESENT) | *A concept of responsibility is in process...* (SIMPLE PRESENT)

Table 2 provides the percentage of clauses in the dataset for each categories. The majority of cases are past (60.82%) and simple tenses (48.97%). This dataset has also been manually annotated for clause dependency anchoring. It was observed that 26.89% of the anchors are not linear, i.e. the head and tail of a coordinated or subordinated clause do not occur consecutively. Moreover, in terms of SOT, both S::R and E::R relations remained the same across sequential clauses in 59.69% of the cases; only S::R remained in 24.82%; and S::R changed in 15.50%.

	Simple	Anterior	Posterior	Subtotal
Present	24.29%	3.30%	9.45%	37.04%
Past	48.97%	3.69%	8.17%	60.82%
Future	1.86%	0.03%	0.25%	2.14%
Subtotal	75.12%	7.02%	17.86%	

Table 2: Percentage of clauses for each tense category (excluding clauses with no verbs)

Since tense theory might still evolve, eventual changes in the model would affect only the annotated data for classification. As a result, the annotation effort by (Derczynski and Gaizauskas, 2011) might greatly contribute to this work, especially if it is integrated to the TimeML effort.

The baseline considered for tense translation is Google Translate for the language pairs EN→PT and EN→JP. When evaluating the statistical translation, only the correctness according to Reichenbach's categories was assessed. In other words, errors concerning verb choice, passive voice usage, etc. were disregarded. In the example, the first translation would be considered correct from the tense perspective, whereas the second would not.

- Correct: *He runs everyday* (present) → *Kare wa mainichi jikkō saremasu*, lit. *He is put into execution everyday* (present)
- Incorrect: *He is running tomorrow* (future) → *Kare wa ashita jikkō sareteiru*, lit. *He is being put into execution tomorrow* (present continuous)

In open domain, EN→PT produces satisfactory translation, whereas EN→JP does not. However, in tense translation, accuracy values are 83.98% and 81.83% respectively. Although at first counterintuitive, these values indicate that tense translation is largely dependent on the source language. It is expected that for source languages whose tenses present ambiguity in verb form according to the target language, translation accuracy is lower.

6 Evaluation and Discussion

The evaluation regards the accuracy of the tense analysis into Reichenbach's categories, compared against the SMT baseline. The proposed method is evaluated using 4-cross validation. The following settings are compared: (1) non-sequential classifier SVM; (2) CRF using linear anchoring; and CRF using (3) proposed automatic and (4) manual dependency anchoring. The software packages CRFSuite (Okazaki, 2007) and LibSVM (Chang and Lin, 2011) were used.

Under all settings, two combinations were compared: using only one classifier for classifying the nine tenses (simple present, anterior past, etc.); or using two separate classifiers, one for present/past/future, and the other for simple/anterior/posterior. From the results in table 3, it is observed that using separate classifiers has lower accuracies in all cases, indicating that they are not able to properly model the interaction between S::R and E::R.

In addition, CRF produces better results than SVM, as they are able to model sequencing. When comparing CRF-based approaches, the results from the proposed anchoring are better than

Evaluation Setting	Accuracy	
	Unified Classifier	Separate Classifiers
SVM	83.63%	83.11%
CRF-linear	89.50%	87.95%
CRF-dependency(automatic)	90.80%	89.36%
CRF-dependency(manual)	91.08%	89.54%
SMT Baseline	83.98% (EN→PT), 81.83% (EN→JP)	

Table 3: Accuracy of analysis according to Reichenbach's tenses

linear anchoring as expected, with accuracies of 90.80% and 89.50% respectively. Considering that the two anchoring structures differ only in 26.89% of the clauses as previously stated, this difference of 1.30% is substantial. Moreover, counting only the clauses in which there is a break in SOT (40.31% of all clauses), the accuracies become 88.66% and 85.34%. This demonstrates that the proposed anchoring provides better modeling of the behavior of temporal markers, with accuracy values comparable to manual anchoring (difference of 0.28%), the theoretical maximum using a fixed feature set and training data.

Most of the obtained errors concern changes in R and S in cases when there is no explicit context from which to infer the new position of the markers. In the first example below, there is no indication of the simple present in "*No telling*". Other errors occurred because of component failure. In the second example, the shift of perspective is not properly addressed because the verb form in c_2 is not identified. However, component errors in clause boundary detector are not propagated when verbs and tempexes are consistently grouped within the same clause, as tense is inherited from the previous clause in 59.69% of the cases due to SOT.

- "... *Mike lifted him (...).* | 'No telling | *how good this horse is*'"
  Obtained: SIMPLE PAST; Expected: SIMPLE PRESENT
- "... *he believed* | there are a number of qualified city residents..."
  Obtained: POSTERIOR PAST; Expected: SIMPLE PRESENT

The obtained results indicate that this interlingua may improve SMT, using hybrid approaches such as modular interlingual generation systems (Singh et al., 2007) and factored models for source information (Avramidis and Koehn, 2008). In the latter, translation accuracy from morphologically poor to rich languages, which is often the case of tense, is shown to improve.

Conclusion

This paper studied the interlingual analysis of verb tense using Reichenbach's system, which describes tense in a language-independent manner. Several difficulties arise from the required deep analysis: the behavior of temporal markers were modeled by supervised learning and proper feature selection; concerning the phenomenon of SOT, different clause anchoring methods were compared regarding their effect on tense analysis, with the proposed algorithm providing considerably higher accuracy than linear anchoring.

Finally, experimental results showed that the proposed analytical method is able to better abstract verb temporality than statistical approaches, which suggests that in domains that are governed by well-defined rules as is the case of verb tense, interlingual translation is able to complement SMT techniques by providing an additional layer of semantic information, which in turn can be integrated into a hybrid translation approach with existing models.

References

Avramidis, E. and Koehn, P. (2008). Enriching morphologically poor languages for statistical machine translation. *Proceedings of ACL-08: HLT*, pages 763–770.

Behrens, H. (2001). Cognitive-conceptual development and the acquisition of grammatical morphemes: The development of time concepts and verb tense. *Language Acquisition and Conceptual Development*, 3:450.

Binnick, R. I. (1991). *Time and the Verb: A guide to tense and aspect*. Oxford University Press.

Carreras, X. and Márquez, L. (2003). Phrase recognition by filtering and ranking with perceptrons. In *Proceedings of RANLP-2003*, pages 205–216.

Chambers, N. (2012). Labeling documents with timestamps: Learning from their time expressions. In *Proceedings of ACL-2012*. ACL.

Chang, C. and Lin, C. (2011). LIBSVM: A library for Support Vector Machines. *ACM Transactions on Intelligent Systems and Technology (TIST)*, 2(3):27.

Comrie, B. (1985). *Tense*. Cambridge University Press.

Derczynski, L. and Gaizauskas, R. (2011). An annotation scheme for Reichenbach's verbal tense structure. In *Workshop on Interoperable Semantic Annotation*, page 10.

Dorr, B., Hovy, E., and Levin, L. (2004). Machine translation: Interlingual methods. *Natural Language Processing and Machine Translation Encyclopedia of Language and Linguistics*.

Dowty, D. (1979). *Word Meaning and Montague Grammar: The semantics of verbs and times in generative semantics and in Montague's PTQ*, volume 7. Springer.

Hinkel, E. (1992). L2 tense and time reference. *TESOL Quarterly*, 26(3):557–572.

Hopper, P. (1979). Aspect and foregrounding in discourse. *Discourse and Syntax*.

Koehn, P. (2010). *Statistical Machine Translation*. Cambridge University Press, New York, NY, USA, 1st edition.

Kolomiyets, O., Bethard, S., and Moens, M. (2012). Extracting narrative timelines as temporal dependency structures. In *Proceedings of ACL-2012*. ACL.

Kučera, H. and Francis, W. (1967). *Computational Analysis of Present-Day American English*. Dartmouth Publishing Group.

Mani, I. and Wilson, G. (2000). Robust temporal processing of news. In *Proceedings of ACL-2000*, pages 69–76. ACL.

Moulin, B. and Dumas, S. (1994). The temporal structure of a discourse and verb tense determination. *Conceptual Structures: Current Practices*, pages 45–68.

Okazaki, N. (2007). CRFsuite: A fast implementation of conditional random fields (CRFs).

Pustejovsky, J., Castano, J., Ingria, R., Sauri, R., Gaizauskas, R., Setzer, A., Katz, G., and Radev, D. (2003). TimeML: Robust specification of event and temporal expressions in text. *New Directions in Question Answering*, 2003:28–34.

Reichenbach, H. (1947). *Elements of Symbolic Logic.*

Saurí, R., Knippen, R., Verhagen, M., and Pustejovsky, J. (2005). Evita: A robust event recognizer for QA systems. In *Proceedings of HLT/EMNLP-2005*, pages 700–707. Association for Computational Linguistics.

Singh, A., Husain, S., Surana, H., Gorla, J., Sharma, D., and Guggilla, C. (2007). Disambiguating tense, aspect and modality markers for correcting machine translation errors. In *Proceedings of RANLP-2007.*

Tjong, E., Sang, K., and Déjean, H. (2001). Introduction to the CoNLL-2001 Shared Task: Clause identification. In *Proceedings of ACL-2001 Workshop on Computational Natural Language Learning (CoNLL)*, page 8. ACL.

Tomlin, R. (1985). Foreground-background information and the syntax of subordination. *Text-Interdisciplinary Journal for the Study of Discourse*, 5(1-2):85–122.

Vauquois, B. (1968). A survey of formal grammars and algorithms for recognition and transformation in machine translation. In *IFIP Congress*, volume 68, pages 254–260.

Verhagen, M., Mani, I., Sauri, R., Knippen, R., Jang, S., Littman, J., Rumshisky, A., Phillips, J., and Pustejovsky, J. (2005). Automating temporal annotation with TARSQI. In *Proceedings of ACL-2005 on Interactive Poster and Demonstration Sessions*, pages 81–84. ACL.

A Metric for Evaluating Discourse Coherence based on Coreference Resolution

Ryu Iida[1] *Takenobu Tokunaga*[1]
(1) Tokyo Institute of Technology, W8-73, 2-12-1 Ohokayama Meguro Tokyo, 152-8552 Japan
[redacted]

ABSTRACT
We propose a simple and effective metric for automatically evaluating discourse coherence of a text using the outputs of a coreference resolution model. According to the idea that a writer tends to appropriately utilise coreference relations when writing a coherent text, we introduce a metric of discourse coherence based on automatically identified coreference relations. We empirically evaluated our metric by comparing it to the entity grid modelling by Barzilay and Lapata (2008) using Japanese newspaper articles as a target data set. The results indicate that our metric better reflects discourse coherence of texts than the existing model.

KEYWORDS: discourse coherence, coreference resolution, evaluation metric.

Proceedings of COLING 2012: Posters, pages 483–494,
COLING 2012, Mumbai, December 2012.

1 Introduction

The task of automatically evaluating discourse coherence has recently received much attention (Karamanis et al., 2004; Barzilay and Lapata, 2008; Lin et al., 2011, etc.) because it is essential for several NLP applications such as generation (Soricut and Marcu, 2006), summarisation (Lapata, 2003; Okazaki et al., 2004; Bollegala et al., 2006) and automated essay scoring (Miltsakaki and Kukich, 2000; Higgins et al., 2004). Researchers in these areas have mainly been concerned with introducing the linguistic notions of cohesion or coherence addressed in discourse theories, such as Centering Theory (Grosz et al., 1995) and Rhetorical Structure Theory (Mann and Thompson, 1988), into computational models for each task, ranging from heuristic rule-based to sophisticated machine learning-based approaches.

Some of this research has relied on the occurrence of discourse entities (e.g. NPs and pronouns) to capture cohesion of a text for indirectly estimating discourse coherence. Barzilay and Lapata (2008)'s approach, for instance, models the transition of discourse entities appearing in adjacent sentences for capturing local discourse coherence, which is derived from the notion of Centering Theory. In their approach, the plausible transition of discourse entities in a coherent text is trained together with a set of incoherent texts by using a ranking SVM (Joachims, 2002), making use of a grid of each discourse entity with regard to its grammatical role, called an *entity grid* representation.

Their approach to evaluating discourse coherence is quite useful when discourse entities explicitly appear in languages such as English. In their evaluation, they reported their coherence modeling based on the entity grid representation contributes to drastically improving accuracy on the information ordering task, which is the pairwise ranking problem given a pair of coherent and incoherent texts in English. However, in languages such as Japanese and Italian, capturing the transition of discourse entities is relatively difficult due to the frequent use of ellipses. As an example of employing the entity grid model in Japanese, Yokono and Okumura (2010) directly attempted this for representing grid using typical Japanese grammatical roles (*wa* (topic), *ga* (subj), *o* / *ni* (obj / i-obj) and others). They conducted an empirical evaluation of pairwise ranking of Japanese texts, replicating the experimental settings by Barzilay and Lapata (2008). Their result shows their model achieved around 70% in accuracy, whereas the evaluation result on the English data set reaches around 90%. This difference of performance might be caused by the frequent occurrence of ellipses. In Japanese, for example, subjects in a sentence are frequently unrealised, resulting in the less frequent occurrence of adjacent discourse entities in a same coreference, which are essential for capturing the transition of discourse entities in entity grid modelling (Barzilay and Lapata, 2008).

Against this background, we propose a metric of discourse coherence, which takes into account any pair of discourse entities in a text to capture the relationship of the entities distantly appeared in a text, which cannot not be directly exploited in the entity grid approaches. In order to evaluate discourse coherence using our metric, we utilise the outputs of a coreference resolution model (especially, the reliability of each output of the model). The assumption behind it is that one tends to appropriately utilise coreference relations when writing a coherent text, i.e. the better use of coreference relations is considered as a good indicator of coherent texts.

This paper is organised as follows. Section 2 briefly reviews the previous work on automatically evaluating discourse (local) coherence. Section 3 explains the proposed metric of evaluating discourse coherence exploiting the outputs of coreference resolution and Section 4

s_1: [John] bought [iPad2] as [a gift] for [Lucy].
s_2: However, [it] has [something amiss] with [the sound system].
s_3: As a result, [he] went to [[Lucy]'s birthday party] with no [gift].

Square-bracketed words (or phrases) stand for discourse entities.

Figure 1: Coherent input example for entity computation

introduces an NP coreference resolution model employed in the metric. Section 5 reports performance of NP coreference resolution on coherent and incoherent texts in Japanese and the effectiveness of the proposed metric on the task of information ordering comparing to an existing model. Section 6 concludes the paper and discuss our future directions.

2 Related work

There has been an increase in recent work for evaluating discourse (local) coherence of a text (Barzilay and Lapata, 2008; Karamanis et al., 2004; Lin et al., 2011; Miltsakaki and Kukich, 2000; Higgins et al., 2004, etc.), which strongly relates to the cohesion of discourse entities appearing in the text from the theoretical perspective mainly based on Centering Theory (Grosz et al., 1995). For example, Karamanis et al. (2004) and Miltsakaki and Kukich (2000) proposed a metric of coherence directly utilising the transition of centers in a text, as Centering Theory does. According to the analysis by Poesio et al. (2004), Karamanis et al. (2004) define a metric based on the numbers of missing *backward-looking centers*, each of which is a discourse entity appearing in the current utterance and was realised as most salient in the previous utterance. On the other hand, Miltsakaki and Kukich (2000) focused on investigating the relationship of the coherence of a text and the transition of centers and revealed that the rough-shift transition of centers correlates to incoherence of a text.

In these studies, one of the most important work was to represent the relationship of discourse entities and their occurrences in a text based on the transition of discourse entities, which was done in a series of studies (Barzilay and Lee, 2004; Barzilay and Lapata, 2005; Lapata and Barzilay, 2005; Barzilay and Lapata, 2008). In Barzilay and Lapata (2008), the transition of discourse entities in adjacent discourse units (e.g. sentences) is formalised as an *entity grid*, which is a matrix of discourse entities and their realised grammatical roles, because a grammatical role of a discourse entity is a good indicator of its salience. For example, a given input text shown in Figure 1, consisting of the three sentences, each discourse entity is represented in the entity grid shown in Table 1. In the entity grid, each column is filled with the corresponding label (e.g. S (subject), O (object), X (others) and – (not realised)). In the grid, the local transition of entities with regard to the labels can be seen as a generalisation of the center transition discussed in a series of Centering studies (Walker et al., 1997; Grosz et al., 1995). Therefore, exploiting the transition becomes a good indicator of (local) discourse coherence. In their work, the transition of each entity was used as a feature for distinguishing a coherent text from an incoherent one.

As an extension of Barzilay and Lapata (2008), Lin et al. (2011) took into account the use of discourse relations to revise the formulation of an entity grid. They used the four types of discourse relations (Temporal, Contingency, Comparison and Expansion) defined in the Penn Discourse Treebank (PDTB) instead of grammatical roles, which are automatically acquired by the discourse parser by Lin et al. (2011). For grid representation, they calculated the tran-

	John	iPad2	gift	Lucy	sound system	birthday party
s_1	S	O	X	X	–	–
s_2	–	S	–	–	X	–
s_3	S	–	X	X	–	X

Table 1: Entity grid of the input example in Figure 1

$s'_1=(s_1)$: [John] bought [iPad2] as [a gift] for [Lucy].
$s'_2=(s_3)$: As a result, [he] went to [[Lucy]'s birthday party] with no [gift].
$s'_3=(s_2)$: However, [it] has [something amiss] with [the sound system].

Figure 2: Incoherent input example for entity computation obtained by random reordering

sition probabilities of discourse entities in a text based on the PDTB-style discourse relations (e.g. $P(S_i : Comp.Arg_1 \rightarrow S_{i+1} : Exp.Arg2)$), and then these probabilities are exploited as features in a ranking SVM (Joachims, 2002). Through their empirical evaluation they reported their extension of the entity grid representation contributes to improving performance on the pairwise ordering task compared to the original entity grid model.

3 A metric for evaluating coherence based on coreference resolution

As explained in Section 2, typical approaches to modeling discourse coherence have exploited the transition of discourse entities in terms of grammatical roles or discourse relations defined in PDTB. In contrast, we estimate discourse coherence by a metric relying on the outputs of an NP coreference resolution model.

For instance, from the coherent text shown in Figure 1, the corresponding incoherent text is generated by randomly reordering sentences, one of which is as shown in Figure 2. In this incoherent text, as the pronoun "it" is placed relatively far from its antecedent "iPad2" and a distractor "birthday party" is inserted between these two expressions, the interpretation of "it" is more difficult than the case of the coherent text. As a result, applying a typical coreference resolution model to coherent and incoherent texts gives rise to the difference in the number of correctly identified coreference relations. In addition, if there is no difference in terms of the number, there may be a difference in the reliability score (i.e. predicted probability outputted by a classifier) of the resolved relations. Based on these differences, we propose a metric for evaluating discourse coherence, which is calculated according to the following two steps:

1. a coreference (or anaphora) resolution model trained with annotated coherent texts is applied to a target text T.

2. the coherence score of T is calculated from the outputs of step1 by

$$\text{coherence}(T) = \frac{1}{N}\sum_{j}^{N} \text{score}_{ana}(i, j), \qquad (1)$$

where T is a target text, j is a candidate anaphor appearing in T and i is the most likely candidate antecedent of j. N is the number of candidate anaphors appearing in T. The reliability score of the coreference relation of i and j, $\text{score}_{ana}(i, j)$, is the output score (e.g. predicted probability) obtained after a coreference model is applied to T in step1.

Note that the proposed metric can also be used as one of the features for the entity grid model because it is obtained from a different perspective from the entity grid (i.e. information of the discourse entity transition). In Section 5.3 we will also demonstrate the results of the entity grid model employing our metric as a feature.

4 Coreference resolution model for a coherence metric

The proposed metric introduced in Section 3 is designed for the use of any anaphora (or coreference) resolution model. In this work, we employ an NP coreference resolution model.

According to formula (1) in Section 3, calculating our metric needs a reliability score of each anaphor and candidate antecedent pair. Recent sophisticated approaches to NP coreference range from considering the transitivity of discourse entities (Denis and Baldridge, 2007) to clustering-based approaches (Cardie and Wagstaf, 1999; Cai and Strube, 2010), but these approaches aim at obtaining globally optimised scores for a set of mentions. Therefore, it is generally difficult using such models to get a reliability score for a pair of two mentions though they typically achieved better performance than simple pairwise coreference resolution models such as Soon et al. (2001) and Ng and Cardie (2002),

In the work on Japanese anaphora resolution by Iida and Poesio (2011), they employed an ILP-based approach to optimise final outputs of NP coreference resolution in Japanese and reported it achieved better performance than simple pairwise baselines. In spite of the global optimisation by ILP, their formulation can be easily reinterpreted as follows due to the best-first constraint used in their ILP formula, which is for avoiding the redundant choice of more than one candidate antecedent:

$$\text{coref}(i,j) = \frac{P(coref|i,j) + P(anaph|j)}{2} \quad (2)$$

where j is a candidate anaphor and i is the most likely candidate antecedent of j. $P(coref|i,j)$ is calculated by a simple coreference classifier such as Ng and Cardie (2002) and $P(anaph|j)$ is the score of anaphoricity of j, which is used to exclude typical non-anaphoric mentions such as pleonastic *it*. Given equation (2), their anaphora resolution model judge as anaphoric if $\text{coref}(i,j) \geq 0.5$; otherwise non-anaphoric.

In this work, we adopt the above approach to obtain $\text{score}_{ana}(i,j)$ needed in equation (1). By using $coref(i,j)$ we define $\text{score}_{ana}(i,j)$ as follows:

$$\text{score}_{ana}(i,j) = -\log(1 - \max_i \text{coref}(i,j)) \quad (3)$$

The feature set and detailed configuration for model creation generally follows the original work by Iida and Poesio (2011). For creating a classifier, we used MegaM [1], an implementation of the Maximum Entropy model, with default parameter settings. As an anaphoricity determination model (Iida et al., 2005), we used the selection-then-classification model, which first selects a most likely candidate antecedent i and then determines the anaphoricity of candidate anaphor j referring to the information from a pair of i and j, because Iida et al. (2005) reported their model determines anaphoricity more precisely than a simple anaphoricity model (e.g. Ng and Cardie (2002)).

[1] http://cs.utah.edu/~hal/megam/

type	#article	#sentence	#word	coreference
train	1,753	24,263	651,986	10,206
test	696	9,287	250,901	4,396

Table 2: Statistics of annotated information in NAIST text corpus

5 Empirical Evaluation

This section first evaluates performance of NP coreference resolution on coherent and incoherent texts for exploring the possible use of these results on evaluating discourse coherence; we then conduct an empirical evaluation on ranking a pair of coherent and incoherent texts by comparing our metric with the entity grid model.

5.1 Data set

For our evaluation, we used the NAIST text corpus, which consists of Japanese newspaper articles containing manually annotated NP coreference relations. Because the corpus has no explicit boundary between training and test sets, articles published from January 1st to January 11th and the editorials from January to August were used for training and articles dated January 14th to 17th and editorials dated October to December are used for testing as done by Taira et al. (2008) and Imamura et al. (2009). Table 2 summarises the statistics of annotated coreference relations in the corpus.

Because the data set contains some texts consisting of only a sentence[2], we excluded them for our evaluation of information ordering. In line with the experiments done by Barzilay and Lapata (2008), we created 20 different texts by randomly scrambling the order of the sentences in an original text, each of which is henceforth called an *incoherent text*, while the original text is called a *coherent text*. In this evaluation, we followed Barzilay and Lapata (2008)'s experimental setting, that is, the task of pairwise ordering, i.e., to detect a coherent text given a coherent and incoherent text pair.

5.2 Experiment 1: NP coreference resolution on incoherent texts

We first evaluate performance of NP coreference resolution on both coherent and incoherent texts. During the training phase, we use only coherent texts as the training instances for creating a classifier used in each model. By using only coherent texts for training, we expect that a model appropriately identifies coreference (or anaphoric) relations in coherent texts, while it is less successful in incoherent texts. Next, classifiers induced from coherent texts are applied to either coherent or incoherent texts to investigate the difference of performance on coreference resolution.

Table 3 shows the results for the recall, precision and F-score of pairwise classification on NP coreference resolution on evaluating coherent or incoherent texts, where the 'coherent' which stands for the results on coherent texts, the 'incoherent:μ' and 'incoherent:σ' which mean the averaged score of the results on incoherent texts and its standard deviation. Table 3 demonstrates that the 'coherent' obtains better performance in F-score than 'incoherent:μ' on NP coreference resolution. It indicates that the performance of NP coreference resolution strongly correlates to discourse coherence, that is, this relative difference of performance between co-

[2]In the NAIST text corpus, 213 articles in the training set and 156 articles in the test set consist of a sentence.

	Recall	Precision	F-score
coherent	0.624	0.508	**0.560**
incoherent	0.538± 0.004	0.496 ± 0.004	0.516 ± 0.004

Table 3: Results using NP coreference resolution

herent and incoherent texts is expected to lead to better discrimination on information ordering which we discuss in Section 5.3.

5.3 Experiment 2: pairwise information ordering

We next investigate the effects of the metric proposed in Section 3 for the task of pairwise information ordering comparing the results with the entity grid model.

As a baseline model, we use a model which randomly selects a text from two given texts. Alternative baselines are variants of the entity grid model; one captures the transition of discourse entities based on lexical chaining (i.e. NPs which have identical head strings are grouped as a cluster), and the other uses the outputs of a NP coreference resolution model for the entity grid representation instead of using lexical chaining. As for the coreference resolution model for obtaining the entity grid representation, we employed the original selection-then-classification model (SCM) described in Section 4 because it performed better in the final evaluation (i.e. pairwise ordering). This may be because the original SCM tends to accurately identify coreference relations in incoherent texts as well as coherent ones, and as a result those relations are considered as less noisy inputs to the entity grid model.

For the entity grid representation in Japanese, we employed the work by Yokono and Okumura (2010), which is based on Japanese case-makers (e.g. *wa* (topic), *ga* (subject), *o* (object)) to simply identify grammatical roles of discourse entities[3]. Note that we excluded the extensions of the base entity grid modeling (e.g. separating discourse entities into two classes based on the salience of each, introduced by Barzilay and Lapata (2008)) for simplification. To create a pairwise ranker based on the entity grid modelling, we used a ranking SVM (Joachims, 2002) as Barzilay and Lapata (2008) did. In this evaluation, we also compared the entity grid models using the coherence metric based on NP coreference as a feature.

The results are shown in Table 4. These results demonstrate the entity grid models and the models based on our coherence metric achieved better accuracy than the random baseline. By comparing the entity grid models with and without coreference resolution, the results show that the former outperforms the latter. It indicates Japanese NP coreference resolution is also useful for grid representation, the same as for English coreference resolution adopted in Barzilay and Lapata (2008).

Furthermore, ranking based on our metric achieved better accuracy than the entity grid models. This is because our metric has an advantage of being able to capture the coherence and incoherence resulting from the use of long-distance coreference relations, while the entity grid model focuses on the local coherence based on discourse entities appearing in the adjacent two or three sentences.

[3]In addition to the three labels (i.e. S, O and X) in the original work by Barzilay and Lapata (2008), we also use a T(opic) label to distinguish topical words from subjects done by Yokono and Okumura (2010) to capture the Japanese grammatical aspect.

	model	accuracy (%)
	random	50.0
	entity grid (−coref)	67.3
(a)	entity grid (+coref)	70.7
(b)	proposed metric	76.1
(c)	(a) + (b)	**78.2**

Table 4: Results of pairwise information ordering

Our metric utilises the appropriateness of anaphoric functions, one of characteristics of coherence which was not directly integrated in the entity grid model. Therefore, by combining them we can expect to see an improvement in accuracy. The last row in Table 4 shows the result of the entity grid model using coreference resolution integrated with our metric as a feature. As expected, the result ((c) in Table 4) obtained the best accuracy out of all the results shown in Table 4 [4]. It indicates that long-distant coreference relations are also important for evaluating discourse coherence in a text.

6 Conclusion

In this paper we proposed a metric for evaluating discourse coherence based on the outputs of a coreference resolution model to reflect the idea that a writer tends to appropriately utilise anaphoric or coreference relations when writing a coherent text. In order to investigate the effects of the proposed metric, we conducted an empirical evaluation on a pairwise ordering task, taking the NAIST text corpus as a target data set. The results of our evaluation demonstrated that the metric calculated using the outputs of NP coreference resolution achieved better accuracy than the entity grid model (Barzilay and Lapata, 2008). Moreover, the result of integrating the metric with the entity grid model shows the improvement of 7 points in accuracy.

In this work, we focused on the use of NP coreference resolution as cues for evaluating discourse coherence in a text. However, even if we refer to coreference relations as indicators of discourse coherence, the relations are sometime sparse in a text, resulting in assigning an inappropriate score to it. One simple way to avoid this problem is to take into account other types of reference behaviour, such as zero anaphora and bridging anaphora, because this type of reference function can often relate distant discourse fragments (e.g. two clauses placed far from each other). In addition, although we focused on exploiting the relationship of discourse entities in terms of anaphoric functions, the (latent) topic transition in a text is another key for capturing text coherence, as discussed by Chen et al. (2009). Therefore, one interesting issue for discourse coherence is how to integrate the above factors into existing coherence models.

References

Barzilay, R. and Lapata, M. (2005). Modeling local coherence: An entity-based approach. In *Proceedings of the 43rd Annual Meeting of the Association for Computational Linguistics (ACL 2005)*, pages 141–148.

Barzilay, R. and Lapata, M. (2008). Modeling local coherence: An entity-based approach. *Computational Linguistics*, 34(1):1–34.

[4] Note that the difference of (b) and (c) is statistically significant (McNemar's test, $p < 0.05$)

Barzilay, R. and Lee, L. (2004). Catching the drift: Probabilistic content models, with applications to generation and summarization. In *Proceedings of the Human Language Technology Conference of the North American Chapter of the Association for Computational Linguistics (HLT-NAACL 2004)*, pages 113–120.

Bollegala, D., Okazaki, N., and Ishizuka, M. (2006). A bottom-up approach to sentence ordering for multi-document summarization. In *Proceedings of the 21st International Conference on Computational Linguistics and 44th Annual Meeting of the Association for Computational Linguistics (COLING-ACL 2006)*, pages 385–392.

Cai, J. and Strube, M. (2010). End-to-end coreference resolution via hypergraph partitioning. In *Proceedings of the 23rd International Conference on Computational Linguistics (COLING 2010)*, pages 143–151.

Cardie, C. and Wagstaf, K. (1999). Noun phrase coreference as clustering. In *Proceedings of 1999 Joint SIGDAT Conference on Empirical Methods in Natural Language Processing and Very Large Corpora*, pages 82–89.

Chen, H., Branavan, S. R. K., Barzilay, R., and Karger, D. R. (2009). Global models of document structure using latent permutations. In *Proceedings of Human Language Technologies: The 2009 Annual Conference of the North American Chapter of the Association for Computational Linguistics (HLT-NAACL 2009)*, pages 371–379.

Denis, P. and Baldridge, J. (2007). Joint determination of anaphoricity and coreference resolution using integer programming. In *Proceedings of Human Language Technologies 2007: The Conference of the North American Chapter of the Association for Computational Linguistics (HLT-NAACL 2007)*, pages 236–243.

Grosz, B. J., Joshi, A. K., and Weinstein, S. (1995). Centering: A framework for modeling the local coherence of discourse. *Computational Linguistics*, 21(2):203–226.

Higgins, D., Burstein, J., Marcu, D., and Gentile, C. (2004). Evaluating multiple aspects of coherence in student essays. In *Proceedings of the Human Language Technology Conference of the North American Chapter of the Association for Computational Linguistics (HLT-NAACL 2004)*, pages 185–192.

Iida, R., Inui, K., and Matsumoto, Y. (2005). Anaphora resolution by antecedent identification followed by anaphoricity determination. *ACM Transactions on Asian Language Information Processing (TALIP)*, 4(4):417–434.

Iida, R. and Poesio, M. (2011). A cross-lingual ilp solution to zero anaphora resolution. In *Proceedings of the 49th Annual Meeting of the Association for Computational Linguistics: Human Language Technologies (ACL-HLT 2011)*, pages 804–813.

Imamura, K., Saito, K., and Izumi, T. (2009). Discriminative approach to predicate-argument structure analysis with zero-anaphora resolution. In *Proceedings of the Joint Conference of the 47th Annual Meeting of the ACL and the 4th International Joint Conference on Natural Language Processing of the AFNLP (ACL-IJCNLP 2009)*, pages 85–88.

Joachims, T. (2002). Optimizing search engines using clickthrough data. In *Proceedings of the ACM Conference on Knowledge Discovery and Data Mining (KDD 2002)*, pages 133–142.

Karamanis, N., Poesio, M., Mellish, C., and Oberlander, J. (2004). Evaluating centering-based metrics of coherence using a reliably annotated corpus. In *Proceedings of the 42nd Annual Meeting of the Association for Computational Linguistics (ACL 2004)*, pages 391–398.

Lapata, M. (2003). Probabilistic text structuring: Experiments with sentence ordering. In *Proceedings of the 41st Annual Meeting of the Association for Computational Linguistics (ACL 2003)*, pages 545–552.

Lapata, M. and Barzilay, R. (2005). Automatic evaluation of text coherence: Models and representations. In *Proceedings of 2005 International Joint Conferences on Artificial Intelligence (IJCAI 2005)*, pages 1085–1090.

Lin, Z., Ng, H. T., and Kan, M.-Y. (2011). Automatically evaluating text coherence using discourse relations. In *Proceeding of the 49th Annual Meeting of the Association for Computational Linguistics: Human Language TEchnologies (ACL-HLT 2011)*, pages 997–1006.

Mann, W. C. and Thompson, S. A. (1988). Rhetorical structure theory: Toward a functional theory of text organization. *Text*, 8(3):243–281.

Miltsakaki, E. and Kukich, K. (2000). Automated evaluation of coherence in student essays. In *Proceedings of the 2nd International Conference on Language Resources and Evaluation (LREC 2000)*.

Ng, V. and Cardie, C. (2002). Improving machine learning approaches to coreference resolution. In *Proceedings of the 40th Annual Meeting of the Association for Computational Linguistics (ACL 2002)*, pages 104–111.

Ng, V. and Cardie, C. (2002). Identifying anaphoric and non-anaphoric noun phrases to improve coreference resolution. In *Proceedings of the 19th International Conference on Computational Linguistics (COLING 2002)*, pages 730–736.

Okazaki, N., Matsuo, Y., and Ishizuka, M. (2004). Improving chronological sentence ordering by precedence relation. In *Proceedings of the 20th International Conference on Computational Linguistics (COLING 2004)*, pages 750–756.

Poesio, M., Stevenson, R., Eugenio, B. D., and Hitzeman, J. (2004). Centering: A parametric theory and its instantiations. *Computational Linguistics*, 30(3):309–363.

Soon, W. M., Ng, H. T., and Lim, D. C. Y. (2001). A machine learning approach to coreference resolution of noun phrases. *Computational Linguistics*, 27(4):521–544.

Soricut, R. and Marcu, D. (2006). Discourse generation using utility-trained coherence models. In *Proceedings of the 21st International Conference on Computational Linguistics and 44th Annual Meeting of the Association for Computational Linguistics (COLING-ACL 2006)*, pages 803–810.

Taira, H., Fujita, S., and Nagata, M. (2008). A Japanese predicate argument structure analysis using decision lists. In *Proceedings of the 2008 Conference on Empirical Methods in Natural Language Processing (EMNLP 2008)*, pages 523–532.

Walker, M., Joshi, A. K., and (eds.), E. P. (1997). *Centering Theory in Discourse*. Oxford Univ. Press.

Yokono, H. and Okumura, M. (2010). Incorporating cohesive devices into entity grid model in evaluating local coherence of Japanese text. In *Proceedings of the 11th International Conference on Intelligent Text Processing and Computational Linguistics (CICLing 2010)*, pages 303–314.

Comparing Word Relatedness Measures Based on Google n-grams

Aminul ISLAM *Evangelos MILIOS* *Vlado KEŠELJ*
Faculty of Computer Science
Dalhousie University, Halifax, Canada
islam@cs.dal.ca, eem@cs.dal.ca, vlado@cs.dal.ca

Abstract

Estimating word relatedness is essential in natural language processing (NLP), and in many other related areas. Corpus-based word relatedness has its advantages over knowledge-based supervised measures. There are many corpus-based measures in the literature that can not be compared to each other as they use a different corpus. The purpose of this paper is to show how to evaluate different corpus-based measures of word relatedness by calculating them over a common corpus (i.e., the Google n-grams) and then assessing their performance with respect to gold standard relatedness datasets. We evaluate six of these measures as a starting point, all of which are re-implemented using the Google n-gram corpus as their only resource, by comparing their performance in five different data sets. We also show how a word relatedness measure based on a web search engine can be implemented using the Google n-gram corpus.

Keywords: Word Relatedness, Similarity, Corpus, Unsupervised, Google n-grams, Trigrams.

Proceedings of COLING 2012: Posters, pages 495–506,
COLING 2012, Mumbai, December 2012.

1 Introduction

Word relatedness between two words refers to the degree of how much one word has to do with another word whereas word similarity is a special case or a subset of word relatedness. A word relatedness method has many applications in NLP, and related areas such as information retrieval (Xu and Croft, 2000), image retrieval (Coelho et al., 2004), paraphrase recognition (Islam and Inkpen, 2008), malapropism detection and correction (Budanitsky and Hirst, 2006), word sense disambiguation (Schutze, 1998), automatic creation of thesauri (Lin, 1998a; Li, 2002), predicting user click behavior (Kaur and Hornof, 2005), building language models and natural spoken dialogue systems (Fosler-Lussier and Kuo, 2001), automatic indexing, text annotation and summarization (Lin and Hovy, 2003). Most of the approaches of determining text similarity use word similarity (Islam and Inkpen, 2008; Li et al., 2006). There are other areas where word similarity plays an important role. Gauch et al. (1999) and Gauch and Wang (1997) applied word similarity in query expansion to provide *conceptual retrieval* which ultimately increases the relevance of retrieved documents. Many approaches to spoken language understanding and spoken language systems require a grammar for parsing the input utterance to acquire its semantics. Meng and Siu (2002) used word similarity for semi-automatic grammar induction from unannotated corpora where the grammar contains both semantic and syntactic structures. An example in other areas is database schema matching (Islam et al., 2008).

Existing work on determining word relatedness is broadly categorized into three major groups: corpus-based (e.g., Cilibrasi and Vitanyi, 2007; Islam and Inkpen, 2006; Lin et al., 2003; Weeds et al., 2004; Landauer et al., 1998), knowledge-based (e.g., Radinsky et al., 2011; Gabrilovich and Markovitch, 2007; Jarmasz and Szpakowicz, 2003; Hirst and St-Onge, 1998; Resnik, 1995), and hybrid methods (e.g., Li et al., 2003; Lin, 1998b; Jiang and Conrath, 1997). Corpus-based could be either supervised (e.g., Bollegala et al., 2011) or unsupervised (e.g., Iosif and Potamianos, 2010; Islam and Inkpen, 2006). In this paper, we will focus only on unsupervised corpus-based measures.

Many unsupervised corpus-based measures of word relatedness, implemented on different corpora as resources (e.g., Islam and Inkpen, 2006; Lin et al., 2003; Weeds et al., 2004; Landauer et al., 1998; Landauer and Dumais, 1997), can be found in literature. These measures generally use co-occurrence statistics (mostly word n-grams and their frequencies) of target words generated from a corpus to form probability estimates. As the co-occurrence statistics are corpus-specific, most of the existing corpus-based measures of word relatedness implemented on different corpora are not fairly comparable to each other even on the same task. In practice, most corpora do not have readily available co-occurrence statistics usable by these measures. Again, it is very expensive to precompute co-occurrence statistics for all possible word tuples using the corpus as the word relatedness measures do not know the target words in advance. Thus, one of the main drawbacks of many corpus-based measures is that they are not feasible to be used on-line. There are other corpus-based measures that use web page count of target words from search engine as co-occurrence statistics (e.g., Iosif and Potamianos, 2010; Cilibrasi and Vitanyi, 2007; Turney, 2001). The performance of these measures are not static as the contents and the number of web pages are constantly changing. As a result, it is hard to fairly compare any new measure to these measures.

Thus, the research question arises: How can we compare a new word relatedness measure that is based on co-occurrence statistics of a corpus or a web search engine with the existing measures? We find that the use of a common corpus with co-occurrence statistics—e.g., the Google n-grams (Brants and Franz, 2006)—as the resource could be a good answer to this question. We experimentally evaluated six unsupervised corpus-based measures of word relatedness using the Google n-gram corpus on different tasks. The Google n-gram dataset[1] is a publicly available corpus with co-occurrence statistics of a large volume of web text. This will allow any new corpus based word relatedness measure to use the common corpus and compare with different existing measures on the same tasks. This will also facilitate a measure based on the Google n-gram corpus to be used on-line. Another motivation is to find an indirect mapping of co-occurrence statistics between the Google n-gram corpus and a web search engine. This is also to show that the Google n-gram corpus could be a good resource to many of the existing and future word relatedness measures. One of the previous works of this nature is (Budanitsky and Hirst, 2006), where they evaluate five knowledge-based measures of word relatedness using WordNet as their central resource.

The reasons of using corpus-based measures are threefold. First, to create, maintain and update lexical databases or resources—such as WordNet (Fellbaum, 1998) or Roget's Thesaurus (Roget, 1852)—requires significant expertise and efforts (Radinsky et al., 2011). Second, coverage of words in lexical resources is not quite enough for many NLP tasks. Third, such lexical resources are language specific, whereas Google n-gram corpora are available in English and in 10 European Languages (Brants and Franz, 2009).

The rest of this paper is organized as follows: Six corpus-based measures of word relatedness are briefly described in Section 2. Evaluation methods are discussed in Section 3. Section 4 and 5 present the experimental results from two evaluation approaches to compare several measures. We address some contributions and future related work in Conclusion.

2 Unsupervised corpus-based Approaches

Corpus-based approaches to measuring word relatedness generally use co-occurrence statistics (mostly word n-grams) of a target word from a corpus in which it occurs and then these co-occurrence statistics may be used to form probability estimates. Different corpus-based measures use different corpora to collect these co-occurrence statistics. The notation used in all the measures of word relatedness described in this section are shown in Table 1. Corpus-

Notation	Description
$C(w_1 \cdots w_n)$	frequency of the n-gram, $w_1 \cdots w_n$, where $n \in \{1, \cdots, 5\}$
$D(w_1 \cdots w_n)$	number of web documents having n-gram, $w_1 \cdots w_n$, where $n \in \{1, \cdots, 5\}$
$M(w_1, w_2)$	number of tri-grams that start with w_1 and end with w_2
$\mu_T(w_1, w_2)$	$\frac{1}{2}(\sum_{i=3}^{M(w_1,w_2)+2} C(w_1 w_i w_2) + \sum_{i=3}^{M(w_2,w_1)+2} C(w_2 w_i w_1))$, which represents the mean frequency of $M(w_1, w_2)$ tri-grams that start with w_1 and end with w_2, and $M(w_2, w_1)$ tri-grams that start with w_2 and end with w_1
N	total number of web documents used in Google n-grams
$\|V\|$	total number of uni-grams in Google n-grams
$C_{\max}$	maximum frequency possible among all Google uni-grams, i.e., $C_{\max} = \max(\{C(w_i)\}_{i=1}^{\|V\|})$

Table 1: Notation used for all the measures

[1]Details can be found at www.ldc.upenn.edu/Catalog/docs/LDC2006T13/readme.txt

based measures of word relatedness that use co-occurrence statistics directly collected from the web using a search engine (e.g., Iosif and Potamianos, 2010; Cilibrasi and Vitanyi, 2007; Turney, 2001) can not directly be implemented using the Google n-gram corpus. This is because these measures use some co-occurrence statistics which are not available in the Google n-gram corpus. Though there is no direct mapping between the Google n-gram corpus and a web search engine, it is possible to get an indirect mapping using some assumptions. It is obvious that based on the notation of Table 1, $C(w_1) \geq D(w_1)$ and $C(w_1w_2) \geq D(w_1w_2)$. This is because a uni-gram or a bi-gram may occur multiple times in a single document. Thus, considering the lower limits of $C(w_1)$ and $C(w_1w_2)$, two assumptions could be: (1) $C(w_1) \approx D(w_1)$ and (2) $C(w_1w_2) \approx D(w_1w_2)$. Based on these assumptions, we will use $C(w_1)$ and $C(w_1w_2)$ instead of using $D(w_1)$ and $D(w_1w_2)$, respectively to implement measures using the Google n-gram corpus.

2.1 Jaccard Coefficient

Jaccard coefficient (Salton and McGill, 1983) is defined as:

$$\text{Jaccard}(w_1, w_2) = \frac{D(w_1w_2)}{D(w_1) + D(w_2) - D(w_1w_2)} \approx \frac{C(w_1w_2)}{C(w_1) + C(w_2) - C(w_1w_2)} \tag{1}$$

In probability terms, Equation (1) represents the maximum likelihood estimate of the ratio of the probability of finding a web document where words w_1 and w_2 co-occur over the probability of finding a web document where either w_1 or w_2 occurs[2].

2.2 Simpson Coefficient

The Simpson coefficient is useful in minimizing the effect of unequal size of the number of web documents where the occurrence of w_1 and w_2 are mutually exclusive. Simpson or overlap coefficient (Bollegala et al., 2011) is defined as:

$$\text{Simpson}(w_1, w_2) = \frac{D(w_1w_2)}{\min(D(w_1), D(w_2))} \approx \frac{C(w_1w_2)}{\min(C(w_1), C(w_2))} \tag{2}$$

which represents the maximum likelihood estimate of the ratio of the probability of finding a web document where words w_1 and w_2 co-occur over the probability of finding a web document where the word with the lower frequency occurs.

2.3 Dice Coefficient

Dice coefficient (Smadja et al., 1996; Lin, 1998b,a) is defined as:

$$\text{Dice}(w_1, w_2) = \frac{2D(w_1w_2)}{D(w_1) + D(w_2)} \approx \frac{2C(w_1w_2)}{C(w_1) + C(w_2)} \tag{3}$$

which represents the maximum likelihood estimate of the ratio of twice the probability of finding a web document where words w_1 and w_2 co-occur over the probability of finding a web document where either w_1 or w_2 or both occurs.

[2]Normalization by the total number of web documents, N, is the same for the nominator and denominator, and can be ignored.

2.4 Pointwise Mutual Information

Pointwise Mutual Information (PMI) is a measure of how much one word tells us about the other. PMI is defined as:

$$\mathrm{PMI}(w_1, w_2) = \log_2\left(\frac{\frac{D(w_1w_2)}{N}}{\frac{D(w_1)}{N}\frac{D(w_2)}{N}}\right) \approx \log_2\left(\frac{\frac{C(w_1w_2)}{N}}{\frac{C(w_1)}{N}\frac{C(w_2)}{N}}\right) \tag{4}$$

where N is the total number of web documents. PMI between two words w_1 and w_2 compares the probability of observing the two words together (i.e., their joint probability) to the probabilities of observing w_1 and w_2 independently. PMI was first used to measure word similarity by Church and Hanks (1990). Turney (2001) used PMI, based on statistical data acquired by querying a Web search engine to measure the similarity of pairs of words.

2.5 Normalized Google Distance (NGD)

Cilibrasi and Vitanyi (2007) proposed a page-count-based distance metric between words, called the Normalized Google Distance (NGD). Normalized Google Distance relatedness between w_1 and w_2, $\mathrm{NGD}(w_1, w_2)$ is defined as:

$$\mathrm{NGD}(w_1, w_2) = \frac{\max(\log D(w_1), \log D(w_2)) - \log D(w_1w_2)}{\log N - \min(\log D(w_1), \log D(w_2))} \tag{5}$$

$$\approx \frac{\max(\log C(w_1), \log C(w_2)) - \log C(w_1w_2)}{\log N - \min(\log C(w_1), \log C(w_2))} \tag{6}$$

NGD is based on normalized information distance (Li et al., 2004), which is motivated by Kolmogorov complexity. The values of Equation (5) and (6) are unbounded, ranging from 0 to ∞. Gracia et al. (2006) proposed a variation of Normalized Google Distance in order to bound the similarity value in between 0 and 1, which is:

$$\mathrm{NGD}'(w_1, w_2) = e^{-2\times\mathrm{NGD}(w_1,w_2)} \tag{7}$$

2.6 Relatedness based on Tri-grams (RT)

Islam et al. (2012) used Google n-grams, the Google tri-grams in particular, for determining the similarity of a pair of words. Their tri-gram word relatedness model can be generalized to n-gram word relatedness model. The main idea of the tri-gram relatedness model is to take into account all the tri-grams that start and end with the given pair of words and then normalize their mean frequency using uni-gram frequency of each of the words as well as the most frequent uni-gram in the corpus used. Word relatedness between w_1 and w_2 based on Tri-grams, $\mathrm{RT}(w_1, w_2) \in [0, 1]$ is defined as:

$$\mathrm{RT}(w_1, w_2) = \begin{cases} \dfrac{\log \frac{\mu_T(w_1,w_2)C_{\max}^2}{C(w_1)C(w_2)\min(C(w_1),C(w_2))}}{-2\times\log\frac{\min(C(w_1),C(w_2))}{C_{\max}}} & \text{if } \frac{\mu_T(w_1,w_2)C_{\max}^2}{C(w_1)C(w_2)\min(C(w_1),C(w_2))} > 1 \\ \dfrac{\log 1.01}{-2\times\log\frac{\min(C(w_1),C(w_2))}{C_{\max}}} & \text{if } \frac{\mu_T(w_1,w_2)C_{\max}^2}{C(w_1)C(w_2)\min(C(w_1),C(w_2))} \leq 1 \\ 0 & \text{if } \mu_T(w_1, w_2) = 0 \end{cases} \tag{8}$$

3 Evaluation Methods

One of the commonly accepted approaches to evaluate word relatedness measures is a comparison with human judgments. Considering human judgments of similarity or relatedness as the upper limit, this approach gives the best assessment of the 'closeness' and 'goodness' of a measure with respect to human judgments. Another approach is to evaluate the measures with respect to a particular application. If a system uses a measure of word relatedness (often in back end) in one of the phases, it is possible to evaluate different measure of word relatedness by finding which one the system is most effective with, while keeping all other phases of the system constant. In the remainder of this paper, we will use these two approaches to compare measures mentioned in sections 2.1 to 2.6.

4 Comparison with Human Ratings of Semantic Relatedness

4.1 Rubenstein and Goodenough's 65 Word Pairs

Rubenstein and Goodenough (1965) conducted quantitative experiments with a group of 51 human judges who were asked to rate 65 pairs of word (English) on the scale of 0.0 to 4.0, according to their similarity of meaning. A word relatedness measure is evaluated using the correlation between the relatedness scores it produces for the word pairs in the benchmark dataset and the human ratings. The correlation coefficients of the six implemented measures with the human judges for the 65 word pairs from Rubenstein and Goodenough (1965) dataset (henceforth, R&G dataset) are shown in Figure 1.

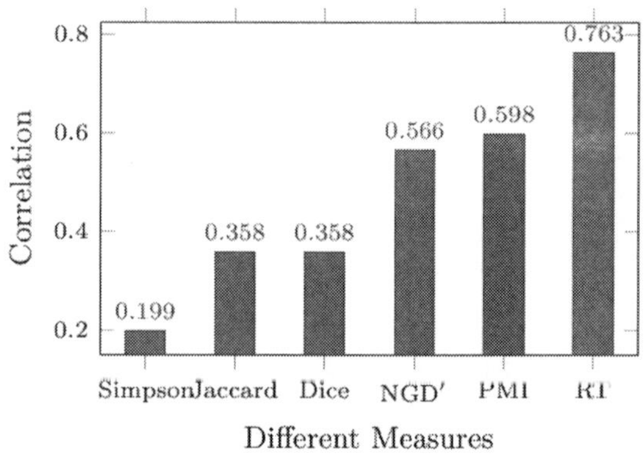

Figure 1: Similarity correlations on RG's 65 noun pairs.

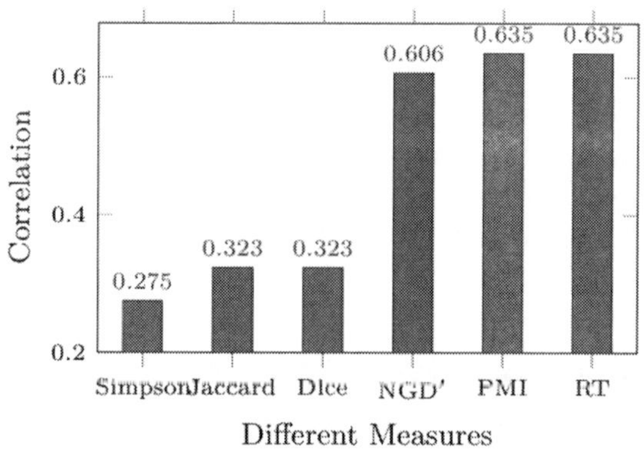

Figure 2: Similarity correlations on MC's 28 noun pairs.

4.2 Miller and Charles' 28 Noun Pairs

Miller and Charles (1991) repeated the same experiment (done by Rubenstein and Goodenough, 1965) restricting themselves to 30 pairs from the original 65, and then obtained similarity judgments from 38 human judges. Most researchers used 28 word pairs of the Miller and Charles (1991) dataset (henceforth, M&C dataset), because two word pairs were omitted from the earlier version of WordNet. The correlation coefficient of different measures with the human judges for 28 word pairs from M&C dataset are shown in Figure 2. It is shown in Figure 2 that the correlation coefficients for both PMI and RT on M&C dataset are same, whereas Figure 1 shows RT's improvement of 16.5 percentage points over PMI on R&G dataset.

5 Application-based Evaluation of Measures of Relatedness

5.1 TOEFL's 80 Synonym Questions

Consider the following synonym test question which is one of the 80 TOEFL (Test of English as a Foreign Language) questions from Landauer and Dumais (1997): Given the problem word *infinite* and the four alternative words *limitless*, *relative*, *unusual*, *structural*, the task is to choose the alternative word which is most similar in meaning to the problem word. The number of correct answers for different word relatedness measures on 80 TOEFL questions is shown in Figure 3. RT measure gets 65 per cent correct answers. A human average score on the same question set is 64.5 per cent (Landauer and Dumais, 1997).

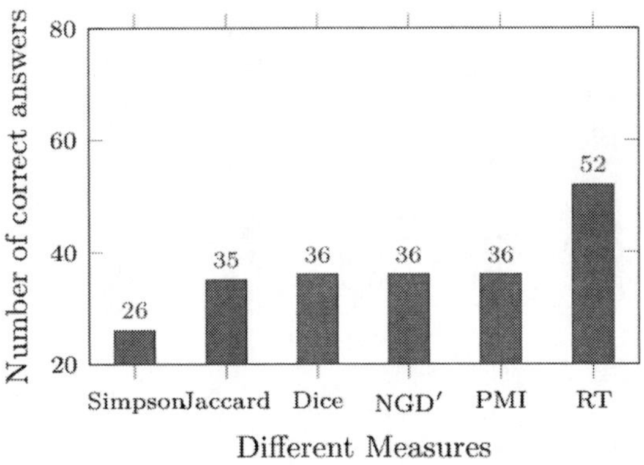

Figure 3: Results on TOEFL's 80 synonym questions.

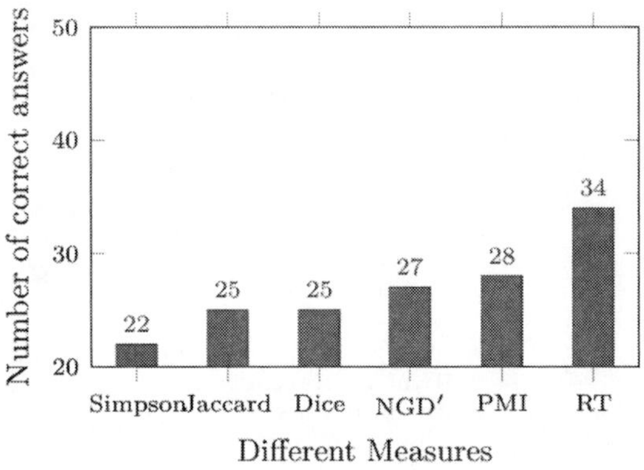

Figure 4: Results on ESL's 50 synonym questions.

5.2 ESL's 50 Synonym Questions

The task here is the same as TOEFL's 80 synonym questions task, except that the synonym questions are from the English as a Second Language (ESL) tests. The number of correct answers for different measures on 50 ESL synonym questions is shown in Figure 4.

5.3 Text Similarity

The task of text similarity is to find the similarity between two text items. The idea is to use all the discussed word relatedness measures separately on a single text similarity measure and then evaluate the results of the text similarity measure based on a standard data set used for the task to see which word relatedness measure works better. There are many text similarity measures, both supervised and unsupervised, in the literature that use word similarity in the back end (e.g., Li et al., 2006; Liu et al., 2007; Feng et al., 2008; O'Shea et al., 2008; Islam and Inkpen, 2008; Ho et al., 2010; Tsatsaronis et al., 2010; Islam et al., 2012). We use one of the state-of-the-art unsupervised text similarity measures proposed by Islam et al. (2012) to evaluate all the discussed word relatedness measures. One of the reasons of using this text similarity measure is that it only uses the relatedness scores of different word pairs in the back end. The main idea of the text similarity measure proposed by Islam et al. (2012) is to find for each word in the shorter text, some most similar matchings at the word level, in the longer text, and then aggregate their similarity scores and normalize the result.

In order to evaluate the text similarity measure, we compute the similarity score for 30 sentence pairs from Li et al. (2006) and find the correlation with human judges. The details of this data set preparation are in (Li et al., 2006). This is one of the most used data sets for evaluating the task. For example, Li et al. (2006); Liu et al. (2007); Feng et al. (2008); O'Shea et al. (2008); Islam and Inkpen (2008); Ho et al. (2010); Tsatsaronis et al. (2010); Islam et al. (2012) used the same 30 sentence pairs and computed the correlation with human judges. The correlation coefficients of Islam et al. (2012) text similarity measures (based on the discussed word relatedness measures) with the human judges for 30 sentence pairs are shown in Figure 5. On the 30 sentence pairs, Ho et al. (2010) used one of the

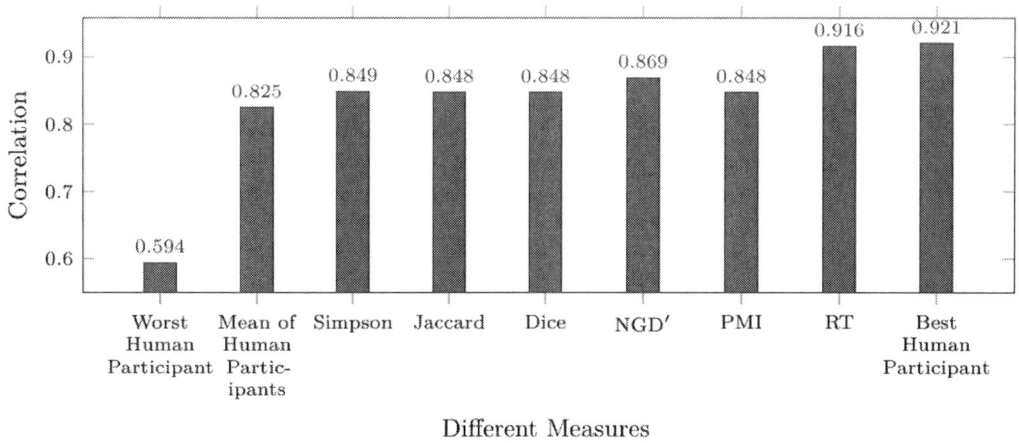

Figure 5: Similarity correlations on Li's 30 sentence pairs.

state-of-the-art word relatedness measures using WordNet to determine the relatedness scores of word pairs, then applied those scores in Islam and Inkpen (2008) text similarity measure, and achieved a Pearson correlation coefficient of 0.895 with the mean human similarity ratings. On the same dataset, Tsatsaronis et al. (2010) achieved a Pearson correlation coefficient of 0.856 with the mean human similarity ratings. Islam et al. (2012) text similarity measure using RT achieves a high Pearson correlation coefficient of 0.916 with the mean human similarity ratings which is close to that of the best human participant. The improvement achieved over Ho et al. (2010) is statistically significant at 0.05 level.

Conclusion

This paper shows that any new corpus-based measure of word relatedness that uses n-gram statistics can easily be implemented on the Google n-gram corpus and be *fairly* evaluated with existing works on standard data sets of different tasks. We also show how to find an indirect mapping of co-occurrence statistics between the Google n-gram corpus and a web search engine using some assumptions. One of the advantages of measures based on n-gram statistics is that they are language independent. Although English is the focus of this paper, none of the word relatedness measures discussed in this paper depends on any specific language, and could be used with almost no change with many other languages that have a sufficiently large n-gram corpus available. Future work could be to evaluate other corpus-based measures using the common Google n-gram corpus and the standard data sets for different tasks.

References

Bollegala, D., Matsuo, Y., and Ishizuka, M. (2011). A web search engine-based approach to measure semantic similarity between words. *IEEE Trans. on Knowl. and Data Eng.*, 23(7):977–990.

Brants, T. and Franz, A. (2006). Web 1T 5-gram corpus version 1.1. Technical report, Google Research.

Brants, T. and Franz, A. (2009). Web 1T 5-gram, 10 European languages version 1. Technical report, Linguistic Data Consortium, Philadelphia.

Budanitsky, A. and Hirst, G. (2006). Evaluating WordNet-based measures of lexical semantic relatedness. *Computational Linguistics*, 32(1):13–47.

Church, K. and Hanks, P. (1990). Word association norms, mutual information, and lexicography. *Computational Linguistics*, 16(1):22–29.

Cilibrasi, R. L. and Vitanyi, P. M. B. (2007). The google similarity distance. *IEEE Trans. on Knowl. and Data Eng.*, 19(3):370–383.

Coelho, T., Calado, P., Souza, L., Ribeiro-Neto, B., and Muntz, R. (2004). Image retrieval using multiple evidence ranking. *IEEE Transaction on Knowledge and Data Engineering*, 16(4):408–417.

Fellbaum, C., editor (1998). *WordNet: An electronic lexical database.* MIT Press.

Feng, J., Zhou, Y.-M., and Martin, T. (2008). Sentence similarity based on relevance. In Magdalena, L., Ojeda-Aciego, M., and Verdegay, J., editors, *IPMU*, pages 832–839.

Fosler-Lussier, E. and Kuo, H.-K. (2001). Using semantic class information for rapid development of language models within ASR dialogue systems. *Acoustics, Speech, and Signal Processing, IEEE International Conference on*, 1:553–556.

Gabrilovich, E. and Markovitch, S. (2007). Computing semantic relatedness using wikipedia-based explicit semantic analysis. In *Proceedings of the 20th international joint conference on Artifical intelligence*, IJCAI'07, pages 1606–1611, San Francisco, CA, USA. Morgan Kaufmann Publishers Inc.

Gauch, S. and Wang, J. (1997). A corpus analysis approach for automatic query expansion. In *Proceedings of the sixth international conference on Information and knowledge management*, CIKM '97, pages 278–284, New York, NY, USA. ACM.

Gauch, S., Wang, J., and Rachakonda, S. M. (1999). A corpus analysis approach for automatic query expansion and its extension to multiple databases. *ACM Trans. Inf. Syst.*, 17(3):250–269.

Gracia, J., Trillo, R., Espinoza, M., and Mena, E. (2006). Querying the web: a multiontology disambiguation method. In *Proceedings of the 6th International Conference on Web Engineering*, ICWE '06, pages 241–248, New York, NY, USA. ACM.

Hirst, G. and St-Onge, D. (1998). *WordNet: An electronic lexical database*, chapter Lexical chains as representations of context for the detection and correction of malapropisms, pages 305–332. The MIT Press, Cambridge, MA.

Ho, C., Murad, M. A. A., Kadir, R. A., and Doraisamy, S. C. (2010). Word sense disambiguation-based sentence similarity. In *Proceedings of the 23rd International Conference on Computational Linguistics: Posters*, COLING '10, pages 418–426, Stroudsburg, PA, USA. Association for Computational Linguistics.

Iosif, E. and Potamianos, A. (2010). Unsupervised semantic similarity computation between terms using web documents. *IEEE Trans. on Knowl. and Data Eng.*, 22(11):1637–1647.

Islam, A. and Inkpen, D. (2006). Second order co-occurrence PMI for determining the semantic similarity of words. In *Proceedings of the International Conference on Language Resources and Evaluation*, pages 1033–1038, Genoa, Italy.

Islam, A. and Inkpen, D. (2008). Semantic text similarity using corpus-based word similarity and string similarity. *ACM Trans. Knowl. Discov. Data*, 2:10:1–10:25.

Islam, A., Inkpen, D., and Kiringa, I. (2008). Applications of corpus-based semantic similarity and word segmentation to database schema matching. *The VLDB Journal*, 17(5):1293–1320.

Islam, A., Milios, E. E., and Keselj, V. (2012). Text similarity using google tri-grams. In Kosseim, L. and Inkpen, D., editors, *Canadian Conference on AI*, volume 7310 of *Lecture Notes in Computer Science*, pages 312–317. Springer.

Jarmasz, M. and Szpakowicz, S. (2003). Roget's thesaurus and semantic similarity. In Nicolov, N., Bontcheva, K., Angelova, G., and Mitkov, R., editors, *RANLP*, volume 260 of *Current Issues in Linguistic Theory (CILT)*, pages 111–120. John Benjamins, Amsterdam/Philadelphia.

Jiang, J. and Conrath, D. (1997). Semantic similarity based on corpus statistics and lexical taxonomy. In *Proc. of the Int'l. Conf. on Research in Computational Linguistics*, pages 19–33.

Kaur, I. and Hornof, A. J. (2005). A comparison of LSA, WordNet and PMI-IR for predicting user click behavior. In *Proceedings of the SIGCHI Conference on Human Factors in Computing Systems*, CHI '05, pages 51–60, New York, NY, USA. ACM.

Landauer, T. and Dumais, S. (1997). A solution to plato's problem: The latent semantic analysis theory of the acquisition, induction, and representation of knowledge. *Psychological Review*, 104(2):211–240.

Landauer, T., Foltz, P., and Laham, D. (1998). Introduction to latent semantic analysis. *Discourse Processes*, 25(2-3):259–284.

Li, H. (2002). Word clustering and disambiguation based on co-occurrence data. *Nat. Lang. Eng.*, 8(1):25–42.

Li, M., Chen, X., Li, X., Ma, B., and Vitanyi, P. M. B. (2004). The similarity metric. *IEEE Transactions on Information Theory*, 50(12):3250–3264.

Li, Y., Bandar, Z., and Mclean, D. (2003). An approach for measuring semantic similarity using multiple information sources. *IEEE Transactions on Knowledge and Data Engineering*, 15(4):871–882.

Li, Y., McLean, D., Bandar, Z. A., O'Shea, J. D., and Crockett, K. (2006). Sentence similarity based on semantic nets and corpus statistics. *IEEE Trans. on Knowl. and Data Eng.*, 18:1138–1150.

Lin, C.-Y. and Hovy, E. (2003). Automatic evaluation of summaries using N-gram co-occurrence statistics. In *Proceedings of the 2003 Conference of the North American Chapter of the Association for Computational Linguistics on Human Language Technology - Volume 1*, NAACL '03, pages 71–78, Stroudsburg, PA, USA. Association for Computational Linguistics.

Lin, D. (1998a). Automatic retrieval and clustering of similar words. In *Proceedings of the 17th International Conference on Computational Linguistics*, pages 768–774, Morristown, NJ, USA. Association for Computational Linguistics.

Lin, D. (1998b). An information-theoretic definition of similarity. In *Proceedings of the Fifteenth International Conference on Machine Learning*, ICML '98, pages 296–304, San Francisco, CA, USA. Morgan Kaufmann Publishers Inc.

Lin, D., Zhao, S., Qin, L., and Zhou, M. (2003). Identifying synonyms among distributionally similar words. In *Proceedings of the 18th International Joint Conference on Artificial Intelligence*, IJCAI'03, pages 1492–1493, San Francisco, CA, USA. Morgan Kaufmann Publishers Inc.

Liu, X., Zhou, Y., and Zheng, R. (2007). Sentence similarity based on dynamic time warping. In *Proceedings of the International Conference on Semantic Computing*, pages 250–256, Washington, DC, USA. IEEE Computer Society.

Meng, H. H. and Siu, K. C. (2002). Semiautomatic acquisition of semantic structures for understanding domain-specific natural language queries. *IEEE Trans. on Knowl. and Data Eng.*, 14(1):172–181.

Miller, G. A. and Charles, W. G. (1991). Contextual correlates of semantic similarity. *Language and Cognitive Processes*, 6(1):1–28.

O'Shea, J., Bandar, Z., Crockett, K., and McLean, D. (2008). A comparative study of two short text semantic similarity measures. In *Proceedings of the 2nd KES International Conference on Agent and Multi-Agent Systems: Technologies and Applications*, KES-AMSTA'08, pages 172–181, Berlin, Heidelberg. Springer-Verlag.

Radinsky, K., Agichtein, E., Gabrilovich, E., and Markovitch, S. (2011). A word at a time: computing word relatedness using temporal semantic analysis. In *Proceedings of the 20th International Conference on World Wide Web*, WWW '11, pages 337–346, New York, NY, USA. ACM.

Resnik, P. (1995). Using information content to evaluate semantic similarity in a taxonomy. In *Proceedings of the 14th International Joint Conference on Artificial Intelligence - Volume 1*, IJCAI'95, pages 448–453, San Francisco, CA, USA. Morgan Kaufmann Publishers Inc.

Roget, P. (1852). *Roget's Thesaurus of English Words and Phrases.* Penguin Books; 150th Anniversary edition (July 2007).

Rubenstein, H. and Goodenough, J. B. (1965). Contextual correlates of synonymy. *Communications of the ACM*, 8(10):627–633.

Salton, G. and McGill, M. (1983). *Introduction to Modern Information Retrieval*. McGraw-Hill.

Schutze, H. (1998). Automatic word sense discrimination. *Computational Linguistics*, 24(1):97–124.

Smadja, F., McKeown, K. R., and Hatzivassiloglou, V. (1996). Translating collocations for bilingual lexicons: a statistical approach. *Comput. Linguist.*, 22(1):1–38.

Tsatsaronis, G., Varlamis, I., and Vazirgiannis, M. (2010). Text relatedness based on a word thesaurus. *J. Artif. Int. Res.*, 37(1):1–40.

Turney, P. (2001). Mining the Web for synonyms: PMI-IR versus LSA on TOEFL. In *Proceedings of the Twelfth European Conference on Machine Learning (ECML 2001)*, pages 491–502, Freiburg, Germany.

Weeds, J., Weir, D., and McCarthy, D. (2004). Characterising measures of lexical distributional similarity. In *Proceedings of the 20th International Conference on Computational Linguistics*, COLING '04, Stroudsburg, PA, USA. Association for Computational Linguistics.

Xu, J. and Croft, W. B. (2000). Improving the effectiveness of information retrieval with local context analysis. *ACM Trans. Inf. Syst.*, 18(1):79–112.

Two-Stage Bootstrapping for Anaphora Resolution

Balaji J, T V Geetha, Ranjani Parthasarathi, Madhan Karky

Dept. of CSE & IST,

Anna University, Chennai- 600 025

Abstract:

In this paper, we propose a two-stage bootstrapping approach to resolve various anaphora representing persons, places, plurals and events in Tamil text. The existing approaches dealt with only single pronoun type and not all anaphora using common approach. Moreover, most of the approaches concentrate on syntax- based algorithms and semantics to some extent. Instead in our approach, we tackle various types of pronouns using a semi-supervised bootstrapping approach with uniform pattern representation and by exploring the semantic features in resolving anaphors. In order to aid the semantics, we use Universal Networking Language (UNL), a deep semantic representation for resolving various types of pronouns. The two stages of our bootstrapping approach consists of identification of anaphora and its set of referring expressions in stage 1 and identification of correct antecedent of a pronoun in stage 2. In our approach two patterns are defined – one for anaphora and other for set of referring expressions. In addition, we introduce triggering tuples, which can be word based semantics or context based semantics, represented in the pattern of both anaphora and referring expressions so as to resolve the ambiguities during the identification of correct antecedent. The performance of our bootstrapping approach gives better results and proved.

Keywords: Anaphora resolution, Universal Networking Language, Bootstrapping, Triggering Tuples

Proceedings of COLING 2012: Posters, pages 507–516,
COLING 2012, Mumbai, December 2012.

1. Introduction

Anaphora Resolution commonly called Pronoun resolution is a problem of finding references in the previous utterances of a pronoun. The references can be noun, noun phrase, verb phrase and/or clause. The main aim of anaphora resolution is to find the correct antecedent of a pronoun from the set of referring expressions. The antecedent of a pronoun is identified by the set of features such as number gender agreement features, grammatical relations for person pronouns and verb predicates for plural and event pronouns.

Popular syntax-based approaches include Centering theory (Brennan et al, 1987) and Hobb's algorithm (Hobbs, 1978) in which the both the algorithms are used to resolve person pronouns using agreement features and grammatical ordering of relations. The verb predicate feature has been used to identify event pronouns using a composite kernel method (Bin et al, 2010). In addition, rule-based has been attempted to resolve personal pronouns. The rules do not fit to resolve entire pronoun resolution task. In contrast, machine learning approaches have also been attempted to resolve person pronouns automatically. In particular, most of these techniques dealt with resolving only person pronouns and in some cases plurals and event pronouns (Chen et al, 2009).

In this paper, we propose a two-stage bootstrapping approach to resolve anaphora representing person, place, plural and events automatically from Tamil text. We define a uniform pattern to detect all types of pronouns while for referring expressions we define two types of patterns, one to tackle person and place pronouns and other to tackle plural and event pronouns. To our knowledge, this is the first attempt to tackle all types of pronouns using a single bootstrapping framework. We introduce the concept of triggering tuples in both the patterns of anaphora and its corresponding referring expressions to identify the correct antecedent. In order to aid the semantic compatibility information in anaphora resolution, we use Universal Networking Language (UNL) (UNDL, 2012), a deep semantic representation, to represent the referring expressions in the form of directed acyclic graphs. In this paper, the word level semantics and context level semantics information are utilized to resolve all the pronoun types. In addition, in order to generate new patterns, the semantic similarity of the antecedents is measured using the taxonomy of semantic constraints called UNL Ontology (UNDL 2012). While in our previous rule-based approach, we use three UNL relation based rules to tackle plural and event pronouns, however in this work, we have generalized the semantic relations to tackle more number of instances.

The paper is organized as follows. Section 2 discusses the related works on pronoun resolution. Section 3 describes the semi-supervised learning – bootstrapping of pronoun resolution which includes features, pattern representation and different stages of bootstrapping in finding the antecedent of a pronoun and generation of new patterns. In section 4, we discuss the performance of our approach and compared with another bootstrapping system. Finally, we conclude our approach with future enhancements.

2. Related Work

In this section, we discuss various techniques attempted for resolving different types of anaphora. A modified Centering theory and a rule-based approach has been proposed for resolving pronouns such as person, place, plural and events in which the rules are based on word-level semantics such as semantic constraints and sentence-level semantics such as UNL relations

(Balaji[2] et al, 2011). A robust rule based system has been applied to resolve personal pronouns, subject and dative pronouns in French in which the rules are based on agreement features and syntactic structure (Trouilleux, 2002). A syntactic rule based Hobb's algorithm has been used to resolve possessive and reflexive pronouns of Hindi language (Kamlesh et al, 2008). In contrast to the rule based approaches, machine learning approaches such as conditional random field (CRF) statistical model for chinese(Li & Shi, 2008), Tamil (Murthi et al, 2007) have been attempted. A twin candidate based learning model has been proposed to resolve event pronouns in English in which the verb predicates are considered as antecedents (Bin et al, 2010).

In the existing approach (Balaji[2] et al, 2011), various pronoun types have been resolved using a set of rules. However, rules have limited knowledge and do not provide accurate results for large set of sentences. In contrast, machine learning techniques focused on using syntactic features. to resolve person pronouns and co-reference chains in which the patterns defined are based on syntactic paths and word associations. Moreover, gender/number information and semantic compatibility have been determined using a probabilistic behavior (Bergsma et al, 2006). Another bootstrapping procedure for co-reference resolution uses word association information and are labeled using a self-trained approach (Kobdani et al, 2011).

However, the use of syntactic features and paths are difficult in relatively free-word order languages like Tamil and the approaches described above consider only limited types of anaphora. In order to overcome these difficulties, we propose a semi-supervised, two-stage bootstrapping procedure to resolve person, place, plural and event pronouns. The input to our bootstrapping framework is a set of UNL semantic graphs. The word level and context level information obtained from UNL graphs is utilized to define the example patterns. We introduce various scoring schemes during the filtering of non-referring expressions, choosing the correct antecedent and, the confidence of tuples and dependency relations in resolving pronouns. In addition to the scoring, we measure the semantic similarity between the semantic tuples of the referring expressions and propose a generalized procedure to learn new set coordinating and subordinating UNL relations to find the correct antecedent of a pronoun along with the existing relations proposed in the existing work (Balaji[2] et al, 2011).

3. Bootstrapping for Anaphora Resolution

Bootstrapping is a task of iteratively learning new patterns from unlabeled data, starting with a small labeled data from which the seed patterns are obtained. In this paper, we describe a two stage bootstrapping approach to resolve various types of anaphora. Our bootstrapping approach consists of two stages.

Stage 1: Extraction of anaphora and an associated set of referring expressions

Stage 2: Identification of the correct antecedent of the anaphora from the referring expressions obtained from Stage 1.

3.1 Features used for pattern representation in Anaphora Resolution

The pattern in the anaphora resolution is represented using the word-based features and context-based features. We use two classes of features, one for detecting anaphora and the other to extract the corresponding referring expressions. Here, each class consists of both word-based and context-based features. In addition, we introduce the concept of triggering tuple which forms part of the pattern representation but however does not take part in the actual matching process.

The triggering tuple helps the bootstrapping process to select the correct antecedent of a pronoun from the set of referring expressions obtained for that pronoun. The features are listed in Table-1.

Features for representing Referring Expressions
POS of the word (W_i) (Nouns or Entities) - POS(W_i)
Semantic Constraint associated with the word (W_i) - SC(W_i)
Attributes associated with the word (W_i) - ATTR(W_i)
Semantic Relation connected with the word (W_i) - SR(W_i)
Features for representing Anaphora
Pronoun (P_j)
POS of Pronoun (P_j) - POS(P_j)
Type of Pronoun (P_j) - PT(P_j)
Attributes associated with Pronoun (P_j) - ATTR(P_j)
Semantic Relation connected with Pronoun (P_j) - SR(P_j)
Triggering tuples
Verb (V) - Verb(V)
Attributes associated with the verb (V) - ATTR(V)
Semantic Constraints associated with the verb (V) - SC(V)
Attributes associated with the word (W_i) and Pronoun (P_j)
Semantic Relation connected with the word (W_i) and Pronoun (P_j)

TABLE 1 Features for resolving various types of anaphora

From Table-1, we introduce a new concept called triggering tuples which are used to signal the correct antecedent of a pronoun from the detected set of referring expressions. The triggering tuples are represented in the patterns of both referring expressions and pronouns. The triggering tuples can be a set of word based features and context based features

3.2 Pattern representation

In our approach, patterns are defined with use the graph based features (including both word-based and context-based features. The pattern representation for the set of referring expressions corresponding to anaphora representing persons and places is different from the referring expressions corresponding to anaphora representing plurals and events and thus can be shown in table 2. However, it is to be noted that the pattern representation for anaphora is common to all anaphora types. The pattern representations are described in detail in the following sections.

3.2.1 Pattern representation for Anaphora

The pattern representation is generic to all types of anaphora. Based on the features mentioned in Table-1, the pattern of anaphora is defined as

<Pronoun(W_i)+POS(W_i)+SC(W_i)+ATTR(W_i)+SR(W_i)-[Verb(V)+ATTR(V)+SC(V)]>

where j = 1,2 ….N

3.2.2 Pattern representation for a set of Referring Expressions

As described earlier, the pattern representation for the set of referring expressions corresponding to anaphora representing persons and places is different from the referring expressions of plural and event anaphora which are shown in table 2.

Referring Expressions for	Pattern Representation
Anaphora representing Person and Place	**<POS(W_i)+SC(W_i)+ATTR(W_i)+SR(W_i)-[Verb(V)+ATTR(V)+SC(V)]>** where i= 1, 2, 3 …N
Anaphora representing Plural and Events	**<{POS(W_i)+SC(W_i)+ATTR(W_i)+SR(W_i)-POS(W_k)+SC(W_k)+ATTR(W_k)+SR(W_k)}$_L$-[Verb(V)+ATTR(V)+SC(V)]>** where i, k, L = 1, 2, 3 …N & i~=k

TABLE 2 Pattern representations for referring expressions of various Pronouns

3.3 Stage 1: Extraction of Anaphora and associated referring expressions

During this stage, anaphora and the associated possible set of referring expressions are identified and extracted. The referring expressions are extracted based on the triggering tuple represented in the pattern of anaphora. Moreover, in order to reduce the redundant expressions such as non-referring expressions, a scoring function is introduced. This scoring is used to filter out non-referring expressions from the set.

3.3.1 Filtering of non-referring expressions

One of the important tasks of anaphora resolution is to filter out non-referring expressions that do not take part in resolving the anaphora type. The referring expressions of a pronoun can be nouns and entities. The non-referring expressions are usually filtered out using grammatical relations (Brennan et al, 1987). Instead of using the grammatical ordering for filtering out non-referring expressions, we use a scoring function for filtering. The scoring of referring expressions is based on the number of entities and/or nouns identified as referring expressions for the corresponding pronoun among the total number of referring expressions along with the type of anaphora to be resolved.

$$\text{Filter } RE_{As} = \frac{N\ RE_I + A_s}{RE_I + A_n}$$

Where RE_{As} - set of referring expressions for a specific anaphora, A_n – all types of anaphora, RE_I - referring expressions where I = 1, 2, 3 …N, A_s - specific anaphora to be resolved

Filtering of non-referring expressions can be performed by identifying the occurrence of a referring expression for a specific anaphora among the total occurrence of that regular expression with other anaphora types.

3.4 Stage 2: Identification of correct antecedent of a pronoun

During this stage, the correct antecedent of a pronoun is identified from the set of referring expressions obtained from stage 1 through the selection of complete patterns and partial patterns. The defined patterns represent the anaphora and the set of referring expressions. In order to choose the correct antecedent of a pronoun, the triggering tuples defined in the pattern are exploited using word based features and context based features.

3.4.1 Triggering Tuples

One of the important aspects of our bootstrapping approach is the use of triggering tuples to identify the correct antecedent of a pronoun. The idea behind the use of triggering tuples is to filter out the non-referring expressions among the set of referring expressions of a pronoun. In some cases, most approaches as discussed earlier failed to identify the correct antecedent of a pronoun. This is because the most popular algorithms such as Centering theory (Brennan et al, 1987), Hobb's algorithm (Hobbs, 1978) etc used in the existing approaches for resolving pronouns are syntax-based algorithms and not focused on the semantics of the word and/or context of a pronoun. However, Bin et al (2010) modified the centering theory by incorporating the semantic roles to resolve the pronouns. This approach solves the problem to an extent but only for person pronouns and the problem remains unsolvable in ambiguous cases (i.e. choosing an antecedent is ambiguous). Instead in our approach, this problem can be resolved by examining word based semantics and context based semantics. The following section describes the selection of correct antecedent of a pronoun.

3.4.2 Selection of complete patterns in identifying the antecedents of a corresponding pronoun

Identifying the correct antecedent of a pronoun is achieved by the selection of complete patterns. The triggering tuples of the patterns of anaphora and its referring expressions play a vital role in identifying the correct antecedent of a pronoun. A probabilistic scoring of triggering tuples in the pattern of anaphora and its corresponding referring expressions set is determined. Based on the scoring, confidence of the instances are examined and identified as an antecedent of a corresponding anaphora. The scoring of tuples is given below.

$$\text{Select } AN_{As} = \frac{N \; T_{RE_I + A_s}}{T_{RE_I + A_n}}$$

where AN_{As} – Antecedent of a specific anaphora, A_s - specific anaphora to be resolved, A_n – all types of anaphora, T – Triggering tuples, RE_I - referring expressions where I = 1, 2, 3 ...

3.4.3 Selection of partial patterns to generate new patterns

After the complete pattern matching is performed, instances that are not tackled under exact matching are then partial matched. Partial matching is carried out at different levels. The first level is to modify the word-based features such as semantic constraints of referring expressions to obtain the semantic similarity between the example patterns of the referring expressions and the input instances of the referring expressions. The semantic similarity of semantic constraints is achieved by using the semantic UNL Ontology (UNDL, 2012) in which the semantic constraints are arranged in a hierarchal relations such as "is-a" and "instance-of". The next level of partial matching is performed at the context-based features such as UNL relations. In addition, the confidence of the tuple values is also computed to identify the correct antecedent of a pronoun.

The detailed analysis of semantic similarity of constraints and, coordinating and subordinating relations are described below.

3.4.3a Semantic Similarity of Constraints

The semantic similarity between constraints is useful in identifying the anaphora representing places. As discussed above, adverbs such as “ingu” and “angu” along with its morphological variations can act as pronouns which represent places. Semantic constraints such as city, town, state, country etc all represent places. However it is difficult to list all these semantic variations in a pattern. Instead a semantic abstraction of constraints is needed to tackle these variations. This is achieved by using the semantic abstraction of the semantic constraints which is available through the semantic UNL ontology (UNDL, 2012). Semantic similarity is measured by the distance between the parent semantic constraints in UNL Ontology and is given below.

$$SIM\ C_i, C_j = DIST\ C_{parent}\ C_i, C_j$$

Where C_i – Semantic Constraint of referring expression obtained for an instance, C_j – Semantic constraint of referring expression in an example pattern, C_{parent} – Parent semantic constraint in UNL Ontology, DIST – Distance measure

Next, we will discuss the handling of coordinating and subordinating relations necessary to obtain the correct antecedent of a pronoun.

3.4.3b Coordinating and Subordinating UNL Relations

UNL relations obtained for referring expressions that exactly matches with the UNL relation obtained for anaphors are coordinating UNL relations and UNL relations obtained for anaphors that infer the UNL relations obtained for referring expressions are subordinating UNL relations (Balaji et al, 2011). In addition, we explored more number of coordinating and subordinating relations to resolve various pronouns. The specific rules on UNL relations are also generalized and thus the antecedent of a pronoun can be decided by

1. Participant relations connected with pronoun that exactly matches with Participant relations connected with the referring expressions in the previous utterances. Here, the triggering tuple is a verb and its associated UNL attribute as unaccusative (NACC). Example shown below comes under this category and is resolved using the triggering tuples mentioned above. For example,

   Ram baluvai adiththaan. Avan azhuthaan. Ramhit Balu. He cried.

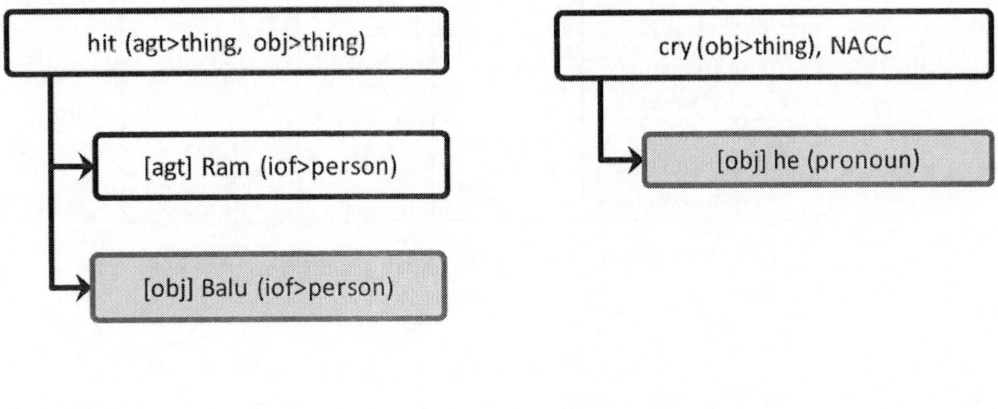

FIGURE 2 UNL Graphs for the sentences "Ram hit Balu. He cried".

The semantic constraints are shown in the braces and the relations connected with the corresponding concepts are shown in square brackets. The attribute "NACC" represents the verb is unaccusative.

The participant relation "obj" connected with pronoun that exactly matches with the participant relation "obj" connected with the concept "balu (iof>person)" in the previous sentence. Here, the triggering tuple is "NACC". And thus the antecedent of a pronoun "he" is identified as "balu". Similarly the other conditions are applied to obtain the correct antecedent of a pronoun.

2. Participant relations connected with pronoun that infers the Participant relations connected with the referring expressions in the previous utterances. Here, the triggering tuples are transitive verbs and its associated information.
3. Modifier relations connected with pronoun that infers the Participant relations connected with the referring expressions in the previous utterances. Here, the triggering tuples are transitive verbs.
4. Location relations connected with pronoun along with the "be" verb infers the Attribute relations connected with referring expressions in the previous utterances.

Using the conditions described above, the coordinating and subordinating relations are identified. In addition, new combination of relations is learned from the above conditions and thus the correct antecedent of a pronoun is obtained.

5. Evaluation

The performance of our bootstrapping approach is investigated using Tourism and News domain. We have considered 10000 sentences from each domain and tagged with the appropriate features such as POS, UNL attributes, UNL semantic constraints and UNL relation. We have taken 1000 tagged sentences for training data and extracted the most frequently occurred example patterns of each pronoun type. During this process we have identified 3025 person pronouns (singular), 2857 place pronouns, 156 plural pronouns and 323 event pronouns. Out of these obtained pronouns, we have achieved the overall result of 84% accuracy. The precision, recall and F-measure for resolving pronouns are shown in the table below. Table-3 shows the precision of various types of pronouns resolved.

Type of Anaphora	Precision	Recall	F-measure
Third Person Singular Pronouns	0.852	0.83	0.84
Third Person Plural Pronouns	0.79	0.74	0.76
Place pronouns	0.842	0.823	0.832
Event pronouns	0.837	0.656	0.735

TABLE 3 Performance of our Bootstrapping approach

We have also compared our bootstrapping approach with the previous rule based approach (Balaji et al, 2011). The comparison is shown in Fig 3. From the results, it is to be noted that our bootstrapping approach performs better than the previous rule based approach. Since the rules are limited in our previous approach, the F-measure is low and this difficulty could be resolved in our bootstrapping approach. We have also compared our bootstrapping approach with the path coreference of (Bergsama et al, 2006) which is a bootstrapping approach. The comparison of baseline system with our approach is shown in Fig 4. The parse tree for Tamil sentences is constructed using the existing Tamil parser (Saravanan et al, 2003). From the results, it can be seen that the performance of our approach gives better results than the existing system and the f-measure of our approach is 84% when compared to the baseline system as 48%.

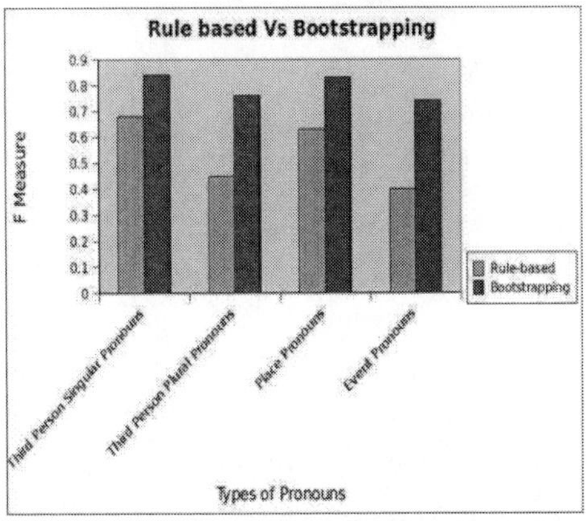

FIGURE 3 Comparison of Bootstrapping and Rule-based approach

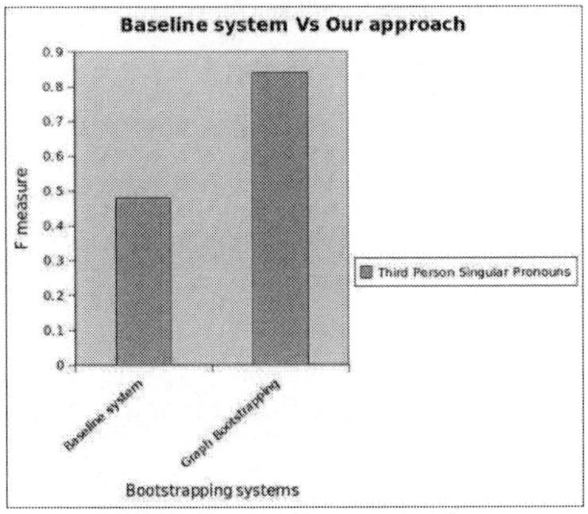

FIGURE 4 Comparison – Baseline system Vs. Graph Bootstrapping

Conclusion

In this paper, a semi-supervised, two-stage bootstrapping approach has been described to resolve all types of anaphora. In stage 1, the anaphora and its referring expressions are identified and in stage 2, the correct antecedent of a pronoun is selected among the set of referring expressions of a corresponding pronoun. This two-stage bootstrapping approach uses two patterns – for anaphora and referring expressions. Both the patterns consist of word based semantics and context based semantics. Moreover, a new concept called triggering tuples has been introduced in our bootstrapping approach so as to identify correct antecedent of a pronoun in case of ambiguities. The performance of our bootstrapping approach produces better results when compared to the baseline bootstrapping system. Further, we enhance this bootstrapping approach for identifying coreference entities by identifying more number of coordinating and subordinating relations.

References

Abney Steven, (2004), Understanding the yarowsky algorithm, Computational Intelligence, pages:365-395

Balaji J[1], T V Geetha, Ranjani and Madhan Karky, (2011), Morpho-Semantic Features for Rule-based Tamil Enconversion, International Journal of Computer Applications 26(6):11-18, July 2011. Published by Foundation of Computer Science, New York, USA

Balaji J[2] and T. V. Geetha and Ranjani Parthasarathi and Madhan Karky, (2011), Anaphora Resolution in Tamil using Universal Networking Language, IICAI-11, pages:1405-1415

Bergsma, Shane and Lin, Dekang, (2006), Bootstrapping path-based pronoun resolution, Proceedings of the 21st International Conference on Computational Linguistics and the 44th annual meeting of the Association for Computational Linguistics, ACL-44, Sydney, Australia, pages: 33--40

Bin, Chen and Jian, Su and Lim, Tan Chew, (2010), A twin-candidate based approach for event pronoun resolution using composite kernel, Proceedings of the 23rd International Conference on Computational Linguistics, COLING '10, Beijing, China, pages: 188—196

Brennan Susan E, Marilyn W. Friedman , Carl J. Pollard, (1987), A centering approach to pronouns, Proceedings of the 25th annual meeting on Association for Computational Linguistics, p.155-162, July 06-09, 1987, Stanford, California

Chen, Zheng and Ji, Heng and Haralick, Robert, (2009), A pairwise event coreference model, feature impact and evaluation for event coreference resolution, Proceedings of the Workshop on Events in Emerging Text Types, eETTs '09, pages: 17—22

Chen, Zheng and Ji, Heng, (2009), Graph-based event coreference resolution, Proceedings of the 2009 Workshop on Graph-based Methods for Natural Language Processing, TextGraphs-4, pages: 54—57

Duan Manjuan and Jiang Ping, (2010), An Empirical study of Centering in Chinese Anaphoric Resolution, International Conference on Artificial Intelligence and Computational Intelligence, IEEE, pages: 373-377

Hobbs, J. R. (1978), Resolving Pronoun references, Lingua 44:311-338

Kamlesh Dutta, Nupur Prakash, and Saroj Kaushik, (2008), Resolving Pronominal Anaphora in Hindi using Hobbs' Algorithm, Web Journal of Formal Computation and Cognitive Linguistics, Vol. 1, No. 10

Kobdani, Hamidreza and Schütze, Hinrich and Schiehlen, Michael and Kamp, Hans, (2011), Bootstrapping coreference resolution using word associations, The Association for Computational Linguistics, ACL, pages: 783-792

Li Fei and Shi Shuicai, (2008), Chinese Pronominal Anaphora Resolution based on Conditional Random Fields, International Conference on Computer Science and Software Engineering, IEEE, pages: 732-734

Narayana Murthi, K.N, Sobha, L, Muthukumari, B. (2007), Pronominal Resolution in Tamil Using Machine Learning Approach, The First Workshop on Anaphora Resolution (WAR I), Ed Christer Johansson, Cambridge Scholars Publishing, 15 Angerton Gardens, Newcastle, NE5 2JA, UK pp.39-50

Saravanan K, Ranjani Parthasarathi and T V Geetha, (2003), Syntactic Parser for Tamil, In INFITT-2003

Shalom Lappin , Herbert J. Leass, (1994), An algorithm for pronominal anaphora resolution, Computational Linguistics, v.20 n.4, p.535-561, December 1994

UNDL, Universal Networking Digital Language, (2012), http: //www.undl.org/ Online; accessed 28 Jan (2012)

Explorations in the Speakers' Interaction Experience and Self-assessments

Kristiina JOKINEN
UNIVERSITY OF TARTU, J.Liivi 2, 50409 Tartu
kjokinen@ut.ee
and
UNIVERSITY OF HELSINKI, PO Box 9 (Siltavuorenpenger 1 A)
Kristiina.Jokinen@helsinki.fi

ABSTRACT

The paper focuses on the interlocutors' self-evaluation in Finnish and Estonian first encounter dialogues. It studies affective and emotive impressions of the participants after they have met the partner for the first time, and presents comparison of the evaluation along the gender, age and education parameters. The results bring forward some statistically significant differences between the two groups, and point to different, culturally determined evaluation scales. The paper discusses the impact of the findings on the complex issues related to the evaluation of automatic interactive systems, and carries over to such applications as intelligent training and tutoring systems, and interactions with robots, encouraging further studies on the interlocutors' engagement in interaction and their evaluation of the success of the interaction.

KEYWORDS : dialogue, conversational engagement, self-assessment, cross-cultural evaluation

Kõnelejate suhtluskogemuse ja enesehinnangute uuringud

KOKKUVÕTE

Artikkel keskendub vestluskaaslaste enesehinnangutele esmakohtumisel peetud dialoogides soome ja eesti keeles. Uuritakse osalejate afektiivseid ja emotiivseid muljeid pärast seda, kui nad on kohtunud partneriga esmakordselt, ja esitatakse hinnangute võrdlus soo, vanuse ja hariduse parameetrite alusel. Tulemused toovad esile statistiliselt olulised erinevused kahe rühma vahel ja viitavad erinevatele, kultuuriliselt determineeritud hinnanguskaaladele. Artikkel analüüsib nende tulemuste mõju keerulistele probleemidele, mis on seotud automaatsete interaktiivsete süsteemide evalveerimisega, ja arendab edasi selliseid rakendusi nagu intelligentsed treenimis- ja õpetamissüsteemid ning suhtlus robotitega, pannes aluse edasistele uuringutele suhtlejate vestlusesse lülitumise ja vestluse edukuse hindamise kohta.

VÕTMESÕNAD : dialoog, vestlusesse lülitumine, enesehinnang, kultuuridevaheline evalveerimine

Proceedings of COLING 2012: Posters, pages 517–526,
COLING 2012, Mumbai, December 2012.

1 Introduction

A growing number of studies concerns how the interlocutors' affective state influences their experience and the interaction as a whole (e.g. Bavelas et al. 1986; Schroeder 2004; Lee et al. 2007; Mancini 2007; Nakano and Nishida, 2007), and how the speakers synchronise and coordinate their actions with each other (e.g. Goodwin, 2000; Krahmer and Swerts 2007; Heldner et al. 2010; Pickering and Garrod 2004; Battersby 2011). These aspects are regarded as signs of the speakers' cooperation and engagement: the speakers align and synchronise their behaviour, and show willingness to listen to their partner and provide coherent contributions. They also provide an important motivation to the design and evaluation of intelligent interactive agents, where user engagement is one of the core issues ranging from service oriented applications to amusing companions. Besides the traditional task completion, user's positive experience with the system is considered important for more natural interaction (Jokinen, 2009; Carlson et al. 2006).

It can be hypothesised that the more active the interlocutors appear to be in their communication, the more engaged they are in the conversation: their speaking frequency, tone of voice and body posture indicate interest and commitment to the topic of the conversation. Previous work has used such measures as utterance density (Campbell and Scherer, 2010; Jokinen, 2011), silence duration (Edlund et al. 2009), speech prosody (Levitan et al. 2011), lexical elements (Pickering and Garrod 2004), and eye-gaze (Levitski et al. 2012), among others. The interlocutors themselves usually describe such interactions afterwards as pleasant, enjoyable, and interesting.

This paper studies engagement and the interlocutors' experience in Finnish and Estonian interactions, and focuses especially on the interlocutor's self-evaluations. Self-evaluations are quick estimates of the interlocutors' conversational experience and provide complementary information to the studies that focus on studying engagement from the point of view of the interlocutors' verbal and non-verbal communicative signalling. It is hypothesised that engagement is related to the interlocutors' experience of the interaction in general, and the more engaged the interlocutors are in the conversation, the more positive their experience is. Such engaging events are described by positive affective adjectives, and thus the speakers' self-evaluation can reveal how they monitored the interaction on the affective level. By comparing the self-evaluations of two linguistically related participant groups, the paper also explores intercultural differences, and draws some interesting results concerning culturally determined interaction evaluation scales.

The paper first introduces the data and the questionnaire, then presents results from the comparison studies, and finishes with discussion and future research topics.

2 The data

2.1 First encounters video corpora

The corpus consists of first encounter dialogues collected in the Estonian MINT project (Jokinen and Tenjes, 2012) and in the Nordic collaboration project NOMCO (Navarretta et al. 2012). The projects aim at providing comparable databases for multimodal interaction studies in Nordic and Baltic languages. Dialogues are conducted between two people who are unfamiliar with each other. They are not given any specific topic to discuss, nor is there any external task to be solved. Each participant took part in two interactions, with a different partner. The Estonian corpus consists of 23 dialogues (12 male and 11 female participants, age range 21-61 years) while the Finnish data consists of 16 dialogues (8 male and 8 female participants, age range 20-59 years).

2.2 Questionnaire

Self-evaluation was conducted via a questionnaire that aims to measure naturalness and homogeneity of the interaction in terms of the speakers' experience. The descriptive features with negative and positive values were chosen following Nezlek (2010). The participants had to describe their experience of the interaction with respect to the given features using a 5-point scale, with 1 indicating that the adjective did not describe their experience at all, and 5 that did so very much. The web-based questionnaire was filled right after the person had had a videotaped interaction, and the participants were asked to fill it in quickly, so as to encourage first impressions rather than carefully considered responses. The adjectives were presented in the participants' mother tongue, and they are translated into English in Table 1.

The questionnaire also asked demographic information like gender, age-group, and education, as well as the person's familiarity with computers and video cameras. To find out how the descriptive features correlate within the two linguistic groups, a series of Student's t-tests were conducted for the two independent samples. Below we briefly go through the correlations along the gender, age, and education.

Descriptive feature	Estonian	Finnish
enjoyable	4.1	3.7
friendly	3.0	2.5
impressive	**3.7**	**2.1**
nice	4.1	4.0
interesting	4.1	3.8
relaxed	3.6	3.0
anxious	2.3	1.9
natural	**3.4**	**2.6**
happy	**4.2**	**2.6**
tense	2.0	1.9
awkward	1.9	2.1
angry	1.0	1.3
Average	3.1	2.6

TABLE 1 – Mean values for the descriptive features of the interaction. Boldface marks statistically significant differences ($p < 0.01$).

3 Self-assessment and experience

As seen in Table 1, Estonian speakers seem to provide more positive evaluations of their first encounters than the Finnish speakers (mean = 3.1, std deviation = 1.0, std error = 0.3 for Estonian, and mean = 2.6, std deviation = 0.8, std error = 0.2 for Finnish). Differences between three features (impressive, natural, and happy) are statistically significant ($p < 0.01$), and other big differences also occur concerning friendly, interesting and relaxed interaction, although these are not statistically significant. It is also interesting that Estonians ranked all 8 positive features over the neutral value 3, while Finns had only 4/8 features ranked so high. The positive views are further supported by the low evaluation of the negative aspects such as awkward and angry. As for the negative impressions in general, Estonians seem to rate their interactions slightly more anxious and tense, while Finns considered interactions slightly more awkward and angry, but these differences are not statistically significant.

3.1 Gender

Gender differences were not significant within either linguistic-cultural group. When the self-evaluation data is analysed across the cultures and languages, however, we find some statistically significant differences. Estonian male participants differ with respect to the features impressive, natural, and happy, from the Finnish male participants ($p < 0.05$). Also the Estonian female participants evaluate their interactions higher than the Finnish female participants with respect to these features, but also consider their interactions more interesting ($p < 0.05$). In general, Finnish and Estonian male participants seem to provide more similar self-evaluations along the different features, whereas the Finnish female participants were more critical of their interactions than the Estonian ones. Finnish female participants tend to rate their interactions lower concerning such features as friendly, interesting, and relaxed, yet also gave lower rates to negative aspects like anxious and tense. The distribution of self-assessment values with respect to male and female participants is given in Figure 1 and Figure 2, respectively.

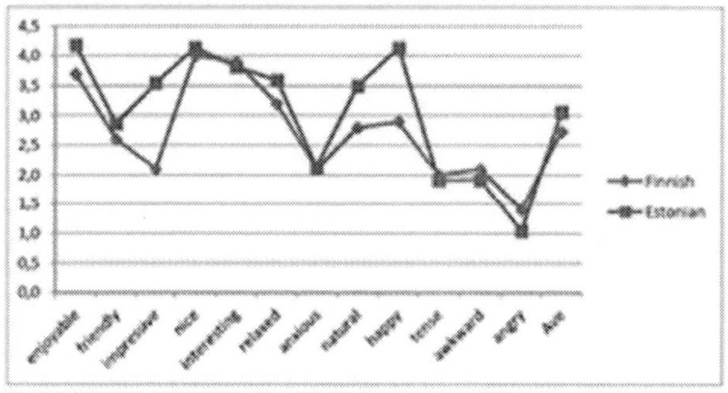

FIGURE 1 – Significant differences between Finnish and Estonian male evaluations concern impressive, natural, and happy interactions.

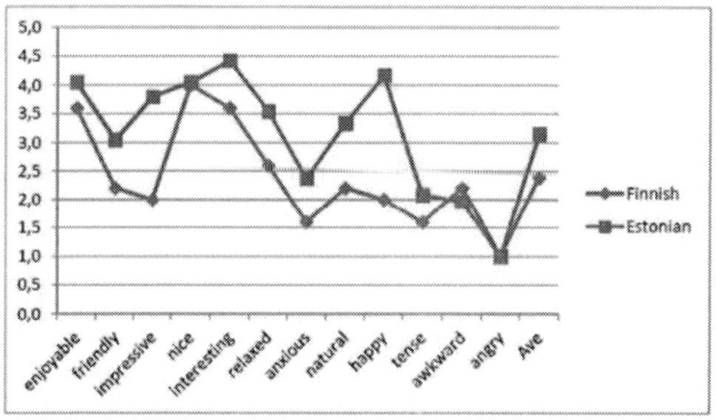

FIGURE 2 – Significant differences between Finnish and Estonian female speakers concern impressive, interesting, natural, and happy interactions.

3.2 Age

The participants were mostly young adults although both populations had one over 55 years of age. Since the two linguistic groups were not balanced with respect to age, it is not possible to draw differences in this respect. However, if we look at the differences across the languages, we can distinguish two age groups, those under 30 years and those above, and we find that the younger Estonians tend to evaluate the interactions significantly ($p < 0.01$) more impressive and happier than the younger Finns, and also more relaxed (significance level $p < 0.05$). Following the same tendency, younger Finns also considered interactions slightly more tense, awkward, and angry than the younger Estonians (Figure 3). Concerning older participants, Figure 4 shows that the older Estonians had stronger experience of their conversations being friendlier, more natural, and happier than what the older Finns do ($p < 0.01$). However, it is interesting, that the older Finns describe their interactions slightly nicer and more relaxed than the old Estonians, and concerning negative impressions, they also find interactions less anxious and tense than the older Estonians, although as mentioned, the differences are not statistically significant. As a summary, it seems that in our first encounter data, the younger and older participants had opposite experiences: the younger Estonians rate their interactions more relaxed and less tense than the younger Finns, while the older Estonians rate interactions less relaxed and more tense than the older Finns.

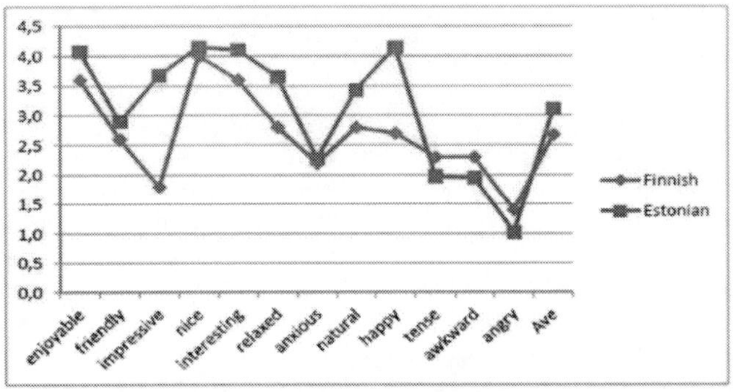

FIGURE 3 – Significant differences between Finnish and Estonian younger interlocutors (age < 30) concern impressive, relax, and happy interactions.

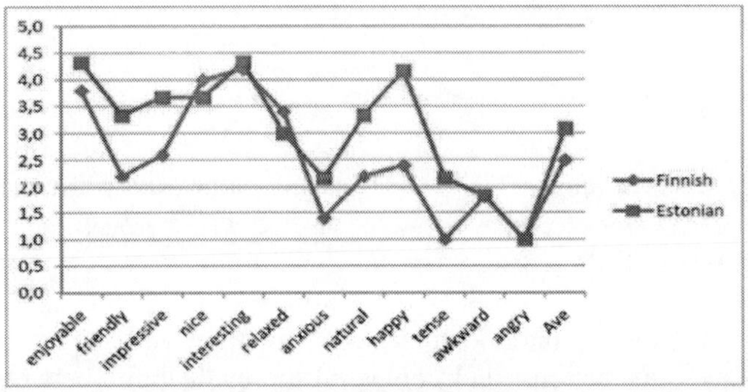

FIGURE 4 – Significant differences between Finnish and Estonian older interlocutors (age > 30) concern friendly and happy interactions.

3.3 Education

The participants' education ranged from undergraduate students to those who had completed Master's degree. It is interesting that this parameter draws statistically significant differences also within the linguistic groups: Estonian students found interactions more relaxed and less anxious than those who had completed their degree, yet also less interesting, while the Finnish students tend to consider interactions less friendly and intereting, yet more anxious and tense than those who had completed their degree.

Across the linguistic groups, Estonian students regarded interactions as more impressive and happier than the Finnish students (Figure 5), while those with a degree, considered interactions also more friendly and natural than the Finns (Figure 6). It is interesting that the student descriptions in both language groups seem to be rather similar, in particular considering the negative features, but the differences grow bigger between those with a degree. This seems to be due to the change in the Finnish participants' evaluation: the Finnish degree holders tend to rate their interactions less anxious, tense and awkward than the Finnish students, while the difference between Estonian students and Estonian degree holders does not vary as much.

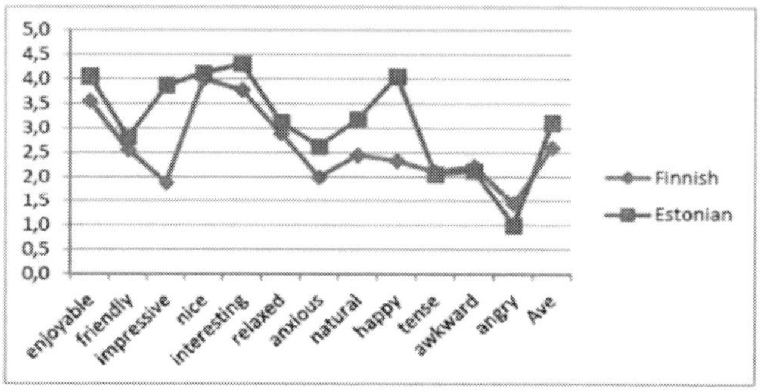

FIGURE 5 – Differences between Finnish and Estonian undergraduate students.

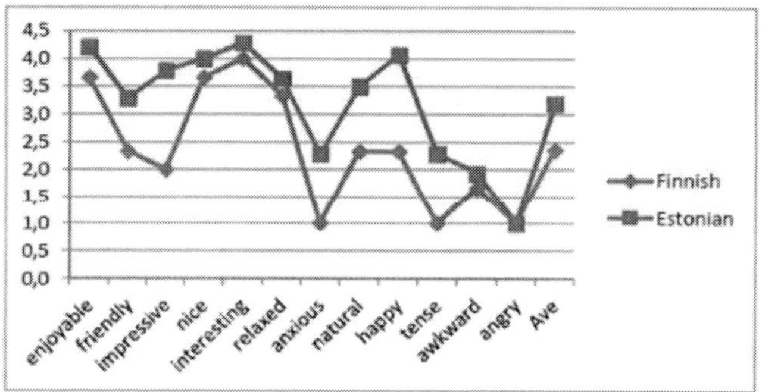

FIGURE 6 – Differences between Finnish and Estonian participants with a master's degree.

Conclusion and perspectives

This paper has focussed on the interlocutors' self-evaluation and impressions on Finnish and Estonian first encounter interactions, and compared the evaluations between two linguistically related participant groups. Statistically significant differences were found between the groups with respect to gender, age, and education, and concerning the evaluation parameters impressive, natural and happy, but due to a small dataset, we refrain from drawing conclusions concerning cultural characteristics.

However, it is noticeable that the Estonian groups consistently give higher evaluation scores for their interactions, and this is consistent regarding all descriptive categories, i.e. also their negative impressions were evaluated more strongly, although the differences were not as big as with the positive ones. We can assume that the differences are due to the different evaluation scales the participants use within their linguistic and cultural contexts. The Estonians' higher scores in all descriptive categories seem to suggest that the starting point of their evaluation scale was set high whereas the Finns tend to describe their impressions of the interaction using less extreme ends of the evaluation scale, thus giving lower scores to their experience compared with the Estonians.

However, even though the assessment scores may be low, the interaction itself may be considered "normal" and typical within the cultural group. In our case, it is impossible to say whether, in absolute terms, the Finns experience their interactions less impressive, natural or happy than the Estonians, or if the Estonians experience their conversations in more extreme terms than the Finns. Nevertheless, there is a clear difference in the way the Finns and Estonians describe their interactive behaviour, and we can only conclude that even within neighbouring countries, with closely related languages, the assessment of one's engagement in interactive situations becomes a complex issue that is not necessarily related to straightforward measurements of overt behaviour. The cultural context deals with social norms and relationships which constrain the appropriateness of interactive behaviour, and also affects the way the behaviour is presented and assessed within the group.

Consequently, this study has impact on the evaluation and annotation methodology for various NL related systems that concern the speakers' attitudes, affection, and emotions: the speaker's judgements do not depend only on the personal characteristics of the users, but also on the different evaluation scales, which seem to depend on a larger cultural context. Annotations dealing with such issues as sentiment analysis, emotion categorisation and intercultural communication, thus need to take into consideration the variation that stems from culturally bound subjective evaluation scales. The design and evaluation of interactive systems also includes modelling of the partner's affective and emotional state, and the correct interpretation of subtle behavioural signals thus requires exposure to the cultural context in which the interaction takes place. For instance, a tutoring system that tries to assess the student's level of interest in intercultural context may reach a wrong conclusion that the student is not interested if the student's self-assessment is not high enough, and this may lead to inappropriate strategies on how to continue the interaction.

Future work concerns more detailed studies of the notion of engagement and its relation to the subjective impressions of the success of interaction. The results can be applied e.g. to robot interaction where the robot tries to engage human in conversations about interesting Wikipedia topics (Jokinen and Wilcock, 2012). It is also important to work on more discriminating self-assessment questionnaires and methods to assess interactions in a more detailed manner, and to refine the set of descriptive parameters to cover the crucial aspects. For instance, it is useful to distinguish parameters that deal with different view-points: the speaker, the partner, and the general view of the interaction as a whole. Related to this it is also possible to extend the work with multimodal features and to correlate self-evaluations with the speakers' multimodal activity, automatically extracted from the video. Finally, to better understand human communication in multicultural contexts, it is necessary to investigate differences in a larger population.

Acknowledgments

Thanks go to all the participants who took part in the video recordings, and to Matti Hocksell and Joonas Toivio in Helsinki and Sven Laater and Anti Torp in Tartu for their assistance in the data collection and analysis. Thanks go also to Mare Koit for her support of the research, and for the translation of the abstract into Estonian.

References

Battersby, S. (2011). Moving Together: the organization of Non-verbal cues during multiparty conversation. PhD Thesis, Queen Mary, University of London.

Bavelas, J. B., A. Black, C. R. Lemery and J. Mullett (1986). "I show how you feel": Motor mimicry as a communicative act. *Journal of Personality and Social Psychology* 50(2): 322-329.

Campbell, N. and Scherer, S. (2010). Comparing Measures of Synchrony and Alignment in Dialogue Speech Timing with respect to Turn-taking Activity. *Proceedings of Interspeech 2010*. Makuhari, Japan

Carlson, R., J. Edlund, M. Heldner, A. Hjalmarsson, D. House and G. Skantze (2006). Towards human-like behaviour in spoken dialog systems. Swedish Language Technology Conference (SLTC). Gothenburg, Sweden.

Edlund, J., M. Heldner and J. Hirschberg (2009). Pause and gap length in face-to-face interaction. *Proceedings of Interspeech 2009*. Brighton, UK.

Goodwin, C. (2000). Action and embodiment within Situated Human Interaction. *Journal of Pragmatics*, 32:1489-1522

Heldner, M., Edlund, J. and Hirschberg, J. (2010). Pitch similarity in the vicinity of backchannels. *Proceedings of Interspeech 2010*, Makuhari, Japan.

Jokinen, K. (2009). *Constructive Dialogue Modelling – Speech Interaction and Rational Agents*. John Wiley & Sons, Chichester, UK.

Jokinen, K. (2011). Turn taking, Utterance Density, and Gaze Patterns as Cues to Conversational Activity. *Proceedings of The International Conference on Multimodal Interaction (ICMI-2011) Workshop on Multimodal Corpora for Machine Learning (MMC)*, Alicante, Spain.

Jokinen, K. and Tenjes, S. (2012). Investigating Engagement – Intercultural and Technological Aspects of the Collection, Analysis, and Use of Estonian Multiparty Conversational Video Data. *Proceedings of the Eight International Conference on Language Resources and Evaluation (LREC'12)*, Istanbul, Turkey. European Language Resources Association (ELRA).

Jokinen, K. and Wilcock, G. (2012). Multimodal open-domain conversations with the Nao robot. *Proceedings of the 4th International Workshop on Spoken Dialogue Systems (IWSDS 2012)*, Paris.

Krahmer, E., and Swerts, M. (2007). The effects of visual beats on prosodic prominence: Acoustic analyses, auditory perception and visual perception. *Journal of Memory and Language*, 57 (3), 396-414.

Lee, J., Marsella, T., Traum, D., Gratch, J., and Lance, B. (2007). The Rickel Gaze Model: A Window on the Mind of a Virtual Human. In C. Pelachaud et al. (Eds.) *Proceedings of the 7th International Conference on Intelligent Virtual Agents (IVA-2007)*. Springer Lecture Notes in Artificial Intelligence 4722, pp. 296-303. SpringerVerlag Berlin Heidelberg.

Levitan, R., Gravano, A. and Hirschberg, J. (2011). Entrainment in Speech Preceding Backchannels. *Proceedings of ACL 2011*, pp. 113-117.

Levitski, A., Radun, J., and Jokinen, K. (2012). Visual interaction and conversational activity. *Proceedings of the 4th Workshop on Eye Gaze in Intelligent Human Machine Interaction: Eye Gaze and Multimodality*. Santa Monica, USA

Mancini, M., Castellano, G., Bevacqua, E. and Peters, C. (2007). Copying Behaviour of Expressive Motion. *Lecture Notes in Computer Science, Computer Vision/Computer Graphics Collaboration Techniques*, 4418:180-191.

Nakano, Y. and Nishida, T. (2007). Attentional Behaviours as Nonverbal Communicative Signals in Situated Interactions with Conversational Agents. In Nishida, T. (Ed.) *Engineering Approaches to Conversational Informatics*, John Wiley.

Navarretta, C., Ahlsén, E., Allwood, J., Jokinen, K., and Paggio, P. (2012). Feedback in Nordic first-encounters: a comparative study. *Proceedings of the Eight International Conference on Language Resources and Evaluation (LREC'12)*, Istanbul, Turkey. European Language Resources Association (ELRA).

Nezlek, J. B. (2010). Multilevel modeling and cross-cultural research. In D. Matsumoto and A. J. R. van de Vijver (Eds.) *Cross-Cultural research methods in psychology*. Oxford.

Pickering, M. and Garrod, S. (2004). Towards a mechanistic psychology of dialogue, *Behavioral and Brain Sciences* 27:169– 226.

Schroeder, M. (2001). Emotional Speech Synthesis: A review. *Proceedings of the 7th European conference on Speech Communication and Technology (Eurospeech'01/Interspeech),* Aalborg.

Multimodal Signals and Holistic Interaction Structuring

Kristiina JOKINEN Graham WILCOCK
UNIVERSITY OF HELSINKI, Finland
kristiina.jokinen@helsinki.fi, graham.wilcock@helsinki.fi

ABSTRACT
This paper focusses on multimodal activity and its functions, especially as a communicative means to structure the discourse among the interlocutors: to give feedback and indicate turn-takings and mutual agreement. Starting from the assumption that natural language communication is a holistic process which aims at creating shared understanding, and requires interpretation of vocal and visual signals as part of successful interaction, the paper aims to form a coherent picture of the participants' multimodal communication strategies and their engagement in the conversation. It presents observations on the conversational feedback and turn-taking functions especially related to head movement, hand gesturing, and body posture. The main claim concerns the meta-discursive function of visual signals, related to their use as unobtrusive means to control the interaction and to construct shared understanding. The paper deals with synchrony between head movements, hand gesturing and body posture, and builds models for the coordination of communication for intelligent and situated autonomous agents.

TITLE AND ABSTRACT IN FINNISH

Multimodaaliset signaalit ja holistinen vuorovaikutuksen jäsennys

Tämä artikkeli keskittyy multimodaalisen aktiivisuuden ja sen viestinnällisten tehtävien tutkimiseen, erityisesti sen käyttöön diskurssin jäsentämisessä keskustelijoiden kesken: palautteen antamiseen, vuoronvaihtojen osoittamiseen sekä yksimielisyyden ilmaisemiseen. Lähtien oletuksesta että kielellinen kommunikointi on holistinen prosessi, joka tähtää yhteisen ymmärryksen luomiseen ja vaatii vokaalisten ja visuaalisten signaalien tulkitsemista osana onnistunutta vuorovaikutusta, artikkeli pyrkii muodostamaan koherentin kuvan puhujien multimodaalisista viestintästrategioista ja keskusteluun osallistumisesta. Se esittelee huomioita, jotka käsittelevät keskustelupalautteen antoa ja vuoronvaihtelua erityisesti pään, käsien, ja vartalon liikkeiden avulla. Keskeinen väite koskee multimodaalisten signaalien meta-diskursiivista funktiota, joka liittyy niiden käyttöön ei-häiritsevinä keinoina keskustelun hallinnassa ja yhteisen ymmärryksen luonnissa. Artikkelissa kuvataan pään, käsien, ja vartalon liikkeiden synkroniaa, sekä kehitetään malleja, joita voidaan käyttää älykkäiden ja tilanteisten autonomisten agenttien viestinnän koordinoimiseksi.

KEYWORDS: discourse structuring, multimodal dialogue management, gesturing, synchrony, feedback, turn-taking.

KEYWORDS IN FINNISH: diskurssin jäsennys, multimodaalinen keskustelun hallinta, elehdintä, synkronia, palaute, vuoronvaihto.

Yhteenveto (Summary in Finnish)

Artikkelissa tarkastellaan multimodaalista viestintää ja erityisesti pään, käsien, ja vartalon liikkeitä osana kielellistä kommunikaatiota. Artikkelin päämäärä on kaksitahoinen: toisaalta se tukee kokonaisvaltaista "gestalt"-näkemystä inhimillisestä kommunikaatiokyvystä ja havainnollistaa tätä käytännön esimerkein, toisaalta se kehittelee malleja ja korrelaatioita puhujien keskustelupalautteen ja vuoronvaihtostrategioiden kuvaamiseksi, joita malleja voidaan käyttää autonomisten agenttien viestinnän koordinoinnin pohjana.

Aineisto on kerätty pohjoismaisessa NOMCO-projektissa (Navarretta et al., 2012), ja se koostuu 16:sta noin 6-10 minuutin ensitapaamiskeskustelusta. Puhujat eivät ole tavanneet toisiaan aikaisemmin, ja heidän ainoa tehtävänsä on tutustua toisiina. Keskustelut on translitteroitu ja käännetty englanniksi, ja ne on annotoitu multimodaalisten elementtien suhteen käyttäen muokattua MUMIN annotointiskeemaa (Allwood et al., 2007). Multimodaalisten elementtien jakauma on esitelty englanninkielisen osuuden taulukossa 1, ja eri elementteihin liittyien piirrearvojen jakauma yksityiskohtaisemmin taulukoissa 2– 4. Korrelaatiotulokset on esitetty alla olevissa kuvioissa Figures 1– 5 ja suhteutettu kokonaismäärään.

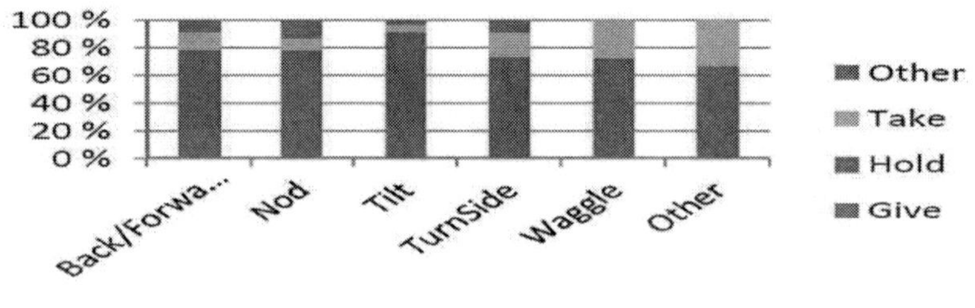

Figure 1: Head movement and turn-taking.

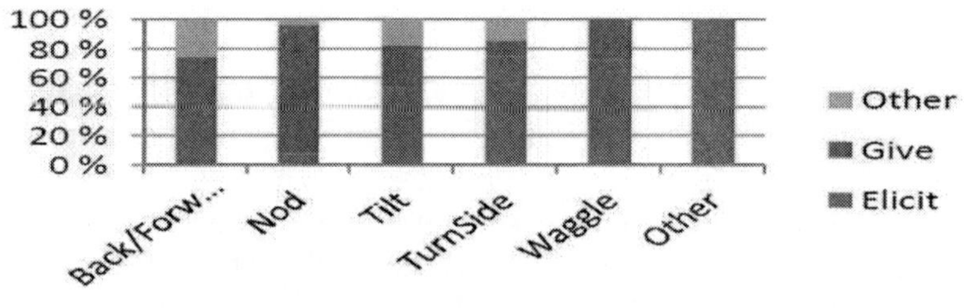

Figure 2: Head movement and feedback.

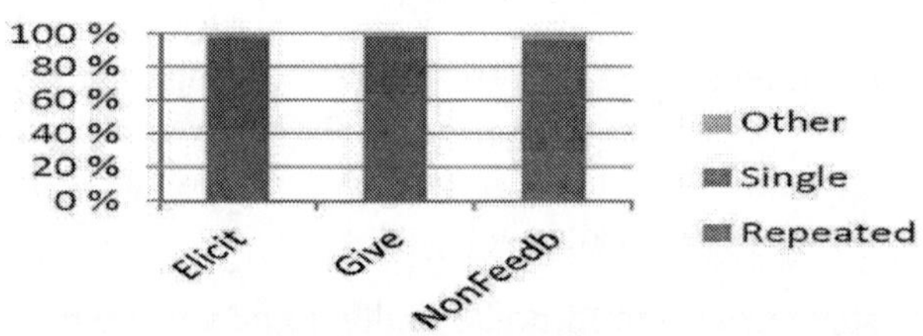

Figure 3: Single stroke vs. repeated hand movement and feedback.

Aineistosta laskettiin korrelaatioita ja yhteisesiintymiä sen selvittämiseksi miten pään, käsien, ja vartalon liikkeet suhteutuvat palautteen antamiseen ja vuoronvaihtoon. Vuoronvaihto oli jaettu kolmeen luokkaan (vuoron ottaminen, pitäminen, ja antaminen) kun taas palaute oli binäärinen luokka (palautteen antaminen vs. saaminen). Kokeelliset hypoteesit olivat seuraavat:

1. pään liikkeet ja palautteen antaminen korreloivat (vrt. Boholm and Allwood (2010))
2. käsieleet ja palautteen saaminen korreloivat (vrt. Battersby (2011))
3. kehon liikkeet ja vuoronvaihto korreloivat (vrt. Kendon (2010) ja f-formaatio)

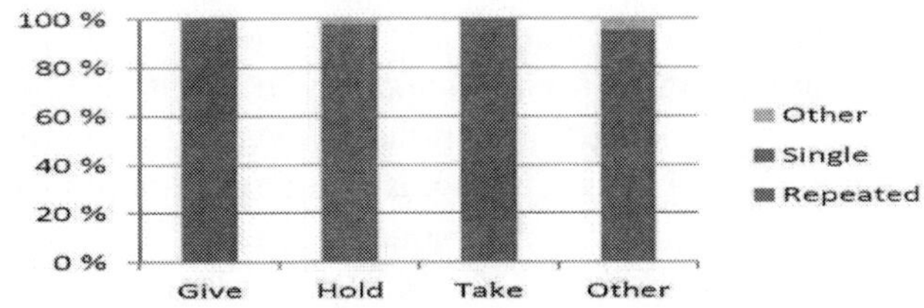

Figure 4: Single stroke vs. repeated hand movement and turn taking.

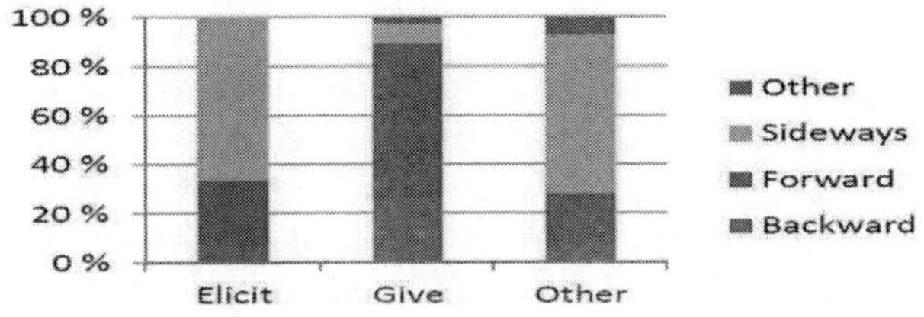

Figure 5: Body movement and feedback.

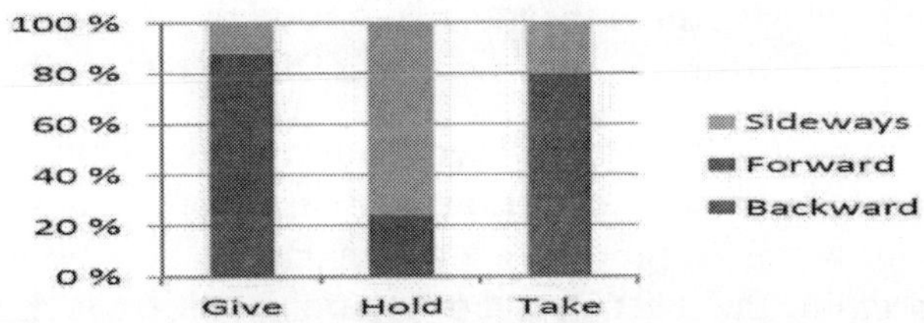

Figure 6: Body movement and turn-taking.

Keskustelijoiden kommunikatiivista aktiivisuutta verrattiin myös heidän itsearviointiinsa keskustelun onnistumisesta. Oletuksena oli, että puhujien itsearviointi liittyy heidän osallisuuteensa vuorovaikutustilanteessa: mitä osallistuvampi ja aktiivisempi puhuja on, sitä positiivisempi on hänen arviointinsa vuorovaikutuksesta. Lisäksi oletettiin, että vuoronvaihtojen määrää voidaan käyttää kriteerinä arvioitaessa keskustelijoiden aktiivisuutta ja osallisuutta keskusteluun: mitä enemmän vuoronvaihtoja, sitä aktiivisemmin puhujat osallistuvat keskusteluun koska he pyrkivät nopeasti koordinoimaan viestejään. Yksittäisten kuvauspiirteiden ja puhujien itsearvioinnin korreloinnissa löytyi statistisesti merkittävä korrelaatio ($p<0.05$) kommunikatiivisen aktiivisuuden ja keskustelukokemuksen onnellisuuden välillä (0.688).

1 Introduction

The paper starts from the assumption that natural language communication is a holistic process which aims at creating shared understanding, and requires perception and interpretation of a wide variety of vocal and visual signals as part of successful interaction. For instance, (Crystal, 1975) has talked about paralanguage, i.e. the 'tone of voice' that bridges non-linguistic forms of communicative behaviour and the core linguistic areas of grammar, vocabulary and pronunciation, whereas (Allwood, 2002) describes on a general level how all body movements that influence the partner can be considered communicative.

We study the use of visual signals, i.e. head movements, hand gestures, and body posture in interaction coordination, and use the term *multimodality* to emphasise the multiple modalities involved in communication. Our approach is holistic: we aim at a coherent picture of the participants' multimodal communication strategies and engagement in interaction. The goal of the paper is two-fold: on one hand, it contributes to the holistic 'gestalt' view of human communication capability, and exemplifies this in practise by examining the interlocutors' multimodal feedback and turn-taking strategies. On the other hand, it studies correlations between head movement, hand gesturing, and body posture so as to develop models for their synergy and synchrony in relation to the giving feedback and taking turns, in order to enable of automatic coordination of communicative functions for autonomous agents.

The main claim concerns the functions of multimodal signals related to their use as unobtrusive means to control the interaction and to construct shared understanding. Following Kendon (2004) we use the term *metadiscursive* to describe gestures that regulate the flow of information rather than express semantic content. Although multimodal aspects have been the subject of many previous studies, the correlation of these particular aspects has not been much discussed in computational linguistics. On the basis of our corpus we argue that body posture is an iconic way to hold the conversational turn, hand gesturing signals turn-taking, and nodding is an effective means to give feedback. Moreover, we hypothesize that the interlocutors' communicative activity gives evidence for their engagement in the interaction, and that engagement positively correlates with the interlocutors' self-assessment of the success of the interaction.

The paper is exploratory in nature, and combines observations of the data into a multimodal interaction model. It is structured as follows. Section 2 discusses previous studies that are confirmed and expanded by our work. Section 3 presents the data and corpus examples used. Section 4 provides results concerning the function and correlation of different visual modalities, and discusses conversational engagement in terms of multimodal activity in the conversation in general. Section 5 describes the interlocutors' own assessment of the interaction. Conclusions are drawn in Section 6.

2 Multimodal aspects of communication

Much of the information related to the basic enablements of communication (being in contact with, and being able to perceive the partner) are conveyed by multimodal means such as eye-gaze, head nods, facial expressions, etc. Multimodal signals also carry emotional and physical feelings, moods, interest, reactions, etc., and they convey social functions of communication: they help the interlocutors to share understanding, bond with their partners, and create social identity (Feldman and Rim, 1991). They also serve to control and coordinate the information flow in interactions. For instance, Kendon (2004) talks about meta-discursive function of hand gestures, while gaze is important in turn-taking (Argyle and Cook, 1976; Goodwin, 2000;

Lee et al., 2007; Jokinen et al., 2010). Body posture can be used to control the interaction: leaning forward often means interest whereas leaning backward signals withdrawing from the conversation (Jokinen and Scherer, 2012). Jokinen and Pärkson (2011) notice that some body movements are used to fill pauses in conversation if the speaker may not want to take the turn or is unable to take the turn. In group conversations, participants create a joint transactional space by forming spatial patterns, f-formations (Kendon, 2010), and they signal contact and availability to take part in the conversation by multimodal activity (Battersby, 2011).

Besides the functions of multimodal signals, there is substantial literature on the signals themselves. Correlation, for instance, between gaze and gesturing has been studied by Gullberg and Holmqvist (1999), and between speech and head movement by Boholm and Allwood (2010). Synchrony between acoustic cues (pitch accents) and visual cues (beat gestures, head nods, and eyebrow movements) is studied in detail by Krahmer and Swerts (2007), while various others have looked at alignment (Pickering and Garrod, 2004) and mimicry (Chartrand and Bargh, 1999).

Computational modelling of multimodal communication has focussed on Embodied Conversational Agents; see an overview in André and Pelachaud (2010). For instance, Nakano and Nishida (2007) experimented with an eye-gaze model to ground information in interactions with an embodied conversational agent, while (Swartout et al., 2010) focused on building realistic and engaging virtual agents for various practical applications. Recently, robots have become an important application domain. Bennewitz et al. (2007) developed a robot companion that can recognize gestures and become engaged in interaction. Jokinen and Wilcock (2012) and Csapo et al. (2012) describe multimodal interaction in conversations with the Nao robot. Non-verbal aspects can also be important in computational and cognitive linguistics: Koller et al. (2012) used eye-tracking in monitoring the hearer's reference resolution process, and Qu and Chai (2009) showed that the coupling of speech and gaze streams in a word acquisition task can improve performance significantly.

3 Data and hypotheses

The data consists of 9 (out of the 16) Finnish first encounter dialogues collected in the NOMCO project (Navarretta et al., 2012): 5 female and 4 male participants, aged 21-40, all native speakers of Finnish. Each participant took part in two conversations with different partners they did not know in advance. The participants were not given any particular topics to discuss but were asked to make acquaintance with the partner they had never met before. After the recordings the participants filled out a web-based questionnaire concerning how they felt about the conversations. Instructions were kept minimal: the participants were only advised to stand in a specific spot, so they would remain in frame throughout the recording. The participants were standing, since recording started when they entered the interaction space through the door, and it was thus a natural posture. It also provided a model of real first encounter situations which often take place standing in a party, lecture hall, etc.

The recordings were made in ambient lighting with three static cameras. Two cameras recorded the participants individually while one camera shot both participants at once. A separate audio recorder was used to obtain a clearer audio track. The encounters are about 6–10 minutes long. They are transcribed and translated into English, and the frontal views were annotated following a modified MUMIN annotation scheme (Allwood et al., 2007). Multimodal features concern the function and form of head, hand, and body movement. Interaction features are related to turn-taking (take, hold, and give the turn) and feedback (give vs. elicit feedback).

Annotation was done by two annotators independently and checked by an expert annotator. Inter-coder agreement between the annotators was checked by calculating kappa co-efficient on two dialogues. The corrected Kappa values varied between 0.71 on head movement to 0.41 on facial display and 0.36 on hand gesturing, while category agreements were 80.7%, 58.1%, and 56.5%, respectively. The main disagreements concern feedback direction (give vs. elicit) of hand gesturing and facial display, as well as trajectory type (complex vs. up vs. side vs. other) on hand gesturing. The body posture annotation was done only by one annotator whose annotations were then selected to be used in the experiments throughout.

Feedback (fb)	Head	Hand	Body	Turn-taking (tt)	Head	Hand	Body
Feedback Elicit	201	205	30	TurnGive	295	72	33
Feedback Give	375	90	38	TurnHold	220	228	41
Unclassified fb	69	107	28	TurnTake	64	37	10
Total	**645**	**402**	**96**	Unclassified tt	66	65	12
Total of all	**56 %**	**35 %**	**9 %**	**Total**	**645**	**402**	**96**
Total of all fb	**61 %**	**32 %**	**7 %**	**Total of all tt**	**58 %**	**34 %**	**8 %**

Table 1: Communicative functions (feedback vs. turn-taking) related to head, hand, and body movements. Unclassified movements are not annotated with respect to the given communicative feature, e.g. of the 645 head movements, 69 are not related to feedback.

Statistics of the multimodal elements (n = 1143) with respect to the communicative functions are given in Table 1, and the statistics of the different annotation features in each category are detailed in Tables 2– 4. Slightly more than half (56%) of all the communicative movements are produced by head, 35% by hand, and only 9% by body. Distributions with respect to feedback and turn-taking have a similar tendency.

Co-occurrences and correlations were calculated on the basis of the data, to find out how hand, head, and body movement were related to feedback and turn-taking functions. The experimental hypotheses were as follows:

1. Correlations can be found with respect to head movements (nods) and feedback giving (cf. Boholm and Allwood (2010)).
2. Correlations can be found with respect to hand gesturing and feedback elicitation (cf. Bavelas and Chovil (2000), Battersby (2011)).
3. Correlations can be found with respect to body movements and turn-taking (cf. f-formation in Kendon (2010)).

4 Experimental results

4.1 Head movement

The majority of head movements are nods (Table 2). We previously showed (Toivio and Jokinen, 2012) that there is a statistically significant difference between up-nods and down-nods, and the difference correlates with different semantics: down-nods are used in situations where common ground is already established, while up-nods are used if the presented information is surprising in the given context. Co-ocurrences normalised with respect to the total numbers and time show that different head movements correlate with turn-taking and feedback functions (Figures 1

Head movements	Count	Percent	Head movements	Count	Percent
Backward	38	6 %	TurnSide	76	12 %
Forward	77	12 %	Waggle	11	2 %
Nod	345	53 %	Other	3	0 %
Tilt	95	15 %	**Total**	**645**	**100 %**

Table 2: Feature values and their frequency in head movements.

and 2 in the Finnish summary). In particular, nodding is a partner oriented signal, used to give feedback, and to signal turn giving. Nodding indicates cooperation: the speaker is engaged in interaction and willing to listen to the partner. The other head gestures, back/forward movements, tilt, sideways turning, and waggle are mostly used to elicit feedback, and also co-occur with turn holding events. We may assume that the speakers use them for regulating the reception of their own speech rather than backchannelling what the partner has said.

In summary, head gestures seem to convey two significantly different visual signalling patterns: nodding is a partner-oriented signal and almost exclusively used to give feedback or the turn to the partner, while other head movements are related to holding one's own turn, during which the speaker's visual signals are interpreted as feedback eliciting signals.

4.2 Hand gesturing

Table 3 shows that hand gestures usually employ both hands, they contain slightly more often single stroke than repeated ones, and they indicate rhythm of the speech (beating). From Table 1 we also notice that 68% of the turn related gestures occur with turn holding, 20% with turn giving, and 10% with turn taking events. Almost 70% of hand gestures are used for eliciting rather than giving feedback, which agrees with Battersby (2011) who demonstrated that the speakers gesture more than the listeners.

Hand movements	Count	Percent	Hand movements	Count	Percent
Handedness			**Interpretation**		
Both hands	265	66 %	Deixis	8	2 %
One hand	137	34 %	Emphasis	19	5 %
Repetition			Rhythm	185	46 %
Repeated	174	43 %	Other	188	47 %
Single stroke	220	55 %			
Other	8	2 %	**Total movements**	**402**	**100 %**

Table 3: Feature values and their frequency in the three hand movement types.

Figures 3 and 4 in the Finnish summary show gesturing patterns with respect to feedback and turn-taking. Most communicative gestures can be one-stroke or repeated, but there is a tendency to give feedback and give turns with repeated gesturing. Single stroke hand gestures co-occur slightly more with feedback elicitation, but the difference is not significant. It is interesting, however, that when taking the turn, 85% of gestures are one-stroke. This suggests that the next speaker prepares for their turn by moving their hands into a kind of "speaking position" which would allow them to gesture in rhythm with their speaking. It has been shown that the gesture peak co-occurs with the speech stress (Krahmer and Swerts, 2007; Kendon, 2004), and thus the non-repetitive turn taking gestures may actually be part of the embodied speech production:

through such gesturing the partners indicate that they are ready to speak. Single stroke gestures signal turn taking and thus effectively prevent the speaker from continuing their turn.

The speaker's turn-holding gestures seem to be rhythmic movements that accompany the speech rather than intend to catch the partner's attention. Gullberg and Holmqvist (1999) showed that the listeners do not look at the speaker's gesturing (but at their face), and that the listener's gaze follows the speaker's hand movement only if the speaker has focussed their attention on their hand, too. Bavelas and Chovil (2000) talk about the meaning of gestures with respect to the degree of redundancy between a gesture and the co-occurring utterance, and notice that reference to the common ground deploys smaller and less explicit gestures, whereas gesturing associated with novel referents is larger and explicit. We can hypothesize that the speaker's continuous gesturing is a behaviour pattern associated with their turn holding and simultaneous feedback elicitation: the speaker can unobtrusively refer to the shared information and elicit feedback by small gesturing, without needing to put the intention into explicit words. We can also speculate that the partner's single stroke gestures are attention catchers that invite the speaker to give the turn, without explicit verbal confrontation or competition for the floor. More gesturing can indicate that the interlocutors are excited and thus active in taking turns and eliciting feedback from their partner.

To summarise, hand gestures in our data are used for feedback eliciting and turn holding. We conform to the assumption that speech and gesturing are closely linked in the production process, and presented an observation concerning gestures and turn-taking to support this view: most turn-taking gestures are single stroke gestures related to the speakers adjusting themselves into a speaking position where beat gesturing is easy to produce.

4.3 Body movement

Only about 9% of the communicative multimodal signalling is assigned to body movements (Table 1), most of them forward or sideways orientations (Table 4). An interesting, novel observation in our data is that sideways orientation relates to turn holding, while the body facing the partner (possibly moving forward and backward) opens up a turn exchange (Tables 5 6). Also, body posture sideways elicits feedback, whereas body movement backward and forward gives feedback.

Body movements	**Count**	**Percent**
Backwards	15	16 %
Forward	37	38 %
LeaningSideways	41	43 %
Other	3	3 %
Total	**96**	**100 %**

Table 4: Feature values and their frequency in body movements.

Body posture seems to have an iconic function in interaction. The posture where the speaker is squarely towards the partner is potentially challenging, but a sideways posture avoids direct face-to-face interaction and gives the speaker a wider transactional space to plan contributions and to hold the turn. Standing sideways locks the space and direct back/forward movement, and consecuently prevents the partner from entering the space. Kendon (2010) describes spatial organization of the speakers in group conversations with the notion of f-formation ('facing formation'). In two-party conversations, we can say that the speakers tend to control turn-taking by similar spatial orientation: by facing or turning away from the partner.

5 Interlocutors' own assessments and communicative activity

We also compared the interlocutors own assessments of the interactions with the observed communicative activity in the same interaction. It is assumed that multimodal activity in giving feedback and taking turns can be used to estimate the interlocutors' communicative activity and engagement in the conversation in general: the more multimodal activity, the more engaged the interlocutors are in the activity. We also hypothesize that the interlocutor's self-assessment of the interaction is related to the amount of their communicative activity: the more engaged (i.e. the more active) the interlocutor is, the more positive impression she has about the interaction.

	Mean	Min	Max		Mean	Min	Max
Enjoyable	3.7	3	4	Anxious	1.9	1	4
Friendly	2.5	1	3	Natural	2.6	1	4
Impressive	2.1	1	4	Happy	2.6	1	4
Nice	4.0	3	5	Tense	1.9	1	4
Interesting	3.8	2	5	Awkward	2.1	1	4
Relaxed	3.0	2	4	Angry	1.3	1	1
				Average	**2.6**		

Table 5: Statistics of the self assessment questionnaire.

Self-assessments were based on a questionnaire where the users rated their interaction with respect to a set of descriptive adjectives on a Likert-scale 1 – 5, with 1 meaning 'I disagree, the interaction was not like this at all' and 5 meaning 'I agree, the interaction was very much like this'. Table 5 shows the mean, minimum and maximum values for each adjective. In general, participants found the interactions enjoyable, nice, and interesting (mean values of 3.5, 3.9, and 3.6). Ratings for the negative impressions, angry, tense and anxious, are clearly lower.

Interlocutor	Gender	Activity	Assessment	Turn-taking
1	F	3.9	2.42	103
2	F	5.5	2.58	106
3	M	1.7	2.58	99
4	F	2.6	2.67	107
5	F	4.8	2.58	123
6	F	7.5	2.92	107
7	F	2.6	2.25	95
8	M	1.7	2.08	96
9	F	1.5	-	93
10	M	0.9	2.17	74
11	M	0.6	2.50	74
Mean		3.0	2.4	

Table 6: The interlocutors' gender, average activity, self assessment mean score and turn-takings.

Table 6 lists the interlocutors' self-assessment mean score, multimodal activity with respect to the length of the interaction (Activity), and the number of turn-takings in the interaction (self assessment from participant 9 is missing). The table shows that the normalized multimodal activity has a rather large variation (mean = 2.7, standard deviation = 2.1), contrary to the interlocutors' self-assessments (mean = 2.2, standard deviation = 0.25). We can also notice that the speakers with most turn-taking activity (the speakers 4, 5, and 6 who all have more than 100 turn-takings in their interactions) have self-assessment values which are above the mean values, i.e. they have positive impressions of the interactions. This allows us to hypothesise that communicative activity and positive evaluation are related. However, we cannot conclude which way the causal relationship goes: maybe the positive impressions are due to the interlocutor's communicative activity, or maybe the large activity is due to the interlocutor's positive attitude. It is likely that the relation is not either-or, since impressions can change during the encounters, and the participants' predisposition may also affect their activity.

Considering the correlations between individual descriptors in the interlocutors' self-assessment and their communicative activity, we found a statistically significant correlation ($p<0.05$) between the activity and 'happiness' (0.688).

6 Conclusion

In this paper we have looked at non-verbal activity from a holistic point of view related to interaction control and feedback. We studied the participants' multimodal behaviour patterns, and correlated them with their engagement in the interaction and their self-reported impressions of the interaction. We found a positive dependence between the objective measures of communicative activity and the speakers' own impressions of the interaction, although the direction of the relation cannot be concluded. Considering the hypotheses set in Section 3, we identified the relation between head movements and feedback to concern nodding, while the other head movements correlated with turn holding. The hypothesis about hand gesturing and feedback elicitation seems to hold, but we also further specified single stroke hand gestures to be used to coordinate the interaction and turn-taking. This is also supported by the fact that motor activity accompanies speech: listener's gestures are related to their intention to take the turn while the speaker's gestures coincide with the stress of their utterances. Finally, correlations were found with respect to body movements and turn-taking, with an observation of the iconic function of body posture: the sideways posture seems to indicate turn-holding. In general, the results are interesting and unique, requiring further investigations.

Future studies can also answer the questions concerning the relative contribution of visual and vocal communication to multimodal interaction in general. Moreover, it is useful to investigate what are the optimal units for information exchange, and what is the role of context in the interpretation of these signals. It is necessary to use a larger corpus (e.g. all 16 dialogues, and even more) to draw more comprehensive conclusions. We are also in the process of exploring automatic analysis techniques for the recognition of visual signals.

Acknowledgments

Thanks to NOMCO partners in Gothenburg and Copenhagen for data collection and comparison, and to Emmi Toivio, Joonas Toivio, and Johanna Reinikainen for analysis of the Finnish data.

References

Allwood, J. (2002). Bodily Communication – Dimensions of Expression and Content. In Granström, B., House, D., and Karlsson, I., editors, *Multimodality in Language and Speech Systems*, pages 7–26. Kluwer Academic Publishers, Dordrecht.

Allwood, J., Cerrato, L., Jokinen, K., Navarretta, C., and Paggio, P. (2007). The MUMIN Coding Scheme for the Annotation of Feedback, Turn Management and Sequencing. *Language Resources and Evaluation*, 41(3–4):273–287.

André, E. and Pelachaud, C. (2010). Interacting with embodied conversational agents. In Cheng, F. and Jokinen, K., editors, *Speech Technology: Theory and Applications*, pages 123–150. Springer.

Argyle, M. and Cook, M. (1976). *Gaze and Mutual Gaze*. Cambridge University Press.

Battersby, S. (2011). *Moving Together: the organization of Non-verbal cues during multiparty conversation*. PhD thesis, Queen Mary, University of London.

Bavelas, J. and Chovil, N. (2000). Visible Acts of Meaning. An Integrated Message Model of Language in Face-to-Face Dialogue. *Journal of Language and Social Psychology*, 19(2):163–194.

Bennewitz, M., Faber, F., Joho, D., and Behnke, S. (2007). Fritz - a humanoid communication robot. In *Proceedings of the 16th IEEE International Symposium on Robot and Human Interactive Communication (RO-MAN)*.

Boholm, M. and Allwood, J. (2010). Repeated head movements, their function and relation to speech. In *Workshop on Multimodal Corpora: Advances in Capturing, Coding and Analyzing Multimodality*.

Chartrand, T. L. and Bargh, J. A. (1999). The chameleon effect: The perception-behavior link and social interaction. *Journal of Personality and Social Psychology*, 76:893–910.

Crystal, D. (1975). Paralinguistics. In Benthall, J. and Polhemus, T., editors, *The body as a medium of expression*, pages 162–174. London: Institute of Conteporary Arts.

Csapo, A., Gilmartin, E., Grizou, J., Han, J., Meena, R., Anastasiou, D., Jokinen, K., and Wilcock, G. (2012). Multimodal conversational interaction with a humanoid robot. In *Proceedings of 3rd IEEE International Conference on Cognitive Infocommunications (CogInfoCom 2012)*, Kosice.

Feldman, R. and Rim, B. (1991). *Fundamentals of Nonverbal Behavior*. Cambridge University Press, Cambridge.

Goodwin, C. (2000). Action and embodiment within situated human interaction. *Journal of Pragmatics*, 32:1489–1522.

Gullberg, M. and Holmqvist, K. (1999). What speakers do and what listeners look at. A comment on visual deixis and mimesis. *Pragmatics and Cognition*, 7:35–63.

Jokinen, K. (2010). Pointing gestures and synchronous communication management. In Esposito, A., Campbell, N., Vogel, C., Hussein, A., and Nijholt, A., editors, *Development of Multimodal Interfaces: Active Listening and Synchrony*, pages 33–49. Springer.

Jokinen, K., Harada, K., Nishida, M., and Yamamoto, S. (2010). Turn-alignment using eye-gaze and speech in conversational interaction. In *Proceedings of 11th International Conference on Spoken Language Processing (Interspeech 2010)*, Makuhari, Japan.

Jokinen, K. and Pärkson, S. (2011). Synchrony and copying in conversational interactions. In *The 3rd Nordic Symposium on Multimodal Interaction*, Helsinki.

Jokinen, K. and Scherer, S. (2012). Embodied communicative activity in cooperative conversational interactions - studies in visual interaction management. In *Acta Polytechnica. Journal of Advanced Engineering*.

Jokinen, K. and Wilcock, G. (2012). Multimodal open-domain conversations with the Nao robot. In *Fourth International Workshop on Spoken Dialogue Systems (IWSDS 2012)*, Paris.

Kendon, A. (2004). *Gesture: Visible action as utterance*. Cambridge University Press.

Kendon, A. (2010). Spacing and orientation in co-present interaction. In *Lecture Notes in Computer Science, 5967*, pages 1–15. Springer.

Koller, A., Garoufi, K., Staudte, M., and Crocker, M. (2012). Enhancing referential success by tracking hearer gaze. In *Proceedings of the 13th Annual Meeting of the Special Interest Group on Discourse and Dialogue (SIGdial)*, Seoul, South Korea.

Krahmer, E. and Swerts, M. (2007). The effects of visual beats on prosodic prominence: Acoustic analyses, auditory perception and visual perception. *Journal of Memory and Language*, 57(3):396–414.

Lee, J., Marsella, T., Traum, D., Gratch, J., and Lance, B. (2007). The Rickel Gaze Model: A Window on the Mind of a Virtual Human. In *Proceedings of the 7th International Conference on Intelligent Virtual Agents (IVA-2007). Springer Lecture Notes in Artificial Intelligence 4722*, pages 296–303, SpringerVerlag Berlin Heidelberg.

Nakano, Y. and Nishida, T. (2007). Attentional behaviours as nonverbal communicative signals in situated interactions with conversational agents. In Nishida, T., editor, *Engineering Approaches to Conversational Informatics*. John Wiley.

Navarretta, C., Ahlsén, E., Allwood, J., Jokinen, K., and Paggio, P. (2012). Feedback in Nordic first-encounters: a comparative study. In *Proceedings of Eighth International Conference on Language Resources and Evaluation (LREC 2010)*, Istanbul.

Paggio, P., Allwood, J., Ahlsén, E., Jokinen, K., and Navarretta, C. (2010). The NOMCO Multimodal Nordic Resource - Goals and Characteristics. In *Proceedings of Seventh International Conference on Language Resources and Evaluation (LREC 2010)*, pages 2968–2973, Valletta, Malta. European Language Resources Association (ELRA).

Pickering, M. and Garrod (2004). Towards a mechanistic psychology of dialogue. *Behavioral and Brain Sciences*, 27:169–226.

Qu, S. and Chai, J. (2009). The role of interactivity in human-machine conversation for automatic word acquisition. In *Proceedings of the SIGDIAL Conference 2009*, pages 188–195.

Swartout, W., Traum, D., Artstein, R., Noren, D., Debevec, P., Bronnenkant, K., Williams, J., Leuski, A., Narayanan, S., and Piepol, D. (2010). Ada and Grace: Toward realistic and engaging virtual museum guides. In *International Conference on Intelligent Virtual Agents (IVA)*, pages 286–300.

Toivio, E. and Jokinen, K. (2012). Multimodal Feedback Signaling in Finnish. In *Proceedings of the Human Language Technologies - The Baltic Perspective*.

New Insights from Coarse Word Sense Disambiguation in the Crowd

Adam Kapelner[1] *Krishna Kaliannan*[1] *H. Andrew Schwartz*[2]
Lyle Ungar[2] *Dean Foster*[1]
(1) The Wharton School of the University of Pennsylvania, Department of Statistics,
3730 Walnut Street, Philadelphia, PA 19104
(2) University of Pennysivania, Department of Computer Science,
200 S. 33rd Street, Philadelphia, PA 19104
kapelner@wharton.upenn.edu, kkali@wharton.upenn.edu, hansens@seas.upenn.edu,
ungar@cis.upenn.edu, foster@wharton.upenn.edu

ABSTRACT
We use crowdsourcing to disambiguate 1000 words from among coarse-grained senses, the most extensive investigation to date. Ten unique participants disambiguate each example, and, using regression, we find surprising features which drive differential WSD accuracy: (a) the number of rephrasings within a sense definition is associated with higher accuracy; (b) as word frequency increases, accuracy decreases even if the number of senses is kept constant; and (c) spending more time is associated with a decrease in accuracy. We also observe that all participants are about equal in ability, practice (without feedback) does not seem to lead to improvement, and that having many participants label the same example provides a partial substitute for more expensive annotation.

KEYWORDS: Word sense disambiguation, crowdsourcing.

Proceedings of COLING 2012: Posters, pages 539–548,
COLING 2012, Mumbai, December 2012.

1 Introduction

Word sense disambiguation (WSD) is the process of identifying the meaning, or "sense," of a word in a written context (Ide and Véronis, 1998). In his comprehensive survey, Navigli (2009) considers WSD an AI-complete problem — a task which is at least as hard as the most difficult problems in artificial intelligence. Why is WSD difficult and what is driving its difficulty? This study examines human WSD performance and tries to identify drivers of accuracy. We hope that our findings can be incorporated into future WSD systems.

To examine human WSD performance, we tap pools of anonymous untrained human labor; this is known as "crowdsourcing." A thriving pool of crowdsourced labor is Amazon's Mechanical Turk (MTurk), an Internet-based microtask marketplace where the workers (called "Turkers") do simple, one-off tasks (called "human intelligence tasks" or "HITs"), for small payments. See Snow et al. (2008); Callison-Burch (2010); and Akkaya et al. (2010) for MTurk's use in NLP, and Chandler and Kapelner (2010) and Mason and Suri (2011) for further reading on MTurk as a research platform.

We performed the first extensive look at coarse-grained WSD on MTurk. We studied a large and variegated set of words: 1,000 contextual examples of 89 distinct words annotated by 10 unique Turkers each. In the closest related literature, Snow et al. (2008) found high Turker annotation accuracy but only annotated a single word, while Passonneau et al. (2011) focused on only a few words and annotated fine-grained senses. The extensive size of our study lends itself to the discovery of new factors affecting annotator accuracy.

Our contribution is three-fold. First, we use regression to identify a variety of factors that drive accuracy such as (a) the number of rephrasings within a sense definition is associated with higher accuracy; (b) as word frequency increases, accuracy decreases even if the number of senses is kept constant; and (c) time-spent on an annotation is associated with lower accuracy. Second, we echo previous findings, mostly from non-WSD experiments, demonstrating that Turkers are respectably accurate (Snow et al., 2008), they're approximately equal in ability (Parent, 2010; Passonneau et al., 2011), spam is virtually non-existent (Akkaya et al., 2010), responses from multiple Turkers can be pooled to achieve high quality results (Snow et al., 2008; Akkaya et al., 2010), and that workers do not improve with experience (Akkaya et al., 2010). Third, we present a system of crowdsourcing WSD boasting a throughput of about 5,000 disambiguations per day at \$0.011 per annotation.

2 Methods and data collection

We selected a subset of the OntoNotes data (Hovy et al., 2006), the SemEval-2007 coarse-grained English Lexical Sample WSD task training data (Pradhan et al., 2007). The coarse-grained senses in OntoNotes address a concern that nuanced differences in sense inventories drives disagreement among annotators (Brown et al., 2010). We picked 1,000 contextual examples at random from the full set of 22,281.[1] Our sample is detailed in table 1. It consisted of 590 nouns and 410 verb examples that had between 2-15 senses each (nouns: 5.7 ± 3.0 senses, verbs: 4.7 ± 3.3 senses). For each snippet, ten annotations were completed by ten *unique* Turkers.

[1]We later disqualified 9 of the 1,000 because they had words with only one sense.

target word	# inst	# senses	target word	# inst	# senses	target word	# inst	# senses
affect-v	1	3	end-v	8	4	policy-n	10	3
allow-v	8	2	enjoy-v	3	2	position-n	13	7
announce-v	4	3	examine-v	3	3	power-n	12	4
approve-v	3	2	exchange-n	17	6	president-n	34	3
area-n	15	5	exist-v	1	2	produce-v	6	3
ask-v	16	6	explain-v	2	2	promise-v	3	2
attempt-v	2	2	express-v	3	3	propose-v	1	3
authority-n	3	6	feel-v	24	3	prove-v	2	6
avoid-v	2	2	find-v	7	6	raise-v	6	9
base-n	5	12	fix-v	2	6	rate-n	49	2
begin-v	7	4	future-n	16	4	recall-v	2	4
believe-v	9	2	go-v	12	14	receive-v	4	2
bill-n	18	9	hold-v	5	10	regard-v	1	3
build-v	1	4	hour-n	9	4	remember-v	8	6
buy-v	7	7	job-n	6	10	remove-v	4	2
capital-n	15	5	join-v	2	4	report-v	7	4
care-v	6	3	keep-v	11	8	rush-v	1	4
carrier-n	4	13	kill-v	5	9	say-v	104	5
chance-n	5	4	lead-v	9	7	see-v	9	10
claim-v	4	4	maintain-v	3	4	set-v	10	12
come-v	7	11	management-n	13	2	share-n	103	3
complain-v	2	2	move-n	19	4	source-n	10	6
complete-v	1	3	need-v	11	2	space-n	2	8
condition-n	7	4	network-n	9	4	start-v	8	7
defense-n	8	8	occur-v	2	4	state-n	33	4
development-n	8	3	order-n	11	9	system-n	15	7
disclose-v	5	2	part-n	14	7	turn-v	19	15
do-v	4	6	people-n	38	6	value-n	16	5
drug-n	7	3	plant-n	12	3	work-v	4	9
effect-n	7	5	point-n	27	14			

Table 1: The 89 words of the sample of 1000 OntoNotes snippets used in this study. "# inst" is the number of instances in the 1,000 with the corresponding target word. "# senses" is the number of sense choices provided by OntoNotes.

2.1 The WSD HIT

We designed a simple WSD task that was rendered inside an MTurk HIT.[2] The Turker read one example in context with the target word emboldened, and then picked the best choice from among a set of coarse-grained senses (see Figure 1). We gave a text box for soliciting optional feedback and there was a submit button below. We term a completed HIT an "annotation."

We employed anti-spam and survey bias minimizing techniques to obtain better data. We faded in each word in the context and the sense choices one-by-one at 300 words/min.[3] Additionally, we randomized the display order of the sense choices. This reduces "first response alternative bias" as explained in Krosnick (1991), but may decrease accuracy when compared to displaying

[2]The HIT was entitled "Tell us the best meaning of a word... do many and earn a lot! Really Easy!", the wage was $0.01, the time limit for each task was seven minutes, and the HITs expired after one hour. We posted batches of 750 new HITs to MTurk hourly upon expiration of the previous batch. Thus, the task was found readily on the homepage which drove the rapid completion.

[3]As Kapelner and Chandler (2010) found, this accomplishes three things: (1) Turkers who plan on cheating will be more likely to leave our task, (2) Turkers will spend more time on the task and, most importantly, (3) Turkers will more carefully read and concentrate on the meaning of the text.

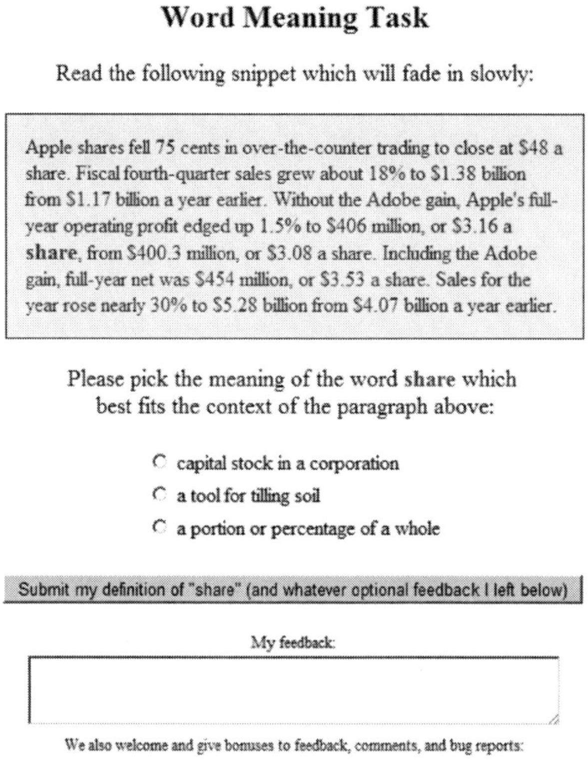

Figure 1: An example of the WSD task that appears inside an MTurk HIT. This was displayed piecewise as each word in the example ("snippet") and senses faded-in slowly.

the senses in descending frequency order as observed by Fellbaum et al. (1997). We also limited participation to US Turkers to encourage fluency in English.

Upon completion, the Turker was given an option to do another of our WSD tasks (this is the MTurk default). A Turker was not limited in the number of annotations they could do.[4] The entire study took 51 hours and cost $110. The code, raw data, and analysis scripts are available under GPL2 at `github.com/kapelner/wordturk_pilot`.

3 Results and data analysis

We were interested in investigating (1) which features in the target word, the context, and sense definition text affect Turker accuracy, (2) which characteristics in the Turker's engagement of the task affect accuracy, (3) heterogeneity in worker performance, and (4) the combination of Turker responses to boost accuracy.

We recruited 595 Turkers to work on our tasks, yielding an average accuracy of 73.4%. We measured inter-tagger agreement (ITA) using the alpha-reliability coefficient (Krippendorff, 1970) to be 0.66 (0.70 for nouns and 0.60 for verbs) which comports with Chklovski and Mihalcea (2003)'s *Open Mind Word Expert* system. However, OntoNotes was specially designed by Hovy et al. (2006) to have 90% ITA by experts. Our measure is significantly less. Untrained Turkers should not be expected to be experts.

[4]The actual upper limit was all 1,000 examples but in practice, not one Turker came close to completing all of them. The most productive Turker completed 405 annotations while the median completed was 4.

3.1 Performance and language characteristics

What makes WSD difficult for untrained Turkers? Are there too many senses to choose from? Is the example difficult to read? With 10,000 instances from 600 workers, we can attempt to answer these questions.

We first construct the features of interest:

- target word part-of-speech (***target word is noun?***)
- target word length in characters (***# chars in target word***)
- target word frequency (***log target word frequency***)
  log of frequency in the contemporary corpus of American English (Davies, 2008).
- number of senses to choose from (***# senses to disambiguate***)
- number of characters in the correct sense definition (***# chars in definition***)
- number of rephrasings in definition text (***# rephrasings in definition***)
  For example, the word "allot" has a sense with definition text "let, make possible, give permission" which would be counted as three rephrasings.
- number of characters in context (***# chars in context***)

We add a fixed intercept for each Turker to account for correlation among tasks completed by the same worker. The result of an ordinary least squares (OLS) regression of correct (as binary) on the variables above is presented in table 2.[5]

	estimate	$\|t\|$
target word is noun?	8.4%	7.5 ***
# chars in target word	-1.0%	3.6 ***
log target word frequency	-3.7%	7.6 ***
# senses to disambiguate	-2.9%	19.8 ***
# chars in definition	-0.063%	2.6**
# rephrasings in definition	3.4%	5.4 ***
# chars in context	-0.0062%	2.6 **

Table 2: OLS regression of instance correctness on features of the target word, context, and senses. Fixed effects for each of the 595 Turkers are not shown. ** indicates significance at the $< .01$ level, *** indicates significance at the <0.001 level.

We found that, controlling for all other variables, nouns have 8% higher disambiguation accuracy. This difference between noun and verb accuracy is also reflected in automatic system performance on the SemEval-2007 task (Pradhan et al., 2007), and often attributed to the idea that nouns "commonly denote concrete, imagible referents" (Fellbaum et al., 1997). For each extra sense, accuracy suffers 3% which also is expected since the Turkers have more choices. We show accuracy by number of senses and part of speech in figure 2. We also found the longer the target word, the more difficult the task, reflecting the fact that longer words are often more complex. Similarly, the longer the context or length of definitions decreased accuracy but the effect was quite small.

Surprisingly, with each extra rephrasing of the definition of the correct sense there is a gain of 3.5%. This suggests untrained annotators benefit from receiving a variety of sense descriptions, or that more rephrasings suggests a more coarse-grained sense which is easier for annotators to understand.

[5]We also ran a variety of fixed and random effects linear and logit models, all of which gave the same significance results. We chose to present the OLS output because of its familiarity and interpretability.

Finally, as the word becomes more common in the English language (controlling for all other variables, including length of word and number of senses) accuracy still suffers. Possibly the more prevalent the word in our language, the more likely it will have senses that overlap conceptually.

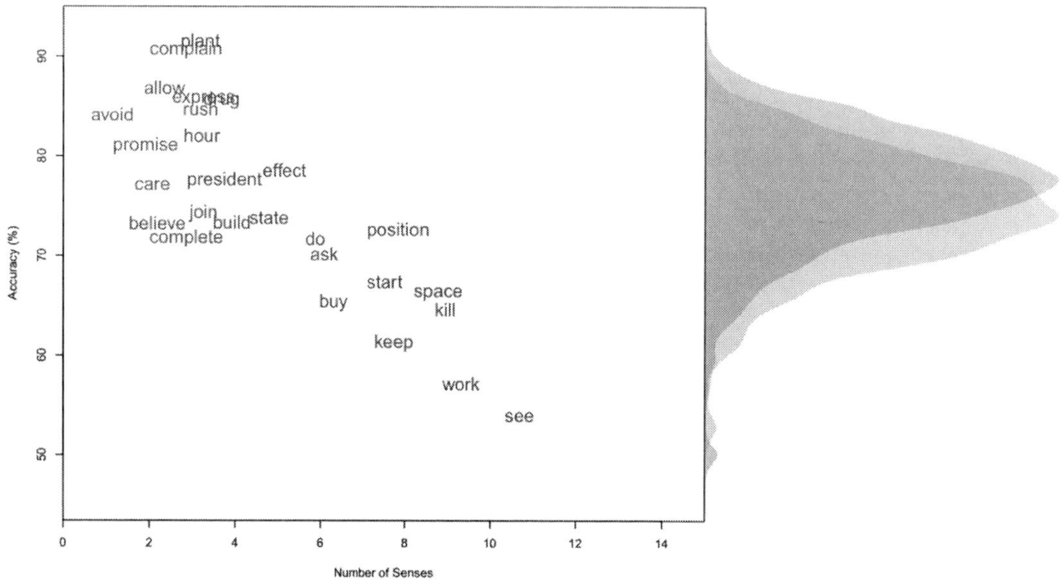

Figure 2: Predicted accuracy vs. number of senses for a sample of the words in our study. Nouns are blue; verbs are red. The densities are smoothed histograms of the noun and verb predicted accuracies. Note that the word display is jittered; there are at least two senses for each word.

3.2 Performance and Turker characteristics

Are there any characteristics about the Turker's engagement with our task that impacts accuracy? We create the following features: time spent on task, the number of words in their optional feedback message, and the number of annotations that worker completed prior to the response being examined. To control for the difficulty of each task, we added 1,000 fixed intercepts — one for each unique task; and to control for correlation among the workers, we added a fixed intercept for each worker. An ordinary least squares regression of the WSD task being correct (as binary) on the variables above[5] was run. We found that for each additional second spent on the task, accuracy drops by 0.06% ($p < 0.001$). We found that, contrary to Kapelner and Chandler (2010), leaving comments does not correspond to higher accuracy, and, in agreement with Akkaya et al. (2010), the number of tasks completed prior does not impact accuracy. This may imply that a learning effect does not exist; practice (without feedback) does *not* make perfect.

Surprisingly, spending more time on the disambiguation task associates with a significant *reduction* in accuracy ($p < 0.001$).[6] Note that this is *after* we non-parametrically control for instance difficulty and worker ability. For every additional minute spent, a Turker is 3.6% less likely to answer correctly. We posit three theories: (1) taking breaks leads to loss of

[6]We validated this linear approximation by regressing time spent as a polynomial and found the effect to be monotonically decreasing with a flat stretch in the middle.

concentration (2) the "knee-jerk" response is best (rumination should be discouraged), and (3) although we control for instance difficulty, an instance may only be difficult for particular workers as evidenced by their taking longer.

3.3 Turker equality

In order to replicate previous work, we investigate Turker equality and the presence of spammers and superstars via plotting the number of annotations correct by the number of annotations completed in figure 3. To test the null hypothesis that all workers are equal (and thus, average), each worker's *total contributions* are assumed to be drawn from independent Binomial random variables with probability of success $p = 73.4\%$ (the experimental average). Does the worker's confidence interval (CI) contain p? Figure 3 reveals that every worker has approximately the same capacity for performing coarse-grained WSD except for two above-average superstars and two below-average.

To test for spammers, we test against the null hypothesis of random answering, $p = 25.5\%$ (determined by simulation). Among workers who did a significant number of tasks,[7] we find only one worker who may be a spammer. We echo Akkaya et al. (2010), Snow et al. (2008), and Singh et al. (2002) and conclude there is minimal spammer contribution. Once again, we do not observe a change in accuracy by quantity of tasks completed, an observation confirmed using regression (table 3).

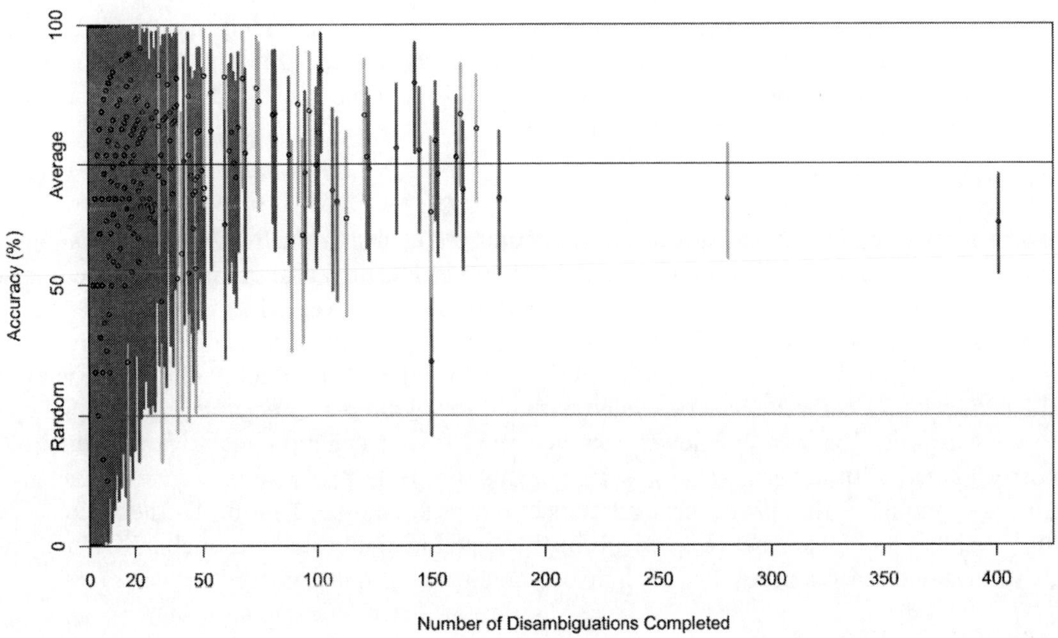

Figure 3: Accuracy of all 595 Turkers. The black line is the average accuracy ($p = 73.4\%$) and the purple line represents random sense choice accuracy (25.5%). We plot the Bonferroni-corrected Binomial proportion confidence intervals in green if they include p, yellow if the non-Bonferroni-corrected confidence intervals do not include p, and red if neither include p.

[7] We do not have significant power to claim a worker has accuracy of even 50% until about $n = 79$ at the Bonferroni-corrected α level.

3.4 Combining responses to optimize prediction

We can combine the 10 unique disambiguation responses for each of the 1000 examples to yield higher accuracy. Our algorithm is naive — we take the plurality vote and arbitrate ties randomly. Snow et al. (2008) found such an approach results in higher accuracy for disambiguating 'president'. We wondered if the same is true for our more extensive dataset and annotations.

# of Annotations	2	3	4	5	6	7	8	9	10	2.4 (1st plurality)
Accuracy	.734	.795	.808	.824	.830	.837	.840	.843	.857	.811

Table 3: Accuracy of the WSD task using plurality voting for different numbers of Turkers. The last column is the accuracy of the variable algorithm: starting with two workers and adding an additional worker until plurality.

Table 4 illustrates our results. There is an overall accuracy of 85.7% when annotations from all workers are aggregated. This is in the ballpark of the best supervised statistical learning techniques which boast almost 90% (Pradhan et al., 2007).[8] We determined the marginal accuracy of each added Turker by simulating random subsets of two Turkers, three Turkers, etc and employed the same plurality vote.

With techniques such as discarding results from annotators who often disagree, and giving the annotators sense choices in order of sense frequency, we could likely achieve higher accuracy.

Given MTurk annotation costs, we believe this system can be extended to accurately disambiguate a million words a year at 80% accuracy for about $25,000. This demonstrates the system's potential for mass annotation, but we reiterate that the main goal of this current work was to gain insight into drivers of WSD accuracy.

Conclusion

We performed the first extensive study of crowdsourced coarse-grained word sense disambiguation in order to gain insight into the behavioral and linguistic features that affect accuracy of the untrained annotations. As expected, we found results improved when there were less sense choices or when the target word was a noun, and that untrained workers did not improve with experience. However, we also discovered surprising insights: (1) the number of rephrasings in the correct sense definition corresponded with improved annotator accuracy, (2) frequency of target word corresponded with lower accuracy, and (3) time-spent on an individual annotation corresponded with lower accuracy. It also seems that time pressure may increase accuracy. Future experiments that prove these relationships causally may be fruitful. Lastly, we looked at Turker ability and found that they are all roughly equal in ability, and although individually not as accurate as experts, many Turkers may be pooled to improve accuracy.

Acknowledgments

We thank Mark Liberman and Lynn Selhat for helpful comments and discussions. Adam Kapelner thanks the National Science Foundation for the Graduate Research Fellowship that made this work possible.

[8]Note that this is not a fair comparison. These supervised algorithms were given all the training data while Turkers were *not* given any previous examples. They also arbitrated based on the senses' frequencies while we randomized the order that the senses appeared in. Finally, they were not limited to polysemous words as we were.

References

Akkaya, C., Conrad, A., and Wiebe, J. (2010). Amazon mechanical turk for subjectivity word sense disambiguation. In *Proceedings of the NAACL HLT 2010 Workshop on Creating Speech and Language Data with Amazon's Mechanical Turk*, pages 195–203.

Brown, S. W., Rood, T., and Palmer, M. (2010). Number or nuance: Which factors restrict reliable word sense annotation? In *LREC: The International Conference on Language Resources and Evaluation*, pages 3237–3243.

Callison-Burch, C. (2010). Creating speech and language data with Amazon's Mechanical Turk. *NAACL HLT Workshop on Creating Speech and Language Data with Amazon's Mechanical Turk*, pages 1–12.

Chandler, D. and Kapelner, A. (2010). Breaking monotony with meaning: Motivation in crowdsourcing markets. *University of Chicago mimeo*.

Chklovski, T. and Mihalcea, R. (2003). Exploiting agreement and disagreement of human annotators for word sense disambiguation. In *Proceedings of the Conference on Recent Advances on Natural Language Processing*.

Davies, M. (2008). *The Corpus of Contemporary American English: 425 million words, 1990-present. Available online at http://corpus.byu.edu/coca/.*

Fellbaum, C., Grabowski, J., Landes, S., and L, S. (1997). Analysis of a hand-tagging task. In *Proceedings of ANLP-97 Workshop on Tagging Text with Lexical Semantics*, pages 34–40.

Hovy, E., Marcus, M., Palmer, M., Ramshaw, L., and Weischedel, R. (2006). OntoNotes: the 90 percent solution. In *Proceedings of the Human Language Technology Conference of the NAACL, Companion Volume: Short Papers on XX*, pages 57–60. Association for Computational Linguistics.

Ide, N. and Véronis, J. (1998). Introduction to the special issue on word sense disambiguation: the state of the art. *Computational Linguistics*, 24(1):2–40.

Kapelner, A. and Chandler, D. (2010). Preventing Satisficing in Online Surveys: A "Kapcha" to Ensure Higher Quality Data. In *CrowdConf ACM Proceedings*.

Krippendorff, K. (1970). Estimating the Reliability, Systematic Error and Random Error of Interval Data. *Educational and Psychological Measurement*, 30(1):61–70.

Krosnick, J. A. (1991). Response strategies for coping with the cognitive demands of attitude measures in surveys. *Applied Cognitive Psychology*, 5(3):213–236.

Mason, W. and Suri, S. (2011). Conducting behavioral research on Amazon's Mechanical Turk. *Behavior research methods, Forthcoming*.

Navigli, R. (2009). Word sense disambiguation: A Survey. *ACM Computing Surveys*, 41(2):1–69.

Parent, G. (2010). Clustering dictionary definitions using Amazon Mechanical Turk. *NAACL HLT 2010 Workshop on Creating Speech and Language Data with Amazon's Mechanical Turk*, pages 21–29.

Passonneau, R. J., Bhardwaj, V., Salleb-Aouissi, A., and Ide, N. (2011). Multiplicity andword sense: Evaluating and learning from multiply labeledword sense annotations. *Language Resources and Evaluation*.

Pradhan, S., Loper, E., and Dligach, D. (2007). Semeval-2007 task-17: English lexical sample, srl and all words. In *Proceedings of the 4th International Workshop on Semantic Evaluations (SemEval-2007)*, pages 87–92.

Singh, P., Lin, T., Mueller, E., Lim, G., Perkins, T., and Li Zhu, W. (2002). Open Mind Common Sense: Knowledge acquisition from the general public. *On the Move to Meaningful Internet Systems 2002: CoopIS, DOA, and ODBASE*, pages 1223–1237.

Snow, R., O'Connor, B., Jurafsky, D., and Ng, A. Y. (2008). Cheap and fast—but is it Good?: Evaluating Non-expert Annotations for Natural Language Tasks. In *EMNLP '08: Proceedings of the Conference on Empirical Methods in Natural Language Processing*, pages 254–263, Morristown, NJ, USA. Association for Computational Linguistics.

A Unified Sentence Space for Categorical Distributional-Compositional Semantics: Theory and Experiments

*Dimitri KARTSAKLIS Mehrnoosh SADRZADEH Stephen PULMAN**
DEPARTMENT OF COMPUTER SCIENCE, UNIVERSITY OF OXFORD
Wolfson Building, Parks Road, Oxford OX1 3QD, UK
firstname.lastname@cs.ox.ac.uk

ABSTRACT
This short paper summarizes a faithful implementation of the categorical framework of Coecke et al. (2010), the aim of which is to provide compositionality in distributional models of lexical semantics. Based on Frobenius Algebras, our method enable us to (1) have a unifying meaning space for phrases and sentences of different structure and word vectors, (2) stay faithful to the linguistic types suggested by the underlying type-logic, and (3) perform the concrete computations in lower dimensions by reducing the space complexity. We experiment with two different parameters of the model and apply the setting to a verb disambiguation and a term/definition classification task with promising results.

KEYWORDS: semantics, compositionality, distributional models, category theory, Frobenius algebra, vector space models, disambiguation, definition classification.

* Support by EPSRC grant EP/F042728/1 is gratefully acknowledged by the first two authors.

Proceedings of COLING 2012: Posters, pages 549–558,
COLING 2012, Mumbai, December 2012.

1 Introduction

Distributional models of meaning work by building co-occurrence vectors for every word in a corpus depending on its context, following Firth's intuition that "you should know a word by the company it keeps" (Firth, 1957). In such models, the co-occurrence vector of each word is built by fixing a set of words as the basis of a vector space and a window of size k, then counting how many times the word in question has co-occurred with each base in that window. This approach has been proved useful in many natural language tasks (Curran, 2004; Schütze, 1998; Landauer and Dumais, 1997; Manning et al., 2008), but until now it lacks any means of compositionality that would allow the combination of two word vectors into a new one following some grammar rule. In fact, compositional abilities of distributional models have been subject of much discussion and research in recent years. For example, Mitchell and Lapata (2008) present results for intransitive sentences, Erk and Padó (2004) work on transitive verb phrases, while Baroni and Zamparelli (2010) and Guevara (2010) provide comprehensive analyses of adjective-noun phrases. Despite the experimental strength of these approaches, most of them only deal with phrases and sentences of two words. On the other hand, Socher et al. (2010, 2011) use recursive neural networks in order to produce vectors for sentences of arbitrary length with good results. However, their method is somehow detached from the formal semantics view, paying little attention to the grammatical relations that hold between the words.

Following a different path, Coecke et al. (2010) provide a solution that offers compositional abilities to distributional models while at the same time avoids all the above pitfalls. Based on the abstract setting of category theory, the authors develop a generic mathematical framework whereby the meaning of a sentence of any length and structure can, in principle, be turned into a vector, following the rules of the grammar. Implementations of this model for transitive and intransitive sentences have been provided by Grefenstette and Sadrzadeh (2011a,b). However, although their method outperforms the multiplicative and additive models of Mitchell and Lapata (2008) on simple transitive sentences, it has a non-scalability problem. Specifically, the concrete structures used in the actual computations are not faithful to the linguistic types of the underlying type-logic, hence the model does not generalize to more complex phrases and sentences where a relational structure can be found nested in another relational structure. Furthermore, the vectors obtained for sentences of different grammatical structures live in different vector spaces: sentences with intransitive verbs live in the same space as context vectors, denoted by N, sentences with transitive verbs in $N^2 = N \otimes N$, and sentences with ditransitive verbs in N^3. A direct consequence of this instantiation is that one cannot compare meanings of sentences unless they have the same grammatical structure.

In this work we outline a solution to the above problems by instantiating the sentence space to be the same space as one in which context vectors live, namely we stipulate that $S = N$. As a result of this decision, we become able to compare lexical meanings of words with compositional meanings of phrases and sentences. We show how the theoretical computations of Coecke et al. (2010) instantiate in this concrete setting, and how the Frobenius Algebras, originating from group theory (Frobenius, 1903) and later extended to vector spaces (Coecke et al., 2008), allow us to not only represent meanings of words with complex roles, such as verbs, adjectives, and prepositions, in an intuitive relational manner, but also to stay faithful to their original linguistic types. Equally as importantly, this model enables us to realize the concrete computations in lower dimensional spaces, thus reduce the space complexity of the implementation.

We experiment in two different tasks with promising results: First, we repeat the disambiguation experiment of Grefenstette and Sadrzadeh (2011a) for transitive verbs. Then we proceed to a novel task: We use The Oxford Junior Dictionary (Sansome et al., 2000), Oxford Concise School Dictionary (Hawkins et al., 2004), and WordNet in order to derive a set of term/definition pairs, measure the similarity of each term with every definition, and use this measurement to classify the definitions to specific terms.

2 An overview of the categorical model

Using the abstract framework of category theory, Coecke et al. (2010) equip the distributional models of meaning with compositionality in a way that every grammatical reduction is in one-to-one correspondence with a linear map defining mathematical manipulations between vector spaces. In other words, given a sentence $s = w_1 w_2 \cdots w_n$ there exists a syntax-driven linear map f from the context vectors of the individual words to a vector for the whole sentence:

$$\overrightarrow{s} = f(\overrightarrow{w_1} \otimes \overrightarrow{w_2} \otimes \cdots \otimes \overrightarrow{w_n}) \tag{1}$$

allowing us to compare the synonymy of two different sentences as if they were words, by constructing their vectors and measuring the distance between them. This result is based on the fact that the base type-logic of the framework, a *pregroup grammar* (Lambek, 2008), shares the same abstract structure with vector spaces, that of a *compact closed category*. If P is the free pregroup generated by such a grammar and **FVect** the category of finite dimensional vector spaces (with linear maps) over $\mathbb{R}$, it is possible then for one to work on the product category **FVect** $\times P$, pairing each grammatical type $\alpha \in P$ with a vector space V to an object (V, α). More importantly, the morphisms of this product category will be pairs of linear maps and pregroup reductions between these objects of the following form:

$$(f, \leq) : (V, p) \to (W, q) \tag{2}$$

leading from the grammatical type p and its corresponding vector space V to type q and the vector space W.

Pregroups A pregroup grammar (Lambek, 2008) is a type-logical grammar built on the rigorous mathematical basis of pregroups, i.e. partially ordered monoids with unit 1, whose each element p has a left adjoint p^l and a right adjoint p^r, that is

$$p^l p \leq 1 \leq p p^l \quad \text{and} \quad p p^r \leq 1 \leq p^r p \tag{3}$$

Each element p represents an atomic type of the grammar, for example n for noun phrases and s for sentences. Atomic types and their adjoints can be combined to form compound types, e.g. $n^r s n^l$ for a transitive verb. The rules of the grammar are prescribed by the mathematical properties of pregroups, and specifically by the inequalities in (3) above. A partial order in the context of a logic denotes implication, so from (3) we derive:

$$p^l p \to 1 \quad \text{and} \quad p p^r \to 1 \tag{4}$$

These cancellation rules to the unit object are called ϵ maps, and linear-algebraically correspond to the inner product between the involved context vectors. It also holds that $1p = p = p1$. We will use the case of a transitive sentence as an example. Here, the subject and the object have the type n, whereas the type of the verb is $n^r s n^l$, denoting that the verb looks for a noun at its left and a noun at its right in order to return an entity of type s (a sentence). The derivation has the form $n(n^r s n^l)n = (nn^r)s(n^l n) \to 1s1 = s$, and corresponds to the morphism $\epsilon_N \otimes 1_S \otimes \epsilon_N : N \otimes N \otimes S \otimes N \otimes N \to S$ which returns a vector living in S.

For details of pregroup grammars and its type dictionary we refer the reader to Lambek (2008). For more information about the compositional-distributional framework, see Coecke et al. (2010); Coecke and Paquette (2011) provide a good introduction to category theory.

3 Instantiating the sentence space

The categorical framework of Coecke et al. (2010) is abstract in the sense that it does not prescribe concrete guidelines for constructing tensors for meanings of words with special roles such as verbs or adjectives. Even more importantly, it does not specify the exact form of the sentence space S, leaving these details as open questions for the implementor.

3.1 Stipulating $S = N \otimes N$

The work of Grefenstette and Sadrzadeh (2011a) was the first large-scale practical implementation of this framework for intransitive and transitive sentences, and thus a first step towards providing some concrete answers to these questions. Following ideas from formal semantics that verbs are actually relations, the authors argue that the distributional meaning of a verb is a weighted relation representing the extent according to which the verb is related to its subjects and objects. In vector spaces, these relations are represented by linear maps, equivalent to matrices for the case of binary relations and to tensors for relations of arity n. Hence transitive verbs can be represented by matrices created by structurally mixing and summing up all the contexts (subject and object pairs) in which the verb appears. More precisely, we have:

$$\overline{verb} = \sum_i (\overrightarrow{sbj_i} \otimes \overrightarrow{obj_i}) \tag{5}$$

where $\overrightarrow{sbj_i}$ and $\overrightarrow{obj_i}$ are the context vectors of subject and object, respectively, and i iterates over all contexts in which the specific verb occurs. This method (which we refer to as "relational") is also extended to other relational words, such as adjectives whose vectors are constructed as the sum of all the nouns that the adjective modifies.

One important design decision was that the meaning of a sentence was represented as a rank-n tensor, where n is the number of arguments for the head word of the sentence. In other words, an intransitive sentence lives in a space $S = N$, a transitive one in $S = N \otimes N$ and so on. Although this approach delivers good results for the disambiguation task on which it was tested, it inherently suffers from two important problems, the most obvious of which is that there is no direct way to compare sentences of different structures, say an intransitive one with a transitive one. Furthermore, the representation of the meaning of a sentence or a phrase as a rank-n tensor with $n > 1$ limits the ability of the model to scale up to larger fragments of the language, where more complex sentences with nested or recursive structure can occur, since the concrete objects used in the actual mathematical operations are not any more faithful to the linguistic types. Finally, the above design decision means that the space complexity of the algorithm is $\Theta(d^n)$, where d is the cardinality of the vector space and n the number of arguments for the head word. This could create certain space problems for complex sentences.

3.2 Stipulating $S = N$

The work presented in this paper stems from the observation that the theory does not impose a special choice of sentence space, in particular it does not impose that tensors for S should have ranks greater than 1. Hence we stipulate that $S = N$ and show how this instantiation works by performing the computations on the example transitive sentence 'dogs chase cats'. Take $\overrightarrow{dog}$ and $\overrightarrow{cat}$ be the context vectors for the subject and the object, both living in N as prescribed by their types. As any vector, these can be expressed as weighted sums of their basis vectors, that is, $\overrightarrow{dog} = \sum_i c_i^{dog} \overrightarrow{n_i}$ and $\overrightarrow{cat} = \sum_k c_k^{cat} \overrightarrow{n_k}$. On the other hand, the type of the verb indicates that this entity should live in N^3, represented by $\overline{chase} = \sum_{ijk} c_{ijk}^{chase} (\overrightarrow{n_i} \otimes \overrightarrow{n_j} \otimes \overrightarrow{n_k})$. By putting everything together, the meaning of the sentence is calculated as follows; this result lives in N, since it is a weighted sum over $\overrightarrow{n_j}$:

$$\epsilon_n^r \otimes 1_s \otimes \epsilon_n^l (\overrightarrow{dog} \otimes \overline{chase} \otimes \overrightarrow{cat}) = \sum_{ijk} c_{ijk}^{chase} \langle \overrightarrow{dog} | \overrightarrow{n_i} \rangle \langle \overrightarrow{n_k} | \overrightarrow{cat} \rangle \overrightarrow{n_j} \tag{6}$$

An important consequence of our design decision is that it enables us to reduce the space complexity of the implementation from $\Theta(d^n)$ (Grefenstette and Sadrzadeh, 2011a) to $\Theta(d)$, making the problem much more tractable. What remains to be solved is a theoretical issue, that in practice the meaning of relational words such as 'chase' as calculated by Equation 5 is a matrix living in N^2—however, the mathematical framework above prescribes that it should be a rank-3 tensor in N^3. The necessary expansions are achieved by using Frobenius algebraic operations, for which the following sections first provide the mathematical definitions and then a linguistic justification.

4 Frobenius Algebras

Frobenius algebras were originally introduced by F. G. Frobenius in group theory (Frobenius, 1903). Since then they have found applications in other fields of mathematics and physics, e.g. see Kock (2003). Carboni and Walters (1987) provided a general categorical definition, according to which a Frobenius algebra over a monoidal category $(\mathscr{C}, \otimes, I)$ is a tuple $(F, \sigma, \iota, \mu, \zeta)$ consisting of an associative coalgebra (σ, ι) and an associative algebra (μ, ζ), respectively given by the following types:

$$\sigma : F \to F \otimes F \qquad \iota : F \to I \qquad \mu : F \otimes F \to F \qquad \zeta : I \to F$$

The above should satisfy the *Frobenius condition*, stating that $(\mu \otimes 1_F) \circ (1_F \otimes \sigma) = (1_F \otimes \mu) \circ (\sigma \otimes 1_F) = \sigma \circ \mu$. For the case of the category **FVect** over a field I (for us $I = \mathbb{R}$), these morphisms become linear maps that form a Frobenius algebra over a vector space N with a fixed set of bases $\{\overrightarrow{n_i}\}_i$, explicitly given as follows (Coecke et al., 2008):

$$\sigma :: \overrightarrow{n_i} \mapsto \overrightarrow{n_i} \otimes \overrightarrow{n_i} \qquad \iota :: \overrightarrow{n_i} \mapsto 1 \qquad \mu :: \overrightarrow{n_i} \otimes \overrightarrow{n_i} \mapsto \overrightarrow{n_i} \qquad \zeta :: 1 \mapsto \overrightarrow{n_i}$$

Since the bases of our vector spaces are orthonormal, these maps moreover form a *special commutative* Frobenius algebra, meaning that they correspond to a uniform copying and uncopying of the basis vectors. When applied to $v \in N$, the copying map σ recovers the bases of v and the unit map ι their corresponding weights. Together, they faithfully encode tensors of a lower dimensional N into a higher dimensional tensor space $N \otimes N$. In linear algebraic terms, $\sigma(v)$ is a diagonal tensor whose diagonal elements consist of weights of v. The uncopying map μ, on the other hand, loses some information when encoding a higher dimensional tensor into a lower dimensional space. For $w \in N \otimes N$, we have that $\mu(w)$ is a tensor consisting only of the diagonal elements of w, hence losing the information encoded in the non-diagonal part.

5 Frobenius parameters in distributional linguistic practice

It would be instructive to see how our decision for taking $S = N$ and the Frobenius constructions affect the meaning of a sentence in practice. We use a pictorial calculus that allows convenient graphical representations of the derivations. In this notation, each tensor is represented by a triangle, and its rank can be determined by the outgoing wires. The tensor product is depicted as juxtaposition of triangles. We also remind to the reader that the relational method for constructing a tensor for the meaning of a verb (Grefenstette and Sadrzadeh, 2011a) provides us with a matrix in N^2. In order to embed this in N^3, as required by the categorical framework, we apply a $\sigma : N^2 \to N^3$ map to it. Now the Frobenius operation σ gives us some options for the form of the resulting tensor, which are presented below:

CpSbj The first option is to copy the "row" dimension of the matrix which, according to Equation 5, corresponds to the subject. In Part (a) below we see how σ transforms the verb this way. Once substituted in Equation 1, we obtain the interaction in Part (b). Linear algebraically, the σ map transforms the matrix of the verb in the way depicted on the right:

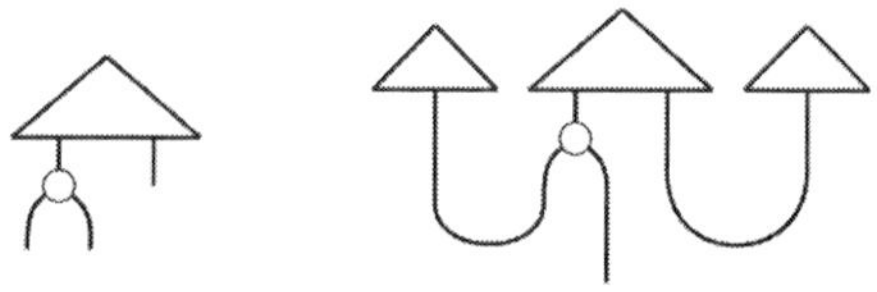

$$\sigma :: \sum_{ij} c_{ij}(\overrightarrow{n_i} \otimes \overrightarrow{n_j}) \mapsto \sum_{iij} c_{ii}(\overrightarrow{n_i} \otimes \overrightarrow{n_i} \otimes \overrightarrow{n_j})$$

(a) (b)

CpObj Our other option is to copy the "column" dimension of the matrix, i.e. the object dimension (the corresponding σ map again on the right):

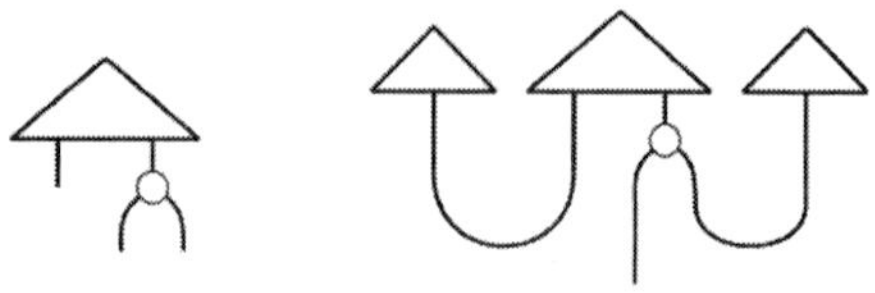

$$\sigma :: \sum_{ij} c_{ij}(\overrightarrow{n_i} \otimes \overrightarrow{n_j}) \mapsto \sum_{ijj} c_{jj}(\overrightarrow{n_i} \otimes \overrightarrow{n_j} \otimes \overrightarrow{n_j})$$

(a) (b)

Geometrically, we can think of these two options as different ways for "diagonally" placing a plane into a cube. The diagrams provide us a direct way to simplify the calculations involved, since they suggest a closed form formula for each case. Taking as an example the diagram of the copy-subject method, we see that: (a) the object interacts with the verb; (b) the result of this interaction serves as input for the σ function; (c) one wire of the output of σ interacts with the object, while the other branch delivers the result. In terms of linear algebra, this corresponds to the computation $\sigma(\overline{verb} \times \overrightarrow{obj}) \times \overrightarrow{sbj}$ (where $\times$ denotes matrix multiplication), which is equivalent to the following:

$$\overrightarrow{sbj\ verb\ obj} = \overrightarrow{sbj} \odot (\overline{verb} \times \overrightarrow{obj}) \tag{7}$$

where the symbol $\odot$ denotes component-wise multiplication and $\times$ is matrix multiplication. Similarly, the meaning of a transitive sentence for the copy-object case is given by:

$$\overrightarrow{sbj\ verb\ obj} = \overrightarrow{obj} \odot (\overline{verb}^T \times \overrightarrow{sbj}) \tag{8}$$

We should bring to the reader's attention the fact that equipped with the above closed forms we do not need to create or manipulate rank-3 tensors at any point of the computation, something that would cause high computational overhead. Furthermore, note that the nesting problem of Grefenstette and Sadrzadeh (2011a) does not arise here, since the linguistic and concrete types are the same.

6 Experiments

We train our vectors from a lemmatised version of the British National Corpus (BNC), following closely the parameters of the setting described in Mitchell and Lapata (2008), later used by Grefenstette and Sadrzadeh (2011a). Specifically, we use the 2000 most frequent words as the basis for our vector space; this single space will serve as a semantic space for both nouns and sentences. The weights of the vectors are set to the ratio of the probability of the context word given the target word to the probability of the context word overall. As our similarity measure we use the cosine distance.

6.1 Disambiguation

We first test our models against the disambiguation task for transitive sentences described in Grefenstette and Sadrzadeh (2011a). The goal is to assess how well a model can discriminate between the different senses of an ambiguous verb, given the context (subject and object) of that verb. The entries of this dataset consist of a target verb, a subject, an object, and a landmark verb used for the comparison. One such entry for example is, "write, pupil, name, spell". A good compositional model should be able to understand that the sentence "pupil write name" is closer to the sentence "pupil spell name" than, for example, to "pupil publish name". On the other hand, given the context "writer, book" these results should be reversed. The dataset contains 200 such entries with verbs from CELEX, hence 400 sentences. The evaluation of this experiment is performed by calculating Spearman's ρ correlation against the judgements of 25 human evaluators. As our baselines we use an additive (ADDTV) and a multiplicative (MULTP) model, where the meaning of a sentence is computed by adding and point-wise multiplying, respectively, the context vectors of its words.

The results are shown in Table 1. The most successful $S = N$ model for this task is the copy-object model, which is performing really close to the original relational model of Grefenstette and Sadrzadeh (2011a), with the difference to be statistically insignificant. This is a promising result, since it suggests that the lower-dimensional new model performs similarly with the richer structure of the old model for transitive sentences, while at the same time allows generalisation to even more complex sentences[1]. More importantly, note that the categorical models are the only ones that respect the word order and grammatical structure of sentences; a feature completely dismissed in the simple multiplicative model.

	Upper-bound	ADDTV	MULTP	CPSBJ	CPOBJ
ρ	0.620	0.050	0.163	0.143	**0.172**

Table 1: Disambiguation results. Upper-bound denotes the inter-annotator agreement.

6.2 Definition classification

The ability of reliably comparing the meaning of single words with larger textual fragments, e.g. phrases or even sentences, can be an invaluable tool for many challenging NLP tasks, such as definition classification, paraphrasing, sentiment analysis, or even the simple everyday search on the Internet. In this task we examine the extent to which our models can correctly match a number of terms (single words) with a number of definitions (phrases). To our knowledge, this is the first time a compositional distributional model is tested for its ability to match words with phrases. Our dataset consists of 112 terms (72 nouns and 40 verbs) and their main definitions, extracted from The Oxford Junior Dictionary (Sansome et al., 2000). For each term, and in order to get a richer dataset, we added two more definitions that expressed the same or an

[1]The original relational model of Grefenstette and Sadrzadeh (2011a) with $S = N^2$, provided a ρ of 0.21. When computed with our program with the exact same parameters (without embedding them in the $S = N$ model), we obtained a ρ of 0.195. The differences between both of these and our best model are statistically insignificant. In Grefenstette and Sadrzadeh (2011b), a direct non-relational model was used to compute verb matrices; this provided a ρ of 0.28. However, as explained by the authors themselves, this method is not general and for instance cannot be used for intransitive verbs.

Term	Main definition	Def. 2	Def. 3
blaze	large strong fire	huge potent flame	substantial heat
husband	married man	partner of a woman	male spouse
apologise	say sorry	express regret or sadness	acknowledge shortcoming or failing
embark	get on a ship	enter boat or vessel	commence trip

Table 2: Sample of the dataset for the term/definition comparison task.

alternative meaning, using the entries from the Oxford Concise School Dictionary (Hawkins et al., 2004) or by paraphrasing with the WordNet synonyms of the words in the definitions. So in total we obtained three definitions per term. In all cases a definition for a noun-term is a noun phrase, whereas the definitions for the verb-terms consist of verb phrases. For the latter case, we construct our verb vectors by summing over all context vectors of objects with which the verb appears in the corpus in a verb phrase; that is, we use $\overline{verb} = \sum_i \overrightarrow{obj_i}$. A sample of the dataset is shown in Table 2; the complete dataset will be made available online.

We approach the evaluation problem as a classification task, where the terms have the role of the classes. Specifically, we calculate the distance between each definition and every term in the dataset, and the definition is assigned to the term that gives the higher similarity. We evaluate the results by calculating accuracy (Table 3). Our model is referred to as the copy-object model (CPOBJ), and is compared with the multiplicative and additive models. The copy-object and multiplicative models perform similarly, with the former to have slightly better performance for nouns and the latter to be slightly better for verbs. We speculate that this lesser ability of our model in verbs terms is due to data sparsity, since the cases of pure verb phrases (from which we build the verb vectors for this task) are limited in BNC and not every verb of our dataset had a well-populated vector representation.

	CPOBJ	MULTP	ADDT	CONT
Nouns	**0.24**	0.22	0.17	0.09
Verbs	0.28	**0.30**	0.25	0.07

Table 3: Accuracy results for the term/definition comparison task.

7 Conclusion

The contribution of this work is that it provides a faithful implementation of the general categorical compositional distributional model of Coecke et al. (2010), with three important advantages compared to previous attempts: (1) it makes possible to compare phrases and sentences with different structures, up to the extreme case of comparing a sentence with a single word; (2) it follows the types suggested by the type-logical approaches, hence enables us to build concrete vectors for nested relational phrases; and (3) drastically reduces the space complexity of previous implementations. We achieved this using operations of Frobenius Algebras over vector spaces to expand and shrink the dimensions of the concrete tensors involved in the actual computations. This theoretical result stands on its own right, since it provides a framework that can be used in conjunction with various compositional-distributional settings and techniques. For example, one could populate the relational matrices using machine-learning techniques, as Baroni and Zamparelli (2010) tried for adjective-noun pairs, and then apply the categorical framework for the composition as described in this paper. As a proof of concept for the viability of our method, we presented experimental results in two tasks involving disambiguation and definition classification.

References

Baroni, M. and Zamparelli, R. (2010). Nouns are Vectors, Adjectives are Matrices. In *Proceedings of Conference on Empirical Methods in Natural Language Processing (EMNLP)*.

Carboni, A. and Walters, R. (1987). Cartesian Bicategories I. *Journal of Pure and Applied Algebra*, 49.

Coecke, B. and Paquette, E. (2011). Categories for the Practicing Physicist. In Coecke, B., editor, *New Structures for Physics*, pages 167–271. Springer.

Coecke, B., Pavlovic, D., and Vicary, J. (2008). A New Description of Orthogonal Bases. *Mathematical Structures in Computer Science*, 1.

Coecke, B., Sadrzadeh, M., and Clark, S. (2010). Mathematical Foundations for Distributed Compositional Model of Meaning. Lambek Festschrift. *Linguistic Analysis*, 36:345–384.

Curran, J. (2004). *From Distributional to Semantic Similarity*. PhD thesis, School of Informatics, University of Edinburgh.

Erk, K. and Padó, S. (2004). A Structured Vector-Space Model for Word Meaning in Context. In *Proceedings of Conference on Empirical Methods in Natural Language Processing (EMNLP)*, pages 897–906.

Firth, J. (1957). A synopsis of linguistic theory 1930–1955. In *Studies in Linguistic Analysis*.

Frobenius, F. (1903). Theorie der Hyperkomplexen Gröβen. *Sitzung der Phys.-Math*, pages 504–538.

Grefenstette, E. and Sadrzadeh, M. (2011a). Experimental Support for a Categorical Compositional Distributional Model of Meaning. In *Proceedings of Conference on Empirical Methods in Natural Language Processing (EMNLP)*.

Grefenstette, E. and Sadrzadeh, M. (2011b). Experimenting with Transitive Verbs in a DisCoCat. In *Proceedings of Workshop on Geometrical Models of Natural Language Semantics (GEMS)*.

Guevara, E. (2010). A Regression Model of Adjective-Noun Compositionality in Distributional Semantics. In *Proceedings of the ACL GEMS Workshop*.

Hawkins, J., Delahunty, A., and McDonald, F. (2004). *Oxford Concise School Dictionary*. Oxford University Press.

Kock, J. (2003). Frobenius Algebras and 2D Topological Quantum Field Theories. In *London Mathematical Society Student Texts*. Cambridge University Press.

Lambek, J. (2008). *From Word to Sentence*. Polimetrica, Milan.

Landauer, T. and Dumais, S. (1997). A Solution to Plato's Problem: The Latent Semantic Analysis Theory of Acquision, Induction, and Representation of Knowledge. *Psychological Review*.

Manning, C., Raghavan, P., and Schütze, H. (2008). *Introduction to Information Retrieval*. Cambridge University Press.

Mitchell, J. and Lapata, M. (2008). Vector-based Models of Semantic Composition. In *Proceedings of the 46th Annual Meeting of the Association for Computational Linguistics*, pages 236–244.

Sansome, R., Reid, D., and Spooner, A. (2000). *The Oxford Junior Dictionary*. Oxford University Press.

Schütze, H. (1998). Automatic Word Sense Discrimination. *Computational Linguistics*, 24:97–123.

Socher, R., Huang, E., Pennington, J., Ng, A., and Manning, C. (2011). Dynamic pooling and unfolding recursive autoencoders for paraphrase detection. *Advances in Neural Information Processing Systems*, 24.

Socher, R., Manning, C., and Ng, A. (2010). Learning continuous phrase representations and syntactic parsing with recursive neural networks. In *Proceedings of the NIPS-2010 Deep Learning and Unsupervised Feature Learning Workshop*.

A Knowledge-Based Approach to Syntactic Disambiguation of Biomedical Noun Compounds

Ramakanth KAVULURU and Daniel HARRIS
Division of Biomedical Informatics, University of Kentucky, Lexington, KY, USA
{ramakanth.kavuluru, daniel.harris}@uky.edu

ABSTRACT
Noun compounds (NCs) provide a convenient way of communicating complex biomedical concepts in natural language. New NCs evolve with scientific progress in various fields and are often not included in standard dictionaries. Thus, semantic analysis of NCs is an important task in applications including ontology alignment, semantic data integration, information extraction, and question answering. A first step in such analysis is the syntactic grouping or bracketing of the constituent nouns. The state-of-the-art in bracketing is mostly limited to compounds with three nouns using empirical studies involving corpora like the Web or Medline biomedical research article citations. Here, we present an alternative knowledge-based approach using the Unified Medical Language System (UMLS) concept labels and definitions for NCs with three or four tokens. Experiments indicate that our method offers comparable accuracy with those that use the Web or Medline for 3-token NCs. Preliminary evaluations with 4-token NCs also point to the potential of our approach to bracketing longer NCs.

KEYWORDS: noun compounds, bracketing, terminologies, knowledge-based methods.

Translation in **Telugu**

Title: జీవ-వైద్య శాస్త్రాలలో ఎదురయ్యే ఆంగ్ల సమ్మేళన నామవాచక వాక్య-నిర్మాణ సందిగ్ధతను తొలగించే ఒక శాస్త్ర-జ్ఞానాధారిత విధానం

Authors: రమాకాంత్ కవులూరు, డేనియల్ హారిస్

Abstract: ఆంగ్లములో క్లిష్టమైన జీవ, వైద్య శాస్త్ర భావనలను సహజ భాషలో వ్యక్తపరచుటకు సమ్మేళన నామవాచకాలు ఒక అనుకూలమైన మార్గాన్ని అందిస్తాయి. శాస్త్రీయ ప్రగతితో పరిణమించే క్రొత్త సమ్మేళన పదాలు ప్రామాణిక నిఘంటువుల్లో సాధారణంగా చేర్చబడవు. అందువలన, జ్ఞాన సంపుటి సంకరణం, జ్ఞానానుసంధానం, జ్ఞాన సంగ్రహణం, మరియు సందేహ నివృత్తి వంటి అనువర్తనాలలో సమ్మేళన వాక్యార్థ విశ్లేషణ ఒక ముఖ్యమైన దశ. అటువంటి విశ్లేషణలో సమ్మేళనం లోని అనుసంధాన నామవాచకాల నిర్మాణ వర్గీకరణ ఒక మొదటి పని. ఆధునిక వర్గీకరణ విధానాలు ఎక్కువగా వెబ్ మరియు వ్యాస సారాంశాల పై అనుభావిక అధ్యయనాల ద్వారా త్రిపద సమ్మేళనాలకే వర్తిస్తాయి. ఈ వ్యాసం లో మేము జీవ-వైద్య పరిభాష సంపుటి - యూనిఫైడ్ మెడికల్ లాంగ్వేజ్ సిస్టం - లో ఉండే భావనల పేర్లు మరియు వాటి నిర్వచనాలను ఉపయోగించి త్రిపద-చతుర్పద సమ్మేళనాలను వర్గీకరించే ఒక జ్ఞానాధారిత ప్రత్యామ్నాయ విధానాన్ని ప్రవేశపెడుతున్నాము. త్రిపద సమ్మేళన ప్రయోగాలలో మా పద్ధతి వెబ్ లేదా వ్యాససారాంశాలు వినియోగించే ఇతర పద్ధతులతో పోల్చదగిన ఖచ్చితత్వం అందిస్తుంది. చతుర్పద సమ్మేళనాలతో జరిపిన ముందస్తు పరిశీలనలు, మా విధానాలు మరింత పొడుగైన సమ్మేళనాల నిర్మాణ వర్గీకరణలో కూడా ఉపయోగపడే సామర్థ్యాన్ని సూచిస్తున్నాయి.

Keywords: సమ్మేళన నామవాచకాలు, వాక్య నిర్మాణ వర్గీకరణ, పరిభాషలు, జ్ఞానాధారిత పద్ధతులు

Proceedings of COLING 2012: Posters, pages 559–568,
COLING 2012, Mumbai, December 2012.

1 Introduction

Noun compounds are noun phrases that are comprised of tokens each of which is a noun. For example `cell count` or `colon cancer` are examples of NCs with two tokens. Although these examples are easy to interpret for a human reader, in general, the semantic content of a noun compound cannot be automatically extracted based on the constituent nouns. In the NCs `olive oil`, `baby oil`, and `fuel oil` the relationship between the second token 'oil' with the corresponding first tokens 'olive', 'baby', and 'fuel' is clearly different. However, in these cases, there is a way of deriving the meaning of the NCs using the constituent words. There are other non-compositional NCs, such as `baby boomer`, `snake oil`, and `olive branch`, where the meaning of the constituent tokens cannot be composed to arrive at the semantic interpretation of the corresponding NCs. In biomedical domains, we often see NCs with 3 or more tokens, where there is additional ambiguity with regards to the syntactic association among the constituent tokens that can lead to different semantic interpretations. Consider the NCs `cancer cell line` and `cancer cell apoptosis`. The first NC is the cell line (immortal cell sample) from a cancerous tumor and the latter is about the apoptosis (programmed cell death) of cancer cells. Thus, we see that, although the part-of-speech tags are exactly the same for both NCs, the syntax trees[1]

(cancer (cell line)) and ((cancer cell) apoptosis)

are different. Since the semantic interpretation closely follows the syntactic interpretation (referred to as bracketing henceforth), it is an important task to correctly bracket NCs.

1.1 Motivation

Biomedical language processing poses several challenges including significant lexical variation, synonymy, polysemy, latent and implicit semantic content, and long sentences with long range compositional dependencies (Friedman and Johnson, 2006). NCs occur frequently in biomedical articles and clinical narratives, and are also found in labels of concepts in biomedical ontologies. Correctly bracketing NCs has applications in ontology alignment, semantic mappings, information extraction, question answering, and other informatics applications in biomedicine. In ontology alignment, identifying concept pairs from two different ontologies that are equivalent or involved in a specific relationship is an essential task. Concept labels together with interrelationships among concepts are used to achieve this goal. But these labels are often NCs and require appropriate interpretation to determine equivalence and identify relationships. NC analysis is also useful in generating semantic mappings where complex biomedical entities in relationships extracted from raw text need to be mapped to appropriate concepts in standard terminologies. Query expansion and modification using relevance feedback for recall oriented search tasks also benefit from NC analysis.

1.2 Related Work

Standard natural language processing tools do not exist for NC bracketing. Both chunkers and deep parsers — including the latest versions of Stanford parser (de Marneffe et al.,

[1] For NCs, these are always binary trees, also representable using binary bracketings. The number of possible ways of binary bracketing n elements is given by the famous n-th Catalan number $\frac{(2n)!}{(n+1)!n!}$.

2006) and Enju parser (Matsuzaki et al., 2007) — do not offer bracketing for NCs. Linguists and computer scientists have been studying NC bracketing mostly in non-biomedical domains in the recent past. Pustejovsky et al. (1993) used the frequencies of adjacent tokens in an NC to determine left or right bracketing for 3-token NCs. Lauer (1995) used the dependency model for NC bracketing based on frequencies of bi-grams in Grolier's encyclopedia achieving 80% accuracy on a dataset of 3-token NCs extracted from the encyclopedia. Recently, Keller and Lapata (2003) used the Web bi-gram counts and Girju et al. (2005) used decision trees for supervised NC bracketing to achieve similar results on Lauer's dataset.

Nakov and Hearst (2005) used new lexical surface features such as possessive markers, hyphenated or concatenated tokens, and capitalization and conducted several experiments using Web n-gram counts to achieve a 90% accuracy using a majority vote on the results of various techniques for Lauer's dataset. Their work is the first and the only attempt to perform bracketing of biomedical NCs. They also constructed a dataset of 430 three-token NCs from Medline[2] abstracts and achieved 95% accuracy using the majority vote of 23 different methods. Bergsma et al. (2010) used support vector machines with n-gram counts and binary lexical features to achieve an accurarcy of 88% with Nakov's dataset. Although these datasets contain NCs outside their original full context (e.g., the full sentences they occur in), the assumption made by all these efforts and our current effort is that effect of the context is not significant to identifying the bracketing option that corresponds to the most frequently used (or well accepted) interpretation. So the correct bracketing of an NC is assumed to be the one that reflects the compositional nature of its most frequent interpretation.

Currently, to the best of our knowledge, there are no attempts on bracketing 4-token NCs, although there were cumulative accuracy results for general noun phrases of arbitrary length by Pitler et al. (2010). Also, earlier 3-token NC bracketing methods are based on large corpora and have only been tested on non-biomedical datasets, with the exception of Nakov and Hearst (2005). Our approach is knowledge-based in that we only use the labels and definitions of UMLS[3] concepts to bracket biomedical NCs. Treating the label and concept definition set as a corpus, we bracketed NCs with techniques based on frequency and relatedness measures. We used the biomedical dataset used in the thesis by Nakov (2007) for 3-token NCs. We also tested our approach on separate 3- and 4-token NC datasets that we constructed by parsing biomedical abstracts (Section 3.1) since Nakov's set was mostly left bracketed. Our results indicate comparable performance to corpus based methods for the 3-token NCs and perform 40% better than random guessing for the 4-token NC dataset.

2 Knowledge-Based NC Bracketing Approach

We use the UMLS Metathesaurus (or just UMLS) as the knowledge base for the bracketing task. UMLS is an ongoing National Library of Medicine (NLM) effort that is an integration of 161 biomedical terminologies with about 2.6 million concepts and 8.6 unique concept names. A new version is released each year with updates from included source vocabularies and additional new terminologies. Besides maintaining the inter-concept relationships provided by the source vocbularies, UMLS also has concept mappings between different terminologies; synonyms for different concepts are also maintained. Thus, UMLS is an excellent source of terminological information in biomedicine. For this paper we particularly

[2]`http://www.nlm.nih.gov/bsd/pmresources.html`
[3]`http://www.nlm.nih.gov/research/umls/`

use the English unique concept names and the definitions (when provided) of concepts in UMLS.

Before we proceed, we enumerate the bracketing possibilities for 3- and 4-token NCs. As seen in example in Section 1, 3-token NCs usually have two options - left and right bracketing. However, 4-token NCs have five options. If $w_1\, w_2\, w_3\, w_4$ is an NC, where each w_i is a single-token noun, we have

$$((w_1 w_2)w_3)w_4, \quad (w_1 w_2)(w_3 w_4), \quad (w_1(w_2 w_3))w_4,$$
$$w_1((w_2 w_3)w_4), \quad \text{and} \quad w_1(w_2(w_3 w_4)),$$

as the five possible bracketing options.

2.1 Frequency Based Greedy Bracketing

There are nearly 6 million unique English concept names (ignoring case) in UMLS that encompass several important topics. We treat the set of these labels as a small corpus and count frequencies of token subsequences (based on word boundaries) of NCs to be bracketed. The first approach is to use the raw frequencies to choose the most frequent groupings. Let $f(x)$ be the frequency of the phrase x in the UMLS concept name corpus. For an NC with n tokens denoted by $w_1\, w_2 \ldots w_n$, the frequency function $f(w_i w_{i+1} \cdots w_j)$, $1 \le i \le j \le n$, is the frequency of the phrase "$w_i\; w_{i+1} \ldots w_j$" in the corpus. For a 3-token NC $w_1\, w_2\, w_3$, if $f(w_1 w_2) > f(w_2 w_3)$, we choose left bracketing; otherwise, it is right bracketed. For 3-token NCs, we also employed the adjacency approach introduced by Pustejovsky et al. (1993) where instead of raw frequencies, simple proportions are used to determine left or right bracketing. Here, left bracketing is selected if $f(w_1 w_2)/f(w_2) > f(w_2 w_3)/f(w_3)$, otherwise right bracketing is chosen.

Algorithm 1 GREEDY-BRACKET-4NC (NC $w_1 w_2 w_3 w_4$)

Set $maxf = \max(f(w_1 w2), f(w_2 w_3), f(w_3 w_4))$
if $maxf = f(w_1 w_2)$ **then**
    if $\log_2(3).f(w_1 w_2 w_3) \ge f(w_3 w_4)$ **then**
        return $((w_1 w_2)w_3)w_4$
    else
        return $(w_1 w_2)(w_3 w_4)$
else if $maxf = f(w_2 w_3)$ **then**
    if $f(w_1 w_2 w_3) \ge f(w_2 w_3 w_4)$ **then**
        return $(w_1(w_2 w_3))w_4$
    else
        return $w_1((w_2 w_3)w_4)$
else
    if $\log_2(3).f(w_2 w_3 w_4) \ge f(w_1 w_2)$ **then**
        return $w_1(w_2(w_3 w_4))$
    else
        return $(w_1 w_2)(w_3 w_4)$

For 4-token NCs, we follow a greedy approach in choosing among the five possible options. Assuming $w_1\, w_2\, w_3\, w_4$ as the four-token NC, we use Algorithm 1 to choose the bracketing.

The intuition behind the algorithm is to use a bottom-up approach to bracket the most frequent adjacent token pair first, before bracketing longer subsequences. The pseudocode is mostly self explanatory, except that since these are raw frequencies, we use $\log_2(3)$ as a factor[4] to give more weight to the occurrence of three-token phrases when comparing them with two-token phrase frequencies.

In addition to using frequencies of NC tokens in the corpus of unique UMLS strings, we also experimented with frequency based and adjacency approaches using the set of all strings in the UMLS without ignoring duplicates arising out of identical concept labels from different terminologies. While considering unique strings gives more importance to the presence of a phrase in multiple unique UMLS labels, considering all strings gives more importance to the overall frequency with which a phrase appears in all labels, thus accounting for the association with multiple UMLS concepts.

2.2 Cohesion Measure Based Non-Greedy Bracketing

Raw frequency based approaches do not fully consider the relative frequencies of other tokens involved in an NC. For example, consider the NC `family health history`. Although the phrase 'family health' is more frequent than 'health history', we see that this NC is right bracketed as it is often interpreted as the health history of a family of an individual. Also, the greedy nature of the bracketing approach outlined in Algorithm 1 might not be ideal. For example, in the compound `liver membrane protein glycosylation`, the frequency of 'membrane protein' is higher than the frequencies of 'liver membrane' or 'protein glycosylation'. Using the greedy approach, (membrane protein) will be chosen as the first grouping. However, it turns out the correct bracketing has (liver membrane) as the first grouping with protein as its modifier. To counter this, we propose *bracketing cohesion* measures that provide a cohesion score based on the full structure of a bracketing choice. Once the cohesion measure is computed for all bracketing choices, the choice with the highest cohesion value is output as the correct bracketing.

Bracketing cohesion is a meta-measure based on other relatedness measures. Let $\mathscr{S}(t_1, t_2) \in [0, 1]$ be a measure that computes relatedness between any two given terms t_1 and t_2. Then, given a bracketing binary tree T, we define the corresponding bracketing cohesion measure

$$\mathbb{C}(T, \mathscr{S}) = \sum_{\text{non-leaf node } n \in T} \mathscr{S}(\text{left-child}(n), \text{right-child}(n)),$$

where left-node(n) and right-node(n) are the subsequences of NC tokens corresponding to the left and right children of node n. For example, let T be the bracketing tree shown in Figure 1 for the example used in this section. Then the cohesion measure value is $\mathscr{S}$(liver, membrane) + $\mathscr{S}$(liver membrane, protein) + $\mathscr{S}$(liver membrane protein, glycosylation).

Based on the cohesion values, the best bracketing is the one that corresponds to the bracketing tree T that maximizes[5] $\mathbb{C}(T, \mathscr{S})$. We note that this approach of using cohesion measures is generic and can be applied to NCs of any length. The intuition behind bracketing

[4]The general strategy is to use $\log_2$(# words in the term) as the weighting factor (Frantzi et al., 1998)

[5]When multiple trees have the same score, other ways of breaking the tie are needed; one can default to the most frequent bracketing tree in the observed data for that length. Also, the highest possible value for the cohesion measure for NCs of length n is $n-1$ since there are $n-1$ internal nodes and each $\mathscr{S}(t_1, t_2) \leq 1$.

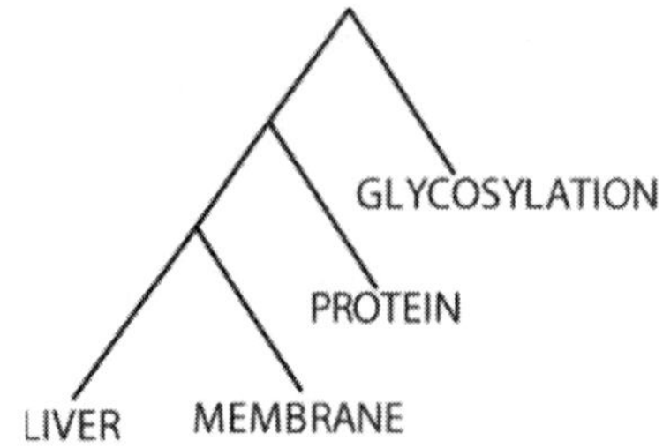

Figure 1: A bracketing tree for "Liver Membrane Protein Glycosylation"

cohesion is based on the observation that token subsequences in an NC that is compositional in nature are related to each other. Otherwise, they would not manifest in textual documents as NCs themselves and as parts of longer NCs. The intuition then is to model the relative suitability/validity of bracketing options for a given NC based on the strength of the relatedness between the subsequences that arise out of the tree structures corresponding to the bracketing options. For example, bracketing the NC in Figure 1 as (liver membrane) (protein glycosylation) would result in the cohesion value $\mathcal{S}$(liver, membrane) + $\mathcal{S}$(protein, glycosylation) + $\mathcal{S}$(liver membrane, protein glycosylation).

We experimented with three symmetric measures for $\mathcal{S}$. The first one is based on the Jaccard index – for two sets A and B, it is the ratio $\frac{|A \cap B|}{|A \cup B|}$, often used to measure resemblance of two sets of items. Translating this to the terms t_i and their frequencies $f(t_i)$, we have a measure

$$\mathcal{S}(t_1, t_2) = \frac{f(t_1 \wedge t_2)}{f(t_1) + f(t_2) - f(t_1 \wedge t_2)}.$$

Since this is a measure based on frequencies, we also used the UMLS label corpus with both unique strings and all strings which give us a total of two measures.

We also use a third measure that uses available concept definitions in the UMLS that are obtained from different source vocabularies and are more descriptive than the concept labels. Pedersen et al. (2007) derived second-order context vectors for UMLS concepts that capture the frequently co-occurring words in the definitions of concepts and certain concept neighbors (nodes reachable by one-hop), hence the name second-order, in the UMLS Metathesaurus relationship graph. They define a relatedness measure using the cosine of the normalized context vectors for any given UMLS concept pair. We call this measure UMLSRel[6] and use this as an option for $\mathcal{S}$ to compute cohesion in our experiments based on a local installation of the Perl modules made available by Pedersen et al. (2007). Other measures, such as mutual information can also be used for $\mathcal{S}$ when computing cohesion measures.

3 Experiments and Evaluation

We applied the methods elaborated in Section 2 to the biomedical 3-token NC dataset constructed by Nakov and Hearst (2005); Nakov (2007). This dataset has 430 biomedical NCs of which 84% are left bracketed. We separately constructed both 3-token and 4-token NC datasets that were bracketed by two biomedical researchers.

[6]If one of the terms does not correspond to a UMLS concept or if neither the term nor its neighbors have a definition, the relatedness value is treated as zero. This usually happens with longer terms with 3 or more tokens.

3.1 Construction of Datasets

We used Natural Language Tool Kit (NLTK (Bird et al., 2009)) to sample and parse approximately 175,000 biomedical research article abstracts from NLM's Pubmed web service. Using NLTK's chunker we sorted 3- and 4-token NCs based on their frequencies and manually selected 100 from each set according to the sorted order. For the 3-token NCs, the selection was done to maintain a rouch balance between possible left and right bracketed NCs while still going in the sorted order. Following the extraction, two biomedical researchers (not the authors) independently bracketed the datasets. The annotator agreement was 90% for our 3 NC dataset (NC) and it was 59% for the 4-token NC set (4NC). We note that expected agreement by chance is only 20% for 4-token NCs because of five possible choices, while it is 50% for the 3-token case. Since we started out with 100 NCs in each data set, we finally have 90 in the 3-token set and 59 in the 4-token set. Of the 90 three-token NCs, 42 are right bracketed; for the 59 NCs in the UK-4NC set, the bracketing choice $((w_1 w_2) w_3) w_4$ is the most frequent, with 32 instances, although, as explained in the next section, for 10 of these 32 cases annotators felt that the bracketing option $(w_1 w_2)(w_3 w_4)$ also applied. These gold standard bracketed NC files used for the experiments are provided here: `http://protocols.netlab.uky.edu/~rvkavu2/bracketing.html`.

3.2 Experiments and Discussion

For the 3-token NCs we used seven techniques to do the bracketing. The first four are the raw frequency based methods and the adjacency model based frequency proportion method outlined in Section 2.1, considering both the unique strings and all strings in the UMLS labels. These are denoted by `Freq`, `Adj`, `Freq_uniq`, `Adj_uniq` in Table 1. The next two methods are based on the bracketing cohesion method when the relatedness measure used in computing cohesion is based on the Jaccard index, again using all labels and only unique labels denoted by `Jaccard` and `Jaccard_uniq` respectively in the table. The final method uses the bracketing cohesion approach based on the context vector based UMLSRel (Pedersen et al., 2007) as discussed in Section 2.2. For the 4-token NCs, we used five techniques where the first two are based on the greedy frequency based bracketing approach outlined in Algorithm 1 using all UMLS strings and then using only unique strings separately. The next two methods pick the best bracketing option based on the cohesion measures of all possible bracketing options using the Jaccard index, again, using all strings and then only unique strings. Finally, the UMLSRel (Pedersen et al., 2007) measure is used for bracketing cohesion as outlined in Section 2.2. We also did a majority vote and defaulted to the most frequent option in the dataset to break ties. The results of these experiments are outlined in Tables 1 and 2.

From the results we see that frequency based approaches slightly outperformed other measures. The cohesion based methods slightly underperformed for the 3-token case compared to the frequency based measures. We attribute this to the nature of the measures chosen – both Jaccard index and UMLSRel are corpus based and moving beyond UMLS labels and definitions to corpus based approaches might be suitable. However, path based similarity measures based on the UMLS graph might be more suitable alternatives to be explored. We also computed majority vote based on our methods, which did not significantly improve the overall accuracy, although there were examples where some methods performed better than others. For the Nakov dataset, the majority vote with left bracketing as the tie-breaker improved the accuracy to 87% (up 3%). Nakov and Hearst (2005) use 23

Method	Nakov-3NC	3NC
Freq	84 %	89%
Freq_uniq	83%	85%
Adj	67%	78%
Adj_uniq	72%	77%
Jaccard	81%	75%
Jaccard_uniq	81%	74%
UMLSRel	79%	74%

Table 1: Accuracy for 3-token NCs

Method	4NC
Freq	63%
Fre_uniq	63%
Jaccard	48%
Jaccard_uniq	44%
UMLSRel	63%

Table 2: Accuracy for 4-token NCs

different methods in their majority vote for 3-token NCs to arrive at an accuracy of 95% on a significantly (84%) left bracketed dataset. It would be interesting future task to see how all those methods perform just by using the UMLS label set as the corpus. Coming to the 4-token NC dataset we constructed, our greedy frequency based approach is 41% more successful than random guessing that can lead to an expected 20% accuracy. In the dataset there were several contentious choices where researchers thought that there are two equally acceptable bracketing options. This happened in about 10 (out of 59) cases where the contention is between the choices $((w_1 w_2) w_3) w_4$ and $(w_1 w_2)(w_3 w_4)$. An example of such an NC is `bone marrow cell proliferation`. Here annotators felt that both interpretations are appropriate. Accuracy improved from 63% to 70% when we allowed either choice for these contentious NCs.

4 Concluding Remarks

We pursued a knowledge-based approach to bracketing biomedical NCs with 3- and 4-tokens. In addition to employing frequency count based approaches, we also proposed the concept of bracketing cohesion that takes as input measures of term pair relatedness. We initially experimented with Jaccard's index and context vector based UMLSRel measures for computing bracketing cohesion. We plan to extend the bracketing cohesion using various other measures of relatedness including mutual information and also compute it over a bigger corpus. We would also like to explore other path based relatedness measures based on the UMLS graph structure. Although we don't have concrete results yet on entire dataset, using

$$\mathcal{S}(t_1, t_2) = \frac{1}{\text{shortest-path-length}(t_1, t_2)}$$

as the relatedness measure for cohesion based method (Section 2.2) produced good results for a smaller subset of the 3-token NCs. Another important frequency based measure that outputs term-hood scores to terms is the C-value method (Frantzi et al., 1998). We are currently in the process of computing C-values for different n-grams. The idea is to use the C-values instead of the frequencies in the greedy approach. We also plan to build and test our methods on a larger 4-token NC dataset and perform a more thorough analysis on inter-annotator agreement and confidence intervals for accuracies on unseen datasets.

Acknowledgements

Many thanks to Jacob Painter and Supriya Prabhala for helping us create the gold standard dataset. The project described was supported by the National Center for Research

Resources, UL1RR033173, and the National Center for Advancing Translational Sciences, UL1TR000117. The content is solely the responsibility of the authors and does not necessarily represent the official views of the NIH.

References

Bergsma, S., Pitler, E., and Lin, D. (2010). Creating robust supervised classifiers via web-scale n-gram data. In *ACL*, pages 865–874.

Bird, S., Klein, E., and Loper, E. (2009). *Natural Language Processing with Python*. O'Reilly Media.

de Marneffe, M., MacCartney, B., and Manning, C. (2006). Generating Typed Dependency Parses from Phrase Structure Parses. In *Proceedings of LREC 2006*.

Frantzi, K. T., Ananiadou, S., and Tsujii, J.-i. (1998). The c-value/nc-value method of automatic recognition for multi-word terms. In *Second European Conf. on Research and Advanced Tech. for Digital Libraries*, ECDL '98, pages 585–604.

Friedman, C. and Johnson, S. B. (2006). Natural language and text processing in biomedicine. In Shortliffe, E. H. and Cimino, J. J., editors, *Biomedical Informatics*, Health Informatics, pages 312–343. Springer New York.

Girju, R., Moldovan, D., Tatu, M., and Antohe, D. (2005). On the semantics of noun compounds. *Comput. Speech Lang.*, 19:479–496.

Keller, F. and Lapata, M. (2003). Using the web to obtain frequencies for unseen bigrams. *Comput. Linguist.*, 29:459–484.

Lauer, M. (1995). *Designing Statistical Language Learners: Experiments on Noun Compounds*. PhD thesis, Macquarie University, Australia.

Matsuzaki, T., Miyao, Y., and Tsujii, J. (2007). Efficient HPSG parsing with supertagging and CFG-filtering. In *Proceedings of the 20th international joint conference on Artificial intelligence*, IJCAI'07, pages 1671–1676.

Nakov, P. and Hearst, M. (2005). Search engine statistics beyond the n-gram: Application to noun compound bracketing. In *Proceedings of CoNLL-05*, pages 17–24.

Nakov, P. I. (2007). *Using the Web as an Implicit Training Set: Application to Noun Compound Syntax and Semantics*. PhD thesis, Univ. of California, Berkeley.

Pedersen, T., Pakhomov, S. V. S., Patwardhan, S., and Chute, C. G. (2007). Measures of semantic similarity and relatedness in the biomedical domain. *J. of Biomedical Informatics*, 40:288–299.

Pitler, E., Bergsma, S., Lin, D., and Church, K. W. (2010). Using web-scale n-grams to improve base np parsing performance. In *COLING*, pages 886–894.

Pustejovsky, J., Anick, P., and Bergler, S. (1993). Lexical semantic techniques for corpus analysis. *Comput. Linguist.*, 19:331–358.

Classification of Inconsistent Sentiment Words Using Syntactic Constructions

Wiltrud KESSLER   Hinrich SCHÜTZE
Institute for Natural Language Processing
University of Stuttgart
wiltrud.kessler@ims.uni-stuttgart.de

ABSTRACT
An important problem in sentiment analysis are *inconsistent* words. We define an inconsistent word as a sentiment word whose dictionary polarity is reversed by the sentence context in which it occurs. We present a supervised machine learning approach to the problem of *inconsistency classification*, the problem of automatically distinguishing inconsistent from consistent sentiment words in context. Our first contribution to inconsistency classification is that we take into account sentence structure and use syntactic constructions as features – in contrast to previous work that has only used word-level features. Our second contribution is a method for learning polarity reversing constructions from sentences annotated with polarity. We show that when we integrate inconsistency classification results into sentence-level polarity classification, performance is significantly increased.

KEYWORDS: sentiment analysis, polarity modifiers, polarity shifters, polarity reversers, negation.

Proceedings of COLING 2012: Posters, pages 569–578,
COLING 2012, Mumbai, December 2012.

1 Introduction

Sentiment analysis or opinion mining is the computational study of opinions and sentiments expressed in text (Liu, 2010). Sentiment analysis is typically performed based on sentiment words – words that indicate the sentiment polarity of a document or sentence. A challenge for this approach is that the dictionary polarity of a sentiment word may be reversed by sentence context (Polanyi and Zaenen, 2004). We call such words *inconsistent* words[1].

A classical example of an inconsistent word is the sentiment word *"worth"* in the sentence *"this player is not* $\textbf{\textit{worth}}_{pos}$ *any price"* where the negation *"not"* reverses the polarity of *"worth"*, so that the final sentiment expressed in the sentence is not positive, but negative. Such polarity reversing expressions are diverse, e.g., *"lack of* $\textbf{\textit{quality}}_{pos}$*"* or *"*$\textbf{\textit{easy}}_{pos}$ *to hit accidentally"*.

In this work we present a supervised machine learning approach to the problem of inconsistency classification, the problem of automatically distinguishing inconsistent from consistent sentiment words in context. Training examples for inconsistency classification are extracted automatically from sentences annotated with polarity. We make two contributions to the state of the art. First, while previous work has used only features at the word level, we take into account sentence structure and use syntactic constructions as features. Second, we present first steps towards automatically extracting polarity reversing constructions (PRCs) from sentences annotated with polarity. PRCs can be used as features for inconsistency classification as well as for directly identifying inconsistent words. We show that our treatment of inconsistent words improves polarity classification performance on sentence-level compared to a baseline.

This paper is structured as follows. The next section discusses related work. Section 3 describes inconsistency classification, the format of syntactic constructions and the extraction of training examples. We then present experimental results for polarity classification (Section 4). The second part of this paper describes our method for automatically extracting PRCs (Section 5), and evaluates their usefulness (Section 6). Finally, we conclude and outline future work.

2 Related Work

Negations, or, more generally, *polarity reversers*, create inconsistent words which are a major source of errors for polarity classification. Polarity reversers are diverse and do not include only negation function words (Choi and Cardie, 2008). Thus, some treatment of inconsistent words in polarity classification is common; for a survey see Wiegand et al. (2010).

Most approaches for polarity classification work on word-level and simply consider a word w as inconsistent if it is preceded by a word out of a fixed list of polarity reversers, this includes rule-based (Polanyi and Zaenen, 2004; Hu and Liu, 2004) as well as statistical approaches (Pang et al., 2002). Unlike these approaches, we use syntactic information.

Some approaches go beyond word-level, e.g., Wilson et al. (2005) use special features to model the existence of polarity modifiers in the syntactic context of a sentiment word, Choi and Cardie (2008) use syntactic patterns to treat content negators, and Nakagawa et al. (2010) integrate polarity reversing words into a dependency tree based method. While these works include some syntactic information, they still use a manually defined list of polarity reversing words. In contrast, we use machine learning to identify polarity reversing constructions (PRCs).

[1] Note that our terminology differs from that used by (Dragut et al., 2012) who use the term "inconsistent" to refer to a word that has conflicting polarity information in a sentiment dictionary or across dictionaries.

An important challenge that most approaches ignore is the detection of the scope of negation. Councill et al. (2010) use dependency parses to predict the scope of polarity reversing words. Our approach goes the opposite way: given a sentiment word, we determine if it is in the scope of any PRC. Our definition of syntactic constructions explicitly includes scope.

The work most closely related to our approach is (Ikeda et al., 2008) who also address the task of inconsistency classification. Their inconsistency classifier uses the local context of three words to the left and right of the target sentiment word as features. Li et al. (2010) extend that method to document level by stacking two classifiers trained on reversed and nonreversed sentences. Both works use only word-level information in their classifiers. We go beyond word-level and use syntactic constructions. We also attempt to explicitly identify and extract the syntactic constructions that are responsible for making a sentiment word inconsistent.

3 Approach

The main component of our approach is the inconsistency classifier, that assigns a score $s_{\text{incons}}(w)$ to each sentiment word token w in context, and classifies w as being `inconsistent` ($s_{\text{incons}}(w) > 0$) or `consistent` ($s_{\text{incons}}(w) \leq 0$) with its dictionary polarity.

The final task we want to improve is sentence-level polarity classification. To determine the polarity of a sentence, we calculate a positivity score $s_{\text{pos}}(S)$ for the sentence S using a dictionary of positive and negative sentiment words (p and n). The sentence is labeled `positive` iff $s_{\text{pos}}(S) \geq 0$, else `negative`. We integrate inconsistency classification by counting a word with its score $s_{\text{incons}}(w)$. Thus, we define $s_{\text{pos}}(S)$ as follows (cf. (Ikeda et al., 2008)):

$$s_{\text{pos}}(S) = \sum_{w \in p} -s_{\text{incons}}(w) + \sum_{w \in n} s_{\text{incons}}(w) \qquad (1)$$

for all $w \in S$. In our proposed **consistency voting** we use a statistical classifier to determine $s_{\text{incons}}(w)$ and use its classification confidence as score. Our first contribution is to include syntactic constructions as defined below as features for inconsistency classification.

We use two baselines with simpler ways of determining $s_{\text{incons}}(w)$: **Standard voting** assumes every word to be consistent, so we set $s_{\text{incons}}(w) = -1$ for all words and Equation 1 is simplified to $s_{\text{pos}}(S) = |\{w \in p\}| - |\{w \in n\}|$. A common way of treating inconsistent words is **negation voting**, which sets $s_{\text{incons}}(w) = 1$ (`inconsistent`) iff an odd number of negation cues occurs in the context of w, else $s_{\text{incons}}(w) = -1$ (`consistent`).

3.1 Syntactic constructions

Polarity modifiers are a syntactic phenomenon and word-level approaches fail to take into account the scope of a polarity reverser (cf. Wiegand et al. (2010)). To integrate syntactic information, we parse all training examples with a dependency parser. The parts of speech (POS) produced by the parser are generalized to the categories N (noun), V (verb), ADJ (adjective), ADV (adverb), PR (preposition), DT (determiner), and * (everything else).

We extract *syntactic constructions* from the parses that describe the syntactic context of a sentiment word. We define a syntactic construction as any path that starts at a sentiment word, ends at another word in the sentence, and contains the POS categories of all nodes that are traversed on the path. An example, the syntactic construction `N<V<V>additionally_ADV`, is given in Figure 1. The sentiment word *"problems"* is represented by POS category (`N`), but is not

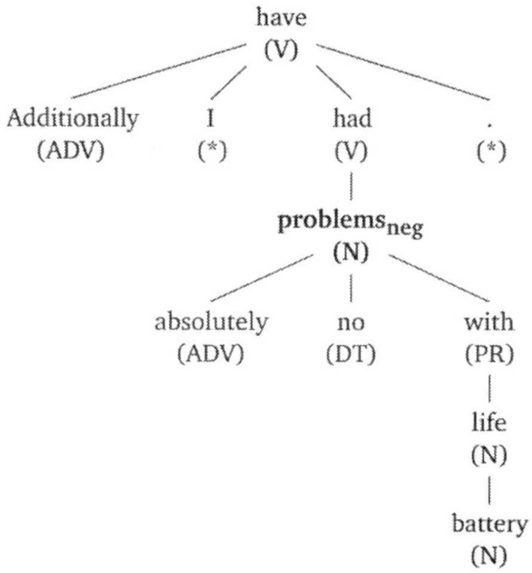


```
k = 0   N

k = 1   N>absolutely_ADV
        N>no_DT
        N>with_PR
        N<have_V

k = 2   N>PR>life_N
        N<V<have_V

k = 3   N>PR>N>battery_N
        N<V<V>additionally_ADV
        N<V<V>i_*
```

Figure 1: Formalization of syntactic constructions. Left: The basis for extracting constructions is a dependency parse, in this case for the sentence *"Additionally I have had absolutely no problems with battery life."* Right: Extracted constructions for the sentiment word *"problems"*.

included, as we are interested in constructions that are independent of specific sentiment words. The path contains the direction in the parse tree (up < or down >), the nodes that are traversed on the way – represented by POS category (V for *"had"* and *"have"*) – and lemma/POS of the final word on the path (*"additionally"*, ADV).

All syntactic constructions extracted from the context of a sentiment word w up to a certain parse tree distance k (defined in number of nodes on the path) are used as features for training the bag-of-constructions inconsistency classifier.

3.2 Finding consistent and inconsistent training examples

For training our inconsistency classifier we need a set of training examples annotated for (in)consistency. We assume that we have a corpus of polarity annotated sentences and a dictionary of positive and negative sentiment words at our disposal.

We follow Ikeda et al. (2008) and extract training examples automatically from the corpus. Given a sentiment word w with dictionary polarity p_w that appears in a sentence s with polarity p_s in the corpus, we label w `consistent` iff $p_w = p_s$, and `inconsistent` otherwise. We ignore words and sentences with any label other than `positive` and `negative` as well as sentiment words occurring with a POS not in the dictionary.

E.g., from the sentence[2] *"The phone isn't* ***hard***$_{neg}$ *to use so its* ***great***$_{pos}$*"* (labeled `positive`), we extract *"hard"* (resp. *"great"*) as an `inconsistent` (resp. `consistent`) training example.

4 Experiments

4.1 Data

We evaluate on the customer review data set[3] (Hu and Liu, 2004). Statistics about the data set can be found in Table 1. The original data set is annotated at aspect level. To create sentence

[2] All example sentences are from user reviews including all errors in spelling and grammar.

[3] `http://www.cs.uic.edu/~liub/FBS/CustomerReviewData.zip`

		all	positive	negative
1	# sentences	1726	1078	648
2	# available sentences	1446	948	498
3	# sentiment words found	2930	2032	898
4	# inconsistent words	824	465	359

Table 1: Statistics of customer review data set.

		A	P_{pos}	R_{pos}	F_{pos}	P_{neg}	R_{neg}	F_{neg}	F
1	standard voting	76.1	76.5	91.7	83.4	74.5	46.4	57.2	70.3 †
2	negation voting	79.0	78.4	**93.7**	85.4	**80.9**	51.0	62.6	74.0*†
3	consistency voting (BoW)	78.5	81.4	87.0	84.1	71.6	62.2	66.6	75.4 †
4	consistency voting (BoC)	**80.9**	**82.1**	90.6	**86.2**	77.8	**62.4**	**69.3**	**77.7***

Table 2: Results of sentence-level polarity classification on customer review data set: **A**ccuracy, **P**recision, **R**ecall, **F**-measure (positive and negative sentences), macro **F**-measure.

polarity annotations, we take the aspect label as sentence label if there is only one aspect or all aspect labels have the same polarity. If a *"but"* separates two aspects of conflicting polarity, the two parts of the sentence are split and separately annotated. If no splitting is possible or there is no annotated aspect, the sentence is ignored.

From the total number of polarity annotated sentences (line 1) we can only compute a useful polarity score for sentences that contain at least one sentiment word (line 2), all other sentences are ignored for the evaluation.

As a dictionary of sentiment words we use the MPQA subjectivity clues[4] (Wilson et al., 2005) containing 2304 positive and 4152 negative words. A word may have several possible POS tags. Sentences have been parsed with the Bohnet dependency parser (Bohnet, 2010). Sentiment words are extracted as (in)consistent (lines 3 and 4) with the method presented in Section 3.2.

4.2 Results of sentence-level polarity classification

We use two different inconsistency classifiers with consistency voting: The bag-of-words classifier **BoW** determines $s_{\text{incons}}(w)$ with the three context words to the left and right of the sentiment word as features. This is a reimplementation of Ikeda et al.'s (2008) "word-wise" learning. The bag-of-constructions classifier **BoC** uses the syntactic constructions described in Section 3.1 up to parse-tree distance $k = 3$ as features for inconsistency classification. In both cases, we use the Stanford MaxEnt classifier (Manning and Klein, 2003) with default settings and train it in a 5-fold cross-validation setting.

As baselines, we include **standard voting** and **negation voting**. For negation voting we define context as the three words to the left and right of the sentiment word and use nine negation cue words from (Ikeda et al., 2008): *no, not, yet, never, none, nobody, nowhere, nothing, neither*.

Ikeda et al. (2008) report an accuracy of 71.6% for the standard voting baseline on the same data set when using sentiment words from General Inquirer (Stone et al., 1996). Our standard voting baseline with MPQA subjectivity clues yields a much higher accuracy of 76.1%. Accuracy is a less suitable performance measure for this task as the data set is skewed (65.6%

[4]`http://www.cs.pitt.edu/mpqa/subj_lexicon.html`

positive sentences). This is why we have reimplemented their approach and restrict our further discussion to our reimplementation and macro F-measure only.

Table 2 shows the result of our experiments. Bold numbers denote the best result in each column. We mark a macro F-measure result with * if it is significantly higher than the previous line and with † if it is significantly worse than consistency voting with the BoC classifier.[5] Determining inconsistency with the BoC classifier significantly outperforms all other methods.

5 Polarity reversing constructions (PRCs)

We define a *polarity reversing construction* (PRC) as a syntactic construction (see Section 3.1) that reverses the polarity of the sentiment word in its scope. Recall that the sentiment word is the first node of the path represented by the construction.

Our goal is the automatic extraction of PRCs. We work on the assumption that in the syntactic context of inconsistent words there is always a PRC present. Syntactic constructions that appear often in the context of inconsistent words are likely to be PRCs. We use the extracted training examples for consistent and inconsistent words (see Section 3.2). All training examples are parsed with a dependency parser and syntactic constructions are extracted from the context (see Section 3.1). All extracted constructions are candidates for PRCs.

The candidates are scored with Mutual Information (**MI**). **MI** measures how much information the presence or absence of a candidate x contributes to making the correct classification decision for a sentiment word. $MI(x,C)$ between candidate x and the classes $C = \{\texttt{consistent}, \texttt{inconsistent}\}$ is defined as

$$MI(x,C) = \sum_{c \in C} P(x,c) \log_2 \frac{P(x,c)}{P(x) \cdot P(c)} + \sum_{c \in C} P(\bar{x},c) \log_2 \frac{P(\bar{x},c)}{P(\bar{x}) \cdot P(c)} \quad (2)$$

where $P(x)$ is the probability that x occurred, and $P(\bar{x})$ the probability that x didn't occur. The n candidates with the highest scores are taken as PRCs.

MI extracts candidates that serve as a good indicator for *one of* the classes, but not necessarily for the class `inconsistent`. For the **MI+** score, we remove candidates with negative association from the final set of PRCs (Dunning, 1993).

6 Experiments with PRCs

6.1 Results of PRC extraction

For the robust extraction of PRCs we need more annotated sentences than the customer review corpus contains. As there is no such corpus in the domain and to avoid manual annotation effort, we use semistructured reviews in which users provide pros (product aspects the user evaluates as positive) and cons (product aspects the user evaluates as negative) in addition to the written text of the review. We automatically create a corpus annotated with polarity at the sentence level as follows: All pros (resp. cons) longer than 3 tokens are extracted as a sentence with label `positive` (resp. `negative`). Shorter pros (resp. cons) are stripped of sentiment words (using the subjectivity clues dictionary) and if the resulting string is found in the review text, the containing sentence is extracted as `positive` (resp. `negative`). This is a somewhat simplistic method, but we still get enough annotated sentences for our purposes.

[5]Statistically significant at $p < .05$ using the approximate randomization test (Noreen, 1989).

		all	positive	negative
1	# extracted sentences	58 503	34 881	23 622
2	# available sentences	42 943	27 510	15 433
3	# sentiment words found	83 258	57 192	26 066
4	# inconsistent words	24 325	12 502	11 823

Table 3: Statistics of automatically annotated camera/cellphone data set.

		A	P_{pos}	R_{pos}	F_{pos}	P_{neg}	R_{neg}	F_{neg}	F
1	negation vot. (words)	79.0	78.4	93.7	85.4	80.9	51.0	62.6	74.0
2	negation vot. (PRC, gold)	80.2	79.6	**93.8**	86.1	**82.1**	54.2	65.3	75.7*
3	negation vot. (PRC, **MI**)	59.1	68.9	68.6	68.7	40.8	41.2	41.0	54.9
4	negation vot. (PRC, **MI+**)	78.8	78.4	93.2	85.2	79.9	51.2	62.4	73.8
5	consist. vot. (BoC)	80.9	**82.1**	90.6	86.2	77.8	**62.4**	69.3	77.7
6	consist. vot. (BoPRC, gold)	**81.3**	81.9	91.7	86.5	79.5	61.4	69.3	**77.9**
7	consist. vot. (BoPRC, **MI**)	81.2	**82.1**	91.2	86.4	78.8	62.0	**69.4**	**77.9**
8	consist. vot. (BoPRC, **MI+**)	**81.3**	81.6	92.4	**86.6**	80.6	60.2	69.0	77.8

Table 4: Sentence-level polarity classification on customer review data set with PRCs.

We perform the annotation on an existing corpus of 17 442 semistructured camera and cellphone reviews[6] (Branavan et al., 2008) from `epinions.com`. Table 3 contains statistics about the data. We use this corpus only for the automatic extraction of PRCs, not to evaluate polarity classification. To judge the quality of the automatic annotation, we hired a graduate student of computational linguistics to manually annotate a random subset of 1271 sentences. The agreement of the automatic and manual annotation is 0.79; Cohen's κ is 0.61.

To directly evaluate the extracted PRCs, the graduate student also annotated some syntactic constructions as PRCs / non-PRCs. This results in a set of 70 gold PRCs.[7]

Comparing the automatically extracted constructions to our set of gold PRCs, we find that few actual PRCs are found when scoring with **MI** (as we expected). Of the top 70 constructions extracted as PRCs with **MI**, only 15 are correct (21%). Results for **MI+** are better, but still noisy: 20 out of 70 are correct (29%). These results do not look very promising, but as we will see, we can still use noisy PRCs successfully in polarity classification.

6.2 Results of sentence-level polarity classification

We use PRCs in two ways: In **negation voting with PRCs**, we define context as the syntactic context of a sentiment word and use PRCs as negation cues. We also use consistency voting with a bag-of-PRC (**BoPRC**) inconsistency classifier that uses only PRCs as features instead of using all constructions (i.e., a feature-selection on BoC). Our intuition is that as only polarity reversal is marked, PRCs should be all that is needed to identify inconsistent words.

Both methods are tested with PRCs extracted using **MI** and **MI+**. We extract these PRCs from the camera/cellphone data described in Section 6.1. We extract the top 70 constructions to match the number of constructions in our manually annotated PRC set. Additionally, we use the manually annotated PRCs (**gold**) as an upper bound of automatic PRC-based performance.

[6]`http://groups.csail.mit.edu/rbg/code/precis/` (camera and cellphone data sets)

[7]Available at `http://www.ims.uni-stuttgart.de/~kesslewd/data/sentiment.html`

To enable comparison with our previous results, we use the evaluation setup described in Section 4.2. Table 4 shows the results. For easier comparison, we have repeated lines 2 (word-level negation voting) and 4 (consistency voting with BoC) from Table 2 as lines 1 resp. 5 in Table 4. Bold numbers denote the best result in each column.

We compare negation voting with PRCs to the word-level negation voting. The improvement in macro F-measure of negation voting with gold PRCs is significant (marked with $*$).[8] Unsurprisingly, the PRCs extracted with **MI** hurt performance instead of improving it. The noisy PRCs extracted with **MI+** achieve a similar performance than word-level negation voting (the difference is not significant). For such a noisy set (only 29% of the PRCs are correct), this is a promising result.

In consistency voting, telling the BoC inconsistency classifier which features are important by some sort of feature selection either manually or automatically improves performance for all variants of BoPRC. Although no improvement is statistically significant, this is still an interesting result, as it shows that even noisy information about the important features can improve performance of inconsistency classification.

Conclusion and perspectives

We have presented a supervised machine learning approach to detect if a sentiment word is consistent or inconsistent with its dictionary polarity in a specific sentence context. We have evaluated our approach on sentence-level polarity classification by integrating the score of such an inconsistency classifier into a majority voting approach. As our first contribution, we have shown that the use of syntactic constructions as features for the inconsistency classifier can improve performance. As a second contribution, we have presented first steps towards automatically extracting polarity reversing constructions from sentences annotated with polarity and demonstrated two possible uses of such constructions in sentence-level polarity classification.

To get sufficient training data for the extraction of polarity reversing constructions, we have automatically annotated sentences from semistructured reviews with polarity. For future work, we plan to improve the quality and coverage of this automatic annotation as a means to get sentence-labeled data from semistructured reviews, which are available in large quantities.

A major problem in sentiment analysis are sentiment words that do not express sentiment in a given context (subjectivity analysis cf. (Wilson et al., 2005)). In a preliminary study, we found that about 50% of words extracted as inconsistent training examples did in fact not express sentiment in the sentence context, e.g., the word *"slow"* in the positive sentence *"easy to hold steady when using slower shutter speeds"*. Identifying and discarding non-subjective phrases like *"slower shutter speeds"* would improve the classification results as well as the quality of the extracted polarity reversing constructions.

Acknowledgments

This research was funded by Deutsche Forschungsgemeinschaft (DFG, SFB 732, D7). We thank Olga Podushko for the annotation. We also thank Andrea Glaser, Charles Jochim, Khalid Al Khatib and Christian Scheible for their suggestions about this work.

[8] Statistically significant at $p < .05$ using the approximate randomization test (Noreen, 1989).

References

Bohnet, B. (2010). Very high accuracy and fast dependency parsing is not a contradiction. In *Proceedings of COLING '10*, pages 89–97.

Branavan, S. R. K., Chen, H., Eisenstein, J., and Barzilay, R. (2008). Learning document-level semantic properties from free-text annotations. In *Proceedings of ACL '08*, pages 263–271.

Choi, Y. and Cardie, C. (2008). Learning with compositional semantics as structural inference for subsentential sentiment analysis. In *Proceedings of EMNLP '08*, pages 793–801.

Councill, I. G., McDonald, R., and Velikovich, L. (2010). What's great and what's not: learning to classify the scope of negation for improved sentiment analysis. In *Proceedings of NeSp-NLP '10*, pages 51–59.

Dragut, E., Wang, H., Yu, C., Sistla, P., and Meng, W. (2012). Polarity consistency checking for sentiment dictionaries. In *Proceedings of ACL '12*, pages 997–1005.

Dunning, T. (1993). Accurate methods for the statistics of surprise and coincidence. *Computational Linguistics*, 19(1):61–74.

Hu, M. and Liu, B. (2004). Mining and summarizing customer reviews. In *Proceedings of KDD '04*, pages 168–177.

Ikeda, D., Takamura, H., Ratinov, L.-A., and Okumura, M. (2008). Learning to shift the polarity of words for sentiment classification. In *Proceedings of IJCNLP '08*, pages 50–57.

Li, S., Lee, S. Y. M., Chen, Y., Huang, C.-R., and Zhou, G. (2010). Sentiment classification and polarity shifting. In *Proceedings of COLING '10*, pages 635–643.

Liu, B. (2010). Sentiment analysis and subjectivity. In Indurkhya, N. and Damerau, F. J., editors, *Handbook of Natural Language Processing, Second Edition*, pages 627–666. Chapman & Hall/CRC.

Manning, C. and Klein, D. (2003). Optimization, maxent models, and conditional estimation without magic. In *Proceedings of NAACL-Tutorials '03*.

Nakagawa, T., Inui, K., and Kurohashi, S. (2010). Dependency tree-based sentiment classification using CRFs with hidden variables. In *Proceedings of HLT '10*, pages 786–794.

Noreen, E. W. (1989). *Computer-intensive methods for testing hypotheses – an introduction*. Wiley & Sons.

Pang, B., Lee, L., and Vaithyanathan, S. (2002). Thumbs up? Sentiment classification using machine learning techniques. In *Proceedings of EMNLP '02*, pages 79–86.

Polanyi, L. and Zaenen, A. (2004). Contextual valence shifters. In *Proceedings of AAAI Spring Symposium on Exploring Attitude and Affect in Text*, pages 106–111.

Stone, P. J., Dunphy, D. C., Smith, M. S., and Ogilvie, D. M. (1996). *General Inquirer: A Computer Approach to Content Analysis*. The MIT Press.

Wiegand, M., Balahur, A., Roth, B., and Klakow, D. (2010). A survey on the role of negation in sentiment analysis. In *Proceedings of NeSp-NLP '10*, pages 60–68.

Wilson, T., Wiebe, J., and Hoffmann, P. (2005). Recognizing contextual polarity in phrase-level sentiment analysis. In *Proceedings of HLT '05*, pages 347–354.

Learning Semantics with Deep Belief Network for Cross-Language Information Retrieval

Jungi Kim[1] *Jinseok Nam*[1] *Iryna Gurevych*[1,2]
(1) Ubiquitous Knowledge Processing Lab (UKP-TUDA)
Department of Computer Science, Technische Universität Darmstadt
(2) Ubiquitous Knowledge Processing Lab (UKP-DIPF)
German Institute for Educational Research and Educational Information
`http://www.ukp.tu-darmstadt.de/`
`{kim,nam,gurevych}@ukp.informatik.tu-darmstadt.de`

ABSTRACT
This paper introduces a cross-language information retrieval (CLIR) framework that combines the state-of-the-art keyword-based approach with a latent semantic-based retrieval model. To capture and analyze the hidden semantics in cross-lingual settings, we construct latent semantic models that map text in different languages into a shared semantic space. Our proposed framework consists of deep belief networks (DBN) for each language and we employ canonical correlation analysis (CCA) to construct a shared semantic space. We evaluated the proposed CLIR approach on a standard ad hoc CLIR dataset, and we show that the cross-lingual semantic analysis with DBN and CCA improves the state-of-the-art keyword-based CLIR performance.

KEYWORDS: Cross-language Information Retrieval, Ad Hoc Retrieval, Deep Learning, Deep Belief Network, Canonical Correlation Analysis, Wikipedia, CLEF.

Proceedings of COLING 2012: Posters, pages 579–588,
COLING 2012, Mumbai, December 2012.

1 Introduction

The state-of-the-art information retrieval (IR) systems of today rely on keyword matching, which suffers from the term mismatch problem. To this end, various techniques such as pseudo-relevance feedback and knowledge-based query expansion have been developed. More recently, a number of semantic analysis approaches such as word sense disambiguation (WSD), latent semantic indexing (LSI), latent dirichlet allocation (LDA), and explicit semantic analysis (ESA) have been utilized in IR (Wolf et al., 2010; Dumais et al., 1996; Vulić et al., 2011; Egozi et al., 2011).

The retrieval task becomes more difficult in the settings of cross-language information retrieval (CLIR), because of additional uncertainty introduced in the cross-lingual matching process. This paper introduces a CLIR framework that combines the state-of-the-art keyword-based approach with a latent semantic-based retrieval model (Fig. 1). To capture and analyze the hidden semantics of source language queries and documents in the target language, we construct latent semantic analysis models that map the texts in the source and the target languages into a shared semantic space, in which the similarities of a query and documents are measured. In addition to the traditional keyword-based CLIR system, our proposed framework consists of deep belief network (DBN)-based semantic analysis models for each language and a canonical correlation analysis (CCA) model for inter-lingual similarity computation. The DBN and the CCA models are trained on a large-scale comparable corpus and use low dimension vectors to represent the semantics of texts. The proposed approach is evaluated on a standard ad hoc CLIR dataset from CLEF workshop, with English as the source language and German as the target language.

2 Related Work

Deep learning is a machine learning approach that utilizes multiple layers of learners for modeling complex and abstract representations of input data. A recent introduction of an efficient deep learning architecture (Hinton et al., 2006) has contributed to its applicability to real world problems. There have been several uses of deep architectures in IR tasks such as mate retrieval (Salakhutdinov and Hinton, 2007; Ranzato and Szummer, 2008) and multimedia retrieval (Hörster and Lienhart, 2008; Krizhevsky and Hinton, 2011). These works find that high-level abstractions through deep networks achieve higher generalization than probabilistic topic models (Blei et al., 2003; Deerwester et al., 1990) in terms of unseen data.

Semantic analysis approaches for CLIR have used the notion of shared semantic space to represent and analyze the semantics across languages. In cross-lingual LSI (CL-LSI) (Dumais et al., 1996), the cross-lingual problem is translated to a monolingual one by merging comparable documents together. Polylingual topic model (Mimno et al., 2009) finds aligned semantics across languages, expanding the notion of the generative process of documents into a multilingual one. In Vulić et al. (2011), LDA-based interlingual topics are utilized in a language modeling approach to CLIR. These cross-lingual latent topic models are extended from monolingual models by blindly concatenating comparable document pairs. Therefore, they suffer from

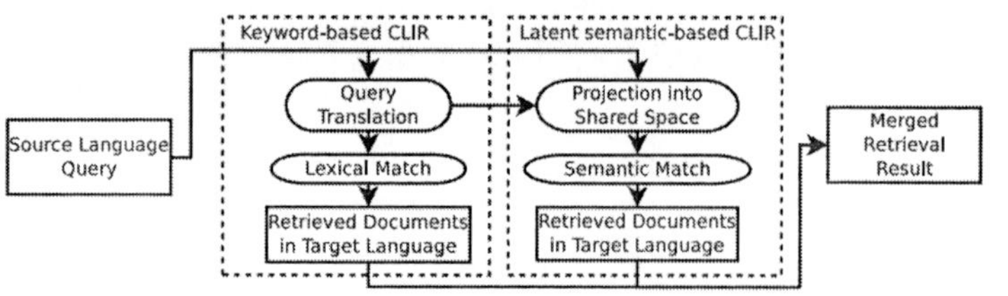

Figure 1: Proposed CLIR framework that combines both the keyword- and the latent semantic-based retrieval models.

reduced feature representations for each language because vocabulary space must be shared across languages.

Another line of research in discovering implicit semantic representation is utilizing CCA (Hotelling, 1936). CCA learns correlations between a pair of comparable representations and projects them into a shared space such that the correlation between the two spaces is maximized. Its recent applications include cross-lingual text analysis (Vinokourov et al., 2002; Hardoon et al., 2004; Li and Shawe-Taylor, 2007) and multi-modal learning (Rasiwasia et al., 2010; Ngiam et al., 2011). The advantage of CCA is that it can easily be generalized to incorporate multiple languages or modalities. Also, it has been shown to out-perform previously known state-of-the-art approaches such as probabilistic LSA and CL-CSI on the cross-lingual mate retrieval task (Platt et al., 2010). However, applying CCA on lexical representation of texts fails to capture complex and abstract relations, because CCA optimizes only on linear correlations.

In contrast to these latent semantic methods, CL-ESA (Potthast et al., 2008; Cimiano et al., 2009) exploits explicit concepts to represent the semantics of texts. ESA methods assume that Wikipedia articles contain distinct topics and a set of Wiki articles can be used as concept features (Gabrilovich and Markovitch, 2007). CL-ESA additionally utilizes interlingual mappings in Wikipedia to find comparable articles, which are considered to be the same concept.

3 Overall approach

We propose a CLIR framework that combines the state-of-the-art keyword matching-based CLIR approach with a DBN-based retrieval model (Fig. 1). The intuition is to exploit the semantics of texts by measuring the similarities of a query and documents in addition to the keyword matching-based similarities. In the following sections, we explain the latent semantic-based (Sec. 3.1) and the keyword-based (Sec. 3.2) CLIR approaches and how the two approaches are merged (Sec. 3.3).

3.1 Deep Belief Network-based CLIR

The task of semantic-based CLIR is to discover a subset of documents in the target language that coincides with a query in the source language in a semantic space. This work utilizes a three-step approach as a latent semantic-based CLIR. First, DBN maps a lexical representation of a document into a latent semantic space (*semantic analysis* step). In the *semantic transformation* step, CCA maps the semantic representations of queries and documents into a shared semantic space. Finally, the *semantic matching* step retrieves relevant documents of a query using a distance metric in the shared semantic space.

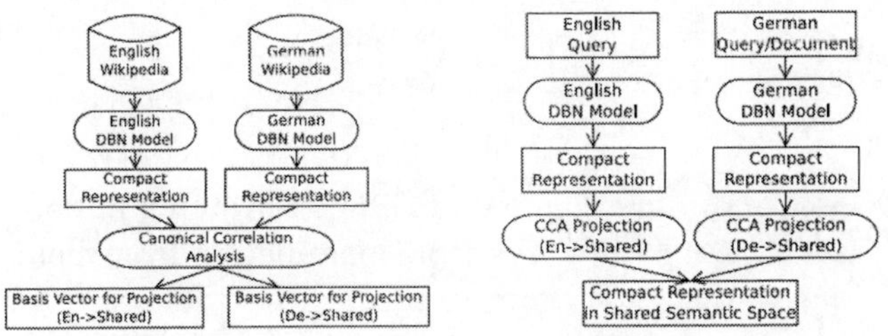

(a) Training DBN and CCA models with a comparable corpus

(b) Mapping query and document into a shared semantic space

Figure 2: Overview of the DBN-based CLIR Framework: offline construction of models (a) and online inference processes (b).

To analyze the semantics of German queries and English documents, we train DBN models on German and English Wikipedia (Fig. 2a) and utilize the compact code resulting from the DBN models as semantic representations (Fig. 2b). Because the outputs from the German and English DBN models are from two different semantic spaces, we train a Canonical Correlation Analysis model (Fig. 2a) to map the German and English compact codes into a shared semantic space (Fig. 2b). To train a CCA model, we create a comparable corpus from Wikipedia using interlingual links between the English and German Wiki articles (Fig. 4).

The shared semantic space can be considered as an intermediate language representation, and the mapping process of the German and the English compact codes into the shared semantic space can be considered as the cross-lingual matching process of the two languages. Once mapped into a shared semantic space, the task of measuring the similarities between the semantic representations becomes trivial.

3.1.1 Semantic analysis with Deep Belief Network

To construct a DBN model, we follow the architecture of the model introduced in (Salakhutdinov and Hinton, 2007). DBN consists of stacked Restricted Boltzmann Machines (RBMs). Each RBM layer is trained in a greedy layer-wise manner (pretraining) and parameters of the entire model are adjusted (fine-tuning).

Pretraining An RBM(Smolensky, 1986) is a special form of Boltzmann Machine with bipartite connectivity constraints in which a set of visible units **v** are connected via symmetric weights **W** to a set of hidden units **h**. In the training step, the edge weights between visible and hidden units are updated iteratively given the input data. In the inference step, when the visible units are activated according to the input data, hidden units activated by the internal stochastic process is considered the hidden representation of the input data.

The bottom-most RBM accepts as input bag-of-word vector representations of texts processed with the replicated softmax model (RSM) (Salakhutdinov and Hinton, 2009). Upper RBMs are inputted with outputs from the binary RBM in the layer below.

An RBM is frequently explained using the *energy*-based analogy borrowed from Physics. The marginal distribution over an input vector **v** in a form of energy-based model (LeCun et al., 2006) is formulated as $p(\mathbf{v}) = \sum_{\mathbf{h}} \frac{e^{-E(\mathbf{v},\mathbf{h})}}{Z}$ where $Z = \sum_{\mathbf{u},\mathbf{g}} e^{-E(\mathbf{u},\mathbf{g})}$ is a normalization factor and $E(\mathbf{v},\mathbf{h}) = -\sum_{i,j} v_i h_j W_{ij} - \sum_i c_i v_i - \alpha \sum_j b_j h_j$ is an energy function of the RBM's state. c_i and b_j are biases for v_i and h_j, and α denotes a scale factor for hidden units and biases. We set α to the document length for discrete valued visible units, and α is set to 1 for binary valued visible units. The conditional distribution of **v** is $p(h_j = 1|\mathbf{v}) = \sigma\left(b_j + \sum_i v_i W_{ij}\right)$. In case of RSM, the

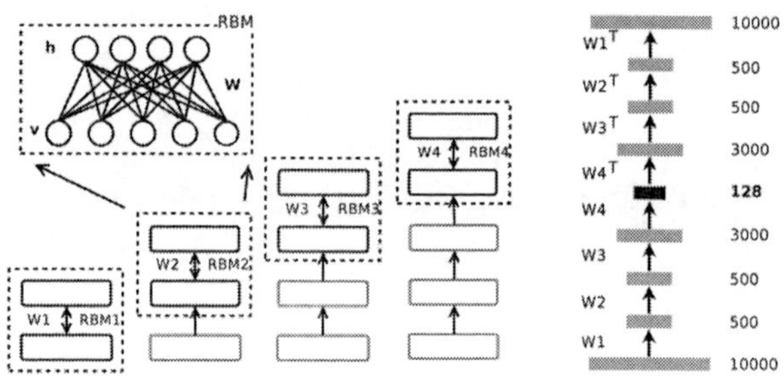

(a) Greedy layer-wise pretraining (b) Fine-tuning

Figure 3: Two-phase learning steps of DBN. Pretraining initializes RBM parameters from bottom to top (a), and fine-tuning optimizes them globally (b).

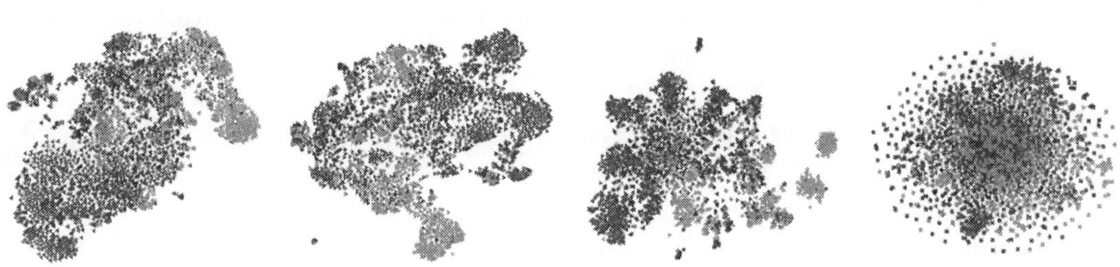

(a) English semantic space (b) German semantic space (c) Shared semantic space (DBN-CCA) (d) Shared lexical space (CCA)

Figure 4: Semantic spaces of English and German DBN models trained on Wikipedia and CCA model. Colors indicate the category of Wiki articles; Red indicates Art, Green is Science, and Blue is Education. The datasets are visualized with a variant of the Stochastic Neighbor Embedding technique (van der Maaten and Hinton, 2008).

conditional distribution of $\mathbf{h}$ is $p(v_i = 1|\mathbf{h}) = \frac{\exp(c_i+\sum_j h_j w_{ij})}{\sum_{k=1}\exp(c_k+\sum_j h_j w_{kj})}$, and in case of binary RBMs, it is $p(v_i = 1|\mathbf{h}) = \sigma(c_i + \sum_j h_j W_{ij})$.

Fine-tuning At the fine-tuning step, pretrained parameters of RBMs are fixed and stacked RBMs are unrolled as a deep autoencoder (Fig. 3b), which learns an identity function with constraints on a small number of hidden units. The constraints enable the autoencoder to find useful hidden representations. The deep autoencoder is trained by backpropagating reconstruction error at the top layer. The activation probability of the central layer (filled rectangle in Fig. 3b, with dimension of 128) is the most abstract and complex representation of the input text, and it is utilized as the latent semantic feature for the text in our work.

3.1.2 Semantic transformation with Canonical Correlation Analysis

CCA (Hotelling, 1936) is a method for discovering a subspace where the correlations of input spaces are maximized when linearly combined. Consider a pair of documents $\{(D_{x1}, D_{y1}), (D_{x2}, D_{y2}), \ldots, (D_{xN}, D_{yN})\} \in \mathbf{D}$ where $D_{xi} \in \mathbf{D}_x$ and $D_{yi} \in \mathbf{D}_y$ and a function $f(x)$ that maps a document into its semantic space. CCA seeks basis vectors w_x and w_y that maximize cross-lingual correlation $\rho = \max_{w_x, w_y} \frac{<w_x f(\mathrm{D}_x), w_y f(\mathrm{D}_y)>}{\|w_x f(\mathrm{D}_x)\|\|w_y f(\mathrm{D}_y)\|}$. We solve this optimization task as a generalized eigenvalue problem using a publicly available toolbox(Hardoon et al., 2004).[1] Figures 4a and 4b illustrate the DBN models trained on the English and German Wikipedia datasets, in which three categories (Art, Science, and Education) are shown for demonstration purposes.

3.1.3 Semantic matching with Cosine similarity

Given a semantic representation of an English query q_x and directions w_x and w_y for English semantics and German semantics, we use Cosine similarity $(f(q_x), f(d_{y_i}); w_x, w_y) = \frac{w_x f(q_x) \cdot w_y f(d_{y_i})}{\|w_x f(q_x)\|\|w_y(d_{y_i})\|}$ to produce the scores of German documents D_y. Note that CCA uses this measure to maximize the correlations of semantics over German and English Wiki articles, hence it is reasonable to use the same measure in the semantic matching phase.

[1] `http://www.davidroihardoon.com/Professional/Code.html`

Table 1: Statistics of the test collections. (T: Title, D: Description, N: Narrative, Cnt: Count)

Collection	Domain	Document			Topic			
		Lang	Cnt	Avg Len	Lang	Cnt	# Rel Doc	Avg Len (T/D/N)
AH 2001-2	News	DE	294,339	323.42	EN	100	4,021	3.38/8.32/18.1
AH 2003						60	1,825	3.83/8.18/17.7

3.2 Keyword matching-based CLIR

As a baseline CLIR framework, we employ a combination of a monolingual IR system with a commercial state-of-the-art MT system to translate English queries into German text.[2]

3.3 Merging Retrieval Results

Overall, there are three sets of retrieved documents: two from the DBN-based CLIR using the original query in the source language and its translation in the target language, and a set of retrieved documents from the keyword-based CLIR.

First, the two sets of retrieved documents from the DBN-based CLIR are linearly combined as:

$$Score_{DBN}(d_i,q) = \beta \cdot \frac{Score_{DBN}(d_i,q_{EN})}{\max_j\{Score_{DBN}(d_j,q_{EN})\}} + (1-\beta)\cdot \frac{Score_{DBN}(d_i,q'_{DE})}{\max_j\{Score_{DBN}(d_j,q'_{DE})\}} \tag{1}$$

in which, the two sets of document scores are first normalized with the maximum scores in each set of scores, and combined together with a ratio optimized on the development data.

Secondly, the document scores in the retrieval results from the BM25 and DBN are merged to produce the final retrieval results.

$$Score(d_i,q) = \lambda \cdot \frac{Score_{BM25}(d_i,q)}{\max_j\{Score_{BM25}(d_j,q)\}} + (1-\lambda)\cdot \frac{Score_{DBN}(d_i,q)}{\max_j\{Score_{DBN}(d_j,q)\}} \tag{2}$$

4 Experiment

Experimental setting We use standard newspaper ad-hoc retrieval datasets[3] for English to German CLIR experiments. General statistics of the test collections are presented in Table 1. As an evaluation measure, we use the mean average precision (MAP), which has been most widely used for evaluating IR systems.

Text preprocessing We obtained English and German comparable articles from Wikipedia dumps from October 07, 2011. For DBN-CLIR, term weights are evaluated with BM25 with an estimation to the nearest integer. After the conversion from texts to real number vectors, all pairs of documents satisfying $|D_{EN}| \geq 3 \times |D_{DE}|$ are dropped where $|D|$ represents the sum of feature values in document D. Out of 700,000 document pairs, 50,000 were randomly selected as training data.

Training DBNs We trained our DBNs with 4 hidden layers, 500-500-3000-128, meaning that 500 hidden units are at the first hidden layer, 500 units at the second, 3000 units at the third, and 128 at the highest level of hidden layer. Each RBM is trained with a mini-batch size of 100 training pairs for 50 epochs. The weights were updated by learning rate 0.1, weight decay 2×10^{-4} and momentum 0.9 except the first RBMs, in which the learning rate was set to 10^{-4}.

[2]Terrier (BM25 with Bo1, `http://terrier.org/`) and Google Translate (`http://translate.google.com/`)
[3]`http://www.clef-initiative.eu/track/series/`

Table 2: Mean average precision (MAP) of CLIR runs with different retrieval models. *%Chg* indicates the relative performance achieved compared to the baseline approach. Significant improvements (Student's paired t-test, $p<0.05$ and $p<0.01$) over the baseline approaches are marked with † and ‡.

Retrieval model	Topic Field					
	T		TD		TDN	
	MAP	*%Chg*	MAP	*%Chg*	MAP	*%Chg*
	AH 2001-2 (λ and β optimized on AH 2003)					
Monolingual (BM25)	24.13	–	28.82	–	30.92	–
Monolingual (BM25Bo1)	28.83	–	33.61	–	35.36	–
BM25	26.04	–	30.92	–	33.29	–
BM25+CCA	26.04	0.00	30.40	−1.68	33.29	0.00
BM25+DBN-CCA	26.32†	+1.07	31.24	+1.03	33.36	+0.21
BM25Bo1	28.97	–	34.64	–	37.35	–
BM25Bo1+CCA	28.82	−0.52	34.64	0.00	37.35	0.00
BM25Bo1+DBN-CCA	29.16	+0.65	35.07‡	+1.24	37.70	+0.94
	AH 2003 (λ and β optimized on AH 2001-2)					
Monolingual (BM25)	31.94	–	35.92	–	39.58	–
Monolingual (BM25Bo1)	39.25	–	40.13	–	44.73	–
BM25	30.40	–	36.01	–	36.43	–
BM25+CCA	30.40	0.00	35.93	−0.22	36.43	0.00
BM25+DBN-CCA	31.25‡	+2.80	36.62	+1.69	37.60†	+3.21
BM25Bo1	33.19	–	43.22	–	40.70	–
BM25Bo1+CCA	33.19	0.00	42.82	−0.93	40.70	0.00
BM25Bo1+DBN-CCA	33.26	+0.21	43.35	+0.30	40.89	+0.47

For fine-tuning phase, parameters of deep autoencoders were trained based on the L-BFGS optimization algorithm[4] with 5 line searches in each iteration.

CLIR results We performed a number of CLIR experiments with different retrieval models and parameter settings, such as the combinations of topic fields for querying (T, TD, and TDN) and whether or not query expansion (Bo1) is applied (Table 2). Performances of monolingual runs are also provided, which provide *soft* upper bounds to the cross-lingual runs. The baseline in our experiments is the state-of-the-art keyword-based CLIR (BM25). Also, we compare DBN-CCA with CCA, which has been shown to achieve top performances among state-of-the-art latent semantic approaches (Platt et al., 2010).

Our proposed approach utilizes a smoothing parameter λ and β to merge BM25 and DBN-based retrieved results (Eqs. 1 and 2). We use AH 2001-2 dataset for parameter estimation for AH 2003, and parameter estimation for AH 2001-2 is carried out on AH 2003.[5]

Table 2 reveals that merging DBN retrieved results with state-of-the-art CLIR approaches further improves the retrieval effectiveness; in all CLIR runs where DBN-CCA is utilized, we observe relative performance improvements in MAP in the range of $+0.21 \sim +3.21$%.We also observe that some improvements are statistically significant. The improvements are consistent over the two test datasets as well as the combinations of topic fields, though utilization of query expansion decreases the effect of DBN, especially for the AH 2003 dataset.

CCA-based retrieval approaches resulted in negative results; in most runs, the optimal value for λ was 1.00, indicating that any portion of retrieval results from CCA only damages the overall performance.

[4]minFunc toolbox for Matlab `http://www.di.ens.fr/~mschmidt/Software/minFunc.html`

[5]For estimation of λ, we used an incremental step 0.05 from 0.0 to 1.0, and β, 0.00 to 1.00 with a step of 0.10.

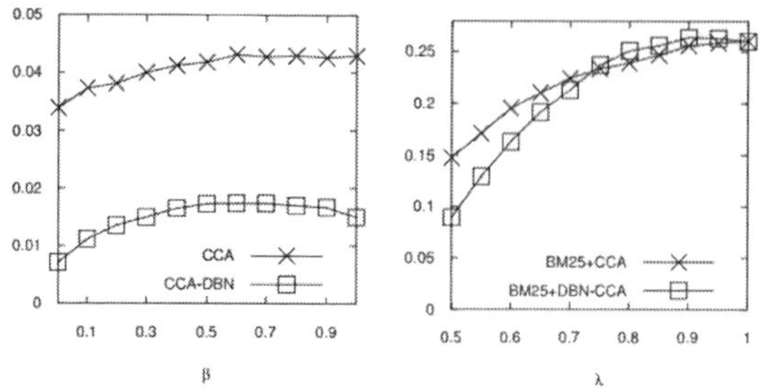

(a) Using latent semantic models alone ($\lambda = 0.0$)

(b) Using keyword and latent semantic fusion models (correspond to rows 4 and 5 in Table 2)

Figure 5: Comparing CLIR performances of CCA vs. DBN-CCA latent semantic methods on AH 2001-2 dataset with Title (T) topic field (x-axis: interpolation parameter, y-axis: MAP). In (b), β for the two runs are fixed to their optimal values (0.1 in both runs).

5 Discussion

Effect of utilizing DBN and CCA models in CLIR We conclude from the experimental results that a DBN-based semantic model helps better represent the query and documents and better matches across the language barrier. We observe, however, that its coverage is limited at its current implementation. This limitation is caused by a number of factors. First, our DBN models have lexicon sizes of only 10,000 terms in each language, which may lead to a lexical coverage problem. Secondly, our framework would not have any effect on topics where the lexical term mismatching problem is not severe. This explains the reduced effectiveness on experiments where query expansion is applied. On the brighter side, applying a DBN semantic model does not harm the overall retrieval performances, even when it is not effective.

CCA vs. DBN-CCA Fig. 4d shows visualization of CCA model trained on the bag-of-word representations of English and German Wikipedia articles with a dimension of 10,000. Compared to the output of DBN-CCA (Fig. 4c), the articles of same topics are scattered over a wider area sporadically and the clusters of topics are less apparent. For capturing underlying semantics, it is clear that DBN-CCA approach is superior over CCA only method.

We observed in our post-experiment analysis that CCA and DBN-CCA have different roles in retrieval; CCA outperforms DBN-CCA when it is used alone in the retrieval process (Fig. 5). However, when combined with a keyword-based retrieval model, CCA only harms the overall performance while DBN-CCA marginally improves the performance. We attribute this to the fact that CCA and keyword-based IR both operate on the lexical level. The combination of DBN-CCA and keyword-based IR is however complementary because DBN-CCA captures topical similarities, introducing a additional information to the task.

Conclusion

This paper introduced a new latent semantic-based CLIR framework based on DBN and CCA. Though our proposed CLIR framework utilizes a relatively simple fusion approach, we showed that the cross-lingual semantic analysis with DBN and CCA improves the state-of-the-art keyword-based and CLIR performance.

Acknowledgments

This work has been supported by the Volkswagen Foundation as part of the Lichtenberg-Professorship Program under grant No. I/82806 and by the German Research Foundation under grant 798/1-5.

References

Blei, D. M., Ng, A. Y., and Jordan, M. I. (2003). Latent Dirichlet Allocation. *The Journal of Machine Learning Research*, 3:993–1022.

Cimiano, P., Schultz, A., Sizov, S., Sorg, P., and Staab, S. (2009). Explicit versus latent concept models for cross-language information retrieval. In *Proceedings of the 21st international jont conference on Artifical intelligence*, pages 1513–1518.

Deerwester, S., Dumais, S. T., Furnas, G. W., Landauer, T. K., and Harshman, R. (1990). Indexing by latent semantic analysis. *Journal of the American society for information science*, 41(6):391–407.

Dumais, S., Landauer, T., and Littman, M. (1996). Automatic cross-language information retrieval using latent semantic indexing. In *Proceedings of the 19th annual international ACM SIGIR conference on Research and development in information retrieval*, pages 16–23.

Egozi, O., Markovitch, S., and Gabrilovich, E. (2011). Concept-based information retrieval using explicit semantic analysis. *ACM Trans. Inf. Syst.*, 29(2):8:1–8:34.

Gabrilovich, E. and Markovitch, S. (2007). Computing semantic relatedness using wikipedia-based explicit semantic analysis. In *Proceedings of the 20th international joint conference on artifical intelligence*, pages 1606–1611, Hyderabad, India.

Hardoon, D., Szedmak, S., and Shawe-Taylor, J. (2004). Canonical correlation analysis: An overview with application to learning methods. *Neural Computation*, 16(12):2639–2664.

Hinton, G., Osindero, S., and Teh, Y. (2006). A fast learning algorithm for deep belief nets. *Neural computation*, 18(7):1527–1554.

Hörster, E. and Lienhart, R. (2008). Deep networks for image retrieval on large-scale databases. In *Proceeding of the 16th ACM international conference on multimedia*, page 643, New York, New York, USA. ACM Press.

Hotelling, H. (1936). Relations Between Two Sets of Variates. *Biometrika*, 28(3/4):pp. 321–377.

Krizhevsky, A. and Hinton, G. E. (2011). Using very deep autoencoders for content-based image retrieval. In *Proceedings of the 18th European Symposium On Artificial Neural Networks, Computational Intelligence and Machine Learning*. ESANN.

LeCun, Y., Chopra, S., Hadsell, R., Ranzato, M. A., and Huang, F.-J. (2006). A Tutorial on Energy-Based Learning. In Bakir, G., Hofman, T., Schölkopf, B., Smola, A., and Taskar, B., editors, *Predicting Structured Data*. MIT Press.

Li, Y. and Shawe-Taylor, J. (2007). Advanced learning algorithms for cross-language patent retrieval and classification: Patent Processing. *Information Processing & Management*, 43(5).

Mimno, D., Wallach, H. M., Naradowsky, J., Smith, D. A., and McCallum, A. (2009). Polylingual topic models. In *Proceedings of the 2009 Conference on Empirical Methods in Natural Language Processing*, pages 880–889, Singapore. Association for Computational Linguistics.

Ngiam, J., Khosla, A., Kim, M., Nam, J., Lee, H., and Ng, A. Y. (2011). Multimodal Deep Learning. In Getoor, L. and Scheffer, T., editors, *Proceedings of the 28th International Conference on Machine Learning (ICML-11)*, ICML '11, pages 689—-696. ACM.

Platt, J., Toutanova, K., and Yih, W.-t. (2010). Translingual Document Representations from Discriminative Projections. In *Proceedings of the 2010 Conference on Empirical Methods in Natural Language Processing*, pages 251–261, Cambridge, MA. Association for Computational Linguistics.

Potthast, M., Stein, B., and Anderka, M. (2008). A wikipedia-based multilingual retrieval model. In Macdonald, C., Ounis, I., Plachouras, V., Ruthven, I., and White, R., editors, *Advances in Information Retrieval*, volume 4956 of *Lecture Notes in Computer Science*, pages 522–530. Springer Berlin/Heidelberg.

Ranzato, M. A. and Szummer, M. (2008). Semi-supervised learning of compact document representations with deep networks. In *Proceedings of the 25th international conference on Machine learning*, pages 792–799, New York, New York, USA. ACM Press.

Rasiwasia, N., Costa Pereira, J., Coviello, E., Doyle, G., Lanckriet, G. R., Levy, R., and Vasconcelos, N. (2010). A new approach to cross-modal multimedia retrieval. In *Proceedings of the international conference on Multimedia*, pages 251–260, New York, New York, USA. ACM Press.

Salakhutdinov, R. and Hinton, G. (2009). Replicated softmax: an undirected topic model. *Advances in Neural Information Processing Systems*, 22:1607–1614.

Salakhutdinov, R. R. and Hinton, G. E. (2007). Semantic Hashing. In *Proceedings of the SIGIR Workshop on Information Retrieval and Applications of Graphical Models*, Amsterdam. Elsevier.

Smolensky, P. (1986). Information processing in dynamical systems: Foundations of harmony theory. In Rumelhart, D. E. and McClelland, J. L., editors, *Parallel Distributed Processing*, chapter 6, pages 194–281. Dept. of Computer Science, University of Colorado, Boulder.

van der Maaten, L. and Hinton, G. E. (2008). Visualizing data using t-SNE. *Journal of Machine Learning Research*, 9:2579–2605.

Vinokourov, A., Shawe-taylor, J., and Cristianini, N. (2002). Inferring a Semantic Representation of Text via Cross-Language Correlation Analysis. In *Advances of Neural Information Processing Systems*, pages 1473–1480, Vancouver, British Columbia, Canada. MIT Press.

Vulić, I., Smet, W. D., and Moens, M.-F. (2011). Cross-Language Information Retrieval with Latent Topic Models Trained on a Comparable Corpus. In Mohamed-Salem, M.-V. O., Shaalan, K. F., Oroumchian, F., Shakery, A., and Khelalfa, H. M., editors, *Proceedings of the 7th Asia Information Retrieval Societies Conference*, volume 7097 of *Lecture Notes in Computer Science*, pages 37–48, Dubai, United Arab Emirates. Springer.

Wolf, E., Bernhard, D., and Gurevych, I. (2010). Combining probabilistic and translation-based models for information retrieval based on word sense annotations. In et al. (Eds.), C. P., editor, *CLEF 2009 Workshop, Part I*, volume 6241 of *Lecture Notes in Computer Science*, pages 120–127. Springer, Berlin/Heidelberg.

Detection of Acoustic-Phonetic Landmarks in Mismatched Conditions Using a Biomimetic Model of Human Auditory Processing

Sarah King   Mark hasegawa − Johnson
University of Illinois, Urbana, Illinois
[redacted]

Abstract

Acoustic-phonetic landmarks provide robust cues for speech recognition and are relatively invariant between speakers, speaking styles, noise conditions and sampling rates. The ability to detect acoustic-phonetic landmarks as a front-end for speech recognition has been shown to improve recognition accuracy. Biomimetic inter-spike intervals and average signal level have been shown to accurately convey information about acoustic-phonetic landmarks. This paper explores the use of inter-spike interval and average signal level as input features for landmark detectors trained and tested on mismatched conditions. These detectors are designed to serve as a front-end for speech recognition systems. Results indicate that landmark detectors trained using inter-spike intervals and signal level are relatively robust to both additive channel noise and changes in sampling rate.

Keywords: Auditory Modeling, Acoustic-Phonetic Landmark, Mismatched Conditions.

Proceedings of COLING 2012: Posters, pages 589–598,
COLING 2012, Mumbai, December 2012.

1 Introduction

Mismatched conditions — differences in channel noise between training audio and testing audio — are problematic for computer speech recognition systems. Signal enhancement, mismatch-resistant acoustic features, and architectural compensation within the recognizer are common solutions (Gong, 1995). The human auditory system implements all three of these solutions by 1.) enhancing the speech signal via the filtering of the head, outer ear, and basilar membrane, 2.) extracting prominent, noise-resistant information from the speech signal, and 3.) implementing dereverberation and noise reduction mechanisms within the cellular architecture of the brain.

Commercial speech recognizers must inevitably deal with mismatched conditions. Such mismatches may include additive channel noise or loss of frequency information. Both of these events occur in the telephone channel. Telephone-band speech recognition (8 KHz) is a difficult task (Bourlard, 1996; Karray and Martin, 2003). Both Gaussian systems (Chigier, 1991; Moreno and Stern, 1994) and non-Gaussian systems (Hasegawa-Johnson et al., 2004) trained on telephone-band speech are not as accurate as systems trained on wide band speech (16 KHz) (Halberstadt and Glass, 1998). This may indicate that a speech recognition system should compensate for channel anomalies before the decoding phase.

The distinctive features [silence, continuant, sonorant, syllabic, and consonantal] are binary valued phonetic descriptors (Stevens, 1999). For example, a sound can either be produced in the nucleus of a syllable ([+syllabic]) or not ([−syllabic]). The vowel /æ/ is a [+syllabic] sound and the consonant /d/ is a [−syllabic] sound. A transition between the two sounds, as in the word "add," is a [+−syllabic] landmark. Detection and recognition of acoustic-phonetic landmarks as a front-end to an HMM-based speech recognition system improves both phone and word recognition accuracy on telephone-band speech (Borys and Hasegawa-Johnson, 2005; Borys, 2008). Landmark-based systems generalize accurately to noisy and mismatched conditions (Kirchhoff, 1999; Juneja and Espy-Wilson, 2004).

Models of the auditory periphery have been used for denoising/enhancing speech (Hunt and Lefebvre, 1989; Virag, 1999), speech recognition in clean (Cohen, 1989; Hunt and Lefebvre, 1989; Ghitza, 1994; Ying et al., 2012) and noisy conditions (Kim et al., 1999), and emotion recognition (Ying et al., 2012). When applied as a front-end, models of the auditory periphery improve speech recognition accuracy (Cohen, 1989; Hunt and Lefebvre, 1989; Ghitza, 1994; Virag, 1999), however, such systems fail to achieve human performance. Current auditory models primarily mimic the cochlea and auditory nerve, both ignoring the effects of head-related filtering and failing to account for neural processing in the brainstem. Neurologists have proposed that the processing in auditory brainstem nuclei, such as the cochlear nucleus and lateral lemniscus, may improve the robustness of human speech recognition to changes in environment (Ehret and Romand, 1997; Winer and Schreiner, 2005; Schnupp et al., 2011).

Both landmark detection and auditory modeling improve recognition accuracy when used as front-ends for speech recognition systems operating in mismatched conditions. This paper proposes an approach that unifies the two methods.

2 Data For Mismatched Speech Recognition

The TIMIT corpus (Garofolo et al., 1993) contains 6300 phonetically rich sentences collected from 630 different male and female speakers from 8 different dialect regions of the United

States. Each utterance is sampled at a rate of 16 KHz. NTIMIT (Jankowski et al., 1990) was constructed by filtering the original TIMIT utterances through a telephone channel and then downsampling to 8 KHz. TIMIT contains detailed, orthographic phonetic transcriptions. NTIMIT is time aligned with TIMIT such that the original transcriptions describe the NTIMIT utterances.

3 The Auditory Model

A diagram of the complete binaural auditory model is shown in Figure 1. Relevant parts of the model are highlighted.

The head, outer, and middle ear are modeled using Tidemann's head-related transfer function (HRTF) measurements (Tidemann, 2011). The output of the HRTF is a set of two acoustic signals — the sound as it is heard at both the left and right ears. HRTF output inputs to the basilar membrane (BM) model.

The BM is modeled using a bank of 2760 parallel gammatone filters. The design of the gammatone filters mimics that in (Patterson and Holdsworth, 1996). The central frequencies of the filters are spaced according to the ERB (equivalent rectangular bandwidth) (Moore and Glasberg, 1983) scale, with 100 filters per ERB, arranged at center frequencies between $f_1 = 60$Hz and $f_{2760} = 8000$Hz. The filter outputs at each time t can be placed side by side to form a topographic map of BM motion from time $t = 0$ to time $t = T$. Examples of such maps for the vowel /i/ are shown in Figure 2.

The location on the BM with the maximal vertical displacement corresponds to a maximum in acoustic pressure (Geisler, 1998) which in turn corresponds to the frequency of the acoustic stimulus (Bekesy, 1960). In Figure 2, a spatio-temporal maximum is equivalent to a pressure maximum. The biomimetic model assumes that processes of lateral inhibition (e.g., as in (Greenberg, 1988)) prevent auditory nerve (AN) fibers from responding to sub-maximal inputs, so that any individual nerve fiber fires only when it is aligned with a spatio-temporal pressure maximum. This aspect of the model is not physiologically accurate, but this approximation is extremely useful for controlling the computational complexity of the biomimetic model. A minimum displacement is required for the inner hair cells (IHCs) to fire. Figure 3 shows which IHCs fire in response to the BM filter outputs of Figure 2. In the figure, an "x" indicates that the IHC corresponding to a given frequency fired at time t. Intensity information is not shown in the figure. A spectrogram of the same audio data used to create Figures 2 and 3 is shown in Figure 4.

The intensity level can be calculated directly from the displacement of the BM model.

$$I(t, f_m) = 20 \log_{10} \frac{y_m(t)}{Y_{ref}} \tag{1}$$

Here, $I(t, f_m)$ is the intensity level in decibels in the mth frequency band at time t, $y_m(t)$ is the observed output at time t from the mth filter given that a maximum has been found, and Y_{ref} is the threshold of hearing of the BM model.

Level, frequency, and timing information for the duration of the acoustic signal are stored as a sparse binary third order tensor A. An individual entry in A is referenced by its time, frequency, and intensity level values and $A(t, f, i) \in \{0, 1\}$. When $A(t, f, i) = 1$, the neuron has fired at time t for an auditory signal at frequency f (in Hz) having level i dB. A value of 0 indicates that

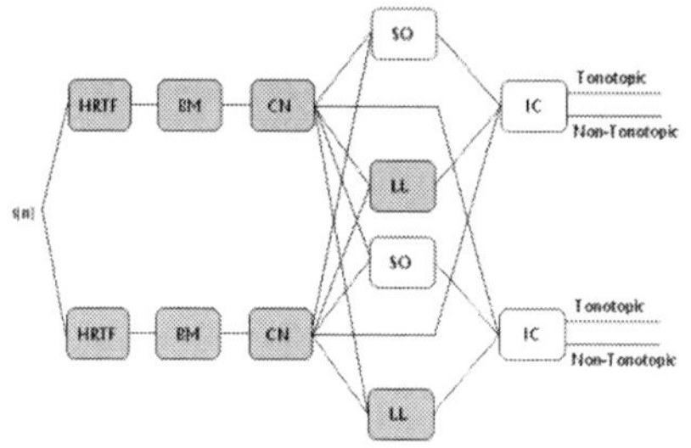

Figure 1: The complete auditory model. The model filters the signal $s[n]$ through a head-related transfer function (HRTF). The HRTF produces a two-channel audio signal that is filtered by the basilar membrane (BM) model. The BM model innervates a cochlear nucleus (CN) model. The CN model innervates a superior olive (SO) model, a lateral lemniscus (LL) model, and a model of the inferior colliculus (IC). The SO model inputs to the LL and the IC. The LL model inputs to the IC. The IC outputs tonotopic and non-tonotopic acoustic features. Only the HRTF, BM, and parts of the CN and LL are described in this paper.

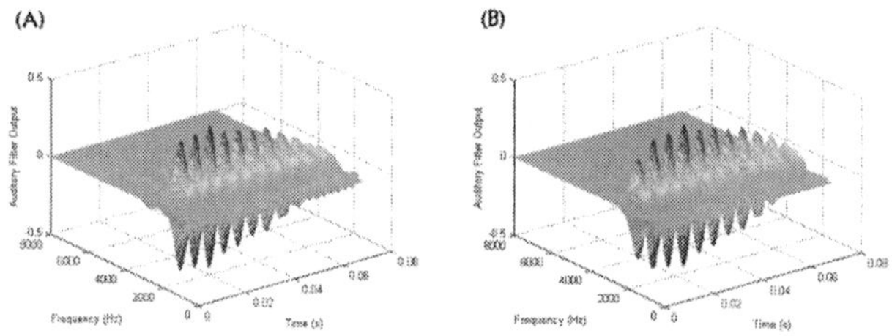

Figure 2: **(A.)** A topographic map of basilar membrane (BM) displacement as a function of time and frequency for the vowel /i/ (as in the word "she") for speaker MMDB0 from the TIMIT corpus. **(B.)** A topographic map of basilar membrane (BM) displacement as a function of time and frequency for the vowel /i/ for speaker MMDB0 from the NTIMIT corpus. For both **(A.)** and **(B.)**, the x-axis is the time in seconds. The y-axis is frequency in Hertz. The z-axis is the amplitude of the the auditory filter outputs.

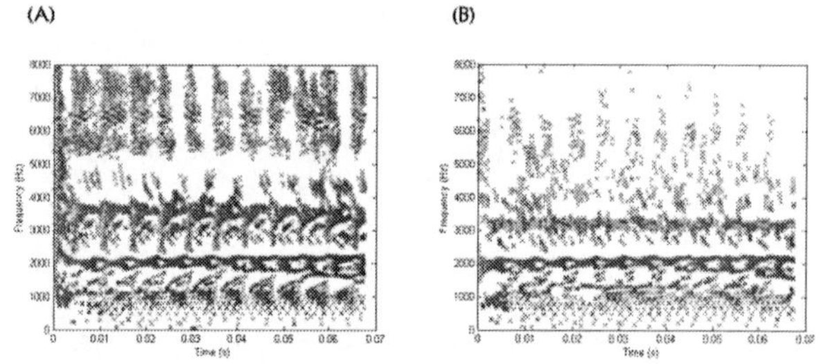

Figure 3: **(A.)** Inner hair cell (IHC) activation as derived from the tonotopic map of the vowel /i/ produced by the speaker MMDB0 from the TIMIT corpus shown in Figure 2A. **(B.)** Inner hair cell (IHC) activation as derived from the tonotopic map of the vowel /i/ produced by the speaker MMDB0 from the NTIMIT corpus shown in Figure 2B. In both **(A.)** and **(B.)**, an "x" indicates that the IHC corresponding to a given frequency (y-axis) has fired at time t (x-axis). The y-axis is spaced according to the ERB scale.

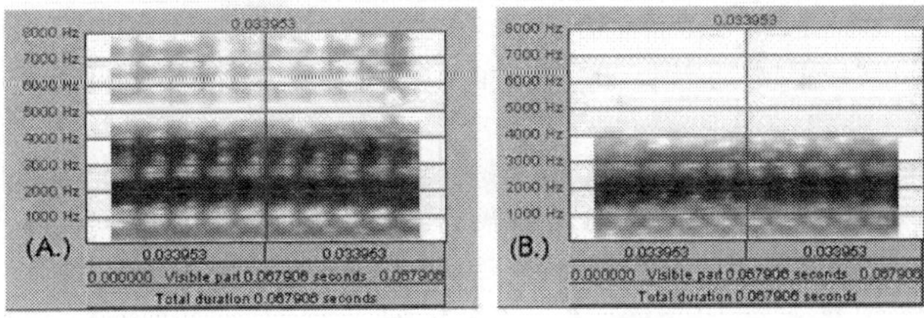

Figure 4: **(A.)** A spectrogram of the vowel /i/ produced by speaker MMDB0 from the TIMIT corpus. **(B.)** A spectrogram of the vowel /i/ produced by speaker MMDB0 from the NTIMIT corpus. corresponding inner hair cell (IHC) maps are shown in Figures 3A and 3B, respectively.

the neuron has not fired at time t. The majority of entries in A will be equal to 0 for any given speech utterance. The left and right ears of the model each produce their own independent tensors (A^l and A^r, respectively), though, for current experiments only the left channel is used. The tensor A is analogous to the information transmitted via the AN.

The octopus cells of the cochlear nucleus (CN) detect synchrony among AN fibers. The tensor A is a more sparse representation than the representation transmitted by the physiological AN. While it is known that octopus fibers are innervated by many AN fibers and that the organization of these fibers is tonotopic, the exact organization of the innervating fibers is unknown. To combat this problem, synchrony is detected using the logical union ($\cup_i$) of the binary variables $A(t,f,i)$ over different values of i, and summing over a time-frequency window of duration T_w and over F_w frequency bands. In other words,

$$S_w(t,f) = \sum_{\tau=0}^{T_w-1} \sum_{\phi=0}^{F_w-1} \cup_{i=I_{min}}^{I_{max}} A(t-\tau, f-\phi, i) \tag{2}$$

and

$$O_w(t,f) = \begin{cases} 1 & S_w(t,f) > \rho \\ 0 & \text{otherwise} \end{cases}$$

where ρ is the minimum number of active neurons in a window w required for the octopus cell to fire. The optimum window size was determined experimentally to be 3 ms by 60 neural inputs (0.6 ERB) with an optimum firing threshold of $\rho = 2$. The frequency step is 0.2 ERB. Each octopus cell overlaps 0.4 ERB with its neighbor. The time step is 1 ms.

The lateral lemniscus (LL) model determines the rate $R_{O_w(t,f)}$ at which the octopus cells corresponding to frequency f fire at time t. The rate (inverse inter-spike interval) is determined as follows

$$R_{O_w(t,f)} = \frac{1}{\tau(O_w(t_m,f)) - \tau(O_w(t_n,f))} \tag{3}$$

where $\tau(O_w(t,f)) = t$, and $O_w(t_m,f)$ and $O_w(t_n,f)$ are two chronologically ordered, nonzero instances of octopus cell activation, i.e., $t_m > t_n$.

The multipolar neurons of the CN calculate the average spectral level of synchronous frequencies. The average spectral level is calculated as follows

$$M_w(t,f) = \frac{\sum_{\tau=0}^{T_w-1} \sum_{\phi=0}^{F_w-1} I(t-\tau, f-\phi)}{T_w F_w} \tag{4}$$

Level is summed from all active nerve fibers in a time-frequency window of duration T_w and over F_w frequency bands. The multipolar cells use the same window as the octopus cells (3 ms by 0.6 ERB) to calculate the average level. The average level feature $M_w(t,f)$ differs from the Mel-frequency spectral coefficients (MFSCs) in at least two ways, and may therefore encode complementary information: 1.) $M_w(t,f)$ averages the log magnitude, whereas MFSC are the logarithm of an averaged magnitude, and 2.) $M_w(t,f)$ averages only detected peaks, whereas MFSC averages all signal components. These properties of the auditory model may make it more resistant to additive noise and channel-dependent filtering.

4 Experiments

Ten support vector machines (SVMs) were trained using the TIMIT corpus to detect the landmarks listed in Table 1. The training set consisted of the SX TIMIT audio files. The two separate test sets contained the SI files from TIMIT and the SI files from NTIMIT. A total of 10000 training tokens (5000 landmark tokens and 5000 non-landmark tokens) were extracted from the TIMIT training data. A total of 8000 tokens (4000 landmark tokens and 4000 non-landmark tokens) were extracted for each of the test sets. No tokens overlap between the training and testing sets.

For the training set and each of the test sets, Mel-frequency cepstral coefficients (MFCCs), the neural firing rate and level features described in this paper (NRL), and a combination set of the MFCCs and NRLs (MFCCNRL) were calculated. The MFCCs were calculated using a 25 ms window with a time-step of 5 ms. NRL features are calculated every millisecond to match the maximal firing rate of the octopus cells of the CN. The NRL feature vector is a 276 dimensional vector composed of 138 instances of $O_w(t,f)$ and 138 instances of $M_w(t,f)$ for the window w at time t.

The training and testing data for each landmark detector SVM in Table 1 consist of feature vectors $\vec{x}_t$ containing 11 concatenated acoustic feature frames. The first frame in $\vec{x}_t$ was sampled at 50 ms before the landmark, the 6th frame was sampled at the landmark time t, and the 11th frame was sampled at 50 ms after the landmark; i.e., $\vec{x}_t \equiv [\vec{y}_{t-50}, \ldots, \vec{y}_t, \ldots, \vec{y}_{t+50}]$ where $\vec{y}_t$ included either MFCCs, NRLs, or a combination of MFCCs and NRL features (MFCC-NRL). In other words, $\vec{x}_t$ is created by concatenating n acoustic feature frames on both sides of the landmark frame $\vec{y}_t$, where the time step between frames is 10 ms and the total number of concatenated frames in $\vec{x}_t$ is $2n+1$.

Radial basis function (RBF) SVMs (Burges, 1998) were trained on TIMIT to detect acoustic landmarks. The TIMIT landmark detectors were tested on TIMIT and NTIMIT. No adaption algorithms were implemented. Results are shown in Table 1. SVM training and testing was performed using LibSVM (Chang and Lin, 2001).

5 Results

Landmark detection results are shown in Table 1. When training and testing conditions are matched, NRL and MFCCNRL-based detectors outperform the MFCC baseline. Detectors trained on MFCCNRLs are not as accurate as those trained on the NRLs alone. When training and testing conditions are mismatched, (i.e., added noise and downsampling), the overall landmark detection accuracy degrades. In mismatched conditions, NRL and MFCCNRL-based landmark detectors generally either outperform the MFCC baseline or do not produce results significantly different from the baseline. SVM landmark detectors trained on the MFCCNRL do not perform as well as the SVMs trained on NRL. Significance is calculated using the binomial

	TIMIT/TIMIT			TIMIT/NTIMIT		
	MFCC	NRL	MFCCNRL	MFCC	NRL	MFCCNRL
−+silence	92.6	**94.7**	93.4	84.3	**86.1**	85.8
+−silence	87.2	**94.9**	91.6	82.3	**87.6**	86.8
−+continuant	81.2	**89.1**	86.4	70.8	**79.4**	**79.4**
+−continuant	92.3	**92.7**	91.5	85.5	**86.5**	85.3
−+sonorant	81.9	**88.8**	86.5	74.0	73.5	**77.9**
+−sonorant	**93.9**	92.6	93.1	86.2	79.1	**88.0**
−+syllabic	85.6	**89.5**	85.5	77.0	**87.1**	80.5
+−syllabic	85.8	**88.1**	84.5	83.0	**86.5**	79.5
−+consonantal	90.8	**92.0**	90.0	86.5	83.2	**87.3**
+−consonantal	80.4	**85.4**	82.2	71.2	71.6	**74.9**

Table 1: Support vector machine (SVM) landmark detection results for SVMs trained and tested on TIMIT (TIMIT/TIMIT), and for SVMs trained on TIMIT and tested on NTIMIT (TIMIT/NTIMIT). SVMs are trained using a Mel-frequency cepstral coefficients (MFCCs), auditory neural rate and level (NRL), and a combination of MFCCs and NRLs (MFCCNRL). Chance is 50%. Underlined values show a significant difference in accuracy from the MFCC baseline for $p = 0.05/20 = 0.0025$. The factor of 20 is necessary because for any given test set, the table above shows the results of 20 simultaneous significance tests.

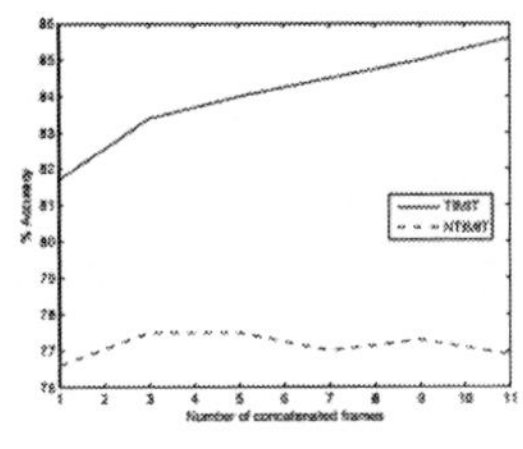

Figure 5: Detection accuracy as a function of the number of concatenated acoustic feature frames in $\vec{x}_t$ for the [−+syllabic] MFCC-based landmark detection SVM. The [−+syllabic] landmark detector was tested on TIMIT (solid line) and NTIMIT (dashed line).

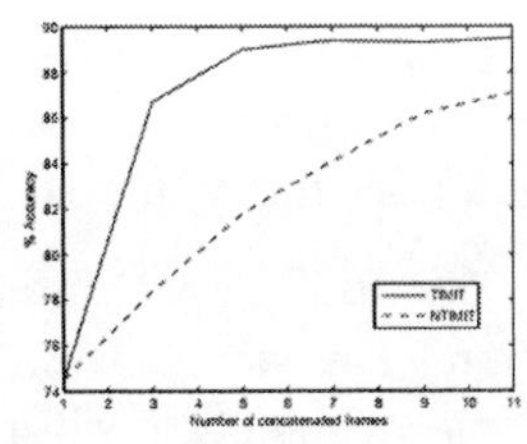

Figure 6: Detection accuracy as a function the number of concatenated acoustic feature frames in $\vec{x}_t$ for the [−+syllabic] rate and level-based landmark detection SVM. The [−+syllabic] landmark detector was tested on TIMIT (solid line) and NTIMIT (dashed line).

test described in (Gillick and Cox, 1989).

Figure 5 shows a plot of detection accuracy vs number of concatenated frames in $\vec{x}_t$ for the MFCC-based [−+syllabic] landmark detector for both test corpora. For MFCC-based SVMs, no significant increase in detection accuracy is observed as a function of the number of concate-

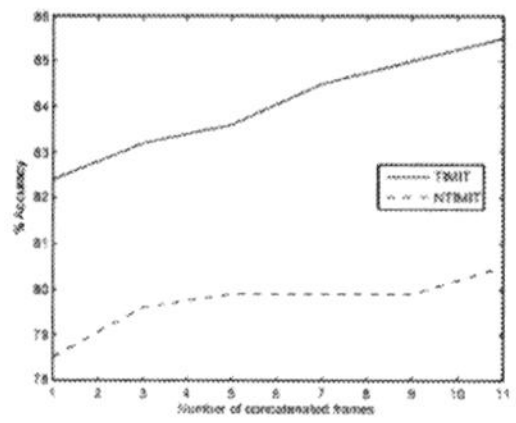

Figure 7: Detection accuracy as a function of the number of concatenated acoustic feature frames in $\vec{x}_t$ for the [−+syllabic] MFCC/rate and level-based landmark detection SVM. The [−+syllabic] landmark detector was tested on TIMIT (solid line) and NTIMIT (dashed line).

nated frames when the training and testing conditions are mismatched. Detection accuracy increases as a function of the number of concatenated frames when the training and testing conditions are matched.

Figure 6 shows a plot of detection accuracy vs number of concatenated frames in $\vec{x}_t$ for the NRL-based [−+syllabic] landmark detector for both test corpora. The detection accuracy of the NRL-based SVMs increases as a function of the number of concatenated frames regardless of whether the training and testing conditions are matched or mismatched.

Figure 7 shows a plot of detection accuracy vs the number of concatenated frames in $\vec{x}_t$ for the MFCCNRL-based [−+syllabic] landmark detector. There is a slight increase in landmark detection accuracy as a function of the number of concatenated frames for both matched and mismatched conditions.

Conclusion

This paper explores the use of octopus cell neural firing rate and average spectral level as acoustic features, and presents an auditory model that can be used to create these features. Neural firing rate and average spectral level accurately represent acoustic-phonetic landmarks in both matched and mismatched conditions.

The current system exploits only the left channel of the model. In the brainstem, input to both ears is essential for signal denoising. Future work will explore methods to combine both channels to increase landmark detection accuracy in mismatched conditions.

Accurate landmark detection may be essential for accurate phonetic segmentation — a process that is essential for speech recognition. The current system provides a building block for an automatic speech segmentation system designed to be integrated with a speech recognizer. Implementation of these systems is the focus of future research.

Acknowledgments

This work was supported in part by a grant from the National Science Foundation (CCF 0807329) and in part by a grant from the Qatar National Research Foundation (NPRP 09-410-1-069). The findings and opinions expressed in this article are those of the authors, and are not endorsed by QNRF or the NSF.

References

Bekesy, G. v. (1960). *Experiments in Hearing*. McGraw-Hill, New York, NY.

Borys, S. (2008). An SVM front end landmark speech recognition system. Master's thesis, University of Illinois, Urbana-Champaign.

Borys, S. and Hasegawa-Johnson, M. (2005). Distinctive feature based discriminant features for improvements to phone recognition on telephone band speech. In *Eurospeech*, pages 679–700.

Bourlard, H. (1996). A new ASR approach based on independent processing and recombination of partial frequency bands. *ICSLP*, 1.

Burges, C. (1998). A tutorial on support vector machines. *Data Mining and Knowledge Recovery*, 2(2).

Chang, C.-C. and Lin, C.-J. (2001). *LIBSVM: a library for support vector machines*. Software available at http://www.csie.ntu.edu.tw/ cjlin/libsvm.

Chigier, B. (1991). Phonetic classification on wide-band and telephone quality speech. In *International Conference on Acoustics, Speech, and Signal Processing*.

Cohen, J. (1989). Application of an auditory model to speech recognition. *JASA*, 85(6).

Ehret, G. and Romand, R., editors (1997). *The Central Auditory System*. Oxford University Press, New York, NY.

Garofolo, J., Lamel, L., Fisher, W., Fiscus, J., Pallett, D., and Dahlgren, N. (1993). The DARPA TIMIT acoustic phonetic speech corpus. Technical report, National Institute of Standards and Technology, Gaithersburg, MD.

Geisler, C. D. (1998). *From Sound To Synapse: Physiology Of The Mammilian Ear*. Oxford University Press, Oxford, NY.

Ghitza, O. (1994). Auditory models and human performance to tasks related to speech coding and speech recognition. *IEEE Transactions on Speech and Audio Processing*, 2(1).

Gillick, L. and Cox, S. (1989). Some statistical issues in the comparison of speech recognition algorithms. In *ICASSP*.

Gong, Y. (1995). Speech recognition in noisy environments: A survey. *Speech Communication*, 16.

Greenberg, S. (1988). The ear as a speech analyzer. *Journal of Phonetics*.

Halberstadt, A. K. and Glass, J. R. (1998). Heterogeneous measurements and multiple classifiers for speech recognition. In *International Conference on Speech and Language Processing*, Sydney, Australia.

Hasegawa-Johnson, M., Baker, J., Greenberg, S., Kirchhoff, K., Muller, J., Sommez, K., Borys, S., Chen, K., Juneja, A., Livescu, K., Mohan, S., Coogan, E., and Wong, T. (2004). Landmark-Based speech recognition: Report of the 2004 Johns Hopkins summer workshop. Technical report, Johns Hopkins University, Center for Speech and Language Processing, Baltimore, MD.

Hunt, M. and Lefebvre, C. (1989). A comparison of several acoustic representations for speech recognition for degraded and undegraded speech. In *ICASSP*, volume 1.

Jankowski, C., Kalyanswamy, J., Basson, S., and Spritz, J. (1990). NTIMIT: A phonetically blaanced, continuous speech, telephone bandwidth speech database. In *International Conference on Acoustics, Speech, and Signal Processing*, volume 1, pages 109–112.

Juneja, A. and Espy-Wilson, C. (2004). Significance of invariant acoustic cues in a probabilistic framework for landmark-based speech recognition. In *From Sound to Sense: 50+ Years of Discoveries in Speech Communication*, pages C–151–C–156. MIT, Cambridge, MA.

Karray, L. and Martin, A. (2003). Towards improving speech detection robustness for speech recognition in adverse conditions. *Speech Communication*, 40.

Kim, D., Lee, S., and Kil, R. (1999). Auditory processing of speech signals for robust speech recognition in real-world noisy environments. *IEEE Transactions on Speech and Audio Processing*, 7(1).

Kirchhoff, K. (1999). *Robust speech recognition using articulatory information*. PhD thesis, University of Bielefield, Germany.

Moore, B. and Glasberg, B. (1983). Suggested formulae for calculating auditory-filter bandwidths and excitation patterns. *JASA*, 74(3).

Moreno, P. and Stern, R. (1994). Sources of degradation of speech recognition in the telephone network. In *IEEE Conference on Acoustics, Speech, and Signal Processing*, volume 1, pages 109–112.

Patterson, R. and Holdsworth, J. (1996). A functional model of neural activity patterns and auditory images. *Advances in Speech, Hearing, and Language Processing*, 3.

Schnupp, J., Nelken, I., and King, A. (2011). *Auditory Neuroscience: Making Sense of Sound*. MIT Press, Cambridge, MA.

Stevens, K. (1999). *Acoustic Phonetics*. MIT Press, Cambridge, MA.

Tidemann, J. (2011). Characterization of the head-related transfer function using chirp and maximum length excitation signals. Master's thesis, University of Illinois.

Virag, N. (1999). Single channel speech enhancement based on masking properties of the human auditory system. *IEEE Transactions on Speech and Audio Processing*, 7(2).

Winer, J. A. and Schreiner, C. E. (2005). *The central auditory system: A functional analysis*, chapter 1. Springer Science+Business Media, Inc., New York, NY.

Ying, S., Werner, V., and Xue-ying, Z. (2012). A robust feature approach based on an auditory model for classification of speech and expressiveness. *J. Cent. South Univ.*, 19.

Learning Verbs on the Fly

Zornitsa Kozareva
USC Information Sciences Institute
4676 Admiralty Way
Marina del Rey, CA 90292-6695
kozareva@isi.edu

ABSTRACT
To answer the question *"What are the duties of a medical doctor?"*, one would require knowledge about verb-based relations. A lot of effort has been invested in developing relation learners, however to our knowledge there is no repository (or system) which can return all verb relations for a given term. This paper describes an automated procedure which can learn and produce such information with minimal effort. To evaluate the performance of our verb harvesting procedure, we have conducted two types of evaluations: (1) in the human based evaluation we found that the accuracy of the described algorithm is .95 at rank 100; (2) in the comparative study with existing relation learner and knowledge bases we found that our approach yields 12 times more verb relations.

KEYWORDS: verb harvesting, relation learning, information extraction, knowledge acquisition.

Proceedings of COLING 2012: Posters, pages 599–610,
COLING 2012, Mumbai, December 2012.

1 Introduction

To be able to answer the questions *"What causes ebola?"*, *"What are the duties of a medical doctor?"*, *"What are the differences between a terrorist and a victim?"*, *"Which are the animals that have wings but cannot fly?"* one requires knowledge about verb-based relations. Over the years, researchers have developed various relation learning algorithms. Some (Ravichandran and Hovy, 2002; Bunescu and Mooney, 2007) targeted specific relations like *BornInYear*, *CorporationAcquired*, others (Wu and Weld, 2010; Fader et al., 2011) extracted any phrase denoting a relation in an English sentence. (Banko, 2009) used labeled data to learn relations, (Suchanek et al., 2007) used information encoded in the structured Wikipedia documents, (Riloff and Jones, 1999) bootstrapped patterns. As a result various knowledge bases have been produced like TopicSignatures (Agirre and Lacalle, 2004), ConceptNet (Liu and Singh, 2004), Yago (Suchanek et al., 2007), NELL (Carlson et al., 2009) and ReVerb (Fader et al., 2011).

Despite the many efforts to date, yet there is no universal repository (or even a system), which for a given term it can immediately return all verb relations related to the term. However, one would still like to dispose of an automated procedure, which on the fly can accurately and quickly produce such information for any term. If available, such resource can aid different natural language processing tasks such as preposition sense disambiguation (Litkowski and Hargraves, 2007), selectional preferences (Resnik, 1996; Ritter et al., 2010), question answering (Ferrucci et al., 2010) and textual entailment (Szpektor et al., 2004).

The question we address in this paper is: *Is it possible to create a procedure which will go beyond existing techniques and learn in a semi-supervised manner for a given term all verb relations associated with it?*

The main contributions of the paper are:

- We develop an automatic procedure, which on the fly can learn a diverse set of *verb* and *verb-preposition* relations for a given term.
- We establish the effectiveness of our approach through human-based evaluation.
- We conduct a comparative study with the verb-based relation extraction system ReVerb (Fader et al., 2011) and show that our approach accurately extracts more verb-based relations.
- We also compare the verb relations produced by our system with those available in existing knowledge bases, and observe that despite their completeness these repositories lack many verb-based relations.

The rest of the paper is organized as follows. Next, we present related work. Section 3 outlines the verb-based relation learner. Section 4 describes the data collection process. Section 5 reports on the experimental results. Finally, we conclude in Section 6.

2 Related Work

Lots of attention has been payed on learning *is-a* and *part-of* relations (Hearst, 1992; Girju et al., 2003; Pasca, 2004; Etzioni et al., 2005; Kozareva et al., 2008; Pantel and Pennacchiotti, 2006; Carlson et al., 2009; Talukdar et al., 2008). Others (Ravichandran and Hovy, 2002; Bunescu and Mooney, 2007) have focused on learning specific relations like *BornInYear*, *EmployedBy* and *CorporationAcquired*. However to build a system that can learn a richer set of relations is not trivial, because often labeled training data is required (Kim and Moldovan, 1993; Soderland et al., 1999) and most methods do not scale to corpora where the number of relations is very large or when the relations are not specified in advance (Fader et al., 2011).

However, recently developed OpenIE systems like TextRunner (Banko et al., 2007; Banko, 2009) and ReVerb (Fader et al., 2011) surmount the necessity of labeled data by extracting arbitrary phrases denoting relations in English sentences. (Banko et al., 2007; Banko, 2009) define relation to be any verb-prep, adj-noun construction. While such systems are great at learning general relations, they are not guided but simply gather in an undifferentiated way whatever happens to be contained in their input. In order to be able to extract all verb relations associated with a given term, such systems need to part-of-speech tag and parse a large document collection, then they have to extract all verb constructions and all arguments matching specific sets of patterns which were written by humans (or experts). Finally, they must filter out the information and retrieve only those verb relations that are associated with the specific term. Once compiled the repository is straightforward to query and use, however if a term is not present in the compiled repository, repeating the whole process on a new document collection becomes time consuming and unpractical. The main objective and contribution of our research is the development of a dynamic and flexible knowledge harvesting procedure, which for any given term can learn on the fly verb based relations associated with the term in a very fast and accurate manner.

3 Learning Verb-based Relations

3.1 Problem Formulation

We define our task as given a term, a relation expressed by a verb and a set of prepositions: (1) learn in bootstrapping fashion new relations (i.e. *verbs*) associated with the initial term and filter out erroneous extractions; (2) form triples of the term, the harvested verbs and the initial set of prepositions to learn additional relations (i.e. *verb-prepositions*) and their argument fillers.

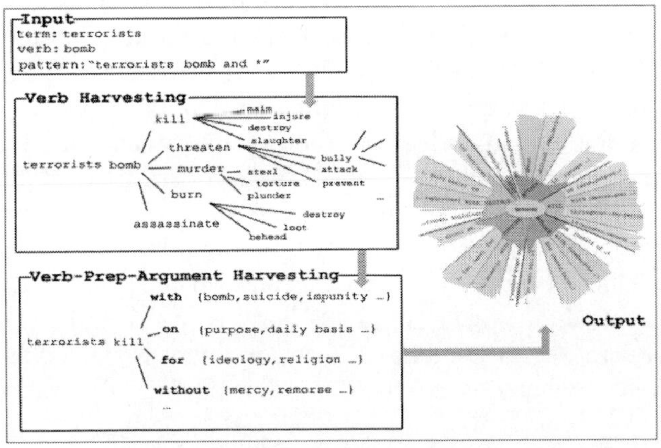

Figure 1: Verb-based Relation Learning.

Figure 1 shows an example for the input term *terrorists*, the verb relation *bomb* and the recursive pattern "*terrorists bomb and* *". The algorithm learns on the * position verbs like *kill, murder, threaten, burn, assassinate*. We denote this phase as *verb* extraction. Then each learned verb is used to form triples of the type *term-verb-preposition* to learn new verb-preposition relations and their argument fillers. For instance, "*terrorists kill with* *" extracts arguments like {*bombs, suicide, impunity*}. We denote this phase as *verb-preposition* extraction. Finally, the learned relations and arguments are ranked and arranged by their ranking score. The output of this harvesting procedure is triples of the kind "*terrorists kill people*", "*terrorists kill on purpose*", "*terrorists bomb buildings*" among others.

3.2 Algorithm Description

Because of their fixed nature, pattern-based methods often fail to extract information from small corpus or single document. However, nowadays we dispose of endless amount of data, which is easily accessible and is making it possible for such systems to work successfully by scanning billions of Web pages to extract the necessary information. Many of the existing and most accurate is-a relation learners rely on lexico-syntactic patterns (Hearst, 1992; Pasca, 2004; Etzioni et al., 2005), therefore we decided to use patterns for the verb extraction procedure.

PHASE1: Learning *Verb* Relations. The first phase of the algorithm focuses on verb extraction. We use (Kozareva et al., 2008) recursive DAP pattern for is-a relation learning and adapted it to verb extraction as follows: "*<seed-term>* *<seed-verb>* and *", where *<seed-term>* is any term (noun) given by the user or taken from an existing knowledge base, *<seed-verb>* is a seed relation expressed through a verb and * indicates the position on which new verbs will be extracted. The generated patterns are submitted to the search engine as a web query and all retrieved snippets are kept. The algorithm extracts on the position of the $*$ all verb constructions and if they were not previously explored by the algorithm, they are placed on the *<seed-verb>* position of DAP and used as seeds in the subsequent verb extraction iteration. The harvesting terminates when there are no more verbs to be explored. Following (Kozareva et al., 2008), we filter out erroneous extractions using graph ranking. We build a directed graph $G = (V, E)$, where each node $v \in V$ is an extracted verb candidate and $(u, v) \in E$ is an edge between two verb nodes indicating that the verb u lead to the extraction of the verb v. Each node u in the graph is ranked as $u = \sum_{\forall(u,v)\in E}(u, v)$. Confidence in u increases when u extracts more verbs.

PHASE2: Learning *Verb-Preposition* Relations. In the second phase, the learned verbs are paired with an initial set of 17 prepositions to learn new relations and argument fillers. The prepositions were taken from the SemEval 2007 task on preposition disambiguation (Litkowski and Hargraves, 2007). To extract more relations, the algorithm uses the pattern "*<seed-term>* *<verb>* *<prep>* *", where *<seed-term>* is the initial term for which we want to learn verb-based relations, *<verb>* are the leaned verbs from the previous phase and * is the position of the argument fillers. Given the relation *kill* for the term *terrorists*, new relations like *terrorists kill on*, *terrorists kill with*, *terrorists kill for* and *terrorists kill without* are instantiated[1]. Similarly to the verb extraction phase, we rank terms by building a bipartite graph $G' = (V', E')$ with two types of nodes. One set represents the verbs and verb-prepositions V, and the other set represents the arguments A. An edge $e'(v, a) \in E'$ between $v \in V$ and $a \in A$ shows that the verb (or verb-prep) v extracted the argument a. Each argument is ranked as $a = \sum_{\forall(v,a)\in E'}(v, a)$. Confidence in a increases when a is extracted multiple times by different verbs.

4 Data Collection

It is impossible to collect and report results for *all* terms in the world. Still to evaluate the effectiveness of our verb-based relation learner, we have randomly selected 36 terms, which capture daily activities like going to a restaurant to unpleasant events like bombing. For the purpose of visualization, we have organized the terms into the following groups (topics): *Bombing*, *Diseases*, *Elections*, *Restaurants*, and *Animals*.

Table 1 shows the terms and seed verbs used to initiate the verb-based relation learning process, and summarizes the obtained results and the total number of iterations which were run to extract the verbs. *#Verbs Unique* shows the number of unique verbs after merging expressions

[1]Some verbs cannot be paired with all prepositions, we filter out those for which no results were found.

Seed Term	Seed Verb	#Verbs Learned	#Verbs Unique	#Iter.	#Args. Learned	#Args. with $a > 5$
BOMBING						
authorities	say	3049	1805	14	7284	151
bomb	explodes	1020	705	11	13454	451
bombers	explode	265	224	19	9097	344
killers	kill	178	163	14	6906	217
soldiers	die	4588	2533	10	34330	1010
terrorists	kill	1401	941	10	13698	468
victims	suffer	1861	1263	13	21982	767
totalDomain	6	12362	7632	–	106751	3408
DISEASE						
bacteria	caused	1439	853	10	39573	1261
cancer	caused	1389	848	7	42640	1585
diseases	caused	792	582	12	38307	1387
doctors	cure	2700	1611	10	56935	1050
drugs	caused	1936	1242	9	60393	1890
nurses	help	1882	1167	8	39305	675
patient	lives	1631	923	9	78946	1668
virus	caused	1835	992	10	43481	1372
totalDomain	4	13604	8218	–	399580	9838
ELECTION						
candidates	vote	2116	1299	8	55009	1078
congressmen	say	92	86	9	5601	123
senators	vote	718	510	16	12385	340
presidents	run	717	535	11	18476	420
voters	vote	1400	935	13	38298	785
totalDomain	3	5043	3365	–	129769	2746
RESTAURANT						
drinks	tasted	881	591	11	39086	1088
food	tasted	984	664	8	74399	1740
meals	tasted	775	562	10	48474	1144
menu	looks	1479	870	11	51278	1041
restaurants	serve	711	532	8	36120	776
waiters	serve	123	107	9	8457	151
totalDomain	3	4953	3326	–	257814	5940
ANIMALS						
ants	eat	827	607	12	25046	753
birds	eat	3623	2064	8	62031	1465
dinosaurs	eat	544	386	11	11013	345
jellyfish	eat	12	11	4	1120	20
lice	eat	42	42	8	3330	131
mammals	eat	338	272	10	14224	527
otters	eat	190	159	8	5051	159
sharks	eat	697	500	12	16942	598
slugs	eat	60	60	11	5223	89
vultures	eat	36	36	5	2757	67
totalDomain	1	6369	4137	–	146737	4154

Table 1: *Tested Terms for Verb-based Relation Learning and Extracted Information.*

like (*were killed, are killed, killed*). For each domain, we also show the total number of verbs used to initiate the harvesting process and the total number of learned information. In total, we have submitted $\sim 101,559$ queries and we have collected 10.3GB snippets, which were cleaned, part-of-speech tagged (Schmid, 1994) and used for the extraction of the verb-based relations and arguments. In total for all terms the algorithm extracted $26,678$ candidate relations and $1,040,651$ candidate arguments of which $26,086$ have rank $a>5$.

5 Evaluation and Results

In this section, we evaluate the results of the verb-based relation learning procedure, which is extremely challenging because there is no universal knowledge repository against which one can compare performance in terms of precision and recall. To the extend to which it is possible, we conduct a human-based evaluation and we compare results to knowledge bases that have been extracted in a similar way (i.e., through pattern application over unstructured text).

5.1 Human-based Evaluation

Among the most common approaches on evaluating the correctness of the harvested information is by using human annotators (Pantel and Pennacchiotti, 2006; Navigli et al., 2011). Conducting such evaluations is very important, because the harvested information is often used by QA, machine reading and IE systems (Ferrucci et al., 2010; Freedman et al., 2011).

Since the evaluation of all $1,067,329$ harvested terms is time consuming and costly, we decided to annotate for each term 100 verb relations and argument fillers. We conducted two separate annotations for the verbs and arguments, which resulted in 7200 annotations. We used two annotators who were instructed to mark as incorrect verbs (and argument fillers) that do not correspond to the term. For instance, "*drugs affect*" is marked as correct, while "*drugs discuss*" is marked as incorrect. We compute *Accuracy* as the number of *Correct* terms, divided by the total number of terms used in the annotation. Table 2 shows the accuracy of each domain at different ranks. The overall performance of our relation learner is .95 at rank 100 for the learned verbs and argument fillers. Tables 3 and 4 show examples of the harvested information.

5.2 Comparison with Existing Knowledge Bases

In this evaluation, we measure the ability of our system to learn verb-based relations of a term with respect to already existing knowledge bases, which have been created in a similar way. However, such comparative evaluations are not always possible to perform, because researchers have not fully explored the same terms and relations we have studied. When we compared results against existing knowledge bases, we noticed that Yago (Suchanek et al., 2007) has more detailed information for the arguments of the verb relations rather than the verb relations themselves. Repositories like ConceptNet[2] (Liu and Singh, 2004) contain 1.6 million assertions, however they only belong to twenty relation types such as *is-a, part-of, made-of, effect-of* among others. The only repository that we found with a diverse set of verb relations is the never-ending language learner NELL[3] (Carlson et al., 2009). However, there were only 11 verb relations for *bomb* and 2 verb relations for *virus*. This analysis shows that despite their completeness and richness, existing knowledge repositories can be further enriched with verb-based relations produced by our learning procedure.

[2] http://web.media.mit.edu/~hugo/conceptnet/#overview

[3] Comparison done in March 2012 with http://rtw.ml.cmu.edu/rtw/kbbrowser/

Term	Accuracy Verbs			Accuracy Arguments		
	@10	@50	@100	@10	@50	@100
BOMBING						
authorities	1	1	1	1	1	.90
soldiers	1	1	1	1	1	.97
killers	1	.98	.99	1	1	.96
Av.Domain	1	.98	.98	1	1	.97
DISEASE						
diseases	1	.98	.95	1	1	.94
virus	1	.94	.93	1	1	.93
drugs	1	.92	.94	1	1	.93
Av.Domain	.99	.97	.96	1	1	.93
ELECTION						
candidates	1	1	1	1	1	1
voters	1	1	1	1	1	1
senators	1	1	.95	1	1	.97
Av.Domain	1	.99	.95	1	1	.96
RESTAURANT						
food	1	1	.93	1	1	.94
restaurants	1	.94	.89	1	1	.98
menu	1	.92	.89	1	1	.95
Av.Domain	1	.94	.89	1	1	.95
ANIMALS						
otters	1	1	.96	1	1	.94
mammals	1	1	.95	1	1	.95
sharks	1	1	.98	1	1	1
Av.Domain	1	.99	.96	1	1	.92

Table 2: *Accuracy of the Harvested Information.*

Term	Learned Verbs
diseases	spread, develop, treat, come, kill, mutate, diagnose, evolve, are caught, survive, grow, occur, carry, cause, are cured, affect, are identified, start, prevent, propagate, are transmitted, thrive, sicken, change, flourish
meals	are prepared, are served, are cooked, are delivered, are planned, are eaten, are tasted, are provided, look, are made, are consumed, are offered, are created, are frozen, are bought, are packed, are paid, smell, are designed, are purchased, are sold, are produced, are prepped, are shared, are catered
soldiers	kill, shoot, beat, fought, fell, destroyed, fired, attacked, are trained, died, took, said, laughed, kicked, die, were humiliating, cheered, mocked, raised, drummed, captured, looted, ran, arrested, buried, defended

Table 3: *Examples of Learned Verbs.*

5.3 Comparison with Existing Relation Learner

For our comparative study with existing systems, we used ReVerb[4] (Fader et al., 2011), which similarly to our approach was specifically designed to learn verb-based relations from unstructured texts. Currently, ReVerb has extracted relations from ClueWeb09[5] and Wikipedia, which have been freely distributed to the public. ReVerb learns relations by taking as input any document and applies POS-tagging, NP-chunking and a set of rules over all sentences in the document to generate triples containing the verbs and the arguments associated with them. According to (Fader et al., 2011) ReVerb outperforms TextRunner (Banko et al., 2007) and the open Wikipedia extractor WOE (Wu and Weld, 2010) in terms of the quantity and quality of the learned relations. For comparison, we took five terms from our experiment: *ant, bomb, president, terrorists, virus* and collected all verbs found by ReVerb in the ClueWeb09 and Wikipedia triples.

Table 5 summarizes the total number of unique verb extractions found by ReVerb in ClueWeb09 since the Wikipedia ones had low coverage. We have also manually validated the correctness of the verbs found by ReVerb and have seen that their accuracy is 100%. With respect to our extractions ReVerb has lower recall.

[4]http://reverb.cs.washington.edu/

[5]http://lemurproject.org/clueweb09.php/

Term-Verb	Preposition	Learned Arguments
terrorists communicate	**through**	violence, micro technology, orkut secure channels, email, internet, internet networks, cellphones
	with	their contacts, each other, the world, other terrorists, US citizens, Korea, governments, America
	in	brief, code, VW, Russian, French, various ways, secret, English
	by	mail, phone, fax, email
	without	detection, tapping calls
birds fly	**above**	earth, castles, our heads, trees, lake, field, river, cloud, city
	through	air, night, sky, park, country club, wind, storm, region, city
	around	her, fish, house, my head, bird feeder, home, your city, ruins, place
	across	sky, gulf, screen, rainbow, sunset, horizon, african savanna, our path, street, hometown
	into	windows, walls, power lines, towers, sun, sea, darkness, mist, house
killers kill	**for**	power, thrill, sexual reasons, money, fun, the sake, rush, sport, cash, fame
	in	ridiculous ways, patterns, cold blood, silence, groups, conflict with, series, certain periods, captivity, sequence
	with	some criteria, knife, brutality, hands, motive, intention, impunity, stealth, purpose, violence
	to	relieve themselves, symbolize, show others, make a statement, just kill, gain money, gain identity, gain control, gain material
	over	a period, time, robberies, course, many months, multiple time

Table 4: *Examples of Learned Arguments.*

Term	ClueWeb (ReVerb)	Web (DAP)
ants	32	607
bomb	46	535
presidents	32	705
terrorists	96	941
virus	128	992

Table 5: *Comparison of Verb-based Relation Learners.*

6 Conclusion

Our key contribution is the development of a semi-supervised procedure, which starts with a term and a verb to learn from Web documents a large and diverse set of verb relations. We have conducted an experimental evaluation with 36 terms and have collected 26,678 unique candidate verbs and 1,040,651 candidate argument fillers. We have evaluated the accuracy of our approach using human based evaluation and have compared results against the ReVerb (Fader et al., 2011) system and existing knowledge bases like NELL (Carlson et al., 2009), Yago (Suchanek et al., 2007) and ConceptNet (Liu and Singh, 2004). Our study showed that despite their completeness these resources lack verb-based information and there is plenty of room for improvement since they can be further enriched with verbs using our harvesting procedure. In the future, we would like to test the usefulness of the generated resources in NLP applications.

Acknowledgements

We would like to thank Ed Hovy for initial comments on the work and the anonymous reviewers.

References

Agirre, E. and Lacalle, O. L. D. (2004). Publicly available topic signatures for all wordnet nominal senses.

Alfonseca, E., Pasca, M., and Robledo-Arnuncio, E. (2010). Acquisition of instance attributes via labeled and related instances. In *Proceedings of the 33rd international ACM SIGIR conference on Research and development in information retrieval*, SIGIR '10, pages 58–65.

Banko, M. (2009). Open information extraction from the web. In *Ph.D. Dissertation from University of Washington*.

Banko, M., Cafarella, M. J., Soderl, S., Broadhead, M., and Etzioni, O. (2007). Open information extraction from the web. In *In IJCAI*, pages 2670–2676.

Buitelaar, P., Cimiano, P., and Magnini, B., editors (2005). *Ontology Learning from Text: Methods, Evaluation and Applications*, volume 123 of *Frontiers in Artificial Intelligence and Applications*. IOS Press, Amsterdam.

Bunescu, R. and Mooney, R. (2007). Learning to extract relations from the web using minimal supervision. In *Proceedings of the 45th Annual Meeting of the Association of Computational Linguistics*, pages 576–583.

Carlson, A., Betteridge, J., Jr., E. R. H., and Mitchell, T. M. (2009). Coupling semi-supervised learning of categories and relations. In *Proceedings of the NAACL HLT 2009 Workskop on Semi-supervised Learning for Natural Language Processing*.

Cuadros, M. and Rigau, G. (2008). KnowNet: A Proposal for Building Highly Connected and Dense Knowledge Bases from the Web. In *Semantics in Text Processing. STEP 2008 Conference Proceedings*, volume 1 of *Research in Computational Semantics*, pages 71–84.

Etzioni, O., Cafarella, M., Downey, D., Popescu, A.-M., Shaked, T., Soderland, S., Weld, D. S., and Yates, A. (2005). Unsupervised named-entity extraction from the web: an experimental study. *Artificial Intelligence*, 165(1):91–134.

Fader, A., Soderland, S., and Etzioni, O. (2011). Identifying relations for open information extraction. In *Proceedings of the 2011 Conference on Empirical Methods in Natural Language Processing, EMNLP 2011*, pages 1535–1545.

Ferrucci, D., Brown, E., Chu-Carroll, J., Fan, J., Gondek, D., Kalyanpur, A. A., Lally, A., Murdock, J. W., Nyberg, E., Prager, J., Schlaefer, N., and Welty, C. (2010). Building watson: An overview of the deepqa project. *AI Magazine*, 31(3):59–79.

Freedman, M., Ramshaw, L. A., Boschee, E., Gabbard, R., Kratkiewicz, G., Ward, N., and Weischedel, R. M. (2011). Extreme extraction - machine reading in a week. In *Proceedings of the 2011 Conference on Empirical Methods in Natural Language Processing, EMNLP 2011*, pages 1437–1446.

Girju, R., Badulescu, A., and Moldovan, D. (2003). Learning semantic constraints for the automatic discovery of part-whole relations. In *Proceedings of the 2003 Conference of the North American Chapter of the Association for Computational Linguistics on Human Language Technology*, pages 1–8.

Girju, R., Nakov, P., Nastaste, V., Szpakowicz, S., Turney, P., and Yuret, D. (2007). SemEval-2007 task 04: Classification of semantic relations between nominals. In *SemEval 2007*.

Hearst, M. (1992). Automatic acquisition of hyponyms from large text corpora. In *Proceedings of the 14th conference on Computational linguistics*, pages 539–545.

Igo, S. and Riloff, E. (2009). Corpus-based semantic lexicon induction with web-based corroboration. In *Proceedings of the Workshop on Unsupervised and Minimally Supervised Learning of Lexical Semantics*.

Jain, A. and Pantel, P. (2010). Factrank: Random walks on a web of facts. In *Proceedings of the 23rd International Conference on Computational Linguistics (Coling 2010)*, pages 501–509.

Katz, B. and Lin, J. (2003). Selectively using relations to improve precision in question answering. In *In Proceedings of the EACL-2003 Workshop on Natural Language Processing for Question Answering*, pages 43–50.

Kim, J. and Moldovan, D. (1993). Acquisition of semantic patterns for information extraction from corpora. In *Proceedings of Ninth IEEE Conference on Artificial Intelligence for Applications*, page 17176.

Kozareva, Z. and Hovy, E. (2010). Learning arguments and supertypes of semantic relations using recursive patterns. In *Proceedings of the 48th Annual Meeting of the Association for Computational Linguistics*, ACL '10, pages 1482–1491.

Kozareva, Z., Riloff, E., and Hovy, E. (2008). Semantic class learning from the web with hyponym pattern linkage graphs. In *Proceedings of ACL-08: HLT*, pages 1048–1056.

Lin, C.-Y. and Hovy, E. (2000). The automated acquisition of topic signatures for text summarization. In *Proceedings of the 18th conference on Computational linguistics - Volume 1*, COLING '00, pages 495–501.

Lin, D. and Pantel, P. (2002). Concept discovery from text. In *Proceedings of the 19th international conference on Computational linguistics*, pages 1–7.

Litkowski, K. C. and Hargraves, O. (2007). Semeval-2007 task 06: Word-sense disambiguation of prepositions. In *Proceedings of the Fourth International Workshop on Semantic Evaluations (SemEval-2007)*, pages 24–29.

Liu, H. and Singh, P. (2004). Focusing on ConceptNet's natural language knowledge representation. In *Commonsense Reasoning in and over Natural Language Proceedings of the 8th International Conference on Knowledge-Based Intelligent Information and Engineering Systems (KES 2004)*, pages 71–84.

Navigli, R., Velardi, P., and Faralli, S. (2011). A graph-based algorithm for inducing lexical taxonomies from scratch. In *IJCAI 2011, Proceedings of the 22nd International Joint Conference on Artificial Intelligence*, pages 1872–1877.

Pantel, P. and Pennacchiotti, M. (2006). Espresso: Leveraging generic patterns for automatically harvesting semantic relations. In *Proceedings of 21st International Conference on Computational Linguistics and 44th Annual Meeting of the Association for Computational Linguistics, ACL 2006*.

Pasca, M. (2004). Acquisition of categorized named entities for web search. In *Proceedings of the thirteenth ACM international conference on Information and knowledge management*, pages 137–145.

Ravichandran, D. and Hovy, E. (2002). Learning surface text patterns for a question answering system. In *Proceedings of the 40th Annual Meeting on Association for Computational Linguistics*, pages 41–47.

Resnik, P. (1996). Selectional constraints: an information-theoretic model and its computational realization.

Riloff, E. (1996). Automatically generating extraction patterns from untagged text. In *Proceedings of the thirteenth national conference on Artificial intelligence - Volume 2*, AAAI'96, pages 1044–1049.

Riloff, E. and Jones, R. (1999). Learning dictionaries for information extraction by multi-level bootstrapping. In *AAAI '99/IAAI '99: Proceedings of the sixteenth national conference on Artificial intelligence and the eleventh Innovative applications of artificial intelligence conference innovative applications of artificial intelligence*.

Ritter, A., Mausam, and Etzioni, O. (2010). A latent dirichlet allocation method for selectional preferences. In *Proceedings of the 48th Annual Meeting of the Association for Computational Linguistics*, ACL 2010, pages 424–434.

Schmid, H. (1994). Probabilistic part-of-speech tagging using decision trees.

Sekine, S. (2006). On-demand information extraction. In *Proceedings of the COLING/ACL on Main conference poster sessions*, COLING-ACL '06, pages 731–738.

Snow, R., Jurafsky, D., and Ng, A. Y. (2006). Semantic taxonomy induction from heterogenous evidence. In *Proceedings of 21st International Conference on Computational Linguistics and 44th Annual Meeting of the Association for Computational Linguistics, ACL*.

Soderland, S., Cardie, C., and Mooney, R. (1999). Learning information extraction rules for semi-structured and free text. In *Machine Learning*, pages 233–272.

Suchanek, F. M., Kasneci, G., and Weikum, G. (2007). Yago: a core of semantic knowledge. In *WWW '07: Proceedings of the 16th international conference on World Wide Web*, pages 697–706.

Szpektor, I., Tanev, H., Dagan, I., and Coppola, B. (2004). Scaling web-based acquisition of entailment relations. In *Proc. Empirical Methods in Natural Language Processing (EMNLP)*.

Talukdar, P. P., Reisinger, J., Pasca, M., Ravichandran, D., Bhagat, R., and Pereira, F. (2008). Weakly-supervised acquisition of labeled class instances using graph random walks. In *Proceedings of the Conference on Empirical Methods in Natural Language Processing, EMNLP 2008*, pages 582–590.

Widdows, D. (2003). Unsupervised methods for developing taxonomies by combining syntactic and statistical information. In *Proceedings of HLT-NAACL*.

Wu, F. and Weld, D. S. (2010). Open information extraction using wikipedia. In *Proceedings of the 48th Annual Meeting of the Association for Computational Linguistics*, ACL '10, pages 118–127.

Decoder-based Discriminative Training of Phrase Segmentation for Statistical Machine Translation

Hyoung – Gyu Lee   *Hae – Chang Rim*
Department of Computer and Radio Communications Engineering
Korea University, Seoul, Korea
{hglee,rim}@nlp.korea.ac.kr

ABSTRACT
In this paper, we propose a new method of training phrase segmentation model for phrase-based statistical machine translation(SMT). We define a good segmentation as the segmentation producing a good translation. According to this definition, we propose a method that can discriminate between a good segmentation and a bad segmentation based on the translation quality. The proposed approach constructs the phrase labeled data by using the SMT decoder, so that the phrase segmentations supporting good translations can be acquired. Furthermore, our iterative training algorithm of the segmentation model can gradually improve the performance of the SMT decoder. Experimental results show that the proposed method is effective in improving the translation quality of the phrase-based SMT system.

TITLE AND ABSTRACT IN ANOTHER LANGUAGE (KOREAN)

통계 기계번역을 위한 디코더 기반 구 분할 차별 학습 방법

본 논문은 구 기반 통계 기계번역을 위한 구 분할 모델의 새로운 학습 방법을 제안한다. 우리는 좋은 번역(good translation)을 생성하는 구 분할을 좋은 분할(good segmentation)이라고 정의한다. 우리는 이 정의에 따라 번역 품질에 기반하여 좋은 분할과 좋지 않은 분할을 차별할 수 있는 방법을 제안한다. 제안하는 접근방법은 통계 기계번역(SMT) 디코더을 이용하여 구 부착 데이터를 구축함으로써, 좋은 번역을 만드는 구 분할을 얻을 수 있다. 또한 SMT 디코더의 성능을 점진적으로 개선시킬 수 있는 반복적인 학습 알고리즘을 제안한다. 실험을 통해, 제안 방법이 구 기반 SMT 시스템의 번역 품질 향상에 효과적이었음을 보인다.

KEYWORDS: phrase-based SMT, phrase segmentation model, decoder-based approach.
KEYWORDS IN KOREAN: 구 기반 통계 기계번역, 구 분할 모델, 디코더 기반 접근방법.

Proceedings of COLING 2012: Posters, pages 611–620,
COLING 2012, Mumbai, December 2012.

1 Introduction

Phrase segmentation model for phrase-based statistical machine translation (SMT) has been studied by several researchers in recent years (Blackwood et al., 2008; Xiong et al., 2010; Lee et al., 2011; Xiong et al., 2011). They have emphasized the necessity of the phrase segmentation model for the following reasons. First, it is required to properly group adjacent words in a sentence so that the system can consider collocation or inter-phrase context (Blackwood et al., 2008; Lee et al., 2011; Xiong et al., 2011). Second, it is also required to properly segment the input sentence to keep the translation fluency despite of the phrase reordering process (Blackwood et al., 2008). Furthermore, there are some observable differences between the segmentations producing high quality translations and low quality translations (Lee et al., 2011).

The existing phrase segmentation models for phrase-based SMT are trained by different methods. Blackwood et al. (2008)'s phrase-level n-gram model is trained through the maximum likelihood estimation from a large monolingual corpus. Lee et al. (2011)'s segmentation model has been designed as multiple scoring functions, whose parameters are obtained from a parallel corpus or a monolingual corpus.

On the other hand, the maximum entropy based segmentation model (Xiong et al., 2011) requires a training data labeled with a segment boundary, because it uses two discriminative probabilistic classifiers. Their approach automatically identifies each phrase boundary of a source sentence by using the shift reduce algorithm (SRA) (Zhang et al., 2008). This study defines good segmentation in terms of cohesiveness of translation and focuses on learning cohesive segments from word aligned training corpus.

In aspects of the training of the phrase segmentation model, any previous studies did not differentiate between a good segmentation and a bad segmentation based on the translation quality. This paper defines a good segmentation as the segmentation producing a good translation. This definition has the goal for improving the performance of the end-to-end SMT system, and thus good segmentations according to this definition may be inconsistent from human translators' point of view.

In this paper, we develop a new decoder-based segmenter for automatically labeling segment boundaries on the training data of phrase segmentation model. This labeler uses the base SMT decoder including the conventional translation model without a phrase segmentation model. In this approach, we assume that there exists a good translation among translation candidates produced by the base decoder.

The advantage of the decoder-based method is that it allows the segmentation model to learn more practically helpful segmentation boundaries. Phrase segmentation boundaries produced by the decoder are obviously helpful in terms of the translation quality, because they have been used in real decoding situations and have been selected by considering the reference translations. In other words, this decoder-based approach can effectively filter the bad phrase segments to train the segmentation model.

In addition to the segmentation labeling method, we design an iterative training algorithm, in which the phrase segmentation model and the decoder are iteratively trained. Through the algorithm, the performance of the phrase segmentation model and the decoder can be gradually improved.

2 System Overview

The proposed system is based on the phrase-based log-linear translation model (Och and Ney, 2004). The decision rule of the model has the following form:

$$\hat{e}_1^I = \arg\max_{e_1^I}\{Pr(e_1^I|f_1^J)\} \quad (1)$$

$$= \arg\max_{e_1^I}\{\sum_{m=1}^{M}\lambda_m h_m(e_1^I, f_1^J)\} \quad (2)$$

where e_1^I denotes a target sentence containing I words, f_1^J denotes a source sentence containing J words, h_m denotes a feature function, and λ_m denotes a weight of a feature function. Conventional phrase-based SMT employs components such as the language model, the phrase translation model, the phrase reordering model, the word penalty, the phrase penalty, and so on, as its feature functions.

Like the previous works for phrase segmentation model (Lee et al., 2011; Xiong et al., 2011), we integrate the phrase segmentation model into the log-linear model as an additional feature function.

The proposed system architecture is shown in Figure 1. In this system, two different sets of parallel sentences are used to train the phrase table and the phrase segmentation model, respectively. Our phrase segmenter using the SMT decoder automatically annotates source phrase boundaries on the training corpus. The phrase segmentation model learns the phrase segments from this labeled data. The SMT decoder employs this learned segmentation model. Our architecture allows a gradual improvement of both the segmentation model and the decoder through an iterative procedure. We describe the detailed training method in section 4.

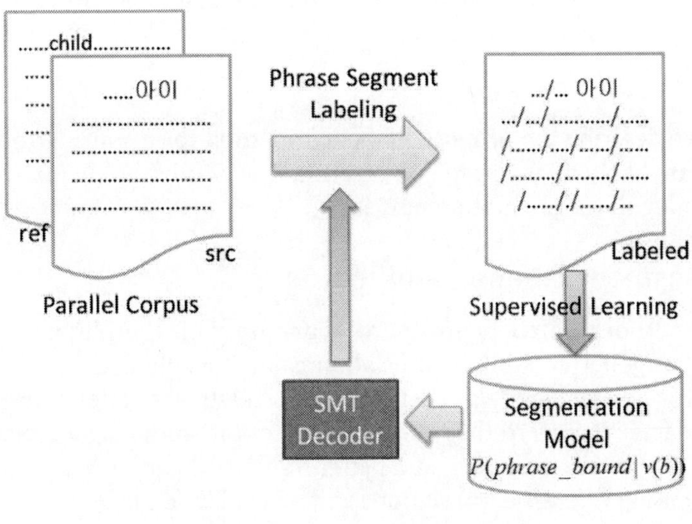

Figure 1: System architecture

3 Phrase Segmentation Model

The phrase segmentation model gives a score to the source segmentation of a given hypothesis. The proposed model outputs a probability that the source segmentation is good given both word boundaries and phrase boundaries of a given hypothesis. This model is simplified as a discriminative probabilistic classifier, which can judge whether each word boundary of a source sentence is a phrase segment boundary or not. The proposed model is described as the following equation:

$$h(x) = P(good\_seg|PB(x), WB(x)) \quad (3)$$

$$\propto \prod_{\forall b \in WB(x)} P(phrase\_bound|v(b))^{I_{PB}(b)} \times \{1 - P(phrase\_bound|v(b))\}^{1-I_{PB}(b)} \quad (4)$$

where $h(x)$ denotes a feature function of a hypothesis x. $PB(x)$ and $WB(x)$ denote a set of source phrase segment boundaries and a set of source word boundaries of a hypothesis x, respectively. The label, $phrase\_bound$ indicates that a given word boundary is a phrase segment boundary, $v(b)$ denotes a function that outputs the feature vector of a word boundary, and $I_{PB}(b)$ denotes an indicator function of the existence of a word boundary b in $PB(x)$.

We simply and intuitively model the phrase segmentation, because this work is more interested in the effective training of the model than in the segmentation modeling. Now, according to this model, we have to train only one classifier, $P(phrase\_bound|v(b))$.

We adopt the maximum entropy log-linear model as a learning model. We propose lexical contexts, part-of-speech contexts, and the collocation score of two adjacent words as the feature set. We use the log likelihood ratio, which is widely used to measure the association of random variables, as the collocation measure. These features known as useful clues for phrase segmentation are used in previous works (Lee et al., 2011; Xiong et al., 2011).

In the decoding process, we use the conventional decoding algorithm of the phrase-based SMT to consider the additional segmentation model feature. The log-probability of good segmentation of current source phrase is added to the total score in every evaluation of translation options.

4 Training

In this section, we describe the proposed labeling method for acquiring the phrase segment boundaries that are likely to generate good translations. And then, we introduce a recursive procedure of training the segmentation model.

4.1 Phrase segment labeling and learning

We use the base decoder to label each word boundary with the phrase segment boundary. Most SMT decoders generate a lot of translation candidates and search the best translation according to their statistical models. There may be a relatively better translation among the translation candidates. We regard the source segmentation producing a better translation as a better segmentation. We also assume that a better translation can be found in the search space of the decoder by using reference translations and an evaluation metric.

Therefore, we try to find the best segmentation among the segmentations producing translation candidates generated by the base decoder. For this, we select the segmentation producing the best translation, whose BLEU score is the highest among the candidates, from the n-best list of translation candidates.[1] Our system set n to 200.

As described in the previous section, the maximum entropy log-linear model is used to estimate the probabilities of the boundaries. This discriminative model requires both the gold-labeled data and the parameter search algorithm. For this requirements, we use the automatically constructed data explained earlier, and the LBFGS algorithm[2].

Our decoder-based approach is similar to the tuning method of the translation model using the algorithms such as MERT (Och, 2003), MIRA (Chiang et al., 2008), or pairwise ranked optimization (Hopkins and May, 2011). Both approaches use a small set of bilingual sentences translated by the base decoder, reference translations and an evaluation metric.

4.2 Iterative training of segmentation model

Once the trained segmentation model is integrated into the base decoder, the improved decoder can be available to train the segmentation model again. In other words, our method utilizes a dependent relationship between the decoder and the phrase segmentation model. Therefore, we propose a recursive training algorithm that can iteratively train the segmentation model. In this algorithm, we assume that if a decoder is improved, the segment-labeled data obtained by the decoder will also be improved. The better segmentations, which were not included in the old n-best list of hypotheses, may be included in the new list.

Figure 2 shows the formal representation of the iterative training algorithm. It uses a decoder D including the pre-constructed phrase table and two equal-sized training sets, B_1, B_2 as inputs. Consequentially, it outputs an improved decoder. $Choose(B_1, B_2)$ alternately selects one training set between two sets. $Label(C, D)$ is a function in which the decoder D annotates segment boundary labels at the source side of the set C, using the method described in section 4.1. $DiffRatio(C_{labled}, C_{old-labled})$ returns the number of different segment boundary labels between two sets. $TrainSM(D, C)$ is a function of training the segmentation model of the decoder D by using the labeled data C. $TuneWeights(D)$ performs the weight optimization of log-linear translation model, by using algorithms such as MERT (Och, 2003), MIRA (Chiang et al., 2008) or pairwise ranked optimization (Hopkins and May, 2011).

The reason of dividing the training set into two sets, B_1 and B_2, is for preventing the decoder from being immediately applied again to the same data that is used for training the segmentation model of the decoder. This algorithm outputs a SMT decoder containing a trained segmentation model for each iteration of the training procedure. This algorithm is terminated when the ratio of the changed labels of the labeled result reaches the threshold θ, compared with the previous labeled result. We empirically determine the threshold.

5 Experimental Results

We have experimented with our method for Korean-to-English (K-E) and Chinese-to-English (C-E) translation tasks. We have used about 1.1M Korean-English parallel sentences[3] to build

[1] We use the Moses toolkit (Koehn et al., 2007) to implement the base decoder, and *-n-best-list* and *-include-alignment-in-n-best* as additional options to obtain n-best outputs and their phrase segmentation results.

[2] Our classifier and its trainer are implemented by using Zhang's MaxEnt Toolkit (*http://homepages.inf.ed.ac.uk/lzhang10/maxent_toolkit.html*).

[3] Part of this corpus is provided by SK Planet CO. only for research purpose. Part of this corpus is automatically constructed by using Hong et al. (2010)'s method. Part of this corpus is released by Kim et al. (2010), and the Sejong corpus (Kang and Kim, 2004) is also used.

$ITA(D, B_1, B_2)$

Input: a decoder D, a set of parallel sentences B_1, another set of parallel sentences B_2

Output: a decoder containing a trained segmentation model

$C = Choose(B_1, B_2)$

$C_{labeled} = Label(C, D)$

if $DiffRatio(C_{labeled}, C_{old-labeled}) < \theta$

Return D

else

$D' = TrainSM(D, C_{labeled})$

$D_{new} = TuneWeights(D')$

$C_{old-labeled} = C_{labeled}$

Return $ITA(D_{new}, B_1, B_2)$

Figure 2: Iterative training algorithm (henceforth ITA)

the K-E SMT system. Among them, 1.1M, 10K, 1K and another 1K sentences were selected as the phrase table training set, the segmentation model training set, the tuning set, and our own test set, respectively. The official evaluation set of NIST OpenMT 2012 Evaluation (MT-12) has been used as another test set for K-E translation. We have also used 475K, 10K and 500 sentences from LDC Chinese-English corpora (LDC2005T10, LDC2005T06, and part of LDC2004T08) as the phrase table training set, the segmentation model training set, and the tuning set for the C-E SMT system, respectively. The official evaluation set of NIST OpenMT 2008 (MT-08) Evaluation has been used as the test set for C-E translation.

In this experiment, we use one half (5K) of the 10K segmentation training set and another one half (5K) as B_1 and B_2 for ITA.

		Korean-English		Chinese-English	
		Korean	English	Chinese	English
Train	Sentences	1,151K		485K	
	Words	27.7M	22.0M	10.5M	11.3M
Tune	Sentences	1,000		500	
	Words	27.6K	22.1K	10.7K	11.2K
Test A (Our own set)	Sentences	1,000		-	
	Words	26.5K	21.6K	-	-
Test B (MT-12/MT-08)	Sentences	3,074		1,357	
	Words	136.0K	90.7K*	32.5K	36.2K*

Table 1: Parallel corpus statistics (*Average of four references)

The SRILM toolkit[4] (Stolcke, 2002) has been used to train a 4-gram language model on 22.1M word tokens of English text. We have also used the morphological analyzer (Lee and Rim, 2009) for Korean tokenization and the Stanford Chinese word segmenter[5] (Tseng et al., 2005) for

[4]http://www.speech.sri.com/projects/srilm

[5]http://nlp.stanford.edu/software/segmenter.shtml

Chinese tokenization. We have used the open source SMT system, Moses[6] (Koehn et al., 2007) to implement the base decoder and the decoder that uses the proposed segmentation model. The minimum error rate training (MERT) (Och, 2003) was used to tune the feature weights. Both the BLEU score (Papineni et al., 2002) and the NIST score (NIST, 2001) are used as the evaluation metric.

We first verify the effectiveness of the proposed phrase segment boundary labeling in phrase-based SMT. We want to know how much the performance of the system can be improved, if the decoder is perfectly aware of the segment boundary information of input sentences. So, we labeled the test set by using the base decoder and the reference translation, and then used only the phrase segments in the labeled data when referring the phrase table during the decoding process. Through this setting, we can directly provide the acquired segmentation boundary information to the decoder. The experimental result is shown in Table 2. From these promising results, we found that if the translation system learns the segmentation boundaries labeled by using the base decoder well, the translation quality can be improved. In other words, these scores can be regarded as the upper bound of the system using the proposed decoder-based segmenter.

System	K-E (Our own)	C-E (MT-08)
Baseline	16.81	17.86
Gold segmentation only	20.16	19.44

Table 2: Effectiveness of the proposed phrase segment boundary labeling (BLEU)

Next, we evaluate the segment boundary classifier by performing 10-fold cross validation on the labeled data. The accuracy was 78% when using the ME model in Korean. This result implies that the learning model and the features adopted in our model are effective enough in finding the phrase segment boundary.

Table 3 shows the performance of the proposed system. In this experiment, all scores of the proposed system were measured after the third iteration, in which the ITA reached the threshold θ, determined by experiments carried out on the development set. Our system outperformed the baseline in both K-E and C-E. From these results, we found that the proposed method can effectively train the segmentation model for the phrase-based translation, even though the system could not achieve the upper bound shown in Table 2. We also found that the performance gain in K-E task is larger than that in C-E task through both Table 2 and Table 3. It implies the relative importance of the phrase segmentation for K-E task, and encourages us to study the linguistically-motivated model of Korean phrase segmentation for Korean-to-X translation as the future work.

Figure 3 shows BLEU scores measured for each iteration up to the fifth iteration of the ITA. From both graphs, we found that the ITA increases the BLEU score until the third iteration, and the score fluctuates in spite of the increase of iterations after the third iteration. We could learn that the proposed iterative training procedure gradually improves the system performance until a certain number of iterations as expected.

[6]http://www.statmt.org/moses

Language pair	K-E				C-E	
Test set	Our own		MT-12		MT-08	
System	BLEU	NIST	BLEU	NIST	BLEU	NIST
Baseline	16.81	5.8053	10.98	5.4596	17.86	6.0822
Proposed	18.04*	6.1020*	12.83*	6.0669*	18.25*	6.2007*

Table 3: Performance of the proposed system. All scores of the proposed system are measured after the third iteration of ITA. The scores marked with * are significantly better than the baseline ($p < 0.05$)

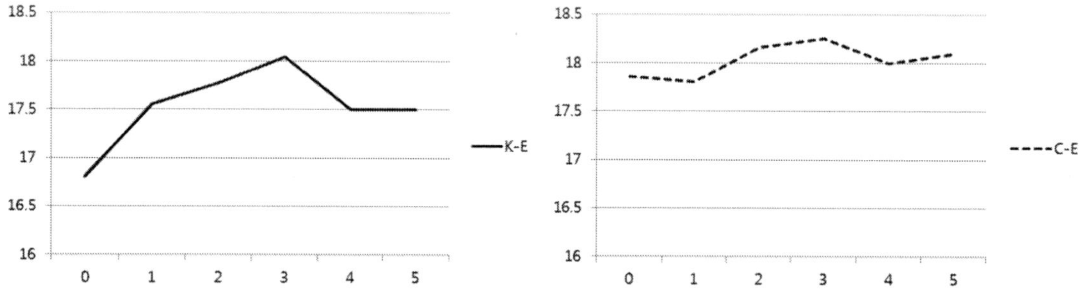

Figure 3: Iteration-BLEU graph

6 Conclusion

In this paper, we propose a new model of decoder based phrase segmentation and a new algorithm which can iteratively train the segmentation model. The main contribution of this paper can be summarized as follows. First, this paper is the first attempt to discriminate between a good segmentation and a bad segmentation based on the evaluation metric of the translation quality. Second, we have shown that the phrase segmentation model supporting the good translation quality can be trained by using the base SMT decoder. Finally, the proposed iterative training algorithm could gradually improve the translation quality of the phrase-based SMT, although the efficiency of the training may be reduced because of its iterative decoding.

For the future work, we try to integrate the decoder-based segmenter into other statistical translation models such as the hierarchical phrase-based model or the syntax-based model. This work is based on the hypothesis that our approach allows the system to select the practically useful boundaries of translation rules in the decoding process in the same way as the phrase-based model.

Acknowledgments

This work was supported by the National Research Foundation of Korea(NRF) grant funded by the Korea government(MEST) (No.2011-0016878).

References

Blackwood, G., de Gispert, A., and Byrne, W. (2008). Phrasal segmentation models for statistical machine translation. In *Proceedings of Coling 2008*.

Chiang, D., Marton, Y., and Resnik, P. (2008). Online large-margin training of syntactic and structural translation features. In *Proceedings of EMNLP 2008*.

Hong, G., Li, C.-H., Zhou, M., and Rim, H.-C. (2010). An empirical study on web mining of parallel data. In *Proceedings of Coling 2010*, pages 474–482.

Hopkins, M. and May, J. (2011). Tuning as ranking. In *Proceedings of EMNLP 2011*, pages 1352–1362.

Kang, B.-M. and Kim, H. (2004). Sejong korean corpora in the making. In *Proceedings of LREC 2004*, pages 1747–1750.

Kim, S., Jeong, M., Lee, J., and Lee, G. G. (2010). A cross-lingual annotation projection approach for relation detection. In *Proceedings of Coling 2010*, pages 564–571.

Koehn, P., Hoang, H., Birch, A., Callison-Burch, C., Federico, M., Bertoldi, N., Cowan, B., Shen, W., Moran, C., Zens, R., Dyer, C., Bojar, O., Constantin, A., and Herbst, E. (2007). Moses: open source toolkit for statistical machine translation. In *Proceedings of ACL 2007*.

Lee, D.-G. and Rim, H.-C. (2009). Probabilistic modeling of korean morphology. *IEEE Transactions on Audio, Speech, and Language Processing*, 17(5):945–955.

Lee, H.-G., Lee, J.-Y., Kim, M.-J., Rim, H.-C., Shin, J.-H., and Hwang, Y.-S. (2011). Phrase segmentation model using collocation and translational entropy. In *Proceedings of MT Summit XIII*.

NIST (2001). Automatic evaluation of machine translation quality using n-gram co-occurrence statistics. In *http://www.nist.gov/speech/tests/mt/doc/ngramstudy.pdf*.

Och, F. J. (2003). Minimum error rate training in statistical machine translation. In *Proceedings of ACL 2003*.

Och, F. J. and Ney, H. (2004). The alignment template approach to statistical machine translation. *Computational Linguistics*, 30(4):417–449.

Papineni, K., Roukos, S., Ward, T., and Zhu, W.-J. (2002). Bleu: a method for automatic evaluation of machine translation. In *Proceedings of ACL 2002*.

Stolcke, A. (2002). Srilm - an extensible language modeling toolkit. In *Proceedings of the 7th International Conference on Spoken Language Processing*.

Tseng, H., Chang, P., Andrew, G., Jurafsky, D., and Manning, C. (2005). A conditional random field word segmenter. In *Proceedings of Fourth SIGHAN Workshop on Chinese Language Processing*.

Xiong, D., Zhang, M., and Li, H. (2010). Learning translation boundaries for phrase-based decoding. In *Proceedings of HLT-NAACL 2010*.

Xiong, D., Zhang, M., and Li, H. (2011). A maximum-entropy segmentation model for statistical machine translation. *IEEE Transactions on Audio, Speech, and Language Processing*, 19(8):2494–2505.

Zhang, H., Gildea, D., and Chiang, D. (2008). Extracting synchronous grammar rules from word-level alignments in linear time. In *Proceedings of Coling 2008*.

Glimpses of Ancient China from Classical Chinese Poems

John LEE WONG Tak-sum
Halliday Centre for Intelligent Applications of Language Studies
Department of Chinese, Translation and Linguistics
City University of Hong Kong
{jsylee,tswong}@cityu.edu.hk

ABSTRACT

While our knowledge about ancient civilizations comes mostly from studies in archaeology and history books, much can also be learned or confirmed from literary texts. Using natural language processing techniques, we present aspects of ancient China as revealed by statistical textual analysis on the Complete Tang Poems, a 2.6-million-character corpus of all surviving poems from the Tang Dynasty (AD 618—907). Using an automatically created treebank of this corpus, we outline the semantic profiles of various poets, and discuss the role of seasons, geography, history, architecture, and colours, as observed through word selection and dependencies.

KEYWORDS : Classical Chinese, poetry, dependency parsing, word selection, semantics.

Proceedings of COLING 2012: Posters, pages 621–632,
COLING 2012, Mumbai, December 2012.

1 Introduction

In Classical Chinese literature, the prestige and popularity of poetry can hardly be overstated. Scholars aspired to master poem composition, not only for career advancement but also as the vehicle for personal expression and social commentary. Common people also liked to memorize, chanted, or even composed poems. The Tang Dynasty (AD 618—907) is widely viewed as the zenith of the art of poetry.

All surviving Tang poems have been preserved in an anthology called the Complete Tang Poems[1]. The whole corpus consists of around 2.6 million Chinese characters, drawn from more than 40,000 poems, composed by 2510 authors, as well as some anonymous ones. The ten most prolific poets, by number of characters, are shown in Table 1.

The sheer size of this corpus means that it would be difficult for any single scholar to analyse all poems by reading. Using a recently compiled digital treebank, we present the first study that exploits the entire corpus to answer questions about semantic content and word usage in the Complete Tang Poems. After outlining previous research (Section 2), we describe our data (Section 3), and then present our textual analysis (Section 4).

Poet	# characters	Poet	# characterss
Bái Jūyì 白居易	187964	Hán Yù 韓愈	41471
Dù Fǔ 杜甫	105930	Guàn Xiū 貫休	40306
Lǐ Bái 李白	84465	Qí Jǐ 齊己	38635
Yuán Zhěn 元稹	66426	Lù Guīméng 陸龜蒙	36590
Liú Yǔxí 劉禹錫	47880	Mèng Jiāo 孟郊	32446

TABLE 1 – The ten most prolific poets in the Complete Tang Poems.

2 Previous Research

2.1 Text Corpora of Classical Chinese

There has been increasing interest in corpus-based research on historical languages (Crane & Lüdeling, 2012). Large-scale corpora for Classical Chinese include the Academia Sinica Ancient Chinese Corpus (Wei et al., 1997), the corpus at the Centre for Chinese Linguistics Corpus at Peking University, the Chinese Ancient Text Database at the Chinese University of Hong Kong (Ho, 2002), and the Sheffield Corpus of Chinese (Hu et al., 2005). Linguistic annotations, if available in these corpora, are limited to part-of-speech (POS) tags. With this constraint, most previous corpus-based studies focused on character frequency distribution (Zhū, 2004; Zhāng, 2004; Qín, 2005), including a concordance for the Complete Tang Poems (Shǐ, 1990).

In terms of syntactic annotations, only two treebanks are currently available: a constituent treebank on 1000 sentences from the pre-Qin period (Huang et al., 2002), and a dependency treebank on a small subset of the Complete Tang Poems (Lee & Kong, 2012). This latter treebank will be used as training data to automatically produce dependency trees for the entire Complete Tang Poems, on which our word analysis will be based.

[1] In Chinese, 全唐詩 *Quántángshī*, (or *Ch'üan T'ang Shi*). The anthology was compiled by a team of scholars in 1705. Our digital version is downloaded from http://www.xysa.com/quantangshi/t-index.htm

2.2 Studies on the Complete Tang Poems

Research on syntactic and semantic issues in the Complete Tang Poems is a venerable subfield in Classical Chinese philology, with a vast literature. We seek to demonstrate a new route of investigation that can be complementary to traditional scholarship: by interrogating the treebank, one can quickly and objectively see broad trends on the entire corpus, which can help validate previous studies based on smaller sample, or point to interesting patterns for further in-depth analysis by hand.

A case in point is the semantic classification scheme of Wáng Lì, listed in Table 2. Wáng proposed 22 semantic categories (Wáng, 1989, p. 184–203), mostly for nouns but also some function words. As part of our analysis, we will apply these categories on the Complete Tang Poems to create semantic profiles of various poets (Section 4.1).

Category	**Representative words**	**Category**	**Representative words**
Celestial	天 sky 日 sun 風 wind	Body Parts	心 heart 目 eye 翼 wing
Seasonal	年 year 秋 fall 晝 day	Human emotions	談 talk 笑 smile 愛 love
Geographic	山 hill 池 pool 道 path	Human relationships	父 dad 王 king 僧 monk
Architectural	房 room 門 door 店 shop	Pronouns	吾 I 汝 you 誰 who
Products of civilization	車 car 弓 bow 杯 cup	Locations	東 east 後 back 上 up
Clothing	衣 cloth 帽 hat 甲 armour	Numbers	一 one 幾 some 半 half
Food	酒 wine 飯 rice 菜 veg	Colours	紅 red 金 gold 素 plain
Instruments	筆 pen 書 book 琴 piano	Calendar coordinates	甲 1st 乙 2nd 丙 3rd 丁 4th
Literary	詩 poem 歌 song	Adverbs	怎 how 不 not 只 only
Flora	木 tree 李 plum 根 root	Conj. & prep.	與 and 於 at 之 of
Fauna	馬 horse 鳥 bird 魚 fish	Particles	也 yě 乎 *hū* 然 rán

TABLE 2 – Semantic categories for nouns in the Complete Tang Poems (Wáng, 1989).

3 Data

A dependency treebank covering a subset of the Complete Tang Poems has been built (Lee & Kong, 2012). It consists of about 32,000 words, annotated with part-of-speech (POS) tags and dependency labels, derived from the Penn Chinese Treebank (Xue et al., 2005) and Stanford dependencies for Modern Chinese (Chang et al., 2009).

Using this treebank as training data, we performed POS tagging[2] on the whole Complete Tang Poems with TreeTagger (Schmid, 1995), and dependency parsing with the Minimum-Spanning Tree (MST) Parser (McDonald et al., 2006). On ten-fold cross-validation on the treebank itself, the average UAS and LAS of dependency parsing are 84.3% and 75.6% respectively[3].

[2] Although word segmentation is provided in the treebank, "in general the syllable, written with a single character, and the word correspond in Classical Chinese" (Pulleyblank, 1995, p. 8); most words to be analysed in this paper (Section 4) are indeed single characters.
[3] Similar experiments with MaltParser (Nivre et al., 2009) yielded similar accuracy rates.

4 Analysis

We first analyze the semantic content of the Complete Tang Poems both globally and by author (section 4.1), then use dependency information to glean aspects of the seasons, geography, architecture, history and use of colours in Ancient China (section 4.2).

4.1 Semantic Profile

To identify the main themes of the poems, we compute the distribution of the semantic categories listed in Table 2; the result is shown in Table 3. The five most frequent categories are 'Geographic', 'Adverbs', 'Celestial', 'Human emotions', and 'Seasonal'. For the most prolific poets, at least four of these five categories also rank among their individual top five, indicating that the topics of interest are rather uniform among Tang poets. Overall, aspects of nature ('Geographic', 'Celestial', 'Seasonal', etc.) dominate the attention of the poets, compared to aspects of humans ('Human emotions', 'Human relationships', 'Body parts', etc.).

Category	Freq.	Category	Freq.	Category	Freq.
Geographic	11.79%	Flora	4.94%	Conj. and prep.	2.54%
Adverbs	9.49%	Pronouns	4.87%	Clothing	1.19%
Celestial	9.48%	Body parts	4.84%	Instruments	1.08%
Human emotions	6.59%	Colours	4.46%	Food	0.78%
Seasonal	6.58%	Architectural	3.76%	Calendar	0.70%
Numbers	6.19%	Products	3.40%	Particles	0.59%
Locations	5.52%	Fauna	3.38%		
Human relationships	5.15%	Literary	2.66%		

TABLE 3 – Distribution of Wáng Lì's semantic categories in the Complete Tang Poems, based on the 864 example characters provided by Wáng. They cover 49% of the tokens in the corpus.

The absolute counts, however, mask some interesting underlying tendencies. To see the extent to which individuals deviate from the average distribution in Table 3, we calculate the z-score for each poet's own distribution. Further, we compute the TF-IDF of words, considering the complete works of each poet as a "document".

As shown in Table 4(a), Bái Jūyì wrote more than the average poet on human themes (e.g., 'Body parts', 'Food'), and less on 'Celestial' and 'Geographic', two of the most common categories related to nature (Table 3). This tendency is confirmed by his words with the highest TF-IDF, listed in Table 5(a), such as 病 bìng 'sick', 衰 shu*āi* 'decline' and 憂 *yōu* 'worry', describing the harshness of life. Another set of high-TF-IDF words involve drinking, such as 杯 *bēi* 'glass', 飲 *yǐn* 'drink', and 酒 ji*ǔ* 'wine'. These statistics concur with the general observation that Bái uses the theme of drinking to illustrate his loneliness and miserableness (Zuǒ, 2011).

Being disrupted by the Ān Lùshān Rebellion, Dù Fǔ was known for his anti-war stance, concern about his country's decline, and sympathy for the common people (Lú, 2009). These themes are confirmed by his set of words about warfare and turmoil, listed in Table 5(b), and his relative disinterest, like Bái Jūyì, in the common themes in nature – in his case, 'Seasonal' and 'Celestial'.

(a) **Bái Jūyì** 白居易		(b) **Dù Fǔ** 杜甫	
Body Parts	1.42	Human relationships	0.92
Food	1.32	Fauna	0.59
Conj. and prep.	1.23	Calendar	0.57
Pronouns	1.07	Food	0.54
Numbers	1.07	Literary	0.53
Adverbs	0.76	Pronouns	0.48
Architectural	-0.64	Seasonal	-0.52
Fauna	-1.17	Celestial	-0.57
Celestial	-1.32	Flora	-0.93
Geographic	-1.35	Human emotions	-1.08
(c) Lǐ Bái 李白		**(d) Wáng Wéi** 王維	
Colours	1.28	Particles	1.75
Human relationships	0.93	Clothing	1.30
Food	0.79	Human relationships	1.30
Conj. and prep.	0.68	Locations	1.19
Pronouns	0.65	Architectural	0.60
Celestial	0.57	Food	0.35
Flora	-0.65	Numbers	-0.65
Calendar	-0.76	Celestial	-0.83
Architectural	-0.85	Seasonal	-0.93
Seasonal	-1.78	Human emotions	-1.21

TABLE 4 – Semantic categories with the highest and lowest z-scores of four well-known poets. The higher the score, the more the poet exceeds the average in the use of the category.

Poet	Characters	Topic
(a) Bái Jūyì	病 'sick' 衰 'decline' 憂 'worry' 苦 貧 臥 杯 'glass' 飲 'drink' 酒 'wine' 歡 醉 弦	Harshness of life Drinking Warfare
(b) Dù Fǔ	衰 'decline' 老 'old' 病 'sick' 胡 兵 亂 泥 失 骨 軍 夫 戰	Harshness of life Warfare and turmoil
(c) Lǐ Bái	胡 劍 陵 嘆 悲 夫 笑 美 顏 女 杯 'glass' 飲 'drink'	Warfare Women Drinking
(d) Wáng Wéi	戶 隱 雞 鳴 田 井 村 川 悠 門 戰	Isolation Warfare

TABLE 5 – Characters with the highest TF-IDF in the works of four poets, grouped into main topics.

In contrast, under the pen of the poet Lǐ Bái, 'Celestial', already a popular category (Table 3), is employed even more frequently. This likely reflects his extensive use of the moon as imagery. His poems are also well recognized for vivid colours and the drinking theme ('Colours' and 'Food' in Table 4(c)), with the characters 杯 *bēi* 'glass' and 飲 *yǐn* 'drink' achieving some of the highest TF-IDF scores.

Lastly, as shown in Table 4(d), the top category for Wáng Wéi is 'Particles', no doubt a result of his frequent use of 兮 *xī*, a particle mainly used in archaic poems. This is a style of which Wáng is known to be fond.

4.2 Word selection

We now exploit dependency information to investigate word selections, centering on three common areas: the seasons, the cardinal directions, and the colours.

4.2.1 Seasons

Among the four seasons, mentions of 春 chūn 'spring' and 秋 *qiū* 'autumn' overwhelmingly outnumber those of 夏 xià 'summer' and 冬 *dōng* 'winter', by a factor of more than ten to one. As seen from the written record in Shang dynasty (circa BC 17c. – 1046), only "spring" and "autumn" were attested in oracle bone inscriptions but "summer" and "winter" were not (Chén, 1988, p. 226 – 227). Thus, the discrepancy may be explained by the fact that the concepts of 'spring' and 'autumn' are much older, and also that these two seasons were bound up with many activities in ancient China. Given this discrepancy, it is more appropriate to use mutual information (MI) than absolute counts to detect significant word selections.

Notable word co-occurrences with the highest MI are shown in Table 6. Reflecting the natural order, both 'summer' and 'autumn' are predominately associated with plant words; 'spring' is associated with significantly fewer ones, and 'winter', hardly any. By the same reasoning, one might expect the word 暉 huī 'sunshine' to relate most strongly with 'summer'. Its relation with 'spring' is in fact stronger since, when poets pay tribute to spring as mother nature, as it were, they often depict the spring sun which is gentle, comforting, and caring for the sprouting of the plants after a severe winter. This tribute also explains the high MI of the direction 'east' for the word 風 fēng 'wind' (section 4.2.2), as wind usually blows from the east during spring. In contrast, summer is more frequently described with words such as 酷 kù 'extreme' and 暑 *shǔ* 'heat', rather than 'sunshine'.

Since peasants formed the majority of the population (Murphey, 1996, p. 5), agriculture was a common way of life. Agricultural activities were highly regulated by the seasons, and naturally the word 耨 nòu 'raking' is significantly related with 'spring', and 稼 jià 'harvest' with 'autumn'. Another major means of subsistence was hunting, especially in the winter, when cooked meat was especially coveted. It is no coincidence that 狩 shòu 'hunting' has the highest MI with 'winter'.

There are two words that both mean 'sleep', namely 睡 shuì and 蟄 zhé. A glance at Table 6, however, shows that the former is highly correlated with 'spring', whereas the latter with 'winter'. The reason is that shuì in general refers to humans, while zhé refers to animals, which tend to go into hibernation during winter.

Scholars were not immune from seasonal cycles, either. National examinations were held annually at the capital city, and passing these exams was critical in climbing the career ladder. Since the examinations were held in spring, the words 闈 wéi 'examination' and 榜 bǎng 'result' only collocate with that season. Candidates who failed the examination sometimes stayed in the capital to take remedial lessons, therefore 課 kè 'lesson' is often modified by 'summer'.

Spring			Summer			Autumn			Winter		
Ch	MI	Meaning	Ch	MI	Meaning	Ch	MI	Meaning	Ch	MI	Meaning
畹	3.41	beauty	汭	4.51	bend of river	旻	3.81	autumn sky	狩	5.56	hunting
闈	2.67	examination	蘖	4.21	sprout	韭	3.56	chives	菁	4.70	flower
韭	2.55	chives	課	4.07	lesson	穟	2.77	ripe grain	蟄	3.19	sleep
耨	2.41	raking	酷	3.39	extreme (hot)	稼	2.70	harvest	筍	3.03	bamboo shoots
暉	2.39	sunshine	筱	3.12	bamboo	荼	2.40	vegetable	霰	2.83	ice
酎	2.33	vintage wine	卉	3.04	grass	蔬	2.34	vegetable	蕊	1.98	bud
醪	2.29	mellow wine	筇	2.95	bamboo	草	1.91	grass			
颪	2.22	wind	苗	2.87	hunting; seed	芋	1.74	taro			
釀	2.10	brew	菜	2.77	vegetable	菰	1.70	taro			
草	2.06	grass	葛	2.68	arrowroot						
酴	1.97	wine	木	2.64	tree						
苜	1.91	clover	暑	2.63	heat						
霖	1.87	heavy rain	麥	2.56	wheat						
畦	1.86	field	果	2.50	fruit						
睡	1.85	sleep	萼	2.29	calyx						
榜	1.72	exam result	蕊	2.18	bud						
蔬	1.67	vegetable	筍	1.85	bamboo shoots						
筍	1.44	bamboo shoots	蘚	1.60	moss						

TABLE 6 – Characters with the highest mutual information (MI) with each of the four seasons. Two characters are considered to co-occur when they are connected by a dependency relation. Characters occurring less than 10 times are excluded.

4.2.2 Cardinal directions

Like the seasons, the four cardinal directions – 東 *dōng* 'east', 南 nán 'south', 西 *xī* 'west', and 北 *běi* 'north' – appear frequently in poems, contributing the bulk of the counts towards the category 'Locations'. Table 7 lists several sets of words with similar meaning but drastically different co-occurrences with the directions. They reveal facets of culture, history and geography of Ancient China.

Geography. The verbs 流 liú 'flow' and 逝 shì 'pass' both like to head eastward. In China, most rivers flow from mountains in the west towards the Pacific Ocean in the east. Since liú and shì tend to be associated with rivers, 'east' is the natural direction for them. Now, given that the ocean is located in the east, one might wonder why 海 hǎi 'sea' has such high MI with 'north'. In fact, in most contexts, the term refers to the remote area in the north far away from the central plain. Likewise, 南國 nánguó 'south country' refers to the remote area in the south, and so 南省 nánshěng 'south province'.

History. The words 都 *dū* and 京 *jīng* both mean 'capital', yet they have diametrically opposing directions, namely 'east' and 'west'. In many dynasties, China had a main capital in the west and also a secondary capital in the east; for example, in the Tang dynasty, they were Cháng'ān and Luòyáng, respectively. The word *jīng* usually refers to the main capital, while *dū* refers to the secondary. Since the Tang capital was located in the west, when an emperor went out on a 巡 xún 'patrol' to tour his domain, he was likely to go 'east' or 'south'. Also, seen from the capital, barbarians on the fringes of the empire were labelled with the name of the tribe that dwelled in that direction during the archaic period. These were 狄 dí in the north, 蠻 mán in the south, 戎 rúng in the west, and 夷 yí in the east or south.

Architecture. The distributions of the cardinal directions also tell us about architectural design. While 'east' and 'west' are the dominant directions of 廂 *xiāng* 'side-room', 'north' has the highest MI with 堂 táng 'hall'. The reason lies with the design of quadrangle courtyards, a common type of residence in ancient China. In a typical courtyard, the main house, or hall, faced the north, while the side-rooms were located along the east-west axes. Furthermore, a small building is often built in the west for moon-viewing. Hence, the word 樓 lóu 'building' is most likely to be modified by 'west'.

Topic	Co-occurring word	East	South	West	North
Geography	流 liú 'flow'	**2.46**	-0.43	0.55	0.89
	逝 shì 'pass'	**2.41**	0.28	/	/
	海 *hǎi* 'sea'	**1.95**	0.98	0.85	**1.55**
	國 guó 'nation'	-0.83	**2.76**	0.06	-1.93
	省 shěng 'province'	0.85	**2.02**	1.42	1.35
	風 fēng 'wind'	**2.01**	0.75	1.53	1.72
History	都 *dū* 'capital'	**2.37**	0.51	0.78	0.09
	京 *jīng* 'capital'	1.84	0.52	**2.78**	1.33
	巡 xún 'patrol'	**2.24**	**2.41**	1.86	0.19
	夷 yí 'tribe'	**0.82**	**0.95**	0.70	-0.28
	蠻 mán 'tribe'	0.37	**1.24**	/	0.18
	戎 rúng 'tribe'	/	-1.06	**2.22**	-0.50
	狄 dí 'tribe'	/	/	/	**3.72**
Architecture	廂 *xiāng* 'side-room'	**4.17**	3.21	**4.45**	/
	堂 táng 'hall'	1.93	-1.33	-0.49	**2.52**
	樓 lóu 'building'	0.72	1.37	**2.00**	1.09

TABLE 7 – Word co-occurrences with the four cardinal directions that have high mutual information. Two characters are considered to co-occur when they are connected by a dependency relation. Characters occurring less than 10 times are excluded.

4.2.3 Colours

Two common words in Classical Chinese both refer to the black colour, namely, 黑 hēi and 玄 xuán. The former tends to be used in negative contexts, and the latter one in positive ones, sometimes indicating an auspicious sign (Yìng, 2004, p.13).

To verify this hypothesis, we compute the mutual information (MI) of characters co-occurring with hēi or xuán. Table 8 lists those characters with the highest MI. Most co-occurrences with xuán involve an exalted or noble entity, such as 玄圃 xuán*pǔ* 'palace of the gods', 玄貺 xuánkuàng 'present from emperor', 玄豹 xuánbào 'leopard' (a rare and thus valuable animal), 玄宗 xuánzōng 'idea on Buddhism', and 玄晏 xuányàn 'ritual'. In contrast, those involving hēi are mostly everyday objects (e.g., 'rice') including some with negative sentiment such as 黑紗 hēishā 'funeral cloth' and 黑蛺 hēijiá 'bug'. These observations lend evidence to the usage of these two characters described in (Yìng, 2004).

玄 xuán 'black'				**黑 hēi 'blank'**			
freq.	Ch	MI	Meaning	freq.	Ch	MI	Meaning
13	牝	5.92	root of everything	9	煤	5.74	ash
207	圃	4.86	gods' palace	170	貂	5.28	sable
48	貺	4.33	present from emperor	42	蛺	4.20	bug
149	豹	4.30	leopard (valuable)	149	米	3.62	rice
434	暉	4.29	sun/moon	129	壤	3.08	fertile earth
541	宗	4.24	idea on Buddhism	277	蛟	3.00	dragon
293	晏	3.91	ritual	337	紗	2.81	cloth for funeral
49	奧	3.90	difficult	176	蟻	2.76	ant
363	兔	3.51	moon	176	鉛	2.76	graphite
234	覽	3.44	foresight	356	裘	2.75	fur coat
39	祉	3.44	kindness from ruler	4090	頭	2.71	young-age
179	冕	3.30	clothes of ruler	3845	龍	2.32	dragon

TABLE 8 – Word co-occurrences with the two words for 'black', hēi and xuán.

Conclusion and Perspectives

This paper presents textual analysis on the entire Complete Tang Poems. We described the overall semantic range of the corpus, as well as the semantic profiles of various poets, via a semantic classification scheme and TF-IDF scores. We then used dependency relations and mutual information to investigate word selections involving the four seasons, the four cardinal directions and the black colour. Our observations lend statistical evidence to previous scholarly assertions, but also reveal aspects of Chinese geography, history, and architecture.

Our analyses represent a new avenue of scholarly enquiry over this treasure trove of Classical Chinese, but they have touched only the tip of an iceberg. It is hoped that the automatically produced treebank will provide useful syntactic features for other research topics, such as the readability of poems (Zhāng et al., 2009) and authorship questions (Matsuoka, 2003).

Acknowledgments

This project was supported in part by a Strategic Research Grant (#7002549) from City University of Hong Kong.

References

Chang, P.-C., Tseng, H., Jurafsky, D. and Manning C. D. (2009). Discriminative Reordering with Chinese Grammatical Relations Features. In Proc. 3rd Workshop on Syntax and Structure in Statistical Translation.

Chén M. (1988). Yīnxū Bǔcí Zòngshù. Zhonghua Book Company, Peking.

Crane, G., and Lüdeling, A. (2012). Introduction to the Special Issue on Corpus and Computational Linguistics, Philology, and the Linguistic Heritage of Humanity. Journal on Computing and Cultural Heritage, 5(1).

Ho, C. W. (2002). CHANT (CHinese ANcient Texts): A Comprehensive Database of All Ancient Chinese Texts up to 600 AD. Journal of Digital Information, 3(2).

Hu, X., Williamson, N., and McLaughlin, J. (2005). Sheffield Corpus of Chinese for Diachronic Linguistic Study. Literary and Linguistic Computing, 20(3):281–293.

Huang, L., Peng, Y., Wang, H., and Wu. Z. (2002). PCFG Parsing for Restricted Classical Chinese Texts. In Proc. 1st SIGHAN Workshop on Chinese Language Processing.

Lee, J. and Kong, Y. H. (2012). A dependency treebank of Classical Chinese poems. In Proc. Conference of the North American Chapter of the Association for Computational Linguistics (NAACL).

Lú, Y. (2009). A Brief Study on Dù Fǔ's Anti-War Poems. Journal of Yunmeng, 4:109–114.

Matsuoka, E. (2003). Are Táo Yuānmíng and Xiè língyùn from the Same Era?: Study in social context after the electronic publication of the Two-Fours. In 1st Literature and Information Technology International Conference, National Tsing Hua University of Taiwan and Yuan Ze University of Taipei, Republic of China.

McDonald, R., Lerman, K. and Pereira F. (2006). Multilingual Dependency Parsing with a Two-Stage Discriminative Parser. In 10th Conference on Computational Natural Language Learning (CoNLL-X).

Murphey, R. (1996). East Asia: A New History. Addison-Wesley Educational Publishers Inc., New York.

Nivre, J., Kuhlmann, M. and Hall, J. (2009). An Improved Oracle for Dependency Parsing with Online Reordering. In Proc. 11th International Conference on Parsing Technologies (IWPT), pages 73–76.

Pulleyblank, E. (1995). Outline of Classical Chinese Grammar. UBC Press, Vancouver.

Qín, Q. (2005). A Statistical Study on Character Frequency of Pre-Qin Books. Studies in Language and Linguistics, 25(4):112–116.

Schmid, H. (1995). Improvements in Part-of-Speech Tagging with an Application to German. In Proc. ACL SIGDAT-Workshop, Dublin, Ireland.

Shǐ, C. (1990). Indexes of Complete Tang Poems. Shanghai Guji, Shanghai.

Wáng, L. (1989). Versification in Chinese. Wáng Lì Collection, vol. 14, 15. Shandong Jiaoyu Chubanshe, Ji'nan.

Wei, P., Thompson, P. M., Liu, C., Huang, C., and Sun, C. (1997). Historical Corpora for Synchronic and Diachronic Linguistics Studies. Computational Linguistics and Chinese Language Processing, 2(1):131–145.

Xue, N., Xia, F., Chiou, F.-D., and Palmer, M. (2005). The Penn Chinese Treebank: Phrase Structure Annotation of a Large Corpus. Natural Language Engineering, 11:207–238.

Yìng, L. (2004). "The whole poems in Tang dynasty" colour words and expressions research. M.A. thesis. Chongqing: Southwest University.

Zhū, Y. (2004). A statistical account of the frequency and distribution of the character usage in the ancient Chinese classics. Journal of the National Library of China, 49:91–93.

Zhāng, J., Ān P. and Sū N. (2009). An analysis of the entropy of the character frequency and the grading of readability by the general public of the Tang poems. Science and Technology Information, 2009(6):241–243.

Zhāng, Z. (2004). A large scale statistical report on the usage of characters in ancient Chinese classics. In 3rd Conference of Database of Chinese Literature and History.

Zuǒ, C. (2011). A Look at the experience and cognition of Bái Jūyì towards wine from Xiào Táo Qián Tǐ Shī Shíliù Shǒu. Young Litterateur, 24.

Conversion between Scripts of Punjabi: Beyond Simple Transliteration

Gurpreet Singh LEHAL[1] *Tejinder Singh SAINI*[2]
(1) DCS, Punjabi University, Patiala
(2) ACTDPL, Punjabi University, Patiala

gslehal@gmail.com, tej@pbi.ac.in

ABSTRACT

This paper describes statistical techniques used for modelling transliteration systems between the scripts of Punjabi language. Punjabi is one of the unique languages, which are written in more than one script. In India, Punjabi is written in Gurmukhi script, while in Pakistan it is written in Shahmukhi (Perso-Arabic) script. Shahmukhi script has its origin in the ancient Phoenician script whereas Gurmukhi script has its origin in the ancient Brahmi script. Whilst in speech Punjabi spoken in the Eastern and the Western parts is mutually comprehensible, in the written form it is not so. This has created a script wedge as majority of Punjabi speaking people in Pakistan cannot read Gurmukhi script, and similarly the majority of Punjabi speaking people in India cannot comprehend Shahmukhi script. In this paper, we present an advanced and highly accurate transliteration system between Gurmukhi and Shahmukhi scripts of Punjabi language which addresses various challenges such as multiple/zero character mappings, missing vowels, word segmentation, variations in pronunciations and orthography and transliteration of proper nouns etc. by generating efficient algorithms along with special rules and using various lexical resources such as Gurmukhi spell checker, corpora of both scripts, Gurmukhi-Shahmukhi transliteration dictionaries, statistical language models etc. The proposed system attains more than 98.6% accuracy at word level while transliterating Gurmukhi text to Shahmukhi. The reverse part i.e. transliterating from Shahmukhi text to Gurmukhi is more complex and challenging but our system has achieved 97% accuracy at word level in this part too.

KEYWORDS: n-gram language model, Shahmukhi, Gurmukhi, Punjabi, Machine Transliteration, Word disambiguation, HMM

Proceedings of COLING 2012: Posters, pages 633–642,
COLING 2012, Mumbai, December 2012.

1 Introduction

There are more that six thousand living languages in the world and some languages are written in different scripts in different regions of the world. The multitude of foreign languages and mutually incomprehensible scripts of the same language pose a barrier to information exchange. Incidentally, the existence of Shahmukhi and Gurmukhi scripts for Punjabi has created a script barrier between the Punjabi literature written in India and in Pakistan. Notably, more than 60 per cent of Punjabi literature of medieval period (500-1450 AD) is available in Shahmukhi script only, while most of the modern Punjabi writings are available in both scripts. Hence, a machine transliteration system that overcomes script barriers is needed to handle these Punjabi scripts with different origins, different direction of writings, different set of alphabet, and different kind of writing system conventions. Already some work in this direction has been reported by Malik, 2006; Saini and Lehal, 2008; Saini et al., 2008 and Lehal, 2009.

2 Transliteration Issues with Punjabi Scripts

- **Missing Short Vowels in Shahmukhi Script:** Most Semitic languages in both ancient and contemporary times are usually written without short vowels and other diacritic marks, often leading to potential ambiguity (Nelken and Shieber, 2005). Similarly, in the written Shahmukhi script, it is not mandatory to put short vowels. In our findings, Shahmukhi corpus has just 1.66% coverage of short vowels ◌ُ[ʊ] (0.81415%), ◌ِ[ɪ] (0.7295%), and ◌َ (0.1234%) whereas the equivalent ਿ◌[ɪ] (4.5462%) and ◌ੁ[ʊ] (1.5844%) in Gurmukhi corpus has 6.13% usage. This leads to potential ambiguous transliteration from Shahmukhi to Gurmukhi script.
- **Multiple Mappings:** It is observed that there are multiple possible mappings between the two scripts. The Shahmukhi characters Vav و [v], Yeh ی[j] and noon ن[n] have shown vowel-vowel, vowel-consonant and consonant-consonant mapping in Gurmukhi script. On the other hand, Gurmukhi characters ਹ[h], ਸ[s], ਕ[k], ਤ[t̪] and ਜ਼[z] have multiple similar sounding character in Shahmukhi.
- **Missing Script Maps:** There are many characters or symbols in the Shahmukhi script, corresponding to which there are no characters in Gurmukhi, e.g. Hamza ء [ɪ], Do-Zabar ً [ən], Do-Zer ٍ [ɪn], Aen ع[ʔ] etc.
- **Word Boundary Issues**: Like Urdu, Shahmukhi is written in Nastalique style. Due to Nastalique style and irregular use of space, Shahmukhi word segmentation has both space omission and space insertion problems (Durrani and Hussain, 2010; Lehal, 2009, 2010). The space within a word is used more as a tool to control the correct letter shaping rather than to consistently separate words and many times the user omits word boundary space between the consecutive Shahmukhi words when the first word ends with a non-joiner character.
- **Shahmukhi Word with Izafat Form:** There are many compound words or combinations of Shahmukhi words written as a multi-word expression in Gurmukhi script e.g. وزیرِاعظم, ਵਜ਼ੀਰ-ਏ-ਆਜ਼ਮ/vazīr-ē-āzam/; قتلِ عام, ਕਤਲ-ਏ-ਆਮ/katal-ē-ām/.
- **Foreign or Complex Spelling Words:** Shahmukhi words including foreign words have typical spellings such as اسکول, ਸਕੂਲ /sakūl/; اسٹوڈیو, ਸਟੂਡਿਓ /saṭūḍiō/; اوپسٹنٹ,

ਇਨਵੈਸਟਮੈਂਟ /invaisṭamaiṇṭ/; جماعت, ਜਮਾਤ /Jamāt/; وکتی, ਵਿਅਕਤੀ/ Viaktī/; عبداللہ, ਅਬਦੁੱਲਾ /abdullā/; رحمٰن, ਰਹਿਮਾਨ /rahimān/ etc.

- **Wrong Spellings due to Missing Gurmukhi Nukta Sign:** In order to accommodate foreign words from Urdu and Persian domain, five consonants (ਸ, ਖ, ਗ, ਜ, ਫ) of Gurmukhi alphabet are extended to ਸ਼[ʃ], ਖ਼[x], ਗ਼[ɣ], ਜ਼[z], ਫ਼[f] with Gurmukhi sign Nukta (pairin bindi). But over the years, the usage of these characters particularly, ਖ਼, ਗ਼, ਜ਼, and ਫ਼ has been on the decline as many Punjabi speakers do not make a distinction between ਖ ਖ਼, ਗ ਗ਼ and ਫ ਫ਼. The result is that most of the words in Gurmukhi are now written without nukta symbol. The symbol ਸ਼ is an exception. When this word is converted to Shahmukhi using character to character based mapping it results in wrong spellings.
- **Difference between Pronunciation and Orthography:** In certain cases, the Gurmukhi words are written with short vowels e.g. ਗੁਰੂ/gurū/, while they are pronounced with long vowels as ਗੁਰੂ /gūrū/. The equivalent words in Shahmukhi are also written with long vowels گورو /gūrū/. Therefore, simple rule based transliteration of such words resulting in wrong transliteration.
- **Ambiguity at word level:** There are many Shahmukhi words which map to multiple Gurmukhi words e.g. گل (ਗੱਲ /gall/, ਗਿੱਲ /gill/, ਗੁੱਲ /gull/, ਗੁਲ /gul/); تک (ਤਕ /tak/, ਤੱਕ /takk/, ਤੁਕ /tuk/) etc. Similarly, Gurmukhi word ਅਰਬ /arab/ has two Shahmukhi spellings with different senses as عرب (Arabia; native of Arabia) and ارب (one billion).

3 Punjabi Machine Transliteration System

The architecture of the Punjabi machine transliteration system is shown in Figure 1.

3.1 Rule-based Transliteration Model

Using the direct method, we have followed manual Consonant-Vowel (CV) approach for character alignments between the source and target scripts.

Dependency Rule for Shahmukhi	Gurmukhi	Example
Alef-Madda آ[ɑ] Vav with hamza ؤ [o] at the beginning	ਆਊ	آؤٹ → ਆਊਟ (āūṭ)
Alef Madda آ[ɑ] followed by Vav و[o] at the beginning	ਆਵ	آواز → ਆਵਾਜ਼ (āvāz)
Alef ا[ə] followed by hamza ء [ɪ] and Choti Yeh ی[i] and Alef ا[ə] and Noongunna ں [ɲ]	◌ਾਈਆਂ	ودھائیاں → ਵਧਾਈਆਂ (vadhāīāṃ)

TABLE 1– Sample of some dependency rules for Shahmukhi characters

After that context dependent transformation rules are generated to resolve zero or multiple mappings into the target script (see Table 1). Similarly, special pronunciation based rules have been developed for Gurmukhi characters while transliterating to Shahmukhi as shown in Table 2.

Char1		Char2		Shahmukhi	Example		
ਇ [e]	+	ਆ[ɑ]	→	یا	ਲਾਇਆ /lāiā/	→	یال
ਿ◌ [ɪ]	+	ਓ[o]	→	یو	ਵਾਲਿਓ /vāliō/	→	یووال
◌ਂ [ɲ]	+	ਪ[p]	→	مپ	ਪੰਪ /pamp/	→	مپ

TABLE 2 – Sample of some Pronunciation based Mapping Rules

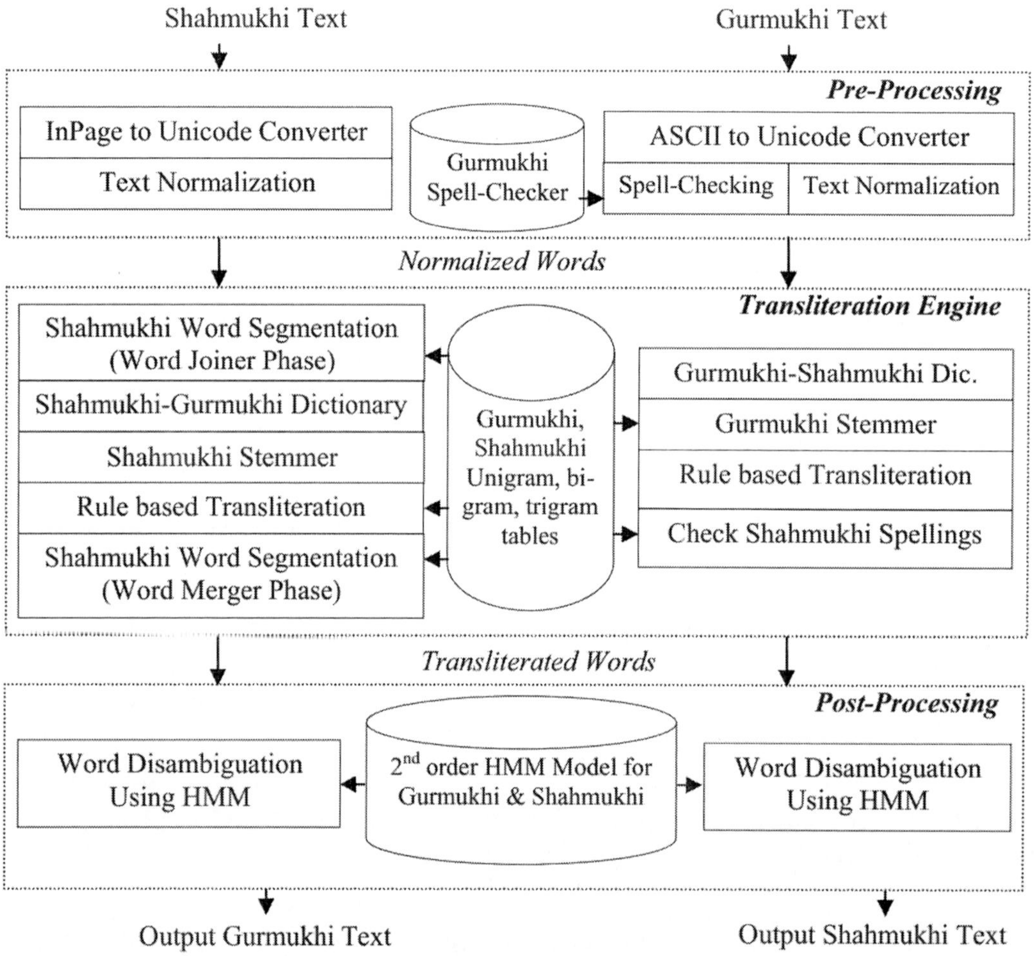

FIGURE 1– System Architecture

3.2 Transliteration using Lexical Resources

3.2.1 Pre-Processing

In the pre-processing stage input text is transformed into Unicode, cleaned and prepared for transliteration in the following manner:

Unicode Conversion: Shahmukhi text in InPage file and Gurmukhi text in traditional fonts is converted into Unicode.

Gurmukhi Spell Checker: Gurmukhi Spell-Checker is used to correct missing Gurmukhi nukta sign problem in Gurmukhi text as discussed earlier.

Text Normalization: The text normalization rules for input Shahmukhi text are formulated with reference to the Urdu Normalization Utility v1.0. (2009). Like Urdu, the normalization of Shahmukhi characters is required for visually indistinguishable glyphs that have a different, but canonically equivalent, code point representation in Unicode character set. On the other hand, to overcome the pronunciation and orthographical differences, we normalize the Gurmukhi word by changing its orthography according to the Shahmukhi spellings and pronunciation after Gurmukhi spell-checking.

3.2.2 Transliteration Engine

Shahmukhi word Segmentation: As discussed by Lehal and Saini, (2011), the proposed transliteration model handles both types of word boundary issues at different phases. The first phase of transliteration handles space insertion problem and the space omission problem is addressed at the final phase of transliteration engine. On the other hand, Gurmukhi script is not affected with any segmentation problem.

Dictionary based Transliteration: A one to one Shahmukhi-to-Gurmukhi and Gurmukhi-to-Shahmukhi dictionary of the most frequent words are developed to speed up the transliteration process as well as to handle words with complex spellings as discussed earlier. In addition to this a special Shahmukhi-to-Gurmukhi bi-gram parallel resource is also developed for handling words with Izafat form (compound word) in Shahmukhi.

Light weight Stemmer for Punjabi Language: The size of any lexical resource is limited. It could happen as at times, though inflection may not be present in the respective script dictionary but its root word maybe present. In order to use this idea, we use a light weight stemmer to obtain the root word. Therefore, in our case, stemming is primarily a process of suffix removal. A list of common suffixes has been created. We have taken only the most common Gurmukhi and Shahmukhi suffixes such as ੇਂ, ਉ, ਿਉ, ੀਂ, ੇ etc and ے‘یں‘اوں‘وں etc.

Finally, rule-based transliteration is used for transliterating the input words that are not fruitfully processed by these developed lexical resources of the transliteration engine. We have proposed the following algorithm for character-level ambiguity and supplying missing short vowels.

Algorithm for Handling Short Vowels and Character-level Ambiguity: While transforming the Shahmukhi word token into Gurmukhi equivalent in the rule-based transliteration phase, we have proposed the following algorithm.
Step1: Convert Shahmukhi word to Gurmukhi by using predefined character mapping with dependency or contextual rules.
Step2: Format Gurmukhi word according to Unicode formatting like ਅ + ਾ → ਆ, ਅ + ੈ → ਐ and ਅ + ੌ → ਔ, ੳ + ੁ → ਉ, ੳ + ੂ → ਊ, ੳ + ੋ → ਓ etc.

Step3: In the converted and formatted Gurmukhi word, at each valid character location, insert short vowels and generate unigram weighted list of all possible combinations.
Step4: Select the word with highest weight of occurrence.

For example, consider the Shahmukhi word سنگھ /saṅgh/ transliterated as ਸਿੰਘ /siṅgh/

Input characters:	س[s]	ں[ɲ]	گھ[g^h]
Character mapping:	ਸ	ਨ | ਂ | ਣ	ਘ
Supply short vowels:	ਸ | ਸੁ | ਸਿ	ਨ | ਨੁ | ਨਿ | ਂ | ਣ | ਣੁ | ਣਿ	ਘ | ਘੁ | ਘਿ

Weighted list: ਸਨਘ(0), ਸਿਨਘ(0), ਸੁਨਘ(0), ਸਨਿਘ(0), ਸਨੁਘ(0), ਸਿਨੁਘ(0), ਸੰਘ(547), ਸੁੰਘ(45), ਸਿੰਘ(55,338), ਸਣਘ(0),ਸਣਿਘ(0), ਸਣੁਘ(0), ਸਿਣੁਘ(0), ਸਣਘ(0) etc.

Valid Unigrams: ਸੰਘ(547), ਸੁੰਘ(45), **ਸਿੰਘ(55,338)**[most frequent]

Similar approach is applied for handling the Gurmukhi characters with multiple Shahmukhi mappings. For example, consider the Gurmukhi word ਸਾਹਿਬ. It has two ambiguous character ਸ[s] → {س|ص|ث} and ਹ[h] → {ہ | ح}. The system will generate all the possible forms and then choose the most frequent صاحب (6432) unigram as output.

3.2.3 Post-processing

The word level ambiguity is still present in the transliteration output generated by transliteration engine. The ambiguous Shahmukhi word /mall/مل with missing diacritics has four valid Gurmukhi interpretations ਮੁੱਲ/mull/, ਮਿਲ/mil/, ਮਿੱਲ/mill/, and ਮੱਲ/mall/ within different contexts. On the other hand, the transliteration of Gurmukhi word ਹਾਲ has two Shahmukhi spellings with different senses as حال (state, condition, circumstance) and ہال (Hall; big room). But correct spellings can be selected after context analysis only. At the outset, all we have is the raw corpora for each script of Punjabi language. We have modelled 2nd order HMM for word level ambiguity as proposed by Thede and Harper (1999) for part of speech tagging. Rather than using fixed smoothing technique, they have discussed their new method of calculating contextual probabilities using the linear interpolation. The formula to estimate contextual probability $P(\tau_p = w_k \mid \tau_{p-1} = w_j, \tau_{p-2} = w_i)$ is:

$$P = k_3.\frac{N_3}{C_2} + (1-k_3)k_2.\frac{N_2}{C_1} + (1-k_3)(1\quad k_2).\frac{N_1}{C_0} \tag{1}$$

where

$$k_3 = \frac{\log_2(N_3+1)+1}{\log_2(N_3+1)+2}; \qquad k_2 = \frac{\log_2(N_2+1)+1}{\log_2(N_2+1)+2}$$

N_3	Freq. of trigram $w_i w_j w_k$	C_2	Occurrence of bi-gram $w_i w_j$
N_2	Freq. of bi-gram $w_j w_k$ in corpus	C_1	Occurrence of unigram w_j
N_1	Freq. of unigram w_k in corpus	C_0	Total vocabulary

The disambiguation of ambiguous words ਹਾਲ and ਅਰਬ is performed using 2nd order HMM and output results are shown in Table 3. On the other hand, the HMM disambiguation for Gurmukhi word ambiguity is shown in Table 4.

Sr.	Before WSD	Ambiguity	After WSD
1	فیصل مختار حال وکھے میٹنگ دا اکھی ویکھیا حال	حال | ہال	فیصل مختار ہال وِکھے میٹنگ دا اکھی ویکھیا حال
2	اس سال عرب دیشاں نال آپسی وپار چار عرب تک پھیلیا	عرب | ارب	اس سال عرب دیشاں نال آپسی وپار چار ارب تک پھیلیا

TABLE 3 – Shahmukhi Word Sense Disambiguation (WSD) using HMM

Sr.	Input Shahmukhi Text	Ambiguity	After WSD
1	تحصیل ترن تارن	{ਤੁਰਨ, ਤਰਨ}	ਤਹਿਸੀਲ ਤਰਨ ਤਾਰਨ
2	لوک اس طرحاں اس دی گرفت وچ	{ਉਸ, ਇਸ}	ਲੋਕ ਇਸ ਤਰਾਂ ਉਸ ਦੀ ਗ੍ਰਿਫ਼ਤ ਵਿਚ

TABLE 4 – Gurmukhi Word Sense Disambiguation (WSD) using HMM

4 Evaluation and Results

4.1 Step-by-Step Evaluation of Shahmukhi-to-Gurmukhi System

A set of ten examples from various online and offline sources are collected for step-by-step evaluation of the system stages. The size of each example ranges from 94 to 246 words per example and the total size of this collection is 1,422 words. The transliteration output from each evaluation stage of the system is manually evaluated. The transliteration steps and Accuracy of the system in the various evaluation stages are shown in Table 5.

Transliteration Steps	Evaluation Stages				
	1st	2nd	3rd	4th	5th
Rule-based approach	☑	☑	☑	☑	☑
Dictionary		☑	☑	☑	☑
Handling missing vowels and char ambiguity			☑	☑	☑
Word segmentation + Light weight Stemmer				☑	☑
Word disambiguation using HMM					☑
Transliteration Accuracy (%)	**47.63**	**87.69**	**92.44**	**95.46**	**97.04**

TABLE 5 – Step-by-Step Evaluation and System Accuracy

4.2 Step-by-Step Evaluation of Gurmukhi-to-Shahmukhi System

A set of eight examples are collected for step-by-step evaluation of the system stages. The size of this collection is 906 words. The transliteration steps and system accuracy with improvement are shown in Table 6 and Figure 4 respectively.

Transliteration Steps	Evaluation Stages		
	1st	2nd	3rd
Rule-based approach	☑	☑	☑
Dictionary + Light weight Stemmer + char ambiguity		☑	☑
Word disambiguation using HMM			☑
Transliteration Accuracy (%)	**75.42**	**97.46**	**98.03**

TABLE 6 – Step-by-Step Evaluation and System Accuracy

4.3 System Evaluation

Shahmukhi-to-Gurmukhi: The natural sources of Shahmukhi text are very limited. With this limitation we have identified the available online and offline sources and three different test sets are taken from different domains. The data Set-1 is a Shahmukhi book of having 37,620 words. The Set-2 consist of online articles, stories and current issues form www.likhari.org having total size of 39,714 words and the Set-3 is a collection news, articles, stories, novels, poetry etc. published on www.wichaar.com and having total size of 46,678 words. The output of the system is manually evaluated by the person having the knowledge of both the scripts and has Punjabi language as a mother tongue. After manual evaluation the word accuracy is calculated as shown in Table 7. The overall transliteration accuracy of the system is fairly high at 97%. Amongst datasets, the word accuracy for the Set-3 (wichaar.com) is less than Set-2 (likhari.org) which in turn is less that the Set-1 (book). One contributory reason might be that the Pakistani dialect of Punjabi language is frequently used by the writers of wichaar.com. Another possible reason may be the diversity within the dataset.

Table 7 shows an average occurrence of 0.67% words marked as out-of-vocabulary (OOV) by the system. We call them OOV because while transliterating such words our system fails to identify them in any form and the output produced by the system is produced by a hybrid system based on rule-based conversion and a tri-gram character language model. We observed that these types of words mostly include words not present in system corpus, wrong input and foreign words mostly from English or Urdu domain. After manual evaluation of the OOV words with correct input, the average word level transliteration accuracy is calculated as 63.04% as shown in Table 7.

Test Data	Total Words	Found	OOV	Accuracy (Found)	Accuracy (OOV)
Set-1 (book)	37,620	99.468%	0.532%	98.49%	50.00%
Set-2 (likhari.org)	39,714	98.927%	1.073%	96.64%	50.00%
Set-3 (wichaar.com)	46,678	99.595%	0.405%	95.68%	87.5%
Total	**1,24,012**	**99.33%**	**0.67%**	**96.94%**	**63.04%**

TABLE 7– Word Accuracy with Test Data

Gurmukhi-to-Shahmukhi: We have tested our system on more that 100 pages of text compiled from newspapers, books and poetry. The overall transliteration accuracy of this system is 98.6% at word level, which is quite high and actually more then its reverse system. The major source of errors are typical and multiple spellings in Shahmukhi. The accuracy of this word disambiguation task is highly dependent on the training corpus. The accuracy of this system can be increased further by increasing the size of the training corpus and having plentiful of data covering maximum senses of all ambiguous words in the target script.

5 Conclusion

The paper proposes a transliteration system model between the scripts of Punjabi language and incorporates various challenges which were hitherto not dealt with by existing rule based system. The paper describes the proposed high accuracy Gurmukhi-to-Shahmukhi transliteration system which can transliterate any Gurmukhi text to Shahmukhi at more than 98.6% accuracy at word level. Both the systems are complex and challenging. The proposed Shahmukhi-to-Gurmukhi transliteration system has more than 97% accuracy at word level. The various challenges such as multiple/zero character mappings, missing vowels, word segmentation, variations in pronunciations and orthography and transliteration of proper nouns etc. have been handled by generating efficient algorithms along with special rules and using various lexical resources such as Gurmukhi spell checker, corpora of both scripts, Gurmukhi-Shahmukhi transliteration dictionaries.

References

Al-Onaizan, Y. and Knight, K. (2002). Machine transliteration of names in Arabic text. In *Proceedings of the ACL workshop on Computational approaches to Semitic languages*, pages 1–13, Philadelphia, PA.

Ananthakrishnan, S., Narayanan, S. and Bangalore, S. (2005). Automatic diacritization of Arabic transcripts for automatic speech recognition. In *Proceedings of ICON-05,* Kanpur, India.

Durrani, N. and Hussain, S. (2010). Urdu Word Segmentation. In *Proceedings of the 2010 Annual Conference of the North American Chapter of the ACL*, pages 528–536, Los Angeles, California.

Jelinek, F. and Mercer, R.L. (1980). Interpolated estimation of Markov source parameters from sparse data. In *Proceedings of the Workshop on Pattern Recognition in Practice*, Amsterdam, The Netherlands: North-Holland.

Katz, S.M. (1987). Estimation of probabilities from sparse data for the language model component of a speech recognizer. *IEEE Transactions on Acoustics, Speech and Signal Processing, ASSP*, 35(3): 400-401.

Lehal, G. S. (2009). A Two Stage Word Segmentation System for Handling Space Insertion Problem in Urdu Script, In *Proceedings of World Academy of Science, Engineering and Technology*, pages 321-324, Bangkok, Thailand.

Lehal, G. S. (2009). A Gurmukhi to Shahmukhi Transliteration System. In *Proceedings of ICON-2009: 7th International Conference on Natural Language Processing*, pages 167-173, Hyderabad, India.

Lehal, G. S. (2010). A Word Segmentation System for Handling Space Omission Problem in Urdu Script, In *Proceedings of the 1st Workshop on South and Southeast Asian Natural Language Processing (WSSANLP) and 23rd COLIN*, pages 43–50, Beijing.

Lehal, G. S. and Saini, T. S. (2011). A Transliteration based Word Segmentation System for Shahmukhi Script. In *Proceedings of ICISIL.* Springer, Communication in Computer and Information Science, CCIS-139, pages 136-143, India.

Malik, M.G.A. (2006). Punjabi Machine Transliteration. In *Proceedings of the 21st International Conference on Computational Linguistics and 44th Annual Meeting of the ACL*, pages 1137-1144.

Naseem, T. and Hussain, S. (2007). Spelling Error Trends in Urdu. In *Proceedings of Conference on Language Technology (CLT07)*, University of Peshawar, Pakistan.

Nelken, R. and Shieber, S. M. (2005). Arabic Diacritization Using Weighted Finite-State Transducers. In *Proceedings of ACL Workshop on Computational Approaches to Semitic Languages,* pages 79-86, Ann Arbor, Michigan.

Oh, J.-H., Choi, K.-S. and Isahara, H. (2006). A comparison of different Machine Transliteration Models. *Journal of Artificial Intelligence Research*, 27:119-151.

Saini, T. S., Lehal, G. S. and Kalra, V. S. (2008). Shahmukhi to Gurmukhi Transliteration System. In *Proceedings of 22nd international Conference on Computational Linguistics (Coling)*, pages 177-180, Manchester, UK.

Saini, T. S. and Lehal, G. S. (2008). Shahmukhi to Gurmukhi Transliteration System: A Corpus based Approach. *Research in Computing Science*, 33:151-162, Mexico.

Thede, S.M. and Harper, M.P. (1999). A Second-Order Hidden Markov Model for Part-of-speech Tagging, In *Proceedings of the 37th annual meeting of the ACL on Computational Linguistics,* pages 175-182.

Urdu Normalization Utility v1.0. (2009). Centre for Research in Urdu Language Processing, National University of Computer and Emerging Sciences, Lahore, Pakistan. Retrieved April 14, 2011 from http://www.crulp.org/software/langproc/urdunormalization.htm

Development of a Complete Urdu-Hindi Transliteration System

Gurpreet Singh LEHAL[1] *Tejinder Singh SAINI*[2]
(1) Department of Computer Science, Punjabi University, Patiala
(2) ACTDPL, Punjabi University, Patiala
gslehal@gmail.com, tej74i@gmail.com

ABSTRACT

Hindi and Urdu are variants of the same language, but while Hindi is written in the Devnagri script from left to right, Urdu is written in a script derived from a Persian modification of Arabic script written from right to left. The difference in the two scripts has created a script wedge as majority of Urdu speaking people in Pakistan cannot read Devnagri, and similarly the majority of Hindi speaking people in India cannot comprehend Urdu script. To break this script barrier, it becomes necessary to develop a high accuracy Urdu-Devnagri transliteration system. The major challenges in developing such system are handling missing diacritic marks and short vowels in Urdu, zero/multiple character mappings of Urdu in Hindi, absence of half characters in Urdu, multiple mappings of Urdu words in Hindi and word segmentation issues in Urdu including broken and merged words. Already a few Urdu-Hindi transliteration systems have developed but their accuracy is not very high and they have failed to address all the above issues. For the first time, we present a complete Urdu-Hindi transliteration system which takes care of all the above issues and has reported a transliteration accuracy of more than 97% at word level.

KEYWORDS : Urdu, Hindi, Devnagri, Machine Transliteration, Language Models

Proceedings of COLING 2012: Posters, pages 643–652,
COLING 2012, Mumbai, December 2012.

1 Introduction

Hindi and Urdu are variants of the same language, but while Hindi is written in the Devnagri script from left to right, Urdu is written in a script derived from a Persian modification of Arabic script written from right to left. Hindi is the official language of India, while Urdu is the national language of Pakistan, and also one of the state languages in India. The spoken form of the two languages is very similar. Since Urdu and Hindi are grammatically same language and they also share a very good number of words, it is easier for both speakers to understand each others' language. The only obstacle is the script. Thus there is an urgent need to develop a high accuracy Urdu-Devnagri transliteration system. Already some work in this direction has been reported (Malik at el. 2008, Malik at el. 2009), but these systems suffer from low accuracy and have not handled some of the major transliteration issues such as resolving word ambiguity. Some work has also been reported on the reverse Hindi-Urdu transliteration (Bushra and Tafseer, 2009; Duranni et al., 2010; Lehal and Saini, 2010; Sajjad et al., 2011; Visweswariah et al., 2010).

In the following sections, we shall be discussing the major challenges in developing a high accuracy Urdu-Hindi transliteration system. The linguistics and language models along with the algorithms developed to meet these challenges are also discussed in detail, followed by experimental results. When there is no confusion, we use the terms Devnagri and Hindi interchangeably.

2 Challenges in Urdu-Hindi Transliteration

The major challenges of transliteration of Urdu to Hindi are as follows:

- **Recognition of Urdu Text without Diacritical Marks:** Diacritical marks are sparingly used in Urdu, even though they are critical for correct pronunciation and disambiguation of certain words. These missing diacritical marks create substantial difficulties for transliteration systems.

- **Filling the Missing Script Maps:** There are many characters which are present in the Urdu script, corresponding to those having no character in Devnagri, e.g. Hamza ء , Do-Zabar ً, Aen ع, Khadi Zabar ٰetc.

- **Multiple mappings for Urdu characters:** It is observed that corresponding to many Urdu characters there are multiple mappings into Devnagri script (example و -> व, ो, ौ, ु, ू, ऊ, ओ, औ). Grammar rules and context are needed to select the appropriate Devnagri character for such Urdu characters.

- **Transliteration ambiguity at word level:** There are many Urdu words which map to multiple Hindi words. For example: میل (मेल, मील, मैल) / بچے (बचे, बच्चे) / کیا (क्या, किया) / ہوا (हुआ, हवा). Higher level language information will be needed to choose the most relevant Hindi word.

- **Word-Segmentation Issues:** Space is not consistently used in Urdu words, which makes word segmentation a non-trivial task. Many times the space is deleted resulting in many Urdu words being jumbled together and many other times extra space is put in word resulting in over segmentation of that word. These words can still be easily understood by Urdu readers, but complicate the transliteration task.

- **Compound words in Urdu:** There are many compound words or combinations of Urdu words written as a multi-word expression in Hindi. For example: نقش قدم (नक्श-ए-क़दम), جوش و خروش (जोश-ओ-ख़रोश).

3 Our Approach

3.1 Lexical Resources Used

In order to perform statistical analysis during the various phases of the transliteration system we have developed lexical resources from Urdu and Hindi Corpora. The resources include a parallel corpus of Urdu-Hindi words/compound words/phrases, Urdu word based unigram language model, a statistical trigram character model for Hindi Language and Hindi word based unigram, bigram and trigram language models.

3.2 System Architecture

The system architecture of the Urdu-Hindi transliteration system is shown in Figure 1. The complete Urdu-Hindi transliteration system is divided into three stages: pre-processing, processing and post-processing. The three stages are discussed in detail in the following sections.

3.3 Pre-processing

In the pre-processing stage, the Urdu words are cleaned and prepared for transliteration by normalizing the Urdu words as well as joining the broken Urdu words. The two main stages in pre-processing are:

3.3.1 Normalizing Urdu words

There are a few Urdu characters that have multiple equivalent Unicodes. As for example, from transliteration point of view, ى(0649), ي(064a) and ی(06cc) represent the same Urdu character, similarly آ (0622) can be also be represented by the combination ا (0627)+ ٓ (0653). All such forms are normalized to have only one representation.

3.3.2 Joining the broken Urdu words

The Urdu-Hindi transliteration system faces many problems related to word segmentation of Urdu script, as in many cases space is not properly put between Urdu words. Sometimes it is deleted resulting in many Urdu words being jumbled together and many other times extra space is put in word resulting in over segmentation of that word. The Urdu text can still be easily read by the reader, but when such words are transliterated to Hindi they produce erroneous results. So it is necessary to handle such space related errors. The space insertion problem is handled in both pre-processing and post-processing stage, while the space deletion problem is handled in the processing stage. The space insertion problem usually occurs due to conventional way of writing in Urdu or due to extra space being inserted during typing. The typing related space insertion problems are handled by using the algorithm suggested by Lehal (Lehal, 2009) in the pre-processing.

3.4 Processing Stage

In this stage, corresponding to each Urdu word, one or several possible Hindi words are generated. For multiple alternatives, the final decision is taken in the post processing stage. In the first pass, the Urdu sentence is parsed word by word and the Urdu word combinations are replaced with equivalent Hindi word combinations in the source Urdu sentence.

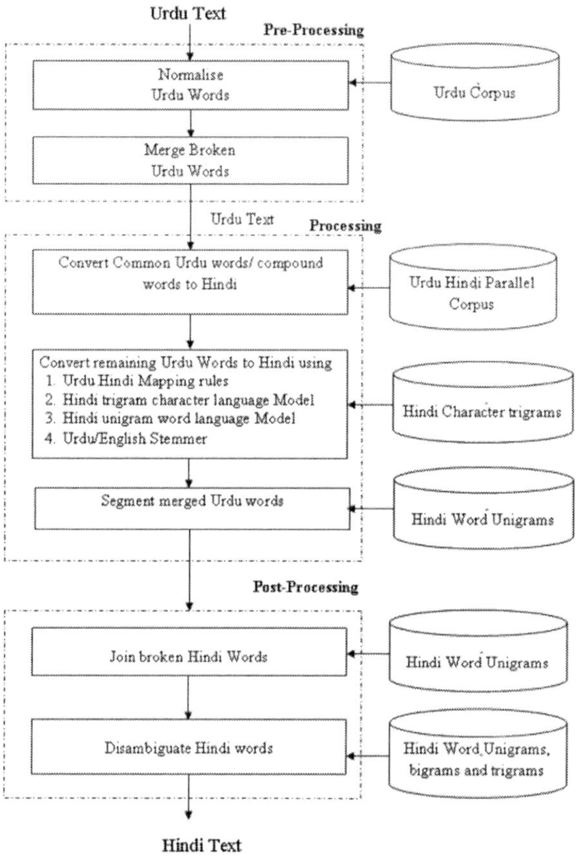

FIGURE 1 –System Architecture

In the next pass, the remaining Urdu words in the sentence, which could not be transliterated to Hindi in the first pass are processed. A multi-stage transliteration engine has been developed, to convert each Urdu. The Urdu words passes through each stage, till it gets converted to a non-empty set of Hindi words. The four stages are:

Stage 1: This stage uses a Language-model-based-generator(LMG) to convert the Urdu word. The LMG uses Urdu-Hindi character rules and a trigram character language model to generate a set of Hindi words from the Urdu word. A unigram word language model is then used to rank these words. If there is no word with non-zero probability, then we move to next stage.

Stage 2: In this stage, an attempt is made to extract the root form of the Urdu word using stemming rules for Urdu and English. If the root is found, then LMG is used to generate set of Hindi words corresponding to the Urdu root word. If root cannot be extracted or LMG returns an empty set, then we go to the next stage.

Stage 3: In this stage, the Urdu word is inspected for presence of merged words which can be transliterated to non empty sets of Hindi words. If no such sets can be generated then the word is sent to the next stage.

Stage 4: An Urdu word reaches this stage, if it cannot be transliterated to Hindi in the above 3 stages. In practice, very few words (only 0.39%) reach this stage. This stage uses the simple character mapping rules to convert the word to Hindi.

3.4.1 Language-model-based-generator (LMG)

This is the major module in the transliteration engine. It generates multiple Hindi transliterations for an Urdu word. The sequence of probable Hindi words is produced by a hybrid system based on rule based character mapping table between Urdu and Hindi characters and a trigram character Language Model. The Urdu word is processed character by character and the Urdu characters are mapped directly to their corresponding similar sounding Hindi characters (snippet shown in the Table 1).

Unicode	Urdu	Hindi
0627	ا	अ, ◌ा
062a+06be	تھ	थ
0646	ن	न, ण, ◌ं, ◌ँ
0648	و	व, ◌ो, ◌ौ, ◌ु, ◌ू, ऊ, ओ, औ
06cc	ی	य, ◌ी, ◌े, ◌ै, इ, ई, ए, ऐ

TABLE 1– Portion of Urdu-Hindi character mapping Table

In most of the cases, there is a 1-1 mapping from Urdu to Hindi characters. But there are a few characters such as و ن, ی, which have multiple mappings. Special rules have been written to handle such cases, for example for character ی(o6cc):

- if ی(o6cc) is preceded by ء (0621), then replace both characters by ई
- if ی(o6cc) is followed by ا (0627), then replace ی by य
- if ی(o6cc) is preceded by ا (0627), then replace ی by ए
- if ی(o6cc) is preceded by a consonant, then replace ی by ◌ी

More than 100 such rules have been written. But it was found that these rules have proved successful only in producing crude transliteration (54.19% accuracy) which is refined in subsequent stages. The first refinement we made was by using a character-based trigram language model, to decide between the various possible alternatives, as shown in Table 1. As a result, the transliteration accuracy increased to 72.62%, but it is still much behind the desired goal. The major reason was this poor accuracy was that in Urdu there are no half characters and also the diacritical marks are usually omitted in written text. The challenge is to fill these missing diacritical marks and put half characters at appropriate locations in Hindi word.

To solve this problem, for each Urdu character, we consider all its possible mappings in Hindi which include the missing short vowels and half characters. As an example, the Urdu character د, which we had mapped only to Devnagri character द, could practically map to द, दु, दि, द्, द्द, द्दु and द्दि (دلدل -> दलदल, دنیا -> दुनिया, دل -> दिल, گدگد -> गद्गद्, مدت -> मुद्दत, تشدد -> तशद्दुद, مجدد -> मुजद्दिद).

So we modify our mapping table to include all such forms for all the Urdu consonants resulting in multiple mappings. As a result, the 66 Urdu characters are mapped to 302 Hindi character combinations. We form all possible combinations, which could be generated from these multiple mappings and the top N combinations are retained. The character based trigram language model for Hindi is used to select the top N combinations. Each character combination may contain upto 4 Hindi characters. As for example, the Urdu character د (062F) can be mapped to Hindi character combination द्दि (0926+094D+0926+093F). These 302 possible mappings in Hindi, lead to 302^3 = 18,514,412 possible character trigrams.

As an example, consider the Urdu word کینسر(cancer). The five characters in the word : ک(क कि कु क् क्क क्कि क्कु), ی (य य् य्य य्यि य्यु यि यु ि ी े ै), ن (न न् न्न नि नु ण् ण णु णि ं ँ), س (स स् स्स सु सि स्सि स्सु) and ر (र र् रि रु र्र र्रु र्रि) have multiple mappings in Hindi, as shown in brackets. Hence a total of 7*11*11*7*7 = 41,503 transliteration candidates have to be considered (Example: कैंसर किन्नसर केणसुर्र केन्सर etc.). After removing the combinations containing zero probability trigrams, the top five suggestions output by the trigram character language model are: केंसर, केंसरि, कींसर, कैंसर, कींसरु. We can see that not all the suggestions generated by the character language model are valid Hindi words. To further rank these words, we use the Unigram Word Model for Hindi. Words with non-zero probability in the Unigram word model are ranked based on their probabilities. In above example, we found that only two words had probability greater than zero and the ranked sequence of words produced by Unigram word model is: कैंसर, केंसर. It could also happen that all the top N alternatives suggested by the character level trigram may be having zero probabilities, in which case no alternative is returned by LMG.

3.4.2 Urdu/English Stemmer

It often happens that the root word maybe present in Hindi corpus but its inflections may not be present in Hindi corpus. In that case, the unigram language model will give zero probability for any such inflection and the word will not be considered for transliteration. To take care of situations, we use a light weight stemmer to obtain the root word and then transliterate it. A novelty in our stemmer has been that besides Urdu words, we also cover the English words which are also now frequently being used in Urdu.

3.4.3 Merged word segmentation

As already discussed above, space is not consistently used in Urdu, which gives rise to both space omission and space insertion errors. Due to the space deletion problem, a sequence of words is jumbled together as a single word and when the LMG tries to generate the equivalent Hindi alternatives it fails. The sequence of Urdu words written together without space is still readable because of the character joining property in Urdu. As for example, consider the word cluster انکارکردیاہے , which is composed of four words انکار, کر , دیا and ہے . The Urdu readers can very easily segment and read the four words separately, but the computer will read them as a single word since there is no space in between, the LMG module fails to produce valid Hindi word. So it becomes necessary to break the jumbled word into individual words. We have used the space deletion algorithm presented by Lehal (Lehal, 2010) to split the Urdu words and then transliterate them.

For out of vocabulary words, the Hindi word is generated by using the trigram character language model and the top alternative is selected for further processing.

3.5 Post Processing Stage

Two main tasks are performed in the post processing stage. The first task is to join the broken words in Hindi and the second and more important task is to choose the best alternative, where ever multiple alternatives for Hindi words exist. The broken words are joined using the algorithm suggested by Lehal (Lehal, 2009). To choose between the different Hindi word alternatives we have used the word trigram probability. To take care of the sparseness in the trigram model, we have used deleted interpolation, which offers the solution of backing away from low count trigrams by augmenting the estimate using bigram and unigram counts. The deleted interpolation trigram model assigns a probability to each trigram which is the linear interpolation of the trigram, bigram, unigram and uniform models as follows:

$$\Pr(w_i \mid w_{i-2} w_{i-1}) = \lambda_3 \frac{c(w_{i-2} w_{i-1} w_i)}{c(w_{i-2} w_{i-1})} + \lambda_2 \frac{c(w_{i-1} w_i)}{c(w_{i-1})} + \lambda \frac{c(w_i)}{\mathrm{N}} + \lambda_0 \frac{1}{V}$$

Where N = Number of words in the training corpus, V = Size of the vocabulary. The weights are set automatically using the Expectation-Maximization (EM) algorithm.

4 Results and Examples

We show with an example, the various stages of our Urdu-Hindi transliteration system in Table 2. The multiple transliteration options generated by the system are shown in braces.

Source Urdu Sentence: استوڈینٹس نے گیارہ مارچ کوپریس میں کہا کہ موسٰی احمد بے قصور ہے اور دہشت کا دور ختم ہو
After Pass1 : Searching Parallel Corpus استوڈینٹس نے گیارہ مارچ کوپریس میں کہا कि मूसा احمد بے قصور ہے اور دہشت کا دور ختم ہو
After Stage 1 : LMG استوڈینٹس ने ग्यारह मार्च کوپریس < में, मैं > कहा कि मूसा < अहमद, एहमद > बे < क़सूर, कुसूर > < है, हे > < और, ओर, अवर > < दहशत, दहश्त > का < दूर, दौर, दवर, दोर > < ख़त्म, ख़तम> <हो, ह, हौ >
After Stage 2 : Urdu/English Stemmer स्टूडैंटस ने ग्यारह मार्च کوپریس < में, मैं > कहा कि मूसा < अहमद, एहमद > बे < क़सूर, कुसूर > < है, हे > < और, ओर, अवर > < दहशत, दहश्त > का < दूर, दौर, दवर, दोर > < ख़त्म, ख़तम> <हो, हृ, हौ >
After Stage 3 : Splitting merged words स्टूडैंटस ने ग्यारह मार्च < को, कौ, कू > <प्रेस, प्रैस > < में, मैं > कहा कि मूसा < अहमद, एहमद > बे < क़सूर, कुसूर > < है, हे > < और, ओर, अवर > < दहशत, दहश्त > का < दूर, दौर, दवर, दोर > < ख़त्म, ख़तम> < हो, हृ, हौ
Post Processing Stage 1 : After Joining broken Hindi words स्टूडैंटस ने ग्यारह मार्च < को, कौ, कू > <प्रेस, प्रैस > < में, मैं > कहा कि मूसा < अहमद, एहमद> बेक़सूर < है, हे > < और, ओर, अवर > < दहशत, दहश्त > का < दूर, दौर, दवर, दोर > <ख़त्म, ख़तम> <हो, ह, हौ >
Post Processing Stage 2 : After selecting the best alternative स्टूडैंटस ने ग्यारह मार्च को प्रैस में कहा कि मूसा अहमद बेक़सूर है और दहशत का दौर ख़त्म हो

TABLE 2–Various transliteration stages

We compare our transliteration output with other available online systems. The transliteration/translation produced by these systems is shown in Table 3. The wrong translations and transliterations are marked in red colour.

5 Experimental Results

We have tested our system on 45 pages of Urdu Unicode text compiled from three Urdu websites. The text contained 18403 words. The transliterated text has been manually evaluated. The results are tabulated in Table 4. We can see how the transliteration accuracy increases in each stage with the addition of new language models and other linguistic resources. The initial transliteration accuracy obtained when the text was transliterated using the simple rule based character mapping is 54.19%. The accuracy improved to 72.62% after application of trigram character language model. Later when the word based unigram language model was applied on the N words returned by the trigram character language model to select the word with highest unigram probability, the accuracy further improved to 82.58%. On combining the parallel Urdu-Hindi corpus, the accuracy increased to 92.81%. A further improvement in the accuracy was observed when the Urdu/English stemmer and word segmentation routines were added and the accuracy went upto 95.24%. And finally on applying the Hindi trigram word language model the accuracy reached 97.74%.

Urdu Sentence: اسٹوڈینٹس نے گیارہ مارچ کوپریس میں کہا کہ موسٰی احمد بے قصور ہے اور دہشت کا دور ختم ہو
Transliterated Hindi Sentence by Puran (http://www.sanlp.org/humt/HUMT.aspx) असटोडेंटस ने गयारा मारच कोपरेस में कहा कि मोसाय अहमद बे क़सोर हे ओर दहशत का दोर ख़तम हो
Translated Hindi Sentence by Sampark (http://www.tdil-dc.in/components/com_mtsystem/CommonUI/homeMT.php) असटोडीनटस ने ग्यारह मार्च कोपरीस में कहा ख मोस?ई अह़मद बे अपराध है और आतंक का समय समाप्त हो
Translated Hindi Sentence by Google Translation (http://translate.google.com) ास्टोडीनटस ने ग्यारह मार्च कोपरेस कहा कह मूसा अहमद निर्दोष है और आतंक का युग समाप्त हो
Transliteration by our system (http://uh.learnpunjabi.org) स्टूडैंटस ने ग्यारह मार्च को प्रैस में कहा कि मूसा अहमद बेक़सूर है और दहशत का दौर ख़त्म हो

TABLE 3– Transliteration/Translation by some of the existing systems

6 Conclusion

In this research paper we have presented an Urdu to Hindi transliteration system which has achieved an accuracy of 97.74% at word level. The various challenges such as multiple/zero character mappings, missing diacritic marks in Urdu, multiple Hindi words mapped to an Urdu word, word segmentation issues in Urdu text etc. have been handled by generating special rules and using various lexical resources such as Hindi character trigram model, Hindi unigram, bigram and trigram word models, Urdu unigram model, Urdu-Hindi parallel corpus etc.

Linguistic/Statistical Resources Used	Transliteration Accuracy
Character based Mapping	54.19 %
Hindi Trigram Character Language Model	72.62 %
Hindi Word Based Unigram Language Model	82.58 %
Parallel Urdu-Hindi Corpus	92.81 %
Urdu/English Stemmer	92.93 %
Word Segmentation	95.24 %
Hindi Trigram Word Language Model	97.74%

TABLE 4 – Transliteration Accuracy in different stages

Acknowledgement

The authors would like to acknowledge the support provided by ISIF grants for carrying out this research.

References

Bushra J., Tafseer A. (2009). Hindi to Urdu Conversion: Beyond Simple Transliteration. In *Proceedings of the Conference on Language & Technology*, pages 24-31, Lahore, Pakistan.

Durrani, N., Sajjad, H., Fraser, A. and Schmid, H. (2010). Hindi-to-Urdu machine translation through transliteration. In *Proceedings of the 48th Annual Conference of the Association for Computational Linguistics*, pages 465–474, Uppsala, Sweden.

Lehal, G. S. and Saini, T. S. (2010). A Hindi to Urdu Transliteration System. In *Proceedings of 8th International Conference on Natural Language Processing*, pages 235-240, Kharagpur, India.

Lehal, G. S. (2009). A Two Stage Word Segmentation System For Handling Space Insertion Problem In Urdu Script, In *Proceedings of World Academy of Science, Engineering and Technology*, volume 60, pages 321-324, Bangkok, Thailand.

Lehal, G. S. (2010) A Word Segmentation System for Handling Space Omission Problem in Urdu Script. In *Proceedings of the 1st Workshop on South and Southeast Asian Natural Language Processing (WSSANLP)*, pages 43–50, the 23rd International Conference on Computational Linguistics (COLING), Beijing.

Malik, A., Boitet, C. and Bhattacharyya, P. (2008). Hindi Urdu machine transliteration using finite-state transducers. In *Proceedings of the 22nd International Conference on Computational Linguistics*, pages 537–544, Manchester, UK.

Malik, A., Besacier, L., Boitet, C. and Bhattacharyya, P. (2009). A hybrid model for Urdu Hindi transliteration. In *Proceedings of the 2009 Named Entities Workshop: Shared Task on Transliteration (NEWS 2009)*, pages 177–185, Singapore.

Sajjad, H., Durrani N., Schmid, H. and Fraser, A. (2011). Comparing Two Techniques for Learning Transliteration Models Using a Parallel Corpus. In *Proceedings of the 5th International Joint Conference on Natural Language Processing (IJCNLP2011)*, pages 129-137, Chiang Mai, Thailand.

Visweswariah, K., Chenthamarakshan, V. and Kambhatla, N., (2010) Urdu and Hindi: Translation and sharing of linguistic resources In *Proceedings of the 23rd International Conference on Computational Linguistics (Coling 2010)*: Poster Volume, pages 1283–1291, Beijing.

Random Walks on Context-Aware Relation Graphs for Ranking Social Tags

*Han Li** *Zhiyuan Liu** *Maosong Sun*
Department of Computer Science and Technology
State Key Lab on Intelligent Technology and Systems
National Lab for Information Science and Technology
Tsinghua University, Beijing 100084, China
{lihan.thu,lzy.thu}@gmail.com, sms@tsinghua.edu.cn

ABSTRACT

Social tagging provides an efficient way to manage online resources. In order to collect more social tags, many research efforts aim to automatically suggest tags to help users annotate tags. Many content-based methods assume tags are independent and suggest tags one by one independently. Although it makes suggestion easier, the independence assumption does not confirm to reality, and the suggested tags are usually inconsistent and incoherent with each other. To address this problem, we propose to model context-aware relations of tags for suggestion: (1) By regarding resource content as context of tags, we propose Tag Context Model to identify specific context words in resource content for tags. (2) Given a new resource, we build a context-aware relation graph of candidate tags, and propose a random walk algorithm to rank tags for suggestion. Experiment results demonstrate our method outperforms other state-of-the-art methods.

TITLE AND ABSTRACT IN CHINESE

在上下文感知的关系网络中随机游走进行社会标签排序

社会标签是一种有效的管理在线资源的方式。为了获取更多的社会标签，许多研究致力于自动推荐标签来帮助人们标注。很多基于内容的方法认为标签之间是独立的，因此孤立地推荐每个标签。虽然这让推荐方法更简单，但是独立性假设并不符合真实情况，从而导致推荐的标签互相之间存在不一致和不协调。为了解决这一问题，我们提出对标签之间的上下文感知的关系进行建模：（1）我们将资源内容作为标签的上下文，通过标签上下文模型从内容中发现标签的特定上下文。（2）当给定一个新的资源，我们建立候选标签之间的上下文关系图，通过随机游走算法对标签排序并推荐。实验结果证明我们的方法优于已有方法。

KEYWORDS: tag ranking, context-aware relation, random walk, social tag suggestion.
KEYWORDS IN CHINESE: 标签排序, 上下文感知的关系, 随机游走, 社会标签推荐.

∗ indicates equal contributions from these authors.

Proceedings of COLING 2012: Posters, pages 653–662,
COLING 2012, Mumbai, December 2012.

1 Introduction

Web 2.0 technologies provide a new scheme, social tagging, for users to collect, manage and share online resources (Gupta et al., 2010). In a social tagging system, each user can freely use any words to annotate resources. Figure 1a shows an exemplary book, *The Catcher in the Rye* from Douban, a review website in China. For the book, many tags have been annotated by thousands of users. For example, the tag "Salinger" is annotated by 1,224 users, which indicates the author J. D. Salinger. The figure also shows some meta-data such as the title, the author and a brief introduction. In this paper, we refer to the meta-data of a resource as *content* and the user-annotated tags as *annotation*.

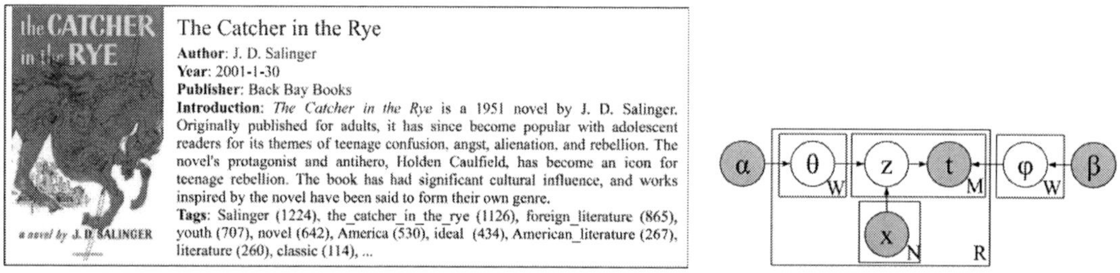

(a) An example book. (b) TCM

Figure 1: (a) An example book. (b) Graphical model of TCM.

Social tagging provides a convenient management scheme compared to strict taxonomy in libraries. In order to attract more users to contribute social annotations, many social tagging systems facilitate users through automatic tag suggestion. There are two main approaches: graph-based and content-based. The former approach (Jaschke et al., 2008; Rendle et al., 2009) suggests tags according to users' annotation history, while the latter approach (Si et al., 2009, 2010; Liu et al., 2011) according to resource meta-data. Since graph-based methods often suffer from the cold-start problem when they face new users or resources, content-based methods are usually regarded as an important component in social tagging systems especially in the initial stage. In this paper we focus on the content-based approach.

Many social tagging methods are based on *independence assumption*, which is widely adopted in computational linguistics (Manning and Schutze, 2000) and information retrieval (Manning et al., 2008). Under this assumption, tags are regarded independent with each other given the resource. Although this makes methods easier to implement, it does not accord with the real world, in which the annotated tags of a resource are usually semantically correlated with each other. Hence, if we can find an effective approach to model tag relations, it may improve the suggestion quality significantly.

It is non-trivial to model tag relations. Given a resource, the tag relations are *context-aware*. Two tags may be more related with each other given a resource but less given another one. Moreover, tag relations are complex for modeling. Since tags are not restricted within a pre-defined vocabulary, their relations cannot be well covered by manually-annotated dictionaries such as WordNet (Miller et al., 1990). Hence, we have to statistically learn the semantic relations of tags from a set of annotated data. This will better guarantee the semantic consistency of suggested tags.

To consider the context-aware relations of tags given a resource, tag graphs are a straightforward representation. We consider a random walk method on context-aware tag relation graphs to rank social tags. There are two critical challenges for this method: (1) How to statistically model the context-aware relations of tags from a large collection of annotation data? (2) After obtaining the context-aware relations of tags, how to construct a tag graph given a resource for random walks? To address the challenges, we propose a probabilistic model to learn the context-aware relations of tags, and propose a random walk algorithm over context-aware relation graphs to suggest tags. To investigate the efficiency of our method, we carry out experiments using real-world datasets.

Related work. Measuring semantic relations have been studied in many tasks such as measuring term similarities (Lin, 1998; Gabrilovich and Markovitch, 2007) and query similarities (Wen et al., 2002; Mei et al., 2008). Meanwhile, context-aware setting is being considered in many applications including recommender systems (Adomavicius and Tuzhilin, 2011) and query suggestion (Brown and Jones, 2001), which is a critical research issue for all applications under real-world complex scene. In social tagging, co-occurrence-based tag relations have been explored to group tags into clusters (Wu et al., 2006b; Brooks and Montanez, 2006; Shepitsen et al., 2008), and have been adopted in personalized tag suggestion (Shepitsen et al., 2008) and extending ontology (Mika, 2005; Wu et al., 2006a). Some specific relations of tags such as subsumption are also studied in social tagging (Si et al., 2010). These relations are mostly context-free. There has been little work on modeling context-aware tag relations for content-based social tag suggestion.

2 Learning Context-Aware Relations of Tags

A resource is denoted as $r \in R$, where R is the set of all resources in the social tagging system. Each resource is composed of the content (meta-data) and the annotation (a set of tags). The content is represented as a sequence of words $\mathbf{x}_r = \{x_i\}_{i=1}^{N_r}$, where N_r is the number of words in $\mathbf{x}_r$. The vocabulary of the words in contents is W, and each word $x_i = w \in W$. The annotation of resource r is represented as $\mathbf{a}_r = \{a_i\}_{i=1}^{M_r}$, where M_r is the number of annotated tags in $\mathbf{a}_r$. The vocabulary of annotations is T, and each annotation $a_i = t \in T$. Tag relations can be either context-free or context-aware, and either symmetric or asymmetric. Without loss of generality, we consider symmetric relations all through the paper and introduce context-free and -aware relations in detail.

2.1 Context-Free Relations

Context-free relations of tags leave context information out. There are various methods to statistically measure context-free relations of tags. The basic idea is regarding two tags are correlated with each other if they tend to be assigned to the same resources. For example, the tags "the_catcher_in_the_rye" and "Salinger" can be found correlated since they are usually assigned to the same resources. In this paper, we measure context-free relations of two tags t_1 and t_2 using joint probability $\Pr(t_1, t_2)$, estimated according to co-occurrences of tags as $\Pr(t_1, t_2) = N_{t_1,t_2}/|R|$, where N_{t_1,t_2} is the number of resources where both t_1 and t_2 appear together, and $|R|$ is the total number of resources.

2.2 Co-Occurrence-based Context-Aware Relations

In this paper, we regard words in resources as the crucial context of tags. The context-aware relation between tags t_1 and t_2 given a context word w can be represented as the conditional probability $\Pr(t_1, t_2|w)$.

We first introduce a naive method to measure context-aware tag relations, i.e., co-occurrence-based context-aware relations. In this method, the conditional probability $\Pr(t_1, t_2|w)$ is estimated according to the co-occurrences of t_1, t_2 and w within a collection of annotated resources as $\Pr(t_1, t_2|w) = N_{w,t_1,t_2}/N_w$, where N_w is the number of resources where w appears, N_{w,t_1,t_2} is the number of resources where w, t_1 and t_2 appear together.

The co-occurrence-based context-aware tag relations are straightforward and easy for implementation. However, empirical experiments show that this type of relations usually suffers from poor performance. The reason is that, in many cases, given two tags of a resource, not all words in the resource can be regarded as their context. It is obvious that each annotated tag usually represents some aspects of a resource, and thus may only correspond to some specific words in the resource.

In order to better model context-aware relations of tags, it is crucial to exactly find corresponding context words for tags. Therefore, we propose a probabilistic graphical model, Tag Context Model (TCM), to learn context words for tags.

2.3 TCM and TCM-based Context-Aware Relations

Tag Context Model (TCM). We propose TCM to find context words of tags. TCM can be regarded as a generative process of each resource r as shown in Figure 1b. Essentially, TCM models semantic relations between words and tags, similar to WTM (Liu et al., 2011) and TAM (Si et al., 2010). We denote the context word sequence as $\mathbf{z}_r = \{z_i\}_1^{M_r}$, corresponding to the tag sequence $\mathbf{a}_r$. The learning goal of TCM is to infer the multinomial distribution of each tag t given word w (i.e., ϕ with $\phi_{tw} = \Pr(t|w)$) and the multinomial distribution of each word w being selected as context word in resource r(i.e., θ with $\theta_{wr} = \Pr(w|r)$). α and β are hyper-parameters of θ and ϕ following Dirichlet distributions.

Given the observed words in resource content $\mathbf{x}$, the joint distribution of θ, ϕ, context words $\mathbf{z}$, and tags $\mathbf{a}$ is $\Pr(\mathbf{z}, \theta, \phi, \mathbf{a}|\mathbf{x}, \alpha, \beta) = \Pr(\theta|\alpha)\prod_{i=1}^{M}\Pr(a_i|z_i, \mathbf{x}, \phi)\Pr(\phi|\beta)\Pr(z_i|\mathbf{x}, \theta)$. The key inference problem of TCM learning is computing posterior distribution of the hidden variables given resource content and tags. The hidden variables in TCM are $\mathbf{z}$, i.e., the context words that correspond to the annotated tags of resources. Here we integrate out the parameters θ and ϕ because it can be regarded as the statistics of the associations between the observed annotations $\mathbf{a}$ and the corresponding $\mathbf{z}$.

In this paper we select Gibbs Sampling for inference, which has been widely adopted in graphical models such as LDA (Griffiths and Steyvers, 2004). Since we integrate out θ and ϕ, the inference algorithm is also referred to as *collapsed* Gibbs Sampling. In Gibbs Sampling, we compute the conditional probability as

$$\Pr(z_i = w|\mathbf{z}_{\neg i}, a_i = t, \mathbf{a}, \mathbf{x}, \alpha, \beta) = \frac{\Pr(\mathbf{z}, \mathbf{a}|\mathbf{x}, \alpha, \beta)}{\Pr(\mathbf{z}_{\neg i}, \mathbf{a}|\mathbf{x}, \alpha, \beta)} \propto \frac{N_{tw}^{\neg i} + \beta}{\sum_t N_{tw}^{\neg i} + |T|\beta} \times \frac{N_{wr}^{\neg i} + \alpha}{\sum_w N_{wr}^{\neg i} + |W|\alpha}, \quad (1)$$

where $N_*^{\neg i}$ indicates the annotation a_i is excluded, N_{tw} is the number of times that tag t takes w as its context word, and N_{wr} is the number of times that word w is selected as a context word within resource r. Note that the probability shown in Equation (1) is unnormalized. The actual probability of assigning a tag to context word w is computed by dividing the quantity in Equation (1) for word w by summing over all unique words in the resource content. Gibbs Sampling outputs the estimation of $\mathbf{z}$ for annotated tags. We further estimate ϕ and θ as $\phi_{tw} = \Pr(t|w) = \frac{N_{tw}+\beta}{\sum_t N_{tw}+|T|\beta}$ and $\phi_{wr} = \Pr(w|r) = \frac{N_{wr}+\alpha}{\sum_w N_{wr}+|W|\alpha}$. With the estimated ϕ, we can obtain all context words of each tag t, i.e., the words that have higher values of $\phi_{tw} = \Pr(t|w)$. Based on the estimations, we further measure context-aware relations of tags.

TCM-based Context-Aware Relations. We define a function $\delta(x)$ as $\delta(x) = 1$ if x is true, otherwise $\delta(x) = 0$. We calculate TCM-based context-aware relations of two tags t_1 and t_2 using **a** and **z** as follows:

$$\Pr(t_1, t_2|w) = \frac{\sum_{r\in R} \delta_r(z_i = w \cap z_j = w \cap a_i = t_1 \cap a_j = t_2)}{\sum_{r\in R} \delta_r(z_i = w)}. \quad (2)$$

In this equation, if $\delta_r(z_i = w \cap z_j = w \cap a_i = t_1 \cap a_j = t_2) = 1$, it indicates the resource $r \in R$ has two tags t_1 and t_2 and both of them are assigned to w as their context word; if $\delta_r(z_i = w) = 1$, it indicates the resource $r \in R$ has w being assigned as context word.

The TCM-based context-aware relations calculated in Equation (2) have a potential size of $|T|^2|W|$, where $|T|$ is the vocabulary size of tags and $|W|$ is the vocabulary size of words. The estimation of context-aware relations suffers from more serious problem of sparsity compared to context-free relations. To alleviate the sparsity problem, we introduce a remedy solution: linear interpolation smoothing. We use the conditional-independent context-aware relations for interpolation. Suppose two tags t_1 and t_2 are conditionally independent given w, the context-aware relations will be $\Pr^+(t_1, t_2|w) = \Pr(t_1|w)\Pr(t_2|w)$, and the interpolation smoothing is performed as $\Pr^*(t_1, t_2|w) = \lambda \Pr(t_1, t_2|w) + (1-\lambda)\Pr(t_1|w)\Pr(t_2|w)$, where λ is the interpolation factor. In this paper, we simply set $\lambda = 0.5$.

Given a resource r with its content $\mathbf{x}_r$ as context, the context-aware relation of two tags t_1 and t_2 can be calculated according to their context-aware relation given each word in the resource content as context word, $\Pr(t_1, t_2|r) = \Pr(t_1, t_2|\mathbf{x}_r) = \sum_{w\in\mathbf{x}} \Pr(t_1, t_2|w)\Pr(w|\mathbf{x})$.

3 Random Walks for Ranking Tags

After modeling the context-aware relations of tags, we can build a context-aware relation graph of tags and rank tags by random walks over the graph.

3.1 Context-Aware Relation Graph Building

Here we focus on building undirected graphs which correspond to symmetric context-aware relations. For a resource r with its content $\mathbf{x}$, we first rank tags according to the conditional probability of each tag estimated by TCM, i.e., $\Pr(t|r) = \sum_{w\in\mathbf{x}} \Pr(t|w)\Pr(w|\mathbf{x})$, where $\Pr(w|\mathbf{x})$ is the probability of w being selected as context words within resource content $\mathbf{x}$, and $\phi_{tw} = \Pr(t|w)$ is the probability of w working as context word of t. The measure assumes each tag is conditionally independent given the resource and thus can be calculated separately. With $\Pr(t|r)$ we select top-ranked tags as candidate tags, denoted as T_c. The number of candidate tags, $|T_c|$, can be manually pre-defined, which should be much larger than the number of suggested tags M_r, but much smaller than the size of tag vocabulary $|T|$.

With candidate tags T_c, we build the context-aware relation graph of tags. We denote the graph as $G = \{V, E\}$, where V is the set of nodes with each node $v_i = t_i \in T_c$, and E is the set of edges with each edge links two nodes in V, e.g., $e_{ij} = (v_i, v_j)$. In an undirected graph, e_{ij} indicates the edge between v_i and v_j with $e_{ij} = e_{ji}$. We set the edge weight using symmetric context-aware relation probability, i.e., $e_{ij} = \Pr(t_i, t_j|r)$, which indicates the semantic relatedness between t_i and t_j given r as context. With G, we represent the context-aware relations of candidate tags given the resource within a unified graph. The next step is performing random walks over the graph to rank tags.

3.2 Random Walks over Context-Aware Relation Graphs

We conduct random walks over context-aware tag relation graphs to rank and suggest social tags. Random walks have been widely used in many tasks of computational linguistics and information retrieval, which can take the knowledge of the whole graph together for ranking nodes (Liu et al., 2009, 2010).

The basic idea of random walks is that a node is important if there are other important nodes connecting with it. Given a tag graph, we denote the ranking score of a node v_i at iteration k as $r_k(i)$. The random walk process is formulated as

$$r_{k+1}(j) = \gamma \sum_{v_i \in N(v_j)} \frac{e_{ij}}{\sum_j e_{ij}} r_k(i) + (1-\gamma)\frac{1}{|V|}, \quad (3)$$

where $\sum_j e_{ij}$ is the out-degree of node v_i, γ is the damping factor ranging from 0 to 1, and $|V|$ is the number of nodes in G. In this paper, we follow most work and set $\gamma = 0.85$ (Langville and Meyer, 2004). The random jump probability in Equation (3) can also be set non-uniformly. Suppose we assign larger scores to some nodes, the final ranking scores will prefer these nodes and their neighbors. The new method is referred to as random walks with restart (RWR) (Tong et al., 2006). RWR takes node preferences into consideration during random walks, which can be written as $r_{k+1}(j) = \gamma \sum_{v_i \in N(v_j)} \frac{e_{ij}}{\sum_j e_{ij}} r_k(i) + (1-\gamma)\Pr(j)$, where $\Pr(j)$ is the preference of node v_j. In this paper, we set $\Pr(j) = \Pr(t_j|r)$ estimated by TCM. Note that $\sum_{v_i \in V} \Pr(i) = 1$. For tag suggestion, we simply use RWR scores to rank candidate tags and select top-ranked ones for suggestion. For this task, we denote the random walk method over context-free relation graphs as CFR; the method over co-occurrence context-aware relation graphs as CCR; and the method over TCM-based context-aware relation graphs as TCM.

4 Experiments

In the previous sections, we introduced the framework of suggesting social tags based on context-aware relations of tags given the resource. To investigate the efficiency of our method, in this section, we carry out experiments on real-world datasets.

4.1 Datasets and Experiment Setting

In our experiments, we select two real world datasets for evaluation. In Table 1 we show statistics of these datasets, where $|R|$, $|W|$, $|T|$, $\hat{N}_r$ and $\hat{M}_r$ are the number of resources, the vocabulary of contents, the vocabulary of tags, the average number of words in each resource content and the average number of tags in each resource, respectively. The two datasets, denoted as BOOK and MUSIC, contain book and music descriptions as content respectively, together with their annotated tags. Both of them are crawled from Douban (`www.douban.com`), the largest Chinese product review service.

Data	$\|R\|$	$\|W\|$	$\|T\|$	$\hat{N}_r$	$\hat{M}_r$
BOOK	26,807	82,420	41,199	368.69	8.95
MUSIC	25,785	107,100	31,288	541.13	8.13

Table 1: Statistical information of two datasets.

We use precision/recall for evaluation. For a resource, we denote gold standard tags as $\mathbf{a}_g$, the suggested tags as $\mathbf{a}_s$, and thus the correctly suggested tags as $\mathbf{a}_g \cap \mathbf{a}_s$. Precision and recall are defined as $P = |\mathbf{a}_g \cap \mathbf{a}_s|/|\mathbf{a}_s|$ and $R = |\mathbf{a}_g \cap \mathbf{a}_s|/|\mathbf{a}_g|$. In experiments, we perform 5-fold cross validation for each method, and the evaluation scores are computed by micro-averaging over resources of test set. We will evaluate the performance when the number of suggested tags M ranges from 1 to 10.

4.2 Evaluation Results

We select Naive Bayes (NB) (Garg and Weber, 2008), *k*NN (Li et al., 2009), CRM (Iwata et al., 2009) and TAM (Si et al., 2010) as baseline methods for comparison. NB and *k*NN are representative classification-based methods; while CRM and TAM are representative topic-based methods. We set the parameters of the baselines as follows, by which these methods achieve their best performance: the number of topics $T = 1,024$ for CRM, the number of nearest neighbors $k = 5$. We will also compare three types of tag relations for tag suggestion, i.e., CFR (Section 2.1), CCR (Section 2.2) and TCM (Section 2.3).

In Figure 2a and Figure 2b we show the precision-recall curves of NB, *k*NN, CRM, TAM, CFR, CCR and TCM on BOOK and MUSIC datasets. Each point of a precision-recall curve represents suggesting different number of tags ranging from $M = 1$ (bottom right, with higher precision and lower recall) to $M = 10$ (upper left, with higher recall but lower precision), respectively. The closer the curve to the upper right, the better the overall performance of the method.

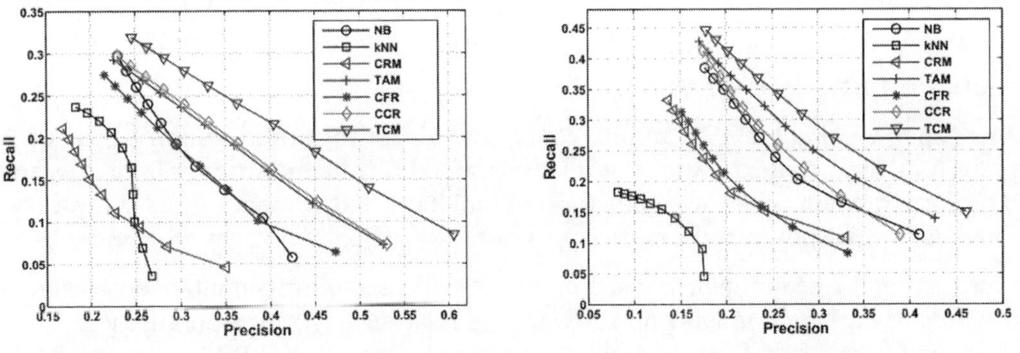

(a) BOOK (b) MUSIC

Figure 2: Precision-recall curves for social tag suggestion on BOOK and MUSIC.

From Figure 2a and Figure 2b, we find that: (1) TCM performs consistently better than other methods for social tag suggestion on both datasets. This indicates the effectiveness and efficiency of TCM. (2) CFR, the method based on context-free tag relations, fails to suggest good tags compared to TCM and some baselines. This indicates the insufficiency of context-free relations and the necessity of modeling context-aware relations for social tag suggestion. (3) TCM is superior to CCR. It reveals that measuring context-aware relations simply based on co-occurrences between words and tags may introduce many noises because each tag of a resource mostly reflects only some specific words of the resource instead of all of them. This suggests that modeling context-aware tag relations is a non-trivial task, and we have to find corresponding context words for tags so as to build accurate context-aware relations. This is what we do by proposing TCM.

In Table 2, we show top-10 tags suggested by several methods for book *The Catcher in the Rye*, the example in Figure 1a. Here we do not show the results of *k*NN because its performance is too poor to compare with others. The number in the brackets after each method is the count of correctly suggested tags. The correctness of suggested tags are marked with +/−, and the incorrect tags are also highlighted in boldface. From Table 2, we can see that NB, CRM and TAM tend to suggest inconsistent and unrelated tags due to independence assumption, such as "philosophy" and "history". CFR is context-free and its suggested tags are also inconsistent. CCR and TCM take the given resource as context, and thus achieve better performance especially for several top tags. TCM is obviously better than CCR, and can suggest specific tags such as "Salinger" and "the_catcher_in_the_rye".

Method	Suggested Tags
NB(5)	novel (+), foreign_literature (+), literature (+), **history** (-), **philosophy** (-), America (+), classic (+), **China** (-), **Japan** (-), **Chinese_literature** (-)
CRM(5)	novel (+), foreign_literature (+), literature (+), **history** (-), **China** (-), culture (+), **Chinese_literature** (-), classic (+), **Britain** (-), **philosophy** (-)
TAM(5)	novel (+), foreign_literature (+), literature (+), America (+), **Britain** (-), **Chinese_literature** (-), **China** (-), **history** (-), classic (+), **British_literature** (-)
CFR(5)	novel (+), literature (+), foreign_literature (+), **China** (-), **Chinese_literature** (-), classic (+), America (+), **history** (-), **love** (-), **Britain** (-)
CCR(6)	novel (+), foreign_literature (+), literature (+), America (+), classic (+), **Britain** (-), American_literature (+), **Chinese_literature** (-), **China** (-), **Britain_literature** (-)
TCM(10)	novel (+), foreign_literature (+), Salinger (+), literature (+), the_catcher_in_the_rye (+), America (+), American_literature (+), foreign_novel (+), classic (+), youth (+)

Table 2: Suggested tags for book *The Catcher in the Rye* (example in Figure 1a).

Conclusion and Future Work

In this paper, we propose TCM to find context words for tags from resource content. We model TCM-based context-aware tag relations, build a context-aware relation tag graph, and perform random walks over the graph to rank tags. Experiment results show that our method can sufficiently suggest more consistent tags compared to other methods.

We have several research plans: (1) Build a unified method to simultaneously find context words of tags and model context-aware tag relations. (2) Incorporate more context, such as time-stamps and geographical information of annotation. (3) Model context-aware tag relations for other applications to investigate their effectiveness, such as personalized information retrieval and recommender systems.

Acknowledgments

This work is supported by the National Natural Science Foundation of China (NSFC) under the grant No. 61170196 and 61202140. The authors would like to thank Douban for providing data.

References

Adomavicius, G. and Tuzhilin, A. (2011). Context-aware recommender systems. *Recommender Systems Handbook*, pages 217–253.

Brooks, C. and Montanez, N. (2006). Improved annotation of the blogosphere via autotagging and hierarchical clustering. In *Proceedings of WWW*, pages 625–632. ACM.

Brown, P. and Jones, G. (2001). Context-aware retrieval: Exploring a new environment for information retrieval and information filtering. *Personal and Ubiquitous Computing*, 5(4):253–263.

Gabrilovich, E. and Markovitch, S. (2007). Computing semantic relatedness using wikipedia-based explicit semantic analysis. In *Proceedings of IJCAI*, pages 6–12.

Garg, N. and Weber, I. (2008). Personalized, interactive tag recommendation for flickr. In *Proceedings of RecSys*, pages 67–74.

Griffiths, T. and Steyvers, M. (2004). Finding scientific topics. *PNAS*, 101(Suppl 1):5228.

Gupta, M., Li, R., Yin, Z., and Han, J. (2010). Survey on social tagging techniques. *ACM SIGKDD Explorations Newsletter*, 12(1):58–72.

Iwata, T., Yamada, T., and Ueda, N. (2009). Modeling social annotation data with content relevance using a topic model. In *Proceedings of NIPS*, pages 835–843.

Jaschke, R., Marinho, L., Hotho, A., Schmidt-Thieme, L., and Stumme, G. (2008). Tag recommendations in social bookmarking systems. *AI Communications*, 21(4):231–247.

Langville, A. and Meyer, C. (2004). Deeper inside pagerank. *Internet Mathematics*, 1(3):335–380.

Li, X., Snoek, C., and Worring, M. (2009). Learning social tag relevance by neighbor voting. *IEEE Transactions on Multimedia*, 11(7):1310–1322.

Lin, D. (1998). Automatic retrieval and clustering of similar words. In *Proceedings of COLING*, pages 768–774.

Liu, D., Hua, X., Yang, L., Wang, M., and Zhang, H. (2009). Tag ranking. In *Proceedings of WWW*, pages 351–360.

Liu, Z., Chen, X., and Sun, M. (2011). A simple word trigger method for social tag suggestion. In *Proceedings of EMNLP*, pages 1577–1588. Association for Computational Linguistics.

Liu, Z., Huang, W., Zheng, Y., and Sun, M. (2010). Automatic keyphrase extraction via topic decomposition. In *Proceedings of EMNLP*, pages 366–376.

Manning, C., Raghavan, P., and Schtze, H. (2008). *Introduction to information retrieval*. Cambridge University Press New York, NY, USA.

Manning, C. and Schutze, H. (2000). *Foundations of statistical natural language processing*. MIT Press.

Mei, Q., Zhou, D., and Church, K. (2008). Query suggestion using hitting time. In *Proceedings of the 17th ACM conference on Information and knowledge management*, pages 469–478. ACM.

Mika, P. (2005). Ontologies are us: A unified model of social networks and semantics. *Proceedings of ISWC*, pages 522–536.

Miller, G., Beckwith, R., Fellbaum, C., Gross, D., and Miller, K. (1990). WordNet: An on-line lexical database. *International Journal of Lexicography*, 3:235–244.

Rendle, S., Balby Marinho, L., Nanopoulos, A., and Schmidt-Thieme, L. (2009). Learning optimal ranking with tensor factorization for tag recommendation. In *Proceedings of KDD*, pages 727–736.

Shepitsen, A., Gemmell, J., Mobasher, B., and Burke, R. (2008). Personalized recommendation in social tagging systems using hierarchical clustering. In *Proceedings of RecSys*, pages 259–266.

Si, X., Liu, Z., Li, P., Jiang, Q., and Sun, M. (2009). Content-based and graph-based tag suggestion. *ECML PKDD Discovery Challenge 2009*, page 243.

Si, X., Liu, Z., and Sun, M. (2010). Modeling social annotations via latent reason identification. *IEEE Intelligent Systems*, 25(6):42–49.

Tong, H., Faloutsos, C., and Pan, J.-Y. (2006). Fast random walk with restart and its applications. In *Proceedings of ICDM*, pages 613–622.

Wen, J., Nie, J., and Zhang, H. (2002). Query clustering using user logs. *ACM Transactions on Information Systems*, 20(1):59–81.

Wu, H., Zubair, M., and Maly, K. (2006a). Harvesting social knowledge from folksonomies. In *Proceedings of the seventeenth conference on Hypertext and hypermedia*, pages 111–114. ACM.

Wu, X., Zhang, L., and Yu, Y. (2006b). Exploring social annotations for the semantic web. In *Proceedings of the 15th international conference on World Wide Web*, pages 417–426. ACM.

Phrase-Based Evaluation for Machine Translation

LI LiangYou GONG ZhengXian ZHOU GuoDong*
School of Computer Science and Technology, Soochow University, Suzhou, China 215006
{20104227013,zhxgong,gdzhou}@suda.edu.cn

ABSTRACT
This paper presents the utilization of chunk phrases to facilitate evaluation of machine translation. Since most of current researches on evaluation take great effects to evaluate translation quality on content relevance and readability, we further introduce high-level abstract information such as semantic similarity and topic model into this phrase-based evaluation metric. The proposed metric mainly involves three parts: calculating phrase similarity, determining weight to each phrase, and finding maximum similarity map. Experiments on MTC Part 2 (LDC2003T17) show our metric, compared with other popular metrics such as BLEU, MAXSIM and METEOR, achieves comparable correlation with human judgements at segment-level and significant higher correlation at document-level.

TITLE AND ABSTRACT IN ANOTHER LANGUAGE (CHINESE)

基于短语的机器翻译自动评价

本文提出了基于短语的机器翻译自动评价方法，并将高层次抽象信息加入到此方法中，如语义相似度，主题模型．本文提出的方法主要有三个部分：计算短语相似度，为短语分配权重和寻找最大相似度匹配．在MTC Part 2 (LDC2003T17)上的实验表明，与BLEU, MAXSIM, METEOR等主流方法相比，本文的方法与人工评价的相关性在句子级评价上取得了相当的效果，在文档级评价上显著地高于其他方法．

KEYWORDS: phrase similarity, topic model, machine translation, automatic evaluation.

KEYWORDS IN CHINESE: 短语相似度，主题模型，机器翻译，自动评价．

*Corresponding author.

Proceedings of COLING 2012: Posters, pages 663–672,
COLING 2012, Mumbai, December 2012.

1 Introduction

In recent years, machine translation (MT) has benefited a lot from the advancement of automatic evaluation which, compared with manual evaluation, can give quick and objective feedback on the quality of translation. So most of current MT systems need one or more automatic metrics to frequently update their models. Among all automatic evaluation metrics, those based on ngrams are most widely used. A basic mode of ngram-based metric is to estimate whether ngrams from system translation (also called **candidate**) can match with those from references or not. However, most of such metrics suffer from one or more following problems: 1) nonsense ngrams in evaluation; 2) same weight for different ngrams; 3) lack of fuzzy matching; 4) absence of context information.

Therefore, this paper proposes a new automatic MT evaluation metric which uses linguistic phrase rather than ngram as the basic unit of evaluation. In linguistics, a phrase is a group of words (or sometimes a single word) that form a constituent and so function as a single unit in the syntax of a sentence.[1] There are some different types of phrases, such as Noun Phrase (NP), Verb Phrase (VP), Adverb Phrase (ADVP), Adjective Phrase (ADJP), and Preposition Phrase (PP) and so forth. In this paper, only NP and VP are used in our experiments, and all phrases are obtained by chunker[2].

Given phrases, our metric evaluates translations with three key parts, including calculating phrase similarity, allocating weight to each phrase, and finding a maximum similarity map. For the first part, we not only adopt a semantic similarity function based on WordNet but also explore a topic similarity function based on a popular topic model. And we present a novel framework to unify the two similarity measures successfully. To the second part, we examine several different weight functions, including phrase length (i.e. ngram weight), tf.idf and topic relevance to distinguish informativeness of phrases. To the last part, we address how to establish a maximum similarity map between phrases of candidates and references and further analyze its working mechanism by experiments.

It is worth to mention that our metric has a great flexibility such that any other similarity and weight functions could be incorporated easily. Experiments also show the metric, compared with some popular metrics, achieves comparable correlation with human judgements at segment-level and significant higher correlation at document-level.

2 Related works

In recent years, numerous ngram-based metrics have been proposed. BLEU (Papineni et al., 2002) as the most famous evaluation metric calculates an overall score via geometric mean of precisions on different ngrams. NIST (Doddington, 2002) improves BLEU with arithmetic mean and weight for different ngrams. However both BLEU and NIST do not consider synonyms. In METEOR (Banerjee and Lavie, 2005), three modules, "exact", "porter stem" and "WN synonymy", are used to create word-alignment successively. And a penalty for word-order is integrated into the final score. MAXSIM (Chan and Ng, 2008) constructs a bipartite graph for unmatched ngrams. And Kuhn-Munkres algorithm (Kuhn, 1955; Munkres, 1957) is used to find a maximum weighted matching. However, synonyms in METEOR and MAXSIM are viewed as equivalent completely. Furthermore, nonsense ngrams are still used in these metrics. By contrast, in our metric, phrases are considered as the unit of evaluation and a fine similarity

[1] `http://en.wikipedia.org/wiki/Phrase`
[2] `http://jtextpro.sourceforge.net/`

function is defined. And context information contributes to our metric as well.

Phrase information has been used in several evaluation methods. In the work of Giménez and Màrquez (2007), overlapping is calculated on the set of words within a same phrase type, and sequences of phrase types are used in the metric of NIST to score phrase-order. However, this work does not distinguish different phrases with the same type and ignores the fact that different types of phrases can be established a correspondence. Echizen-ya and Araki (2010) propose to establish correspondence of phrases for which mutual similarity score is highest. But this method just takes NP into consideration since similarity based on PER (Su et al., 1992) cannot determine the correspondence of VP correctly. Zhou et al. (2008) diagnoses translations based on check-points where each phrase can be scored by ngram matching. However, it ignores the order of phrases in a translation and phrase correspondence relies on word-alignment trained on parallel corpus. Different with these works, this paper treats a phrase as a single unit and integrates explicit measurement of phrase-order into metric and correspondence is established by fine similarities between phrases.

3 Phrase-based evaluation metric

Phrase-based evaluation (PBE) metric proposed by this paper compares a pair of candidate-reference translation by identifying phrase correspondence between them. Firstly, this metric extracts phrases from them using chunking tool; then each phrase is assigned a weight to indicate its informativeness. After that, according to similarities between phrases, the metric find a maximum similarity map between two phrase sequences so that each phrase of one translation is correspondent with at most one in the other. Figure 1 gives two examples of mapping.

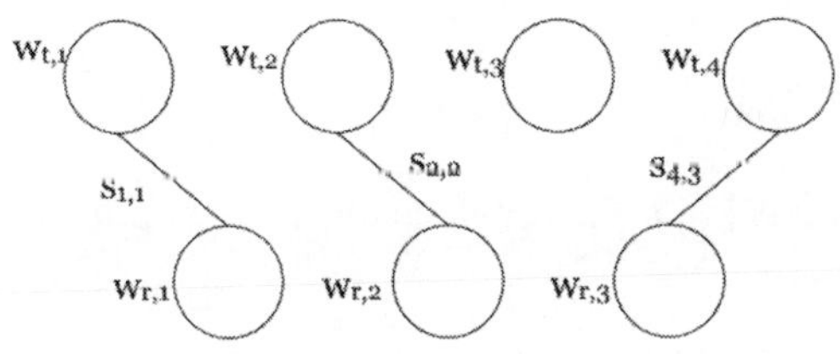

(a) Map with 2 blocks

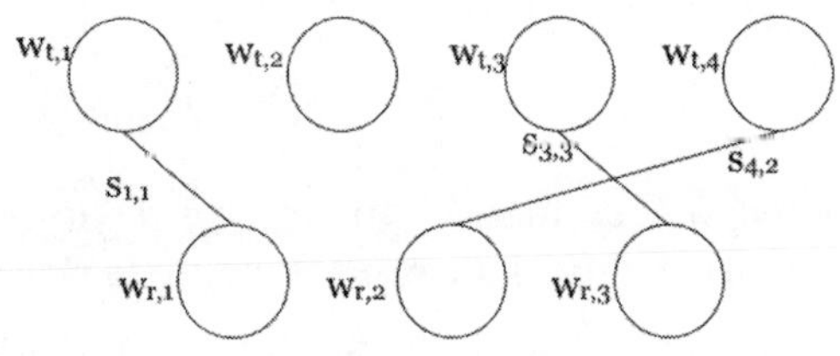

(b) Map with 3 blocks

Figure 1: Examples of mapping. w is the weight of a phrase in candidate t or reference r; and s is the similarity between two phrases

Given a maximum map, we can calculate precision scores for candidate t and reference r respectively and a penalty factor, similar to Banerjee and Lavie (2005), to measure phrase-order:

$$P_t = \sum_{i\in t} w_i s_i / \sum_{i\in t} w_i \qquad P_r = \sum_{j\in r} w_j s_j / \sum_{j\in r} w_j \qquad pen = \gamma(\#blocks - 1/m)^{\beta}$$

where w_i is the weight of the ith phrase and s_i is the similarity related to this phrase, γ and β are constant, m and $\#blocks$ are the number of matchings and blocks[3] in the map. Then final score for evaluation is:

$$score = \left(\alpha P_t + (1-\alpha) P_r\right) \cdot \left(1 - pen\right)$$

[3]A block in a map consists of only as more consecutive matchings as possible. For example, in Figure 1(a), there are two blocks: one consists of $s_{1,1}$ and $s_{2,2}$; $s_{4,3}$ is the other one; Figure 1(b) has three blocks.

where α is a constant varying from zero to one.

In this paper, similar to METEOR, document-level score is obtained by integrating fragments of scores from segments. However, in our metric, context information is also used to improve the performance of document-level evaluation.

4 Phrase similarity

In this paper, phrase similarity consists of two parts and can be represented by an interpolation:

$$SIM = \theta SIM_{in} + (1-\theta) SIM_{ctxt}$$

where θ is a constant ranging from zero to one; SIM_{in}, called internal or general function, is only related to phrases and separated from their contexts; external SIM_{ctxt} is also called context similarity which is circumstance-specific.

In this paper, internal similarity is based on WordNet, defined as SIM_{WN} and external similarity is measured by topic similarity SIM_t. The rest of this section will describe the two functions.

4.1 Similarity function based on WordNet

Ignoring word-order, each pair of words between two phrases can have a lexical similarity. So similarity between phrases can be measured by similarities of words.

Lexical Similarity: Given two words, their similarity is one if they have the same lemma or porter stem. Otherwise, WordNet is used to compute a semantic similarity. However, different with other metrics where similarity of any two synonyms is one, our metric uses a fine function proposed by Lin (1998)[4]:

$$lin(c_1, c_2) = 2\log P(c_0) / [\log P(c_1) + \log P(c_2)]$$

where c_1 and c_2 are two synsets, c_0 is the lowest level of synset which subsumes c_1 and c_2, $P(c)$ is the probability of a word belonging to synset c.

Similarity between two phrases: For two phrases $phr_1 = w_1 w_2 \cdots w_m$ and $phr_2 = v_1 v_2 \cdots v_n$, there would be in total $m \times n$ lexical similarities. According to Liu et al. (2008), these similarities can be presented in a matrix where the element at position of (i, j) corresponds to the value of lexical similarity $sim(w_i, v_j)$. Then, a similarity between the two phrases can be obtained by:

$$SIM_{wn}(phr_1, phr_2) = [S(phr_1, phr_2) + S(phr_2, phr_1)]/2$$

where $S(phr_1, phr_2) = \sum_{i=1}^{m} \max\{sim(w_i, v_1) \cdots sim(w_i, v_n)\}/m$.

4.2 Similarity function based on topic model

There are three steps to use topic model as external similarity for phrases: topic model estimation, obtaining topic distributions of phrases and calculating topic similarity of phrases.

Topic model estimation: In this paper, We use Latent Dirichlet Allocation[5] (LDA) (Blei et al., 2003), an unsupervised machine learning technique, to obtain topic model from data collection.

[4] `http://www.sussex.ac.uk/Users/drh21/`
[5] `http://jgibblda.sourceforge.net/`

This model could give two type of distributions: $p(w \mid z)$ and $p(z \mid d)$. It is worth to mention that we build separate topic models for references and candidate translations of each system. This is because separate models can prevent unknown or semantically equivalent words between different systems from being underestimated.

Topic distributions of phrases: For a phrase $phr = w_1 \cdots w_n$, its probability on topic z can be calculated as follows:

$$\begin{aligned} P\left(topic = z \mid phr = w_1 \cdots w_n\right) &= P\left(w_1 \cdots w_n \mid z\right) \cdot P(z) / P\left(w_1 \cdots w_n\right) \\ &= \prod_{i=1}^{n} P\left(w_i \mid z\right) \cdot P(z) / \prod_{i=1}^{n} P\left(w_i\right) \\ &= \prod_{i=1}^{n} P\left(w_i \mid z\right) \cdot P(z) / \prod_{i=1}^{n} \sum_{k=1}^{K} P\left(w_i \mid Z_k\right) P\left(Z_k\right) \end{aligned}$$

where K is the number of topics and Z is the set of topics. In this paper, $p(z) = 1/K$. Note that this equation treats phrase as bag of words and the same phrases in different documents within a topic model have the same topic distribution. Thus such distribution is topic-specific rather than document-specific.

Topic similarity of phrases: Generally, similarity between topic distributions of two phrases can be calculated by cosine function. However, in this paper, topic is not aligned between different models and thus two distributions from different models cannot be used in cosine function directly. In this paper, we adopt a simplified method. Given two phrases phr_t and phr_r from document d_t of one system and d_r of one reference, their topic similarity is:

$$SIM_t\left(phr_t, phr_r\right) = 1 - \mid cos\left(phr_r, d_r\right) - cos\left(phr_t, d_t\right) \mid$$

where $cos\left(phr, d\right)$ denotes cosine value between topic distributions of phrase phr and document d. This Equation suggests that if two phrases have approximate phrase-document similarity, so does their mutual similarity. Such topic similarity is document-specific. Of course, it is possible that two translations differ too much while two phrases in them get a higher final similarity. However, our experiment shows that a bias to internal similarity can reduce such influence.

5 Phrase weight

In this section, we will present two basic functions: ngram, tf.idf. Then a method of improving them with topic model is described.

5.1 Basic weight functions

In our metric, **ngram,** length of a phrase, is the default weight function. However, this function ignores the contexts of a phrase. Thus another function, **tf.idf** which has been used in information retrieval widely, is also presented:

$$tf.idf_{t,d} = (1 + \log(tf_{t,d})) \log\left(N/df_t\right)$$

where $tf_{t,d}$ is the number of occurrence of the term t in the document d, df_t is the number of documents which contains term t, N is the number of documents.

It is worth noting that in this paper, we build their own tf.idf dictionaries for references and candidates of each system. This is different from other works, such as Babych and Hartley

(2004) and Wong and Kit (2009), where tf.idf value of a word in candidate is directly taken from references and thus unmatched words in the candidate are ignored.

5.2 Topic-based weight

With close scrutiny, phrase weight can be divided into two parts:

$$Weight(phr, t) = Rel(phr, t) \cdot Info(phr) \quad (1)$$

where $Info(phr)$ denotes informativeness of phrase phr, $Rel(phr, t)$ measures the correlation between the phrase and its text t. Ideally, we expect the function $Info(phr)$ has little correlation with t.

In general, we could measure the correlation between phr and t from different perspectives, such as topic relevance, probability of co-occurring and so on. In this paper, we define: $Rel(phr, t) = cos(phr, t)$. And functions in section 5.1 can serve as $Info$. However, It should be noted that tf.idf value of a word or phrase relys on its contexts to some extent.

6 Maximum similarity map

Similar to Chan and Ng (2008), we view matching between phrases as a bipartite graph and Kuhn-Munkres (KM) algorithm is use to find a map which has a maximum sum of similarities. However, our metric needs to calculate a penalty score for phrase-order. Thus when there are multiple such maps, we need to select one from them.

In this paper, facing with multi-options, KM algorithm will select the maps in which the first phrase of current reference has the minimal correspondent position in candidate; and this process will continue in the phrase sequence of the reference until there's only one map left. This stratagem would keep the relative order of phrases in some situations which will be illustrated in section 7.3.

Take Figure 1 as an example. KM will choose Figure 1(a), because in both maps $w_{r,1}$ has the same correspondence $w_{t,1}$ while $w_{r,2}$ has the correspondence $w_{t,2}$ in Figure 1(a) and $w_{t,4}$ in Figure 1(b).

7 Experiments

We conduct experiments on MTC Part 2 (LDC2003T17) which contains 100 source documents (878 segments in total) in Chinese and 4 English references for each segment. Translations of three systems were assessed by human judges on each segments in terms of adequacy (Adq) and fluency (Flu). We normalize the human raw scores according to Blatz et al. (2004) and average scores for segments. Document score is the average of scores of its segments. Before evaluation, translations are tokenized and lower-cased.

In our default metric PBE (or $\text{PBE}_{\text{ngram}}$), α is set to 0.2, both β and γ are 0.5, θ is 1 and phrase weight function is ngram. In this paper, only NP and VP are taken into consideration since they contain more information and give a stable evaluation in our preliminary experiments. Pearson correlation coefficient is used to measure correlation between automatic evaluation and human judgements.

7.1 Performance of default metric

According to Table 1[6], our metric PBE is significantly better than other three popular metrics only with an exception on METEOR[7] at segment-level. We guess the reason of relative lower performance of our metric at segment-level than document-level is that short segments do not contain enough phrases and thus PBE can not perform well on them. Furthermore, Table 1 shows tf.idf brings the best metric PBE_{tfidf}, suggesting that context information can help to improve evaluation effectively. In addition, since these metrics put more effort on matching between candidates and references, they are more correlated with Adq than Flu score.

Metric	Segment-Level		Document-Level	
	Adq	Flu	Adq	Flu
BLEU	0.2379	0.2184	–	–
MAXSIM	0.2677	0.2235	0.2722	0.2600
METEOR	0.3489	0.3014	0.3025	0.2938
PBE	0.3262	0.3199	0.3807	0.3291
PBE_{tfidf}	–	–	0.4153	0.3471

Table 1: Pearson coefficient for automatic evaluation metrics

7.2 Effect of topic model in evaluation

Table 2 is the result of evaluation based on topic model.[8] We can find that topic model can improve metrics significantly. An exception happens on PBE_{tfidf}: topic-based weight function "Weight" seems helpless. We guess this results from the potential relevance between tf.idf and our topic model: both rely on context information within a document and corpus.

Metric	Topic-Based Func.	Document-Level	
		Adq	Flu
PBE_{ngram}		0.3807	0.3291
	+Weight	0.4065	0.3503
	+SIM	0.4007	0.3380
	+Weight+SIM	0.4285	0.3648
PBE_{tfidf}		0.4153	0.3471
	+Weight	0.4176	0.3439
	+SIM	0.4428	0.3626
	+Weight+SIM	0.4324	0.3519

Table 2: Pearson coefficient for metrics based on topic model with K=50 and θ=0.8

[6]Tf.idf is tested only on document since document is more suitable for it to make estimation for phrase weight. And we do not report performance of BLEU at document-level because it's unfair to compare it with other metrics since BLEU considers impact of sentence length.

[7]METEOR (Denkowski and Lavie, 2011) uses parameters tuned to adequacy scores.

[8]LDA is trained on documents, thus only results at document-level evaluation are presented. And preliminary experiments suggest that metrics based on topic model perform better when K=50 and θ=0.8. Thus this setting is also used in this paper.

7.3 Selection of maximum similarity map

For comparing with our selection strategy for multi-options, we use beam search to find a "better" map which has less blocks without changing the maximum similarity. Our experiment shows that there is only one maximum similarity map in most cases; otherwise, in most situations of multi-options, our strategy will give a better and reasonable results.

For example, in Figure 2, each translation has two "peace" and beam search finds a different map with KM where the number of blocks declines by 1. However, this result seems to lead to an overestimation since it destroys the original order of "peace" for the sake of lower *pen* value (see related equation in section 3).

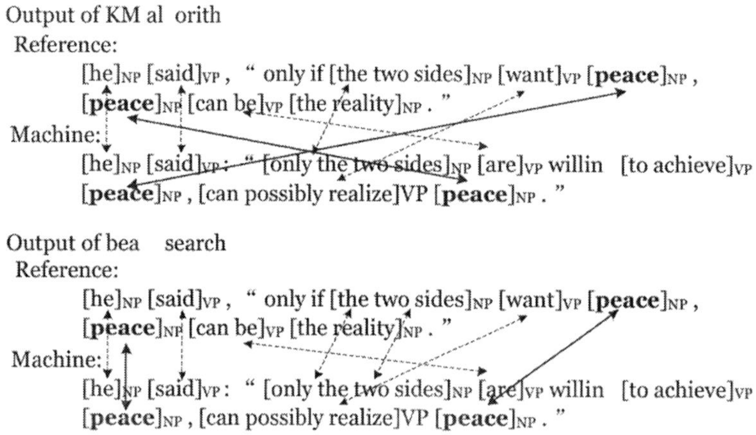

Figure 2: An example of comparison between results of KM and beam search

Conclusion and Future Work

This paper present a new automatic MT evaluation metric which is based on linguistic phrase. This metric incorporates high-level abstract information such as semantic similarity based on WordNet and topic model into phrase similarity and explores several functions such as ngram, tf.idf and topic relevance to allocate weight for each phrase. And a method of finding a maximum similarity map is presented. Experiments show our metric is more suitable for long translation and achieves significant higher correlation with human judgements than several other popular metrics at document-level and comparable results at segment-level. Experimental results also show that context information and topic model can improve the performance of evaluation effectively.

In the future, we would examine in details how chunker performs on translations with various qualities, use syntactic information or structure in evaluation and explore utilization of more sophisticated model instead of bag-of-word etc. We expect our metric could be performed on document-level SMT systems (Gong et al., 2011) to measure their quality rightly.

Acknowledgments

This research is supported by the National Natural Science Foundation of China under grant No.61273320 and 61003155, the National High Technology Research and Development Program of China (863 Program) under grant No.2012AA011102, and the Preliminary Research Project of Soochow University.

References

Babych, B. and Hartley, A. (2004). Extending the BLEU MT evaluation method with frequency weightings. In *Proceedings of ACL 2004*. Association for Computational Linguistics.

Banerjee, S. and Lavie, A. (2005). METEOR: An automatic metric for MT evaluation with improved correlation with human judgments. In *Proceedings of the ACL 2005 Workshop on Intrinsic and Extrinsic Evaluation Measures for Machine Translation and/or Summarization*, pages 65–72. Association for Computational Linguistics.

Blatz, J., Fitzgerald, E., Foster, G., Gandrabur, S., Goutte, C., Kulesza, A., Sanchis, A., and Ueffing, N. (2004). Confidence estimation for machine translation. In *Proceedings of COLING 2004*. Association for Computational Linguistics.

Blei, D. M., Ng, A. Y., and Jordan, M. I. (2003). Latent dirichlet allocation. *Journal of Machine Learning Research*, 3:993–1022.

Chan, Y. S. and Ng, H. T. (2008). MAXSIM: A maximum similarity metric for machine translation evaluation. In *Proceedings of ACL 2008: HLT*, pages 55–62. Association for Computational Linguistics.

Denkowski, M. and Lavie, A. (2011). Meteor 1.3: automatic metric for reliable optimization and evaluation of machine translation systems. In *Proceedings of WMT 2011*, pages 85–91. Association for Computational Linguistics.

Doddington, G. (2002). Automatic evaluation of machine translation quality using n-gram co-occurrence statistics. In *Proceedings of HLT 2002*, pages 138–145. Morgan Kaufmann Publishers Inc.

Echizen-ya, H. and Araki, K. (2010). Automatic evaluation method for machine translation using noun-phrase chunking. In *Proceedings of ACL 2010*, pages 108–117. Association for Computational Linguistics.

Giménez, J. and Màrquez, L. (2007). Linguistic features for automatic evaluation of heterogenous MT systems. In *Proceedings of WMT 2007*, pages 256–264. Association for Computational Linguistics.

Gong, Z., Zhang, M., and Zhou, G. (2011). Cache-based document-level statistical machine translation. In *Proceedings of EMNLP 2011*, pages 909–919. Association for Computational Linguistics.

Kuhn, H. W. (1955). The Hungarian method for the assignment problem. *Naval research logistics quarterly*, 2:83–97.

Lin, D. (1998). An information-theoretic definition of similarity. In *Proceedings of ICML 1998*, pages 296–304. Morgan Kaufmann Publishers Inc.

Liu, Y., Li, C., Zhang, P., and Xiong, Z. (2008). A query expansion algorithm based on phrases semantic similarity. In *Proceedings of ISIP 2008*, pages 31–35. IEEE Computer Society.

Munkres, J. (1957). Algorithms for the Assignment and Transportation Problems. *Journal of the Society for Industrial and Applied Mathematics*, 5:32–38.

Papineni, K., Roukos, S., Ward, T., and Zhu, W.-J. (2002). BLEU: a method for automatic evaluation of machine translation. In *Proceedings of ACL 2002*, pages 311–318. Association for Computational Linguistics.

Su, K.-Y., Wu, M.-W., and Chang, J.-S. (1992). A new quantitative quality measure for machine translation systems. In *Proceedings of COLING 1992*, pages 433–439. Association for Computational Linguistics.

Wong, B. and Kit, C. (2009). ATEC: automatic evaluation of machine translation via word choice and word order. *Machine Translation*, 23:141–155.

Zhou, M., Wang, B., Liu, S., Li, M., Zhang, D., and Zhao, T. (2008). Diagnostic evaluation of machine translation systems using automatically constructed linguistic check-points. In *Proceedings of COLING 2008*, pages 1121–1128. Association for Computational Linguistics.

A Beam Search Algorithm for ITG Word Alignment

Peng Li Yang Liu Maosong Sun
State Key Laboratory of Intelligent Technology and Systems
Tsinghua National Laboratory for Information Science and Technology
Department of Computer Science and Technology, Tsinghua University, Beijing 100084, China
pengli09@gmail.com, {liuyang2011,sms}@tsinghua.edu.cn

Abstract

Inversion transduction grammar (ITG) provides a syntactically motivated solution to modeling the distortion of words between two languages. Although the Viterbi ITG alignments can be found in polynomial time using a bilingual parsing algorithm, the computational complexity is still too high to handle real-world data, especially for long sentences. Alternatively, we propose a simple and effective beam search algorithm. The algorithm starts with an empty alignment and keeps adding single promising links as early as possible until the model probability does not increase. Experiments on Chinese-English data show that our algorithm is one order of magnitude faster than the bilingual parsing algorithm with bitext cell pruning without loss in alignment and translation quality.

Title and Abstract in another language, Chinese

一种ITG词语对齐的柱搜索算法

反向转录语法为两种语言间的词语调序提供了一种句法驱动的解决方案。虽然双语句法分析算法可以在多项式时间内搜索到Viterbi对齐，其计算复杂度依然太高，难以处理包含很多长句子的真实数据。为此，我们提出一种简单有效的柱搜索算法。该算法以空对齐为起点，优先选择最好的连线添加到对齐中，直至无法提高模型概率为止。在汉英数据上的实验结果表明，我们的算法比使用剪枝技术的双语分析算法快一个数量级，同时保持了对齐和翻译的质量。

Keywords: word alignment, inversion transduction grammar, beam search.

Keywords in L_2: 词语对齐, 反向转录语法, 柱搜索.

Proceedings of COLING 2012: Posters, pages 673–682,
COLING 2012, Mumbai, December 2012.

1 Introduction

Word alignment plays an important role in statistical machine translation (SMT) as it indicates the correspondence between two languages. The parameter estimation of many SMT models rely heavily on word alignment. Och and Ney (2004) firstly introduce alignment consistency to identify equivalent phrase pairs. Simple and effective, rule extraction algorithms based on word alignment have also been extended to hierarchial phrase-based (Chiang, 2007) and syntax-based (Galley et al., 2004) SMT systems successfully. Studies reveal that word alignment has a profound effect on the performance of SMT systems (Ayan and Dorr, 2006; Fraser and Marcu, 2007).

One major challenge in word alignment is modeling the permutations of words between source and target sentences. Due to the diversity of natural languages, the word orders of source and target sentences are usually quite different, especially for distantly-related language pairs such as Chinese and English. While most word alignment approaches either use distortion models (Brown et al., 1993; Vogel and Ney, 1996) or features (Taskar et al., 2005; Moore, 2005; Moore et al., 2006; Liu et al., 2010c) to capture reordering of words, *inversion transduction grammar* (ITG) (Wu, 1997) provides a syntactically motivated solution. ITG is a synchronous grammar of which a derivation explains how a source sentence and a target sentence are generated synchronously. By recursively merging blocks (i.e., consecutive word sequences) either in a monotone order or an inverted order, ITG constrains the search space of distortion in a way that proves to be effective in both alignment (Zhang and Gildea, 2005, 2006; Haghighi et al., 2009; Liu et al., 2010a,b) and translation (Zens and Ney, 2003; Xiong et al., 2006) benchmark tests.

Although ITG only requires $O(n^6)$ time for finding Viterbi alignment, which is a significant improvement over the intractable search problem faced by most alignment models (Brown et al., 1993; Moore et al., 2006; Liu et al., 2010c), the degree of the polynomial is still too high for practical use. For example, the maximal sentence length of bilingual corpus is often set to 100 words in Moses (Koehn et al., 2007), a state-of-the-art SMT system. Synchronous parsing of such long sentences can be prohibitively slow, making ITG alignment methods hard to deal with large scale real-world data.

To alleviate this problem, many pruning methods have been proposed to reduce the computational complexity of synchronous parsing by pruning less promising cells. Zhang and Gildea (2005) introduce a tic-tac-toe pruning method based on IBM model 1 probabilities. Haghighi et al. (2009) use posterior predictions from simpler alignment models for identifying degenerate cells. Liu et al. (2010a) propose a discriminative framework to integrate all informative features to constrain the search space of ITG alignment.

Instead of using synchronous parsing to search for Viterbi ITG alignments, we propose a simple and effective search algorithm extended from the beam search algorithm proposed by Liu et al. (2010c). The algorithm starts with an empty alignment and keeps adding single links until the model probability does not increase. During the search process, a shift-reduce algorithm is used to verify the ITG constraint. As our algorithm runs in $O(bn^3)$ time, where b is the beam size, it is about 1000 times faster than the $O(n^6)$ time bilingual parsing algorithm empirically. More importantly, experiments on Chinese-English data show that our algorithm is 20 times faster than bilingual parsing with tic-tac-toe pruning (Zhang and Gildea, 2005) when achieving comparable alignment and translation quality.

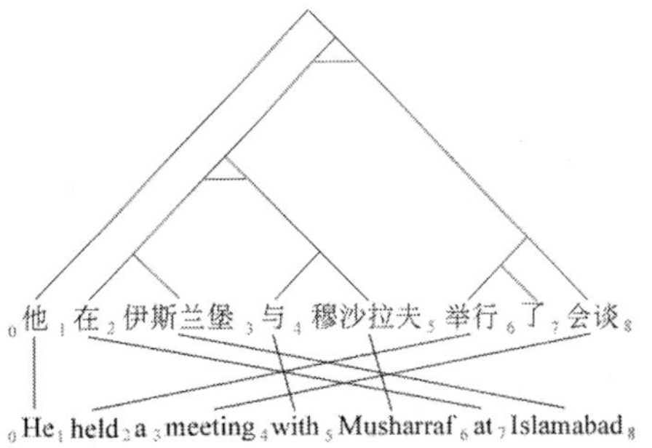

1) $X_{[0,8,0,8]} \rightarrow [X_{[0,1,0,1]}\ X_{[1,8,1,8]}]$
2) $X_{[0,1,0,1]} \rightarrow$ 他/he
3) $X_{[1,8,1,8]} \rightarrow \langle X_{[1,5,4,8]}\ X_{[5,8,1,4]} \rangle$
4) $X_{[1,5,4,8]} \rightarrow \langle X_{[1,3,6,8]}\ X_{[3,5,4,6]} \rangle$
5) $X_{[1,3,6,8]} \rightarrow [X_{[1,2,6,7]}\ X_{[2,3,7,8]}]$
6) $X_{[1,2,6,7]} \rightarrow$ 在/at
7) $X_{[2,3,7,8]} \rightarrow$ 伊斯兰堡/Islamabad
8) $X_{[3,5,4,6]} \rightarrow [X_{[3,4,4,5]}\ X_{[4,5,5,6]}]$
9) $X_{[3,4,4,5]} \rightarrow$ 与/with
10) $X_{[4,5,5,6]} \rightarrow$ 穆沙拉夫/Musharraf
11) $X_{[5,8,1,4]} \rightarrow [X_{[5,7,1,3]}\ X_{[7,8,3,4]}]$
12) $X_{[5,7,1,3]} \rightarrow [X_{[5,6,1,2]}\ X_{[6,7,2,3]}]$
13) $X_{[5,6,1,2]} \rightarrow$ 举行/held
14) $X_{[6,7,2,3]} \rightarrow [X_{[6,7,2,2]}\ X_{7,7,2,3}]$
15) $X_{[6,7,2,2]} \rightarrow$ 了/ϵ
16) $X_{[7,7,2,3]} \rightarrow \epsilon$/a
17) $X_{[7,8,3,4]} \rightarrow$ 会谈/meeting

Figure 1: An ITG derivation for a Chinese-English sentence pair.

2 Beam Search for ITG Word Alignment

Inversion transduction grammar (ITG) (Wu, 1997) is a synchronous grammar for synchronous parsing of source and target language sentences. It builds a synchronous parse tree that indicates the correspondence as well as permutation of blocks (i.e., consecutive word sequences) based on the following production rules:

$$(1)\ X \rightarrow [X\ X],\ (2)\ X \rightarrow \langle X\ X \rangle,\ (3)\ X \rightarrow f/e,\ (4)\ X \rightarrow f/\epsilon,\ (5)\ X \rightarrow \epsilon/e,$$

where X is a non-terminal, f is a source word, e is a target word, and ϵ is an empty word. While rule (1) merges two blocks in a monotone order, rule (2) merges in an inverted order. Rules (3) – (5) are responsible for aligning source and target words.

Figure 1 shows an ITG derivation for a Chinese-English sentence pair $\langle \mathbf{f}_0^J, \mathbf{e}_0^I \rangle$. The subscript of a non-terminal X denotes a bilingual span $[s,t,u,v]$ that corresponds to a block pair $\langle \mathbf{f}_s^t, \mathbf{e}_u^v \rangle$, where $\mathbf{f}_s^t = \mathbf{f}_{s+1} \dots \mathbf{f}_t$ and $\mathbf{e}_u^v = \mathbf{e}_{u+1} \dots \mathbf{e}_v$. An empty source word is represented as $\mathbf{f}_s^s$ and $\mathbf{e}_u^u$ for the target case.

The decision rule of finding the Viterbi alignment $\hat{\mathbf{a}}$ for a sentence pair $\langle \mathbf{f}_0^J, \mathbf{e}_0^I \rangle$ is given by [1]

$$\hat{\mathbf{a}} = \arg\max_{\mathbf{a}} \Big\{ \prod_{(j,i)\in\mathbf{a}} p(\mathbf{f}_j, \mathbf{e}_i) \times \prod_{j \notin \mathbf{a}} p(\mathbf{f}_j, \epsilon) \times \prod_{i \notin \mathbf{a}} p(\epsilon, \mathbf{e}_i) \Big\} \quad (1)$$

Traditionally, this can be done in $O(n^6)$ time using bilingual parsing (Wu, 1997).

In this paper, we extend a beam search algorithm (Liu et al., 2010c) to search for Viterbi ITG word alignment. Starting from an empty word alignment, the beam search algorithm

[1] For simplicity, we assume the distribution for the binary rules $X \rightarrow [X\ X]$ and $X \rightarrow \langle X\ X \rangle$ is uniform. Xiong et al. (2006) propose a maximal entropy model to distinguish between two merging options based on lexical evidence. We leave this for future work.

Algorithm 1 A beam search algorithm for ITG alignment.

```
1: procedure ALIGNITG(f, e)
2:     â → ∅                                          ▷ the alignment with highest probability
3:     𝓛 → {(j, i) : p(f_j, e_i) > p(f, ε) × p(ε, e)}          ▷ a set of promising links
4:     open ← ∅                                              ▷ a list of active alignments
5:     a ← ∅                                            ▷ begin with an empty alignment
6:     ADD(open, a, β, b)                                             ▷ initialize the list
7:     while open ≠ ∅ do
8:         closed ← ∅                                      ▷ a list of expanded alignments
9:         for all a ∈ open do
10:            for all l ∈ 𝓛 − a do                      ▷ enumerate all possible new links
11:                a′ ← a ∪ {l}                                ▷ produce a new alignment
12:                if ITG(a′) then                            ▷ ensure the ITG constraint
13:                    ADD(closed, a′, β, b)               ▷ update expanded alignments
14:                    if a′ > â then
15:                        â = a′                              ▷ update the best alignment
16:                    end if
17:                end if
18:            end for
19:        end for
20:        open ← closed                                     ▷ update active alignments
21:    end while
22:    return â                         ▷ return the alignment with highest probability
23: end procedure
```

proposed by Liu et al. (2010c) keeps adding single links to current alignments until all expanded alignments do not have higher probabilities. From a graphical point of view, the search space is organized as a directed acyclic graph[2] that consists of $2^{J \times I}$ nodes and $J \times I \times 2^{J \times I - 1}$ edges. The nodes are divided into $J \times I + 1$ layers. The number of nodes in the kth layer ($k = 0, \ldots, J \times I$) is $\binom{J \times I}{k}$. The maximum of layer width is given by $\binom{J \times I}{\lfloor \frac{J \times I}{2} \rfloor}$. The goal of word alignment is to find a node that has the highest probability in the graph.

The major difference of our algorithm from (Liu et al., 2010c) is that we only consider ITG alignments. Wu (1997) shows that ITG alignments only account for 0.1% in the full search space. The percentage is even lower for long sentences. As the worst-case running time is $O(bn^4)$ (b is a beam size) for the beam search algorithm of Liu et al. (2010c), this can be reduced to $O(bn^3)$ for the beam search algorithm that searches for ITG word alignment. [3]

Algorithm 1 shows the beam search algorithm for ITG alignment. The best alignment is set to empty at the beginning (line 2). The algorithm collects *promising* links $\mathcal{L}$ before alignment expansion (line 3). By promising, we mean that adding a link will increase the probability of current alignment. The gains keep fixed during the search process: [4]

$$\forall \mathbf{a} \in \mathcal{A} : gain(\mathbf{a}, \mathbf{f}, \mathbf{e}, l) \equiv \frac{p(\mathbf{f}_j, \mathbf{e}_i)}{p(\mathbf{f}_j, \epsilon) \times p(\epsilon, \mathbf{e}_i)}, \tag{2}$$

[2]For space limitation, please refer to Figure 3 in (Liu et al., 2010c) for example.

[3]If the Viterbi alignment is a full alignment, i.e., there is a link between any pair of source and target words, and the beam size is 1, $\frac{(J \times I) \times (J \times I + 1)}{2}$ nodes will be explored. Apparently, this can hardly happen in practice. For ITG alignments, however, our algorithm can reach at most the $min(J, I)$-th layer because ITG only allows for one-to-one links.

[4]As ITG alignments are strictly one-to-one, the gain of adding a link $l = (j, i)$ only depends on the associated source word $\mathbf{f}_j$ and target word $\mathbf{e}_i$.

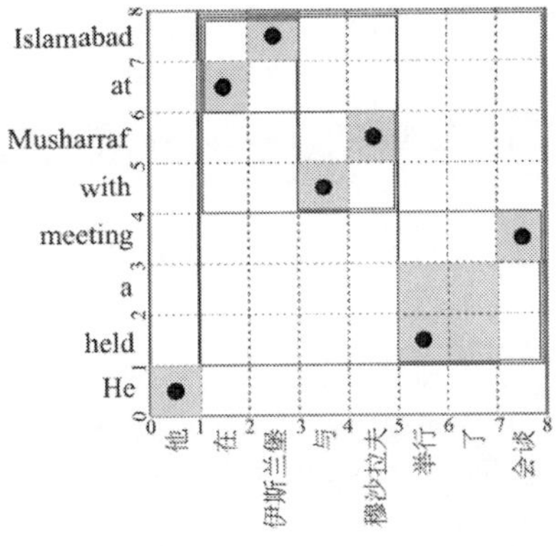

step	operation	stack
1	S	[0, 1, 0, 1]
2	S	[0, 1, 0, 1] [1, 2, 6, 7]
3	S	[0, 1, 0, 1] [1, 2, 6, 7] [2, 3, 7, 8]
4	R_M	[0, 1, 0, 1] [1, 3, 6, 8]
5	S	[0, 1, 0, 1] [1, 3, 6, 8] [3, 4, 4, 5]
6	S	[0, 1, 0, 1] [1, 3, 6, 8] [3, 4, 4, 5] [4, 5, 5, 6]
7	R_M	[0, 1, 0, 1] [1, 3, 6, 8] [3, 5, 4, 6]
8	R_I	[0, 1, 0, 1] [1, 5, 4, 8]
9	S	[0, 1, 0, 1] [1, 5, 4, 8] [5, 7, 1, 3]
10	S	[0, 1, 0, 1] [1, 5, 4, 8] [5, 7, 1, 3] [7, 8, 3, 4]
11	R_M	[0, 1, 0, 1] [1, 5, 4, 8] [5, 8, 1, 4]
12	R_I	[0, 1, 0, 1] [1, 8, 1, 8]
13	R_M	[0, 8, 0, 8]

Figure 2: A shift-reduce algorithm for judging ITG alignment.

where $\mathscr{A}$ is the set of all possible alignments. So our algorithm can safely take the computation of gains out of the loop (i.e., lines 7-21), which can not be done in (Liu et al., 2010c).

For each alignment, the algorithm calls a procedure ITG($\mathbf{a}$) to verify whether it is an ITG alignment or not (line 12). We use a shift-reduce algorithm for ITG verification. As shown in Figure 2, the shift-reduce algorithm scans links from left to right on the source side. Each link (j, i) is treated as an atomic block $[j-1, j, i-1, i]$. The algorithm maintains a stack of blocks, on which three operators are defined:

1. S: shift a block into the stack;
2. R_M: merge two blocks in a monotone order;
3. R_I: merge two blocks in an inverted order.

The algorithm runs in a reduce-eager manner: merge blocks as soon as possible (e.g., [5, 7, 1, 3] in step 9). Unaligned words are attached to the left nearest aligned words deterministically. The alignment satisfies the ITG constraint if and only if the algorithm manages to find a block corresponding to the input sentence pair. The shift-reduce algorithm runs in linear time. [5]

At each level, the algorithm at most retains b alignments (line 13). As ITG only allows for one-to-one links, the beam search algorithm runs for at most $min(J, I) + 1$ iterations (lines 7-21)[6]. Therefore, the running time of our beam search algorithm is $O(bn^3)$.

3 Experiments

We evaluated our algorithm on Chinese-English data for both alignment and translation. As Haghighi et al. (2009) has already compared ITG alignment with GIZA++ and discriminative methods, we only focus on comparing the search algorithms for ITG alignment. Our algorithm is compared with two baseline methods:

1. *biparsing*: the bilingual parsing algorithm as described in (Wu, 1997);

[5]In practice, the algorithm can be even more efficient by recording the sequence of blocks in each hypothesis without unaligned word attachment. Therefore, block merging needs not to start from scratch for each hypothesis.

[6]In the worst case, $min(J, I)$ links will be added in $min(J, I)$ iterations, in the $min(J, I) + 1$ iteration, all the expanded alignments will validate the ITG constrain and the algorithm terminates.

algorithm	setting	average time (s)↓	average model score↑	AER↓
biparsing		126.164	**-127.17**	**29.13**
biparsing+pruning	$t = 10^{-3}$	2.404	-167.44	34.92
	$t = 10^{-4}$	3.002	-152.68	33.13
	$t = 10^{-5}$	3.571	-144.27	31.93
	$t = 10^{-6}$	5.427	-138.23	31.12
beam search	$b = 1$	**0.019**	-142.27	33.00
	$b = 10$	0.126	**-131.73**	**30.52**

Table 1: Comparison with bilingual parsing algorithms in terms of average time per sentence pair, average model score per sentence pair and AER (length ≤ 50 words on both sides). Note that t is the beam ratio in tic-tac-toe pruning (Zhang and Gildea, 2005).

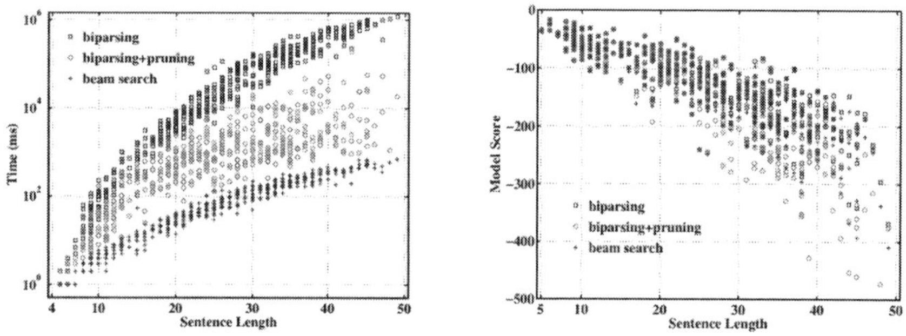

(a) Comparison of aligning time.

(b) Comparison of model score.

Figure 3: Comparison of aligning time and model score over various sentence lengths.

2. *biparsing + pruning*: the bilingual parsing algorithm with tic-tac-toe pruning (Zhang and Gildea, 2005).

For simplicity, we used the IBM model 4 translation probabilities trained on the FBIS corpus (6.5M+8.4M words) to approximate ITG lexical probabilities in the following experiments: $p(f,e) \approx p_{m4}(f|e) \times p_{m4}(e|f)/2$, $p(f,\epsilon) \approx p_{m4}(f|\epsilon)$, $p(\epsilon,e) \approx p_{m4}(e|\epsilon)$.

3.1 Alignment Evaluation

For the alignment evaluation, we selected 461 sentence pairs that contain at most 50 words on both sides from the hand-aligned dataset of (Liu et al., 2005). The three ITG alignment methods are compared in terms of average time per sentence pair, average model score per sentence pair, and AER. The results are shown in Table 1. Although achieving the best model score and AER, the *biparsing* algorithm runs too slow: 126.164 seconds per sentence pair on average. This is impractical for dealing with large scale real-world data that usually contains millions of sentence pairs. The tic-tac-toe pruning method (*biparsing + pruning*) does increase the speed by two orders of magnitude (3.571 seconds per sentence pair), which confirms the effectiveness of cell pruning (Zhang and Gildea, 2005; Haghighi et al., 2009; Liu et al., 2010a). Our beam search algorithm is one order of magnitude faster than the *biparsing+pruning* algorithm with significantly less search error.

Figure 3 compares aligning time of the three algorithms over different sentence lengths ranging

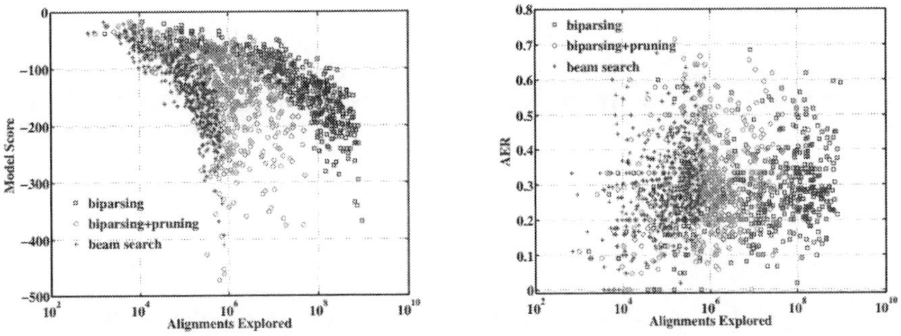

(a) Comparison of model score over alignments explored.

(b) Comparison of AER over alignments explored.

Figure 4: The scatter diagram of model score and AER over alignments explored for the 461 evaluation sentence pairs.

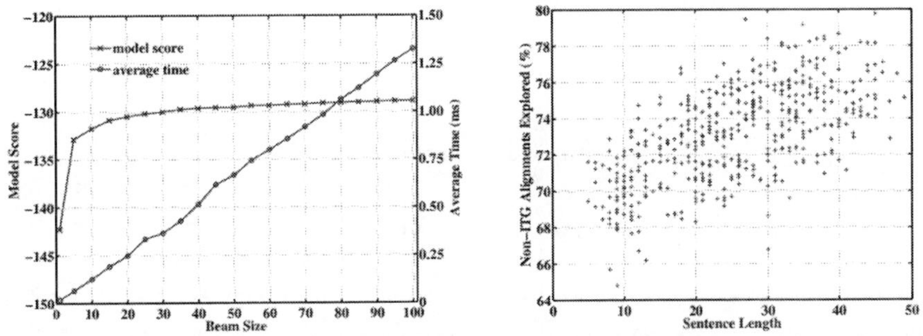

(a) Effect of beam size on average time per sentence pair and model score per sentence pair.

(b) Percentages of non-ITG alignments explored.

Figure 5: Investigation on different properties of our algorithm.

from 5 to 50 words. Clearly, our beam search algorithm is faster than the *biparsing* and *biparsing + pruning* algorithms for all lengths. More importantly, the gap enlarges with the increase of sentence length. We observe that our search algorithm almost achieves the same model scores with *biparsing* and *biparsing + pruning* for short sentences. For long sentences, however, the differences are increasingly significant because it is hard to find Viterbi alignments for long sentences. In most cases, our algorithm achieves higher model scores than *biparsing+pruning*, which is consistent with Table 1.

Figure 4 shows the model score and AER over alignments explored. Generally, our beam search algorithm explores less alignments before reaching the same level of model score and AER than *biparsing* and *biparsing + pruning*. And the diversity between different sentences is much smaller than the other two algorithms. So our beam search algorithm is more efficient.

Figure 5(a) shows the effect of beam size on average time per sentence pair and average model score per sentence pair. While the theoretical running time is $O(bn^3)$, the empirical average time does increase linearly with the beam size. The model score also generally rises with the increase of beam size but grows insignificantly when $b > 20$.

Figure 5(b) shows the percentages of non-ITG alignments explored during the search process. We observe that generally over 68% alignments expanded are non-ITG alignments and the percentage increases for long sentences. This finding suggests that most of expanded alignments are verified as non-ITG, especially for long sentences. Our algorithm can be significantly improved if it manages to know which link will result in an ITG alignment before calling the ITG(**a**) procedure. We leave this for future work.

3.2 Translation Evaluation

For the translation evaluation, we used 138K sentence pairs that have at most 40 words from the FBIS corpus as the training set, NIST 2002 dataset as the development set, and NIST 2005 dataset as the test set. As the *biparsing* algorithm runs too slow on the training data, we only compared our algorithm with *biparsing+pruning* in terms of average time per sentence pair and BLEU. *Moses* (Koehn et al., 2007) (a state-of-the-art phrase-based SMT system) and *Joshua* (Li et al., 2009) (a state-of-the-art hierarchial phrase-based SMT system) are used in our experiments. Both of them are used with default settings, except that word alignments are produced by "*biparsing+pruning*" and "*beam search*" respectively rather than GIZA++. Table 2 shows the average aligning time as well as the BLEU scores obtained by Moses and Joshua. Our system runs 20 times faster than the baseline without significant loss in translation quality.

algorithm	setting	average time (s)	Moses	Joshua
biparsing+pruning	$t = 10^{-5}$	7.57	23.86	**23.77**
beam search	$b = 10$	**0.35**	**23.95**	23.38

Table 2: Comparison of average time per sentence pair and BLEU scores (trained on the sentence pairs with no more than 40 words of FBIS corpus). Our system runs 20 times faster than the baseline without significant loss in translation quality.

Conclusion

We have presented a simple and effective algorithm for finding Viterbi ITG alignments. With a time complexity of $O(bn^3)$, the algorithm starts with an empty alignment and keeps adding single links until the model probability does not increase. Our experiments on Chinese-English data show that the proposed beam search algorithm is one order of magnitude faster than the conventional bilingual parsing algorithm with tic-tac-toe pruning without loss in alignment and translation quality.

In the future, we plan to extend our algorithm to the block-based ITG with discriminative training (Haghighi et al., 2009; Liu et al., 2010a), which proves to deliver state-of-the-art alignment and translation performance. It is interesting to include maximum entropy reordering models (Xiong et al., 2006) to make better predictions for binary rules. In addition, adding an estimate of future cost will help reduce search error further.

Acknowledgments

This research is supported by the Boeing Tsinghua Joint Research Project "English-Chinese Bilingual Text Alignment and Study of English-Chinese Translation" and National High-tech R&D Program (863 Program) under the grant no. 2011AA01A207 and 2012AA011102. We are grateful to Dr. Ping Xue for his inspirational suggestions in early discussions.

References

Ayan, N. F. and Dorr, B. J. (2006). Going beyond AER: An extensive analysis of word alignments and their impact on MT. In *Proceedings of COLING-ACL 2006*, pages 9–16.

Brown, P. F., Della Pietra, S. A., Della Pietra, V. J., and Mercer, R. L. (1993). The mathematics of statistical machine translation: Parameter estimation. *Computational Linguistics*, 19(2):263–311.

Chiang, D. (2007). Hierarchical phrase-based translation. *Computational Linguistics*, 33(2):201–228.

Fraser, A. and Marcu, D. (2007). Measuring word alignment quality for statistical machine translation. *Computational Linguistics*, 33(3):293–302.

Galley, M., Hopkins, M., Knight, K., and Marcu, D. (2004). What's in a translation rule? In *Proceedings of NAACL 2004*, pages 273–280.

Haghighi, A., Blitzer, J., DeNero, J., and Klein, D. (2009). Better word alignments with supervised ITG models. In *Proceedings of ACL-IJCNLP 2009*, pages 923–931.

Koehn, P., Hoang, H., Birch, A., Callison-Burch, C., Federico, M., Bertoldi, N., Cowan, B., Shen, W., Moran, C., Zens, R., Dyer, C., Bojar, O., Constantin, A., and Herbst, E. (2007). Moses: Open source toolkit for statistical machine translation. In *Proceedings of ACL 2007 (the Demo and Poster Sessions)*, pages 177–180.

Li, Z., Callison-Burch, C., Dyer, C., Ganitkevitch, J., Khudanpur, S., Schwartz, L., Thornton, W. N. G., Weese, J., and Zaidan, O. F. (2009). Joshua: An open source toolkit for parsing-based machine translation. In *Proceedings of WMT 2009*, pages 135–139.

Liu, S., Li, C.-H., and Zhou, M. (2010a). Discriminative pruning for discriminative ITG alignment. In *Proceedings of ACL 2010*, pages 316–324.

Liu, S., Li, C.-H., and Zhou, M. (2010b). Improved discriminative ITG alignment using hierarchical phrase pairs and semi-supervised training. In *Proceedings of COLING 2010*, pages 730–738.

Liu, Y., Liu, Q., and Lin, S. (2005). Log-linear models for word alignment. In *Proceedings of ACL 2005*, pages 459–466.

Liu, Y., Liu, Q., and Lin, S. (2010c). Discriminative word alignment by linear modeling. *Computational Linguistics*, 36(3):303–339.

Moore, R. C. (2005). A discriminative framework for bilingual word alignment. In *Proceedings of EMNLP 2005*, pages 81–88.

Moore, R. C., Yih, W.-t., and Bode, A. (2006). Improved discriminative bilingual word alignment. In *Proceedings of COLING-ACL 2006*, pages 513–520.

Och, F. and Ney, H. (2004). The alignment template approach to statistical machine translation. *Computational Linguistics*, 30(4):417–449.

Taskar, B., Lacoste-Julien, S., and Klein, D. (2005). A discriminative matching approach to word alignment. In *Proceedings of EMNLP 2005*, pages 73–80.

Vogel, S. and Ney, H. (1996). HMM-based word alignment in statistical translation. In *Proceedings of COLING 1996*, pages 836–841.

Wu, D. (1997). Stochastic inversion transduction grammars and bilingual parsing of parallel corpora. *Computational Linguistics*, 23(3):377–403.

Xiong, D., Liu, Q., and Lin, S. (2006). Maximum entropy based phrase reordering model for statistical machine translation. In *Proceedings of COLING-ACL 2006*, pages 521–528.

Zens, R. and Ney, H. (2003). A comparative study on reordering constraints in statistical machine translation. In *Proceedings of ACL 2003*, pages 144–151.

Zhang, H. and Gildea, D. (2005). Stochastic lexicalized inversion transduction grammar for alignment. In *Proceedings of ACL 2005*, pages 475–482.

Zhang, H. and Gildea, D. (2006). Efficient search for inversion transduction grammar. In *Proceedings of EMNLP 2006*, pages 224–231.

Active Learning for Chinese Word Segmentation

Shoushan Li[1] *Guodong Zhou*[1] *Chu-Ren Huang*[2]
(1) Natural Language Processing Lab, Soochow University, China
(2) Department of Chinese and Bilingual Studies, The Hong Kong Polytechnic University, Hong Kong
{lishoushan, gdzhou}@suda.edu.cn, churenhuang@gmail.com

ABSTRACT

Currently, the best performing models for Chinese word segmentation (CWS) are extremely resource intensive in terms of annotation data quantity. One promising solution to minimize the cost of data acquisition is active learning, which aims to actively select the most useful instances to annotate for learning. Active learning on CWS, however, remains challenging due to its inherent nature. In this paper, we propose a Word Boundary Annotation (WBA) model to make effective active learning on CWS possible. This is achieved by annotating only those uncertain boundaries. In this way, the manual annotation cost is largely reduced, compared to annotating the whole character sequence. To further minimize the annotation effort, a diversity measurement among the instances is considered to avoid duplicate annotation. Experimental results show that employing the WBA model and the diversity measurement into active learning on CWS can save much annotation cost with little loss in the performance.

KEYWORDS: Chinese Word Segmentation; Active Learning; Word Boundary Annotation

Proceedings of COLING 2012: Posters, pages 683–692,
COLING 2012, Mumbai, December 2012.

1 Introduction

Chinese word segmentation (CWS) is an indispensable pre-processing requirement for many Chinese language processing tasks, such as named entity recognition, syntactic parsing, semantic parsing, information extraction, and machine translation. Although state-of-the-art CWS systems report a high performance at the level of 95-97%, these systems typically require a large scale of pre-segmented corpus of tens (if not hundreds) of millions of words for training. However, the collection of the data on such a scale is very time-consuming and resource-intensive.

One possible solution to handle this dilemma is to deploy active learning, where only a small scale of instances are actively selected to serve as training data so that the annotation effort can be highly reduced (Settles and Craven, 2008). Although active learning has been widely employed to many NLP tasks, such as word sense disambiguation (Chan and Ng, 2007; Chen et al., 2006; Fujii et al., 1998), text categorization (Lewis and Gale, 1994; Liere and Tadepalli, 1997; McCallum and Nigam, 1998; Li et al., 2012), and named entity recognition (Shen et al., 2004), there are few studies of active learning on CWS, probably due to the strong challenges inherent in performing active learning on CWS.

First, the state-of-the-art methods treat CWS as a sequence labelling task (Jiang et al., 2008; Ng and Low, 2004; Tseng et al., 2005; Zhang et al., 2006), i.e. labelling characters with tags from a pre-defined tag set, representing the position of a character in a word. Different from traditional classification tasks, each character is tagged sequentially according to its corresponding context. Under this circumstance, a character cannot be determined as a single unit to query in active learning. One possible solution is to select one sentence as a unit for annotation, as Sassano (2002) does for Japanese word segmentation. However, such solution is expensive for annotation and since one sentence might contain some words which can be easily segmented correctly by existing models with high confidence, annotating them becomes a waste of time and manual effort.

Second, the number of the characters in a CWS corpus is normally extremely huge. For example, among the four corpora in SIGHAN Bakeoff 2 (Emerson, 2005), even the smallest corpus contains more than 1,800,000 characters while others are much larger in the order of tens of millions of characters. Compared to other tasks like text classification, normally with less than 20,000 instances (McCallum and Nigam, 1998), or named entity recognition, normally with less than 80,000 instances (Shen et al., 2004), CWS with such tremendous amount of instances makes it impossible to iteratively select one most informative instance for manual annotation in the active learning process. Instead, in each iteration, many informative instances are selected at the same time in practice. Under this circumstance, the selected informative instances are very likely overlapping when a standard uncertainty query strategy is used. For example, one unknown word may appear many times and a few sentences containing the unknown word may be selected for manual annotation at the same time according to the uncertainty strategy.

In this paper, we address the above challenges in active learning for CWS. In particular, for the first challenge, we propose a word boundary annotation (WBA) model, where the boundary between a character pair is considered the annotation unit. Specifically, we actively select the most informative boundaries to label manually and leave their easy and non-informative surrounding boundaries automatically labelled. Compared to using the sentence as the annotation unit, using the boundary is capable of reducing much annotation cost. For the second challenge, we propose a diversity measurement among the instances to avoid duplicate annotation, so as to further reduce the annotation efforts.

2 Related Work

Research on CWS has a long history and various methods have been proposed in the literature. Basically, these methods are mainly focus on two categories: unsupervised and supervised.

Unsupervised methods aim to build a segmentation system without any lexicon or labelled data. They often start from an empirical definition of a word and then use some statistical measures, e.g. mutual information (Sproat and Shih, 1990; Sun et al., 1998), to learn words from a large unlabelled data resource. Although these unsupervised methods can capture many strong words, their performance is often not high enough for the practical use.

Supervised methods, such as HMM tagging (Xue, 2003), character-based classification (Wang et al., 2008) and morpheme-based lexical chunking (Fu et al., 2008), attempt to acquire a model based on a dictionary or a labelled data set. Among them, character-based classification has drawn most attention recently and been further implemented with sequence labelling algorithms (Tseng et al., 2005), e.g., conditional random fields (CRF), which perform well in both in-vocabulary (IV) recall and out-of-vocabulary (OOV) recall. Based on the character labelling approach, many related studies make efforts to improve the performance by various means, such as using more tags and features (Tang et al., 2009; Zhao et al., 2006), employing word-based tagging without tagging (Zhang and Clark, 2007), employing some joint models that combines a generative model and a discriminative model (Wang et al., 2010; Wang et al., 2011) or Markov and semi-Markov CRF (Andrew, 2006), and integrating unsupervised segmentation features (Zhao and Kit, 2011).

Although there are various studies CWS individually, there are few studies of active learning on CWS. One related work is about active learning on Japanese word segmentation via Support Vector Machines (SVM) (Sassano, 2002). However, both the two challenging problems mentioned above are unsolved. Specifically, that study annotates the whole sentence as a basic unit, which means much more annotation effort than our model. Furthermore, our corpus scale is much larger than the one in Sassano (2002). This makes SVM impractical in terms of the training time for active learning on CWS. Meanwhile, they do not give an explicit diversity measurement, although their two-pool strategy implicitly considers the diversity.

3 Our Approach

3.1 Framework of Active Learning for CWS

Figure 1 illustrates the framework of our active learning approach for CWS. In the following subsections, we address the two remaining key issues.

1) The Word Boundary Annotation (WBA) model, which cares boundary annotation instead of the whole sentence.

2) The sample selection strategy $\phi(x)$, which evaluates the informativeness of one instance x. An efficient selection strategy is essential for active learning on CWS, where a huge number of unlabeled instances are involved.

Input:

Labeled set L, unlabeled pool U, selection strategy $\phi(x)$

Procedure:

Repeat until the predefined stopping criterion is met

(1). Learn a segmenter using current L with WBA

(2). Use current segmenter to label all the unlabeled boundaries

(3). Use the selection strategy $\phi(x)$ to select a batch of most informative boundaries for oracle labelling

(4). Put the new labeled boundaries together with their context (automatically labeled) into L

Figure 1: WBA-based active learning for CWS

3.2 Word Boundary Annotation (WBA) Model

3.2.1 Boundary Labelling

Formally, a Chinese text can be formalized as a sequence of characters and intervals

$$c_1 I_1 c_2 I_2, \ldots, c_{n-1} I_{n-1} c_n$$

where c_i means a character and I_i means an interval between two characters. Since there is no indication of word boundaries in a Chinese text, each interval might be a word boundary ($I_i = 1$) or not ($I_i = 0$). Accordingly, the objective of manual annotation is to label the word boundaries given the sequence of characters.

Take following sentence **E-A** as an example, where '/' in the output indicates a word boundary. The annotation process is to indicate that the intervals of I_{A3}, I_{A5}, I_{A7}, I_{A8}, I_{A10}, I_{A12}, I_{A13}, I_{A16}, I_{A18}, and I_{A19}.

E-A. Input: 索 I_{A1} 拉 I_{A2} 纳 I_{A3} 今 I_{A4} 天 I_{A5} 下 I_{A6} 午 I_{A7} 在 I_{A8} 波 I_{A9} 兰 I_{A10} 议 I_{A11} 会 I_{A12} 上 I_{A13} 发 I_{A14} 表 I_{A15} 了 I_{A16} 演 I_{A17} 说 I_{A18} 。 I_{A19}

Output: 索拉纳/ 今天/ 下午/ 在/ 波兰/ 议会/ 上/ 发表了/ 演说/ 。/

(*Solana gave a speech in the Polish parliament this afternoon .*)

From the above example, we can see that the annotation cost of CWS is very high because too many of boundaries (samples) need to be manually labeled. To overcome this problem, our active learning strategy labels those informative boundaries only.

3.2.2 Context Collection

In the training phase, the context of a selected boundary is essential for learning in that the nearby boundary categories are required to obtain the transition features. Consequently, not only the most informative boundaries but also their surrounding characters and boundaries are required to be collected for generating the new training data. In this paper, the nearby boundaries are automatically determined via the basic segmenter and don't need manual annotation.

In our approach, the context of a manually labelled boundary is defined as the character sequence between the first previous word boundary and the first following word boundary. In particular, if the selected boundary is manually labelled as a word boundary, i.e. $y_k = 1$, the two words around it are considered as its context. For examples, in the example sentence **E-A**, I_{A1}, I_{A2}, I_{A3} and I_{A9} are among the most informative boundaries. Since I_{A3} is manually labelled as a word boundary, '索拉纳/今天/' are considered as its context with I_{A4} and I_{A5} automatically labelled. In contrast, if the selected boundary is not manually labelled as a word boundary, i.e. $y_k = 0$, only the word containing the selected boundary is considered as its context. For example, I_{A9} is not manually labelled as word boundary and thus only '波兰/' is considered as its context with I_{A8} and I_{A10} automatically labelled.

3.3 Sample Selection Strategy with Diversity Measurement

In the literature, uncertainty sampling (Lewis and Gale, 1994) and Query-By-Committee (QBC) (Seung et al., 1992) are two popular selection schemes in active learning. This paper focuses on uncertainty sampling.

In uncertainty sampling, a learner queries the instance which is most uncertain to label. As WBA is a binary classification problem, uncertainty can simply be measured by querying the boundary whose posterior probability is nearest to 0.5. Therefore, we can define the uncertainty confidence value as follows:

$$\phi^{Un}(b_k) = \max_{y \in \{0,1\}} P(y \mid I_k) - 0.5$$

where $P(y \mid I_k)$ denotes the posterior probability that boundary I_k is labelled as y. The lower the confidence value is, the more informative the boundary is thought to be. After computing the confidences, all the boundaries in the unlabeled pool U are ranked according to their uncertainty values. In this way, a batch of top uncertain boundaries can be picked as the most informative ones for oracle labelling.

A major problem with uncertainty sampling is that it may cause duplicate annotation. That is to say, some instances in the "*N*-best" queries may be similar. To minimize the manual annotation effort, some diversity measurement among the instances should be taken into account to avoid duplicate annotation. For example, in the example **E-A** above, both the words '索拉纳' and '波兰' are unknown words for the initial segmenter learned by the initial labelled set L with the boundaries of I_{A1}, I_{A2}, I_{A9}, I_{B1}, I_{B2}, and I_{B9}, among the top uncertain instances. Obviously, some boundaries share the same segmentation information, e.g., I_{A1} and I_{B1}. Therefore, labelling both of them is a waste.

One straightforward way to handle such duplicate annotation is to compute the similarity between every two instances and then pick those with the highest diversities (Settles and Craven, 2008). This method, however, requires $O(N^2)$ in computational complexity where N is the number of all boundaries. When N is huge (e.g. N>1,800,000 in our experiments), the high computational burden is simply unacceptable. Fortunately, we find that the similarity between two boundaries is highly related to their surrounding character *N*-grams (in particular bigrams) and we can better evaluate the diversity with the help of the surrounding character bigrams.

This is done in this paper by recording the frequencies of all surrounding bigrams in a set S_{cc}, where $f_{c_i c_{i+1}} \in S_{cc}$ indicates the frequency of the character bigram $c_i c_{i+1}$ and is initialized to 0.

During training, we go through all the boundaries in the unlabeled data only once and the frequency of the surrounding bigram is updated serially as:

$$f_{c_k c_{k+1}} += 1$$

Where $c_k c_{k+1}$ is the surrounding character bigram of current boundary I_k. Meanwhile, the diversity of boundary I_k can be measured exactly by the frequency of its surrounding bigram:

$$\phi^{Div}(I_k) = f_{c_k c_{k+1}}$$

It is worth mentioning that above diversity measure is a dynamic one. It is possible that two boundaries with the same character bigram context, e.g., I_{A1} and I_{B1} in the above examples, are assigned with different diversity values during training. Specifically, the boundary with a first appearing bigram has the lowest diversity value while the boundaries appearing afterwards have higher values and thus are not likely to be picked as the top informative ones. In this way, the duplicate-annotated words can be avoided to some extent.

In summary, uncertainty sampling with diversity (in short, uncertainty-diversity sampling) ranks the boundaries according to the following formula:

$$\phi^{Un\_Div}(I_k) = \phi^{Un}(I_k) \cdot \phi^{Div}(I_k)$$

The lower the value is, the more informative the boundary is thought to be. Obviously, uncertainty-diversity sampling requires only $O(N)$ in computational complexity.

Therefore, active learning on CWS can be implemented in the following two ways: **Uncertainty sampling**: In each iteration, all the instances in the unlabeled data U are ranked according to their uncertainty values and top instances are selected for oracle labelling; **Uncertainty-Diversity sampling**: In each iteration, all the instances in the unlabeled data U are ranked according to their uncertainty-diversity values and top instances are selected for oracle labeling.

4 Experimentation

4.1 Experimental Setting

The SIGHAN Bakeoff 2 dataset consists of four different corpora: PKU, MSR, CityU, and AS. But we only report the performance on three of the corpora except AS due to its significant large scale in causing the out-of-memory error. The basic segmenter in the active learning process is trained with a 2-tag labelling model (Huang et al., 2007; Huang and Xue, 2012) and implemented with a public tool for CRF implementation, i.e. CRF++ (Kudo, 2005). For the feature template, we adopt the one by Li and Huang (2009). In all experiments, we use the standard F1 score as our main performance measurement. Besides, the out-of-vocabulary (OOV) recall is used to evaluate the OOV issue.

4.2 Experimental Results

In this experiment, we compare the random selection strategy and the two sampling strategies as illustrated in Section 3.3: uncertainty sampling and uncertainty-diversity sampling. To fairly compare the performances of different sampling strategies, we make sure that the number of annotated boundaries in either uncertainty sampling or uncertainty-diversity sampling is the same as random selection. Figure 2 indicates that either uncertainty or uncertainty-diversity greatly outperforms random selection. Among them, uncertainty-diversity sampling always performs best, which verifies the effectiveness of considering the diversity in uncertainty sampling. The success of the diversity measurement is mainly due to the fact that it can effectively avoid duplicate annotation. For example, while the word "企業/enterprise" occurs 392 times in the newly-obtained training data of CityU after using uncertainty sampling, it only occurs 144 times after using uncertainty-diversity sampling.

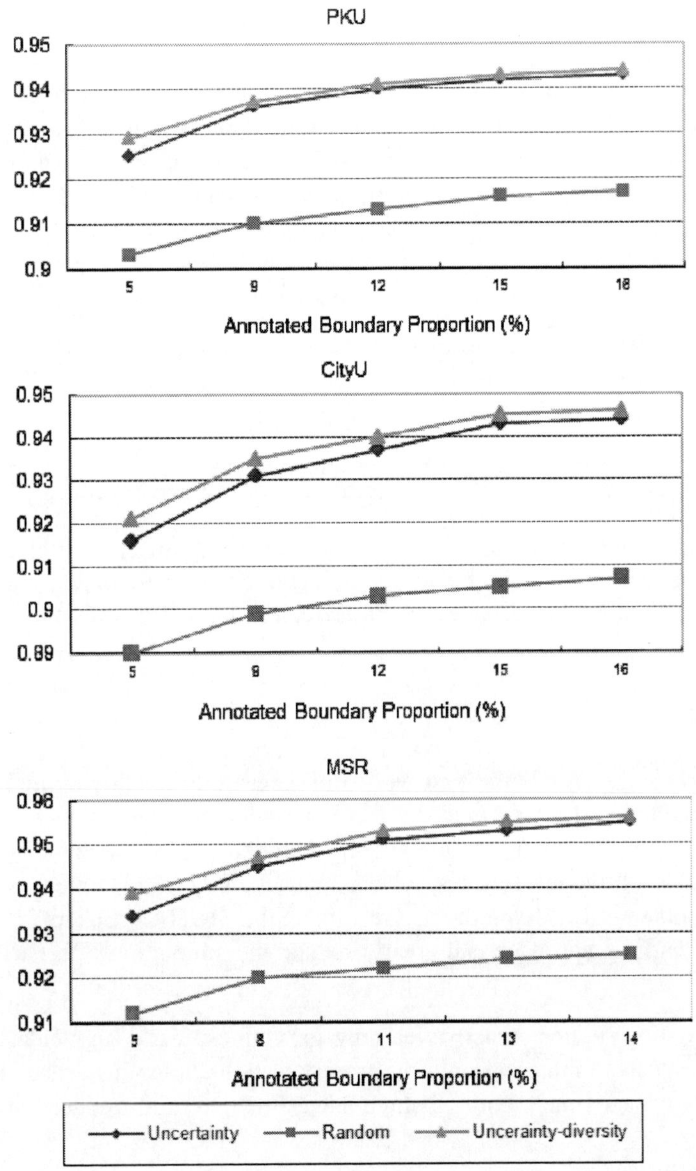

Figure 2: Performance (F1-score) comparison of active learning with different sampling strategies

WBA on Annotation Effort

In this experiment, we randomly draw three different data sets from training data in PKU and ask three students to annotate. Here, each data set has 50 sentences, containing 2186, 2556 and 2528 characters respectively. For a quick annotation, we design an annotation tool where the boundary between two neighbouring Chinese characters is shown for annotation as a word boundary or not. In particular, three different strategies are used to annotate the data: the first one annotates all sentences; the second one annotates the sentences that contain one or more uncertain boundaries, and the third one only annotates uncertain boundaries (our WBA model).

Here, the main differences between the second and third ones are the context range of the uncertain boundaries. The second one needs the whole sentence as its context and needs to annotate the whole sentence. The third one (used in our approach) only needs part of the sentence as the context (see Section 3.2 in detail) and thus only needs to annotate the uncertain boundary. Table 1 shows real annotation time and the proportion to that of annotating all sentences. From this table, we can see that our active learning approach could save averagely 85% of annotation time and is obviously preferable to the way of annotating the whole sentence.

	All Sentences		Selected Sentences		Selected Boundaries (Our approach)	
	Time	Proportion	Time	Proportion	Time	Proportion
Data Set 1	1232s	100%	790s	64.1%	239s	19.4%
Data Set 2	1746s	100%	1162s	66.6%	320s	18.3%
Data Set 3	1967s	100%	1124s	57.1%	178s	9.0%
AVERAGE	*1648s*	*100%*	*1025s*	*62.6%*	*246s*	*15.6%*

Table 1: Time of annotating three different data sets using different strategies. **All Sentences**: annotating all sentences in the each data set; **Selected Sentences**: annotating only the sentences containing uncertain boundaries; **Selected Boundaries**: annotating only the uncertain boundaries.

5 Conclusion

To our best knowledge, this is the first work in successfully employing active learning on Chinese word segmentation. In particular, our active learning approach aims to annotate only uncertain boundaries with the context automatically labelled. This is achieved via a WBA (Word Boundary Annotation) model. Besides, an efficient diversity measurement is proposed to further reduce the annotation effort. Experimental results on the SIGHAN Bakeoff 2 dataset demonstrate that our active learning approach can greatly reduce the annotation effort with little loss in performance.

Compared to existing studies on active learning for Chinese word segmentation, our approach is unique in two aspects: annotating only the uncertain boundaries instead of the whole sentence, and the diversity measurement, both of which have shown to fairly reduce the annotation cost.

Acknowledgments

The research work described in this paper has been partially supported by three NSFC grants, No.61003155, No.60873150 and No. 61273320, one National High-tech Research and Development Program of China No.2012AA011102, Open Projects Program of National Laboratory of Pattern Recognition. We also thank the three anonymous reviewers for their helpful comments.

References

Andrew G. 2006. A Hybrid Markov/Semi-Markov Conditional Random Field for Sequence Segmentation. In Proceedings of EMNLP-2006, pages 465–472.

Chan Y. and H. Ng. 2007. Domain Adaptation with Active Learning for Word Sense Disambiguation. In Proceedings of ACL-2007, pages 49-56.

Chen J., A. Schein, L. Ungar and M. Palmer. 2006. An Empirical Study of the Behavior of Active Learning for Word Sense Disambiguation. In Proceedings of HLT/NAACL-2006, pages 120–127.

Emerson T. 2005. The Second International Chinese Word Segmentation Bakeoff. In Proceedings of SIGHAN-2005, pages 123-133.

Fu G., C. Kit, J.Webster. 2008. Chinese Word Segmentation as Morpheme-based Lexical Chunking. Information Sciences, 178,(9): 2282-2296.

Fujii A., K. Inui, T. Tokunaga and H. Tanaka. 1998. Selective Sampling for Example-based Word Sense Disambiguation. Computational Linguistics, 24(4): 573-597.

Huang C. and N. Xue. 2012. Words Without Boundaries: Computational approaches to Chinese Word Segmentation. Language and Linguistics Compass. (to appear).

Huang C., P. Šimon, S. Hsieh and L. Prevot. 2007. Rethinking Chinese Word Segmentation: Tokenization, Character Classification, or Wordbreak identification. In Proceedings of ACL-2007 (poster), pages 69-72.

Jiang W., L. Huang, Q. Liu and Y. Lv. 2008. A Cascaded Linear Model for Joint Chinese Word Segmentation and Part-of-Speech Tagging. In Proceedings of ACL-HLT-2008, pages 897–904.

Kudo T. 2005. CRF++: http://crfpp.sourceforge.net/

Laws F. and H. Schütze. 2008. Stopping Criteria for Active Learning of Named Entity Recognition. In Proceedings of COLING-2008, pages 465-472.

Lewis D. and W. Gale. 1994. A Sequential Algorithm for Training Text Classifiers. In Proceedings of SIGIR-1994, pages 3-12.

Li S. and C. Huang. 2009. Word Boundary Decision with CRF for Chinese Word Segmentation. In Proceedings of PACLIC-2009, pages 726-732.

Li S., S. Ju, G. Zhou, and X. Li. 2012. Active Learning for Imbalanced Sentiment Classification. In Proceedings of EMNLP-CoNLL-2012, pages 139-148.

Liere R. and P. Tadepalli. 1997. Active Learning with Committees for Text Categorization. In Proceedings of AAAI-1997, pages 591-596.

McCallum A. and Nigam K. 1998. Employing EM in Pool-based Active Learning for Text Classification. In Proceedings of ICML-1998, pages 350-358.

Ng H. and J. Low. 2004. Chinese Part-of-speech Tagging: One-at-a-time or All-at-once? Word-Based or Character-based. In Proceedings of EMNLP-2004, pages 277–284.

Sassano M. 2002. An Empirical Study of Active Learning with Support Vector Machines for Japanese Word Segmentation. In Proceedings of ACL-2002, pages 505-512.

Settles B. and M. Craven. 2008. An Analysis of Active Learning Strategies for Sequence Labeling Tasks. In Proceedings of EMNLP-2008, pages 1070–1079.

Seung H., M. Opper and H. Sompolinsky. 1992. Query by Committee. In Proceedings of the ACM Workshop on Computational Learning Theory, pages 287–294.

Shen D., J. Zhang, J. Su, G. Zhou and C. Tan. 2004. Multi-criteria-based Active Learning for Named Entity Recognition. In Proceedings of ACL-2004, pages 589-596.

Sproat R. and C. Shih. 1990. A Statistical Method for Finding Word Boundaries in Chinese Text. Computer Processing of Chinese and Oriental Languages, 4(4):336–351.

Sun M., D. Shen and B. Tsou. 1998. Chinese Word Segmentation without Using Lexicon and Handcrafted Training Data. In Proceedings of ACL-COLING-1998, pages 1265-1271.

Tang B., X. Wang and X. Wang. 2009. Chinese Word Segmentation Based on Large Margin Methods. International Journal of Asian Language Processing, 19(1): 55-68.

Tseng H., P. Chang, G. Andrew, D. Jurafsky and C. Manning. 2005. A Conditional Random Field Word Segmenter for Sighan Bakeoff 2005. In Proceedings of SIGHAN-2005, pages 168-171.

Wang K., C. Zong, and K. Su. 2010. A Character-Based Joint Model for Chinese Word Segmentation. In Proceedings of COLING-2010, pages 1173-1181.

Wang K., C. Zong and K. Su. 2012. Integrating Generative and Discriminative Character-Based Models for Chinese Word Segmentation. ACM Transactions on Asian Language Information Processing, vol.11, no.2, pages 7:1-7:41.

Wang Z., C. Huang and J. Zhu. 2008. The Character-based CRF Segmenter of MSRA&NEU for the 4th Bakeoff. In Proceedings of SIGHAN-2008, pages 98-108.

Xue N. 2003. Chinese Word Segmentation as Character Tagging. Computational Linguistics and Chinese Language Processing, 8 (1): 29-48.

Zhang H., H. Yu, D. Xiong and Q. Liu. 2003. HHMM-based Chinese Lexical Analyzer ICTCLAS. In Proceedings of SIGHAN-2003, pages 184-187.

Zhang R., G. Kikui and E. Sumita. 2006. Subword-Based Tagging for Confidence-Dependent Chinese Word Segmentation. In Proceedings of ACL-COLING-2006, pages 961-968.

Zhang Y. and S. Clark. 2007. Chinese Segmentation with a Word-based Perceptron Algorithm. In Proceedings of ACL-2007, pages 840-847.

Zhao H. and C. Kit. 2008. Unsupervised Segmentation Helps Supervised Learning of Character Tagging for Word Segmentation and Named Entity Recognition. In Proceedings of SIGHAN-2008, pages 106-111.

Zhao H. and C. Kit. 2011. Integrating Unsupervised and Supervised Word Segmentation: The Role of Goodness Measures. Information Sciences, 181(1):163-183.

Zhao H., C. Huang, M. Li and B. Lu. 2006. Effective Tag Set Selection in Chinese Word Segmentation via Conditional Random Field Modeling. In Proceedings of PACLIC-2006, pages 87-94.

Fine-Grained Classification of Named Entities by Fusing Multi-features

Wenjie Li   Jiwei Li   Ye Tian   Zhifang Sui[*]
Key Laboratory of Computational Linguistics, Peking University, Beijing, 100871, China
{lwj, bdlijiwei, ytian, szf}@pku.edu.cn

ABSTRACT

Due to the increase in the number of classes and the decrease in the semantic differences between classes, fine-grained classification of Named Entities is a more difficult task than classic classification of NEs. Using only simple local context features for this fine-grained task cannot yield a good classification performance. This paper proposes a method exploiting Multi-features for fine-grained classification of Named Entities. In addition to adopting the context features, we introduce three new features into our classification model: the cluster-based features, the entity-related features and the class-specific features. We experiment on them separately and also fused with prior ones on the subcategorization of person names. Results show that our method achieves a significant improvement for the fine-grained classification task when the new features are fused with others.

KEYWORDS : Named Entities, fine-grained classification, cluster-based features, entity-related features, class-specific features.

* Corresponding author.

Proceedings of COLING 2012: Posters, pages 693–702,
COLING 2012, Mumbai, December 2012.

1 Introduction

The named entity categories defined by the classic Named Entity Classification (NEC) task are coarse grained, typically PERS, LOC, ORG, MISC. The results obtained from coarse grained NEC are insufficient for complex applications such as Information Retrieval, Question-Answering or Ontology Population. Consequently, some researchers turn to address the problem of recognizing and categorizing fine-grained NE classes. Fleischman (2001) presents a preliminary study on the subcategorization of location names, and more recent work focuses on the subcategorization of person names (Fleischman et al., 2002; Giuliano, 2009; Asif Ekbal et al., 2010).

Fine-grained NEC (FG-NEC) is a more difficult task than classic NEC, due to the increase in the number of classes and the decrease in the semantic differences between classes. The classic NEC can yield a good classification performance using only simple local context features. While for the FG-NEC, just using these features is far from enough to meet the requirements.

Take the following sentence for example,

"*Dennis Rodman*, a close friend of *Pippen*'s who won three NBA Champions with *Jordan*'s Bulls, was shocked to hear of *Pippen*'s comments.",

Based on the context information "NBA Champions", it is easy to recognize "*Pippen*" as an athlete. However for the person "*Dennis Rodman*", using simple context information is difficult to classify it. Therefore FG-NERC needs extended context and semantic features. Acquiring more context information from other related entity mentions in the same text for each entity mention (like "*Pippen*" for "*Dennis Rodman*") and extracting the class-specific feature words (like "NBA Champions" for athlete) may improve the classification results.

In addition, many prior works indicate that the performance of the model just using the lexical features is always limited by the data sparsity. Classic bag-of-words model does not work when there are few matching terms between feature word vectors. For example, there are two context word sets: set1={kitten, nyc} and set2={cat, new, york}. There is no similarity between the terms in each set. Address this limitation, prior works use word clusters from large unannotated corpora as additional features (Ang Sun et al., 2011). These features have been proved to be very useful for alleviating such data sparsity problem. Inspired by this, we also intend to introduce this cluster-based features into our model.

Combining these motivations, we present a method exploiting Multi-features for fine-grained classification of NEs in this paper. The only input data for our algorithm is a few manually annotated entities for each class. In addition to adopting the context word features and the word sense disambiguation features proposed by prior work, this paper puts forward three new features: the cluster-based features, the entity-related features and the class-specific features.

1. *Cluster-based features are generated by the Brown clustering algorithm (Peter F. Brown et al., 1992) from a large unlabeled corpus.*
2. *Entity-related features are context features introduced by other related entities.*
3. *Class-specific features are words extracted for each class. Each word is given a class-specific score denoting its ability to indicate the relevant class.*

Our work presented here concentrates on the subcategorization of person names, since the previous researches have indicated that the classification of person names which relies on much more contextual information are often more challenging. The person instances are already identified as entities, and only being classified into the fine-grained classes here. We choose Maximum Entropy (MaxEnt) model[1] which has already been widely used for a variety of NLP tasks, and proven to be a viable and competitive algorithm in the classification domain. In the following sections, we will describe the proposed features in detail.

2 Features

2.1 Context Features

Context words are the most frequently used features in the prior work. This is based on the assumption that entities occurring in similar contexts belong to the same class. In order to exclude the interference of unrelated words, we extract the words within a window for each entity mention. Only three individual word tokens and their PoS tags before and after the occurrence of the mention will be added into the feature set. In this paper, a context word and its PoS tag are tied together as an ensemble feature. For an entity mention W_i, its context words will be represented as: $fc_{i-3}^{i+3}=(wi\text{-}3\&posi\text{-}3)\cdots(wi\text{+}3\&posi\text{+}3)$.

2.2 Cluster-based Features

Bag-of-words model cannot deal with synonyms. To address this flaw, some work took advantage of the cluster-based features. The preliminary idea of using word clusters as features was presented by Miller et al. (2004), who augmented name tagging training data with hierarchical word clusters generated by the Brown clustering algorithm (Peter F. Brown et al., 1992) from a large unlabeled corpus.

Ang Sun et al. (2011) use the Brown algorithm to generate the word clusters as additional features which are applying to improve the performance of the relation extraction system. They use the English portion of the TDT5 corpora as their unlabeled data for inducing word clusters. The result of this word clusters is a binary tree. A particular word can be assigned a binary string by following the path from the root to itself in the tree, assigning a 0 for each left branch, and a 1 for each right branch. Each word occupies a leaf in the hierarchy, but each leaf might contain more than one word. The example bit strings of word clusters can be seen from Table 1.

Bit string	Word examples
11111110010111	Poland, Sweden, Australia ...
1111001110000	preventing, protecting ...
110010011	spokespeople, spokesmen ...
110110110001	cup, finals, champions ...
1101111101100	senator, citizen ...
1101111101110	legislator, lawmaker ...

TABLE 1 – Sample bit strings and their corresponding words

[1] In this paper we use the OpenNLP MaxEnt package (http://maxent.sourceforge.net).

In our work, we directly adopt this word clusters result supplied by Ang Sun et al. (2011)[2] to expanding the context features. Without further processing, we exploit the smallest granularity of clusters, just considering the leaf node in the binary tree in our method. For the features extracted in Section 2.1, if a feature word can be found as a leaf in the binary tree, the bit string of this leaf will be added as the additional features into the final feature set.

2.3 Entity-Related Features

The traditional classification methods focus only on the local context features described in Section 2.1. Actually, the local context might not provide sufficient information. In order to improve the performance of fine-grained classification, we want to find more context information.

Gale et al. (1992) state and quantify the observation that words strongly tend to exhibit only one sense in a given discourse or document. Inspired by the view, we discover that in the same passage the person instances appearing together are very likely belong to the same class. We expect to take advantage of this regularity to obtain more contexts for each entity mention.

Looking back to the example mentioned in Section 1, for the person "*Dennis Rodman*", there is no useful local contextual information and we can hardly recognize it as an athlete. However, in that sentence, appearing together with another person "*Pippen*" which can be easily identified as an athlete is a clue that "*Dennis Rodman*" is an athlete too.

Entity-related features are selected based on the assumption that if two entity mentions *A* and *B* often appear together in the same passage, then *A* and *B* are most likely to be the instances of the same class. Before feature sets construction, we can add the local context features of *A* into the feature set of *B*, and vice versa. From such features expanding process, each mention will obtain more sufficient context information. We extract entity-related features as follows:

1. ***Related contexts.*** *For an entity mention A and the text T that contains A, if another mention B appears in T and the distance between A and B is within a length of K, the context features of B which are introduced in Section 2.1 will be added into the feature set of A. In this paper we consider two mentions separated by not more than 10 words are highly related. We set K to 10.*
2. ***Relativity.*** *A binary feature that identifies whether the mentions are related. Since not all entities appear together are actually related, we try to extract the words which always co-occur with instances of the same class, and utilize these words to judge whether multi-mentions appearing together are related. This is based on the fact that when instances of the same class appear in the same text, some words always co-occur with high frequency, e.g. words representing coordination like and or along. For the training corpus, we collect all words co-occur with the same class instances, choosing the top M most frequent words into a word set. Empirically, we set M to 2000 in our work. Given a classification mention A and its related mention B, if their context words hit the word in the word set, this binary feature is set to 1.*

2.4 Class-Specific Features

For the classification task, the feature words representing the semantic information for each class are very important. Similar to the example mentioned in Section 1, the person "*Pippen*" co-

[2] http://www.cs.nyu.edu/~asun/data/TDT5_BrownWC.tar.gz.

occurs in the context with "NBA Champions", we know the proper word "NBA Champions" always co-occurs with the *athlete* instances rather than other class instances, so we regard this proper word as a class-specific feature for class *athlete*.

Therefore, we create the class-specific word sets for each class. The class-specific word set for a class is a list of words, in which each word is given a class-specific score denoting its ability to indicate the relevant class. Each class-specific word set constructs a relevant domain resource for the corresponding class.

Afterwards, we will describe how to choose the class-specific feature word sets for each class. These feature words are derived from the context word features described in Section 2.1. For all unigrams in a window of 3 surrounding the entity mentions in the entire training data, only nouns and verbs are kept as the candidate class-specific feature words. In our work, the same word with different PoS tags will be regarded as different ones. Assuming that there are n classes, namely $C_1C_2\cdots C_n$, the class-specific score of the candidate word m for the class C_j is computed as follows.

$$Weight_{C_j}(m) = \frac{Frequency_{cj}(m)}{\sum_{k=1}^{n} Frequency_{ck}(m)}$$

$Frequency_{cj}(m)$ represents the frequency of the word m co-occurring with instances of class C_j; the denominator is the frequency of m co-occurs with all class instances. For the class C_j, only those candidate words of which class-specific scores exceed the threshold t are kept; the retained words constitute the class-specific word set for C_j. In our experiments, the threshold t is empirically set to 0.8.

This weight formula shows that the word occurring with instances of the specific class C_j more times than other class instances will achieve a bigger score. This word represents strong semantic domain information for C_j. We know the domain distribution knowledge is very important for classification. If a mention co-occurs with this word, it would be very likely an instance of C_j.

Class	Word	PoS tag	Weight
Musician	ballet	NNS	1.0
	symphony	NN	0.94
	…	…	…
Poet	ode	NNS	1.0
	sonnet	NN	0.9
	…	…	…
Physicist	mercury	NN	1.0
	equation	NN	0.9
	…	…	…

TABLE 2 – Subset of class-specific feature words generated from training data

After constructing the class-specific word sets (see Table 2), we define a binary feature for each class that checks whether the context of entity mention W_i contains the word in the relevant class-specific word set. If context words surrounding W_i hit the word in the class-specific feature set of C_j, the binary feature corresponding to C_j is set to 1.

3 Experiments

3.1 Experimental Settings

We test our approach on UKWAC[3](M. Baroni et al., 2009), a 2 billion word English corpora constructed from the Web limiting the crawl to the *.uk* domain which has been PoS-tagged and lemmatized. The input person instances for each class are the same as used by Giuliano (2009) based on the People Ontology defined by Giuliano and Gliozzo (2008). The ontology extracted from WordNet is arranged in a multi-level taxonomy with 21 fine-grained classes, containing 1,657 distinct person instances. The taxonomy has a maximum depth of 4.

We extract all entity mentions together with their contexts in the entire corpus. All the contexts in which NEs occur are randomly partitioned into two equally sized subsets. One is used for training and the other for testing, and vice versa. Like other hierarchical classification tasks, the hypernym classes contain all instances of their hyponym classes when constructing the datasets. For example, *Mozart* is an instance of class *Musician* and also regarded as an instance of *Artist*.

The evaluation for hierarchical classification tasks is more complicated. The serious misclassification errors (e.g., an entity mention of class *Musician* is classified as the irrelevant class *Writer*) will be treated differently as the minor errors (e.g., an entity mention of class *Musician* is classified as the super-class *Artist*). In this paper we use the evaluation metric proposed by Melamed and Resnik (2000).

3.2 Experimental Results

We take the model only applying the context features as the baseline, and try to observe the different performance of mixing other features described in Section 2 with the context features. The results are reported in Table 3.

Feature set	Micro-F_1	Macro-F_1
Context Features	50.8	42.1
Context Features & Cluster-based Features	55.2	46.5
Context Features & Entity-related Features	52.4	43.6
Context Features & Class-specific Features	65.2	62.9
All features	79.6	76.5

TABLE 3 – Comparison among the different composite features sets

According to Table 3, the performances of all the composite feature sets are better than the baseline. The baseline using only local context features has the worst performance, achieving an F_1 value of about 50.8%. However, for the coarse grained classification of NEs, currently proposed works (William J. Black et al., 2009) show that using these local context features can achieve an F_1 value of above 80%. In Table 3, the model combining all the features achieves the best performance, a Micro-F_1 of about 79.6%.

Comparison among different features: According to Table 3, the composite feature set applying the class-specific features overperforms the others. Let us review the definition of these

[3] http://wacky.sslmit.unibo.it/doku.php?id=corpora

features. Class-specific features are words that we extract for each class. Each word is given a class-specific score denoting its ability to indicate the relevant class. Actually, these words construct a relevant domain resource for the classification task. Therefore, using these feature words can improve the performance significantly. Since the cluster-based features and entity-related features attempt to expand more information from just the local context window words, the performance of them is not as good as class-specific features. The cluster-based features can expand lexical representation of the feature words. The entity-related features bring in wider contexts through expanding the features from other related entity mentions. For the fine-grained classification task, larger contexts are expected to be employed. For this reason, when the cluster-based features and entity-related features are introduced, their performance is still better than the baseline in Table 3.

Comparison on different levels: Then, we want to evaluate the classification performance on different levels of granularities. According to the People Ontology, the general class person is on the level 1. Table 5 shows the levels which each class belongs to. For each level, both training and test entity mentions belong to the classes from the topmost level to the current level. Table 4 shows the results for different levels. The performance decreases as the level getting lower. Coarser grained classification on higher level has a better performance. For the six classes at level 2, fusing all the features achieves a high Micro-F_1 value of about 92.1%. This indicates that fine grained classification is more difficult.

Level	Context Features		Context Features & Cluster-based Features		Context Features & Entity-related Features		Context Features & Class-specific Features		All features	
	Micro -F_1	Macro -F_1	Micro -F_1	Macro -F_1	Micro -F_1	Macro -F_1	Micro -F_1	Macro -F_1	Micro -F_1	Macro -F_1
1	100.0	100.0	100.0	100.0	100.0	100.0	100.0	100.0	100.0	100.0
2	59.5	48.7	61.2	51.4	61.0	50.7	77.9	73.0	92.1	91.6
3	52.2	41.6	56.3	46.7	55.0	44.9	67.1	64.0	81.6	78.2
4	50.8	42.1	55.2	46.5	52.4	43.6	65.2	62.9	79.6	76.5

TABLE 4 – Comparison of performance of the different composite feature sets on different levels

Comparison to other work: We compare our best performance against the other systems. Fleischman and Hovy (2002) uses the decision trees algorithms and achieve an F_1 value of about 70.4% on held-out data. Claudio Giuliano (2009) classifies person instances into one of the People Ontology classes. They collect more semantic information for the entity instances from the search engines and Wikipedia, achieving an F_1 value of about 80.2%. For the same 21 fine-grained classes, our method classifies each person instance mention in context, while acquire a comparable performance. Asif Ekbal et al. (2010) use an unsupervised pattern-based method to automatically construct a gold standard dataset for this task, the system solely using the context features achieves the F_1 value of 82.6%. They also use UKWAC as their corpus. However, the automatically generated training and test datasets are only based on the appositional patterns, not including all the mentions which can be found in context. These datasets are not representative. Because of different settings and corpus used, the comparison is not convincing. Nevertheless, our experimental results demonstrate that combining these multi-features can achieve a better performance for NEs classification. Table 5 shows the overall view of the best result for each class combining all the features.

Class	Confusion all the features		
	Prec.	Recall	F_1
Creator (2)	63.8	92.1	75.4
Artist (3)	73.9	81.6	77.6
Musician (4)	90.3	57.6	70.3
Painter (4)	92.9	58.5	71.8
Film Maker (3)	89.5	73.1	80.5
Communicator (2)	71.7	86.0	78.2
Representative (3)	97.7	72.9	83.5
Writer (3)	78.9	82.5	80.7
Poet (4)	96.4	58.0	72.4
Dramatist (4)	94.7	57.5	71.6
Scientist (2)	54.3	90.4	67.8
Physicist (3)	87.7	60.0	71.3
Chemist (3)	87.9	58.2	70.0
Social scientist (3)	88.0	59.8	71.2
Mathematician (3)	87.8	59.8	71.1
Biologist (3)	87.3	58.5	70.1
Health professional (2)	84.4	97.7	90.5
Businessperson (2)	89.3	100.0	94.4
Performer (2)	70.2	86.2	77.4
Musician (3)	88.8	74.0	80.7
Actor (3)	88.3	73.4	80.2

TABLE 5 – The results for each class combining all the features (Number *n* in brackets means the corresponding class is arranged in the *n*-th level)

Conclusion and perspectives

This paper presents a method exploiting multi-features for fine-grained classification of Named Entities. We test our approach on UKWAC corpus and classify a candidate entity instance into one of a multi-level taxonomy with 21 fine-grained classes. We experiment on the different composite feature sets and compare the performance on different levels. The results show that these features are useful for this fine-grained classification task.

The remaining problem is that the instance seeds as input should be unambiguous. We need to manually specify them. Though Asif Ekbal et al. (2010) propose a method to automatically construct a dataset, the entity mentions are extracted based only on appositional patterns. The dataset dose not include all the mentions which can be found in context. In order to automatically build training examples for NEs classification, we consider applying more class labels and using these labels to extract the unambiguous entities. This is based on the assumption that ambiguous entity instances for one class always have common labels with other classes.

Acknowledgments

This work is supported by NSFC Project 61075067 and National Key Technology R&D Program (No: 2011BAH10B04-03). We thank Claudio Giuliano for their input person instances and the anonymous reviewers for their insightful comments.

References

Michael Fleischman. (2001). Automated subcategorization of named entities. In *Proceedings of the ACL 2001 Student Workshop*.

Michael Fleischman and Eduard Hovy. (2002). Fine grained classification of named entities. In *Proceedings Of COLING-02*, pages 1–7.

Claudio Giuliano and Alfio Gliozzo. (2008). Instance-based ontology population exploiting named-entity substitution. In *Proceedings of COLING-ACL-08*, pages 265–272.

Claudio Giuliano. (2009). Fine-grained classification of named entities exploiting latent semantic kernels. In *Proceedings of CoNLL-09*, pages 201–209.

Asif Ekbal, Eva Sourjikova, Anette Frank, and Simone Ponzetto. (2010). Assessing the Challenge of Fine-grained Named Entity Recognition and Classification. In *Proceedings of the ACL 2010 Named Entity Workshop (NEWS)*.

Ang Sun , Ralph Grishman , Satoshi Sekine. (2011). Semi-supervised relation extraction with large-scale word clustering. In *Proceedings of ACL-11*, pages 521–529.

Peter F. Brown, Vincent J. Della Pietra, Peter V. deSouza, Jenifer C. Lai, and Robert L. Mercer. (1992). Class-based n-gram models of natural language. *Computational Linguistics*, pages 467–479.

Scott Miller, Jethran Guinness and Alex Zamanian. (2004). Name Tagging with Word Clusters and Discriminative Training. In *Proceedings of HLT-NAACL*, pages 337–342.

Gale, W., K. Church, and D. Yarowsky. (1992). A Method for Disambiguating Word Senses in a Large Corpus. *Computers and the Humanities*, pages 415–439.

M. Baroni, S. Bernardini, A. Ferraresi and E. Zanchetta. (2009). The WaCky Wide Web: A Collection of Very Large Linguistically Processed Web-Crawled Corpora. *Language Resources and Evaluation*, pages 209–226.

Dan Melamed and Philip Resnik. (2000). Tagger evaluation given hierarchical tag sets. *Computers and the Humanities*, pages 79–84.

William J. Black , Argyrios Vasilakopoulos. (2002). Language independent named entity classification by modified transformation-based learning and by decision tree induction. In *proceeding of CoNLL*, pages1–4.

Expert Finding for Microblog Misinformation Identification

Chen Liang[*] *Zhiyuan Liu*[*] *Maosong Sun*
Department of Computer Science and Technology
State Key Lab on Intelligent Technology and Systems
National Lab for Information Science and Technology
Tsinghua University, Beijing 100084, China
{chenliang.harry,lzy.thu}@gmail.com, sms@tsinghua.edu.cn

ABSTRACT
The growth of social media provides a convenient communication scheme for people, but at the same time it becomes a hotbed of misinformation. The wide spread of misinformation over social media is injurious to public interest. We design a framework, which integrates collective intelligence and machine intelligence, to help identify misinformation. The basic idea is: (1) automatically index the expertise of users according to their microblog contents; and (2) match the experts with given suspected misinformation. By sending the suspected misinformation to appropriate experts, we can collect the assessments of experts to judge the credibility of information, and help refute misinformation. In this paper, we focus on expert finding for misinformation identification. We propose a tag-based method to index the expertise of microblog users with social tags. Experiments on a real world dataset demonstrate the effectiveness of our method for expert finding with respect to misinformation identification in microblogs.

TITLE AND ABSTRACT IN CHINESE

面向微博不实信息识别的专家发现

在为人们提供了便利的交流方式的同时，社会媒体也成为不实信息传播的温床。不实信息在社会媒体中的广泛传播将对公共利益造成损害。这里，我们提出综合利用群体智能和机器智能帮助识别不实信息，基本思想是：（1）根据微博用户产生内容自动分析和索引用户的专长；（2）自动将可疑的不实信息与相应的专家匹配。通过将不实信息发送给合适的专家，我们可以收集专家们对信息可信性的评估，帮助识别不实信息和辟谣。本论文将主要探讨面向不实信息识别的专家发现问题。我们采用基于标签的方法来索引微博用户的专长。在真实数据上的实验表明，我们的方法可以有效进行微博专家发现用于不实信息识别。

KEYWORDS: misinformation identification, expert finding, microblog.
KEYWORDS IN CHINESE: 不实信息识别, 专家发现, 微博.

∗ indicates equal contributions from these authors.

Proceedings of COLING 2012: Posters, pages 703–712,
COLING 2012, Mumbai, December 2012.

1 Introduction

Although rumors lack a specific definition, most theories agree that a rumor is a statement of information, whose veracity is not quickly or ever confirmed, spreading from person to person and pertaining to an object, event or issue in public concern (Peterson and Gist, 1951). Rumors are regarded as a type of misinformation. In recent years, online social media is growing rapidly. Social media provides a convenient communication scheme between people. Meanwhile, the scheme enables unreliable sources to spread large amounts of unverified information among people. Rumors are thus possible to spread more quickly and widely through online social media compared to traditional offline social communities. The wide spread of misinformation may bring disorder to people especially when they are facing crises. This indicates that it is crucial for social media to identify misinformation in time so as to limit the spread of rumors.

Most existing research efforts on rumors in social media focus on their external features, such as spread and conversation patterns. It is a consensus that automatically identifying rumors via in-depth content analysis is a challenging task. Social media still lacks solutions to effectively identify and refute misinformation to stop it from wide spread. Although fully-automatic identification of misinformation is currently a mission impossible for computer programs, most rumors can be easily identified by human experts with corresponding knowledge or experiences. Due to the popularity of social media, most experts can be found in social media. Under such a scenario, we design a framework to identify misinformation with the help of experts in microblogs. We automatically route suspected misinformation to a set of experts who can assess the credibility. With the assessments from experts, we can help determine the credibility of the information, identify and refute misinformation, and eventually stop the wide spread of rumors.

The most crucial part of the framework is finding appropriate experts for suspected misinformation. A relevant task has been studied as expert finding. However finding experts for suspected misinformation is different from the traditional task in many aspects, which make it more challenging. In this paper, we focus on expert finding for misinformation identification. With the help of experts, we incorporate the power of natural language processing techniques and the knowledge of human experts. With the method, we may help social media achieve self-management and self-organization.

2 Empirical Analysis of Rumors

We give empirical analysis of rumors on Sina Weibo, the largest microblog service in China. Sina Weibo has more than 250 million registered users as of October 2011, over 60% network users have accounts of Sina Weibo, and 31% Weibo users post more than 3 messages per day. Due to the overflow of rumors, Sina Weibo maintains a team to refute rumors. Since the process is carried out manually, it is manpower intensive while the refutation is usually delayed and the scope is limited.

We collect 859 rumors identified by both Sina Weibo team and a public interest organization (guokr.com) for empirical analysis. All the rumors have widely spread over Sina Weibo ranging from 18 November, 2010 to 29 December, 2011. By studying the real-world rumors, according to what restricts people from identifying them as rumors, we manually categorize rumors into two classes: (1) 588 out of 859 rumors are **domain knowledge constrained (DKC) misinformation.** This type of information usually talks about some domain-specific topics. Most people do not master the corresponding professional knowledge and thus cannot verify the correctness. For example, a rumor claimed that "A nutritionist finds that if you eat a bag of instant noodles, the liver will need 32 days for detoxification", which is related to the knowledge of food hygiene and nutrition. (2) 271 out of 859 rumors are **time-space constrained (TSC) misinformation**. This type of misinformation is usually related to some events that occur in some places and time. Most people have not experienced these events and thus cannot check the authenticity. For example, a rumor claimed that "Some mentally retarded children in Xiangyang, Hubei were cut out tongues and genitals". The people not living in that city will not be able to verify the reliability of the information. According to the analysis, we summarize that the two types of rumors are different in: (1) Their topics are quite different. DKC rumors focus on the topics of science and technologies, while TSC rumors focus on the topics of public security, society and politics. (2) TSC rumors usually talk about events and thus often mention specific names of persons, places or organizations; while DKC rumors seldom mention specific names.

We build a two-class classifier using the occurrences of names and topics as features to quantitatively identify the differences between the two types of misinformation. The classifier is built using LIBLINEAR (Fan et al., 2008). For each message, features are boolean values indicating the appearance of names and topics. We perform 5-cross validation for evaluation and the prediction accuracies are 0.848, 0.804, and 0.865 when using names, topics or both as features. We can see that most misinformation can be well distinguished according to these features. Based on the characteristics of DKC and TSC misinformation, we propose a unified method to find applicable experts for them.

3 Tag-based Method for Expert Finding

Suppose all microblog users are candidate experts denoted as a set E. These users may be either people or organizations. Given a suspected misinformation m, the probability of selecting a microblog user e from E being an expert on m can be estimated as

$$\Pr(e|m) = \frac{\Pr(m|e)\Pr(e)}{\Pr(m)} \propto \Pr(m|e)\Pr(e), \tag{1}$$

where $\Pr(e)$ is the prior probability of an expert; $\Pr(m)$ is the prior probability of m, which remains the same for all candidate experts and thus is ignored for expert ranking. Here, $\Pr(e)$ is estimated as the authority of e, and $\Pr(m|e)$ is as the expertise of the expert e on m. We adopt social tags annotated by microblog users to model expertise.

For DKC misinformation, we use Eq.(1) to find experts from E directly; while for TSC misinformation, we have to restrict the set of candidate experts with respect to the named entities that have appeared in m. We introduce our method in details in the following three aspects: (1) modeling expertise with tag-based method to compute $\Pr(e|m)$; (2) computing authorities of experts, i.e., $\Pr(e)$; and (3) restricting candidate set of experts for TSC.

3.1 Modeling Expertise with Tag-based Method

Social tagging is an iconic application in social media (Gupta et al., 2010). Sina Weibo allows users to annotate tags for themselves, which may attract users with similar interests to follow them. Expertise of experts can be represented in terms of social tags because tags represent the interests or characteristics of users to some extent. For example, a user whose occupation is ophthalmologist may annotate itself with the tag "ophthalmology".

We denote the set of tags as T. Suppose $\Pr(m|e)$ is a generation process as follows. An expert e first generates a tag $t \in T$, and then t generates the message m. Given the generation process, the probability $\Pr(m|e)$ can thus be estimated as follows:

$$\Pr(m|e) = \sum_t \Pr(m|t)\Pr(t|e) = \sum_t \frac{\Pr(t|m)\Pr(m)}{\Pr(t)}\Pr(t|e) \propto \sum_t \frac{\Pr(t|m)}{\Pr(t)}\Pr(t|e), \tag{2}$$

where $\Pr(t)$ indicates the prior probability for the tag t, $\Pr(t|m)$ measures the probability of t given the message m, and $\Pr(t|e)$ computes the probability of expertise t given the expert e. The prior $\Pr(t)$ can be estimated using the number of microblog users who annotate themselves with the tag t; while $\Pr(t|m)$ and $\Pr(t|e)$ are modeled as a problem of social tag suggestion task. $\Pr(t|e)$ can be decomposed into two parts: one is the suggestion score of t given the messages posted by e, and the other is whether e has annotated itself with t. The two parts are combined with a smoothing factor γ ranging from 0 to 1, $\Pr(t|e) = \gamma \sum_{m \in M_e} \Pr(t|m)\Pr(m|e) + (1-\gamma)\mathbf{1}_{t \in T_e}$, where M_e is the set of messages that are posted by e, $\Pr(t|m)$ is the ranking score of t given the message m, $\Pr(m|e)$ indicates the weight of message m within all messages posted by e, and $\mathbf{1}_{t \in T_e}$ equals 1 if the tag set T_e annotated by e contains t and 0 otherwise. In this paper, we simply set the weights of all messages $\Pr(m|e)$ for e to be equal, and set $\gamma = 0.5$.

Based on the above analysis to $\Pr(t|m)$ and $\Pr(t|e)$, the essential task is to suggest social tags for a message m. As the rapid growth of social media, social tag suggestion has been well studied (Gupta et al., 2010). There are two approaches for social tag suggestion: graph-based approach and content-based approach. Since we have to suggest tags according to the content of m, we follow the content-based approach. The specialty of our problem compared to previous problems lies in: (1) the method should be robust to noise and informal format of microblog messages; and (2) m is short with no more than 140 Chinese characters in Sina Weibo.

Taking the specialty in consideration, we propose to use word alignment model (WAM) in statistical machine translation (Brown et al., 1993) for social tag suggestion, which has been verified to outperform other existing content-based methods (Liu et al., 2011, 2012). Here we give a brief introduction to WAM, and introduce some important extensions to make the method appropriate to suggest social tags for microblog messages.

WAM for Social Tag Suggestion. Given a message m, WAM ranks candidate tags by computing their likelihood $\Pr_{\text{WAM}}(t|m) = \sum_{w \in m} \Pr(t|w)\Pr(w|m)$, where $\Pr(w|m)$ is the weight of the word w in m, and $\Pr(t|w)$ is the translation probability from w to t obtained from the translation models. $\Pr(w|m)$ is estimated using term-frequency and inverse message frequency (TFIMF), which is similar to TFIDF. According to the ranking scores, we suggest the top-M as tags for m. WAM can avoid the problem caused by noise and informal format of microblogs. Moreover, WAM can suggest tags that have not appeared in the given message. However, a tag that appears in the given message may be more important. Therefore, we improve WAM by combining WAM with frequency-based methods. A simple and effective frequency-based method is using TFIMF to rank candidate tags in a given message. We thus compute the ranking score using improved WAM (IWAM) for a candidate tag as follows, $\Pr_{\text{IWAM}}(t|m) = \alpha \Pr_{\text{WAM}}(t|m) + (1-\alpha)\Pr_{\text{TFIMF}}(t|m)$, where α is a smoothing factor with range $\alpha \in [0.0, 1.0]$. In experiments we set $\alpha = 0.5$ which achieves the best performance.

Training Translation Models for WAM. Training WAM for tag suggestion consists of two steps: preparing translation pairs and training translation models. The training set for traditional WAM consists of a number of translation pairs written in two languages. In our task, we have to collect sufficient translation pairs of microblog messages and their tags to capture the semantic relationship between them. However, microblogs are usually not annotated with tags. We thus propose to prepare translation pairs by automatically extracting tags using a simple and effective method for each message. The basic idea is that most results of the simple method are correct, while the errors can be filtered out by WAM. The preparation process is as follows. We first collect all tags annotated by microblog users in Sina Weibo. For each tag t, we record the users that annotate tag t as E_t. We group all tags with $|E_t| > 10$ as a tag list. After that, we collect a large set of microblog messages. For each message m, we extract several tags according to the score of tag-frequency and inverse expert-frequency $\mathrm{TFIEF}_{(t,m)} = \mathrm{TF}_{(t,m)}|E|/|E_t|$. Similar to TFIDF, $\mathrm{TF}_{(t,m)}$ indicates the significance of the tag t in m, and $|E|/|E_t|$ indicates the discriminative ability of the tag t. Using messages and their corresponding extracted tags, we build the translation pairs for WAM training.

We use IBM Model 1 (Brown et al., 1993) for WAM training. IBM Model 1 is a widely used word alignment algorithm which does not require linguistic knowledge for two languages. We have also tested more sophisticated word alignment algorithms such as IBM Model 3 for tag suggestion. However, these methods do not achieve better performance than IBM Model 1. Therefore, in this paper we only demonstrate the experimental results using IBM Model 1. In experiments, we select GIZA++ (Och and Ney, 2003) to train IBM Model 1.

3.2 Measuring Authority

Some works have been devoted to authority analysis of social media (Pal and Counts, 2011). The basic conclusion is that a microblog user has more authority if it has more followers and posts more original messages. Therefore, in this paper, we simply compute authority of a user e as:

$$\Pr(e) = \frac{\log\left(\frac{|F_e|}{|A_e|}\right) \times \log(|M_e|)}{\sum_{e\in E_m} \log\left(\frac{|F_e|}{|A_e|}\right) \times \log(|M_e|)}, \tag{3}$$

where F_e is the follower set of e and A_e is the user set followed by e. The score is normalized over all experts in E_m.

3.3 Restricting Candidate Expert Set for TSC

We denote the names of each user $e \in E$ as N_e and the names in m as N_m. We perform named entity disambiguation for N_m according to microblog users, and link each name n in N_m to all relevant microblog users that n really mentions. We denote the restricted candidate experts as a set E_m. To restrict candidate expert set for TSC, we perform the following three steps.

Extracting Names for Microblog Experts. We extract and index the names N_e of each microblog user $e \in E$ according to its nickname, introduction and authentication reason. This problem is addressed as a sequence labeling task solved by conditional random fields (CRF) (Lafferty et al., 2001)[1]. Since nicknames, introductions and authentication reasons

[1]We use CRF++ for implementation, which can be obtained in `http://crfpp.sourceforge.net/`.

have obvious patterns, we can obtain the labeling accuracy of above 90% by training on a set of 500 manually annotated users.

Named Entity Recognition for m. Since Sina Weibo is in Chinese, we first perform Chinese word segmentation (CWS) and part-of-speech (POS) tagging for messages using the algorithm originally proposed in (Jiang et al., 2008). After that, we perform named entity recognition (NER). Since misinformation always pretends to be credible by written in a formal style, we can thus achieve high accuracy using the algorithm CRF (Nadeau and Sekine, 2007) based on the CWS and POS tagging output.

Named Entity Disambiguation. We disambiguate the names in m with respect to microblog users, and thus restrict candidate expert set from E to $E_m = \{e|N_e \cap N_m \neq \emptyset\}$. First, we find all microblog users by substring match between the names of microblog users and the names extracted from the message, denoted as E_s. These users are not all relevant to the names in m. The following task is to disambiguate the names in m to microblog users in E_s according to the relevance of these users with m. We follow the state-of-the-art algorithm in (Zheng et al., 2010), and use list-wise learning to rank (L2R) framework to address the problem. After investigating various combinations of features, we use the following effective features for L2R: (1) Follow-attention ratio which indicates the popularity of e. (2) The number of original messages that e has posted which indicates the vitality of e. (3) The numbers of comments and reposts for recent 100 messages which also indicates the recent vitality of e. (4) The number of microblog user names that appear in both recent 100 messages of e and m. This measures the semantic relatedness between e and m.

Since the number of TSC rumors are limited for training and testing, we instead manually annotate 6394 names in news articles ranging from June to December, 2011 as dataset, with each name linked to a microblog user. By training on 3,985 instances and testing on 2,409 instances, we obtain accuracy of 96.3%, which indicates the effectiveness of L2R for named entity disambiguation to microblog users. With the trained model on the dataset, we perform named entity disambiguation to names in given message m and restrict the candidate expert set to E_m.

4 Experiments and Analysis

We perform experiments on 859 rumors manually collected from Sina Weibo. We also collect 5 million the most active microblog users with their profiles and messages to build expert database. For each rumor, we recommend 10 experts from microblog users. We ask two editors to manually annotate the correctness of the results, who discussed and finally achieved final agreement on annotation. For the inconsistent annotations, the two editors discuss to achieve agreement. We use P@N for evaluation where N ranges from 1 to 10.

Evaluation Results on DKC Rumors. To investigate the effectiveness of tag-based method, we compare our method with language model, the state-of-the-art method for expert finding, on 588 DKC rumors. For each DKC rumor, we suggest maximum 10 microblog experts.

In language model, a candidate expert e is represented by a multinomial probability distribution over the vocabulary of words, i.e., $\Pr(w|\theta_e)$. A message m is represented by a bag of words with each word generated independently. Therefore, the probability of m being generated by the language model θ_e can be obtained by taking the product across all words in m: $\Pr(m|e) = \prod_{w \in m} \Pr(w|\theta_e)^{n(w,m)}$, where $\Pr(w|\theta_e)$ is the probability of a word w given θ_e, and $n(w,m)$ is the number of times word w appears in m. The language model of e, $\Pr(w|\theta_e)$, is estimated as $\Pr(w|\theta_e) = \sum_{m \in M_e} \Pr(w|m)\Pr(m|e)$, where $\Pr(m|e)$ is the weight of an message posted by e, and $\Pr(w|m)$ is the generation probability by the message m. We set $\Pr(m|e)$ equal for all messages posted by e; while $\Pr(w|m)$ is estimated using the TFIMF score of w. We also apply the Jelinek-Mercer method to smooth language model (Zhou et al., 2009), which is not introduced in detail for space limit.

We show the evaluation results in Fig. 1. From Fig. 1 we observe that: (1) The tag-based method consistently and significantly outperforms language model for expert finding. This indicates the effectiveness of the tag-based method. The reason is that tags are annotated by microblog users and provide sufficient information. (2) Although the performance of expert finding is far from perfection, it can help find experts and reduce manual work to a great extent. Moreover, the performance of expert finding can be further improved as more knowledge are taken into consideration, which will be our future work.

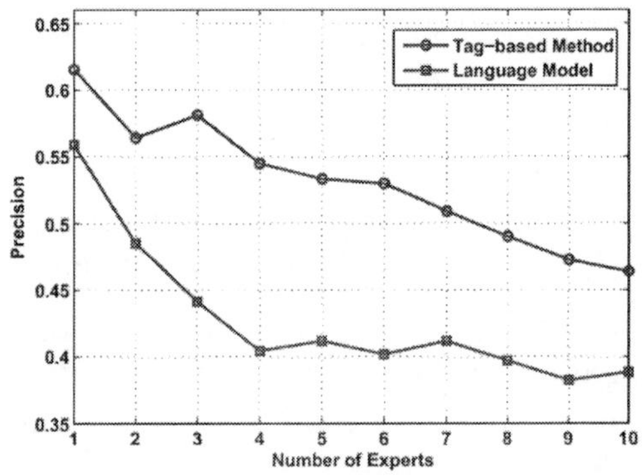

Figure 1: Evaluation results on expert finding for DKC rumors.

We also analyze the sample errors in expert finding for DKC rumors. The main reasons for these errors are: (1) Some tags are ambiguous and we may find experts that are irrelevant to m. For example, the tag "apple" may refer to either a type of fruits or an IT company. Although the tag-based method takes the topics of m into consideration, it still cannot thoroughly solve the problem. In future work, we may adopt tag disambiguation (Yeung et al., 2007) in our method. (2) We treat all tags annotated by experts equally. However, microblog users may annotate tags arbitrarily, which will thus import noise to our method. In future work, we will estimate confidence scores to the tags annotated by microblog users.

Evaluation Results on TSC Rumors. Different from DKC rumors, for TSC rumors our method will identify named entities in the suspected message to restrict the candidate expert set. In experiments, we set a person name may correspond to only one microblog user, while a place/organization name may refer to multiple microblog users. We evaluate the disambiguation for person names to demonstrate the performance of named entity disambiguation. The accuracy achieves 0.818 for all person names occurred in 271 TSC rumors. The precisions of expert finding for TSC rumors are 0.760 and 0.592 when suggesting 1 and 10 experts. The performance is slightly better than DKC rumors due to the impact of restricting candidate expert set, and is also much better than language model.

Take the rumor "Some mentally retarded children in Xiangyang, Hubei were cut out tongues and genitals" for example. We extract the named entities "Xiangyang, Hubei". By substring matching, we find microblog users such as "Unicom Xiangyang" (a mobile company), "PSB Xiangyang", and "News Broadcast Xiangyang". According to the relatedness between the given message and microblog experts, we rank "PSB Xiangyang" and "News Broadcast Xiangyang" higher than other microblog experts, which are more probable to refute the rumor.

Discussion. From the above evaluation and analysis, we validate the effectiveness of our tag-based method for expert finding from microblog users. This will greatly improve the efficiency of refuting misinformation and further prevent rumors from wide spread.

5 Related Work

Rumors have been extensively studied in sociology (Pendleton, 1998). However, quantitative studies of rumors have just begun, and microblog services provide a chance. Recently, researchers have developed different approaches to study rumors or misinformation. Some researchers devoted to finding information diffusion patterns over social networks (Kempe et al., 2003; Gruhl et al., 2004; Leskovec et al., 2009; Romero et al., 2011) and limiting the spread of misinformation by means of network structure (Budak et al., 2011). The spread patterns of rumors with respect to the content and conversations were also studied (Ennals et al., 2010; Mendoza et al., 2010; Qazvinian et al., 2011; Castillo et al., 2011). On one hand, most of these methods all focused on *external* features of rumors, which cannot ultimately determine whether a message is misinformation. On the other hand, the features can be obtained only after the information has spread over social networks.

Existing methods find experts based on either people relations (graph-based approach) or people meta-data (content-based approach). In the graph-based approach, users are ranked according to their authority scores computed by the algorithms such as HITS and PageRank (Zhang et al., 2007; Jurczyk and Agichtein, 2007). In the content-based approach, topic models (Mimno and McCallum, 2007) and language models (Balog et al., 2006; Petkova and Croft, 2006; Zhou et al., 2009; Li et al., 2011) have been explored. Due to sound foundations in statistical theory and sufficient performance, language models have been dominating techniques for expert finding (Balog, 2012). Different from existing methods, this paper proposes a tag-based method to find experts for suspected misinformation.

Conclusion and Future Work

This paper proposes a novel framework for microblog misinformation identification with the favor of experts. We focus on the task of finding experts for suspected misinformation. By categorizing rumors into two types, i.e. domain-knowledge constrained and time-space constrained, we propose a unified tag-based method to find experts from microblog users and match suspected misinformation to appropriate experts. Experiments on the real-world dataset indicate the effectiveness of our method.

This is an initial step to fight against microblog misinformation. We plan the following future work. (1) Build a real-world system to fight against rumors and evaluate the effectiveness of our method. (2) Extend the work by considering more factors, such as the spread patterns (Budak et al., 2011) and conversation patterns (Ennals et al., 2010) of rumors. (3) Improve our method by considering social networks and tag disambiguation.

Acknowledgments

This work is supported by the National Natural Science Foundation of China (NSFC) under the grant No. 61170196 and 61202140.

References

Balog, K. (2012). Expertise retrieval. *Foundations and Trends in Information Retrieval*, 6(2-3):127–256.

Balog, K., Azzopardi, L., and De Rijke, M. (2006). Formal models for expert finding in enterprise corpora. In *Proceedings of SIGIR*, pages 43–50.

Brown, P., Pietra, V., Pietra, S., and Mercer, R. (1993). The mathematics of statistical machine translation: Parameter estimation. *Computational linguistics*, 19(2):263–311.

Budak, C., Agrawal, D., and El Abbadi, A. (2011). Limiting the spread of misinformation in social networks. In *Proceedings of WWW*, pages 665–674.

Castillo, C., Mendoza, M., and Poblete, B. (2011). Information credibility on twitter. In *Proceedings of WWW*, pages 675–684.

Ennals, R., Byler, D., Agosta, J., and Rosario, B. (2010). What is disputed on the web? In *Proceedings of the 4th workshop on Information credibility*, pages 67–74.

Fan, R., Chang, K., Hsieh, C., Wang, X., and Lin, C. (2008). Liblinear: A library for large linear classification. *The Journal of Machine Learning Research*, 9:1871–1874.

Gruhl, D., Guha, R., Liben-Nowell, D., and Tomkins, A. (2004). Information diffusion through blogspace. In *Proceedings of WWW*, pages 491–501.

Gupta, M., Li, R., Yin, Z., and Han, J. (2010). Survey on social tagging techniques. *ACM SIGKDD Explorations Newsletter*, 12(1):58–72.

Jiang, W., Mi, H., and Liu, Q. (2008). Word lattice reranking for chinese word segmentation and part-of-speech tagging. In *Proceedings of COLING*, pages 385–392.

Jurczyk, P. and Agichtein, E. (2007). Discovering authorities in question answer communities by using link analysis. In *Proceedings of CIKM*, pages 919–922.

Kempe, D., Kleinberg, J., and Tardos, É. (2003). Maximizing the spread of influence through a social network. In *Proceedings of SIGKDD*, pages 137–146.

Lafferty, J., McCallum, A., and Pereira, F. (2001). Conditional random fields: Probabilistic models for segmenting and labeling sequence data. In *Proceedings of ICML*, pages 282–289.

Leskovec, J., Backstrom, L., and Kleinberg, J. (2009). Meme-tracking and the dynamics of the news cycle. In *Proceedings of SIGKDD*, pages 497–506. ACM.

Li, B., King, I., and Lyu, M. (2011). Question routing in community question answering: putting category in its place. In *Proceedings of CIKM*, pages 2041–2044.

Liu, Z., Chen, X., and Sun, M. (2011). A simple word trigger method for social tag suggestion. In *Proceedings of EMNLP*, pages 1577–1588.

Liu, Z., Chen, X., and Sun, M. (2012). Mining the interests of chinese microbloggers via keyword extraction. *Frontiers of Computer Science*, 6(1):76–87.

Mendoza, M., Poblete, B., and Castillo, C. (2010). Twitter under crisis: can we trust what we rt? In *Proceedings of the 1st workshop on social media analytics*, pages 71–79.

Mimno, D. and McCallum, A. (2007). Expertise modeling for matching papers with reviewers. In *Proceedings of SIGKDD*, pages 500–509.

Nadeau, D. and Sekine, S. (2007). A survey of named entity recognition and classification. *Lingvisticae Investigationes*, 30(1):3–26.

Och, F. and Ney, H. (2003). A systematic comparison of various statistical alignment models. *Computational linguistics*, 29(1):19–51.

Pal, A. and Counts, S. (2011). Identifying topical authorities in microblogs. In *Proceedings of WSDM*, pages 45–54.

Pendleton, S. (1998). Rumor research revisited and expanded. *Language & Communication*, pages 69–86.

Peterson, W. and Gist, N. (1951). Rumor and public opinion. *American Journal of Sociology*, pages 159–167.

Petkova, D. and Croft, W. (2006). Hierarchical language models for expert finding in enterprise corpora. In *Proceedings of ICTAI*, pages 599–608.

Qazvinian, V., Rosengren, E., Radev, D., and Mei, Q. (2011). Rumor has it: Identifying misinformation in microblogs. In *Proceedings of EMNLP*, pages 1589–1599.

Romero, D., Meeder, B., and Kleinberg, J. (2011). Differences in the mechanics of information diffusion across topics: Idioms, political hashtags, and complex contagion on twitter. In *Proceedings of WWW*, pages 695–704. ACM.

Yeung, C., Gibbins, N., and Shadbolt, N. (2007). Tag meaning disambiguation through analysis of tripartite structure of folksonomies. In *Proceedings of WI*, pages 3–6. IEEE Computer Society.

Zhang, J., Ackerman, M., and Adamic, L. (2007). Expertise networks in online communities: structure and algorithms. In *Proceedings of WWW*, pages 221–230.

Zheng, Z., Li, F., Huang, M., and Zhu, X. (2010). Learning to link entities with knowledge base. In *Proceedings of HLT-NAACL*, pages 483–491.

Zhou, Y., Cong, G., Cui, B., Jensen, C., and Yao, J. (2009). Routing questions to the right users in online communities. In *Proceedings of ICDE*, pages 700–711.

Printed from e-media with permission by:

Curran Associates, Inc.
57 Morehouse Lane
Red Hook, NY 12571

CURRAN ASSOCIATES INC. proceedings.com

Some format issues inherent in the e-media version may also appear in this print version.

Printed by Curran Associates, Inc. (2013)

Association for Computational Linguistics
209 N. Eighth Street
Stroudsburg, Pennsylvania 18360

Phone: 1-570-476-8006
Fax: 1-570-476-0860

acl@aclweb.org

Additional copies of this publication are available from:

Curran Associates, Inc.
57 Morehouse Lane
Red Hook, NY 12571 USA
Phone: 845-758-0400
Fax: 845-758-2634
Email: curran@proceedings.com
Web: www.proceedings.com

COLING 2012

24th International Conference on Computational Linguistics

Proceedings of COLING 2012: Posters

Program chairs:
Martin Kay and Christian Boitet

8-15 December 2012
Mumbai, India

Diamond sponsors

Tata Consultancy Services
Linguistic Data Consortium for Indian Languages (LDC-IL)

Gold Sponsors

Microsoft Research
Beijing Baidu Netcon Science Technology Co. Ltd.

Silver sponsors

IBM, India Private Limited
Crimson Interactive Pvt. Ltd.
Yahoo
Easy Transcription & Software Pvt. Ltd.

Table of Contents

Author Index

Improving Relative-Entropy Pruning using Statistical Significance

Wang Ling[1,2] *Nadi Tomeh*[3]
Guang Xiang[1] *Alan Black*[1] *Isabel Trancoso*[2]
(1)Language Technologies Institute, Carnegie Mellon University, Pittsburgh, PA, USA
(2)L^2F Spoken Systems Lab, INESC-ID, Lisboa, Portugal
(3)LIMSI-CNRS and Université Paris-Sud Orsay, France
{lingwang,guangx,awb}@cs.cmu.edu, nadi.tomeh@limsi.fr,
isabel.trancoso@inesc-id.pt

Abstract

Relative Entropy-based pruning has been shown to be efficient for pruning language models for more than a decade ago. Recently, this method has been applied to Phrase-based Machine Translation, and results suggest that this method is comparable the state-of-art pruning method based on significance tests. In this work, we show that these 2 methods are effective in pruning different types of phrase pairs. On one hand, relative entropy pruning searches for phrase pairs that can be composed using smaller constituents with a small or no loss in probability. On the other hand, significance pruning removes phrase pairs that are likely to be spurious. Then, we show that these methods can be combined in order to produce better results, over both metrics when used individually.

Proceedings of COLING 2012: Posters, pages 713–722,
COLING 2012, Mumbai, December 2012.

1 Introduction

Statistical Machine Translation systems are generally built on large amounts of parallel data. Typically, the training sentences are first aligned at the word level, then all phrase pairs that are consistent with the word alignment are extracted, scored and stored in the phrase table. While such extraction criterion performs well in practice, it produces translation models that are unnecessarily large with many phrase pairs that are useless for translation. This is undesirable at decoding time, since it leads to more search errors due to the large search space. Furthermore, larger models are more expensive to store, which limits the portability of such models to smaller devices.

Pruning is one approach to address this problem, where models are made more compact by discarding entries from the model, based on additional selection criteria. The challenge in this task is to choose the entries that will least degenerate the quality of the task for which the model is used. For language models, an effective algorithm based on relative entropy is described in (Seymore and Rosenfeld, 1996; Stolcke, 1998; Moore and Quirk, 2009). In these approaches, a criteria based on the KL divergence is applied, so that higher order n-grams are only included in the model when they provide enough additional information to the model, given the lower order n-grams. Recently, this concept was applied for translation model pruning (Ling et al., 2012; Zens et al., 2012), and results indicate that this method yields a better phrase table size and translation quality ratio than previous methods, such as the well known method in (Johnson et al., 2007), which uses the Fisher's exact test to calculate how well a phrase pair is supported by data.

In this work, we attempt to improve the relative entropy model, by combining it with the significance based approach presented in (Johnson et al., 2007).The main motivation is that, as suggested in (Ling et al., 2012), relative entropy and significance based methods are complementary. On one hand, relative entropy aims at pruning phrase pairs that can be reproduced using smaller constituents with a small or no loss in terms of the models predictions. On the other hand, significance pruning aims at removing phrase pairs that are spurious, and are originated from incorrect alignments at sentence or word level. This indicates that both methods can be combined to obtain better results. We propose a log-linear interpolation of the two metrics to achieve a better trade off between the number of phrase pairs and the translation quality.

This paper is structured as follows: Section 2 includes a brief summary of relative entropy and significance pruning approaches in sub-sections 2.1 and 2.2. Sub-section 2.3 analyses both algorithms and preceeds our combination approach in sub-section 2.4. The results obtained with the EUROPARL corpus (Koehn, 2005) are shown in Section 3. Finally, we conclude and present directions for future research in Section 4.

2 Combining Relative Entropy and Significance Pruning

In principle, any method of evaluation of phrase pairs can be used as the basis for pruning. This includes phrase counts and probabilities (Koehn et al., 2003), statistical significance tests (Johnson et al., 2007), and relative entropy scores (Ling et al., 2012; Zens et al., 2012) and many others (Deng et al., 2008; Venugopal et al., 2003; Tomeh et al., 2011), in addition to the features typically found in phrase tables (Och et al., 2004; Chiang et al., 2009). Each method reflects some characteristics of phrase pairs that are not sought by the other, and hence trying to combine them is a tempting idea. (Deng et al., 2008) incorporate several features into a log-linear model parametrized with y_k that are tuned, along with the extraction threshold, to maximize a translation quality, which makes the procedure extremely expensive. A similar model is used in (Venugopal et al., 2003) without any parameter tuning. (Zettlemoyer and Moore, 2007) use an already tuned model (using MERT) in a competitive linking algorithm to keep the best one-to-one phrase matching in each training sentence. In our work we favor efficiency and we focus on relative entropy and significance pruning, which can be efficiently computed, without the need to external information. They also deliver good practical performance.

2.1 Relative Entropy Pruning

Relative entropy pruning for translation models (Ling et al., 2012; Zens et al., 2012) has a solid foundation on information theory. The goal in these methods is to find a pruned model $P_p(t|s)$ that yields predictions that are as close as possible as the original model $P(t|s)$. More formally, we want to minimize the relative entropy or KL divergence between these models, expressed as follows:

$$D(P_p||P) = -\sum_{s,t} P(s,t) log \frac{P_p(t|s)}{P(t|s)} \tag{1}$$

In another words, for each phrase pair with source s and target t, we calculate the log difference between their probabilities $log \frac{P_p(t|s)}{P(t|s)}$. This value is then weighted by the empirical distribution $P(s,t)$, so that phrase pairs that are more likely to be observed in the data are less likely to be pruned. The empirical distribution is given as:

$$P(s,t) = \frac{C(s,t)}{N} \tag{2}$$

Where $C(s,t)$ denotes, the number of sentence pairs where s and t are observed, and N denotes the number of sentence pairs.

Computing $P_p(t|s)$ is the most computationally expensive operation in this model, since it involves finding all possible derivations of a phrase pair using smaller units, which involves a forced decoding step (Schwartz, 2008).

While minimizing $D(P_p||P)$ would lead to optimal results, such optimization is computationally infeasible. Thus, an approximation is the find the local values for each phrase pair:

$$\text{RelEnt(s,t)} = -P(s,t) log \frac{P_p(t|s)}{P(t|s)} \tag{3}$$

This score can be viewed as the relative entropy between $P_p(t|s)$ and $P(t|s)$, if only the phrase pair with source s and target t is pruned. The problem with this approximation is that, we might assume a given phrase pair A can be pruned, because it can be composed by phrase pairs B and C, only to discover later that B is also pruned.

2.2 Significance Pruning

Significance pruning of phrase tables (Johnson et al., 2007; Tomeh et al., 2009) relies on a statistical test that assesses the strength of the association between the source and target phrases in a phrase pair. Such association can be represented using a two-by-two contingency table:

$C(s,t)$	$C(s)-C(s,t)$
$C(t)-C(s,t)$	$N-C(s)-C(t)+C(s,t)$

where N is the size of the training parallel corpus, $C(s)$ is the count of the source phrase, $C(t)$ is the count of the target phrase, and $C(s,t)$ is the count of the co-occurences of s and t. The probability of this particular table is given by the the hypergeometric distribution:

$$p_h(C(s,t)) = \frac{\binom{C(s)}{C(s,t)}\binom{N-C(s)}{C(t)-C(s,t)}}{\binom{N}{C(t)}}.$$

The p-value correponds to the probability that s and t co-occur at least $C(s,t)$ times only due to chance. It is computed by Fisher's exact test by summing the probabilities of all contingency tables that are at least as extreme:

$$\text{p-value}(C(s,t)) = \sum_{k=C(s,t)}^{\infty} p_h(k).$$

We define the association score to be $-$ log(p-value) which varies between 0 and $infty$. The higher the association score, the less likely this phrases s and t co-occurred with the observed count $C(s,t)$ by chance.

2.3 Error Analysis

Table 1 shows examples of phrase table entries that are likely to be pruned for each method for a translation model using he EUROPARL dataset with 1.2M sentence pairs. The phrase pairs were chosen from the list of phrase pairs that would be pruned if we only pruned 1% of the table. We can see that both methods aim at pruning different types of phrase pairs.

In significance pruning, we observe that most of the filtered phrase pairs are spurious phrase pairs. These phrase pairs are generally originated from sentence level mis-alignments, which can occur in automatically aligned corpora. Another possible origin for spurious phrase pairs are Word-alignment errors. We can see that relative entropy pruning is not the best approach to address with these problems. For instance, if we calculate the divergence $log\frac{P_p(t|s)}{P(t|s)}$ for the phrase pair with source "it" and target "+", we will obtain $log(0)$, since it is cannot be composed using smaller units. Thus, it is unlikely that these phrase pairs will be pruned by relative pruning. Note, that while it is true that spurious phrase pairs will have a low empirical distribution probability, the same is true will longer and sparser phrase pairs that are actually correct, and in such cases the relative entropy model will prefer to prune the longer phrase pairs, since they can be composed using smaller constituents, which is not desired.

On the other hand, there is nothing intrinsically wrong in the phrase pairs that are pruned by relative entropy pruning. However, these phrase pairs are redundant and can be easily translated using smaller units. For instance, it is not surprising that the source phrase "0.005 %" can be translated "0.005 %", using the smaller units, "0.005" to "0.005" and "%" to "%", since it is unlikely that "0.005" or "%" to be translated another target phrase, or have a non-monotonous reordering. In significance pruning, for a moderately large corpora, it is unlikely that this phrase pair would be pruned early, since it is likely that the phrase pair is well supported by data.

Significance		Relative Entropy	
English	French	English	French
it	+	2 6 8 10 and	2 6 8 10 et
with	, entre	0,005 %	0.005 %
a	, un accord a été	! ! !	! ! !

Table 1: Selected examples of phrase pairs that have low scores according to Significance pruning (Left) and Relative Entropy pruning (Right). The examples are selected from the model built using the EUROPARL training dataset for French and English.

Thus, we can see that it is prominent that relative entropy and significance methods are complementary in terms of what types of phrase pairs that are pruned. We can see that all the phrase pairs pruned by significance pruning in the table would be unlikely to be pruned by relative entropy pruning, since these phrase pairs only have one word in the target side and so they cannot be decomposed into smaller units. On the other hand, it is also unlikely that the phrase pairs that are pruned using relative entropy, are pruned by significance pruning, since these phrases are well aligned and likely to be well supported by data.

2.4 Combination Method

In our work, we will attempt to achieve a better trade off between the number of phrase pairs that are pruned due to their redundancy and due to their spurious nature.

There are many different approaches that can be taken to combine these two scores. For instance, in Phrase-based machine translation multiple features are combined using a log-linear model. Thus, we could use a similar approach and set a weight α and combine the two scores as follows:

$$Score(s,t) = \alpha RelEnt(s,t) + (1-\alpha)Sig(s,t) \tag{4}$$

Where $RelEnt(s,t) = -P(\tilde{s},\tilde{t})log\frac{P_p(t|s)}{P(t|s)}$ is the relative entropy score and $Sig(s,t) = -log$ p-value$(C(s,t))$ is the significance score of the phrase pair with source s and target t.

However, one problem with this approach is that classification boundary for these two features does not seem to be linear from our analysis, especially since these features seem to be orthogonal. For instance, suppose that we have a phrase pair with a very high score using relative entropy (for instance 300), meaning that the phrase pair is definitely not redundant. However, in terms of p-value, the phrase pair is scored with a with a extremely low value (such as 10), which means that it is very likely that the phrase pair is not well-formed. If we simply interpolate the scores, we would expect the score of the phrase pair to be 155, with $\alpha = 0.5$, which is an average score. This is not necessarily a good decision, because regardless of how unique a phrase pair is, if the phrase pair is spurious it should not be kept in the model. The opposite is also true, if a phrase pair is well-formed, but it can be built using smaller phrase pairs, it means that it can be removed, since it is not useful in the model.

In another words, good phrase pairs must be well-formed and not redundant. Thus, we propose to select the minimum of the two scores rather than their average. More formally, we score each phrase pair as:

$$Score(s,t) = min(\alpha RelEnt(s,t), (1-\alpha)Sig(s,t)) \quad (5)$$

We still apply the scaling factor α, so that we can specify which score has a higher weight.

Using this score, for the example above, the phrase pair would be scored with the significance score of 10.

3 Experimental Results

3.1 Data Sets

Experiments were performed using the publicly available EUROPARL (Koehn, 2005) corpora for the English-French language pair. From this corpus, 1.2M sentence pairs were selected for training, 2000 for tuning and another 2000 for testing.

3.2 Baseline System

The baseline translation system was trained using a conventional pipeline similar to the one described in (Koehn et al., 2003).

First, the word alignments were generated using IBM model 4.

Then, the translation model was generate using the phrase extraction algorithm (Paul et al., 2010)(Koehn et al., 2007). The maximum size of the phrase pairs is set to 7, both for the source and the target language. The model uses as features:

- Translation probability
- Reverse translation probability
- Lexical translation probability
- Reverse lexical translation probability
- Phrase penalty

The reordering model is built using the lexicalized reordering model described in (Axelrod et al., 2005), with MSD (mono, swap and discontinuous) reordering features for orientations.

All the translation and reordering features are considered during the calculation of the relative entropy. As in (Zens et al., 2012), we removed all singleton phrase pairs from the phrase table. This will lower the effectiveness of significance pruning, since a large amount of least significant phrase pairs will be removed a priori. The filtered translation model contains, approximately 50 million phrase pairs.

As language model, a 5-gram model with Kneser-ney smoothing was used.

The baseline model was tuned using MERT tuning (Och, 2003). We did not rerun tuning again after pruning to avoid adding noise to the results.

Finally, we present the results evaluated with BLEU-4 (Papineni et al., 2002).

After computing the negative log likelihood of both scores, we also rescale both score's values by mean, so that scores will have similar values. This step is performed so the interpolation weights, in the results appear more intuitive.

3.3 Results

We can see the results in table 2, where the first two rows, represent the BLEU scores for relative entropy pruning and significance pruning, respectively. Then, we have the scores obtained using the scorer in 4 of these 2 scores, with α weights at intervals of 0.1. Finally, we have the scores using the scorer 5, also with the weight α set at intervals of 0.1.

From the results, we observe that using relative entropy pruning, we obtain better translation quality in terms of BLEU than significance pruning until 20%, where significance pruning works considerably better. This is because, at 20%, relative entropy pruning starts having to discard phrase pairs that have no smaller constituents, relying only on the empirical distribution. Thus, we would like to perform better by considering both scores.

However, we can see that using linear interpolation does not improve the results. This is because, as stated before, the two scores evaluate different aspects of phrase pairs. Thus, performing a weighted average of these two scores will simply degenerate the precision of the pruning decision. For instance, if one phrase pair has a 0 value according to relative entropy, implying that it is redundant, while the significance score is 300, because the phrase pair is well aligned, a uniform linear interpolation would give this phrase pair the score of 150. This is not the effect we desire, since if a phrase pair is classified is classified as redundant, it can be discarded regardless of how well-formed it is. The same applies to phrase pairs that are not-redundant but not significant. As we can see from the results, we can obtain results that range between the scores for using significance pruning and relative entropy pruning separately, but not improve over both of them.

On the other hand, we can see that using an weighted minimum of the 2 scores achieves much better results. We can see that results are equally good at higher phrase table sizes as the relative entropy. This indicates that at higher phrase table sizes, the pruning choices are governed by relative entropy pruning. At lower phrase tables sizes, we can see that we can achieve better results than each of the methods separately, where the 2 scores are combined to make better pruning decisions. Specifically, 20% of the phrase table size, the combined method for the best α (0.5) achives 27.16 BLEU points which is 0.3(1%) points over the significance pruning method and 1.51(6%) points over relative entropy pruning.

Conclusion

In this work, we evaluated two state of the art methods for translation model pruning, one based on significance tests and one based on relative entropy. While the former is effective at removing phrase pairs that are result of misalignments, the latter aims at removing phrase pairs that are redundant, since they can be formed using other phrase pairs. We showed that 2 the methods are complementary and a better pruning methodology can be obtained by combining them. We showed empirically that using linear interpolation is not the best approach to combine these scores, and better results can be obtained by taking the minimum from both scores at each data point.

The code used for calculating relative entropy and combining scores presented in this paper is currently integrated with MOSES[1].

Acknowledgments

This work was partially supported by FCT (INESC-ID multiannual funding) through the PIDDAC Program funds, and also through projects CMU-PT/HuMach/0039/2008 and CMU-PT/0005/2007. The PhD thesis of Wang Ling is supported by FCT grant SFRH/BD/51157/2010.

[1] available at https://github.com/moses-smt/mosesdecoder

Experiment	100%	80%	60%	40%	20%
Relative Entropy	27.50	**27.50**	**27.51**	27.37	25.65
Significance	27.50	27.39	27.24	27.20	26.86
Avg($\alpha = 0.9$)	27.50	27.48	27.48	27.35	26.21
Avg($\alpha = 0.8$)	27.50	27.48	27.46	27.36	26.21
Avg($\alpha = 0.7$)	27.50	27.49	27.46	27.34	26.21
Avg($\alpha = 0.6$)	27.50	27.49	27.43	27.32	26.21
Avg($\alpha = 0.5$)	27.50	27.48	27.43	27.33	26.21
Avg($\alpha = 0.4$)	27.50	27.47	27.44	27.31	26.21
Avg($\alpha = 0.3$)	27.50	27.48	27.36	27.31	26.21
Avg($\alpha = 0.2$)	27.50	27.47	27.38	27.31	26.21
Avg($\alpha = 0.1$)	27.50	27.46	27.37	27.31	26.21
Min($\alpha = 0.9$)	27.50	**27.50**	**27.51**	27.37	27.06
Min($\alpha = 0.8$)	27.50	**27.50**	**27.51**	**27.42**	27.15
Min($\alpha = 0.7$)	27.50	**27.50**	**27.51**	27.39	27.12
Min($\alpha = 0.6$)	27.50	**27.50**	**27.51**	27.38	27.11
Min($\alpha = 0.5$)	27.50	**27.50**	**27.51**	27.35	**27.16**
Min($\alpha = 0.4$)	27.50	**27.50**	**27.51**	27.36	27.14
Min($\alpha = 0.3$)	27.50	**27.50**	27.49	27.39	27.11
Min($\alpha = 0.2$)	27.50	**27.50**	27.49	27.41	27.15
Min($\alpha = 0.1$)	27.50	**27.50**	27.48	27.37	27.11

Table 2: Results for the EN-FR EUROPARL CORPORA. Each Column represents the size of the phrase table and each row represents a different pruning score. Each cell represents the BLEU score using a 2000 sentence pair test set.

References

Axelrod, A., Mayne, R. B., Callison-burch, C., Osborne, M., and Talbot, D. (2005). Edinburgh system description for the 2005 iwslt speech translation evaluation. In *Proc. International Workshop on Spoken Language Translation (IWSLT)*.

Chiang, D., Knight, K., and Wang, W. (2009). 11,001 new features for statistical machine translation. In *Proceedings of Human Language Technologies: The 2009 Annual Conference of the North American Chapter of the Association for Computational Linguistics*, NAACL '09, pages 218–226. Association for Computational Linguistics.

Deng, Y., Xu, J., and Gao, Y. (2008). Phrase table training for precision and recall: What makes a good phrase and a good phrase pair? In *Proceedings of ACL-08: HLT*, pages 81–88, Columbus, Ohio. Association for Computational Linguistics.

Johnson, J. H., Martin, J., Foster, G., and Kuhn, R. (2007). Improving translation quality by discarding most of the phrasetable. In *Proceedings of EMNLP-CoNLL 07*, pages 967–975.

Koehn, P. (2005). Europarl: A Parallel Corpus for Statistical Machine Translation. In *Conference Proceedings: the tenth Machine Translation Summit*, pages 79–86, Phuket, Thailand. AAMT, AAMT.

Koehn, P., Hoang, H., Birch, A., Callison-Burch, C., Zens, R., Aachen, R., Constantin, A., Federico, M., Bertoldi, N., Dyer, C., Cowan, B., Shen, W., Moran, C., and Bojar, O. (2007). Moses: Open source toolkit for statistical machine translation. In *Proceedings of the 45th Annual Meeting of the Association for Computational Linguistics Companion Volume Proceedings of the Demo and Poster Sessions*, pages 177–180, Prague, Czech Republic. Association for Computational Linguistics.

Koehn, P., Och, F. J., and Marcu, D. (2003). Statistical phrase-based translation. In *Proceedings of the 2003 Conference of the North American Chapter of the Association for Computational Linguistics on Human Language Technology - Volume 1*, NAACL '03, pages 48–54, Morristown, NJ, USA. Association for Computational Linguistics.

Ling, W., Graça, J., Trancoso, I., and Black, A. (2012). Entropy-based pruning for phrase-based machine translation. In *EMNLP-CoNLL*, pages 962–971.

Moore, R. C. and Quirk, C. (2009). Less is more: significance-based n-gram selection for smaller, better language models. In *Proceedings of the 2009 Conference on Empirical Methods in Natural Language Processing: Volume 2 - Volume 2*, EMNLP '09, pages 746–755, Stroudsburg, PA, USA. Association for Computational Linguistics.

Och, F. J. (2003). Minimum error rate training in statistical machine translation. In *Proceedings of the 41st Annual Meeting on Association for Computational Linguistics - Volume 1*, ACL '03, pages 160–167, Stroudsburg, PA, USA. Association for Computational Linguistics.

Och, F. J., Gildea, D., Khudanpur, S., Sarkar, A., Yamada, K., Fraser, A., Kumar, S., Shen, L., Smith, D. A., Eng, K., Jain, V., Jin, Z., and Radev, D. (2004). A smorgasbord of features for statistical machine translation. In *Proceedings of the Joint Conference on Human Language Technologies and the Annual Meeting of the North American Chapter of the Association of Computational Linguistics (HLT-NAACL)*.

Papineni, K., Roukos, S., Ward, T., and Zhu, W.-J. (2002). Bleu: a method for automatic evaluation of machine translation. In *Proc. of the 40th Annual Meeting on ACL*, pages 311–318.

Paul, M., Federico, M., and StÃ¼ker, S. (2010). Overview of the iwslt 2010 evaluation campaign. In *IWSLT '10: International Workshop on Spoken Language Translation*, pages 3–27.

Schwartz, L. (2008). Multi-source translation methods. In *Proceedings of AMTA*, pages 279–288.

Seymore, K. and Rosenfeld, R. (1996). Scalable backoff language models. In *Proceedings of ICSLP*, pages 232–235.

Stolcke, A. (1998). Entropy-based pruning of backoff language models. In *Proc. DARPA Broadcast News Transcription and Understanding Workshop*, pages 270–274.

Tomeh, N., Cancedda, N., and Dymetman, M. (2009). Complexity-based phrase-table filtering for statistical machine translation. In *MT Summit XII: proceedings of the twelfth Machine Translation Summit*, pages 144–151, Ottawa, Ontario, Canada.

Tomeh, N., Turchi, M., Wisniewski, G., Allauzen, A., and Yvon, F. (2011). How good are your phrases? assessing phrase quality with single class classification. In Hwang, M.-Y. and Stueker, S., editors, *Proceedings of the eigth International Workshop on Spoken Language Translation (IWSLT)*, pages 261–268, San Francisco, CA.

Venugopal, A., Vogel, S., and Waibel, A. (2003). Effective phrase translation extraction from alignment models. In Hinrichs, E. and Roth, D., editors, *Proceedings of the 41st Annual Meeting of the Association for Computational Linguistics*, pages 319–326.

Zens, R., Stanton, D., and Xu, P. (2012). A systematic comparison of phrase table pruning techniques. In *Proceedings of the 2012 Joint Conference on Empirical Methods in Natural Language Processing and Computational Natural Language Learning*, pages 972–983, Jeju Island, Korea.

Zettlemoyer, L. S. and Moore, R. C. (2007). Selective phrase pair extraction for improved statistical machine translation. In *Human Language Technologies 2007: The Conference of the North American Chapter of the Association for Computational Linguistics; Companion Volume, Short Papers on XX*, NAACL '07, pages 209–212, Morristown, NJ, USA. Association for Computational Linguistics.

Expected Error Minimization with Ultraconservative Update for SMT

Lemao LIU[1], *Tiejun ZHAO*[1], *Taro WATANABE*[2], *Hailong CAO*[1], *Conghui ZHU*[1]
(1) School of Computer Science and Technology
Harbin Institute of Technology, Harbin, China
(2) National Institute of Information and Communication Technology
3-5 Hikari-dai, Seika-cho, Soraku-gun, Kyoto, Japan
{lmliu,tjzhao,hailong,chzhu}@mtlab.hit.edu.cn, taro.watanabe@nict.go.jp

ABSTRACT
Minimum error rate training is a popular method for parameter tuning in statistical machine translation (SMT). However, the optimization objective function may change drastically at each optimization step, which may induce MERT instability. We propose an alternative tuning method based on an ultraconservative update, in which the combination of an expected task loss and the distance from the parameters in the previous round are minimized with a variant of gradient descent. Experiments on test datasets of both Chinese-to-English and Spanish-to-English translation show that our method can achieve improvements over MERT under the Moses system.

KEYWORDS: statistical machine translation; tuning; minimum error rate training; ultraconservative update; expected BLEU.

Proceedings of COLING 2012: Posters, pages 723–732,
COLING 2012, Mumbai, December 2012.

1 Introduction

Minimum error rate training (Och, 2003), MERT, is an important component of statistical machine translation (SMT), and it has been the most popular method for tuning parameters for SMT systems. One of its major contributions is the use of an evaluation metric, such as BLEU (Papineni et al., 2002), as a direct loss function during its optimization procedure by interchanging decoding and optimization steps in each round.

While MERT is successful in practice, it is known to be unstable (Clark et al., 2011). At the optimization step in each round, MERT tries to repeatedly optimize a loss function defined by the k-best candidate lists. Since new k-best lists are generated and merged with the previously generated lists at each round, the optimization objective function may change drastically between two adjacent rounds (Pauls et al., 2009), and the optimized weights of these two rounds may also be far from each other.

Motivated by the above observation, this paper investigates a new tuning approach under the k-best lists framework, instead of the lattices or hypergraphs framework as Macherey et al. (2008) and Kumar et al. (2009), to achieve a more stable loss function between optimization steps. We propose an expected loss-based ultraconservative update method, in which an expected loss is minimized using an ultraconservative update strategy (Crammer and Singer, 2003; Crammer et al., 2006). In the optimization step, we iteratively learn the weight which should not only minimize the error rates as in MERT but also not be far from the weight learned at the previous optimization step. Instead of using the L_2 in Euclidean space to describe the distances between the two weights as in the Margin Infused Relaxed Algorithm (MIRA), we define a new distance metric inspired by the max-posterior probability decoding strategy in translation.

Compared with MERT, in which an exact line search is difficult to implement, our method is easier since we employ a gradient-based algorithm, which is simple but proved to be successful in other tasks such as tagging or parsing. Further, experiments on Chinese-to-English and Spanish-to-English show that our method outperforms MERT.

2 MERT Revisited

MERT is the most popular method to tune parameters for SMT systems. The main idea behind it is that it iteratively optimizes the weight such that, after re-ranking a k-best list of a given development set with this weight, the error of the resulting 1-best list is minimal.

The whole tuning algorithm with MERT is described in Algorithm 1. It requires a development set $\{\langle f_i; \mathbf{r}_i \rangle\}_{i=1}^{n}$ with f_i as the source sentence and $\mathbf{r}_i$ as its reference, initial weight W_{init} and the maximal iterations K. It initializes some parameters in line 1: iteration index k; the current weight W_k; the accumulated k-best list $\mathbf{c}_i$. For each optimization step $k \leq K$, it repeatedly performs decoding and training during the loop from line 2 to line 9: for each sentence f_i, it decodes to get $\mathbf{tc}_i$ and updates $\mathbf{c}_i$; it minimizes the error rates to obtain W_{k+1}. At the end of the algorithm, it returns W_K.

The definition of **Loss** in line 7 of Algorithm 1 is formalized as follows:

$$\mathbf{Loss}_{error}\Big(\big\{\mathbf{r}_i; \hat{e}(f_i; W)\big\}_{i=1}^{n}\Big), \tag{1}$$

Algorithm 1 TUNING WITH MERT

Input: $\{\langle f_i; \mathbf{r}_i \rangle\}_{i=1}^n; W_{init}; K$
Output: W

$k = 1; W_k = W_{init}; \{\mathbf{c}_i = \emptyset\}_{i=1}^n$ //initialization, $\mathbf{c}_i$ the accumulated k-best list for f_i
while $k \leq K$ **do**
  for all sentence f_i such that $1 \leq i \leq n$ **do**
    Decode f_i with W_k to get $\mathbf{tc}_i$; // $\mathbf{tc}_i$ translation candidates of k-best decoding
    $\mathbf{c}_i = \mathbf{c}_i \bigcup \mathbf{tc}_i$;
  end for
  Set W_{k+1} as the weight according to a **Loss** of error rates defined on $\mathbf{tc}_i$ and W;
  k++;
end while
$W = W_K$;

with

$$\hat{e}(f; W) = \text{argmax}_e \mathbf{P}(e|f; W) = \text{argmax}_e \frac{\exp\{W \cdot h(f,e)\}}{\sum_{e'} \exp\{W \cdot h(f,e')\}} = \text{argmax}_e \{W \cdot h(f,e)\}, \quad (2)$$

where $h(f, e)$ denotes the feature vector of f and its translation e. $\mathbf{Loss}_{error}$ is usually set as Corpus-BLEU (exactly speaking, minus BLEU). Eq. 2 describes the maximal posterior decoding strategy.

As mentioned in Section 1, since at each optimization step a new k-best list $\mathbf{tc}_i$ is generated and merged with $\mathbf{c}_i$, the optimization objective will change between two adjacent optimization steps. This can increase the instability of MERT. In the next section, we will investigate the strategy of ultraconservative update to address this issue.

3 Expected Loss Based Ultraconservative Update

Ultraconservative Update is an efficient way to consider the trade-off between the amount of progress made on each round and the amount of information retained from previous rounds. On one hand, the weight update should assure better performance to improve optimization. On the other hand, the new weight must stay as close as possible to the weight optimized on the last round, thus retaining the information learned on previous rounds.

3.1 Objective Function

Suppose W_k be the weight learnt from last optimization step, $\{\langle f_i; \mathbf{c}_i; \mathbf{r}_i \rangle\}_{i=1}^n$ a translation space obtained with W_k, where f_i is a source sentence, $\mathbf{c}_i$ is a set of translation candidates and $\mathbf{r}_i$ is a set of references for f_i. Now we want to optimize W_{k+1} using the idea of ultraconservative update to the objective of MERT, and we obtain the following objective function:

$$\mathbf{d}(W, W_k) + \lambda \mathbf{Loss}_{error}\Big(\{\mathbf{r}_i; \hat{e}(f_i; W)\}_{i=1}^n\Big), \quad (3)$$

where $\mathbf{d}(W, W_k)$ is a distance function of a pair of weights and it is used to penalize a weight far away from W_k. $\mathbf{Loss}_{error}$ is the objective function of MERT as defined in Eq. 1. $\lambda \geq 0$ is the regularization penalty. When $\lambda \rightarrow \infty$ Eq. 3 goes back to the objective function of MERT.

Because the first term $\mathbf{d}$ in Eq. 3 is not piecewise linear in respect to W, the exact line search routine in MERT does not hold anymore. Generally, it is not easy to directly minimize Eq. 3. Motivated by (Och, 2003; Smith and Eisner, 2006; Zens et al., 2007), we use the expected loss to substitute the direct loss in Eq. 3 and we obtain the objective function as follows:

$$\mathbf{d}(W, W_k) + \frac{\lambda}{n}\sum_{i=1}^{n}\sum_{e\in\mathbf{c}_i}\mathbf{Loss}_{error}(\mathbf{r}_i; e)\mathbf{P}_{\alpha}(e|f_i; W), \tag{4}$$

with

$$\mathbf{P}_{\alpha}(e|f_i; W) = \frac{\exp[\alpha W \cdot h(f_i, e)]}{\sum_{e'\in\mathbf{c}_i}\exp[\alpha W \cdot h(f_i, e')]},$$

where $\alpha > 0$ is a real number, each $h(f_i, e)$ is a feature vector, and $\mathbf{d}$ is a distance metric defined on a pair of weights. $\mathbf{Loss}_{error}(\mathbf{r}_i; e)$ in Eq. 4 is a sentence-wise direct loss, and in this paper we used a variant of sentence BLEU proposed by Chiang et al. (2008) which smoothes BLEU statistics with pseudo-document.

3.2 Distance Metric Based on Projection

Euclidean distance (L_2 norm) is usually employed as in MIRA (Watanabe et al., 2007; Chiang et al., 2008). In this section we will specifically investigate another metric for ultraconservative update in SMT.

In log-linear based translation models, since the decoding strategy is the maximal posterior probability, the translation results are the same for the weight W and its positive multiplication (see Eq. 2). Therefore, for a translation decoder, we wish that the distance of two weights satisfies the following property: the smaller the distance between them is, the more similar the translation results decoded with them are. However, L_2 norm does not satisfy this property. Inspired by this observation, we define the distance[1] between W and W' as follows:

$$\mathbf{d}(W, W') = \begin{cases} 0, \text{ either } W \text{ or } W' \text{ is } 0 & , \\ \frac{1}{2}\|\frac{W}{\|W\|} - \frac{W'}{\|W'\|}\|^2, \text{ otherwise} & , \end{cases} \tag{5}$$

For the sake of simplicity, if we constrain the feasible region to $\{W : \|W\| = 1\}$ and substitute the above $\mathbf{d}$ in Eq. 4, we derive the following optimization problem:

$$\begin{aligned} &\min_{W}\left\{\frac{1}{2}\|W - W_k\|^2 + \frac{\lambda}{n}\sum_{i=1}^{n}\sum_{e\in\mathbf{c}_i}\mathbf{Loss}_{error}(\mathbf{r}_i; e)\mathbf{P}_{\alpha}(e|f_i; W)\right\} \\ s.t. & \\ &\|W\| = 1, \end{aligned} \tag{6}$$

where we assume $\|W_k\| = 1$, otherwise we can normalize it instead. Since Eq. 6 is defined on the expected loss and ultraconservative update, we call it the expected loss based ultraconservative update, or ELBUU.

[1] Strictly speaking, it is not the traditional distance metric because it violates the property of positive definiteness. For example, when one of W and W' is zero and the other is not, it does not hold that $\mathbf{d}(W, W') = 0$ induces $W = W'$. However, in this paper, our attention is focused on the non-zero weights.

3.3 Gradient Descent with Projection

We employ the gradient projection method (Horst and Tuy, 1996) to optimize Eq. 6. The gradient projection method contains two main operations, one of which is the gradient descent for the objective function and the other is the projection of the weight into the constraint area. The first operation is easy to implement. For the second one, taking the derivative of $\mathbf{P}_\alpha(e|f_i;W)$ with respect to W , the following equation holds:

$$\nabla_W \mathbf{P}_\alpha(e|f;W) = \alpha \mathbf{P}_\alpha(e|f;W)\Big(h(f,e) - E_{\mathbf{P}_\alpha(\cdot|f;W)}(h(f,\cdot)\Big), \tag{7}$$

with

$$E_{\mathbf{P}_\alpha(\cdot|f;W)}(h(f,\cdot)) = \sum_{e'} \mathbf{P}_\alpha(e'|f;W) * h(f,e'),$$

where $E_{\mathbf{P}_\alpha(\cdot|f;W)}$ can be interpreted as the expectation of feature function $h(f,\cdot)$ according to the distribution of $\mathbf{P}_\alpha(\cdot|f;W)$. Then, the derivative of the objective function in Eq. 6 is as follows:

$$\Delta = W - W_k + \frac{\lambda}{n}\sum_{i=1}^{n}\sum_{e} \mathbf{Loss}_{error}(\mathbf{r}_i,e)\nabla_W \mathbf{P}_\alpha(e|f;W). \tag{8}$$

Algorithm 2 gives the pseudo-code of the gradient projection method to optimize Eq. 6. In the Algorithm,$\eta > 0$ is the learning rate , $\epsilon > 0$ is the threshold, and other notations are the same as before. The loop (line 2-10) is the whole iteration step, which contains a gradient descent operation in line 3 and a projection operation[2] in line 4-8. At the end of this algorithm, it returns W_{k+1}.

Algorithm 2 Gradient Descent with Projection

Input: $W_k, \lambda, \epsilon, \alpha, \eta,$

Output: W_{k+1}

1: $W_k^0 \neq W_k; W_k^1 = W_k; t = 1; \eta_1 = 1/\eta;$ // initialization
2: **while** $(||W_k^t - W_k^{t-1}|| > \epsilon)$ **do**
3: $W_k^{t+1} = W_k^t - \eta_t \Delta$ according to Eq. 8; // gradient operation
4: **if** $W_k^{t+1} \neq 0$ **then**
5: $W_k^{t+1} = W_k^{t+1}/||W_k^{t+1}||$; //projection operation
6: **else**
7: Reset W_k^{t+1} $s.t.$ $||W_k^{t+1}|| = 1$;
8: **end if**
9: $t{+}{+}; \eta_t = 1/(\eta \cdot t)$;
10: **end while**
11: $W_{k+1} = W_k^t$;

[2]Actually, in our experiments, W does not arrive at the point 0 during the iteration steps.

Methods	NIST02(Dev)	NIST03	NIST04	NIST05	NIST06	NIST08
MERT	30.39	26.45	29.47	26.31	25.34	19.07
ELBUU	30.06	27.36^{++}	29.89	27.03^{+}	26.30^{++}	19.79^{+}

Table 1: Comparison of two tuning methods, MERT and ELBUU, on Chinese-to-English translation tasks. + or ++ means the ELBUU method is significantly better than MERT with confidence $p < 0.05$ or $p < 0.01$, respectively.

3.4 Tuning with ELBUU

Similar to tuning algorithm MERT, i.e. **Algorithm** 1, our tuning algorithm ELBUU repeatedly performs decoding and optimization. In detail, Our ELBUU can be obtained from **Algorithm** 1 as follows: by inserting the **Algorithm** 2 to substitute for line 7 in **Algorithm** 1, and modifying the returned weight as averaged weight[3] at the end of the algorithm, one can obtain the ELBUU tuning algorithm.

Our method ELBUU is similar to the MIRA in (Watanabe et al., 2007; Chiang et al., 2008), since both of them employ a strategy of ultraconservative update. However, there are also some differences between them. ELBUU optimizes the expected BLEU, a loss more approximate towards Corpus-BLEU compared with the generalized hinge loss, and it utilizes the projection distance metric instead of L_2 as with MIRA. Further, ELBUU is a MERT-like batch mode which ultraconservatively updates the weight with all training examples, but MIRA is an online one which updates with each example (Watanabe et al., 2007) or parts of examples (Chiang et al., 2008). The batch mode has some advantages over online mode: more accurate sentence-wise BLEU towards Corpus-BLEU (Watanabe, 2012) and more promising experimental performance (Cherry and Foster, 2012). Additionally, our method is similar to (Liu et al., 2012). However, the main difference is that ours is a global training method instead of a local training method.

4 Experiments and Results

4.1 Experimental Setting

We conduct our translation experiments on two language pairs: Chinese-to-English and Spanish-to-English. For the Chinese-to-English task, the training data is FBIS corpus consisting of about 240k sentence pairs; the development set is NIST02 evaluation data; the test set NIST05 is used as the development test set for tuning hyperparameter λ in Eq. 6; and the test datasets are NIST03, NIST04, NIST05, NIST06, and NIST08. For the Spanish-to-English task, all the datasets are from WMT2011: the training data is the first 200k sentence pairs of Europarl corpus; the development set is dev06; and the test datasets are test07, test08,test09, test10, test11.

We run GIZA++ (Och and Ney, 2000) on the training corpus in both directions (Koehn et al., 2003) to obtain the word alignment for each sentence pair. We train a 4-gram language model on the Xinhua portion of the English Gigaword corpus using the SRILM Toolkits (Stolcke, 2002) with modified Kneser-Ney smoothing (Chen and Goodman, 1998). In our experiments, the translation performances are measured by the case-insensitive BLEU4 metric (Papineni et al., 2002) and we use mteval-v13a.pl as the evaluation tool. The significance testing is performed by paired bootstrap re-sampling (Koehn, 2004).

[3]At the end of tuning, we average the weights as (Collins, 2002). The norm of the averaged weight may nolonger be equal to 1, but it is irrelevant for testing, see discussion in Section 3.2.

Methods	dev06(Dev)	test08	test09	test10	test11
MERT	28.85	19.68	21.36	23.35	23.65
ELBUU	28.67	20.23	21.72	23.90^{+}	24.18^{+}

Table 2: Comparison of two tuning methods, MERT and ELBUU, on Spanish-to-English translation tasks. + means the ELBUU method is significantly better than MERT with confidence $p < 0.05$.

Distance metrics	NIST02(Dev)	NIST03	NIST04	NIST05	NIST06	NIST08
L_2	29.95	27.09	29.65	26.79	25.98	19.54
Projection	30.06	27.36	29.89	27.03	26.30	19.79

Table 3: Comparison of two distance metrics L_2 and projection on Chinese-to-English translation tasks.

The translation system is a phrase-based translation model (Koehn et al., 2003) and we use the open source toolkit **MOSES** (Koehn et al., 2007) as its implementation. In the experiments, the default setting is used for MOSES. The baseline tuning method is the standard algorithm MERT and the k-best-list size is set as 100 for tuning. For ELBUU, we empirically set $\alpha = 3.0$ as (Och, 2003), $\eta = 1$, $\epsilon = 10^{-5}$, $K = 20$, and we do not tune them further. We tune λ on NIST05 with $\lambda = 1.0$ for the Chinese-to-English translation tasks and we do not tune it again for the Spanish-to-English translation tasks.

4.2 Results

Table 1 and Table 2 give the main results of ELBUU compared with the baseline MERT on Chinese-to-English and Spanish-to-English translation tasks, respectively. Overall, we can see that the proposed ELBUU achieves consistent improvements on both language pairs: ELBUU is better than MERT, although some of the comparisons are not significant. In detail, for Chinese-to-English tasks, ELBUU achieves improvements from 0.42 BLEU points on NIST04 to 0.96 BLEU points on NIST06; and for Spanish-to-English tasks, ELBUU also outperforms MERT with improvements up to 0.5 BLEU points on both the test10 and test11 test sets.

Table 3 shows the performance of the distance metric defined in section 3.3, and L_2 is used as its comparison[4]. We also tune it on NIST05 and set it to 0.1 for the case of L_2 distance. Although the comparison results are not significant, we can see that the performance of projection distance is slightly better than that of L_2 distance.

Figure 1 shows the learning curves during tuning for Chinese-to-English translation tasks. It shows that the performances over the test datasets do not decrease as iterations increase and the weights can achieve stable performances within 20 iterations.

To further testify to the advantage of the ultraconservative update, we fix the k-best-list results as those produced by MERT and compare ELBUU with MERT: when running ELBUU, we do not perform the decoding step to generate the k-best list $\mathbf{tc}_i$, and instead we set it as the k-best list

[4]The algorithm of ELBUU with L_2 as its distance is the same as ELBUU with projection distance after deleting the projection step in line 4-8 of Algorithm 2

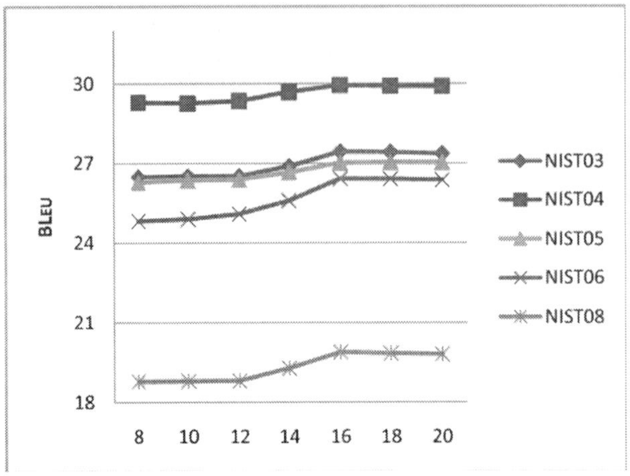

Figure 1: The learning curves for ELBUU as tuning algorithm on all the test sets of Chinese-to-English translation. The horizontal axis denotes the number of iterations during tuning, and the vertical one denotes the BLEU points.

Methods	NIST05	NIST06	NIST08
MERT	26.31	25.34	19.07
ELBUU	26.65	25.85	19.41

Table 4: The comparison of ELBUU and MERT with the same k-best-list results for optimization under the Chinese-to-English translation tasks.

exactly obtained by MERT tuning at the corresponding decoding step. Table 4 shows that the ELBUU is slightly better than MERT. This fact also directly indicates the advantages of ELBUU over MERT.

Conclusion and Future Work

This paper proposes a new tuning algorithm which minimizes the expected BLEU with ultraconservative update. By taking the progress made in previous rounds during the training process, our method obtains significant improvements over MERT on many test sets for both the Chinese-to-English and Spanish-to-English translation over the MOSES system. In future work, we will investigate our method on large training data.

Acknowledgments

We would like to thank Muyun Yang and Hongfei Jiang for many valuable discussions and thank three anonymous reviewers for many valuable comments and helpful suggestions. This work was supported by National Natural Science Foundation of China (61173073,61100093,61073130,61272384), the Key Project of the National High Technology Research and Development Program of China (2011AA01A207), and and the Fundamental Research Funds for Central Universites (HIT.NSRIF.2013065).

References

Chen, S. F. and Goodman, J. (1998). An empirical study of smoothing techniques for language modeling. In *Technical Report TR-10-98*. Harvard University.

Cherry, C. and Foster, G. (2012). Batch tuning strategies for statistical machine translation. In *Proceedings of the 2012 Conference of the North American Chapter of the Association for Computational Linguistics: Human Language Technologies*, pages 427–436, Montréal, Canada. Association for Computational Linguistics.

Chiang, D., Marton, Y., and Resnik, P. (2008). Online large-margin training of syntactic and structural translation features. In *Proc. of EMNLP*. ACL.

Clark, J. H., Dyer, C., Lavie, A., and Smith, N. A. (2011). Better hypothesis testing for statistical machine translation: controlling for optimizer instability. In *Proceedings of the 49th Annual Meeting of the Association for Computational Linguistics: Human Language Technologies: short papers - Volume 2*, HLT '11, pages 176–181, Stroudsburg, PA, USA. Association for Computational Linguistics.

Collins, M. (2002). Discriminative training methods for hidden markov models: Theory and experiments with perceptron algorithms. In *Proc. of EMNLP*. ACL.

Crammer, K., Dekel, O., Keshet, J., Shalev-Shwartz, S., and Singer, Y. (2006). Online passive-aggressive algorithms. *J. Mach. Learn. Res.*, 7:551–585.

Crammer, K. and Singer, Y. (2003). Ultraconservative online algorithms for multiclass problems. *J. Mach. Learn. Res.*, 3:951–991.

Horst, R. and Tuy, H. (1996). Global optimization: Deterministic approaches. Springer.

Koehn, P. (2004). Statistical significance tests for machine translation evaluation. In *Proc. of EMNLP*. ACL.

Koehn, P., Hoang, H., Birch, A., Callison-Burch, C., Federico, M., Bertoldi, N., Cowan, B., Shen, W., Moran, C., Zens, R., Dyer, C., Bojar, O., Constantin, A., and Herbst, E. (2007). Moses: open source toolkit for statistical machine translation. In *Proceedings of the 45th Annual Meeting of the ACL on Interactive Poster and Demonstration Sessions*, ACL '07, pages 177–180, Stroudsburg, PA, USA. Association for Computational Linguistics.

Koehn, P., Och, F. J., and Marcu, D. (2003). Statistical phrase-based translation. In *Proc. of HLT-NAACL*. ACL.

Kumar, S., Macherey, W., Dyer, C., and Och, F. (2009). Efficient minimum error rate training and minimum bayes-risk decoding for translation hypergraphs and lattices. In *Proceedings of the Joint Conference of the 47th Annual Meeting of the ACL and the 4th International Joint Conference on Natural Language Processing of the AFNLP: Volume 1 - Volume 1*, ACL '09, pages 163–171, Stroudsburg, PA, USA. Association for Computational Linguistics.

Liu, L., Cao, H., Watanabe, T., Zhao, T., Yu, M., and Zhu, C. (2012). Locally training the log-linear model for smt. In *Proceedings of the 2012 Joint Conference on Empirical Methods in Natural Language Processing and Computational Natural Language Learning*, pages 402–411, Jeju Island, Korea. Association for Computational Linguistics.

Macherey, W., Och, F. J., Thayer, I., and Uszkoreit, J. (2008). Lattice-based minimum error rate training for statistical machine translation. In *Proceedings of the Conference on Empirical Methods in Natural Language Processing*, EMNLP '08, pages 725–734, Stroudsburg, PA, USA. Association for Computational Linguistics.

Och, F. J. (2003). Minimum error rate training in statistical machine translation. In *Proceedings of the 41st Annual Meeting of the Association for Computational Linguistics*, pages 160–167, Sapporo, Japan. Association for Computational Linguistics.

Och, F. J. and Ney, H. (2000). Improved statistical alignment models. In *Proceedings of the 38th Annual Meeting on Association for Computational Linguistics*, ACL '00, pages 440–447, Stroudsburg, PA, USA. Association for Computational Linguistics.

Papineni, K., Roukos, S., Ward, T., and Zhu, W.-J. (2002). Bleu: a method for automatic evaluation of machine translation. In *Proceedings of 40th Annual Meeting of the Association for Computational Linguistics*, pages 311–318, Philadelphia, Pennsylvania, USA. Association for Computational Linguistics.

Pauls, A., Denero, J., and Klein, D. (2009). Consensus training for consensus decoding in machine translation. In *Proceedings of the 2009 Conference on Empirical Methods in Natural Language Processing*, pages 1418–1427, Singapore. Association for Computational Linguistics.

Smith, D. A. and Eisner, J. (2006). Minimum risk annealing for training log-linear models. In *Proceedings of the COLING/ACL 2006 Main Conference Poster Sessions*, pages 787–794, Sydney, Australia. Association for Computational Linguistics.

Stolcke, A. (2002). Srilm - an extensible language modeling toolkit. In *Proc. of ICSLP*.

Watanabe, T. (2012). Optimized online rank learning for machine translation. In *Proceedings of the 2012 Conference of the North American Chapter of the Association for Computational Linguistics: Human Language Technologies*, pages 253–262, Montréal, Canada. Association for Computational Linguistics.

Watanabe, T., Suzuki, J., Tsukada, H., and Isozaki, H. (2007). Online large-margin training for statistical machine translation. In *Proceedings of the 2007 Joint Conference on Empirical Methods in Natural Language Processing and Computational Natural Language Learning (EMNLP-CoNLL)*, pages 764–773, Prague, Czech Republic. Association for Computational Linguistics.

Zens, R., Hasan, S., and Ney, H. (2007). A systematic comparison of training criteria for statistical machine translation. In *Proceedings of the 2007 Joint Conference on Empirical Methods in Natural Language Processing and Computational Natural Language Learning (EMNLP-CoNLL)*, pages 524–532, Prague, Czech Republic. Association for Computational Linguistics.

Generalized Sentiment-Bearing Expression Features for Sentiment Analysis

Shizhu Liu   Gady Agam   David Grossman
Computer Science Department, Illinois Institute of Technology
sliu28, agam, grossman@iit.edu

ABSTRACT
In this work, we propose a novel approach to extract sentiment-bearing expression features derived from dependency structures. Rather than directly use dependency relations generated by a parser, we propose a set of heuristic rules to detect both explicit and implicit negations in the text. Then, three patterns are defined to support generalized sentiment-bearing expressions. By altering existing dependency features with detected negations and generalized sentiment-bearing expressions we are able to achieve more accurate sentiment polarity classification. We evaluate the proposed approach on three labeled collections of different lengths, and measure the gain from the generalized dependency features when used in addition to the bag-of-words features. Our results demonstrate that generalized dependency-based features are more effective when compared to standard features. Using these we are able to surpass the state-of-the-art in sentiment classification.

KEYWORDS: Sentiment analysis, Natural Language Processing, Classification.

Proceedings of COLING 2012: Posters, pages 733–744,
COLING 2012, Mumbai, December 2012.

1 Introduction

With the proliferation of Web 2.0 tools and applications on the Internet, there is an exponential increase in the number of online postings submitted by web users on their opinions, experiences, etc. This trend drawn the attention of organizations, companies and researchers who are interested in opinions expressed by people on various topics. Sentiment analysis, the task of identifying sentimental aspect of a text, has been a popular direction in the field of language technologies.

Recent work in supervised sentiment analysis has focused on innovative approaches to feature creation, which aim to improve the performance with features that capture the essence of linguistic constructs used to express sentiment. A straightforward way to extend the traditional bag-of-words representation is to heuristically add new types of features, such as fixed-length n-gram (e.g., bigram or trigram) or pairwise syntactic relations (e.g., typed dependencies).

However, the performance of joint features is still far from satisfactory. N-grams which cover only co-occurrences of N continuous words in a sentence has problems with capturing long dependencies, and the performance of a dependency relation feature set is reported to be inferior to N-grams. We conjecture that this reduced performance is in part due to the following two reasons: 1) pairwise dependency features sometimes fail to reflect the correct sentiment polarity by neglecting to consider the influence of other terms, especially negations, in the given sentence; 2) in dependency relation features, features lack sentiment oriented generalizations.

The main contribution of this paper is in the construction of more accurate generalized sentiment-bearing expression features for the sentiment classification. We propose a set of heuristic rules to detect implicit negation relations and propose three patterns as the basis for generalized dependency-based sentiment oriented features:

Explicit patterns Many terms directly reflect the sentiment. e.g. "great camera", "love this movie". The parsed dependency relations amod(camera, great), and obj(love, movie) can already capture these explicit sentiment expressions.

Range patterns In some cases, there is an assumed standard and sentiment is indicated by describing the distance from the standard. For example, in the sentence "The quality of this product is above average", "above average" indicates distance from the standard.

Trend patterns In some cases, sentiment is conveyed by describing the trend of how the object changes. For example, in the sentence "The popularity of this band have continuously decreased from their peak in 2000", "decreased from" indicates a trend.

For each type of sentiment expression, we propose a corresponding generalization strategy. We show that when trained on such revised generalized features, machine learning classification algorithms achieve better sentiment classification accuracy.

The remainder of this paper is organized as follows. Section 2 presents related work on the topic of sentiment analysis. Section 3 introduces the proposed approach using some motivating examples and a set of heuristic rules with generalization strategies. Experimental results are discussed and compared to known techniques in Section 4. Section 5 concludes the paper and outlines future directions.

2 Related Work

Sentiment has been studied at three different levels: word, sentence, and document level. On document level, previous work (Pang et al., 2002) (Pang and Lee, 2004) have shown that traditional text classification approaches can be quite effective when applied to sentiment analysis. On word level, Wilson et al.(Wilson et al., 2005) extract phrase-level clues by identifying polarity shifter words to adjust the polarity of opinion phrases. Kim et al.(Kim et al., 2009) shows how various term weighting schemes improve the performance of sentiment analysis systems. Choi et al.(Choi et al., 2009) validated that topic-specific features would enhance existing sentiment classifiers. On sentence level, linguistic approaches are used to discover the interaction between words that may switch a sentence's sentiment polarity (Wilson et al., 2004) (Choi et al., 2005).

A prominent polarity shifter clue in sentences is negation. Pang et al. (Pang et al., 2002) employ the technique of Das and Chen (Das and Chen, 2001) to add the tag "NOT_" to every word between a negation word and the first following punctuation mark. Negation and its scope in the context of sentiment analysis has been studied in (Moilanen and Pulman, 2007). Choi and Cardie (Choi and Cardie, 2008) combine different kinds of negations with lexical polarity items through various compositional semantic models to improve phrasal sentiment analysis. A recent study by Danescu-Niculescu-Mizil et al. (Danescu-Niculescu-Mizil et al., 2009) looked at the problem of finding downward-entailing operators that include a wider range of lexical items, including soft negation such as adverbs "rarely" and "hardly". Councill et al. (Councill et al., 2010) focus on explicit negation mentions and investigate how to identify the scope of negation in free text.

There have been some attempts at using features for polarity classification from dependency parses. Dave et al. (Dave et al., 2003) found that adding adjective-noun dependency relationships as features does not provide any benefit over a simple bag-of-words based feature space. Arora et al.(Arora et al., 2010) use a subgraph mining algorithm to automatically derive frequent subgraph features in addition to the bag-of-words features. Moilanen et al.(Moilanen and Pulman, 2007) discuss sentiment propagation, polarity reversal, and polarity conflict resolution within various linguistic constituent types. Ng et al. (Ng et al., 2006) proposed that the subjective-verb and verb-object relationships should also be considered for polarity classification. However, they observed that the addition of these dependency relationships does not improve performance over a feature space that includes unigrams, bigrams.

To solve the sparse-data problem for machine learning classifiers, there were attempts at finding better generalized dependency features. (Gamon, 2004) back off words in N-gram (and semantic relations) to their respective POS tags. (Joshi and Penstein-Rose, 2009) proposed a method by only backing off head word in dependency relation pairs to its POS tag. Xia and Zong (Xia and Zong, 2010) further propose to back off the word in each word relation pairs to its corresponding POS cluster to make the feature space smarter and more effective.

3 Methodology

In this section, we first motivate our approach using sample sentences. We then demonstrate the application of heuristic rules for negation and pattern detection. Finally, we describe how to generalize the extracted sentiment-bearing expressions.

3.1 Motivation for our Approach

To facilitate the discussion, consider the following examples:

1. *Avatar is a great movie!*
2. *This is not a great movie.*
3. *No one likes these extra functions.*
4. *This news is too good to be true.*
5. *The leading actors' sterling performances raise this far above the level of the usual maudlin disease movie .*
6. *The lack of training exposed truck drivers to an increased risk of injury.*
7. *This accessory can abate the damage.*
8. *New regulations increase accountability and boost quality in head start.*

By applying the dependency parser to the first two sentences, the extracted dependency relations in both sentences contain the dependency relation *amod(movie, great)* which is used to express both positive (in the first sentence) and negative (in the second sentence) sentiments. If all pairwise dependency relations are directly appended to unigram features, *amod-movie-great* becomes a common feature for positive and negative examples and the sentiment classifier cannot benefit from it. We propose to keep all negated word as negation indicator terms and present them in their negated status as composite dependency features (e.g. not-amod-movie-great for the second sentence).

Besides explicit negation relations that can be detected by a dependency parser directly, implicit negation which does not use negation terms is hard to detect. For example, "no one" in the third sentence shifts the polarity of the verb "likes", and "too" in the fourth sentence shows the implicit negation for the term after the word "to". To construct accurate dependency features for sentiment classification, we propose a set of heuristics for the detection of implicit negation relations.

Sentiment may be expressed implicitly by referring to an assumed standard. For example, consider the fifth and sixth sentences where sentiment information is expressed by describing the target object as being above or below an ordinary level. In the seventh and eighth sentences, sentiment may also be expressed by describing how an object changed. For the construction of composite back off features for the range and trend patterns, related indicator terms are backed off as status info instead of its POS tags (e.g. "prep(lack, training)" backed off as "prep-blw-training" and backed off as "dobj(abate, damage)" as "dobj-dec-damage").

3.2 Heuristics-Based Sentiment Detection Methods

This section describes a set of heuristic rules for detecting sentiment-bearing expressions. For a given sentence, we first parse it and get its corresponding dependency tree represented as a list of dependency relation list. We then attempt to detect negation, range, and trend indicator terms. These are used for generalized sentiment expression construction in the next step.

WordNet [1] is used to construct range and trend pattern indicator term synset. e.g. all the

[1]http://wordnet.princeton.edu/

synonyms of “above” will be included in the range indicator synset and all the synonyms of “increase” will be in the trend pattern indicator synset.

Table 1 shows the definition of sentiment indicator detection rules along with motivating examples. In order to apply a rule, we first detect the a dependency relation and then apply the *Detect* function as defined in Table 2. The *Detect* function first checks whether the first argument is a negation indicator term, and if so, insert a negation dependency relation for the second argument. If the first argument is a range or trend indicator term, we keep it in the indicator term list for the next step of generalized feature construction.

	Rules	Examples
1	$neg(arg1, not) = \neg(arg1)$	not $[bad]_{arg1}$
2	$subj(V,N) = Detect(N,V,subj)$	$[Nobody]_N[likes]_V$ this product
3	$obj(V,N) = Detect(N,V,obj)$	He is $[supported]_V$ by $[none]_N$.
4	$advmod(V,R) = Detect(V,R,advmod)$	PM2.5 $[rarely]_R[decreased]_V$ recently.
5	$ccomp(J,V) = Detect(J,V,ccomp)$	It is $[impossible]_J$ to $[overrate]_V$ it.
6	$xcomp(J,V) = Detect(J,V,xcomp)$	This news is too $[good]_J$ to $[believe]_V$.
7	$amod(N,J) = Detect(N,J,amod)$	$[high]_J[interestrate]_N$.
8	$advmod(J,R) = Detect(J,R,advmod)$	$[too]_R[fast]_N$.
9	$prep(N_1,N_2) = Detect(N_1,N_2,prep)$	$[lack]_{N_1}$ of $[training]_{N_2}$
10	$obj(V,N) = Detect(N,V,obj)$	This accessory can $[abate]_V[damage]_N$.

Table 1: Sentiment indicator term detection rules

if($arg3 == subjANDarg1 \in negatedsubject$)	then insert neg(arg2, not)
else if($arg3 == objANDarg1 \in negatedsubjects$)	then insert neg(arg2, not)
else if($arg3 == advmodANDarg2 \in negatedadv$)	then insert neg(arg1, not)
else if($arg3 == ccompANDarg1 \in negatedadj$)	then insert neg(arg2, not)
else if($arg3 == xcompANDarg1existinadvmod(arg1, too)$)	then insert neg(arg2, not)
else if($arg3 == amodANDarg2 \in abovesynset$)	then label arg1 as abv
else if($arg3 == amodANDarg2 \in belowsynset$)	then label arg1 as blw
else if($arg3 == advmodANDarg2 \in abovesynset$)	then label arg1 as abv
else if($arg3 == advmodANDarg2 \in belowsynset$)	then label arg1 as blw
else if($arg3 == prepANDarg1 \in abovesynset$)	then label arg2 as abv
else if($arg3 == prepANDarg1 \in belowsynset$)	then label arg2 as blw
else if($arg3 == objANDarg1 \in increasesynset$)	then label arg1 as inc
else if($arg3 == objANDarg1 \in decreasesynset$)	then label arg1 as dec

Table 2: Definition of Detect(arg1, arg2, arg3)

3.3 Generalized Sentiment-bearing Expression Features

In order to make a further generalization, we conduct POS and grammatical relation clustering. The POS tags and grammatical relations are categorized as shown in Table 3

For negation indicator terms, we add the tag “not-” to all the dependency relations where it occurred. For the range and trend pattern indicator terms, a status tag based on its semantic meaning will used in the corresponding relations. Table 4 present some examples for these type of specific generalizations.

POS-cluster	Contained POS tags
J	JJ, JJS, JJR
R	RB, RBS, RBR
V	VB,VBZ, VBD, VBN, VBG, VBP
N	NN, NNS, NNP, NNPS, PRP
O	The other POS tags
Relation-cluster	**Contained grammatical relations**
mod	amod, advmod, partmod, rcmod, acomp
subj	nsubj, nsubjpass, xsubj, agent
obj	dobj, iobj, xcomp
prep	prep, prepc

Table 3: POS clustering (the Penn Corpus Style) and grammatical relation clustering.

Dep	Indicator	G-Feature
amod(camera, great)	not-great	not-mod-N-great
amod(interest, high)	high	mod-abv-interest
prep(level, below)	below	prep-blw-level
dobj(abate, damage)	abate	obj-dec-damage
dobj(improve, quality)	improve	obj-inc-quality

Table 4: Different types of generalized sentiment-bearing expression feature.

4 Experiments

Details of our experimental evaluation and results follow.

4.1 Experimental Setup

Datasets: Three datasets are used in our sentiment polarity classification experiments:

1. NPS survey dataset v1.0 to which we refer to as "surveys" (3000 promoter and 3000 detractor survey entries, with avg. 10 words)
2. sentences/snippets polarity dataset v1.0 (Pang and Lee, 2005) to which we refer to as "short reviews" (5331 positive and 5331 negative reviews, with avg. 21 words)[2].
3. polarity dataset v2.0 (Pang and Lee, 2004) to which we refer to as "long reviews" (1000 positive and 1000 negative reviews, with avg. 780 words)[3].

The three datasets are of different lengths. The polarity dataset is composed of relatively long movie reviews. The sentence/snippets polarity dataset v1.0 is composed of formal written sentence level examples and text in survey sentences are usually short and incomplete. We conduct polarity classification experiments over these three datasets to evaluate the proposed method and investigate the effect of text length on classification performance.

Classifier: We performed n-fold cross-validation experiments on the above datasets, using Joachims' SVM-light (Joachims, 1999) [4] package to train an SVM polarity classifier. All

[2]http://www.cs.cornell.edu/people/pabo/movie-review-data/rt-polaritydata.tar.gz
[3]http://www.cs.cornell.edu/people/pabo/movie-review-data/review-polarity.tar.gz
[4]http://svmlight.joachims.org

	Negation	Range	Trend
review	261	142	8
survey	308	162	47

Table 5: Negation, Range, Trend Pattern Occurrence Information

Patterns	Precision/Recall(%)	
	review	survey
Negation	74.9/70.9	88.3/75.6
Range	75.8/79.6	82.4/86.4
Trend	88.9/100.0	100.0/97.9
Average	75.6/74.5	87.3/81.0

Table 6: Negation, Range, Trend Pattern Detection Accuracy

learning parameters were left at their default values. Following (Pang et al., 2002), we use frequency to determine word presence. Each document is first tokenized and downcased, and then represented as a vector of features with 2-norm. A χ^2 feature selection strategy (Yang and Pedersen, 1997) is applied to back-off sentiment-bearing expression features, where we reject features if their χ^2 score is not significant at the 0.2 level.

4.2 Pattern Detection Evaluation

Considering the critical role of sentiment-bearing expression detection in the proposed approach, we evaluated the accuracy of this step separately. For this purpose, we annotated several subsets of the datasets. Specifically, we created a subset which consists of 200 positive and 200 negative sentences from the sentences/snippets polarity dataset v1.0 and a subset which consists of 200 positive and 200 negative sentences from the NPS survey dataset v1.0. Table 5 presents information of negation, range, and trend patterns in the labeled subsets. We see that negation patterns are in general the most frequent, and occur in a majority of the documents whereas trend patterns are in general less frequent.

The Stanford parser[5] was used to extract dependency relations in our experiments. Table 6 shows the performance of the sentiment-bearing expression detection component. As can be observed, our detection component performs better on sentences of the survey dataset compared with the review dataset. This is related to fact that sentences from the review set are longer and more complex compared with sentences from the survey set, which indicates increase in complexity for the review set.

4.3 Results and Discussion

Finally, the accuracy of an SVM classifier using different sets of features is shown in Table 7. We used the the SVM-light classifier over unigram (uni), unigram with bigram (uni+bi), unigram with all dependencies (uni+dep), and an ensemble with the proposed sentiment-bearing expression features (uni+gdep) using 10-fold cross-valuation. As can be observed the proposed feature set yields the best results when compared with several baseline techniques. Compared with the baseline of bag-of-words expression, the proposed feature set yields a significant performance improvement with the sentence and review datasets. And a minor

[5]http://nlp.stanford.edu/software/lex-parser.shtml

Features	Accuracy(%)		
	survey	sentence	review
uni	90.4	76.6	87.1
uni+bi	91.5	77.8	88.0
uni+dep	91.1	77.4	87.7
uni+gdep	**91.7**	**84.4**	**93.3**

Table 7: Sentiment Classification Accuracy using 10-fold Cross-evaluation

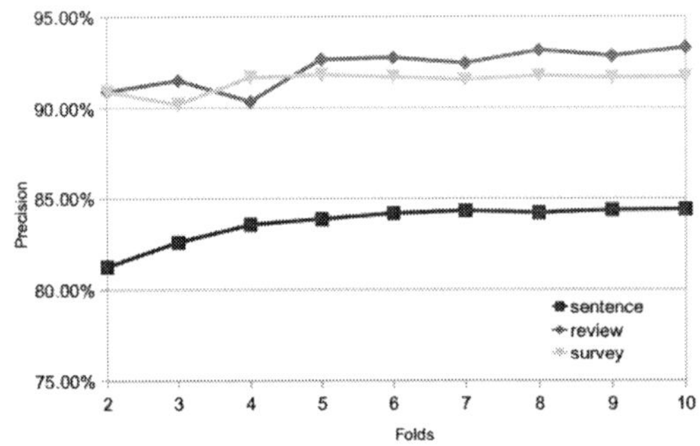

Figure 1: Sentiment classification accuracy using variable cross-validation

improvement is achieved by both bigram and generalized sentiment-bearing features for the survey dataset. The minor improvement in the survey dataset is due to the fact that sentences in this dataset are simpler and shorter, and some of the negation, range, and trend pattern have already been captured by bigrams.

A comparison between our results and results reported in the literature for the movie review polarity dataset v2.0 (Pang and Lee, 2004) (Ng et al., 2006) (Matsumoto et al., 2005) indicate that our results surpass the known state-of-the-art regarding this dataset.

To evaluate the influence of the training set size on performance, we performed evaluation using from 2 to 10-fold cross-validation using three datasets. The results shown in Figure 1 indicate that the accuracy of the proposed approach improves with increase in the training set size. As can be observed, the precision fluctuates under 4 folds and stays steady above the 5 folds.

5 Conclusions

The focus of this paper is the construction of more accurate composite sentiment-bearing expression features for sentiment classification. Three patterns are defined to cover more sentiment-bearing expressions and we investigate how to construct more sentiment feature by considering both explicit and implicit negations in the sentence. We propose a set of heuristic rules to detect negations and sentiment-bearing expressions and a dataset is manually annotated for the evaluation of the pattern detection component. Results show that the performance of the pattern detection components can meet the practical applications' requirement and the proposed methods can improve the accuracy significantly.

References

Aho, A. V. and Ullman, J. (1972). *The Theory of Parsing, Translation and Compiling*, volume 1. Prentice-Hall, EngleWood Cliffs, NJ.

Arora, S., Mayfield, E., Penstein-Rose, C., and Nyberg, E. (2010). Sentiment classification using automatically extracted subgraph features. In *Proc. NAACL HLT Workshop on Computational Approaches to Analysis and Generation of Emotion in Text*, pages 131–139.

Ashok K. Chandra, D. C. K. and J.Stockmeyer, L. (1981). Alternation. *Journal of the Association for Computing Machinery*, 28(1):114–133.

Benarmara, F., Hatout, N., Muller, P., and Ozdowska, S., editors (2007). *Actes de TALN 2007 (Traitement automatique des langues naturelles)*, Toulouse. ATALA, IRIT.

Choi, Y. and Cardie, C. (2008). Learning with compositional semantics as structural inference for subsentential sentiment analysis. In *Proc. EMNLP*, pages 793–801.

Choi, Y., Cardie, C., Riloff, E., and Patwardhan, S. (2005). Identifying sources of opinions with conditional random fields and extraction patterns. In *Proc. conf. Human Language Technology and Empirical Methods in Natural Language Processing*, pages 355–362.

Choi, Y., Kim, Y., and Myaeng, S.-H. (2009). Domain-specific sentiment analysis using contextual feature generation. In *Proc. 1st intl. CIKM workshop on Topic-sentiment analysis for mass opinion*, pages 37–44.

Councill, I. G., McDonald, R., and Velikovich, L. (2010). What's great and what's not: learning to classify the scope of negation for improved sentiment analysis. In *Proc. Workshop on Negation and Speculation in Natural Language Processing*, pages 51–59.

Danescu-Niculescu-Mizil, C., Lee, L., and Ducott, R. (2009). Without a doubt?: unsupervised discovery of downward-entailing operators. In *Proc. Human Language Technologies: NAACL*, pages 137–145.

Das, S. and Chen, M. (2001). Yahoo! for amazon: Extracting market sentiment from stock message boards. In *Proc. Asia Pacific Finance Association Annual Conf. (APFA)*.

Dave, K., Lawrence, S., and Pennock, D. M. (2003). Mining the peanut gallery: opinion extraction and semantic classification of product reviews. In *Proc. 12th intl. conf. on World Wide Web*, pages 519–528.

Engstrom, C. (2004). *Topic Dependence in Sentiment Classification*. PhD thesis, University of Cambridge.

Gamon, M. (2004). Sentiment classification on customer feedback data: noisy data, large feature vectors, and the role of linguistic analysis. In *Proc. 20th intl. conf. on Computational Linguistics (COLING)*.

Joachims, T. (1999). Making large-scale support vector machine learning practical. In Scholkopf, B., Burges, C. J. C., and Smola, A. J., editors, *Advances in kernel methods*, pages 169–184. MIT Press.

Joshi, M. and Penstein-Rose, C. (2009). Generalizing dependency features for opinion mining. In *Proc. ACL-IJCNLP Conf. Short Papers*, pages 313–316.

Kim, J., Li, J.-J., and Lee, J.-H. (2009). Discovering the discriminative views: measuring term weights for sentiment analysis. In *Proc. Joint Conf. Annual Meeting ACL and Intl. Joint Conf. Natural Language Processing of the AFNLP*, pages 253–261.

Laignelet, M. and Rioult, F. (2009). Repérer automatiquement les segments obsolescents à l'aide d'indices sémantiques et discursifs. In *Actes de TALN 2009 (Traitement automatique des langues naturelles)*, Senlis. ATALA, LIPN.

Langlais, P. and Patry, A. (2007). Enrichissement d'un lexique bilingue par analogie. In (Benarmara et al., 2007), pages 101–110.

Matsumoto, S., Takamura, H., and Okumura, M. (2005). Sentiment classification using word sub-sequences and dependency sub-trees. In *Proc. 9th Pacific-Asia conference on Advances in Knowledge Discovery and Data Mining*, pages 301–311.

Moilanen, K. and Pulman, S. (2007). Sentiment composition. In *Proc. of RANLP*.

Mukherjee, S. and Bhattacharyya, P. (2012). Wikisent : Weakly supervised sentiment analysis through extractive summarization with wikipedia. In *European Conference on Machine Learning (ECML-PKDD 2012)*, pages 250–260, Bristol, U.K. Springer.

Ng, V., Dasgupta, S., and Arifin, S. M. N. (2006). Examining the role of linguistic knowledge sources in the automatic identification and classification of reviews. In *Proc. Intl. Conf. on Computational Linguistics (COLING): Posters*, pages 611–618.

Pang, B. and Lee, L. (2004). A sentimental education: sentiment analysis using subjectivity summarization based on minimum cuts. In *Proceedings of the 42nd Annual Meeting on Association for Computational Linguistics*, Proc. ACL.

Pang, B. and Lee, L. (2005). Seeing stars: Exploiting class relationships for sentiment categorization with respect to rating scales. In *Proc. ACL*, pages 115–124.

Pang, B., Lee, L., and Vaithyanathan, S. (2002). Thumbs up?: sentiment classification using machine learning techniques. In *Proc. EMNLP*, pages 79–86.

Turney, P. D. (2002). Thumbs up or thumbs down?: semantic orientation applied to unsupervised classification of reviews. In *Proceedings of the 40th Annual Meeting on Association for Computational Linguistics*, Proc. ACL, pages 417–424.

Wilson, T., Wiebe, J., and Hoffmann, P. (2005). Recognizing contextual polarity in phrase-level sentiment analysis. In *Proc. conf. on Human Language Technology and Empirical Methods in Natural Language Processing*, pages 347–354.

Wilson, T., Wiebe, J., and Hwa, R. (2004). Just how mad are you? finding strong and weak opinion clauses. In *Proc. 19th national conference on Artifical intelligence (AAAI)*, pages 761–767.

Xia, R. and Zong, C. (2010). Exploring the use of word relation features for sentiment classification. In *Proc. Intl. Conf. on Computational Linguistics (COLING): Posters*, pages 1336–1344.

Yang, Y. and Pedersen, J. O. (1997). A comparative study on feature selection in text categorization. In *Proc. 14th Intl. Conf. on Machine Learning (ICML)*, pages 412–420.

Unsupervised domain adaptation for joint segmentation and POS-tagging

Yang Liu[1] *Yue Zhang*[2]
(1) University of Cambridge
(2) Singapore University of Technology and Design
yang.liu@cantab.net, yue_zhang@sutd.edu.sg

ABSTRACT
Sophisticated models have been developed for joint word segmentation and part-of-speech tagging, with increasing accuracies reported on the Chinese Treebank data. These systems, which rely on supervised learning, typically perform worse on texts from a different domain, for which little annotation is available. We consider self-training and character clustering for domain adaptation. Both methods use only unannotated target-domain data, and are relatively straightforward to implement upon a baseline supervised system. Our results show that both methods can effectively improve target-domain performance. In addition, a combination of the two orthogonal methods leads to further improvement.

TITLE AND ABSTRACT IN CHINESE

分词与词性标注联合模型的领域适应

分词与词性标注的联合模型是一个正在被广泛研究的问题，随着复杂模型的应用，其在宾大中文数据库上的测试精度不断提升。这些方法通常使用有监督学习，致使在不同领域下的效果不如单一领域满意。我们用自学习和字聚类实现领域适应。这两个方法使用未标注领域训练数据，而且易于实现。我们的实验结果表明，这两种方法都可以提高领域适应。同时，这两种方法可以结合使用达到更高性能。

KEYWORDS: Semi-supervised learning, domain adaptation, word segmentation, POS-tagging.
KEYWORDS IN CHINESE: 分词，词性标注，领域适应，半监督学习，聚类，自学习

Proceedings of COLING 2012: Posters, pages 745–754,
COLING 2012, Mumbai, December 2012.

1 Introduction

Joint segmentation and POS-tagging can improve upon a pipelined baseline by reducing error propagation and accommodating features that represent combined word and POS information. Three general approaches have been taken to perform joint inference, namely two-stage ensemble methods (Jiang et al., 2008a; Sun, 2011), reranking (Jiang et al., 2008b; Shi and Wang, 2007) and single joint models with heuristic search (Ng and Low, 2004; Zhang and Clark, 2008; Kruengkrai et al., 2009; Zhang and Clark, 2010), leading to improved accuracies on the Chinese Treebank data.

All these methods rely on supervised learning, and are expected to perform worse when the test domain shifts from CTB to blogs, computer forums, and internet literature, which are written in a different genre, and for which little manual annotation is available. In this paper, we choose internet literature as the target domain, and study domain adaptation for joint segmentation and POS-tagging. We consider the single model approach of Zhang and Clark (2010), trained using the CTB, as our baseline system, and apply self-training and character clustering to improve its performance on our test data from an internet novel.

Much work has been done on domain adaptation for POS-tagging (Blitzer et al., 2006; Daumé III and Marcu, 2006; Jiang and Zhai, 2007). However, relatively little attention has been paid to the domain adaptation for joint segmentation and POS-tagging. Among the range of methods that have been developed for domain adaptation, self-training and character clustering are applicable to a comparatively large number of baseline supervised model types, including feature-based probability models and large-margin discriminative models, and are fairly straightforward to implement. We focus on unsupervised domain adaptation, using fully unannotated data in the target-domain.

We evaluate our system on a set of manually annotated target-domain data. Our baseline system, trained using the CTB, gave an overall segmentation and POS-tagging F-score of 82.20% on this set. Application of self-training and character clustering improved the overall F-score to 83.17% and 82.56%, respectively. Since these two methods are orthogonal, they were combined to further improve the overall F-score to 83.99%.

2 Self-training

Self-training is a general semi-supervised learning approach. It has been applied to several NLP tasks with mixed results reported. Clark et al. (2003) apply self-training to POS-tagging and achieve minor improvements. Steedman et al. (2003) report that self-training can either slightly improve or significantly harm the parsing accuracy. McClosky et al. (2006) achieves improved parsing accuracies using self-training, and Reichart and Rappoport (2007) has obtained significant improvement on small datasets with lexicalized parser.

In this paper, we focus on the use of self-training for unsupervised domain adaptation. Self-training has been applied to the domain adaptation of several NLP tasks, including parsing (Roark and Bacchiani, 2003; Sagae, 2010), POS-tagging (Jiang and Zhai, 2007) and cross-language text classification (Shi et al., 2010). It improves system performance on the target domain by simultaneously modelling annotated source-domain data and unannotated target-domain data in the training process. Theoretically, self-training has a strong relationship with the EM algorithm, where tagging unlabeled data corresponds to the expectation step, and supervised parameter estimation corresponds to the maximization step. There are various factors that affects the effectiveness of self-training, such as the difference in the distributions of

Data set	chap. IDs	# of sen.	# of words
Training	1-270, 400-931, 1001-1151	18089	493939
Development	301-325	350	6821
Test	271-300	348	8008

Table 1: CTB training, development and test data.

labeled and unlabeled data, the supervised training algorithm, and additional reranking and filtering of output predictions.

Modifications can be made to the standard self-training process for domain adaptation to address the difference in source and target distributions (Margolis, 2011). In Tan et al. (2009), the weights on the target-domain data is increased at each iteration; in Saerens et al. (2002), EM is applied to the target-domain only, and the source data is used for an initial estimation. In this paper, we apply the standard self-training process, but with target-domain data point selection (Rehbein, 2011; Søgaard, 2011).

3 Character clustering

Word/character clustering is an unsupervised approach that groups similar words/characters according to their context. Clusters can be used as features instead of the original words/characters for the reduction of data sparsity. Word clustering has been applied to many NLP problems (Miller et al., 2004; Liang, 2005; Koo et al., 2008).

For our domain adaptation problem, clusters are created from large unannotated target-domain data, and applied as features in our joint segmentor and POS-tagger during both training and testing. The weights of the cluster features are estimated during training using source-domain data. During testing, they can help to alleviate the out-of-vocabulary (OOV) problem in the target-domain when a rare input has not been seen in the training data but belongs to a known cluster.

We use Liang's implementation (Liang, 2005) of the bottom-up agglomerative Brown algorithm (Brown et al., 1992) to generate character clusters, choosing the numbers of clusters according to development experiments.

4 Experiments

Software We use ZPar (Zhang and Clark, 2010, 2011) as the baseline system[1]. The system uses a single discriminative model for joint segmentation and tagging, trained using the generalized perceptron algorithm. Standard beam search is applied to ensure efficient decoding.

Source-domain data We use the CTB 5 for source-domain training, making the same training, development and test sections as Kruengkrai et al. (2009) (Table 1).

Target-domain data We collect the target-domain data from a Chinese Internet novel "*Jade dynasty*"[2] (also known as "*Zhuxian*") by Ding Xiao. The first 18 chapters (927K words in 25413 sentences) have been collected. Section 1 of chapter 6 is used as the development data, and

[1] www.sourceforge.net/project/zpar; version 0.4

[2] An electronic version of the book is free for download from the Internet.

Data set	chap. IDs	# of sen.	# of words
Training	1-5, 8-18	25413	927405
Development	6.1	159	5077
Test	7.2	226	5173

Table 2: Target-domain training, development and test data.

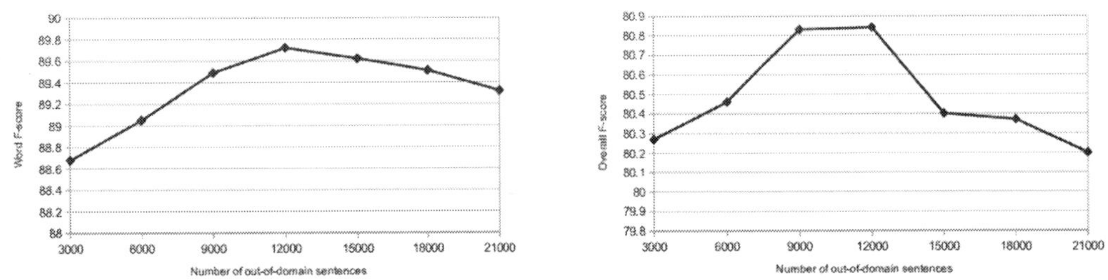

Figure 1: Development word F-scores (left) and overall word and POS F-scores (right) of self-training.

section 2 of chapter 7 is used as the test data. The remaining 16 chapters are used as the training data, as shown in Table 2. We manually annotate the development and test data to produce the gold standard reference.

Evaluation We follow Zhang and Clark (2008) and Kruengkrai et al. (2009), and use standard F-scores to measure both the word segmentation accuracy and the overall word segmentation and POS tagging accuracy. The F-score is $TF = \frac{2pr}{p+r}$ where p is the precision and r is the recall. The precision p is calculated as the percentage of correct tokens in the output, and the recall r as the percentage of golden-standard tokens that are correctly identified by the program. For word F-score, a correct token is identified as a word with the correct word boundary. For overall word and POS F-score, both the word boundary and the POS tag must be correct to make the word a correct token.

4.1 Self-training development experiments

We produce different amounts of target-domain training data by taking the first n sentences of the internet novel, with n ranging from 3000 to 21000. The sentences are automatically annotated and then combined with the CTB training data. Development test results achieved with the optimal numbers of training iterations are shown in Figure 1. The results are consistently higher than the baseline (79.64%), and the best accuracy (80.83%) is achieved with 12000 target-domain sentences (424K words).

Figure 1 also suggests that more raw text does not always lead to improved target-domain test accuracies for self-training. When the number of target-domain sentences exceeds 12000, the accuracies start to decrease. Similar observations have been reported for a cross-domain parsing task (Zhang et al., 2010). Possible reasons include the difference between source- and target-domain texts, and the intrinsic nature of self-training. To further study the problem, we conduct data-point selection (Søgaard, 2011; Rehbein, 2011), choosing to use those target-

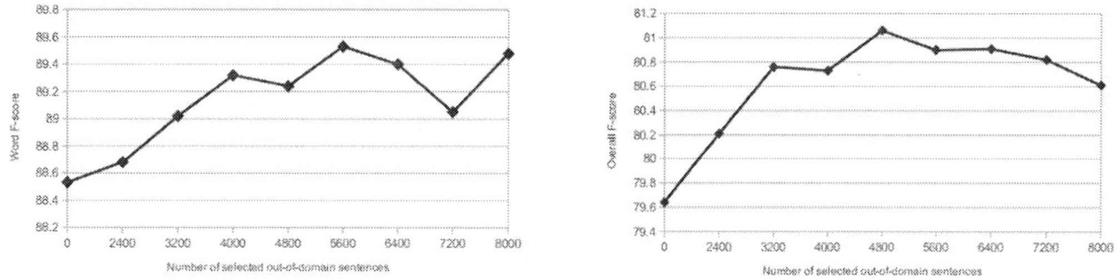

Figure 2: Development word F-scores (left) and overall word and POS F-scores (right) of self-training with data-point selection.

domain sentences that are most similar to the source-domain data for self-training, so that we can separate out the effect of text dissimilarity to some extent. To measure similarity, we use the source-domain training data to train a trigram character language model, and use perplexity per character to measure the similarity to source-domain data for target-domain sentences.

We produce different amounts of training data by selecting the top n sentences from the target domain with the lowest perplexity per character, with n ranging from 2400 to 8000, and combining them with the CTB training data. Figure 2 shows our development test results with respect to the number of target-domain sentences. The best result (F-score = 81.06%) is achieved with 4800 selected target domain sentences, which is slightly better than our previous result of self-training (F-score = 80.83%). The "self-training (perplexity)" rows in Tables 4 and 5 show the development and final test results of this method.

As Figure 2 shows, the F-scores increase when the amount of target-domain unannotated data increases from 0 to 4800, demonstrating the effect of sentences that are most similar to the source-domain data. When the amount of data increases, the perplexity of the additional data starts to increase, and the target-domain sentences are less similar to the source-domain sentences. After the peak point, the accuracy of self-training starts to decrease with more unannotated sentences. These observations suggest that data distribution does influence the effect of self-training on domain adaptation, and also partly explains why more unannotated data do not necessarily lead to improved target-domain accuracies in previous experiments.

4.2 Clustering development experiments

To include cluster information in the tagger, we add 10 cluster-based features to the feature templates used by ZPar, as shown in Table 3. Templates 1-6 contain only word information and templates 7-10 contain both word and POS information. w, t and c represent a word, a POS tag and a cluster bit-string, respectively. The subscripts in the templates are based on the current character, e.g. w_{-2} is the second word to the left of the current character. All templates are instantiated when the current character starts a new word. We select these feature templates based on the feature templates of Zhang and Clark (2010) and our development experiments.

Our clusters are extracted from the combined source- and target-domain data using the Brown algorithm. Following Koo et al. (2008) and Miller et al. (2004), we use specific prefixes of the cluster hierarchy to produce clusterings of varying granularity. Koo et al. (2008) used short

ID	Features	ID	Features
1	$w_{-2}c\_start(w_{-1})$	6	$c_{-2}c_{-1}c_0$
2	$w_{-1}c_{-1}$	7	$c_0t_{-1}t_0$
3	$w_{-1}c_0$	8	$c_0t_{-2}t_{-1}t_0$
4	c_{-1}	9	$c_{-1}t_0$
5	$c_{-1}c_0$	10	$c\_start(w_{-1})t_{-2}$

Table 3: Cluster-based feature templates.

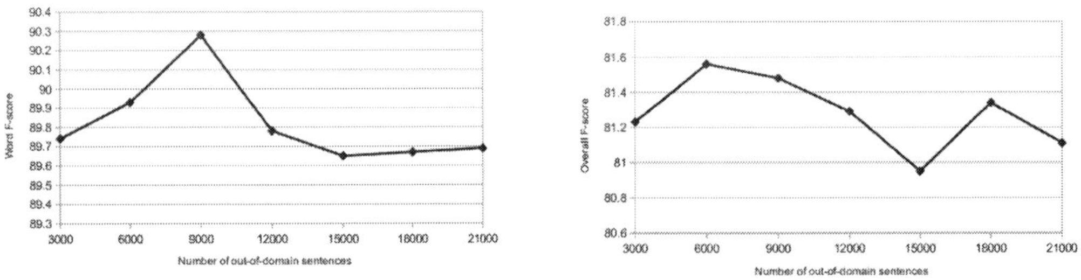

Figure 3: Development word F-scores (left) and overall word and POS F-scores (right) of the combined method.

bit-string and full bit prefixes for dependency parsing; Miller et al. (2004) used longer prefixes (12 to 20 bits) for the named-entity tagging task. In our case, we try every possible prefix length ranging from 4 to 18, both individually and jointly, and choose to use the combination of 14- and 16-bit prefixes.

Our development tests suggest that the best accuracy is achieved with the clustering extracted from the combined dataset consisting of 1000 clusters. We achieve an overall F-score of 80.26% on the Internet literature development data, which is higher than the baseline and proves the effectiveness of character clustering on this task.

4.3 Combining the two methods

Since the two methods are orthogonal to each other, they can be combined to achieve further improvement. In each of the following experiments, the same target-domain sentence set is used for both self-training and clustering. Figure 3 shows the development test results with respect to the amount of target-domain data. The highest accuracy (81.49%) is achieved with 9000 target-domain sentences, which we choose to use in our final test. Table 4 gives a summary of our development experiments.

4.4 Final test results

Table 5 shows our final test results. Similar to the development experiments, both self-training and character clustering improve the performance of the system on the target-domain, and the combined method achieves further improvement. Character clustering gives less improvements over the baseline than self-training in both the development tests and the final test. We give discussions on possible reasons in the next section.

	F-score
baseline	79.64
character clustering	80.26
self-training	80.83
self-training (perplexity)	81.06
combined method	81.49

Table 4: Development test summary.

	F-score
baseline	82.20
character clustering	82.56
self-training	83.17
self-training (perplexity)	83.32
combined method	83.99

Table 5: Final test results.

5 Discussions

In this section we give error analysis and some intuitions about the effect of the methods that have been applied in our experiments.

Self-training The most important improvement with self-training is the more accurate handling of proper nouns such as the names of persons or locations. For example, the following sentence is from the target-domain dataset: "萧逸才转头对田不易道 (Yicai Xiao turns his head towards Buyi Tian and says)". The correct segmentation and tagging of the sentence should be:

"萧逸才_NR (Yicai Xiao) 转头_VV (turn one's head) 对_P (towards) 田不易_NR (Buyi Tian) 道_VV (say)"

The output from the baseline system is:

"萧逸_NR (XiaoYi) 才_AD (Cai) 转头_VV (turn one's head) 对_P (towards) 田_NN (Tian) 不_AD (Bu) 易道_VV (Yi say),"

with both segmentation and POS-tagging errors. Using the self-trained model, the output sentence becomes:

"萧逸才_NN (Yicai Xiao) 转头_VV (turn one's head) 对_P (towards) 田不易_NR (Buyi Tian) 道_VV (say),"

which contains only one tagging error and no segmentation error — a significant improvement over the baseline result.

The two OOV personal names contribute to all baseline errors. The three characters of the second name, "田不易", are more likely to be used individually (田→ field, 不→ not, 易→ easy), which is a possible explanation to the errors made by the baseline model. In the automatically annotated target-domain data, however, in-vocabulary local context can lead "田不易" to be tagged as a single word most of the time, which could then improve the self-trained model.

Character clustering Compared to self-training, character clustering helps joint word segmentation and POS tagging in a different way, by improving the recognition of words containing rare characters and single-character words.

For example, the rare character "鼇", which stands for a legendary animal, was tagged as FW (foreign word) by the baseline tagger. The cluster-based tagger, on the other hand, is able to identify it as a noun, since it appears in the same cluster with many nouns, which indicates its syntactical similarity with nouns.

For another example, the character "而" can appear as a part of an adverb (AD). Such cases including the word "然而 (however)" or "从而 (so that)". It could also be used as a single-character conjunction or part of a conjunction, e.g. "而 (and)" and "而且 (besides)", with the POS tag "CC". Yet another less frequent use of "而" is as an auxiliary that connects an adverb to a verb, as in "侃侃 (confidently) 而 (auxiliary) 谈 (talk)", whose POS tag is "MSP". Since the first two cases are more likely to happen, the baseline model mostly treats "而" as a conjunction or an adverb, rather than an auxiliary. With the clustering information, the tagger receives more information from single-character words, therefore could tag the character "而" as "MSP" rather than "CC" or "AD" when it appears alone.

The combined method One explanation for the comparatively less effect of the character clustering method compared to the self-training method is that, although data sparsity is reduced, the weights to the cluster-based features are trained on annotated data, therefore capturing the distribution of source-domain data. When the two methods are combined, some target-domain data are used to train the feature weights of the clusters, and therefore they can play a better role in improving target-domain accuracies.

The combined method does combine the advantages of both self-training and clustering. We find that both the handling of personal names and the identification of rare characters are improved.

6 Conclusion

We studied the domain adaptation problem for joint segmentation and POS-tagging. Trained using the Chinese Treebank, the baseline system gave significantly lower accuracies on test data from internet literature. We applied self-training and unsupervised clustering to improve target-domain accuracies, both of which require comparatively small changes to the supervised baseline system, and use fully unannotated target-domain data. We observed positive results using both methods, and a combination of the methods led to further improvements. Future work remain to further reduce the gap between in-domain and out-of-domain performances for joint segmentation and tagging.

References

Blitzer, J., McDonald, R., and Pereira, F. (2006). Domain adaptation with structural correspondence learning. In *Proceedings of EMNLP*, pages 120–128, Sydney, Australia.

Brown, P. F., Pietra, V. J. D., deSouza, P. V., Lai, J. C., and Mercer, R. L. (1992). Class-based n-gram models of natural language. *Computational Linguistics*, 18(4):467–479.

Clark, S., Curran, J., and Osborne, M. (2003). Bootstrapping POS-taggers using unlabelled data. In *Proceedings of CoNLL-2003*, pages 49–55.

Daumé III, H. and Marcu, D. (2006). Domain adaptation for statistical classifiers. *Artificial Intelligence Research*, 26:101–126.

Jiang, J. and Zhai, C. (2007). Instance weighting for domain adaptation in nlp. In *Proceedings of the 45th Annual Meeting of the Association of Computational Linguistics*, pages 264–271, Prague, Czech Republic. Association for Computational Linguistics.

Jiang, W., Huang, L., Liu, Q., and Lü, Y. (2008a). A cascaded linear model for joint Chinese word segmentation and part-of-speech tagging. In *Proceedings of ACL/HLT*, pages 897–904, Columbus, Ohio.

Jiang, W., Mi, H., and Liu, Q. (2008b). Word lattice reranking for Chinese word segmentation and part-of-speech tagging. In *Proceedings of COLING*, pages 385–392, Manchester, UK.

Koo, T., Carreras, X., and Collins, M. (2008). Simple semi-supervised dependency parsing. In *Proceedings of ACL/HLT*, pages 595–603, Cambridge, MA.

Kruengkrai, C., Uchimoto, K., Kazama, J., Wang, Y., Torisawa, K., and Isahara, H. (2009). An error-driven word-character hybrid model for joint Chinese word segmentation and POS tagging. In *Proceedings of ACL/AFNLP*, pages 513–521, Suntec, Singapore.

Liang, P. (2005). Semi-supervised learning for natural language. Master's thesis, Massachusetts Institute of Technology.

Margolis, A. (2011). A literature review of domain adaptation using unlabeled data.

McClosky, D., Charniak, E., and Johnson, M. (2006). Effective self-training for parsing. In *Proceedings of HLT-NAACL*, pages 152–159.

Miller, S., Guinness, J., and Zamanian, A. (2004). Name tagging with word clusters and discriminative training. In *Proceedings of HLT-NAACL*, Cambridge, MA.

Ng, H. T. and Low, J. K. (2004). Chinese part-of-speech tagging: One-at-a-time or all-at-once? word-based or character-based? In *Proceedings of EMNLP*, Barcelona, Spain.

Rehbein, I. (2011). Data point selection for self-training. In *Proceedings of the Second Workshop on Statistical Parsing of Morphologically Rich Languages*.

Reichart, R. and Rappoport, A. (2007). Self-training for enhancement and domain adaptation of statistical parsers trained on small datasets. In *Proceedings of ACL*.

Roark, B. and Bacchiani, M. (2003). Supervised and unsupervised pcfg adaptation to novel domains. In *HLT-NAACL'03*, pages -1–1.

Saerens, M., Latinne, P., and Decaestecker, C. (2002). Adjusting the outputs of a classifier to new a priori probabilities: A simple procedure. *Neural Computation*, pages 21–41.

Sagae, K. (2010). Self-training without reranking for parser domain adaptation and its impact on semantic role labeling. In *Proceedings of the 2010 Workshop on Domain Adaptation for Natural Language Processing*, pages 37–44, Uppsala, Sweden. Association for Computational Linguistics.

Shi, L., Mihalcea, R., and Tian, M. (2010). Cross language text classification by model translation and semi-supervised learning. In *Proceedings of the 2010 Conference on Empirical Methods in Natural Language Processing*, pages 1057–1067, Cambridge, MA. Association for Computational Linguistics.

Shi, Y. and Wang, M. (2007). A dual-layer CRF based joint decoding method for cascade segmentation and labelling tasks. In *Proceedings of IJCAI*, Hyderabad, India.

Søgaard, A. (2011). Data point selection for cross-language adaptation of dependency parsers. In *49th Annual Meeting of the Association for Computational Linguistics: Human Language Technologies (ACL-HLT)*.

Steedman, M., Osborne, M., Sarkar, A., Clark, S., Hwa, R., Hockenmaier, J., Ruhlen, P., Baker, S., and Crim, J. (2003). Bootstrapping statistical parsers from small datasets. In *Proceedings of EACL*, Budapest, Hungary.

Sun, W. (2011). A stacked sub-word model for joint Chinese word segmentation and part-of-speech tagging. In *Proceedings of ACL/HLT*, pages 1385–1394, Portland, Oregon, USA. Association for Computational Linguistics.

Tan, S., Cheng, X., Wang, Y., and Xu, H. (2009). Adapting naive bayes to domain adaptation for sentiment analysis. In *ECIR'09*, pages 337–349.

Zhang, Y., Ahn, B.-G., Clark, S., Van Wyk, C., Curran, J. R., and Rimell, L. (2010). Chart pruning for fast lexicalised-grammar parsing. In *Coling 2010: Posters*, pages 1471–1479, Beijing, China. Coling 2010 Organizing Committee.

Zhang, Y. and Clark, S. (2008). Joint word segmentation and POS tagging using a single perceptron. In *Proceedings of ACL/HLT*, pages 888–896, Columbus, Ohio.

Zhang, Y. and Clark, S. (2010). A fast decoder for joint word segmentation and POS-tagging using a single discriminative model. In *Proceedings of EMNLP*, pages 843–852, Cambridge, MA.

Zhang, Y. and Clark, S. (2011). Syntactic processing using the generalized perceptron and beam search. *Computational Linguistics*, 37(1):105–151.

Tag Dispatch Model with Social Network Regularization for Microblog User Tag Suggestion

Zhiyuan Liu   Cunchao Tu   Maosong Sun
Department of Computer Science and Technology
State Key Lab on Intelligent Technology and Systems
National Lab for Information Science and Technology
Tsinghua University, Beijing 100084, China
{lzy.thu,tucunchao}@gmail.com, sms@tsinghua.edu.cn

ABSTRACT
Microblog is a popular Web 2.0 service which reserves rich information about Web users. In a microblog service, it is a simple and effective way to annotate tags for users to represent their interests and attributes. The attributes and interests of a microblog user usually hide behind the text and network information of the user. In this paper, we propose a probabilistic model, Network-Regularized Tag Dispatch Model (NTDM), for microblog user tag suggestion. NTDM models the semantic relations between words in user descriptions and tags, and takes the social network structure as regularization. Experiments on a real-world dataset demonstrate the effectiveness and efficiency of NTDM compared to other baseline methods.

TITLE AND ABSTRACT IN CHINESE

用于微博用户标签推荐的社会网络正则化的标签分发模型

微博是Web2.0的重要应用，其中包含了丰富的网络用户信息。在微博中，标签是一种表示用户兴趣和属性的简单有效的方式。一个微博用户的属性和兴趣也通常隐藏在他/她的文本和网络中。本文提出一种概率模型，网络正则化的标签分发模型（NTDM），用来进行微博用户标签推荐。NTDM对用户个人介绍中的词和标签之间的语义关系进行建模，同时将其所在的网络结构信息通过正则化的方式考虑进来。在真实数据上的实验表明，NTDM与其他方法相比更加有效。

KEYWORDS: user tag suggestion, microblog, tag dispatch model, random walks.

KEYWORDS IN CHINESE: 用户标签推荐, 微博, 标签分发模型, 随机游走.

Proceedings of COLING 2012: Posters, pages 755–764,
COLING 2012, Mumbai, December 2012.

1 Introduction

As a popular application in Web 2.0 era, microblog provides a new scheme for sharing information and expressing opinion (Java et al., 2007). Microblog users are able to post short messages within a certain length, and may also follow other users that they are interested in. A microblog service is a typical social network of microblog users with rich text information.

In order to better model user profile and provide high-quality personalized services, many microblog services (e.g., Sina Weibo) allow a user to annotate itself with several tags, which may either describe their interests or attributes. As shown in Fig. 1a, we take Kai-Fu Lee as an example, who is the CEO of Innovation Works and also a famous IT activist. Lee describes himself with several short sentences under his name and also assigns ten tags for himself.

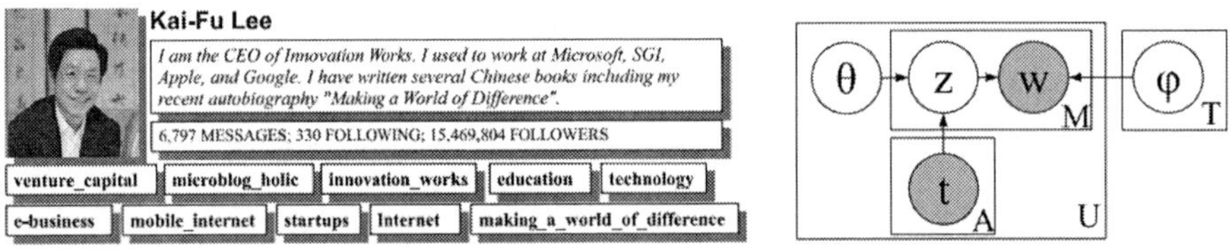

(a) Kai-Fu Lee (b) TDM

Figure 1: (a) The example of Kai-Fu Lee. (b) Graphical model of TDM.

In order to collect more accurate tags, many Web services provide tag suggestion to help users annotate. Many studies have been done to suggest tags for products such as books, movies and restaurants (Jaschke et al., 2008; Rendle et al., 2009; Iwata et al., 2009; Si et al., 2010; Liu et al., 2011). However, it is still rarely explored to suggest tags for microblog users. Due to the huge gap between the hidden attributes/interests of microblog users and their tags, it is non-trivial to build an efficient tag suggestion system. In this paper, we focus on this problem and propose a framework for efficient user tag suggestion.

Microblog services contain rich information of users, which can be roughly divided into two major types: (1) **Text Information**. A microblog user may fill a short description about itself and also post many messages. Both of them reveal the attributes or interests of the user (Liu et al., 2012). (2) **Network Information**. A user may follow other users that it is interested in, and can also be followed by other users. Following-behaviors form a social network of microblog users. The neighborhood of a user in this social network also indicates the interests of the user (McPherson et al., 2001). It is intuitive to suggest tags for a user by comprehensively considering both text and network information of the user. The idea of incorporating text and network information has been explored in many tasks such as news recommendation (De Francisci Morales et al., 2012).

In this paper, we first propose Tag Dispatch Model (TDM) for user tag suggestion based on text information. In TDM, each user is represented as a probabilistic distribution over tags, while each tag is represented as a distribution over words. For each user, TDM will learn to dispatch the most appropriate tag to each word in the description. TDM does not take network information into consideration. By assuming that tag distributions do not change dramatically from a user to its neighbors all over the social network, we define a regularizer based on social network structure for TDM, and propose Network-Regularized

TDM (NTDM). In NTDM, the distributions of user tags are smoothed all over social network. When given a new user, NTDM will suggest tags based on its text and neighbors.

2 The Framework

In this section, we present Network-Regularized Tag Dispatch Model as our framework for user tag suggestion. The data to be analyzed is a set of microblog users with their text and network information. Without loss of generality, we use the description of a user as text information, and use the following-relation to build the network. We now formally give some related concepts.

Suppose we have a set of microblog users U. Each user $u \in U$ provides a short description d_u, which can be represented as a sequence of words $x_1, x_2, \ldots, x_{N_u}$, where N_u is the number of words in the description, and each word token x_i is from a fixed word vocabulary W, i.e., $x_i = w \in W$. Following the assumption of bag-of-words, d_u is represented as $\mathbf{x}_u = \{x_i\}_{i=1}^{M_u}$, where M_u is the number of unique words that occur in the description, and we use $c(d_u, w)$ to represent the number of times that word w occurs in the description. Microblog users also form a social network according to their following-behaviors. We denote the network as $G_U = (U, E)$, where U denotes the network nodes (i.e., microblog users) and E denotes the network edges. We denote the weight of an edge (u_i, u_j) as $e(u_i, u_j)$. We define the weights of all edges in E are equal. A microblog user may annotate itself with some tags. For a user u, we denote the annotated tags as $\mathbf{a}_u = \{z_i\}_{i=1}^{A_u}$, where A_u is the number of tags in $\mathbf{a}_u$ and each tag token z_i is from a fixed tag vocabulary T, i.e., $z_i = t \in T$.

The task of user tag suggestion is formalized as follows. Given a user u with no annotated tags, we have to find a set of tags $\mathbf{a}_u$ to maximize $\Pr(\mathbf{a}_u | u, \mathbf{x}_u, G)$. Under independent assumption of tags, we have $\arg\max_{\mathbf{a}_u} \Pr(\mathbf{a}_u | u, \mathbf{x}_u, G) = \arg\max_{\mathbf{a}_u} \prod_{t \in \mathbf{a}_u} \Pr(t | u, \mathbf{x}_u, G)$. Suppose the number of suggested tags A_u is pre-defined, the task becomes a problem of ranking tags according to $\Pr(t | u, \mathbf{x}_u, G)$, and select top-$A_u$ ones as user tags.

2.1 Tag Dispatch Model (TDM)

Tag Dispatch Model (TDM) is a probabilistic graphical model. Like Probabilistic Latent Semantic Analysis (PLSA) (Hofmann, 1999) and Latent Dirichlet Allocation (LDA) (Blei et al., 2003), TDM models each user description as a distribution over tags and generates each word from a tag. Hence, TDM is different from PLSA and LDA in the following two aspects. (1) TDM considers each tag as an *explicit* topic. In other words, TDM models with *explicit tags* rather than latent topics. TDM incorporates user-annotated tags by regarding each word in user descriptions as generated from a tag. This is similar to the setting of Labeled LDA (Ramage et al., 2009). (2) When learning the mixture of tags for the description of a user, TDM constrains the distribution only having values on those tags that have been annotated by the user.

PLSA and LDA are two popular statistical topic models in information retrieval and natural language processing. In this paper, we build TDM inspired by the idea of PLSA and incorporate the advantages of LDA to avoid over-fitting. Suppose descriptions of all users in U form a collection of documents D_U. The graphical model of TDM is shown in Fig. 1b, where the observed variables are shaded. Since the generative process is to select and dispatch a tag to each word in user descriptions, we name the model as Tag *Dispatch* Model. In order to fulfill the requirement that the tag distribution of a user is restricted to its annotated tags, we set $\Pr(t|u,\mathbf{a}_u) = 0$ for all $t \notin a_u$. In other words, $\sum_{t\in\mathbf{a}_u} \Pr(t|u,\mathbf{a}_u) = 1$. The log likelihood of generating a collection D_U in TDM is formalized as $L(D_U) = \sum_{d_u\in D_U} \sum_{w\in\mathbf{x}_u} c(\mathbf{x}_u, w) \sum_{t\in T} \Pr(w|t)\Pr(t|u,\mathbf{a}_u)$. In TDM, the parameters are θ and ϕ, where $\theta_{tu} = \Pr(t|u,\mathbf{a}_u)$ and $\phi_{wt} = \Pr(w|t)$. Since each d_u belongs to a user u, we also say $\Pr(t|u) = \Pr(t|u,\mathbf{a}_u)$, which indicates the probabilistic distribution over tags given a user.

The parameters of TDM (i.e., θ and ϕ) can be estimated using the Expectation Maximization (EM) algorithm (Dempster et al., 1977). EM algorithm will iteratively computes a local maximum of $L(D_U)$. In the E-step of $(p+1)$th iteration of TDM, the posterior probabilities of latent variables (i.e., the distribution over tags on each z_i corresponding to word $x_i = w$ in $\mathbf{x}_u$ with $\mathbf{a}_u$) are calculated according to the parameters estimated in the pth iteration (i.e., $\theta^{(p)}$ and $\phi^{(p)}$) as follows,

$$\Pr(z_i = t|x_i = w, u, \mathbf{a}_u) = \frac{\Pr^{(p)}(w|t)\Pr^{(p)}(t|u,\mathbf{a}_u)}{\sum_{t\in\mathbf{a}_u} \Pr^{(p)}(w|t)\Pr^{(p)}(t|u,\mathbf{a}_u)}. \tag{1}$$

Following the common practice as shown in PLSA (Hofmann, 1999), we obtain the update equations for the M-step of the $(p+1)$th iteration in TDM as follows:

$$\phi_{wt}^{(p+1)} = \Pr^{(p+1)}(w|t) = \frac{\sum_{u\in U} c(\mathbf{x}_u, w)\Pr(t|w,u,\mathbf{a}_u) + \beta}{\sum_{w\in W}\sum_{u\in U} c(\mathbf{x}_u, w)\Pr(t|w,u,\mathbf{a}_u) + |W|\beta}, \tag{2}$$

$$\theta_{tu}^{(p+1)} = \Pr^{(p+1)}(t|u,\mathbf{a}_u) = \frac{\sum_{w\in W} c(\mathbf{x}_u, w)\Pr(t|w,u,\mathbf{a}_u) + \alpha}{\sum_{t\in\mathbf{a}_u}\sum_{w\in W} c(\mathbf{x}_u, w)\Pr(t|w,u,\mathbf{a}_u) + A_u\alpha}. \tag{3}$$

In Equation (2) and Equation (3), we follow the comparative analysis of latent Dirichlet allocation (Blei et al., 2003), and introduce hyper-parameters α and β to avoid over-fitting. In this paper, we set $\alpha = 50/|T|$ and $\beta = 0.01$. EM algorithm of TDM will run iteratively until a termination condition is satisfied.

After estimating parameters θ and ϕ of TDM, we can suggest tags for a new microblog user u with description $\mathbf{x}_u$ as follows. Suppose all tags in T are candidates for this user. We perform EM algorithm to estimate $\Pr(t|u,\mathbf{x}_u)$ while keeping $\Pr(t|w)$ fixed. Then we rank candidate tags according to $\Pr(t|u,\mathbf{x}_u)$ and select top-A_u as suggested tags.

We have $c(\mathbf{x}_u, w)$ in Equation (2) and (3), which indicates the importance of w in $\mathbf{x}_u$. In practice, a word that occurs frequently doest not indicate it is important. In this paper, we estimate the importance of a word w in $\mathbf{x}_u$ using term frequency and inverse user frequency (TFIUF) as follows:

$$\Pr(w|\mathbf{x}_u) = \frac{c(\mathbf{x}_u, w)}{\sum_{w\in\mathbf{x}_u} c(\mathbf{x}_u, w)} \times \log\frac{|U|}{|\{w\in\mathbf{x}_u\}_{u\in U}|}. \tag{4}$$

Here the first part is term frequency of word w in $\mathbf{x}_u$, and the second is the inverse user frequency, where user frequency is the proportion of users who use word w in their descriptions. The idea of TFIUF is similar to term frequency and inverse document frequency (TFIDF) (Salton and Buckley, 1988) which is widely adopted in information retrieval.

2.2 Network-Regularized Tag Dispatch Model (NTDM)

We take the network structure into account as a regularization for TDM. In the context of social network, we assume that the users who are connected with each other should share more interests and attributes, and thus should have similar tag distributions, i.e., for a connected user pair $(u, v) \in E$, $\Pr(t|u, \mathbf{a}_u)$ is similar to $\Pr(t|v, \mathbf{a}_v)$.

Formally, given a collection of microblog users U with their descriptions D_U and social network G_U, we define the regularized likelihood as $L(D_U, G_U) = (1-\alpha)L(D_U) - \alpha R(D_U, G_U)$, where $L(D_U)$ is the log likelihood of generating user descriptions, and $R(D_U, G_U)$ is a harmonic regularizer defined on the social network G_U. Similar to graph harmonic function (Zhu et al., 2003), we define $R(D_U, G_U)$ as $R(D_U, G_U) = \frac{1}{2}\sum_{(u,v)\in E} e(u,v) \sum_{t\in T} \left(\Pr(t|u,\mathbf{a}_u) - \Pr(t|v,\mathbf{a}_v)\right)^2$, where $e(u, v)$ is the weight of edge (u, v), and α is the harmonic factor ranging from 0 to 1. Since $L(D_U)$ indicates the probability that user descriptions are generated from the model, we can maximize $L(D_U)$ to find optimal model parameters (i.e., θ and ϕ) with respect to user descriptions. $R(D_U, G_U)$ indicates the weighted average distance in terms of tag distributions between any two connected users in the social network. We maximize $-R(D_U, G_U)$ (i.e., minimizing $R(D_U, G_U)$) to smooth the tag distributions over the social network, i.e., the neighbored users will tend to share similar tag distributions. The harmonic factor α controls trade-off between data likelihood and regularization. When $\alpha = 0$, the regularized likelihood will be the same to TDM. When $\alpha = 1$, the regularized likelihood will only consider the network structure, which likes clustering based on network structure.

We will also use EM algorithms to estimate parameters of NTDM. We can see that NTDM and TDM share the same latent variables, i.e., tag distribution conditional over a word in user description $\Pr(t|w, u, \mathbf{a}_u)$. We can also use Equation (1) to compute the latent variables for NTDM. The M-step in NTDM is more complicated than that in TDM due to the harmonic regularization. The estimation of $\Pr(w|t)$ does not have relations to regularization. Hence we can update $\phi_{wt} = \Pr(w|t)$ in the same way as in Equation (2). Since θ is involved in the regularizer, we do not have a closed form solution to update θ. As proposed in (Mei et al., 2008; Cai et al., 2008), we can iteratively update and obtain

$$\Pr_{i+1}^{(p+1)}(t|u,\mathbf{a}_u) = (1-\lambda)\Pr_{i}^{(p+1)}(t|u,\mathbf{a}_u) + \lambda \frac{\sum_{(v,u)\in E} e(v,u)\Pr_{i}^{(p+1)}(t|v,\mathbf{a}_v)}{\sum_{(v,u)\in E} e(v,u)}, \tag{5}$$

where i is the number of the inner iterations, and λ is a damping factor ranging from 0 to 1. When $\lambda = 0$, NTDM becomes into TDM without considering network structure. When $\lambda = 1$, it indicates that the new tag distribution of u is the average of the old tag distributions of its neighbors. In experiments, we set $\lambda = 0.15$ which follows most settings in random walks (Langville and Meyer, 2004). The iterative random walks with Equation (5) will make the tag distributions smoother over the microblog social network. In practice, not all users in the dataset have annotated themselves with tags. For a user u that has not annotated itself with tags, we set $\mathbf{a}_u = T$. In Equation (5) of NTDM, we set $\Pr_{i+1}^{(p+1)}(t|u,\mathbf{a}_u) = 0$ if $t \notin \mathbf{a}_u$. This will avoid tag drift during iteration.

2.3 User Tag Suggestion based on NTDM

Given a user u with its description $\mathbf{x}_u$, NTDM suggests tags as follows. If u belongs to the dataset (i.e., $u \in U$), we have obtained its tag distribution with Equation (5) with learning of NTDM, and can suggest top-ranked tags according to $\Pr^{(p+1)}(t|u,\mathbf{a}_u)$.

If the new user u does not belong to the dataset (i.e., $u \notin U$), we estimate $\Pr(t|u, \mathbf{a}_u)$ in two ways: (1) We use EM algorithm to estimate the tag distribution of u based on user description $\mathbf{x}_u$ and NTDM parameters ϕ. The difference is in the process we do not necessarily modify ϕ and just update θ_u. We denote the text-based tag distribution as $\Pr_T(t|u,\mathbf{a}_u)$. (2) We estimate the tag distribution of u based on its neighbors. We assume that all neighbors of u belong to U, and denote the set of neighbors as U_u. We estimate the tag distribution as $\Pr(t|u,\mathbf{a}_u) = \sum_{v\in U_u} e(v,u)\Pr(t|v,\mathbf{a}_v)/\sum_{v\in U_u} e(v,u)$, where $\Pr(t|v,\mathbf{a}_v)$ is the tag distribution of $v \in U$ estimated in NTDM. We denote the network-based tag distribution as $\Pr_N(t|u,\mathbf{a}_u)$. Finally, we integrate the text-based and network-based tag distribution together with smoothing factor λ: $\Pr(t|u,\mathbf{a}_u) = (1-\lambda)\Pr_T(t|u,\mathbf{a}_u) + \lambda\Pr_N(t|u,\mathbf{a}_u)$. Similar to Equation (5), we also set $\lambda = 0.15$.

3 Experiments

We crawled 2 million users from Sina Weibo for experiments. These users are all active and post messages frequently. In order to better demonstrate the effectiveness of our method, from these users we select 341,353 users who have both descriptions and tags as the dataset. We further divide the dataset by randomly selecting 10,000 users as test set and the rest users as training set. We use precision/recall for evaluation. For a user, we denote the original tags (gold standard) as T_a, the suggested tags as T_s, and the correctly suggested tags as $T_s \cap T_a$. Then, precision and recall are defined as $p = (T_s \cap T_a)/T_s$ and $r = (T_s \cap T_a)/T_a$.

3.1 Evaluation on User Tag Suggestion

To evaluate the performance of NTDM for social tag suggestion, we select two major types of baseline methods for comparison: context-based methods which suggest tags relying on user descriptions, and network-based methods which suggest tags according to the neighborhood information of users.

Text-Based Methods. There are many text-based methods proposed for social tag suggestion. In this paper, we use the following text-based methods as baselines. (1) *Feature Driven Methods*. We regard user tag suggestion as a multi-label classification task, and use feature driven methods to train classifiers. In these methods, the probability of a user u being annotated with tag t is computed as $\Pr(t|u) = \sum_{w\in\mathbf{x}_u} \Pr(t|w)\Pr(w|\mathbf{x}_u)$. We use TFIUF defined in Equation (4) to measure $\Pr(w|\mathbf{x}_u)$. There are various statistical measures to estimate $\Pr(t|w)$. We select Pointwise Mutual Information (PMI) (Lin, 1998) and Normalized Google Distance (NGD) (Cilibrasi and Vitanyi, 2007) for estimation. In experiments, we denote the two feature driven methods as PMI-T and NGD-T, respectively. (2) *k Nearest Neighbor (kNN)*. kNN is a classification method based on closest training instances in the feature space (Mishne, 2006; Li et al., 2009). In user tag suggestion, given a user u, kNN finds k nearest neighbors according to their description similarities with u and selects tags by majority vote of neighbors for suggestion. In experiments, we set $k = 5$ which achieves the best performance of kNN. In experiments, we denote the method as kNN-T. (3) *TagLDA*. TagLDA (Krestel et al., 2009; Si and Sun, 2009) is a representative latent topic model by extending latent Dirichlet allocation (LDA) (Blei et al., 2003). Using a collection of annotated users, TagLDA will learn the distributions over words and tags for each topic. Given a novel user, TagLDA will first infer the topic distribution according to the user's description and then suggest tags based on the topic distribution. (4) *Tag Dispatch Model (TDM)*. TDM can be regarded as a text-based version of NTDM, which only considers user descriptions for user tag suggestion. Different from TagLDA, TDM uses tags as *explicit* topics to directly build semantic relations between words and tags.

Network-Based Methods. Network-based methods consider the network structure for social tag suggestion. The basic idea is that a tag will be suggested to a user if the tag is widely annotated by the neighbors of the user. Similar to text-based methods, we use the tags annotated by neighbors as features to build feature-driven classifiers. We formalize the probability of t given a user u as $\Pr(t|u) = \sum_{s\in T} \Pr(s|t)\Pr(s|U_u)$, where U_u is the neighbors of u, $\Pr(s|U_u)$ is the importance of a tag s in neighbors of u, and $\Pr(s|t)$ indicates the probability of s given t. In this equation, $\Pr(s|U_u)$ is estimated as $\Pr(s|U_u) = (|U_{tu}|)/(|U_u|)$, where $|U_{tu}|$ is the number of neighbors that annotate tag s, and $|U_u|$ is the total number of neighbors. $\Pr(s|t)$ can be measured using either PMI or NGD. In experiments, we denote the two methods as PMI-N and NGD-N, respectively.

Hybrid Methods. We can also take text features and network features together and use NB, PMI and NGD as classifiers. Under the assumption of naive Bayes, it is straightforward to combine the two types of features as $\Pr(t|u) = \sum_{w\in \mathbf{x}_u} \Pr(t|w)\Pr(w|\mathbf{x}_u) + \sum_{s\in T} \Pr(t|s)\Pr(s|U_u)$. In hybrid methods, we can also use either PMI or NGD. Hence, in experiments, we denote the two hybrid methods as PMI-H and NGD-H.

3.1.1 Evaluation Results and Analysis

In Figure 2 we show the precision-recall curves of various baseline methods and NTDM on test set. Each point of a precision-recall curve represents different numbers of suggested tags from $M = 1$ (bottom right, with higher precision and lower recall) to $M = 6$ (upper left, with higher recall but lower precision) respectively. The closer the curve to the upper right, the better the overall performance of the method. Hence, in experiments we focus on evaluating the performance when $M \leq 6$ since the average number of tags per user in the dataset is 6.0.

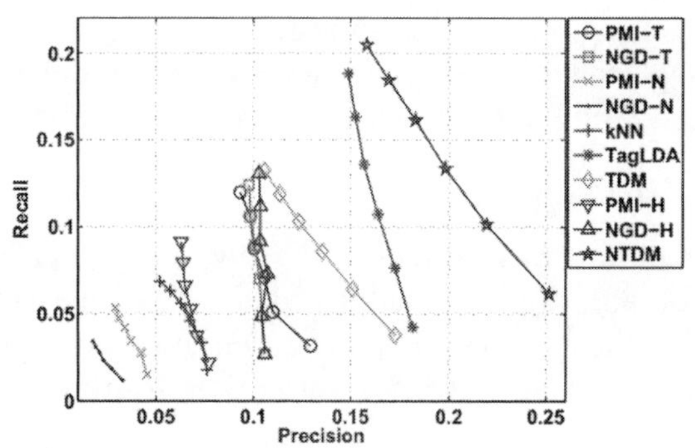

Figure 2: Evaluation results when suggesting tags from $M = 1$ to $M = 6$.

From Figure 2 we have the following observations. (1) NTDM significantly outperforms other methods when M ranges from 1 to 6. The significance test is performed by using bootstrap re-sampling with 95% confidence. This indicates that NTDM is efficient and effective for user tag suggestion. Other text-based and network-based methods perform poorly because independently using either text information or network information will be insufficient to capture the attributes and interests of users. Although TagLDA performs better than TDM, NTDM outperforms TagLDA significantly. This indicates that it is crucial to take network structure into consideration. (2) PMI-H and NGD-H perform poor compared to NTDM. Both methods are even worse than PMI-T and NGD-T. This suggests that naive hybrid of text and network information will not eventually lead to better results. Essentially, we have to find a smart way to combine the two types of information. This is what NTDM is proposed to do, and the experiment results demonstrate its effectiveness.

3.1.2 Case Studies

In Table 1 we show top words ranked by $\Pr(w|t)$ for several tags of Kai-Fu Lee. We observe that NTDM can sufficiently capture the semantic relations between words and tags, while TDM introduces noise. For example, in TDM the top words "optimization", "factory" and "Jinan" of the tag "e-business" are, to some extent, not tightly correlated with the tag.

Tag	Top Words Ranked by $\Pr(w\|t)$
venture_capital	venture_capital, VC, early_stage, copartner, minor_enterprises
education	parents, children, coaching, normal_university, admission
e-business	B2C, supply, Alibaba, supermarket, B2B
mobile_Internet	Internet, terminal, LBS, summit, android

Table 1: Top words ranked by $\Pr(w|t)$ for some tags of Kai-Fu Lee.

With accurate semantic relations, NTDM suggests better tags for microblog users. Take Kai-Fu Lee for example, top-5 tags suggested by NTDM are "startups","Internet", "Google", "e-business" and "mobile_Internet". In this list, although "Google" is not annotated by Lee, it reflects the fact that Lee used to work as President of Google China from 2005 to 2009. Meanwhile, TDM suggests "Google", "Apple", "startups", "photographing" and "post_80s"; TagLDA suggests "post_80s", "Internet", "music", "movie" and "travel". We have the following observations: (1) TagLDA tends to suggest common tags irrelevant to the user. This is the common issue shared by latent topic models, which project both descriptions and tags into topic space for measuring relatedness and suffer from the over-generalization problem. (2) The last two tags suggested by TDM are roughly not correlated to Lee, which is a natural consequence of not considering network structure for regularization.

Conclusion and Future Work

This paper presents NTDM for microblog user tag suggestion. NTDM models the semantic relations between words and tags, as well as taking social network structure as regularization. Experiments on the real-world dataset demonstrate that NTDM is sufficient to combine the text information and network information of users for user tag suggestion.

We design the following research plans. (1) NTDM considers edge weights of all connected users being equal for simplicity. In future, we plan to incorporate more microblog information to estimate edge weights, and further make the network regularization more accurate. (2) This paper does not take user posts into consideration. We plan to model more complex text and network information for user tag suggestion.

Acknowledgments

This work is supported by the National Natural Science Foundation of China (NSFC) under the grant No. 61170196 and 61202140. The authors would like to thank Mr. Bin Liang for providing data.

References

Blei, D., Ng, A., and Jordan, M. (2003). Latent dirichlet allocation. *JMLR*, 3:993–1022.

Cai, D., Mei, Q., Han, J., and Zhai, C. (2008). Modeling hidden topics on document manifold. In *Proceedings of CIKM*, pages 911–920.

Cilibrasi, R. and Vitanyi, P. (2007). The google similarity distance. *IEEE Transactions on Knowledge and Data Engineering*, 19(3):370–383.

De Francisci Morales, G., Gionis, A., and Lucchese, C. (2012). From chatter to headlines: harnessing the real-time web for personalized news recommendation. In *Proceedings of WSDM*, pages 153–162.

Dempster, A., Laird, N., Rubin, D., et al. (1977). Maximum likelihood from incomplete data via the em algorithm. *Journal of the Royal Statistical Society. Series B (Methodological)*, 39(1):1–38.

Hofmann, T. (1999). Probabilistic latent semantic indexing. In *Proceedings of SIGIR*, pages 50–57.

Iwata, T., Yamada, T., and Ueda, N. (2009). Modeling social annotation data with content relevance using a topic model. In *Proceedings of NIPS*, pages 835–843.

Jaschke, R., Marinho, L., Hotho, A., Schmidt-Thieme, L., and Stumme, G. (2008). Tag recommendations in social bookmarking systems. *AI Communications*, 21(4):231–247.

Java, A., Song, X., Finin, T., and Tseng, B. (2007). Why we twitter: understanding microblogging usage and communities. In *Proceedings of the 9th WebKDD and 1st SNA-KDD 2007 workshop on Web mining and social network analysis*, pages 56–65.

Krestel, R., Fankhauser, P., and Nejdl, W. (2009). Latent dirichlet allocation for tag recommendation. In *Proceedings of ACM RecSys*, pages 61–68.

Langville, A. and Meyer, C. (2004). Deeper inside pagerank. *Internet Mathematics*, 1(3):335–380.

Li, X., Snoek, C., and Worring, M. (2009). Learning social tag relevance by neighbor voting. *IEEE Transactions on Multimedia*, 11(7):1310–1322.

Lin, D. (1998). An information-theoretic definition of similarity. In *Proceedings of ICML*, pages 296–304.

Liu, Z., Chen, X., and Sun, M. (2011). A simple word trigger method for social tag suggestion. In *Proceedings of EMNLP*, pages 1577–1588.

Liu, Z., Chen, X., and Sun, M. (2012). Mining the interests of chinese microbloggers via keyword extraction. *Frontiers of Computer Science*, 6(1):76–87.

McPherson, M., Smith-Lovin, L., and Cook, J. (2001). Birds of a feather: Homophily in social networks. *Annual review of sociology*, pages 415–444.

Mei, Q., Cai, D., Zhang, D., and Zhai, C. (2008). Topic modeling with network regularization. In *Proceedings of WWW*, pages 101–110.

Mishne, G. (2006). Autotag: a collaborative approach to automated tag assignment for weblog posts. In *Proceedings of WWW*, pages 953–954.

Ramage, D., Hall, D., Nallapati, R., and Manning, C. (2009). Labeled lda: A supervised topic model for credit attribution in multi-labeled corpora. In *Proceedings of EMNLP*, pages 248–256.

Rendle, S., Balby Marinho, L., Nanopoulos, A., and Schmidt-Thieme, L. (2009). Learning optimal ranking with tensor factorization for tag recommendation. In *Proceedings of KDD*, pages 727–736.

Salton, G. and Buckley, C. (1988). Term-weighting approaches in automatic text retrieval. *Information processing and management*, 24(5):513–523.

Si, X., Liu, Z., and Sun, M. (2010). Modeling social annotations via latent reason identification. *IEEE Intelligent Systems*, 25(6):42 – 49.

Si, X. and Sun, M. (2009). Tag-LDA for scalable real-time tag recommendation. *Journal of Computational Information Systems*, 6(1):23–31.

Zhu, X., Ghahramani, Z., and Lafferty, J. (2003). Semi-supervised learning using gaussian fields and harmonic functions. In *Proceedings of ICML*, pages 912–919.

Summarization of Business-related Tweets: A Concept-based Approach

Annie LOUIS[1] *Todd NEWMAN*[2]
(1) University of Pennsylvania, Philadelphia PA 19104, USA
(2) FUSE Labs Microsoft Research, Redmond WA 98052, USA
lannie@seas.upenn.edu, todd.newman@microsoft.com

ABSTRACT
We present a method for summarizing the collection of tweets related to a business. Our procedure aggregates tweets into subtopic clusters which are then ranked and summarized by a few representative tweets from each cluster. Central to our approach is the ability to group diverse tweets into clusters. The broad clustering is induced by first learning a small set of business-related concepts automatically from free text and then subdividing the tweets into these concepts. Cluster ranking is performed using an importance score which combines topic coherence and sentiment value of the tweets. We also discuss alternative methods to summarize these tweets and evaluate the approaches using a small user study. Results show that the concept-based summaries are ranked favourably by the users.

KEYWORDS: tweets, twitter, summarization, business, concepts, domain-specific.

Proceedings of COLING 2012: Posters, pages 765–774,
COLING 2012, Mumbai, December 2012.

1 Introduction

In this work, we focus on tweets that mention a company name. Such company-related tweets are useful to multiple audiences. Tweets are a good source of public opinion. Hence company analysts and internal users can benefit from an overview of social chatter about the company. On the other hand, consumers are interested in reviews about a company for product, job-related and financial aspects. Other non-opinion content in tweets such as deals, job postings and advertisements are also useful to consumers. But the volume of tweets and their unconnected nature make browsing a stream of tweets rather difficult. This paper explores how to categorize tweets into subtopics and create a representative summary for each subtopic.

The challenge for this task is the diversity of the tweets. Tweets related to a company range from current news involving the company to job postings, advertisements, and cursory mentions. Moreover, tweets are short and contain informal language. As a result, there is little word overlap between tweets making it difficult to categorize them. We introduce an innovative method that performs broad clustering and does not rely solely on word overlap. Central to the method is the automatic acquisition and use of business-specific concepts. Our three-step approach is briefly summarized below:

1. Concept learning. Firstly, we acquire possible business concepts which are related to any company. For example, a company would have people in its management, customers, products, stocks and financial matters, events related to the company etc. Each of these 'people', 'products', 'assets' and 'events' could be a possible aspect for dividing the tweets. Our innovation is to learn such a set of business aspects automatically from an external source other than tweets—business news articles. Each concept is a group of related words identified from business news articles but also includes flexibility to handle new words in tweets that were unseen during concept extraction. Further this procedure is done offline only once and does not rely on any tweets.

2. Tweet clustering. All companies are assumed to have the same set of concepts indentified above. The tweets for each company get mapped to these concepts forming clusters. This mapping process allows even tweets with non-overlapping words to map to the same cluster.

3. Cluster ranking and summarization. These clusters are ranked using properties such as influential subtopic and sentiment associated with it. For this purpose, we also develop a sentiment classifier for business tweets.

We compare our method with other ways of summarizing the tweets and provide a small annotation study to understand user preferences. We found that the concept-based approach is able to provide useful summaries of tweets.

2 Dataset and types of business tweets

This section describes how we obtain the input tweets for our summarization system. We used an existing Microsoft crowdsourcing framework to obtain keywords related to different companies. We gave a company's name and asked people to add any keyword related to the company. Most keywords were related to products, people in its management, and affiliated businesses. There was a maximum of 5 keywords for a company and we also include the company name in keyword set. Each keyword is used to collect matching tweets from the past three days. The set of tweets for *all* the keywords for each company is the collection we wish to summarize for that company. The number of tweets for the companies in our development and test sets are shown in Table 1.

The tweets vary in their source as well as content. Some broad categories are shown in Table 2.

	Development set					Test set	
Bank of America	695	RBS	197	Supervalu	108	Wells Fargo	1020
Sams Club	359	Costco	140	Abbot Labs	97	Lowes	887
JP Morgan Chase	351	Comcast	150	Sage Summit	87	Johnson & Johnson	811
Samsung	314	Delta Airlines	129	Att wireless	68	Northrop Grumman	280
Exxon Mobil	287	Prudential	128	Trader Joes	33	LinkedIn	280
Goldman Sachs	256	Safeway	125	Easy Jet	39	Nokia	158

Table 1: Companies and number of associated tweets

1. Related to news	**2. Comments on products/services**
RT @user1: Goldman Sachs: Calling for Greater Oil Price Speculation, Again http://.../ "vampire squid", indeed	Walmart orange chicken is digustin!!! My mom learned her lesson only the SAMs club version now on
3. On company aspects (eg. financial matters, people)	**4. Comments not related to any particular aspect**
Sen. Rubio: we don't need new taxes, we need new taxpayers Agreed, how about we start with GE and Exxon/Mobil.	I JUST LOVE WHEN BANK OF AMERICA LIESSSS TO MEEEE!
5. Postings from other applications such as 4Square	**6. Advertisements, job postings**
I'm at JPMorgan Chase in Lake Mary, FL http://	AZ Jobs | North Phoenix- Part time Teller - 67th Ave
7. Mentions but not really about the company	
My little bro just asked me was uncle Sam the owner of Sams club...	

Table 2: Types of business-related tweets. The company-related keyword is underlined.

3 Related work

Most methods for summarizing tweets have either focused on tweets matching a generic search query (O'Connor et al., 2010), or on tweets related to sports and celebrity events (Sharifi et al., 2010; Chakrabarti and Punera, 2011; Liu et al., 2011; Inouye and Kalita, 2011; Nichols et al., 2012). We focus on summarizing the tweets that show up in the search for a company.

In fact, our work is more related to aspect-based summarization methods commonly employed on product reviews (Hu and Liu, 2004; Gamon et al., 2005; Sauper et al., 2011; Zhai et al., 2011). These methods first obtain a set of attributes for the product. For example, for a camera, the attributes may be "lens", "focus" and "zoom". Then positive and negative sentences in the reviews are divided according to these attributes and their aggregate are shown for each category. Some approaches obtain the attributes through manual annotations and domain resources (Gamon et al., 2005; Zhuang et al., 2006). Others learn the attributes automatically using the review text (Hu and Liu, 2004; Titov and McDonald, 2008; Sauper et al., 2011; Zhai et al., 2011). Frequently occurring phrases in the reviews and also which often tend to be associated with sentiment as chosen as attributes. But while product review archives have significant overlap in topics, the informal nature of twitter conversation creates diverse tweets and also mixes review and non-review content. Identifying frequent attributes from tweet streams becomes difficult and unreliable. So we use an external resource, news articles, to learn concepts for the business domain and use these concepts to guide clustering of tweets. Our procedure for learning concepts is fully automatic and without reference to individual companies whereas product review attributes are usually specific to the product.

Our cluster ranking procedure is also novel compared to prior approaches that either do not rank the clusters explicitly or use only sentiment information for ranking (Gamon et al., 2005; Zhuang et al., 2006; Blair-Goldensohn et al., 2008; Sauper et al., 2011). In our work, we merge sentiment information with a score to identify if a subtopic discusses an overwhelming issue.

packages	pay	bonus	profits	examples	wiring	kiosks
talent	telecommunication	stability	bookstores	cancellation	pilot	supplies
prize	investigation	equals	applicant	shutdown	savings	earnings
actuary	reports	plant	notice	vehicle	pilots	brands

Table 3: Samples from the company-word dictionary

4 Concept-based summarization

We present our three-step approach in this section.

4.1 Concept creation

This step creates a dictionary of business-related concepts using one year's worth of news articles from the New York Times (NYT) corpus (Sandhaus, 2008).

We first identify company names in these articles. A named entity tagger is used to automatically mark all mentions of 'organizations'. Using the metadata in the NYT corpus, we identify articles that appeared in the business section of the newspaper and only the 'organization' mentions in these articles are considered as possible company names. These company names are replaced with a generic token "COMPANY" because we are interested in words associated with company mentions in general without reference to individual companies.

Then the nouns (proper nouns are excluded) in a window of 20 words each before and after all COMPANY tokens are obtained as a list of candidates for the dictionary. For each candidate word w_i, we compute its association with COMPANY tokens in the corpus using mutual information.

$$\mathrm{MI}(w_i, \mathrm{COMPANY}) = \log \frac{p(w_i, \mathrm{COMPANY})}{p(w_i)p(\mathrm{COMPANY})}$$

p(w_i, COMPANY) is the probability with which w_i is found in the vicinity (20 word window before and after) of COMPANY tokens. p(w_i) is the probability of w_i in the full corpus and p(COMPANY) is computed likewise.

The top 2000 nouns in this ranking are selected to create a company-word dictionary (a random sample is shown in Table 3). Next we group these words using WordNet (Miller, 1995) to obtain more general concepts. We obtain the list of synsets on the hypernym path between each company-word and the root of WordNet. Then we record the synset names for a word at levels 3, 4 and 5 from the root. (Root is considered as level 1.) The sequence of these 3 synsets is considered as the SEMANTIC TAG for the word. Word that map to the same SEMANTIC TAG are grouped and correspond to a concept. We choose levels 3, 4 and 5 to obtain a concept that is neither too specific nor too general. The resulting set has 57 diverse concepts and most of them can be intuitively understood to be business-related. We manually assigned a name for each concept based on the SEMANTIC TAG and the group of words. Each concept is a triple (T, L, D) where T is its SEMANTIC TAG and L is the MANUAL LABEL. D represents the grouped words (called PRIOR WORDS) for that concept. Table 4 shows example concepts with different number of PRIOR WORDS.

All the above processing is done offline and only once. Note that up to this step, we have used only the news articles and WordNet for concept extraction.

4.2 Mapping tweets into concepts

For each company, we assume that the same set of 57 concepts are the possible subtopics for its tweets. We assign each tweet to one of these concepts.

Semantic tag [T] (Levels 3 - 4 - 5)	Size	Example prior words [D]	Manual label [L]
[psychological feature] - [event] - [human activity]	341	merger, consultancy, takeover	Activities
[physical object] - [unit] - [animate thing]	208	acquirer, creditor, sibling, analyst	People
[physical object] - [unit] - [artefact]	189	airline, appliance apparel, auto	Artefacts
[group] - [social_group] - [organization]	54	carmaker, insurer, division, firm	Group
[matter] - [substance] - food	23	beer, provisions, candy, snack	Food
[relation] - [possession] - [property]	5	trust, effects, estate, property	Property
[attribute] - [quality] - [asset]	5	specialty, asset, advantage	Plus/Quality

Table 4: Some company-related semantic concepts. 'Size' indicates total number of prior words.

This process involves computing a membership score for each tweet and concept pair (t_i, C_k). The score has two components—exact and fuzzy. We first record words from t_i which directly match any of the PRIOR WORDS D of the concept C_k. We call these words as exact matches, set E, for that concept. For each of the remaining words in the tweet, we compute its SEMANTIC TAG from WordNet as before and check if it matches the tag T of C_k. In the event of a match, we add the word to the set of fuzzy matches F. The remaining words are ignored. The membership score for the tweet-concept pair is computed as:

$$score(t_i, C_j) = \lambda * |E| + (1 - \lambda) * |F|$$

Here λ is set to 0.8 to give higher weight to exact matches. The union of exact and fuzzy matches $E \cup F$ are stored as the MATCHING WORDS for that tweet-concept pair. The tweet is assigned to the concept with which it has maximum membership score. Where there is a tie, the tweet is assigned to the concept that has the most non-zero membership values across all tweets. In this way, the tweet is assigned to the more general of the candidate concepts.

4.3 Cluster ranking and summarization

We summarize the resulting clusters using two modules.

4.3.1 Cluster ranking

We introduce a method to rank clusters by combining sentiment value and entropy of word distribution in the cluster. The intuition is that when the tweets in a cluster discuss a common issue, we should rank it higher than a cluster which has diverse content. For example, on a given day when the CEO of a company resigns, many users discuss the event and so the "people" concept cluster of the company would have homogenous content on that day. In addition, the tweets in such a cluster will also have a lot of sentiment.

We use the entropy of the word distribution in a cluster as a measure of homogeneity and also adapt the score to consider the sentiment of words. Further, rather than use all the words in the cluster, we utilize only a smaller set of topical words which we obtain by combining all the MATCHING WORDS (see Section 4.2) for tweets belonging to that cluster.

Consider a cluster C_j and the union of MATCHING WORDS for its constituent tweets is the set M. The probability of a word $w_i \in M$ is given as:

$$p(w_i) = \frac{wtcount(w_i)}{\sum_{w_k \in M} wtcount(w_k)}$$

where $wtcount(w_i) = \sum_m sentimentValue(S_m)$. Here S_m is a tweet MATCHED to C_j by w_i.

The sentiment value of a tweet ranges between 0 and 1 and is obtained from a sentiment classifier. The classifier does a 3-way division of tweets into positive, negative and neutral

(+57) People: customer, banker, employee, man
Wells Fargo holding a daylong seminar to help customers having problems with mortgage http://../
I swear Wachovia care more about customer service than anything
Wells Fargo decided to exit reverse mortgages after federal officials insisted it foreclose on elderly customers http://../
(+14) Amount: money, cash, fund
Wells Fargo act like they are mad about their little money
Wells Fargo lost cash off my card. #smh I am sewing someone

Table 5: Snippet from a concept-summary for *Wells Fargo*. (+x) indicates cluster size.

categories and outputs a probability distribution over these 3 classes. The sentiment value is the absolute difference in positive and negative confidence value from the classifier. This score indicates the degree to which the tweet is oriented towards one kind of sentiment—positive or negative and takes the highest value of 1 when the tweet is predicted as fully positive or negative. Using these sentiment-aware probabilities, we compute the entropy of C_j.

$$H(C_j) = -\sum_i p(w_i) \log p(w_i)$$

Lower values of entropy indicate a skewed distribution of MATCHING WORDS and therefore a better cluster. But a large cluster is likely to get higher entropy even if it is cohesive, compared with a smaller cluster. So we apply a weighting factor to reduce the entropy of large clusters.

$$H_{adjusted}(C_j) = (1 - \frac{|C_j|}{\sum_k |C_k|})H(C_j)$$

This score $H_{adjusted}$ is the final score for a cluster. Lower scores indicate higher ranked clusters.[1]

4.3.2 Faceted summarization

This step generates a summary for the top-ranked clusters. First we obtain the top four MATCHING WORDS of the cluster that have highest probability (also incorporating sentiment as in the previous step). These words are displayed as a headline for the cluster.

For each headline word, we identify all the tweets containing that word. We compute average probability of words in each tweet and rank them in descending order of score. The average probability scoring is a popular and successful method for automatic summarization (Nenkova et al., 2006). The probability value is computed as in the previous section by also incorporating sentiment information. We only use the first two headline words for summary generation. For the first headline word we pick the top two sentences from its ranked list and we choose one sentence for the second word. For the final interface, the clusters are shown in rank order up to a certain limit on the number of tweets displayed. Table 5 shows an example summary.

5 Sentiment classification

We built a 3-way sentiment classifier for our task. We annotated 2470 tweets from the development set as positive, negative or neutral in sentiment. Exact retweets were removed and when the main topic of a tweet was not the company, it was annotated as neutral regardless of other sentiment. Annotators include the authors and six software engineers. The resulting data had 49.5% neutral, 22.8% positive and 27.6% negative tweets.

[1]But when the entropy is zero (only one MATCHING WORD), we lose information about sentiment value. For such zero-entropy clusters, check the average sentiment value on the MATCHING WORD and if below a threshold, we demote the cluster and assign to it the largest entropy value across all clusters.

CN is first word of tweet	CN has dependency link to main/some verb
POS of words within two words around CN	CN has positive/negative modifier or sibling
POS of CN's parent	Modifier of CN's sibling is positive/negative
Sentiment of CN's parent and grandparent	Positive/Negative word within two words around CN

Table 6: Target-based features for sentiment prediction

Our features include counts of unigrams, bigrams as well as parts of speech (POS) tags and punctuations. We also count the sentiment words using two lexicons (MPQA (Wilson et al., 2005) and General Inquirer (Stone et al., 1966)) and a hand-built dictionary of sentiment-related slang words. We also added features specifically aimed to identify if the company is the main target of the tweet. These features were computed from a dependency parse of the tweet and are briefly listed in Table 6. In this list, 'CN' indicates the company keyword present in the tweet. We used a MaxEnt classifier for training and performed 10-fold cross validation.

The n-gram, sentiment words and POS features gave an accuracy of 64%. Target-based features increased the accuracy to 82.6% showing that such features are valuable for our task.

6 Alternative summarization methods

We introduce three other methods of summarizing tweets for comparison with our approach.

a) Sentiment only (Sen). A simple summary for our task is showing the top positive and negative tweets (according to classifier confidence).

b) Frequency only (Frq). This summary aims to show the most discussed tweets in the stream. For each tweet, we compute the number of similar tweets. Two tweets are considered similar when the cosine similarity based on unigram counts is above 0.8. The tweets with the largest number of similar tweets are displayed along with the number of similar tweets.

c) No categorization but sentiment + frequency (Prb). We apply the same summarization method as used in our concept method. The probabilities of words (also using sentiment) are computed over the full set of tweets. Then sentences are ranked by the average probability of words. But the sentences are not categorized into positive/negative or frequency sets. The average probability method works remarkably well for summarizing newswire (Nenkova et al., 2006), the domain where more mature systems exist. So we include it for comparison.

Table 7 shows snippets from alternative summaries for "Wells Fargo".

7 Annotation experiment

For each of the four approaches, we generated summaries containing a maximum of 20 tweets. In the case of the concept approach (**con**), this limit is for the total tweets across all clusters.

1. Sentiment summary (Sen)	**2. Frequency summary (Frq)**
(+) I love Wells Fargo. They let you customize your debit card!	(+19) Banks financing Mexico drug gangs admitted in Wells Fargo deal
(-) Wells Fargo has pissed me off one too many times. Time to move my money	(+14) Wells Fargo to pay $125 million in mortgage suit http://t.co/
3. Average probability summary (Prb)	
Wachovia banks to become Wells Fargo	
Wells Fargo, Goldmann Sachs and all other banks don't come close	

Table 7: Snippets from other summary approaches for "Wells Fargo". (+) and (-) indicate polarity. (+x) indicates cluster size.

	Useful for analysts			Informative for consumers			Interesting for consumers		
	sen/con	**prb/con**	**frq/con**	**sen/con**	**prb/con**	**frq/con**	**sen/con**	**prb/con**	**frq/con**
well fargo	sen	**con**	**frq/con**	sen	**con**	frq	sen	**con**	frq
johnson	**con**	**con**	**con**	**con**	**con**	-	sen	**con**	-
linkedin	sen	**con**	**con**	sen	**con**	-	sen	**con**	frq
nokia	**con**	**con**	frq	**con**	**con**	frq	**con**	-	frq
northup	sen	**con**	-	sen	**con**	**con**	**con**	**con**	**con**
lowes	**con**	prb	**con**	**con**	prb	**con**	**con**	prb	**con**
% con		61.1			55.6			50.0	

Table 8: Evaluation results. The header indicates the pair that was compared and cells indicate user judgement. '-' denotes no preference and x/y indicates both x and y are preferred.

We use the 6 companies listed in Table 1 as the test set. For each company, we paired the output of the concept approach with each of the alternative summaries. Judges were asked to provide their preference between the summaries in each pair. Our judges were 14 software developers and had no prior computational linguistics experience. Each judged two or three random pairs of summaries and did not see more than one pair from the same company. They were asked to answer three questions.

If you were an analyst working for the company,
Q1) Which summary would be more useful for you?
Imagine you are a consumer interested in learning about a company. From your viewpoint,
Q2) Which summary was more informative? It gave you a useful overview about the relevant tweets.
Q3) Which summary was more interesting to read?

The judges had 4 options "summary A", "summary B", "prefer both", "none". Table 8 shows the judgements provided for our test set. The last row indicates for each question, how often the concept approach summary was preferred in the 18 judgements that were made.

In the analyst view, concept summaries are highly preferred. 61% of the comparisons noted this summary as better than an alternative method. For informativeness quality, the concept summary was preferred 55% of the time and 50% of the cases for interest value. When all three questions are put together, there are 54 judgements and the concept summary was preferred 30 times, 55%. Our test set is small, still these results indicate that judges find the concept summaries useful. The concept summary was almost always better than the PRB option where there was no clustering into subtopics. But judges noted that the SEN summary was fairly intuitive and easy to interpret.

8 Conclusion

We showed that use of domain concepts can provide a useful summarization method for diverse tweets. Since we only rely on unannotated news articles and WordNet which are available in other languages as well, our method is also easily portable. Another attractive feature of our approach is that the same concepts are used for all companies. So one could track what happened in the "people" cluster across different companies or over time for the same company. On the other hand, fine-grained concepts for different classes of companies such as technology versus finance could also be interesting to obtain. We plan to explore these ideas in future.

We also found that properties of the tweet stream influenced the quality of the summary. Some companies' tweets were mostly offers and deals and here concept summaries were less useful. Frequency or sentiment summaries displayed more interesting tweets. So we want to explore how to vary the summarization approach depending on the type of tweets in the input set.

References

Blair-Goldensohn, S., Neylon, T., Hannan, K., Reis, G. A., Mcdonald, R., and Reynar, J. (2008). Building a sentiment summarizer for local service reviews. In *In NLP in the Information Explosion Era*.

Chakrabarti, D. and Punera, K. (2011). Event summarization using tweets. In *Proceedings of ICWSM*.

Gamon, M., Aue, A., Corston-Oliver, S., and Ringger, E. K. (2005). Pulse: Mining customer opinions from free text. In *Proceedings of IDA*, pages 121–132.

Hu, M. and Liu, B. (2004). Mining opinion features in customer reviews. In *Proceedings of AAAI*, pages 755–760.

Inouye, D. and Kalita, J. (2011). Comparing twitter summarization algorithms for multiple post summaries. In *Proceedings of IEEE Third International Conference on Social Computing*, pages 298 –306.

Liu, F., Liu, Y., and Weng, F. (2011). Why is "sxsw" trending? exploring multiple text sources for twitter topic summarization. In *Proceedings of the ACL Workshop on Language in Social Media (LSM 2011)*, pages 66–75.

Miller, G. A. (1995). Wordnet: a lexical database for english. *Communication of the ACM*, 38(11):39–41.

Nenkova, A., Vanderwende, L., and McKeown, K. (2006). A compositional context sensitive multi-document summarizer: exploring the factors that influence summarization. In *Proceedings of SIGIR*.

Nichols, J., Mahmud, J., and Drews, C. (2012). Summarizing sporting events using twitter. In *Proceedings of the ACM International Conference on Intelligent User Interfaces*, pages 189–198.

O'Connor, B., Krieger, M., , and Ahn, D. (2010). Tweetmotif: Exploratory search and topic summarization for twitter. In *Proceedings of ICWSM*.

Popescu, A. and Jain, A. (2011). Understanding the functions of business accounts on twitter. In *Proceedings of WWW*, pages 107–108.

Sandhaus, E. (2008). The new york times annotated corpus. *Corpus number LDC2008T19, Linguistic Data Consortium, Philadelphia*.

Sauper, C., Haghighi, A., and Barzilay, R. (2011). Content models with attitude. In *Proceedings of ACL HLT*, pages 350–358.

Sharifi, B., Hutton, M., and Kalita, J. (2010). Summarizing microblogs automatically. In *Proceedings of HLT-NAACL*, pages 685–688.

Stone, P., Kirsh, J., and Associates, C. C. (1966). *The General Inquirer: A Computer Approach to Content Analysis*. MIT Press.

Titov, I. and McDonald, R. (2008). A joint model of text and aspect ratings for sentiment summarization. In *Proceedings of ACL*, pages 308–316.

Wilson, T., Wiebe, J., and Hoffmann, P. (2005). Recognizing contextual polarity in phrase-level sentiment analysis. In *Proceedings of HLT-EMNLP*, pages 347–354.

Zhai, Z., Liu, B., Xu, H., and Jia, P. (2011). Clustering product features for opinion mining. In *Proceedings of WSDM*, pages 347–354.

Zhuang, L., Jing, F., and Zhu, X. (2006). Movie review mining and summarization. In *Proceedings of CIKM*, pages 43–50.

Towards the automatic detection of the source language of a literary translation

Gerard Lynch[1,2] & Carl Vogel[1,2,3]
(1) School of Computer Science and Statistics$_1$, Trinity College, Dublin 2, Ireland
(2) Centre For Next Generation Localisation$_2$,
(3) Centre for Computing and Language Studies$_3$
gplynch@scss.tcd.ie, vogel@scss.tcd.ie

ABSTRACT
Experiments on the detection of the source language of literary translations are described. Two feature types are exploited, n-gram based features and document-level statistics. Cross-validation results on a corpus of twenty 19th-century texts including translations from Russian, French, German and texts written in English are promising: single feature classifiers yield significant gains on the baseline, although classifiers containing a combination of feature types outperform these, bringing L1 detection accuracy to ~80% using ten-fold training set cross validation. Average test set results are slightly lower but still comparable to the cross-validation results. Relative frequencies of a number of salient features are studied, including several English contractions (*I'll*, *that's*, etc.) and uncontracted forms; we articulate hypotheses, anchored in source languages, towards explaining differences.

KEYWORDS: Computational stylometry, translation studies, source language detection, text classification.

Proceedings of COLING 2012: Posters, pages 775–784,
COLING 2012, Mumbai, December 2012.

1 Introduction

This study focuses on experimentation towards the detection of source language influence in literary translations into English from the late nineteeth and early twentieth centuries. We assembled a corpus of novels from this period, consisting of fifteen translations, five each from Russian, German and French, and five works written originally in English.[1] We carry out cross-validation experiments to determine robust features which identify the L1 of the texts.

We use document-level metrics such as sentence length and readability scores together with n-gram features such as the frequency of sequences of POS tags and closed-class words, features which are not directly related to the topics and themes contained within the texts. The present experiments attempt to correctly attribute the L1 of texts; this entails correctly classifying a text as translated or not. In order to minimize the effect of authorial or translatorial style in this study, we have not selected more than one work by the same author or translator.

Four criteria for corpus selection were as follows. Firstly, text should be available in an machine-readable format and in the public domain. Secondly, from the previous point, this dictates that text will most likely stem from prior to the early twentieth century, due to US copyright law. Thirdly, each text should have a unique author and in the case of translations, translator, i.e. no repeated authors or translators. Finally, text should be of sufficient length, at least two hundred kilobytes in size, i.e. preferably a novel or novella. In many cases, particular translators had translated numerous works by a single author and indeed also occasionally by several authors. Thus, it was necessary to choose texts so that each author and translator remained unique.[2] Table 1 lists the texts, all sourced from Project Gutenberg.[3]

Section 2 describes prior research. Section 3 explains our own experimental methodology. Section 4 details the results of experiments carried out on detection of the L1 of a corpus of texts translated from Russian, German and French together with texts in original English.

2 Previous research

Recent work in computational and corpus linguistics has focused on the analysis of comparable corpora[4] of translated and original text (see Kilgarriff (2001) on comparability assessment).

Olohan (2001) identifies patterns in *optional* usage in comparable English corpora, citing examples such as the use of complementizer *that*[5] as discriminatory between translations and original texts, with translations containing a higher incidence of the complementizer construction, using t-tests to identify features which differ with statistical significance. This method depends on selective expert hypotheses about which features discriminate texts of L2 English.

Guthrie, Guthrie, Allison, and Wilks (2007) evaluated their general method of ranked feature differences on the problem of assessing whether translations of L1 Chinese newspaper texts

[1] We will henceforth refer to the source language of the text as the L1.

[2] This was more complicated for Russian, for example, with the translator Constance Garnett having translated works by Dosteyevsky and Turgenev, amongst others, resulting in the bypassing of a title of such repute as *Anna Karenina* for the less well-known novella *The Cossacks* by Tolstoy, due to the fact that Garnett was already represented as the sole available translator of Turgenev.

[3] www.gutenberg.org, last verified August 2012

[4] These are corpora of the same style and genre, containing a proportional amount of translated and original text.

[5] *He said* ***that*** *he was ill* vs. *he said he was ill* vs. *the illness* ***that*** *killed him was swift*: the first contains a complementizer-that and the last, a relativizer-that.

Title	Author	Source	Pub.	Translator	T.pub.
Great Expectations	Charles Dickens	English	1861	n/a	n/a
The Picture of Dorian Gray	Oscar Wilde	English	1891	n/a	n/a
Jude the Obscure	Thomas Hardy	English	1895	n/a	n/a
Treasure Island	R.L Stevenson	English	1883	n/a	n/a
Middlemarch	George Eliot(M. Evans)	English	1874	n/a	n/a
The Idiot	Fyodor Dostoyevsky	Russian	1869	Eva Martin	1915
The Man Who Was Afraid	Maxim Gorky	Russian	1899	Hermann Bernstein	1901
Fathers and Children	Ivan Turgenev	Russian	1862	Constance Garnett	1917
The Cossacks	Leo Tolstoy	Russian	1863	Louise and Alymer Maude	n/a
A Man of our Time	Mikhail Lermontov	Russian	1841	J.H Wisdom/M. Murray	1917
The Count of Monte Cristo	Alexandre Dumas	French	1844	Anon	1846
Madame Bovary	Gustave Flaubert	French	1857	Eleanor Marx-Aveling	1898
Fr Goriot	Honoré de Balzac	French	1853	Ellen Marriage	1901
The Hunchback of Notre Dame	Victor Hugo	French	1831	Isabel F. Hapgood	1888
Around the World in Eighty Days	Jules Verne	French	1873	George M. Towle	1873
Effi Briest	Theodor Fontane	German	1896	William A. Cooper	1914
The Merchant of Berlin	Luise Mühlbach	German	1896	Amory Coffin	1910
Venus in Furs	Leopold V. Sacher-Masoch	German	1870	Fernanda Savage	1921
The Rider on the White Horse	Theodor Storm	German	1888	Margarete Münsterberg	1917
Debit and Credit	Gustave Freytag	German	1855	Georgiana Harcourt	1857

Table 1: Corpus of texts

in L2 English could be identified in a set of L1 English news texts (35K words of Chinese translated to English and 50K words of English L1). Features focused on what we consider document-level features (ie. percentages of words in major grammatical categories, ratios of frequencies between grammatical categories, most frequent POS trigrams and bigrams, etc). Feature vectors are constructed to represent each text and its relative complement, with separate vectors for the percentages and ratios and the ranked frequency features. A derived vector records a score based on the Spearman rank correlation coefficient between the text and its complement for each of the sorts of frequency list. Two texts are compared by calculating the average differences between feature vectors and adjusting with the derived scores from the ranked frequency list differences. In each configuration of the evaluation, one translation was presented without annotation along with 50 L1 English texts, texts separated as 1000 word samples. The translated text appeared in the top three ranked positions, representing greatest anomaly, in 93% of experiments, and in the top ten positions in 100%. Our own work is comparable in the features analyzed, but uses a classification approach that labels the source language of each text. rather than giving each text a rank in its evidence of being a translation.

Baroni and Bernardini (2006) explore whether machine learning methods may discover translated texts more robustly than people. They investigate a corpus of translated and original articles from the Italian current affairs publication *Limes* using machine learning methods similar to this study, and report high degrees (≥85%) of classification accuracy between the two categories, identifying features such as clitic pronouns and adverbial forms as distinguishing features between the translated and original sections of the corpus. Only one of ten humans in an evaluation exercise outperformed the ML system on all measures.

In previous work on detecting the L1 of translations using computational methods similar to those used in our study, van Halteren (2008) examined source language markers in the Europarl corpus, obtaining high accuracy in L1 detection($\geq$ 90%) across translations and original texts in multiple European languages, using features such as n-grams of words and POS tags alone. Frequent n-grams included *framework conditions* in the English corpus translated from German, and the n-gram *certain number*, which occurred to a higher extent in the translations from French and Spanish than the German, Italian and Dutch texts. However more recent work by Ilisei, Inkpen, Corpas Pastor, and Mitkov (2010) on stylistics of translations in Spanish technical and medical translations motivated the use of features other than simple n-grams in our work. These comprise of a number of statistics calculated on a document level, features which are listed in Table 2 We also broaden the scope of our study to literary translations, which we believe will pose a greater challenge to the task of L1 detection than the Europarl corpus which is more homogenous in style and comprising only parliamentary transcriptions.

3 Methods

We use Weka (Hall et al. (2009)) as a machine-learning toolkit, coupled with the TagHelperTools package (Dönmez et al. (2005)) which provides support for processing natural language data in Weka. We calculated values for the document-level features (Table 2) using our own script which relies on the TreeTagger POS tagger (Schmid (1994)) for the tagging of text. Within Weka, we use the Ranker algorithm coupled with the χ^2 metric to rank the features by classification power. These rankings are then listed in Tables 4 and 5 For the experiments, we used the Weka SMO classifier, which is an implementation of a Support Vector Machine (SVM) classifier, the Simple Logistic classifier and the Naive Bayes classifier.

Feature	Description	Feature	Ratio Description
Avgsent	Average sentence length	*Typetoken*	word types : total words
Avgwordlength	Average word length	*Numratio*	numerals : total words
CLI	Readability metric	*Fverbratio*	finite verbs : total words
ARI	Readability metric	*Prepratio*	prepositions : total words
		Conjratio	conjunctions : total words
		Infoload	open-class words : total words
		dmarkratio	discourse markers : total words
		Nounratio	nouns : total words
		Grammlex	open-class words : closed-class words
		simplecomplex	simple sentences : complex sentences
		Pnounratio	pronouns : total words
		lexrichness	lemmas : total words
		simplecomplex	simple sentences : complex sentences
		simpletotal	simple sentences : total sentences
		complextotal	complex sentences : total sentences

Table 2: Document-level features

3.1 Features and corpus treatment

We use 19 document-level features in this analysis listed in Table 2. Two readability indices, the Automated Readability Index, (Smith and Senter (1967)) and the Coleman-Liau Index,

(Coleman and Liau (1975)) were used. We also use n-gram features such as word-unigrams and part-of-speech bigrams. We remove any proper nouns in the word n-gram feature list, as any character or place-names could unambiguously distinguish a text. We do this after the word unigram features are calculated. The frequency of untranslated terms and titles from the source language, place-names or names of characters could prove highly useful in predicting the source language of a text, however these we would expect to vary depending on the topics and themes within the text.[6] We therefore focus on highly frequent n-grams, such as prepositions, determiners and frequent verb forms, which we expect to be more robust predictors of the source language of a text.

To balance the corpus for each source language, we selected a random contiguous section of 200 kb of text from each work in the study and divided this up into 20 chunks of 10 kb each. This results in 100 textual segments per source language. Corpus balancing is important when using metrics such as type-token ratio which vary with relation to text length. We trained on 360 of the text chunks retained a separate set of 40 chunks from the corpus divided evenly across the four languages and works[7] for test purposes.

3.2 Classification tasks

The features described are used to label texts written in English according to their source language. This is more refined than labelling a text as translated or not since we want to know not just whether it is a translation, but further, if it is a translation, the identity of its L1.

4 Experiments

4.1 Single and combined feature sets

Using the SVM classifier we obtain 66% accuracy using ten-fold cross validation for the four categories using our 19 document level statistics only. The Naive Bayes classifier performs worse, giving 54% accuracy. The Simple Logistic classifier performs the best here, with 68% accuracy. Given that the baseline for this task is 25%, 68% can be deemed a promising result, although the results are lower for the hold-out set, at 62% for the Simple Logistic classifier. The merged feature sets produce better results in this task, the best performing combination being Run 13, which consists of the top 50 features as ranked by the chi-squared metric in Weka taken from: (i) the top one hundred POS bigrams; (ii) all 19 document-level features; (iii) the top fifteen word unigrams. This yielded an overall classification accuracy average after ten-fold cross validation of 86.3% using the Simple Logistic classifier, with a test set classification accuracy of 80% using the SVM classifier.

4.2 Discussion of distinguishing features

Table 9 shows that the German translations have a much higher frequency of the word *toward* as opposed to the other texts. A likely explanation for this is dialectal: two translators of the German texts were American,[8] while the other translations from German were published in the US, by translators whose nationality is not defined.

Table 7 displays the relative frequencies of both *that's* and *it's* and the expanded versions of the same. Olohan (2001) has shown that these forms tend to be less prevalent in translated English

[6]A novel translated from French may be set in a Francophone locale and contain tokens like *Madame, Rue,* etc.

[7]This consists of two segments from each work.

[8]Amory Coffin and William Cooper

Run	Training	Test	Classifier	Feature Set	Accuracy
1	Full	10-f cv	Baseline	n/a	25%
2	Full	Test	NB	19 doc-level	55%
3	Full	Test	SVM	19 doc-level	60%
4	Full	Test	SimpLog	19 doc-level	62%
5	Full	10-f cv	NB	19 doc-level	54%
6	Full	10-f cv	SVM	19 doc-level	66%
7	Full	10-f cv	SimpLog	19 doc-level	**68%**
8	Full	Test	NB	Top50(100 POS-bi+19doc+15wuni)	72%
9	Full	Test	SVM	Top50(100 POS-bi+19doc+15wuni)	80%
10	Full	Test	SimpLog	Top50(100 POS-bi+19doc+15wuni)	67%
11	Full	10-f cv	NB	Top50(100 POS-bi+19doc+15wuni)	81%
12	Full	10-f cv	SVM	Top50(100 POS-bi+19doc+15wuni)	80%
13	Full	10-f cv	SimpLog	Top50(100 POS-bi+19doc+15wuni)	**86.3%**
14	Full	Test	NB	30(100 POS-bi+19doc+15wuni)	60%
15	Full	Test	SVM	30(100 POS-bi+19doc+15wuni)	70%
16	Full	Test	SimpLog	30(100 POS-bi+19doc+15wuni)	72.5%
17	Full	10-f cv	NB	30(100 POS-bi+19doc+15wuni)	70%
18	Full	10-f cv	SVM	30(100 POS-bi+19doc+15wuni)	75%
19	Full	10-f cv	SimpLog	30(100 POS-bi+19doc+15wuni)	75%

Table 3: Summary of classification accuracy: Full corpus

in general, however in this case they may be less/more prevalent in translations from different languages. Russian has a much larger proportion of *that's* and *it's*, although it's proportion of *it is* is also relatively high. One possible explanation for this is that in French and German, *that is* and *it is* are two words,[9] whereas in the Russian language, one word zto serves both purposes.

Table 8 displays the frequencies for the contractions *I'm* and *I'll* in the four corpora. Again Russian contains the highest frequency for the two contractions among the languages. This may again be a source language artifact: In German there is no equivalent contraction, *Ich bin* for I am, and in French *je suis*, both two word phrases. In Russian *I am* is corresponds to ya,[10] with

[9]Ger. *es ist* or *das ist* and Fre. *il est* or *qui est*.
[10]Pronounced *ya* with a short a sound.

Chi	Rank	Token	Chi	Rank	Token
191.1184	1	toward	60.2458	11	though
101.8571	2	prepratio	56.4456	12	that's
79.6687	3	nounratio	54.1083	13	RB-CC
78.6035	4	lexrich	52.0254	14	i'll
78.1577	5	thousand	50.1781	15	PRP-CC
69.6095	6	it's	49.9458	16	conjratio
66.4622	7	towards	49.868	17	nodded
62.1622	8	numratio	49.224	18	i'm
62.1324	9	fverbratio	48.7354	19	law
61.1304	10	ari	48.6329	20	FW-FW

Table 4: Features 1-20 for Table 3, run 13

Chi	Rank	Token	Chi	Rank	Token
48.3455	21	VBP-VB	33.2283	36	typetoken
47.5911	22	suddenly	33.1439	37	simpletotal
47.1891	23	scream	32.2981	38	complextotal
46.9136	24	CD-CD	30.9333	39	simplecomplex
46.7665	25	don't	27.0928	40	what's
46.6164	26	resumed	26.4912	41	somewhere
43.3339	27	got	26.2167	42	you're
42.7951	28	drink	26.16	43	thought
37.8411	29	sense	25.7212	44	ain't
37.8411	30	infoload	25.6271	45	gazed
37.8411	31	presently	25.6141	46	beneath
37.8409	32	he's	25.3143	47	there's
37.6963	33	whispered	25.2518	48	say
36.2862	34	avgsent	24.1848	49	won't
35.8047	35	anyone	24.125	50	now

Table 5: Features 21-50 for Table 3, run 13

L1	No. of tokens
German	185413
French	180813
English	148565
Russian	183448

Table 6: Number of tokens in each L1 sub-corpus

I will also being one word, budu.[11] This is a possible reason for the abundance of contracted forms in the translations with Russian as L1.

Table 9 displays the frequencies for the next four words in the list. It is difficult to ascertain whether these are true source language artifacts, although the frequency of *drink* in the translations from Russian may reflect a rather unsavoury national stereotype. It is interesting also that the characters in the German translations tend to agree with an affirmative head movement more often than French or Russian. The high frequency of *thousand* in the French corpus is likely as a result of references to large denominations of the French *franc*.

[11]Pronounced *boodoo*.

Text	**it is**	**it's**	**that is**	**that's**
English	0.002358	0.000361	0.000754	0.000538
German	0.002931	0.000194	0.001106	0.000116
French	**0.003236**	0.000092	**0.001370**	0.000167
Russian	0.003216	**0.001058**	0.001112	**0.001052**

Table 7: Relative frequency of that's/it's

Language	I am	I will	I'm	I'll
English	0.003112	0.000452	0.000318	0.000555
French	0.002500	**0.001416**	0.000061	0.000088
German	0.003463	0.001219	0.000092	0.000205
Russian	**0.003598**	0.000883	**0.000627**	**0.000725**

Table 8: Relative frequency of I'll/I'm

Text	drink	nodded	resumed	thousand	toward	toward
English	0.000194	0.000075	0.000048	0.000075	0.000000	**0.000441**
French	0.000083	0.000011	**0.000227**	**0.000785**	0.00002	0.00038
German	0.000129	**0.000248**	0.000027	0.000167	**0.0006**	0.000010
Russian	**0.000627**	0.000033	0.000016	0.000076	0.00015	0.00029

Table 9: Common word frequencies

Conclusion

Our hybrid approach towards detecting the source language of a literary translation resulted in high classification accuracies using ten-fold cross validation on our translation corpus and also comparably high accuracies on our test set from the same corpus. We have identified a number of trends in our corpus, such as the frequency of certain English contractions (*I'm*, *it's* etc) which may be attributable to source language influence.

As noted at the outset, our work is comparable to research published by Guthrie et al. (2007). If one were to derive a classification of each item from the point at which their method achieved 100% inclusion of the translated item among the top ten items in terms of anomalies pointed out using the vectors of document level features, then precision is at 9%, but recall is at 100%, and accuracy is at 80%. However, note that this depends on two categories: L1 English or L2 English (translated from L1 Chinese). Our experiments provide a further label for which language provided the texts L1 source.

Comparing our results to the work by Baroni and Bernardini (2006), there are similarities, although the tasks were different, we focused on source language detection and they focused on detecting whether a text was a translation or original. Classification results for our task were lower than theirs, they obtained ca. 87.5% accuracy using an ensemble of classifiers and two categories, we obtained ca. 80% accuracy with four categories. Comparing discriminating features, we found optional contractions in English to be discriminatory amongst source languages, while they found optional items in Italian such as clitic pronouns to be markers of *translationese*.

Ongoing work focuses on corpora containing a variety of genres, as well as more source languages, and cross-validation experiments on unseen texts. We also wish to examine longer n-gram sequences such as bigrams and trigrams of words and parts-of-speech, with the possibility of supporting non-contiguous sequences or skip-grams, as used by van Halteren (2008).

Acknowledgments

We are grateful for support from the Science Foundation Ireland (Grant 07/CE/I1142) to the Centre for Next Generation Localisation (`www.cngl.ie`) and for anonymous review feedback.

References

Baroni, M., & Bernardini, S. (2006). A new approach to the study of translationese: Machine-learning the difference between original and translated text. *Literary and Linguistic Computing*, *21*(3), 259.

Coleman, M., & Liau, T. (1975). A computer readability formula designed for machine scoring.. *Journal of Applied Psychology*, *60*(2), 283.

Dönmez, P., Rosé, C., Stegmann, K., Weinberger, A., & Fischer, F. (2005). Supporting CSCL with automatic corpus analysis technology. In *Proceedings of th 2005 conference on Computer support for collaborative learning: learning 2005: the next 10 years!*, pp. 125–134. International Society of the Learning Sciences.

Guthrie, D., Guthrie, L., Allison, B., & Wilks, Y. (2007). Unsupervised Anomaly Detection. In *IJCAI*, pp. 1624–1628.

Hall, M., Frank, E., Holmes, G., Pfahringer, B., Reutemann, P., & Witten, I. (2009). The WEKA data mining software: an update. *ACM SIGKDD Explorations Newsletter*, *11*(1), 10–18.

Ilisei, I., Inkpen, D., Corpas Pastor, G., & Mitkov, R. (2010). Identification of Translationese: A Machine Learning Approach. *Computational Linguistics and Intelligent Text Processing*, 503–511.

Kilgarriff, A. (2001). Comparing Corpora. *International Journal of Corpus Linguistics*, *6*(1), 97–133.

Olohan, M. (2001). Spelling out the optionals in translation: a corpus study. *UCREL Technical Papers*, *13*, 423–432.

Schmid, H. (1994). Probabilistic part-of-speech tagging using decision trees. In *Proceedings of international conference on new methods in language processing*, Vol. 12, pp. 44–49. Manchester, UK.

Smith, E., & Senter, R. (1967). Automated readability index.. *AMRL-TR. Aerospace Medical Research Laboratories (6570th)*, 1.

van Halteren, H. (2008). Source Language Markers in EUROPARL Translations. In *Proceedings of the 22nd International Conference on Computational Linguistics (Coling 2008)*, pp. 937–944. Coling 2008 Organizing Committee.

Fourth-Order Dependency Parsing*

Xuezhe Ma[1,2] *Hai Zhao*[1,2†]
(1) Center for Brain-Like Computing and Machine Intelligence
Department of Computer Science and Engineering, Shanghai Jiao Tong University
(2) MOE-Microsoft Key Laboratory for Intelligent Computing and Intelligent Systems
Shanghai Jiao Tong University
800 Dong Chuan Rd., Shanghai 200240, China
`xuezhe.ma@gmail.com, zhaohai@cs.sjtu.edu.cn`

ABSTRACT
We present and implement a fourth-order projective dependency parsing algorithm that effectively utilizes both "grand-sibling" style and "tri-sibling" style interactions of third-order and "grand-tri-sibling" style interactions of forth-order factored parts for performance enhancement. This algorithm requires $O(n^5)$ time and $O(n^4)$ space. We implement and evaluate the parser on two languages—English and Chinese, both achieving state-of-the-art accuracy. This results show that a higher-order ($\geq$4) dependency parser gives performance improvement over all previous lower-order parsers.

KEYWORDS: Dependency Parsing, Fourth-order.

*This work was partially supported by the National Natural Science Foundation of China (Grant No. 60903119 and Grant No. 61170114), the National Research Foundation for the Doctoral Program of Higher Education of China under Grant No.20110073120022, the National Basic Research Program of China (Grant No. 2009CB320901), and the European Union Seventh Framework Program (Grant No. 247619).
†Corresponding author

Proceedings of COLING 2012: Posters, pages 785–796,
COLING 2012, Mumbai, December 2012.

1 Introduction

In recent years, dependency parsing has gained universal interest due to its usefulness in a wide range of applications such as synonym generation (Shinyama et al., 2002), relation extraction (Nguyen et al., 2009) and machine translation (Katz-Brown et al., 2011; Xie et al., 2011).

CoNLL-X shared task on dependency parsing (Buchholz and Marsi, 2006; Nivre et al., 2007) made a comparison of many algorithms, and graph-based parsing models have achieved state-of-the-art accuracy for a wide range of languages. Graph-based dependency parsing algorithms usually use the factored representations of dependency trees: a set of small *parts* with special structures. The types of features that the model can exploit depend on the information included in the factorizations. Several previous works have shown that higher-order parsers utilizing richer contextual information achieve higher accuracy than lower-order ones—Chen et al. (2010) illustrated that a wide range of decision history can lead to significant improvements in accuracy for graph-based dependency parsing models. Meanwhile, several previous works (Carreras, 2007; Koo and Collins, 2010) have shown that grandchild interactions provide important information for dependency parsing. However, the computational cost of the parsing algorithm increases with the need for more expressive factorizations. Consequently, the existing most powerful parser (Koo and Collins, 2010) is limited to third-order parts, which requires $O(n^4)$ time and $O(n^3)$ space.

In this paper, we further present a fourth-order parsing algorithm that can utilize more richer information by enclosing grand-sibling and tri-sibling parts into a grand-tri-sibling part. Koo and Collins (2010) discussed the possibility that the third-order parsers are extended to fourth-order by increasing vertical context (e.g. from grand-siblings to "great-grand-siblings") or horizontal context (e.g. from grand-siblings to "grand-tri-siblings"), and Koo (2010) first described this algorithm. In this work, we show that grand-tri-siblings can effectively work. The computational requirements of this algorithm are $O(n^5)$ time and $O(n^4)$ space. To achieve empirical evaluations of our parser, we implement and evaluate the proposed parsing algorithm on the Penn WSJ Treebank (Marcus et al., 1993) for English, and Penn Chinese Treebank (Xue et al., 2005) for Chinese, both achieving state-of-the-art accuracy. A free distribution of our implementation in C++ has been put on the Internet.[1]

2 Related Work

There have been several existing graph-based dependency parsing algorithms, which are the backbones of the new fourth-order dependency parser. In this section, we mainly describe four graph-based dependency parsers with different types of factorization.

The first-order parser (McDonald et al., 2005) decomposes a dependency tree into its individual edges. Eisner (2000) introduced a widely-used dynamic programming algorithm for first-order parsing, which is to parse the left and right dependents of a word independently, and combine them at a later stage. This algorithm introduces two types of dynamic programming structures: *complete* spans, and *incomplete* spans (McDonald, 2006). Larger spans are created from two smaller, adjacent spans by recursive combination in a bottom-up procedure.

McDonald and Pereira (2006) defined a second-order sibling dependency parser in which interactions between adjacent siblings are allowed. Koo and Collins (2010) proposed an algorithm

[1] `http://sourceforge.net/projects/maxparser/`

that factors each dependency tree into a set of *grandchild* parts. Formally, a grandchild part is a triple of indices (g,s,t) where g is the head of s and s is the head of t. In order to parse this factorization, it is necessary to augment both complete and incomplete spans with grandparent indices. Following Koo and Collins (2010), we refer to these augmented structures as *g-spans*. The second-order parser proposed in Carreras (2007) is capable of scoring both sibling and grandchild parts with complexities of $O(n^4)$ time and $O(n^3)$ space. However, the parser suffers a crucial limitation that it can only evaluate events of grandchild parts for outermost grandchildren.

Koo and Collins (2010) proposed a third-order grand-sibling parser that decomposes each tree into set of *grand-sibling* parts—parts combined with sibling parts and grandchild parts. This factorization defines all grandchild and sibling parts and still requires $O(n^4)$ time and $O(n^3)$ space. Koo and Collins (2010) also discussed the possibility that the third-order parsers are extended to fourth-order by increasing vertical context or horizontal context and Koo (2010) first described this algorithm.

Zhang and McDonald (2012) generalized the Eisner (1996) algorithm to handle arbitrary features over higher-order dependencies. However, their generalizing algorithm suffers quite high complexities of time and space – for instance, the parsing complexity of time is $O(n^5)$ for a third-order factored model. In order to achieve asymptotic efficiency of cost, cube pruning for decoding is utilized (Chiang, 2007).

Another dominant category of data-driven dependency parsing systems is local-and-greedy transition-based parsing (Yamada and Matsumoto, 2003; Nivre and Scholz, 2004; Attardi, 2006; McDonald and Nivre, 2007) which parameterizes models over transitions from state to another in an abstract state-machine. In these models, dependency trees are constructed by making a series of incremental decisions. Parameters in these models are typically learned using standard classification techniques.

3 Fourth-Order Parsing Algorithm

In this section, we propose our fourth-order dependency parsing algorithm, which factors each dependency tree into a set of *grand-tri-sibling* parts. Specifically, a grand-tri-sibling is a 5-tuple of indices (g,s,r,m,t) where (s,r,m,t) is a tri-sibling part and (g,s,r,m) and (g,s,m,t) are grand-sibling parts.

The algorithm is characterized by introducing a new type incomplete g-spans structure: grand-sibling-spans or *gs-spans*, by augmenting incomplete g-spans with a sibling index. Formally, we denote gs-spans as $[g,s,m,t]$ where $[g,s,t]$ is a normal incomplete g-span and m is an index lying in the strict interior of the range $[s,t]$, such that (s,m,t) forms a valid sibling part.

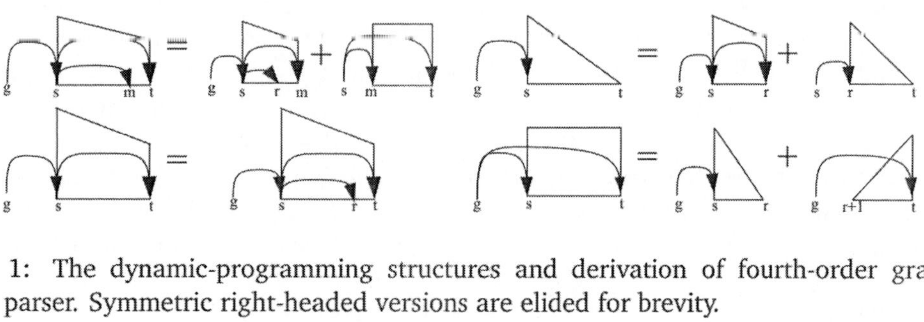

Figure 1: The dynamic-programming structures and derivation of fourth-order grand-tri-sibling parser. Symmetric right-headed versions are elided for brevity.

Initialization: $C[g][s][s][d][c] = 0.0 \quad \forall g, s, d, c$

for $k : 1..n$

  for $s : 0..n - k$

    $t = s + k$

    for $g < s$ or $g > t$

      for $m > s$ and $m < t$

$$D[g][s][m][t][\rightarrow] = C[s][s+1][m][\leftarrow][1] + S(g, s, -, -, m) + C[s][m][t][-][2] + S(g, s, -, m, t)$$
$$D[g][s][m][t][\leftarrow] = C[t][m][t-1][\rightarrow][1] + S(g, t, -, -, m) + C[t][s][m][-][2] + S(g, t, -, m, s)$$

$$D[g][s][m][t][\rightarrow] = \max\{D[g][s][m][t][\rightarrow], \max_{s<r<m}\{D[g][s][r][m][\rightarrow] + C[s][m][t][-][2] + S(g, s, r, m, t)\}\}$$
$$D[g][s][m][t][\leftarrow] = \max\{D[g][s][m][t][\leftarrow], \max_{m<r<t}\{D[g][m][r][t][\leftarrow] + C[t][s][m][-][2] + S(g, t, r, m, s)\}\}$$

      end for

$$C[g][s][t][-][2] = \max_{s\leq r<t}\{C[g][s][r][\rightarrow][1] + C[g][r+1][t][\leftarrow][1]\}$$

$$C[g][s][t][\rightarrow][0] = C[g][s][s][\leftarrow][1] + C[s][s+1][t] \leftarrow][1] + S(g, s, -, -, t)$$
$$C[g][s][t][\leftarrow][0] = C[g][t][t][\rightarrow][1] + C[t][s][t-1][\rightarrow][1] + S(g, t, -, -, s)$$

$$C[g][s][t][\rightarrow][0] = \max\{C[g][s][t][\rightarrow][0], \max_{s<r<t}\{D[g][s][r][t][\rightarrow]\}\}$$
$$C[g][s][t][\leftarrow][0] = \max\{C[g][s][t][\leftarrow][0], \max_{s<r<t}\{D[g][s][r][t][\leftarrow]\}\}$$

$$C[g][s][t][\rightarrow][1] = \max_{s<r\leq t}\{C[g][s][r][\rightarrow][0] + C[s][r][t][\rightarrow][1]\}$$
$$C[g][s][t][\leftarrow][1] = \max_{s\leq r<t}\{C[g][r][t][\leftarrow][0] + C[t][s][r][\leftarrow][1]\}$$

    end for

  end for

end for

Figure 2: Pseudo-code of bottom-up chart parser for fourth-order grand-tri-sibling parsing algorithm

Figure 1 provides a graphical specification of the fourth-order grand-tri-sibling parsing algorithm. An incomplete gs-span is constructed by combining a smaller incomplete gs-span, representing the next-innermost pair of modifiers, with a sibling g-span. The algorithm resembles the third-order grand-sibling parser except that the incomplete g-spans are constructed by an incomplete gs-span with the same region.

We will now describe the fourth-order grand-tri-sibling parsing algorithm in more detail. Like factored parsing algorithms presented in the previous section, this parsing algorithm can be parsed via adaptations of standard chart-parsing techniques. Following McDonald (2006), let $C[g][s][t][d][c]$ be a dynamic programming table that stores the score of the best subtree from position s to position t, $s < t$, with grandparent position g, direction d and complete value c. The variable $d \in \{\leftarrow, \rightarrow\}$ indicates the direction of the subtree (gathering left or right dependents). The variable $c \in \{0, 1, 2\}$ indicates if a subtree is complete ($c = 1$), incomplete ($c = 0$) or represents sibling subtrees ($c = 2$). Sibling types have no inherent direction, so it will be always able to assume that when $c = 2$ then $d = null(-)$. We introduce another dynamic programming table $D[g][s][m][t][d]$ to store the score of the best gs-span from position s to position t, $s < t$, with grandparent position g, sibling position m and direction d. Since gs-spans are all incomplete ($c = 1$), the complete value can be omitted. Pseudo code for filling up the dynamic programming tables is in Figure 2. Since the introduction of gs-span, this parsing algorithm requires $O(n^5)$ time and $O(n^4)$ space.

grand-sibling features for part (g,s,m,t)	
4-gram features	**context features**
L(g)·P(s)·P(m)·P(t)	P(g)·P(s)·P(m)·P(t)·P(g+1)·P(s+1)·P(t+1)
P(g)·L(s)·P(m)·P(t)	P(g)·P(s)·P(m)·P(t)·P(g-1)·P(s-1)·P(t-1)
P(g)·P(s)·L(m)·P(t)	P(g)·P(s)·P(m)·P(t)·P(g+1)·P(s+1)
P(g)·P(s)·P(m)·L(t)	P(g)·P(s)·P(m)·P(t)·P(g-1)·P(s-1)
L(g)·L(s)·P(m)·P(t)	P(g)·P(m)·P(t)·P(g+1)·P(m+1)·P(t+1)
L(g)·P(s)·L(m)·P(t)	P(g)·P(m)·P(t)·P(g+1)·P(m-1)·P(t-1)
L(g)·P(s)·P(m)·L(t)	P(g)·P(m)·P(g+1)·P(m+1)
P(g)·L(s)·L(m)·P(t)	P(g)·P(m)·P(g-1)·P(m-1)
L(g)·L(s)·P(m)·L(t)	P(g)·P(t)·P(g+1)·P(t+1)
P(g)·P(s)·L(m)·L(t)	P(g)·P(t)·P(g-1)·P(t-1)
P(g)·P(s)·P(m)·P(t)	P(m)·P(t)·P(m+1)·P(t+1)
	P(m)·P(t)·P(m-1)·P(t-1)

coordination features			backed-off features	
L(g)·L(s)·L(t)	L(g)·P(s)	P(s)·P(t)	L(g)·P(m)·P(t)	L(g)·P(m)·L(t)
L(g)·P(s)·P(t)	P(g)·L(s)	P(g)·P(s)	P(g)·L(m)·P(t)	P(g)·L(m)·L(t)
P(g)·L(s)·P(t)	L(g)·P(t)	P(g)·L(t)	P(g)·P(m)·L(t)	P(g)·P(m)·P(t)
P(g)·P(s)·L(t)	P(g)·P(t)	L(s)·P(t)	L(g)·L(m)·P(t)	
L(g)·L(s)·P(t)	P(g)·P(s)·P(t)	P(s)·L(t)		
L(g)·P(s)·L(t)	P(g)·L(s)·L(t)			

tri-sibling features for part (s,r,m,t)			
4-gram features		**backed-off features**	
L(s)·P(r)·P(m)·P(t)	L(s)·P(r)·P(m)·L(t)	L(r)·P(m)·P(t)	P(r)·P(m)·P(t)
P(s)·L(r)·P(m)·P(t)	P(s)·L(r)·L(m)·P(t)	P(r)·L(m)·P(t)	L(r)·L(t)
P(s)·P(r)·L(m)·P(t)	P(s)·L(r)·P(m)·L(t)	P(r)·P(m)·L(t)	L(r)·P(t)
P(s)·P(r)·P(m)·L(t)	P(s)·P(r)·L(m)·L(t)	L(r)·L(m)·P(t)	P(r)·L(t)
L(s)·L(r)·P(m)·P(t)	P(s)·P(r)·P(m)·P(t)	L(r)·P(m)·L(t)	P(r)·P(t)
L(s)·P(r)·L(m)·P(t)		P(r)·L(m)·L(t)	

context features	
P(r)·P(m)·P(t)·P(r+1)·P(m+1)·P(t+1)	P(r)·P(m)·P(r+1)·P(m+1)
P(r)·P(m)·P(t)·P(r-1)·P(m-1)·P(t-1)	P(r)·P(m)·P(r-1)·P(m-1)
P(s)·P(r)·P(m)·P(t)·P(s+1)·P(r+1)	P(r)·P(t)·P(r+1)·P(t+1)
P(s)·P(r)·P(m)·P(t)·P(s-1)·P(r-1)	P(r)·P(t)·P(r-1)·P(t-1)
P(s)·P(r)·P(m)·P(t)·P(r+1)·P(t+1)	P(m)·P(t)·P(m+1)·P(t+1)
P(s)·P(r)·P(m)·P(t)·P(r-1)·P(t-1)	P(m)·P(t)·P(m-1)·P(t-1)
P(s)·P(r)·P(m)·P(t)·P(s+1)·P(r+1)·P(t+1)	P(s)·P(r)·P(m)·P(t)·P(s+1)·P(t+1)
P(s)·P(r)·P(m)·P(t)·P(s-1)·P(r-1)·P(t-1)	P(s)·P(r)·P(m)·P(t)·P(s-1)·P(t-1)

grand-tri-sibling features for part (g,s,r,m,t)			
5-gram features		**4-gram backed-off features**	
L(g)·P(s)·P(r)·P(m)·P(t)	P(g)·L(s)·P(r)·P(m)·P(t)	L(g)·P(r)·P(m)·P(t)	P(g)·L(r)·P(m)·P(t)
P(g)·P(s)·L(r)·P(m)·P(t)	P(g)·P(s)·P(r)·L(m)·P(t)	P(g)·P(r)·L(m)·P(t)	P(g)·P(r)·P(m)·L(t)
P(g)·P(s)·P(r)·P(m)·L(t)	P(g)·P(s)·P(r)·P(m)·P(t)	P(g)·P(r)·P(m)·P(t)	

Table 1: All feature templates used by the fourth-order grand-tri-sibling parser. L(·) and P(·) are the lexicon and POS tag of each token.

4 Feature Space

Following previous works (McDonald and Pereira, 2006; Koo and Collins, 2010), the fourth-order parser captures not only features associated with corresponding fourth-order grand-tri-sibling parts, but also the features of relevant lower-order parts that are enclosed in its factorization.

The lower-order features (first-order features of dependency parts and second-order features of grandchild and sibling parts) are based on feature sets from previous work (McDonald et al., 2005; McDonald and Pereira, 2006; Carreras, 2007). We added lexicalized versions of several features. For example, second-order grandchild feature set defines lexical trigram features, while previous work only used POS trigram features.

Table 1 outlines all feature templates of third-order grand-sibling, third-order tri-sibling, and fourth-order grand-tri-sibling parts. The fourth-order feature set consists of two sets of features. The first set of features is defined to be *5-gram features* that is a 5-tuple consisting of five relevant indices using words and POS tags. The second set of features is defined as *backed-off features* (Koo and Collins, 2010) for grand-tri-sibling part (g, s, r, m, t)—the 4-gram (g, r, m, t), which never exist in any lower-order part. The determination of this feature set is based on on experiments on the development data for both English and Chinese. In section 5.1 we examine the impact of these new features on parsing performance.

According to Table 1, several features in our parser depend on part-of-speech (POS) tags of input sentences. For English, POS tags are automatically assigned by the SVMTool tagger (Gimenez and Marquez, 2004). The accuracy of the SVMTool tagger on PTB is 97.3%; For Chinese, we used gold-standard POS tags in CTB. Following Koo and Collins (2010), two versions of POS tags are used for any features involve POS: one using is normal POS tags and another is a coarsened version of the POS tags. [2]

5 Experiments

The proposed fourth-order dependency parsing algorithm is evaluated on the Penn English Treebank (PTB 3.0) (Marcus et al., 1993) and the Penn Chinese Treebank (CTB 5.0).

For English, the PTB data is prepared by using the standard split: sections 2-21 are used for training, section 22 is for development, and section 23 for test. For Chinese, we adopt the identical training/validation/testing data split and experimental set-up as Zhang and Clark (2009). Dependencies are extracted by using Penn2Malt[3] tool.

Parsing accuracy is measured with unlabeled attachment score (UAS): the percentage of words with the correct head, and the percentage of complete matches (CM).[4]

The k-best version of the Margin Infused Relaxed Algorithm (MIRA) (Crammer and Singer, 2003; Crammer et al., 2006; McDonald, 2006) for the max-margin models (Taskar et al., 2003) is chosen for parameter estimation of our parsing model, In practice, we set $k = 10$ and exclude the sentences containing more than 100 words in both the training data sets of English and Chinese in all experiments.[5]

[2]For English, we used first two characters of the tag, except PRP$; For Chinese, we dropped the last character, except PU and CD

[3]http://w3.msi.vxu.se/~nivre/research/Penn2Malt.html

[4]As in previous work, English evaluation ignores any token whose gold-standard POS tag is one of { “ ” : , .}, and Chinese evaluation ignores any token whose tag is "PU".

[5]The number of sentences with more than 100 words is 3 for PTB and 67 for CTB.

	Eng		Chn	
Feature	UAS	CM	UAS	CM
baseline	93.45	49.06	87.38	38.85
+tri-sibling	93.62	49.42	87.60	38.94
+grand-tri-sibling	93.70	49.76	87.69	39.12
+4-gram backed-off	93.77	50.82	87.74	39.23

Table 2: The effect of different types of features on the development sets for English and Chinese.

5.1 Development Experiments

In this section, we dissect the contributions of each type of features. Table 2 shows the effect of different types of features on the development data sets for English and Chinese. Each row in Table 2 uses a super set of features than the previous one. Third-order grand-sibling parser is used as the baseline, and third-order tri-sibling, 5-gram grand-tri-sibling and 4-gram backed-off feature templates in Table 1 are incrementally added. All systems use our proposed fourth-order parsing algorithm. Since the only difference between systems is the set of features used, we can analyze the improvement from additional features.

From Table 2, we can see that each of the following parser capturing a group of new feature templates makes improvement on parsing performance over the previous one. Thus, we can conclude that the improvements come from the factorization's ability of capturing richer features which contains more context information.The parser with all these features achieves UAS of 93.77% and CM of 50.82% on PTB and UAS of 87.74%, CM of 39.23% on CTB.

5.2 Results and Analysis

Our parser obtains UAS of 93.4% and CM 50.3% of on PTB, and UAS of 87.4%, CM of 36.8% on CTB. Both of the results are state-of-the-art performance on these two treebanks.

Table 3 illustrates the UAS and CM of the fourth-order parser on PTB, together with some relevant results from related work. We compare our method to first-order and second-order sibling dependency parsers (McDonald and Pereira, 2006), and two third-order graph-based parsers (Koo and Collins, 2010). Additionally, we compare to a state-of-the-art graph-based parser (Zhang and McDonald, 2012) as well as a state-of-the-art transition-based parser (Zhang and Nivre, 2011).

Our experimental results show an improvement in performance over the results in Zhang and Nivre (2011), which are based on a transition-based dependency parser with rich non-local features. Our results are also better than the results of the two third-order graph-based dependency parsing models in Koo and Collins (2010). Moreover, our algorithm achieves better parsing performance than the generalized higher-order parser with cube-pruning (Zhang and McDonald, 2012), which is the state-of-the-art graph-based dependency parser so far. The models marked † or ‡ are not directly comparable to our work. The models marked † use semi-supervised methods with large amount of unlabeled data, and those marked ‡ utilize phrase-structure annotations, whiling our parser obtains results competitive with these works. All three models marked † or ‡ are based on the Carreras (2007) parser, which might be replaced by our fourth-order parser to get an even better performance.

Parser	UAS	CM
McDonald and Pereira (2006), 1^{st}order	90.9	36.7
McDonald and Pereira (2006), 2^{nd}order	91.5	42.1
Zhang and Clark (2008)	92.1	45.4
Zhang and Nivre (2011)	92.9	48.0
Koo and Collins (2010), model 2	92.9	–
Koo and Collins (2010), model 1	93.0	–
Zhang and McDonald (2012)	93.1	–
this paper	**93.4**	**50.3**
Koo et al. (2008)†	93.2	–
Carreras et al. (2008)‡	93.5	–
Suzuki et al. (2009)†	93.8	–

Table 3: UAS and CM of different parsers on PTB 3.0

Parser	UAS	CM
Huang and Sagae (2010)	85.2	33.7
Zhang and Clark (2008)	85.7	34.4
Zhang and Nivre (2011)	86.0	36.9
3^{rd}order grand-sibling	86.8	35.5
Zhang and McDonald (2012)	86.9	–
this paper	**87.4**	**36.8**
Zhang and Clark (2009)‡	86.6	36.1

Table 4: UAS and CM of different parsers on CTB 5.0

Next, we turn to the impact of our fourth-order parser on Chinese. Table 4 shows the comparative results for Chinese. Here we compare our method to an implement of the third-order grand-sibling parser — whose parsing performance on CTB is not reported in Koo and Collins (2010), and the dynamic programming transition-based parser of Huang and Sagae (2010). Additionally, we compare to the state-of-the-art graph-based dependency parser (Zhang and McDonald, 2012) as well as a state-of-the-art transition-based parser (Zhang and Nivre, 2011). The results indicates that our parser achieved significant improvement of the previous systems on this data set. The parsing model of Zhang and Clark (2009), which is marked ‡, also depends on phrase-structure annotations. So it cannot compare with ours directly, even through our results are better.

6 Conclusion

We have presented an even higher-order projective dependency parsing algorithm that can evaluate the fourth-order sub-structures of grand-tri-siblings. This algorithm achieves stage-of-the-art performance on both PTB and CTB, which demonstrates that the fourth-order grand-tri-sibling features have important contribution to dependency parsing.

A wide range of further research involving the fourth-order parsing algorithm is available. One idea would be to identify the highest n for which the information of nth-order part still improves parsing performance. Moreover, as the fourth-order parser has achieved state-of-the-art accuracy on standard parsing benchmarks, many NLP tasks may benefit from it.

References

Attardi, G. (2006). Experiments with a multilanguage non-projective dependency parser. In *Proceedings of the Tenth Conference on Natural Language Learning (CoNLL-2006)*, pages 166–170, New York, USA.

Buchholz, S. and Marsi, E. (2006). CoNLL-X shared task on multilingual dependency parsing. In *Proceeding of the 10th Conference on Computational Natural Language Learning (CoNLL'06)*, pages 149–164, New York, NY.

Carreras, X. (2007). Experiments with a higher-order projective dependency parser. In *Proceedings of the CoNLL Shared Task Session of EMNLP-CONLL*, pages 957–961.

Carreras, X., Collins, M., and Koo, T. (2008). Tag, dynamic programming, and the perceptron for efficient, feature-rich parsing. In *Proceedings of CoNLL*, pages 9–16, Manchester, England.

Chen, W., Kazama, J., Tsuruoka, Y., and Torisawa, K. (2010). Improving graph-based dependency parsing with decision history. In *Proceeding of the 23rd International Conference on Computional Linguistics (COLING'10)*, pages 126–134, BeiJing, China.

Chiang, D. (2007). Hierarchical phrase-based translation. *Computational linguistics*, 33(2).

Crammer, K., Dekel, O., Keshet, J., Shalev-Shwartz, S., and Singer, Y. (2006). Online passive-aggressive algorithms. *Jornal of Machine Learning Research*, 7:551–585.

Crammer, K. and Singer, Y. (2003). Ultraconservative online algorithms for multiclass problems. *Journal of Machine Learining Research*, 3:951–991.

Eisner, J. (1996). Three new probabilistic models for dependency parsing: An exploration. In *Proceedings of the 9th International Conference on Computational Linguistics (COLING'06)*, pages 340–345.

Eisner, J. (2000). Bilexical grammars and their cubic-time parsing algorithms. In Bunt, H. and Nijholt, A., editors, *Advances in Probabilistic and Other Parsing Technologies*, pages 29–62. Kluwer Academic Publishers.

Gimenez and Marquez (2004). Svmtool: A general pos tagger generator based on support vector machines. In *Proceedings of the 4th International Conference of Language Resources and Evaluation (IREC'04)*, Lisbon, Portugal.

Huang, L. and Sagae, K. (2010). Dynamic programming for linear-time incremental parsing. In *Proceeding of ACL 2010*, pages 1077–1086, Uppsala, Sweden.

Katz-Brown, J., Petrov, S., McDonald, R., Och, F., Talbot, D., Ichikawa, H., Seno, M., and Kazawa, H. (2011). Training a parser for machine translation reordering. In *Proceedings of the 2011 Conference on Empirical Methods in Natural Language Processing*, pages 183–192, Edinburgh, Scotland, UK. Association for Computational Linguistics.

Koo, T. (2010). *Advances in Discriminative Dependency Parsing*. PhD thesis, Massachusetts Institute of Technology.

Koo, T., Carreras, X., and Collins, M. (2008). Simple semi-supervised dependency parsing. In *Proceedings of ACL-08: HLT*, pages 595–603, Columbus, Ohio, USA.

Koo, T. and Collins, M. (2010). Efficient third-order dependency parsers. In *Proceedings of 48th Meeting of the Association for Computional Linguistics (ACL'10)*, pages 1–11, Uppsala, Sweden.

Marcus, M., Santorini, B., and Marcinkiewicz, M. A. (1993). Building a large annotated corpus of English: the Penn Treebank. *Computational Linguistics*, 19(2):313–330.

McDonald, R. (2006). *Discriminative learning spanning tree algorithm for dependency parsing*. PhD thesis, University of Pennsylvania.

McDonald, R., Crammer, K., and Pereira, F. (2005). Online large-margin training of dependency parsers. In *Proceedings of the 43rd Annual Meeting on Association for Computational Linguistics (ACL-2005)*, pages 91–98, Ann Arbor, Michigan, USA.

McDonald, R. and Nivre, J. (2007). Characterizing the errors of data-driven dependency parsing models. In *Proceedings of the 2007 Joint Conference on Empirical Methods in Natural Language Processing and Computational Natural Language Learning (EMNLP-CoNLL 2007)*, pages 122–131, Prague, Czech.

McDonald, R. and Pereira, F. (2006). Online learning of approximate dependency parsing algorithms. In *European Association for Computational Linguistics (EACL-2006)*, pages 81–88, Trento, Italy.

Nguyen, T.-V. T., Moschitti, A., and Riccardi, G. (2009). Convolution kernels on constituent, dependency and sequential structures for relation extraction. In *Proceedings of the 2009 Conference on Empirical Methods in Natural Language Processing*, pages 1378–1387, Singapore. Association for Computational Linguistics.

Nivre, J., Hall, J., Kübler, S., Mcdonald, R., Nilsson, J., Riedel, S., and Yuret, D. (2007). The CoNLL 2007 shared task on dependency parsing. In *Proceeding of EMNLP-CoNLL 2007*, pages 915–932, Prague, Czech.

Nivre, J. and Scholz, M. (2004). Deterministic dependency parsing of english text. In *Proceedings of the 20th international conference on Computational Linguistics (COLING'04)*, pages 64–70, Geneva, Switzerland.

Shinyama, Y., Sekine, S., and Sudo, K. (2002). Automatic paraphrase acquisition from news articles. In *Proceeding of the 2nd International Conference on Human Language Technology Research (HLT'02)*, pages 313–318.

Suzuki, J., Isozaki, H., Carreras, X., and Collins, M. (2009). An empirial study of semi-supervised structured conditional models for dependency parsing. In *Proceedings of EMNLP*, pages 551–560.

Taskar, B., Guestrin, C., and Koller, D. (2003). Max margin markov networks. In Sebastian Thrun, L. K. S. and Scholköopf, B., editors, *NIPS*. MIT Press.

Xie, J., Mi, H., and Liu, Q. (2011). A novel dependency-to-string model for statistical machine translation. In *Proceedings of the 2011 Conference on Empirical Methods in Natural Language Processing*, pages 216–226, Edinburgh, Scotland, UK. Association for Computational Linguistics.

Xue, N., Xia, F., Chiou, F.-D., and Palmer, M. (2005). The Penn Chinese TreeBank: Phrase structure annotation of a large corpus. *Natural Language Engineering*, 11(2):207–238.

Yamada, H. and Matsumoto, Y. (2003). Statistical dependency analysis with support vector machines. In *Proceedings of the 8th International Workshop on Parsing Technologies (IWPT-2003)*, pages 195–206, Nancy, France.

Zhang, H. and McDonald, R. (2012). Generalized higher-order dependency parsing with cube pruning. In *Proceedings of the 2012 Joint Conference on Empirical Methods in Natural Language Processing and Computational Natural Language Learning*, pages 320–331, Jeju Island, Korea. Association for Computational Linguistics.

Zhang, Y. and Clark, S. (2008). A tale of two parsers: investigating and combining graph-based and transition-based dependency parsing using beam search. In *Proceedings of EMNLP*, pages 562–571.

Zhang, Y. and Clark, S. (2009). Transition-based parsing of Chinese treebank using a global discriminative model. In *Proceedings of the 11th International Conference on Parsing Technologies (IWPT'09)*, pages 162–171, Paris, France.

Zhang, Y. and Nivre, J. (2011). Transition-based dependency parsing with rich non-local features. In *Proceeding of ACL 2011*, pages 188–193, Portland, Oregon.

A Subjective Logic Framework for Multi-Document Summarization

Sukanya Manna[1] *Byron J. Gao*[1] *Reed Coke*[2]
(1) Department of Computer Science, Texas State University, San Marcos, TX 78666
(2) Department of Computer Science, Swarthmore College, Swarthmore, PA 19081
s_m201@txstate.edu, bgao@txstate.edu, rcoke1@swarthmore.edu

ABSTRACT
In this paper we propose SubSum, a subjective logic framework for sentence-based extractive multi-document summarization. Document summaries perceived by humans are subjective in nature as human judgements of sentence relevancy are inconsistent and laden with uncertainty. SubSum captures this uncertainty and extracts significant sentences from a document cluster to generate extractive summaries. In particular, SubSum represents the sentences of a document cluster as propositions and computes *opinions*, a probability measure containing secondary uncertainty, for these propositions. Sentences with stronger opinions are considered more significant and used as candidate sentences. The key advantage of SubSum over other techniques is its ability to quantify uncertainty. In addition, SubSum is a completely unsupervised approach and is highly portable across different domains and languages.

KEYWORDS: multi-document summarization, subjective logic, belief measures, uncertainty.

Proceedings of COLING 2012: Posters, pages 797–808,
COLING 2012, Mumbai, December 2012.

1 Introduction

Automatic multi-document summarization can effectively condense information found in multiple documents into a short, readable synopsis, allowing users to quickly familiarize themselves with the main ideas of the information. It has vast applications, especially for online documents where redundancy abounds (Harabagiu and Lacatusu, 2010). Example source documents include news articles, email threads, blogs, reviews, and search results, just to name a few. There has been an increasing research effort towards multi-document summarization in recent years (McKeown and Radev, 1995; Radev and McKeown, 1998; Radev et al.; Carbonell and Goldstein, 1998; Barzilay et al., 1999; Conroy et al., 2004; Barzilay and McKeown, 2005; Daumé III and Marcu, 2005; Nenkova and Vanderwende, 2005; Nenkova et al., 2006; Ji, 2006; Park et al., 2007; Wei et al., 2008; Wan, 2008; Wang et al., 2008; Li et al., 2010; Zhang et al., 2010; Shen and Li, 2010; Xia et al., 2011; Ribaldo et al., 2012).

Document summaries perceived by humans are subjective in nature. Judgments of sentence importance can be affected by user interests, preferences and viewpoints, which may vary from person to person. Any given portion of a document can be interpreted in different fashions by different people, especially in the way they understand and interpret the context (Pardo et al., 2002). For example, for the news of "a small plane smashed into the tallest building in Milan Thursday evening ...", a user could perceive its main idea as a tragic accident, whereas another user could interpret it as a topic about a terrorist attack. Therefore, people arrive at their judgements based on *subjective* information which is not completely certain or reliable.

SubSum Framework: In order to capture the uncertainty of human judgements in summarizing documents, in this paper we propose SubSum, a subjective logic framework for multi-document summarization. SubSum represents the sentences of a document cluster as propositions and computes *opinions*, a probability measure containing secondary uncertainty, for these propositions. Sentences with stronger opinions are considered more significant and used as candidate sentences to summarize a document.

While standard logic deals with propositions that are either true or false, subjective logic (Josang, 2001) is a type of probabilistic logic that explicitly takes uncertainty and belief into account. It can be seen as an extension of probability calculus and binary logic. Subjective logic is particularly suitable for modeling and analyzing situations involving uncertainty and incomplete knowledge (Josang and McAnally, 2010; Josang, 2001).

SubSum is an evidence-based method. It formulates opinions using evidence derived or found in a document, which can be terms, phrases, sentences, co-occurrences of words or phrases, or any syntactic or semantic features. Opinions can clearly classify sentences based on their importance and can be used to select significant sentences in summarizing a document.

SubSum differs significantly from many existing summarization approaches. Existing approaches typically use corpus statistics (Luhn, 1958), linguistic features (Hovy and Lin, 1998), linear algebra methods (Gong and Liu, 2001), or graphical methods (Mihalcea and Tarau, 2005) to find out relevant sentences within documents. These methods do not focus on capturing or quantifying uncertainty as SubSum does.

SubSum is completely based on belief measures adapted from Dempster-Shafer theory (Shafer, 1976) and independent of lexical databases, making it easily portable across different domains and languages. Additionally, it does not require any training data as in many existing summarizers (Conroy et al., 2004; Kupiec et al., 1995).

Contributions: (1) We propose SubSum, the first subjective logic-based framework for multi-document summarization, leveraging belief measures to capture uncertainty of human judgements on significance of sentences. (2) SubSum does not require training data, and is highly portable across different domains and languages. (3) We perform extensive experiments on benchmark datasets, demonstrating the advantages and effectiveness of the SubSum framework.

2 Subjective Logic Preliminaries

Subjective logic (Josang, 2001) operates on subjective beliefs about the world, and uses *opinions* to denote the representations of subjective beliefs. In subjective logic, first order measure of evidence is expressed as belief mass distribution functions over the *frame of discernment*. An *opinion* can be interpreted as a probability measure containing secondary uncertainty, and as such subjective logic can be seen as an extension of both probability calculus and binary logic (Josang, 2001). *Belief*, *disbelief*, *uncertainty*, and *base rates* are the four main belief representations used to express opinions of propositions in subjective logic. The following definitions of subjective logic concepts are adapted from Josang's draft book (folk.uio.no/josang/papers/subjective_logic.pdf) and (Josang, 2001).

Belief Mass Assignment: Let Θ be a frame of discernment. For each sub-state $x \in 2^\Theta$, if a number $m_\Theta(x)$ is associated such that, $m_\Theta(x) \geq 0$, $m_\Theta(\emptyset) = 0$, $\sum_{x \in 2^\Theta} m_\Theta(x) = 1$, then m_Θ is called a belief mass assignment in Θ, or *BMA* for short. For each sub-state $x \in 2^\Theta$, the number $m_\Theta(x)$ is called the belief mass of x.

Belief Function: Let Θ be a frame of discernment, and let m_Θ be a *BMA* on Θ. Then the belief function corresponding to m_Θ is the function $b: 2^\Theta \rightarrow [0,1]$ defined by:

$$b(x) = \sum_{y \subseteq x} m_\Theta(y), \quad x, y \in 2^\Theta \tag{1}$$

Disbelief Function: Let Θ be a frame of discernment, and let m_Θ be a *BMA* on Θ. Then the disbelief function corresponding to m_Θ is the function $d: 2^\Theta \rightarrow [0,1]$ defined by:

$$d(x) = \sum_{y \cap x = \emptyset} m_\Theta(y), \quad x, y \in 2^\Theta. \tag{2}$$

Uncertainty Function: Let Θ be a frame of discernment, and let m_Θ be a *BMA* on Θ. Then the uncertainty function corresponding to m_Θ is the function $u: 2^\Theta$ $[0,1]$ defined by:

$$u(x) = \sum_{y \cap x \neq \emptyset, y \quad x} m_\Theta(y), \quad x, y \in 2^\Theta. \tag{3}$$

Base Rate Function: Let Θ be a frame of cardinality k, and let a_Θ be the function from Θ to $[0,1]^k$ satisfying, $a_\Theta(\emptyset) = 0$, $a_\Theta(x_i) \in [0,1]$ *and* $\sum_{i=1}^{k} a_\Theta(x_i) = 1$ Then a_Θ is a base rate distribution over Θ.

Relative Atomicity or Relative Base Rate: Let Θ be a frame of discernment and let $x, y \in 2^\Theta$. Then for any given $y \neq \emptyset$ the relative atomicity of x to y is the function $a: 2^\Theta \rightarrow [0,1]$,

$$a(x/y) = \frac{|x \cap y|}{|y|}, \quad x, y \in 2^\Theta, \ y \neq \emptyset. \tag{4}$$

It can be observed that $x \cap y = \emptyset \Rightarrow a(x/y) = 0$ and $y \subseteq x \Rightarrow a(x/y) = 1$. In all other cases relative atomicity will be a value between 0 and 1.

Binomial Opinion: Let $\Theta = \{x, \neg x\}$ be either a binary frame or a binary partitioning of an n-ary frame. A binomial opinion about the truth of state x is an ordered quadruple $\omega_x = (b, d, u, a)$, where b is belief, d is disbelief, u is uncertainty, and a is base rate respectively. These components satisfy $b + d + u = 1$ and $b, d, u, a \in [0, 1]$.

Probability Expectation of a binomial opinion of proposition x: Let Θ be a frame of discernment with *BMA* m_Θ then the probability expectation function corresponding to m_Θ is the function $E : 2^\Theta \rightarrow [0, 1]$ defined by:

$$E(x) = b(x) + a(x)u(x) \tag{5}$$

Ordering of Opinions: Let ω_x and ω_y be two opinions. They can be ordered according to the following criteria by priority: (1) The opinion with the greatest probability expectation is the greatest opinion. (2) The opinion with the least uncertainty is the greatest opinion. (3) The opinion with the least relative atomicity is the greatest opinion.

3 SubSum Framework For Multi-Document Summarization

In this section, we first formally define the multi-document summarization problem, then we present the SubSum framework. In SubSum, sentences are considered as propositions. The *opinions* of these propositions are computed, which signify their importance in the document cluster and are used to select candidate sentences for summarization purposes.

Multi-Document Summarization Problem: Given a cluster of documents D consisting of a set of sentences $S = \{s_1, s_2, ..., s_m\}$ and a set of words $W = \{w_1, w_2, ..., w_n\}$, the task of multi-document summarization is to extract a subset of sentences from S, denoted by S_r ($S_r \subset S$), that best represent the content of document cluster D.

3.1 Formulation

Concept of States: A cluster of related documents consisting of n unique words represent an n-ary frame of discernment Θ. Words are elementary states or atomic states. Sentences and phrases on the other hand are composite states, which can be represented as the union of multiple atomic states.

Assumptions: The following framework is proposed for the practical application of subjective logic in a document analysis/summarization context: (1) Documents in a cluster are related. (2) All the words or terms (stop words excluded) in a document cluster are atomic. (3) The sentences are unique, i.e., each sentence occurs only once in given document cluster. Single-word sentences can also exist.

Document Representation: Sentences of a document cluster are considered as a set of words separated by a stop mark ".", "!" or "?". These sentences are tokenized to generate words (stop words excluded). These words and sentences represent atomic and composite states.

We discuss here different notations used in this paper. Θ is the frame of discernment, a document cluster D can be represented as a set of words, which is denoted by $W = \{w_1, w_2, ..., w_n\}$, where W is a set of words present in the document cluster D. $|W| = n$. Since there are n words in D, Θ is an $n-ary$ frame of discernment. Thus, $\rho(\Theta) = \{\{w_1\}, \{w_2\}, ..., \{w_1, w_2, w_3, ..., w_n\}\} \equiv 2^\Theta$, where $|\rho(\Theta)| = 2^n$.

A document cluster D can also be represented by a set of sentences S such that $S = \{s_1, s_2, ..., s_m\}$, where $|S| = m$ and $s_i (i \in |S|)$ is an element of $\rho(\Theta)$, because each sentence can be represented as $S_i = \{w_j \cup w_k \cup ... \cup w_r\} \in \Theta$ where $S_i \in \rho(\Theta)$. Note that for practical reasons, $|\rho(\Theta)| = 2^n - 2$, excluding Θ and $\emptyset$, which is also known as *reduced frame of discernment*. If there are n words in the document cluster, then there can be at maximum $2^n - 2$ possible states (words and their co-occurrences). For example, suppose a document cluster D has words a, b, c, d, then $\{a\}$, $\{b\}$, $\{c\}$, $\{d\}$, $\{a, b, c, d\}$, are the states we use for our analysis (to avoid computational expenses, we do not consider all the states of $|\rho(\Theta)|$, such as, $\{ab\}$, $\{bc\}$... $\{abc\}$...).

Frequency of States: Before computing Belief Mass Assignment (*BMA*), frequency of each states should be computed.

$$F_x = \Sigma_{i=1}^{m} f_x, \quad x \in 2^{\Theta},\ f_x > 0,\ m = |S|, \tag{6}$$

where f_x is the frequency of the state x in each sentence and m is the total number of sentences in the document cluster D.

$$Z = \Sigma_{j=1}^{M} F_x, \quad M \in |\rho(\Theta)|, \tag{7}$$

where Z is the sum of the frequencies of all states in the document cluster D.

Belief Mass Assignment (*BMA*): Belief mass assignment (*BMA*) is computed in this case by

$$m(x) = F_x / Z, \tag{8}$$

where F_x, computed by Eq.(6), is the total frequency of that sub-state in all the sentences (or the whole document), and Z, computed by Eq. (7), is the total frequency of all the existing states in the document cluster D. The other parameters of belief measure will follow the definitions presented in Section 2.

Belief Representations of Subjective Opinions: The basic definitions of belief, disbelief, uncertainty and relative atomicity remain the same as in Section 2. We re-define some of the other definitions in the following.

Propositional Atomicity: Let Θ be a frame of discernment and $x, y \in 2^{\Theta}$. Then for any given $y \neq \emptyset$, the propositional atomicity of x is the average relative atomicity values of all x to y. Precisely,

$$a_p(x) = \frac{\sum_{\forall |a(x/y) \neq 0|} a(x/y)}{|a(x/y) \neq 0|}, \quad x, y \in 2^{\Theta}, y \neq \emptyset \tag{9}$$

Accordingly, *Probability Expectation* for a given proposition (sentence in this case) x can be re-written as

$$PE(x) = b(x) + a_p(x)u(x), \tag{10}$$

where $b(x)$, $u(x)$, and $a_p(x)$ are belief, uncertainty and propositional atomicity of proposition x. Opinions of a sentence can be measured by this probability expectation as in Eq.(10) using propositional atomicity.

3.2 Procedures

Generally, there are three major problems associated with multi-document summaries: (1) recognizing and coping with redundancy, (2) identifying important differences among documents, and (3) ensuring summary coherence, even when material stems from different source documents (Radev et al., 2002). We have addressed problem (1) in our method. Problems (2) and (3) are not very significant for us, as our proposed method is applicable for a cluster of related or coherent documents. Multi-document summary generation using SubSum involves the following steps:

Step 1 Compute opinions as representativeness scores for the sentences in S.

Step 2 Pick the sentence $s \in S$ with the greatest opinion based on 'ordering of opinions'.

Step 3 For each state x in s, update its belief mass by setting it to a small number close to zero.
Step 4 If the desired summary length has not been reached, go back to step 1.
Steps 1 and 3 are explained in the following.

Computation of Opinions: A key step of SubSum is to assign a representativeness score (opinion) for each sentence $s_i \in S$, for the document cluster D. Algorithm 1 explains how SubSum computes opinions.

ALGORITHM 1: Computing Opinions of Sentences

Input: A document cluster D containing a set S of sentences.
Output: A weighted list of sentences $S_{weighted} \in S$ for D.

Pre-process D;
Extract the states X, where $X \in 2^{\Theta}$;
Assign *belief masses* to the states using Eq.(8);
foreach *sentence* $s \in S$ **do**
  Apply Eq.(1) to compute *belief* $b(s)$;
  Apply Eq.(3) to compute *uncertainty* $u(s)$;
  Apply Eq.(9) to compute *propositional atomicity* $a_p(s)$;
  Apply Eq.(10) to compute *probability expectation* $PE(s)$;
end
$S_{weighted}$ = weighted list of sentences.

Context Adjustment: Using frequency-based approaches to determine summary content in multi-document summarization results in a repetitive summary (Nenkova et al., 2006). In SubSum, the assignment of belief masses is dependent on frequency of occurrence of words. Thus, we need to consider removal of redundant contexts. The basic intuition of redundancy removal has been taken from (Nenkova et al., 2006). For each state (atomic or composite) x in the sentence s chosen at step 3, we update its belief masses by setting it to a very small number close to 0. Here we use 0.00001 for this number.

4 Evaluation

Qualitative analysis of summarizers is done by comparing them against human abstracts using ROUGE (Lin, 2004). For evaluation of our SubSum framework, we have compared ROUGE-generated recall, precision, and F-measure with baseline summaries and other summarizers using standard benchmarks of DUC (Document Understanding Conference `duc.nist.gov`)-DUC2001, DUC2002, and DUC2004 datasets.

4.1 Methodology

Frequency is a good predictor of content in human summaries according to (Nenkova et al., 2006). The word frequency feature forms the basis of the SubSum framework as we use the frequency of each state of Θ to assign that state's belief mass (Eq. 8). This belief mass further contributes to the computation of opinion, which is the main sentence scoring function of SubSum. Through the experiments discussed below, we focus on how well SubSum corresponds to human-generated summaries and observe its performance when compared to other methods.

Pre-processing of Documents: Documents of each cluster are pre-processed by tokenizing them into words, removing stop-words and then by stemming (using Snowball `snowball.tartarus.org/index.php`) to retain the root form of the words. Unique instances of sentences are selected by removing the duplicates if at all they occur in the document cluster. The processed word list and the sentence list are then used by SubSum for summarization.

Comparison Partners: The human-generated summaries provided by DUC datasets have been used as reference summaries for qualitative evaluation of automatic summarizers. These datasets also provide baseline summaries that can be used for comparison purposes. In addition, we have used the 16 system summaries from DUC2004. These summaries are referred to as *peer* followed by a reference number provided by the dataset.

Beyond the baselines, we have implemented a summarizer based on Composition Functions (CF) (Nenkova et al., 2006) as an additional comparison partner. Nenkova et al., (Nenkova et al., 2006) proposed a context-sensitive frequency-based summarizer that uses a composition function to assign importance weights to sentences. Out of the three proposed composition functions, we have chosen the best one, *Avr*, as our comparison partner.

In addition, to test the effect of context adjustments in multi-document summarization, we have also included comparisons with with *SubSum_NoAdj* and *CF_NoAdj*, which are the modified versions of SubSum and CF without performing any context adjustments (basically omitting Step 3 of the procedures mentioned in Sec.3.2).

Evaluation Metrics: Our evaluation was done using 1-gram setting of ROUGE (Lin, 2004), which was found to have the highest correlation with human judgments, namely at a confidence level of 95%. ROUGE calculates Precision, Recall, and F-measure values. In our experiments, summary length was set to 100 words. The exact parameters we used were *-c 95 -n 4 -x -m -r 1000 -w 1.2 -l 100 -a -z*.

4.2 Results

Performance Comparison: Since the length of summaries was set to 100 words, the performance of summarizers was determined by examining the ROUGE recall scores.

Table 1 presents the average performance (recall, precision, and F-measure) of the summarizers over all the 30 DUC2001 and 59 DUC2002 sub-datasets. From table 1, we can observe that SubSum corresponds well to the human reference summaries, outperforming the baseline and CF. In particular, for DUC2001, SubSum outperformed the baseline by 3.4% and CF by 0.6% in terms of recall. For DUC2002, SubSum outperformed the baseline by 4.2% and CF by 2.1% in terms of recall.

	DUC2001			DUC2002		
Methods	Recall	Precision	F-measure	Recall	Precision	F-measure
SubSum	0.3306	0.2836	0.3051	0.3294	0.3331	0.3312
SubSum_NoAdj	0.3244	0.2784	0.2995	0.3371	0.3393	0.3381
Baseline	0.2967	0.2558	0.2746	0.2872	0.2938	0.2901
CF	0.3246	0.2792	0.3001	0.3084	0.3362	0.3216
CF_NoAdj	0.3150	0.2703	0.2909	0.2927	0.3165	0.3040

Table 1: Average ROUGE-1 values on DUC2001 and DUC2002

Note that the DUC2001 and DUC2002 datasets have extremely strong baselines. As analyzed by (Nenkova, 2005), these baselines correspond to the selection of first n sentences of a news article. (Sarkar, 2012) has pointed out that beating DUC2001 and DUC2002 baseline summaries is difficult. According to (Das and Martins, 2007), many of the best performing summarization systems could not outperform the DUC2001 and DUC2002 baselines with statistical significance.

For example, the summarizers in (Nenkova et al., 2006) and (Erkan and Radev, 2004) either reached the baselines or outperformed them with a small margin.

Methods	Recall	Precision	F-measure
SubSum	0.3849	0.3418	0.3621
SubSum_NoAdj	0.3814	0.3382	0.3584
Baseline	0.3215	0.2954	0.3049
CF	0.3765	0.3347	0.3543
CF_NoAdj	0.3632	0.3213	0.3409
peer11	0.3254	0.3452	0.3317
peer27	0.3154	0.2987	0.3061
peer34	0.3830	0.3429	0.3618
peer44	0.3694	0.3365	0.3520
peer55	0.3694	0.3281	0.3474
peer65	0.3913	0.3462	0.3674
peer81	0.3764	0.3353	0.3546
peer93	0.3432	0.3391	0.3375
peer102	0.3857	0.3467	0.3651
peer111	0.2336	0.2097	0.2209
peer117	0.3476	0.3126	0.3291
peer120	0.3248	0.3765	0.3423
peer123	0.3056	0.3195	0.3097
peer124	0.3784	0.3375	0.3567
peer138	0.3422	0.3090	0.3247

Table 2: Average ROUGE-1 values on DUC2004

Table 2 presents the average performance (recall, precision, and F-measure) of the summarizers over all the 50 DUC2004 sub-datasets. From the results we can have similar observations that SubSum corresponds well to the human reference summaries, outperforming the baseline by 6.3% and CF by 0.8% in terms of recall.

SubSum performed extremely well compared to other DUC2004 peer summarization systems. It significantly outperformed most systems, roughly tied with peer34 and peer102, and slightly lost to peer65. Note that peer65 is a supervised HMM system (Conroy et al., 2004) that requires training data and parameter adjustment, while SubSum is non-supervised and totally data-driven. Overall, SubSum is among the best of DUC2004 participants.

Effect of Context Adjustment: Tables 1 and 2 have included the ROUGE evaluation scores for SubSum_NoAdj and CF_NoAdj as two other comparison partners of SubSum and CF. SubSum_NoAdj and CF_NoAdj are the modified versions of SubSum and CF without context adjustment in the summarization process. As discussed in Sec. 3.2, one of the main purposes of context adjustment is to remove context redundancy, which is a typical issue in multi-document summarization. From the results we can observe that CF outperformed CF_NoAdj in all the three datasets, showing that the content selection capability of CF would be affected by the removal of the context adjustment step. On the contrary, SubSum_NoAdj performed comparably to SubSum, where it slightly lost to SubSum for DUC2001 and DUC2004 and won by a small margin for DUC2002. This reflects the fact that SubSum can handle redundancy to some extent even without applying context adjustments separately.

5 Acknowledgement

This work was supported in part by the Texas Norman Hackerman Advanced Research Program (003656-0035-2009) and the National Science Foundation (OCI-1062439, CNS-1058724).

References

Barzilay, R. and McKeown, K. (2005). Sentence fusion for multidocument news summarization. *Computational Linguistics*, 31(3):297–328.

Barzilay, R., McKeown, K., and Elhadad, M. (1999). Information fusion in the context of multi-document summarization. In *Proceedings of the 37th annual meeting of the Association for Computational Linguistics on Computational Linguistics*.

Carbonell, J. and Goldstein, J. (1998). The use of mmr, diversity-based reranking for reordering documents and producing summaries. In *Proceedings of the 21st annual international ACM SIGIR conference on Research and development in information retrieval*.

Conroy, J., Schlesinger, J., Goldstein, J., and O'leary, D. (2004). Left-brain/right-brain multi-document summarization. In *Proceedings of the Document Understanding Conference (DUC 2004)*.

Das, D. and Martins, A. (2007). A survey on automatic text summarization. *Literature Survey for the Language and Statistics II course at CMU*, 4:192–195.

Daumé III, H. and Marcu, D. (2005). Bayesian multi-document summarization at mse. In *ACL 2005, Workshop on Multilingual Summarization Evaluation*.

Erkan, G. and Radev, D. (2004). Lexrank: Graph-based lexical centrality as salience in text summarization. *J. Artif. Intell. Res. (JAIR)*, 22:457–479.

Gong, Y. and Liu, X. (2001). Generic text summarization using relevance measure and latent semantic analysis. In *Proceedings of the 24th annual international ACM SIGIR conference on Research and development in information retrieval*.

Harabagiu, S. and Lacatusu, F. (2010). Using topic themes for multi-document summarization. *ACM Transactions on Information Systems (TOIS)*, 28(3):13.

Hovy, E. and Lin, C. (1998). Automated text summarization and the summarist system. In *Proceedings of a workshop on held at Baltimore, Maryland: October 13-15, 1998*.

Ji, P. (2006). Multi-document summarization based on unsupervised clustering. In *Proceedings of the Third Asia conference on Information Retrieval Technology*. Springer-Verlag.

Josang, A. (2001). A logic for uncertain probabilities. *International Journal of Uncertainty, Fuzziness and Knowledge-Based Systems*, 9(3):279–311.

Josang, A. and McAnally, D. (2010). Multiplication and comultiplication of beliefs. *International Journal of Approximate Reasoning*, 38(1):19–51.

Kupiec, J., Pedersen, J., and Chen, F. (1995). A trainable document summarizer. In *Proceedings of the 18th annual international ACM SIGIR conference on Research and development in information retrieval*.

Li, L., Wang, D., Shen, C., and Li, T. (2010). Ontology-enriched multi-document summarization in disaster management. In *Proceedings of the 33rd international ACM SIGIR conference on Research and development in information retrieval*.

Lin, C.-Y. (2004). Rouge: A package for automatic evaluation of summaries. Barcelona, Spain. Association for Computational Linguistics.

Luhn, H. (1958). The automatic creation of literature abstracts. *IBM Journal of research and development*, 2(2):159–165.

McKeown, K. and Radev, D. (1995). Generating summaries of multiple news articles. In *Proceedings of the 18th annual international ACM SIGIR conference on Research and development in information retrieval*.

Mihalcea, R. and Tarau, P. (2005). A language independent algorithm for single and multiple document summarization. In *Proceedings of IJCNLP*.

Nenkova, A. (2005). Automatic text summarization of newswire: Lessons learned from the document understanding conference. In *Proceedings of the National Conference on Artificial Intelligence*.

Nenkova, A. and Vanderwende, L. (2005). The impact of frequency on summarization. *Microsoft Research, Redmond, Washington, Tech. Rep. MSR-TR-2005-101*.

Nenkova, A., Vanderwende, L., and McKeown, K. (2006). A compositional context sensitive multi-document summarizer: exploring the factors that influence summarization. In *Proceedings of the 29th annual international ACM SIGIR conference on Research and development in information retrieval*.

Pardo, T., Rino, L., and Nunes, M. (2002). Extractive summarization: how to identify the gist of a text. In *the Proceedings of the 1st International Information Technology Symposium–I2TS*.

Park, S., Lee, J.-H., Kim, D.-H., and Ahn, C.-M. (2007). Multi-document summarization using weighted similarity between topic and clustering-based non-negative semantic feature. In *Proceedings of the joint 9th Asia-Pacific web and 8th international conference on web-age information management conference on Advances in data and web management*. Springer-Verlag.

Radev, D., Jing, H., and Budzikowska, M. Centroid-based summarization of multiple documents: sentence extraction, utility-based evaluation, and user studies. *Ann Arbor*, 1001:48103.

Radev, D. and McKeown, K. (1998). Generating natural language summaries from multiple on-line sources. *Computational Linguistics*, 24(3):469–500.

Radev, D. R., Hovy, E., and McKeown, K. (2002). Introduction to the special issue on summarization. *Computational Linguistics*, 28(4):399–408.

Ribaldo, R., Akabane, A. T., Rino, L. H. M., and Pardo, T. A. S. (2012). Graph-based methods for multi-document summarization: exploring relationship maps, complex networks and discourse information. In *Proceedings of the 10th international conference on Computational Processing of the Portuguese Language*.

Sarkar, K. (2012). Bengali text summarization by sentence extraction. *Arxiv preprint arXiv:1201.2240*.

Shafer, G. (1976). *A mathematical theory of evidence*. Princeton University Press Princeton, NJ.

Shen, C. and Li, T. (2010). Multi-document summarization via the minimum dominating set. In *Proceedings of the 23rd International Conference on Computational Linguistics*.

Wan, X. (2008). An exploration of document impact on graph-based multi-document summarization. In *Proceedings of the Conference on Empirical Methods in Natural Language Processing*. Association for Computational Linguistics.

Wang, D., Li, T., Zhu, S., and Ding, C. (2008). Multi-document summarization via sentence-level semantic analysis and symmetric matrix factorization. In *Proceedings of the 31st annual international ACM SIGIR conference on Research and development in information retrieval.*

Wei, F., Li, W., Lu, Q., and He, Y. (2008). A cluster-sensitive graph model for query-oriented multi-document summarization. In *Proceedings of the IR research, 30th European conference on Advances in information retrieval*. Springer-Verlag.

Xia, Y., Zhang, Y., and Yao, J. (2011). Co-clustering sentences and terms for multi-document summarization. In *Proceedings of the 12th international conference on Computational linguistics and intelligent text processing - Volume Part II*.

Zhang, R., Li, W., and Lu, Q. (2010). Sentence ordering with event-enriched semantics and two-layered clustering for multi-document news summarization. In *Proceedings of the 23rd International Conference on Computational Linguistics: Posters*.

Manual Corpus Annotation:
Giving Meaning to the Evaluation Metrics

Yann MATHET [1,2,3] *Antoine WIDLÖCHER* [1,2,3] *Karën FORT* [4,5]
Claire FRANÇOIS [6] *Olivier GALIBERT* [7] *Cyril GROUIN* [8,9]
Juliette KAHN [7] *Sophie ROSSET* [8] *Pierre ZWEIGENBAUM* [8]

(1) Université de Caen Basse-Normandie, UMR 6072 GREYC, Caen, France
(2) ENSICAEN, UMR 6072 GREYC, Caen, France (3) CNRS, UMR 6072 GREYC, Caen, France
(4) LIPN, Villetaneuse, France (5) LORIA, Vandœuvre, France (6) INIST–CNRS, Vandœuvre, France
(7) LNE, Trappes, France (8) LIMSI–CNRS, Orsay, France
(9) INSERM, UMR_S 872, Eq 20 & UPMC, Paris, France

`{yann.mathet, antoine.widlocher}@unicaen.fr,`
`karen.fort@loria.fr, claire.francois@inist.fr,`
`{olivier.galibert, juliette.kahn}@lne.fr,`
`{cyril.grouin, sophie.rosset, pierre.zweigenbaum}@limsi.fr`

ABSTRACT

Computing inter-annotator agreement measures on a manually annotated corpus is necessary to evaluate the reliability of its annotation. However, the interpretation of the obtained results is recognized as highly arbitrary. We describe in this article a method and a tool that we developed which "shuffles" a reference annotation according to different error paradigms, thereby creating artificial annotations with controlled errors. Agreement measures are computed on these corpora, and the obtained results are used to model the behavior of these measures and understand their actual meaning.

KEYWORDS: inter-annotator agreement, manual corpus annotation, evaluation.

Proceedings of COLING 2012: Posters, pages 809–818,
COLING 2012, Mumbai, December 2012.

1 Introduction

The quality of manual annotations has a direct impact on the applications using them. For example, it was demonstrated that machine learning tools learn to make the same mistakes as the human annotators, if these mistakes follow a certain regular pattern and do not correspond to simple annotation noise (Reidsma and Carletta, 2008; Schluter, 2011). Furthermore, errors in a manually annotated reference corpus (a "gold-standard") can obviously bias an evaluation performed using this corpus as a reference. Finally, a bad quality annotation would lead to misleading clues in a linguistic analysis used to create rule-based systems.

However, it is not possible to directly evaluate the validity of manual annotations. Instead, inter-annotator agreement measures are used: at least two annotators are asked to annotate the same sample of text in parallel, their annotations are compared and a coefficient is computed. The latter can be of many types and the well-known Kappa-family is described in details in (Artstein and Poesio, 2008). However, as pointed out by the authors of this article, the obtained results are difficult to interpret. Kappa coefficients, for example, are difficult to compare, even within the same annotation task, as they imply a definition of the markables that can vary from one campaign to the other (Grouin et al., 2011). More generally, we lack clues to know if a Kappa of 0.75 is a "good" result, or if a Kappa of 0.8 is twice as good as one of 0.4 or if a result of 0.6 obtained using one coefficient is better than 0.5 with another one, and for which annotation task.

We first briefly present the state of the art (Section 2), then detail the principles of our method to benchmark measures (Section 3) and show on some examples how different coefficients can be compared (Section 4). We finally discuss current limitations and point out future developments.

2 State of the art

A quite detailed analysis of the most commonly used inter-annotator agreement coefficients is provided by Artstein and Poesio (2008). They present the pros and cons of these methods, from the statistical and mathematical points of view, with some hints about specific issues raised in some annotation campaigns, like the prevalence of one category. A section of their article is dedicated to various attempts at providing an interpretation scale for the Kappa family coefficients and how they failed to converge. Works such as (Gwet, 2012) are also to be mentioned. They present various inter-rater reliability coefficients and insist on benchmarking issues related to their interpretation.

Many authors, among whom (Grouin et al., 2011; Fort et al., 2012), tried to obtain a more precise assessment of the quality of the annotation in their campaigns by computing different coefficients and analyzing the obtained results. However, their analyses lack robustness, as they only apply to similar campaigns. Other studies concerning the evaluation of the quality of manual annotation identified some factors that influence inter- and intra-annotator agreements, thereby giving clues on their behavior. Gut and Bayerl (2004) thus demonstrated that the inter-annotator agreement and the complexity of the annotation task are correlated: the larger the number of categories, the lower the inter-annotator agreement. However, categories prone to confusion are in limited number. The meta-analysis presented by Bayerl and Paul (2011) extends this research on the factors influencing agreement results, identifying 8 such factors and proposing useful recommendations to improve manual annotation reliability. However, neither of these studies provides a clear picture of the behavior of the agreement coefficients

[0]This work has been partially financed by OSEO, the French State Agency for Innovation, under the Quaero program.

or of their meanings. The experiments detailed in (Reidsma and Carletta, 2008) constitute an interesting step in this direction, focusing on the effect of annotation errors on machine learning systems and showing the impact of the form of disagreements on the obtained quality (random noise disagreement being tolerable, but not patterns in disagreements). This work puts Kappa-like coefficients results into perspective but presents a tool-oriented view, limited to these coefficients. In summary, the domain lacks a tool providing a clear and generic picture of the agreement coefficients behavior, allowing to better qualify the obtained agreement results.

3 Generating benchmarking corpora: the Corpus Shuffling Tool

The method presented in this section is currently restricted to annotation campaigns consisting in delimiting a span of text and characterizing it. It will be extended in the future to relations and more complex structures.

3.1 Objectives and principles

Manual annotation, as already mentioned, is subject to human errors. Except for very simple annotation tasks, these errors may involve several paradigms. Indeed, each manually annotated element may diverge from what it should be (which is called the reference, see below), in one or multiple ways, including: (i) the location is not correct (the frontiers of an element do not exactly match those of the reference); (ii) the characterization is not correct (wrong category, or wrong feature value); (iii) the annotation does not belong to the reference (false positive); or (iv), on the contrary, a reference element is missing (false negative). All of these error paradigms tend to damage the annotations, so each of them should be taken into account by agreement measures. We propose here to apply each measure to a set of corpora, each of which embeds errors from one or more paradigms, and with a certain magnitude (the higher the magnitude, the higher the number of errors). This experiment should allow us to observe how the measures behave w.r.t. the different paradigms, and with a full range of magnitudes. The idea of creating artificial damaged corpora is inspired by Pevzner and Hearst (2002), then Bestgen (2009) in thematic segmentation, but our goal (giving meaning to measures) and our method (e.g. applying progressive magnitudes) are very different.

3.2 Protocol

Reference. A reference annotation set (called *reference*) is provided to the system: a true Gold Standard or an automatically generated set based on a statistical model. It is assumed to correspond exactly to what annotations should be, with respect to the annotation guidelines.

Shuffling. A shuffling process is an algorithm that automatically generates a multi-annotated corpus given three parameters: a reference annotation, a number n of annotators to simulate, and a coefficient $0 \leq m \leq 1$ called magnitude (in reference to earthquake measures). Each time it is run, it creates a set of n parallel annotations (simulating n different annotators) on the corpus, but with a quality damaged according to magnitude m.

Process. The system iteratively runs a given shuffling process on the full range of possible magnitudes (from 0 to 1) with a parametrizable step (default is 0.05).

Agreement measure graph. For each of these annotation sets, i.e., for each magnitude, we submit each agreement measure we want to evaluate, and record its score. At the end of the process, we obtain a graph showing how a given measure reacts to a progressive shuffling, where the x-axis represents the magnitude from 0 to 1, and the y-axis represents the agreement.

3.3 Overview of the implemented shuffling processes

All processes described here come from real observations of various corpora: *false positives* and *false negatives* are usual in many campaigns, *fragmentation* and *shift* are observed in thematic segmentation, *category mistake* is so usual that most agreement measures (e.g. Kappa) address it, and *combination* of them appear for instance in discourse annotation.

3.3.1 False negative

A *false negative* is the fact for an annotator not to annotate an element belonging to the reference. It is simulated as follows: (i) magnitude $m = 0$: the annotator did not miss any annotation; (ii) magnitude $m = 1$: the annotator missed all the annotations and therefore did not produce any; and (iii) $0 < m < 1$: each element to be annotated has a probability m of being missed.

3.3.2 False positive

Reversely, a *false positive* is the fact for an annotator to annotate an element not belonging to the reference. We made the following decisions: (i) the maximum shuffling corresponds to adding x times the number of elements of the reference, x default value being 1; (ii) for $0 \leq m \leq 1$, $m \cdot x$ elements are added; (iii) the way annotations are added is done with respect to the characteristics of the reference (statistical distribution of categories, etc.)

3.3.3 Fragmentation

Sometimes, annotators have the choice between using several contiguous elements (of the same category), or just one (covering the same text spans). Fragmentation simulates this by splitting up reference elements. The protocol is as follows, n being the number of reference elements: (i) the number of fragmentations to apply is $n_{frag} = n \cdot x \cdot m$, where x is settable (its default value is 1); (ii) for each fragmentation to apply, one element is chosen at random, and is split (not necessarily in its center); (iii) the fragment of a split may be re-split next time, so that we finally get several levels of fragmentation.

3.3.4 Shift

In some annotation campaigns, annotators manage to properly identify the phenomenon to annotate, but have trouble locating it perfectly. We try to reproduce this error paradigm with the *shift* shuffling, that moves the frontiers of the reference annotations. It is defined as follows: (i) for magnitude m, we take into account the average length of the elements (w.r.t. their category), using for instance a statistical model as described in section 3.2, called *maxlength*, to compute the possible shifting latitude of each frontier, called *maxlat*, as follows: $maxlat = maxlength \cdot m \cdot x$, where m is the magnitude and x is a parameter whose default value is 2; (ii) a number is chosen at random for each frontier, in the range from *-maxlat* to *+maxlat*, and the frontier is shifted by this algebraic value. This shuffling process is conceptually more difficult to design than the previous ones because the shuffling space being finite (the text length), it is difficult to know to what extent it is actually possible to shuffle the annotations.

3.3.5 Category mistake

A frequent annotation mistake is to assign a wrong category to an annotated element. Two important phenomena are to be mentioned, that are quite frequent and lead to some important differences among current measurement methods: **Prevalence** is the fact that some categories are more frequent than others. Some measures take this phenomenon into account in their definition of so-called (and controversial) chance correction in order not to overrate the observed agreement. **Overlapping** is the fact for two categories to cover, even slightly, a same phenomenon: in such cases, annotators happen to choose a wrong but not so different category, and some measures consider them as less important mistakes. The question now is to define how best to simulate, the more gradually possible, a progressive category assignation mistake. To define such a simulation, we rely, for a given magnitude, on a matrix that indicates, for each category of the reference annotation, what is the probabilistic distribution of the chosen categories for 100 annotations. We have made the following choices: (i) for $m = 0$, we use the **perfect matrix** A (as given in table 1); (ii) for $m = 1$, we use the worst matrix B or C depending on the choice of simulating prevalence (B) or not (C). The **prevalence matrix** B simulates a (semi) random behavior with respect of the prevalence observed in the reference, while the **noPrevalence matrix** C reflects a full random choice; (iii) Besides, overlapping is simulated by the **overlapping matrix** D, which describes the way an annotator, for a given category in the reference, makes mistakes more often in favor of friendly categories than in favor of others; (iv) then, for each $0 < m < 1$, we built a matrix by weighted averaging of perfect matrix (100% weighted at $m = 0$) and worst matrix (100% weighted at $m = 1$), as shown in Figure 1 (right). When the overlapping option is chosen, the overlapping matrix is integrated in the averaging, with a weight distribution being zero at $m = 0$ and $m = 1$, and a maximum in the intermediate magnitudes, as shown in Figure 1 (left). Indeed, we consider such errors as neither belonging to perfect annotation, nor to worst annotation.

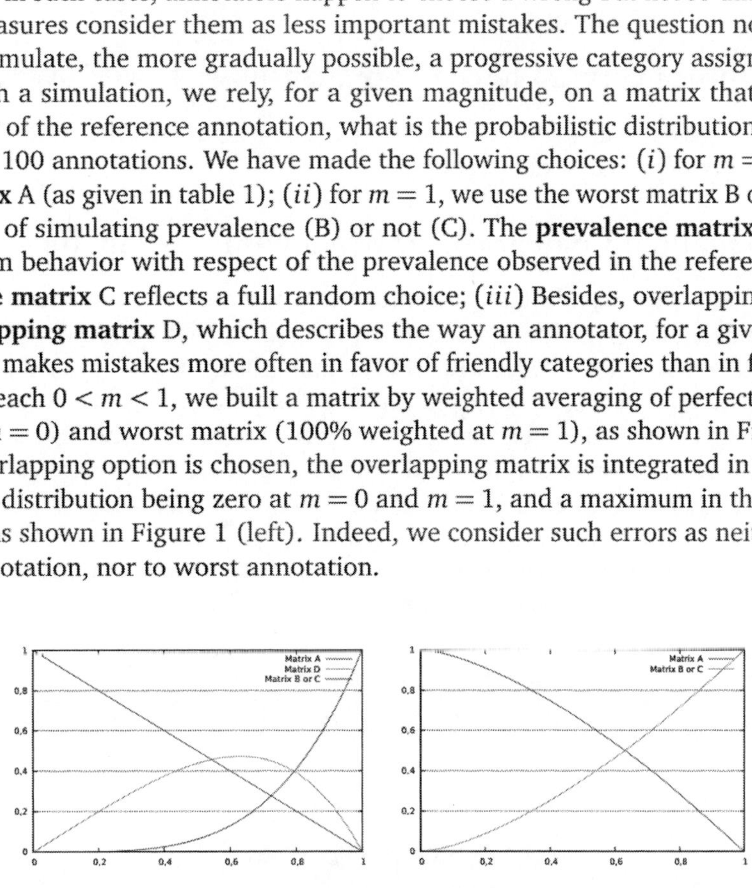

Figure 1: Weight distributions for averaging with overlapping (left) or without it (right)

	A:Perfect				B:Prevalence				C:NoPrevalence				D:Overlapping			
	Noun	Verb	Adj	Prep	Noun	Verb	Adj	Prep	Noun	Verb	Adj	Prep	Noun	Verb	Adj	Prep
Noun	100	0	0	0	27	9	18	45	25	25	25	25	0	80	15	5
Verb	0	100	0	0	27	9	18	45	25	25	25	25	80	0	0	20
Adj	0	0	100	0	27	9	18	45	25	25	25	25	15	10	0	75
Prep	0	0	0	100	27	9	18	45	25	25	25	25	5	20	75	0

Table 1: The four confusion matrices used for interpolation

Combining the two options, 4 different experiments can be built: with or without overlapping and with or without prevalence.

3.3.6 Combination

Each previously defined shuffling process involves a particular paradigm. However, in the real world, human annotation errors in a given campaign may involve several paradigms at the same time, sometimes on the same annotated element (e.g. a slight shift and a category mistake). To address this situation, we provide a shuffling process that combines as many shuffling processes as needed, defined as follows: (i) n sub-processes are chosen in a given order; (ii) for a magnitude m, the main process shuffles the reference annotation, successively applying each sub-process (in the given order) with magnitude m/n (hence, this multi-shuffling is not n times faster as classic ones).

4 Using shuffled corpora to compare measures: a brief overview

To demonstrate the consistency of the method we briefly show in this section how it can be used with two types of annotation paradigms.

4.1 Segmentation: Comparison of WindowDiff, G-Hamming and GM

Segmentation consists in determining frontiers between contiguous textual segments. We compare here two metrics already compared by (Bestgen, 2009): WindowDiff (WD) described in (Pevzner and Hearst, 2002) and Generalized Hamming Distance (GH) described in (Bookstein et al., 2002), as well as a new versatile measure, the Glozz Measure (GM), described in (Mathet and Widlöcher, 2011), which can be adapted to several paradigms, including segmentation. WD and GH cannot exactly be considered as agreement measures, as they are distances between a reference and a human annotation. These distances equal 0 when annotations are the same, and 1 in the worst case. We have adapted the results as follows: $agreement = 1 - distance$. Moreover, since these metrics consider two annotators only, we have averaged the one-to-one results when working with 3 or more annotators.

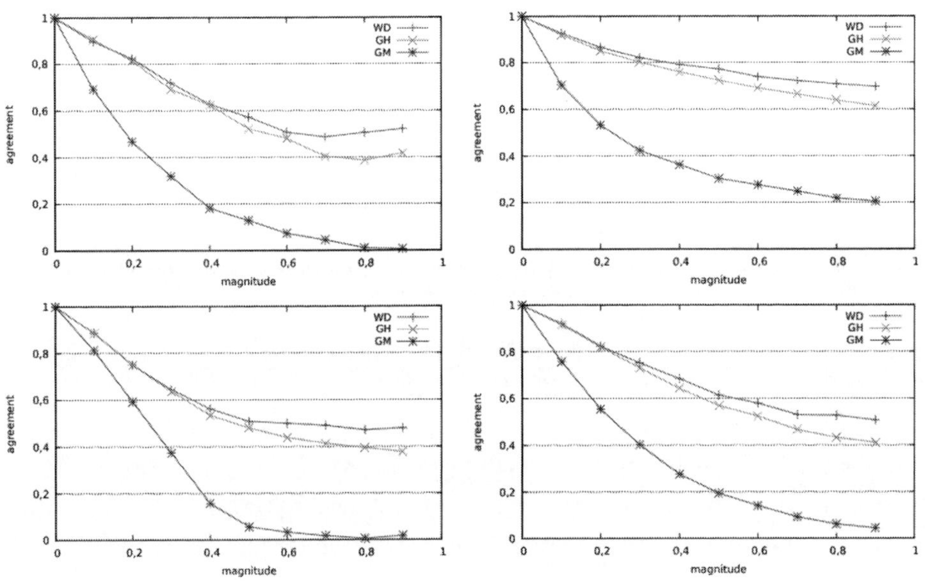

Figure 2: False negatives (upper left), false positives (upper right), shift (lower left) and combination (lower right)

Figure 2 shows the behavior of these three measures for three paradigms and their combination: for **false negatives** WD and GH are quite close, with an almost linear response until magnitude 0.6. Their drawback is that their responses are limited by an asymptote, while GM shows a full range of agreements, but is not linear; again, for **false positives**, WD and GH are very similar, and their responses, if not asymptotic, show a lower limit at a quite high value (resp. 0.7 and 0.6). GM behaves in the same way as for false negatives, but with an asymptote at $agreement = 0.2$ much lower than WD and GH; once again, for **shifts**, WD and GH show an asymptote at about $agreement = 0.4$, when GM shows values from 1 to 0. Not surprisingly, when using **combination**, the overall responses look like an average of the other paradigms. This very first and brief comparison reveals that WD and GH are quite close, but GH scores are a little more severe, and with a wider range. For these reasons, according to this experiment, GH seems slightly better. GM is quite different, with almost a full range of agreements, probably because it takes chance into account.

4.2 Categorization: Comparison of Kappa, W-Kappa and GM

We focus here on categorization only, assuming a situation where the elements to annotate are pre-located. Four sets of corpora were created, with respect to the two available options described in section 3.3.5. The measures we compare here are Cohen's Kappa (Cohen, 1960), the weighted Kappa (Cohen, 1968), with two different weight matrices (W-Kappa 1 being much more forgiving than W-Kappa 2); and GM (Mathet and Widlöcher, 2011), with two different options, GM1 which has overlapping capabilities, and GM2 which has not. We also add a very simple percentage agreement value as a baseline (called BM, for Baseline Measure) for all the other measures. The results are shown in Figure 3. First of all, when neither overlapping

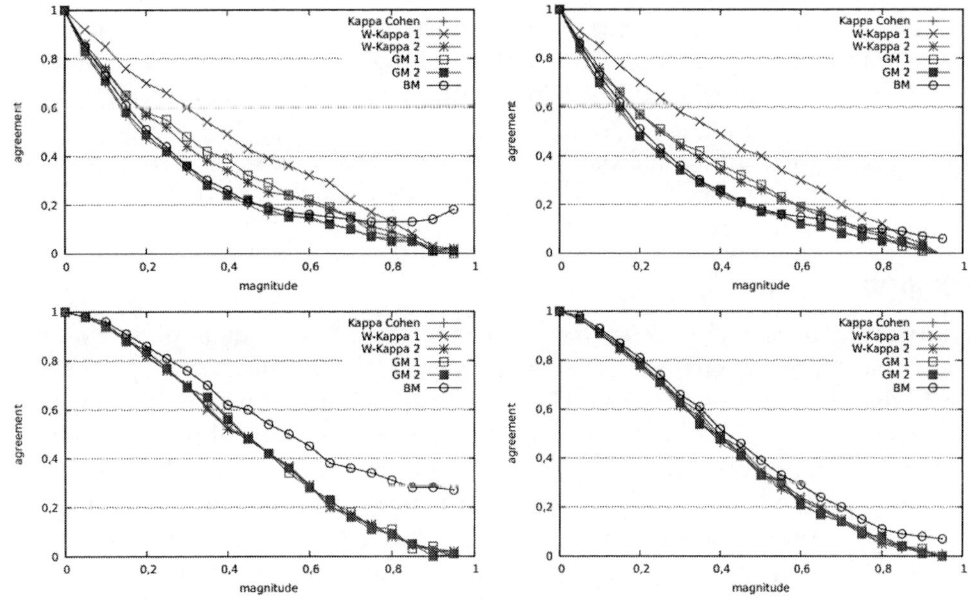

Figure 3: Results of different measures with prevalence (bottom-left), overlapping (top-right), overlapping+prevalence (top-left), and none (bottom-right)

nor prevalence is involved, all the measures behave almost in the same way (even though BM slightly overrates the agreement as magnitude increases, because it does not take chance into account). When a **prevalence** phenomenon occurs, all the measures (except BM) still perform equivalently, but BM increasingly overrates the agreement by up to about 0.25. Taking chance into account has more impact here. The **overlapping** phenomenon clearly opposes W-Kappa and GM to others. Whatever the prevalence option (top-left and top-right figures), the differences are important in the 0.1 to 0.6 magnitude range (where the overlapping matrix has more influence), with a difference of up to 0.15 for GM, and up to about 0.25 for W-Kappa-1. The latter reacts with more strength because we set it with a very forgiving weight matrix, while W-Kappa-2 is set with a less forgiving one, and is very close to GM whose weight matrix is data-driven. Besides, it is interesting to note that when applying these two measures to non-overlapping data (bottom figures), they behave almost exactly the same way as their basic versions not taking overlapping into account.

5 Limitations and future work

Enhancing annotators' simulation. We shall try in the future to get closer to real annotation constraints. For instance, shifting is currently free, whereas in some campaigns annotating overlapping entities is prohibited. We will also address the question of differences of behavior between annotators.

Using real Gold Standard corpora. It is also possible to use a real Gold Standard corpus as a reference for the system, and then to shuffle it. We started this work with the TCOF-POS-tagged corpus (Benzitoun et al., 2012), for which annotators reached a 0.96 Kappa agreement, which corresponds to a magnitude of 0.1 in the Shuffling Tool, i.e., to a matrix averaged between the perfect one at 95% and the worst one at 5%.

Playing with more parameters. For each experiment this tool makes possible, it will be possible to generate sub-experiments, each of which taking into account a given parameter, including: (*i*) the number of annotators, (*ii*) the number of categories, (*iii*) the number of annotated elements, as already studied with statistical considerations by (Gwet, 2012).

Relations and more complex structures. Finally, we shall extend the current work, focused on entities as textual segments, to relations and sets of entities, in order to address other annotation types such as co-reference chains and discourse relations.

Conclusion

According to the results on various types of paradigms, and with quite different agreement measures, the proposed method and corpora happen to be consistent: as expected, it is confirmed that the different measures provide decreasing scores from 1 to 0. Some important differences as well as some similarities, appear between the studied methods. This seems promising for further comparisons, in particular for measures with multi error paradigms capabilities, e.g. Krippendorff's α_U (Krippendorff, 1995) and GM. To sum up, this tool will help to (i) objectively compare the behavior of different agreement measures, (ii) obtain a new and enhanced interpretation of their results: a given result of a given method corresponds to a certain magnitude, of which we have a clear and formal definition, (iii) set and enhance existing or future measures (checking improvements and regressions). The shuffling tool used in this work to generate the damaged corpora is written in Java and is freely available[1] under the GPL license and all the corpora we generated and used for this paper are also freely available.

[1] http://www.glozz.org/shufflingtool

References

Artstein, R. and Poesio, M. (2008). Inter-coder agreement for Computational Linguistics. *Computational Linguistics*, 34(4):555–596.

Bayerl, P. S. and Paul, K. I. (2011). What determines inter-coder agreement in manual annotations? A meta-analytic investigation. *Computational Linguistics*, 37(4):699–725.

Benzitoun, C., Fort, K., and Sagot, B. (2012). TCOF-POS : un corpus libre de français parlé annoté en morphosyntaxe. In *Proceedings of the Traitement Automatique des Langues Naturelles (TALN)*, pages 99–112, Grenoble, France.

Bestgen, Y. (2009). Quels indices pour mesurer l'efficacité en segmentation thématique? In *Actes de TALN'09*, page p. 10, Senlis (France).

Bookstein, A., Kulyukin, V. A., and Raita, T. (2002). Generalized Hamming distance. *Information Retrieval*, (5):353–375.

Cohen, J. (1960). A coefficient of agreement for nominal scales. *Educational and Psychological Measurement*, 20(1):37–46.

Cohen, J. (1968). Weighted kappa: Nominal scale agreement with provision for scaled disagreement or partial credit. *Psychological Bulletin*, 70(4):213–220.

Fort, K., François, C., Galibert, O., and Ghribi, M. (2012). Analyzing the impact of prevalence on the evaluation of a manual annotation campaign. In *Proceedings of the Eighth International Conference on Language Resources and Evaluation (LREC 2012)*, Istanbul, Turkey. 7 pages.

Grouin, C., Rosset, S., Zweigenbaum, P., Fort, K., Galibert, O., and Quintard, L. (2011). Proposal for an extension of traditional named entities: From guidelines to evaluation, an overview. In *Proceedings of the 5th Linguistic Annotation Workshop*, pages 92–100, Portland, Oregon, USA. (poster).

Gut, U. and Bayerl, P. S. (2004). Measuring the reliability of manual annotations of speech corpora. In *Proceedings of the Speech Prosody*, pages 565–568, Nara, Japan.

Gwet, K. L. (2012). *Handbook of Inter-rater Reliability*. Advanced Analytics, LLC, third edition.

Krippendorff, K. (1995). On the reliability of unitizing contiguous data. *Sociological Methodology*, (25):47–76.

Mathet, Y. and Widlöcher, A. (2011). Une approche holiste et unifiée de l'alignement et de la mesure d'accord inter-annotateurs. In *Proceedings of the Traitement Automatique des Langues Naturelles 2011 (TALN 2011)*, Montpellier, France.

Pevzner, L. and Hearst, M. A. (2002). A critique and improvement of an evaluation metric for text segmentation. *Computational Linguistics*, 28(1):19–36.

Reidsma, D. and Carletta, J. (2008). Reliability measurement without limits. *Computational Linguistics*, 34(3):319–326.

Schluter, N. (2011). *Treebank-Based Deep Grammar Acquisition for French Probabilistic Parsing Resources*. PhD thesis, Dublin City University - Faculty of Engineering and Computing, School of Computing.

Discriminative Boosting from Dictionary and Raw Text – A Novel Approach to Build A Chinese Word Segmenter

Fandong Meng Wenbin Jiang Hao Xiong Qun Liu
Key Laboratory of Intelligent Information Processing
Institute of Computing Technology
Chinese Academy of Sciences
{mengfandong, jiangwenbin, xionghao, liuqun}@ict.ac.cn

ABSTRACT
Chinese word segmentation (CWS) is a basic and important task for Chinese information processing. Standard approaches to CWS treat it as a sequence labelling task. Without manually annotated corpora, these approaches are ineffective. When a dictionary is available, dictionary maximum matching (DMM) is a good alternative. However, its performance is far from perfect due to the poor ability on out-of-vocabulary (OOV) words recognition. In this paper, we propose a novel approach that integrates the advantages of discriminative training and DMM, to build a high quality word segmenter with only a dictionary and a raw text. Experiments in CWS on different domains show that, compared with DMM, our approach brings significant improvements in both the news domain and the Chinese medicine patent domain, with error reductions of 21.50% and 13.66%, respectively. Furthermore, our approach achieves recall rate increments of OOV words by 42.54% and 23.72%, respectively in both domains.

KEYWORDS: discriminative model, word segmentation, dictionary maximum matching.

Proceedings of COLING 2012: Posters, pages 819–828,
COLING 2012, Mumbai, December 2012.

1 Introduction

Word segmentation is a basic and important task for information processing of Chinese. Most effective approaches (Xue and Shen, 2003; Ng and Low, 2004) to CWS treat it as a character tagging task, in which the model used to make tagging decisions can be trained by discriminative methods, such as Maximum Entropy (ME) (Ratnaparkhi and Adwait, 1996), Conditional Random Fields (Lafferty et al., 2001), perceptron training algorithm (Collins, 2002; Collins and Roark, 2004), etc. These methods have achieved good results, but rely on large scale high quality annotated corpora, which are rare in resource-poor languages and domains. Besides, directly adapting a classifier trained on one domain to another domain leads to poorer performance [1]. Given a dictionary, dictionary maximum matching (DMM) is an alternative in the case of no available annotated corpora, but its performance is not satisfying due to the poor ability on OOV words recognition.

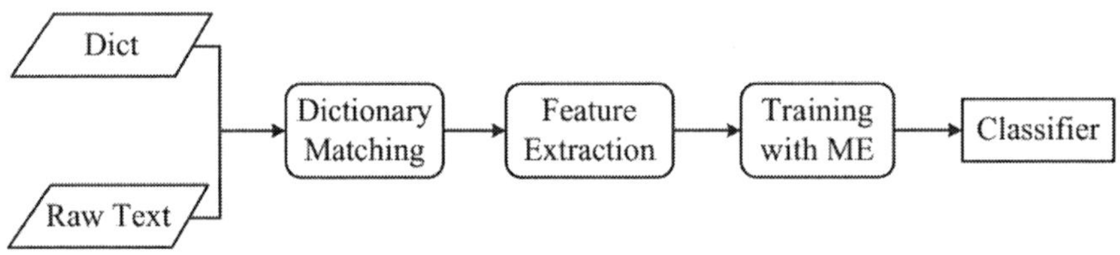

Figure 1: The pipeline of our method.

In this paper, we propose a novel approach of integrating the advantages of discriminative training and DMM, that enables us to utilize only a domain dictionary and a raw corpus to build a high quality word segmenter. Figure 1 describes the pipeline of our method. First, we scan each sentence in the raw corpus, and compare the continuous characters with the words in dictionary by reliable dictionary matching strategy. If successfully matched, we extract feature instances from the matching parts and construct reliable feature instance set. Finally, we train a classifier using all the reliable feature instances by Maximum Entropy approach.

To test the efficacy of our method, we do experiments in CWS, with Penn Chinese Treebank 5.0 (CTB) (Xue et al., 2005) and Chinese medicine patent (CMP) corpus. When we use the classifier trained on CTB to process the CMP testing set, the performance is poorer than DMM with dictionary of CMP. Besides, compared with DMM, our method achieves significant improvements with error reductions of 21.50% and 13.66%, respectively. Besides, the recall rate increments of OOV words are 42.54% and 23.72%, respectively (Section 4).

2 Segmentation as Gap Tagging Classification

Before describing the method of dictionary matching based feature instances extraction, we give a brief introduction of gap tagging classification strategy for segmentation. Formally, a Chinese sentence can be represented as a character sequence: $C_{1:n} = C_1C_2\cdots C_n$, where $C_i(i = 1,\cdots,n)$ is a character. We explicitly add the gap $G_i(i = 1,\cdots,n-1)$ of character C_i and C_{i+1} to the sentence $C_{1:n}$, denoted as $C_{1:n}|G_{1:n-1} = C_1G_1C_2G_2\cdots G_{n-1}C_n$. Then the segmented results with gaps represented as follows:

$$C_{1:e_1}|G_{1:e_1-1}, G_{e_1}, C_{e_1+1:e_2}|G_{e_1+1:e_2-1}, G_{e_2}, \cdots, G_{e_{m-1}}, C_{e_{m-1}+1:e_m}|G_{e_{m-1}+1:e_m-1}$$

[1] Jiang et al. (2009) describe a similar situation. We also tried to directly adapt a classifier trained with news corpus to Chinese medicine patent corpus, which led to dramatic decrease in accuracy.

where $C_{i:j}|G_{i:j-1}$ denotes the character-gap sequence with gaps $G_{i:j-1}$. As is shown above, there are two kinds of gaps, one occurs inside a word, such as $G_1 \cdots G_{e_1-1}$; the other occurs between two words, such as G_{e_1}. Word Segmentation can be treated as a gap tagging problem.

2.1 From Character Tagging to Gap Tagging

Ng and Low (2004) give a boundary tag to each character denoting its relative position in a word. There are four boundary tags: "b" for a character that begins a word, "m" for a character that occurs in the middle of a word, "e" for a character that ends a word, and "s" for a character that occurs as a single-character word. Following Ng and Low (2004), the feature templates and the corresponding instances are listed in Table 1.

Feature Template	Instances
$C_i(i=-2,\cdots,2)$	$C_{-2}=$美$, C_{-1}=$国$, C_0=$商$, C_1=$务$, C_2=$部
$C_iC_{i+1}(i=-2,\cdots,1)$	$C_{-2}C_{-1}=$美国$, C_{-1}C_0=$国商$, C_0C_1=$商务$, C_1C_2=$务部
$C_{-1}C_1$	$C_{-1}C_1=$国务
$Pu(C_0)$	$Pu(C_0)=0$
$T(C_{-2})T(C_{-1})T(C_0)T(C_1)T(C_2)$	$T(C_{-2})T(C_{-1})T(C_0)T(C_1)T(C_2)=44444$

Table 1: Character tagging feature templates and the corresponding instances, suppose we are considering the third character "商" in "美国商务部".

Actually, the classical character tagging method can be explained by gap tagging. Given a character-tag sequence $\cdots G_{i-1}C_iG_i\cdots$, tagging $G_{i-1}G_i$ to "AA" is equivalent to assigning C_i to "m", "AS" is equal to "e", "SA" is equal to "b" and "SS" is equal to "s".

2.2 N-Gram Markov Gap Tagging

For n-gram markov gap tagging, the number of decisions is 2^{N+1} when we consider N+1 gaps in one step. These decisions compose a decision set, denoted as $\{A,S\}^{\otimes N+1}$. The operator $\otimes$ stands for the cartesian product between different decision sets. Gap sequence $G_{i-N:i}$ will be tagged in the position G_i with n-gram markov gap classification. Given a character-gap sequence: $x=C_{1:n}|G_{1:n-1}$, we aim to find an output $F(x)$ that satisfies:

$$F(x)=\underset{y\in\{A,S\}^{\otimes n-1}}{\arg\max}\ Score(x,y) \tag{1}$$

where $Score$ stands for the score of the tagging sequence y evaluated by the classifier.

$$Score(x,y)=\sum_i Eval(y_{i-N:i},\Phi(x,i)) \tag{2}$$

$\Phi(x,i)$ denotes the feature vector extracted from position G_i of character-gap sequence x. $Eval$ denotes the evaluated score to $y_{i-N:i}$ selected by classifier, based on feature vector $\Phi(x,i)$.

We use the Maximum Entropy approach to train the classifier, with dynamic programming decoding algorithm to find the highest score. In our experiments, we use 2-gram markov gap tagging, with trading off the performance and speed.

Gap tagging features are denoted by the characters around the gap. When we consider the current gap G_0, the ith character to the left of G_0 is C_{1-i}, and to the right is C_i. The gap tagging feature templates and the corresponding instances are listed in Table 2.

Feature Template	Instances
$C_i(i=0,\cdots,1)$	$C_0=$商$, C_1=$务
$C_iC_{i+1}(i=-1,\cdots,1)$	$C_{-1}C_0=$国商$, C_0C_1=$商务$, C_1C_2=$务部

Table 2: Gap tagging feature templates and the corresponding instances, suppose we are considering the gap between the character " 商" and the character "务" in "美国商务部".

3 Dictionary-Based Feature Extraction

With annotated corpora, discriminative training approaches for CWS have two stages. Extracting feature instances and training a model with them. Since the training algorithm has been described in the last section, now we describe the method of dictionary matching based feature extraction by a dictionary and a raw corpus. This method contains two key points, the dictionary matching strategy (Section 3.1) and the tagging strategy (character tagging or gap tagging) of extracting feature instances (Section 3.2).

3.1 Dictionary Bi-direction Maximum Matching

Noting that the dictionary we used does not contain time words, numerals and English strings, which can be accurately recognized by some manual rules. Besides, single-character words are not included in the dictionary for two reasons: First, the single-character word is very flexible and usually appears as a character in a multi-character word. Second, the scale of dictionary is limited and single-character words are in high frequence, a lot of matching errors will occur during dictionary matching. [2]

To minimize errors caused by the dictionary matching ambiguity, we use forward maximum matching (FMM) and backward maximum matching (BMM) to match the raw corpus with the dictionary, to generate feature instances sets S_{fmm} and S_{bmm}, respectively. Then, we reserves the intersection of the two feature instances sets to the reliable set $S_{fmm\&bmm}$.

The dictionary matching procedure is that, we scan each sentence S in the raw corpus R, suppose $S = C_{1:N}(C_q(q = 1,\cdots,N)$ is character), and compare the continuous characters $C_{i:k}(0 \le i < k \le N)$ with the words in dictionary D by FMM and BMM, respectively. If successfully matched, it means that the character sequence $C_{i:k}$ is matched with the word W_j ($W_j = C_{i:k}$) in dictionary. Then we transform the character sequence $C_{i:k}$ and its context (*preceding-text* and *following-text* are both made up of two characters, $C_{i-2}C_{i-1}$ is the *preceding-text*, $C_{k+1}C_{k+2}$ is the *following-text*) to a *text fragment* P with the structure of "*preceding-text*($C_{i-2}C_{i-1}$)+*word*($C_{i:k}$)+*following-text*($C_{k+1}C_{k+2}$)".

3.2 Gap Tagging Feature Extraction

3.2.1 Features from Multi-Character Words

It is worth mentioning that the feature instances extracted by the method described in Section 3.1 are from multi-character words. For each *text fragment* "*P=preceding-text*($C_{i-2}C_{i-1}$)+*word*($C_{i:k}$)+*following-text*($C_{k+1}C_{k+2}$)" extracted by FMM and BMM, we extract feature instances from the gap in three kinds:

1. Gap between the last character of the *preceding-text* and the first character of the *word*

[2] We test the performance of our method, with the dictionary containing single-character words. As single-character words lead to errors during dictionary matching, the performance is poorer than DMM method.

2. Gap between every pair of characters in the *word*
3. Gap between the last character of the *word* and the first character of the *following-text*

DMM Strategy	FMM	BMM
Result	美国 商务部 长 访问 上海	美国 商务 部长 访问 上海

Table 3: Results of sentence "美国商务部长访问上海" by FMM and BMM, suppose words "美国","商务部","商务","部长","访问","上海" are included in the dictionary.

Method	Fragments	Feature Instance
FMM	美国 商务部 长访	$S: C_0 = \text{国}, C_1 = \text{商}, C_{-1}C_0 = \text{美国}, C_0C_1 = \text{国商}, C_1C_2 = \text{商务}$ $A: C_0 = \text{商}, C_1 = \text{务}, C_{-1}C_0 = \text{国商}, C_0C_1 = \text{商务}, C_1C_2 = \text{务部}$ $A: C_0 = \text{务}, C_1 = \text{部}, C_{-1}C_0 = \text{商务}, C_0C_1 = \text{务部}, C_1C_2 = \text{部长}$ $S: C_0 = \text{部}, C_1 = \text{长}, C_{-1}C_0 = \text{务部}, C_0C_1 = \text{部长}, C_1C_2 = \text{长访}$
BMM	美国 商务 部长	$S: C_0 = \text{国}, C_1 = \text{商}, C_{-1}C_0 = \text{美国}, C_0C_1 = \text{国商}, C_1C_2 = \text{商务}$ $A: C_0 = \text{商}, C_1 = \text{务}, C_{-1}C_0 = \text{国商}, C_0C_1 = \text{商务}, C_1C_2 = \text{务部}$ $S: C_0 = \text{务}, C_1 = \text{部}, C_{-1}C_0 = \text{商务}, C_0C_1 = \text{务部}, C_1C_2 = \text{部长}$
	商务 部长 访问	$S: C_0 = \text{务}, C_1 = \text{部}, C_{-1}C_0 = \text{商务}, C_0C_1 = \text{务部}, C_1C_2 = \text{部长}$ $A: C_0 = \text{部}, C_1 = \text{长}, C_{-1}C_0 = \text{务部}, C_0C_1 = \text{部长}, C_1C_2 = \text{长访}$ $S: C_0 = \text{长}, C_1 = \text{访}, C_{-1}C_0 = \text{部长}, C_0C_1 = \text{长访}, C_1C_2 = \text{访问}$
FMM &BMM	—	$S: C_0 = \text{国}, C_1 = \text{商}, C_{-1}C_0 = \text{美国}, C_0C_1 = \text{国商}, C_1C_2 = \text{商务}$ $A: C_0 = \text{商}, C_1 = \text{务}, C_{-1}C_0 = \text{国商}, C_0C_1 = \text{商务}, C_1C_2 = \text{务部}$

Table 4: Gap tagging feature instances sets extracted by FMM, BMM and the intersection of the two sets, for two matching results of character sequence "商务部长" listed in Table 3. "S" means "split", and "A" means "adjoin". "—" means the corresponding "Fragments" are undefined.

For example, Table 3 lists the segment results of the sentence "美国商务部长访问上海", by FMM and BMM. It is difficult to distinguish which one is better. So we extract feature instances from both the matching results, and take the intersection of the two feature instances sets. For the two results listed in Table 3, only four characters' ("商", " 务", "部", " 长") segmentation results are different. We only list the feature instances sets of "商务部长" extracted by FMM and BMM and the intersection (corresponding to "FMM&BMM") of the two sets in Table 4. As the segmented results of "商务部长" generated by BMM are " 商务" and " 部长", two fragments are constructed. Besides, features of "长" (single-character word) are not extracted by FMM.

Since we can generate feature instances from each character in the matching word ($C_{i:k}$), we can also extract character tagging feature instances from the *text fragment*.

3.2.2 Features from Single-Character Words

As we have described in section 3.1, single-character words are not included in the dictionary. Lacking feature instances from single-character words, the ability of character tagging classifier weakened a lot, since the feature instances with tagger "s" can not be extracted. Gap tagging does not need to distinguish whether a character is a single-character word, so we do not have to extract feature instances of single-character words.

However, single-character words account for a large proportion in actual corpora. The ability of classifier will be stronger if adding feature instances of single-character words. We propose a simple strategy to extract feature instances of single-character words. Given a Character "C", if its left part and right part are words in dictionary, or time words, or numerals, or English strings, or the beginning tag of the sentence, or the ending tag of the sentence, then we take "C" as a single-character word. Next, we can extract feature instances from single-character words as described in section 3.1.

4 Experiments

4.1 Setup

We conducted experiments mainly on two domains:

1. In news domain, we use Penn Chinese Treebank 5.0 (CTB). The dictionary D_{ctb} (33500 words) consists of words extracted from chapters 1-270 (18K sentences). The raw corpus[3] is mainly in news domain with 10M sentences. In order to compare with CMP, we also extract a smaller scale raw text with 2M sentences from the raw corpus (10M).
2. In Chinese medicine patent (CMP) domain, the dictionary D_{cmp} (21800 words) is from our internal resource, consists of words in Chinese medicine patent domain. As the dictionary D_{cmp} is so specialized with few common words, we combine D_{cmp} and D_{ctb} to a new dictionary $D_{cmp+ctb}$ (55100 words after duplicate removal). The raw corpus is from our internal resource. We extract 300 sentences from the raw corpus, and annotate them manually to form the testing set, the others (2M sentences) are used for training.

Dictionaries in both domains do not contain time words, numerals, English strings and single-character words.

We use the Maximum Entropy Toolkit developed by Zhang[4] to train the discriminative model. Empirically, the number of training iterations is 150 with gaussian prior 3.0 on training process. The performance measurement indicators for word segmentation is balanced *F-measure*, $F = 2PR/(P+R)$, a function of *Precision* P and *Recall* R. *Precision* is the relative amount of correct words in the system output. *Recall* is the relative amount of correct words compared to the gold standard annotations.

4.2 Dictionary Based Discriminative Training Results

Given a sentence, we first recognize time words, numerals and English strings by manual rules, then process other parts by the discriminative classifier.

Train On		**Test On (F_1%)**	
Dictionary	S-W	Character-tagging	Gap-tagging
D_{cmp}	No	56.21	67.55
D_{cmp}	Yes	56.21	67.51
$D_{cmp+ctb}$	No	53.13	76.23
$D_{cmp+ctb}$	Yes	55.47	76.37

Table 5: Results on CMP by dictionary matching based discriminative classifier with gap tagging and character tagging. "S-W" means feature instances of single-character words, "Yes" stands for containing these feature instances, "No" for not.

First, we check which tagging strategy is more suitable for our method, gap-tagging or character-tagging? In Table 5, it is clear from each row that results generated by gap-tagging

[3]The raw corpus includes People's Daily corpus(removing spaces); LDC2002E18, LDC2003E07, LDC2003E14; Hansards portion of LDC2004T07, LDC2004T08 , LDC2005T06; and other raw corpora of our internal resource.

[4]homepages.inf.ed.ac.uk/lzhang10/maxent_toolkit.html

classifier achieve much higher F_1 scores than those generated by character-tagging, with +16.66 points on average. Although, adding features instances of single-character words does improve the performance of both gap-tagging (from 76.23 to 76.37) and character-tagging (from 53.13 to 55.47)[5]. But the accuracy increment brought by this strategy can not compensate for the defects of character-tagging. Thereby, gap-tagging classification is more suitable for our method.

Method		Test On (F_1%)	
		CTB	CMP
FMM		91.05	72.30
BMM		91.44	72.63
Dictionary	**Raw corpus / scale**		
D_{ctb}	News / 2M	92.98	—
D_{ctb}	News / 10M	**93.28**	—
D_{cmp}	CMP / 2M	—	67.51
$D_{cmp+ctb}$	CMP / 2M	—	**76.37**

Table 6: Comparisons between DMM and our method (including feature instances of single-character words).

Then, we propose the comparisons between DMM and our method. In Table 6, when we use FMM or BMM on CTB testing set, the corresponding dictionary is D_{ctb}, and $D_{cmp+ctb}$ for CMP testing set. Comparing row 1 and row 2, we can see that BMM achieves better performance than FMM in both CTB and CMP. On CTB test, our method achieves an increment of 1.54 points on F_1 score than BMM (from 91.44 to 92.98), with small scale raw corpus. Using the larger scale raw corpus (10M sentences) leads to a further increment of 0.3 points (93.28), with error reduction[6] of 21.50%. The result of row 5 (67.51) is lower than row 1 (72.30), the reason is that D_{cmp} contains few common words, so that few feature instances of common words can be extracted. When using $D_{cmp+ctb}$, we get higher performance (76.37).

Dictionary	Raw corpus / scale	Test On (Recall %)	
		CTB	CMP
D_{ctb}	News / 10M	**42.54**	—
$D_{cmp+ctb}$	CMP / 2M	—	**23.72**

Table 7: Recall rate of OOV words by our method.

To compare with DMM on the ability of OOV words recognition, we show the recall rate of OOV words by our method in Table 7. As time words, numerals and English strings can be recognized by manual rules, we do not consider them when computing recall rate of OOV words. Besides, we do not consider single-character words which are not included in the dictionary. For DMM method, the recall rates of OOV words are zero both in CTB and CMP. Compared with DMM, our method shows much stronger ability on OOV words recognition, with the recall rate increments of 42.54% and 23.72%, respectively in CTB and CMP.

Due to the obvious improvement brought by our method, we can safely conclude that our dictionary matching based discriminative training approach is better than DMM method. With no available annotated corpora, our method achieves considerable performance.

[5]Results of row 1 and row 2 are not consistent with this situation, as the dictionary D_{cmp} contains much more specialized vocabulary than common words, resulting in much fewer feature instances of common words.

[6]Error rate is defined as $1 - F_1$, which has been described in many previous works.

5 Related Work

Many works have been devoted to the word segmentation task in recent years, including the word-based perceptron algorithm (Zhang and Clark, 2007); taking punctuation as implicit annotations (Li and Sun, 2009); the strategies of stacked modeling (Sun, 2011); the investigation of word structures (Li, 2011); the approach of automatic adaptation between different corpora (Jiang et al., 2009, 2012); joint model on word segmentation and new word detection (Sun et al., 2012) and other single-model approach (Zhang and Clark, 2008, 2010; Kruengkrai et al., 2009; Wang et al., 2010).

There are also some unsupervised approaches with raw text. Peng and Schuurmans (2001) propose an unsupervised approach based on an improved expectation maximum learning algorithm and a pruning algorithm based on mutual information. Non-parametric Bayesian techniques (Johnson and Goldwater, 2009; Mochihashi et al., 2009) have been introduced to word segmentation. Bootstrapped voting experts algorithm paired with minimum description length is used to for word segmentation (Hewlett and Cohen, 2011). Wang et al. (2011) propose an ESA (Evaluation, Selection, and Adjustment) unsupervised approach to word segmentation.

Our method is different from above methods, as we integrate the advantages of discriminative training and DMM. Moreover, we only use a dictionary[7] and a raw text.

Conclusion

In this paper, we propose an effective approach of integrating the advantages of discriminative training and DMM, to build a high quality word segmenter with only a dictionary and a raw text. We conduct experiments in CWS on both news domain and Chinese medicine patent domain. Our method gains much higher word segmentation accuracy than DMM in both domains, with error reductions of 21.50% and 13.66%, respectively. The capability of OOV words recognition of our method is stronger than DMM by a large margin, with the increments of recall rate 42.54% and 23.72%, respectively.

Our method does not use annotated corpora, we only use a small scale dictionary and a raw text, which are easier to get in resource-poor languages and domains compared with annotated corpora. Theoretically, our method is not only effective in Chinese, but also in languages with no obvious word delimiters in sentences, such as Japanese and some other Asian languages.

In the future, we will explore better strategies of extracting high quality features from raw text. Besides, we will try to integrate some unsupervised approaches to our method, which may help us learn more knowledge from raw text.

Acknowledgments

The authors were supported by National Natural Science Foundation of China, Contracts 61202216, and 863 State Key Project No. 2011AA01A207. We are grateful to the anonymous reviewers for their thorough reviewing and informative comments.

References

Collins, M. (2002). Discriminative training methods for hidden markov models: Theory and experiments with perceptron algorithms. In *Proceedings of the ACL-02 conference on Empirical*

[7]The dictionaries used in this paper are available resources. To our knowledge, we can produce a dictionary for a novel domain/language from Wikipedia or Baidupedia (Chinese).

methods in natural language processing-Volume 10, pages 1–8. Association for Computational Linguistics.

Collins, M. and Roark, B. (2004). Incremental parsing with the perceptron algorithm. In *Proceedings of ACL*, volume 2004.

Hewlett, D. and Cohen, P. (2011). Fully unsupervised word segmentation with bve and mdl. In *Proceedings of the 49th Annual Meeting of the Association for Computational Linguistics: Human Language Technologies: short papers-Volume 2*, pages 540–545. Association for Computational Linguistics.

Jiang, W., Huang, L., and Liu, Q. (2009). Automatic adaptation of annotation standards: Chinese word segmentation and pos tagging: a case study. In *Proceedings of the Joint Conference of the 47th Annual Meeting of the ACL and the 4th International Joint Conference on Natural Language Processing of the AFNLP: Volume 1-Volume 1*, pages 522–530. Association for Computational Linguistics.

Jiang, W., Meng, F., Liu, Q., and Lü, Y. (2012). Iterative annotation transformation with predict-self reestimation for chinese word segmentation. In *Proceedings of the 2012 Joint Conference on Empirical Methods in Natural Language Processing and Computational Natural Language Learning*, pages 412–420.

Johnson, M. and Goldwater, S. (2009). Improving nonparameteric bayesian inference: experiments on unsupervised word segmentation with adaptor grammars. In *Proceedings of Human Language Technologies: The 2009 Annual Conference of the North American Chapter of the Association for Computational Linguistics*, pages 317–325. Association for Computational Linguistics.

Kruengkrai, C., Uchimoto, K., Kazama, J., Wang, Y., Torisawa, K., and Isahara, H. (2009). An error-driven word-character hybrid model for joint chinese word segmentation and pos tagging. In *Proceedings of the Joint Conference of the 47th Annual Meeting of the ACL and the 4th International Joint Conference on Natural Language Processing of the AFNLP: Volume 1-Volume 1*, pages 513–521. Association for Computational Linguistics.

Lafferty, J., McCallum, A., and Pereira, F. (2001). Conditional random fields: Probabilistic models for segmenting and labeling sequence data. In *Proceedings of the 18th ICML*, pages 282–289.

Li, Z. (2011). Parsing the internal structure of words: a new paradigm for chinese word segmentation. In *Proceedings of the 49th Annual Meeting of the Association for Computational Linguistics: Human Language Technologies. Portland, Oregon, USA: Association for Computational Linguistics.*

Li, Z. and Sun, M. (2009). Punctuation as implicit annotations for chinese word segmentation. *Computational Linguistics*, 35(4):505–512.

Mochihashi, D., Yamada, T., and Ueda, N. (2009). Bayesian unsupervised word segmentation with nested pitman-yor language modeling. In *Proceedings of the Joint Conference of the 47th Annual Meeting of the ACL and the 4th International Joint Conference on Natural Language Processing of the AFNLP: Volume 1-Volume 1*, pages 100–108. Association for Computational Linguistics.

Ng, H. and Low, J. (2004). Chinese part-of-speech tagging: One-at-a-time or all-at-once? word-based or character-based. In *Proceedings of EMNLP*, volume 4.

Peng, F. and Schuurmans, D. (2001). Self-supervised chinese word segmentation. *Advances in Intelligent Data Analysis*, pages 238–247.

Ratnaparkhi and Adwait (1996). A maximum entropy model for part-of-speech tagging. In *Proceedings of the conference on empirical methods in natural language processing*, volume 1, pages 133–142.

Sun, W. (2011). A stacked sub-word model for joint chinese word segmentation and part-of-speech tagging. In *Proceedings of the 49th Annual Meeting of the Association for Computational Linguistics*, pages 1385–1394.

Sun, X., Wang, H., and Li, W. (2012). Fast online training with frequency-adaptive learning rates for chinese word segmentation and new word detection. In *Proceedings of the 50th Annual Meeting of the Association for Computational Linguistics*, pages 253–262.

Wang, H., Zhu, J., Tang, S., and Fan, X. (2011). A new unsupervised approach to word segmentation. *Computational Linguistics*, 37(3):421–454.

Wang, K., Zong, C., and Su, K. (2010). A character-based joint model for chinese word segmentation. In *Proceedings of the 23rd International Conference on Computational Linguistics*, pages 1173–1181. Association for Computational Linguistics.

Xue, N. and Shen, L. (2003). Chinese word segmentation as lmr tagging. In *Proceedings of the second SIGHAN workshop on Chinese language processing-Volume 17*, pages 176–179. Association for Computational Linguistics.

Xue, N., Xia, F., Chiou, F., and Palmer, M. (2005). The penn chinese treebank: Phrase structure annotation of a large corpus. *Natural Language Engineering*, 11(02):207–238.

Zhang, Y. and Clark, S. (2007). Chinese segmentation with a word-based perceptron algorithm. In *Anual Meeting-Association for Computational Linguistics*, volume 45, page 840.

Zhang, Y. and Clark, S. (2008). Joint word segmentation and pos tagging using a single perceptron. In *Proceedings of ACL*, volume 8, pages 888–896.

Zhang, Y. and Clark, S. (2010). A fast decoder for joint word segmentation and pos-tagging using a single discriminative model. In *Proceedings of the 2010 Conference on Empirical Methods in Natural Language Processing*, pages 843–852. Association for Computational Linguistics.

Lost in Translations? Building Sentiment Lexicons Using Context Based Machine Translation

Xinfan Meng[1] *Furu Wei*[2] *Ge Xu*[1,3] *Longkai Zhang*[1]
Xiaohua Liu[2] *Ming Zhou*[2] *Houfeng Wang*[1*]
(1) MOE Key Lab of Computational Linguistics, Peking University
(2) Microsoft Research Asia
(3) Department of Computer Science, Minjiang University
mxf@pku.edu.cn, xuge@pku.edu.cn, fuwei@microsoft.com, zhlongk@qq.com,
xiaoliu@microsoft.com, mingzhou@microsoft.com, wanghf@pku.edu.cn

Abstract
In this paper, we propose a simple yet effective approach to automatically building sentiment lexicons from English sentiment lexicons using publicly available online machine translation services. The method does not rely on any semantic resources or bilingual dictionaries, and can be applied to many languages. We propose to overcome the low coverage problem through putting each English sentiment word into different contexts to generate different phrases, which effectively prompts the machine translation engine to return different translations for the same English sentiment word. Experiment results on building a Chinese sentiment lexicon (available at https://github.com/fannix/Chinese-Sentiment-Lexicon) show that the proposed approach significantly improves the coverage of the sentiment lexicon while achieving relatively high precision.

KEYWORDS: Sentiment analysis, Multilingual, Dictionary.

*corresponding author

Proceedings of COLING 2012: Posters, pages 829–838,
COLING 2012, Mumbai, December 2012.

1 Introduction and Related Work

Sentiment lexicons are valuable resources for sentiment analysis; they can be used to identify sentiment words and expression, and they can also be used to generate informative features for sentiment classification of documents. Several sentiment lexicons have been compiled (Stone et al., 1966; Hu and Liu, 2004; Wilson et al., 2005) for English. They are widely used in the research on sentiment analysis. By contrast, due to the high cost of manually compiling a lexicon, sentiment lexicons in many other languages are very few or even unavailable. The shortage of sentiment lexicons limits our capability to analyze the sentiment conveyed in the documents written in other languages; it is estimated that as of May 31 2011, only 26.8% of Internet users speak English [1].

There is some research on automatically building sentiment lexicons for other languages using translation based methods or bootstrapping methods. Straightforward translation methods make use of multilingual dictionaries, and bootstrapping methods enlarge the sentiment lexicons from English sentiment seed words using semantic resources. However, straightforward translation methods suffer from low sentiment word coverage in the bilingual dictionaries. Moreover, in many cases, two or more English sentiment words often are translated to the same foreign word. Both factors lead to smaller translated sentiment lexicons than the original ones. (Mihalcea et al., 2007) study the effectiveness of translating English sentiment lexicon to Romanian using two bilingual dictionaries. The original English sentiment lexicon contains 6,856 entries; after translation, only 4,983 entries are left in the Romanian sentiment lexicon. About 2000 entries are lost or conflated into other entries during the translation process. The translation method is also used in (Wan, 2008, 2011).

On the other hand, though bootstrapping methods don't use bilingual dictionaries and hence are not subject to the limitation of the translation methods, they have relatively high demands for semantic resources such as WordNet (Fellbaum, 1998). Bootstrapping methods enlarge the sentiment lexicons from English sentiment seed words. (Hassan et al., 2011) present a method to identify the sentiment polarity of foreign words by using WordNet (or similar semantic resources) in the target foreign language. (Ku and Chen, 2007) create a Chinese Lexicon by translating the General Inquirer, combining with Chinese Network Sentiment Dictionary, and conducting expansion using two thesauri. Other semi-supervised lexicon construction methods such as random walk (Esuli and Sebastiani, 2006), label propagation (Rao and Ravichandran, 2009; Xu et al., 2010) or graph propagation (Kerry and McDonald, 2010) can also be used here. However, all those methods require high quality lexicon seed words in the target languages and/or some semantic resources, which are not always available in the target languages.

Besides automatic methods, semi-automatic approaches are also studied. (Steinberger et al., 2012) first produce high-level gold-standard sentiment dictionaries for two languages, then translate them automatically into third languages respectively and obtain overlap of translated lexicon. The experiment suggests that this triangulation method works significantly better than simple translation method. However, in some intermediate stages, the dictionaries need to be filtered and expanded manually.

In this paper, we present a simple yet effective approach to creating high quality sentiment lexicons using English sentiment lexicons. Instead of relying on bilingual dictionaries or

[1] http://www.internetworldstats.com/stats7.htm

Context	English	Translation
None	elegant	优雅
	graceful	优雅
Collocation	graceful voice	优美的声音
	graceful dance	曼妙的舞姿
Coordinated phrase	elegant and graceful	典雅大方
	graceful and elegant	雍容典雅
Punctuation	graceful.	优美。
	elegant.	优雅。
	graceful and elegant.	婉约和优雅。

Table 1: Chinese Translations of "graceful" and "elegant" in different contexts

semantic resources, we leverage online machine translation services, which are readily accessible. In order to overcome the word coverage problem, we put each English sentiment word in different contexts to generate different phrases, which can prompt translation engines to return different translations for the same English sentiment word. In particular, we develop three techniques for constructing contexts and generating different phrases. It should also be emphasized that leveraging online machine translation service enables us to easily construct lexicons in many languages; as an empirical study, we use this approach to construct a Chinese sentiment lexicon, and the obtained lexicon is both large and accurate.

2 Our Approach

Formally, our task is to build a sentiment lexicon for a target language, such as Chinese, given an English sentiment lexicon. We use Table 1 to illustrate the idea. As an example, we translate two English positive words, "graceful" and "elegant", to Chinese. When we translate "graceful" or "elegant" individually, they are translated to the same Chinese word, "优雅" [2]. Though the two Chinese translations are generally correct, two distinct English words are conflated into only one Chinese word. This phenomenon is very common in translation. Many English sentiment words have identical or similar meaning. Corresponding to this meaning, there are also many possible translations in the target language, among which one translation is often dominant. As a result, when those English sentiment words are translated individually, this dominant translation are very likely to be picked out, whether by using bilingual dictionary or machine translation engine. In this circumstance, many translation variations are lost.

In order to recover the lost translation variations, we put the English words into different contexts. By using different contexts, we effectively prompt the machine translation engine to query the large scale parallel corpora that it is trained on, and then to return the most accurate translations in the target language. Furthermore, we can take advantage of the polysemy of words; one word can mean different things and it usually has various target language translations. Our context-based method effectively lead to translation diversity.

The flow chart of our approach is provided in Figure 1. As seen, we divide the overall process into three steps: (1) Generating the context; (2) Translation; (3) Extraction.

[2] All the following translation examples are obtained by using Google Translate (http://translate.google.com/)

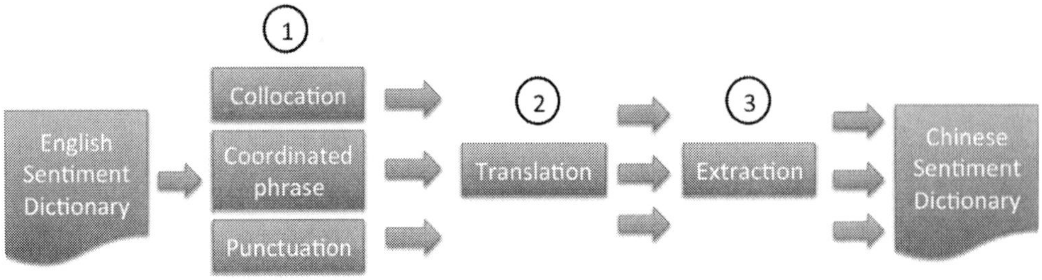

Figure 1: The Flow Chart of Our Approach

First, We devise the following three methods to generate contexts for translation.

- **Collocation**: We obtain the most frequent bi-grams containing the English word. This technique effectively makes the word meaning more specific and concrete, which helps the translation engine to pick out more accurate and diverse translations. For example, we generate "graceful voice" and "graceful dance". Given the contexts, "voice" and "dance", two "graceful" are translated to "优美" and "曼妙", respectively, which are more natural Chinese translations.
- **Coordinated phrase**: We combine two English words that have the same Chinese translations. This makes the translation engine less likely to return the same translations for both words. For example, we create a coordinated phrase by joining "elegant" and "graceful" with the word "and". Joining together, the translations for both words are different from the original translation. More interestingly, putting the two English words in different orders lead to different translations.
- **Punctuation**: We place a punctuation mark, such as period or question mark, at the end of the English word. We use this simple rule to limit the possible parts-of-speech of the translations. For example, "effusive." is translated to "热情洋溢", while "effusive" is translated to "感情奔放的"; after adding punctuation context, "effusive" is translated to words that have different parts-of-speech. We can also combine this technique with the coordinated phrase technique.

Concretely, We use a bi-gram language model for generating possible collocations. Instead of creating our own language model from large corpora, we leverage the Microsoft Web N-gram Services (Wang et al., 2010)[3], an online N-gram corpus that built from Web documents. We choose the bi-gram language model trained on document titles. Given each English polarity word w_1, we use the language model to generate up to the 1000 most frequent bi-grams $w_1 w_2$.

To create coordinated phrases, we first translate all sentiment words using Google Translate. And then we create coordinated phrases for the English sentiment words which are translated into the same Chinese word. We select those English words and join them with the word "and". The punctuation context are generated by appending a period after the given English word. By combining and using both rules simultaneously, we can generate even more queries.

[3]http://research.microsoft.com/web-ngram

Lexicon	#POS	#NEG	#TOTAL
MPQA(EN)	1,481	3,080	4,561
DICT	742	1,139	1,881
DICT + Stem	814	1,230	2,044
DICT + Multiple	2,811	3,799	6,610
MT	1078	2,104	3,182
CONTEXT	**3,511**	**5,210**	**8,721**

Table 2: Vocabulary Size of Different Lexicons

Then we translate the resulted queries. We use Google Translate[4] as the online machine translation service. After that, we extract the foreign sentiment words from machine translation results. This step is language dependent but is often straight-forward. In this paper, we conduct experiment on Chinese. We first use Stanford Chinese Word Segmenter[5] for segmentation, and then use the position of the words and the punctuation between the words to locate the sentiment polarity word candidates. Finally we prune the candidates list by removing the words have less than 3 occurrences.

Discussion Our approach can be applied to construct sentiment dictionaries in other languages as well. Depending on the target language, we might need to make some small modifications. Word segmentation is unnecessary for most European languages. And in some languages, we need to consider the word order issues when extracting the sentiment words from the translation results, since translation engine might reorder the queries. For example, in Arabic, the modifying adjectives are placed before the nouns, which is different from English; and also in Arabic, the words are written from right to left.

3 Experimental Study

We use the MPQA subjective lexicon (Wilson et al., 2005) as the English lexicon. We only keep the strong subjective entries, which include 1,481 positive and 3,080 negative entries. For the purpose of comparison, we implemented the following baseline approaches. The first three baselines rely on a bilingual dictionary. We use the LDC (Linguistic Data Consortium) English-Chinese bilingual wordlists[6], which is also used in (Wan, 2008). This dictionary contains 18,195 entries. Each English entry is mapped to a list of Chinese words or expressions.

As shown in Table 2, the first baseline (DICT) looks up the English entry in the bilingual dictionary and use the first translation in the corresponding Chinese translation lists. Only 1,148 positive and 2,004 negative entries can be found in the bilingual dictionary, while about 1,500 entries are lost in the bilingual dictionary. After removing duplicate Chinese entries in the translated Chinese sentiment lexicon, only 742 unique positive entries and 1,139 negative entries remain. To improve the chances of finding English sentiment words in the bilingual dictionary, we use the Porter stemmer[7] to first obtain the lemmatization forms of the English sentiment words and then search them again in the bilingual dictionary. The results (DICT + Stem) show that the recall slightly improves, but the size

[4] http://translate.google.com/
[5] http://nlp.stanford.edu/software/segmenter.shtml
[6] http://projects.ldc.upenn.edu/Chinese/LDC_ch.htm
[7] http://tartarus.org/~martin/PorterStemmer/

Lexicon	Precision
DICT	93%
DICT + Stem	93%
DICT + Multiple	82%
MT	91%
CONTEXT	91.5%

Table 3: Precision of Different Lexicons

of the Chinese sentiment lexicon is still much smaller than the English sentiment lexicon. We further expand the sentiment lexicon by including all translations of each English entry, with the exception of the translations that contain punctuations and are longer than 6 characters; we filter translations longer than 6 characters since most of these sentiment words or phrases are merely the combinations of the shorter words and phrases. From the results of this baseline (DICT + Multiple), we can see that this approach can remarkably expand the lexicon. However, This method introduces many noises, as described later. Instead of using bilingual dictionary, we can use the machine translation engine to directly translate the English sentiment words. The results of this baseline (denoted by MT) show that the it is superior to the DICT baseline, but the vocabulary it covers is still too limited. The results of our approach (denoted by CONTEXT) are shown at the bottom. The lexicon generated are significantly larger than all other lexicons.

3.1 Lexicon Quality

To evaluate the precision of the sentiment lexicons generated by using our approach and the baselines, we sample 200 entries for each polarity (positive and negative) from each lexicon and compute their precision. Table 3 depicts the comparison, from which we can see that the positive lexicon generated by DICT + Multiple is very noisy. By contrast, our approach can generate a large lexicon with high precision. Though other lexicons have very high precisions, the vocabularies are too small.

To investigate why Dictionary-based translation methods lead to relatively low coverage lexicon, we look into the generated Chinese sentiment lexicon and identify three causes. First, the bilingual dictionary is not a comprehensive list of the Chinese translations of each English word. Instead it just includes a few translations to help people to understand the meaning of the English word. Second, the bilingual dictionary often translates different English words to one Chinese word. Third, the bilingual dictionary does not include translations of multi-word expressions. The MT baseline alleviates the problem of multi-word expressions, but it still suffers from the first two problems. We also study the noise words introduced by DICT + Multiple. Most of noise words are direct translations of one particular sense of some polarity English words. For example, “吸入” , which means “breathe in” , is included because the polarity word “inspire” has this sense as a technical term.

One other possible approach to enlarging the lexicon is to use N-best translations for English polarity words. We do not explore this approach in this paper for two reasons. First, online machine translation services often do not provide convenient interfaces for retrieving N-best translation results. Second, based on our observation, N-best translations of individual sentiment words are similar to multiple translations using a bilingual

Lexicon	NTCIR	Weibo
DICT	61.9%	57.6%
DICT + Stem	61.9%	57.5%
DICT + Multiple	64.7%	61.7%
MT	66.2%	64.6%
CONTEXT	**70.1%**	**73.5%**

Table 4: Classifier Accuracy Using Different Lexicons

dictionary. Both approaches tend to produce general and abstract words like "高兴" and "快乐" (both mean "happy"), but have difficulties in generating Chinese idioms such as "兴高采烈", which also expresses "happy", but in a more vivid way. One interesting fact of the CONTEXT lexicon is that it includes many four-characters idioms, which are widely used in Chinese but rarely found in bilingual dictionaries. By contrast, dictionary-based approaches often fail to generate those idioms.

3.2 Lexicon Usefulness in Sentiment Classification

One important application of sentiment lexicons is document sentiment classification, predicting whether a given document to express a positive or negative attitude. Sentiment lexicons can be used either as the basic resources for dictionary-based classifiers, or as a preprocessing step to generate augmented features for corpus-based classifiers. Therefore, we evaluate the usefulness of the lexicons by evaluating the performance of classifiers using different lexicons.

We use a dictionary-based sentiment classification approach. Besides the sentiment lexicon, we also use a negation lexicon, which collect the terms that can reverse the sentiment. The negation lexicon we use is the Chinese translation of negation lexicon from OpinionFinder[8]. The polarity score of each document is the sum of all the polarity of sentiment words in the document; if a negation word is in the context window of the sentiment word[9], we inverse the polarity of this sentiment word. If the overall polarity score is less than 0, we label this document as negative; otherwise the document is predicted as positive.

We test the classifiers on two data sets, which belong to different genres. The first test data set comes from the NTCIR Opinion Analysis Pilot Task data set (Seki et al., 2007, 2008). This data set contains 4,294 Chinese sentences, 2,378 being positive sentences and 1,916 being negative. Those sentences are all extracted from news. The second data set is collected from Weibo[10], a micro-blogging service website in China. We sample 5,000 messages from Weibo, and label them manually. To be consistent with the NTCIR data set, we only keep the positive and negative message. The resulting Weibo data set contains 906 positive messages and 807 negative messages. Each sentence/message is segmented into Chinese words by using Stanford Chinese word segmenter.

We report the results in Table 4. As seen, the classifier using our CONTEXT lexicon obtains the highest accuracy on both data sets. Comparing the results in the NTCIR and

[8] http://www.cs.pitt.edu/mpqa/opinionfinder.html

[9] We use a distance window of two words

[10] http://weibo.com

the Weibo column, it is interesting to note that the Weibo data set decreases the accuracy of classifiers using all lexicon but CONTEXT lexicon. As described in the previous section, our CONTEXT lexicon contains many Chinese idioms, which are seldom used in news. Hence our lexicon performs even better in user generated contents, such as blogs and user reviews.

We also note that bilingual dictionary is not an effective method for adapting resources cross-lingually, since classifiers with MT lexicon performs better than all the ones with DICT variants. Another interesting fact is that using larger lexicon do not always lead to better classifier accuracy; the classifier with MT lexicon performs better than the one with DICT+Multiple, despite the fact that the DICT+Multiple lexicon is much larger than the MT lexicon.

Conclusion and Future Work

In this paper, we propose an approach to leveraging publicly available machine translation services for creating sentiment lexicons from English sentiment lexicons. By placing English sentiment words in carefully crafted contexts, we effective prompt the translation engine to translate the same sentiment words differently. The experiment results show that our approach can obtain a high sentiment word coverage while achieving relatively high precision. This approach treats the machine translation engine as a black box. In the future, we will experiment with the ideas of directly using the underlying parallel corpus for creating sentiment lexicons.

Acknowledgment

This work was partially supported by National High Technology Research and Development Program of China (863 Program) (No. 2012AA011101), National Natural Science Foundation of China (No.91024009, No.60973053), the Specialized Research Fund for the Doctoral Program of Higher Education of China (Grant No. 20090001110047), and 2009 Chiang Ching-kuo Foundation for International Scholarly Exchange (under Grant No. RG013-D-09).

References

Esuli, A. and Sebastiani, F. (2006). SentiWordNet: a publicly available lexical resource for opinion mining. In *Proceedings of LREC-06, the 5th Conference on Language Resources and Evaluation*, Genova, IT.

Fellbaum, C. (1998). *WordNet: An electronic lexical database*. The MIT press.

Hassan, A., Abu-Jbara, A., Jha, R., and Radev, D. (2011). Identifying the semantic orientation of foreign words. In *Proceedings of the 49th Annual Meeting of the Association for Computational Linguistics: Human Language Technologies: short papers-Volume 2*, pages 592---597.

Hu, M. and Liu, B. (2004). Mining and summarizing customer reviews. In *Proceedings of KDD '04, the ACM SIGKDD international conference on Knowledge discovery and data mining*, pages 168---177, Seattle, US. ACM Press.

Kerry, L. V. and McDonald, H. R. (2010). The viability of web-derived polarity lexicons. In *Annual Conference of the North American Chapter of the ACL*.

Ku, L. and Chen, H. (2007). Mining opinions from the web: Beyond relevance retrieval. *Journal of the American Society for Information Science and Technology*, 58(12):1838---1850.

Mihalcea, R., Banea, C., and Wiebe, J. (2007). Learning multilingual subjective language via cross-lingual projections. In *ANNUAL MEETING-ASSOCIATION FOR COMPUTATIONAL LINGUISTICS*, volume 45, page 976.

Rao, D. and Ravichandran, D. (2009). Semi-supervised polarity lexicon induction. In *Proceedings of the 12th Conference of the European Chapter of the Association for Computational Linguistics*, EACL '09, pages 675---682, Athens, Greece. Association for Computational Linguistics. ACM ID: 1609142.

Seki, Y., Evans, D. K., Ku, L.-W., Chen, H.-H., Kando, N., and Lin, C.-Y. (2007). Overview of opinion analysis pilot task at NTCIR-6. In *Proceedings of NTCIR-6 Workshop Meeting*, page 265–278.

Seki, Y., Evans, D. K., Ku, L.-W., Sun, L., Chen, H.-H., Kando, N., and Lin, C.-Y. (2008). Overview of multilingual opinion analysis task at NTCIR-7. In *Proc. of the Seventh NTCIR Workshop*.

Steinberger, J., Ebrahim, M., Ehrmann, M., Hurriyetoglu, A., Kabadjov, M., Lenkova, P., Steinberger, R., Tanev, H., Vuez, S., and Zavarella, V. (2012). Creating sentiment dictionariesvia triangulation. *Decision Support Systems*.

Stone, P. J., Dunphy, D. C., Smith, M. S., and Ogilvie, D. M. (1966). *The General Inquirer: A Computer Approach to Content Analysis*. MIT Press.

Wan, X. (2008). Using bilingual knowledge and ensemble techniques for unsupervised chinese sentiment analysis. In *Proceedings of the Conference on Empirical Methods in Natural Language Processing*, EMNLP '08, pages 553---561, Stroudsburg, PA, USA. Association for Computational Linguistics.

Wan, X. (2011). Bilingual co-training for sentiment classification of chinese product reviews. *Computational Linguistics*, 37(3):587–616.

Wang, K., Thrasher, C., Viegas, E., Li, X., and Hsu, B. (2010). An overview of microsoft web n-gram corpus and applications. In *Proceedings of the NAACL HLT 2010 Demonstration Session*, page 45–48.

Wilson, T., Wiebe, J., and Hoffmann, P. (2005). Recognizing contextual polarity in phrase-level sentiment analysis. In *Proceedings of Human Language Technologies Conference/Conference on Empirical Methods in Natural Language Processing (HLT/EMNLP 2005)*, Vancouver, CA.

Xu, G., Meng, X., and Wang, H. (2010). Build chinese emotion lexicons using a graph-based algorithm and multiple resources. In *Proceedings of the 23rd International Conference on Computational Linguistics (Coling 2010)*, pages 1209---1217, Beijing, China. Coling 2010 Organizing Committee.

How Does the Granularity of an Annotation Scheme Influence Dependency Parsing Performance?

Simon Mille[1] *Alicia Burga*[1] *Gabriela Ferraro*[1] *Leo Wanner*[1,2]
[1]Universitat Pompeu Fabra Barcelona; [2]ICREA
firstname.lastname@upf.edu

ABSTRACT
The common use of a single *de facto* standard annotation scheme for dependency treebank creation leaves the question open to what extent the performance of an application trained on a treebank depends on this annotation scheme and whether a linguistically richer scheme would imply a decrease of the performance of the application. We investigate the effect of the variation of the number of grammatical relations in a tagset on the performance of dependency parsers. In order to obtain several levels of granularity of the annotation, we design a hierarchical annotation scheme exclusively based on syntactic criteria. The richest annotation contains 60 relations. The more coarse-grained annotations are derived from the richest. As a result, all annotations and thus also the performance of a parser trained on different annotations remain comparable. We carried out experiments with four state-of-the-art dependency parsers. The results support the claim that annotating with more fine-grained syntactic relations does not necessarily imply a significant loss of accuracy. We also show the limits of this approach by giving details on the fine-grained relations that do have a negative impact on the performance of the parsers.

TITLE AND ABSTRACT IN SPANISH

¿Cómo influye la granularidad de un esquema de anotación en el rendimiento de parsers de dependencia?

El uso frecuente de un único esquema de anotación estándar para crear corpus de análisis sintáctico de dependencias genera las preguntas de hasta qué punto el rendimiento de una aplicación entrenada con dichos corpus depende del esquema de anotación, y si un esquema lingüísticamente más rico implica que la calidad de la aplicación disminuya. Investigamos aquí el efecto de la granularidad de la anotación sobre el rendimiento de parsers de dependencia. Para obtener distintos niveles de granularidad, diseñamos un esquema de anotación jerárquico basado exclusivamente en criterios sintácticos. La anotación más detallada incluye 60 relaciones, y de ésta derivamos los conjuntos menos detallados. Así, las anotaciones—y el rendimiento de parsers entrenados con ellas—se mantienen comparables. Los experimentos utilizan cuatro parsers del estado del arte. Los resultados apoyan la hipótesis de que una anotación más detallada no implica una pérdida de precisión del parser. Presentamos también las limitaciones de este enfoque, ofreciendo detalles acerca de aquellas relaciones que sí tienen un impacto negativo en la calidad de los parsers.

KEYWORDS: dependencies, syntax, annotation, tagset granularity, parsing.

KEYWORDS IN SPANISH: dependencias, sintaxis, anotación, granularidad del tagset, parsing.

Proceedings of COLING 2012: Posters, pages 839–852,
COLING 2012, Mumbai, December 2012.

SYNOPSIS IN SPANISH

Para medir la precisión de los parsers en función del detalle de los tagsets, se diseñó un esquema jerárquico de anotación de relaciones de dependencia que permite expandir o contraer el número de relaciones a utilizar. La idea general tras este esquema es la aplicación de criterios sólo sintácticos (más que semánticos), más o menos finos, que permiten identificar cada etiqueta gramatical a ser introducida en la anotación, así como agrupar relaciones en una etiqueta más amplia. Así, por ejemplo, para dependientes verbales, necesitamos capturar si éstos pueden pronominalizar, si su movimiento es limitado, etc. En la Tabla 1 se muestra qué relaciones del tagset más detallado son agrupadas bajo la misma etiqueta en el siguiente, y menos detallado, conjunto. Estas agrupaciones se basan en propiedades sintácticas compartidas por un grupo de relaciones.

60 Rels	44 Rels	31 Rels	15 Rels
abs pred	abs pred	abs pred	NMOD
det	det	det	
quant	quant	quant	
compl adnom	compl adnom	compl adnom	
appos	appos	modif	
abbrev	abbrev		
attr	attr		
modif	modif		
relat	relat		
adjunct	adv	adv	ADV
adv			
restr			
relat expl	relat expl		
prolep	prolep		
adv mod	copred		
obj copred			
subj copred			
analyt fut	analyt fut	analyt fut	AUX
analyt pass	analyt pass	analyt pass	
analyt perf	analyt perf	analyt perf	
analyt prog	analyt prog	analyt prog	
modal	modal	modal	
dobj clitic	dobj clitic	dobj clitic	DOBJ
dobj	dobj	dobj	
copul	copul	copul	COPUL
copul clitic	copul clitic	copul clitic	
iobj1	iobj	iobj	IOBJ
iobj2			
iobj3			
iobj clitic1	iobj clitic	iobj clitic	
iobj clitic2			
iobj clitic3			

60 Rels	44 Rels	31 Rels	15 Rels
obl obj1	obl obj	obl obj	OOBJ
obl obj2			
obl obj3			
noun compl			
agent	agent		
compar	compar	compar	
compl1	compl	compl	
compl2			
elect	elect	elect	
subj	subj	subj	SUBJ
quasi subj	quasi subj	quasi subj	QSUBJ
compar conj	conj	prepos	PREPOS
sub conj			
coord conj	coord conj		
prepos	prepos		
coord	coord	coord	COORD
num junct	num junct		
juxtapos	juxtapos	juxtapos	
quasi coord	quasi coord		
sequent	sequent	sequent	BIN
bin junct	bin junct	bin junct	
aux phras	aux phras	aux phras	NAME
aux refl lex	aux refl	aux refl	AUX REFL
aux refl pass			
aux refl dir			
aux refl indir			
punc	punc	punc	PUNC
punc init	punc init		

Table 1: Tag groupings for a hierarchy of syntactic tags/Jerarquía de agrupación de etiquetas sintácticas (Left=top, right=bottom of table)

Para los experimentos, se utilizaron cuatro tagsets de relaciones sintácticas. El más detallado (60 relaciones) se obtuvo a partir de una adaptación, revisión y enriquecimiento de la anotación original de AnCora, desde la cual se derivaron automáticamente los otros tres tagsets (44, 31 y 15 relaciones), obteniendo así cuatro anotaciones distintas del mismo corpus. Se evaluaron cuatro parsers de referencia. Tres de ellos son los parsers con mejores resultados para español en la CoNLL Shared Task 2009: Che, Merlo y Bohnet; el cuarto es el muy conocido Malt Parser. El corpus fue dividido al azar en un grupo de entrenamiento (3200 oraciones) y un grupo de evaluación (313 oraciones). Cada parser fue entrenado con los cuatro conjuntos de relaciones y los dieciséis modelos de parsing obtenidos fueron aplicados a los correspondientes conjuntos de evaluación.

Los resultados para el Labelled Attachment Score (LAS)—es decir, la proporción de asignación de relaciones con la adecuada etiqueta y el gobernador y el dependiente correctos—se muestran en la Tabla 2. Observamos que los cuatro parsers se comportan de modo similar: su precisión

tags# >	60	44	31	15
Bohnet	81.95	84.11	84.28	84.69
Che	75.14	84.24	84.67	85.11
Malt	79.7	81.9	82.1	82.2
Merlo	82.32	84.53	84.05	84.52

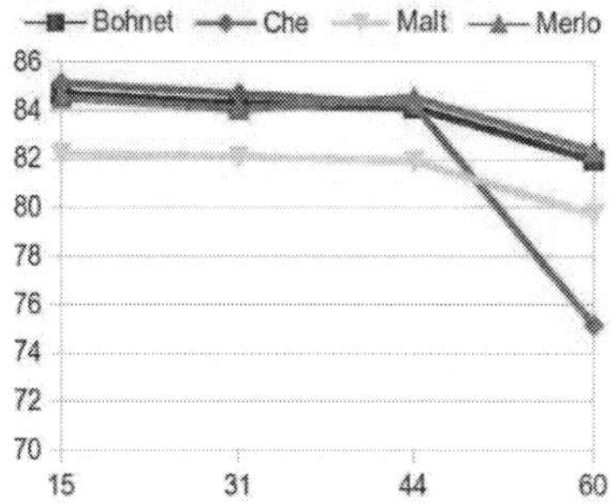

Table 2: LAS (%) of the parsers depending on tag granularity; right: graphical illustration/LAS de los parsers en función de la granularidad del tagset; derecha: ilustración

es constante de 15 a 44 relaciones, pero disminuye con 60 relaciones. Asimismo, notamos una diferencia entre las curvas de Bohnet, Merlo y Malt (prácticamente paralelas) y la de Che, que cae significativamente con 60 relaciones. Todos los parsers logran el mejor rendimiento con el tagset más pequeño y menos detallado. Sin embargo, sorprendentemente, el LAS disminuye muy poco cuando el número de relaciones se duplica, y menos aun entre 31 y 44 relaciones. Con 60 relaciones, no obstante, el LAS cae significativamente alrededor de al menos 2 puntos. También calculamos el UnLabelled Attachment Score (ULA)(ver Tabla 3). Para Bohnet, el ULA aumenta leve pero constantemente de 15 relaciones (90.27%) a 60 relaciones (90.49%). Che, en cambio, presenta la tendencia contraria, y sus resultados decrecen de 15 a 60 relaciones (habiendo una caída mayor con 60). Malt es tan estable como Bohnet, pero no presenta una clara mejora al trabajar con un número mayor de etiquetas. Asimismo, para evaluar si con 15 relaciones la calidad mejora si el parser es entrenado con un tagset más detallado, todos los outputs fueron transformados a 15 relaciones. Como vemos en la Tabla 4, en términos generales, la tendencia es la misma que para el ULA, de modo que podemos concluir que la anotación con más relaciones no parece mejorar la calidad del parser al trabajar con 15 relaciones.

Observamos que aquellas relaciones que se diferencian gracias a rasgos sintácticos muy finos (como los diferentes tipos de objetos oblicuos, completivos, o auxiliares reflexivos) son las que más influyen en la disminución de la calidad del parser. Consecuentemente, no separar estas relaciones en relaciones más finas puede ser beneficioso para el parser. Al contrario, observamos que las dependencias que implican diferentes tipos de coordinaciones entre grupos o frases se parsean mejor si no se juntan.

tags# >	60	44	31	15
Bohnet	90.49	90.39	90.31	90.27
Che	86.28	90.37	90.57	90.6
Malt	87.91	88	87.83	87.75
Merlo	90.11	90.67	90.39	-

Table 3: ULA of the parsers depending on tag granularity/ULA de los parsers en función de la granularidad del tagset (%)

tags# >	15	31→15	44→15	60→15
Bohnet	84.69	84.56	84.51	84.54
Che	85.11	84.93	84.71	77.91
Malt	82.2	82.3	82.2	82.2
Merlo	84.52	84.33	84.92	84.12

Table 4: LAS of the parsers (with 15 SyntRels) trained on fine-grained tagsets/LAS de los parsers (con 15 SyntRels) entrenados con anotaciones más finas (%)

1 Introduction

As already pointed out by some researchers (see, e.g., Kübler (2005), Rehbein and van Genabith (2007), Bosco et al. (2010), Bosco and Lavelli (2010)), the use of a single annotation scheme for treebank creation leaves the question open to what extent the performance of an application trained on a treebank depends on the annotation scheme in question. Or, in other words, whether the annotation scheme in use is the best for a given application. To answer this question, Kübler (2005) and Rehbein and van Genabith (2007) compared the performance of a PCFG parser trained on two comparable corpora of German, annotated following different annotation schemes, while Bosco et al. (2010) trained three dependency parsers on two different Italian corpora. In contrast, we are interested in a comparison of the change of the performance of a dependency parser when trained on the same corpus, but annotated with gradually more fine-grained annotation schemes, that is, with gradually more arc labels in the tagset. Our approach differs from (Bosco and Lavelli, 2010) in that we only retain functional syntax for the design of our tagsets. The background of our research is that standard annotation schemes such as the scheme underlying the dependency conversion from the Penn Treebank.[1] tend to be minimal in order to facilitate the process of annotation and to improve the readability of the resulting annotation.[2] This tendency is reinforced by the general assumption that the less fine-grained the annotation, the better the parser performance. However, this has a major drawback, namely that the parsed structure is often too poor to serve well, e.g., semantic role labeling, deep summarization, content extraction, word sense disambiguation, etc.

To the best of our knowledge, no study actually compares the performance of a dependency parser trained on annotations of varying syntactic granularity, so there are no figures that would demonstrate that it is worth to sacrifice grammatical accuracy and detail for the sake of an acceptable parser accuracy. We carried out such a study on Spanish material. We developed a hierarchical syntactic dependency annotation scheme that allows us to expand and contract syntactic relation branches into larger, more fine-grained, or smaller, more coarse-grained, annotation schemes. The results of parsing experiments demonstrate that it is possible to reach a good balance between the accuracy of a parser and the richness of the linguistic annotation. They also show that the principles that we applied when designing the hierarchical annotation schema are valid and may be used for the design of other annotation schemes in the future.

2 Hierarchical syntactic annotation scheme

The hierarchical annotation scheme in Table 1 has been developed for Spanish on a small corpus of 3513 sentences (100892 words, see (Mille et al., 2009); corpus available at UPF-TALN webpage), which constitutes a section of the Spanish corpus AnCora (Taulé et al., 2008). The general idea underlying this scheme is to apply only syntactic (rather than also semantic) criteria in order to identify each grammatical tag that is to be introduced into the scheme. Using more or less fine-grained criteria allows us to control the level of granularity of the tagset. We do not orientate our scheme towards any particular linguistic theory; the selected criteria are dictated by syntactic behaviour observed in the language in question (in our case, Spanish). For instance, for dependents of verbs, we need to capture whether they can be cliticized, promoted

[1]The dependency annotation scheme of the Penn Treebank has served as blueprint for annotation schemes of a series of treebanks in different languages and is thus a *de facto* standard. See (Marcus et al., 1993) for the original consituency annotation, and (Johansson and Nugues, 2007) for the conversion to one-word-per-line dependency representations.

[2]"Minimal" refers here not only to the number of tags, but also to the level of precision of the syntactic tags. Indeed, many corpora mix several levels of representation (e.g., syntax, semantics, lexicon, etc.) such that the number of syntactic relations does not necessarily reflect the level of idiosyncracy of the annotation.

or demoted, etc. For any kind of dependent, we need to capture the canonical order with respect to its governor, the part-of-speech of the governor, the part-of-speech of the prototypical element that appears in that paradigm, the existence or absence of some agreement between the prototypical dependent and another element of the sentence, the presence/absence and type of required features of the dependent (e.g., governed preposition, imposed finiteness or case, etc.), the possibility to remove a dependent or not without hampering sentence grammaticality, etc.; see (Burga et al., 2011) for examples and details.

The leftmost column in Table 1 represents the most detailed (and thus linguistically richest) tagset of 60 syntactic relations (henceforth *SyntRels*) we defined for Spanish: the distinction between one relation and another is, in general, very fine-grained. For instance, there are three types of oblique objects (*obl-obj1/2/3*), differentiated only by their default order of appearance in a neutral sentence; *noun-compl* is reserved for constructions in which the object cannot move to the left of its governor. The tags in this detailed tagset can be summarized under more generic tags, which would lead to a more coarse-grained, smaller tagset. The obtained more coarse-grained tagset can again be contracted, and so on. In Table 1, we illustrate this procedure for four tagsets in total. The brackets indicate which relations at one level were grouped together under the same label at the following level. Thus, in the second column (44 SyntRels), we group under the label *obl-obj* any non-agentive prepositional object which cannot be pronominalized, bringing together *obl-obj1/2/3* and *noun-compl*. In the third column (31 SyntRels), *obl-obj* and *agent* are fused into one relation *obl-obj*, defined as "prepositional object which cannot be pronominalized". Finally, in the last column (15 SyntRels), one tag *OOBJ* gathers any object which cannot be pronominalized, as opposed to *IOBJ* and *DOBJ*, which can be replaced by a dative and an accusative pronoun, respectively.

3 Experiments

3.1 Background

A number of experiments on different granularities of annotation and their impact on the performance of probabilistic parsers are known from the literature; see in particular Klein and Manning (2003) and Petrov et al. (2006), who show the benefits of splitting generic part-of-speech tags (e.g., NP, VP, etc.) into more precise subcategories for the derivation of accurate probabilistic context-free grammars (PCFG). Our proposal differs from these works in that they focus on constituency parsing and part-of-speech tags, whereas we tackle dependency parsing and edge labels.[3] But more importantly, the goals are different. Thus, they target the improvement of parsing accuracy, and for that they infer, with simple rules, from the training data (categorial) information which is more specific than what is directly available. Closer to our work, Bosco and Lavelli (2010) use an Italian corpus in which the dependency relations encode information on morphology, functional syntax and semantics. They discuss the influence of the annotation policies on the evaluation of the parsers and show that the precision and recall of hard-to-parse relations can be quite different, depending on the tag granularity in the annotation, that is, if the annotation contains or not morphological and/or semantic information. In contrast, our goal is to provide evidence that the creation of annotations that capture significant fine-grained distinctive features of the grammar (and only the grammar) of a language does not need to harm significantly the performance of the parsers. Consider as two

[3]Some other works present a hierarchical organization of grammatical relations (in particular (Bosco et al., 2000), (Briscoe et al., 2002), and (Marneffe et al., 2006)), but those hierarchies are not used to test the impact of the tagset granularity on the results of a parser.

such fine-grained distinctive features the relations *modal* and *direct-object* in the following two sentences. As indicated, only the direct object can be pronominalized by a clitic pronoun and moved before the governing verb, without that a pro-verb is needed: *Juan puede*-modal→ *venir mañana*, lit. 'John might come tomorrow' (*Juan lo puede *(hacer)*), and *Juan puede*-dobj→ *venir mañana*, lit. 'John is able to come tomorrow' (*Juan lo puede (hacer)*). If the annotation of the relations does not encode these phenomena, they are, in fact, lost.[4] Since this information is of primary relevance to applications related to natural language understanding, it would be an advantage to include it in the syntactic annotation. In the next sections, we show that its inclusion does not harm a parser's accuracy.

3.2 Setup of the experiments

In our experiments, we used the four tagsets introduced in Section 2. The annotation of the corpus with the most detailed tagset of 60 SyntRels has been obtained from the original annotation in AnCora (Taulé et al., 2008), which has been adapted, revised and enriched manually. Starting from the most fine-grained annotation, we derived automatically the other three, ending up with four different treebanks for the same corpus. Four reference parsers have been used. Three of them are the top three parsers for Spanish in the CoNLL Shared Task 2009 (Hajič et al., 2009): Che's (Che et al., 2009), henceforth *Che*, Merlo's (Gesmundo et al., 2009), henceforth *Merlo*, and Bohnet's (Bohnet, 2009), henceforth *Bohnet*. The fourth, the Malt Parser (Nivre et al., 2007), henceforth *Malt*, has been chosen because it is a very broadly used syntactic dependency parser. Malt and Merlo are transition based, while Bohnet and Che are graph based. In our experiments, all of them processed non-projective dependency trees. Each parser contains its own configuration options, which depend on the parsing approach, the learning techniques, etc. Therefore, it was not possible to apply the same setup to all parsers. Instead, we used for each parser its own default configuration, which does not guarantee an optimal performance. However, as the goal of this paper is not to compare the results of the parsers, but rather the performance of the same parser with different tagsets, optimized configurations are not needed for our purpose.

To train the parsers, the corpus has been divided randomly into a training set (3200 sentences) and a test set (313 sentences).[5] Each parser has been trained on each of the four annotations of the training set. The obtained sixteen parsing models were applied to the corresponding test sets. Also, in order to see whether or not the performance improved with respect to the smallest tagset when training with more fine-grained tagsets, we mapped the output of each parser onto the smallest tagset. The training and the test sets were the same as in the first experiment.

3.3 Results

For Malt, the assessment of the *Labelled Attachment Score* (LAS) (that is, the proportion of edges with correct governor and dependent and the right label on the edge) was carried out using the evaluation toolkit provided with the parser. For the other parsers, we used the official CoNLL'06 evaluation toolkit. The LAS figures for each parser and for each version of the annotation are

[4]One can always imagine some statistical "disambiguation" based on the context in which the construction is used, but the amount of data needed could be prohibitive—at least for Spanish—and eventually, the only way would probably be to imply human experts for the revision of the annotation.

[5]Bohnet's parser uses CoNLL'09 14-column format, while the other three need to be trained on the CoNLL'06 10-column format (Buchholz and Marsi, 2006), but the available information is exactly the same, whatever the format: word positions, word forms, PoS, lemmas, (all of which kept the same in our experiments), and dependencies.

shown in Table 2. The graphic on the right of Table 2 shows how each parser reacts to and how its performance varies with the increasing number of relations in the tagset. We can observe that all four parsers behave similarly: their accuracy is very constant from 15 to 44 SyntRels, and decreases with 60 SyntRels. We also notice that there is a significant difference between Bohnet, Merlo and Malt's LAS progressions (which are rather parallel) and the progression of Che, which drops when trained with 60 relations (see Section 4). As expected, all parsers reach the highest accuracy with the smallest tagset (15 SyntRels). But surprisingly, the LAS decreases only little with twice as many SyntRels in the tagset (namely 31 SyntRels): 0.1 for Malt, 0.41 for Bohnet, 0.44 for Che, and 0.47 for Merlo. Even more surprisingly, the drop is also rather small between 31 and 44 SyntRels (0.2 for Malt, 0.17 for Bohnet, 0.43 for Che). Merlo even gets better with 44 SyntRels, obtaining a LAS of 84.53%, comparable to that with 15 SyntRels and higher than that with 31 SyntRels. As a result, the decrease of performance from 15 to 44 tags in the tagset is surprisingly small for Malt, Bohnet and Che: 0.3 points for Malt, 0.6 points for Bohnet, 0.9 points for Che, and no decrease at all for Merlo. However, Bohnet, Malt and Merlo see their LAS drop significantly by around 2 points when trained with 60 SyntRels. Che drops by even more than 2 points. The in depth analysis of the behaviour of the parsers with respect to the groups of relations is presented in Section 4.

We also calculated the *UnLabelled Attachment* (ULA) score for all four parsers (see Table 3). For a reason beyond our control, we could not get the ULA for Merlo with 15 relations (however, even if incomplete, the ULA figures for Merlo are useful from the perspective of one of our experiments described below). For Bohnet, we observe that the ULA scores slightly but steadily increase in the range from 15 SyntRels (90.27%) to 60 SyntRels (90.49%). Opposite to this tendency, the scores for Che slightly decrease in the range from 15 SyntRels (90.6%) to 44 SyntRels (90.37%), and drop then with 60 SyntRels (86.28%). Malt is as stable as Bohnet, but does not show a regular improvement when dealing with higher numbers of tags. Note that the observed slight variation of the performance numbers of the different parsers across tagsets of varying sizes (always lower than 0.25 points, except Che with 60 relations) could be due to the small size of our training and test sets. In other words, it is possible that with more data, the parsers would give quite stable unlabeled attachment scores across tagsets of varying sizes.

In order to verify the effects of training a parser on a fine-grained tagset and using it then to parse with a coarse annotation, we took the test sets parsed with the models trained on 31, 44, and 60 relations, and mapped them to the coarse-grained tagset (15 different tags), following the hierarchy presented in Table 1. Then, we ran the evaluation of the resulting output against the gold standard of the 15-tag annotation; the results are presented in Table 4. In the first column, the figures obtained with the original 15-tag annotated test set for each parser are repeated in order to facilitate the comparison. Table 4 shows that there does not seem to be a benefit in annotating with fine-grained arc labels if one wants a coarse annotation. The only case in which a fine-grained annotation makes the parser improve significantly with 15 SyntRels (0.4 points) is the 44 SyntRel annotation for Merlo. Table 4 is actually very similar to Table 3, which contains the unlabeled attachment scores: all the figures for each parser are quite similar, with two exceptions: the fall of Che trained with 60 SyntRels, and a peak for Merlo trained with 44 relations. The correlation between ULA and LAS is obvious, but unfortunately, we cannnot explain so far those two deviations of ULA.

4 Evaluation of selected parsers with respect to specific SyntRels

In the previous section, we saw that the figures of all four parsers drop when trained on the most fine-grained tagset. In this section, we try to identify which relations particularly affect the performance of the parsers and thus obtain information on how the composition of the tagset has an impact on the figures of the evaluation.[6]

4.1 Impact of distinctive properties of SyntRels

Due to the relatively small amount of data we have at hand[7], there are only 8025 relation instances in the test set[8]. Some relations do not appear in it at all: *prolep, adv-mod, copul-clitic, num-junct* and *aux-refl-indir*. On the other side, it is not possible to generalize along the lines that the less a relation appears in the training set, the worse the performance of the parser on this relation is. Some relations (*compl-adnom, analyt-fut, analyt-progr, analyt-perf, compar, compar-conj,* and *compl1*) are scarce in the training set (<200 instances) and in the test set (<20 instances) and, in spite of this, they are parsed with a high accuracy (78%–100%) at least by one of the parsers.

Interestingly, as opposed to the example about objects and modals in Section 3, either the governor or the dependent (or both) of these relations have very distinctive features:

- *compl-adnom* implies a determiner followed by a preposition; cf. *la*-compl-adnom→*del sombrero azul*, lit. 'the of-the hat blue', 'that one with the blue hat';
- *analyt-fut, analyt-progr* and *analyt-perf* always presuppose the same auxiliary as governor and a governed preposition or a non-finite verb as dependent; cf. *voy*-analyt-fut→*a cocinar*, lit. 'I-will [to] cook'; *estoy*-analyt-progr→*cocinando*, lit. 'I-am cooking'; *fue*-analyt-pass→*cocinado*, lit. 'I-was cooked';
- *compar* and *compar-conj* require a comparative adjective governing a fixed conjunction, itself governing another element (*compar-conj*); cf. *mejor*-compar→*que*-compar-conj→*Juan*, lit. 'better than John';
- *compl1* requires an adjective on the right of a non-copular verb which undergoes agreement with the subject; cf. *la frase resulta*-compl1→*buena*, lit. 'the sentence$_{FEM.SG}$ ends up correct$_{FEM.SG}$.

There are also some relations that are not parsed well by either of the parsers, even if the number of their instances in the training and test sets is significant (see Table 5). There are two main explanations of the poor figures for the SyntRels in Table 5. First, the morpho-syntactic features of such relations (e.g., PoS of the head, PoS of the dependent) can vary a lot throughout the corpus: an adverbial or an adjunctive can be an adverb, a common noun, a non-finite verb, a prepositional group, etc. An appositive is usually a common or a proper noun, sometimes introduced by a preposition; an attributive can be a prepositional group or a gerund. Second, these relations also tend to share their basic syntactic configuration with other SyntRels; consider, e.g., *casa*-attr→*de Barcelona*, lit. 'house from Barcelona' vs. *hermano*-obl-obj1→*de*

[6]The problematic SyntRels were the same for all four parsers. Due to space restrictions, we chose to focus on the two graph-based parsers, since the graph-based approach becomes increasingly popular in parsing research.

[7]Still, we believe that our results are already quite reliable since the average accuracies (without tuning the parsers) get close to the accuracies obtained by the same parsers at the Shared Task 2009 with much larger data sets (http://ufal.mff.cuni.cz/conll2009-st/results/results.php).

[8]The dependencies to punctuation signs were not considered in the figures of the evaluation because they are parsed with the same (very high) accuracy whatever the tagset; considering them would boost the parser figures by 0.5% but it would not bring anything to our experiment.

	Training Set (instances)	Test Set (instances)	Bohnet (%)	Che (%)
adjunct	830	87	37.93	31.03
adv	5751	549	62.3	56.83
appos	1060	100	54	34
attr	2165	213	37.56	41
obl-obj1	3551	384	50.78	26.82

Table 5: Poorly parsed frequent SyntRels

Juan 'John's brother'. Thus, even if the two syntactic constructions seem to be the same (the governor is a noun, the dependent is a preposition, and the dependent of it is a proper noun), only the attributive dependent can be replaced by an adverb, and only the oblique objective is introduced by a preposition which cannot be changed (i.e., a governed preposition; in this case, *de* 'of'). As far as the SyntRels in Table 5 are concerned, an appositive (and even an adverbial in some cases) can also be confused with them: *nebulosa*-appos→*de Orion*, lit. 'nebula of Orion'. The other SyntRels that share the same N-Prep-N configuration are: *abs-pred*, *obl-obj2*, *obl-obj3*, and *noun-compl*; all of these SyntRels obtain poor scores in the evaluation of both parsers. Similarly, the only difference between adverbials and adjunctives is that adjunctives operate at a sentential level while the scope of adverbials is restricted to their governor: [*por ejemplo*]←adjunct-,-*funciona*-,-adv→ *con una silla*, lit. 'for instance, it-works, with a chair'. The two dependents of the verb are prepositional groups that could be found in any position of the sentence; in other words, there is no superficial clue that would differentiate one from the other.

This general absence of clear distinctive features for each particular SyntRel makes it hard for the parsers to find patterns in their learning phases. Grouping the SyntRels with similar configurations is the main factor that makes the parsers improve. In the next subsection, we give more details about the groupings made in the 60 label tagset.

4.2 Detailed analysis of the evaluations results

In this subsection, we take a close look at the SyntRels which trigger the decrease of performance of the parsers between the tagsets containing 44 and 60 labels, respectively. In order to make an adequate comparison of the tagsets, we calculate the weighted average (*WA* in Table 6) of the grouped relations and compare it with the score of the corresponding single edge label in the smaller tagset. We focus on the comparison between those two tagsets, given that the LAS variation of the parsers trained on them is higher than when trained on any other pair of tagsets. Table 6 does not show the results for the relations that have a one-to-one correspondence in both tagsets: *abs-pred*, *det*, *quant*, *compl-adnom*, *appos*, etc. This is because we observed that these relations show the same figures, or their figures only slightly improve or decrease from one tagset to another. In the end, these relations as a whole have almost no impact on the difference between the results obtained with the two tagsets. Instead, the two tables show the relations from the 60 relation tagset which are grouped together in the 44 relation tagset. Among them, only one grouping (*copred* for both parsers) does not lead to a better performance of the parser (16.67%, against 18.75% in average when separated into *obj-* and *subj-copred* for Bohnet, and 16.67% in both configurations for Che). The low number of occurrences of the relations grouped in *copred*, 25 in total, does not allow for a more profound analysis.

For all other relations in the 60 relation tagset, the weighted average in Bohnet and Che is significantly lower than the score of their corresponding group label in the 44 relation tagset:

SyntRels (60)	train #	test #	$LAS_{Boh/Che}$ (%)	$WA_{Boh/Che}$ (%)	SyntRels (44)	$LAS_{Boh/Che}$ (%)
iobj1	46	7	0/0			
iobj2	195	13	30.77/15.38	19.05/5.13	iobj	28.57/57.14
iobj3	1	1	0/0			
iobj-clitic1	81	5	20/40			
iobj-clitic2	262	21	76.19/61.9	62.96/55.55	iobj-clitic	81.48/77.78
iobj-clitic3	5	1	0/0			
obl-obj1	3551	384	50.78/26.82			
obl-obj2	662	62	20.97/8.06	52.24/26.58	obl-obj	71.1/73.57
obl-obj3	17	2	50/0			
noun-compl	1912	199	64.82/32.16			
compl1	141	9	66.67/77.78	50/45	compl	70/65
compl2	121	11	36.36/18.18			
aux-refl-pass	405	43	62.79/62.79			
aux-refl-lex	625	69	84.06/42.03	72.27/49.64	aux-refl	92.44/91.6
aux-refl-dir	102	7	14.29/42.86			
adjunct	830	87	37.93/31.03			
adv	5751	549	62.3/56.83	65.91/59.51	adv	69.64/67.71
restr	1913	194	88.66/79.9			
obj-copred	36	3	0/66.67	18.75/16.67	copred	16.67/16.67
subj-copred	76	9	25/0			

Table 6: Comparison between 60 and 44 SyntRels for Bohnet's and Che's parser

- *iobj1*, *iobj2*, and *iobj3* give an average weighted LAS of 19.05% and 5.13% for the two parsers, whereas when they are grouped under one single label *iobj*, the LAS reaches 28.57% and 57.14%; in other words, the LAS drops 9.52 and 52.01 points respectively when training with the most fine-grained relations relations.
- The weighted average of *iobj-clitic1*, *iobj-clitic2*, and *iobj-clitic3* is 18.52 / 22.23 points lower than when those labels are grouped under the generic label *iobj-clitic*.
- The weighted average of *obl-obj1*, *obl-obj2*, *obl-obj3* and *noun-compl* is 18.86 / 46.99 points lower than when they are grouped under the label *obl-obj*. There are 647 instances of this relation in our test set, which means more than 8% of the total number of edges. This subset of SyntRels is largely responsible for the bigger drop of Che when trained with 60 relations.
- For *compl1* and *compl2*, the drop is also important compared to when they are grouped under *compl*: exactly 20 points for both parsers;
- The different types of reflexive auxiliaries that appear in the test set (passive, lexical, and direct) also work much better as one single label *aux-refl*: when they are separated, the LAS drops 20.17 and 41.96 points.
- Finally, for the other very important group by the number of instances in the test set (more than 10% of the edges), the comparison is similar, even if the amplitude is more reduced: *adjunct*, *adv* and *restr* see their LAS 3.73 and 8.2 points inferior to the LAS of the generic label *adv*, which includes them all in the 44 label tagset. Here too the drop is more important for Che than for Bohnet and largely accounts for the global LAS as seen in Table 2.

The performance drop of the 60 relation tagset when compared to the 44 relation tagset could, actually, be expected since some relations of the 60-tagset not only have superficially identical configurations (see Section 4.1), but the properties that differentiate them are closely related to semantics: the different kinds of oblique objects, completives, or reflexive auxiliaries actually behave among each other extremely similarly at the syntactic level, but reflect very distinct semantic realities. In fact, the number appended to the oblique object relation label not only stands for the order by default in a neutral sentence (with all the objects being present), but it also directly correlates with the slot in the valency pattern of the governor occupied by the corresponding dependent.[9] Although there is a relation between the default order of the objects and their (semantic) numbering, when several oblique objects of the same verb are used at the same time, there usually are information structure features that constrain their order. As a result, the objects are never instantiated in the same order, and the parser has almost no clue for guessing to which slot to assign an object.

From the bird's eye view of the composition of SyntRel-tagsets, it seems that grouping together SyntRels based on their syntactic properties helps the parsers. But not all relation groupings turn out to be beneficiary for the performance of the parsers. Consider the relations that connect two parallel clauses related by a coordination conjunction: *juxtapos*, *quasi-coord* and *coord*. In the 60 and 44 label tagsets, those three SyntRels are kept separated, and the average weighted LAS is 71.5% and 72.58% for Bohnet, and 61.85% and 68.63% for Che respectively. When *juxtapos* and *quasi-coord* are grouped in the 31 label tagset, Bohnet drops by more than 2 points to 70.31%, while Che slightly rises to 69.33%. However, when *coord* is also grouped with the other two under the label *COORD*, both parsers have more difficulties: Bohnet drops by one point and Che by more than six points. We believe that with these three SyntRels, the syntactic constructions at stake are too different for the parsers to be able to find strong common features: a juxtaposition involves a punctuation sign (colon or semi-colon), while a coordination involves a conjunction or a comma, and a quasi-coordination nothing but the two coordinated elements (e.g.*¡Estoy aquí*-,-quasi-coord→ *en mi cuarto!*, lit. 'I'm here, in my room!'). Therefore, we believe that even if it is tempting to annotate with a same label any coordinate structure, it is better to keep the different types annotated with different labels.

5 Conclusions

The evaluation of the performance of four state-of-the-art parsers trained on a corpus that was annotated following schemes of different granularity revealed that the loss of accuracy as a consequence of the increase of the size of the tagset, in particular, from 15 to 44 tags, is surprisingly small. This outcome supports the claim that an annotation with more fine-grained syntactic relations does not necessarily imply a significant loss in accuracy. It also supports the argumentation that it is useful to compile a detailed annotation scheme, which then allows for the derivation of a variety of more or less detailed annotations. Our study also suggests that there seems to be a limit with respect to the degree of detail of the tagset beyond which a parser's accuracy suffers significantly, and that there are some tags which provoke a drop of the LAS more than others. These are, in particular, the very fine-grained divisions which directly reflect semantic valency information. Another conclusion that can be drawn is that training a parser on a fine-grained annotation does not lead to a better performance of this parser when parsing with a coarse-grained tagset. However, it still remains unclear whether the unlabeled attachment score can improve when training on a fine-grained annotation. Experiments with more data would be necessary in order to draw more solid conclusions.

Acknowledgments

We would like to thank B. Bohnet and the anonymous reviewers for their very helpful comments.

[9] This goes along the lines of Bosco et al. (2010), who mention that semantic distinctions are problematic in their experiments, and that merging locative and temporal complements under the same label, for example, increases the f-scores of the parsers.

References

Bohnet, B. (2009). Efficient Parsing of Syntactic and Semantic Dependency Structures. In *Proceedings of CoNLL '09*, pages 67–72, Boulder, Colorado, USA.

Bosco, C. and Lavelli, A. (2010). Annotation Schema Oriented Evaluation for Parsing Validation. In *Proceedings of TLT-9*, pages 19–30, Tartu, Estonia.

Bosco, C., Lombardo, V., Vassallo, D., and Lesmo, L. (2000). Building a Treebank for Italian: a Data-Driven Annotation Schema. In *Proceedings of LREC '00*, pages 99–105, Athens, Greece.

Bosco, C., Montemagni, S., Mazzei, A., Lombardo, V., Dell'Orletta, F., Lenci, A., Lesmo, L., Attardi, G., Simi, M., Lavelli, A., Hall, J., Nilsson, J., and Nivre, J. (2010). Comparing the Influence of Different Treebank Annotations on Dependency Parsing. In *Proceedings of LREC '10*, pages 1794–1801, Valletta, Malta.

Briscoe, T., Carroll, J., Graham, J., and Copestake, A. (2002). Relational Evaluation Schemes. In *Proceedings of the Workshop at LREC '02 on Beyond PARSEVAL: Towards Improved Evaluation Measures for Parsing Systems*, pages 4–6, Gran Canaria, Spain.

Buchholz, S. and Marsi, E. (2006). CoNLL-X Shared Task on Multilingual Dependency Parsing. In *Proceedings of CoNLL '06*, pages 149–164, New York City, USA.

Burga, A., Mille, S., and Wanner, L. (2011). Looking Behind the Scenes of Syntactic Dependency Corpus Annotation: Towards a Motivated Annotation Schema of Surface-Syntax in Spanish. In *Proceedings of DepLing '11*, pages 104–114, Barcelona, Spain.

Che, W., Li, Z., Li, Y., Guo, Y., Qin, B., and Liu, T. (2009). Multilingual Dependency-based Syntactic and Semantic Parsing. In *Proceedings of CoNLL '09: Shared Task*, pages 49–54, Boulder, Colorado, USA.

Gesmundo, A., Henderson, J., Merlo, P., and Titov, I. (2009). A Latent Variable Model of Synchronous Syntactic-Semantic Parsing for Multiple Languages. In *Proceedings of CoNLL '09: Shared Task*, pages 37–42, Boulder, Colorado, USA.

Hajič, J., Ciaramita, M., Johansson, R., Kawahara, D., Martí, M. A., Màrquez, L., Meyers, A., Nivre, J., Padó, S., Štěpánek, J., Straňák, P., Surdeanu, M., Xue, N., and Zhang, Y. (2009). The CoNLL-2009 Shared Task: Syntactic and Semantic Dependencies in Multiple Languages. In *Proceedings of CoNLL '09: Shared Task*, pages 1–18, Boulder, Colorado, USA.

Johansson, R. and Nugues, P. (2007). Extended Constituent-to-dependency Conversion for English. In *Proceedings of NODALIDA '07*, pages 105–112, Tartu, Estonia.

Klein, D. and Manning, C. D. (2003). Accurate Unlexicalized Parsing. In *Proceedings of ACL '03*, volume 1, pages 423–430, Sapporo, Japan.

Kübler, S. (2005). How Do Treebank Annotation Schemes Influence Parsing Results? Or How Not to Compare Apples And Oranges. In *Proceedings of RANLP '05*, pages 293–300, Borovets, Bulgaria.

Marcus, M. P., Santorini, B., and Marcinkiewicz, M. A. (1993). Building a Large Annotated Corpus of English: The Penn Treebank. *Computational Linguistics*, 19(2):313–330.

Marneffe, M.-C. D., MacCartney, B., and Manning, C. D. (2006). Generating Typed Dependency Parses from Phrase Structure Parses. In *Proceedings of LREC '06*, pages 449–454, Genoa, Italy.

Mille, S., Burga, A., Vidal, V., and Wanner, L. (2009). Towards a Rich Dependency Annotation of Spanish Corpora. In *Proceedings of SEPLN '09*, pages 325–333, San Sebastian, Spain.

Nivre, J., Hall, J., Nilsson, J., Chanev, A., Eryiğit, G., Kübler, S., Marinov, S., and Marsi, E. (2007). MaltParser: A Language-Independent System for Data-Driven Dependency Parsing. *Natural Language Engineering Journal*, 13(2):99–135.

Petrov, S., Barrett, L., Thibaux, R., and Klein, D. (2006). Learning Accurate, Compact, and Interpretable Tree Annotation. In *Proceedings of COLING/ACL '06*, pages 433–440, Sydney, Australia.

Rehbein, I. and van Genabith, J. (2007). Treebank Annotation Schemes and Parser Evaluation for German. In *Proceedings of EMNLP-CoNLL '07*, pages 630–639, Prague, Czeck Republic.

Taulé, M., Martí, M. A., and Recasens, M. (2008). AnCora: Multilevel Annotated Corpora for Catalan and Spanish. In *Proceedings of the LREC '08*, pages 96–101, Marrakesh, Morroco.

Does Tectogrammatics Help the Annotation of Discourse?

Jiří Mírovský, Pavlína Jínová and Lucie Poláková
Charles University in Prague
Institute of Formal and Applied Linguistics

{mirovsky|jinova|polakova}@ufal.mff.cuni.cz

Abstract

In the following paper, we discuss and evaluate the benefits that deep syntactic trees (tectogrammatics) and all the rich annotation of the Prague Dependency Treebank bring to the process of annotating the discourse structure, i.e. discourse relations, connectives and their arguments. The decision to annotate discourse structure directly on the trees contrasts with the majority of similarly aimed projects, usually based on the annotation of linear texts. Our basic assumption is that some syntactic features of a sentence analysis correspond to certain discourse-level features. Hence, we use some properties of the dependency-based large-scale treebank of Czech to help establish an independent annotation layer of discourse. The question that we answer in the paper is how much did we gain by employing this approach.

Title and abstract in Czech

Pomáhá tektogramatika při anotaci diskurzních vztahů?

Abstrakt

V tomto příspěvku hodnotíme přínos, který představují syntacticko-sémantické stromy (tektogramatická rovina anotace) a celá bohatá anotace Pražského závislostního korpusu pro anotaci diskurzní struktury textu, tedy pro anotaci diskurzních vztahů, jejich konektorů a argumentů. Rozhodnutím anotovat diskurzní strukturu přímo na stromech se náš přístup liší od většiny podobně zaměřených projektů, které jsou obvykle založeny na anotaci lineárního textu. Naším základním předpokladem je, že některé syntaktické rysy větné analýzy odpovídají jistým rysům z roviny diskurzní struktury. Proto využíváme některé vlastnosti rozsáhlého závislostního korpusu češtiny k ustanovení nezávislé diskurzní anotační vrstvy. V tomto příspěvku odpovídáme na otázku, jaké výhody tento přístup přináší.

Keywords : Tectogrammatics, PDT, Discourse annotation

Keywords in Czech: Tektogramatika, PDT, Diskurzní anotace

Proceedings of COLING 2012: Posters, pages 853–862,
COLING 2012, Mumbai, December 2012.

1 Introduction

In recent years, there has been an increasing interest in studying linguistic phenomena going beyond the sentence boundary. Corpora of different languages conveying discourse-relevant annotation start to appear, e.g. RST Discourse Treebank (Carlson, Marcu and Okurowski, 2002), Penn Discourse Treebank (Prasad et al., 2008) – both for English, Hindi Discourse Relation Bank (Oza et al., 2009), Potsdam Commentary Corpus for German (Stede, 2004) etc. They usually have raw written documents as the annotation basis and the authors use and adjust for their purposes some of the well known discourse methodologies. In the discourse project for Czech, on the contrary to the majority, syntactic (tectogrammatical) trees have been used as the basis for the discourse annotation. Thus, the project makes use of the theoretical framework of the functional generative description (Sgall, Panevová and Hajičová, 1986), which gave rise to the dependency treebanking in Prague. The main goal of this paper is to report in detail on exploitations we were able to make of the syntactic annotation to establish an independent level of the discourse annotation. Annotation of the discourse structure here is understood as analyzing semantic relations between discourse units, in this phase of the project exclusively relations signalled by a specific discourse connective (henceforth DC). Some of the (not only) syntactic features were very helpful and enabled us to perform automatic extractions and conversions. The tectogrammatical layer of the Prague Dependency Treebank 2.0 (henceforth PDT, Hajič et al., 2006) provided most of the information we used, in less extent we used some features from the analytical layer and also the annotation of coreference.

1.1 Layers of Annotation in PDT

The data in our project come from the Prague Dependency Treebank 2.0, which is a manually annotated treebank of Czech journalistic texts, consisting of almost 50 thousand sentences. It is already provided with several layers of manual annotation: the morphological layer (where each token from the sentence gets a lemma and a morphological tag), the analytical layer (surface syntax in the form of a dependency tree, where each node corresponds to a token in the sentence), and the tectogrammatical layer (henceforth TR; underlying syntax and semantics, also in the form of a dependency tree). There is also a separate layer of manually annotated coreference and bridging anaphora (Nedoluzhko et al., 2011b), published as an extension to PDT.

1.2 Discourse Annotation in Two Steps

In our project so far, we have focused on discourse relations anchored by an explicit (surface-present) discourse connective. These relations and their connectives have been annotated throughout the whole treebank. However, all numbers reported in the paper refer to the training and development test parts of the whole data, i.e. 43,955 sentences (approx. 9/10 of the treebank).[1]

The annotation of discourse relations proceeded in two major steps. The first phase of the annotation was a thorough manual processing of the treebank focused on the inter-sentential relations (relations between sentences) signalled by explicit discourse connectives. Intra-sentential relations were only marked manually in cases where the TR did not provide enough or correct information for the subsequent automatic extraction of discourse relations. Other cases of intra-sentential relations, where the tectogrammatical annotation was adequate for the discourse interpretation, were left to the second phase.

The second phase of the annotation consisted predominantly of an automatic procedure that extracted mostly tectogrammatical features and used them directly for the annotation of the intra-sentential discourse relations. A detailed description of the second phase can be found in Jínová, Mírovský and Poláková (2012b).

The main theoretical principle of the annotation was naturally the same for both the phases. It has been inspired partially by the lexical approach of the Penn Discourse Treebank project (Prasad et al., 2008), and partially by the already mentioned tectogrammatical approach and the functional generative description (Sgall, Panevová and Hajičová, 1986, Mikulová et al., 2005). A discourse connective in this view takes two discourse arguments (verbal clauses) as its arguments. The semantic relation between the arguments is represented by a discourse arrow (link), the direction of which also uniformly defines the nature of the argument (e.g. *reason - result*).[2] However, the annotation itself proceeded in each of the phases differently. During the manual annotation (phase 1), the annotators first searched for possible discourse connectives in the texts and then assigned relations, arguments, connectives and discourse types to the tree structures. In the automated annotation (phase 2), the relations and their discourse types were identified and annotated first (mostly automatically), then we searched for their connectives (also mostly automatically).

[1] Thus the last tenth of the treebank, evaluation test data, remains (as far as possible) unobserved.
[2] For further information on the annotation guidelines, see the annotation manual (Poláková et al., 2012) or http://ufal.mff.cuni.cz/discourse/

Type of the relation	number
Intra-sentential relations	**12,673**
- automatic vertical	3,090 (2,599+491)
- automatic horizontal	7,392
- manual vertical	510
- manual horizontal	1,681
Inter-sentential (all manual)	**5,514**
Total	**18,187**

TABLE 1 – Overview of discourse relations annotated in PDT

Table 1 shows the summary of all relations annotated during both phases. The intra-sentential relations are divided into two categories – vertical and horizontal. Vertical relations correspond to dependency relations, horizontal relations correspond to coordinations. Also the number of inter-sentential relations (relations between sentences) and the total number of all relations are presented.[3]

2 Intra-sentential Relations

In this Section, we focus on the annotation of the intra-sentential discourse relations (mostly phase 2) and discuss and evaluate features that helped automatize the annotation. All topics are discussed only briefly here, a detailed analyses is given in Jínová, Mírovský and Poláková (2012b).

Concerning the intra-sentential relations, i.e. the syntax-based ones, we were able to automatically convert 10,482 (3,090 vertical and 7,392 horizontal) tectogrammatical relations to discourse relations. However, for 491 of them, the discourse type had to be set manually, as explained below (second number in the parenthesis in the second row of Table 1). Mostly during the first phase of the annotation, 2,191 (510 vertical and 1,681 horizontal) intra-sentential discourse relations were annotated completely manually.

2.1 Discourse Types

An ideal case for the automatic treatment was a tectogrammatical relation with an exact semantic counterpart on the level of discourse analysis, e.g. *reason-result* (signaled by functors REAS, CSQ, CAUS), *concession* (CNCS),

[3] Let us emphasize again: all numbers refer to the training and development test parts of the data (9/10 of the treebank, 43,955 sentences).

conjunction (CONJ) (all automatic horizontal relations and 2,599 completely automatic vertical relations). Because of rich variety of connectives, some manual work preceded in case of temporal relations (491 relations).

2.2 Detection of Discourse Connectives

In most cases, the discourse connectives of intra-sentential discourse relations could be automatically detected on the basis of the information on the tectogrammatical and analytical layers. With the exception of 31 atypical cases (which were fixed manually), discourse connectives could be detected automatically for all 10,482 intra-sentential discourse relations.

2.2.1 Grammatical Coreference and Expression *což*

Pronoun-like expression *což*[4] (roughly *which* in English) represents an intra-sentential connective with the conjunction meaning and is, at the same time, inflected and plays a role of a participant of the clause structure. To make it possible to associate this connective with the discourse relation automatically, the grammatical coreference[5] had to be used. The deictic part of the expression *což* can refer both to a verbal phrase (*the war unites us* in Example 1), and to a nominal phrase (*a love to war* in Example 2). However, it functions as a DC only when it refers to a verbal phrase (Example 1).

(1) *Válka nás sjednocuje, což pro nás není přirozené.*
The war unites us, which is not natural for us.

(2) *Cítil jsem z nich lásku k válce, což je něco proti přírodě.*
I felt from them a love to war, which is something against nature.

There are a total of 355 occurrences of the expression *což* in our data, 220 occurrences have a grammatical coreference link to a finite-verb node, 11 occurrences have this link to a coordination of finite-verb nodes. Therefore, thanks to the grammatical coreference, it was possible to automatically distinguish these 231 (220+11) occurrences from the rest and identify the expression *což* as a discourse connective in these contexts.

2.3 Scope of Arguments

In all intra-sentential relations, the scope of arguments is defined as the effective

[4] It has arisen from relative pronoun *co* (*what*) and particle *-ž* which is no longer used as a separate word in Czech.
[5] Grammatical coreference has been annotated in the PDT for expressions for which it is possible to identify the coreferred part of the text on the basis of grammatical rules (this applies e.g. for relative pronouns, reflexive pronouns or for participants of control verbs (see Mikulová et. al, 2005)).

subtree[6] of the root node of the argument (the root node of the argument can either be a finite verb or a node coordinating finite verbs[7]), excluding all nodes of the other argument of the relation. In all 10,482 automatically annotated intra-sentential relations, the tectogrammatical tree structure correctly defined the scope of the arguments, independently of the fact whether the argument was formed on the surface by a continuous sequence of words or not.

For the 2,191 manually annotated relations, in all but 146 cases the scope of arguments was also equal to the effective subtree of the root node, in the 146 cases the annotator had to define a different scope of the argument.

3 Inter-sentential Relations

In this section, we focus on the annotation of the inter-sentential discourse relations (phase 1). Unlike for the intra-sentential relations, the inter-sentential discourse relations (relations between sentences) had to be annotated completely manually.[8] However, in the following subsections, we discuss and evaluate features of the tectogrammatical layer that contributed notably to the annotation.

3.1 Expressions with the PREC Label

Although the annotation on the tectogrammatical layer does not in principle surpass sentence boundaries (i.e. each sentence is represented by an individual tree), one special mark has been adopted for expressions that signal (mostly) an inter-sentential relation (it is often the case with connectives such as *proto* (*therefore*), *ovšem* (*however*), *tedy* (*hence*)), see Mladová (2008). An expression marked with the functor PREC (a reference to PREceding Context) on the tectogrammatical layer thus indicates a possible presence of a discourse relation, but, at the same time, it does not interpret the semantic type of the relation, neither says anything about the scope and the position of the other discourse argument (see Example 3).

(3) *Rádi bychom ale začali u středních odborných učilišť.*
V jejich případě ***ovšem*** *záleží také na domluvě s ministerstvem hospodářství.*

But we would like to start with the vocational schools.
In their case, ***however,*** *also the arrangement with the Ministry of Economy matters.*

Expressions with label PREC proved to be a very important clue during the annotation process – they served as a clear signal of a possible discourse relation

---

[6] Effective subtree of a node is a set of nodes that linguistically depend (transitively) on the given node, taking all effects of coordinations etc. into account.
[7] possibly transitively, i.e. through other coordinating nodes
[8] See Jínová, Mírovský and Poláková (2012a) for the evaluation and analysis of the inter-annotator agreement.

in the context and were used after each part of the annotation to check the completeness of the annotation. The total number of occurrences of expressions with label PREC in our data is 5,441. The vast majority of them – 4,313 – were added as a connective to a discourse arrow (3,910 to inter-sentential relations, 403 to intra-sentential relations). The remaining occurrences of these expressions were marked by an annotator´s comment in the data and will be analyzed according to their function in some next phase of the work.

3.2 Role of Textual Coreference

In the PDT, textual coreference has been annotated for all syntactic nouns (substantives and pronouns behaving as nouns) and some adjectives throughout the whole corpus. Coreferred expressions are not necessarily only other nouns, they can also be verbs or other parts of text, if it is an appropriate interpretation of the context (for details see Nedoluzhko, 2011a). From the theoretical point of view, textual coreference is not a part of the tectogrammatical layer of the PDT but it contributes largely to the representation of meaning.

3.2.1 Connectives with a Deictic Part

One aspect of textual coreference proved to be partly helpful in determining discourse connectives. Many connectives in Czech (and also in other languages) have arisen from a connection of a preposition and a deictic element.[9] The deictic part of these prepositional phrases refers to some previous context and the coreference link helps decide if the phrase in a given context functions as a DC or not. For the DC function of such prepositional phrases, verbal antecedent of the deictic part is characteristic (for a detailed analysis, see Poláková, Jínová, Mírovský, 2012). In Example 4, the deictic element *tomu* (dative form of *that*) of the phrase *naproti tomu* (*in contrast with that*, lit. *opposite that*) has in the PDT annotation a referential link to the verb *dosáhnout* (*to achieve*) in the sentence 1.

(4) 1. *Velmi dobrých výsledků* ***dosáhly*** *divize Montáže, Klimatizace a Dodavatelská divize.*
2. ***Naproti tomu*** *divize Odlučování měla za první tři měsíce ztrátu 1,8 milionu korun a divize Ventilátory tři miliony korun.*

1. *Very good results* ***were achieved*** *by the divisions of Assembly, Air Conditioning and Delivery.*
2. *In contrast with that [lit.* ***opposite that****], the division of Separation lost 1.8 million in the first three months and the division of Fans three million.*

We encountered 103 occurrences of a preposition plus a deictic element during

[9] These connectives were called alternative lexicalizations in the PDTB approach to the annotation of discourse (see Prasad et al., 2010).

the discourse annotation that can function as a DC in Czech. Only 11 instances of them had a referential link to a syntactic noun and therefore (besides other criteria such as the impossibility to replace the phrase in the given context by a regular connective) were not considered to be DCs.

4 Ellipsis Resolution

Missing or omitted nodes in structures with an ellipsis have been reconstructed on the tectogrammatical layer of the PDT. It proved to be helpful both in the annotation of intra-sentential and inter-sentential discourse relations, namely in case of reconstructed verbal nodes. Thus, we were able to mark 1,630 relations that have in one or both arguments an elided verb. Without the ellipsis resolved, the relations could be easily overlooked in the text or it would not be possible to annotate them in the trees at all. Example 5 shows a relation with an elided verb.

(5) *Zloději nechodí po horách, ale po domácnostech.*
Thieves do not visit mountains but households.

Conclusions and Perspectives

We have presented a discourse annotation project and discussed and evaluated how it benefited from the previous annotation of the underlying syntactic structure of sentences in PDT. Its main contribution was to the partially automatic annotation of the intra-sentential discourse relations; it helped find the arguments of the discourse relations, identify the connectives and assign the discourse senses. Resolved cases of ellipses in the trees made it possible to annotate relations with no surface-present finite verb and also made it easier to determine the argument extent, both for intra- and inter-sentential relations. As for the inter-sentential discourse relations alone, the marking of a majority of discourse connectives with the semantic label PREC (reference to PREceding Context) was a helpful feature. Grammatical and textual coreference helped distinguish some of the less typical connectives.

Acknowledgments

We gratefully acknowledge support from the Grant Agency of the Czech Republic (grants P406/12/0658 and P406/2010/0875) and from the Ministry of Education, Youth and Sports in the Czech Republic, program KONTAKT (ME10018) and the LINDAT-Clarin project (LM2010013).

References

Carlson, L., Marcu, D., and Okurowski, M.E. (2002). *RST Discourse Treebank*, LDC2002T07 [Corpus]. *Linguistic Data Consortium*, Philadelphia, PA, USA.

Hajič, J., Panevová, J., Hajičová, E., Sgall, P., Pajas, P., Štěpánek, J., Havelka, J., Mikulová, M., Žabokrtský, Z. and Ševčíková-Razímová, M. (2006). Prague Dependency Treebank 2.0. *Software prototype, Linguistic Data Consortium*, Philadelphia, PA, USA, ISBN 1-58563-370-4, www.ldc.upenn.edu, Jul 2006.

Mikulová, M., Bémová, A., Hajič, J., Hajičová, E., Havelka, J., Kolářová-Řezníčková, V., Kučová, L., Lopatková, M., Pajas, P., Panevová, J., Razímová, M., Sgall, P., Štěpánek, J., Urešová, Z., Veselá, K. and Žabokrtský, Z. (2005). Anotace na tektogramatické rovině Pražského závislostního korpusu. Anotátorská příručka. *Praha: UFAL MFF.* Available at: http://ufal.mff.cuni.cz/pdt2.0/doc/manuals/cz/t-layer/html/index.html.

Jínová, P., Mírovský J. and Poláková, L. (2012a). Analyzing the Most Common Errors in the Discourse Annotation of the Prague Dependency Treebank. In *Proceedings of the 11th International Workshop on Treebanks and Linguistic Theories (TLT 11),* Lisbon, Portugal, November 2012.

Jínová, P., Mírovský J. and Poláková, L. (2012b). Semi-Automatic Annotation of Intra-sentential Discourse Relations in PDT. In *Procedings of the 24th International Conference on Computational Linguistics (COLING 2012), ADACA Discourse Workshop,* Mumbai, India, December 2012.

Mladová, L. (2008). Diskurzní vztahy v češtině a jejich zachycení v anotovaném korpusu. *Technical report no. 2008/TR-2008-40, Faculty of Mathematics and Physics, Charles University in Prague,* Czech Republic, ISSN 1214–5521, 136 pp., Dec 2008.

Nedoluzhko, A. (2011a). Rozšířená textová koreference a asociační anafora (Koncepce anotace českých dat v Pražském závislostním korpusu). *Institute of Formal and Applied Linguistics, Charles University in Prague*, Czech Republic, ISBN 978-80-904571-2-6, 268 pp., Dec 2011.

Nedoluzhko, A., Mírovský, J., Hajičová, E., Pergler, J. and Ocelák, R. (2011b). Extended Textual Coreference and Bridging Relations in PDT 2.0. *Data/software, ÚFAL MFF UK, Prague, Czech Republic*, Dec. 2011. Available at: https://ufal-point.mff.cuni.cz/xmlui/handle/11858/00-097C-0000-0005-BCCF-3, Dec 2011.

Oza, U., Prasad, R., Kolachina S., Sharma, D.M. and Joshi, A.K. (2009). The Hindi Discourse Relation Bank. In *Proc. Linguistic Annotation Workshop (LAW 2009)*, Suntec, Singapore, August 2009, pp.158-161.

Poláková (Mladová), L., Jínová, P. and Mírovský, J. (2012). Interplay of Coreference and Discourse Relations: Discourse Connectives with a Referential Component. In *Proceedings of the 8th International Conference on Language Resources and Evaluation (LREC 2012)*, Eropean Language Resources Association, Istanbul, Turkey, ISBN 978-2-9517408-7-7, pp. 146–153.

Poláková L., Jínová, P., Zikánová, Š., Bedřichová, Z., Mírovský, J., Rysová, M., Zdeňková, J., Pavlíková, V. and Hajičová, E. (2012). Manual for Annotation of Discourse Relations in the Prague Dependency Treebank. *Technical report, UFAL MFF UK, Prague, Czech Republic.* Available at: http://ufal.mff.cuni.cz/techrep/tr47.pdf.

Prasad, R., Dinesh, N., Lee, A., Miltsakaki, E., Robaldo, L., Joshi, A. and Webber, B. (2007). The Penn Discourse TreeBank 2.0 Annotation Manual. Available at: http://www.seas.upenn.edu/~pdtb/PDTBAPI/pdtb-annotation-manual.pdf.

Prasad, R., Dinesh, N., Lee, A., Miltsakaki, E., Robaldo, L., Joshi, A. and Webber, B. (2008). The Penn Discourse Treebank 2.0. In *Proceedings of the 6th International Conference on Language Resources and Evaluation (LREC 2008)*, Marrakech, Morocco.

Prasad, R., Joshi, A. and Webber, B. (2010). Realization of Discourse Relation by Other Means: Alternative Lexicalizations. In *Proceedings of the 23rd International Conference on Computational Linguistics (Coling 2010)*, Beijing, China, pp. 1023–1031.

Stede, M. (2004). The Potsdam Commentary Corpus. In *Proceedings of the ACL-04 Workshop on Discourse Annotation*, Barcelona, Spain.

Sgall, P., Hajičová, E. and Panevová, J. (1986). The Meaning of the Sentence in Its Semantic and Pragmatic Aspects, *Dordrecht: Reidel Publishing Company,* Praha: Academia.

The Effect of Learner Corpus Size in Grammatical Error Correction of ESL Writings

Tomoya Mizumoto[1] *Yuta Hayashibe*[1]
Mamoru Komachi[1] *Masaaki Nagata*[2] *Yuji Matsumoto*[1]
(1) Nara Institute of Science and Technology, Nara, Japan
(2) NTT Communication Science Laboratories, Kyoto, Japan
tomoya-m@is.naist.jp, yuta-h@is.naist.jp, komachi@is.naist.jp,
nagata.masaaki@lab.ntt.co.jp, matsu@is.naist.jp

ABSTRACT
English as a Second Language (ESL) learners' writings contain various grammatical errors. Previous research on automatic error correction for ESL learners' grammatical errors deals with restricted types of learners' errors. Some types of errors can be corrected by rules using heuristics, while others are difficult to correct without statistical models using native corpora and/or learner corpora. Since adding error annotation to learners' text is time-consuming, it was not until recently that large scale learner corpora became publicly available. However, little is known about the effect of learner corpus size in ESL grammatical error correction. Thus, in this paper, we investigate the effect of learner corpus size on various types of grammatical errors, using an error correction system based on phrase-based statistical machine translation (SMT) trained on a large scale error-tagged learner corpus. We show that the phrase-based SMT approach is effective in correcting frequent errors that can be identified by local context, and that it is difficult for phrase-based SMT to correct errors that need long range contextual information.

KEYWORDS: ESL, grammatical error correction, statistical machine translation.

Proceedings of COLING 2012: Posters, pages 863–872,
COLING 2012, Mumbai, December 2012.

1 Introduction

English as a Second Language (ESL) learners' writings contain various kinds of grammatical errors. Recent growth in corpus annotation of learner English allows detailed analysis of grammatical errors in learners' writings. Konan-JIEM Learner Corpus (hereafter referred to as KJ Corpus)[1] is one such corpus composed of English essays written by Japanese college students. Table 1 shows the distribution of errors found in KJ Corpus[2]. The most frequent error type is *article* errors, followed by *noun number* and *preposition* errors. It is not surprising that frequent types of errors account for the most errors, but it should be noted that there are many different types of errors in learner corpus.

Thus far, a lot of studies have been made on automated error correction in regard to errors ESL learners make. However, most previous studies of second language learning deal with one or a few restricted types of learners' errors. For example, there are studies on *preposition* errors (Rozovskaya and Roth, 2011), *verb selection* errors (Liu et al., 2011), *tense* errors (Tajiri et al., 2012), *verb form* errors (*agreement* and *tense*) (Lee and Seneff, 2008), *preposition* and *article* errors (Dahlmeier and Ng, 2011) and *spelling*, *article*, *preposition* and *word form* (*agreement* and *tense*) errors (Park and Levy, 2011). Recently, Swanson and Yamangil (2012) presented a detailed analysis on correcting all types of errors in the Cambridge Learner Corpus, but their task is different from the others in that their goal is to detect errors and select error types given both the original and corrected text, which is not often available in practice.

Some types of errors like agreement errors can be corrected by simple rules using heuristics, while others like preposition errors are difficult to correct without statistical model trained on native corpora and/or learner corpora. It was not until recently that large scale learner corpora became widely available for grammatical error correction. However, little is known about the effect of learner corpus size in ESL grammatical error correction.

In this paper, we conduct experiments in error correction targeting all types of errors using a large scale error-annotated learner corpus to see the effect of corpus size in grammatical error correction. We build an error correction system with phrase-based statistical machine translation (SMT) technique. Also, we create a large scale error-tagged corpus of learner English from the web. We then analyze the results of error correction by breaking down the error types and discuss the strength and weakness of the example based approach using a large scale but noisy learner corpus.

The main contribution of this work is two-fold:

- To our knowledge, it is the first attempt to use a large scale learner corpus to correct all types of errors.
- We show the effect of learner corpus size on the phrase-based SMT approach and show its advantages and disadvantages.

In the following, we briefly overview related work of grammatical error correction in Section 2. Then we describe our grammatical error correction system and large scale error-annotated learner corpus in Section 3. Section 4 shows our experimental results and discusses the effect of corpus size on different error types.

2 Related work

Even though there are many works on error correction in learners' English, only a few target multiple various kinds of grammatical errors.

[1] `http://www.gsk.or.jp/catalog/GSK2012-A/catalog_e.html`

[2] Spelling errors are excluded from target of annotation in KJ Corpus.

Types	Proportion (%)	Types	Proportion (%)
article	19.23	verb other	4.09
noun number	13.88	adverb	3.59
preposition	13.56	conjunction	2.04
tense	8.77	word order	1.34
lexical choice of noun	7.04	noun other	1.30
lexical choice of verb	6.90	auxiliary verb	0.88
pronoun	6.62	other lexical choice	0.74
agreement	5.25	relative	0.42
adjective	4.30	interrogative	0.04

Table 1: The distribution of errors on KJ Corpus.

First, Brockett et al. (2006) proposed an error correction model with phrase-based SMT. Even though their model can deal with all types of errors, they evaluated their method only on noun number errors using an artificial data, partly because there was no large scale learner corpus available at the time. We would like to emphasize that our work is the first attempt to use a real world large learner corpus with phrase-based SMT technique. We will show that phrase-based SMT especially suffers from data sparseness.

Second, Park and Levy (2011) attempted to correct various kinds of errors with a noisy channel model using a large scale unannotated corpus of learner English. Ours differs from their work in that we use a large scale error-tagged corpus annotated by the wisdom of crowds. In addition, they targeted only spelling, article, preposition and word form errors, while we do not restrict error types.

Third, Han et al. (2010) developed a preposition correction system using a large scale error-tagged corpus of learner English. They built a maximum entropy-based model for preposition errors trained on learner and native corpora. We also take advantage of a large scale error-tagged corpus of learner English, but use phrase-based SMT to deal with various kinds of errors and to fully exploit the learner corpus.

Recently, Dahlmeier and Ng (2012) presented a beam-search decoder for correcting spelling, article, preposition, punctuation and noun number errors. They reported that their discriminative model achieves considerably better results than an SMT baseline trained on a few hundreds of sentences. As we will see later, we observed a similar tendency in preposition error correction when we trained a phrase-based SMT system on a small learner corpus. However, in this work, we exploit a large scale error-annotated corpus extracted from the web to overcome the data sparseness problem.

3 Using a large scale learner corpus with phrase-based SMT for grammatical error correction

3.1 Error correction with phrase-based SMT

We use phrase-based statistical machine translation (Koehn et al., 2003) to conduct unrestricted error correction. There are several studies about grammatical error correction using phrase-based statistical machine translation (Brockett et al., 2006; Mizumoto et al., 2011; Ehsan and Faili, 2012). Although Brockett et al. (2006) corrected English learners' error using phrase-based statistical machine translation, they only targeted mass noun errors. Mizumoto et al. (2011) dealt with unrestricted types of learners' errors, but their target is not English but Japanese. Ehsan and Faili (2012) applied an SMT framework to English and Persian grammatical error correction, but used artificially created learner corpora.

The well-known statistical machine translation formulation using a log-linear model (Och and Ney, 2002) is defined by:

$$\hat{e} = \arg\max_{e} P(e|f) = \arg\max_{e} \sum_{m=1}^{M} \lambda_m h_m(e,f) \quad (1)$$

where e represents target sentences (corrected sentences) and f represents source sentences (sentences written by learners). $h_m(e,f)$ is a feature function and λ_m is a model parameter for each feature function. This formulation finds a target sentence e that maximizes a weighted linear combination of feature functions for source sentence f. A translation model and a language model can be used as feature functions. The translation model is commonly represented as conditional probability $P(f|e)$ factored into the translation probability between phrases. The language model is represented as probability $P(e)$. The translation model is learned from sentence-aligned parallel corpus while the language model is learned from target raw corpus.

3.2 Crowdsourcing annotation of a large scale corpus of learner English

We use data from a language learning social networking service Lang-8 [3] to train the error correction system using statistical machine translation. In Lang-8, language learners post their writing on the Lang-8 site to be corrected by native speakers. We can obtain pairs of learner's sentence and corrected sentence in large scale from Lang-8. Mizumoto et al. (2011) first presented an approach to extract a learner corpus from the web, but we differ from them in that we create a learner corpus of English rather than Japanese. Also, unlike (Tajiri et al., 2012), we propose to use metadata of users to determine the L1 of English learners. Because our test corpus (KJ Corpus) is written by Japanese college students, we would like to use the same kind of data; it is out side of the scope of this paper to see the effect of learners' L1.

We crawled blog entries found in Lang-8 as of December 2010. We used writings in Lang-8 written by Japanese ESL learners for translation model and language model of error correction system with SMT. There are 509,116 sentence pairs in English writings written by Japanese L1 English learners. However, we need to filter noisy sentences because it may be hard to align them if the sentences are drastically changed from the original learner's sentences, resulting in degraded performance on phrase-based SMT approach. Therefore, we calculate the edit distance between a learner sentence and the corrected sentence using a dynamic programming algorithm, and retain sentences whose numbers of both insertions and deletions is equal to or less than 5 words [4]. As a result, we obtain 391,699 sentence pairs.

4 Experiment: Effect of learner corpus size in grammatical error correction

We carried out an experiment on grammatical error correction with SMT-based system using a large scale learner corpus. To see the effect of corpus size, we compare a system using Lang-8 Corpus (large scale learner corpus) with different sizes and a system using KJ Corpus (small scale corpus). In order to get a closer look at the effect of error correction methods, we also experimented on the preposition error correction task using a maximum entropy model as a discriminative baseline and SMT-based models as our proposal for all error correction.

[3] `http://lang-8.com/`

[4] We use 6 as a distortion-limit for Moses, therefore we chose the edit distance to be smaller than the distortion-limit.

4.1 Tools and experimental data

We used Moses 2010-08-13 [5] with default parameters as a decoder and GIZA++ 1.0.5 [6] as an alignment tool to implement an error correction system with phrase-based SMT. We applied grow-diag-final-and (Och and Ney, 2003) heuristics for phrase extraction. The number of extracted phrases are 1,050,070 (245 MB) using all data of Lang-8 Corpus. We used 3-gram as a language model trained on the corrected text of Lang-8 Corpus.

Next, we built the maximum entropy model (Berger et al., 1996) as a multi-class classifier baseline for preposition error correction (Sakaguchi et al., 2012). We used the implementation of Maximum Entropy Modeling Toolkit [7] with its default parameters. We incorporated surface, POS, WordNet, parse and language model features described in (Tetreault et al., 2010) and (De Felice and Pulman, 2008). POS and parse features were extracted using the Stanford Parser 2.0.2. This system achieves recall of 18.44, precision of 34.88 and F-measure of 24.12 trained and tested on the CLC FCE dataset (Yannakoudakis et al., 2011), which ranked the 4th out of 13 systems at the HOO 2012 Shared Task (Dale et al., 2012).

We use KJ Corpus as a test data. KJ Corpus consist of 170 essays, containing 2,411 sentences. When we experiment on a system using KJ Corpus, we perform 5-fold cross validation.

4.2 Evaluation metrics

For the evaluation metrics, we use automatic evaluation criteria. To be precise, we use recall, precision and F-measure.

Recall and precision for each type of errors are calculated from true positive, false positive and false negative based on error tags in KJ Corpus. The word which does not have any tag in KJ Corpus does not affect precision for each type of errors [8]. For example, let us consider the following:

learner: He talked to me _ his life of Kyoto, and he took me _ Kyoto university.
correct: He talked to me about his life in Kyoto and he took me to Kyoto university.
system: He talked _ me _ his life on Kyoto, and he took me to Kyoto university.

In this example, the system deletes preposition "to", which does not have any tag. Thus, precision = 1/2, recall = 1/2 for *preposition* errors and precision = 1/3, recall = 1/2 for Total scores.

4.3 Experimental results

Table 2 shows error correction results for each type of errors on different corpora. We compared SMT systems trained on KJ Corpus, Lang-8 Corpus with the same amount of data with KJ Corpus, and full Lang-8 Corpus. With very few exceptions, the larger the size of learner corpus, the higher the accuracy. In addition, using the larger corpus, precision tends to increase more than recall.

Table 3 presents F-measures for each type of error varying the corpus sizes (2K, 10K, 20K, 100K, 200K, 300K, All (390K)). As we will see later in the next section, there are two types of errors in which learner corpus size matters.

Table 4 shows the performance of preposition error correction. Perhaps not surprising, but it still deserves attention that SMT model trained on all Lang-8 Corpus clearly outperformed other two

[5] `http://http://www.statmt.org/moses/`
[6] `http://code.google.com/p/giza-pp/`
[7] `https://github.com/lzhang10/maxent`
[8] The total score is calculated using all the correction output with and without any tag.

Training Corpus	KJ Corpus			Lang-8 Corpus (2K)			Lang-8 Corpus (390K)		
	Recall	Prec	F	Recall	Prec	F	Recall	Prec	F
article	0.187	0.531	0.277	0.187	0.571	0.282	**0.359**	**0.761**	**0.488**
noun number	0.207	0.603	0.308	0.136	0.671	0.226	0.199	**0.710**	0.311
preposition	0.137	0.375	0.201	0.092	0.319	0.143	**0.262**	**0.585**	**0.361**
tense	0.102	0.170	0.128	0.043	0.088	0.058	0.080	0.149	0.104
lexical choice of noun	0.035	0.114	0.054	0.033	0.152	0.054	**0.182**	**0.443**	**0.258**
lexical choice of verb	0.070	0.161	0.098	0.065	0.200	0.098	**0.192**	**0.324**	**0.241**
pronoun	0.075	0.220	0.112	0.040	0.143	0.063	0.150	**0.367**	**0.213**
agreement	0.236	**0.604**	0.340	0.125	0.483	0.199	0.228	0.469	0.307
adjective	0.151	0.326	0.206	0.056	0.286	0.094	**0.389**	**0.522**	**0.446**
verb other	0.089	0.139	0.109	0.147	0.333	0.204	**0.286**	**0.419**	**0.340**
adverb	0.265	0.450	0.333	0.214	0.429	0.286	0.292	0.432	0.349
conjunction	0.100	0.417	0.161	0.091	0.714	0.161	0.115	**0.546**	0.190
word order	0.500	0.025	0.048	0.667	0.050	0.093	**0.750**	0.075	0.136
noun other	0.182	0.222	0.200	0.143	0.167	0.154	**0.571**	**0.429**	**0.490**
auxiliary verb	0.056	0.167	0.083	0.100	0.400	0.160	0.100	**0.400**	0.160
other lexical choice	0.167	0.200	0.182	0.000	0.000	0.000	**0.357**	**0.455**	**0.400**
relative	0.111	0.250	0.154	0.182	0.667	0.286	0.091	**0.500**	0.154
interrogative	0.000	0.000	0.000	0.000	0.000	0.000	0.000	0.000	0.000
Total	0.149	0.147	0.148	0.113	0.205	0.146	0.247	**0.275**	**0.260**

Table 2: Result for each type of errors by statistical machine translation. Bold face indicates that one system's result is equal or greater by more than 0.1 points than the other systems' result.

systems. MaxEnt does slightly better than SMT when they are trained on the same small corpus. Unfortunately, we were not able to use Lang-8 Corpus since it took too long to train.

4.4 Discussion

We can classify errors into two types: (1) errors which get better correction by increasing corpus size and (2) errors which have little relationship with corpus size. The first type of errors includes *article*, *preposition*, *lexical choice of noun*, *lexical choice of verb*, *adjective*, and *noun other*. On the other hand, the second type of errors comprises *noun number*, *tense*, *agreement*, *adverb*, *conjunction*, *word order*, *auxiliary verb*, *relative* and *interrogative*. We can expect to improve performance (both recall and precision) for errors that require wide coverage lexical knowledge, such as lexical choice errors, by using a much larger corpus with phrase-based SMT. In contrast, we may say that errors which involve larger context such as tense errors are difficult to correct with phrase-based SMT. We discuss the result while looking at examples of two of the former type of errors (*article* and *lexical choice of noun*) whose F-measures improve with increasing corpus size, and three of the latter type of errors (*noun number*, *tense* and *agreement*), whose F-measures do not change or even degrade.

Table 5 shows examples of article and lexical choice of noun. These are the examples that phrase-based SMT failed to correct using KJ Corpus. Because we can acquire a lot of pairs of an error phrase and its correction by increasing the size of the learner corpus, the phrase-based SMT was able to correct them using Lang-8 Corpus.

Table 6 shows examples of noun number, tense and agreement errors. The first example of noun

Training Corpus	**KJ**	**Lang-8**						
		2K	10K	20K	100K	200K	300K	390K
article	0.277	0.282	*0.390	*0.420	*0.443	*0.459	*0.475	*0.488
noun number	0.308	0.226	0.214	0.238	0.270	0.300	0.319	0.311
preposition	0.201	0.143	0.192	0.226	*0.333	*0.336	*0.344	*0.362
tense	0.128	0.058	0.066	0.058	0.081	0.096	0.089	0.104
lexical choice of noun	0.054	0.054	0.124	0.133	*0.189	*0.216	*0.250	*0.258
lexical choice of verb	0.098	0.098	0.087	0.138	*0.196	*0.232	*0.232	*0.241
pronoun	0.112	0.063	0.131	0.150	0.177	0.195	0.213	0.213
agreement	0.340	0.197	0.224	0.248	0.260	0.284	0.307	0.307
adjective	0.206	0.094	0.165	0.219	*0.413	*0.426	*0.426	*0.446
verb other	0.109	0.204	0.240	0.311	0.291	*0.340	0.308	0.340
adverb	0.333	0.286	0.286	0.302	0.333	0.349	0.349	0.349
conjunction	0.161	0.161	0.161	0.191	0.161	0.191	0.191	0.191
word order	0.048	0.093	0.093	0.091	0.091	0.091	0.091	0.136
noun other	0.200	0.154	0.286	0.286	*0.531	*0.490	*0.490	*0.490
auxiliary verb	0.083	0.160	0.160	0.083	0.083	0.160	0.160	0.160
other lexical choice	0.182	0.000	0.095	0.095	0.400	0.400	0.400	0.400
relative	0.154	0.285	0.154	0.154	0.154	0.154	0.154	0.154
interrogative	0.000	0.000	0.000	0.000	0.000	0.000	0.000	0.000
Total	0.148	0.146	0.180	0.200	0.239	0.247	0.254	0.260

Table 3: Results (F-measure) for error correction by SMT varying the learner corpus sizes. Asterisks indicate that the difference of result using Lang-8 Corpus and result using KJ Corpus is statistically significant ($p < 0.01$).

System	**Training corpus**	**Recall**	**Precision**	**F-measure**
Maximum entropy-based model	KJ Corpus	0.165	0.407	0.235
Phrase based SMT	KJ Corpus	0.137	0.375	0.201
Phrase-based SMT	Lang-8 Corpus (390K)	**0.262**	**0.585**	**0.362**

Table 4: Result for preposition error correction on KJ Corpus.

number was corrected using Lang-8 Corpus with phrase-based SMT since the error is one of the common learners' expressions. The second was not corrected using Lang-8 Corpus with phrase-based SMT because "dools" [9] is slightly displaced from "a big", and a proper noun "snoopy" is inserted between "dools" and "a big". It is hard to correct this kind of error with Phrase-based SMT, even using artificial data such as in Brockett et al. (2006). To solve this problem, we need to conduct generalization using POS or consider dependency relations.

The first example of a tense error was corrected using both KJ Corpus and Lang-8 Corpus with phrase-based SMT. One of the reasons why the baseline system was able to correct the error is that it requires only local context to correct and is very frequent even in a small leaner corpus. In the second example, the system fails to find tense agreement in the complex sentence. Tense error is difficult to correct for phrase-based SMT since it involves global context (Tajiri et al., 2012).

The first example of agreement error was corrected using Lang-8 Corpus with phrase-based SMT. This is because the phrase pair correcting "Flowers is" to "Flowers are" is frequent and the language

[9] The word "dools" written by a learner is also a spelling error.

	learner	correct
article	I like a chocolate very much.	I like _ chocolate very much.
lexical choice of noun	my cycle was injured, but i wasn't.	my bicycle was damaged, but i wasn't.

Table 5: Examples of system output for article and lexical choice of noun error

	learner	correct
noun number 1	I read various type books.	I read various types of books.
*noun number 2	There is a big snoopy dools in my room.	There is a big snoopy doll in my room.
tense 1	If I 'll live in saitama, I must have ...	If I _ live in saitama, I must have ...
*tense 2	The weather is very sunny, so we were ...	The weather was very sunny, so we were ...
agreement 1	Flowers is very beautiful.	Flowers are very beautiful.
*agreement 2	I think, reading comics are not "reading"	I think, reading comics is not "reading"

Table 6: Examples of system results for noun number, tense and agreement errors. Asterisks indicate that the SMT system using full Lang-8 Corpus failed to correct the errors.

model probability of "Flowers are" is also higher than "Flowers is". The second example is one that the system failed to correct since the pattern is unseen in the learner corpus and thus the system has no way to capture the relation between the subject "reading" and "are". To solve this problem, it needs to get the subject-verb relation considering a dependency structure.

As for prepostion error correction, we suspect that there are two reasons why the SMT-based model using full Lang-8 Corpus outperformed the MaxEnt model. First, due to the small amount of training data in KJ Corpus (2,000 sentences), the MaxEnt model failed to build a high performance system. Second, the high performance of the SMT system may be attributed to the fact that both KJ Corpus and Lang-8 Corpus were written by Japanese native speakers. Also, the reason why the MaxEnt model achieved better result than SMT when trained on the same small corpus is possibly because KJ Corpus is too small to learn variations in learner English by phrase-based SMT approach, while a discriminative model can exploit a small dataset using rich features.

Conclusion

We tackled the task of ESL grammatical error correction of all types of errors using a large scale corpus of learner English with phrase-based SMT technique. Previous research focused on restricted types of errors due to the small amount of learner corpora. We overcome this problem by training an error correction system on a large scale error tagged corpus extracted from the web.

We found that the size of corpus is critical to improve phrase-based SMT approach. However, the degree of improvement varies across error types. Phrase-based SMT is effective in correcting frequent errors which require only local context. For example, there is a clear improvement in increasing the size of learner corpus for correcting *article*, *preposition*, *lexical choice* and *adjective* errors, while there is little improvement for correcting *agreement* and *tense* errors.

Acknowledgement

We would like to thank Yangyang Xi for granting permission to use text from Lang-8.

References

Berger, A. L., Pietra, V. J. D., and Pietra, S. A. D. (1996). A Maximum Entropy Approach to Natural Language Processing. *Computational Linguistics*, 22(1):39–71.

Brockett, C., Dolan, W. B., and Gamon, M. (2006). Correcting ESL Errors Using Phrasal SMT Techniques. In *Proceedings of COLING-ACL*, pages 249–256.

Dahlmeier, D. and Ng, H. T. (2011). Grammatical Error Correction with Alternating Structure Optimization. In *Proceedings of ACL-HLT*, pages 915–923.

Dahlmeier, D. and Ng, H. T. (2012). A Beam-Search Decoder for Grammatical Error Correction. In *Proceedings of EMNLP*, pages 568–578.

Dale, R., Anisimoff, I., and Narroway, G. (2012). HOO 2012: A Report on the Preposition and Determiner Error Correction Shared Task. In *Proceedings of BEA*, pages 54–62.

De Felice, R. and Pulman, S. G. (2008). A Classifier-Based Approach to Preposition and Determiner Error Correction in L2 English. In *Proceedings of COLING*, pages 169–176.

Ehsan, N. and Faili, H. (2012). Grammatical and Context-Sensitive Error Correction Using a Statistical Machine Translation Framework. *Software: Practice and Experience*.

Han, N.-R., Tetreault, J., Lee, S.-H., and Ha, J.-Y. (2010). Using an Error-Annotated Learner Corpus to Develop an ESL/EFL Error Correction System. In *Proceedings of LREC*, pages 763–770.

Koehn, P., Och, F. J., and Marcu, D. (2003). Statistical Phrase-Based Translation. In *Proceedings of HLT-NAACL*, pages 48–54.

Lee, J. and Seneff, S. (2008). Correcting Misuse of Verb Forms. In *Proceedings of ACL-HLT*, pages 174–182.

Liu, X., Han, B., and Zhou, M. (2011). Correcting Verb Selection Errors for ESL with the Perceptron. In *Proceedings of CICLing*, pages 411–423.

Mizumoto, T., Komachi, M., Nagata, M., and Matsumoto, Y. (2011). Mining Revision Log of Language Learning SNS for Automated Japanese Error Correction of Second Language Learners. In *Proceedings of IJCNLP*, pages 147–155.

Och, F. J. and Ney, H. (2002). Discriminative Training and Maximum Entropy Models for Statistical Machine Translation. In *Proceedings of ACL*, pages 295–302.

Och, F. J. and Ney, H. (2003). A Systematic Comparison of Various Statistical Alignment Models. *Computational Linguistics*, 29(1):19–51.

Park, Y. A. and Levy, R. (2011). Automated Whole Sentence Grammar Correction Using a Noisy Channel Model. In *Proceedings of ACL*, pages 934–944.

Rozovskaya, A. and Roth, D. (2011). Algorithm Selection and Model Adaptation for ESL Correction Tasks. In *Proceedings of ACL*, pages 924–933.

Sakaguchi, K., Hayashibe, Y., Kondo, S., Kanashiro, L., Mizumoto, T., Komachi, M., and Matsumoto, Y. (2012). Naist at the hoo 2012 shared task. In *Proceedings of the Seventh Workshop on Building Educational Applications Using NLP*, pages 281–288.

Swanson, B. and Yamangil, E. (2012). Correction Detection and Error Type Selection as an ESL Educational Aid. In *Proceedings of NAACL: HLT*, pages 357–361.

Tajiri, T., Komachi, M., and Matsumoto, Y. (2012). Tense and Aspect Error Correction for ESL Learners Using Global Context. In *Proceedings of ACL*, pages 198–202.

Tetreault, J., Foster, J., and Chodorow, M. (2010). Using Parse Features for Preposition Selection and Error Detection. In *Proceedings of ACL*, pages 353–358.

Yannakoudakis, H., Briscoe, T., and Medlock, B. (2011). A New Dataset and Method for Automatically Grading ESOL Texts. In *Proceedings of ACL*, pages 180–189.

GRAFIX: Automated Rule-Based Post Editing System to Improve English-Persian SMT Output

Mahsa Mohaghegh[1] *Abdolhossein Sarrafzadeh*[2] *Mehdi Mohammadi*[3]
(1) Massey University, School of Engineering and Advanced Technology, Auckland, New Zealand
(2) Unitec, Department of Computing, Auckland, New Zealand
(3) SheikhBahaee University, Department of Computer Engineering, Isfahan, Iran
M.mohaghegh@massey.ac.nz, Hsarrafzadeh@unitec.ac.nz
mehdi.mka@gmail.com

ABSTRACT

This paper describes the latest developments in the PeEn-SMT system, specifically covering experiments with Grafix, an APE component developed for PeEn-SMT.

The success of well-designed SMT systems has made this approach one of the most popular MT approaches. However, MT output is often seriously grammatically incorrect. This is more prevalent in SMT since this approach is not language-specific. This system works with Persian, a morphologically rich language, so post-editing output is an important step in maintaining translation fluency.

Grafix performs a range of corrections on sentences, from lexical transformation to complex syntactical rearrangement. It analyzes the target sentence (the SMT output in Persian language) and attempts to correct it by applying a number of rules which enforce consistency with Persian grammar.

We show that the proposed system is able to improve the quality of the state-of-the-art English-Persian SMT systems, yielding promising results from both automatic and manual evaluation techniques.

KEYWORDS : Machine Translation, Post-editing of Machine Translation, Evaluation of Machine Translation

Proceedings of COLING 2012: Posters, pages 873–882,
COLING 2012, Mumbai, December 2012.

1 Introduction

Since most mistakes associated with machine translation are of a repetitive nature, the task of post-editing can be made automatic (Allen & Hogan, 2000). Furthermore, the process of automatic post-editing (APE) is very similar in nature to a machine translation process (Simard, Goutte, & Isabelle, 2007). Because of this, certain MT systems can be used to model the APE process.

The advantages and disadvantages of RBMT and SMT approaches may be summarised as follows: RBMT is strong in syntax, morphology, structural semantics, and lexical reliability, but demonstrates weakness in the areas of lexical semantics and lexical adaptivity. SMT, while being weak in the areas of syntax, morphology, and structural semantics, is superior to RBMT in areas of lexical semantics and adaptability, although the advantage of adaptability to other language pairs is only valuable when the system is to be used with a wider range of languages.

The Grafix APE system's main algorithm follows a Transfer-based approach. Transfer-based MT is among the most commonly used approaches for MT. This method involves capturing the meaning of a source sentence using intermediate representations, and from it generating a target output (Mohamed, 2000). The Grafix system developed by the authors attempts to correct some frequently occurring grammatical SMT system errors in English-to-Persian translations.

2 Related Work

Simard et al. (2007), Lagarda, Alabau, Casacuberta, Silva, and Diaz-de-Liano (2009) present APE systems that are added to commercial RBMT systems. Their APE components utilise a phrase-based SMT system using Moses as a decoder.

In his recent work, Pilevar (2011) demonstrates a statistical post-editing (SPE) module that is used to improve RBMT output for the English-Persian language pair in order to improve the translation of subtitles for movies. The results show that the SPE module can improve the performance of the RBMT system's output when used in a new domain. However, they found that the use of the SMT system alone yields a better result compared to the combination of RBMT + SPE. To our knowledge this is the only post-editing system reported for the English-Persian language pair, and it did not succeed in improving the output of the main system.

Marecek, Rosa, and Bojar (2011) report on experimental work in correcting the output of an English-Czech MT system by performing several rule-based grammatical corrections on sentences parsed to dependency trees. Their baseline SMT system relies on Moses, a phrase-based translation system. In their post-processing system, DEPFIX, they used a two-step translation that is a setup in which, the English source is first translated into simplified Czech, and then the simplified Czech is monotonically translated to fully inflected Czech. Both steps are simple phrase-based models. Rosa, Marecek, and Du˘sek (2012) enriched the rule set of DEPFIX and used a modified version of MST Parser. Their results show that both modifications led to better performance of DEPFIX 2012; however, they mention that since the effect of DEPFIX on the output in terms of BLEU score is not significant, the results are not as reliable as results obtained through manual evaluation.

3 Description of the System

Our approach to the system architecture differs from what is commonly used in most other systems in that the APE does not use an SMT system to automatically post-edit the output of an MT system, as described, for example, in Simard et al. (2007) and Lagarda et al. (2009).

In this study, we couple the PeEn-SMT system we previously developed (Mohaghegh, Sarrafzadeh, & Moir, 2011)with an RBMT-based APE. Since post-editing an MT system's output usually seeks to improve grammatical structure in order to render sentences and phrases with greater fluency, the advantage of RBMT's linguistic knowledge can be utilised well here.

3.1 The Underlying SMT System

Most recent research in the area of statistical machine translation has been targeted at modelling translation based on phrases in the source language and matching them with their statistically-determined equivalents in the target language ("phrase-based" translation) – (Koehn, Och, & Marcu, 2003; Marcu & Wong, 2002; Och & Ney, 2004; Och, Tillmann, & Ney, 1999). After conducting numerous experiments with Moses, we decided to experiment with some modifications of the Joshua 4.0 toolkit, to compare them and see if a better score could be achieved. To the best of our knowledge, this is the first time a hierarchical SMT system is being used for the Persian-English language pair. One motivation for this is the fact that since Persian is a morphologically rich language, word disordering is a common issue that we face. Hierarchical SMT takes syntax into account to some extent, with phrases being used to learn word reordering. This improvement is due to the word order differences between Persian and English, which are better handled with a hierarchical phrase based system than a standard phrase-based approach. Hierarchical phrase-based translation (Chiang, 2005) expands on phrase-based translation by allowing phrases with gaps, modelled as synchronous context-free grammars (SCFGs). Joshua is a well-known open source machine translation toolkit based on the hierarchical approach (Li, Callison-Burch, Khudanpur, & Thornton, 2009). In the latest version of Joshua (Version 4.0), the main changes include implementation of Thrax, which enables extended extraction of Hiero grammars, and a modified hypothesis exploration method (Ganitkevitch, Cao, Weese, Post, & Callison-Burch, 2012).

3.2 The Proposed APE Model

The proposed rule-based APE module consists of three levels of transformation.

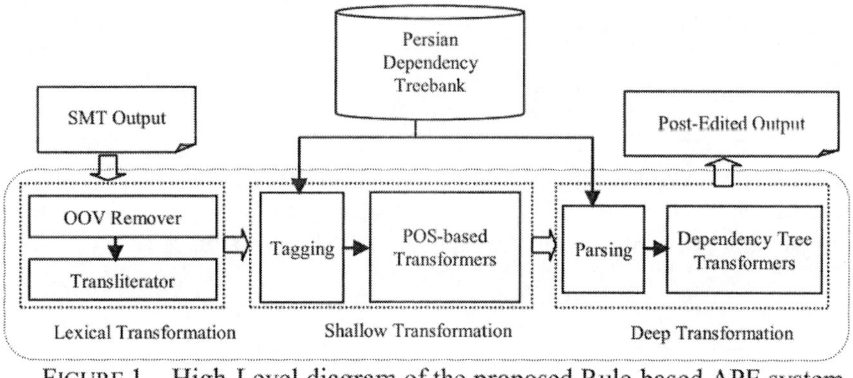

FIGURE 1 – High-Level diagram of the proposed Rule-based APE system

As shown in Figure 1, these three levels are lexical transformers, shallow transformers and deep transformers. First OOVRemover and Transliterator as lexical transformers are run using a bilingual dictionary, after which some shallow transformers are run based on POS tag patterns. Deep transformation at the third level is applied in which the rules exploit the tree dependecy structure of sentences.

Lexical Transformation: The first level benefits from the outcome of two components. OOV[1] remover is a simple substitute rule to replace an English word with the correct translation in Persian. However, there are instances like named entities where OOV remover could not find equivalent Persian translations for English words appearing as OOV in the output. In this case, a transliterator is used to replace English words by their equivalents in Persian scripts. The transliterator component uses a training data set containing over 4600 of the most frequently used Persian words and named entities written using English letters, and also the equivalent in Persian script.

Shallow Transformation: The second stage of the system involves a shallow transfer module. POS-tagging the input text is a pre-requisite process for both shallow and deep transformation levels. The MLE POS-tagger is used in this stage and trained with the Persian Dependency Treebank[2] data. Shallow transformers are developed, based on some POS patterns identified as wrong ones.

Deep Transformation: In the third level, the input is parsed by a dependency parser. Once the text is tagged, some preparation is performed to parse the input, based on the parsing input format (McDonald, Pereira, Ribarov, & Hajic, 2005). The Persian Dependency Treebank is also used in the parser training process.

We used MSTParser, which is an implementation of Dependency Parsing using, the Maximum Spanning Tree (Kübler, McDonald, & Nivre, 2009). The rules here are used for examination of the sentence's dependency tree in order to have some syntactical and grammatical constraints.

3.3 Training Data Source

In a sentence dependency tree, words and relations are graphed, with each word either modifying or being modified by another word, and the root in each tree being the only word which does not modify any other word. We have used Persian Dependency Treebank as our main source of training data for both tagging and data-driven parsing. It contains about 125,500 annotated sentences. The data format is based on CoNLL Shared Task on Dependency Parsing (Buchholz & Marsi, 2006). The sentences are manually annotated in the corpus, which contains about 12,500 sentences and 189,000 tokens

3.4 Pre-Processing and Tagging

The pre-processing of input Persian sentences consists of tokenizing the sentences using our implemented tokenizer. We chose the Maximum Likelihood Estimation (MLE) approach as the POS-tagging component for our APE, due to its ability to be implemented easily and its consistency in yielding promising results for tagging the Persian language (Raja et al., 2007).

---

[1] Out Of Vocabulary
[2] http://dadegan.ir/en

3.5 Parsing

In dependency parsing, words are linked to their arguments by dependency representations (Hudson, 1984). These representations have been in use for many years. In Figure 2, the sentence, shown in sentence tree form, is a dependency tree. Each word depends on a "parent" word or a root symbol.

Label	PUNC	ROOT	OBJ	PREDEP	NPREMOD	SBJ
Token	.	می خوانم	را	نامه	یک	من
Pronunciation	.	/mi:khãnam/	/rã/	/nãmæ/	/yek/	/man/
POS	PUNC	V	POSTP	N	PRENUM	PR
English Equivalent	.	read		letter	a	I

FIGURE 2 – Dependency Parsing Example

3.6 Rule-based Transformers

The translation rules were gathered manually by investigating a broad range of incorrect translations. By considering the dependency parser output for these sentences, and determining frequent wrong patterns among them, we have defined the most common incorrect patterns under four rules in the shallow transformers, and six in the deep transformers. The following sections cover some of them regarding the transfer level.

3.6.1 Shallow Transformers

IncompleteDependentTransformer: In Persian, as in English, dependent clauses are usually connected by relative pronouns such as«که»(English *"that"*). The rule below identifies a lack of verb in a dependent sentence and corrects it by adding a verb. Currently, in most instances the verb «است» (English *"is"*) is suggested. In the notation below, * denotes any number of POS, and ^ denotes 'except'.

If POS-sequence matches [SUBR *^V PUNC] → modify as [* SUBR V(است) PUNC]*

IncompleteEndedPREMTransformer: Pre-modifiers (denoted by PREM) are a class of noun modifiers that precede nouns and are in complementary distribution with other members of the class. In the POS sequence in which a pre-modifier precedes a punctuation mark (PUNC) deemed as incorrect. Since there is no logical translation for given inputs with this pattern, these sequences were removed from the sentence altogether. The rule is described as:

If POS-sequence matches [$*_a$ N PREP PREM PUNC $*_b$] → modify as [$*_a$ $*_b$]

3.6.2 Deep Transformers

NoSubjectSentenceTransformer: SMT output occasionally contains instances of sentences with a third person verb, no definite subject and an object labelled as OBJ in the parse tree and tagged as POSTP (postposition) in the POS sequence. Compared to known reference sentences, it was seen that what was parsed as the object in the sentence was actually the subject. The transformer is designed to revise the sentence by removing the postposition «را» which is the indicator of a direct object in the sentence. Removal of this postposition changes the sentence to one with a subject.

VerbArrangementTransformer: As a natural language, Persian has a preferred word order, with SOV (subject-object-verb) followed by SVO. One frequently violating case is sentences in which a main verb as Root does not occur immediately before the period punctuation. The matching procedure is as follows: For the verb of the sentence tagged as Root, reordering is performed by moving the root verb and its NVE dependants (in the case of compound verbs) to the end of the sentence, immediately before the period punctuation.

MissingVerbTransformer: In this transformer, any subject with a referred verb preceding the subject is identified as an incorrect linked subject to any verb, since the sentence does not follow the standard SOV structure. In this case, it can be assumed that the last word in the sentence can act as a candidate in order to find the non-verbal element in the verb Valency Lexicon (Rasooli, Moloodi, Kouhestani, & Minaei-Bidgoli, 2011). If such a verb is found, that verb will be suggested to fill the space of the missing verb. The tense of the verb is then modified to match that of the subject of the sentence.

MozafOfAlefEndedTokenTransformer: In Persian, there are certain nouns or pronouns following a head noun which signify relationships with the head noun, such as possession or name relation. Such nouns/pronouns are known as Ezafe dependents. Indication of such in the language is given as the vowel sound /e/, coming immediately after pronunciation of the head noun. If the head-word ends in «ا »/a/, then the character « ی» must be added to the end of that word. This character is a representation of the /e/ vowel that is written in such cases to ease the pronunciation. This transformer recognizes the Ezafe dependents which require a « ي» character between them and add it properly.

4 Experiments and Results

The SMT system evaluated in this paper is based on Joshua 4.0 with default setting. The parallel corpus used for the training set was based on the NPEC corpus tested by (Mohaghegh & Sarrafzadeh, 2012), but we built a modified version consisted of almost 85,000 sentence pairs in which we removed the subtitle addition. The language model was extracted from IRNA[3] website. The details of the components of the baseline system prior to alignment are shown in Table 1.

	English		Persian	
Training Set	Sentences	83042	Sentences	82496
	Words	1322470	Words	1399759
Tunings Set	Sentences	1578	Sentences	1578
	Words	40044	Words	41287
		Language Model	Sentences	5852532
			Words	66331086

TABLE 1 – Baseline System Components

[3] http://www.irna.ir/ENIndex.htm

4.1 Test Data Set

We used eight test sets based on text extracted from certain bilingual websites for our experiments, as shown in Table 2.

Testing Data Set #		1	2	3	4	5	6	7	8	Total
English	Word	163	218	371	362	101	354	555	259	2383
	Character	878	1381	1941	1922	589	1887	2902	1325	12825
Persian	Word	158	222	403	337	115	386	653	297	2571
	Character	551	955	1663	1230	430	1717	2551	1063	10160

TABLE 2 – Statistics of eight test set used in automatic and manual evaluation

Test sentences have been selected randomly covering different domains, regardless of whether or not they had potential to be covered by any post-editing rules. We performed translation in the English-Persian translation direction. The Persian side of the test sets was used as the translation reference when using scoring metrics to evaluate the output quality of both the baseline system and the final post-APE output.

4.2 Automatic Evaluation

The translation output before and after the APE is scored with BLEU, the results of which are shown in Table 3.

Input	1	2	3	4	5	6	7	8
Before APE	0.6523	0.2232	0.5914	0.1365	0.7925	0.2738	0.2945	0.4048
After APE	0.6770	0.2187	0.7388	0.1214	0.8716	0.2779	0.2951	0.4089
BLEU Difference	0.0247	-0.0045	0.1474	-0.0151	0.0791	0.0041	0.0006	0.0041

TABLE 3 - Scores of APE based on SMT Joshua version 4.0

The results generally show increases in BLEU metric, which is also shown in Figure 3. The greatest increase in BLEU score due to the APE was achieved in test set #3, with an increase of about 0.15 BLEU. However, in certain test sets the scoring metrics report a decrease in output quality, the worst BLUE score being at a difference of -0.0151.

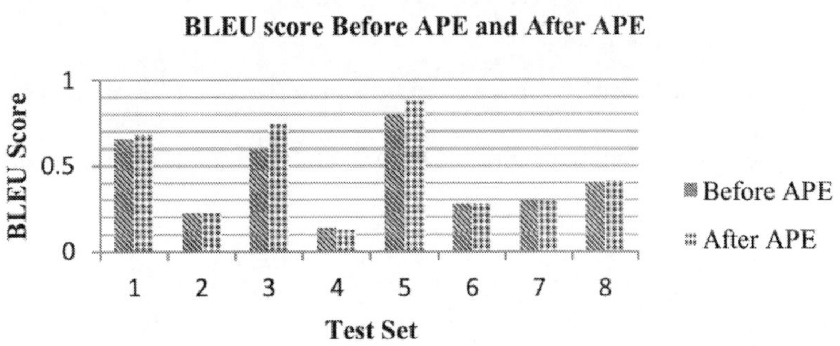

FIGURE 3 –Difference of BLEU score after applying APE on eight test sets

We propose that the weakened results are mainly due to the lack of training data for the Transliterator module in which some proper names and terms are scripted incorrectly in Persian.

Since we use the output of the SMT system, the quality of statistical translation (in terms of BLEU metric score) affects the APE module directly. Test set #4 yielded poor quality since the parallel corpus contained much less data in the religious genre. Furthermore, where there were some English words in the SMT output that OOVRemover was unable to correct, Transliterator generated a Persian script which completely changed the meaning of the original sentence.

4.3 Manual Evaluation

Marecek et al. (2011) show that grammatical correctness cannot simply be drawn from BLEU metrics alone. Because of this, we manually evaluated the proposed model. We used the same test sets as the automatic evaluation containing 153 sentences and the sentences were translated using SMT and post-edited by the proposed APE system. We assigned the APE output to two separate annotators, who were to rank the APE output based on the following criteria:

No Change: There is no difference to APE output and SMT output.
Improved: There are certain changes improving fluency.
Weakened: There are certain changes decreasing fluency.

The results of the manual evaluation are shown in Table 4.

Annotator/Rank	Improved	No Change	Weakened
Annotator 1	47	95	11
Annotator 2	43	99	11

TABLE 4 – Scores of two human evaluators for 153 test sentences

Both annotators completed the evaluation separately, but had very similar judgments of the APE system's output. The results show an improvement of the quality of the baseline SMT system output by 29.4% and that the rules developed in the APE system are not applicable to more than a half (63.4%) of the SMT output. On the other hand, human evaluation also shows that in some cases, the output is weakened after applying APE.

Both annotators' scores (Table 5) show a sentence quality improvement of 25% due to the APE.

I / II	Improved	No Change	Weakened
Improved	39	5	5
No Change	3	90	2
Weakened	3	4	4

TABLE 5 – Mutual score for both human evaluator I and evaluator II

Conclusion

We present an uncommon APE model for English-Persian statistical machine translation modeled on a rule-based approach in different levels of transformation. The automatic and manual evaluation results show encouraging improvement in quality of translation after post editing. While the improvement in some test sets is small, it still improves the SMT output up to 0.15 BLEU. Manual evaluation scores show that a rule-based APE system can yield even better results. From our results we can see at least a 25% improved output for a loss of at most 7%.

References

Allen, J., & Hogan, C. (2000). *Toward the Development of a Post editing Module for Raw Machine Translation Output: A Controlled Language Perspective*.

Buchholz, S., & Marsi, E. (2006). *CoNLL-X shared task on multilingual dependency parsing*.

Chiang, D. (2005). *A hierarchical phrase-based model for statistical machine translation*.

Ganitkevitch, J., Cao, Y., Weese, J., Post, M., & Callison-Burch, C. (2012). Joshua 4.0: Packing, PRO, and paraphrases.

Hudson, R. A. (1984). *Word grammar*: Blackwell Oxford.

Koehn, P., Och, F., & Marcu, D. (2003). *Statistical phrase-based translation*.

Kübler, S., McDonald, R., & Nivre, J. (2009). Dependency parsing. *Synthesis Lectures on Human Language Technologies, 1*(1), 1-127.

Lagarda, A. L., Alabau, V., Casacuberta, F., Silva, R., & Diaz-de-Liano, E. (2009). *Statistical post-editing of a rule-based machine translation system*.

Li, Z., Callison-Burch, C., Khudanpur, S., & Thornton, W. (2009). Decoding in Joshua. *The Prague Bulletin of Mathematical Linguistics, 91*, 47-56.

Marcu, D., & Wong, W. (2002). *A phrase-based, joint probability model for statistical machine translation*.

Marecek, D., Rosa, R., & Bojar, O. (2011). *Two-step translation with grammatical post-processing*.

McDonald, R., Pereira, F., Ribarov, K., & Hajic, J. (2005). *Non-projective dependency parsing using spanning tree algorithms*.

Mohaghegh, M., & Sarrafzadeh, A. (2012). *A hierarchical phrase-based model for English-Persian statistical machine translation*.

Mohaghegh, M., Sarrafzadeh, A., & Moir, T. (2011). *Improving Persian-English Statistical Machine Translation: Experiments in Domain Adaptation*.

Mohamed, A. A. E. M. (2000). Machine Translation of Noun Phrases from English to Arabic. *Faculty of Engineering, Cairo University, Giza*.

Och, F., & Ney, H. (2004). The alignment template approach to statistical machine translation. *Computational Linguistics, 30*(4), 417-449.

Och, F., Tillmann, C., & Ney, H. (1999). *Improved alignment models for statistical machine translation.*

Pilevar, A. H. (2011). USING STATISTICAL POST-EDITING TO IMPROVE THE OUTPUT OF RULE-BASED MACHINE TRANSLATION SYSTEM. *Training, 330*, 330,000.

Raja, F., Amiri, H., Tasharofi, S., Sarmadi, M., Hojjat, H., & Oroumchian, F. (2007). Evaluation of part of speech tagging on Persian text. *University of Wollongong in Dubai-Papers*, 8.

Rasooli, M. S., Moloodi, A., Kouhestani, M., & Minaei-Bidgoli, B. (2011). *A syntactic valency lexicon for Persian verbs: The first steps towards Persian dependency treebank.*

Rosa, R., Marecek, D., & Duˇsek, O. (2012). *DEPFIX: A System for Automatic Correction of Czech MT Outputs.*

Simard, M., Goutte, C., & Isabelle, P. (2007). Statistical phrase-based post-editing.

Relational Structures and Models for Coreference Resolution

Truc-Vien T. Nguyen[1] *Massimo Poesio*[1,2]
(1) CIMeC, University of Trento, Rovereto (TN), 38068, Italy
(2) University of Essex, Wivenhoe Park, Colchester CO4 3SQ, UK
{trucvien.nguyenthi,massimo.poesio}@unitn.it

Abstract

Coreference resolution is the task of identifying the sets of mentions referring to the same entity. Although modern machine learning approaches to coreference resolution exploit a variety of semantic information, the literature on the effect of relational information on coreference is still very limited. In this paper, we discuss and compare two methods for incorporating relational information into a coreference resolver. One approach is to use a filtering algorithm to rerank the output of coreference hypotheses. The filter is based on the relational structures between mentions and their corresponding relationships. The second approach is to use a joint model enriched with a set of relational features derived from semantic relations of each mention. Both methods have shown to improve the performance of a learning-based state-of-the-art coreference resolver.

Keywords: coreference resolution, relation extraction, machine learning.

Proceedings of COLING 2012: Posters, pages 883–892,
COLING 2012, Mumbai, December 2012.

1 Introduction

Much of the recent progress in statistical models of coreference resolution (Rahman and Ng, 2009, 2011; Ng, 2010) has come from the adoption of richer models of this interpretive task that overcome the limitations and simplifications of earlier models (Soon et al., 2001; Ng and Cardie, 2002), such as the assumption that resolving coreference involves linking mentions. There has also been some progress towards taking advantage of richer forms of information in general and of semantic knowledge in particular. Lexical knowledge has been shown to be clearly useful (Ponzetto and Strube, 2006) and is exploited by most state-of-the-art systems (Bengtson and Roth, 2008; Lee et al., 2011); it has been shown that encyclopedic knowledge as contained e.g., in Wikipedia can help as well (Ponzetto and Strube, 2006; Uryupina et al., 2011). But the ultimate goal is to develop a statistic-based integrated model of semantic interpretation in which coreference interacts with other aspects of interpretation such as predicate-argument structure recognition or discourse structure resolution, as argued in particular by (Hobbs, 1979) and implemented on a small-scale basis in the early, pre-statistical systems (Wilks, 1975; Hobbs et al., 1993; Alshawi, 1992).

Most work to this end has been concerned with the use of semantic role information to improve in particular the resolution of pronouns (Yang and Su, 2007; Ponzetto and Strube, 2006; Bean and Riloff, 2004). However, there has been much more limited investigation of the effect on coreference of the information provided by ACE-style relations. This is surprising given, first, that *prima facie*, such information should be very useful, and second, that annotated containing both coreference and relational information exist, most notably ACE-05. ACE-style relational information could be useful to increase precision, by ruling out coreference relations between entities already known to be related by other relations: if Jack is related by a 'colleague' relation with Mr. Smith, then most likely Jack and Mr. Smith are not coreferent. Such information could also be useful to increase recall: if Jack is related by a 'works-for' relation to an entity mentioned as 'Foobar Inc.' and by a 'colleague' relation with Mr. Smith, and Mr. Smith is related by a 'works-for' relation to an entity mentioned as 'the international conglomerate', then most likely 'Foobar Inc.' and 'the international conglomerate' are mentions of the same entity. Yet we are only aware of one study exploring the use of such information to improve coreference, namely (Ji et al., 2005), whose approach however was rule-based. In this paper we revisit the topic and compare rule-based methods with machine-learning approaches to integrating relational and coreference information.

The structure of the paper is as follows. In Section 2 we discuss previous work on using relational information for coreference. In Section 3 we describe relational information in the ACE corpora. In Section 4 we propose three methods for integrating relational information in a coreference resolver; the experimental setting used to evaluate these methods and the results we obtained are discussed in Section 5.

2 Related Work

The most closely related work to ours is the proposal by (Ji et al., 2005), who use heuristics to integrate constraints from relations between mentions with a coreference resolver. Their methodology involves a two-stage approach where the probabilities output from a MaxEnt classifier are rescored by adding information about the semantic relations between the two candidate mentions. These relations are automatically output by a relation tagger, which is trained on a corpus annotated with the semantic relations from the ACE 2004 relation ontology. Given a candidate pair 1.B and 2.B and the respective mentions 1.A and 2.A they are related to in the same document, Ji et al identify three lightweight rules to identify configurations informative of coreference:

1. If the relation between 1.A and 1.B is the same as the relation between 2.A and 2.B, and 1A and 2A don't corefer, then 1.B and 2.B are less likely to corefer.

2. If the relation between 1.A and 1.B is different from the relation between 2.A and 2.B, and 1.A is coreferent with 2.A, then 1.B and 2.B are less likely to corefer.

3. If the relation between 1.A and 1.B is the same as the relation between 2.A and 2.B and 1.A is coreferent with 2.A, then 1.B and 2.B are more likely to corefer.

While Ji et al. argue that the second rule usually has high accuracy independently of the particular relation, the accuracy of the other two rules depends on the particular relation. For example, the chairman of a company, which has a EMP- ORG/Employ-Executive relation, may be more likely to remain the same chairman across the text than a spokesperson of that company, which is in the EMP- ORG/Employ-Staff relation to it. Accordingly, the system retain only those rule instantiated with a specific ACE relation which have a precision of 70% or more, yielding 58 rule instances. For instances that still have lower precision, they try conjoining additional preconditions such as the absence of temporal modifiers such as "current" and "former," high confidence for the original coreference decisions, substring matching and/or head matching. In this way, they can recover 24 additional reliable rules that consist of one of the weaker rules plus combinations of at most 3 of the additional restrictions. They evaluate the system, trained on the ACE 2002 and ACE 2003 training corpora, on the ACE 2004 evaluation data and provide two types of evaluation: the first uses Vilain et al's scoring scheme, but uses perfect mentions, whereas the second uses system mentions, but ignore in the evaluation any mention that is not both in the system and key response. Using these two evaluation methods, they get an improvement in F-measure of about 2% in every case. In the main text of the paper, Ji et al. report an improvement in F-measure from 80.1% to 82.4%, largely due to a large gain in recall. These numbers are relatively high due to the fact that Ji et al. use a relaxed evaluation setting disregarding spurious links. A strict evaluation on exact mentions is able instead to yield an improvement in F-measure from 62.8% to 64.2% on the newswire section of the ACE corpus.

3 Relational Information in the ACE corpora

The ACE effort (Doddington et al., 2004) (Automatic Content Extraction) aims at developing technology for automatically carrying out inference in natural language text. The data includes the entities being mentioned, the relations among these entities that are directly expressed, and the events in which these entities participate. The program began with a pilot study in 1999. Moreover, data includes various source types (image, audio, text) and languages (English, Arabic).

We use the ACE 2005 Multilingual Training Corpus[1]. ACE defines 7 major entity types: FAC (Facility), GPE (Geo-Political Entity: countries, cities, etc.), LOC (Location), ORG (Organization), PER (Person), VEH (Vehicle) and WEA (Weapon). Relationship is defined in ACE as semantic relations between pairs of entities in texts. Note that relations in ACE are mostly directional (i.e., asymmetric), very few are symmetric, such as PHYS.Near that characterizes the two locations are nearby and PER-SOC.Family-Colleague that characterizes a family or colleague relationship.

Table 1 shows examples of ACE relations, the pair of arguments participating in the relation with their directionality, according to ACE guidelines and standards. In the models that integrate relational features, we mainly take the relation's direction into account to compute the features. In the following, we use the term *head* and *tail* to indicate the mentions where the relations are directed from and to, respectively.

[1]http://www.ldc.upenn.edu/Catalog/catalogEntry.jsp?catalogId=LDC2006T06

Relation type	Example	From	To
ART(artifact)	*My house is in West Philadelphia* ART.User-Owner("my", "my house")	"my"	"my house"
GEN-AFF	*U.S. businessman* GEN-AFF.Citizen("businessman", "U.S")	"businessman"	"U.S"
ORF-AFF	*the CEO of Yahoo* ORF-AFF.Employment("the CEO", "Yahoo")	"the CEO"	"Yahoo"
PART-WHOLE	*Northern Ireland in Belfast* PART-WHOLE.Geographical("Belfast", "Northern Ireland")	"Belfast"	"Northern Ireland"
PER-SOC*	*their colleagues* PER-SOC.Business("their", "their colleagues")	"their"	"their colleagues"
PHYS*	*a news conference in Paris* PHYS.Located("conference", "Paris")	"conference"	"Paris"

Table 1: Relation types in ACE 2005 and their directionality

4 Embedding Relational Information

In this section, we describe three methods for integrating relational information in a coreference resolver: the reranker, the enriched model and the joint model.

In traditional mention-pair coreference resolvers (Soon et al., 2001), the training and testing units are pairs $< x, y >$ of candidate antecedent and anaphor. The system extracts a vector v which contains syntactic and semantic features from these two mentions. A coreference resolver then learns a mapping function $v \rightarrow c$ where $c = (0, 1)$ indicates if x and y belong to the same coreference chain. In other words, a coreference resolver estimates $p(c|v)$, the probability that x is the antecedent of y given the feature vector v.

4.1 Reranking

The coreference reranker operates by first applying a baseline model trained using a maximum entropy classifier with the features proposed in (Soon et al., 2001) to determine whether two mentions $(antecedent, anaphor)$ are coreferent or not. We then use the resulting coreference chains c in combination with the relationships between mentions to construct a set of *relational structures*. We then extract from those structures a vector r of *relational features*. The coreference reranker then integrates v and r and improves the mapping function $(v, r) \rightarrow c$.

In other words, when integrated with relational information, the system extracts a vector r of relational features, which are derived from both the coreference chains c of the base model and relationships between pairs of mentions. The coreference reranker then integrates v and r and improves the mapping function $(v, r) \rightarrow c$.

Figure 1 shows the relational structure for the coreference chain on the left. The directionality specified in Table 1 is used to determine the relations belonging to the structure: only the relations whose first argument ('from' in Table 1) belongs to the coreference chain on the left are considered part of the relational structure for that coreference chain; which represents the coreference chains as group of mentions on the left, their relationships and other participants on the right. These structures are used to infer if it is likely that two mentions corefer, as described in the following.

From the relational structure we extract features that can supplement the information available to the base coreference resolver. Our set of features are inspired from those used by (Ji et al., 2005), but the method discussed in this subsection differs from theirs in three important respects, as discussed below.

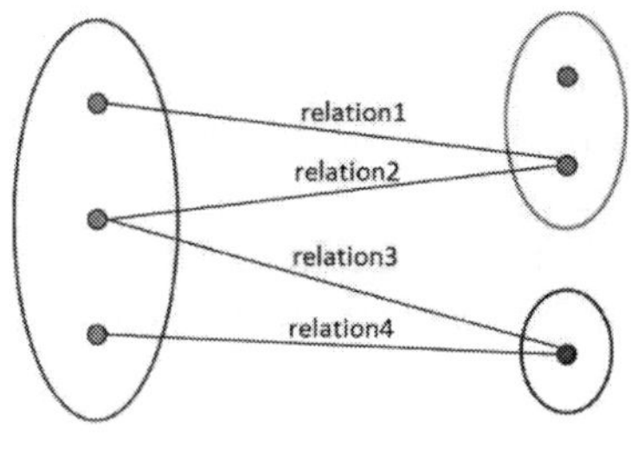

Figure 1: Relational structure

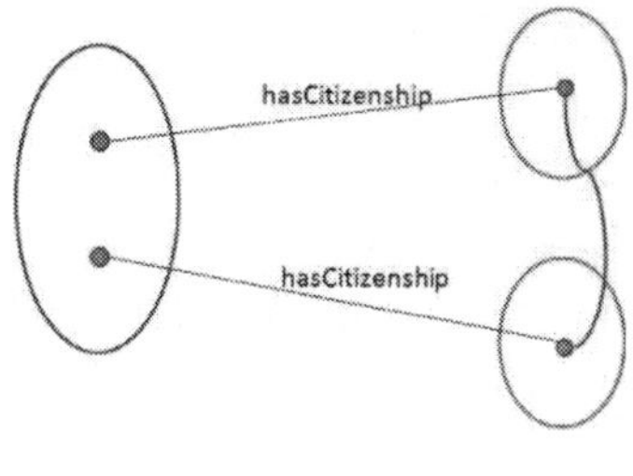

Figure 2: Coref_SameRelation

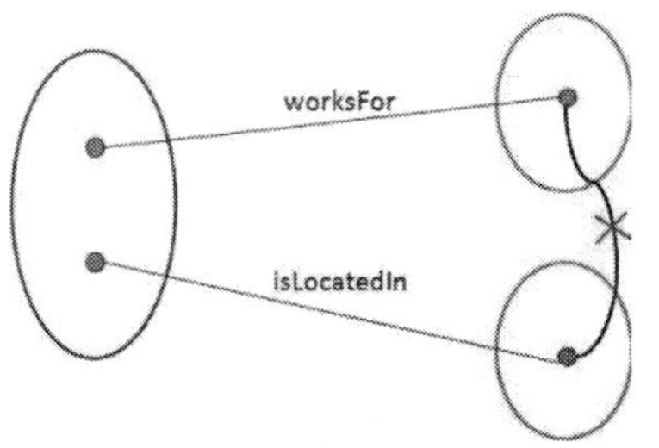

Figure 3: Coref_NotSameRelation

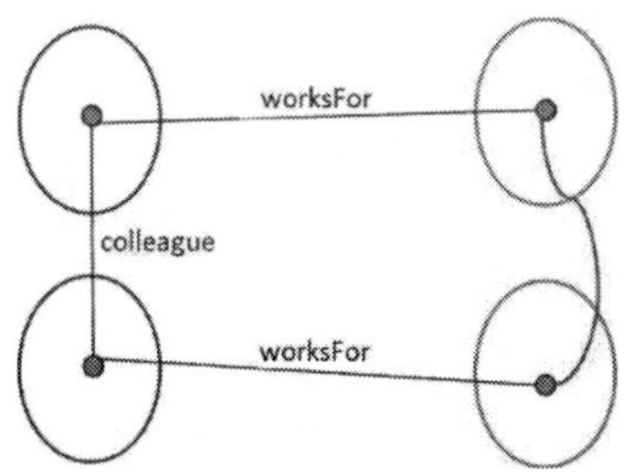

Figure 4: Coref_Transitivity

1. **Coref_SameRelation**: if two mentions in the same coreference chain have two relations directed from them with the same relation type and direction, then the two participants in those relations are likely to corefer, as illustrated in Figure 2.

2. **Coref_NotSameRelation**: if two mentions in the same coreference chain have two relations directed from them with different relation type and the same direction, or the same relation type but different direction, then the two participants in those relations are unlikely to corefer, as illustrated in Figure 3.

3. **Coref_Transitivity**: : if two mentions in different coreference chains have two relations directed from them with the same relation type and the same direction, and if these two mentions have the same semantic classes and participate in "maybe peer" relation (such as PHYS.Near or PER-SOC.Colleague), then the two participants in those relations are likely to corefer, as illustrated in Figure 4.

Our proposal differs from the work of (Ji et al., 2005) in three aspects. First, our approach is not rule-based but learning based. Second, we do not compute the reliability weight for each rule; instead, we integrate each feature with relation type/direction directly to the learning model and let the model learn automatically. Finally, whereas their second and third rules are similar to our feature $FE\_Coref\_SameRelation$ and $FE\_Coref\_NotSameRelation$, we do not use the first rule (discussed in section 2) that refers to the two mentions in two different chains that have the same relation type/direction, since that rule is problematic. For example, the fact that *Bush* and *Obama* are mentions in different coreference chains with the same relation types/direction *leadership* with mentions of the entity *US*, doesn't mean that the two mentions *US* participating in the relationships cannot corefer.

4.2 Relational Features

An alternative approach is to use relational information to define features. Relational features are derived from relationships between mentions. As shown in Table 1, a relationship in ACE is defined between a pair of mentions, with a corresponding relation. In Table 1, each relationship is directed from one mention to another, the direction, as we notice, is *many-to-one* in most of cases and should be taken into account. Given a pair of *(antecedent, anaphor)*, we then extract relations for each mention and define the following features.

1. **FE_Related** characterizes relationships hold between a anaphor with its potential antecedent. Reasonably, relationships should not be hold between mentions of the same coreference chain.

2. **FE_SameRelation** determines if the pair *(anaphor, antecedent)* has two relations starting from them with the same relation type and direction. We argue that if the two mentions *(anaphor, antecedent)* have relationships of the same type/direction (e.g., *hasCitizenship* or *worksFor*), then it is more likely they are corefered.

3. **FE_SameRelationEntity** determines if the pair *(anaphor, antecedent)* has two relations starting from them with the same relation type/direction and directed to the same mention.

4. **FE_SameRelationWithPeer** determines if the pair *(anaphor, antecedent)* has two relations starting from them with the same relation type/direction and if the relations are directed to the two mentions of the same semantic type and connected by a "peer" relation, such as PHYS.Near or PER-SOC.

5. **FE_LeftRelation** describes the set of relation types in common between *antecedent* and *anaphor* where relations are those with these two mentions as *head*, as described in Table 1. We construct a vector from set of relations where *antecedent* and *anaphor* are the head, respectively, then compute the *dot-product* between the two vectors.

6. **FE_RightRelation** is the same as above, but applied for relations are those with these two mentions as *tail*.

7. **FE_SumRelation** computes the sum of FE_LeftRelation and FE_RightRelation.

8. **FE_SubtractRelation** computes the subtraction of FE_RightRelation and FE_LeftRelation. Given that the relation' direction is almost *many-to-one*, we argue that the *tail mention* promise to be more effective. Therefore, we compute the *dot-product* of *tail mention* and of *head mention* with respect to the pair *(antecedent, anaphor)* and take the subtraction of these two.

9. **FE_MultiplyRelation** computes the multiplication of FE_LeftRelation and FE_RightRelation.

4.3 Enriched Model and Joint Model

Given the baseline and set of additional relational features as described in the previous section, the enriched model works simply by adding those features into the baseline. Although the features *FE_Related, FE_SameRelationEntity, FE_SameRelationWithPeer* and *FE_SubtractRelation* are the best performers, the performance is almost consistent amongst the nine relational features.

However, we notice that, when integrated with each of nine relational features r_i (which we call 'individual model'), the increase in the performance is not always consistent amongst different documents. Therefore, we proceed with a joint model that learns jointly among separate individual models and picks the one with the highest score as the final answer. To train the basic models, we add each relational feature into the baseline and re-train. At testing time the model receiving the highest score is selected as the final answer.

5 Experiments and Results

5.1 Experimental Setup

Corpus. We use the ACE 2005 coreference corpus released by the LDC, which consists of the 599 training documents used in the official ACE evaluation. The corpus was created by selecting documents from six different sources: Broadcast News (bn), Broadcast Conversations (bc), Newswire (nw), Webblog (wb), Usenet (un), and conversational telephone speech (cts). For evaluation, we reuse the partition done by (Rahman and Ng, 2009) that splits the 599 documents into a training set and a test set following a 80/20 ratio, resulting in a partition of 482/117 documents.

In our experiments, we use the relation extraction model[2] proposed in (Nguyen and Moschitti, 2011). To extract mentions from both the training and test set, we used the model defined in (Nguyen et al., 2010, 2009) to train a mention extractor. When evaluated on the ACE 2005 data sets, since documents in the corpus are from six different sources with equivalent number of documents in each source, we perform 6-fold cross-validation where each fold consists of documents from one source. The performance of the relation and mention extractor is given in Table 2.

Task	Precision	Recall	F_1
Relation extractor	57.9%	59.4%	58.5%
Mention extractor	75.3%	67.7%	71.3%

Table 2: Performance of relation extraction and mention extraction

Baseline. As a baseline we train a maximum entropy classifier to generate the coreference chains. We use (Soon et al., 2001) set of features as implemented in the BART coreference toolkit[3]. The base model makes use of a maximum entropy classifier to train a *mention-pair* model, which determines whether two mentions are coreferent or not. Our baseline results are shown in Table 3 which also includes the results of another state-of-the-art coreference system of (Rahman and Ng, 2009). For this and the following experiments, all the results were computed using *MUC-score* with standard precision, recall, and *F-measure*.

	Gold mentions			System mentions		
System	Recall	Precision	F_1	Recall	Precision	F_1
Our Baseline	65.7	87.9	75.2	50.8	76.7	61.1
(Rahman and Ng, 2009)	71.7	69.2	70.4	70.0	56.4	62.5

Table 3: Performance comparison on the ACE 2005

5.2 Results

In this section, we report the results of different relationals model with the reranker, the enriched model and the joint model. Results with the reranking approach is shown in the second line of Table 4. Results of the enriched model with separate features and with the combination of all features, and results with the joint model are shown in Table 4.

[2]http://sourceforge.net/projects/reck/files/reck_v1.0.0.tar.gz/download
[3]http://www.bart-coref.org/

First, the *reranker* improves to 76.1 with *gold mentions* and 62.7 with *system mentions* when relational information is added. This suggests that the relational structures are effectively exploited with the three features as desribed in section 4.1 and that such information is somewhat complementary to the basic feature set as defined in (Soon et al., 2001).

	Gold mentions			System mentions		
Setting	Recall	Precision	F_1	Recall	Precision	F_1
Baseline	65.7	87.9	75.2	50.8	76.7	61.1
Reranking	**66.8**	**88.4**	**76.1**	**52.6**	**77.5**	**62.7**
FE_Related	65.7	88.2	75.3	51.0	77.0	61.4
FE_SameRelation	65.7	88.2	75.3	50.9	77.0	61.3
FE_SameRelationEntity	65.7	88.1	75.3	51.1	77.0	61.4
FE_SameRelationWithPeer	65.8	88.1	75.3	51.1	77.0	61.4
FE_LeftRelation	65.8	88.1	75.3	51.0	76.7	61.2
FE_RightRelation	65.8	88.0	75.3	50.9	77.0	61.3
FE_SumRelation	65.8	88.0	75.3	50.9	77.0	61.3
FE_SubtractRelation	65.8	88.0	75.3	51.0	77.0	61.4
FE_MultiplyRelation	65.7	88.0	75.3	51.2	77.0	61.4
Enriched Model	**66.3**	**88.7**	**76.0**	**52.1**	**76.7**	**62.0**
Joint Model	**67.0**	**88.9**	**76.4**	**54.5**	**75.7**	**63.3**

Table 4: Results with reranking, enriched and joint models

Second, the enriched model improves to 76.0 with *gold mentions* and 62.0 with *system mentions* when the base model is enriched with nine relational features. This suggests that the relation information between pairs of mentions can be encoded together with information merely from the mentions themselves.

Third, the joint model improves to 76.4 with *gold mentions* and 63.3 with *system mentions* when the enriched models are trained with separate relational features and the joint model chooses the best score for each testing instance. This suggests that the relational information, when possible to be encoded to yield better results as in the case of the *enriched model*, are not exploited as better as the *joint model* strategy. We also conducted *sign test* to measure the difference between the best model (i.e., joint model) and the baseline. The significance results are $\rho = 0.0047$ with *gold mentions* and $\rho = 0.0033$ with *system mentions*, which means that our results are statistically significant.

6 Conclusion

Previous results suggest that relational features are clearly helpful for coreference resolution in ACE. However, as we showed, there has been much more limited investigation of the effect on coreference of the information provided by ACE-style relations. Such information should be very useful, and that annotated containing both coreference and relational information exist, most notably ACE-05.

The *joint model* performs the best. That would suggest 1. relational features are helpful in linking one anaphor to its antecedent; 2. the integration of machine learning methods outperforms the merely addition of relational features, as in the enriched model.

We analyzed the impact of relational structures and features for coreference resolution. Our study demonstrates that both kinds of structures and features clearly give improvement to the coreference resolver. Most interestingly, as we shown, the integration of relational features, in combination of the ranking method, yields the best results. The joint model, that is taken by comparing the enriched models one with each other, turns out as very effective for both *gold mentions* and *system mentions*.

References

Alshawi, H., editor (1992). *The Core Language Engine*. The MIT Press.

Bean, D. and Riloff, E. (2004). Unsupervised learning of contextual role knowledge for coreference resolution. In Susan Dumais, D. M. and Roukos, S., editors, *HLT-NAACL 2004: Main Proceedings*, pages 297–304, Boston, Massachusetts, USA. Association for Computational Linguistics.

Bengtson, E. and Roth, D. (2008). Understanding the value of features for coreference resolution. In *Proceedings of the 2008 Conference on Empirical Methods in Natural Language Processing*, pages 294–303, Honolulu, Hawaii. Association for Computational Linguistics.

Doddington, G., Mitchell, A., Przybocki, M., Ramshaw, L., Strassel, S., and Weischedel, R. (2004). The automatic content extraction (ACE) program tasks, data, and evaluation. In *Proceedings of LREC*, pages 837–840, Barcelona, Spain.

Hobbs, J. R. (1979). Resolving pronoun references. *Coherence and Coreference*, 3:67–90.

Hobbs, J. R., Stickel, M., Appelt, D., and Martin, P. (1993). Interpretation as abduction. *Artificial Intelligence Journal*, 63:69–142.

Ji, H., Westbrook, D., and Grishman, R. (2005). Using semantic relations to refine coreference decisions. In *Proceedings of Human Language Technology Conference and Conference on Empirical Methods in Natural Language Processing*, pages 17–24, Vancouver, British Columbia, Canada. Association for Computational Linguistics.

Lee, H., Peirsman, Y., Chang, A., Chambers, N., Surdeanu, M., and Jurafsky, D. (2011). Stanford's multi-pass sieve coreference resolution system at the conll-2011 shared task. In *Proceedings of the Fifteenth Conference on Computational Natural Language Learning: Shared Task*, pages 28–34, Portland, Oregon, USA. Association for Computational Linguistics.

Ng, V. (2010). Supervised noun phrase coreference research: The first fifteen years. In *Proceedings of the 48th Annual Meeting of the Association for Computational Linguistics*, pages 1396–1411, Uppsala, Sweden. Association for Computational Linguistics.

Ng, V. and Cardie, C. (2002). Improving machine learning approaches to coreference resolution. In *Proceedings of 40th Annual Meeting of the Association for Computational Linguistics*, pages 104–111, Philadelphia, Pennsylvania, USA. Association for Computational Linguistics.

Nguyen, T. V. T. and Moschitti, A. (2011). Joint distant and direct supervision for relation extraction. In *Proceedings of the 5th International Joint Conference on Natural Language Processing*, Chiang Mai, Thailand.

Nguyen, T.-V. T., Moschitti, A., and Riccardi, G. (2009). Conditional random fields: Discriminative training over statistical features for named entity recognition. In *Proceedings of EVALITA 2009 workshop, the 11st International Conference of the Italian Association for Artificial Intelligence (AI*IA)*, Reggio Emilia, Italy.

Nguyen, T.-V. T., Moschitti, A., and Riccardi, G. (2010). Kernel-based reranking for named-entity extraction. In *Coling 2010: Posters*, pages 901–909, Beijing, China. Coling 2010 Organizing Committee.

Ponzetto, S. P. and Strube, M. (2006). Exploiting semantic role labeling, wordnet and wikipedia for coreference resolution. In *Proceedings of the Human Language Technology Conference of the NAACL, Main Conference*, pages 192–199, New York City, USA. Association for Computational Linguistics.

Rahman, A. and Ng, V. (2009). Supervised models for coreference resolution. In *Proceedings of the 2009 Conference on Empirical Methods in Natural Language Processing*, pages 968–977, Singapore. Association for Computational Linguistics.

Rahman, A. and Ng, V. (2011). Ensemble-based coreference resolution. In *Proceedings of the Twenty-Second international joint conference on Artificial Intelligence - Volume Volume Three*, IJCAI'11, pages 1884–1889. AAAI Press.

Soon, W. M., Ng, H. T., and Lim, D. C. Y. (2001). A machine learning approach to coreference resolution of noun phrases. *Computational Linguistics*, 27(4):521–544.

Uryupina, O., Poesio, M., Giuliano, C., and Tymoshenko, K. (2011). Using wikipedia for coreference resolution. In *Proceedings of the 24th Florida Artificial Intelligence Research Society Conference*.

Wilks, Y. (1975). A preferential pattern-matching semantics for natural language. *AIJ*, 6:53–74.

Yang, X. and Su, J. (2007). Coreference resolution using semantic relatedness information from automatically discovered patterns. In *Proceedings of the 45th Annual Meeting of the Association of Computational Linguistics*, pages 528–535, Prague, Czech Republic. Association for Computational Linguistics.

Text Summarization Model based on Redundancy-Constrained Knapsack Problem

Hitoshi Nishikawa[1], *Tsutomu Hirao*[2], *Toshiro Makino*[1] *and Yoshihiro Matsuo*[1]
(1) NTT Media Intelligence Laboratories, NTT Corporation
1-1 Hikarinooka Yokosuka-shi, Kanagawa 239-0847 Japan
(2) NTT Communication Science Laboratories, NTT Corporation
2-4 Hikaridai Seika-cho, Soraku-gun, Kyoto 619-0237 Japan
{ nishikawa.hitoshi, hirao.tsutomu, makino.toshiro, matsuo.yoshihiro }@lab.ntt.co.jp

ABSTRACT

In this paper we propose a novel text summarization model, the redundancy-constrained knapsack model. We add to the Knapsack problem a constraint to curb redundancy in the summary. We also propose a fast decoding method based on the Lagrange heuristic. Experiments based on ROUGE evaluations show that our proposals outperform a state-of-the-art text summarization model, the maximum coverage model, in finding the optimal solution. We also show that our decoding method quickly finds a good approximate solution comparable to the optimal solution of the maximum coverage model.

KEYWORDS: Text summarization, Knapsack problem, Maximum coverage problem, Lagrange heuristics.

Proceedings of COLING 2012: Posters, pages 893–902,
COLING 2012, Mumbai, December 2012.

1 Introduction

Many text summarization studies in recent years formulate text summarization as the maximum coverage problem (Filatova and Hatzivassiloglou, 2004; Yih et al., 2007; Takamura and Okumura, 2009; Gillick and Favre, 2009; Nishikawa et al., 2010; Higashinaka et al., 2010). The maximum coverage model, based on the maximum coverage problem, generates a summary by selecting sentences to cover as many information units (such as unigrams and bigrams) as possible. Takamura and Okumura (2009) and Gillick and Favre (2009) demonstrated that the maximum coverage problem offers great performance as a text summarization model. Unfortunately, its potential is hindered by the fact that it is NP-hard (Khuller et al., 1999). There is little hope that a polynomial time algorithm for the problem exists.

Another theoretical framework for text summarization, the knapsack problem, avoids trying to cover unigrams or bigrams, and instead emphasizes the selection of important sentences under the constraint of summary length. The knapsack problem can be solved by a dynamic programming algorithm in pseudo-polynomial time (Korte and Vygen, 2008). However, the knapsack model, a text summarization model based on the knapsack problem, scores each sentence independently. While it can easily maximizes the sum of their scores, it threatens to generate redundant summaries unlike the maximum coverage model.

To tackle this trade-off between summary quality and decoding speed, we propose a novel text summarization model, the redundancy-constrained knapsack model. Starting with the advantage of the knapsack model, it uses dynamic programming to achieve optimization in pseudo-polynomial time. We add to it a constraint that curbs summary redundancy. Although this constraint can suppress summary redundancy, finding the optimal solution again becomes a challenge.

To ensure that our proposed model can find good approximate solutions, we turn to the Lagrange heuristic (Haddadi, 1997). This is an algorithm that finds a feasible solution from the relaxed, infeasible solution induced by Lagrange relaxation. It is known to be effective in finding good approximate solutions for the set covering problem (Haddadi, 1997).

We present the novelty and contribution of this paper as follows:

- In this paper we define a novel objective function and decoding algorithm for multi-document summarization. The model and algorithm presented in this paper are new in the context of automatic summarization research.
- Our proposal, the redundancy-constrained knapsack model, outperforms the maximum coverage model on the ROUGE (Lin, 2004) evaluation.
- The approximate solution of our proposed model, found by our proposed decoding method, is comparable with the optimal solution of the maximum coverage model. We also show that this approximate solution is found far faster than the optimal solution of the maximum coverage model.

This paper is organized as follows. In Section 2, we describe related work. In Section 3, we elaborate our proposed model. In Section 4, we explain the algorithm that finds a good approximate solution for our proposed model. In Section 5, we show results of experiments conducted to evaluate our proposal. In Section 6 we conclude this paper.

2 Related Work

The text summarization model based on the maximum coverage problem was proposed by Filatova and Hatzivassiloglou (2004). They solved their model by a greedy algorithm (Khuller et al., 1999). Yih et al. (2007) solved the model by a stack decoder. Takamura and Okumura (2009) and Gillick and Favre (2009) formulated the model as Integer Linear Programming (ILP) and solved the model using a branch-and-bound method.

The maximum coverage model has a trade-off between its performance and decoding speed. Although simple decoding algorithm like the greedy algorithm and the stack decoder can find an approximate solution quickly, in many cases it is far from optimal. The ILP-based approach can find the optimal solution but it spends too long in doing so. In contrast to the maximum coverage model, our proposed decoding algorithm uses the Lagrange heuristic to quickly find a good approximate solution comparable to the optimal solution of the maximum coverage model.

McDonald (2007) showed that the text summarization model based on the knapsack problem can be solved by dynamic programming in pseudo-polynomial time. We leverage this knowledge to develop a novel algorithm that can find good approximate solutions for our proposed model.

3 Redundancy-Constrained Knapsack Model

In this section we elaborate our proposed text summarization model, the redundancy-constrained knapsack model. We first introduce the maximum coverage model and show its relationship with the knapsack model. We then explain the redundancy-constrained knapsack model and a variant that includes the Lagrange multipliers.

We consider there are n input sentences containing m unique information units, such as unigrams and bigrams. Let $\mathbf{x} = (x_1, \ldots, x_n)$ be a binary vector whose element x_i is a decision variable indicating whether sentence i is contained in the summary. If sentence i is contained in the summary, $x_i = 1$. Let $\mathbf{z} = (z_1, \ldots, z_m)$ be a binary vector whose element z_j is a decision variable indicating whether information unit j is contained in the summary. If information unit j is contained in the summary, $z_j = 1$. Let $\mathbf{w} = (w_1, \ldots, w_m)$ be a vector whose element w_j indicates the importance of information unit j. Let $\mathbf{A}$ be a matrix whose element a_{ji} indicates the number of information units, j, contained in sentence i. If sentence i contains two information units j, $a_{ji} = 2$. Let $\mathbf{l} = (l_1, \ldots, l_n)$ be a vector whose element l_i indicates the length of sentence i. Let K be the maximum summary length desired.

The maximum coverage model can be formulated as follows:

$$\max_{\mathbf{z}} \quad \mathbf{w}^{\mathrm{T}}\mathbf{z} \tag{1}$$

$$s.t. \quad \mathbf{A}\mathbf{x} \geq \mathbf{z} \tag{2}$$

$$\mathbf{x} \in \{0,1\}^n \tag{3}$$

$$\mathbf{z} \in \{0,1\}^m \tag{4}$$

$$\mathbf{l}^{\mathrm{T}}\mathbf{x} \leq K \tag{5}$$

As mentioned above, the maximum coverage model selects sentences to cover as many information units as possible. If the summary contains information units 3 and 4, the value of the objective function is the sum of w_3 and w_4. To maximize the objective function, the summary has to cover as many information units with high w values as possible.

Next, we describe the knapsack model. If constraint (2) is $\mathbf{Ax} = \mathbf{z}$ and constraint (4) is $\mathbf{z} \in \{\mathbb{N}^0\}^{\mathrm{m}}$, which is an m-dimensional vector whose elements are the natural numbers including 0, the model is the knapsack model. The knapsack model can be solved by dynamic programming in pseudo-polynomial time O(nK). However, due to the change of constraint (4) which prevents redundancy in the summary, the summary generated by the knapsack model is likely to be redundant. We suppress this redundancy through the addition of a constraint.

We describe our novel proposal, the redundancy-constrained knapsack model, below.

$$\max_{\mathbf{z}} \quad \mathbf{w}^{\mathrm{T}}\mathbf{z} \tag{6}$$

$$s.t. \quad \mathbf{Ax} = \mathbf{z} \tag{7}$$

$$\mathbf{x} \in \{0,1\}^n \tag{8}$$

$$\mathbf{z} \in \{z_j | \mathbb{N}^0 \cap [0, r_j]\}^m \tag{9}$$

$$\mathbf{l}^{\mathrm{T}}\mathbf{x} \leq K \tag{10}$$

$r_j \in \mathbf{r}$ in constraint (9) is an integer more than or equal to 0, and is the upper bound of z_j, the number of information units, j, contained in the summary. That is, in the redundancy-constrained knapsack model, constraint (9) limits z_j to lie in the range 0 to r_j. Thus redundancy in the summary can be reduced by vector $\mathbf{r}$. Although the model originally can be solved easily, constraint (9) explodes the search space so fining the optimal solution under redundancy constraint (9) is difficult[1].

To make the model tractable, we draw on Lagrangian relaxation. We add Lagrange multipliers to objective function (6) and relax constraint (9).

$$\max_{\mathbf{z}} \quad \mathbf{w}^{\mathrm{T}}\mathbf{z} + \boldsymbol{\lambda}^{\mathrm{T}}(\mathbf{r} - \mathbf{z}) \tag{11}$$

$$s.t. \quad \mathbf{Ax} = \mathbf{z} \tag{12}$$

$$\mathbf{x} \in \{0,1\}^n \tag{13}$$

$$\mathbf{z} \in \{\mathbb{N}^0\}^m \tag{14}$$

$$\mathbf{l}^{\mathrm{T}}\mathbf{x} \leq K \tag{15}$$

Non-negative Lagrange multipliers $\boldsymbol{\lambda} = (\lambda_1, \lambda_2, \ldots, \lambda_m)$ impose a penalty on objective function (11) when constraint (9) is violated. If the summary contains more than r_j information units, j, its importance w_j is reduced by Lagrange multiplier λ_j. Therefore, the number of information units, j, contained in the summary will decrease when the model is solved again by dynamic programming and the redundancy in the summary will be reduced (we detail our algorithm in the

[1] The redundancy-constrained knapsack problem can also be solved in pseudo-polynomial time. However its runtime is $O(nk \prod_{j=1}^{m} r_j)$, which is in effect exponential time.

next section). The Lagrange multipliers $\boldsymbol{\lambda}$ are calculated by solving the Lagrange dual problem of $L(\boldsymbol{\lambda}) = \min_{\boldsymbol{\lambda}}\{\max_{\mathbf{z}} \mathbf{w}^{\mathrm{T}}\mathbf{z} + \boldsymbol{\lambda}^{\mathrm{T}}(\mathbf{r} - \mathbf{z})\}$ using the subgradient method. Constraint (9) is an inequality constraint, so an optimal solution on the model can't be found unlike dependency parsing (Koo and Collins, 2010) and statistical machine translation (Chang and Collins, 2011), but an approximate solution can, however, be found by the decoding algorithm proposed below.

4 Decoding with Lagrange heuristic

We propose the following algorithm to find an approximate solution on objective function (11) in Algorithm 1. We outline our decoding algorithm below.

(1). Let all Lagrange multipliers λ_j be 0.
(2). Iterate following steps T times.
   A) Find the optimal solution on objective function (11) by dynamic programming.
   B) If the solution by (A) satisfies all constraints, return the solution. If not, use the heuristic to find a feasible solution from the optimal solution by (A).
   C) If solution (B) exceeds the lower bound, update the lower bound.
   D) Update the Lagrange multipliers.
(3). Output the solution corresponding to the lower bound.

```
input A, K, l, m, n, w
input α, r
initialize λ = 0, s = 0, x = 0, z = 0
initialize b_l = −∞, b_u = +∞, x_l = 0
for t = 1...T
        s = sentence(A, λ, m, n, w)
        x = dpkp(K, l, n, s)
        if score(A, m, n, x, w) ≤ b_u
                b_u = score(A, m, n, x, w)
        z = count(A, m, n, x)
        if z violates r
                x = heuristic(A, K, l, m, n, w)
                if score(A, m, n, x, w) ≥ b_l
                        b_l = score(A, m, n, x, w)
                        x_l = x
                λ = update(α, b_l, b_u, λ, m, r, z)
        else
                return x
return x_l
```

Algorithm 1: An iterative decoding algorithm with Lagrange heuristic. α is a parameter that controls the step size of λ. **s** is a vector whose element, s_i, indicates the score of sentence i. The score is calculated by function *sentence*. Function *dpkp* implements the dynamic programming algorithm for the knapsack problem in Algorithm 2. b_l and b_u indicate the lower bound and upper bound of the objective function, respectively, and are also used to decide the step size of λ. Function *score* calculates the score of summary **x**. Function *count* counts the information units contained in summary **x**, which is indicated by vector **z**. $\mathbf{x}_l$ preserves the solution corresponding to the lower bound b_l.

This iterative algorithm based on the Lagrange heuristics (Haddadi, 1997) can find a feasible solution at each iteration. If the algorithm doesn't converge in T iterations, the algorithm returns the most recent lower bound, which is the best feasible solution. If convergence is achieved, the solution is feasible. We show a dynamic programming algorithm to solve the knapsack problem in Algorithm 2. The Lagrange multipliers are updated by the following formula (Korte and

Vygen, 2008):

$$\lambda_j \leftarrow \max\,(\lambda_j + \alpha \frac{b_u - b_l}{||\mathbf{d}||^2}(z_j - r_j), 0) \tag{16}$$

where α is a parameter that controls the step size of λ_j; b_u and b_l are the lower and upper bounds; **d** is a subgradient of the Lagrange dual problem. This formula is based on the following search strategy:

(1). If the gap between the upper and lower bounds is large, λ_j should be updated substantially.
(2). λ_j should be updated in proportion to the gap between z_j and r_j.

Our heuristic, which recovers a feasible solution from the infeasible solution, is implemented as a greedy algorithm. We outline it below:

(1). Remove iteratively a sentence from the summary until the summary satisfies the redundancy constraint. The sentence whose score divided by its length is the least among the sentences that have information units violating the redundancy constraint is removed.
(2). If the summary satisfies the constraint, remove the sentences contained in the summary and its length from the original problem, generate a sub-problem, and then solve this sub-problem by the greedy method (Khuller et al., 1999).

```
input K, l, n, s
initialize x = 0
for j = 0...K
        T[0][j] = 0
for i = 1...n
        for j = 0...K
                T[i][j] = T[i - 1][j]
                U[i][j] = 0
        for j = l[i]...K
                if T[i - 1][j - l[i]] + s[i] ≥ T[i][j]
                        T[i][j] = T[i - 1][j - l[i]] + s[i]
                        U[i][j] = 1
j = K
for i = n...1
        if U[i][j] = 1
                x_i = 1
                j = j - l[i]

return x
```

Algorithm 2: A dynamic programming algorithm for the knapsack problem. The algorithm fills out two dimensional arrays T and U. $T[i][j]$ preserves the maximum score achieved at the time of i and j. $U[i][j]$ remembers whether sentence i is added to achieve the maximum score at the time of i and j. After filling out T and U, the best solution can be found by backtracking U.

5 Experiment

We evaluate our proposed method in terms of two criteria.

(1). **ROUGE**: We evaluate the quality of summaries produced from ROUGE (Lin, 2004).
(2). **Time**: We measure the time taken to generate the summaries of 30 input document sets.

We compare the following four methods:

(1). **Redundancy-constrained knapsack model (RCKM)**: Our proposed method. Find the optimal solution of Equation (11) using `lp_solve`[2] solver.
(2). **Redundancy-constrained knapsack model with the Lagrange heuristic (RCKM-LH)**: Our proposed method. Find the approximate solution of Equation (11) by our proposed algorithm shown in Algorithm 1. We evaluate the proposed algorithm with 10 iterations ($T = 10$) and 100 ($T = 100$) iterations.
(3). **Maximum coverage model (MCM)**: Baseline. Find the optimal solution using `lp_solve`.
(4). **Knapsack model (KM)**: Baseline. Find the optimal solution using the algorithm shown in Algorithm 2.

5.1 Data

We use the TSC-3 corpus (Hirao et al., 2004) for evaluation. It is an evaluation corpus for multi-document summarization and was used in Text Summarization Challenge 3[3]. It contains 30 Japanese news article sets, 352 articles and 3587 sentences. Each set has three reference summaries. Detailed information of the corpus is shown in (Hirao et al, 2004).

5.2 Parameter settings

We set the three essential parameters as follows:

- α: We set α as the inverse of the number of times that Lagrange multipliers have been updated.
- **r**: The allowed redundancy r_j can be set for each information unit j. We set $r_j = \lfloor\sqrt{\mathrm{tf}_j}\rfloor$ where tf_j is the number of information units, j, contained in the input document set and $\lfloor\ \rfloor$ is the floor function.
- **w**: we simply set j as a content word, and weight w_j based on tf-idf (Filatova and Hatzivassiloglou, 2004; Clarke and Lapata, 2007), $\mathrm{tf}_j \log\left(\frac{N}{\mathrm{df}_j}\right)$. N and df_j are the total number of documents and the number of documents containing word j in the corpus, respectively. They are calculated from the Mainichi Shimbun corpora[4] 2003 and 2004.

α is used only by RCKM-LH. **r** is used by RCKM and RCKM-LH. **w** is used by all methods. Although **r** and **w** are can be estimated in a more sophisticated fashion such as the supervised approach, in this paper we simply estimate these parameters from just the input documents, i.e. the unsupervised approach. The use of the supervised approach is a future topic.

5.3 Results and Discussions

We show the results of the ROUGE evaluation in Table 1. Our proposed method, RCKM, yielded the top score. The differences between RCKM and other methods are significant[5] according to the Wilcoxon signed-rank test (Wilcoxon, 1945). The differences between KM and other methods are also significant. One reason for the success of the proposal is that the references usually contain some redundant information units. Interestingly, reference summaries contain two or more instances of the same word. In Figure 1, we show the frequency distribution of content word occurrence. Obviously, some of words occur more than once in the document. The study of

---

[2] http://lpsolve.sourceforge.net/
[3] http://lr-www.pi.titech.ac.jp/tsc/tsc3-en.html
[4] http://mainichi.jp/
[5] $P < 0.01$

text coherence evaluation leverages this repetition to capture the coherence (Barzilay and Lapata, 2005); to make a text coherent, sometimes the same words are used in two successive sentences. In the context of automatic text summarization research, this repetition is referred to as Lexical Chain and can be leveraged to find important sentences (Barzilay and Elhadad, 1997). While MCM considers these repetitions as redundant information, RCKM can permit some redundancy in the summary. In view of this, redundancy parameter **r** can be estimated from the aspect of text coherence.

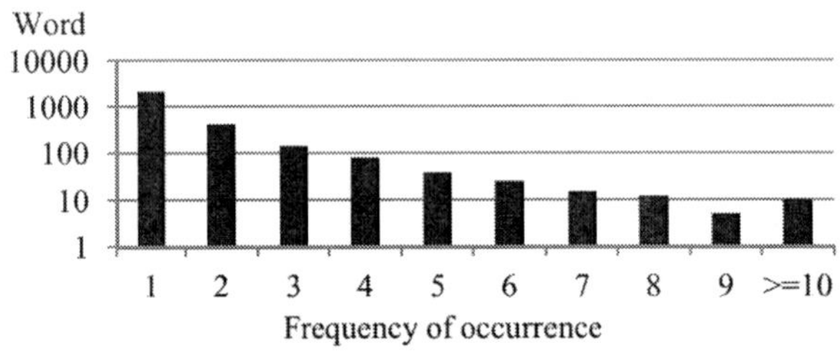

Figure 1: Frequency distribution of content word occurrence in the references. The horizontal axis indicates the frequency of content word occurrence in one reference; the vertical axis indicates the number of words. For example, there are 2093 words that occur once in one reference; there are 10 words that occur more than 9 times in one reference. This graph shows that some words occur more than once in one reference.

We also show the time spent for decoding in Table 1. MCM decoding took more than one week. KM can be quickly decoded by dynamic programming. The solver can decode RCKM far faster than MCM. RCKM-LH solves the dynamic programming iteratively. Hence the time is roughly proportional to the number of iterations.

	ROUGE-1	ROUGE-2	Time (sec.)
RCKM	**0.493**	**0.238**	2642.4
RCKM-LH (10)	0.454	0.217	72.4
RCKM-LH (100)	0.466	0.223	649.8
MCM	0.459	0.218	924349.3
KM	0.443	0.204	8.1

Table 1: ROUGE evaluation results and time taken to summarize 30 input document sets.

6 Conclusion

Our proposed model, the redundancy-constrained knapsack model, improves the quality of summaries significantly compared to a state-of-the-art system, the maximum coverage model. Our model can be decoded by the Lagrange heuristic, and the algorithm proposed here can quickly find approximate solutions of good quality.

Immediate future work is to estimate redundancy parameter **r** from large corpora. Although there are a lot of studies on estimating the weight of units, the allowed redundancy for each word has received less attention. We also plan to test our proposal on other corpora and evaluation criteria.

Acknowledgements

We would like to sincerely thank the reviewers for their comments.

References

Barzilay, R. and Elhadad, M. (1997). Using Lexical Chains for Text Summarization. In *Proceedings of the Intelligent Scalable Text Summarization Workshop (ISTS)*. Pages 10—17.

Barzilay, R. and Lapata, M. (2005). Modeling Local Coherence: An Entity-Based Approach. In *Proceedings of the 43rd Annual Meeting of the Association for Computational Linguistics (ACL)*, pages 141—148.

Chang, Y.-W. and Collins, M. (2011). Exact Decoding of Phrase-Based Translation Models through Lagrangian Relaxation. In *Proceedings of the Conference on Empirical Methods in Natural Language Processing (EMNLP)*, pages 26—37.

Clarke, J. and Lapata, M. (2007). Modelling Compression with Discourse Constraints. In *Proceedings of the Conference on Empirical Methods in Natural Language Processing and on Computational Natural Language Learning (EMNLP-CoNLL)*, pages 1—11.

Filatova, E. and Hatzivassiloglou, V. (2004). A formal model for information selection in multi-sentence text extraction. In *Proceedings of Coling 2004*, pages 397–403.

Gillick, D and Favre, B. (2009). A scalable global model for summarization. In *Proceedings of the Workshop on Integer Linear Programming for Natural Language Processing*, pages 10–18.

Haddadi, S. (1997). Simple Lagrangian heuristic for the set covering problem. *European Journal of Operational Research*, 97:200–204.

Higashinaka, R., Minami, Y., Nishikawa, H., Dohsaka, K., Meguro, T., Kobashikawa, S., Masataki, H., Yoshioka, O., Takahashi, S. and Kikui, G. 2010. Improving hmm-based extractive summarization for multi-domain contact center dialogues. In *Proceedings of the IEEE Workshop on Spoken Language Technology*.

Hirao, T., Fukushima, T., Okumura, M., Nobata, C., and Nanba, H. (2004) Corpus and Evaluation Measures for Multiple Document Summarization with Multiple Sources. In *Proceedings of the 20th International Conference on Computational Linguistics (Coling)*, pages 535—541.

Khuller, S., Moss, A. and Naor, J. (1999). The budgeted maximum coverage problem. *Information Processing Letters*, 70(1):39–45.

Koo, T. and Collins, M. (2010). Efficient third order dependency parsers. In *Proceedings of the 48th Annual Meeting of the Association for Computational Linguistics (ACL)*, pages 1—11.

Korte, B. and Vygen, J. (2008). *Combinatorial Optimization*. Springer-Verlag, third edition.

Lin, C.-Y. (2004). Rouge: A package for automatic evaluation of summaries. In *Text Summarization Branches Out: Proceedings of the ACL-04 Workshop*, pages 74–81.

McDonald, R. (2007). A study of global inference algorithms in multi-document summarization. In *ECIR'07: Proceedings of the 29th European conference on IR research*, pages 557–564.

Nishikawa, H., Hasegawa, T., Matsuo, Y. and Kikui, G. (2010). Opinion summarization with integer linear programming formulation for sentence extraction and ordering. In *Coling 2010:Posters*, pages 910–918.

Takamura, H. and Okumura, M. (2009). Text summarization model based on maximum coverage problem and its variant. In *Proceedings of the 12th Conference of the European*

Chapter of the ACL (EACL), pages 781–789.

Wilcoxon, F. (1945). Individual comparisons by ranking methods. *Biometrics Bulletin,* 1(6):80—83.

Yih, W.-t., Goodman, J., Vanderwende, L. and Suzuki, H. (2007). Multi-document summarization by maximizing informative content-words. In *IJCAI'07: Proceedings of the 20th international joint conference on Artificial intelligence*, pages 1776–1782.

Lexical categories for improved parsing of web data

Lilja ØVRELID Arne SKJÆRHOLT
Department of Informatics
University of Oslo
{liljao,arnskj}@ifi.uio.no

ABSTRACT
We investigate the use of features expressing lexical generalizations over word forms when parsing web data and experiment with a range of web text samples, taken from the Ontonotes corpus, as well as the web 2.0 data sets described in Foster et al. (2011b). We obtain significant improvements for a standard data-driven dependency parser when incorporating features expressing these lexical categories, and in fact find that we may dispense with word form features altogether and still observe the same levels of improvement.

KEYWORDS: Syntactic parsing, data-driven dependency parsing, web language, clustering, lemmatization, delexicalization.

Proceedings of COLING 2012: Posters, pages 903–912,
COLING 2012, Mumbai, December 2012.

1 Introduction

Syntactic analysis of web language has been shown to pose several challenges for traditional parsers trained on edited news text. First of all, web text does not represent a uniform domain or genre, but varies greatly, both in terms of topics and level of formality, where texts may range from edited articles to increasingly informal genres like blogs, user fora and tweets. It is well known that lexical statistics employed by the parser become less reliable when moving to a new domain (Gildea, 2001), and for web text like user forums and twitter data, the amount of unknown words may be as high as 17% (Foster et al., 2011a). In the same way, the performance of other post processing tools, such as part-of-speech taggers, also suffer (Foster et al., 2011b).

Even though parser lexicalization has been a topic of some debate, features incorporating information regarding lexical co-occurrence are employed in most state-of-the-art syntactic parsers in some form or other. Since the task of assigning word-to-word relations is at the core of dependency parsing, statistics regarding relations between different word forms in the training data provide vital information. These lexical statistics are, however, often sparse, and there exists a growing body of work which examines various strategies for generalizing over the distributions of words and using different kinds of lexical categories in syntactic parsing. Word clusters derived from unlabeled data have been shown to improve parsing accuracy for dependency parsing of English (Koo et al., 2008; Suzuki et al., 2009) and so have clusters derived from parsed data (Sagae and Gordon, 2009). Zhou et al. (2011) show that co-occurence based measures of word-to-word selectional preference derived from web-scale data sets can improve statistical dependency parsing. Furthermore, other types of lexical semantic information, such as named entity classes (Ciaramita and Attardi, 2007) and word sense information from WordNet (Agirre et al., 2011), have recently been shown to improve dependency parsing for English.

In this article, we investigate the use of different lexical categories when parsing a range of different types of web data with a state-of-the-art data-driven dependency parser. We examine the effect of enriching the parser with features detailing information about word cluster labels as well as lemma information. We furthermore revisit the role of parser lexicalization in the light of our findings.

The article is structured as follows: Section 2 presents the data used in our experiments and its enrichment with two types of lexical categories, whereas Section 3 describes the extended feature models used in order to enable the parser to take these categories into account. In Section 4 we go on to describe the experiments investigating the effects of these categories, as well as the effect of delexicalization. Finally, we conclude and outline some plans for future work.

2 Data

In the following, we present the different corpora used in our experiments, the preprocessing performed prior to experimentation and the enrichment of the data with automatically derived cluster labels and lemma information.

2.1 Corpora

We use the Wall Street Journal portion of the Penn Treebank sections 2-23, with the standard splits for training (2-21) and testing (23). Due to tokenization differences we train on both the original LDC version, as well as the version released with the Ontonotes corpus. Moreover, we use a wide range of treebanked web data in our experiments. First, the Ontonotes corpus, release 4.0, contains web data from different sources. This portion of the Ontonotes corpus amounts to around 500,000 tokens (including punctuation) and 23,000 sentences split into six different data sets: translated Arabic-to-English (a2e; 55,000 tokens) and Chinese-to-English (c2e; 74,000 tokens) web text, P2.5 translated Arabic-to-English (p2.5_a2e; 16,000 tokens) and Chinese-to-English (p2.5_c2e; 22,000 tokens), as well as general English web data (eng; 71,500 tokens) and a large set of sentences originally selected to improve sense coverage in the corpus (sel; 279,000 tokens). Second, we use the user forum and twitter data sets described in Foster et al. (2011b), which contain a total of 1000 sentences split into development and test sets for user forums (on football topics) and twitter data.

As mentioned earlier, the amount of unknown words for a parser trained on the standard training sections of the Wall Street Journal has been reported to increase notably when moving to web data. For the data sets described above, this is also the case. Compared to a 2.5% proportion of unknown words for the test section of Wall Street Journal (section 23), we observe proportions ranging from 5.5% to 8.1% for the Ontonotes web data. The user forum data on football has 8% unknown words, whereas the twitter data has as much as 17.9% unknown words.

2.2 Preprocessing

The treebank data sets are converted to dependency representations using the Stanford parser, version 2.0, and its *basic* setting which performs a conversion of PTB-style phrase structure trees and provides a dependency graph which is a directed tree (de Marneffe et al., 2006). The dependency representations result from a conversion of PTB-style phrase structure trees, combining 'classic' head finding rules with rules that target specific linguistic constructions.

The data is subsequently PoS-tagged using SVMTool (Gimenez and Marquez, 2004) and the pretrained model for English available from the tool web page. In the Ontonotes data set all hyphens were in addition converted to the HYPH tag which is used in this data set.

2.3 Lexical categories

The data sets described above were enriched with information about the *lemma* of each token using the NLTK WordNet lemmatizer (Bird et al., 2009). The lemmatizer requires information about part-of-speech, hence lemmatization was performed separately on gold and automatically tagged data sets.

Following lemmatization, the data sets were further enriched with the *cluster labels* described in Turian et al. (2010), created using the Brown clustering algorithm (Brown et al., 1992) and induced from the RCV1 corpus, a corpus containing Reuters English newswire text, with approximately 63 million words and 3.3 million sentences. The Brown algorithm is a hierarchical clustering algorithm which clusters words by maximizing the mutual information of bigrams. Since the algorithm is hierarchical, cluster labels are simply unique identifiers of each node within the tree, expressing the path from the root, where 0 indicates a right branch and 1 a left branch. Furthermore, clusters may be extracted at various depths, giving clusters of different sizes. Brown clusters have previously been shown to improve statistical dependency parsing (Koo et al., 2008; Suzuki et al., 2009), as well as other NLP tasks such as Chunking and Named Entity Recognition (Turian et al., 2010).

Feature model	Features
Baseline	S_0p, S_1p, S_2p, S_3p, L_0p, L_1p, L_2p, I_0p, $S_{0l}p$, $S_{0r}p$, $S_{1r}p$, $S_{0l}d$, $S_{1r}d$, S_0w, S_1w, S_2w, L_0w, L_1w, $S_{0l}w$, $S_{1r}w$, S_0pS_1p, S_0wL_0w, S_0pS_0w, S_1pS_1w, L_0pL_0w, $S_{1r}dS_{0l}d$, $S_{1r}pS_{1l}p$, $S_0pS_1pL_0p$, $S_0pS_1pS_2p$, $S_0pL_0pL_1p$, $L_0pL_1pL_2p$, $L_1pL_2pL_3p$, $S_0pL_0pI_0p$, $S_1pS_{1l}dS_{1r}d$
+ PoS simple	S_0l, S_l1l, S_2l, S_3l, L_0l, L_1l, L_2l, I_0l, $S_{0l}l$, $S_{0r}l$, $S_{1r}l$
+ Form simple	S_0l, S_1l, S_2l, L_0l, L_1l, $S_{0l}l$, $S_{1r}l$
+ Form all	S_0l, S_1l, S_2l, L_0l, L_1l, $S_{0l}l$, $S_{1r}l$, S_0lL_0l, S_0pS_0l, S_1pS_1l, L_0pL_0l,

Table 1: Baseline and extended feature models, where p=PoS-tag, w=word form, d=dependency label in the graph constructed so far (if any), and l=lexical category, i.e., either cluster labels or lemma.

We experiment with several techniques for the introduction of cluster labels. First of all, we vary the number of clusters to be either 100, 320, 1000 or 3200 clusters. This means that the number of clusters is fixed prior to clustering. Koo et al. (2008) found the use prefixes of the cluster labels of various lengths (4 to 6) to be beneficial for parsing, so we adopt this approach in addition to using full-length labels. A third method for generalizing over the cluster labels is to use the lemma information directly in the assignment of clusters, so that all word forms with the same lemma are assigned identical cluster labels.

3 Parser features

We use Maltparser (Nivre et al., 2006) (v. 1.4.1), a system for data-driven dependency parsing which is based on a deterministic parsing strategy in combination with treebank-induced classifiers for predicting parse transitions. It supports a rich feature representation of the parse history and may easily be extended to take additional features into account. We choose to use Maltparser primarily due to its extendible feature model which facilitates experimentation with additional features during parsing.

As our baseline parser, we use the parse model described in Foster et al. (2011a), where Maltparser was employed to parse web 2.0 data. It employs the stacklazy algorithm (Nivre, 2009), along with the liblinear package (Fan et al., 2008) for inducing parse transition classifiers. The stacklazy algorithm operates over three data structures: a stack (S) of partially processed tokens, a list (I) of nodes that have been on the stack, and a "lookahead" list (L) of nodes that have not been on the stack. We refer to the top of the stack using S_0 and subsequent nodes using S_1, S_2, etc., and the leftmost/rightmost dependent of S_0 with S_{0l}/S_{0r}.

Lexical categories – Ontonotes							
Parser	wsj23$_{onto}$	a2e	c2e	p2.5a2e	p2.5c2e	eng	sel
BaseGold	**89.27**	**84.85**	**82.22**	**84.99**	**86.11**	**83.89**	**83.61**
ClstGold	89.05$_{fa320}$	84.46$_{fs100}$	82.02$_{fs320}$	84.59$_{fs320}$	86.07$_{fs320}$	83.36$_{fs320}$	83.09$_{fs100}$
LemmGold	88.91$_{ps}$	84.38$_{ps}$	81.93$_{ps}$	84.46$_{ps}$	85.81$_{fa}$	83.41$_{ps}$	82.96$_{ps}$
BaseTag	86.24	78.35	75.38	79.40	79.38	76.99	74.84
ClstTag	**86.67**$_{fa320}$	**79.97**$_{fa100}$	**76.71**$_{fa100}$	**80.48**$_{fa100}$	**80.78**$_{fs100}$	**78.30**$_{fa320}$	**75.82**$_{fs100}$
LemmTag	86.49$_{ps}$	79.50$_{fs}$	76.41$_{ps}$	80.17$_{fa}$	80.60$_{fs}$	78.02$_{ps}$	75.43$_{fs}$

Table 2: Labeled accuracy scores (proportion of tokens with correct head *and* dependency label) for parsers trained on wsj02-21 and tested on wsj23 and Ontonotes web data sets, as well as web 2.0 (football and twitter) data sets using gold (Gold) and automatic (Tag) PoS-tags, for baseline (Base), as well as extended (Clst, Lemm) parsers, where results indicate the best configuration of feature model (ps=pos simple, fs=form simple, fa=form all) and cluster set size (100, 320, 1000 or 3200).

Table 1 provides the baseline feature model, along with three sets of additional features (PoS simple, Form simple, Form all), which are constructed by copying the full feature set ("all") or only the features that pertain to a single token ("simple") and involve either the PoS-tag or the word form. Note that the "PoS all" feature set proved to be too large for practical experimentation with lexical features derived from clusters or lemmas.

4 Experiments

We train two pairs of baseline parsers on the standard sections 2-21 of the WSJ data both with gold PoS-tags and automatically assigned PoS-tags, for the original tokenization and for the Ontonotes tokenization. The results for these parsers, evaluated on section 23 with original and Ontonotes tokenization are presented in Table 2 and 3, respectively (BaseGold, BaseTag). All results are provided as labeled accuracy scores (LAS), which express the proportion of tokens which were assigned correct head *and* dependency label by the parser. Statistical significance is checked using Bikel's randomized parsing evaluation comparator.

4.1 Lexical categories

The baseline parsers are subsequently applied to the different web data sets, as detailed in Section 2 above. We find that results vary with the degree of formality, ranging from LAS 85-86% for some of the more edited web data (Table 4), to LAS 76% for the twitter data (Table 4)). Just like Foster et al. (2011b), we find that the drop in performance following PoS tagging is considerably larger for the web data than the WSJ data (5-10 vs. 2-3 percentage points, respectively).

Tables 2 and 3 also show the results for the parsers with additional features: cluster labels (Clst) and lemmas (Lemm) over gold and tagged data, indicating the feature model (ps=pos simple, fs=form simple, fa=form all) and cluster set size (100, 320, 1000 or 3200) that produced the result. The addition of the cluster and lemma features are beneficial largely for

Lexical categories – Web 2.0			
Parser	**wsj23$_{orig}$**	**football**	**twitter**
BaseGold	89.83	79.62	**76.15**
ClstGold	**90.13**$_{fa1000}$	79.87$_{fs1000}$	75.93$_{fs3200}$
LemmGold	89.92$_{ps}$	**79.89**$_{fs}$	76.05$_{fs}$
BaseTag	87.83	73.86	65.57
ClstTag	**87.94**$_{fa100}$	**74.50**$_{fa100}$	**66.18**$_{fs100}$
LemmTag	87.76$_{fs}$	74.23$_{fs}$	65.55$_{fa}$

Table 3: Labeled accuracy scores (proportion of tokens with correct head *and* dependency label) for parsers trained on wsj02-21 and tested on wsj23 and web 2.0 data sets, using gold (Gold) and automatic (Tag) PoS-tags, for baseline (Base), as well as extended (Clst, Lemm) parsers, where results indicate the best configuration of feature model (ps=pos simple, fs=form simple, fa=form all) and cluster set size (100, 320, 1000 or 3200).

the parsers trained and tested with automatically assigned PoS-tags, and more so on the web data than the WSJ data. For the web data, the addition of cluster labels lead to improvements of 1-1.5 percentage points for the Ontonotes web data (Table 4), all differences being statistically significant ($p < 0.0001$).

We furthermore find that the cluster features provide significant improvements for the user forum data (football; $p < 0.05$), and small, but non-significant, improvements for the twitter data, see Table 3. The models that perform the best are the models copying the form features and using the smaller cluster sizes (100, 320) and exclusively the models which use the lemmatized assignment of full cluster labels described above. The prefix labels do not perform as well on these data sets and show best results on average 0.5 percentage points lower than the results presented in Table 2 and 3.

4.2 Delexicalization

Seeing that the lexical categories employed above gave clear improvements and knowing that the proportion of unknown words typically rises dramatically for web language texts, we investigate the role of lexicalization in the parsing of web language. We therefore train *delexicalized* parsers, i.e., where we modify the baseline feature model in Table 1 by removing all features involving word forms (w).

As shown by the results in Table 4 and 5, delexicalization causes an expected drop in performance over all data sets. We then add our cluster features and lemma features, using a fixed feature model, the "Form simple" model, and vary the cluster sizes as before. Not surprisingly, the results show that with a delexicalized model, the largest cluster size (3200) provides the best performing model throughout.

We furthermore observe that the delexicalized models including either clusters or lemmas significantly out-perform the lexicalized baseline for the automatically tagged web data sets ($p < 0.0001$) (Table 4) and the user forum data ($p < 0.01$) (Table 5), indicating that the

	Delexicalization – Ontonotes						
Parser	**wsj23$_{onto}$**	**a2e**	**c2e**	**p2.5a2e**	**p2.5c2e**	**eng**	**sel**
BaseGold	**89.27**	**84.85**	**82.22**	**84.99**	**86.11**	**83.89**	**83.61**
DelexGold	81.02	77.07	73.72	77.75	76.36	75.65	75.92
DelexClstGold	88.99	84.44	81.74	84.41	85.41	83.27	82.86
DelexLemmGold	88.94	84.47	81.81	84.63	85.77	83.66	83.22
BaseTag	86.24	78.35	75.38	79.40	79.38	76.99	74.84
DelexTag	78.15	70.57	66.75	72.31	70.01	68.52	67.34
DelexClstTag	86.31	79.48	**76.51**	79.88	**80.55**	77.70	74.90
DelexLemmTag	**86.34**	**79.66**	76.32	**80.24**	80.44	**78.23**	**75.48**

Table 4: Labeled accuracy scores (proportion of tokens with correct head *and* dependency label) for delexicalized parsers trained on wsj02-21 and tested on wsj23 and Ontonotes web data sets, using gold (Gold) and automatic (Tag) PoS-tags, for baseline (Base), as well as extended (Clst, Lemm) parsers. All delexicalized extended experiments were performed using the form simple feature model and a cluster set size of 3200.

	Delexicalization – Web 2.0		
Parser	**wsj23$_{orig}$**	**football**	**twitter**
BaseGold	89.83	79.62	76.15
DelexGold	81.37	70.84	68.72
DelexClstGold	89.91	79.53	76.19
DelexLemmGold	**89.97**	**79.93**	**76.37**
BaseTag	**87.83**	73.86	**65.57**
DelexTag	79.14	65.90	58.77
DelexClstTag	87.60	73.98	65.18
DelexLemmTag	87.83	**74.47**	65.51

Table 5: Labeled accuracy scores (proportion of tokens with correct head *and* dependency label) for delexicalized parsers trained on wsj02-21 and tested on wsj23, Ontonotes web data and web 2.0 (football and twitter) data sets, using gold (Gold) and automatic (Tag) PoS-tags, for baseline (Base), as well as extended (Clst, Lemm) parsers. All delexicalized extended experiments were performed using the form simple feature model and a cluster set size of 3200.

generalizations provided by clustering and/or lemmatization help overcome some of the sparsity problems mentioned initially. We furthermore observe that the delexicalized models including clusters and/or lemmas perform only marginally worse than their lexicalized counterparts. Seeing that word token features are used in most state-of-the-art parsers today, the finding that we may dispense of these completely and still observe the same level of improvements using the cluster label and/or lemma information is highly interesting. Our work indicates that these types of lexical categories capture many important properties of word tokens and even generalize over these so that lexical constraints may be acquired even when individual word features prove too sparse due to domain and genre differences.

Conclusion and future work

We have shown how lexical features derived from clusters and lemmas may improve data-driven dependency parsing of web data and even replace individual word forms during parsing. The addition of the cluster and lemma features are beneficial largely for the parsers trained and tested with automatically assigned PoS-tags, and more so on the web data than the WSJ data. We furthermore find that the delexicalized models including information about either clusters or lemmas significantly out-perform the lexicalized baseline for the automatically tagged web data sets.

In terms of future work, we plan to experiment with other parsers and other clustering algorithms. We would also like to perform similar experiment with data taken from other genres and/or domains.

Acknowledgments

Our thanks go to Jennifer Foster for sharing her Web 2.0 (football and twitter) data. Thanks also to our colleagues at UiO and the anonymous reviewers for their comments.

References

Agirre, E., Bengoetxa, K., Gojenola, K., and Nivre, J. (2011). Improving dependency parsing with semantic classes. In *Proceedings of the 49th Meeting of the Association for Computational Linguistics*.

Bird, S., Klein, E., and Loper, E. (2009). *Natural Language Processing with Python*. O'Reilly, Beijing.

Brown, P., deSouza, P., Mercer, R., Pietra, V., and Lai, J. (1992). Class-based n-gram models of natural language. *Computational Linguistics*, 18.

Ciaramita, M. and Attardi, G. (2007). Dependency parsing with second-order feature maps and annotated semantic information. In *Proceedings of the 10th International Conference on Parsing Technologies*.

de Marneffe, M.-C., MacCartney, B., and Manning, C. D. (2006). Generating typed dependency parses from phrase structure parses. In *Proceedings of the International Conference on Language Resources and Evaluation (LREC)*.

Fan, R., Chang, K., Hsieh, C., Wang, X., and Lin, C. (2008). Liblinear: A library for large linear classification. *Journal of Machine Learning Research*, (9).

Foster, J., Çetinoglu, Ö., Wagner, J., Roux, J. L., Hogan, S., Nivre, J., Hogan, D., and van Genabith, J. (2011a). hardtoparse: Pos tagging and parsing the twitterverse. In *Proceedings of AAAI-11 Workshop on Analysing Microtext*.

Foster, J., Çetinoglu, Ö., Wagner, J., Roux, J. L., Nivre, J., Hogan, D., and van Genabith, J. (2011b). From news to comment: Resources and benchmarks for parsing the language of web 2.0. In *Proceedings of IJCNLP*.

Gildea, D. (2001). Corpus variation and parser performance. In *Proceedings of the 2001 Conference on Empirical Methods in Natural Language Processing (EMNLP)*, pages 167–202.

Gimenez, J. and Marquez, L. (2004). SVMTool: A general POS tagger generator based on Support Vector Machines. In *Proceedings of the 4th International Conference on Language Resources and Evaluation (LREC)*.

Koo, T., Carreras, X., and Collins, M. (2008). Simple semi-supervised dependency parsing. In *Proceedings of the 46th Meeting of the Association for Computational Linguistics*.

Nivre, J. (2009). Non-projective dependency parsing in expected linear time. In *Proceedings of the 47th Meeting of the Association for Computational Linguistics*.

Nivre, J., Hall, J., and Nilsson, J. (2006). MaltParser: A data-driven parser-generator for dependency parsing. In *Proceedings of the International Conference on Language Resources and Evaluation (LREC)*.

Sagae, K. and Gordon, A. S. (2009). Clustering words by syntactic similarity improves dependency parsing of predicate argument structures. In *Proceedings of the 11th International Conference on Parsing Technologies (IWPT)*, pages 192–201.

Suzuki, J., Isozaki, H., Carreras, X., and Collins, M. (2009). An empirical study of semi-supervised structured conditional models for dependency parsing. In *Proceedings of the 2009 Conference on Empirical Methods in Natural Language Processing*.

Turian, J., Ratinov, L., and Bengio, Y. (2010). Word representations: a simple and general method for semi-supervised learning. In *Proceedings of the 48th Meeting of the Association for Computational Linguistics*.

Zhou, G., Zhao, J., Liu, K., and Cai, L. (2011). Exploiting web-derived selectional preference to improve statistical dependency parsing. In *Proceedings of the 49th Meeting of the Association for Computational Linguistics*.

Text-To-Speech for Languages without an Orthography

Sukhada Palkar   *Alan W Black*   *Alok Parlikar*
Language Technologies Institute
Carnegie Mellon University
Pittsburgh (PA), USA
{spalkar, awb, aup} @cs.cmu.edu

ABSTRACT
Speech synthesis models are typically built from a corpus of speech that has accurate transcriptions. However, many of the languages of the world do not have a standardized writing system. This paper is an initial attempt at building synthetic voices for such languages. It may seem useless to develop a text-to-speech system when there is no text available. But we will discuss some well defined use cases where we need these models. We will present our method to build synthetic voices from only speech data. We will present experimental results and oracle studies that show that we can automatically devise an artificial writing system for these languages, and build synthetic voices that are understandable and usable.

TITLE AND ABSTRACT IN MARATHI

अक्षरपद्धती नसलेल्या भाषांसाठी वाणी संस्लेषण

ध्वनिमुद्रित वाक्यांच्या कोषापासून वाणी संस्लेषणाची संगणकीय प्रतिरुपे बनविण्यासाठी त्या कोषाची अचूक लिखित प्रतिलिपी उपलब्ध असावी लागते. जगातील अनेक भाषा मात्र मानांकित अक्षरपद्धती वापरत नाहीत. प्रस्तुत काम हे अशा भाषांसाठी संस्लेषित आवाज बनविण्याचा एक पहिला प्रयास आहे. मुळात अक्षरपद्धतीच नसताना त्या भाषेच्या लिखित पाठ्याचे वाणी संस्लेषण करण्याचे तंत्र हे व्यर्थ वाटू शकते. पण प्रस्तुत लेखात आम्ही या संस्लेषण प्रणालीचे काही प्रमुख उपयोग सुचवीत आहोत. केवळ ध्वनिमुद्रित वाक्यांचा कोष वापरून संस्लेषित आवाज बनविण्याची आमची पद्धत या लेखात आपण पाहू. आम्ही केलेले प्रयोग व विश्लेषण असे दर्शवितात की आपण एखादी अक्षरपद्धती आपोआप शोधू शकतो, जिचा वापर करून केलेले वाणी संस्लेषण सुगम व वापरण्याजोगे असते.

KEYWORDS: Speech Synthesis, Synthesis Without Text, Low Resource Languages, Languages without an Orthography.

KEYWORDS IN L_2: वाणी संस्लेषण, पाठ्याशिवाय संस्लेषण, संसाधन-दुर्लभ भाषा, अक्षरपद्धती नसलेल्या भाषा.

Proceedings of COLING 2012: Posters, pages 913–922,
COLING 2012, Mumbai, December 2012.

1 Introduction

Of the many languages in the world, most actually are only spoken, and do not have a writing system. Even for many of the languages that do have writing systems, the orthography is poorly standardized. Such languages typically have speakers that are not literate in those languages, even if they may be literate in other languages such as English.

Speech processing should offer the opportunity to communicate in all languages, and is perhaps even more valuable for languages where a written form is not well defined. This paper investigates how to build a text-to-speech system in languages where no well-defined writing system exists.

If text is fundamental to speech synthesis, what does it even mean to synthesize in a language that does not have text? We propose the following: Given a speech corpus in such a language, we automatically derive a writing system appropriate for that language. This could be a phonetic writing system that uses either a universal phone set, or a phone set from a closely related language. We use Automatic Speech Recognition technology to develop this writing system. This automatically derived, artificial writing system can then be used as "text" that is input to our text-to-speech system.

At first it might seem futile to develop a speech synthesis system without a related writing system. But consider these two use cases that highlight the need of such a system. The clearest use case, that underlies the reason for this work, is the development of a speech to speech translation system from a language that has a written form, into a language that does not. If we attempt to collect "parallel data" for training translation systems, we will end up with text in the source language, and only speech in the target language. But standard methods of machine translation require text to be present on both source and target sides. Our proposed artificial phonetic orthography can be used as the text in the target language to enable training of machine translation models. Note that such a system will essentially translate words in the source language into phonetic units of our artificial writing system. But such translation systems have been shown (Stueker and Waibel, 2008) to be possible. Another use case of our proposed method is in dialog systems. If the language of a dialog system does not have a written form, how will people write the prompts? And how will the synthesis happen? Our proposal will allow system developers to use the automatically derived writing system to write prompts that can then be synthesized.

Our goal is to develop synthetic voices in languages without orthography. However, in order to test our methods and illustrate our techniques, we have in fact used languages that do have well defined written forms, and speech and text corpora available. We have particularly used Marathi as the language in this research, built synthetic voices by pretending it did not have a writing system, and we will show results about how well these models do. We will also present similar results for Hindi and Telugu.

This paper is organized as follows. Section 2 describes all the data we have used in this research. Section 3 describes the basic strategy of developing a synthetic voice from speech data that has no transcriptions. In Section 4, we discuss a novel method of improving the quality of the synthetic voice. In Section 5, we comment on the nature of the artificial writing system we devise for languages at hand, and present conclusions towards the end.

2 Data and Resources

We used Indian languages (Marathi, Hindi, Telugu) in this work. Our method uses two resources: (i) Speech data in the target language, and (ii) Text data in a related high resource language.

For Marathi, we used about 30 minutes of speech data made available by Parlikar and Black (2012). For Hindi and Telugu, we used the speech corpora collected by Prahallad et al. (2012). These have about an hour each of single speaker speech. We used a corpus for Hindi and Marathi text made available by IIT Bombay CFILT, and crawled wikipedia articles for Telugu text. All the speech data we used is single channel clean speech, recorded in a studio setting at 16KHz.

Note that these three languages all have well defined written forms. Hindi and Marathi use the Devanagari script, and Telugu uses its own script. The speech corpora described above all have an associated transcript. For purposes of this research, we did not use the transcripts except to run an oracle evaluation of our models.

We used publicly available tools for speech recognition and speech synthesis. For recognition, we used the CMU Sphinx3 (Placeway et al., 1996) system. For building synthetic voices, we used the Festvox (Black and Lenzo, 2002) suite of tools. The voices we build use the clustergen (Black, 2006) method of statistical parametric synthesis. We used the Festival (Black and Taylor, 1997) system for speech synthesis.

3 Basic Approach to Synthetic Voices without Orthography

We have speech data in our target language, and there is no well defined orthography for transcriptions. A simple method to deal with this situation is to run an automatic speech recognizer over available speech data and use its output as transcriptions.

The caveat with using a speech recognizer is that because our target language does not have a text form, a speech recognizer will not exist in that language. We hence have to use a speech recognizer in another language: a language that has an orthography, and large corpora to train speech recognizers. This presents another caveat: we are recognizing in a different language than the models are trained for. Using the default language model is thus not ideal, and we need to adapt it so that it is suitable for our target language. We also use **phonetic** decoding instead of word level decoding.

We propose the following: (i) Choose an appropriate acoustic model for speech recognition, then (ii) Choose a language that has an orthography and is phonetically close to our target language, and then build a phonetic language model on text in this language. (iii) Run phonetic decoder on our target speech data with these two models and obtain transcripts. (iv) Build a voice using the speech data and the phonetic transcripts just obtained. Figure 1 illustrates this method.

We used this method and ran experiments on our Marathi data. We assumed Marathi to be the language that has no orthography. We considered English and Hindi to be the languages that have high resources available, and those that have an orthography.

3.1 Decoding with an English Acoustic Model

We used an English acoustic model trained on the Wall Street Journal data that we obtained from the CMU-Sphinx website. This model uses the CMU-DICT US English phone set, which

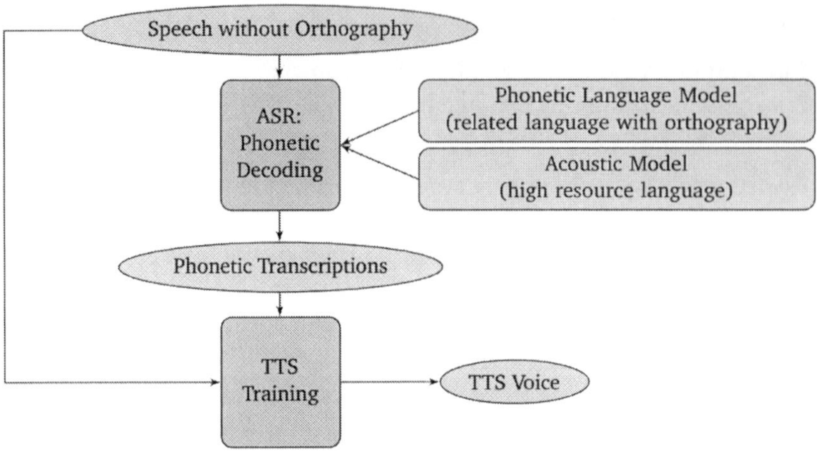

Figure 1: An overview of our basic approach

consists of 39 phones.

Keeping the acoustic model fixed, we decoded our speech with three different language models: (i) An English Phonetic Language Model trained on part of the BTEC Data , (ii) A Hindi Phonetic Language Model trained on the Hindi text corpus, and (iii) A Marathi Phonetic Language Model trained on the Marathi text, for oracle comparison.

Since the phone set of the acoustic model is CMU-DICT, we wrote a tool that converts Indic Unicode Script into CMU-Dict phone strings. The language models from Hindi and Marathi text mentioned above were built on this phonetized text.

With these acoustic and language models, we decoded the Marathi speech data and obtained transcriptions. We then built a phone-based clustergen voice using this data. We held out 10% of the data for evaluating the synthetic voice. We synthesized the test set, aligned it using dynamic-time-warping to the original speech, and computed the spectral distance (MCD) (Mashimo et al., 2001) between the two as the evaluation measure. Since this is a distance, lower is better. Kominek (2009) has showed that a difference of 0.1 in the MCD is perceptually significant.

Table 1 shows the quality of synthesis obtained using the different language models. We see that using a language model trained on Hindi is better than one trained on English. This could be because Marathi is phonetically much closer to Hindi than to English. Notice also that the model obtained with Hindi language model is almost as good as the oracle result of using a Marathi language model. This shows promise in the use of sister languages for language modeling.

Language Model	**MCD of Synthesis**
Phonetic English	7.391
Phonetic Hindi	7.124
Phonetic Marathi (Oracle Result)	7.117

Table 1: MCD of Synthesis using English acoustic model and different language models

3.2 Decoding with an Hindi Acoustic Model

The CMU-DICT phone set is very different from the set of phones that Marathi uses. We investigated whether using an acoustic model from a closely-related language could yield improvements. We used the Hindi speech data we have to train an acoustic model. However, this data was only an hour of female speech. Our Marathi data is recorded by a male speaker. The gender mismatch, and the small size of training data yielded a very weak acoustic model. After decoding with this acoustic model and a language model trained on the larger Hindi text corpus and repeating our voice build, we were left with a synthesizer that had an MCD of 7.868. We believe that with more training data for a Hindi acoustic model, we might have a better voice than with an English acoustic model.

3.3 Extended CMU-DICT phone set

CMU-DICT is an English phone set, and English is not very similar phonetically to Marathi. We hence explored enhancing the CMU-DICT phoneset. Specifically, we investigated whether splitting English vowels into finer groups of short and long vowels could improve our models. We decoded the speech data with the previous English acoustic model. We then aligned the speech to these phonetic transcripts using an EHMM alignment tool (Prahallad et al., 2006). We determined the duration of different vowels and clustered them into two groups based on the duration. We then labeled these vowel clusters as being two different vowels when training the synthetic voice. We saw marginal improvements to the MCD of synthesis using this method, but did not yet explore this in more detail.

4 Targeted Acoustic Model for Improved Synthetic Voices

In the previous section, we saw that our best baseline synthetic voice comes from transcriptions derived using an English acoustic model. We explored if we could target the acoustic model to the speech database at hand and get an improved result over all.

4.1 Method Description

We use a bootstrapping method. First, we use the English acoustic model and obtain baseline transcriptions for our target speech. Using these transcriptions and the speech data, we train a targeted acoustic model. This model is a small acoustic model, but it is specific to the data we are using. Using this new acoustic model, keeping rest of the decoding process similar, we decode our speech data again. We get a new set of transcriptions. We train another targeted acoustic model with these new transcriptions and repeat the iterations until the MCD on a held out test set stops improving. Figure 2 shows a flow diagram for this training.

4.2 Experiments and Results

We started with our Marathi speech data (assumed again, that Marathi had no writing system). We used the baseline speech recognition system as described in Section 3. We then applied the described iterative method to build and use a targeted acoustic model. We obtained very good improvements as evaluated objectively using the MCD distance. We then repeated similar experiments for Hindi and Telugu. We assumed that Hindi had no orthography, used the Wall Street Journal acoustic model and a Marathi Phonetic Language Model for recognition. For Telugu, we used the same acoustic model and the Hindi Phonetic Language Model.

The results of these experiments are plotted in Figure 3. We see that for all three languages,

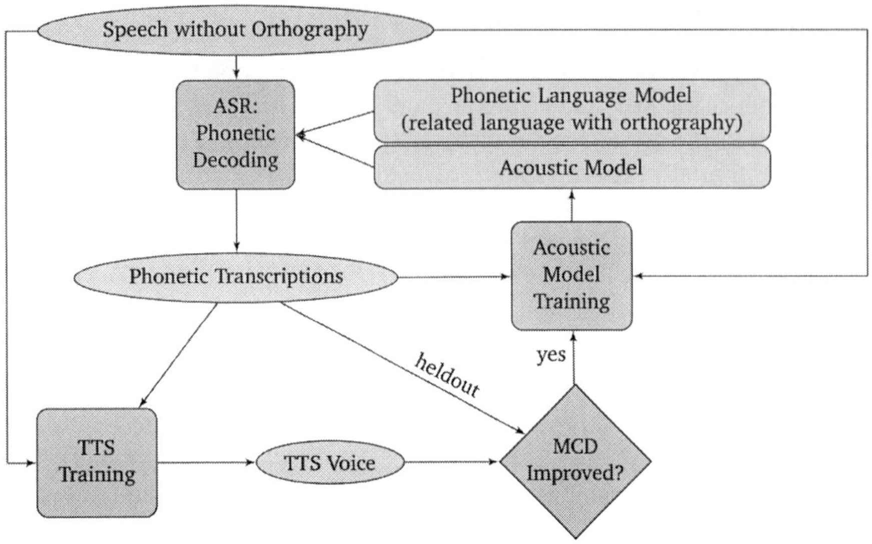

Figure 2: Building a targeted acoustic model for improved synthesis

the iterative targeting of acoustic model ultimately produces a synthesizer that is better than the baseline. The range of MCD values in each language depends on the recording conditions and the speaker. We see that the improvement over the baseline is more for Telugu, compared to the other two languages and we are investigating why.

Given that we see consistent improvements in MCD using the proposed method, we evaluated whether these improvements are perceptually meaningful. We ran listening tests on the Marathi data. We compared the baseline Marathi voice to the voice after 6 iterations of acoustic model targeting. We synthesized 20 utterances using both voices and ran an A/B test. Each participant was presented with the utterance in both voices and they had to pick the utterence that they thought was more understandable. We had 6 native speakers of Marathi take the test. Figure 4 shows that the improvements we obtain out of the proposed method are indeed perceptually significant.

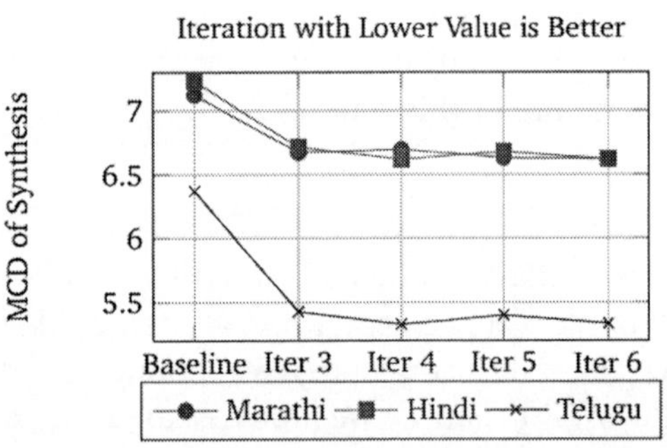

Figure 3: Objective Improvements using Iterative Targeted Acoustic Models

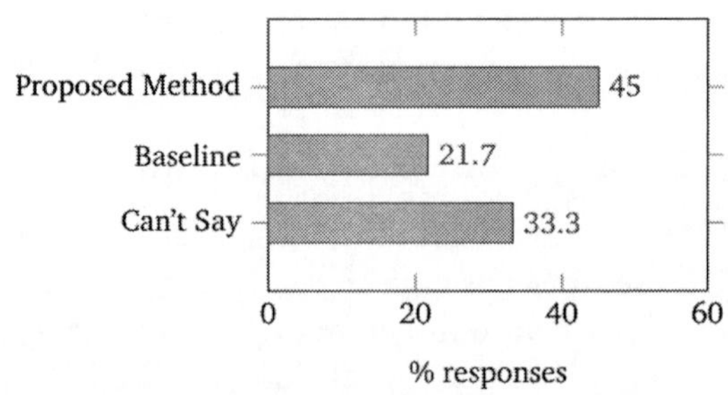

Figure 4: Subjective Preference between Synthetic Voices

5 Phonetic Writing System: Discussion

Our goal is to build synthetic voices for languages without an orthography. Our proposal is to automatically invent a phonetic writing system in that language, and then use it to build synthesis systems. We have used speech recognition techniques to devise these writing systems. This raises the questions of whether the artificially invented writing system is valid, or even useful.

In our experiments we used an English acoustic model for speech recognition. The output of the recognition decoder became the new writing system for the language at hand, Marathi. There are two main issues with using this writing system. (i) A smaller phone set (CMU-DICT) where Marathi actually has more phonemes. and (ii) Errors that speech recognition introduces in the phone strings. These two issues are explained below.

5.1 Effect of Phone-set Divergences on Synthesis Quality

The actual Marathi phone set is bigger than the CMU-DICT phone set that the English models have used. This leads to multiple Marathi phones getting mapped down to the same English phone. We looked at how using our ASR-based script for Marathi compares to using real Marathi text for building synthetic voices.

We built a standard Grapheme-based clustergen voice for Marathi. Each Unicode grapheme of the Devanagari alphabet was considered to be an independent phone. Because Devanagari is a phonetic alphabet, this voice provides us with an oracle data point: if we had an artificial language with a very good phone set, how good could our synthesis be?

Table 2 shows the comparison of the models we built in our work against the oracle voice. We observe that while our proposed method of acoustic model targeting gives good improvements over the baseline, there is a big gap in synthesis quality between using a CMU-DICT based writing system and the oracle writing system. This suggests that we should explore using more sophisticated acoustic models, such as those that use globalphone (Schultz and Waibel, 2001), or investigate phone splitting and phone joining techniques in future work.

Writing System	MCD of Synthesis
ASR-Based (CMU-DICT)	7.124
ASR-Based (CMU-DICT) (Targeted Acoustic Model)	6.620
Devanagari (Actual Marathi) (Oracle Result)	5.780

Table 2: Comparing ASR-based writing system to actual Marathi orthography

5.2 Effect of Errors Introduced by Speech Recognizers

Speech Recognition is often not perfect. Well-trained phonetic decoding can make mistakes when decoding speech in a language it was trained in. In our work, we are using a CMU-DICT based English acoustic model to decode a different language: Marathi. This discrepancy can introduce gross errors in the transcriptions generated. The writing system we invent is thus tainted.

We performed an oracle experiment to study the effect of noisy ASR on the quality of synthesis we ultimately achieve. We used the CMU-DICT as the phone set for our writing method. We used our own tool to map the original Indic script for Marathi into the CMU-DICT phone set. These transcriptions can be thought of as the output of a "perfect ASR" system. We then built an oracle voice using these transcripts and compared it to the voices built using automatically derived transcription language.

Table 3 shows the comparison of our models to the oracle voice. We observe that our baseline model is quite a bit weaker than the oracle voice. The targeted acoustic model helps build a voice that is better, but there is a good scope for future improvements in this direction. Good ways to detect noise introduced by ASR and methods to ignore the noise can potentially help bridge this gap and make synthesis even better.

Writing System	**MCD of Synthesis**
ASR-Based (CMU-DICT)	7.124
ASR-Based (CMU-DICT) (Targeted Acoustic Model)	6.620
Phonetized Devanagari (CMU-DICT) (Oracle Result)	6.006

Table 3: Effect of ASR noise on synthesis quality

5.3 Validity of the Phonetic Writing System

The automatically generated ASR-based writing system does generate understandable synthesis. It could thus be used as an intermediate language in speech to speech translation if the target language has no orthography. However, if we were building a dialog system in the target language, some person will have to write down text in the language as designed by ASR. No matter what phone set we use, ASR language can potentially be tainted by ASR errors. We need to measure the effort that a human would require in generating prompts in the artificial phonetic language. However, this is outside the scope of this paper.

6 Conclusions and Future Work

We have addressed a novel problem of building speech synthesizers for languages without an orthography. In our solution, we proposed automatically developing a writing system for the language, using a speech recognition system. Our iterative method to build targeted acoustic models yield very good improvements in synthesis quality. We showed objective and subjective results, as well as oracle results on Marathi, which show that our direction to building synthesis models without written text is promising. We also showed similar results on Hindi and Telugu, thus showing that our methods are language independent.

We have shown that the ASR-based writing system helps us build understandable synthesis. Two improvements we want to explore are: (i) using a large acoustic model trained on a larger phone set, or a universal phone recognizer such as (Siniscalchi et al., 2008), and (ii) Detecting noise in ASR transcript and mitigating the effects of that noise in synthesis output. We also plan to build speech translation systems for languages without orthography. The idea is to use the writing system we developed in this work and train statistical machine translation. We also plan to develop a written system for a real world language that has no orthography, and evaluate the user effort required in using the system to type real text.

References

Black, A. W. (2006). CLUSTERGEN: A statistical parametric synthesizer using trajectory modeling. In *Proceedings of Interspeech*, pages 194–197, Pittsburgh, Pennsylvania.

Black, A. W. and Lenzo, K. (2002). Building voices in the festival speech synthesis system.

Black, A. W. and Taylor, P. (1997). The festival speech synthesis system: system documentation. Technical report, Human Communication Research Centre, University of Edinburgh.

Kominek, J. (2009). *TTS From Zero: Building Synthetic Voices for New Languages*. PhD thesis, Carnegie Mellon University.

Mashimo, M., Toda, T., Shikano, K., and Campbell, W. N. (2001). Evaluation of cross-language voice conversion based on GMM and straight. In *Proceedings of Eurospeech*, pages 361–364, Aalborg, Denmark.

Parlikar, A. and Black, A. W. (2012). Data-driven phrasing for speech synthesis in low-resource languages. In *Proceedings of IEEE International Conference on Acoustics, Speech and Signal Processing*, Kyoto, Japan.

Placeway, P., Chen, S. F., Eskenazi, M., Jain, U., Parikh, V., Raj, B., Mosur, R., Rosenfeld, R., Seymore, K., Siegler, M. A., Stern, R. M., and Thayer, E. (1996). The 1996 hub-4 sphinx-3 system. In *Proceedings of the DARPA Speech Recognition Workshop*.

Prahallad, K., Black, A. W., and Mosur, R. (2006). Sub-phonetic modeling for capturing pronunciation variations for conversational speech synthesis. In *Proceedings of IEEE International Conference on Acoustics, Speech and Signal Processing*, volume 1, pages 853–856, Toulouse, France.

Prahallad, K., Kumar, E. N., Keri, V., Rajendran, S., and Black, A. W. (2012). The iiit-h indic speech databases. In *Proceedings of Interspeech*, Portland, OR, USA.

Schultz, T. and Waibel, A. (2001). Language-independent and language-adaptive acoustic modeling for speech recognition. *Speech Communication*, 35(1):31–51.

Siniscalchi, S. M., Svendsen, T., and Lee, C.-H. (2008). Toward a detector-based universal phone recognizer. In *Proceedings of IEEE International Conference on Acoustics, Speech and Signal Processing*, Las Vegas, USA.

Stueker, S. and Waibel, A. (2008). Towards human translations guided language discovery for asr systems. In *Proceedings of Spoken Language Technologies for Under-Resourced Languages*.

Part of Speech (POS) Tagger for Kokborok

Braja Gopal Patra[1] Khumbar Debbarma[2] Dipankar Das[3] Sivaji Bandyopadhyay[1]
(1) Department of Compute Science & Engineering, Jadavpur University, Kolkata, India
(2) Department of Compute Science & Engineering, TIT, Agartala, India
(3) Department of Compute Science & Engineering, NIT Meghalaya, Shillong, India
brajagopal.cse@gmail.com, khum_10jan@yahoo.co.in,
dipankar.dipnil2005@gmail.com, sivaji_cse_ju@yahoo.com

ABSTRACT

The Part of Speech (POS) tagging refers to the process of assigning appropriate lexical category to individual word in a sentence of a natural language. This paper describes the development of a POS tagger using rule based and supervised methods in Kokborok, a resource constrained and less computerized Indian language. In case of rule based POS tagging, we took the help of a morphological analyzer while for supervised methods, we employed two machine learning classifiers, Conditional Random Field (CRF) and Support Vector Machines (SVM). A total of 42,537 words were POS tagged. Manual checking achieves the accuracies of 70% and 84% in case of rule based and supervised POS tagging, respectively.

KEYWORDS : Kokborok, POS Tagger, Suffix, Prefix, CRF, SVM, Morph analyser.

Proceedings of COLING 2012: Posters, pages 923–932,
COLING 2012, Mumbai, December 2012.

1 Introduction

From the very beginning, POS tagging has been playing its significant roles in several Natural Language Processing (NLP) applications such as chunking, parsing, developing Information Extraction systems, semantic processing, Question Answering (QA), Summarization, Event Tracking etc. To the best of our knowledge, no prior work on POS tagging has been done for Kokborok except the development of a stemmer (Patra et al., 2012). Thus, in this paper, we have basically described the development of a POS tagger in Kokborok, a less privileged native language of the Borok people of Tripura, a state in North Eastern part of India. Kokborok is also spoken by neighboring states such as Assam, Manipur, Mizoram and the countries like Bangladesh, Myanmar etc. The language comprises of more than 2.5 millions of people[1] and belongs to Tibeto-Burman (TB) language family. It has several unique features if compared with other South-Asian Tibeto-Burman languages. Kokborok literatures were written in Koloma or Swithaih borok script which suffered massive destruction. Overall, the Kokborok language is very scientific and the people use a script similar to Roman script to project the tonal effect. As the language follows the Subject-Object-Verb (SOV) pattern and its agglutinative verb morphology is enriched by the Indo-Aryan languages of Sanskrit origin. The affixes play an important role in framing the structure of the language, e.g., prefixing, suffixing and compounding form new words in this language. In case of compound words, some infixing are also seen where no specific demarcation and morphology is found. Mainly, the root words appear in bounded forms and are joined together to form the compound words.

In general, the POS tagger for the natural languages are developed using linguistic rules, probabilistic models and combination of both. To the best of our knowledge, the POS tag set is not available in Kokborok as no prior work has been carried out in this language. Thus, we prepared a POS tag set by ourselves with the help of linguists by considering different characteristics of the similar Indian languages.

Several POS taggers have been developed in different languages using both rule based and statistical methods. Different approaches to POS tagging for English have already been developed such as Transformation based error-driven learning (Brill, 1995), Decision tree (Black et al., 1992), Hidden Markov Model (Cutting et al., 1992), Maximum Entropy model (Ratnaparkhi, 1996) etc. It was also found that in a practical Part-of-Speech Tagger (Cutting et al., 1992), the accuracy exceeds 96%.

The rule based systems require handcrafted rules and are typically not very robust (Brill, 1992). POS tagger in different Indian languages such as in Hindi (Dalal et al., 2007; Shrivastav et al., 2006; Singh et al., 2006), Bengali (Dandapat et al., 2007; Ekbal et al., 2007; Ekbal and Bandyopadhyay, 2008a), and Manipuri (Kishorjit et al., 2011; Singh and Bandyopadhyay 2008; Singh et al., 2008) etc. have also been developed using both rule based and machine learning approaches. In case of rule based POS Tagging, we considered the help of three dictionaries, namely prefix, suffix and root dictionary. It is also observed that the Probabilistic models have been widely used in POS tagging as they are simple to use and language independent (Dandapat et al., 2007). Among the probabilistic models, Hidden Markov Models (HMMs) are quite popular but it performs poor when less tagged data is used to estimate the parameters of the model. Due to the scarcity of POS tagged corpus in Kokborok, among different machine learning algorithms,

---

[1] http://tripura.nic.in

we have used only CRF and SVM to accomplish the POS tagging task. CRF is a widely used probabilistic framework for sequence labelling tasks. In our case, we observed that the accuracies achieved in the rule based POS tagger is less than the CRF based POS tagger whereas the accuracy of CRF based POS tagger is less than SVM based POS tagger.

The rest of the paper is organized in the following manner. Section 2 gives a brief discussion about word features in Kokborok whereas Section 3 details about resources preparation. Section 4 describes the implementation of rule based POS tagger and Section 5 gives the detail study of Machine learning algorithms, feature selection, implementation and their results while the conclusion is drawn at the end.

2 Word Features in Kokborok

In general, Kokborok possesses unique features like agglutination and compounding. Specially, it has both free and bound root words and has more numbers of bound root words compared to English. In Kokborok, the inflections play the major role and almost all verbs and many of noun root words are bound. It is found that the free root words are nouns, pronouns, some adjectives, numerals etc. The compound words are formed by joining multiple root words affixed with multiple suffixes or prefixes. It is found by the linguistic observations that we can classify the Kokborok words into following seven categories as given below.

i) Only root word (RW). For e.g., Naithok (beautiful)
ii) Root words (RW) having a prefix (P). For e.g., **Bu**pha (my father)
iii) Root words having a suffix (S). For e.g., Braja**no** (to Braja)
iv) P+RW+S. For e.g. **Bu**kumui**ni** (His/Her Brother In Law's)
v) P+RW+S+S… For e.g., Ma(P)+thang (to go)+lai(S)+nai(S)→**Ma**thang**lainai**(need to go)
vi) RW+RW… For e.g., Khwn (Flower)+Lwng(Garden)→Khwmlwng(Flowergarden)
vii) RW+S+RW+S. For e.g., Hui(RW)(to hide)+jak(S)+hui(RW)+jak(S)+wi(S) → Hujakhujakwi (Without Being Seen)

We observed that there is less number of free root words. In Kokborok, affixes are of two types, i.e. derivational affixes and inflectional affixes (Debbarma et al., 2012). In Kokborok, the prefixes are very limited in numbers, generally inflectional and do not change the syntactic category when added to a root word but the suffixes are of both inflectional and derivational. A total of 19 prefixes and 72 suffixes are found in Kokborok.

3 Resource Preparation

In the following sections, we have discussed about the basic requirements of our experiments. The first section discusses about the dictionaries used in the experiments and their formats and in the final section, we have presented the POS tagset for Kokborok which is used for our experiments.

3.1 Dictionaries

We used three dictionaries namely prefix, suffix and root. Prefix and suffix dictionaries contain the list of prefixes and suffixes along with the word features like TAM (Tense, Aspect and Modality), gender, number and person etc. Root dictionary is a bilingual dictionary containing

1895 root words. The format of root dictionary is <root><lexical category><English meaning>. This bilingual dictionary is used for testing of the POS tagger.

3.2 The Tagset

The Kokborok language is one of the agglutinative languages in India and its word formation technique is quite different from other Indian languages. Thus, the POS tagset for Kokborok has been developed keeping the similarity of the POS tagset with other Indian languages[2] in mind. The POS tagset used in this task is given below in Table 1.

POS	Types/ Tag	Examples
Noun	Proper (NNP), Common (NNC), Verbal (NNV)	Aguli, yachakrai (All names), Chwla(boy), bwrwi(girl), khaina(to do), phaina(to come)
Pronoun	Personal (PRP)	Ang(I), Nwng(you), Bo(He/she), Ani(my)
Adjective	JJ	Naithok(beautiful), kwchwng(bright)
Determiner	Singular (DTS), Plural (DTP)	Khoroksa(a), Joto(all), bebak(every)
Predeterminer	PDT	Aa(that), o(this)
Conjunction	CC	Bai(and), tei(or)
Verb	Root (VB), Present (VBP), Past (VBD), Gerund (VBG), Progression (PROG), Future (VBF)	Cha (to eat), khai (to do), Chao (eat), khaio (do), Chakha (ate), phaikha (came), Chawi (eating), khaiwi (doing), Tongo (is/am/are), tongmani (was/were), Chanai(will eat), khainai (will do)
Inflectors	*D	O (to), Rok([charai(child)rok]-children
Quantifiers	QF	Kisa(less), kwbang(more)
Cardinal	CD	Sa(one), nwi(two)
Adverb	RB	Twrwk(slow), dakti(fast)
Interjection	UH	Bah(wao), uh(huh)
Indeclinable	ID	Haiphano(still), Abonibagwi(that's why)
Onomatopes	ON	Sini-sini, sek-sek,sep-sep
Question Words	QW	boh(which), sabo(who), Saboni(whose)
Compound word	CW	
Unknown	UNK	
Symbol	SYM	`,~,@,#,$,%,^,&,*,_,+,-,=,<,>,.,', etc.

Table 1 – POS Tagset for Kokborok.

4 Rule Based POS Tagger

In case of rule based POS tagger, the basic POS tags are assigned to each of the words in a natural language sentence using the morphological rules. The descriptions of the different modules as shown in Figure.1 are as follows:

- **Tokenizer**: Based on the space in between consecutive words, each word of a sentence is separated or tokenized.

[2] http://shiva.iiit.ac.in/SPSAL2007/iiit_tagset_guidelines.pdf

- **Stemmer (Patra et al., 2012):** It identifies the prefixes and suffixes using the affix dictionaries and finds the root words.
- **Morphological Analyzer & Tag generator:** Different analysis on the stemmed words and suffixes are performed using the lexical rules and morpho-syntactic features. Then, the POS tags are assigned to the words based on the tagset and morphology rules.
- **Dictionary:** Prefix, suffix and root dictionaries are described in Section 3.
- **Morpho syntactic Rules:** These are the heuristic rules based morphological characteristics of the words. For e.g., VB + kha (suffix) = VBD, VB + o(suffix)=VBP etc.

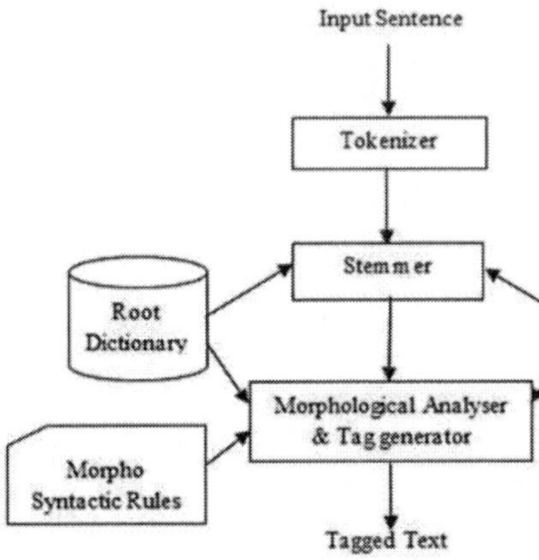

FIGURE 1 –System Diagram of Rule based Morphology driven POS Tagger.

4.1 Algorithm

1. Give input text to the tokenizer module.
2. Repeat step 3 and 4 until each token is tagged.
3. Check for prefixes and suffixes and separate them with the help of affix dictionaries and check if the stemmed word occurs in the root dictionary or not. The words which are not stemmed are sent to the complex word handler module.
4. The complex words are stemmed separately, if these words are not stemmed by complex word handler and tag them as the Named Entities (NEs).
5. Apply the morphological rules on the affixes and root words for identifying the POS tag of the words according to the output of the morphological analyzer.

4.2 Evaluation and Result Discussion

In Kokborok, word categories are not distinct; all the verbs are under the bound categories whereas another problem is to classify basic root forms according to their word classes as the distinction between noun and adjectives is often vague while the distinction between the noun and verb classes is relatively clear. It is found that distinction between a noun and an adjective becomes unclear because structurally a word may be a noun but contextually it is an adjective. For e.g., Uttor Bharato watwi kwbang wakha ("North" "India" "lots" "rain" "happened"). Here north is an adjective where as in the sentence, "Abo uttor" (that is north) the word 'uttor' is a noun. Thus, the word 'uttor' may be an adjective or a noun but the POS of the word in lexicon is noun there by making it difficult to extract the exact POS for the word appearing in various sentences.

The assumption made for the word categories depends upon the root category and affix information that are available from the dictionaries. Further a part of root may also be a prefix which leads to wrong tagging. It is found that the verb morphology is more complex than that of noun. When multiple suffixes added to a verb, it's difficult to find the POS category of the word as the specific rules are not available. The input of 2525 Kokborok sentences of 42537 words was supplied to the tagger . Sometimes, two words get fused to form a complete word and handling such collocations is difficult. Table 2 shows the percentage of tagging output based on the actual and correctly tagged words. There are some unknown words which could not be tagged based on rules available. Due to the unavailability of root dictionary, the performance of POS tagger was reduced effectively. A word can be easily formed by affixation or compounding in Kokborok, so the number of unknown words are relatively large. The accuracy of the tagging can be further improved by introducing more numbers of linguistic rules and adding more root words to the dictionary.

Items	**Percentage**
Correctly tagged words	70%
Wrongly tagged words	22%
Wrongly tagged unknown words	8%

TABLE 2 – Results of the Rule Based POS Tagger.

5 Stochastic POS Taggers

Stochastic models are more popular than rule based POS taggers as these are language independent and easy to use. Among the entire stochastic models, HMMs is quite popular but it requires a huge amount of annotated corpus. Simple HMMs do not work well when small amount of labelled data are used to estimate the model parameters. Incorporating diverse features in an HMM-based tagger is also difficult and complicates the smoothing typically used in such taggers (Ekbal and Bandyopadhyay, 2008b). Thus, we have used Conditional Random Fields (CRF) (Lafferty et al., 2001) and Support Vector Machines (SVM) (Cortes and Vapnik, 1995) frameworks to develop Stochastic POS taggers for the resource constrained Kokborok language.

5.1 Feature Selection

Feature selection plays important role in CRF based machine learning framework. The main features for POS tagging are selected based on the different combinations of available words and tags. As the Kokborok is one of the highly inflected and agglutinative Indian languages, the suffix and prefix features are the effective features in POS tagging task. We have considered different combinations of features to get the best feature set for POS tagging task. Following are the sample and the details of the set of features that have been included in the above list for POS tagging in Kokborok:

F={$w_{(i-m)}$,$w_{(i-m+1)}$,......$w_{(i-1)}$, w_i, $w_{(i+1)}$,........$w_{(i+n)}$, |prefix|=n, |suffix|=n, Context word feature, Digit information, Symbol, Length of the word, Frequent word}

Word suffix: Kokborok is highly inflected language. So, the word suffix information is one of the most important features as it is very helpful to identify the POS classes. This feature can be used in two different ways. The first way is to check whether a word has a suffix or not. If yes, then set the suffix feature 1 else set 0. The second way is to check whether a suffix is changing the POS class of the root word. If yes, then set change POS feature 1 else set 0.
Word prefix: Word prefix information is also helpful to identify the POS class of the word. This feature has been introduced with the observation that the words of the same category POS tags contain some common prefix. This feature has been used in a similar way as word suffixes.
Context word Feature: The immediate previous and next word of a particular word can also be used as feature, i.e., the surrounding words can play an important role in deciding the POS tag of the current word.
Digit information: If any word consists of any digit, then set the digit feature to 1 otherwise 0. It helps to identify the QF (Quantifier) tag.
Symbol: If the token consists of symbols like (%, $,. etc.), then set the symbol feature to 1, otherwise set it to 0. This helps to identify the SYM tag.
Length of a word: It is found that length of a word is an effective feature in deciding POS tag of the word (Singh et al., 2008). If the length of a word is four or less, set the length word feature to 1, otherwise set it as 0. The motivation of using this feature is to distinguish the Personal pronoun from the nouns. We observed that words of very short length are generally Personal pronoun.
Frequent Word: A list for frequently occurring word is prepared for the training corpus. The words that occur more than 10 times in the entire training corpus are considered as the frequent words. The feature for the frequent word is set to 1 if they are in the list else set it as 0. This has been observed that frequently occurring words are rarely proper nouns.

5.2 Evaluation

For applying the statistical models in Kokborok, we required huge amount of annotated corpus in order to achieve good result. But, Kokborok is less computerized language and the corpora for training and testing were not available. During the manually annotation, we faced the problems due to agglutinative structure of the Kokborok language.

5.2.1 Experimental Results of CRF

We have conducted several experiments by considering the different combination of features to find out the best combination of features and feature templates. From the analysis, we observed that our proposed features as mentioned in Section 5.1 give the best results for testing purpose.

We have designed three types of modules based on the CRF Frameworks. The first module makes use of simple contextual features (i.e. CRF), whereas the second module uses the information of affixes along with contextual information (i.e. CRF+suf.). In order to increase the accuracy of the system, we have integrated the morphological information with the model (i.e. CRF + suf. +MA_F). The tagging accuracy of the CRF based POS tagging model has been evaluated as the ratio of correctly tagged words with respect to the total numbers of words. We have trained the system on different data size and the result is shown in Table 3.

The above experiment leads us to the following observations that the use of suffix information plays an important role in achieving the accuracy of the system, especially when the training data is less. Furthermore, the morphology of the word gives significant improvement in the accuracy over the CRF and CRF+suf models.

It was found that the CRF based POS tagger performs far better than the morphology driven POS tagger and has less computational complexity. We have also conducted the experiments with large number of features but, the inclusion of the features decreases the accuracy. It is found that large number of features works well when large amount of annotated corpus is available for training. The other reason was the biasness of noun tags in the corpus.

	10K	20K	40K
CRF baseline model	59.67	63.51	65.72
CRF + suf.	67.23	73.57	76.25
CRF + suf. + MA_F	74.57	79.53	81.67
SVM baseline model	60.51	64.26	68.32
SVM + suf.	69.38	72.66	76.97
SVM + suf. + MA_F	75.52	80.47	84.46

TABLE 3 – Tagging Accuracies In %age With Different Template For CRF & SVM.

5.2.2 Experimental Results of SVM

Same training set which was used for CRF is also used for SVM based experiments. We also conducted several experiments considering the different combination of features to find out the best combination of features and feature templates. From the analysis, we found that the similar features of CRF also produced the best results for testing of SVM based POS Tagger.

We have also conducted several experiments for the various polynomial kernel functions and found that the system is giving the best result for the second degree kernel functions. It has been also observed that the pair wise multi-class decision strategy performs better than the than the one-vs.-rest strategy. The models described here are simple and quite good for automatic POS tagging even less amount of tagged corpus was available. The best performance is achieved when suffix information and morphological information is added to the system.

SVM performs far better than the CRF based POS tagger. The performance in SVM can be improved significantly by including the language specific resources such as lexicon and inflection lists. It is found that a Named Entity Recognizer (NER) and a Multiword Identification Systems are necessary to reduce the large number of errors that involve proper nouns and different multiword expressions. The experiments of SVMs are also conducted on same type of data set and same features as shown in Table 3.

Conclusion and Future works

In this paper, we have described the development of POS taggers using both rule based and statistical models. We achieved the accuracies of 69%, 81.67% and 84.46% in rule based, CRF based and SVM based POS taggers, respectively with respect to 26 different POS tags.

Future work includes the development of language specific resources such as lexicon and inflection lists. The Named Entity recognition module may be included to improve the accuracy in the POS taggers. Some language specific rules should be implemented to handle the Complex words in rule based POS tagger. Other experiments like voting technique for two or more models may be an interesting research direction.

References

Black, E., Jelinek, F., Lafferty, J., Mercer, R., and Roukos, S. (1992). Decision tree models applied to the labeling of text with parts-of-speech. In Proceedings of the DARPA Speech and Natural Language Workshop, pages 117-121.

Brants, T. (2000). TnT: a statistical part-of-speech tagger. In Proceedings of the sixth conference on Applied natural language processing, pages 224-231, Association for Computational Linguistics.

Brill, E. (1992). A simple rule-based part of speech tagger. In Proceedings of the workshop on Speech and Natural Language, pages 112-116, Association for Computational Linguistics.

Brill, E. (1995). Transformation-based error-driven learning and natural language processing: A case study in part-of-speech tagging. Computational linguistics, 21(4):543-565.

Carlos, C. S., Choudhury, M., and Dandapat, S. (2009). Large-coverage root lexicon extraction for Hindi. In Proceedings of the 12th Conference of the European Chapter of the Association for Computational Linguistics, pages 121-129, Association for Computational Linguistics.

Choudhury, S., Singh, L., Borgohain, S., and Das, P. (2004). Morphological Analyzer for Manipuri: Design and Implementation. Applied Computing, 123-129.

Cortes, C., and Vapnik, V. (1995). Support-vector networks. Machine learning, 20(3): 273-297.

Cutting, D., Kupiec, J., Pedersen, J., and Sibun, P. (1992). A practical part-of-speech tagger. In Proceedings of the third conference on Applied natural language processing, pages 133-140. Association for Computational Linguistics.

Debbarma, Binoy and Debbarma, Bijesh (2001). Kokborok Terminology P-I, II, III, English-Kokborok-Bengali. Language Wing, Education Dept., TTAADC, Khumulwng, Tripura.

Debbarma, K., Patra, B. G., Debbarma, S., Kumari, L., and Purkayastha, B. S. (2012). Morphological analysis of Kokborok for universal networking language dictionary. In Proceedings of First International Conference on Recent Advances in Information Technology, pages 474-477. IEEE.

Dalal, A., Nagaraj, K., Swant, U., Shelke, S., and Bhattacharyya, P. (2007). Building feature rich pos tagger for morphologically rich languages: Experience in Hindi. In Proceedings of ICON.

Dandapat, S., Sarkar, S., and Basu, A. (2007). Automatic Part-of-Speech tagging for Bengali: An approach for morphologically rich languages in a poor resource scenario. In Proceedings of the 45th Annual Meeting of the ACL on Interactive Poster and Demonstration Sessions, pages 221-224. Association for Computational Linguistics.

Ekbal, A., and Bandyopadhyay, S. (2008a). Part of speech tagging in Bengali using Support Vector Machine. In proceedings of the International Conference on Information Technology, 2008. ICIT'08, pages 106-111. IEEE.

Ekbal, A., and Bandyopadhyay, S. (2008). Web-based Bengali News Corpus for lexicon Development and POS tagging. POLIBITS, ISSN 1870, 9044(37):20-29.

Ekbal, A., Haque, R., and Bandyopadhyay, S. (2007). Bengali Part of Speech Tagging using

Conditional Random Field. In Proceedings of Seventh International Symposium on Natural Language Processing (SNLP2007), pages 131-136.

Kishorjit, N., Laishram, J., Haobam, V., Soibam, A., Longjam, N., Lourembam, S. and Bandyopadhyay, S. (2009). Unsupervised POS Tagging for Manipuri Text. In Reso-illusion 2009, MIT, Imphal, India.

Kishorjit, N., Salam, B., Romina, M., Chanu, N. M., and Bandyopadhyay, S. (2011). A Light Weight Manipuri Stemmer. In The Proceedings of National Conference on Indian Language Computing (NCILC), Chochin, India.

Kumar, D., and Josan, G. S. (2010). Part of Speech Taggers for Morphologically Rich Indian Languages: A Survey. International Journal of Computer Applications IJCA, 6(5):1-9.

Lafferty, J., McCallum, A., and Pereira, F. C. (2001). Conditional random fields: Probabilistic models for segmenting and labeling sequence data. In Proceedings of the Eighteenth International Conference on Machine Learning, pages 282–289.

Patra, B. G., Debbarma, K., Debabarma, S., Das, D., Das, A. and Bandyopadhyay, S. (2012). A light Weight Stemmer for Kokborok. In Proceedings of the 24th Conference on Computational Linguistics and Speech Processing (ROCLING 2012), Yuan Ze University, Chung-Li, Taiwan, pages 318-325.

Ratnaparkhi, A. (1996). A maximum entropy model for part-of-speech tagging. In Proceedings of the conference on empirical methods in natural language processing, volume 1, pages 133-142.

Shrivastav, M., Melz, R., Singh, S., Gupta, K. and Bhattacharyya, P. (2006). Conditional Random Field Based POS Tagger for Hindi. In Proceedings of the MSPIL, pages 63-68.

Singh, S., Gupta, K., Shrivastava, M., and Bhattacharyya, P. (2006). Morphological richness offsets resource demand-experiences in constructing a POS tagger for Hindi. In Proceedings of the COLING/ACL 2006 Main Conference Poster Sessions, pages 779-786.

Singh, T. D. and Bandyopadhyay, S. (2005). Manipuri Morphological Analyzer. In Proceedings of the Platinum Jubilee International Conference of LSI, University of Hyderabad, India.

Singh, T. D., and Bandyopadhyay, S. (2008). Morphology driven Manipuri POS tagger. IJCNLP-08 Workshop on NLP for Less Privileged Languages, pages 91-98, IIIT, Hyderabad, India.

Singh, T. D., Ekbal, A., and Bandyopadhyay, S. (2008). Manipuri POS tagging using CRF and SVM: A language independent approach. In proceeding of 6th International conference on Natural Language Processing (ICON-2008), pages 240-245.

Forced Derivations for Hierarchical Machine Translation

Stephan Peitz   Arne Mauser   Joern Wuebker   Hermann Ney
Human Language Technology and Pattern Recognition Group
Computer Science Department
RWTH Aachen University
D-52056 Aachen, Germany
`<surname>@cs.rwth-aachen.de`

ABSTRACT
We present an efficient framework to estimate the rule probabilities for a hierarchical phrase-based statistical machine translation system from parallel data. In previous work, this was done with bilingual parsing. We use a more efficient approach splitting the bilingual parsing into two stages, which allows us to train a hierarchical translation model on larger tasks. Furthermore, we apply leave-one-out to counteract over-fitting and use the expected count from the inside-outside algorithm to prune the rule set. On the WMT12 Europarl German→English and French→English tasks, we improve translation quality by up to 1.0 BLEU and 0.9 TER while simultaneously reducing the rule set to 5% of the original size.

KEYWORDS: statistical machine translation, hierarchical decoding, translation model training, forced derivation.

Proceedings of COLING 2012: Posters, pages 933–942,
COLING 2012, Mumbai, December 2012.

1 Introduction

In hierarchical machine translation, discontinuous phrases with "gaps" are allowed and the model is formalized as a synchronous context-free grammar (SCFG). This grammar consists of bilingual rules, which are based on bilingual standard phrases and discontinuous phrases. Each bilingual rule rewrites a generic non-terminal X into a pair of strings $\tilde{f}$ and $\tilde{e}$ with both terminals and non-terminals in both languages

$$X \rightarrow \langle \tilde{f}, \tilde{e} \rangle. \tag{1}$$

In the following, we denote $\tilde{f}$ as *source side* and $\tilde{e}$ as *target side* of a bilingual rule. Obtaining these rules is based on a heuristic extraction from automatically word-aligned bilingual training data. Just like in the phrase-based approach, all bilingual rules of a sentence pair are extracted given an alignment. The standard phrases are stored as *lexical rules* in the rule set. In addition, whenever a phrase contains a sub-phrase, this sub-phrase is replaced by a generic non-terminal X. With these hierarchical phrases we can define the *hierarchical rules* in the SCFG. However, this extraction method causes two problems. First, this approach does not consider, whether a rule is extracted from a likely alignment or not. The rule probabilities which are in general defined as relative frequencies are computed based on the joint counts $C(X \rightarrow \langle \tilde{f}, \tilde{e} \rangle)$ of a bilingual rule $X \rightarrow \langle \tilde{f}, \tilde{e} \rangle$

$$p_H(\tilde{f}|\tilde{e}) = \frac{C(X \rightarrow \langle \tilde{f}, \tilde{e} \rangle)}{\sum_{\tilde{f}'} C(X \rightarrow \langle \tilde{f}', \tilde{e} \rangle)}. \tag{2}$$

Thus, the probabilities depend only on simple counts from a word alignment. Another issue is the large number of extracted rules which is exponential in sentence length (Lopez, 2008). To reduce the size of the hierarchical translation model, threshold pruning, which is based on the counts of the rules, can be applied. However, this is connected to the first mentioned difficulty. Using these counts to prune the rule set may reduce the rule set size, but the translation quality can get worse (Zens et al., 2012). An alternative is a more consistent pruning regarding the translation process.

In this work, we present an approach to directly estimate the rule probabilities by applying an expectation-maximization (EM) inspired algorithm. The rule probabilities are computed in both translation directions, i.e. source-to-target $p_H(\tilde{f}|\tilde{e})$ and target-to-source $p_H(\tilde{e}|\tilde{f})$, and are combined in a weighted log-linear model with other features to find the best translation. Similar to the classical EM algorithm, our algorithm is divided into an expectation step and a maximization step. For the expectation step, we parse the training data to get all possible synchronous derivations between the source and target sentences. The parsing is done with a two-parse algorithm where separately first the source sentence and then the target sentence is parsed. From the resulting parse tree of the target parse, the used rules are extracted. Both parsing steps are done with the CYK+ parsing algorithm. After parsing, we apply the inside-outside algorithm on the generated target parse tree to compute expected counts for each applied rule. As maximization step, we update the rule probabilities using the expected counts.

On the German→English and French→English Europarl task from *NAACL 2012 Workshop on Statistical Machine Translation* (WMT12), we show that our presented approach improves the translation quality by up to 1.0 Bleu and 0.9 Ter while the rule set is reduced by 95% of the original size.

The paper is organized as follows. In the following Section, we give a short overview of related work. In Section 3, we describe our forced derivation step in detail. Finally, we discuss the experimental results in Section 4, followed by a conclusion.

2 Related Work

In recent years, several works have investigated the direct training of the translation model to close the gap between the extraction and the translation process.

In (Marcu and Wong, 2002), a joint probability model is presented which estimates phrase translation probabilities from a parallel corpus. For aligning the phrases and estimating the probabilities, the EM algorithm is applied. In (Birch et al., 2006) the joint probability model is constrained by a word alignment to limit the complexity.

The problem of over-fitting due to the EM algorithm is analyzed in (DeNero et al., 2006) and a solution is proposed in (Wuebker et al., 2010) by applying leave-one-out. We will adopt the leave-one-out method in this work and show that its benefits translate to the hierarchical case.

Another approach to learn from decoding on the training data is presented in (Duan et al., 2012). In this work, a training method based on forced derivation trees is described. This structure is used to train apart from a translation model, a distortion model, a source language model and a rule sequence model. As first step, they verified their method on a phrase-based system. However, this method can be adapted for the hierarchical approach.

Besides these publications about phrase training for the phrase-based approach, several works have been presented for hierarchical machine translation during the past years. In most of these papers the idea of bilingual parsing on parallel corpora is described.

In (Blunsom et al., 2008) a discriminative model using derivations as a hidden variable is presented. In training, they perform a synchronous parsing of the source and target sentences using a modified CYK algorithm over two dimensions with a time complexity of $\mathcal{O}(J^3 I^3)$ where J is the source sentence length and I the target sentence length. Further, the inside-outside algorithm is employed. The experiments were carried out on a subset of the French→English Europarl corpus (170K sentences) and show comparable results. Another observation is that their model improves as they increase the number of parsable training sentences. Starting from this observation, we will apply our approach on a larger training corpus and show, that we improve the translation quality on a recent task.

Bilingual parsing on parallel corpora is also described in (Huang and Zhou, 2009), (Čmejrek et al., 2009) and (Čmejrek and Zhou, 2010). They also use the EM algorithm to recompute the translation probabilities. In order to do that, in (Huang and Zhou, 2009) the EM algorithm for SCFG is introduced. In the maximization step, the expected counts from the inside-outside algorithm are used to update the translation probabilities for non-lexical rules only. Experiments on the Chinese→English IWSLT 2006 task (40K sentences without punctuation and case information) result in a significantly better Bleu score. In (Čmejrek et al., 2009) and (Čmejrek and Zhou, 2010), this work is extended and they report improvement on a subset of the German→English Europarl corpus (300K sentences without punctuation and case information).

In (Heger et al., 2010), a standard hierarchical machine translation system is combined with phrases trained as in (Wuebker et al., 2010). Experimental results on Arabic→English IWSLT and English→German WMT task show improvements in translation quality and motivate to investigate the impact of phrase training for the hierarchical approach.

In (Dyer, 2010) a synchronous parsing algorithm is introduced that is based on two successive monolingual parses. Instead of performing one bilingual parse for a given sentences pair, a two-parse algorithm is applied. This improves the average run-time. The authors reported speed improvement on the same task as in (Blunsom et al., 2008). We apply this approach to reduce the run-time of our forced derivation procedure.

Compared to previous described approaches for training the hierarchical translation model, we are now able to employ forced derivation on larger task. Furthermore, we estimate the inside-outside probabilities on the target chart only and calculate the expected count for all type of rules. We also apply a threshold pruning on the rule set using the estimated expected counts. This leads to a more consistent pruning and a smaller rule set. Another difference is that we perform leave-one-out to counteract over-fitting. Further, in the forced derivation procedure, we include the log-linear combination of all features which are used in the translation process except for the language model.

3 Forced Derivation

In the forced derivation procedure, the two-parse algorithm and the inside-outside algorithm are the expectation step of the EM-inspired algorithm. During the expectation step, the expected counts are calculated. First, we need all possible synchronous derivations given the parallel training data. From the resulting parse trees, all applied rules are extracted and the expected count of each rule is estimated with the inside-outside algorithm. In general, a bilingual parser parses all parallel sentences of the training data based on the full extracted rule set of the training data (Huang and Zhou, 2009). However, to calculate all parses efficiently, we apply the two-parse algorithm instead of full bilingual parsing. The two-parse algorithm performs two monolingual parses, one on the source language sentence f_1^J and one on the target language sentence e_1^I. Each parse is done using the CYK+ algorithm as described in (Chappelier and Rajman, 1998). The main advantage of the CYK+ algorithm is that it does not require the grammar to be in Chomsky Normal Form and we can use hierarchical translation rules directly. of the grammar in the algorithm itself. Similar to the CYK algorithm, the basic data structure is a chart with $\frac{J(J+1)}{2}$ cells where J is in this case the size of the source sentence f_1^J. The source sentence can be generated by the grammar if the start symbol of the grammar S is found in top cell $(J,1)$, i.e. $S \Rightarrow^* f_1^J$. The time complexity is $\mathcal{O}(J^3)$ and $\mathcal{O}(I^3)$ respectively. The resulting charts have a space complexity of $\mathcal{O}(J^2)$ and $\mathcal{O}(I^2)$ for the representation of all derivations. In the hierarchical approach of (Chiang, 2005), the set of non-terminals consists of a start symbol S and a generic non-terminal X. Furthermore, the number of non-terminals n on the right hand side of the rules is limited to two. In addition to the hierarchical and lexical rules, a rule set $\mathcal{R}$ is extended with an initial rule and a glue rule

$$S \to \langle X, X \rangle, S \to \langle SX, SX \rangle. \tag{3}$$

Given $\mathcal{R}$, the parallel training corpus is parsed with the two-parse algorithm. First, we parse the source sentence f_1^J with the source sides of the rules of the given rule set $\mathcal{R}$ and a sentence pair (f_1^J, e_1^I). Note, we ensure that each source sentence can always be parsed by employing several heuristics during the extraction process to get all necessary rules. From the chart we extract the target side of the used rules. This is done by simply traversing from the top cell $(J,1)$ through the chart. Then the non-terminals on the left hand side and the non-terminals of the target side are annotated with the source span of the corresponding non-terminals in the chart. The annotated rules are stored in a new rule set $\mathscr{R}_t$. Moreover, we annotate applied initial rules and glue rules. Hence, the set of non-terminals now consists of several annotated start symbols and generic non-terminals. In our implementation, the left hand side with the annotated target side of the bilingual rule and a pointer to the corresponding original rule including all features is stored. Further, to keep the time and memory usage low, we limit the number of target sides for each rule in the described extraction step.

In the second pass, the target sentence e_1^I is parsed using the annotated target sides of the bilingual rules in the new rule set $\mathscr{R}_t$. The annotation of non-terminals of the rules in the first parse ensures that rules applied in the target parse cover only one span in the source sentence. The target sentence is generated by the new grammar and the forced derivation procedure is successful, if the start symbol S_1^J is found in cell $(I, 1)$. In contrast to the source parse, it is possible that a target parse is not found due to the fact that we prune necessary target sides as describe before. If a target sentence can not be parsed, we discard the sentence pair. The generated parse tree represents all possible synchronous derivations between the source and target sentence and the used rules are extracted from the chart as we save a pointer to the corresponding source side of the rule. Again, the extraction procedure starts from the top cell $(I, 1)$ and traverses through the chart of the target parse.

3.1 Inside-Outside Algorithm

For the estimation of the rule probabilities we employ the inside-outside algorithm to calculate the expected count for each rule used in the forced derivation step. In the maximization step the expected counts are used to update the rule probabilities. As described in (Čmejrek et al., 2009), we calculate the expected count based on the inside and outside probabilities depending on the number of non-terminals in the rule. Due to the fact that we do not perform full bilingual parsing, we apply the inside-outside algorithm on the target parse only. Considering a sentence pair (f_1^J, e_1^I), the expected count $C_{FD}(r_n)$ is computed for a rule r_n applied in target parse. Note, the expected counts for a rule are summed up over all sentence pairs of the training data. For the maximization step, we use the expected counts $C_{FD}(r_n)$ of a rule $r_n = X \rightarrow \langle \tilde{f}, \tilde{e} \rangle$ to update the rule probability $p_{FD}(\tilde{f} | \tilde{e})$

$$p_{FD}(\tilde{f} | \tilde{e}) = \frac{C_{FD}(X \rightarrow \langle \tilde{f}, \tilde{e} \rangle)}{\sum_{\tilde{f}'} C_{FD}(X \rightarrow \langle \tilde{f}', \tilde{e} \rangle)}. \quad (4)$$

This is also done for the target-to-source translation probability $p_{FD}(\tilde{e} | \tilde{f})$.

3.2 Leave-one-out

Another issue of phrase model training in general is over-fitting. Due to the fact that all rules which are extracted from a sentence pair are used in the forced derivation step, longer rules are often preferred. Even though those long rules only match for a few sentences of the training data and do not generalize very well, they tend to be assigned very high translation probabilities. In (Wuebker et al., 2010) a leave-one-out method is described which counteracts the over-fitting. This method modifies the translation probabilities in the forced derivation step for each sentence pair. The occurrences of a given rule in a sentence pair (f_n, e_n) are subtracted from the rule counts obtained from the full training data resulting in the modified translation probability

$$p_{l1o,n}(\tilde{f}|\tilde{e}) = \frac{C(X \to \langle \tilde{f},\tilde{e}\rangle) - C_n(X \to \langle \tilde{f},\tilde{e}\rangle)}{\sum_{\tilde{f}'} C(X \to \langle \tilde{f}',\tilde{e}\rangle) - C_n(X \to \langle \tilde{f}',\tilde{e}\rangle)} \quad (5)$$

where $C_n(X \to \langle \tilde{f},\tilde{e}\rangle)$ is the count for the rule $X \to \langle \tilde{f},\tilde{e}\rangle$, that was extracted from this sentence pair. Singleton rules, which are rules occurring only in one sentence, are handled differently. These rules get a low probability depending on the source and target rule lengths. Note, the non-terminals on the right hand side of the rules are treated such as terminals. Without leave-one-out, the longer rule

$$X \to \langle \text{Und } [\ldots] \text{ Strafen}, \text{It } [\ldots] \text{ should}\rangle \quad (6)$$

is applied. Such long rules are used only in few sentence pairs and will hardly generalize well to unseen test data. Using leave-one-out, three shorter, more general rules are used for generating this part of the sentence pair

$$X \to \langle \text{Und zwar } X, \text{It } X\rangle, X \to \langle \text{sollen } X, X \text{ should}\rangle, X \to \langle \text{derartige Strafen}, \text{says that this}\rangle. \quad (7)$$

4 Experiments

Our experiments were carried out on the German→English and French→English Europarl task from the *NAACL 2012 Workshop on Statistical Machine Translation*. For both tasks, we selected parallel sentences according to two criteria: Only sentences of maximum 100 tokens are considered and the ratio of the vocabulary size of a sentence and the number of its tokens is minimum 80% i.e. we remove sentences that have too many repeated words. The German text was further preprocessed by splitting German compound words using the frequency-based method described in (Koehn and Knight, 2003). For the experiments, we used the open source translation toolkit Jane (Vilar et al., 2010), which has been developed at RWTH and is freely available for non-commercial use. We extended the hierarchical phrase-based machine translation system based on (Chiang, 2005) with the two-parse algorithm and the inside-outside algorithm as described in Section 3.

4.1 Experimental Setup

Given the training data, we created a word alignment with GIZA++ (Och and Ney, 2003). The resulting alignment was used to extract the initial rule set. As the initial rule set is extracted heuristically, we name it *heuristic rule set* in the following. In contrast, the produced rule set after the forced derivation procedure is called *learned rule set*. First, we built a baseline system which is a standard hierarchical phrase-based SMT system with ten features in a log-linear model: translation and word lexicon probabilities in both translation directions (source-to-target and target-to-source), rule penalty, word penalty, language model score and three binary features for hierarchical rules. Furthermore, we used the heuristic rule set to perform our proposed forced derivation procedure and initialized the weights of each rule in the EM-inspired algorithm with log-linear combination of all features. We used a standard set of non-optimized parameters for the log-linear combination. We applied length-based leave-one-out as described in Section 3 and compared to a setup without leave-one-out. For all experiments, we used a 4-gram language model with modified Kneser-Ney smoothing which was trained with the SRILM toolkit (Stolcke, 2002). Further, we used the cube prune algorithm (Huang and Chiang, 2007) to perform the search. The scaling factors of the features were optimized for BLEU (Papineni et al., 2001) on the development set with Minimum Error Rate Training (Och, 2003) on 100-best lists. The performance of the different setup was evaluated on the development (newstest2010) and the test set (newstest2011) using the two metrics BLEU and TER (Snover et al., 2006).

4.2 Experimental Results

The results of our different experiments are presented in Table 2. Our approach is abbreviated to *FD* (forced derivation). First, we did different preliminary experiments on the German→English task. We then applied the best methods on the French→English task to verify our proposed approach.

During the forced derivation procedure, around 93% of the parallel sentences of the German→English corpus and around 97% of French→English corpus were parsed with the two-parse algorithm. The non-parsable sentences were skipped. In general, those are longer sentences, which are misaligned usually caused by liberal or wrong translation. For a batch of 2000 sentences, the parsing took on average 2.5 hours (without rule set loading time) on a single machine.

First, we performed our proposed method with and without leave-one-out (Table 1). The length-based leave-one-out (*lbl1o*) method outperforms forced derivation without leave-one-out in terms of BLEU and is also slightly better than the baseline. Further, we pruned the final learned rule set by dropping all rules which got a summed up expected count lower than a given threshold. The results for different threshold values are shown in Table 1. Discarding such rules seems to improve the translation quality and in addition reduces the size of the rule set. We ran several setups using different thresholds and compared them on the development set. Even the full learned rule set does not contain all rules of the initial rule set. The reason for that is the pruning in the forced derivation procedure and the skipped non-parsable sentences. Note, that the pruning settings are weaker then in the translation process. We tested the best setup (*cutoff 0.1*) on the test translation set and achieved an improvement of 0.4 points in BLEU and 0.3 points in TER. The final rule set size is reduced by more than 95%. It seems that the greatest improvement is achieved by this reduction. The results of the experiment using the heuristic rule set filtered to contain the same rules as the pruned learned rule set (*baseline filtered*) are similar to the setup using the translation probabilities learned with the EM-inspired algorithm. This observation shows that using filtered rules performs as least as good as using the full rule set. However, due to the reduced rule set, following experiments were consuming less computation time and memory.

We achieved further improvement applying a log-linear interpolation of the learned rule set with the heuristic one as proposed in (DeNero et al., 2006). The log-linear interpolations $p_{int}(\tilde{f}\,|\,\tilde{e})$ are computed as

$$p_{int}(\tilde{f}\,|\,\tilde{e}) = \left(p_H(\tilde{f}\,|\,\tilde{e})\right)^{1-\omega} \cdot \left(p_{FD}(\tilde{f}\,|\,\tilde{e})\right)^{\omega} \quad (8)$$

where ω is the interpolation weight, p_H the heuristic rule set and p_{FD} the learned rule set. Only the intersection of both tables is retained. The interpolation weight was adjusted on the development set and set to $\omega = 0.2$. Our final result shows an improvement of 0.7 BLEU points and 0.8 TER points over the baseline on the test translation set of the German→English task.

For the the French-English task, we applied forced derivation with length-based leave-one-out and a cutoff threshold of 0.1. Similar to the German→English task, we got an improvement of

cutoff threshold	dev Bleu [%]	% of full rule set: all type of rules	% of full rule set: hierarchical only
0.2	21.0	3.2	3.0
0.15	21.4	3.9	3.6
0.1	**21.4**	**4.9**	**4.7**
0.01	21.2	13.2	15.0
full (length-based l1o)	21.0	92.0	94.3
full (without l1o)	20.3	92.0	94.3
baseline	20.8	100	100

Table 1: Preliminary experiments on the development set of the German→English WMT12 task.

setup	German→English		French→English	
	Bleu [%]	Ter [%]	Bleu [%]	Ter [%]
baseline	19.1	63.4	24.6	57.2
baseline (filtered)	19.5	63.3	-	-
FD +lbl1o +cutoff 0.1	19.5	63.1	25.0	57.2
fixed interpolation $\omega = 0.2$	**19.8**	**62.6**	**25.6**	**56.3**

Table 2: Final results for the German→English and French→English WMT12 task.

0.4 points in Bleu while the rule set size was reduced by more than 95%. With the log-linear interpolation, we gained further 0.6 Bleu points. In sum, we achieved an improvement of 1.0 points in Bleu and 0.9 points in Ter over the baseline on the French-English task.

Conclusion

In this paper, we have introduced an efficient method to perform the direct estimation of rule probabilities for hierarchical machine translation. Based on an EM-inspired algorithm, the expectation is computed with the two-parse algorithm that generates all possible synchronous derivations between a source and target sentence. We applied the inside-outside algorithm to calculate the expected counts and to estimate rules probabilities. To avoid over-fitting, we used length-based leave-one-out. By pruning rules with a low expected count, it is possible to significantly reduce the rule set size.

Compared to previous work, we have also shown improvements on an medium sized task. On the WMT12 Europarl German→English task we improved translation quality by 0.4 Bleu points with the trained rule set and 0.7 Bleu points using the interpolation. Furthermore, the rule set size was reduced by over 95%. In addition, we showed improvements of up to 1.0 Bleu and 0.9 Ter on the WMT12 Europarl French→English task.

In future work, a leave-one-out strategy considering non-terminals in a more sophisticated way could further improve forced derivation.

Acknowledgments

This work was partly funded by the European Union under the FP7 project T4ME Net, Contract n° 249119. The research leading to these results has also received funding from the European Union Seventh Framework Programme (FP7/2007-2013) under grant agreement n° 287658.

References

Birch, A., Callison-Burch, C., Osborne, M., and Koehn, P. (2006). Constraining the Phrase-Based, Joint Probability Statistical Translation Model. In *Human Language Technology Conf. (HLT-NAACL): Proc. Workshop on Statistical Machine Translation*, pages 154–157, New York City, NY.

Blunsom, P., Cohn, T., and Osborne, M. (2008). A discriminative latent variable model for statistical machine translation. In *Proceedings of ACL-08: HLT*, pages 200–208, Columbus, Ohio. Association for Computational Linguistics.

Chappelier, J.-C. and Rajman, M. (1998). A generalized CYK algorithm for parsing stochastic CFG. In *Proceedings of the First Workshop on Tabulation in Parsing and Deduction*, pages 133–137.

Chiang, D. (2005). A Hierarchical Phrase-Based Model for Statistical Machine Translation. In *Proc. of the 43rd Annual Meeting of the Association for Computational Linguistics (ACL)*, pages 263–270, Ann Arbor, Michigan.

DeNero, J., Gillick, D., Zhang, J., and Klein, D. (2006). Why generative phrase models underperform surface heuristics. In *Workshop on Statistical Machine Translation at HLT-NAACL*.

Duan, N., Li, M., and Zhou, M. (2012). Forced derivation tree based model training to statistical machine translation. In *Proceedings of the 2012 Joint Conference on Empirical Methods in Natural Language Processing and Computational Natural Language Learning*, pages 445–454, Jeju Island, Korea. Association for Computational Linguistics.

Dyer, C. (2010). Two monolingual parses are better than one (synchronous parse). In *In Proc. of HLT-NAACL*.

Heger, C., Wuebker, J., Vilar, D., and Ney, H. (2010). A combination of hierarchical systems with forced alignments from phrase-based systems. In *International Workshop on Spoken Language Translation*, pages 291–297, Paris, France.

Huang, L. and Chiang, D. (2007). Forest rescoring: Faster decoding with integrated language models. *Proceedings of ACL 2007*, 45(1):144.

Huang, S. and Zhou, B. (2009). An em algorithm for scfg in formal syntax-based translation. In *Acoustics, Speech and Signal Processing, 2009. ICASSP 2009. IEEE International Conference on*, pages 4813–4816.

Koehn, P. and Knight, K. (2003). Empirical Methods for Compound Splitting. In *Proc. 10th Conf. of the Europ. Chapter of the Assoc. for Computational Linguistics (EACL)*, pages 347–354, Budapest, Hungary.

Lopez, A. (2008). Tera-scale translation models via pattern matching. In *Proceedings of the 22nd International Conference on Computational Linguistics - Volume 1*, COLING '08, pages 505–512, Stroudsburg, PA, USA. Association for Computational Linguistics.

Marcu, D. and Wong, W. (2002). A Phrase-Based, Joint Probability Model for Statistical Machine Translation. In *Proc. of the Conf. on Empirical Methods for Natural Language Processing (EMNLP)*, pages 133–139, Philadelphia, PA.

Och, F. J. (2003). Minimum Error Rate Training for Statistical Machine Translation. In *Proc. of the 41th Annual Meeting of the Association for Computational Linguistics (ACL)*, Sapporo, Japan.

Och, F. J. and Ney, H. (2003). A Systematic Comparison of Various Statistical Alignment Models. *Computational Linguistics*, 29(1):19–51.

Papineni, K., Roukos, S., Ward, T., and Zhu, W.-J. (2001). Bleu: a Method for Automatic Evaluation of Machine Translation. IBM Research Report RC22176 (W0109-022), IBM Research Division, Thomas J. Watson Research Center, P.O. Box 218, Yorktown Heights, NY 10598.

Snover, M., Dorr, B., Schwartz, R., Micciulla, L., and Makhoul, J. (2006). A Study of Translation Edit Rate with Targeted Human Annotation. In *Proceedings of the 7th Conference of the Association for Machine Translation in the Americas*, pages 223–231, Cambridge, Massachusetts, USA.

Stolcke, A. (2002). SRILM – An Extensible Language Modeling Toolkit. In *Proc. of the Int. Conf. on Speech and Language Processing (ICSLP)*, volume 2, pages 901–904, Denver, CO.

Čmejrek, M. and Zhou, B. (2010). Two methods for extending hierarchical rules from the bilingual chart parsing. In *Proceedings of the 23rd International Conference on Computational Linguistics: Posters*, COLING '10, pages 180–188, Stroudsburg, PA, USA. Association for Computational Linguistics.

Čmejrek, M., Zhou, B., and Xiang, B. (2009). Enriching scfg rules directly from efficient bilingual chart parsing. In *IWSLT'09*, pages 136–143.

Vilar, D., Stein, D., Huck, M., and Ney, H. (2010). Jane: Open source hierarchical translation, extended with reordering and lexicon models. In *ACL 2010 Joint Fifth Workshop on Statistical Machine Translation and Metrics MATR*, pages 262–270, Uppsala, Sweden.

Wuebker, J., Mauser, A., and Ney, H. (2010). Training phrase translation models with leaving-one-out. In *Proceedings of the 48th Annual Meeting of the Assoc. for Computational Linguistics*, pages 475–484, Uppsala, Sweden.

Zens, R., Stanton, D., and Xu, P. (2012). A systematic comparison of phrase table pruning techniques. In *Proceedings of the 2012 Joint Conference on Empirical Methods in Natural Language Processing and Computational Natural Language Learning*, pages 972–983, Jeju Island, Korea.

On Pāṇini and the Generative Capacity of Contextualized Replacement Systems

Gerald PENN[1] *Paul KIPARSKY*[2]
(1) University of Toronto
(2) Stanford University
`gpenn@cs.toronto.edu, kiparsky@csli.stanford.edu`

Abstract

This paper re-examines the widely held belief that the formalism underlying the rule system propounded by the ancient Indian grammarian, Pāṇini (ca. 450–350 BCE), either anticipates or converges upon the same expressive power found in finite state control systems or the context-free languages that are used in programming language theory and computational linguistics. While there is indeed a striking but cosmetic resemblance to the contextualized rewriting systems used by modern morphologists and phonologists, a subtle difference in how rules are prevented from applying cyclically leads to a massive difference in generative capacity. The formalism behind Pāṇinian grammar, in fact, generates string languages not even contained within any of the multiple-component tree-adjoining languages, MCTAL(k), for any k. There is ample evidence, nevertheless, that Pāṇini's grammar itself judiciously avoided the potential pitfalls of this unconstrained formalism to articulate a large-coverage, but seemingly very tractable grammar of the Sanskrit language.

Keywords: generative capacity, grammar formalisms, Pāṇini, morphophonological rewriting systems.

Proceedings of COLING 2012: Posters, pages 943–950,
COLING 2012, Mumbai, December 2012.

1 Background: Formal Language Complexity

Assuming that every language can be characterised as the set of all and only those strings that are grammatical in that language, Chomsky (1959) defined a chain of language classes (sets of languages, thus sets of sets of strings) now called the Chomsky Hierarchy, each class of which is defined by a kind of grammar that can characterise every language in that class. The chain, as Chomsky (1959) defined it, is:

$$RL \subset CFL \subset CSL \subset UL$$

where RL are the regular languages, CFL are the context-free languages, CSL are the context-sensitive languages, and UL are the unrestricted languages.

Note that we are discussing *languages* and not *grammars*. A language is regular (resp. context-free, context-sensitive, unrestricted) if and only if there exists a regular (resp. context-free, context-sensitive, unrestricted) grammar that generates it. Even regular languages have presentations as context-free or context-sensitive grammars, for example, because regular languages are also context-free languages and context-sensitive languages. Even if the context-sensitive rules in a grammar have non-empty contexts, this does not guarantee, *pace* Staal (1965), that the language defined by the grammar is in fact properly context-sensitive. There may be a different presentation of the same language that is a regular grammar. In this case, the language would in fact be a regular language.

Membership in a language class has practical consequences because it determines the worst-case running time of an algorithm that receives a grammar G and string w as input and determines whether w belongs to the language characterised by G. It also arguably has psycholinguistic consequences in that the precise position(s) of human languages relative to these classes has not yet been determined. There are proofs that at least one human language is not syntactically context-free (Swiss-German; Huybregts, 1984, Shieber, 1985) and that at least one human language is not morphologically context-free (Bambara; Culy, 1985).

Normally, within the field of formal language theory, we investigate abstract, nonsensical languages that have simple, precise definitions. The well-known language $\{a^n b^n \mid n \geq 0\}$, for example, is comprised of the strings *ab*, *aabb*, *aaabbb*, etc. This language belongs to CFL, but not to RL. Note that string membership can still be determined in time linear in the length of an input string for this fixed language. But a general CFL membership algorithm would take roughly cubic time.

2 Two Essential Questions of Formal Language Complexity for Pāṇinian Grammar

There are two principal question schemes that we can distinguish with respect to the study of Pāṇinian grammar as a computational device:

A: Given the specific, fixed grammar that Pāṇini articulated in the Aṣṭādhyāyī, which formal language class(es) does it belong to?

B: Given the grammar formalism that Pāṇini used for this grammar, what kind of grammars can we write in general? That is to say, where does the class of Pāṇinian languages fit within the Chomsky hierarchy?

The answer to (A) has been argued by Hyman (2007) to be RL. (B) is much more difficult to answer conclusively because Pāṇini did not define this class formally. But we do have a very thorough example, as well as the benefit of several traditional commentators who speculated as to the unstated conventions that Pāṇini must have assumed in order for the Aṣṭādhyāyī to make correct predictions about Sanskrit grammar.

There have been 2 replies to (B) thus far:

(i) the Pāṇinian languages are the CFL. This answer is widely assumed within computer science circles, probably as a result of a claim by Ingerman (1967) that Pāṇini had anticipated the invention of Backus-Naur form, a means of specifying context-free grammars. Even to the trifling extent that the Aṣṭādhyāyī looks anything like BNF, it would be a strident oversimplification to claim that the two are equivalent in a formal-language-theoretic sense.

(ii) the Pāṇinian languages are either RL or UL. There is an unmistakable similarity between the form of many of the rules in the Aṣṭādhyāyī and the more recent occidental tradition of formulating rules in both phonology and morphology as instances of:

$$\phi \longrightarrow \psi \,/\, \lambda \_\_ \rho,$$

which signifies that an instance of ϕ rewrites to an instance of ψ when preceded by an instance of λ and followed by an instance of ρ. ϕ, ψ, λ and ρ are either strings or (regular) sets of strings. Johnson (1970) proved (without reference to Pāṇini) that systems of these rules generate UL in general, but that with one restriction, which modern morphophonologists seem willing to follow, they only generate RL. That restriction is acyclicity.

The purpose of this paper is to set the record straight on (B). Section 3 discusses the acyclicity restriction in more detail. It turns out that Pāṇini observes a related condition that we shall call Nīlakaṇṭhadīkṣitar's condition. Section 4 proves that the two restrictions, while related, are not equivalent, as can be seen prominently when the redex lengths in individual rules are greater than 1. Section 5 shows that Pāṇini does in fact use redexes of length greater than 1 in his grammar. Section 6 then shows that the Pāṇinian formalism recognizes all of the count languages, placing it well above context-free on the Chomsky hierarchy.

3 Acyclicity

In every derivation in one of these contextualized replacement systems, it is possible to relate the rule application instances of the derivation such that $r_1 < r_2$ iff the input redex of r_2 contains at least 1 of the output characters of r_1. The transitive closure of this relation is a partial order, which can be decomposed into totally ordered chains of rule application instances, each successive member of which rewrites some of the output of the previous member. The aforementioned restriction is that there must exist a natural number k such that no rule has more than k application instances in any chain in any derivation.

Often it is assumed by linguists that k must be 1. This is not actually necessary. But often this restriction is paraphrased as: 'no rule may rewrite its own output.' This paraphrase is simply inaccurate; it does not capture how these rules are allowed to interact, even when $k = 1$.

It appears that this "acyclicity" condition does in fact hold of derivations induced by the Aṣṭādhyāyī. But it does so contingently: there are explicit meta-rules in the Aṣṭādhyāyī that seem to have been placed there to establish this restriction (Joshi and Kiparsky, 1979). This means that, unless otherwise stated, Pāṇini's contextualized rules can apply in cycles (and possibly to their own output).

These pre-emptory meta-rules are only used where a prohibition on re-using the same context to apply the same rule would not already have accomplished the prohibition. Such a prohibition is nowhere explicitly stated in the Aṣṭādhyāyī. Thus the prohibition on re-using contexts does seem to be part of the underlying formalism, and it has been acknowledged as such by at least one traditional commentator (Nīlakaṇṭhadīkṣitar: lakṣye lakṣaṇam sakṛd eva pravartate).

"Context," as Nīlakaṇṭhadīkṣitar describes it, refers to a specific replacement instance within a given input string that is denoted by a grammar rule. That includes both λ and ρ, but it also includes other information that can be mentioned as conditions on the rules of the Aṣṭādhyāyī, e.g., whether a candidate context is contained with a reduplicated verbal stem, the presence of culturally determined levels of respect in the dialogue, and even earlier steps in the derivational history. There is seemingly no limit to the allowable sources of such information.

It is known, however, from specific example derivations (*prakriya*) adduced by traditional commentators, that for either the string matching λ or the string matching ρ in a new candidate context to be the same string instance as in a previous context is enough to violate Nīlakaṇṭhadīkṣitar's condition. That is, "same context" does not necessarily mean that both λ and ρ are the same. Reusing just one of them is sufficient to violate the condition.

Note that for both Johnson (1970) and Pāṇini, the rules:

$$\phi \longrightarrow \psi \,/\, \lambda \_\_ \rho$$

and:

$$\lambda\phi\rho \longrightarrow \lambda\psi\rho$$

are potentially very different in their effects, as a result. If there even are any rules in the Aṣṭādhyāyī that should be interpreted as having no conditions whatsoever on their application, it is uncertain whether such rules could then never reapply because every context trivially satisfies those conditions, or always reapply because no specified contextual information is reused between the previous and subsequent contexts. We will assume the latter, because rules that have an empty λ and a non-empty ρ or a non-empty λ and an empty ρ may apply more than once within a single derivation — even to adjacent consonants. In other words, an unstated left/right context means "no left/right context," not "trivial left/right context."

4 Is Nīlakaṇṭhadīkṣitar's condition equivalent to Acyclicity?

No. Acyclicity implies the former.

Nīlakaṇṭhadīkṣitar's condition only prevents cyclicity when, in a chain of rule applications, the left and right contexts conspire to prevent partial overlaps between the output of a rule application and the input of a later application of the same rule. To consider a chain of length 2, for example, the rules:

$$\begin{array}{l} aa \longrightarrow bb \;/\; c\,\_\,d \\ bb \longrightarrow aa \;/\; c\,\_\,d \end{array}$$

by themselves constitute a system that will not accept any string with the substrings *caad* or *cbbd*, and passes through any other input unchanged, if neither of these restrictions is in force. With either acyclicity or Nīlakaṇṭhadīkṣitar's condition (it does not matter which), all input is passed through unchanged, even when it contains caad or cbbd. In this rule system, however:

$$\begin{array}{l} aa \longrightarrow bb \;/\; b\,\_\,a \\ b \longrightarrow a \;/\; b\,\_\,a \\ b \longrightarrow a \;/\; \_\,bb \end{array}$$

Nīlakaṇṭhadīkṣitar's condition would not be sufficient to prevent cyclic rule applications. On the input string *baaaa*, for example, acyclicity produces *baaaa* and *abaaa*, whereas Nīlakaṇṭhadīkṣitar's condition allows *baaaa*, *aabaa*, *babaa*, and *abbaa*. With neither condition in force, the system produces *aabaa* and *babaa*.

It is interesting that Kaplan and Kay (1994), in their improved presentation of Johnson's 1970 result, present many examples where ϕ and ψ are sets of larger cardinality than 1, but not even one where they contain a string of greater length than 1. String length is essential to our understanding of the effects of Nīlakaṇṭhadīkṣitar's condition on contextualized replacement systems.

5 Replacement string length in the Aṣṭādhyāyī

The rules of the Aṣṭādhyāyī use input and output strings of length greater than 1, but it is clear that these sequences can and often do have derivational histories attached to them, i.e., not just any matching sequence will actually serve as a redex for the given rule. The English translations provided below are based upon those given in Sharma (2003).

5.1 Input

- 6.1.84: *ekaḥ pūrvaparayoḥ*, "[when saṃhitā obtains,] one comes in place of both the preceding and following." The Sanskrit *pūrvaparayoḥ* here refers to a sequence of two contiguous elements as redexes (*sthāni*) simultaneously (*yugapat*). The presence of *ekaḥ* implies that the alternative, in which there are two separate replacements of the preceding and following sounds, respectively, admits the possibility of either one being blocked independently; cf. Aṣṭādhyāyī 8.2.42 in which:

  $$t \longrightarrow n \;/\; rd\,\_\,,$$

  but the preceding *d* can nevertheless be replaced with *n*.

  Saṃhitā here means that the articulation of the sounds in question is closely spaced in time, defined by the traditional commentators as a pause length (*kāla*) of no more than half of a syllabic mora (*ardha-mātrā*).

- 6.1.85: "simultaneous replacement of two sounds in saṃhitā will be treated as both a final of the preceding context and an initial of the following context," e.g.:

  $$khaṭvā + indraḥ \longrightarrow [khaṭv{<}e]ndraḥ{>}$$

This elaborates upon the how the simultaneous replacements of 6.1.84 are treated with respect to their derivational histories.

5.2 Output

Perhaps the clearest examples of these are the optional gemination rules of Aṣṭādhyāyī 8.4.46 and 47:

- 8.4.46: "A sound denoted by [the non-terminal] *yaR*, when occurring in close proximity after a vowel followed by *r* and *h*, is optionally replaced with two," e.g. $arka \longrightarrow arkka$. Perhaps this one can apply to itself (*arkkka?*): the rule states no constraints on the context that follows the duplication, but we are unable to think of an occasion when this rule would apply to a consonant that does not immediately precede a vowel.

- 8.4.47: "A sound denoted by *yaR* and occurring after [a vowel] is, optionally, replaced with two, even when [a vowel] does not follow," e.g. $dadhy{+}atra \longrightarrow daddhy{+}atra$, in which gemination of *dh* is licensed in part by the following *y*. This one only applies to itself in the case of gemination of *y, v, r* or *l* in the so-called *paryudāsa* reading of the Sanskrit word *anacaḥ*, in which it is not translated as 'non-vowel' but rather as 'not quite a vowel.' On the other hand, Nīlakaṇṭhadīkṣitar's condition has been cited as the reason that $atra \longrightarrow attra \not\rightarrow attttra$ [*sic*] is blocked (Joshi and Kiparsky, 1979) under the more literal 'non-vowel' reading of this word.

- 8.1.1: "Two occur in place of one whole form ..." This is an *adhikāra* (meta-rule) that takes scope over the next 14 rules, which license the repetition of a word or certain prefixes under specific circumstances. Sharma (2003) debates whether the repetition (*āmreḍita*) of a word that results from this rule has come about through a process of "1 ⟶ 2" (a single instance rewrites to two instances) or a special process of "repetition of a single word." The traditional commentator, Kāśikā, says "1 ⟶ 2," largely on the basis of how the genitive case in "of one whole form" (*sarvasya*) must be interpreted. *āmreḍita* refers here to the second of two repeated words, not consonants. It definitely cannot refer simply to the last (*param*) instance of several repeated forms because of Aṣṭādhyāyī 6.1.99, wherein we must know that the repetition was the result of an *āmreḍita* with respect to meaning (*artha*), in order to justify exempting it from Aṣṭādhyāyī 6.1.98. This is evidence that a derivational history is somehow being maintained.

Repeated application of rules (*āvṛtti*) and derivational history are perhaps the most crucial pieces of evidence that we have for understanding the restricted use of the rewriting of long sequences in the Aṣṭādhyāyī.

6 The Generative Capacity of Contextualized Replacement Systems

Let $C(j) = \{a_1^n a_2^n ... a_j^n \mid n \geq 0\}$. The set, $\{a^n b^n \mid n \geq 0\}$, presented above, is a notational variant of $C(2)$. These are the so-called count languages.

Now consider this contextualized replacement system, which generates $C(2)$:

$$\begin{aligned} S &\longrightarrow A \,/\, \_\_ \\ A &\longrightarrow abA \,/\, \_\_ \\ A &\longrightarrow ab \,/\, \_\_ \\ ba &\longrightarrow X \,/\, \_\_ \\ X &\longrightarrow ab \,/\, \_\_ \end{aligned}$$

There are analogous systems for every other $C(j)$. They rely on cycles in derivations, but they never violate Nīlakaṇṭhadīkṣitar's condition. So the Pāṇinian language class includes all of the count languages.

In the years since Chomsky (1959), many language classes have been added to the Chomsky hierarchy. Some well-known ones are k-MCFL, which are generated by k CFGs in parallel, and MCTAL(k), which are generated by k parallel tree-adjoining grammars. These all lie between CFL (= 1-MCFL) and CSL, and form chains ordered by their parameter k, e.g. 1−MCFL ⊂ 2−MCFL ⊂ 3−MCFL ⊂ ...

Each k-MCFL recognizes $C(j)$ for all $j \leq 2k$ and no more. Each MCTAG(k) recognizes $C(j)$ for all $j \leq 4k$ and no more. So the class of Pāṇinian languages is not even close to being CFL. On the other hand, Pāṇini himself uses this expressive power very sparingly in his grammar. His grammar may in fact require far fewer computational resources than membership in MCTAG(k) for a large value of k would suggest.

7 Concluding Remarks

The underlying formalism to Pāṇinian grammar, while our knowledge of it is incomplete, presents enough evidence to conclusively demonstrate that it is far greater in its expressive power than either RL or CFL. Pāṇini has nevertheless anticipated modern generative-syntactic practice in defining for himself a very versatile tool which he then applies very thriftily to advance his own objectives of grammatical brevity and elegance. As a result, his Aṣṭādhyāyī may even be amenable to an RL-style analysis, as Hyman (2007) has claimed. But in light of this investigation, the result of this analysis certainly could not be a grammar in Pāṇini's own style, but rather Pāṇini's grammar recast into someone else's style.

No proof is presented here, however, that the Pāṇinian framework is complete in the sense that it can generate any context-sensitive language. This remains an open question.

We have not even touched upon perhaps the greatest difference between Pāṇini's own formalism and the standard string-rewriting systems concomitant with Chomsky's hierarchy, which is its built-in capacity for disambiguation. Pāṇini's grammar, through its use of rule precedence and other meta-conventions, generates a single derivation for every grammatical sentence of Sanskrit.

Not even a single one of the standard Chomskyan systems possesses this property, and it is this lack of theirs, rather than some inherent quality of the syntax of human languages that is responsible for the now-widespread use of numerical reasoning and statistical pattern recognition methods in natural language processing. These are required in order to curb the natural propensity of these algebras to overgenerate. Through the lens of contemporary NLP, the most amazing fact about the Aṣṭādhyāyī is not that it produces so many correct derivations, after all, but that it simultaneously avoids so many incorrect ones.

References

Chomsky, N. (1959). On certain formal properties of grammars. *Information and Control*, 2:137–167.

Culy, C. (1985). The complexity of the vocabulary of Bambara. *Linguistics and Philosophy*, 8:345–351.

Huybregts, M. A. C. (1984). The weak adequacy of context-free phrase structure grammar. In de Haan, G. J., Trommelen, M., and Zonneveld, W., editors, *Van periferie naar kern*, pages 81–99. Foris.

Hyman, M. D. (2007). From Pāṇinian sandhi to finite state calculus. In Huet, G. and Kulkarni, A., editors, *Proceedings of the First International Symposium on Sanskrit Computational Linguistics*, pages 13–21.

Ingerman, P. Z. (1967). "Pāṇini-Backus Form" suggested. *Communications of the ACM*, 10(3):137. Letter to the Editor.

Johnson, C. D. (1970). *Formal Aspects of Phonological Description*. PhD thesis, University of California, Berkeley.

Joshi, S. D. and Kiparsky, P. (1979). Siddha and asiddha in Pāṇinian phonology. In Dinnsen, D., ed., *Current Approaches to Phonological Theory*, pages 223–250. Indiana University Press.

Kaplan, R. M. and Kay, M. (1994). Regular models of phonological rule systems. *Computational Linguistics*, 20(3):331–378.

Sharma, R. N. (1987–2003). *The Astadhyayi of Panini*, volume I–VI. Munshiram Manoharlal Publishers Pvt. Ltd.

Shieber, S. M. (1985). Evidence against the context-freeness of natural language. *Linguistics and Philosophy*, 8(3):333–344.

Staal, F. (1965). Context-sensitive rules in Pāṇini. *Foundations of Language*, 1:63–72.

Joint Segmentation and Tagging with Coupled Sequences Labeling

Xipeng Qiu[1], *Feng Ji*[1,2], *Jiayi Zhao*[1] *and Xuanjing Huang*[1]
(1) School of Computer Science, Fudan University
(2) Suntec Software (Shanghai) Co. Ltd.
{xpqiu,fengji,11210240073,xjhuang}@fudan.edu.cn

ABSTRACT

Segmentation and tagging task is the fundamental problem in natural language processing (NLP). Traditional methods solve this problem in either pipeline or joint cross-label ways, which suffer from error propagation and large number of labels respectively. In this paper, we present a novel joint model for segmentation and tagging, which integrates two dependent Markov chains. One chain is used for segmentation, and the other is for tagging. The model parameters can be estimated simultaneously. Besides, we can optimize the whole model by improving the single chain. The experiments show that our model could achieve higher performance over traditional models on both English shallow parsing and Chinese word segmentation and POS tagging tasks.

TITLE AND ABSTRACT IN CHINESE

基于双链序列标注的联合切分和标注模型

在自然语言处理中，序列标注模型是最常见的模型，也有着广泛地应用。针对常见的可分解为分段和标注两个子任务的复杂序列标注问题，我们提出了双链序列标注模型。该模型中存在着两条相互联系的马尔科夫链。为此我们提出了一个同时求解这两条链上最优序列的解码算法。同时利用这两条链，针对不同的实际应用场景可以组合出不同的标注模型，使用不同的解码算法完成实际的标注任务。为了能够适应不同的解码算法，我们还提出了一个能够利用异构语料训练模型的参数学习算法。在多个语料上的实验表明，我们提出的模型性能要优于其他模型，并能在同一个模型内完成多种标注任务。

KEYWORDS: Coupled Sequences Labeling, Segmentation, Tagging.

KEYWORDS IN CHINESE: 双链序列标注, 切分, 标注.

Proceedings of COLING 2012: Posters, pages 951–964,
COLING 2012, Mumbai, December 2012.

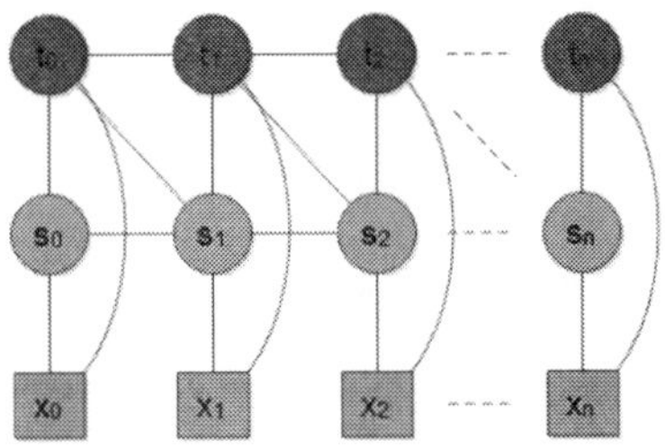

Figure 1: Coupled Sequences Labeling Model (双链序列标注模型)

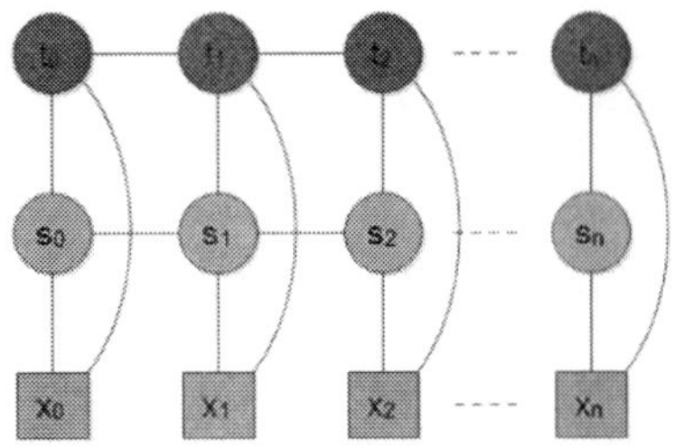

Figure 2: Factorial CRF Model (FCRF 模型)

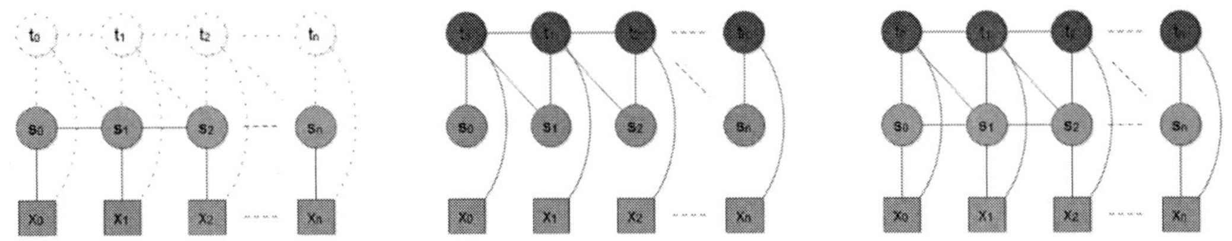

(a) segment by only using the linear chain s

(b) label a segmented sentence

(c) simultaneously segment and label a sentence

Figure 3: Coupled Sequences Labeling Model for Different Tasks (处理不同任务时的双链序列标注模型变换), where gray nodes are observed nodes.

Table 1: Feature templates for shallow parsing (浅层句法分析特征模板)

Joint Cross-Product Model	Coupled Sequence Labeling Model
$w_{i-2}y_i, w_{i-1}y_i, w_iy_i, w_{i+1}y_i, w_{i+2}y_i$	$w_{i-1}s_i, w_is_i, w_{i+1}s_i$
	$w_{i-2}t_i, w_{i-1}t_i, w_it_i, w_{i+1}t_i, w_{i+2}t_i$
$w_{i-1}w_iy_i, w_iw_{i+1}y_i$	$w_{i-1}w_is_i, w_iw_{i+1}s_i$
	$w_{i-1}w_it_i, w_iw_{i+1}t_i$
$p_{i-2}y_i, p_{i-1}y_i, p_iy_i, p_{i+1}y_i, p_{i+2}y_i$	$p_{i-1}s_i, p_is_i, w_{i+1}s_i$
	$p_{i-2}t_i, p_{i-1}t_i, p_it_i, p_{i+1}t_i, p_{i+2}t_i$
$p_{i-2}p_{i-1}y_i, p_{i-1}p_iy_i, p_ip_{i+1}y_i, p_{i+1}p_{i+2}y_i$	$p_{i-2}p_{i-1}s_i, p_{i-1}p_is_i, p_ip_{i+1}s_i, p_{i+1}p_{i+2}s_i$
	$p_{i-3}p_{i-2}t_i, p_{i-2}p_{i-1}t_i, p_{i-1}p_it_i, p_ip_{i+1}t_i,$ $p_{i+1}p_{i+2}t_i, p_{i+2}p_{i+3}t_i, p_{i-1}p_{i+1}t_i$
$p_{i-2}p_{i-1}p_iy_i, p_{i-1}p_ip_{i+1}y_i, p_ip_{i+1}p_{i+2}y_i$	$p_{i-2}p_{i-1}p_is_i, p_{i-1}p_ip_{i+1}s_i, p_ip_{i+1}p_{i+2}s_i$
$y_{i-1}y_i$	$w_is_it_i$
	$w_is_{i-1}s_i$
	$w_{i-1}t_{i-1}t_i, w_it_{i-1}t_i, p_{i-1}t_{i-1}t_i, p_it_{i-1}t_i$
	$s_{i-1}t_{i-1}s_i, t_{i-1}s_it_i$

Table 2: Feature templates for Chinese S&T (中文分词、词性标注特征模板)

Joint Cross-Label Model	Coupled Sequence Labeling Model
$c_{i-2}y_i, c_{i-1}y_i, c_iy_i, c_{i+1}y_i, c_{i+2}y_i$	$c_{i-2}s_i, c_{i-1}s_i, c_is_i, c_{i+1}s_i, c_{i+2}s_i$
	$c_{i-3}t_i, c_{i-2}t_i, c_{i-1}t_i, c_it_i, c_{i+1}t_i, c_{i+2}t_i, c_{i+3}t_i$
$c_{i-1}c_iy_i, c_ic_{i+1}y_i, c_{i-1}c_{i+1}y_i$	$c_{i-1}c_is_i, c_ic_{i+1}s_i, c_{i-1}c_{i+1}s_i$
	$c_{i-3}c_{i-2}t_i, c_{i-2}c_{i-1}t_i, c_{i-1}c_it_i, c_ic_{i+1}t_i,$ $c_{i+1}c_{i+2}t_i, c_{i+2}c_{i+3}t_i, c_{i-2}c_it_i, c_ic_{i+2}t_i$
$y_{i-1}y_i$	$c_is_it_i$
	$c_{i-1}t_{i-1}t_i, s_{i-1}s_i$
	$s_{i-1}t_{i-1}s_i, t_{i-1}s_it_i$

input : Taggging training dataset: $(\mathbf{x}_i, \mathbf{s}_i, \mathbf{t}_i), i = 1, \cdots, M,$;
input : Segmentation training dataset (optional): $(\mathbf{x}_i, \mathbf{s}_i), i = M+1, \cdots, M+N,$;
input : Parameters: $\mathcal{C}, K$.
output: **w**

```
Initialize: cw ← 0, w ← 0;
for k = 0 ··· K − 1 do
    random select an integer number l ∈ (1, ..., M + N) with no repeat;
    if l ≤ M then
        receive an example (x_l, s_l, t_l);
        predict (2nd Viterbi): (ŝ_l, t̂_l) = arg max_{s,t} ⟨w, Φ^{st}(x_l, s, t)⟩;
        if (ŝ_l, t̂_l) ≠ (s_l, t_l) then
            update with w with Eq. 10, where (·) is (x_l, s_l, t_l) and (∗) is (x_l, ŝ_l, t̂_l);
        end
    else
        receive an example (x_l, s_l);
        predict (1st Viterbi): ŝ_l = arg max_s ⟨w, Φ^s(x_l, s)⟩;
        if ŝ_l ≠ s_i then
            update with w with Eq. 10, where (·) is (x_l, s_l) and (∗) is (x_l, ŝ_l);
        end
    end
end
w = cw/K ;
```

Algorithm 1: Online Learning Algorithm for Coupled Sequences Labeling Model. (双链序列标注在线学习算法)

1 Introduction

In the fields of natural language processing (NLP), joint segmentation and tagging (S&T) task is an important research topic. Many NLP problems can be transformed to joint S&T task, such as shallow parsing(Sha and Pereira, 2003), named entity recognition(Zhou and Su, 2002), Chinese part-of-speech (POS) tagging(Ratnaparkhi, 1996) and so on. For example, there are no explicitly boundaries between words in Chinese sentence. Therefore, sentence must be segmented into sequence of words, in which each word would be assigned with a POS tag.

Recently many research works focused on joint S&T tasks, which can be categorized into two ways: pipeline and cross-label.

The pipeline approaches are to solve two subtasks in order, segmentation and tagging. However, the obvious disadvantage of these approaches is error propagation, which significantly affects the whole performance.

The cross-label approaches can avoid the problem of error propagation and achieve more higher performance on both subtasks (Ng and Low, 2004). However, due to the large number of labels, two problems arise: (1) The amount of parameters increases rapidly and would be apt to overfit to the training corpus; (2) The decoding efficiency by dynamic programming would decrease.

In addition, joint cross-label approaches cannot segment or tag sentences separately. For example, in Chinese POS tagging task, the joint model cannot segment sentences individually without tagging the sentences. Moreover, if the sentences are already segmented, the joint model can not tag individually with the existing segmentation information.

In this paper, we present a novel joint model for S&T task with coupled sequences labeling. The proposed model integrates two linear Markov chains with a two dimensional structure. One chain is used for segmentation, and the other is for tagging. These two chains are labeled simultaneously, so our method does not suffer from error propagation. Unlike cross-label model, the number of labels in our model is much smaller. Experiments on two tasks, shallow parsing and Chinese POS tagging, demonstrate the effectiveness of our model.

The contributions of our methods are as follows:

1. Instead of cross-product labels, two types of nodes in our model make us represent features more flexibly.
2. Exact decoding algorithm can be employed to find the best S&T sequences simultaneously.
3. Our method not only can do joint S&T task, it can also segment or tag sentences separately.
4. Our model can be trained simultaneously with the heterogeneous data sources.

It is very important in practice that to utilize the heterogeneous data sources. For example in Chinese POS tagging, we can use two datasets (segmentation dataset and POS tagging dataset) for training parameters. This character is especially useful since the segmentation dataset is more easily annotated than POS tagging dataset.

The rest of the paper is organized as follows: In section 2, we describe the general sequence labeling method. In section 3 we present our novel model with coupled sequences labeling, then we analysis its complexity and discuss its applications. The experimental results are shown in section 4. In section 5, we introduce the related works. Finally, we conclude our work in section 6.

2 Joint Sequences Labeling Model

In this section, we first introduce and analyze joint S&T task with common sequence labeling model. Then, we present the joint cross-label approach and analyze its complexity.

2.1 Sequence Labeling Model

Sequence labeling is the task of assigning labels $\mathbf{y} = y_1, \ldots, y_L$ to an input sequence $\mathbf{x} = x_1, \ldots, x_L$.

Give a sample $\mathbf{x}$, we define the feature vector as $\Phi(\mathbf{x}, \mathbf{y})$. Thus, we can label $\mathbf{x}$ with a score function,

$$\hat{\mathbf{y}} = \arg\max_{\mathbf{y}} F(\mathbf{w}, \Phi(\mathbf{x}, \mathbf{y})), \tag{1}$$

where $\mathbf{w}$ is the parameter of function $F(\cdot)$. The feature vector $\Phi(\mathbf{x}, \mathbf{y})$ consists of lots of overlapping features, which is the chief benefit of discriminative model.

For example, in first-order Markov sequence labeling model, the feature can be denoted as $\phi_k(y_{i-1}, y_i, \mathbf{x}, i)$, where i is the position in the sequence. Then the score function can be rewritten as

$$\hat{\mathbf{y}} = \arg\max_{\mathbf{y}} F(\sum_{i=1}^{L} \sum_{k} w_k \phi_k(y_{i-1}, y_i, \mathbf{x}, i)), \tag{2}$$

where L is length of $\mathbf{x}$.

2.2 Joint S&T with Cross-Label Sequence Labeling Model

In the traditional approach for joint S&T, each label y_i is the cross-product of segmentation label s_i and tagging label t_i, usually with the form of s_i-t_i. Therefore, the state space of cross-labels is $|\mathcal{Y}| = |\mathcal{S}| \times |\mathcal{T}|$, where $|\mathcal{S}|$, $|\mathcal{T}|$ is the number of segmentation labels and tagging labels, respectively.

In real applications, $|\mathcal{S}|$ is always small, while $|\mathcal{T}|$ will be very large. In segmentation task, there are several commonly used label sets such as {B, I}, {B, I, O}, {B, I, E, S}, etc. For example, {B, I, E, S} represent *Begin, Inside, End* of a multi-node segmentation, and *Single* node segmentation respectively. In tagging task, the label set depends on the detail definition of the task, such as {PER, LOC, ORG, MISC} in classic name entity recognition task, and {NNS, NNPS, NNP, ...} in Part-of-Speech tagging task.

Although joint learning with cross-label can avoid error propagation, which usually occurs in pipeline frameworks, the complexity of decoding algorithm would be increased rapidly due to the increased state space. Suppose we use first order Viterbi algorithm for decoding in linear chain model, the complexity is $(|\mathcal{S}||\mathcal{T}|)^2 L$ in such joint labeling frameworks, while $(|\mathcal{S}|^2 + |\mathcal{T}|^2)L$ in pipeline frameworks.

3 Coupled Sequences Labeling Model

In this section, we will describe the coupled sequences labeling model in detail, and propose an exact inference algorithm for finding two best sequences simultaneously. Then we apply this model to the problems mentioned in the beginning of this paper. Finally an online training algorithm is proposed to learn the parameters of our model by optimizing two difference inference algorithms.

3.1 Model Description

Different from the cross-label model, we define two sequences $\mathbf{s} = s_1, \ldots, s_L$ and $\mathbf{t} = t_1, \ldots, t_L$ for an input sequence $\mathbf{x} = x_1, \ldots, x_L$. $\mathbf{s}$ and $\mathbf{t}$ represent the segmentation and tagging labels respectively.

Then we employ a hybrid model by integrating these two linear chains. While keeping relative independence and completeness of these two chains, we also consider the interactions between them in order to cope with error propagation. The graphic structure of our model is shown in Figure 1.

Besides the original undirected edges (hereinafter to be referred as edges) existed in two linear chains, corresponding to $e(s_{i-1}, s_i)$ and $e(t_{i-1}, t_i)$, we also append two kinds of edges between different chains. $e(s_i, t_i)$ is equivalent to the representation of "Cross-Label" mentioned in section 2.2. Meanwhile, we also add an edge $e(t_{i-1}, s_i)$ into the model. This change brings about two new different cliques, respectively associated with variables $C_1 = \{s_{i-1}, t_{i-1}, s_i\}$ and $C_2 = \{t_{i-1}, s_i, t_i\}$,which essentially gives rise to the increment of the complexity of our model.

The reason for this change is to avoid the "label bias" problem citeLafferty:2001 in factorial CRF (FCRF) (Sutton et al., 2004). FCRF model has a similar graphic structure to our model, shown in Figure 2. As in the case of Chinese POS tagging, if given a context s_{i-1} = "B", t_{i-1} = "NN" and s_i = "E", t_i would be assigned to "JJ" instead of "NN" with a higher probability, since the transition from "NN" to "JJ" defeats against the transition to "NN" while s_i = "E" has no effect. However, s_i = "M" provides a strong clue, which implies that word w_{i-1} and w_i are in the same segmentation and would be assigned to the same label.

3.2 Inference Algorithm

According to the theory of probabilistic graphical models (Koller and Friedman, 2009), we can define a score function $F(\cdot)$ as the logarithmic potential function:

$$F(\mathbf{w}, \Phi(\mathbf{x}, \mathbf{s}, \mathbf{t})) = \sum_{i}^{L} \{\mathbf{w}^T \Phi_{C_1}(s_{i-1}, t_{i-1}, s_i, \mathbf{x}, i) + \mathbf{w}^T \Phi_{C_2}(t_{i-1}, s_i, t_i, \mathbf{x}, i)\}, \quad (3)$$

Given an observed sequence $\mathbf{x}$, the aim of inference algorithm is to find two best label sequences simultaneously with the highest score. In order to adapt to our model with two kinds of 3-variable cliques, we make some modifications of a second order Viterbi algorithm (Thede and Harper, 1999). We define two functions for recording the score of the best partial path from the beginning of the sequence to the position i:

$$\begin{aligned} \delta_i(t_{i-1}, s_i) \triangleq F(\mathbf{w}, \Phi(\mathbf{x}, s_{0:i}, t_{0:i-1})) &= \arg\max_{s_{i-1}} \{\eta_{i-1}(s_{i-1}, t_{i-1}) + \mathbf{w}^T \Phi_{C_1}(s_{i-1}, t_{i-1}, s_i, \mathbf{x}, i)\} \quad (4) \\ \eta_i(s_i, t_i) \triangleq F(\mathbf{w}, \Phi(\mathbf{x}, s_{0:i}, t_{0:i})) &= \arg\max_{t_{i-1}} \{\delta_i(t_{i-1}, s_i) + \mathbf{w}^T \Phi_{C_2}(t_{i-1}, s_i, t_i, \mathbf{x}, i)\}, \end{aligned}$$

Initially, only features associated with variables s_0 and t_0 are hired. Without loss of generality, we set s_{-1} = "BoS" [1], t_{-1} = "BoT" [2] and $\eta_{-1}(s_{-1}, t_{-1}) = 0$. Then iteratively calculate these two

[1] denotes "Beginning of Segmentation"
[2] denotes "Beginning of Tagging"

score functions for any possible partial path. At last, the final score of two label sequences is

$$F(\mathbf{w}, \Phi(\mathbf{x}, \mathbf{s}, \mathbf{t})) = \eta_L(s_L, t_L), \tag{5}$$

Compared with the complexity of other joint models, the complexity of our model is $O((|\mathcal{S}|^2|\mathcal{T}| + |\mathcal{T}|^2|\mathcal{S}|)L)$, which is lower than cross-label model but higher than pipeline model. Although the asymptotic complexity is higher than pipeline model, the advantage is that our model would not suffer from error propagation and could make use of label information more efficiently.

3.3 Discussion of Coupled Sequences Labeling Model

As shown in Figure 1, our model can label two sequences simultaneously. However, we hope our model can be applied to solve the "inconsistent" problem (Section 1). Although two linear chains **s** and **t** are modeled in a hybrid framework, they still retain its complete structure. This means that we can independently use the linear chain **s** to segment a sentence (Figure 3a), while use the linear chain **t** to label a segmented sentence (Figure 3b) or use the whole structure to label two sequences together (Figure 3c). Therefore, we need two inference algorithms, respectively a first order Viterbi algorithm for segmenting a sentence when only using the linear chain **s**, and a second order Viterbi algorithm (see Section 3.2) for other two applications. The main idea behind this method is the fact that there are many overlapping features used in both segmentation and tagging tasks since most of the features are extracted from a local context.

Another reason to employ different inference algorithms is to maintain the decoding speed for different applications. If only used in the segmentation task, the complexity of our method is $O(|\mathcal{S}|^2L)$. If applied to tag a segmented sentence, the complexity is $O((|\mathcal{T}| + |\mathcal{T}|^2)L) = O(|\mathcal{T}|^2L)$. If used in the joint labeling task, its complexity is still $O((|\mathcal{S}|^2|\mathcal{T}| + |\mathcal{T}|^2|\mathcal{S}|)L)$.

However, in the coupled sequences labeling model, two linear chains are highly dependent due to the edge $e(t_{i-1}, s_i)$. It implies that if we train a model by using the whole structure, we cannot directly use the segmentation features, which are only related to the segmentation chain **s**. Therefore, we need to optimize the whole structure together with the segmentation chain.

Besides training a model with a corpus annotated segmentation and tagging labels, we can also use heterogeneous corpora because two inference algorithms are jointly optimized. It is very meaningful in real applications. As we all known, difficulties of annotating corpus for different tasks are different. In our setting, segmentation corpus are easy to annotate while tagging corpus are difficulty. As a result, we can easily obtain a large segmentation corpus while a small tagging corpus. Because we aim to optimize two chains simultaneously, it is possible for us to training a unified model with these two different scale corpora. We can learn parameters from a small tagging corpus for two chains, and learn parameters from a large segmentation corpus for the segmentation chain.

3.4 Learning Parameters with Passive-Aggressive Algorithm

In the training stage, we use passive-aggressive algorithm to learn the model parameters. Passive-aggressive (PA) algorithm (Crammer and Singer, 2003; Crammer et al., 2006) was proposed for normal multi-class classification and can be easily extended to structure learning (Crammer et al., 2005). Like perceptron, PA is an online learning algorithm.

Because two inference algorithms are needed to optimize in our framework, without loss of generality, we use $(\cdot)$ to represent the gold answer while $(*)$ to the response of an inference algorithm with the highest score. In the segmentation task, $(\cdot)$ equals to $(\mathbf{x}, \mathbf{s})$ and $(*)$ is $(\mathbf{x}, \hat{\mathbf{s}})$. In the joint task, $(\cdot)$ denotes $(\mathbf{x}, \mathbf{s}, \mathbf{t})$ and $(*)$ is $(\mathbf{x}, \hat{\mathbf{s}}, \hat{\mathbf{t}})$. Here $\hat{\mathbf{s}}, \hat{\mathbf{t}}$ are the incorrect labels with the highest scores.

We can define the **margin** $\gamma(\mathbf{w}; (\cdot))$ as

$$\gamma(\mathbf{w}; (\cdot)) = F(\mathbf{w}, \Phi(\cdot)) - F(\mathbf{w}, \Phi(*)), \tag{6}$$

Thus, we calculate the **hinge loss** $\ell(\mathbf{w}; (\cdot))$ (abbreviated as ℓ_w) by

$$\ell_w = \begin{cases} 0, & \gamma(\mathbf{w}; (\cdot)) > 1 \\ 1 - \gamma(\mathbf{w}; (\cdot)), & \text{otherwise} \end{cases} \tag{7}$$

In round k, the new weight vector $\mathbf{w}_{k+1}$ is calculated by

$$\mathbf{w}_{k+1} = \arg\min_{\mathbf{w}} \frac{1}{2}||\mathbf{w} - \mathbf{w}_k||^2 + C \cdot \xi, \tag{8}$$

$$\textbf{s.t. } \ell(\mathbf{w}; (\cdot)) <= \xi \textbf{ and } \xi >= 0 \tag{9}$$

where ξ is a non-negative slack variable, and C is a positive parameter which controls the influence of the slack term on the objective function.

Following the derivation in PA (Crammer et al., 2006), we can get the update rule,

$$\mathbf{w}_{k+1} = \mathbf{w}_k + \tau_k(\Phi(\cdot) - \Phi(*)), \tag{10}$$

where

$$\tau_k = \min(C, \frac{\ell_k(\mathbf{w}; (\cdot))}{||\Phi(\cdot) - \Phi(*)||^2}) \tag{11}$$

Our training algorithm is based on PA algorithm and shown in Algorithm 1. In our algorithm, the input examples are randomly selected in each round k. According to the source of the selected example, we obtain the best response by using the proper inference algorithm, and finally update the parameters $\mathbf{w}$. Following (Collins, 2002), the average strategy is also adopted to avoid overfitting problem.

4 Experiments

We employ two joint sequence labeling tasks to show the performance of our model. In the following section, we would report our experiment settings and discuss the experiment results.

We compare our method with cross-label model and factorial model with PA algorithm. The factorial model is similar with Factorial CRF(Sutton et al., 2007), but its parameters are learning with PA algorithm.

We use the standard evaluation metrics $F1$ score, which is the harmonic mean of precision P (percentage of predict phrases that exactly match the reference phrases) and recall R (percentage of reference phrases that returned by system).

4.1 Datasets

In order to demonstrate the performance of our proposed model, we employ two joint segmentation and tagging tasks, respectively English shallow parsing and Chinese word segmentation and POS tagging (Chinese S&T).

In English shallow parsing, the corpus from CoNLL 2000 shared task is commonly used, which contains 8936 sentences for training and 2012 sentences for testing. We employ the commonly used label set $\{B, M, E, S\}$ in the segmentation task. 12 tagging labels, such as noun phrase (NP), verb phrase (VP),...and others (O), are used in the sequence tagging task.

In Chinese S&T, we employ the Chinese Treebank (CTB) corpus, obtained from the Fourth International SIGHAN Bakeoff datasets (Jin and Chen, 2008). The label set $\{B, M, E, S\}$ is also used for segmentation task.

4.2 Performance of Coupled Sequences Labeling Model

In the first experiment, we aim to compare the performances of our coupled sequences labeling model with other traditional joint models. Feature templates used in this experiment are summarized in Table 1 for English shallow parsing and in Table 2 for Chinese word segmenation and POS tagging, in which w_i denotes i^{th} word, p_i denotes i^{th} POS tag, c_i denotes i^{th} Chinese character.

We compare the total performance between traditional joint cross-label model, factorial model and our model. To learn the parameters of these models, we employ PA algorithm with an average parameter strategy to avoid the overfitting problem. The maximum amount of iterations is fixed to be 50.

The experiment results are shown in Table 3 for English shallow parsing, and in Table 4 for Chinese S&T. We also provides the performances of other methods reported in papers.

Table 3: Performances in English Shallow Parsing

Method	F1
Cross-Label CRFs	93.88
Voted Perceptrons (Carreras and Marquez, 2004)	93.74
Cross-Label model	93.47
Factorial model	93.11
Our model	93.94

Table 4: Performances in Chinese S&T

Method	$F1$
Pipeline	89.04
100-best reranking	89.23
Cross-label model	89.18
Factorial model	88.64
Our model	89.32

In English shallow parsing, our coupled sequences labeling model achieves the best performance than other two methods. We are surprised to find that the performance of the factorial model is lower than the joint cross-label model because of the "label bias" problem. However, a cross edge $e(t_{i-1}, si)$ is added into our coupled sequences model and shows its ability to avoid this problem. Experimental results in Chinese S&T show the similar conclusions.

4.3 Performance on Heterogeneous Corpora

The second experiment is to jointly train a unified model with heterogeneous corpora. In this experiment, we are expected to find out whether additional resources could increase the performance simultaneously on two different tasks.

We randomly divide the training corpus into two equal parts. One part is used as the joint S&T training corpus while another part is used for just segmentation training corpus.

For joint sequence labeling task, we employ our second order decoding algorithm (see 3.2) and the same feature templates (listed in Table 1 and Table 2) to extract features. For segmentation task, we use the first order Viterbi algorithm to find the most possible segmentation. Only feature templates (listed in Table 1) irrelevant to tagging task are used for the segmentation task. Therefore template such as $w_{i-1}t_i$ would not be used to extract the segmentation features. Moreover this means two different tasks would share many common features in the training stage. The final test performances are shown in Table 5.

We experiment three real scenarios, respectively only segmenting a sentence, tagging a segmented sentence and jointly labeling a sentence. Notice that these different tasks use the same model in this experiment. Joint cross-label approach is chosen as the baseline, but this method cannot segment a sentence individually or tag a segmented sentence. However, our coupled sequences labeling model can handle these tasks in a unified model.

The experimental results are shown in Table 5 for English shallow parsing, and in Table 6 for Chinese S&T.

Table 5: Performances on English shallow parsing

	Corpus 1	Corpus 2	Segments	Segments(Joint)	Joint	Tagging
Cross-label	used	-	-	94.97	92.67	-
Cross-label	used	used	-	95.56	93.47	-
Our model	used	-	94.24	95.14	93.02	95.20
Our model	used	used	94.89	95.65	93.94	96.02
Our model	used	used as Seg	94.68	95.56	93.61	95.73

Note 1: "used" means that the corpus is used joint S&T task with both segmentation and tagging labels, "used as Seg" means that the corpus is just used with segmentation labels.

Note 2: "Segments" means the performance of segmentation which just used the segmentation chain, "Segments(joint)" means the performance of segmentation in joint labeling, "Tagging" is the performance of tagging when given gold segmentation labels.

Table 6: Performances on Chinese S&T

	Corpus1	Corpus2	Segments	Segments(Joint)	Joint	Tagging
Cross-label	used	-	-	93.53	87.05	-
Cross-label	used	used	-	94.85	89.18	-
Our model	used	-	92.56	93.70	87.39	89.28
Our model	used	used	94.37	94.71	89.32	91.87
Our model	used	used as Seg	94.15	95.03	89.21	91.30

In Chinese S&T, we can find that our coupled model on joint labeling task can outperform the cross-label model in both the experiments of using half of the corpus and full corpus. With using the second corpus, all models have better performances. This result demonstrates a common sense in machine learning community "more data, more performance". However, after adding the second corpus, the performance of the joint task is promoted, but still lower than using the full annotations. It is reasonable because the second corpus is only used as a segmentation corpus. This means we only employ half of the POS annotations to train our model. Experimental results on segmentation task show that after adding the second corpus, our model improves the performance and slightly behind the model trained with the full annotations. With the performance increases on segmentation, the performance of tagging a segmented sentence is increased as well.

Similar conclusions can be found in the experiments of English shallow parsing.

The results also indicate that two different tasks efficiently help each other via shared features.

Therefore, we believe that additional resources could be introduced into our model more flexible and be helpful to the final performance.

4.4 Decoding Speed

At last, we also list the decoding speed for different tasks in Table 7.

Table 7: Decoding speed on English Shallow Parsing and Chinese S&T task. (sentences/second)

	English Shallow Parsing				Chinese S&T			
	Seg	Seg(Joint)	Joint	Tagging	Seg	Seg(Joint)	Joint	Tagging
Cross-label	-	1503	1453	-	-	117	113	-
Our model	22995	1467	1435	1601	17572	130	124	153

Compared to the joint cross-label approach in both corpora, our model has the equivalent decoding speed on the joint task. While on the task of tagging a segmented sentence, our model provides a slight decoding speedup. The reason is that the states of segmentation are much less than tagging. However, on the only segmentation task, our model provides a decoding speedup over 10 times, since we can use the segmentation chain independently in our model.

5 Related Works

Several methods have been proposed to cope with the problems of joint S&T task.

Sutton et al. (2004, 2007) proposed Dynamic Conditional Random Fields (DCRF) to jointly represent the different tasks in a single graphical model. However, the exact training and inference for DCRF are time-consuming.

Duh (2005) proposed a model for jointly labeling multiple sequences. The model is based on the Factorial Hidden Markov Model (FHMM). Since FHMM is directed graphical model, FHMM requires considerably less computation than DCRFs and exact inference is easily achievable. However, the FHMM's generative framework cannot take full advantage of context features, so its performance is lower than DCRF.

Different with our model applied in joint S&T task, both the DCRF and FHMM are used in POS tagging and NP Chunking tasks. These two tasks are not strongly dependent on each other. Therefore, their models are relatively simplified for joint S&T task.

6 Conclusion

In this paper, we propose a novel joint S&T model by integrating two linear chains into a coupled sequence labeling model. Our approach does not suffer from the problem of error propagation, which usually occurs in pipeline models. Meanwhile, our proposed model would not result in the rapid increase of states as cross-label models. Our model also takes the advantage of more flexible feature representation, a uniform model with a flexible combination of labeling tasks, etc.

Acknowledgments

We would like to thank the anonymous reviewers for their valuable comments. This work was funded by NSFC (No.61003091 and No.61073069), 863 Program (No.2011AA010604) and 973 Program (No.2010CB327900).

References

Carreras, X. and Marquez, L. (2004). Phrase recognition by filtering and ranking with perceptrons. *Recent advances in natural language processing III: selected papers from RANLP 2003*, 260:205.

Collins, M. (2002). Discriminative training methods for hidden markov models: Theory and experiments with perceptron algorithms. In *Proceedings of the 2002 Conference on Empirical Methods in Natural Language Processing*.

Crammer, K., Dekel, O., Keshet, J., Shalev-Shwartz, S., and Singer, Y. (2006). Online passive-aggressive algorithms. *Journal of Machine Learning Research*, 7:551–585.

Crammer, K., McDonald, R., and Pereira, F. (2005). Scalable large-margin online learning for structured classification. In *NIPS Workshop on Learning With Structured Outputs*. Citeseer.

Crammer, K. and Singer, Y. (2003). Ultraconservative online algorithms for multiclass problems. *Journal of Machine Learning Research*, 3:951–991.

Duh, K. (2005). Jointly labeling multiple sequences: A factorial HMM approach. In *Proceedings of the ACL Student Research Workshop*, pages 19–24, Ann Arbor, Michigan. Association for Computational Linguistics.

Jin, C. and Chen, X. (2008). The fourth international chinese language processing bakeoff: Chinese word segmentation, named entity recognition and chinese pos tagging. In *Sixth SIGHAN Workshop on Chinese Language Processing*, page 69.

Koller, D. and Friedman, N. (2009). *Probabilistic Graphical Models: Principles and Techniques*. MIT Press.

Ng, H. and Low, J. (2004). Chinese part-of-speech tagging: one-at-a-time or all-at-once? word-based or character-based. In *Proceedings of EMNLP*, volume 4.

Ratnaparkhi, A. (1996). A maximum entropy model for part-of-speech tagging. In Brill, E. and Church, K., editors, *Proceedings of the Empirical Methods in Natural Language Processing*, pages 133–142.

Sha, F. and Pereira, F. (2003). Shallow parsing with conditional random fields. In *Proceedings of the 2003 Conference of the North American Chapter of the Association for Computational Linguistics on Human Language Technology-Volume 1*, pages 134–141. Association for Computational Linguistics.

Sutton, C., McCallum, A., and Rohanimanesh, K. (2007). Dynamic conditional random fields: Factorized probabilistic models for labeling and segmenting sequence data. *J. Mach. Learn. Res.*, 8:693–723.

Sutton, C., Rohanimanesh, K., and McCallum, A. (2004). Dynamic conditional random fields: Factorized probabilistic models for labeling and segmenting sequence data. In *Proceedings of the twenty-first international conference on Machine learning*, page 99. ACM.

Thede, S. M. and Harper, M. P. (1999). A second-order hidden markov model for part-of-speech tagging. In *Proceedings of the 37th annual meeting of the Association for Computational Linguistics on Computational Linguistics*, pages 175–182. Association for Computational Linguistics.

Zhou, G. and Su, J. (2002). Named entity recognition using an HMM-based chunk tagger. In *Proceedings of the 40th Annual Meeting on Association for Computational Linguistics*, pages 473–480. Association for Computational Linguistics.

Defining syntax for learner language annotation

Marwa RAGHEB[1] *Markus DICKINSON*[1]
(1) Indiana University, Bloomington, IN USA
mragheb@indiana.edu, md7@indiana.edu

ABSTRACT
We discuss making syntactic annotation for learner language more precise, by clarifying the properties which the layers of annotation refer to. Building from previous proposals which split linguistic annotation into multiple layers to capture non-canonical properties of learner language, we lay out the questions which must be asked for grammatical annotation and provide some answers. Our investigation points to the layer of distributional syntax being based on properties of the target language (L2) and largely redundant with the other layers. We show, for example, that subcategorization seems to better be able to underspecify annotation for situations where no single correct solution can be found. While this paves the way for applying the annotation to larger corpus efforts, it also represents a significant step in elucidating syntax for non-canonical language.

KEYWORDS: syntactic annotation, dependency syntax, learner language.

Proceedings of COLING 2012: Posters, pages 965–974,
COLING 2012, Mumbai, December 2012.

1 Introduction

Learner corpora are increasingly gaining attention due to the potential wealth of data they present for a variety of purposes, including the investigation of different aspects of *interlanguage*, the developing language of second language learners. Interlanguage (IL) often differs from the target language (L2), and the annotation of such corpora is an important means of accessing its unique characteristics (Granger, 2003). Such annotation has practical benefits for developing error detection systems and intelligent tutoring systems (e.g., Nagata et al., 2011; Rozovskaya and Roth, 2010), by providing data and insights for the parsing of learner language. While many benefits have been derived from error annotation, a recent approach to annotating learner language is to annotate the linguistic properties of a text to provide direct access to grammatical properties of interest (e.g., Díaz-Negrillo et al., 2010; Dickinson and Ragheb, 2009; Rastelli, 2009; Pienemann, 1992). To account for IL, multiple layers of analysis—e.g., three separate part-of-speech (POS) layers—have been proposed to capture learner innovations. These layers have yet to be properly defined for syntax, however. Our aim is to probe syntactic annotation for learner language, making precise what decisions annotation efforts must make.

Recent work on learner corpora has underscored the importance of providing a linguistic description of learner text for second language acquisition (SLA) (Ragheb and Dickinson, 2011). To see the need more broadly, consider that there has been very little work investigating POS tagging (Thouësny, 2009; van Rooy and Schäfer, 2002; de Haan, 2000) or parsing (Rehbein et al., 2012; Krivanek and Meurers, 2011; Ott and Ziai, 2010) of learner language, due to a lack of annotated data or clear standards. Furthermore, the studies on parsing often first map to a target form, while many situations—such as extracting parse features for error detection (Tetreault et al., 2010) or identifying criterial features indicating learner proficiency level (Hawkins and Buttery, 2010)—require direct parsing of learner language. Defining and applying syntactic annotation provides a clearer picture of the goal for parsing learner language, and evaluation data to do so. Only by developing such annotation can research into POS tagging and syntactic parsing for learner language make serious advancements.

As mentioned, proposals for linguistic annotation split categories into multiple layers. In proliferating categories, however, we must ask what these categories denote and whether they should all be marked by annotators. We specifically look at syntactic dependency annotation, each layer based on different evidence: morphological dependencies, distributional dependencies, and subcategorization (Dickinson and Ragheb, 2011) . In order to define these layers, we must revisit core syntactic principles, to clearly delineate the different layers and their realizations for the in-progress language of learners. Our most important contribution is to outline the questions which need to be addressed for grammatical annotation of learner language.

2 Annotation for Learner Language

Since learner language includes non-native-like constructions, an annotation scheme with single categories for each native-like property does not seem to be adequate (Dickinson and Ragheb, 2011, 2009; Díaz-Negrillo et al., 2010). We thus adopt a multi-layer annotation approach (cf., e.g., Lüdeling et al., 2005), which allows us to capture different pieces of evidence, some of which might conflict for the same token. We thus need to be clear on what the evidence is.

Although we focus on syntactic dependencies, we start by examining part-of-speech (POS) information. Consider two POS layers, one for *morphological* evidence and one for *distributional*. For most native constructions, the layers include the same information, but mismatches arise with non-canonical structures. For example, in *I have see a movie,*[1] the word *see* has conflicting evidence. The morphological form is the base form or the non-3rd person singular present tense; distributionally, the position is of a dependent of *have*, i.e., a past participle. The use of two POS layers captures the mismatch between morphology and distribution without referencing a unified POS. In this framework, errors are often derivable from mismatches between layers.

Focusing on the evidence relevant for dependency annotation, we build from the POS layers, with a morphosyntactic and a distributional layer of dependencies. We also include subcategorization information, to capture issues relating to the presence or absence of arguments (Dickinson and Ragheb, 2011, 2009). Most of the paper will be spent on defining these three layers of annotation, but we can see the impetus for them by continuing this example. Figure 1 shows the morphosyntactic dependency tree,[2] where the relations are based on the surface form of the tokens and the morphological POS tags.[3] We also see subcategorization frames.

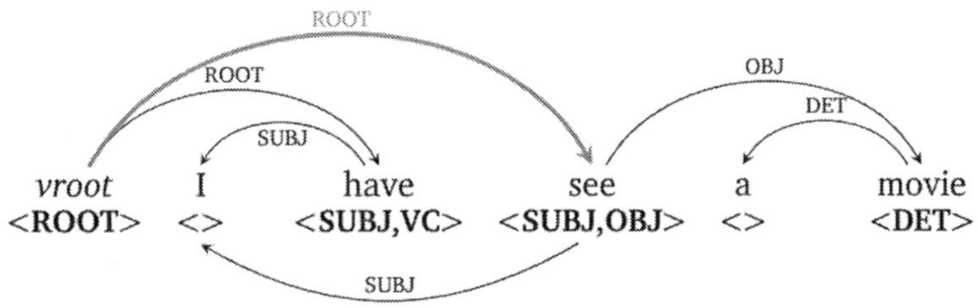

Figure 1: Morphosyntactic dependency tree

By contrast, figure 2 shows the distributional dependency tree. The two trees feature discrepancies in how *see* is treated, as the morphological and distributional evidence diverge.

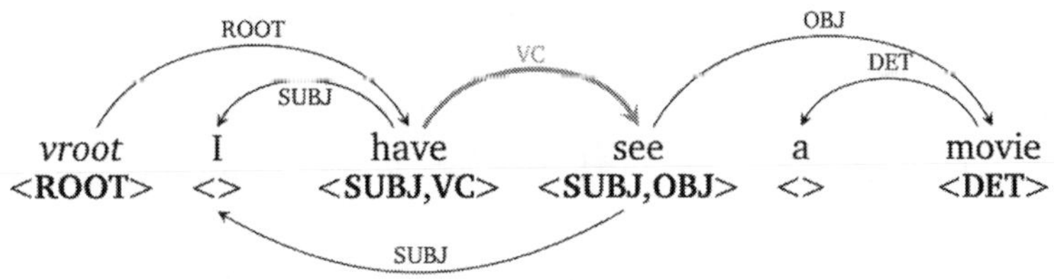

Figure 2: Distributional dependency tree

We can note: a) distribution and morphology often coincide, with four out of five dependency relations repeated; and b) with subcategorization, there is already a mismatch within the morphosyntactic tree (figure 1), as *have* does not realize its verbal complement (vc). We return to issues of redundancy in section 6 after clarifying the three different layers.

3 Defining Subcategorization

While dependencies model what is realized, learner language often contains violations of argument structure (e.g., a missing subject); to capture the nature of these cases, we need to model what is *selected*, in order to identify mismatches (see Dickinson and Ragheb, 2011). Encoding subcategorization does this. As one example, in (1), *house* requires a determiner.

[1]Unless stated, examples are from two corpora collected from English L2 learners, used for developing annotation.
[2]We refer to this layer as *morphosyntactic*, as it incorporates some syntactic information, as described in section 4.
[3]We illustrate with adaptations of the CHILDES dependency scheme (Sagae et al., 2010, 2007).

One way to capture this is as in figure 3, where *house* selects for a determiner on the level of subcategorization (<DET>), though no determiner is present.

(1) . . . we moved again to other **house** . . .

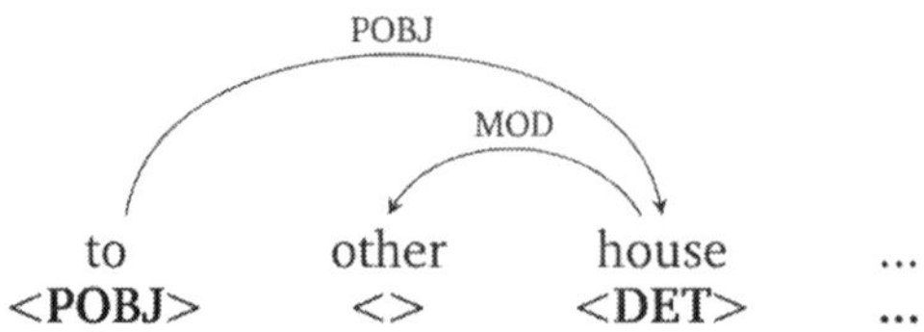

Figure 3: Partial tree with morphosyntactic dependencies and subcategorization frames

Whether derived from the L1, L2, or IL, subcategorization encodes general constraints in the language. This is a different perspective than with annotating dependencies, as dependencies are based on the (local) *evidence* in the sentence (see sections 4 and 5)—e.g., in figure 2, the subcategorization of *see* is for the word in general, while the dependency reflects its immediate context. We model subcategorization on the basis of the requirements in the target language (L2), as constraints most naturally coincide with the language being learned (see also section 5). To say that *house* selects for a determiner in (1) is a fact derived from the L2.

An important question—as with lexical stem information on the POS level (Díaz-Negrillo et al., 2010)—is: what do we do about ambiguity? Words may have many subcategorization frames (Levin, 1993), and we could annotate all of them, since they represent lexical constraints equally well. For a given sentence, however, not all are equally relevant. In (2), for instance, the use of *community* in the whole essay is as a count noun, even though *community* can have uses where a determiner is not required. If we annotate all subcategorizations, then both <DET> and <> are marked, thereby making it unclear whether the learner is doing anything novel.

(2) One [goal] is to contribute to both global and local **community** through my job .

We thus choose to annotate the subcategorization frame which best fits the context of a given sentence. Note what this means: subcategorization annotation is now not totally lexical. It is a lexical property combined with some *contextual* information. Space precludes discussing exactly how context is used to whittle the subcategorization possibilities down to one.

To sum, annotating subcategorization requires answering: 1) What is the source of information? (L1? L2? IL?) 2) How does one handle lexical ambiguity, in particular how much context should be incorporated? Future work can also investigate: 3) how does one disambiguate for an ambiguous context? Our answers of using the L2 as a reference frame and incoporating sentence context means that we will overlap with distribution, as discussed in section 6.

4 Defining Morphosyntax

Morphosyntactic dependencies are based on the visible forms of words. In (3), for instance, regardless of the distribution of *chooses*, its morphology is a third singular present tense verb.

(3) I had a problem a bout **chooses** my car . . .

While this is relatively clear for POS, we must work out what it means to annotate a dependency graph based on morphology, given that dependencies are normally either syntactic or semantic entities (though, see Mel'čuk, 1988). By *morphosyntactic* dependencies, we refer to the syntactic functions derived from the morphological forms. Back in figure 1, for instance, *see* is morphologically a candidate for a ROOT dependency, as it occurs in a (possibly) tensed form.

It is important to distinguish the task: do we base trees on context-sensitive morphological analysis (cf. POS tagging) or context-independent analysis, with multiple analyses? Keeping every possible analysis makes fewer assumptions, but becomes infeasible. If every word in a sentence of n words had 2 possible morphological POS tags, there would potentially be a different tree for every unique sequence of tags—2^n trees. Thus, we choose to annotate only the most contextually-relevant morphological dependency. This is also in line with the idea that some morphological tags are too distant to annotate. Considering (1), for example, VERB is one possibility for the word *house*. Yet in this sentence, the usage is clearly nominal—an orthogonal fact to any non-native properties of the phrase.

How then do we determine which of multiple tags to annotate? As with subcategorization (section 3), we propose annotating the closest fit to the context. In figure 1, for instance, we annotate the correctly-used *have* as ROOT—appropriate for this tensed finite verb, but not for its alternative category of base form verb (depending upon one's definition of ROOT).

We leave open to what degree *context* is defined by syntax, semantics, discourse, or even extra-linguistic factors. For a non-native case, consider (4), an example where the morphological form is ambiguous between base form verb and non-third person singular present tense. Neither exactly matches the context, but as the head of the entire sentence, the tensed form could take precedence, as sentences syntactically require tense, leading to an annotation based on the morphological form of a non-third singular present verb.

(4) This first year **have** been wonderful ... (Díaz-Negrillo et al., 2010)

Importantly, the occurence of this phenomenon has led us to define morphosyntax to include some degree of contextual information, as was done with subcategorization. While we choose to base decisions on context, one may use other properties to disambiguate morphosyntax, e.g., taking the base form as more "basic" in (4), relying on an error taxonomy, etc.

There are further issues in defining morphosyntax which, due to space limitations, we only mention here. For example, returning to (3) and ignoring the space in *a bout* (=*about*), the dependency relation between *about* and *chooses* should be one appropriate for a verb, as this is the morphological form of *chooses*, but should the label be consistent with the head (in this case, a preposition, normally taking a noun phrase as its complement)?

To sum, annotating morphosyntax requires answering: 1) Is the analysis context-sensitive? 2) How does one disambiguate in context? Future work can also investigate: 3) How compatible with the head does a dependency relation need to be? 4) Is this dependency relation based more on lexical or categorical properties? With a contextually-influenced layer, we again overlap with distribution, which we now turn to.

5 Defining Distribution

We define a syntactic distributional slot as a position where a token with particular properties (e.g., singular noun) is predicted to occur, on the (syntactic) basis of its surrounding tokens. In the constructed *Him sleep*, for instance, the presence of a verb (*sleep*) predicts a nominative noun functioning as subject to its left, while the presence of a third singular pronoun at the beginning of the sentence can be said to predict a third singular verb to the right. The pronoun predicts some set of properties (agreement) and the verb an orthogonal set of properties (case). Parts of those slots are satisfied, and parts are not.

As with subcategorization (section 3), we need to make precise the basis for the linguistic categories being used. Since all learners are learning the same L2, there are common aspects to their interlanguage development, in spite of the potential influence of the native language (L1) (Ellis, 2008). We thus use the L2 as a reference frame for the annotation, to define properties such as: "this verb requires a nominative subject to the left." While one might want to directly encode IL, it is not clear what terms like "subject" mean in such a case. Additionally, annotation reliability would be an issue for L1-based or IL-based annotation, as the same sentence can have different analyses depending upon the L1 (Gass and Selinker, 2008, p. 106).

Distributional syntax can be disambiguated by morphology to get a single layer, just as morphosyntax can be disambiguated by context. In *having an experience*, the slot before the noun could be either a determiner (DET) or a quantifier (QUANT), e.g., *some experience*. If this were purely distribution, we would need to mark both possibilities, in addition to noun modifier (MOD). The fact that the word *an* is present, though, leads to DET as the best relation.

Complements Looking at what drives distributional predictions, complements can be government-based or agreement-based. In a case of syntactic government, a head selects its dependents and determines specific properties which need to be true of them. In these cases, the definition of a distributional slot follows from the head's subcategorization (see section 6). For example, in (5), *with* selects for a prepositional object, governing the case of the object. Distributionally, then, *he* is in a prepositional object position, regardless of its actual form.

(5) I must play with **he**.

For cases of agreement, the head may not be the locus of agreement. Consider (6), where the subject-verb disagreement affects the forms of both tokens. In this case, the verb is the head, but the subject could be considered the source of the agreement features. This is why, instead of being head-driven, we speak of one token predicting another token's properties.

(6) **He play** by toys.

The exact treatment for cases of agreement depends upon defining the source of agreement in one's syntactic theory—as annotation depends upon the theory employed (Leech, 2004; Rambow, 2010). For most label inventories, there is no distinction for agreement, but if there were (e.g., SUBJ3s vs. SUBJp), one could choose to use the relation driven by the *dependent* (SUBJ3s), since the prediction works "backwards." This would directly contradict the head-driven subcategorization (SUBJpl), specifying that the L2 requires a verb which agrees. The interaction with morphosyntax—which would underspecify (to SUBJ or to nothing)—is then similar to the case of adjuncts, as in section 6 (see the discussion around *He runs quick*).

Adjuncts Adjuncts select for their heads (Pollard and Sag, 1994), yet at the same time, heads delimit the properties of adjuncts (cf. selective adjunction, Abeillé and Rambow, 2000).

Annotation is straightforward if the selective properties do not conflict. Unlike complements, adjunction cases are not mediated via subcategorization; we discuss them in section 6.

To sum, annotating distributional dependencies requires answering: 1) What is the basis of the categories? (L1? L2? IL?) 2) How does one disambiguate in context, specifically what is the role of morphology? 3) What information drives the distributional predictions? Our answers led us to conclude that subcategorization drives the predictions in part, but not in whole.

6 Annotation Redundancies

Consider again the trees in figures 1 and 2: 1) the *vroot* selects for one ROOT and finds two in the morphosyntactic tree; 2) *have* selects for a verbal complement (VC), not realized morphosyntactically; and 3) the head and label of *see* differs between the trees. But with a better understanding of distribution, note what the third mismatch means: *see* is in the distributional slot of a verbal complement in figure 2, defined by virtue of the subcategorization list of *have*. In other words, this mismatch is already in mismatch #2, where *have* selects for VC. Based on the treatment of complements and adjuncts, we are more inclined towards removing distributional dependencies. We briefly outline some cases which led to this conclusion here.

Complements In terms of argument structure, non-canonical constructions center around a mismatch between what is subcategorized for and what is realized (cf. consistency, completeness, and coherence (Bresnan, 2001)). In these cases, distributional dependencies require annotating more than is known from the evidence available in the sentence, as we will illustrate.

For mismatched requirements, consider (7), where a non-finite clause (*what success to be*) appears as the complement of *wondered*, where one would expect a finite clause.

(7) I wondered what success **to be**.

Morphologically, *to be* has non-finite marking and the clause is thus a non-finite complement (XCOMP), as shown in the left side of figure 4, assuming *to* is the head. The subcategorization selects for a finite complement (COMP), making for a clear mismatch.

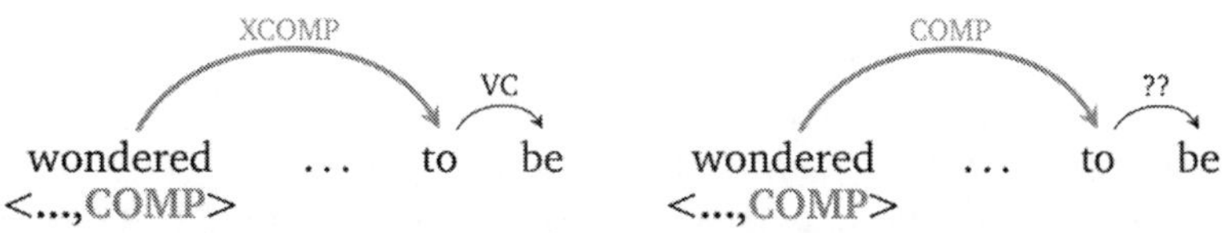

Figure 4: Morphosyntactic (left) and distributional (right) trees for a complement mismatch

Based on subcategorization predictions, in a distributional tree we use COMP as a label. The subtree, however, is unclear, as shown on the right side. If *to be* is in a finite distributional position, is *to* a finite modal verb with a verbal complement? Is *be* the finite verb with an extraneous *to* marking? Annotating subcategorization does not force such an internal analysis.

Missing arguments illustrate how subcategorization captures information distributional dependencies cannot. Consider (8), for example, where the learner wrote *shakes*. Neither verb has an object, but *shakes* here requires an object that *runs* does not. Both, however, have the exact same distributional trees (not shown), with only a SUBJ from the verb.

(8) As he saw it, at once he takes it and { **shakes** | **runs** }

This difference is easily captured via subcategorization, distinguishing <SUBJ> (*runs*) from <SUBJ,OBJ,> (*shakes*). Extra arguments work in a similar fashion. Missing heads (e.g., copulas) are more complicated, but the challenge is for all layers; space precludes a discussion here.

Adjuncts Non-native use of adjuncts are cases where distributional dependencies seem to be required, as subcategorization does not include adjuncts. We sketch some of the issues here.

Consider an adjective modifying a verb, as in the constructed *He runs quick* (cf. real examples like *It is quickly*). In this case, if we ignore the morphology of the dependent, the distributional layer would reflect the selectional properties of the head, encoding *quick* as a verbal modifier (JCT) of *runs*, whereas the morphosyntactic layer lacks a label which fits with both the head (e.g., JCT) and the dependent (MOD) (cf. (3)). With no adjunct subcategorization, the morphosyntactic layer does not convey that the L2 requires something like a JCT relation here.

This is not the entire story, though. First, once POS is taken into account, we have more information than an unspecified relation between *runs* and *quick*; namely, it is verb+adjective which has an undefined relation. Secondly, defining a distributional label makes more assumptions than it may at first appear. In this case, this is also an appropriate slot for CJCT (clausal adjunct) or XJCT (non-finite adjunct); it is only because *quick* is similar to *quickly* that we assume a label appropriate for adverbs. Working out which label to use when the morphology is not a totally valid piece of evidence requires more analysis (cf. (7)).

7 Conclusion & Outlook

We started with a proposal for learner language to annotate: 1) subcategorization, 2) morphosyntactic dependencies, and 3) distributional dependencies. By precisely defining each layer, we uncovered several questions that need to be addressed, including the degree of context to incorporate into subcategorization and morphosyntax in order to arrive at a single annotation. We suggested that it may be preferable to annotate subcategorization *instead of* distribution, as subcategorization is a source of distribution; such a decision prevents annotators from having to specify distributional trees in cases where they are indeterminate. Based on our ongoing annotation efforts, we have developed extensive annotation guidelines reflecting our decisions and examining various constructions, which will be made publicly available in the near future.

The decisions discussed here raise questions for the future, the foremost one being to definitively answer the questions raised about each layer here. Where, for example, does semantic evidence fit and what is the precise role of word order in defining each layer? We have only scratched the surface, and to carry out automatic analysis, for instance, will require a deeper look into the connections between different pieces of evidence. Secondly, how does such a division of layers of syntax bear on other non-canonical language use, such as web data, or the annotation of native language (cf. the discussion in Rehbein et al., 2012)? It is an open question as to whether the elucidation of layers for learner language can impact annotation schemes for syntax more broadly. Thirdly, there is a need to work out the exact connection between this annotation and the annotation of target hypotheses for learner language, building from annotation mismatches. Mismatches in annotation layers point to errors (Dickinson and Ragheb, 2009), an insight used for creating multiple parsing models for learner language (e.g., Dickinson and Lee, 2009).

Acknowledgments

We would like to thank Detmar Meurers, the IU CL discussion group, and the three anonymous reviewers for helpful feedback.

References

Abeillé, A. and Rambow, O. (2000). Tree adjoining grammar: An overview. In Abeillé, A. and Rambow, O., editors, *Tree Adjoining Grammars: Formalisms, Linguistic Analyses and Processing*, pages 1–68. CSLI Publications, Stanford, CA.

Bresnan, J. (2001). *Lexical-Functional Syntax*. Blackwell Publising, Oxford.

de Haan, P. (2000). Tagging non-native english with the tosca-icle tagger. In Mair, C. and Hundt, M., editors, *Corpus Linguistics and Linguistic Theory*, pages 69–79. Rodopi, Amsterdam.

Díaz-Negrillo, A., Meurers, D., Valera, S., and Wunsch, H. (2010). Towards interlanguage POS annotation for effective learner corpora in SLA and FLT. *Language Forum*, 36(1–2). Special Issue on New Trends in Language Teaching.

Dickinson, M. and Lee, C. M. (2009). Modifying corpus annotation to support the analysis of learner language. *CALICO Journal*, 26(3).

Dickinson, M. and Ragheb, M. (2009). Dependency annotation for learner corpora. In *Proceedings of the Eighth Workshop on Treebanks and Linguistic Theories (TLT-8)*, pages 59–70, Milan, Italy.

Dickinson, M. and Ragheb, M. (2011). Dependency annotation of coordination for learner language. In *Proceedings of the International Conference on Dependency Linguistics (Depling 2011)*, Barcelona, Spain.

Ellis, R. (2008). *The Study of Second Language Acquisition*. Oxford University Press, Oxford, second edition.

Gass, S. M. and Selinker, L. (2008). *Second Language Acquisition: An Introductory Course*. Taylor & Francis, New York, third edition.

Granger, S. (2003). Error-tagged learner corpora and CALL: A promising synergy. *CALICO Journal*, 20(3):465–480.

Hawkins, J. A. and Buttery, P. (2010). Criterial features in learner corpora: Theory and illustrations. *English Profile Journal*, 1(1):1–23.

Krivanek, J. and Meurers, D. (2011). Comparing rule-based and data-driven dependency parsing of learner language. In *Proceedings of the Int. Conference on Dependency Linguistics (Depling 2011)*, Barcelona.

Leech, G. (2004). Adding linguistic annotation. In Wynne, M., editor, *Developing Linguistic Corpora: a Guide to Good Practice*, pages 17–29. Oxbow Books, Oxford.

Levin, B. (1993). *English Verb Classes and Alternations: A Preliminary Investigation*. University of Chicago Press, Chicago, IL.

Lüdeling, A., Walter, M., Kroymann, E., and Adolphs, P. (2005). Multi-level error annotation in learner corpora. In *Proceedings of Corpus Linguistics 2005*, Birmingham.

Mel'čuk, I. (1988). *Dependency Syntax: Theory and Practice*. State University of New York Press.

Nagata, R., Whittaker, E., and Sheinman, V. (2011). Creating a manually error-tagged and shallow-parsed learner corpus. In *Proceedings of the 49th Annual Meeting of the Association for Computational Linguistics: Human Language Technologies*, pages 1210–1219, Portland, OR.

Ott, N. and Ziai, R. (2010). Evaluating dependency parsing performance on German learner language. In *Proceedings of TLT-9*, volume 9, pages 175–186.

Pienemann, M. (1992). Coala-a computational system for interlanguage analysis. *Second Language Research*, 8(1):59–92.

Pollard, C. and Sag, I. A. (1994). *Head-Driven Phrase Structure Grammar*. The University of Chicago Press.

Ragheb, M. and Dickinson, M. (2011). Avoiding the comparative fallacy in the annotation of learner corpora. In *Selected Proceedings of the 2010 Second Language Research Forum: Reconsidering SLA Research, Dimensions, and Directions*, pages 114–124, Somerville, MA. Cascadilla Proceedings Project.

Rambow, O. (2010). The simple truth about dependency and phrase structure representations: An opinion piece. In *Human Language Technologies: The 2010 Annual Conference of the North American Chapter of the Association for Computational Linguistics*, pages 337–340, Los Angeles, CA.

Rastelli, S. (2009). Learner corpora without error tagging. *Linguistik online*, 38.

Rehbein, I., Hirschmann, H., Lüdeling, A., and Reznicek, M. (2012). Better tags give better trees - or do they? *Linguistic Issues in Language Technology (LiLT)*, 7(10).

Rozovskaya, A. and Roth, D. (2010). Annotating ESL errors: Challenges and rewards. In *Proceedings of the NAACL HLT 2010 Fifth Workshop on Innovative Use of NLP for Building Educational Applications*, pages 28–36, Los Angeles, California.

Sagae, K., Davis, E., Lavie, A., and an Shuly Wintner, B. M. (2010). Morphosyntactic annotation of childes transcripts. *Journal of Child Language*, 37(3):705–729.

Sagae, K., Davis, E., Lavie, A., MacWhinney, B., and Wintner, S. (2007). High-accuracy annotation and parsing of childes transcripts. In *Proceedings of the Workshop on Cognitive Aspects of Computational Language Acquisition*, pages 25–32, Prague.

Tetreault, J., Foster, J., and Chodorow, M. (2010). Using parse features for preposition selection and error detection. In *Proceedings of the ACL 2010 Conference Short Papers*, pages 353–358, Uppsala, Sweden.

Thouësny, S. (2009). Increasing the reliability of a part-of-speech tagging tool for use with learner language. Presentation given at the Automatic Analysis of Learner Language (AALL'09) workshop on automatic analysis of learner language: from a better understanding of annotation needs to the development and standardization of annotation schemes.

van Rooy, B. and Schäfer, L. (2002). The effect of learner errors on pos tag errors during automatic pos tagging. *Southern African Linguistics and Applied Language Studies*, 20:325–335.

How good are Typological Distances for determining Genealogical Relationships among Languages?

Taraka Rama[1] *KOLACHINA Prasanth*[2]
(1) Språkbanken, Department of Swedish Language, University of Gothenburg, Gothenburg, Sweden
(2) Language Technologies Research Centre, IIIT-Hyderabad, Hyderabad, India
`taraka.rama.kasicheyanula@gu.se`, `prasanth_k@research.iiit.ac.in`

ABSTRACT
The recent availability of typological databases such as World Atlas of Language Structures (WALS) has spurred investigations regarding their utility for language classification, the stability of typological features in genetic linguistics and typological universals across the language families of the world. Existing work on building NLP resources such as parallel corpora, treebanks for under-resourced languages has a lot to gain by taking into consideration insights about inter-language relationships. Since Yarowsky et al. (2001), there have been a number of attempts to create resources for resource-poor languages by projecting information from resource-rich languages using comparable corpora. An important intuition in such work is that syntactic information can be transferred with higher accuracy between languages if they are similar. In this paper, we compare typological distances derived from fifteen vector similarity measures with family internal classifications and also lexical divergence. These results are only a first step towards the use of WALS database in the projection of NLP resources for typologically or genetically similar, yet resource-poor languages.

KEYWORDS: WALS, ASJP, Vector similarity, Internal classification, Typological features.

Proceedings of COLING 2012: Posters, pages 975–984,
COLING 2012, Mumbai, December 2012.

1 Introduction

There are around 7000 languages in this world (Lewis, 2009) which fall into more than 140 genetic families having descended from a common ancestor. The aim of traditional historical linguistics is to trace the evolutionary path, a tree of extant languages to their extinct common ancestor. Genealogical relationship is not the only characteristic which relates languages; languages can also share structurally common features such as *word order*, *similar phoneme inventory size* and *morphology*. It would be a grave error to posit that two languages are genetically related due to a single common structural feature. There have been attempts in the past (Nichols, 1995) to rank the stability of structural features. Stability implies the resistance of a structural feature to change across space and time. For instance, Dravidian languages have adhered to subject-object-verb (SOV) word order for the last two thousand years (Krishnamurti, 2003; Dunn et al.). Hence, it can be claimed that the structural feature SOV is very stable in the Dravidian language family. Also, structural features have recently been used for inferring the evolutionary tree of a small group of Papuan languages of the Pacific (Dunn et al., 2005).

In the area of computational linguistics, existing work on building NLP resources such as parallel corpora, treebanks for under-resourced languages has a lot to gain by taking into consideration insights about inter-language relationships. For example, Birch et al. (2008) is an interesting example of a work that uses genealogical distances between two language families to predict the difficulty of machine translation. However, the use of typological distances in the development of various NLP tools largely remains unexplored. In this paper, we feed such research by providing robust estimates of inter-language distances and comparing them with family internal classification and also within-family lexical divergence.

The paper is structured as followed. In Section 2, we summarize the related work. Section 3 lists the contributions of this work. Section 4 describes the typological database, lexical database and the criteria for preparing the final dataset. Section 5 presents the different vector similarity measures and the evaluation procedure. The results of our experiments are given in Section 6.

2 Related Work

Dunn et al. (2005) were the first to apply a well-tested computational phylogenetic method (from computational biology), Maximum Parsimony (MP; Felsenstein 2004) to typological features (phonological, syntactic and morphological). They use MP to classify a set of unrelated languages – in Oceania – belonging to two different families. In another related work, Wichmann and Saunders (2007) apply three different phylogenetic algorithms – Neighbor Joining (Saitou and Nei, 1987), MP and Bayesian inference (Huelsenbeck et al., 2001) – to the typological features (from WALS) of 63 native American languages. They also ranked the typological features in terms of stability. Nichols and Warnow (2008) survey the use of typological features for language classification in computational historical linguistics. In a novel work, Bakker et al. (2009) combine typological distances with lexical similarity to boost the language classification accuracy. As a first step, they compute the pair-wise typological distances for 355 languages, obtained through the application of length normalized Hamming distance to 85 typological features (ranked by Wichmann and Holman 2009). They combine the typological distances with lexical divergence, derived from lexicostatistical lists, to boost language classification accuracy. Unfortunately, these works seem to have gone unnoticed in computational linguistics.

Typological feature such as phoneme inventory size (extracted from WALS database; Haspelmath et al. 2011) was used by Atkinson (2011) to claim that the phoneme inventory size shows a negative correlation as one moves away from Africa[1]. In another work, Dunn et al. (2011) make an effort towards demonstrating that there are lineage specific trends in the word order universals across the families of the world.

In computational linguistics, Daume III (2009) and Georgi et al. (2010) use typological features from WALS for investigating relation between phylogenetic groups and feature stability. Georgi et al. (2010) motivate the use of typological features for projecting linguistic resources such as treebanks and bootstrapping NLP tools from "resource-rich" to "low-resource" languages which are genetically unrelated yet, share similar syntactic features due to contact (ex., Swedish to Finnish or vice-versa). Georgi et al. (2010) compute pair-wise distances from typological feature vectors using cosine similarity and a shared overlap measure (ratio of number of shared features to the total number of features, between a pair of feature vectors). They apply three different clustering algorithms – k-means, partitional, agglomerative – to the WALS dataset with number of clusters as testing parameter and observe that the clustering performance measure (in terms of F-score) is not the best when the number of clusters agree with the exact number of families (121) in the whole-world dataset. They find that the simplest clustering algorithm, k-means, wins across all the three datasets. However, the authors do not correct for geographical bias in the dataset.

3 Contributions

In this article, we do not investigate the topic of feature stability or prediction accuracy of clustering methods discussed in Georgi et al. (2010). Instead, we try to answer the following questions:

- Do we really need a clustering algorithm to measure the internal classification accuracy of a language family?
- How well do the typological distances within a family correlate with the lexical distances derived from lexicostatistical lists (Swadesh, 1952; Wichmann et al., 2011b), originally proposed for language classification?
- Given that there are more than dozen vector similarity measures, which vector similarity measure is best suited for the above mentioned tasks?

4 Database

In this section, we describe a database of typological features, referred to as WALS and a lexicostatistical database called *Automated Similarity Judgment Program* (ASJP), which are used in our experiments.

4.1 WALS

The WALS database[2] has 144 feature classes for 2676 languages distributed across the world. As noted in Hammarström (2009), the WALS database is sparse across many language families of the world and the dataset needs to be pruned before it is used for further investigations. The database is represented as matrix of languages vs. features. The pruning of the dataset has to be done in both the directions to avoid sparsity when computing the pair-wise distances between languages. Following Georgi et al. (2010), we remove all the languages which have less than 25 attested features. We also remove features with less than 10% attestations. This leaves the

[1]Assuming a mono-genesis hypothesis of language similar to the mono-genesis hypothesis of *homo sapiens*.
[2]Accessed on 2011-09-22.

dataset with 1159 languages and 193 features. Our dataset includes only those families having more than 10 languages (following Wichmann et al. 2010), shown in Table 1. Georgi et al. (2010) work with a pruned dataset of 735 languages and two major families Indo-European and Sino-Tibetan whereas, we stick to investigating the questions in Section 3 for the well-defined language families – Austronesian, Afro-Asiatic – given in Table 1.

Family	Count	Family	Count
Austronesian	150 (141)	Austro-Asiatic	22 (21)
Niger-Congo	143 (123)	Oto-Manguean	18 (14)
Sino-Tibetan	81 (68)	Arawakan	17 (17)
Australian	73 (65)	Uralic	15 (12)
Nilo-Saharan	69 (62)	Penutian	14 (11)
Afro-Asiatic	68 (57)	Nakh-Daghestanian	13 (13)
Indo-European	60 (56)	Tupian	13 (12)
Trans-New Guinea	43 (33)	Hokan	12 (12)
Uto-Aztecan	28 (26)	Dravidian	10 (9)
Altaic	27 (26)	Mayan	10 (7)

Table 1: Number of languages in each family. The number in parenthesis for each family gives the number of languages present in the database after mapping with ASJP database.

4.2 ASJP

A international consortium of scholars (calling themselves ASJP; Brown et al. 2008) started collecting Swadesh word lists (Swadesh, 1952) (a short concept meaning list usually ranging from 40–200) for most of the world's languages (more than 58%), in the hope of automatizing the language classification of world's languages [3]. The ASJP lexical items are transcribed using a broad phonetic transcription called ASJP Code (Brown et al., 2008). The ASJP Code collapses distinctions in vowel length, stress, tone and reduces all click sounds to a single click symbol. This database has word lists for a language (given by its unique ISO 693-3 code as well as WALS code) and its dialects. We use the WALS code to map the languages in WALS database with that of ASJP database. Whenever a language with a WALS code has more than one word list in ASJP database, we chose to retain the first language for our experiments. An excerpt of word list for Russian is shown in Figure 1. The first line consists of name of language, WALS classification (Indo-European family and Slavic genus), followed by Ethnologue classification (informing that Russian belongs to Eastern Slavic subgroup of Indo-European family). The second line consists of the latitude, longitude, number of speakers, WALS code and ISO 639-3 code. Lexical items begin from the third line.

4.3 Binarization

Each feature in the WALS dataset is either a binary feature (presence or absence of the feature in a language) or a multi-valued feature, coded as a discrete integers over a finite range. Georgi et al. (2010) binarize the feature values by recording the presence or absence of a feature value in a language. This binarization greatly expands the length of the feature vector for a language but allows to represent a wide-ranged feature such as *word order* (which has 7 feature values) in terms of a sequence of 1's and 0's. The issue of binary vs. multi-valued features has been a

[3] Available at: `http://email.eva.mpg.de/~wichmann/listss14.zip`

```
RUSSIAN{IE.SLAVIC|Indo-European,Slavic,East}
 1   56.00   38.00   145031551   rus   rus
1 I      ya //
2 you    t3, v3 //
3 we     m3 //
4 this   iEt3 //
5 that   to //
6 who    kto //
7 what   tato //
8 not    ny~E //
9 all    fsy~e //
10 many imnogy~i //
```

Figure 1: 10 lexical items in Russian.

point of debate in genetic linguistics and has been shown to not give very different results for the Indo-European classification (Atkinson and Gray, 2006).

5 Measures

In this section, we list the 15 vector similarity measures (shown in Table 2), followed by a description of the evaluation measure used in our work to compare the typological distances to WALS classification. We also describe the procedure used to compute lexical divergence from the ASJP lists.

Vector similarity	
euclidean	$\sqrt[2]{\Sigma_{i=1}^{n}(v_1^i - v_2^i)^2}$
seuclidean	$\Sigma_{i=1}^{n}(v_1^i - v_2^i)^2$
nseuclidean	$\frac{\lVert\sigma_1 - \sigma_2\rVert}{2 * \lVert\sigma_1\rVert + \lVert\sigma_2\rVert}$
manhattan	$\Sigma_{i=1}^{n}\lvert v_1^i - v_2^i\rvert$
chessboard	$max((v_1^i - v_2^i)\forall i \in (1,n))$
braycurtis	$\frac{\Sigma_{i=1}^{n}\lvert v_1^i - v_2^i\rvert}{\Sigma_{i=1}^{n}\lvert v_1^i + v_2^i\rvert}$
cosine	$\frac{v_1 \cdot v_2}{\lVert v_1\rVert * \lVert v_2\rVert}$
correlation	$1 - \frac{\sigma_1 \cdot \sigma_2}{\lVert\sigma_1\rVert * \lVert\sigma_2\rVert}$

Boolean similarity	
hamming	$\#_{\neq 0}(v_1 \,\hat{}\, v_2)$
jaccard	$\frac{\#_{\neq 0}(v_1 \,\hat{}\, v_2)}{\#_{\neq 0}(v_1 \,\hat{}\, v_2) + \#_{\neq 0}(v_1 \& v_2)}$
tanimoto	$\frac{2 * \#_{\neq 0}(v_1 \,\hat{}\, v_2)}{\#_{\neq 0}(v_1 \& v_2) + \#_{=0}(v_1 \Vert v_2) + 2 * \#_{\neq 0}(v_1 \,\hat{}\, v_2)}$
matching	$\frac{\#_{\neq 0}(v_1 \,\hat{}\, v_2)}{\# v_1}$
dice	$\frac{\#_{\neq 0}(v_1 \,\hat{}\, v_2)}{\#_{\neq 0}(v_1 \,\hat{}\, v_2) + 2 * \#_{\neq 0}(v_1 \& v_2)}$
sokalsneath	$\frac{2 * \#_{\neq 0}(v_1 \,\hat{}\, v_2)}{2 * \#_{\neq 0}(v_1 \,\hat{}\, v_2) + \#_{\neq 0}(v_1 \& v_2)}$
russellrao	$\frac{\#_{\neq 0}(v_1 \,\hat{}\, v_2) + \#_{=0}(v_1 \Vert v_2)}{\# v_1}$
yule	$\frac{2 * \#_{\neq 0}(v_1 - v_2) * \#_{=0}(v_1 - v_2)}{\#_{\neq 0}(v_1 - v_2) * \#_{=0}(v_1 - v_2) + \#_{\neq 0}(v_1 \& v_2) * \#_{=0}(v_1 \Vert v_2)}$

Table 2: Different vector similarity measures used in our experiments (distance computed between v_1 and v_2). In vector similarity measures, $\|\|$ represents the L_2 norm of the vector, and σ represents the difference from mean of vector (μ_1) i.e. ($v_1 - \mu_1$). Similarly, for the boolean similarity measures, $\hat{}$ stands for the logical XOR operation between bit vectors while & and $\|$ stand for logical AND and OR operations respectively. $\#_{\neq 0}(\cdot)$ stands for number of non-zero bits in a boolean vector.

5.1 Internal classification accuracy

Apart from typological information for the world's languages, WALS also provides a two-level classification of a language family. In the WALS classification, the top level is the family name, the next level is genus and a language rests at the bottom. For instance, Indo-European family has 10 genera. Genus is a consensually defined unit and not a rigorously established genealogical unit (Hammarström, 2009). Rather, a genus corresponds to a group of languages which are supposed to have descended from a proto-language which is about 3500 to 4000 years old. For instance, WALS lists Indic and Iranian languages as separate genera whereas, both the genera are actually descendants of Proto-Indo-Iranian which in turn descended from Proto-Indo-European – a fact well-known in historical linguistics (Campbell and Poser, 2008).

The WALS classification for each language family listed in Table 1, can be represented as a 2D-matrix with languages along both rows and columns. Each cell of such a matrix represents the WALS relationship in a language pair in the family. A cell has 0 if a language pair belong to the same genus and 1 if they belong to different genera. The pair-wise distance matrix obtained from each vector similarity measure is compared to the 2D-matrix using a special case of pearson's r, called point-biserial correlation [4].

5.2 Lexical distance

The ASJP program computes the distance between two languages as the average pair-wise length-normalized Levenshtein distance, called Levenshtein Distance Normalized (LDN) (Levenshtein, 1965). LDN is further modified to account for chance resemblance such as accidental phoneme inventory similarity between a pair of languages to yield LDND (Levenshtein Distance Normalized Divided; Holman et al. 2008). The performance of LDND distance matrices was evaluated against two expert classifications of world's languages in at least two recent works (Pompei et al., 2011; Wichmann et al., 2011a). Their findings confirm that the LDND matrices largely agree with the classification given by historical linguists. This result puts us on a strong ground to use ASJP's LDND as a measure of lexical divergence within a family.

The distribution of the languages included in this study is plotted in Figure 2.

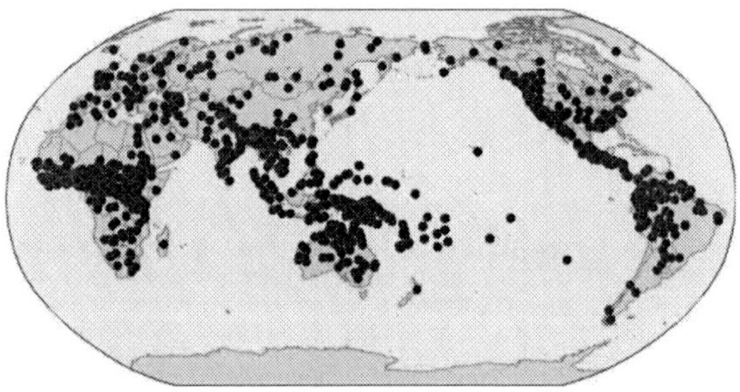

Figure 2: Visual representation of world's languages in the final dataset.

The correlation between typological distances and lexical distances is (within a family) computed as the spearman's rank correlation ρ between the typological and lexical distances for all language pairs in the family. It is worth noting that Bakker et al. (2009) also compare LDND distance matrices with WALS distance matrices for 355 languages from various families using a pearson's r whereas, we compare within-family LDND matrices with WALS distance matrices derived from 15 similarity measures.

6 Results

In this section, we present and discuss the results of our experiments in internal classification and correlation with lexical divergence. We use heat maps to visualize the correlation matrices resulting from both experiments.

[4] http://en.wikipedia.org/wiki/Point-biserial_correlation_coefficient

6.1 Internal classification

The point bi-serial correlation, r, introduced in Section 5, lies in the range of -1 to $+1$. The value of r is blank for Arawakan and Mayan families since both families have a single genus in their respective WALS classifications. Subsequently, r is shown in white for both of these families. Chessboard measure is blank across all language families since it gives a single score of 1 between two different binary vectors. Interestingly, all vector similarity measures perform well for Australian, Austro-Asiatic, Indo-European and Sino-Tibetan language families, except for 'russellrao'. We take this result to be encouraging since they consist of more than 33% of the total languages in the sample given in Table 1. Among the measures, 'matching', 'seuclidean', 'tanimoto', 'euclidean', 'hamming' and 'manhattan' perform the best across the four families. Interestingly, the widely used 'cosine' measure does not perform as well as 'hamming'. None of the vector similarity measures seem to perform well for Austronesian and Niger-Congo families which have more than 14% and 11% of the world's languages respectively. The worst performing language family is Tupian. This does not come as a surprise, since Tupian has 5 genera with one language in each and a single genus comprising the rest of family. Australian and Austro-Asiatic families shows the maximum correlation across 'seuclidean', 'tanimoto', 'euclidean', 'hamming' and 'manhattan'.

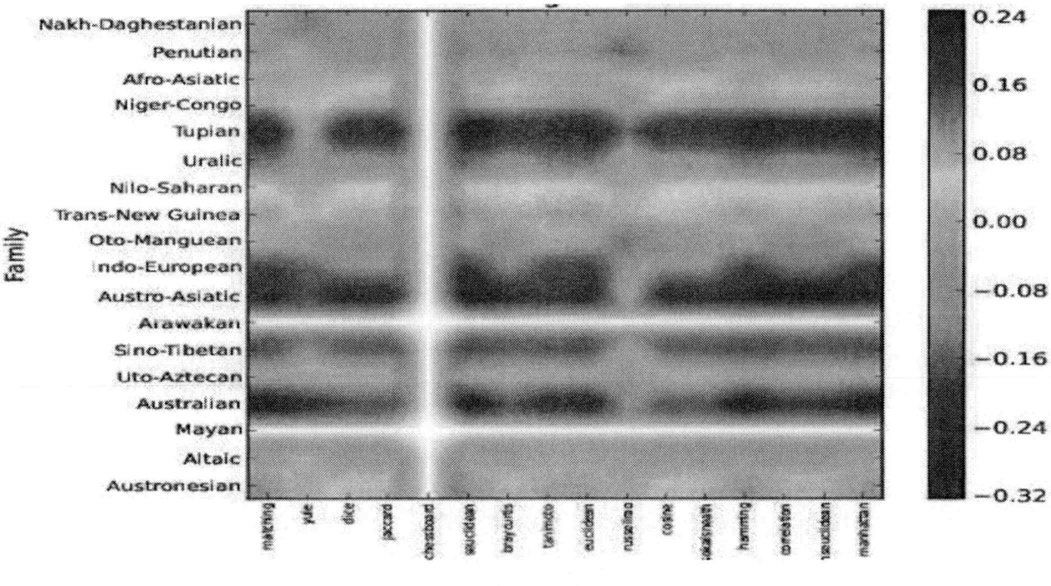

Figure 3: Heatmap showing the gradience of r across different language families and vector similarity measures.

6.2 Lexical divergence

The rank correlation between LDND and vector similarity measures is high across Australian, Sino-Tibetan, Uralic, Indo-European and Niger-Congo families. The 'Russel-Rao' measure works the best for families – Arawakan, Austro-Asiatic, Tupian and Afro-Asiatic – which otherwise have poor correlation scores for the rest of measures. The maximum correlation is for 'yule' measure in Uralic family. Indo-European, the well-studied family, shows a correlation from 0.08 to the maximum possible correlation across all measures, except for 'Russell-Rao' and 'Bray-Curtis' distances. The Hokan family shows the lowest amount of correlations across all distance measures. One possible reason for this could be the controversial nature of the family, with a lack of proper consensus among historical linguistics regarding its status as a seperate language family.

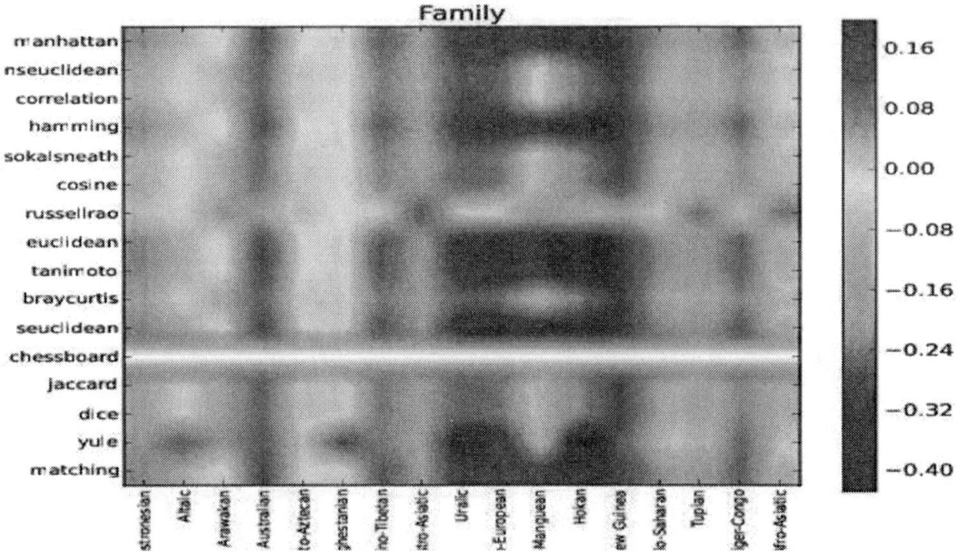

Figure 4: Heatmap showing the gradience of ρ across different families and vector similarity measures.

Conclusion

In summary, choosing the right vector similarity measure when calculating typological distances makes a difference in the internal classification accuracy. The choice of similarity measure does not influence the correlation between WALS distances and LDND distances within a family. The internal classification accuracies are similar to the accuracies reported in Bakker et al. (2009). Our correlation matrix suggests that internal classification accuracies of LDND matrices (reported in Bakker et al. 2009) can be boosted through the right combination of typological distances and lexical distances. There is also a need to investigate the effect of geographical proximity and time depth of the language families on typological distances. In fact, our work in this paper is a starting point to tease apart the influence of geographical proximity and time depth factors from typological similarity. In our experiments, we did not control for feature stability and experimented on all available features. By choosing a smaller set of typological features (from the ranking of Wichmann and Holman (2009)) and right similarity measure one might achieve higher accuracies. The current rate of language extinction is unprecedented in human history. Our findings might be helpful in speeding up the language classification of many small dying families by serving as a springboard for traditional historical linguists.

Acknowledgments

The research presented here was supported by the Swedish Research Council (the project Digital areal linguistics, VR dnr 2009-1448) and by the University of Gothenburg through its support of the Centre for Language Technology and of Språkbanken. We would like to thank Harald Hammarström, Lars Borin and Søren Wichmann for the discussions and their insights into this work. We would also like to thank the anonymous reviewers for their comments on the paper.

References

Atkinson, Q. and Gray, R. (2006). How old is the Indo-European language family? Progress or more moths to the flame. *Phylogenetic Methods and the Prehistory of Languages (Forster P, Renfrew C, eds)*, pages 91–109.

Atkinson, Q. D. (2011). Phonemic diversity supports a serial founder effect model of language expansion from Africa. *Science*, 332(6027):346.

Bakker, D., Müller, A., Velupillai, V., Wichmann, S., Brown, C. H., Brown, P., Egorov, D., Mailhammer, R., Grant, A., and Holman, E. W. (2009). Adding typology to lexicostatistics: A combined approach to language classification. *Linguistic Typology*, 13(1):169–181.

Birch, A., Osborne, M., and Koehn, P. (2008). Predicting Success in Machine Translation. In *Proceedings of the 2008 Conference on Empirical Methods in Natural Language Processing*, pages 745–754, Honolulu, Hawaii. Association for Computational Linguistics.

Brown, C., Holman, E., Wichmann, S., and Velupillai, V. (2008). Automated classification of the world's languages: a description of the method and preliminary results. *Sprachtypologie und Universalienforschung*, 61(4):285–308.

Campbell, L. and Poser, W. (2008). *Language classification: history and method*. Cambridge University Press.

Daume III, H. (2009). Non-parametric bayesian areal linguistics. In *Proceedings of Human Language Technologies: The 2009 Annual Conference of the North American Chapter of the Association for Computational Linguistics*, pages 593–601. Association for Computational Linguistics.

Dunn, M., Greenhill, S., Levinson, S., and Gray, R. (2011). Evolved structure of language shows lineage-specific trends in word-order universals. *Nature*, 473(7345):79–82.

Dunn, M., Levinson, S., and Lindström, E. Ger reesink and angela terrill 2008. structural phylogeny in historical linguistics: Methodological explorations applied in island melanesia. *Language*, 84(4):710–59.

Dunn, M., Terrill, A., Reesink, G., Foley, R., and Levinson, S. (2005). Structural phylogenetics and the reconstruction of ancient language history. *Science*, 309(5743):2072–2075.

Felsenstein, J. (2004). Inferring phytogenies. *Sunderland, Massachusetts: Sinauer Associates*.

Georgi, R., Xia, F., and Lewis, W. (2010). Comparing language similarity across genetic and typologically-based groupings. In *Proceedings of the 23rd International Conference on Computational Linguistics*, pages 385–393. Association for Computational Linguistics.

Hammarström, H. (2009). Sampling and genealogical coverage in the wals. *Linguistic Typology*, 13(1):105–119. Plus 198pp appendix.

Haspelmath, M., Dryer, M. S., Gil, D., and Comrie, B. (2011). *WALS online*. Munich: Max Planck Digital Library. http://wals.info.

Holman, E. W., Wichmann, S., Brown, C. H., Velupillai, V., Müller, A., and Bakker, D. (2008). Advances in automated language classification. In Arppe, A., Sinnemäki, K., and Nikanne, U., editors, *Quantitative Investigations in Theoretical Linguistics*, pages 40–43, Helsinki: University of Helsinki.

Huelsenbeck, J., Ronquist, F., et al. (2001). Mrbayes: Bayesian inference of phylogenetic trees. *Bioinformatics*, 17(8):754–755.

Krishnamurti, B. (2003). *The Dravidian languages*. Cambridge Univ. Press.

Levenshtein, V. (1965). Binary codes capable of correcting spurious insertions and reversals. *Cybernetics and Control Theory*, 10:707–710.

Lewis, P. M., editor (2009). *Ethnologue: Languages of the World*. SIL International, Dallas, TX, USA, Sixteenth edition.

Nichols, J. (1995). Diachronically stable structural features. *Historical Linguistics 1993. Selected Papers from the 11th International Conference on Historical Linguistics*, pages 337–355.

Nichols, J. and Warnow, T. (2008). Tutorial on computational linguistic phylogeny. *Language and Linguistics Compass*, 2(5):760–820.

Pompei, S., Loreto, V., and Tria, F. (2011). On the accuracy of language trees. *PloS one*, 6(6):e20109.

Saitou, N. and Nei, M. (1987). The neighbor-joining method: a new method for reconstructing phylogenetic trees. *Molecular biology and evolution*, 4(4):406–425.

Swadesh, M. (1952). Lexico-statistic dating of prehistoric ethnic contacts: with special reference to North American Indians and Eskimos. *Proceedings of the American philosophical society*, 96(4):452–463.

Wichmann, S. and Holman, E. (2009). Assessing temporal stability for linguistic typological features. *München: LINCOM Europa*.

Wichmann, S., Holman, E. W., Bakker, D., and Brown, C. H. (2010). Evaluating linguistic distance measures. *Physica A: Statistical Mechanics and its Applications*, 389:3632–3639.

Wichmann, S., Holman, E. W., Rama, T., and Walker, R. S. (2011a). Correlates of reticulation in linguistic phylogenies. *Language Dynamics and Change*, 2. In press.

Wichmann, S., Müller, A., Velupillai, V., Wett, A., Brown, C. H., Molochieva, Z., Sauppe, S., Holman, E. W., Brown, P., Bishoffberger, J., Bakker, D., List, J.-M., Egorov, D., Belyaev, O., Urban, M., Mailhammer, R., Geyer, H., Beck, D., Korovina, E., Epps, P., Valenzuela, P., Grant, A., and Hammarström, H. (2011b). The ASJP database (version 14). http://email.eva.mpg.de/ wichmann/listss14.zip.

Wichmann, S. and Saunders, A. (2007). How to use typological databases in historical linguistic research. *Diachronica*, 24(2):373–404.

Yarowsky, D., Ngai, G., and Wicentowski, R. (2001). Inducing multilingual text analysis tools via robust projection across aligned corpora. In *Proceedings of the first international conference on Human language technology research*, pages 1–8. Association for Computational Linguistics.

Sentence Boundary Detection: A Long Solved Problem?

Jonathon READ, Rebecca DRIDAN, Stephan OEPEN, Lars Jørgen SOLBERG
University of Oslo, Department of Informatics
{jread|rdridan|oe|larsjol}@ifi.uio.no

ABSTRACT
We review the state of the art in automated sentence boundary detection (SBD) for English and call for a renewed research interest in this foundational first step in natural language processing. We observe severe limitations in comparability and reproducibility of earlier work and a general lack of knowledge about genre- and domain-specific variations. To overcome these barriers, we conduct a systematic empirical survey of a large number of extant approaches, across a broad range of diverse corpora. We further observe that much previous work interpreted the SBD task too narrowly, leading to overly optimistic estimates of SBD performance on running text. To better relate SBD to practical NLP use cases, we thus propose a generalized definition of the task, eliminating text- or language-specific assumptions about candidate boundary points. More specifically, we quantify degrees of variation across 'standard' corpora of edited, relatively formal language, as well as performance degradation when moving to less formal language, viz. various samples of user-generated Web content. For these latter types of text, we demonstrate how moderate interpretation of document structure (as is now often available more or less explicitly through mark-up) can substantially contribute to overall SBD performance.

KEYWORDS: Sentence Boundary Detection, Segmentation, Comparability, Reproducibility.

Proceedings of COLING 2012: Posters, pages 985–994,
COLING 2012, Mumbai, December 2012.

1 Motivation and Introduction

Sentence Boundary Detection (SBD) is not widely counted among the grand challenges in NLP. Even though there were comparatively few studies on SBD in the past decades, the assessment of extant techniques for English is hindered by variation in the task definition, choice of evaluation metrics, and test data used. Furthermore, two development trends in NLP pose new challenges for SBD, viz. (a) a shift of emphasis from formal, edited text towards more spontaneous language samples, e.g. Web content; and (b) a gradual move from 'bare' ASCII to *rich* text, exploiting the much wider Unicode character range as well as mark-up of text structure. The impact of such textual variation on SBD is hardly explored, and off-the-shelf technologies may perform poorly on text that is not very newswire-like, i.e. different from the venerable Wall Street Journal (WSJ) collection of the Penn Treebank (PTB; Marcus et al., 1993).

In this work, we seek to provide a comprehensive, up-to-date, and fully reproducible assessment of the state of the art in SBD. In much NLP research, the 'sentence' (in a suitable interpretation; see below) is a *foundational* unit, for example in aligning parallel texts; PoS tagging; syntactic, semantic, and discourse parsing; or machine translation. Assuming gold-standard sentence boundaries (and possibly tokenisation)—as provided by standard data sets like the PTB—has been common practice for many isolated studies. However, strong effects of error propagation must be expected in standard NLP pipelines, for example of imperfect SBD into morpho-syntactic, semantic, or discourse analysis (Walker et al., 2001; Kiss and Strunk, 2002). For these reasons, we aim to determine (a) what levels of performance can be expected from extant SBD techniques; (b) to which degree SBD performance is sensitive to variation in text types; and (c) whether there are relevant differences in observed behavior across different SBD approaches.

Our own motivation in this work is twofold: First, working in the context of semi-automated parser adaptation to domain and genre variation, we would hope to encourage a shift of emphasis towards parsing as an end-to-end task, i.e. taking as its point of departure the running text of a document collection rather than idealized resources comprised of 'pure' text with manually annotated, gold-standard sentence and token boundaries. Second, in preparing new annotated language resources (encompassing a broader range of different text types), we wish to identify and adapt extant preprocessing tool(s) that are best suited to our specific needs—both to minimize the need for correction in manual annotation and to maximize quality in automatically produced annotations. Finally, we felt prompted into systematizing this work by a recent query (for SBD technology, a recurrent topic) to the CORPORA mailing list[1], where a wealth of subjective recommendations were offered, but very few 'hard' empirical results.

This article first offers a concise summary of previous SBD work (§ 2) and data sets and evaluation metrics applicable to SBD (§ 3).[2] For nine publicly available SBD technologies and against four 'standard' data sets, § 4 surveys the current state of the art. Next, § 5 turns to trends in 'Web-scale' NLP sketched earlier, viz. processing more informal, more varied language: here, we extend the experimental SBD survey with results on a variety of samples of user-generated content and quantify the potential contribution of mark-up analysis to SBD. Throughout the text, we use the term *sentence* in a non-syntactic sense, viz. to refer to all types of root-level utterances (including, for example, noun or verb phrases), i.e. text units whose relations to surrounding context are not primarily of a syntactic but rather of a rhetorical, discourse-level nature. Nunberg (1990) coins the term *text-sentence* for this unit, and his definition seems to capture well the variation of segment types we find in our various gold-standard SBD data sets.

[1] See `http://listserv.linguistlist.org/cgi-bin/wa?A2=CORPORA;545fc67c.1208`.

[2] For comparability in future work, all our resources are available at `http://svn.delph-in.net/odc/`.

2 Previous Work on Sentence Segmentation

Approaches to sentence segmentation broadly fall into three classes: (a) *rule-based* SBD, using hand-crafted heuristics and lists (of abbreviations, for example); (b) machine learning approaches to SBD trained in a *supervised* setup, i.e. on text annotated with gold-standard boundaries; and (c) *unsupervised* applications of machine learning, requiring only raw, unannotated corpora. There is comparatively little SBD research literature, and with some notable exceptions, published studies focus on machine learning approaches. Conversely, as we see in § 4 below, many existing tools actually rely on heuristic approaches, but these have very rarely been compared empirically to each other or to the performance of machine learning techniques. As such, despite an imbalance in available literature, the choice of SBD approach and relevant trade-offs—e.g. in terms of maximum accuracy vs. robustness to variations in text types—have remained open questions, both methodologically and technologically.

Riley (1989) presents an early application of machine learning to SBD, investigating the use of decision tree classifiers in determining whether instances of full stops (periods, in American English) mark sentence boundaries. As we argue in § 3 below, limiting SBD to the disambiguation of a single punctuation mark (or a small set of such) is an overly narrow interpretation of the task—even for formal, edited language—albeit quite characteristic for the vast majority of SBD research reports. The approach of Riley (1989) utilizes features including the probabilities of words being sentence-final or -initial, word length, and word case. When training on 25 million words of AP newswire and testing on the Brown Corpus (Francis and Kucera, 1982), they report an accuracy of 99.8%.

The SATZ system (Palmer and Hearst, 1997) performs sentence segmentation using models of the part-of-speech distribution of the context surrounding a potential sentence boundary. The basis of the system involves representing contextual words as vectors of binary values with elements that indicate whether or not a part-of-speech tag is plausible for that word. Evaluating their system against WSJ text, they report an error rate of 1.1% using a neural net, and 1.0% using a decision tree. Creating a hybrid system by integrating their classifier with a heuristics-based approach, reduces the error rate to 0.5%.

Reynar and Ratnaparkhi (1997) employ supervised Maximum Entropy learning. Both their system variants treat segmentation as a disambiguation task, wherein every token containing '!', '.' or '?' is a potential sentence boundary. The first system aims for premium in-domain performance, using features targeting English financial use (e.g. identification of honorifics and corporate designations). The second system is designed to be more portable and uses domain-independent features, including a list of abbreviations derived from the training data. Testing on both WSJ text and the Brown Corpus, they report accuracies of 98.8% and 97.9%, respectively, for the domain-dependent system, and of 98.0% and 97.5%, respectively, for the portable system. More recently, Gillick (2009) discusses further feature development for supervised classification, but concentrates on the narrower problem of full stops as candidate boundaries. The best configuration of his system, `Splitta`, employs Support Vector Machines as a learning framework, with reported error rates of 0.25% on WSJ and 0.36% on Brown.

Mikheev (2002) treats sentence segmentation with a small set of rules based on determining whether the words to the left or right of a potential sentence boundary are abbreviations or proper names (which are derived from heuristics on unlabeled training data). Mikheev (2002) reports an error rate of 0.45% on WSJ text and 0.28% on the Brown Corpus. Combining this approach with a supervised part-of-speech tagger that includes tags for end of sentence markers (Mikheev, 2000) further reduces the error rates to 0.31% and 0.20%, respectively.

A fully unsupervised system, Punkt, is presented by Kiss and Strunk (2006). The approach is rooted in the identification of abbreviations, by finding collocational bonds between candidates and full stops. Their reported rate of errors on 'classic' test sets is 1.02% (Brown) and 1.65% (WSJ), but further experiments on other data sets demonstrate the system's usefulness across a broad variety of text types and languages.

3 Reflections: SBD Resources and Metrics

Comparability and reproducibility are lacking in previous work, due to divergent interpretations of the SBD task and often vaguely specified test sets and evaluation metrics. Different assumptions about which and how many candidate boundary points to consider, for example, directly impact the relative difficulty of the task; likewise, although much previous work involved one or both of WSJ and Brown texts, historically there have been different (more or less) annotated versions of these resources, and several published studies indicate that preparation of SBD test data from these sources involved some amount of manual 'correction'. In order to conduct a more systematic survey, we assembled various publicly available data sets where both raw text and gold-standard sentence segmentation were possible to download or reconstruct. We also suggest a formal, generalized definition of the SBD task that we feel better represents the practical problem, from the point of view of an NLP pipeline.

Gold-Standard Data Sets Our aim is to produce data sets that are as faithful as possible to the original text form, including paragraph breaks. For some continuity with previous work, we use both WSJ and Brown Corpus data, which required some corpus archaeology and reconstruction. An alignment between the original text of the WSJ (last released in 1995 as LDC #95T07) and the annotations in the PTB has recently been published (Dridan and Oepen, 2012), and we thus start from raw, untokenised text and superimpose onto it 7,706 PTB gold-standard sentence boundaries (from Sections 3–6, the 'classic' SBD subset). Various versions of the Brown Corpus exist, but none correspond exactly to the original raw text. For our SBD tests, we combine sentence segmentation in the tagged Brown Corpus (distributed with the Natural Language Toolkit, NLTK) with the 'raw', so-called *Bergen Form I*[3] as a reference for automatically reversing tokenisation, quote disambiguation, and some artifacts that appear only in the tagged version. As in previous work, we also occasionally corrected the segmentation (often related to paragraph-initial quote marks, which in the tagged data can occur as a 'sentence' by themselves), and restored punctuation to better match the original raw text—for a total of 57,275 sentences.

We also used more recently released data, to explore a wider range of edited text types and introduce 'fresh' test data. The Conan Doyle Corpus (CDC) was used in the 2012 *SEM Shared Task (Morante and Blanco, 2012), and provides various Sherlock Holmes stories in both raw and segmented versions, albeit for only 5,692 sentences. Then, from quite a different domain, the GENIA Corpus, a collection of 16,392 sentences from biomedical research abstracts (Kim et al., 2003), also contains the required boundary annotation. The use of these additional corpora allows us to assess the generality of the various tools, which is particularly important as WSJ and Brown data has been central in much previous SBD development.

Task Definition and Evaluation In much previous work, SBD was operationalized as a binary classification of a fixed number of candidate boundary points—restricted to, for example, full stops, token-final full stops, or a small set of sentence-terminating punctuation. While this makes for a clean machine learning task, we consider that it over-simplifies the SBD problem, specifically in not directly penalizing for missing gold-standard boundary points that do not fall

[3] As described at `http://icame.uib.no/brown/bcm.html`.

CoreNLP	R	18.7	http://nlp.stanford.edu/software/corenlp.shtml
GATE	R	60.6	http://gate.ac.uk
LingPipe	R	1.7	http://alias-i.com/lingpipe/
MxTerminator	S	2.8	ftp://ftp.cis.upenn.edu/pub/adwait/jmx/
OpenNLP	S	2.2	http://opennlp.apache.org/
Punkt	U	7.1	http://nltk.org/api/nltk.tokenize.html
RASP	R	0.3	http://ilexir.co.uk/applications/rasp/
Splitta	S	31.5	http://code.google.com/p/splitta
tokenizer	R	0.3	http://www.cis.uni-muenchen.de/~wastl/misc/

Table 1: Overview of publicly available SBD systems in our survey. The table columns indicate, from left to right, the general approach (rule-based, supervised, or unsupervised); total (wall-clock) number of seconds to segment the Brown Corpus on an unloaded workstation; and download site.

onto a classification candidate. Even on the edited 'standard' texts in our survey, the percentage of sentences ending in a full stop is only 87.7 (91.9% for sentence-final '.', '?', or '!'). We anticipate that this percentage will drop further in less formal texts. Thus, to give a more representative picture of how the sentence segmenters succeed in segmenting raw running text, we propose a more general definition of the task, which considers the positions after *every* character as a potential boundary point. Hence, any gold-standard boundary missed will be counted as a false negative, even if there was no punctuation mark at that point. This makes the set of candidate boundaries not only much larger, but also very heavily weighted towards the negative, uninteresting class. As such, we evaluate SBD in terms of precision, recall, and F_1 over boundary points, since accuracy or error rate (used in much of the previous work) would be both less informative and more difficult to compare for the task as defined here.

4 Surveying the State of the Art

Our survey covers nine publicly-available SBD systems and toolkits with sentence segmentation components, as summarized in Table 1.[4] Although purely technical aspects (e.g. supported platforms or available APIs) are not in focus here, we seek to provide a coarse indication of run-time efficiency in terms of total processing time when segmenting the Brown Corpus as one single document. For high-throughput use cases, the comparatively 'lean', heuristic systems RASP and tokenizer—building on the Un*x (f)lex tool in the tradition of Grefenstette and Tapanainen (1994)—may have an advantage. Note that one tool offers two pre-packaged configurations: one for 'general' text, here dubbed $\texttt{LingPipe}_1$, and another tuned to bio-medical literature and specifically the GENIA Corpus, $\texttt{LingPipe}_2$. We were unable to obtain implementations for the earlier studies of Palmer and Hearst (1997) and Mikheev (2002).

Table 2 presents SBD performance levels for our nine systems and four corpora in a first, off-the-shelf experiment. Here, we sought to run each tool in its default configuration—often instantiating sample invocations or API calls, where available—and in a setup we consider representative for an NLP pipeline: processing each corpus as a contiguous text stream. For Punkt, we rely on the implementation and pre-trained model for English that ships with NLTK (Bird et al., 2009). Recall from § 3 above that our corpus preparation preserves in-text paragraph boundaries (as indicated in plain raw text by consecutive double line breaks); where a corpus internally is comprised of multiple segments (e.g. the distinct sections of the PTB or separate stories in CDC), we inserted paragraph breaks between segments.

In this first experiment, we see stark variation between tools and across corpora. We were

[4] The table also includes a tenth system, the GATE text processing environment. However, we have not been able to empirically determine its SBD performance, as GATE (at least in its standard configuration) often fails to reproduce the full input in its output (for example dropping parts of date expressions or sentence-initial quote marks).

	Brown	CDC	GENIA	WSJ	All
`CoreNLP`	87.7	72.1	98.8	91.3	89.1
`LingPipe`$_1$	94.9	87.6	98.3	97.3	95.2
`LingPipe`$_2$	93.0	86.3	**99.6**	88.0	93.2
`MxTerminator`	94.7	97.9	98.3	97.4	95.8
`OpenNLP`	96.6	**98.6**	98.8	99.1	**97.4**
`Punkt`	96.4	98.7	99.3	98.3	97.3
`RASP`	**96.8**	96.1	98.9	99.0	**97.4**
`Splitta`	95.4	96.1	99.0	**99.2**	96.5
`tokenizer`	94.9	**98.6**	98.6	97.9	96.2

Table 2: Out-of-the-box SBD performance (F_1 over sentence boundary points) over a sample of edited English corpora. Note that many of the tools were trained on or tuned towards variants of WSJ, Brown, or GENIA, and hence some of the scores may overestimate general performance on these text types.

surprised at comparatively low performance levels for some of the tools (e.g. `CoreNLP` and `MxTerminator`), and further note that some systems seem far less robust to corpus variation than others, in particular showing relatively drastic performance drops on CDC (e.g. `CoreNLP`, `LingPipe`, `RASP`, or `Splitta`). To investigate this variation, we performed a coarse error analysis and found two main issues: First, not all SBD tools interpret paragraph boundaries, whereas forcing sentence boundaries there would seem a strong and practical heuristic rule. Second, sentence-final punctuation can of course be followed by closing quotation marks,[5] and it appears that the ‘modern’ Unicode quotes in CDC are not recognized by all tools.

To control for these factors, we ran a second batch of experiments and allowed what we consider a reasonable amount of preprocessing of input texts, to better match tool-internal assumptions: (a) slicing our corpora into separate ‘documents’ at paragraph boundaries, i.e. effectively forcing sentence boundaries there; (b) substituting Unicode directional quote marks ⟨‘ ’ “ ”⟩ with straight ASCII quotes ⟨' "⟩ or (c) substituting Unicode quotes with the directional variants used in LaTeX and the PTB ⟨` ' `` ''⟩.[6] Table 3 shows resulting SBD performance, where for each system we ran an additional four configurations—with or without paragraph slicing, and applying either scheme of quote substitution—and report the best-performing setup.

The results in Table 3 no longer show surprising outliers and, in our view, offer better indicators of available performance levels across text types. Only in very few cases do we observe performance levels as suggested by some previous reports (e.g. 99.8 for `LingPipe`$_2$ on GENIA and 99.1 and 99.2 for `OpenNLP` and `Splitta`, respectively, on WSJ)—and these are very likely owed to training or tuning against these very data sets. In this regard, CDC may be our most independent indicator of SBD performance, although we note that due to its fictional nature it is especially rich in quoted speech. The unsupervised system in this survey, `Punkt`, appears reasonably competitive on Brown, CDC, and GENIA and achieves an overall fifth rank (outperforming `CoreNLP`, `LingPipe`$_2$, `MxTerminator`, and `Splitta`). In our view, these results bode well for adaptability to new text types or languages. At the same time, comparatively poor performance of `Punkt` on WSJ text may be a key reason for its ‘not quite state-of-the-art’ reputation. In future work, it would be interesting to break down corpus properties that affect SBD performance and, thus, seek to identify which WSJ characteristics prove especially challenging for the unsupervised machine-learning approach.

[5]This is the case for question marks and exclamation points in both prevalent typographic conventions for quotations, which are at times called American- and British-style. Further, full stops (and also commas, though these are not typically sentence boundary cues) can precede a closing quotation mark in American-style typography.

[6]We note that either quote substitution scheme may introduce low-level technical hurdles into the NLP pipeline, as scheme (b) loses the distinction between opening and closing quote marks, while scheme (c) substitutes two characters for one, which may complicate book-keeping of character points against the original document.

	Brown	CDC	GENIA	WSJ	All
CoreNLP	$^{+}$93.6	$^{L+}$98.3	$^{+}$99.0	$^{+}$94.8	95.0
LingPipe$_1$	$^{+}$96.6	$^{A+}$99.1	$^{+}$98.6	$^{+}$98.7	97.4
LingPipe$_2$	$^{+}$94.5	$^{+}$97.2	$^{+}$**99.8**	$^{+}$90.9	95.3
MxTerminator	$^{+}$96.5	$^{+}$98.6	$^{+}$98.5	$^{+}$98.5	97.2
OpenNLP	96.6	98.6	98.8	99.1	97.4
Punkt	96.4	98.7	99.3	98.3	97.3
RASP	96.8	^{A}99.1	98.9	99.0	**97.6**
Splitta	95.4	^{A}96.7	99.0	**99.2**	96.5
tokenizer	$^{+}$**96.9**	$^{+}$**99.2**	$^{+}$98.9	$^{+}$**99.2**	**97.6**

Table 3: Best-case SBD performance. Results prefixed with '+' indicate forcing sentence boundaries at paragraph breaks, while the '*A*' and '*L*' prefixes mark substitution of Unicode quotes to ASCII or LaTeX-style, respectively. Non-prefixed scores are repeated from Table 2 for ease of comparison.

Among the supervised machine-learning tools, MxTerminator and OpenNLP show very similar results, confirming OpenNLP as essentially a reimplementation of Reynar and Ratnaparkhi (1997), if maybe with a slight edge over the original. Splitta, representing the most recent SBD study applying supervised learning, on the other hand, is outranked by OpenNLP by almost one full F_1 point. It further shows comparatively larger drops on Brown and CDC, which taken together with its premium performance on WSJ could be suggestive of limited robustness to text variation (or over-tuning effects). Three of the rule-based tools, in this survey, show comparable behavior: LingPipe$_1$ (the 'generic' variant), RASP, and tokenizer all deliver relatively good results across the board and show comparatively limited sensitivity to variation in text types. Keeping in mind the caveat of being developed against the exact same type of texts, LingPipe$_2$ on GENIA confirms the potential benefits from SBD adaptation to a specific genre and domain. Finally, CoreNLP and LingPipe differ in architecture from the other rule-based systems, in that they apply SBD to a stream of tokens rather than a raw text stream. Hence, overall lower performance in CoreNLP could in principle be an effect of error propagation from the preceding tokenisation phase (Dridan and Oepen, 2012), or may just be owed to this (part of a larger) system not being as thoroughly engineered as the specialized RASP or tokenizer rule sets.

5 SBD for More Informal, User-Generated Content

To extend our survey to rather different types of text—user-generated Web content (UGC)—we ran similar experiments on two recent corpora that come with gold-standard sentence boundary annotations: First, the WeScience Corpus of Ytrestøl et al. (2009) comprises some 12,000 sentences from Wikipedia, drawing on a sample of articles in the NLP domain. Second, the WeSearch Data Collection (WDC; Read et al., 2012) includes gold-standard annotations for two smaller samples of Web blogs, some 1,000 sentences each in the NLP and Linux domains, respectively (dubbed WNB and WLB in Table 4 below). As none of our SBD tools fully supports mark-up processing, we reduced the WeScience and WDC corpora into a pure text form, only keeping paragraph breaks from the original mark-up in a first experimental setup dubbed *A* in Table 4. A variant experiment, dubbed *B* below, aims to gauge the potential contribution of mark-up to SBD, where we insert additional paragraph boundaries around block elements like headings, pre-formatted text, and individual elements of lists.

Comparing variants *A* and *B* in Table 4, there is no doubt that forcing sentence boundaries around select mark-up elements much improves SBD on the two blog fragments, even if our WNB and WLB scores draw on comparatively small test sets. Therefore, we focus on setup *B* in the subsequent discussion. Intuitively, there is a decline in linguistic formality along the horizontal dimension of Table 4: in spite of greater author diversity in Wikipedia, personal blogs are likely less thoroughly edited and possibly more creative in their language use; furthermore,

	WeScience		WNB		WLB	
	A	*B*	*A*	*B*	*A*	*B*
`CoreNLP`$^{+L}$	90.0	97.9	95.3	96.4	89.1	90.9
`LingPipe`$_1^{+A}$	90.0	98.1	94.8	96.1	92.4	94.2
`LingPipe`$_2^{+}$	89.8	98.0	94.4	95.6	92.7	94.5
`MxTerminator`$^{+}$	89.5	97.2	94.7	95.9	90.3	92.2
`OpenNLP`	90.2	97.9	95.3	96.5	90.2	92.0
`Punkt`	89.9	97.7	**95.6**	96.7	92.8	94.5
`RASP`^{A}	**91.0**	99.1	95.4	96.6	92.8	94.6
`Splitta`^{A}	**91.0**	98.9	94.0	95.5	91.2	93.4
`tokenizer`$^{+}$	**91.0**	**99.2**	**95.6**	**96.8**	**93.1**	**94.9**

Table 4: SBD performance over a sample of user-generated English content. Paragraph slicing and quote substitution were applied as per the individual best-case configurations on CDC, as indicated in Table 3.

bloggers in the Linux domain may care less about linguistic form than NLP bloggers, and quite possibly make more use of technical 'slang'. Average SBD performance levels appear to match these intuitions, where top Wikipedia scores in fact are higher than the best average F_1 over our 'formal' corpora in Table 3 above. We conjecture that this difference is probably owed to our mark-up processing and a relatively high proportion of headings and list elements.

While average performance levels on WNB and especially WLB are markedly lower, the magnitudes of differences in system scores seem somewhat reduced in all UGC experiments. However, we see several earlier observations confirmed, with `tokenizer` first and `RASP` (in total) a close second—consistently across data sets (despite a potential bias in favour of `tokenizer` on WeScience due to its use in the construction of that corpus). Relative ranks of most other tools vary somewhat with the data sets, suggesting variable robustness to pertinent stylistic elements. Still, `OpenNLP` (on average) improves mildly over `MxTerminator`, whereas among the rule-based systems `LingPipe`$_1$ now often patterns more with `CoreNLP` than with the top performers. Maybe most notably, the unsupervised `Punkt` performs close to the top scores for WDC. It would be interesting to extend the survey further towards more 'noisy' Web text.

6 Conclusions—Future Work

In this work, we have sought to compile a comprehensive and fair assessment of the state of the art in sentence boundary detection—both for our own benefit and in the hope that this survey may be of wider interest. To better relate to practical use cases of SBD as a foundational element in the NLP pipeline, we generalize the task definition to recovering *all* gold-standard sentence boundaries in *running* text. For this more realistic definition of the task, performance levels upwards of 99% (as previously reported) are not generally available. Our results establish, for the first time, comparability and reproducibility across a broad range of approaches and text types, including novel test corpora and a systematic exploration of performance degradation along the dimension of linguistic formality. We anticipate possible further calibration in dialogue with tool developers and plan on publishing our data sets and results as part of the *State of the Art* Section on the ACL Wiki. In doing so, we hope to stimulate new research in SBD, particularly aiming to improve performance on 'noisy' language, increase robustness to domain and genre variation, and take better advantage of rich text properties and structure.

In ongoing work, we aim to combine some of the attractions in unsupervised learning with the robustness of heuristic rules, for example extending a tool like `tokenizer` with automatically acquired and domain-adapted lists of abbreviations. Furthermore, we believe that tighter integration of mark-up processing and SBD is a prerequisite to better results on user-generated Web content. Some of the tools in our survey (notably `GATE`) provide some HTML support, and we hope to assess the efficacy of mark-up modes, where available, in the near future.

References

Bird, S., Klein, E., and Loper, E. (2009). *Natural Language Processing with Python*. O'Reilly, Beijing.

Dridan, R. and Oepen, S. (2012). Tokenization. Returning to a long solved problem. A survey, contrastive experiment, recommendations, and toolkit. In *Proceedings of the 50th Meeting of the Association for Computational Linguistics*, page 378–382, Jeju, Republic of Korea.

Francis, W. N. and Kucera, H. (1982). *Frequency Analysis of English Usage*. Houghton Mifflin Co., New York.

Gillick, D. (2009). Sentence boundary detection and the problem with the U.S. In *Proceedings of Human Language Technologies: The 2009 Annual Conference of the North American Chapter of the Association for Computational Linguistics, Companion Volume: Short Papers*, page 241–244, Boulder, CO, USA.

Grefenstette, G. and Tapanainen, P. (1994). What is a word, what is a sentence? Problems of tokenization. In *Proceedings of the 3rd Conference on Computational Lexicography and Text Research*, page 79–87, Budapest, Hungary.

Kim, J.-D., Ohta, T., Teteisi, Y., and Tsujii, J. (2003). GENIA corpus — a semantically annotated corpus for bio-textmining. *Bioinformatics*, 19:i180–i182.

Kiss, T. and Strunk, J. (2002). Viewing sentence boundary detection as collocation identification. In *Proceedings of 6. Konferenz zur Varabeitung natürlicher Sprache*, page 75–82, Saarbrücken, Germany.

Kiss, T. and Strunk, J. (2006). Unsupervised multilingual sentence boundary detection. *Computational Linguistics*, 32(4):485–525.

Marcus, M., Santorini, B., and Marcinkiewicz, M. A. (1993). Building a large annotated corpora of English: The Penn Treebank. *Computational Linguistics*, 19:313–330.

Mikheev, A. (2000). Tagging sentence boundaries. In *Proceedings of the 1st Meeting of the North American Chapter of the Association for Computational Linguistics*, page 264–271, Seattle, WA, USA.

Mikheev, A. (2002). Periods, capitalized words, etc. *Computational Linguistics*, 28(3):289–318.

Morante, R. and Blanco, E. (2012). *SEM 2012 shared task: Resolving the scope and focus of negation. In *Proceedings of the 1st Joint Conference on Lexical and Computational Semantics*, page 265–274, Montréal, Canada.

Nunberg, G. (1990). *The Linguistics of Punctuation*. Number 18 in Lecture Notes. CSLI Publications, Stanford, CA.

Palmer, D. D. and Hearst, M. A. (1997). Adaptive multilingual sentence boundary disambiguation. *Computational Linguistics*, 23(2):242–267.

Read, J., Flickinger, D., Dridan, R., Oepen, S., and Øvrelid, L. (2012). The WeSearch Corpus, Treebank, and Treecache. A comprehensive sample of user-generated content. In *Proceedings of the 8th International Conference on Language Resources and Evaluation*, Istanbul, Turkey.

Reynar, J. C. and Ratnaparkhi, A. (1997). A maximum entropy approach to identifying sentence boundaries. In *Proceedings of the 5th Conference on Applied Natural Language Processing*, page 16–19, Washington, D.C., USA.

Riley, M. D. (1989). Some applications of tree-based modelling to speech and language. In *Proceedings of the DARPA Speech and Natural Language Workshop*, page 339–352.

Walker, D. J., Clements, D. E., Darwin, M., and Amtrup, J. W. (2001). Sentence boundary detection: A comparison of paradigms for improving MT quality. In *Proceedings of the MT Summit VIII*, Santiago de Compostela, Spain.

Ytrestøl, G., Oepen, S., and Flickinger, D. (2009). Extracting and annotating Wikipedia sub-domains. In *Proceedings of the 7th International Workshop on Treebanks and Linguistic Theories*, page 185–197, Groningen, The Netherlands.

Document and Corpus Level Inference For Unsupervised and Transductive Learning of Information Structure of Scientific Documents

Roi Reichart *Anna Korhonen*
The Computer Laboratory, University of Cambridge, UK
Roi.Reichart@cl.cam.ac.uk, alk23@cam.ac.uk

ABSTRACT
Inferring the information structure of scientific documents has proved useful for supporting information access across scientific disciplines. Current approaches are largely supervised and expensive to port to new disciplines. We investigate primarily unsupervised discovery of information structure. We introduce a novel graphical model that can consider different types of prior knowledge about the task: within-document discourse patterns, cross-document sentence similarity information based on linguistic features, and prior knowledge about the correct classification of some of the input sentences when this information is available. We apply the model to Argumentative Zoning (AZ) scheme and evaluate it on a fully unsupervised learning scenario and two transduction scenarios where the categories of some test sentences are known. The model substantially outperforms similarity and topic model based clustering approaches as well as traditional transduction algorithms.

TITLE AND ABSTRACT IN FINNISH

Dokumentti- ja korpustason inferenssiin perustuva ohjaamattomankoneoppimisen tekniikka tieteellisen julkaisujen rakenteen analyysissa

Tieteellisten julkaisujen rakenteen analyysi voi tukea tietojen saatavuutta eri tieteenaloilta. Nykyiset koneoppimismetodit ovat pitkälti ohjattuja ja niiden soveltaminen uusille tieteenaloille on kallista. Tämä artikkeli tutkii pääasiassa ohjaamatonta julkaisujen rakenteen analyysia. Lähtökohtana on uusi graafinen malli, joka pystyy integoimaan erilaista etukäteistietoa tehtävästä: dokumenttien sisäisen diskurssin, dokumenttienvälisten samankaltaisuuden kielellisten ominaisuuksien suhteen, ja tietoa joidenkin lauseiden oikeasta luokittelusta, silloin kun tämänkaltaista tietoa on saatavilla. Malli sovellettiin Argumentative Zoning (AZ) -analyysiin ja sen soveltuvuutta täysin ohjaamattomaan oppimiseen sekä transduktio-oppimiseen, jossa joidenkin testilauseiden luokat on tiedossa, tutkittiin. Malli osoittautuu huomattavasti tarkemmaksi kuin samankaltaisuuteen ja klusterointiin perustuvat vertailumallit sekä perinteiset transduktio-algoritmit.

KEYWORDS: Information structure, Argumentative Zoning , Approximate Inference.

FINNISH KEYWORDS: Rakenteen analyysi, Argumentative Zoning , Approksimoitu Inferenssi.

Proceedings of COLING 2012: Posters, pages 995–1006,
COLING 2012, Mumbai, December 2012.

1 Introduction

Information structure of scientific literature (i.e. the way scientists communicate their ideas, methods, results, conclusions, and so forth, to their audience) has been a topic of intense research within different disciplines (Taboada and Mann, 2006; Argamon et al., 2008; Deane et al., 2008; Lungen et al., 2010). Within Natural Language Processing (NLP), various schemes have been proposed for describing the information structure of scientific documents. These have been based on, for example, section names found in documents (Lin et al., 2006; Hirohata et al., 2008), rhetorical or argumentative zones (AZ) of sentences (Teufel and Moens, 2002; Mizuta et al., 2006; Teufel et al., 2009), qualitative aspects of scientific information (Shatkay et al., 2008) or core scientific concepts (Liakata et al., 2010).

Previous works have shown that it is possible to classify sentences in scientific documents according to the categories of such schemes (e.g. the Background, Method, Results and Conclusions categories of the AZ scheme) using supervised methods. These methods perform very well and their output has proved useful for important tasks such as information retrieval and extraction (Teufel, 2001; Teufel and Moens, 2002; Mizuta et al., 2006; Tbahriti et al., 2006; Ruch et al., 2007). This comes, however, with a heavy cost of requiring thousands of manually annotated sentences to achieve good performance. Even the weakly supervised approach by (Guo and Korhonen, 2011) requires hundreds of annotated sentences for optimal performance.

In this paper we focus on a primarily unsupervised approach to inferring information structure which avoids the high annotation cost of the supervised approaches. The only previous work on this topic that we are aware of is that of (Varge et al., 2012) who proposed a simple word-level Latent Dirichlet Allocation (LDA) model to the task, assuming that the phenomenon is mostly lexical. As we show in this paper, the information structure of scientific documents is governed by a number of additional factors, which calls for a more expressive model.

We propose a more sophisticated and flexible model capable of integrating different types of task knowledge, depending on the knowledge available in a real-life situation. We investigate two scenarios: (1) the fully unsupervised scenario where no manually annotated sentences are available; and (2) the transductive scenario (Gammerman et al., 1998) where the classes of some of the test set sentences are given. The transductive scenario is of particular interest when some test time knowledge about the document collection is available that could benefit learning. Examples of such knowledge are lexical cues (e.g. key words associated with a database index) for test sentences from a particular target category or sentence annotations that can be obtained fast for a small fraction of test data (e.g. using mechanical turk annotators).

Our model can take into account three types of knowledge about the task: (1) within-document discourse patterns; (2) linguistic feature representation used to model cross-document sentence similarity; and (3) in the transductive scenario, prior knowledge about the correct classification of some of the input sentences. Importantly, none of these knowledge types are actually required by the model, but the flexibility of the model enables us to consider all of them or only a subset.

We formulate our approach as a graphical model that encodes sentence-level knowledge via single-vertex potentials and knowledge about sets of sentences, both within and between documents, via global potentials. While these potentials encode important linguistic properties, they complicate the inference process. We therefore apply a linear-programming (LP) relaxation method (Sontag et al., 2008) which approximates the maximum aposteriori (MAP) assignment of our model. In our experiments the algorithm provably finds the exact MAP assignment.

We compare the predictions of our model to those of argumentative zoning (AZ) – a widely used information structure scheme (Teufel and Moens, 2002) where the core categories are argued to be domain-independent and which has been used to analyse texts in various disciplines such as computational linguistics (Teufel and Moens, 2002), law (Hachey and Grover, 2006), biology (Mizuta et al., 2006) and chemistry (Teufel et al., 2009). We experiment with the only publicly available AZ corpus: the corpus of 792 biomedical abstracts by (Guo et al., 2010) which provides AZ annotations for 7886 sentences. Our experimental evaluation shows that the model outperforms traditional algorithms for both the unsupervised and the transductive setups. by a large margin Our results show that it is possible to infer high quality knowledge about the information structure of scientific documents even when only little or no human annotation effort is involved.

2 Previous Work

Machine Learning for Information Structure Nearly all previous work on automatic detection of information structure has relied on supervised algorithms and, consequently, on corpora consisting of thousands of manually annotated sentences (Teufel and Moens, 2002; Lin et al., 2006; Hirohata et al., 2008; Shatkay et al., 2008; Teufel et al., 2009; Guo and Korhonen, 2011).

Recently, (Varge et al., 2012) were the first to apply unsupervised learning to the information structure of scientific documents. They applied standard word-level LDA models to the IMRAD scheme for the biomedical domain (along with their own information structure scheme for the aerospace domain). This purely lexical approach ignores other important linguistic phenomena, such as discourse patterns and syntactic properties, which play a role in information structure. The 35 F-score performance of their model indeed show that there is much scope for improvement. Our model integrates a much wider range of linguistic knowledge about the task at both within-document (e.g. discourse patterns) and cross-document (e.g. sentence similarity) levels, and can be flexibly applied to both fully unsupervised and transductive learning scenarios, depending on how much prior knowledge about the task is actually available. Although the transductive learning scenario can realistically occur when developing new corpora or applications, it has not been addressed in previous work on our task.

Corpus level Inference A number of recent models have obtained improved performance by sharing information between sentences and documents in large text collections (Sutton and McCallum, 2004; Taskar et al., 2002; Bunescu and Mooney, 2004; Finkel et al., 2005; Gupta et al., 2010; Rush et al., 2012; Reichart and Barzilay, 2012; Ganchev et al., 2010; Gillenwater et al., 2010; Mann and McCallum, 2010; Liang et al., 2009; Roth and Yih, 2005). We follow these works and model inter-sentence similarity across multiple scientific documents. To the best of our knowledge, this is the first model for the AZ classification task that explicitly shares information among sentences in different documents.

3 Model

Given a set of scientific documents our goal is to assign each sentence in these documents into a category that represents its role in the information structure of the document. As our data is biomedical, we use the version of the AZ scheme adapted for biology by (Mizuta et al., 2006). This version has ten zone categories. We focus on the five that appear in abstracts (as opposed to full papers): BACKGROUND, OBJECTIVE, METHODS, RESULTS, and CONCLUSIONS.[1] For a detailed

[1]Two additional categories – RELATED and FUTURE work – appear only occasionally in abstracts. Since in our corpus only 2% of the sentences were tagged with one these categories we left their exploration for future work.

definition of the zone categories and an example annotated abstract see (Guo et al., 2010).

3.1 Model Structure

We denote the number of sentences in the document collection with n and the number of target categories with K. We define an undirected graphical model (Markov Random Field, MRF) with the vertex set $V = X \cup A$, where $X = \{x_1, \ldots, x_n\}$ consists of one vertex for every sentence in the document collection, and $A = \{a_1 \ldots a_K\}$ is a set of agreement vertices.

We integrate knowledge in the model through *singleton potentials* (defined over individual vertices) as well as *pairwise potentials* (defined between pairs of vertices). We consider the following types of knowledge: **(1) Within-Document Discourse Patterns** which encode the information conveyed by discourse patterns about the progress of information categories along a document. The discourse knowledge is encoded through within-document pairwise potentials as well as singleton potentials, both defined over vertices in X. **(2) Cross-Document Sentence Similarity** which encourages similar sentences in different documents to be assigned in the same category. This knowledge is encoded through cross-document pairwise potentials, defined over vertices in X, and through potentials between sentence vertices (X) and the agreement vertices (A). **(3) Class-Specific Lexical Cues** Encode lexical cues for the cluster of a given sentence through within-document pairwise potentials. **(4) Prior Knowledge on Sentence Categorization** which encodes prior knowledge about the categories of a predefined set of sentences through local potentials.

We use five types of potentials: (1) The singleton potentials encode context-free knowledge that does not depend on neighbouring vertices. (2) The pairwise potentials between sentence vertices in the same document encode discourse patterns that govern the information flow in the document. (3) The pairwise potentials between sentence vertices (X) in different documents encode the similarity between the sentences. The more similar a pair of sentences, the stronger the tendency of its members to be assigned to the same category. (4) The pairwise potentials between sentence vertices (X) and agreement vertices (A) encoded a tendency of sentences in different documents to be assigned to the same category based on sentence similarity patterns in their documents. In the last two potential types, the similarity between sentences is based on linguistic features. Finally, (5) the pairwise potentials between agreement vertices ensure that $category(a_i) = category(a_{i-1}) + 1$ by giving an infinite bonus to those assignments.

The resulting maximum aposteriori problem (MAP) takes the form of:

$$MAP(V) = \sum_{i=1}^{n} \theta_i(x_i) + \sum_{i=1}^{n}\sum_{j=1}^{n} \theta_{i,j}(x_i, x_j) + \sum_{i=1}^{n}\sum_{j=1}^{K} \phi_{i,j}(x_i, a_j) + \sum_{i=1}^{K}\sum_{j=1}^{K} \xi_{i,j}(a_i, a_j)$$

We define the singleton and the pairwise potentials to take the following forms[2]:

$$\theta_i(x_i) = \left\{ \begin{array}{ll} \alpha & \text{if discourse pattern holds} \\ \infty & \text{if prior sentence-classification condition holds} \\ 0 & \text{otherwise} \end{array} \right\}$$

$$\theta_{i,j}(x_i, x_j) = \left\{ \begin{array}{ll} \beta & \text{if discourse pattern holds} \\ SimScore_{i,j} & \text{if similarity condition holds} \\ 0 & \text{otherwise} \end{array} \right\}$$

$$\phi_{i,j}(x_i, a_j) = \left\{ \begin{array}{ll} \gamma & \text{if similarity pattern holds} \\ 0 & \text{otherwise} \end{array} \right\}$$

Where $SimScore_{i,j}$ are the feature-based similarity scores computed between sentences in different documents and α, β and γ are the model parameters representing the relative strength

[2]To avoid clutter we omit the explicit definition of the pairwise potential between agreement nodes (ξ).

of the different types of knowledge. In section 3.2 we give a detailed description of the information encoded into these potentials.

3.2 Potentials and Encoded Knowledge

Within Document Discourse Patterns $\theta_{i,j}(x_i, x_j)$ and $\theta_i(x_i)$. We encode different types of knowledge through the pairwise and the singleton potentials. The pairwise potentials encode a number of discourse cues for the progress of information categories in the document: (1) Passive verbs tend to indicate category change; (2) Category change is highly likely in the opening part of a document; and (3) The closing part of a document is devoted mainly to reporting results and conclusions.

Therefore, if a sentence contains a passive verb or appears in the opening part[3] of a document, the pairwise potentials of that sentence and of its predecessor give a bonus to assignments in which a category change occur. Likewise, when moving from the opening part to the closing part of the document, the corresponding pairwise potentials encourage transition to a predefined set of clusters. [4]. The singleton potentials encode the tendency of scientific documents to start with a background knowledge related to the article, and to end with conclusions. They do so by encouraging the first sentence in each document to be in the first output category and, likewise, the last sentence in each document to be in the last output category.

Cross-Document Sentence Similarity. We build a feature representation for each vertex in X. We consider three of the feature sets described in (Guo and Korhonen, 2011): *POS* – the part-of-speech tags of the verbs in the sentence; *Location* – each document is divided into 10 parts, the location feature takes two values: the part where the sentence starts and the part where it ends; and *Object* – the words that appear as verb objects in the sentence .

We use this representation to encourage identical category assignment for similar sentences. We do this by two types of pairwise potentials: **(1) Pairwise potentials between sentence vertices ($\theta_{i,j}(x_i, x_j)$).** We define the similarity between the $i-th$ and the $j-th$ sentences, $SimScore_{i,j}$, as the number of features that have the same value in their representation. The similarity condition in the potential definition holds if the similarity score between the sentences is among the top M scores for the $i-th$ sentence; **(2) Pairwise potentials between sentence and agreement vertices ($\phi_{i,j}(x_i, a_j)$).** The similarity scores between sentences that belong to the same category tend to concentrate around the same value. Consequently a significant change in similarity between consecutive sentences is an indication of a category change. To encode this potential we scan the document from the beginning and compute the similarity between consecutive sentences. A similarity score that exceeds the maximum or deceeds the minimum of the previously observed similarity scores by a pre-defined threshold, is considered to be a class change indication [5]. For a sentence i that appears before the $j-th$ change we write $\phi(x_i, a_j) = \gamma$. The other values of this potential are set to zero. An example of two documents where a similarity pattern exists and of one document in which it does not exist (and therefore the ϕ values for its sentences with all agreement vertices are set to zero) is given in Figure 1.

[3]The opening part of a document is defined to be the first m^1 sentences, the rest of the sentences are considered to be its closing part. The average number of sentences in our abstracts is 10.3 and we set $m^1 = 4$.

[4]In our experiments we associated the last two clusters of the output scheme with the last part of the document as the AZ scheme we use for evaluation contains one cluster for results and one for conclusions.

[5]The maximum and minimum scores are computed over the sentence vertices from the previous change. For the first change the sentence vertices from the beginning of the document are considered.

Prior knowledge about Sentence Classification (Transduction) $\theta_i(x_i)$. We experiment with the conditions where we have oracle knowledge (i.e. knowledge that is taken from the gold standard) of the categories of some of the test set sentences and the model should predict the categories of the other sentences. The prior sentence-classification condition in the definition of $\theta_i(x_i)$ is simply that the category of the i-th sentence is known to be x_i.

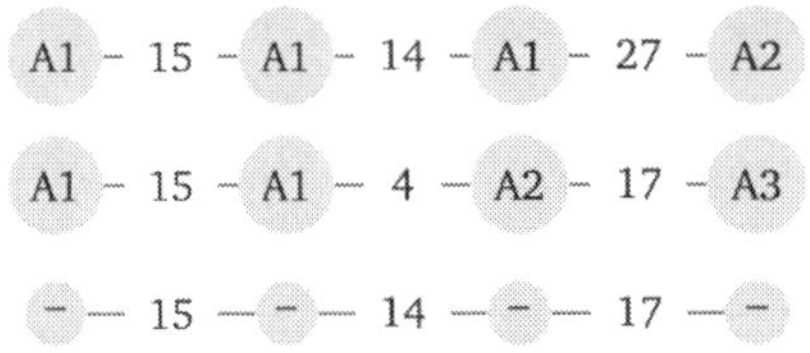

Figure 1: Three examples of similarity patterns in the beginning of documents. Lines represent documents, vertices represent sentences and the label inside a vertex corresponds to the agreement vertex to which this vertex is connected. Edges are labeled with the similarity score between the vertices they connect. The similarity difference threshold in this example is 10.

Inference Our model is a pairwise MRF. When cross-document sentence similarity knowledge is encoded, the model is very likely to have cycles which make exact inference NP-hard (see Section 3.1). When this knowledge is not encoded, the model becomes a simple linear chain model with edges between each pair of consecutive sentences in the same document. In such a model, exact inference can be done efficiently using dynamic programming. We addressed this problem by using the message passing algorithm for linear-programming (LP) relaxation of the MAP assignment (MPLP) described in (Sontag et al., 2008). LP relaxation algorithms for the MAP problem define an upper bound on the original objective which takes the form of a linear program. Consequently, a minimum of this upper bound can be found using standard LP solvers or, more efficiently, using specialised message passing algorithms (Yanover et al., 2006). The algorithm comes with an optimality guarantee: when the solution to the linear program is integral it is guaranteed to give the global optimum of the MAP problem. The MPLP algorithm described in (Sontag et al., 2008) is attractive in that it iteratively computes tighter upper bounds on the MAP problem.

4 Experiments

Data and Scenarios We experimented with the biomedical abstracts from the data set of (Guo et al., 2010) consisting of 1000 AZ-annotated abstracts (7985 sentences, 225785 words). We used the 792 abstract (7886 sentences) test set of (Guo and Korhonen, 2011). We consider two scenarios: a fully unsupervised scenario, and a transduction. For the latter we consider two conditions: (1) the identity of all the sentences that belong to one of the clusters is known; and (2) the oracle cluster assignment of randomly selected 5% or 10% of the sentences is known. In all cases our model as well as the baselines induce $K = 5$ categories.

Baselines Our first baseline is the K-means algorithm (Bishop, 2006) where sentences are represented by the same features that are used for constructing our similarity scores. In the fully unsupervised scenario we use the standard K-means. For transduction, in the condition where all the sentences of one of the classes are known, we run K-means only for the rest of the sentences and induce K-1 clusters; In the condition where the labels of a randomly selected sentence subset are known, we fix the classes of these sentences during the run of the algorithm (so that they affect their class centroid over the iterations) and use the mean of the vectors that are known to belong to each class as its initial centroid.

For the fully unsupervised scenario we also compare to the Hidden Topic Markov Model (HTMM) (Gruber et al., 2007) , a fully unsupervised, topic-model based algorithm. Like our within-document pairwise potentials, this algorithm models the sequential progress of topics in an abstract. However, in contrast to our model, it aims to maximize the lexical coherence of the induced categories. For the transduction scenario our second baseline is the transductive SVM algorithm (T-SVM from (Sinz, 2011)), where the feature-based representation is similar to the one we use in our model and in K-means. Being a classifier, this baseline is only useful in the second transduction condition where the categories of 5% or 10% of the sentences are given. T-SVM is a transductive classifier. To better understand the effect of each of these properties we also compare our model to the performance of a standard SVM . In addition to these baselines, we compare our full model to models created by omitting all the potentials related to a specific type of encoded knowledge: feature-based similarity or discourse patterns.

Parameter Tuning Our model governs the relative weight of its components with three potential parameters α, β and γ, and with M, the connectivity degree of the graph (Section 3). We manually set these parameters on 10 abstracts to the values that give the best performance in the unsupervised scenario and used them across all experiments. The potential parameters used are: $\alpha = 10^5$, $\beta = 10^2$, $\gamma = 10^7$ and M was set to 50.

We run K-means 100 times, randomly selecting the cluster centers from the set of clustered vectors, and selected the output clustering with the highest objective values. For HTMM, we assumed symmetric prior and ran the algorithm 10 times for each hyperparameter value in $\{0.01, 0.05, 0.1, 0.15 \ldots 1\}$. For each parameter assignment we selected the solution with the highest likelihood and the results we report are of oracle selection of the best of these solutions. The SVM algorithms were trained with the default setting of UniversSVM (Sinz, 2011).

Evaluation We uses greedy 1-1 mapping for evaluation. We mapped each induced category in the test set to one of the gold classes in a greedy 1-1 manner using the Kuhn-munkres algorithm for maximum matching in a bi-partite graph (Munkres, 1957). We then report the sentence level accuracy across the entire test set. In addition, we report per-class F-score (adjusted to a 0-100 scale) after the greedy 1-1 mapping is performed.

5 Results

The Fully Unsupervised Scenario Table 1 (left) presents results for the unsupervised setup. The top line shows results for the full test set: our model outperforms the K-means and HTMM baselines by 7% and 17.3%, respectively. The bottom lines present a similar pattern for the per-class F-score: our model is better for the BACKGROUND, RESULTS and CONCLUSIONS zones by up to 52%. This result demonstrates the importance of modelling linguistic similarity between sentences jointly with the sequential progression of the abstract discourse. While K-means clusters sentences together according to their linguistic similarity and HTMM models the progression of lexical topics in the abstract, our approach is to model linguistic similarity and sequential category progress jointly. Furthermore, unlike HTMM, we capitalize on discourse elements rather than on lexical cohesion when modelling the sequential progress.

The Transduction Scenario Results for this setup are in Table 2 (left). The first five rows correspond to the condition where all the sentences belonging to one of the gold classes are known. The SVM classifiers are not applicable to this condition as they cannot learn categories

	Results			Ablation Analysis		
Class	Full Model	K-means	HTMM	Full Model	Model - Similarity	Model - Disc.
All classes	**61.5**	54.5	44.2	**61.5**	58.5	53.0
Background (14.1%)	**58.4**	44.5	12.0	**58.4**	51.0	58.3
Objective (8.8%)	18.9	32.5	**33.0**	18.9	**22.7**	4.6
Methods (15.4%)	32.0	0	**46.0**	**32.0**	23.0	5.4
Results (45.3%)	**71.8**	66.6	57.6	**71.8**	70.2	58.3
Conclusions (15.4%)	**70.0**	50.8	18.0	**70.0**	64.3	57.5

Table 1: Results for the fully unsupervised scenario. Top line is for 1-1 accuracy for the full data set. Bottom lines are for per-class F-score.

	Results				Ablation Analysis		
Condition	Full Model	K-means	SVM	T-SVM	Full Model	Model - Similarity	Model - Disc.
Known background	**72.3**	65.6	—	—	**72.3**	70.7	58.5
known Obj.	**70.9**	63.3	—	—	**70.9**	66.5	59.4
Known Method	**77.6**	72.9	—	—	**77.6**	72.3	65.3
Known Results	**79.6**	74.5	—	—	79.6	72.7	**80.3**
Known Conclusion	**69.0**	63.2	—	—	**69.0**	64.5	67.9
Known 5% Sen.	**63.4**	59.0	59.9	54.2	**63.4**	61.2	52.5
Known 10% Sen.	**65.0**	60.5	61.9	55.8	**65.0**	63.2	56.5

Table 2: Results for the transduction scenario. In each of the first five lines the identity of all the sentences that belong to one of the classes is given to the models. In the last two lines the classes of a random sample of 5% or 10% of the sentences are known.

that do not appear in the training data. Our model is better than K-means in propagating this knowledge achieving 5.1% - 7.6% performance gain. The next two lines of the table compare the performance of the models when the categories of randomly selected 5% or 10% of the test-set sentences are known. Our model is superior again beating the baslines by 3.1% or more.

Model Components The right sections of the tables present an ablation analysis where we compare the performance of our full model to that of its components. When excluding the potentials that model between-document similarity from our model (Model - Similarity), the performance drops by 3% for the full test set (Table 1 top) and by up to 9% for four of the zone classes (Table 1 bottom) in the unsupervised scenario. Our full model further outperforms its discourse component in the seven transduction scenarios by up to 6.9%. When excluding these potentials from the model (Model - Discourse), the performance in the unsupervised scenario drops by 8.5% for the full test set and by up to 26.6% for the per-class F-score. Similarly, the performance drops in six of the seven transductive scenarios, by up to 13.8%.

Convergence The MPLP algorithm minimizes an upper bound on the MAP objective. Since this bound is convex, the MPLP algorithm is promised to converge to its global minimum, but the bound is promised to be tight only if the solution is integral – i.e. if every vertex is assigned to the same category by all the potentials that take it as an argument. In practice, in all the experimental conditions for all test subsets our model converges to an integral exact solution.

Conclusion and perspectives

We presented a novel unsupervised model for inferring information structure of scientific documents. The model integrates within-document discourse patterns and cross-document, feature-based linguistic information in a flexible way that enables to control the relative importance of different knowledge types by parameter setting. In the future we intend to extend our model to address more information sources and to use it for data-driven analysis of the various existing AZ schemes.

Acknowledgments

The work in this paper was funded by the Royal Society, (UK), EPSRC (UK) grant EP/G051070/1 and EU grant 7FP-ITC-248064.

References

Argamon, S., Dodick, J., and Chase, P. (2008). Language use reflects scientific methodology: A corpus-based study of peer reviewed journal articles. *Scientometrics*, 75(2):203–238.

Bishop, C. M. (2006). *Pattern Recognition and Machine Learning*. Springer-Verlag, New-York.

Bunescu, R. and Mooney, R. (2004). Collective information extrction with relational markov networks. In *Proceedings of ACL*.

Deane, P., Odendahl, N., Quinlan, T., Fowles, M., Welsh, C., and Bivens-Tatum, J. (2008). Cognitive models of writing: Writing proficiency as a complex integrated skill. *ETS RR-08-55*.

Finkel, J., Grenager, T., and Manning, C. (2005). Incorporating non-local information into information extraction systems by gibbs sampling. In *Proceedings of ACL*.

Gammerman, A., Volk, V., and Vapnik, V. (1998). Learning by transduction. In *Proceedings of UAI*.

Ganchev, K., Graca, J., Gillenwater, J., and Taskar, B. (2010). Posterior regularization for structured latent variable models. *Journal of Machine Learning Research*, 11:2001–2049.

Gillenwater, J., Ganchev, K., Graca, J., Pereira, F., and Taskar, B. (2010). Sparsity in dependency grammar induction. In *Proceedings of ACL Short Papers*.

Gruber, A., Rosen-Zvi, M., and Weiss, Y. (2007). The hidden topic markov model. In *Proceedings of AISTAT*.

Guo, Y. and Korhonen, A. (2011). A weakly supervised approach to argumantative zoning of scientific documents. In *Proceedings of EMNLP*.

Guo, Y., Korhonen, A., Liakata, M., Karolinska, I. S., Sun, L., and Stenius, U. (2010). Identifying the information structure of scientific abstracts: an investigation of three different schemes. In *Proceedings of the 2010 Workshop on Biomedical Natural Language Processing*.

Gupta, R., Sarawagi, S., and Diwan, A. (2010). Collective inference for extraction mrfs coupled with symmetric clique potentials. *Journal of Machine Learning Research*.

Hachey, B. and Grover, C. (2006). Extractive summarisation of legal texts. *Artif. Intell. Law*, 14:305–345.

Hirohata, K., Okazaki, N., Anaiadou, S., and Ishikika, M. (2008). Identifying sections in scientific abstracts using conditional random fields. In *Proceedings of IJCNLP*.

Liakata, M., Teufel, S., Siddharthan, A., and Batchelor, C. (2010). Corpora for the conceptualisation and zoning of scientific papers. In *Proceedings of the Seventh conference on International Language Resources and Evaluation (LREC'10)*.

Liang, P., Jordan, M., and Klein, D. (2009). Learning from measurements in exponential families. In *Proceedings ICML*.

Lin, J., Karakos, D., Demner-Fushman, D., and Khudanpur, S. (2006). Generative content models for structural analysis of medical abstracts. In *Proceedings of BioNLP-06*.

Lungen, H., Barenfanger, M., Hilbert, M., Lobin, H., and Puskas, C. (2010). Discourse relations and document structure. *Text, Speech and Language Technology*, 41:97–123.

Mann, G. and McCallum, A. (2010). Generalized expectation criteria for semi-supervised learning with weakly labeled data. *Journal of Machine Learning Research*, 11:955–984.

Mizuta, Y., Korhonen, A., Mullen, T., and Collier, N. (2006). Zone analysis in biology articles as a basis for information extraction. *International Journal of Medical Informatics on Natural Language Processing in Biomedicine and Its Applications*, 75(6):468–487.

Munkres, J. (1957). Algorithms for the assignment and transportation problems. *Journal of the SIAM*, 5(1):32–38.

Reichart, R. and Barzilay, R. (2012). Multi event extraction guided by global constraints. In *Proceedings of NAACL-HLT*.

Roth, D. and Yih, W. (2005). Integer linear programming inference for conditional random fields. In *Proceedings of ICML*.

Ruch, P., Boyer, C., Chichester, C., Tbahriti, I., Geissbuhler, A., Fabry, P., Gobeill, J., Pillet, V., Rebholz-Schuhmann, D., Lovis, C., and Veuthey, A. L. (2007). Using argumentation to extract key sentences from biomedical abstracts. *Int J Med Inform*, 76(2-3):195–200.

Rush, A., Reichart, R., Collins, M., and Globerson, A. (2012). Improved parsing and pos tagging using inter-sentence consistency constraints. In *Proceedings of EMNLP*.

Shatkay, H., Pan, F., Rzhetsky, A., and Wilbur, W. J. (2008). Multi-dimensional classification of biomedical text: Toward automated, practical provision of high-utility text to diverse users. *Bioinformatics*, 24(18):2086–2093.

Sinz, F. (2011). *UniverSVM Support Vector Machine with Large Scale CCCP Functionality*. http://www.kyb.mpg.de/bs/people/fabee/universvm.html.

Sontag, D., Meltzer, T., Globerson, A., Jaakkola, T., and Weiss, Y. (2008). Tightening lp relxations for map using message passing. In *UAI*.

Sutton, C. and McCallum, A. (2004). Collective segmentation and labeling of distant entities in information extractions. In *ICML workshop on Statistical Relational Learning and its Applications*.

Taboada, M. and Mann, W. (2006). Applications of rhetorical structure theory. *Applications of Rhetorical Structure Theory*, 8(4):567–588.

Taskar, B., Abbeel, P., and Koller, D. (2002). Discriminative probabilistic models for relational data. In *Proceedings of UAI*.

Tbahriti, I., Chichester, C., Lisacek, F., and Ruch, P. (2006). Using argumentation to retrieve articles with similar citations. *Int J Med Inform*, 75(6):488–495.

Teufel, S. (2001). Task based evaluation of summary quality: Describing relationships between scientific papars. In *NAACL workshop on Automatic Text Summarization*.

Teufel, S. and Moens, M. (2002). Summarizing scientific articles: Experiments with relevance and rhetorical status. *Computational Linguistics*, 28:409–445.

Teufel, S., Siddharthan, A., and Batchelor, C. (2009). Towards domain-independent argumentative zoning: Evidence from chemistry and computational linguistics. In *Proceedings of EMNLP*.

Varge, A., Preotiuc-Pietro, D., and Ciravegna, F. (2012). Unsupervised document zone identification using probabilistic graphical models. In *Proceedings of LREC*.

Yanover, C., Meltzer, T., and Weiss, Y. (2006). Linear programming relazations and belief propogataion – and empitical study. *JMLR Special Issue on Machine Learning and Large Scale Optimization*.

Light Textual Inference for Semantic Parsing

Kyle Richardson *Jonas Kuhn*
Institute for Natural Language Processing,
University of Stuttgart
{kyle,jonas}@ims.uni-stuttgart.de

Abstract
There has been a lot of recent interest in Semantic Parsing, centering on using data-driven techniques for mapping natural language to full semantic representations (Mooney, 2007). One particular focus has been on learning with ambiguous supervision (Chen and Mooney, 2008; Kim and Mooney, 2012), where the goal is to model language learning within broader perceptual contexts (Mooney, 2008). We look at learning light inference patterns for Semantic Parsing within this paradigm, focusing on detecting speaker commitments about events under discussion (Nairn et al., 2006; Karttunen, 2012). We adapt PCFG induction techniques (Börschinger et al., 2011; Johnson et al., 2012) for learning inference using event polarity and context as supervision, and demonstrate the effectiveness of our approach on a modified portion of the Grounded World corpus (Bordes et al., 2010).

Keywords: Semantic Parsing, Computational Semantics, Detecting Textual Entailment, Grammar Induction.

Proceedings of COLING 2012: Posters, pages 1007–1018,
COLING 2012, Mumbai, December 2012.

1 Overview and Motivation

Semantic Parsing is a subfield in NLP that looks at using data-driven techniques for mapping language expressions to complete semantic representations (Mooney, 2007). A variety of corpora and learning techniques have been developed for these purposes, both for doing supervised learning (Kate et al., 2005; Kwiatkowski et al., 2010) and learning in more complex (ambiguous) settings (Chen and Mooney, 2008, 2011). In many studies, the learning is done by finding alignments between (latent) syntactic patterns in language and parts of the target semantic representations, often using techniques from Statistical Machine Translation (Wong and Mooney, 2006; Jones et al., 2012). Despite achieving impressive results in different domains, learning semantic inference patterns is often not addressed, making it unclear how to apply these methods to tasks like Detecting Textual Entailment. In this work, we show how to learn light (syntactic) inference patterns for textual entailment using loosely-supervised Semantic Parsing methods.

Detecting Textual Entailment is a topic that has received considerable attention in NLP, largely because of its connection to applications such as question answering, summarization, paraphrase generation, and many others. The goal, loosely speaking, is to detect entailment inference relationships between pairs of sentences (Dagan et al., 2005). More recent work on Hedge and Event Detection (Farkas et al., 2010) has focused on similar issues related to determining event certainty, especially in the biomedical domain (Example 3 (Thompson et al., 2011)). Four inferences are shown in Examples 1-4, and relate to implied speaker commitments (Karttunen, 2012; Nairn et al., 2006) about events under discussion.

1. John forgot to help Mary organize the meeting
   (a) $\models$ John didn't help Mary organize the meeting
2. John remembered (to not neglect) to turn off the lights before leaving work
   (a) $\models$ John turned off some lights
3. NF-kappa B p50 alone *fails to* (=*doesn't*) stimulate kappa B-directed transcription
4. The camera {didn't manage, managed} to impress me (=*negative/positive* opinion)

In Example 1, the speaker of the sentence is committed to the belief that the main event (i.e. *helping Mary organize the meeting*) did not occur, whereas the opposite is true in Example 2. This is triggered by the implicative phrases *Forget to X* and *Remember to X*, which affect the polarity of the modified event X. These inferences relate to the semantics of English complement constructions, a topic well studied in Linguistics (Karttunen, 1971; Kiparsky and Kiparsky, 1970). They are also part of a wider range of inference patterns that are syntactic in nature, or visible from language surface form (Dowty, 1994). They have been of interest to studies in proof-theoretic semantics and Natural Logic, which look at doing inference on natural language directly (MacCartney and Manning, 2007; Moss, 2010; Valencia, 1991).

We aim to learn these implicative patterns, building on existing computational work. (Nairn et al., 2006; Karttunen, 2012) provide a classification of implicative verbs according to the effect they have on their surrounding context. They observe that implicative constructions differ in terms of the polarity contexts they occur in, and the effect they have in these contexts.

As illustrated in Table 1, one-way implicatives occur in a single polarity, whereas two-way implicatives occur in both. For example, *Forget to X* in Example 1 switches polarity in a positive context to negative, and has the opposite effect in a negative context, giving it the implicative signature (+)(-), (-)(+) (i.e. start context, result).

Implicatives can be productively stacked together as shown in Example 2. Determining the resulting inference for an arbitrary nesting of implicatives requires computing the relative polarity of each smaller phrase, which is the idea behind the polarity propagation algorithm (Nairn et al., 2006). This can be done directly from syntax by traversing a tree annotated with polarity information and calculating the polarity interactions incrementally. This general strategy for doing inference, which relies on syntactic and lexical features alone, avoids a full semantic analysis and translation into logic (Bos and Markert, 2005), and has been successfully applied to more general textual entailment tasks (MacCartney and Manning, 2007, 2008).

One problem with the approach of (Nairn et al., 2006), however, is that the implicative signatures of verbs must be manually compiled, as there are no standard datasets available for doing learning. To our knowledge, there has been little work on learning these specific patterns (some related studies (Danescu-Niculescu-Mizil et al., 2009; Cheung and Penn, 2012)), which would be useful for applying these methods to languages and domains where resources are not available. Further, their algorithm encodes the lexical properties as hard facts, making it hard to model potential uncertainty and ambiguity associated with these inferences (e.g. if *John was* able to *do X*, how certain are we that he actually *did X*?)

The semantics of implicative expressions can often be inferred from non-linguistic context. Knowing that *managed to X* implies X is something we can learn from hearing this utterance in contexts where X holds. Recent studies on learning from ambiguous supervision for Semantic Parsing (Chen and Mooney, 2008, 2011) has looked at incorporating perceptual context (Mooney, 2008) of this sort into the learning process (see also (Johnson et al., 2012)). Work on the Sportscaster Corpus (Chen and Mooney, 2008) considers interpreting soccer commentary in ambiguous contexts where several closely occurring events are taking place. Their data is taken from a set of simulated soccer games extended with human commentary. Each comment is paired with a set of grounded events occurring in the game around the time of the comment. Using these ambiguous contexts as supervision, they learn how to map novel sentences to the correct grounded semantic representations.

We look at learning implicative inference in a similar grounded learning scenario, using ambiguous contexts and the polarity of events as supervision. We use a modified portion of the Grounded World corpus (Bordes et al., 2010), which was extended to have phrasal implicatives and ambiguous contexts. Three training examples are displayed in Figure 1, and an illustration of the analysis we aim to learn. Each example is situated in a virtual house environment and a context, and describes events taking place in the house. Details of the corpus and learning procedure are described in the next section.

2 Experiments

2.1 Materials

The original Grounded World corpus (Bordes et al., 2010) is a set of English descriptions situated within a virtual house, and was designed for doing named entity recognition and situated pronoun resolution. Inside the house is a fixed set of domain objects, including a set of actors (e.g. *father, brother*), a set of furniture pieces (e.g. *couch, table*), a set of rooms (e.g.

Type	Examples	Effect on Polarity
Two-way implicatives	*manage to*	(+)(+) | (–)(–)
	forget to	(+)(–) | (–)(+)
One-way +implicatives	*force to*	(+)(+)
	refuse to	(+)(–)
One-way -implicatives	*attempt to*	(–) (–)
	hesitate to	(–)(+)

Table 1: Types of Implicative Verbs from (Nairn et al., 2006; Karttunen, 2012)

# Sentences	# Token Gold Relations	Aver. Context Size
7,010 Total *(6,065 (85%) unique)*	**2,444** *(63 unique concepts)*	**2.17** *(90% > 1)*
1,863 Implicative Sentences *(26%)*		

Frequent Verb Tokens: refuse to, manage to, decline to, admit to, remember to, dare to
Complex Constructions: fail to neglect to, didn't refrain from, refuse to remember to
Examples:
Their grandmother [admitted$_{++}$ *to]*$_{+}$ *drinking a little wine.*
The brother [didn't$_{+-}$ *dare*$_{++}$ *to]*$_{-}$ *move into the bedroom.*
Their mom [remembered$_{++}$ *to not*$_{-+}$ *forget*$_{+-}$ *to]*$_{+}$ *grab their toy from the closet*

Table 2: Details of the extended Grounded World Corpus. The average context size is the average number of events in the ambiguous training contexts. On the bottom are some corpus examples with implicative constructions.

living room, bathroom), and a set of small objects (e.g. *doll, chocolate*), plus a set of 15 event types (e.g. *eating, sleeping, and drinking*).

For our study, we used a subset of 7,010 examples from the original training set, and modified the sentences to have syntactic alternations and paraphrases not seen in the initial corpus. 1,863 of these sentences were modified to have implicative constructions (using 70 unique constructions from 20 verb types, see examples in Table 2)[1] that relate to the original content of the sentence, in some cases creating negated forms of the original sentences. We expanded the original named-entity annotations to normalized semantic representations, and produced a set of distractor events (or observable contexts) for each example to make the data ambiguous.

Three training examples are shown in Figure 1. In the first example, the sentence is situated in three observable events (*sleeping, getting* and *bringing*). These can be viewed as events in the current context or the speaker's belief state. Additional information about the world state (i.e. location of objects) is provided from the original corpus for pronoun resolution, which we ignore. The last two examples have implicative constructions, the first one leading to a negative inference (*the sister is not sleeping in the bedroom/guestroom*). The last example leads to a positive inference (*the sister got a toy from the closet/storage*). We show the annotations from the original corpus for comparison.

Expanding the relations from the overall corpus and situating them within ambiguous contexts

[1] we used the phrasal implicative lexicon available at http://www.stanford.edu/group/csli_lnr/Lexical_Resources /phrasal-implicatives/, compiled by the authors of (Nairn et al., 2006; Karttunen, 2012)

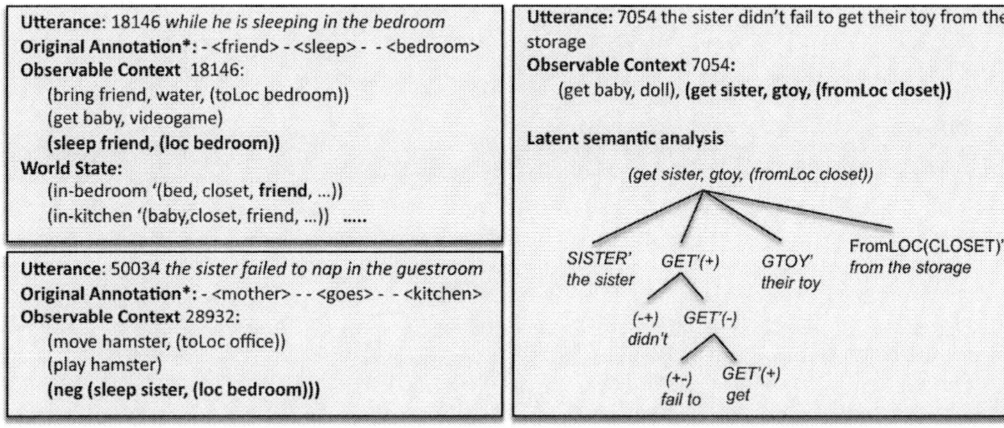

Figure 1: Ambiguous training examples from the extended corpus. The *latent semantic analysis* on the right is the representation we aim to learn from the observable context.

makes the learning task much harder. The overall aim is to use the ambiguous contexts and event polarity to construct a latent semantic analysis (see Figure 1), that derives the appropriate relation and inference (for a similar idea, see (Angeli et al., 2012)). In other words, we want to learn, merely from ambiguous supervision, how to map novel sentences to their correct semantic representations (the typical goal in Semantic Parsing), while also making the correct inferences. Notice that the target analysis is a kind of syntactic analysis, keeping to the idea that such inferences are visible from the surface.

2.2 Method

Many approaches to Semantic Parsing start by assigning rich structure to the target semantic representations, which can be used for finding alignments with latent structures in the language. Well known work by (Wong and Mooney, 2006) uses Statistical Machine Translation methods for finding alignments between semantic representations structured as trees and syntactic patterns in language. These alignments constitute the domain lexicon, and can be modeled using synchronous grammars. A number of such alignment-based learning methods have been proposed, using a variety of tools (Kate and Mooney, 2006; Jones et al., 2012; Wong and Mooney, 2006; Liang et al., 2011; Kwiatkowski et al., 2010).

(Börschinger et al., 2011) recast the problem in terms of an unsupervised PCFG induction problem, an idea also explored in (Johnson et al., 2012; Angeli et al., 2012; Kim and Mooney, 2012). They develop a method for automatically generating PCFGs from semantic relations, by decomposing parts of the relations into rewrite rules. Formally, a semantic PCFG G is $\langle V_{Non}, V_{Term}, Con, S_R, R, P \rangle$, where $S_R \in V_{Non}$ is the set of start symbols corresponding to the full semantic representations in a corpus, $Con \in V_{Non}$ is the set of contexts, R is the set of productions $X \rightarrow \beta$ for $X \in V_{Non}, \beta \in V^*$, and P is a probability function over R. A schema of the rules in R is shown at the top of Figure 2. Words in the training data (in V_{Term}) are assigned to all pre-terminals (i.e. semantic concepts) with equal probability, and the parameters are learned using EM and the ambiguous contexts as supervision.

We build a large PCFG from the semantic relations in our data using the method above. Rules

$S\text{-}Rel(arg_1,...,arg_n)$	$\longrightarrow$	$Contexts\ \{Phrase_{Rel},\ Phrase_{arg_1},\ ...,\ Phrase_{arg_n}\}$	
$Phrase_O$	$\longrightarrow$	$Word_O$	$Rel\ (arg_1 ..., arg_n) \in Corpus$
$Phrase_O$	$\longrightarrow$	$PhX_O\ Word_O$	$O \in \{Rels, args\}$
PhX_O	$\longrightarrow$	$Word_O$	
PhX_O	$\longrightarrow$	$PhX_O\ Word_O$	
PhX_O	$\longrightarrow$	$PhX_O\ Word_{null}$	
PhX_O	$\longrightarrow$	$Word_{null}$	
$Word_O$	$\longrightarrow$	w	$w \in \{words\ in\ corpus\}$
$Word_{null}$	$\longrightarrow$	w	
		....	
$Phrase_{Rel}$	$\longrightarrow$	$Phrase_{pos-pos}\ Phrase_{Rel}$	
$Phrase_{Rel}$	$\longrightarrow$	$Phrase_{neg-pos}\ Phrase_{negRel}$	
$Phrase_{negRel}$	$\longrightarrow$	$Phrase_{pos-neg}\ Phrase_{Rel}$	
$Phrase_{negRel}$	$\longrightarrow$	$Phrase_{neg-neg}\ Phrase_{negRel}$	
$Phrase_Z$	$\longrightarrow$	$Phrase_{MON}$	$Z \in \{pos-pos, neg-neg\}$
$Phrase_W$	$\longrightarrow$	$Phrase_{NMON}$	$W \in \{pos-neg, neg-pos\}$
$Phrase_P$	$\longrightarrow$	$Word_P$	$P \in \{NMON, MON\}$
$Phrase_P$	$\longrightarrow$	$PhX_P\ Word_P$	
PhX_P	$\longrightarrow$	$PhX_P\ Word_P$	
....			
....			
$Word_P$	$\longrightarrow$	w	

Figure 2: PCFG schema (Börschinger et al., 2011) extended with rules for implicative phrases shown under the dotted lines. Note that word order is not modeled. The top most rule encodes all combinations of rules on the right in the brackets.

for detecting implicative patterns are specified at the bottom of Figure 2. Like the rules in the top part of the figure, every word in the corpus has an equal chance of being in an implicative phrase. We distinguish between two types of implicative phrases, ones that reverse polarity in the opposite direction (NMONPhrase), and ones that keep the polarity the same (MONPhrase). The rules $Phrase_Z$ and $Phrase_W$ specify that both types can have different effects (e.g. MONPhrase can be (+)(+), (-)(-)), which gets settled once the neighboring polarity is determined. The top rules specify that each event or relation is subject to modification by an implicative phrase, which allows for an arbitrary nesting of implicative phrases.

For example, in the fragment *didn't bother to remember to eat*, *didn't* reverses polarity (NMON-Phrase), whereas *bother* and *remember* preserve polarity (MONPhrase). Equation (1) shows how the polarity of the verb is propagated through a derivation in our grammar. Because the verb gets transformed back into its original phrase when it encounters a MONPhrase with the signature *pp*, it is again subject to modification. This is consistent with how inferences are computed in the polarity propagation algorithm, and stays within the syntactic analysis.

$$notEat \leftarrow \Big[Eat_n \leftarrow (didn't_{pn}\Big(Eat_p \leftarrow \Big(bother_{pp}\Big(Eat_p \leftarrow \Big(remember_{pp}\Big(Eat_p\Big)\Big)\Big)\Big)\Big)\Big] \tag{1}$$

For training, we perform cross validation by making four different splits in our 7,010 sentence set (5,010 for training, and 2,000 for testing). As in (Börschinger et al., 2011), we train the

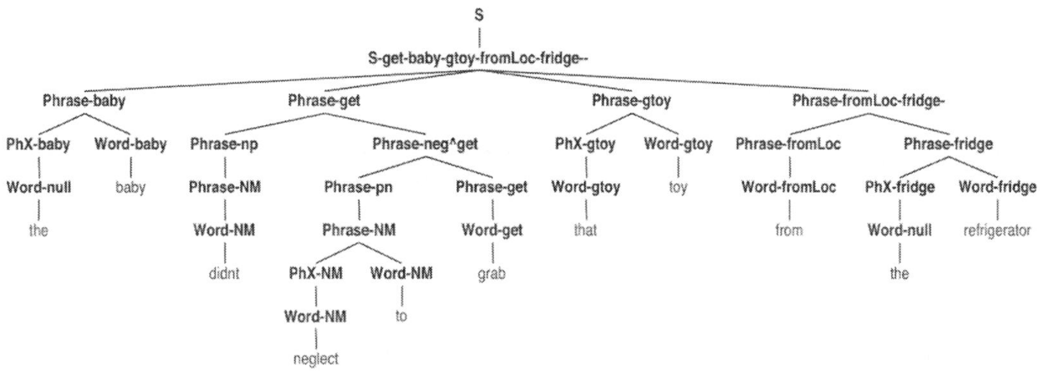

Figure 3: Example output of an analysis after training

Set	Pronoun Precision	Implicative Precision	Overall Precision	Recall	F-Score
1	**0.3859** (203/526)	**0.8277** (471/569)	**0.788** (1576/2000)	1.0	0.8814
2	**0.38878** (208/535)	**0.7489** (373/498)	**0.769** (1538/2000)	1.0	0.8694
3	**0.39405** (199/505)	**0.83116** (448/539)	**0.8005** (1601/2000)	1.0	0.8891
4	**0.333** (177/531)	**0.730** (376/515)	**0.75** (1500/2000)	1.0	0.8571
Av.	**0.3755**	**0.7845**	**0.7768**		**0.874**

Table 3: Results on extended Grounded World data

grammars on each split using the Inside-Out Algorithm (Lari and Young, 1990) [1], a variant of the EM algorithm often used for PCFG induction. The main thrust of the learning algorithm is that sentences are parsed with their contexts, which provides a top-down constraint on the possible analyses. Implicatives that lead to negative inference, for example, will consistently be observed in negative contexts, which forces the learner to construct latent parses that lead to such inferences. Over time, the probability that the associated words receive the correct analysis increases.

Once the grammars are trained on the different splits, information about the original contexts is removed, and the remaining unseen sentences are parsed. Like in (Börschinger et al., 2011), the derived relation (or S-node) for each parse is evaluated against a gold standard relation and marked correct if it matches this relation exactly. An example parse after training is shown in Figure 3, where the resulting relation is *(get baby, gtoy, (fromLoc fridge))*. All words related to the inference, in addition to words corresponding to other semantic concepts, were learned to have the correct analysis (e.g. *didn't*$_{-+}$, *neglect to*$_{+-}$, *grab*$_{get'}$) , which allows us to recursively compute the inference in the manner described above.

2.3 Results and Discussion

The results are provided in Table 3 and are broken down into each training-testing split. Sentences are counted as correct when the main relation in the parse matches exactly a gold-standard annotation. In terms of evaluating inference, getting the right relation means that

[1] we used Mark Johnson's CKY and Inside-Out implementation available at http://web.science.mq.edu.au/ mjohnson/Software.htm.

the correct inference is achieved. As mentioned above, a large portion of the original corpus contains sentences with pronouns, and we isolate sentences with pronouns, as well as with implicative phrases, and measure the overall precision for each set.

The average overall precision is 0.7768, with 0.7845 average precision on implicative phrases and 0.3755 on sentences with pronouns. The latter precision is the lowest, and is to be expected since we simply assign pronouns the most probable referent based on training (no further resolution is done). Recall in all cases is 1.0, since we build the semantic relations from the total corpus following (Börschinger et al., 2011). This avoids having out-of-grammar issues when parsing test sentences, but limits the parsers to only the relations seen in the corpus. This is one downside to a grammar approach, which is discussed and improved upon in (Kim and Mooney, 2012) and will be a main focus of future work.

We emphasize that the evaluation, following (Börschinger et al., 2011; Kim and Mooney, 2012) and others, is done by looking at the resulting semantic relations (S-Node), and ignores the rest of the syntactic analysis. The parser therefore might make wrong decisions while arriving at the correct inference and relations. For example, the analysis in Figure 3 might have *didn't neglect to* as a single implicative phrase marked as *pp* (as opposed to two), which leads to the same inference. Future work will look at evaluating this and employing unsupervised learning methods for ensuring that the domain lexicon is properly inferred.

Despite these issues, the results are encouraging and show that learning light inference can be done using standard Semantic Parsing techniques with loose ambiguous supervision. This result is not altogether surprising, given that the inference patterns we consider are types of syntactic patterns, and are therefore similar to the other patterns we induce. Future work will look at scaling this up to more complex types of inference in an open-domain. One particular direction might be looking at more complex forms of negation, as studied in, for example, (Blanco and Moldovan, 2012). Another direction is using these techniques, which require very little supervision, to help learn inference patterns for unresourced languages and domains.

3 Conclusions

This work complements recent work on Semantic Parsing, specifically within the ambiguous learning paradigm, and shows how to integrate light syntactic inference into the learning using event polarity and context as loose supervision. The main focus has been on learning implicative verb constructions, which have well-understood semantic properties relating to speaker commitment. The strategy we adopted follows that of (Nairn et al., 2006), and keeps inference computation within the syntax. We adapted current PCFG-based grammar induction techniques for Semantic Parsing, and demonstrated the effectiveness of our inference learning method on a modified portion of the Grounded World corpus. Future work will concentrate on extending these results to open-domain textual entailment problems, and on inference learning for unresourced languages and domains.

Acknowledgments

This work was funded by the Deutsche Forschungsgemeinschaft (DFG) on the project SFB 732, "Incremental Specification in Context". We thank Sina Zarriess for useful suggestions and discussions, and Annie Zaenen and Cleo Condoravdi for earlier discussions about the overall idea and method.

References

Angeli, G., Manning, C. D., and Jurafsky, D. (2012). Parsing time: Learning to interpret time expressions. In *Proceedings of NAACL-HLT-12*, pages 446–455, Montreal, Canada.

Blanco, E. and Moldovan, D. (2012). Fine-grained focus for pinpointing positive implicit meaning from negated statements. In *Proceedings of NAACL-HLT-12*, pages 456–465, Montreal, Canada.

Bordes, A., Usunier, N., Collobert, R., and Weston, J. (2010). Towards understanding situated natural language. In *Proceedings of AISTATS-10*, pages 628–635, Sardinia, Italy.

Börschinger, B., Jones, B. K., and Johnson, M. (2011). Reducing grounded learning tasks to grammatical inference. In *Proceedings of EMNLP-11*, pages 1416–1425, Edinburgh, United Kingdom.

Bos, J. and Markert, K. (2005). Recognising textual entailment with logical inference. In *Proceedings of HLT-EMNLP-05*, pages 628–635, Vancouver, Canada.

Chen, D. L. and Mooney, R. J. (2008). Learning to sportscast: A test of grounded language acquisition. In *Proceedings of the ICML-08*, pages 128–135, Helsinki, Finland.

Chen, D. L. and Mooney, R. J. (2011). Learning to interpret natural language navigation instructions from observations. In *Proceedings of the AAAI-11*, pages 859–865, San Francisco, CA.

Cheung, J. C. K. and Penn, G. (2012). Unsupervised detection of downward-entailing operators by maximizing classification certainty. In *Proceedings of EACL-12*, pages 696–705, Avignon, France.

Dagan, I., Glickman, O., and Magnini, B. (2005). The pascal recognizing textual entailment challenge. In *Proceedings of PASCAL Challenges Workshop on Recognizing Textual Entailment*, pages 177–190.

Danescu-Niculescu-Mizil, C., Lee, L., and Ducott, R. (2009). Without a "doubt"? unsupervised discovery of downward-entailing operators. In *Proceedings of HLT-NAACL-09*, pages 137–145, Boulder, Colorado.

Dowty, D. (1994). The role of negative polarity and concord marking in natural language reasoning. In *Proceedings of Semantics and Linguistics Theory (SALT)*, pages 114–144, Ithaca, New York.

Farkas, R., Vincze, V., Móra, G., Csirik, J., and Szarvas, G. (2010). The conll-2010 shared task: learning to detect hedges and their scope in natural language text. In *Proceedings of CoNNL-10: Shared Task*, pages 1–12, Uppsala, Sweden.

Johnson, M., Demuth, K., and Frank, M. (2012). Exploiting social information in grounded language learning via grammatical reduction. In *Proceedings of the ACL-12*, pages 883–891, Jeju Island, Korea.

Jones, B. K., Johnson, M., and Goldwater, S. (2012). Semantic parsing with bayesian tree transducers. In *Proceedings of ACL-12*, pages 488–496, Jeju Island, Korea.

Karttunen, L. (1971). Implicative verbs. *Language*, 47(2):340–358.

Karttunen, L. (2012). Simple and phrasal implicatives. In *Proceedings of *SEM-12*, pages 124–131, Montreal, Canada.

Kate, R. and Mooney, R. (2006). Learning language semantics using string kernels. In *Proceedings of Coling-ACL-06*, pages 913–920, Sydney, Australia.

Kate, R. J., Wong, Y. W., and Mooney, R. J. (2005). Learning to transform natural to formal languages. In *Proceedings of AAAI-05*, pages 1062–1068, Pittsburgh, Pennsylvania.

Kim, J. and Mooney, R. J. (2012). Unsupervised pcfg induction for grounded language learning with highly ambiguous supervision. In *Proceedings of EMNLP-CoNLL-12*, pages 883–891, Jeju Island, Korea.

Kiparsky, P. and Kiparsky, C. (1970). Fact. In Bierwisch, M. and Heidolph, K., editors, *Progress in Linguistics*, pages 143–173. Mouton,Hague.

Kwiatkowski, T., Zettlemoyer, L., Goldwater, S., and Steedman, M. (2010). Inducing probabilistic ccg grammars from logical form with higher-order unification. In *Proceedings of EMNLP-10*, pages 1223–1233, Cambridge, Massachusetts.

Lari, K. and Young, S. (1990). The estimation of stochastic context-free grammars using the inside-outside algorithm. *Computer Speech and Language*, 4(1):35–56.

Liang, P., Jordan, M. I., and Klein, D. (2011). Learning dependency-based compositional semantics. In *Proceedings of ACL-11*, pages 590–599, Portland, Oregon.

MacCartney, B. and Manning, C. (2008). Modeling semantic containment and exclusion in natural language inference. In *Proceedings of Coling-08*, pages 521–528, Manchester, United Kingdom.

MacCartney, B. and Manning, C. D. (2007). Natural logic for textual inference. In *Proceedings of ACL-PASCAL Workshop on Textual Entailment and Paraphrasing*, pages 193–200, Prague, Czech Republic.

Mooney, R. (2007). Learning for semantic parsing. In *Proceedings of CICLing-07*, pages 311–324, Mexico City, Mexico.

Mooney, R. (2008). Learning to connect language and perception. In *Proceedings of AAAI-08*, pages 1598–1601, Chicago, Illinois.

Moss, L. (2010). Natural logic and semantics. In *Proceedings of 17th Amsterdam Colloquium*, pages 84–93.

Nairn, R., Condoravdi, C., and Karttunen, L. (2006). Computing relative polarity for textual inference. In *Proceedings of ICoS-5 (Inference in Computational Semantics)*, pages 63–76, Buxton, UK.

Thompson, P., Nawaz, R., McNaught, J., and Ananiadou, S. (2011). Enriching a biomedical event corpus with meta-knowledge annotation. *BMC Bioinformatics*, 12:393.

Valencia, V. S. (1991). *Studies on Natural Logic and Categorial Grammar*. PhD thesis, University of Amsterdam.

Wong, Y. W. and Mooney, R. J. (2006). Learning for semantic parsing with statistical machine translation. In *Proceedings of HLT-NAACL-06*, pages 439–446, New York City, NY.

Korektor – A System for Contextual Spell-checking and Diacritics Completion

Michal RICHTER[*] *Pavel STRAŇÁK*[*] *Alexandr ROSEN*[†]
[*]Charles University in Prague, Faculty of Mathematics and Physics
[†]Charles University in Prague, Faculty of Arts
{richter,stranak}@ufal.mff.cuni.cz, alexandr.rosen@ff.cuni.cz

ABSTRACT
We present *Korektor* – a flexible and powerful purely statistical text correction tool for Czech that goes beyond a traditional spell checker. We use a combination of several language models and an error model to offer the best ordering of correction proposals and also to find errors that cannot be detected by simple spell checkers, namely spelling errors that happen to be homographs of existing word forms. Our system works also without any adaptation as a diacritics generator with the best reported results for Czech text. The design of *Korektor* contains no language-specific parts other than trained statistical models, which makes it highly suitable to be trained for other languages with available resources. The evaluation demonstrates that the system is a state-of-the-art tool for Czech, both as a spell checker and as a diacritics generator. We also show that these functions combine into a potential aid in the error annotation of a learner corpus of Czech.

TITLE AND ABSTRACT IN CZECH

Korektor – systém pro kontextovou opravu pravopisu a doplnění diakritiky

Představujeme *Korektor* – flexibilní statistický nástroj pro opravu českých textů, jehož schopnosti přesahují tradiční nástroje pro kontrolu pravopisu. *Korektor* využívá kombinace jazykových modelů a chybového modelu jak k tomu, aby setřídil pořadí nabízených náhrad pro neznámé slovo podle pravděpodobnosti výskytu na daném místě v textu, tak také, aby nalezl i překlepy, které se nahodile shodují s existujícím českým slovním tvarem. Prostou náhradou chybového modelu náš pracuje *Korektor* také jako systém pro doplnění diakritiky („oháčkování textu“) s nejvyšší publikovanou úspěšností. Systém neobsahuje žádné významné jazykově specifické komponenty s výjimkou natrénovaných statistických modelů. Je tedy možné jej snadno natrénovat i pro jiné jazyky. Ukážeme, jakých zlepšení náš systém dosahuje v porovnání se stávajícími českými korektory pravopisu i systémy pro doplnění diakritiky. Ukážeme také, že kombinace těchto schopností pomáhá při anotaci chyb v korpusu češtiny jako druhého jazyka.

KEYWORDS: spellchecking, diacritics completion, language model, error model.

CZECH KEYWORDS: kontrola pravopisu, oprava pravopisu, doplnění diakritiky, jazykový model, chybový model.

Proceedings of COLING 2012: Posters, pages 1019–1028,
COLING 2012, Mumbai, December 2012.

1 Introduction

The idea of using context of a misspelled word to improve the performance of a spell checker is not new (Mays et al., 1991), moreover, recent years have seen the advance of context-aware spell checkers such as *Google Suggest*, offering reasonable corrections of search queries. Errors detected by such advanced spell checkers have a natural overlap with those of rule-based grammar checkers – grammatical errors are also manifested as unlikely n-grams.

Methods used in such spell checkers usually employ the *noisy-channel* or *winnow-based* approach (Golding and Roth, 1999). The system described here also belongs to the *noisy-channel* class. It makes extensive use of language models based on several morphological factors, exploiting the morphological richness of the target language.

The purpose of this work was to implement a flexible system, capable of performing diverse tasks such as spelling correction, diacritics completion and abbreviated text expansion by simple module replacement. Rather than presenting a scientific prototype we aimed at a practical system providing a better spell-checking for Czech than systems currently available.

Section 2 introduces the statistical models used here and describes their application to the tasks of spell-checking and diacritics completion. In Section 3 results of performance evaluation are presented. Section 4 discusses the system's performance, while Section 5 provides conclusions and outlines our plans for the future.

2 Statistical Model

The task of context-sensitive spelling correction and diacritics completion can be seen as a problem of sequence decoding, which is often formulated in terms of the noisy-channel model. A transmitter sends a sequence of symbols to a receiver. During the transfer, though, certain symbols of the transmitted sequence are garbled due to the deficiencies of the transmission channel. The receiver's goal is to reconstruct the original sequence using the knowledge of the *source* (i.e. how a Czech sentence looks like) and the transmission channel properties.

2.1 Source Modeling

Several feature functions[1] were used to model the source:

- Word forms feature F_f – based on language model probability $P(f_i|f_{i-2}, f_{i-1})$, where f_i denotes the next word form and f_{i-2} and f_{i-1} are the previous word forms.
- Morphological lemma feature F_l – based on language model probability $P(l_i|l_{i-2}, l_{i-1})$ and emission model probability $P(f_i|l_i)$, where l_i stands for the next lemma, l_{i-1}, l_{i-2} are the previous lemmas and f_i is the next word form.
- morphological tag feature F_t – which is, analogically to the morphological lemma feature, based on $P(t_i|t_{i-2}, t_{i-1})$ and $P(f_i|t_i)$.

The source feature functions are task independent. Their role is to approximate grammaticality of the output sentence. The probability measures were estimated on the basis of n-gram

[1] For the convenience of the reader, the feature functions are based on trigram statistic in the descriptions. However, higher order n-grams are supported as well.

counts collected from a training corpus, using interpolated Kneser-Ney (Kneser and Ney, 1995) smoothing.

A large text corpus was needed in order to produce well-estimated language models and word emission models. This need was met by the *Czech Web Documents Collection* (henceforth *WebColl*) (Marek et al., 2007), a 111 million words resource consisting of 223,000 articles, downloaded from news servers and on-line archives of Czech newspapers, lemmatized and tagged with detailed morphological tags as described in the paper. N-gram counts for each morphological factor and counts of `form-lemma` and `form-tag` combinations were collected. For the word forms and lemmas, n-grams up to order 3 were collected. For morphological tags, 4-grams were collected as well.

2.2 Channel Modeling

A single channel feature F_{ch} estimates the probability $P(f|f')$ of word form f' being transferred as word form f. The channel feature links the input and the output words. The score is assigned according to the similarity of the output words to the input words according to the task specific similarity measure – for the spelling correction problem, it takes into account the probabilities of specific typing errors. Transmission channel for the diacritics completion is constructed in such a way that it assigns a uniform cost to all variants of an output word with diacritics and the infinite cost to all other words.

2.3 Log-linear Model and Viterbi algorithm

A log-linear model (Jurafsky and Martin, 2008) was used to combine all feature functions into a single statistical model. The search space of the model is enormous – $|V|^{|S|}$, where $|V|$ is the vocabulary size and $|S|$ is the sentence length. However, since all the features use only limited history, we could use Viterbi algorithm (Viterbi, 1967) to find the optimal hypothesis.

2.4 Error Model For Spelling Correction

The error model used in this work is based on the model of (Church and Gale, 1991). They consider only candidate words obtained by a single edit operation – insertion, deletion, substitution, or swap. This model is a good fit for Czech language. Since Czech has mostly phonetic spelling, the errors tend to be local, limited to one of these operations. Edit operations have their distinct probabilities, i.e. the probability of the letter substitution $s \rightarrow d$ may differ from the probability of $e \rightarrow a$. Letter insertion and deletion probabilities are also context-conditioned.

These probabilities were estimated from the large text corpus. They considered each word that did not appear in the dictionary and was not farther than one edit operation from a word included in the dictionary as a spelling error, and built their error corpus out of such words. First, they set the probabilities of all edit operations uniformly. Later on, they iteratively spell-checked their error corpus, found the best correction for each word and updated the edit probabilities according to the proposed *error* $\rightarrow$ *suggestion* pairs.

This method of finding spelling errors was tested on the *WebColl* corpus (see Section 2.1), but turned out to be useless. The reason was that the vast majority of words identified as spelling errors were correct words or colloquial word forms.

The modified version builds an error corpus out of words recognized by the spell checker as spelling errors, however there must be a significant evidence that the proposed correction is

Error Type	Cost	Error Type	Cost
Substitution – horizontally adjacent letters	2.290	Substitution – diacritic redundancy	2.250
Substitution – vertically adjacent letters	2.661	Substitution – other cases	4.285
Substitution – $z \rightarrow s$	2.747	Insertion – horizontally adjacent letter	2.290
Substitution – $s \rightarrow z$	1.854	Insertion – vertically adjacent letter	2.661
Substitution – $y \rightarrow i$	3.167	Insertion – same letter as previous	1.227
Substitution – $i \rightarrow y$	2.679	Insertion – other cases	2.975
Substitution – non-adjacent vocals	3.706	Deletion	4.140
Substitution – diacritic omission	2.235	Swap letters	3.278

Table 1: Spelling Error Types together with their costs ($-log$ of their probabilities)

right, otherwise the spelling error is not added to the error corpus. More specifically, both bigrams (w_{i-1}, s) and (w_{i+1}, s), where w_{i-1} is the predecessor of a misspelled word e, w_{i+1} is the successive word and s is the correction suggestion, must be present in the language model, otherwise the error-correction pair $e \rightarrow s$ is not included in the error corpus. Recall of this method is rather small, but the precision is quite satisfactory and most of the recognized error-correction pairs were correct. This method identified 12,761 words out of 111,000,000 words in *WebColl* as spelling errors. A classification of these errors is shown in Table 1. The granularity of spelling error types being distinguished is much smaller than in (Church and Gale, 1991).

2.5 Letter Language Model For Diacritics Completion

It may happen that for a given word of the input sentence, no candidate word is found. An example of such a word is *nemeckofrancouzsky* 'German-French', which remains untouched without any added diacritics. However, an error, here a missing hyphen, is very likely. The present example should receive diacritics as in *německofrancouzský* (adjective) or *německofrancouzsky* (adverb).

In order to cut down the number of errors made on unknown words, a custom implementation of the Viterbi decoder was provided. The states on the underlying HMM are tuplets of letters and the transition probabilities are given by a letter n-gram language model (it estimates the probability of next letter on the basis of previous letters). The aim of this Viterbi decoder is to find the most probable letter sequence given the input letter sequence. The only substitutions allowed are the substitutions that add diacritics. Using this approach, diacritics can be added correctly even to the unknown words.

Given that the vocabulary of letter n-gram language model is extremely small (the size of the alphabet), it is possible to train letter LMs of a very high order. In this work, letter LMs of the order up to 7 were trained. The letter LMs were trained on the training part of *WebColl*.

During the evaluation the contribution of using letter LMs was examined. Table 4 shows a significant accuracy improvement when this feature is used.

3 Evaluation

3.1 Diacritics Completion Results

Diacritics completion was evaluated on three different data sets: the development part of the *WebColl* corpus and the Czech translations of two books: by Martin Gilbert's *A History of the Twentieth Century* (non-fiction) and Lion Feuchtwanger's *Foxes in the Vineyard* (fiction). All the diacritics in the testing data were simply removed. Then the system generated it back and the

α_l	non-fiction	fiction	*WebColl*
0.1	97.45%	96.82%	98.16%
0.3	97.49%	96.86%	98.21%
0.5	97.51%	96.85%	98.20%
0.7	97.45%	96.77%	98.09%
0.9	97.18%	96.48%	97.79%

Table 2: Results of *form – lemma* experiments. Only F_l and F_f are used for source modeling and $\alpha_f = (1 - \alpha_l)$.

α_t	non-fiction	fiction	*WebColl*
0.1	97.66%	97.20%	98.35%
0.3	97.83%	97.60%	98.53%
0.5	97.88%	97.74%	98.57%
0.7	97.85%	97.71%	98.52%
0.9	97.62%	97.53%	98.26%

Table 3: Results of *form – tag* experiments. Only F_t and F_f are used for source modeling and $\alpha_f = (1 - \alpha_t)$.

data set	α_f	α_l	α_t	accuracy – no Letter LM	accuracy – with Letter LM
non-fiction	0.31	0.28	0.41	97.9%	98.3%
fiction	0.31	0.14	0.55	97.7%	97.9%
WebColl	0.34	0.33	0.33	98.6%	99.1%

Table 4: The best accuracy values achieved on each testing set.

results wece compared to the originals.

The main parameters are the weights α_f, α_l and α_t of features F_f, F_l and F_t.

First, the contributions F_l and F_t were examined separately. In these experiments α_f was ranging from 0 to 1 and the weight $(1 - \alpha_f)$ was given either F_l or F_t, all the language models used were trigrams. The results of such experiments are shown in Tables 2, 3. It is clear from the plots that both features F_l, F_t improve the system performance. However the contribution of F_t is more significant. Surprisingly, it seems to be better to give all the weight to F_t than to give all the weight to F_f.

The performance boost achieved by using F_t is most visible on a comparison of results achieved on history domain and fiction domain data. For baseline setup ($\alpha_f = 1, \alpha_t = 0$), the accuracy is 97.39% on non-fiction data and 96.74% on fiction data, which means that the error rate is 25% bigger on fiction data. Nevertheless, by increasing the weight of F_t the difference in performance was becoming less significant and for the best parameter settings ($\alpha_f = 0.4, \alpha_t = 0.6$), the error rate on fiction data was only 7% bigger (97.72% accuracy on fiction data and 97.89 on non-fiction data).

Next, the estimation of the best parameter setting for each data set was done using a simple hill-climbing algorithm (see (Russell and Norvig, 2003) for details). As the starting point, all the weights were set equally. The resulting parameters and the accuracy values are shown in the Table 4. Experiments with the letter LM feature turned on were made also for the particular settings. It can be seen that the use of letter LM for the completion of unknown words improves the results significantly.

Results of the diacritics completion provided by *Korektor* were compared with those of *CZACCENT*[2], the diacritics completion tool developed by the NLP Center of Masaryk University in Brno, using the non-fiction data set. The accuracy achieved by *CZACCENT* was 95.85%, while the accuracy achieved by *Korektor* reached 98.3%. The error rate of *Korektor* is thus almost 2.5 times smaller.

[2]http://nlp.fi.muni.cz/cz_accent/index.php

3.2 Spell-checking Results

The quality of spell checkers is usually measured by the spelling correction error rate (i.e., the probability that the first given suggestion is correct, or that the correct suggestion is included in the list of first three suggestions, etc.). If a context-sensitive spell checker is considered and the ability of recognizing the real-word errors is to be tested, *F-measure* based on *precision* and *recall* can be used. It is a good indicator of a quality of a classifier.

During the evaluation of spelling correction, the optimal parameter settings (weights of distinct feature functions), estimated for the diacritic completion task, were used on the assumption that the features F_f, F_l and F_t are task independent and that their weighting obtained for one task will perform well for other tasks as well. The reason why we made no separate parameter tuning was that the size of available annotated spelling error data was too small. The weights were set according to the optimal setting for diacritics completion on non-fiction, i.e. $\alpha_f = 0.31$, $\alpha_l = 0.28$ and $\alpha_t = 0.41$. Channel feature F_{ch} was set to the weight $\alpha_{ch} = 1.0$, which assigns the same importance to both the source and the channel models.

For the evaluation of spell-checking, three different data sets were used: 1. *Chyby* – an error corpus (Pala et al., 2003); 2. *Audio* – transcription of an audio book; 3. *WebColl* test set – semi-automatically recognized spelling errors in the part of *WebColl* not used during the training. 4. *CzeSL* – a corpus of short essays written by learners of Czech as a foreign language

The error corpus *Chyby* (Pala et al., 2003) is a collection of essays written by students of Brno University of Technology, annotated for errors including spelling, morphological, syntactic and stylistic errors. Spell checking was tested on spelling and morphological errors since these types of errors are potentially recognizable by the system. There were 744 such errors, 321 of them were real-word errors. The high ratio of real-word errors show that most of the student works were already spell-checked.

The *Audio* test set, including the total of 1371 words, has 218 spelling errors, 12 of them real-word errors. The data set was built by transcribing an audio version of Jaroslav Hašek's novel *Osudy dobrého vojáka Švejka* 'The Good Soldier Švejk'.[3] The transcribed text was not post-corrected and the spelling error rate in the resulting text is relatively high.

The *WebColl* testing set was extracted from the part of *WebColl* not used during the system training. Spelling errors were collected semi-automatically using *Korektor*. Words identified by the spell-checker[4] as spelling errors were examined manually and the words that were flagged as spelling errors by mistake were filtered out. The result was a set of sentences containing spelling errors authorized by a human. The golden standard data were created manually in the next step. This approach made the collection of errors in the *WebColl* testing data feasible, but all real-word errors were missed (they were ignored, because they were not flagged as spelling errors by the spell checker in the first step). Thus, only the evaluation of suggestion accuracy could be done for this data.

The results of spelling correction accuracy evaluation for *Chyby*, *Audio* and *WebColl* are shown in Table 5 and the results of real-word error detection evaluation are shown in Table 6. For

[3]The audio extracts can be downloaded for free from the website of the Czech Radio: `http://www.rozhlas.cz/ctenarskydenik`.

[4]The spell checker made look-up for the out–of–vocabulary words easier. The correction suggestions provided by the spell checker were not taken into consideration during the creation of the golden standard data, so the fact that the spell checker to be tested participated in the creation of the testing set does not invalidate the testing set.

Number of suggestions	*WebColl*	*Chyby* 1	*Chyby* 2	*Audio (Korektor)*	*Audio (MS Word)*
1	91.4%	73.5%	82.3%	91.6%	71.2%
2	95.1%	80.1%	80.9%	97.2%	-
5	96.3%	80.9%	90.5%	98.6%	-

Table 5: Spelling correction rates achieved on the different data sets. For the *Chyby* corpus, two measurements were taken. In *Chyby 1,* all spelling errors are considered. For *Chyby 2,* only those spelling errors for which an appropriate correct version is in the lexicon are taken into account.

	Chyby	*Audio (Korektor)*	*Audio (MS Word)*
Precision	0.41	1.0	0.5
Recall	0.24	0.77	0.08
F-measure	0.31	0.87	0.14

Table 6: Real-word error correction statistics for *Audio* data set and *Chyby* corpus.

the *Audio* data set, comparison with the *Microsoft Word 2007* spell checker with grammar checking features turned on was made. For *MS Word* spell checker only the accuracy on the first suggestion was considered since there is no API that would allow to do the evaluation automatically. We are not certain how exactly the MS system works, since as far as we know no details have been published. However, we think that it is a conventional spell checker without any statistical model (for Czech) and a rule based grammar checker. Since the components seem to be separate, the grammar checker assumes the text has already been spell checked. This assumption, combined with what looks like a minimum edit distance algorithm to pick the first suggestion of the spelling module provides a disadvantage for MS Word system in the fully automated setting.

The results suggest that *Korektor* has a much higher accuracy on a single suggestion and ability to detect real-word spelling errors. The cases when the *MS Word* spell checker marked a grammar error were all because of capitalization problems, which suggests that there is no statistical real-word error detection in the Czech version of *MS Word* [5] Significantly lower spelling correction rate on the *Chyby* corpus can be caused by the fact that the properties of the texts in this corpus (technical topics) differ significantly from the training data properties (newspapers).

Finally, *Korektor*'s performance was tested on a sample from *CzeSL*, a learner corpus consisting of texts produced by learners of Czech as a second or foreign language. A part of the corpus is manually annotated in two stages with correct versions of deviant forms and relevant error codes. The annotators are instructed to correct both non-words (stage/Tier 1) and real-word errors (stage/Tier 2) to arrive at a grammatically correct sentence.[6]

In a pilot study of 67 short, doubly-annotated essays, *Korektor* was used to see whether automatic correction of learner texts is viable as a way to assist the annotator or even as a fully automatic annotation procedure.

Among the total 9,372 tokens, 918 (10%) were not recognized by a tagger (Spoustová et al., 2007) we used to find incorrect word forms. Even more forms were judged as faulty by the

[5]However, the *MS Word* spell checker for Czech is equipped with other capabilities that *Korektor* does not possess, such as punctuation checking.

[6]See (Hana et al., 2010).

annotators: 1,189 (13%) were corrected in the same way by both annotators at Tier 1 (T1) and 1,519 (16%) at Tier 2 (T2). Results of *Korektor* were compared with those of the tagger and with forms at T1 and T2, provided both annotators were in agreement. In the case of the tagger *Korektor* was deemed to be successful if it agrees with the tagger in the correct/incorrect status of the form. The results in terms of F-measure show 0.86 in comparison with the tagger, 0.72 in comparison with T1 and 0.53 in comparison with T2. The results support the idea to integrate *Korektor* into the learner corpus annotation workflow, either as suggestions to the annotator or as a solution to obtain fully automatic large-scale annotation at the cost of a higher error rate. In fact, the entire *CzeSL* corpus (2 mil. words, including unannotated parts) has been processed by *Korektor* to help querying the corpus.

4 Discussion

The results for spelling correction accuracy are not as good as those reported in (Brill and Moore, 2000) – around 95% on the first suggestion. However, those results were achieved for English and are not directly comparable. Czech with its rich morphology may be more challenging. For the *Chyby* corpus, significantly lower performance (73% on the first suggestion) may be caused by the heavy usage of technical terminology, such as names of software products, including their inflected forms. On the other hand, the fact that *Korektor* clearly outperformed the spell checker integrated in *Microsoft Word 2007* indicates the qualities of the system.

5 Conclusion and Future Work

We have designed and implemented a context-sensitive method of spell-checking and diacritics completion. The result is a spell checker that is freely available and ready for use.

Our primary concern was a robust, purely statistical, language-independent design. As a result, the system can be re-trained for any language. The only limitation is the availability of an annotated error corpus to train the error model, the availability of a general corpus to train the language model, and (depending on the language) a lemmatizer / POS tagger.

As for the spell-checking task, we focussed on the ability of the system to recognize real-word spelling errors and also to suggest the most likely corrections of spelling errors. In the spell-checking evaluation, *Korektor* achieved much better performance than the *MS Word 2007* spell checker.

Diacritics completion module was implemented on top of the spell checker. The accuracy of diacritics completion was about 98% with training and test data coming from different domains. Such performance is acceptable for many tasks, the best reported for Czech so far, and among the best reported for any language.

Korektor was also applied to texts produced by non-native speakers of Czech to provide anotation of a learner corpus. The result will soon be available for on-line searching via a concordancer.

In the future, we want to train *Korektor* for other languages by creating language and error models for the individual languages. In that setting a possible improvement could be achieved by utilization of more fine-grained error models as proposed by (Brill and Moore, 2000). In standard Czech it has a limited value as explained in Section 2.4, but the experiments on a learner corpus show that even in Czech it could still be useful for non-native speakers. For languages with less straightforward orthography, such as English, it would be even more valuable.

References

Brill, E. and Moore, R. C. (2000). An improved error model for noisy channel spelling correction. In *ACL '00: Proceedings of the 38th Annual Meeting on Association for Computational Linguistics*, pages 286–293, Morristown, NJ, USA. Association for Computational Linguistics.

Church, K. and Gale, W. (1991). Probability scoring for spelling correction. *Statistics and Computing*, 1(7):93–103.

Golding, A. R. and Roth, D. (1999). A winnow-based approach to context-sensitive spelling correction. *Machine Learning*, 34:107–130. 10.1023/A:1007545901558.

Hana, J., Rosen, A., Škodová, S., and Štindlová, B. (2010). Error-tagged learner corpus of Czech. In *Proceedings of the Fourth Linguistic Annotation Workshop*, Uppsala, Sweden. Association for Computational Linguistics.

Jurafsky, D. and Martin, J. H. (2008). *Speech and Language Processing: An Introduction to Natural Language Processing, Computational Linguistics and Speech Recognition*. Prentice Hall, second edition.

Kneser, R. and Ney, H. (1995). Improved backing-off for M-gram language modeling. In *Acoustics, Speech, and Signal Processing, 1995. ICASSP-95., 1995 International Conference on*, volume 1, pages 181–184 vol.1.

Marek, M., Pecina, P., and Spousta, M. (2007). Web page cleaning with conditional random fields. In Fairon, C., Naets, H., Kilgarriff, A., and de Schryver, G.-M., editors, *Proceedings of the 3rd Web As a Corpus Workshop, Incorporating CLEANEVAL*, pages 155–162, Louvain-la-Neuve, Belgium. UCL Pressess Universitaires de Louvain.

Mays, E., Damerau, F. J., and Mercer, R. L. (1991). Context based spelling correction. *Information Processing & Management*, 27(5):517 – 522.

Pala, K., Rychlý, P., and Smrž, P. (2003). Text corpus with errors. In *TEXT, SPEECH AND DIALOGUE*, volume 2807/2003 of *Lecture Notes in Computer Science*, pages 90–97. Springer.

Russell, S. and Norvig, P. (2003). *Artificial Intelligence: A Modern Approach*. Prentice-Hall, Englewood Cliffs, NJ, 2nd edition edition.

Spoustová, D., Hajič, J., Votrubec, J., Krbec, P., and Květoň, P. (2007). The best of two worlds: Cooperation of statistical and rule-based taggers for Czech. In *Proceedings of the Workshop on Balto-Slavonic Natural Language Processing 2007*, pages 67–74, Praha, Czechia. Association for Computational Linguistics.

Viterbi, A. J. (1967). Error bounds for convolutional codes and an asymptotically optimal decoding algorithm. *IEEE Transactions on Information Theory*, 13:260–269.

Using qualia information to identify lexical semantic classes in an unsupervised clustering task

Lauren ROMEO[1] *Sara MENDES*[1,2] *Núria BEL*[1]

(1) Universitat Pompeu Fabra
Roc Boronat, 138, Barcelona, Spain

(2) Centro de Linguística da Universidade de Lisboa
Avenida Professor Gama Pinto, 2, Lisboa, Portugal

{lauren.romeo,sara.mendes,nuria.bel}@upf.edu

ABSTRACT

Acquiring lexical information is a complex problem, typically approached by relying on a number of contexts to contribute information for classification. One of the first issues to address in this domain is the determination of such contexts. The work presented here proposes the use of automatically obtained FORMAL role descriptors as features used to draw nouns from the same lexical semantic class together in an unsupervised clustering task. We have dealt with three lexical semantic classes (HUMAN, LOCATION and EVENT) in English. The results obtained show that it is possible to discriminate between elements from different lexical semantic classes using only FORMAL role information, hence validating our initial hypothesis. Also, iterating our method accurately accounts for fine-grained distinctions within lexical classes, namely distinctions involving ambiguous expressions. Moreover, a filtering and bootstrapping strategy employed in extracting FORMAL role descriptors proved to minimize effects of sparse data and noise in our task.

KEYWORDS : lexical semantic classes, qualia roles, unsupervised clustering, automatic extraction of lexical information

Proceedings of COLING 2012: Posters, pages 1029–1038,
COLING 2012, Mumbai, December 2012.

1 Introduction

Acquiring lexical information is a complex problem, typically approached by relying on a number of contexts to contribute information for classification, following the Distributional Hypothesis (Harris, 1954) and the idea of distributional similarity. In this domain it is crucial to determine which distributional information is significant to characterize lexical items. In line with Pustejovsky and Ježek (2008), we will make apparent how focusing on occurrences indicative of the FORMAL role of the Generative Lexicon (GL) theory (Pustejovsky, 1995) allows for identifying lexical semantic classes.

Lexical classes are linguistic generalizations regarding characteristics of meaning that correspond to sets of properties shared by groups of words. Bybee and Hopper (2001) and Bybee (2010) state that words are organized in lexical-semantic classes defined as emergent properties of words that recurrently occur in a set of particular contexts. Though many NLP tasks rely on rich lexica annotated with lexical semantic classes, reliable lexical resources including this type of lexical information are mostly manually developed, which is unsustainable, costly and time-consuming, and makes conceiving methods to automatically acquire such information crucial. An approach for acquiring lexical semantic classes proposes to classify words according to their occurrences in contexts where other lexical items belonging to a known class also occur. Yet, this approach has some limitations, such as data sparseness and noise (see Section 2), which underline the importance of developing new strategies to improve its effectiveness. Authors such as Pustejovsky and Ježek (2008) have shown how distributional analysis and theoretical modeling interact to account for rich variation in linguistic meaning. In line with this proposal, we evaluate the significance of specific co-occurrences whose selection was motivated by aspects of GL.

This work attempts to evaluate whether information provided by qualia roles, in specific the FORMAL role, is sufficient to discriminate lexical semantic classes of English nouns. With the experiments depicted in this paper, we aim to empirically demonstrate to which extent these features draw together nouns from the same lexical semantic class in an unsupervised clustering task. In this paper, Section 2 depicts background and motivation of this work. Section 3 presents relevant information on the GL and dot-objects. Section 4 describes the methodology to automatically obtain and cluster FORMAL role descriptors of nouns. Section 5 and 6, respectively, describe and discuss results. Section 7 reflects upon lexical classes and logical polysemy and is followed by final remarks.

2 Background and Motivation

Mainstream approaches to lexical semantic class acquisition classify words according to occurrences, i.e. they use the entire set of occurrences of a word to determine class membership. Yet, this approach has some limitations. Blind-theory distributional approaches have been shown to fail to account for the wide range of linguistic behavior displayed by words in language data (see Pustejovsky and Ježek (2008)), while authors such as Bel et al. (2010) reported problems caused by sparse data, or lack of evidence, and noise, or information obtained though not aimed at. Concerning sparse data in classification tasks, nouns that appear only once or twice in a corpus, and not in sought contexts, can render ineffective any classifier or clustering algorithm by not providing sufficient information for classification. We aim to soften effects of sparse data in the context of a clustering task by using a bootstrapping technique reliant on natural language inference properties (see Section 4.1). Noise, another pervasive issue in lexical semantic class acquisition, can be due to different factors: the occurrence of very general nominal expressions (e.g. "kind of"), which do not provide distinguishing lexical information; misleading corpus features; and the use of low-level tools (see Bel et al. (2012)). We assume noise resulting from errors generated by NLP tools to be typically characterized by unique occurrences and we employ a filtering strategy to overcome its possible effects (see Section 4.1). Concerning misleading corpus features, these are often caused by ambiguity of lexical items, resulting in nouns occurring in contexts not corresponding to their assumed lexical class. This presents challenging problems in classification tasks, as most authors do not distinguish among related senses of the same word, i.e. they either consider it as part of the class or not (Hindle, 1990; Bullinaria, 2008; Bel et al., 2012). This is particularly problematic when words allow for multiple selection, i.e. when different senses of the same lexical item can be simultaneously selected for in one sentence (see (1)). Known as logical polysemy, this type of ambiguity has been shown to have well-defined properties (see Pustejovsky (1995) and Buitelaar (1998)) and has been consistently reported as a factor in lexical semantic acquisition tasks.

The newly constructed (LOCATION) *bank offers special conditions* (ORGANIZATION) *to new clients.* (1)

Approaches in this domain have usually tried to distinguish and isolate each word sense. We address this phenomenon differently, considering polysemous nouns as members of a given ambiguity class (within a wider lexical semantic class) and making apparent the relation between members of different classes by identifying shared properties beyond class limits. Given these considerations, we assume lexical units are complex objects that display rich variations of meaning in language use, placing ourselves within a theoretical framework that provides us the tools to account for this fact. Using the levels of representation and generative mechanisms in GL, we attempt to soften the effects of the aforementioned limitations in the automatic acquisition of lexical information.

3 Generative Lexicon theory

GL models the internal structure of lexical items in a computational perspective (Pustejovsky, 1995), proposing various levels of representation to semantically represent words, while allowing for the computation of meaning in context. Qualia Structure (QS) is one of these levels, consisting of 4 roles (FORMAL: what an object is; CONSTITUTIVE: what it is composed of; TELIC: its purpose; AGENTIVE: its origin), which model the predicative potential of lexical items. Here, we focus on the FORMAL role, defined as the role that distinguishes a lexical object within a larger domain (Pustejovsky, 1991).

QS also models phenomena such as polysemy of lexical items inherently complex in their meaning. These instances, *dot objects*, are the logical pairing of senses denoted by individual types in a complex type (Pustejovsky, 1995), which can pick up distinct aspects of the object, as well as properties of more than one class (Pustejovsky and Ježek, 2008), typically allowing for multiple selection (see (1)). Being able to represent lexical items as complex objects is useful in the context of our work as it provides a formal explanation for words belonging to more than one type, and essentially to more than one class.

Our experiment uses FORMAL role information as features for identifying lexical class membership. However, as there are no lexica available annotated with such information, we needed to obtain it automatically. Automatically extracting qualia roles with lexico-syntactic patterns has been receiving considerable attention for its success: Hearst (1992) identified lexico-syntactic patterns to acquire noun hyponyms, corresponding to the FORMAL role, whereas Cimiano and Wenderoth (2007) identified lexico-syntactic patterns to obtain information regarding semantic relations that correspond to each qualia role. As we needed information regarding the FORMAL role, not full lexical entries, in order for clusters to emerge, following Celli and Nissim (2009), we bypassed the representation of the entire QS, assuming semantic relations can be induced by matching lexico-syntactic patterns that convey a relation of interest.

4 Methodology

Given the unavailability of lexica annotated with FORMAL role information, and considering our basic goal of evaluating whether this information is enough to cluster together nouns of the same class, we extracted it from a corpus using lexico-syntactic patterns, following Cimiano and Wenderoth (2007), and then used it as features for a clustering task. In the experiment performed, we employed two steps: the extraction of FORMAL role descriptors from corpus data; and the clustering of this information. To obtain FORMAL role descriptors for our unsupervised clustering task, we used a part of the UkWaC Corpus (Baroni et al., 2009), consisting of 150 million tokens. We employed 60 seed nouns pertaining to three lexical semantic classes: HUMAN, LOCATION, and EVENT. The seed nouns were said to belong to a class if they contained a sense in WordNet (Miller et al., 1990) corresponding to one of the three classes. Seed nouns were not contrasted with actual occurrences in the corpus.

4.1 Extraction of FORMAL role descriptors using lexico-syntactic patterns

Firstly, seed nouns were used in handcrafted lexico-syntactic patterns, adapted from Hearst (1992) patterns and the list proposed by Cimiano and Wenderoth (2007), to extract FORMAL role descriptors. These patterns were specified through regular expressions with PoS tags given after each token.

*x*_(or/and)_other_*y*
*x*_such_as_*y*
*x*_(is/are)_(a/an/the)_(kind(s)/type(s))_of_*y*
*x*_(is/are)_also_known_as_*y*

TABLE 1 – Clues on which patterns used to detect FORMAL role information in corpus data were built

The information obtained was stored in vectors representing co-occurrences with seed nouns in relevant contexts (patterns), where each element corresponds to occurrences of a particular seed noun (*x*) with a possible FORMAL role descriptor (*y*), following Katrenko and Adriaans (2008). Using the clues in Table 1, we obtained 185 FORMAL role descriptors for 55 of the 60 seed nouns in 353 occurrences. Considering this, and given the properties of the clustering algorithm used (see Section 4.2) a random value would be provided to nouns not sharing feature information with any other noun in our data set. To avoid random cluster assignations and provide more significant information to the system, we filtered out the features not shared between at least two seed nouns, without controlling which class the shared features belonged to, thus maintaining an unsupervised environment. Though we employed a large set of data, there were not enough shared FORMAL role descriptors for an important part of our data set, leading us to devise a strategy to increase the information available to the clustering algorithm.

a. A mammal is a [type of] animal.
b. A zebra is a [type of] mammal.
c. Therefore, a zebra is a [type of] animal. (2)

To increase the amount of FORMAL role descriptors, we employed a bootstrapping technique (Hearst, 1998) relying on monotonic patterns for natural language inference (Hoeksema, 1986; van Behthem, 1991; Valencia, 1991), illustrated in (2). This strategy is consistent with GL lexical inheritance structure (Pustejovsky, 1995; 2001), which assumes lexical items obtain their semantic representation by accessing a hierarchy of types and inheriting information according to their QS, meaning qualia elements are viewed as categories hierarchically organized. To illustrate how this applies in our case, the HUMAN noun *treasurer* obtained *officer* as a FORMAL role descriptor, whereas *officer* extracted *person* and *employee* as its own FORMAL role descriptors. Assuming this lexical organization, we consider FORMAL role descriptors extracted for *officer* to also be features of *treasurer*. Thus, we gathered additional information regarding the nouns to cluster, using originally obtained FORMAL role descriptors as "seed nouns" to extract more elements in an attempt to overcome biases due to sparse data (see Section 6), as well as to reinforce information already obtained. Employing the original patterns and original extractions as seeds, we obtained information that was added to the vectors. We conducted one iteration of the bootstrapping technique, going up one level of generalization to obtain the final distribution of information below. Newly obtained information was unified with previously extracted features, filtering out any additional noise attained. Table 2 presents the final distribution of this information.

Class	Elements	Occurrences
HUMAN	61 elements	841 occurrences
LOCATION	43 elements	225 occurrences
EVENT	36 elements	216 occurrences

TABLE 2 – Distribution of FORMAL role descriptors extracted (after filtering and bootstrapping) per class of seed noun

4.1.1 Error Analysis

Basing our clustering experiment on automatically extracted FORMAL role descriptors, the accuracy of the information obtained was a concern. To assess the accuracy of the information obtained, the FORMAL role descriptors extracted were revised manually. Extractions were considered erroneous if they provided information not in accordance with the class that the seed nouns pertained to. Table 3 presents the results of this analysis. Erroneous extractions were due to faults of the extraction mechanism (i.e. problems handling phenomena such as PP attachment), PoS tagging errors, lexical ambiguity or erroneous statements in text (Katrenko and Adriaans, 2008), as well as errors due to logical polysemy (see Section 6). Note that although errors were identified, they were not filtered for the clustering task, i.e. all information (erroneous or not) was included (on the impact of errors in results see Section 6).

Class	**% of accurate FORMAL role descriptors extracted**
HUMAN	87.60%
LOCATION	63.54%
EVENT	75.96%

TABLE 3 – Percentage (%) of accurate FORMAL role descriptors obtained per class

4.2 Clustering nouns using FORMAL role information

The second step of our experiment consisted in clustering nouns using the FORMAL role descriptors extracted. Given the nature of our data, we selected the sIB clustering algorithm (see Slonim et al. (2002) for a formal definition) for the manner it manages large data sets. This algorithm calculates similarity between two vectors using the *Jensen-Shannon* divergence, which measures similarity between probability distributions, rather than the Euclidean distance, which can bias the results when the number of attributes representing the factors is unequal (Davidson, 2002). This was our case as our feature spaces depend on the number of FORMAL role descriptors each seed noun occurred with in the corpus. To empirically demonstrate to which extent FORMAL role descriptors draw together nouns from the same class, we designed an experiment using the sIB algorithm in WEKA (Witten and Frank, 2005) to cluster seed nouns into lexical semantic classes, based only on the FORMAL role information obtained.

5 Results

As mentioned, our goal was to cluster together nouns from the same lexical semantic class using only FORMAL role descriptors. As the evaluation of unsupervised distributional clustering algorithms is usually done by comparing results to manually constructed resources (see Rumshsiky et al. (2007), among others), we employed our list of pre-classified seed-words to determine if nouns of the same class clustered together. Tables 4 and 5 present clustering results. The distribution of nouns across each cluster is given by the percentage of nouns pertaining to each lexical class included in it. The total number of seed nouns in each cluster is also given.

Cluster 0	Cluster 1	Cluster 2	**Class**
0.9285	0	**0.5714**	HUMAN
0.0769	0.3913	0.1429	LOCATION
0	**0.6087**	0.2857	EVENT
14	**23**	7	TOTAL NUMBER OF SEED NOUNS PER CLUSTER

TABLE 4 – Distribution of nouns in a 3-way clustering solution

We experimented with a 3-way and a 4-way clustering solution. In the first, the number of clusters was defined by the number of known classes, and resulted in the clustering of HUMAN nouns (Cluster 0). LOCATION and EVENT nouns grouped together in Cluster 1, the remaining cluster being composed of nouns from all classes with very few features available (less than three), i.e. insufficient information for classification. Considering this, we employed a 4-way solution to see whether LOCATION and EVENT nouns could be discriminated. This solution distinguished between the three classes (Cluster 0, 1 and 3 in Table 5) with a fourth cluster containing the "sparse data" nouns also affecting the 3-way solution.

Cluster 0	Cluster 1	Cluster 2	Cluster 3	**Class**
0	0	**0.5714**	**0.9286**	HUMAN
0	**0.9**	0.1429	0.0769	LOCATION
1	0.1	0.2857	0	EVENT
13	10	7	14	TOTAL NUMBER OF SEED NOUNS PER CLUSTER

TABLE 5 – Distribution of nouns in a 4-way clustering solution

The results show that even after filtering and bootstrapping the features extracted, sparse data still affected the results. However, nouns whose most salient common trait was the lack of sufficient information were consistently grouped together. Thus, the clustering is able to both discriminate between lexical semantic classes and act as a filter to detect those nouns for which there is not sufficient information using only FORMAL role information extracted from corpus data.

6 Discussion

As shown, the clustering algorithm discriminated between the three classes considered, using only the FORMAL role descriptors extracted from corpora data as features. Leaving aside the nouns for which there was not enough information available (12.7% of our data set), EVENT, HUMAN and LOCATION nouns were discriminated in the 4-way clustering solution (Clusters 0, 1 and 3 in Table 5, respectively). In this section we analyze misclassified nouns, to understand the reasons behind their misclassification, aiming to evaluate to which extent they correspond to recurring phenomena in language, which can possibly be accounted for by additional strategies.

Although their impact is not significant, noisy extractions (see Section 4.1.1) play a role in misclassification. In the 4-way clustering results, for instance, an EVENT noun is included in the cluster dominated by LOCATION nouns due to errors in extraction, specifically the incorrect identification as a FORMAL role descriptor of the noun in a PP modifying the head noun of an NP, which should be the one extracted. This type of noise is mostly generated by the use of low-level NLP tools. Overall, however, the existence of some noise in the data did not significantly affect the clustering, as demonstrated by the accuracy of the results presented in the previous section.

Concurrently, although general patterns can be identified in language use, one of the main characteristics of language data is its heterogeneity, which means that elements of a given lexical class do not necessarily share all their features or show perfectly matching linguistic behavior. Moreover, considering lexical items are complex objects with different semantic dimensions, they may share properties with elements of more than one lexical class. This type of phenomenon is behind some of the misclassifications in our data, such as the inclusion of *factory*, whose expected lexical class was LOCATION, in the HUMAN nouns cluster. This misclassification seems to be related to the fact that a part of HUMAN class members tended to obtain FORMAL role descriptors typical of HUMAN nouns, as well as of ORGANIZATION nouns, making apparent that nouns do not always occur in the sense considered in our pre-classified list of seed nouns.

7 Lexical classes and logical polysemy

As aforementioned, some HUMAN nouns in our list of seed nouns obtain FORMAL role descriptors typical of ORGANIZATION nouns. This is a type of polysemy that occurred in our data only with plural HUMAN nouns, alluding to the work of Copestake (1995) and Caudal (1998), according to whom some HUMAN nouns show a specific type of polysemy when heading definite plural NPs: the polysemy between the individual HUMAN sense and the collection of HUMANs sense, which in turn is polysemous between the HUMANGROUP and ORGANIZATION senses. In (3) we see how the definite plural NP *the doctors* can select for the two senses typically denoted by collective nouns, while having also the possibility to denote individual entities, which is not possible with collectives (see (4a)) that cannot occur in contexts that force a distinct individual entity reading.

a. *The doctors lay in the sun.* (several individual HUMAN entities)
b. *The doctors protested in front of the hospital.* (HUMANGROUP)
c. *The administration negotiated with the doctors.* (ORGANIZATION) (3)

a. *# The staff lay in the sun.* (several individual HUMAN entities)
b. *The employees lay in the sun.* (several individual HUMAN entities)
c. *The staff protested in front of the hospital.* (HUMANGROUP)
d. *The administration negotiated with the staff.* (ORGANIZATION) (4)

As both collectives and definite plural NPs denote collections, Caudal (1998) states that it is desirable to account for the polysemy of such items morpho-syntactically. This analysis is further strengthened by the observation that, unlike pairs such as *employee* and *staff,* for nouns like *doctor* there is no lexicalization for "group of doctors" in English, the same being true for collective nouns like *audience* or *committee,* whose individual members are not lexicalized. Given such lexical gaps, morpho-syntax is the strategy available. However, though logically polysemous, plural definite NPs like *the doctors* do not allow for multiple selection as is typical of complex types: once the individual HUMAN sense has been selected for there is no access to the HUMANGROUP·ORGANIZATION sense, as suggested by (5) (see Buitelaar (1998) and Rumshisky et al. (2007)).

The administration negotiated with the doctors, which later lay in the sun. (several individual HUMAN entities) (5)

Pustejovsky (1995:155) claims these patterns of linguistic behavior are due to the information in the QS. In the case of expressions like *the doctors,* the dot element denoting the individual HUMAN entity and the complex type HUMANGROUP·ORGANIZATION correspond to different qualia roles, as represented in (6). Hence, the different senses of the expression cannot be selected at the same time.

$$\begin{bmatrix} \textbf{the doctors} & \\ \text{ARGSTR} = & \begin{bmatrix} \text{ARG1} = \textbf{x: human} \\ \text{ARG2} = \textbf{y: humangroup}\cdot\textbf{organization} \end{bmatrix} \\ \text{QUALIA} = & \begin{bmatrix} \text{FORMAL} = \textbf{x} \\ \text{CONST} = \textbf{is\_part\_of(x,y)} \end{bmatrix} \end{bmatrix} \quad (6)$$

Going back to the case of *factory,* which was clustered with HUMAN nouns (see Section 6), we will see how the polysemy described above partially applies to this noun. Among the descriptors obtained for *factory* we found, alongside descriptors typical of LOCATION nouns, nouns such as *sector, organization* and *profession,* also extracted for HUMAN nouns showing the HUMANGROUP·ORGANIZATION logical polysemy, indicating that nouns like *factory* are also complex objects, as illustrated below by (7):

a. *The factory on the corner of Main Street is big and brown.* (LOCATION)
b. *The factory summoned a protest against the new government sanctions.* (ORGANIZATION)
c. *There was a protest organized* (ORGANIZATION) *by the factory that burned down* (LOCATION) *last week.* (7)

In our data, *factory* shared features both with definite plural NPs headed by HUMAN nouns like *teacher* and *employee* and LOCATION nouns such as *kitchen* and *resort.* The linguistic behavior of *factory* can, therefore, be assumed to reflect the logical polysemy of ORGANIZATION·LOCATION·HUMANGROUP dot types identified by Rumshisky et al. (2007), and represented as follows:

$$\begin{bmatrix} \textbf{factory} & \\ \text{ARGSTR} = & \begin{bmatrix} \text{ARG1} = \textbf{x: location} \\ \text{ARG2} = \textbf{y: organization} \\ \text{ARG3} = \textbf{z: human} \end{bmatrix} \\ \text{QUALIA} = & \begin{bmatrix} \text{FORMAL} = \textbf{x}\cdot\textbf{y}\cdot\textbf{z} \end{bmatrix} \end{bmatrix} \quad (8)$$

For our work, the most relevant aspect of the behavior displayed by nouns like *factory* is that it makes apparent how our strategy to extract FORMAL role descriptors reflects the ambiguity of nouns to be clustered, which is often difficult to handle in NLP, particularly in classification tasks. The clustering solutions we obtained (see Section 5) grouped together HUMAN nouns, both those that display the ambiguity discussed in this section and those that do not, the same being true for LOCATION nouns. And yet, polysemous nouns display features that clearly point towards the existence of finer-grained distinctions, i.e. sub-classes within lexical semantic classes. This way, particularly given that these fine-grained distinctions are mirrored in FORMAL role descriptors, we assume it should also be possible to automatically recognize groups of nouns within the same ambiguity class, i.e. dot objects.

Hence, we expected the clustering algorithm to identify polysemous lexical items and distinguish them from other members of the same class. To validate this hypothesis we performed an additional iteration of the clustering using the same features and algorithm over previously identified clusters. The iteration was run individually over Clusters 1 and 3 (LOCATION and HUMAN noun clusters, respectively) from our 4-way clustering solution, as both clusters contained logically polysemous nouns. We obtained a 2-way clustering solution for each class, aiming to discriminate nouns strictly containing the LOCATION sense and those reflecting the polysemy described above for *factory*, on one hand, and nouns in the HUMAN·HUMANGROUP·ORGANIZATION ambiguity class from those strictly denoting human individuals on the other. Cluster 1 split into 2 clusters distinguishing between polysemous LOCATION nouns and those that are not, whereas for Cluster 3 the clustering algorithm arrived at a near perfect distinction of dot object nouns and non-ambiguous HUMAN nouns. The noun *factory* clustered with polysemous HUMAN nouns, once more confirming its semantic proximity with nouns of the HUMAN·HUMANGROUP·ORGANIZATION type. Hence, a second iteration of the same clustering algorithm over the same feature vectors was able to identify finer-grained distinctions within lexical classes, automatically recognizing groups of nouns in the same ambiguity class. In doing this, we validate our analysis regarding the role of logical polysemy and dot object types in the clustering solutions obtained, and further strengthen our original hypothesis.

Final remarks

In this paper, we proposed using automatically obtained FORMAL role descriptors as features to draw together nouns from the same lexical semantic class in an unsupervised clustering task. As there were no available lexica annotated with such information, we obtained it automatically and carried out clustering experiments. In line with the results, our initial hypothesis was supported: in an unsupervised clustering task using FORMAL role descriptors automatically extracted from corpora data as features, we showed it was possible to discriminate between elements of different lexical semantic classes. The filtering and bootstrapping strategy employed proved to minimize effects of sparse data and noise in our task. As shown in the 4-way clustering solution (see Table 5), the clustering exercise, as we designed it, also discriminated the nouns for which there was not sufficient information for a decision to be made on their membership to a cluster corresponding to one of the classes considered. Finally, we explained misclassifications through logical polysemy and showed how the method outlined in this paper allows for making finer-grained distinctions within lexical classes, recognizing lexical items in the same ambiguity class.

The results depicted in this paper demonstrate the validity of our hypothesis, while simultaneously showing that it is possible to incorporate the polysemous behavior of nouns in classification tasks (Hindle, 1990; Bullinaria, 2008) by using an approach that minimizes the effects of sparse data and noise (Bel et al., 2010; 2012). Considering these promising results, in future work we will address the possibility of extending our experiments to other qualia roles, as well as to other lexical semantic classes. At a more applied level, a further step consists in evaluating the feasibility of this approach to automatically extract lexical semantic classes in the automatic acquisition of rich language resources.

Acknowledgments

This work was funded by the EU 7FP project 248064 PANACEA and the UPF-IULA PhD grant program, with the support of DURSI, and by FCT post-doctoral fellowship SFRH/BPD/79900/2011.

References

Baroni, M., Bernardini, S., Ferraresi, A. and Zanchetta, E. (2009). The WaCky Wide Web: A Collection of Very Large Linguistically Processed Web-Crawled Corpora. *Language Resources and Evaluation, 43*(3), 209-226.

Bel, N., Coll, M. and Resnik, G. (2010). Automatic detection of non-deverbal event nouns for quick lexicon production. In *Proceedings of the 23rd International Conference on Computational Linguistics, (COLING 2010)*, Beijing, China (pp. 46-52).

Bel, N., Romeo, L. and Padró, M. (2012). Automatic Lexical Semantic Classification of Nouns. In *Proceedings of the Language Resources and Evaluation Conference (LREC 2012)*, Istanbul, Turkey.

Buitelaar, P. (1998). *CoreLex: Systematic Polysemy and Underspecification.* Doctoral dissertation, Brandeis University.

Bullinaria, J.A. (2008). Semantic Categorization Using Simple Word Co-occurrence Statistics. In M. Baroni, S. Evert and A. Lenci (Eds.), *Proceedings of the ESSLLI Workshop on Distributional Lexical Semantics*, 1-8. Hamburg, Germany.

Bybee, J. L. and Hopper, P. (2001). *Frequency and the emergence of language structure.* Amsterdam: John Benjamins.

Bybee, J. (2010). *Language, usage and cognition*. Cambridge: Cambridge University Press.

Caudal, P. (1998). Using complex lexical types to model the polysemy of collective nouns within the Generative Lexicon. In *Proceedings of the Ninth International Workshop on Database and Expert Systems Applications,* Viena, Austria (pp.154-159).

Celli, F., Nissim, M., (2009) Automatic Identification of semantic relation in Italian complex nominals, *In Proceedings of the 8th International Conference on Computational Semantics (IWCS-8)*, Tilburg, Netherlands.

Cimiano, P. and Wenderoth, J. (2007). Automatic Acquisition of Ranked Qualia Structures from the Web. In *Proceedings of the 45th Annual Meeting of the Association of Computational Linguistics*, Prague, Czech Republic (pp.888-895).

Copestake, A. (1995). The representation of group denoting nouns in a lexical knowledge base. In P. Saint Dizier and E. Viegas (Eds.) *Computation Lexical Semantics* (pp. 207-230). Cambridge: Cambridge University Press.

Davidson, I. (2002). *Understanding K-means non-hierarchical clustering.* (Tech. Rep. 02-2). Albany: State University of New York.

Harris, Z. (1954). *Structural Linguistics*. Chicago: Chicago University Press.

Hearst, M. (1992). Automatic acquisition of hyponyms from large text data. In *Proceedings of the 14th International Conference on Computational Linguistics (COLING 92)*, Nantes, France (pp. 539-545).

Hearst, M. (1998). Automated Discovery of Word-Net relations. In C. Fellbaum (Ed.), *An Electronic Lexical Database and Some of Its Applications* (pp. 131-153). Cambridge: The MIT Press.

Hindle, D. (1990). Noun classification from predicate-argument structures. In *Proceedings of the 28th Annual Meeting of the Association for Computational Linguistics*, Pittsburgh. Pennsylvania (pp. 268-275).

Hoeksema J. (1986). Monotonicity Phenomena in Natural Language. *Linguistic Analysis, 16,* 25-40.

Katrenko, S. and Adriaans, P. (2008). *Qualia Structures and their Impact on the Concrete Noun Categorization Task.* In *Proceedings of the "Bridging the gap between semantic theory and computational simulations" workshop (ESSLLI 2008),* Hamburg, Germany.

Miller, G.A., Beckwith, R., Fellbaum, C., Gross, D. and Miller, K.J. (1990). Introduction to WordNet: An online lexical database. *International Journal of Lexicography, 3*(4), 235-44.

Pustejovsky, J. (1991). The Generative Lexicon. *Computational Linguistics. 17*(4), 409–41.

Pustejovsky, J. (1995). *Generative Lexicon.* Cambridge: The MIT Press.

Pustejovsky, J. (2001). Type Construction and the Logic of Concepts. In P. Bouillon and F. Busa (Eds.), *The Language of Word Meaning* (pp. 91-123). Cambridge: Cambridge University Press.

Pustejovsky, J. and Ježek, E. (2008). Semantic coercion in language. beyond distributional analysis. *Italian Journal of Linguistics*, *20*(1), 175-208.

Rumshisky, A., Grinberg, V. and Pustejovsky, J. (2007). Detecting Selectional Behavior of Complex Types in Text. In *4th International Workshop on Generative Lexicon*, Paris, France.

Slonim, N., Friedman, N. and Tishby, N. (2002). Unsupervised document classification using sequential information maximization. In *Proceedings of the 25th International ACM SIGIR Conference on Research and Development in Information Retrieval*, Tampere, Finland (pp.129-136).

Valencia, V. (1991). *Studies on Natural Logic and Categorial Grammar.* Doctoral dissertation, University of Amsterdam.

van Benthem, J. (1991). *Language in Action: Categories Lambdas and Dynamic Logic.* North Holland: Elsevier Science Publishers.

Witten, I.H. and Frank, E. (2005). *Data Mining: Practical machine learning tools and techniques* (2nd ed.). San Francisco: Morgan Kaufmann.

A strategy of Mapping Polish WordNet onto Princeton WordNet [+]

Ewa Rudnicka[1], *Marek Maziarz*[1], *Maciej Piasecki*[1], *Stanisław Szpakowicz*[2,3]
1) Institute of Informatics, Wrocław University of Technology
2) School of Electrical Engineering and Computer Science, University of Ottawa
3) Institute of Computer Science, Polish Academy of Sciences
{rudnicka,maziarz,piasecki}@pwr.wroc.pl, szpak@eecs.uottawa.ca

ABSTRACT

We present a strategy and the early results of the mapping of *plWordNet* – one of the largest such language resources in existence – onto Princeton WordNet. The fundamental structural premise of *plWordNet* differs from those of most other wordnets: lexical units rather than synsets are the basic building blocks. The addition of new material to *plWordNet* is consistently informed by semantic relations and by various analyses of large corpora. The mapping is difficult because of the subtly distinct structures and because of WordNet's focus on synsets. We have designed a set of inter-lingual semantic relations and an effective mapping procedure. In the course of mapping, we have discovered a range of systematic differences between *plWordNet* and WordNet, and proposed ways of accounting for such differences.

Strategia rzutowania polskiego WordNetu na WordNet princetoński

STRESZCZENIE

Przedstawiamy strategię i wstępne wyniki rzutowania *plWordNetu* (Słowosieci) – jednego z największych takich zasobów językowych na świecie – na WordNet princetoński. Struktura *plWordNetu* różni się zasadniczo od struktury większości innych wordnetów: najmniejszym elementem sieci jest w nim nie synset, tylko jednostka leksykalna. Nowy materiał wprowadza się do *plWordNetu* po konsekwentnym i systematycznym rozpoznaniu relacji semantycznych, wynikającym z wielostronnej analizy dużych korpusów tekstu. Subtelne różnice w strukturze i specjalne miejsce synsetu w WordNecie sprawiają, że rzutowanie jest zadaniem trudnym. Zaprojektowaliśmy zbiór międzyjęzykowych relacji semantycznych i skuteczną procedurę rzutowania. W toku prac nad rzutowaniem wykryliśmy szereg systematycznych różnic między *plWordNetem* i WordNetem, po czym zaproponowaliśmy sposoby opisywania i wyjaśniania takich różnic.

KEYWORDS: wordnet, bilingual wordnet, wordnet-to-wordnet mapping, synset, lexical unit

SŁOWA KLUCZOWE: wordnet, wordnet dwujęzyczny, rzutowanie wordnetów, synset, jednostka leksykalna

[+] Work financed by the EU, the European Innovative Economy Programme Project POIG.01.01.02-14-013/09

Proceedings of COLING 2012: Posters, pages 1039–1048,
COLING 2012, Mumbai, December 2012.

1 Introduction

We present a strategy and the preliminary results of the mapping of Polish WordNet [*plWordNet*] onto Princeton WordNet [PWN] (Fellbaum 1998). There have been many attempts to build such mappings for wordnets, including EuroWordNet [EWN] (Vossen 1998, Vossen 2002), MultiWordNet (Bentivogli, et al. 2000; Bentivogli & Pianta 2000), AsianWordNet (Robkop et al. 2010) and IndoWordNet (Sinha, et al. 2006, Bhattacharyya 2010). Those projects usually took advantage of EWN's transfer-and-merge method, which largely consisted in the translation of most of PWN's structure and content into the target language. In contrast with this, *plWordNet*'s design and construction are independent of EWN or PWN, though inevitably substantially influenced by both. A unique corpus-based method was employed (Maziarz et al. 2012, Piasecki et al. 2009). Synsets in *plWordNet* are merely groups of similarly interconnected lexical units [LUs], and it is the LU that is the basic element of the network. We aim at linking two largely independent lexical systems. An inter-lingual mapping procedure connects *plWordNet* synsets with PWN synsets via an ordered set of inter-lingual semantic relations. Mapping is manual, but it is very strongly supported by automatic prompting and bookkeeping. Nouns are by far the most numerous class in PWN and in *plWordNet*, so we decided to test our procedure by the mapping of *plWordNet* nouns in specific domains: people*, artefacts*, places*, family relationships, food, drinks, time units, illnesses, economic vocabulary*, scientific disciplines and names connected with thinking and communication*. (The domains marked with * have been covered selectively.)

2 The mapping procedure

Our mapping procedure has three steps: recognize the sense of a source language synset S, search for candidate target-language synset(s) to link S with, and select the target-language synset and the appropriate inter-lingual relation [*I*-relation]. The mapping goes from *plWordNet*, so our source synsets are Polish synsets. The relations are applied in the following order: synonymy, hyponymy, hypernymy, meronymy, holonymy, near-synonymy, inter-register synonymy (Rudnicka et al. 2012). Once the highest possible relation has been established, others are no longer searched for and applied.

The procedure's first step is the proper identification of the source synset's sense. While very few *plWordNet* synsets have glosses, the considerably more frequent comments partly make up for the absence of glosses. Still, *plWordNet* is largely relation-based, so the key (sense) denominator will be the position of the given set of synonymous LUs in the overall wordnet structure. Nevertheless, the *plWordNet* editor begins with reading all LUs in the synset, plus the glosses or comments if there are any. For example, consider the Polish synset {zagranica 1, obczyzna 1, obce terytorium 1} (countries abroad, foreign lands, foreign territory):

(**Example 1**) {**zagranica** 1, obczyzna 1, obce terytorium 1} —*I*-holonymy→ {**foreign country** 1}
{**zagranica** 1} —hypo→ {strefa 2} {**foreign country** 1} —hypo→ {state 4}
{**zagranica** 1} —meronymy→ {świat 2}

The editor now considers the wordnet structure: the immediate hypernyms/hyponyms and meronyms and holonyms, if there are any. These are *strefa* and *świat* (zone, world). In case of doubts or difficulties with determining the synset sense, the editor considers the direct and indirect hypernyms (or other relations). Once the sense of the analysed synset has been established ('area located beyond the borders of a given country'), the editor can move to the next stage: seek the equivalent target synset in PWN. First, automatic prompts are checked if they are present. We re-implemented an automated mapping algorithm described in (Daudé et al. 2003, Daudé et al. 2000). If there is no prompt, the editor's language intuitions help select among target-language LUs one or two candidates which share the sense of the source-language synset ('foreign country'). These candidate LUs are located in PWN and their synsets are analysed with respect to their sense and position in the wordnet structure (hypernym *state*). Special attention must be paid to their immediate hypernym(s) and hyponyms (or other relations if there are any), since these are going to be juxtaposed with the equivalent relations of the target synset. The editor must check if there already exist, or are likely to be posited, inter-lingual synonymy links between any of the immediate relations of the source and the target synset. When such links exist or are likely to be established for most of the immediate relations, and the gloss of the target synset also matches the sense of the source synset, the inter-lingual synonymy is granted between the two synsets in question; otherwise, the next candidate is considered.

When the editor has exhausted the list of candidates to test, the previously chosen candidates are checked for their potential of linking via other relations. In Example 1, we could try linking our source synset with {world 4, earth 9, Earth 1, globe 1} and then {terrestial planet 1}; or with {solar system} via *I*-meronymy, because this synset can be a synonym of {świat 2}, a meronym of our source synset. That is not correct: the source synset {zagranica 1, obczyzna 1, obce terytorium 1} is in the domain of political organization, while the target synset is in the domain of geography, so the link must be dismissed. Next, we check the potential for linking of the candidate target synset {foreign country 1} —hyper→ {state 4} and decide that the source synset can be linked to this target synset via *I*-holonymy.

Since the start of our project in March 2012 we have introduced 28061 *I*-relation instances, see Table 1. The frequency of specific relations almost ideally agrees with the proposed ranking, based on our intuitions, concerning meaning closeness and the identity and inclusion of *denotata* sets. Surprisingly, *I*-hyponymy and *I*-hypernymy account for half of all inter-lingual relations. This suggests that the structures of *plWordNet* and PWN differ non-trivially.

I-synonymy	*I*-hyponymy	*I*-hypernymy	*I*-meronymy	*I*-holonymy	*I*-near-synonymy	*I*-inter-register synonymy
11173	12092	2622	927	332	649	266

Table 1. The number of inter-lingual relation instances

3 Mapping dilemmas and their solutions

In the course of mapping, we have faced dilemmas resulting both from the differences in the conceptual and lexico-grammatical structure of English and Polish, and from different methodological assumptions which underlie the construction of *plWordNet* and PWN.

3.1 Lexico-grammatical differences

The existence of lexical gaps is an obvious problem: concepts either are not lexicalised in one of the languages or do not exist in its extra-linguistic reality and conceptual structure (cultural gaps). An example of the former is the English word *chantry* meaning "a chapel endowed for singing Masses for the soul of the donor" (adopted from PWN's definition of {chantry 2}). The concept is not lexicalised in Polish, though it exists in its extra-linguistic reality, so {chantry 2} is linked to its closest Polish equivalent {kaplica wotywna 1} via *I*-near synonymy which signals partial correspondence in meaning and/or structure:

(Example 2) {**chantry** 2} —hypo→ {**chapel** 1} —hypo→ {**place of worship** 1}
{**kaplica wotywna** 1} —hypo→ {**miejsce kultu** 1} {**place of worship** 1} —*I*-hypo→ {**miejsce kultu** 1}
{**chantry** 2} ←*I*-near-synonymy→ {**kaplica wotywna** 1}

Cultural gaps can be the names of occupations or administrative functions never present in the other language's reality, thus not lexicalised. An apt example is {kaowiec 1}, a Polish term denoting an institution's employee responsible for the organization of cultural and recreational events in the Communist times. It is linked to the PWN synset {organizer 1 ...} meaning "a person who brings order and organization to an enterprise" via the *I*-hyponymy relation, which is the most often used relation in such cases:

(Example 3) {**kaowiec** 1} —hypo→ {**pracownik oświaty** 1}; {**organizator** 1}
{**organizator** 1 } —*I*-hyper→ {**organizer** 1 ...} {**kaowiec** 1} —*I*-hypo→ {**organizer** 1 ...}

The last type of lexical gaps is a mismatch resulting from different structuring of information, as in the case of English and Polish family relation hierarchies. Polish lexicalizes the distinction between the brother of one's father (*stryj* or *stryjek*) and one's mother (*wuj* or *wujek*), although the former term is marked and slowly becomes obsolete. Both terms are present in *plWordNet*. The unmarked term {wujek 2} is linked to its English equivalent {uncle 1} via the *I*-synonymy relation, while the marked term {stryj 1} is linked to {uncle 1} via *I*-hyponymy:

(Example 4) {**stryj** 1} —hypo→ {**wujek** 2}
{**wujek** 2} —*I*-near-synonymy→ {**uncle** 1} {**stryj** 1} —*I*-hypo→ {**uncle** 1}

The contrast can be expressed in English using the premodifying adjectives *paternal* and *maternal*, but the phrases *paternal uncle* and *maternal uncle* are not LUs in PWN. It is important to distinguish all these gaps from dictionary-content gaps due to differences in sources or methodology of building the two wordnets. (We repair most dictionary-content gaps in *plWordNet* and catalogue such gaps in PWN for possible future use.) Clearly, our most preferred I-synonymy relation cannot be used in either instance. Still, most of these cases can be handled by the I-hyponymy/hypernymy relation which we treat as the second option. Occasionally, we resort to I-meronymy/holonymy and *I*-near-synonymy.

Another type of dilemma is to do with the divergent degree of gender lexicalisation in English and Polish. Polish feminine nominal forms are frequent, while most of English nouns are not marked for gender, e.g., the English word *cousin* and Polish *kuzyn* '$\text{cousin}_{\text{masc}}$' and *kuzynka* '$\text{cousin}_{\text{fem}}$'. The most natural strategy to adopt here is again to resort to *I*-hyponymy, making the English {cousin 1} the hypernym of both Polish {kuzyn 1} and {kuzynka 1}, which can easily be construed as two sub-types of a more general concept. Interestingly, there are also mixed English synsets consisting of feminine and masculine forms (and sometimes also unmarked forms), as in {bondswoman 1, bondsman 2} or {chairman 1, chairwoman 1, chairperson 1}. I-hypernymy links such synsets to the corresponding Polish synsets lexically differentiated for gender.

(Example 5) {**bondswoman** 1, bondsman 2} —*I*-hyper→ {**gwarant** 1, poręczyciel 1}; {**poręczycielka** 2}

Apart from lexically marked gender, Polish has a variety of other marked forms such as diminutives and augmentatives, which either do not appear or are very rare in English. *plWordNet* has a special relation of *markedness* (*nacechowanie* in Polish) to show the links between base forms and their derivatives. Crucially, it is a relation between LUs, not synsets. It has three variants: *istota młoda* 'young creature', *diminutywność* 'diminutiveness' and *augmentatywność i ekspresywność* 'augmentativeness and expressiveness'. Polish LUs which denote young creatures but are not derivative forms, such as *cielę* or *cielak* 'calf', *prosię* or *prosiak* 'piglet', are linked to {młodzik, młodziak 2} 'young animal' via hyponymy. Analogically in PWN, synsets denoting young animals are attached by hyponymy to synsets denoting young sub-kinds of animals, such as {young mammal 1}. Now, PWN often places LUs denoting young animals with diminutive forms, when such forms exist, e.g., {kitten 1, kitty 3}, or {piglet 1, piggy 1, shoat 1, shote 1}. Since LUs denoting young creatures and diminutive LUs are not always in the same synsets, they are linked to PWN synsets via *I*-hyponymy relation, e.g.,

(Example 6) {**prosiaczek** 1} —dimin→ {**prosiak** 1}
{**kitten** 1, kitty 3}, {**piglet** 1, piggy 1, shoat 1, shote 1 } —hypo→ {**young mammal** 1}
{**piglet** 1, ..} —*I*-hypernymy→ {**prosiak** 1, prosię 2}; {**prosiaczek** 1, prosiątko 2}

In the rare cases without direct equivalents, *I*-synonymy will be applied. If an item has no English equivalents, we opt for *I*-hyponymy to link it to its English hypernyms.

3.2 Structural differences

3.2.1 Synonymy and synsets

The different strategy of synset construction and the resulting different idea of intra-lingual synonymy have led to systematic structural discrepancies. To begin with, *plWordNet* systematically distinguishes between count and mass nouns and never places them in the same synset. Conversely, PWN often neutralises this distinction at the synset level, putting both mass and count LUs into one synset (e.g. {furniture 1, piece of furniture 1, article of furniture 1}) (Miller 1998: 36). Such cases may cause problems for mapping, because it is hard to determine which *plWordNet* synset should be linked via *I*-synonymy, if any. *I*-hyponymy could be also applied to link the count nouns and mass noun *plWordNet* synsets to such "mixed" PWN synset.

(Example 7) {**mebel** 1} —*I*-hypo→ {**furniture** 1, piece of furniture 1, article of furniture 1}
{**mebel** 1} —hypo→ {**element wyposażenia** 1}, {**sprzęt** 2} {**mebel** 1} —meronymy→ {**umeblowanie** 1}
{**umeblowanie** 1} —*I*-hypo→ {**furniture** 1, piece of furniture 1, article of furniture 1}

There also are PWN synsets with singular and plural forms of the same lemma, e.g., {dumpling, dumplings 1} with singular and plural hyponyms such as {matzo ball 1}, {wonton 1}, {gnocchi 1}. These are also linked via *I*-hyponymy to their corresponding *plWordNet* synsets:

(Example 8) {**pierog** 1, pieróg 2} —*I*-hypo→ {**dumpling** 1, dumplings 1}
{**pierogi** 1} —*I*-hypo→ {**dumpling** 1, dumplings 1}
{**matzo ball** 1}, {**wonton** 1}, {**gnocchi** 1} —hypo→ {**dumpling** 1, dumplings 1}

The differently defined synonymy affects the definition of hyponymy in *plWordNet* and PWN. In PWN, singular and collective nouns (*pluralia tantum*) may be hyponyms/hypernyms of each other. This is impossible in *plWordNet*: {dumpling 1, dumplings 1} 'small balls or strips of boiled or steamed dough' is a hypernym of synsets {gnocchi} '(Italian) a small dumpling made of potato or flour or semolina that is boiled or baked and is usually served with a sauce or with grated cheese', {matzo ball, matzoh ball, matzah ball} 'a Jewish dumpling made of matzo meal; usually served in soup' and {won ton, wonton} 'a Chinese dumpling filled with spiced minced pork; usually served in soup'. A somewhat drastic, though maybe not unmotivated, case of using a broad notion of synonymy in PWN is the synset {monte 1, four-card monte 1, three-card monte 1} 'a gambling card game of Spanish origin; 3 or 4 cards are dealt face up and players bet that one of them will be matched before the others as the cards are dealt from the pack one at a time'. It is obvious that a *four-card monte* is not a synonym of a *three-card monte*, they are just both hyponyms of *monte*. In Poland *monte* is not so popular. There only is a three-card monte – *trzy karty* (literally 'three cards'). The synsets were joined by inter-language hyponymy, since the English equivalent *three-card monte* of the Polish LU is in the PWN synset:

(**Example 9**) {**trzy karty** 1} —*I*-hypo→ {**monte** 1, four-card monte 1, three-card monte 1}

To sum up, we consistently use *I*-hyponymy in all cases of mixed PWN synsets.

3.2.2 Differently defined relations

There is a lot of correspondence between the set of linguistic relations employed by PWN and *plWordNet* and their respective construction, but there are differences. They are reflected in the structure of both wordnets and may have consequences for the mapping. To give an example, PWN uses the conjunction *or* in its definitions, thus allowing for the hypernymy *and/or*, while *plWordNet* restricts its hypernymy to *and*. For example, the PWN synset {musical 1, ...} was given the gloss 'a play or film whose action and dialogue is interspersed with singing and dancing'; it received the following relational description in PWN (two instances of hyponymy):

(**Example 10**) {**musical**, musical comedy, musical theater} —hypo→ {movie, film, picture, ...},
{**musical**, musical comedy, musical theater} —hypo→ {play 2}.

The word *musical* gained a similar definition in (Dubisz 2004): "a theatre or film spectacle with comedic or melodramatic content, consisting of oral, sung or danced parts". We had to split the concept into theatrical musical and musical film in order to avoid *or*-hyponymy:

(**Example 11**) {**musical** 1, komedia muzyczna} —hypo→ {**film** 1, obraz 6} 'movie, picture',
{**musical** 2} —hypo→ {**przedstawienie** 7} 'play'

Or-hyponymy was banned from *plWordNet* in order to preserve the transitivity of hyponymy. For example, the English synset {musical 1, ...} also contains synonyms *musical comedy* and *musical theatre.* The first is a synonym of *musical* (Merriam-Webster Dictionary Online). The second clearly refers to theatrical musical (Oxford English Dictionary). In fact, the latter LU should be a hyponym, not a synonym, of *musical* in the broader sense. This leads to a paradox: two synonyms of the synset have both hyponymy relations (to a play and to a film), while *music(al) theatre* has only one (to a play). The opposite could be noted in *plWordNet* where the LU *komedia muzyczna* could be found in the meaning *film musical.* It is linked to {film 1, obraz 6} 'movie, picture' with hyponymy and is, of course, a synonym of Polish *musical 1.* It seems that in PWN hyponymy is only partly transitive and in some cases synonymy captures cases of hyponymy. *Musicals* from PWN and *plWordNet* had to be, naturally, linked with *I*-hyponymy:

(**Example 12**) Pol. {**musical** 1, komedia muzyczna} —*I*-hypo→ Eng. {**musical** 1, ...}
Pol. {**musical** 2} —*I*-hypo→ Eng. {**musical** 1, ...}

Relations are not the only source of difficulty. Glosses also pose dilemmas during mapping. A case of *thriller* 'a suspenseful adventure story or play or movie' is somehow similar to *musical.* Here the connective *or* appears twice, surprisingly followed by only one hyponymy:

(**Example 13**) {**thriller** 1} —hypo→ {**adventure story** 1, heroic tale 1}

(Dubisz 2004) gives a very similar definition: "a movie, novel or play whose sensational and supenseful action is imbued with elements of mystery, horror and eeriness; a thriller". In *plWordNet* we distinguish three senses according to the medium: (a) 'movie', (b) 'novel', (c) 'play'. Unfortunately the English gloss does not fit the English relation instance for *thriller*, so we are not sure whether Polish {thriller 1} should be linked to English {thriller} with *I*-synonymy (according to the English relation instance) or whether all three Polish *thrillers* ought to be connected with the English synset with *I-hyponymy* (according to the English gloss). We chose the former solution, assuming that for a wordnet relations are more important than glosses:

(**Example 14**) Pol. {**thriller** 1} 'novel' —*I*-syn→ Eng. {**thriller** 1},
Pol. {**thriller** 2, dreszczowiec 1} 'movie' —*I*-hypo→ Eng. {**movie**, film, picture, ...},
Pol. {**thriller** 3} 'play' —*I*-hypo→ Eng. {**play** 2}

3.2.3 Different relations to code the same conceptual dependencies

Sometimes equivalent synsets are differently interlinked within the two wordnets, e.g., {jewelry, jewellery} is linked via *hyponymy* to synsets {bracelet, bangle} 'jewelry worn around the wrist for decoration', {ring, band} 'consisting of a circlet of precious metal (often set with jewels) worn on the finger', {earring} 'jewelry to ornament the ear; usually clipped to the earlobe or fastened through a hole in the lobe' and many others. The Polish counterpart of *jewellery* – *biżuteria* – is linked to the equivalents of *ring* (*pierścionek*, *pierścień*), *bracelet* (*bransoletka*) and *earring* (*kolczyki*, *klipsy*) and so on. Linking is with a different relation type, *holonymy* (the *part* subtype). So, the equivalent synsets appear in different structures:

(**Example 15**) {**jewellery**} —hyper→ {**bracelet**} vs. {**biżuteria**} —holonymy→ {**bransoletka**}.

We have discussed in Section 3.1 *plWordNet*'s *markedness* relation, which has no exact counterpart in PWN (*is-a-derivative-of*, is too broad for our purposes). There are a few more nominal relations specific to *plWordNet*. The *inhabitant* relation is quite instructive. In PWN, the synset {American 1} 'native or inhabitant of the United States' is linked to the synset {United States, United States of America, America, the States, US, U.S., USA, U.S.A.} via the *member* meronymy relation. In *plWordNet*, {Amerykanin 2} and {USA, Ameryka, Stany Zjednoczone, Stany} are connected via the inhabitant relation, because *Amerykanie* (Americans$_{plural}$) inhabit *Ameryka* and this is expressed by the systematic derivational relation (Maziarz et al. 2011). Despite this difference, the synsets will be linked via *I*-synonymy:

(**Example 16**) {**United States**, ...} ←*I*-synonymy→ {**USA**, Ameryka, Stany Zjednoczone, Stany}
↑meronymy (member) ↑ ↑inhabitant↑
{**American** 1} ←*I*-synonymy→ {**Amerykanin** 2}

The two wordnets differ not only in the repertory of lexico-semantic relations but also in sense distinctions. We have already discussed the case of English *thriller*, strongly interrelated with three '*thrillers*' in *plWordNet*, and *musical* which in *plWordNet* gained two equivalent *musicals* (its *I*-hyponyms). The case of *chapel* and *kaplica* is similar. In PWN *chapel* was given a definition 'a place of worship that has its own altar'. Because in *plWordNet* senses are distinguished by relations in which a particular word-sense pair is involved, Polish *kaplica* had two meanings: 'autonomous building with its own altar' and 'part of another building (church or cloister) with its own altar'. Relation instances of the two synsets are illustrated below:

(**Example 17**) {**kaplica** 1} 'chapel, autonomous building' —hypo→ {**świątynia**} 'temple'
{**kaplica** 1} —hyper→ {**kaplica przycmentarna**, …} 'cemetery chapel'
{**kaplica** 2} 'chapel, part of another building' —hypo→ {**pomieszczenie** 3} 'room'
{**kaplica** 2} —mero:place→ {**klasztor** 1} 'monastery' {**kaplica** 2} —mero:place→ {**kościół** 2} 'church'

The two senses do have different lexical neighbourhoods, so we assume that they should stay separate. PWN shows an alternative way of describing the concept 'chapel'. Instead of splitting the sense, it was kept intact and linked to a higher hypernym {place of worship, …}. At a first glance the two approaches appear justified. Unfortunately, the hypernym {place of worship, house of prayer, house of God, house of worship} was itself linked to {building, edifice} and was given too narrow a definition 'any building where congregations gather for prayer', although {chapel} has two hyponyms which clearly are not buildings: {lady church} 'a small chapel in a church; dedicated to the Virgin Mary' and {side chapel} 'a small chapel off the side aisle of a church'. Despite this inconsistency we decided to link our {kaplica 1} and {kaplica 2} with *I-hyponymy* with {chapel 1}, assuming that it has both meanings:

(**Example 18**) {**kaplica** 1} 'building' —I-hypo→ {**chapel** 1} 'a place of worship',
{**kaplica** 2} 'room' —I-hypo→ {**chapel** 1} 'a place of worship'.

3.2.4 Dictionary-content mismatches

Mapping is also made more difficult by *dictionary content gaps*. We have decided that, though we could improve *plWordNet*, we were not supposed to make any changes inside PWN. What is a dictionary gap? Lexical gaps are caused by specificities of the two languages, dictionary gaps are produced by limitations of any dictionary/thesaurus/wordnet size. For example, in PWN names of artists are restricted to only one domain of art even in cases when they apply quite systematically to more than one domain. For example, {impressionist 1} 'a painter who follows the theories of Impressionism' has one hypernym relation instance to {painter 1}, although there is a clear evidence that the word could be used also to indicate impressionist musicians (see the entry in (Procter 1978)) or poets (see *impressionism* in (Myers, Wukasch 2003)). Polish *impresjonista* 'impressionist painter, musician or poet' is defined using two *and*-hypernyms *artysta* 'artist' and *przedstawiciel* 'exponent (of an artistic trend)'. We cope with the lexical database mismatch between PWN and *plWordNet* simply using *I*-hyponymy between more specific English {impressionist 1} and broader Polish {impresjonista 1}.

Conclusion and perspectives

The system of inter-lingual relations and the mapping procedure proposed in this paper have been shown to work successfully. We have managed to map about 28000 *plWordNet* synsets onto PWN synsets. All edited *plWordNet* synsets have been linked to PWN's synsets by one of the proposed inter-lingual relations. The manual mapping was enhanced by an automatic prompt system, which turned out to be useful. The created mapping is especially valuable in that we have been linking two completely independently created large-scale wordnets. It enabled a systematic comparison of *plWordNet*'s and PWN's structure and content, but also *plWordNet*'s verification and correction. We have encountered mapping dilemmas which boil down to lexico-grammatical differences between English and Polish and to structural incompatibilities resulting from different methodologies which underlie the construction of the two wordnets; we have proposed systematic solutions.

References[*]

Bentivogli, L., Pianta, E., Pianesi, F. (2000). *Coping with lexical gaps when building aligned multilingual wordnets. Proceedings of LREC 2000.* Athens, Greece. 993-997.

Bentivogli, L., Pianta, E. (2000). *Looking for lexical gaps. Proceedings of Euralex 2000,* Stuttgart, Germany. multiwordnet.fbk.eu/paper/wordnet-euralex2000.pdf

Bhattacharyya, P. (2010). *IndoWordNet. Lexical Resources and Evaluation Conference LREC 2010,* Malta. www.cse.iitb.ac.in/~pb/papers/lrec2010-indowordnet.pdf

Daudé, J., Padró, L., Rigau, G. (2003). *Making Wordnet mappings robust. Proceedings of the 19th Congreso de la Sociedad Española para el Procesamiento del Lenguage Natural.* Madrid, Spain. 47-54.

Daudé, J., Padró, L., Rigau, G. (2000). *Mapping Wordnets Using Structural Information. Proceedings of the 38th Annual Meeting of the Association for Computational Linguistics ACL'00.* Hong Kong. www.aclweb.org/anthology-new/P/P00/P00-1064.pdf

UDP = Dubisz, S. (Ed.). (2004). *Uniwersalny słownik języka polskiego* [*Universal Dictionary of Polish Language*], electronic version 1.0. Wydawnictwo Naukowe PWN.

Hamp, B., Feldweg H. (1997). *GermaNet – a Lexical-Semantic Net for German. Proceedings of the ACL Workshop on Automatic Information Extraction and Building of Lexical Semantic Resources for NLP Applications.* Madrid. 9-15.

Fellbaum, Ch. (Ed). (1998). *WordNet: An Electronic Lexical Database.* MIT Press: Cambridge, Massachusets.

Maziarz, M., Piasecki, M., Szpakowicz., S., Rabiega-Wiśniewska, J. (2011). *Semantic Relations Among Nouns in Polish WordNet Grounded in Lexicographic and Semantic Tradition. Cognitive Studies, 11,* 161-182.

Maziarz, M., Piasecki, M., Szpakowicz, S. (2012). *Approaching* plWordNet *2.0. Proceedings of the 6th Global Wordnet Conference,* Matsue. 189-196.

Miller, G.A. (1998). *Nouns in WordNet.* In Fellbaum, Ch. (Ed.). *WordNet. An Electronic Lexical Database.* The MIT Press. 23-46.

Myers, J, Wukasch D. C. (2003). Dictionary of Poetic Terms. University of North Texas Press.

Piasecki, M., Marcińczuk, M., Musiał, A., Ramocki, R. and Maziarz, M. (2010), *WordnetLoom: a Graph-based Visual Wordnet Development Framework,* Proceedings of International Multiconference on Computer Science and Information Technology - IMCSIT 2010, Wisla, Poland, 18-20 October 2010, 469-476.

Piasecki, M., Szpakowicz, S., Broda, B. (2009). *A Wordnet from the Ground Up.* Oficyna Wydawnicza Politechniki Wrocławskiej: Wrocław.

Piotrowski, T., Saloni, Z. (2002). *Słownik angielsko-polski, polsko-angielski.*

Polish Wikipedia: pl.wikipedia.org

[*] (Rudnicka et al. 2012) is a much more complete version of this paper.

Polish Wiktionary: pl.wiktionary.org

Procter P., ed. (1978) Longman Dictionary of Contemporary English. www.ldoceonline.com/

Robkop, K., Thoongsup, S., Charoenporn, T., Sornlertlamvanich, V., Isahara, H. (2010). *WNMS: Connecting the Distributed WordNet in the Case of Asian WordNet. The 5th International Conference of the Global WordNet Association (GWC-2010).* Mumbai, India, 31st Jan. - 4th February.

Rudnicka, E., Maziarz, M., Piasecki, M., Szpakowicz, S. (2012) "Mapping *plWordNet* onto Princeton WordNet". www.nlp.pwr.wroc.pl/pl/slowosiec-20/130/show/publication (Technical Report).

Sinha, M., Reddy, M., Bhattacharyya, P. (2006). *An Approach towards Construction and Application of Multilingual Indo-WordNet. 3rd Global WordNet Conference (GWC 06).* Jeju Island, Korea. www.cse.iitb.ac.in/~pb/papers/gwc06_IITB_IndoWN.pdf

Vossen, P. (2002). *EuroWordNet General Document.* EuroWordNet Project LE2-4003 & LE4-8328 report. University of Amsterdam.

Vossen Piek (Ed.). (1998). *EuroWordNet: a multilingual database with lexical semantic networks for European Languages*. Kluwer, Dordrecht.

A Hierarchical Domain Model-Based Multi-Domain Selection Framework for Multi-Domain Dialog Systems

Seonghan Ryu[1] *Donghyeon Lee*[1] *Injae Lee*[1] *Sangdo Han*[1] *Gary Geunbae Lee*[1]
Myungjae Kim[2] *Kyungduk Kim*[2]
(1) Pohang University of Science and Technology
(2) Samsung Electronics
{ryush,semko,lij1984,hansd,gblee}@postech.ac.kr
{koong.kim,kduk.kim}@samsung.com

ABSTRACT

We proposed a hierarchical domain model (HDM)-based multi-domain selection framework (MDSF) for multi-domain dialog systems. The HDM-based MDSF statistically detects one or more candidate domains and heuristically determines one or more final domains from among the candidate domains. The HDM is used in both the candidate domain detection and final domain determination components. Multi-domain dialog systems that employ the HDM-based MDSF provide service to one or more domains at the same time, whereas traditional multi-domain dialog systems provide service to only one domain at a time. To validate the HDM-based MDSF, we developed a multi-domain dialog system for TV program, video-on-demand, and TV device domains. The experimental results show that the HDM-based MDSF correctly selects one or more domains and enables multi-domain dialog systems to provide more accurate and rapid dialog service than traditional multi-domain dialog systems.

TITLE AND ABSTRACT IN KOREAN

다중 도메인 대화 시스템을 위한 계층적 도메인 모델 기반의 다중 도메인 선택 프레임워크

본 논문은 다중 도메인 대화 시스템을 위한 계층적 도메인 모델 기반의 다중 도메인 선택 프레임워크를 제안한다. 계층적 도메인 모델 기반의 다중 도메인 선택 프레임워크는 통계적 방법으로 한 개 이상의 후보 도메인을 검출하고, 규칙으로 후보 도메인 중 한 개 이상의 최종 도메인을 결정한다. 후보 도메인 검출 및 최종 도메인 결정 단계에서 계층적 도메인 모델이 사용된다. 기존의 다중 도메인 대화 시스템이 한 번에 한 개의 도메인에 대한 서비스만을 제공하는 반면, 계층적 도메인 모델 기반의 다중 도메인 선택 프레임워크를 적용한 다중 도메인 대화 시스템은 한 번에 한 개 이상의 도메인에 대한 서비스를 제공한다. TV 프로그램, 주문형 비디오, TV 장치에 대한 다중 도메인 대화 시스템에 대한 실험을 통해 계층적 도메인 모델 기반의 다중 도메인 선택 프레임워크는 한 번에 한 개 이상의 도메인을 정확하게 선택할 수 있고, 다중 도메인 대화 시스템이 기존 다중 도메인 대화 시스템에 비해 정확하고 신속한 대화 서비스를 제공할 수 있게 함을 확인할 수 있었다.

KEYWORDS : Multi-domain dialog system; Multi-domain selection; Hierarchical domain model; Candidate domain detection; Final domain determination
KEYWORDS IN KOREAN : 다중 도메인 대화 시스템; 다중 도메인 선택; 계층적 도메인 모델; 후보 도메인 검출; 최종 도메인 결정

1 Introduction

A dialog system is a natural and effective interface between humans and machines because dialog is a natural method of human communication. Recently, multi-domain dialog systems that provide service to multiple domains have become widely employed in real-life situations (Allen et al., 2000; Komatani et al., 2006; Larsson and Ericsson, 2002; Pakucs, 2003). Multi-domain dialog systems that employ the distributed architecture first select a domain based on a user utterance, and then execute the domain-specific processes of the selected domain (Lin et al., 1999). Therefore, previous research has focused on the correct selection of a single domain based on a user utterance (Çelikyilmaz et al., 2011; Ikeda et al., 2008; Nakano et al., 2011).

However, to our knowledge, no previous research has focused on the selection of one or more domains at the same time for multi-domain dialog systems that provide service to closely related domains. For example, suppose that a multi-domain dialog system provides service to a TV program and video-on-demand (VOD) domains. When a user asks "*Are there any animation programs?*" the system should select both the TV program and the VOD domains. In contrast, when the user says "*Play it.*" in the middle of a dialog for the VOD domain, the system should select the VOD domain based on the dialog history, although the user utterance could be accepted by both the TV program and the VOD domains. However, traditional multi-domain dialog systems have no method of selecting one or more domains at the same time.

In this paper, we proposed a hierarchical domain model (HDM)-based multi-domain selection framework (MDSF). The HDM-based MDSF selects one or more domains at the same time. The HDM-based MDSF consist of two processes: statistically detecting one or more candidate domains based on a user utterance and heuristically determining one or more final domains from among the candidate domains based on the previous domains and the type of the dialog act of the user utterance. The HDM is used in both the candidate domain detection component and the final domain determination component. We developed a multi-domain dialog system using the HDM-based MDSF for TV program, VOD, and TV device domains to validate the HDM-based MDSF.

This paper is organized as follows: Section 2 briefly introduces related work. Section 3 introduces multi-domain dialog systems that employ the MDSF. Section 4 describes the detailed method of the HDM-based MDSF. Section 5 demonstrates the experimental results of the HDM-based MDSF. Finally, we draw conclusions and make suggestions for future work.

2 Related work

Most research on domain selection has focused on selecting a domain correctly. To avoid erroneous domain switching, a two-stage domain selection framework determines whether the previous domain is continued, and then selects another domain only if the previous domain is determined to not be continued (Nakano et al. 2011). To cope with speech recognition errors and grammatically incorrect user utterances, a robust domain selection method integrates topic estimation results and dialog history (Ikeda et al., 2011).

Most research on domain selection has not considered the scenario of encountering a user utterance that can be served by several domains together at the same time. In contrast, we consider multi-domain dialog systems that provide service to one or more domains at the same time. Therefore, we proposed the HDM-based MDSF.

3 Multi-domain dialog systems

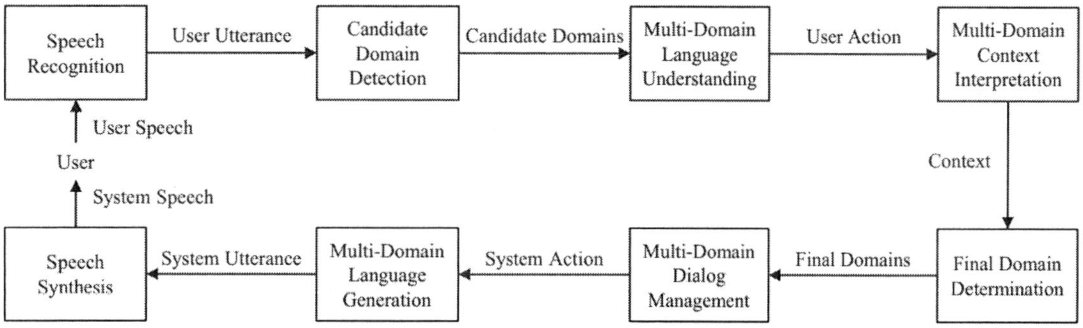

Figure 1 - The architecture of a multi-domain dialog system.

A dialog system is a computer software program that provides natural and effective interaction between humans and machines (McTear, 2002). Users ask dialog systems for services using natural language, and the dialog systems respond using natural language. Some multi-domain dialog systems select one or more domains based on a user utterance and provide service to the selected domains at the same time. The architecture of these multi-domain dialog systems (Figure 1) consists of eight main components:

- **Speech recognition**: the recognition of a user utterance from a user speech.
- **Candidate domain detection**: the detection of one or more candidate domains based on a user utterance.
- **Multi-domain language understanding**: the classification of a dialog act and recognition of a named entity sequence based on a user utterance for the candidate domains.
- **Multi-domain context interpretation**: the determination of either continuing a previous context or setting a new context for the candidate domains.
- **Final domain determination**: the determination of one or more final domains from among the candidate domains.
- **Multi-domain dialog management**: the management of dialog flow by deciding a next system for the final domains.
- **Multi-domain language generation**: the generation of the textual representation of a system action for the final domains.
- **Speech synthesis**: the synthesis of a system speech from the system utterance.

The MDSF consists of the candidate domain detection and final domain determination components. If the MDSF misunderstands the domains of a user utterance, the multi-domain dialog system would perform unexpected behaviors. Therefore, the MDSF should correctly select one or more domains and enable the multi-domain dialog system to provide service to one or more domains at the same time.

Turn	Speaker	Utterance	Domain
1	User	Play "The Closer."	TV program
	System	Do you mean a TV program or a VOD?	TV program and VOD
2	User	TV program.	TV program
	System	The TV program has been started.	TV program

Table 1 - The dialog in a single-domain scenario in a multi-domain dialog system.

For example, in the dialog in a single-domain scenario in a multi-domain dialog system (Table 1), a user tells the system "*Play 'The Closer'*." in the first turn. The system understands the domains of the user utterance as being either TV program or VOD, and then asks the user to select the desired domain. This is because playing both TV program and VOD at the same time is impossible to the system.

Turn	Speaker	Utterance	Domain
1	User	Are there any animation programs?	TV program and VOD
	System	This is the list of the related TV programs: (...). This is the list of the related VODs: "Ice Age", (...).	TV program and VOD
2	User	Who starred in "Ice Age"?	VOD
	System	No such TV program is available. Denis Leary, (...) starred in the VOD.	TV program and VOD
3	User	I want to watch it.	VOD
	System	The VOD has been started.	VOD

Table 2 - A dialog in a multi-domain scenario in a multi-domain dialog system.

In contrast, in the dialog in a multi-domain scenario in a multi-domain dialog system (Table 2), a user asks the system "*Are there any animation programs?*" in the first turn. The system understands the domains of the user utterance as being both TV program and VOD and presents the user with the list of related TV programs and VODs. In the second turn, the user asks the system "*Who starred in 'Ice Age'?*" The system understands the domains of the user utterance as being both TV program and VOD. However, the system presents the user with only the stars of the VOD because no such TV program is available in the system. In the third turn, the user says "*I want to watch it.*" The system understands the domains of the user utterance as being either TV program or VOD. However, by considering dialog history, the system regards the domains of the user utterance as being VOD without asking a domain to the user; the system then plays the VOD.

4 Hierarchical domain model-based multi-domain selection framework

4.1 Hierarchical domain model

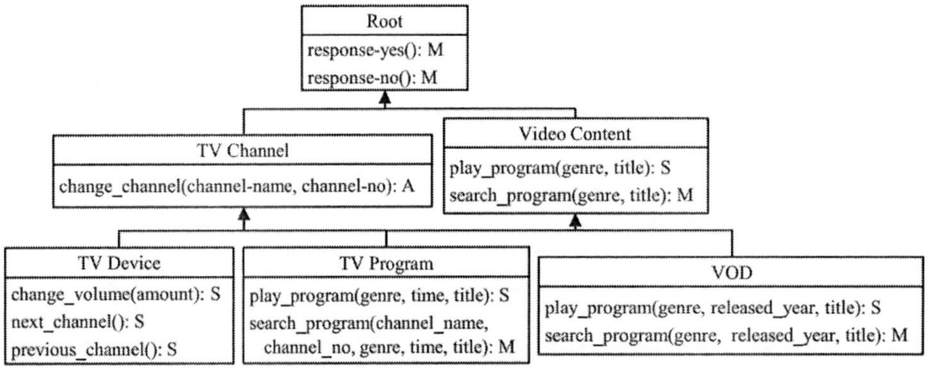

Figure 2 - An example of the hierarchical domain model. TV device, TV program, and VOD are the base domains; root, TV channel, and video content are the expanded domains. (M stands for MULTIPLE; S stands for SINGLE; A stands for ARBITRARY)

We used the HDM in both the candidate domain detection and final domain determination components. The HDM is a formal description of the capabilities of domains and the hierarchical relationships among the domains (Figure 2). The capability of a domain means the dialog acts of the domain, the types of the dialog acts, and the parameters for the dialog acts. The characteristics of the dialog acts of each type are as follows:

- ***MULTIPLE***: the dialog acts can be served by multiple domains at the same time.
- ***SINGLE***: the dialog acts should be served by only one domain.
- ***ARBITRARY***: the dialog acts should be served by only one domain, but the result of the action is equal in all domains.

In the HDM, each domain is either a base domain or a virtual expanded domain. A base domain is the basic unit of functionality designed for the multi-domain dialog system. A virtual expanded domain has multiple child domains, which inherit the definition of the virtual expanded domain. A domain can define a new dialog act or redefine an existing dialog act of the parent domain by adding more parameters to the dialog act. When the domain does not redefine the inherited dialog act of the parent domain, the dialog act does not need to be explicitly described.

4.2 Candidate domain detection

The candidate domain detection component takes a user utterance for its input and detects one or more candidate domains for its output. The candidate domain detection component consists of the in-domain verification components of all the domains; the output of the candidate domain detection component is an integration of the outputs of the in-domain verification components.

4.2.1 Training phase

The basic method for training an in-domain verification component of the candidate domain detection components is to use an in-domain corpus as a positive example and out-domain corpora as negative examples. The in-domain verification component is then trained using a keyword-based approach or a feature-based approach (Chelba et al., 2003; Komatani et al. 2006).

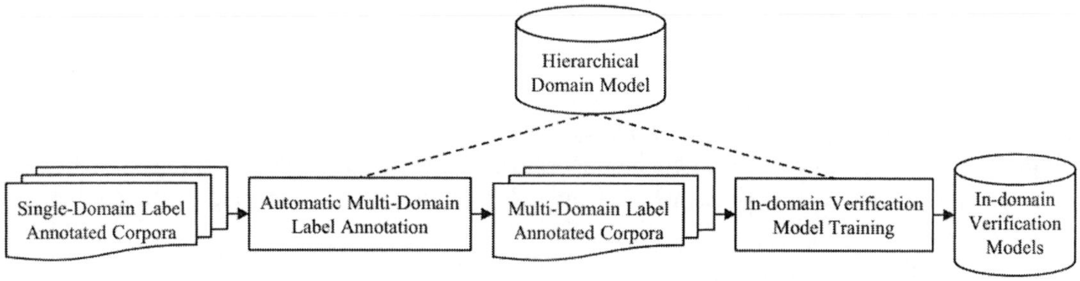

Figure 3 - Candidate domain detection component training.

However, the domain of the corpus to utterances belong cannot be used directly to train the in-domain verification component. This is because some user utterances of the other domains are not negative examples but are positive examples when the domains are closely related to each other. For example, a user utterance "*Are there any animation programs?*" in the TV program corpus is a positive example of both the TV program and VOD domains. Therefore, multi-domain labels on corpora should be automatically annotated before training in-domain verification components (Figure 3).

In the automatic multi-domain label annotation process, multi-domain labels for all user utterances in corpora are automatically annotated using the HDM. More specifically, when several multi-domains can accept a user utterance by considering the dialog act and the named entity sequence of the user utterance, the multi-domain label of the user utterance is annotated as the most general one from among the multi-domains. For example, a user utterance "*Do you have action?*" [*search_program(genre='action')*] can be accepted by the video content, the TV program, and the VOD domains. The video content domain is the most general domain from among these domains; therefore, the multi-domain label of the user utterance is annotated as video content.

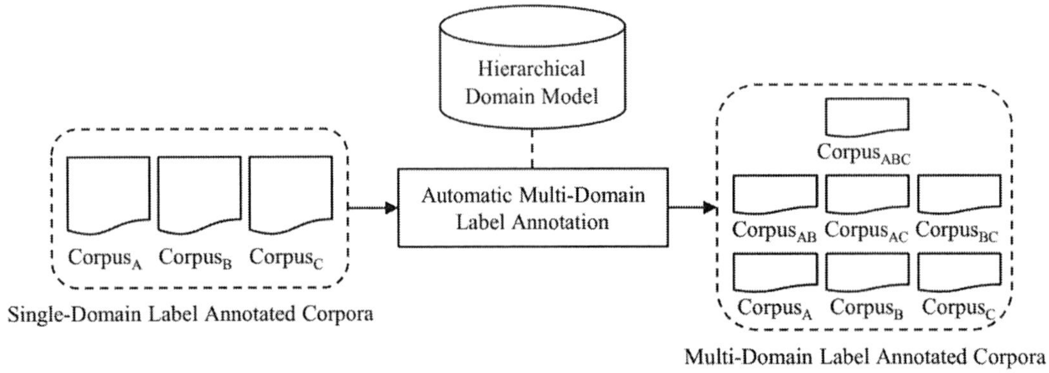

Figure 4 - An example of automatic multi-domain label annotation for domain A, B, and C.

After the automatic multi-domain label annotation, the multi-domain labels of positive examples of a single-domain are the domain or its parent domains; the multi-domain labels of negative examples of the single-domain are remaining domains. For example, when the single domains are A, B, and C, the automatically annotated multi-domain labels are A, B, C, AB, AC, BC, and ABC (Figure 4). The multi-domain labels of the positive examples of single-domain A are A, AB, AC, and ABC; the multi-domain labels of negative examples of single-domain A are remaining domains.

4.2.2 Decoding phase

The candidate domain detection component takes user utterance for its input and detects one or more candidate domains for its output. The candidate domain detection component integrates the outputs of the in-domain verification components of all the domains. The in-domain verification component of each domain verifies whether the user utterance can be accepted by the domain.

4.3 Final domain determination

The final domain determination component takes the candidate domains, a dialog act, a named entity sequence, and a context interpretation result for its input and determines one or more final domains from among the candidate domains for its output. Two cases exist in final domain determination according to the relationship between a set of previous domains and a set of candidate domains.

Case 1: When the previous domain set is a proper subset of the candidate domain set and the multi-domain context interpretation component continues a previous context, the final domain determination component ignores the candidate domains and determines the previous domains as the final domains. This is because the dialog history implies that the domains do not changed in this case. For example, a user utterance "*Play it.*" can be accepted by both the TV program and VOD domains, but domain switching should not occur for the user utterance in the middle of dialog in the TV program domain.

In addition, to avoid unnecessarily asking a domain, the failed domains are not considered to be previous domains in the next turn. This is because the intended domain of a user utterance within a continued context is only successful domains. For example, suppose a user asks "*Do you have animation programs for adult?*" and no such TV program is available. The system should then inform the user that no such TV program is available and present the user with the list of related VODs. When the user says "*Play the first one.*" in the next turn, the intended domain of the user is VOD not both TV program and VOD.

Case 2: Otherwise, the final domain determination component determines final domains from among the candidate domains based on the type of dialog act described in Section 4.1.

- ***MULTIPLE***: determines all candidate domains as final domains.
- ***SINGLE***: asks the user to select one domain from among the candidate domains.
- ***ARBITRARY***: determines an arbitrary candidate, but priority is given to the previous domain.

5 Experiments

5.1 Candidate domain detection

We used 5-fold cross validation to evaluate the candidate domain detection component of the proposed HDM-based MDSF using the corpora of three base domains, which consist of 2628 user utterances. In the corpora, 52.6% of user utterances belong to only one domain; the others belong to more than one domain. The multi-domain label answers were annotated by hands for evaluation. For the evaluation metrics, we used precision, recall, and F-1 score. We used the Maximum entropy classifier (Ratnaparkhi, 1998) to implement the in-domain verification components of the proposed candidate domain detection component. The baseline is the traditional domain detection component that the domains of the corpora to the user utterances belong are used directly to train the domain detection component.

Component	Precision	Recall	F-1 score
Baseline	97.1%	65.2%	78.0%
Proposed	95.6%	96.2%	95.9%

Table 3 - The result of the candidate domain detection experiments.

The proposed candidate domain detection component had much higher accuracy, recall, and F-1 score, but slightly lower precision than did the baseline component; the recall increased from 65.2% to 96.2%, the precision decreased from 97.1% to 95.6%, and the F-1 score increased from 78.0% to 95.9% (Table 3). The recall of the baseline component was too low because it made numerous false negative errors; i.e. it cannot detect the domains to which a user utterance may refer when the user utterance can be accepted by more than one domain. In contrast, the recall of the proposed candidate domain detection component was high because it made very few false negative errors.

5.2 Multi-domain dialog systems

We used human user experiments to evaluate the multi-domain dialog system that employed the proposed HDM-based MDSF to validate its effectiveness. We exclude the speech recognition component and speech synthesis component in the experiments because these components are independent to the domain. We asked 10 student volunteers to complete 10 dialog tasks involving TV program, VOD, TV device, or combinations of them. For the evaluation metrics, we used successful turn rate (STR), task completion rate (TCR), and average turn length (ATL). STR indicates the average success turn rate of user utterances; TCR indicates the average success rate of the tasks; ATL indicates the average turn length of the dialogs. We excluded the top-most and the bottom-most outliers for each task. The baseline is the traditional multi-domain dialog system that selects only one domain at a time.

System	STR	TCR	ATL
Baseline	55.0%	58.8%	4.7
Proposed	91.1%	95.0%	3.5

Table 4 - The result of the multi-domain dialog system experiments.

The proposed system had higher STR and TCR and lower ATL than did the baseline system; the STR increased from 55.0% to 91.1%, the TCR increased from 58.8% to 95.0%, and the ATL decreased from 4.7 to 3.5 (Table 4). More specifically, the STR, the TCR, and the ATL of each task were improved in all tasks. The STR and the TCR of the proposed system were high because the HDM-based MDSF correctly selects the domains of interest of users. The ATL of the proposed system was low because the HDM-based MDSF enables the proposed system to provide service to one or more domains at the same time.

Conclusion and future work

Is this paper, we proposed the HDM-based MDSF. The experimental results show that the HDM-based MDSF correctly selects one or more domains and enables multi-domain dialog systems to provide more accurate and rapid dialog service than traditional multi-domain dialog systems. To our knowledge, this paper is the first work on the selection of one or more domains in multi-domain dialog systems.

We plan to research multi-domain user simulation. A simulated user experiment is a useful method for evaluating dialog systems with large number of dialogs because a human user experiment is time-consuming and expensive; however, no existing user simulator can simulate users within multi-domain dialog systems that employ the MDSF. Therefore, multi-domain user simulation is an important part of future research on domain selection.

Acknowledgments

This research was supported by the Basic Science Research Program through National Research Foundation of Korea (NRF) funded by the Ministry of Education, Science and Technology (2011-0027953).

This research was supported by the MKE(The Ministry of Knowledge Economy), Korea, under the ITRC(Information Technology Research Center) support program supervised by the NIPA(National IT Industry Promotion Agency) (NIPA-2012-H0301-12-3002).

References

Allen, J., Byron, D., Dzikovska, M., Ferguson, G., Galescu, L., and Stent, A. (2000). An architecture for a generic dialogue shell, *Natural Language Engineering*, 6(3): 213-228.

Çelikyilmaz, A., Hakkani-Tür, D. Z., and Tür, G. (2011). Approximate inference for domain detection in spoken language understanding, In *Proceedings of the Interspeech 2011*, pages 713-716, Florence, Italy.

Chelba, C., Mahajan, M., and Acero, A. (2003). Speech utterance classification, In *Proceedings of the ICASSP 2003*, pages 69-72, Hong Kong, China.

Ikeda, S., Komatani, K., Ogata, T., and Okuno, H. G. (2008). Extensibility verification of robust domain selection against out-of-grammar utterances in multi-domain spoken dialogue system, In *Proceedings of the Interspeech 2008*, pages 487-490, Pittsburgh, Pennsylvania, USA.

Komatani, K., Kanda, N., Nakano, M., Nakadai, K., Tsujino, H., Ogata, T., and Okuno, H. G. (2006). Multi-domain spoken dialogue system with extensibility and robustness against speech recognition errors, In *Proceedings of the SIGdial 2006*, pages 9-17, Sydney, Australia.

Larsson, S. and Ericsson, S. (2002). GoDiS – issue-based dialogue management in a multi-domain, multi-language dialogue system, In *Proceedings of the ACL 2002 Demonstration Abstracts*, pages 104-105, Philadelphia, Pennsylvania, USA.

Lee, C., Jung. S., Kim, S., and Lee, G. G. (2009). Example-based dialog modelling for practical multi-domain dialog system, *Speech Communication*, 51(5): 466-484.

Lin, B., Wang, H., and Lee, L. (1999). A distributed architecture for cooperative spoken dialogue agents with coherent dialogue state and history, In *Proceedings of the ASRU 1999*, Keystone, Colorado, USA.

McTear, F. M. (2004). Spoken Dialogue Technology: Towards the Conversational User Interface, Springer.

Nakano, M., Sata, S., Komatani, K., Matsuyama, K., Funakoshi, K., and Okuno, H. G. (2011). A two-stage domain selection framework for extensible multi-domain spoken dialogue systems, In *Proceedings of the SIGdial 2011*, pages 18-29, Portland, Oregon, USA.

Pakucs, B. (2003). Towards dynamic multi-domain dialogue processing, In *Proceedings of the Interspeech 2003*, pages 741-744, Geneva, Switzerland.

Ratnaparkhi, A. (1998). Maximum entropy models for natural language ambiguity resolution, Doctoral Dissertation, University of Pennsylvania, Philadelphia, USA.

A Fully Coreference-annotated Corpus of Scholarly Papers from the ACL Anthology

Ulrich Schäfer Christian Spurk Jörg Steffen
German Research Center for Artificial Intelligence (DFKI), Language Technology Lab
Campus D 3 1, D-66123 Saarbrücken, Germany
{ulrich.schaefer,christian.spurk,joerg.steffen}@dfki.de

ABSTRACT
We describe a large coreference annotation task performed on a corpus of 266 papers from the ACL Anthology, a publicly, electronically available collection of scientific papers in the domain of computational linguistics and language technology. The annotation comprises mainly noun phrase coreference of the full textual content of each paper in the Anthology subset. It has been performed carefully and at least twice for each paper (initial annotation and secondary correction phase). The purpose of this paper is to summarize the comprehensive annotation schema and release the corpus publicly, along with this paper. The corpus is by far larger than the ACE coreference corpora. It can be used to train coreference resolution systems in the Computational Linguistics and Language Technology domain for semantic search, taxonomy extraction, question answering, citation analysis, scientific discourse analysis, etc.

KEYWORDS: Coreference Resolution, Resource, Annotated Corpus, Scientific Papers, eScience.

1 Introduction and Motivation

Coreference resolution (CR), mostly on newspaper text, has been studied *in extenso* during the last decades. The task consists in finding all mentions of real-world entities such as persons or organizations in a text, regardless of their textual representation. It could be a proper name, a role (e.g. 'the director'), a pronoun, or a similar circumscribing expression (mention).

Related (with an overlap) to this task is anaphora resolution. Here, the interpretation of a mention, called anaphor (e.g. a pronoun), depends on a previous mention, called antecendent, or on context. Different relations may hold between an anaphor and its antecedent, e.g. part-of, subset, etc. If both refer to the same entity, the anaphoric relation is also coreferential. In contrast to coreference, the order matters, but in general, not every anaphoric relation is coreferential and vice versa. A more detailed discussion of the coreference vs. anaphora distinction can be found in van Deemter and Kibble (2000).

For 15 years, significant progress in terms of robustness and coverage has been made by applying machine learning and including semantic information. Instead of enumerating the history of CR literature, we refer the interested reader to Ng (2010) and Mitkov (1999). They present comprehensive, though compact, surveys of the CR research for this period. However, most of the research so far was done in the news text domain only, as the largest available annotated corpora such as MUC (Grishman and Sundheim, 1996) and ACE (Doddington et al., 2004) mostly were of this origin.

The purpose of our endeavor is to move to a different domain, namely scientific texts, extracted

Proceedings of COLING 2012: Posters, pages 1059–1070,
COLING 2012, Mumbai, December 2012.

from proceedings papers and journal articles. We do this because our evaluations have shown that systems trained on news text, where mainly persons and organizations are the subject of coreference phenomena, perform worse on scientific text.

We observe a general rising research interest in applying CR to real-world texts other than newswire, e.g. the CoNLL Shared Task on Modeling Unrestricted Coreference in OntoNotes (Pradhan et al., 2011) and the BioNLP Shared Task supporting task: Protein/Gene Coreference Task (Nguyen et al., 2011).

Watson et al. (2003) argue that CR in scientific text may be harder than in newspaper text, as scientific text tends to be more complex and contains relatively high proportions of definite descriptions, which are the most challenging to resolve. Conversely, the proportion of easier-to-determine entities such as person names, is inferior in papers.

In scientific texts, anaphoric expression referring to named entities are less frequent. Instead, references to domain terminology and abstract entities such as results, variables and values are more important.

Motivation for improving CR in scientific text is manifold. Applications such as Question Answering (Watson et al., 2003), Information Extraction (Gaizauskas and Humphreys, 2000), ontology extraction, or accurate semantic search in digital libraries (Schäfer et al., 2011) can benefit from identified coreferences in running text.

On the one hand, making implicit or hidden relations explicit and complete by resolving e.g. anaphora may increase redundancy and hence the chance for answer candidates to be found. On the other hand, coreferences, if resolved correctly, may help to increase precision. Without anaphora replaced by their antecedents, certain propositions simply cannot be found. The same holds for variants of coreferring expressions. A recent work also shows the benefits of CR for biomedical event extraction from scientific literature (Miwa et al., 2012).

The paper is structured as follows. In Section 2, we discuss recent related work. We present details of the coreference annotation task and parts of the annotation guidelines in Section 3. Section 4 discusses error analysis, inter-annotator agreement and correction. Finally, we give a conclusion.

2 Related Work

While a considerable part of previous and current research concentrates on news texts as provided by the MUC and ACE corpora, coreference annotation of scientific papers is a relatively new area. In particular, work on coreference phenomena in scientific text mostly seems to focus on the biomedical domain. There is only a small number of publications dealing with other science domains.

One of the earliest approaches is performed in the context of the Genia project and corpus of medical texts from MEDLINE. In a first stage, only MEDLINE abstracts are used (Yang et al., 2004), later *other*-anaphora, a very specific sub-task, are investigated using full paper content (Chen et al., 2008).

Gasperin (2009) presents a full annotation of anaphora and coreference in biomedical text, but only noun phrases referring to biomedical entities are considered. On the basis of this annotation, she implements a probabilistic anaphora resolution system.

In contrast, Cohen et al. (2010) build a corpus of 97 full-text journal articles in the biomedical domain where every co-referring noun phrase is annotated (CRAFT – Colorado Richly Annotated Full Text). Their annotation guidelines follow those of the OntoNotes project (Hovy et al., 2006), adapted to the biomedical domain. OntoNotes itself is a text corpus of approx. one million words from mainly news texts (newswire, magazines, broadcast conversations, web pages). It also contains general anaphoric coreference annotations (Pradhan et al., 2007): events and (like in our annotation) unlimited noun phrase entity types.

Kim and Webber (2006) investigate a special aspect, citation sentences where a pronoun such as "they" refers to a previous citation. The study is performed on astronomy journal articles and a maximum-entropy classifier is trained.

Kaplan et al. (2009) investigate coreferences and citations as well, but only at a very small scale (4 articles from the *Computational Linguistics* journal). They focus on so-called c-sites which are the sentences following a citation that also refer to the same paper (typically by anaphora). The authors train a specific coreference model for this phenomenon. They show that exploitation of coreference chains improves the extraction of citation contexts which they then use for research paper summarization.

3 Corpus Creation

Our corpus comprises 266 scientific papers from the ACL Anthology (Bird et al., 2008) sections P08 (ACL-2008 long papers), D07 (EMNLP-CoNLL-2007) and C02 (COLING 2002). Texts were extracted from PDF using a commercial OCR program which gurantees uniform, though not perfect, quality of the resulting text files. We did not rely on the original ACL-ARC text files converted with PDFBox because they contained considerable extraction errors depending on the (various) PDF tools that were used to generate the PDFs. Hence quality of extraction would have dependent on the PDF generator, and OCR-based extraction is much more independent from the generation process.

Moreover, PDFBox cannot reliably recover reading order from text typeset in multiple columns (again, depending on the PDF generator used). OCR introduces sporadic character and layout recognition errors, but overall works robustly, cf. discussion and a recent and even more accurate approach in Schäfer et al. (2012). The main part of the corpus creation endeavor consisted in manual annotation assisted by a customized version of the MMAX2 annotation tool (Müller and Strube, 2006), operating on the extracted raw texts (the annotators had the possibility to open and view the original PDF files). In a second step, the corpus was then augmented with automatically created annotations.

3.1 Manual Annotations

The annotators were not trained in the Computational Linguistics domain, but as advanced students of English language and literature studies, they had some prior knowledge of general linguistics.

We gave our human annotators the same task that a coreference resolution system shall solve. This task is similar to the core annotation task of the ACE program: in the so-called "entity detection and tracking (EDT) task, all mentions of an entity, whether a name, a description, or a pronoun, are to be found and collected into equivalence classes based on reference to the same entity" (Doddington et al., 2004, p. 837). However, unlike in ACE, we did not restrict the type of entities to be annotated. Because of this we do not even distinguish entity types in our annotation scheme.

In terms of ACE entity classes, we only consider referential mentions for annotation, i.e. only "Specific Referential (SPC)", "Generic Referential (GEN)", and "Under-specified Referential (USP)" (LDC, 2004, p. 17f.) entities, but we do not explicitly differentiate between these classes in our corpus.

Only noun phrases (NPs, including coordinations of NPs), possessive determiners ("my", "your", ...) and proper names (which may be part of NPs as in "Sheffield's GATE system") were considered as possible entity mentions. As for mention types we asked our annotators to classify each mention as one of the types listed in Table 1. It also contains the different kinds of pronouns and other noun phrases that can be mentions.

Just like the annotators in ACE, our annotators were advised to identify the maximal extent of entity mentions. The mention extent thus includes all modifiers of the mention's head, i.e. any preceding adjectives and determiners, post-modifying phrases like prepositional phrases and relative clauses or parenthetical modifiers.

Coreferences between mention pairs were marked, i.e. coreferential entity mentions were put into the same coreference set. Only those entity mentions were marked which are coreferential with any other mention in the text, i.e. a coreference set always contains at least two mentions.

The annotators were asked to annotate *maximal coreference sets*, i.e., whenever they found two coreferential markables, they only created a new coreference set if there was not any other coreference set whose elements refer to the same referent as the two newly found markables. In other words, for every pair of document and real-world referent there should be only one coreference set with markables of the document refering to the referent. In the extreme case, coreferential markables in the abstract at the beginning of a paper and in the conclusion at the end, and all markables refering to the same entity in between were to be put into the same set. This is useful because subsets for smaller ranges (e.g. for paragraphs or sections) can easily be derived from the complete annotation.

Our manually annotated corpus contains 1,326,147 tokens (ACE 2004: 189,620) in 48,960 sentences (ACE: 5,654). The number of coreferring mentions in non-singleton coreference sets is 65,293 (ACE: 22,293). This number is plausible because scientific text typically contains less person and organization mentions than newspaper text.

Mention Type	Amount
`def-np` (definite NPs)	32,547
`pper` (personal pronouns)	5,921
`ne` (proper names incl. citations)	14,451
`ppos` (possessive pronouns/determiners)	3,407
`indef-np` (indefinite NPs)	6,820
`conj-np` (coordinations)	1,446
`pds` (demonstrative pronouns)	435
`prefl` (reflexive pronouns)	266
Σ	65,293

Table 1: Annotated mention types and their frequency in the manually annotated corpus. Only mentions appearing in non-singleton coreference sets are counted.

3.2 Annotation Guidelines and Corpus Data

The full annotation guidelines (approx. 20 printed pages) with many examples and special hints for the corpus-specific phenomena such as citations, as well as user guides for the annotation tool MMAX2 are too comprehensive to be discussed here in detail. Therefore, they are part of the attached, compressed archive in file `AnnotationGuidelines.html` (along with A4 and letter paper versions in PDF format for printing). Independently of the conference proceedings, the data will be made available on `http://take.dfki.de/#2012` and in the ACL Anthology as supplementary material to the electronic version of this publication.

The archive also contains the complete annotated data in MMAX2 format for each of the 266 papers in the subdirectory `annotation`. The file `README.txt` contains instructions on how to download, install and run MMAX2 and open the annoted corpus files for inspection. MMAX2 needs to be downloaded separately[1], a screenshot is depicted in Figure 1.

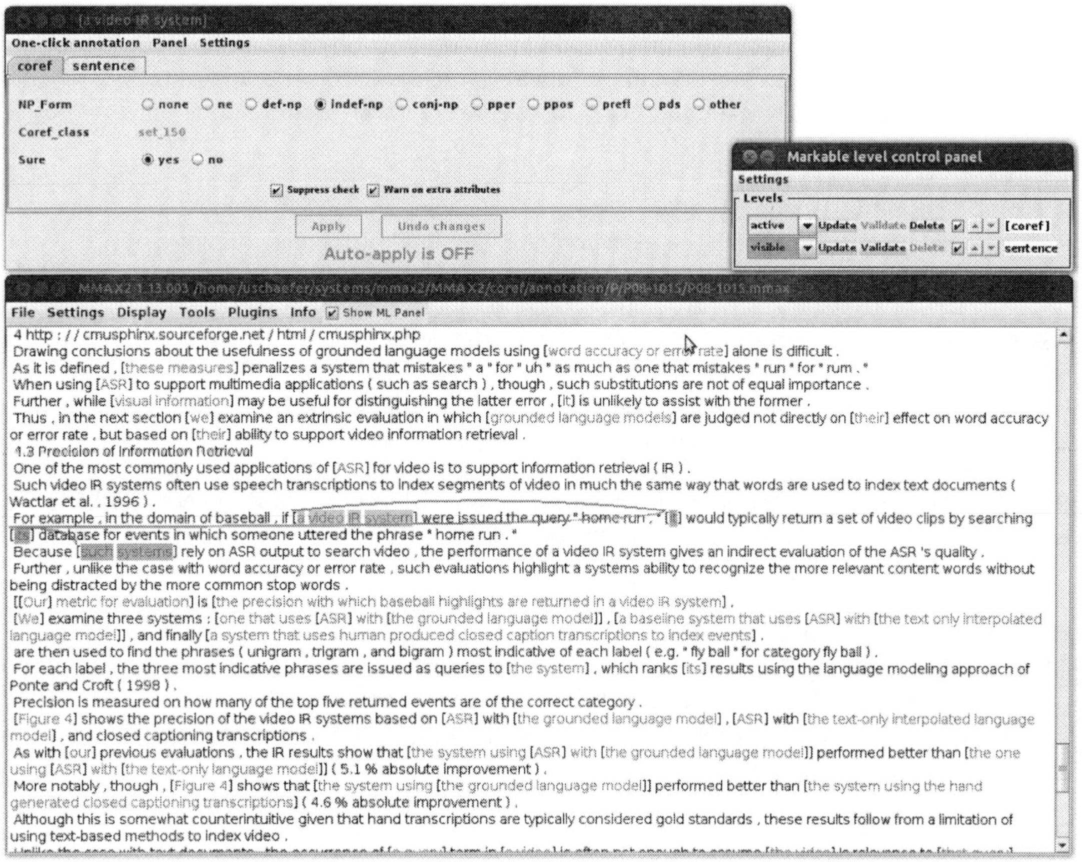

Figure 1: ACL Anthology paper annotation in the MMAX2 user interface.

The annotation guidelines introduce terminology, explain which markables to annotate and which not, both with many examples, summarize general annotation principles, and present an introduction to the MMAX2 annotation tool.

[1]`http://sourceforge.net/projects/mmax2/files/`

3.2.1 Markables to Annotate

Named Entities. Names and named entities (NEs) are usually (definite) NPs and as such can enter into coreference relations, i.e., they are relevant markables. NEs may be, among others, names of companies, organizations, persons, locations, languages, currencies, programming languages, standards, scientific fields, systems, frameworks, etc. As a special case for our ACL Anthology corpus, we consider citations in scientific papers as NEs, too.

Definite Noun Phrases. Definite noun phrases are NPs which correspond to a specific and identifiable entity in a given context. In many cases this definiteness is marked by the definite article "the" or a demonstrative determiner such as "these" or "that".

Indefinite Noun Phrases. Indefinite noun phrases are NPs which do not correspond to a specific and identifiable entity in a given context. In many cases this indefiniteness is marked by the indefinite articles "a" and "an" or it is indicated by the lack of a certain determiner.

Conjunctions. For our annotation task, we define a conjunction to be an NP which results by conjoining other NPs. The most common junctor which is used for conjoining NPs is "and". Other junctors include, for example, "or", "as well as" or the discontinuous junctor "both ... and".

Personal Pronouns. Personal pronouns are pronouns which stand for other NPs and which are even complete NPs themselves. The most common personal pronouns in English are "I", "you", "he", "she", "they", "it", "me", "him", "us", "them", "her" and "we".

Possessive Pronouns. Possessive pronouns in a strict sense are NPs which stand for another NP and which attribute ownership to the NP they substitute, e.g., "mine", "hers" or "ours". In our annotation task, we assume a broader sense in which possessive determiners are also considered to be possessive pronouns, e.g., "his", "her" or "my".

Reflexive Pronouns. Reflexive pronouns are pronouns that substitute the NP to which they refer in the same clause as the NP. The most common reflexive pronouns in English are "myself", "yourself", "himself", "herself", "themself", "itself", "ourselves", "yourselves" and "themselves".

Demonstrative Pronouns. In our annotation task, demonstrative pronouns are pronouns which are NPs that stand for some other NP of the discourse. As such they are very similar to personal pronouns. The most common demonstrative pronouns in English are "this", "that", "these" and "those" while for the annotations in our corpus, "these" will mostly be found as markable.

Relative Pronouns. Relative pronouns are pronouns which introduce relative clauses. We are only interested in relative pronouns that introduce non-restrictive relative clauses. In restrictive relative clauses, the relative pronoun does not refer to any real-world entity and therefore it can't be a coreferential markable (The relative pronoun refers syntactically to the head noun of the noun phrase (NP) to which the relative clause belongs, however, this is no coreference; the NP is semantically incomplete without the relative clause). In non-restrictive clauses, the relative pronoun really corefers with the noun phrase (NP) to which the relative clause belongs. The relative pronouns in English which are also relevant for annotation are "who", "which", "whose", "where", "whom" and "when" as well as sometimes "that" and rarely "why".

3.2.2 Markables not to Annotate

Our detailed annotation guidelines do not only give definitions, explanations and examples of markables and coreference phenomena to annotate, they also explain what shouldn't be annotated. Here is an excerpt.

Relative Clauses. In general, relative clauses alone are not markables themselves, but only part of other markables.

Restrictive relative pronouns and clauses should not be annotated, as the NP the relative pronoun refers to is semantically incomplete without the relative clause.

Only Definite Predicate Nominatives with Definite Subjects. A predicate nominative can only be a coreferential markable if it is definite and connected to a definite subject.

Predicate nominatives are only to be annotated if they are definite and connected with a definite subject ("A mason is a workman" is indefinite and thus not coreferential).

Bound anaphora (e.g. in "Every teacher likes his job.") should not be annotated because the referents do not necessarily refer to the same.

Indirect anaphora or **bridging references** (e.g. in "The bar is crowded. The waitress is stressed out.") should not be annotated because the referents are not identical.

3.3 Automatic Annotations

Because the main purpose of the corpus will be training machine learning systems, we also need examples of mentions that are not coreferential with any other mention in the text – as kind of negative examples. These single mentions were automatically annotated. To achieve this, we looked up all NPs (including coordinations functioning as NPs), possessive determiners and proper names (including citations as a special case) in the corpus that were not part of any entity mention, yet. All these were then automatically classified into the above-mentioned mention types and stored with the manually annotated mentions.

The automatic annotations were generateed using the Stanford Parser (Klein and Manning, 2003) in version 1.6.3 for NPs and possessive determiners. Proper nouns are detected using the SProUT system (Drożdżyński et al., 2004) with its generic named entity grammar for English. SProUT robustly recognizes *inter alia* person names and locations in MUC style in running text, without any domain-specific adaptations or extensions except for citations. For the detection of citations, we have created an elaborate regular expression that reliably matches all kinds of citation patterns.

3.4 Citations

Coreferences in citation context have special properties (Kim and Webber, 2006). When they exist, they are in most cases anaphoric pairs, typically the antecedent is a name. Roughly 10 % of the sentences in the corpus contain citations. Therefore, special care has been taken to coreference phenomena in conjunction with citations.

In the ACL Anthology, citations could be quite reliably identified automatically by regular expression patterns, as the citation styles are restricted. The annotators then only had to connect with e.g. pronouns in follow-up sentences.

4 Error Analysis, Inter-annotator Agreement and Correction

In the initial annotation phase, 13 % of our corpus was annotated twice by different annotators in order to measure inter-annotator agreement. We did this measurement as it was done for MUC (Hirschman et al., 1997) and in the same way as a coreference resolution system is evaluated against some gold standard: one annotation was set to be the gold standard ("key") and the second annotation was set to be the "response". Herewith we reached an inter-annotator agreement of 49.5 MUC points (for MUC score calculation see Vilain et al. (1995)). Although the MUC measure is questionable (Luo, 2005) and the task is difficult, this number is too low and asked for improvements.

Therefore in a second phase, the annotation guidelines have been improved in order to cover more corner cases and to resolve possible ambiguities. Additionally, all annotations were checked and corrected at least a second time in order to find accidental annotation mistakes and to be consistent with the updated guidelines. This procedure has also been suggested by Hirschman et al. (1997) for the MUC data, who – after optimizing their annotation guidelines and changing the annotation process to a two-step process – could improve their inter-annotator agreement by about 12 %.

The second round has been performed by a single person over approx. 9 months part-time (8–10 hrs/week). Therefore we did not measure the inter-annotator agreement a second time, but on the other hand a single corrector ensures the annotation is of uniform quality throughout the whole corpus.

Conclusion

We have developed a comprehensive annotation schema and annotation guidelines for coreference in scientific text and fully annotated a 266 paper subset of the ACL Anthology. The corpus is publicly available along with this paper. By a coreference resolution system built on top of it, e.g. training available tools such as LBJ (Bengtson and Roth, 2008; Rizzolo and Roth, 2010), Reconcile (Stoyanov et al., 2010, 2011), Stanford's dcoref (Raghunathan et al., 2010; Lee et al., 2011), or (Haghighi and Klein, 2009, 2010), it could serve to improve other NLP tasks such as semantic search, taxonomy extraction, question answering, citation analysis, scientific discourse analysis, etc.

The corpus in its current state is not perfect. It will probably be necessary to add a further round of annotation assessment and correction. At this point, our project ends and we release the annotation data to the public along with the hope that the scientific community finds it useful and further improves the corpus.

Acknowledgments

We would like to thank the student annotators, most notably Leonie Grön and Philipp Schu, for their intelligent, careful and patient work. We also thank the three anonymous reviewers for helpful comments. The work described in this paper has been funded by the German Federal Ministry of Education and Research, projects TAKE (FKZ 01IW08003) and Deependance (FKZ 01IW11003), and under the Seventh Framework Programme of the European Commission through the T4ME contract (grant agreement no.: 249119).

References

Bengtson, E. and Roth, D. (2008). Understanding the value of features for coreference resolution. In *Proceedings of the Conference on Empirical Methods in Natural Language Processing*, EMNLP-2008, pages 294–303, Morristown, NJ, USA.

Bird, S., Dale, R., Dorr, B., Gibson, B., Joseph, M., Kan, M.-Y., Lee, D., Powley, B., Radev, D., and Tan, Y. F. (2008). The ACL anthology reference corpus: A reference dataset for bibliographic research. In *Proceedings of the 6th International Conference on Language Resources and Evaluation (LREC-2008)*, Marrakesh, Morocco.

Chen, B., Yang, X., Su, J., and Tan, C. L. (2008). Other-anaphora resolution in biomedical texts with automatically mined patterns. In *Proceedings of the 22nd International Conference on Computational Linguistics (COLING-2008)*, pages 121–128, Manchester, UK.

Cohen, K. B., Lanfranchi, A., Corvey, W., Jr., W. A. B., Roeder, C., Ogren, P. V., Palmer, M., and Hunter, L. (2010). Annotation of all coreference in biomedical text: Guideline selection and adaptation. In *Proceedings of the 2nd Workshop on Building and Evaluating Resources for Biomedical Text Mining (BioTxtM-2010)*.

Doddington, G., Mitchell, A., Przybocki, M., Ramshaw, L., Strassel, S., and Weischedel, R. (2004). The automatic content extraction (ACE) program – tasks, data, and evaluation. In *Proceedings of the 4th International Conference on Language Resources and Evaluation (LREC-2004)*, pages 837–840.

Drożdżyński, W., Krieger, H.-U., Piskorski, J., Schäfer, U., and Xu, F. (2004). Shallow processing with unification and typed feature structures – foundations and applications. *Künstliche Intelligenz*, 2004(1):17–23.

Gaizauskas, R. and Humphreys, K. (2000). Quantitative evaluation of coreference algorithms in an information extraction system. In Botley, S. and McEnery, T., editors, *Corpus-based and Computational Approaches to Discourse Anaphora*, pages 145–169. John Benjamins, Amsterdam.

Gasperin, C. V. (2009). *Statistical anaphora resolution in biomedical texts*. PhD thesis, University of Cambridge, Cambridge, UK.

Grishman, R. and Sundheim, B. (1996). Message understanding conference - 6: A brief history. In *Proceedings of COLING-96*, pages 466–471.

Haghighi, A. and Klein, D. (2009). Simple coreference resolution with rich syntactic and semantic features. In *Proceedings of the 2009 Conference on Empirical Methods in Natural Language Processing*, pages 1152–1161, Singapore.

Haghighi, A. and Klein, D. (2010). Coreference resolution in a modular, entity-centered model. In *Human Language Technologies: The 2010 Annual Conference of the North American Chapter of the Association for Computational Linguistics*, pages 385–393, Los Angeles, California.

Hirschman, L., Robinson, P., Burger, J., and Vilain, M. (1997). Automating coreference: The role of annotated training data. In *Proceedings of the AAAI Spring Symposium on Applying Machine Learning to Discourse Processing*.

Hovy, E., Marcus, M., Palmer, M., Ramshaw, L., and Weischedel, R. (2006). OntoNotes: The 90% solution. In *Proceedings of the HLT-NAACL 2006 Companion Volume*.

Kaplan, D., Iida, R., and Tokunaga, T. (2009). Automatic extraction of citation contexts for research paper summarization: A coreference-chain based approach. In *Workshop on text and citation analysis for scholarly digital libraries (NLPIR4DL), ACL-IJCNLP-09*, pages 88–95, Singapore.

Kim, Y. and Webber, B. (2006). Implicit references to citations: A study of astronomy papers. In *Proceedings of the 20th International CODATA Conference: Scientific Data and Knowledge within the Information Society*.

Klein, D. and Manning, C. D. (2003). Accurate unlexicalized parsing. In *Proceedings of the 41st Meeting of the Association for Computational Linguistics (ACL-2003)*, pages 423–430. Association for Computational Linguistics.

LDC (2004). Annotation guidelines for entity detection and tracking (EDT) – version 4.2.6.

Lee, H., Peirsman, Y., Chang, A., Chambers, N., Surdeanu, M., and Jurafsky, D. (2011). Stanford's multi-pass sieve coreference resolution system at the CoNLL-2011 shared task. In *15th CoNLL: Shared Task*, pages 28–34.

Luo, X. (2005). On coreference resolution performance metrics. In *Proceedings of Human Language Technology Conference and Conference on Empirical Methods in Natural Language Processing*, pages 25–32, Vancouver, British Columbia, Canada. Association for Computational Linguistics.

Mitkov, R. (1999). Anaphora resolution: The state of the art. Technical report, School of Languages and European Studies, University of Wolverhampton.

Miwa, M., Thompson, P., and Ananiadou, S. (2012). Boosting automatic event extraction from the literature using domain adaptation and coreference resolution. *Bioinformatics*.

Müller, C. and Strube, M. (2006). Multi-level annotation of linguistic data with MMAX2. In Braun, S., Kohn, K., and Mukherjee, J., editors, *Corpus Technology and Language Pedagogy: New Resources, New Tools, New Methods*, pages 197–214. Peter Lang, Frankfurt a.M., Germany.

Ng, V. (2010). Supervised noun phrase coreference research: The first fifteen years. In *Proceedings of the 48th Annual Meeting of the Association for Computational Linguistics*, pages 1396–1411, Uppsala, Sweden.

Nguyen, N., Kim, J.-D., and Tsujii, J. (2011). Overview of BioNLP 2011 protein coreference shared task. In *Proceedings of BioNLP Shared Task 2011 Workshop*, pages 74–82, Portland, Oregon, USA.

Pradhan, S., Ramshaw, L., Marcus, M., Palmer, M., Weischedel, R., and Xue, N. (2011). CoNLL-2011 shared task: Modeling unrestricted coreference in ontonotes. In *Proceedings of the Fifteenth Conference on Computational Natural Language Learning: Shared Task*, pages 1–27, Portland, Oregon, USA.

Pradhan, S. S., Ramshaw, L., Ralph, Weischedel, MacBride, J., and Micciulla, L. (2007). Unrestricted coreference: Identifying entities and events in OntoNotes. In *Proceedings of the International Conference on Semantic Computing*, pages 446–453. IEEE.

Raghunathan, K., Lee, H., Rangarajan, S., Chambers, N., Surdeanu, M., Jurafsky, D., and Manning, C. (2010). A multi-pass sieve for coreference resolution. In *Proceedings of EMNLP-2010*, pages 492–501, Cambridge, MA.

Rizzolo, N. and Roth, D. (2010). Learning based Java for rapid development of NLP systems. In *Proceedings of the 7th International Conference on Language Resources and Evaluation (LREC-2010)*, Valletta, Malta.

Schäfer, U., Kiefer, B., Spurk, C., Steffen, J., and Wang, R. (2011). The ACL Anthology Searchbench. In *Proceedings of the ACL-HLT 2011 System Demonstrations*, pages 7–13, Portland, Oregon. Association for Computational Linguistics.

Schäfer, U., Read, J., and Oepen, S. (2012). Towards an ACL Anthology Corpus with logical document structure. An overview of the ACL 2012 contributed task. In *Proceedings of the ACL-2012 Special Workshop on Rediscovering 50 Years of Discoveries*, pages 88–97, Jeju Island, Korea. Association for Computational Linguistics.

Stoyanov, V., Babbar, U., Gupta, P., and Cardie, C. (2011). Reconciling OntoNotes: Unrestricted coreference resolution in OntoNotes with Reconcile. In *Proceedings of 15th CoNLL: Shared Task*, pages 122–126.

Stoyanov, V., Cardie, C., Gilbert, N., Riloff, E., Buttler, D., and Hysom, D. (2010). Coreference resolution with Reconcile. In *Proceedings of the ACL 2010 Conference Short Papers*, pages 156–161, Uppsala, Sweden.

van Deemter, K. and Kibble, R. (2000). On coreferring: coreference in MUC and related annotation schemes. *Computational Linguistics*, 26(4).

Vilain, M., Burger, J., Aberdeen, J., Connolly, D., and Hirschman, L. (1995). A model-theoretic coreference scoring scheme. In *Proceedings of the Fourth Message Understanding Conference (MUC-4)*, San Mateo, CA. Morgan Kaufmann.

Watson, R., Preiss, J., and Briscoe, E. J. (2003). Contribution of domain-independent robust pronominal anaphora resolution to open-domain question answering. In *Proceedings of the International Symposium on Reference Resolution*.

Yang, X., Su, J., Zhou, G., and Tan, C. L. (2004). An NP-cluster based approach to coreference resolution. In *Proceedings of COLING-2004*, pages 226–232, Geneva, Switzerland.

Continuous Space Translation Models for Phrase-Based Statistical Machine Translation

Holger Schwenk
University of Le Mans
Avenue Laennec
72085 Le Mans Cedex, France
Holger.Schwenk@lium.univ-lemans.fr

ABSTRACT
This paper presents a new approach to perform the estimation of the translation model probabilities of a phrase-based statistical machine translation system. We use neural networks to directly learn the translation probability of phrase pairs using continuous representations. The system can be easily trained on the same data used to build standard phrase-based systems. We provide experimental evidence that the approach seems to be able to infer meaningful translation probabilities for phrase pairs not seen in the training data, or even predict a list of the most likely translations given a source phrase. The approach can be used to rescore n-best lists, but we also discuss an integration into the Moses decoder. A preliminary evaluation on the English/French IWSLT task achieved improvements in the BLEU score and a human analysis showed that the new model often chooses semantically better translations. Several extensions of this work are discussed.

KEYWORDS: Statistical machine translation, phrase probability estimation, continuous space models, neural network.

Proceedings of COLING 2012: Posters, pages 1071–1080,
COLING 2012, Mumbai, December 2012.

1 Introduction

In the statistical approach to machine translation (SMT), all models are automatically estimated from examples. Let us assume that we want to translate a sentence in the source language **s** to a sentence in the target language **t**. Then, the fundamental equation of SMT is:

$$\mathbf{t}^* = \arg\max_{\mathbf{t}} P(\mathbf{t}|\mathbf{s}) = \arg\max_{\mathbf{t}} P(\mathbf{s}|\mathbf{t})P(\mathbf{t})/P(\mathbf{s}) = \arg\max_{\mathbf{t}} P(\mathbf{s}|\mathbf{t})P(\mathbf{t}) \quad (1)$$

The translation model $P(\mathbf{s}|\mathbf{t})$ is estimated from bitexts and the language model $P(\mathbf{t})$ from monolingual data. A popular approach are phrase-based models which translate short sequences of words together (Koehn et al., 2003; Och and Ney, 2003). The translation probabilities of these phrase pairs are usually estimated by simple relative frequency. We are only aware of few works to perform more sophisticated smoothing techniques, for instance (Foster et al., 2006). The log-linear approach is commonly used to consider more *feature functions* (Och, 2003). In the Moses system, four feature functions are usually used for the translation model: the forward and backward phrase translation probabilities and lexical probabilities in both directions. These four feature functions together could be seen as a particular smoothing technique of the translation model. In other works, hundreds or thousands of features are used.

The dominant approach in language modeling are so-called back-off n-gram models. An alternative approach was proposed by (Bengio and Ducharme, 2001; Bengio et al., 2003). The basic idea is to project the words into a continuous space and to perform the probability estimation in that space. The projection as well as the estimation can be jointly performed by a multi-layer neural network. The continuous space language model (CSLM) was very successfully applied to large vocabulary speech recognition, and more recently to SMT, e.g. (Schwenk et al., 2006; Le et al., 2010; Zamora-Martínez et al., 2010; Schwenk et al., 2012).

Given this success for language modeling, there were also two attempts to apply the same ideas to the translation model. Both were developed for tuple-based translation systems, e.g. based on bilingual units. This allows to to see the translations model like a standard n-gram LM task and it is straight forward to apply the CSLM (Schwenk et al., 2007). In the second work, this idea was improved by considering different factorization of the joint probability, in particular word-based ones: the principal idea is to predict the probability of a target word given the context of the previous source and target words (Le et al., 2012). The authors report good improvements in the BLEU scores for several tasks, but the approach seems to be complicated, in particular with respect to the training of the model or direct integration into the decoder.

In this work we propose a generic architecture which can be used in the standard pipeline to build a phrase-based SMT system. The continuous space translation model (CSTM) is trained on exactly the same data, i.e. the so-called `extract` files and no additional word alignments, segmentation, etc is necessary. In machine learning, we are generally not interested in memorizing perfectly the training data, but in learning the underlying structure of the data, and being able to generalize well to unseen events. We give experimental evidence that the architecture proposed in this paper can provide meaningful probability estimations for new *phrase pairs* which were not seen in the training data. The architecture can be also used to provide a list of the most likely translations given (an unseen) source phrase.
Our implementation is based on the open-source CSLM toolkit described in (Schwenk, 2010; Schwenk et al., 2012). This allows us to take advantage of all the possibilities of this software, in particular weighted resampling of large corpora and fast training on GPU cards.[1].

[1] `http://www.lium.univ-lemans.fr/~cslm`

2 Architecture

Let us first the recall the principles of the CSLM, using the same notion as (Schwenk, 2007). The inputs to the neural network are the indices of the $n-1$ previous words in the vocabulary h_j and the outputs are the posterior probabilities of *all* words of the vocabulary: $P(w_j = i|h_j), \forall i \in [1, N]$, where N is the size of the vocabulary. The input uses the so-called 1-of-n coding, i.e., the ith word of the vocabulary is coded by setting the ith element of the vector to 1 and all the other elements to 0. The ith line of the $N \times P$ dimensional projection matrix corresponds to the continuous representation of the ith word. These continuous projections of the words are concatenated. This layer is followed by one or more tanh hidden layers. The output layer uses a softmax normalization. The value of the ith output neuron is used as the probability $P(w_j = i|h_j)$. Training is performed with the standard back-propagation algorithm minimizing the cross-entropy between the output and the target probability distributions and a weight decay regularization term. The CSLM has a much higher complexity than a back-off LM, in particular because of the high dimension of the output layer. We use the option proposed by the CSLM toolkit to limit the size of the output layer to the most frequent words (short list). All the words are still considered at the input layer. Other options are explored in (Le et al., 2011).

2.1 Continuous space translation model

The central question of a phrase-based SMT system is how to estimate the probability of a phrase-pair. In practice, the length of the phrases is limited to a small value, e.g. $p, q \in [1, 7]$.

$$P(\bar{\mathbf{t}}|\bar{\mathbf{s}}) = P(t_1 \ldots t_p|s_1 \ldots s_q) \tag{2}$$

This equation can be factorized as follows:

$$\begin{aligned} P(t_1, \ldots, t_p|s_1, \ldots, s_q) &= P(t_1|t_2, \ldots, t_p, s_1, \ldots, s_q) \times P(t_2, \ldots, t_p|s_1, \ldots, s_q) \\ &= P(t_1|t_2, \ldots, t_p, s_1, \ldots, s_q) \times P(t_2|t_3, \ldots, t_p, s_1, \ldots, s_q) \times P(t_3, \ldots, t_p|s_1, \ldots, s_q) \quad (3) \\ &= \prod_{k=1}^{p} P(t_k|t_{k+1}, \ldots, t_p, s_1, \ldots, s_q) \approx \prod_{k=1}^{p} P(t_k|s_1, \ldots, s_q) = \prod_{k=1}^{p} P(t_k|\bar{\mathbf{s}}) \quad (4) \end{aligned}$$

At a first look, our model seems to be based on the approximation in the last line of the above equation, i.e. we drop the dependence between the target words. By these means we actually get p independent "n-gram models" which try to predict the kth word in the target phrase given all the words of the source phrase $\bar{\mathbf{s}}$. This naturally leads to the neural network architecture depicted in Figure 1 left. Note that there are no constraints to use the same vocabulary at the input and the output of the neural network. In this first architecture, we do not use p completely independent neural networks, but all the target words share the same projection of the words of the source phrase into the continuous space. This idea can be pushed further by adding one common hidden layer (see Figure 1 middle). Both architectures are trained by the same back-propagation algorithm than the CSLM – we just have a target vector for each output layer. The common hidden layer forces the neural network to learn a distributed representation suitable to predict each one of the p words in the target phrase. We argue that this re-introduces a dependence between the target words which we had initially dropped in equation 4. This can even be made more explicit with neural network architectures like the one in Figure 1 right.

Currently, we have only performed experiments with architecture depicted in the middle of Figure 1, using seven words at the input and output respectively. In practice, many phrase

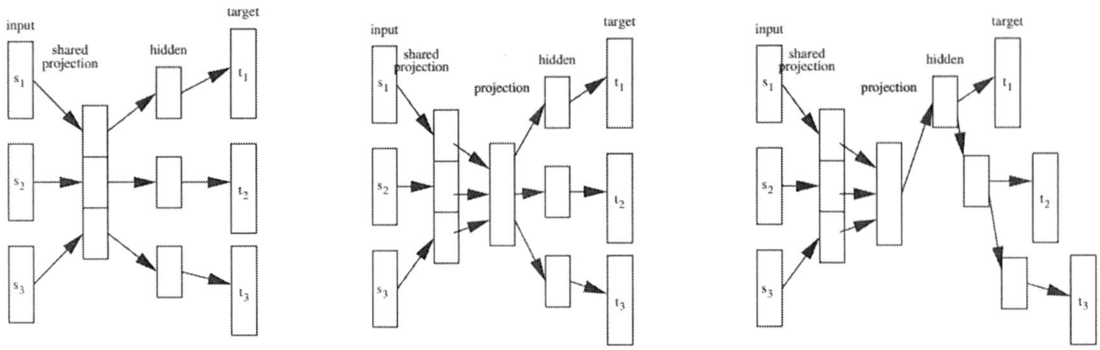

Figure 1: Different neural network architectures for a continuous space translation model. In this example, the input and output phrases are limited to a size of three words each. Left: simple extension of the CSLM. Middle: addition of a common hidden layer in order to introduce a dependence between the target words. Right: hierarchical dependence.

pairs are shorter since long phrases rarely match new test data. This is handled as follows. For an incomplete source phrase, i.e. with less than seven words, we set the projections of the "missing" words to zero. By these means, they have no influence on the calculation of the subsequent neural network layers. We could also use a special NULL word token whose projections are initialized to zero. This may enable the neural network to learn a different, more suitable, projection. Incomplete target phrases at the output layer are handled by simply not back-propagating a gradient for the "missing" words. In future work, we will also investigate the use of a special NULL word token at the output layer. By these means, we can try to learn the length of the target phrase for a given input phrase.

We have performed some initial experiments to analyze whether predicting multiple words is a difficult task for the neural network. For these experiments, we took a small corpus of phrase pairs of length of up to three source and two target words. We first trained a neural network with only one output layer to predict the first target word. This is actually a continuous space *language* model with different input and output vocabularies. Therefore, we can calculate the perplexity to measure its quality. Another neural network of the same architecture is used to predict the second target word. The results are given in Table 1, first two rows. We then trained a neural network on the same data to predict both target words, but evaluating the perplexity of only one target word (first or second). As can be seen in Table 1, 3rd row, this led to lower perplexities. From these experiments we can conclude that predicting multiple words is actually better than predicting separately individual words. The individual output layers of the NN seem to benefit of the gradient back-propagated to the common hidden and projection layer.

To measure the quality of the prediction of a phrase, i.e. a sequence of words, we define the *multi-word perplexity* as $ppl = e^{-H}$, using the approximation of equation 4:

$$
\begin{aligned}
H &= \frac{1}{n}\sum_{e}\log P(\bar{\mathbf{t}}^{(e)}|\bar{\mathbf{s}}^{(e)}) \approx \frac{1}{n}\sum_{e}\log \sqrt[p]{\prod_{k=1}^{p} P(t_k^{(e)}|\bar{\mathbf{s}}^{(e)})} = \frac{1}{n}\sum_{e}\frac{1}{p}\sum_{k=1}^{p}\log P(t_k^{(e)}|\bar{\mathbf{s}}^{(e)}) \\
&= \frac{1}{p}\sum_{k=1}^{p} H_k \quad \text{with} \quad H_k = \frac{1}{n}\sum_{e}\log P(t_k^{(e)}|\bar{\mathbf{s}}^{(e)}) \qquad (5)
\end{aligned}
$$

Therefore, the multi-word perplexity of a phrase pair is identical to the geometric mean of

Architecture	Perplexity Target 1	Target 2
Separate network which predicts first target word only	64.0	n/a
Separate network which predicts second target word only	n/a	81.9
One network which predicts both target words	62.8	80.8
multi-word perplexity:	71.3	

Table 1: Comparison of single and multi-word prediction (networks with 1 or 2 output layers)

the perplexity when predicting the individual target words separately. This is experimentally verified (see last line of Table 1). Note that this measure is pretty meaningless for classical phrase-tables with probability estimates obtained by relative frequency. Many phrase-pairs are singletons and their translation probability is estimated to be 1.0.

3 Experimental evaluation

First experimental results were performed on the data of the 2011 IWSLT evaluation which addressed translation of public lectures from English into French. The main resource provided for this task is a parallel corpus of about 100k sentences (2M words). A development and test corpus with one reference translation is also available (see Table 2). For LM we used the French side of the bitext and about 1.3G words of the LDC Gigaword corpus and other provided news corpora. According to the system description of the best performing system (Rousseau et al., 2011), adding more (out-of domain) parallel training data yields only small improvements. Our baseline phrase-based system achieves a BLEU score of 23.12 on the development and 24.84 on the test data, respectively. This system is build with the Moses toolkit using default parameters. Fourteen feature functions were used: five scores for the reordering model, four scores for translation model, a LM score, a distortion, phrase and word penalty. The coefficients of these feature functions are tuned with MERT to maximize the BLEU score.

In our initial experiments, we trained a neural network to estimate the forward phrase translation probability $P(\bar{\mathbf{t}}|\bar{\mathbf{s}})$. The maximal phrase length was set to seven words, as it is also used during the standard phrase extraction process. The extraction process of the Moses toolkit produced 7M phrase pairs after word alignment of the 100k parallel sentences. The resulting phrase table has five 5M phrase-pairs. Our neural network has the following architecture: a 320 dimensional projection layer for each input word, one common hidden layer of dimension 768, one 512 dimensional additional hidden layer for each output, and seven output layers of dimension 16384 (we use the mechanism of a short list provided by the CSLM toolkit). In our case, a phrase is processed by the neural network when all the target words fall into the short list. This was the case for about 93% of the observed phrases in the training data. Note that the source and target vocabulary of the translation model are much smaller than the one of the LM (about 50k). Phrase pairs which are not processed by the CSTM are obtained from a classical phrase table. We used binary phrase-tables which are kept on disk. Training of this configuration takes about 2 days on a standard multi-core server and less than 10 hours on a GPU card.

We experimented with three different possibilities to use the translation model probabilities provided by the neural network: 1) evaluation of the CSTM to provide meaningful probabilities for unseen phrase pairs; 2) rescoring of n-best lists provided by Moses; and 3) direct integration into the decoding algorithm of Moses. These options are discussed in the following sections.

Corpus	#lines	#words English	French
Train (TED)	107k	1.8M	2.0M
Dev	2026	36.6k	39.0k
Test	572	9.0k	9.1k

Table 2: Statistics of the parallel corpora provided for the 2011 IWSLT evaluation.

Source phrase	Translation provided by the CSTM
a nice car	une jolie voiture
a nice bike	un vélo sympa
a nice woman	une jolie femme
a nice garden	un joli jardin
a nice man	un homme sympa

Table 3: Example translations proposed by the CSTM. All these phrase-pairs were not in the training data. No target LM was used.

3.1 Generalization to new phrase-pairs

Table 3 shows some examples of phrase pairs and the most likely translation provided by the CSTM. These translations are obtained by selecting the output target words with the highest probability. It is important to note that none of these phrase pairs are included in the training data. The standard Moses phrase table only contains many single word-to-word translations of the words *nice*, *car*, *bike*, *woman*, *garden* and *man*. Therefore, the full translation process must completely rely on the LM to select the best individual translations of the three words so that a correct French sentence will be created. It can be clearly seen that the CSTM does not seem to perform a simple word-by-word translation. In our setting, we translate from English into French, a morphologically rich language. French has two genders and the adjectives must be adapted to the noun. In our example, the source phrases only differ by the third word, but this induces changes of all the three words in the target phrase because of the morphology of the French language. The CSTM was able to produce in all cases the correct translation and to adapt the article and adjective to the noun. Note that this is obtained without an additional LM on the target words. We interpret this is as experimental evidence that our architecture is able to capture relations between the target words. The CSTM can also propose *word reorderings*: in some translations the adjective is correctly placed in front of the noun (e.g. *une jolie voiture*), and in others behind the noun (e.g. *un vélo sympa*).

3.2 Rescoring n-best lists

The CSTM can be used to rescore n-best lists produced by the baseline system. This is in analogy to the use of the continuous space *language* model which is usually not integrated into beam search. Rescoring the translation model probabilities requires the phrase alignments in the n-best list. Table 4 gives some statistics on this process. Although there are almost 17M requests for phrase translation probabilities, only 53k were actually different. We take advantage of this redundancy to speed-up the translation model rescoring. In our case, this takes less than five minutes, but half of the time is actually needed to load and parse the n-best lists. The CSTM processes almost 95% of the probability requests, this means using a short list is not a limitation. The forward phrase probability estimated by the neural network is added as 15th score and the coefficients are retuned with MERT. By these means we were able to achieve an improvement of about 0.3 BLEU on the development and 0.2 BLEU on the test set (see Table 5). This is not a huge improvement, but we have changed only one score of the phrase-table. Exactly the same approach can be used to estimate the inverse phrase translation probability $P(\bar{\mathbf{s}}|\bar{\mathbf{t}})$.

3.3 Integration into the decoder

As far as we know, there is only one attempt to integrate the CSLM directly into the translation process (Zamora-Martínez et al., 2010). This is in fact tricky since many LM probabilities are requested and it is not straight forward to delay a bunch of requests so that we can use the CSLM more efficiently. A possible implementation could be based on the work on distributed LMs, for instance (Brants et al., 2007). Previous works on continuous space translation models in an bilingual tuple system only used rescoring (Schwenk et al., 2007; Le et al., 2012). On the other hand, it seems to be easier to integrate the approach proposed in this paper directly into the decoder. When translating a sentence, Moses first enumerates all the possible segmentations of the source sentence, given the known phrases in the phrase-table. Once all those probabilities are obtained, the translation model is not queried any more. This process largely simplifies the use of continuous space methods. Two options come to mind: 1) keep the segmentations proposed by the classical phrase table, but get the translation probabilities from the CSTM instead of the phrase-table; or 2) don't use a classical phrase-table any more, but request all possible phrase-pairs directly from the CSTM. The integration of the phrase-table into the decoder according to the first option can be in fact simulated by creating a "fake" phrase-table that has the same form than the standard Moses phrase-table, but replacing the probabilities with the ones calculated by the CSTM. Alternatively, we could add the CSTM probability as an additional feature function. The results of these experiments are summarized in Table 5. When replacing the forward translation model probability in the phrase-table, we achieve a slight improvement of the BLEU score on the test data, in comparison to rescoring n-best lists (25.03→25.13). This seems to indicate that the CSTM probabilities trigger the exploration of new paths during the beam search which were pruned in the n-best list.

Some example translations are provided in Figure 2. In the first example, the English word *"right"* can have several translations which have different meanings: *"à droite"* if we are referring to a direction, *"correct"*, etc if we approve something, and *"pas vrai ?"* or *"non ?"* if we ask for confirmation. The CSTM made the right choice, but this did not improve the BLEU score. The same observations hold for the second example where the CSTM selects the correct translation of *"little"*. In the third example, the phrase-based baseline system fails and performs a very bad word by word translation. The CSTM provides a much better translation.

When using the CSTM to completely replace a phrase-table, we are able to apply phrases of any length at each position in the source phrase. Limiting the source phrase length to the usual seven words, there are at most $7 \times q$ possible segmentations of the source sentence into phrases, where q is the length of the source sentence. For each of these segmentations, the CSTM could provide a large number of translations. The goal would be to obtain an ordered list of the most likely translations given an input source. Initial work has shown that the CSTM can provide a meaningful list of possible translations, but this list also contains wrong translations. We

Nb of sentences	2026
Nb of phrase pairs	16.8M
Nb of different phrase pairs	53k
Aver. nb of phrases per sentence	10.3
Phrases processed by CSTM	94.9%

Table 4: Statistics of rescoring 1000-best lists with the CSTM.

System	Dev	Test
Baseline	23.12	24.84
CSTM rescoring	23.45	25.03
CSTM decode	23.13	25.13

Table 5: n-best rescoring versus integrating the CSTM into beam-search (BLEU scores).

SRC:	now this sounds crazy **right**
BASE:	cela peut paraître fou **à droite**
CSTM:	c'est fou **pas vrai**
REF:	cela paraît incroyable **non**
SRC:	and sometimes a **little** prototype of this experience is all that it takes to ...
BASE:	et parfois un **peu** prototype de cette expérience est qu'il faut pour ...
CSTM:	et parfois un **petit** prototype de cette expérience est qu'il faut pour ...
REF:	et parfois un **petit** prototype de cette expérience sera la seule chose qui ...
SRC:	but the things i constantly hear far too many chemicals pesticides ...
BASE:	mais **les choses je constamment entendre** bien trop de produits chimiques ...
CSTM:	mais **ce que j'entends constamment** beaucoup trop de produits chimiques ...
REF:	**ce que j'entends souvent** c'est trop de produits chimiques ...

Figure 2: Example translations of the test set: English source, translation provided by the baseline systems, decoding with a CSTM, and reference translation.

are currently experimenting with various thresholds to discard unreliable translation options. Finally, it is also possible to combine both options to integrate the CSTM into the beam-search: keep the original segmentations of the source sentence into phrases, only add the most reliable new phrase pairs proposed by the CSTM and calculate all the translation model probabilities with the neural network. This research is ongoing.

Conclusion and perspectives

This paper has presented a new technique to estimate the translation probabilities in a phrase-based SMT system. This can be seen as an extension of the continuous space language model: all the words of the source phrase are projected onto a continuous space and the neural network predicts the joint probability of all the words in the target phrase. To the best of our knowledge, previous research to apply continuous space methods to the translation model, were limited to tuple-based translation models (Schwenk et al., 2007; Le et al., 2012). The system proposed in this paper is trained on the same data than a standard phrase-based systems.

An interesting feature of the approach is the ability to provide translation model probabilities for any possible phrase-pair. We have provided experimental evidence that the system actually seems to be able to provide meaningful translations for source phrase which were not seen in the training data. An interesting extension of this idea is to use large amounts of *monolingual* data to pre-train the projections of the source words onto the continuous space. The neural network could learn from the monolingual data that words are synonyms since they often appear in similar contexts. This could be used in the CSTM to provide translations for source words not seen in the bitexts. This could be also interesting when translating from a morphologically rich language into English since many verb forms actually translate into the same English word.

The implementation of the continuous space translation model is based on an extension of the CSLM toolkit and it will be freely available. By these means, we can benefit of all the infrastructure of the toolkit, in particular training on large amounts of data using resampling techniques and a fast implementation on GPU cards, or weighting of the training data.

Acknowledgments

This work was partially financed by the French government (CosMAT, ANR-09-CORD-004), the European Commission (MATECAT, ICT-2011.4.2 – 287688) and the DARPA BOLT project.

References

Bengio, Y. and Ducharme, R. (2001). A neural probabilistic language model. In *NIPS*, volume 13, pages 932–938.

Bengio, Y., Ducharme, R., Vincent, P., and Jauvin, C. (2003). A neural probabilistic language model. *JMLR*, 3(2):1137–1155.

Brants, T., Popat, A. C., Xu, P., Och, F. J., and Dean, J. (2007). Large language models in machine translation. In *EMNLP*, pages 858–867.

Foster, G., Kuhn, R., and Johnson, H. (2006). Phrasetable smoothing for statistical machine translation. In *EMNLP*, pages 53–61.

Koehn, P., Och, F. J., and Marcu, D. (2003). Statistical phrase-based machine translation. In *HLT/NACL*, pages 127–133.

Le, H.-S., Allauzen, A., Wisniewski, G., and Yvon, F. (2010). Training continuous space language models: Some practical issues. In *EMNLP*, pages 778–788.

Le, H.-S., Allauzen, A., and Yvon, F. (2012). Continuous space translation models with neural networks. In *NAACL*.

Le, H.-S., Oparin, I., Allauzen, A., Gauvain, J.-L., and Yvon, F. (2011). Structured output layer neural network language model. In *ICASSP*, pages 5524–5527.

Och, F. J. (2003). Minimum error rate training in statistical machine translation. In *ACL*, pages 160–167.

Och, F. J. and Ney, H. (2003). A systematic comparison of various statistical alignement models. *Computational Linguistics*, 29(1):19–51.

Rousseau, A., Bougares, F., Deléglise, P., Schwenk, H., and Estève, Y. (2011). Lium's systems for the IWSLT 2011 speech translation tasks. In *International Workshop on Spoken Language Translation*.

Schwenk, H. (2007). Continuous space language models. *Computer Speech and Language*, 21:492–518.

Schwenk, H. (2010). Continuous space language models for statistical machine translation. *The Prague Bulletin of Mathematical Linguistics*, (93):137–146.

Schwenk, H., Costa-jussà, M. R., and Fonollosa, J. A. R. (2007). Smooth bilingual n-gram translation. In *EMNLP*, pages 430–438.

Schwenk, H., Déchelotte, D., and Gauvain, J.-L. (2006). Continuous space language models for statistical machine translation. In *Proceedings of the COLING/ACL 2006 Main Conference Poster Sessions*, pages 723–730.

Schwenk, H., Rousseau, A., and Attik, M. (2012). Large, pruned or continuous space language models on a GPU for statistical machine translation. In *NAACL Workshop on the Future of Language Modeling for HLT*.

Zamora-Martínez, F., Castro-Bleda, M. J., and Schwenk, H. (2010). N-gram-based machine translation enhanced with neural networks for the French-English BTEC-IWSLT'10 task. In *IWSLT*, pages 45–52.

Data-driven Dependency Parsing With Empty Heads

Wolfgang Seeker Richárd Farkas Bernd Bohnet
Helmut Schmid Jonas Kuhn
Institut für Maschinelle Sprachverarbeitung
University of Stuttgart
firstname.lastname@ims.uni-stuttgart.de

ABSTRACT
Syntactic dependency structures are based on the assumption that there is exactly one node in the structure for each word in the sentence. However representing elliptical constructions (e.g. missing verbs) is problematic as the question where the dependents of the elided material should be attached to has to be solved. In this paper, we present an in-depth study into the challenges of introducing *empty heads* into dependency structures during automatic parsing. Structurally, empty heads provide an attachment site for the dependents of the non-overt material and thus preserve the linguistically plausible structure of the sentence. We compare three different (computational) approaches to the introduction of empty heads and evaluate them against German and Hungarian data. We then conduct a fine-grained error analysis on the output of one of the approaches to highlight some of the difficulties of the task. We find that while a clearly defined part of the phenomena can be learned by the parser, more involved elliptical structures are still mostly out of reach of the automatic tools.

KEYWORDS: Empty heads, statistical dependency parsing, German, Hungarian.

Proceedings of COLING 2012: Posters, pages 1081–1090,
COLING 2012, Mumbai, December 2012.

1 Introduction

Dependency structures (Mel'čuk, 1988) are a versatile formalism if one wants to represent syntactic structures for languages with free word order. Elliptical structures however can cause problems for this formalism because they violate a basic assumption, namely that there is exactly one node in the structure for each word in the sentence. In verbal ellipsis for example, this problem can break the entire structure because verbs often have dependents, but if the verb is not present in the sentence and subsequently not present in the structure, where should the dependents of the verb be attached to? One possibility that has been proposed is the introduction of *zero word forms* (Mel'čuk, 2009, 47), i. e. phonetically empty heads that appear in the structure but not on the surface string and provide an attachment site for the dependents of the ellipsis. In many languages, these constructions are rather frequent and should be handled by dependency parsers in a way that makes them easy to use in downstream applications.

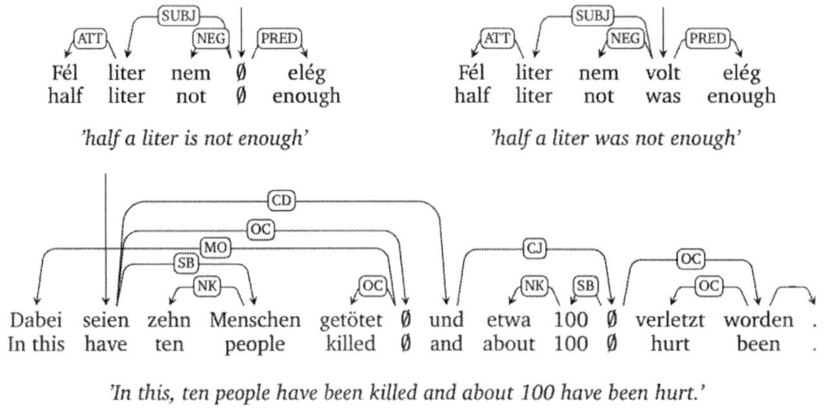

Figure 1: Empty heads in Hungarian (top) and German (bottom).

Figure 1 shows examples for two languages, Hungarian and German, where empty heads are annotated to ensure a linguistically plausible structure. In the top examples, a Hungarian copula construction is shown. In present tense (the sentence to the left), the copula is not overtly expressed and therefore represented as a phonetically empty head (Ø), while in all other tenses (right example), the copula would be expressed overtly. Since we would like the structure to be the same for both sentences, an empty head can be used to preserve the parallelism. The German example on the bottom shows a coordination of two sentences that share the finite and the passive auxiliary with each other, both represented as a phonetically empty head in the structure. By introducing empty nodes into the annotation, the parallelism in the underlying syntactic structure of the two conjuncts is preserved.

We would like to stress that the problem of empty heads in dependency syntax is rather different from the problem of introducing trace elements previously addressed by work on the English Penn Treebank (Johnson, 2002; Dienes and Dubey, 2003; Campbell, 2004). The PTB encodes a lot of different elements that do not show on the surface, but most of these would be leaf nodes in dependency representation.[1]

[1]There is a small number of cases, where the PTB annotates a missing verb (marked as *?*, see Section 4.6 in Bies et al. (1995)). We found 581 instances of those in the whole corpus, 293 of which were dominated by a VP node. Only those empty elements correspond to empty heads in a dependency representation since they would normally have dependents on their own. But in contrast to dependency formalisms, it is not a problem to annotate a head-less phrase in a phrase-structure formalism.

The aim of this paper is to investigate the problem of automatically predicting these empty heads in the process of statistical dependency parsing and to shed some light on the challenges of this problem. For this, we present and evaluate three different methods of introducing empty heads into dependency structures, one direct approach, where the parser itself decides when to annotate an empty head, one approach where the information about empty heads is encoded into the label set of the structure, and one approach where the presence of empty heads is determined by a classifier run prior to parsing.

The paper is structured as follows: we first review some related work and continue with the presentation of the three different methods. We then define the metric that we use to measure the quality of the empty head prediction and use it to evaluate parsing experiments on German and Hungarian. We conclude with an error analysis and a discussion of the results.

2 Related Work

We are aware of two previous papers where the issue of empty heads has been addressed in the context of dependency parsing: One is Dukes and Habash (2011) who present a parser for the Quranic Arabic Dependency Treebank, which also contains empty heads. Unfortunately, they do not evaluate or discuss the role of empty heads. Their solution of the problem – introducing a new transition into a transition-based parser – is similar to one of our proposed procedures (the in-parsing approach). The other work is by Chaitanya et al. (2011), who use hand-crafted rules to recover empty nodes from the output of a rule-based dependency parser for the Hindi Dependency Treebank. They achieve good results on some phenomena and a bit lower results on others, proving that it is indeed possible to treat this problem in syntactic processing. However, given that their data base is very small, and they used a rule-based, language-specific approach, the question remains if we can use statistical learning to address this problem.

3 Approaches for Parsing with Empty Heads

The parser that we use for our experiment is basically a best-first parser like the ones described in (Goldberg and Elhadad, 2010; Tratz and Hovy, 2011), which is trained with the Guided Learning technique proposed in Shen et al. (2007) embedded in a MIRA framework (Crammer et al., 2003). The best-first parsing approach has the advantage that it is easy to modify in order to allow for the introduction of empty heads, while for graph-based parsers (McDonald et al., 2005) it is not even clear how to do it. The approach is also more suitable here than the standard transition-based approach (Nivre et al., 2004), since it can build context on both sides of the current attachment site while it achieves competitive results.

In contrast to the best-first parser in Goldberg and Elhadad (2010), the decoding algorithm is modified so that it works like the LTAG dependency parser described in Shen and Joshi (2008), which allows an edge to attach to an inside node of an already built structure. This difference makes it possible to directly produce a large portion of non-projective structures (e. g. sentence extraposition or WH-extraction) without having to resort to a swap operation as is done in Tratz and Hovy (2011). It also increases theoretical decoding complexity to $O(n^2)$. However, there are non-projective structures that cannot be produced by this approach.[2] To allow the derivation of these structures, we reintroduce the swap operation from the parser in Tratz and Hovy (2011), but during training, the parser is only allowed to apply the swap operation in case of an ill-nested structure, which leads to a very small number of swaps.

[2]These structures do not fulfill the *well-nestedness condition* that is described in Bodirsky et al. (2005); Kuhlmann and Nivre (2006) and appear for example in German centerfield scrambling structures.

The **feature set** of the parser uses the word forms, lemmata, POS tags, and already predicted dependency labels for the head and its prospective dependent, as well as combinations thereof for up to three surrounding tokens in the sentence. The same features and combinations are extracted for up to three surrounding partially built structures. We also add features for the left-most and right-most dependent of a token, the labels of the dependents, distance features, and valency features as proposed by Zhang and Nivre (2011) but adapted to the best-first decoder. For internal feature representation and combination the parser implements the hash kernel method by Bohnet (2010).

3.1 Empty Head Introduction during Parsing

For the first method, we change the parser so that it can decide for an empty head during the parsing itself. To the three moves that the standard parser can perform – attach_left(label), attach_right(label), and swap – we add a fourth move (see Figure 2), that allows the parser to introduce an empty head for a particular dependent (together with a dependency label). This is similar in spirit to the parser presented in Dukes and Habash (2011), although they use a transition-based left to right approach for decoding. When training the parser, the empty heads in the training data are skipped in the feature extraction as long as they have not been predicted by the parser, and then added to the sentence as an additional node. If the parser makes a mistake during training, and the oracle is asked to provide the currently best-scoring valid action, we force it to defer proposing the introduction of an empty head as long as there is any other valid action available. This way we ensure that the decision to introduce an empty head is made only when the maximum syntactic context is available for the decision. During test time, we do not allow the parser to introduce two empty heads in a row to make sure that the parser does not enter an infinite loop of predicting empty heads over and over.

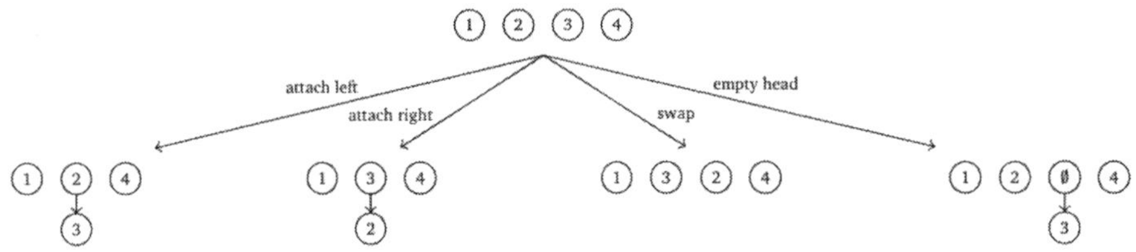

Figure 2: The four possible moves to extend the top configuration (unlabeled).

We add three basic features to the parser that are meant to capture some features of the empty heads. (1) we add a boolean feature that is true if there is a verb following the current token in the sentence. (2) we add a boolean feature that is true if there is at least one verb in the sentence. (3) we add a boolean feature that is true if there is at least one finite verb in the sentence. All three features are computed based on the POS tags of the tokens in the sentence. Finally, we also extract features (word form, pos, etc.) from the closest verb to the right and to the left of the current dependent. The boolean features are supposed to give information if there is any verb available in the sentence that could play the role of the main verb. Furthermore, since we assume for some of the elliptical constructions, that the verb that is missing is actually taking up another verb in the sentence, the latter features may capture this.

3.2 Standard Dependency Parsing with Complex Labels

In the second method, we encode information about empty heads in the label set of the treebank. Dependents of an empty head are attached to its head and their labels are combined with the label of the empty head (see Figure 3). All the trees remain proper dependency trees where each node in the structure corresponds to a token in the input. The method is thus compatible with any standard parsing strategy. We apply the best-first parser to the complex-label data in order to gain a fair comparison with the previous approach. When the parser model with complex labels is applied to unseen data, it predicts the complex labels in the output, which then allow us to recover the empty heads. The recovery algorithm simply looks for all daughters of a node that are labeled with a complex label and introduces an empty node for each subset of nodes whose label prefixes match.[3]

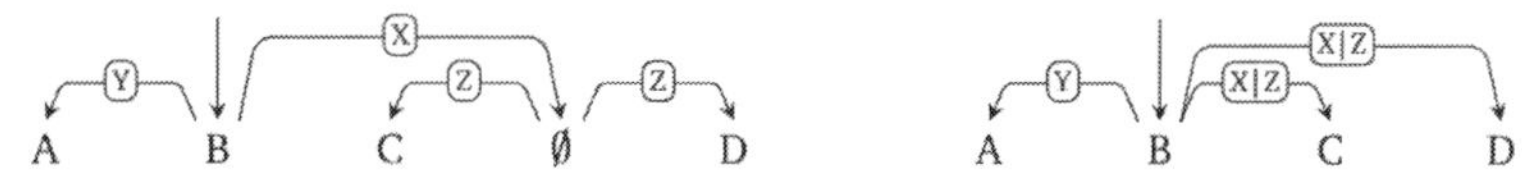

Figure 3: Encoding scheme for complex labels.

The complex label approach allows us to use any standard dependency parser. However, encoding information into labels needs to be done with caution. The label set can grow quickly, so the parsers will become much slower and will have a hard time learning the rare labels.

3.3 Preinserting Empty Heads

Besides the in-parsing approaches, we also experimented with a preinserting procedure as a third method. Here, the empty heads are automatically inserted into the sentence before parsing based on surface information. The advantage of this approach is again that we can use any standard dependency parser for parsing the input tokens and inserted empty word forms.

Our first attempt following the approach by (Dienes and Dubey, 2003) from the phrase-structure parsing literature shows very low accuracies. We attribute this to the different nature of the empty elements in the standard Penn Treebank setting and our data. The Penn Treebank traces can be modeled by local features and have fixed string positions (e. g. before to-infinitive constructions) whereas our empty heads can occur more freely due to the free word order of German and Hungarian.

We therefore pursue here a clause-based empty head preinsertion procedure since we think that the decision about inserting an empty head (which is basically the identification of the absence of the verb) can be made on the clause-level. For this, we implemented a clause boundary identification module and a classifier that predicts whether an empty word form should be inserted into a particular clause. Clause boundary identification is a difficult problem (cf. (Sang and Déjean, 2001)) as clauses usually form a hierarchy – and this hierarchy is important for predicting the insertion of empty heads. Our clause boundary detector achieves f-scores of 92.6 and 86.8 on the German and Hungarian development datasets respectively. These results are in line with the state-of-the-art results on the English Penn Treebank (Carreras et al., 2005; Ram and Lalitha Devi, 2008). If we evaluate only the in-sentence clauses, we get f-scores of 85.4 and 78.2 for German and Hungarian respectively.

In order to decide whether to insert an empty head, we implemented a classifier that decides for the insertion based on the output of the clause detector. The classifier utilizes the tokens, POS tags and morphological features of the clause and their patterns (bi- and trigrams) along with information about the hierarchy of the clauses (the depth of the clause and covered clauses).

[3]This is not a completely reversible procedure since we cannot recover two different empty nodes if they are sisters and happen to be labeled by the same label. However, this is a rare case in the treebanks (twice in the German treebank, five times in the Hungarian treebank).

The classifier achieves f-scores of 42.3 and 70.1 on the German and Hungarian development datasets respectively.

We use simple rules for finding the position inside the clause where the empty head should be inserted. For German, we insert it after the first noun sequence (which is an approximation of the place of the verb in the verb-second word order of German). For Hungarian, the manual annotation of the position of the empty word forms is quite irregular and we insert them at the beginning of the clause. Finally, we train the best-first parser on the original training dataset containing the gold standard empty heads and use it to parse the sentences that contain the automatically inserted empty heads from the preinserter.

4 Experiments

In order to test the parsing methods, we performed two experiments each: we trained the parser on the German TiGer corpus using the dependency representation by Seeker and Kuhn (2012) , and on the Szeged Dependency Treebank of Hungarian (Vincze et al., 2010), both of which data sets explicitly represent empty heads in the dependency trees. Table 1 shows the data sizes and the splits we used for the experiment. The German data was preprocessed (lemma, POS, morphology) with the mate-tools,[4] the Hungarian data comes with automatic annotation.[5]

		training		development		test	
data set	# sentences	# sents	# empty	# sents	# empty	# sents	# empty
German	50,474	36,000	2,618	2,000	117	10,472	722
Hungarian	81,960	61,034	14,850	11,688	2,536	9,238	2,106

Table 1: Data sets

4.1 Evaluation Method

Since the number of edges in the gold standard does not always equal the number of edges in the parser output if we allow the introduction of empty heads, we cannot use attachment accuracy anymore. To evaluate the recovery of empty heads, we therefore introduce three measures, which focus on different characteristics of the empty heads.[6]

The first metric (**ATTe**) is the labeled attachment score for empty heads only, where we count the correct attachment to the head as well as the correct attachment of the daughters of the empty head. A correct edge is thereby an edge that connects the same two tokens as in the gold standard, and that has the same label as the gold-standard edge, similar as in the ELAS score proposed by Dukes and Habash (2011), disregarding however the POS tag. One problem with the ELAS score is that it is not clear what happens if there is more than one empty head in the output of the parser or in the gold standard. In these cases, we compute the mapping of parser output empty heads to gold standard empty heads that maximizes the final score. This way, the evaluation is not skewed if the empty head is at the wrong string position, or if the number of empty heads in the gold standard differs from the number of empty heads in the parser output. As an extension to this metric, we define **ATTall**, which applies the ATTe to the whole node set in order to see the complete picture including the empty heads. For both metrics, we compute precision, recall, and f-score. In the last measure, **cLAS**, we use standard LAS by collapsing the

[4]http://code.google.com/p/mate-tools

[5]Our data sets and the evaluation tool will be made available on `www.ims.uni-stuttgart.de/~seeker`

[6]We do not evaluate string position since empty heads are only important for the structure.

empty heads in both parser output and gold standard using the complex label encoding. cLAS is a way of applying LAS to our parser output.

4.2 Experimental Results

The parser was trained on the training sets using 10 iterations and was then tested on the test sets. Table 2 presents the results in terms of the measures that we defined in Section 4.1.

		German				Hungarian			
		prec	rec	f1	acc	prec	rec	f1	acc
direct parsing	ATTe	56.81	24.46	34.20		69.08	63.07	65.94	
	ATTall	88.90	88.66	88.78		85.67	85.56	85.61	
	cLAS				88.90				85.28
complex labels	ATTe	58.82	28.77	38.64		67.56	59.36	63.20	
	ATTall	88.85	88.68	88.76		85.36	85.36	85.36	
	cLAS				88.90				85.18
preinsertion	ATTe	23.22	25.75	24.42		68.40	56.67	61.98	
	ATTall	88.09	88.11	88.10		85.25	85.02	85.14	
	cLAS				88.31				84.89

Table 2: Evaluation results on test sets.

Two general trends can be seen from the results. First, the preinsertion approach performs worse than the other two approaches. It is however not clear which of the other two is superior since for German, the complex label approach performs better while for Hungarian, the direct parsing approach comes out first. The second trend is that generally, the precision of the approach is much better than the recall, indicating that there are some phenomena that are relatively easy to learn resulting in a high precision, but most of the empty heads are not even recognized in the first place, hence the low recall. We also see that all approaches operate on a much higher level for Hungarian than for German.

5 Error Analysis

In this section, we perform a short error analysis to hint at some of the problems. We use the development sets of both data sets and the output of the direct parsing approach. Table 3 shows the performance on the development sets.

	German				Hungarian			
	prec	rec	f1	acc	prec	rec	f1	acc
ATTe	59.35	25.21	35.38		65.53	64.90	65.21	
ATTall	89.17	88.94	89.05		85.17	85.17	85.17	
cLAS				89.15				84.89

Table 3: Evaluation results on development sets.

One problem that we find when reviewing the output is that the parser often fails because of incorrect part-of-speech tagging. Sometimes, verbs are not recognized, which then prompts the parser to predict an empty head instead. Sometimes, other words are mistagged as verbs, which then prevents the parser from predicting an empty head. Table 4 shows the performance of the direct parsing approach when run on gold POS tags. The effect is greater for German than for Hungarian, but it is not substantial in both languages, showing that the parser relies strongly on POS information.

Another effect we find in the output is that some empty heads seem to be easier to predict than others. We illustrate this on the Hungarian data, where a coarse classification into empty copula (VAN) and other ellipsis (ELL) is annotated in the gold standard. Table 5 shows the

		German			Hungarian		
		prec	rec	f1	prec	rec	f1
predicted POS	ATTe	59.35	25.21	35.38	65.53	64.90	65.21
gold POS	ATTe	70.59	32.88	44.86	68.57	68.68	68.62

Table 4: Evaluation results on development sets using gold POS annotation.

performance on sentences that contain exactly one empty head in the gold standard.[7] The results indicate that empty copula are easier to learn for the parser than the more involved ellipses, which could be explained by the stronger grammaticalization of the former. Generally, the parser seems to rely heavily on lexical cues that do not vary much.

		ATTe		
	#sentence	prec	rec	f1
VAN	1760	83.64	69.23	75.76
ELL	307	80.18	42.56	55.61

Table 5: Results achieved on two different types of empty heads (Hungarian).

	prec	rec	f1	acc
ATTe	95.37	66.16	78.13	
ATTall	98.88	98.73	98.81	
cLAS				98.85

Table 6: Applying the direct parsing approach to its own training set (German).

Finally, we show the performance of the direct parsing approach when applied to its own training set in German. This can be instructive to see if the features of the statistical model actually capture the correct information to identify empty heads. The results (Table 6) suggest that they do not. A standard statistical dependency parser (without empty heads) usually achieves scores in the high 90s on its own training data. Results clearly show that work in the feature set of the parser is necessary to predict empty heads more accurately, but also that the standard syntactic features are not capable of modeling the phenomenon.

Conclusion and Future Work

Empty heads represent material that is missing on the surface of the sentence but is understood and usually easily reconstructible by humans. Formally, empty heads provide attachment sites for their overtly expressed dependents and thus help representing syntactic structures of elliptic constructions in the same way as their non-elliptic counterparts. In this paper, we evaluated three methods of introducing empty heads into a dependency structure, a direct approach during parsing, an encoding scheme that allows the reconstruction of empty heads after standard parsing, and a preinsertion approach where the empty heads are predicted prior to parsing. All three methods were evaluated on German and Hungarian.

The preinsertion method is outperformed by the two other approaches, but which of these is superior remains to be seen. In general, no method performs on a satisfactory level indicating that empty heads are a difficult phenomenon. Our error analysis shows that standard features for statistical dependency parsing are not able to model empty heads convincingly. One thing that we can learn from our investigation is, that it is probably wise to separate the empty heads that we have in the data into at least two parts, namely the part that contains constructions like the Hungarian copula (and probably similar local, more grammaticized constructions), and the other more involved ellipses. The parser seems to be able to predict missing copula reasonably well and this can be used to predict more accessible output structures. Since the construction also appears in other languages, e. g. the Slavic languages, this may turn out useful.

[7] We only choose these sentences, because the type of a predicted empty head is not straight forward to determine automatically.

Acknowledgments

We would like to thank Bernadette Rauschenberger for her help. This work was funded by the Deutsche Forschungsgemeinschaft (DFG) via Projects D4 and D8 of the SFB 732 "Incremental Specification in Context".

References

Bies, A., Ferguson, M., Katz, K., and MacIntyre, R. (1995). Bracketing Guidelines for Treebank II style Penn Treebank Project. Technical report, Linguistic Data Consortium.

Bodirsky, M., Kuhlmann, M., and Möhl, M. (2005). Well-nested drawings as models of syntactic structure. In *Proceedings of the 10th Conference on Formal Grammar and 9th Meeting on Mathematics of Language*, pages 195–204.

Bohnet, B. (2010). Very high accuracy and fast dependency parsing is not a contradiction. In *Proceedings of the 23rd International Conference on Computational Linguistics (Coling 2010)*, pages 89–97, Beijing, China. International Committee on Computational Linguistics.

Campbell, R. (2004). Using linguistic principles to recover empty categories. In *Proceedings of the 42nd Annual Meeting on Association for Computational Linguistics - ACL 2004*, pages 645–es, Morristown, NJ, USA. Association for Computational Linguistics.

Carreras, A. X., Màrquez, B. L., and Castro, C. J. (2005). Filtering-ranking perceptron learning for partial parsing. *Machine Learning*, 60:41–71. 10.1007/s10994-005-0917-x.

Chaitanya, G., Husain, S., and Mannem, P. (2011). Empty categories in Hindi dependency treebank: analysis and recovery. In *Proceedings of the 5th Linguistic Annotation Workshop (LAW 2011)*, Portland, USA. Association for Computational Linguistics.

Crammer, K., Dekel, O., Shalev-Shwartz, S., and Singer, Y. (2003). Online passive-aggressive algorithms. In *Proceedings of the 16th Annual Conference on Neural Information Processing Systems (NIPS)*, volume 7. MIT Press.

Dienes, P. and Dubey, A. (2003). Deep syntactic processing by combining shallow methods. In *Proceedings of the 41st Annual Meeting on Association for Computational Linguistics-Volume 1*, volume 1, pages 431–438, Sapporo, Japan. Association for Computational Linguistics.

Dukes, K. and Habash, N. (2011). One-Step Statistical Parsing of Hybrid Dependency-Constituency Syntactic Representations. In *Proceedings of the International Conference on Parsing Technology (IWPT 2011)*, pages 92–104, Dublin, Ireland. Association for Computational Linguistics.

Goldberg, Y. and Elhadad, M. (2010). An efficient algorithm for easy-first non-directional dependency parsing. In *Human Language Technologies: The 2010 Annual Conference of the North American Chapter of the Association for Computational Linguistics (NAACL 2010)*, pages 742–750. Association for Computational Linguistics.

Johnson, M. (2002). A simple pattern-matching algorithm for recovering empty nodes and their antecedents. In *Proceedings of the 40th Annual Meeting on Association for Computational Linguistics - ACL '02*, page 136, Morristown, NJ, USA. Association for Computational Linguistics.

Kuhlmann, M. and Nivre, J. (2006). Mildly non-projective dependency structures. In *Proceedings of the COLING/ACL on Main conference poster sessions*, pages 507–514, Morristown, NJ, USA. Association for Computational Linguistics.

McDonald, R., Crammer, K., and Pereira, F. (2005). Online large-margin training of dependency parsers. In *Proceedings of ACL 2005*, pages 91–98, Morristown, NJ, USA. Association for Computational Linguistics.

Mel'čuk, I. (1988). *Dependency Syntax: Theory and Practice*. State University Press of New York, suny serie edition.

Mel'čuk, I. (2009). *Dependency in linguistic description*.

Nivre, J., Hall, J., and Nilsson, J. (2004). Memory-based dependency parsing. In *Proceedings of the 8th Conference on Computational Natural Language Learning (CoNLL 2004)*, pages 49–56, Boston, Massachusetts.

Ram, R. and Lalitha Devi, S. (2008). Clause boundary identification using conditional random fields. In Gelbukh, A., editor, *Computational Linguistics and Intelligent Text Processing*, volume 4919 of *Lecture Notes in Computer Science*, pages 140–150. Springer Berlin Heidelberg.

Sang, E. F. T. K. and Déjean, H. (2001). Introduction to the conll-2001 shared task: clause identification. In *Proceedings of the ACL 2001 Workshop on Computational Natural Language Learning (ConLL)*.

Seeker, W. and Kuhn, J. (2012). Making Ellipses Explicit in Dependency Conversion for a German Treebank. In *Proceedings of the 8th Language Resources and Evaluation Conference (LREC 2012)*, pages 3132–3139, Istanbul, Turkey. European Language Resources Association (ELRA).

Shen, L. and Joshi, A. K. (2008). Ltag dependency parsing with bidirectional incremental construction. In *Proceedings of the Conference on Empirical Methods in Natural Language Processing (EMNLP 2008)*, pages 495–504, Honolulu, Hawaii. Association for Computational Linguistics.

Shen, L., Satta, G., and Joshi, A. K. (2007). Guided Learning for Bidirectional Sequence Classification. In *Proceedings of the 45th Annual Meeting of the Association for Computational Linguistics (ACL 2007)*, pages 760–767. Association for Computational Linguistics.

Tratz, S. and Hovy, E. (2011). A Fast, Accurate, Non-Projective, Semantically-Enriched Parser. In *Proceedings of the Conference on Empirical Methods in Natural Language Processing (EMNLP 2011)*, pages 1257–1268, Edinburgh, UK.

Vincze, V., Szauter, D., Almási, A., Móra, G., Alexin, Z., and Csirik, J. (2010). Hungarian Dependency Treebank. In *Proceedings of the Seventh conference on International Language Resources and Evaluation (LREC 2010)*, pages 1855–1862, Valletta, Malta.

Zhang, Y. and Nivre, J. (2011). Transition-based Dependency Parsing with Rich Non-local Features. In *Proceedings of the 49th Annual Meeting of the Association for Computational Linguistics: Human Language Technologies: short papers*, pages 188–193, Portland, USA. Association for Computational Linguistics.

Extension of TSVM to Multi-Class and Hierarchical Text Classification Problems With General Losses

S.Sathiya Keerthi[(1)] *S.Sundararajan*[(2)] *Shirish Shevade*[(3)]
(1) Cloud and Information Services Lab, Microsoft, Mountain View, CA 94043
(2) Microsoft Research India, Bangalore, India
(3) Computer Science and Automation, Indian Institute of Science, Bangalore, India
keerthi@microsoft.com, ssrajan@microsoft.com, shirish@csa.iisc.ernet.in

Abstract

Transductive SVM (TSVM) is a well known semi-supervised large margin learning method for binary text classification. In this paper we extend this method to multi-class and hierarchical classification problems. We point out that the determination of labels of unlabeled examples with fixed classifier weights is a linear programming problem. We devise an efficient technique for solving it. The method is applicable to general loss functions. We demonstrate the value of the new method using large margin loss on a number of multi-class and hierarchical classification datasets.

Proceedings of COLING 2012: Posters, pages 1091–1100,
COLING 2012, Mumbai, December 2012.

1 Introduction

Consider the following supervised learning problem corresponding to a general structured output prediction problem:

$$\min_{\mathbf{w},\xi^s} F^s(\mathbf{w}) = \frac{\lambda}{2}\|\mathbf{w}\|^2 + \frac{1}{l}\sum_{i=1}^{l}\xi_i^s \tag{1}$$

where $\xi_i^s = \xi(\mathbf{w}, \mathbf{x}_i^s, y_i^s)$ is the loss term and $\{(\mathbf{x}_i^s, y_i^s)\}_{i=1}^l$ is the set of labeled examples. For example, in large margin and maxent models respectively we have

$$\xi(\mathbf{w}, \mathbf{x}_i, y_i) = \max_y L(y, y_i) - \mathbf{w}^T \Delta\mathbf{f}(y, y_i; \mathbf{x}_i) \; and \; \xi(\mathbf{w}, \mathbf{x}_i, y_i) = -\mathbf{w}^T \mathbf{f}(y_i; \mathbf{x}_i) + \log Z \tag{2}$$

where $\Delta\mathbf{f}(y, y_i; \mathbf{x}_i) = \mathbf{f}(y_i; \mathbf{x}_i) - \mathbf{f}(y; \mathbf{x}_i)$ and $Z = \sum_y \exp(\mathbf{w}^T \mathbf{f}(y; \mathbf{x}_i))$. Text classification problems involve a rich and large feature space (e.g., bag-of-words features) and so linear classifiers work very well (Joachims, 1999). We particularly focus on multi-class and hierarchical classification problems (and hence our use of scalar notation for y). In multi-class problems y runs over the classes and, $\mathbf{w}$ and $\mathbf{f}(y; \mathbf{x}_i)$ have one component for each class, with the component corresponding to y turned on. More generally, in hierarchical classification problems, y runs over the set of leaf nodes of the hierarchy and, $\mathbf{w}$ and $\mathbf{f}(y; \mathbf{x}_i)$ consist of one component for each node of the hierarchy, with the node components in the path to leaf node y turned on. $\lambda > 0$ is a regularization parameter. A good default value for λ can be chosen depending on the loss function used.[1] The superscript s denotes 'supervised'; we will use superscript u to denote elements corresponding to unlabeled examples.

In semi-supervised learning we use a set of unlabeled examples, $\{\mathbf{x}_i^u\}_{i=1}^n$ and include the determination of the labels of these examples as part of the training process:

$$\min_{\mathbf{w},\mathbf{y}^u} F^s(\mathbf{w}) + \frac{C^u}{n}\sum_{i=1}^{n}\xi_i^u \;\; \text{s.t.} \;\; \sum_{i=1}^{n}\delta(y, y_i^u) = n(y) \;\; \forall y \tag{3}$$

where $\mathbf{y}^u = \{y_i^u\}$, $\xi_i^u = \xi(\mathbf{w}, \mathbf{x}_i^u, y_i^u)$ and δ is the Kronecker delta function. C^u is a regularization parameter for the unlabeled part. A good default value is $C^u = 1$; we use this value in all our experiments. (3) consists of constraints on the label counts that come from domain knowledge. (In practice, one specifies $\phi(y)$, the fraction of examples in class y; then the values in $\{\phi(y)n\}$ are rounded to integers $\{n(y)\}$ in a suitable way so that $\sum_y n(y) = n$.[2]) Such constraints are crucial for the effective solution of the semi-supervised learning problem; without them the semi-supervised solution tends to move towards assigning the majority class label to most unlabeled examples. In more general structured prediction problems (3) may include other domain constraints (Chang et al., 2007). In this paper we will use just the label constraints in (3).

Inspired by the effectiveness of the TSVM model of Joachims (1999), there have been a number of works on the solution of (3) for binary classification with large margin losses. These methods fall into one of two types: (a) combinatorial optimization; and (b) continuous optimization.

[1] In the experiments of this paper, for multi-class and hierarchical classification with large margin loss, we use $\lambda = 10$.

[2] We will assume that quite precise values are given for $\{n(y)\}$. The effect of noise in these values on the semi-supervised solution needs a separate study.

See (Chapelle et al., 2008, 2006) for a detailed coverage of various specific methods falling into these two types. In combinatorial optimization the label set $\mathbf{y}^u$ is determined together with $\mathbf{w}$. It is usual to use a sequence of alternating optimization steps (fix $\mathbf{y}^u$ and solve for $\mathbf{w}$, and then fix $\mathbf{w}$ and solve for $\mathbf{y}^u$) to obtain the solution. An important advantage of doing this is that each of the sub-optimization problems can be solved using simple and/or standard solvers. In continuous optimization $\mathbf{y}^u$ is eliminated and the resulting (non-convex) optimization problem is solved for $\mathbf{w}$ by minimizing

$$F^s(\mathbf{w}) + \frac{C^u}{n}\sum_{i=1}^{n}\rho(\mathbf{w},\mathbf{x}_i^u) \quad (4)$$

where $\rho(\mathbf{w},\mathbf{x}_i^u) = \min_{y^u} \xi(\mathbf{w},\mathbf{x}_i^u,y_i^u)$. The loss function ξ as well as ρ are usually smoothed so that the objective function is differentiable and gradient-based optimization techniques can be employed. Further, the constraints in (3) involving $\mathbf{y}^u$ are replaced by smooth constraints on $\mathbf{w}$ expressing balance of the mean outputs of each label over the labeled and unlabeled sets.

Zien et al. (2007) extended the continuous optimization approach to (4) for multi-class and structured output problems. But their experiments only showed limited improvement over supervised learning. The combinatorial optimization approach, on the other hand, has not been carefully explored beyond binary classification. Methods based on semi-definite programming (Xu et al., 2006; De Bie and Cristianini, 2004) are impractical, even for medium size problems. One-versus-rest and one-versus-one ideas have been tried, but it is unclear if they work well: Zien et al. (2007) and Zubiaga et al. (2009) report failure while Bruzzone et al. (2006) use a heuristic implementation and report success in one application domain. Unlike these methods which have binary TSVM as the basis, we take up an implementation of the approach for the direct multi-class and hierarchical classification formulation in (3). The special structure in constraints allows the $\mathbf{y}^u$ determination step to reduce to a degenerate transportation linear programming problem. So the well-known transportation simplex method can be used to obtain $\mathbf{y}^u$. We show that even this method is not efficient enough. As an alternative we suggest an effective and much more efficient heuristic label switching algorithm. For binary classification problems this algorithm is an improved version of the multiple switching algorithm developed by Sindhwani and Keerthi (2006) for TSVM. Experiments on a number of multi-class and hierarchical classification datasets show that, like the TSVM method of binary classification, our method yields a strong lift in performance over supervised learning, especially when the number of labeled examples is not sufficiently large. Although we demonstrate our method using hinge loss, the applicability of our approach to general loss functions (e.g., maxent loss) is a key advantage. The reader is referred to the longer version of this paper (Keerthi et al., 2012) for details on specialization to maxent losses ((Gärtner et al., 2005), (Graca et al., 2007), (Ganchev et al., 2009) and (Mann and McCallum, 2010)) and more experimental results.

2 Semi-Supervised Learning Algorithm

The semi-supervised learning algorithm for multi-class and hierarchical classification problems follows the spirit of the TSVM algorithm (Joachims, 1999). Algorithm 1 gives the steps. It consists of an initialization part (steps 1-9) that sets starting values for $\mathbf{w}$ and $\mathbf{y}^u$, followed by an iterative part (steps 10-15) where $\mathbf{w}$ and $\mathbf{y}^u$ are refined by semi-supervised learning. Using exactly the same arguments as those in (Joachims, 1999; Sindhwani and Keerthi, 2006) it can be proved that Algorithm 1 is convergent.

Initialization of $\mathbf{w}$ is done by solving the supervised learning problem. This $\mathbf{w}$ can be used to predict $\mathbf{y}^u$. However such a $\mathbf{y}^u$ usually violates the constraints in (3). To choose a $\mathbf{y}^u$ that satisfies (3), we do a greedy modification of the predicted $\mathbf{y}^u$. Steps 3-9 of Algorithm 1 give the details.

The iterative part of the algorithm consists of an outer loop and an inner loop. In the outer loop (steps 10-15) the regularization parameter C^u is varied from a small value to the final value of 1 in annealing steps. This is done to avoid drastic switchings of the labels in $\mathbf{y}^u$, which helps the algorithm reach a better minimum of (3) and hence achieve better performance. For example, on ten runs of the multi-class dataset, *20NG* (see Table 1) with 100 labeled examples and 10,000 unlabeled examples, the average macro F values on test data achieved by supervised learning, Algorithm 1 without annealing and Algorithm 1 with annealing are, respectively, 0.4577, 0.5377 and 0.6253. Similar performance differences are seen on other datasets too.

The inner loop (steps 11-14) does alternating optimization of $\mathbf{w}$ and $\mathbf{y}^u$ for a given C^u. In steps 12 and 13 we use the most recent $\mathbf{w}$ and $\mathbf{y}^u$ as the starting points for the respective sub-optimization problems. Because of this, the overall algorithm remains very efficient in spite of the many annealing steps involving C^u. Typically, the overall cost of the algorithm is only about 3-5 times that of solving a supervised learning problem involving $(n+l)$ examples. For step 12 one can employ any standard algorithm suited to the chosen loss function. In the rest of the section we will focus on step 13.

Algorithm 1 *Semi-Supervised Learning Algorithm*

1: Solve the supervised learning problem, (1) and get $\mathbf{w}$.
2: Set initial labels for unlabeled examples, $\mathbf{y}^u$ using steps 3-9 below.
3: Set $Y = \{y\}$, the set of all classes, $A_y = \emptyset \ \forall y$, and $I = \{1, \ldots, n\}$.
4: **repeat**
5:    $S_i = \max_{y \in Y} \mathbf{w}^T \mathbf{f}(y; \mathbf{x}_i^u)$ and $y_i = \arg\max_{y \in Y} \mathbf{w}^T \mathbf{f}(y; \mathbf{x}_i^u) \ \forall i \in I$.
6:    Sort I by decreasing order of S_i.
7:    By order allocate i to A_{y_i} while not exceeding sizes specified by $n(y_i)$.
8:    Remove all allocated i from I and remove all saturated y (i.e., $|A_y| = n(y)$) from Y.
9: **until** $Y = \emptyset$
10: **for** $C^u = \{10^{-4}, 3 \times 10^{-4}, 10^{-3}, 3 \times 10^{-3}, \ldots, 1\}$ (in that order) **do**
11:    **repeat**
12:       Solve (3) for $\mathbf{w}$ with $\mathbf{y}^u$ fixed (i.e., without constraints).
13:       Solve (3) for $\mathbf{y}^u$ with $\mathbf{w}$ fixed.
14:    **until** step 13 does not alter $\mathbf{y}^u$
15: **end for**

2.1 Linear programming formulation

Let us now consider optimizing $\mathbf{y}^u$ with fixed $\mathbf{w}$. Let us represent each y_i^u in a 1-of-m representation by defining boolean variables z_{iy} and requiring that, for each i, exactly one z_{iy} takes the value 1. This can be done by using the constraint $\sum_y z_{iy} = 1$ for all i. The label constraints become $\sum_i z_{iy} = n(y)$ for all y. Let $c_{iy} = \xi(\mathbf{w}, \mathbf{x}_i^u, y)$. With these definitions the optimization problem of step 13 becomes (irrespective of the type of loss function used) the integer linear programming problem,

$$\min \sum_{i,y} c_{iy} z_{iy} \ \text{ s.t. } \sum_y z_{iy} = 1 \ \forall i, \ \sum_i z_{iy} = n(y) \ \forall y, \ z_{iy} \in \{0,1\} \ \forall i, y \qquad (5)$$

This is a special case of the well known Transportation problem (Hadley, 1963) in which the constraint matrix satisfies unimodularity conditions; hence, the solution of the integer linear programming problem (5) is same as the solution of the linear programming (LP) problem (i.e., with the integer constraints left out), i.e., the integer constraints hold automatically at LP optimality. Previous works (Joachims, 1999; Sindhwani and Keerthi, 2006) do not make this neat connection to linear programming. The constraints $\sum_y z_{iy} = 1 \ \forall i$ allow exactly n non-zero elements in $\{z_{iy}\}_{iy}$; thus there is degeneracy of order m, i.e., there are $(n+m)$ constraints but only n non-zero solution elements.

2.2 Transportation simplex method

The transportation simplex method (a.k.a., stepping stone method) (Hadley, 1963) is a standard and generally efficient way of solving LPs such as (5). However, it is not efficient enough for typical large scale learning situations in which n, the number of unlabeled examples is large and m, the number of classes, is small. Let us see why. Each iteration of this method starts with a basis set of $n+m-1$ basis elements. Then it computes reduced costs for all remaining elements. This step requires $O(nm)$ effort. If all reduced costs are non-negative then it implies that the current solution is optimal. If this condition does not hold, elements which have negative reduced costs are potential elements for entering the basis.[3] One non-basis element with a negative reduced cost (say, the element with the most negative reduced cost) is chosen. The algorithm now moves the solution to a new basis in which an element of the previous basis is replaced by the newly entering element. This operation corresponds to moving a chosen set of examples between classes in a loop so that the label constraints are not violated. The number of such iterations is observed to be $O(nm)$ and so, the algorithm requires $O(n^2m^2)$ time. Since n can be large in semi-supervised learning, the transportation simplex algorithm is not sufficiently efficient. The main cause of inefficiency is that the step (one basis element changed) is too small for the amount of work put in (computing all reduced costs)!

2.3 Switching algorithm

We now propose an efficient heuristic *switching algorithm* for solving (5) that is suited to the case where n is large but m is small. The main idea is to use only pairwise switching of labels between classes in order to improve the objective function. (Note that switching makes sure that the label constraints are not violated.) This algorithm is sub-optimal for $m \geq 3$, but still quite powerful because of two reasons: (a) the solution obtained by the algorithm is usually close to the true optimal solution; and (b) reaching optimality precisely is not crucial for the alternating optimization approach (steps 12 and 13 of Algorithm 1) to be effective.

Let us now give the details of the switching algorithm. Suppose, in the current solution, example i is in class y. Let us say we move this example to class $\bar{y}$. The change in objective function due to the move is given by $\delta c(i,y,\bar{y}) = c_{i\bar{y}} - c_{iy}$. Suppose we have another example $\bar{i}$ which is currently in class $\bar{y}$ and we switch i and $\bar{i}$, i.e., move i to class $\bar{y}$ and move $\bar{i}$ to class y. The resulting change in objective function is given by $\rho(i,y,\bar{i},\bar{y}) = \delta c(i,y,\bar{y}) + \delta c(\bar{i},\bar{y},y)$. The more negative $\rho(i,y,\bar{i},\bar{y})$ is, the better will be the objective function reduction due to the switching of i and $\bar{i}$. The algorithm looks greedily for finding as many good switches as possible

[3] Presence of negative reduced costs may not mean that the current solution is non-optimal. This is due to degeneracy. It is usually the case that, even when an optimal solution is reached, the transportation algorithm requires several end steps to move the basis elements around to reach an end state where positive reduced costs are seen.

Algorithm 2 *Switching Algorithm to solve* (5)

1: **repeat**
2:   **for** each class pair $(y, \bar{y})$ **do**
3:     Compute $\delta c(i, y, \bar{y})$ for all i in class y and sort the elements in increasing order of δc values.
4:     Compute $\delta c(\bar{i}, \bar{y}, y)$ for all $\bar{i}$ in class $\bar{y}$ and sort the elements in increasing order of δc values.
5:     Align these two lists (so that the best pair is at the top) to form a switch list of 5-tuples, $\{(i, y, \bar{i}, \bar{y}, \rho(i, y, \bar{i}, \bar{y})\}$.
6:     Remove any 5-tuple with $\rho(i, y, \bar{i}, \bar{y}) \geq 0$.
7:   **end for**
8:   Merge all the switch lists into one and sort the 5-tuples by increasing order of ρ values.
9:   **while** switch list is non-empty **do**
10:     Pick the top 5-tuple from the switch list; let's say it is $(i, y, \bar{i}, \bar{y}, \rho(i, y, \bar{i}, \bar{y}))$. Move i to class $\bar{y}$ and move $\bar{i}$ to class y.
11:     From the remaining switch list remove all 5-tuples involving either i or $\bar{i}$.
12:   **end while**
13: **until** the merged switch list from step 8 is empty

at a time. Algorithm 2 gives the details. Steps 2-12 consist of one major greedy iteration and has cost $O(nm^2)$. Steps 2-7 consist of the background work needed to do the greedy switching of several pairs of examples in steps 9-12. Step 11 is included because, when i and $\bar{i}$ are switched, data related to any 5-tuple in the remaining switch list that involves either i or $\bar{i}$ is messed up. Removing such elements from the remaining switched list allows the algorithm to continue finding more pairs to apply switching without a need for repeating steps 2-7. It is this multiple switching idea that gives the needed efficiency lift over the transportation simplex algorithm.

The algorithm is convergent due to the following reasons: the algorithm only performs switchings which reduce the objective function; thus, once a pair of examples is switched, that pair will not be switched again; and, the number of possible switchings is finite. A typical run of Algorithm 2 requires about 3 loops through steps 2-12. Since this algorithm only allows pairwise switching of examples, it cannot assure that the class assignments resulting from it will be optimal for (5) if $m \geq 3$. However, in practice the objective function achieved by the algorithm is very close to the true optimal value; also, as pointed out earlier, reaching true optimality turns out to be not crucial for good performance of the semi-supervised algorithm.

We compared the speed performance of transportation simplex and switching algorithms on real-world datasets such as *Ohscal* and found that the switching algorithm is faster by two orders of magnitude. Note that if m is large then steps 2-7 of Algorithm 2 can become expensive. We have applied the switching algorithm to datasets that have $m \leq 105$, but haven't observed any inefficiency. If m happens to be much larger then steps 2-7 can be modified to work with a suitably chosen subset of class pairs instead of all possible pairs.

3 Experiments with large margin loss

In this section we give results of experiments on our method as applied to multi-class and hierarchical classification problems using the large margin loss function, (2). We used the loss, $L(y, y_i) = \delta(y, y_i)$. Eight multi-class datasets and two hierarchical classification datasets were

Table 1: Properties of datasets. N : number of examples, d : number of features, m : number of classes, Type: M=Multi-Class; H=Hierarchical, with D=Depth and I=# Internal Nodes

	20NG	*la1*	*webkb*	*ohscal*	*reut8*	*sector*	*mnist*	*usps*	*20NG*	*rcv-mcat*
N	19928	3204	8277	11162	8201	9619	70000	9298	19928	154706
d	62061	31472	3000	11465	10783	55197	779	256	62061	11429
m	20	6	7	10	8	105	10	10	20	7
Type D/I	M	M	M	M	M	M	M	M	H 3/8	H 2/10

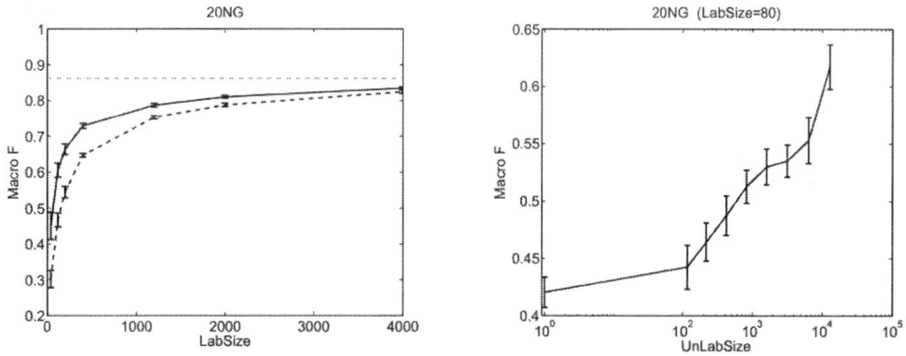

Figure 1: Hierarchical classification dataset - Variation of performance (Macro F): **Left** - as a function of the number of labeled examples (LabSize). Dashed black line corresponds to supervised learning; Continuous black line corresponds to the semi-supervised method; Dashed horizontal red line corresponds to the supervised classifier built using L and U with their labels known. **Right** - as a function of the number of unlabeled examples (UnLabSize), with the number of labeled examples fixed at 80.

used. Due to lack of space, performance results are given only for some datasets. The reader is referred to the longer version of this paper (Keerthi et al., 2012) for details on other data sets. Properties of these datasets (Lang, 1995; Forman, 2003; McCallum and Nigam, 1998; Lewis et al., 2006; LeCun, 2011; Tibshirani, 2011) are given in Table 1. Most of these datasets are standard text classification benchmarks. We include two image datasets, *mnist* and *usps* to point out that our methods are useful in other application domains too. *rcv-mcat* is a subset of rcv1 (Lewis et al., 2006) corresponding to the sub-tree belonging to the high level category MCAT with seven leaf nodes consisting of the categories, Equity, Bond, Forex, Commodity, Soft, Metal and Energy. In one run of each dataset, 50% of the examples were randomly chosen to form the unlabeled set, U; 20% of the examples were put aside in a set L to form labeled data; the remaining data formed the test set. Ten such runs were done to compute the mean and standard deviation of (test) performance. Performance was measured in terms of Macro F (mean of the F values associated with various classes).

In the first experiment, we fixed the number of labeled examples (to 80) and varied the number of unlabeled examples from small to big values. The variation of performance as a function of the number of unlabeled examples, for the multi-class dataset, *20NG*, is given in Figure 1 (Right). Performance steadily improves as more unlabeled data is added. Next we fixed the unlabeled data to U and varied the labeled data size from small values up to $|L|$. This is an important study for semi-supervised learning methods since their main value is when labeled

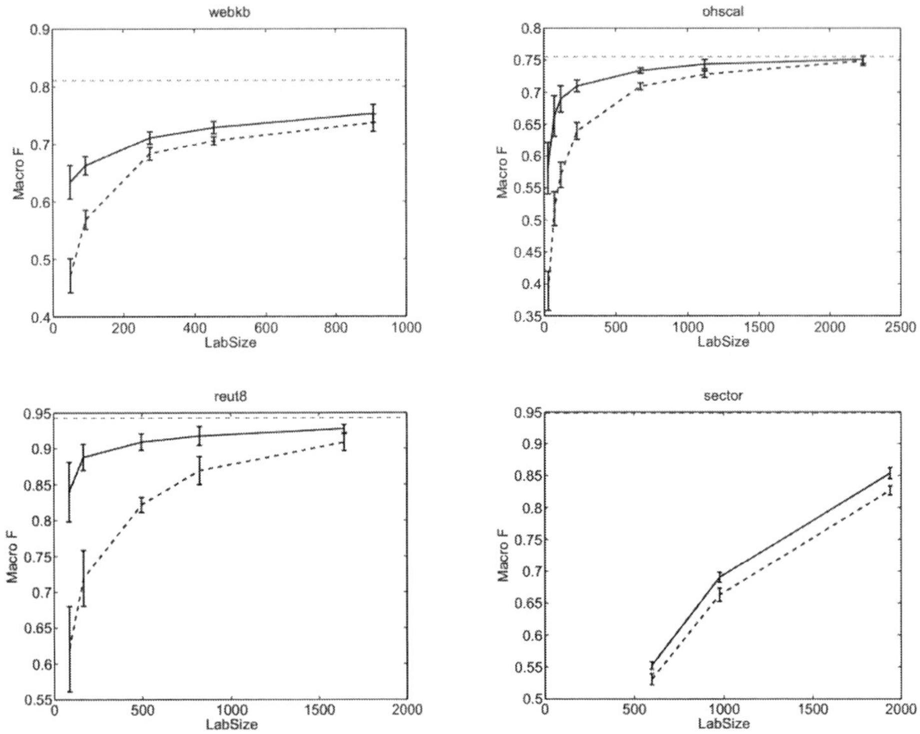

Figure 2: Multi-class datasets: Variation of performance (Macro F) as a function of the number of labeled examples (LabSize). Dashed black line corresponds to supervised learning; Continuous black line corresponds to the semi-supervised method; Dashed horizontal red line corresponds to the supervised classifier built using L and U with their labels known.

data is sparse (lower side of the learning curve). The variation of performance as a function of the number of labeled examples is shown in Figure 1 (Left). The same holds in other datasets too. The results for four multi-class datasets are given in Figure 2. Clearly, semi-supervised learning is very useful and yields good improvement over supervised learning especially when labeled data is sparse. The degree of improvement is sharp in some datasets (e.g., *reut8*) and mild in some datasets (e.g., *sector*). While the semi-supervised method is successful in linear classifier settings such as in text classification and natural language processing, we want to caution, like (Chapelle et al., 2008), that it may not work well on datasets originating from nonlinear manifold structure.

4 Conclusion

In this paper we extended the TSVM approach of semi-supervised binary classification to multi-class and hierarchical classification problems with general loss functions, and demonstrated the effectiveness of the extended approach. As a natural next step we are exploring the approach for structured output prediction. The $\mathbf{y}^u$ determination process is harder in this case since reduction to linear programming is not automatic. But good solutions are still possible. In many applications of structured output prediction, labeled data consists of examples with partial labels. This can be handled in our approach by including all unknown labels as a part of $\mathbf{y}^u$.

References

Bruzzone, L., Chi, M., and Marconcini, M. (2006). A novel transductive SVM for semisupervised classification of remote-sensing images. volume 44, pages 3363–3373.

Chang, M. W., Ratinov, L., and Roth, D. (2007). Guiding semi-supervision with constraint-driven learning. In *ACL*.

Chapelle, O., Chi, M., and Zien, A. (2006). A continuation method for semi-supervised SVMs. In *ICML*.

Chapelle, O., Sindhwani, V., and Keerthi, S. S. (2008). Optimization techniques for semi-supervised support vector machines. In *JMLR*, volume 9, pages 203–233.

De Bie, T. and Cristianini, N. (2004). Convex methods for transduction. In *NIPS*.

Forman, G. (2003). An extensive empirical study of feature selection metrics for text classification. In *JMLR*, volume 3, pages 1289–1305.

Ganchev, K., Graca, J., Gillenwater, J., and Taskar, B. (2009). Posterior regularization for structured latent variable models. Technical report, Dept. of Computer & Information Science, University of Pennsylvania.

Gärtner, T., Le, Q. V., Burton, S., Smola, A. J., and Vishwanathan, S. V. N. (2005). Large-scale multiclass transduction. In *NIPS*.

Graca, J., Ganchev, K., and Taskar, B. (2007). Expectation maximization and posterior constraints. In *NIPS*.

Hadley, G. (1963). *Linear Programming*. Addison-Wesley, 2nd edition.

Joachims, T. (1999). Transductive inference for text classification using support vector machines. In *ICML*.

Keerthi, S. S., Sundararajan, S., and Shevade, S. (2012). Extension of TSVM to multi-class and hierarchical text classification problems with general losses. http://arxiv.org/abs/1211.0210.

Lang, K. (1995). Newsweeder: Learning to filter netnews. In *ICML*.

LeCun, Y. (2011). The MNIST database of handwritten digits.

Lewis, D., Yang, Y., Rose, T., and Li, F. (2006). Rcv1: A new benchmark collection for text categorization research. In *JMLR*, volume 5, pages 361–397.

Mann, G. S. and McCallum, A. (2010). Generalized expectation criteria for semi-supervised learning with weakly labeled data. In *JMLR*, volume 11, pages 955–984.

McCallum, A. and Nigam, K. (1998). A comparison of event models for naive Bayes text classification. In *AAAI Workshop on Learning for Text Categorization*.

Sindhwani, V. and Keerthi, S. (2006). Large-scale semi-supervised linear SVMs. In *SIGIR*.

Tibshirani, R. (2011). USPS handwritten digits dataset. http://www-stat-class.stanford.edu/~tibs/ElemStatLearn/datasets/zip.info.

Xu, L., Wilkinson, D., Southey, F., and Schuurmans, D. (2006). Discriminative unsupervised learning of structured predictors. In *ICML*.

Zien, A., Brefeld, U., and Scheffer, T. (2007). Transductive support vector machines for structured variables. In *ICML*.

Zubiaga, A., Fresno, V., and Martinez, R. (2009). Is unlabeled data suitable for multiclass SVM-based web page classification? In *NAACL HLT Workshop on Semi-supervised Learning for Natural Language Processing*.

Calculation of phrase probabilities for Statistical Machine Translation by using belief functions

Christophe SERVAN Simon PETITRENAUD
University of Le Mans, Avenue Laënnec 72085 Le Mans Cedex 9, France
first-name.last-name@lium.univ-lemans.fr

ABSTRACT
In this paper, we consider a specific part of statistical machine translation: feature estimation for the translation model. The classical way to estimate these features is based on relative frequencies. In this new approach, we propose to use the concept of belief masses to estimate the phrase translation probabilities. The Belief Function theory has proven to be suitable and adapted for dealing with uncertainties in many domains. We have performed a series of experiments to translate from English into French and from Arabic into English showing that our approach performs, at least as well as and at times better than, the classical approach.

KEYWORDS: Belief function, Statistical Machine Translation.

Proceedings of COLING 2012: Posters, pages 1101–1110,
COLING 2012, Mumbai, December 2012.

1 Introduction

In statistical machine translation (SMT), there have been many works on smoothing translation model probabilities (Foster et al., 2006; Kuhn et al., 2010), but few work on feature estimation. (Chiang et al., 2009) proposed to add new features outside the translation model, but to the best of our knowledge there is few research on a different way to estimate the features of the translation model (TM). De Nero and Moore (DeNero et al., 2006; Moore and Quirk, 2007) proposed some approaches that did not improve the translation. More recent works based on a smooth Maximum-Likelihood estimate (Sima'an and Mylonakis, 2008) give better results. As we consider the popular phrase-based approach, the TM corresponds to the phrase table in this paper.

The phrase table is basically a list of possible translations and their probabilities for a given source phrase. Each line or event of a phrase table is composed of a source and a target language phrase pair. The events are supposed to be independent from each other. Phrase tables may contain many features like phrase translation and lexical probabilities. In order to estimate these probabilities, SMT uses very large corpora called *bitexts*, which are composed of sentences translated from a source language into a target language. For each sentence, the words of both languages are aligned according to the translation.

In the classical approach, the estimation of the probabilities is performed by the use of simple count functions, based on relative frequencies. But it is possible to use other concepts to estimate the features. In particular, many authors showed that the Dempster-Shafer theory (or Belief Function theory) allows a more flexible representation of uncertainty than a probability model (Smets, 1988; Cobb and Shenoy, 2006). For example, probabilities do not really take into account the conflict between different translation hypotheses, especially in the case of rare examples, or the global confidence in the translations. The belief function theory, as an alternative to the probability theory, can take this into account. In this paper, we present an original way to estimate the feature associated with a set of phrase pairs with the use of belief functions.

This paper presents our first studies and results obtained with this new approach. Firstly, we briefly recall the theory of SMT. In Section 3, we present our approach based on belief functions. Then, we propose several experiments in order to show the effectiveness of our approach. At last we conclude this paper and present some perspectives.

2 Background

2.1 General model for statistical machine translation

Let us assume that we are given a source sentence s to be translated into different target sentences $t_i \in T_s$, where T_s is the set of all observed translations of s in the phrase table. The statistical machine translation (SMT) model uses a set of n feature functions $f_k, k = 1 \ldots, n$, depending on the source and target word sequences, in order to estimate the best translation. Typical feature functions include the translation and distortion model, a language model on the target language and various penalties. Among all possible target sentences, the sentence is chosen as follows:

$$t^* = \arg\max_{t_i \in T_s} \log \left(\prod_{i=1}^{n} f_k(t_i, s)^{\lambda_k} \right), \tag{1}$$

where each parameter λ_k is a coefficient to weight the feature function f_k (Och, 2003). These weights are usually optimized so as to maximize the translation performance on some development dataset. The work presented in this paper focuses on features used to estimate the translation model.

2.2 Feature estimation in statistical machine translation

In the popular Moses toolkit (Koehn et al., 2007), the phrase table contains five features (Koehn, 2010): the phrase translation features and the lexical weighting for both translation directions, and the phrase penalty. The phrase translation features are usually estimated using relative frequency; the lexical weights are estimated by using the word-based IBM Model 1 of each phrase pair. At last, the phrase penalty depends on phrase length. This feature is set by the user to the same value ρ for each phrase. If $\rho > e$, longer phrases will be preferred over shorter ones. Conversely, if $\rho < e$, shorter phrases will be preferred.

Source language (s) - fr	Target language (t) - en
...	...
étant donné un	given a
étant donné un	starting from an
étant donné	given
étant donné	given
étant donné	starting from
étant donné	starting
...	...

Table 1: Example of phrase pairs extracted from a bitext.

Table 1 gives an example of phrase pairs extracted from a bitext and a small part of the corresponding phrase table is presented in Table 2. In this example, the classical estimation of the feature of the phrase translation pair "*starting*" given "*étant donné*" is equal to 0.25 and the probability of "*given*" given "*étant donné*" is equal to 0.5. The inverse phrase translation probability is estimated in the same way.

source (s) - fr	seg cib (t) - en	$p(t\|s)$	$lex(t\|s)$	$p(s\|t)$	$lex(s\|t)$
...	...				
étant donné	given	**0.5**	0.060147	**0.333333**	0.306373
étant donné	starting	**0.25**	7.15882e-06	**0.333333**	5.19278e-05
étant donné	starting from	**0.25**	7.15882e-06	**0.333333**	0.0277778
...	...				

Table 2: Extract of a translation table with parameters.

This classical way to estimate the phrase translation probability may have some drawbacks. When some unique phrase translation pair occurs many times, like the pair "*la maison blanche|the white house*", the phrase translation probability estimation is equal to 1. But in other situations, occurrences are very rare and ambiguous at the same time. For example, let us assume that for the French word "*dents*" (which should be translated as "*teeth*" in English), two contradictory pairs are available in the phrase table: "*dent|teeth*" and "*dents|jaws*". These events may both have a probability estimation equal to 1 because they occur only once.

Even though the estimation of the inverse phrase translation pair may balance this problem, if the event is observed only once in either translation direction, the inverse estimation is useless. The goal of this work is to propose a new way to estimate the translation features in both translation directions. Fortunately, thanks to alternative theories to the probability theory, it is possible to improve these estimations. One of these theories is particularly suited to deal with uncertainties: the theory of belief functions, which has been developed for thirty years. This theory has been successfully applied in several domains such as speaker identification

$$m_s(\text{starting}) = p(\text{starting}|\text{étant donné}) * \overline{p(\text{given}|\text{étant donné})} * \overline{p(\text{starting from}|\text{étant donné})}$$
$$m_s(\text{starting}) = 0.09375$$
$$m_s(\text{starting from}) = 0.09375$$
$$m_s(\text{given}) = 0.28125$$

Table 3: Example of the estimation of some phrase pair features with the TBM Theory (s ="étant donné")

(Petitrenaud et al., 2010) or classification (Elouedi et al., 2000). In this paper, we adapt some concepts of this theory to our feature estimation problem.

3 Belief functions for SMT

In this section, we briefly present some notions of the belief function theory (Shafer, 1976; Smets and Kennes, 1994) and we apply it to the problem of feature estimation. In this article, we adopt the point of view proposed by Smets: the Transferable Belief Model (TBM) (Smets and Kennes, 1994). The aim of this model is to determine the belief concerning different propositions, from some available information.

3.1 Belief function theory

Let Ω be a finite set, called frame of discernment of the experience. The representation of uncertainty is made by the means of the concept of belief function, defined as a function m from 2^Ω to $[0,1]$ as $\sum_{A \subseteq \Omega} m(A) = 1$. The quantity $m(A)$ represents the belief exactly allowed to proposition A. The subsets A of Ω such that $m(A) > 0$ are called focal elements of m. In the very particular case when Ω is the only focal element (i.e. $m(\Omega) = 1$ and $\forall A \neq \Omega, m(A) = 0$), the belief function expresses a total lack of information on the frame of discernment. This is one of the essential differences with the probability theory. In general, the total absence of information would be represented by a uniform distribution on Ω in probability theory. One of the most important operations in the TBM is the procedure of aggregating information to combine several belief functions defined in a same frame of discernment (Smets and Kennes, 1994). In particular, the combination of two belief functions m_1 and m_2 independently defined on Ω using the conjunctive binary operator $\cap$, denoted as $m' = m_1 \cap m_2$, is defined as (Smets and Kennes, 1994) :

$$\forall A \subseteq \Omega, m'(A) = \sum_{B \cap C = A} m_1(B) * m_2(C). \tag{2}$$

Note that this combination operation may produce a non-null mass on the empty set $\emptyset$. The quantity $m'(\emptyset)$ represents the mass that cannot be allocated to any proposition of Ω. In this case, $m'(\emptyset)$ also measures the conflict between the belief functions m_1 an m_2. Since the operator $\cap$ is commutative and associative, it is easy to define the combination of n functions $m_1, \ldots, m_n$ on Ω by:

$$m = m_1 \cap \ldots \cap m_n = \bigcap_{i=1}^{n} m_i, \tag{3}$$

with $m(A) = \sum_{A_1 \cap \ldots \cap A_n = A} \prod_{i=1}^{n} m_i(A_i), \quad \forall A \subseteq \Omega$. Finally the function m captures the global information concerning the experience.

3.2 Belief functions as features for the translation model

Here, we propose to use the TBM to estimate the phrase translation features. First, for a given source s, each target $t_i \in T_s$ gives a piece of information for the translation and can be described by a belief function m_s^i, such as:

$$\begin{cases} m_s^i(\{t_i\}) = p(t_i|s) \\ m_s^i(T_s) = \overline{p(t_i|s)}, \end{cases} \tag{4}$$

where $\overline{p(t_i|s)} = 1 - p(t_i|s)$. The belief function m_s^i has only two focal elements: t_i, and T_s. The mass on T_s expresses a confidence degree for this piece of information. We combine the information defined by all the translation hypotheses concerning s, thanks to the conjunctive obtained by the following straightforward formula:

$$m_s = \bigcap_{t \in T_s} m_s^i. \tag{5}$$

The resulting mass concerning t_i is obtained by the following formula (cf. Equation 3):

$$m_s(\{t_i\}) = p(t_i|s) * \prod_{t_k \in T_s \setminus \{t_i\}} \overline{p(t_k|s)}. \tag{6}$$

Note that $\sum_{t_i \in T_s} m_s(\{t_i\}) = 1 - m(T_s) - m(\emptyset) < 1$ generally. The mass $m(T_s)$ and $m(\emptyset)$ can be interpreted respectively as the general ignorance degree and the level of information conflicting concerning the translation of s. Then we obtain our feature estimation defined in Equation 1 by: $f(t_i, s_j) = m_{s_j}(\{t_i\})$. In the same way, we obtain the inverse feature estimation by the following equation:

$$m_t^I(\{s_j\}) = p(s_j|t) * \prod_{s_k \in S_t \setminus \{s_j\}} \overline{p(s_k|t)}, \tag{7}$$

where S_t is the set of possible sources for target t. If we apply these formulas to the example presented in Tables 1 and 2, the new estimation of the features associated with the phrase translation pairs are computed in Table 3. Note that if $p(t_i|s) = 1$, the belief masses for the other hypotheses become zero (cf. Equation 6). The belief mass indicated in this equation may be modified as follows: $m_s(\{t_i\}) = \frac{1}{1 + \frac{1}{|s|}}$, where $|s|$ denotes the count of s. Thus, $m_s(t_i) < 1$ but $m_s(t_i)$ tends to 1 when the information concerning s increases. Finally, the optimized target sentences are obtained by Equation 1.

4 Experimental design

As presented before, the new approach with the TBM is applied only on the phrase translation features. Therefore, in all our experiments, we have removed the lexical features from the phrase tables of all the translation models. We performed several experiments on various language pairs with various kinds of corpus kind described in the next part. The metrics used are the BLEU score (Papineni et al., 2002) and the TER metric (Snover et al., 2006).

4.1 Data

Several data sets were used in our experiments, with various language pairs and various kind of data (*e.g.* news, scientific papers). A complete description of all the corpora presented in this part is shown in Table 4. The framework used in the evaluation of the WMT task contains a set of several corpora. The corpora used in our experiments are described in Table 4. The training corpora used are Europarl 7 (eparl7), News-commentary 7 (nc7).

Task				
Task COSMAT	corpus	AbsTrain	AbsDev	AbsTest
	language	fr en	fr en	fr en
	# of sentences	5141	1083	1102
	# of words	135K 120K	28K 25K	28K 25K
Task WMT	corpus	nc7+eparl7	nwtst2010	nwtst2011
	language	fr en	fr en	fr en
	# of sentences	2M	2489	3003
	# of words	65,7M 59M	62k 70k	75k 84,5k
Task Ar-En	corpus	train	nist09-nw	nist08-nw
	language	ar en	ar en	ar en
	# of sentences	184K	586	813
	# of words	4.8M 5M	23K 23K	29K 28K

Table 4: Description of the bitexts and development (or tuning) and test corpora.

The corpus from the French ANR project COSMAT[1] is composed of a collection of abstracts of PhD Theses in both French and English (Lambert et al., 2012). These abstracts have been classified according to several topics. In our experiments, we selected only the topic of computer science.

The last set of data concerns the translation of Arabic news into English. Following the GALE program, the DARPA launched a new 5 year language technology program called Broad Operational Language Translation program (BOLT). The goal of this project is to create a technology capable of translating multiple foreign languages in all genres, to retrieve information from the translated material, and to enable a bilingual communication via speech or text from Arabic and Mandarin into English. We used as the development corpus the news part of the NIST 2009 evaluation (*nist09-nw*) and as the test corpus the NIST 2008 evaluation (*nist08-nw*). The system ensue from this corpus could be used in the NIST evaluation.

4.2 Stability test

In order to have a more reliable precision in our experiments, we performed several optimizations with random initialisation toward the BLEU score for each experiment (Clark et al., 2011). Following this method, three runs of Minimum Error Rate Training (MERT) (Och, 2003) and Margin Infused Relaxed Algorithm (MIRA) (Chiang et al., 2008, 2009) were made. Then, the result is an average of these three runs and the standard deviation is given between parenthesis next to the scores. Both optimization approaches were used to observe how these features are influenced by the process.

4.3 Results

Tables 5, 6 and 8 show the results obtained with the classical approach and with our approach based on the TBM theory. The Brevity Penalty is about 0.99 (0.01) for the two approaches in each experiment.

First, we compare the classical ($Proba.$) and the TBM ($Belief$) approaches with the tuning thought MERT. According to the French-English WMT (Table 5), we can observe a slight improvement of the BLEU score when the translation is from French into English. The $Belief$

[1] http://www.cosmat.fr

optimization process		MERT		MIRA	
corpus	approach	BLEU	TER	BLEU	TER
Translation direction: fr→en					
nwtst2010	Proba.	27.42 (0.04)	54.50 (0.03)	27.22 (0.04)	54.48 (0.04)
(Dev)	Belief	27.47 (0.06)	54.46 (0.03)	27.21 (0.04)	54.53 (0.03)
	Proba.+Belief	27.43 (0.05)	54.61 (0.09)	**27.34** (0.01)	**54.54** (0.05)
nwtst2011	Proba.	27.69 (0.07)	53.85 (0.04)	27.73 (0.04)	53.75 (0.05)
(Test)	Belief	27.72 (0.03)	53.87 (0.06)	27.79 (0.03)	53.74 (0.04)
	Proba.+Belief	27.59 (0.11)	53.95 (0.12)	27.79 (0.04)	53.80 (0.06)
Translation direction: en→fr					
nwtst2010	Proba.	26.55 (0.05)	58.67 (0.03)	26.41 (0.04)	58.44 (0.21)
(Dev)	Belief	26.51 (0.09)	58.88 (0.06)	26.42 (0.08)	58.58 (0.11)
	Proba.+Belief	**26.64 (0.05)**	**58.66** (0.20)	**26.53** (0.06)	**58.42** (0.07)
nwtst2011	Proba.	28.29 (0.31)	56.74 (0.19)	28.59 (0.05)	56.18 (0.15)
(Test)	Belief	28.39 (0.07)	56.88 (0.06)	28.72 (0.03)	56.28 (0.05)
	Proba.+Belief	**28.47** (0.06)	**56.72** (0.21)	**28.74** (0.06)	**56.06** (0.12)

Table 5: BLEU and TER scores obtained on the WMT task.

approach can be considered as efficient as the classical one. The performance gain is more visible when the translation is from English to French and can reach about 0.18 BLEU point on the test corpus. In Table 6, the experiment shows a decrease of the two scores (respectively 0.1 and 0.15) on the tuning corpus. Contrary to the tuning corpus, an improvement of 0.1 BLEU point and 0.08 point of TER is visible on the test corpus. In the last experiment proposed on the COSMAT corpus (Table 8), we can observe a decrease only on the tuning corpus when we translate French into English. On the test corpus, the improvement is about 0.1 point on both BLEU and TER score. When the translation is from English into French, the increase is about 0.04 BLEU point on both development and test corpus.

optimization process		MERT		MIRA	
corpus	approach	BLEU	TER	BLEU	TER
nist09-nw	Proba.	**33.81** (0.14)	**47.27** (0.13)	34.04 (0.07)	48.51 (0.19)
(Dev)	Belief	33.71 (0.07)	47.42 (0.03)	34.11 (0.03)	48.08 (0.34)
	Proba.+Belief	33.74 (0.14)	47.56 (0.33)	**34.30** (0.06)	**48.14** (0.12)
nist08-nw	Proba.	26.99 (0.09)	57.37 (0.18)	26.51 (0.09)	58.54 (0.25)
(Test)	Belief	**27.10** (0.08)	**57.29** (0.10)	**26.83** (0.14)	**57.71** (0.32)
	Proba.+Belief	26.90 (0.09)	57.65 (0.28)	26.73 (0.13)	58.24 (0.36)

Table 6: Results for the translation from Arabic into English.

Regarding the results, the new approach is at least as efficient as the classical one. When we look at the entropy of each phrase table, and the various translations produced by the systems, we can observe better translations in the two approaches like in the example given in Table 7. This example shows us how the combination takes the best of the two approaches.

Source	ils permettent la réutilisation du code de gestion de la duplication et de la cohérence .
Reference	they allow reuse of replication and consistency management code .
Proba.	they allow the reuse of the code of management and replication consistency .
Belief	they allow the reuse of the code of replication and the consistency .
Proba.+Belief	they allow the reuse of the code of replication management and consistency .

Table 7: Example of translation from French into English.

This has lead us to combine the two approaches ($Proba. + Belief$) in all experiments. The increase is visible in the WMT task on the translation of English into French about 0.2 BLEU point on the tuning corpus and 0.15 BLEU point on the test corpus. With the COSMAT experiment in table 8, in both translation directions when using the combined approaches, we observe an increase of the BLEU score.

These experiments show us this novel approach can be considered as comparable to the classical

optimization process		MERT		MIRA	
corpus	approach	BLEU	TER	BLEU	TER
Translation direction: fr→en					
AbsDev	Proba.	35.83 (0.03)	47.64 (0.20)	35.54 (0.03)	47.98 (0.05)
	Belief	35.82 (0.06)	47.89 (0.04)	35.66 (0.04)	**47.71** (0.03)
	Proba.+Belief	**35.93 (0.06)**	47.80 (0.05)	**35.72** (0.04)	47.72 (0.04)
AbsTest	Proba.	43.02 (0.11)	42.73 (0.17)	**43.00** (0.01)	**42.61** (0.03)
	Belief	43.13 (0.09)	42.66 (0.05)	42.81 (0.10)	42.64 (0.00)
	Proba.+Belief	**43.27** (0.17)	42.62 (0.12)	42.95 (0.04)	42.63 (0.01)
Translation direction: en→fr					
AbsDev	Proba.	41.95 (0.20)	45.68 (0.39)	42.06 (0.01)	46.23 (0.03)
	Belief	41.99 (0.18)	46.25 (0.20)	42.06 (0.07)	46.17 (0.06)
	Proba.+Belief	42.12 (0.10)	46.08 (0.10)	**42.18** (0.12)	**46.03** (0.04)
AbsTest	Proba.	33.33 (0.09)	**52.22** (0.82)	33.15 (0.05)	53.04 (0.05)
	Belief	33.37 (0.08)	52.83 (0.28)	33.26 (0.08)	52.92 (0.03)
	Proba.+Belief	**33.56** (0.10)	52.72 (0.20)	**33.45** (0.06)	**52.81** (0.08)

Table 8: Results obtains on the COSMAT Task.

approach and can be more efficient under certain conditions. But for all the systems tuned with MERT, there is sometimes a high standard deviation of about 0.2 BLEU point and 0.3 TER point. Recent MIRA experiments (Cherry and Foster, 2012) show a lower deviation of the score and a better robustness than MERT. All the experiments were rerun with MIRA in order to observe a smaller deviation and a better precision in our experiments; this is the second set of experiments shown in the various tables.

The new set of experiment shows an improvement especially for the WMT results (Table 5): the combination of the two approaches obtains 0.15 BLEU point and 0.1 TER point more than the classical approach. The improvement, visible in Table 6, reach respectively 0.26 and 0.2 BLEU point and 0.37 and 0.3 TER point on the tuning corpus and the test corpus. At last, in the COSMAT experiment, a decrease is visible when we translate French into English on the test corpus of 0.05 BLEU point. But when we translate English into French, the increase can reach 0.3 BLEU point and 0.23 TER point on the test corpus. It seems the MIRA process give a better advantage to the combination of the two approaches over the classical approach. We can also observe better results comparing the two optimizations in the WMT task when we translate from English into French.

Conclusions and Further Work

In this paper, we presented our first results on the application of the Transferable Belief Model to Statistical Machine Translation. The approach was used to estimate only the phrase translation pair features. The results obtained on the different experiments lead us to combine the new and the classical approaches. The score of the translations obtained with this combination is improved, and this also leads to better translation quality according our experiments. This combination of approaches encourages us to work further. For example, this new approach could be applied as a secondary phase-table in order to rescore the first one. This rescoring could be done during the decoding process on the graph of hypothesis or on the n-best translations output as proposed in several works on language model adaptation and rescoring (Bacchiani and Roark, 2003; Schwenk et al., 2006; Bulyko et al., 2007).

Acknowledgments

This work has been partially funded by the European Union under the EuroMatrixPlus project ICT-2007.2.2-FP7-231720, the French government under the ANR project COSMAT ANR-09-CORD-004 and the DARPA Bolt project.

References

Bacchiani, M. and Roark, B. (2003). Unsupervised language model adaptation. In *International Conference on Acoustics, Speech, and Signal Processing (ICASSP'03)*, Hong Kong, China.

Bulyko, I., Matsoukas, S., Schwartz, R., Nguyen, L., and Makhoul, J. (2007). Language model adaptation in machine translation from speech. In *International Conference on Acoustics, Speech, and Signal Processing (ICASSP'07)*, Honolulu, Hawaii, USA.

Cherry, C. and Foster, G. (2012). Batch tuning strategies for statistical machine translation. In *Proceedings of the 2012 Conference of the North American Chapter of the Association for Computational Linguistics: Human Language Technologies*, pages 427–436, Montréal, Canada. Association for Computational Linguistics.

Chiang, D., Knight, K., and Wang, W. (2009). 11,001 new features for statistical machine translation. In *Proceedings of Human Language Technologies: The 2009 Annual Conference of the North American Chapter of the Association for Computational Linguistics*, pages 218–226, Boulder, Colorado, USA. Association for Computational Linguistics.

Chiang, D., Marton, Y., and Resnik, P. (2008). Online large-margin training of syntactic and structural translation features. In *Proceedings of the 2008 Conference on Empirical Methods in Natural Language Processing*, pages 224–233, Honolulu, Hawaii, USA. Association for Computational Linguistics.

Clark, J. H., Dyer, C., Lavie, A., and Smith, N. A. (2011). Better hypothesis testing for statistical machine translation: Controlling for optimizer instability. In *Proceedings of the 49th Annual Meeting of the Association for Computational Linguistics: Human Language Technologies*, pages 176–181, Portland, Oregon, USA. Association for Computational Linguistics.

Cobb, B. R. and Shenoy, P. P. (2006). A comparison of methods for transforming belief function models to probability models. *International Journal of Approximate Reasoning*, 41(3):255–266.

DeNero, J., Gillick, D., Zhang, J., and Klein, D. (2006). Why generative phrase models underperform surface heuristics. In *Proceedings of the Workshop on Statistical Machine Translation*, StatMT '06, pages 31–38, Stroudsburg, PA, USA. Association for Computational Linguistics.

Elouedi, Z., Mellouli, K., and Smets, P. (2000). Classification with belief decision trees. In *Proceedings of the 9th International Conference on Artificial Intelligence : Methodology, Systems, Architectures.*, Varna, Bulgaria. AIMSA 2000, Springer Lecture Notes on Articial Intelligence.

Foster, G., Kuhn, R., and Johnson, H. (2006). Phrasetable smoothing for statistical machine translation. In *Proceedings of the 2006 Conference on Empirical Methods in Natural Language Processing*, pages 53–61, Sydney, Australia. Association for Computational Linguistics.

Koehn, P. (2010). *Statistical Machine Translation*. Cambridge University Press.

Koehn, P., Hoang, H., Birch, A., Callison-Burch, C., Federico, M., Bertoldi, N., Cowan, B., Shen, W., Moran, C., Zens, R., Dyer, C., Bojar, O., Constantin, A., and Herbst, E. (2007). Moses: Open source toolkit for statistical machine translation. In *Proceedings of the 45th Annual Meeting of the Association for Computational Linguistics Companion Volume Proceedings of the Demo and Poster Sessions*, pages 177–180, Prague, Czech Republic. Association for Computational Linguistics.

Kuhn, R., Chen, B., Foster, G., and Stratford, E. (2010). Phrase clustering for smoothing tm probabilities: or, how to extract paraphrases from phrase tables. In *Proceedings of the 23rd International Conference on Computational Linguistics*, COLING '10, pages 608–616, Stroudsburg, PA, USA. Association for Computational Linguistics.

Lambert, P., Senellart, J., Romary, L., Schwenk, H., Zipser, F., Lopez, P., and Blain, F. (2012). Collaborative machine translation service for scientific texts. In *Proceedings of the Demonstrations at the 13th Conference of the European Chapter of the Association for Computational Linguistics*, pages 11–15, Avignon, France. Association for Computational Linguistics.

Moore, R. C. and Quirk, C. (2007). An iteratively-trained segmentation-free phrase translation model for statistical machine translation. In *Proceedings of the Second Workshop on Statistical Machine Translation*, StatMT '07, pages 112–119, Stroudsburg, PA, USA. Association for Computational Linguistics.

Och, F. J. (2003). Minimum error rate training in statistical machine translation. In *Proceedings of the 41st Annual Meeting of the Association for Computational Linguistics*, pages 160–167, Sapporo, Japan. Association for Computational Linguistics.

Papineni, K., Roukos, S., Ward, T., and Zhu, W.-J. (2002). Bleu: a method for automatic evaluation of machine translation. In *Proceedings of the 40th Annual Meeting of the Association for Computational Linguistics*, pages 311–318, Philadelphia, USA.

Petitrenaud, S., Jousse, V., Meignier, S., and Estève, Y. (2010). Automatic named identification of speakers using belief functions. In *Information Processing and Management of Uncertainty (IPMU'10)*, Dortmund, Germany.

Schwenk, H., Déchelotte, D., and Gauvain, J.-L. (2006). Continuous space language models for statistical machine translation. In *Proceedings of the COLING/ACL 2006 Main Conference Poster Sessions*, pages 723–730.

Shafer, G. (1976). *A Mathematical Theory of Evidence*. Princeton University Press.

Sima'an, K. and Mylonakis, M. (2008). Better statistical estimation can benefit all phrases in phrase-based statistical machine translation. In *Proceedings of the IEEE Workshop on Spoken Language Technology (SLT) 2008*, pages 237–240, Goa, India.

Smets, P. (1988). Belief functions versus probability functions. In Bouchon, B., Saitta, L., and Yager, R., editors, *Uncertainty and Intelligent Systems*, volume 313 of *Lecture Notes in Computer Science*, pages 17–24. Springer Berlin / Heidelberg.

Smets, P. and Kennes, R. (1994). The transferable belief model. *Artificial Intelligence*, 66:191–234.

Snover, M., Dorr, B., Schwartz, R., Micciulla, L., and Makhoul, J. (2006). A study of translation edit rate with targeted human annotation. In *Proceedings of the 7th Conference of the Association for Machine Translation in the Americas*, Cambridge, Massachusetts, USA.

Sense and Reference Disambiguation in Wikipedia

Hui SHEN[1] *Razvan BUNESCU*[1] *Rada MIHALCEA*[2]
(1) School of Electrical Engineering and Computer Science, Ohio University, Athens, OH
(2) Department of Computer Science, University of North Texas, Denton, TX
hs138609@ohio.edu, bunescu@ohio.edu, rada@cs.unt.edu

ABSTRACT
Wikipedia articles are annotated by volunteer contributors with numerous links that connect words and phrases to relevant titles in Wikipedia. In this paper, we identify inconsistencies in the user annotation of links and show that they can have a substantial impact on the performance of word sense disambiguation systems that are trained on Wikipedia links. We describe two major types of link annotations – *sense* and *reference* – that are frequently used without being explicitly distinguished in Wikipedia, and present an approach to training sense and reference disambiguation systems in the presence of such annotation inconsistencies. Experimental results demonstrate that accounting for annotation ambiguity in Wikipedia links leads to significant improvements in disambiguation accuracy.

KEYWORDS: word sense disambiguation, Wikipedia.

TITLE AND ABSTRACT IN ROMANIAN

Dezambiguizare de Sensuri si Referinte in Wikipedia

Articolele din Wikipedia sunt adnotate de editori voluntari cu numeroase link-uri ce conecteaza fraze din articol cu titluri relevante in Wikipedia. In acest articol descriem inconsecvente in adnotarile editorilor si aratam ca ele pot avea un impact substantial asupra performantei sistemelor de dezambiguizare care sunt antrenate cu link-uri din Wikipedia. Descriem doua tipuri majore de adnotari – *sensuri* si *referinte* – care sunt folosite frecvent fara a fi diferentiate explicit in Wikipedia. Prezentam modele de invatare automata pentru dezambiguizare de sensuri si referinte care pot fi antrenate in prezenta acestor ambiguitati de adnotare. Evaluarea experimentala a acestor modele confirma o imbunatatire semnificativa a performantei de dezambiguizare.

KEYWORDS: dezambiguizare de sensuri, Wikipedia.

Proceedings of COLING 2012: Posters, pages 1111–1120,
COLING 2012, Mumbai, December 2012.

1 Introduction and Motivation

The vast amount of world knowledge available in Wikipedia has been shown to benefit many types of text processing tasks, such as coreference resolution (Ponzetto and Strube, 2006; Haghighi and Klein, 2009; Bryl et al., 2010; Rahman and Ng, 2011), information retrieval (Milne, 2007; Li et al., 2007; Potthast et al., 2008; Cimiano et al., 2009), or question answering (Ahn et al., 2004; Kaisser, 2008; Ferrucci et al., 2010). In particular, the user contributed link structure of Wikipedia has been shown to provide useful supervision for training named entity disambiguation (Bunescu and Pasca, 2006; Cucerzan, 2007) and word sense disambiguation (Mihalcea, 2007; Mihalcea and Csomai, 2007) systems. Articles in Wikipedia often contain mentions of concepts or entities that already have a corresponding article. When contributing authors mention an existing Wikipedia entity inside an article, they are required to link at least its first mention to the corresponding article, by using *links* or *piped links*. Consider, for example, the following Wikipedia annotations from the article about Palermo: *"Palermo is a city in [[Southern Italy]], the [[capital city | capital]] of the [[autonomous area | autonomous region]] of [[Sicily]]"*. The bracketed strings *[[Southern Italy]]* and *[[Sicily]]* identify the title of the Wikipedia articles that describe the corresponding named entities. The same strings are also used in the displayed HTML version of the sentence. If the author wants a different string displayed (e.g., *"autonomous region"* instead of the title string *"autonomous area"*), then the alternative string is included in a piped link, after the title string. Using these rules for expanding simple or piped links, the HTML string that is displayed for the aforementioned example is: *"Palermo is a city in Southern Italy, the capital of the autonomous region of Sicily"*.

Since many words and names mentioned in Wikipedia articles are inherently ambiguous, their corresponding links can be seen as a useful source of supervision for training named entity and word sense disambiguation systems. For example, Wikipedia contains articles that describe possible senses of the word "capital", such as CAPITAL CITY, CAPITAL (ECONOMICS), FINANCIAL CAPITAL, or HUMAN CAPITAL, to name only a few. When disambiguating a word or a phrase in Wikipedia, a contributor uses the context to determine the appropriate Wikipedia title to include in the link. In the example above, the editor of the article determined that the word "capital" was mentioned in that context with the political center meaning, consequently it was mapped to the article CAPITAL CITY through a piped link.

In order to use Wikipedia links for training a WSD system for a given word, one needs first to define a sense repository that specifies the possible meanings for that word, and then use the Wikipedia links to create training examples for each sense in the repository. Taking the word "atmosphere" as an example, the process might be implemented using the following sequence of steps:

1. Collect all Wikipedia titles that are linked from the anchor word "atmosphere". This results in a wide array of titles, ranging from the general ATMOSPHERE and its instantiations ATMOSPHERE OF EARTH or ATMOSPHERE OF MARS, to titles as diverse as ATMOSPHERE (UNIT), MOOD (PSYCHOLOGY), or ATMOSPHERE (MUSIC GROUP).

2. Create a repository of senses from all titles that have sufficient support in Wikipedia i.e., titles that are referenced at least a predefined minimum number of times using the ambiguous word as anchor. The most frequent titles for the anchor word "atmosphere" are thus assembled into a repository $\mathcal{R}$ = {ATMOSPHERE, ATMOSPHERE OF EARTH, ATMOSPHERE OF MARS, ATMOSPHERE OF VENUS, STELLAR ATMOSPHERE, ATMOSPHERE (UNIT), ATMOSPHERE (MUSIC GROUP)}.

The Beagle 2 lander objectives were to characterize the physical properties of the [[atmosphere]] and surface layers
Sense = **Atmosphere**; *Reference* = Atmosphere of Mars; *Label* = A → A(S) → AM

The Orbiter has been successfully performing scientific measurements and study of the interaction of the [[Atmosphere of Mars|atmosphere]] with
Sense = Atmosphere; *Reference* = **Atmosphere of Mars**; *Label* = A → A(S) → AM

In global climate models, the state and properties of the [[atmosphere]] are specified or computed at a number of discrete locations
Sense = **Atmosphere**; *Reference* = Atmosphere of Earth; *Label* = A → A(S) → AE

The principal natural phenomena that contribute acid-producing gases to the [[Atmosphere of Earth|atmosphere]] are emissions from volcanoes
Sense = Atmosphere; *Reference* = **Atmosphere of Earth**; *Label* = A → A(S) → AE

An aerogravity assist, or AGA, is a spacecraft maneuver designed to change velocity when arriving at a body with an [[atmosphere]]
Sense = **Atmosphere**; *Reference* = Atmosphere ▷ *generic*; *Label* = A → A(O)

Assuming the planet's [[atmosphere]] is close to chemical equilibrium, it is predicted that 55 Cancri d is covered in a layer of water clouds
Sense = **Atmosphere**; *Reference* = Atmosphere of Cancri ▷ *missing*; A → A(O)

Figure 1: A(S) = Atmosphere (S), A(O) = Atmosphere (O), A = Atmosphere, AE = Atmosphere of Earth, AM = Atmosphere of Mars.

3. Use the links extracted for each sense in the repository as labeled examples for that sense and train a WSD model to distinguish between alternative senses of the ambiguous word "atmosphere" based on features extracted from the word context.

This Wikipedia-based approach to creating training data for word sense disambiguation has a major shortcoming. Many of the training examples extracted for the title Atmosphere could very well belong to more specific titles such as Atmosphere of Earth or Atmosphere of Mars. Whenever the word "atmosphere" is used in a context with the sense of "a layer of gases that may surround a material body of sufficient mass, and that is held in place by the gravity of the body," the contributor has the option of adding a link either to the title Atmosphere that describes this sense of the word, or to the title of an article that describes the atmosphere of the actual celestial body that is referred in that particular context, as shown in the first 4 examples in Figure 1. We will call the more general link a *sense* annotation, and the more specific link a *reference* annotation. Correspondingly, Atmosphere will be a sense for the word "atmosphere", whereas Atmosphere of Earth, Atmosphere of Mars, and Atmosphere of Venus will all be references associated with this sense. As shown in bold in Figure 1, different occurrences of the same word may be tagged with a sense or a reference link, an ambiguity that is pervasive in Wikipedia for words like "atmosphere" that have senses with multiple, popular references. There does not seem to be a clear, general rule underlying the decision to tag a word or a phrase with a sense or a reference link in Wikipedia. We hypothesize that, in some cases, editors may be unaware that an article exists in Wikipedia for the actual reference of a word or for a more specific sense of the word, and therefore they end up using a link to an article describing the general sense of the word. There is also the possibility that more specific articles are introduced only in newer versions of Wikipedia, and thus earlier annotations were not aware of these recent articles. Furthermore, since annotating words with the most specific sense or reference available in Wikipedia may require substantial cognitive effort, editors may often choose to link to a general sense of the word, a choice that is still correct, yet less informative than the more specific sense or reference.

atmosphere	Size
ATMOSPHERE	932
Atmosphere (S)	*559*
Atmosphere of Earth	*518*
Atmosphere of Mars	*19*
Atmosphere of Venus	*9*
Stellar Atmosphere	*13*
Atmosphere (O)	*373*
ATMOSPHERE OF EARTH	345
ATMOSPHERE OF MARS	37
ATMOSPHERE OF VENUS	26
STELLAR ATMOSPHERE	29
ATMOSPHERE (UNIT)	96
ATMOSPHERE (MUSIC GROUP)	104

game	Size
GAME	819
Game (S)	*99*
Video game	*55*
PC game	*44*
Game (O)	*720*
VIDEO GAME	312
PC GAME	24
GAME (FOOD)	232
GAME (RAPPER)	154

Table 1: Wikipedia annotations (normal) and manual annotations (*italics*).

To estimate the magnitude of the sense vs. reference annotation ambiguity, we extracted all link annotations for the words “atmosphere” and “game” that were labeled with the sense links ATMOSPHERE and GAME, respectively. We then used the context to manually determine for each sense link annotation the corresponding more specific title, when such a title exists in Wikipedia. The statistics in Table 1 show a significant overlap between the sense and reference categories for words like "atmosphere" that have senses with multiple, popular references. For example, out of the 932 ATMOSPHERE links that were extracted in total, 518 were actually about the ATMOSPHERE OF EARTH, but the user linked them to the more general sense category ATMOSPHERE. On the other hand, there are 345 links to ATMOSPHERE OF EARTH that were explicitly made by the user. The table also shows that sometimes the ambiguous word is linked to a more specific sense, such as STELLAR ATMOSPHERE. We manually assigned *other* links (O) whenever the word is used with a generic sense, or when the reference is not available in the repository of Wikipedia titles collected for that word because either the reference title does not exist in Wikipedia or the reference title exists, but it does not have sufficient support – at least 20 linked anchors – in Wikipedia. We grouped all references and more specific links for any given sense into a special category suffixed with (S), to distinguish them from the other links (generic use, or missing reference) that were grouped into the category suffixed with (O).

A supervised learning algorithm that uses the extracted links for training a WSD classification model to distinguish between categories in the sense repository assumes implicitly that the categories, and hence their training examples, are mutually disjoint. This assumption is clearly violated for words like “atmosphere,” consequently the learned model will have a poor performance on distinguishing between the overlapping categories. Alternatively, we can say that sense categories like ATMOSPHERE are ill defined, since their supporting dataset contains examples that could also belong to more specific, reference categories such as ATMOSPHERE OF EARTH or ATMOSPHERE OF MARS. We see two possible solutions to the problem of inconsistent link annotations:

1. Group related senses and references into one general sense, such that all categories in the resulting repository become disjoint. For the word "atmosphere", we could augment the general category ATMOSPHERE to contain all the links previously annotated as ATMOSPHERE, ATMOSPHERE OF EARTH, ATMOSPHERE OF MARS, ATMOSPHERE OF VENUS, or STELLAR ATMOSPHERE. Correspondingly, the new sense repository would be reduced to $\mathscr{R}$ = {ATMOSPHERE, ATMOSPHERE (UNIT), ATMOSPHERE (MUSIC GROUP)}.

2. Keep the original sense and reference repository, but change the definition of some sense categories such that all categories in the repository become mutually disjoint. Correspondingly, the WSD model will be trained to categorize as ATMOSPHERE (O) all contexts of the word "atmosphere" in which either the word is used with a generic sense, or the corresponding reference does not belong to the Wikipedia title repository. The sense repository then becomes $\mathscr{R}$ = {ATMOSPHERE (O), ATMOSPHERE OF EARTH, ATMOSPHERE OF MARS, ATMOSPHERE OF VENUS, STELLAR ATMOSPHERE, ATMOSPHERE (UNIT), ATMOSPHERE (MUSIC GROUP)}.

The first solution is straightforward, however it has the disadvantage that the resulting WSD model will never link words to specific reference titles in Wikipedia like ATMOSPHERE OF EARTH or ATMOSPHERE OF MARS. The rest of this paper describes a feasible implementation for the second solution, which has the advantage that it results in a WSD system that can make more fine grained annotations, down to the reference level. While leading to a more useful system, this second approach is however complicated by the link annotation ambiguity. A WSD system that is trained on sense and reference links extracted automatically from Wikipedia needs to account for the fact that links annotated as ATMOSPHERE may belong either to the general ATMOSPHERE (O) sense category, to the more specific sense STELLAR ATMOSPHERE, or to one of the reference categories ATMOSPHERE OF EARTH, ATMOSPHERE OF MARS, ATMOSPHERE OF VENUS. The distinction between the general sense category ATMOSPHERE and the more specific categories is missing in the Wikipedia link annotations. Since performing an extra step of manual annotation cannot scale to the whole word and phrase vocabulary of Wikipedia, the system needs to be trained with incomplete label information.

2 Learning for Sense and Reference Disambiguation

Figure 2 shows our proposed hierarchical classification scheme for disambiguation, using "atmosphere" as the ambiguous word. Shaded leaf nodes show the final categories in the sense repository for each word, whereas the doted frames on the second level in the hierarchy denote artificial categories introduced to enable a finer grained classification into more specific senses or references. Thick arrows illustrate the classification decisions that are made in order to obtain a fine grained disambiguation of the word. Thus, the word "atmosphere" is first classified to have the general sense ATMOSPHERE i.e., "a layer of gases that may surround a material body of sufficient mass, and that is held in place by the gravity of the body". In the first solution, the disambiguation process would stop here and output the general sense ATMOSPHERE. In the second solution, the disambiguation process continues and further classifies the word to

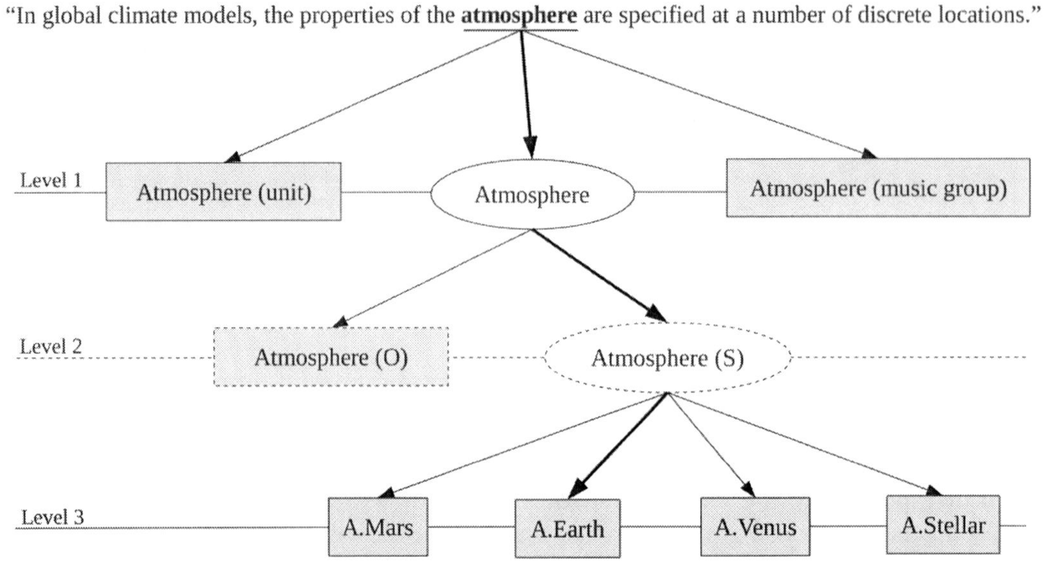

Figure 2: Hierarchical classification for sense and reference disambiguation.

be a reference to ATMOSPHERE OF EARTH. To get to this final classification, the process passes through an intermediate binary classification level where it determines whether the word has a generic sense or a sense that is not covered in the Wikipedia repository, corresponding to the artificial leaf category ATMOSPHERE (O). In such cases, the system stops the disambiguation process and outputs the general sense category ATMOSPHERE. This disambiguation scheme could be used to relabel the ATMOSPHERE links in Wikipedia with more specific, and therefore more informative, references such as ATMOSPHERE OF EARTH. According to the statistics from Table 1, for ambiguous words like "atmosphere" there is a significant number of instances where a more specific annotation is possible: out of all 933 instances annotated as ATMOSPHERE in Wikipedia, about 60% (559 of them) could have been labeled with more specific titles.

Training word sense classifiers for Levels 1 and 3 is straightforward. For Level 1, Wikipedia links that are annotated by users as ATMOSPHERE, ATMOSPHERE OF EARTH, ATMOSPHERE OF MARS, ATMOSPHERE OF VENUS, or STELLAR ATMOSPHERE are collected as training examples for the general sense category ATMOSPHERE. Similarly, Wikipedia links that are annotated as ATMOSPHERE (UNIT) and ATMOSPHERE (MUSIC GROUP) will be used as training examples for the two categories, respectively. A binary or multiclass classifier is then trained to distinguish between the two or more categories at this level. For Level 3, binary or multiclass classifiers are trained on Wikipedia links collected for each of the specific senses or references.

For the binary classifier at Level 2, we could use as training examples for the category ATMOSPHERE (O) all Wikipedia links that were annotated as ATMOSPHERE, whereas for the category ATMOSPHERE (S) we will use as training examples all Wikipedia links that were annotated specifically as ATMOSPHERE OF EARTH, ATMOSPHERE OF MARS, ATMOSPHERE OF VENUS, or STELLAR ATMOSPHERE. Using this dataset, we could train a traditional binary classification SVM to distinguish between the two categories. We call this approach *Naive SVM*, since it does not account for the fact that a significant number of the links that are annotated by Wikipedia contributors as ATMOSPHERE should actually belong to the ATMOSPHERE (S) category – about 60% of them, according to Table 1. Alternatively, we could treat all ATMOSPHERE examples as unlabeled examples. If we consider the examples in ATMOSPHERE (S) to be positive examples, then the problem becomes one of *learning with positive and unlabeled examples.*

2.1 Learning with positive and unlabeled examples

This general type of semi-supervised learning has been studied before in the context of tasks such as text classification and information retrieval (Lee and Liu, 2003; Liu et al., 2003), or bioinformatics (Elkan and Noto, 2008; Noto et al., 2008). In this setting, the training data consists of positive examples $x \in P$ and unlabeled examples $x \in U$. Following the notation of Elkan and Noto (2008), $s(x) = 1$ if the example is positive and $s(x) = -1$ if the example is unlabeled. The true label of an example is $y(x) = 1$ if the example is positive and $y(x) = -1$ if the example is negative. Thus, $x \in P \Rightarrow s(x) = y(x) = 1$ and $x \in U \Rightarrow s(x) = -1$ i.e., the true label $y(x)$ of an unlabeled example is unknown. In the *Biased SVM* formulation of Lee and Liu (2003), a soft-margin SVM is trained on the $s(x)$ values to optimize an estimate of pr, the product between the precision and the recall with respect to the partially hidden true labels $y(x)$. Lee and Liu (2003) show that pr can be estimated using only the observed labels $s(x)$. The other approach used in our experiments is based on the *Weighted Samples SVM* formulation of Elkan and Noto (2008), which assumes that labeled examples $\{x|s(x) = 1\}$ are selected at random from the positive examples $\{x|y(x) = 1\}$ i.e., $p(s = 1|x, y = 1) = p(s = 1|y = 1)$. Correspondingly, a first classifier $g(x)$ is trained on the labeling s to approximate the label distribution i.e., $g(x) = p(s = 1|x)$. The probabilistic output of this classifier is used to create a weighted sample of the original training data, and then a second classifier is trained on the weighted sample to approximate the true labels $y(x)$.

3 Experimental Evaluation

We ran disambiguation experiments on the two ambiguous words *atmosphere* and *game*. Their repository of senses and references have been summarized previously in Table 1. All the WSD classifiers evaluated here use the same set of standard WSD features, such as words and their part-of-speech tags in a window of 3 words around the ambiguous keyword, the unigram and bigram content words that are within 2 sentences of the current sentence, the syntactic governor of the keyword, and its chains of syntactic dependencies of lengths up to two. Furthermore, for each example, a Wikipedia specific feature was computed as the cosine similarity between the context of the ambiguous word and the text of the article for the target sense or reference.

The Level_1 and Level_3 classifiers were trained using the SVM^{multi} component of the SVM^{light} package.[1] The WSD classifiers were evaluated in a 4-fold cross validation scenario in which 50% of the data was used for training, 25% for tuning the capacity parameter C, and 25% for testing. The final accuracy numbers were computed by averaging the results over the 4 folds. For *atmosphere*, the accuracy was 93.1% at Level_1 and 85.6% at Level_3. For *game*, the accuracy was 82.9% at Level_1 and 92.9% at Level_3.

For the binary classifier at Level_2 we follow the same 4-fold cross validation scheme. We emphasize that our manual labels are used only for testing purposes – the manual labels are ignored during training and tuning, when the data is assumed to contain only positive and unlabeled examples that are automatically collected from Wikipedia without any manual effort. We compare the Naive SVM, Biased SVM, and Weighted SVM, using for all of them the same train/development/test splits of the data and the same features.

[1]http://svmlight.joachims.org

Accuracy	Naive SVM	Biased SVM	Weighted SVM
atmosphere	39.9%	**79.6%**	75.0%
game	83.8%	**87.1%**	84.6%

F-measure	Naive SVM	Biased SVM	Weighted SVM
atmosphere	30.5%	**86.0%**	83.2%
game	75.1%	**81.8%**	77.5%

Table 2: Disambiguation results at Level_2.

Table 2 shows the accuracy and F-measure results of the three methods for Level_2. The Biased SVM and the Weighted Samples SVM outperform the Naive SVM on both accuracy and F-measure. The improvement in performance is particularly substantial for the Biased SVM. Based on these initial results, the Biased SVM could be seen as the method of choice for learning with positive and unlabeled examples in the task of sense and reference disambiguation in Wikipedia.

Conclusion and Future Work

Sense and *reference* annotations of words are frequently used without being explicitly distinguished in Wikipedia. Correspondingly, we showed that inconsistencies in link annotations can have a significant impact on the performance of word sense disambiguation systems that are trained on Wikipedia links. We presented an approach to training sense and reference disambiguation systems that treats annotation inconsistencies under the framework of learning with positive and unlabeled examples. Experimental results on two ambiguous words demonstrate that accounting for annotation ambiguity in Wikipedia links leads to consistent improvements in disambiguation accuracy. An accurate sense and reference disambiguation system has the advantage of enabling finer sense distinctions over a generic word sense disambiguation system. It can be used, for example, to annotate general sense links in Wikipedia with more fine grained annotations, down to the reference level.

Annotation inconsistencies in Wikipedia were circumvented by adapting two existing approaches that use only positive and unlabeled data to train binary classifiers. This binary classification constraint led to the introduction of the artificial specific (S) category on Level_2 in our disambiguation framework. In future work, we plan to investigate a more direct extension of learning with positive and unlabeled data to the case of multiclass classification, which will reduce the number of classification levels from three to two. We also plan to evaluate the new disambiguation method on a larger collection of ambiguous words.

Acknowledgments

This material is based in part upon work supported by the National Science Foundation IIS awards #1018613 and #1018590 and CAREER award #0747340. Any opinions, findings, and conclusions or recommendations expressed in this material are those of the authors and do not necessarily reflect the views of the National Science Foundation.

References

Ahn, D., Jijkoun, V., Mishne, G., Muller, K., de Rijke, M., and Schlobach, S. (2004). Using Wikipedia at the TREC QA track. In *Proceedings of the 13th Text Retrieval Conference (TREC 2004)*.

Bryl, V., Giuliano, C., Serafini, L., and Tymoshenko, K. (2010). Using background knowledge to support coreference resolution. In *Proceedings of the 2010 conference on ECAI 2010: 19th European Conference on Artificial Intelligence*, pages 759–764, Amsterdam, The Netherlands.

Bunescu, R. and Pasca, M. (2006). Using encyclopedic knowledge for named entity disambiguation. In *Proceesings of the 11th Conference of the European Chapter of the Association for Computational Linguistics (EACL-06)*, pages 9–16, Trento, Italy.

Cimiano, P., Schultz, A., Sizov, S., Sorg, P., and Staab, S. (2009). Explicit versus latent concept models for cross-language information retrieval. In *International Joint Conference on Artificial Intelligence (IJCAI-09*, pages 1513–1518, Pasadena, CA.

Cucerzan, S. (2007). Large-scale named entity disambiguation based on Wikipedia data. In *Proceedings of the Conference on Empirical Methods in Natural Language Processing*, pages 708–716.

Elkan, C. and Noto, K. (2008). Learning classifiers from only positive and unlabeled data. In *Proceedings of the 14th ACM SIGKDD international conference on Knowledge discovery and data mining*, KDD '08, pages 213–220.

Ferrucci, D. A., Brown, E. W., Chu-Carroll, J., Fan, J., Gondek, D., Kalyanpur, A., Lally, A., Murdock, J. W., Nyberg, E., Prager, J. M., Schlaefer, N., and Welty, C. A. (2010). Building watson: An overview of the deepqa project. *AI Magazine*, 31(3):59–79.

Haghighi, A. and Klein, D. (2009). Simple coreference resolution with rich syntactic and semantic features. In *Proceedings of the 2009 Conference on Empirical Methods in Natural Language Processing*, pages 1152–1161, Singapore.

Kaisser, M. (2008). The QuALiM question answering demo: Supplementing answers with paragraphs drawn from Wikipedia. In *Proceedings of the ACL-08 Human Language Technology Demo Session*, pages 32–35, Columbus, Ohio.

Lee, W. S. and Liu, B. (2003). Learning with positive and unlabeled examples using weighted logistic regression. In *Proceedings of the Twentieth International Conference on Machine Learning (ICML*, pages 448–455, Washington, DC.

Li, Y., Luk, R., Ho, E., and Chung, K. (2007). Improving weak ad-hoc queries using Wikipedia as external corpus. In *Proceedings of the 30th Annual International ACM SIGIR Conference on Research and Development in Information Retrieval*, pages 797–798, Amsterdam, Netherlands.

Liu, B., Dai, Y., Li, X., Lee, W. S., and Yu, P. S. (2003). Building text classifiers using positive and unlabeled examples. In *Proceedings of the Third IEEE International Conference on Data Mining*, ICDM '03, pages 179–186, Washington, DC, USA.

Mihalcea, R. (2007). Using Wikipedia for automatic word sense disambiguation. In *Human Language Technologies 2007: The Conference of the North American Chapter of the Association for Computational Linguistics*, pages 196–203, Rochester, New York.

Mihalcea, R. and Csomai, A. (2007). Wikify!: linking documents to encyclopedic knowledge. In *Proceedings of the Sixteenth ACM Conference on Information and Knowledge Management*, Lisbon, Portugal.

Milne, D. (2007). Computing semantic relatedness using Wikipedia link structure. In *Proceedings of the New Zealand Computer Science Research Student Conference*, Hamilton, New Zealand.

Noto, K., Saier, Jr., M. H., and Elkan, C. (2008). Learning to find relevant biological articles without negative training examples. In *Proceedings of the 21st Australasian Joint Conference on Artificial Intelligence: Advances in Artificial Intelligence*, AI '08, pages 202–213.

Ponzetto, S. P. and Strube, M. (2006). Exploiting semantic role labeling, wordnet and wikipedia for coreference resolution. In *Proceedings of the Human Language Technology Conference of the North American Chapter of the Association of Computational Linguistics*, pages 192–199.

Potthast, M., Stein, B., and Anderka, M. A. (2008). Wikipedia-based multilingual retrieval model. In *Proceedings of the 30th European Conference on IR Research*, Glasgow.

Rahman, A. and Ng, V. (2011). Coreference resolution with world knowledge. In *Proceedings of the 49th Annual Meeting of the Association for Computational Linguistics: Human Language Technologies - Volume 1*, pages 814–824, Stroudsburg, PA, USA. Association for Computational Linguistics.

Unsupervised Metaphor Paraphrasing using a Vector Space Model

Ekaterina Shutova[1,2,3] Tim Van de Cruys[1,4] Anna Korhonen[1,2]
(1) DTAL, University of Cambridge, UK
(2) Computer Laboratory, University of Cambridge, UK
(3) ICSI and ICBS, University of California at Berkeley, USA
(4) IRIT, UMR 5505, CNRS, Toulouse, France
katia@icsi.berkeley.edu, tim.vandecruys@irit.fr, anna.korhonen@cl.cam.ac.uk

ABSTRACT
We present the first fully unsupervised approach to metaphor interpretation, and a system that produces literal paraphrases for metaphorical expressions. Such a form of interpretation is directly transferable to other NLP applications that can benefit from a metaphor processing component. Our method is different from previous work in that it does not rely on any manually annotated data or lexical resources. First, our method computes candidate paraphrases according to the context in which the metaphor appears, using a vector space model. It then uses a selectional preference model to measure the degree of literalness of the paraphrases. The system identifies correct paraphrases with a precision of 0.52 at top rank, which is a promising result for a fully unsupervised approach.

KEYWORDS: Metaphor, paraphrasing, lexical substitution, vector space model.

Proceedings of COLING 2012: Posters, pages 1121–1130,
COLING 2012, Mumbai, December 2012.

1 Introduction

Metaphor has traditionally been viewed as an artistic device that lends vividness and distinction to its author's style. This view was first challenged by Lakoff and Johnson (1980), who claimed that it is a productive phenomenon that operates at the level of mental processes. Humans often use metaphor to describe abstract concepts through reference to more concrete experiences.

Being a characteristic property of human thought and communication, metaphor becomes an important problem for natural language processing. Shutova and Teufel (2010) have shown in an empirical study that the use of metaphor is ubiquitous in natural language text (according to their data, on average every third sentence in general domain text contains a metaphorical expression). Due to this high frequency usage, a system capable of recognizing and interpreting metaphorical expressions in unrestricted text would become an invaluable component of many semantics-oriented NLP applications.

The majority of previous computational approaches to metaphor rely on manually created knowledge and thus operate on a limited domain and are expensive to build and extend. Hand-coded knowledge has proved useful for both *metaphor identification*, i.e. distinguishing between literal and metaphorical language in text (Fass, 1991; Martin, 1990; Krishnakumaran and Zhu, 2007; Gedigian et al., 2006) and *metaphor interpretation*, i.e. identifying the intended literal meaning of a metaphorical expression (Fass, 1991; Martin, 1990; Narayanan, 1997; Barnden and Lee, 2002). However, to be applicable in a real-world setting a metaphor processing system needs to be able to identify and interpret metaphorical expressions in unrestricted text. The recent metaphor paraphrasing approach of Shutova (2010) was designed with this requirement in mind and used statistical methods, but still relied on the WordNet (Fellbaum, 1998) database to generate the initial set of paraphrases. In this paper, we take the metaphor paraphrasing task a step further and present a fully unsupervised approach to this problem. In our method, candidate substitutes for the metaphorical term are generated using a vector space model. Vector space models have been previously used in the general lexical substitution task (Mitchell and Lapata, 2008; Erk and Padó, 2008, 2009; Thater et al., 2009, 2010; Erk and Padó, 2010; Van de Cruys et al., 2011). However, (to the best of our knowledge) they have not yet been deployed in tasks involving figurative meaning transfers, such as interpretation of metonymy or metaphor. In this paper, we address this problem and apply a vector space model of word meaning in context to metaphor paraphrasing, appropriately adapting it to the task.

In comparison to lexical substitution, metaphor paraphrasing presents an additional challenge, namely that of discriminating between literal and metaphorical substitutes. Shutova (2010) used a selectional preference-based model for this purpose, obtaining encouraging results in a supervised setting. We evaluate the capacity of our vector space model to discriminate between literal and figurative paraphrases on its own, as well as integrating it with a selectional preference-based model similar to that of Shutova (2010) and thus evaluating the latter in an unsupervised setting. Our system thus operates in two steps. It first computes candidate paraphrases according to a latent model of semantic similarity based on the context of the metaphorically used word, and then measures the literalness of the candidates using a selectional preference model.

We focus on paraphrasing metaphorical verbs and evaluate our system using the dataset of Shutova (2010) especially designed for this task. The comparison against a paraphrasing gold standard provided by Shutova (2010) is complemented by an evaluation against direct human judgements of system output.

2 Method

2.1 Generation of candidate paraphrases using a vector space model

Paraphrase candidates are generated by first computing the specific meaning of the metaphorical term in its context. The meaning of a word instance in context is computed by adapting its original (global) meaning vector according to the dependency relations in which the word instance participates. For this purpose, we build a factorization model in which words, together with their window-based context words and their dependency relations, are linked to latent dimensions. Both types of contexts are combined to be able to induce broad, topical semantics as well as tight, synonym-like semantics. The factorization model allows us to determine which dimensions are important for a particular context, and adapt the dependency-based feature vector of the word accordingly. The model uses non-negative matrix factorization (NMF) (Lee and Seung, 2000) in order to find latent dimensions, using the minimization of the Kullback-Leibler divergence as an objective function. A more detailed description of the factorization model can be found in Van de Cruys et al. (2011).

Our paraphrase generation model has been trained on part of the UKWAC corpus (Baroni et al., 2009), covering about 500M words. The corpus has been part of speech tagged and lemmatized with Stanford Part-Of-Speech Tagger (Toutanova and Manning, 2000; Toutanova et al., 2003), and parsed with MaltParser (Nivre et al., 2006), so that dependency triples could be extracted.

Using the latent distributions yielded by our factorization model, it is now possible to compute the meaning vector for a particular word in context, and subsequently the most similar words to this meaning vector, which will be our candidate paraphrases.

Intuitively, the contextual features of the word (i.e. the dependency-based context features) will highlight the important semantic dimensions of the particular instance, creating a probability distribution over latent factors $p(\mathbf{z}|d_j)$. Using this probability distribution, a new probability distribution is determined over dependency features given the context, following equation 1.

$$p(\mathbf{d}|d_j) = p(\mathbf{z}|d_j)p(\mathbf{d}|\mathbf{z}) \tag{1}$$

The last step is to weight the original probability vector of the word according to the probability vector of the dependency features given the word's context, by taking the pointwise multiplication of probability vectors $p(\mathbf{d}|w_i)$ and $p(\mathbf{d}|d_j)$.

$$p(\mathbf{d}|w_i, d_j) = p(\mathbf{d}|w_i) \cdot p(\mathbf{d}|d_j) \tag{2}$$

This final step is a crucial one in the model. The model is not just based on latent factors; rather, the latent factors are used to determine which of the features in the original word vector are the salient ones given a particular context. This allows us to compute an accurate adaptation of the original word vector in context.

As an example, take the metaphorical expression *reflect concern*. We want to compute the meaning vector for the verb *reflect* (w_i) in the context of its direct object, $concern_{dobj}$ (d_j). Using the probability distribution over latent factors given the dependency context $p(\mathbf{z}|d_j)$ (a result that comes out of the factorization), we can compute the probability of dependency features given the context – $p(\mathbf{d}|d_j)$.

The former step yields a general probability distribution over dependency features that tells us how likely a particular dependency feature is given the context $concern_{dobj}$ that the verb appears in. Our last step is now to weight the original probability vector of the target word (the aggregate of dependency-based context features over all contexts of the target word) according to the new distribution given the context in which the verb appears. Features associated with *concern* (or more specifically, the dependency features associated with latent factors that are related to the feature $concern_{dobj}$) will be emphasized, while features associated with unrelated latent factors are leveled out. We can now return to our original matrix **A** and compute the top similar words for the adapted vector of *reflect* given the dependency feature $concern_{dobj}$, which yields the results presented in 1. If we instead compute the meaning vector for *reflect* given the dependency feature $light_{dobj}$ (as in the non-metaphorical expression *reflect light*), we get the results in 2.

1. **reflect**$_V$, *concern*$_{dobj}$: *address, highlight, express, ...*

2. **reflect**$_V$, *light*$_{dobj}$: *emit, shine, flash, ...*

The top 6 candidate paraphrases the model produces for some example metaphorical expressions are shown in Table 1.

similarity score	replacement
verb – direct object	
reflect concern	
0.1657	address
0.1638	highlight
0.1608	*express*
0.1488	focus
0.1473	outline
0.1415	comment
subject – verb	
campaign *surge*	
0.1492	subside
0.1214	*intensify*
0.1146	erupt
0.0967	plummet
0.0935	swell
0.0928	slump

Table 1: The list of paraphrases with the initial ranking. The correct paraphrases are printed in italic.

association	replacement
verb – direct object	
reflect concern	
0.1822	*express*
0.0809	nurture
0.0771	share
0.0522	reinforce
0.0088	demonstrate
0.0088	lack
subject – verb	
campaign *surge*	
0.0377	*intensify*
0.0028	sweep
0.0009	boom
≈ 0	grow
≈ 0	sweep
≈ 0	plunge

Table 2: Paraphrases re-ranked by the selectional preference model. Correct paraphrases are printed in italic.

2.2 Reranking of candidate paraphrases using a selectional preference model

The candidate lists which are generated by the vector space model contain a number of substitutes that retain the meaning of a metaphorical expression as closely as possible. However, due to the fact that the model favours the substitutes that are similar to the metaphorical verb, the highly-ranked substitutes are sometimes also metaphorically used. For example, "*speed up* change" is the top-ranked paraphrase for "*accelerate* change" and the literal paraphrase "*facilitate* change" appears only in rank 10. As the task is to identify the literal interpretation, this ranking still needs to be refined.

Following Shutova (2010), we use a selectional preference model to discriminate between literally and metaphorically used substitutes. Verbs used metaphorically are likely to demonstrate semantic preference for the source domain, e.g. *speed up* would select for MACHINES, or VEHICLES, rather than CHANGE (the target domain), whereas the ones used literally for the target domain, e.g. *facilitate* would select for PROCESSES (including CHANGE). We therefore expect that selecting the verbs whose preferences the noun in the metaphorical expression matches best should allow us to filter out non-literalness.

We automatically acquired selectional preference (SP) distributions of the candidate substitutes (for subject-verb and verb-object relations) from the British National Corpus (BNC) (Burnard, 2007) parsed by the RASP parser (Briscoe et al., 2006). We obtained SP classes by clustering the 2000 most frequent nouns in the BNC into 200 clusters using the algorithm of Sun and Korhonen (2009). We quantified selectional preferences using the association measure proposed by Resnik (1993). It represents SPs as the difference between the posterior distribution of noun classes in a particular relation with the verb and their prior distribution in that syntactic position irrespective of the identity of the verb. This difference then defines the *selectional preference strength* (SPS) of the verb, quantified in terms of Kullback-Leibler divergence as follows.

$$S_R(v) = D(P(c|v)||P(c)) = \sum_c P(c|v) \log \frac{P(c|v)}{P(c)}, \tag{3}$$

where $P(c)$ is the prior probability of the noun class, $P(c|v)$ is the posterior probability of the noun class given the verb and R is the grammatical relation. SPS measures how strongly the predicate constrains its arguments. Resnik then quantifies how well a particular argument class fits the verb using another measure called *selectional association*:

$$A_R(v,c) = \frac{1}{S_R(v)} P(c|v) \log \frac{P(c|v)}{P(c)} \tag{4}$$

We use selectional association as a measure of semantic fitness, i.e. literalness, of the paraphrases. The selectional preference model was applied to the top 20 substitutes suggested by the vector space model. The threshold of 20 substitutes was set experimentally on a small development set. The paraphrases were re-ranked based on their selectional association with the noun in the context. Those paraphrases that are not well suited or used metaphorically are dispreferred within this ranking. The new ranking (top 6 paraphrases) is shown in Table 2. The expectation is that the paraphrase in the first rank (i.e. the verb with which the noun in the context has the highest association) represents a literal interpretation.

3 Evaluation and Discussion

We compared the rankings of the initial candidate generation by the vector space model (**VS**) and the selectional preference-based reranking (**SP**) to that of an unsupervised paraphrasing baseline. We thus evaluated the ability of **VS** on its own to detect literal paraphrases, as well as the effectiveness of the **SP** model of Shutova (2010) in an unsupervised setting and in combination with **VS**.

3.1 Dataset

To our knowledge, the only metaphor paraphrasing dataset and gold standard available to date is that of Shutova (2010). We used this dataset to develop and test our system. Shutova (2010) annotated metaphorical expressions in a subset of the BNC sampling various genres: literature, newspaper/journal articles, essays on politics, international relations and sociology, radio broadcast (transcribed speech). The dataset consists of 62 phrases that include a metaphorical verb and either a subject or a direct object. The metaphorical expressions in the dataset include e.g. *stir excitement, reflect enthusiasm, accelerate change, grasp theory, cast doubt, suppress memory, throw remark* (verb-object constructions) and *campaign surged, factor shaped [..], tension mounted, ideology embraces, changes operated, approach focuses, example illustrates* (subject-verb constructions). 10 phrases in the dataset were used during development to observe the behavior of the system, and the remaining 52 constituted the test set. 11 of them were subject-verb constructions and 41 were verb-direct object constructions.

3.2 Baseline system

The baseline system is also unsupervised and incorporates two methods: that of generating most similar substitutes for the metaphorical verb regardless of its context and a method for their re-ranking based on the likelihood of their co-occurrence with the noun in the metaphorical expression. Thus a list of most similar substitutes is first generated using a standard dependency-based vector space model (Padó and Lapata, 2007). The likelihood of a paraphrase is then calculated as a joint probability of the candidate substitutes and the noun in the context as follows:

$$L_v = P(v,n)) = P(v) \cdot P(n|v) = \frac{f(v)}{\sum_k f(v_k)} \cdot \frac{f(v,n)}{f(v)} = \frac{f(v,n)}{\sum_k f(v_k)} \qquad (5)$$

where $f(v,n)$ is the frequency of the co-occurrence of the substitute with the context and $\sum_k f(v_k)$ is the total number of verbs in the corpus.

3.3 Evaluation method and results

We evaluated the paraphrases with the aid of human judges and against a human-created gold standard in two different experimental settings.

Setting 1 Human judges were presented with a set of sentences containing metaphorical expressions and their rank 1 paraphrases produced by **VS**, by **SP** and by the baseline, randomised. They were asked to mark the ones that have the same meaning as the metaphorically used term – and are used literally in the context of the paraphrase expression – as correct.

We had 4 volunteer annotators who were all native speakers of English and had no or sparse linguistic expertise. Their agreement on the task was $\kappa = 0.54$ ($n = 2, N = 115, k = 4$), whereby the main source of disagreement was the presence of highly conventionalised metaphorical paraphrases. We then evaluated the system performance against their judgements in terms of precision at rank 1, $P(1)$. Precision at rank 1 measures the proportion of correct literal interpretations among the paraphrases in rank 1. A paraphrase was considered correct if at least 3 judges out of 4 marked it as such. The results are demonstrated in Table 3. The **VS** model identifies literal paraphrases with $P(1) = 0.48$ and the **SP** model with $P(1) = 0.52$. Both models outperform the baseline that only achieves $P(1) = 0.40$.

Setting 2 We then also evaluated **VS**, **SP** and baseline rankings against a human-constructed paraphrasing gold standard. The gold standard was created by Shutova (2010) as follows. Five independent annotators were presented with a set of sentences containing metaphorical

relation	baseline $P(1)$	**VS** $P(1)$	**SP** $P(1)$	Shutova (2010) $P(1)$
verb – direct object	0.37	0.43	0.48	0.79
verb – subject	0.54	0.64	0.72	0.83
Average across dataset	0.40	0.48	0.52	0.81

Table 3: Results in the evaluation setting 1

expressions and asked to write down all suitable literal paraphrases for the metaphorical verbs. The annotators were all native speakers of English and had some linguistics background. Shutova (2010) then compiled a gold standard incorporating all of their annotations. For example, the gold standard for the phrase *brushed aside the accusations* contained the verbs *rejected, ignored, disregarded, dismissed, overlooked, discarded.*

However, given that the metaphor paraphrasing task is open-ended, it is hard to construct a comprehensive gold standard. For example, for the phrase *stir excitement* the gold standard includes the paraphrase *create excitement*, but not *provoke excitement* or *stimulate excitement*, which are more precise paraphrases. Thus the gold standard evaluation may unfairly penalise the system, which motivates our two-phase evaluation against both the gold standard and direct judgements of system output.

The system output was compared against the gold standard using *mean average precision* (MAP) as a measure. MAP is defined as follows:

$$MAP = \frac{1}{M}\sum_{j=1}^{M}\frac{1}{N_j}\sum_{i=1}^{N_j}P_{ji}, \qquad (6)$$

where M is the number of metaphorical expressions, N_j is the number of correct paraphrases for the metaphorical expression, P_{ji} is the precision at each correct paraphrase (the number of correct paraphrases among the top i ranks). First, average precision is estimated for individual metaphorical expressions, and then the mean is computed across the dataset. This measure allows us to assess ranking quality beyond rank 1, as well as the recall of the system. As compared to the gold standard, MAP of **VS** is 0.40, MAP of **SP** is 0.41 and that of the baseline is 0.37.

3.4 Discussion

Our system consistently produces better results than the baseline, with an improvement of 12% in precision on our human evaluation (**SP**) and an improvement of 4% MAP on the gold standard (**SP**). At first sight, these improvements of our unsupervised system may not seem very high, in particular when compared to the results of the supervised system of Shutova (2010). Note, however, that our results are in line with the performance of unsupervised approaches on the lexical substitution task. Unsupervised approaches to lexical substitution perform well below their supervised counterparts (which are usually based on WordNet), and often have difficulties getting significant improvements over a baseline of a simple dependency-based vector space model of semantic similarity (Erk and Padó, 2008; Van de Cruys et al., 2011). We therefore think that the method presented here takes a promising step in the direction of unsupervised metaphor paraphrasing.

The **SP** re-ranking of the candidates yields an improvement over the **VS** model used on its own, as expected. Our data analysis has shown that **SP** produces higher quality top paraphrases with respect to their literalness, however the two models perform similarly on the meaning retention task (according to our own judgements 55% of the top ranked paraphrases had a similar meaning to that of a metaphorical verb for both models). The difference in MAP scores of the two models is, however, not as high as that of the respective $P(1)$ scores. This can be explained by the fact that the **VS** model produces a number of antonymous candidates. The candidates are then re-ranked by the **SP** model which does not consider meaning retention, but rather the semantic fit of a candidate interpretation in the context. As a result, a number of antonymous paraphrases that are highly associated with the noun in the context get ranked above some of the correct literal paraphrases, lowering the method's MAP score. For example, the antonymous paraphrase *tension eased* for the metaphorical expression *tension mounted* is ranked higher than the correct paraphrase *tension intensified*. In general, antonymous paraphrasing was the most common type of error. Antonyms are known to attract high similarity scores within a distributional similarity framework. This is an issue that needs to be addressed in the future, in lexical substitution in general and metaphor paraphrasing in particular.

Although the **SP** model generally improves the initial **VS** ranking, there were some instances where this was not the case. One such example is the metaphorical expression *break agreement*. The top ranked paraphrases suggested in the first step, *breach* and *violate*, were overrun by the well matching paraphrases *ratify* and *sign*, that have a different – almost opposite – meaning.

The baseline tends to produce metaphorical paraphrases rather than literal ones. However, in a few cases the baseline suggests better rank 1 paraphrases than the system. For example, it interprets the expression *leak a report* as *circulate a report*, as opposed to *print a report* incorrectly suggested by the system. This is due to the fact that the paraphrase generation relies entirely on one single context word (in this case *report*); taking a broader context into account might alleviate this problem.

4 Conclusion

In this paper we presented the first fully unsupervised approach to metaphor interpretation. Our system produces literal paraphrases for metaphorical expressions in unrestricted text. Producing metaphorical interpretations in textual format makes our system directly usable by other NLP applications that can benefit from a metaphor processing component. The fact that, unlike all previous approaches to this problem, our system does not use any supervision makes it easily scalable to new domains and applications, as well as portable to a wider range of languages.

Our method identifies literal paraphrases for metaphorical expressions with a precision of 0.52 measured at top-ranked paraphrases. Given the unsupervised nature of our system and considering the state-of-the-art in unsupervised lexical substitution, we consider this a promising result. Following Shutova (2010), the current experimental design and test set focuses on subject-verb and verb-object metaphors only, but we expect the method to be equally applicable to other parts of speech and a wider range of syntactic constructions. Our context-based vector space model is suited to all part-of-speech classes and types of relations. Selectional preferences have been previously successfully acquired not only for verbs, but also for nouns, adjectives and even prepositions (Brockmann and Lapata, 2003; Zapirain et al., 2009; Ó Séaghdha, 2010). Extending the system to deal with further syntactic constructions is thus part of our future work.

Acknowledgements

The work in this paper was funded by the Royal Society (UK), the Isaac Newton Trust (Cambridge, UK), and EU grant 7FP-ITC-248064 'PANACEA'.

References

Barnden, J. and Lee, M. (2002). An artificial intelligence approach to metaphor understanding. *Theoria et Historia Scientiarum*, 6(1):399–412.

Baroni, M., Bernardini, S., Ferraresi, A., and Zanchetta, E. (2009). The wacky wide web: A collection of very large linguistically processed web-crawled corpora. *Language Resources and Evaluation*, 43(3):209–226.

Briscoe, E., Carroll, J., and Watson, R. (2006). The second release of the rasp system. In *Proceedings of the COLING/ACL on Interactive presentation sessions*, pages 77–80.

Brockmann, C. and Lapata, M. (2003). Evaluating and combining approaches to selectional preference acquisition. In *Proceedings of the tenth conference on European chapter of the Association for Computational Linguistics - Volume 1*, EACL '03, pages 27–34, Budapest, Hungary.

Burnard, L. (2007). *Reference Guide for the British National Corpus (XML Edition)*.

Erk, K. and Padó, S. (2008). A structured vector space model for word meaning in context. In *Proceedings of the Conference on Empirical Methods in Natural Language Processing*, pages 897–906, Waikiki, Hawaii, USA.

Erk, K. and Padó, S. (2009). Paraphrase assessment in structured vector space: Exploring parameters and datasets. In *Proceedings of the Workshop on Geometrical Models of Natural Language Semantics*, pages 57–65, Athens, Greece.

Erk, K. and Padó, S. (2010). Exemplar-based models for word meaning in context. In *Proceedings of the ACL 2010 Conference Short Papers*, pages 92–97, Uppsala, Sweden.

Fass, D. (1991). met*: A method for discriminating metonymy and metaphor by computer. *Computational Linguistics*, 17(1):49–90.

Fellbaum, C., editor (1998). *WordNet: An Electronic Lexical Database (ISBN: 0-262-06197-X)*. MIT Press, first edition.

Gedigian, M., Bryant, J., Narayanan, S., and Ciric, B. (2006). Catching metaphors. In *In Proceedings of the 3rd Workshop on Scalable Natural Language Understanding*, pages 41–48, New York.

Krishnakumaran, S. and Zhu, X. (2007). Hunting elusive metaphors using lexical resources. In *Proceedings of the Workshop on Computational Approaches to Figurative Language*, pages 13–20, Rochester, NY.

Lakoff, G. and Johnson, M. (1980). *Metaphors We Live By*. University of Chicago Press, Chicago.

Lee, D. D. and Seung, H. S. (2000). Algorithms for non-negative matrix factorization. In *Advances in Neural Information Processing Systems 13*, pages 556–562.

Martin, J. H. (1990). *A Computational Model of Metaphor Interpretation*. Academic Press Professional, Inc., San Diego, CA, USA.

Mitchell, J. and Lapata, M. (2008). Vector-based models of semantic composition. *proceedings of ACL-08: HLT*, pages 236–244.

Narayanan, S. (1997). Knowledge-based Action Representations for Metaphor and Aspect (KARMA). Technical report, PhD thesis, University of California at Berkeley.

Nivre, J., Hall, J., and Nilsson, J. (2006). Maltparser: A data-driven parser-generator for dependency parsing. In *Proceedings of LREC-2006*, pages 2216–2219.

Ó Séaghdha, D. (2010). Latent variable models of selectional preference. In *Proceedings of the 48th Annual Meeting of the Association for Computational Linguistics*, Uppsala, Sweden.

Padó, S. and Lapata, M. (2007). Dependency-based construction of semantic space models. *Computational Linguistics*, 33(2):161–199.

Resnik, P. (1993). *Selection and Information: A Class-based Approach to Lexical Relationships*. PhD thesis, Philadelphia, PA, USA.

Shutova, E. (2010). Automatic metaphor interpretation as a paraphrasing task. In *Proceedings of NAACL 2010*, Los Angeles, USA.

Shutova, E. and Teufel, S. (2010). Metaphor corpus annotated for source - target domain mappings. In *Proceedings of LREC 2010*, Malta.

Sun, L. and Korhonen, A. (2009). Improving verb clustering with automatically acquired selectional preferences. In *Proceedings of EMNLP 2009*, pages 638–647, Singapore.

Thater, S., Dinu, G., and Pinkal, M. (2009). Ranking paraphrases in context. In *Proceedings of the 2009 Workshop on Applied Textual Inference*, pages 44–47, Suntec, Singapore.

Thater, S., Fürstenau, H., and Pinkal, M. (2010). Contextualizing semantic representations using syntactically enriched vector models. In *Proceedings of the 48th Annual Meeting of the Association for Computational Linguistics*, pages 948–957, Uppsala, Sweden.

Toutanova, K., Klein, D., Manning, C. D., and Singer, Y. (2003). Feature-rich part-of-speech tagging with a cyclic dependency network. In *Proceedings of HLT-NAACL 2003*, pages 252–259.

Toutanova, K. and Manning, C. D. (2000). Enriching the knowledge sources used in a maximum entropy part-of-speech tagger. In *Proceedings of the Joint SIGDAT Conference on Empirical Methods in Natural Language Processing and Very Large Corpora (EMNLP/VLC-2000)*, pages 63–70.

Van de Cruys, T., Poibeau, T., and Korhonen, A. (2011). Latent vector weighting for word meaning in context. In *Proceedings of the 2011 Conference on Empirical Methods in Natural Language Processing*, pages 1012–1022, Edinburgh, Scotland, UK. Association for Computational Linguistics.

Zapirain, B., Agirre, E., and Màrquez, L. (2009). Generalizing over lexical features: selectional preferences for semantic role classification. In *Proceedings of the ACL-IJCNLP 2009 Conference Short Papers*, pages 73–76.

Memory-Efficient Katakana Compound Segmentation Using Conditional Random Fields

KRAUCHANKA Siarhei[1,2] *ARTSYMENIA Artsiom*[3]
(1) MINSK STATE LINGUISTIC UNIVERSITY, Belarus, Minsk, Zakharova st. 21
(2) IHS Inc., Japan, Tokyo, Minato-ku, Toranomon 5-13-1
(3) IHS Inc., Belarus, Minsk, Starovilenskaya st. 131
Sergey.Kravchenko@ihs.com, Artsiom.Artsymenia@ihs.com

ABSTRACT

The absence of explicit word boundary delimiters, such as spaces, in Japanese texts causes all kinds of troubles for Japanese morphological analysis systems. Particularly, out-of-vocabulary words represent a very serious problem for the systems which rely on dictionary data to establish word boundaries. In this paper we present a solution for decompounding of katakana sequences (one of the main sources of the out-of-vocabulary words) using a discriminative model based on Conditional Random Fields. One of the notable features of the proposed approach is its simplicity and memory efficiency.

KEYWORDS : Japanese language, Tokenization, Katakana Compound Segmentation, Conditional Random Fields

Proceedings of COLING 2012: Posters, pages 1131–1140,
COLING 2012, Mumbai, December 2012.

1 Introduction

It is well known that in Japanese language the absence of word boundary delimiters, such as spaces, adds to the morphological ambiguity, which, in turn, causes many difficulties for the language processing systems, which rely on precise tokenization and POS tagging. This problem is especially grave in compound nouns of Japanese and foreign origin. A number of morphological analysis systems were developed to resolve this problem and a number of such systems show some relatively good results. It is reported, however, that one of the biggest problems in most of these researches is related to the out-of-vocabulary (OOV) words. In some cases, an OOV word can be a sign of an insufficient core lexicon, which simply needs to be updated to correspond to the requirements of the processing system, while in other cases, an OOV word can be related to the constantly changing and growing peripheral lexicon, which cannot be reflected in any existing dictionary, and, therefore, it needs to be identified by non-vocabulary means.

In relation to Japanese language, this duality has its own specifics. In general, the Japanese texts consist of different types of writings – kanji, hiragana, katakana and a small amount of non-Japanese characters (for words and abbreviations coming from foreign languages). Most of the words of Japanese origin are written using kanji and hiragana, while katakana is usually used to transcribe the words of a foreign language (mostly, English) origin. When it comes to compound nouns, each of these two types of writings have their own specifics of formation of new expressions. For Japanese compound nouns, the most common way of formation is the concatenation of simple nouns (which can also be accompanied by abbreviation):

磁気共鳴画像 (Magnetic Resonance Imaging, MRI)

where 磁気 - "magnetism", 共鳴 - "resonance, sympathy", 画像 - "image, picture".

The compound nouns of non-Japanese origin are formed by transliteration of foreign words using katakana syllables and then concatenation of the elements:

プリントダイポールアレイアンテナ (printed dipole array antenna)

where プリント - "print" (here, "printed"), ダイポール - "dipole", アレイ - "array", アンテナ - "antenna".

These two are by far the richest sources of OOV words and, consequently, of the problems for many morphological analysis systems. Therefore, by solving the problem of correct identification of words in these expressions, it is possible to significantly reduce the bad influence of OOV words on the results of morphological analysis in general.

The method described in this paper focuses primarily on katakana expressions, and the possibility of applying a similar approach to the kanji-based expression segmentation will be left for another research.

2 Related work

Our research can be characterized as a discriminative approach to katakana compound segmentation. It can be viewed as both – as a specific task aimed at a narrow problematic area of the Japanese morphological analysis, and as a part of the Japanese text tokenization problem in general.

The specific problem of katakana compound segmentation has received an extra attention in the works of (Nakazawa, 2005) and (Kaji, 2011). Both of these researches present a number of techniques, such as dictionary and corpus validation, back-transliteration, web search, which, when combined, do a really good work of identifying the words in compound expressions. It should be noted, though, that in order to de-compound katakana expressions, these systems rely on large external resources like large vocabulary, "huge" English or Japanese corpora, parallel corpora or Web search results. Because of that, these approaches can be very efficient for the task of extraction of new vocabulary data, but it is doubtful, that they can be efficiently implemented in a morphological analysis system to solve the problem of constantly appearing OOV words.

As for the Japanese text tokenization problem in general, a number of researches have been performed for many years (Kurohashi, 1994; Kudo, 2004; Asahara, Matsumoto, 2000), some of them culminating in working morphological analysis systems such as Juman, Chasen or Mecab. It has been noted on numerous occasions that one of the weaknesses of these systems is their very tight connection to their respective dictionaries, which results in poor performance when it comes to the OOV words. Traditional vocabulary-based approaches using Hidden Markov Model (such as Chasen) preform quite well on texts with fewer OOV words. More advanced approaches using Maximum Entropy Markov Models (Uchimoto, 2001) or Conditional Random Fields (Kudo, 2004) take better care of OOV words, but still underperform when it comes to processing the texts out of training domain. As opposed to sequential vocabulary-based approaches, advances in pointwise modeling for Japanese morphological analysis have been made recently. The method described in (Neubig, Nakata, Mori, 2011) combines character context and dictionary information in one model to get good results on both – vocabulary and OOV words. Our research is very closely related to these works, but in our paper we focus exclusively on the problem of word segmentation, because POS tagging of katakana expressions does not require highly complex models. By doing that, we concentrate on one of the most problematic areas of Japanese morphological analysis and try to solve this problem using minimal resources with maximum efficiency. In perspective, it could mean that even using a less complicated (and, therefore, less resource demanding) model for such task as morphological analysis, it might be possible to achieve superior results by solving some of the problems with their own dedicated methods.

3 Research environment

For the general morphological analysis we have been using our original system, whose resource base includes a POS dictionary, which consists of more than 210000 unique entries (out of which, at least 21000 entries are katakana words), and a morphologically annotated corpus of technical and scientific documents with 33,134 sentences, which contains 6,909 unique katakana single- and multi-word expressions. Here, morphological annotation means word boundary and POS tag assignment. For the Japanese POS tagset, we use our own original formalism which is close to that of the well-known Penn Treebank project.

Additionally, in order to train and test our model, we needed a much larger and more representative corpus of katakana expressions with explicitly indicated word boundaries. For this purpose, we have developed a simple method of katakana expression extraction based on back-transliteration and employing parallel sentence-aligned Japanese-English text corpora. We have managed to automatically acquire a corpus of 4,977,790 non-unique katakana (both, single- and multi-word) expressions matched to their English translations with explicitly indicated word boundaries. We used this result for both - training (4,000,000 katakana expressions which after unification turned into 80,550 expressions) and testing (977,790 non-unique katakana expressions).

4 CRF model for katakana decompounding

For splitting of katakana compounds into words we use a method where each katakana character is treated as a separate token with a label assigned to it depending on the position of the character in the word it belongs to, similar to that of (Ng, Low, 2004). The following labels are used for marking the word boundaries:

F - First character of the word

M - Middle character of the word

L - Last character of the word

S - Single character word

This way the task of katakana compound segmentation can be defined as a label tagging problem. For parameter training we use Conditional Random Fields as described in (Lafferty, 2001). For each katakana character in the sequence with each possible label a number of features are assigned based on the dictionary and context information about the word the character may belong to. The set of features is provided in table 1, where T_i is one of the labels (F, M, L, S) for the i-th character (katakana syllable) in the compound.

Feature form	Description
$T_i\_C_i$	Character itself
$T_i\_C_{i-1}$	Previous character in the sequence
$T_i\_C_{i+1}$	Next character in the sequence
$T_i\_C_{i-2}\_C_{i-1}$	Context character pairs
$T_i\_C_{i-1}\_C_i$	-
$T_i\_C_i\_C_{i+1}$	-
$T_i\_C_{i+1}\_C_{i+2}$	-
$T_i\_C_{i-3}\_C_{i-2}\_C_{i-1}$	Context character triples
$T_i\_C_{i-2}\_C_{i-1}\_C_i$	-
$T_i\_C_{i-1}\_C_i\_C_{i+1}$	-
$T_i\_C_i\_C_{i+1}\_C_{i+2}$	-
$T_i\_C_{i+1}\_C_{i+2}\_C_{i+3}$	-
T_i_D	Dictionary information
$T_{i-1}\_ T_i$	Label bi-gram feature, which takes into account the label of the previous character to avoid impossible label sequences (F F, M F, L L and so on)

TABLE 1 – Feature set.

The dictionary information feature T_i_D is assigned to a character based on pre-splitting of the katakana sequence using some dictionary-based heuristic. For example the greedy algorithm may be used where, at first, the longest dictionary word is selected starting at the first syllable of katakana expression, then the longest dictionary word is chosen from the position next to the first word and so on. Any other dictionary-based method of word segmentation can also be used. After splitting of the word with heuristics each character gets a feature $T_i\_WL\_WP$ where WP – position of the character in the word, WL – length of the word.

For example, the word キャンセレーション which is absent from our system dictionary will be split by the greedy algorithm into キャン + セレーション. So the dictionary feature T_i_D will be assigned the following way during the training procedure:

キ → F_3_0

ャ → M_3_1

ン → M_3_2

セ → M_6_0

レ → M_6_1

ー → M_6_2

シ → M_6_3

ョ → M_6_4

ン → L_6_5

During the testing, the features M_3_2 and L_3_2, M_6_0 and F_6_0 will compete with each other and together with other features will vote towards M M or L F chain of labels. T_{i-1}_T_i feature will also add the weight of M M and L F transitions to get the final decision whether the word should be split into two or not.

5 Experiments and results

The training data for our experiments included the following resources (all described in section 3):

- approx. 21,000 katakana words from our POS dictionary to train the dictionary feature;
- 6,909 unique katakana expressions from our POS corpus, and 80,550 unique automatically extracted katakana expressions from English-Japanese parallel corpora (originally - 4,000,000 non-uniqued expressions) to train the context features;

One of the characteristics which allowed us to achieve a high memory-efficiency in our approach is the usage of regularization techinque described in (Vail, Lafferty, Veloso, 2007). All of the training for our model was performed at L1 regularization. L2 regularization shows slightly better results, but it also produces a very large number of features (45,484 features for L1 against 638,472 for L2), which we did not consider as efficient implementation.

In order to test our method we used the following corpora:

- automatically extracted katakana compounds from parallel English-Japanese texts of the same domain as the training corpus (PAR) containing 977,790 non-unique compounds with 1,160,770 words, out of which 54% (631,168) are OOV words;
- out-of-domain manually annotated corpus of general newspaper articles (NEWS) containing 4,986 non-unique katakana expressions with 5,338 words, out of which 44% (2,390) are OOV words.

While the results received using our approach were satisfactory for our original task (improvement of OOV words processing in katakana compounds), we also needed to compare them with those of other existing systems. We compared our approach with the most common methods of Japanese morphological analysis – a simple dictionary-based Hidden Markov Model approach (HMM), and a more sophisticated Conditional Random Fields approach from Mecab morphological analysis system (MECAB). For training of HMM and MECAB we used the same training data which was used for our system. The results of comparison are presented in the table 2.

System	**PAR**	**NEWS**
HMM	84.01%	82.73%
MECAB	87.50%	91.45%
Our approach	98.27%	96.67%

TABLE 2 – Comparison with other systems (F-Measure).

The results show that our approach heavily outperforms some of the most popular morphological analysis methods used in katakana compound segmentation task. The reason for that is the usage of character-based feature assignment and boundary labelling, which, instead of dictionary data, relies on more robust syllable sequence data. Because of that, the influence of OOV words is significantly reduced. However, as it was mentioned earlier, our approach also uses the dictionary information, which gives it additional domain specific training data. The influence of dictionary data (D-feature) on performance of our model is explored in table 3.

Model variation	**PAR**	**NEWS**
Model without D-feature	98.10%	95.89%
D-feature, greedy	98.21%	96.49%
D-feature, smart	98.27%	96.67%

TABLE 3 – Influence of the dictionary feature on the decompounding results (F-Measure).

In the table, "D-feature, greedy" relates to the greedy dictionary-based algorithm of compound pre-splitting, "D-feature, smart" relates to the dictionary-based pre-splitting algorithm which chooses the splitting variant with as few splittings as possible (longest words from the dictionary). As we can see from the results, the influence of D-feature is very small, which suggests that it is possible to employ our method without using any dictionary data at all, and still reach high level of performance, thus reducing the total amount of features required for this task, and contributing to the memory-efficiency of the system. The usage of D-feature would most certainly improve performance on texts "familiar" to the dictionary, which have very few OOV words. The difference in results between greedy and smart way of using dictionary is not significant – a slight advantage goes to the latter.

Finally, we decided to evaluate the impact of employing our approach for katakana compound segmentation (KAT) within a general morphological analysis system based on a first order Hidden Markov Model (HMM). The testing was performed on the NEWS corpus, which was used in the out-of-domain testing of katakana compound segmentation earlier. The results are presented in table 4.

System configuration	Segmentation F-Measure	Segmentation +Tagging F-Measure
HMM only	93.24%	90.12%
HMM + KAT	93.64%	90.44%

TABLE 4 – The impact of the proposed katakana compound segmentation approach on the performance of a morphological analysis system.

As seen in the table, the overall performance of a morphological analysis system shows a small but notable improvement in overall performance after implementation of our approach for the processing of katakana expressions. While the overall performance itself might not be so high due to the simplicity of the test model (first order dictionary-based HMM), the difference of approx. 0.35% gained on katakana expressions rich with OOV words, cannot be discounted.

Conclusions

In this paper we have presented a new solution for katakana compound segmentation problem. Such characteristics as limited lexicon (only 50 syllables of katakana, instead of thousands of vocabulary words), possibility to implement the model without using any vocabulary data at all (without D-Feature), and a small number of resulting features due to a corresponding regularization technique make our approach very memory-efficient. This simplicity is a great advantage to other existing approaches especially considering the gravity of such problem as katakana decompounding in the overall performance of a morphological analysis system. As a result, our approach can be implemented as a dedicated solution for katakana expression tokenization within a general morphological analysis system of any complexity.

For the future work, we plan to explore the possibility of applying a similar dedicated approach for kanji-based multi-word expression tokenization and POS-tagging.

References

T. Nakazawa, D. Kawahara, and S. Kurohashi. (2005). Automatic acquisition of basic Katakana lexicon from a given corpus. In Proceedings of IJCNLP, pages 682–693.

N. Kaji, M. Kitsuregawa. (2011). Splitting noun compounds via monolingual and bilingual paraphrasing: a study on Japanese katakana words. In Proceedings of EMNLP, pages 959–969.

S. Kurohashi, M. Nagao. (1994). Improvements of Japanese morphological analyzer JUMAN. In Proceedings of the International Workshop on Sharable Natural Language Resources, pages 22–38.

T. Kudo, K. Yamamoto, and Y. Matsumoto. (2004). Applying conditional random fields to Japanese morphological analysis. In Proceedings of EMNLP, pages 230–237.

K. Uchimoto, S. Sekine, and H. Isahara. (2001). The unknown word problem: a morphological analysis of Japanese using maximum entropy aided by a dictionary. In Proceedings Of EMNLP, pages 91–99.

M. Asahara and Y. Matsumoto. (2000). Extended models and tools for high-performance part-of-speech tagger. In Proceedings of COLING, pages 21–27.

G. Neubig, Y. Nakata, S. Mori. (2011). Pointwise Prediction for Robust, Adaptable Japanese Morphological Analysis. In Proceedings of the 49th Annual Meeting of the Association for Computational Linguistics: Human Language Technologies (ACL HLT 2011), pages 529-533.

J. Lafferty, A. McCallum, and F. Pereira. (2001). Conditional random fields: Probabilistic models for segmenting and labeling sequence data. In Intl. Conf. on Machine Learning.

H. T. Ng, J. K. Low. (2004). Chinese Part-of-Speech Tagging: One-at-a-Time or All-at-Once? Word-Based or Character-Based? In EMNLP 9.

D. Vail, J. Lafferty, and M. Veloso. (2007). Feature Selection in Conditional Random Fields for Activity Recognition. IEEE/RSJ International Conference on Intelligent Robots and Systems (IROS).

New Readability Measures for Bangla and Hindi Texts

Manjira Sinha Sakshi Sharma Tirthankar Dasgupta Anupam Basu
Indian Institute of Technology Kharagpur, Kharagpur 721302
manjira87@gmail.com, sakshisharma4u@gmail.com,
iamtirthankar@gmail.com, anupambas@gmail.

ABSTRACT

In this paper we present computational models to compute readability of Indian language text documents. We first demonstrate the inadequacy and the consequent inapplicability of some of the popular readability metrics in English to Hindi and Bangla. Next, we present user experiments to identify important structural parameters of Bangla and Hindi that affect readability of texts in these two languages. Accordingly, we propose two different readability models for each Bangla and Hindi. The models are tested against a second round of user studies with completely new set of data. The results validate the propose models. Compared to the handful of existing works in Hindi and Bangla text readability, this paper presents the first ever definitive readability models for these languages incorporating their salient structural features.

KEYWORDS : Text Readability, Indian Language Texts , Structural Features, Readability Metrics

Proceedings of COLING 2012: Posters, pages 1141–1150,
COLING 2012, Mumbai, December 2012.

1 Introduction

Readability of a text generally refers to how well a reader is able to comprehend the content of a text, through reading. Studies have shown that easy to read texts improve comprehension, retention, reading speed and reading persistence. In this paper we have used the terms readability and comprehensibility interchangeably. Readability is a complex cognitive phenomenon. The cognitive load of a text for a reader depends on the characteristics of a text like lexical choice, syntactic and semantic complexity, discourse level complexity as well as on the background of the user.

The quantitative analysis of English text readability started with L.A. Sherman in 1880 (Sherman, 1893). Till date, English has got over 200 readability metrics. Now there are formulas for Spanish, French, German, Dutch, Swedish, Russian, Hebrew, Chinese, Vietnamese and Korean (Rabin et al., 1988). The existing quantitative approaches towards predicting readability of a text can be broadly classified into three categories (Benjamin, 2012): **traditional methods** incorporate the easy to compute syntactic features of a text like sentence length, paragraph length etc. The examples are Flesch Reading Ease Score (Flesch, 1948), FOG index (Gunning, 1968), Fry graph (Fry, 1968), SMOG (McLaughlin, 1969) etc. The chronologically newer formulas like new Dale-Chall index (Chall, 1995), lexile framework(Stenner, 1996), ATOS-TASA(Learning, 2001), Read-X (Miltsakaki and Troutt, 2007) consider the readers' background and text semantics; **cognitively motivated methods** use high level text parameters like cohesion and cognitive aspects of the reader. Proposition and inference model (Kintsch and Van Dijk, 1978), prototype theory (Rosch, 1978), latent semantic analysis (Landauer et al., 1998), semantic networks (Foltz et al., 1998) are examples of this category. This type of approach introduced text levelling or text revising methods (Kemper, 1983; Britton and Gülgöz, 1991). Two distinguished instances of this class are Coh-metrix (Graesser et al., 2004), and the DeLite software (vor der Brück et al., 2008); the third class of approaches incorporate the power of **machine learning methods** and probabilistic analysis. They are useful in determining online readability based on user queries (Liu et al., 2004) and predicting readability of web texts (Collins-Thompson and Callan, 2005; Collins-Thompson and Callan, 2004; Si and Callan, 2003). Sophisticated machine learning methods like support vector machines have been used to identify grammatical patterns within a text and classification based on it (Heilman et al., 2008).

However, we posit that language plays an important role in the study of readability and the corresponding measures. It has been seen that the first language proficiency increases learning skill and comprehension (Oakland and Lane, 2004). Every language has its own unique properties and any effective metric of readability should be tailored to address language specificities. Some of the specialties of Bangla and Hindi, as compared with English are that these languages are very reach in morphology; they have different grapheme characteristics and their orthography is more phonemic than English; they are head-final and allow free order sentence generation.

Research towards development of readability measures for Bangla and Hindi is still in its infancy. No definitive model of predicting readability in Hindi or Bangla has been proposed in literature yet. Bhagoliwal (1961) applied the Johnson (Johnson and Bond, 1950), Flesch Reading Ease, Farr-Jenkins-Paterson (Farr et al., 1951), and Gunning FOG formulas to 31 short stories in Hindi. In 1965, he examined the features of Hindi typography affecting the legibility of Hindi texts (Bhagoliwal, 1965). Agnihotri and Khanna (1991) applied the classical English formulas to

Hindi textbooks and studied the relative ordering of the predictions against user evaluations. They concluded that along with surface features, readability of a text depends on its linguistic and conceptual organisation. In Bangla, Das and Roychoudhury (2006) studied a miniature model with respect to one parametric and two parametric fits with respect to two structural features of a text: average sentence length and number of syllables per 100 words. Seven paragraphs for seven different texts were used. They found the two-parametric fit as better performer.

In this paper, we first show that the distinguishing features of Bangla and Hindi render the readability models for English untenable for these languages. We next proceed to develop readability indicators for Bangla and Hindi to predict overall difficulty of a text perceived by a native user of the concerned language. Our study is based on the structural features of a text. We have identified three major parameters that contribute to text readability in these languages. Finally we propose two models for each of Bangla (RB1, RB2) and Hindi (RH1, RH2) involving those features.

The organization of the paper is as follows: section 2 defines the features of a text considered in this study, section 3 details the Indian language texts used; section 4 shows the problem of using English readability model in Bangla or Hindi, section 5 deals with the details of user studies and model building. Finally section 6 offers validation and discussion followed by conclusion and perspective.

2 Structural parameters of a text considered in the study

We have considered the following standard structural parameters of a text but customized them to accommodate the specificities of Hindi and Bangla:

1. **Average Sentence Length (ASL):** Total number of words divided by total number of sentences.
2. **Average Word Length (AWL)**: in terms of visual units: Along with dedicated graphemes for consonants and vowels, Bangla and Hindi scripts have some additional graphemes corresponding to the vowel modifiers (diacritic) and consonant conjuncts (jukta-akshars). We consider each kind as a separate visual unit of a word which is equivalent to each alphabet in an English word. The length of a word corresponds to total number of visual units in that word. Average Word Length is equal to total word length divided by number of words.

   Example: शारीरिक = शा + री + रि + क Length = 4

   দিবানিশি=দি + বা+ নি+ শি Length = 4
3. **Average number of Syllables per Word (ASW):** Average number of Syllable per word is equal to total syllable count divided by number of words.
4. **Number of PolySyllabic Words (PSW):** Polysyllabic words are the words whose count of syllable exceeds 2.
5. **Number of PolySyllabic Words per 30 sentences (PSW30):** PSW normalized for 30 sentences.
6. **Number of Jukta-akshars (JUK):** jukta-akshar or consonant-conjunct is consonants occuring together in clusters. When a consonant with a halant (hasanta) is followed by

another consonant, we consider it as one jukta-akshar. The number of jukta-akshars count is the total number jukta-akshars present in the text. The measure is normalized for 50 sentences. Jukta-akshars are not present in English, so the relation between juktakshars and text readability has not been examined before.

Example: साक्षी = स + ◌ा + क + ◌् + ष + ◌ी (jukta-akshars count=1)
শিক্ষা = ◌ি + শ + ক + ◌্ + ষ + ◌া (jukta-akshars count=1)

3 Text selection

Sixteen Hindi and sixteen Bangla texts are selected for the experiment (11 texts) and validation (5 texts) purpose. They cover a broad range of documents types starting from new paper article, short stories, interviews, and blogs to philosophical articles. So we can generalize the model for a variety of text types. Excerpts of length varying from 400 to 1000 words are chosen randomly from the texts to examine the parameters responsible for text readability in case of short as well as long documents. The texts are numbered from 1 to 16 arbitrarily and henceforth will be referred by the text number only.

4 English readability models applied to Hindi and Bangla documents

We have considered the following four models to examine their applicability in Bangla and Hindi, the reason being their high correlation with the established comprehension tests in English (DuBay, 2007; McLaughlin, 1969):

1.	**Flesch Reading Ease** = 206.835 – (1.015 × ASL) – (84.6 × ASW)	3.	**Gunning FOG grade** = 0.4 (ASL+ PSW)
2.	**Flesch-Kincaid Grade-Level** = (0.39× ASL)+(11.8 × ASW)—15.59	4.	**SMOG grading** = 3 + square root of PSW30

TABLE 1-English readability formulas

Although these readability models have been applied to several languages with satisfactory results (Bamberger and Rabin, 1984), in our case, out of bound results are found. As an instance, reading score of Flesch Reading Ease should lie in the range of 0-100, whereas for the Hindi or Bangla texts, its value is more than 150. Grade levels of Flesch-Kincaid Grade Level are not even positive. Grade levels evaluated by Gunning Fog Index and SMOG Index lie far from the expected grades as obtained from user study. The disagreement on the values can be attributed to the significant differences in the language structure of English and Hindi, Bangla as pointed out in introduction. Therefore, we need to start from the scratch in order to develop readability metrics for Bangla and Hindi texts based on structural properties of text.

5 Readability indicator for Bangla and Hindi

As discussed at the end of the previous section, we have developed entirely new readability metrics for Bangla and Hindi based on structural features of a text. In order to achieve this, we have conducted user studies and subsequently built models based on the test results.

5.1.1 Participants

24 native speakers of Hindi and 24 native speakers of Bangla participated in the user studies. Their age group ranges from 24 years to 37 years. 37 of them are from science and engineering background, 10 are from the humanities stream and 1 person is from the commerce stream. 26 of them hold post graduate degrees in their respective fields.

5.1.2 Procedure

Each participant was given the same 16 texts in their native languages in two different sessions: 11 texts during the experiment and 5 texts for the validation. They were asked to rate each on a ten point scale (1=easiest, 10=hardest) depending on its overall comprehension difficulty as perceived by the reader. These results are used to build the readability metrics. Refer to table below (the table contains both experiment and validation texts for sake of convenience):

Text	1	2	3	4	5	6	7	8
Hindi	1.33	5.23	4.44	5.27	3.67	5.21	4.06	4.08
Bangla	3.92	1.54	2.83	1.29	4.23	1.42	2.77	4.83
Text	**9**	**10**	**11**	**12**	**13**	**14**	**15**	**16**
Hindi	5.58	4.65	3.35	3.4	4.67	2.31	3.73	3
Bangla	6.08	5.75	5.92	1.38	2.96	2.29	5.33	5.58

TABLE 2- Average grade by each user

5.1.3 User data analysis

The user data have been analysed statistically. To check the degree of variation of different linguistic features to the evaluation done by the users, the Spearman's rank correlate (Zar, 1998) has been computed between them. Table 3 lists correlation between the features and the user study for the 11 experimental texts:

Feature	Flesch	SMOG	ASL	AWL	ASW	PSW	PSW30	JUK
Hindi	-0.37	0.3	0.4	0.28	0.26	0.21	0.3	0.45
Bangla	-0.76	0.7	0.75	0.8	0.8	0.81	0.75	0.87

TABLE 3-Correlation of textual features, readability scores calculated by Flesch Reading Ease and Smog Index with user evaluation (square-root of PSW30 is omitted as it will have values same as PSW30)

From the above table, it is fairly visible that the best correlated factor with the user's perception of hardness of a text is the number of jukta-akshars present per 50 sentences in the text. There are some interesting findings to be observed. For Hindi the correlation coefficient for ASL is comparatively high but that for ASW is lower. Opposite is the case for Bangla. In both the cases the correlation of user values with the Flesch Reading Ease score is comparatively lower which is based on the assumption that both ASL and ASW are the important factors determining text difficulty. We can see that the assumption does not hold for Bangla or Hindi.

5.2 Feature selection for model building

To make a selection of the features or text parameters that should be incorporated in our models, we have analysed the Spearman' rank correlation among the structural features.

		Bangla					
		ASL	AWL	ASW	PSW	PSW30	JUK
Hindi	ASL		0.53	0.55	0.58	0.91	0.79
	AWL	0.32		0.93	0.75	0.71	0.69
	ASW	0.24	0.85		0.86	0.76	0.79
	PSW	0.48	0.04	0.28		0.74	0.86
	PSW30	0.84	0.51	0.55	0.67		0.92
	JUK	0.83	0.57	0.32	0.34	0.72	

TABLE 4- correlation among structural features of a text for Bangla and Hindi (square-root of PSW30 is omitted as it will have values same as PSW30)

From table 3, we can see that for Hindi, the four mostly correlated text parameters are JUK, ASL, PSW30 and AWL and for Bangla these are JUK, PSW, ASW/AWL and ASL. From 4, we can see that in case of Hindi, ASL and AWL as well as AWL and JUK are loosely correlated (below 0.8), so we have to consider all three in our model as any one of them cannot well represent the trend for the others. PSW30 will anyway be checked while calculating SMOG equivalence. For Bangla, table 4 shows that except for ASW and PSW, the correlation among JUK, PSW, ASL and AWL is less (below 0.8). Therefore, we have to consider all four of them for the same reason as described in case of Hindi.

5.3 Model Building

We have used regression analysis (Montgomery et al., 2007) for model building. In the previous section, we have identified some text parameters which seem as important contributors towards the comprehensibility of a text; we have checked each parameter to obtain an optimized model while giving preference to those. We have used Coefficient of determination[1] or R^2 and Estimate of the error varience (EEV)[2] as measures of goodness of fit of a model. The table 5 below document the short-listed Models (including Flesch (Model 1) and SMOG (Model 2) equivalence) in Hindi and Bangla for which the fittings are optimal from each category.

Model	Expression	R^2	*EEV*
Hindi			
Model 1	-3.72+0.078*ASL+3.36*ASW	0.35	1.19
Model 2	2.26 + 0.19 * sqrt(PSW30)	0.25	Not calculated

[1] http://en.wikipedia.org/wiki/Coefficient_of_determination
[2] http://en.wikipedia.org/wiki/Mean_squared_error

Model 3	-2.34+2.14*AWL+0.01*PSW	0.44	1.02
Model 4	0.211+1.37*AWL+.005*JUK	0.36	1.17
Model 5	2.78-0.21*ASL+0.03*PSW+0.01*JUK	0.50	1.07
Model 6	-2.94+.01*PSW+2.77*ASW+.01*JUK	0.46	1.13
Bangla			
Model 1	-10.4+.11*ASL+5.22*ASW	0.58	1.77
Model 2	0.44*sqrt(PSW30) -1.79	0.53	Not Calculated
Model 3	-5.23+1.43*AWL+.01*PSW	0.80	0.82
Model 4	1.15+.02*JUK-.01*PSW30	0.67	1.40
Model 5	5.37+.01*PSW-2.29*ASW+.01*JUK	0.83	0.83
Model 6	5.71+.18*ASL-1.49*ASW+.01*PSW	0.83	0.84

TABLE 5- First round of readability metrics for Bangla and Hindi

6 Validation and Discussion

To carry out the validation study we took the same 24 users for Bangla and 24 users for Hindi and a completely new set of 5 texts for each of the two languages. The users were asked to perform the same operations on each text as described in the Procedure part. We have applied our 6 shortlisted readability models (refer Table 5) to the validation texts. The comparative analysis of prediction made by our readability models to the actual scores given by the users are summarized below. From the results it can be inferred clearly that root mean square errors for model 3 and model 4 stand out as the bottoms among their respective groups. So, we propose these two models as our readability metric for Bangla and Hindi.

		Model 1	Model 2	Model 3	Model 4	Model 5	Model 6
RMSE(square-root(MSE))	**Hindi**	1.086	1.085	1.04	0.81	2.06	2.23
	Bangla	1.32	1.19	0.85	1.13	1.19	3.51

TABLE 6- Summary of validation results

One interesting thing to be noted here, although the two selected models are the two top fits for both Bangla and Hindi, model 3 in Bangla is the best fit whereas, model 4 is the best fit for Hindi. Model 3 in both the cases comprise of AWL and PSW, but for Hindi model 4 has AWL and JUK, whereas for Bangla it consists of JUK and PSW30. These once again prove our initial assumptions that for different language, different textual features contribute to readability and an effective readability indicator is language dependent.

We name the two models for Hindi as RH1 (model 3), RH2 (model4) and for Bangla they are RB1 (model 3), RB2 (model 4). The figure 1 below graphically represents the comparison of user scores with that of the proposed model for Hindi and Bangla; the straight lines represent the trendlines of the respective curves. We can see that in both cases, the models closely follow the users' response curves. The models differ very slightly in accuracy and they feature different text parameters, so, any model alone may not suffice to correctly predict text difficulty. Therefore, we have decided to keep both the models as measure of how the three different structural dimensions of a text contribute to its comprehensibility.

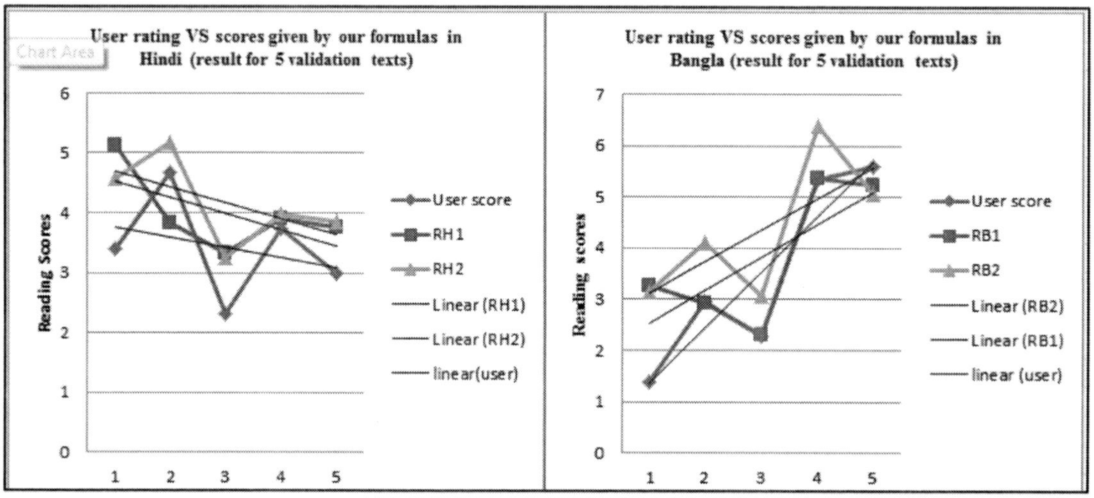

Figure 1: Graph representing the predicted scores versus user evaluation

Conclusion and perspective

In this study, we have developed two new readability measures: RH1, RH2 and RB1, RB2 for Hindi and Bangla text documents respectively. We have also identified AWL, PSW, JUK and PSW30 as major factors affecting readability in Hindi and Bangla. We have shown that for these languages, English readability formulas are not helpful as text difficulty. The two previous studies in Hindi (Bhagoliwai, 1961; Bhagoliwal, 1965; Agnihotri and Khanna, 1991) have applied English readability formulas like Flesch on Hindi passages and school level textbooks, but none of them proposed any definitive model for Hindi text readability like ours. In case of Bangla readability (Das and Roychoudhury, 2006) have compared one and two parametric fits for a miniature model, but they have not considered parameters like AWL, JUK; we have found these parameters to be the major players. The proposed readability models for Bangla and Hindi incorporating features like AWL, JUK have been validated against extensive user studies. In future, we plan to extend this work to different sections of users to obtain readability models, more appropriately related to different user groups.

References

Agnihotri, R. K. and Khanna, A. L. (1991). Evaluating the readability of school textbooks: An indian study. Journal of Reading, 35(4):pp. 282–288.

Bamberger, R. and Rabin, A. T. (1984). New approaches to readability: Austrian research. The Reading Teacher, 37(6):pp. 512–519.

Benjamin, R. (2012). Reconstructing readability: Recent developments and recommendations in the analysis of text difficulty. Educational Psychology Review, 24:1–26.

Bhagoliwal, B. (1961). Readability formulae: Their reliability, validity and applicability in hindi. Journal of Education and Psychology, 19:13–26.

Bhagoliwal, B. (1965). Typographic dimensions affecting the legibility of hindi print: a factorial experiment. Journal of Education and Psychology.

Britton, B. and Gülgöz, S. (1991). Using kintsch's computational model to improve instructional text: Effects of repairing inference calls on recall and cognitive structures. Journal of Educational Psychology, 83(3):329.

Chall, J. (1995). Readability revisited: The new Dale-Chall readability formula, volume 118. Brookline Books Cambridge, MA.

Collins-Thompson, K. and Callan, J. (2004). A language modeling approach to predicting reading difficulty. In Proceedings of HLT/NAACL, volume 4.

Collins-Thompson, K. and Callan, J. (2005). Predicting reading difficulty with statistical language models. Journal of the American Society for Information Science and Technology, 56(13):1448–1462.

Das, S. and Roychoudhury, R. (2006). Readability modelling and comparison of one and two parametric fit: A case study in bangla*. Journal of Quantitative Linguistics, 13(01):17–34.

DuBay, W. (2007). Smart Language: Readers, Readability, and the Grading of Text. ERIC.

Farr, J., Jenkins, J., and Paterson, D. (1951). Simplification of flesch reading ease formula. Journal of applied psychology, 35(5):333.

Flesch, R. (1948). A new readability yardstick. Journal of applied psychology, 32(3):221.

Foltz, P., Kintsch, W., and Landauer, T. (1998). The measurement of textual coherence with latent semantic analysis. Discourse processes, 25(2-3):285–307.

Fry, E. (1968). A readability formula that saves time. Journal of reading, 11(7):513–578.

Graesser, A., McNamara, D., Louwerse, M., and Cai, Z. (2004). Coh-metrix: Analysis of text on cohesion and language. Behavior Research Methods, 36(2):193–202.

Gunning, R. (1968). The technique of clear writing. McGraw-Hill NewYork, NY.

Heilman, M., Collins-Thompson, K., and Eskenazi, M. (2008). An analysis of statistical models and features for reading difficulty prediction. In Proceedings of the Third Workshop on Innovative Use of NLP for Building Educational Applications, pages 71–79. Association for Computational Linguistics.

Johnson, R. and Bond, G. (1950). Reading ease of commonly used tests. Journal of Applied Psychology, 34(5):319.

Kemper, S. (1983). Measuring the inference load of a text. Journal of educational psychology, 75(3):391.

Kintsch, W. and Van Dijk, T. (1978). Toward a model of text comprehension and production. Psychological review, 85(5):363.

Landauer, T., Foltz, P., and Laham, D. (1998). An introduction to latent semantic analysis. Discourse processes, 25(2-3):259–284.

Learning, R. (2001). The atos readability formula for books and how it compares to other formulas. Madison, WI: School Renaissance Institute.

Liu, X., Croft, W., Oh, P., and Hart, D. (2004). Automatic recognition of reading levels from user queries. In Proceedings of the 27th annual international ACM SIGIR conference on Research and development in information retrieval, pages 548–549. ACM.

McLaughlin, G. (1969). Smog grading: A new readability formula. Journal of reading, 12(8):639–646.

Miltsakaki, E. and Troutt, A. (2007). Read-x: Automatic evaluation of reading difficulty of web text. In Proceedings of E-Learn.

Montgomery, D., Peck, E., and Vining, G. (2007). Introduction to linear regression analysis, volume 49. John Wiley & Sons.

Oakland, T. and Lane, H. (2004). Language, reading, and readability formulas: Implications for developing and adapting tests. International Journal of Testing, 4(3):239–252.

Rabin, A., Zakaluk, B., and Samuels, S. (1988). Determining difficulty levels of text written in languages other than english. Readability: Its past, present & future. Newark DE: International Reading Association, pages 46–76.

Rosch, E. (1978). Principles of categorization. Fuzzy grammar: a reader, pages 91–108.

Sherman, L. (1893). Analytics of literature: A manual for the objective study of english poetry and prose. Boston: Ginn.

Si, L. and Callan, J. (2003). A semisupervised learning method to merge search engine results. ACM Transactions on Information Systems (TOIS), 21(4):457–491.

Stenner, A. (1996). Measuring reading comprehension with the lexile framework.

vor der Brück, T., Helbig, H., Leveling, J., and Kommunikationssysteme, I. (2008). The Readability Checker Delite: Technical Report. FernUniv., Fak. für Mathematik und Informatik.

Zar, J. (1998). Spearman rank correlation. Encyclopedia of Biostatistics.

Automatic question generation in multimedia-based learning

Yvonne SKALBAN[1], *Le An HA*[1], *Lucia SPECIA*[2], *Ruslan MITKOV*[1]
(1) UNIVERSITY OF WOLVERHAMPTON, Stafford Street, Wolverhampton, WV1 1LY, UK
(2)UNIVERSITY OF SHEFFIELD, 211 Portobello, Sheffield, S1 4DP, UK
Yvonne.Skalban@wlv.ac.uk

Ha.L.A@wlv.ac.uk

l.specia@dcs.shef.ac.uk

R.Mitkov@wlv.ac.uk

ABSTRACT

We investigate whether questions generated automatically by two Natural Language Processing (NLP) based systems (one developed by the authors, the other a state-of-the-art system) can successfully be used to assist multimedia-based learning. We examine the feasibility of using a Question Generation (QG) system's output as pre-questions; with different types of pre-questions used: text-based and with images. We also compare the psychometric parameters of the automatically generated questions by the two systems and of those generated manually. Specifically, we analyse the effect such pre-questions have on test-takers' performance on a comprehension test about a scientific video documentary. We also compare the discrimination power of the questions generated automatically against that of questions generated manually. The results indicate that the presence of pre-questions (preferably with images) improves the performance of test-takers. They indicate that the psychometric parameters of the questions generated by our system are comparable if not better than those of the state-of-the-art system.

KEYWORDS: Automatic question generation, question evaluation, psychometric parameters

Proceedings of COLING 2012: Posters, pages 1151–1160,
COLING 2012, Mumbai, December 2012.

1 Introduction

Questions are an integral part of teachers' instructional activities. Teachers spend between 35% to 50% of their instructional time conducting questioning sessions (Cotton, 2001). Research in education (Hamilton, 1985; Klauer, 1984; Rothkopf, 1982; Hamaker, 1986; Anderson & Biddle, 1975) has shown that pre-questions, i.e. questions which are supplied to test-takers before receiving learning material, can have beneficial effects on student learning in reading activities. Pre-questions can help focus learners' attention on the learning material targeted by the questions and they also increase the learning effect through repetition (Thalheimer, 2003). The manual creation of questions is time-consuming and requires the knowledge of domain experts. Research in Natural Language Processing (NLP), indicates that systems for Question Generation (QG) can assist teachers in this laborious task, thus saving time and resources. Semi-automatic QG systems can produce test questions up to 4 times faster than a human expert, without compromising quality (Mitkov et. al, 2006). In this experiment, we examine whether the questions produced by our system can be successfully used as pre-questions and thus support creators of assessment materials. Two different types of pre-questions are investigated: text-based and with supporting image. This experiment also serves to test whether pre-questions have a beneficial effect in combination with audio-visual learning material as opposed to reading material; we analyse the effect pre-questions have on test-takers' performance on a comprehension test about a scientific video documentary. We also examine whether or not questions generated automatically (by two systems) have the same psychometric parameters as those generated manually. The psychometric parameters of questions, such as their discrimination power, are among the most important measures of the quality of the questions.

2 Related Work

QG has frequently been employed in educational contexts. Applications include systems which automatically create learning resources such as multiple-choice question (MCQ) tests (Mitkov, 2003, Mitkov et. al., 2006), vocabulary exercises (Brown et. al., 2005, Hoshino and Nakagawa, 2007), as well as solutions which promote reading comprehension (Feeney and Heilman, 2008; Gates, 2008). QG systems help promote student learning by providing learning content and forms of assessment which allow for convenient and fast evaluation of student performance. Several systems have been developed to automatically generate questions from texts using NLP techniques, with a system developed by Heilman (2011) showcasing the state-of-the-art. The system generates questions from reading material for educational practice and assessment using existing tools such as the Stanford parser (Klein and Manning, 2003), Tregex expressions for T-Surgeon (Levy and Andrew, 2006), and BBN Identifinder (Bikel, et. al., 1998). The QG process follows several stages. Firstly, sentences are simplified by removing certain discourse markers and adjunct modifiers and by breaking sentences down into clauses. Next, pronoun resolution is performed using the ARKref coreference system (Heilman, 2011). A complex set of transformational rules implemented in Tregex is then used to form *who*, *what*, *where*, *when* and *how much* questions from declarative statements. Since one sentence in the source text can give rise to a number of questions, the questions are statistically ranked in terms of quality before being displayed to the user.

3 Methodology

This section describes the author's QG system and the experimental setup and execution of the in-class experiment.

3.1 A QG system for documentary videos

The QG system we developed employs existing NLP tools (GATE, Cunningham, et. al., 2002) for pre-processing and a rule-based approach to generate factual questions from documentary videos, utilizing the subtitles accompanying a documentary. Several of GATE's processing resources (PRs) are employed to pre-process the subtitles; steps include tokenization, sentence splitting, POS tagging, dependency parsing, NE recognition, gazetteer look-up, morphological analysis and co-reference resolution. The PRs enrich the text with linguistic information in the form of annotations, which is exploited in the subsequent steps. Pronoun resolution is performed, based on information provided by GATE's pronominal co-referencer. First-mention pronouns are replaced with the longest co-referent in the co-reference chain. In independent clauses in compound sentences, not only first-mention pronouns, but all subject personal pronouns are replaced with their co-referents. Then the compound sentences are split into several sentences with initial conjunctions deleted. Next, several transformational rules, written in a GATE-specific format (JAPE), are applied. These rules consist of a left hand side (LHS), which is used to match a pattern in a GATE corpus (in our case subtitles) and a right hand side (RHS) which is used to perform actions and to manipulate the text and parse trees. We distinguish between question rules and helper rules. Question rules are used to identify question candidates in the source text. By using the linguistic information made available in the pre-processing steps and the application of syntactic transformations (such as WH-movement and subject-auxiliary inversion) declarative sentences are transformed into questions. Currently, six types of 'wh-questions' can be generated: questions about persons (*who*, *whom*), temporal questions (*when*), questions about possessives (*whose*), location questions (*where*) and questions about inanimate entities (*what*). It has been designed to work with video subtitles, and as a result, is able to explore their unique attribute: each utterance has a time-stamp. These time-stamps can be used to link the texts with their relevant video section. In this experiment, we use this feature to extract relevant screenshots for the questions.

3.2 Definitions

Pre-questions are supplied to test-takers before receiving learning material (here: the documentary video). Pre-questions are non-scoring and do not require an answer. Pre-questions can be text-only or can be accompanied by a relevant image. In this experiment, images are screenshots extracted from the video.

Post-questions are presented to the test-takers after receiving learning material (here: after watching a documentary). Post-questions are generated either manually by a human expert or automatically. The post-questions employed in this experiment are short answer style questions.

System A is the QG system designed by the authors, as described in section .

System B is the QG system developed by Heilman (2011). Its methodology is explained in section 2.

3.3 Research questions

The aim of the experiment is to answer the following research questions:

1. a) Whether the presence of text-based pre-questions helps test-takers to answer post-questions more accurately (i.e. more questions are answered correctly).

   b) Whether the presence of pre-questions *with screenshots extracted from the video* helps the test-takers to answer post-questions more accurately.

2. a) Whether the presence of text-based pre-questions affects the time taken to answer post-questions.

   b) Whether the presence of pre-questions *with screenshots extracted from the video* affects the time taken to answer post-questions.

3. What are the psychometric parameters of questions generated by system A when compared to system B and manually generated questions?

3.4 Selection of system-generated post-questions

Due to the nature of their QG approach, both QG systems produced more questions (A: 139, B: 567) than required for the experiment. Only 9 questions were needed from each method for the participants to complete the experiment in approximately one hour. As system B uses certain heuristics to output questions ranked in terms of quality, the top 3 questions corresponding to the respective parts of the video were selected for use in the experiment. From system A's pool of questions, 3 questions per part were selected by a human expert.

3.5 Generation and selection of human-generated questions

The manually generated questions were obtained from a high school teacher of English and Media. The teacher was given access to the documentary video and a transcript and was asked to produce comprehension questions that they would also use in their classroom were they to utilize this video in one of their teaching sessions. The teacher was also instructed to generate the questions in such a way that they could be answered solely with information from the video and did not require any additional knowledge. The human expert generated 22 questions in about 80 minutes, 9 of which were selected for the experiment at random.

3.6 Selection of pre-questions

For the first two hypotheses, the focus is on whether or not pre-questions help the performance of test-takers, rather than the generation method of pre-questions. As a result, pre-questions were selected manually from system A's pool of generated questions. Pre-questions were selected based on two premises. Firstly, a question was deemed a suitable pre-question if it revolved around an important concept in the documentary. Secondly, a question was selected as a pre-question if the same or a similar question was also generated by one or more of the other systems. For example, the question "What is nuclear fusion?" was selected as a pre-question because it revolves around a central concept in the documentary. In addition, the same question was generated by the human expert. An example for similar questions generated by all three methods can be seen in Table 1. The development of automatic selection methods for pre-questions and their evaluation will be left to future research.

System A	What did some scientists suspect that Rusi Taleyarkhan's fusion neutrons could in fact be coming from?	From his own neutron generator
System B	What did Mike Saltmarsh think that any fusion finding could be explained by?	From the pulse neutron generator
Manual	What did the other scientists criticise about Taleyarkhan's first experiment?	Other scientists criticised that the neutrons detected in the experiment might be background neutrons from the neutron generator.

TABLE 1 Questions with similar content generated by all three QG methods

3.7 Selection of images

The screenshots are extracted using the following process. After questions have been generated, the source sentence of a question (i.e. the sentence which gave rise to a question) is mapped to the time stamp contained in the subtitles. Then a screenshot is taken from the video at the respective time a source sentence occurs in the video. For example, the sentence "It was Mike Saltmarsh's task to work out whether the neutrons detected could indeed be from fusion or were simply background neutrons from the neutron generator" which occurred 29 minutes and 15 seconds into the video gave rise to the first question and screenshot in Table 2.

Whose task was to work out whether the neutrons detected could indeed be from fusion or were simply background neutrons from the neutron generator?	Mike Saltmarsh	
What should be produced at exactly the same billionth of a second if fusion was happening?	Fusion neutrons	
What is nuclear fusion?	A nuclear reaction in which atoms are forced together until they fuse, giving off massive amounts of heat, light and energy.	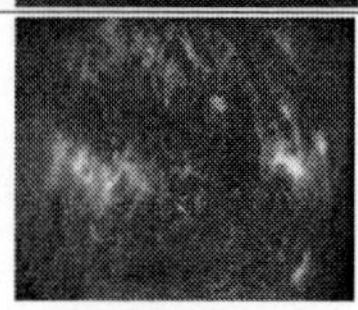

TABLE 2 Pre-questions with screenshots extracted from the video

3.8 Participants and interface

29 students took part in the experiment. All participants were final year undergraduate students at a university Spain reading translation with a major in English. The participants had access to the experiment via an online interface[1]. Instructions for the experiment (e.g. note-taking was allowed, but participants should watch the video only once) were displayed in the interface. The interface provided access to the video and tracked each participant's answers and time spent to answer each question.

[1] The experiment can be accessed at: http://www.bootlace.eu/quiz/randq/

3.9 Procedure

The video used was a documentary on 'nuclear fusion' (Horizon, 2005). The experiment consisted of three parts, each corresponding to a 10-minute section of the documentary. The participants were divided into three groups. Before each part of the video was shown, participants were given either three pre-questions containing a screenshot extracted from the video, three text-only pre-questions or no pre-questions, depending on their group (cf. Table 3). After each part of the video, the students were asked to answer nine comprehension questions (post-questions) about what they had just seen in the video. Three of those questions had been generated by system A, three by system B and three by a human expert. The post-questions were identical for all participants. This group scenario was used in order to eliminate the problem of cross group performance comparison and cross-question performance comparison.

	Group 1	Group 2	Group 3
Part 1	Pre-questions + screenshots	Pre-questions no screenshots	No pre-questions
Part 2	Pre-questions no screenshots	No pre-questions	Pre-questions + screenshots
Part 3	No pre-questions	Pre-questions + screenshots	Pre-questions no screenshots

TABLE 3 Pre-question scenarios

4 Results

4.1 Answering research question 1: accuracy

Firstly, a χ^2 test of independence was used to determine whether the performance across the groups differed significantly; there was no evidence to suggest so. Table 4 shows the breakdown of correctly and incorrectly answered post-questions for each pre-question type (Q_{np}=no pre-questions, Q_{tp}=text-based pre-questions, Q_{sp}=pre-questions with screenshots). Due to time constraints, not all test-takers answered all questions, which is the reason for the total number of questions answered varying for each pre-question type. Proportionally, the highest number of correctly answered questions is observed where test-takers were given pre-questions with screenshots, followed by text-based pre-questions. Test-takers who did not receive any pre-questions at all produced the smallest proportion of correct answers.

Pre-question type	Correct	Incorrect	Total	% correct
Q_{np}	75	113	188	39.83
Q_{tp}	86	85	171	50.29
Q_{sp}	84	60	144	58.33
(Q_{tp}+Q_{sp})	(170)	(145)	(315)	(53.97)

TABLE 4 Breakdown of correct and incorrect answers per pre-question type

A χ^2 test was performed to determine whether these results are statistically significant. When comparing the performance of students who did not receive pre-questions (Q_{np}) to the performance of students who received only text-based pre-questions (Q_{tp}), the result is statistically significant (p= 0.047). The same applies when the performance of students who did not receive pre-questions is compared with that of students who that received pre-questions with screenshots (Q_{sp}); we observed a better statistically significant difference (p=0.00085). When text-based pre-questions and pre-questions with screenshots are grouped together ($Q_{tp}+Q_{sp}$) and compared to no pre-questions (Q_{np}), the result is also statistically significant (p=0.00225). However, when comparing the performance of students who received text-based pre-questions with that of those who received pre-questions with screenshots, we found no statistically significant difference (p=0.1537). We can thus conclude that test-takers who receive pre-questions (with or without image) tend to perform better on a comprehension test than those who receive no pre-questions at all. Supplying a screenshot alongside a pre-question results in a more significant difference of correctly answered questions when compared to text-based pre-questions.

4.2 Answering research question 2: time taken to answer post-questions

For each test taker, the time to answer a question was measured. We hypothesized that the presence of pre-questions would affect the time taken to answer post-questions. We observed that the highest mean value (cf. Table 5) occurred in the pre-questions with screenshots condition (Q_{sp}), followed by text-based pre-questions (Q_{tp}). The lowest average time required to answer a question was observed in the no pre-questions condition (Q_{np}). However, there appears to be no significant difference between the means of the different conditions, which is confirmed by a single-factor analysis of variance. We can thus conclude that the presence of pre-questions, with or without screenshot, does not affect the time taken to answer post-questions.

	Min t in s	Max t in s	Mean	SD
Q_{np}	2	237	53.26	44.38
Q_{tp}	3	403	54.84	55.07
Q_{sp}	5	306	58.57	46.49

TABLE 5 Seconds taken to answer post-questions depending on pre-question type

4.3 Answering research questions 3: psychometric parameters

Classical test theory can provide information about the effectiveness of a question (also referred to as 'item'). One measure is item discriminating power (DP) (Gronlund, 1982). DP describes the relationship between student performance on a particular item and their total exam score. DP ranges from -1.0 to 1.0; the higher the value, the more discriminating the item. A high DP means that test takers with overall high scores answered the item correctly, whereas test takers who performed poorly overall did not answer the item correctly. On the converse, a low DP indicates that poorly performing test takers answered an item correctly whereas test takers with overall high scores did not answer an item correctly; this means that the item may be confusing for better scoring test takers. Items with near zero or negative DP should not be used for assessment. To calculate DP, test results need to be ranked from highest to lowest score. Two equal-sized groups are formed, the 'upper group' containing the tests with the highest scores, and the 'lower group' containing those with the lowest scores. DP is calculated as follows:

$$DP = \frac{R_U - R_L}{\frac{1}{2}P}$$

Where DP is the discriminating power, R_U is the number of right answers from the upper group, R_L is the number of right answers from the lower group, P is the number of total participants. The results for the discriminating power for the three QG methods can be seen in Table 6.

	Min	Max	Mean DP
System A	-0.15	0.44	0.16
System B	-0.22	0.22	0.07
Manual	0.15	0.59	0.37

TABLE 6 Discriminating powers for all three QG methods

The manually created questions exhibit the highest average DP, followed by system A and lastly system B. The application of Student's t-test shows that there is a statistically significant difference between system A's mean DP and the manual questions' mean DP (p=0.0434). The same applies when comparing system B's mean DP to that of the manual questions. However, no statistically significant difference could be observed between system A's and system B's mean DPs (p=0.356988). While this means that neither automatic system's questions are as good as questions generated by human experts at distinguishing between well and poorly performing students, it also means that system A's questions are as good as, if not better than, those generated by the state-of-the-art system.

Conclusion and directions for future research

Our findings show that both text-based pre-questions and pre-questions with images lead to a larger number of correctly answered post-questions (as opposed to using no pre-questions). Supplying a screenshot alongside a pre-question will result in a statistically more significant difference of correctly answered questions when comparing to no pre-questions. The ability to supply a screenshot alongside a question is unique to our system. The average time taken to answer a question is not statistically significantly different between the pre-question settings. We analysed whether questions generated by our system have a discriminating power (DP), comparable to that of questions generated by human experts and a state-of-the-art system. We found that manually created questions exhibit the highest DP and there is no statistically significant difference between our system and the state-of-the-art system, implying that questions generated by our system are as good as, if not better than, questions generated by the state-of-the-art system. A number of issues need to be addressed in future research. The feasibility of automatically or semi-automatically choosing pre-questions needs to be explored. Furthermore, we aim to investigate whether other images taken from other sources (e.g. Google Image search) can also be used in pre-questions. A large-scale experiment investigating the productivity of generating questions (time taken to post-edit questions vs. time taken to generate questions from scratch) is planned.

References

Anderson, R. C., & Biddle, W. B. (1975). On asking people questions about what they are reading. In G. H. Bower (Ed.) *The psychology of learning and motivation: Advances in research and theory* (Vol. 9). New York: Academic Press.

Bikel, D., Schwartz, R., Weischedel, R. (1999). An Algorithm that Learns what's in a Name. *Machine Learning- Special Issue on NL Learning*, 34, 1–3.

Brown, J.C., Frishkoff, G.A, Eskenazi, M. (2005). *Automatic question generation for vocabulary assessment.* In Proceedings of the Conference on Human Language Technology and Empirical Methods in Natural Language Processing. Vancouver, Canada, 2005.

Cotton, K. (2001). *Classroom questioning.* School Improvement Research Series.

Cunningham, H., Maynard, D., Bontcheva, K., Tablan, V. (2002). *GATE: A Framework and Graphical Development Environment for Robust NLP Tools and Applications.* Proceedings of the 40th Anniversary Meeting of the Association for Computational Linguistics (ACL'02). Philadelphia, July 2002.

Dantonio, M. (2001). Developing effective teacher questioning practices. *Learning to Question, Questioning to Learn*, 1, 6-10.

Feeney, C. and Heilman, M. (2008). *Automatically generating and validating reading-check questions.* In Proc. of the Young Researcher's Track. Ninth International Conference on Intelligent Tutoring Systems.

Gates, D. M. (2008). *Generating reading comprehension look-back strategy questions from expository texts.* Master's thesis, Carnegie Mellon University.

Hamaker, C. (1986). The effects of adjunct questions on prose learning. *Review of Educational Research*, 56, 212-242.

Hamilton, R. J. (1985). A framework for the evaluation of the effectiveness of adjunct questions and objectives. *Review of Educational Research*, 55, 47-85.

Heilman, M. (2011). *Automatic Factual Question Generation from Text.* Ph.D. Dissertation, Carnegie Mellon University. B-LTI-11-004.

Horizon (2005). [online]. Accessed 30/05/2012 < http://www.bbc.co.uk/iplayer>.

Klein, D., Manning, C. (2003). *Fast Exact Inference with a Factored Model for Natural Language Parsing.* In Advances in Neural Information Processing Systems 15 (NIPS 2002), 3-10, Cambridge, MA.

Levy, R., Galen, A. (2006). *Tregex and Tsurgeon: tools for querying and manipulating tree data structures.* Proceedings of LREC 2006.

Mitkov, R. and Ha, L. A. (2003). *Computer-Aided Generation of Multiple-Choice Tests.* In Proceedings of the HLT-NAACL 2003 Workshop on Building Educational Applications Using Natural Language Processing. Edmonton, Canada, 2003.

Mitkov, R., Ha, L. A., Karamanis, N. (2006). A computer-aided environment for generating multiple-choice test items. *Natural Language Engineering*, 12(2), pp.177-94.

Hoshino, A., Nakagawa, H. (2007). *Assisting cloze test making with a web application.* In Proceedings of Society for Information Technology and Teacher Education International Conference. Chesapeake, VA, 2007. AACE.

Rothkopf, E. Z. (1982). *Adjunct aids and the control of mathemagenic activities during purposeful reading.* In W. Otto & S. White (Eds.) Reading expository material. New York: Academic Press.

Thalheimer, W. (2003). *The learning benefits of questions.* [online]. Accessed 30/08/2012. <http://www.learningadvantage.co.za/pdfs/questionmark/LearningBenefitsOfQuestions.pdf>.

A More Cohesive Summarizer

Christian Smith[1], *Henrik Danielsson*[1], *Arne Jönsson*[1]
(1) Santa Anna IT Research Institute AB, Linköping, Sweden
christian.smith@liu.se, henrik.danielsson@liu.se, arnjo@ida.liu.se

Abstract

We have developed a cohesive extraction based single document summarizer (COHSUM) based on coreference links in a document. The sentences providing the most references to other sentences and that other sentences are referring to, are considered the most important and are therefore extracted. Additionally, before evaluations of summary quality, a corpus analysis was performed on the original documents in the dataset in order to investigate the distribution of coreferences. The quality of the summaries is evaluated in terms of content coverage and cohesion. Content coverage is measured by comparing the summaries to manually created gold standards and cohesion is measured by calculating the amount of broken and intact coreferences in the summary compared to the original texts. The summarizer is compared to the summarizers from DUC 2002 and a baseline consisting of the first 100 words. The results show that COHSUM, aimed only at maintaining a cohesive text, performed better regarding text cohesion compared to the other summarizers and on par with the other summarizers and the baseline regarding content coverage.

Keywords: Summarization, Coreference resolution, Cohesion.

Proceedings of COLING 2012: Posters, pages 1161–1170,
COLING 2012, Mumbai, December 2012.

1 Introduction

Extraction based summarizers are often prone to create texts that are fragmented, where sentences are extracted without considering the context, resulting in for instance broken anaphoric references. As pointed out by Nenkova (2006), the linguistic quality of automatically generated summaries can be improved a lot. For current popular measures summarizers often score relatively well on measures regarding content coverage that incorporates a comparison to humanly created gold standard summaries. The cohesiveness of the summaries is often left out in the evaluations since the measures favor inclusion of certain information, disregarding how well the text fits together. Brandow et al. (1995) revealed that summaries of news articles consisting only of the lead sentences are difficult to beat; when it comes to newspaper articles this type of summary fits well since the structure of the text is built around first presenting the gist in the lead sentences and then focusing the rest of the article on elaborating the information. These texts will of course also be cohesive since the sentences are extracted in the order they were written.

Barzilay and Elhadad (1999) proposed to improve cohesion in summaries by using lexical chains to decide which sentences to extract and Bergler et al. (2003) used coreference chains. Other attempts propose the use of a variety of revisions to the text based on cohesion and discourse relations (Mani et al., 1998; Otterbacher et al., 2002) or using both revisions and lexical chains (Alonso i Alemany and Fuentes Fort, 2003). Such approaches require a thesaurus, e.g. WordNet (Barzilay and Elhadad, 1999). Boguraev and Neff (2000) show that cohesion can be improved by utilizing lexical repetition. Coreference information has also been used, for instance, for creating summaries with a focus on answering queries on a text (Baldwin and Morton, 1998).

Pitler et al. (2010) attempted to develop and validate methods for automatic evaluation of linguistic quality in text summarization. They concluded that the topics of Referential clarity and Structure/Coherence seems to be most important when dealing with extraction based single document summarization. Furthermore, anaphoric expressions are important for a text's cohesion (Mani et al., 1998). Errors regarding broken anaphoric references are, however, common in extraction based summaries, especially (not surprisingly) in short summaries (Kaspersson et al., 2012), and in particular for summarizers that focus on content coverage and disregard how sentences are related to each other.

In this paper, we focus on cohesion and referential clarity, creating summaries that hopefully are more readable in that they maintain text cohesion. This can be contrasted to summarizers that are focused only on extracting the most important information in the text, without taking into account cohesion e.g. (DUC, 2002; Smith and Jönsson, 2011b; Chatterjee and Mohan, 2007; Hassel and Sjöbergh, 2007; Gong, 2001; Mihalcea and Tarau, 2004). Such summarizers have performed well when compared to gold standards, the studies lack however results on how cohesive the summaries are. The hypothesis is that a summarizer focused on creating a cohesive text without regarding content coverage will score well on cohesive measures while scoring worse at measures aimed at summary content, and vice versa.

2 Coreferences in Newspaper Texts

Coreferences are commonly used as a feature when evaluating cohesion and coherence (Graesser et al., 2004; Pitler et al., 2010) and we therefore conducted experiments on the distribution of coreferences in summaries. We analyzed the 533 news paper texts used for single text summarization at the 2002 Document Understanding Conference (DUC, 2002). The original documents were

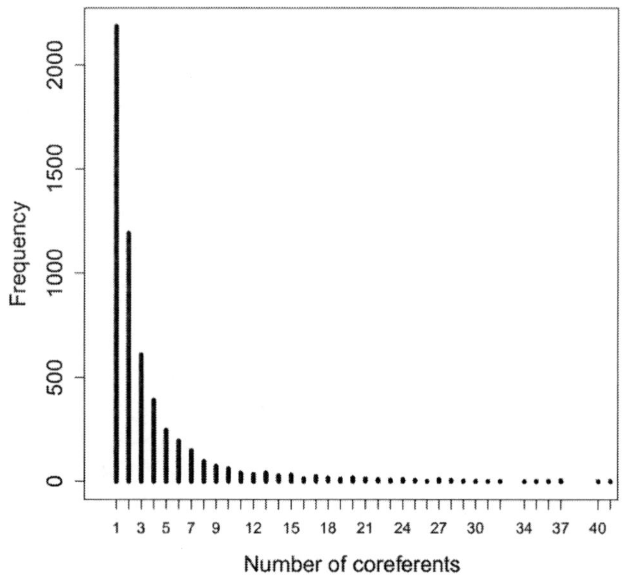

Figure 1: Frequency of the number of coreferents. The X-axis depicts the number of coreferents. The Y-axis shows the frequency for each number of coreferents for all 533 news paper texts. For example, most of the coreferents are between two sentences (one representative mention and one refererent).

tagged for coreference using the Stanford CoreNLP package (Lee et al., 2011)[1]. The coreference resolution system first extracts mentions together with relevant information such as gender and number. These mentions are processed in multiple steps (sieves), which are sorted from highest to lowest precision. For example, the first sieve (i.e., highest precision) requires an exact string match between a mention and its antecedent, whereas the last one (i.e., lowest precision) implements pronominal coreference resolution. At this stage, noun phrases, possessive pronouns and named entities have been considered for reference. In the last step, after coreference resolution has been done, a post-processing step is performed where singletons are removed. The results from the experiments are summarized in Figures 1, 2, and 3.

Figure 1 shows the length of the coreference chains (the number of sentences in the chains) that are most frequent. Note, however, that most sentences, 7281, does not have a reference at all (not included in the figure). Most references, 2185, are between two sentences; one with the representative mention and one additional mention. Approximately 1200 reference chains include three sentences and so on. There are very few reference chains of length 10 or more.

Figure 2 shows the average distance of the coreferences, that is, how many sentence indices are between a current sentence and the sentence it references. The X-axis shows the sentence index and the Y-axis shows the distance or number of sentences between the referents. In the beginning of the document the distance between referring sentences is around 4, increasing until index (sentence) 20 where the distance is approximately 8, probably because they refer to the first sentences. Then the

[1] `nlp.stanford.edu/software/index.shtml`

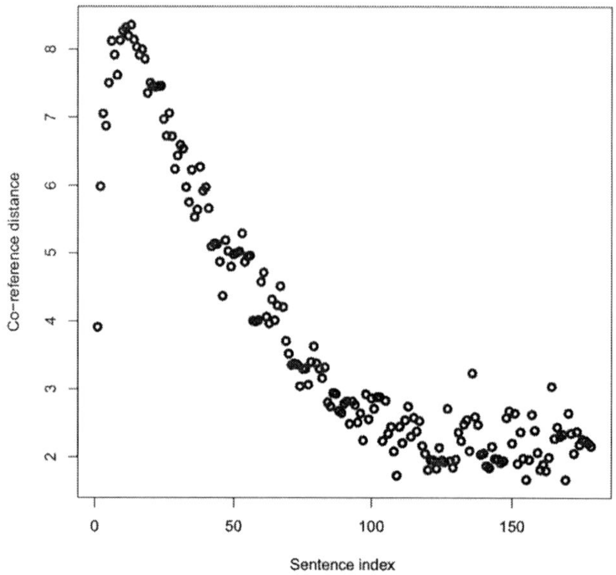

Figure 2: Coref distances, text. The earliest sentences have short distances, quickly followed by long distances in middle sentences and a shorter distance again concerning sentences further into the document.

distance decreases rapidly.

Figure 3 shows a plot where the sentence indices are on the X- and Y-axis and the size of the circle depicts the number of times a coreference exists in a given sentence pair. This figure shows that sentences early in the document have the most coreferences and that they corefer to each other. In the later parts of the document the sentences are mostly referring to the sentence before. Looking back at Figure 2 we see that long distance references occur mostly in the middle (around sentence number 20) of the document and is referring to the beginning of the document.

To summarize, the results reveal that, for news texts, the beginning of the document is terse with sentences coreferring each other. In the middle of the document, sentences are most often coreferring to the sentence before. Also, in the middle of the document, there is a longer average coreference distance, meaning that the sentences in the middle probably refers to the beginning of the document. This means that many of the coreferences can not be captured by, for instance, picking the previous sentence in an effort to glue together a summary to increase its cohesion.

3 The Summarizer

Based on the results from our investigations of coreferences in news paper texts presented above, we have developed a summarizer (COHSUM) that takes into account the distribution of coreferences indirectly, by calculating a rank for the sentences based on how many out-links (how many other sentences are a representative sentence referring to) and in-links (how many sentences are referring to a current sentence). To calculate the ranks, a variant of PageRank (Brin and Page, 1998) is used, similar to TextRank (Mihalcea, 2004). Mihalcea (2004) further notes that the nature of PageRank is probably enough for summaries to exhibit some kind of coherence, since sentences that contain

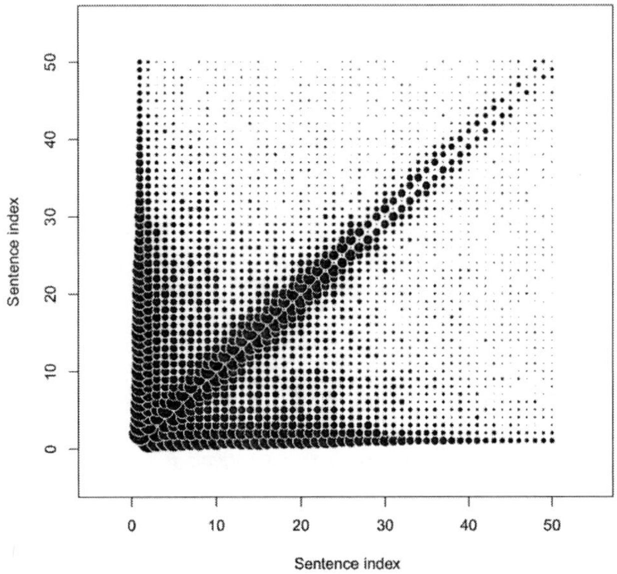

Figure 3: The figure shows a sentence by sentence matrix, where the radii of the circles depicts the number of times in average over 370 texts that a sentence corefers to another sentence. Early sentences and adjacent sentences corefer the most. The first 50 sentences are plotted. Coreferences within sentences are omitted.

similar information will be extracted. In COHSUM we take this one step further and extract coreferring sentences only. Coreferences have, as previously discussed, been used when creating summaries, however, using coreference chains in graph based ranking algorithms for summarization has not been done to our knowledge.

Each document that was to be summarized was first parsed and tagged using the CoreNLP-toolkit for coreference resolution. The coreference chains provided by the parser were used to create a graph, were each sentence is a node and all sentences having a referential relation to the sentence being in-/out links in the graph. In more detail; for each sentence, check if it exists in any coreference chain. For every coreference chain it exists in, count the number of sentences it refers to (with regards to noun phrases, possessive pronouns and named entities as mention earlier). Let these be the number of links. A reference consists, in the simplest case, of a two-way link, that is, if sentence A is referencing sentence B, then sentence A is also referenced by sentence B. A sentence can exist in multiple coreference chains but possible references within a sentence are not considered.

It is also possible for the parser to select the *representative mention*. In COHSUM mentions headed by proper nouns are preferred to mentions headed by common nouns, and nominal mentions are preferred to pronominal ones. In case of ties, the longer string is selected. The representative mention in the coreference chain can be considered as the preferred mention, or the most elaborate. The edges in the graph are weighted to prefer sentences with representative mentions; only sentences with representative mentions can be considered to have out links. Thus, sentences in a coreference chain that does not have the representative mention, will have 0 out links and X in-links, where X is the number of sentences in the chain minus one.

The sentences were ranked according to the number of links provided by the coreference chains using Equation 1, c.f. PageRank, which recursively calculates the number of links for a number of iterations (50 in our experiments, with d set to .85, c.f. Smith and Jönsson (2011a)). For our purposes, sentences containing the representative mention contain out-links while sentences lacking representative mentions only have in-links. Sentences with representative mentions referencing a high number of other sentences that are also referenced by a high number of sentences will thus receive a high rank. This means that sentences existing in multiple coreference chains will receive a higher rank, especially if that sentence has the representative mention for several chains.

$$PR^W(s_i) = \frac{1-d}{N} + d \sum_{s_j \in In(s_i)} w_{ji} \frac{PR^W(s_j)}{\sum_{s_k \in Out(s_k)} w_{kj}} \quad (1)$$

From the graph, weighted using Equation 1, COHSUM extracted the highest ranked sentences one sentence at a time until the summary consisted of roughly 100 words, to match the output from other systems and models. Focus was thus not for the summaries to retain the highest amount of coreference chains, but to be in comparable size to the resource data.

4 Evaluation

The summaries were evaluated using two measures; content coverage and cohesion. Content coverage is used to compare our summarizer with the systems from DUC (2002) as well as a baseline consisting of the first part of the documents. For evaluation of content coverage, ROUGE 1-gram F-measure (Lin, 2004) was used to compare summaries created by COHSUM to the summarization systems from DUC 2002. Other ROUGE measures are possible, but for this part of the DUC 2002 dataset (single document, 100 word summaries), ROUGE-1 has been shown not to differ significantly from other ROUGE measures. In total 533 texts were used[2], summarized by all 13 systems from DUC (concerned with producing single document 100 word abstracts), COHSUM and the baseline, FIRST, consisting of the first 100 words.

Cohesion is meant to be contrasted to content coverage; if content coverage is up to par, how cohesive are the texts? Looking at summaries as cohesive units and measuring the cohesion in them based on first parsing them with current parsers may be erroneous (Pitler et al., 2010). Current metrics may work for texts that are produced the way they are supposed to be read; in its entirety. Measures utilizing parsers (a common way of measuring cohesion, e.g through coreferences) used directly on summaries might not provide expected results, since the parsers expect the input texts to be correct. Thus, we have chosen to compare the summaries to the original documents. To calculate text cohesion when summarizing them, the coreferences in the summaries were logged in terms of what sentences coreferenced each other in the original documents. Depending on what sentences were retained in the summary, a coreference in the original document could be intact or broken:

Intact The amount of intact coreferences, that is, the amount of sentences that were retained in the summary that are coreferencing in the original document.

Broken Broken coreferences, sentences not extracted that contain the representative mention in the coreference chains. This case often leaves dangling anaphoric expressions without antecedent, leading to less cohesion.

[2]Duplicate texts from the corpus were removed.

Using the Stanford CoreNLP-toolkit, the original documents were parsed, followed by the DUC summaries, the 100 word summary, and the summaries created by COHSUM. The parser was used for the summaries even though coreference information from the summaries were not. This was to ensure that comparable outputs from the original documents and the summaries were created. By calculating the number of sentences in the summaries compared to the coreference chains in the original texts, we achieve a measure on how much of the cohesion that has been retained, given our measures of cohesion.

Table 1: Results on content coverage and cohesion. Results significantly worse than COHSUM in boldface.

System	Content	Intact	Broken
15	**0.442**	**3.318**	**3.775**
16	**0.425**	**2.991**	**3.294**
17	**0.158**	**1.959**	1.986
18	**0.432**	**2.973**	3.218
19	0.459	**3.531**	**3.878**
21	0.459	**3.805**	**4.292**
23	**0.410**	**4.409**	**4.939**
25	**0.443**	-	-
27	0.446	**3.806**	**4.282**
28	0.465	**4.231**	**4.692**
29	0.45	**4.217**	**4.817**
30	**0.114**	-	-
31	**0.443**	**2.505**	2.796
COHSUM	0.458	5.276	2.528
FIRST	0.459	10.587	0.417

5 Results

Table 1 shows the results from running the DUC summarizers, FIRST, and COHSUM on the 533 DUC 2002 news paper texts. The table shows the systems and their performance on gold standard comparison (Content) and cohesion (Intact and Broken). The blanks in the table are due to the systems 25 and 30 altering the summaries[3], making a coreference comparison fruitless.

We see that COHSUM is the fifth best system compared to FIRST and the DUC summarizers with regards to content coverage. The systems 28, 19, COHSUM 21, 29, 27 and FIRST perform best and compared to COHSUM no significant difference is obtained. COHSUM however, performs significantly better ($p < .05$) than the rest of the systems, 15, 16, 17, 18, 23, 25, 30, and 31, with regards to content coverage.

Comparing COHSUM to the DUC-systems with regards to coreference chains, reveals that one system's summary has fewer coreference chain breaks than COHSUM, no. 17. Compared to COHSUM there is a significant difference to all systems except systems 31, 18 and 17 with regards to broken coreferences ($p < .05$). Again, systems that perform significantly worse than COHSUM are marked as bold in Table 1. COHSUM has the most intact coreferences compared to the DUC systems. The number of intact coreferences is significantly higher in COHSUM than in all other summarisers ($p < .05$). FIRST is significantly better than all summarizers on both number of broken coreferences and intact coreferences.

[3]System 25 was a multi-document summarizer that was also tried on the single document summarization task, while system 30 focused on producing informative headlines.

6 Discussion

The performance on content coverage for COHSUM is surprisingly on par to the systems from the DUC 2002 competition (Table 1). Actually, most systems perform well on content coverage, the differences between the top systems were not significant. While performing on par with the DUC systems, the COHSUM summaries also have the highest amount of intact coreferences, and the second fewest breaks of coreference chains. The system with least broken coreferences, number 17, scores, however, low on content coverage. This indicates that by only taking into account the coreferences in a newspaper text, a summary that contains a high degree of important information can be created that also have a more cohesive structure in that they have fewer breaks in the coreference chains compared to other systems.

The baseline, FIRST, is still the clear winner. The nature in which newspaper articles are produced (where the gist of the story is presented first, with the rest of the article containing more detailed explanations, quotes and general development of the text) makes this kind of summary function well. COHSUM, making use of coreferences, will also often extract the beginning of the document, since this is where most of the coreferences are (c.f. Figure 3). The sentences in a document is often referring to the sentence before, however, most of the content seems to be introduced in the beginning which later parts of the document refer to. Thus, only doing a flat pick of the sentence before when trying to improve cohesion on a summary is not feasible (Smith et al., 2012).

The coreferences used in COHSUM are not weighted in any way, all sentences with coreferences are possible candidate sentences for inclusion in the summary. An informed decision on the type of coreference that should be allowed/weighted might affect the results. Our simplistic approach does not make this distinction since we were interested in sentences "being about" other sentences regardless of type. Currently all coreferences are considered as both in- and out-links if they contain a representative mention. The type of coreference could be further used to decide whether a link should be in one direction or another.

Using news texts has its limitations, as also pointed out by Over et al. (2007), but this is where most current research is conducted, and is, thus, important for benchmarking. It is, however, time for a new single text summarization competition where other text types are considered, texts that are important for the public to read and understand but where e.g. persons with reading disabilities have difficulties, such as authority texts and information texts, but also academic texts. Summarizing such texts (in Swedish) is in our focus of research, c.f. Smith and Jönsson (2011a) and our next step is to use COHSUM on these texts.

When it comes to other text types, the beginning of the document might not be as important. We have carried out some initial experiments on a variety of other text types. Looking at plots of the distribution of coreferences, similar to Figure 3, for other genres we find that scientific texts and financial publications seem even more terse with coreferences across the entire document, even though the first couple of sentences seem to contain a lot of coreferences in all the genres. This indicates that for these genres, the distribution of coreferences is different and taking for instance the lead sentences will break more coreferences and thus cohesion of the texts.

To summarize, COHSUM performs comparatively well with regards to content coverage, not significantly beaten by any system or the baseline but it has significantly fewer broken coreference chains and more intact coreferences compared to the other summarizers. It, thus, seems that coreferences are an important factor that can be tied to important sentences when summarizing news texts.

References

Alonso i Alemany, L. and Fuentes Fort, M. (2003). Integrating cohesion and coherence for automatic summarization. In *Proceedings of the tenth conference on European chapter of the Association for Computational Linguistics - Volume 2*, EACL '03, pages 1–8, Stroudsburg, PA, USA. Association for Computational Linguistics.

Baldwin, B. and Morton, T. S. (1998). Dynamic coreference-based summarization. In *In Proceedings of the Third Conference on Empirical Methods in Natural Language Processing (EMNLP-3*.

Barzilay, R. and Elhadad, M. (1999). Using lexical chains for text summarization. In Mani, I. and Maybury, M. T., editors, *Advances in Automatic Text Summarization*. The MIT Press.

Bergler, S., Witte, R., Khalife, M., Li, Z., and Rudzicz, F. (2003). Using knowledge-poor coreference resolution for text summarization. In *in DUC, Workshop on Text Summarization, May-June*, pages 85–92.

Boguraev, B. and Neff, M. S. (2000). The effects of analysing cohesion on document summarisation. In *COLING*, pages 76–82. Morgan Kaufmann.

Brandow, R., Mitze, K., and Rau, L. F. (1995). Automatic condensation of electronic publications by sentence selection. *Information Processing and Management*, 31(5):675 – 685.

Brin, S. and Page, L. (1998). The anatomy of a large-scale hypertextual web search engine. *Computer Networks and ISDN Systems*, 30(1-7):107–117.

Chatterjee, N. and Mohan, S. (2007). Extraction-based single-document summarization using random indexing. In *Proceedings of the 19th IEEE international Conference on Tools with Artificial intelligence – (ICTAI 2007)*, pages 448–455.

DUC (2002). Document understanding conference. `http://duc.nist.gov/pubs.html#2002`.

Gong, Y. (2001). Generic text summarization using relevance measure and latent semantic analysis. In *Proceedings of the 24th Annual International ACM SIGIR Conference on Research and Development in Information Retrieval*.

Graesser, A. C., McNamara, D. S., Louwerse, M. M., and Cai, Z. (2004). Coh-metrix: Analysis of text on cohesion and language. *Behavior Research Methods, Instruments, & Computers*, 36(2):193–202.

Hassel, M. and Sjöbergh, J. (2007). Widening the holsum search scope. In *Proceedings of the 16th Nordic Conference of Computational Linguistics (Nodalida)*, Tartu, Estonia.

Kaspersson, T., Smith, C., Danielsson, H., and Jönsson, A. (2012). This also affects the context - errors in extraction based summaries. In *Proceedings of the eighth international conference on Language Resources and Evaluation (LREC), Istanbul, Turkey*.

Lee, H., Peirsman, Y., Chang, A., Chambers, N., Surdeanu, M., and Jurafsky, D. (2011). Stanford's multi-pass sieve coreference resolution system at the conll-2011 shared task. In *Proceedings of the Fifteenth Conference on Computational Natural Language Learning: Shared Task*, CONLL Shared Task '11, pages 28–34, Stroudsburg, PA, USA. Association for Computational Linguistics.

Lin, C.-y. (2004). Rouge: a package for automatic evaluation of summaries. In *ACL Text Summarization Workshop*, pages 25–26.

Mani, I., Bloedorn, E., and Gates, B. (1998). Using cohesion and coherence models for text summarization. In *AAAI Technical Report SS-98-06*.

Mihalcea, R. (2004). Graph-based ranking algorithms for sentence extraction, applied to text summarization. In *Proceedings of the ACL 2004 on Interactive poster and demonstration sessions*, ACLdemo '04, Morristown, NJ, USA. Association for Computational Linguistics.

Mihalcea, R. and Tarau, P. (2004). TextRank: Bringing order into texts. In *Conference on Empirical Methods in Natural Language Processing*, Barcelona, Spain.

Nenkova, A. (2006). *Understanding the process of multi-document summarization: Content selection, rewriting and evaluation*. PhD thesis, Columbia University.

Otterbacher, J. C., Radev, D. R., and Luo, A. (2002). Revisions that improve cohesion in multi-document summaries: A preliminary study. In *Proceedings of the Workshop on Automatic Summarization (including DUC 2002), Philadelphia*, pages 27–36.

Over, P., Dang, H., and Harman, D. (2007). Duc in context. *Information Processing & Management*, 43:1506–1520.

Pitler, E., Louis, A., and Nenkova, A. (2010). Automatic evaluation of linguistic quality inmulti-document summarization. In *Proceedings of the 48th Annual Meeting of the Association for Computational Linguistics, Uppsala, Sweden*, pages 544–554.

Smith, C., Danielsson, H., and Jönsson, A. (2012). Cohesion in automatically created summaries. In *Proceedings of the Fourth Swedish Language Technology Conference, Lund, Sweden.*

Smith, C. and Jönsson, A. (2011a). Automatic summarization as means of simplifying texts, an evaluation for swedish. In *Proceedings of the 18th Nordic Conference of Computational Linguistics (NoDaLiDa-2010), Riga, Latvia.*

Smith, C. and Jönsson, A. (2011b). Enhancing extraction based summarization with outside word space. In *Proceedings of the 5th International Joint Conference on Natural Language Processing, Chiang Mai, Thailand.*

Robust learning in random subspaces: equipping NLP for OOV effects

Anders Søgaard and Anders Johannsen
Center for Language Technology
University of Copenhagen
DK-2300 Copenhagen S
{soegaard|ajohannsen}@hum.ku.dk

ABSTRACT
Inspired by work on robust optimization we introduce a subspace method for learning linear classifiers for natural language processing that are robust to out-of-vocabulary effects. The method is applicable in live-stream settings where new instances may be sampled from different and possibly also previously unseen domains. In text classification and part-of-speech (POS) tagging, robust perceptrons and robust stochastic gradient descent (SGD) with hinge loss achieve average error reductions of up to 18% when evaluated on out-of-domain data.

KEYWORDS: robust learning, regularization, document classification, part-of-speech tagging.

Proceedings of COLING 2012: Posters, pages 1171–1180,
COLING 2012, Mumbai, December 2012.

1 Introduction

In natural language processing (NLP), data is rarely drawn independently and identically at random. In particular we often apply models learned from available labeled data to data that differs from the original labeled data in several respects. Supervised learning without the assumption that data is drawn identically is sometimes referred to as *transfer learning*, i.e. learning to make predictions about data sampled from a target distribution using labeled data from a *related, but different source distribution* or under a strong *sample bias*.

Domain adaptation refers to a prominent class of transfer learning problems in NLP. Two domain adaptation scenarios are typically considered: (a) *semi-supervised* domain adaption, where a small sample of data from the target domain is available, as well as large pool of unlabeled target data, and (b) *unsupervised* domain adaptation where only unlabeled data is available from the target domain. In this paper we do *not even* assume the latter, but consider the more difficult scenario where the target domain is unknown.

The assumption that a large pool of unlabeled data is available from a relatively homogeneous target domain holds only if the target domain is known in advance. In a lot of applications of NLP, this is not the case. When we design publicly available software such as the Stanford Parser, or when we set up online services such as Google Translate, we do not know much about the input in advance. A user will apply the Stanford Parser to any kind of text from any textual domain and expect it to do well.[1] Recent work has extended domain adaptation with domain *identification* (Dredze et al., 2010; McClosky et al., 2010), but this still requires that we know the possible domains in advance and are able to relate each instance to one of them, and in many cases we do not. If the possible target domains are *not* known in advance, the transfer learning problem reduces to the problem of learning robust models that are as insensitive as possible to domain shifts. This is the problem considered in this paper.

One of the main reasons for performance drops when evaluating supervised NLP models on out-of-domain data is out-of-vocabulary (OOV) effects (Blitzer et al., 2007; Daumé and Jagarlamudi, 2011). Several techniques for reducing OOV effects have been introduced in the literature, including spelling expansion, morphological expansion, dictionary term expansion, proper name transliteration, correlation analysis, and word clustering (Blitzer et al., 2007; Habash, 2008; Turian et al., 2010; Daumé and Jagarlamudi, 2011), but most of these techniques still leave us with a lot of "empty dimensions", i.e. features that are always 0 in the test data. While these features are not uninstantiated in the sense of missing values, we will nevertheless refer to OOV effects as *removing dimensions* from our datasets, since a subset of dimensions become uninformative as we leave our source domain.

This is a potential source of error, since the best decision boundary in n dimensions is not necessarily the best boundary in $m < n$ dimensions. If we remove dimensions, our optimal decision boundaries may suddenly be far from optimal. Consider, for example, the plot in Figure 1. 2D-SVC is the optimal decision boundary for this two-dimensional dataset (the non-horizontal, solid line). If we remove one dimension, however, say because this variable is never instantiated in our test data, the learned weight vector will give us the decision boundary TEST(2D-SVC) (the dashed line). Compare this to the optimal decision boundary for the reduced, one-dimensional dataset, 1D-SVC (the horizontal, solid line).

OOV effects "remove" dimensions from our data. In robust learning, we do not know which di-

[1] Chris Manning previously raised this point in an invited talk at a NAACL workshop.

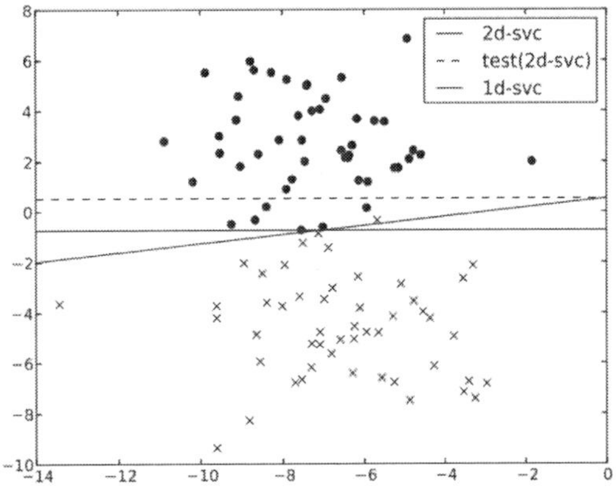

Figure 1: Optimal decision boundary is not optimal when one dimension is removed

mensions are to be removed in our target data in advance, however. In this paper we therefore, inspired by previous work on robust optimization (Ben-Tal and Nemirovski, 1998), suggest to minimize our expected loss under all (or K random) possible removals. We will implement this strategy for perceptron learning and SGD with hinge loss and apply it to text classification, as well as POS tagging. Results are very promising, with error reductions up to 70% and average error reductions up to 18%.

2 Robust learning under random subspaces

In robust optimization (Ben-Tal and Nemirovski, 1998) we aim to find a solution $\mathbf{w}$ that minimizes a (parameterized) cost function $f(\mathbf{w}, \xi)$, where the true parameter ξ may differ from the observed $\hat{\xi}$. The task is to solve

$$\min_{\mathbf{w}} \max_{\hat{\xi} \in \Delta} f(\mathbf{w}, \hat{\xi}) \tag{1}$$

with Δ all possible realizations of ξ. An alternative to minimizing loss in the worst case is minimizing loss in the average case, or the sum of losses:

$$\min_{\mathbf{w}} \sum_{\hat{\xi} \in \Delta} f(\mathbf{w}, \hat{\xi}) \tag{2}$$

The learning algorithms considered in this paper aim to learn models $\mathbf{w}$ from finite samples (of size N) that minimize the expected loss on a distribution ρ (with, say, M dimensions):

$$\min_{\mathbf{w}} \mathbb{E}_{\langle y, \mathbf{x} \rangle \sim \rho} L(y, \text{sign}(\mathbf{w} \cdot \mathbf{x})) \tag{3}$$

OOV effects can be seen as introducing an extra parameter into this equation. Let ξ be a binary vector of length M selecting what dimensions are removed. In NLP we typically assume that $\xi = \langle 1, \ldots, 1 \rangle$ and minimize the expected loss in the usual way, but if we have a set Δ of possible instantiations of ξ such that ξ can be any binary vector, minimizing expected loss is

```
X = {(y_i, x_i)}_{i=1}^N
for k ∈ K do
    w^0 = 0, v = 0, i = 0
    ξ ← random.bits(M)
    for n ∈ N do
        if sign(w · x ∘ ξ) ≠ y_n then
            w^{i+1} ← update(w^i)
            i ← i + 1
        end if
    end for
    v ← v + w^i
end for
return w = v/(N × K)
```

Figure 2: Robust learning in random subspaces

likely to be suboptimal, as discussed in the introduction. In this paper we will instead minimize average expected loss *under random subspaces*:

$$\min_{\mathbf{w}} \sum_{\xi \in \Delta} \mathbb{E}_{\langle y,\mathbf{x}\rangle \sim \rho} L(y, \text{sign}(\mathbf{w} \cdot \mathbf{x} \circ \xi)) \tag{4}$$

We refer to this idea as robust learning in random subspaces (RLRS). Since the number of possible instantiations of ξ is 2^M we randomly sample K instantiations removing 10% of the dimensions, with $K \leq 250$.[2]

RLRS can be applied to any linear model, and we present the general form in Figure 2. Given a dataset $X = \{\langle y_i, \mathbf{x}_i \rangle\}_{i=1}^N$ we randomly draw ξ from the set of binary vectors of length M. We now pass over $\{\langle y_i, \mathbf{x}_i \circ \xi \rangle\}_{i=1}^N$ K times, updating our linear model according to the learning algorithm. The weights of the K models are averaged to minimize the average expected loss in random subspaces. In our experiments we will use perceptron (Rosenblatt, 1958) and SGD with hinge loss (Zhang, 2004) as our learning algorithms. A perceptron c consists of a weight vector $\mathbf{w}$ with a weight for each feature, a bias term b and a learning rate α. For a data point $\mathbf{x}_j$, $c(\mathbf{x}_j) = 1$ iff $\mathbf{w} \cdot \mathbf{x} + b > 0$, else 0. The threshold for classifying something as positive is thus $-b$. The bias term is left out by adding an extra variable to our data with fixed value -1. The perceptron learning algorithm now works by maintaining $\mathbf{w}$ in several passes over the data (see Figure 2). Say the algorithm at time i is presented with a labeled data point $\langle \mathbf{x}_j, y_j \rangle$. The current weight vector $\mathbf{w}^i$ is used to calculate $\mathbf{x}_j \cdot \mathbf{w}^i$. If the prediction is wrong, an update occurs:

$$\mathbf{w}^{i+1} \leftarrow \mathbf{w}^i + \alpha(y_j - \text{sign}(\mathbf{w}^i \cdot \mathbf{x}_j))\mathbf{x}_j \tag{5}$$

The numbers of passes K the learning algorithm does (if it does not arrive at a perfect separator any earlier) is typically fixed by a hyper-parameter. The number of passes is fixed to 5 in our experiments below. The RLRS variant of the perceptron (P-RLRS) is obtained by replacing

[2] Our choice to constrain ourselves to instantiations of ξ removing 10% of the dimensions was somewhat arbitrary, and we briefly discuss the effect of this hyper-parameter after presenting our main results.

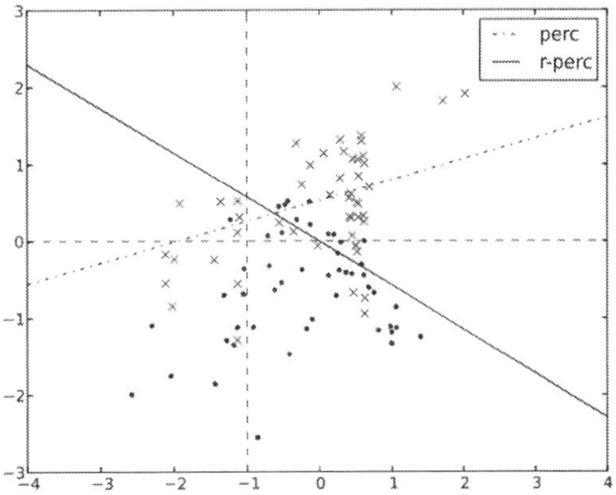

Figure 3: Robust learning in random subspaces (Perceptron on artificial data)

line 8 in Figure 2 with Equation 5. The application of P-RLRS to an artificial two-dimensional dataset in Figure 3 (the solid line) illustrates how P-RLRS can lead to very different decision boundaries than the regular perceptron (the black dashed line) by averaging decision boundaries learned in random subspaces (red dashed lines).

A perceptron finds the vector $\mathbf{w}$ that minimizes the expected loss on training data where the loss function is given by:

$$L(y, \text{sign}(\mathbf{w} \cdot \mathbf{x})) = \max\{0, -y(\mathbf{w} \cdot \mathbf{x})\} \tag{6}$$

which is 0 when y is predicted correctly, and otherwise the confidence in the mis-prediction. This reflects the fact that perceptron learning is conservative and does not update on correctly classified data points. Equation 6 is the hinge loss with $\gamma = 0$. SGD uses hinge loss with $\gamma = 1$ (like SVMs) (Zhang, 2004). Our objective function thus becomes:

$$\min_{\mathbf{w}} \sum_{\hat{\xi} \in \Delta} \mathbb{E}_{\langle y, \mathbf{x} \rangle \sim \rho} \max\{0, \gamma - y(\mathbf{w} \cdot \mathbf{x} \circ \hat{\xi})\} \tag{7}$$

with $\gamma = 0$ for the perceptron and $\gamma = 1$ for SGD. We call the RLRS variant of SGD SGD-RLRS.

3 Evaluation

In our experiments we use perceptron and SGD with hinge loss, regularized using the L_2-norm. Since we want to demonstrate the general applicability of RLRS, we use the default parameters in a publicly available implementation of both algorithms.[3] Both algorithms do five passes over the data. SGD uses 'optimal' learning rate, and perceptron uses a learning rate of 1.

Text classification. The goal of text classification is the automatic assignment of documents into predefined semantic classes. The input is a set of labeled documents $\langle y_1, \mathbf{x}_1 \rangle, \ldots, \langle y_N, \mathbf{x}_N \rangle$, and the task is to learn a function $f : \mathcal{X} \mapsto \mathcal{Y}$ that is able to correctly classify previously unseen documents. It has previously been noted that robustness is important for the success of text

[3] http://scikit-learn.org/stable/

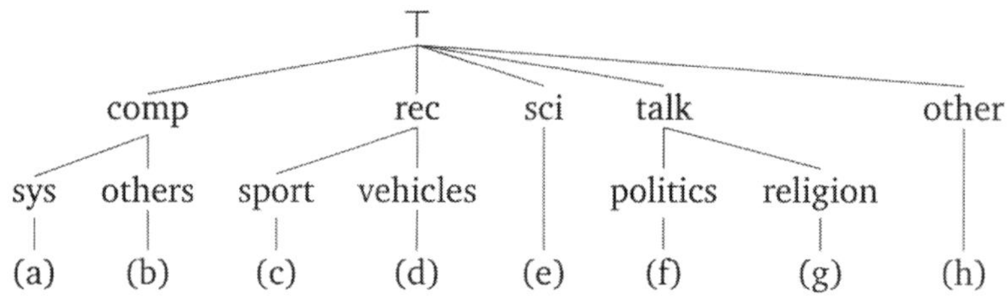

Figure 4: Hierarchical structure of 20 Newsgroups. (a) IBM, Mac, (b) Graphics, MS-Windows, X-Windows, (c) Baseball, Hockey, (d) Autos, Motorcycles, (e) Cryptography, Electronics, Medicine, Space, (f) Guns, Mideast, Miscellaneous, (g) Atheism, Christianity, Miscellaneous, (h) Forsale

classification in down-stream applications (Lipka and Stein, 2011). In this paper we use the 20 Newsgroups dataset.[4] The topics in 20 Newsgroups are hierarchically structured, which enables us to do domain adaptation experiments (Chen et al., 2009; Sun et al., 2011) (except that we will not assume unlabeled data is available in the target domain). See the hierarchy in Figure 4. We extract 20 high-level binary classification problems by considering all pairs of top-level categories, e.g. Computers-Recreative (comp-rec). For each of these 20 problems, we have different possible datasets, e.g. IBM-Baseball, Mac-Motorcycles, etc. A *problem instance* takes training and test data from two *different* datasets belong to the same high-level problem, e.g. Mac-Motorcycles and IBM-Baseball. In total we have 280 available problem instances in the 20 Newsgroups dataset. For each problem instance, we create a sparse matrix of occurrence counts of lowercased tokens and normalize the counts using TF-IDF in the usual way. Otherwise we did not do any preprocessing or feature selection. The code necessary to replicate our text classification experiments is available from the main author's website.[5]

POS tagging. To supplement our experiments on the 20 Newsgroups corpus, we also evaluate our approach to robust learning in the context of discriminative HMM training for POS tagging using averaged perceptron (Collins, 2002). The goal of POS tagging is to assign sequences of labels to words reflecting their syntactic categories. We use a publicly available and easy-to-modify reimplementation of the model proposed by Collins (2002).[6] We evaluate our tagger on the English Web Treebank (EWT; LDC2012T13). We use the original PTB tag set, and our results are therefore not comparable to those reported in the SANCL 2012 Shared Task of Parsing the Web. Our model is trained on the WSJ portion of the Ontonotes 4.0 (Sect. 2-21). Our initial experiments used the Email development data, but we simply applied document classification parameters with no tuning. We evaluate our model on test data in the remaining sections of EWT: Answers, Newsgroups, Reviews and Weblogs.

3.1 Results and discussion

Figure 1 presents our main results on text classification. The left column is the number of extracted subspaces (K in Figure 2). Note that rows are not comparable, since the 20/280 problem instances were randomly selected for each experiment. Neither are the perceptron and SGD results. We observe that P-RLRS consistently outperforms the regular perceptron

[4]http://people.csail.mit.edu/jrennie/20Newsgroups/
[5]http://cst.dk/anders
[6]https://github.com/gracaninja/lxmls-toolkit

K	P	P-RLRS	err.red	p-value	SGD	SGD-RLRS	err.red	p-value
25	67.2	70.1	0.09	< 0.01	75.2	75.7	0.02	~ 0.17
50	63.8	66.2	0.07	< 0.01	68.6	70.9	0.07	~ 0.02
75	73.2	75.3	0.08	< 0.01	76.3	78.9	0.11	< 0.01
100	72.0	73.3	0.05	~ 0.06	73.6	77.1	0.15	< 0.01
150	72.3	76.2	0.14	< 0.01	74.6	79.2	0.18	< 0.01
250	70.4	72.6	0.07	~ 0.02	75.0	78.7	0.15	< 0.01

Table 1: Results on 20 Newsgroups

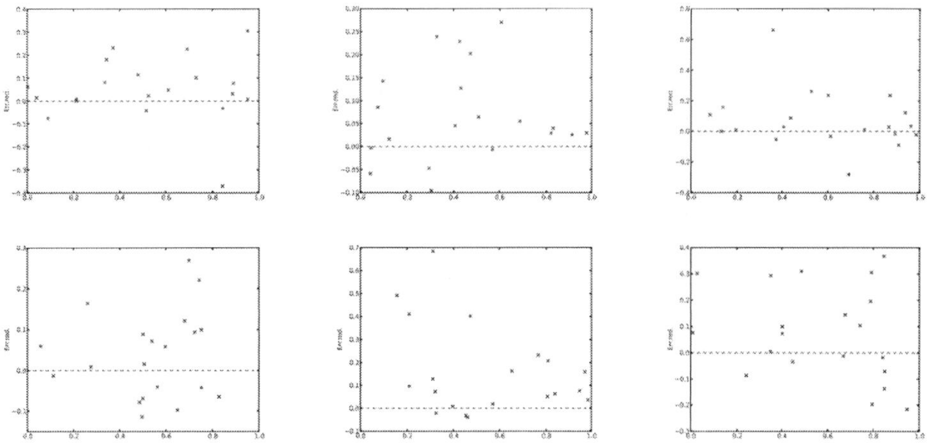

Figure 5: Plots of P-RLRS error reductions with $K = 25$ (upper left), $K = 50$ (upper right), $K = 75$ (lower left), $K = 100$ (lower mid), $K = 150$ (lower mid) and $K = 250$ (lower right).

(P), with error reductions of 7–14%. SGD-RSRL consistently outperforms SGD, with error reductions of 2–18%. Note that statistical significance is *across datasets*, not across data points. Since we are interested in the probability of success on new datasets, we believe this is the right way to evaluate our model, putting our results to a much stronger test. All results, except two, are still statistically significant, however. As one would expect our models become more robust the more instantiations of ξ we sample. The error reductions for each problem instance in the P/P-RLRS experiments are plotted in Figure 5. The plots show that error reductions are up to 70% on some problem instances, and that RLRS seldom hurts (in 3-8 out of 20 cases).

We include a comparison with state-of-the-art learning algorithms for completeness. In Figure 6 (left), we compare SGD-RLRS to passive-aggressive learning (PA) (Crammer et al., 2006) and confidence-weighted learning (CW) (Dredze et al., 2008), using a publicly available implementation,[7] on randomly chosen 20 Newsgroups problem instances. CW is known to be relatively robust to sample bias, reducing weights under-training for correlating features. All algorithms did five passes over the data. Our results indicate that RLRS is more robust than other algorithms, but on some datasets algorithms CW performs much better that RLRS.

The results on the EWT are similar to those for 20 Newsgroups, and we observe consistent improvements with both robust averaged perceptron. The results are presented in Table 2. All

[7]http://code.google.com/p/oll/ (using default parameters)

	AP	AP-RLRS$_{K=25}$	AP-RLRS$_{K=50}$	AP-RLRS$_{K=100}$
EWT-Answers	85.22	85.63	**85.69**	85.68
EWT-Newsgroups	86.82	87.26	**87.36**	87.26
EWT-Reviews	84.92	85.32	85.31	**85.35**
EWT-Weblogs	87.00	87.54	87.52	**87.61**

Table 2: Results on the EWT

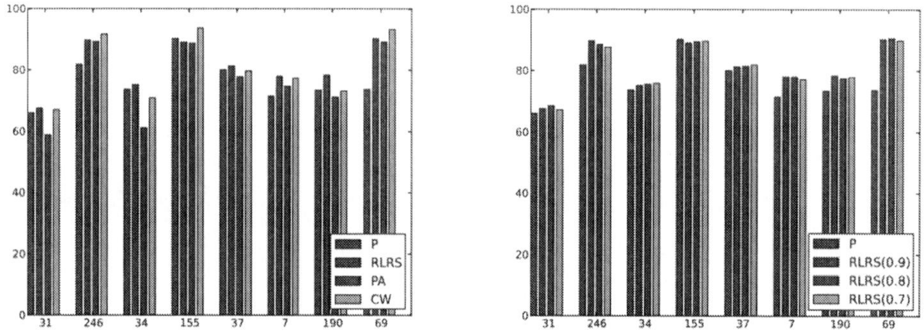

Figure 6: Left: Classifier comparison. Right: Using increased removal rates when sampling ξ.

improvements are statistically significant across data points.

As mentioned, fixing the removal rate to 10% when randomly sampling $\xi \in \Delta$ was a relatively arbitrary choice. RLRS actually benefits slightly from increasing the removal rate. See Figure 6 (right) for results on the selection of problem instances we used in our classifier comparison. In order to explain this we investigated and found a statistically significant correlation between the empirical removal rate and the difference in performance of a model with removal rate 0.8 over a model with removal rate 0.9. This, in our view, suggests that the intuition behind RLRS is correct. Learning under random subspaces *is* a way of equipping NLP for OOV effects.

Related work. The RLRS algorithm in Figure 2 is essentially an ensemble learning algorithm, similar in spirit to the random subspace method (Ho, 1998), except averaging over multiple models rather than taking majority votes. Ensemble learning is known to lead to more robust models and therefore to performance gains in domain adaptation (Gao et al., 2008; Duan et al., 2009), so in a way our results are maybe not that surprising. There is also a connection between RLRS and feature bagging (Sutton et al., 2006), a method proposed to reduce weights under-training as an effect of indicative features swamping less indicative features. Weights under-training makes models vulnerable to OOV effects, and feature bagging, in which several models are trained on subsets of features and combined using a mixture of experts, is very similar to RLRS. Sutton et al. 2006 use manually defined rather than random subspaces. See Smith et al. 2005 for an interesting predecessor.

4 Conclusion

We have presented a novel subspace method for robust learning with applications to document classification and POS tagging, aimed specifically at out-of-vocabulary effects arising in the context of domain adaptation. We have reported average error reductions of up to 18%.

References

Ben-Tal, A. and Nemirovski, A. (1998). Robust convex optimization. *Mathematics of Operations Research*, 23(4).

Blitzer, J., Dredze, M., and Pereira, F. (2007). Biographies, bollywood, boom-boxes and blenders: Domain adaptation for sentiment classification. In *ACL*.

Chen, B., Lam, W., Tsang, I., and Wong, T.-L. (2009). Extracting discriminative concepts for domain adaptation in text mining. In *KDD*.

Collins, M. (2002). Discriminative training methods for hidden markov models. In *EMNLP*.

Crammer, K., Dekel, O., Keshet, J., Shalev-Shwartz, S., and Singer, Y. (2006). Online passive-agressive algorithms. *Journal of Machine Learning Research*, 7:551–585.

Daumé, H. and Jagarlamudi, J. (2011). Domain adaptation for machine translation by mining unseen words. In *ACL*.

Dredze, M., Crammer, K., and Pereira, F. (2008). Confidence-weighted linear classification. In *ICML*.

Dredze, M., Oates, T., and Piatko, C. (2010). We're not in Kansas anymore: detecting domain changes in streams. In *EMNLP*.

Duan, L., Tsang, I., Xu, D., and Chua, T.-S. (2009). Domain adaptation from multiple sources via auxilliary classifiers. In *ICML*.

Gao, J., Fan, W., Jiang, J., and Han, J. (2008). Knowledge transfer via multiple model local structure mapping. In *KDD*.

Habash, N. (2008). Four techniques for online handling of out-of-vocabulary words in Arabic-English statistical machine translation. In *ACL*.

Ho, T. K. (1998). The random subspace method for constructing decision forests. *IEEE Transactions on Pattern Analysis and Machine Intelligence*, 20(8):832–844.

Lipka, N. and Stein, B. (2011). Robust models in information retrieval. In *DEXA*.

McClosky, D., Charniak, E., and Johnson, M. (2010). Automatic domain adaptation for parsing. In *NAACL-HLT*.

Rosenblatt, F. (1958). The perceptron: a probabilistic model for information storage and organization in the brain. *Psychological Review*, 65(6):386–408.

Smith, A., Cohn, T., and Osborne, M. (2005). Logarithmic opinion pools for conditional random fields. In *ACL*.

Sun, Q., Chattopadhyay, R., Panchanathan, S., and Ye, J. (2011). Two-stage weighting framework for multi-source domain adaptation. In *NIPS*.

Sutton, C., Sindelar, M., and McCallum, A. (2006). Reducing weight undertraining in structured discriminative learning. In *NAACL*.

Turian, J., Ratinov, L., and Bengio, Y. (2010). Word representations: a simple and general method for semi-supervised learning. In *ACL*.

Zhang, T. (2004). Solving large scale linear prediction problems using stochastic gradient descent algorithms. In *ICML*.

An empirical study of non-lexical extensions to delexicalized transfer

Anders Søgaard and Julie Wulff
Center for Language Technology
University of Copenhagen
DK-2300 Copenhagen S
soegaard@hum.ku.dk

ABSTRACT
We propose a simple cross-language parser adaptation strategy for discriminative parsers and apply it to easy-first transition-based dependency parsing (Goldberg and Elhadad, 2010). We evaluate our parsers on the Indo-European corpora in the CoNLL-X and CoNLL 2007 shared tasks. Using the remaining languages as source data we average under-fitted weights learned from each source language and apply the resulting linear classifier to the target language. Of course some source languages and some sentences in these languages are more relevant than others for the target language in question. We therefore explore improvements of our cross-language adaptation model involving source language and instance weighting, as well as unsupervised model selection. Overall our cross-language adaptation strategies provide better results than previous strategies for direct transfer, with near-linear time parsing and much faster training times than other approaches.

KEYWORDS: cross-language dependency parsing, regularization, importance weighting, typological information.

Proceedings of COLING 2012: Posters, pages 1181–1190,
COLING 2012, Mumbai, December 2012.

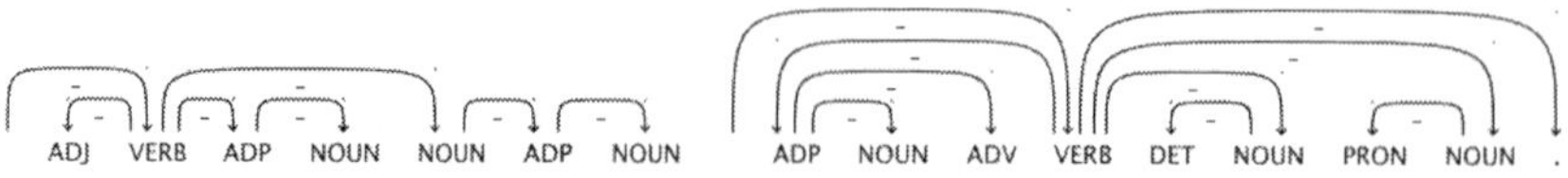

Figure 1: Bulgarian and German dependency structures, delexicalized

1 Introduction

High-quality syntactic parsing is important for advanced language technologies such as question-answering, machine translation between distant languages, and sentiment analysis. State-of-the-art parsers provide accurate syntactic analyses in languages for which annotated resources known as *treebanks* exist, although significant and sometimes prohibitive performance drops are observed when parsing text that differs in domain or genre from the available treebank(s). However, there are still many languages for which no treebanks exist, and for which we therefore do not have parsers available.

Unsupervised parsing has seen considerable progress over the last ten years (Gelling et al., 2012), but recently several authors have demonstrated that better results can be achieved transferring linguistic knowledge from treebanks from other languages rather than inducing this knowledge from unannotated text (Zeman and Resnik, 2008; Smith and Eisner, 2009; Spreyer and Kuhn, 2009; Søgaard, 2011; Cohen et al., 2011; McDonald et al., 2011; Täckström et al., 2012; Naseem et al., 2012). Some of these authors have projected syntactic structures across word aligned parallel text (Smith and Eisner, 2009; Spreyer and Kuhn, 2009; McDonald et al., 2011), while others have used a much simpler technique sometimes referred to as *delexicalized transfer* (Zeman and Resnik, 2008; Søgaard, 2011; Cohen et al., 2011; McDonald et al., 2011; Täckström et al., 2012; Naseem et al., 2012). This work presents a new approach to delexicalized transfer and explores possible improvements.

Sect. 2 covers related work on delexicalized transfer for cross-language parser adaptation. We explore delexicalized transfer in the context of easy-first transition-based dependency parsing (Goldberg and Elhadad, 2010), which is introduced in Sect. 3. Sect. 4 introduces our implementation of delexicalized transfer which differs from other approaches by doing model averaging of under-fitted models rather than concatenating data when learning from multiple source languages. Sect. 4 also introduces the possible improvements of this model we explore in our experiments. Sect. 5 and 6 present the experiments and results.

2 Cross-language adaptation with delexicalized transfer

Delexicalized transfer refers to a simple idea first introduced in Zeman and Resnik (2008). In unsupervised parsing, you hope to learn that nouns tend to attach to verbs, determiners tend to attach to nouns, adverbs to verbs, etc. Many of these tendencies are cross-linguistic tendencies, a fact also exploited in unsupervised parsing by Naseem et al. (2010) and Søgaard (2012). Since this knowledge is reflected in most treebanks, can't we extract this knowledge from a treebank in *one* language and apply the resulting model to another language for which we do not have a treebank? There are certainly differences between distant languages in, for example, how likely adjectives are to modify adverbs rather than nouns, but as mentioned in McDonald et al. (2011) using multiple source languages may reduce such biases on average.

Zeman and Resnik (2008), in their seminal paper, considered a pair of closely related languages, namely Danish and Swedish. They removed the words from the source treebank and learned a parsing model from the distribution of parts of speech (POS) only. In order to parse the target language they devised a mapping of the different POS tag sets into a common feature representation.

Consider the two delexicalized dependency structures in Figure 1 to see how this makes sense. The left structure is from the Bulgarian treebank, and the right one from the German. However, the left structure contains many edges that also occur in the right structure, e.g. from root to verb, from verb to noun, and from adposition to noun. A dependency parser can learn such dependencies are likely in Bulgarian, but apply this knowledge when parsing German.

Independently of each other, three papers revisited the idea of delexicalized transfer in 2011. Søgaard (2011) used the tag set mappings in Zeman and Resnik (2008), but also used instance weighting to do a form of outlier detection. In a way similar to Jiang and Zhai (2007) he did not make use of the actual weights, but simply used all labeled instances with weights greater than some fixed threshold. McDonald et al. (2011) used the more recent tag set mappings by Petrov et al. (2011), explored combinations of delexicalized transfer and structure projection (Smith and Eisner, 2009; Spreyer and Kuhn, 2009) and were able to improve delexicalized transfer averaging across several languages. They also were the first to explicitly introduce the idea of using multiple source languages as a kind of regularization. Finally, Cohen et al. (2011) used the delexicalized transfer models to initialize unsupervised parameter estimation on unlabeled target data.

Naseem et al. (2012) subsequently explored a more complex transfer model where only hierarchical information is transferred directly to reflect that languages have very different word orders.

Täckström et al. (2012) augment delexicalized transfer with bilingual clusters, while Durrett et al. (2012) use a bilingual dictionary to project lexical features. Täckström (2012) used self-training to supply the bilingual word clusters with monolingual clusters, but evaluated the idea on named entity recognition rather than cross-language parser adaptation.

3 Easy-first transition-based parsing with averaged perceptron

The parser we apply in this study is a non-directional easy-first transition-based dependency parser (Goldberg and Elhadad, 2010). The parser consecutively applies one of two actions, AttachLeft(i) and AttachRight(i), to a list of partial structures initialized as the words in the sentence. Each action connects the heads of two neighboring structures, making one the head of the other. The dependent partial structure is removed from the list. The parsing algorithm is obviously projective.

The next action is chosen by a score function $score(\text{Action})(i)$ that assigns a weight to all pairs of actions and locations. The scoring function ideally ranks possible actions from easy to hard. The scoring function is learned from data using a variant of the averaged perceptron learning algorithm (Freund and Schapire, 1999; Collins, 2002) similar to the one used in Shen et al. (2007). While the ordering from easy to hard is not known in advance, the ordering is implicitly learned by decreasing weights associated with invalid actions and increasing weights associated with the currently highest scoring valid action.

The major advantage of using easy-first parsing is the efficient $\mathcal{O}(n \log n)$ parsing algorithm, but training is also a lot faster than with comparable dependency parsers (Goldberg and Elhadad, 2010); e.g. training an experiment for Spanish-Italian on a Macbook Pro takes less than a minute. The easy-first learning algorithm is used throughout our experiments, except that we modify the update function when using easy-first with importance weighting.

4 Cross-language adaptation of easy-first parsing

The easy-first dependency parser (Goldberg and Elhadad, 2010) by default does 20 passes over the data and returns an averaged weight vector as our parsing model. Since our training data in cross-language adaptation is heavily biased, we do not want to over-fit our models to source data and only do a single round over data for each source language. This hyper-parameter is kept constant in all experiments. We use the feature model proposed for English in Goldberg and Elhadad (2010) for all languages (see Discussion). There are no other hyper-parameters to the parsing model. In our experiments we consider some possible extensions of this simple model. The extensions are discussed in the following subsections:

4.1 Language-level weighted learning

Intuitively some languages are more relevant as source languages for some language than others. While results in the literature show that good source languages may be geographically distant and unrelated to the target language (e.g. Arabic and Danish (Søgaard, 2011)), genealogically related languages should in general be better source languages for each other. This idea was first explored by Berg-Kirkpatrick and Klein (2010) who used genealogical relations to impose contraints on models in multi-lingual grammar inductions.

In the experiments below we use a language genealogy to take a weighted average of the models obtained from our set of source languages. Each model is weighted by $4-d$ where d is the distance between the source language and a node dominating the target language node in a genealogical tree (see Figure 2). If two languages belong to the same subfamily such as the Western Germanic languages Dutch and German, $d = 1$, but for Dutch to Greek, for example, $d = 3$.

We also try using a typological database to weight languages by their typological properties. The database lists basic typological properties of languages such as order of plural and noun, or whether the language has anti-passive constructions, and we simply let the weight of each target language be the inverse of the Hamming distance between the source language property vector and its own property vector.

$$f_w(L_S) = \frac{5}{H(L_S, L_T)}$$

The constant was chosen such that the number of weight vectors used in averaging was comparable to the experiments using linguistic genealogy to weight source languages.

Naseem et al. (2012) explore a similar idea (using the same typological database we do), but (a) they only use a subset of features (without specifying how this subset was selected), and (b) they use the typological features in a generative model rather than distances between property vectors.

4.2 Unsupervised model selection

Our models for the source languages are comparable weight vectors, i.e. the ith weight encodes the importance of the same feature across all models. So models with similar weights will lead to similar decisions. Like with data points in graph-based semi-supervised learning, we can build a graph out of our models with edges representing similarity of models. We can then use random walk algorithms to select diverse or homogeneous subsets of models.

In our experiments we explore the following idea: Using a random walk we compute the probability of reaching a node in our graph of source language models. We then compute the average of the three lower quartiles in order to optimize diversity and thereby regularization in the final model. In principle we want to optimize diversity and individual accuracy (Brown et al., 2005), but this method does unsupervised model selection not taking accuracy into account. Combining this technique with the weighting techniques introduced here which are intended to optimize for individual accuracy is theoretically an appealing option.

4.3 Sentence-level weighted learning

Some sentences in a source language may be more like the target language than others. Søgaard (2011) introduces a very simple idea to reflect this intuition. He uses a language model over POS sequences to remove outliers, discarding the 10% source language labeled sentences with highest perplexity per word according to a target language model. We go beyond Søgaard (2011) by learning from *weighted* data, where each weight estimates the relevance of a labeled sentence by the perplexity by word of the corresponding POS sequence in a target language model over its perplexity by word in a source language model.

In weighted perceptron learning (Cavallanti et al., 2006), we make the learning rate dependent on the current instance, using the following update rule on $\mathbf{x}_n$:

$$\mathbf{w}^{i+1} \leftarrow \mathbf{w}^i + \beta_n \alpha (y_n - \text{sign}(\mathbf{w}^i \cdot \mathbf{x}_n))\mathbf{x}_n \quad (1)$$

where $\beta_1, \ldots, \beta_n$ are importance weights.

Søgaard and Haulrich (2011) present an application of an importance weighted version of the MIRA algorithm (Crammer and Singer, 2003) and apply it to dependency parsing. Huang et al. (2007) present an instance-weighted learning algorithm for support vector machines. Under the assumption that differences between source and target distributions are due to sample bias only (which is clearly not the case here) we should weight a data point by its probability in the target domain over its probability in the source domain (Shimodaira, 2000), but since it is not possible to estimate densities in our case, we resort to a heuristic combining the insights from Shimodaira (2000) and Søgaard (2011), weighting each sentence in every source language treebank by:

$$f_w(\mathbf{x}) = \frac{\sqrt{ppw_S(\mathbf{x})}}{\sqrt{ppw_T(\mathbf{x})}}$$

where $ppw_D(\cdot)$ is the perplexity per word given a language model trained on a corpus sampled from domain D.

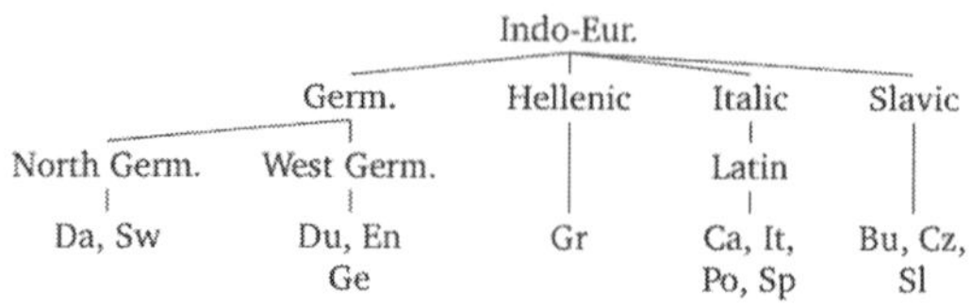

Figure 2: Language genealogy.

5 Experiments

Our parser is a modification of the publicly available implementation of the easy-first parser.[1] In our main experiments, we used the English feature model *as is* with no modifications. This is not entirely meaningful as the feature model refers to POS tags specific to the English Penn Treebank (PTB) (see Discussion). We used the datasets from the CoNLL-X (Buchholz and Marsi, 2006) and CoNLL 2007 (Nivre et al., 2007) shared tasks with standard train-test splits, but mapped all POS tags into Google's universal tag set (Petrov et al., 2011). See the shared task descriptions for dataset characteristics.

We used a publicly available language genealogy[2] and a publicly available database of typological properties[3] to obtain our weights. See Figure 2 for the linguistic genealogy. In the typological table, we disregarded phonological properties (properties 1–20) when computing Hamming distances between languages. We also report results obtained using voting. These results are obtained using the reparsing technique first described in Sagae and Lavie (2006) with our various weighted parsers as committee members.

6 Results

We note that our macro-average results are the best reported results for a fully delexicalized model, i.e. without lexical projections or bilingual word clusters. That being said recent results show that using cross-language projection or bilingual clustering to obtain lexical knowledge is beneficial, and we will explore different ways of augmenting the models presented here with such knowledge.

7 Discussion

We have tried to prevent over-fitting doing only a single pass over the data. While the averaged perceptron is less prone to over-fitting than the original perceptron learning algorithm (Rosenblatt, 1958), there is no guarantee that it does not over-fit the training data, and in our case where there is a considerable bias in the training data, over-fitting is more likely to happen. Averaging over several source languages provides implicit regularization.

Averaging has several advantages over just concatenating data. First of all we assign equal weights to all source languages (unless taking a weighted average), which means our model is not biased by the size of the linguistic resources used. More importantly, if we want to deliberately under-fit our models, learning with concatenated data is risky, especially if we do not shuffle the data.

Arguably our method to prevent over-fitting is crude, and we would like to explore more

[1] http://www.cs.bgu.ac.il/~yoavg/software/easyfirst/
[2] http://andromeda.rutgers.edu
[3] http://wals.info

source/target	Bu	Ca	Cz	Da	Du	Ge	Gr	It	Po	Sl	Sp	Sw	AV	AV_M	p-value
Bulgarian	68.5	55.7	45.0	44.1	50.4	49.2	47.8	55.7	67.0	35.8	51.7	61.1			
Catalan	59.7	77.8	43.2	45.9	49.4	57.0	59.1	**74.4**	71.3	51.6	**70.2**	52.5			
Czech	29.6	24.8	33.8	28.1	23.6	24.0	26.2	26.0	23.0	23.3	22.7	21.9			
Danish	36.9	30.0	29.5	45.4	25.5	22.9	18.7	37.7	30.5	26.0	29.5	26.6			
Dutch	59.6	59.4	43.4	46.6	71.2	57.6	63.1	59.5	67.4	44.1	53.1	57.4			
German	54.2	51.7	41.7	40.8	43.7	81.2	53.4	55.5	55.0	41.3	49.3	57.9			
Greek	56.5	67.6	45.8	42.3	60.5	52.3	70.6	66.9	67.9	**55.2**	58.0	57.5			
Italian	61.6	**79.5**	41.1	47.0	49.6	55.1	61.9	77.0	71.6	52.2	67.5	51.7			
Portuguese	49.5	59.7	34.5	25.8	49.0	37.9	50.6	59.3	58.1	34.1	50.6	39.7			
Slovene	20.8	16.6	19.5	33.1	19.2	20.4	23.9	18.7	19.3	24.0	17.2	22.8			
Spanish	46.0	74.8	30.5	42.1	41.3	46.6	42.6	64.1	67.2	42.1	72.9	46.9			
Swedish	58.6	58.3	36.5	45.0	50.8	54.2	56.7	57.6	68.3	37.5	55.1	80.6			
flat	62.1	68.9	45.5	46.0	54.0	**58.0**	63.4	67.4	76.5	44.7	64.4	60.7	59.2	61.2	
gtree	62.1	67.0	**46.9**	45.8	54.3	57.7	63.4	69.4	75.5	47.4	66.0	61.6	59.8	61.7	
typology	62.1	68.9	45.5	46.0	54.3	56.3	62.8	67.7	76.5	44.7	64.7	58.4	59.0	60.8	
pr	62.6	69.3	46.1	45.8	53.2	57.4	63.2	68.0	76.0	46.4	65.3	60.1	59.4	61.1	
vote (a)	62.7	69.3	45.8	46.3	54.0	57.7	63.4	68.8	76.4	45.8	65.6	61.2	60.5	62.6	
weighted	64.6	68.5	**46.9**	48.6	57.2	56.3	65.0	67.2	**77.6**	44.6	62.9	62.4	60.1	62.1	~ 0.005
w-typ	64.6	68.5	**46.9**	48.6	58.6	55.7	**66.2**	68.3	**77.6**	44.6	62.8	61.4	60.3	62.4	< 0.001
w-gtree	64.2	69.1	46.7	48.3	57.2	56.3	65.0	68.3	76.9	46.1	63.8	63.1	60.4	62.4	< 0.001
vote (b)	64.2	68.9	46.9	48.6	57.3	57.4	65.3	69.0	77.3	45.7	63.6	62.6	60.6	62.6	< 0.001
MPH11(dir)	-	-	-	48.9	55.8	56.7	60.1	64.1	74.0	-	64.2	65.3		61.2	
MPH11(proj)	-	-	-	**49.5**	**65.7**	56.6	65.1	65.0	75.6	-	64.5	**68.0**		**63.8**	
TMU12(dir)	-	-	-	36.7	52.8	48.9	-	64.6	66.8	-	60.2	55.4		55.1*	
TMU12(clust)	-	-	-	38.7	54.3	50.7	-	68.8	71.0	-	62.9	56.9		57.6*	
NBO12(best)	**66.8**	71.8	44.6	-	55.9	53.7	67.4	65.6	73.5	-	62.1	61.5			

Figure 3: Results, incl. language-level weighting (gtree and typology), unsupervised model selection (pr), instance-weighted extensions (w–) and a comparison with recent work. AV is macro-average, and AV_M is macro-average on the 8 languages used in McDonald et al. (2011). The voted systems (a) and (b) take non-weighted votes over the systems in the above rows.

advanced methods in the future.

Since we average over languages - which in a domain adaptation setting corresponds to distinct source domains - our model is very similar to multi-source domain adaptation models that use mixtures of experts (McClosky et al., 2010; Spinello and Arras, 2012). In future work we would also like to explore the idea of using smoothness assumptions in the target domain to select models based on source languages (Gao et al., 2008). Another option would be to view multi-source language learning as multi-task learning and apply a multi-task perceptron learning algorithm (Cavallanti et al., 2008) rather than just averaged perceptron learning.

On a more technical note, as already mentioned, readers familiar with the easy-first parser may wonder what we did with the POS-tag specific features in the English feature model distributed with the parser. We did not change anything in the feature model specification, keeping features that refer to PTB-specific tags. Changing the PTB-specific tags to their Google tag set translations yielded worse results on average with only small improvements for four languages (Catalan, Italian, Slovene and Spanish). Instead of optimizing the feature model we therefore chose to keep the original feature specification file *as is* for reproducibility.

References

Berg-Kirkpatrick, T. and Klein, D. (2010). Phylogenetic grammar induction. In *ACL*.

Brown, G., Wyatt, J., and Tino, P. (2005). Managing diversity in regression ensembles. *Journal of Machine Learning Research*, 6:1621–1650.

Buchholz, S. and Marsi, E. (2006). CoNLL-X shared task on multilingual dependency parsing. In *CoNLL*.

Cavallanti, G., Cesa-Bianchi, N., and Gentile, C. (2006). Tracking the best hyperplane with a simple budget perceptron. In *COLT*.

Cavallanti, G., Cesa-Bianchi, N., and Gentile, C. (2008). Linear algorithms for online multi-task classification. In *COLT*.

Cohen, S., Das, D., and Smith, N. (2011). Unsupervised structure prediction with non-parallel multilingual guidance. In *EMNLP*.

Collins, M. (2002). Discriminative training methods for hidden markov models. In *EMNLP*.

Crammer, K. and Singer, Y. (2003). Ultraconservative algorithms for multiclass problems. In *JMLR*.

Durrett, G., Pauls, A., and Klein, D. (2012). Syntactic transfer using a bilingual lexicon. In *EMNLP*.

Freund, Y. and Schapire, R. (1999). Large margin classification using the perceptron algorithm. *Machine Learning*, 37:277–296.

Gao, J., Fan, W., Jiang, J., and Han, J. (2008). Knowledge transfer via multiple model local structure mapping. In *KDD*.

Gelling, D., Cohn, T., Blunsom, P., and Graca, J. (2012). The pascal challenge on grammar induction. In *WILS-NAACL*.

Goldberg, Y. and Elhadad, M. (2010). An efficient algorithm for easy-first non-directional dependency parsing. In *NAACL*.

Huang, J., Smola, A., Gretton, A., Borgwardt, K., and Schölkopf, B. (2007). Correcting sample bias by unlabeled data. In *NIPS*.

Jiang, J. and Zhai, C. (2007). Instance weighting for domain adaptation in nlp. In *ACL*.

McClosky, D., Charniak, E., and Johnson, M. (2010). Automatic domain adaptation for parsing. In *NAACL-HLT*.

McDonald, R., Petrov, S., and Hall, K. (2011). Multi-source transfer of delexicalized dependency parsers. In *EMNLP*.

Naseem, T., Barzilay, R., and Globerson, A. (2012). Selective shargin for multilingual dependency parsing. In *ACL*.

Naseem, T., Chen, H., Barzilay, R., and Johnson, M. (2010). Using universal linguistic knowledge to guide grammar induction. In *EMNLP*.

Nivre, J., Hall, J., Kübler, S., McDonald, R., Nilsson, J., Riedel, S., and Yuret, D. (2007). The CoNLL 2007 shared task on dependency parsing. In *EMNLP-CoNLL*.

Petrov, S., Das, D., and McDonald, R. (2011). A universal part-of-speech tagset. CoRR abs/1104.2086.

Rosenblatt, F. (1958). The perceptron: a probabilistic model for information storage and organization in the brain. *Psychological Review*, 65(6):386–408.

Sagae, K. and Lavie, A. (2006). Parser combination by reparsing. In *HLT-NAACL*.

Shen, L., Satta, G., and Joshi, A. (2007). Guided learning for bidirectional sequence classification. In *ACL*.

Shimodaira, H. (2000). Improving predictive inference under covariate shift by weighting the log-likelihood function. *Journal of Statistical Planning and Inference*, 90:227–244.

Smith, D. and Eisner, J. (2009). Parser adaptation and projection with quasi-synchronous grammar features. In *EMNLP*.

Søgaard, A. (2011). Data point selection for cross-language adaptation of dependency parsers. In *ACL*.

Søgaard, A. (2012). Unsupervised dependency parsing without training. *Natural Language Engineering*, 18(1):187–203.

Søgaard, A. and Haulrich, M. (2011). Sentence-level instance-weighting for graph-based and transition-based dependency parsing. In *IWPT*.

Spinello, L. and Arras, K. (2012). Leveraging RGB-D data: adaptive fusion and domain adaptation for object detection. In *CRA*.

Spreyer, K. and Kuhn, J. (2009). Data-driven dependency parsing of new languages using incomplete and noisy training data. In *CoNLL*.

Täckström, O. (2012). Nudging the envelope of direct transfer methods for multilingual named entity recognition. In *WILS-NAACL*.

Täckström, O., McDonald, R., and Uszkoreit, J. (2012). Cross-lingual word clusters for direct transfer of linguistic structure. In *NAACL*.

Zeman, D. and Resnik, P. (2008). Cross-language parser adaptation between related languages. In *IJCNLP*.

Entropy-based Training Data Selection for Domain Adaptation

Yan Song[1,2] *Prescott Klassen*[1] *Fei Xia*[1] *Chunyu Kit*[2]
[1] University of Washington, Seattle, WA 98195, USA
[2] City University of Hong Kong, Kowloon, Hong Kong SAR, China
{yansong,klassp,fxia}@uw.edu, ctckit@cityu.edu.hk

ABSTRACT
Training data selection is a common method for domain adaptation, the goal of which is to choose a subset of training data that works well for a given test set. It has been shown to be effective for tasks such as machine translation and parsing. In this paper, we propose several entropy-based measures for training data selection and test their effectiveness on two tasks: Chinese word segmentation and part-of-speech tagging. The experimental results on the Chinese Penn Treebank indicate that some of the measures provide a statistically significant improvement over random selection for both tasks.

KEYWORDS: Domain Adaptation, Training Data Selection, Entropy-based measures.

Proceedings of COLING 2012: Posters, pages 1191–1200,
COLING 2012, Mumbai, December 2012.

1 Introduction

The performance of Natural Language Processing (NLP) systems often degrades significantly when training and testing data come from different domains. There has been extensive research on methods for domain adaptation including training data selection (e.g.,(Moore and Lewis, 2010; Plank and van Noord, 2011)), model combination (e.g., (McClosky et al., 2010)), feature copying (Daume III, 2007), semi-supervised learning (e.g., (McClosky et al., 2006)), and many more.

The goal of training data selection is to choose a subset of training data that was similar to a given test data set. The challenge is to find a good measure for calculating the similarity between training sentences and the test data set. Moore and Lewis (2010) calculated the difference of the cross entropy values for a given sentence, based on language models from the source domain and the target domain. Axelrod et al. (2011) adopted the idea of cross entropy measurement for training data selection for machine translation, in three different ways: the first directly measured cross entropy for the source side of the text; the second is similar to (Moore and Lewis, 2010) and ranked the data using cross entropy difference; and the third, took into account the bilingual data on both the source and target side of translations. Both studies showed that the selected subset of training data worked better than the entire training corpus for machine translation. Plank and van Noord (2011) investigated several different training data selection methods aimed at enhancing dependency parsing and part-of-speech (POS) tagging. These methods were classified into two categories, probabilistically-motivated and geometrically-motivated. Their work proved again that models trained on data selected by data selection methods outperform those trained on randomly selected data.

In this paper, we explore the use of entropy-based methods for training data selection and evaluate their effect on the tasks of Chinese word segmentation (CWS) and POS tagging.

2 Methodology

In this study, we first test whether there is a strong correlation between system performance and cross entropy of two probability distributions estimated from the training data and the test data. If that is the case, it implies that entropy-based measures could be effective for training data selection. We then propose several new entropy-based measures and test their effects on two NLP tasks: CWS and POS tagging. For evaluation, we use the Chinese Penn Treebank as described below.

2.1 Data

The Chinese Penn Treebank (CTB) was developed in the late 1990s (Xia et al., 2000) and each sentence is word segmented, part-of-speech tagged, and bracketed with a scheme similar to the English Penn Treebank (Marcus et al., 1993). Its latest release is version 7.0 [1], which contains more than one million words from five genres: Broadcast Conversation (BC), Broadcast News (BN), Magazine (MZ), Newswire (NW), and Weblog (WB). Some statistics of CTB7 are given in Table 1.

We have used CTB 7.0 for multiple experiments, some of them not directly related to this study. To prepare the data for all of our experiments, we divide the data in each genre into

[1] Linguistic Data Consortium No. LDC2010T07

Genre	# of chars	# of words	# of files	Source
Broadcast Conversation (BC)	275,289	184,161	86	China Central TV, CNN, MSNBC, Phoenix TV, etc.
Broadcast News (BN)	482,667	287,442	1,146	China Broadcasting System, China Central TV, China National Radio, Voice of America, etc.
Magazine (MZ)	402,979	256,305	137	Sinaroma
Newswire (NW)	442,993	260,164	790	Xinhua News, Guangming Daily, People's Daily, etc.
Weblog (WB)	342,116	208,257	214	Newsgroups, Weblogs
Total	1,946,044	1,196,329	2,373	

Table 1: Statistics of the CTB 7.0.

ten folds based on character counts, and use the first eight folds for training, the next fold for development, and the last fold for testing. In order to study the effect of genre variation on system performance, we want the size of the training data for each genre to be the same, so we set the training size to be the size of the training folds in the BC genre (the smallest genre in the CTB 7.0). We do the same for the development data. For testing, we use the whole test fold for each genre. The sizes of the data sets used in the experiments are shown in Table 2. Although we are not using the development fold for the experiments in this study, we chose to use the same data split for training and test to facilitate comparison with our other experiments.

	BC	BN	MZ	NW	WB
Training	211,795	211,826	211,834	211,853	211,796
Development	30,678	30,760	30,708	30,726	30,746
Test	32,816	48,317	37,531	44,543	33,623

Table 2: CTB 7.0 Genre character counts for data splitting.

2.2 System performance and cross entropy

In order to determine whether entropy-based measures are helpful in training data selection, we first check whether cross entropy correlates with system performance. For this, we first trained and tested the Stanford POS Tagger[2] (Toutanova et al., 2003) on the CTB 7.0. The results are in Table 3, in which the training and testing genres are indicated by row labels and column labels, respectively.

In the top part of the table, each cell (i, j) has two numbers, where i is the row and j is the column. The first number is the tagging accuracy, when the tagger is trained on the training data of the genre i, and tested on the test data of the genre j. The second number is cross entropy of the test data, estimated by a trigram language model built from the training data using the CMU-Cambridge LM Toolkit[3]. The final row in the table lists the

[2]http://nlp.stanford.edu/software/tagger.shtml
[3]http://www.speech.cs.cmu.edu/SLM/toolkit.html

Pearson Correlation Coefficient (PCC) between tagging accuracy and the cross-entropy for each column.

	BC	BN	MZ	NW	WB
BC	91.90/8.09	89.11/9.82	82.39/9.79	85.98/10.50	87.45/9.06
BN	88.42/9.04	91.42/9.28	84.90/9.62	89.71/9.88	87.48/9.38
MZ	85.34/9.01	85.91/9.84	91.64/9.31	87.43/10.09	84.68/9.35
NW	83.83/9.86	88.87/9.60	85.38/9.94	91.26/8.89	83.71/9.68
WB	90.38/8.75	88.07/9.78	86.93/9.78	88.40/10.10	89.24/9.10
PCC	-0.9023	-0.8344	-0.7594	-0.9252	-0.8178

Table 3: Results of Stanford POS Tagger on CTB 7.0 genre sub corpora with trigram cross entropy calculated on training and test and Pearson Correlation Coefficient on columns.

Table 3 indicates there is a strong inverse correlation between cross entropy and performance for POS tagging. Based on this result, we propose to use entropy-based measures for training data selection and test their effect on the tasks of Chinese word segmentation and POS tagging.

3 Entropy-based Measures

In this section, we propose several new entropy-based measures for training data selection.

3.1 Difference of Entropy (DE)

Eq 1 shows the standard definition of entropy in information theory, where X is a discrete random variable with m possible outcomes $\{x_1, ..., x_m\}$ and p is a probability distribution of X.

$$H(X) = -\sum_{i=1}^{m} p(x_i) \log p(x_i) \tag{1}$$

Given a sentence s, we represent s as a set of information units $\{x_1, ..., x_n\}$, where an information unit can be a word/character unigram or a bigram.[4] Let p be the probability distribution over all the information units collected from a data set C. Instead of calculating the entropy of the random variable X as in Eq 1 which uses all the possible x_i in C, we want to focus only on the x_i in s; therefore, we define a new function $H(s,p)$ as in Eq 2.

$$H(s,p) = -\sum_{i=1}^{n} p(x_i) \log p(x_i) \tag{2}$$

Now let p and q be the probability distributions estimated from the training data and the test data, respectively. Let s be a sentence in the training data. We define the difference of sentence entropy, $DE(s,p,q)$, as in Eq 3. Intuitively, choosing sentences with low DE values means we prefer sentences whose information units x_i have similar values with respect to p and q.

$$DE(s,p,q) = | H(s,p) - H(s,q) | \tag{3}$$

[4] We use character ngrams for CWS and word ngrams for POS tagging.

3.2 Cross Entropy (CE)

Similar to the difference between Eq 1 and 2, one could use a variation of cross entropy (CE) to calculate the cross entropy for a sentence s over two discrete probability distributions p and q, where p and q are estimated from the training and test data, respectively.

$$CE(s,p,q) = -\sum_{i=1}^{n} p(x_i)\log q(x_i) \tag{4}$$

3.3 Average Entropy Gain (AEG)

Let C be the test corpus and s be a sentence. The third measure, entropy gain (EG), is defined as in Eq 5, where q is a probability distribution estimated from C and $q1$ is one estimated from $C+s$, a new corpus formed by adding s to C. Intuitively, if s is similar to C, $q1$ will be very similar to q and $EG(s,c)$ will be small.

$$EG(s,C) = \mid H(C+s,q1) - H(C,q) \mid \tag{5}$$

The measures in Eq 3-5 can all be normalized by sentence length. For instance, Eq 6 shows the normalized entropy gain. We call it Average Entropy Gain (AEG).

$$AEG(s,C) = \frac{EG(s,C)}{length(s)} \tag{6}$$

3.4 Descriptive Length Gain (DLG)

Description length gain (DLG) is a goodness measure proposed by (Kit and Wilks, 1999) as an unsupervised learning approach to lexical acquisition (Kit, 2005; Kit and Zhao, 2007). Intuitively, the DLG of a string *str* w.r.t. a corpus *C*, *DLG(str, C)*, indicates the reduction of description length of *C* when the characters in *str* are treated as a unit and all the occurrences of *str* in *C* are replaced by the index of the unit. Therefore, the more frequent *str* is in *C* and the longer *str* is, the higher *DLG(str,C)* is. The DLG calculation resorts to a re-implementation of the suffix array approach to counting n-grams (Kit and Wilks, 1998).

Based on this property, we define a similarity measure, $Sim(s,C)$, between a training sentence s and the test corpus C as the average of DLG scores of substrings in s, as shown in Eq 7. Here, $Substr(s)$ is the set of substrings in s, and n is the size of the set. High $Sim(s,C)$ scores indicate that s is closer to C in the sense that the substrings in s tend to have high DLG scores with respect to C.

$$Sim(s,C) = \frac{1}{n} \sum_{str \in Substr(s)} DLG(str,C) \tag{7}$$

4 Experiments

In the previous section, we defined four entropy-based measures: difference of entropy (DE), cross entropy (CE), average entropy gain (AEG), and a DLG-based similarity measure. For DE, the information unit can be a unigram (*DE-1*), a bigram with joint probability

$P(w_{i-1}, w_i)$ (*DE-2J*), a bigram with conditional probability $P(w_i \mid w_{i-1})$ (*DE-2C*), or other ngrams. The same is true for CE and AEG. We use each measure to rank training sentences (in ascending order for DE, CE, and AEG and in descending order for the DLG-based measures), choose the top x% of the training data, train a word segmenter or a POS tagger (as described below), and compare the results with the system trained on x% of randomly selected training data (RDM).

The results of our experiments were tested for significance using a ten-partition two-tailed paired Student t-test, comparing each entropy-based measure with the average of three random experiments. To be more specific, the t-test was conducted in the following steps: (1) split the test data into N chunks (N is set to 10 in these experiments). (2) calculate the system performance on each chunk when using random selection vs. a particular selection method (e.g., DLG). That gives us 10 pairs of scores. (3) compute t-test scores to determine whether the difference between random selection and a particular selection method is statistically significant. In Tables 4 and 5, 95% confidence for significance is indicated by a single asterisk and 99% confidence by two asterisks.

Of the five genres in the CTB 7.0, we use BC as the test genre and BN, MZ, NW, WB as training genres. [5] The test data is the test portion of BC; the training data is the union of the training portions of the other four genres.

4.1 Chinese Word Segmentation

For word segmentation, we used a Conditional Random Fields word segmenter as described in (Song and Xia, 2012), which uses similar character tags and features as in (Zhao and Kit, 2011). We train the segmenter with a fixed percentage of training data and test the segmenter on the test data. The results are in Table 4.[6] The table shows that the performances of these entropy-based measures vary a lot: while some measures (e.g., DE-2J) are not better than random selection, others (e.g., DLG) provide a modest gain. For instance, seven of the ten results for DLG are statistically significant better than random selection at p=0.05, and four of these seven are significant at p=0.01.

4.2 POS Tagging

For POS tagging, we used the Stanford POS Tagger (Toutanova et al., 2003). The training and test data are the same as in word segmentation. The results are in Table 5. They show similar patterns as the ones for word segmentation: while measures such as DE-2J are not better than random selection, other measures such as DLG and AEG-2J often provide a small, but statistically significant gain.

5 Discussion

In the previous section, we use four entropy-based measures to select training data and show their performance on two tasks: Chinese word segmentation and POS tagging. Some

[5] BC was randomly selected as the test genre. Results for other genres are not included due to the page limit.

[6] We have experimented with other measure variants such as normalized DE-2J and normalized CE-2J, whose results are similar to their non-normalized counterparts. We also used DCE-2J, where DCE stands for difference of cross entropy, as defined in (Moore and Lewis, 2010). The f-scores when using DCE-2J to select x% of training data (x=5, 10, ..., 90) are 84.24, 87.54, 89.57,90.47, 92.44, 92.75, 93.22, 93.63, and 93.89%, respectively, and these results are not as good as DLG for most *x*'s. We did not include these numbers due to the space limit.

	AEG-1	AEG-2J	AEG-2C	CE-1	CE-2J	CE-2C	DE-1	DE-2J	DE-2C	DLG	RDM
5%	88.41*	**89.28****	87.28	87.12	86.11	88.43*	88.41*	84.74	86.28	88.98**	85.56
10%	90.03	90.82**	89.42	89.89*	88.35	90.66**	90.13	87.64	89.52	**91.29****	89.12
20%	91.60	92.08*	91.95**	91.00	90.97	91.87**	91.49	89.74	90.91	**92.49****	91.19
30%	92.29	92.55*	92.52**	92.11*	91.74	92.65**	92.23	90.86	92.06	**92.79****	91.71
40%	92.35	92.53	92.88**	92.40	92.37	93.01*	**93.08****	91.17	92.54	92.80*	92.21
50%	92.76	93.22	93.10	93.09	92.71	93.16	92.23	91.58	93.15	**93.31**	93.01
60%	92.84	93.42	93.36	93.34	93.01	93.31*	93.43	91.92	93.61*	**93.47****	93.12
70%	93.45*	93.43**	93.32	93.43	93.33	93.30	**93.56****	92.12	93.47	**93.56***	93.21
80%	93.50	93.54	**93.66**	93.51	93.51	93.40	93.58	92.58	93.59	**93.66**	93.59
90%	93.57	93.44	**93.96***	93.84*	93.58	93.73	93.74	93.33	93.68	93.80	93.68
100%	93.83	93.83	93.83	93.83	93.83	93.83	93.83	93.83	93.83	93.83	93.83

Table 4: Word segmentation results (in f-score): tested on *BC* and trained on the other four genres. * and ** indicate significance at 0.05 and 0.01, respectively. The highest score in each row is in bold.

	AEG-1	AEG-2J	AEG-2C	CE-1	CE-2J	CE-2C	DE-1	DE-2J	DE-2C	DLG	RDM
5%	86.44	**88.38****	86.73	87.11	86.80	86.70	86.23	84.06	86.78	86.80	87.02
10%	88.25	**89.61****	88.90	88.84	88.52	88.89	88.24	86.09	88.66	89.18*	88.60
20%	90.71**	**91.01****	90.61**	90.00	89.85	90.23	89.46	88.23	89.93	90.70**	89.74
30%	91.37**	91.40**	91.28**	90.80	90.80	90.85**	90.94**	88.98	90.81*	**91.49****	90.59
40%	91.64**	91.67	91.61**	91.36	91.45	91.60*	91.28	89.70	91.37	**91.79***	91.25
50%	91.86	91.94**	91.91*	91.68	91.58	91.81	91.69	89.96	91.57	**92.06****	91.37
60%	91.96	**92.31****	92.25*	91.73	91.63	92.20*	92.12	91.40	91.75	92.19*	91.84
70%	92.10	**92.53****	92.19	91.94	91.89	92.15	92.35*	91.64	91.97	92.30	91.84
80%	92.37	92.41	**92.51***	92.22	92.24	92.30	92.47*	91.89	92.24	92.43	92.11
90%	92.46	92.45	92.35	92.14	92.43*	92.38	**92.47***	92.40	92.18	92.26	92.22
100%	92.30	92.30	92.30	92.30	92.30	92.30	92.30	92.30	92.30	92.30	92.30

Table 5: POS tagging results (in tagging accuracy): tested on *BC* and trained on the other four genres. * and ** indicate significance at 0.05 and 0.01, respectively. The highest score in each row is in bold.

measures (e.g., AEG and DLG) provide a small, but statistically significant, improvement over random selection, while others do not. The question is why are some methods better than random selection and others are not.

While it requires more study to provide an adequate answer to the question, a few points are worth noting. First, there are several variants for each of the first three measures (i.e., CE, DE, and EG): the measures can be normalized by sentence length or not normalized; the information unit can a unigram, a bigram, or a higher ngram; probability distribution can be a joint probability or a conditional probability. All these could affect the system performance. Due to the space limit, Tables 4 and 5 list the results of only some of the variants. Second, while all the four measures use the test data to select training sentences, CE and DE also use the entire training data to calculate the scores (see Eq 3 and 4 where p is estimated from the training data). If the training data consists of data from multiple genres, as in our experiments, p would be a mixture of the distributions for several genres in the training data. If p is similar to the distribution q estimated from the test data,

CE and DE would not be very effective in training data selection, even when individual training sentences are very different with respect to their similarity to the test data. Third, as mentioned above, the t-test results are based on the scores from ten chunks of the test data; therefore, the variance of the scores for the ten chunks would affect the significant test results. That means, when we compare two measures, we should consider not only the overall evaluation scores on a test set, but also whether the system performance is stable across different subsets of the test data.

Finally, it is quite possible that the effectiveness of a domain adaptation technology in general (and a training data selection measure in particular) would vary depending on NLP tasks, languages, and training/test data sets, because those factors lead to different causes of low system performance when the training and test data come from different domains. For example, in Chinese word segmentation, the out-of-vocabulary word (OOV) problem is usually the main cause of low performance when training and test data come from different domains; whereas in machine translation different word senses could be one factor. All these imply that it is unlikely that one measure is always better than another, for all the tasks, all the languages, and all the data sets.

6 Conclusion and future work

Training data selection is a common approach to domain adaptation. The challenge is to find a good measure for calculating the similarity between training sentences and the test data to improve selection. In this paper, we propose four entropy-based measures for training data selection and test their effectiveness on two tasks: Chinese word segmentation and POS tagging. The experiments show that some measures such as AEG-2J and DLG often provide statistically significant improvement over random selection for both tasks, especially when a small percentage of training data is used.

As illustrated in our experiments, not all the measures we used outperform random selection with statistical significance. This is not surprising given that we know the effectiveness of a domain adaptation method can be influenced by many factors such as the NLP task itself, language, and the differences between the training and the test data. For our future work, we want to study the link between these factors and the behavior of our entropy-based measures and determine whether it is possible to predict what measures work well in particular settings.

Acknowledgments

The work is partly supported by the Intelligence Advanced Research Projects Activity (IARPA) via Department of Interior National Business Center (DoI/NBC) contract number D11PC20153. The U.S. Government is authorized to reproduce and distribute reprints for Governmental purposes notwithstanding any copyright annotation thereon. The views and conclusions contained herein are those of the authors and should not be interpreted as necessarily representing the official policies or endorsements, either expressed or implied, of IARPA, DoI/NBC, or the U.S. Government. This work is also partly supported by the Research Grants Council (RGC) of HKSAR, China, through the GRF Grant 9041597 (CityU 144410). We also thank three anonymous reviewers for very helpful comments.

References

Axelrod, A., He, X., and Gao, J. (2011). Domain adaptation via pseudo in-domain data selection. In *Proceedings of the Conference on Empirical Methods in Natural Language Processing*, pages 355–362.

Daume III, H. (2007). Frustratingly easy domain adaptation. In *Proceedings of the 45th Annual Meeting of the Association of Computational Linguistics*, pages 256–263.

Kit, C. (2005). Unsupervised lexical learning as inductive inference via compression. In Minett, J. W. and Wang, W. S., editors, *Language Acquisition, Change and Emergence*, pages 251–296. City University of Hong Kong Press.

Kit, C. and Wilks, Y. (1998). The virtual corpus approach to deriving n-gram statistics from large scale corpora. In Chang-Ning Huang, editor, *Proceedings of 1998 International Conference on Chinese Information Processing Conference*, pages 223–229, Beijing, China.

Kit, C. and Wilks, Y. (1999). Unsupervised Learning of Word Boundary with Description Length Gain. In *CoNLL-99*, pages 1–6.

Kit, C. and Zhao, H. (2007). Improving Chinese Word Segmentation with Description Length Gain. In *The 2007 International Conference on Artificial Intelligence (ICAI-2007)*, Monte Carlo Resort, Las Vegas, Nevada, USA.

Marcus, M., Marcinkiewicz, M. A., and Santorini, B. (1993). Building a large annotated corpus of English: the Penn Treebank. *Computational Linguistics*, 19(2):313–330.

McClosky, D., Charniak, E., and Johnson, M. (2006). Reranking and self-training for parser adaptation. In *Proceedings of the 21st International Conference on Computational Linguistics and the 44th annual meeting of the Association for Computational Linguistics*, pages 337–344.

McClosky, D., Charniak, E., and Johnson, M. (2010). Automatic Domain Adaptation for Parsing. In *Proceedings of HLT-NAACL*, pages 28–36.

Moore, R. and Lewis, W. (2010). Intelligent selection of language model training data. In *Proceedings of the ACL 2010 Conference Short Papers*, pages 220–224.

Plank, B. and van Noord, G. (2011). Effective measures of domain similarity for parsing. In *Proceedings of the 49th Annual Meeting of the Association for Computational Linguistics: Human Language Technologies-Volume 1*, pages 1566–1576.

Song, Y. and Xia, F. (2012). Using a Goodness Measurement for Domain Adaptation: A Case Study on Chinese Word Segmentation. In *Proceedings of the Eight International Conference on Language Resources and Evaluation (LREC'12)*.

Toutanova, K., Klein, D., Manning, C. D., and Singer, Y. (2003). Feature-rich part-of-speech tagging with a cyclic dependency network. In *Proceedings of the 2003 Conference of the North American Chapter of the Association for Computational Linguistics on Human Language Technology - Volume 1*, pages 173–180.

Xia, F., Palmer, M., Xue, N., Okurowski, M. E., Kovarik, J., Chiou, F., Huang, S., Kroch, T., and Marcus, M. (2000). Developing Guidelines and Ensuring Consistency for Chinese Text Annotation. In *In Proceedings of the Second Language Resources and Evaluation Conference*.

Zhao, H. and Kit, C. (2011). Integrating unsupervised and supervised word segmentation: The role of goodness measures. *Information Sciences*, 181(1):163–183.

Corpus-based Explorations of Affective Load Differences in Arabic-Hebrew-English

Carlo Strapparava[1] *Oliviero Stock*[1] *Ilai Alon*[2]

(1) FBK-irst, via Sommarive 18, Trento, Italy
(2) Department of Philosophy, Tel Aviv University, Israel
strappa@fbk.eu,stock@fbk.eu,ilaialon@post.tau.ac.il

ABSTRACT
This work is about connotative aspects of words, often not carried over in translation, which depend on specific cultures. A cross-language computational study is presented, based on exploitation of similarity techniques on large corpora of news documents in English, Arabic, and Hebrew. In particular, focus of the exploration is on specific terms expressing emotion, negotiation and conflict.

KEYWORDS: Multilinguality, Affective Language, Emotions in Language.

KEYWORDS IN L_2: Here a list of keywords in L_2 (if option used).

1 Introduction

Even an excellent human translator has problems in carrying over the target language all the culture-related aspects that go with words. If focus is put into emotion-related aspects the matter is even subtler. The relation of a word to emotion concepts may depend on ideology and in general on cultural aspects that can be inferred from extensive word usage rather than from what can be found in dictionaries. Of course it also depends on genres, different periods of text production, sociolinguistic characteristics of the text originators and so on.

In this paper, we describe a cross-language computational study based on exploitation of similarity techniques on large corpora of news documents in English, Arabic, and Hebrew. In particular, we focus our exploration on specific terms expressing emotion, negotiation and conflict.

Aside of the general scientific motivation, we had a specific motivation for starting this work: help overcoming unnecessary language problems in international negotiations involving different languages. In fact, perhaps the most damaging mistake in any negotiation is misunderstanding, especially that which is the result of ignorance and disregard. The need is to reduce one aspect of such misunderstanding.

During negotiations between Israelis and Palestinians for example, more than once the latter used the expression "the final solution" with reference to the Israeli-Palestinian conflict. For Israelis, as for many Westerners, this expression most importantly refers to the Holocaust. Thus, almost automatically it creates aversion, and is sometimes even interpreted as a threat. Or just consider the different valence of the word "honor" in an Arabic, English or Hebrew expression, particularly in an emotionally tense situation.

The aim of this work is to assess the emotional connotations of words which have more or less the same denotation in Arabic, Hebrew and English. Although Arabic and Hebrew have been studied for centuries by both Arab and foreign scholars, their emotive aspects have been rather neglected, at least from the semantic point of view. An exception among Arab scholars is Abdullah-T Shunnaq (Shunnaq, 1993). The view that emotions take part in the meaning of words was already made by McDougall during the Twenties' of the last century (Gregg, 2005). (Ogden and Richards, 1923) and more recently (Kövecses, 2000) call attention on how emotions are treated in language. Davitz's early work in the area of lexicography (Davitz, 1969) has recently gained greater interest with the advent of electronic media (Heise, 2001). (Kövecses, 2000) divides "emotion language" into expressive terms, terms literally denoting particular kinds of emotions, and figurative expressions, of which the latter "is the largest by far". On a similar line goes the cognitive approach of (Ortony et al., 1987).

On the other hand, cultures, and thus, languages, differ in the degree of emotionality, Arabic being considered high in this criterion (Shunnaq, 1993). This is even more evident for political terms, and in particular for those associated with conflict. In negotiation, recognition of the emotions of the other party is the first step on the road to conciliation. As (Irani, 1999) say "A first step in the process of healing, then, is the mutual acknowledgment by all parties of their emotions, viewpoints and needs.". On the negative side it has been said that "representing outcomes in affective terms leads to longer negotiation times and higher impasse rates" (Conlon and Hunt, 2002).

The important role of emotions in Middle East politics is also eloquently pointed to in an article by (Moïsi, 2007). In it he coined the phrase "clash of emotions", and argued that the Arab world manifests a culture of humiliation. Others in the Middle East argue too, that the role of emotions is greater than that of civilizations in explaining violence in the region (Fattaha and Fierke, 2009). On the Social-personal level, emotion is closely tied to moral system of a culture, and thus plays a decisive role in communicating with that culture. As (Fattaha and Fierke, 2009) put it: "In this view, emotion finds expression only in a language and a culture, which is linked to a moral order and moral appraisal. In the Middle East, feelings are always "situated in configurations of interpersonal relationships." These are connected in turn with the honor-modesty system (honor, shame, and modesty) (Gregg, 2005).

Coming to us, as said, we had the goal of establishing a methodology and eventually reaching concrete results concerning the different connotations of corresponding terms in Arabic, Hebrew and English. For one of us the initial strategy was to proceed via questionnaires in Arabic, and Hebrew, with different populations.The initial attempt at getting results via questionnaires could not get very far, mainly because of small numbers. The subtlety of the questions and situations suggested crowdsourcing techniques were not appropriate as well. The idea then came of following a computational approach very much in line with the experience of the other two authors. In particular, we used corpus-based similarity techniques for exploring affective significance of words in different languages, with relevant practical implications.

2 Corpora and terms in focus

In the experiment of exploring similarity, we exploited three corpora in the respective languages.

Arabic: Arabic Gigaword Third Edition is a comprehensive archive of newswire text data acquired from Arabic news sources. The six distinct sources of Arabic newswire are: Agence France Presse, Assabah, Al Hayat, An Nahar, Ummah Press, and Xinhua News Agency. The total number of documents is about 1.500.000 in a span time from 1995 until 2007. The preprocessing on this corpus consisted of a conversion from Arabic to Buckwalter ascii encoding and of a postagging process with the AMIRA tool (Diab et al., 2004).

English: We collected about 400.000 Google-News in the years 2008/2009. The documents have been pos-tagged with the TextPro tool (Pianta et al., 2008).

Hebrew: We used a collection of news documents from three newspapers in the span time 1990 - 2002: Arutz7, The Marker, and HaAretz.The corpus includes 11.474 documents and it has been preprocessed with a pos-tagger (Itai and Wintner, 2008).

In building the datasets from the documents of the three corpora, we considered as parts of speech nouns, verbs, adjectives and adverbs.

In order to select a suitable set of terms of conflict and emotion terms, questionnaires were distributed among native speakers of Arabic and Hebrew respectively, i.e. students of universities (Tel Aviv, Haifa), colleges (al-Qasemi) and high-schools (Palestinian East Jerusalem). For English we felt it was not strictly necessary. Respondents were asked to provide words in the categories of emotion, conflict, conciliation and trust terms. Among the emotion terms, some would not be considered "emotions" by English speakers, but were still included by us. This method was employed in order to avoid contamination of the list by Western culture researchers (Wierzbicka, 1997), e.g. by only referring to the "universal" emotions, i.e., anger, fear, disgust, sadness,

Emotion Terms	
English	Frustration Respecting Contempt Faithfulness Humiliation Satisfaction Revulsion Security Taking-Interest Faith Abhorrence Tolerance Determination Extremism Empathy Mutual-Understanding Emergency Love Sadness Grudge Kindness Perplexion Fear Mercy Contentedness Fright Happiness Tenderness Friendship Weakness Persecution Compassion Violence Anger Fervor Amicability Hardheartedness Worry Subdue Power Hatred Pin Indifference Suffering Boredom Cordiality Despair Fondness Disgust
Arabic	تعاطف تطرف تصميم تسامح بغض ايمان اهتمام امان اشمئزاز ارتياح اذلال اخلاص احتقار احترام احباط ظلم ضعف صداقة شفقة سعادة سرور رعب رضا رحمة خوف حيرة حنان حقد حزن حب توتر تفاهم يأس مودة ملل معاناة محبة مبالاة، عدم الم كره كراهية قوة قهر قلق قسوة فرح الفة غيرة غضب عنف عطف إشمِئزاز ميل إلى
Hebrew	תעוב אמונה התענינות בטחון סלידה נחת רוח השפלה נאמנות זלזול כבוד תסכול מבוכה רוך טינה עצב אהבה חרום הבנה הדדית אמפתיה קיצוניות נחישות סובלנות אלימות חבה עוול חולשה חברות חמלה אושר שמחה חרדה שביעות רצון רחמים פחד סבל אדישות כאב שנאה שנאה כח הכנעה ראגה אכזריות ששון ידידותיות קנאות כעס גועל אהדה לבביות שעמום
Conflict Terms	
English	Racialism Coalition Innocent-people Respecting Fraternity Land Americanism Revenge-taking Degeneration Decline Humanism Solidarity Transfer Intimidation Clash-of-Civilizations Solidarity Normalization Cooperation Competition Expulsion Nationality Unlawful War Right-of-Return Blood Religion Peace Politics Struggle Zionism Oppressive Enmity Arab Secularism Globalization Racialism Killing Force Nationality Equality Muslim Confiscation Jews
Arabic	الترهيب ترانسفير ترابط الانسانية انحطاط انحطاط انتقام ارض اخوة احترام أبرياء ائتلاف عنصرية سياسة سلام دين دم حق العودة حرب حرام جنسية تهجير تنافس تعاون التطبيع تضامن تصادم الحضرات مساواة قومية قوة قتل عنصرية عولمة علمانية عربي العداوة - آخر شيء في النزاع ظالم صهيزنية صراع يهود مصادرة مسلم
Hebrew	שקיעה התנקמות אמריקאיות אדמה אחווה כבוד חפים מפשע קואליציה גזענות נורמליזציה סולידריות התנגשות היות טרור טראנספר סולידריות אנושיות מדיניות שלום דת דם זכות השיבה מלחמה לאומיות גרוש תחרות שתוף פעולה לאומיות כח הרג גזענות גלובליזציה חילוניות ערבי איבה עושק ציונות מאבק יהודים החרמה מסלם שויון
Conciliation Terms	
English	Compromise Concessions Conciliation Negotiating Deal
Arabic	صفقة أخذ وعطاء تصالح تنازلات تسوية
Hebrew	עסקה משא ומתן פיוס ויתורים פשרה
Trust Terms	
English	Double-cross Betrayal Treason Loyalty Confidence Trust Deceit Credibility Treachery Reliability Fraud
Arabic	غش إخلاص خيانة مصداقية خدعة ثقة أمانة وفاء خيانة غدر خداع
Hebrew	מעל מהימנות בגידה נאמנות אמינות רמאות אמון אמון נאמנות בגידה בגידה הונאה

Table 1: Emotion, conflict, conciliation, and trust terms in the three languages

happiness, surprise. The terms that emerged as important in the questionnaires in Arabic and Hebrew were in the focus list of the computational experiment. Their translations (selected by a human expert) in the two other languages were picked out as well. In Table 1 the terms used in our experiments are reported.

Frustration	*Land*	0.311	*Anger*	*Politics*	0.376	*Extremism*	*Zionism*	0.101
احباط	ارض	0.640	غضب	سياسة	0.341	تطرف	صهيونية	0.316
תסכול	אדמה	0.184	כעס	מדיניות	0.132	קיצוניות	ציונות	0.157
Mercy	*Respecting*	0.149	*Fear*	*Double-cross*	0.154	*Extremism*	*Arab*	0.114
رحمة	احترام	0.021	خوف	خداع	0.691	تطرف	عربي	0.068
רחמים	כבוד	0.500	אהבה	הונאה	0.059	קיצוניות	ערבי	0.404
Hatred	*Fraud*	0.057	*Fright*	*Double-cross*	0.305	*Extremism*	*Blood*	0.029
كراهية	غش	0.209	رعب	خداع	0.645	تطرف	دم	0.261
שנאה	מעל	0.325	חרדה	הונאה	0.001	קיצוניות	דם	0.092
Sadness	*War*	0.074	*Anger*	*Double-cross*	0.105	*Extremism*	*Intimidation*	0.297
حزن	حرب	0.096	غضب	خداع	0.717	تطرف	الترهيب	0.436
עצב	מלחמה	0.209	כעס	הונאה	0.150	קיצוניות	טרור	0.085
Fright	*Killing*	0.078	*Fright*	*Globalization*	0.089	*Love*	*Zionism*	0.045
رعب	قتل	0.545	رعب	عولة	0.224	حب	صهيونية	0.057
חרדה	הרג	0.220	חרדה	גלובליזציה	0.016	אהבה	ציונות	0.237
Fear	*Politics*	0.366	*Fright*	*Confiscation*	0.008	*Love*	*Arab*	0.025
خوف	سياسة	0.330	رعب	مصادرة	0.250	حب	عربي	0.247
פחד	מדיניות	0.079	חרדה	החרמה	0.064	אהבה	ערבי	0.056

Table 2: Some similarity values in the three corpora

3 Technique

As a corpus-based measure of semantic similarity we exploited latent semantic analysis (LSA) proposed by Landauer (Landauer et al., 1998). In LSA, term co-occurrences in a corpus are captured by means of a dimensionality reduction operated by a singular value decomposition (SVD) on the term-by-document matrix **T** representing the corpus.

SVD is a well-known operation in linear algebra, which can be applied to any rectangular matrix in order to find correlations among its rows and columns. In our case, SVD decomposes the term-by-document matrix **T** into three matrices $\mathbf{T} = \mathbf{U}\Sigma_k\mathbf{V}^T$ where Σ_k is the diagonal $k \times k$ matrix containing the k singular values of **T**, $\sigma_1 \geq \sigma_2 \geq \ldots \geq \sigma_k$, and **U** and **V** are column-orthogonal matrices. When the three matrices are multiplied together the original term-by-document matrix is re-composed. Typically we can choose $k' \ll k$ obtaining the approximation $\mathbf{T} \simeq \mathbf{U}\Sigma_{k'}\mathbf{V}^T$.

LSA can be viewed as a way to overcome some of the drawbacks of the standard vector space model (sparseness and high dimensionality). In fact, the LSA similarity is computed in a lower dimensional space, in which second-order relations among terms and texts are exploited. The similarity in the resulting vector space is then measured with the standard *cosine* similarity. Note also that LSA yields a vector space model that allows for a *homogeneous* representation (and hence comparison) of words, word sets, and texts. It is possible to represent set of words in the semantic space using the *pseudo-document* text representation for LSA computation, as described by Berry (Berry, 1992). In practice, each text segment is represented in the LSA space by summing up the normalized LSA vectors of all the constituent words, using also a *tf.idf* weighting scheme. For the experiments reported in this paper, we run the SVD operation respectively on the three preprocessed corpora described in the previous section, using $k' = 400$ dimensions.

4 Results and discussion

To give an idea about different behaviors of corresponding terms in the three languages, in Table 2 we report some similarity values. In the initial part of the list we show similarity measures between emotion terms and some generic terms. The entries that follow in the list include more opinionated terms. The differences among values in the three languages are quite noticeable and can be considered as evidence of different sociocultural perceptions of the involved terms.

These results suggest that the proposed techniques are a viable tool for approaching cultural differences that emerge in different languages.

Of course, in the future, more specialized and, when possible, strictly aligned corpora can be used for the involved languages, as the applied context may require.

The computational approach we have presented has proven to be very promising: looking at specifically critical words for a sensitive situation like a multilingual negotiation in a bitter conflict, different emotional connotations of words, which are considered as the right translation, tend to appear clearly. From the applied point of view we are taking into consideration the development of an interface that would offer a quick perception of these different connotations across the involved languages, yielding an immediate feeling of the emotional aspect often lost in translation.

Acknowledgments

We thank Shuly Wintner, Noam Ordan, and Yulia Tsvetkov for providing and preprocessing the Hebrew corpus, and Arianna Bisazza for her hints regarding Arabic preprocessing. Carlo Strapparava was partially supported by Eurosentiment FP7 EU-project.

References

Berry, M. (1992). Large-scale sparse singular value computations. *International Journal of Supercomputer Applications*, 6(1).

Conlon, D. and Hunt, C. (2002). Dealing with feeling: the influence of outcome representations on negotiation. *International Journal of Conflict Management*, 13(1):38–58.

Davitz, J. R. (1969). *The Language of Emotion*. Academic Press.

Diab, M., Hacioglu, K., and Jurafsky, D. (2004). Automatic Tagging of Arabic Text: From Raw Text to Base Phrase Chunks. In Susan Dumais, D. M. and Roukos, S., editors, *HLT-NAACL 2004: Short Papers*, pages 149–152, Boston, Massachusetts, USA. Association for Computational Linguistics.

Fattaha, K. and Fierke, K. (2009). A clash of emotions: The politics of humiliation and political violence in the middle east. *European Journal of International Relations*, 15(1):67–93.

Gregg, G. S. (2005). *The Middle East: A Cultural Psychology*. Oxford University Press.

Heise, D. R. (2001). Project magellan: Collecting cross-cultural affective meanings via the internet. *Electronic Journal of Sociology*.

Irani, G. E. (1999). Islamic mediation techniques for middle east conflicts. *Middle East Review of International Affairs*, 3(2).

Itai, A. and Wintner, S. (2008). Language resources for hebrew. *Language Resources and Evaluation*, 42(1):75–98.

Kövecses, Z. (2000). *Metaphor and Emotion: Language, Culture, and Body in Human Feeling.* Cambridge University Press.

Landauer, T. K., Foltz, P., and Laham, D. (1998). Introduction to latent semantic analysis. *Discourse Processes*, 25.

Moïsi, D. (2007). The clash of emotions-fear, humiliation, hope, and the new world order. *Foreign Affairs*, 86.

Ogden, C. K. and Richards, I. A. (1923). *The Meaning of Meaning*. Harcourt, Brace & World.

Ortony, A., Clore, G. L., and Foss, M. A. (1987). The psychological foundations of the affective lexicon. *Journal of Personality and Social Psychology*, 53:751–766.

Pianta, E., Girardi, C., and Zanoli, R. (2008). The TextPro tool suite. In *Proceedings of 6th edition of the Language Resources and Evaluation Conference (LREC)*.

Shunnaq, A. (1993). Lexical incongruence in arabic-english translation due to emotiveness in arabic. *Turjuman*, 2:237–263.

Wierzbicka, A. (1997). *Understanding cultures through their key words.* Oxford University Press.

Acquiring and Generalizing Causal Inference Rules from Deverbal Noun Constructions

Shohei Tanaka[1] *Naoaki Okazaki*[2,3] *Mitsuru Ishizuka*[1]
(1) University of Tokyo, 7-3-1 Hongo, Bunkyo-ku, Tokyo, 113-8656, Japan
(2) Tohoku University, 6-3-09 Aramaki Aza Aoba, Aobaku, Sendai 980-8579, Japan
(3) PREST, Japan Science and Technology Agency (JST), Japan
`shh.tanaka at gmail.com, okazaki at ecei.tohoku.ac.jp, ishizuka at i.u-tokyo.ac.jp`

ABSTRACT
This paper presents a novel approach for inducing causal rules by using deverbal nouns as a clue for finding causal relations. We collect verbs and their deverbal forms from FrameNet, and extract pairs of sentences in which event verbs and their corresponding deverbal forms co-occur in documents. The most challenging part of this work is to generalize an instance of causal relation into a rule. This paper proposes a method to generalize and constrain causal rules so that the obtained rules have the high chance of applicability and reusability. In order to find a suitable constraint for a causal rule, we utilize relation instances extracted by an open-information extractor, and build a classifier to choose the most suitable constraint. We demonstrate that deverbal nouns provide a good clue for causal relations and that the proposed method can induce causal rules from deverbal noun constructions.

KEYWORDS: causal relation, rules, pattern generalization, semantic inference, knowledge acquisition.

Proceedings of COLING 2012: Posters, pages 1209–1218,
COLING 2012, Mumbai, December 2012.

1 Introduction

Performing semantic inference is important for natural language applications such as Question Answering (QA), Information Extraction, and Discourse Analysis. One of the missing links for semantic inference is the availability of commonsense knowledge in computers. In this paper, we focus on acquiring knowledge about causal relations between events.

Previous work on causal rule acquisition targeted at simple rules each of whose head is represented by a single literal or n-ary predicate: for example, Girju (2003) collected causal rules between nouns (e.g., *hunger* ⇒ *headache*); and Pantel et al. (2007) acquired causal rules between verbs (e.g., Y *announced the arrest of* X ⇒ X *is charged by* Y). However, humans perform more complicated inferences to predict outcomes of an event.

Let us consider the following example: *Google acquires Android Inc. The acquisition will enhance Google's competition in mobile phones.* The first sentence mentions an acquisition event with the verb *acquire*. Starting with its deverbal noun *acquisition*, the second sentence describes the possible outcome of the acquisition event. Referring to events explained in the preceding sentences, deverbal nouns often provide good clues for identifying cause-effect relations. However, acquiring the following causal rule from the above example is of no use:

$$\texttt{acquire}(\mathrm{X}, \textit{Android}) \Rightarrow \texttt{compete-in}(\mathrm{X}, \textit{mobile phones}) \tag{1}$$

Even though we generalize the causal relation by replacing the company name *Google* with a variable X, it is unlikely to reuse the causal knowledge that *if a company acquires Android, the company will compete in mobile phones.* Having said that, the following rule may be too generic:

$$\texttt{acquire}(\mathrm{X},\mathrm{Y}) \Rightarrow \texttt{compete-in}(\mathrm{X},\mathrm{Z}) \tag{2}$$

This rule only expresses that *if a company acquires something, the company will compete in some area.* This causality may be supported by a lot of activities in the real world, but it does not provide a good hint for predicting the value of Z. In contrast, inducing the following causal rule would be more preferable in terms of the reusability and predictability:

$$\texttt{acquire}(\mathrm{X},\mathrm{Y}) \land \texttt{specialized-in}(\mathrm{Y},\mathrm{Z}) \Rightarrow \texttt{compete-in}(\mathrm{X},\mathrm{Z}) \tag{3}$$

Here, we complemented a predicate specialized-in(Y, Z) as a constraint, i.e., as a premise in the head (left-hand side) of the rule, even though this is not explicit in the original text. Humans accept the causal relation mentioned in the above text because we have a prior knowledge about Rule 3 and the truth of the predicate specialized-in(*Android*, *mobile phone*).

This paper presents a novel approach for inducing causal rules like Rule 3 from the sentences with deverbal nouns (as in the above example). The contributions of this paper are twofold:

1. We focus on verbs and their deverbal nouns that co-refer to the same events. The use of deverbal nouns was not explored in the previous work on causal knowledge acquisition. We investigate the advantage of this approach empirically.
2. We present a method for generalizing and constraining causal relations by making use of relation instances acquired automatically from a large corpus. Previous work replaced the same mention (string) in a pattern with a variable to induce an inference rule (template). In contrast, this work unveils hidden predicates and variables that are not stated explicitly in text, but are crucial for explaining causal relations. This part is very challenging because we need to combine pieces of predicates obtained from different texts.

2 Proposed Method

The proposed system uses FrameNet[1] (Fillmore, 1976; Baker et al., 1998) for obtaining a list of verbs and their deverbal nouns (e.g., *acquisition* and *purchase* as deverbal nouns of verbs *buy* and *acquire*). Finding documents containing both verbs and their deverbal nouns in the corpus, the system extracts text fragments in which causal relations are expressed by pairs of sentences, "*A verb B* ..." and "*Deverbal-noun* ...". Here, *A* and *B* present named entities[2], and "*Deverbal-noun* ..." denotes a sentence starting with the deverbal noun of *verb*. We call the former sentence "*A verb B* ..." a *head sentence* and the latter sentence "*Deverbal-noun* ..." a *body sentence*. We apply several NLP analyses including part-of-speech tagging, dependency parsing, named entity recognition, and coreference resolution for obtaining causal relation instances as dependency trees with variables (Section 2.1). Independently of this process, the system extracts relation instances from the corpus by using ReVerb[3] (Fader et al., 2011) (Section 2.2). Searching for candidates of relation instances that can be inserted to a causal rule as a constraint, the system chooses the best relation instance as a constraint (Section 2.3).

2.1 Extracting causal relations using deverbal nouns

Using the list of verbs and their deverbal nouns extracted from FrameNet, the proposed system finds documents that contain both verbs and their corresponding deverbal nouns. For example, we extract a document when it contains a verb *buy* and its deverbal nouns (*purchase*, *acquisition*, *procurement*, etc). We employ Stanford Core NLP[4] for fundamental NLP analyses including sentence splitting, tokenization, part-of-speech tagging, named entity recognition, dependency parsing, and coreference resolution. The system extracts a causal relation from every sentence pair containing a verb and its deverbal noun. In this section, we use the following example to explain the process of generalizing causal relations into causal rules.

UnitedHealth buys Pacificare. The acquisition also gives UnitedHealth new operations in Nevada.

Firstly, the proposed method extracts a predicate and its arguments as the event referred to by the head (first) sentence. We define that: a predicate is a verb; arguments are a subject and object of the verb in the dependency tree; and arguments must mention named entities. For instance, the system extracts buy(*UnitedHealth*, *Pacificare*) from the example. In this study, we assume that a named entity presents either a person, location, or organization recognized by Stanford Core NLP. We replace mentions of each argument with a variable such as A and B, and generalize the predicate into a pattern buy(A, B). We call the pattern and variables extracted from the head sentence *head pattern* and *entity variables*, respectively.

2.1.1 Simplifying a pattern from the sentence with a deverbal noun

Sentences with deverbal nouns are often so specific that we cannot reuse corresponding patterns as bodies of causal rules. For example, the pattern from the example, *the acquisition also gives* A *new operations in Nevada*, is too specific. Therefore, we simplify a pattern from the body sentence (*body pattern* hereafter) by applying the following procedure.

[1] `https://framenet.icsi.berkeley.edu/fndrupal/`

[2] We use newswire text as a corpus, where the current NLP tools (e.g., POS tagger and NER) were designed to perform well. Because articles in the newswire domain mostly describe events occurring with named entities (e.g., companies, organizations, people), we do not think the requirement of variables *A* and *B* was strong.

[3] `http://reverb.cs.washington.edu/`

[4] `http://nlp.stanford.edu/software/corenlp.shtml`

1. Remove nodes whose depths (distances from the root node) are more than three in the dependency tree. We assume that these words are unnecessary for body patterns.
2. Replace every noun node with a variable (e.g., X) whose depth is no more than three. These variables will be used for generalizing the causal relation.
3. Keep nodes whose depths are one or two.
4. For each variable X, resolve it to a variable in the head pattern, A or B, if the variable X satisfies the following rules:
    - The variable X is a part of the named entity in the head pattern. For example, when X is *Google* and A is *Google Inc*, we replace X with A.
    - The variable is the initials of the named entity. For example, when X is *HP* and A is *Hewlett-Packard*, we replace X with A.
5. If a node is recognized as a numerical expression (tagged as either "Time", "Money", "Percent", "Date" and "Number" by Stanford Core NLP), replace the node with a special variable representing its semantic class. For example, we replace *$1,500,000* with MONEY.
6. Remove nodes that have certain syntactic relations (adverbial modifiers, appositional modifiers, adjectival modifiers and complementizers) with their parents. Nodes under these relations unnecessary for body patterns, describing specific/additional information.
7. Remove a body pattern if it ends with words other than nouns. This rule removes body patterns in passive voice, for example, *the acquisition of A was announced.*

We call variables that were unresolved to entity variables after this procedure *unconstrained variables*. The procedure yields a body pattern *the acquisition gives* A *operations in* X. Combining the head and body patterns, we obtain the following causal relation,

$$\texttt{buy(A,B)} \Rightarrow \textit{the acquisition gives } \texttt{A} \textit{ operations in } \texttt{X} \quad (4)$$

Meanwhile, it would be better for the usability of causal rules if we could paraphrase the body pattern *the acquisition gives* A *operations in* X into a predicate representation operate-in(A,X) or a simpler textual pattern like A *will operate in* X. As the first attempt for using deverbal nouns, we leave the task as a future work; in this study we focus on generalizing causal rules.

2.2 Finding possible constraints for causal rules

So far, we obtained generalized causal rules with variables. However, these rules are too generic to represent a causal relation; for example, it is inadequate to fill any location name (e.g., *Tokyo* and *London*) in the unconstrained variable X of the rule, buy(A,B) ⇒ *The acquisition gives* A *operations in* X. Therefore, we would like to find constraints for unconstrained variables so that a rule is likely to instantiate a causal relation. The basic idea for inducing constraints is to associate unconstrained variables (e.g., X) with entity variables (e.g., A and/or B). In other words, if we found a relation associating either of the pairs (X, A) or (X, B), we could use the relation as the constraint for the variable X.

For example, if we were aware of a relation instance headquartered-in(*Pacificare, Nevada*), we could transform Rule 4 into:

$$\texttt{buy(A,B)} \wedge \texttt{headquartered-in(B,X)} \Rightarrow \textit{The acquisition gives } \texttt{A} \textit{ operations in } \texttt{X} \quad (5)$$

With the predicate headquartered-in(B,X) as a constraint (premise), Rule 5 has a higher chance of realizing the causality than Rule 4. In this way, we solve the problem of inducing

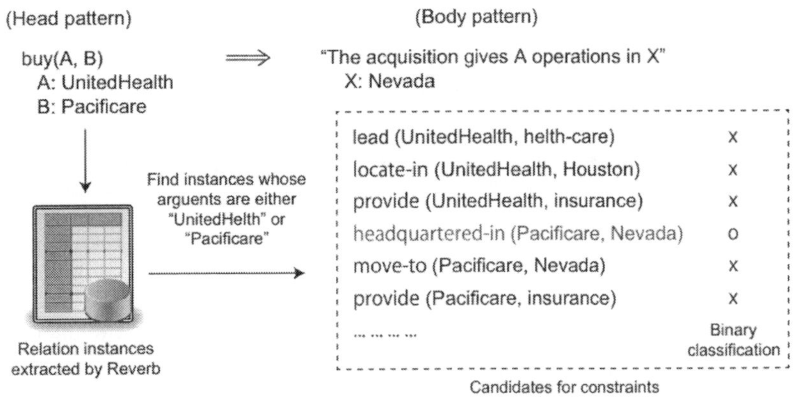

Figure 1: Choosing a constraint as a binary classification problem.

constraints by finding relation instances that associate unconstrained variables with entity variables. An easy and secure approach for the problem would be to extract a relation instance from the target document from which body and head patterns are extracted. However, there is no guarantee that a target document has a sentence associating unconstrained variables with entity variables. For example, the target document may not include a sentence like *Pacificare maintains headquarters in Nevada.* Therefore, we extract relation instances by applying ReVerb, an Open Information Extractor, to a large text corpus. We use the collection of relation instances as a knowledge base to explain unconstrained variables. In this study, we use the ClueWeb09 corpus[5] as a large text corpus.

2.3 Choosing a relation instance for inducing a constraint

A naive approach for associating unconstrained variables (e.g., X) with entity variables (e.g., A and B) would be to find relation instances that match to the query *(A,X) or *(B,X), where * denotes a wildcard. However, this query is inflexible in that it assumes an exact match for the value of X. In addition, if the query finds multiple relation instances (see "Candidates for constraints" in Figure 1), we need a mechanism to rank the relation instances. Therefore, we formalize the problem of choosing a relation instance for a constraint as a binary classification problem: choose a relation instance that yields the highest confidence score in the candidate relation instances. In order to allow flexible matching on the value of unconstrained variables (e.g., X), we relax the query such that it retrieves relation instances containing either the value of A or B,

$$*(\mathtt{A},*) \text{ or } *(\mathtt{B},*) \text{ or } *(*,\mathtt{A}) \text{ or } *(*,\mathtt{A}) \tag{6}$$

Figure 1 illustrates this process. Because we relaxed the query, the retrieved relation instances may not refer to the value of X (e.g., *Nevada*). At the same time, the retrieved instances may include multiple relations (e.g., `headquartered-in` and `move-to`) that refer to the value of X. Thus, we design several features to choose a relation instance that is suitable for the causal rule as a constraint. In the descriptions of the features, we denote: X as the value of the unconstrained variable; X' as the value of the argument other than A and B in the retrieved relation instance; R as the text representation of the retrieved relation (e.g., *has a headquarter in* for `headquarter-in` relation).

[5] `http://lemurproject.org/clueweb09.php/`

1. Word overlap between X and X'. Representing an argument X as a vector w_X whose elements present occurrences of words in X, and $w_{X'}$ similarly, this feature computes a cosine similarity between the vectors w_X and $w_{X'}$.
2. Word overlap between R and the target document. Representing the relation R as a vector w_R whose elements present occurrences of words in R and the vector of target document w_D similarly, this feature computes a cosine similarity between the vectors w_R and w_D.
3. Overlap of documents supporting the relation R and the body pattern. We define d_R as the set of documents containing the relation R, in other words, documents from which ReVerb yields the relation R. We also define d_b containing all the words in the body pattern. This feature measures the overlap of the two sets d_R and d_b by using the Jaccard coefficient.
4. Overlap of documents supporting the relation R and X'. This feature measures the overlap of two sets of documents that containing the relation R and the value of X', respectively, by using the Jaccard coefficient.
5. Overlap of documents supporting the relation R and X. This feature measures the overlap of two sets of documents that containing the relation R and the value of X, respectively, using the Jaccard coefficient.
6. Overlap of documents supporting X and X'. This feature measures the overlap of two sets of documents containing the values of X and X' by using the Jaccard coefficient.
7. Context similarity between X and X'. We represent an argument X as a vector c_X whose elements present frequencies of words that co-occur with X within sentences. We also define $c_{X'}$ similarly. This feature computes a cosine similarity between the vectors c_X and $c_{X'}$ as a distributional similarity between X and X'.

In order to build a classifier for ranking constraints, we manually prepared a training set. In this study, we used a verb *acquire* (belonging to the frame "Getting") as the target verb. Using its deverbal nouns, the system extracted ten causal relations from the corpus. The system found 100 relation instances for each causal relation. Then we asked a human annotator to label each relation instance as: positive if a relation is suitable as a constraint for the causal relation; and negative otherwise. In this way, we obtained 1,000 training instances for the classifier. Although the training set might look small in numbers, we think this is sufficient because the designed features do not include lexicalized features. We use liblinear[6] as an implementation of linear kernel SVMs for modeling the classifier. The system computes the dot product of the feature vector and the weight vector to compute the score of a relation instance.

3 Experiments

We conducted two experiments to evaluate the proposed method. The first experiment investigates the ability of deverbal nouns as clues for causal relations (without any generalization). The second experiment evaluates the correctness of causal rules. In these experiments, we used the portion of L.A. Times (about 300,000 articles) in English Gigaword Corpus Third Edition[7].

3.1 Deverbal nouns as clues for causal relations

Because no resource exists for evaluating causal relations between verbs, we built an evaluation set manually, selecting 10 verbs (frames) for this evaluation[8]. For each verb in the target verb

[6] http://www.csie.ntu.edu.tw/~cjlin/liblinear/

[7] http://www.ldc.upenn.edu/Catalog/CatalogEntry.jsp?catalogId=LDC2007T07

[8] We chose verbs that are frequent in the ClueWeb09 corpus, but excluded some verbs that do not have deverbal nouns (e.g., *be*), and that do not introduce causal relations (e.g., *like*).

Method	Precision	Recall	F_1
Baseline method (causal)	0.0445	0.1574	0.0694
Baseline method (causal + other)	0.1440	0.2165	0.1730
Proposed method (causal)	0.5357	0.2778	0.3659
Proposed method (causal + other)	0.6607	0.1457	0.2387

Table 1: Precision and recall on locating causal relations

set, we randomly sampled five documents in which both the verb and one of its deverbal nouns appear. This process obtained 50 documents (five for each verb) as an evaluation set. Then we asked a human annotator to mark pairs of verbs and other expressions (including verbs and nouns) that have causal relations in the documents. In addition, we also asked the annotator to mark pairs if they do not have causal relations but other relations (e.g., similar and associated). In this way, we obtained 108 pairs in causal relations and 146 pairs in other relations.

We prepared a baseline method that assumes a pair of relations sharing the same argument to have a causal relation. The baseline method uses ReVerb to extract relation instances in each document in the test set. For example, when ReVerb finds relation instances visit(*the prime minister, US*) and meet(*the prime minister, the president*) from the same document, the baseline method yields *visit* $\Rightarrow$ *meet*.

Table 1 reports precision and recall of the proposed and baseline methods for locating causal relations. In the table, "causal" uses causal relations identified by the annotator as the gold standard, and "causal + other" uses causal and other relations as the gold standard. Our method performed much better than the baseline method in terms of precision and F_1 score. The baseline method did not work well for finding causal relations (0.0694 F_1 score), but found causal and other relations to some extent (0.1730 F_1 score). In contrast, the proposed method gained 0.3659 F_1 score in finding causal relations, but the F_1 score decreased to 0.2387 when we include other relations for the evaluation. This fact suggests that deverbal nouns can locate causal relations selectively, separating from other types of associations.

3.2 Extraction of causal rules

Using the same set of the 50 documents in Section 3.1, we evaluated the correctness of the rules extracted by a system. We asked the human subject to mark each rule extracted by a system into: *causal* if the rule presents a causal relation; *related* if the head and body of the rule does not present a causal relation but have some relation; and *incorrect* if the rule is incorrect.

We compare four methods including a baseline and the proposed method and their variants. "ReVerb+ReVerb" applies ReVerb to a target document, and finds causal rules such as verb1(A, B) $\Rightarrow$ verb2(B, X), using the identical argument B as the bridge to connect *verb1* and *verb2*. In order to insert a constraint for the causal rule, it searches for relation instances verb3(A, X), verb3(B, X), verb3(X, A), or verb3(X, B) in the database constructed in Section 2.2. This method selects the relation instance with the highest score (computed by ReVerb) as a constraint. "ReVerb+SVM" extracts causal rules similarly to "ReVerb+ReVerb", but selects a relation for a constraint for a causal rule by using the SVM classifier described in Section 2.3. "Proposed method+ReVerb" extracts causality rules by using the proposed method. When this method selects a constraint for a causal rule, it selects the relation instance with the highest score computed by ReVerb. "Proposed method+SVM" is identical to the proposed method; this

Method	Causal	Causal + Related
ReVerb+ReVerb	0.1667	0.4902
ReVerb+SVM	0.1176	0.4804
Proposed method+ReVerb	0.2946	0.5982
Proposed method+SVM	0.3750	0.6339

Table 2: Accuracy of causal rules extracted by the systems

setting uses the SVM classifier to select a relation instance as a constraint for a causal rule.

Table 2 reports the average of accuracy values computed on the gold standard prepared by a human subject. The proposed method using SVM achieved the highest performance (0.3750 for causality). The SVM-based constraint selector boosted the correctness of causal rules for the proposed method (0.2946 → 0.3750). The baseline method could yield rules representing some association (0.4902 for causal and other relations), but failed to produce causal rules (0.1667). The SVM-based constraint selector did not contribute to the baseline method. This is probably because we trained the constraint selector for the proposed method. We observed that the half of rules extracted by the proposed method were judged incorrect. Analyzing these false cases, we found that these errors appeared in the phase of selecting constraints.

4 Related Work

The previous work on automatic acquisition of causal knowledge can be categorized into three groups in terms of types of inference rules: noun-noun causality (Girju, 2003; Chang and Choi, 2006; Saeger et al., 2011), verb-verb causality (Lin and Pantel, 2001; Chklovski and Pantel, 2004; Torisawa, 2006; Pantel et al., 2007; Abe et al., 2008; Beamer and Girju, 2009; Do et al., 2011; Hashimoto et al., 2012), and inference rules of other types (e.g., entailment) (Pekar, 2006; Szpektor and Dagan, 2008; Aharon et al., 2010; Schoenmackers et al., 2010; Berant et al., 2010, 2011; Gordon and Schubert, 2011; Berant et al., 2012). However, causal rules extracted by the previous work were limited to those without variables (e.g., *lean* ⇒ *kiss*) or those with the same set of variables (e.g., X *leaves for* Y ⇒ X *gets to* Y) in the head and body of a rule. In contrast, our work is the first approach that leverages deverbal nouns that directly express causal relations, and generalizes causal relations into causal rules with multiple variables.

5 Conclusion

In this paper, we presented a novel approach for inducing causal rules from the sentences with deverbal nouns. We conducted two experiments, and demonstrated that deverbal nouns present a good clue for causal relations and that the proposed method can generalize causal relations into causal rules. In this work, we did not address the problem of paraphrasing the body pattern (e.g., *the acquisition gives* A *operations in* X) into a predicate representation (e.g., `operate-in(A,X)`) or a simpler textual pattern (e.g., A *will operate in* B). This task would be an immediate future work of this study. In addition, we would like to extend the approach of rule generalization to causal relations identified by other clues (e.g., distributional similarity of verbs) and to other types of semantic relations, for example, entailment relations.

Acknowledgments

This research was partly supported by JST, PRESTO. This work was partly supported by JSPS KAKENHI Grant Numbers 23240018 and 23700159.

References

Abe, S., Inui, K., and Matsumoto, Y. (2008). Acquiring event relation knowledge by learning cooccurrence patterns and fertilizing cooccurrence samples with verbal nouns. In *Proceedings of the Third International Joint Conference on Natural Language Processing*, IJCNLP 2008, pages 497–504.

Aharon, R. B., Szpektor, I., and Dagan, I. (2010). Generating entailment rules from FrameNet. In *Proceedings of the ACL 2010 Conference Short Papers*, ACL 2010 (short), pages 241–246.

Baker, C. F., Fillmore, C. J., and Lowe, J. B. (1998). The Berkeley FrameNet project. In *Proceedings of the 17th international conference on Computational linguistics (Coling 1998) and the 36th Annual Meeting of the Association for Computational Linguistics and 17th International Conference on Computational Linguistics*, ACL 1998, pages 86–90.

Beamer, B. and Girju, R. (2009). Using a bigram event model to predict causal potential. In *Proceedings of the 10th International Conference on Intelligent Text Processing and Computational Linguistics*, CICLing 2009, pages 430–441.

Berant, J., Dagan, I., Adler, M., and Goldberger, J. (2012). Efficient tree-based approximation for entailment graph learning. In *Proceedings of the 50th Annual Meeting of the Association for Computational Linguistics*, ACL 2012, pages 117–125.

Berant, J., Dagan, I., and Goldberger, J. (2010). Global learning of focused entailment graphs. In *Proceedings of the 48th Annual Meeting of the Association for Computational Linguistics*, ACL 2010, pages 1220–1229.

Berant, J., Dagan, I., and Goldberger, J. (2011). Global learning of typed entailment rules. In *Proceedings of the 49th Annual Meeting of the Association for Computational Linguistics: Human Language Technologies*, ACL HLT 2011, pages 610–619.

Chang, D.-S. and Choi, K.-S. (2006). Incremental cue phrase learning and bootstrapping method for causality extraction using cue phrase and word pair probabilities. *Information Processing and Management*, 42(3):662–678.

Chklovski, T. and Pantel, P. (2004). VerbOcean: Mining the web for fine-grained semantic verb relations. In *Proceedings of the 2004 Conference on Empirical Methods in Natural Language Processing*, EMNLP 2004, pages 33–40.

Do, Q. X., Chan, Y. S., and Roth, D. (2011). Minimally supervised event causality identification. In *Proceedings of the 2011 Conference on Empirical Methods in Natural Language Processing*, EMNLP 2011, pages 294–303.

Fader, A., Soderland, S., and Etzioni, O. (2011). Identifying relations for open information extraction. In *Proceedings of the 2011 Conference on Empirical Methods in Natural Language Processing*, EMNLP 2011, pages 1535–1545.

Fillmore, C. J. (1976). Frame semantics and the nature of language. *Annals of the New York Academy of Sciences: Conference on the Origin and Development of Language and Speech*, 280(1):20–32.

Girju, R. (2003). Automatic detection of causal relations for question answering. In *Proceedings of the ACL 2003 workshop on multilingual summarization and question answering*, pages 76–83.

Gordon, J. and Schubert, L. K. (2011). Discovering commonsense entailment rules implicit in sentences. In *Proceedings of the TextInfer 2011 Workshop on Textual Entailment*, TIWTE 2011, pages 59–63.

Hashimoto, C., Torisawa, K., De Saeger, S., Oh, J.-H., and Kazama, J. (2012). Excitatory or inhibitory: A new semantic orientation extracts contradiction and causality from the web. In *Proceedings of the 2012 Joint Conference on Empirical Methods in Natural Language Processing and Computational Natural Language Learning*, EMNLP-CoNLL 2012, pages 619–630.

Lin, D. and Pantel, P. (2001). DIRT – Discovery of inference rules from text. In *Proceedings of ACM Conference on Knowledge Discovery and Data Mining*, KDD 2001, pages 323–328.

Pantel, P., Bhagat, R., Chklovski, T., and Hovy, E. (2007). ISP: Learning inferential selectional preferences. In *In Proceedings of Human Language Technologies: The Annual Conference of the North American Chapter of the Association for Computational Linguistics*, NAACL HLT 2007, pages 564–571.

Pekar, V. (2006). Acquisition of verb entailment from text. In *Proceedings of the main conference on Human Language Technology Conference of the North American Chapter of the Association of Computational Linguistics*, HLT-NAACL '06, pages 49–56.

Saeger, S. D., Torisawa, K., Tsuchida, M., Kazama, J., Hashimoto, C., Yamada, I., Oh, J.-H., Varga, I., and Yan, Y. (2011). Relation acquisition using word classes and partial patterns. In *Proceedings of the 2011 Conference on Empirical Methods in Natural Language Processing*, EMNLP 2011, pages 825–835.

Schoenmackers, S., Etzioni, O., Weld, D. S., and Davis, J. (2010). Learning first-order Horn clauses from web text. In *Proceedings of the 2010 Conference on Empirical Methods in Natural Language Processing*, EMNLP 2010, pages 1088–1098.

Szpektor, I. and Dagan, I. (2008). Learning entailment rules for unary templates. In *Proceedings of the 22nd International Conference on Computational Linguistics*, Coling 2008, pages 849–856.

Torisawa, K. (2006). Acquiring inference rules with temporal constraints by using Japanese coordinated sentences and noun-verb co-occurrences. In *Proceedings of the Human Language Technology Conference of North American chapter of the Association for Computational Linguistics*, HLT NAACL 2006, pages 57–64.

Advertising Legality Recognition

Yi-jie Tang, Cong-kai Lin, Hsin-Hsi Chen
Department of Computer Science and Information Engineering, National Taiwan University
#1, Sec.4, Roosevelt Road, Taipei, 10617 Taiwan
tangyj@nlg.csie.ntu.edu.tw, r00922106@ntu.edu.tw, hhchen@ntu.edu.tw

ABSTRACT

As online marketing and advertising keep growing on the Internet, a large amount of advertisements are presented to consumers. How consumers, advertisers and the authorities identify false and overstated advertisements becomes a critical issue. In this paper, we address this problem, and propose various classification models to detect illegal advertisements. Illegal advertisement lists announced by the government and legal advertising data crawled from an online shopping website are used for training and testing the classification models. Naïve Bayes and SVM classifiers with various feature settings are explored on food and cosmetic datasets to demonstrate their feasibility. The experimental results show that log relative frequency ratio can be used as weights for unigram features to achieve the best accuracy. The accuracies of SVM classifiers on food and cosmetic datasets are 93.433% and 86.037%; the false alarm rates are 0.083 and 0.166; and the missing rates are 0.053 and 0.115, respectively. Log relative frequency ratio is further used to mine verb phrases consisting of a transitive verb and an object noun from the illegal datasets. The mined verb phrases, which form an illegal advertising statement list, can be used as a reference for both the advertisers and the authority.

廣告合法性偵測

隨著線上廣告和行銷活動的快速發展，每天都有大量的廣告內容透過網際網路呈現在使用者眼前。因此，不論對於消費者、廣告主、或是政府相關單位來說，如何辨識誇大不實或具誤導性質的廣告，都已成為一項重要的課題。本研究提出數種分類模型來進行廣告合法性偵測。為了取得具有合法性標記的語料，我們採用政府單位公布的違規廣告資料，並從購物網站擷取合法廣告內容，以作為訓練和測試資料。資料分為食品廣告資料集和化粧品廣告資料集，分別以 Naive Bayes 和 SVM 分類器搭配不同特徵進行合法性偵測。實驗結果顯示使用相對頻率比率對數 (log relative frequency ratio) 來代表單字組 (unigram) 的權重並作為特徵時，能達到最佳準確率；在此模型下，食品和化粧品資料集的 SVM 分類準確率分別達到 94.433% 與 86.037%，其錯認率 (false alarm rate) 分別為 0.083 與 0.166，誤失率 (missing rate) 分別為 0.053 與 0.115。相對頻率比率對數也用於對非法廣告資料集進行動詞組的探勘，這些動詞組皆由動詞與其受詞組成，所形成的非法廣告用詞表可讓廣告主和政府單位作為辨識廣告合法性的參考依據。

KEYWORDS: Ad classification, collocation mining, computational advertising, legality recognition
關鍵詞 : 廣告分類, 詞語搭配探勘, 計算式廣告, 合法性辨識

Proceedings of COLING 2012: Posters, pages 1219–1228,
COLING 2012, Mumbai, December 2012.

1 Introduction

As online advertising keeps growing on the Internet, this new form of marketing has started to be regulated by advertising law. Two forms of advertising regulation exist, namely statutory regulation and self-regulation, to protect consumers from fraudulent and misleading advertising (FTC, 2000; CFIA, 2010; DOH, 2009). Under the food and cosmetic advertising regulations of Taiwan, food-related and cosmetic-related advertisements cannot be false, overstated or misleading, and should not mention any curative effects. Advertising statements that violate the regulations are called *illegal statements*. Advertisements containing illegal statements are regarded as illegal advertisements. Because of a large amount of advertisements are presented to consumers, how to recognize advertising legality automatically becomes an important task.

Besides consumers, several parties who are involved in online advertising can benefit from the automatic illegal advertisement recognition (*IDR*). On the one hand, the authority has to examine advertisements to decide which can be presented to Internet users. That requires a lot of time. An advertising legality recognition system not only saves much human effort, but also reports the illegal advertisements in real time. On the other hand, advertisers need to avoid legal issues while maximizing the effectiveness of their advertising. Even weblog and auction website users may need to take care of legal issues. Texts and images from their websites and auctions may be related to products, and thus may also be regarded as online advertising by the authority. Websites that deliver marketing messages from other companies may want to show only truthful advertisements to their users and avoid providing illegal and misleading ones.

Computational advertising has attracted much attention in recent years. How to "best match" between a given user in a given context and a suitable advertisement is one of the major issues. Gabrilovich, Josifovski and Pang (2008, 2009) gave tutorials on this trend in ACL 2008 and IJCAI 2009. Previous Internet advertising focuses on bidding (selecting) advertisements and placing them in the best (right) positions. Ghosh et al. (2009) proposed bidding strategies for the allocations of advertisements. Edelman, Ostrovsky and Schwarz (2007) investigated generalized second-price (GSP) auction for online advertising. Huang, Lin, and Chen (2008) classified instant messaging dialogues into the Yahoo categories, and applied the method to advertisement recommendation. Cheng and Cantú-Paz (2010) proposed a framework to predict the probability that individual users click on ads. Scaiano and Inkpen (2011) used Wikipedia as an annotated corpus to find negative key phrases to avoid displaying advertisements to non-target audience.

Unlike advertisement bidding, matching and recommendation in computational advertising, this paper deals with illegal advertisement recognition. Illegal advertising is similar to ad spam[1] in financial gain, but the former exploits false, overstated or misleading statements to defraud customers, and the latter creates artificial ad traffic, inflates click/impression, and so on, to defraud online advertising systems like AdWords. To the best of our knowledge, advertising legality recognition is a pilot study in this research direction. Food, cosmetic, and medicine are three major sources of illegal advertising. Since advertisements that make health claims are highly regulated in many countries, we focus on food-related and cosmetic-related advertising in this paper. We introduce NLP techniques to extract critical features for illegal statement detection. Section 2 introduces the experimental datasets. Section 3 presents legality recognition methods. Section 4 proposes an approach to illegal verb phrase mining. The last concludes the remarks.

[1] http://support.google.com/adwordspolicy/bin/answer.py?hl=en&answer=50424

2 Datasets

The first step for the advertising legality recognition research is to obtain advertisements with appropriate labels. Since advertising legality can only be determined by the authority, we need to obtain official announcements regarding illegal advertisements. We collect the illegal food and cosmetic advertisement lists made public by the Taipei City Government[2] from July 2009 to November 2011. Each item in the list contains a product name and the corresponding problematic advertising statements. Figure 1 shows a food advertisement consisting of a product name (the 1st line) and illegal food advertising statements (the 2nd-4th lines). The legal parts are removed and denoted by "…". English translation is listed after Chinese food advertisement for reference.

活百O2高溶氧水
可潤腸通便，改善腸胃道的血行，清除宿便，預防痔瘡及治療高血壓、低血壓、肥胖症…活化細胞…改善腦細胞的血液體環境，血液黏稠度…增加唾液之分泌，血液的循環和 血紅球隊氧合(活血)…減少代謝廢物的堆積…失眠及疼痛…消除宿醉…

HOPPER High Oxygen Water
Can remove intestinal obstruction, improve blood flow of the stomach and intestines, prevent hemorrhoid, and cure hypertension, hypotension, and obesity … Activates cells … Improves blood conditions of brain cells and blood concentration … Increases saliva and promotes blood circulation … Reduces waste produced by metabolism process … Stops insomnia and pain … Stops hangover

FIGURE 1– An Example of an illegal food advertisement

The above example shows the fact that the government prohibits the use of statements related to curative effects and improvement of physical conditions. Most illegal statements listed by the government are verb phrases consisting of a verb and an object noun. According to the observed patterns, we propose methods to expand these terms and find similar phrases in the datasets, as described in Section 3.2 and Section 4. This can improve the recognition tasks and help the authorities and advertisers to find problematic expressions.

Since the government web site does not announce the legal advertisements, we need to collect legal advertising data from other sources. An online shopping website in Taiwan[3] is used to collect legal food and cosmetic advertising items. We assume most of these advertisements comply with advertising regulations, and these data are examined by human to make sure that unsuitable data are removed. Food and cosmetic product descriptions are used to build two legal advertising datasets: FOOD and COS, respectively. To obtain a balanced dataset, each dataset is collected from all related categories listed on the website.

All data are separated into sentences according to punctuations, including period, question mark, and exclamation. Only sentences with more than 3 characters are collected. Any expressions containing only product names are filtered out because product names cannot be used to determine its legality. All sentences are in Traditional Chinese. We perform Chinese word segmentation and part-of-speech tagging using the CKIP segmentation and POS tagging system.[4]

[2]http://www.health.gov.tw/Portals/0/%E8%97%A5%E7%89%A9%E9%A3%9F%E5%93%81%E8%99%95/10010food.pdf
[3] http://www.7net.com.tw
[4] http://ckipsvr.iis.sinica.edu.tw/

Thus, we have four datasets for legal food advertising, illegal food advertising, legal cosmetic advertising, and illegal cosmetic advertising. For clarity, they are named as FOOD_LEGAL, FOOD_ILLEGAL, COS_LEGAL, and COS_ILLEGAL. The numbers of instances in the four datasets are 5,059, 7,033, 10,520, and 11,381, respectively.

3 Advertising Legality Recognition

Advertising legality statement recognition aims at determining if an advertising statement is legal or illegal, so that it can be regarded as a binary classification problem. In the development processes, Naïve Bayes classifiers and SVM classifiers implemented with libSVM (Chang & Lin, 2001) are adopted. All training and test processes are based on 10-fold cross validation and every training model was tuned with the optimized parameters to achieve the best performance. Accuracy is adopted as an evaluation metric. Table 1 shows the experimental results. Two classification models (Naïve Bayes and SVM) with different feature settings are explored on food (FOOD) and cosmetic (COS) datasets. The following sections describe how various features are extracted for legality classification.

Classification Models →	Naïve Bayes		SVM	
Features ↓ Materials →	FOOD	COS	FOOD	COS
Unigram	89.148%	81.357%	88.851%	82.416%
Unigram + CILIN	88.950%	81.311%	89.728%	82.759%
Unigram + DOH	89.182%	81.553%	89.554%	83.658%
Unigram + CILIN + DOH	89.000%	81.439%	89.727%	83.325%
Unigram + logRF	**90.695%**	**85.179%**	**93.433%**	**86.037%**

TABLE 1 – Accuracies of advertising legality recognition models

3.1 Feature Set 1: Unigrams

Unigrams are considered as a fundamental feature set. We select the top 1,000 most frequent words from the legal and the illegal advertising datasets as features. Only content words including verbs, nouns and adjectives are included in order to remove the words that may not be relevant. Every sentence separated by punctuations forms an instance of the datasets, and each instance is represented by a word vector (w_1, w_2, …, w_{1000}), where w_i is a binary value indicating whether a word occurs in the sentence or not. The 3rd row of Table 1 shows the accuracies of Naïve Bayes classifiers and SVM classifiers on FOOD and COS datasets are (89.148%, 81.357%) and (88.851%, 82.416%), respectively. Bigram features are also tested, but the performance is lower than that of unigrams, so the results of bigram features are not included in this paper.

3.2 Feature Set 2: Health Related Terms

Advertising regulations are announced along with illegal advertising statement examples for advertisers' reference. Table 2 shows some illegal examples for food related regulations. The 1st type listed in the 1st column denotes mention of any curative effects and the 2nd type denotes false, overstated or misleading cases. Several subtypes along with the corresponding examples are listed in the 2nd and the 3rd columns, respectively.

Advertisers should not mention any curative effects on food and cosmetic advertisements under advertising regulations. We expand the words related to curative effects by a thesaurus to increase the coverage of the feature sets. These statements are used as auxiliary features, and are

Type	Sub-Type	Example
1	宣稱預防、改善、減輕、診斷或治療疾病或特定生理情形 (Claim of prevention, improvement, reduction, diagnosis or cure of diseases or physical conditions)	減輕過敏性皮膚病 (reduce allergic skin disease)
	宣稱減輕或降低導致疾病有關之體內成分 (Claim of elimination of substances that cause diseases)	解肝毒, 降肝脂 (remove poison and fat in liver)
	宣稱產品對疾病及疾病症候群或症狀有效 (Claim of effectiveness to diseases and symptoms)	消除心律不整 (cure arrhythmia)
	涉及中藥材之效能者 (Related to effects of Chinese medicine)	補腎 (improve health condition of kidney)
	引用或摘錄出版品、典籍或以他人名義並述及醫藥效能 (Reference to publications, books or statements by others with medical effects)	「本草綱目」記載：黑豆可止痛 (according to the book "Bencao Gangmu," black beans can ease pain)
2	涉及生理功能者 (Related to physiological functions)	分解有害物質 (decompose toxicants)
	涉及五官臟器者 (Related to organs)	增加血管彈性 (increase elasticity of blood vessel)
	涉及改變身體外觀者 (Related to change of appearance of human body)	防止老化 (prevent aging)
	引用本署衛署食字號或相當意義詞句者 (Reference to DOH permission numbers or related expressions)	通過衛生署配方審查 (pass formula review by DOH)

TABLE 2 – Illegal advertising statement examples announced by the government

combined with unigram features. Two kinds of auxiliary features shown as follows are used.

(1) All verbs related to curative effects from a Chinese thesaurus *Tongyicicilin* (Mei et al., 1984): This feature set is called CILIN in Table 1.

(2) Illegal statement examples listed by Department of Health (DOH) of Taiwan: This feature set is called DOH in Table 1.

The 4th-6th rows of Table 1 show the accuracies of using the above feature sets. Thesaurus expansion (Unigram + CILIN) has some positive effects in SVM classifiers. Comparing with pure unigram feature sets, integrating features selected from illegal advertising statement examples of DOH is also useful (refer to Unigram + DOH). However, the accuracy is not further improved, when all the three kinds of features are combined (refer to Unigram + CILIN + DOH). A possible reason is that the number of terms in the CILIN feature set is high, and a thesaurus always tries to collect as many terms as possible. Thus, many uncommon words are included as incorrect expansion. The DOH feature set includes lists that are edited by professionals in the government, so it captures illegal advertising statements that are in actual use. However, the coverage is an issue. Section 4 discusses how to expand this list.

3.3 Feature Set 3: Log Relative Frequency Ratio

Relative frequency ratio between two datasets has been shown to be useful to discover collocations that are characteristic of a dataset when compared to the other dataset (Damerau, 1993). It is also used to model emotion transition between writers and readers (Tang and Chen, 2012). We extend this idea to select the critical features that capture the legality transition. The log relative frequency ratio *lr* of words in two datasets *A* and *B* are defined as follows. For each $w^i \in A \cup B$, we compute

$$lr_{AB}(w^i) = \log \frac{\frac{f_A(w^i)}{|A|}}{\frac{f_B(w^i)}{|B|}}$$

where $lr_{AB}(w^i)$ is a log ratio of relative frequencies of word w^i in *A* and *B*, $f_A(w^i)$ and $f_B(w^i)$ are frequencies of w^i in *A* and in *B*, and $|A|$ and $|B|$ are total words in *A* and in *B*, respectively. The log relative frequency ratios are used to estimate the distribution of the words in datasets *A* and *B*.

The interpretations of $lr_{AB}(w^i)$ are shown as follows.

(1) If w^i has higher relative frequency in *A* than in *B*, then $lr_{AB}(w^i)>0$. Those words of positive ratio form a set *A-B*.
(2) If w^i has higher relative frequency in *B* than in *A*, then $lr_{AB}(w^i)<0$. Those words of negative ratio form a set *B-A*.
(3) If w^i has similar relative frequency in both sets, then $lr_{AB}(w^i)\cong 0$.

In our experiments for food advertising, *A*=FOOD_LEGAL and *B*=FOOD_ILLEGAL. As for the experiments for cosmetic advertising, *A*=COS_LEGAL and *B*=COS_ILLEGAL. We employ the log relative frequency ratio as a weight of each unigram in a dataset. Each sentence in the datasets is represented by a vector $(w_1, w_2, \ldots, w_n)$, where w_i is the weight of ith word from the unigram feature set. The 7th row of Table 1 lists the accuracy of the log relative frequency ratio feature set for the FOOD and COS advertising legality classification. The performance of both Naïve Bayes and SVM classifiers with Unigram + logRF feature settings are higher than those with the unigram and the auxiliary feature settings on both FOOD and COS datasets. The differences of accuracies between Unigram + logRF and all the other feature settings for both datasets are statistically significant ($p<0.01$).

3.4 Discussion

We further examine the individual accuracies of illegal advertising detection and legal advertising detection. Tables 3 and 4 show the experimental results of Naïve Bayes and SVM classifiers with different feature settings on food and cosmetic datasets, respectively. We can summarize some conclusions from these two tables. Firstly, Unigram+CILIN does not improve the accuracy of Unigram. The *Cilin* thesaurus contains many words that are not commonly used. Besides, its purpose is to help people find similar and related words conveniently. Thus, its organization of lexical terms may not be suitable for our classification tasks. Secondly, the accuracies of illegal advertising detection with both classifiers on both datasets are better than

Classification Models → Features ↓ Illegal vs. Legal →	Naïve Bayes		SVM	
	Illegal	Legal	Illegal	Legal
Unigram	92.592%	85.058%	89.463%	88.000%
Unigram + CILIN	93.367%	83.851%	90.330%	88.889%
Unigram + DOH	92.705%	84.994%	89.875%	89.106%
Unigram + CILIN + DOH	93.421%	83.902%	90.159%	89.126%
Unigram + logRF	**94.317%**	**86.371%**	**94.696%**	**91.677%**

TABLE 3 – Individual accuracies of illegal and legal advertising recognition on food dataset

Classification Models → Features ↓ Illegal vs. Legal →	Naïve Bayes		SVM	
	Illegal	Legal	Illegal	Legal
Unigram	86.479%	77.632%	82.470%	82.357%
Unigram + CILIN	86.812%	77.374%	83.287%	82.186%
Unigram + DOH	86.944%	77.658%	83.375%	83.964%
Unigram + CILIN + DOH	87.075%	77.431%	83.384%	83.260%
Unigram + logRF	**88.197%**	**83.060%**	**88.463%**	**83.413%**

TABLE 4 – Individual accuracies of illegal and legal advertising recognition on cosmetic dataset

those of legal advertising detection with the same classifiers on the same datasets. The accuracy difference between illegal and legal advertising recognition with SVM classifier is comparatively smaller than that with Naïve Bayes classifier. Note that the ratio of legal instances versus illegal instances in the food dataset is 41.84:58.16, and the ratio in the cosmetic dataset is 48.03:51.97. Thirdly, in the first four feature settings, Naïve Bayes classifiers perform illegal advertising detection better than SVM classifiers in both datasets. In contrast, SVM classifiers achieve better legal advertising detection than Naïve Bayes classifiers. Fourthly, when log relative frequency ratio is introduced, i.e., the Unigram+logRF feature setting, SVM classifier achieves the best performance in both illegal and legal advertising recognition on both datasets. The false alarm rates, a ratio of legal statements mis-recognized as illegal ones among all the legal statements, in food and cosmetic datasets are 0.083 and 0.166, respectively. The missing rates, a ratio of illegal statements mis-recognized as legal ones among all the illegal statements, in food and cosmetic datasets are 0.053 and 0.115, respectively. That illustrates the feasibility of log relative frequency ratio and SVM classifier.

4 Illegal Verb Phrase Mining

Effective identification of illegal advertising is a challenge for the authority and advertisers. Table 2 shows that almost all illegal advertising statements listed by DOH are verb phrases consisting of a transitive verb and an object noun. Thus, the usage of these verb phrases is a key criterion. To realize how illegal advertising uses verb phrases, we mine illegal advertising verb phrases from the illegal food and cosmetic datasets. The results can be used to extend the official list of illegal statements to improve illegal advertising recognition processes by the authority, and to help advertisers prepare legal advertisements.

The first step of mining illegal advertising verb phrases is to obtain the words that present more frequently in the illegal datasets. We adopt the same formula of log relative frequency ratio mentioned in Section 3.3. If $lr_{AB}(w^i)$ is a negative value, then w^i is more frequently used in illegal advertising. In our experiments, only the words with a log relative frequency lower than -0.1 and with appropriate POS tags will be selected. The verb must be a transitive verb or nominalize verb, and the noun must be a common noun.

Then, we examine each sentence in the datasets to determine whether it contains a verb phrase consisting of a verb and a noun from our word list or not. Since we do not use a parser in the current stage, and an object noun does not necessarily immediately follow its verb, we identify a VP by the following criteria.

(1) The verb should occur before the noun.
(2) The distance between the verb and the noun should not exceed 3 words.

The noun should be the head of the noun phrase where it presents. That is, the noun should be the last word in the noun phrase. In Chinese, the head of a noun phrase is preceded by its adjectives and noun modifiers in most cases.

There are 979 and 2,302 verb phrases mined from the FOOD and the COS datasets, respectively. Some examples of these phrases are listed in Table 5. Log relative frequency ratio can be used with a POS tagger to mine illegal verb phrases consisting of a transitive verb and an object noun. We can observe that most verbs in the verb phrase lists are related to curative effects, and the objects are related to the human body, nutrients and diet. Similar structure and properties can been seen in the sample illegal expressions provided by the government. Thus we can conclude that log relative frequency ratio is an effective method to mine illegal expression lists.

Dataset	Illegal advertising verb phrases
FOOD	增強體質 (improve physical condition) 抑制細菌 (inactivate bacteria) 對抗年齡 (fight against aging) 分解膽固醇 (decompose cholesterol)
COS	淨化體質 (purify human body) 舒緩疼痛 (ease pain) 供給氧氣 (provide oxygen) 治療面皰 (cure acne vulgaris)

TABLE 5 – Examples of illegal advertising verb phrases mined from the FOOD and COS datasets.

Conclusion

This paper addresses the importance of legality recognition in Internet advertising. We use Naïve Bayes and SVM classifiers to perform the recognition tasks. The experimental results show that log relative frequency ratio can be used as weights for unigrams to improve performance of advertising legality recognition, and achieve the best accuracy in our experiments. We also use log relative frequency ratio to mine verb phrases consisting of a transitive verb and an object noun from illegal advertising statements. We find that this is an effective way to obtain a list of verb phrases that are related to problematic advertisements.

The recognition models proposed in this paper can be employed to build an automated illegal advertising recognition system in order to identify a huge number of advertisements automatically. The illegal verb phrase lists can also be used in a computer assisted system to help both the authority speed up the illegal advertising identification processes, and the advertisers to prepare suitable advertisements. As future work, we will extend the methodology to other types of advertising legality recognition task such as medicine domain.

Acknowledgments

This research was partially supported by Excellent Research Projects of National Taiwan University under contract 101R890858.

References

CFIA (2010). Advertising Requirements. Canadian Food Inspection Agency. Available at http://www.inspection.gc.ca/english/fssa/labeti/advpube.shtml.

Chang, C. and Lin, C. (2001). LIBSVM: a Library for Support Vector Machines. Available at http://www.csie.ntu.edu.tw/~cjlin/libsvm.

Cheng, H and Cantú-Paz, E. (2010). Personalized click prediction in sponsored search. In *Third ACM International Conference on Web Search and Data Mining* (*WSDM 2010*), pages 351-359, New York, USA.

Damerau, Fred J. (1993). Generating and Evaluating Domain-Oriented Multi-Word Terms from Text, *Information Processing and Management*, 29:433-477.

DOH (2009). Legal and Illegal Advertising Statements for Cosmetic Regulations. Department of Health of Taiwan, Available at http://www.doh.gov.tw/ufile/doc/0980305527.pdf.

Edelman, B., Ostrovsky, M., Schwarz, M. (2007). Internet Advertising and the Generalized Second Price Auction: Selling Billions of Dollars Worth of Keywords, *American Economic Review*, American Economic Association, 97(1):242-259.

FTC (2000). Advertising and Marketing on the Internet: Rules of the Road, Bureau of Consumer Protection. Federal Trade Commission, September 2000, Available at http://business.ftc.gov/sites/default/files/pdf/bus28-advertising-and-marketing-internet-rules-road.pdf.

Gabrilovich, E., Josifovski, V. and Pang, B. (2008). Introduction to Computational Advertising. Tutorial Abstracts of ACL-08: HLT, page 1.

Gabrilovich, E., Josifovski, V. and Pang, B. (2009). Introduction to Computational Advertising. IJCAI 2009 Tutorial, http://research.yahoo.com/tutorials/ijcai09_compadv/

Ghosh, A., McAfee, P., Papineni, K., and Vassilvitskii, S. (2009). Bidding for Representative Allocations for Display Advertising. CoRR, abs/0910-0880, 2009.

Huang, H.C., Lin, M.S. and Chen H.H. (2008). Analysis of intention in dialogues using category trees and its application to advertisement recommendation. In *the Third International Joint Conference on Natural Language Processing* (*IJCNLP 2008*), pages 625-630, Hyderabad, India.

Mei, J., Zhu, Y., Gao, Y. and Yin, H. (1982). *Tóngyìcícílín*. Shanghai Dictionary Press.

Scaiano, M. and Inkpen, D. (2011). Finding negative key phrases for internet advertising campaigns using wikipedia. In *Recent Advances in Natural Language Processing* (*RANLP 2011*), pages 648–653, Hissar, Bulgaria.

Tang, Y.J. and Chen, H.H. (2012). Mining sentiment words from microblogs for predicting writer-reader emotion transition. In *the 8th International Conference on Language Resources and Evaluation* (*LREC 2012*), pages 1226-1229, Istanbul, Turkey.

A Joint Phrasal and Dependency Model for Paraphrase Alignment

Kapil THADANI[1] *Scott MARTIN*[2] *Michael WHITE*[2]
(1) COLUMBIA UNIVERSITY, New York NY 10027
(2) OHIO STATE UNIVERSITY, Columbus OH 43210
kapil@cs.columbia.edu, {scott,mwhite}@ling.ohio-state.edu

ABSTRACT

Monolingual alignment is frequently required for natural language tasks that involve similar or comparable sentences. We present a new model for monolingual alignment in which the score of an alignment decomposes over both the set of aligned phrases as well as a set of aligned dependency arcs. Optimal alignments under this scoring function are decoded using integer linear programming while model parameters are learned using standard structured prediction approaches. We evaluate our joint aligner on the Edinburgh paraphrase corpus and show significant gains over a Meteor baseline and a state-of-the-art phrase-based aligner.

TITLE AND ABSTRACT IN FRENCH

Un modèle de phrases et de dépendances pour l'alignement des paraphrases

L'alignement monolingue s'impose fréquemment dans les tâches de langue naturelle qui comprennent des phrases similaires. Nous présentons un nouveau modèle pour l'alignement monolingue dans lequel le score d'un alignement tient compte de l'ensemble de phrases alignées et d'un ensemble d'arcs de dépendance alignés. Cette fonction de score donne des alignements en utilisant l'optimisation linéaire, et nous effectuons l'apprentissage des paramètres du modèle avec des méthodes standardes de prédiction structurée. Nous évaluons notre système mixte par rapport au corpus de paraphrases d'Edinburgh et nous démonstron un avantage significatif par rapport á Meteor et á un système de pointe fondé sur l'alignement des phrases.

KEYWORDS: monolingual alignment, integer linear programming, structured prediction.

KEYWORDS IN FRENCH: alignement monolingue, optimisation linéaire, prediction structurée.

Proceedings of COLING 2012: Posters, pages 1229–1238,
COLING 2012, Mumbai, December 2012.

1 Introduction

Textual alignment involves the identification of links between words or phrases which are effectively semantically equivalent in their respective input sentences. *Monolingual* alignment in particular is often needed in natural language problems which involve pairs or groups of related sentences such as textual entailment recognition, multidocument summarization, text-to-text generation and the evaluation of machine translation systems. For example, paraphrase recognition systems can use alignments between input sentences to identify mentions of repeated concepts and determine the degree to which the input sentences overlap.

Recent work on monolingual alignment problems (MacCartney et al., 2008; Thadani and McKeown, 2011) has focused on phrase-based techniques in which the alignment between a pair of sentences is represented through a set of aligned phrase pairs; this has demonstrated advantages over token-based aligners such as Chambers et al. (2007) as well as standard aligners used in machine translation (Och and Ney, 2003; Liang et al., 2006). This paper presents an improved model for monolingual phrase-based alignment that elegantly accounts for syntactic relationships between tokens by additionally considering an *arc-based* alignment representation comprising a set of aligned pairs of dependency arcs consistent with the phrase-based representation. Under this formulation, the score of any alignment is simply defined to factor over all aligned phrase pairs and arc pairs in the alignment. However, recovering a full sentence alignment that optimizes this joint scoring function is non-trivial due to both the interdependence among individual phrase alignments as well as the interaction between phrase-based and arc-based alignments to ensure consistency between the two representations.

In this paper, we describe a technique to recover joint phrasal and arc-based alignments by using integer linear programming (ILP). Given a feature-based scoring function, standard structured prediction techniques can be leveraged to learn parameters that weight features over phrasal and arc-based alignments. We evaluate this joint aligner on a human-annotated paraphrase corpus (Cohn et al., 2008) and show significant gains over phrase-based alignments generated by the Meteor metric for machine translation (Denkowski and Lavie, 2011) as well as a state-of-the-art discriminatively-trained phrase-based aligner (Thadani and McKeown, 2011).

2 Related Work

Text alignment is a crucial component of machine translation (MT) systems (Vogel et al., 1996; Och and Ney, 2003; Liang et al., 2006; DeNero and Klein, 2008); however, the general goal of multilingual aligners is the production of wide-coverage phrase tables for translation. In contrast, monolingual alignment is often consumed directly in applications like paraphrasing and textual entailment recognition; this task therefore involves substantially different challenges and tradeoffs.[1] Nevertheless, modern MT evaluation metrics have recently been found to be remarkably effective for tasks requiring monolingual alignments (Bouamor et al., 2011; Madnani et al., 2012; Heilman and Madnani, 2012)—even used off-the-shelf with their default parameter settings—and for this reason we use Meteor as a baseline in this paper.

Monolingual token-based alignment has been used for many natural language processing applications such as paraphrase generation (Barzilay and Lee, 2003; Quirk et al., 2004). Dependency arc-based alignment has seen similar widespread use in applications such as sentence fusion (Barzilay and McKeown, 2005; Marsi and Krahmer, 2005), redundancy removal (Thadani and McKeown, 2008) and textual entailment recognition (Dagan et al., 2005). Furthermore,

[1] See MacCartney et al. (2008) for an enumeration of these challenges in the context of entailment recognition.

joint aligners that simultaneously account for the similarity of tokens and dependency arcs have also been explored (Chambers et al., 2007; Chang et al., 2010). Monolingual phrase-based alignment was first tackled by the MANLI system of MacCartney et al. (2008) and was subsequently expanded upon by Thadani and McKeown (2011) to incorporate exact inference.

ILP has seen widespread use in natural language problems involving formulations which cannot be decoded efficiently with dynamic programming but can be expressed as relatively compact linear programs. DeNero and Klein (2008) and Thadani and McKeown (2011) proposed ILP approaches to finding phrase-based alignments in a multilingual and monolingual context respectively. Chang et al. (2010) describe a joint token-based and arc-based alignment technique using ILP to ensure consistency between the two alignment representations. Our proposed joint phrasal and arc-based aligner generalizes over both these alignment techniques.

3 Corpus

As our dataset, we use a modified version of the human-aligned corpus of paraphrases described by Cohn et al. (2008), which we call the *Edinburgh corpus*. We derive this dataset from the original corpus first by standardizing the treatment of quotes (both single and double) and by truecasing the text (Lita et al., 2003). Following MacCartney et al. (2006), we collapse named entities using the Stanford named entity recognizer[2] trained on the pre-built models distributed with it (Finkel et al., 2005). For example, the corpus contains a sentence with the named entity *Bank of Holland*, which we collapse to the single token *Bank_of_Holland*. In future work, we plan to leave the original corpus uncollapsed and annotate named entities by token index.

Our training/testing splits are as follows. We use all of the nonoverlapping portions of the Edinburgh corpus (those only aligned by a single human annotator) as training data. We then randomly sample training instances from the overlapping portions of the corpus: 45 instances from the 'trial' portion drawn from the 'mtc' subcorpus, 19 from the 'news' portion, and 10 from the 'novels' portion. The testing data includes all of the instances in the overlapping portions of the corpus that are not selected as training data, plus the five remaining 'trial' instances. The resulting splits yield 70% for training and 30% for testing, with identical ratios from the three subcorpora ('mtc', 'news', and 'novels') in both training and testing. The training set has 715 paraphrase pairs with a total of 29,827 tokens and an average of 20.9 tokens per sentence, while the test set has 305 paraphrase pairs with 14,391 tokens and 23.6 tokens/sentence on average. Finally, rather than using the merged alignments from the Edinburgh corpus for the overlapping portions, we randomly select one of the two annotators to use as the reference alignment in an unbiased way, with each annotator chosen exactly half of the time.[3]

4 Corpus Analysis and Example

Figure 1 shows an example paraphrase pair from the training portion of the corpus. At the top are the Meteor alignments as visualized by the Meteor X-ray tool using shaded boxes, along with the gold standard alignments using filled circles for SURE alignments and open circles for POSSIBLE alignments. Below the alignment grid, the recall errors (SURE only) in the Meteor alignments that are supported by Stanford parser dependencies are shown in bold. These recall errors are supported in the sense that the missed aligned tokens participate in dependencies with other aligned tokens. For example, Meteor fails to align *scout* with *monitor*. This token-level alignment is supported by two aligned dependencies, namely the alignment of

[2] `http://nlp.stanford.edu/software/CRF-NER.shtml`

[3] The modified corpus is available at `http://www.ling.ohio-state.edu/~mwhite/data/coling12/`.

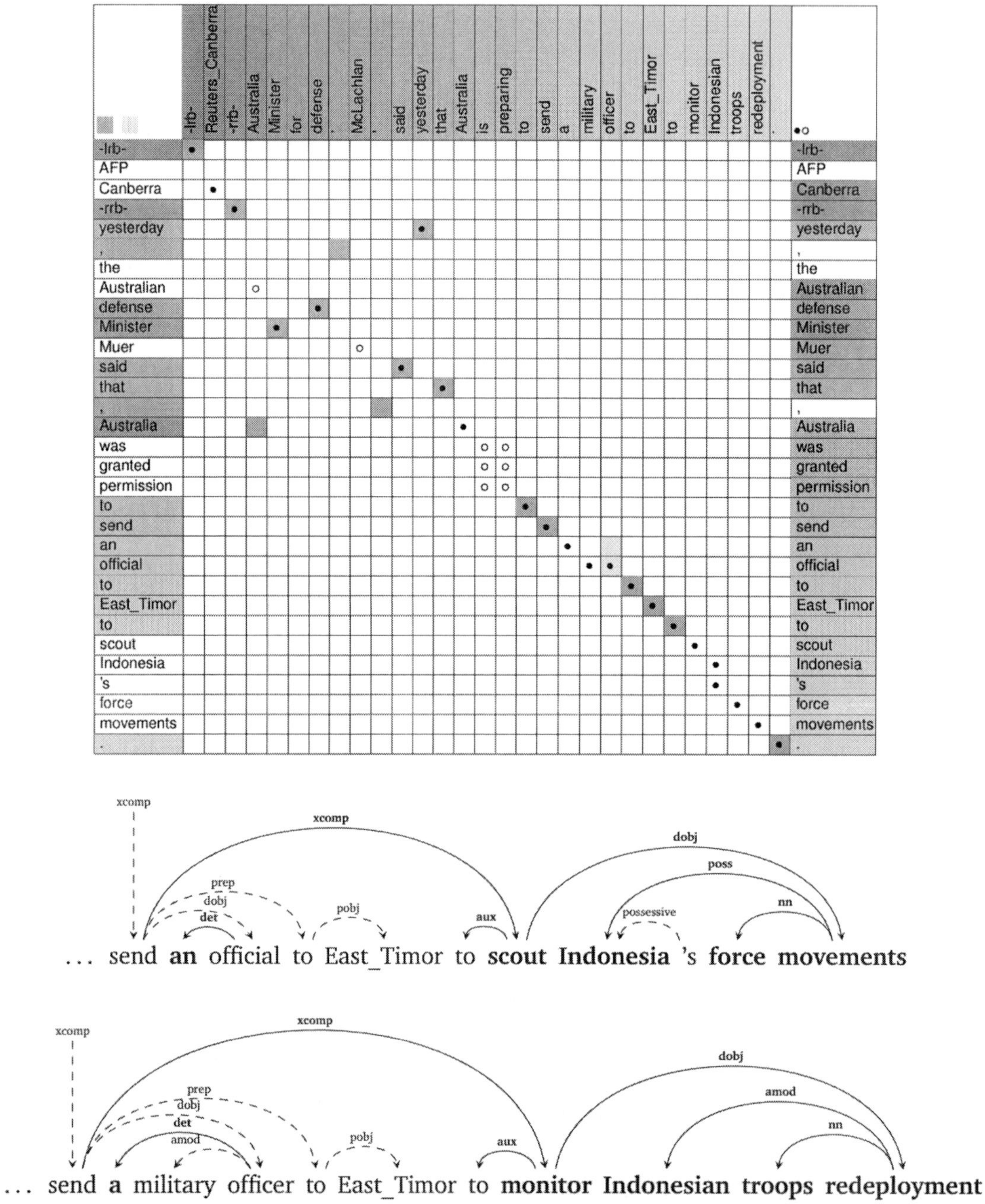

Figure 1: At top, example Meteor alignments (shaded boxes, gray for exact matches and yellow for stem/synonym/paraphrase matches) along with gold SURE and POSSIBLE alignments (circles, filled for SURE and open for POSSIBLE); at bottom, Meteor recall errors (SURE only, in bold) that are supported by aligned Stanford parser dependencies (solid lines).

$send \xrightarrow{xcomp} scout$ with $send \xrightarrow{xcomp} monitor$ and $scout \xrightarrow{aux} to$ with $monitor \xrightarrow{aux} to$. Here, the other tokens in the dependencies are identical, and thus the dependencies provide strong evidence for the token-level alignment. Interestingly, the final three recall errors involve interrelated dependencies, suggesting the need for joint inference.

Using this notion of dependency arc alignments supporting token-level alignments, we counted how frequently the token alignments were supported by dependency alignments, and found that 64% of the SURE alignments and 65% of the SURE+POSSIBLE alignments in the training corpus were supported in this way. We also tabulated how often the dependencies were aligned, and found that 54% of the dependency arcs were aligned based on the SURE token alignments, and 62% were aligned based on the SURE+POSSIBLE alignments, thus indicating the greater potential of dependencies to aid alignment when including the POSSIBLES. The alignment percentages varied considerably by type: of the non-rare dependency types, 74% of the *aux* dependencies were aligned (including the POSSIBLES), while only 38% of the *rcmod* dependencies were aligned, with most core dependency types such as *xcomp* and *dobj* in the 64-70% range.[4]

5 Joint alignment framework

Consider a pair of text segments $\langle T_1, T_2 \rangle$ where each T_s represents a set of n_s tokens. We denote $T_s \triangleq \{t_i^s : 1 \leq i \leq n_s\}$ where each t_i^s represents a token in the ith position of segment s. We also use the notation $t_{i\ldots j}^s \triangleq \{t_k : t_k \in T_s, i \leq k \leq j\}$ to indicate the subsequence of contiguous tokens from positions i to j (inclusive) in T_s. Each T_s is also associated with a dependency graph D_s which is treated as a set of labeled arcs, i.e., $D_s \triangleq \{d_{ij}^s : t_j^s \text{ is a dependent of } t_i^s \in T_s \cup \{\text{ROOT}\}\}$.

5.1 Alignment representations

Our proposed alignment formulation has its roots in the phrase-based representation proposed in MacCartney et al. (2008) and Thadani and McKeown (2011). An alignment E between T_1 and T_2 is represented by a set of edits $\{e_1, e_2, \ldots\}$ which indicate the modifications that would be needed to convert T_1 to T_2. We consider two types of edits:

1. *Phrase edits* capture the changes that would need to be made to subsequences of tokens to transform T_1 to T_2 and vice versa. These are of two types: the first represents the *alignment* of equivalent phrases in T_1 and T_2 while the other denotes *deletion* or non-alignment of phrases from either T_s. A valid phrase-based alignment configuration, denoted by E_{phr} must have every token participating in exactly one edit.

2. *Arc edits* similarly capture the alignments or deletions of edges in a dependency graph. For a dependency alignment configuration E_{arc} to be meaningful, the edits in it must be kept *consistent* with the phrase-based alignment configuration E_{phr}. Specifically, two edges that have both their source and target tokens aligned (i.e., participating in the same alignment edit) must also participate in an alignment edit.

We assume that the score for an alignment E factors over the phrase and arc edits present in E. Using e^* to represent alignment edits and e^- to represent deletion edits, this can be written as:

$$score(E) = \sum_{e^*_{\text{phr}} \in E} \alpha_{\text{phr}}(e^*_{\text{phr}}) + \sum_{e^-_{\text{phr}} \in E} \delta_{\text{phr}}(e^-_{\text{phr}}) + \sum_{e^*_{\text{arc}} \in E} \alpha_{\text{arc}}(e^*_{\text{arc}}) + \sum_{e^-_{\text{arc}} \in E} \delta_{\text{arc}}(e^-_{\text{arc}}) \qquad (1)$$

[4] Note that dependencies can fail to be aligned for a variety of reasons, including parse errors, head-dependent inversions (not taken into account in this paper) and more large-scale structural divergences.

where scoring functions $\alpha_{\text{phr}} : \langle t^1_{i...j}, t^2_{k...l}\rangle \to \mathbb{R}$ indicate the score of aligning a pair of token sequences, and $\delta_{\text{phr}} : t^s_{i...j} \to \mathbb{R}$ indicate the score of deleting any token sequence of segment s from the alignment. $\alpha_{\text{arc}} : \langle d^1_{ij}, d^2_{kl}\rangle \to \mathbb{R}$ and $\delta_{\text{arc}} : d^s_{ij} \to \mathbb{R}$ are defined analogously for scoring alignments and deletions of arc edits respectively.

5.2 Features and learning

The scoring function described above is parameterized by features over the different categories of edits, i.e., $score(E) = \sum_{e \in E} \mathbf{w} \cdot \Phi(e)$ where $\Phi(e)$ is a feature vector for edit e and $\mathbf{w}$ is a vector of parameter weights. The features defined over phrase edits are similar to MacCartney et al. (2008); these encode the type of edit (alignment or deletion), the size of the phrases in alignment edits, the similarity of the phrases determined by leveraging various lexical resources, as well as contextual and positional features. Features for arc edits simply encode the type of edit for an arc of a given class of dependency label, e.g., whether an alignment edit involves two *subj* dependencies, or whether a deletion edit involves a *det* dependency.

Given a inference technique for alignments under the parameterized scoring function, feature weights $\mathbf{w}$ can be learned using any appropriate structured prediction technique. We employ the structured perceptron (Collins, 2002) in our experiments.

5.3 Inference via ILP

We now describe an integer linear program that recovers optimal solutions to the problem of jointly recovering a phrasal and arc alignment given any parameter configuration $\mathbf{w}$. Although ILPs in general do not have guarantees on returning solutions efficiently, the programs for alignment problems over text segments consisting of a few sentences are relatively small and can be easily tackled with highly optimized general-purpose solvers.[5]

First, we define indicator variables for all potential phrase and arc edits in an alignment, as well as indicators that denote which pairs of tokens are aligned.

- $y^s_{ij\sim kl} \in \{0,1\}$ represents an alignment between the token sequence $t^s_{i...j}$ from T_s and $t^{s'}_{k...l}$ from $T_{s'}$. We use s' as shorthand for the segment index other than s, i.e., $s' = 3 - s$. Note that $y^s_{ij\sim kl}$ and $y^{s'}_{kl\sim ij}$ are equivalent for a given i, j, k, l and refer to the same indicator.
- $\bar{y}^s_{ij} \in \{0,1\}$ represents a non-alignment or deletion of the token sequence $t^s_{i...j}$ from either segment T_s.
- $z^s_{ij\sim kl} \in \{0,1\}$ represents an alignment between the dependency $d^s_{ij} \in D_s$ and $d^{s'}_{kl} \in D_{s'}$. Note that $z^s_{ij\sim kl}$ and $z^{s'}_{kl\sim ij}$ are equivalent for a given i, j, k, l and refer to the same indicator.
- $\bar{z}^s_{ij} \in \{0,1\}$ represents a non-alignment or deletion of the dependency $d^s_{ij} \in D_s$.
- Finally, $x^s_{p\sim q} \in \{0,1\}$ indicates whether the token $t^s_p \in T_s$ participates in some phrase-based alignment with $t^{s'}_q \in T_{s'}$.

$$x^s_{p\sim q} = \begin{cases} 1, & \text{iff } \exists i,j,k,l \text{ s.t. } y^s_{ij\sim kl} = 1,\ i \le p \le j,\ k \le q \le l \\ 0, & \text{otherwise} \end{cases} \tag{2}$$

[5] We use Gurobi: `http://www.gurobi.com`

Now, finding the optimal alignment between any sentence pair $\langle T_1, T_2 \rangle$ is equivalent to solving the following optimization problem over the edit indicator variables:

$$\max_{y,z} \sum_{i=1}^{n_1} \sum_{j=i}^{\min(n_1,i+\lambda)} \sum_{k=1}^{n_2} \sum_{l=k}^{\min(n_2,k+\lambda)} y_{ij\sim kl}\, \alpha_{\text{phr}}(\langle t^1_{i\ldots j}, t^2_{k\ldots l}\rangle)$$
$$+ \sum_{\substack{i,j:\\ d^1_{ij}\in D_1}} \sum_{\substack{k,l:\\ d^2_{kl}\in D_2}} z_{ij\sim kl}\, \alpha_{\text{arc}}(\langle d^1_{ij}, d^2_{kl}\rangle)$$
$$+ \sum_{s\in\{1,2\}} \left(\sum_{i=1}^{n_s} \sum_{j=i}^{\min(n_s,i+\lambda)} \bar{y}^s_{ij}\, \delta_{\text{phr}}(t^s_{i\ldots j}) + \sum_{d^s_{ij}\in D_s} \bar{z}^s_{ij}\, \delta_{\text{arc}}(d^s_{ij}) \right) \tag{3}$$

where the parameter λ controls the maximum number of tokens permitted in a phrase for alignment. The optimization problem requires some linear constraints in order to specify a complete and consistent alignment. The following constraints are applied for all $i = 1\ldots n_s$, $j = i\ldots\min(n_s, i+\lambda)$, $k = 1\ldots n_{s'}$, and $l = k\ldots\min(n_{s'}, k+\lambda)$ where $s \in \{1,2\}$.

1. Exactly one phrase edit must be active per token, ensuring a consistent segmentation for the phrase-based solution. Similarly, only one arc edit can be active per dependency.

$$\sum_{\substack{i,j:\\ i\le p\le j}} \sum_{k,l} y^s_{ij\sim kl} + \bar{y}^s_{ij} = 1 \qquad \forall p \in 1\ldots n_s \tag{4}$$

$$\sum_{k,l} z^s_{ij\sim kl} + \bar{z}^s_{ij} = 1 \qquad \forall i,j,k,l \text{ s.t. } d^s_{ij} \in D_s,\ d^{s'}_{kl} \in D_{s'} \tag{5}$$

2. An activated token pair indicator must participate in exactly one phrase alignment.

$$\sum_{\substack{i,j:\\ i\le p\le j}} \sum_{\substack{k,l:\\ k\le q\le l}} y^s_{ij\sim kl} = x^s_{p\sim q} \qquad \forall p \in 1\ldots n_s,\ q \in 1\ldots n_{s'} \tag{6}$$

3. In order to ensure that the phrase-based solution is consistent with the arc-based solution, arc alignments must activate corresponding token-pair alignment indicators.

$$z^s_{ij\sim kl} \le x^s_{i\sim k} \qquad \forall i,j,k,l \in 1,\ldots n_s \tag{7}$$

$$z^s_{ij\sim kl} \le x^s_{j\sim l} \qquad \forall i,j,k,l \in 1,\ldots n_s \tag{8}$$

4. If the governor and dependent of a dependency arc in one sentence are aligned to those of an arc in the other sentence, the corresponding arc alignment must be active.

$$x^s_{i\sim k} + x^s_{j\sim l} \le z^s_{ij\sim kl} + 1 \qquad \forall i,j,k,l \text{ s.t. } d^s_{ij} \in D_s,\ d^{s'}_{kl} \in D_{s'} \tag{9}$$

6 Experiments

We trained models with and without the dependency features using 20 epochs of averaged perceptron learning. Separate models were trained on the training corpus with just the SURE alignments and with the SURE+POSSIBLE alignments.[6] We used the unconstrained approach of Thadani and McKeown (2011) as a phrase-based baseline; this is an extension of MacCartney

[6]Note that all alignments are considered equally when evaluating on the SURE+POSSIBLE alignments.

Alignments	System	Prec%	Rec%	F_1%	Exact%
	Meteor	81.82	71.90	75.49	11.22
Tokens/SURE	Phrase-based	74.83	83.25	**77.85**	12.21
	Phrase+Arc	76.57	83.79	**79.20**	12.21
	Meteor	85.40	64.76	72.32	10.56
Tokens/SURE+POSSIBLE	Phrase-based	70.84	82.54	**75.37**	13.53
	Phrase+Arc	73.03	84.60	**77.57**	14.85
	Meteor	84.64	58.03	65.60	17.49
Deps/SURE	Phrase-based	76.07	78.42	**75.10**	23.10
	Phrase+Arc	73.56	84.27	**76.30**	20.79
	Meteor	91.19	51.80	62.57	12.87
Deps/SURE+POSSIBLE	Phrase-based	80.09	80.74	**78.79**	22.11
	Phrase+Arc	77.04	88.76	**80.92**	22.44

Table 1: Test set macro-averaged results on token alignments and projected dependency alignments over Stanford parses. F_1 increases are statistically significant in each case (see text).

et al. (2008) which outperforms a number of other alignment techniques (Och and Ney, 2003; Liang et al., 2006; Chambers et al., 2007). As an additional baseline, we ran Meteor on the test corpus using its precision-focused *max accuracy* setting, which we found to yield higher F-measure on the training corpus than the *max coverage* option. Table 1 shows the results.

It is evident that the feature-based aligners have much higher recall than Meteor, with some unsurprising loss in precision due to the conservative *max accuracy* matching. Compellingly, the joint model increases both precision and recall on aligned tokens over the phrasal model, with greater increases using the SURE+POSSIBLE alignments as expected. Jointly aligning arcs also helps considerably in recovering the dependency alignments projected onto Stanford parses from the gold standard phrase alignments. Wilcoxon signed-rank tests on F_1 indicate that all increases are statistically significant, with $p < 0.001$ in all cases except one, namely the increase on the SURE syntactic dependencies of the joint model over the phrasal model, where $p < 0.05$.

Conclusion

We have presented a monolingual alignment strategy that jointly produces phrasal and syntactic dependency alignments using a discriminative structured prediction framework and an exact inference technique using ILP. Our alignment technique shows significant gains over recent phrase-based aligners and alignments obtained via the well-known Meteor metric. In future work, we intend to apply joint alignment approaches to additional corpora and develop more powerful similarity features over phrases and arcs.

Acknowledgments

This work was supported in part by the Air Force Research Laboratory under a subcontract to FA8750-09-C-0179 and in part by the Intelligence Advanced Research Projects Activity (IARPA) via Department of Interior National Business Center (DoI/NBC) contract number D11PC20153. The U.S. Government is authorized to reproduce and distribute reprints for Governmental purposes notwithstanding any copyright annotation thereon.

Disclaimer: The views and conclusions contained herein are those of the authors and should not be interpreted as necessarily representing the official policies or endorsements, either expressed or implied, of IARPA, DoI/NBC, or the U.S. Government.

References

Barzilay, R. and Lee, L. (2003). Learning to paraphrase: an unsupervised approach using multiple-sequence alignment. In *Proceedings of HLT-NAACL*, NAACL '03, pages 16–23.

Barzilay, R. and McKeown, K. R. (2005). Sentence fusion for multidocument news summarization. *Computational Linguistics*, 31(3):297–328.

Bouamor, H., Max, A., and Vilnat, A. (2011). Monolingual alignment by edit rate computation on sentential paraphrase pairs. In *Proceedings of ACL-HLT*, pages 395–400.

Chambers, N., Cer, D., Grenager, T., Hall, D., Kiddon, C., MacCartney, B., de Marneffe, M.-C., Ramage, D., Yeh, E., and Manning, C. D. (2007). Learning alignments and leveraging natural logic. In *Proceedings of the ACL-PASCAL Workshop on Textual Entailment and Paraphrasing*, pages 165–170.

Chang, M.-W., Goldwasser, D., Roth, D., and Srikumar, V. (2010). Discriminative learning over constrained latent representations. In *Proceedings of HLT-NAACL*, HLT '10, pages 429–437.

Cohn, T., Callison-Burch, C., and Lapata, M. (2008). Constructing corpora for the development and evaluation of paraphrase systems. *Computational Linguistics*, 34(4):597–614.

Collins, M. (2002). Discriminative training methods for hidden Markov models. In *Proceedings of EMNLP*, pages 1–8.

Dagan, I., Glickman, O., and Magnini, B. (2005). The pascal recognising textual entailment challenge. In *Proceedings of the PASCAL Challenges Workshop on Recognising Textual Entailment*.

DeNero, J. and Klein, D. (2008). The complexity of phrase alignment problems. In *Proceedings of ACL-HLT*, pages 25–28.

Denkowski, M. and Lavie, A. (2011). Meteor 1.3: Automatic Metric for Reliable Optimization and Evaluation of Machine Translation Systems. In *Proceedings of the EMNLP 2011 Workshop on Statistical Machine Translation*.

Finkel, J. R., Grenager, T., and Manning, C. (2005). Incorporating non-local information into information extraction systems by Gibbs sampling. In *Proceedings of the 43rd Annual Meeting of the Association for Computational Linguistics*.

Heilman, M. and Madnani, N. (2012). ETS: Discriminative edit models for paraphrase scoring. In *Proceedings of *SEM: The First Joint Conference on Lexical and Computational Semantics*, pages 529–535.

Liang, P., Taskar, B., and Klein, D. (2006). Alignment by agreement. In *Proceedings of HLT-NAACL*, HLT-NAACL '06, pages 104–111.

Lita, L. V., Ittycheriah, A., Roukos, S., and Kambhatla, N. (2003). tRuEcasIng. In *Proceedings of the 41st Annual Meeting of the Association for Computational Linguistics*.

MacCartney, B., Galley, M., and Manning, C. D. (2008). A phrase-based alignment model for natural language inference. In *Proceedings of EMNLP*, EMNLP '08, pages 802–811.

MacCartney, B., Grenager, T., de Marneffe, M.-C., Cer, D., and Manning, C. D. (2006). Learning to recognize features of valid textual entailments. In *Proceedings of the Human Language Technology Conference of the NAACL, Main Conference*, pages 41–48.

Madnani, N., Tetreault, J., and Chodorow, M. (2012). Re-examining machine translation metrics for paraphrase identification. In *Proceedings of HLT-NAACL*, pages 182–190.

Marsi, E. and Krahmer, E. (2005). Explorations in sentence fusion. In *Proceedings of the European Workshop on Natural Language Generation*, pages 109–117.

Och, F. J. and Ney, H. (2003). A systematic comparison of various statistical alignment models. *Computational Linguistics*, 29:19–51.

Quirk, C., Brockett, C., and Dolan, W. B. (2004). Monolingual machine translation for paraphrase generation. In *Proceedings of EMNLP*, pages 142–149.

Thadani, K. and McKeown, K. (2008). A framework for identifying textual redundancy. In *Proceedings of COLING*, pages 873–880.

Thadani, K. and McKeown, K. (2011). Optimal and syntactically-informed decoding for monolingual phrase-based alignment. In *Proceedings of ACL-HLT*, HLT '11, pages 254–259.

Vogel, S., Ney, H., and Tillmann, C. (1996). HMM-based word alignment in statistical translation. In *Proceedings of COLING*, COLING '96, pages 836–841.

Sourcing the Crowd for a Few Good Ones: Event Type Detection

Tommaso CASELLI[1] *Chu − Ren HUANG*[2]
(1) TrentoRise, Via Sommarive 18, Povo I-38123, Povo (TN) Italy
(2) Dept. of Chinese and Bilingual Studies, Hong Kong Polytechnic University, Hung Hom, Hong-Kong SAR
t.caselli@trentorise.eu, churen.huang@polyu.edu.hk

ABSTRACT
This paper reports a crowdsourcing experiment on the identification and classification of event types in Italian. The data collected show that the task is not trivial (360 trusted judgments collected *vs.* 475 untrsuted ones) but it has been shown to be linguistically felicitous. The overall accuracy of the annotation is 61.6%. A reliability threshold assigned to the workers allows us to indentify the sub-population who has the awareness to perform this complex task and the accuracy of this sub-population is raised to 93%. Our hypothesis is that although the initial crowdsourced data is necessarily noisy, it can yield high quality results if the sub-population of 'good' workers can be identified. In other words, crowdsourcing offers a solution to difficult annotation tasks as long as there is an effective way to identify the reliable workers.

TITLE AND ABSTRACT IN ANOTHER LANGUAGE, L_2 (OPTIONAL, AND ON SAME PAGE)

Identificare Annotatori Affidabili: Riconoscimento di Tipi di Evento

Questo articolo descrive un esperimento di *crowdsourcing* per il riconoscimento e la classificazione dei tipi di evento in Italiano. I dati raccolti mostrano che il compito non è banale (360 giudizi affidabili *vs.* 475 giudizi non affidabili), ma dimostra di essere linguisticamente "felice". L'accuratezza globale della annotazione è del 61,6%. Una soglia di affidabilità assegnata ai lavoratori ci permette di identificare la sotto-popolazione che ha la consapevolezza di svolgere questo compito complesso la cui accuratezza arriva fino al 93%. La nostra ipotesi è che, sebbene i dati iniziali ottenuti tramite tecniche di *crowdsourcing* siano necessariamente rumorosi, dei risultati di buona qualità possono essere ottenuti se la sotto-popolazione di "buoni" lavoratori è identificabile. In altre parole, il *crowdsourcing* offre una soluzione per compiti di annotazione difficili finché vi è un modo efficace per identificare i lavoratori affidabili.

KEYWORDS: crowdsourcing, semantic annotation, event types, quality assessment.

KEYWORDS IN L_2: *crowdsourcing*, annotazione semantica, tipi di evento, valutazione della qualità.

Proceedings of COLING 2012: Posters, pages 1239–1248,
COLING 2012, Mumbai, December 2012.

1 Introduction

Many Natural Language Processing (NLP) systems are based on supervised learning approaches relying on large amounts of manually annotated training data collected by domain experts. Such annotation process is highly expensive both in terms of money and time. However, the absence of manually annotated Language Resources (LRs) makes supervised NLP systems subject to the so-called knowledge acquisition bottleneck. In recent years, in order to facilitate the development of LRs, two different approaches have been tackled. The first aims at automatically acquiring LRs, such as lexica, from large corpus data (Briscoe and Carroll, 1997; Korhonen et al., 2006, among others). The second investigates the exploitation of the Web 2.0 through the use of crowdsourcing techniques, i.e. by using non-expert annotators recruited on the Web. The crucial motivation of crowdsourcing is that when a simple linguistic task is performed by a population much larger than the sampling allowable by traditional experiments, interesting and hitherto unobserved distributional properties of human behaviors may emerge. In addition to this, for Language Technology, the additional motivation is that a web-based crowd can provide data for the construction of large-scale LRs in a faster, cheaper and still reliable way.
So far, annotation works conducted by means of crowsourcing techniques have focused on rather simple linguistic tasks, such as the evaluation of automatic translations (Callison-Burch, 2009), word sense disambiguation (Snow et al., 2008; Akkaya et al., 2010, Rumshinsky, 2011), textual entailment (Snow et.al., 2008; Wang and Callison-Burch, 2010), commonsense knowledge (Gordon et al., 2010), text alignment for machine translations (Ambati and Vogel, 2010) and speech transcriptions (Callison-Burch and Dredze, 2010) among others. Such choices are in line with the idea of using the "wisdom of the crowd" as the tasks can be simplified and presented to the workers as a sort of online game such that a large percentage of the population can be expected to perform the task reliably.
In this work we explore the untapped strength of crowdsourcing when the linguistic task is a complex and challenging one, trying to understand "how far can go the crowd?". As mentioned, the received wisdom is that when the tasks are complex, crowdsourced data may be too noisy to use. However, the noise may come in two ways. One possibility is that the data is noisy across the board. The other possibility is that the data is noisy from those who are not able to perform these tasks well but clean from those who perform well. The latter scenario seems promising since we learn from our experience that regardless of how difficult a task is, there will be someone good at it if a big enough population is searched. In other words, by sheer size, crowdsourcing should in principle be able to provide good quality data for more complex tasks difficult to obtain otherwise. The challenge is to separate the reliable crowd from the unreliable one.
In this paper, we study the complex task of event type classification and detection. The remainder of this work will be structured as follows: in Section 2 we will report the theoretical framework we have adopted for the analysis of the event type. In Section 3 the task of event type classification through crowdsourcing techniques will be described. Section 4 analyzes and comments on the results obtained. Finally, we reports on the conclusions and future work.

2 Event Types: theoretical background

The event type, lexical aspect or *aktionsaart*, is a lexical category and represents the intrinsic temporal structure associated with eventualities. Though strictly interconnected, the notion of event type is not to be confused with that of (viewpoint) aspect, which, on the other hand, is a grammatical category and contributes to the description of an eventuality as being bounded or unbounded.

The event type is commonly associated with verbs since the range of linguistic tests elaborated so far in literature are based on syntactic criteria with the aim of identifying homogeneous classes. As Moens (1987) points out, what is needed as a starting point in an aspectual classification of verbs are tests based on co-occurrence possibilities of the verb with certain adverbial expressions or with the progressive and perfect aspect. However, we want to depart from this perspective, and we claim that the event type applies to all eventualities, independently of their linguistic realizations. This means that event nouns, like "*assemblea*" [meeting], can be associated with a specific event type value.

Vendler's (1967) seminal work proposed four main classes of event types, namely *states*, *activities*, *accomplishments* and *achievements*. Each of these classes can be described in terms of three basic sematic features such as [+/- homogeneous], [+/- durative] and [+/- dynamic]. For clarity's sake, one example per class is provided below.

1 The door is closed [*state*];

2 John ran. [*activity*]

3 John closed the door [*accomplishment*]

4 John died [*achievement*]

In this work we depart from the original approach proposed by Vendler and adopt a different theoretical backgound following Pustejovsky's proposals (1991; 1995). With respect to previous studies based on semantic primitives (Vendler, 1967; Dowty, 1970; Lakoff, 1970 among others), the theoretical model adopted assumes:

- the existence of a complex subeventual structure for predicates which provides a template for verbal decomposition and lexical semantics;
- that adverbial modification is described in terms of scope assignement on the event structure; and
- that semantic arguments within an event structure expression can be mapped on argument structure in a predictable and systematic way.

Vendler's classes are thus reorganized from four to three basic event type values, namely: *state*, *process* and *transition* and defined as follows:

- State: a single event which is evaluated relative to no other event (Example 1);
- Process: a sequence of events which identify the same semantic expression (Example 2);
- Transition: an event which identifies a semantic expression which can be evaluated only relative to its opponent (Examples 3 and 4).

For the current study, we will not enter into the details of the phenomenon of event composition, which accounts for the interaction of the basic event types with syntactic constituents and grammatical categories to form derived event representations (e.g.: the fact that a transition event occurring at the progressive viewpoint is to be re-classified as a process event).

3 Crowdsourcing the identification of event type in context

Our goal is the identification and classification of the actual event types of predicates. In this work, we concentrated on verbs, but we are aiming at extending the work to all predicative elements, including nominals and adjectives.

Recognizing the event type of a verb in context is not a trivial task (Klavans and Chodorow 1992). Recently, Zarcone and Lenci (2009) have conducted an experiment on the identification and classification of verb event types in Italian by using three expert annotators. They report results on classification accuracy ranging between 44% to 73%.

As for our experiment we collected a subset of 100 sentences from a 2,000 sentence corpus automatically extracted from La Repubblica (Baroni et al., 2004), a large corpus of Italian newspaper articles containing more that 300 million tokens. The 2,000 sentence corpus has been created by selecting the 20 most frequent verbs in the corpus La Repubblica which satisfy the following criteria:

- they must belong to WordNet semantic class of *motion* or *change*; and
- they must belong to at least one of the following semantic types in the SIMPLE/CLIPS Ontology (Ruimy et al., 2003): *change of location, move, cause change of location* and *cause motion*.

For each verb a set of 100 random sentences has been collected. The verbs are: ARRIVARE [arrive], TORNARE [come back], PASSARE [pass/go], ENTRARE [enter], USCIRE [exit/leave], SEGUIRE [follow], CORRERE [run], INCONTRARE [meet], SALIRE [climb/rise/go up], MUOVERE [move/raise], TIRARE [throw/pull], PARTIRE [leave/go/depart], SUPERARE [overcome/get over], CADERE [fall], GIRARE [turn/spin/rotate], ALZARE [raise/get up/turn up], SALTARE [jump], VIAGGIARE [travel], CONDURRE [lead], PROCEDERE [proceed/go on].

The subcorpus of 100 sentences was uploaded on the Crowdflower platform (CF[1]) with the task name "Classify the verbs". Following the basic philosophy of crowdsourcing, we have tried to keep the annotation task for the workers as simple as possible. Thus, we have simplified the definitions of Pustejovsky's basic event types in a way that the workers could easily understand them. The participants were asked to "classify the verbs according to their meaning". In particular, we have focused the explanation of the task on the idea that each verb meaning could be grouped into a class which corresponds to one of Pustejovsky's event type. The annotators were presented with the following definitions:

- State: the verb describes a condition of something or someone;
- Process: the verb describes/reports that a certain action has taken place, is taking place or will take place;
- Transition: the verb describes/reports that a certain action has taken place or will take place and as a consequence of the occurrence of this action there has been a change of state in the world.

The definitions were accompanied by a number of examples which aimed at clarifying the task. For each example we provided a paraphrasis of the verb meaning which tried to match the

[1] http://crowdflower.com/

event type definition and the associated event type. For clarity's sake we report one example of the instruction below. The verb which the workers have to assign the event type class is in bold.

5 Marco **arrivo'** al negozio.
[Marco arrived at the shop.]
Verb meaning: Marco has moved form a place to another and now he's at the shop.
Event type: TRANSITION

The experiment was set along the following parameters: a.) each worker could analyze a maximum of 20 sentences; and b.) each sentence could receive a maximum of 10 judgments from the workers. As for this latter aspect, we considered 10 judgments per sentence as a good top threshold for validating the annotation quality of the final answers following Snow et al. (2008)'s analysis.

3.1 Quality control: Gold Standard and worker recruitment

One of the central issues in crowdsourcing is the quality control of the data. In order to filter non reliable workers and possible spammers, we adopted two strategies. The first strategy exploits the "Gold Standard" functionality of the CF platform. 15 random sentences were annotated by an expert with respect to their event type. The Gold Standard will help us in assuring that the worker' answers are correct with respect to the instructions. The second strategy is to rely on altruism instead of monetary reward in recruiting to discourage spammers. For this task, we did not offer any compensation and recruited our workers by means of a campaign on social networks such as Facebook and Twitter.

On the basis of the answers to the Gold Standard, each worker receives a reliability score. This reliability score is useful for evaluating the annotation of subsequent data, i.e. non Gold Standard items, since it allows to filter out those instances with low values, thus excluding them from the final data set.

4 Evaluation

Our purpose in the evaluation is twofold: on the one hand, we are interested in determining if crowdsourcing can be used to obtain high quality information for complex semantic tasks or if there is a limit over which expert annotation is required, and, on the other hand, we are interested in understanding what is the level of awareness of average speakers when involved in the identification of complex linguistic phenomena like event types.

4.1 Reliability of the crowd

In Table 1 we report the aggregated results. The experiment was available on the Web through CF for a period of two weeks starting on Feb. 29th this year. 46 people took part in the experiment providing a total of 835 judgements. Each sentence received at least one judgement.

The first result is the difference between trusted and untrusted judgments. By computing the judgement percentage per judgement, more than 56% (475 out of 835) of the judgments expressed have been considered as not reliable according to the Gold Standard filter, thus providing a first cue on the complexity of this task. On the other hand, it is interesting to notice

Analytics	Results
number of judgments	835
number of trusted judgments	360
number of untrusted judgments	475
judgments on gold standard data	67
average trusted judgments per sentence	3.82
number of participants	46
overall accuracy	61.6%
overall accuracy of gold standard	53%
accuracy of gold of trusted workers	93%

Table 1: Overall breakdown of the experiment.

that: a.) the accuracy of the trusted workers on the Gold Standard data is surprisingly high (93%); and b.) the overall accuracy is 61.6%, which qualify the data as reliable, although noisy. These figures allow a first important generalization: although the task is complex and the possibility of reducing its complexity are limited due to the task itself (i.e. event type detection), it is still doable and it is possible to identify a relatively high number of reliable workers. Further data in support of this analysis can be obtained by observing the distribution of the selected verbs among the three classes. Provided the verbs'characteristics, the classes of *Transition* and *Process* are by far the most selected event types (48 and 42 assignments out of 100 sentences, respectively), while the *State* class is very low (only 10 assigenements of of 100).
As a pre-test for determining the worker's qualification, an initial reliability score of 1.0 is assigned to each worker and it is reduced by 0.25 for each wrong answer to the Gold Standard items. The final reliable judgments provided by the CF platform can be grouped along four main clusters on the basis of this score. Table 2 reports the figures.

Group	# sentences	Reliability score
Cluster 1	43	1.0
Cluster 2	24	0.95 -0.7
Cluster 3	21	0.67 - 0.52
Cluster 4	11	0.5 - 0.33

Table 2: Reliability clusters of the trusted judgments.

A manual analysis of the data has shown that there is no error in the assignment of the event type for the items belonging to the first two clusters, i.e. reliability ranging from 1.0 to 0.7. On the other hand, in the last two clusters, i.e. reliability ranging from 0.67 to 0.33, we have identified 11 wrong answers. The distribution of the mistakes appears to be balanced between the two groups as there are 5 mistakes in Cluster 3 and 6 in Cluster 4. Nevertheless, by observing the corresponding percentages, it clearly appears that the items in the last group, Cluster 4, are those with the highest error rate and, thus, the least reliable (54.5% error rate in Cluster 4 *vs.* 23.8% error rate in Cluster 3). This suggests that the assignment of the event type cannot be determined only on the basis of a majority voting of the reliable workers and that not all the data provided by the workers for this specific task can be used as they are. Although the CF system assigns the event types to non Gold Standard items on the basis of a majority vote among the judgments of the trusted workers, the reliability score plays a much more important role in identifying those clusters of data which are problematic. As a consequence for

the development of LRs for complex linguistic information, such as the identification of event types, the results of this experiment provide some insights. The first is that, in principle, no linguistic task is too complex to be performed by non-experts, even though the amount of noisy data is expected to be higher than for easy tasks. In addition to this, reliability scores are more important that majority voting thus providing support to the development of well-balanced but small Gold Standards whose main purpose is the identification of those clusters of data which are more "prone" to contain errors and for which expert post-processing is required. As for our data, we propose to to set the reliability threshold to 0.7.
Finally, it appears that the correct class can be identified with a minimum of three/four judgments from reliable workers, as reported in Table 1 where the average number of trusted judgments per sentence is 3.82.

4.2 Awareness of the crowd

On the basis of the results, we can perform a further analysis on the awareness of the average speakers on the phenomenon of event type **identification and classification**. The analysis we report in this section is preliminary, although in line with what described in Zarcone and Lenci (2009). Although, average speakers seem to understand the notion of event type, the identification and classification of this property in the actual linguistic context is not trivial. As already stated, the fact that we have collected more untrusted judgements than trusted ones is a direct proof of this fact.
A further element of analysis on this aspect is provided by the the agreement on the correct class (i.e. majority voting). We have restricted the analysis to the Gold Standard items. The figures ranges between 43% to 88%. It is interesting to observe that the highest percentages of agreement are on those cases which express in a more clearcut way the event type. When facing more complex cases, including also instances of event type shifting, the percentages tend to split on all three possible classes with small differences.

Finally, it is interesting to observe that the results we have obtained are in line with those of Zarcone and Lenci (2009). As already stated, Zarcone and Lenci (2009) obtained an agreement on event type identification and classification ranging from 44% to 73%. In our experiment we have obtained an agreement per class ranging from 43% to 88%. One of the most interesting aspect is that they have used three expert annotators while we have used naive ones. These data support our conclusions on the awareness of the speaker with respect to the event types.

Conclusion and future work

This paper has explored the possibility of using crowdsourcing techniques to collect data for the identification and classification of event types in context. The most characteristic feature of this work with respect to previous studies is the difficulty of the task which is proposed to the non-expert annotators through a crowdsourcing platform.
The results collected provide empirical support to the claim that the identification and classification of event type is not easy (360 trusted judgments *vs.* 475 untrusted judgments) but, at the same time, it suggests that crowdsourcing techniques can be applied also to collect complex semantic information. As a matter of fact, we have obtained an overall accuracy of 61.6% which can be considered a good threshold for such a complex semantic task, with a top accuracy of 93% on Gold Standard data from trusted workers.
The data collected cannot be used as they are but require an expert post-processing analysis. However, the expert post-processing can be reduced to a subset of the data, in particular to those

which are below a certain reliability threshold. As for the event type identification, we claim that such a reliabiliy threshold can be put at 0.7. In this way, the development of annotated corpora both for testing and training can be facilitated with useful results in terms of reducing the efforts and costs for the creation of new Language Resources.

As for the issue of quality control, we have exploited the use of Gold Standard data and recruited motivated workers by means of a campaign on social platforms such as Facebook and Twitter. This latter element has proved important in avoiding the presence of spammers. As for the data collected, the combination of majority voting and reliability scores has proven useful for the identification both of reliable workers and correct data. However, the identification of the reliable crowd is still an open issue (see Ipeirotis et al., 2010) and better mechanisms of crowd selection should be integrated into existing (and new) crowdsourcing platforms. The solution we have adopted is partial though it proved to be efficient.

Finally, it is interesting to notice that average speakers are aware of the notion of event type, but as the results prove, they have problems to project the event type category on the actual context of occurrence.

In order to get better results in terms of quality and quantity, we are planning to further exploit the Gold Standard to identify the subset(s) of participants who is good at the sub-tasks of annotating each event type separately (i.e. state, activity, and transition respectively). This may even include workers whose reliability is below the threshold for the whole task (i.e. identify the three event types), but, on the contrary, is (almost) perfect on the sub-tasks. Moreover, we will extend this experiment with data from other languages such as English and Chinese to provide further support to our observations and, most importantly, to the reliability threshold. Finally, we aim at using the collected data for testing a classifier of event types in context. This will be the first step of a more complex task involving the identification of event internal structures (Im and Pustejovsky, 2009; 2010), which will contribute to the development of a new lexicon on events for complex NLP systems such as Question Answering and Recognizing Textual Entailment.

Acknowledgments

This research was supported in part by the Erasmus Mundus Action 2 program MULTI of the European Union, grant agreement number 2009-5259-5.

References

Akkaya, C., Alexander, C., Janyce, W., and Mihalcea, R. (2010). Amazon mechanical turk for subjectivity word sense disambiguation. In *Proceedings of the NAACL HLT 2010 Workshop on Creating Speech and Language Data with Amazon's Mechanical Turk.*

Akkaya, C., Janyce, W., and Rada, M. (2009). Subjectivity word sense disambiguation. In *Proceedings of the 2009 Conference on Empirical Methods in Natural Language Processing (EMNLP'09).*

Ambati, V. and Vogel, S. (2010). Can crowds build parallel corpora for machine translation systems? In *Proceedings of the NAACL HLT 2010 Workshop on Creating Speech and Language Data with Amazon's Mechanical Turk.*

Bertinetto, P. and Delfitto, D. (1996). Aspect vs. actionality. In Bertinetto, P., editor, *Il dominio tempo-aspettuale*, Torino. Rosebnerg Sellier.

Bertinetto, P. M. (1986). *Tempo, Aspetto e Azione nel verbo italiano. Il sistema dell'indicativo*. Accademia della Crusca., Firenze.

Briscoe, T. and Carroll, J. (1997). Automatic extraction of subcategorization from corpora. In *Proceedings of the 5th Conference on Applied Natural Language Processing*.

Callison-Burch, C. (2009). Fast, cheap, and creative: evaluating translation quality using amazon mechanical turk. In *Proceedings of the 2009 Conference on Empirical Methods in Natural Language Processing (EMNLP'09)*.

Callison-Burch, C. and Dredze, M. (2010). Creating speech and language data with amazon's mechanical turk. In *Proceedings of the NAACL HLT 2010 Workshop on Creating Speech and Language Data with Amazon's Mechanical Turk*.

Dowty, D. (1979). *Word Meaning and Montague Grammar*. D. Reidel,, Dordrecht, W. Germany.

Im, S. and Pustejovsky, J. (2009). Annotating event implicatures for textual inference tasks. In *Proceedings of G.L. 2009*.

Im, S. and Pustejovsky, J. (2010). Annotating lexically entailed subevents for textual inference tasks. In *Proceedings of FLAIRS-2010*.

Ipeirotis, P., Provost, F., and Wang, J. (2010). Quality management on amazon mechanical turk. In *Proceedings of KDD-HCOMP '10*.

Jonathan, G., Benjamin, V. D., and Schubert, L. (2010). Evaluation of commonsense knowledge with mechanical turk. In *Proceedings of the NAACL HLT 2010 Workshop on Creating Speech and Language Data with Amazon's Mechanical Turk*.

Klavans, J. and Chodorow, L. (1992). Degrees of stativity: The lexical representation of verb aspect. In *Proceedings of the 14th International Conference on Computational Linguistics (COLING'92)*.

Korhonen, A., Krimolowsky, Y., and Briscoe, T. (2006). A large subcategorization lexicon for natural language processing applications. In *Proceedings of the 5th International Language Resources and Evaluation (LREC'06)*.

Lakoff, G. (1970). *Irregularity in syntax*. Holt, Rinchart and Winston, New York.

Moens, M. (1987). *Tense, Aspect and Temporal Reference*. Centre for Cognitive Science, University of Edinburgh, Edinburgh, Scotland.

Pustejovsky, J. (1991). The generative lexicon. *Computational Linguistics*, 17(4):409–441.

Pustejovsky, J. (1995). *The Generative Lexicon*. The MIT Press.

Ruimy, N., Monachini, M., Gola, E., Calzolari, N., Fiorentino, M. D., Ulivieri, M., and Rossi, S. (2003). A computational semantic lexicon of italian: Simple. *Linguistica Computazionale*, XVIII-XIX:821–864.

Rumshisky, A. (2011). Crowdsourcing word sense definition. In *Proceedings of the 5th Linguistic Annotation Workshop (LAW V)*.

Snow, R., Connor, B. O., Jurafsky, D., and Ng, A. Y. (2008). Cheap and fastut is it good?: Evaluating non-expert annotations for natural language tasks. In *Proceedings of the 2008 Conference on Empirical Methods in Natural Language Processing (EMNLP'08)*.

Vendler, Z. (1995). *Linguistics in Philosophy*. Cornell University Press, Ithaca, NY.

von Ahn, L. and Dabbish, L. (2004). Labeling images with a computer game. In *ACM Conference on Human Factors in Computing Systems, CHI 2004*.

Wang, R. and Callison-Burch, C. (2010). Cheap facts and counter-facts. In *Proceedings of the NAACL HLT 2010 Workshop on Creating Speech and Language Data with Amazon's Mechanical Turk*.

Zarcone, A. and Lenci, A. (2006). Un modello stocastico della classificazione azionale. In G., F., Benatti, R., and Mosca, M., editors, *Linguistica e modelli tecnologici della ricerca. Atti del XL Congresso SLI - Vercelli, Settembre 2006*.

Zarcone, A. and Lenci, A. (2008). Computational models of event type classification in context. In *Proceedings of the 6th International Language Resources and Evaluation (LREC8)*.

Combining Multiple Alignments to Improve Machine Translation

Zhaopeng Tu[1] *Yang Liu*[2] *Yifan He*[3] *Josef van Genabith*[4]
Qun Liu[1,4] *Shouxun Lin*[1]

(1) Key Laboratory of Intelligent Information Processing, Institute of Computing Technology, Chinese Academy of Sciences, China
{tuzhaopeng, liuqun, sxlin}@ict.ac.cn

(2) Department of Computer Science and Technology, State Key Lab on Intelligent Technology and Systems, National Lab for Information Science and Technology, Tsinghua University, China
liuyang2011@tsinghua.edu.cn

(3) Computer Science Department, New York University, USA
yhe@cs.nyu.edu

(4) Centre for Next Generation Localisation, School of Computing, Dublin City University, Ireland
josef@computing.dcu.ie

ABSTRACT
Word alignment is a critical component of machine translation systems. Various methods for word alignment have been proposed, and different models can produce significantly different outputs. To exploit the advantages of different models, we propose three ways to combine multiple alignments for machine translation: (1) *alignment selection*, a novel method to select an alignment with the least expected loss from multiple alignments within the minimum Bayes risk framework; (2) *alignment refinement*, an improved algorithm to refine multiple alignments into a new alignment that favors the consensus of various models; (3) *alignment compaction*, a compact representation that encodes all alignments generated by different methods (including (1) and (2) above) using a novel calculation of link probabilities. Experiments show that our approach not only improves the alignment quality, but also significantly improves translation performance by up to 1.96 BLEU points over single best alignments, and 1.28 points over merging rules extracted from multiple alignments individually.

KEYWORDS: alignment combination, minimum Bayes risk, alignment refinement, weighted alignment matrix.

Proceedings of COLING 2012: Posters, pages 1249–1260,
COLING 2012, Mumbai, December 2012.

Alignments	GIZA++	Berkeley	Vigne
GIZA++	–	70.29%	75.17%
Berkeley	70.29%	–	73.25%
Vigne	75.17%	73.25%	–

Table 1: Agreement of alignment links between different alignment models. Here we use three different alignment models: GIZA++ (Och and Ney, 2003), the unsupervised Berkeley aligner (Liang et al., 2006), and a discriminative aligner Vigne (Liu et al., 2010).

1 Introduction

Word alignment is a preliminary step for statistical machine translation (SMT). Most SMT systems, not only phrase-based models (Och and Ney, 2004; Koehn et al., 2003; Chiang, 2005; Xiong et al., 2006), but also syntax-based models (Galley et al., 2006; Shen et al., 2008; Liu et al., 2006; Huang et al., 2006), rely heavily on word-aligned bilingual corpora.

Various methods for word alignment, including generative methods (Brown et al., 1993; Vogel et al., 1996; Liang et al., 2006) and discriminative methods (Moore et al., 2006; Taskar et al., 2005; Blunsom and Cohn, 2006; Liu et al., 2010), have been proposed in the literature. Different models produce significantly different alignments. [1] Table 1 shows the *agreement* between each pair of alignments on 1.5M Chinese-English parallel sentence pairs. Here *agreement* is computed by using one alignment model's output as a gold standard to evaluate the other alignment model's output in terms of F1 score (Xiao et al., 2010). The higher the agreement score is, the more similar two alignments are. Table 1 shows that the agreement scores are always below 76%.

Therefore, it is natural to combine multiple alignments to improve both alignment quality and translation quality. In this paper, we propose three ways to exploit multiple alignments for machine translation: alignment selection, refinement and compaction. Alignment selection chooses high quality alignments while refinement generates new and more reliable alignments. Alignment compaction encodes multiple possible alignments. We show that these methods work well together: alignment refinement e.g. offers high quality alignment choices, that can be exploited by alignment compaction.

2 Related Work

Our research builds on previous work in the field of minimum Bayes risk (MBR) decision, system combination and model compaction. MBR decision aims to find the candidate hypothesis that has the least expected loss under a probability model when the true reference is not known (Brickel and Doksum, 1977). Diverse loss functions have been described by using different evaluation criteria for loss calculation, e.g. edit distance and sentence-level BLEU in SMT (Kumar and Byrne, 2004; Tromble et al., 2008; González-Rubio et al., 2011). In our work, we select an alignment within the MBR framework using a number of loss functions at both alignment and phrase levels.

System combination, the process which integrates fragment outputs from multiple systems, has produced substantial improvements in many natural language processing tasks, including parsing (Henderson and Brill, 1999; Sagae and Lavie, 2006; Fossum and Knight, 2009), word segmentation (Sun and Wan, 2012) and machine translation (Rosti et al., 2007; He et al.,

[1] These alignments have equivalent qualities compared to a true gold standard (see in Table 2).

2008; Feng et al., 2009), just to name a few. Alignment combination has also been explored previously (Och and Ney, 2003; Koehn et al., 2003; Ayan et al., 2005; DeNero and Macherey, 2011). We draw inspiration from (Och and Ney, 2003; Koehn et al., 2003) but our technique differs from previous work in that (1) they require exactly two bidirectional alignments while our approach can use an arbitrary number of alignments; (2) we take into account the occurrences of potential links, which turns out to be important.

Previous research has demonstrated that compact representations can produce improved results by offering more alternatives, e.g. using forests over 1-best trees (Mi and Huang, 2008; Tu et al., 2010), word lattices over 1-best segmentations (Dyer et al., 2008), and weighted alignment matrices (WAMs) over 1-best alignments (Liu et al., 2009; Tu et al., 2011). Instead of using k-best alignments from the same model, as in (Liu et al., 2009; Tu et al., 2011), here we construct WAMs from multiple alignments generated by different models (including MBR-based and refined models). As the alignment probabilities are generally incomparable between different alignment models, we propose a novel calculation of link probabilities in WAMs.

3 Approach

3.1 Alignment Selection

Alignment selection refers to selecting one alignment from multiple alignments using minimum Bayes risk. If the reference alignment a was known, we could measure each alignment a_i using the loss function $\mathscr{L}(a_i, a)$. In the MBR framework, although the true reference alignment is unknown, we assume that the individual alignment models' output forms a reasonable distribution over possible reference alignments. The MBR decision aims to find the candidate alignment that has the least expected loss under the distribution (Brickel and Doksum, 1977).

3.1.1 MBR Decision

MBR decision has the following form:

$$\hat{a} = \arg\min_{a_i \in A} \mathscr{R}(a_i) = \arg\min_{a_i \in A} \sum_{a_j \in A} \mathscr{L}(a_i, a_j) \cdot p(a_j | f, e) \tag{1}$$

where $\mathscr{R}(a_i)$ denotes the Bayes risk of candidate alignment a_i under loss function $\mathscr{L}$, A indicates the set of alignments generated by different models. In general, for different alignment models, the probabilities $p(a|f, e)$ are not directly comparable. For simplicity, in our work below we assume that they are in fact comparable and have the same value. [2]

3.1.2 Loss Functions

The loss function $\mathscr{L}(a_i, a_j)$ is used to measure the quality of alignments. Here we introduce a set of metrics for the evaluation of alignments at both alignment and phrase levels.

AER

Alignment error rate (Och and Ney, 2003) has been used as the official evaluation criterion in most alignment shared tasks (Liu et al., 2009). AER scores are given by:

$$AER(S, P, A) = 1 - (|A \cap S| + |A \cap P|)/(|A| + |S|) \tag{2}$$

[2] Alignment probabilities can be set empirically based on (expected overall) performance (Fossum and Knight, 2009), or uniformly without any bias (Xiao et al., 2010; Duan et al., 2010). We tried a few other settings and found them to be less effective.

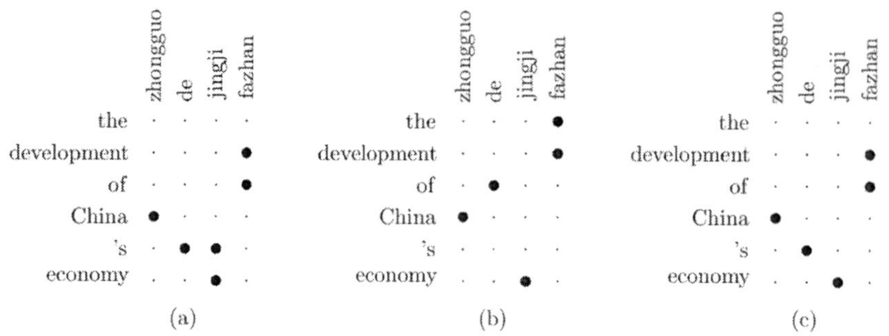

Figure 1: (a) Alignment of a sentence pair generated by GIZA++ (a_1), (b) alignment of the same sentence by Berkeley aligner (a_2), (c) another alignment by Vigne (a_3).

where S and P are sets of sure and possible links in a hand-aligned reference alignment respectively, and A is a candidate alignment. Note that S is a subset of P: $S \subseteq P$. As there is no reference alignment that is hand-aligned by human experts in our work, we cannot distinguish sure links from possible links. Therefore, we regard all links to be sure links: $S = P$. With this, the AER score is calculated by:

$$AER(a_i, a_j) = 1 - (2 \times |a_i \cap a_j|)/(|a_i| + |a_j|) \tag{3}$$

CPER

Although widely used, AER is criticized for correlating poorly with translation performance (Ayan and Dorr, 2006; Fraser and Marcu, 2007). Therefore, Ayan and Dorr (2006) have proposed *constituent phrase error rate* (CPER) for evaluating word alignments at the phrase level instead of the alignment level. CPER can be computed as:

$$CPER(a_i, a_j) = 1 - (2 \times |P_{a_i} \cap P_{a_j}|)/(|P_{a_i}| + |P_{a_j}|) \tag{4}$$

where P_a denotes the set of phrases that are consistent with a given alignment a. Compared with AER, CPER penalizes dissimilar alignment links more heavily. As a dissimilar link reduces the number of intersected links of two alignments by 1 in AER, it might lead to more than one different phrase pair added to or removed from the set of phrases (Ayan and Dorr, 2006).

CHER

As CPER evaluates word alignments in the context of phrase-based MT, we propose a similar metric called *constituent hierarchical-phrase error rate* (CHER) for hierarchical-phrase models. The difference between them is that we use H_a instead of P_a, where H_a denotes the hierarchical phrases extracted. Hierarchical phrases are more sensitive to word alignments because they are sensitive to inside (i.e. subtracted) phrases.

3.2 Alignment Refinement

Alignment refinement refers to extracting parts of multiple alignments and constructing a new alignment instead of selecting the best one from existing alignments. A simple way to refine multiple alignments is to employ their intersection or union. However, using intersection will result in a high-precision but low-recall alignment, while using union will result in a high-recall but low-precision alignment. Koehn et al. (2003) show performance improvements by finding a balance between the intersection and union with the *grow-diag-final* algorithm.

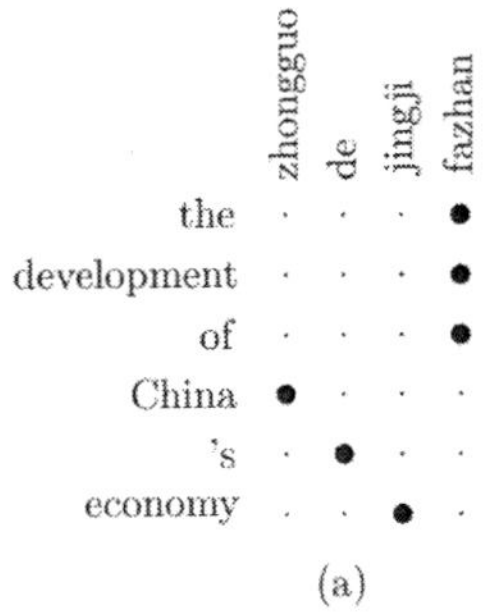

	zhongguo	de	jingji	fazhan
the	0	0	0	0.3
development	0	0	0	1.0
of	0	0.3	0	0.7
China	1.0	0	0	0
's	0	0.7	0.3	0
economy	0	0	1.0	0

(b)

Figure 2: (a) The refined alignment generated from multiple alignments in Figure 1, (b) the resulting weighted alignment matrix that samples the same alignments, where the number in the cells are the probabilities of the corresponding link.

Unfortunately, this algorithm cannot be applied to our approach. This is because the *grow-diag-final* algorithm requires exactly two bidirectional alignments, while we would use more than two alignments. Therefore, we propose a variation of the *grow-diag-final* algorithm named *grow-diag-final-rank* adapted for multiple alignments. The difference between the two algorithms is that we take into account the occurrences of *conflicting links*. Conflicting links refer to triples $<l_i, l_j, l_k>$, in which l_i and l_j are the links that share the same source side, and l_j and l_k share the same target side. For example, the triple < *(de, 's)*, *(de, of)*, *(fazhan, of)*> is conflicting because the first two share the same source side while the latter two share the same target side.

Alignment refinement chooses the links with the most occurrences when there are conflicting links. Intuitively, our approach is motivated by the following observation: the links that occur more often in different alignments frequently have a higher confidence than those that occur less often. Our algorithm favors the links that occur frequently. As an example, consider the conflicting links < *(de, 's)*, *(de, of)*, *(fazhan, of)*>: without considering the number of their occurrences, we would retain the first two links if we run grow-diag-final greedily. In contrast, considering that the links *(de, 's)* and *(fazhan, of)* occur twice while *(de, of)* only occurs once, we prefer to retain *(de, 's)* and *(fazhan, of)*. Figure 2(a) shows the refined alignment generated from the three alignments in Figure 1 using the *grow-diag-final-rank* algorithm.

3.3 Alignment Compaction

Given the original alignments and the alignments generated by alignment refinement, it is quite natural to try to encode them in a compact representation. In this paper, we use weighted alignment matrices for this purpose. A weighted alignment matrix (Liu et al., 2009) is a matrix to encode the probabilities of k-best alignments of the same sentence pair. Each element in the matrix stores a link probability which is estimated from a k-best list.

$$p_m(j,i) = \frac{\sum_{k=1}^{K} p(a_k|f,e) \cdot \delta(a_k,j,i)}{\sum_{k=1}^{K} p(a_k|f,e)} \tag{5}$$

where

$$\delta(a_k,j,i) = \begin{cases} 1 & (j,i) \in a_k \\ 0 & \text{otherwise} \end{cases} \tag{6}$$

Here $a_k \in \mathcal{K}$ is a k-best list, $p(a_k|f,e)$ is the probability of an alignment a_k in the k-best list. Intuitively, a higher link probability $p_m(j,i)$ indicates high agreement between different alignments, thereby high quality.

(Liu et al., 2009; Tu et al., 2011) have shown that WAMs yield encouraging results by making good use of k-best alignments from a single alignment model. Unlike in this previous work, in our approach we construct WAMs from alignments generated by different models (including MBR-based and refined models). In a k-best list, each alignment is weighted using their probabilities since they are obtained from the same model, and a higher weight denotes that the alignment model has higher confidence in the output. In contrast, the alignments in our work are generated by different models and their probabilities are generally incomparable. As noted above, we assume that all the alignments have the same probabilities. Then, we obtain:

$$p_m(j,i) = \frac{\sum_{k=1}^{N} \delta(a_k, j, i)}{N} \tag{7}$$

Figure 2(b) shows the WAM that captures the three alignments in Figure 1.[3]

We then follow (Tu et al., 2011) to extract hierarchical phrases from WAM and calculate their translation and lexical probabilities. Instead of extracting phrase pairs that respect the word alignment, Tu et al. (2011) enumerate all potential phrase pairs and calculate their fractional counts. As they soften the alignment consistency constraint, there exists a massive number of phrase pairs extracted from the training corpus. To maintain a reasonable phrase table size, they discard any phrase pair that has a fractional count lower than a threshold t. For further details, see (Tu et al., 2011).

4 Experiments

4.1 Setup

We carry out our experiments using a reimplementation of the hierarchical phrase-based system (Chiang, 2005) on the NIST Chinese-English translation tasks. Our training data contains 1.5M sentence pairs from LDC dataset.[4] We train a 4-gram language model on the Xinhua portion of the GIGAWORD corpus using the SRI Language Toolkit (Stolcke, 2002) with modified Kneser-Ney Smoothing (Kneser and Ney, 1995). We use minimum error rate training (Och, 2003) to optimize the feature weights on the MT02 testset, and test on the MT03/04/05 testsets. For evaluation, case-insensitive NIST BLEU (Papineni et al., 2002) is used to measure translation performance.

Three alignment models are chosen for our experiments with default settings: GIZA++ (Och and Ney, 2003), the unsupervised Berkeley aligner (Liang et al., 2006), and the linear modeling alignment Vigne (Liu et al., 2010). We use the three baseline alignments to select MBR alignments and to generate a refined alignment. We use all three baseline alignments, as well as all of the MBR and refined alignments in the WAM-based compaction approach. When extracting rules from WAM, we follow (Tu et al., 2011) to set the pruning threshold t=0.5.

[3]In practice, alignment compaction encodes both baseline alignments and the new alignments in Section 3.1 and 3.2.

[4]The corpus includes LDC2002E18, LDC2003E07, LDC2003E14, Hansards portion of LDC2004T07, LDC2004T08 and LDC2005T06.

Alignments	AER	BAER	CPER	CHER
GIZA++	22.50	27.92	24.11	33.23
Berkeley	21.11	26.41	23.35	34.44
Vigne	19.13	24.05	23.54	34.02
Selection$_{AER}$	**17.93**	**23.29**	22.10	31.47
Selection$_{CPER}$	18.32	23.72	**21.53**	30.56
Selection$_{CHER}$	18.52	23.93	21.68	30.84
Refinement	18.79	24.43	**21.50**	**30.31**

Table 2: Evaluation of alignment quality. Here "Selection$_{\mathscr{L}}$" indicates the alignment selected from multiple single alignments using MBR decision under the loss function $\mathscr{L}$ (e.g. AER, CPER and CHER). For all metrics, the lower the score is, the better the alignment quality is.

4.2 Evaluation of Alignment Quality

In this section, we investigate the quality of different alignments on the Chinese-English language pair data. We annotated 1007 sentences with annotations that distinguish between sure and possible links.[5] We used 502 sentences as the tuning set, and 505 sentences as the test set. We run GIZA++ and the Berkeley aligner on the training corpus as well as the test set. We tune the feature weights of Vigne on the tuning set using AER as the optimization criterion. We evaluate alignments in terms of AER, CPER and CHER as described in Section 3.1.2. Inspired by Fraser and Marcu (2007), we also employ a new metric called **balanced AER** (BAER) that considers only the sure links in the reference alignments:

$$BAER(S,A) = 1 - (2 \times |A \cap S|)/(|A| + |S|) \tag{8}$$

For all metrics, lower score indicates better alignment quality.

Table 2 lists the alignment quality results for different alignment strategies. We find that both selection and refinement methods outperform single alignments at all metrics, indicating that our methods improve the quality of alignment in a certain way. One finding is that the selection method usually achieves the best score at the metric it uses as loss function. For example, the selection method using AER as loss function outperforms other alignments at the AER and BAER metrics while underperforming at other metrics. This is intuitive, since the method always selects the alignment with the minimum expected loss under the metric.

4.3 Evaluation of Translation Quality

Table 3 summaries the results of translation performance with different alignment methods.

- **Baseline results.** We have three baseline systems: GIZA++, Berkeley and Vigne. The results show that GIZA++ achieves the best performance among the baseline systems. Therefore, we compare our methods with GIZA++ system in the following analysis.
- **Rule Merging.** Different alignments generally result in very different sets of hierarchical rules. As one would expect, merging them outperforms using any of them individually through enlarging the rule coverage. Experimental results show that merging rules indeed outperforms using single best alignments, at the cost of a much larger rule table.

[5] available at http://nlp.ict.ac.cn/~tuzhaopeng/.

Alignments	Links	Rules	DEV	MT03	MT04	MT05	Avg.
GIZA++	45.4M	143M	35.07	33.11	35.06	32.98	33.72
Berkeley	33.7M	270M	34.72	32.64	34.93	32.58	33.38
Vigne	35.6M	140M	34.64	33.16	34.29	32.45	33.30
Rule Merging	–	553M	35.55	34.12**	35.88**	33.66*	34.55
Inter	24.5M	178M	34.10	32.35	34.17	32.47	33.00
Union	55.6M	94M	34.83	33.42	35.04	33.05	33.84
Selection_{AER}	37.9M	175M	35.35	33.65**	35.82**	33.56*	34.34
Selection_{CPER}	38.9M	187M	35.36	34.21**	36.05**	33.71**	34.66
Selection_{CHER}	39.1M	182M	35.71	34.16**	35.88**	33.94**	34.66
Refinement	45.5M	210M	35.44	33.81**	35.98**	33.95**	34.58
Compaction	55.6M	319M	**36.64**	**35.01****	**36.81****	**34.94****	**35.59**

Table 3: Evaluation of translation quality. "Links" denotes the number of links in the alignment and "Rules" denotes the number of rules (Chiang, 2005) extracted from the corresponding alignment. "Avg." is the average BLEU score on the three test sets. Significance tests are done against GIZA++ on test sets following the *sign-test* approach (Collins et al., 2005), and "**" and "*" denote p-value less than 0.01 and 0.05, respectively. Furthermore, Compaction is significantly better than Rule Merging for p-value less than 0.01 on all test sets.

- **Alignment Selection.** Concerning selection methods, the results show that using loss functions at phrase level (i.e. CPER and CHER) outperforms loss function at alignment level (i.e AER). One possible reason is that CPER and CHER relate more tightly to the translation performance, because they care about the phrases which are used directly in machine translation. In brief, using selection methods with different loss functions improves translation performance in BLEU score by up to 0.92 points on average.

- **Alignment Refinement.** Table 3 shows that simply using the intersection (Inter) or union (Union) does not achieve any improvement. This is in accord with intuition, because intersection discards many useful links while union includes many incorrect links. By contrast, alignment refinement finds a good balance between them, and achieves significant improvement in BLEU score ranging from 0.70 to 0.97 points.

- **Alignment Compaction.** Alignment compaction encodes all alignments and achieves the best result, which improves BLEU scores by between 1.75 and 1.96 points. Compared with rule merging, alignment combination produces substantial improvements in both translation performance and rule table size.

5 Conclusion

In this paper, we have presented three simple and effective methods to make use of multiple alignments. First, we select the alignments with minimum Bayes risk using different loss functions at both alignment and phrase levels. Then, we refine multiple alignments using an improved *grow-diag-final-rank* algorithm that considers the occurrences of alignment links. Finally, we use a compact representation named weighted alignment matrix to represent all alignments (including MBR-based and refined alignments) and propose a novel calculation of link probabilities. Experimental results show that our method not only improves the alignment quality, but also significantly improves translation performance over both single best alignments and merging rules extracted from different single alignments individually.

Acknowledgement

The authors were supported by 863 State Key Project No. 2011AA01A207, 863 Project No. 2012AA011102 and Science Foundation Ireland (Grant No. 07/CE/I1142). We thank the anonymous reviewers for their insightful comments.

References

Ayan, N. F. and Dorr, B. J. (2006). Going beyond aer: An extensive analysis of word alignments and their impact on mt. In *Proceedings of the 21st International Conference on Computational Linguistics and 44th Annual Meeting of the Association for Computational Linguistics*, pages 9–16, Sydney, Australia. Association for Computational Linguistics.

Ayan, N. F., Dorr, B. J., and Monz, C. (2005). Neuralign: Combining word alignments using neural networks. In *Proceedings of Human Language Technology Conference and Conference on Empirical Methods in Natural Language Processing*, pages 65–72, Vancouver, British Columbia, Canada. Association for Computational Linguistics.

Blunsom, P. and Cohn, T. (2006). Discriminative word alignment with conditional random fields. In *Proceedings of the 21st International Conference on Computational Linguistics and 44th Annual Meeting of the Association for Computational Linguistics*, pages 65–72, Sydney, Australia. Association for Computational Linguistics.

Brickel, P. J. and Doksum, K. A. (1977). Mathematical statistics: basic ideas and selected topics.

Brown, P. E., Pietra, S. A. D., Pietra, V. J. D., and Mercer, R. L. (1993). The mathematics of statistical machine translation: Parameter estimation. *Computational linguistics*, 19(2):263–311.

Chiang, D. (2005). A hierarchical phrase-based model for statistical machine translation. In *Proceedings of the 43rd Annual Meeting on Association for Computational Linguistics*, pages 263–270. Association for Computational Linguistics.

Collins, M., Koehn, P., and Kučerová, I. (2005). Clause restructuring for statistical machine translation. In *Proceedings of the 43rd Annual Meeting on Association for Computational Linguistics*, pages 531–540. Association for Computational Linguistics.

DeNero, J. and Macherey, K. (2011). Model-based aligner combination using dual decomposition. In *Proceedings of the 49th Annual Meeting of the Association for Computational Linguistics: Human Language Technologies*, pages 420–429, Portland, Oregon, USA. Association for Computational Linguistics.

Duan, N., Li, M., Zhang, D., and Zhou, M. (2010). Mixture model-based minimum bayes risk decoding using multiple machine translation systems. In *Proceedings of the 23rd International Conference on Computational Linguistics (Coling 2010)*, pages 313–321, Beijing, China. International Committee on Computational Linguistics.

Dyer, C., Muresan, S., and Resnik, P. (2008). Generalizing word lattice translation. In *Proceedings of ACL-08: HLT*, pages 1012–1020, Columbus, Ohio. Association for Computational Linguistics.

Feng, Y., Liu, Y., Mi, H., Liu, Q., and Lü, Y. (2009). Lattice-based system combination for statistical machine translation. In *Proceedings of the 2009 Conference on Empirical Methods in Natural Language Processing*, pages 1105–1113, Singapore. Association for Computational Linguistics.

Fossum, V. and Knight, K. (2009). Combining constituent parsers. In *Proceedings of Human Language Technologies: The 2009 Annual Conference of the North American Chapter of the Association for Computational Linguistics, Companion Volume: Short Papers*, pages 253–256, Boulder, Colorado. Association for Computational Linguistics.

Fraser, A. and Marcu, D. (2007). Measuring word alignment quality for statistical machine translation. *Computational Linguistics*, 33(3):293–303.

Galley, M., Graehl, J., Knight, K., Marcu, D., DeNeefe, S., Wang, W., and Thayer, I. (2006). Scalable inference and training of context-rich syntactic translation models. In *Proceedings of the 21st International Conference on Computational Linguistics and 44th Annual Meeting of the Association for Computational Linguistics*, pages 961–968, Sydney, Australia. Association for Computational Linguistics.

González-Rubio, J., Juan, A., and Casacuberta, F. (2011). Minimum bayes-risk system combination. In *Proceedings of the 49th Annual Meeting of the Association for Computational Linguistics: Human Language Technologies*, pages 1268–1277, Portland, Oregon, USA. Association for Computational Linguistics.

He, X., Yang, M., Gao, J., Nguyen, P., and Moore, R. (2008). Indirect-hmm-based hypothesis alignment for computing outputs from machine translation systems. In *Proceedings of the 2008 Conference on Empirical Methods in Natural Language Processing*, pages 98–107, Honolulu, Hawaii. Association for Computational Linguistics.

Henderson, J. C. and Brill, E. (1999). Exploiting diversity in natural language processing: Combining parsers. In *Proceedings of the Fourth Conference on Empirical Methods in Natural Language Processing*, pages 187–194.

Huang, L., Knight, K., and Joshi, A. (2006). Statistical syntax-directed translation with extended domain of locality. In *Proceedings of AMTA*, pages 66–73. Citeseer.

Kneser, R. and Ney, H. (1995). Improved backing-off for m-gram language modeling. In *ICASSP IEEE INT CONF ACOUST SPEECH SIGNAL PROCESS PROC*, volume 1, pages 181–184.

Koehn, P., Och, F. J., and Marcu, D. (2003). Statistical phrase-based translation. In *Proceedings of the 2003 Conference of the North American Chapter of the Association for Computational Linguistics on Human Language Technology-Volume 1*, pages 48–54. Association for Computational Linguistics.

Kumar, S. and Byrne, W. (2004). Minimum bayes-risk decoding for statistical machine translation. In Susan Dumais, D. M. and Roukos, S., editors, *HLT-NAACL 2004: Main Proceedings*, pages 169–176, Boston, Massachusetts, USA. Association for Computational Linguistics.

Liang, P., Taskar, B., and Klein, D. (2006). Alignment by agreement. In *Proceedings of the Human Language Technology Conference of the NAACL, Main Conference*, pages 104–111, New York City, USA. Association for Computational Linguistics.

Liu, Y., Liu, Q., and Lin, S. (2006). Tree-to-string alignment template for statistical machine translation. In *Proceedings of the 21st International Conference on Computational Linguistics and 44th Annual Meeting of the Association for Computational Linguistics*, pages 609–616, Sydney, Australia. Association for Computational Linguistics.

Liu, Y., Liu, Q., and Lin, S. (2010). Discriminative word alignment by linear modeling. *Computational Linguistics*, 36(3):303–339.

Liu, Y., Xia, T., Xiao, X., and Liu, Q. (2009). Weighted alignment matrices for statistical machine translation. In *Proceedings of the 2009 Conference on Empirical Methods in Natural Language Processing*, pages 1017–1026, Singapore. Association for Computational Linguistics.

Mi, H. and Huang, L. (2008). Forest-based translation rule extraction. In *Proceedings of the 2008 Conference on Empirical Methods in Natural Language Processing*, pages 206–214, Honolulu, Hawaii. Association for Computational Linguistics.

Moore, R. C., Yih, W.-t., and Bode, A. (2006). Improved discriminative bilingual word alignment. In *Proceedings of the 21st International Conference on Computational Linguistics and 44th Annual Meeting of the Association for Computational Linguistics*, pages 513–520, Sydney, Australia. Association for Computational Linguistics.

Och, F. J. (2003). Minimum error rate training in statistical machine translation. In *Proceedings of the 41st Annual Meeting of the Association for Computational Linguistics*, pages 160–167, Sapporo, Japan. Association for Computational Linguistics.

Och, F. J. and Ney, H. (2003). A systematic comparison of various statistical alignment models. *Computational Linguistics*, 29(1):19–51.

Och, F. J. and Ney, H. (2004). The alignment template approach to statistical machine translation. *Computational Linguistics*, 30(4):417–449.

Papineni, K., Roukos, S., Ward, T., and Zhu, W.-J. (2002). Bleu: a method for automatic evaluation of machine translation. In *Proceedings of 40th Annual Meeting of the Association for Computational Linguistics*, pages 311–318, Philadelphia, Pennsylvania, USA. Association for Computational Linguistics.

Rosti, A.-V., Ayan, N. F., Xiang, B., Matsoukas, S., Schwartz, R., and Dorr, B. (2007). Combining outputs from multiple machine translation systems. In *Human Language Technologies 2007: The Conference of the North American Chapter of the Association for Computational Linguistics; Proceedings of the Main Conference*, pages 228–235, Rochester, New York. Association for Computational Linguistics.

Sagae, K. and Lavie, A. (2006). Parser combination by reparsing. In *Proceedings of the Human Language Technology Conference of the NAACL, Companion Volume: Short Papers*, pages 129–132, New York City, USA. Association for Computational Linguistics.

Shen, L., Xu, J., and Weischedel, R. (2008). A new string-to-dependency machine translation algorithm with a target dependency language model. In *Proceedings of ACL-08: HLT*, pages 577–585, Columbus, Ohio. Association for Computational Linguistics.

Stolcke, A. (2002). Srilm - an extensible language modeling toolkit. In *Proceedings of Seventh International Conference on Spoken Language Processing*, volume 3, pages 901–904. Citeseer.

Sun, W. and Wan, X. (2012). Reducing approximation and estimation errors for chinese lexical processing with heterogeneous annotations. In *Proceedings of the 50th Annual Meeting of the Association for Computational Linguistics (Volume 1: Long Papers)*, pages 232–241, Jeju Island, Korea. Association for Computational Linguistics.

Taskar, B., Simon, L.-J., and Dan, K. (2005). A discriminative matching approach to word alignment. In *Proceedings of Human Language Technology Conference and Conference on Empirical Methods in Natural Language Processing*, pages 73–80, Vancouver, British Columbia, Canada. Association for Computational Linguistics.

Tromble, R., Kumar, S., Och, F., and Macherey, W. (2008). Lattice Minimum Bayes-Risk decoding for statistical machine translation. In *Proceedings of the 2008 Conference on Empirical Methods in Natural Language Processing*, pages 620–629, Honolulu, Hawaii. Association for Computational Linguistics.

Tu, Z., Liu, Y., Hwang, Y.-S., Liu, Q., and Lin, S. (2010). Dependency forest for statistical machine translation. In *Proceedings of the 23rd International Conference on Computational Linguistics (Coling 2010)*, pages 1092–1100, Beijing, China. International Committee on Computational Linguistics.

Tu, Z., Liu, Y., Liu, Q., and Lin, S. (2011). Extracting Hierarchical Rules from a Weighted Alignment Matrix. In *Proceedings of 5th International Joint Conference on Natural Language Processing*, pages 1294–1303, Chiang Mai, Thailand. Asian Federation of Natural Language Processing.

Vogel, S., Ney, H., and Tillmann, C. (1996). Hmm-based word alignment in statistical translation. In *Proceedings of the 16th conference on Computational linguistics*, pages 836–841. Association for Computational Linguistics.

Xiao, T., Zhu, J., Zhang, H., and Zhu, M. (2010). An empirical study of translation rule extraction with multiple parsers. In *Coling 2010: Posters*, pages 1345–1353, Beijing, China. International Committee on Computational Linguistics.

Xiong, D., Liu, Q., and Lin, S. (2006). Maximum entropy based phrase reordering model for statistical machine translation. In *Proceedings of the 21st International Conference on Computational Linguistics and 44th Annual Meeting of the Association for Computational Linguistics*, pages 521–528, Sydney, Australia. Association for Computational Linguistics.

A new search approach for interactive-predictive computer-assisted translation

Zeinab VAKIL Shahram KHADIVI
Human Language Technology Lab,
Computer Engineering Department, Amirkabir University of Technology, Tehran, Iran
{Z.Vakil,Khadivi}@aut.ac.ir

ABSTRACT

Although significant improvements have been achieved in statistical machine translation (SMT), even the best machine translation technology is far from competing with human translators. An alternative approach to obtain high quality translation is to use a human translator who is assisted by an SMT. In interactive-predictive computer-assisted translation (IPCAT) paradigm, the human translator begins to type the translation of a given source text; by typing each character the MT system interactively offers the choices to complete the translation. Human translator may continue typing or accept the whole completion or part of it. In this paper, we propose a new search approach for increasing the performance of the IPCAT. This new search approach consists of a new search method and a hybrid back-off model. We achieve 2.3% and 1.16% absolute improvements by using the proposed search approach for two different corpora.

KEYWORDS : Statistical Machine Translation (SMT), Computer-Assisted Translation (CAT), Interactive-Predictive Computer-Assisted Translation (IPCAT), Prefix Search.

Proceedings of COLING 2012: Posters, pages 1261–1270,
COLING 2012, Mumbai, December 2012.

1 Introduction

Nowadays, with the expansion of global communications, the need for the translation has become a basic and important requirement, especially for international institutions and news agencies. Consider the following example to illustrate the importance of the translation in today world. In 2003, after the enlargement of the European Union, with a population of 453 million, the cost of the translation at all institutions, once translators are operating at full speed, was estimated at 807 M€ per year.

Recently, significant improvements have been achieved in statistical machine translation (MT), but still even the best machine translation technology is far from replacing or even competing with human translators. Because of the inability of existing MT systems for giving the correct and perfect translation, Researchers began to provide tools to facilitate and accelerate the translation process, instead of automatic translation. Already, Interactive computer-assisted translation systems are the latest version of these tools.

Interactive machine translation (IMT), first appeared as part of Kay's MIND system (Kay, 1973), where the user's role was to help with source-text disambiguation by answering questions about word sense, pronominal reference, prepositional-phrase attachment, etc. Later work on IMT, eg (Brown and Nirenburg, 1990; Maruyama and Watanabe, 1990; Whitelock et al., 1986), has followed in this vein, concentrating on improving the question/answer process by having less questions, more friendly ones, etc. Despite progress in these endeavors, the question/answer process remained in the systems of this sort. Finally these systems are only used where the cost of manually producing a translation is high enough to justify the extra effort. With introducing TransType project by (Foster et al., 1997), a major change in how the user interacts with the machine had occurred. In such an environment, human translators interact with a translation system that acts as an assistance tool and dynamically provides a list of translations (suffixes) which complete the part of the source sentence already translated (prefix). Also from 1997 to 2004, most of the given papers related to the various versions of the TransType project such as (Langlais et al., 2000 and 2002; Foster, 2002; Cubel et al., 2004).

In 2005, a new search strategy for giving suffix was proposed in (Bender et al., 2005). Also in (Barrachina et al., 2007), for creating search graph has been used finite state automata. Another important project in field of the interactive translation is Caitra project. Caitra is a web base project which is provided from an online platform and is based on the AJAX Web.2 technologies and the Moses decoder (Koehn, 2009a and 2009b). Another option which was added to the CAT is online learning; this option has been suggested in (Ortiz-Martínez et al., 2010). By this option, the interactive system can learn from user feedback and update itself statistical models.

In this paper, we will propose two new approaches to improve the performance of the interactive CAT system. To implement the interactive machine translation system, we use Moses as a statistical machine translation system. We extract of the Moses a search graph and offer a new search way of the graph which increases the quality of the suggestions of the interactive system. Also we offer a new back-off model which helps the system to suggest a suffix to the user in the some cases which the search graph does not consistent with the user prefix.

In the follow sections, the first we introduce the translation engine of our system. Next in the section three we describe interactive part of the system and our proposed approaches then we evaluate our system in section four.

2 Engine of translation

As mentioned in the introduction, we develop an interactive CAT for English to Germany by Moses system. Moses (Koehn et al., 2007) is a statistical machine translation system that allows us to automatically train translation models for English-Germany language pair. Indeed, Moses is translation engine of our interactive CAT. Also we use from Moses for offering a complementary translation to human translator. For giving a suitable suffix according to prefix, we created a graph by using hypotheses of Moses which are produced in decoding phase of the translation process of Moses. For better definition of the translation engine of our interactive CAT, we need to define statistical machine translation system and decoding phase of the Moses.

2.1 Statistical Machine Translation System

A statistical machine translation system allows us to automatically train translation models for any language pair by using parallel bilingual corpus and statistical theories. In statistical machine translation, we are given a source language sentence $F = f_1^J = f_1, \ldots, f_j, \ldots, f_J$, which is to be translated into a target language sentence $E = e_1^I = e_1, \ldots, e_i, \ldots, e_I$. Among all possible target language sentences, we will choose the sentence with the highest probability:

$$\hat{e}_1^I = \operatorname{argmax}\{Pr(e_1^I | f_1^J)\} \quad (1)$$

$$= \operatorname{argmax}\{Pr(e_1^I) \cdot Pr(f_1^J | e_1^I)\} \quad (2)$$

The decomposition into two knowledge sources in Equation 2 is known as the source channel approach to statistical machine translation (Brown et al., 1990). It allows an independent modelling of the target language model $Pr(e_1^I)$ and the translation model $Pr(f_1^J | e_1^I)$. The target language model describes the well-formedness of the target language sentence. The translation model links the source language sentence to the target language sentence. It can be further decomposed into the alignment and the lexicon models. The argmax operation denotes the search problem, i.e. the generation of the output sentence in the target language. We have to maximize over all possible target language sentences.

2.2 Decoding phase

The task of decoding in a machine translation system is to find the best scoring translation according to probabilistic scores of the language model and the translation model. This is a hard problem, since there are an exponential number of choices, given a specific input sentence. In fact, it has been shown that the decoding problem for the presented machine translation models is NP-complete (Knight, 1999; Udupa and Maji, 2006). In order to reduce the search space, we have to resort to a search heuristic. To this end, Moses organizes hypotheses into hypothesis stacks. If the stacks get too large, Moses prune out the worst hypotheses in the stack. One way to organize hypothesis stacks is based on the number of foreign words translated. One stack contains all hypotheses that have translated one foreign word; another stack contains all hypotheses that have translated two foreign words in their path, and so on.

3 Engine of Interaction

As described in the introduction, whenever user apply any change by keyboard in the translation, the system according to the modified translation, offers the completed translation. Now in this section, we want to investigate how the system is able to provide the completed translation based on the prefix translation. For providing a completed translation, the system should seek the graph which is produced from hypotheses of the Moses decoder. As described in section 2-2, in decoding process of Moses, Hypotheses are organized in the stacks while we need to graph structure. Therefore the first task of the interactive component is to create a search graph from the Hypotheses into stacks of Moses. For creating the search graph, we reinstruct the organization of the hypotheses of the Moses from stacks to the graph by map data structure of C++. After finding the hypothesis which consistent with the prefix, the interactive component should give a completed translation to the user by using completed optimal path of that hypothesis in the search graph. In the next subsections, we will describe common search way and new our search way.

3.1 Edit Distance-Based Search

According to (Barrachina et al., 2007; Koehn, 2009a), for giving a completed translation to the user, we should find a node of the graph which has minimum edit distance with prefix; we call this approach, *edit distance-based search.* The purpose of the edit distance between two strings is the Levenshtein distance (Levenshtein, 1965) that defined as the minimum number of edits needed to transform one string into the other, with the allowable edit operations being insertion, deletion, or substitution of a single character.

This method is based on the assumption that a hypothesis which has minimum edit distance with prefix, has a greater chance to consistent with the desired translation of the user in the future than other hypotheses. If there are several hypotheses with minimum edit distance, we should compare cost of translation of the hypotheses together. The purpose of the cost of translation is summation of the current cost and the future cost of the hypothesis translation.

3.2 Using the translation cost in the search

The search method based on the edit distance has a fundamental inconsistency with the translation word graphs. The translation word graph has different hypotheses in terms of the orderings of the words (phrases); but not all the reordering possibilities due to the pruning that is applied during the generation of the word graph. Therefore, since the edit distance is only based on the deletion, insertion and substitution operations, this distance is not able to handle different ordering between the hypothesis and the reference sentences. I.e., we are only able to find those hypotheses which have similar ordering of words to the prefix of the user.

We explain this problem by using an example. We assume that the desired translation of the user is "**Newton is one of the greatest scientists who discovered gravity**" and our prefix is "**Newton is one of the greatest scientists w**". We also assume that only two translation hypotheses are available. The first hypothesis is "**one of the greatest scientists is Newton who discovered gravity**" which its translation cost is 0.0015. The second hypothesis is "**Newton gravity one of the greatest discovered which the greatest**" which its translation cost is 0.6812. In table 1, the edit distance between the first and the second hypotheses with the prefix is calculated. The numbers of this table are calculated according to Levenshtein algorithm (Levenshtein, 1965). Since the last word of the prefix is incomplete, we should find a complement to this prefix that its first word matches the last incomplete word of the prefix. According to the result of the Table 1 and the search method based on the edit distance, the second hypothesis is selected, while this hypothesis syntactically and semantically does not correct. The suffix which is offered according to the second hypothesis, is **"which the greatest"**. Obviously, this suffix is not compatible with the correct translation of the user.

Prefix	Hyp 1	one	of	the	greatest	scientists	is	Newton	who	Hyp 2	Newton	gravity	one	of	the	greatest	discovered	which
Prefix	0	1	2	3	4	5	6	7	8	0	1	2	3	4	5	6	7	8
Newton	1	1	2	3	4	5	6	6	7	1	0	1	2	3	4	5	6	7
Is	2	2	2	3	4	5	5	6	7	2	1	1	2	3	4	5	6	7
one	3	2	3	3	4	5	6	6	7	3	2	2	1	2	3	4	5	6
Of	4	3	2	3	4	5	6	7	7	4	3	3	2	1	2	3	4	5
the	5	4	3	2	3	4	5	6	7	5	4	4	3	2	1	2	3	4
greatest	6	5	4	3	2	3	4	5	6	6	5	5	4	3	2	1	2	3
scientists	7	6	5	4	3	2	3	4	5	7	6	6	5	4	3	2	2	3
w?	8	7	6	5	4	3	3	4	4	8	7	7	6	5	4	3	3	2

TABLE 1 - The edit distance matrix between the first hypothesis and the user prefix.

According to the results obtained in the previous example, we can conclude that edit distance measure is not enough for finding a correct suffix. If we only emphasis on edit distance measure, our search may lead to find a hypothesis which the scores of the language and translation models is low; rationally, such hypothesis would not be acceptable in opinion of the user. To overcome this problem, we propose a new search approach. In this way, we use the weighted summation of the edit distance and the cost of the translation of the hypothesis in search process, that is:

$$compare\ measure\ = (\alpha \times D) + ((1-\alpha) \times C) \quad (3)$$

Where D is edit distance between the hypothesis and prefix and C is the summation of the current and future translation cost of the hypothesis; this cost include both language and translation models.

The idea of this approach is stemmed from the reality that a translation hypothesis which its cost of translation and language models is lower than other hypotheses has more chance to be a correct translation and to be consistent with desired translation of the user in the future. We should note that, this search method might find hypotheses that do not match with the prefix at all due to the reordering of phrases like the previous example, and therefore we cannot generate a good offer to the user. However, we hope this method generates better offers to the user in overall. In the previous example, if we use new approach and set $\alpha = 0.2$, we will have:

$$Hyp1 = (0.2 \times 4) + (0.8 \times 0.0015) = 0.8, \quad Hyp2 = (0.2 \times 2) + (0.8 \times 0.6812) = 0.96 \quad (4)$$

According to above result, the first hypothesis has lower cost than the second hypothesis, thus the first hypothesis will be selected.

The weights related to the edit distance and the cost of the translation, are empirically determined by development set of the bilingual corpus. Since we allow any amount of edit distance between the prefix and the word graph hypotheses and although we do not directly use the reordering of phrases, our IPCAT system is able to generate offers even there is not any hypotheses in the word graph with similar ordering to the user prefix. The results of the experiments are presented in Section 4. In the experiments, the weight of the edit distance and the translation cost are set to 0.2 and 0.8, respectively.

3.3 Back-Off models

In some cases, it is possible that any of the search method which are described in pervious sections, are not able to offer a suggestion to the user. This problem often occurs when the last word of the prefix is incomplete and there is not any phrase in the search graph that contains that partial word. This problem is solved in (Barrachina et al., 2007), by searching for a completion of the last word with the highest probability using only the language model. In this way isn't used any translation models, thus the degree of certainty of the suggestions which are produced by this way would be low. Now, we will propose a new approach which heightens the degree of certainty of the suggestions, but before explain it, we illustrate the problem of the pervious approach by an example.

Assume, we want to translate the Germany sentence **"het geluid van de muziek was luid"** to the English sentence "**the sound of music was loud**". Also we assume that the prefix is "**the sound of mu"** and there isn't any word in the search graph of the interactive system that contains the partial word of the prefix. If the interactive system only use language model, it will be possible that offers any word which starts with "mu" (such as **mu**sic, **mu**mmy, **mu**rmur, **mu**sketeer, **mu**tter, etc.), based on posterior probability of their occurrence after the penultimate word(s) of the prefix. According to the corpus which the language model has been trained it, each of the mentioned words can be selected. if the frequency of the phrase "sound of murmur" is more than others, then word **"murmur"** will be offered to the user; while if we attended to source sentence and translation model, we would select **"music"** word.

As we have explained, the selection process in above example was done only based on probability of the language model of the n-grams in the target language, without considering source sentence. In our proposed approach, we use IBM Model 1 (Brown et al., 1993) in addition to language model, to estimate the translation likelihood of the source sentence and candidate words (the purpose of candidate words is the words which start with the last partial word of the prefix). To achieve this goal, we use the weighted summation of the probability of the language model and the probability of the IBM-1 translation model.

Although using the IBM Model 1 in addition to the language model, has been proposed by (Ueffing and Ney, 2005), but its application is different from where we stand. They have used IBM Model-1 as a confidence measure for sub-sentences in the word graph, while we use the IBM Model-1 as a back-off model for words which are not available in the search graph.

IBM model 1 estimates the translation likelihood of a source language sentence $F = f_1^J = f_1 \ldots f_j \ldots f_J$, and a target language sentence $E = e_1^I = e_1 \ldots e_i \ldots e_I$, as:

$$Pr_{IBM-1}(E|F) = Pr(e_1^I|f_1^J) = \prod_{i=1}^{I} \frac{1}{J+1} \sum_{j=1}^{J} p(e_i|f_j) \tag{5}$$

According to equation 5, for obtaining the probability which a word e_i, be part of the translation of the source sentence f_1^J, we have:

$$Pr_{IBM-1}(e_i|f_1^J) = \frac{1}{J+1} \sum_{j=1}^{J} p(e_i|f_j) \tag{6}$$

In a hybrid model that has consisted of the both the language model and IBM-1 model, we have:

$$Pr_{IBM-1,LM}(e_i|f_1^J) = (\alpha \times Pr_{LM}(e_i|e_{i-1})) + ((1-\alpha) \times Pr_{IBM-1}(e_i|f_1^J)) \tag{7}$$

Also we can use the higher IBM models such as IBM-2 or HMM instead of IBM model 1.

4 Evaluation of the purposed approach

For evaluating the performance of the interactive computer-assisted translation system, we need to estimate the effort of a human translator to produce the correct translations using the interactive system. To this end, the target translations which a real user would have in mind are simulated by the given reference(s). For each given source sentence, first the translation is produced by IPCAT system, then it is compared with a single reference translation to find the longest common character prefix. Afterwards, the first non-matching character is replaced by the corresponding reference character and then IPMT system offers a new complement to the given prefix. This process is iterated until a full match with the reference is obtained.

In order to evaluate the IPCAT system, we use KSR and KSMR metrics. The KSR is the number of key-strokes required to produce the single reference translation using the IPCAT system divided by the number of keystrokes needed to type the reference translation. The KSMR measure is the summation of KSR and MAR, which is the amount of all required actions either by keyboard or by mouse to generate the reference translation using the interactive machine translation system divided by the total number of reference characters.

We conduct the experiments on two different tasks: Xerox and Verbmobil. The Xerox is an English-German corpus, and the Verbmobil corpus is an English-Persian corpus, the Verbmobil corpus is originally an English-German corpus that we advanced it to an English-German-Persian corpus by translating a large part of English sentences to Persian. The statistics of these corpora are depicted in Table 2. The term OOVs in the table denotes the total number of occurrences of unknown words, the words which were not seen in the training corpus.

		Xerox		Verbmobil	
		English	Germany	English	Persian
Train	Sentences	47 619		22 642	
	Running words	528 779	467 633	254 665	233 948
	Vocabulary size	9 816	16 716	2 696	5 405
	Singletons	2 302	6 064	1 016	2 501
Dev	Sentences	700		276	
	Running words	8 823	8 050	5358	3 339
	OOVs	56	108	198	200
Eval	Sentences	862		250	
	Running words	10 019	10 094	2 871	2 692
	OOVs	58	100	142	193

TABLE 2 - The statistics of the Xerox and Verbmobil corpora.

4.1 Evaluation of the experiment result

In the first experiment, we evaluate the proposed search method which described in section 3-2. This method is based on the weighted summation of the edit distance and the cost of generating the complement translation for a given prefix in the word graph. In contrast, the previous method is only based on the edit distance measure. The results of the experiments are shown in table 3. According to the results, the proposed method is superior to the previous method and both the KSR and the KSMR measures are decreased. Therefore, we could conclude using the hypotheses which have the lower cost in terms of the language and translation models in addition to the edit distance with a given prefix, lead to improve the results of the IPCAT systems.

The second experiment is conducted to evaluate the proposed back-off model. The new back-off model is a hybrid model which consists of IBM-1 and language models. The experimental results are shown in table 3, in the rows where the back-off models set to 'No'. As we expected, the proposed back-off model obtained better results than the previous back-off model, which is purely based on the language model. This improvement is due to the use of two knowledge sources namely source sentence and target language to estimate the back-off model, instead of just using the target language. Obviously with more information, our system gives better suffix to the user. Although, the result of the hybrid back-off model has been better than language model, but the difference between the results of these models is very small. The cause of this small difference may be that the desired translation of the user has the words which are not available in the training corpus. In such cases, neither language model nor IBM-1 model could suggest any suffix to the user.

Also we used IBM-2 model instead of IBM-1, but unfortunately, we it does not lead to obtain a better result, the reason of this result may be that the IBM-2 model apply more restriction than IBM-1 model.

	Back-off model	Xerox En→De		Verbmobil En→Pe	
		KSR	KSMR	KSR	KSMR
Edit distance	No	20.46	28.57	29.27	40.09
	IBM-1	16.13	25.43	25.47	37.66
	LM	15.25	24.31	24.39	36.68
	IBM-1 + LM	15.27	24.31	24.18	36.47
Edit distance + Translation cost	No	19.10	26.27	28.58	38.93
	IBM-1	14.46	22.67	24.64	36.35
	LM	13.88	22.00	23.59	35.46
	IBM-1 + LM	13.87	21.97	23.31	35.14

TABLE 3 - The results of various types of back-off models and search methods.

5 Conclusion

The goal of this paper was to develop an interactive computer assisted translation system. We recognized the defect of the edit distance measurement and offered new search way based on a combined measurement which consisted of edit distance and cost of translation. Edit distance measure does not consider reordering of phrase; thus by using this measure, two sentences "**Newton is one of the greatest scientists**" and "**one of the greatest scientists is Newton**" would have four edit distance. While by considering the reordering operation, the edit distance between these sentences would be only two. In this paper we didn't insert the reordering of the phrase operation, but we tried to decrease the defect of the edit distance measure by considering translation cost. We could achieve 2.3% and 1.16% improvements by using our offered measure search in Xerox and Verbmobil corpora respectively. Also we obtained 0.3% improvement by using new back-off model in the Verbmobil corpus.

Reference

Barrachina, S., Bender, O., Casacuberta, F., Civera, J., Cubel, E., Khadivi, S., Lagarda, A., Ney, H., Tomás, J., Vidal, E. and Vilar, J. M. (2007). *Statistical Approaches to Computer-Assisted Translation*, Computational Linguistics, Volume 35, pp. 3-28.

Bender, O., Hasan, S., Vilar, D., Zens, R. and Ney, H. (2005). *Comparison of generation strategies for interactive machine translation*, In Proceedings of the 10th Annual Conference of the European Association for Machine Translation (EAMT 05), pp. 33–40.

Brown, R.D., Nirenburg, S. (1990). *Human-computer interaction for semantic disambiguation,* In Processing of the International Conference on Computational Linguistics (COLING), PP. 42-47.

Brown, P.F., Cocke, J., Della Pietra, S.A., Della Pietra, V.J., Jelinek, F., Lafferty, J.D., Mercer, R.L., Roossin, P.S. (1990). *A Statistical Approach to Machine Translation*, Computational Linguistics, Vol. 16, No. 2, pp. 79–85.

Brown, P. F., Della Pietra, S. A., Della Pietra, V. J. and Mercer, R. L. (1993). *The mathematics of statistical machine translation: Parameter estimation*, Computational Linguistics, pp. 263–311.

Cubel, E., González, J., Lagarda, A. L., Casacuberta, F., Juan, A. and Vidal, E. (2004). *Adapting finite-state translation to the TransType2 project,* Proceedings of the Joint Conference combining the 8th International Workshop of the European Association for Machine Translation.

Foster, G., Isabelle, P. and Plamondon, P. (1997). *Target-Text Mediated Interactive Machine translation*, in Kluwer Academic Publishers, pp. 175–194.

Foster, G. (2002). *Text Prediction for Translators,* Ph.D. thesis, Universit´e de Montr´eal, Canada.

Kay, M. (1973). *The MIND system,* in Natural Language Processing, pp. 155-188.

Knight, K. (1999). *Decoding complexity in word replacement translation models*, Computational Linguistics, 25(4):607–615.

Koehn, P., Hoang, H., Birch, A., Callison-Burch, C., Federico, M., Bertoldi, N., Cowan, B., Shen, W., Moran, C., Zens, R., Dyer, C. J., Bojar, O., Constantin, A. and Herbst, E. (2007). *Moses: Open source toolkit for statistical machine translation*, In ACL Demo and Poster Session, Available: http://www.statmt.org/moses/.

Koehn, P. (2009a). *A Process Study of Computed Aided Translation*, Kluwer Academic Publishers.

Koehn, P. (2009b). *A web-based interactive computer aided translation tool*, In Proceedings of the ACL Interactive Poster and Demonstration Sessions.

Levenshtein, V. I. (1965). *Binary Codes Capable of Correcting Deletions, Insertions, and Reversals*. Soviet Physics - Doklady, Vol. 10 No. 8 pp. 707-710.

Langlais, P., Foster, G., and Lapalme, G. (2000). *TransType: a computer-aided translation typing system*, In Proceedings of the NAACL/ANLP Workshop on Embedded Machine Translation Systems, pp. 46–52.

Langlais, P., Lapalme G. and Loranger, M. (2002). *TRANSTYPE: Development–Evaluation Cycles to Boost Translator's Productivity*, in Kluwer Academic Publishers, pp. 77–98.

Maruyama, H., Watanabe, H. (1990). *An interactive Japanese parser for machine translation,* In Processing of the International Conference on Computational Linguistics (COLING), pp. 257-262.

Ortiz-Martínez, D., García-Varea, I. and Casacuberta, F. (2010). *Online Learning for Interactive Statistical Machine Translation*, In The 2010 Annual Conference of the North American Chapter of the ACL, pp. 546–554.

Tillmann, C. (2001). *Word re-ordering and dynamic programming based search algorithms for statistical machine translation*, PhDthesis, Computer Science Department, RWTH Aachen, Germany.

Ueffing, N. and Ney, H. (2005). *Application of Word-Level Confidence Measures in Interactive Statistical Machine Translation*, In Proceedings of EAMT 2005 (10th Annual Conference of the European Association for Machine Translation), pp. 262-270, Budapest, Hungary.

Udupa, U. and Maji, H. K. (2006). *Computational Complexity of Statistical Machine Translation*, 11st Conference of the European Chapter of the Association for Computational Linguistics, Proceedings of the Conference, Italy.

Whitelock, P. J., McGee Wood, M., Chandler, B. J., Holden, N. and Horsfall, H. J. (1986). *Strategies for interactive machine translation: the experience and implications of the UMIST Japanese project*, In Proceedings of the International Conference on Computational Linguistics (COLING), pages 329-334.

Zens, R., Och, F. J. and Ney, H. (2002). *Phrase-Based Statistical Machine Translation*, in Springer-Verlag Berlin Heidelberg, pp. 18–32.

Automatic extraction of polar adjectives for the creation of polarity lexicons

Silvia VÁZQUEZ[1] Muntsa PADRÓ[1] Núria BEL[1] Julio GONZALO[2]

(1)UNIVERSITAT POMPEU FABRA, Roc Boronat, 138, Barcelona, Spain
(2) E.T.S.I. INFORMÁTICA UNED, Juan del Rosal, 16, Madrid, Spain
{silvia.vazquez, muntsa.padro, nuria.bel}@upf.edu, julio@lsi.uned.es

ABSTRACT

Automatic creation of polarity lexicons is a crucial issue to be solved in order to reduce time and efforts in the first steps of Sentiment Analysis. In this paper we present a methodology based on linguistic cues that allows us to automatically discover, extract and label subjective adjectives that should be collected in a domain-based polarity lexicon. For this purpose, we designed a bootstrapping algorithm that, from a small set of seed polar adjectives, is capable to iteratively identify, extract and annotate positive and negative adjectives. Additionally, the method automatically creates lists of highly subjective elements that change their prior polarity even within the same domain. The algorithm proposed reached a precision of 97.5% for positive adjectives and 71.4% for negative ones in the semantic orientation identification task.

KEYWORDS: Sentiment Analysis, Opinion Mining, Polarity Lexicon, Subjectivity Detection

Proceedings of COLING 2012: Posters, pages 1271–1280,
COLING 2012, Mumbai, December 2012.

1 Introduction

In recent years, Sentiment Analysis has become one of the most important applications of Natural Language Processing. In the beginning, the discipline tried to reutilize techniques used in fields like Document Classification, Information Extraction or Question-Answering, but soon researchers realized that the typology of the texts in Sentiment Analysis was very different from those studied in these areas (Cardie, 1997), (Stoyanov, Cardie, & Wiebe, 2005). In this sense, for the summarization of subjective texts, the most important issue is to discover what is the general and predominant opinion, evaluation, emotion or speculation expressed by the author, and not the identification of the main topic of the text, the main interest of the cited areas. This task can only be done with information about the polarity of words.

Discovery and extraction of the vocabulary used to express subjectivity is crucial to start the development of any complex sentiment analysis tool. For example, knowing that an old film could be positive for some people but negative for others is very important in order to summarize the global opinion of that product. Therefore, designing algorithms that allow us to automatically build these kinds of language resources is very important.

There are three main approaches to create polarity lexicons: manual, dictionary based and corpus based. Early works in the field of Sentiment Analysis manually compiled lists of subjective words but this task was very time consuming and needed great human efforts. Some examples of this approach are The General Inquirer (Stone, Dunphy, Smith, & Ogilvie, 1966) and some of the lists of verbs annotated by Levin (Levin, 1993).

Dictionary based approach utilizes external language resources as lexicons and thesaurus which, although not collecting polarity relations, can help to increase the number of a set of opinion seeds by different methods. The majority of the works that follow this procedure make use of WordNet (Miller, 1995) to carry out this task. In the work of (Hu & Liu, 2004) the authors hypothesized that synonyms of a seed adjective have the same semantic orientation while the antonymous would have the opposite one, employing WordNet synsets to find out these relations. Lexical resources like SentiWordNet (Esuli & Sebastiani, 2005) (Baccianella, Esuli, & Sebastiani, 2010) classified polarity elements into Positive, Negative or Objective by analyzing the similarity between the glosses or definitions of the words and also by studying the relations established among them in the thesaurus. Valitutti (Valitutti, Strapparava, & Stock, 2004) tried to adapt WordNet to Sentiment Analysis purposes through the identification and subsequent annotation of all the elements having a high load of emotion or affective content.

Although the dictionary based approach achieved great results, it has two main shortcomings. On the one hand, it does not take into account the polarity changes due to different domains. As some works demonstrated (Vázquez & Bel, 2012), a great majority of the adjectives are domain dependent: they could be positive in one domain but negative or even neutral in another. On the other hand, this approach suffers from a lack of scalability since it does not take into account words not appearing in the language resources used. Actually, it falls down on the analysis of colloquial words or different kinds of slang expressions that are not collected in WordNet or any thesaurus.

Corpus based approach starts, as dictionary based one, with a manually built list of seed words but unlike it, this approach does not rely on the availability of external language resources (that for some languages could even not exist) but on linguistic cues which systematically appear in opinionated texts. The main idea behind this approach is that there are actually linguistic constraints that allow automatically identifying opinion-bearing words. One of the most early and well-known work that followed this method was proposed by Hatzivassiloglou and McKeown (1997). This work will be commented in more detail in Section 2. Other important works based on this approach are (Kanayama & Nasukawa, 2006), (Kaji & Kitsuregawa, 2007) and (Riloff, Wiebe, & Wilson, 2003). Kanayama and Nasukama tried to expand a set of polar atoms (words and expressions) starting from an unannotated corpus and an initial lexicon. Their main assumption was that opinion words with the same prior polarity appear successively in the text, unless this context changed through an adversative expression. Kaji and Kitsuregawa addressed the polarity lexicon building from the lexico-syntactic patterns found in a large collection of documents. They achieved high precision for positive (92%) and negative (88%) elements but their recall is low. The work of Riloff et al. was not restricted to adjectives but they collected subjective nouns (they managed to learn 1000 new subjective nouns) by a bootstrapping process.

In this paper, we follow the corpus-based approach and propose a bootstrapping method to automatically and iteratively extract polar adjectives as well as their prior polarity. Additionally, this bootstrapping method permits to identify all of the polar adjectives that, exclusively depending on the context (i.e. surrounding words), can behave as positive or negative polar elements. The proposed method achieved a precision of 97.5% for positive adjectives and 71.4% for negative ones in the semantic orientation identification task and significantly increased recall to 67%.

The remainder of this paper is organized as follows. Section 2 introduces the methodology followed in our experiment, the bootstrapping process carried out and the results achieved. Section 3 details the evaluation of the bootstrapping method proposed. Finally, we present the conclusions and outline the future work.

2 Methodology

The contribution of our method to automatically identify, extract and label subjective adjectives is that we introduce a bootstrapping approach to gain coverage, and a new category of adjectives, i.e. "highly subjective adjectives", to gain precision. Our method is based, basically, on the following two works.

We based our method on the approach presented in Hatzivassiloglou & McKeown (1997) where the authors hypothesized that two adjectives joined by "and" have the same semantic orientation while two adjectives joined by "but" have the opposite one. They used this idea along with a log-linear regression model and a set of supplementary morphological rules to predict whether a pair of adjectives joined by any of these conjunctions has the same or different semantic orientation. Once pairs of adjectives are extracted, they utilized a clustering method to separate all the adjectives conjoined into two groups. The group with more elements was labeled as positive adjectives and the other as negative. This final labeling task, based on the normal frequency of positive elements, it is right if we work with a balanced corpus (with the same number of positive and negative reviews). However, in the case we worked with a corpus with more negative than positive texts, the number of negative words tended to be higher, and, therefore, the results of the tagging could be biased.

In this work, they achieved a 92% of accuracy in the classification of positive and negative adjectives.

The second work in which our research is based on is (Vázquez & Bel, 2012). This work is a case study where the authors introduced a taxonomy of polar adjectives. The results of their study showed that a great majority of polar adjectives change their prior polarity values when occurring in different domains, that is, an adjective could be positive in a domain but negative or even irrelevant in other. For example "entertaining" is very positive in a film review, but has no sense, for instance, in a car review. Besides, the authors proposed a new type of polar adjectives, called "highly subjective adjectives", which could change their prior polarity not only among different domains but even within the same domain. For instance, a "big" car, could be positive for some customers (easy to park) but negative for others (any space inside).

To consider the existence of these "highly subjective" adjectives turned out to be very important in our experiments to gain precision. Taking into account the existence of these kinds of units in our bootstrapping process, it was possible to automatically discover not only domain dependent positive and negative adjectives but also to identify highly subjective adjectives that had caused mistakes in our final lexicon if we had not identified them.

The bootstrapping algorithm that we propose automatically extracts all of the polar adjectives joined by "y" ("and") or "pero" ("but") in a given corpus. A small set of seed adjectives as well as their corresponding prior polarity values is used for initializing the algorithm. This initial seed list was made from domain independent adjectives, therefore these elements could be used as initial list of seeds not only in the domain of cars, but also in any domain that we want to work with.

Our methodology differs from the one proposed by Hatzivassiloglou and McKeown since we hypothesized that after the first detection step, the new adjectives and their corresponding prior polarity can be iteratively reused to discover more new polar adjectives. We utilized the adjectives that were in our seed polarity lexicon as input for our algorithm to find new adjectives joined with them, identifying also the prior polarity of those. Therefore, we propose that polar adjectives and their corresponding polarity values can be automatically identified if they are found in a coordinated construction with the appropriate conjunctions and with other adjectives that were not in our seed lexicon. The process will continue until any adjective of our lexicon is not found joined with any new adjective or until there is no more conjunctive relation of this type.

Additionally, following the taxonomy of polar adjectives proposed in (Vázquez & Bel, 2012), we also automatically built lists of elements that should be treated differently in order to avoid important mistakes in the precision of automatically built polarity lexicons. As Vázquez & Bel (2012) we have worked with Spanish. However the method can be applied to any language where the conjunctive constructions work in the same manner.

Therefore, our algorithm operates on the following conditions:

- If a seed adjective is joined by "y" ("and") with an unknown adjective (that is, it is not in our seed list) and did not appear in contradictory constructions[1], we will conclude that the unknown adjective will have the same semantic orientation of the seed adjective and can be added, along with its corresponding prior polarity, to our polarity lexicon.
- If a seed adjective is joined by "pero" ("but") with an unknown adjective and did not appear in contradictory constructions, we will conclude that the unknown adjective will have the opposite semantic orientation of the seed adjective and can be added, along with its prior polarity, to our polarity lexicon.

[1] Positive adjective + and + negative adjective; negative adjective + and + positive adjective; positive adjective + but + positive adjective ; negative adjective + but + negative adjective

- If a seed adjective appears in conjunctive patterns which imply that its semantic orientation is positive but also appears in conjunctive patterns which imply that its semantic orientation is negative, the polar adjective will be added to the highly subjective adjective list.

See a diagram of the process in FIGURE 1.

2.1 Bootstrapping experiment

As explained before, the bootstrapping algorithm was meant to iteratively increase the number of polar adjectives collected for our polarity lexicon as well as to separate elements in our highly subjective adjective lists.

The experiment was carried out using a corpus of 250,000 words from car reviews. This corpus was extracted from a wider corpus (8 million of words) consisting of texts of different domains (cars, movies, mobile phones, video games and sport teams).

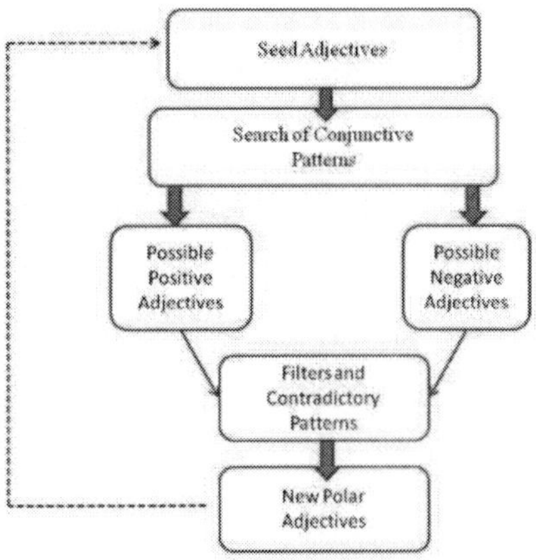

FIGURE 1 – Diagram of the bootstrapping process

All of the texts were collected from Ciao[2], a website specialized in reviews where the users write in Spanish, the language studied in this work, and where they are paid for doing this task. This last aspect guaranteed us a minimum level of correctness in all the texts, minimizing the amount of noisy text in the study.

The corpus was annotated with Part-Of-Speech tags and lemmatized using Freeling[3] POS tagger (Padró, Collado, Reese, Lloberes, & Castellón, 2010) and indexed using Corpus Query Processor (CQP)[4] (Christ, 1994) in order to facilitate the search of coordinated adjectives.

The process started by searching adjectives in the corpus occurring in a set of conjunction patterns, in order to find all the adjectives that were conjoined. 482 pairs of adjectives joined by the conjunctions "y" ("and") or "pero" ("but") were found. These pairs were the input for the identification of polarity if joined with an adjective of a known polarity; in a first step if the pair contains an adjective of the seed list, and later if containing an adjective identified and labeled by the algorithm.

[2] http://www.ciao.es/
[3] http://nlp.lsi.upc.edu/freeling/
[4] http://www.ims.uni-stuttgart.de/projekte/CorpusWorkbench/

We started the iterative process with 28 positive and 7 negative seed adjectives. These elements were taken from the list of Bel and Vázquez (2012). Seeds were very reliable polar words that five annotators manually labeled as domain independent in a previous work. See the lists of positive and negative seeds in TABLE 1.

The procedure was iteratively repeated until no more polar adjectives were extracted, and it finished in 7 iterations.

2.2 Results

As a result of the bootstrapping process proposed in the last subsection, we increased six times the number of polar adjectives that there were in the seed polarity dictionary. We augmented the positive adjectives from 28 (seeds) to 173 and the negative ones from 7 (seeds) to 37. Crucially, we identified 13 highly subjective adjectives that indeed appeared with positive polarity in some contexts and with negative in others.

Positive Seeds[5]	alucinante, bello, bueno, chulo, cojonudo, elegante, espectacular, estupendo, excelente, excepcional, extraordinario, fantástico, genial, hermoso, impecable, impresionante, increíble, inmejorable, insuperable, lindo, magnífico, maravilloso, novedoso, perfecto, precioso, recomendable, sensacional, único
Negative Seeds[6]	terrible, pésimo, malo, horrible, feo, cutre, chungo

TABLE 1- Lists of positive and negative seeds

The growth in the number of adjectives in connection with the number of iterations is detailed in FIGURE 2.

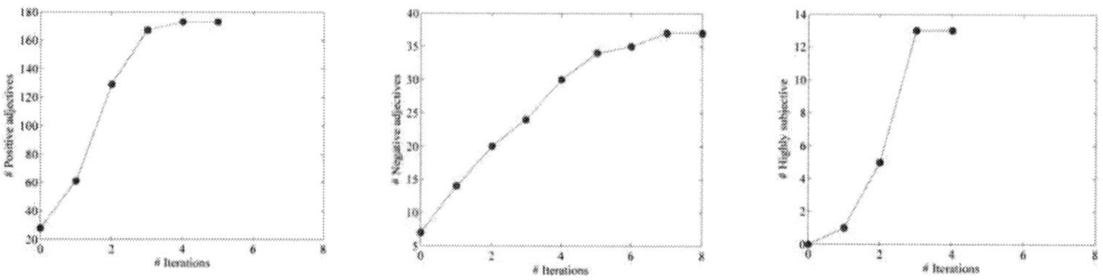

FIGURE 2 – Positive, negative and highly subjective adjectives collected and number of iterations

3 Evaluation

In this section, we report on the evaluation of the bootstrapping method proposed in the Section 3. To carry out this evaluation, we manually annotated a Gold Standard which consisted of the 12% of the whole car corpus; 200 documents in total. In each text, all the polar adjectives that should be in the final polarity lexicon were identified and labeled with their corresponding semantic orientation (positive or negative) in the particular context where they appeared. For the

[5] Amazing, beautiful, good, lovely, brilliant, elegant, spectacular, excellent, exceptional, extraordinary, fantastic, terrific, impeccable, impressive, incredible, unbeatable, pretty, superb, marvellous, original, perfect, gorgeous, sensational (some of them are synonyms so we avoided to repeat them in the translation)

[6] Terrible, dreadful, bad, horrible, ugly, shabby, dicey

annotation task we used Brat[7] (Stenetorp et al., 2012), a web-based annotation tool that allowed us to create our own labels, adapted to the experiment.

The instructions given to the annotator were the following: "If an adjective is used to describe a positive or negative speaker's evaluation, opinion, emotion or speculation of some of the objects reviewed, then this word should be in our polarity lexicon and annotated with the label that better describe it according to its semantic orientation".

It is important to note that some words that are typically used as subjective elements can also be found as objective ones. For example, "pequeño" ("small") behaves as a subjective adjective in sentences like "este coche es pequeño y aburrido" ("this car is small and boring") where we can easily understand than the writer does not like the car, since he joined the adjective "pequeño" ("small") with a negative adjective, in this case, "aburrido" ("boring"). However, if the writer was enumerating the general characteristics of the car, for example in "este coche es pequeño ya que solo tiene dos plazas, tiene 3 puertas y los vidrios tintados..." ("this car is small because it only has two seats, has three doors and dyed glasses..."), it does not imply that "pequeño" ("small") was positive or negative. In this last example, the writer performed a merely informative function, the adjective acting as an objective unit. In these cases, if the adjective had a subjective behavior, it was annotated with its corresponding tag, while if it was objective remained untagged.

The Gold Standard contained 263 words annotated as polar adjectives, being 199 of them tagged as positive and 52 of them as negative. See some examples of the annotated adjectives in TABLE 2.

It is important to note that 12 of them were identified as highly subjective elements since they were tagged as positive in some occasions and as negative in others. Some examples are "alto" ("high"), "grande" ("big") or "pequeño" ("small").

Label	Examples
Positive Adjective	afortunado, bestial, deportivo, poderoso[8]
Negative Adjective	despreciable, renqueante, molesto, prohibitivo[9]

TABLE 2 – Examples of annotation in the Gold Standard

In order to evaluate the bootstrapping process proposed in Section 2.1, we repeated the experiment only with the texts that formed the Gold Standard. We searched for all the conjunctive patterns and found 64 pairs of adjectives joined by "y" ("and") or "pero" ("but"). Therefore, we collected 64 pairs of adjectives of the total of 482 appearing in the car corpus. Then, we repeated the bootstrapping process carried out for the conjunctive pairs extracted from the car corpus, over the pairs of conjoined adjectives extracted from the Gold Standard.

Obviously, in this case, the growth in the number of adjectives collected is smaller, since we worked only with a 13% of the total pairs of adjectives joined by a conjunction. We augmented the positive adjectives from 28 (seeds) to 55 and the negative ones from 7 (seeds) to 14. In these data, we did not identify any highly subjective adjective due to the reduction of the corpus.

[7] http://brat.nlplab.org/

[8] Lucky, terrific, sports, powerful

[9] Despicable, ailing, annoying, prohibitive

The recall of the bootstrapping process proposed was calculated comparing the total number of adjectives that appeared in the conjunction pairs with the number of polar adjectives that our method was capable to extract. We identified the 67% of all the adjectives that appear in the 64 pairs of adjectives.

In order to know the precision of the method, we calculated the number of adjectives that were correctly labeled (as positive or negative) over all of the adjectives extracted by the bootstrapping process. In the Gold Standard, of all the 51 adjectives identified, 41 of them were tagged as positive, 7 of them were tagged as negative and 3 of them were extracted of these lists as highly subjective because they appeared labelled as positive or as negative depending on the context. This yields a precision for positives of 97.6% and 71.5% for negatives. See all the results in TABLE 3.

Recall	Precision for Positives	Precision for Negatives
67%	97.6%	71.5%

TABLE 3 – Recall and precision of the extraction and annotation of the polar adjectives

The results of the experiment and the data obtained with the evaluation show that our bootstrapping algorithm is able to identify and label most of the polarity adjectives contained in a corpus. The evaluation shows that our method achieves better rates of precision than other published works reported in Section 1 while maintaining recall.

Conclusions and future work

In this paper we present a bootstrapping method to automatically identify, extract and label polar adjectives, not only as positive or negative but also as highly subjective elements. Our method is based on the hypothesis that two adjectives joined by "y" ("and") have the same prior polarity and two adjectives joined by "pero" ("but") have the opposite one. Additionally, it labels as "highly subjective" all of the adjectives that can behave as positive as well as negative depending on the context. This triple classification of the polar adjectives improves the methods based on the same hypothesis and achieves a precision of 97.6% in the identification and labeling of positive elements and of 71.5% in the classification of negative ones.

Moreover, our method is capable to extract some slang polar adjectives, (for example, "cojonudo" ("insane"), "fardón" ("showy")) since it is not based on external language resources but in the real language usages of the writers. Apart from that, it is possible to reutilize the bootstrapping method because the process is simple and replicable for other domains and languages.

In future works, we will adapt the bootstrapping method proposed in order to extract and annotate polar nouns joined with the appropriate conjunctions and we also plan to study the possible extractions of polar verbs and adverbs.

Acknowledgments

This work was funded by the EU 7FP project 248064 PANACEA and the UPF-IULA PhD grant program.

References

Baccianella, S., Esuli, A., & Sebastiani, F. (2010). SentiWordNet 3.0: An Enhanced Lexical Resource for Sentiment Analysis and Opinion Mining. In N. C. C. Chair, K. Choukri, B. Maegaard, J. Mariani, J. Odijk, S. Piperidis, M. Rosner, et al. (Eds.), Proceedings of the Seventh conference on International Language Resources and Evaluation LREC10 (Vol. 0, pp. 2200–2204). European Language Resources Association (ELRA). Retrieved from http://www.lrec-conf.org/proceedings/lrec2010/pdf/769_Paper.pdf

Cardie, C. (1997). Empirical Methods in Information Extraction. AI Magazine, 18(4), 65–79. Retrieved from http://www.aaai.org/ojs/index.php/aimagazine/article/viewArticle/1322

Christ, O. (1994). A Modular and Flexible Architecture for an Integrated Corpus Query System, 10. Computation and Language. Retrieved from http://arxiv.org/abs/cmp-lg/9408005

Esuli, A., & Sebastiani, F. (2005). Determining the semantic orientation of terms through gloss classification. Proceedings of the 14th ACM international conference on Information and knowledge management CIKM 05, 617–624. doi:10.1145/1099554.1099713

Hatzivassiloglou, V., & McKeown, K. R. (1997). Predicting the semantic orientation of adjectives. Proceedings of the 35th annual meeting on Association for Computational Linguistics, pages(2), 174–181. doi:10.3115/976909.979640

Hu, M., & Liu, B. (2004). Mining and summarizing customer reviews. Proceedings of the 2004 ACM SIGKDD international conference on Knowledge discovery and data mining - KDD *'04* (p. 168). New York, New York, USA: ACM Press. doi:10.1145/1014052.1014073

Kaji, N., & Kitsuregawa, M. (2007). Building Lexicon for Sentiment Analysis from Massive Collection of HTML Documents. Computational Linguistics, 43(June), 1075–1083. Retrieved from http://www.aclweb.org/anthology/D/D07/D07-1115

Kanayama, H., & Nasukawa, T. (2006). Fully automatic lexicon expansion for domain-oriented sentiment analysis. Proceedings of the 2006 Conference on Empirical Methods in Natural Language Processing EMNLP 06, (July), 355–363. doi:10.3115/1610075.1610125

Levin, B. (1993). English Verb Classes and Alternations: A Preliminary Investigation. Chicago Il (p. 366). University of Chicago Press. Retrieved from http://www.amazon.com/English-Verb-Classes-Alternations-Investigation/dp/0226475336

Miller, G. A. (1995). WordNet: a lexical database for English. Communications of the ACM, 38(11), 39–41. doi:10.1145/219717.219748

Padró, L., Collado, M., Reese, S., Lloberes, M., & Castellón, I. (2010). FreeLing 2.1: Five Years of Open-Source Language Processing Tools. Retrieved from http://upcommons.upc.edu/e-prints/handle/2117/7616

Riloff, E., Wiebe, J., & Wilson, T. (2003). Learning subjective nouns using extraction pattern bootstrapping. In E. Riloff, J. Wiebe, & T. Wilson (Eds.), Proceedings of the seventh conference on Natural language learning at HLTNAACL 2003 (Vol. 4, pp. 25–32). Association for Computational Linguistics. doi:10.3115/1119176.1119180

Stenetorp, P., Pyysalo, S., Topić, G., Ohta, T., Ananiadou, S., & Tsujii, J. (2012). brat: a Web-based Tool for NLP-Assisted Text Annotation. Proceedings of the Demonstrations at the 13th Conference of the European Chapter of the Association for Computational Linguistics (pp. 102–107). Avignon: Association for Computational Linguistics. Retrieved from http://www.aclweb.org/anthology/E12-2021

Stone, P. J., Dunphy, D. C., Smith, M. S., & Ogilvie, D. M. (1966). The General Inquirer: A Computer Approach to Content Analysis. (M. I. T. Press, Ed.)The MIT Press (Vol. 08, p. 651). MIT Press. Retrieved from http://www.webuse.umd.edu:9090/

Stoyanov, V., Cardie, C., & Wiebe, J. (2005). Multi-Perspective Question Answering Using the OpQA Corpus. Proceedings of HLT-EMNLP 2005. Retrieved from http://www.cs.cornell.edu/home/cardie/papers/hlt-emnlp05-ves.pdf

Valitutti, A., Strapparava, C., & Stock, O. (2004). Developing Affective Lexical Resources. PsychNology Journal, 2(1), 2004.

Vázquez, S., & Bel, N. (2012). A Classification of Adjectives for Polarity Lexicons Enhancement. Proceedings of the Eight International Conference on Language Resources and Evaluation (LREC'12). Retrieved from http://www.lrec-conf.org/proceedings/lrec2012/pdf/223_Paper.pdf

Optimal Scheduling of Information Extraction Algorithms

Henning WACHSMUTH[1] *Benno STEIN*[2]
(1) UNIVERSITÄT PADERBORN, s-lab – Software Quality Lab, Paderborn, Germany
(2) BAUHAUS-UNIVERSITÄT WEIMAR, Web Technology and Information Systems, Weimar, Germany
hwachsmuth@s-lab.upb.de, benno.stein@uni-weimar.de

ABSTRACT
Most research on run-time efficiency in information extraction is of empirical nature. This paper analyzes the efficiency of information extraction pipelines from a theoretical point of view in order to explain empirical findings. We argue that information extraction can, at its heart, be viewed as a relevance filtering task whose efficiency traces back to the run-times and selectivities of the employed algorithms. To better understand the intricate behavior of information extraction pipelines, we develop a sequence model for scheduling a pipeline's algorithms. In theory, the most efficient schedule corresponds to the Viterbi path through this model and can hence be found by dynamic programming. For real-time applications, it might be too expensive to compute all run-times and selectivities beforehand. However, our model implies the benchmarks of filtering tasks and illustrates that the optimal schedule depends on the distribution of relevant information in the input texts. We give formal and experimental evidence where necessary.

TITLE AND ABSTRACT IN GERMAN

Optimales Scheduling von Information-Extraction-Verfahren

Nahezu alle Forschung zur Laufzeiteffizienz in der Information Extraction ist empirischer Natur. Die vorliegende Arbeit analysiert die Effizienz von Information-Extraction-Pipelines aus theoretischer Sicht, um empirische Erkenntnisse zu erklären. Wir sehen Information Extraction im Kern als Relevanz-Filteraufgabe an, deren Effizienz auf die Laufzeiten und Selektivitäten der eingesetzten Algorithmen zurückgeht. Zum besseren Verständnis des komplexen Verhaltens von Information-Extraction-Pipelines entwickeln wir ein Sequenzmodell für das Scheduling der Algorithmen einer Pipeline. Theoretisch entspricht der effizienteste Schedule dem Viterbi-Pfad durch dieses Modell und lässt sich daher mittels dynamischer Programmierung finden. Für Echtzeitanwendungen kann es zu teuer sein, alle Laufzeiten und Selektivitäten im Vorhinein zu berechnen. Unser Modell impliziert jedoch die Benchmarks von Filteraufgaben und zeigt, dass der optimale Schedule von der Verteilung relevanter Informationen in den Eingabetexten abhängt. Wo nötig, führen wir sowohl formale als auch experimentelle Belege an.

KEYWORDS: information extraction, theory, efficiency, scheduling.

KEYWORDS IN GERMAN: Information Extraction, Theorie, Effizienz, Scheduling.

Proceedings of COLING 2012: Posters, pages 1281–1290,
COLING 2012, Mumbai, December 2012.

1 Introduction

Information extraction deals with the analysis of natural language text in order to find relevant information about entities, relations, and events. Relations typically involve two named or numeric entities, such as "Apple was founded in 1976", whereas events model more complex dependencies between a number of entities, as for example: "IBM ended Q1 2011 with $13.2 billion of cash on hand and free cash flow of $0.8 billion." If event templates with three or more arguments have to be filled, several analysis steps are performed. In terms of run-time efficiency, it is reasonable to filter only those portions of text after each step that contain the information sought for and, thus, may be relevant for one of the events in question. In this respect, a *conjunctive filtering task* is to be solved for each event type. Consequently, the organization of the analysis will have a noticeable impact on the efficiency of the extraction process.[1]

In information extraction, a conjunctive filtering task is addressed with an algorithm pipeline $\Pi = \langle \mathbf{A}, \pi \rangle$, comprised of a set of algorithms **A** and a schedule π that prescribes the order of algorithm application. Each algorithm in **A** filters an argument of the event in question by classifying a portion of its input text as relevant. In the first example above, both "Apple" and "1976" are such arguments. The output of Π is given by the arguments in the intersection of the filtered portions. In order to work properly, an algorithm may require as input a preprocessing of the text by other algorithms. As in (Wachsmuth et al., 2011), we call a pipeline *admissible* if its schedule ensures that the input constraints of all algorithms are fulfilled. Accordingly, all admissible pipelines $\langle \mathbf{A}, \pi_1 \rangle, \ldots, \langle \mathbf{A}, \pi_l \rangle$ classify the same portion of text as relevant. I.e., they entail the same effectiveness, e.g. quantified as F_1-score, in solving an extraction task.

We observe an increasing demand to extract complex information structures in applications of computational linguistics, e.g. the *BioNLP Shared Task 2011* included event types where entities of three types had to be related to an event in four roles (Kim et al., 2011). Our research question refers to the outlined efficiency potential and can be stated as optimization problem:

Given an algorithm set **A** *that solves an information extraction task. Determine a schedule* π^* *such that the pipeline* $\langle \mathbf{A}, \pi^* \rangle$ *is run-time optimal under all admissible pipelines* $\langle \mathbf{A}, \pi_1 \rangle, \ldots, \langle \mathbf{A}, \pi_l \rangle$.

While a few practical scheduling approaches exist, in this paper we discuss the problem's nature. We consider a text as an ordered set of atomic text units. The efficiency of a pipeline $\Pi = \langle \mathbf{A}, \pi \rangle$ depends on the run-times and selectivities of the algorithms in **A** when being applied to the text units. The *selectivity* defines the portion of text units classified as relevant by an algorithm in **A**. Only this portion forms the input of the next algorithm in π. Hence, the optimization problem consists in finding the schedule that minimizes the sum of the algorithms' run-times. An optimal solution requires a global analysis due to the recurrent structure of the run-times and selectivities. We represent this structure in a sequence model and solve it with dynamic programming. The optimization view raises an important question: To what extent does the optimality of a schedule depend on the distribution of relevant information in input texts?

Contributions. We provide a theoretical approach and the theoretically optimal solution to the construction of run-time efficient information extraction pipelines. First, we model the scheduling of a set of extraction algorithms as a dynamic program, which yields the optimal pipeline schedule (Section 3). Then, we offer formal and quantitative evidence that the distribution of relevant information is decisive for the efficiency of a pipeline (Section 4).

[1] Different event types imply disjunctions of conjunctive filtering tasks. Filtering is common in information extraction (Cowie and Lehnert, 1996; Agichtein, 2005), but until today most approaches rely only on heuristics (Sarawagi, 2008).

2 Related Work

One of the most recognized approaches to efficient information extraction refers to the open domain system TextRunner (Banko et al., 2007). TextRunner employs special index structures and fast extraction algorithms, but it is restricted to simple relations. In contrast, we target at template filling tasks that relate several entities to events (Cunningham, 2006). We approach such tasks with classic pipelines where each algorithm takes on one analysis, e.g. a certain type of entity recognition (Grishman, 1997). The decisions within a pipeline can be viewed as irreversible, which allows to perform filtering. Hence, an algorithm can never make up for false classifications of its predecessors, as in iterative or probabilistic pipeline approaches (Finkel et al., 2006; Hollingshead and Roark, 2007). Accordingly, we do not deal with joint extraction, which often suffers from its computational cost (Poon and Domingos, 2007).

In (Wachsmuth et al., 2011), we introduced a generic method to construct efficient pipelines that achieves run-time improvements of one order of magnitude without harming a pipeline's effectiveness. Similarly, Shen et al. (2007) and Doan et al. (2009) optimize schedules in a declarative extraction framework. These works give only heuristic hints on the reasons behind empirical results. While some algebraic foundations of scheduling are established for rule-based approaches by Chiticariu et al. (2010), we explain the determinants of efficiency for any set of extraction algorithms. To the best of our knowledge, we are the first to address scheduling in information extraction with dynamic programming, which relies on dividing a problem into smaller subproblems and solving recurring subproblems only once (Cormen et al., 2009).

In our research we analyze the impact of text types on the efficiency of information extraction pipelines. Existing work on text types in information extraction mainly deals with the filtering of promising documents, such as (Agichtein and Gravano, 2003). Instead, we identify the properties of a text that influence run-time optimality. For optimizing rule-based pipelines, samples from a text corpus are analyzed by Wang et al. (2011) in order to collect statistics similar to the ones used for optimizing database queries.

In the database community, run-time optimization has a long tradition. While dynamic programming is used for *join* operations since the pioneer System R (Selinger et al., 1979), template filling corresponds to processing *And*-conditioned queries that select those tuples of a database table whose values fulfill a desired attribute conjunction. The optimal schedule for such a query is obtained by ordering the involved attribute tests according to their increasing number of expected matches, i.e., without having to solve a dynamic program (Ioannidis, 1997). The filtering problem in information extraction looks pretty similar, but a simple ordering strategy fails because the effort for extracting one type of information (which is the analog of an attribute test) is not constant; it depends on the applied extraction algorithm.

3 Optimal Scheduling of Information Extraction Algorithms

We now develop a theoretical model for the efficiency of scheduling a fixed set of extraction algorithms. In order to maintain effectiveness, we consider only *admissible* information extraction pipelines, i.e., pipelines where the input constraints of all algorithms are fulfilled (cf. Section 1). For an algorithm set $\mathbf{A}$, different admissible pipelines can vary in efficiency if they apply the algorithms in $\mathbf{A}$ to different numbers of text units. The run-time $t(\Pi)$ of a pipeline $\Pi = \langle \mathbf{A}, \pi \rangle$ on an ordered set of text units U depends on the run-time t_i and the filtered portion of text units R_i of each algorithm $A_i \in \mathbf{A}$ within the schedule π. Assume that π schedules $\mathbf{A}$ as $(A_1, \ldots, A_m)$. If Π analyzes only the filtered portions of text units, then A_1 processes U, while A_2

processes $R_1(U)$, A_3 processes $R_1(U) \cap R_2(U)$, and so on. Therefore, the run-time of Π is

$$t(\Pi) = t_1(U) + \sum_{i=2}^{m} t_i(\bigcap_{k=1}^{i-1} R_k(U)). \quad (3.1)$$

From (Wachsmuth et al., 2011) we infer that, in the optimal schedule of two independent extraction algorithms A_1 and A_2, A_1 precedes A_2 on an ordered set of text units U if and only if

$$t_1(U) + t_2(R_1(U)) < t_2(U) + t_1(R_2(U)). \quad (3.2)$$

Obviously, the run-time of an algorithm within a pipeline results from the portion of text units filtered by its preceding algorithm. Hence, the run-time $t(\Pi^{(m)})$ of a pipeline $\Pi^{(m)} = (A_1, \ldots, A_m)$ is the sum of the run-time $t(\Pi^{(m-1)})$ of $\Pi^{(m-1)} = (A_1, \ldots, A_{m-1})$ and the run-time of A_m on the text units $R(\Pi^{(m-1)})$ filtered by $\Pi^{(m-1)}$. This recursive definition resembles the one used by the Viterbi algorithm (Viterbi, 1967), which operates on hidden Markov models to compute the *Viterbi path*, i.e. the most likely sequence of states for a given sequence of observations. In the following, we adapt the Viterbi algorithm to schedule an algorithm set $\mathbf{A}$, such that the Viterbi path corresponds to the run-time optimal schedule for an ordered set of text units U.

The Sequence Model. To represent scheduling, we define a sequence model similar to a hidden Markov model. Each state a_i in the model corresponds to having applied an algorithm $A_i \in \mathbf{A}$, $i \in \{1, \ldots, m\}$. A transition to a_i denotes the application of A_i with run-time t_i. Instead of observations, the model contains the positions $p^{(1)}, \ldots, p^{(m)}$ of a schedule, and having applied A_i at $p^{(j)}$ means having filtered a portion of text units R_i. In contrast to the state and emission probabilities of a hidden Markov model, however, t_i and R_i are not directly influenced by the preceding state or the current position, but they depend on the currently filtered portion of text units. For this reason, we include a running variable $R(\Pi_k^{(j-1)})$ in the model that stores the filtered portion of A_k at position $p^{(j-1)}$. Initially, the running variable is set to the ordered set of text units U. Figure 1(a) illustrates the described sequence model.[2]

In classic information extraction pipelines, no algorithm is applied multiple times. This means that each state must occur exactly once in a path through the model. Also, for admissibility, a state may only be reached if all input constraints of the associated algorithm are fulfilled. Hence, we define that an algorithm $A_i \in \mathbf{A}$ is *applicable* at position $p^{(j)}$ if A_i has not been applied at $p^{(1)}$ to $p^{(j-1)}$, and if all input constraints of A_i are fulfilled by the algorithms at these positions.

The Pipeline Viterbi Algorithm. For an observation x_j, the original Viterbi algorithm computes the most likely path with state y_i at x_j in an iterative (dynamic programming) manner. Accordingly, we store for each position $p^{(j)}$ the run-time optimal pipeline from $p^{(1)}$ to $p^{(j)}$ and algorithm A_i at $p^{(j)}$. To this end, we iteratively compute the run-time of each $\Pi_i^{(j)}$ based on the set of run-time optimal pipelines $\mathbf{\Pi}^{(j-1)}$ after which A_i is applicable. If $\mathbf{\Pi}^{(j-1)}$ is empty, then A_i is not applicable, denoted as $\perp$. The recursive function of the *Pipeline Viterbi algorithm* can be derived from Equation 3.1 and Inequality 3.2:

$$t(\Pi_i^{(j)}) = t_i(U) \quad \text{if } j = 1 \qquad t(\Pi_i^{(j)}) = \min_{\Pi_l \in \mathbf{\Pi}^{(j-1)}} \big(t(\Pi_l) + t_i(R(\Pi_l)) \big) \quad \text{else}$$

To solve the problem of optimal scheduling with dynamic programming, we keep track of all values $t(\Pi_i^{(j)})$ and $R(\Pi_i^{(j)})$. Additionally, we store $\Pi_i^{(j)}$ to finally obtain the optimal pipeline $\langle \mathbf{A}, \pi^* \rangle$ for $\mathbf{A} = \{A_1, \ldots, A_m\}$ and a set of text units U, as sketched in the following pseudocode.

[2]Notice that the sequence model does not have the Markov property (Manning and Schütze, 1999), but we define the sequence model accordingly in order to make it viable for the Viterbi algorithm.

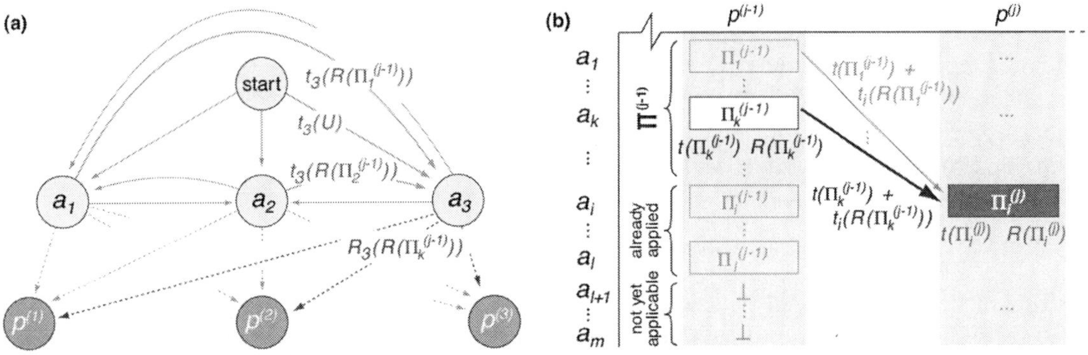

Figure 1: (a) The sequence model for three algorithms. Transitions *to* a state a_i are labeled with the run-time t_i of the algorithm A_i on its input. A dashed transition *from* a_i to a position $p^{(j)}$ refers to the text units filtered by A_i. (b) Determination of pipeline $\Pi_i^{(j)}$ of the Pipeline Viterbi algorithm. For illustration, $a_1,\ldots,a_m$ are ordered by applicability of the respective algorithm A_i after the pipelines of length $j-1$.

Pseudocode Pipeline Viterbi algorithm (U, $\{A_1,\ldots,A_m\}$)

1: **for each** $i \in \{1,\ldots,m\}$ **do** ▷ position $p^{(1)}$, state a_1 to a_m
2: **if** A_i is applicable in position $p^{(1)}$ **then**
3: $\Pi_i^{(1)} \leftarrow (A_i)$
4: $t(\Pi_i^{(1)}) \leftarrow t_i(U)$
5: $R(\Pi_i^{(1)}) \leftarrow R_i(U)$
6: **for each** j from 2 to m **do** ▷ position $p^{(2)}$ to $p^{(m)}$
7: **for each** $i \in \{1,\ldots,m\}$ **do** ▷ state a_1 to a_m
8: $\Pi^{(j-1)} \leftarrow \{\Pi_l^{(j-1)} \mid A_i \text{ is applicable after } \Pi_l^{(j-1)}\}$
9: $\Pi_k^{(j-1)} \leftarrow \underset{\Pi_l \in \Pi^{(j-1)}}{\arg\min} \Big(t(\Pi_l) + t_i(R(\Pi_l)) \Big)$
10: $\Pi_i^{(j)} \leftarrow \Pi_k^{(j-1)} \,\|\, (A_i)$
11: $t(\Pi_i^{(j)}) \leftarrow t(\Pi_k^{(j-1)}) + t_i(R(\Pi_k^{(j-1)}))$
12: $R(\Pi_i^{(j)}) \leftarrow R_i(R(\Pi_k^{(j-1)}))$
13: **return** $\underset{\Pi_i^{(m)},\, i \in \{1,\ldots,m\}}{\arg\min} t(\Pi_i^{(m)})$

Lines 1 to 5 of the pseudocode initialize a pipeline $\Pi_i^{(1)}$ for each applicable algorithm A_i. The pipeline's run-time and its filtered portion of text units are set to the according values of A_i. The remaining lines compute $\Pi_i^{(j)}$, $t(\Pi_i^{(j)})$, and $R(\Pi_i^{(j)})$ for position $p^{(2)}$ to $p^{(m)}$. Here, the best predecessor pipeline $\Pi_k^{(j-1)}$ is determined in lines 8 and 9. $\Pi_k^{(j-1)}$ is then used to update $\Pi_i^{(j)}$ and its values. Finally, the optimal pipeline is returned in line 13. A trellis diagram that visualizes the operations of the Pipeline Viterbi algorithm is shown in Figure 1(b).

Correctness. The optimality of the returned pipeline follows from the optimal solutions to all subproblems, i.e., all pipelines $\Pi_i^{(j)}$. We do not prove the correctness of the Pipeline Viterbi algorithm formally here. The proof idea is that, by definition, the order of any two algorithms $A_1, A_2 \in \mathbf{A}$ is only variable if neither A_1 depends on A_2 nor vice versa. In this case, applying A_1 and A_2 in sequence is a commutative operation. Thus, $\Pi_k^{(j-1)}$ will always be optimal for A_i at position $p^{(j)}$, no matter what comes afterwards. Consequently, $\Pi_i^{(j)}$ is optimal.

Computational Cost. The cost of running the developed algorithm for an algorithm set $\mathbf{A} = \{A_1,\ldots,A_m\}$ can be inferred from the pseudocode above: if both the run-times t_i and the filtered portions of text units R_i of all algorithms $A_i \in \mathbf{A}$ were given, the cost would follow from the m^2 loop iterations, where $\Pi_i^{(j)}$ is determined based on at most $m-1$ pipelines $\Pi_l^{(j-1)}$. This results in $O(m^3)$ operations. Practically, these values are not known beforehand but need to be measured during execution. In the worst case, all algorithms have an equal run-time $t_{max}(U)$ on U and they filter the whole text, i.e., $R_i(U) = U$ for each A_i. So, all algorithms must indeed be applied to U, which leads to an overall upper bound of $O(m^3 \cdot t_{max}(U))$.[3]

4 The Impact of Text Types on the Efficiency of Pipelines

In this section, we first analyze the influence of text types on the optimality of schedules. Then, we reveal that the efficiency of an information extraction pipeline is governed by the distribution of relevant entities, relations, and events in the input texts. In all experiments, we evaluated the following set-up on a 2 GHz Intel Core 2 Duo MacBook with 4 GB memory:

Data. We processed the training sets of two German text corpora: the *Revenue corpus* introduced in (Wachsmuth et al., 2010) and the corpus of the *CoNLL'03 shared task* (Tjong Kim Sang and De Meulder, 2003).[4] The former contains 752 online business news articles with 21,586 sentences, whereas 553 mixed classic newspaper articles with 12,713 sentences refer to the latter.

Task. The conjunctive filtering task that we consider emanates from the purpose of the Revenue corpus, namely, we define a text unit to be classified as relevant as a sentence that represents a forecast and that contains a money entity, a time entity, and an organization name.

Algorithms. We employed four algorithms that filter text units: regex-based money and time entity recognizers A_M and A_T, the CRF-based STANFORD NER system A_N (Finkel et al., 2005; Faruqui and Padó, 2010) for organization names, and the SVM-based forecast event detector A_F from (Wachsmuth et al., 2011) that needs time entities as input. Further algorithms were used only as preprocessors. In all experiments we executed each preprocessing algorithm right before its output was needed. Hence, we simply speak of the algorithm set $\mathbf{A}_1 = \{A_M, A_T, A_N, A_F\}$ in the following without loss of generality. All algorithms in $\mathbf{A}_1$ operate on sentence-level.

Application of the Pipeline Viterbi Algorithm. On both corpora, we executed all applicable pipelines $\Pi_i^{(j)}$ for $\mathbf{A}_1$ to obtain the filtered portions $R(\Pi_i^{(j)})$ and to measure all run-times $t(\Pi_i^{(j)})$, averaged over ten runs. All standard deviations were lower than 1.0s on the Revenue corpus and 0.5s on the CoNLL'03 corpus, respectively. For clarity, we omitted them in Figure 2 and 3, which visualize the Pipeline Viterbi algorithm as a trellis. Also, the two figures state only the number of sentences of each filtered portion of text units instead of the portions themselves. In the trellises the bold arrows denote the Viterbi paths. A_T is scheduled first and A_N is scheduled last in both optimal cases, but only on the Revenue corpus it is more efficient to apply A_F before A_M. So, the run-time optimality of schedules is corpus-dependent.

Seemingly, one reason lies in the text units classified as relevant by $\mathbf{A}_1$: 215 of the sentences in the Revenue corpus are returned by each admissible pipeline, which is about 1%, as opposed to 2 sentences of the CoNLL'03 corpus (0.01%). A closer look uncovers significant differences between the trellises, e.g. the pipeline (A_T, A_M) filters 3818 sentences of the Revenue corpus (17.7%), but only 82 CoNLL'03 sentences (0.6%). These values originate in the distribution of entities in the two corpora. Additionally, the run-times of A_N (Revenue: 91.63s, CoNLL'03: 48.03s) emphasize the general importance of optimizing the efficiency of pipelines.

[3]Besides the unrealistic nature of the worst case, the value m^3 ignores that an algorithm is applied only once and only if its input constraints are fulfilled. Thus, the cost of the Pipeline Viterbi algorithm will be much lower in practice.

[4]In general, the evaluated determination of optimal schedules works on input texts of any language, of course.

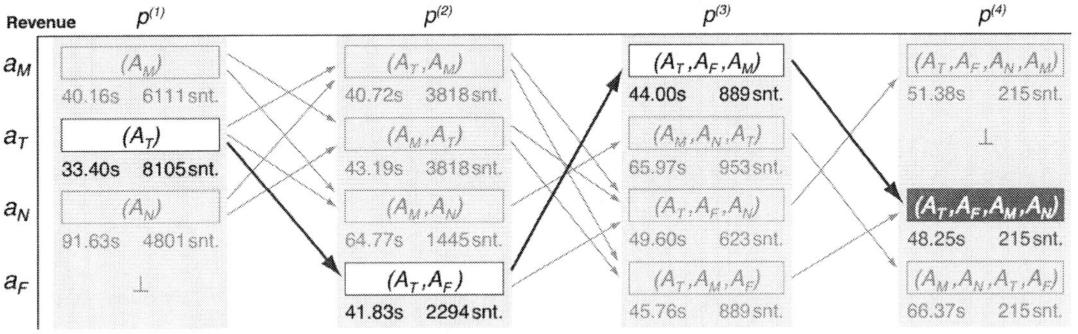

Figure 2: Illustration of the Pipeline Viterbi algorithm for $\mathbf{A}_1$ on the training set of the Revenue corpus. Below each pipeline $\Pi_i^{(j)}$, $t(\Pi_i^{(j)})$ is given in seconds next to the number of filtered sentences (snt.) in $R(\Pi_i^{(j)})$. The bold arrows denote the Viterbi path resulting in the run-time optimal pipeline (A_T, A_F, A_M, A_N).

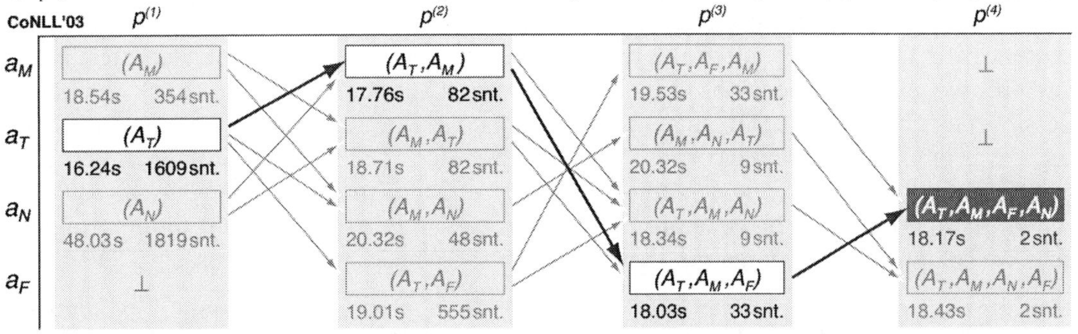

Figure 3: Illustration of the Pipeline Viterbi algorithm for $\mathbf{A}_1$ on the training set of the CoNLL'03 corpus.

The Distribution of Relevant Information. It seems reasonable to assume that the fraction of text units, which are classified as relevant, influences the run-time optimality of a schedule. In fact, it is not the relevant but the irrelevant text units that matter as follows from Theorem 1.

Theorem 1. *Let $\Pi^* = \langle \mathbf{A}, \pi^* \rangle$ be run-time optimal on a set of text units U under all admissible pipelines for a set of extraction algorithms $\mathbf{A}$. Let $R \subseteq U$ be the set of text units classified as relevant by Π^*. Now let $R' \subseteq U'$ be any other set of text units classified as relevant by Π^*. Then Π^* is run-time optimal on $(U \setminus R) \cup R'$.*

Proof. Within the proof, we denote the run-time of an arbitrary pipeline Π on U as $t^{(U)}(\Pi)$ and accordingly on other sets of text units. By hypothesis, $\Pi^* = \langle \mathbf{A}, \pi^* \rangle$ is run-time optimal on U, i.e., for any pipeline $\Pi' = \langle \mathbf{A}, \pi' \rangle$ with $\pi' \neq \pi^*$, we have

$$t^{(U)}(\Pi^*) \quad \leq \quad t^{(U)}(\Pi'). \tag{4.1}$$

Now, for an algorithm set $\mathbf{A}$, all admissible pipelines classify the same set of text units $R \subseteq U$ as relevant. So, on each text unit in R, all algorithms must be applied irrespective of the schedule. Hence, for any two admissible pipelines $\Pi_1 = \langle \mathbf{A}, \pi_1 \rangle$ and $\Pi_2 = \langle \mathbf{A}, \pi_2 \rangle$, we can expect

$$t^{(R)}(\Pi_1) \quad = \quad t^{(R)}(\Pi_2). \tag{4.2}$$

Obviously, the same holds for R'. Thus, from Equation 4.1 and 4.2, Theorem 1 follows:

$$\begin{aligned} t^{((U \setminus R) \cup R')}(\Pi^*) &= t^{(U)}(\Pi^*) - t^{(R)}(\Pi^*) + t^{(R')}(\Pi^*) \\ &\overset{(4.1)}{\leq} t^{(U)}(\Pi') - t^{(R)}(\Pi^*) + t^{(R')}(\Pi^*) \\ &\overset{(4.2)}{=} t^{(U)}(\Pi') - t^{(R)}(\Pi') + t^{(R')}(\Pi') \quad = \quad t^{((U \setminus R) \cup R')}(\Pi') \end{aligned}$$ □

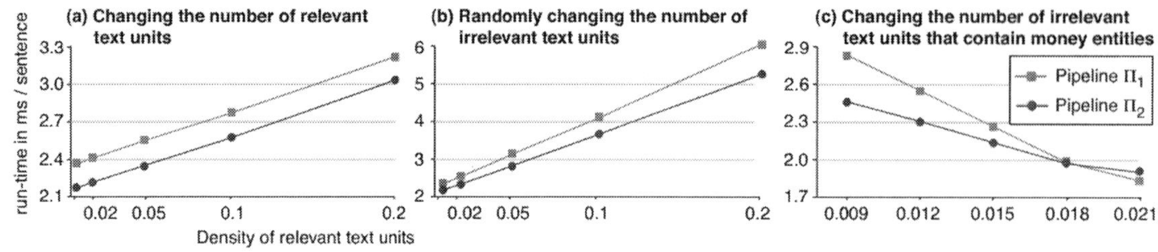

Figure 4: Average run-time per sentence of Π_1 and Π_2 under different densities of relevant information in the training set of the Revenue corpus. The densities were generated by duplicating or deleting sentences.

Consequently, two pipelines $\Pi = \langle \mathbf{A}, \pi \rangle$ and $\Pi' = \langle \mathbf{A}, \pi' \rangle$ differ in efficiency if they apply the algorithms in $\mathbf{A}$ to different numbers of the irrelevant text units in $U \setminus R$. To analyze this further, we altered the *density* of relevant information (i.e., the fraction of relevant text units) of the Revenue corpus by randomly duplicating or deleting sentences of one of three types: (a) relevant sentences, (b) irrelevant sentences, and (c) irrelevant sentences with money entities. For (a) and (b), we generated densities of 0.01, 0.02, 0.05, 0.1, and 0.2. In case of (c), the highest possible density is about 0.021; under that density, no irrelevant sentence that contains money entities is left in the Revenue corpus. Now, we executed the pipelines $\Pi_1 = (A_M, A_T, A_F, A_N)$ and $\Pi_2 = (A_T, A_F, A_M, A_N)$, which are comparably efficient though employing very different schedules, ten times on the generated text collections. As these collections differ strongly in size, we computed the average run-times *per sentence* to make all results comparable.

Figure 4(a-c) plot the run-times for all densities. In Figure 4(a), the absolute gap between Π_1 and Π_2 remains the same under changing density, which gives additional evidence for Theorem 1. In contrast, the interpolated curves in Figure 4(b) increase proportionally, since the two pipelines spend a proportional amount of time processing irrelevant text. Finally, Figure 4(c) shows a change in optimality: Whereas Π_2 is faster on densities lower than about 0.018, Π_1 outperforms Π_2 on higher densities.[5] Π_1 applies A_M first, so it benefits from deleting irrelevant sentences with money entities, which represents a shift in the distribution of information. While other influencing factors exist, we cancelled out many of them by only reusing sentences from the evaluated corpus. Hence, we conclude that the distribution of relevant entities, relations, and events is decisive for the optimal scheduling of information extraction algorithms.

Conclusion

We provide a theoretical model to explain empirical findings when optimizing a pipeline's run-time efficiency at a given effectiveness. Based on this model, we propose a dynamic programming algorithm to determine the optimal schedule of a fixed set of extraction algorithms on input texts of any language. Together, the model and the algorithm give a comprehensive insight into the scheduling problem of conjunctive filtering tasks, such as template filling. Also, they represent a fast means to compute the theoretically optimal solution for benchmarks in future research and applications of computational linguistics. Our experiments showed that different types of texts may lead to different optimal schedules. For homogeneous input texts, a solution is to transform dynamic programming into an A* algorithm (Huang, 2008) with a heuristic based on run-time estimations of the employed algorithms. A* can then be executed on a sample of texts in order to find a near-optimal schedule. For more heterogeneous texts, a schedule should be chosen in respect of a classification of the input text at hand.

[5]The declining curves in Figure 4(c) seem counterintuitive. However, sentences with money entities often also contained other relevant information such as time entities. So, the average time to process them was rather high.

References

Eugene Agichtein and Luis Gravano (2003). Querying Text Databases for Efficient Information Extraction. In *Proceedings of the 19th International Conference on Data Engineering*, pages 113–124.

Eugene Agichtein (2005). Scaling Information Extraction to Large Document Collections. *Bulletin of the IEEE Computer Society Technical Committee on Data Engineering*, 28:3–10.

Michele Banko, Michael J. Cafarella, Stephen Soderland, Matt Broadhead, and Oren Etzioni (2007). Open Information Extraction from the Web. In *Proceedings of the 20th International Joint Conference on Artificial Intelligence*, pages 2670–2676.

Laura Chiticariu, Rajasekar Krishnamurthy, Yunyao Li, Sriram Raghavan Frederick R. Reiss, and Shivakumar Vaithyanathan (2010). SystemT: An Algebraic Approach to Declarative Information Extraction. In *Proceedings of the 48th Annual Meeting of the Association for Computational Linguistics*, pages 128–137.

Thomas H. Cormen, Charles E. Leiserson, Ronald L. Rivest, and Clifford Stein (2009). *Introduction to Algorithms*, third edition, MIT Press, Cambridge, MA, USA.

Jim Cowie and Wendy Lehnert (1996). Information Extraction. *Communications of the ACM*, 39(1):80–91.

Hamish Cunningham (2006). Information Extraction, Automatic. *Encyclopedia of Language & Linguistics*, 4:665–677.

AnHai Doan, Jeffrey F. Naughton, Raghu Ramakrishnan, Akanksha Baid, Xiaoyong Chai, Fei Chen, Ting Chen, Eric Chu, Pedro DeRose, Byron Gao, Chaitanya Gokhale, Jiansheng Huang, Warren Shen, and Ba-Quy Vuong (2009). Information Extraction Challenges in Managing Unstructured Data. In *SIGMOD Records*, 37(4):14–20.

Jenny R. Finkel, Trond Grenager, and Christopher D. Manning (2005). Incorporating Non-local Information into Information Extraction Systems by Gibbs Sampling. In *Proceedings of the 43nd Annual Meeting of the Association for Computational Linguistics*, pages 363–370.

Jenny R. Finkel, Christopher D. Manning, and Andrew Y. Ng (2006). Solving the Problem of Cascading Errors: Approximate Bayesian Inference for Linguistic Annotation Pipelines. In *Proceedings of the 2006 Conference on Empirical Methods in Natural Language Processing*, pages 618–626.

Manaal Faruqui and Sebastian Padó (2010). Training and Evaluating a German Named Entity Recognizer with Semantic Generalization. In *Proceedings of KONVENS 2010*, pages 129–133.

Ralph Grishman (1997). Information Extraction: Techniques and Challenges, In *International Summer School on Information Extraction: A Multidisciplinary Approach to an Emerging Information Technology*, pages 10–27.

Daniel Gruhl, Laurent Chavet, David Gibson, Jörg Meyer, Pradhan Pattanayak, Andrew Tomkins, and Jason Y. Zien (2004). How to Build a WebFountain: An Architecture for Very Large-scale Text Analytics. IBM Systems Journal, 43(1):64–77.

Kristy Hollingshead and Brian Roark (2007). Pipeline Iteration. In *Proceedings of the 45th Annual Meeting of the Association for Computational Linguistics*, pages 952–959.

Lian Huang (2008). Advanced Dynamic Programming in Semiring and Hypergraph Frameworks. In *COLING 2008: Advanced Dynamic Programming in Computational Linguistics: Theory, Algorithms and Applications – Tutorial notes*, pages 1–18.

Yannis Ioannidis (1997). Query optimization. In *Handbook for Computer Science*, CRC Press.

Jin-Dong Kim, Yue Wang, Toshihisa Takagi, and Akinori Yonezawa (2011). Overview of Genia event task in BioNLP Shared Task 2011. In *Proceedings of the BioNLP Shared Task 2011 Workshop*, pages 7–15.

Christopher D. Manning and Hinrich Schütze (1999). *Foundations of Statistical Natural Language Processing*, MIT Press, Cambridge, MA, USA.

Hoifung Poon and Pedro Domingos (2007). Joint Inference in Information Extraction. In *Proceedings of the 22nd National Conference on Artificial Intelligence*, pages 913–918.

Sunita Sarawagi (2008). Information Extraction. *Foundations and Trends in Databases*, 1(3):261–377.

Patricia G. Selinger, Morton M. Astrahan, Donald D. Chamberlin, Raymond A. Lorie, and Thomas G. Price (1979). Access Path Selection in a Relational Database Management System. In *Proceedings of the 1979 ACM SIGMOD International Conference on Management of Data*, pages 23–34.

Warren Shen, AnHai Doan, Jeffrey F. Naughton, and Raghu Ramakrishnan (2007). Declarative Information Extraction using Datalog with Embedded Extraction Predicates. In *Proceedings of the 33rd International Conference on Very Large Data Bases*, pages 1033–1044.

Erik F. Tjong Kim Sang and Fien De Meulder (2003). Introduction to the CoNLL-2003 Shared Task: Language-independent Named Entity Recognition In *Proceedings of the Seventh Conference on Natural Language Learning at HLT-NAACL 2003*, pages 142–147.

Andrew J. Viterbi (1967). Error Bounds for Convolutional Codes and an Asymptotically Optimum Decoding Algorithm. *IEEE Transactions on Information Theory*, 13(2):260–267.

Henning Wachsmuth, Peter Prettenhofer, and Benno Stein (2010). Efficient Statement Identification for Automatic Market Forecasting. In *Proceedings of the 23rd International Conference on Computational Linguistics*, pages 1128–1136.

Henning Wachsmuth, Benno Stein, and Gregor Engels (2011). Constructing Efficient Information Extraction Pipelines. In *Proceedings of the 20th ACM Conference on Information and Knowledge Management*, pages 2237–2240.

Daisy Z. Wang, Long Wei, Yunyao Li, Frederick R. Reiss, and Shivakumar Vaithyanathan (2011). Selectivity Estimation for Extraction Operators over Text Data. In *Proceedings of the 2011 IEEE 27th International Conference on Data Engineering*, pages 685–696.

Update Summarization Based on Co-Ranking with Constraints

Xiaojun Wan
Institute of Computer Science and Technology
The MOE Key Laboratory of Computational Linguistics
Peking University, Beijing 100871, China
wanxiaojun@pku.edu.cn

ABSTRACT

Update summarization is an emerging summarization task of creating a short summary of a set of news articles, under the assumption that the user has already read a given set of earlier articles. In this paper, we propose a new co-ranking method to address the update summarization task. The proposed method integrates two co-ranking processes by adding strict constraints. In comparison with the original co-ranking method, the proposed method can compute more accurate scores of sentences for the purpose of update summarization. Evaluation results on the most recent TAC2011 dataset demonstrate that our proposed method can outperform the original co-ranking method and other baselines.

KEYWORDS : Update Summarization, Multi-document summarization, Co-Ranking

Proceedings of COLING 2012: Posters, pages 1291–1300,
COLING 2012, Mumbai, December 2012.

1 Introduction

Update summarization is an emerging new summarization task of creating a short summary of a set of news articles, under the assumption that the user has already read a given set of earlier articles. The purpose of update summarization is to inform the reader of new information about a particular topic. Update summary is very useful for the user to know about a chronic topic. For example, given a topic of "Haiti earthquake", the earlier articles mainly talk about the occurrence of the earthquake and the consequence of the earthquake, and the later articles talk about the consequence of the earthquake and the rescue issues. In this case, the reader will read the later articles to know about the rescue issues after he/she has read the earlier articles. Therefore, an update summary of the later articles may facilitate the reader to grasp the "update" information in a very convenient way.

The update summarization task can be formulated as follows: Given an earlier document set D^A and a later document set D^B about a topic q, the sentence set for D^A is denoted as S^A and the sentence set for D^B is denoted as S^B. The update summary with a predefined length for D^B after reading D^A is denoted as SUM^B, where the sentences in SUM^B must meet the following requirements:

1) The summary sentences must be representative of D^B, i.e., the summary sentences in SUM^B must reflect important information in D^B. Moreover, the sentences must be biased to the topic q.

2) The summary sentences must be the least redundant with the sentences in D^A, i.e., the summary must not contain important information in D^A.

The task of update summarization was piloted in DUC2007, and it has been the fundamental task through TAC2008~TAC2011. The "update" characteristic makes the task more challenging than traditional document summarization tasks. Till now, most existing update summarization methods are adaptations of multi-document summarization methods by considering the redundancy information between the earlier and later document sets (Boudin et al. 2008; Fisher and Roark 2008; Nastase et al. 2008). In addition, several new methods have been proposed for addressing this task (Du et al. 2010; Wang and Li 2010; Li et al. 2008), and graph-based co-ranking is a typical one, where the sentences in the two document sets are ranked simultaneously by considering the sentence relationships across the document sets. Based on the co-ranking framework, Li et al. (2008) propose a graph-based sentence ranking algorithm named PNR^2 for update summarization, and it models both the positive and negative mutual reinforcement between sentences in the ranking process. In addition, Wan et al. (2011) apply the co-ranking algorithm for multilingual news summarization.

In this study, we propose a new co-ranking method, which is inspired by (Wan et al. 2011), to address the update summarization task. The proposed method integrates two co-ranking processes by adding strict constraints. In comparison with the original co-ranking method, the proposed method can compute more accurate scores of sentences for the purpose of update summarization. We perform experiments on the most recent TAC2011 dataset, and the evaluation results demonstrate that out proposed method can outperform the original co-ranking method and a few other baselines.

2 Our proposed method

Given the two document sets D^A and D^B about a topic q, we introduce two kinds of scores for each sentence: an update score and a consistency score. In our proposed method, each kind of score is computed with a co-ranking process, and the two kinds of scores are adjusted by adding strict constraints. Finally, the refined update scores are used for summary extraction.

We assign each sentence an update score to indicate how much the sentence contains significant and new information after knowing about the sentences in the other document set. The update score of each sentence relies not only on the sentences in the same document set, but also on the sentences in the other document set. In particular, the co-ranking method is based on the following assumption:

> *The update score of a sentence is positively associated with the sentences with high update scores in the same document set, and is negatively associated with the sentences with high update scores in the other document set.*

We introduce a consistency score for each sentence to indicate how much a sentence contains important and shared information in the two document sets. In particular, the consistency scores of the sentences can be computed based on the following assumption:

> *The consistency score of a sentence is positively associated with the sentences with high consistency scores in the same document set, and is also positively associated with the sentences with high consistency scores in the other document set.*

Formally, let $G=(S^A, S^B, E^A, E^B, E^{AB})$ be an undirected graph for the sentences in the two document sets D^A and D^B. $S^A=\{s^A_i \mid 1\leq i\leq m\}$ is the set of earlier sentences. $S^B=\{s^B_j \mid 1\leq j\leq n\}$ is the set of later sentences. m, n are the sentence numbers in the two document sets, respectively. Each sentence s^A_i or s^B_j is represented by a term vector $\vec{s}_i^{\,A}$ or $\vec{s}_j^{\,B}$ in the VSM model. E^A is the edge set to reflect the similarity relationships between the sentences in the earlier document set. E^B is the edge set to reflect the similarity relationships between the sentences in the later document set. E^{AB} is the edge set to reflect the similarity or dissimilarity relationships between the sentences in the two different document sets. The following matrices are required to be computed to reflect the three kinds of sentence relationships:

$\boldsymbol{M}^A=[M^A_{ij}]_{m\times m}$: This matrix aims to reflect the similarity relationships between the sentences in S^A. Each entry in the matrix corresponds to the cosine similarity between two sentences, and we let $M^A_{ii}=0$. Then $\boldsymbol{M}^A$ is normalized to $\tilde{\boldsymbol{M}}^A$ to make the sum of each row equal to 1.

$\boldsymbol{M}^B=[M^B_{ij}]_{n\times n}$: This matrix aims to reflect the similarity relationships between the sentences in S^B. Each entry in the matrix corresponds to the cosine similarity between two sentences, and we let $M^B_{ii}=0$. Then $\boldsymbol{M}^B$ is normalized to $\tilde{\boldsymbol{M}}^B$ to make the sum of each row equal to 1.

$\boldsymbol{W}^{AB}=[W^{AB}_{ij}]_{m\times n}$: This matrix aims to reflect the similarity relationships between the two sets of sentences. Each entry W^{AB}_{ij} in the matrix corresponds to the cosine similarity value between the sentence s^A_i and the sentence s^B_j. Then $\boldsymbol{W}^{AB}$ is normalized to $\tilde{\boldsymbol{W}}^{AB}$ to make the sum of each row equal to 1. In addition, we use $\boldsymbol{W}^{BA}=[W^{BA}_{ij}]_{n\times m}$ to denote the transpose of $\boldsymbol{W}^{AB}$, i.e., $\boldsymbol{W}^{BA}=(\boldsymbol{W}^{AB})^{\mathrm{T}}$. Then $\boldsymbol{W}^{BA}$ is normalized to $\tilde{\boldsymbol{W}}^{BA}$ to make the sum of each row equal to 1.

$M^{AB}=[M^{AB}_{ij}]_{m\times n}$: This matrix aims to reflect the dissimilarity relationships between the sentences in S^A and the sentences in S^B. Each entry M^{AB}_{ij} in the matrix corresponds to the dissimilarity between the sentence s^A_i and the sentence s^B_j.

$$M^{AB}_{ij} = \frac{\left\| \vec{s}^{\,A}_i - \vec{s}^{\,B}_j \right\|}{\left\| \vec{s}^{\,A}_i \right\| \times \left\| \vec{s}^{\,B}_j \right\|}$$

Then M^{AB} is normalized to $\widetilde{M}^{AB}$ to make the sum of each row equal to 1. In addition, we use $M^{BA}=[M^{BA}_{ij}]_{n\times m}$ to denote the transpose of M^{AB}, i.e., $M^{BA}= (M^{AB})^T$. Then M^{BA} is normalized to $\widetilde{M}^{BA}$ to make the sum of each row equal to 1.Note that $\widetilde{M}^{AB}$ and $\widetilde{M}^{BA}$ directly embody the negative association between the sentences in the two sets.

In order to compute the query-biased scores of the sentences, the relevance values of the sentences to the query also need to be computed. We use two column vectors $r^A=[r^A_i]_{m\times 1}$ and $r^B=[r^B_j]_{n\times 1}$ to reflect the query-biased scores, where each entry in r^A corresponds to the cosine similarity between a sentence and the given topic description. Then r^A is normalized to $\widetilde{r}^{\,A}$ to make the sum of all elements equal to 1. Each entry in r^B is computed in the same way, and r^B is normalized to $\widetilde{r}^{\,B}$.

After computing the above matrices and vectors, we can compute the update scores of the sentences in the two sets in a co-ranking process. We use two column vectors $u^A=[u^A_j]_{m\times 1}$ and $u^B=[u^B_i]_{n\times 1}$ to denote the update scores of the sentences in S^A and the sentences in S^B, respectively. Based on the first assumption, we can obtain the following equations:

$$u^A_j = \alpha_1 \sum_i \widetilde{M}^A_{ij} u^A_i + \beta_1 \sum_i \widetilde{M}^{BA}_{ij} u^B_i + \gamma_1 \cdot r^A_j$$

$$u^B_i = \alpha_1 \sum_j \widetilde{M}^B_{ji} u^B_j + \beta_1 \sum_j \widetilde{M}^{AB}_{ji} u^A_j + \gamma_1 \cdot r^B_i$$

where $\alpha_1, \beta_1, \gamma_1 \in [0, 1]$ specify the relative contributions to the final scores from different sources and we have $\alpha_1+\beta_1+\gamma_1=1$. Note that since $\widetilde{M}^{AB}$ and $\widetilde{M}^{BA}$ contain the dissimilarity values between the two sets of sentences, the second terms in the right hands of the above equations actually embody the negative reinforcement between the two sets of sentences. Different from (Li et al. 2008), the addition of all the terms in the right hands of the equations makes the algorithm more convenient to be solved in an iterative way.

We can also compute the consistency scores of the sentences in the two sets in a co-ranking process. We use two column vectors $v^A=[v^A_j]_{m\times 1}$ and $v^B=[v^B_i]_{n\times 1}$ to denote the consistency scores of the sentences in S^A and the sentences in S^B, respectively. Based on the second assumption, we can obtain the following equations:

$$v^A_j = \alpha_2 \sum_i \widetilde{M}^A_{ij} v^A_i + \beta_2 \sum_i \widetilde{W}^{BA}_{ij} v^B_i + \gamma_2 \cdot r^A_j$$

$$v^B_i = \alpha_2 \sum_j \widetilde{M}^B_{ji} v^B_j + \beta_2 \sum_j \widetilde{W}^{AB}_{ji} v^A_j + \gamma_2 \cdot r^B_i$$

where $\alpha_2, \beta_2, \gamma_2 \in [0, 1]$ specify the relative contributions to the final scores from different sources and we have $\alpha_2+\beta_2+\gamma_2=1$.

Then, we interconnect the two co-ranking processes based on our key assumption that the update score and the consistency score of each sentence is mutually exclusive. If the update score of a sentence is high, then the sentence contains significant and new information, which is not contained in the other document set; but if the consistency score of a sentence is high, then the sentence contains significant and shared information with the other document set. Therefore, the update score and the consistency score of a sentence are conflicting with each other, and they cannot be high at the same time.

The sum of the update score and the consistency score of each sentence is fixed to a particular value.

This assumption can be used to adjust the inaccurately assigned scores for the sentences.

Till now, the update scores and the consistency scores are computed by using a co-ranking process separately. Based on our new assumption, we can add the following constraints to interconnect the two co-ranking processes:

$$u_j^A + v_j^A = \varepsilon_j^A \qquad u_i^B + v_i^B = \varepsilon_i^B$$

where ε_j^A and ε_i^B are the specified fixed sum values for the sentences s^A_i and s^B_i. The values for different sentences may be different since they are unequally important in the document sets. In this study, we use the generic informativeness score of each sentence as the fixed sum value for the sentence. The generic informativeness score of a sentence is computed by using the basic graph-based ranking algorithm. Taking a sentence s^B_i in S^B as an example, the value can be computed in a recursive form as follows:

$$\varepsilon_i^B = \mu \cdot \sum_{all\, j \neq i} \varepsilon_j^B \cdot \widetilde{M}_{ji}^B + \frac{(1-\mu)}{\mathrm{n}}$$

where μ is the damping factor usually set to 0.85, as in the PageRank algorithm. The generic informativeness score of a sentence in S^A can be computed based on $\widetilde{M}^A$ in the same way.

In order to add the constraints to interconnect the two co-ranking processes, the constraints are executed as a normalization step. In particular, the following steps are iteratively performed until convergence. Note that all the scores are simply initialized to 1, and (t+1), (t) means the (t+1)-th and (t)-th iterations, respectively.

1) Compute the update scores of the sentences with the following equations:

$$(u_j^A)^{(t+1)} = \alpha_1 \sum_i \widetilde{M}_{ij}^A (u_i^A)^{(t)} + \beta_1 \sum_i \widetilde{M}_{ij}^{BA} (u_i^B)^{(t)} + \gamma_1 \cdot r_j^A$$

$$(u_i^B)^{(t+1)} = \alpha_1 \sum_j \widetilde{M}_{ji}^B (u_j^B)^{(t)} + \beta_1 \sum_j \widetilde{M}_{ji}^{AB} (u_j^A)^{(t)} + \gamma_1 \cdot r_i^B$$

$$(\boldsymbol{u}^A)^{(t+1)} = (\boldsymbol{u}^A)^{(t+1)} / \left\|(\boldsymbol{u}^A)^{(t+1)}\right\| \qquad (\boldsymbol{u}^B)^{(t+1)} = (\boldsymbol{u}^B)^{(t+1)} / \left\|(\boldsymbol{u}^B)^{(t+1)}\right\|$$

2) Compute the consistency scores of the sentences with the following equations:

$$(v_j^A)^{(t+1)} = \alpha_2 \sum_i \widetilde{M}_{ij}^A (v_i^A)^{(t)} + \beta_2 \sum_i \widetilde{W}_{ij}^{BA} (v_i^B)^{(t)} + \gamma_2 \cdot r_j^A$$

$$(v_i^B)^{(t+1)} = \alpha_2 \sum_j \widetilde{M}_{ji}^B (v_j^B)^{(t)} + \beta_2 \sum_j \widetilde{W}_{ji}^{AB} (v_j^A)^{(t)} + \gamma_2 \cdot r_i^B$$

$$(\boldsymbol{v}^A)^{(t+1)} = (\boldsymbol{v}^A)^{(t+1)} / \left\|(\boldsymbol{v}^A)^{(t+1)}\right\| \qquad (\boldsymbol{v}^B)^{(t+1)} = (\boldsymbol{v}^B)^{(t+1)} / \left\|(\boldsymbol{v}^B)^{(t+1)}\right\|$$

3) Add the constraints on the update scores and the consistency scores of the sentences by normalization with the following equations ($\boldsymbol{\zeta}^A$, $\boldsymbol{\eta}^B$ are temporary vectors):

$$\xi_j^A = (u_j^A)^{(t+1)} + (v_j^A)^{(t+1)} \qquad \eta_i^B = (u_i^B)^{(t+1)} + (v_i^B)^{(t+1)}$$

$$(u_j^A)^{(t+1)} = \varepsilon_j^A \cdot \frac{(u_j^A)^{(t+1)}}{\xi_j^A} \qquad (v_j^A)^{(t+1)} = \varepsilon_j^A \cdot \frac{(v_j^A)^{(t+1)}}{\xi_j^A}$$

$$(u_i^B)^{(t+1)} = \varepsilon_i^B \cdot \frac{(u_i^B)^{(t+1)}}{\eta_i^B} \qquad (v_i^B)^{(t+1)} = \varepsilon_i^B \cdot \frac{(v_i^B)^{(t+1)}}{\eta_i^B}$$

Finally, we obtain the update scores $\boldsymbol{u}^B$ for the sentences in the later document set D^B, and we apply the simple greedy algorithm in (Wan et al. 2007) to remove redundant sentences and select summary sentences until the summary length reaches the given limit. Note that in the experiments, the iteration number of the above algorithm is mostly around10, which is very efficient.

3 Empirical evaluation

3.1 Evaluation setup

In this study, we used the most recent update summarization task on TAC 2011 for evaluation purpose. NIST selected 44 topics, and two sets of 10 documents (set A and set B) were provided for each topic. The update task aims to create a 100-word summary of 10 documents in set B, with the assumption that the content of the first 10 documents in set A is already know to the reader. For each document set, NIST assessors have created 4 human summaries as reference (model) summaries. The sentences have already been split for the documents.

For each topic, we only used the topic title as the topic description. As a pre-processing step, we removed the very long or very short sentences, which are usually not good summary sentences. We also polished some sentences to make them more concise by applying simple rules, e.g. removing some clauses in the sentences. The sentences in the documents were then stemmed by using Porter's stemmer. Our proposed summarization method and the baseline methods were performed on the pre-processed document sets.

We used the ROUGE-1.5.5 toolkit[1] for evaluation, which was officially adopted by DUC for automatic summarization evaluation. The toolkit measures summary quality by counting overlapping units such as the n-gram, word sequences and word pairs between the candidate summary and the reference summary. The ROUGE toolkit reports separate scores for 1, 2, 3 and 4-gram, and also for longest common subsequence co-occurrences. In this study, we show three ROUGE scores in the experimental results[2]: ROUGE-1 (unigram-based), ROUGE-2 (bigram-based), and ROUGE-SU4 (based on skip bigram with a maximum skip distance of 4).

[1] http://www.berouge.com

[2] We used the options: -n 4 -w 1.2 -m -2 4 -u -c 95 -r 1000 -f A -p 0.5 -t 0 -a -l 100.

In the experiments, our proposed method is compared with the following baseline methods:

Lead: This baseline is provided by NIST, and it returns all the leading sentences (up to 100 words) in the most recent document. Baseline 1 provides a lower bound on what can be achieved with a simple fully automatic extractive summarizer.

Mead: This baseline is also provided by NIST, and it uses the MEAD automatic summarizer with all default settings, to produce summaries.

MMR: This baseline is based on the MMR criterion for selecting summary sentences with new information.

SinkManifoldRank: This baseline is a new graph based ranking method for update summarization, which is based on manifold ranking with sink points (Du et al. 2010).

CoRank: This baseline is the basic co-ranking method for update summarization, and it directly uses the co-ranking algorithm to compute the update score for each sentence, without considering the constraints between the update score and the consistency score.

For the baseline co-ranking method, we let $\gamma_1 = 0.15$, as in the PageRank algorithm, and thus we have $\alpha_1+\beta_1 = 0.85$, and $\alpha_1:\beta_1$ is empirically set to 0.7:0.3. For our method, we also let $\gamma_1=\gamma_2=0.15$. Thus we have $\alpha_1+\beta_1=\alpha_2+\beta_2= 0.85$, and $\alpha_1:\beta_1$ is set to 0.5:0.5 and $\alpha_2:\beta_2$ is set to 0.7:0.3.

3.2 Evaluation results

First, our proposed method is compared with the baseline methods, and the comparison results are shown in Table 1. In the table, the 95% confidence interval of each ROUGE score is given in brackets, which is reported by the ROUGE toolkit.

We can see from the table that our proposed method outperforms all the baseline methods over all three metrics. In particular, the baseline co-ranking method performs better than other baselines, and our proposed method can achieve better performance than the co-ranking method. The results demonstrate the good effectiveness of our proposed method.

Method	ROUGE-1	ROUGE-2	ROUGE-SU4
Our Method	**0.36795** [0.35673 - 0.37893]	**0.08838** [0.07894 - 0.09812]	**0.12716** [0.11931 - 0.13544]
CoRank	0.36143 [0.34755 - 0.37588]	0.07994 [0.06960 - 0.09048]	0.12164 [0.11274 - 0.13151]
SinkManifoldRank	0.31112 [0.29678 - 0.32543]	0.06198 [0.05456 - 0.06946]	0.10106 [0.09373 - 0.10878]
MMR	0.34724 [0.33493 - 0.36005]	0.07450 [0.06548 - 0.08367]	0.11529 [0.10780 - 0.12326]
Mead	0.28347 [0.27062 - 0.29696]	0.05903 [0.05037 - 0.06781]	0.09132 [0.08444 - 0.09850]
Lead	0.29378 [0.27684 - 0.30969]	0.05685 [0.04769 - 0.06680]	0.09449 [0.08637 - 0.10289]

TABLE 1 – Comparison results

Second, our proposed method is compared with the participating systems on TAC 2011. On TAC 2011, NIST received 48 runs from 24 participating teams. We rank the runs based on the ROUGE-2 scores, and list the top five runs for comparison. In addition, we also compute the average ROUGE scores. The comparison results are shown in Table 2.

We can see from the table that our proposed method ranks 4th out of all the runs over the ROUGE-2 metric. The performance of our proposed method is comparable with the top run's performance. We can also see that the performance values of our proposed method are much better than the average scores. Note that the top runs have leveraged world knowledge or various features, for example, the NUS1 run has used category knowledge in a supervised machine learning approach. However, our proposed method only uses the similarity/dissimilarity relationships between sentences in an unsupervised approach. The comparison results demonstrate that our proposed method is a competitive method for the update summarization task.

ID & Run Name	ROUGE-2	ROUGE-SU4
43 (NUS1)	0.09581	0.13080
25 (CLASSY2)	0.09259	0.12759
17 (NUS2)	0.08855	0.12792
Our Method	0.08838	0.12716
24 (PolyCom2)	0.08643	0.12803
35 (SIEL_IIITH2)	0.08538	0.12376
TAC Average	0.07053	0.11009

TABLE 2 – Comparison with top five runs (out of 48 runs, ranked by ROUGE-2) on TAC 2011

Conclusion and future work

In this paper, we propose a new method for update summarization, and it improves the basic co-ranking method by adding strict constraints and interconnecting two co-ranking processes. Evaluation results on the most recent TAC 2011 dataset demonstrate the good effectiveness of the proposed method, which can outperform a few baseline methods, and the performance is comparable to the top participating systems on TAC 2011.

In this study, we only use the topic title as the topic description, however, the title is usually very short, and we will investigate query expansion techniques to get a clearer topic description. We will also make use of the topic category specific features (i.e. the guided information) to improve our update summarization method in future work.

Acknowledgments

The work was supported by NSFC (61170166), Beijing Nova Program (2008B03) and National High-Tech R&D Program (2012AA011101).

References

Boudin, F., El-Bèze, M., and Torres-Moreno, J.-M. (2008). The LIA update summarization systems at TAC-2008. In *Proceedings of TAC2008.*

Du, P., Guo, J., Zhang, J., and Cheng, X. (2010). Manifold ranking with sink points for update summarization. In *Proceedings of CIKM2010.*

Fisher, S. and Roark, B. (2008). Query-focused supervised sentence ranking for update summaries. In *Proceeding of TAC2008.*

Li, W., Wei, F., Lu, Q., and He, Y. (2008). PNR^2: Ranking sentences with positive and negative reinforcement for query-oriented update summarization. In *Proceedings of COLING2008.*

Nastase, V., Filippova, K., and Ponzetto, S. P. (2008). Generating update summaries with spreading activation. In *Proceedings of TAC2008.*

Wan, X., Jia, H., Huang, S., and Xiao, J. (2011). Summarizing the Differences in Multilingual News. In *Proceedings of SIGIR2011.*

Wan, X., Yang, J., and Xiao, J. (2007). Manifold-ranking based topic-focused multi-document summarization. In *Proceedings of IJCAI-07.*

Wang, D. and Li, T. (2010). Document update summarization using incremental hierarchical clustering. In *Proceedings of CIKM2010.*

Sentence Realization with Unlexicalized Tree Linearization Grammars

Rui WANG   Yi ZHANG
DFKI GmbH, Germany
{ruiwang,yizhang}@dfki.de

Abstract

Sentence realization, as one of the important components in natural language generation, has taken a statistical swing in recent years. While most previous approaches make heavy usage of lexical information in terms of N-gram language models, we propose a novel method based on unlexicalized tree linearization grammars. We formally define the grammar representation and demonstrate learning from either treebanks with gold-standard annotations, or automatically parsed corpora. For the testing phase, we present a linear time deterministic algorithm to obtain the 1-best word order and further extend it to perform *exact* search for n-best linearizations. We carry out experiments on various languages and report state-of-the-art performance. In addition, we discuss the advantages of our method on both empirical aspects and its linguistic interpretability.

Keywords: Tree Linearization Grammar, Sentence Realization, Dependency Tree.

Proceedings of COLING 2012: Posters, pages 1301–1310,
COLING 2012, Mumbai, December 2012.

1 Introduction

Natural language generation (NLG) is the key processing task of producing natural language from some level of abstract representation, either syntactic or (more often) semantic. The long-standing research in NLG has gone through in-depth investigation into various sub-steps, including content planning, document structuring, lexical choices, surface realization, etc. The traditional generation systems typically rely on a rich set of annotation as input and is tightened to specific frameworks or internal representation, making the reuse of other natural language processing components difficult. Inspired by the successful application of statistical methods in natural language analysis, researchers shifted towards using standardized linguistic annotations to learn generation models. In particular, the now ever-so-popular dependency representation for syntacto-semantic structures has made its way into the sentence realization task, as evident by the recent Generation Challenge 2011 Surface Realization Shared Task (Belz et al., 2011). Given the full-connectedness of the input structure, the task of surface realization concerns mainly about the linearization process[1], which shall determine the ordering of words in the dependency structures.

While the earlier work like Langkilde and Knight (1998) showed that the N-gram language models can work well on the tree linearization, more recent study shows that improvements can be achieved by combining the language model outputs with discriminative classifiers (Filippova and Strube, 2009; Bohnet et al., 2010). On the other hand, we see that relatively few results have been reported on a grammar-based approach, where linearization rules are used instead to determine the word order within a given structured input.

In this paper, we use **tree linearization grammars** to specify the local linearization constraints in bilexical single-headed dependency trees. Unlexicalized linearization rules and their probabilities can be learned easily from the treebank. By using a dependency parser, we expand the grammar extraction to **automatically parsed** dependency structures as well. The linearization model is **fully generative**, which can produce N-best word orders for each dependency input. Detailed evaluation and error analysis on **multiple languages** show that our grammar-based linearization approach achieves state-of-the-art performance without language specific tuning or detailed feature engineering. The resulting linearization rules are comprehensible and reflect linguistic intuitions.

2 Unlexicalized Tree Linearization Grammar

The task of tree linearization takes the unordered single-headed bilexical dependency tree as input, and produces the surface sentence with determined word order. We define the tree linearization grammar to be a set of rules that licenses the legitimate linearization of the tree.

More specifically, we define a *local configuration* $\mathscr{C} = \langle w_0, \{\langle r_1, w_1\rangle, \cdots, \langle r_n, w_n\rangle\}\rangle$ to be an unordered dependency tree of height 1, with w_0 as the *head*, and $\{w_1, w_2, \cdots, w_n\}$ as the immediate *dependents* (daughters) with corresponding dependency relations $\{r_1, r_2, \cdots, r_n\}$. A linearization rule $\mathscr{L}$ is defined to be:

$$\mathscr{L} : \mathscr{C} \Rightarrow \langle w'_0, w'_1, \cdots, w'_n\rangle \quad s.t. \quad \begin{array}{l} \forall i, 0 \le i \le n, w'_i \in \{w_0, \cdots, w_n\} \\ \forall i, j, 0 \le i, j \le n, w'_i = w'_j \text{iff } i = j \end{array} \tag{1}$$

which determines the complete order of all the words on the LHS of the local configuration. For an unlexicalized tree linearization rule, w_i are syntactic categories instead of words. In our later experiments, we use either coarse- or fine-grained parts-of-speech as representation of words in the configurations. Below is an example local configuration with two alternative linearization rules:

[1]For morphologically-rich languages, an additional inflection realizer is needed as a postprocessor.

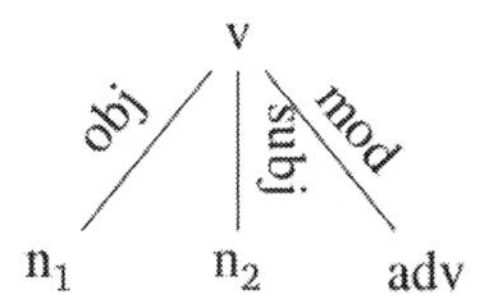

$\Rightarrow\langle n_2, adv, v, n_1\rangle$

$\Rightarrow\langle n_2, v, n_1, adv\rangle$

Assuming the projectivity of the dependency structure, we can find the linearization of the complete sentence if the linearization of each local configuration is determined by one of the rules. In practice, the linearization of many local configurations are ambiguous. We define a probabilistic tree linearization grammar by attaching a conditional probability distribution to the rules:

$$\mathbf{Pr}: \mathscr{L} \rightarrow [0,1] s.t. \forall \mathscr{C} \in \mathscr{C}, \sum_{\forall \mathscr{L} \in \mathscr{L}, LHS(\mathscr{L})=\mathscr{C}} \mathtt{Pr}(\mathscr{L}) = 1 \tag{2}$$

where $\mathscr{C}$ is the set of all local configurations, and $\mathscr{L}$ the set of all linearization rules in the grammar. The probability of a sentence linearization given an input dependency structure $\mathscr{D}$ is then defined as: $P(\mathscr{L}_{\mathscr{D}}) = \prod_{\mathscr{L} \in \mathscr{L}_{\mathscr{D}}} \mathtt{Pr}(\mathscr{L})$, where $\mathscr{L}_{\mathscr{D}}$ is the linearization of the complete sentence with the application of one linearization rule $\mathscr{L}$ on each local configuration in the input $\mathscr{D}$.

Note that although we assume the projectivity of the dependency structure in this paper, it is possible to extend the definition of the tree linearization grammar to also encode the discontinuities in the syntactic structure (e.g., by explicitly marking the gaps in the structure and pointers to their fillers). Thorough investigation in this direction belongs to our future work. Nevertheless, empirical results from section 4 suggest that non-projectivity is not a major source of errors for the languages and datasets used in our experiments.

Similar to the treebank-based approach to grammar extraction for parsing, we extract linearization rules from the annotated dependency treebank with determined word order. Each local configuration and its linearization is then gathered as a rule. Due to the unlexicalized approach we take, this produces a relatively small grammar which can be manually interpreted. To estimate the rule probabilities **Pr**, we simply use the maximum likelihood estimation: $\mathtt{Pr}(\mathscr{L}) = \frac{Freq(\mathscr{L})}{Freq(LHS(\mathscr{L}))}$.

3 *N*-Best Tree Linearization

We start with the grammar-based deterministic tree linearization algorithm which outputs 1-best linearization by recursively finding the best linearization for each local configuration. The time complexity of the algorithm is $\mathscr{O}(n)$, where n is the number of words in the dependency tree.

The n-best linearization algorithm is an extension to the 1-best procedure. Each `hypothesis` represents a state in the search for the n-best linearizations for the sub-tree under a given `node`. It further relies on a vector `indices`, where `indices[0]` identifies the index of the linearization rule, and the remaining elements `indices[1..k]` point to the sub-states in the n-best linearization of the dependents. Top level procedure `linearize-node(root,n)` will iteratively instantiate the top-n linearization hypothesis of the root. The main procedure `hypothesize-node(node, i)` creates the $\mathtt{i}^{th}$ best hypothesis of `node`, which recursively finds the linearization of the sub-trees.

According to our definition, the linearization probability of a given node n can be calculated by multiplying the rule probability with the sub-linearization probabilities of the dependents:

$$P(\mathscr{L}_n) = \mathtt{Pr}(rule(\mathscr{L}_n)) * \prod_{d \in dependents(n)} P(\mathscr{L}_d) \tag{3}$$

```
procedure linearize-node(root, n) ≡
  results ← ⟨⟩; i ← 0;
  do
    hypothesis ← hypothesize-node(root, i); i ← i + 1;
    if (not hypothesis) break;
    new ← instantiate-hypothesis(hypothesis);
    n ← n − 1; results ← results ⊕ ⟨new⟩;
  while (n ≥ 1);
  return results;

procedure hypothesize-node(node, i) ≡
  if (node.hypotheses[i]) return node.hypotheses[i];
  if (i = 0) then
    node.rules ←sorted-rules(node.config); indices ← ⟨0⟩
    daughters ← ⟨⟩;
    for each (dnode in node.dependents) do
      daughters ← daughters ⊕ ⟨hypothesize-node(dnode, 0)⟩;
      indices ← indices ⊕ ⟨0⟩;
    new-hypothesis(node, daughters, indices);
  if (hypothesis ← node.agenda.pop()) then
    for each (indices in advance-indices(hypothesis.indices)) do
      daughters ← ⟨⟩;
      for each (dnode in node.dependents) each (j in indices[1..k]) do
        daughter ← hypothesize-node(dnode, j);
        if (not daughter) then daughters ← ⟨⟩; break
        daughters ← daughters ⊕ ⟨daughter⟩;
      if (daughters) then new-hypothesis(node, daughters, indices)
    node.hypotheses[i] ← hypothesis;
    return hypothesis;

procedure new-hypothesis(node, daughters, indices) ≡
  hypothesis ← new hypothesis(node, daughters, indices);
  node.agenda.insert(score-hypothesis(hypothesis), hypothesis);
```

Figure 1: N-best tree linearization algorithm

This calculation is achieved within the procedure `score-hypothesis`. Since the nth best linearization must be different from one of the top $n-1$ linearizations in just one position (either one of the dependents' sub-linearization or the linearization rule chosen for the top node), `advance-indices` will find all such possibilities. With such *lazy* expansion of the search frontier, only the immediate candidates are added to the local agenda of each node.

4 Experiments

For the evaluation, we use the dependency treebanks for multiple languages from the CoNLL-shared task 2009[2] (Hajič et al., 2009). Additional unlabeled English texts from L.A. Times & Washington Post of the North American News Text (NANC) (Supplement)[3] are used for training the English models. Testing results are reported on the development sets of the CoNLL dependency treebanks. In addition to the automatic metrics such as BLEU (Papineni et al., 2002) and Ulam's distance (Birch et al., 2010), we also manually evaluate the quality of the system outputs (Section 4.3).

4.1 Basic Models

For the basic models, we compare our grammar-based approaches with three baselines, Random, N-Gram, and Rank. The first baseline simply produces a random order of the words; the second model can be viewed as a simplified version of (Guo et al., 2011)'s basic model[4]; and the third model

[2] `http://ufal.mff.cuni.cz/conll2009-st/index.html`

[3] `http://www.ldc.upenn.edu/Catalog/CatalogEntry.jsp?catalogId=LDC98T30`

[4] Instead of using grammatical functions derived from lexical functional grammar (LFG), we use the dependency relation and the parts-of-speech as our syntactic categories. For the previous example, we obtain N-gram counts from

is a log-linear model, which is trained on each word's relative position in its local configuration[5]. For the main approach based on linearization grammars, we have two configurations using either coarse- or fine-grained part-of-speech (CPOS vs. POS)[6]. Notice that the baseline system N-Gram can also choose between CPOS and POS.

In Table 1, 'Covered' rows report the results on the subcorpus whose sentences are fully covered by the grammar, and 'Overall' rows report the results on the complete test corpus with Rank baseline as the backoff model for the out-of-grammar configurations. As Rank can only produce 1-best linearization, we set the score for that configuration as 1 for further calculation in Equation (3). '1-best' is the deterministic tree linearization result, while 'upper bound (1000)' gives the upper bound of n-best linearization with $n = 1000$.

Models		POS	CPOS	Baselines		
				Rank	N-Gram	Random
Coverage	Sent. (1334)	451 (33.8%)	711 (53.3%)	-	-	-
	Config. (17282)	15843 (91.7%)	16423 (95.0%)			
BLEU						
Covered	1-best	92.65	90.64	-	-	-
	upper bound (1000)	96.31	95.31			
Overall	1-best	81.63	**83.28**	73.09	43.22	32.34
	upper bound (1000)	84.08	87.13	-	66.55	44.90

Table 1: Performance of the basic models

We observe that although the grammar with fine-grained POS achieves better performance on the data covered by the grammar, the coverage is relatively low. On the overall results, when combined with the Rank backoff model, the CPOS model achieves a good balance between 'precision' and 'recall', and also outperforms all the baselines with large margins (10+ BLEU points). We will refer to this system as our Base model for the rest of this section.

While the configuration level coverage is over 95%, the Base grammar only achieves full coverage on 53% of the sentences. We investigate the possible ways of expanding the coverage of the linearization grammar in Section 4.2. Also, when comparing the Base model with the n-best upper bound, the difference of 4 BLEU points suggests that a better ranking model can potentially achieve further improvements on the linearization. This will be discussed in Section 4.3.

4.2 Experiments with Automatically Parsed Data

Self-training has been shown to be effective for parser training (McClosky et al., 2006). It expands the training observations on new texts with hypothesized annotation produced by a base model. In our case, we can obtain further linearization observations from unannotated sentences, and rely on a parser to produce the dependency structures[7].

We use a state-of-the-art dependency parser, MSTParser (McDonald et al., 2005), and train it with the same data with gold-standard dependency annotations using the second order features and a projective decoder. For the additional data, we use a fragment of the NANC corpus (765670

sequences $\langle n|subj, adv|mod, v|hd, n_1|obj\rangle$ and $\langle n_2|subj, v|hd, n_1|obj, adv|mod\rangle$. On top of such instances from all the configurations, we train a tri-gram model.

[5]The features we use include token features, lemma and part-of-speech, and the dependency relation. We differentiate parent and children nodes by adding different prefixes.

[6]In the CoNLL data, the coarse-grained POS is the first character of the fine-grained POS.

[7]Unlike parser self-training, we do not update the parsing model, but expect the extra observations to help improve the coverage of the linearization grammar.

sentences in total). The 1-best linearization with the additional corpus improved from 83.28 to 83.94 BLEU, with the oracle (1000) upper-bound improved from 87.13 to 88.82 BLEU.

Although the performance on the grammar-covered sentences drops slightly, the overall performance improves steadily for both 1-best and the upper bound. We also notice that on such high range BLEU scores (above 80), the differences are less indicative of the actual quality of the linearization. We will address this issue in the next section.

4.3 Manual Analysis

In the previous experiments, we have observed the performance difference between the 1-best result and the n-best upper bound. In an attempt to improve the selection of the best linearization, we incorporate a simple tri-gram language model at the surface level to re-rank the n-best output of the Base model (LM-Rerank), and hope it will compensate for the lack of lexical information in our unlexicalized linearization grammar. We train the language model on the same data and choose $n = 1000$.

When we perform a pair-wise comparison of the output from these two systems, the results show that in 28% of the cases Base is better; and only in 14% of the cases LM-Rerank is better. To further investigate the difference between the two systems, we carry out a manual analysis on two aspects: 1) *comprehensiveness* and 2) *grammaticality*, which are similar to the measurements used in the surface realization evaluation (Belz et al., 2011). In particular, we have three levels of judgement for both criteria, ranging from 0 to 2. As both systems output exactly the same gold standard linearizations in almost half of the cases, we calculate the BLEU score for each sentence and randomly sample 100 sentences between the range $(75.0, 90.0]$. This allows us to 'zoom in' on the (error) characteristics of the two systems.

Each sentence from both systems is annotated by two annotators on two criteria with reference to the gold standard linearization. For both criteria, the annotations are mostly agreed, with Cohen's Kappa scores (Cohen, 1960) $\kappa = 0.83$ for *comprehensiveness* and $\kappa = 0.87$ for *grammaticality*. Table 2 shows the results only on the agreed cases.

	Comprehensiveness	*Grammaticality*	Perfect
Base	84.1%	**77.1%**	28.8%
LM-Rerank	**90.1%**	73.2%	36.7%

Table 2: Agreed manual evaluation results on sentences within BLEU range $(75.0, 90.0]$

We sum up the scores for both criteria separately, and divide by a sum of maximal scores. The 'Perfect' column indicates the portion of sentences which get full scores for both criteria, i.e., they are correct and fluent, though being different from the gold standard.

Notice that the sampled sentences do not reflect the performance of two configurations as a whole due to the selection process. However, the differences on two criteria reflect different characteristics of the two systems. Base tends to output grammatical linearization, though the results could be less fluent and hard to comprehend; LM-Rerank is more fluent and comprehensible, though might violate grammaticality. Furthermore, the result indicates that within this BLEU range about 1/3 of the output sentences are perfect linearization, although the BLEU scores are not 1. We view this issue as the inadequacy of 1-best evaluation for this task, as among the n-best output, we have observed more than one correct realizations. However, proposing a better evaluation method is out of the scope of this paper, which we will leave for our future work.

Sentences
Gold: *[" **The market is overvalued , not cheap ,** " **says**] Alan Gaines of the New York money - management firm Gaines Berland .*
System: *Alan Gaines of the New York money - management firm Gaines Berland [**says** , " **The market is overvalued , not cheap .** "]*
Gold: ... *than many taxpayers working at the same kinds of jobs and [**perhaps**] supporting families .*
System: ... *than many taxpayers [**perhaps**] working at the same kinds of jobs and supporting families .*
Gold: ... *to set [**aside**] provisions covering all its C$ 1.17 billion in non - Mexican LDC debt .*
System: ... *to set provisions covering all C$ its 1.17 billion in non - Mexican LDC debt [**aside**] .*
Gold: *Good service programs require recruitment , screening , training and supervision – [**all of high quality**] .*
System: *[**all of high quality**] – Good service programs require recruitment , screening , training and supervision .*

Table 3: Examples of the system output compared with the gold standard

We list several examples of the system output in Table 3. One major source of errors is the clustering of punctuations, in particular, commas, as they are not differentiable at the configuration level for the backoff model Rank. This occurs less with the LM-Rerank model. The free movement of modifiers (adjectives, adverbs, modifying prepositional phrases, etc.) poses a serious challenge for automatic evaluation, as in most cases the meaning does not change. However, in the second example in the table, due to the coordinate structure, the movement of *"perhaps"* does change the meaning of the sentence. Furthermore, the context-freeness of the linearization rules do not concern the *'heaviness'* of the dependent NP, hence (wrongly) preferring the unnatural placement of *"aside"* to the end of the sentence in the third example. The last example shows that even when the generated sentence is perfectly grammatical, the discourse semantics could change drastically.

4.4 Multilinguality

To investigate the multilingual applicability of our approach, we further experiment with five more languages: Catalan (CA), Chinese (CN), Czech (CZ), German (DE), and Spanish (ES). There is no language-specific tuning, so this is achieved easily with the availability of the CoNLL 2009 Shared Task datasets. We show some basic statistics of the datasets in Table 4 as well as the system performance under two automatic measurements: BLEU and Ulam's distance. The latter is the minimum number of single item movements of arbitrary length required to transform one permutation into another (Ulam, 1972), which is the same as the 'di' measurement used by Bohnet et al. (2010) and others.

Languages		CA	CN	CZ	EN	DE	ES
No. of CPOS Tag		12	13	12	24	10	12
Avg. Token / Sent.		31.0	30.0	16.8	25.0	16.0	30.4
Grammar							
Avg. Config. / Sent.		13.1	14.0	8.3	12.4	6.0	13.2
Coverage	Sent.	578 / 1724 (33.5%)	790 / 1762 (44.8%)	498 / 5228 (9.5%)	724 / 1334 (54.3%)	1512 / 2000 (**75.6%**)	650 / 1655 (39.3%)
	Config.	22526 / 24546 (91.8%)	24749 / 26250 (94.3%)	43552 / 49751 (87.5%)	16536 / 17369 (95.2%)	11925 / 12503 (**95.4%**)	21920 / 23511 (93.2%)
BLEU							
Covered	1-best	84.51	88.67	82.00	91.95	78.52	79.93
	upper bound (1000)	91.77	94.49	93.60	96.20	88.01	89.78
Overall	1-best	75.79	**81.48**	66.59	**84.89**	73.85	73.10
	upper bound (1000)	80.61	86.52	76.85	88.75	82.09	79.75
Ulam's distance							
Covered	1-best	0.890	0.946	0.867	0.950	0.857	0.871
	upper bound (1000)	0.949	0.973	0.965	0.978	0.934	0.941
Overall	1-best	0.838	**0.891**	0.771	**0.911**	0.829	0.820
	upper bound (1000)	0.875	0.914	0.856	0.934	0.897	0.869

Table 4: Performance of the multilingual models

Notice that the best coverage of the grammar is on the German data, which is mainly due to the short average sentence length (16.0 tokens / sentence) and the flatness of the tree (6.0 configurations / sentence). However, the high coverage does not guarantee good performance, as for each configuration, the linearization selection could still be ambiguous. Overall, the best performances come from English and Chinese, whose word orders are relatively strict; while Czech has the worst performance due to its relatively free word order, and the coverage of the grammar is also the lowest.

We observe 803 non-projective inputs from the Czech test set (15.4%), and 106 sentences from German (5.3%); for the other languages, almost all the trees are projective. The proposal of Bohnet et al. (2012) to use a separate classifier to predict the lifting of non-projective edges in a dependency tree can be combined with the use of linearization rules in our approach in the future.

Note that although we test our models on the same data source as the surface realization shared task[8], subtle differences in the preprocessing of the data and/or the evaluation scripts make the direct comparison to previously reported results difficult. Some comparison of different approaches and reported results will be discussed in the next section.

5 Discussion and Future Work

Several works on statistical surface realization have been reported recently. Ringger et al. (2004) proposed several models, and achieved 83.6 BLEU score on the same data source.They also tested their approaches on French and German data, but with predicate-argument structures as input. One of the interesting features of our approach is the generative nature of the model. Unlike the previous work of (Filippova and Strube, 2009; Bohnet et al., 2010) who relied on discriminative modeling for the selection of the realization, our approach actually produces the realization probabilities, and does not rely on ad hoc pruning of the search space. Filippova and Strube (2009) (and their previous paper) reported 0.88 Ulam's distance for English and 0.87 for German, but their evaluation is at the clause level instead of full sentences. Bohnet et al. (2010)'s experiments were also on the CoNLL datasets, achieving 85 BLEU score for Chinese, 89.4 for English, 73.5 for German, and 78 for Spanish. Their system was ranked the first place in the surface realization shared task, followed by Guo et al. (2011)'s dependency-based N-gram approach. The permutation filtering technique they use is essentially similar to our linearization rules. As we show in the manual evaluation, the BLEU scores are not always indicative (especially at the higher range) of the generation quality, in the future, we are interested in a more elaborate manual analysis of their results.

While we are achieving satisfying results with our method on multiple languages without language-specific tuning, it should be noted that the dependency tree linearization task is only part of the sentence realization workflow, along with other subtasks such as lexical choices, morphological realizer, etc. The linearization rules learned are not a full-fledged grammar covering the entire syntactic layer of the language, but rather the complements to the morphological or grammatical relations given by the dependency inputs and they specify the linear precedence of the words. In comparison to the other sentence realization systems which relies on richer frameworks and accept more abstract semantic inputs, our task does not touch the syntacto-semantic interface. Nevertheless, it is interesting to note that one of the key challenges in semantics-based sentence realization is the lack of word-order constraints, hence the inefficiency (Carroll et al., 1999; Carroll and Oepen, 2005; Espinosa et al., 2008). With our efficient grammar-based linearization algorithms, extra efficiency boost to the deeper generation workflow can be achieved by pruning the implausible orderings.

Acknowledgments

The work is partially supported by the *Deependance* project funded by BMBF (01IW11003).

[8]Unfortunately, we were not able to acquire the datasets after the shared task has ended.

References

Belz, A., White, M., Espinosa, D., Kow, E., Hogan, D., and Stent, A. (2011). The first surface realisation shared task: Overview and evaluation results. In *Proceedings of the Generation Challenges Session at the 13th European Workshop on Natural Language Generation*, pages 217–226, Nancy, France. Association for Computational Linguistics.

Birch, A., Osborne, M., and Blunsom, P. (2010). Metrics for MT evaluation: evaluating reordering. *Machine Translation*, pages 1–12.

Bohnet, B., Björkelund, A., Kuhn, J., Seeker, W., and Zarriess, S. (2012). Generating non-projective word order in statistical linearization. In *Proceedings of the 2012 Joint Conference on Empirical Methods in Natural Language Processing and Computational Natural Language Learning*, pages 928–939, Jeju Island, Korea. Association for Computational Linguistics.

Bohnet, B., Wanner, L., Mill, S., and Burga, A. (2010). Broad coverage multilingual deep sentence generation with a stochastic multi-level realizer. In *Proceedings of the 23rd International Conference on Computational Linguistics (Coling 2010)*, pages 98–106, Beijing, China.

Carroll, J., Copestake, A., Flickinger, D., and Poznanski, V. (1999). An efficient chart generator for (semi-)lexicalist grammars. In *Proceedings of the 7th European Workshop on Natural Language Generation*, pages 86–95, Toulouse, France.

Carroll, J. and Oepen, S. (2005). High-efficiency realization for a wide-coverage unification grammar. In Dale, R. and Wong, K. F., editors, *Proceedings of the 2nd International Joint Conference on Natural Language Processing*, pages 165–176, Jeju, Korea.

Cohen, J. (1960). A Coefficient of Agreement for Nominal Scales. *Educational and Psychological Measurement*, 20(1):37.

Espinosa, D., White, M., and Mehay, D. (2008). Hypertagging: Supertagging for surface realization with CCG. In *Proceedings of ACL-08: HLT*, pages 183–191, Columbus, Ohio. Association for Computational Linguistics.

Filippova, K. and Strube, M. (2009). Tree linearization in english: Improving language model based approaches. In *Proceedings of Human Language Technologies: The 2009 Annual Conference of the North American Chapter of the Association for Computational Linguistics, Companion Volume: Short Papers*, pages 225–228, Boulder, Colorado.

Guo, Y., Wang, H., and van Genabith, J. (2011). Dependency-based n-gram models for general purpose sentence realisation. *Natural Language Engineering*, 17(04):455–483.

Hajič, J., Ciaramita, M., Johansson, R., Kawahara, D., Martí, M. A., Màrquez, L., Meyers, A., Nivre, J., Padó, S., Štěpánek, J., Straňák, P., Surdeanu, M., Xue, N., and Zhang, Y. (2009). The conll-2009 shared task: Syntactic and semantic dependencies in multiple languages. In *Proceedings of the Thirteenth Conference on Computational Natural Language Learning (CoNLL 2009): Shared Task*, pages 1–18, Boulder, Colorado. Association for Computational Linguistics.

Langkilde, I. and Knight, K. (1998). Generation that exploits corpus-based statistical knowledge. In *Proceedings of the 36th Annual Meeting of the Association for Computational Linguistics and 17th International Conference on Computational Linguistics, Volume 1*, pages 704–710, Montreal, Quebec, Canada.

McClosky, D., Charniak, E., and Johnson, M. (2006). Effective self-training for parsing. In *Proceedings of the Conference on Human Language Technology and North American chapter of the Association for Computational Linguistics (HLT-NAACL 2006)*, Brooklyn, New York, USA. Association for Computational Linguistics.

McDonald, R., Pereira, F., Ribarov, K., and Hajic, J. (2005). Non-Projective Dependency Parsing using Spanning Tree Algorithms. In *Proceedings of HLT-EMNLP 2005*, pages 523–530.

Papineni, K., Roukos, S., Ward, T., and Zhu, W.-J. (2002). Bleu: a method for automatic evaluation of machine translation. In *Proceedings of 40th Annual Meeting of the Association for Computational Linguistics*, pages 311–318, Philadelphia, Pennsylvania, USA.

Ringger, E., Gamon, M., Moore, R. C., Rojas, D., Smets, M., and Corston-Oliver, S. (2004). Linguistically informed statistical models of constituent structure for ordering in sentence realization. In *Proceedings of Coling 2004*, pages 673–679, Geneva, Switzerland. COLING.

Ulam, S. M. (1972). Some ideas and prospects in biomathematics. *Annual Review of Biophysics and Bioengineering*, pages 277–292.

Exploiting Discourse Relations for Sentiment Analysis

Fei Wang[1] Yunfang Wu [1] Likun Qiu[2]
(1) Institute of Computational Linguistics, Peking University
(2) School of Chinese Language and Literature, Ludong University
sxjzwangfei@163.com, wuyf@pku.edu.cn, qiulikun@gmail.com

ABSTRACT

The overall sentiment of a text is critically affected by its discourse structure. By splitting a text into text spans with different discourse relations, we automatically train the weights of different relations in accordance with their importance, and then make use of discourse structure knowledge to improve sentiment classification. In this paper, we utilize explicit connectives to predict discourse relations, and then propose several methods to incorporate discourse relation knowledge to the task of sentiment analysis. All our methods integrating discourse relations perform better than the baseline methods, validating the effectiveness of using discourse relations in Chinese sentiment analysis. We also automatically find out the most influential discourse relations and connectives in sentiment analysis.

TITLE AND ABSTRACT IN CHINESE

基于句际关系的情感分析方法

文档情感与其篇章结构息息相关。将一篇文档切分成具有不同句际关系的文本语段，可以自动训练并获得表征不同句际关系重要性的权重，进而利用这些篇章结构信息来提升情感分析的性能。本文利用显性关联标记来预测句际关系，继而提出了多种不同的方法利用句际关系来进行情感分析。实验结果表明，融合句际关系的方法均优于前人的情感分析方法，证明了句际关系对于汉语篇章情感分析的重要作用。本文还自动发现了情感计算中显要的句际关系类型和显要的关联标记。

KEYWORDS: sentiment analysis; discourse relation; connective.
KEYWORDS IN CHINESE：情感分析；句际关系；关联标记

Proceedings of COLING 2012: Posters, pages 1311–1320,
COLING 2012, Mumbai, December 2012.

1 Introduction

Sentiment analysis has attracted considerable attention in the field of natural language processing. Previous work on this problem falls into three groups: opinion mining of documents, sentiment classification of sentences and polarity prediction of words. Recently, the importance of discourse relations in sentiment analysis has been increasingly recognized.

In traditional lexicon-based methods, all words and sentences are treated equally, ignoring the structural aspects of a text. However, discourse structure knowledge is vital to some texts for polarity prediction. Take (1) as an example:

(1) 诺基亚5800屏幕很好| Nokia 5800's screen is very good, 操作也很方便| the operation is convenient, 通话质量也不错| the call quality is good, 但是外形偏女性化| but the shape is feminine, 而且电池不耐用| and the battery life is short, 总之我觉得不值| in general, I think it is not worth buying.

Three words "很好|very good", "方便|convenient" and "不错|good" are positive, and three words "女性化|feminine", "不耐用|short" and "不值|not worth" are negative. The overall sentiment of document (1) would be predicted as neutral using the lexicon-based method, however, it is negative.

By analysing a text's discourse structure, a text is split into spans with different semantic relations. With this discourse knowledge, we assign text spans with different weights in accordance with their contribution to the overall sentiment of a document. For example in document (1), the span introduced by connective "但是|but" has higher degree of importance, denoting a Contrast relation; the span introduced by connective "总之|in general" has the highest degree of importance, denoting a Generalization relation. This leads to the overall negative sentiment.

This paper exploits discourse relations by using explicit connectives for sentiment classification of texts, achieving better results than state of the art method. Our contributions are: (1) For the first time, we propose a relatively complete discourse relation hierarchy and list their corresponding connectives in Chinese, and validate their effectiveness in sentiment analysis; (2) We conduct weighting schemes at various granularities of discourse relations; (3) We find out the influential discourse relations and connectives that contribute most to the overall meaning of texts.

2 Related Work

In sentiment analysis, we can refer to Pang and Lee (2008) for an in-depth survey. For discourse parsing, we can refer to Joty et al. (2012), Hernault et al. (2010) and Wang et al. (2010) for recent progresses. Polanyi and Zaenen (2006) argue that polarity calculation is critically affected by discourse structure. In applying discourse relations to sentiment analysis, previous work can be divided into two groups: constraint-based approaches and weight-based schemes.

Somasundaran et al. (2008) and Somasundaran et al (2009) represent reinforce and non-reinforce relations in opinion frame. For example, text spans targeted at the same entity with reinforce relations are constrained to have same polarities, while text spans targeted at opposing entities with reinforce relations are constrained to have opposite polarities. Narayanan et al. (2009) apply conditional relations to improve sentiment analysis. Zhou et al. (2011) describe several constrains to eliminate the intra-sentence polarity ambiguities. For example, a sentence holding Contrast relation contains two text spans with opposite polarities.

Taboada et al. (2008) hypothesize that sentiment words expressed in nuclei are more important than words in satellites, and thus give different weights (1.5 vs. 0.5) to words in nuclei and satellites. Heerschop et al. (2011) hypothesize that not only nuclei and satellites should be weighted differently; satellites of different discourse relations should also be weighted differently.

In this paper, we adopt Rhetorical Structure Theory (RST) (Mann and Thompson, 1988) as the basis of discourse relations, and we follow the weighting scheme. Different from previous work, we hypothesize: (1) nuclei of different relations and satellites of different relations should all be weighted differently; (2) some relations are more important than other relations in sentiment classification.

3 Our Method

3.1 Overview

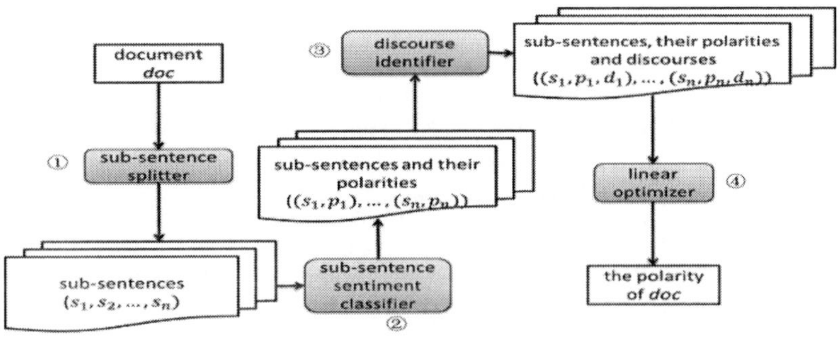

FIGURE 1 – Overview of our method

The proposed method consists of 4 main steps, as shown in Figure 1. First, a document doc is divided into sub-sentences $(s_1, s_2, ...s_n)$ by sub-sentence splitter. Second, a polarity p_i is assigned to each sub-sentence s_i by sub-sentence sentiment classifier. Third, discourse identifier identifies the discourse type d_i holding by sub-sentence s_i. Last, linear optimizer generates the polarity of the document by calculating the weighted sum of sub-sentences in accordance with their discourse types.

3.2 Sub-sentence Splitter

Sub-sentence splitter utilizes punctuation marks, including comma, period, semicolon, exclamation mark and question mark, to divide a sentence into sub-sentences. A document consists of one or more sentences, and a sentence consists of one or more sub-sentences. For example in document (1), it consists 6 sub-sentences. We treat intra-sentence and inter-sentence relations equally, because Chinese comma can signal both intra- and inter- sentence boundaries (Yang and Xue, 2012).

3.3 Sub-sentence Sentiment Classifier

The polarity of each sub-sentence p_i is generated by the Basic SELC model proposed by Qiu et al. (2009), a state of the art work. In Basic SELC model, some documents are initially classified based on a sentiment dictionary (HowNet[1]); and then more sentiment-bearing n-grams are learned and more documents are classified through an iterative process with negative/positive ratio control.

For each sub-sentence s_i, the polarity p_i is assigned with +1 if the sub-sentence is positive, and −1 if the sub-sentence is negative, and 0 if the sub-sentence is neutral.

Our method is a little different from the work of Taboada et al. (2008) and Heerschop et al. (2011), where discourse weights are multiplied with individual sentiment-bearing words (word-based method for short). However in our method, relation weights are multiplied directly with sub-sentences (sub-sentence-based method for short).

We also conduct a word-based method using HowNet, but it gives us a poor baseline with an F-score of 56.9% without using discourse relations. So we adopt the sub-sentence-based method that provides a relatively high baseline with an F-score of 83.55% (as shown in Table 3). What's more, the sub-sentence-based method is more consistent with people's intuition on discourse structure.

3.4 Discourse Identifier

Discourse identifier tags each sub-sentence s_i with a discourse type d_i. Discourse relation defines the relationship between two adjacent sub-sentences, while discourse type represents the relationship from the view of each component sub-sentence. For example, there is a Contrast relation between the two sub-sentences in sentence (2).

(2) 虽说是大牌| although it is a famous brand, 但是没感觉出大牌的味道| (but) I didn't feel anything extraordinary.

In sentence (2), the second sub-sentence is the Head (nucleus) of the sentence while the first sub-sentence is the Modifier (satellite). Thus, we will assign discourse type ContrastH to the second sub-sentence and ContrastM to the first one. For those relations with multi-nucleus, we assign all the component sub-sentences with the same relation type.

The research on Chinese discourse parsing has just begun, and there isn't a gold standard for Chinese discourse relation annotation in previous work. So we develop a specification of Chinese discourse relation hierarchy, as shown in Table 1. In this task, we remove a few connectives that may cause relation ambiguities, and we only list the discourse types that have explicit connectives. In the absence of Chinese discourse parser, we exploit explicit connectives to predict the discourse types. Sub-sentences introduced with specific connectives (Table 1) will be assigned with the corresponding discourse types, and sub-sentences without explicit connectives will be tagged with None.

For single-nucleus relations (except List), a head sub-sentence can appear by itself, while a modifier sub-sentence must co-occur with its corresponding head. So, if one modifier sub-sentence appears alone, we will guess the subsequent sub-sentence as its head. For example:

（3）如果拿它看书| if you want to read e-books on this mp4，眼睛会非常累|your eyes would be very tired.

The first sub-sentences is tagged as HypotheticalM because of connective "如果|if". Though the second sub-sentence contains no connective, it would still be guessed as the head of the first sub-sentence and thus labelled as HypotheticalH. As a result, for a specific relation, there are more head instances than modifier ones, as shown in Table 2.

[1] http://www.keenage.com/download/sentiment.rar

	Discourse relation	Discourse type	Connectives
联合关系 Multi-nucleus	等立Coordinate	Coordinate	同时|于此同时|另外|此外|再则|另一方面|一边|时而
	时序 Temporal	Temporal	尔后|接下来|起初|而后|随即|随后|继而
	选择 Alternative	Alternative	或|或者|或是|或者说|抑或|要么|或则|宁可|宁肯|宁愿|不如说|不如
	递进 Progression	Progression	不但|不光|不仅|不止|且不说|并且|何况|况且|而且|再说|在这|并|甚至
	重述 Equivalence	Equivalence	换言之|就是说|事实上|实际上
	顺承 Succession	Succession	N/A
主从关系 Single-nucleus	转折Contrast	ContrastH	不过|但|但是|而是|反之|可是|然而|转而|恰恰相反|反倒|反而|却|仍旧|仍
		ContrastM	虽说|固然|非但|虽然|尽管
	让步 Concession	ConcessionH	也
		ConcessionM	即便|即使|即或|即令|即若|纵然|纵使|就算
	因果 Cause	CauseH	之所以|因此|故而|那么|那末|所以|于是|进而|则|乃至于|因而|难怪|显而
		CauseM	因|因为|由于|既然|是因为|既|也许|或许|兴许
	结果 Result	ResultH	从而|以至|以致|以至于|致使
	目的 Purpose	PurposeH	以免|以便
	假设 Hypothetical	HypotheticalM	假如|假若|假使|倘若|如果|如若|要是|如果说|万一|一旦
	条件Condition	ConditionH	否则|要不|要不然|不然
		ConditionM	要不是|除非|不管|不论|无论|只要|只有|任|哪怕|多亏|幸而|幸好|幸亏
	解证 Explanation	ExplanationM	具体地说|具体来说|具体来讲|一方面
	分述 List	ListM	首先|其次|然后
	总括Generalization	GeneralizationH	总之|总的来说|总的看|综上所述|总的来看|总而言之

TABLE 1 – Discourse relation, discourse types and explicit connectives

3.5 Linear Optimizer

Linear optimizer generates the polarity of a document by calculating the weighted sum of its sub-sentences in accordance with their discourse types.

$$\text{score} = \left(\sum_{(s_i, p_i, d_i)} \text{weight}(d_i) \times p_i\right) + b \qquad (1)$$

where $\text{weight}(d_i)$ is the weight of discourse type d_i, p_i is the polarity score of sub-sentence s_i, and b is an offset adjustment factor. The offset corrects a possible bias in sentiment scores caused by people's tendency to write negative reviews with positive words. Both Taboada et al. (2008) and Heerschop et al. (2011) validated that an offset can improve experiment results. We use a linear kernel SVM to train $\text{weight}(d_i)$ and b. The document would be classified as positive/negative/neutral if score is larger than/less than/equals zero.

4 Influential Discourse Relation Detecting

Intuitively, some discourse relations are more influential on the overall sentiment of a document. We apply a greedy search method to detect the most influential discourse relations, and the corresponding discourse types are considered as influential discourse types. When predicting the sentiment of a document, sub-sentences of influential discourse types are identified and weighted differently; the weight of remained sub-sentences are constrained to be equal. Figure 2 shows the procedure of detecting influential discourse relations.

Definitions: Define DR as the set of discourse relations, $DR = [dis_1, dis_2 .. dis_m]$

Define IDR as the set of influential discourse relations, initialized as $IDR = \varnothing$

Algorithm: while true:

$dis = \text{argmax}_{dis_i \in DR}(\text{Performance}(IDR \cup [dis_i]) - \text{Performance}(IDR))$ which meets

$\text{Performance}(IDR \cup [dis_i]) - \text{Performance}(IDR) > 0$

//find dis which could get the highest performance gain

if $\exists dis$: $IDR = IDR \cup [dis]$; $DR = DR - [dis]$

else: break

return IDR

FIGURE 2 – Greedy search for influential discourse relations

5 Experiment

5.1 Data

Our data is collected from 360buy (http://www.360buy.com/). Reviews on 360buy are structured, elaborating the strong points and shortcomings of the products. Reviews collected from the strong point column are automatically tagged as positive, and reviews collected from the shortcoming column are automatically tagged as negative. In our task, all the extracted reviews should meet two requirements: (1) contain at least two sub-sentences; (2) contain at least one connective. There are 53,040 reviews in our collected corpus, including 24,532 positive reviews and 28,508 negative reviews. Each review consists of 5.06 sub-sentences on average. Table 2 illustrates the occurrences of each discourse type in our collected data.

Discourse type	#times	discourse type	#times	discourse type	#times	discourse type	#times
None	46645	HypotheticalH	4060	ConditionM	2023	Alternative	365
ContrastH	22303	HypotheticalM	4060	Coordinate	1840	ConcessionM	231
Progression	8339	CauseM	3257	Equivalence	1460	ResultH	60
ConcessionH	5541	ContrastM	2727	ListM	789	PurposeH	47
CauseH	5062	ConditionH	2147	GeneralizationH	595	Temporal	35

TABLE 2- Distribution of Discourse Types

Discourse types whose occurrence is less than 100 are merged into "None" type. 3/4 of the collected data is used to train the linear optimizer, and the rest is used as test data. In the case of detecting influential discourse relations, we further divide 1/4 from the training data as the development data (development data is used to tune the most influential discourse relations), and the test data remains the same.

5.2 Experiment Set

We conduct 6 types of experiments, described as follows.

Baseline1. We implemented Qiu et al. (2009) as our baseline.

Baseline2. All the sub-sentences are equally weighted in Formula (1). No discourse knowledge is applied.

SNSS. (Single Nucleus Single Satellite Method.) Following the idea of Taboada et al. (2008), all discourse types denoting the Heads of relations are grouped as "nucleus", and other discourse types are grouped as "satellite". In this method, we have only two distinguishing categories: nucleus and satellite.

SNMS. (Single Nucleus Multiple Satellites Method.) Following the idea of Heerschop et al. (2011), all discourse types denoting the Heads of relations are grouped as "nucleus", while all discourse types denoting the Modifiers of discourse relations are reserved. In this method, we hypothesize that nucleus types contribute equally while different satellite types contribute differently to the overall polarity of documents.

MNMS. (Multiple Nuclei Multiple Satellites Method.) All the discourse types specified in Table 1 are reserved and weighted differently in calculating a document's sentiment. In this method, we hypothesize that both different nucleus types and different satellite types contribute differently to the overall polarity of the documents.

GDR. (Greedy Discourse Relation Method.) Following Figure 2, influential discourse relations are identified. The corresponding discourse types are reserved and weighted differently, and others are grouped as "None".

GCW. (Greedy Connective Word Method.) Explicit connectives are objective language usage, while relation types are subjective induction. Following the same procedure as Figure 2, we hypothesize that the weight of each sub-sentence depends directly on its connective. That means, only influential connectives are identified and weighted differently in calculating a document's sentiment, while others are grouped as "None".

5.3 Experiment Results

Performance is evaluated in terms of Precision (Pre), Recall (Rec) and F score.

	Positive			Negative			Overall	Comments &
Method	Pre	Rec	F	Pre	Rec	F	F	Influential discourse relations or connectives
Baseline1	85.0	**84.8**	84.9	**81.9**	82.0	81.9	83.55	The performance gain of baseline2 than baseline1 indicates the effectiveness of offset b in Formula (1).
Baseline2	**91.5**	77.6	84.0	77.2	**91.4**	83.7	83.86	
SNSS	89.1	82.0	85.4	80.4	88.0	84.0	84.76	The performance gain of SNSS, SNMS, MNMS, GDR and GCW than baseline2 indicates the effectiveness of our weighting scheme which exploits discourse knowledge.
SNMS	89.4	82.7	**85.9**	80.9	88.2	84.4	85.20	
MNMS	89.2	82.2	85.5	80.5	88.1	84.1	84.86	
GDR	89.9	82.2	**85.9**	80.7	89.0	**84.6**	**85.28**	Contrast, Cause, Condition, Generalization
GCW	90.4	81.4	85.6	80.1	89.6	**84.6**	85.13	不过|however, 虽然|although,但|but, 同时|at the same time, 总的来说|in general,但是|but

TABLE 3- Experiment results

As shown in Table 3, all our methods integrating discourse knowledge perform better than both baselines in overall F score. To test for significance, we conduct t-test which meets $p<0.01$. GDR achieves the best result, 1.42% higher than baseline2. This validates the effectiveness of using discourse relations in Chinese sentiment analysis. In English data, Heerschop et al. (2011) yield an improvement of 4.7% in F score when using discourse structure, but their baseline is quite low with an F score of 68.7%.

The overall F value of SNSS is 0.9% higher than baseline2, validating the effectiveness of the simple distinction between nuclei and satellites. Both SNMS and MNMS perform better than SNSS, indicating that more discourse knowledge is helpful in calculating the overall polarity. Note that MNMS performs slightly worse than SNMS, perhaps this is because too many weights have to be trained in MNMS.

GDR, which differentiates Contrast, Cause, Condition and Generalization from other discourse relations, harvests the best result. It is consistent with our intuition that these relations have great impact on the meaning of the texts. The influential discourse relations that we find out are partly consistent with previous work: Narayanan et al. (2009) exploit Conditional sentences for sentiment analysis; Zhou et al. (2011) focus their attention on Contrast, Condition, Cause, Continuation and Purpose in polarity classification.

To our surprise, GCW, which utilizes only 6 explicit connectives, obtains a rather promising result, with a performance of 1.27% higher than baseline2. Among these 6 connectives, "不过|however", "虽然|although","但|but", "但是|but" denote a Contrast relation; "同时|at the same time" denotes a Coordinate relation; and "总的来说|in general" denotes an Generalization relation.

Conclusion and Future Work

In this paper, we utilize explicit connectives to predict discourse relations, and then conduct several methods to incorporate discourse structure knowledge to the task of sentiment analysis. We define discourse relations in different granularities: nucleus-satellite, nucleus-different satellites and different nuclei-different satellites. The experimental results validate the effectiveness of using discourse relations in Chinese sentiment analysis. Furthermore, we automatically detect the most influential discourse relations and connectives. Experimental results show that Contrast, Cause, Condition and Generalization are the most influential relations, and "不过|however", "虽然|although", "但|but", "同时|at the same time", "总的来说|in general", "但是|but" are the most influential connectives.

This is only a preliminary study on discourse relation and Chinese sentiment analysis. The future work includes the following aspects. (1) We would like to develop a Chinese discourse parser to automatically parse the discourse structure, to get both explicit and implicit relations and their argument spans. (2) We will apply more sophisticated methods to get more reliable polarity scores for sub-sentences. (3) We will incorporate discourse structure knowledge to other tasks such as summarization.

Acknowledgments

This paper was supported by National High Technology Research and Development Program of China (No.2012AA011101), 2009 Chiang Ching-kuo Foundation for International Scholarly Exchange (No.RG013-D-09) and National Natural Science Foundation of China (No. 61103089).

References

Heerschop, B., Goossen, F., Hogenboom, A., Frasincar, F., Kaymak, U. and de Jong, F. (2011). Polarity analysis of texts using discourse structure. In Proceedings of CIMK-2011, pages 1061-1070.

Hernault, H., Bollegala, D. and Ishizuka, M. (2010). A semi-supervised approach to improve classification of infrequent discourse relations using feature vector extension. In Proceedings of the EMNLP-2010, pages 399-409.

Joty, S., Carenini, G. and Ng, R.T. (2012). A novel discriminative framework for sentence-level discourse analysis. In Proceedings of EMNLP-2012, page 904-915

Mann, W.C. and Thompson, S.A. (1988). Rhetorial structure theory: towards a functional theory of text organization. Text, 8(3):243-281.

Narayanan, R., Liu, B. and Choudhary, A. (2009). Sentiment analysis of conditional sentences. In Proceedings of EMNLP-2009, pages 180-189.

Pang, B. and Lee, L. (2008). Opinion mining and sentiment analysis. Information Retrieval, 2(1-2): 1-135.

Polanyi, L. and Zaenen, A. (2006). Contextual valence shifters, Computing attitude and affect in text: Theory and applications, page 1-10.

Qiu, L., Zhang, W., Hu, C. and Zhao, K. (2009). SELC: a self-supervised model for sentiment classification. In Proceedings of CIKM-2009, pages 929-936.

Somasundaran, S., Namata, G. , Wiebe, J. and Getoor, L. (2009). Supervised and unsupervised methods in employing discourse relations for improving opinion polarity classification, In Proceedings of the ENMLP-2009, pages 170-179.

Somasundaran, S., Wiebe, J. and Ruppenhofer, J. (2008). Discourse level opinion interpretation, In Proceedings of COLING-08, pages 801-808.

Taboada, M., Voll, K. and Brooke, J. (2008). Extracting sentiment as a function of discourse structure and topically. Technical Report No. 2008-20, Simon Fraser University.

Wang, W.T., Su, J. and Tan, C.L. (2010). Kernel based discourse relation recognition with temporal ordering information. In Proceedings of ACL-2010, pages 710-719.

Yang, Y. and Xue, N. (2012). Chinese comma disambiguation for discourse analysis. In Proceedings of ACL-2012, pages 786-794.

Zhou, L., Li, B., Gao, W., Wei, Z. and Wong, K.F. (2011). Unsupervised discovery of discourse relations for eliminating intra-sentence polarity ambiguities, In Proceedings of EMNLP-2011, pages 162-171.

Expansion Methods for Job-Candidate Matching Amidst Unreliable and Sparse Data

Jerome WHITE   Krishna KUMMAMURU   Nitendra RAJPUT
IBM Research, India
`{jerome.white,kummamuru,rnitendra}@in.ibm.com`

ABSTRACT
We address the problem of matching jobs with workers when information about both elements is incomplete and in some cases inaccurate. Such a situation occurs, for example, when profile information is generated from recorded audio, rather than typed or written sources. We present various methods of dealing with such post-processed voice information and show how it compares to human generated matches over the same data. Our analysis includes both SQL- and ontological-based methods that provide higher recall over a sparse data. A probabilistic weighted ontology model is proposed that enables assignment of realistic weights to different attributes and considers probabilistic conversion of audio to text. The evaluation is performed on real-life data from 1,100 candidates and 48 jobs spanning more than 3,000 vacancies.

KEYWORDS: Spoken Web, job search, resume matching, ontology.

Proceedings of COLING 2012: Posters, pages 1321–1330,
COLING 2012, Mumbai, December 2012.

1 Introduction

While job websites such as Dice and Monster have proven useful for a variety of job seekers, such technologies have not been suitable for unorganized, low-skilled workers in developing countries. To take full advantage of websites, users are required to have reliable Internet access, and some amount of technological savvy. To bring the benefits of the Internet to a larger population we have developed a *VoiceSite* (see Kumar et al., 2007a) to enable users to create and advertise their resumes through voice. Candidates and employers can listen to VoiceSites through telephone—including low-end mobiles that are prevalent in rural communities—in local languages. One of the challenges in developing such a system lies in data capture: being that we are dealing with voice audio, data is often noisy and not well structured. This paper presents various methods of generating "good" matches between candidates and employers amidst such unreliable information.

The difficulty of matching in this context is two-fold: first, attribute similarity is domain specific, not necessarily captured by traditional string or numeric distances; second, elements may have a subset of attributes defined due to the problems around voice-based data capture. Specifically, given that underlying values are taken from voice-data, they are both imprecise and lie within a wide range; resulting in a very sparse data set where exact matches are rare. Thus, to increase user satisfaction, we must look beyond exact matches.

While our results were developed for, and subsequently tailored to, low-skilled job matching, the methodologies discussed herein are applicable within the broader context of voice-driven market places. That is, environments where a supply must be matched to a demand, and the specifics of both are drawn from voice records. In many rural regions of developing countries, this is becoming a popular method of information exchange given the rate of mobile penetration versus the rate of Internet and literacy growth.

2 Related work

Recommender systems have been used to tackle pre-selection of candidates (Malinowski et al., 2008), as well as improve job-candidate match rankings (Keim, 2007). Automated methods have also been used to ease the burden on human decision making (Yu et al., 2005a). One novel approach has been to generate filters based on the information that is available in resumes (Singh et al., 2010). While most of these studies are performed either on synthetic data or on text data, our work is performed on real-world, semi-structured audio data.

Much of the work on spoken document retrieval (SDR) has been done on English language broadband speech (16–24 KHz audio) (Singhal and Pereira, 1999; Mamou et al., 2006; Garofolo et al., 1999). Speech recognition accuracies for such languages are usually more than 60 percent. However, this is not directly applicable to resource constrained languages and telephony speech (8 KHz audio), which is the domain of our work.

Over the last five years, researchers have started to look at searching speech not through speech recognition, but by indexing speech at a subword level (Yu et al., 2005b; Chelba and Acero, 2005). Such techniques are more robust to speech recognition errors since they consider multiple recognition hypotheses in the index (Chia et al., 2008). Most systems for audio search use a visual query interface for accessing content indexed from audio. This is typical of a web based search system for searching video content (Alberti et al., 2009), and in call centers where supervisors wish to monitor offline content of the call center agents (Mishne et al., 2005). In such situations, the query is still textual. What differentiates our work is that both the query

ID	City	Qualification	Skill	Salary	Experience
669	Mandya	Diploma		5000	5
670	Mandya	Diploma		10000	5
681	Mandya	ITI	Mechanical	6000	4
684	Bangalore*	PUC	COPA	5500400	0
685	Kodagu*	PUC		6000	0
695	Bangalore*	BDes		6000	2
711	Bijapur*	MTech	Technician*	15000	2
712	Bijapur	PUC		8000	1
718	Bangalore	PUC	Data Entry Operator	7000	1
723	Bangalore	BCom		5000	5

Table 1: Job profiles used for matching. "Experience" is denoted in years; salary values are in denominations of Indian Rupees per month. The salary specification for job 684 is presumably a mistake in user input. Starred entries ($\star$) are values obtained from offline speech recognition. Missing values are pieces of information that could be recognised neither during the call, nor during offline processing.

and the content are in audio.

Ontology based information extraction systems use semantic information to enrich the existing content for improving the understanding of the system (Chandrasekaran et al., 1999). Such systems are being increasingly used for various information extraction tasks: understanding the context (Cimiano et al., 2005), extracting content from Wikipedia (Wu et al., 2008), next-page prediction (Mabroukeh and Ezeife, 2009), and business intelligence (Saggion et al., 2007), among others. This paper uses the information in ontologies with respect to location, skill and qualification to improve recall in job-candidate matching scenario.

3 System Setup

Candidates and employers create their resume and job profiles, respectively, by calling into an interactive voice platform driven by Spoken Web (Kumar et al., 2007b). When a party calls into the system, they are presented with a series of prompts to collect their information. Addressing these prompts is done either by dual-tone multi-frequency signaling (DTMF), or by speaking an answer. For example, "please speak your highest qualification," versus "using your phone keypad, please enter the monthly salary you are seeking." The audio content is stored as 8 KHz data, and is in a mix of English and Kannada, the language native to the area in which the system was deployed.

There are five structured fields common to both candidates and employers: location, qualification (degree), skill, salary, and experience. Location, qualification, and skill were spoken input; salary and experience were DTMF. Structured fields are converted to text and stored in a database. In the case of spoken fields, audio is first run through an online speech recognizer to perform the conversion. In the event that the recognizer cannot confidently produce a single answer, a list of probable answers is maintained, and the recorded audio is stored.[1]

[1]The list of probable answers is stored in a location that is separate from confident answers. Thus, database analysis can easily distinguish between the two.

3.1 Job Selection

Our analysis was performed over a subset of 10 jobs; Table 1 provides details of each. These jobs were randomly selected from a subset of the 48 jobs that had similar candidate-distance distributions. Selected jobs fell into one of three categories: jobs with complete information (681, 718); jobs with incomplete but speech augmented information (684, 711); and jobs with information that have at least one attribute is incomplete (669, 670, 685, 695, 712, 723)—where speech recognition could not determine one or more of their attributes. This subset provided volunteers with room for personal subjectivity, and enough choices within the candidate pool that such subjectivity could be realized.

3.2 Ground Truth

The ground truth was established by asking a set of volunteers to manually match candidates to jobs. Ten volunteers were presented with three job openings. For redundancy, job was assigned to three separate volunteers; thus, each job had three sets of independently matched candidates.[2] All volunteers were presented with the same set of available candidates. Where candidate information was missing, textual results from the speech recognizer, along with recorded audio from candidates, were presented. It was clear to the volunteer, from presentation of the candidate database, where such information was included in place of standard database information. For example, if a candidates location was missing, the value would be empty; however, another value within the database would be filled with the recognized text and the recorded speech. Further, volunteers were made aware of the nature of this information—that it was inexact and perhaps not clear—and instructed to use their best judgment.

4 Methodology

We compare two job matching algorithms with a set of ground truth. Throughout, we denote the set of attributes as A, the set of jobs as J, and the set of candidates as C. It is sometimes convenient to talk about jobs and candidates as generic elements from the same set; in such cases $E = J \cup S$.

4.1 SQL Queries

Sets of job matches were generated directly from the database using structured query language (SQL). Two separate queries were performed: one that operated over DTMF and high confidence speech recognition values, and another operating over DTMF and probable speech recognition values. In the case of the former, if a particular attribute had a missing value, that attribute was not taken into account when performing the query. In the case of the latter, the highest probable recognized value was taken in place of missing values.[3]

In both cases, results were ranked by the number of attributes containing exact matches. For example, if there were n number of attributes to match, entries with n exact matches were ranked highest; matches with $n-1$ entries were ranked second, and so forth. For entries with $n' < n$ exact attribute matches, a pre-defined priority was established for which n' subset was matched. Specifically, if two of three attributes matched, there were three different combinations of two-match pairings—a priority within that two-match set was specified. Based

[2]Volunteers were not only unaware of one another, but unaware that others might be investigating the same job.

[3]Ties were broken by selecting a value at random. If there was no value even in the probable set, then the attribute was not taken into account.

on prior research that involved interviews with the employers (White et al., 2012), qualification, location, and skill were prioritized in that order. As an example, an exact match of qualification and location will be ranked higher than an exact match of qualification and skill.

Our database was designed such that two independent tables contained job and candidate information. The SELECT and FROM portions of the SQL statement were straightforward, including the attributes of interest and the table of interest, respectively. A WHERE clause was used to combine pairs of attributes, while an ORDER BY clause was used to rank the results. Let $\mathscr{P}_{=2}(A)$ be the set of all attribute pairs, and $\mathscr{P}_{>1}(A)$ be the set of attributes where the cardinality is greater than one. The WHERE clause is the conjunction of $\mathscr{P}_{=2}(A)$ equalities,

$$\bigwedge_{(a_1,a_2)\in\mathscr{P}_{=2}(A)} \left(a_1 = v_e(a_1) \vee a_2 = v_e(a_2)\right),$$

where v_e is the value of an element $e \in E$ for a given attribute.

The ORDER BY clause consists of a case statement such that the more matching attributes that exist in a row, the higher the rows rank in the result set. Formally,

$$\forall A' \in \mathscr{P}_{>1}(A)\colon \text{WHEN} \left[\bigwedge_{a\in A'} a = v_e(a)\right] \text{THEN}\ i,$$

where $i = \max_{A^\star\in\mathscr{P}_{>1}(A)}(A^\star) - |A'|$. In practice, some augmentation is required as priority must be specified among subsets of $\mathscr{P}_{>1}(A)$ that have the same cardinality. Also, a final ELSE-clause must be specified with a value greater-than the cardinality of the largest set in $\mathscr{P}_{>1}(A)$.

As an example, consider a candidate whose location is Bangalore, skill is plumber, and qualification is PUC. The resulting SQL statement would be:

```
SELECT [columns] FROM [job_table] WHERE
 (location='Bangalore' OR skill='plumber') AND
 (skill='plumber' OR qualification='PUC') AND
 (qualification='PUC' OR location='Bangalore')
ORDER BY CASE
 WHEN location='Bangalore' AND skill='plumber' AND qualification='PUC' THEN 0
 WHEN location='Bangalore' AND skill='plumber' THEN 1
 WHEN location='Bangalore' AND qualification='PUC' THEN 2
 WHEN skill='plumber' AND qualification='PUC' THEN 3
 ELSE 4
END
```

4.2 Weighted Ontological Search

To broaden the scope of matches beyond exact string equality, we employed attribute-specific ontologies. These ontologies were applied to location, qualification, and skill. In particular, a notion of distance was developed for each pair of valid entries in each set. For location, the distance calculation corresponded to the Euclidean distance between two points. Distance between qualifications was developed based on the lattice that they formed. That is, when taken in order of academic completion—one must obtain a bachelors degree, for example, before obtaining a masters degree—qualifications form a tree. To determine a value for distance between qualifications, we used distance between their common parent.

Skills are a collection of arbitrary nouns. To establish distances between them we relied on WordNet (Miller, 1995). In particular, we used the methodology defined by Leacock et al. (1998) since, for our particular set of words, their algorithm provided highest variance among distances, with least number of zero values.

Let $j \in J$ and $c \in C$. Further, let w represent the weight of a given attribute for a particular element. The aggregate distance between a candidate and a job is thus the summation of the weighted distances between attributes,

$$D'(j,c) = \sum_{a \in A} w_a(j) \cdot d_a(j,c),$$

Attribute distances are normalized such that $d_a \in [0,1]$ for all attributes a; thus, $D \in [0, |A|]$. Note that comparisons that are exact matches, as in the case of SQL, will lie at the upper bound of this space ($D = |A|$).

For each attribute, weights were established by finding the variance of the distance between all elements. Formally, let $X_a(j) = \{d_a(j,c)\}_{c \in C}$, and $j \in J$,

$$\forall a \in A \colon w_a(j) = \begin{cases} 1 & \text{if } \operatorname{Var}\left(X_a(j)\right) = 0, \\ \operatorname{Var}\left(X_a(j)\right)^{-1} & \text{otherwise.} \end{cases} \quad (1)$$

Equation 1 looks at the variance of a given attribute distances across all elements within a common set.[4] It reduces the weight of a given attribute if there are several different distances for that attribute, giving precedence of attributes that are uniform. The logic being that searching between too many different people is difficult; by distributing that diversity among the common population, higher quality results arise.

5 Results

5.1 Evaluation

Because of the nature of our data, as well as the nature in which it is consumed, it is prudent to use a variety of retrieval metrics to establish the quality of our query methods. The inaccuracies in the data allow for a variety opinions when establishing matches; this was especially clear when evaluating the results within the ground truth itself. Thus, set-based metrics that do not consider rank have a place in our evaluation metrics, since there was no consensus even among human opinion. Further, in the context of job search, set inclusion is as important as rank. Because candidate search comes early in the recruitment stage, it is often a good idea for employers to select several candidates before beginning the initial screening process. Simply because a candidate is a good fit in theory does not mean they are a suitable fit in practice. Thus, an employer often wants to know a plurality of "best" matches, which make measures of unranked inclusion useful.

However, as previously mentioned, this data was acquired, and is meant to be consumed, via telephone. Such a medium not only has mental limitations, as audio data takes more patience to consume than visual data, but physical limitations as well. The longer a user waits to get results they are satisfied with, the longer they are tying up their line. This puts a strain on battery life, air-time charges, and ultimately user patience. Thus, comparing result rankings is also important.

[4] By "common" we mean candidates in the case of candidates, and jobs in the case of jobs

		SQL				Weighted Ontology			
ID	N	Prec@10	Rec@10	Avg Pr	ERR	Prec@10	Rec@10	Avg Pr	ERR
669	21	**0.2500**	0.0476	0.0159	0.0129	0.2000	**0.0952**	**0.0417**	**0.0252**
670	27	0.2500	0.0370	0.0093	0.0163	**0.3000**	**0.1111**	**0.1069**	**0.0309**
681	20	**0.5000**	**0.1000**	**0.1833**	0.0000	0.3000	0.0500	0.1500	0.0000
684	15	0.0000	0.0000	0.0000	0.0000	0.0000	0.0000	0.0000	0.0000
685	34	0.0000	0.0000	0.0009	0.0000	**1.0000**	**0.2941**	**0.6279**	**0.1202**
695	25	0.0000	0.0000	0.0000	0.0000	**0.4000**	**0.1600**	**0.1733**	**0.0884**
711	6	0.0000	0.0000	0.0000	0.0000	0.0000	0.0000	0.0000	0.0000
712	22	0.3000	0.1364	0.1297	0.0116	0.3000	0.1364	0.1297	0.0116
718	24	0.1000	0.0417	**0.0469**	0.0016	0.1000	0.0417	0.0117	**0.0027**
723	8	**0.2857**	0.2500	0.2083	0.0093	0.2500	0.2500	0.2083	0.0093
MAP				0.0594				0.1450	

Table 2: Retrieval metrics when when searching over non-speech corrected data.

To capture these concepts, we use four metrics for evaluating our algorithms: recall, precision, average precision, and expected reciprocal rank (ERR) (Chapelle et al., 2009). Precision and recall are good measures for basic query similarity. Moreover, for documents retrieved via SQL, these metrics are in some ways a fairer perspective, as SQLs ability to rank is not as granular as the ontological-based methods.

Average precision and ERR are our ranked evaluation metrics. Again, given our context and environment, both metrics are relevant. On the one hand, when searching for candidates an employer is likely to go through a large set, choosing to continue their search irrespective of the goodness the current document provides. Of course, this is under the assumption that a majority of the returned set contains relevant documents. However, given that the employer is consuming these documents over the phone, they are likely to base some of their decision to continue on the quality of the current, or previous n, results, where n is small. We use the combination of average precision and ERR to capture these characteristics.

Note, that our use of metrics are primarily as a tool to compare our methodology. As such we are not necessarily concerned with their absolute value, but more so with their respective, or comparative, values. Further, when producing metrics, we used the number of results returned in the ground truth set as the number of documents we limited our searches to returning.

5.2 Evaluation Over Raw Data

We first apply our match heuristics to *raw data*. Raw data is data in which there is no attempt to correct the speech anomalies; thus, we ignore portions of the data for which there is no reliably accurate information. For example, if a candidate or employer spoke a particular attribute that our system did not recognize, we treat the data as missing. Comparing our results to the ground truth in this context was not entirely fair, as volunteers had access to spoken audio files and were not told to produce two sets of matches based on whether or not they listened to them. However, performing the comparison allows us to establish a baseline, and gives us an idea of how accurate the additional recognition information is.

Despite the lack of information, the ontology methods were able to outperform SQL queries

		SQL				Weighted Ontology			
ID	N	Prec@10	Rec@10	Avg Pr	ERR	Prec@10	Rec@10	Avg Pr	ERR
669	21	0.2500	0.0476	0.0159	0.0129	**0.4000**	**0.1905**	**0.1317**	**0.0414**
670	27	0.2500	0.0370	0.0093	**0.0163**	**0.3000**	**0.0741**	**0.0966**	0.0143
681	20	**0.5000**	**0.1000**	**0.1833**	0.0000	0.3000	0.0500	0.0300	0.0000
684	15	**0.2500**	0.0667	**0.0222**	0.0000	0.1000	0.0667	0.0095	0.0000
685	34	0.0000	0.0000	0.0000	0.0000	0.0000	0.0000	**0.0845**	**0.0152**
695	25	**1.0000**	0.0800	0.0800	0.0435	0.3000	**0.1200**	**0.1784**	**0.0605**
711	6	**1.0000**	0.1667	0.1667	0.0000	0.1667	0.1667	0.1667	0.0000
712	22	0.3000	0.1364	**0.1297**	**0.0116**	0.3000	0.1364	0.1157	0.0097
718	24	0.1000	0.0417	0.0469	0.0016	**0.2000**	**0.0883**	**0.0571**	**0.0290**
723	8	**0.2857**	0.2500	**0.2083**	0.0093	0.2500	0.2500	0.1250	**0.0319**
MAP				0.0862				0.0995	

Table 3: Retrieval metrics when when searching over speech corrected data.

in rank evaluations for many of the job profiles; this trend is also see in recall and average precision. See Table 2 for a comparison.

5.3 Evaluation with Noise Reduction

To reduce the amount of missing data in the system, we replaced non-existent values with estimates from the offline speech recognition engine. For each attribute, we first considered the value, or set of values, that the speech recognizer returned, taking the value with the highest probability as the authority. If, however, the recognition engine was unable to produce any values for a given attribute, we looked at recognition values of other attributes for that job or candidate. In some cases, we were actually able to find proper values in non-proper fields. As an example, consider a candidate that does not have a real-time recognized value for location. We would first check the offline recognition values for the recorded location. In the event that there were no values or valid values found, we would move to another speech attribute that was unrecognized, searching through that set for what could be considered a location. The premise was that some users might have had confusion during their usage of the system, giving valid input at incorrect times. These techniques for removing noise more than doubled the amount of overall information available for querying.

Table 3 lists retrieval evaluation values for noise reduction. SQL performance was notably better, with respect to its own performance in the raw tests, as well as ontological methods within noise-reduced tests. In fact, recall measures aside, there is no clear winner between the two methods when offline speech recognition is present.

Conclusion and Future Work

Voice-based information processing, as tackled herein, is an important step in the success of mobile data collection. To this end, we have developed an algorithm to match jobs with candidates that considers both issues of noise in the data, as well as proximity of the attributes in matching. In the future, we would like to augment our matching function to consider all probable values presented by offline speech recognition, and to apply "active learning" to our weight calculation.

References

Alberti, C., Bacchiani, M., Bezman, A., Chelba, C., Drofa, A., Liao, H., Moreno, P., Power, T., Sahuguet, A., Shugrina, M., and Siohan, O. (2009). An audio indexing system for election video material. In *International Conference on Acoustics, Speech, and Signal Processing*.

Chandrasekaran, B., Josephson, J., and Banjamins, V. R. (1999). What are ontologies, and why do we need them? *IEEE Transactions on Intelligent Systems and their Applications*, 14(1).

Chapelle, O., Metlzer, D., Zhang, Y., and Grinspan, P. (2009). Expected reciprocal rank for graded relevance. In *Proceedings of the 18th ACM conference on Information and knowledge management*, pages 621–630.

Chelba, C. and Acero, A. (2005). Position specific posterior lattices for indexing speech. In *Annual Meeting on Association for Computational Linguistics*, pages 443–450.

Chia, T. K., Sim, K. C., Li, H., and Ng, H. T. (2008). A lattice-based approach to query-by-example spoken document retrieval. In *International Conference on Research and Development in Information Retrieval*, pages 363–370. ACM.

Cimiano, P., Ladwig, G., and Staab, S. (2005). Gimme' the context: context-driven automatic semantic annotation with c-pankow. In *international conference on World Wide Web*, pages 332–341, New York, NY, USA. ACM.

Garofolo, J., Auzanne, C., and Voorhees, E. (1999). The trec spoken document retrieval track: A success story. In *TREC*.

Keim, T. (2007). Extending the applicability of recommender systems: A multilayer framework for matching human resources. In *Annual Hawaii International Conference on System Sciences*, HICSS '07, pages 169–, Washington, DC, USA. IEEE Computer Society.

Kumar, A., Rajput, N., Chakraborty, D., Agarwal, S., and Nanavati, A. A. (2007a). Voiserv: Creation and delivery of converged services through voice for emerging economies. In *International Symposium on a World of Wireless, Mobile and Multimedia Networks*, Finland.

Kumar, A., Rajput, N., Chakraborty, D., Agarwal, S., and Nanavati, A. A. (2007b). WWTW: A World Wide Telecom Web for Developing Regions. In *SIGCOMM Workshop on Networked Systems For Developing Regions*. ACM.

Leacock, C., Miller, G. A., and Chodorow, M. (1998). Using corpus statistics and WordNet relations for sense identification. *Computational Linguistics—Special issue on word sense disambiguation*, 24(1):147–165.

Mabroukeh, N. and Ezeife, C. (2009). Using domain ontology for semantic web usage mining and next page prediction. In *Conference on Information and Knowledge Management*, pages 1677–1680, New York, NY, USA. ACM.

Malinowski, J., Weitzel, T., and Keim, T. (2008). Decision support for team staffing: An automated relational recommendation approach. *Decision Support Systems*, 45(3):429 – 447.

Mamou, J., Carmel, D., and Hoory, R. (2006). Spoken document retrieval from call-center conversations. In *International Conference on Research and Development in Information Retrieval*, pages 51–58, New York, NY, USA. ACM.

Miller, G. (1995). WordNet: a lexical database for english. *Communications of the ACM*, 38(11):39–41.

Mishne, G., Carmel, D., Hoory, R., Roytman, A., and Soffer, A. (2005). Automatic analysis of call-center conversations. In *International conference on Information and knowledge management*, pages 453–459.

Saggion, H., Funk, A., Maynard, D., and Bontcheva, K. (2007). Ontology-based information extraction for business intelligence. In *International Semantic Web Conference and Asian Semantic Web Conference*, pages 843–856, Berlin, Heidelberg. Springer-Verlag.

Singh, A., Catherine, R., Visweswariah, K., Chenthamarakshan, V., and Kambhatla, N. (2010). PROSPECT: a system for screening candidates for recruitment. In Huang, J., Koudas, N., Jones, G. J. F., Wu, X., Collins-Thompson, K., and An, A., editors, *International Conference on Information and Knowledge Management*, pages 659–668. ACM.

Singhal, A. and Pereira, F. (1999). Document expansion for speech retrieval. In *International Conference on Research and Development in Information Retrieval*, pages 34–41, New York, NY, USA. ACM.

White, J., Duggirala, M., Kummamuru, K., and Srivastava, S. (2012). Designing a voice-based employment exchange for rural india. In *International Conference on Information and Communication Technologies and Development*, pages 367–373, New York, NY, USA. ACM.

Wu, F., Hoffmann, R., and Weld, D. S. (2008). Information extraction from wikipedia: moving down the long tail. In *International conference on Knowledge discovery and data mining*, pages 731–739, New York, NY, USA. ACM.

Yu, K., Guan, G., and Zhou, M. (2005a). Resume information extraction with cascaded hybrid model. In *Annual Meeting on Association for Computational Linguistics*, pages 499–506, Stroudsburg, PA, USA. Association for Computational Linguistics.

Yu, K. C., Ma, C., and Seide, F. (2005b). Vocabulary independent indexing of spontaneous speech. *IEEE Transactions on Speech and Audio Processing*, 13(5).

A Unified Framework for Discourse Argument Identification via Shallow Semantic Parsing

XU Fan ZHU Qiao Ming[*] *ZHOU Guo Dong*
School of Computer Science and Technology
Soochow University, Suzhou, China 215006
{20104027010, qmzhu, gdzhou}@suda.edu.cn

ABSTRACT

This paper deals with Discourse Argument Identification (DAI) from both intra-sentence and inter-sentence perspectives. For intra-sentence cases, we approach it via a simplified shallow semantic parsing framework, which recasts the discourse connective as the predicate and its scope into several constituents as the argument of the predicate. Different from state-of-the-art chunking approaches, our parsing approach extends DAI from the chunking level to the parse tree level, where rich syntactic information is available, and focuses on determining whether a constituent, rather than a token, is an argument or not. For inter-sentence cases, we present a lightweight heuristic rule-based solution. Evaluation using Penn Discourse Treebank (PDTB) shows that the current research's parsing approach significantly outperforms the state-of-the-art chunking alternatives.

TITLE AND ABSTRACT IN CHINESE

基于浅层语义分析的篇章论元识别统一框架

本文从句内和句外两种角度处理篇章论元识别问题. 针对句内情况, 我们采用浅层语义分析框架来处理, 将篇章连接词看作谓词, 并将谓词的论元映射成一些组块. 不同于现有的基于组块方法, 我们的语义分析方法将组块层次提升为富于句法信息的句法树层次, 同时将组块而不是单词作为处理单元. 针对句外情况, 我们提出了一种轻量级的规则解决方案. 通过宾州篇章树库上的实验, 说明我们提出的基于语义分析方法在性能上显著优于现有的基于组块方法.

KEYWORDS : Argument Pruning, Discourse Argument Identification, Shallow Semantic Parsing.
KEYWORDS IN CHINESE : 论元过滤, 篇章论元识别, 浅层语义分析.

[*] Corresponding author

Proceedings of COLING 2012: Posters, pages 1331–1340,
COLING 2012, Mumbai, December 2012.

1 Introduction

Discourse parsing is considered one of the most challenging Natural Language Processing (NLP) tasks. It is essential in many downstream NLP applications, such as statistical machine translation (Meyer, 2011), information retrieval (Huttunen et al., 2011), opinion mining (Somasundaran et al., 2009) and so on.

Generally, Discourse Argument Identification (DAI) involves two sub-tasks: Discourse Connective Identification (DCI) and Argument Scope Identification (ASI). ASI is much more complex than DCI, which has been comprehensively reported in literature with, for example, F-measure of 94.19% on the Penn Discourse Treebank (PDTB) Prasad et al. (2008). Compared with DCI, the performance of ASI is much lower. For example, Ghosh et al. (2012) only got F-measure of 59.39% on exact Arg1 identification, on golden tree structures. Most previous studies on DAI focus on token level, such as Ghosh et al. (2012) (2011a) (2011b) and Lin et al. (2010) and suffer from the limitation of focusing on determining whether a token in a discourse simply either belongs to the argument of a connective or not. However, such a strong independence assumption among the tokens may result in poor performance. The tokens should not be independent and sometimes they combine together and play the specific role for the discourse connective.

Accordingly, this paper focuses on PDTB-style exact argument identification, from both intra-sentence and inter-sentence perspectives. For intra-sentence cases, we approach it via a simplified shallow semantic parsing framework, which recasts the discourse connective as the predicate and its scope into several constituents as the argument of the predicate. Different from state-of-the-art chunking approaches, our parsing approach extends DAI from the chunking level to the parse tree level, where rich syntactic information is available, and focuses on determining whether a constituent, rather than a token, is an argument or not. For inter-sentence cases, we present a lightweight heuristic rule-based solution. Evaluation on the PDTB shows that our parsing approach significantly outperforms the afore-mentioned chunking alternatives.

The rest of this paper is organized as follows. Section 2 reviews related work on discourse parsing and on shallow semantic parsing. In Section 3 the PDTB corpus is briefly introduced. Section 4 describes the methodology used for exact argument identification. In Section 5 the results of the research experiment are presented. Finally, some conclusions are drawn.

2 Related Work

Related work on PDTB-style discourse parsing and shallow semantic parsing is presented in this section.

PDTB-style discourse parsing consists of two major sub-tasks: Discourse Argument Identification (DAI) and Discourse Relation Identification (DRI). Related work for PDTB-style DAI can be mainly classified into three categories: rule-based approach, Dinesh et al. (2005); Prasad et al., (2010), classification-based method, Wellner et al. (2007); Elwell et al. (2008); Lin et al. (2010) and chunking-based approach, Ghosh et al. (2011a) (2011b) (2012). To be more specific, Dinesh et al. (2005) proposed a tree subtraction method for restricted subordinating connectives. Prasad et al. (2010) provided a set of scope-based filters for argument identification. Wellner et al. (2007) and Elwell et al. (2008) investigated the matching of head-words located in the argument. However, a potential issue of their work is that no golden head-words were annotated in the PDTB. Lin et al. (2010) proposed a token-level argument node identifier, which determined whether each internal node was an Arg1, Arg2 or Non-argument, and then conducted a tree subtraction algorithm to extract the argument of connectives. Ghosh et al. (2012) which integrated the n-best result of the previous token-level approach (Ghosh et al, 2011a) into their global sentence-level method, significantly improved the method's DAI performance.

Compared with DAI, explicit and implicit discourse relation identification has been studied more recently, such as Pitler et al. (2009a); Lin et al. (2009); Wang et al. (2010); Zhou et al. (2010); Hong et al. (2012). However, due to inherent difficulties within the implicit discourse relation, its performance is still very low.

Shallow semantic parsing, used to answer 'the five Ws' (Who, What, When, Where and Why) questions in a sentence, has been extensively studied in recent years, such as Moschitti (2004) and Li et al. (2010a). Scope learning, a specific shallow semantic parsing problem is also related to DAI. Most existing research on scope learning can be further classified by methodology into rule-based, Chapman et al. (2001), chunking-based, Morante et al. (2009) and shallow semantic parsing-based, Li et al. (2010b) and Zhu et al. (2010).

3 Penn Discourse Treebank (PDTB): an Introduction

Currently, PDTB is the largest available discourse corpus. It has annotated 40,600 discourse relations, presented as five relation types: Explicit, Implicit, Alternative Lexicalization (AltLex), Entity-based coherence Relation(EntRel) and No Relation (NoRel). PDTB regards connectives as the discourse predicate, taking two text spans as two arguments, Arg1 and Arg2, which describe the events, facts and/or propositions. Of the two arguments Arg2 is syntactically bound to the connective, while Arg 1 is not. In addition, 3-layered hierarchy, semantic senses have been annotated for Explicit, Implicit and AltLex relations, with 4,16 and 23 kinds of senses for each level, respectively. Due to space limitation, we only give an instance of Explicit relation in this paper. Sentence '*In addition, its machines are typically easier to operate*, <u>so</u> **customers require less assistance from software**. (CONTINGENCY: Cause: result).' (According to PDTB, an Arg1 is indicated by italics, Arg2 indicated in bold, a discourse connective underlined and the sense annotated by parentheses.) is an Explicit instance of where there is an overt connective occurrence between the two arguments.

4 Discourse Argument Identification Framework

Similar to Lin et al. (2010), we also separate the DAI into intra-sentence and inter-sentence cases. The entire framework is shown in Figure 1. We run our classifiers in Arg1 position identification and argument identification steps in Figure 1. The performance of DCI is considered reliable, therefore we just integrate AddDiscourse, Pitler et al. (2009b) as the module of connective identification, as shown in Figure 1.

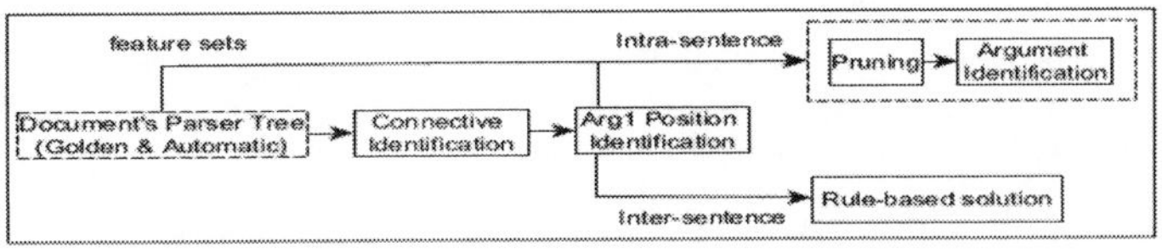

FIGURE 1 – Pipeline framework for discourse argument identification

For Arg1 position identification, Lin et al. (2010) showed that contextual features for connective *C* were useful when identifying Arg1's position. In addition, we can observe that the first and second next words ($next_1$ and $next_2$) of *C* also give a strong insight into Arg1's position. For example, the pronoun 'that', as contained within 'and ensure that', after the connective 'and', sometimes denotes abstract objects located in the previous sentence. Based on this observation, we add 8 new features: $next_1$, $next_1$ POS, $next_1$+C, $next_1$ POS+C POS, $next_2$, $next_2$ POS, $next_2$+C, $next_2$ POS+C POS. It is hard to decide which feature-set is more effective for Arg1 position identification, even if we use the Hill-climbing (greedy) feature selection technique, Caruana and Freitag (1994), due to the combination of a large number of different features. Therefore, we adopt the Information Gain (IG), which is widely used in text classification, Li et al. (2009), to calculate the efficacy of features and select an approximate optimal feature-set.

After Arg1's position is identified, we handle the DAI according to intra-sentence and inter-sentence cases methodologies, as follows.

4.1 Formulating Intra-sentence DAI as a Simplified Semantic Parsing Problem

Given a parse tree and a predicate, shallow semantic parsing detects and classifies each of the constituents in the sentence into either their corresponding semantic argument (role) for the predicate, or as a non-argument. Similarly, the discourse connective can be taken as the predicate, while its scope can be mapped into several constituents dominated by the connective and thus can be regarded as the argument of the connective. Take this sentence as an example 'Shorter maturities are considered a sign of rising rates because portfolio managers can capture higher rates sooner.'. The connective 'because' has the Arg1 'Shorter maturities are considered a sign of rising rates' and 'portfolio managers can capture higher rates sooner' the Arg2. As shown in Figure 2 below, the node "$IN_{9,9}$" represents the connective "because" while its Arg1 includes four constituents {$NP\text{-}SBJ\text{-}9_{0,1}$,$VBP_{2,2}$,$VBN_{3,3}$,$S_{4,8}$}, and its Arg2 includes only one constituent {$S_{10,16}$}. Similar to common shallow semantic parsing, our DAI consist of two pipeline phases: argument pruning and argument identification. Currently, we leave post-processing phase as one of our future works.

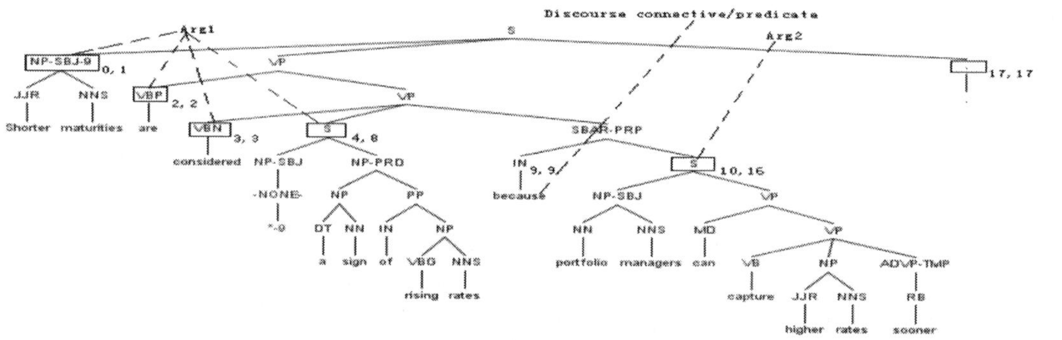

FIGURE 2 – An example of a connective and its argument in a parse tree

Argument pruning: Our discourse argument pruning strategy, being similar to that of Xue et al. (2004), which is widely used in common shallow semantic parsing, is detailed as follows.

(1) Designate the connective as the current node and collect its siblings.

(2) Reset the current node to its parent and repeat Step (1) until it reaches a threshold *Level* (tree level distance between the current node and the connective).

Argument identification: We divide the argument identification into the following two phases. Firstly, a binary classifier is applied to determine whether or not, after pruning, the argument candidates constitute valid arguments. Secondly, a multiclass classifier is adopted to assign a valid argument candidate with a label, e.g. Arg1 or Arg2 or Null.

Most features listed in Table 1 are commonly used in shallow semantic parsing, and most of them are semantic driven(We adopt the head-finding rules described in Collins (1999) and the function type of connection listed in appendix A of Knott (1996).). We categorize the features into three groups as lexical, syntactic and connective-driven features, as shown in Table 1. For the connective-driven features, for example, statistics of connective positions in PDTB tells us that the connective positions are suitable as start, before and back of middle. Therefore, we separate these 3 situations into either lesser or greater than middle, F14, as shown in Table 1.

Features	**Remarks**	**Feature value**
Lexical features		
F1	Connective itself	because
F2	Part-of-speech of the connective	IN
F3	The headword and its POS of constituent candidate	sign, NN
F4	The left and right word of the connective	rates, portfolio
F5	The left and right word of the constituent candidate	considered, because
Syntactic features		
F6	The syntactic category of the constituent candidate.	S
F7	The syntactic path from the constituent candidate to the connective.	S<VP>SBAR-PRP>IN
F8	The subcategory of the connective.	SBAR-PRP:IN+S
F9	The phrase type of the connective's parent node.	SBAR-PRP
F10	The subcategory of the constituent candidate.	VP:VBN+S+SBAR-PRP
F11	The phrase type of the constituent candidate's parent node.	VP
F12	The phrase type of the constituent candidate's left and right sibling.	VBN,SBAR-PRP
Connective-driven features		
F13	The position of the constituent candidate with the connective. "left" or "right"	left
F14	The position of the connective in sentence. "lesser than middle" or "greater than middle"	greater than middle
F15	The function type of the connective. "subordinator" or "Coordinator" or "Conj-adverb"	subordinator

TABLE 1 – Features and their instantiations for argument identification within DAI, with "because" as the connective, and $S_{4,8}$, as shown in Figure 2, as the focus constituent.

We don't use features provided by AddDiscourse tool because it was designed for discourse connective and relation identification. In this paper, we formulate the DAI as a shallow semantic parsing problem, and our main goal is to verify the effectiveness of shallow semantic parsing driven features in DAI. The relationship between the constituents and arguments can be embodied within the shallow semantic parsing framework if we regard connective as predicate.

4.2 Rule-based Inter-sentence DAI

According to Prasad et al. (2008)'s statistics, Arg1 in previous, adjacent sentence account for 30.1% in the whole PDTB corpus. Based on this observation, a lightweight heuristic rule-based solution is adopted. Therefore, we assign the preceding adjacent sentence as Arg1, which has already given F1-measures of 76.90% overall in the PDTB, as mentioned in Lin et al. (2010). In addition, we assign the entire sentence excluding the connective as Arg2.

5 Experiment

In this section, we describe the experiment settings, together with the experiment results.

5.1 Experiment Settings

Similar to Lin et al.(2010)'s evaluation settings, we evaluate our system with GS_noEP(Gold Standard parsers without Error Propagation), GS_EP and Auto(Automatic parsers)_EP settings. All the results use the Johansson and Moschitti (2010)'s exact matching scoring of argument. For the intra-sentence cases, we remove parenthesis and keep subordinate clause for spans to comply with minimality principle on the PDTB, normalize all spans by removing leading or trailing punctuation, and evaluate the system on three main tasks: (1) argument detection, (2)independently classifying phase of known to be discourse arguments into the specific categories, Arg1 and Arg2, and (3) the combined task of detection of the discourse argument and then assigning respective labels (Arg1, Arg2, Null) to them. The Maximum Entropy software package Mallet (http://mallet.cs.umass.edu/) is selected as our classifier, and Berkley parser (http://code.google.com/p/berkeleyparser/downloads/list) is used to generate the automatic parser tree. For feature selection, we set *IG_rate* (a threshold value for IG) at a value of 0.5 which is widely used in the common text classification task.

5.2 Experiment Results

For the Arg1 position classification phase, we get F-measure of 97.55% using our new added features and feature selection process trained on Section 02-22 and tested on Section 23-24 under GS_noEP setting. A paired t-test shows that the improvement is significantly superior to Lin's 96.45% with p<0.01. The output of final feature sets after using our feature selection are {*C*; *C*'s position; *C* POS; $prev_1$; $prev_1$+*C*; $prev_1$ POS+*C* POS; $prev_2$; $prev_2$ POS; $next_2$; $next_2$ POS; $next_2$ + C; $next_2$ POS+*C* POS}. They show that the new added features along with the feature selection process are useful for determining Arg1's position and they can mitigate the effect of cascaded error propagation.

Experiments on development sets (Section 00-01) show the proper value of *Level* for intra-sentence cases, resulting in an average value of *Level* equal to 3.73. Therefore, we set *Level*=3 *and Level*=4 to check their influence on the parameter *Level* for the argument identification phase. We get F-measure of 86.70% for argument detection when Level equals to 4 trained on Section 02-22 and tested on Section 23-24 under GS_noEP setting, improvements of 1.10% over the Level equals to 3. For the heuristic rules in argument pruning, we also tried the pruning strategy (no Level consideration) as adopted in Xue et al.(2004). However, its performance was about 2.0% lower than our extended pruning strategy. Due to space limitation, we do not give the detail comparison. The result also verifies our assumption that the argument of a connective consists of a constituent in the parser tree, which is always located at a specific level, near the connective.

For the independently classifying phase of Arg1, Arg2 and Both (exact match of both Arg1 and Arg2 simultaneously) for intra-sentence cases, we get Accuracy of 94.15%, 88.72% and 83.28% for Arg1, Arg2 and Both, respectively. With the performance of Level equals to 4 is greater than *Level* equals to 3, therefore, we conduct the following experiments using a parameter *Level* equals to 4.

Table 2, below, compares the performance for the combined task, between our system and Ghosh's system. As is shown, the performance of Arg1 exact matching of our system significantly outperforms Ghosh's system, and the performance of Arg2 with our system slightly outperforms or comparable with theirs. In addition, the performance on automatic syntactic parsing is lower than on the golden parser tree. As expected, some nodes in the automatic parser tree cannot be mapped into corresponding nodes in the golden parser tree, which result in error propagation within the argument pruning and identification phases. Generally, the Precision of Ghosh's system is higher than our system, while the Recall of their system is lower than ours, which is maybe caused by the features listed in the Table 1 are fine-grained, most of them can capture the relationship between constituent and discourse connective, while features adopted in Ghosh's system are coarse-grained. Thus, the total F-measure of our system is higher than theirs.

	Our system			Ghosh's system		
	Arg1	Arg2	Both	Arg1	Arg2	Both
	GS_noEP			(Ghosh et al.,2012)		
Precision(%)	66.28	82.64	58.38	66.10	82.96	-
Recall(%)	59.99	78.24	58.05	53.92	76.28	-
F-measure	**62.98***	80.38	58.21	59.39	79.48	-
	GS_EP			(Ghosh et al.,2011b)		
Precision(%)	65.61	83.14	58.44	67.00	82.00	-
Recall(%)	53.36	68.65	50.22	31.00	70.00	-
F-measure	**58.85***	75.20	54.02	43.00	76.00	-
	Auto_EP			(Ghosh et al.,2011b)		
Precision(%)	58.45	75.64	56.41	63.00	78.00	-
Recall(%)	40.88	59.12	39.06	28.00	58.00	-
F-measure	**48.11***	66.37	46.16	39.00	67.00	-

TABLE 2 – Performance of combined task trained on Section 02-22 and tested on Section 23-24. Performance that is significantly superior to Ghosh's system ($p<0.01$,using paired t-test for significance) is denoted by *.

Table 3 illustrates the performance comparison, for combined task, between our system and Lin's system. As is shown, the performance of Arg1 and Both of our system significantly outperforms Lin's system under GS_noEP setting. Furthermore, the performance of Arg1 and Both of our system slightly outperforms Lin's system under GS_EP setting. The performance of Arg2 of our system is lower than Lin's system, which may be caused by the following two reasons: firstly,

Lin et al. (2010) significantly improved the connective identification performance by incorporating their own features and further processing; secondly, the data distribution of intra-sentence and inter-sentence in Section 23 is not coincident with that in Section 23-24. In addition, we can observe that the performance of Arg1 and Both of our system significantly outperforms Lin's system under Auto_EP setting. This also verifies our framework is robust when facing parser tree error. For example, if the $S_{10,16}$(Arg2) of the connective in Figure 2 is incorrectly expanded by the rule $S_{10,16}$->NP-SB$J_{10,11}$+M$D_{12,12}$+V$P_{13,16}$, the scope of Arg2 of the connective "because" can still be correctly detected.

	Our system			Lin's system(Lin et al.,2010)		
	Arg1	Arg2	Both	Arg1	Arg2	Both
GS_noEP						
Precision(%)	64.36	83.30	56.16	-	-	-
Recall(%)	57.42	78.66	55.69	-	-	-
F-measure	**60.69***	81.00	**55.92***	59.15	82.23	53.85
GS_EP						
Precision(%)	62.36	81.15	54.75	-	-	-
Recall(%)	55.04	71.61	51.35	-	-	-
F-measure	58.47	76.08	53.00	57.64	79.80	52.29
Auto_EP						
Precision(%)	62.48	80.86	60.41	-	-	-
Recall(%)	42.36	61.97	40.74	-	-	-
F-measure	**50.48***	70.17	**48.66***	47.68	70.27	40.37

TABLE 3 – Results of combined task trained on Section 02-21 and tested on Section 23. Performance that is significantly superior to Lin's system (p<0.01,using paired t-test for significance) is denoted by *.

Conclusions and Future Work

In this paper, we have presented a new approach to PDTB-style discourse argument identification from intra-sentence and inter-sentence perspectives. For the intra-sentence cases, we formulate it as a simplified shallow semantic parsing problem. In particular, we regard the discourse connective as the predicate and map its scope into several constituents, which are deemed as argument of the predicate. For the inter-sentence cases, we present a lightweight heuristic rule-based solution. Evaluation on the PDTB shows the appropriateness of our approach. It also shows that our approach significantly outperforms the state-of-the-art chunking alternatives.

Our future work will be to improve the performance further, through exploring tree kernel-based method, together with more feature engineering.

Acknowledgments

This research was supported by Projects 60970056, 90920004, 61273320 under the National Natural Science Foundation of China, Project CXZZ11_0101 under the Program Granted for Scientific Innovation Research of College Graduate of Jiangsu province, Project 2012AA011102 under the National High-Tech Research and Development Plan of China, Project 20093201110006 under the Specialized Research Fund for the Doctoral Program of Higher Education of China, Project BK2011282, 11KIJ520003 under the National Natural Science Foundation of Jiangsu province.

References

Caruana, R. and Freitag, D. (1994). Greedy attribute selection. In *Proceedings of ML 1994*, pages 28-36.

Chapman, W. W., Bridewell, W., Hanbury, P., Cooper, G. F. and Buchanan, B. G. (2001). A simple algorithm for identifying negated findings and diseases in discharge summaries. *Journal of Biomedical Informatics*,34(2001):301-310.

Collins, M. (1999). Head-driven statistical models for natural language parsing. *Ph.D thesis, USA: University of Pennsyivania*, 1999:1-296.

Dinesh, N.,Lee, A.,Miltsakaki, E.,Prasad, R. and Joshi, A. (2005). Attribution and the (non-)alignment of syntactic and discourse arguments of connectives. In *Proceedings of Workshop on Frontiers in Corpus Annotation II:Pie in the Sky 2005*, pages 29-36.

Elwell, R. and Baldridge, J. (2008). Discourse connective argument identification with connective specific rankers. In *Proceedings of ICSC 2008*, pages 198-205.

Ghosh, S., Johansson, R., Riccardi, G. and Tonelli, S. (2011a). Shallow discourse parsing with conditional random fields. In *Proceedings of IJCNLP 2011*, pages 1071-1079.

Ghosh, S., Riccardi, G. and Johansson, R. (2012). Global features for shallow discourse parsing. In *Proceedings of SIGDIAL 2012*, pages 150-159.

Ghosh, S.,Tonelli, S., Riccardi, G. and Johansson, R. (2011b). End-to-end discourse parser evaluation. In *Proceedings of ICSC 2011*, pages 169-172.

Hong, Y., Zhou, X., Che, T., Yao, J., Zhu, Q. and Zhou, G. (2012). Cross-argument inference for implicit relation extraction. In *Proceedings of CIKM 2012*:accepted.

Huttunen, S., Vihavainen, A., Etter, P. V. and Yangarber, R. (2011). Relevance prediction in information extraction using discourse and lexical features. In *Proceedings of NCCL 2011*, pages 114-121.

Johansson, R. and Moschitti, A. (2010). Syntactic and semantic structure for opinion expression detection. In *Proceedings of CoNLL 2010*, pages 67-76.

Knott, A. (1996). A data-driven methodology for motivating a set of coherence relations. *Ph.D thesis, Scotland: University of Edinburgh*, 1996:1-216.

Li, S., Xia, R., Zong, C. and Huang, C. (2009). A framework of feature selection methods for text categorization. In *Proceedings of ACL-IJCNLP 2009*, pages 692-700.

Li, J., Zhou, G., Ng, H. (2010a). Joint Syntactic and Semantic Parsing of Chinese. In *Proceedings of ACL 2010*, pages 1108-1117.

Li, J., Zhou, G., Wang, H. and Zhu, Q. (2010b). Learning the scope of negation via shallow semantic parsing. In *Proceedings of COLING 2010*, pages 671-679.

Lin, Z., Kan, M. and Ng H. (2009). Recognizing implicit discourse relations in the penn discourse treebank. In *Proceedings of EMNLP 2009*, pages 343-351.

Lin, Z., Ng, H. T. and Kan, M. (2010). A pdtb-styled end-to-end discourse parser. *Technical report TRB8/10, Singapore: National University of Singapore*, 2010:1-15.

Meyer, T. (2011). Disambiguating temporal-contrastive discourse connectives for machine translation. In *Proceedings of ACL-HLT 2011*, pages 46-51.

Morante, R. and Daelemans,W. (2009). A metalearning approach to proceeding the scope of negation. In *Proceedings of CoNLL 2009*, pages 21-29.

Moschitti, A. (2004). A study on convolution kernels for shallow semantic parsing. In *Proceedings of ACL 2004*, pages 335-342.

Pitler, E., Louis, A. and Nenkova, A. (2009a). Automatic sense prediction for implicit discourse relations in text. In *Proceedings of ACL-IJCNLP 2009*, pages 683-691.

Pitler, E. and Nenkova, A. (2009b). Using syntax to disambiguate explicit discourse connectives in text. In *Proceedings of ACL-IJCNLP 2009*, pages 13-16.

Prasad, R., Dinesh, N., Lee, A., Miltsakaki, E., Robaldo, L., Joshi, A. and Webber, B. (2008). The penn discourse treebank 2.0. In *Proceedings of LREC 2008*, pages 2961-2968.

Prasad, R., Joshi, A. and Webber, B. (2010). Exploiting scope for shallow discourse parsing. In *Proceedings of LREC2010*, pages 2076-2083.

Somasundaran, S., Namata, G., Wiebe, J. and Getoor, L. (2009). Supervised and unsupervised methods in employing discourse relations for improving opinion polarity classification. In *Proceedings of EMNLP 2009*, pages 170-179.

Wang, W., Su, J. and Tan, C. (2010). Kernel based discourse relation recognition with temporal ordering information. In *Proceedings of ACL 2010*, pages 710-719.

Wellner, B. and Pustejovsky, J. (2007). Automatically identifying the arguments of discourse connectives. In *Proceedings of EMNLP-CoNLL 2007*, pages 92-101.

Xue, N. and Palmer, M. (2004). Calibrating features for semantic role labeling. In *Proceedings of EMNLP 2004*, pages 88-94.

Zhou, Z., Xu, Y., Niu, Z., Lan, M., Su, J., Tan, C. (2010). Predicting of discourse connectives for implicit discourse relation recognition. In *Proceedings of COLING 2010*, pages 1507-1514.

Zhu, Q., Li J., Wang H. and Zhou G. (2010). A unified framework for scope learning via simplified shallow semantic parsing. In *Proceedings of EMNLP 2010*, pages 714-724.

Using Deep Linguistic Features for Finding Deceptive Opinion Spam*

Qiongkai Xu[1,2] Hai Zhao[1,2†]
(1) MOE-Microsoft Key Laboratory of Intelligent Computing and Intelligent System;
(2) Department of Computer Science and Engineering, Shanghai Jiao Tong University,
#800 Dongchuan Road, Shanghai, China, 200240
xuqiongkai@sjtu.edu.cn, zhaohai@cs.sjtu.edu.cn

ABSTRACT

While most recent work has focused on instances of opinion spam which are manually identifiable or deceptive opinion spam which are written by paid writers separately, in this work we study both of these interesting topics and propose an effective framework which has good performance on both datasets. Based on the golden-standard opinion spam dataset, we propose a novel model which integrates some deep linguistic features derived from a syntactic dependency parsing tree to discriminate deceptive opinions from normal ones. On a background of multiple language tasks, our model is evaluated on both English (gold-standard) and Chinese (non-gold) datasets. The experimental results show that our model produces state-of-the-art results on both of the topics.

TITLE AND ABSTRACT IN ANOTHER LANGUAGE (MANDARIN)

欺骗性垃圾信息中的高级语言特征探索

最近，许多研究工作分别着重研究了可手动识别的意见垃圾和由收费写手编写的欺骗性意见垃圾。本文中，我们提出了一个行之有效的框架，并在这两个不同的主题的数据集上都获得了良好的处理效果。基于标准的意见垃圾数据集，本文提出了一个集成了依存句法树等高级语言特征的新模型，用于欺骗性垃圾意见的识别。在多语言任务背景下，所提出的模型分别在英文数据集（职业写手编写的）和中文（手工标注的）数据集上进行了评估。实验结果表明，所提出的模型均能获得目前为止的最优结果。

KEYWORDS: Opinion Spam, Multi-Language, Deep Linguistic Features.

KEYWORDS IN MANDARIN: 意见垃圾, 多语言, 深度语言特征.

† Corresponding author

* This work was partially supported by the National Natural Science Foundation of China (Grant No. 60903119 and Grant No. 61170114), the National Research Foundation for the Doctoral Program of Higher Education of China under Grant No. 20110073120022, the National Basic Research Program of China (Grant No. 2009CB320901), and the European Union Seventh Framework Program (Grant No. 247619).

Proceedings of COLING 2012: Posters, pages 1341–1350,
COLING 2012, Mumbai, December 2012.

1 Introduction

With the growing number of review websites where users can express opinions (e.g.,TripAdvisor [1]), there is an increasing potential to gain money through opinion spam–inappropriate or fraudulent reviews. The large benefits of this result in the occurrence of a group of writers who only write articles that deceive the users. Their comments always mislead readers to buy or use their products. Our goal is to find the hidden features of the deceptive opinions written by these writers. In Chinese, paid writers who flood websites are called "water army" and recognizing them is called "Water Army detection".

Till now, considerable attentions have been paid to other kinds of spam, such as web spam, e-mail spam and so on. Research focused on opinion spam is rarely reported till now. Jindal and Liu (2007) was one of the earliest work about Internet review spam. Further more, most previous work in this area focused on finding methods of detecting opinion spam which can be identified by a human reader. Only detecting this kind of opinion spam is not enough, because users can easily recognize the useless information by themselves and will not be misled. A much more challenging task, detection of deceptive opinion has been proposed by (Yoo and Gretzel, 2009; Ott et al., 2011) which is based on a gold-standard dataset. They have done the data selection and initial analysis work on this interesting topic.

Our work uses gold-standard dataset collected by (Ott et al., 2011) and non-gold standard Chinese dataset collected by ourselves. We give a machine learning model which is about 2 percent better than previous works on gold standard dataset and is also very effective on non-gold standard dataset. Later, we analyze the close relationship between sentence structure and deceptive opinion. Finally, statistical methodologies have been used to analyze all the feature sets and some theoretical contributions are summarized.

Our work mainly focuses on deceptive opinion spam. They are fictitious opinions that have been deliberately written by paid writers to sound authentic, in order to deceive the reader. If a deceptive opinion is mixed with a huge amount of truthful opinions, it is very hard for users to ignore or even identify it. The existing study proved that even a native speaker cannot identify most deceptive opinions. However, automatic classifiers have really good performance on these disturbing texts.

To obtain better performance on this task, we optimize it in two parts. Firstly, we test some other machine learning models. We use a support vector machine (SVM) as baseline to compare with the maximum entropy model (MEM). The result is that MEM performs better. Secondly, we try other approaches on this dataset and find that sentence structure features give really good performance. We combine all these improvements and train a final model that outputs state-of-the-art performance on gold-standard dataset. Later, this model is used on Chinese dataset collected by our group and also obtain good performance. Finally, we make some theoretical contributions to this topic.

2 Related Work

Most Internet spam detection work can be divided into two stages of development. The earliest work tried to detect spam which contained little useful information. They focused on the media of e-mail spam (Sahami et al., 1998; Drucker et al., 1999), web spam (Fetterly et al., 2004; Ntoulas et al., 2006),blog spam (Bhattarai et al., 2009), Twitter spam (Grier et al., 2010) and

[1] http://tripadvisor.com

review spam (Jindal and Liu, 2008). They used statistics and machine learning methodologies to analyze and investigate this topic extensively. In recent years, some researchers have begun to pay attention to the detection of spam which is deceptive. They analyzed review spam (Yoo and Gretzel, 2009; Wu et al., 2010; Ott et al., 2011; Li et al., 2011; Lau et al., 2012) and rumors on microblogs (Qazvinian et al., 2011). Following these works, our work deals with the second problem, deceptive opinion detection.

Although, opinion spam is widely spread on the Internet(Jindal and Liu, 2008). It is quite difficult to obtain a first-hand deceptive opinion dataset. Jindal and Liu (2008) used duplicate reviews as positive data and other views as negative examples[2]. Wu et al. (2010) tried to detect deceptive opinion spam by comparing popularity rankings. Qazvinian et al. (2011) annotated rumors (a similar concept to deceptive opinion) by experts manually which is a huge project. Our work may save such human judgement as we use gold-standard deceptive opinions.

Yoo and Gretzel (2009) first tried to collect a small gold-standard dataset from a group of tourism marketing students and statistical methods were used to analyze the difference between them from a psychological viewpoint. Ott et al. (2011) extended their work and collected a gold-standard dataset of 400 truthful and 400 deceptive opinions to develop automated deception classifiers. Following them, we also collect two datasets, 800 gold-standard opinions in English and 1800 non-gold standard opinions in Chinese (See section 3). We try to find the sentence structure or deep linguistic characteristics of deceptive opinions. By this effort, we improve the automated deceptive classifier by about 2 percent on gold-standard dataset and our model also works well on non-gold standard Chinese dataset collected by our group.

Chen et al. (2011) introduced the spam detection work into Chinese forums. They focus on detecting deceptive writers by using both semantic and non-semantic analysis. Spam writer detection was also investigated by (Lim et al., 2010; Mukherjee et al., 2011). Different from their works, our work only focuses on the content of opinions themselves with no additional information.

3 Dataset Construction

It is pointed that most of the opinions online are truthful(Jindal and Liu, 2008). Insidious deceptive opinions are very difficult to obtain. In this part, we describe where our English gold-standard deceptive opinions and Chinese manually annotated dataset come from.

3.1 Gold-standard English Dataset

Since Ott et al. (2011) have already provided a dataset which contains deceptive and truthful opinions, we use their dataset as our English gold standard dataset for our research. Bellow, we describe the detailed methods of collection.

3.1.1 Deceptive Opinions

To obtain a credible deceptive dataset, data collection procedure imitates the real way how these deceptive opinions are collected by asking those true deceptive opinion authors to do their jobs again. They created 400 Human Intelligence Tasks (HITs) using the Amazon Mechanical Turk[3](AMT)[4] with a one dollar award and allocated them to Turkers located in the United

[2]They suppose duplicate opinions are likely to be deceptive opinions

[3]http://mturk.com

[4]20 HITs for each of the 20 hotels they selected.

		TRUTHFUL			DECEPTIVE		
	Accuracy	P	R	F	P	R	F
META-old(native)	60.6%	60.8%	60.0%	60.4%	60.5%	61.3%	60.9%
META-new(non-native)	54.5%	52.8%	54.7%	53.7%	56.3%	61.5%	58.8%

Table 1: Performance of meta judgement of three college students, corresponding to the cross-validation experiment in Section 5.

States. They imposed a restriction that all the opinions should be written by unique authors to avoid that classifiers are over-tuned by different author styles, and all the tasks should be finished in 30 minutes.

They told the Turkers the name and website of a hotel. The Turkers were asked to assume that they worked for the hotel and write a deceptive, realistic-sounding and positive review for the hotel. Finally, they filtered out all the insufficient quality reviews(e.g., unreasonably short, plagiarized and so on) and obtained 400 golden deceptive opinions. These opinions were used as the deceptive part of the dataset.

3.1.2 Truthful Opinions

For truthful part, they first got all 6,977 opinions of the 20 most popular hotels (Same as the 20 hotels chosen for HIT) form TripAdvisor. To balance the number of truthful opinions and deceptive opinions, 20 opinions for each of the 20 hotels that meet the following conditions were selected[5]:

- 5-star[6] review;
- Only English reviews;
- More than 150 characters, because most deceptive opinions have at least 150 characters;
- Not written by first-time authors (new users who have not previously posted an opinion);[7]

3.1.3 Human Performance

Ott et al. (2011) have proved the human performance on their dataset is low and made this a baseline for further discussion. The highest result is from meta-judge[8] of the three students, as presented in Table 1. We also ask three Chinese college students who have passed CET6 (College English Test Level 6) for help to make the judgement on a subset of this data. We label the review deceptive when any of the students believe that the review is deceptive. The result is shown in the second line of Table 1.

The result in Table 1 shows that non-native speakers perform even worse than native speakers. Both these meta judges will be used as baselines to compare with the automatic approach of detecting deceptive opinions.

[5]Same as the hotels selected for deceptive opinion dataset

[6]Score given by user from 1-star to 5-star shows the support of the user for the hotel.

[7]First-time authors are more likely to give opinion spam(Wu et al., 2010)

[8]Meta judge labels a review deceptive when any human judge believes the review to be deceptive.

total	DECEPTIVE	TRUTHFUL
23397	22337	1060

Table 2: Number of each class of instances.

3.2 Chinese Dataset

Chinese dataset is collected from a famous Chinese online forum [9]. Since it is very hard to find qualified deceptive opinion authors, we use a collection-and-annotation method. We collected over 20000 reviews and asked two experts who are very familiar with photography to go through all these reviews and marked each review a spam or not, see Table 2. Finally, we get a dataset of 1800 reviews (900 positive and 900 negative opinions) for the balance of data.

To evaluate the accuracy of our Chinese non-gold dataset, we annotated 800 reviews randomly selected instances twice and Kappa coefficient (κ) was calculated to compare the result of each annotator by the following formula:

$$\kappa = \frac{Pr(a) - Pr(e)}{1 - Pr(e)} \quad (1)$$

where $Pr(a)$ is the proportion of times that the two annotators agree and $Pr(e)$ is the proportion of times that they would are expected to agree by chance(Carletta, 1996). The Kappa coefficient result is 0.97. This result shows that our annotators reach a high agreement in our deceptive opinion annotation task.

4 Deceptive Opinion Detection

To train an effective classifier, Ott et al. (2011) mainly focus on the following three approaches:

- Genre identification;
- Psycholinguist deceptive detection;
- Text categorization;

Another approach to identify deceptive opinion spam is using structural features of sentences. We are inspired by the idea that the genre of the text can be used to detect deceptive opinion spam. The structure of the sentence shows the genre of a writer, in some sense. We use the following two approaches to describe the structure of the sentence :

- BIPOS($POS_{-1} + POS$)
- DEP($DEP\_label + form + head\_form$)

Since the frequency distribution of part-of-speech (POS) tags in a text is often dependent on the genre of the text (Newman et al., 2003) and POS tag bigrams (BIPOS) will not only show frequency information of POS, but also show the structure of the sentence, we suppose that POS tag bigrams will give a better performance than pure POS features. By counting the frequency

[9] http://bbs.fengniao.com/forum/. Most topics on this forum are about photography.

of different structural features of the sentence, we get the hidden genre information of the text. These features also provide a baseline with which to compare our other sentence structure features.

The structure of the sentence is usually represented by a parsing tree. Among various existing syntactic parsers, the dependency parser is chosen for this work due to its simplicity. We extract the corresponding feature from the output of the Stanford parser (De Marneffe et al., 2006). Three dependency parsing features are integrated, dependency label (*DEP_label*), word forms (*form*) of the current word and the head word (*head_form*). These features are used as part of a sentence structure feature set in our classifier.

4.1 Classifiers

Features from the approaches just introduced are used to train support vector machine and maximum entropy classifiers, both of which are well known machine learning models which have performed well in related work (Zhang and Yao, 2003; Ott et al., 2011).

We train a support vector machine (SVM) classifier, which finds a high-dimensional separating hyperplane between two groups of data. This method is proved useful in (Ott et al., 2011). Instances can be classified by the following formula:

$$y(x) = sign\left[\sum_{k=1}^{N} \alpha_k y_k \Phi(x, x_k) + b\right] \tag{2}$$

Where N is the number of instance, x_k is the kth input pattern and y_k is the kth output pattern. Φ is the kernel function : $\Phi(x, x_k) = x_k^T x$ (linear SVM).

We use LIBSVM(Chang and Lin, 2011) to train our linear support vector machine (SVM) models on all the approaches mentioned in Section 4.

We also train a maximum entropy model (MEM), which finds the probability distribution that satisfies the constraints and minimizes the relative entropy. In general, a conditional Maximum Entropy model is an exponential (log-linear) model which has the form:

$$p(a|b) = \frac{1}{Z(b)} \prod_{j=1}^{k} \alpha_j^{f_j(a,b)} \tag{3}$$

where $p(a|b)$ denotes the probability of predicting an outcome a in the given context b with constraint or "feature" functions $f_j(a, b)$. Here k is the number of features and $Z(b) = \sum_a \prod_{j=1}^{k} \alpha_j^{f_j(a,b)}$.

We use openNLP MAXENT[10] (Berger et al., 1996) and iterate 200 times to train our models on all the approaches mentioned in Section 4, the same as the approaches used for the support vector machine (SVM) model.

5 Experiment and Discussion

5.1 Experiment

We use a five-fold nested cross validation (CV) (Quadrianto et al., 2009) procedure to evaluate the performance of each feature set. The result is given in Table 3. SVM-linear line is the result

[10]http://incubator.apache.org/opennlp/

			TRUTHFUL			DECEPTIVE		
Model	Feature	Accuracy	P	R	F	P	R	F
SVM-linear (baseline)	UNIGRAM	88.4%	89.9	86.5	88.2	87.0	90.3	88.6
	BIGRAM$^+$	89.6%	**90.1**	89.0	89.6	89.1	**90.3**	89.7
	BIGRAM$^+$ + LIWC	**89.8%**	89.8	**89.8**	**89.8**	**89.8**	89.8	**89.8**
MEM	POS	74.0%	72.0	75.0	73.5	76.0	73.1	74.5
	BIPOS	76.9%	76.3	77.2	76.7	77.5	76.5	77.0
	DEP	86.3%	86.3	86.3	86.3	86.3	86.3	86.3
	UNIGRAM	90.6%	89.0	92.0	90.5	92.2	89.3	90.8
	UNIGRAM + DEP	**91.6%**	**90.8**	92.4	**91.6**	92.5	**90.9**	**91.7**
	UNIGRAM + LIWC	91.4%	89.8	**92.8**	91.2	**93.0**	90.1	91.5
	BIGRAM$^+$	90.5%	89.3	91.5	90.4	91.8	89.5	90.6
META_JUDGEMENT_old		60.6%	60.8	60.0	60.4	60.5	61.3	60.9
META_JUDGEMENT_new		58.1%	53.1	56.3	55.5	56.3	54.4	55.3

Table 3: Performance of our approaches based on 5-fold cross-validation (CV) experiments with accuracy, precision, recall and F-score. Baseline is the performance of the approaches according to (Ott et al., 2011) on our dataset.

		TRUTHFUL			DECEPTIVE		
Feature	Accuracy	P	R	F	P	R	F
UNIGRAM+DET	79.1%	89.8	74.0	81.1	68.5	87.0	76.6
BIGRAM$^+$	78.3%	89.8	73.0	80.5	66.8	86.7	75.4
BIGRAM$^+$ +DET	78.8%	89.8	73.6	80.9	67.8	86.9	76.1

Table 4: Performance of 5-fold cross-validation (CV) experiments with accuracy, precision, recall and F-score on Chinese dataset

POS		UNIGRAM		DEPENDENCY label only	
DECEPTIVE	TRUTHFUL	DECEPTIVE	TRUTHFUL	DECEPTIVE	TRUTHFUL
-LRB-	JJ	prime_JJ	why_WRB	punct	mwe
,	WP	home_NN	etc._NN	prt	purpcl
PRP	NN	well_NN	commented_VBD	possessive	advmod
-RRB-	MD	convention_NN	extras_NNS	iobj	aux
CC	.	round_NN	downstairs_NNS	nsubj	amod
BIPOS		**BIGRAM**		**DEPENDENCY detail**	
DECEPTIVE	TRUTHFUL	DECEPTIVE	TRUTHFUL	DECEPTIVE	TRUTHFUL
WRB_FW	RB_,	checking_VBG_out_PRP	was_VBD_worth_IN	pobj(for&members)	pobj(with&amenity)
VBG_PDT	IN_$	want_VB_to_TO	Just_RB_returned_VBN	mark(visiting&while)	nn(Michigan&Lake)
NNP_DT	VBD_RP	the_DT_wine_NN	feeling_NN_._.	cop(spacious&is)	prep(surrounded&by)
VBN_VBP	WP_PRP	next_JJ_year_NN	level_NN_._.	root(ROOT&leave)	xcomp(in&check)
IN_VBZ	CC_FW	a_DT_breakfast_NN	and_CC_take_VB	amod(staff&excellent)	prep(reminded&of)

Table 5: 15 most frequently occurring features of each feature set. Ranks of deceptive and truthful opinion are separated.

of the approach in (Ott et al., 2011). MEM line is our new model which outperforms previous work.

We also give the results of non-native speaker performance on gold-standard dataset in Table 1. We find that they do worse work than native speaker. We attribute this to the reason that the students that we asked for help are Chinese college students and English is not their native language. That suggests that deceptive text can mislead foreigners more easily.

On a background of multiple language tasks, our model is also tested on our Chinese dataset. All the approaches described in Section 4 were used on the MEM. We use BaseSeg (Zhao et al., 2006) as word segmenter, BasePos[11] as POS (part of speech) tagger and FudanNLP tools [12] as dependency parser. The highest three results are shown in Table 4. BIGRAM$^+$+DEP outperforms BIGRAM$^+$ shows that sentence structure features also give good performance on Chinese and our model keeps effective.

5.2 Discussion

Comparing POS feature alone with POS tag bigram (BIPOS) features, we find BIPOS always performs better. That means POS feature alone cannot fully represent the genre of an opinion. On the other hand, the BIPOS feature set has much richer features and can classify the genre more easily. Since sentence structure also indicates the genre of a text, we will use this feature set as an optimization feature set.

We have tested different combinations of feature sets and listed the representative results, see Table 3. We find that UNIGRAM+DEP works best on maximum entropy model(MEM), about 2% higher than best result of SVM-linear model(BIGRAM$^+$+LIWC). This proves that sentence structure can decide the genre of a text and detect deceptive opinions.

To make the following analysis clear, the 5 highest weighted features (learned by MEM) for each feature set for deceptive opinion and truthful opinion are listed in Table 5. Observation results are shown below: (1) PRP has a high weight in deceptive opinion spam, which means that deceptive opinions are more likely to use personal words. (2) Such forms, nn(Michigan&Lake) weights high showing that truthful opinion always provided concrete information like a location. (3) Words like home, well, wine, breakfast, excellent which are normally used in daily life get higher weight in deceptive opinion, while words like feeling, downstairs which can reflect self feeling are more likely to occur in truthful opinion. (4) etc. obtain high weight in truthful opinion detection meaning that truth authors can sometimes give concrete examples to elaborate their views.

6 Conclusion

In this work, we made an extensive annotation based on the existing dataset for deceptive opinion spam detection. We tried a new approach, using deep linguistic features, for this task and proved it useful. We also tested some other classifiers and improved the classification models for the task. The proposed model outperforms the baseline system by about 2%. On the background of multiple language tasks, our new model was tested on both English and Chinese datasets and proved to be useful.

[11] http://bcmi.sjtu.edu.cn/ zhaohai/index.html
[12] http://code.google.com/p/fudannlp/

References

Berger, A., Pietra, V., and Pietra, S. (1996). A maximum entropy approach to natural language processing. *Computational linguistics*, 22(1):39–71.

Bhattarai, A., Rus, V., and Dasgupta, D. (2009). Characterizing comment spam in the blogosphere through content analysis. In *Computational Intelligence in Cyber Security, 2009. CICS'09. IEEE Symposium on*, pages 37–44. IEEE.

Carletta, J. (1996). Assessing agreement on classification tasks: the kappa statistic. *Computational linguistics*, 22(2):249–254.

Chang, C. and Lin, C. (2011). Libsvm: a library for support vector machines. *ACM Transactions on Intelligent Systems and Technology (TIST)*, 2(3):27.

Chen, C., Wu, K., Srinivasan, V., and Zhang, X. (2011). Battling the internet water army: Detection of hidden paid posters. *CoRR*, abs/1111.4297.

De Marneffe, M., MacCartney, B., and Manning, C. (2006). Generating typed dependency parses from phrase structure parses. In *Proceedings of LREC*, volume 6, pages 449–454.

Drucker, H., Wu, D., and Vapnik, V. (1999). Support vector machines for spam categorization. *Neural Networks, IEEE Transactions on*, 10(5):1048–1054.

Fetterly, D., Manasse, M., and Najork, M. (2004). Spam, damn spam, and statistics: Using statistical analysis to locate spam web pages. In *Proceedings of the 7th International Workshop on the Web and Databases: colocated with ACM SIGMOD/PODS 2004*, pages 1–6. ACM.

Grier, C., Thomas, K., Paxson, V., and Zhang, M. (2010). @ spam: the underground on 140 characters or less. In *Proceedings of the 17th ACM conference on Computer and communications security*, pages 27–37. ACM.

Jindal, N. and Liu, B. (2007). Analyzing and detecting review spam. In *Data Mining, 2007. ICDM 2007. Seventh IEEE International Conference on*, pages 547–552. IEEE.

Jindal, N. and Liu, B. (2008). Opinion spam and analysis. In *Proceedings of the international conference on Web search and web data mining*, pages 219–230. ACM.

Lau, R. Y. K., Liao, S. Y., Kwok, R. C.-W., Xu, K., Xia, Y., and Li, Y. (2012). Text mining and probabilistic language modeling for online review spam detection. *ACM Trans. Manage. Inf. Syst.*, 2:25:1–25:30.

Li, F., Huang, M., Yang, Y., and Zhu, X. (2011). Learning to identify review spam. In *Twenty-Second International Joint Conference on Artificial Intelligence*.

Lim, E., Nguyen, V., Jindal, N., Liu, B., and Lauw, H. (2010). Detecting product review spammers using rating behaviors. In *Proceedings of the 19th ACM international conference on Information and knowledge management*, pages 939–948. ACM.

Mukherjee, A., Liu, B., Wang, J., Glance, N., and Jindal, N. (2011). Detecting group review spam. In *Proceedings of the 20th international conference companion on World wide web*, pages 93–94. ACM.

Newman, M., Pennebaker, J., Berry, D., and Richards, J. (2003). Lying words: Predicting deception from linguistic styles. *Personality and Social Psychology Bulletin*, 29(5):665.

Ntoulas, A., Najork, M., Manasse, M., and Fetterly, D. (2006). Detecting spam web pages through content analysis. In *Proceedings of the 15th international conference on World Wide Web*, pages 83–92. ACM.

Ott, M., Choi, Y., Cardie, C., and Hancock, J. T. (2011). Finding deceptive opinion spam by any stretch of the imagination. In *Proceedings of the 49th Annual Meeting of the Association for Computational Linguistics: Human Language Technologies*, pages 309–319, Portland, Oregon, USA. Association for Computational Linguistics.

Qazvinian, V., Rosengren, E., Radev, D. R., and Mei, Q. (2011). Rumor has it: Identifying misinformation in microblogs. In *Proceedings of the 2011 Conference on Empirical Methods in Natural Language Processing*, pages 1589–1599, Edinburgh, Scotland, UK. Association for Computational Linguistics.

Quadrianto, N., Smola, A., Caetano, T., and Le, Q. (2009). Estimating labels from label proportions. *The Journal of Machine Learning Research*, 10:2349–2374.

Sahami, M., Dumais, S., Heckerman, D., and Horvitz, E. (1998). A bayesian approach to filtering junk e-mail. In *Learning for Text Categorization: Papers from the 1998 workshop*, volume 62, pages 98–105. Madison, Wisconsin: AAAI Technical Report WS-98-05.

Wu, G., Greene, D., Smyth, B., and Cunningham, P. (2010). Distortion as a validation criterion in the identification of suspicious reviews. In *Proceedings of the First Workshop on Social Media Analytics*, pages 10–13. ACM.

Yoo, K. and Gretzel, U. (2009). Comparison of deceptive and truthful travel reviews. *Information and Communication Technologies in Tourism 2009*, pages 37–47.

Zhang, L. and Yao, T. (2003). Filtering junk mail with a maximum entropy model. In *Proceeding of 20th international conference on computer processing of oriental languages (ICCPOL03)*, pages 446–453.

Zhao, H., Huang, C., and Li, M. (2006). An improved chinese word segmentation system with conditional random field. In *Proceedings of the Fifth SIGHAN Workshop on Chinese Language Processing*, volume 1082117. Sydney: July.

Latent community discovery with network regularization for core actors clustering

XUN GuangXu[1], *YANG YuJiu*[2], *WANG LiangWei*[3], *LIU WenHuang*[4]
(1,2,4) Shenzhen Key Laboratory of Information Science and Technology,
Graduate School at Shenzhen, Tsinghua University, P.R.China
(3)Noah's Ark Laboratory, HUAWEI, Shenzhen, P.R.China
xgxo_atbash@yahoo.com.cn[1], {yang.yujiu, liuwh}@sz.tsinghua.edu.cn[2,4],
wangliangwei@huawei.com[3]

ABSTRACT

Community structure is a common attribute of many social networks, which would give us a better understanding of the networks. However, as the social networks grow lager and lager nowadays, the Pareto Principle becomes more and more notable which makes traditional community discovery algorithms no longer suitable for them. This principle explains the unbalanced existence of two different types of network actors. Specifically, the core actors usually occupy only a small proportion of the population, but have a large influence. In this paper, we propose a novel algorithm LCDN (Latent Community Discovery with Network Structure) for dividing the core actors. This is a hierarchical probabilistic model based on statistical topic model and regularized by network structure in data. We had experiments on three large networks which show that this new model performs much better than the traditional statistical models and network partitioning algorithms.

KEYWORDS: community discovery, statistical topic models, social networks, core actors, regularization.

Proceedings of COLING 2012: Posters, pages 1351–1360,
COLING 2012, Mumbai, December 2012.

1 Introduction

Social network has been studied for a long time in both empirical ways and theoretical ways. A common attribute of many networks is community structure. Discovering this inherent attribute can lead us to a deeper understanding of the networks (Scott, 1988). The study of community structure in networks is mainly related to the graph partitioning of graph theory and statistical model. Most of the graph partitioning and statistical model algorithms have been proved effective. However, a new problem which is known as the Pareto principle arose, especially in large networks. For many events, roughly 80% of the effects come from 20% of the causes (Wikipedia, 2001). This also fits many large social networks. In these networks, there exist two different kinds of actors with disparate social behaviors and social influence. The core actors get a small proportion of population but make a big proportion of social influence. See figure 1 for an example. Core actors get more attention than the ordinary ones.

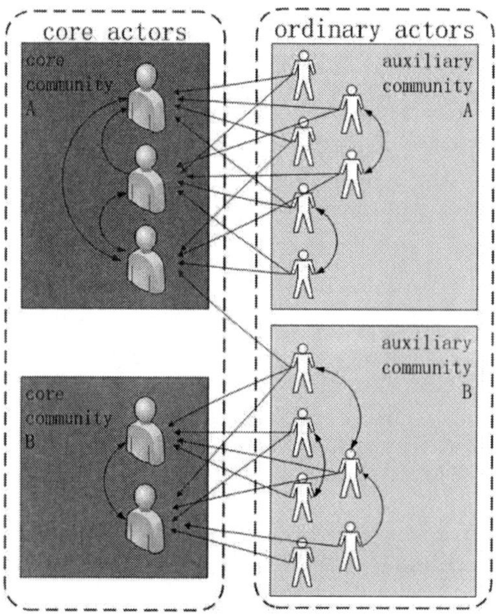

Figure 1: Two different kinds of actors

Because of the Pareto principle, the existed community discovery algorithms do not perform very well about core actors. In order to address this problem, we design a regularized model LCDN (Latent Community Discovery with Network Structure). The rest of this paper is organized as follows. We present related work in section 2. In section 3, we define the problem of community discovery on core network. And In section 4, we propose the novel algorithm LCDN. Finally in section 5 we discuss the experiments and evaluation.

2 Related work

Community discovery is a problem that arise in, for example, the Social Network Service (SNS). It is mainly related to the graph partitioning of graph theory and statistical model. For the graph partitioning of graph theory, its solutions fall into two main classes, agglomerative and divisive, depending on whether the procedure is to add or to remove the edges in the network to form communities, such as the k-means algorithm (Hartigan and Wong, 1979) and the

Girvan-Newman algorithm (Newman and Girvan, 2004). Statistical model is another way to discover community structure (Zhang et al., 2007b). Statistical model, especially topic model, has been applied to many domains such as information retrieval successfully (Chang and Blei, 2009). Compared with the graph partitioning of graph theory, statistical model for community detection introduces probability, which means one actor in the network could belong to more than one community and the boundaries between different communities could be blurry (Zhang et al., 2007a). That makes it more explainable (Chang et al., 2009).

3 Problem formulation

We assume that the network to be analyzed is influenced by Pareto Efficiency. These networks that we are going to handle conspicuously separated the actors into two groups, namely the core actors and the ordinary actors. Now we introduce the related definitions of LCDN:

Definition 1 (core actor): core actors are more influential. For example, in scientific coauthors, they publish most of the papers, and in a SNS, they get the highest in-degrees.

Definition 2 (association document): an association document d in a network n is a sequence of core actors $a_1, a_2 ... a_{|d|}$ that are associated with the current actor, where a_i is an element from a fixed core actor map. And c(a,d) means the occurrences of actor a in d.

Definition 3 (core network): a network is a graph G=<V, E>, where V is a set of vertices and E is a set of edges. A vertex $u \in V$ represents a single actor of the network associated with its association document. An edge <u, v> is a connection between vertices u and v. It can be either directed or undirected. A core network is an extraction of the whole network, a sub network that its vertices only consist of the core actors.

Definition 4 (latent community): a latent community in our model corresponds to a topic in the topic model. We represent it with z, then we have $\sum_z P(z|d) = 1$ and $\sum_a P(a|z) = 1$. And we assume that there are k latent communities in this network.

Definition 5 (community map): for each core actor in the association document, its community map is a weighting function $f(z, a)$ that shows the probabilistic relevance between core actor and latent community. For example, we may define $f(z, a) = P(z|a)$. And we expect that the adjacent actors have similar community maps.

4 Latent Community Discovery with Network Structure

4.1 Probabilistic latent semantic analysis

First of all, we introduce the PLSA (Probabilistic Latent Semantic Analysis) topic model which our statistical part is based on. The PLSA model assumes that there are k topics in the corpora, where k is a fixed parameter, and every document in the corpora corresponds to one distribution of topics. This is a hierarchical model. We can describe its generative process as:

- Select a document d with probability $P(d)$.
- Pick a latent topic z with probability $P(z|d)$.
- Generate a word w with probability $P(w|z)$.

So we obtain an observed pair $P(d, w_n) = P(d) \sum_z P(z|d)P(w_n|z)$ (Hofmann, 1999). When this statistical model is used to do community detecting, documents are replaced by association documents, and words in a document correspond to actors in an association document. So, the log likelihood of a network n to be generated with PLSA model is given by:

$$L = \sum_{d=1}^{M} \sum_{a=1}^{N_d} C(a, d) * \log \sum_{j=1}^{T} P(z_j|d) * P(a|z_j) \quad (1)$$

4.2 The probabilistic community discovery framework

By regularizing the statistical model with network structure, we propose a framework that takes both the statistical model and the network structure into consideration. As we expect that the adjacent actors have similar community maps, the criterion function is succinct and natural:

$$O(N,G) = x*(-L(N)) + (1-x)*R(N,G) \tag{2}$$

Where $L(N)$ is the log likelihood of an association corpora with statistical model, and $R(N,G)$ is the regularizer defined on the network structure. This criterion function is very general, where $L(N)$ can be the log likelihood of any statistical model and $R(N,G)$ can be any regularizer to make the community map smoother. In this paper, we choose PLSA as the statistical model, and define the regularizer $R(N,G)$ as (Zhu et al., 2003):

$$R(N,G) = \frac{1}{2}\sum_{(a_1,a_2)\in E}\sum_{z}(P(z|a_1) - P(z|a_2))^2 \tag{3}$$

By maximizing $L(N)$, we will get the $P(z|d)$ and $P(a|z)$ that fit our association document the best, and by minimizing $R(N,G)$, we will get the $P(z|a)$ that smooth our network structure the most. The parameter x will be set between 0 and 1 to control the balance between statistical log likelihood and smooth regularizer. Then we have the following optimization problem:

$$\begin{aligned} O(N,G) = x*(-\sum_{d=1}^{M}\sum_{a=1}^{N_d} C(a,d)*\log\sum_{j=1}^{T} P(z_j|d)*P(a|z_j)) \\ +(1-x)*\frac{1}{2}\sum_{(a_1,a_2)\in E}\sum_{z}(P(z|a_1) - P(z|a_2))^2 \end{aligned} \tag{4}$$

4.3 Parameter inference

When $x = 0$, the criterion function turns into a standard log likelihood of the PLSA model. The way to infer and estimate parameters for PLSA is the EM (Expectation Maximization) algorithm (Dempster et al., 1977), so we can find a local maximum of $L(N)$ in this iterative way. In the PLSA model, the E-step boils down to computing the probability of latent variables:

$$P(z|a,d) = \frac{P(z|d)*P(a|z)}{\sum_{j'=1}^{T} P(z_{j'}|d)*P(a|z_{j'})} \tag{5}$$

Take the latent variables into consideration, and then we have its complete likelihood:

$$Q(N) = \sum_{d=1}^{M}\sum_{a=1}^{N_d} C(a,d)*\sum_{z} P(z|a,d)\log(P(z|d)P(a|z)) \tag{6}$$

By maximizing the complete likelihood in the-M step, we obtain the following updated equations:

$$P(a|z) = \frac{\sum_d C(a,d)*P(z|a,d)}{\sum_{d,a} C(a,d)*P(z|a,d)} \qquad P(z|d) = \frac{\sum_a C(a,d)*P(z|a,d)}{\sum_{a,z} C(a,d)*P(z|a,d)} \tag{7}$$

When $x \neq 0$, it becomes more complicated. Then we consider the constraints:

$$\sum_z P(z|d) - 1 = 0, \qquad \sum_a P(a|z) - 1 = 0, \qquad \sum_z P(z|a) - 1 = 0$$

Add Lagrange multipliers corresponding to the constraints, we obtain the following complete likelihood with network structure information:

$$\begin{aligned} Q(N,G) &= x * (-\sum_{d=1}^{M}\sum_{a=1}^{N_d} C(a,d) * \sum_z P(z|a,d)\log(P(z|d)P(a|z))) \\ &+ \sum_d \alpha_d(\sum_z P(z|d) - 1) + \sum_z \alpha_z(\sum_a P(a|z) - 1) + \sum_a \alpha_a(\sum_z P(z|a) - 1) \\ &+ (1-x) * \frac{1}{2}\sum_{(a_1,a_2)\in E}\sum_z (P(z|a_1) - P(z|a_2))^2 \end{aligned} \tag{8}$$

Where α_d,α_z and α_a are all Lagrange multipliers. Continue our EM process to seek the local minimum of $Q(N,G)$. It is easy to see that the latent variables do not change from equation 6 to equation 9 compared with PLSA model, so the E-step of LCDN is still the same as equation 5. The introduction of network structural $R(N,G)$ do not affect the $P(z|d)$, so the estimation of $P(z|d)$ remains as equation 8. However, $P(a|z)$ and $P(z|a)$ are no longer calculable directly by minimizing $Q(N,G)$. The Newton-Raphson method is a good way to solve this kind of problem. Suppose x_n is the variable to be updated by the Newton-Raphson method at n-th iteration, corresponding to the unknown parameters $P(a|z)$ and $P(z|a)$ in our model. Specifically applied to our task:

$$x_{n+1} = x_n - \frac{f(x_n)}{f'(x_n)} = x_n - HQ(x_n;N,G)^{-1} \bigtriangledown Q(x_n;N,G) \tag{9}$$

Where $\bigtriangledown Q(x_n;N,G)$ is the gradient of $Q(x_n;N,G)$ and $HQ(x_n;N,G)$ is the Hessian matrix of $Q(x_n;N,G)$.

4.4 An efficient algorithm

In fact, we could achieve the expected effect by ensuring $Q_{n+1}(N,G) < Q_n(N,G)$ at every M-step. So we can optimize the statistical complete likelihood part and network structural regularizer of the objective function separately. In each M-step, we could maximize the complete likelihood by equation 7 and equation 8 as before, but this does not necessarily mean $Q_{n+1}(N,G) < Q_n(N,G)$, so we have to continue optimizing the structural part $R(N,G)$. Obviously, random walk on the network is a simple and effective choice to minimize $R(N,G)$. Thus for $P(z|a)$:

$$P_{n+1}(z|a) = x * P_n(z|a) + (1-x) * \frac{\sum_{(a,a')\in E} C(a,a') * P_n(z|a')}{\sum_{(a,a')\in E} C(a,a')} \tag{10}$$

It is easy to see that $\sum_z P_{n+1}(z|a) = 1$ and $P_{n+1}(z|a) \geq 0$ always hold in equation 11. Here, x is the random walk parameter. Every iteration of random walk makes the network smoother (Jamali and Ester, 2009). Note that, the random walk process is based on $P(z|a)$ of each actor in the network, so we have to use the Bayes' theorem to obtain $P(a|z)$ for next EM algorithm iteration:

$$P(a|z) = \frac{P(z|a) * P(a)}{P(z)} = \frac{P(z|a) * P(a)}{\sum_a P(z|a) * P(a)} \tag{11}$$

5 Experiments and evaluation

In this section, we experiment on three large networks. Since the LCDN is unsupervised, pairwise comparison is a good choice to measure our experiment results (Menestrina et al., 2010). So we get the pairwise $precision$, $recall$ and $F1$:

$$precision(E,G) = \frac{|pair_E \bigcap pair_G|}{|pair_E|} \qquad recall(E,G) = \frac{|pair_E \bigcap pair_G|}{|pair_G|} \tag{12}$$

$$F1(E,G) = \frac{|2 * precision * recall|}{|precision + recall|} \tag{13}$$

Besides, in order to obtain a more comprehensive evaluation of the model, we add two comparison indexes: time cost to measure efficiency and community size to measure partitioning balance. We pick two statistical models (PLSA and Ball-Karrer-Newman models) and two graph partitioning models (k-means and Newman-Girvan models) as the comparative algorithms.

5.1 DBLP co-authorship network

In DBLP co-authorship network, the actors represent authors, and the edges represent the collaboration relation between authors. This benchmark co-authorship network contains the co-authorship of more than 50000 papers published at 27 computer science conferences from 2008 to 2010. And the whole network gets 59073 actors and 151399 edges. These conferences can be mainly divided into five research groups (Wang et al., 2011):

1. AI: artificial intelligence, including IJCAI, AAAI, ICML, UAI, NIPS, UMAP and AAMAS.
2. DB: database, including EDBT, ICDT, ICDE, PODS, SIGMOD and VLDB.
3. DP: distributed and parallel computing, including ICCP, IPDPS, PACT, PPoPP and Euro-Par.
4. GV: graphics, vision and HCI, including I3DG, ICCV, CVPR and SIGGRAPH.
5. NC: networks communications and performance, including MOBICOM, INFOCOM, SIGMETRICS, PERFORMANCE and SIGCOMM.

Intuitively, we believe that the program committee members are academically active in their respective areas, so that these program committee members (1241 actors, including 406 AI members, 282 DB members, 323 NC members, 79 GV members and 188 DP members) constitute the core actor group. In PLSA and LCDN model, the input weight in the association document is the number of collaboration times between current actor and target actor. And NG is short for Newman-Girvan algorithm and BKN is short for Ball-Karrer-Newman algorithm. The core community discovery result comparison of these algorithms is given in table 1:

	Pairwise precision	Pairwise recall	Pairwise F1	Time cost(s)	Community size C1	C2	C3	C4	C5
PLSA	0.276	0.238	0.265	**19**	243	199	244	256	299
k-means	0.257	**0.978**	0.406	569	2	19	1218	1	1
NG	Unavailable since this network is not fully interconnected								
BKN	0.156	0.306	0.206	799	852	100	80	126	83
LCDN	**0.456**	0.434	**0.445**	114	**136**	**370**	**108**	**251**	**376**

Table 1: Algorithm performance comparison on the DBLP co-authorship network

And then we move on to the fully interconnected DBLP co-authorship network. This is the biggest sub network extracted from the DBLP co-authorship network, whose actors are fully interconnected. So the Newman-Girvan algorithm would work on it. This extraction contains 42956 actors and 130132 edges. And the number of core actors is reduced to 1222, including 402 AI members, 281 DB members, 319 NC members, 79 GV members and 178 DB members. The core community discovery result comparison of these algorithms is given in table 2:

	Pairwise precision	Pairwise recall	Pairwise F1	Time cost(s)	Community size				
					C1	C2	C3	C4	C5
PLSA	0.309	0.245	0.273	**18**	221	252	242	213	294
k-means	0.258	0.979	0.409	432	1199	19	1	1	2
NG	0.253	**0.988**	0.403	8625	1217	1	1	1	2
BKN	0.287	0.480	0.359	755	764	102	104	125	127
LCDN	**0.501**	0.465	**0.483**	267	**394**	**298**	**171**	**92**	**267**

Table 2: Comparison on the fully interconnected DBLP co-authorship network

We can see from table 1 and 2 that LCDN achieves an 8% $\sim$ 20% improvement in terms of pairwise $F1$ value over the other comparative algorithms. And the k-means algorithm and Newman-Girvan algorithm are confronted with the problem of unbalanced partitioning.

5.2 WEIBO network

Compared with the DBLP co-authorship network, WEIBO network is a much larger one with 164524 actors and 14444794 edges. WEIBO is a directed graph whose actors are fully interconnected. And there are two kinds of edges in it, strong and weak. This will influence the actor weight in association documents. In this paper, we set the weight to 1 for the weak ones and to 11 for the strong ones. Since the actors of WEIBO network get far more neighbors than the ones of DBLP co-authorship network, the random walk parameter is set smaller to keep the regularization balance of LCDN model. And in fact, to achieve a better performance, the denser the network, the smaller value of random walk parameter x we should set. In this paper, we set the random walk parameter of DBLP co-authorship network to $x = 0.9$, and set the random walk parameter of WEIBO network to $x = 0.1$.

Intuitively, we believe that in a SNS the more followers mean the more influence, so we pick actors whose in-degree is greater than 2000 to constitute the core actor group. These actors can be mainly divided into 5 social groups according to their tags and verification information:

1. Entertainment and sports, including 244 members.
2. Grass roots and leisure, including 333 members.
3. Finance and technology, including 297 members.
4. Culture and religion, including 185 members.
5. Newspapers and media, including 163 members.

The core community discovery result comparison of these algorithms is given in table 3:

We can see that LCDN still gets a much better performance than the other algorithms. For the k-means algorithm and Newman-Girvan algorithm, the problem of unbalanced partitioning remains. Besides, compared with the other algorithms, the time cost of Newman-Girvan algorithm is really unacceptable. Empirically, the Newman-Girvan algorithm should not partition a network so unbalanced as a divisive method. So we traced the actor Li Kaifu, who had the

	Pairwise precision	Pairwise recall	Pairwise F1	Time cost(s)	Community size				
					C1	C2	C3	C4	C5
PLSA	0.627	0.567	0.596	1098	176	200	235	299	271
k-means	0.227	0.715	0.345	**558**	77	108	2	992	2
NG	0.201	**0.873**	0.326	85084	11	1124	21	10	15
BKN	0.528	0.478	0.502	4164	184	270	227	304	196
LCDN	**0.682**	0.611	**0.645**	2067	**282**	**185**	**221**	**277**	**216**

Table 3: Algorithm performance comparison on the WEIBO network

highest in-degree in WEIBO network but was assigned to a small community. Actually, we found that, the community that Li Kaifu was assigned to was not really small because it also contained thousands of ordinary actors. As Li Kaifu and other famous actors have numerous followers, this will surely lead to an very high betweenness score of the edges between these core actors. Thus edges between core actors tend to be cut with a very high priority, and it is indeed so according to our observation of Li.

Conclusion and perspectives

A structure of communities with Pareto Principle exists in many real-world social networks. Every individual does not get the same social influence. Naturally, we pay more attention to the core actors, since they are the kernel of a network. In this paper, we define the problem of community detection among the core actors in large social networks. Taking both the statistical model and the network structure into consideration, we propose a probabilistic community discovery framework LCDN. The experimental results show that LCDN model performs much better than the other algorithms.

For future work, we would like to try to make this framework multifunctional, for example to collaborative filtering, and develop this framework into a fuller Bayesian model. Since we can obtain the association document parameters $P(z|d)$ which could properly represent the interest of current actor. So we can do collaborative recommendation based on either the community map or association document parameter $P(z|d)$ (Su and Khoshgoftaar, 2009). The PLSA model gets limitations that there is no constraint on the association document parameters $P(z|d)$. This leads to overfitting: the number of association document parameters grows linearly with the data size (Mei et al., 2008). The LDA (Latent Dirichlet Allocation) model is a good choice to alleviate this problem (Blei et al., 2003; Griffiths, 2002). Moreover, the LDA model is more general. It gets plenty of variations which pay different emphases so that it is applicable to many different situations (Ramage et al., 2009; Blei and Lafferty, 2006; Blei and McAuliffe, 2007; Blei and Lafferty, 2005).

Acknowledgments

The work was supported by Guangdong Natural Science Foundation (No.9451805702004046) and the cooperation project in industry, education and research of Guangdong province and Ministry of Education of P.R. China (No.2010B090400527). In addition, we thank the anonymous reviewers for their careful read and valuable comments.

References

Blei, D. M. and Lafferty, J. D. (2005). Correlated topic models. In *NIPS*.

Blei, D. M. and Lafferty, J. D. (2006). Dynamic topic models. In Cohen, W. W. and Moore, A., editors, *ICML*, volume 148 of *ACM International Conference Proceeding Series*, pages 113–120. ACM.

Blei, D. M. and McAuliffe, J. D. (2007). Supervised topic models. In Platt, J. C., Koller, D., Singer, Y., and Roweis, S. T., editors, *NIPS*. Curran Associates, Inc.

Blei, D. M., Ng, A. Y., and Jordan, M. I. (2003). Latent dirichlet allocation. *Journal of Machine Learning Research*, 3:993–1022.

Chang, J. and Blei, D. M. (2009). Relational topic models for document networks. *Journal of Machine Learning Research - Proceedings Track*, 5:81–88.

Chang, J., Boyd-Graber, J. L., Gerrish, S., Wang, C., and Blei, D. M. (2009). Reading tea leaves: How humans interpret topic models. In Bengio, Y., Schuurmans, D., Lafferty, J. D., Williams, C. K. I., and Culotta, A., editors, *NIPS*, pages 288–296. Curran Associates, Inc.

Dempster, A. P., Laird, N. M., and Rubin, D. B. (1977). Maximum likelihood from incomplete data via the em algorithm. *Journal of the Royal Statistical Society*, 39(1):1–38.

Griffiths, T. (2002). Gibbs sampling in the generative model of latent dirichlet allocation.

Hartigan, J. A. and Wong, M. A. (1979). A k-means clustering algorithm. *Journal of the Royal Statistical Society*, 28(1):100–108.

Hofmann, T. (1999). Probabilistic latent semantic indexing. In *SIGIR*, pages 50–57. ACM.

Jamali, M. and Ester, M. (2009). *TrustWalker*: a random walk model for combining trust-based and item-based recommendation. In IV, J. F. E., Fogelman-Soulié, F., Flach, P. A., and Zaki, M. J., editors, *KDD*, pages 397–406. ACM.

Mei, Q., Cai, D., Zhang, D., and Zhai, C. (2008). Topic modeling with network regularization. In Huai, J., Chen, R., Hon, H.-W., Liu, Y., Ma, W.-Y., Tomkins, A., and Zhang, X., editors, *WWW*, pages 101–110. ACM.

Menestrina, D., Whang, S., and Garcia-Molina, H. (2010). Evaluating entity resolution results. *PVLDB*, 3(1):208–219.

Newman, M. E. J. and Girvan, M. (2004). Finding and evaluating community structure in networks. *Physical Review E*.

Ramage, D., Hall, D., Nallapati, R., and Manning, C. D. (2009). Labeled lda: A supervised topic model for credit attribution in multi-labeled corpora. In *EMNLP*, pages 248–256. ACL.

Scott, J. (1988). Social network analysis. *Sociology*, 22(1):109–127.

Steyvers, M. and Griffiths, T. (2007). *Probabilistic Topic Models*. Handbook of Latent Semantic Analysis.

Su, X. and Khoshgoftaar, T. M. (2009). A survey of collaborative filtering techniques. *Adv. Artificial Intellegence*, 2009.

Wang, L., Lou, T., Tang, J., and Hopcroft, J. E. (2011). Detecting community kernels in large social networks. In Cook, D. J., Pei, J., Wang, W., Zaïane, O. R., and Wu, X., editors, *ICDM*, pages 784–793. IEEE.

Wikipedia (2001). Pareto principle. `http://en.wikipedia.org/wiki/Pareto_principle`.

Zhang, H., Giles, C. L., Foley, H. C., and Yen, J. (2007a). Probabilistic community discovery using hierarchical latent gaussian mixture model. In *AAAI*, pages 663–668. AAAI Press.

Zhang, H., Qiu, B., Giles, C. L., Foley, H. C., and Yen, J. (2007b). An lda-based community structure discovery approach for large-scale social networks. In *ISI*, pages 200–207. IEEE.

Zhu, X., Ghahramani, Z., and Lafferty, J. D. (2003). Semi-supervised learning using gaussian fields and harmonic functions. In Fawcett, T. and Mishra, N., editors, *ICML*, pages 912–919. AAAI Press.

HYENA: Hierarchical Type Classification for Entity Names

Mohamed Amir Yosef[1] *Sandro Bauer*[2] *Johannes Hoffart*[1]
Marc Spaniol[1] *Gerhard Weikum*[1]
(1) Max-Planck-Institut für Informatik, Saarbrücken, Germany
(2) Computer Laboratory, University of Cambridge, UK
{mamir|jhoffart|mspaniol|weikum}@mpi-inf.mpg.de, sandro.bauer@cl.cam.ac.uk

ABSTRACT
Inferring lexical type labels for entity mentions in texts is an important asset for NLP tasks like semantic role labeling and named entity disambiguation (NED). Prior work has focused on flat and relatively small type systems where most entities belong to exactly one type. This paper addresses very fine-grained types organized in a hierarchical taxonomy, with several hundreds of types at different levels. We present HYENA for multi-label hierarchical classification. HYENA exploits gazetteer features and accounts for the joint evidence for types at different levels. Experiments and an extrinsic study on NED demonstrate the practical viability of HYENA.

KEYWORDS: Fine-grained entity types, multi-labeling, hierarchical classification, meta-classification.

Proceedings of COLING 2012: Posters, pages 1361–1370,
COLING 2012, Mumbai, December 2012.

1 Introduction

Motivation: Web contents such as news, blogs, etc. are full of named entities. Recognizing them and disambiguating them has been intensively studied (see, e.g., (Finkel et al., 2005; Cucerzan, 2007; Milne and Witten, 2008; Hoffart et al., 2011; Ratinov et al., 2011)). Each entity belongs to one or more *lexical types* associated with it. For instance, an entity such as *Bob Dylan* should be assigned labels of type `Singer`, `Musician`, `Poet`, etc., and also the corresponding supertype(s) (hypernyms) in a type hierarchy, in this case `Person`. Such fine-grained typing of entities can be a great asset for various NLP tasks, e.g. semantic role labeling. Most notably, named entity disambiguation (NED) can be boosted by knowing or inferring a mention's lexical types. For example, noun phrases such as "songwriter Dylan", "Google founder Page", or "rock legend Page" can be easily mapped to the entities Bob Dylan, Larry Page, and Jimmy Page if their respective types `Singer`, `BusinessPerson`, and `Guitarist` are available.

Problem Statement: State-of-the-art tools for named entity recognition like the Stanford NER Tagger (Finkel et al., 2005) compute such lexical tags only for a small set of coarse-grained types: `Person`, `Location`, and `Organization` (plus tags for non-entity phrases of type time, money, percent, and date). There is little literature on *fine-grained typing* of entity mentions (Fleischman and Hovy, 2002; Ekbal et al., 2010; Rahman and Ng, 2010; Ling and Weld, 2012), and these approaches are pretty much limited to flat sets of several dozens of types. Because of the relatively small number of types, an entity or mention is typically mapped to one type only. The goal that we address in this paper is to extend such methods by automatically computing lexical types for entity mentions, using a large set of types from a hierarchical taxonomy with multiple levels. In this setting, many entities naturally belong to multiple types. So we face a *hierarchical multi-label classification* problem (Tsoumakas et al., 2012).

Contribution: This paper introduces *HYENA* (Hierarchical tYpe classification for Entity NAmes). HYENA is a multi-label classifier for entity types based on hierarchical taxonomies derived from WordNet (Fellbaum, 1998) or knowledge bases like YAGO (Suchanek et al., 2007) or Freebase (Bollacker et al., 2008). HYENA's salient contributions are the following:

- the first method for entity-mention type classification that can handle multi-level type hierarchies with hundreds of types and multiple labels per mention;
- extensions to consider cross-evidence and constraints between different types, by developing a meta-classifier demonstrating the superiority of HYENA;
- experiments against state-of-the-art baselines, demonstrating the superiority of HYENA;
- an extrinsic study on boosting NED by harnessing type information.

2 Type Hierarchy and Feature Set

2.1 Fine-grained Type Hierarchy

We have systematically derived a very fine-grained type taxonomy from the YAGO knowledge base (Suchanek et al., 2007; Hoffart et al., 2012) which comes with a highly accurate mapping of Wikipedia categories to WordNet synsets. We start with five broad classes namely `PERSON`, `LOCATION`, `ORGANIZATION`, `EVENT` and `ARTIFACT`. Under each of these superclasses, we pick 100 prominent subclasses. The selection of subclasses is based on the population of the classes: we rank them in descending order of the number of YAGO entities that belong to a class, and pick the top 100 for each of the top-level superclasses. This results in a very fine-grained reference taxonomy of 505 types, organized into a directed acyclic graph with 9 levels in its deepest parts. For instance, this includes fine-grained classifications of an `Adminstrative`

District in order to distinguish between Municipality, Township, Commune, etc. or differentiations of Publications into Books, Periodicals and Magazines.

We are not aware of any similarly rich type hierarchies used in prior work on NER and entity typing. Our approach can easily plug in alternative type taxonomies (e.g. derived from Freebase or DBpedia as in (Ling and Weld, 2012), or from hand-crafted resources such as WordNet).

2.2 Feature Set

For a general approach and for applicability to arbitrary texts, we use only features that are automatically extracted from input texts. We do not use any features that require manual annotations, such as sense-tagging of general words and phrases in training documents. This discriminates our method from some of the prior work which used WordNet senses as features (e.g., (Rahman and Ng, 2010)).

Mention String: We derive the mention string itself (a noun phrase of one or more consecutive words) as well as unigrams, bigrams, and trigrams that overlap with the mention string.

Sentence Surrounding Mention: We derive from a bounded window (size 3) around the mention: all unigrams, bigrams, and trigrams in the sentence along with their distance to the mention, and all unigrams along with their absolute distance to the mention.

Mention Paragraph: We consider the mention paragraph in order to obtain additional topical cues about the mention type. We extract unigrams, bigrams, and trigrams in a bounded window (2000 characters) around the mention (truncated at the paragraph boundaries).

Grammatical Features: We use part-of-speech tags (with/without distance) of the tokens within a bounded window. Further, we resolve the first "he" or "she" pronoun in the same and in the subsequent sentence (including distance) and the closest preceding verb-preposition pair.

Gazetteer Features: We build type-specific gazetteers of words occurring in entity names derived from the YAGO knowledge base. YAGO has a huge dictionary of name-entity pairs extracted from Wikipedia. We automatically construct a binary feature whether the mention contains a word in this type's gazetteer or not. This does not mean determining the mention type(s) (e.g. "Alice" occurs in person subclasses but also in locations, songs, organizations, etc.).

3 Classifier

3.1 Hierarchical Classifier

Based on the feature set defined in the previous section, we build a set of type-specific classifiers using the SVM software liblinear (Fan et al., 2008; Chang and Lin, 2011). As our YAGO-based type system integrates WordNet and Wikipedia categories, we obtain ample training data from Wikipedia effortlessly, by following Wikipedia anchor texts to the corresponding YAGO entities.

For each type, we consider Wikipedia mentions (and their context, cf. Section 2.2) of the type's instances as positive training samples. For discriminative learning, we use all siblings in the type hierarchy as negative samples. As the subclasses of type t do not necessarily cover all entities, we add a subclass Others to each non-leaf type. Positive samples for Others are instances of type t that do not belong to any of its subclasses. Conversely, the classifiers for non-leaf nodes include all instances of their subtypes as positive samples (with full weight). HYENA performs type-specific classification in a top-down manner. A mention is assigned to all types for which the classifier signals acceptance. If rejected, classification is stopped at this level.

3.2 Meta Classifier

HYENA uses a global threshold θ for accepting to a class. Using a single parameter for all types is not fully satisfying, as different types may exhibit very different characteristics. So the optimal acceptance threshold may be highly type-dependent. To overcome this limitation, we devised a meta classifier that ranks the types for each test mention by decreasing confidence values and then predicts the "right" number of top-n labels to be assigned to a mention, similar to the methodology of (Tang et al., 2009). We use the confidence values of the type-specific classifier ensemble as meta-features, and train a multi-class logistic regression classifier to obtain a suitable value n of features. We combine the base classifiers and the meta classifier by first running the entire ensemble top-down along the type hierarchy, and then letting the meta model decide on how many of the highest-scoring types we accept for a mention.

4 Experiments

4.1 Setup

System: The described methods are implemented in HYENA. The Stanford NLP tools are used to identify mentions of named entities and to extract grammatical features from the context.
Data: We used the English Wikipedia edition as of 2012-05-02. In order to obtain ground-truth type labels, we exploited the links to other Wikipedia articles, resolved the corresponding YAGO2 entity and retrieved the semantic types. For example, from the Wikipedia markup:

> "In June 1989, Obama met [[Michelle Obama|Michelle Robinson]] when he was employed as a summer associate at the Chicago law firm of [[Sidley Austin]]"

the following YAGO2 entities are assigned:

> Michelle Robinson → http://yago-knowledge.org/resource/Michelle_Obama
> Sidley Austin → http://yago-knowledge.org/resource/Sidley_Austin

HYENA is trained on 50,000 randomly Wikipedia articles selected, containing around 1.6 million entity mentions. 92% of the corresponding entities belong to at least one of our 5 top-level types, with 11% belonging to at least two top-level types. Testing of HYENA is performed on 10,000 randomly selected Wikipedia articles withheld from the same Wikipedia edition and disjoint from the training data. All experimental data is available at http://www.mpi-inf.mpg.de/yago-naga/hyena/.
Performance Measures: We report micro- and macro-evaluation numbers for precision, recall and F1 scores. Let T be the set of all types in our hierarchy, and let I_t be the set of instances tagged with type t, and let $\hat{I}_t$ the set of instances that are predicted to be of type t. The measures used are:

$$Precision_{micro} = \frac{\sum_{t \in T} |I_t \cap \hat{I}_t|}{\sum_{t \in T} |\hat{I}_t|} \quad and \quad Recall_{micro} = \frac{\sum_{t \in T} |I_t \cap \hat{I}_t|}{\sum_{t \in T} |I_t|}$$

$$Precision_{macro} = \frac{1}{|T|} \sum_{t \in T} \frac{|I_t \cap \hat{I}_t|}{|\hat{I}_t|} \quad and \quad Recall_{macro} = \frac{1}{|T|} \sum_{t \in T} \frac{|I_t \cap \hat{I}_t|}{|I_t|}$$

Competitors: We identified the methods by (Fleischman and Hovy, 2002) referred to as *HOVY*, (Rahman and Ng, 2010) referred to as *NG*, and *FIGER* by (Ling and Weld, 2012) for comparison (cf. Section 6). We conducted experiments on the competitors' datasets to avoid re-implementation and to give them the benefit of their original optimization and tuning.

	Macro			Micro		
	Prec.	Rec.	F1	Prec.	Rec.	F1
5 Top-level Types	0.941	0.922	0.932	0.949	0.936	0.943
All 505 Types	0.878	0.863	0.87	0.913	0.932	0.922

Table 1: Overall Experimental Results for HYENA on Wikipedia 10000 articles

		Macro			Micro		
		Prec.	Rec.	F1	Prec.	Rec.	F1
5 Top-level Types	*HOVY*	0.522	0.464	0.491	0.568	0.51	0.537
	HYENA	**0.941**	**0.922**	**0.932**	**0.949**	**0.936**	**0.943**
All 505 Types	*HOVY*	0.253	0.18	0.21	0.405	0.355	0.378
	HYENA	**0.878**	**0.863**	**0.87**	**0.913**	**0.932**	**0.922**

Table 2: Results of HYENA vs *HOVY* (trained and tested on Wikipedia 10000 articles)

4.2 Multi-label Classification

We present multi-label experiments that are geared for high precision and high recall. Experiments are performed against ground truth coming from Wikipedia, the BBN Pronoun Coreference Corpus and Entity Type Corpus (LDC2005T33)and the FIGER-Gold dataset.

4.2.1 HYENA experiments on Wikipedia

The results of our HYENA approach on Wikipedia are shown in Table 1. HYENA achieves very high F1 scores of around 94% for its 5 top-level types. Evaluated against the entire hierarchy, F1 scores are still remarkably high with F1 scores of 87% and 92% for macro and micro evaluations, respectively. The slightly weaker results for the macro evaluation are explainable by our fine-grained hierarchy, which also contains a few "long-tail" types.

In order to compare against *HOVY*, we emulated their method within the HYENA framework. This is done by specifically configuring the feature set, and using the same training and testing instances as for HYENA. Results are shown in Table 2. HYENA significantly outperforms *HOVY*. Similar to the results reported in (Fleischman and Hovy, 2002) *HOVY* shows decent performance for the 5 top-level types, but performance sharply drops for subtypes at deeper levels.

4.2.2 HYENA Experiments on FIGER-GOLD

The FIGER-GOLD dataset consists of 18 news reports from a university website, as well as local newspapers and specialized magazines (Ling and Weld, 2012). The test dataset was annotated with at least one label per mention. This resulted in a total of 434 sentences with 563 entities having 771 labels coming from 42 out of the 112 types. The original evaluation for FIGER was instance-based. In order to compare against HYENA, a per-type evaluation is needed. To this end, we created a per-type based classification of FIGER based on their output data. Since the distribution of mentions on different types in the FIGER dataset is heavily skewed (e.g. 217 of the 562 entities are of type `PERSON` without finer-grained subtype annotation) we cover in our evaluation the most 10% populated classes (covering around 70% of the tags). These classes were then mapped onto the hierarchy of HYENA. Since all instances in the FIGER-GOLD dataset are tagged with at least one class, we ran HYENA in two configurations: without any modification as before (using a classifier trained to deal with abstract concepts, e.g. `Chinese Philosophy`, that are of generic type `ENTITY_OTHER`) as well as by enforcing the assignment

	Macro			Micro		
	Prec.	Rec.	F1	Prec.	Rec.	F1
FIGER	**0.75**	0.743	0.743	**0.828**	**0.838**	**0.833**
HYENA	0.745	0.631	0.684	0.815	0.645	0.72
HYENA (at least one tag)	0.724	**0.801**	**0.75**	0.788	0.814	0.801

Table 3: Results of HYENA vs *FIGER* (trained on Wikipedia and tested on FIGER-Gold)

	Macro			Micro		
	Prec.	Rec.	F1	Prec.	Rec.	F1
NG (trained on BBN)	0.859	0.864	0.862	0.812	0.871	0.84
HYENA (trained on Wikipedia)	**0.943**	0.406	0.568	**0.932**	0.371	0.531
HYENA (trained on Wikipedia, at least one tag)	0.818	0.671	0.737	0.835	0.632	0.719
HYENA (trained on BBN)	0.916	**0.909**	**0.911**	0.919	**0.881**	**0.899**

Table 4: Results of HYENA vs *NG* (tested on BBN Corpus)

of at least one class for all instances (referred to as "at least one tag").

Results are shown in Table 3. In the standard configuration, HYENA shows precision scores close to *FIGER*. However, HYENA suffers from the training against abstract concepts. In the second configuration, both systems achieve results in the same range with slight advantages for *FIGER* on micro-average and overall better results of HYENA on macro-average. However, 771 type labels for 562 entity mentions (not entities) is only a very moderate amount of multi-label classification. This is disadvantageous for HYENA, which has been designed for data where the number of labels per mention is higher.

4.2.3 HYENA Experiments on BBN

The BBN Pronoun Coreference and Entity Type Corpus consists of 2311 manually annotated documents. Since *NG* exploits WordNet word-senses for disambiguation, the corpus is restricted to those 200 documents (160 training, 40 testing) that have corresponding annotations. For comparison against *NG* we performed a mapping onto the hierarchy of HYENA. Among the 16 types for the *NG* dataset (cf. (Rahman and Ng, 2010)), there are 8 non-entity types (e.g. `Date`) and 5 descriptor types (`_DESC`) which cannot be mapped. This resulted in mapping the 3 top-level types: `Person`, `Organization` and `GPE` (country, city, states, etc.). Similar to the FIGER-GOLD dataset, there are no unclassified mentions in the BBN corpus. Hence we ran HYENA in three configurations: standard ("trained on Wikipedia"), enforcing at least one type label to be assigned ("trained on Wikipedia, at least one tag") and HYENA trained on the *NG* training set ("trained on BBN").

Results on the BBN dataset exhibit high precision of HYENA already with its standard configuration (cf. Table 4). However, it suffers from low recall in this setting, due to training against abstract concepts. When enforcing HYENA to assign at least one tag, F1 scores strongly improve. In the third configuration, the fairest side-by-side comparison, we clearly outperform *NG*.

4.3 Meta-Classification

In use-cases for type labeling (e.g. NED), precision is often more important than recall. This is particularly demanding for types that suffer from data sparsity (less prominent and/or less populated types) deep in the type hierarchy. For example in NED, it may be crucial to distinguish

		Macro			Micro		
		Prec.	Rec.	F1	Prec.	Rec.	F1
All 505 Types	HYENA	0.878	**0.863**	**0.87**	0.913	**0.932**	**0.922**
	HYENA + meta-classifier	**0.89**	0.837	0.862	**0.916**	0.914	0.915

Table 5: Performance gain in precision by meta-classification

	Macro			Micro		
	Prec.	Rec.	F1	Prec.	Rec.	F1
HYENA	0.673	**0.638**	**0.644**	0.659	**0.681**	**0.67**
HYENA + meta-classifier	**0.693**	0.619	0.638	**0.674**	0.66	0.667

Table 6: Meta-classifier impact on the 5% worst-performing classes

a `Painter` from a `Musician`. When applied, meta classification (see Section 3.2 for details) improves macro-precision over all 505 types by more than 1% (cf. Table 5). When focusing on the 5% types that performed worst without it, we even gained more than 2% in precision, as shown in Table 6. The top-5 winners in this group gain from 5% up to 13%.

4.4 HYENA Feature Analysis

In addition to a comprehensive feature set, HYENA exploits a large amount of training data and the gazetteer features derived from YAGO. To assess the impact of each asset, we varied the number of training instances and en-/disabled gazetteer features (cf. Table 7). Precision and recall improve from a larger training corpus, particularly for sparsely populated types. When gazetteer features are disabled, performance drops significantly.

5 Extrinsic Study on Named Entity Disambiguation

We conducted an extrinsic study on harnessing HYENA for NED, based on a state-of-the-art NED tool, AIDA by (Hoffart et al., 2011). This NED method uses a combination of contextual similarity and entity-entity coherence for disambiguation. In order to speed up its computationally expensive graph algorithms, it is desirable to prune the search space. Hence, we use the type predictions by HYENA for pruning (e.g. for the sentence "He was born in Victoria" and the mention "Victoria", the entities of type `Person`, `River` and `Lake` should be dropped). To this end, we use the confidence scores of HYENA to remove entities of types with type scores below some threshold θ. Our technique proceeds in three steps:

1. Invoke HYENA on the mention to obtain the predicted types and confidence scores.
2. Generate entity candidates using AIDA and its underlying name-entity dictionary.
3. For each candidate, if there is no overlap between the entity types and the predicted mention types with confidence greater than or equal to θ, drop the candidate.
4. Run AIDA on the reduced candidate space.

When dropping the correct entity, a mention becomes *unsolvable*. We vary the relaxation parameter θ to investigate search space rdecution versus mentions that are rendered *unsolvable*. We performed our experiment on the extended CoNLL 2003 NER dataset with manual entity annotations from (Hoffart et al., 2011). With a pruning threshold of $\theta = -1$, we can prune almost 40% of all entities while rendering less than 8% of the mentions unsolvable (cf. Table 8). The search space reduction of 40% actually results in a much larger saving in run-time because the graph algorithm that AIDA uses for NED has super-linear complexity (NP-hard in the worst case, but typically $O(n \log n)$ or $O(n^2)$ with appropriate approximation algorithms).

Size of training set (# of articles)	5 Top-level Types			All 505 Types		
	Prec.	Rec.	F1	Prec.	Rec.	F1
50,000	0.949	0.936	0.942	0.913	0.932	0.922
20,000	0.937	0.924	0.93	0.893	0.917	0.905
5,000	0.92	0.903	0.912	0.869	0.89	0.879
50,000 (without gazetteers)	0.915	0.825	0.868	0.82	0.718	0.766

Table 7: Micro-average impact of varying the number of Wikipedia articles used for training

Threshold	% dropped Entities	% unsolvable Mentions	avg. Document Prec.	avg. Mention Prec.
0.0	49.2	16.1	0.659	0.639
−0.5	45.7	12.3	0.738	0.713
−1.5	28.8	4.7	0.791	0.779
−2.5	17.7	2.2	0.802	0.798
AIDA	0	0	0.82	0.823

Table 8: Impact of Varying Type Prediction Confidence Threshold on NED Results

6 Related Work

There is little prior work on the task of classifying named entities, given in the form of (still ambiguous) noun phrases, onto fine-grained lexical types. (Fleischman and Hovy, 2002) has been the first work to address type granularities that are finer than the handful of tags used in classical NER work (person, organization, location, date, money, other – see, e.g., (Wacholder et al., 1997; Alfonseca and Manandhar, 2002; Cunningham, 2002; Finkel et al., 2005)). It considered 8 sub-classes of the `Person` class, and developed a decision-tree classifier. (Ekbal et al., 2010) developed a maximum entropy classifier using word-level features from the mention contexts, but experimental results are flagged as non-reproducible in the ACL Anthology. (Rahman and Ng, 2010) considered a two-level type hierarchy consisting of 29 top-level classes and a total of 92 sub-classes. These include many non-entity types such as date, time, percent, money, quantity, ordinal, cardinal, etc. The method uses a rich set of features, including WordNet senses of noun-phrase head words in mention contexts. (Giuliano, 2009) proposed an SVD-based latent topic model with a semantic kernel that captures word proximities. The method was applied to a set of 21 different types; each mention is assigned to exactly one type. The work of (Ling and Weld, 2012) considered a two-level taxonomy with 112 tags taken from the Freebase knowledge base, forming a two-level hierarchy with top-level topics and 112 types (with entity instances). (Ling and Weld, 2012) trained a CRF for the joint task of recognizing entity mentions and inferring type tags. The feature set included the ones used in earlier work (see above) plus patterns from ReVerb (Fader et al., 2011).

7 Conclusions

We presented HYENA for fine-grained type classification of entity mentions. In contrast to prior methods, we can deal with hundreds of types in a multi-level hierarchy, and consider that a mention can have many different types. In experiments, HYENA outperformed state-of-the-art competitors even on their original datasets and improved efficiency of NED by reducing the search space.

Acknowledgements

This work is supported by the 7th Framework IST programme of the European Union through the focused research project (STREP) on Longitudinal Analytics of Web Archive data (LAWA) – contract no. 258105.

References

Alfonseca, E. and Manandharm, S. (2002). An Unsupervised Method for General Named Entity Recognition and Automated Concept Discovery. In *Proc. of the 1st International Conference on General WordNet.*

Bollacker, K. D., Evans, C., Paritosh, P., Sturge, T., and Taylor, J. (2008). Freebase: a collaboratively created graph database for structuring human knowledge. In *Proc. of SIGMOD Conference*, pages 1247–1250.

Bunescu, R. and Pasca, M. (2006). Using Encyclopedic Knowledge for Named Entity Disambiguation. In *Proc. of the 11th Conference of the European Chapter of the Association for Computational Linguistics (EACL '06)*, pages 9–16.

Chang, C.-C. and Lin, C.-J. (2011). Libsvm: A library for support vector machines. *ACM Transactions on Intelligent Systems and Technology (TIST)*, 2(3):27.

Cucerzan, S. (2007). Large-scale named entity disambiguation based on wikipedia data. In *Proc. of the 2007 Joint Conference on Empirical Methods in Natural Language Processing and Computational Natural Language Learning* (EMNLP-CoNLL), pages 708–716.

Cunningham, H. (2002). Gate, a general architecture for text engineering. *Computers and the Humanities*, 36(2):223–254.

Ekbal, A., Sourjikova, E., Frank, A., and Ponzetto, S. P. (2010). Assessing the challenge of fine-grained named entity recognition and classification. In *Proc. of the 2010 Named Entities Workshop*, (NEWS '10), in conjunction with *the 48th Annual meeting of the Association for Computational Linguistics.* (ACL '10), pages 93–101, Stroudsburg, PA, USA.

Fader, A., Soderland, S., and Etzioni, O. (2011). Identifying relations for open information extraction. In *Proc. of the Conference on Empirical Methods in Natural Language Processing* (EMNLP '11), pages 1535–1545.

Fan, R.-E., Chang, K.-W., Hsieh, C.-J., Wang, X.-R., and Lin, C.-J. (2008). LIBLINEAR: A library for large linear classification. *Journal of Machine Learning Research*, 9:1871–1874.

Fellbaum, C., editor (1998). *WordNet: An Electronic Lexical Database.* MIT Press, Cambridge, MA.

Finkel, J. R., Grenager, T., and Manning, C. (2005). Incorporating non-local information into information extraction systems by gibbs sampling. In *Proc. of the 43rd Annual Meeting on Association for Computational Linguistics*, (ACL '05), pages 363–370, Stroudsburg, PA, USA.

Fleischman, M. and Hovy, E. (2002). Fine grained classification of named entities. In *Proc. of the 19th International Conference on Computational Linguistics - Volume 1*, (COLING '02), pages 1–7, Stroudsburg, PA, USA. Association for Computational Linguistics.

Giuliano, C. (2009). Fine-Grained Classification of Named Entities Exploiting Latent Semantic Kernels. In *Proc. of the 13th Conference on Computational Natural Language Learning*, (CoNLL '09) pages 201–209.

Hoffart, J., Yosef, M. A., Bordino, I., Fürstenau, H., Pinkal, M., Spaniol, M., Taneva, B., Thater, S., and Weikum, G. (2011). Robust disambiguation of named entities in text. In *Proc. of the Conference on Empirical Methods in Natural Language Processing* (EMNLP '11), pages 782–792, Edinburgh, Scotland, United Kingdom 2011.

Hoffart, J., Suchanek, F., Berberich, K. and Weikum, G. (2012). YAGO2: A Spatially and Temporally Enhanced Knowledge Base from Wikipedia. *Special issue of the Artificial Intelligence Journal* 2012.

Lesk, M. (1986). Automatic sense disambiguation using machine readable dictionaries: how to tell a pine cone from an ice cream cone. In *Proc. of the 5th annual International Conference on Systems Documentation*, (SIGDOC '86), pages 24–26, New York, NY, USA. ACM.

Ling, X. and Weld, D. S. (2012). Fine-grained entity recognition. In *Proc. of the 26th AAAI Conference on Artificial Intelligence*, Toronto, Ontario, Canada.

Miller, G. A. (1995). Wordnet: A lexical database for english. *Communications of the ACM*, 38:39–41.

Milne, D. and Witten, I. H. (2008). Learning to link with wikipedia. In *Proc. of the 17th ACM conference on Information and knowledge management*, (CIKM '08), pages 509–518, New York, NY, USA. ACM.

Rahman, A. and Ng, V. (2010). Inducing fine-grained semantic classes via hierarchical and collective classification. In *Proc. of the 23rd International Conference on Computational Linguistics* (COLING 2010), pages 931–939.

Ratinov, L.-A., Roth, D., Downey, D., and Anderson, M. (2011). Local and global algorithms for disambiguation to wikipedia. In *Proc. of the 49th Annual Meeting of the Association for Computational Linguistics* (ACL '11), pages 1375–1384.

Suchanek, F., Kasneci, G., and Weikum, G. (2007). YAGO: A core of semantic knowledge - unifying WordNet and Wikipedia. In Williamson, C. L., Zurko, M. E., and Patel-Schneider, Peter F. Shenoy, P. J., editors, In *Proc. of the 16th International World Wide Web Conference* (WWW '07), pages 697–706, Banff, Canada. ACM.

Tang, L., Rajan, S., and Narayanan, V. K. (2009). Large scale multi-label classification via metalabeler. In *Proc. of the 18th International World Wide Web Conference*, (WWW '09), pages 211–220, New York, NY, USA. ACM.

Tsoumakas, G., Zhang, M.-L., and Zhou, Z.-H. (2012). Introduction to the special issue on learning from multi-label data. *Machine Learning*, 88(1-2):1–4.

Wacholder, N., Ravin, Y., and Choi, M. (1997): Disambiguation of Proper Names in Text. In *Proc. of the 5th Conference on Applied Natural Language Processing* (ANLP '97), pages 202-208.

Identifying Temporal Relations by Sentence and Document Optimizations

Katsumasa Yoshikawa[1] *Masayuki Asahara*[2] *Ryu Iida*[3]
(1) IBM Research, Tokyo, Japan
(2) National Institute for Japanese Language and Linguistics, Japan
(3) Tokyo Institute of Technology, Japan
katsumasay@gmail.com, masayu-a@ninjal.ac.jp, ryu-i@cl.cs.titech.ac.jp

Abstract

This paper presents a temporal relation identification method optimizing relations at sentence and document levels. Temporal relation identification is to identify temporal orders between events and time expressions. Various approaches of this task have been studied through the shared tasks TempEval (Verhagen et al., 2007, 2010). Not only identifying each temporal relation independently, some works also try to find multiple temporal relations jointly by logical constraints in Integer Linear Programming (Chambers and Jurafsky, 2008; Do et al., 2012) or Markov Logic Networks (Yoshikawa et al., 2009; Ling and Weld, 2010; Ha et al., 2010).

Though previous joint approaches optimize temporal relations in an entire document, we first optimize our model at sentence level and then extend it to document level. We consider that different types of temporal relations require different types of optimizations. By evaluating our sentence and document optimized model on the TempEval-2 data, we show that our approaches can achieve competitive performance in comparison to other state-of-the-art systems. We find that the sentence and document optimized model has strong tasks in TempEval-2, respectively.

Keywords: temporal relation identification, time, markov logic, semantic role.

Keywords in L_2: .

Proceedings of COLING 2012: Posters, pages 1371–1380,
COLING 2012, Mumbai, December 2012.

1 Introduction

Recent work on temporal analysis has focused on several sub-tasks, such as event (time) recognition, event (time) classification, time normalization, and temporal relation identification. Temporal relation identification (or temporal ordering) has especially been given much attention among studies in recent years. Since temporal orders often effect causal relations (*cause and effect*), identifying them is an essential task for deep language understanding.

Various approaches to temporal ordering have been proposed through shared tasks called *TempEval* (Verhagen et al., 2007, 2010). TempEval-2 involved four temporal ordering tasks corresponding to four types of temporal relations: between events and time expressions in a sentence (Task C), [1] between events of a document and the document creation time (DCT) (Task D), between two main events in two consecutive sentences (Task E), and between two events where one event syntactically dominates the other event (Task F).

Figure 1 shows an example of temporal relations. This example has five events and one time expression and includes the four types of relations corresponding to Tasks C, D, E, and F of TempEval-2. The temporal relations (TLINKs) are annotated as shown in Table 1 and we have to estimate these TLINK labels such as BEFORE, OVERLAP, and AFTER.

task	relation
Task C	e53 (change) OVERLAP t10 (a couple of years)
Task D	e50 (think) OVERLAP t0 (DCT)
Task D	e52 (think) OVERLAP t0 (DCT)
Task D	e53 (change) AFTER t0 (DCT)
Task E	e50 (think) OVERLAP e57 (reposition)
Task F	e50 (think) OVERLAP e51 (gloomy)
Task F	e52 (think) BEFORE e53 (change)

Table 1: Temporal Relations (TLINKs) in Figure 1

While the first studies handled this task as local classification problems (Boguraev and Ando, 2005; Mani et al., 2006), some recent works regard temporal relation identification as a global optimization problem in an entire document. Global optimization approaches take into account several relations and jointly identify all relations within a document. In order to ensure the consistencies among relations, previous work exploited global approaches with *transitivity* constraints in Integer Linear Programming (Chambers and Jurafsky, 2008; Do et al., 2012) or Markov Logic (Yoshikawa et al., 2009; Ling and Weld, 2010).

In this paper, we propose a new approach to temporal relation identification by optimizing temporal relations at sentence or document levels. We have two motivations to improve conventional global approaches. First, we consider that identifying each type of temporal relations requires different type of optimization. Optimizing at sentence level are suitable for some types of TLINKs rather than optimizing at document level. In addition, optimizing at sentence level allows us to effectively utilize rich syntactic and semantic features.

Secondly, it is difficult to construct global model by controlling many global constraints simultaneously. It is well-known that overly strong constraints hurt the performance of

[1]Note, Task C of TempEval-2 is further restricted by requiring that either the event syntactically dominates the time expression or the event and time expression occur in the same noun phrase.

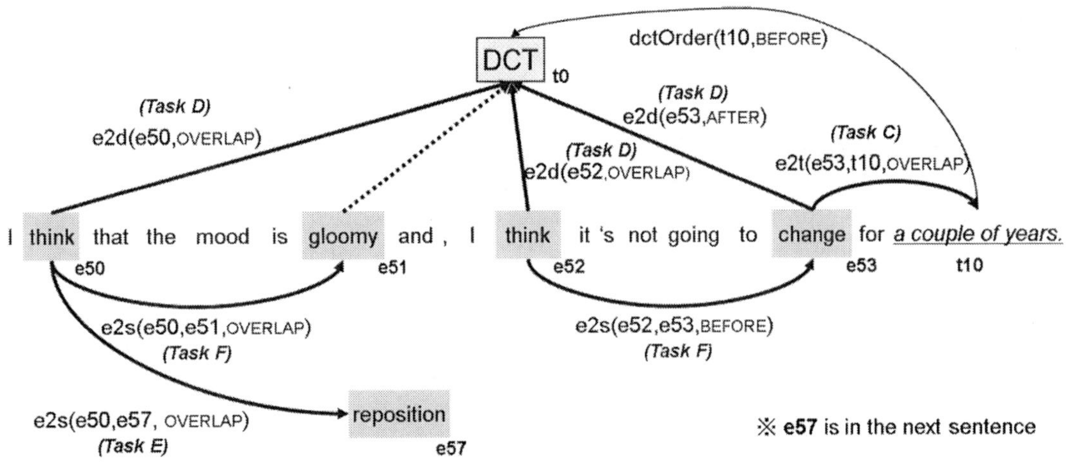

Figure 1: Temporal Relations

identification. Ha et al. adopted a Markov Logic for identifying temporal relations in TempEval-2 (Ha et al., 2010), but their global model at document level could not improve upon their local model in the majority of tasks. Especially in Tasks D and F, the results of their global model were much worse than those of their local model. According to their analysis, utilizing *hard* constraints caused many errors. Though Markov Logic (Richardson and Domingos, 2006) makes it possible to utilize both *hard* and *soft* constraints, both types of constraints are very sensitive and hard to be controlled well. It is possible for even a *soft* constraint to drastically improve (or hurt) the performance of temporal relation identification. Thus, finding effective constraints sometimes becomes more difficult task than feature selection for general machine learning.

To effectively control the sensitivity of constraints, we need first to reduce our large problem down to a smaller one. We construct our models optimized at two levels, sentence and document. First, we create a model which optimizes temporal relations at sentence level and then extend it to a model for document optimization. The *sentence-optimized* model focuses on only the temporal relations within the same sentence. The *document-optimized* model covers all relations in a document. For both models, we employ Markov Logic and control sensitive soft constraints. Each optimized model has respective advantages. The sentence-optimized model is good at handling TLINKs inside sentences (Tasks C and F) by exploiting rich syntactic and semantic features. The document-optimized model is strong at solving TLINKs beyond sentence boundaries (Task E). We evaluate our models on TempEval-2 data. As a result of advantages above, our sentence and document-optimized models outperform TempEval-2 participants on Tasks C and E, respectively.

2 Proposed Method

In this section we introduce the Markov Logic Network designed for our global models. Marlov Logic is a combination of first-order logic and Markov Networks (Richardson and Domingos, 2006). It can be understood as a formalism that extends first-order logic to allow formulae that can be violated with some penalties. From an alternative point of view, it is an expressive template language that uses first order logic formulae to instantiate Markov Networks of repetitive structure. Unfortunately, we do not have enough space to explain the details about Markov Logic. Since we can refer various previous works with Markov Logic (Singla and Domingos, 2006; Poon and Domingos, 2007, 2008), this section focuses on model constructions by Markov Logic Network.

First, we define four *hidden* predicates, corresponding to Tasks C, D, E, and F listed in Table 2. We do not know their extensions at test time. Our *observed* predicates reflect observed information extracted from the corpus (such as words, POS, etc.). Note that the TempEval data also contains temporal relations that were not supposed to be predicted. These relations are represented using an *observed* predicate: $dctOrder(t, R)$ for the relation R between a time expression t and a fixed DCT. An illustration of all "temporal" predicates can be seen in Figure 1.

In the following parts, we describe our three models: (1) *local* model which solves each task independently, (2) *sentence-optimized* model which targets Tasks C, D and F by sentence level optimization, and (3) *document-optimized* model which solves Tasks C-F by document level optimization. The sentence-optimized model also includes local features same as local model. The document-optimized model utilizes both features of local and sentence-optimized. So, the document-optimized model is a full version which contains all the local and global features.

2.1 Local Model

Our local model utilizes only local features and solves each task independently as a local classification problem. In the Markov Logic framework, local features are represented as *local formulae*. We say that a formula is local if it only considers the *hidden* temporal relation of a single event-event, event-time or event-DCT pair. The formulae in the second class are *global*: they involve two or more temporal relations at the same time.

The local features are based on features employed in previous work (UzZaman and Allen, 2010; Llorens et al., 2010) and are listed in Table 3. In order to illustrate how we implement each feature as a formula, we show a simple example. Consider the tense-feature for Task F. For this feature we introduce a predicate $tense(e, te)$ that denotes the tense te for an event e. In Table 3, this feature corresponds to the second row "EVENT-tense". For Task F, we employ the tense combinations of two events (e1 x e2). Then we add a formula such as

$$tense(e1, +te1) \wedge tense(e2, +te2) \Rightarrow e2s(e1, e2, +R) \tag{1}$$

which represents the properties of combinations between tense and event-event relations. Note, "+" sign means that the ground formulae derived from this formula have different weights for each label. Formula (1) are grounded for all possible combinations of tenses and temporal relations such as

$$tense(e1, \mathrm{PRESENT}) \wedge tense(e2, \mathrm{FUTURE}) \Rightarrow e2s(e1, e2, \mathrm{BEFORE}) \tag{2a}$$

$$tense(e1, \mathrm{PRESENT}) \wedge tense(e2, \mathrm{PRESENT}) \Rightarrow e2s(e1, e2, \mathrm{BEFORE}). \tag{2b}$$

This type of "template-based" formulae generation can be performed automatically by the Markov Logic Engine. Markov Logic Engine assigns different weights to Formulae (2a) and (2b). For example, Formula (2a) possibly obtains higher weight than Formula (2b). Actually, Formula (2a) matches the example in Figure 1 (Consider it replacing $e1$ with e52 and $e2$ with e53, respectively).

For Tasks E and F, there is no time expression directly related to the targeted events. So, we employ the time expressions which are syntactically dominated by the events or which are identified as arguments of them by a semantic role labeler. We also apply semantic role features (SR-Label) as a rich semantic feature introduced in (Llorens et al., 2010).

Task	predicate	description
Task C	$e2t(e, t, R)$	temporal relation between an event e and a time expression t is R
Task D	$e2d(e, R)$	temporal relation between an event e and DCT is R
Task E	$e2e(e1, e2, R)$	temporal relation between two main events of the adjacent sentences, $e1$ and $e2$ is R
Task F	$e2s(e1, e2, R)$	temporal relation between two events where one event $e1$ syntactically dominates the other event $e2$ is R

Table 2: Hidden Predicates and Targeted Temporal Relations

Feature	MLN predicate	C	D	E	F
EVENT-class	$class(e, c)$	Y	Y	e1 x e2	e1 x e2
EVENT-tense	$tense(e, te)$	Y	Y	e1 x e2	e1 x e2
EVENT-aspect	$aspect(e, a)$	Y	Y	e1 x e2	e1 x e2
EVENT-tense-aspect	$tense(e, te)\&aspect(e, a)$	Y	Y	e1 x e2	e1 x e2
EVENT-polarity	$polarity(e, p)$	Y	Y	e1 x e2	e1 x e2
EVENT-stem	$stem(e, s)$	Y	Y	e1 x e2	e1 x e2
EVENT-word	$wordEvent(e, w)$	Y	Y	Y	Y
EVENT-POS	$eventPos(e, p)$	Y	Y	e1 x e2	e1 x e2
TIME-type	$type(t, ty)$	Y	Y	Y	Y
TIME-value	$value(t, ty)$	Y	Y	Y	Y
TIME-word	$wordTime(t, w)$	Y			
TIME-POS	$posTime(t, p)$	Y			
TIME-DCT order	$dctOrder(t, r)$	Y	Y	Y	Y
Dependency-Word	$depWord(e(\text{or } t), w)$	Y	Y	Y	
Dependency-POS	$depPos(e(\text{or } t), p)$	Y	Y	Y	
Dependency-Label	$dep(e1, e2(\text{or } t), l)$	Y			Y
SR-Word	$srlWord(c(\text{or } t), w)$	Y	Y	Y	Y
SR-POS	$srlPOS(e, (\text{or } t), p)$	Y	Y	Y	Y
SR-Label	$srl(e1, e2(\text{or } t), l)$	Y			Y

Table 3: Local Features

2.2 Sentence-optimized Model

The original Markov Logic approach to temporal relation identification solves problems in a document-by-document manner (Yoshikawa et al., 2009). On the other hand, our sentence-optimized model is a global model optimized at sentence level and solves problems in a sentence-by-sentence manner. Optimizing at sentence level gives us at least two advantages: (1) it allows us to keep a problem simple and control sensitive constraints well, (2) we can exploit rich syntactic and semantic features and constraints. The first advantage is an original motivation of sentence-optimized model. Even though our models have only several global formulae, they are very sensitive and it is difficult for us to control them well. In addition, since the optimization at document level is sometimes computationally hard, we cannot employ large number of features. The sentence-optimized model provides us with a solution to overcome these difficulties.

Though we need to solve four types of relations in TempEval-2, the sentence-optimized model focuses on only three of them corresponding to Tasks C, D, and F. Our global formulae are designed to enforce consistency between the three *hidden* predicates $e2t, e2d$, and $e2s$. In the following parts, we show the set of formula templates we use to generate the global formulae. Here each template produces several instantiations, one for each assignment of temporal relation classes to the variables R1, R2, etc.

Our global formulae mainly employ DCT as a reference time. First, the global formulae between Tasks C and D are,

$$dctOrder(t, +R1) \wedge e2t(e, t, +R2) \Rightarrow e2d(e, +R3) \quad (3)$$

$$dctOrder(t, +R1) \wedge e2d(e, +R2) \Rightarrow e2t(e, t, +R3) \quad (4)$$

which ensure the consistency between $e2t$ and $e2d$. We implement these formulae as *soft* constraints. If a possible world violates some soft constraints, they give it some penalties with corresponding weights. In contrast to hard constraints, a possible world which causes some violation of soft constraints is *less* probable (not prohibited). Soft constraints are good way to control ambiguous transition rules. For example, Formula (4) can be instantiated as,

$$dctOrder(t, \text{BEFORE}) \wedge e2d(e, \text{AFTER}) \Rightarrow e2t(e, t, \text{AFTER}), \quad (5a)$$

$$dctOrder(t, \text{BEFORE}) \wedge e2d(e, \text{AFTER}) \Rightarrow e2t(e, t, \text{OVERLAP}) \quad (5b)$$

which possibly hold but not always do. [2] Fortunately, this type of soft rule poses no problem for Markov Logic: after training, Formula (5b) will have a lower weight than Formula (5a).

The global formulae for Tasks D and F are,

$$e2d(e1, +R1) \wedge e2d(e2, +R2) \Rightarrow e2s(e1, e2, +R3), \quad (6)$$

$$e2d(e1, +R1) \wedge e2s(e1, e2, +R2) \Rightarrow e2d(e2, +R3) \quad (7)$$

which enforce the consistency between $e2d$ and $e2s$. Formula (6) is especially effective because the results of $e2d$ (Task D) are much higher than $e2s$ (Task F).

Since some events share the same time expression, we add the following global formulae,

$$e2t(e1, t, +R1) \wedge e2t(e2, t, +R2) \Rightarrow e2s(e1, e2, +R3), \quad (8)$$

$$e2t(e1, t, +R1) \wedge e2s(e1, e2, +R2) \Rightarrow e2t(e2, t, +R3) \quad (9)$$

which ensure the consistency between Tasks C and F.

With event-argument relations (semantic roles), we construct some more global formulae. For $e2d$, we assume that the relations sharing the same time expression have the same relations. Such properties can be expressed as,

$$srl(e1, t, \text{AM-TMP}) \wedge srl(e2, t, \text{AM-TMP}) \Rightarrow e2d(e1, R1) \wedge e2d(e2, R2) \wedge R1 = R2. \quad (10)$$

Likewise, for $e2t$, we assume that the relations sharing the same time expression affect each other:

$$srl(e1, t, \text{AM-TMP}) \wedge srl(e2, t, \text{AM-TMP}) \wedge e2t(e1, t, +R1) \Rightarrow e2t(e2, t, +R2). \quad (11)$$

It is easy for the sentence-optimized model to implement much more features and constraints as in other tasks (Meza-Ruiz and Riedel, 2009; Yoshikawa et al., 2011).

2.3 Document-optimized Model

The last model is the method which optimizes problems at document level. We add another hidden predicate $e2e$ which handles Task E of TempEval-2. Note, in order to pursue computational efficiency, we should deal with $e2t$, $e2d$, and $e2s$ as *observed* predicates and solve only $e2e$ in this phase. However, we only add a few global formulae and can construct

[2] Formula (5b) is instantiated by the relations in Figure 1

a global model which jointly optimizes four tasks. We no longer change the formulae we constructed for the sentence-optimized model. So, what we have to make is constructing global formulae for only $e2e$. Transition rules also apply to $e2e$ in a similar way to $e2s$.

$$e2d(e1, +R1) \land e2d(e2, +R2) \Rightarrow e2e(e1, e2, +R3) \quad (12)$$

$$e2d(e1, +R1) \land e2e(e1, e2, +R2) \Rightarrow e2d(e2, +R3) \quad (13)$$

which represent the transitive relations between $e2e$ and $e2d$. We can add more constraints such as relations between $e2e$ and $e2t$ or $e2s$. However, these constraints sometimes cause error propagations because $e2t$ and $e2s$ are difficult to solve and possibly include many errors. Thus, we add only the two formulae above for document-optimized model.

3 Experiments and Results

With our experiments we want to answer two questions: (1) do optimizations at sentence and document levels help to increase the overall accuracy of temporal relation identification? (2) How does our approach compare to the state-of-the-art results? In the following we will first present the experimental set-up we chose to answer these questions.

In our experiments we used the test and training sets provided by the TempEval-2 shared task. The language we target is only English. We further split the original training data into a training and a development set, used for optimizing parameters and formulae. We employ 147 documents for training, 15 for development, and 20 for testing.

For feature generation we use the following tools. POS tagging is performed with the stanford-POS-tagger; [3] as parser and semantic role labeler for our syntactic and semantic features we employ LTH semantic parser. [4] As a Markov Logic Engine, we employ *Markov thebeast*, which is tailored for NLP applications. For evaluation of temporal relation identification, we employ an accuracy-based scoring of TempEval-2. It is a simple metric: the number of correct answers divided by the number of answers.

3.1 Impact of Sentence and Document Optimizations

Here we present our comparison of three models. Let us show the results on TEST set in Table 4. We can find four columns corresponding to Tasks C–F, for our models of "Local", "Sentence-optimized" and "Document-optimized".

Both optimized models outperform the local model (Local). The scores with bold characters are the best scores of the tasks. The sentence-optimized model got the best position in Task C and the document-optimized model won the other tasks D–F. The sentence-optimized model also outputs competitive results to the document-optimized model in Task F. Unfortunately, our improvements are not statistically significant. But can our joint modelling help to reach or improve state-of-the-art results? We will try to answer this question in the next section.

3.2 Comparison to State-of-the-art

In order to put our results into context, Table 5 shows them alongside those of other TempEval-2 participants. We show only five teams: the winners of Tasks C–F in TempEval-2 and NCSU-joint which a global model with Markov Logic. The best result of each task is

[3] http://nlp.stanford.edu/software/tagger.shtml

[4] http://nlp.cs.lth.se/

	C	D	E	F
Local	0.652	0.745	0.553	0.520
Sentence-optimized	**0.674**	0.742	-	0.546
Document-optimized	0.652	**0.759**	**0.569**	**0.556**

Table 4: Results of the All Models

team	C	D	E	F
TRIOS*	**0.65**	0.79	0.56	0.60
TIPSem	0.55	**0.82**	0.55	0.59
TRIPS*	0.63	0.76	**0.58**	0.59
NCSU-indi	0.63	0.68	0.48	**0.66**
NCSU-joint	0.62	0.21	0.51	0.25
Sentence-optimized	**0.67**	0.74	-	0.55
Document-optimized	0.65	0.76	**0.57**	0.56

Table 5: Results with Other Systems (Systems with * have recall errors)

shown with bold characters. As shown in the last two rows, our Sentence and Document-optimized won Tasks C and E, respectively. Note, for Task E TRIPS (UzZaman and Allen, 2010) got 0.58 on precision but 0.50 on recall. Hence our Document-optimized outperforms TRIPS system on F-measure (0.57 vs 0.54). These results fit our intuitions that Task C requires rich linguistic knowledge inside sentences and Task E requires global knowledge such as inter-sentential logical constraints or ontological features. In TempEval-2's final report, it is not clear why the results on Task C (event-time) have not improved compared with the corresponding task in TempEval-1, notwithstanding TempEval-2 is added restriction that the event and time expression had to be syntactically adjacent. However, our system achieved over 0.67 pt and was better than TempEval-1's participants.

For Tasks D and F our results cannot reach the best TempEval-2 scores. But our results have some interesting points compared with the best results. TIPSem (Llorens et al., 2010), the best team of Task D, also employed semantic roles as features. Their learning classifiers are CRF with local features. So, a global joint approach is not always advantageous for event-DCT classifications. NCSU-indi (Ha et al., 2010), the best system for Task F, outperformed other participants (at more than 6 pt margins for all). This point suggests that ontological features NCSU-indi applied are more effective than global optimization. Compared with NCSU-joint which is a global model applied hard constraints in Markov Logic, we can find that our Markov Logic approach successfully controls soft constraints.

4 Conclusion

In this paper we presented a novel global approach to temporal relation identification. Our approach first optimized our model at sentence level and then extended it at document level. We revealed that the sentence-optimized model is better than the document-optimized model at least for identifying event-time relations (Task C) in TempEval-2 data. The document-optimized model is also strong at identifying relations between two events (Task E). As future work we are planning to use external or untagged data along with methods for unsupervised learning in Markov Logic (Poon and Domingos, 2008). We would also like to investigate the utility of our models for multilingual temporal ordering.

References

Boguraev, B. and Ando, R. K. (2005). Timeml-compliant text analysis for temporal reasoning. In *Proceedings of the 19th International Joint Conference on Artificial Intelligence*, pages 997–1003.

Chambers, N. and Jurafsky, D. (2008). Jointly combining implicit constraints improves temporal ordering. In *Proceedings of the 2008 Conference on Empirical Methods in Natural Language Processing*, pages 698–706, Honolulu, Hawaii. Association for Computational Linguistics.

Do, Q., Lu, W., and Roth, D. (2012). Joint inference for event timeline construction. In *Proceedings of the 2012 Joint Conference on Empirical Methods in Natural Language Processing and Computational Natural Language Learning*, pages 677–687, Jeju Island, Korea. Association for Computational Linguistics.

Ha, E., Baikadi, A., Licata, C., and Lester, J. (2010). Ncsu: Modeling temporal relations with markov logic and lexical ontology. In *Proceedings of the 5th International Workshop on Semantic Evaluation*, pages 341–344, Uppsala, Sweden. Association for Computational Linguistics.

Ling, X. and Weld, D. S. (2010). Temporal information extraction. In *Proceedings of the Twenty Fifth National Conference on Artificial Intelligence.*

Llorens, H., Saquete, E., and Navarro, B. (2010). Tipsem (english and spanish): Evaluating crfs and semantic roles in tempeval-2. In *Proceedings of the 5th International Workshop on Semantic Evaluation*, pages 284–291, Uppsala, Sweden. Association for Computational Linguistics.

Mani, I., Verhagen, M., Wellner, B., Lee, C. M., and Pustejovsky, J. (2006). Machine learning of temporal relations. In *ACL-44: Proceedings of the 21st International Conference on Computational Linguistics and the 44th annual meeting of the Association for Computational Linguistics*, pages 753–760, Morristown, NJ, USA. Association for Computational Linguistics.

Meza-Ruiz, I. and Riedel, S. (2009). Jointly identifying predicates, arguments and senses using markov logic. In *Proceedings of Human Language Technologies: The 2009 Annual Conference of the North American Chapter of the Association for Computational Linguistics*, pages 155–163, Boulder, CO, USA. Association for Computational Linguistics.

Poon, H. and Domingos, P. (2007). Joint inference in information extraction. In *Proceedings of the Twenty-Second National Conference on Artificial Intelligence*, pages 913–918, Vancouver, Canada. AAAI Press.

Poon, H. and Domingos, P. (2008). Joint unsupervised coreference resolution with Markov Logic. In *Proceedings of the 2008 Conference on Empirical Methods in Natural Language Processing*, pages 650–659, Honolulu, Hawaii. Association for Computational Linguistics.

Richardson, M. and Domingos, P. (2006). Markov logic networks. *Machine Learning*, 62(1-2):107–136.

Singla, P. and Domingos, P. (2006). Entity resolution with markov logic. In *Proceedings of the Sixth International Conference on Data Mining (ICDM)*, pages 572–582, Washington, DC, USA. IEEE Computer Society.

UzZaman, N. and Allen, J. (2010). Trips and trios system for tempeval-2: Extracting temporal information from text. In *Proceedings of the 5th International Workshop on Semantic Evaluation*, pages 276–283, Uppsala, Sweden. Association for Computational Linguistics.

Verhagen, M., Gaizaukas, R., Schilder, F., Hepple, M., Katz, G., and Pustejovsky, J. (2007). Semeval-2007 task 15: Tempeval temporal relation identification. In *Proceedings of the 4th International Workshop on SemEval-2007.*, pages 75–80.

Verhagen, M., Sauri, R., Caselli, T., and Pustejovsky, J. (2010). Semeval-2010 task 13: Tempeval-2. In *Proceedings of the 5th International Workshop on Semantic Evaluation*, pages 57–62, Uppsala, Sweden. Association for Computational Linguistics.

Yoshikawa, K., Asahara, M., and Matsumoto, Y. (2011). Jointly extracting japanese predicate-argument relation with markov logic. In *Proceedings of 5th International Joint Conference on Natural Language Processing*, pages 1125–1133, Chiang Mai, Thailand. Asian Federation of Natural Language Processing.

Yoshikawa, K., Riedel, S., Asahara, M., and Matsumoto, Y. (2009). Jointly identifying temporal relations with markov logic. In *Proceedings of the Joint Conference of the 47th Annual Meeting of the ACL and the 4th International Joint Conference on Natural Language Processing of the AFNLP*, pages 405–413, Suntec, Singapore. Association for Computational Linguistics.

Affect Detection from Semantic Interpretation of Drama Improvisation

Li ZHANG[1] Ming JIANG[2]
(1) NORTHUMBRIA UNIVERSITY, Faculty of Engineering and Environment, Newcastle, UK
(2) UNIVERSITY OF LEEDS, School of Computer Science, UK
li.zhang@northumbria.ac.uk

ABSTRACT

We have developed an intelligent agent to engage with users in virtual drama improvisation previously. The intelligent agent was able to perform sentence-level affect detection from user inputs with strong emotional indicators. However, we noticed that many inputs with weak or no affect indicators also contain emotional implication but were regarded as neutral expressions by the previous interpretation. In this paper, we employ latent semantic analysis to go beyond linguistic restrictions and to perform topic theme detection and identify target audiences for those inputs with vague affect indicators and ambiguous target audiences. We also discuss how emotions embedded in such emotionally ambiguous inputs are detected with the consideration of interpersonal relationships, special sentence types and emotions experienced by the target audiences using a neural network based contextual affect detection. The work contributes to the conference themes on discourse and pragmatics, semantics and sentiment and text classification.

TITLE AND ABSTRACT IN CHINESE

对于戏剧即席创作语义解析的情感识别

我们曾开发了一个能跟用户进行虚拟戏剧即席创作交流的智能代理. 它能从有明显情感迹象的单句话中检测情感. 然而, 很多不具有情感词的句子也有很强的情感寓意却被认为是中性. 在这里, 我们使用 Latent Semantic Analysis, 摆脱语言特征的限制, 用话题和目标听众的检测去识别情感隐含在那些只具有微弱情感信号的输入中. 并讨论怎样从这样的输入中, 使用基于神经网络的上下文检测去识别情感.

KEYWORDS : Affect detection, semantic interpretation, drama improvisation
KEYWORDS IN CHINESE : 情感检测, 语义解析, 戏剧即席创作

Proceedings of COLING 2012: Posters, pages 1381–1390,
COLING 2012, Mumbai, December 2012.

1 Introduction

It is a long-term research goal to build a 'thinking' machine in the AI field. This endeavour has given rise to agent-based user interfaces (Endrass et al., 2011; Zhang et al., 2009). Moreover, we believe it will make intelligent agents possess human-like behaviour and narrow the communicative gap between machines and human-beings if they are equipped to interpret human emotions during social interaction. Thus in this research, we equip our AI agent with emotion and social intelligence. According to Kappas (2010), human emotions are psychological constructs with notoriously noisy, murky, and fuzzy boundaries. These natural features of emotion also make it difficult for a single modal recognition, such as via acoustic-prosodic features of speech or facial expressions. Since human being's reasoning process takes related context into consideration, in our research, we intend to make our agent take multi-channels of subtle emotional expressions embedded in social interaction contexts into consideration to draw reliable affect interpretation. The research presented here focuses on the production of intelligent agents with the abilities of interpreting dialogue contexts semantically to support affect detection as our first step of building an agent-based interface within this application domain.

The research presented here is conducted within a previously developed online multi-user role-play virtual drama framework, which allows school children aged 14 – 16 to perform drama performance training. In this platform young people could interact online in a 3D virtual drama stage with others under the guidance of a human director. In one session, up to five virtual characters are controlled on a virtual stage by human users ("actors"). The actors are given a loose scenario around which to improvise, but are at liberty to be creative. An intelligent agent is also involved in improvisation. It included an affect detection component, which detected affect from human characters' each individual text-based turn-taking input. This previous affect detection component was able to detect 15 emotions including basic and complex emotions, but the detection has not taken any context into consideration. The agent also made attempts to produce appropriate responses to help stimulate the improvisation based on the detected affect. The detected emotions are also used to generate emotional animations of the avatars.

This original affect detection processing was mainly built using pattern-matching rules that looked for simple grammatical patterns or templates. A syntactic parser, Rasp (Briscoe and Carroll, 2002), was also used to provide syntactical processing of each input. From the analysis of the collected transcripts, the original affect interpretation without any contextual inference proved to be effective enough for those inputs containing strong clear emotional indictors such as 'yes/no', 'haha', 'thanks' etc. There are also situations that users' inputs contain very weak or even no affect signals, thus contextual inference is needed to further derive the affect conveyed in such inputs. Moreover, it is noticed that in the collected transcripts the improvisational dialogues are often multi-threaded. This refers to the situation that conversational responses of different discussion themes to previous several speakers are mixed up due to the nature of the online chat setting. Therefore the detection of the most related discussion themes using semantic analysis is very crucial for the accurate interpretation of emotions implied in those inputs with ambiguous audiences and weak affect indicators.

2 Related work

There is much well-known research work in the field of intelligent conversational agents. Aylett et al. (2006) focused on the development of affective behaviour planning for their synthetic characters. Endrass, Rehm and André (2011) carried out study on the culture-related differences in the domain of small talk behaviour. Their agents were equipped to generate culture specific dialogues. Recently textual affect sensing has also drawn researchers' attention. Neviarouskaya et al. (2010) provided a sentence-level rule-based textual affect sensing system to recognize judgments, appreciation and affective states. But the detection was still limited to the analysis of individual inputs. Ptaszynski et al. (2009) employed context-sensitive affect detection with the integration of a web-mining technique to detect affect from users' input and verify its contextual appropriateness. However, their system targeted interaction only between an agent and one human user, which reduced the complexity of the modelling of the interaction context.

There is also research related to building opinion-related lexical resources beneficial to opinion mining applications. E.g. Esuli (2008) employed a semi-supervised term classification model with quantitative analysis of definitions of terms provided by on-line dictionaries. The research generated a lexical resource, SentiWordNet. It provided positive, negative and objective orientations for a general category of terms and senses. Cambria and Hussain (2012) proposed a sentic computing framework for open-domain opinion mining and sentiment analysis based on the integration of common sense knowledge and graph mining and multi-dimensionality reduction techniques. Generally, they employed common sense computing techniques to bridge the semantic gap between word-level data and their corresponding concept-level opinions. Moreover, as mentioned earlier, naturalistic emotion expressions usually consist of a complex and continuously changed symphony of multimodal expressions. Kappas (2010) argued that it is inappropriate to conclude a smiling user is really happy. In fact, the same expression can be interpreted completely differently depending on the context that is given. Thus it also motivates us to use semantic interpretation of social contexts to inform affect detection in this research.

3 Semantic interpretation of social interaction contexts

In the collected transcripts, we noticed that the language used in our application domain is often complex, idiosyncratic and invariably ungrammatical. Most importantly, the language also contains a large number of weak cues to the affect that is being expressed. These cues may be contradictory or they may work together to enable a stronger interpretation of the affective state. In order to build a reliable and robust analyser of affect it is necessary to undertake several diverse forms of analysis and to enable these to work together to build stronger interpretations. Therefore, in this work, we integrate contextual information to further derive the affect embedded in contexts and to provide affect interpretation for those without strong affect indicators.

In our original affect detection processing, we relied on keywords and partial phrases matching with simple semantic analysis using WordNet. However, we notice many concepts and emotional expressions can be described in various ways. Especially if the inputs contain no strong affect indicators, other approaches focusing on underlying semantic structures should be considered. Thus in this section we discuss the approaches of using latent semantic analysis (LSA) (Landauer and Dumais, 2008) and its related packages for terms and documents comparison to recover the most related discussion themes and target audiences to benefit affect detection.

LSA generally identifies relationships between a set of documents and the terms they contain by producing a set of concepts related to the documents and terms. In order to compare the meanings behind the words, LSA maps both words and documents into a 'concept' space and performs comparison in this space. In detail, LSA assumes that there are some underlying latent semantic structures in the data which are partially obscured by the randomness of the word choice. This random choice of words also introduces noise into the word-concept relationship. LSA aims to find the smallest set of concepts that spans all the documents. It employs singular value decomposition to estimate the hidden concept space and to remove the noise. This concept space associates syntactically different but semantically similar terms and documents. We use these transformed terms and documents in the concept space for retrieval rather than the original ones.

In our work, we employ the semantic vectors package (Widdows and Cohen, 2010) to perform LSA and analyze underlying relationships between documents and their similarities. This package provides APIs for concept space creation. It applies concept mapping algorithms to term-document matrices using Apache Lucene, a high-performance, full-featured text search engine library implemented in Java. We integrate this package with the AI agent's affect detection component to calculate semantic similarities between those inputs without strong affect signals and training documents with clear discussion themes. In this paper, we target the transcripts of the school bullying scenario[1] for context-based affect analysis.

In order to perform semantic comparison between user inputs and documents belonging to different topic categories, sample documents with strong topic themes are collected. Personal articles from the Experience project (www.experienceproject.com) are used for this purpose. These articles belong to 12 categories including Education, Family & Friends, Health & Wellness, etc. Since we intend to perform discussion theme detection for the transcripts of those employed testing scenarios (including school bullying and Crohn's disease), we extracted documents close enough to these scenarios including articles of Crohn's disease (five articles), school bullying (five), family care for children (five), food choice (three), school life including school uniform (10) and school lunch (10) etc. Phrase and sentence level expressions implying 'disagreement' and 'suggestion' were also gathered from several other articles published on the website. Thus we have training documents with eight discussion themes including 'Crohn's disease', 'bullying', 'family care', 'food choice', 'school lunch', 'school uniform', 'suggestions' and 'disagreement'. The first six themes are sensitive and crucial discussion topics to the employed scenarios, while the last two themes are intended to capture arguments expressed in multiple ways. Affect detection from metaphorical expressions often poses great challenges to automatic linguistic processing systems. In order to detect a few metaphorical phenomena, we include four types of metaphorical examples published on the following website: http://knowgramming.com, in our training corpus. These include cooking, family, weather, and farm metaphors. We also borrowed a group of 'Ideas as External Entities' metaphor examples from the ATT-Meta databank (http://www.cs.bham.ac.uk/~jab/ATT-Meta/Databank/) to enrich the metaphor categories. Individual files are used to store each type of the metaphorical expressions. All the sample documents of the above 13 categories are regarded as training files.

We also added some training documents with broader topic themes as noise training data in order to evaluate the robustness of topic theme detection. Five articles of each of the following themes are employed: 'alcoholism', 'voluntary work', 'self-employment', 'politics', and 'hobbies'. These are also added to the training corpus for topic theme detection. The following example interaction of the school bullying scenario is used to demonstrate how we detect the discussion themes for those inputs with weak affect indicators and ambiguous target audiences.

---

[1] The bully, Mayid, is picking on a new schoolmate, Lisa. Elise and Dave (Lisa's friends), and Mrs Parton (the school teacher) are trying to stop the bullying.

1. Mrs Parton: children, stop arguing! [disapproval]
2. Mayid: u shut up, how the hell does that sound like a gal, u twat!!! [angry]
3. Elise: Stop it, Mayid. Lisa how r u? [disapproval]
4. Mayid: do ya even have any brain to think about that one! [Topic: bullying and disease, Target audience: Elise, Emotion: angry]
5. Lisa: hi, elise, *I'm alright*. [neutral]
6. Elise: cuz it jus does. Actually I'm cleverer than u think, u wus. [angry]
7. Mayid: ur da most ugly wus face! [angry]
8. Dave: could u please all tune ur voice down. [Played by the AI agent]
9. Elise: look at ur face u twat. [angry]
10. Mayid: my face is beautiful and wot, u jealous!! [angry]
11. Elise: I think the mirror breaks all da time u look in it. [Topic: bullying, Target audience: Mayid, Emotion: angry]
12. Mayid: hahaha. [happy]
13. Dave: Are these all desperate people? [Played by the AI agent]
14. Mayid: u looking in da mirror rite now, but u probably can't see urself with all the cracks. [Topic: bullying, family care and suggestion, Target audience: Elise, Emotion: angry]

The original affect detection focuses on inputs with strong emotion signals and provides affect annotation for such inputs in the above example. The emotion indicators are also illustrated in italics in the above interaction. The inputs without an affect label followed straightaway are those with weak affect indicators (4th, 11th and 14th inputs). Therefore further processing is needed to recover their discussion themes and identify their most likely audiences in order to identify implied emotions more accurately. The general idea for the detection of discussion themes is to use LSA to calculate semantic distances between each test input and all the training files with clear topic themes. Semantic distances between the test input and the 13 valid topic terms (e.g. 'disease') are also calculated. The detected topics are derived from the integration of these semantic similarity outputs. We start with the 4th input to demonstrate the theme detection.

Documents	Similarity scores for document vectors closest to the vector for the topic theme, 'bullying'
bullied1.txt	0.733
bullied2.txt	0.472
bullied3.txt	0.285
family_care4.txt	0.232
school_uniform.txt	0.231
crohn2.txt	0.230
test_corpus1.txt (the 4th input)	0.220

TABLE 1 – Partial scores for document vectors closest to the vector of the theme 'bullying'

In order to produce a concept space, the corresponding semantic vector APIs are used to create a Lucene index for all the training samples and the test file ('test_corpus1.txt' contains the 4th input). This generated index is then used to create term and document vectors, i.e. the concept space. First of all, we provide rankings for all the training files and the test input based on their semantic distances to a topic theme by searching for document vectors closest to that of a specific term (e.g. 'bullying'). The 4th input thus semantically relates to the topic theme, 'bullying', the most among all the 13 topics. Table 1 shows the partial outputs of such semantic calculation. Moreover, another effective approach for topic detection is to find the semantic similarity between documents. If the semantic distances between training files and the test file are calculated, then it provides another source of information for topic detection. Therefore we use the CompareTerms semantic vector API to calculate semantic similarities between documents.

The similarity results show there are three training files (bullied3.txt, bullied2.txt and crohn3.txt) semantically most similar to the test file. These three files respectively recommend the following two themes: 'bullying' and 'disease'. In the processing of finding documents closest to a topic theme vector (see Table 1), the test input also achieves the best ranking for the 'bullying' theme. With the integration of the semantic similarity results between document vectors, the processing concludes that the 4th input relates most closely to topics of 'bullying' and 'disease'. In order to identify its target audiences, we start from the 3rd input to derive topic themes until retrieving the input with at least partially the same themes as those of the 4th input. The original affect processing detects the 3rd input is most likely to indicate 'bullying' with a rude attitude. It shares one of the themes embedded in the 4th input. The 3rd input from Elise also mentions Mayid as its audience. Thus the target audience of the 4th input is Elise, who started the conversation in the first place.

In a similar way, the topic detection processing also identifies the 11th input from Elise indicates a theme of 'bullying'. In order to find its target audience, the theme detection starts from the 10th input from Mayid. The original affect processing identifies the 10th input shows an 'angry' emotion indicated by a strong affect indicator, thus it contains a 'bullying' theme. Moreover, the 9th input is the last round input from the same speaker, Elise. The original affect detection also identifies it as an 'angry' aggressive input. Based on the above reasoning, Elise showed aggressive behaviour in the last round input, followed by Mayid's angry response. Therefore this new round input from Elise with a strong 'bullying' theme most likely continues the previous bullying discussion. Thus the 11th input from Elise regards Mayid as the most intended audience.

By searching for document vectors closest to those of the topics 'family care' and 'bullying', the 14th input from Mayid shows high semantic closeness to these two topics. The similarity calculation between document vectors indicates that it is also most closely related to 'bullied3.txt (0.813)' and 'suggestion1.txt (0.788)'. Thus the 14th input is most likely to indicate topics of 'bullying', 'family care' and 'suggestion'. Since the 13th input from Dave, played by the AI agent, indicates 'disapproval', it is regarded to indicate 'bullying'. Thus Dave is one of the audiences of this 14th input. Moreover, as discussed earlier, the 11th input from Elise contains a 'bullying' theme with Mayid as the audience. Thus the 14th input from Mayid is unlikely to indicate topics of 'family care' or 'suggestion', but more likely to indicate 'bullying' with Elise and Dave as the intended audiences. In general, the semantic-based theme detection is able to help the AI agent derive the most related discussion themes and identify the most intended audiences for those inputs without strong affect indicators. We believe these are very important aspects for the accurate interpretation of the emotion contexts.

4 A neural network-based contextual affect detection

The research of Wang et al. (2011) discussed that feedback of artificial listeners can be influenced by relationships, personalities and culture. The research of Hareli and Rafaeli (2008) also pointed out that "one person's emotion is a factor that can shape the behaviours, thoughts and emotions of other people". Thus in this work such interpersonal (positive (friendly) or negative (hostile)) relationships are also employed to advise affect detection in social contexts.

In the example mentioned in section 3, the topic detection identifies the most likely audience of the 4th input from Mayid is Elise. That is, the most related social context of the 4th input is the 3rd input indicating a 'bullying' negative theme contributed by Elise. Especially, the speaker, Mayid (the bully) and the audience, Elise (the bullied victim's best friend) have a tense relationship, thus the 4th input from Mayid with the themes of 'bullying' and 'disease' will be most likely to show 'sad' or 'outrageous/angry' indication. Moreover, the processing also reveals that the 11th input from Elise is mainly related to the 'bullying' topic and its target audience is Mayid. Since Mayid and Elise share a tense relationship and the bully, Mayid, has expressed an 'angry' emotion in the most related context (i.e. the 10th input), this 11th bullying input from Elise most probably indicates 'anger'. In a similar way, the 14th input from Mayid is also embedded in a negative context contributed by the 11th and 13th inputs with strong bullying themes. Thus this last input is more likely to continue the 'bullying' discussion theme rather than focusing on any other topics such as 'family care' and 'suggestion'. Therefore it most probably indicates 'anger'. Moreover, in this work, we also employ sentence types as another dimension for context-based affect detection. Especially we detect rhetorical questions using LSA. E.g., the semantic vector API is used to perform semantic similarity comparison between rhetorical & normal training document vectors and the 4th input from Mayid. The processing recognizes the 4th input as a rhetorical question with a high confidence score.

Moreover, we implement the above reasoning of emotional influences between characters using a supervised neural network algorithm, Backpropagation. The neural network we used employs a three-layer topology: one input, one hidden and one output layer, with six nodes in the input layer and 10 nodes respectively in the hidden and output layers. The six nodes in the input layer indicate the most recent emotions expressed by potential up to four target audiences, a sentence type and an averaged relationship value between the speaker and audiences. The 10 nodes in the output layer represent the 10 output detected affective states ('neutral', 'approval', 'disapproval', 'angry', 'grateful', 'regretful', 'happy', 'sad', 'worried' and 'caring'). They are chosen because of their high occurrences in the annotation of the training set. These emotion labels are mainly borrowed from Ekman (1992) and the OCC emotion model (Ortony et al., 1988). We also notice that the semantic boundaries between some of the emotions are rather fuzzy, e.g., 'regret' overlapping with 'sadness'. However, although these two emotions both belong to the appraising of events (consequences for self), 'sadness' reflects more generally on one's well-being while 'regret' is a specific kind of distress involving more specific events about which the experiencing person is displeased. In this application, 'sadness' is used for context-based general emotion appraisal while 'regret' is used only when the input contains specific strong affective indicators such as 'sorry' and 'I should*n't* have done that'. Moreover, the output emotion with the highest weighting is regarded as the most probable emotion implied in the current input.

500 example inputs with agreed annotations from the bullying scenario are used to train the neural network. After it is trained to reach a reasonable error rate (< 0.05 with an average training time: 3.5s), it is used for testing to predict emotional influence of other participant characters towards the speaking character. In the example discussed in section 3, for the 4th input, the neural net considers the following as inputs: the implied 'angry' emotion by the audience, Elise, 'a negative relationship' and a rhetorical question input. The algorithm detects 'anger' implied in the 4th input. Similarly, it interprets both the 11th and 14th inputs indicating 'angry' emotions.

In order to improve the system's robustness, we use semantic orientations of words/phrases embedded in sentences and min-margin based active learning to detect emotions from open-ended inputs without the constraints of pre-defined scenarios. Especially it helps to interpret emotions when daily-life discussion outside of the scenarios is less heated with diverse number of audiences, or emotion contexts of audiences or relationships between characters are not available.

5 Evaluation and conclusion

User testing was conducted previously with 200 British secondary school students to evaluate the affect detection and the AI agent's performance. We use previously collected transcripts to evaluate the efficiency of the updated affect detection with contextual inference. In order to evaluate the performances of the topic theme detection and the neural network based affect detection, three transcripts of another scenario, Crohn's disease, are used. Two human judges are employed to annotate the topic themes of the extracted 300 inputs from the test transcripts using the 13 topics. We used Cohen's Kappa to measure the agreement level between human judges for the topic annotation and obtained 0.813. Then the 250 inputs with agreed annotations are used as the gold standards to test the performance of the theme detection. A pattern matching baseline system is used to compare the performance with that of the LSA. We obtain an averaged precision, 0.783, and an averaged recall, 0.753, using the LSA while the baseline system achieves an averaged precision of 0.609 and an averaged recall of 0.587 for the 13 topic theme detection. Generally the semantic-based interpretation achieves better performances than the baseline system.

The human judges also annotated these 250 inputs with the output 10 emotions. The inter-annotator agreement between human judge A/B is 0.65. While the previous version of the affect detection achieves 0.43 in good cases, the new version achieves agreement levels with human judge A/B respectively 0.55 and 0.58. The new version achieves inter-annotator agreements generally fairly close to the agreement level between human annotators themselves.

Moreover, in order to provide evaluation results for the neural network-based affect detection, the human judges' previous annotations are converted into positive, negative and neutral. Then 203 inputs with agreed annotations are used as the gold standards. The annotations achieved by the neural net are also converted into solely positive and negative. A baseline system is built using simple Bayesian networks in order to further measure the neural network-based detection. The Bayesian network used emotions implied in the last two inputs as its inputs. The output is the predicted affect implied in the current input. The neural network inference with the consideration of relationships, sentence types and audiences' emotions achieved an average precision of 0.833 and an average recall of 0.827 while the baseline system achieved a precision of 0.609 and a recall of 0.633. Especially our approach coped well with the sudden change of emotions due to unexpected topic change, while such situations challenged the baseline system greatly.

We also noticed that the training and test transcripts contained imbalanced class categories, e.g. more negative inputs presented than positive and neutral ones. In order to deal with such imbalanced classifications, we employ min-margin based active learning. It proved to be efficient in dealing with open-ended and imbalanced affect classifications in our application. In future work, we aim to equip the AI agent with culturally related small talk behaviour in order to ease the interaction. The presented semantic analysis also shows great potential to automatically recognize emotional metaphorical expressions and contribute to the responding regimes for the AI agent's development. Other uncertainty sampling techniques will also be employed. We believe these are crucial aspects for the development of effective agent-based interfaces.

References

Aylett, A., Louchart, S. Dias, J., Paiva, A., Vala, M., Woods, S. and Hall, L.E. (2006). Unscripted Narrative for Affectively Driven Characters. IEEE Computer Graphics and Applications. 26(3):42-52.

Briscoe, E. and Carroll, J. (2002). Robust Accurate Statistical Annotation of General Text. In Proceedings of the 3rd International Conference on Language Resources and Evaluation, Las Palmas, Gran Canaria. 1499-1504.

Cambria, E. and Hussain, A. (2012). Sentic Computing: Techniques, Tools, and Applications. Springer, 2012 Edition. ISBN-10: 9400750692.

Ekman, P. (1992). An Argument for Basic Emotions. In Cognition and Emotion, 6, 169-200.

Endrass, B., Rehm, M. & André, E. (2011). Planning Small Talk Behavior with Cultural Influences for Multiagent Systems. Computer Speech and Language. 25(2):158-174.

Esuli, A. (2008). Automatic Generation of Lexical Resources for Opinion Mining: Models, Algorithms and Applications. PhD thesis. PhD School "Leonardo da Vinci", University of Pisa.

Hareli, S. and Rafaeli, A. (2008). Emotion cycles: On the social influence of emotion in organizations. Research in Organizational Behavior, 28, 35-59.

Kappas, A. (2010). Smile when you read this, whether you like it or not: Conceptual challenges to affect detection. IEEE Transactions on Affective Computing, 1 (1), 38-41.

Landauer, T.K. and Dumais, S. (2008). Latent semantic analysis. Scholarpedia, 3(11):4356.

Neviarouskaya, A., Prendinger, H. and Ishizuka, M. (2010). Recognition of Affect, Judgment, and Appreciation in Text. In Proceedings of the 23rd International Conference on Computational Linguistics, Beijing, China, pp. 806-814.

Ortony, A., Clore, G.L. & Collins, A. (1988). The Cognitive Structure of Emotions. Cambridge U. Press.

Ptaszynski, M., Dybala, P., Shi, W., Rzepka, R. and Araki, K. (2009). Towards Context Aware Emotional Intelligence in Machines: Computing Contextual Appropriateness of Affective States. In Proceeding of IJCAI.

Wang, Z., Lee, J. and Marsella, S. (2011). Towards More Comprehensive Listening Behavior: Beyond the Bobble Head. In Proceedings of International Conference on Intelligent Virtual Agents.

Widdows, D. and Cohen, T. (2010). The Semantic Vectors Package: New Algorithms and Public Tools for Distributional Semantics. In Proceedings of IEEE International Conference on Semantic Computing.

Zhang, L., Gillies, M., Dhaliwal, K., Gower, A., Robertson, D. and Crabtree, B. (2009). E-drama: Facilitating Online Role-play using an AI Actor and Emotionally Expressive Characters. International Journal of Artificial Intelligence in Education. Vol 19(1), pp.5-38.

Analyzing the Effect of Global Learning and Beam-search on Transition-based Dependency Parsing

Yue Zhang[1] *Joakim Nivre*[2]
(1) Singapore University of Technology and Design
(2) Uppsala University, Sweden
yue_zhang@sutd.edu.sg, joakim.nivre@lingfil.uu.se

ABSTRACT

Beam-search and global models have been applied to transition-based dependency parsing, leading to state-of-the-art accuracies that are comparable to the best graph-based parsers. In this paper, we analyze the effects of global learning and beam-search on the overall accuracy and error distribution of a transition-based dependency parser. First, we show that global learning and beam-search must be jointly applied to give improvements over greedy, locally trained parsing. We then show that in addition to the reduction of error propagation, an important advantage of the combination of global learning and beam-search is that it accommodates more powerful parsing models without overfitting. Finally, we characterize the errors of a global, beam-search, transition-based parser, relating it to the classic contrast between "local, greedy, transition-based parsing" and "global, exhaustive, graph-based parsing".

TITLE AND ABSTRACT IN CHINESE

分析全局模型和柱搜索对基于转移依存分析器的影响

柱搜索和全局模型被应用于基于转移的依存分析，可以取得与最好的基于图的依存分析器同一水平的精度。我们分析全局学习和柱搜索对基于转移的依存分析器的精度与错误分布的影响。首先，全局学习和柱搜索需要同时使用才能达到显著优于局部学习和贪婪搜索的效果。此外，全局学习和柱搜索的联合使用不仅可以减少错误蔓延，还可以支持更为复杂的模型训练而不过拟合。最后，我们对应用了全局学习和柱搜索的基于转移的依存分析器进行错误分析，且将此分析与对MaltParser与MSTParser的错误对比相比较。

KEYWORDS: Dependency parsing, error analysis, ZPar, MaltParser, MSTParser.

KEYWORDS IN CHINESE: 依存分析, 错误分析, ZPar, MaltParser, MSTParser

Proceedings of COLING 2012: Posters, pages 1391–1400,
COLING 2012, Mumbai, December 2012.

1 Introduction

Beam-search has been applied to transition-based dependency parsing in recent studies (Zhang and Clark, 2008; Huang and Sagae, 2010; Hatori et al., 2011). In addition to reducing search errors compared to greedy search, it also enables the use of global models that accommodate richer non-local features without overfitting, leading to recent state-of-the-art accuracies of transition-based dependency parsing (Zhang and Nivre, 2011; Bohnet and Kuhn, 2012; Bohnet and Nivre, 2012) that are competitive with the best graph-based dependency parsers.

It has been known that a transition-based parser using global learning, beam-search and rich features gives significantly higher accuracies than one with local learning and greedy search. However, the effects of global learning, beam-search and rich features have not been separately studied. Apart from the natural conclusion that beam-search reduces error propagation compared to greedy search, exactly how these techniques help to improve parsing has not been discussed, and many interesting questions remain unanswered. For example, the contribution of global learning in improving the accuracies has not been separately studied. It has not been shown how global learning affects the accuracies, or whether it is important at all. For another example, it would be interesting to know whether a local, greedy, transition-based parser can be equipped with the rich features of Zhang and Nivre (2011) to improve its accuracy, and in particular whether MaltParser (Nivre et al., 2006) can achieve the same level of accuracies as ZPar (Zhang and Nivre, 2011) by using the same range of rich feature definitions.

In this paper, we answer the above questions empirically. First, we separate out global learning and beam-search, and study the effect of each technique by comparison with a local greedy baseline. Our results show that significant improvements are achieved only when the two are jointly applied. Second, we show that the accuracies of a local, greedy transition-based parser cannot be improved by adding the rich features of Zhang and Nivre (2011). Our result suggests that global learning with beam-search accommodates more complex models with richer features than a local model with greedy search and therefore enables higher accuracies.

One interesting aspect of using a global model with beam-search is that it narrows down the contrast between "local, greedy, transition-based parsing" and "global, exhaustive, graph-based parsing" as exemplified by McDonald and Nivre (2007). On the one hand, global beam-search parsing is more similar to global, exhaustive parsing than local, greedy parsing in the use of global models and non-greedy search. On the other hand, beam-search does not affect the fundamental transition-based parsing process, which allows the use of rich non-local features, and is very different from graph-based parsing.

An interesting question is how such differences in models and algorithms affect empirical errors. McDonald and Nivre (2007) make a comparative analysis of local greedy transition-based MaltParser and global near-exhaustive graph-based MSTParser (McDonald and Pereira, 2006) using the CoNLL-X Shared Task data (Buchholz and Marsi, 2006), showing that the parsers give near identical overall accuracies, but have very different error distributions according to various metrics. While MaltParser is more accurate on frequently occurring short sentences and dependencies, it performs worse on long sentences and dependencies due to search errors.

We present empirical studies of the error distribution of global, beam-search transition-based dependency parsing, using ZPar (Zhang and Nivre, 2011) as a representative system. We follow McDonald and Nivre (2007) and perform a comparative error analysis of ZPar, MSTParser and MaltParser using the CoNLL-X shared task data. Our results show that beam-search improves the precision on long sentences and dependencies compared to greedy search, while the advantage of transition-based parsing on short dependencies is preserved. Under particular measures, such as precision for arcs at different levels of the trees, ZPar shows characteristics surprisingly similar to MSTParser.

2 Analyzing the effect of global learning and beam-search

In this section we study the effects of global learning and beam-search on the accuracies of transition-based dependency parsing. Our experiments are performed using the Penn Treebank (PTB). We follow the standard approach to split PTB3 into training (sections 2–21), development (section 22) and final testing (section 23) sections. Bracketed sentences from the treebank are transformed into dependency structures using the Penn2Malt tool.[1] POS-tags are assigned using a perceptron tagger (Collins, 2002), with an accuracy of 97.3% on a standard Penn Treebank test. We assign automatic POS-tags to the training data using ten-way jacknifing. Accuracies are measured using the *unlabeled attached score* (UAS) metric, which is defined as the percentage of words (excluding punctuation) that are assigned the correct heads.

2.1 The effects of global learning and beam-search

In this subsection, we study the effects of global learning and beam-search separately. Our experiments are performed using ZPar, which uses global learning and beam-search. To make comparisons with local learning under different settings, we make configurations and modifications to ZPar where necessary. Global learning is implemented in the same way as Zhang and Nivre (2011), using the averaged perceptron algorithm (Collins, 2002) and early update (Collins and Roark, 2004). This is a global learning method in the sense that it tries to maximize accuracy over the entire sentence and not on isolated local transitions. Unless explicitly specified, the same beam size is applied for training and testing when beam-search is applied. Local learning is implemented as a multi-class classifier that predicts the next transition action given a parser configuration (i.e. a stack and an incoming queue), trained using the averaged perceptron algorithm. In local learning, each transition is considered in isolation and there is no global view of the transition sequence needed to parse an entire sentence.

Figure 1 shows the UAS of ZPar under different settings, where 'global' refers to a global model trained using the same method as Zhang and Nivre (2011), 'local' refers to a local classifier trained using the averaged perceptron, 'base features' refers to the set of base feature templates in Zhang and Nivre (2011), and 'all features' refers to the set of base and all extended feature templates in Zhang and Nivre (2011).

When the size of the beam is 1, the decoding algorithm is greedy local search. Using base features, a locally trained model gives a UAS of 89.15%, higher than that of a globally trained model (89.04%). Here a global model does not give better accuracies compared to a local model under greedy search.

As the size of the beam increses, the UAS of the global model increases, but the UAS of the local model decreases. Global learning gives significantly better accuracies than local learning under beam-search. There are two ways to explain the reason that beam-search hurts the UAS of a locally trained model. First, the perceptron can be viewed as a large-margin training algorithm that finds a separation margin between the scores of positive examples (gold-standard structures) and negative examples (non-gold structures from the decoder). The online learning

[1]http://w3.msi.vxu.se/ñivre/research/Penn2Malt.html.

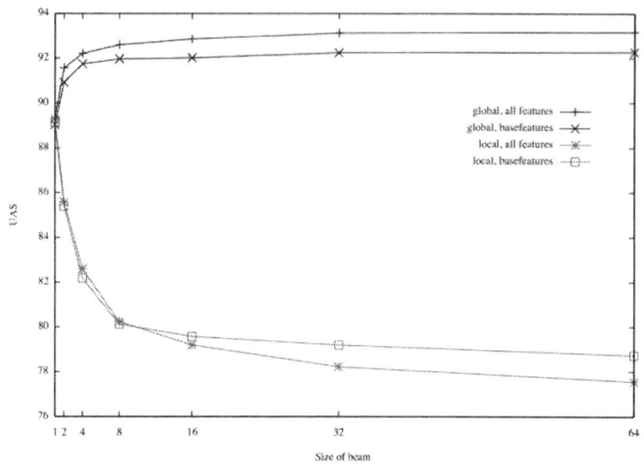

Figure 1: The effect of global learning and beam-search.

training beam	testing beam	UAS
1	1	89.04
1	64	79.34
64	1	87.07
64	64	92.27

Table 1: The effect of different settings between training and testing.

process runs the decoding algorithm to generate a space of negative examples, which is used together with its corresponding positive example space for parameter udpates. If the negative example space during training is different from that during testing, the trained model will not separate the test examples as effectively as when the negative example spaces for training and testing are similar, since there are more unseen negative examples in the model.

To further illustrate this, we conduct an additional set of development experiments by training two global models with different beam sizes. Each of the models is tested using its own training beam size and the training beam size of the other model. The results are shown in Table 1. As can be seen from the table, a global model trained with a size-1 beam gives a higher UAS when tested with a size-1 beam than with a size-64 beam. Similarly, a global model trained with a size-64 beam gives a higher UAS when tested using a size-64 beam than using a size-1 beam. Our observations are consistent with those of Daumé III and Marcu (2005), which show that the accuracies of another online large-margin model are lower when the training and testing beam sizes are different than when they are the same. These results show the negative effect of a mismatch between training and testing negative example spaces, which also happens when a locally trained model is tested using beam-search.

To take a second perspective, a local model is trained to disambiguate different transition actions under the same parser configuration, but not different transitions under different parser configurations. This means that the scores of two sequences of transition actions may not be comparable with each other when they consist of very different parser configuration sequences. This is reminiscent of the label bias problem (Lafferty et al., 2001), and partly explains the performance degradation of the local model when tested with beam-search.

	ZPar	Malt
Baseline	92.18	89.37
+distance	+0.07	−0.14
+valency	+0.24	0.00
+unigrams	+0.40	−0.29
+third-order	+0.18	0.00
+label set	+0.07	+0.06
Extended	93.14	89.00

Table 2: The effect of adding rich non-local features to ZPar and MaltParser. Row 'Baseline' shows the scores of ZPar and MaltParser before extended features are applied. Rows '+distance', '+valency', '+unigrams', '+third-order' and '+label set' show the effect of each group of extended features of Zhang and Nivre (2011), respectively. Row 'Extended' shows the scores with all extended features.

To summarize the above discussion, a global model does not improve over a local model for greedy parsing, and beam-search does not improve the performance of a parser trained locally using the perceptron algorithm. However, the combination of global learning and beam-search can significantly improve the performance compared to a local, greedy transition-based parser.

2.2 Benefits from global learning and beam-search

An additional benefit of global learning and beam-search is the accommodation of rich non-local features. Again in Figure 1, the use of rich non-local features improves the UAS of the global models with all beam sizes, while the improvement brought by rich non-local features also increases with increased size of the beam. With greedy local search, the accuracy improves from 89.04% with base features to 89.35% with all features; with the size of the beam being 64, the accuracy improves form 92.27% with base features to 93.18% with all features. The absolute improvement increased from 0.3% to 0.89%.

The above fact shows that rich non-local features are more effective on a global model with a large beam-size. This is a consequence of the interaction between learning and search: a large beam not only reduces search errors, but also enables a more complex model to be trained without overfitting. In contrast to a globally trained model, a local model cannot benefit as much from the power of rich features. With greedy local search, the UAS of a local model improves from 89.15% with base features to 89.28% with all features. Beam-search does not bring additional improvements.

For further evidence, we add rich non-local features in the same increments as Zhang and Nivre (2011) to both ZPar and MaltParser, and evaluate UAS on the same development data set. Original settings are applied to both parsers, with ZPar using global learning and beam-search, and MaltParser using local learning and greedy search. Table 2 shows that while ZPar's accuracy consistently improves with the addition of each new set of features, there is very little impact on MaltParser's accuracy and in some cases the effect is in fact negative, indicating that the locally trained greedy parser cannot benefit from the rich non-local features.

Yet another evidence for the support of more complex models by global learning and beam-search is the work of Bohnet and Nivre (2012), where non-projective parsing using online reordering (Nivre, 2009) and rich features led to significant improvements over greedy search (Nivre, 2009), achieving state-of-the-art on a range of typologically diverse languages.

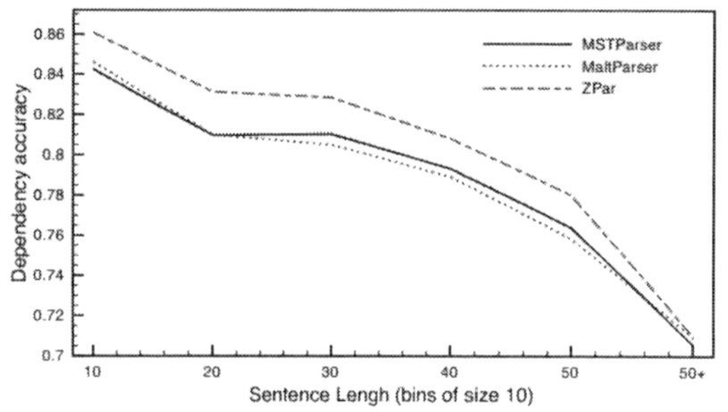

Figure 2: Accuracy relative to sentence length.

3 Characterizing the errors

3.1 The parsers and evaluation data

In this section we study the effect of global learning and beam-search on the error distributions of transition-based dependency parsing. We characterize the errors of ZPar and add it to the error comparison between MaltParser and MSTParser (McDonald and Nivre, 2007).

Following McDonald and Nivre (2007) we evaluate the parsers on the CoNLL-X Shared Task data (Buchholz and Marsi, 2006), which include training and test sentences for 13 different languages. For each parser, we conjoin the outputs for all 13 languages in the same way as McDonald and Nivre (2007), and calculate error distributions over the aggregated output. Accuracies are measured using the *labeled attached score* (LAS) evaluation metric, which is defined as the percentage of words (excluding punctuation) that are assigned both the correct head word and the correct arc label.

To handle non-projectivity, pseudo-projective parsing (Nivre and Nilsson, 2005) is applied to ZPar and MaltParser, transforming non-projective trees into pseudo-projective trees in the training data, and post-processing pseudo-projective outputs by the parser to transform them into non-projective trees. MSTParser produces non-projective trees from projective trees by score-based rearrangements of arcs.

3.2 Error distributions

We take a range of different perspectives to characterize the errors of ZPar, comparing them with those of MaltParser and MSTParser by measuring the accuracies against various types of metrics, including the size of the sentences and dependency arcs, the distance to the root of the dependency tree, and the number of siblings. The parsers show different empirical performances over these measures, demonstrating the comparative advantages and disadvantages of their design discussed in Section 3.1.

Figure 2 shows the accuracy of the parsers relative to sentence length (the number of words in a sentence, in bins of size 10). All three parsers perform comparatively better on short sentences. The performance of MaltParser and MSTParser is very similar, with MaltParser performing better on very short sentences ($\leq$ 20) due to richer feature representations, and worse on longer sentences (20 to 50) due to the propagation of search errors. Because short sentences are much more frequent in the test data, MaltParser and MSTParser give almost identical overall accuracies.

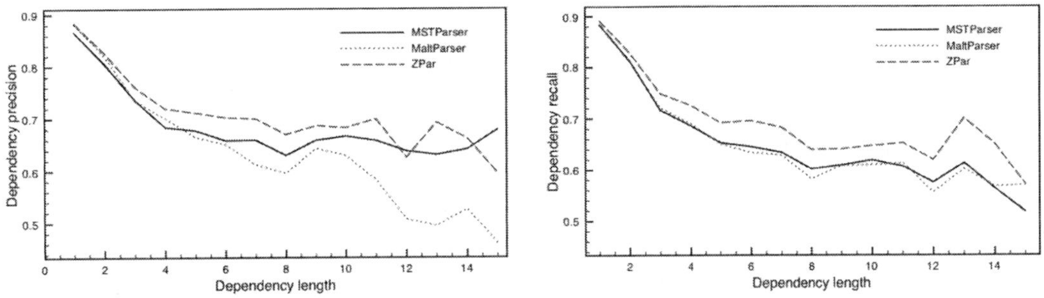

Figure 3: Dependency arc precision/recall relative to predicted/gold dependency length.

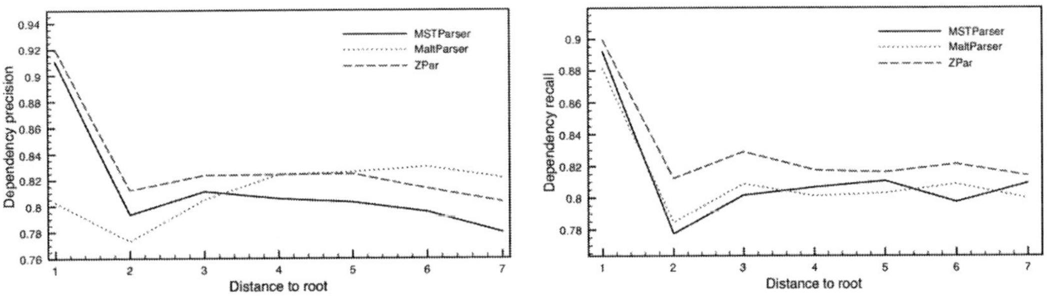

Figure 4: Dependency arc precision/recall relative to predicted/gold distance to root.

ZPar performs better than MaltParser and MSTParser, particularly on short sentences (≤ 30), due to the richest feature representation. For longer sentences (20 to 50), the performance of ZPar drops as quickly as that of MaltParser. One possible reason is that the effect of a fixed-size beam on the reduction of error propagation becomes less obvious when the number of possible parse trees grows exponentially with sentence size. The performance of MSTParser decreases less quickly as the size of the sentence increases, demonstrating the advantage of exact inference. Sentences with 50+ words are relatively rare in the test set.

The three parsers show larger variance in performance when evaluated against specific properties of the dependency tree. Figure 3 shows the precision and recall for each parser relative to the arc lengths in the predicted and gold-standard dependency trees. Here the length of an arc is defined as the absolute difference between the indices of the head and modifier. Precision represents the percentage of predicted arcs with a particular length that are correct, and recall represents the percentage of gold arcs of a particular length that are correctly predicted.

MaltParser gives higher precision than MSTParser for short dependency arcs (≤ 4), but its precision drops rapidly for arcs with increased lengths. These arcs take more shift-reduce actions to build, and are hence more prone to error propagation. The precision of ZPar drops much slower compared to MaltParser, demonstrating the effect of beam-search for the reduction of error propagation. Another important factor is the use of rich non-local features by ZPar, which is a likely reason for its precision to drop slower even than that of MSTParser when the arc size increases from 1 to 8. Interestingly, the precision of ZPar is almost indistinguishable from that of MaltParser for size 1 arcs (arcs between neighbouring words), showing that the wider range of features in ZPar is the most helpful in arcs that take more than one, but not too many shift-reduce actions to build. The recall curves of the three parsers are similar, with ZPar having higher recall than MSTParser and MaltParser, particularly when the dependency size is greater than 2. This shows that particular gold-standard dependencies are hard for all parsers to build, but ZPar is better in recovering hard gold dependencies probably due to its rich features.

To take another perspective, we compare the performance of the three parsers at different levels of a dependency tree by measuring accuracies for arcs relative to their distance to the root. Here the distance of an arc to the root is defined as the number of arcs in the path from the root to the modifier in the arc. Figure 4 shows the precision and recall of each system for arcs of varying distances to the root.

Here the precision of MaltParser and MSTParser is very different, with MaltParser being more precise for arcs nearer to the leaves, but less precise for those nearer to the root. One possible reason is that arcs near the bottom of the tree require comparatively fewer shift-reduce actions to build, and are therefore less prone to the propagation of search errors. Another important reason, as pointed out by McDonald and Nivre (2007), is the default single-root mechanism by MaltParser: all words that have not been attached as a modifier when the shift-reduce process finishes are attached as modifiers to the pseudo-root. Although the vast majority of sentences have only one root-modifier, there is no global control for the number of root-modifiers in the greedy shift-reduce process, and each action is made locally and independently. As a result, MaltParser tends to over-predict root modifiers, leading to the comparatively low precision.

Surprisingly, the precision curve of ZPar is much more similar to that of MSTParser than that of MaltParser, although ZPar is based on the same shift-reduce parsing process, and even has a similar default single-root mechanism as MaltParser. This result is perhaps the most powerful demonstration of the effect of global learning and beam-search compared to local learning and greedy search. The model which scores whole sequences of shift-reduce actions, plus the reduction of search error propagation, lead to significantly reduced over-prediction of root-modifiers. In addition, rich features used by ZPar, such as the valency (number of modifiers for a head) and set of modifier labels for a head, can also be useful in reducing over-prediction of modifiers. Because of these, ZPar effectively pushes the predictions of difficult arcs down the tree, which is exactly the behavior of MSTParser. Interestingly, the recall curve of ZPar is more similar to that of MaltParser than that of MSTParser, showing that arcs at particular levels are harder to recover using the shift-reduce process than a global tree search.

4 Conclusion

We studied empirically the effect of global learning and beam-search on the overall accuracies and error distributions of transition-based dependency parsing. We first analyzed the ways in which global learning and beam-search improved parsing accuracies over local learning and greedy search, showing that they allow more complex parsing models without overfitting, including the use of rich non-local features and online reordering for non-projective parsing, which result in state-of-the-art accuracies (Zhang and Nivre, 2011; Zhang and Clark, 2011; Bohnet and Nivre, 2012). We also showed that the effects result from the interaction between global learning and beam-search, and that applying either of the techniques by itself does not lead to improvements over local learning and greedy search. We then performed a detailed error analysis of a global, beam-search transition-based dependency parser, relating it to the classic comparison of local greedy transition-based and global near-exhaustive graph-based parsing (McDonald and Nivre, 2007). Our results might serve to inspire further parser developments by providing more insights into these techniques.

References

Bohnet, B. and Kuhn, J. (2012). The best of bothworlds – a graph-based completion model for transition-based parsers. In *Proceedings of the 13th Conference of the European Chapter of the Association for Computational Linguistics*, pages 77–87, Avignon, France. Association for Computational Linguistics.

Bohnet, B. and Nivre, J. (2012). A transition-based system for joint part-of-speech tagging and labeled non-projective dependency parsing. In *Proceedings of the 2012 Joint Conference on Empirical Methods in Natural Language Processing and Computational Natural Language Learning*, pages 1455–1465, Jeju Island, Korea. Association for Computational Linguistics.

Buchholz, S. and Marsi, E. (2006). Conll-X shared task on multilingual dependency parsing. In *Proceedings of CoNLL*, pages 149–164, New York City.

Collins, M. (2002). Discriminative training methods for hidden Markov models: Theory and experiments with perceptron algorithms. In *Proceedings of EMNLP*, pages 1–8, Philadelphia, USA.

Collins, M. and Roark, B. (2004). Incremental parsing with the perceptron algorithm. In *Proceedings of ACL*, pages 111–118, Barcelona, Spain.

Daumé III, H. and Marcu, D. (2005). Learning as search optimization: approximate large margin methods for structured prediction. In *ICML*, pages 169–176.

Hatori, J., Matsuzaki, T., Miyao, Y., and Tsujii, J. (2011). Incremental joint POS tagging and dependency parsing in chinese. In *Proceedings of 5th International Joint Conference on Natural Language Processing*, pages 1216–1224, Chiang Mai, Thailand. Asian Federation of Natural Language Processing.

Huang, L. and Sagae, K. (2010). Dynamic programming for linear-time incremental parsing. In *Proceedings of ACL*, pages 1077–1086, Uppsala, Sweden.

Lafferty, J., McCallum, A., and Pereira, F. (2001). Conditional random fields: Probabilistic models for segmenting and labeling sequence data. In *Proceedings of ICML*, pages 282–289, Massachusetts, USA.

McDonald, R. and Nivre, J. (2007). Characterizing the errors of data-driven dependency parsing models. In *Proceedings of EMNLP/CoNLL*, pages 122–131, Prague, Czech Republic.

McDonald, R. and Pereira, F. (2006). Online learning of approximate dependency parsing algorithms. In *Proceedings of EACL*, pages 81–88, Trento, Italy.

Nivre, J. (2009). Non-projective dependency parsing in expected linear time. In *Proceedings of the Joint Conference of the 47th Annual Meeting of the ACL and the 4th International Joint Conference on Natural Language Processing of the AFNLP*, pages 351–359, Suntec, Singapore. Association for Computational Linguistics.

Nivre, J., Hall, J., Nilsson, J., Eryiğit, G., and Marinov, S. (2006). Labeled pseudo-projective dependency parsing with support vector machines. In *Proceedings of CoNLL*, pages 221–225, New York, USA.

Nivre, J. and Nilsson, J. (2005). Pseudo-projective dependency parsing. In *Proceedings of the 43rd Annual Meeting of the Association for Computational Linguistics (ACL'05)*, pages 99–106, Ann Arbor, Michigan. Association for Computational Linguistics.

Zhang, Y. and Clark, S. (2008). A tale of two parsers: investigating and combining graph-based and transition-based dependency parsing using beam-search. In *Proceedings of EMNLP*, Hawaii, USA.

Zhang, Y. and Clark, S. (2011). Syntactic processing using the generalized perceptron and beam search. *Computational Linguistics*, 37(1):105–151.

Zhang, Y. and Nivre, J. (2011). Transition-based dependency parsing with rich non-local features. In *Proceedings of the 49th Annual Meeting of the Association for Computational Linguistics: Human Language Technologies*, pages 188–193, Portland, Oregon, USA. Association for Computational Linguistics.

Chinese Word Sense Disambiguation based on Context Expansion

Zhizhuo Yang [1,2] *Heyan Huang* [1,2]
(1) Department of Computer Science, Beijing Institute of Technology, No.5 Yard, Zhong Guan Cun South Street Haidian District, Beijing, 100081,ChinaNo.5 Yard, Zhong Guan Cun South Street Haidian District, Beijing, 100081,China
(2) Beijing Engineering Applications Research Center of High Volume Language Information Processing and Cloud Computing, Beijing Institute of Technology
10907029@bit.edu.cn, hhy@bit.edu.cn

ABSTRACT

Word Sense Disambiguation (WSD) is one of the key issues in natural language processing. Currently, supervised WSD methods are effective ways to solve the ambiguity problem. However, due to lacking of large-scale training data, they cannot achieve satisfactory results. In this paper, we suppose synonyms for context words that can provide more knowledge for WSD task, and present two different WSD methods based on context expansion. The first method regards Synonyms as topic contextual feature to train Bayesian model. The second method treats context words made up of synonyms as pseudo training data, and then derives the meaning of ambiguous words using the knowledge from both training and pseudo training data. Experimental results show that the second method can significantly improve traditional WSD accuracy by 2.21%. Furthermore, it also outperforms the best system in SemEval-2007.

KEYWORDS: Data sparseness, Context expansion, Bayesian model, Synonym, Parameter estimation

Proceedings of COLING 2012: Posters, pages 1401–1408,
COLING 2012, Mumbai, December 2012.

1. Introduction

Word Sense Disambiguation (WSD), the task of identifying the intended meaning (sense) of words in a given context is one of the most important problem in natural language processing. Various approaches have been proposed to deal with the WSD problem. Hwee found that the supervised machine learning methods are the most successful approach to WSD when contextual features have been used to distinguish ambiguous words in these methods (Hwee and Bin Wang, 2003). However, word occurrences in the context are too diverse to capture the correct pattern, which means that the dimension of contextual words will be very large when all words are used in robust WSD system. It has been proved that expanding context window size around the target ambiguous word can help to enhance the WSD performance. However, expanding window size unboundedly will bring not only useful information but also some noise which may deteriorate the WSD performance. Can we find another way to expand context words without bringing too much noise?

In this paper, we propose to conduct WSD based on context expansion, which acquires WSD knowledge from synonymy dictionary. The assumption of our approach is that contextual words around ambiguous word can be substituted by synonymy, and the new context represented by synonymy expresses the same meaning, thus the sense of the ambiguous word in new context remains unchanged. Therefore, the new context can provide more knowledge for us to improving WSD performance. Under this assumption, we propose two methods to integrate the contribution of synonymy into supervised WSD model. The first method directly considers synonymy as contextual feature, and exploit synonymy feature to train supervised WSD model. The second method treats the new context represented by synonymy as pseudo training data. In the method, the pseudo and authentic training data are both utilized to train supervised model. Consequently, the sense of ambiguous word is not only determined by authentic training data, but also pseudo training data. Experiments are carried out on dataset and the results confirm the effectiveness of our approach. The synonym for context word can significantly improve the performance of WSD.

The rest of paper is organized as follows: Section 2 briefly introduces the related work. The proposed method is described in detail in Section 3, and experimental results are presented in Section 4. Lastly we conclude this paper in Section 5.

2. Related Work

Generally speaking, Word Sense Disambiguation methods are either knowledge-based or corpus-based. In addition, the latter can further be further divided into two kinds: unsupervised ones and supervised ones. In this paper we focus on supervised WSD method.

More recently, WSD approaches based on pseudo word have gained much attention in the NLP community (Yarowsky, 1995; Leacock et al, 1998; Mihalcea and Moldovan, 1999; Agirre and Marinez, 2004; Brody and Lapata, 2008; Lu et al, 2006). The pseudo words can simulate the function of the real ambiguous words. In most cases, synonyms are used as pseudo words to acquire semantic knowledge as the real ambiguous word does. Specifically, These approaches exploits a sense inventory such as WordNet or corpus to collect pseudo words for ambiguous words, and use pseudo words to automatically create sense label data which can subsequently serve to train any supervised classifier. Such approaches are often regarded as weakly supervised learning or semi-supervised learning methods. Inspired by these approaches, we use synonymy of context to provide more knowledge for WSD task. Different from previous approach, we generate training data from another perspective. Instead of utilizing synonymy of ambiguous word to acquire instance form corpus, context words around ambiguous word are extended by synonymy to produce training data in our method 2. Moreover, the method 2 and previous pseudo words based approach can be applied simultaneously in WSD task.

3. Proposed Approach

3.1 The Bayesian Classifier

Naïve Bayesian model have been widely used in most classification task, and was first used in WSD by Gale et al. The classifier works under the assumption that all the feature variables are conditionally independent given the classes. For word sense disambiguation, the context in which an ambiguous word occurs is represented by a vector of feature variables $F = \{f_1, f_2, \dots, f_n\}$. The sense of ambiguous word is represented by variables $S = \{s_1, s_2, \dots, s_n\}$. Finding the right sense of the ambiguous word equal to choosing the sense s' that maximizes the conditional probability as follow:

$$s' = \arg\max_{s_i \; S} \; \underset{f_j \; F}{} P(f_j \mid s_i) P(s_i) \qquad (1)$$

The probability of sense $P(s_i)$ and the conditional probability of feature f_j with observation of sense $P(f_j \mid s_i)$ are computed via Maximum-Likelihood Estimation:

$$P(s_i) = \frac{C(s_i)}{\underset{s_i \; S}{\square} C(s_i)} \qquad (2)$$

$$P(f_j \mid s_i) = \frac{C(f_j, s_i)}{C(s_i)} \qquad (3)$$

where $C(s_i)$ is the number of sense s_i that appears in training corpus. $C(f_j, s_i)$ is the number of occurrences of feature f_j in context with sense s_i in the training corpus. We use "add one" data smooth strategies to avoid data sparse problem when estimating the conditional probabilities of the model.

3.2 WSD Methods based on Context Expansion

Synonyms are different words with almost identical or similar meanings. In this paper, we extend context around ambiguous word into a larger dimension using synonyms, which could provide more knowledge and clues for WSD task. In the previous study of WSD, the most widely used assumption is that words of the same meaning usually play the same role in a language. The assumption can be further extended as words of the same meaning often occur in similar context. Base on the above assumptions, we propose basic assumption in this study, synonyms of context express similar meaning to that of original context, thus the sense of ambiguous word appear in the two similar contexts remains unchanged. For example, in Chinese sentence “可以使消费者清楚地知道自己的钱花在何处” (makes consumers to clearly know where your money goes), the target ambiguous word is “使” , it has two meanings as a verb in HowNet (Dong, 2000) which are “make” and “use”. We can easily infer the meaning of ambiguous word as “make” based on the context. After word segmentation, the context around ambiguous word can be expanded into synonyms set as figure 1. Since the context nearby ambiguous word has the largest impact to the sense of ambiguous word, only three contextual word “可以，消费者，清楚地” are listed and expanded with synonyms in the figure. We simply expand each contextual word with only four synonyms in the figure, actually more synonyms could be added into the synonyms set. Given ambiguous word and synonyms set for each contextual word, some reliable training data could be generated. For example, “可使顾主明白地” ,“足以使购买者明晰地” and “得以使买主清晰地” , etc. The ambiguous word “使” express the same meaning “make” in all of these training examples. It is obvious that synonyms provide additional knowledge for training model, and the knowledge can be exploited to improve the WSD performance.

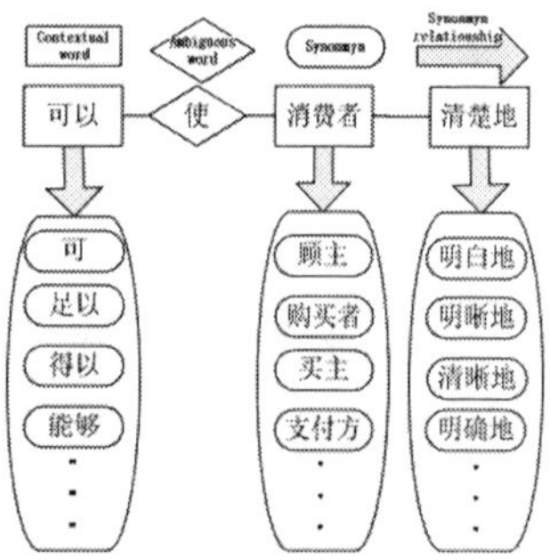

FIGURE 1 – WSD Method base on Context Expansion

The first method we proposed is that treating these expanded synonyms as topic feature. Then, we use these features together with other features to train the classifier. The method is quite straightforward. If contextual words near ambiguous word appear once in training data, synonyms of these contextual words are supposed to appear once in the corpus at the same time. For example, in the previous example, if the testing instance contain contextual word “可” or “顾主”, it is likely that the sense of ambiguous word "使" could be inferred as "make" by Bayesian classifier. But it should be noted that the method has its own shortcomings. The authentic training data is labeled by human while the training data which consists of synonyms is generated automatically by machine. Thus the latter training data contain some noise compared to former training data, and should not play the same role while deducing the sense of the ambiguous word.

In order to overcome the disadvantage of method 1, we proposed method 2. The data which consist of synonyms are regarded as pseudo training data in method 2. The pseudo and authentic training data are both utilized to train the classifier. Instead of using formula (3) to compute the conditional probability of feature with sense, we apply follow formula to compute $P(f_j \mid s_i)$:

$$P(f_j \mid s_i) = \frac{C_a(f_j, s_i)}{C_a(s_i)} + \lambda \frac{C_p(f_j, s_i)}{C_p(s_i)} \quad (4)$$

Here, $C_a(s_i)$ and $C_p(s_i)$ are the number of sense s_i that appears in authentic and pseudo training corpus respectively. $C_a(f_j, s_i)$ and $C_p(f_j, s_i)$ are the number of occurrences of feature f_j with sense s_i in authentic and pseudo training corpus respectively. Parameter λ adjusts the influence of two different kinds of training data. We can set λ to a larger value to let the pseudo training data play a stronger role, and vice versa. In the model, pseudo training data always play a lesser role to determine the sense of ambiguous word. Furthermore, we can set different value to λ for different kinds of ambiguous word.

We encounter two problems when expanding the contextual word with synonyms. The first problem is that not all the synonyms are suitable for generating training data. For example, contextual word "清楚" has synonyms such as "清晰","明晰","历历" and "不可磨灭" in dictionary. It is obvious that "历历" and "不可磨灭" should not be added into the expanded synonyms set, since the collocations of those synonyms with ambiguous word are rarely occur in large-scale corpus. In addition, the contextual words are not monotonous in most cases, and we do not know which sense of the ambiguous word should be expanded by synonyms. For example , Chinese word "可以" has three meanings in dictionary. They are "不错","认可" and "可" respectively. Which sense should be expanded by synonyms in order to generate appropriate training data? To solve the above problems, we exploit word collocation relationship to restrict expansion of synonyms, i.e., only synonyms co-occurrence with ambiguous word that exceeded a certain number are used to train classifier. This strategy can not only filter out uncommonly used collocations, but also solve the problem of noise caused by ambiguity of contextual word. The collocation parameter threshold $threshold\_cooc$ will be adjusted in the experiment.

4. Experiment

4.1 Experimental Setup

Synonyms dictionary: The extended TongYiCiCiLin[1] which was developed by HIT-SCIR is applied to look up synonyms. The items in Cilin are organized as hierarchy of five levels. From the root level to the leaf level, the lower the level is, the more specific the sense is. Since the words in fifth level have similar sense and linguistic function, they can be substituted for each other without changing the meaning of the sentence.
Collocation relationship: In the experiment, Sogou Chinese collocation relation[2]was used to filter out uncommonly used collocations. The collocation corpus involves more than 20 million collocation relations and more than 15000 high-frequency words, which was extracted from over 100 million internet pages on web in October 2006.
Training and testing data: In SemEval-2007, the 4th international workshop on semantic evaluations under conference of ACL-2007 (Jin et al, 2007), we used task#5 multilingual Chinese English lexical sample to test our methods. Macro-average precision (Liu et al., 2007) was used to evaluate word sense disambiguation performance.
Since we aim to evaluate discriminating power of synonymy feature, in the experiment, only some basic features such as topic words, collocations, and words assigned with their positions were used. We compare two baseline methods with our methods, the two baseline methods are as follows:
(1) Original: WSD method based on traditional Bayesian Classifier.
(2) SRCP_WSD (Xing Y, 2007): The system participated in semeval-2007 and won the first place in multilingual Chinese English lexical sample task.($p_{mar} = 74.9\%$)
Our methods:
(1) Method_1: The first method we proposed. This method was based on traditional Bayesian classifiers, which use synonym feature and basic features to train model.
(2) Method_2: The second method we proposed. This method was also based on Bayesian classifiers, which use Basic features to train model. But this method computed the conditional probability using formula (4) .

4.2 Evaluation Results

Because not all words in the sentence are useful for WSD, the contextual words are restricted by syntactic filters, i.e., only the words with a certain part of speech are added.
(1) In order to compare the performances of various methods, table 1 gives the average precision of four methods. It can be seen that method_1 and method_2 obtain improvement over original method, which shows that the methods we propose are

---

1 It is located at http://ir.hit.edu.cn/.

2 http://www.sogou.com/labs/dl/r.html

effective. Moreover, method_2 also outperforms the best system participated in SemEval-2007.

	Original	Method_1	SRCP_WSD	Method_2
Average precision (p_{mar})	0.7336	0.7447	0.7490	**0.7557**
Improving performance (%)	0	1.11	1.54	2.21

TABLE 1 –Experimental result of 4 methods

(3) In order to investigate how the threshold of co-occurrences number influence the performance, experiment on different $threshold\_cooc$ was conducted, and the results are shown in Figure 2. The figure shows the curves for two methods when $threshold\_cooc$ ranges from 5 to 35. We can see that the performance of the two methods first increases and then decreases with the increase of $threshold\_cooc$. The trend demonstrates that extremely small or large co-occurrences number will deteriorate the results. Because a small number means that too many synonyms co-occur with ambiguous word and the number of synonyms exceeds the number that are used to train the classifier. These synonyms introduce noisy knowledge. On the other hand, a large number means very few synonyms are used to train the classifier and this cannot provide sufficient knowledge. The best performance was achieved when set $threshold\_cooc$ to 25.

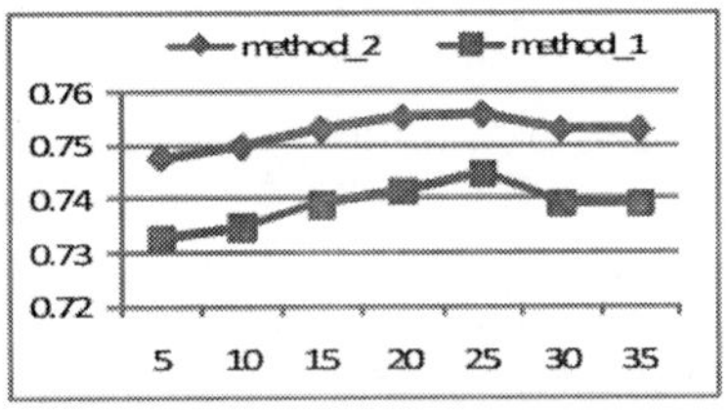

FIGURE 2 – Comparison result of different $threshold\_cooc$

(4) In order to investigate how the λ parameter in formula (4) influences the performance, we conduct experiment with different value of λ as shown in figure 3. In this experiment, we set different λ to different values for ambiguous nouns and verbs contained in testing instance. The red curve represent verb while blue curve represent noun. We can see from the figure, the best experimental results were achieved when λ is set to (0, 1), and the optimal value of λ for noun and verb were set to 0.8 and 0.5 respectively. Because the collocation relationship between noun ambiguous and contextual word would be different with that relationship between verb ambiguous and contextual word, the synonym of contextual word should have larger impact on ambiguous nouns and smaller impact on ambiguous verbs.

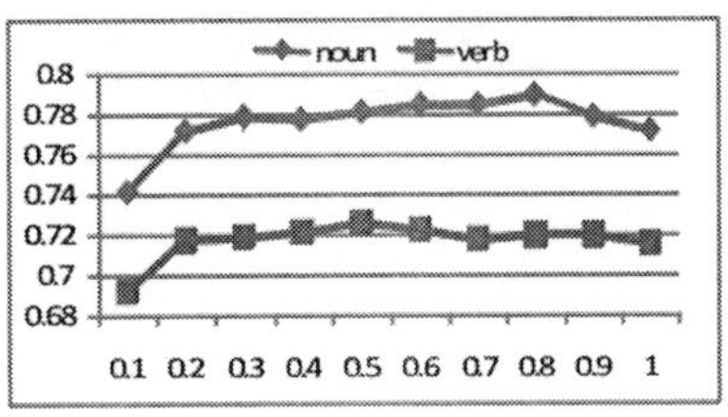

FIGURE 3 – Comparison result of different λ_noun and λ_verb using method_2

Conclusion and perspectives

In this paper, we proposed two novel methods for supervised word sense disambiguation by leveraging synonym for context around ambiguous word. The experimental results on dataset demonstrate the effectiveness of our methods. In current study, we search synonym by extended TongYiCiCiLin. In future work, we will retrieve more synonyms from HowNet and large-scale corpus to expand context nearby ambiguous word, attempting to further improve the performance of WSD.

Acknowledgments

This work is supported by the National Natural Science Foundation of China under Grant No.61132009, the Primary Funds of National Defense.

References

Hwee Tou Ng, Bin Wang, Yee Seng Chan. (2003). Exploiting Parallel Texts for Word Sense Disambiguation. In *Proceedings of the 41st Annual Meeting of the Association for Computational Linguistics*. pages 455--462.

David Yarowsky. (1995). Unsupervised word sense disambiguation rivalling supervised methods. In *Proceedings of the 33rd Annual Meeting of the Association for Computational Linguistics*, pages 189–196, Cambridge, MA, June.

C. Leacock, M.Chodorow, and G.A. Miller. (1998). Using Corpus Statistics and WordNet Relations for Sense Identification. *Computational Linguistics*, 24(1):147-166.

R. Mihalcea and I. Moldovan. (1999). A Method for Word Sense Disambiguation of Unrestricted Text. In *Proceedings of the 37th annual meeting of the Association for Computational Linguistics*, pages 152-158.

E. Agirre and D. Mart'inez. (2004). Unsupervised WSD based on automatically retrieved examples: The importance of bias. In *Proceedings of the International Conference on Empirical Methods in Natural Language Processing*, pages 25-32.

Samuel Brody and Mirella Lapata. (2008). Good Neighbors Make Good Senses: Exploiting Distributional Similarity for Unsupervised WSD. In *Proceedings of COLING*, pages 65-72.

Lu, Zhimao, Wang Haifeng and Yao Jianmin. (2006). An Equivalent Pseudoword Solution to Chinese Word Sense Disambiguation. In *Proceedings of the 44th annual meeting of the Association for Computational Linguistics*, pages 457-464.

Dong ZD, Dong Q. Hownet. 2000. http://keenage.com.

Peng Jin, YunfangWu, and Shiwen Yu. (2007). SemEval-2007 task 05: Multilingual Chinese-English lexical sample task. In: Eneko Agirre, ed. *Proceedings of the Fourth International Workshop on the Evaluation of Systems for the Semantic Analysis of Text*, Prague, Czech Republic: Association for Computational Linguistics. pages 19-23.

Xing Y. (2007). SRCB-WSD : Supervised Chinese Word Sense Disambiguation with Key Features. In : *Proceedings of the 4th in Workshop on Semantic Evaluations*. pages 300-303.

Cross-lingual Identification of Ambiguous Discourse Connectives for Resource-Poor Language

Lanjun Zhou[1] *Wei Gao*[2] *Binyang Li*[1] *Zhongyu Wei*[1] *Kam-Fai Wong*[1]
[1] Dept. of Systems Engineering and Engineering Management, The Chinese University of Hong Kong
[2] Qatar Computing Research Institute, Qatar Foundation
`{ljzhou,byli,zywei,kfwong}@se.cuhk.edu.hk, wgao@qf.org.qa`

Abstract
The lack of annotated corpora brings limitations in research of discourse classification for many languages. In this paper, we present the first effort towards recognizing ambiguities of discourse connectives, which is fundamental to discourse classification for resource-poor language such as Chinese. A language independent framework is proposed utilizing bilingual dictionaries, Penn Discourse Treebank and parallel data between English and Chinese. We start from translating the English connectives to Chinese using a bi-lingual dictionary. Then, the ambiguities in terms of senses a connective may signal are estimated based on the ambiguities of English connectives and word alignment information. Finally, the ambiguity between discourse usage and non-discourse usage were disambiguated using the co-training algorithm. Experimental results showed the proposed method not only built a high quality connective lexicon for Chinese but also achieved a high performance in recognizing the ambiguities. We also present a discourse corpus for Chinese which will soon become the first Chinese discourse corpus publicly available.

Keywords: Discourse, Explicit Connectives, Ambiguity of Connectives.

Proceedings of COLING 2012: Posters, pages 1409–1418,
COLING 2012, Mumbai, December 2012.

1 Introduction

Discourse classification with its applications in many natural language processing tasks such as automatic summarization (Spärck Jones, 2007), text generation (McKeown, 1992) and sentiment analysis (Zhou et al., 2011) etc., has attracted much attention in recent years. However, the lack of annotated corpora brings limitations in research of discourse for many languages (e.g., Chinese).

The Penn Discourse Tree Bank 2.0 (PDTB2) (Prasad et al., 2008a) divided the English discourse connectives into two categories: explicit connectives and implicit connectives. Explicit discourse connectives could be found within a sentence or between sentence pairs while implicit connectives appear only between paragraph-internal adjacent sentence pairs. We focus on the explicit connectives in this work.

Pitler et al. (2008) argued that discourse senses triggered by explicit connectives were easy to be identified in English PDTB2. However, their conclusions may not be true for other languages (Alsaif and Markert, 2011). The ambiguities of explicit connectives could vary among different languages. For many other languages (e.g., Chinese), there is no published discourse corpus available rendering even the identification of explicit discourse difficult. In this work, we focus on the problem of identifying explicit discourse connectives and recognizing their ambiguities for languages without annotated corpus, where the problem is dealt with from cross-lingual perspective. We set English as the source language and Chinese as the target language and we attempt to get answers to the following two questions: (1) Is it possible to build a high quality discourse connective lexicon for the target language (i.e., Chinese) from the source language (i.e., English)? (2) How to disambiguate the ambiguities of each discourse connective in the target language, including the ambiguities between discourse usage to non-discourse usage (e.g., 'for' serves both discourse function and non-discourse function) and ambiguities among the discourse relations it may signal (e.g., 'since' could signal both *Temporal* and *Causal* relations)? To the best of our knowledge, our work is the first that addresses the identification of two different kinds of ambiguities for resource-poor language.

To answer the above questions, we propose a language independent framework using bilingual dictionaries, annotated corpora from the source language and parallel data. The framework mainly consists of the following steps: (1) translate the English connectives to Chinese using a bi-lingual dictionary and expand the connective set by adding synonyms; (2) extract all English connectives aligned with each of the Chinese connectives in large amount of bilingual parallel data; (3) recognize and disambiguate the ambiguities of Chinese connectives. The experimental results showed the effectiveness of the proposed method.

We also present the Discourse Treebank for Chinese (DTBC) project as there is no published discourse corpus in Chinese. Currently, DTBC contains discourse annotations for 500 articles selected from the Penn Chinese Tree Bank 6 (Xue et al., 2005). We annotated 2,549 explicit relations with connectives and arguments. DTBC will soon become the first Chinese discourse corpus publicly available.

2 Related Work

Ambiguity of Connectives. Pitler et al. (2008) argued that the overall degree of ambiguity for English connectives were low. Alsaif and Markert (2011) showed that Arabic connectives are more ambiguous. The most closely related work was Versley (2010). They treated the two kinds of connective ambiguities without necessary differentiation. However, these two kinds of ambiguities should be studied individually since they are essentially different (Pitler and Nenkova, 2009b). Therefore, the way we dealt with ambiguities was very different from theirs. To the best of our knowledge, there is little work that focuses on the problem of cross-lingual identification of ambiguities of discourse connectives for discourse classification.

Discourse corpus annotation. For English, there are mainly two corpora: (1) RST Discourse Treebank (RST-DT) (Carlson et al., 2001) following the RST (Mann and Thompson, 1988); (2) Penn Discourse Treebank (PDTB) (Miltsakaki et al., 2004)(Prasad et al., 2008a). Based on the RST or PDTB, corpora for other languages such as Spanish (da Cunha et al., 2011), Hindi (Prasad et al., 2008b), Arabic (Al-Saif and Markert, 2010) etc. were developed. However, for most of the other languages, there is no published discourse corpus.

For Chinese, Xue (2005) proposed the Chinese Discourse Treebank (CDTB) Project. However, they mainly discussed the issues that arise from the annotation process and the annotated corpus was not published. Zhou et al. (2011) annotated 1,225 intra-sentence discourse instances for improving the performance of polarity classification for Chinese. However, the discourse scheme proposed by them was specially for sentiment analysis. Zhou and Xue (2012) presented a PDTB-style discourse corpus for Chinese. Nevertheless, their data was not publicly available. As far as we know, there is no published discourse corpus in Chinese.

3 Methods

3.1 Finding possible discourse connectives

Utilizing the most frequent discourse relation a connective may signal, Pitler et al. (2008) achieved over 90% of accuracy in recognizing explicit relations in PDTB2 and Alsaif and Markert (2011) reported 82.7% of accuracy in Arabic. As a result, building a high quality connective lexicon is crucial for recognizing explicit relations in the target language.

Since English explicit connectives could be extracted directly from PDTB2, the most intuitive way of finding discourse connectives in the target language is the dictionary based approach. Thus, we adopt an English-Chinese bilingual dictionary[1]. Similar resources could be found between other language pairs. We first extract the Chinese translations for all English connectives using the bilingual dictionary. Then, the connectives are extended using the Chinese synonym list extended version (Che et al., 2010). Note that we adopt part-of-speech restrictions according to the settings of PDTB2 during the translation and extension process. However, many of the connectives in the list are noisy or ambiguous (See section 4). Hence, the connective list need to be refined to preserve only high quality connectives.

3.2 Filtering and estimating the ambiguities of discourse connectives

During the translation process of Section 3.1, we found that the ambiguity of a connective in English could usually be eliminated when translated to Chinese. For example, 'since' could be translated to unambiguous Chinese connectives signaling different discourse relations (e.g., (因为, *Contingency*), (自从, *Temporal*)). Although this observation is between

[1]The 21st Century Unabridged English-Chinese Dictionary

English and Chinese, we believe that similar findings also occur between other language pairs. This observation inspired us to use word alignment information for estimating the ambiguities of Chinese discourse connectives. Fortunately, there are large amount of parallel data available between Chinese and English.

The general idea of the proposed method is to estimate the ambiguities of Chinese connectives by calculating the entropy over its probability distribution on parallel data. Suppose S denotes the source language, T denotes the target language, $E=\{e_1, e_2...e_n\}$ denotes all discourse connectives in T, $E'=\{e'_1, e'_2...e'_m\}$ denotes all discourse connectives in S and $R=\{r_1, r_2, r_3, r_4\}$ denotes the top level relation (i.e., *Temporal, Contingency, Comparison* and *Expansion*) in PDTB2. For $e'_i \in E'$ and $r_k \in R$, we estimate $P(r_k|(e'_i, S))$ using the distribution of occurrences for e'_i over R.

Given a discourse connective $e_j \in E$ from the target language, suppose $C_j=\{c_1, c_2...c_m\}$ denotes the frequency of occurrences for each connective in E' aligned with e_j in the parallel data. The probability for e_j signals relation r_k in T is estimated using the following equation:

$$P(r_k|(e_j, T)) = \sum_i P(r_k|(e'_i, S))\frac{c_i}{||C_j||} \tag{1}$$

in which $||C_j|| = \sum c_i$. As entropy is a measure of uncertainty, the ambiguity of e_j in T is estimated using the following equation:

$$Amb(e_j, T) = -\sum_k P(r_k|(e_j, T)) \cdot \log P(r_k|(e_j, T)) \tag{2}$$

Finally, we rank all connectives in E and use a threshold value $max\text{-}e$ to control the quality of E. $max\text{-}e$ will be determined experimentally to achieve the best performance in recognizing the explicit relations in Chinese.

3.3 Identifying discourse usage of connectives

Given a discourse connective, it could be ambiguous between discourse usage and non-discourse usage in different contexts. For example, in most of the cases, the English connective 'for' does not act as a discourse connective. Since we assume that there is no annotated corpus for the target language, we adopt the co-training algorithm(McKeown, 1992). The main idea of our method is to start from annotated data in English (i.e., the source distribution) and then increase the size of training data by incrementally adding the unlabeled data from Chinese (i.e., the target distribution). We outline the steps of proposed co-training based method in Algorithm 1.

Note that all labeled and unlabeled instances will have two versions: an English version and a Chinese version. We adopt the Baidu Translator[2] for the translation process between English and Chinese. c_1 and c_2 will output probabilities of every testing instance for whether it will serve a discourse function. We take the average of the probabilities given by c_1 and c_2 as the prediction of Algorithm 1.

Since the performance of discourse vs non-discourse usage classification reported by Pitler and Nenkova (2009a) had already reached near human results for English, we adopt their

[2]http://translate.baidu.com/

Algorithm 1 Co-training algorithm for identifying discourse usage of connectives

Given:
- a feature set F_e for the English view
- a feature set F_c for the Chinese view
- a set L of labeled instances from PDTB2;
- a set U of unlabeled instances from DTBC;

Create a pool U' of examples by choosing u examples randomly from U
Loop for k iterations:
  Use L to train a classifier c_1 that uses the feature set F_e
  Use L to train a classifier c_2 that uses the feature set F_c
  Allow c_1 to label U' and choose p most-confident positive instances and n negative instances
  Allow c_2 to label U' and choose p most-confident positive instances and n negative instances
  Add these self-labeled examples to L
  Replenish U' by randomly choose $2 * (p + n)$ from U

	Temporal	*Contingency*	*Comparison*	*Expansion*
DTBC	10%	17%	13%	61%
PDTB2	19%	19%	29%	33%

Table 1: Distribution of explicit relations in DTBC and PDTB2.

feature set for the English view. The Chinese view comprises syntactic features, lexical features and word alignment features. Lexical features and syntactic features are inspired by previous work (Pitler and Nenkova, 2009a; Alsaif and Markert, 2011). The word alignment features are new. Intuitively, given a sentence (or sentence pair) from the source language, if a connective signals a discourse relation, the translation of this connective (if any) will signal the same relation in the target language. Hence, word alignment information will be useful for recognizing discourse usage for the target languages.

4 Experiments and Discussion

4.1 Data

PDTB2. We utilized the Penn Discourse Treebank 2 (PDTB2) (Prasad et al., 2008a), the largest annotated corpora available for English.

DTBC: We presented the Discourse Treebank for Chinese (DTBC). DTBC followed the observations of CDTB (Xue, 2005) and principles of PDTB2 as far as possible. At the current stage, we only annotated explicit discourse relations with their corresponding connective and arguments. DTBC consists of discourse annotations for 500 Chinese news texts selected from Penn Chinese Tree Bank 6 (CTB6) (Xue et al., 2005). It contains annotations for 2,549 explicit relations with connectives and arguments. 2 human annotators were trained to annotate discourse information for all articles. The *kappa-value* is $k_e = 0.78$ for relation identification for the top-level relations. A statistics of DTBC is shown in Table 1. We adopt this corpus to evaluate the performance of discourse usage vs non-discourse usage and explicit discourse relation classification.

NiuTrans: An open-source English-Chinese statistical machine translation system[3]. It contains a sample data of 199,630 English-Chinese parallel sentences. The word alignment

[3]http://www.nlplab.com/NiuPlan/NiuTrans.html

results were the output of GIZA++ (Och and Ney, 2003).

4.2 Experimental settings

4.2.1 Building discourse connective lexicons for Chinese

DIC-1 & DIC-2: The method described in Section 3.1. If a Chinese connective was translations of multiple English connectives, we chose the English connective appeared most frequently in PDTB2 for DIC-1 while the connective will be removed in DIC-2.

DIC+ENT: Different with DIC-2, we did not drop the ambiguous connectives. Instead, the ambiguities in terms of different relations a connective may signal were estimated using the method proposed in Section 3.2. Note that we only estimated the ambiguities in this paper, disambiguating the ambiguities would be another work.

DIC-1, DIC-2 and DIC+ENT output three different discourse connective lexicons. Then, three annotators were trained to label all the connectives as 'discourse connective' or 'not discourse connective'.The golden set was built according to the majority voting.

It was also interesting to evaluate the performance of discourse classification using the lexicons generated by above methods. Note that in this experiment, we used annotated discourse usage information for all connectives in DTBC. A connective based classifier (Pitler et al., 2008) was utilized to evaluate the performance of discourse classification for Chinese. Moreover, we compared the performance of the above methods to the following machine translation based method.

MT-1: We adopted the Baidu Translator[4] to translate all the Chinese text to English. Then, we find discourse relations in the translated English texts.

4.2.2 Identifying discourse usage of connectives

In this experiment, we utilized all sentences containing connectives in DTBC. Since many of the sentences contained more than one discourse connective, the annotated connectives were added to the positive set and others were added to the negative set. We adopted a maximum entropy classifier[5] with iteration number of $i = 15$. We empirically set $|U'| = |U| = u$, $p = 5$, $n = 5$ for the co-training based methods.

CON : A connective would serve a discourse function when it appeared.

MT-2 : We implemented the state-of-the-art method proposed by Pitler and Nenkova (2009b). We adopted PDTB2 as the training data and English translation of DTBC as the testing data.

COT-1 & COT-2 : The method described in Section 3.3. In COT-1, we adopted the same feature set for English and Chinese. The feature set included connectives and syntactic information. The Stanford Parser[6] was adopted to get the syntax structures for translated English sentences and all Chinese sentences. COT-2 added lexical features and alignment features to the Chinese view.

[4]http://translate.baidu.com/
[5]http://mallet.cs.umass.edu
[6]http://nlp.stanford.edu/software/lex-parser.shtml

	Size	*Precision*	*Recall*	*F-score*
DIC-1	561	0.5009	**1.0000**	0.6675
DIC-2	413	0.4649	0.6833	0.5533
DIC+ENT	231	**0.8615**	0.7082	**0.7773**

Table 2: Performance of different connective lexicons. Note that we set *max-e*=1 for DIC+ENT because we did not need to drop any ambiguous connectives in this experiment

	DIC-1	**DIC-2**	**MT-1**	**DIC+ENT**
Precision	0.7948	**0.9253**	0.9082	0.8119
Recall	0.5982	0.3967	0.4287	**0.6937**
F-score	0.6827	0.5554	0.5825	**0.7481**

Table 3: Performance of discourse classification on DTBC. The result of DIC+ENT was acquired by setting *max-e* = 0.3.

4.3 Results

4.3.1 Results of building discourse connective lexicons

Refer to Table 2, DIC+ENT significantly outperformed DIC-1 and DIC-2 in both *precision* and *F-score*. Although the recall of DIC+ENT was not high, the most common discourse connectives in Chinese were all recognized (Refer to Table 3). We believed that the *recall* of DIC+ENT will be further improved by adding more parallel data. Moreover, the size of connective lexicon was greatly reduced in DIC+ENT. Noticeably, the performance of DIC-2 was poor comparing to DIC-1. The recall of DIC-2 dropped to 0.6833 since we filtered 148 connectives which were ambiguous. The result of DIC-2 indicated that over 30% of the Chinese connectives were ambiguous. Accordingly, it was important to recognize the ambiguity of each connective before the discourse classification task.

4.3.2 Results of discourse classification

We introduced *max-e* to control the quality of discourse connectives in DIC+ENT. If *max-e*= 0, the proposed method became DIC-2. This threshold was tuned using the development data (20% of DTBC). The best performance was observed when *max-e*=0.3 (*F-score*= 0.7481). Accordingly, we adopted this optimal value for *max-e* in the following experiment.

Table 3 shows the experimental results of explicit relation classification. Consider Table 3, following conclusions could be drawn: (1) DIC+ENT reached the best result for *recall* and *F-score*. Note that the performance of DIC+ENT outperformed DIC-1 in both *precision* and *recall* . This observation indicated the effectiveness of proposed method. (2) The comparison between DIC-2 and DIC+ENT showed that the drop of recall for DIC-2 comparing with DIC+ENT is up to 0.26. This indicated that ambiguous connectives cannot to be neglected in explicit relation classification. (3) The performance of MT-1 was poor comparing to DIC+ENT. The reason mainly lies in two aspects: (a) the machine translation results were far from perfect; (b) the PDTB2 only contained annotations for 100 different English connectives, resulting to a low recall.

	CON	MT-2	COT-1 ($k = 41$)	COT-2 ($k = 34$)	PDTB2* (reported*)
Accuracy	0.2470	0.6404	**0.7043**	0.7428	0.8586
F-score	0.3961	0.6814	**0.7590**	0.7933	0.7533

Table 4: Experimental results of discourse usage identification for Chinese. The best results of COT-1 and COT-2 during the iteration were presented in the table. *The result was reported by (Pitler and Nenkova, 2009b) on PDTB2.

4.3.3 Results of identifying discourse usage of connectives

Table 4 presents the results of discourse usage identification for Chinese. Refer to Table 4, the co-training based methods significantly ($p < 0.05$) outperformed CON and MT-2 in identification of discourse usages for Chinese connectives.

The performance of CON which predicted discourse usage for every occurrence of connective was poor. However, Pitler and Nenkova (2009b) reported 85.86% of *accuracy* and 75.33% of *F-score* for the connective only method on English PDTB2. We performed a simple error analysis for CON and found that some Chinese connective served as non-discourse function appeared very frequently in DTBC. For example, ' 和 (and)' and ' 在 (in, at, etc.)' appeared thousands of times in DTBC but served as discourse function less than 5% of the time. Thus, the disambiguation between discourse usage to non-discourse usage in Chinese DTBC was essential and more challenging than in English.

MT-2 performed better than the connective only method. However, it only achieved less than 50% of *recall* since the English translations of some common Chinese connectives not belonged to the PDTB2 connective list. Moreover, the parsing results were inaccurate because of the imperfect translations and long sentences. Thus, the overall performance of MT-2 was not satisfactory.

The comparison between COT-1 and COT-2 showed that lexical features and alignment features were effective. One possible explanation was that the performance of proposed method highly relied on the results of machine translation and syntactic parsers. The lexical features and alignment features could still provide useful information when accurate machine translation or syntactic information were unavailable.

Conclusion and perspectives

In this paper, we proposed a language independent framework for building discourse connective lexicons and recognizing their ambiguities for languages without annotated corpora; Experimental results showed the effectiveness of our method. The future work includes: (1) Adapt the proposed method to other languages such as Arabic, Hindi, etc; (2) continue the annotation work of DTBC to include journal articles and well written reviews.

Acknowledgments

This work is partially supported by National 863 program of China (No. 2009AA01Z150), Innovation and Technology Fund of Hong Kong (No. InP/255/10, GHP/036/09SZ) and CUHK Direct Grants (No. 2050525).

References

Al-Saif, A. and Markert, K. (2010). The leeds arabic discourse treebank: Annotating discourse connectives for arabic. In *Language Resources and Evaluation Conference (LREC)*.

Alsaif, A. and Markert, K. (2011). Modelling discourse relations for arabic. In *Proceedings of the 2011 Conference on Empirical Methods in Natural Language Processing*, pages 736--747.

Carlson, L., Marcu, D., and Okurowski, M. (2001). Building a discourse-tagged corpus in the framework of rhetorical structure theory. In *Proceedings of the Second SIGdial Workshop on Discourse and Dialogue-Volume 16*, pages 1--10. Association for Computational Linguistics.

Che, W., Li, Z., and Liu, T. (2010). Ltp: A chinese language technology platform. In *Proceedings of the 23rd International Conference on Computational Linguistics: Demonstrations*, pages 13--16. Association for Computational Linguistics.

da Cunha, I., Torres-Moreno, J., and Sierra, G. (2011). On the development of the rst spanish treebank. *ACL HLT 2011*, page 1.

Mann, W. and Thompson, S. (1988). Rhetorical structure theory: Toward a functional theory of text organization. *Text-Interdisciplinary Journal for the Study of Discourse*, 8(3):243--281.

McKeown, K. (1992). *Text generation: using discourse strategies and focus constraints to generate natural language text*. Cambridge Univ Pr.

Miltsakaki, E., Prasad, R., Joshi, A., and Webber, B. (2004). The penn discourse treebank. In *Proceedings of the 4th International Conference on Language Resources and Evaluation*. Citeseer.

Och, F. and Ney, H. (2003). A systematic comparison of various statistical alignment models. *Computational linguistics*, 29(1):19--51.

Pitler, E. and Nenkova, A. (2009a). Using syntax to disambiguate explicit discourse connectives in text. In *Proceedings of the ACL-IJCNLP 2009 Conference Short Papers*, pages 13--16, Suntec, Singapore. Association for Computational Linguistics.

Pitler, E. and Nenkova, A. (2009b). Using syntax to disambiguate explicit discourse connectives in text. In *Proceedings of the ACL-IJCNLP 2009 Conference Short Papers*, pages 13--16. Association for Computational Linguistics.

Pitler, E., Raghupathy, M., Mehta, H., Nenkova, A., Lee, A., and Joshi, A. (2008). Easily identifiable discourse relations. *Proceedings of COLING 2008, Posters Proceedings*, pages 87--90.

Prasad, R., Dinesh, N., Lee, A., Miltsakaki, E., Robaldo, L., Joshi, A., and Webber, B. (2008a). The penn discourse treebank 2.0. In *Proceedings of the 6th International Conference on Language Resources and Evaluation (LREC 2008)*, pages 2961--2968. Citeseer.

Prasad, R., Husain, S., Sharma, D., and Joshi, A. (2008b). Towards an annotated corpus of discourse relations in hindi. *Proceedings of IJCNLP-2008*.

Spärck Jones, K. (2007). Automatic summarising: The state of the art. *Information Processing & Management*, 43(6):1449--1481.

Versley, Y. (2010). Discovery of ambiguous and unambiguous discourse connectives via annotation projection. In *Proceedings of Workshop on Annotation and Exploitation of Parallel Corpora (AEPC)*, pages 83--82.

Xue, N. (2005). Annotating discourse connectives in the chinese treebank. In *Proceedings of the Workshop on Frontiers in Corpus Annotations II: Pie in the Sky*, pages 84--91. Association for Computational Linguistics.

Xue, N., Xia, F., Chiou, F., and Palmer, M. (2005). The penn chinese treebank: Phrase structure annotation of a large corpus. *Natural Language Engineering*, 11(02):207--238.

Zhou, L., Li, B., Gao, W., Wei, Z., and Wong, K. (2011). Unsupervised discovery of discourse relations for eliminating intra-sentence polarity ambiguities. In *Proceedings of the 2011 Conference on Empirical methods in natural language processing*, pages 162--171. Association for Computational Linguistics.

Zhou, Y. and Xue, N. (2012). Pdtb-style discourse annotation of chinese text. In *Proceedings of the 50th Annual Meeting of the Association for Computational Linguistics (Volume 1: Long Papers)*, pages 69--77, Jeju Island, Korea. Association for Computational Linguistics.